ENCYCLOPEDIA OF

CHINESE PHILOSOPHY

中國哲學

中國哲學

ENCYCLOPEDIA OF CHINESE PHILOSOPHY

中國哲學

ANTONIO S. CUA
EDITOR

Routledge
New York London

Published in 2003 by
Routledge
29 West 35 Street
New York, NY 10001-2299
www.routledge-ny.com

Published in Great Britain by
Routledge
11 New Fetter Lane
London EC4P 4EE
www.routledge.co.uk

Routledge is an imprint of Taylor & Francis Books, Inc.

Project Editor: Susan Gamer
Production Editor: Jeanne Shu
Editorial Assistants: Loren Cappelson, Mary Funchion, Shveta Thakrar
Copyediting and proofreading: Rebecca Condit, Geoff Gneuhs, Arline Keith, Richard Mickey
Glossary: Andrew Schwartz, Ed Noval
Orthography: Frederick Lau
Cover: Pearl Chang; calligraphy by Tin-cheng Zhang
Production Manager: Anthony Mancini, Jr.
Production Director: Dennis P. Teston
Director of Development: Kate Aker
Publishing Director, Reference: Sylvia K. Miller

10 9 8 7 6 5 4 3 2 1

Printed on acid-free, 250-year-life paper

Library of Congress Cataloging-in-Publication Data
Encyclopedia of Chinese philosophy / edited by Antonio S. Cua.
p. cm.
Includes bibliographical references and index.
ISBN 0-415-93913-5 (alk. paper)
1. Philosophy, Chinese—Encyclopedias. I. Cua, A. S. (Antonio S.), 1932-
B126 .E496 2002
181'.11'03–dc21

2002010760

Permission acknowledgments appear on page 973, and on this copyright page by reference.

For Shoke-Hwee Khaw and Athene Cua

Qingshen yizhong

中國哲學

CONTENTS

Board of Editorial Consultants ii

Preface xvii

Contributors xix

Map xxi

Chronology xxii

Aesthetics 1
by Kuang-ming WU

Buddhism in China: A Historical Survey 7
by Whalen LAI

禪宗 Buddhism: Zen (Chan Zong, Ch'an Tsung) 19
by Hsueh-li CHENG

Calligraphy 25
by Jiuan HENG

陳大齊 Chen Daqi (Ch'en Ta-ch'i) 29
by Vincent SHEN

陳確 Chen Que (Ch'en Ch'üeh) 32
by Kai-wing CHOW

陳獻章 Chen Xianzhang (Ch'en Hsien-chang) 35
by William Yau-nang NG

誠 *Cheng* (*Ch'eng*): Wholeness or Sincerity 37
by Kwong-loi SHUN

程顥 Cheng Hao (Ch'eng Hao) 39
by Tze-ki HON

程頤 Cheng Yi (Ch'eng I) 43
by Tze-ki HON

誠意 *Chengyi* (*Ch'eng-i*): Making One's Thoughts Sincere 47
by Kwong-loi SHUN

蔣介石 Chiang Kai-shek (Jiang Jieshi) 48
by Ke-wen WANG

Comparative Philosophy 51
by David B. WONG

孔子 Confucianism: Confucius (Kongzi, K'ung Tzu) 58
by Roger T. Ames

Confucianism: Constructs of Classical Thought 64
by Pei-jung Fu

Confucianism: Dialogues 69
by John Berthrong

Confucianism: Ethics 72
by A. S. Cua

Confucianism: Ethics and Law 80
by Fuldien Li

漢儒學 Confucianism: Han 82
by Chi-yun Chen

Confucianism: Humanism and the Enlightenment 89
by Weiming Tu

Confucianism: Japan 97
by Mary Evelyn Tucker

Confucianism: Korea 102
by Young-chan Ro

明儒學 Confucianism: Ming 107
by Thomas A. Wilson

清儒學 Confucianism: Qing (Ch'ing) 115
by Ying-shih Yü

Confucianism: Rhetoric 126
by A. S. Cua

宋儒學 Confucianism: Song (Sung) 135
by Tzi-ki Hon

唐儒學 Confucianism: Tang (T'ang) 140
by David McMullen

郭籍 Confucianism: Texts in Guodian (Kuo-tien) Bamboo Slips 149
by Xiaogan Liu

道統 Confucianism: Tradition—*Daotong* (*Tao-t'ung*) 153
by A. S. Cua

Confucianism: Twentieth Century 160
by Chung-ying Cheng

Confucianism: Vietnam 173
by Van Doan Tran

Confucianism: Vision 177
by A. S. Cua

元儒學 Confucianism: Yuan (Yüan) 182
by David Gedalecia

Cosmology 187
by John B. Henderson

戴震	Dai Zhen (Tai Chen) by Chung-ying CHENG	195
道	*Dao* (*Tao*): The Way by Chung-ying CHENG	202
道家	Daoism (Taoism): Classical (*Dao Jia*, *Tao Chia*) by Vincent SHEN	206
玄學	Daoism (Taoism): Neo-Daoism (*Xuanxue*, *Hsüan-hsüeh*) by Alan K. L. CHAN	214
	Daoism (Taoism): Religious by Livia KOHN	222
郭籍	Daoism: Texts in Guodian (Kuo-tien) Bamboo Slips by Xiaogan LIU	229
大學	*Daxue* (*Ta Hsüeh*): The Great Learning by Yanming AN	232
德	*De* (*Te*): Virtue or Power by David S. NIVISON	234
董仲舒	Dong Zhongshu (Tung Chung-shu) by Roger T. AMES	238
	Egoism in Chinese Ethics by Kim Chong CHONG	241
法	*Fa*: Model, Law, Doctrine by Roger T. AMES	247
方東美	Fang Dongmei (Thomé H. Fang) by Vincent SHEN	249
法藏	Fazang (Fa-tsang) by Ming-wood LIU	252
馮友蘭	Feng Youlan (Fung Yu-lan) by Lujun YIN	258
馮友蘭	Feng Youlan (Fung Yu-lan): Works on the History of Chinese Philosophy by Nicholas STANDAERT and Bie GIEVER	261
格物; 致知	*Gewu* (*Ke-wu*) and *Zhizhi* (*Chih-chih*): Investigation of Things and Extension of Knowledge by Kwong-loi SHUN	267
公孫龍	Gongsun Long (Kung-sun Lung) by Whalen LAI	270
顧炎武	Gu Yanwu (Ku Yen-wu) by Thomas BARTLETT	272
管子	*Guanzi* (*Kuan Tzu*): The Book of Master Guan by W. Allyn RICKETT	277
郭象	Guo Xiang (Kuo Hsiang) by Alan K. L. CHAN	280
韓非子	Han Feizi (Han Fei Tzu) by Yuk WONG	285

韓愈	Han Yu (Han Yü) by Jo-shui CHEN	288
鶡冠子	The *Heguanzi* (*Ho Kuan Tzu*) Treatise by Carine DEFOORT	291
胡宏	Hu Hong (Hu Hung) by Conrad SCHIROKAUER	294
胡適	Hu Shi (Hu Shih) by Min-chih CHOU	297
淮南子	The *Huainanzi* (*Huai-nan Tzu*) Text by Griet VANKEERBERGHEN	303
黃宗羲	Huang Zongxi (Huang Tsung-hsi) by Lynn STRUVE	306
惠施	Hui Shi (Hui Shih) by Whalen LAI	309
惠能	Huineng (Hui-neng): The Sixth Patriarch by Hsueh-li CHENG	312
	Intercultural Hermeneutics by Robert E. ALLINSON	315
賈誼	Jia Yi (Chia I) by Mark CSIKSZENTMIHALYI	321
吉藏	Jizang (Chi-tsang) by Hsueh-li CHENG	323
君子	*Junzi* (*Chün-tzu*): The Moral Person by A. S. CUA	329
康有爲	Kang Youwei (K'ang Yu-wei) by Lauren PFISTER	337
	Language and Logic by Chung-ying CHENG	343
老子	Laozi (Lao Tzu) by Vincent SHEN	355
	Legalism by Yuk WONG	361
理	*Li*: Principle, Pattern, Reason by Shu-hsien LIU	364
禮	*Li*: Rites or Propriety by A. S. CUA	370
李翺	Li Ao by Jo-shui CHEN	385
梁啓超	Liang Qichao (Liang Ch'i-ch'ao) by Min-chih CHOU	388
梁漱溟	Liang Shuming (Liang Shu-ming) by Guy ALITTO	395

列子	Liezi (Lieh Tzu) by T. H. Barrett	397
林語堂	Lin Yutang by Dian Li	400
凌廷堪	Ling Ting-kan (Ling T'ing-k'an) by Kai-wing Chow	403
劉宗周	Liu Zhongzhou (Liu Tsung-chou) by Lynn Struve	405
理一分殊	*Liyi fenshu* (*Li-i fen-shu*): Principle and Manifestations by Shu-hsien Liu	409
陸賈	Lu Jia (Lu Chia) by Mark Csikszentmihalyi	411
陸象山	Lu Xiangshan (Lu Hsiang-shan) by Joanne D. Birdwhistell	413
羅欽順	Luo Qinshun (Lo Ch'in-shun) by William Yau-nang Ng	420
毛澤東	Mao Zedong (Mao Tse-tung) by Stuart R. Schram	423
	Marxism in China by David Kelly	431
馬祖道一	Mazu Daoyi (Ma-tsu Tao-i) by Whalen Lai	438
孟子	Mencius (Mengzi, Meng Tzu) by Chung-ying Cheng	440
	Metaphysics by Vincent Shen	449
墨子	Mohism: The Founder, Mozi (Mo Tzu) by David B. Wong	453
墨家	Mohism: Later (*Mo Jia*, *Mo Chia*) by Chad Hansen	461
	Moral Philosophy by Kwong-loi Shun	469
	Moral Psychology by Kwong-loi Shun	475
牟宗三	Mou Zongsan (Mou Tsung-san) by Shu-hsien Liu	480
	Mythology and Early Chinese Thought by Whalen Lai	486
名家	Names, School of (*Ming Jia*, *Ming Chia*) by John Makeham	491
	Philosophy in China: Historiography by A. S. Cua	499

Philosophy of Art 511
by Stanley MURASHIGE

Philosophy of Change 517
by Chung-ying CHENG

Philosophy of Culture 525
by Robert C. NEVILLE

Philosophy of Governance 534
by Stephen ANGLE

Philosophy of History 540
by David S. NIVISON

Philosophy of Human Nature 554
by Kwong-loi SHUN

Philosophy of Knowledge 558
by Chung-ying CHENG

Philosophy of Language 569
by Chad HANSEN

Philosophy of Literature 576
by Dian LI

Philosophy of Mind 581
by Chad HANSEN

Philosophy: Recent Trends in China since Mao 588
by Tongqi LIN

Philosophy: Recent Trends Overseas 598
by Chung-ying CHENG

Philosophy: Recent Trends in Taiwan 608
by Vincent SHEN

氣 *Qi* (*Ch'i*): Vital Force 615
by Chung-ying CHENG

錢穆 Qian Mu (Ch'ien Mu) 617
by Kirill O. THOMPSON

情 *Qing* (*Ch'ing*): Reality or Feeling 620
by Chad HANSEN

窮理 *Qiongli* (*Ch'iung-li*): Exhaustive Inquiry into Principles 623
by Chung-ying CHENG

權 *Quan* (*Ch'üan*): Weighing Circumstances 625
by A. S. CUA

權利 *Quanli* (*Ch'üan-li*): Rights 628
by Stephen ANGLE

Reason and Principle 631
by A. S. CUA

Religions 638
by Pei-jung FU

仁 *Ren* (*Jen*): Humanity 643
by Vincent SHEN

	Ritualism by Kai-wing CHOW	646
阮籍	Ruan Ji (Juan Chi) by Alan K. L. CHAN	653
	Science and Technology by Robin D. S. YATES	657
	Scientism and Humanism by Shiping HUA	663
	Self-Deception by A. S. CUA	670
僧肇	Sengzhao (Seng-chao) by Hsueh-li CHENG	678
商鞅	Shang Yang by Chad HANSEN	680
邵雍	Shao Yong (Shao Yung) by Joanne D. BIRDWHISTELL	683
申不害	Shen Buhai (Shen Pu-hai) by Chad HANSEN	689
慎到	Shen Dao (Shen Tao) by Chad HANSEN	692
生	*Sheng*: Life or Creativity by Shu-hsien LIU	695
聖	*Sheng*: Sage by Pei-jung FU	697
神會	Shenhui (Shen-hui) by Hsueh-li CHENG	699
神明	*Shenming* (*Shen-ming*): Gods or Godlike Intelligence by Edward MACHLE	701
是非	*Shifei* (*Shih-fei*): This and Not, Right and Wrong by Chad HANSEN	703
孫逸仙	Sun Yat-sen (Sun Yixian) by Ke-wen WANG	706
譚嗣同	Tan Sitong (T'an Ssu-t'ung) by Lauren PFISTER	709
唐君毅	Tang Junyi (T'ang Chün-i) by Tu LI	712
體	*Ti*: Body or Embodiment by Chung-ying CHENG	717
體用	*Ti* and *Yong* (*T'i* and *Yung*): Substance and Function by A. S. CUA	720
體用	*Ti-Yong* (*Tiyong*, *T'i-yung*) Metaphysics by Chung-ying CHENG	723
天	*Tian* (*T'ien*): Heaven by Pei-jung FU	726

時中	Time and Timeliness (*Shizhong, Shih-chung*) by Chung-ying CHENG	728
	Translation and Its Problems by Lauren PFISTER	734
王弼	Wang Bi (Wang Pi) by Alan K. L. CHAN	741
王充	Wang Chong (Wang Ch'ung) by Michael NYLAN	745
王夫之	Wang Fuzhi (Wang Fu-chih) by JeeLoo LIU	748
王國維	Wang Guowei (Wang Kuo-wei) by Min-chih CHOU	755
王陽明	Wang Yangming (Wang Yang-ming) by A. S. CUA	760
王陽明	Wang Yangming (Wang Yang-ming): Rivals and Followers by William Yau-nang NG	775
文子	The *Wenzi* (*Wen Tzu*) Treatise by Paul VAN ELS	781
無爲	*Wuwei* (*Wu-wei*): Taking No Action by Chad HANSEN	784
五行	*Wuxing* (*Wu-hsing*): Five Phases by John B. HENDERSON	786
嵇康	Xi Kang (Hsi K'ang) by Alan K. L. CHAN	789
孝	*Xiao* (*Hsiao*): Filial Piety by Kwong-loi SHUN	793
心	*Xin* (*Hsin*): Heart and Mind by John BERTHRONG	795
性	*Xing* (*Hsing*): Human Nature by Kwong-loi SHUN	798
熊十力	Xiong Shili (Hsiung Shih-li) by Shu-hsien LIU	801
修身	*Xiushen* (*Hsiu-shen*): Self-Cultivation by Kwong-loi SHUN	807
虛	*Xu* (*Hsü*): Emptiness by Xiaogan LIU	809
徐復觀	Xu Fuguan (Hsü Fu-kuan) by Su-san LEE	811
玄奘	Xuanzang (Hsüan-tsang) by Bruce WILLIAMS	814
荀子	Xunzi (Hsün Tzu) by A. S. CUA	821

嚴復	Yan Fu (Yen Fu) by Kirill O. THOMPSON	831
顏元	Yan Yuan (Yen Yüan) by Ying-shih YÜ	834
揚雄	Yang Xiong (Yang Hsiung) by Michael NYLAN	837
楊朱	Yang Zhu (Yang Chu) by Vincent SHEN	840
義禮	*Yi* (*I*) and *Li*: Rightness and Rites by A. S. CUA	842
陰陽	*Yin* and *Yang* by Roger T. AMES	846
有無	*Youwu* (*Yu-wu*): Being and Nonbeing by Chad HANSEN	847
湛若水	Zhan Ruoshui (Chan Jo-shui) by Annping CHIN	851
章炳麟	Zhang Binglin (Chang Ping-lin) by Fan-sen WANG	854
張東蓀	Zhang Dongsun (Chang Tung-sun) by Key-chong YAP	857
章學誠	Zhang Xuecheng (Chang Hsüeh-ch'eng) by David S. NIVISON	861
張載	Zhang Zai (Chang Tsai) by Chung-ying CHENG	864
正名	*Zhengming* (*Cheng-ming*): Rectifying Names by Chung-ying CHENG	870
眞人	*Zhenren* (*Chen-jen*): The True, Authentic Person by Vincent SHEN	872
知	*Zhi* (*Chih*): To Know, To Realize by Roger T. AMES	874
知行合一	*Zhixing Heyi* (*Chih-hsing Ho-i*): Unity of Knowledge and Action by A. S. CUA	876
智顗	Zhiyi (Chih-i) by David CHAPPELL	879
忠恕	*Zhong* (*Chung*) and *Shu*: Loyalty and Reciprocity by David S. NIVISON	882
忠信	*Zhong* (*Chung*) and *Xin* (*Hsin*): Loyalty and Trustworthiness by Kwong-loi SHUN	885
中庸	*Zhongyong* (*Chung yung*): The Doctrine of the Mean by Yanming AN	888
周敦頤	Zhou Dunyi (Chou Tun-i) by Tze-ki HON	891
朱熹	Zhu Xi (Chu Hsi) by Shu-hsien LIU	895

朱熹 Zhu Xi (Chu Hsi): Rivals and Followers 903
by Hoyt C. Tillman

莊子 Zhuangzi (Chuang Tzu) 911
by Chad Hansen

莊子 Zhuangzi (Chuang Tzu): Schools 919
by Xiaogan Liu

Glossary 925

Permission Acknowledgments 973

Index 975

中國哲學

PREFACE

The *Encyclopedia of Chinese Philosophy* is a reference work addressed primarily to an audience of college and university students and scholars, but it is fully accessible to other interested readers. Seventy-six scholars from around the world have contributed 187 entries; ten of these contributors have also served as editorial consultants. The scope of the work encompasses major periods in the history of Chinese philosophy and systematic discussions of major thinkers from Confucius to Mou Zongsan. In addition, readers will find entries that explain central concepts and problems in Chinese philosophy, by writers who have made original contributions to its development. Readers who are especially interested in the history of Confucianism will find a fairly comprehensive treatment of principal figures from the classical period and the Han, Tang, Song, Yuan, Ming, and Qing dynasties, as well as trends in the late twentieth century.

The contributors were asked to write their articles with general readers in mind, from a broadly philosophical standpoint and from both Chinese and western perspectives, with reference to as many actual examples as were appropriate and as length permitted. Because of their theoretical nature, a few entries may appeal most to upper-division undergraduate and graduate students in philosophy. In appropriate cases there are also entries emphasizing conceptual explanations and supporting arguments for philosophical theses that the contributors considered significant for contemporary Chinese philosophy and comparative Chinese and western philosophy. It should be noted that the entries included, and their length, reflect selective decisions. The final list of entries represents the consensus of the Board of Editorial Consultants and is an outcome of extensive communication. Typically, entries on important thinkers and philosophical topics range from 5,000 to 9,000 words in length.

Originally, the contributors were asked to use the Wade-Giles system for romanization of Chinese characters. In late 1999, after consultation with the board, I decided to use pinyin instead, and the contributors kindly sent updated versions of the articles incorporating pinyin. Professor Chong Kim Chong of the University of Singapore was most helpful in converting and editing some twenty entries. For the readers' convenience and information, the Wade-Giles versions of certain terms appear as alternative spellings in entry titles, occasionally in the text, and in the glossary.

Acknowledgments

The idea for this encyclopedia came from Christopher Collins, in the fall of 1992. Over the next three years—interrupted by a year when I was recovering from an illness—I developed a list of entries and writers, with the generous help of the Board of Editorial Consultants. Work on the final list of entries and the assignment of writers was completed over four years; this aspect of the work was also a product of extensive correspondence with the editorial consultants. I am very grateful to the board and to the contributors for their participation in this project.

After Garland, the original publisher, became part of Taylor and Francis, the encyclopedia eventually was assigned to Routledge. I am thankful for the help of several people at Garland: my first project editor, Christopher Collins; Vice President Leo Balk; and the project editors Marianne Lown and Paula Manzanero. At Routledge, I am especially grateful to Sylvia Miller, Publishing Director of the Reference group, for her valuable aid as I worked on the final version of the manuscripts; and most especially to Susan Gamer, Senior Project Editor, who helped organize the manuscript and saw it through the early stages of publication.

I am also grateful to my friend and former colleague Daniel Dahstrom, who has been a constructive critic of many papers I wrote in the 1980s and the early 1990s.

Nearer to home, I am grateful to Jude P. Dougherty, Dean Emeritus, and Kurt Pritzl, the present dean of the School of Philosophy at the Catholic University of America, for their constant encouragement and their support with secretarial assistance. Over a decade before her retirement from our university in 1998, Eunice Rice spent innumerable hours, above and beyond the call of duty, typing manuscripts and class materials, managing correspondence, and organizing files. I am deeply indebted to her for her care and expertise. I am also thankful to Gabrielle Fenlon, an office manager at our school, for help on various matters regarding the encyclopedia. And I owe much to my brother Benito and my brother-in-law Dr. Kon-taik Khaw, for their special care and concern.

Finally, with deep affection and a sense of profound obligation, I dedicate this work to my wife Shoke-Hwee Khaw and my daughter Athene. Without their loving care and concern and constant encouragement, this work would not have seen the light of day. In the first few years after I became committed to this project, on many occasions, because of ill health, I thought of abandoning it. My wife was mainly responsible for maintaining my good health, freeing me from having to deal with family matters, and making it possible for me to continue writing and working on the encyclopedia. In much the same spirit, my daughter was constantly supportive and a comfort to me during hours when I thought that I might not live long enough to finish the work.

Antonio S. Cua
Bethesda, Maryland

中國哲學

CONTRIBUTORS

Guy Alitto
University of Chicago

Robert E. Allinson
Chinese University of Hong Kong

Roger T. Ames
University of Hawaii at Manoa

Yanming An
Clemson University

Stephen Angle
Wesleyan University

T. H. Barrett
University of London

Thomas Bartlett
La Trobe University

John Berthrong
Boston University

Joanne D. Birdwhistell
The Richard Stockton College of New Jersey

Alan K. L. Chan
University of Singapore

David Chappell
University of Hawaii at Manoa

Chi-yun Chen
University of California at Santa Barbara

Jo-shui Chen
Academia Sinica, Taiwan

Chung-ying Cheng
University of Hawaii at Manoa

Hsueh-li Cheng
University of Hawaii at Hilo

Annping Chin
New Haven, Connecticut

Kim Chong Chong
University of Singapore

Min-chih Chou
University of Washington

Kai-wing Chow
University of Illinois at Urbana-Champaign

Mark Csikszentmihalyi
University of Wisconsin at Madison

Antonio S. Cua
Catholic University of America

Carine Defoort
Katholieke Universiteit Leuven

Pei-jung Fu
National Taiwan University

David Gedalecia
College of Wooster

Bie Geiver
Katholieke Universiteit Leuven

Chad Hansen
University of Hong Kong

John B. Henderson
Louisiana State University

Jiuan Heng
University of Singapore

Tze-ki Hon
College of Geneseo, State University of New York

Shiping Hua
Eckerd College

David Kelly
China Academy of Social Science

Livia Kohn
Boston University

Whalen Lai
University of California at Davis

Su-san Lee
Taipei Municipal Teachers College

Dian LI
University of Arizona

Fuldien LI
Taipei, Taiwan

Tu LI
New Asia Research Institute, Hong Kong

Tongqi LIN
Harvard-Yenching Institute

JeeLoo LIU
College at Geneseo, State University of New York

Ming-wood LIU
University of Hong Kong

Shu-hsien LIU
Academia Sinica, Taiwan

Xiaogan LIU
Chinese University of Hong Kong

Edward MACHLE
University of Colorado at Boulder

John MAKEHAM
University of Adelaide

David MCMULLEN
University of Cambridge

Stanley MURASHIGE
School of the Art Institute of Chicago

Robert C. NEVILLE
Boston University

William Yau-nang NG
National Chang-hua University of Education, Taiwan

David S. NIVISON
Stanford University

Michael NYLAN
Bryn Mawr College

Lauren PFISTER
Hong Kong Baptist University

W. Allyn RICKETT
University of Pennsylvania

Young-chan RO
George Mason University

Conrad SCHIROKAUER
City University of New York

Stuart R. SCHRAM
Harvard University

Vincent SHEN
University of Toronto

Kwong-loi SHUN
University of California at Berkeley

Nicolas STANDAERT
Katholieke Universiteit Leuven

Lynn STRUVE
University of Indiana

Kirill O. THOMPSON
National Taiwan University

Hoyt C. TILLMAN
University of Arizona

Van Doan TRAN
National Taiwan University

Weiming TU
Harvard University

Mary Evelyn TUCKER
Bucknell University

Paul VAN ELS
Leiden University

Griet VANKEERBERGHEN
California State University at Pomona

Fan-sen WANG
Academia Sinica, Taiwan

Ke-wen WANG
Saint Michael's College

Bruce WILLIAMS
University of California at Berkeley

Thomas A. WILSON
Hamilton College

David B. WONG
Duke University

Yuk WONG
Chinese University of Hong Kong

Kuang-ming WU
University of Missouri at Columbia

Key-chong YAP
Academia Sinica, Taiwan

Robin D. S. YATES
McGill University

Lujun YIN
Beijing, China

Ying-shih YÜ
Princeton University

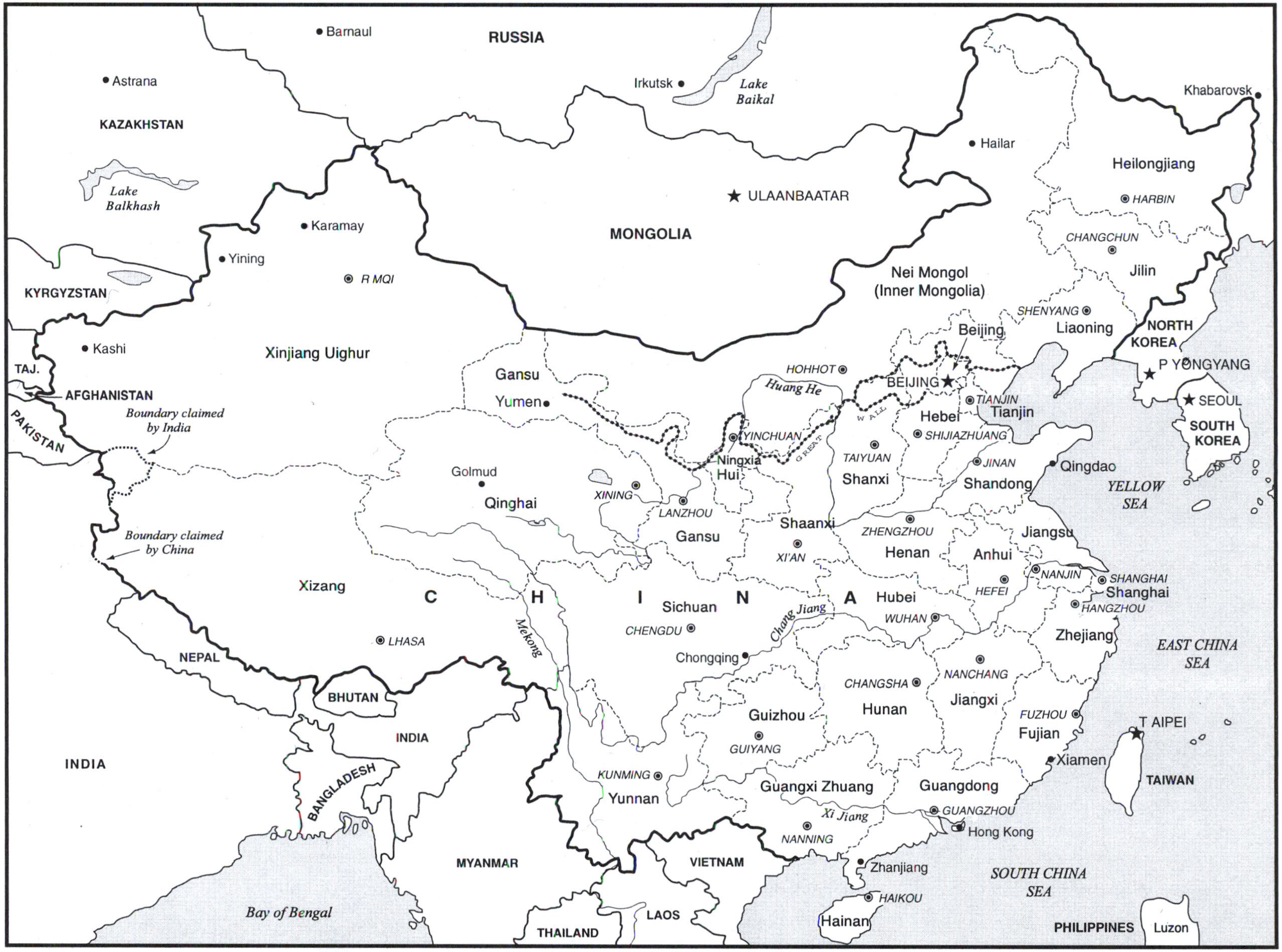

China. (Map prepared by Graphic Services at Indiana University, Bloomington.)

CHRONOLOGY

Antiquity

Xia (Hsia) c. 2100–1600 B.C.E.
Shang (Yin) c. 1600–1066 or 1045 B.C.E.
Zhou (Chou) 1066 or 1045–256 B.C.E.
  Western Zhou c. 1066–771 B.C.E.
  Eastern Zhou 770–256 B.C.E.
Spring and Autumn (Chunqiu, Ch'un Ch'iu) 770–476 B.C.E.
Warring States (Zhanguo) 484 or 475–221 B.C.E.

Dynasties of Imperial China

Qin (Ch'in) 221–206 B.C.E.
Han 206 or 202 B.C.E.–220 C.E.
  Western Han 206 B.C.E.–23 or 8 C.E.
  Xin (Hsin) 9–23
  Eastern Han 25–220 C.E.
Three Kingdoms (Sanguo) 220–280 C.E.
  Wei 220–265
  Shu (Shu-Han) 221–263
  Wu 222–280
Western Jin (Chin) 265 or 266–316
Eastern Jin (Chin) 317–420
Southern and Northern Dynasties
  Southern Song (Sung) 420–479
  Southern Qi (Ch'i) 479–502
  Southern and Later Liang 502–557
  Southern Chen (Ch'en) 557–589
  Northern Wei 386–534
  Eastern Wei 534–550; Western Wei 535–557
  Northern Qi (Ch'i) 550–577
  Northern Zhou (Chou) 557–581
Sui 581–618
Tang (T'ang) 618–907
Five Dynasties and Ten Kingdoms
  Later Liang 907–923
  Later Tang (T'ang) 923–936
  Later Jin (Chin) 936–946
  Later Han 947–950
  Later Zhou 951–960
  Ten Kingdoms 902–979
Liao (Qidan, Khitan) 907 or 916–1125
Song (Sung) 960–1279
  Northern Song 960–1127
  Southern Song 1127–1279
Western Xia (Xi Xia, Hsi Hsia) 882 or 1032–1227
Jin (Chin, Nüzhen, Juchen) 1115–1234
Yuan (Mongol) 1206, 1271, or 1279–1368
Ming 1368–1643 or 1644
Qing (Ch'ing, Manchu) 1644–1911

Modern China

Republic of China 1911–
People's Republic of China 1949–

中國哲學

A

Aesthetics

Kuang-ming Wu

In China, "beauty" is a sentiment more than views—that is, spontaneous views infusing actual performances or informing everyday attitudes. For the Chinese, beauty is a sentiment that pervades life and represents a reaching toward the noble, the true, and the right and an uplifting of all life's interactions. The ugly, the horrendous, the tragic, and the base are utilized to enhance what is beautiful and uplifting. There is no room to indulge in the absurd for its own sake—that would be considered pointless—and thus there is no Chinese Beckett.

The vitality of beauty breathes (*qi*) throughout the interlocking universe of *yin* and *yang*. The Chinese treasure harmony that is at the same time filled with tension; they treasure what might be described as dynamic integrative happiness. These values are not only praised but meditated on, and sacrifices are made for their sake. They are at the base of metaphysics, sentiments, attitudes, and performances in *yin-yang* coincidences of patterns: the five elements (*wuxing*) and the sixty-four hexagrams of the *Yijing*. They infuse all sorts of daily pursuits—politics, cuisine, martial arts, music, painting, calligraphy, religion, architecture, augury, and so on. Even cosmology and morality take on aesthetic undertones.

These characteristics, which are both pragmatic and universal, help us to understand the fascinating panorama of Chinese aesthetics. It starts at the the basic level of expression, writing units or ideographs—what Todo (1965, 19) called *manga*, "cartoons"—then goes on to expressive stories and notions, compressed exempla, and finally literature that is meant to enthrall, entertain, enlighten, and ennoble by representing, concentrating, and typifying memorable events that can be rendered as beautiful and then applied to and diffused through all of life.

In China, the true is the right and the beautiful. What reflects and is true to reality is right and uplifting. Heaven and earth, sky and fields, are considered to be alive and to contain forces—in the most generic sense—that move (*xing*) in the most general way and constitute an intriguing and sometimes bewildering array of perspectives, processes, and seasonal actualities. They intermix and interact, manifesting themselves as sociopolitical and harmonious. To be truly human is to join in their harmony, to join in the mutual workings of the *wuxing*: the five elementary forces, fire, water, wood, metal, and soil. They are an elaboration of the basic conviction that the negative force *yin* and the positive *yang* are forever in conflict with each other and forever give birth to each other. Their interactions form a sort of tapestry (*wen*) of the five elementary forces (or phases), which develop into sixty-four hexagrammatic modes. These modes consist of sixty-four systematic juxtapositions of the *yin* and the *yang*; each hexagram is typified by a paradigmatic situation encapsulated in a story characterized by a "pregnant phrase." Confucius is said to have used the *Book of*

Poetry (*Shijing*) as an exemplar to explicate these (1.15, 17.8).

The Chinese are enthralled by the cosmic interweaving of forces, processes, phases, and activities, and from time immemorial they have engaged in ingenious, observant, concentrated representations of these diverse phenomena. Thus were born the ideographic symbols for writing, the Chinese characters. Xu Shen (30–124 B.C.E.), in the afterword to his *Shuowen jiezi*, the first etymological dictionary in China, said that our writings began with the legendary sage Fu Xi tying knots in a cord to symbolize events and situations and serve as a mnemonic device. How did the tying or knotting occur? Actual tying or knotting was done by another sage, Cang Jie, who in effect painted a specific situation, by developing a paradigm and tying it up in the "knot" of an ideograph or character. This operation fuses two performances: painting or morphemic shaping (*hua*, *xiangxing*) and rhyming or phonemic coupling (*yin, yun*).

Shaping characters by painting (*xiangxing*) with assigned sounds (*shengyun*) is a process of concrete delineation: for instance, drawing a person with spread legs, pronounced *da* and meaning "big"; or drawing a standing person, pronounced *li* and meaning "stand" or "establish." The people of ancient China symbolized an impalpable and therefore unpaintable situation or referred to an event (*zhishi*) by, for example, making a triangle for the character *si*, meaning "private." Then this character would be coupled with other homophones (*xiesheng*) to produce a range of meanings that would effect an understanding of the situation: thus, according to Xu Shen, *hu* (door) stands for *hu* (protection). Liu Shipei (1884–1919) was convinced that meaning arises out of the sound of a word (Todo, 21). Thus characters that are similar in sound, or similar in shape, cross-reference each other, and each elucidates the other: according to Liu Xie, for instance, *li* (rites, decorum) is to be *ti* (embodied). To put this another way, similarity in shape or sound indicates related meanings—a familial relationship. Deciphering meaning according to this principle is called *huiyi* (associative understanding); it is a recognition of a family resemblance among characters, in the form of notions expressed as painterly rhythms.

That is, a character is already a compact story of a situation, "knotted" and made into a paradigm, a notion; a character is inherently a "story-notion." Characters serving compact exempla then became fixed or established with regard to their meaning. Often, a meaning is so pregnant, so complex, that expressing it requires a complex story. Thus a four-character phrase developed to explain it and to deal with similar situations in the future, by *zhuanzhu* (extending meaning) and *jiajie* (lending meaning). Let us consider an example. *Zhudou ranqi* (cooking beans, burning stalks) compresses or "knots" a sad story of the jealous Cao Pi, who ordered his brother, the poet Cao Zhi (192–232), to compose, on pain of death, a poem within seven steps. Cao Zhi at once created a poem that ended, "Beans in a pot crying, stalks under a pot burning, originally born of the same root; why is their common cooking so dire?" The pathos of a family feud is laid bare: the four-character phrase "cooking beans, burning stalks," which would ordinarily be so trite as to seem almost meaningless, reminds us of the story as nothing else could. In this way a "story-notion" graphically knots the cord of actuality and truthfully reflects the world, enabling us to deal with it.

Story-characters and story-notions weave a tapestry (*wen*) of literature, letting us describe situations faithfully. Chinese poets are in a sense painters: characters are the brush they wield. A great calligrapher and essayist, Su Shi (1036–1101), said of Wang Wei (699–759) that his "poems are paintings and his paintings, poems." The best essayists expressed themselves as compactly and powerfully as poets and painters; their essays are terse but full of imagery, musical, pulsating with the rhythm (*yun*) of actuality. Prose-poems (*fu*) seem to have developed spontaneously, originally to reflect actuality; later, however, they leaned toward the intoxicated lyricism of *pianwen* (parallel prose). Consciously shying away from that trend, the great essayists of the Tang and Song eras developed a lean discourse, *sanwen* (free prose), that joined hands with *baihua wen* (folk prose). Significantly, though, this terse prose style was still full of tacit imagery and rhyme, and it was called *guwen* (archaic prose). We can see, in this, that styles of writing and attitudes toward writing in China are closely aligned—if not imbued—with lyrical and figurative beauty, and that there is a consistent historical tendency to continue the best of a tradition. Aristotle claimed that prose was not "destitute of rhythm," and indeed poetic rhythm (*yun*) is ubiquitous in Chinese prose. Chinese literature is more spontaneously poetic and rhythmic than western literature in reflecting, and reflecting on, matters at hand. As Nienhauser said:

> The basic unit of prose is generally accepted to be a four-word (or four-graph) phrase or sentence. Although on the surface this parallels nicely the *paeon* which Western critics have claimed is the basic rhythm of classical Western prose . . ., actually it is a much more "natural" configuration (witness the usual length of an aphorism). Besides, because of the impact of parallelism on Chinese prose of all sorts, there is a tendency for primary rhythm (that based on syntactical and thought patterns) to be more in concert with secondary rhythm (that based on sound and prosody)

> than is the case in the West. A more regular rhythm and attention to oral presentation, therefore, was able to perform another important function by substituting for punctuation and paragraphing, which were unknown in traditional prose. (1986, 95)

Liu (1962, 3) and many others rejected the view of Chinese characters as ideographic, painterly, or packed with ideas, for two reasons: first, many characters are now purely phonetic (like the letters of an alphabet); second, it is very difficult to determine definitely which characters originally meant what. However, their objections can be answered as follows.

With regard to their first point: Almost no one is now aware that in the alphabet the letter A was originally an ox's head, inverted, or that B was a house, whereas most important Chinese characters do retain their ideographic connotations. To treat them as phonetic signs interrupts the flow of a sentence and makes it unwieldy, for they are, after all, more images than signs (Wu 1991, 163).

With regard to the second point: To "paint" or to "sound forth" actuality is part of creative art. Creativity can neither be checked nor be definitive, because creation involves groping and experimenting, with nothing to follow as a norm or a guide. The creation of a character—a compact story, an exemplum—is a creative art; to discern how it happened is also a creative art, which is no less exciting. Who could claim to have discovered the definitive "route" that, say, Picasso took in creating a specific painting? By the same token, etymology is beyond mechanical, critical measurement. We can also think of the legion of synonyms in Chinese writings; this is why Todo had to design *waku* (frames) of shapes and sounds for *tango-kazoku* (word families). We find an effulgence of "knotting"—identifying and expressing paradigms—and, as a consequence, richly varied connotations in characters. This wealth of synonyms puts roadblocks in the way of our etymological exploration.

Still, to recognize creative effulgence is one thing; to let loose irresponsible imagination, as Ezra Pound or Ernest Fenollosa did, is quite another. Somewhere, there needs to be a framework of tradition and a guide to style. As regards etymological propriety, whether or not there is an agreed-on guide, two things are clear: scientific critical methods alone are inadequate to discern a "route" of semantic creativity; and the very elusiveness of creativity has its own definiteness, if not definitiveness. Usually, we can see at once see that a certain interpretation is on the right etymological track, just as we can see integrity in a painting or in calligraphy—a thrust, a coherent sense, a uniquely consistent, penetrating *qi*. We cannot define it, but we can see it when we meet it. When we see a certain origin for a word, we think, "Eureka!"—and we do not react this way when we see another origin.

For literary propriety at the level of the essay, we find many proposals, usually lumped together under the heading "literary criticism," although this actually involves, or should involve, methods of appreciative discernment more than judgmental criticism. The first such work in Chinese history is *Wenfu* (*Rhyme-Prose on Letters*), by Lu Ji (261–303), who rhapsodizes over the inspiring process of creating lively poetry and pulsating prose. Literature inspires the reader because an essay or a poem breathes with life—a life that integrates it, invigorates it, gives it its typical integrity. The breath (*qi*) of a piece of writing is joined by and blended with the reader's breath in a cosmic breath flooding (*haoran zhi qi*) the sky and the fields. This appreciative description of a lively essay later comes to be the norm whereby we judge the works of other writers, past and present.

How do true "living letters" come about? The writer, the artist, watches how things go (*dao*), selects a series of scenes, captures them in a series of knots, and then ties the knots together in a compact story or essay. Through these knots, the writing preserves the events and leads us to learn a typical thrust (*qi*)—a sense of how things go at the moment, conveying the dynamics of a situation (*haoran zhi qi*). All this, the work of art, requires discernment and inspiration. Lu Ji described the process with singular beauty.

Conveying a scene requires us to enhance the situation, and to exalt cosmic harmony. Writing is a musical sounding forth (*ming*) evoked by things that are not "pacific" or not in harmony (*buping*), as Han Yu said in *Song Meng Dongye shu* (*Letter to Meng Tung-yeh*). It is to sound forth the "wooden bell" (*Analects* 3.24), to capture one notable corner, to alert us to "revert" to another yet-to-happen "three" so as to obtain (*juyi fansan*) the yet-to-happen square of things, as Confucius also advised us (*Analects* 7.8).

Significantly, in the creation of good artworks, artistic creativity is joined to morality. This is why the classics (or canon) and other well-known literature are a moral exhortation to posterity as well as a literary tapestry. Even fiction depicting "small talk" (*minjian xiaoshuo*) in which people let down their hair, even grotesque stories (as in *Liaozhai zhiyi*), have a tacit moral agenda. *Shuihu zhuan, Xiyou ji, Jin ping mei*, and *Honglou meng*, as well as the literary humor and joking that pervades Daoist and many Confucian writings, are all historical, futuristic, ethical, sociopolitical, and ecological.

This cosmic, social, and ethical character of literature—the tapestry formed by a series of knots—is supported by a firm vision of the operation of heaven and earth as a coincidence of *yin* and *yang*, in the patterns of the five elementary forces and the sixty-four hexagrams, in the *Book of Changes* (*Yi jing*), a magnificent, artistically coherent work consisting of story situations rendered poetically, many of them patterned after the *Book of Poetry* (*Shi jing*; Nienhauser, 59). Composing an essay about a dire situation amounts to picturing it so as to fit it into one of the hexagrams, and envisioning how it leads to the next hexagram or situation. We might also paraphrase contemporary jargon and say that literary interpretation of the "text" of events is an extrapolation from those events and an interpolation of ourselves into them, creating situational or intertextual dynamics (*qi*) that push the events forward. It was natural for Confucius to confess that he came to understand the decree and bidding of heaven (*tianming*) at age fifty (2.3), when he studied the *Book of Changes* (*Yi jing*) in order to be free of error (7.17); and it was natural for Mencius to sigh, when he calculated a 500-year cycle of sagely rulers, that as yet he saw no sign that such a ruler was coming (7B.38). These writings and sayings sparkle; they are clothed in beauty, a beauty that pervades not only letters, essays, epitaphs, and poetry but even bureaucratic proposals. As Cao Pi (187–226) says in his *Essay on Literature* (*Lun wen*), they all belong to literature. Moreover, cosmology is as ethical and literary as literature is moral and metaphysical. The thrust (*qi*) of Chinese literature is ethical, social, political, historical, and prophetic, spreading from the paragons of the past to the performances of the future, inspiring us to join in its cosmic, hexagrammatic progress.

Once we recognize the universal hortatory beauty of Chinese literature, we can understand how it is invariably a symbol for other arts in all activities of life. Literature (*wen*) is rhythmic sounds and paradigmatic shapes crisscrossed (*jiaocuo*) and interwoven into a texture of letters that will mirror nature—the *yin-yang* tapestry (*wen*) of the five elements or phases of the dynamic sixty-four hexagrams, themselves the interwoven texts, three times over, of *yin* and *yang*. Literary expression is perhaps the tersest but at the same time the most articulate of our tying of knots as a mnemonic for, and a reflection of, the universe and its history. In his *Wenxin diaolong* (*Literary Mind-Heart Etching Dragon*), the first comprehensive and systematic treatise on literature in China, Liu Xie (465–522) spared no words to emphasize this point: literature mirrors cosmic dynamics, and that is its cosmological foundation and its raison d'être. Good essays are poetic; good poetry is a true expression of life; and a good life is the paragon for our existence. Literature, then, is the ideal of life, joining paragons of the past and the beauty of the cosmos in a scene or an event. By faithfully, empathically mirroring the world, literature paints and chants the norm and the ideal of our life.

It is no accident that all Chinese writers use musical and poetic intonations and tend toward painterly calligraphy. To write is to recite, to poeticize, to paint, to be a calligrapher; and writing alludes to other forms that mirror actuality—to the tapestry of shapes we call paintings, to the rhythmic texture of music, to the blending of materials, through water and fire, that we call the art of cooking. Furthermore, governing people through the mouthpieces of heaven is an art of music making that must fall into the rhythms of the music of the heavens, as the *Liji* (*Book of Rites*) insists; and an art of nourishing the community, as the *Daodejing* (60) remarks. The art of rulership, then, patterns itself after other arts that mirror the dynamics of things, the *qi* of the *dao* of heaven and earth. We might also say that these arts, which involve aesthetic and pragmatic performance, must themselves incarnate or be a microcosm of nature; otherwise, they lead to perdition (Wu 1990). The dancing art of the "timely knife" is graphically presented by the Daoist Zhuangzi (ch. 3): the knife of nutrition, dancing with an ox that thereby loosens itself (*jieniu*), also dances with the knifelike art of rulership in the politically mutilated "commander of the right," and with the art of timely death in Lao Dan, the senior Daoist. Finally, martial art clearly patterns itself on all this; it is as alive, and as deathly, as the rhythm of nature. All this embodies the "Lordly Principle of Nourishing Life" (*Yangsheng zhu*)—the title Zhuangzi gave his chapter.

This brings us to the Daoist contribution, without which Chinese aesthetics is not complete. The world includes scenes that are beyond description—inchoate buddings (*ji*, *duan*) of nature and the sheer "thereness" of things; attempts to describe these will miss, or destroy, their fresh concreteness. How, then, do we capture them? By showing. "Don't say it; show it," the beloved urges the lover. How? By using words not as direct referents or pointers but as echoes in a valley (*Daodejing* 28, 41, 66; *Zhuangzi* 11.64), as shadows flickering over the real thing, even as a penumbra, if the real is the umbra (*Zhuangzi* 2.92–94; Wu, 172–173, 215–216, 222–225, etc.). All exempla or stories and gnomic sayings have an adumbrative flavor, touch, and tone. In the world of praxis, such as love (lingering memories of a scene, love of a person, nostalgia for a paragon, yearning for morality, a ruler's parental concern for the people), to say something is to spoil it. Also, to do something is to spoil it, according to the Daoists. Nongovernment—an unknown "small state, few people," in the words of Laozi (80)—is the best government; leaving things as they are expresses the most concentrated solicitude. Practice nondoing, *wei wuwei* (*Daodejing* 3), and things will come to be there, in all their "thereness." Zhuangzi says (12.80–83) that this is the age and the world of the ultimate virtue, *zhide zhi shi*:

> Age of ultimate virtue: No honoring the wise, no employing the capable; [rulers] as tree branches above, people as wild deer below; decent and right and not knowing wherewith to make righteousness, mutually loving and not knowing wherewith to make benevolence, solid and not knowing wherewith to make loyalty, fitting and not knowing wherewith to make fidelity, moving insectlike and mutually employing, not knowing wherewith to make gifts. Thus going and making traces, happenings and no records.

Here, everyone is a friend. Zhuangzi sighed, "Get the rabbit and forget the trap; get the intention and forget the talk. How do I get at all a man of talk-forgotten and with him talk?" (26.49), and he told a story (6.45–66):

> Messieurs Oblation, Carriage, Plow, Coming, these four talked, saying, "Those who take nothing as their heads, birth as their backs, death as their bottoms, who know how dying, birthing, existing, perishing are one body, we befriend them." Four men looked at one another, smiled. Nothing opposed their minds-and-hearts; they became friends. . . . Mr. Mulberry-Door, Elder Return, Mr. Lute-Stretch, these three were friends, saying, "Who can be with one another in not being so, doing with one another in not doing so? Who can mount skies, wander through mists, bounce in No-Bound, mutually forgetting, nowhere exhausting?" The three looked at one another, smiled. Nothing opposed their minds-and-hearts; they became friends.

The beauty and spontaneity of a passage like this suggest the friendliness and the effectiveness of Chinese ecological aesthetics. Here nothing can be said; it must be done in nondoing—following Elder Return.

See also Calligraphy; Laozi; Philosophy of Art; Philosophy of Change; *Qi*; *Yin* and *Yang*; Zhuangzi.

Bibliography

Liu, James. *The Art of Chinese Poetry*. Chicago, Ill.: University of Chicago Press, 1962.

Nienhauser, William H., Jr., ed. and comp. *The Indiana Companion to Traditional Chinese Literature*. Bloomington: Indiana University Press, 1986.

Todo, Akiyasu. *Kanji gogen jiten* (Etymological Dictionary of Chinese Characters). Tokyo: Gakutosha, 1965.

Wu, Kuang-ming. *The Butterfly as Companion: Meditations on the First Three Chapters of the Chuang Tzu*. Albany: State University of New York Press, 1990.

———. *History, Thinking, and Literature in Chinese Philosophy*. Taipei: Academia Sinica, 1991.

中國哲學

B

Buddhism in China: A Historical Survey

Whalen Lai

Buddhism occupies a central place in the history of Chinese thought, as the system that attracted some of the best minds in the millennium between the Han and the Song (second to twelfth centuries). However, integrating Buddhist thought into Chinese philosophy poses some problems, because Buddhists worked from a different set of texts and spoke what seems to be a different language. Christianity began as a hellenized biblical faith whose theology combined *theos* and *logos* from the start; by contrast, long before Buddhism found its way into China there was an extensive history of reflection by Indians on the Buddhist *dharma*—so that Chinese Buddhists had to think through an inherited tradition before they could embark on their own Sinitic reading. As a result, much of the convoluted scholastic detail in Buddhism remains alien to most Chinese. The fact that the neo-Confucian Zhuxi (1130–1200) openly advised his students against debating with Buddhists (lest they be seduced into the Buddhists' mind-boggling dialectics and thus defeated) also means that there was a calculated break between the two traditions. To this day, Chinese Buddhism remains isolated and is often left to Buddhologists. Also, because of the way the field has developed, Chinese Buddhism is often treated as an interim in a pan-Asian development beginning in India and ending in Japan. Integrating Chinese Buddhist thought into the history of Chinese philosophy did not begin until Fung Yu-lan. It is a formidable challenge to attempt integration while fully recognizing the emerging findings of Buddhologists.

Certain paradigms describing the overall cultural interaction are still in use. People still speak of initial Indianization and subsequent Sinicization; of Buddhist conquest and Chinese transformation; of Indians as proverbially otherworldly and Chinese as, by inclination, down-to-earth. Under scrutiny, such generalizations often seem simplistic; but at some macrocosmic level they remain useful heuristic devices, and for certain ends they can even lend overall clarity. The same can be said of several periodization schemes. They all depict a rise, growth, and decline of Buddhism—that is, looking at it from the outside. For adherents of the faith, and for others who still perceive its vitality, the story is one of seeding, flowering, and continual tension or consolidation. The present overview will minimize historic and political details in order to suggest larger sociocultural implications. It will focus on the major developments and their contributions to a history of Chinese ideas and ideals.

A Cultural History

Buddhism came into China sometime in the first century C.E. At first, it remained within the pariah communities of foreign traders and made few inroads into the larger Han Chinese society. Around 150 C.E., translators such as An Shigao began to leave a literary trace of this tradition. Judging from the reception by the Han of the Hinayana works and from the early commentaries, it appears that Buddhism was being perceived and digested through the medium of religious Daoism (Taoism). Buddha was seen as a foreign immortal who had achieved some form of Daoist nondeath. The Buddhists' mindfulness of the breath was regarded as an extension of Daoist breathing exercises. The Buddhist law of karmic retribution impressed many and is said to have struck fear into the ruling elite; but it was also thought that to break free of the horror of multiple rebirths, a person had only to refine his vital force until his spirit realized nirvanic immortality.

Emptiness and Nonbeing

The collapse of the Han dynasty in 220 C.E. weakened the Han Confucian state ideology. The message of Buddhism then became timely and attractive. As there was a revival of Daoism during the Wei-Jin era (third century), there arose a philosophical appreciation of the Mahayana doctrine of emptiness. Since Laozi (ch. 40) had asserted that being comes from nonbeing, the neo-Daoist Wang Bi now made nonbeing the substance of being. And since the *Prajnaparamita* (*Transcendental Wisdom*) *Sutras* also declared that all forms are empty, it was widely held by the Chinese Buddhists that Laozi and Buddha had taught the same need to return to the roots of nonbeing, or emptiness.

Zhuangzi had praised the freedom of going along with nature (*jiran*, "self-being"). Now the Mahayana sutras seemed to speak of the same freedom as the ability of a bodhisattva to see or to abide with things just as they are. The term for this, *tathata*, or "thusness," was accordingly translated as *ru*, suggesting naturalness. With that, the Mahayana idea of a nonabiding nirvana (nirvana being anywhere) came to be associated with roving freely with the *dao*. The freedom exemplified by the householder bodhisattva Vimalakirti was especially appealing. A wealthy layman in the mercantile city of Vaisali, Vimalakirti lived in samsara as if it were nirvana. Since the neo-Daoist gentleman claimed to be dwelling in the forest even while holding political office, the urbane monks of renown then also claimed to be transcending the world even as they circulated among the wealthy and the powerful.

From such confluences of Buddhist and Daoist ideas came the *keyi* ("concept matching") Buddhism of the fourth century. Although Dao'an (312–388) objected to this dilution of *dharma* and urged his fellow monks to undertake a more diligent study of the analytical subtleties of *abhidharma* (Hinayana scholastics), he himself was not entirely free of Daoist assumptions. Only after the learned translator Kumarajiva arrived in Chang'an in 401 would that situation be substantially changed. Only then did the treatises of Nagarjuna (c.150), architect of the philosophy of the "middle path" or emptiness, become available in translation. Only then was the special status of the *Lotus Sutra* made known. Subsequently Sengzhao (374–414) became the first Chinese to master that Madhyamika philosophy, although—because he believed in the centrality of emptiness—he did not grasp the full import of the *Lotus Sutra*'s teaching about the "singular reality" of the eternal Buddha.

The Beginning of a Tenet-Classification Scheme

Another major doctrine, an extension of Buddha's omnipresence, concerns the universal "Buddha-nature." But this teaching was not known to Kumarajiva. It came in only after his death, when the Mahayana *Nirvana Sutra* was translated by Dharmaksema in northern Liangzhou. This, together with the later translation of the *Queen Srimala Sutra* in the south, proclaimed that the Buddha-nature or *tathagatagarbha* (embryo or seed of the Buddha) was Buddha's final, positive teaching. Instead of the Hinayanist no-self or no-soul (*anatman*), Mahayana finally revealed the "self" or "great soul" that is the Buddha-nature. Ultimate reality was not just empty (*sunya*) of self-nature but, in a more important sense, also not-empty (*asunya*) of the infinitely positive attributes of Buddha. With this, the stage was set for postulating a progression in Buddha's teaching following this basic teleological format.

1. Hinayana teaching of the "four noble truths": samsaric realities are many and impermanent.
2. Mahayana initial teaching of universal emptiness.
3. *Lotus Sutra*'s further teaching of the "one vehicle" (that is, reality) of Buddha.
4. *Nirvana Sutra*'s final doctrine of permanence.

There are variations to this scheme. Sometimes the *Vimalakirti Sutra* is placed between stages 2 and 3, mediating the "empty" and the "one vehicle," because Vimalakirti taught with his noble silence the truth of the nondual: that samsara and nirvana as well as any and all distinctions are "not two." Whatever the variance, the basic teleology of this tenet-classification scheme is to move from the impermanent, multiple realities of the mundane, through their universal emptying and the nondual, to seeing some transcendental, permanent principle.

Gradual and Sudden Enlightenment

Although Daosheng (c. 360–430) had an inkling of this progression in the teachings, credit usually went to his contemporary Huiguan for producing the seminal scheme. Daosheng, the last of the great neo-Daoistic Buddhists, had some notion of the doctrine of universal Buddha-nature even before the final chapters of the *Nirvana Sutra* arrived in the south. On the basis of the *Lotus Sutra*, he had already argued that if the truth is one, then enlightened realization of this truth of the "one vehicle" must also be sudden and total. He was opposed by Huiguan (and Sengzhao), who successfully defended gradual enlightenment. That Huiguan won the debate is not unjust. Tibetan Buddhism also adhered to that general consensus, which can be traced back to Indian Buddhism. Daosheng was ahead of his time. (Chan, or Zen, Buddhism later endorsed sudden enlightenment.) But then the southern Buddhists were also putting aside his type of neo-Daoist intuitionism and were showing a new patience in working through the intricacies of Indian Buddhist thought step by step. The Lushan circle under Huiyuan (344–416) had previously taken Dao'an's advice and began studying Abhidharma with Sanghadeva, so much so that Kumarajiva saw them as sliding back into the analytical realism of Sarvastivada—a Hinayana atomist school which insisted that everything conceivable must be real in itself. The realist legacy survived Kumarajiva's critique, and the southern Buddhists would spend the next century interpreting Nagarjuna through a lesser figure: Harivarman, author of the *Chengshilun* (*Satyasiddhi*, *Treatise on Establishing the Real*), which the Chinese mistook as somehow overcoming the nihilism of the mundane by confirming as real the truth of a transmundane nirvana. (More on this later.)

Should Monks Bow before Kings?

Meanwhile, from 316 on, the north had been overrun by barbarians. War and chaos were hardly the ideal environment for philosophical speculation, but they were a perfect setting for seeking out quietude and rebuilding a community life that could withstand them. Fotudeng, the founder of the northern Sangha, did not sit down and translate even a single text, but he was instrumental in converting the Chinese population en masse. The Chinese literally took refuge with this holy man, whose aura of sanctity held the bloody killers at bay. He could protect his flock and mediate effectively on its behalf before the barbarian rulers, who, being Buddhists, honored Deng as the "great reverent" and pillar of the state. This was based on a Buddhocratic ideal that kings who supported *dharma* would be protected by it and by the powers of the "four heavenly guardians." Moral precepts, ascetic living, and social reconstruction became the forte of the northern monk leaders, whose Sangha flourished under strong state patronage.

In this regard, the difference between north and south is seen in the careers of Faguo and Huiyuan. The north did not record any debates on the immortality of the soul; the south had many. Although Buddha had renounced the Hindu notion of a soul (*atman*), Chinese Buddhists long presumed that if there was to be rebirth, there must be a soul to be reborn, and if a person could attain nirvana, his soul must be what entered nirvana. They knew that the religious Daoists also taught a doctrine of an immortal soul, but they would have held that the Daoist soul sought a materialistic longevity whereas the Buddhist "soul" aspired to a transcendental, spiritual nirvana. Although this was an imperfect understanding, Huiyuan used it to justify the Buddhist calling. The quest for spiritual transcendence is what impels the monk to leave the world. And because the monk lives beyond the mundane, he is also beyond the jurisdiction of the "son of heaven" who ruled over everything within the mundane sphere. Thus would Huiyuan defend the monk's autonomy (spiritual self-rule) and the Sangha's right not to bow to the king. If anything, even the ruler should be grateful to the monk for working for the welfare of the world. With strong support from the magnate families, the southern Sangha successfully defied the state that wanted to subordinate it.

The Sangha in the north was well aware of the monastic rule that prohibited paying homage to kings. But then the relationship between king and Buddha—the two wheels of *dharma*—was much more intricate there. A custom had been established since the Kushan Empire in northwest India in the first century C.E. of paying homage to both king and Buddha. The idea that the ruling king is a bodhisattva destined for future buddhahood (e.g., Maitreya) was nothing new. What might have been new was that the barbarian ruler Holin Bobo went further and declared himself a living buddha. The idea of a *tathagata*-king was also endorsed by the Doba who founded the Wei dynasty in the north. The Wei emperor Taizu (r. 386–409) commanded the homage due him from Faguo; the leader of the Sangha he appointed around 396–398 acquiesced. This set a norm for the north, where the king would assume the dual roles of king of the domain and effectively also the vicar of the Sangha.

What scholars called state Buddhism can easily give the wrong impression that the state was in full control of the Sangha. Although it has become proverbial that *dharma* flourishes and declines according to the fortunes of the state, this does not mean that state support translated into state control or even into the Sangha's prosperity. One clear proof that state Buddhism repeatedly failed to police the Sangha is, of course, the state's repeated persecution of the faith. If the Sangha had been under the state's control, the use of force—the last political resort—would not have been necessary. In fact, often a pious ruler woke up one morning to find on his hands a state within a state. And even after persecution, the Sangha frequently rebounded. But all that belongs more to a sociopolitical history than to our concerns here.

The *Huahu* Controversy

In 520, in Loyang, there was a court-sponsored public debate between the Daoists and the Buddhists over the *huahu* thesis: did Laozi leave China and reappear in India as Buddha? Or did Buddha will his own rebirth in China as Laozi? This debate was a product of the Han perception of Buddha and Laozi as equal sages, and each side sought to absorb the other. (Centuries later, the Hindus would also claim that Vishnu had masqueraded as a heretical Buddha in order to deceive and weaken the demonic hosts.) In the process of the debate, the Chinese Buddhists and Daoists pushed the relative dates of their respective founders farther and farther back until Buddha was said to have died in 1052 B.C.E. The Buddhists won the debate, but that also moved the date of the demise of the *dharma*, set by one popular count as coming 1,500 years after Buddha's death, which would move the beginning of the last age to 552 C.E. When 552 came around, reality seemed to confirm that prophecy. A civil war was raging, and the temples of Loyang had gone up in smoke. The darkest hour came with the anti-Buddhist persecution of 574–577. Yet out of that trial by fire, the Buddha *dharma* would rise like a phoenix, and a result would be the Sinitic Mahayana schools that flourished in the Sui and the Tang dynasties.

The mature Sinitic Mahayana synthesis was not like the earlier "concept-matching" syncretism. The period of digesting Indian subtleties had ended; a time of independent creativity had begun. But before we consider a philosophical analysis of the Sinitic Mahayana schools, we need to consider the building blocks of that edifice.

Paradigm Shifts before 600 C.E.

The four major concerns of Chinese Buddhist thought before the Sui and Tang era were as follows.

1. Before 400: emptiness and the immortal soul.
2. After 420: "two truths and one reality."
3. Around 500: speculations on Buddha-nature.
4. Around 550: synthesis under the "one" of *ekayana* ("one vehicle").

Although these do represent significant shifts, their unfolding naturally overlapped.

1. Beyond nihilism. For the Han Chinese, the doctrine of karmic rebirth entailed the transmigration of the soul—a presumption that they could not do away with even when they accepted the doctrine of emptiness. Since *nirvana* was seen as a return to a pure origin, it was believed to be achieved by discarding the defiled. Refining one's inner self was thought to be a process of attaining a sublime *shen* (spirit) that would realize nirvanic immortality or nondeath.

Nearly all the early *keyi* Buddhists believed in refining the spirit by reducing being to nonbeing. The monk Mindu (fl. 340) was an exception, however. He became aware, first, that, Buddha had no doctrine of a soul; second, that emptiness was not a Daoist, nihilistic void; and third, that since emptiness was not other than form, one should never empty reality but could only empty the mind—and only if the mind was emptied would the world appear empty. A prophet is, proverbially, without honor in his own country, and Mindu was vilified for denying the existence of the soul. Still, because his daring concept of *xinwu* (emptiness of mind) challenged the concept of *benwu* (original nothingness), he provided the momentum for what are called the six *prajna* schools—each of which proposed how emptiness might be better understood.

Mindu, to repeat, held that there is no soul but that there is a real outer world, and thus that one should empty the mind, not objects or forms. The other schools never conceded the "no-self," but they all knew better than to endorse naive nihilism, and nearly all of them incorporated Mindu's psychological argument. Zhi Dun (Zhi Daolin, 314–366) probably developed the most complex synthesis of opinions of his time. In three steps, he first reduced being to nonbeing ontologically; then blamed the distinction between being and nonbeing on a discriminating mind, which he duly emptied; and finally united this refined mind or spirit with the *dao*. Thus Zhi Dun roamed psychically in emptiness while abiding physically in the world of forms. In a sense, he combined the nonbeing of Laozi and the roving freedom of Zhuangzi.

The six *prajna* schools did not have the benefit of Kumarajiva's guidance. Sengzhao (374–414), who was tutored by the Kuchan master in the dialectics of Nagarjuna, reviewed the past attempts and found them all one-sided—they missed the "middle path." He selected three schools to analyze, taking *benwu* to task for valuing nonbeing over being, faulting *xinwu* for emptying the mind without facing up to the problem of form, and accusing Zhi Dun of having espoused a causalist or a relativist reduction of form by form without tackling the inherent emptiness of all form. All three, Sengzhao held, failed to see the inherent emptiness of the unreal. Sengzhao was well received in his own time but thereafter was soon forgotten. He was not even counted within the Madhyamika lineage by either the Sanlun or the Tiantai school and was not to be rediscovered later.

2. Detour into a higher reality. One reason for Sengzhao's eclipse is that when Nagarjuna introduced the notion of the "two truths," the Chinese evolved a new discourse. Instead of talking about being and emptiness at just one level, they became preoccupied with investigating two layers. As a result, the problem of form and emptiness was elevated to a problem of the mundane and the highest truth. An amateurish reading would consider the real to be the mundane truth and the empty to be the highest truth. But since that reading seemed to create a new dualism—between *samsara* and *nirvana*—it led to a search for a still higher, nondual truth. We begin to hear of a third truth, and soon of higher and higher unions of two truths.

Zhou Yong once disputed with the Daoist Zhang Rong, arguing that whereas Buddha knew the emptiness of both being and nonbeing, Laozi knew only the reduction of being to nonbeing. In his treatise *Three Schools of Two Truths*, Zhou Yong exposed the biases of his contemporaries, avoiding the two extremes and staying with the middle path. After Zhou Yong, the southerners evolved more fanciful unities of the two truths. The early *prajna* schools, faced with the problem of explaining how things could be both real and not real, could offer only relatively simple metaphors such as dreams and magical illusions. The new theorists compared this duality to rolling and unrolling a lotus leaf, bobbing a melon into and out of water, or flipping a coin from front to back and vice versa. In this way, the Chinese were sharpening their earlier cosmogonic speculations on how the unity of the great ultimate (*taiji*) could evolve into the two aspects of *yin* and *yang*. Later, this would affect the way the Huayan school handled its pan-cosmic-Buddhist metaphysics.

Nagarjuna, however, never taught a third truth. Nor would the Chinese have taught this, if they had realized that the two truths were epistemic, not ontologic—that is, two ways of looking at the world and not two sides, aspects, or levels of some singular reality. It was Jizang (549–623) of the Sanlun (Three Treatises, Madhyamika) school who exposed that mistake. He reminded the Chinese that the two truths pertained to two modes of discourse; they did not denote principles in reality. Even so, Jizang himself had to fight fire with fire; he had to go along with an opponent's wrong assumptions in order to expose the fallacy. Jizang even developed a "fourfold two truths" (one more than the standard three), but his goal was not to pile up more ontic unities: he called for an end to fixation on the *yin-yang* synthesis.

The Chinese did not embark on their quest for a higher "one truth" without a reason. They had gathered from the *Nirvana Sutra* that the final Buddhist teaching of a universal Buddha-nature constituted the one truth. This suggested to them that there was a "positive truth" above emptiness and the two truths. It was while they were looking for a way to reconcile emptiness and this one truth that they came across Harivarman's treatise *Chengshilun* (*On Establishing the Real*). Harivarman reduced all elements to their finest parts until a virtual nil was reached. Also, among the Four Noble Truths, he considered the third one—about nirvana—the one truth. The other three—describing the nature, the cause, and the way out of the world of suffering—were too mundane to be considered transcendental truths. But using Harivarman's basically Hinayanist scheme to explicate the Mahayana emptiness of Nagarjuna and the one truth of Buddha-nature turned out to be a mistake, which Jizang, again, would later undo.

3. Locating the Buddha-nature. China was attracted especially to the doctrine of the universal Buddha-nature, so much so that Xuanzang's Yogacara school was later called Hinayanist simply for deviating from it. By teaching the Buddha-nature, the *Nirvana Sutra* seems to reverse the earlier Buddhist teaching of no-self and the initial Mahayana teaching of universal emptiness. Daosheng circumvented the problem, noting succinctly that there was no samsaric self of life and death but there was a nirvanic self, which was the Buddha-nature. Still, it was not always easy to keep the Buddha-self from being confused with the Daoist immortal soul, despite all cautions against this.

Emperor Wu of the Liang dynasty (r. 502–549), the King Asoka of China, once presided over a court debate that sought to refute Fan Zhen's denial of an immortal soul. The emperor wrote an essay establishing the spirit as that which would one day become enlightened. This essay has been criticized for confusing the transmigrating soul—a ghost tainted by karma and ignorance—with the transcendental seed of enlightenment that is the Buddha-nature. But the essay did forge a synthesis that anticipated a formula in the *Awakening of Faith in Mahayana*, a text compiled within the next half century in China that became a cornerstone of Buddhist philosophy: in this text, the "one mind" has two aspects—suchness (or thusness), and birth and death (samsara). The emperor's essay also postulated a pure core (the enlightened spirit) that is somehow, inexplicably, trapped in darkness (ignorance). The spirit itself, being one with suchness, is destined for enlightenment; ignorance is what mires a person in birth and death. The emperor probably came up with this ambiguous mixture by drawing on canonical references to the Buddha-nature as the innately pure mind that is somehow accidentally polluted, or on the idea that, like *tathagatagarbha*, it encompasses samsara and nirvana. The *Awakening of Faith* might have done nothing more than express this paradox in a more sophisticated way.

The similarities do not end there. The poet Shen Yue was asked along with other courtiers to comment on the emperor's essay. In Shen Yue's response—which was miscataloged by the *Guang hongmingji* and broken into a number of independent short essays—enlightenment was a matter of putting an end to momentary thoughts. The same psychology is found in the *Awakening of Faith*, where *wunien* (no-thought, or a stripping away of delusions) is equated with suchness. This equation would later appear in the *Platform Sutra* of the sixth patriarch as a slogan of the southern Chan school. Sudden enlightenment is based on this sudden cessation of the thought process. To what extent Emperor Wu, who was a patron of both Daoism and Buddhism, had actually fostered a Sino-Buddhist synthesis of consequence still awaits investigation. But it is perhaps telling that he is also said to have written a commentary on the *Doctrine of the Mean*. The Buddhists were among the first to discover in this Confucian text, which later entered the neo-Confucianists' canon as one of the Four Books, a psychic depth that Buddhists could identify with and that neo-Confucians would regard as a distinct feature of their own philosophy.

Because humans are said to possess Buddha-nature, there was considerable speculation on its exact location in man. And because the *Nirvana Sutra* noted that this *atman* was somehow related to as well as separate from the human personality, there was ample room for debate. Like western attempts to locate the seat of the soul, this speculation could be stimulating but could also prove ultimately futile. In hindsight, any location is an expedient. As a synonym for emptiness and for wisdom, Buddha-nature is not an ontic entity but a function of intuition, not so much a knowable object as a metaphor for knowledge, awakening, and realization. The mistake of the nirvana school is that it read the text too literally—as Jizang was to explain.

4. Resurgence of the Lotus ekayana. If the early sixth century was known for its synthesis of the two truths and Buddha-nature, the century ended with a rediscovery of the unity of the middle path and the "one vehicle." Both Jizang and Zhiyi of the Tiantai school underscored this. It is customary to consider southern China as having excelled in theory while the barbaric north excelled in practice, but by the early sixth century that was no longer true. After the Tuoba Wei had reunited the north in 439 and, by 493, moved the capital to Loyang, a sinicized emperor, Gaozu (Xiaoywendi, r. 471–500), initiated a cultural renaissance; and judging from the fragments of northern works that have survived, the north became at least equal to the south in intellectual achievements.

Unlike southerners—who worked almost exclusively on the *Nirvana Sutra* and followed the authority of Harivarman—northerners maintained their appreciation of the *Lotus Sutra* and Nagarjuna. Both the Sanlun school and the Tiantai school had roots in the north, and both criticized the southerners' shortcomings and won. A merging of the northern and southern traditions was brought about in part by the anti-Buddhist persecution of 574–577 in the north. The Northern Zhou emperor Wu out-Chinesed the Chinese by returning to the ancient Zhou ideal, supporting only Confucianism, and banning Buddhism and Daoism. Many northern monks migrated to the south, and the Sinitic Mahayana schools were born in response to this historical crisis. North and south were reunited under the Sui emperor Wendi in 589. And the Parthian Jizang was honored in the capital. He took Harivarman to task, demolished various current theories of two truths, and returned the dialectics of the middle path to a neither-nor format that avoided both extremes. With a sharp eye for internal contradictions in the various theories on the what, how, and whereof of Buddha-nature, Jizang demolished their biases and revealed the true. Properly understood, positive Buddha-nature was none other than emptiness. In the end, there was nothing to gain (nil to ascertain) but the freedom that comes with the denial of pros and cons. Though committed to emptiness, Jizang also recognized the *Lotus ekayana*, or "one vehicle."

The metaphor of the one vehicle came from the *Lotus Sutra*. In the parable of the world as a burning house, the Buddha as father lured his children out of danger by a promise of three carts awaiting them outside. His final gift to them all is the large, white bullock cart. The parable is meant to show how the one Buddha vehicle (*ekayana*) replaces the three vehicles of the listener, the solitary buddha, and the bodhisattva. Kumarajiva's translation had referred to this *ekayana*—also known as Mahayana—as the Buddha vehicle. Kumarajiva also considered the *Lotus Sutra* as teaching Buddha's secret store, a teaching more profound than the bodhisattva vehicle of the *Emptiness* sutras.

By preferring the *Nirvana Sutra* to the *Lotus Sutra*, the Nirvana school missed the import of *ekayana*. It knew the one truth of the Buddha-nature as Buddha's final teaching. That "one" is a teleological one which came at the end of a progression of teachings. With regard to the parable of the burning house, this is like saying that the three carts were once real options; it is only in the end that they were superseded by the white bullock cart. The preferred reading is that the three vehicles were never real; they were only expedients (white lies). From the very beginning, the truth was that there is only one vehicle, which subsumes all the other vehicles.

As a philosophical discourse, this means qualifying the ultimate "one" (the teleological cause) by making it also a genealogical and omnipresent one (the material and the efficient cause). As a gift of an all-pervasive Buddha-wisdom, it is a priori enlightenment that brings about a seemingly incipient enlightenment. If the one is the beginning, the middle, and the end, that would make an end of all the mundane, karma-driven, causal realities. Realizing the one would then bring an insight into the emptiness of one and all. It would entail dissolving the distinction between past, present, and future. *Ekayana*, then, absorbs all Buddhist teachings into one holistic teaching. In terms of intellectual history, it would imply that as China was reunited under the Sui, the fragmentation of reality that accompanied the age of disunity had been overcome by a synthesis of ideas and a realized harmony. The world as disparate elements and the self as the product of karma were no longer too far removed from the nirvanic "beyond." In the words of the *Awakening of Faith*—which summarizes the essentials of Mahayana—self and world, mind and suchness, are integrally one. Everything is a carrier of that a priori enlightenment; all incipient enlightenment is predicated on it. The mystery of existence is, then, not, "How may we overcome alienation?" The challenge is, rather, "Why do we think we are lost in the first place?"

The Sinitic Mahayana Schools

Four Buddhist schools emerged in China that had no direct, exact precedents in India. India produced the *Lotus Sutra*; Central Asia put together the *Avatamsaka* ("garland," "wreath") corpus; but only China produced the distinct schools of Tiantai and Huayan. Although it is customary to regard these schools, especially Chan (Zen), as Chinese, it should be kept in mind that they are first and foremost Buddhist. Not even Kamalasila at the debate in Lhasa, in Tibet, would deny that Chan was Mahayana or label it Chinese the way Hu Shi would.

Chinese Buddhism is often said to have reached its apogee in the Tang era. But in one sense, it only shared with Confucianism and Daoism the glory, the power, and the prosperity of the Tang. Confucianism would enjoy a revival, especially in the second half of Tang; religious Daoism had the patronage of the ruling house, which considered itself descended from Laozi. Thus, during the Tang, Buddhism had to contend with serious rivals. Earlier, in the Six Dynasties, Buddhism was responsible for new social experiments. During the Tang, it had to come up with more sutras of filial piety, to accord with the family values of Confucianism. Buddhist monks in the Tang could still withstand the pressure to pay homage to rulers (as to parents), but the Sangha had by then lost much of its old autonomy. In the Northern Wei, the Sangha had a leader at the court; by the Sui, that office was replaced by a committee of ten elders; and during the Tang many of the vacancies were left unfilled. When the Japanese pilgrim Ennin came to China in the early ninth century, he needed permission to travel from the local authorities. The Sangha was effectively under the control of the civil authorities. Thus the Sangha—which had once been the mover and shaker—had become part of an entrenched establishment. It owned land and had peasants as tenants; as a result, it lost their support in the anti-Buddhist persecution of 845. This is not to say that Buddhism did not innovate during the Tang—it did, especially with regard to lay devotion and bodhisattvic vocation—but the most daring innovations came from the extraordinarily successful Three Periods sect. The state, however, disestablished this sect, with no protest from any of the major schools.

In the realm of ideas, we will focus on the Tiantai, the Huayan, and the Chan schools. The Pure Land school in China, which did not develop a philosophy of faith, will be covered only in passing, as an adjunct to Tiantai and Chan.

Tiantai (*Lotus*, *Saddharmapundarika*) *school*. The first Sinitic Mahayana school was Tiantai, whose third patriarch, Zhiyi (538–597), found favor with the Sui rulers (581–618). These rulers sought to live up to the Asokan ideal. They revered Buddha, divided the relics, and built a network of state temples. Zhiyi finally became a resident holy man in the capital, his hopes of returning to a meditative life at Mount Tiantai having been repeatedly dashed. Still, the capital was then once more the cultural center of a united China; as a trendsetter, it would also be the home of the later major Sinitic Mahayana schools.

Unlike the Tibetan Buddhists, who followed the Indian *sastra* (commentary) tradition in forming their schools, Chinese Buddhists built their schools directly on the words of Buddha in the sutras. By regarding a sutra as self-revelatory, they in effect produced their own style of commentary that, when necessary, could bypass the Indian authorities. For example, the Tiantai school—named after Mount Tiantai, where Zhiyi (Master Zhizhe) lived—claimed direct inspiration from Buddha (to Zhiyi in a former life). It also claimed a direct transmission from Nagarjuna, so that it could circumvent Indian authorities such as Aryadeva and even discount Kumarajiva, who was the translator of the *Lotus Sutra* but was not considered a patriarch. Jizang, earlier, would not have made such presumptions.

The *Lotus Sutra* is an inspired work, but it is not a systematic treatise. To develop a philosophy out of it requires nothing short of turning mythopoeic narratives into rational discourse. To do that, first, a basic unity is assumed for the sutra; this principle had already been set by Tao'an in the fourth century. Second, a basic teleology is postulated for all sutras; this method of classifying tenets was initiated by Huiguan in the fifth century. To this Zhiyi added something new, a common essence for all Mahayana sutras; this ensured that they all would preach the "one form" of the real.

Zhiyi also innovated a new reading of the *Lotus Sutra*. He broke this work into two parts and located two principles instead of one. The first has to do with the "trace aspect"; this pertains to the absorption by the one vehicle (a singular truth) of three vehicles. The second has to do with the "root aspect"; this pertains to the revelation of the boundless life span of Buddha. This formula—original root and manifest trace—allowed the same one substance to be present in all three vehicles as functions. It solved the problems of the two truths of the transmundane, formless *Dharmakaya* (*Body of Law*) and the mundane, physical *Rupakaya* (*Body of Form*). It subsumed all other sutras under the *Lotus Sutra*. It proclaimed the presence of the omnipresent Buddha-wisdom (another term for Buddha-nature) in all things. It collapsed into the eternal Buddha the "three times"—past, present, and future. Whereas all sutras share this essence, only the *Lotus Sutra* knows it fully. In Hegelian terms, in this work Mahayana attains *ekayana* self-consciousness. That teleology, when spelled out, becomes the theory of the Four Periods and the Five Teachings.

Zhiyi developed a new Buddhist hermeneutics. He distinguished the words and sentences from the hidden meaning of the *Lotus Sutra*. He transformed *mythos* into *logos* by an extensive use of allegories. The budding, flowering, and falling of a lotus blossom carry many more shades of meaning for Zhiyi than the rather arid correlative paradigm of the five processes (*wuxing*) used in the Han. In his *Fahua xuanyi* (*The Hidden Meaning of the Dharma Flower*), he laid out the final mystery, wisdom, and insight: the telescoping of the limit of reality (3,000 worlds) into a single moment of thought. Scholarly details aside, this says that all realities in time and space crisscross, and all can be made present to the mind at any time.

According to this cosmic vision, Buddha must be present at every level of reality, from the highest (nirvana) to the lowest (hell), the top and bottom of the "ten realms." From that came the Tiantai theory of essential evil. Even Buddha has this evil as an element of his nature. If he did not, he would be unable to manifest himself in the evil paths to help deliver sentient beings trapped there. Christian critics have accused the *Lotus Sutra* of Docetism; Zhiyi's reading here is an important corrective. His reading is firmly committed to an existential analysis of evil. It does not opt for a gnostic escape from the fallen world but instead works hard at accumulating merits in this life for realizing enlightenment in the here and now. All Sinitic Mahayana schools have this innerworldly activistic component.

The cornerstone of Tiantai philosophy is the "harmony of three in one." China was already familiar with *yin-yang* harmony, but that is the harmony of a complementary pair, either member of which, by itself, would be considered a cause of discord. Tiantai "harmonism" depicts perfection: a triadic round (*yuan*, "circle") in which all three members are equally holistic. This formula—three-*qua*-one—is the Chinese counterpart of Christian Trinitarianism, or three in one. However, there is a difference: the Chinese formula has no possibility of a procession (analogous to the Holy Spirit proceeding from the Son and the Father); in Tiantai, there is no "first person in the three"—no apex but only the round. Any one of the three is equally eligible to be alpha or omega.

The framework of the round is provided by Zhiyi's reading of the following verse (as translated by Kumarajiva) in Nagarjuna's *Madhyamika-karika* (*Middle Treatise*):

> What is produced by cause and condition
> Is what I mean by the Empty
> Known also as conditioned coarising.
> It is also what is meant by the Middle Path.

Nagarjuna intends the four descriptions—causation, emptiness, interdependence, and the middle—to be synonymous. Zhiyi, however, reads the passage as noting that (1) reality is (2) empty and (3) real yet (4) neither. This should not be considered a distortion of the original; it is Zhiyi's way of reconfiguring Nagarjuna's four-cornered dialectics. Instead of piling up a pyramid of two truths as the Chengshi masters would do or aiming at an ultimate negation as Jizang would require, Zhiyi rounded everything off.

Everything in the universe is thus seen as simultaneously empty, real, and neither. Any one of the three, taken as a starting point, will be in sequence negated, affirmed, transcended, and returned to itself in a full circle, a perfect round. This became the Tiantai formula of the three truths: three perspectives on the one form of the real (*dharmata*). These three modes of knowledge are correlated with the "three wisdoms of one mind." In order make the picture complete, Zhiyi would insist that a person should always learn to look at reality from all sides: the positive, the negative, and neither. Ingeniously, Zhiyi had turned the four corners of an empty square into three points on an endlessly revolving round.

In so doing, Tiantai liberated the practitioner's mind from all conceptual bias and gave him an exhilarating sense of utter freedom before the nondual. In that vision, every color, every aroma (any object that can be smelled or seen) is, as such, the middle path. Centuries earlier, Zhuangzi had pondered the question of the truth about things and the many theories of things. Are things different? Are they the same? Do I have the truth? Or do you? Do we just think we do? Does thinking makes it so? And how can we ever be sure? In the history of ideas, it would appear that Zhiyi had reformulated and then resolved those questions, giving an answer that is clearly of the Mahayana and Madhyamika. He might have been inspired by Zhuangzi to "forget the pros and cons," but he was, clearly, also more reassuring than Zhuangzi. In relatively recent times, Mou Zongsan's philosophy produced something of a stir by reversing the traditional judgment, considering Tiantai with its perfect round as a more perfect teaching than Huayan. Unknowingly, Mou had revived an old controversy surrounding the advent of these two schools.

Huayan (*Garland, Avatamsaka*) *school.* Tiantai was patronized by the Sui rulers, and so when the Sui dynasty fell, it too fell into disfavor. The new Tang rulers, whose surname was Li, considered themselves the descendants of Laozi and gave Daoism official recognition and support. During the reign (627–650) of Emperor Taizong, the pilgrim Xuanzang (Master Tripitaka) returned from India and was much honored. A new, large-scale translation project began under him, with imperial auspices. Xuanzang had brought back the new Yogacara philosophy of "consciousness only," which for a while was the rage of the capital, until it was superseded by the Huayan school supported by Empress Wu of Zhou (r. 684–705). To appreciate this ideological upheaval, we need to backtrack a little.

In India, Hinayana produced its own scholasticism, called Abhidharma, that reduced reality to a multiplicity of elements. Repudiating that, the Mahayana *Wisdom* sutras deemed all such ontic distinctions empty, and Nagarjuna (in 150 C.E.) systematized this into the philosophy of emptiness. His "middle path" school taught universal emptiness. Around 400, the brothers Asanga and Vasubandhu built on other, later Mahayana sutras and founded Yogacara, the idealist school of Yoga masters who, while accepting the doctrine of universal emptiness, qualified it by declaring that everything is empty because it is of the mind or is known through representations only (*vijnaptimatrata*, "consciousness only"). This school of thought entered China in the early sixth century but was rejected by many because it seemed to have a subjective bias—i.e., it seemed to claim that there are no cognized objects; there is only cognition itself.

Zhiyi of the Tiantai school shared this opinion, so even though he knew Yogacara, he kept to Madhyamika. He held that his "round" would avoid both extremes: subjectivism and objectivism. He then pitted form against mind and subject against object, working out his threefold dialectics to ensure perfect harmony. That was important, for when it is applied to the problem of whether the "pure land," the paradise that devotees of the Buddha Amitabha would seek to be born into, is real or not real, the Tiantai would typically answer yes-no-both-neither. Accepting it as real supports the piety of the Pure Land school. Reducing it to a correlate of the mind entails seeing the realm as pure only to the extent that the mind is pure; this accommodates what would be Vimalakirti's understanding, a view typical of Chan (Zen). The Tiantai school on principle avoids both extremes of faith and wisdom; it observes the middle path and incorporates both. It regards the "pure land" as a real icon of perfection that can induce (or be induced by) a parallel perfection in the mind. Although it considers the mindless chanting of Amitabha's name an expedient for lesser intellects, the Tiantai school has traditionally been supportive of Pure Land piety. That is true also of the Tendai school in Heian Japan. But in the Kamakura period in Japan, a sectarian Pure Land school developed that broke away from Tendai and produced a well-thought-out argument for relying solely on faith. Japan also developed an equally sectarian Zen school that in theory would not practice Pure Land devotion. In China, by contrast, Pure Land devotion and Chan wisdom went hand in hand. (For lack of a systematic critique, the Pure Land school will not be discussed further here.)

By the early Tang, Yogacara was gaining a sizable following. But it was divided by a difference of opinion concerning the status of the "storehouse" consciousness (*alayavijnana*, the deepest stratum of the mind, where all experiences and forms of knowledge are stored). The question was, Is this core psyche tainted or pure? Is it essentially defiled, in which case it cannot reach the fruition of enlightenment? Or is it the pure

Buddha-nature, destined for self-awakening? Tradition has it that Xuanzang, unable to find a definitive answer in China, sought one in India. What he learned at the Nalanda university, from an existing school headed by Dharmapala, was that the storehouse consciousness as such was tainted; the possibility of enlightenment existed in it as seeds, so that this eighth consciousness would not itself subsist as buddhahood. Also, there was—logically—a class of people devoid of this seed of enlightenment; in other words, Buddha-nature was not universal. Chinese had accepted Buddha-nature for a long time, so it is understandable that this new teaching of Xuanzang's would eventually be rejected and even condemned as less than Mahayana.

The thinker largely responsible for that was the Huayan patriarch Fazang (643–712). According to legend, Fazang was a member of Xuanzang's translation project but left after an open disagreement with Xuanzang. A change in political fortunes—the usurpation of Tang rule by Empress Wu, who founded her own Zhou dynasty—saw the rise of Fazang and the Huayan school. For Fazang, the right understanding of mind was found in the *Awakening of Faith in Mahayana*, which postulated a "suchness" mind (a true consciousness) at the heart of all realities. The Huayan formula—that the three realms are of mind only—is taken to mean that everything is derived from this "true mind." As in the classic debate on whether human nature is evil (Xunzi) or good (Mencius), in this case the proponent of good, Huayan, won and the "consciousness only" school lost; the Tiantai doctrine of essential evil also lost. This victory of the "pure mind" would anticipate the later Mencian revival among the Song neo-Confucians.

Huayan philosophy is usually condensed into the formula "all is one; one is all." It is called totalism, and it holds that any one part of the universe is immediately the numinous whole of that universe. To understand how this pan-cosmic-Buddhism came about, it is perhaps instructive to analyze how Huayan had remade the metaphor of the water and the waves that in the *Awakening of Faith* explains how delusion arose from the pure mind. The argument is that the wind of ignorance ruffled up the calm ocean of the suchness mind; thereupon, the waves of phenomenal forms appeared. Although the rising and falling of the waves may create an illusion of samsaric change, in truth the waves, being no less watery, are identical in substance with the suchness of the pure mind. In this way, the Mahayana dictum "samsara is nirvana" is affirmed, but it is also given a new twist. Since in this paradigm, the forms (waves) and the abiding essence (water) are of the same substance, appearance and essence, phenomenon and noumenon, are fundamentally one.

However, this metaphor was from the *Lankavatara sutra*, where it served a slightly different end. There, the wind of phenomenal forms stirs up the waves of the corresponding six senses. The sutra describes a relationship between the (once calm) storehouse consciousness and the other (now active) consciousness; it is not about the consubstantiality of the suchness mind and samsaric reality. The latter came from a reinscribing of that metaphor in the *Awakening of Faith*, which is most likely a Chinese, not an Indian, compilation. Relying on this text, Fazang was able to undermine Xuanzang. Because it separated essence and form, the new teaching from India was called *faxiang* or *dharma-laksana*, while the old teaching (championed by Fazang) was credited with knowing *faxing* or *dharmata*. The former—"consciousness only"—was criticized, metaphorically, for separating a house from the ground that supports it (this is the classic Sanskrit reading of *dharma*). The latter was praised for seeing that fluidity between water and waves alone qualified as the (pure) "mind only" school. That Sinitic understanding of the nature and function of mind led to the following tenets in Huayan philosophy:

1. The mind is pure; everything generated from this suchness mind is likewise pure.
2. The genesis of the world is due to this interaction between ignorance (the wind) and wisdom (the sea). The true and the false interact, somewhat like *yang* and *yin*.
3. The discrete forms of things in the world (waves) may delude the unsuspecting but not the wise. The waves being no less watery, the wise can find in any form (such as Wordsworth's blade of grass) a token of eternity (suchness).
4. Since pure suchness is the substance of the mind, the forms of things and the essence of mind, *dharma-laksana* and *dharmata*, are ultimately one.
5. Since every single wave encapsulates the wetness of the whole ocean, each wave is at the same time all other waves and the sum of all waves.

Thus the Huayan formula: "one is all and all is one." With it, Huayan superseded the Tiantai harmonism based on three-*qua*-one, upholding instead the totalism of all-*qua*-one.

The final vision is hard to put into words. But if we imagine the ocean to be boundless and churning out wave after wave, incessantly, by itself, without even the aid of an external wind of ignorance, so that at any one time each part of this whole is contributing to the regeneration of itself and the whole, that would approximate what Huayan calls *dharmadhatu* causation. At one point, Fazang explained this perfect, sudden, tenfold (instead of threefold) mystery at court. He pointed to a golden lion, saying that every speck of gold contained the whole lion, every hair encapsulated the whole, and every part reflected and captured every other part. It is like the jewels woven into Indra's net: every jewel reflects every other jewel. Totalism, which presumes a perfect fusion and interpenetration of part and whole, is predicated on the idea of the infinite. In an infinite universe, every part is identically infinite. This vision is inspired by a hologramic universe revealed in the rich mythopoeic language of the *Huayan sutra*. A faint echo can be detected in the philosophy of Hui Shi, the first Chinese thinker to become aware of the infinite.

The extravagant Huayan philosophy was patronized by Empress Wu, who ruled as a female Maitreya and who saw her realm as, and turned it into, an incarnation of Indra's net. She had a gigantic Sun Buddha built in the capital and miniature versions enshrined in every provincial state temple, symbolically creating an all-penetrating *dharmadhatu*, a Buddha-kingdom on earth. This vision was too good to be true, too perfect to last; when her dynasty fell, the Huayan school had to adjust itself to an imperfect reality. Just as Tiantai had always supported the Pure Land faith, Huayan had traditionally advocated Chan. The adjustment of Huayan theory to the more practical ends of Chan meditation was later completed by Zongmi (780–841), who was considered a patriarch by both the Huayan school and the Chan school.

The Chan (*Zen*) *school*. The Chan school is often said to be the most Chinese of all schools. In legend, Bodhidharma brought this teaching to China in the early sixth century. A certain Bodhidharma did arrive in Loyang, and the *Record of the Loyang Temples* described him as singing the praises of the spectacular Yongning pagoda. A different picture emerged a hundred years later, when Chan legends described a Bodhidharma who was highly critical of the kind of merit-making temple piety he saw in the southern capital. Instead of trying to decide which image of Bodhidharma is more authentic, we would do well to recognize that Chan was a school which claimed to rely on secret transmission, and so its early history cannot be determined one way or another by pitting esoteric against exoteric records. In other words, the Chan tradition is created by its own legends. These narratives depict Chan primarily as a school that began with monks of the forests and ascetics of the mountains who conflicted with city monks and popular lecturers—a very familiar tale in the history of Buddhism, and a conflict that went all the way back to the post-Asokan Sangha and to the birth of Mahayana itself.

What modern historians can ascertain is that Huike (487–593), a disciple of Bodhidharma (d. 532), was an ascetic of some renown. This lover of the forest life was eclipsed by popular Buddhist lecturers in the city, according to the records, which blame one leading Loyang elder monk in particular. But then the anti-Buddhist persecution of 574–577 in the north effectively undermined this monk's urban base of support. It drove monks to take refuge in the hills, where, in retrospect, they criticized urban temple piety as superficial or shallow. The soul-searching undertaken in response to persecution called for a return to the fundamentals of the faith, and especially to meditation.

This beginning—asceticism—is clear. Huike was a *dhuta* (extreme ascetic) who schooled others, and one of his disciples was Sengzan (d. 606). However, the link between this pair and Daoxin (580–651, now deemed the fourth Chan patriarch) is far from clear and remains tenuous. This is perhaps unsurprising, because with Daoxin a new style emerged. A sizable fellowship now gathered at his East Mountain. It was supported by a powerful local lay patron. Extreme asceticism became outmoded; Daoxin even criticized a lone wayfarer who visited him—when the man left, Daoxin said he was not of Mahayana stock, i.e., not ready to rejoin the world. Daoxin's burgeoning community would rejoin the world, following a set of precepts he had compiled for bodhisattvas. Daoxin also taught a more relaxed form of meditation that would bring peace of mind to a wider and less hardy circle of monks and lay practitioners.

Daoxin and his disciple Hongren (601–674) co-taught at the Twin Peaks, from which their fame spread to the capital. Around 700 C.E., Empress Wu invited Shenxiu (c. 605–706), who had apparently succeeded Hongren, to come to Chang'an. Whether or not the tradition had actually begun with forest monks who rejected the world, it had by then matured into a force which the world had to reckon with—and which, in turn, had to reckon with the world. Considering the politicization of the tradition, it is not surprising that soon afterward, Shenhui (670–762), seeking imperial patronage, began a campaign in which he argued that the real sixth patriarch was not Shenxiu but his own master, Huineng (638–713).

Up to that point, the school did not call itself Chan (meditation), a rather colorless name. It was in fact still looking for a name, and the custom then was to tie a new teaching to a sutra. Huike used the *Srimala sutra*, but Daoxin later drew inspiration from the *Awakening of Faith*. Members of the East Mountain Teaching, realizing that the *Awakening of Faith* was a *sastra*, came up with the next best; they conjured up a lineage of *Lankavatara sutra* masters, this being the sutra that informed the *Awakening of Faith*. Shenhui then perpetuated the myth that Huineng favored the

Diamond Sutra. Actually, none of these labels really indentifies the school's ideological affiliation, because this tradition apparently never used one sutra to legitimize itself.

Shenxiu, who used five *upayas* (expedients)—five formulas for wisdom excerpted freely from five or more sutras—is a good example of the school's typically loose practice. The formulas are the means; wisdom is the end. The intention was to bring meditation out of the cloister and make it accessible to the larger populace. Short, catchy dicta were used to encapsulate the teaching. The *Platform Sutra* describes itself, for example, as teaching no-thought, no-abiding, no-form. A school in Sichuan (Szechwan) would distinguish itself by modifing this slightly; there, even the unlettered could join large but intensive sessions lasting fourteen days over the new year and be tutored, receiving certified enlightenment with *dharma* names (previously given only to monks) as well. Today we might call this pop Zen or instant Zen; it was to bring many into a form of wisdom hitherto reserved for a few. This was accomplished by lectures on *dharma* like the one Huineng gave in the Dafan Temple in Canton, and by massive precept "platforms" like the one Shenhui presided over to raise money for the throne.

The *Platform Sutra* of the sixth patriarch gives the southern school's account of how Huineng composed the better "mind verse," for which he received—in secret, at midnight—a transmission from Hongren. The decline of the northern school, the success of Shenhui's campaign, and later the destruction of major temples (especially in the north during the anti-Buddhist persecution of 845) guaranteed the preeminence of two surviving southern lineages. Regional styles emerged, and an infusion of folk wisdom created a folk Zen tradition, which has rarely been studied.

Much has been written on the depth of Chan wisdom, and most of it is true. If we take a longer view, though, we see that there is nothing in Chan which was not present before. What was new in Chan is its effective and dramatic teaching. Whether one wanted to see one's own nature, achieve sudden enlightenment, or cut off all thought, these formulas for wisdom under the personal guidance of a master could provide liberation. Much as Luther's dictum "By faith alone" condensed a lifetime of profound reflection on the scriptures, so Chan slogans reduced Mahayana wisdom to its essentials. The following four lines are said to capture the essence of Chan:

> No reliance on words.
> Transmission outside the scriptures.
> Point directly at the minds of men.
> See your (Buddha) nature and be enlightened.

This passage is attributed to Bodhidharma or to Huineng, but it actually appeared after Mazu Daoyi (709–788) and may better describe his innovation. In any case, however, the four lines would free many from the letter of Buddhist law and, with their reference to mind and nature, bring the Buddhist discourse back to an important Mencian concern. The fact that by now Buddhism—in decline in India—could offer little further inspiration to China meant that Chan would evolve its own indigenous, secondary scriptures: the colloquial Yulu and the Gong'an that would even more effectively connect the two traditions.

Conclusion

What did Buddhism contribute to Chinese thought? Neo-Confucians in the Song era denied that they owed any debt to Buddhists, but their denial only underscored their indebtedness. The friendships some of them had with Chan monks tell us that, public polemics against Buddhism notwithstanding, personal exchanges continued. Buddhist terminology appears here and there in their writings, but it is often given a reading that is as much nonclassical as non-Buddhist. In fact, the intercultural dialogue had a hybrid nature. Drawing a line between what is Buddhist and what is Confucian is not easy. For example, it is well known that Li Ao (d. c. 844), a disciple of Han Yu (768–824), gave an evaluation to human emotions so negative that it was deemed too Buddhist by the Song masters. In turn, the Song masters were considered crypto-Buddhists by the Qing scholars who sought a return to Han scholarship. So the question remains.

In retrospect, the major innovation of medieval Buddhist thought had to do with probing the structure of the mind and the grandeur of metaphysical reality and considering how one reflected the other. In that sense, Buddhist thought is inherently idealist; it is—as Lovejoy recalled of William James—the mind taking a holiday from the seemingly fragmented realities of a world in chaos and discovering a refuge in monistic pathos. Over the long term, however, the strength of this inner self would return to, and bear on, changing reality for the better. The standard complaint of the Confucians is that the Buddhists neglect social ethics. That is not true—the Buddhists also had a sense of moral behavior and a moral code—but this is not the point. Rather, the point is that, to follow Foucault's last writings on ethics, the Buddhists delve into ethics understood (by Foucault) as the self's relationship to itself. In that internal arena of spiritual exercises seeking self-transformation, there are four concerns: ethical substance, mode of subjection, self-forming activity, and telos. For the Buddhist, the substance is desire;

the mode of control is dispassion; the activities are largely ascetic; the goal is liberation. It is ultimately this art of self-analysis and self-transformation that the Buddhists would leave as a gift to all those who came after.

See also Buddhism: Zen (Chan); Fazang; Hui Shi; Huineng: The Sixth Patriarch; Jizang; Mazu Daoyi; Shenhui; Shengzhao; Xuanzang; Zhiyi.

Bibliography

Chen, Kenneth. *Buddhism in China*. Princeton, N.J.: Princeton University Press, 1964.
Cook, Francis H. *Hua-yen Buddhism: The Jewel Net of Indra*. University Park and London: Pennsylvania State University Press, 1977.
Hakeda, Yoshito. *The Awakening of Faith*. New York: Columbia University Press, 1967.
Hurvitz, Leon. "Chih-i (538–597): An Introduction to the Life and Ideas of a Chinese Monk." *Melanges chinois et bouddhiques*, 12, pp. 1960–1962.
Liebenthal, Walter. *The Treatise of Seng-chao*, 2nd ed. Hong Kong: Hong Kong University Press, 1968.
McRae, John. *The Northern School and the Formation of Early Chan Buddhism*. Honolulu: University of Hawaii Press, 1986.
Robinson, Richard. *Early Madhyamika in India and China*. Madison: University of Wisconsin Press, 1967.
Swanson, Paul. *Foundations of T'ien-t'ai Philosophy*. Berkeley, Calif.: Asian Humanities, 1989.
Takakusu, Junjiro. *The Essentials of Buddhist Philosophy*. Honolulu: University of Hawaii Press, 1947.
Zurcher, Erik. *The Buddhist Conquest of China*, 2 vols. Leiden: Brill, 1959.

Buddhism: Zen (Chan Zong, Ch'an Tsung)

Hsueh-li CHENG

I

Buddhism was founded by Gautama Buddha (563–483 B.C.E.) in India about 2,500 years ago. It became popular inside and outside India, and it developed from early Buddhism into Hinayana (Small Vehicle, also known as Theravada) and then Mahayana (Great Vehicle) Buddhism. Both conservative Hinayana and liberal Mahayana Buddhist teachings were introduced from India to China in the first century C.E. Chinese people have generally preferred Mahayana to Hinayana Buddhism. Since the fifth century, Chinese Buddhist masters have transformed Indian Buddhism to Chinese Buddhism and created many new Buddhist schools in China. Chan, or Zen (the Japanese transcription of the Chinese term), is a new Mahayana Buddhist school founded in China; one cannot find a counterpart in India.

Although Chan Buddhism—hereafter Chan—as established in China is a new school, orthodox Chan Buddhists have claimed that it is the real, original teaching of Buddha. According to Chan tradition, Gautama Buddha was the first patriarch of Chan Buddhism in India. He is said to have gathered his disciples to hear his holiest message at the Mount of the Holy Vulture. But instead of giving a verbal statement, he simply held up a bouquet of flowers before the assemblage. No one understood the meaning of his gesture except the elderly Mahakasyapa, who smiled at Buddha as if he completely realized the master's teaching. At this moment, it is said, Buddha appointed Mahakasyapa as his successor by proclaiming, "I have the most precious treasure, spiritual and transcendental, which this moment I hand over to you, O venerable Mahakasyapa!" In Chan tradition this incident has been taken as the origin of the Chan school.

After Mahakasyapa, Chan Buddhism is said to have been transmitted through twenty-six chief masters. Bodhidharma (d. 532) was regarded as the twenty-eighth patriarch of Chan Buddhism in India. Yet he has been revered as the first patriarch of Chan in China because he came from India to China to bring the following special Chan teaching:

> A special transmission outside the scriptures,
> No dependence upon words and letters.
> Direct pointing at the human mind,
> Seeing into the nature to attain buddhahood.

Bodhidharma came to south China during the reign of Emperor Wu (520–550). He is said to have crossed the Yangtze (Chang) River on a reed, and he taught a new way of meditation. He lived at Shaolinsi monastery, sat facing a wall, and meditated for nine years.

Bodhidharma is well known as a great master of meditation. His way of meditation is called *biguan*, "wall-gazing." Bodhidharma's sitting meditation became a trademark of Chan Buddhism in China, Japan, and Korea.

In the Chan tradition the question why Bodhidharma came from the west is often posed, and Chan writings frequently use Bodhidharma's journey from India to China to point to the essence of Chan. In the *Wumenguan* (*Gateless Gate*) we read: Zhaozhou was once asked by a monk, "What is the meaning of the first patriarch's coming from the west?" Zhaozhou answered, "The tree of life in the front garden." The same question has been answered by saying, "Hand me that support over there" or "No meaning."

The Mahayana doctrine of emptiness is the important message Bodhidharma taught. In his first encounter with Emperor Wu of Liang, he conveyed the idea that all things, including good deeds and meritorious virtues, are empty. The emperor asked Bodhidharma, "Ever since the beginning of my reign I have built so many temples, copied so many sacred books, and supported so many monks and nuns; what do you think my merit might be?" Bodhidharma bluntly answered, "No merit whatsoever, sire!" The emperor then asked, "Why no merit whatever?" Bodhidharma said, "All these are inferior deeds, which would cause their doer to be born in the heavens or on this earth again. They still show the traces of worldliness. They are like shadows, but have no reality. As to true merit, it is full of pure wisdom and is perfect and wonderful. Its essence is emptiness. One cannot obtain such merit by any worldly achievement."

The emperor thereupon asked, "What is the first principle of the holy doctrine?" Bodhidharma replied, "Vast emptiness, nothing holy." "Who is it then that now stands before me?" "I do not know," was the answer.

Chan is not a doctrine, theory, or dogma, but a way of avoiding dogmatic views and assertions. Chan *dharma* is not a body of fixed truths, but rather the stoppage of all thoughts. This is illustrated by the following familiar account.

After his nine-year stay in China, Bodhidharma wished to return to India. He called in all his disciples and said, "The time has now come for me to depart, and I want to see what you know about Chan." The disciple Taofu (Daofu) replied, "As I see it, the truth is above affirmation and negation, for this is the way it moves." Bodhidharma said, "You have got my skin." Next came the nun Zongchi, who said, "As I understand it, the truth is like Ananda's viewing of the Buddha land of Akshobhya: it is seen once and never again." Bodhidharma replied, "You have attained my flesh." Taofu presented his view, saying, "The four great elements are originally empty; the five skandhas have no existence. According to my view, there is no *dharma* to be grasped." Bodhidharma said, "You have got my bones." Finally, Huike bowed respectfully and stood silent. Bodhidharma claimed, "You have attained my marrow." Huike inherited the robe from the master and became the second patriarch of Chinese Chan Buddhism.

II

After Bodhidharma, the best-known Chan patriarch is Huineng (638–713), the sixth patriarch. He was born in Canton. As a child he sold firewood to support his mother. One day, on his way to deliver firewood to a customer's home, he encountered a man reciting the *Diamond sutra*. It is said that as soon as Huineng heard the text, his mind became enlightened. He was advised to study Buddhism with Hongren (601–674), the fifth patriarch, who was then living at Yellow Plum in Qinzhou.

The master asked him where he came from and what he wanted. Huineng replied, "I am a commoner from Xinzhou of Canton. I have traveled far to pay you respect, and ask I for nothing but buddhahood." The master rejected him. "You are a native of Canton, a barbarian? How can you expect to be a buddha?" Huineng answered, "Although there are northern men and southern men, north and south make no difference as to their Buddha-nature. A barbarian is different from Your Holiness physically, but there is no difference in our Buddha-nature." The fifth patriarch was impressed by the boy's statement and let him stay at the monastery. However, Huineng was accepted not as a regular disciple, but merely as a worker to pound rice in the barn.

One day Master Hongren, wanting to appoint a successor, asked his disciples to compose poems that would show their understanding of Buddhist *dharma*. Shenxiu (d. 762), the most outstanding disciple in the monastery, wrote the following poem on the wall in the temple hall:

> The body is the Bodhi tree,
> The mind is like a clear mirror on a stand.
> Take care to wipe it all the time,
> Allow no speck of dust to cling.

Master Hongren praised the poem publicly and ordered all disciples to memorize it. But in private he told Shenxiu to write another one, since the verse expressed Hinayana *vinaya*, gradual moral discipline, rather than the Mahayana philosophy of emptiness. Huineng, an uneducated man, seemed to be the only one who knew what the flaw in Shenxiu's verse was. He composed his own poem and asked a temple boy to write it on the wall:

> There is no Bodhi-tree,
> Nor is there a stand with a bright mirror.
> All things are originally empty,
> Where can the dust alight?

This poem is an excellent expression of Mahayana philosophy; it teaches that all things, including meditation, religious discipline, enlightenment, good and evil, are empty.

Chan is indeed the practice of *sunyata*, emptiness. Publicly, Master Hongren said that Huineng's poem was no good, yet privately he called Huineng to his side and appointed him as his successor. Huineng, following the master's order, fled south to avoid jealousy and persecution by the other disciples.

While Shenxiu's teaching of gradual enlightenment was popular in northern China, Huineng promoted Chan *dharma* as abrupt enlightenment in the south. Eventually, Huineng was recognized as the sixth patriarch, and his teachings became the orthodox message of Chinese Chan Buddhism. The *Sutra Spoken by the Sixth Patriarch from the High Seat of the Treasure of the Law* is the only Chinese Buddhist writing which is called sutra—that is, scripture.

Meditation is the most important practice in Chan. Yet Chan should not be identified with the physical act of sitting in contemplation. This lesson is exemplified by a tale.

Mazu (709–788) was a diligent and gifted monk. He sat constantly in meditation. Master Huairang (677–744) asked, "Virtuous one, why are you sitting in meditation?" Mazu replied, "I want to become a buddha." Thereupon Huairang picked up a tile and rubbed it continuously in front of the hermitage. Mazu asked, "What is the master doing?" The master replied, "I am polishing this to make a mirror." The monk exclaimed, "How can you make a mirror by polishing a tile?" The master responded, "How can you make a buddha by practicing *zuochan* (*zazen* in Japanese), sitting meditation?"

Biguan (wall-gazing), *zuochan*, and other religious disciplines are all fine. But enlightenment depends on inner nature; it is the opening of one's inner mind flower.

III

According to Madhyamika Buddhism, all things are devoid of definite nature, character, and function, and one should not be attached to anything. Now, since all things are equally empty, any incident, for Chan, can be an appropriate occasion for awakening. The meditation hall is not the only place where one becomes enlightened. According to Chan, one can have *wu*—enlightenment—while hearing an inchoate voice, listening to a senseless remark, seeing a plant grow, or experiencing a trivial event such as opening a door, reading a book, or drinking tea. The great Chan masters did not stick to fixed patterns to express themselves; they used every possible means, including unconventional shouting, kicking, and beating, to enlighten sentient beings. Enlightenment can be attained in many different ways, even without formal education or religious discipline.

One needs to be liberated from traditional valuation, and unconventional approaches can be an effective means to free us from enslavement to conventional values, institutions, and establishments. For example, the monk Linji (d. 867) studied under Huangpo (d. 847). For a long time, Linji received no instruction from the master, but he was a diligent disciple and was very eager to learn. One day he asked the master, "What is the great meaning of Buddha's *dharma*?" The master kept silent. Linji asked the same question three times. Three times the master told him not to ask questions, beat him, and drove him out. Linji was disappointed and could not comprehend the master's behavior. He left Huangpo and went to study under Dayu. Linji complained to his new master about his previous experience with Huangpo: "I do not know where my fault was." Instead of comforting him, the master praised Huangpo and stated, "Huangpo was so kind. He exerted himself to the utmost for you. Why do you go on speaking of fault or no fault?" Linji was said to be awakened immediately, and later he became the founder of the Linji Chan school (in Japanese, Rinzai).

An enlightened person is not one who faithfully follows a master and blindly accepts his teachings. Thus a Chan master taught: "When you meet the Buddha, kill the Buddha. When you meet the patriarch, kill the patriarch." Chan Buddhists often reject the deification of Buddha and even deliberately downplay the ontic status of Buddha. For example, a monk asked Master Dongshan (807–869), "Who is the Buddha?" The master replied, "Three pounds of flax." A monk asked Master Yunmen, "What is the Buddha?" Yunmen said, "A stick of dry dung."

Yet for Chan, Buddhist *dharma* is not a teaching of negativity or passivity. Rather, it means being open-minded and creative. Whenever people asked Master Judi questions, such as "Why does the patriarch come from the west?" or "What is the essence of Buddhism?" he would simply raise one finger. His way of teaching is known as one-finger Chan. His actions appear to say nothing but really proclaim an important *dharma* teaching: "Penetrate one place, and at once you penetrate a thousand places, ten thousand places." Clearly apprehend one device, and at once you apprehend a thousand devices, ten thousand devices.

One of Judi's disciples is said to have imitated the master. When someone asked him, "What method does your master usually use to teach people?" he raised one finger. If the boy was asked, "What is it the Chan master teaches?" he would stick up one finger. Judi learned of this and cut off the disciple's finger with a knife. As the disciple ran out screaming, the master called to him. As soon as the disciple looked back, Judi raised one finger. The disciple was said to have been enlightened immediately.

Chan is a dynamic, living, imbued experience. Physically, the raising of the master's finger and the disciple's finger looked alike. Yet spiritually one was living Chan, and the other a dead practice.

Chan enlightenment is an individual activity. It has to be done by the individual personally and creatively. In the strict sense what is created in one's personal experience is not a new thing, but rather an old thing comprehended from a new, unattached perspective. Again, an example serves.

Once a monk came to see Master Ciming (986–1040) for instruction. The master asked, "What is the fundamental principle of Buddhism?" The monk replied:

> No clouds are gathering over the mountain peaks,
> And how serenely the moon is reflected on the waves!

Master Ciming appeared unhappy with the answer and scolded the monk, shouting, "Shame on you! For such an old, seasoned man to have such a view! How can you expect to be delivered from birth and death?" The monk humbly requested more instruction. The master said, "You ask me." The monk repeated the same question, "What is the fundamental principle of Buddhism?" Ciming replied:

> No clouds are gathering over the mountain peaks,
> And how serenely the moon is reflected on the waves!

Immediately, the story goes, the monk was awakened. Objectively, nothing new occurred, but internally the monk's mind was opened.

In Chan, nirvana is samsara, and vice versa. An enlightened person does not live outside this universe, and Chan is a way of seeing the same old things in this world from a new perspective. Enlightenment involves a change of outlook, not obtaining any new, external thing. Master Qingyuan (d. 740) expressed his experience of enlightenment as follows:

> Before I had studied Chan for thirty years, I saw mountains as mountains, and waters as waters. When I arrived at a more intimate knowledge, I came to the point where I saw that mountains are not mountains, and waters are not waters. But now that I have got its very substance I am at rest. For it is just that I see mountains once again as mountains, and waters once again as waters.

Enlightenment is not something remote from us. Master Nanquan taught: "Dao is everyday-mindedness."

IV

Chan is also the practice of the Buddhist teachings of the middle way and the twofold truth. After Buddha attained his own enlightenment, the first sermon he gave was on the doctrine of the middle way. He advised the five mendicants not to live a pessimistic ascetic life or a hedonistic, worldly life, but to go beyond the two extremes. Chan masters followed Buddha's doctrine of the middle way and extended it to cover not only extreme views of life but also all extreme philosophical and religious positions.

For Chan, the middle way is a way to avoid all conceptual and dualistic thinking by eschewing "is" and "is not." People may describe the reality of the universe as something permanent or impermanent, going or coming, internal or external, appearing or disappearing. But Chan masters may dismiss all such concepts as extreme views. Huineng stated:

> The true nature of an event is marked by
> No permanence, no impermanence;
> No arrival, no departure;
> No exterior, no interior;
> No origination, no extinction.

Chan negation, of which this is an example, is a wholesale negation of all limited views. Truth, for Chan, is not a new view but an absence of views. Huineng taught that right is "that which is without any view" and wrong is "that which is with some view."

Teachings and practices in Chan Buddhism can be comprehended by means of the "twofold truth," a convenient term for the standpoints of worldly and ultimate truth. The twofold truth expresses a difference about the way we perceive things. Worldly truth involves emotional and intellectual attachment to what we perceive, while ultimate truth eliminates all attachment. Comprehended in this light, many paradoxical words and actions in Chan do not appear so illogical and absurd as one might at first believe. For example, the sixth patriarch beat Shenhui with a stick and asked, "Do you feel pain?" Shenhui replied, "I am both pained and painless." From the ordinary standpoint, anyone would feel pain when he is beaten. However, if examined from the higher point of view, all things, including pain, are empty. So Shenhui, the brilliant disciple of

Huineng, expressed the twofold truth by stating, "I am both pained and painless."

Chan paradoxes are essentially tactical devices. They are given to awaken people. As long as they can help sentient beings toward enlightenment, these expressions, no matter how absurd they may appear, can be accepted as "true." Truth, for Chan masters, is practical and pragmatic, and its value consists in its effectiveness as a means to achieve nirvana.

Ultimately, no claim to truth should be made, and often no words apply. For example, a monk asked Master Nanquan (748–834), "Please tell me what it is that goes beyond the four alternatives and the hundredfold negations." The master made no answer but went back to his room. A monk asked Master Kueishan (771–853), "When the great action is taking place, how do you determine it?" The master came down from his seat and went to his chamber. For Chan, silence like this is often the best answer to questions about *dharma*.

Yet the masters have spoken out and sometimes written extensively. How could Chan masters be silent and open at the same time? Their seemingly inconsistent behavior may be apprehended by means of the twofold truth. From a transcendental standpoint, one should keep silent. But from the conventional standpoint, discursive expression is a good means to attract sentient beings to the *dharma*. Chan masters have the mind of compassion to help all sentient beings, so they might be silent and open at same time. Many of Chan's paradoxical teachings and practices are really a manifestation of Chan compassion.

V

Indeed, Chan is an outcome of cultural communication between India and China. In many ways it reflects the Chinese way of thinking and feeling. The great Chan masters were often well versed in both Indian and Chinese culture. They selected from Mahayana, Confucian, and Daoist (Taoist) thought, and beautifully blended the parts together to create a new religious-philosophical ethos that is quite original.

Like many other Chan writings, Bodhidharma's poem, his special message from India to the Chinese people, is really a product of the Chinese mind rather than the Indian mind. In many ways its philosophy is more like Chinese Confucian thought than Indian Mahayana. Its key philosophical term is *xing* ("nature," a thing's own nature or self-nature). To know the *dharma* and hence to become a buddha is to see into one's own nature.

According to Indian Mahayana Buddhism, all things are empty or devoid of their own nature or self-nature. The Indian doctrine of emptiness is *wuxing* (no nature, without nature, elimination of nature). Seeing into nature is the very idea the Indian Mahayana masters tried to repudiate. According to them, all things are causally conditioned and hence nothing has its own nature. Opposed to this view, Chan teaches that to become a buddha one should see into nature. This is something new and quite different from the message of Indian Buddhist scriptures. Therefore, Chan is said to be a "special transmission outside the scriptures." If one interprets traditional Indian Buddhist writings literally, one would never obtain enlightenment, Chan advises. So it counsels: "no dependence on words and letters."

Chan's doctrine of seeing into nature is actually a practical application of Chinese Confucian philosophy. Since ancient times, the *xing* has been an important issue in Chinese thought. Confucius and Mencius pondered the problem and are known for their thesis that human nature is "good." For them, all human beings are alike in nature and become different owing to their external environment. In its original state, human nature is sound and innocent. Each person has a mind (*xin*) that cannot bear to see the suffering of others.

In Confucianism, *xin* (mind) is *xing*, and vice versa. This nature or mind is not an ontological substance such as the Greek *substratum*, Hindu *atman*, or Theravada *svabhava*, but a quality or ability inherent in human beings. Axiologically, it is a value or qualitative attribute that makes human beings moral and valuable. Without this nature or mind, a person would be merely a beast. With this nature, a person can become a sage, since the mind is the spring of all virtues.

Following this vein of thought, Chan masters skillfully absorbed the Confucian sense of mind, nature, and sagehood into Buddhist *dharma*. The outcome of this skillful measure (*fangbian, upaya*) is the teaching, "Direct pointing at the human mind; seeing into the nature to attain buddhahood." The same teaching is stated in the opening passage of Huineng's *Platform Sutra of the Sixth Patriarch*: "Virtuous ones! The Bodhi-nature is originally pure. To make use of this mind alone, one can directly become a buddha." In this respect, the human mind, nature, and the goal of spiritual discipline are similar in Confucianism and Chan Buddhism. The attainment of buddhahood in Chan is an opening of the human mind. In Mencius's words, it is "all already complete in oneself" and is "not far to seek, but right by oneself." Therefore, an abrupt enlightenment is possible.

VI

There was an extensive religious persecution against Buddhism in 845 C.E. After this anti-Buddhist movement, most Buddhist schools in China disappeared, but Chan continued to flourish. During the Song and Ming dynasties it influenced Confucianism and inspired Confucian scholars to reexamine traditional Confucian philosophy and develop neo-Confucianism, which has had a strong impact on intellectual, social, and political life in China, Korea, and Japan.

Chan has produced a wealth of distinguished literature. Collections concerning the words and deeds of Chan masters and practitioners are often known as collections of *gong'an* (in Japanese, *koan*). They are new religious writings in Buddhism. The brief Chan *gong'an* is used not just for comprehending Buddhist *dharma* but also as a means of achieving enlightenment. For Chan the Buddhist scriptures are not paramount, yet they may provide an occasion for opening the mind's flower. The way to express enlightenment is not just to write poems or *koan*. Nonverbal actions such as painting, arranging flowers, and drinking tea—and even the martial arts—can also be forms for developing spiritual life and conveying religious experience. In such modes Chan has exercised a lasting influence on Chinese cultural life.

During the Kamakura period (1185–1336) Chan was introduced from China to Japan. Since then, the Japanese have been enriched culturally and artistically by Chan Buddhism. It would be difficult to have a proper understanding of the east Asian mind and east Asian culture without knowing Chan.

See also Buddhism in China; Huineng: The Sixth Patriarch; Mazu Daoyi; Philosophy of Human Nature; *Xin*; *Xing*.

Bibliography

Abe, Masao. *Zen and Western Thought*. Honolulu: University of Hawaii Press, 1985.

Cheng, Hsueh-li. *Empty Logic: Madhyamika Buddhism from Chinese Sources*. Delhi, India: Motilal Banarsidass, 1991.

———. *Exploring Zen*. New York: Peter Lang, 1996.

Cleary, Thomas, and J. C. Cleary. *The Blue Cliff Record*, 3 vols. Boulder, Colo., and London: Shambhala, 1977.

Cua, A. S. "Uses of Dialogues and Moral Understanding." *Journal of Chinese Philosophy*, 2(2), 1975, pp. 131–148.

Dumoulin, Heinrich. *Zen Buddhism: A History*, Vol. 1, *India and China*. New York: Macmillan, 1988.

———. *Zen Buddhism: A History*, Vol. 2, *Japan*. New York: Macmillan, 1990.

Kasulis, T. P. *Zen Action/Zen Person*, Honolulu: University of Hawaii Press, 1981.

McRae, John R. *The Northern School and the Formation of Early Chan Buddhism*. Honolulu: University of Hawaii Press, 1986.

Sekida, Katsuki. *Two Zen Classics: Mumonkan and Hekigaroku*. New York: Weatherhill, 1977.

Suzuki, D. T. *Essays in Zen Buddhism*. New York: Grove, 1949.

———. *Manual of Zen Buddhism*. New York: Grove, 1978.

———. *Zen and Japanese Culture*. Princeton, N.J.: Princeton University Press, 1973.

———. *Zen Buddhism*. Garden City, N.Y.: Doubleday, 1956.

Yampolsky, Philip B., trans. *The Platform Sutra of the Sixth Patriarch*. New York: Columbia University Press, 1967.

Yinshun (Shi Yinshun). *Zhongguo chanzong shi* (History of Chinese Chan Buddhism). Taipei: Chengwen, 1988.

Zhang, Mantao, ed. *Chanzong dianji yanjiu* (Studies in Chan Documents). Taipei: Dacheng wenhua, 1977.

中國哲學

C

Calligraphy

Jiuan HENG

To understand the significance of Chinese calligraphy, think of how a medium that is used by every educated Chinese to formulate and communicate ideas, feelings, and values might itself be used to embody these expressions of the mind-heart. Insofar as calligraphy integrates the content and form of thought, bridging the gap between saying and showing, it may be seen as an embodied philosophy. The aesthetic values that theorists have emphasized in the practice of calligraphy have changed from period to period, reflecting changing philosophical agendas. Nevertheless, certain features of the practice and assumptions about it have remained constant.

Fundamental Aesthetics of Calligraphy

Calligraphy is the art of movement captured in script, not merely a means of transcribing characters. The ninth-century theorist Zhang Huaiguan, in his systematic approach to calligraphy, revived a distinction between *zi*, the character, and *shu*, the gesture of writing (*Zhongguo meixueshi* 1983, 259). To have made this distinction is to have separated, in theory, the utilitarian and the aesthetic functions of writing. In viewing calligraphy aesthetically, as art, the reader finds meaning in the act of writing itself. In reading it functionally, as one might read a newspaper, one regards the inscription as a means of grasping thoughts expressed in words. The meaning of the thoughts is not affected by whether they are written, recited, or "composed in the head," because meaning resides in the grasp of the language in which the thought is expressed. Zhang (*Zhongguo meixueshi*, 261) goes so far as to pronounce that the connoisseur of calligraphy beholds only its vivacity of spirit (*shen cai*) and does not see the shapes of its characters (*zi xing*).

Yet Chinese characters are the building blocks of the art of calligraphy. They determine the composition—the strokes, the sequence, the direction of reading and writing—and, of course, contribute to the literal meaning of the text. The aesthetic dimension builds on these semiotic markers of the Chinese character system, even if it is possible to overlook semantics. Looking for meaning in the gesture of writing may be likened to listening for tone in a telephone conversation: it gives us immediate clues to the other party's state of being, regardless of what he affirms or denies, supplying a subtext to and a context for the explicit text. Somehow, the act of expressing ourselves in words inevitably reveals even as we conceal ourselves, and conceals even as we reveal. The body, by contrast, is guileless. Zhang's defense of calligraphy hinges on the notion that the gesture of writing can accomplish directly what a sign system does indirectly:

> Literary composition needs several characters to complete the meaning, whereas calligraphy can reveal the mind with only one character. This is certainly the ultimate attainment of economy and simplicity. (Kao 1991, 75)

Under the aesthetic gaze, gesture becomes the grammar of the body and the mind simultaneously, insofar as the movement of the calligrapher's mind is connected at once to the movement of his energy (*qi*) and his brush. The connection between the state of mind of the calligrapher and the calligraphy is kinetic. The brush and its traces are manifestations of the body and its energy.

Calligraphy is the supreme art of variation. The four basic script styles developed sequentially, and all of them remain in use today: the seal scripts (*da zhuan* and *xiao zhuan*) of the Shang, Zhou, and Qin periods (c. sixteenth century to 206 B.C.E.); the clerical script (*li shu*) of the Han (206 B.C.E. to 220 C.E.); a running script (*xing shu*) of the fourth century; and the final version of the standard script (*kai shu*) in the Tang (618–907). No other script style has been invented or accepted since. The calligrapher must accept as given the form of the characters and the script style in which he will compose; sometimes the text of his composition is not his own. The calligrapher's contribution lies in the nuances of style that he introduces to the writing—the way he inflects his strokes, the subtleties of spacing between strokes and characters, the variations in the size and appearance of each stroke and character. Sun Guoting, the Tang author of the *Treatise on Calligraphy* (*Shu pu*), notes: "Within a single stroke, changes result from alternately raising and lowering the tip; inside a single dot, movement rebounds at the very end of the brush" (Chang and Frankel 1995, 4). He raises variation to the level of philosophy: calligraphy is an attempt to model the process of transformation that is fundamental to Chinese ontology, integrating movement within rest and rest within movement.

Variation introduces a dimension of ritual to the art: because of the limits prescribed by the form, every variation is identifiable and thereby definitive of the individual calligrapher. The practice of "copying" the texts of celebrated calligraphers creates opportunities for a later calligrapher to recall his influences, display his depth of learning and his inventiveness, test his versatility, and continue a tradition. The *Thousand-Character Essay*, for instance, transcribed by calligraphers for centuries, becomes a rich intertext in which calligraphers refer to one another while expanding the possibilities of the art.

For writing to be adequate to the expression of mind and body, the materials of writing had to evolve into a performance medium. It is no accident that brush and paper replaced the earlier instruments of the scribe—tortoiseshell, bamboo slips, and silk. On these other surfaces, writing had to be incised or carved, and even when written with the brush it served ritual and monumental functions. The brush, when it had improved to the point where it could be pliable and still hold most of the ink in reserve, could modulate strokes and respond to every movement of the calligrapher's hand. The invention of an absorbent paper, which registers each ink trace as movement in time, provided the final catalyst. Calligraphy became an art for personal expression. Yang Xiong (53–18 B.C.E.) described calligraphy as the image of the heart-mind (*Zhongguo meixueshi*, 118).

The sensitivity of the medium enabled the calligrapher to literally compose on paper, to link characters in a running script, to improvise the placement of his characters as the flow of writing and space demanded. Writing could then become a performance art that transcended the ephemeral moment of the performance, as each reader could reenact, by following the order of writing, the calligrapher's movements.

Writing Inspired by Forces of Nature

The emphasis on movement can be traced to one of the earliest theoretical texts on calligraphy: *Bi zhen tu* (*Strategic Plan of Battle for the Brush*), by Madam Wei (272–349). Writing, she says, comes from the body: each stroke must be executed with the full strength of the body. She then models the appreciation of writing on the body, equating strength of the brush with "having bone" and weakness of the brush—that is, ink without structure—with "having much flesh." Calligraphers who have an excess of "bone" over "flesh" are "sinewy" writers. Ideally, "bone" and "flesh" should be balanced: she calls a calligrapher who achieves this "sagely." This balance forms the basis of calligraphy—a point that constitutes the background of her contribution to the theory of calligraphy. She relates each of the seven fundamental calligraphic strokes to an image of dynamism in nature:

> [The horizontal stroke is] Like a cloud formation stretching a thousand li; indistinct, but not formless.
> [The dot is] Like a stone falling from a high peak, bouncing and crashing, about to shatter.
> [The left diagonal stroke is] The tusk of an elephant or rhinoceros thrust into and broken by the ground.
> [The right diagonal hook is] Fired from a three thousand pound crossbow.
> [The vertical stroke is] A weathered vine, ten thousand years old.
> [The right diagonal stroke is like] Crashing waves or rolling thunder.
> [The angular stroke is like] The sinews and joints of a mighty bow. (Barnhart 1964, 16)

By this period, dots and strokes were not mere dabs on paper but had become models of the vital forces in nature that calligraphers wanted to enact.

Madam Wei's essay could not, by itself, have maneuvered calligraphy into an arena of creative forces, but she probably modulated the expressive possibilities of each stroke and reinforced the idea that the combination of strokes had to be a matter of strategy, like a battle plan, for maximum efficacy. A difference between calligraphy (*shu*) and characters (*zi*) is that while the calligrapher may vary the order of strokes of his characters to maximize his kinesthetic advantage, so that the stroke order of the character in each script type (*shu ti*) may vary, the stroke order of a character (*zi*) is prescribed.

In the Song dynasty, the poet and calligrapher Su Shi extended the critical vocabulary of calligraphy based on human physiology to include blood, *shen* (spirit), and *qi* (breath or physical energy)—the dynamic energy that distinguishes a living body from a corpse (*Zhongguo meixueshi*, 373).

As the notion took hold that calligraphy manifests the heart-mind, movement acquired a psychological significance. Sun Guoting writes about the need to match technical mastery with mastery of the heart-mind:

> Force combined with speed is the key to superb beauty, and deliberate lingering leads to perfect appreciation and comprehension. If you proceed from lingering to speed, you will reach a world of consummate beauty; but if you get stuck lingering, you will miss the ultimate perfection. Being able to move without haste—this may be called true lingering; but lingering for the sake of delay—how can this be considered appreciative understanding? Unless the mind is at ease and the hand skilled, it is difficult to achieve both speed and lingering. (Chang and Frankel, 13)

Moreover, calligraphy discloses the character of the man through style, essentially his manner of movement:

> If a person is straight, the writing will be rigid and lacking in vigorous beauty; if a person is hard and ruthless, it will be stubbornly unsubmissive and lacking in suppleness; those who are overly careful will have the defect of being unrelaxed; those who are careless and superficial will be lacking in exactitude; those who are genial and gentle will suffer from softness; those who are impetuous will be excessively hasty; those who hesitate will get stuck; those who are clumsy will limp and lack sharpness; those who are trivial and petty will have the style of vulgar clerks. (Chang and Frankel, 13)

Calligraphy as a Means of Cultivating the Self: The Discipline of Brushwork

In an aesthetics of manifestation, the inner reveals itself, unintentionally and ineluctably, on the surface, and writing is read as a map of the psyche. The hermeneutics of self-manifestation, superimposed on the inherently demanding art of calligraphy, gave its technical demands an ethical dimension. The self could be cultivated through the discipline of art. For instance, while the vertically held brush is ideally poised to move in any direction, thus allowing the greatest spontaneity of response, it also projects an effect of serenity, of the controlled power of the brushwork. These are not just aesthetic values but qualities that a Confucian gentleman should cultivate. The vertical brush holds most of its ink in reserve, symbolizing the moral strength and energy that the gentleman harbors within. Or again, while writing a stroke by beginning in the opposite direction increases the dynamic force of the stroke, it also produces an effect of containment.

Sun links the cycle of training in calligraphy to the cycle of self-cultivation. It is the process of exposing oneself to extremes of experience that permits self-mastery, spontaneously doing what is right:

> When you first learn to structure your writing, seek only the level and straight. After the level and straight, seek the daring and precipitous, but after that, return to the level and straight. In the beginning, you do not go far enough, halfway through, you overstep the bounds. When you have achieved thorough mastery, both man and calligraphy would have matured. Confucius said, "At fifty, I knew the decree, at seventy, I followed my heart." Only when you have encountered the level and the precipitous will you be able to act without deliberation and without error. (adapted from Chang and Frankel, 12)

The Tang dynasty saw a consolidation of technical methods as well as the establishment of a state-sponsored orthodox tradition, derived from two calligraphers of the Six Dynasties, Wang Xizhi and his son Xianzhi. The *Eight Laws of Yong*, an analysis of the brushstrokes in the character *yong*, were first formulated at that time, to instruct the student in the dynamics of each stroke. Subsequently, variations on these eight amounted to as many as seventy-two laws. Essentially based on the standard script, Tang calligraphy sought an objective, ideal standard of beauty. Consider the long list of criteria found in an anonymous essay on Ouyang Xun's methods:

> Every brushstroke must be centred. . . . Investigate the momentum of the character: it should be balanced on four sides, complete in eight directions. Lengths should be proportionate, thickness evenly distributed, the disposition level, the spacing correct. . . . Leaning or standing upright like a gentleman, the upper half sits comfortably, while the bottom half supports it. (Wang et al. 1708, *chuan* 3: 3b–4a, translation adapted from Harrist and Fong 1999, 45)

The conviction that man can be shaped in the image of art—that aesthetics could be put to the service of ethics—resulted in a proliferation of standards, methods, and laws in calligraphy. Once instituted, the prescriptions made for a thoroughly absorbing practice, a veritable training ground for patience and a cathartic outlet for obsession. Ouyang Xiu, the Song statesman and poet, explains:

> Whenever I am free I practise my calligraphy. It is not that I seek to excel at this art, it's simply better than exerting myself at other activities. Those who do not need to lodge their minds in any material thing are "sages." Those who lodge their minds in things that improve them are superior men. But those who lodge their minds in things that assail their nature and convulse their emotions, doing injury to them, are stupid and confused men. To practise calligraphy does require exertion but at least it does not injure one's nature and emotions. If you would attain the joy found in quietude, there is only this. (*Zhongguo meixueshi*, 334, as translated by Egan)

From Self-Cultivation to Self-Expression: The Emergence of Spontaneity

Although calligraphers of the Tang and the Song shared a vision of calligraphy as a means of self-cultivation, Song calligraphers rejected the preoccupation of their Tang counterparts with rigor, symmetry, and perfect balance in favor of spontaneous, natural expression. These qualities could be better explored through the running and cursive scripts than the regular script. Reversing the Tang tenet of training the mind through calligraphy, the Song calligraphers emphasized the importance of establishing one's intent (*yi*). The notion of intent is that of an orientation of the heart-mind, the incipient energy that has yet to crystallize into an emotion, a thought, an idea, or a form. It goes to the core of the making of a self, for once we train our intent in a particular direction, our lives gain a focus; opportunities and challenges follow. Mi Fu writes of how, when his intent (*yi*) is abundant, he naturally follows it, releasing his brush in ink play. Su Shi, in an enthusiastic, if not uncharacteristic, moment, pronounced that if one could penetrate intent, one could discard learning. He took as his guides the "primordial lack of models" and "naturalness and spontaneity" rather than orthodox calligraphic models. What makes these aesthetic ideals particularly interesting is that they stem from a philosophical-religious syncretism. Note, for instance, the Buddhist logic behind the rejection of models in this fragment: "Calligraphy relies on form for its excellence; when there is form, there will be irregularities. It is better to arrive at emptiness, to rejoice in the moment" (*Zhongguo meixueshi*, 365).

In fact, the Song calligraphers did not reject models as such; they rejected only a strict fidelity to models that hampered the development of an individual style. Mi Fu forged a highly individualistic style, after undertaking a highly systematic study of models ranging from Yan Zhenqing of the Tang to bronze inscriptions. Huang Tingjian modeled his work on the two Wangs of the Sui dynasty—a very orthodox choice, but he used it lightly. According to Wen Fong (1984, 83), he "borrowed a single element from [Wang Xizhi's] *Burying a Crane*—two horizontal strokes, the roof radical from the character *qin*—as the hallmark of his personal style."

Influence of Calligraphy on Painting

The idea of establishing one's intent in calligraphy paved the way for the final realization, in the Yuan dynasty, of the "three perfections"—painting, calligraphy, and poetry—within the same work. This concept freed painting from its representational function and from conformity to an objective measure of truth; and it transformed painting into an extension of calligraphy. A literati painting commonly goes by the term *xie yi*: writing intent.

The Yuan calligrapher, painter, and statesman Zhao Mengfu pioneered a revolutionary type of painting, systematically grafting calligraphic brushwork onto pictorial forms. He codified his program for integrating painting and calligraphy in a colophon to his *Elegant Rocks and Sparse Trees*:

> Rocks as flying white, trees as seal script;
> When painting bamboo, one should master the spreading-eight method.
> Those who understand this principle thoroughly
> Will recognize that calligraphy and painting have always been one. (Fong 1992, 440)

Painters before the Yuan painters chose their brushwork to suit the subject; Yuan painters, by contrast, adapted the subject to the brushwork they had chosen. The brushwork prototype of a literati painting retains its integrity, uncompromised by painterly effects. This meant that a painting could be read, and reading the symbolic values of calligraphic brushstrokes into painting transformed painting into an art of personal expression, a declaration of the self.

See also Aesthetics; Philosophy of Art.

Bibliography

Barnhart, Richard. "Wei Fu-jen's *Bi zhen tu* and Early Texts on Calligraphy." *Archives of the Chinese Art Society of America*, 18, 1964, pp. 13–25.

Cahill, James. *Hills beyond a River*. New York: Weatherhill, 1976.

Chang, Ch'ung-ho, and Hans H. Frankel, eds. *Two Chinese Treatises on Calligraphy: Treatise on Calligraphy (Shu pu) and Sequel to the "Treatise on Calligraphy" (Xu shu pu)*. New Haven, Conn., and London: Yale University Press, 1995.

Fong, Wen. *Beyond Representation: Chinese Painting and Calligraphy, Eighth–Fourteenth Century*. New Haven, Conn.: Yale University Press, 1992.

———. *Images of the Mind: Selections from the Edward L. Elliot Family and John B. Elliot Collections of Chinese Calligraphy and Painting at the Art Museum, Princeton University*. Princeton, N.J.: Princeton University Press, 1984.

Harrist, Robert E., and Fong Wen, eds. *The Embodied Image*. Princeton, N.J.: Princeton University Art Museum, Princeton University, in association with Abrams, 1999.

Hay, John. "The Body as a Microcosmic Source of Macrocosmic Values in Calligraphy." In *Theories of the Arts in China*, ed. Susan Bush and Christian Murck. Princeton, N.J.: Princeton University Press, 1983.

Kao, Yu-kung. "Chinese Lyric Aesthetics." In *Words and Images: Chinese Poetry, Calligraphy, and Painting*, ed. Alfreda Murck and Wen Fong. New York and Princeton, N.J.: Metropolitan Museum of Art and Princeton University Press, 1991, pp. 47–90.

Ledderose, Lothar. *Mi Fu and the Classical Tradition of Chinese Calligraphy*. Princeton, N.J.: Princeton University Press, 1979.

Stanley-Baker, Joan. "The Development of Brush-Modes in Sung and Yüan." *Artibus Asiae*, 39(1), 1977, pp. 13–59.

Sturman, Peter. *Mi Fu: Style and the Art of Calligraphy in Northern Song China*. New Haven, Conn., and London: Yale University Press, 1997.

Wang, Yuanqi, et al., eds. *Peiwenzhai shuhua pu*. Beijing, 1708.

Zhongguo meixueshi. Taipei: Guangmei shuju, 1983.

Chen Daqi (Ch'en Ta-ch'i)

Vincent SHEN

Chen Daqi (1887–1983) is a very significant figure among contemporary Chinese Confucians, because his logical and ethical approaches to Confucianism differ from the transcendental and ontological approaches of Mou Zongsan (Mou Tsung-san) and Tang Junyi (T'ang Chün-i). As a scholar of psychology and logic, Chen conducted a serious and profound program of research in basic Confucian concepts, ethical argumentation, and virtue ethics. He can be considered a pathfinder in these domains: "The pioneering study of the conceptual aspects of Confucian ethics has been Chen Daqi's *Kongzi xueshuo* [*Doctrines of Confucius*]" (Cua 1998).

From Logic to Confucianism

Chen started his study of psychology and logic in the early twentieth century, and then—when he began to teach at Beijing University in 1914—concentrated on logical inquiries. With his training in logic, he extended his research first to Indian logic and next to Chinese logic. After he moved to Taiwan in 1948 with the government of the Republic of China, he turned to Chinese philosophy—perhaps motivated by the cultural crisis that had been caused by the communists' takeover of mainland China. He began to conduct research in the logical and conceptual aspects of Confucianism, beginning with Xunzi, tracing the sources back to Mencius and finally to Confucius, going deeper and deeper into Confucian ethics. Thus his academic career moved from psychology to comparative logic to classical Confucianism.

Among Chen Daqi's works, those in classical Confucianism are probably the most interesting, though much can, of course, be said for his studies in comparative logic. He was the first Chinese scholar to introduce western formal logic for the purpose of expounding the method of debate and the argumentative character of Indian logic. Also, he identified two weaknesses of Indian logic. First, because it is an argumentative logic in which winning a debate is the only point of argumentation, its truth becomes situational and lacks absolute necessity. Second, it depends to some extent on psychology rather than on formal structure.

Chen's Confucian studies moved from Xunzi, the classical analytic, argumentative Confucian; to Mencius, an argumentative yet ethical thinker; to Confucius himself, a purely ethical thinker. His philosophy could therefore be characterized as founded on an analytical, conceptual approach to virtue ethics, which is quite different from the transcendental approach to Confucianism represented by Mou Zongsan and Tang Junyi, who may have overemphasized the transcendental structure and dynamism of human subjectivity.

Chen Daqi's Confucian studies focus on the philosophical significance of Confucius, Mencius, and Xunzi, through logical and conceptual analysis of the notions and ideas implicit in their philosophical texts. His earlier study of Xunzi's ethical, conceptual structure and argumentation culminates in an explication of Confucius's ethics, supplemented by his critical evaluation of Mencius's thought. His approach may be described as a version of the realist approach to Confucian logic, theory of human nature, and ethics.

This essay will concentrate only on Chen's creative interpretations of classical Confucianism: (1) his studies on Xunzi's logic, (2) his conceptual studies of Confucian ethics, (3) his comparison of Xunzi's and Mencius's theories of human nature, and (4) his status as a pioneer of virtue ethics.

Studies on Xunzi's Logic

Chen Daqi's Confucian studies begin with research on Xunzi's logic, or *mingxue*. With his psychological and logical background, he discusses Xunzi's doctrine of human nature based on the human capacity to discern right and wrong. For him, Xunzi's doctrine of human nature belongs to a kind of intellectualism that emphasizes a psychological ability, *bian*—"discernment" or "discriminating." This ability is displayed in what may be called discerning discourse or argumentation. The objective of argumentation is to make a decision about right and wrong, for which criteria must first be set up. According to Chen's interpretation, Xunzi's concept of *dao* represents the ultimate criterion or standard of right or wrong; it includes *lei* (kind, class), *tong* (unity, coherence), and *fen* (division, distinction) as subcriteria. In order to distinguish right from wrong, one has to keep one's mind in a state of "great and pure enlightenment" (*da qing ming*), that is, one's mind must be "empty, united, and still" (*xu yi er jing*). Negatively, one must discard all obscuring factors (*jie bi*); positively, one must always be alert to another, easily neglected aspect of an issue. According to Chen, "name" (*ming*) means almost the same as the concept in western philosophy, and "discernment" seems to be functionally equivalent to *logos*, reason, or reasoning.

To analyze Xunzi, Chen Daqi applies the distinction between "intension" and "extension" of terms in western formal logic. With regard to intension, he finds in Xunzi a distinction between names for superiority-inferiority and names for identity-difference. According to Chen, these represent, respectively, concepts indicating values and concepts indicating facts—the former being higher than the latter. With regard to extension, Xunzi distinguishes between generic names (*gongming*) and specific names (*bieming*); according to Chen, these can be analyzed by the relations of inclusion or "belonging" between classes and subclasses. Finally, concerning reasoning, for Xunzi, *dao* is the ultimate criterion of right and wrong, and *dao* can be sorted into different classes (*lei*); therefore *lei* can be seen as the basis of all deductive and inductive reasoning.

Conceptual Studies of Confucian Ethics

Chen Daqi's studies of Confucius's thought led him to ethics. He differs from Mou Zongsan, a contemporary neo-Confucian who, in developing a "moral metaphysics" of Confucianism, neglected the importance of praxis in Confucian ethics. Chen takes ethics as the core of Confucius's thought—which he sees not as a theoretical philosophy but rather as a practical philosophy. When applied to education, say, it becomes an educational philosophy; when applied to politics, it becomes a political philosophy.

Other contemporary interpreters understand *ren* (humanness, goodness) and *yi* (rightness, appropriateness) as the ultimate values in Confucianism. Chen Daqi, by contrast, assumes that *an* (calm happiness) is Confucius's ultimate value, whereas *ren* and *yi* are merely two instrumental or secondary values contributing to calm happiness. But he does think that *ren* and *yi* have a necessary relation to *an*, to the extent that when *ren* and *yi* are realized, *an* will be attained as a consequence.

Also, Chen takes the position that *ren* and *yi* should be united. *Ren* can be seen as both a collective and an individual concept. As a collective concept, it means the summation of all virtues; as an individual concept, it means love—love of self and love of others, establishing oneself and establishing others, achieving oneself and achieving others. *Ren* as love, when applied to one's parents, becomes "filiality"; when applied to brethren, it means *di*, "brotherhood"; when applied to executing obligations, it means loyalty; when applied to keeping one's promises, it means trustworthiness.

Yi can be seen as having a positive aspect and a negative aspect. Negatively, it means not being fixated on one point of view or not being obstinate. Positively, it means using one thing properly—being appropriate or, better, "hitting the mark."

According to Chen Daqi, *ren* and *yi* are best when united because *ren* means love, yet love without appropriateness could result in silly acts. And appropriateness comes from *yi*; *yi* should hit the mark, but to hit the mark without satisfying ethical conditions would invite evildoing—here, the condition comes from *ren*. *Yi* when united with *ren* becomes true *yi*, and *ren* when united with *yi* becomes true *ren*. Chen believes that Confucius, in positing calm happiness as the ultimate aim of human life, takes *ren* and *yi*—united—as the most necessary means toward this end.

Comparing Xunzi's and Mencius's Doctrines of Human Nature

A dominant traditional interpretation assumes that Mencius's and Xunzi's theories of human nature are contradictory, that the one supposed human nature to be innately good and the other supposed it to be innately evil. Chen Daqi, through conceptual and textual analysis, argued that they are not contradictory, and indeed that they are complementary.

Conceptually, he pointed out that these two thinkers use the term "human nature" (*xing*) identically with regard to name but differently with regard to reference. Mencius uses *xing* to refer to three levels of human nature. On the lowest level we find four beginnings of goodness: the senses of (1) sympathy, (2) yielding to or respecting others, (3) discerning right and wrong, and (4) shame about doing wrong. On the middle level these four senses develop into four beginnings: *ren, yi, li* (ritual propriety), and *zhi* (wisdom). On the highest level we find the virtues of *ren, yi, li*, and *zhi* as a fulfillment of those four beginnings. Mencius never took desire as an element of *xing*.

Xunzi, on the other hand, examines human psychological capacity in terms of three functions: *xing* (human nature), *zhi* (knowledge), and *neng* (abilities). He never understands the sense of yielding to or respecting others as belonging to *xing*. On the contrary, he presumes that competition or struggle is a necessary evil consequent to the human desire for "self-profit." Xunzi sees the sense of right and wrong as belonging to the capacity of knowing, not to human nature. As for *yi* and *li*, they have to do with deliberate efforts of sages and are by no means innate. Also, Xunzi considers desire an important constituent of human nature.

In short, since Mencius sees four good beginnings as belonging to human nature whereas Xunzi takes desire—the beginning of evil—to be part of human nature, their references for *xing* differ. Therefore, their views on human nature should not be considered contradictory. On the other hand, both take *ren, yi, li*, and *zhi* as good and sensuous desire as evil, so their theories of human nature are different merely in name, not in logic.

Further, Mencius and Xunzi can be seen as complementary in at least two ways. First, the a priori goodness of human nature needs human effort a posteriori, and human perfectibility in the process of education and culture presupposes some sort of good ability in human nature. Second, according to their effective consequences, Mencius's theory of the goodness of human nature can encourage those who feel frustrated and abandoned, and Xunzi's theory of human nature as evil can be a calming, clarifying remedy for those who are self-complacent and self-limiting—helping them overcome laziness and practice self-cultivation.

Chen as a Pioneer of Virtue Ethics

Chen Daqi can be described as a pioneer in interpreting Confucian ethics according to virtue ethics. In western philosophy, though the movement began as early as the 1960s, it was not until the 1980s that the ethics of virtue became a serious contender with the ethics of obligation and Aristotelian ethics became a serious rival to Kantian ethics. Contemporary neo-Confucians such as Mou Zongsan and his followers use Kant's categorical imperative to interpret Confucian ethics, neglecting the importance of ethical praxis. Chen Daqi, recognizing the importance of utilitarian ethics (in positing calm happiness as the ultimate human value) and ethics of obligation (in formulating a list of minimal ethical obligations), integrated them into an ethics of virtue, emphasizing virtuous praxis and the formation of character.

Chen Daqi addressed the problems of conflict between vice and virtue and the need to establish certain criteria for distinguishing between true virtue and vice. For him, true virtue should first of all direct itself to the attainment of calm happiness. This is the most important of all criteria. Other, secondary criteria consist in (1) not going beyond and not falling short, which means holding to the principle of *zhong*, understood not as the middle but rather as the pertinent principle; (2) acting according to the demands of a situation, in keeping with the principles; (3) considering the positions of others and, especially, considering the consequences of one's acts and words from others' point of view; and (4) adopting the right or legitimate means. In all these criteria, Chen Daqi emphasizes the consequences of an act—he seldom touches on motivation. Therefore, we can say that he is a consequentialist.

In brief, Chen put forward a consequentialist, intellectual virtue ethics that presupposes a correct knowledge of what is best for others and what is to be done. For Chen, the act of discerning right and wrong always presupposes a knowledge of true and false.

Conclusion

Chen Daqi represents a pioneering logical and conceptual approach in contemporary Confucianism. His conceptual and argumentative studies laid an analytic foundation for contemporary Confucian studies. Notably, these studies inspired Antonio Cua's reconstruction of Confucian argumentation and rhetoric (1985; 1998, Essays 1 and 10). He does not go on to unfold the transcendental and ontological dimensions of Confucianism for self-awareness and speculative discourse. Chen Daqi's own interest is in science rather than in speculative philosophy, and he posits an ethical consciousness based on praxis, although he does not discuss the transcendental structure or dynamism of human subjectivity. It should be noted that those who do take up transcendental subjectivity are not necessarily moving toward a true ethical consciousness, which presupposes recognition of the other. We might even say that where there is no recognition of the other, there is no ethics worthy of the term. In Chen Daqi's ethics there is always a recognition of others; his ethical praxis is in a context of "being-with" others. Ultimately, in ethical matters praxis is more important than any discourse. More than any contemporary new Confucianists, Chen Daqi, in emphasizing ethical praxis and the formation of virtues, goes directly to the essence of ethics.

See also Confucianism: Ethics; Confucianism: Rhetoric; Confucianism: Tradition; Mou Zongsan; Tang Junyi; Xunzi.

Bibliography

Cua, A. S. *Ethical Argumentation: A Study in Hsün Tzu's Moral Epistemology*. Honolulu: University of Hawaii Press, 1985.

———. *Moral Vision and Tradition: Essays in Chinese Ethics*. Washington, D.C.: Catholic University of America Press, 1998.

Chen, Daqi. *Chen Daqi xiansheng wenji* (Collected Essays of Mr. Ch'en Ta-ch'i), Vols. 1–3. Taipei: Commercial Press, 1987, 1990, 1994.

———. *Kongzi xueshuo* (Confucius's Doctrines). Taipei: Zhengzhong, 1964.

———. *Kongzi xueshuo lunji* (Collected Essays on Confucius's Doctrines). Taipei: Zhengzhong, 1958.

———. *Mengzi mingli sixiang ji qi bianshuo shi kuang* (Mencius's Logical Thought and the Actual Process of His Argumentation). Taipei: Commercial Press, 1968.

———. *Mengzi xingshan shuo yu Xunzi xing'e shuo di bijiao yanjiu* (A Comparative Study of Mencius's Theory of Human Nature as Good and Xunzi's Theory of Human Nature as Evil). Taipei: Central, 1953.

———. *Mingli luncong* (Collected Essays on Logic). Taipei: Cheng-zhong, 1957.

———. *Pingfan di daode guan* (An Ordinary Vision of Morality). Taipei: Zhonghua, 1970.

———. *Shiyong lizexue* (Practical Logic). Taipei: Yuantong, 1953.

———. *Xunzi xueshuo* (Xunzi's Doctrines). Taipei: Chinese Culture Publication Enterprise, 1954.

———. *Yindu lizexue* (Indian Logic). Taipei: Chinese Culture Publication Enterprise, 1952.

Shen, Vincent. "Yu mingxue zouxiang ruxue zhi lu: Chen Daqi dui Taiwan ruxue di gongxian (The Way from Logic to Confucianism: Chen Daqi's Contribution to Confucian Studies in Taiwan)." *Chinese Studies*, 16(2), 1998, pp. 1–27.

Chen Que (Ch'en Ch'üeh)

Kai-wing Chow

Chen Que (Ch'en Ch'üeh, 1604–1677) was a native of Haining County in Zhejiang. His life spanned the most tumultous period of the transition from the Ming to the Qing. His philosophy marks the beginning of a reorientation of Confucianism in the Qing period. He studied with the renowned philosopher Liu Zongzhou (1578–1645), who was an avid student of Wang Yangming. Although he was Liu Zongzhou's student, Chen was repelled by the subjectivistic and syncretic tendencies in ethical thought characteristic of many followers of Wang Yangming in the late Ming period. Chen's own philosophy is distinguished by a monistic ontology and a ritualist approach to the cultivation of morals. He is important in Qing thought for at least two reasons. First, Chen's philosophy was informed by two powerful currents in the early Qing: ritualist ethics and Confucian purism. Second, his efforts to purify the Confucian classics by identifying heterodox texts and concepts presaged the eventual triumph of the purist hermeneutics of the Han "learning movement" in the second half of the eighteenth century.

Chen Que takes a monistic view of human nature. Like many of his contemporaries, Chen criticized the dualistic concept of human nature that was generally associated with Cheng-Zhu Confucianism. For Chen, it was erroneous to speak of human nature in terms of essence (*benti*) and physical embodiment (*qizhi zhi xing*). This was a result of applying Buddhist ideas to Confucian teachings by the Song *Daoxue* Confucians. Human nature is nothing but the corporeal (*qi*), sentiments (*qing*), and faculties (*cai*). They are all good (*shan*). But man's good nature, Chen insisted, could be discerned only after its "full extension" (*kuochong*). By extension he meant moral exertion (*gongfu*). To put this differently, one's nature in lived experience depended exclusively on the totality of one's moral exertions. Those who dwelled on vacuous speculation on the abstract nature prior to man's physical existence could easily lead people into believing Chan Buddhism. The problem with the dualistic notion of human nature is that it provides an excuse—the inferior physical constitution—for not actively cultivating morality.

In his attempt to foreground on Confucian ethics in ritual, Chen drew textual evidence from the *Book of Changes* and the *Mencius*. In his treatise *Explaining Human Nature* (*xingjie*), he cited from the *Book of Changes* the phrase *ji shan cheng xing* ("sustained effort in doing good to establish one's nature") and from the *Mencius* the expression *jin xin zhi xing* ("exhaust the mind to discover the fullest extent of one's nature"). Both phrases, according to Chen, explain Confucius's view of the "similarity of human nature" (*xing xiang jin*). Both phrases point to an ethics that stresses effort in the dynamic cultivation of the good nature of human beings. While he reiterated Mencius's view that humans are born with a good nature, he insisted that the full actualization of the good is a result of human effort. The good is not a given, nor is it fixed at birth and immutable thereafter. It is not something that can be sought before birth (*qiu zhih fumu wei sheng zhiqian*) but something that humans themselves have to develop (*renxing wu bushan, yu kuochong hou jian zhi*). Chen is making a distinction between potential good and actualized good—that is, good conduct. In other words, there is no morality without human action. Morality has to be practiced. One simply does not know whether a person *is* good even though he or she is capable of goodness. The phrase *ji shan cheng xing* from the *Book of Changes* emphasizes sustained effort in actualizing the good. Only through an unceasing sustained moral effort can one's good nature be firmly established. This implies that good nature needs to be actualized and can be lost when actualization stops. When it stops, human nature is incomplete. Without actualization, there is no demonstration of the full endowment of the good by heaven.

Significantly—and reminiscent of the ritualist ethics of the Song *Daoxue* Confucian Zhang Zai—Chen Que's ethics stresses the need to develop good habits in accordance with moral standards encoded in rituals. Nowhere is Chen's regard for rituals more forcefully expressed than in his instruction to his son: "What distinguishes man from beast is man's capacity to devote himself to ritual practice. Man also set himself apart from beasts by practicing ritual in earnest." For Chen, ritual practice provided the solid, sure ground for the development of good habits.

Cheng-Zhu Confucianism reemerged as the dominant school in the second half of the seventeenth century. When exponents of *Daoxue* Confucianism of the Cheng-Zhu school rejected Wang Yangming's teachings and all forms of syncretism as heterodox, a more "radical" strain of purism was taking shape in the 1650s that worked to undermine the theoretical and textual basis of Song *Daoxue* Confucianism. This purism came to focus on identifying heterodox elements in the Confucian classics at the level of commentary. The correct understanding of Confucian texts would be possible when non-Confucian phrases and expressions were identified and excised. Chen's effort to ground his ethics in the *Mencius* and the *Book of Changes* was an integral part of his attempt to purify the Confucian canon. He was among the first to launch a full-scale attack on Song *Daoxue* Confucianism in the early Qing. Through identifying texts, terms, and concepts, Chen sought to purify the Confucian canon and doctrine.

Chen Que was deliberately polemical in his philosophical treatises, for he believed that Confucian ethics had been deeply flawed by the pernicious influence of Buddhism. He believed that a "correction" of the wayward interpretation of Confucian doctrine had to begin with a comprehensive purging of heterodox ideas and textual corruption. He disputed the idea of self-sufficiency of the moral will (*benti*), which he believed to be essentially a Buddhist teaching, introduced into Confucianism later by the Song *Daoxue* Confucians. Anticipating the methodology of the eighteenth-century Han "learning school," Chen pointed out that the term *benti* (original substance), denoting the essential rather than the experiential aspect of human nature, was not to be found in the classics. It had its origin in Buddhism. Man's good nature could not exist in abstraction, any more than moral acts could spring naturally from a sheer "discovery" of the essential nature of the mind, i.e., the moral will. Moreover, moral will is not in itself sufficient to ensure moral conduct. Chen therefore opposed seeking good nature in abstraction, which he associated with Buddhism and the various trends of syncretism of the late Ming.

The most disturbing of Chen Que's writings was the treatise *Distinguishing the Great Learning* (*Daxue bian*), a critique that he began to work on as early as 1654. The basic Confucian text *Daxue*, he argued, was in origin a crass writing by a Han scholar. Strangely, he argued that the teaching of the text is that of Chan Buddhism. The primary reason was its exclusive focus on "knowing" (*yan zhi bu yan xing*) without concern for practice (*xing*). He singled out the phrase *zhizhi* ("knowing where to stop") as evidence for Chan Buddhism. "How could a scholar's quest for knowledge stop?" Chen asked. To aver that "knowing where to stop" was, for him, to entertain the Chan Buddhist idea that once one attained perfect knowledge, no further knowledge was necessary. For Chen, the teaching of *zhizhi* (extension of knowledge) resulted in two ethical problems: first, the belief that once one knows, there is no more to know; second, that knowing is sufficient without practice.

The strategies or textual methods Chen used to discredit the *Great Learning* involve both ordinary methods of textual criticism and interpretive devices. Chen declared that the *Great Learning* was not written by Confucius or his disciple and tried to prove that there is no evidence for attributing the *Great Learning* to Confucius. Nor is there any reference to the term *Daxue* in other, indisputable Confucian texts such as the *Spring and Autumn Annals*, the *Book of Odes*, and the *Book of Documents*. Chen then explained how Cheng Yi and Zhu Xi contributed to turning this heterodox text into the most important text of *Daoxue* Confucianism.

In dismissing the *Great Learning* as a doubtful piece of writing, he rendered the controversy about the textual structure and the meaning of *gewu* irrelevant to the proper understanding of Confucianism. Chen clearly had no concern for possible damage done to *Daoxue* Confucianism. Despite his admiration for Wang Yangming, who venerated the *Great Learning*, Chen did not apologize for his vehement attack on this central text of *Daoxue* Confucianism. His iconoclastic treatise immediately elicited protests, even from his friends. Chen was moving ahead of his contemporaries in abandoning Song exegetical traditions. He called for a return to the classics for the authentic Confucian teachings. Chen was among the first in the early Qing to call for a demarcation between Song *Daoxue* Confucianism and classical Confucianism. He criticized the teachings of Zhou Dunyi, Cheng Yi, and Zhu Xi for having assimilated a strong dose of Chan Buddhism.

Chen Que's ritualist ethics and Confucian purism were not meant to be merely polemical. They informed his own ritual practice at both the family level and the lineage level. From the 1660s on, the efforts to restore the house of Ming were channeled into the preservation and glorification of Chinese rituals, and of Chinese culture in general. Chen Que, Zhang Lüxiang, and their inner circle of friends had been striving to rectify ritual abuses in accordance with canonical rituals. They came to realize that the canonical ritual of the descent-line system (*zongfa*) formed the basis of Zhu Xi's *Family Rituals*. Chen Que, on learning the descent-line principle that "secondary sons do not make sacrifice" (*zhizi bu ji*), renounced his right to worship his father, since he was not the eldest son. It is apparent that Chen regarded classical ritual not as arbitrary rules but as sacred principles that transcended variations in dynastic institutions. Whether or not the Manchus granted the right to worship "four ancestors," it remained everyone's obligation to abide by the classical regulations. The classical rituals were meant to be strictly followed, for Chen equated them with "heavenly principle" (*tianli*). Any action going beyond the specific boundary, which was "heavenly principle," was nothing but human desire (*renyu*).

The principle of the descent line lies at the heart of the controversy regarding the canonical model of lineage. Chen Que saw the ancestral hall and the descent-line system as important institutions to bring together otherwise loosely linked kin. Chen took exception to Cheng Yi's idea that all could worship their "four ancestors" by virtue of their mourning obligation. By granting privilege to all descendants to worship their own four ancestors, Cheng Yi's view presented a theoretical obstacle to creating lineages through centralization of ritual authority in the heir of the line of descent.

In addition to his treatises on proper burial, weddings, mourning, and worship, Chen Que compiled a list of rules for his family called the "family covenant" (*jia yue*). He also wrote a supplement to Lü Qi's *New Manual for Women* (*Bu xinfu pu*), in which he expressed his objection to many activities popular among women in the late Ming. He exhorted women not to watch drama or invite matchmakers and nuns into their homes. Women should not be allowed to watch religious and festival parades in public, nor should they be allowed to visit monasteries and make pleasure trips.

Chen Que's radical attack on the *Great Learning* and his ritualist ethics have not received as much attention as the scholarship and anti-Manchu activism of Gu Yanwu and Huang Zongxi. But Chen was no less important in his contribution to the reorientation of Confucian ethics and classical scholarship in the early Qing.

See also Cheng Yi; Huang Zongxi; *Li*: Rites or Propriety; Liu Zongzhou; Ritualism; Wang Yangming; Zhu Xi.

Bibliography

Chan, Haiyun. *Chen Qianchu Daxue bian yanjiu*. Taipei: Mingwen shuju, 1986.

Chen Que. *Chen Que ji* (Collected Writings of Chen Que). Beijing: Zhonghua shuju, 1979.

Chow, Kai-wing. *The Rise of Confucian Ritualism in Late Imperial China: Ethics, Classics, and Lineage Discourse*. Stanford, Calif.: Stanford University Press, 1994.

Lin, Qingzhang. *Qing chu di qunjing bianwei xue* (A Study of the Critical Examination of Falsified Classical Texts in the Early Qing). Taipei: Lianjing shuju, 1990.

Qian, Mu. *Zhongguo jin sanbai nian xueshu shi* (History of Chinese Scholarship during the Past Three Centuries). Taipei: Shangwu yinshu guan, 1957.

Chen Xianzhang (Ch'en Hsien-chang)

William Yau-nang NG

Chen Xianzhang (1428–1500) was a famous Confucian scholar of great philosophical originality in the early Ming period. He came from Xinhui, Guangdong, and was better known as Chen Baisha, after the name of the village where he lived. In 1447, he passed the provincial examinations in Guangdong. After failing the metropolitan examinations in the next year, he entered the national university.

In 1454, Chen went to Jiangxi, where he studied under Wu Yubi (1397–1469), the founder of the Chongren school. Chen reported that he failed to find the "entrance gate" to truth. However, he learned much from Wu regarding the study of the classics and was particularly inspired by Wu's personal example. Thus Chen made up his mind to seek sagehood.

After returning to Guangdong, he spent years on extensive book learning, the customary approach of the school of Cheng-Zhu. However, his futile efforts eventually convinced him that learning was a matter of self-realization and spiritual cultivation should be the real basis of learning—not vice versa. He then led a hermit's life and spent years in tranquillity. In the experience of enlightenment Chen discovered that mind-heart (*xin*) is the master and the basis of the universe. This discovery was crucial to the new philosophy he eventually developed. Meanwhile, his new teaching, together with the great success of his spiritual pursuit, attracted many followers, among whom Zhan Ruoshui (1466–1560) was the most important.

In 1466, Chen went back to Beijing to try for public office and reenrolled in the national university. Three years later, he failed again in the metropolitan examinations and returned home. On the recommendation of the governor, Zhu Ying, Chen was summoned to Beijing in 1482 and finally received the title of Hanlin corrector from the emperor. Shortly afterward, Chen returned to Guangdong, where he died in 1500. In 1585, the honorific title "Wen Gong" was conferred on him, and his tablet was enshrined in the Confucian temple—the highest posthumous honor for a Confucian scholar.

Chen believed that the *dao* could be grasped only by a purified mind that had reached the utmost tranquillity. However, the *dao*, according to Chen, is ineffable, and thus any attempt at theorizing or analysis would simply lead nowhere. Chen said, "If you talk about *dao* in words, you end up referring only to its crude and trivial aspects." Thus he saw book learning, an important part in the teaching of the school of Cheng-Zhu, as a hindrance to the pursuit of *dao*. Chen himself did not even attempt to write books. In Chen's philosophy, if we take it to its logical extreme, the only sensible attitude is silence.

Chen believed that the right path for a spiritual pursuit was to nourish the *duanni* in tranquillity. Here, *duanni* refers to "indications" of the presence or the "beginnings" (*kaiduan*) of the unfolding of mind-heart. After years of practicing spiritual cultivation, Chen finally experienced an inner world of peace and tranquillity through which he acquired a sense of the oneness of all things. However, he held that this stage of spiritual pursuit was attained not so much by strenuous efforts as by the "effort" of the natural (*ziran*).

In fact, *ziran* is the basis of Chen's philosophy. Chen stated clearly: "My learning is based on the natural." But what is the "natural"? Chen's understanding of the term was heavily influenced by Daoist as well as Chan Buddhist and other Neo-Confucian scholars, especially Cheng Hao (1032–1085). Jen Yu-wen, a modern expert on Chen's philosophy, pointed out that "his general concept of the natural was similar to that of the Neo-Daoists in recognizing that it was at once self-caused, self-completing, self-existing, self-reproducing, and self-perpetuating" (1970). While all these adjectives point to important aspects of the "natural," one should not ignore the basic meaning that expressed the very nature of Chen's understanding of the mind-heart—spontaneity.

The mind-heart, according to Chen, is a source of spontaneous creativity. It is an inexhaustible reservoir of potentialities and possibilities. One important manifestation of the creative power of the mind-heart is to correlate everything into one universal whole, which is a kind of spiritual experience rather than a result of intellectual activity. Paul Yun-ming Jiang has pointed out that in Chen's philosophy, "to cultivate the self is to pursue (or rather to recruit) its inner spontaneity in order that the Mind will unfold its primordial functioning in the process of creativity" (1980). Functioning in a creative way, the mind-heart, in this sense, is actually the *dao* or the "principle," the ultimate ontological reality in the Confucian tradition. Thus one can say that the principle is both immanent and transcendent.

By identifying the mind-heart with the principle, Chen took a radically different position from that of the school of Cheng-Zhu, which separated the mind-heart from the principle. By emphasizing the importance of spontaneity, Chen also discarded any artificial effort to acquire wisdom. He went so far as to say that it is wrong even to talk about how to learn. Again, this view directly contradicts the teachings of the school of Cheng-Zhu. Chen's emphasis on focusing inward marked a break from the school of Cheng-Zhu. Naturally, Chen's philosophy met with serious criticism from scholars influenced by Zhu Xi. Among them, the most famous one was Hu Juren (1434–1484), who—like Chen—was a student of Wu Yubi. In his *Juyelu*, Hu accused Chen of mistaking *qi*, which is commonly translated as material force, for *li* (principle). According to Zhu Xi, *li* is attached to but separable from *qi*. Hu also said that Chen's position—embracing myriad things in one mind-heart and nourishing the *duanni* in one's tranquillity—was heretical, being influenced by Daoism and Buddhism. Chen, consistently with his concept of tranquillity, did not respond.

While it is clear that Chen's philosophy differs drastically from Zhu Xi's, Chen's inward turn in his spiritual pursuit was not a complete break from the dominant trend of thought in his time. Modern scholars, like Wing-tsit Chan, Yamanoi Yu, and Peiyuan Meng, reach a consensus in pointing out that the school of Cheng-Zhu in the early Ming period had shifted its emphasis from the investigation of external things to the pursuit of the inner realm of the mind-heart. In this respect, Chen's position was in line with the new development within the Cheng-Zhu school. However, the difference between the school of Cheng-Zhu and the school of Lu-Wang is traditionally interpreted as a contrast between the principle and the mind-heart. Chen's inward pursuit of the mind-heart is viewed as foreshadowing Wang Yangming's philosophy, which emphasized the pursuit of one's moral sense (*liangzhi*). Thus Wang's philosophy was viewed as a further development of Chen's. This understanding of the relationship between the two philosophers was popularized by Huang Zongxi's *Mingru xue'an* (*Records of Ming Scholars*), which held that Ming learning had started to become precise with Chen and had started to become mature with Wang Yangming. This may be so, but there is no conclusive evidence for the assertion that Wang Yangming was directly influenced by Chen. Wing-tsit Chan held that Wang Yangming never read Chen's works, and Paul Jiang pointed out that Wang Yangming mentioned Chen's name on only three occasions.

If the relation between Chen and Wang remains unclear, it is clear that Chen's philosophy became influential in the early years of the Ming dynasty. This was to a considerable extent because of the contributions of Zhan Ruoshui, who had studied under Chen's supervision for six years. Chen was delighted to have such a gifted disciple and openly declared Zhan his successor. Zhan was eventually very successful in his political career. With his tremendous resources, Zhan built academies spreading Chen's teachings wherever he worked.

As Wang Yangming's philosophy eventually came to dominate the academic arena, the influence of Chen's teaching continued to diminish. Yet the Chinese from Guangdong, and naturally those from Xinhui County in particular, continued to honor Chen. In 1745, to pay tribute to him, a local Confucian academy, Baisha Shuyuan, was built next to the Confucius Temple in Zhanghua, a city in central Taiwan. This academy eventually became the National Chang-hua University of Education. In the 1960s there was a resurgence of interest in Chen in Hong Kong that eventually led to the publication of his complete works. In 1982 the San Wui Commercial Society (SWCS) Chan Pak Sha Secondary School was founded in Hong Kong.

See also Wang Yangming; Wang Yangming: Rivals and Followers; Zhan Ruoshui; Zhu Xi: Rivals and Followers.

Bibliography

Chan, Wing-tsit. *Zhuxue lunji* (Collected Works on Zhu Xi's Scholarship). Taipei: Xuesheng, 1982.

Chang, Carsun. *The Development of Neo-Confucian Thought*, 2 vols. New York: Bookman, 1957, 1962.

Chen, Xianzhang. *Baisha xiansheng quanji* (Complete Works of Chen Baisha), comp. Luo Qiao. Taipei: Commercial Press, 1973. (Reprint.)

———. *Chen Xianzhangji* (Collected Works of Chen Xianzhang). Beijing: Zhonghua, 1987.

Chen, Yufu, ed. *Ming Chen Baisha xiansheng xianzhang nianpu* (A Chronological Record of Chen Baisha). Taipei: Taiwan shangwu yinshuguan, 1970.

de Bary, William Theodore, ed. *Self and Society in Ming Thought*. New York: Columbia University Press, 1970.

Fung, Yu-lan. *A History of Chinese Philosophy*, trans. Derk Bodde, 2 vols. Princeton, N.J.: Princeton University Press, 1953.

Goodrich, L. Carrington, and Gang Chaoying, eds. *Dictionary of Ming Biography 1368–1644*. New York: Columbia University Press, 1976.

Huang, Guilan. *Baisha xueshuo jiqishi zhiyanjiu* (A Study of Baisha's Teachings and His Poems). Taipei: Wenshizhe chubanshe, 1981.

Huang, Mingtong. *Chen Xianzhang pingzhuan* (Critical Biography of Chen Xianzhang). Nanjing: Nanjing daxue chubanshe, 1998.

Huang, Zongxi. *Mingru xue'an* (Records of Ming Scholars). *Sibu beiyao* edition—SBBY (Ssu-pu pei-yao—SPPY). (For selected English translations of this work, see Julia Ching, ed. *The Records of Ming Scholars*. Honolulu: University of Hawaii Press, 1987.)

Jen, Yu-wen. *Baishazi yanjiu* (A Study of Baisha). Hong Kong: Mengjin shuwu, 1972.

———. "Ch'en Hsien-chang's Philosophy of the Natural." In *Self and Society in Ming Thought*, ed. W. T. de Bary. New York: Columbia University Press, 1970, pp. 53–92.

Jiang, Paul Yun-ming. *The Search for Mind: Ch'en Pai-sha, Philosopher-Poet*. Singapore: Singapore University Press, 1980. (Jiang's work was still, at this writing, the only full-length study of Chen's philosophy in English. It includes, at the end, inspiring comparisons between Chen and western philosophers.)

———. *Xinxuedi xiandaiquanshi* (Modern Interpretation on the Learning of Mind-Heart). Taipei: Dongdai tushu chubanshe, 1988.

Lyu, Miaofen. *Hu Juren yu Chen Xianzhang* (Hu Juren and Chen Xianzhang). Taipei: Wenjin chubanshe, 1996.

Meng, Peiyuan. *Lixue di yanbian* (The Evolution of Neo-Confucianism). Taipei: Wenjin chubanshe, 1990.

Yamanoi, Yu. *Minshin shisoshi no kenkyu* (A Study of the History of Ming and Qing Thought). Tokyo: Tokyo University Press, 1980.

Zhang, Pei. *Chen Baisha zhexue sixiang yanjiu* (A Study of the Philosophical Thought of Chen Baisha). Guangdong: Guangdong renmin chubanshe, 1984.

Cheng (*Ch'eng*): Wholeness or Sincerity

Kwong-loi SHUN

Cheng has the meaning of something's being truly or really the case and is contrasted with *wei*, meaning "false appearance." It is used in early Confucian texts, including *Mengzi* (*Mencius*), *Xunzi*, *Daxue* (*Great Learning*), and *Zhongyong* (*Centrality and Commonality*), to refer to an ideal state of the heart (*xin*) in which the heart is completely directed toward ethics; in such contexts, *cheng* is often translated as "wholeness" or "sincerity." It becomes a key concept in the thinking of several later Confucian thinkers, including Li Ao (eighth to ninth century), Zhou Dunyi (1017–1073), Zhu Xi (1130–1200), and Wang Yangming (1472–1529).

Cheng occurs in two passages of *Mengzi*. Passage 7A.4 observes that the ten thousand things are already one, and there is no greater joy than realizing, upon self-reflection, that one has *cheng*. Passage 4A.12, a variation of which is also found in *Zhongyong* (ch. 20), describes *cheng* as dependent on understanding goodness and as necessary for pleasing one's parents, being trusted by friends, obtaining the confidence of superiors, and bringing order to the people. It describes *cheng* as the way of heaven (*tian*) and as reflected in the way of human beings, and observes that *cheng* is necessary for moving or affecting others. *Daxue* also describes *cheng* as something inevitably manifested on the outside and detected by others (ch. 6). *Xunzi* describes *cheng* as a method for nourishing the heart, as necessary if one is to transform others, and as the ideal basis for government (3.26–34). The most elaborate discussion of *cheng*, however, is in *Zhongyong*, the second half of which is devoted primarily to this subject.

Although the beginning of *Zhongyong* (ch. 1) does not explicitly mention *cheng*, it refers to the idea of being watchful over *du* (solitude, privacy), an idea also found in *Daxue* (ch. 6), in the context of discussing what it is to make one's thoughts and inclinations *cheng* and how *cheng* is manifested on the outside. This indicates that the idea of being watchful over *du* is related to *cheng*, and the discussion of the idea in these two texts shows that it concerns one's being watchful over the innermost part of oneself, in which the minute and subtle activities of the heart first arise. By being watchful over oneself, one ensures *cheng* in the sense of being completely directed toward ethics, so that there is not even a single thought or inclination in oneself that could lead to the slightest reluctance or hesitation in doing good.

In the second half of *Zhongyong, cheng*—as noted above—is presented as the basis of the social and political order: it is only when one is *cheng* that one can please one's parents, be trusted by friends, obtain the confidence of superiors, and bring order to the people. Furthermore, the effect of *cheng* transforms and nourishes everything in the universe; a person who has *cheng* will have a transformative effect on the character of others, and in government, such a person will also ensure that the ten thousand things take their proper places. This effect comes about naturally and without deliberate effort; in this regard, the person is like heaven, which also nourishes the ten thousand things without deliberate effort. *Cheng* as the way of heaven is contrasted with making oneself *cheng* ("whole" or "sincere"), which is the way of human beings. Efforts are required to make oneself *cheng*—one has to understand what is good and choose the good. This contrast between someone who is *cheng* and someone who tries to become *cheng* is described in terms of the relation between *cheng* and *ming* (illumination or understanding). Someone who is *cheng* will *ming* ("understand," "illuminate"), meaning either that the person will understand goodness or that he will illuminate everything. Someone who is *ming*, presumably in the sense of understanding goodness, can thereby become *cheng*.

The notion of *cheng* is taken up by later Confucians and elaborated on in the context of their metaphysical thinking and views of human nature, in a way that goes beyond the *Zhongyong*. In his "Essay on Restoring Nature" (*Fuxing shu*), Li Ao described human nature (*xing*) as the same in everyone and as perfectly good. Emotions (*qing*) are the activities of nature when it comes into contact with things, and emotions can be impure, accounting for people's failure to be ethical. The perfectly good nature he identified with *cheng*, a complete inclination toward goodness, which transforms, nourishes, and illuminates everything. Furthermore, drawing on ideas in the *Yijing* (*Book of Changes*), Li Ao characterized *cheng* as unmoving and without deliberate thought, presumably in the sense that the person who is or has *cheng* responds spontaneously to situations without effort or deliberation. Thus everyone originally is or has *cheng*, and the task of self-cultivation is to restore this original state by ridding the heart of distorting emotions and thoughts, just as one can restore the original purity of water by letting the sediment settle.

A similar view of the relation between *cheng* and human nature is found in the thinking of Zhou Dunyi and Zhu Xi, but with a metaphysical twist. Whereas *Zhongyong* described *cheng* as the way heaven operates, Zhou identified *cheng* with the "great ultimate" (*taiji*), a notion found in the *Yijing* and characterized as the source of everything. *Cheng* as the source of everything is supremely good, as can be seen from its transformative and nourishing effect, and Zhou characterized it in terms of nonaction (*wuwei*) because of the effortless way in which it accomplishes its work. *Cheng* is also present in every human being, taking the form of the five virtues (*de*): humaneness (*ren*), propriety (*yi*), observance of the rites (*li*), wisdom (*zhi*), and trustworthiness (*xin*). *Ji* (subtle incipient activation) refers to the activation of *cheng* when one comes into contact with external things, and it is in these emerging activities of the heart that the distinction between good and evil arises. So one should carefully examine *ji* to ensure that it is properly directed, an idea closely related to the idea of being watchful over *du* in *Zhongyong* and *Daxue*.

Drawing on Zhou's ideas, Zhu Xi identified *cheng* not just with the great ultimate but also with pattern (*li*). Drawing on ideas of Cheng Yi (1033–1107), Zhu regarded everything as consisting of pattern and material force (*qi*). Pattern is abstract and is what explains the way things operate as well as that to which their operation should conform. Material force, on the other hand, is the concrete but freely flowing stuff of which things are made. Pattern in human beings comprises the Confucian virtues; the nature (*xing*) of human beings, which is identical with pattern and with *cheng*, is therefore perfectly good. In identifying human nature with *cheng*, Zhu emphasizes that in the original state everyone is completely inclined toward the Confucian virtues. These virtues are fully or really (*shi*) there in that, in the original state, not the slightest thought or inclination in one is incongruent with them, and one acts effortlessly in accordance with them. Like Li Ao, he regarded ethical failure as a matter of deviation from this original state due to erroneous thoughts or problematic desires, and self-cultivation as a matter of restoring the original state.

Whereas *cheng* is presented in early Confucian texts as an ideal state of existence toward which one should strive, for later Confucians it is the original state of human beings to which one should return. For both early and later Confucians, *cheng* is an ideal state in which one fully embodies the Confucian virtues, and only when one is or has *cheng* will one have the transformative and nourishing effect on others that provides the ideal basis for government.

See also *Chengyi*; *Daxue*; Li Ao; *Zhongyong*; Zhou Dunyi; Zhu Xi.

Bibliography

Cheng, Yi. *Ercheng quanshu*. Sibu beiyao series.

Daxue (Great Learning). In *Confucius: Confucian Analects, The Great Learning, and The Doctrine of the Mean*, trans. James Legge, 2nd ed. Oxford: Clarendon, 1893. (References in the present article are by chapter numbers, following Zhu Xi's division of the text.)

Li, Ao. *Li wengong ji*. Siku quanshu series.

Mengzi (Mencius). *Mengzi yizhu*, trans. Yang Bojun. Beijing: Zhonghua shuju, 1984. (In modern Chinese. References are by book and passage numbers, with book numbers 1A to 7B substituted for 1 to 14. See also D. C. Lau, trans. *Mencius*. London: Penguin, 1970.)

Xunzi. Harvard-Yenching Institute Sinological Index Series. (References are by chapter and line numbers. See also John Knoblock, trans. *Xunzi: A Translation and Study of the Complete Works*, 3 vols. Stanford, Calif.: Stanford University Press, 1988–1994.)

Yijing (Book of Changes). (See *The I Ching: The Book of Changes*, trans. James Legge, 2nd ed. Oxford: Clarendon, 1899.)

Zhongyong (Centrality and Commonality, or Doctrine of the Mean). In *Confucius: Confucian Analects, The Great Learning, and The Doctrine of the Mean*, trans. James Legge, 2nd ed. Oxford: Clarendon, 1893. (References are by chapter numbers, following Zhu Xi's division of the text.)

Zhou, Dunyi. *Zhou Dunyi ji*. Beijing: Zhonghua shuju, 1990.

Zhu, Xi. *Daxue zhangju* (Commentary on the *Daxue*).

———. *Zhongyong zhangju* (Commentary on the *Zhongyong*).

———. *Zhuzi yulei*. Beijing: Zhonghua shuju, 1986. (See also Wing-tsit Chan, trans. and comp. *A Source Book in Chinese Philosophy*. Princeton, N.J.: Princeton University Press, 1963, ch. 34.)

Cheng Hao (Ch'eng Hao)

Tze-ki Hon

To historians of Chinese philosophy, Cheng Hao (1032–1085) and his younger brother, Cheng Yi (1033–1107), are known as *Er Cheng* (the two Chengs). They and Zhou Dunyi (1017–1073), Shao Yong (1011–1077), and Zhang Zai (1020–1077) are called the "five masters of eleventh-century Chinese philosophy" for their role in neo-Confucianism. The writings of the Chengs, collected in *Er Cheng quanshu* (*The Complete Work of the Two Cheng Brothers*), are the major works in the neo-Confucian canon.

The Chengs were born into a scholar-official's family in Henan. When he was fifteeen, Cheng Hao, along with his brother, studied under Zhou Dunyi. Influenced by Zhou, Cheng Hao radically changed his view of learning. Instead of seeing learning as a way to pass the civil service examinations—which was the common view of educated people who aspired to upward social mobility—Cheng Hao set his mind to learning as an end in itself. Describing his learning as "the learning of the Way," Cheng Hao sought to be a fulfilled person morally and philosophically. In this quest, he first studied Buddhism and Daoism, as was typical of early neo-Confucianists. It took ten years of soul-searching to convert to him to Confucianism. Thereafter he expounded his thought, based on his own understanding of Confucian doctrine.

Cheng Hao's intellectual development suggests an ambiguous relationship between neo-Confucianism on the one hand and Buddhism and Daoism on the other. On the surface, the rise of neo-Confucianism countered Buddhism and Daoism. The goal of the neo-Confucianists was to revive Confucianism, making it competitive with the other two schools of thought. Thus it was common for them to openly condemn Buddhism and Daoism as heresies. In their internal debates, the neo-Confucianists sometimes called one another Buddhists and Daoists to make a rhetorical point. Yet many neo-Confucianists, such as Cheng Hao, had been students of Buddhism and Daoism before converting to Confucianism. Their understanding of Confucianism had been shaped significantly by their own exposure to Buddhism and Daoism, and their revival of Confucianism was aimed at conveying Confucian doctrine to an audience steeped in Buddhism and Daoism.

Cheng Hao and Cheng Yi broke new ground in Chinese philosophy by making *li* (principle, pattern, reason) the central concept of neo-Confucianism. For Cheng Hao, a single principle governed the universe—a universe that was continuously undergoing self-transformation and self-regeneration. But although he emphasized that one principle underlay this self-transformation of the multitude of beings, he also stressed that such transformations were nothing but concrete manifestations of the principle. With regard to transformation, Cheng Hao saw no ontological difference between the "one" and the "many." As a general principle of transformation, the *li* of the one remains empty until it is particularized in unique instances of self-transformation, the *li* of the many. Conversely, the *li* of the many would be, in essence, particular manifestations of the *li* of the one.

Scholars have not yet identified the sources of Cheng Hao's concept of *li*. Some scholars, who want to underscore Cheng Hao's Confucianism, trace *li* back to the *Book of Rites*, one of the Confucian Five Classics. Others, focusing on Cheng Hao's possible neo-Daoist roots, argue that he borrowed the term from neo-Daoist thinkers such as Wang Bi (226–249). Still others contend that Cheng Hao was influenced by Huayan Buddhism, which taught the interaction and interpenetration of the four realms of *dharma*: (1) facts; (2) principle, *li*; (3) principle and facts harmonized; and (4) all facts. Although none of the three sources is considered definitive, it is certain that Cheng Hao had access to a variety of resources in formulating his concept of *li*.

In arguing for an ontological identity of the one and the many, Cheng Hao wanted to show that ethics has a basis in metaphysics. In comparison with Buddhism and Daoism, classical Confucianism is strong in ethics but weak in metaphysics. Confucius (551–479 B.C.E.) himself seems to have been reluctant to discuss metaphysical issues such as the nature of the universe, life after death, and the human role in the cosmos; in some cases, he apparently avoided metaphysical issues rather than confronting them. In the *Analects*, for instance, he responded to a student's inquiry about the worship of ghosts and spirits by saying, "We don't know yet how to serve men; how can we know about serving the spirits?" (11.11). Similarly, responding to an inquiry on death, Confucius said: "We don't know yet about life; how can we know about death?" (11.11). Confucius's vagueness regarding metaphysics is sometimes said to have been partially responsible for the popularity of Buddhism and Daoism in medieval China.

To revive Confucianism, in contradistinction to Buddhism and Daoism, Cheng Hao found it imperative to strengthen Confucian metaphysics. By arguing that the one and the many are ontologically identical, Cheng Hao turned the Confucian weakness in metaphysics into a strength. Since the same principle of self-transformation underlies the one and the many, Confucius's attitude toward—or avoidance of—metaphysics can be interpreted as a profound recognition of the relationship of humankind and the cosmos. Instead of discussing the cosmos as an entity separate from humankind, Confucius focused on ethics to emphasize that what is human is, as such, metaphysical. Since the *li* in human daily practices is the same *li* that governs the universe's self-regeneration, human beings need not go beyond themselves to know the cosmos. If they simply concentrate on their everyday moral practices, those practices will have an impact on the universe as a whole.

In his essay "On Understanding the Nature of *Ren*," Cheng Hao explains the intimate connection between ethics and metaphysics by offering a fresh interpretation of the Confucian concept *ren*, "humanity." In classical Confucianism, *ren* is understood as proper regulation of human relations based on love, respect, and reciprocity. In the *Analects*, for instance, Confucius remarks that *ren* consists in "loving men" (12.22). He also regards the person characterized by *ren* as someone who seeks to establish himself by establishing others, and who achieves success by helping others succeed (6.28). In both cases, *ren* is understood primarily as altruism and reciprocity in human relationships.

In Cheng Hao's version, however, *ren* is understood as having both moral and metaphysical significance. The person of *ren* is someone who not only loves his fellow human beings but also "forms one body with all things without any differentiation" (*Er Cheng quanshu*, 2A.3a). The person of *ren* sees himself as carrying out a cosmic mission in human relationships. He regards his fellowship with humankind as part of his fellowship with all beings of the universe.

Applying this novel understanding of *ren*, Cheng Hao discusses how a human being can embrace all beings in this universe. He addresses the issue through a paradox. He emphasizes, on the one hand, the vastness of the universe, which is beyond human comprehension. On the other hand, he stresses that all operations of the universe are in fact human operations. How can a finite part possibly embody the infinite whole?

Cheng Hao offers a resolution to this paradox by quoting the *Mencius* (7A.4): "All things are already complete in oneself." If we consider the size and complexity of the universe, we must conclude that no human being can comprehend it. However, because the *li* governing the universe's self-transformation is the same *li* governing the transformation of human life, it follows that by coming to grips with the problems of their lives, humans become in tune with the rhythm of the universe's self-regeneration (*Er Cheng quanshu, Yishu*, 2A.3b). To illustrate this point, Cheng Hao once told his students that even sweeping a floor or answering a question has metaphysical significance. By themselves, such acts are mundane. But in performing them we concentrate the mind on things at hand and begin to listen to the rhythm of the universe. That experience is metaphysical, he said, because we are performing more as members of the cosmic family of beings than as members of the human community (13.1b).

Regarding the connection between ethics and metaphysics, Cheng Hao seems to have much in common with Zhou Dunyi, his early teacher. Zhou, in his essay "An Explanation of the Diagram of the Great Ultimate" (especially its second half), goes so far as to argue that a sage is half human and half cosmic. Despite their similarity, though, Cheng Hao did not acknowledge his intellectual debt to Zhou, nor did he mention Zhou's essay in his own writings—a striking omission. Evidently, Cheng Hao wanted to keep his distance from Zhou Dunyi.

One way to understand why this was so is to compare Cheng Hao's concept of *li* with Zhou's concept of *taiji* (the "great ultimate"). For Cheng Hao, to repeat, *li* is the principle underlying the self-transformation of the universe. The key to this concept is that part and whole are organically connected and affect each other in the process of transformation: "There is only one principle [*li*] in this world. You may extend it to the four seas and it is everywhere true. . . . Therefore to be serious is merely to be serious with this principle. To be humane [*ren*] is to be humane with this principle. And to be faithful is to be faithful to this principle" (*Er Cheng quanshu, Yishu*, 2A.19a; Chan 1963, 534).

By contrast, in Zhou's concept of *taiji* the relationship between part and whole is less important. Zhou maintains that *taiji* is the final source of the entire universe. *Taiji* first gives birth to the yielding cosmic force *yin* and the assertive cosmic force *yang*—the source of motion in the universe. The interaction of *yin* and *yang* gives birth to the "five phases" (water, fire, wood, metal, and earth); then, the mutual causation and mutual checking of the five phases create the many beings. *Taiji*, in short, sets into motion a sequential process of creation that finally brings the universe into being. Through this cosmogony, Zhou maintains that human beings share an ontology with the universe, but he does see all existent things as dependent on *taiji*. It seems that *taiji* is the precondition for any relationship between part and whole.

If Cheng Hao wanted to distance himself from Zhou Dunyi, he thought highly of the essay "Western Inscription" (*Xi ming*) by Zhang Zai, who was the Chengs' maternal uncle. Zhang Zai offered a holistic vision of the universe as the organic unity, and of the intrinsic connection between ethics and metaphysics:

> Heaven is my father and Earth is my mother, and even such a small creature as I finds an intimate place in their midst. Therefore that which fills the universe I regard as my body and that which directs the universe I consider as my nature. All people are my brothers and sisters, and all things are my companions. (*Song Yuan xue an*, 17.3a; Chan, 497)

In bold language, Zhang Zai describes the universe in ethical terms. Unlike Zhou Dunyi, who prefaced his discussion of ethics with a cosmogony, Zhang Zai treats ethics as a branch of metaphysics. He calls heaven and earth his parents and all beings in the universe his relatives. He loves the universe in the same way that he loves his actual parents and relatives, and he takes care of the universe in the same way that he takes care of his family. For Zhang Zai, ethics is not just a matter of proper behavior in the human community; it also has to do with proper human behavior in the universal family of beings. This anthropic-cosmic approach, as Tu Wei-ming (1979) calls it, was what Cheng Hao had attempted to articulate in "On Understanding the Nature of *Ren*."

Traditionally, Cheng Hao and Cheng Yi have been considered together, but more recent scholarship has identified fundamental differences between them. Scholars such as Feng Youlan (Fung Yu-lan), Mou Zongsan, and A. C. Graham describe Cheng Hao as an idealist because he regarded the mind as the sole agent in understanding moral principles, and Cheng Yi as a rationalist because he gave equal importance to the intuition of the mind and the empirical study of the external world in discovering such principles. In fact, for many scholars, the difference between the Chengs went beyond this: it was a fundamental difference between two schools of neo-Confucianism—the idealistic "mind and heart" school (*xinxue*) of Lu Xiangshan (1139–1193) and Wang Yangming (1472–1529), and the rationalistic "principle" school (*lixue*) of Cheng Yi and Zhu Xi (1130–1200).

A fundamental difference between the Chengs was their understanding of the intrinsic connection between the *li* in one's body and the *li* in the universe. For Cheng Hao, since ontologically a part is an element of an organic whole, there is no need to do anything except remind oneself of this organic unity. Learning is more an inner task than an outer task; it is a matter not of seeking knowledge from without but of attaining spiritual enlightenment from within. The goal of learning is to activate one's innate ability to feel connected with all beings in the universe.

What some scholars call Cheng Hao's "idealism" is found near the end of "On Understanding the Nature of *Ren*," where Cheng Hao argues that moral cultivation is simple and easy, involving nothing more than the preservation of *ren* in one's mind (*Er Cheng quanshu*, *Yishu*, 2A.3b). We have seen that Cheng Hao modified the classical Confucian concept of *ren* as a matter of human relations, making it instead a concept that emphasized the organic unity of part and whole, of humankind and the cosmos. In this essay, however, Cheng Hao goes a step further, arguing that in order to be complete and fulfilled, a person needs to keep in mind the inseparability of humankind and the cosmos. This is why moral cultivation is so easy—it requires only that we remember our roots in the universe. It is simply a return to our inner self for a deeper understanding of who we are.

To emphasize that moral cultivation is a return to one's inner self, Cheng Hao describes it as "preserving *ren*." Since *ren* is an innate human ability, we do not need to acquire *ren* from without; we need only preserve what is already given to us. This is like inheriting property—we do not need to earn it; we need only put it to good use. On some occasions, Cheng Hao used a metaphor from medicine to explain the preservation of *ren*. He compares a lack of *ren* to a paralysis of all four limbs (*Er Cheng quanshu*, *Yishu*, 2A.2a–b). In Chinese medicine, every being in this world is invigorated by *qi* (vital force). Just as the *li* of the one and the *li* of the many are connected, *qi* in the universe is the same as *qi* in any single being. By sharing the same *qi*, all beings in the universe are connected as a family. Similarly, the human body as a whole and its parts are connected by *qi*. The limbs become paralyzed not because they have been separated from the body but because *qi* has ceased to penetrate them. The cure is to reactivate *qi* by applying such measures as acupuncture. Moral cultivation has much the same purpose: it adds nothing new to the human mind; rather, it awakens a paralyzed sensitivity so that humans will again see themselves as an integral part of the universe.

Cheng Hao's emphasis on inner transformation in moral cultivation is also shown in his discussion with Zhang Zai, who acknowledged that Cheng Hao was ahead in learning the Way and sought advice from him. Despite his admiration of "Western Inscriptions," Cheng Hao disagreed with Zhang Zai regarding the degree to which the external environment influences the human mind. In a letter responding to Zhang Zai's queries, "Reply to Master Hengzhu's Letter on Calming Human Nature," Cheng Hao counseled that no special care is necessary to protect onesef from the influence of one's surroundings (*Er Cheng quanshu*, *Mingdao wenji*, 3.1a–b). For Cheng Hao, the question whether or not the external environment has an impact on the mind is wrongly posed. First, is not the external environment a perception of the mind? If there are temptations, they are manifestations of an impure mind far more than they are external or real. Second, is it not the goal of moral cultivation to reawaken the human mind so that it can see the universe as a family of beings? For the person of *ren*, the mind encompasses all beings in the universe. Such a person will never separate (as Zhang Zai did) the internal from the external, or the human mind from the human feelings. He is never worried about external temptation. Much in the spirit of Zhuangzi's sage, he responds spontaneously to things as they come.

Unlike Cheng Hao, Cheng Yi emphasizes both internal awakening and external conformity to ritual. In his essay "A Treatise on What Yanzi [Yan Hui] Loved to Learn," Cheng Yi expresses the same concern about external temptations as one finds in Zhang Zai. He agrees that human beings are, by nature, pure at birth. But he stresses that after birth humankind encounters many temptations from without—temptations so powerful that they can pervert human nature. To counter these temptations, Cheng Yi suggests two steps. First, one cultivates one's mind (this is similar to what Cheng Hao suggested). Second, one practices daily rites to create a positive external environment. For Cheng Yi, Confucius's favorite student, Yanzi, best exemplified the second step: he did not see, hear, speak, or do what was contrary to propriety. By carefully controlling his seeing, listening, speaking, and movement, Yanzi "learned" to be a sage (*Er Cheng quanshu*, *Yichuan wenji*, 4.1a–2a).

With regard to learning, then, the Chengs shared something but also differed. For Cheng Hao, learning involves only learning to have a "right mind." But for Cheng Yi, learning includes, as well, following the right *li*—principles of action. Whereas the Cheng Hao's "monism" paved the way for the *xin* or "mind-and-heart" school of neo-Confucianism, Cheng Yi's "dualism" set the stage for the *li* or "principle" school.

See also Cheng Yi; Confucianism: Song; *Li* (Principle); *Qi*; Zhang Zai; Zhou Dunyi.

Bibliography

Chan, Wing-tsit, trans. *A Source Book in Chinese Philosophy*. Princeton, N.J.: Princeton University Press, 1963.

Cheng, Hao, and Cheng Yi. *Er Cheng quanshu*. Taipei: Taiwan Zhonghua. (Reprint.)

Cua, A. S. "Harmony and the Neo-Confucian Sage." In *Moral Vision and Tradition: Essays in Chinese Ethics*. Washington, D.C.: Catholic University of America Press, 1998.

Fung, Yu-lan. *A History of Chinese Philosophy*, trans. Derk Bodde, Vol. 2. Princeton, N.J.: Princeton University Press, 1953.

Graham, A. C. *Two Chinese Philosophers: Ch'eng Ming-tao and Ch'eng Yi-ch'uan.* La Salle, Ill.: Open Court, 1992.

Huang, Zongxi. *Song Yuan xuean.* Taipei: Taiwan Zhonghua. (Reprint.)

Mou, Zongsan. *Xinti yu xingti* (The Substance of the Mind and the Substance of Human Nature), Vol. 2. Taipei: Zhengzhong, 1969.

Tu, Wei-ming. *Humanity and Self-Cultivation: Essays in Confucian Thought.* Berkeley, Calif.: Asian Humanities, 1979.

Cheng Yi (Ch'eng I)

Tze-ki Hon

At age twenty-four, Cheng Yi (1033–1107) entered the imperial academy in the capital, Kaifeng, and quickly became an outstanding student. His student essay, "A Treatise on What Yanzi Loved to Learn," won the admiration of his teacher, Hu Yuan (993–1056), and earned Cheng a reputation as a moral philosopher. At twenty-five, Cheng Yi wrote long exhortations to Emperor Renzong (r. 1023–1063), to practice the kingly way. A few years later, in the capacity of expositor-in-waiting, Cheng Yi had the opportunity to lecture the emperor regularly on moral cultivation. But Cheng's strong opinions on political reform soon involved him in factional struggles at the court; as a result, he was blacklisted, his property was confiscated, and he was forced to leave the capital. Like his older brother, Cheng Hao (1032–1085), Cheng Yi spent most of his life as a private teacher. He taught mostly in the Yi River area in Henan, and for this reason he was often called Master Yichuan (Yi River). As a teacher, Cheng Yi was highly respected; two of his students once spent hours standing in the snow rather than disturb his nap.

The Cheng brothers are known as *Er Cheng* (the two Chengs) for their shared role in founding neo-Confucianism. However, Cheng Yi differed from his brother in several respects. One difference was in temperament: while Cheng Hao was warm, approachable, and agreeable, Cheng Yi was stern, strict, and demanding. Once, when the brothers entered a hall and went to opposite sides of it, everyone else in the room followed Cheng Hao—no one followed Cheng Yi.

Another difference between the two Cheng brothers was their moral philosophies. In general, they had the same vision of the universe as an organic whole. Both maintained that *li* (principle) was the common ontological root of all beings in the universe. And in the formulation "The principle is one and its manifestations are many" (*liyi fenshu*), they both argued that ethics was intimately connected with metaphysics. But they differed with regard to methods of moral cultivation: Cheng Hao emphasized the illumination of the mind as the sole means of moral cultivation; Cheng Yi stressed a pairing of inner illumination with an outer quest for objective knowledge. Behind this difference lay a disagreement on whether the human mind alone is capable of achieving moral perfection—a disagreement that prepared the way for the intensive debate between the idealist "mind-and-heart" school and the rational "principle" school of neo-Confucianism.

The difference between the Chengs' moral philosophies is evident in Cheng Yi's early essay "A Treatise on What Yanzi Loved to Learn," which addresses the human propensity for evil. Cheng Yi argues that although human nature in its original form is pure and tranquil, it is easily perverted when it comes into contact with external stimuli. Once stimulated, human nature will express the "seven feelings": pleasure, anger, sorrow, joy, love, hate, and desire. Many people, according to Cheng Yi, lose their original purity when they allow the seven feelings to shape their lives (*Er Cheng quanshu*, *Yishu*, 4.1a–2a).

What is important about this essay is that Cheng Yi modifies Mencius's notion of the innate goodness of human nature. On the ontological level, Cheng Yi agrees with Mencius that at birth human nature is good, because *li* is manifested and particularized in the human body. Xunzi, the archrival of Mencius, was wrong in teaching that original human nature is evil. But for Cheng Yi, accepting Mencius's notion of the innate goodness of human nature does not necessarily lead to the conclusion that moral cultivation is simple or easy. What is ontologically given is at best a potential awaiting activation. There is a vast gulf between what is ontologically given and what is manifested.

For this reason (which is somewhat similar to the dichotomy between nature and nurture in western philosophy), Cheng Yi modifies Mencius's thesis, distinguishing between human nature *by* birth, which, as a manifestation of *li*, is innately good; and human nature *after* birth, which is contingent on one's social environment and one's efforts at moral cultivation. If the social environment nurtures innate human goodness and adequate efforts are made to preserve this innate goodness, then it will develop fully. In this case, human nature by birth and after birth will be the same. Cheng Yi calls this "turning the feelings into the original nature." However, if the social environment impedes the full manifestation of innate goodness and efforts to preserve innate goodness are inadequate, then innate goodness will not develop or function properly, and human nature by birth and after birth will differ. Cheng Yi calls this "turning one's nature into feelings."

In this concept of the fragility of innate goodness, Cheng Yi disagrees with his brother. Cheng Yi argues that moral cultivation must be strenuous and time-consuming, because it is a constant struggle against an adverse environment, a ceaseless attempt to ward off temptation. In seeking guidance for moral cultivation, one cannot rely solely on a mental recognition of the potential goodness of human nature. One must combine this recognition with actual experience if innate goodness is to be fully realized. For this reason, Cheng Yi argues that moral cultivation must be a dual process. Inwardly, it is a "rectification of the mind" (*zhengxin*). Outwardly, it is a "nourishment of one's nature" (*yangxing*) in order to create an external environment conducive to the realization of innate goodness (*Er Cheng quanshu*, *Yishu*, 4.1a).

Cheng Yi considered Confucius's student Yanzi (Yan Hui) the prime example of this dual process of inward awakening and outward nourishment. Yanzi's moral cultivation was extremely self-disciplined and included both "firm faith in the Way" and a determination to practice a series of proper behaviors: right seeing, right listening, right speech, and right movement. One of Yanzi's virtues—for which he was famous—was not committing the same mistake twice. Cheng Yi believed that it was Yanzi's inward self-reflection and outward conformity to strict rituals that made him so dear to Confucius, who wept over his untimely death (*Er Cheng quanshu*, *Yishu*, 4.1b).

In later life, Cheng Yi developed sets of binary categories to highlight the importance of controlling one's external environment. For instance, he juxtaposed *li* (principle) with *qi*—the vital force that propels the universe, a gigantic system of relations that brings the whole universe together. While *li* is structured and orderly, *qi* is dynamic and creative. While *li* provides the universe with a system of operation, *qi* sets the universe in motion, propelled by the duality of *yin* and *yang*. To move unceasingly, the universe requires both the structure of *li* and the dynamism of *qi*.

From the human perspective, *li* is a given. No human being can change the cosmic pattern or his role in it. What a human being can change is the configuration of *qi* in his body and the process by which *qi* will help him nourish his life. By carefully nurturing *qi*, human beings can be more effective members of the cosmic family. To explain the importance of nurturing *qi*, Cheng Yi used the example of a fish in water. A fish's existence does not come from water, and human existence does not come directly from *qi*. But a fish does require water to survive, and, similarly, human beings depend on *qi* for nourishment. To better their lives, human beings need to take special care in nurturing *qi* (*Er Cheng quanshu*, *Yishu*, 15.17b).

Another set of binaries is nature (*xing*), an innate human potential endowed by the universe; and capacity (*cai*), a specific configuration of human characteristics and social setting that makes a person unique. *Xing* is universal among human beings, but *cai* varies from person to person. Everyone is the same in having an innately good nature; differences arise from humans' efforts to come to grips with an adverse environment so that they can fully manifest their innate goodness. To explain the difference between nature and capacity, Cheng Yi takes wood as an example. A piece of wood is by nature straight or crooked; whether it can be used as a beam or a truss is determined by its capacity. While the nature of wood is always good in general, the capacity of a particular piece of wood may be good or bad, depending on how it is treated and how it is to be used (*Er Cheng quanshu*, *Yishu*, 19.4b).

By formulating binary categories to express the dynamism and materiality of the universe, Cheng Yi was implicitly criticizing Buddhism. In eleventh-century China, Buddhism as an ethical and religious doctrine (especially Chan Buddhism) competed with neo-Confucianism and posed a threat to it. In many respects, neo-Confucianism was a response to Buddhism, particularly to Buddhist metaphysics, which had proved to be far more sophisticated than Confucian metaphysics. By stressing the dynamism and materiality of the universe, Cheng Yi joined other neo-Confucianists (such as Zhou Dunyi and Zhang Zai) in affirming that the universe is a living entity and human existence is not illusory.

An example of Cheng Yi's anti-Buddhist stance is found in a conversation with a student on avoiding external stimulation:

> Question: How about hating external things?
> Answer: This is due to ignorance of the Way. How can things be hated? That is the doctrine of the Buddhists.

> They want to cast aside affairs, and do not ask whether according to *li* [principle, reason] they exist or not. If they exist, how can you cast them aside? (*Er Cheng quanshu, Yishu*, 18.10b; Chan 1963, 564)

By emphasizing mastery of the external environment in moral cultivation, Cheng Yi indicates the neo-Confucian belief that the universe is organic.

To clarify similarities and differences between him and his brother, we can consider a statement in which Cheng Yi summarized his moral philosophy: "Self-cultivation requires seriousness; the pursuit of learning depends on the extension of knowledge" (*Er Cheng quanshu, Yishu*, 18.5b). The first half of the statement is what Cheng Hao advocates—introspection to return to one's innate goodness. In the second half, Cheng Yi adds something to Cheng Hao's suggestion: he calls for sincere efforts to increase one's knowledge of the external world. The statement as a whole gives equal weight to the inner and outer, or spiritual and practical, dimensions of moral cultivation. It helps to define the position of the *li* school (*lixue*) of neo-Confucianism.

Cheng Yi's statement is also significant in that it incorporates the *Great Learning* (*Daxue*) into the neo-Confucian discourse. Thus far, eleventh-century neo-Confucianists had based their philosophies on four texts: the *Book of Changes*, *Analects*, *Mencius*, and *Doctrine of the Mean*. Zhou Dunyi and Zhang Zai, for instance, founded their moral metaphysics on their reading of the *Book of Changes* (especially the *Great Appendix*) and the *Doctrine of the Mean* (especially the concept of *cheng*, "sincerity"). Cheng Hao had made frequent reference to the *Analects* and the *Mencius* to elucidate his concept of cultivation of the mind. But the *Great Learning* (originally a chapter in the *Book of Rites*) did not have a prominent role in neo-Confucian discourse until Cheng Yi built his moral philosophy on it.

In the second half of Cheng Yi's statement, "extension of knowledge" (*zhizhi*) is adopted from the *Great Learning*. Strikingly similar to Cheng Yi's moral thought, the *Great Learning* speaks of a dual process of outward expansion and inward deepening in moral cultivation. Regarding outward expansion, the *Great Learning* suggests four steps: cultivating one's life, regulating one's family, ordering one's state, and clearly manifesting one's character to the world. The four steps are like concentric circles that extend outward, enlarging one's social space—from self to family to state to universe. Parallel to them are four steps of inward deepening: rectification of the mind, sincerity of the will, extension of knowledge, and investigation of things (*gewu*). These steps lead one back to the inner world in a search for the true self—a search that is a process of unlearning and uncovering. By rectifying one's mind and making one's will sincere, one unlearns what society has imposed, liberating the social self to catch a glimpse of the natural self. Then, by the extension of knowledge, one finds one's common roots with all beings in the universe and regains a true identity as a cosmic being.

Cheng Yi chooses "extension of knowledge" as the exemplar of the four steps of inward deepening in the *Great Learning*—significantly, because this choice implies, at least in part, a critique of Cheng Hao's almost exclusive emphasis on the inner cultivation of the mind. It should be noted that Cheng Yi had great respect for his brother and may not have been aware that his own interpretation differed from Cheng Hao's. Still, by highlighting "extension of knowledge" rather than "rectification of the mind" as the most important step in the quest for the true self, Cheng Yi sees the quest as more experiential than introspective. One may know one's true self intellectually, but this knowledge must be put into practice: one must integrate oneself with the universe in daily life—otherwise, one cannot claim full self-knowledge.

To illustrate the distinction between knowledge acquired intellectually and knowledge gained from experience, Cheng Yi gives the example of being afraid of tigers. Virtually everyone, child or adult, knows that a tiger is dangerous; but no one is more "terror-filled" than the man who has been bitten by a tiger (*Er Cheng quanshu, Yishu*, 18.5a). Similarly, in moral cultivation, "rectification of the mind" gives only a mental picture of oneself. For a full, true understanding, one needs to combine this mental picture with the living experience of being a part of the cosmic family. In this regard, Cheng Yi anticipates Wang Yangming's distinction between prospective and retrospective moral knowledge, or knowledge anterior to action and knowledge posterior to action (Cua 1982).

Cheng Yi emphasizes not only extension of knowledge (*zhizhi*) but also investigation of things (*gewu*). When he was asked about the foundation of learning, he answered unequivocally that it was to rectify the mind and make the will sincere—adding, however, that rectification of the mind and sincerity of the will depended on the extension of knowledge, and extension of knowledge depended on investigation of things (*Er Cheng quanshu, Yishu*, 18.5b). When Cheng Yi asked his students to extend knowledge by investigating things, his purpose was not empirical knowledge. What he intended was a search for the *li* manifest in all beings. Since "the principle is one and its manifestations are many" (*liyi fenshu*), all things are manifestations of the cosmic principle. One may meditate on the nature of that cosmic principle, but for Cheng Yi, it is better to gain a sense of the principle by participating in its unfolding in life.

Since all beings in this world are manifestations of *li*, Cheng Yi sees "investigation of things" as a dynamic, all-inclusive activity. It is an investigation not of one or two specific things but of the general pattern that brings all things together. Comparing the universe to a tree, Cheng Yi says that there is a universal principle running through all myriad beings, just as a tree's lifeblood runs through the roots, trunk, branches, and leaves. Investigation of things can involve reading books, discussing moral issues, analyzing historical events, handling daily affairs, and so on. In any case, the end remains the same—uncovering the universal principle that underlies the transformation of things (*Er Cheng quanshu*, *Yishu*, 18.5a–b).

Concerning the investigation of things, *gewu*, Cheng Yi has confidence in his interpretation of *ge*. Literally, *ge* means "to examine." But Cheng Yi fears that this suggests an idle observer analyzing the world around him, and so he interprets *ge* as "to arrive," which has a different connotation—an image of an active participant interacting with things in the world.

To support this interpretation of *ge*, Cheng Yi cites, tellingly, a classic statement: "The spirits of imperial progenitors have arrived" (*Er Cheng quanshu*, *Yishu*, 18.5b). As the spirits of one's ancestors (though invisible) are always present, one does not need to go outside the home or even intellectualize laboriously to commune with them. What one needs to do is participate earnestly in the daily ancestral worship and the management of the house. If indeed "the principle (*li*) is one and its manifestations are many," what is ordinary is already spiritual, and what is mundane is already transcendent. One does not need to separate the mundane from the transcendent or reach transcendence through pure thought.

One way in which neo-Confucianists distinguished themselves from classical Confucianists was by restoring the Confucian texts to the canon. To replace the five texts of classical Confucianism (*Book of Changes*, *Book of Documents*, *Book of Rites*, *Book of Poetry*, and *Spring and Autumn Annals*), the neo-Confucianists put together their own classics, the Four Books: *Great Learning*, *Doctrine of the Mean* (these first two were originally chapters in the *Book of Rites*), *Analects*, and *Mencius*. The establishment of the Four Books was not completed until Zhu Xi (1130–1200), but Cheng Yi was instrumental in bringing the *Great Learning* into the neo-Confucian discourse. His emphasis on the last two steps of inward deepening in the *Great Learning* helped make this text a canon of neo-Confucian moral thought.

See also Cheng Hao; Confucianism: Song; *Daxue*; *Li* (Principle); *Liyi fenshu*; *Qi*; *Zhongyong*.

Bibliography

Chan, Wing-tsit, trans. *A Source Book in Chinese Philosophy*. Princeton, N.J.: Princeton University Press, 1963.

Cheng, Hao, and Cheng Yi. *Er Cheng quanshu*. Taipei: Zhonghua. (Reprint.)

Cua, A. S. "Harmony and the Neo-Confucian Sage." In *Moral Vision and Tradition: Essays in Chinese Ethics*. Washington, D.C.: Catholic University of America Press, 1998.

———. *The Unity of Knowledge and Action: A Study in Wang Yang-ming's Moral Psychology*. Honolulu: University of Hawaii Press, 1982.

Fung, Yu-lan. *A History of Chinese Philosophy*, trans. Derk Bodde, Vol. 2. Princeton, N.J.: Princeton University Press, 1953.

Graham, A. C. *Two Chinese Philosophers: Ch'eng Ming-tao and Ch'eng Yi-ch'uan*. La Salle, Ill.: Open Court, 1992.

Huang, Zongxi. *Sung Yuan xue'an*. Taipei: Zhonghua. (Reprint.)

Mou, Zongsan. *Xinti yu xingti* (The Substance of the Mind and the Substance of Human Nature), Vol. 2. Taipei: Zhengzhong, 1969.

Munro, Donald, ed. *Individualism and Holism: Studies in Confucian and Taoist Values*. Ann Arbor: University of Michigan Press, 1985.

Tu, Wei-ming. *Humanity and Self-Cultivation: Essays in Confucian Thought*. Berkeley, Calif.: Asian Humanities, 1979.

Chengyi (Ch'eng-i): Making One's Thoughts Sincere

Kwong-loi Shun

Chengyi (making one's thoughts sincere) is presented in the *Daxue* (*Great Learning*) along with *gewu* (investigation of things), *zhizhi* (extension of knowledge), and *zhengxin* (rectification of the heart), as four steps in the process of self-cultivation. The *Daxue* was originally a chapter in the *Liji* (*Record of Rites*), which was probably compiled in the early Han. It explains *chengyi* in terms of fully satisfying oneself and not deceiving onself, and it depicts the petty person as someone who does bad things when alone but tries to conceal his badness in the presence of a superior person. It also describes how what is on the inside is inevitably manifested on the outside, so that one cannot conceal from others the way one is. In the context of these observations, it refers twice to how a superior person is always watchful over *du* (solitude, privacy); this suggests that there is a close connection between *chengyi* and watchfulness over *du* (*Daxue*, ch. 6).

The character *yi*, often translated as "thought" or "will," is used in early texts to refer to one's thoughts and opinions, the meaning behind what one says, or the meaning behind certain words or practices (such as rituals). It can also refer to one's inclinations—wanting to see certain things happen or thinking of bringing about certain things—and thus *yi* is something one can attain or fail to attain. *Yi* in the sense of inclinations is closely related to *yu* (desire) and *zhi* (intentions, aims, directions of the heart), and the terms are sometimes used together. For example, the *Mozi* refers to one's *zhi* and *yi* (70.39) and to the *yu* of one's *yi* (47.27–28). Still, these terms have different connotations. *Yu* can refer to certain inclinations (such as the tendency of the senses to seek objects) that simply exist without our having reflective awareness of wanting specific things. *Yi*, however, is more reflective, in that one is aware of the object of one's *yi* as part of one's thoughts, which pertain to the heart (*xin*). And *yi* is a less focused or less directed state than *zhi*: while *yi* can be no more than a thought in favor of something, without any actual decision to act on it, *zhi* does involve forming an aim or an intention to act.

Cheng, often translated as "making sincere" or "making real," indicates that something is true, or really the case. In early Confucian texts, such as *Mengzi* (*Mencius*), *Xunzi, Daxue*, and *Zhongyong* (*Centrality and Commonality*; this, like *Daxue*, was originally a chapter in the *Liji*), *cheng* is used to refer to an ideal state in which the heart is completely inclined or directed toward ethics. Sometimes *cheng* is contrasted with false appearances (*wei*); for instance, the *Xunzi* refers to making one's *cheng* manifest and getting rid of false appearances (20.34). The combination *chengyi*, then, refers to a process of directing one's thoughts and inclinations truly and fully toward ethics—an idea that Zhu Xi (1130–1200) described as making real (*shi*) what emanates from the heart.

The idea of being watchful over *du* also occurs in the *Xunzi* (3.26–34), in the context of discussing *cheng* as a way of nourishing the heart and as a precondition for having a transforming effect on others. The text says that there will be no *du* without *cheng*. Watchfulness over *du* also occurs in the *Zhongyong* (ch. 1); here the context is a discussion of how the superior person is cautious about what is not perceptible and how nothing is more manifest than what is hidden and minute. Although the idea is not explicitly related to *cheng* in the *Zhongyong, cheng* is the main subject of discussion of the second half of that text.

The interpretation of *du*, which has the meaning of being alone, is a matter of scholarly disagreement. However, given the context in which it occurs in the *Daxue*, *Xunzi*, and *Zhongyong*, it probably refers to the innermost self, where the minute and subtle activities of the heart first emerge. The *Zhongyong* relates being watchful over *du* to being cautious and watchful over what is imperceptible; this is the point at which it goes on to say (as mentioned above) that nothing is more manifest than what is hidden and minute. The commentary by Zhu Xi notes that here, *du* probably refers to what one alone (*du*) knows about, which is not known to others—the minute and subtle activities of the heart that are not yet manifested outwardly. Zhu relates watchfulness *du* to the idea of cautiously examining *ji*. This term, *ji*, is highlighted in the thinking of Zhou Dunyi (1017–1073); Zhu interprets it as referring to the minute activities of the heart that are in a state of transition from what does not yet exist to what exists—that is, the very subtle tendencies that have just started to emerge from the heart. A similar interpretation can be found in other Confucian thinkers. For example, in commenting on the *Zhongyong*, Li Ao (eighth to ninth century) explains being watchful over *du* in terms of guarding one's innermost self (2.7a–7b).

A common theme in Confucian texts is that the condition of the heart will inevitably be manifested on the outside and be perceivable by others, and that one's power to transform others depends on the heart's being truly and fully inclined in an ethical direction. Thus, although initially the minute and subtle tendencies of the heart are known to oneself alone and not yet perceived by others, they will eventually become manifest, and one's power to transform depends on ensuring that they are fully directed toward ethics. In emphasizing the need to be watchful over *du*, the *Daxue* and the *Zhongyong* both highlight the eventual and inevitable manifestation of these subtle, minute tendencies, whereas the *Xunzi* and the *Zhongyong* stress that one's transforming effect on others depends on the complete ethical inclination of these tendencies.

In the *Daxue*, the idea of being watchful over *du* and the idea of *chengyi* are related: it is by being watchful over the minute tendencies of the heart when they first arise that one can direct one's thoughts and inclinations truly and fully toward ethics. Thus there will be no self-deception: not a single thought or inclination will be incongruous with what is ethical; there will be nothing that could cause the slightest reluctance or hesitation about doing good. In Zhu Xi's commentary, self-deception is illustrated by the petty person; that he should try to conceal his badness in the presence of a moral superior shows that he is aware of what is good but cannot fully devote himself to it. Also, despite his attempts to conceal his badness, it will inevitably be perceivable by others, since what is in oneself will eventually be manifested outwardly.

Chengyi, then, describes the aspect of self-cultivation that involves cautiously watching over the subtle operations of the heart to ensure that the heart is fully inclined toward ethics. This is needed if one is to have a transforming effect on others; in turn, that effect constitutes the ideal basis for government. Later Confucians disagree about the relative importance of different aspects self-cultivation—they do not agree, for example, about the importance of studying the classics—but they would continue to regard watchfulness over one's own heart as a significant part of the process.

See also *Cheng*; *Daxue*; Self-Deception; *Zhongyong*.

Bibliography

Daxue (Great Learning). In *Confucius: Confucian Analects, The Great Learning, and The Doctrine of the Mean*, trans. James Legge, 2nd ed. Oxford: Clarendon, 1893. (References are by chapter numbers, following Zhu Xi's division of the text.)

Li, Ao. *Li wengong ji*. Siku chuanshu series. (References are by volume and page numbers.)

Mengzi (Mencius). See D. C. Lau, trans. *Mencius*. London: Penguin, 1970.

Mozi. Harvard-Yenching Institute Sinological Index Series. (References are by chapter and line numbers.)

Xunzi. Harvard-Yenching Institute Sinological Index Series. (References are by chapter and line numbers. See also John Knoblock, trans. *Xunzi: A Translation and Study of the Complete Works*, 3 vols. Stanford, Calif.: Stanford University Press, 1988–1994.)

Zhongyong (Centrality and Commonality, or Doctrine of the Mean). In *Confucius: Confucian Analects, The Great Learning, and The Doctrine of the Mean*, trans. James Legge, 2nd ed. Oxford: Clarendon, 1893. (References are by chapter numbers, following Zhu Xi's division of the text.)

Zhou, Dunyi. *Zhou Dunyi ji*. Beijing: Zhonghua shuju, 1990.

Zhu, Xi. *Daxue zhangju* (Commentary on the *Daxue*).

———. *Zhongyong zhangju* (Commentary on the *Zhongyong*).

———. *Zhuzi yulei*. Beijing: Zhonghua shuju, 1986. (See also Wing-tsit Chan, trans. and comp. *A Source Book in Chinese Philosophy*. Princeton, N.J.: Princeton University Press, 1963, ch. 34.)

Chiang Kai-shek (Jiang Jieshi)

Ke-wen WANG

Chiang Kai-shek (1887–1975), also known as Jiang Zhongzheng, was the leader of Nationalist China. He was born in Fenghua, Zhejiang Province, and joined Sun Yat-sen's anti-Manchu revolutionary movement while studying at a military school in Japan in 1908. When the revolution of 1911 broke out, Chiang returned to China and took part in the uprisings in his home province. After the establishment of the republic, he again followed Sun in the failed "second revolution" against President Yuan Shikai. During the late

1910s, Chiang lived in Shanghai while occasionally offering his services to Sun's efforts against the warlord government in Beijing. In 1922, he came to Sun's assistance when Sun was ousted from Guangzhou by the local ruler Chen Jiongming. Chiang's relationship with Sun was said to have been strengthened after this incident.

In 1923 Sun, advised by the Comintern, instructed his Nationalist Party to form a United Front with the Chinese Communist Party. He sent Chiang on a study tour in the Soviet Union and then appointed Chiang commandant of the newly established military academy at Whampoa. This military position helped Chiang defeat other contenders for party leadership and assume control of the Guangzhou regime after Sun's death in 1925. The following year Chiang began the "northern expedition" to overthrow the warlords and reunify the country. As his troops entered the lower Yangtze (Changjiang) region in early 1927, Chiang, long dissatisfied with the United Front, broke off with the communists and massacred them in the thousands. In late 1928, the "northern expedition" was successfully completed and Chiang became the new leader of China.

In the next decade, Chiang's Nationalist government in Nanjing ruled the country as a party dictatorship. It faced constant threats from residual warlordism, communist insurgency, and Japanese aggression. Adopting a strategy of "domestic pacification before external resistance," Chiang made a series of territorial concessions to Japan while concentrating on crushing his domestic rivals. He waged several civil wars against the rebelling warlords and organized five "bandit-suppression" campaigns that eventually uprooted the communists from their base in Jiangxi. With help from western countries, the Nanjing government also improved the infrastructure of China's economy, especially in the coastal cities where the government's control was relatively stable.

Chiang's leadership, however, came under increasing criticism for its weak-kneed policy toward Japan. In December 1936, Chiang was placed under house arrest by one of his generals while visiting the northwestern city of Xi'an. He was released weeks later, after giving in to the general's demand that he stop his anticommunist campaigns and begin preparations for a war against Japan. That war came in July 1937. Although Chiang's forces suffered disastrous defeats in the first year of the war, losing the entire coastal areas to the invading Japanese, his prestige as the leader of national resistance rose. A second United Front with the Chinese communists was formed, in which the communists were allowed to keep their army and joined the Nationalists in the war effort. Chiang's wartime government in Chongqing (Chungking) fought a strenuous war with limited foreign help, until the Japanese attack on Pearl Harbor in 1941 brought the United States into the conflict. After that Chiang relied on American assistance for the continuation of the war while preparing for a showdown with his temporary communist ally.

As soon as Japan surrendered in 1945, a full-scale civil war broke out between the Nationalist government and the communists. To Chiang's surprise, the long war against Japan had left his party and army demoralized and corrupt but had transformed the communists into an experienced and popular force. The Nationalists lost almost every battle in the civil war and were driven out of the mainland by the communists in late 1949. Seeking refuge on the island of Taiwan, Chiang and remnants of his following were saved from total defeat by the outbreak of the Korean War in 1950. The United States, which had given up on Chiang a year earlier, decided to provide military and financial aid to Taiwan as part of its global strategy of "containment" of communism. For the next two decades, American protection and assistance ensured the survival of Chiang and his government in exile in Taiwan.

On the island, Chiang resumed his presidency of the "Republic of China" and was "reelected" four times, until his death. He ruled the island with an iron fist while continuing to claim sovereignty over the mainland. Political stability, American aid, and appropriate development strategies produced rapid economic growth in Taiwan during the 1960s and 1970s, while international support for Chiang's regime gradually faded. As the United States improved its relations with the People's Republic of China in the early 1970s, Taiwan lost its seat in the United Nations as well as its diplomatic ties with many countries. Chiang died, of an illness, amid this diplomatic crisis. His leadership on the island was passed on to his son, Jingguo (Chiang Ching-kuo).

Among the numerous books and treatises published under Chiang's name, the most famous may be *China's Destiny* (1943), an interpretation of China's recent past and a blueprint of its "revolutionary reconstruction"; and *Soviet Russia in China* (1956), a review of Sino-Soviet relations since the 1920s with an exposition of anticommunist strategies. Both works convey Chiang's strong anti-imperialist and nationalist sentiments. Chiang was certainly not alone among China's modern leaders in his desire for a strong and unified state. The interests of the state, in his view, take precedence over, and represent the ultimate realization of, the interests of the individual. However, the nationalism that Chiang (unlike many others of his generation) espoused was closely linked to an affirmation of China's cultural heritage.

Educated in Chinese classics, Chiang was traditional, and traditionalistic, in his worldview. Although he had been briefly attracted to social Darwinism in his youth, he was scarcely touched by the "new culture" of the May Fourth era. His leftist stance under the United Front of the early 1920s was largely motivated by political opportunism. Later, in *China's Destiny*, he would lament the erosive effects of western ideas such as communism and liberalism on China's social order. Despite his conversion to Christianity in the late 1920s—in order to marry Song Meiling, who had been educated in America—western culture was on the whole alien to Chiang. As commandant of the Whampoa Academy, he considered the writings of the Confucian generals Zeng Guofan and Hu Lingyi essential military and ideological texts. After assuming leadership of the Nationalist Party, he reinterpreted Sun Yat-sen's political doctrines as an embodiment of the Chinese "moral tradition" (*daotong*) and presented his anticommunism as a defense of that tradition.

The Chinese moral tradition, according to Chiang, was based primarily on Confucian ethics. A student of the Wang Yangming school of neo-Confucianism, Chiang believed that the "rectification of mind" (*zhengxin*) was the fundamental approach to all human problems. He regarded China's modern social and political crisis as at least in part a result of its moral decline. The key to the revolutionary reconstruction of China, therefore, should be a moral renewal. "The goal of our revolution," Chiang once proclaimed, "is to revive our cultural heritage; . . . specifically, it is to continuously promote the Chinese moral tradition." A collective rectification of the minds of the Chinese people, through the practice of Confucian ethics in daily life, would lead to what he described as a revival of China's "national spirit" (*minzu jingshen*), or the "soul of China" (*Zhongguohun*). Only when this "national spirit" was imbued in every Chinese could the survival of China be truly secured.

Chiang's vision of national renewal and reconstruction may be best seen in the "new life" movement he launched in 1934. In part an effort to cleanse the areas recently recovered from the communists of dangerous subversive influences, the movement aimed to restore social order by reforming the daily life of the populace. Its approaches combined elements of Confucianism, fascism, and the reformism of the Young Men's Christian Association (YMCA). The movement advocated moral renewal, with attention to attitudinal and behavioral details, as a substitute for socioeconomic programs in tackling China's rural problems. Chiang identified "four cardinal bonds" (decorum, righteousness, integrity, and a sense of shame) and "eight virtues" (loyalty, filial piety, benevolence, love, sincerity, righteousness, harmony, and peace), all derived from Confucian doctrines, as the essential moral principles that must be reintroduced into the thought and actions of the Chinese. His method of measuring the application of these principles by the people, however, was rather superficial—he expected them to be "tidy" and "clean" in their daily routines and habits. This apparently reflected his own military background and his militaristic approach to governing.

The "new life" movement failed miserably to accomplish its intended objectives, but Chiang remained convinced of the critical role of moral renewal in revolutionary reconstruction. After his retreat to Taiwan in 1949, he concluded that the fundamental cause of the Nationalist defeat on the mainland was in fact a failure in "education and culture." When Mao Zedong launched the Cultural Revolution in 1966, Chiang quickly responded by initiating the "Chinese cultural revival" movement on the island. The movement displayed much of the same concerns and approaches as the "new life" movement three decades earlier. It explicitly promoted Confucianism as the foundation of modern Chinese society and portrayed the Nationalist regime as the defender of China's tradition.

In an effort to affirm his status as Sun Yat-sen's intellectual heir, Chiang completed Sun's unfinished lectures, the "Three Peoples' Principles," by adding a treatise on education, recreation, and culture to Sun's principle of people's livelihood (*minsheng zhuyi*). He also provided his own interpretations of some of Sun's philosophical formulations. Sun had criticized the neo-Confucianist idea that "to know is easy, to act is difficult" and proposed instead that "to know is difficult, to act is easy" (*zhinan xingyi*). An admirer of Wang Yangming, Chiang attempted to find a compromise between the two propositions. He argued that Wang and Sun defined "knowledge" in different ways. Sun was referring to practical and specific knowledge, Chiang said, while Wang concerned himself with the innate human ability of "knowing." Thus their different observations did not contradict each other. On the basis of this theoretical compromise, Chiang developed his own "philosophy of action" (*lixing zhexue*). Since it is easy to act, as Sun had proposed, and since Wang had advised "unity of action and knowledge" (*zhixing heyi*), Chiang believed that the utmost emphasis should be placed on action. "In all of the universe, from past to present," he declared, "everything has been created by action. . . . Even thought and speech can be regarded as parts of (human) action." To exist is therefore to act; one rediscovers one's "innate knowledge" (*liangzhi*) only through action. At times

Chiang even broadened the connotation of "action" and equated it with "eternal movement" in the natural world. Yet epistemological clarity was never Chiang's primary concern; his main interests were social and political. Not unlike Sun before him, Chiang hoped that his philosophical exposition would convince his followers of the necessity of political action, of "practicing" (*shijian*) the revolution.

In his last years, facing new political situations in Taiwan, Chiang appeared to have moderated his attitude toward modern western intellectual trends. He suggested that the "essence" of the three peoples' principles could be summarized as "ethics, democracy and science," each corresponding to one of the three principles. The latter two, representing the "essence" of the principle of people's rights (*minquan zhuyi*) and the principle of people's livelihood, respectively, had been popular slogans of the May Fourth era. He now gave them credence. Nevertheless, Chiang continued to uphold "ethics" (*lunli*), defined in terms based on Confucianism as the "essence" of the first principle, the principle of people's national consciousness, or nationalism (*minzu zhuyi*). Ethics remained the deepest concern in his vision of nation-building.

See also Confucianism: Ethics; Confucianism: Tradition; Sun Yat-sen; Wang Yangming; *Zhixing Heyi*.

Bibliography

Chen, Tiejian, and Huang Daoxuan. *Jiang Jieshi yu Zhongguo wenhua* (Jiang Jieshi and Chinese Culture). Hong Kong: Zhonghua Bookstore, 1992.

Eastman, Lloyd E. *The Abortive Revolution: China under Nationalist Rule, 1927–1937*. Cambridge, Mass.: Harvard University Press, 1972.

———. *Seeds of Destruction: Nationalist China in War and Revolution, 1937–1949*. Stanford, Calif.: Stanford University Press, 1984.

Loh, Pichon. *The Early Chiang Kai-shek: A Study of His Personality and Politics, 1887–1924*. New York: Columbia University Press, 1971.

Qin, Xiaoyi, ed. *Xianzongtong Jianggong sixiang yanlun zongji* (A Comprehensive Collection of the Writings and Speeches of the Late President Chiang). Taipei: Guomindang dangshihui, 1984.

———, ed. *Zongtong Jianggong dashi changbian chugao* (A Preliminary Draft of the Chronology of President Chiang). Taipei: Guomindang dangshihui, 1978.

Comparative Philosophy

David B. Wong

Doing comparative philosophy compels one to examine one's deepest assumptions about value, knowledge, the structure of reality, and the proper way to do philosophy itself. The comparison of Chinese and western traditions has yielded fresh and illuminating perspectives on the basic assumptions of each tradition. Comparative philosophy, however, presents special pitfalls as well as special benefits. The desire to draw an interesting and dramatic contrast between traditions often leads to overgeneralization and oversimplification of each tradition, making both appear more different than they are. On the other hand, the desire to make another tradition speak to the problems of one's own tradition often leads to a blurring of genuine differences.

Comparisons in Ethical Philosophy

Zigong said, "What I do not wish others to impose on me, I also do not wish to impose on others" (*Lunyu*, 5.11). "A man of *ren* [humanity, benevolence], wishing to establish himself [to establish his character], helps others to establish themselves, and wishing to gain perception [to gain a thorough understanding of the *dao* or Way], helps others to gain perception" (6.28). It is impossible to ignore the resemblance of these sayings of Confucius to the western "golden rule" (for the Christian version, see Matthew 7:12). This point of convergence suggests that a frequent (if not invariable) function of ethical codes is to encourage consideration of others' interest and to keep in check the most socially harmful impulses of the "dear self," as Kant put it.

Two important themes with cross-cultural resonance emerge from Confucius's comment on a student who questions the need for a lengthy mourning period for one's parents: "Was Yu not given three years of love by his parents?" (17.21). One theme is an ethical norm of reciprocity, the duty to return good for good.

This theme is virtually universal across cultures, and it is not difficult to see why the theme would play an essential role in the life of creatures who survive and flourish through social cooperation but do not possess unlimited amounts of selfless goodwill toward their fellows. Another theme emerging from the passage is special duties toward those with whom one has some particular relationship—for example, duties that one has toward others not just because they are human but because they are one's family. As is well known, the Confucians defended the doctrine of "graded love" or "love with distinctions" (that one owes more to family members, say, than to strangers) against the Mohist doctrine of "universal" or equal and impartial love. A strikingly similar debate occurs within contemporary Anglo-American philosophy between utilitarians who see our fundamental duties as transcending the boundaries of special relationships (e.g., Singer 1972) and those who defend the irreducibility of special duties (e.g., MacIntyre 1984). A parallel conflict between duties to kin and duties to the state appears in *Antigone*, and it is the occasion for Socratic reflections on the nature of piety in the *Euthyphro*. Interestingly, Plato's motivations for eliminating the family in his ideal state are very much Mohist in spirit: to permit the family to survive is to encourage particularistic loyalties that undermine a wider concern for the common good (*Republic* 449c–d). Such conflicts may well be an inevitable feature of the ethical life across many different cultures: on the one hand, human beings depend on small groups for their survival, nurturance, and flourishing, and this gives rise to strong ethical ties within these groups; but on the other hand, these groups typically interact and cooperate, forming larger social units joined by the recognition of duties that transcend the boundaries of family, friendship, and local community. Perpetual debate about the relative priorities of these potentially conflicting duties would seem an inevitable result.

Confucian ethics fits into the category of "virtue ethics" and can appropriately be compared with ancient Greek ethics in this regard. As exemplified by the *junzi* (the superior person, the gentleman) and virtues such as *ren* (humanity, benevolence), *yi* (righteousness), and *li* (conformity to rules of propriety or of ritual), virtue ethics provides guidance to the individual primarily through description of ideal personhood and character traits to be realized rather than the application of general principles purporting to identify general characteristics of right or dutiful action. The very concept of *yi* connotes the ability to identify and perform the action that is appropriate to the particular context. While the traditional rules of ritual provide one with a sense of what is appropriate given standard contexts, the virtue of *yi* allows one to identify when those rules need to be set aside in exigent circumstances (Cua 1998). The parallel with Aristotelian practical wisdom (*phronesis*) is striking. The contemporary revival of virtue ethics is premised partly on a reaction against the ambition of modern ethical theory to guide primarily through general principles of action rather than through the specification of ideal character traits. That ambition has been judged overreaching and insufficiently heedful of the need to judge what is required in the particular context. Virtue ethics also tends to embody the theme that the ethical life is necessary for flourishing as a human being. This theme emerges most clearly in Mencius, who identifies distinctively human potential with incipient tendencies to develop the moral virtues (*Mengzi*, 2A.6, 6A.1, 3, 7). Aristotle held that reason makes us distinctively human, and that reason and our social nature compel recognition of the desirability of the ethical life for human beings (*Nicomachean Ethics*, 1097b, 1103b; see also Nivison 1996 for comparisons of Aristotle and Mencius and Yearley 1990 for comparisons of Aquinas and Mencius).

The similarities coexist with significant differences, however. Even if both Chinese and Greek virtue ethics emphasize the desirability of the ethical life, the Greeks seem to have been drawn to a quest for theoretical truth for its own sake, as exemplified by Aristotle's claim that a life focused on theoretical contemplation is best, while the social life of responsibility to others is secondary (*Nicomachean Ethics* 1179a). The Confucians are comparatively unequivocal about the primacy of the social life in individual flourishing, and this perhaps reflects a difference in the value placed on theoretical truth for its own sake. (It is a good possibility, furthermore, that in the Confucian tradition no importance was placed on the distinction between truth for its own sake and its practical consequences; see the discussion below on epistemology and metaphysics.)

Another contrast arises from the focus in modern western morality on individual rights to liberty and to other goods, where the basis for such rights to persons lies in attributing moral worth to each individual independently of what conduces to his or her responsibilities to self and others. Confucianism lacks a comparable concept, given its assumption that the ethical life of responsibility to others and individual flourishing are inextricably intertwined. There is little space for the idea that individuals may have ethically legitimate interests that conflict with the interests of the communities to which they belong. This sort of contrast has prompted such views as Hegel (1956) had to the effect that Chinese Confucian ethics exemplifies a less advanced stage in moral thinking than moralities with modern European origins. On the other side, some advocates of Confucian ethics criticize rights-focused morality for ignoring the social nature of human beings and portraying human life in terms of an excessively "atomistic" or "individualist" concept of persons (e.g., Rosemont 1986).

Such criticisms may not do justice to the complexity of comparing and evaluating traditions. Against the rights-oriented critics of Confucianism, it could be said that the framework of rights is not the only way to tend to the needs of individuals and protect them against mistreatment; the framework of responsibilities to others can afford significant protections and arguably addresses the human need for community and belonging better than rights frameworks (Rosemont 1991). Moreover, it is possible that rights in some sense did play a role in the Confucian tradition, even if such rights were not grounded in the idea of the independent moral worth of the autonomous individual. Rights in the sense of morally justified claims to be protected in certain kinds of action or morally justified entitlement to certain kinds of goods can be justified as necessary for individual flourishing and the life of responsibility to others. Mencius recognized a right to revolution against tyrannical kings (*Mengzi* 1B.8); furthermore, he advised kings to attach more weight to the opinions of their people than to those of their ministers and officers in making certain crucial decisions, implying that the people have a right to speak up (1B.7). Mencius's Confucian rival, Xunzi, recognized the need for subordinates to speak their views freely to their superiors and hence, by implication, their right to speak (*Xunzi, Zidao, Way of the Son*). On the other side, one must be wary of oversimplifications of western rights-oriented ethical codes. The social nature of persons is not denied by all such codes. (Of the major theorists, only Hobbes seems to take an unambiguously "atomistic" view of human beings, and Rousseau and Locke seem to require no such view.) It could further be argued that rights-oriented codes provide individuals greater protection when their interests collide with communal or social interests.

An evaluative stance different from asserting the superiority of one or the other tradition is that each tradition has something important to learn from the other. Chinese philosophy emphasizes the need to pay attention to the concrete details of the situation at hand and displays healthy skepticism about the power of general principle to reveal what sort of action is suitable to the situation. It displays an appreciation for the power of tradition, and in particular the *li*, in helping to make vivid and concrete and therefore meaningful such ethical abstractions as love, respect, and care for others. On the other hand, an appreciation for the concrete and for the culturally specific may obscure the possibility of general and transcultural principles that help to evaluate the concrete and culturally specific (Cua 1985).

A fourth possible attitude toward difference is that each tradition is not wrong to emphasize different values. The argument for such a pluralistic or relativistic answer may start with the claim that each sort of ethics focuses on a good that may reasonably occupy the center of an ethical ideal for human life. On one hand, there is the good of belonging to and contributing to a community; on the other, there is the good of respect for the individual apart from any potential contribution to community. It would be surprising, the argument goes, if there were just one justifiable way of setting a priority with respect to the two goods. On this view, comparative ethics teaches us about the diversity and richness of what human beings may reasonably prize, and about the impossibility of reconciling all they prize in just a single ethical ideal (e.g., Wong 1984).

Buddhism and Daoism are often adduced as evidence for a wide ethical gulf between east and west. There are, however, some important parallels in these philosophies to the Hellenistic Stoics and Epicureans, who argued for the need to accept the inevitable in human life, the need to dampen one's desires to achieve tranquillity in the face of the inevitable, and an identification with the world that makes acceptance and dampening of desires possible (Nussbaum 1994). These important parallels coexist with the equally important contrast over the Stoic belief in *logos* as the basis of the order of the world.

Some striking parallels and contrasts appear when Nietzsche is compared with Daoist and Buddhist thinkers. On one hand, there is a common wariness of the use of ethical categories. More specifically, Nietzsche and Zhuangzi share an awareness of the possible use of such categories to assert power over others and to dominate them (*Zhuangzi*, ch. 5; Nietzsche, *On the Genealogy of Morals*). On the other hand, the contrasts between Nietzsche and these eastern philosophies are perhaps more striking. Nietzsche ends up proposing a radically individualistic break from ethical relation to others to a single-minded dedication to the aesthetic project of fashioning a life for oneself that is like a work of art. Given his emphatic rejection of conventional ethical values and his relatively low interest in refashioning Chinese society (at least compared with the *Daodejing*), Zhuangzi might be the closest the Chinese tradition comes to Nietzsche. Even Zhuangzi, however, advocates a kind of acceptance of the low and the lowly that seems anathema to Nietzsche's celebration of the *Übermensch*. Moreover, Nietzsche is well known for his scorn for the Buddhist theme of the oneness and interdependence of all life and of the resulting universal compassion. He would have rejected similarly the *Daodejing*'s embrace of compassion (ch. 67). More fundamentally, Nietzsche proposes strong, vital desire as the heart of the individual's aesthetic project, rather than its dampening. Nietzsche seems to represent a kind of radical individualism that did not find a congenial home in the Chinese tradition (Solomon 1995).

Some might argue that comparisons like those articulated above are fundamentally misguided in presupposing that various thinkers in the Chinese and western traditions are all talking about the same sort of thing, which is called "morality" in the west. Some contemporary thinkers (e.g., Williams 1985) have tended to confine the "moral" to a relatively narrow set of characteristics associated with Kant's moral philosophy—a belief in universal laws validated by pure reason, a belief that responsibility for one's actions requires freedom from determination by external causes. On this view of the moral, it could be argued that there is no equivalent in Chinese philosophy (Rosemont 1988). Yet such a conception of the moral seems to give Kant and his followers too much credit for having captured all that people in the west have meant by "morality," neglecting, for example, those filial duties and character traits recognized in western morality that overlap with Chinese virtue ethics such as Confucianism.

Cultures that emphasize the moral rights of individuals are also cultures that recognize duties between parents and children and such virtues as kindness, for example. Indeed, some Anglo-American philosophers have criticized modern western moral *theory* precisely for its neglect of the special duties and virtues that make possible a decent life with others (Baier 1987; MacIntyre 1981). Indeed, this overlap between a revival of interest in western virtue ethics and the virtue features of Confucian ethics accounts for much of the current surge of western interest in Chinese philosophy. Here it is absolutely crucial to keep in mind the difference between theories put forward by thinkers in a culture and the complex phenomena these theories are meant to explain. Such theories typically highlight certain aspects of the phenomena but obscure others. Comparative Chinese and western writers intent on portraying dramatic contrasts between cultures sometimes choose theories that conveniently support their case, paying insufficient attention to whether or not the theories are adequate explanations. One error of comparative philosophy is imposing an alien conceptual framework on another tradition, but a complementary error is extreme contextualism, under which any attempt to note broad thematic similarities across cultures is condemned as an unacceptable distortion of meaning uprooted from the surrounding web of belief and practice. The possibility of doing comparative philosophy squeezes in somewhere between these two errors.

To consider another example, the way in which Daoism and certain schools of Buddhism seem to reject conventional ethical values (for this theme in Chan Buddhism, see Huineng, *Liu zutanjing*, and *Recorded Conversations of Yixuan*) might make the Chinese tradition seem dramatically different from the west, but one must keep in mind that these philosophies seem to espouse a certain way of life that in many respects coincides with what might be called an ethic. Moreover, it is not difficult to find counterparts such as Nietzsche in the west to this combination of rejection of conventional ethics and espousal of unconventional ethics.

Comparisons in Epistemology and Metaphysics

Points of divergence over epistemology are perhaps best introduced through a contrast between Chinese and western conceptions of the modes and aims of philosophy. Confucius's *Lunyu* opens not with an argument but with a series of questions:

> To learn something and regularly practice it—is it not a joy? To have friends come from distant states—is it not a pleasure? Not to complain when men do not know you—is it not like a *junzi* [superior person, gentleman]? (1.1)

Such passages exemplify a method of persuasion that is not argumentative but invitational (Naess and Hannay 1972). Confucius was not propounding a set of doctrines and defending them with systematic argument but portraying a way of life to which a person would be drawn once it was properly understood. The *Daodejing* uses a similar method of persuasion to endorse an empty way of life free of contention with others and things (ch. 8). The *Zhuangzi* exemplifies not only an invitational mode of persuasion but the sort of therapeutic aim for philosophy that has parallels in Nietzsche and Wittgenstein but has occupied a more central place in mainstream Chinese philosophy than in western philosophy. The therapeutic aim typically presupposes skepticism about the power of argumentative and analytical methods of discovering the truth, or at least (in Wittgenstein's case) the kind of truth philosophers have sought. It is controversial whether *Zhuangzi* offers some other way of finding the truth in place of argumentative and analytical methods. What is clear is that it offers a way of being at home in the world which does not depend on these methods. That is what makes its aim therapeutic.

The argumentative mode is by no means absent from Chinese philosophy. It was Mozi's enduring contribution to the Chinese tradition to have explicitly introduced modes of critical analysis and argumentation. Mencius responded to Mo's critique of Confucianism through counterargumentation (Shun 1997), and Xunzi countered Mencius within the Confucian tradition with perhaps the most sophisticated and self-conscious methods of argumentation in the classical period (Cua 1985). The invitational mode of persuasion, however, is still strongly present in Mencius, as is evidenced by his discussion of the kind of courage that allows one to go forward against men in the thousands as long as one is in the right, a courage that allows tranquillity in the face of danger, the kind of courage that comes of cultivating one's heaven-sent sprouts of goodness and that allows one to cultivate the "flood-like *qi* [energy-stuff] that fills the space between Heaven and Earth" (*Mengzi* 2A.2). This is not argumentation but an invitation to realize a state of being.

The relative centrality of invitational method in Chinese philosophy may reflect a trait that is shared in varying degrees between Confucianism, Daoism, and Chinese Buddhism: a certain humility about human powers of theorizing, rational analysis, and argumentation in the face of the fullness of experience. Confucianism emphasizes that the particular cannot be eliminated from ethical judgment, especially as regards its virtue of *yi* (righteousness or rightness) and the way it constitutes the ultimate ground and basis for correcting or setting aside the general rules of *li* (ritual, propriety). Daoism emphasizes the way that experience invariably overflows the artificial and rigid boundaries of human names and categories of opposites. Chinese Buddhism turns this humility into a full-blown skepticism about the ultimate reality of the human self and a positive metaphysical view about the ultimate oneness and interdependence of things that our analytical powers would lead us to believe are ultimately distinct.

This humility about the human powers of theorizing, analysis, and argumentation corresponds to a confidence in practical human wisdom, a wisdom that apparently greatly exceeds human discursive resources for grounding and explaining its successes. This is the truth behind the common observation that Chinese philosophy is comparatively concrete, worldly, and practical. Given such epistemological themes, then, it should not be surprising if therapeutic aims and nonargumentative modes of persuasion should be more central to the Chinese tradition than to the western tradition.

It is important to note, however, that such features distinguish Chinese philosophy through their comparative centrality to the tradition as a whole. Similar features, after all, do appear in the western tradition, and sometimes in the most central of thinkers. Nietzsche and Wittgenstein, as indicated above, apply nonargumentative modes of persuasion and have therapeutic aims. David Hume's skeptical doubts about the unitary and stable self (*Treatise of Human Nature*, Book 1, sec. 6) would have fit nicely with Buddhist and Daoist themes. The theme of intuitive apprehension of reality as a unity underlying sensible diversity is of course found in mystical literature of the Christian and Jewish traditions.

Most traditions worth studying are complex and to a significant degree heterogeneous. Generalizations about the ways that Chinese movements such as the Confucian and the Buddhist differ from the ancient Greek or the modern western European tradition, for instance, are at best generalizations about the ways that dominant or frequently accepted themes differ. Themes that sound strangely familiar can emerge from the most exotic traditions. For example, a significant internal counterpoint to the dominant Confucian theme of nature as containing ethical qualities is represented by Xunzi's conception of nature as neutral to human aspirations and as a thing to be understood for the sake of satisfying these aspirations (*Xunzi, tianlun*). Part of the value of doing comparative philosophy may, in fact, lie not in confronting some totally alien system of thought but in recognizing how themes that are not currently dominant in one's own tradition are combined in unfamiliar ways and given enduringly dominant places in other traditions.

An issue about truth arises from the fact that in the Chinese tradition one rarely finds an appreciation of discovering the way things *really* are, divorced from all questions of how such a discovery would fit into a desirable way of life. Some hold that the lack of distinction between truth and desirability reflects a radical difference between western and Chinese conceptions of language and reality. One possible view along these lines (Hansen 1992) is that the classical Chinese thinkers conceived of the primary function of language not as descriptive or as attempting to match propositions with states of affairs, but rather as a pragmatic instrument for guiding behavior. A related interpretation is that the *dao* or Way in a thinker such as Confucius was conceived not as a reality independent of tradition and language, against which linguistically formulated beliefs were to be measured and judged reliable or unreliable, but in fact as a cumulative creation of individuals working from within a context provided by tradition (Hall and Ames 1987).

Such interpretations would align the classical Chinese thinkers with critics in the western tradition who have criticized the mainstream assumptions of a propositional theory of language, a correspondence theory of truth, and a realistic view of the relation between language and reality. While Confucius does show tolerance and flexibility in judging where the Way lies, it seems going too far to present him as a clear alternative to the western mainstream of thought about truth. When Confucius says that filial piety and brotherly love are at the root of humanity (1.2), there is no indication that he is limiting the claim to Chinese culture; rather, he means to say something about human beings generally. He is talking about the way human beings must learn to respond to authority that is based not on force or coercion but on love, respect, and care. Furthermore, Confucius clearly believes that rulers cannot hold power simply on the basis of law and punishment and that they need a kind of moral authority. He condemns the abuse of power for the sake of personal ambition or conspicuous consumption. There is no sign that such judgments are limited in scope to his own time and place.

Similarly, an urge to present the classical thinkers as a clearly pragmatic and antimetaphysical alternative to western mainstream metaphysics leads to some serious distortions. One must be very creative in explaining away all those apparently metaphysical passages in the *Daodejing* such as Chapter 4, where *dao* is described as empty, as seeming something like the ancestor of all things, as appearing to precede the *di*, "lord" (LaFargue 1992). Moreover, the passage on the "floodlike" *qi* in the *Mengzi* seems clearly metaphysical and links the *dao* of humanity with the *dao* of Heaven (*tian*).

However this issue is resolved, no one has denied that nonbeing *eventually* acquired frankly metaphysical meanings in the Chinese tradition, where it refers at the least to an indeterminate ground in which the determinate "ten thousand things" are incipient (Neville 1989). This embrace of an indeterminate ground of the determinate may reflect a decision to give a fundamental place in ontology to the phenomenon of change, rather than to an absolutely stable being as in Parmenidean ontology and as later reflected in Aristotelian and Cartesian notions of substance (Cheng 1989, 1991). The revival of interest in Chinese metaphysics has been fueled partly by a perception that twentieth-century physics undermined the strategy of giving determinate being ontological primacy (Zukav 1979).

The neo-Confucians Zhu Xi and Wang Yangming represent, respectively, the metaphysical and pragmatic bents present in the Chinese tradition. Zhu Xi (*Zhuzi yulei*) reinterpreted ethical themes inherited from the classical thinkers and grounded them in a cosmology and metaphysics. On his conception of *ren* as an all-inclusive virtue, it constitutes the Way (*dao*) and consists of the fact that the mind of heaven and earth to produce things is present in everything, including the mind of human beings. Wang Yangming (*Chuanxi lu*) taught of the sage who formed one body with heaven and earth and the "ten thousand things," but he showed little of Zhu's interest in the *li* or principle of existent things. The investigation of things prescribed in the *Great Learning* (*Daxue*) was not the empirical inquiry Zhu envisioned but a rectification of the mind, ridding it of evil thoughts. Neither Zhu nor Wang constitutes an anomalous development of the classical tradition. Rather, both of them represent a development of tendencies which were present from the beginning and between which there was never conceived to be a mutually exclusive choice.

The temptation to see an interest in the metaphysical and culturally transcendent as anomalous or exported into the Chinese tradition is a temptation to see its thinkers as representing the path not taken by western philosophy, a path the interpreter might see as better or worse. Ironically, the path not taken in China is often taken in the western tradition, even if it is less trodden. The danger behind this temptation is that Chinese thinkers are enlisted in a fight that was not theirs and that perhaps they do not even regard as a fight. The alternative path the classical thinkers represent may rather be the *absence* of a division between the metaphysical and the pragmatic or the transcendent and the culturally particular. What is striking about the discussion of truth in the mainstream tradition is that it is highly theoretical and on a meta-level. To place oneself on one side or another of this debate, one must have the relevant theoretical concerns, and it is not clear that such concerns were present in the Chinese tradition. One simply does not find in China the discussions of the nature of truth that one finds early in the western tradition—in Plato and Aristotle, for instance. There is plenty of discussion that amounts to a search for *truths* about how to live and, as some might hold, the nature of the world; but there is none about the abstract concept of truth itself. Sometimes the search for truths lead to claims that seem to be concerned with things existing independently of human thought, and sometimes the main concern is how truths encourage human beings to lead a desirable life, but the anomalous element in the Chinese tradition may be, not an exclusive focus on one or the other, but rather the thought that one must somehow make a choice between these concerns.

Another topic that involves similar questions concerns the different ways in which the human being is "parsed" by traditions. Much of classical Confucian ethics contains no division between the rational, the emotional, and the appetitive parts comparable to the division that played such a large role in ancient Greek ethics, for example, and that in some form or another continues to play a role in the western tradition. For example, Mencius's inborn moral sprouts (*duan*) exhibit characteristics we associate with feeling or emotion but also possess a cognitive dimension of judgment. The sprout he calls the sense of right and wrong obviously possesses the cognitive dimension, but so does the sense of shame (Wong 1991a, b). The parable he tells (3A.5) about the ancients who did not bury their parents illustrates both the conative and the cognitive aspects of the sprouts. When the sons passed by the bodies of their parents they had thrown into gullies, a sweat broke out on their brows, they could not bear to look, and they buried their parents' bodies. Mencius presents their reactions, clearly conative in nature, as revealing the rightness of burying their parents. Feeling can be a guide to what is right and appropriate. Consider, by contrast, Plato's story in the *Republic* (440a) about Leontius, whose eyes (standing in for the appetitive part of the soul) desired to look at the corpses of human beings, whose reason told him that looking would be shameful, and whose spirited part became furious when his eyes defied his reason. Feeling (or, at least, anger) can be an ally of reason, but it is reason that discerns what is right.

A common and popular reaction to the difference between Mencius and, say, Plato is to conclude that Chinese philosophy is much more "intuitive" and "nonrational" than western philosophy. But again, this might be a mistaken enlisting of Chinese thinkers into an intramural fight within the western tradition between the "rationalist" mainstream and dissenters. As was noted above, Mencius certainly knows how to use argument. Reason is not absent from his philosophy; rather, the boundaries between reasoning, wanting, and feeling are not drawn sharply, and an issue is not made of whatever division can be made.

Xunzi's picture of moral motivation makes it even harder to see the Chinese tradition as emphasizing the intuitive and nonrational in its picture of the person. In his conception of human nature as containing desires for gain that lead to a self-destructive conflict with others, and in his conception of morality as born of the sages' reasoned reflection on what rules most effectively curb and transform this nature, Xunzi anticipates Hobbes. In his emphasis on the capacity of the mind to approve or disapprove of its inborn desires for gain and to prevent action on those desires when it runs against the self's overall interests to do so, Xunzi gets as close as many thinkers in the western tradition to Plato (or, for that matter, Kant). It is not clear how Xunzi conceives of the mind's power over desire, however. The original impetus for the sages to try to change human nature is rational self-interest, and he has a problem explaining how one can become a Confucian *junzi* whose motivations are of an altogether different kind (Nivison 1996). The solution to Xunzi's problem may lie in his chapter on ritual, where he further explains how acting according to the rules of ritual (*li*) can inculcate moral desires in human beings. His story seems to depend on positing in human nature some original feelings for family members such as parents (*Xunzi, Lilun pian*—"Discussion of Rites"). The power of the mind over desire, then, may rest in part on natural human feelings that are strengthened and trained according to the rules of morality. Here again, the temptation to see Xunzi as a Chinese version of Plato or Kant probably entails mapping philosophical divisions originating in the western tradition onto a thinker who did not make quite the same divisions.

See also Confucianism: Ethics; *Daxue*; *Junzi*; Mencius; Xunzi; Zhuangzi.

Bibliography

Allinson, Robert E., ed. *Understanding the Chinese Mind: Philosophical Roots*. Hong Kong: Oxford University Press, 1989.

Baier, Annette. "Hume, the Women's Moral Theorist." In *Women and Moral Theory*, ed. Eva Feder Kitay and Diana T. Meyers. Totowa, N.J.: Rowman and Littlefield, 1987.

Cheng, Chung-ying. "Chinese Metaphysics as Non-Metaphysics: Confucian and Daoist Insights into the Nature of Reality." In *Understanding the Chinese Mind: The Philosophical Roots*, ed. Robert E. Allinson. Hong Kong: Oxford University Press, 1989.

———. *New Dimensions of Confucian and Neo-Confucian Philosophy*. Albany: State University of New York Press, 1991.

Cua, Antonio S. "Confucian Vision and Human Community." *Journal of Chinese Philosophy*, 11, 1984.

———. *Ethical Argumentation: A Study in Hsün Tzu's Moral Epistemology*. Honolulu: University of Hawaii Press, 1985.

———. *Moral Vision and Tradition: Essays in Chinese Ethics*. Washington, D.C.: Catholic University of America Press, 1998.

Hall, David L., and Roger T. Ames. *Thinking through Confucius*. Albany: State University of New York Press, 1987.

Hansen, Chad. *A Daoist Theory of Chinese Thought: A Philosophical Interpretation*. New York: Oxford University Press, 1992.

Hegel, Georg Wilhelm Friedrich. *The Philosophy of History*. New York: Dover, 1956.

Hume, David. *A Treatise of Human Nature*. Oxford: Clarendon, 1951.

LaFargue, Michael. *The Tao of the Tao Te Ching*. Albany: State University of New York Press, 1992.

MacIntyre, Alasdair. *After Virtue*. Notre Dame, Ind.: University of Notre Dame Press, 1981.
———. "Is Patriotism a Virtue?" Lindley Lectures, University of Kansas, 1984.
Naess, Arne, and Alastair Hannay, eds. *Invitation to Chinese Philosophy: Eight Studies*. Oslo: Universitetsforlaget, 1972.
Neville, Robert. "The Chinese Case in a Philosophy of World Religions." In *Understanding the Chinese Mind: The Philosophical Roots*, ed. Robert E. Allinson. Hong Kong: Oxford University Press, 1989.
Nivison, David S. "Two Roots or One?" *Proceedings and Addresses of the American Philosophical Association*, 53, 1980, pp. 739–761.
———. *The Ways of Confucianism*, ed. Bryan Van Norden. La Salle, Ill.: Open Court, 1996.
Nussbaum, Martha C. *The Therapy of Desire: Theory and Practice in Hellenistic Ethics*. Princeton, N.J.: Princeton University Press, 1994.
Rosemont, Henry. "Against Relativism." In *Interpreting across Boundaries*. Princeton, N.J.: Princeton University Press, 1988.
———. *A Chinese Mirror: Moral Reflections on Political Economy and Society*. La Salle, Ill.: Open Court, 1991.
———. "Kierkegaard and Confucius: On Finding the Way." *Philosophy East and West*, 36, 1986, pp. 208–209.
Shun, Kwong-loi. "*Jen* and *Li* in the Analects." *Philosophy East and West*, 43, 1993, pp. 457–479.
———. *Mencius and Early Chinese Thought*. Stanford, Calif.: Stanford University Press, 1997.
Singer, Peter. "Famine, Affluence, and Morality." *Philosophy and Public Affairs*, 1, 1972, pp. 29–43.
Smart, J. J. C. "Extreme and Restricted Utilitarianism." *Philosophical Quarterly*, 6, 1956.
Solomon, Robert C. "The Cross-Cultural Comparison of Emotion." In *Emotions in Asian Thought*, ed. Joel Marks and Roger T. Ames. Albany: State University of New York Press, 1995.
Tu, Wei-ming. *Humanity and Self-Cultivation: Essays in Confucian Thought*. Berkeley, Calif.: Asian Humanities, 1979.
Williams, Bernard. *Ethics and the Limits of Philosophy*. Cambridge, Mass.: Harvard University Press, 1985.
Wong, David. "Is There a Distinction between Reason and Emotion in Mencius?" *Philosophy East and West*, 41, 1991a.
———. *Moral Relativity*. Berkeley, Calif.: University of California Press, 1984.
———. "Universal Love versus Love with Distinctions: An Ancient Debate Revived." *Journal of Chinese Philosophy*, 16, 1989.
———. "Xunzi on Moral Motivation." In *Chinese Language, Thought, and Culture: Nivison and His Critics*, ed. Philip J. Ivanhoe. Chicago, Ill.: Open Court, 1991b.
Yearley, Lee H. *Mencius and Aquinas: Theories of Virtue and Conceptions of Courage*. Albany: State University of New York Press, 1990.
Zukav, Gary. 1979. *The Dancing Wu Li Masters*. New York: Morrow, 1979.

Confucianism: Confucius (Kongzi, K'ung Tzu)

Roger T. Ames

Confucius (551–479 B.C.E.) is arguably the most influential philosopher in human history—"is" rather than "was" because Confucius is still very much alive. He is recognized as China's first teacher both chronologically and in importance, and his ideas have been the rich soil in which the Chinese cultural tradition has grown and flourished. In fact, whatever we might mean by "Chineseness" today, some 2,500 years after his death, is inseparable from the example of personal character that Confucius provided for posterity. And his influence did not end with China. All the Sinitic cultures—especially (outside China) Korea, Japan, and Vietnam—have evolved around ways of living and thinking derived from the wisdom of the sage.

The Historical Context

Confucius was born in the state of Lu in one of the most formative periods of Chinese culture. Two centuries before his birth, scores of small city-states owing allegiance to the house of Zhou filled the Yellow River basin. This was the Zhou dynasty (c. 1100–256 B.C.E.), out of which the empire of China was to emerge. By the time of Confucius's birth in the middle of the sixth century B.C.E., only fourteen independent states remained, with seven of the strongest elbowing each other militarily for hegemony over the central plains. It was a period of escalating internal violence, driven by the knowledge that no state was exempt, and that all comers were competing in a zero-sum game—to fail to win was to perish. The accelerating ferocity of battle was like the increasing frequency and severity of labor pains, anticipating the eventual birth of the Chinese empire.

Not only was the landscape diverse politically. Intellectually, Confucius set a pattern for the "hundred schools" that emerged during these centuries in their competition for doctrinal supremacy. Confucius began the practice of independent philosophers' traveling from state to state in an effort to persuade political leaders that their particular teachings were a practicable formula for social and political success. In the decades that followed the death of Confucius, intellectuals of every stripe—Confucians, legalists, Mohists, *yinyang* theorists, militarists—would take to the road, attracted by court academies which sprang up to be their hosts. Within these seats of learning, the viability of their various strategies for political and social unity would be hotly debated.

Confucius as Teacher

A couple of centuries before Plato was to found his Academy to train statesmen for the political life of Athens, Confucius had established a school with the explicit purpose of educating the next generation for political leadership. As his curriculum, Confucius is credited with having over his lifetime edited what were to become the Chinese classics, a collection of poetry, music, historical documents, and annals that chronicled events at the Lu court, along with an extensive commentary on the *Book of Changes*. These classics provided a shared cultural vocabulary for his students, and they were to become the standard curriculum for Chinese literati in subsequent centuries. Although Confucius was deferred to as a man of wisdom and culture by those around him, he described himself modestly as an avid student, and as a person who loved learning more than most.

As a teacher, Confucius expected this same degree of commitment to learning from his students. On the one hand, he was tolerant and inclusive. He made no distinction among economic classes in selecting his students, and he would take whatever they could afford as payment for his services. His favorite student, Yan Hui (Yanzi), was desperately poor, a fact that simply added to Confucius's admiration for him. On the other hand, Confucius set high standards, and if students did not approach their lessons with seriousness and enthusiasm, Confucius would not suffer them.

One stereotype of Chinese society and of Confucius in particular that is exploded by a careful reading of the *Analects* is the supposed reverence for age. Confucius did not promote an uncritical respect for age; instead, he respected accomplishment. In reflecting on the youth of his day, he said, "Young people should be regarded with awe—how do we know that those of today are better than those yet to come?" And on confronting an old acquaintance who had lived a worthless life, Confucius rapped him with his cane, saying, "In your youth, you were neither modest nor deferential. As an adult you had nothing to pass on to others; and now being old you will not die. What a scoundrel!"

Over his lifetime, Confucius attracted a large group of young and able students, and provided them not only with book learning but with a curriculum that encouraged personal articulation and refinement on several fronts. His "six arts" included propriety and ceremony, music making, archery, charioteering, writing, and mathematics and, in sum, were directed at developing the moral character of his charges rather than any set of practical skills. In the Chinese tradition broadly, proficiency in the "arts" has been seen as the medium through which one reveals quality of one's person.

Although Confucius enjoyed great popularity as a teacher and many of his students found their way into political office, his enduring frustration was that personally he achieved only marginal influence in the practical politics of the day. He was a *philosophe* rather than a theoretical philosopher; he wanted desperately to hold sway over intellectual and social trends, and to improve the quality of life that was dependent on them. Although there were occasions on which important political figures sought his advice and services, over his years in the state of Lu, he held only minor offices at court. When finally Confucius was appointed as police commissioner of Lu late in his career, his advice was not heeded, and he was not treated by the Lu court with appropriate courtesy. During his lifetime, Confucius had made several trips to neighboring states, and after being mistreated in the performance of court sacrifices at home, he determined to take his message on the road and try to influence the world outside. These were troubled times, and there was great adventure and much danger in offering counsel to the competing political centers of his day. In his early fifties, he traveled abroad as an itinerant counselor, and several times came under the threat of death. Having served briefly in Wei, he moved on to the states of Song and Cai and took up office in the small state of Chen, only later to return to service in the state of Wei. After his return to Wei, he was summoned back to Lu, where he lived out his last few years as a counselor of the lower rank and continued his compilation of the classics.

Confucius as God

The early philosophical literature has a catalog of mostly apocryphal stories that purport to tell the events in the life of a remarkable man. Early on, and certainly by the time of his death, Confucius had risen in reputation to become a model of erudition, attracting attention from all segments of society. Many of the stories that surround his life are intent on demonstrating how special a person Confucius was, and how different he was from the common run. Much of this material is an attempt to rationalize the few details that were known of his life. For example, there are several stories describing the peculiar concave shape of his head, an attempt to explain his given name, *qiu*, meaning "mound" or "hill." Elaborate stories emerge out of offhand allusions in the historical records.

Another feature of this literature is Confucius's encounters with important men of his time. The assumption was that any sage worth his salt would certainly have attracted the attention of other sages. For example, in several historical texts and some of the Daoist literature, Confucius visits Laozi, sometimes receiving instruction from him, but more often being discomfited.

As time passes and Confucius's stock rises, the historical records "recall" details about his official career that had supposedly been lost. Over time, his later disciples alter the wording of his biographical record in his favor, effectively promoting him from a minor official to several of the highest positions in the land. He achieves the exalted rank first of acting prime minister of the state of Lu, and then prime minister. The later the record, the higher the position. What drives this exaggeration of Confucius's achievements is the conviction of his later admirers that a person of his extraordinary talent could not possibly have lived in his community and been overlooked by the rulers of his day.

But the story does not end here. As the record moves into the Han dynasty, Confucius is celebrated as the "uncrowned king" of the state of Lu, and by the fourth century C.E., any prefecture wanting to define itself as a political entity is required by imperial decree to erect a temple to Confucius. Confucius is not being treated *like* a god; rather, gods in China are dead people. They are local cultural heroes who are remembered by history as having contributed meaning and value to the tradition. And of these revered ancestors, the god called Confucius has been remembered best.

Confucius: His Influence

Confucius was certainly a flesh-and-blood historical figure, as real as George Washington was or as Jesus is believed to have been. But the received Confucius was and still is a "living corporate person" in the sense that generation after generation of descendants have written commentary on his legacy in an effort to make his teachings appropriate for their own times and places. "Confucianism" is a lineage of scholars who have continued to elaborate on the canonical texts passed on after the life of Confucius came to an end, extending the way of living that Confucius had begun. It is wave after wave of teachers who hold Confucius up as an exemplar of what it means to become truly human.

Although the exaltation of Confucius began early in the tradition with the continuation of his work by his many disciples, it was not until Confucianism was established as the state ideology during the Han dynasty (206 B.C.E.–220 C.E.) that his school of thought became an unchallenged orthodoxy. By developing his insights into the most basic and enduring aspects of the human experience—family, friendship, education, community, and so on—Confucius had guaranteed their continuing relevance.

One characteristic of Confucianism that began with Confucius himself, and made it so resilient in the Chinese tradition, is its porousness and adaptability. Confucius said of himself that he only transmitted traditional culture, he did not create it—his contribution was simply to take ownership of the tradition and adapt the wisdom of the past to his own present historical moment. Confucius harks back to the duke of Zhou, an idealized ruler who helped to establish the high culture of the Zhou dynasty in its first century, and on a bad day when things are not going well for Confucius, he laments, "It is a long time since I have dreamt of the duke of Zhou."

Just as Confucius reinvented the culture of the Zhou and earlier dynasties for his own era, Confucianism of the Han dynasty draws into itself many of the ideas owned by competing schools in the earlier centuries, and in so doing, fortifies itself against their challenge. This pattern—absorbing competing ideas and adapting them to the specific conditions of the time—sustained Confucianism across the centuries as the official doctrine of the Chinese empire until the fall of the Qing dynasty in 1911. In fact, an argument can be made that just as the composite of Buddhism and Confucianism produced neo-Confucianism, the combination of Marxism and Confucianism in the twentieth century, and into the twenty-first, created a kind of neo-neo-Confucianism.

As recently as the Cultural Revolution (1966–1976), Jiang Qing, the wife of Mao Zedong, and her associates mounted an anti-Confucius campaign that swept the country. Although the struggle was ostensibly between "legalists" backed by the Gang of Four and the reactionary "Confucians," the real target was Premier Zhou Enlai—a modern reincarnation of Confucius's cultural hero, the duke of Zhou. The irony of the anti-Confucius campaign was that during this period one could not buy a copy of the *Analects* for love or money—the entire country had been put to work reading the teachings of Confucius in order to criticize them.

The *Analects*: Sagely Leftovers

Many sources for the teachings of Confucius have been passed down to us. For the actual teachings of Confucius, the most authoritative among them is the *Analects*. The "analects" is a good translation of *Lunyu*—literally, "discourses"—because it comes from the Greek *analekta*, which has the root meaning "leftovers after a feast." Probably, the first fifteen books of these literary "leftovers" were assembled and edited by a congress of Confucius's disciples shortly after his death. The disciples seem to have concluded that a very special person had walked among them, and that his way—what he said and did—should be preserved for future generations. Much of this portion of the text is devoted to remembering Confucius; it is a personal narrative of what he had to say, to whom he said it, and how he said it. The middle three chapters are like snapshots of his habits: Confucius never sat down without first straightening his mat; he never slept in the position of a corpse; he never sang on a day that he attended a funeral; he drank freely but never to the point of confusion.

The last five books of the *Analects* appear to have been compiled sometime later, after the most prominent disciples of Confucius had launched their own teaching careers and had undertaken to elaborate on the philosophy of their late master. Confucius is less prominent in these chapters, though he is referred to in more honorific terms, while the now mature disciples are themselves often quoted.

There were many versions of the *Analects*, with three important editions surviving into the Han dynasty: the Lu version from the state of Lu, the Qi version from the state of Qi, and the "ancient" version reportedly recovered from within the walls of Confucius's old home. While the presently extant text is eclectic, having had access to all three versions, its editor had to make choices among them.

There is exciting news on this front. In 1971 a version of the *Analects* was recovered from a tomb dating from 55 B.C.E. in an archaeological dig just outside Peking (Beijing). This *Analects* is a thousand years older than our received text, and it is probably the Lu edition. It is substantially the same as the text in circulation today, containing twenty books and having significant variations in the readings of extant passages. Although badly damaged by fire and only fragmentary, this find holds significant potential for revising our understanding of one of the most canonical texts in human history.

In addition to the *Analects*, the other two most important resources for the life and teachings of Confucius are the Zuo commentary on the *Spring and Autumn Annals*, and the *Mencius*. The Zuo commentary is a narrative history that purports to interpret the chronicle of the court history of the state of Lu up to the death of Confucius. *Mencius* is a text named after a disciple who elaborated the doctrines of Confucius some 150 years after his death; it became one of the Four Books in the Song dynasty—from then on, the core of the Confucian classics.

One thing is clear about the *Analects* and these supplementary texts: they do not purport to lay out a formula that everyone should live by. Rather, they provide an account of one man: how he cultivated his humanity, and how he lived a satisfying life, much to the admiration of those around him.

The Teachings of Confucius

The *dao*—the "way" or Way—of Confucius is nothing more or less than the way in which he as a particular person chose to live his life. The power and lasting value of his ideas lie in the fact that they are intuitively persuasive and readily adaptable. Confucius begins with the insight that the life of every human being is played out in the context of a particular family, for better or for worse. For Confucius and generations of Chinese to come, it is one's family and the complex of relationships that constitute it, rather than the solitary individual, that is the basic unit of humanity. In fact, for Confucius, there is no individual—no "self" or "soul"—that remains once layer after layer of social relations are peeled away. One is one's roles and relationships. The goal of living, then, is to achieve harmony and enjoyment for oneself and others through acting appropriately in those roles and relationships that constitute one.

Given that we all live within the web of family relationships, it is entirely natural that we should project this institution out onto the community, the polity, and the cosmos as an organizing metaphor. The Confucian community is an extension of aunts and uncles, sisters and cousins; the teacher is "teacher-father," and one's senior classmates are "elder-brother students"; "the ruler is father and mother to the people" and is the son of "heaven." "Heaven" itself is a faceless amalgam of ancestors rather than some transcendent creator deity. As Confucius says, "The exemplary person works hard at the root, for where the root has taken firm hold, the way will grow." What then is the root?

He continues: "Treating your family members properly—this is the root of becoming a person."

For Confucius, the way to live is not dictated by some power beyond us; it is something we must all participate in constructing. On one occasion, Confucius said, "It is not the way that broadens people, but people who broaden the way." The way is our passage through life, the road we take. Our forebears mapped out their way and built their roads, and in so doing provided a bearing for succeeding generations. They have given us the culture and institutions that structure our lives and give them value and meaning. But each new generation must be road builders too, continuing the efforts that have gone before.

Confucius saw living as an art rather than a science. There are no blueprints, no formulas, no replications. He once said, "The exemplary person seeks harmony, not sameness." In a family, each member has his or her unique role. Harmony is simply getting the most out of these differences. Similarly, Confucius saw harmony in community emerging out of the uninhibited contributions of its diverse people. Communal enjoyment is like Chinese cooking—getting the most out of your ingredients.

Confucius was extraordinarily fond of good music, because making music conduces to harmony, bringing different voices into productive relationships. Music is tolerant in allowing each voice and instrument to have its own place, its own integrity, while at the same time requiring that each ingredient find a complementary role in which it can add the most to the ensemble. And music is always unique in that each performance has a life of its own.

What Confucius calls "authoritative conduct" or "benevolence" (*ren*)—more literally, "becoming a person"—is the recognition that personal character is a consequence of cultivating one's relationships with others. For Confucius, nothing defines humanity more than the practical consideration of one human being for another. Importantly, benevolence does not precede practical employment—it is not a principle or standard that has some existence beyond the day-to-day lives of the people who realize it in their relationships. Rather, benevolence is fostered in the deepening of relationships that occurs as one takes on the responsibility and obligations of communal living and comes fully to life. Benevolence is human flourishing. It is the achievement of the quality of relationships which, like the lines in calligraphy or landscape painting, collaborate to maximum aesthetic effect.

Wisdom for Confucius is relevant knowledge—not knowing "what" in some abstract or theoretical sense, but knowing "how" to map one's way through life and get the most happiness out of it. And happiness for oneself and for others is isomorphic, or mutual. In discussing knowledge, Confucius says that being fond of something is better than just knowing it, and finding enjoyment in it is better than just being fond of it. "Authoritative conduct" (*ren*) Confucius associates with mountains—spiritual and enduring, a constant geographical marker from which we can all take our bearings. Wisdom is like water—pure, flowing, nurturing. And the gentleman is both benevolent and wise, both mountain and water.

A good way to think about "the way" is as a passage. On one occasion, Confucius was standing on the bank of a river and, waxing philosophical, said, "So it passes, never ceasing day or night." Life is at its very best a pleasant journey, where the inherited body of cultural institutions and the pattern of roles and relationships that locate us within community—what Confucius calls "propriety" (*li*)—is a code of formal behaviors for stabilizing and disciplining our ever-changing circumstances. "Propriety" covers everything from table manners to the three years of mourning a dead parent, from the institution of parenthood to the appropriate posture for expressing commiseration. It is a social syntax that brings the particular members of community into meaningful relationships. Propriety is a discourse, which, like language, enables people to communicate and to locate themselves appropriately relative to one another.

What distinguishes "propriety" from rules and regulations is that these cultural norms must be personalized and are open to refinement. Only I can be father to *my* sons; only I can be *this* son to *my* mother; only I can sacrifice to *my* ancestors. And if I act properly, performing my roles and cultivating my relationships so that they are rich and fruitful, other people in community will see me as a model of appropriate conduct and will defer to me. It is precisely this power of example that Confucius called "virtue" (*de*). Virtue is the propensity to behave a certain way when provided with an inspiring model.

The other side of what Confucius calls "propriety" is the cultivation of a sense of shame. Shame is community based. It is an awareness of and a concern for how others perceive one's conduct. Persons with a sense of shame genuinely care about what other people think of them. Self-sufficient individuals, on the other hand, need not be concerned about the judgments of others—and such individuals can thus be capable of acting shamelessly, using any means at all to take what they want when they want it.

The Disciples

Confucius was tolerant of difference. In fact, on six separate occasions in the *Analects*, he is asked what he means by "authoritative conduct" (*ren*), an idea that is at the heart of his teachings. And six times Confucius gives different answers. For Confucius, instructing disciples in "authoritative conduct" requires that the message be tailored to the conditions of the person asking the question. We have seen that, for Confucius, persons are no more than the sum of their specific familial and communal roles and relationships, and that "authoritative conduct" emerges out of the quality that they are able to achieve in cultivating them. It stands to reason, then, that to know Confucius, we do best to familiarize ourselves with his community of disciples. The teacher can best be known by his students. Some of these disciples come to life in a careful reading of the *Analects*.

Confucius was reluctant to use the term "authoritative conduct" (*ren*) to describe anyone, but he did use it of his favorite disciple, Yan Hui (or Yanzi), also called Yan Yuan, who lived on a bowl of rice and a ladle of water a day. Yan Hui's eagerness to learn and his sincerity endeared him to the master. But there was more, much more. Yan Hui was of incomparable character, and he was so intelligent that Confucius said of him, "When he is told one thing he understands ten." Although Yan Hui was some thirty years younger than Confucius, it was only this one, among his many disciples, that Confucius saw as his equal. It is no surprise, then, that Confucius was devastated when Yan Hui died at age thirty-one.

Min Sun, known as Ziqian, is praised as an exemplary son and was admired by Confucius for the economy and directness of his comments, and for his uncompromising scruples in refusing to serve persons of questionable morals.

Ran Yong, called Zhonggong, like Yan Hui, was three decades younger than Confucius. Although Zhonggong was of humble origins, Confucius thought so highly of him and his refinement that he said, "Zhonggong could be king"—high praise indeed.

Zhong Yu, also known as Zilu, was another of Confucius's best-known and favorite disciples. He was a person of courage and action who was sometimes upbraided by Confucius for being too bold and impetuous. When he asked Confucius if courage was indeed the highest virtue, Confucius tried to rein him in by replying that a person who has courage without a sense of appropriateness will be a troublemaker, and a lesser person will be a thief.

Confucius's feelings for Zilu were mixed. On the one hand, he was constantly critical of Zilu's rashness and immodesty, and impatient with his seeming indifference to book learning. On the other hand, Confucius appreciated Zilu's unswerving loyalty and directness—Zilu never delayed in fulfilling his commitments.

Being nearer Confucius in age, and having a military temper, Zilu was not one to take criticism without giving it back. On several occasions, especially in the apocryphal literature, Zilu challenges Confucius's judgment in associating with political figures of questionable character and immodest reputation—the wife of Duke Ling of Wei, for example. Confucius is left defending himself—honestly, I didn't do anything! At the end of the day, enormous affection for the irrepressible Zilu comes through in the text.

Zai Yu, also called Ziwo, was devoted to Confucius, yet on numerous occasions Confucius criticized him roundly for a lack of character. In a metaphorical reference to attempting to educate Ziwo, Confucius said that you cannot carve rotten wood, nor can you whitewash a wall made from dry manure.

Duanmu Si, known as Zigong, excelled as a statesman and as a merchant and was perhaps second only to Yan Hui in Confucius's affections. Confucius was respectful of Zigong's abilities—in particular, his intellect—but was less impressed with Zigong's use of this intellect to amass personal wealth. Putting the many references to Zigong together, it is clear that Confucius was not entirely comfortable with his lack of commitment to the well-being of others, his choosing to increase his own riches rather than take on the responsibilities of government office. Zigong was aloof, and not a generous man. And in his readiness to pass judgment on others, he acted superior. Coming from a wealthy, educated home, Zigong was well-spoken; Confucius's most persistent criticism of him is that his deeds could not keep pace with his words. Even so, much of the flattering profile of Confucius collected in the *Analects* is cast in the words of the eloquent Zigong.

Bu Shang, known as Zixia, was a man of letters and is remembered by tradition as having had an important role in establishing the Confucian canon. He has a major place in the last five chapters, where he underscores the importance of learning. Confucius allows that he himself has gotten a great deal from his conversations with Zixia.

Although Zixia tries to compensate for his image as a pedant by insisting that virtuous conduct in one's personal relationships is what learning is all about, Confucius criticizes him at times for a being petty and narrow in his aspirations.

Ziyu, whose formal name was Tantai Mieming, was a protégé of the Ziyu described below, and as such invested a great deal of importance in protocol.

Zeng Can, known as Ziyu or Zengzi, is best remembered as a proponent of filial piety—devotion and service to one's parents. A natural extension of this affection for one's family is friendship, and Zengzi is portrayed as being able to distinguish between the sincerity of Yan Hui and the rashness of Zizhang.

If Zixia erred on the side of book learning, Yu Ruo—he too is known as Ziyu—went too far in the direction of the other Ziyu, emphasizing the formal side of the Confucian teachings, the rites and rituals, at the expense of warmth and good humor.

Nangong Kuo, called Zirong, was a person whom Confucius praised as a gentleman and a man of virtue. He held office only when the "way" prevailed in the land, and stayed out of range when it did not. It is not surprising that Confucius gave his niece to Zirong in marriage.

Gongxi Chi, also known as Zihua, has the image of a diplomat—decorous, and careful and concise in his speech.

These and many other disciples came from the central states of China, gravitating to the state of Lu to study with Confucius. In spite of the sometimes severe opinions which Confucius expressed freely about them—and he admonishes almost every one of them—they were devoted to the master and responded to him with reverence. There is no greater proof of this enduring respect for Confucius than the fact that they had a hand in recording Confucius's criticisms of themselves, and then went on to found branch schools based on these same criticisms to perpetuate his teachings.

See also Mencius.

Note: An earlier version of this essay appeared as the introduction to *Confucius Speaks: The Way of Benevolence*, adapted and illus. by Tsai Chih-chung, trans. by Brian Bruya. New York: Anchor/Doubleday, 1996.

Bibliography

Ames, Roger T., and Henry Rosemont Jr. *The Analects of Confucius: A Philosophical Translation*. New York: Ballantine, 1998. (A translation of the *Analects* that takes into account the Dingxian text and attempts to explain the philosophical import of the key terms.)

Fingarette, Herbert A. *Confucius: The Secular as Sacred*. New York: Harper and Row, 1972. (A pioneering reevaluation of the philosophy of Confucius and its relevance to contemporary philosophy.)

Hall, David L., and Roger T. Ames. *Thinking through Confucius*. Albany: State University of New York Press, 1987. (A reconstruction of the philosophical insights of Confucius, comparing the presuppositions of his way of thinking with presuppositions that underlie western philosophical traditions.)

Lau, D. C., trans. *Confucius: The Analects (Lun-yü)*. Hong Kong: Chinese University Press. (A revised bilingual translation, with a philosophical introduction, appendixes on the history of the text, events in the life of Confucius, and a characterization of his disciples.)

Confucianism: Constructs of Classical Thought

Pei-jung Fu

The character *ru* existed before Confucius's time. It consists of two parts: *ren* and *xu*, together implying "the weak people." This understanding gives rise to two kinds of explanations for the origin of the group *ru*. According to one view, *ru* can be traced to the Shang people, whose state had been replaced by the Zhou dynasty. The other view regards *ru* as a legacy of aristocratic families of early Zhou times, who were in decline. These theories have in common the point that the people of *ru* had an affluent cultural background, which would qualify them to serve as assistants in various rituals. Since the special robe of such assistants was called *ru*, it is probable that the group *ru* developed from some such profession. Confucius became a specialist in rituals after a long time of learning and practice. This fact suggests that Confucius himself once worked as an assistant at sacrificial and funeral rites in the early stage of *ru*. Disciples of Confucius seemed to acknowledge this, and Confucius admonished one of them by saying: "Be a *ru* after the style of the superior man (*junzi*), and not after that of the small-minded man" (*Lunyu*, or *Analects*, 6.13).

In any case, it is indisputable that academic Confucianism started as a school and a system of thought because of the acceptance of the teachings of Confucius. Classical Confucianism, which was founded by Confucius and formed into a school of thought, has its own texts, including the *Analects, Mencius, Xunzi, Yizhuan, Great Learning*, and *Doctrine of the Mean*. Let us survey the characteristics and the creed of classical Confucianism before considering the content of these texts.

The Characteristics and Creed of Classical Confucianism

Classical Confucianism has three characteristics. First, because they cherished the heritage of tradition, Confucians stressed the importance of learning and education. Their teaching was based on canonical texts. This educational tradition allowed Confucians to become the main, powerful preservers and transmitters of the cultural heritage. Second, to put their learning into practice, Confucians participated in politics. They expressed their commitment to promoting virtuous government, with special concern for the moral, social, and political welfare of the people. Third, for Confucians individual social success was based on the practice of moral virtues. They thought that people should not be motivated by success in political and social affairs to the point where their joy in—or the significance of—the practice of virtue was affected. This represents the Confucian attitude toward transcendence: the dignity of human nature would not be restrained by historical contexts, and human beings would be able to make a testament to the transcendent "mandate of heaven" (*tianming*).

In addition, Confucians affirmed three creeds. First, human nature has an inclination toward goodness. All individuals are endowed with a capacity to practice virtue such that they are able to advance their morality toward perfection, as exemplified in the lives of the ancient sages. Second, in real life this capacity manifests itself as a categorical claim. The claim imposes a sort of obligation, urging the person to exert efforts to do what is good. In other words, doing good for the sake of the good is the only right path in human life. The committed individual, if necessary, would devote his whole life to this. Third, if an individual sincerely does what is good, his deed will bring about a virtuous response from those in his circle, and enlighten them. For this reason, Confucianism teaches that the practice of virtue is the responsibility of the individual and emphasizes the significance of human relationships.

The *Analects*

The *Analects* (*Lunyu*) record the words and deeds of Confucius (551–479 B.C.E.). This is the most accessible and reliable source for his thought. Although it consists largely of terse dialogues and comments, we can discern an order. Confucius stressed the primacy of learning. The subjects include the Five Classics (*Book of Documents, Book of Odes, Book of Rituals, Book of Music*, and *Book of Changes*) and six arts of living—ritual, music, archery, driving a chariot, calligraphy, and calculation. Confucius's learning was always accompanied by careful thought leading to new insights about the significance of tradition. His most important insight is, perhaps, his conception of *ren* (benevolence) as a basis of the *li* (ritual tradition or ritual propriety).

To understand the implications of *ren*, we must examine *li*. *Li* was cherished in the Three Dynasties of ancient China and mediated between state and society; its functions covered all the important realms of human concern, such as family, social interaction, religion, politics, and morality. With the social transformations of the Spring and Autumn period, a situation described as a "collapse of rituals and music" became salient. For Confucius, this situation could not be rectified merely by recovering the traditional *li*, which by then had degenerated into pure formality. Therefore, he proposed the concept of *ren*, which designates, so to speak, the capacity for benevolence inherent in every human being. If *ren* is practiced by the people, their society will attain harmony. This view seems implicit in his remark: "If a man has no benevolence, what has he to do with the rites or propriety? If a man has no benevolence, what has he to do with music?" (*Analects*, 3.3). Confucius's task may be summed up in one sentence: "In transmitting the *li* of the cultural tradition, he opened the path to *ren*."

The character *ren* consists of *ren* (a person) and *er* (two). This combination depicts the human situation. Ideally, if a person reflects, seriously and sincerely, on the possibility of his existence, he will appreciate that it is possible because of interdependent relationships with and affection for others—which constitute his humanity. Confucius expected that all the human virtues, such as filial piety, fraternal love, loyalty, and truthfulness, would be attained as a consequence of performance based on "appropriate relationships between persons." Given this ideal of human relationships, we may say that human nature has a tendency toward goodness and that goodness can be realized in appropriate relationships among individuals.

This was the foundation for the social concern of Confucianism. The Confucian concept of *ren* or benevolence indicates not only the nature of human beings but also the proper way of life. When Confucius was asked about benevolence, he answered in different ways according to the capacity, level of moral attainment, and personality of each student. This practice suggests that Confucius was looking for an answer to the human predicament in the concrete setting of ordinary human life. The realization of Confucian benevolence would imply the perfect realization of human nature; hence, Confucius did not regard himself or any of his contemporaries as embodying benevolence. However, he did not hesitate to declare that a man of *ren*, in appropriate circumstances, is justified in sacrificing his life for its sake (*Analects*, 15.9). In this sense we may see the practice of *ren* as, ideally, leading to the perfection of human nature.

With regard to the proper way of life, Confucius never overlooked the value of *li*. He said that "to master oneself in line with *li* is *ren*" (*Analects*, 12.1). This passage makes *ren* and *li* interdependent; that is, human nature is perfected only through a union of *ren* and *li*. *Ren* constitutes the inner aspect and *li* the outer aspect of ideal humanity. This balanced perspective suggests an equal emphasis on cultural education and the cultivation of personal moral character. Odes and music are also characteristic of the Confucian style of life.

As regards Confucius's religious concerns, three aspects are worth noting. First, Confucius respected the ancestor worship and sacrificial rites that were prevalent in his time. When he attended such rituals, he was reverential toward the deities. Second, Confucius did not deny the existence of spirits and ghosts, yet he was critical of an atmosphere that fostered superstition. In particular, he was convinced that performing sacrifices to spirits and ghosts was no excuse for neglecting one's ethical responsibilities. Third, Confucius believed that *tian* (heaven) should be construed as the supreme being. He felt that heaven had given him a distinct mission, was mindful of his conduct, accepted his sacrifices, and could even determine his life and death. Yet he realized that the will of heaven was not always expressed in the will of human beings and felt that human destiny was both mysterious and inconceivable. He describes himself as a man who—independently of the will of heaven—"forgets his food while ardently pursuing knowledge, forgets his sorrows while experiencing joy in its attainment, and does not notice the commencement of old age" (*Analects*, 7.19). Confucius does have a spiritual dimension, but his ethical teachings on the significance of cultural tradition and personal moral cultivation do not depend on the will of heaven or other religious beliefs.

Mencius

Mencius (c. 371–289 B.C.E.) highly esteemed Confucius, whom he called the "sage of timeliness." He thought, indeed, that since the beginning of history there had been no greater person than Confucius. The works of Mencius contain longer and more complete discourses than the *Analects*, systematically expounding and developing Confucius's idea of *ren*.

Mencius extends the scope of *ren* (benevolence) and its intrinsic connection with other virtues such as *yi* (righteousness), *li* (ritual propriety), and *zhi* (wisdom). He focuses on the fundamental role of *xin* (heart and mind) in Confucian ethics. For Mencius, *xin* contains "four germs": (1) compassion, (2) shame and dislike, (3) modesty and compliance, and (4) distinction of right from wrong. These four germs can be developed into the virtues of *ren, yi, li*, and *zhi*, which define Mencius's conception of goodness (*shan*). Mencius's interpretation of human nature is based on his conception of the human mind, though without disregarding the significance of the physical. Mencius distinguishes two aspects of human nature: the "great body" (mind and heart) and the "small body" (the physical body). If a person conducts himself according to the great body and practices goodness, he will become a *junzi* (a gentleman, paragon, or exemplar). But a person who allows himself to be governed by the desires of the "small body" will become a "petty man" (*xiaoren*). Since all individuals have mind and heart, all are capable of becoming *junzi*. In general, Mencius's thesis that human nature is good does not mean that actualized goodness is innate. Rather, human nature has an inherent potential for goodness or excellence (*shan*). Notably, Mencius does not deny the influence of the external social environment. In fact, he advocates that a state should properly establish the political institutions and economic plans which are indispensable to the realization of the Confucian ethical ideal.

For Mencius the people are the most important element in the state; next in importance are the altars of land and grain; last in importance is the sovereign (*Mencius*, 7B.14). Although we cannot plausibly claim that Mencius advocated democracy, he does express his faith that "people are the foundation of a country." This is a matter not of individuals' political rights but rather of individual moral dignity: all humans are equal in their potential to become good. Mencius regarded the relationship between a lord and his subjects as reciprocal responsibility. This meant that subjects should not be required to submit absolutely to their lord. According to Mencius, an individual, in his routine of life and work, should make reasonable, principled decisions. In exigent circumstance, the individual is expected to grasp the situation and exercise discretion. For Mencius, since death is inevitable, if a person gives up his life for the sake of justice, or follows the right way of life, he may be said to have a "proper destiny" endowed by heaven.

Mencius's belief in heaven involves little of religious practice; it has to do with a mission in human life, conferred because the human heart-mind (*xin*) is endowed with the "four germs" that enable humans to do what is good. The proper way to observe the decree of heaven is "to strengthen one's righteousness and to nourish one's vital breath." Once a person attains the state of the "floodlike *qi*" (the vital breath of the flowing state), courage will spring forth in his being so that he can confront even a perverted crowd without fear. Mencius remarked: "All things are already complete within me. There is no greater delight than to be conscious of sincerity on self-examination. If one acts with a vigorous effort at promoting reciprocity (*shu*), no way can be closer than this to the attainment of benevolence" (7A.4). Understanding this aspect of Mencius's thought requires profound personal experience, and for that reason some scholars consider Mencius, in a sense, a mystic.

Xunzi

Xunzi (c. 313–238 B.C.E.) professed to be an advocate of Confucianism. However, his view of human nature differs radically from that of Mencius. According to Mencius, human nature is good; Xunzi argued against Mencius and maintained that human nature is evil. Actually, there is no real issue between them on this subject, because their discussions were based on different definitions of human nature (*xing*). For Xunzi, human nature consists of emotions and desire, while for Mencius it is essentially based on his conception of *xin* (mind and heart). Emotion and desire are inborn, and, without proper control, they will inevitably lead human relationships into struggles and violence. Is not this situation "evil"? On the other hand, if human beings are disciplined and educated, they will do what is good. For Xunzi, this reasoning would indicate that goodness cannot be inborn. If we ask why human beings are able to do what is good, Xunzi would reply that the distinction between human beings and other creatures is that human beings are able to distinguish good from evil and do good deeds. This ability renders human morality possible and practicable. His perspective is compatible with the view that human nature has an inclination toward goodness, so that an individual is capable of attaining sagehood.

Xunzi's understanding of *xin* (mind and heart) is not confined to its moral aspect. More fundamentally, the mind is the ruler of the body, including the senses. It exercises its volition with respect to feeling and desires. Further, the mind performs acts of thought and judgment. If the mind attains the states of "emptiness," "stillness," and "unity," it can acquire a quasi-mystical, comprehensive insight into all things (*da qingming*).

Xunzi's *dao*, a moral ideal, is embodied in *li* (ritual, norms, rules of proper conduct). The function of *li* is coextensive with *ren* (benevolence) and *yi* (righteousness). In Xunzi's philosophy, *li* may be construed as the ultimate standard for doing what is good. It was established by the "sage kings," who had examined the rules and regulations of both the human and the natural world. Without *li*, political operations, social organizations, and families cannot be peacefully sustained. However, although *li* clearly comprises indispensable institutions and ceremonies, if they are founded on human nature, what is the basis of its presumed universality? It is difficult to find a clear answer in Xunzi to this question.

The real issue between Mencius and Xunzi lies in their concepts of heaven (*tian*). Xunzi's concept implies a "naturalized" heaven, functioning according to unchangeable rules. This heaven has nothing to do with order and disorder in the human world, or with individual virtue and vice. Xunzi would say that humans, not heaven, should be held responsible for practical social problems. For Xunzi, learning, correct perceptions of society and the world, observance of rituals and social norms, and individual efforts to do what is good are the right path to human well-being.

Yizhuan

Yizhuan (*Ten Wings*) is said to have been compiled between the end of the Warring States period and the early Western Han. If so, it overlaps Xunzi's works. It was a commentary on the *Yijing* (*Book of Changes*), one of the earliest Chinese classics. However, its significance comes largely from its position in Confucian tradition. The *Analects* report that Confucius did not expound his views on human nature and the way of heaven. To fill this gap, *Yizhuan* contains extensive discussions on the relationship between the way of heaven and human beings.

The way of heaven is manifest in the unending interaction between *qian* (representing heaven) and *kun* (representing earth), which have common elements. This interaction results in the transformation of all things according to an invariable standard that also influences all auspicious and inauspicious events in the human world. *Yizhuan* mainly elucidates this standard as expressed in the way of heaven and as determining the way of humanity. We find, for instance, the following: "It is *yin* and *yang* that exhibit the Way of Heaven. It is softness and hardness that exhibit the Way of Earth and *ren* and *yi* that exhibit the Way of human beings" (*Shuogua*). If an individual conducts himself in accordance with the principle of *ren* and *yi*, presumably he will encounter only what is auspicious and become a "gentleman" (*junzi*). The Confucian gentleman must learn from the ancient sages. He must aspire to a virtuous life and make persistent efforts to cultivate his moral capabilities and the pursuit of wisdom.

The *Doctrine of the Mean (Zhongyong)*

The *Book of the Mean* was originally a chapter of the *Book of Rites* (*Li ji* or *Liji*), the final compilation of which probably took place in the Western Han period. In this treatise, we find a well-organized description of the relationship between heaven and human beings. The opening chapter says: "What Heaven has conferred is called [human] nature; the accordance with this nature is called the way [of human beings]; and the cultivation of this way is called education."

The nature of human beings comes from the decree of heaven. All individuals are born with the same potential, but they are able to become "gentlemen" only if they make efforts to know and to practice what is good. Their potential is thus itself an immanent claim, a demand from within. All an individual has to do is to follow his immanent nature and practice what it requires. It is this practice that the *Book of the Mean* designates as the "principal way of humans." In this connection, the purpose of a Confucian education can also be established. There are two clues to a better understanding of this argument: (1) An individual must realize his *cheng* (sincerity, wholeness) so as to perceive his own inner inclination toward goodness. (2) Precisely speaking, "the principal way of humans" is "to choose the good and hold it fast."

The function of *cheng* is not confined to moral sincerity and loyalty; it also enlarges the dimension and scope of human life and breaks through the limitations of time and space. Therefore, a man of *cheng* is able to perceive and communicate with all other people, participates in the providence of heaven and earth, and even removes any barriers between the worlds of humans and spirits. *Cheng* is the right path for human beings to embrace the mandate of heaven. If *cheng* consists in the mind's awareness and openness, then "choosing the good and holding it fast" is the accomplishment of *cheng*. Since human nature has an inborn leaning toward goodness, while one is in the state of *cheng* it should be easy to judge what is good. Two things, then, are required of human beings: the wisdom to choose what is good and the courage to hold to it. The *Book of the Mean* lists "five ethical codes" as the content of goodness; it also designates "wisdom," "benevolence," and "courage" as the "three comprehensive virtues." This point of view forms the mainstream of Confucian thought.

The *Great Learning (Daxue)*

The *Daxue* (*Great Learning*), which was also a chapter of the *Book of Rites*, represents the program of Confucian education. It tersely presents the Confucian idea of education, which envisions a path to *chengde* (the perfection of virtue). According to the *Great Learning*, the purpose of a Confucian education is threefold: to illustrate virtue, to renew the people, and to rest in the highest goodness. This purpose is accomplished by eight steps that are more specific: (1) investigate things; (2) complete knowledge; (3) render thoughts sincere; (4) rectify hearts and minds; (5) cultivate persons; (6) regulate families; (7) govern a state rightly; and (8) attain wordly peace and order. The purpose of the program is to cultivate personal morality, which will then exert a good influence on others—ultimately, on all people.

The *Great Learning* elucidates the concept of *shu* ("reciprocal consideration with compassion"), which was originally advocated by Confucius and Mencius. The *Great Learning* elaborates this concept and formulates a new phrase: "the way of reciprocal understanding." The substance of this idea can be explained as follows. In human society, whenever a person acts in a specific situation, he has to take others into consideration by putting himself in their position. If he is able to do this, he will find that he should not do to others what he does not want others to do to him. Similarly, Confucius's golden rule is: "Do not impose on others what you yourself do not desire."

Ever since Confucius, classical Confucianism has proposed important concepts and ideas, including *ren* and *li*, human nature, and the way of heaven. Through centuries of transmission and evolution, it has developed into a complete, highly sophisticated system of philosophical thought. From the Han dynasty on, it has been a dominant influence on Chinese society, helping to shape the personality and attitudes of the Chinese people, and continuing to make Chinese culture what we see today.

See also Confucianism: Confucius; Confucianism: Tradition; Mencius; Xunzi.

Bibliography

Cua, A. S. "Morality and the Paradigmatic Individuals." *American Philosophical Quarterly*, 6(4), 1969, pp. 324–329.

———. "Reflections on the Structure of Confucian Ethics." *Philosophy East and West*, 21(2), 1971, pp. 125–140.

Finazzo, Giancarlo. *The Principle of T'ien: Essays on Its Theoretical Relevancy in Early Confucian Philosophy*. Taipei: Meiya, 1967.

Fingarette, Herbert. *Confucius—The Secular as Sacred*. New York: Harper and Row, 1972.
Fu, Pei-jung. *Rujia zhexue xinlun* (New Essays on Classical Confucianism). Taipei: Yeqiang, 1985.
Hall, David, and Roger Ames. *Thinking through Confucius*. Albany: State University of New York Press, 1987.
Munro, Donald J. *The Concept of Man in Early China*. Stanford, Calif.: Stanford University Press, 1969.
Tu, Weiming. *Humanity and Self-Cultivation: Essays on Confucian Thought*. Berkeley, Calif.: Asian Humanities, 1979.

Confucianism: Dialogues

John Berthrong

A study of global intellectual history demonstrates that religion and philosophy were always more cross-cultural than has previously been recognized. There has been a constant interchange of ideas and techniques wherever people with different traditions have gathered for the arts of war and peace. The study of Chinese philosophy confirms this fact, through examination of conversations between Confucians, Mohists, Daoists, logicians, and legalists; the medieval incorporation of Buddhism; and finally western modes of thought after the nineteenth century.

However, the term "dialogue" designates something different from a persistent exchange of ideas between different philosophies and religions. Dialogue as a cross-cultural movement refers to a subset of social and cultural exchange marked by some specific characteristics. The most important aims of dialogue are willingness to treat the other tradition as a (1) worthy partner with (2) something positive to contribute to the discussion. For organized religions, a third goal is (3) to encourage social cooperation in charity and social justice. Although quite early on there were individuals such as the Mogul emperor Akbar (r. 1542–1605) and the Qing emperor Kangxi (r. 1662–1723) who were genuinely interested in such exchanges, there was nothing like the organized and global modern religious dialogue movement before the 1960s. It is too early to tell definitively, but many postmodern philosophers have also become committed to dialogue with other traditions, expanding the intellectual range of dialogue beyond theological circles in the late twentieth century.

Confucianism was born in the exchange between the philosophic and religious traditions of classical China and has continued this interaction ever since, expanding its response to include various new movements from outside China such as Buddhism, Islam, and Christianity. For instance, Book 18 of the *Analects* contains an apocryphal story of Confucius's own encounter with the quasi-Daoist recluse of Chu, who admonished Confucius to give up his quest to restore the virtue that had once been Zhou China. Because Confucius refused to flee the duties of the world, later Confucians were forced to talk to other people about the world and everything that is in it. Confucius rejects reclusiveness but also states: "I have no preconceptions about the permissible and the impermissible" (*Analects*, 7.8). Of course, what Confucius meant is that deliberations about matters of right and wrong must be a result of social interaction and the study of the actions and words of the sage kings.

The more common human response to something new is the polemical attitude that the other person is wrong or needs correction in order to find the right opinion or ritual. More often than not, the standard Confucian view of non-Chinese thinkers was that they came to China in order to become civilized. It has always been hard for any culture to acknowledge the contribution of another; often the recognition is grudging and circumscribed by the argument that such truth was actually present in one's own tradition.

The history of Confucian dialogue with other traditions can be divided into three major periods: (1) the classical period, (2) the reception of Buddhism, and (3) the arrival of west Asian religions and philosophies. While Confucians, because of their commitment to the world, have always entered into conversation with other traditions, they have done so with mixed emotions. For instance, Mencius stated that he did not like disputation about philosophic issues. The impression Mencius gives is that he is willing to engage in conversation with other thinkers only in order to vindicate his own Confucian position. Consequently, Mencius is the first great disputer among Confucians and identifies such other thinkers as Yang Chu and the Mohists as representatives of mistaken theories that must be refuted in order for the true teachings of Confucius to flourish.

Another classical Confucian response was Xunzi's arguments against non-Confucian thinkers. He argued that someone like Zhuangzi might well understand the Way as a cosmological ultimate but did not understand the way of ritual action as appropriate to civilized human life. Nonetheless, it is clear from Xunzi's writings that he was indebted to Daoist thinkers like Zhuangzi for the formulation of his own subtle theory of the mind-heart and to the neo-Mohists for the art of disputation. Nonetheless, Xunzi was a member of the famous Jixia academy and would have debated with thinkers representing the other philosophic options of his day.

The coming of Buddhism marked China's first encounter with another great religious and philosophic tradition. As is well known, Confucians maintained a long and complicated interaction with Buddhist scholars. Sometimes the reaction was negative, as when Han Yu condemned Buddhist rituals in the Tang dynasty. On the other hand, the great Song Confucian Su Shi is famous for incorporating Buddhist ideas and images into his own poetry and thought. In fact, many critics of Song moral philosophy and neo-Confucianism in general charge that the Song philosophers borrowed, without adequate attribution, many Buddhist ideas about the cosmos, including the key notion of principle as well as the practice of meditation known as "quiet-sitting."

After Buddhism, the next important foreign religion to arrive was Islam. While the origins of Islam in China are shrouded in the mists of legend, it is clear that Muslims quickly made their way along the famous Silk Road of Central Asia into the vibrant, cosmopolitan world of Tang China. The first official contacts took place in 651, and there was even a great battle between a Tang army and an Arab army at the Talas River in 751. Even though the Muslims won the battle, this did not affect the Muslims' lively trade in China; in fact, Muslims even assisted the Tang rulers in defeating An Lu-shan's rebellion.

The second phase of Confucian-Islamic contact took place under the Mongol Yuan dynasty, when many Muslims were employed by the Mongols in their government. Here again the Chinese reaction was generally negative because the Chinese saw the Muslims as agents of an oppressive regime; but as before, with the founding of the Ming in 1366, there was no attempt to outlaw or penalize the Muslim community, and the Ming were tolerant of the Muslims as long as they remained obedient to Chinese law. The Muslims' response was to practice peaceful coexistence with the Chinese state. In fact, the Muslim community continued to grow with new immigration, intermarriage, and conversions of Chinese to Islam.

The Manchu Qing dynasty continued the historic approach to the Muslim community and attempted to promote good working relations with its Muslim subjects. It is also important to remember that the Qing court conquered large parts of Central Asia and hence greatly increased China's Muslim population. Relations were generally good until a series of Muslim insurrections in the nineteenth century.

What is fascinating is the fact that there were no apologetic Muslim writings in Chinese until the seventeenth century, when a series of Chinese Muslim scholars sought to explain their tradition to the larger Chinese world and to their fellow Muslims. For instance, Wang Daiyu (c. 1580–1650) argued that there was no need for any hostility between Islam and Confucianism. In fact, Wang tried to show that all the major Confucian virtues were also Islamic virtues. The main difference between Islam and Confucianism, according to Wang, was that Confucianism was not monotheistic. But even here Wang tried to show, as later Christian missionaries would do, that archaic Chinese notions of heaven were a common theistic ground between Islam and Confucianism. Slightly later, Liu Zhi (c. 1662–1736) added material from Buddhism and Daoism to Wang's attempt to show how Islam could be understood within a Confucian framework. However, this kind of interaction was one-way in that Confucian intellectuals were never very interested in learning about Islam.

The next foreign tradition to enter China was the Christian missionary effort from the sixteenth century to the nineteenth. In many respects this was more of a dialogue than the Islamic encounter, though never comparable to the entrance of Buddhism into China. In the early phase, except for a few Chinese intellectuals who actually converted to Christianity, most Chinese interest in western thought was focused on science and technology. This kind of scientific interest parallels the earlier Chinese study of Muslim astronomy. The Chinese astronomers were quick, in terms of both Muslim and western astronomy, to recognize excellence when they saw it and were more than willing to incorporate it into their official intellectual life. In the case of the west, selected Chinese intellectuals became interested in medicine, cartography, and other areas of western science where the Chinese perceived that western scholars had something to teach them.

What is intriguing about the early Jesuit missionaries is that they were able, like the Buddhists before them, to convert a few Chinese Confucians to their faith. One thing that the Jesuits did was base their essential arguments for Christianity on Confucian scholarly grounds. What the Jesuits did, paralleling Muslim arguments about religion as well, was to go back to the early Chinese classics and demonstrate to the Confucians that they actually had an articulated doctrine of God as *tian* (heaven) or *shangdi* (lord on high). The Jesuits' strategy was to show, from this fine monotheistic beginning, that the main line of the Confucian tradition lost its theistic roots. The Jesuits were careful and sincere in giving high praise to the ethical system of Confucianism.

The crux of the dialogue was whether or not a belief in God could be added to Confucian teachings. In the Ming and early Qing, many converts to Christianity agreed with the Jesuits that Christian doctrine did revive the lost theistic part of their Confucian Way that never should have been neglected. Sadly, this promising theological and philosophic dialogue came to grief over the famous "rites controversy." Some missionaries disagreed with the accommodationist stance of the Jesuits on the issue of whether or not the Confucian ancestral rites were a violation of the Christian injunction against idolatry. The Jesuits and the Chinese argued that the ancestor rites represented veneration, not worship. Unfortunately, the pope ruled against the Jesuits' interpretation of the rites, and this ban against their use for Christians ended what had been a compelling dialogue about religion and ultimate worldviews. The ban was not rescinded until 1939.

The second phase of western engagement came with the great imperial expansion of the mid-nineteenth century. Unfortunately, positive dialogue was not high on anyone's list of cultural priorities during this period. Offended by the exclusive view of the Christian religion on the part of the Protestant missionaries and the overwhelming secular power of science and military technology, the Chinese elite was faced, for the first time in its history, with a classical role reversal in terms of who viewed whom as civilized. If there was to be any philosophic borrowing, the westerners believed it would be by the Chinese from the enlightened science, philosophy, and religion of the west.

The late nineteenth century and the early twentieth were a time of an enforced dialogue for Chinese intellectuals with the west. In a more compressed time than the reception of Buddhism, and motivated by a fear of total cultural domination, Chinese intellectuals (as well as the Japanese and Koreans) grappled with the rapid appropriation of western science, religion, technology, and philosophy. For instance, the victory of the Chinese Communist Party in 1949 marked a selective appropriation and dialogue with western Marxism. What is evident in retrospect is that any such cross-cultural exchange creates something new, and Maoist thought is certainly distinctive compared with its European origins.

By the 1960s the mainline Christian churches, led by the Roman Catholic Church in the great council known as Vatican II, signaled new willingness to engage in what they called dialogue. Rapidly the Buddhist communities of the diaspora and South, Southeast, and East Asia began the dialogue between the two traditions. More recently, Confucians from their own diaspora and from Taiwan, Hong Kong, Korea, Singapore, and even China have become interested in dialogue with Christian intellectuals.

In many ways the renewed dialogue picks up where the great debate of the seventeenth and eighteenth centuries left off. However, the dialogue has been expanded beyond just Catholic and Protestant religious concerns to include wider cross-cultural philosophic exchange and discussion of pressing issues that affect humanity as a whole, such as the ecological crisis and the nature of human rights. It is evident from the renewed dialogue that Chinese philosophers now have a better general understanding of western thought than do any but a small group of western specialists. One of the tasks of the new dialogue is to educate western intellectuals about the richness of Chinese traditional thought and to demonstrate that East Asian intellectuals have been renewing and modernizing their traditions rapidly over the past century.

In the theological dialogue, two questions tend to become points of contact. The first has to do with the issue of how to understand transcendence and immanence in the Confucian tradition. This entire conversation is preceded by an examination of the religious dimensions of the Confucian tradition. On the whole, Confucians find that their way of defending a notion of mutual implication between the transcendent and immanent nature of divine reality wins a sympathetic hearing from modern Christian theologians. The second question raised by the Confucians is what has come to be called multiple religious participation or dual religious citizenship.

Confucian scholars are exploring the option of incorporating a concept of God or ultimate transcendence into their renewed Confucian worldview. Like the first round of Confucian-Christians, they argue that such an understanding of the "transcendent referent" in no way violates essential Confucian patterns of thought and in fact enriches the corporate notion of the Confucian Way. On the western side, such an idea of religious harmony and multiple religious participation, often said to be an East Asian social norm, is both disturbing and intriguing to many western religious intellectuals who recognize that they live in a culturally pluralistic world. One can only expect the dialogue to become more intense, intricate, and philosophically rewarding as it continues into the twenty-first century.

See also Buddhism in China; Buddhism: Zen (Chan); Confucianism: Tradition; Daoism: Religious; Religions.

Bibliography

Berthrong, John H. *All under Heaven: Transforming Paradigms in Confucian-Christian Dialogue*. Albany: State University of New York Press, 1994.

Ching, Julia. *Confucianism and Christianity: A Comparative Study*. Tokyo: Kodansha International, 1977.

Cracknell, Kenneth. *Justice, Courtesy, and Love: Theologians and Missionaries Encountering World Religions, 1846–1914*. London: Epworth, 1995.

de Bary, William Theodore. *East Asian Civilizations: A Dialogue in Five Stages*. Cambridge, Mass.: Harvard University Press, 1988.

Gernet, Jacques. *China and the Christian Impact: A Conflict of Cultures*, trans. Janet Lloyd. Cambridge: Cambridge University Press, 1985.

Lee, Peter K. H., ed. *Confucian-Christian Encounters in Historical and Contemporary Perspective*. Lewiston, N.Y.: Mellen, 1991.

Mungello, David E. *Curious Land: Jesuit Accommodation and the Origins of Sinology*. Stuttgart: Franz Steiner Verlag, 1985.

Rossabi, Morris. "Islam in China." In *The Encyclopedia of Religion*, ed. Mircea Eliade, Vol. 7. New York: Macmillan, 1987, pp. 377–390.

Rozman, Gilbert, ed. *The East Asian Region: Confucian Heritage and Its Modern Adaptation*. Princeton, N.J.: Princeton University Press, 1991.

Tu, Wei-ming, ed. *Confucian Traditions in East Asian Modernity: Moral Education and Economic Culture in Japan and the Four Mini-Dragons*. Cambridge, Mass.: Harvard University Press, 1996.

Young, John D. *Confucianism and Christianity: The First Encounter*. Hong Kong: Hong Kong University Press, 1983.

Confucianism: Ethics

A. S. Cua

The principal aim of this essay is to present Confucian ethics as an ethics of virtue. The required task involves complex issues on the explication of its conceptual framework. One major obstacle is a lack of definitions of important terms such as *ren*, *li*, and *yi*. William Theodore de Bary remarks that "for the Chinese the idea is not so much to analyze and define concepts precisely as to expand them, to make them suggestive to the widest possible range of meaning" (1970, v). Moreover, many key terms, to borrow an expression from Philip Wheelwright (1968), are plurisignations, suggesting and stimulating different thoughts and interpretations.

This pervasive feature of Confucian discourses, from the point of view of contemporary moral philosophy, may appear to be an anomaly, given the classical Confucian emphasis on the right use of terms (*zhengming*). A serious student of the works of Xunzi, the classical Confucian generally considered the most rationalistic and systematic philosopher, will be frustrated in attempting to find definitions, in the sense of necessary and sufficient conditions, for the application of basic Confucian terms. This is all the more surprising in view of Xunzi's recurrent use of certain definitional locutions or quasi-definitional formulas for explaining his theses on human nature and the mind (Cua 1985a, ch. 3). Xunzi, like most major Confucians, has a pragmatic attitude toward the use of language. That is, the uses of terms that require explanation are those that are liable to misunderstanding in the context of a particular discourse. The Confucian explanation of the use of ethical terms is context-dependent, addressed to a particular rather than universal audience (Perelman and Olbrechts-Tyteca 1969, 31).

Two different assumptions underlying this attitude toward language may account for the lack of interest among Chinese in context-independent explanation of the use of ethical terms. First, there is an assumption of the primacy of practice implicit in the Confucian doctrine of the unity of knowledge and action (Cua 1982). Definition, in the sense of an explanation of meaning, is a matter of practical rather than theoretical necessity. This assumption does not depreciate the importance of theoretical inquiry but focuses instead on its relevance to the requirements of practice, particularly those that promote unity and harmony in the community. Such requirements vary from time to time and place to place. In general, their concrete significance is affected by changing circumstances. A viable ethical theory is subject to pragmatic assessment in the light of changing circumstances. Consequently, ethical requirements cannot be stated in terms of absolute principles or rules. It is this assumption that renders plausible Donald Munro's claim:

> The consideration important to the Chinese is the behavioral implications of belief or proposition in question. What effect does adherence to the belief have on people? What implications for social action can be drawn from the statement? . . . In Confucianism, there was no thought of "knowing" that did not entail some consequence for action. (1969, 55–56).

Related to the primacy of practice is the assumption that reasoned discourse may legitimately appeal to what Nicholas Rescher calls "plausible presumptions," that is, an appeal to shared knowledge, belief, or experience, as well as to the established or operative standards of discourse (1977, 38). For Confucian thinkers most of these presumptions, while defeasible, represent the shared understanding of a common cultural heritage, a living ethical tradition. These presumptions are often suppressed and mainly form the background of practical discourse. Thus, Confucian reasoning and argumentation appear to be highly inexplicit. From the Aristotelian point of view, Confucian argumentation is "rhetorical," as it frequently involves enthymemes and arguments from examples (Kennedy 1991).

Given the primacy of practice and the appeal to plausible presumptions, explication of the conceptual framework of Confucian ethics is a task of philosophical reconstruction, a sort of experiment in conceptual hermeneutics. Such an exploration serves the purposes of reasonable explication and critical development of Confucian ethical thought.

An Ethics of Virtue

While major Confucians (e.g., Mencius and Xunzi) differ in their conceptions of human nature in relation to conduct, most of them adopt Confucius's ideal of a well-ordered society based on good government. Good government is responsive to the basic needs of the people, to issues of wise management of natural and human resources, and to a just distribution of burdens and benefits. In this vision of sociopolitical order, special emphasis is placed on harmonious human relationships (*lun*) in accord with *de*, virtues or standards of excellence. This vision is often called *dao*, a term appropriated by different classical schools of Chinese thought—for example, Daoism and legalism. In the *Analects, dao* is sometimes used as a verb, meaning "to guide"; sometimes it is used as a concrete noun, meaning literally "road." In the latter sense, it can be rendered as "way." But in distinct Confucian ethical usage, as commonly acknowledged by commentators, it is *dao* as an abstract noun that is meant, and more especially in the evaluative rather than descriptive sense, that is, as referring to the ethical ideal of a good human life as a whole.

Throughout its long history, Confucianism has stressed character formation or personal cultivation of virtues, *de* (Chan 1963, "Great Learning"). Thus it seems appropriate to characterize Confucian ethics as an ethics of virtues. To avoid misunderstanding, two explanations are in order. First, the Confucian focus on the centrality of virtues assumes that *de* can be rendered as "virtue." Second, as we shall see later, this focus does not depreciate the importance of rule-governed conduct or the principled interpretation of basic notions.

Sinologists differ in their interpretation of the Confucian use of *de*. Some maintain that *de* is functionally equivalent to "power," "force," or "potency," and, in Confucian usage, should be qualified as moral in contrast to physical force. More commonly, *de* is rendered as "virtue" in the distinctively ethical sense, as pertaining to excellence of a character trait or disposition. Interestingly, these two interpretations of *de* are not incompatible in the light of some English uses of "virtue." We find the first sense in the sixth entry of "virtue" in *Webster's Third New International Dictionary*: "an active quality or power whether of physical or of moral nature: the capacity or power adequate to the production of a given effect"; and in the fifth entry: "a characteristic, quality, or trait known or felt to be excellent." Both these senses of "virtue" are present in the classical Chinese uses of *de*. Of course, there is, as in English, a value-neutral sense of *de* that leaves open the question whether personal traits or qualities merit ethical approval. This question is reflected in the distinction in familiar Chinese between *meide* and *e'de*. The former pertains to "beautiful" or "commendable" *de* and the latter to its contrary. *Meide* are those traits acquired through personal cultivation. *The Encyclopedic Dictionary of the Chinese Language* offers the following two entries for *de* in the ethical sense, one of them suggested by an interpretation of its homophone, meaning "to get" or "to obtain," found in the *Liji* (*Book of Rites*): (1) "that which is obtained in the *xin* (mind/heart) as a result of personal cultivation," and (2) "the nature that is formed after successful personal cultivation." Both these entries involve *meide*, commendable, acquired qualities of character, much in the sense of Hume's "personal merits" (1957).

Also important is the sense of *de* as power or force, in view of the Confucian notion of *junzi* (the ethically paradigmatic individual or paragon). The *junzi* who exercises the virtues possesses the power of attraction or influence indicative of effective agency. Thus the *junzi*, equipped with the various virtues (*de*), has the power or capacity to influence the course of human affairs. This interpretation is suggested by two remarks of Confucius: "Virtue (*de*) never stands alone; it is bound to have neighbors"; and, "The virtue of the *junzi* is like the wind; the virtue of the small man is like grass. Let the wind blow over the grass and it is sure to bend" (*Analects*, 4.25 and 12.19; Lau 1979). Even if the *junzi's* power is limited, he has an indispensable educational role, not only in providing models for competence in *li* or following rules, but also in inculcating a "*ren* attitude" or ethical concern and reasonableness in applying rules (Cua 1998, Essay 8). This educational role provides, at least, a partial account for Confucius's emphasis on the necessity of caution in speech and commitment prior to action in the light of his ideal of harmony of words and deeds, or, in the famous words of Wang Yangming, "the unity of knowledge and action" (Cua 1978, ch. 4).

In sum, the Confucian notion of *de* can be properly rendered as a conception of ethical virtues that has dual aspects: (1) an achieved condition of an ethically well-cultivated person, with commendable character traits in accord with the ideal of *dao*; and (2) a condition that is deemed to have a peculiar potency or power of efficacy in influencing the course of human life. The difficult problem is to present the Confucian *dao* and *de* as an ethics of virtue with a coherent conceptual scheme.

Basic Notions and the Problem of Conceptual Unity

The *Lunyu* (*Analects*), commonly considered the main and most reliable source of Confucius's teachings, bequeathed to the Chinese a large and complex ethical vocabulary. This vocabulary contains a significant number of virtue (*de*) terms with implicit reference to the Confucian ideal of *dao*. Terms such as *ren*, *yi*, and *li* seem to occupy a central position both in the *Lunyu* and throughout the history of Confucian discourse. Until recent times, few philosophical scholars of Confucianism attended to the problem of conceptual explication and the unity of these basic notions, that is, their presumed interconnection or interdependence in the light of *dao* as an ideal, unifying perspective. While most Confucian terms for particular virtues can be rendered into English without elaborate explanation (e.g., filiality, courage, dignity, fidelity, kindness, respectfulness), the apparently basic notions (*ren*, *li*, and *yi*) are not amenable to simple translation and thus pose a problem for conceptual analysis and interpretation. Moreover, existing translations of these terms embody the writer's interpretation, a sort of compendious statement of an implicit commentary, representing the writer's preunderstanding of the translated texts.

Likewise, an explication of basic Confucian notions involves philosophical commentary, a familiar feature in the development of the history of Chinese thought. However, the attempt is beset by a formidable difficulty, especially in explicating the basic concepts of the Confucian framework. To my knowledge, the pioneering study of the conceptual aspect of Confucian ethics is Chen Daqi's *Kongzi xueshuo* (*Doctrines of Confucius*). Chen maintains that before interpreting the ideas of Confucius, it is essential to inquire into the conceptual status of some recurrent terms in the text. For determining the centrality or basic status of notions or concepts, Chen proposes four criteria. Basic concepts are (1) fundamental, (2) leading or guiding, (3) the most important, and (4) the most comprehensive (1976, 98).

Fundamental concepts. Feature 1 suggests the distinction between basic and derivative concepts. However, it is more plausible and accords better with Chen's discussion to construe his distinction as one between basic and dependent concepts. Given our characterization of Confucian ethics as an ethics of virtues, it is a conceptual distinction between basic and dependent virtues. A concept may depend on another for its ethical significance without being a logical derivation. For instance, one cannot derive the concept of love from *ren*, yet its ethical significance depends on its connection with *ren*. This is perhaps the principal basis of Zhu Xi's famous contention that *ren* cannot be equated with love, for it is the rationale of love (*ai zhi li*) (Chan 1963, 595; Qian 1982, 2:55–56).

Leading or guiding concepts. Feature 2 recalls the purport of ethical terms as action guides and informs the Confucian agent that the enduring significance of ethical endeavors lies in *dao* or the ideal of the good human life as a whole, an ideal to be pursued and rendered concrete in particular circumstances.

Cardinal and comprehensive concepts. Feature 3 is the chief mark of basic ethical concepts as cardinal concepts. Feature 4 raises an issue in Confucian scholarship. It seems unproblematic if comprehensiveness is ascribed to *dao* or *ren* in the broad sense as signifying the holistic, ideal unifying perspective of Confucian discourse. Again, consider Zhu Xi's thesis that *ren* (in the broad sense) embraces the four: *ren* (in the narrow sense), *yi*, *li*, and wisdom. In terms of an ethics of virtue, the fundamental distinction is the distinction between cardinal and dependent virtues. Accordingly, Chen proposes that in addition to *dao* and *de*, the Confucian scheme consists of *ren*, *li*, and *yi* as the basic, cardinal concepts. This thesis is well supported by the recurrence of such concepts and their fundamental importance throughout the history of Confucianism.

The foregoing remarks pertain to the question of identifying basic, cardinal concepts as contrasted with dependent concepts. It is important to note that this is an ethical distinction, not a general nonethical distinction between general and subordinate virtues. The ethically dependent virtues are not mere means to the realizations of the basic virtues. In nonethical contexts, dependent virtues such as trustworthiness, compliance with ritual, and honesty are properly considered virtues that promote human welfare. One may even claim that these virtues are intrinsically valuable with no connection to any particular ethical outlook. However, in the context of an ethical ideal that recognizes their value, they may be embraced as dependent ethical virtues. When this is done, their nonethical worth increases their worth, so to speak, particularly when they contribute to the realization of the ethical ideal of the good human life or *ren* in the broad sense. Virtues or values that contribute to such realization are plausibly considered as *constitutive means* of *dao* (Lau 1970, app. 5). A more difficult problem remains: how are these basic concepts related to one another? The following discussion presents a sketch of a philosophical reconstruction. The sketch offers a general characterization of Confucian ethics as a form of virtue ethics and provides a sample of how such basic notions as *li* and *yi* can be shaped in response to questions deemed important for the development of a Confucian moral philosophy.

The Confucian ethical framework comprises five basic concepts: *dao*, *de*, *ren*, *yi*, and *li*. Perhaps the best approach is to regard them initially, with a minimum of interpretation, as "focal notions," that is, terms which function like lenses to convey distinct though not unrelated centers of ethical concern. As generic terms, focal notions are amenable to specification in particular contexts, thus acquiring specific or narrower senses. This is an adaptation of Xunzi's distinction between generic (*gongming*) and specific terms (*bieming*). However, in general, a term used as a specific term in one context may in another context be used as a generic term subject to further specification. In other words, the use of a term in either the generic or the specific sense is entirely relative to the speaker's purpose on a particular occasion, rather than to any theory concerning the intrinsic characters of terms or the essential attributes of things.

As noted earlier, *dao* is an evaluative term. Its focal point lies in the Confucian vision of the good human life as a whole or the ideal of human excellence. Commonly rendered as the "way" or "Way," *dao* is functionally equivalent to the ideal "way of life," an ideal theme that admits of diverse specifications of its concrete significance as befitting individual human life (Cua 1978, ch. 8). Unlike other basic terms, *dao* is most distinctive as an abstract, formal term in the highest generic sense, that is, subject to general specification by way of such virtue (*de*) words as *ren*, *li*, and *yi*. Recall that *de* (virtue, power) is an individual achievement through personal cultivation. When a person succeeds in realizing *dao*, he or she has attained such basic *de* as *ren*, *li*, and *yi*. The specification of *de*, apart from *ren*, *li*, and *yi*, can take a variety of forms or dependent virtues such as filiality, respectfulness, or fidelity. In this sense, *de* is an abstract noun like *dao*, but it depends on *dao* for its distinctive character. *De* is thus functionally equivalent to ethical virtue. Thus, the opening remark in *Daxue* (*Great Learning*) points out that the way of great learning or adult ethical education lies in the clear exemplification of the virtues (*ming mingde*). With its emphasis on *dao* and *de*, Confucian ethics is properly characterized as an ethics of virtue, but more informatively as an ethics of *ren*, *li*, and *yi*, relative to their concrete specification or particularization by terms of dependent virtues (e.g., filiality, respectfulness, integrity). As generic, focal terms *ren*, *li*, and *yi* are specific terms relative to *dao* as a generic term. To put this differently, implicit in Chen's account is a distinction between basic, interdependent virtues (*ren*, *li*, and *yi*) and dependent virtues (e.g., filiality, respectfulness). As indicated earlier, the latter are dependent in the sense that their ethical import depends on direct or indirect reference to one or more of the basic, interdependent virtues of *ren*, *li*, and *yi*, respectively. It must be noted that ethically dependent virtues may be valuable character traits independently of their connection with basic virtues.

While *ren* has a long history of conceptual evolution and interpretation, as a focal notion it suggests an ethical interest centered on love and care for one's fellows, that is, an affectionate concern for the well-being of others—the one persistent idea in the Confucian tradition (Cua 1978, ch. 4). Thus *ren* has been felicitously rendered as "human-heartedness," "humanity," or benevolence—a concrete specification of the abstract ideal of *dao*. This core meaning of *ren* as fellow feeling is found in *Lunyu* (12.22). It is reported that Confucius once said to his disciple Zengzi, "My *dao* has one thread that runs through it" (4.15). Zengzi construed this *dao* as consisting of *zhong* and *shu*, an interpretation widely acknowledged as a method for pursuing *ren*. While the relation between *zhong* and *shu* has divergent interpretations, *zhong* may be rendered as "doing one's best" (Lau 1979, 16) and *shu* as "consideration of other people's feelings and desires." In this light, Confucian ethics displays a concern for both self-regarding and other-regarding virtues.

However, the acquisition of these particular, dependent virtues presupposes a locus in which they are exercised. Thus among dependent virtues, filiality and fraternity are considered primary, for the family is the natural home and the foundation for the extension of *ren*-affection. In Song and Ming Confucianism (e.g., Cheng Hao, Wang Yangming), *dao* is sometimes used interchangeably with *ren*. In this manner, *ren* has attained the status of a supreme, all-embracing ethical ideal of the well-being of every existent thing, human or nonhuman, animate or inanimate. Confucius's vision of a well-ordered human society is transformed into a vision of the universe as a moral community (Cua 1993; 1998, Essays 7 and 9). In this conception anything that is an actual or potential object of human attention is considered an object of human concern. Exploitation of human and natural resources must be subject to evaluation in terms of *dao* as an all-embracing ethical ideal of excellence. This ideal of *dao* makes no specific demands on ordinary humans. For the most part, conflict of values is left to individual determination, though the welfare of parents is always the first consideration. Thus, the concrete significance of *dao* is open to the exercise of *yi*, alternatively moral discretion (*quan*) or the agent's sense of rightness.

The exercise of *yi* depends on ethical education based on *daotong* or the tradition of the community of interpretation. That is, reasoned interpretation by the educated members of the community is informed by *sensus communis*, a sense of common interest, a regard for *dao* as the ideal unifying perspective. Disagreement or dispute on the pragmatic import of *dao* is expected, as members of the community of interpretation have their own conceptions of human excellence (*shan*) and possibilities of fulfillment. The ethical solution of interpretive conflicts lies in transforming the disagreement into agreement in the light of *sensus communis*, not in a solution defined by agonistic debate, which presumes that there are impartial judges who can render their corporate decision in terms of majority vote. Unlike contemporary democratic polity, the majority rule cannot be reasonably accepted as a standard for settling ethical disagreements. Sound ethical decision, contrary to the claim of a recent utilitarian, is not a matter of subjectivity and statistical evaluation (Shiang 1991). It is the ethical tradition that provides the background and guidelines to ethical conduct. Normative ethical theories have value because they provide different ways of assessing the significance of tradition. Like the basic concepts of Confucian ethics, they are focal notions for important centers of ethical concern, e.g., duty and interest (private or public) or, in recent terminology, agent-relative and agent-neutral reasons for action.

The notion of *li* focuses on the ritual code. For this reason, it is commonly rendered as "rites," "ritual," "propriety," or "ceremonials." The ritual code is essentially a set of rules of proper conduct pertaining to the manner or style of performance (Cua 1978; 2002). As *yi* is incompatible with exclusive regard for personal gain, the *li* set forth the rules of ethical responsibility. For Confucius and his followers, the *li* represent an enlightened tradition. As D. C. Lau put it:

> The rites (*li*) were a body of rules governing action in every aspect of life and they were the repository of past insights into morality. It is, therefore, important that one should, unless there are strong reasons to the contrary, observe them. Though there is no guarantee that observance of the rites necessarily leads, in every case, to behaviour that is right, the chances are it will, in fact do so. (1979, 20)

Yet the ethical significance of *li* is determined by the presence of the spirit of *ren*. As Confucius once said, "If a man has no *ren*, what has he to do with *li*?" (*Analects*, 3.3).

Since the ritual code represents a customary practice, the early Confucians, particularly Xunzi and the writers of some chapters in *Record of Rites* (or *Book of Rites*, *Liji*) were concerned with providing a reasoned justification for compliance with *li* or traditional rules of proper conduct. Arthur Waley remarks: "It was with the relation of ritual [*li*] as a whole to morality and not with the details of etiquette and precedence that the early Confucianists were chiefly concerned" (1938, 67; Cua 1983). The same concern with reasoned justification is evident in Song and Ming Confucianists (e.g., Zhu Xi and Wang Yangming) who maintain that the significance of *li* (ritual) lies in its rationale (*li zhi li*).

The ethical significance of *yi*, in part, has to do with an attempt to provide a rationale for the acceptance of *li*. *Yi* focuses principally on what is right or fitting. The equation of *yi* with its homophone meaning "appropriateness" is explicit in the *Doctrine of the Mean* (*Zhongyong* or *Zhong Yong*, sec. 20), and is generally accepted by Confucian thinkers, e.g., Xunzi, Li Gou, and Zhu Xi. However, what is right or fitting depends on reasoned judgment. As Xunzi puts it: "The person concerned with *yi* follows reason" (Li 1979, 605). Thus, *yi* may be construed as reasoned judgment concerning the right thing to do in particular exigencies. As Li Gou, a Song Confucian, put it, *yi* is "decisive judgment" that is appropriate to the situation at hand (Cua 1989).

In light of the foregoing, we may state the interdependence of basic notions in this way. Given *dao* as the ideal of the good human life as a whole, *ren*, *li*, and *yi*, the basic Confucian virtues (*de*), are constitutive rather than mere instrumental means to its actualization. In other words, the actualization of *dao* requires the concurrent satisfaction of the standards expressed in *ren*, *li*, and *yi*. Since these focal notions pertain to different foci of ethical interest, we may also say that the actualization of *dao* requires a coordination of three equally important centers of ethical interest and endeavor. The connection between these foci involves interdependence rather than subordination. Thus, in the ideal case, *ren*, *li*, and *yi* are mutually supportive and adhere to the same ideal of *dao*. When *dao* is in fact realized, *ren*, *li*, and *yi* would be deemed constituents of this condition of achievement. When, on the other hand, one attends to the prospect of *dao*-realization, *ren*, *li*, and *yi* would be regarded as complementary foci and means to *dao* as an end. In sum, *ren*, *li*, and *yi* are complementary foci of human interest.

The Scope and Functions of *Li*

Because of its distinctive character and role in Confucian ethics and its pervasive influence in traditional China and contemporary critique, the notion of *li* requires special attention. Implicit in *li* is an idea of rule-governed conduct. In the *Liji* (*Book of Rites*), the subject matter ranges from formal prescriptions (henceforth, ritual rules) concerning mourning, sacrifices, marriage, and communal festivities to the more ordinary occasions relating to conduct toward ruler, superior, parent, elder, teacher, and guest. Because of its emphasis on the form of behavior, *li* is often translated as religion, ceremony, deportment, decorum, propriety, formality, politeness, courtesy, etiquette, good form, or good behavior. These renderings are misleading without an understanding of the different functions of *li*. At the outset, it is important to note that for Confucians the *li* embody a living cultural tradition, that is, they are subject to modification in response to changing circumstances of society. Thus some writers of the *Liji* point out that the *li* are the prescriptions of reason, that any ritual rule that is deemed right and reasonable can be considered a part of *li*. On one plausible interpretation, the traditional ritual code represents no more than a codification of ethical experiences based on the concern with *ren* and *yi*. In this light, the *li* are in principle subject to revision or replacement. In the spirit of Zhu Xi, we may say that a Confucian must reject ritual rules that are burdensome and superfluous and accept those that are practicable and essential to the maintenance of a harmonious social order. However, any reasoned attempt to revise or replace *li* presupposes an understanding of their functions. It is this understanding that distinguishes the Confucian scholar from a pedant, who may have a mastery of rules without understanding their underlying rationale. For elucidation, we rely mainly on a reconstruction of Xunzi's view, since we find in some of his essays the most articulate concern for and defense of *li* as an embodiment of a living, cultural tradition (Cua 1979; 1998, Essay 13).

With any system of rules governing human conduct, one can always raise questions concerning its purpose. In Confucian ethics, the *li*, as a set of formal prescriptions for proper behavior, have a threefold function: delimiting, supportive, and ennobling. The delimiting function is primary, in that the *li* are fundamentally directed to the prevention of human conflict. They comprise a set of constraints that delineate the boundaries of pursuit of individual needs, desires, and interests. The *li* purport to set forth rules of proceeding in an orderly fashion, ultimately to promote the unity and harmony of human association in a state ruled by a sage king imbued with the spirit of *ren* and *yi*. This orderliness consists of social distinctions or divisions in various kinds of human relationships (*lun*)—distinctions between ruler and minister, father and son, the eminent and the humble, the elder and the younger, the rich and the poor, and the important and unimportant members of society. In abstraction from the connection with *ren* and *yi*, the delimiting function of *li* may be compared with that of negative moral rules or criminal laws. Like rules against killing, stealing, or lying, the *li* impose constraints on conduct. They create, so to speak, paths of obstruction, thus blocking certain moves of agents in the pursuit of their desires or interests. The *li*, in effect, stipulate the conditions of the eligibility or permissibility of actions. They do not prejudge the substantive character or value of individual pursuit. They provide information on the limiting conditions of action but no positive guidance as to how one's desires may be properly satisfied. In other words, the *li* tell agents what goals *not* to pursue, but they do not tell agents how to go about pursuing goals within the prescribed limits of action.

Apart from their delimiting function, the *li* have also a supportive function; that is, they provide conditions or opportunities for satisfaction of desires within the prescribed limits of action. Instead of suppressing desires, the *li* provide acceptable channels or outlets for their fulfillment. In an important sense, the supportive function of *li* acknowledges the integrity of our natural desires. So long as they are satisfied within the bounds of propriety, we accept them for what they are, whether reasonable or unreasonable, wise or foolish, good or bad. The main supportive function of *li* is the redirection of the course of individual self-seeking activities, not the suppression of the motivating desires. Just as the delimiting function of *li* may be compared with that of criminal law, their supportive function may be compared with that of procedural law, which contains rules that *enable* us to carry out our wishes and desires (e.g., the law of contracts). The *li*, like these procedural rules, aid the realization of desires without pronouncing value judgments.

The focus on the ennobling function of *li* is a distinctive feature of Confucian ethics and traditional Chinese culture. The keynote of the ennobling function is "cultural refinement," the education and nourishment (*yang*) of emotions or their transformation in accord with the spirit of *ren* and *yi*. The characteristic concern with the *form* of proper behavior is still present. However, the form stressed is not just a matter of fitting into an established social structure or set of distinctions, nor is it a matter of methodic procedure that facilitates the satisfaction of the agent's desires and wishes; rather, it involves the elegant form (*wen*) for the expression of ethical character. In other words, the ennobling function of *li* is directed primarily to the development of commendable or beautiful virtues (*meide*). The "beauty" (*mei*) of the expression of an ethical character lies in the balance between emotions and forms. Thus, what is deemed admirable in the virtuous conduct of an ethically superior person (*junzi*) is the harmonious fusion of elegant form and feelings. In the ideal case, a *li*-performance may be said to have an aesthetic dimension. In two different and related ways, a *li*-performance may be said to be an object of delight. In the first place, the elegant form is something that delights our senses. It can be contemplated with delight quite apart from the expressed emotional quality. In the second place, when we attend to the emotion or emotional quality expressed by the action, which we perceive as a sign of an ethical virtue or character, the mind is delighted and exalted, provided, of course, that we are also agents interested in the promotion of ethical virtues in general. Doing justice to the ennobling function of *li* requires a complex characterization and evaluation, well beyond the scope of this article. The general idea is stated by Thomé H. Fang. *Li* is:

> cultural refinement, bodying forth either in the prudence of conduct, or the balance of emotion, or the rationality of knowledge, or the intelligent working of order. Especially, it is blended with the excellent spirit of fine arts such as poetry and music. In short, what is called *Li* in Chinese is a standard of measurement for the general cultural values, according to which we can enjoy the beauties of life in the rational order of political societies. (1980, 159)

Problems of rules and exceptions and justification. Appreciating the rationale of the *li* in terms of delimiting, supportive, and ennobling functions does not entail that the *li* provide sufficient guidance in resolving ethical perplexities. The problem of rules and exceptions is not a genuine problem in Confucian ethics, for the notions of *yi* and *quan* can be used in dealing with perplexities concerning what one ought to do in a particular situation. For classical Confucians like Mencius and Xunzi, ethical perplexities arise largely from unanticipated, changing circumstances of human life. As Xunzi succinctly reminds his readers, one must use *yi* to respond to exigent or changing circumstances (*yiyi bianying*). Hard cases for deliberation are those that can be resolved by an appeal, not to an established rule of *li*, but to one's reasoned judgment of what is the right or fitting thing to do. Mencius particularly emphasizes *quan* (weighing of circumstances) in coping with exigent situations. When asked what a person ought to do when his sister-in-law is drowning, given the *li*-requirement that male and female are not to touch one another in giving or receiving anything, Mencius appeals to *quan* rather than to compliance with rules. This appeal has nothing to do with building an exception to a rule of proper conduct but has to do instead with one's sense of rightness in exigent situations. In the light of the crucial function of *yi*, a rule may be judged to be irrelevant to an ethical perplexity, not because it has no authoritative status but rather because the *li* as a set of formal prescriptions for proper behavior are not intended to cover all situations of human life. It is *yi* that responds to ethical perplexities. More explicitly, Zhu Xi, perhaps following Li Gou, considers *yi* a decisive judgment as to what is appropriate (to the situation at hand) and the courage to carry it out (*Zhuzi yulei*, ch. 6, 19a). In view of its emphasis on *yi*, the characterization of Confucian ethics as an ethics of flexibility is apt. Moreover, there are grounds in the *Analects* for this flexible attitude toward changing circumstances. It is recorded, for example, that Confucius once said of himself, "I have no preconception about the permissible and the impermissible" (*Analects*, 18.8).

Quite naturally, one may raise the question of justification for such judgments in exigent circumstances. In normal situations, the *li* are quite sufficient to guide action insofar as they are informed by a concern for *ren*. The problem of reasoned justification for such judgments has not received attention from most Confucian thinkers, except Xunzi. However, even in the works of Xunzi we do not find any articulate answer to this problem, though they provide materials for constructing a response. In the first place, Xunzi is explicit that any discussion is valuable because there exist certain standards for assessment, and these standards pertain principally to conceptual clarity, respect for linguistic practices and evidence, and the requirement of consistency and coherence in discourse. A philosophical reconstruction along the lines of the theory of argumentation presents an interesting Confucian view of justification in terms of rational and empirical standards of competence, along with certain desirable qualities of participants in ethical discourse. In this reconstruction of Xunzi's works, ethical justification is a phase of discourse, preceded by explanatory efforts in the clarification of normative claims responsive to a problem of common concern among participants, which in turn presupposes that queries concerning the proper uses of terms are understood by participants in ethical argumentation (Cua 1985a, b). As widely noted by contemporary writers on Confucian ethics, the Confucians are fond of appeal to historical events and paradigmatic individuals. This ethical use of historical knowledge and beliefs is a pervasive feature of early Confucianism.

In closing, it may be noted that Confucian ethics, like any normative system, presents conceptual problems of interpretation and reconstruction. In this essay, in order to characterize some of the distinctive concerns of classical Confucianism, I have focused on the Confucian framework of basic notions and their interdependence. Complex issues regarding the justification of *li* are elaborated elsewhere (Cua 1998, Essay 13).

See also Confucianism: Confucius; Confucianism: Tradition; *Dao*: The Way; *De*; *Junzi*: The Moral Person; *Quan*; *Ren*; *Yi* and *Li*; *Zhong* and *Shu*: Loyalty and Reciprocity.

Bibliography

Chan, Wing-tsit, trans. *A Source Book in Chinese Philosophy*. Princeton, N.J.: Princeton University Press, 1963.

Chen, Daqi. *Kongzi xueshuo*. Taipei: Zhengzhong, 1976.

Cua, A. S. "Between Commitment and Realization: Wang Yang-ming's Vision of the Universe as a Moral Community." *Philosophy East and West*, 43(4), 1993, pp. 611–647.

———. "Dimensions of *Li* (Propriety): Reflections on an Aspect of Hsün Tzu's Ethics." *Philosophy East and West*, 29(4), 1979, pp. 373–394.

———. *Dimensions of Moral Creativity: Paradigms, Principles, and Ideals*. University Park: Pennsylvania State University Press, 1978.

———. "Ethical and Religious Dimensions of *Li* (Rites)." *Review of Metaphysics*, 55(3), 2002, pp. 501–549.

———. *Ethical Argumentation: A Study in Hsün Tzu's Moral Epistemology*. Honolulu: University of Hawaii Press, 1985a.

———. "Ethical Uses of the Past in Early Confucianism: The Case of Hsün Tzu." *Philosophy East and West*, 35(2), 1985b, pp. 133–156. (Reprinted in *Virtue, Nature, and Moral Agency in the Xunzi*, ed. T. C. Kline and Philip J. Ivanhoe. Indianapolis, Ind.: Hackett, 2000.)

———. "Li and Moral Justification: A Study of the *Li Chi*." *Philosophy East and West*, 33(1), 1983, pp. 1–16.

———. *Moral Vision and Tradition: Essays in Chinese Ethics*. Washington, D.C.: Catholic University of America Press, 1998.

———. "The Problem of Conceptual Unity in Hsün Tzu and Li Kou's Solution." *Philosophy East and West*, 36(2), 1989, pp. 115–134.

———. *The Unity of Knowledge and Action: A Study in Wang Yang-ming's Moral Psychology*. Honolulu: University of Hawaii Press, 1982.

de Bary, William Theodore, ed. *Self and Society in Ming Thought*. New York: Columbia University Press, 1970.

Fang, Thomé H. *The Chinese View of Life*. Taipei: Linking, 1980.

Hume, David. *An Inquiry Concerning the Principles of Morals*. Indianapolis, Ind.: Bobbs-Merrill, 1957.

Kennedy, George A., trans. *Aristotle on Rhetoric: A Theory of Civic Discourse*. New York: Oxford University Press, 1991.

Lau, D. C., trans. *Confucius: The Analects*. New York: Penguin, 1979.

Lau, D. C., trans. *Mencius*. Middlesex, England, 1970.

Li, Disheng. *Xunzi jishi*. Taipei: Xuesheng, 1979.

Munro, Donald J. *The Concept of Man in Early China*. Stanford, Calif.: Stanford University Press, 1969.

Perelman, Chaim, and Anna Olbrechts-Tyteca. *The New Rhetoric: A Treatise in Argumentation*. Notre Dame, Ind.: University of Notre Dame Press, 1969.

Qian, Mu. *Zhuzi xin xue'an*. Taipei: Sanmin, 1982.

Rescher, Nicholas. *Dialectics*. Albany: State University of New York Press, 1977.

Shiang, Ching Lai. *A New Approach to Utilitarianism: A Unified Utilitarian Theory and Its Applications to Distributive Justice*. Dordrecht: Kluwer, 1991.

Waley, Arthur, trans. *The Analects of Confucius*. New York: Vintage, 1938.

Wheelwright, Philip. *The Burning Fountain: A Study in the Language of Symbolism*. Bloomington: Indiana University Press, 1968.

Zhu, Xi. *Zhuzi yulei*, Vol. 1. Taipei: Zhengzhong, 1982.

Confucianism: Ethics and Law

Fuldien Li

Chinese legal philosophy essentially follows the teaching of Confucius. The basic ideas of Confucianism, such as *de* (virtue) and *li* (variously rendered as rules of proper conduct, rites, ceremonies, etc.), have important implications for Chinese legal philosophy.

The "rectification of names" (*zhengming*), to which Confucius gave a high priority, involved not only clear terminology but the acceptance by each level and member of society, from "common people" to king, of its place and proper function (Joblin 1974, 35). Fundamentally, Confucians believe in a society in which each person conducts himself according to his position and status in the family and in the society (Ma 1971, 444). According to the idea of "rectification of names," each level and member of society should know what to do and how to behave. In light of this, self-cultivation is considered the foundation. "From the Son of Heaven down to the mass of the people, all must consider the cultivation of the person the root of everything besides" (*Daxue*, sec. 6; Legge 1893, 1: 359). The roles each individual must assume in a particular relationship are called the *li*, or rules of proper conduct. The dominant role of the *li* is evident in the maintenance of the traditional Chinese duty-oriented social structure. The rules of *li* are not arbitrary; major Confucian thinkers—e.g., Xunzi and Zhu Xi—considered these rules to be in harmony with *ren* (benevolence, humanity) and *yi* (rightness). Moreover, *li* has a homophone that may be rendered as "reason." Ideally, for the Confucian, the *li* provide the principal guidance to a person's ethical thought and conduct in conformity with traditional social norms, which are presumed to be reasonable. As one writer of a chapter in *Liji* points out, what is reasonable may be considered part of *li* (Legge, 2:275).

According to Confucius's conception, there are two major elements of law: (1) *li* (rules of proper conduct), or rules that inspire positive orderly conduct; (2) *xing* (penalties), or rules that discourage and punish disorderly or destructive conduct. To Confucius, government and moral culture are one and the same thing (Wu 1968, 351). Ideally, laws and morals have the same foundation. People who violate the *li*, depending on the gravity of the offense, may be subject to penalties (*xing*). From this point of view, moral duties are ipso facto legal duties in the sense that there are laws providing penalties for violations and breaches. Whatever is immoral is not only illegal but a criminal offense (Wu 1968, 324). For the same reason, civil law in China is not obvious. The *li* are the normative bases for distinguishing right and wrong conduct, determining the nearness and distance of relatives, and resolving doubts about guilt and innocence. More generally, without respect for *li*, the requirements of morality (*daode*), *ren*, and *yi* cannot be completely satisfied.

The subordination of law (*fa*) to *li* is not just a matter of theoretical interest. It has had a tremendous impact on the development of the traditional conception of law and the legal system in China. First, legal codes of the dynasties after the Han were almost invariably formulated by Confucian statesmen. The influence of Confucian ethics, particularly its focus on *li*, therefore, permeated all legislation. Second, the administration of justice was much influenced by the Confucian classics of *li*, such as *Liji*. Not only did the interpretation of legal codes appeal to the teachings of *li*, but judicial officials also referred to Confucian classics as standards for adjudication. We have noted before that traditionally Chinese law and legal processes focused mainly on criminality. As a result, Confucius's moral teaching became entrenched in an official system upheld by laws and punishments. This is what some scholars have called the Confucianization of law or the legalization of Confucianism (Ch'u 1984, 267; Wu 1968, 394). Since the code of the Qin, the stipulations can be roughly divided into criminal law and administrative law. Civil law is not included, but it was not completely neglected—for example, there were cases of litigation involving property (*song*). Civil law is stipulated in the realm of *li* or propriety, an autonomous part of the moral norm (*defa*). A party who disobeys the terms conveyed by an authority in the settlement of a civil dispute will be regarded as a rebel and will be punished by the authority according to the criminal law.

Law and morals are, so to speak, the two wings of a bird (Wu 1968, 351). Confucius saw the source of all the evils of his day in a decay of morals, especially among the ruling classes. He said:

> If you lead the people by political measures and keep them in order by penal law, they will avoid transgressing them but they will lose their sense of honor. If you lead them by virtue (*de*) and keep them in order by ritual and morals (*li*), they will not only preserve their sense of honor but

> also become thoroughly transformed. (*Analects*, 2.3; Wu 1968, 324)

Thus Confucius declared: "In legal proceedings, I am like others. The most important thing was to avoid litigation" (*Analects*, 12.13). Confucius did not exactly despise the penal law, nor did he refuse to hear litigation. However, his main concern was the observance of *li* and music, and the cultivation of personal virtues in promoting good and humane government (*renzheng*). "If ritual and music are not promoted," he said, "then punishments cannot attain the just measure. If punishments do not attain the just measure, then the people would not know where to put their hands and feet" (*Analects*, 13.3; Wu 1968, 325).

Of the six schools of thought classified by Sima Qian, only Confucianism (*Ru jia*) has been accepted by Chinese historians as orthodox. The doctrines of legalists were perhaps those most mercilessly attacked (Ma 1971, 445). When the legalists took up the idea of *fa* or law, they gave it a new interpretation. Instead of being an intuitive notion applied ad hoc, *fa*, in their view, should be promulgated and apply to all people equally—to both the ruler and the ruled irrespective of personal relationships. The *fa* is absolutely compulsory. If it is to be effective, severe punishments must be imposed. The legalists Shang Yang and Han Fei stressed the strict rule of law, supplemented by a system of rewards and punishments. They considered all the moral doctrines irrelevant, dangerous, and harmful to the administration of the state.

In the Han dynasty, Confucian scholars gradually but steadily acquired political power. During the reign of Emperor Wu Di (140–87 B.C.E.), Confucianism was advocated as the authoritative doctrine of the state. By that time, *fa* as an effective instrument for maintaining order and administering justice was generally recognized. The new situation, however, brought about a new relationship between the two concepts, that is, the subordination of *fa* to *li*. Dong Zhongshu, a major Han Confucian thinker, set forth the doctrine that "*De* (virtue) is the master and punishment the assistant (*de zhu xing fu*)."

As is well known, Confucius laid the greatest emphasis on filial piety. This idea has a legitimate place in any system of law. Since the Tang dynasty, family relationships have been an index to degrees of punishment in criminal codes.

Cruel punishments have been common in judicial history worldwide, but in Chinese institutions and administration of justice—in accordance with the Confucian teaching of love and goodness (*ren*)—much emphasis was placed on mercy and pardon. Repeatedly applied are the doctrines of forgiveness for ignorance; pardons for the young, the weak, the old, and the stupid; suspension of execution; reduction of punishment because of extremely hot or cold weather; and probation in order to serve parents.

After the revolution of 1911, a comprehensive judicial reform was established. Civil law was accepted in the modern Chinese legal system, and parts of traditional Chinese legal philosophy were absorbed into the modern legal institutions of the Republic of China.

See also Confucianism: Ethics; Han Feizi; Legalism; Shang Yang; Shen Buhai.

Bibliography

Chen, Kou-yuang. *Introduction to Chinese Legal Institutions*, 4th ed. Taipei: Sanmin, 1970.

Ch'u, Tung-tsu. *Law and Society in Traditional China*. Taipei: Liren, 1984.

Hsieh, Kuen-sheng. "Introduction to Chinese Judicial System and Related Laws." In *Essays on Dr. Sun Yat-sen's Legal Philosophy*, ed. Liang-chien Cha, 2nd ed. Taipei: Chinese Culture University, School of Law, 1966.

Joblin, Kingsley J. "The Humanistic Faith of Confucius." In *Chinese Philosophy*, Vol. 1, *Confucianism and Other Schools*, ed. Y. C. Koo et al. Taipei: China Academy, 1974.

Legge, James. *The Chinese Classics*. Oxford: Clarendon, 1893. (Includes *The Great Learning*, *Ta Hsüeh*.)

Ma, Herbert H. P. "The Chinese Concept of the Individual and the Reception of Foreign Law," *Journal of Chinese Law*, 9, 1995, p. 209.

———. "Law and Morality: Some Reflections on the Chinese Experience Past and Present." *Philosophy East and West*, 21, 1971, pp. 443–460.

Wu, John C. H. "Chinese Legal Philosophy: A Brief Historical Survey." In *Chinese Philosophy*, Vol. 1, *Confucianism and Other Schools*, ed. Y. C. Koo et al. Taipei: China Academy, 1974.

———. "The Individual in Chinese Political Tradition." In *The Status of the Individual in East and West*, ed. Charles A. Moore. Honolulu: University of Hawaii Press, 1968.

Yuan, Shao-chi. "Some Reflections on Shang Yang and His Political Philosophy." In *Chinese Philosophy*, Vol. 1, *Confucianism and Other Schools*, ed. Y. C. Koo et al. Taipei: China Academy, 1974.

Confucianism: Han

Chi-yun CHEN

I

The era of the Han dynasty (Former or Western Han, 202 B.C.E.–2 C.E.; Wang Mang interregnum, 2–25 C.E.; Later or Eastern Han, 25–220 C.E.) poses some perplexing problems for students of Chinese thought and philosophy. (In this essay, Han thought and thinkers, Han Confucian thought and scholars, and Han Confucianism and Confucians are referred to somewhat interchangeably, depending on the context. The reason for this will become clear as the discussion unfolds.)

On the one hand, the Han era is no doubt one of the most important periods in the history of China. It was during this era that many of the political, social, economic, and other cultural developments of the preceding millennium came to fruition and became crystallized in the high civilization of the Han Chinese. In fact, the names of many "schools" of thought of the classical age (sixth to third centuries B.C.E.)—such as Daoism and legalism—were coined by scholars of the Han era; the definitive texts ascribed to these schools were also recompiled or edited by Han scholars. The classification of ancient Chinese thought into "schools" was itself devised by the Han scholars in an effort to define the issues and tenets of diverse ancient traditions and to reorganize them into a unified intellectual legacy. Long after the end of the Han dynasty, the cultural tradition formed during the Han era continues to mold the civilization of China, so much so that the very name Han has become synonymous with "culturally Chinese," and "Han learning" (*Hanxue*) has come to mean Chinese studies or sinology.

On the other hand, many modern Chinese students of philosophy tend to treat the Han era with some contempt. Han thought has been denounced as shallow, confused, superstitious, or downright irrational, representing at best a vulgarization and at worst the death of classical Chinese philosophy of the preceding golden age. The reason for this attitude lies in the fact that most of these students have been strongly influenced by the "Song learning" (*Songxue*) or neo-Confucian legacy, which was historically and intellectually antithetic to the legacy of *Hanxue*.

Historically, the basic tenor of Chinese thought has gone through five epochal changes:

- *Period I.* Classical era (fifth to third centuries B.C.E.), which established the mode and the basic vocabulary of philosophical-ideological discourse in traditional China (classical Confucianism).
- *Period II.* The Han (through Tang) era (third century B.C.E. to ninth century C.E.), during which time the pragmatic, historical, culturally focused mode of Han thought evolved as a reaction to the philosophical, theoretically focused legacy of period I.
- *Period III.* Song (through Ming) era (tenth to seventeenth centuries), during which the tradition of Song learning (neo-Confucianism) developed—returning to the legacy of period I (classical Confucianism) in a reaction against the Han tradition of period II.
- *Period IV.* Qing era (seventeenth to nineteenth centuries), which reverted back to the mode of Han thought of period II, in a reaction against the legacy of period III.
- *Period V.* Protomodern to modern era (late nineteenth century and twentieth century), which witnessed China's rapid opening to the outside world, including the introduction of western philosophy, and, in response to this western challenge, the rise of a nativistic movement to revitalize a countervailing Chinese philosophic tradition. That effort was dominated by but not limited to the so-called modern neo-Confucianists, who, reacting to both the western philosophic challenge and the discredited Han-learning tradition of period IV, espoused a modernized and westernized form of the Song-learning tradition of period III and through it the classical legacy of period I.

This brief survey indicates that Chinese thinkers of period I (classical Confucians), period III (Song neo-Confucians), and period V (modern neo-Confucians) predominate in China's philosophic tradition, not only because they are more philosophically inclined but also because they set the mode and the basic vocabulary of nativistic Chinese philosophic discourses in modern times. Against this, the Han and Han-learning thinkers and scholars (loosely called *ru* Confucians) of periods II and IV tend to lose out in the modernized-westernized enterprise, with only their aphilosophic or antiphilosophic credentials to offer.

To interpret the meaning of Han thought, modern scholars have made use of at least five approaches:

1. The "ideology" approach, taken by Feng Youlan (Fung Yu-lan) and other Marxist scholars, who discuss Han Confucianism in terms of the Marxian superstructure as the ideology of an emerging Han empire or unitary feudal regime.
2. The "mentality" approach, exemplified by Xu Fuguan, who discusses works of major Han thinkers, such as Dong Zhongshu, Yang Xiong, and Wang Chong, mainly in terms of the tension between ideal and reality—i.e., between the legacy of free and independent thinking of the classical era (period I) and the restrictive reality of the expanding Han imperium.
3. The "zeitgeist" approach, attempted by Qian Mu, emphasizing reason, ideals, a value system, or a sense of mission underlying the intellectual, cultural, and political agenda of the Han Confucians.
4. A new effort to get rid of the Marxist straitjacket of approach 1 and treat Han thought on its own terms; this effort, represented by the work of Jin Qunfeng, is still at the level of simple description and narrative, with little in-depth analysis.
5. The syncretic studies, among others, made by Chen Qiyun (Chi-yun Chen, the present author), combining approaches 1–4. This syncretic approach will be taken in the discussion here.

II

The most important feature of Han Confucianism is that, whereas in pre-Han times Confucianism was but one of the competing schools of thought, in Han times it became not only the dominant school of thought and learning but also the only one officially and publicly recognized. Hence its name becomes synonymous with Han thought and scholarship in general. Also for this reason, Han Confucianism is often treated as an official ideology of the Han imperium and blamed for the lamentable demise of the other schools of thought (Daoism, legalism, Mohism, etc.).

Classical Chinese thought, evolving in the preceding Warring States era (fifth to third centuries B.C.E.), revealed a strong tendency toward pragmatism and syncretism, with an urgent agenda of saving the Chinese world from destructive civil war. This imposed a certain limitation on the freedom of the speculative and imaginative mind in its philosophic journey. The tendency culminated in the legalist writing of Han Fei (d. 233 B.C.E.), whose teachings became the guiding principles of the emerging imperial regime of Qin, which unified China in 221 B.C.E., thus ending the divided Warring States and their rampaging warfare. The ensuing legalist undertakings soon plunged the newly unified China into a widespread revolution that destroyed the Qin regime in 206 B.C.E. (barely fifteen years after its founding). As a result of this traumatic experience, philosophical-ideological thinking became discredited in the Chinese mind, which—being pragmatic—was inclined to judge a doctrine or a mode of thought by its practical consequences. In the Han dynastic regime that followed, a much more somber mood and a more practical bent of mind set in.

In reaction to Qin legalism, the early Han regime, from about 202 to about 140 B.C.E., adopted the Daoist teaching of nonaction (*wuwei*) as its guiding ideology. This doctrine of quietism and passivity, as an antidote to the inclination toward excessive governmental action of Qin legalism, carried with it a strongly anti-ideological, anti-intellectualist, or even antirational bent. As an anti-ideological ideology and an anti-intellectual intellectual current, early Han Daoism further strengthened the tendency of Chinese thought toward pragmatism, syncretism, and the concern of salvaging the world. In the long run, its attitude of live and let live, "all-moderating and balancing-all," had the inadvertent effect of discouraging free, untrammeled thinking.

Confucianism, as represented by Xunzi (fl. 298–238 B.C.E.), had become broadly syncretistic as a leading school of thought in the late Warring States period, but it suffered a considerable setback under the Qin regime, especially when the Qin court proscribed learning in 213 B.C.E. It suffered a further setback as a result of the early Han reaction against legalism, because the major champions of legalism, Han Fei and Li Si (the prime minister of Qin, d. 208 B.C.E.), had both been Xunzi's disciples. Han Fei's legalist concepts—such as the evil nature of humans and the importance of external authority and control—were derived directly from Xunzi's teaching. Disfavored and sometimes even strongly disliked by the early Han rulers, Confucianism had to find its own means and depend on its own merits to survive. And it not only survived but developed vigorously in early Han times, thanks to strong currents of reaction against Qin legalism.

The Qin court was notorious for its proscription of learning and its burning of books—it was especially harsh to "ancient traditions" and "records of history" (such as *Shi*, or *Book of Odes*; and *Shu*, or *Book of History*)—as well as for its disdain of moral teaching. In reaction, there was during the early Han a popular yearning for works of these kinds. The Confucians, from Confucius to Mencius to Xunzi, had all emphasized the importance of learning, particularly the moral traditions of ancient times, and the preservation and teaching of these traditions were considered the primary calling of all Confucians. As preservers and teachers of the ancient traditions, the early Han Confucians found themselves winning increasing support among the general public, despite the express wishes of the Han rulers, who favored Daoism. As for other schools of classical thought, they were not severely persecuted in the Qin period, nor were they vigorously supported in the early Han era; they merely survived.

III

The first corpus of the ancient traditions, the canon later known as the Five Confucian Classics (*Wujing*) by the Han court, was recovered by Confucian masters (most of them disciples or disciples of the disciples of Xunzi) who had lived in Qin times and learned these traditions by heart before they were proscribed. These old masters were invited by the early Han court to recite the traditions orally from memory; the traditions were then written down by their students in the prevailing Han script, the *li* (clerical) style. Hence this corpus came to be called the "modern (i.e., Han) texts" of the canonical classics. Some of these masters, or their principal disciples (most likely the ones who wrote down the texts), were appointed official "erudites" (*boshi*) at the Han court.

Later, when some old manuscripts of these classics, written in pre-Han scripts and supposedly having survived the Qin book burning, were discovered, they were called the "ancient" (i.e., pre-Han) texts" of the classics. These "ancient texts" did not have the same pedigree as the "modern texts"—the ancient texts, not having been transmitted from "erudite" master to disciple, were suspected of being spurious and were rejected by the erudites of the "modern texts" school, which in 136 B.C.E. had become the official teaching of the Han court. This remained so, in spite of several attempts by the court to include the "ancient texts" traditions as part of the official teaching. Thus throughout the rest of the Han era, the "modern texts" school represented the official Confucian teaching of the court and the "ancient texts" school represented unofficial teaching.

Actually, the differences between the "modern texts" school and the "ancient texts" school tended to be minor and technical. A more significant distinction between these two Confucian schools is that the former, being officially championed, became more strongly influenced by the political and ideological interests of the Han regime, and since its teaching was originally orally transmitted—without fixed texts—it could be more easily swayed or adjusted to suit the political or mental perspectives of the emerging Han imperium. The most outrageous example was the reinterpretation of the *Classic of Spring-and-Autumn* (or *Annals of the Chaotic Spring-and-Autumn Era*, 721–482 B.C.E.) by Gongyang scholars of the "modern texts" school as a canon morally and spiritually sanctifying the ideal of political "grand unity" and "public-mindedness," or even presaging the rise of the unified Han empire. In general, scholars of "modern texts" Confucianism tended to interpret the classics as recording or preserving the morally superlative traditions of the Western Zhou dynasty (c. 1111–771 B.C.E.) to serve as an exemplar for the fledgling Han world. The "ancient texts" school, with its fixed texts supposedly from pre-Han times, tended to be more faithful to historical reality, especially the feudalistic, kinship-focused Zhou traditions emphasizing filial piety. In a sense, one may compare the "modern texts" Confucians with moral idealists and the "ancient texts" Confucians with historicists.

Beyond their primary calling of preserving (salvaging, re-collecting, compiling, and reediting) and teaching the "morally superlative" ancient traditions, the early Han Confucians were ardent advocates of political, social, and cultural reform. Taking advantage of the general resentment of Qin legalism, these Confucians argued that the Zhou dynasty (including the Eastern Zhou era, 770–249 B.C.E.) had enjoyed a reign of some eight hundred years because of its superior moral culture, whereas the Qin had perished in a mere fifteen years because of its disdain of moral and cultural values—this became the core of moral interpretation of history in traditional China. The fledgling Han regime, these Confucians counseled, must learn this solemn lesson of history in order to avoid the fate of the Qin.

IV

The reform agenda of the early Han Confucians included, most importantly, the promotion of education, especially learning the ancient traditions by studying the transmitted canonical classics. This means that emphasis was now placed on understanding history as "accomplished facts" and "actualized reality" rather than on manipulating "empty words" in abstract theorizing and conceptual analysis, as during the preceding Warring States era. This attitude is exemplified by the saying "Let the facts tell the truth." One reason for this change of mind may be that excessive philosophic reasoning in the Warring States had produced the legalism of Han Fei, which had led China to the disastrous Qin rule. Human reasoning had failed to anticipate its own outcomes or to chart the course of history; it presumed to guide history but was more comfortable being a postmortem judge (i.e., rendering historical verdicts). Another reason may be that most of the thinkers of the Warring States era, beginning with Confucius (551–479 B.C.E.), had been hoping for, contemplating, and reasoning about something that did not yet exist—a mere idea or ideal of a "grand peace" (*taiping*) in a world ("all-under-heaven") of "grand union" (*datong*). The Han thinkers now had to deal with an actual "grand union" in the form of an awesome imperium and had to turn their attention to considering how to handle it, how to bring peace to it, and how to understand its meaning.

With this came another item on the Han Confucian agenda: pragmatic moralization of the conceptualized "will of heaven" or "mandate of heaven." Belief in the mandate of heaven had constituted the core of religious-political tradition in the Western Zhou and had become a sustaining force in Confucian and Mohist idealistic teaching during the Warring States era. Now, with the idealization of the ancient Zhou tradition by the Han Confucians, the will of heaven and mandate of heaven were greatly elaborated and urbanized. The will of heaven was now manifested not only singularly in an ultimate "mandate" founding or dooming a dynasty but also continuously revealed in numerous signs favorable or unfavorable to man. Unfavorable signs included natural disasters such as eclipses of the sun, earthquakes, floods, and droughts, as well as human oddities or mishaps such as bodily abnormalities or horrendous behavior—these indicated heaven's anger at human misconduct. Favorable signs, which tended to be rare, included felicitous natural or human occurrences, such as sweet dews, timely rains, the appearance of fabulous animals like the unicorn, or remarkable human acts of filial piety—these showed heaven's satisfaction with human conduct. Since the emperor was an epitome of the human world and his actions had fateful consequences, heaven's pleasure or displeasure was mostly incurred by, and concerned with, his proper or improper conduct.

The Han Confucians made great efforts to study and interpret such omens, hoping thereby to understand empirically and pragmatically the working of the cosmos, and to guide as well as restrain the reigning emperor in conducting affairs of state. With this effort, the Han Confucians hoped to bring about a genuine harmonious grand union (*datong*) and great peace (*taiping*), realizing the ideal of their predecessors.

V

In their criticism of Qin legalism and their idealization of Zhou moralism, the Han Confucians could not fail to notice, in their own time, the suffering of the poor and lowly, the exploited, the oppressed, and the persecuted. They blamed corrupt government, cruelty, economic inequality, and social injustice on the evil practices left over from Qin legalism, which the nonaction taught by the Daoists—who were favored by the court—had done nothing to change. In advocating reform, the Han Confucians thus assumed the role of champions of the downtrodden, so much so that their ideal of *taiping*—the great peace—was construed to mean "great equality."

The contrast between the reform- or revolution-minded Confucians and the court-supported conservative Daoists becomes clear in the following episode:

> In the reign of Emperor Ching [Jing] (r. 158–141 B.C.E.), the Confucian Master Yuan-ku [Yuangu] and the Taoist Master Huang debated [about political revolution] in front of the Emperor. . . .
>
> Master Yuan-ku said: ". . . The wicked rulers Chieh [Jie] (last ruler of the Hsia [Xia] dynasty) and Tsou [Zou] (last ruler of the Shang dynasty) were cruel and unruly. The mind of all the people turned to T'ang [Tang] and Wu [for help]. T'ang and Wu accorded with the wishes of the people by killing King Chieh and King Tsou . . . thus becoming kings themselves. If this is not the case of [justified revolution] with receipt of the Mandate [of Heaven], what would it be?"
>
> Master Huang said: "A cap, although old and worn, should be put on the head; shoes, though new, should be put under the feet. Why is this so? This is due to the discrimination between the high and the low. King Chieh and King Tsou, though they had lost the Way, were rulers in high positions; T'ang and Wu, though they were sagely, were servitors in lower positions. Although the rulers misbehaved, [it is not right] for the servitors to murder their masters and take over their throne. If this was not regicide, what would it be?"

Jia Yi, an eminent Confucian in the reign of Emperor Wen (r. 180–157 B.C.E.), using the "faults of the Qin" as a lesson of history, persuaded the emperor to employ good Confucians as royal tutors, so that his heirs would become good rulers. Among these heirs, Wu (r. 141–87 B.C.E.) became the first Han emperor with a good Confucian education. Under Emperor Wu, Gongsun Hong, a self-made scholar, was the first Confucian to rise from the status of commoner to be prime minister at the Han court. On his advice, the five Confucian classics were made the official teaching of the court, and the official erudites (*boshi*) were put in charge of this instruction, forming the Grand Imperial Academy (*Taixue*). In 124 B.C.E. fifty official disciples of the erudites were enrolled; these increased to 3,000 in 33–7 B.C.E. By the late first century C.E., there were about 30,000 students at the academy, although some of them may have been only visitors.

Disciples were enrolled in the Grand Imperial Academy on the recommendation of high officials in central and local government. After one year of study, they might take an examination in one of the Five Classics. If they passed, they would be appointed to middle to lower central or local government posts. Thereafter, they would be evaluated and promoted according to a set of standards and criteria inspired by Confucian values. Government schools were later established at the local level. The system of filling government positions by special selection or recommendations was Confucianized, stressing cherished Confucian qualities such as "morally worthy and upright," "filially pious and incorruptible," and "talented in literary learning"; those who had these qualities are called Confucian "worthies." From this time on, the composite label "Confucian scholar-officials" denotes the majority of government administrators in traditional China. Through such mechanisms, numerous former followers of other classical schools of thought (Daoists, legalists, eclectics, etc.) were attracted and converted to Confucianism. As we have seen, Han Confucianism tended to become a generic name for Han scholars and thinkers, and its tenets evolved as a grand synthesis of various ideas from many classical schools of thought of pre-Han times.

VI

Emperor Wu launched many other reform programs aimed at strengthening the imperial government administratively, militarily, and financially by crushing any opponents, especially those from the rank of semi-independent princes of blood (other members of the imperial clan) or excessively wealthy merchants and industrialists. These measures were later considered oppressive, exploitive, and hence legalistic and un-Confucian. But initially the programs tended to accord well with the Han Confucian ideal of a "grand union" (e.g., a strong and expansive central authority) and a "great equality" (e.g., social and economic leveling aimed at the rich and powerful).

Wu's programs proceeded successfully but brought about many unexpected and unwelcome consequences. The emperor's military campaigns against the barbarian hordes that threatened the imperial frontiers in the north were expensive and ineffective. His efforts to crush the local power of the landed interests were stalled because the landowners' strength continued to grow (they would became the all-influential great "gentry" and the cultural elite of post-Han China). One reason why local landed interests not only could survive but challenge Wu's attempts to crush them was the sympathy and support they received from the Confucian scholar-officials. This was so because the Confucian systems of education and selection of civil servants had recruited many members of the local elite into the government service, to the point where even the more unruly local magnates began to style themselves after the Confucian model gentlemen. Besides, it was a basic Confucian belief that a ruler should serve as a moral example and be a kindhearted father figure to the people, and that government should not compete with the general population for profit, much less exploit them through oppressive measures. Since the emperor must rely on officials to execute his orders, the latter were in a position to stall or forestall imperial orders that went against their basic interests or convictions.

The inclination and the courage of the Han Confucians, for better or for worse, to challenge imperial authority also owed much to the fact that Confucianism had survived and prospered on its own in early Han times in spite of the ruler's ill will. The Confucians' open challenge to Emperor Wu's "cruel" measures came in a court conference in 81 B.C.E., in which all the high officials including the prime minister and a number of locally selected Confucian "worthies" took part, reviewing the late emperor's policies. At this conference—as we learn in the preserved records, titled *Discourses on Salt and Iron*—the Confucian worthies severely criticized many of those policies as having been oppressive, exploitative, profiteering, or frankly immoral, and they denounced as wicked and doomed to a bad end the deputy prime minister who had helped formulate and perpetuate these policies. Not long thereafter, this deputy prime minister was accused of high treason and sentenced to death, and many of the measures criticized by the Confucian worthies were nullified or modified by the court.

VII

The Confucians in the third quarter of the first century B.C.E. had every reason to believe that they had done all they could with regard to their reform agenda. The reigning emperor, Yuan (r. 49–33 B.C.E.), was a devoted and accomplished Confucian; most members of government officialdom, from the prime minister down to the clerks, had—like the emperors—received a Confucian education and were selected and promoted in accordance with the Confucian criteria of merits; even the previously unruly local magnates, as we have noted, now modeled themselves on the Confucian gentlemen. But somehow the Confucians were aware that their world was far from a perfect state of "grand union," "great peace," or "great equality."

Modern scholars would explain this by saying that education has limits; it is unrealistic to expect education to perfect the world by perfecting human nature. In fact, we might now conclude that the most important consequences of the Confucian reform were its moderating or undermining of the imperial power of the ruling house, and the formation of the triangular establishment of scholar-official-landlord (the alliance of the cultural, political, and economic elites) as the forebear of the "great gentry" in medieval China. The victorious Confucians, however, were more optimistic; they would not admit such limitations on their cherished reformist doctrines, and indeed they were by then in a position to demand greater perfection through more fundamentalist reforms.

A basic tenet of Confucianism was that the world would reach a state of perfection when each person in it acquired his standing (economic, social, and political stations) not by birthright but by his own accomplishments: his own moral character, knowledge, and ability, developed through education. So far this tenet had worked out rather well in the Han society and state—except where the position of the emperor was concerned. Despite the emperors' Confucian education, their occupation of the throne was due not to that education or to any accomplishments resulting from it but simply to their birth. Thus the Confucians argued that the world had not yet attained perfection because the Han emperor, who, being at the summit of the society and the state, should be the embodiment of consummate Confucian cultivation, fell far short of this ideal. These Confucians became increasingly dissatisfied with the existing reforms, and with the ruling dynasty. They urged the Han emperor to reform himself and the ruling family more thoroughly, or abdicate in favor of someone more truly deserving—e.g., a sage—so as to truly accord with the requirements of the mandate of heaven.

As early as the reign of Emperor Xuan (r. 74–49 B.C.E.), the Confucian scholar-official Gai Kuanrao submitted a memorial to the throne, reading:

> The Five Emperors [in remote antiquity] treated the realm as belonging to the public; the kings of [the more recent] Three Dynasties treated the realm as their family possession. Family possession was passed on to the sons. What belonged to the public should be handed over to the worthiest. This is like the rotation of the four seasons. The one having completed his work should retire from his post. A person unworthy of the position ought not occupy that position.

Gai was accused of high treason for advising the Han emperor to abdicate, and he committed suicide. But severe criticism and reformist demands continued, until a sage acclaimed by the Confucians, Wang Mang, took the throne, ending the Former Han dynasty and founding his New Dynasty (9–23 C.E.).

The triumph of Wang Mang seemed to fulfill the Han Confucian dream that a commoner sage (the worthiest person in the realm) would ascend to the throne (the highest position in the realm). But the triumph turned out to be a disaster. For one reason or another, Wang Mang soon faced widespread disorder and rebellions, which cost him his life. The New Dynasty was overthrown, and the Han dynasty was restored in 25 C.E. (thus the name Later Han). Henceforth the Confucians were in disarray. Wang Mang had given the Han Confucians high hopes and then dealt the severest blow to their ideals—which, as we have seen, were ingrained in the "modern texts" school.

VIII

Profound disillusionment generated a more discriminating and reflective mood among the Later Han thinkers. The "modern texts" school of Confucian learning remained the official teaching of the court. But, with its reformist zeal lost and its lofty stand discredited, it became merely a government mechanism for recruiting Confucian scholar-officials to serve the Later Han court. Many reformist Confucians had stood steadfast in Wang Mang's cause and perished with him; others refused to enter government service in the Later Han dynasty, preferring to preserve their personal moral purity by living in retirement. Still others, more seriously interested in Confucian scholarship, now turned to the unofficial "ancient texts" school of classical learning, which was probably more faithful, textually and contextually, to the old Zhou traditions.

The Confucian vision of a "great peace" and "grand union" that had developed in the Former Han was shattered. Losing interest in the imperial government as an embodiment of these ideals, many Confucians of the Later Han shifted their attention to a private concentric world—self, family, clan, and local and regional community—hoping to find a "lesser peace" there. The Confucians' grand ideational synthesis of Former Han times was breaking down. Many non-Confucian ideas that had been co-opted into the grand synthesis were finding their way out again and regaining their former identity.

The Confucian assumption of the correspondence of the physical, the intellectual, and the moral in a "grand unity" was also called into question. Yang Xiong (53 B.C.E.–18 C.E.), in his *Fayan* (*Model Discourses*), suggested that for a sage, moral virtue and intellectual ability were two distinctly different qualifications, and that human intelligence and luck operated as categorically different determinants of fate. Wang

Chong (c. 27–100 C.E.), in his *Lunheng* (*Balanced Discussions*), further divided the qualities and determinants of human life into the personal (subdivided into the physiological, the intellectual, and the moral), the interpersonal (each person bringing his own set of determinants into a chance encounter with the other person), and the transpersonal (common time, common environment, and common fate). The destiny of a person would be determined by the chance combination of such separate causes or factors. Thus a person might be physically weak and morally bad, though intelligent; and such a person might have a long and successful life, if by chance he served under a person who was also weak, morally bad, and intelligent, and if they were living in a time of peace and prosperity. Wang Chong explicitly decried many Confucian tenets as unsound and many Confucian works as untrustworthy.

Wang Fu (c. 90–165) was less discriminative but more stringent in his criticism of political, socioeconomic, and spiritual conditions in the Later Han. In his *Qianfu lun* (*Discourses by a Recluse*), he emphatically separated the outer, political realm of public affairs from the inner, spiritual world of personal morality. The former culminated in the office of the emperor, with its awesome power and responsibilities, which should be handled with the utmost public-mindedness, worldly intelligence, and statecraft, irrespective of the emperor's personal morality. The inner realm, culminating in the sage, would be concerned with personal moral cultivation merging into spiritual transcendence. The sage, in his consummate moral cultivation, would find himself estranged from the mundane world and misunderstood by the vulgar masses, but he should persevere in his nonconformist spiritual journey, for he alone was safekeeping the world's spiritual values and he alone served as Heaven's spokesman; and when the right time came, he alone would be able to return the world to its original goodness.

IX

The imperial structure tended to break down in parallel with the breakdown of the synthetic Confucian ideational construct. The trend toward defiance of the Han rulers and authorities in favor of the personal, familial, local, or regional interests of the cultural and social elite was greatly accelerated by the corruption and power struggles at the imperial court. This aroused the indignant outcries of the self-styled "morally pure" (*qingyi*, literally "pure criticism") against the court, particularly the eunuchs who as personal servants of the Han emperor came to dominate it after 92 C.E., and especially after 125. In retaliation, the court accused its critics of treacherous partisanship and persecuted them with a series of "antipartisan" measures (*danggu*). From 166 on, these measures were inflicted on an increasingly enlarged circle of the Confucian elite and drove them into alliance with the less compliant local magnates.

In 184, the empire was wrecked by the uprising of the Yellow Turbans (*Huangjin*), which comprised the followers of Taiping Dao (Way of Great Peace). Taiping Dao was commonly considered the first popular organized Daoist religion, but its teaching tended to be highly eclectic, as was characteristic of Han Confucianism (*taiping*, "great peace," was the ideal of Han Confucianism). The uprising received much sympathy and probably strong support from the persecuted "partisans." Most noteworthy in this connection is the commentary by Xun Shuang (128–190) on the Confucian classic *Yi jing* (*Book of Changes*); this commentary was written at about the same time as the Taiping Dao movement was getting under way. Xun Shuang, who came from the family of a Confucianized local magnate, suffered under the court's antipartisan measures and lived in hiding for more than ten years (c. 174–184). During this time, he devoted himself to learning and became a prominent Confucian. In his interpretation of the *Yi jing*, he expressed his sympathy with "the gentleman who was strong and virtuous but was wronged and put in a lowly position" and he vented his unrestrained hatred of those who were wicked and yet in a high position (such as the emperor). A situation like this, Xun Shuang counseled, called for a righteous revolution, in which the virtuous would defeat the wicked and the lowly would take over the positions of those highly placed.

After the Yellow Turbans' uprising, the Later Han court survived for some thirty-six years, in the midst of rampant civil war, until it was officially replaced by the Wei dynasty (house of Cao) in 220. The last Confucian worth mentioning in this period is Xun Yue (148–209), who served as the personal attendant and secretary of Xian, the last, figurehead emperor of the Later Han (r. 190–220). By order of the emperor, Xun Yue finished *Han ji* (*Chronicles of the Former Han*) in 200, ostensibly to glorify the Han ruling house, but the work actually contained many discourses highly critical of the dynasty, reminiscent of the *qingyi* criticism of the court by the self-styled "morally pure" Confucians half a century earlier. In his preface to *Han ji*, Xun Yue wrote:

> What I have recounted here may be examined against the real facts and verified; they rightly constitute counsels of lasting values, which may be applied in a myriad situations without becoming unreasonably muddled.

This aptly summed up the Han Confucians' empirical attitude of "letting the facts tell the truth."

A few years after completing *Han ji*, Xun Yue wrote a philosophical work, *Shenjian* (*Extended Reflections*), in which he hinted at the "mystery" (*ao*) or the "darkly unknown" (*xuan*) lurking underneath the reasonable mind, the manifested world, and the superficial speeches of men. He wrote:

> Words should be simple and straight. Why were the words of our Sage so subtle (*ao*)? That is because truth itself is subtle and intriguing; to communicate this kind of truth, the Sage could not but use subtle words.

This emphasis on *ao* foreshadowed in style and content the new intellectual current of *qingtan* ("pure conversations") in the medieval Wei and Chin eras (220–420).

In conclusion, it may be said that although the true philosophic value and meaning of Han Confucianism has yet to be rediscovered and reevaluated, it cannot be simply dismissed as a mere ideological mouthpiece of the Han rulers, lacking rich or intricate cultural meaning, or lacking the dynamism of changes and developments necessitating intense human mental, ideational and spiritual exertion.

See also Jia Yi; Wang Chong; Yang Xiong.

Bibliography

Chen, Chi-yun. "Confucian, Legalist, and Taoist Thought in Later Han." In *The Cambridge History of China*, Vol. 1, ed. Denis Twitchett and Michael Loewe. Cambridge: Cambridge University Press, 1986.

———. "A Confucian Magnate's Idea of Political Violence: Hsün Shuang's (A.D. 128–190) Interpretation of the Book of Changes." *T'oung-pao*, 54, 1968, pp. 73–115.

———. "Development of Confucianism As Seen in the Taoist Writing, Chuang-tzu." In *Zhongguo wenhua yu Zhongguo zhexue* (Chinese Culture and Chinese Philosophy). Beijing: Sanlian shudian, 1987–1988. (In Chinese.)

———. *Hsün Yüeh (A.D. 148–209): The Life and Reflections of an Early Medieval Confucian*. Cambridge: Cambridge University Press, 1975.

———. *Hsün Yüeh and the Mind of Late Han China*. Princeton, N.J.: Princeton University Press, 1980.

Creel, H. G. *Chinese Thought from Confucius to Mao Tse-tung*. Chicago, Ill.: University of Chicago Press, 1953.

Dubs, Homer H. "The Victory of Han Confucianism." In *The History of the Former Han Dynasty*, Vol. 2. American Council of Learned Societies, 1944.

Forke, Alfred, trans. *Lun-heng*, 2 vols. New York: Paragon Book Gallery, 1962. (Reprint.)

Fung, Yu-lan. *A History of Chinese Philosophy*, trans. Derk Bodde, 2 vols. Princeton, N.J.: Princeton University Press, 1952–1953.

Gale, Esson, trans. *Discourses on Salt and Iron*. Taipei, 1967. (Reprint.)

Hall, David L., and Roger T. Ames. *Anticipating China: Thinking through the Narratives of Chinese and Western Culture*. Albany: State University of New York Press, 1995.

Hall, David L., and Roger T. Ames. *Thinking from the Han: Self, Truth, and Transcendence in Chinese and Western Culture*. Albany: State University of New York Press, 1998.

Kramers, Robert P. "The Development of the Confucian Schools." In *The Cambridge History of China*, Vol. 1, ed. Denis Twitchett and Michael Loewe. Cambridge: Cambridge University Press, 1986.

Confucianism: Humanism and the Enlightenment

Weiming Tu

Since China's first contact with the west, the Confucian tradition has been, in theory if not in practice, thoroughly deconstructed by many aspects of Enlightenment tradition, most notably science and democracy. As east and west together enter a new millennium, and against a background of competing and conflicting theories of international relations, the possibility of an intercivilizational dialogue between Confucian humanism and Enlightenment mentality exists. The question posed to the modern Chinese intellectual is whether Confucian humanism, in its creative modern transformation, can offer an intellectual challenge as a response.

Background

When first encountered by European thinkers, Confucianism posed a challenge that was met by Enlightenment philosophy. Reports of China's humanistic splendor brought back by Matteo Ricci and the seventeenth-century Jesuits contributed cosmological thinking, benevolent autocracy, and secular ethics to intellectuals in France, Italy, England, and Germany, at the same time that they inspired a craze for chinoiserie amongst many other Europeans. To men such as Montesquieu, Voltaire, Quesnay, Diderot, the philosophes, the physiocrats, and the deists, Confucian China represented an intellectual challenge that was met with the first fruits of Enlightenment thinking. Unfortunately, as that mentality evolved into the Eurocentric nineteenth-century model, the effects on China and its understanding of itself as a developing modern state would be devastating. The dichotomy inherent in modern western thinking that pits spirit against matter, mind against body, the sacred against the profane, the creator against the creature, is diametrically opposed to the Chinese understanding of the heart and mind, which sees the two as so integrated that together they are represented by single Chinese character. In its final formulation, informed by Bacon's dictum that knowledge is power and the Darwinian concept of competition for survival, the Enlightenment mentality is so radically different from any style of thought familiar to the Chinese mind that it challenges all facets of the Sinitic world.

The Enlightenment faith in instrumental rationality included a Faustian drive to explore, know, subdue, and control. The scientific method to which it gave birth produced spectacular progress in science, technology, industrial capitalism, nation-building, democratic polity, legal systems, educational institutions, multinational cooperation, and military hardware. A new set of rules of the international game, defined in terms of the wealth and power produced by these tremendous advances, was superimposed on China by gunboat diplomacy in the 1800s, forcing the Chinese intellectuals to countenance the inevitability of westernization and act accordingly.

Yet the urgency that prompted thinkers of the May Fourth (1919) generation in China to advocate China's wholesale westernization was disconcerting and self-defeating. The deliberate choice to undermine rich spiritual resources and to embark on a materialist path to cultural salvation led instead to revolutionary romanticism and populist scientism. The demand for effective action and tangible results was so compelling that the life of the mind was marginalized. There was little room for reflection, let alone meditative thinking.

For philosophy, the outcome was disastrous. The fate of modern Chinese intellectuals was much worse than that of their Indian counterparts. While centuries of colonization did not break the backbone of Indian spirituality, semicolonial status prompted the Chinese intelligentsia to voluntarily reject in toto the spiritual traditions that defined China's soul. Only now do we find indications that Chinese thinkers have begun to recover from this externally imposed but internally inflicted malaise.

Despite its boundless energy and creative impulse, the Enlightenment mentality is incapable of reflection on the human condition from a spiritual perspective, oblivious of the "holy rite" of human-relatedness, and ignorant of the art of self-cultivation. The collapse of the former Soviet Union may have destroyed China's faith in the inevitable historical process of communism, yet the assumption that human beings are rational animals endowed with inalienable rights and motivated by their own self-interest to maximize economic profit is a persuasive, if not inspiring, ideology in the People's Republic of China. A market economy, a democratic polity, and individualism, identified by Talcott Parsons as the three inseparable dimensions of modernity, are likely to loom large in China's intellectual discussion. The Enlightenment mentality is alive and well in cultural China. It is understandable that scholars such as Vera Schwarcz and Li Zhehou can argue that the basic conflict in the tragic history of China's modernization was how a widely shared desire to save the nation overshadowed the need for a deep understanding of the Enlightenment, and that omission made China's march toward modernity lamentably tortuous.

The accepted explanation is that China's effort to learn from the west was thwarted by a burning need for national survival. As a result, the time was too short and the space too limited for Enlightenment ideals such as liberty, equality, rationality, and due process to take root and flourish in China's intellectual soil. It took centuries for science and democracy to become fully established in western Europe and North America, but in China the westernizers, and by implication the modernizers, had only a few decades to try to transform the country into a scientific and democratic model.

That explanation, however, overlooks some difficulties that lay in the ambiguity of the Enlightenment mentality itself. The Chinese westernizers and modernizers, seasoned in the Enlightenment mentality, were committed political activists who passionately desired to save China from its own dark, backward feudal past. The ills of the Chinese family distinguished by the three authoritarian bonds (domination of the father over the son, the ruler over the minister, and the husband over the wife) have been thoroughly critiqued by some of the most articulate and influential writers in modern China. Ba Jin's novel *The Family* represents the iconoclastic ethos of the May Fourth generation and poignantly reminds us that the Confucian idea of "home," when viewed through a contemporary lens informed by western liberal democratic ideas, is a prison that denies the basic rights of the individual and enslaves the creative energy of the young. Indeed, Confucian family ethics as effectively depicted by the indignant pen of Lu Xun are no more than "ritual teaching," an outmoded education that, instead of humanizing, subtly cannibalizes itself (in his graphic phrase: "Eat people!"). The slogan "Down with Confucius and Sons!" was directed against feudalism in general and the Confucian family in particular. It is understandable, then, that even those who advocated the revival of Confucian humanism in the early 1900s acknowledged that the Confucian family ethic was the single most important cultural factor inhibiting Sinitic modernization. Both Kang Youwei and Tan Sitong propounded the destruction of family particularism as a precondition for the revitalization of inclusive Confucian humanism. The Confucian thinker Xiong Shili straightforwardly condemned the family as the source of all evils.

The rise of Maoism as the ruling ideology during China's modernization in the 1950s intensified the critique of Confucian family ethics. Several seemingly incompatible currents of thought were damned under the umbrella phrase "Enlightenment mentality": positivistic scientism, romantic revolutionism, agrarianism, iconoclasm, industrial modernism, and nativistic spiritualism. The philosophy of Mao Zedong was incompatible with Confucian humanism in general and Confucian family ethics in particular. It is possible that totalistic social transformation may be based on the universal laws of historical progress, that continuous revolution in the development of both consciousness and material goods will eventually eliminate China's backwardness, that the peasants are the force motivating China's march toward modernity, and that a naive and distorted vision of the Enlightenment required the destruction of China's feudal legacy to welcome in the brave new world as Chinese Marxists posit. For almost half a century until about 1980, these ideas were taken for granted as a faith by China's leaders. In this peculiar version of the Enlightenment, Confucian concepts of community, not only the family but every relation in human interaction, were relegated to the dustbin of history.

Today, while we are willing to grant that western European and North American modernization is now the common heritage of humanity, we cannot ignore the serious contradictions inherent in modernization and the explosive destructiveness embodied in the dynamics of the modern west. The Enlightenment's legacy is pregnant with disturbing ambiguities. Its values neither cohere nor integrate to recommend a coordinated course of ethical action. As one example, in the west the conflict between liberty and equality is often unresolvable.

Therefore, it behooves those deeply concerned about environmental degradation, social disintegration, and a lack of distributive justice to rethink the heritage of the Enlightenment. In light of its unintended negative consequences for the global community, we must not uncritically accept its inner logic; paradoxically, though, neither can we reject its relevance, with its inherent fruitful ambiguities, to our continued intellectual self-definition. There is no easy either-or choice.

The possibility of radically different ethics or a new value system independent of the Enlightenment mentality is not realistic and may even appear cynical or hypercritical. We need to explore the spiritual resources that may help us to broaden the scope of the Enlightenment project, deepen its moral sensitivity, and, if necessary, creatively transform its constraints in order to fully realize its potential as a positive force for the human community.

A New Ethics for the Global Community

A key to the success of this intellectual joint venture is recognizing that the Enlightenment perspective utterly lacks an idea of community, let alone a global community.

Fraternity, the functional equivalent of community in the three cardinal virtues of the French Revolution, has received scant attention in modern western economic, political, and social thought. Tolerance of inequality, faith in self-interest as a salvific power, and acceptance and even approval of unbridled, aggressive egoism have poisoned the well of progress, reason, and individualism. The need to form a global village and to articulate a possible link between the fragmented world we each experience in our daily existence and the imagined community of the whole human species is deeply felt by an increasing number of concerned intellectuals. Understandably, the family—the basic unit in any society, past or present—looms large in contemporary political discourse. The idea of global stewardship implicit in this line of thinking demands an ethic significantly different from what was espoused by the Enlightenment.

From the Confucian perspective, the first requisite is that the governing principle of self-interest be replaced by the golden rule, stated negatively in classical Chinese as: "Do not do unto others what you would not want others to do unto you." The recognition that what we cherish as the best way to live may not apply to our neighbor is the initial step toward an appreciation of the other's integrity. Such a negative golden rule would have to be augmented by a positive principle: "To establish ourselves, we must help others to establish themselves; to enlarge ourselves, we must help others enlarge themselves." A sense of inclusive community, based on mutual benefit and fruitful interchange, rather than on a zero-sum economic game, needs to be cultivated.

Under the influence of Confucian culture, industrial East Asia has already developed a modern civilization less adversarial, individualistic, and self-interested than its western counterparts. It is now widely acknowledged that market economics and government leadership together provided an important impetus for the rapid economic development of Japan, South Korea, Taiwan, Hong Kong, Singapore, and, more recently, the People's Republic of China. Scholars of comparative politics have also noted that the development of a democratic polity in East Asia is not at all incompatible with meritocracy. Indeed, educational elitism may have been instrumental in enabling the public sector to attract the best talents among college graduates. In short, the synergy of individual initiatives and a focus on groups has made this region the most economically and politically dynamic area of the world since World War II.

In the Confucian view, neither capitalism nor socialism, both of which exemplify the Enlightenment mentality, can deal adequately with the issue of primordial human ties, specifically, the vital roles played by ethnicity, gender, language, land, and religion in defining the concrete living human being within a unique nexus of relationships. The abstract universal principle in both the capitalist and the socialist conception of *Homo economicus* totally fails to account for the complexity and variability of the human settlements that physically constitute the global community. The primordial ties, culturally specific and historically contextualized, diametrically oppose the Enlightenment assumption that modernization naturally leads to homogenization. On the other hand, Confucian inclusive humanism may provide rich resources for us to develop an ethic that celebrates cultural diversity, respects difference, and encourages a plurality of spiritual orientations.

The caveat, of course, is that the rise of industrialism in East Asia—which was humiliated and frustrated by western imperialism and colonization for more than a century from the 1940s on—also symbolizes the instrumental rationality of the Enlightenment heritage: the mentality of Japan and the "four mini-dragons" is characterized by mercantilism, commercialism, and international competitiveness. The possibility of their developing a more humane and sustainable community should be acknowledged, but this need not undermine the persuasive power of the Confucian idea that despite ethnic, linguistic, religious, social, political, and economic diversity, the human community ought to be inclusive.

From a modern liberal-democratic perspective, Confucian humanism suffers from manifold shortcomings, especially its lack of a strong commitment to individualism. The issue of individualism as a reflection of a modern ethos is complex, but undeniably, the dignity, autonomy, and independence of the person is greatly valued in all modern societies. If a Confucian society can use its cherished value of "learning for the sake of oneself" and the moral imperative of continuous self-realization to generate a concept of basic rights and liberties and to develop a legal system to protect its citizens' privacy, its belief in the person as a center of relationships rather than as an isolated individual may be conducive to stable democracy.

The westernization of Confucian Asia (including Japan, the two Koreas, mainland China, Hong Kong, Taiwan, Singapore, and Vietnam) may have forever altered its spiritual landscape, but its indigenous resources (including Mahayana Buddhism, Daoism, Shinto, and shamanism and other folk religions) are resilient enough to resynthesize and resurface. The Confucian tradition lacks ideas of radical transcendence, positive evil, and transcendental rationality. As a result, Confucian societies may not have sufficient resources to check abuses of power by autocratic or paternalistic regimes. Modern Confucian societies must and can learn to appreciate the value of suspicion in defining the proper relationship between the government and the governed. Lord Acton's liberal dictum "Power tends to corrupt, and absolute power corrupts absolutely" is particularly instructive to East Asian intellectuals, who have been too seasoned in the mentality of the Confucian scholar-official to cultivate a critical attitude toward the dictatorial tendencies of strong rulers. The idea of God as the absolute has been, by and large, effective in rendering the worldly power structures of the west relative. The unintended healthy consequence of subsuming political authority under a more transcendent framework is eminently suited to the East Asian vulnerability to authoritarianism. Yet, the Confucian mandate of heaven, based on an ethic of elite responsibility, is more congenial to a democratic polity than, say, the divine right of kings. The Confucian ideas of benevolent government, the "duty-consciousness" of the elite, and the right of the people to revolt are all consistent with democratic demands for civility, impartiality, and public accountability. Actually, Confucians are noted for their commitment to cultivating the value of reasonableness in daily human interaction, for they believe that true social harmony can be attained only through communication and negotiation.

The political philosophy of the Confucian seems to lack the concepts of liberty, human rights, privacy, and due process of law. The Confucian predilection for rightness, duty, public-spiritedness, and ritual may have undermined East Asia's capacity to fully integrate freedom of individual expression, inalienable political and civil rights, respect for the private sphere, and an independent judiciary. However, in a complex modern society, we can no longer afford to stress the value of liberties without considering adequate political protections for the economically disadvantaged. Notwithstanding the ills of an inefficient welfare system, the government must ensure that vicious competitiveness enhanced by market forces does not lead to unbearable inequalities. This requires the cultivation of a strong sense of culpability and the responsibility of business and government elites to answer for the well-being of society at large. Confucian concern for duty is not at variance with the demand for rights. Actually, a salient discourse on self-interest and privacy requires the development of a public sphere that respects the spirit of impartiality. Ironically, the legal formulation of civilized modes of conduct (such as a fiduciary commitment to the public good) may still be the most effective way to curtail unbridled pursuit of self-interest.

Confucian institutions also lack an obvious mechanism against autocracy, such as checks and balances, as well as an adversarial division of labor within a constitutional framework and the political participation of a loyal opposition. Authoritarianism, whether harsh or soft, continues to haunt East Asian democracies. The East Asian political penchant for consensus undermines the dynamism of the creative tension inherent in an adversarial system. The patient tolerance and informed understanding of a loyal opposition, a characteristic of most western democracies, has yet to become a presence in East Asia. Nevertheless, multiparty elections have already become a reality for all politicians in industrial East Asia. Even the People's Republic of China is experienced in suffrage. However, while a political process within a constitutional framework is now being worked out in most industrial East Asian societies, it will take years to create the ethos of civility and openness in intraparty communication that is the ideal if not always the reality of western political systems. The idea of government for, of, and by the people is no longer merely wishful thinking in Japan and the "four mini-dragons," but the democratic polity, far from being an institutionalized mechanism fully integrated into ordinary life, remains contentious, disruptive, and even explosive.

Whether or not a truly functioning public sphere adjudicated by rational communication will arise in these newly industrial countries, the density of the human network and the complexity of their cultural texture make them a remarkably modern example of Durkheim's "organic solidarity," which requires the division of labor as a condition for modernity. In interpersonal praxis, the Confucian tradition apparently lacks the precedents of social contract, civil society, and public sphere. However, the fruitful human interaction of "network capitalism," which has been extended to virtually all corners of the global community, suggests that the ethical requirements of complex business transactions—trust, reliability, responsibility, and obligation—that are salient features of this approach are rooted in Confucian culture. Although this manner of generating wealth cannot be made universal without well-developed legal systems, it has already created a unique style of economic and social development with worldwide implications. The emergence of public institutions in business, the mass media, academia, religion, and the professions, independent of the political center and yet instrumental in shaping its long-term policies, enables industrial East Asia to gradually develop full-fledged civil societies. While it is difficult to predict the future course of these emerging institutions, which have already made the idea of civil society intelligible to East Asian intellectuals, their increasing pluralism inevitably leads to new systems of thought, religion, ethics, aesthetics, and worldviews.

This discussion of the limitations of the Confucian tradition from the liberal-democratic perspective and the possible Confucian responses to the Enlightenment mentality suggests a new ethical horizon. Ethically, Confucian East Asia exemplifies a significantly different form of modernity. A market economy, a democratic polity, and individualism are all of course present in East Asian modernity, but government leadership, meritocracy, and communitarianism have so fundamentally restructured adversarial democracy, Adam Smith's "invisible hand," and the individualistic ethos that they demand a reconsideration of the rules defining western European and North American modernity. The ideal of humankind as beings with rights, motivated by self-interest and attempting to maximize personal profit through rational calculation adjudicated by law, is incompatible with the Confucian understanding of the self as a center of relationships and the eastern emphasis on duty, well-being, rightness, sympathy, and the moral transformation of ritual. The representation of the *Problematik* of community in recent European and American political discourses is symptomatic of the confluence of two apparently incongruous forces of the late twentieth century: the global village as both a virtual reality and an imagined community in the information age, and the disintegration and restructuring of all levels of human relations, from family to nation.

The survival and flourishing of humanity require a thorough reexamination of the global ethic, which in turn demands that the Enlightenment mentality be transcended without deconstructing or abandoning its commitment to rationality, liberty, equality, human rights, and distributive justice. It may not be presumptuous to say that the Confucian tradition can be a rich spiritual resource for developing a new vision of community based in the core of the Enlightenment project.

If we assume, using East Asia as an example, that traditions shape the modernization process and define the meaning of modernity, what becomes of the claim that modernity must be conceived only in terms of market economy, democratic polity, and individualism? Surely the case at hand enhances the conviction that market economy, as an engine of modernization, is a constitutive part of modernity. It is worth noting, however, that East Asian market practices are not at all incompatible with strong and comprehensive participation by government. Political leadership can provide the guidance necessary for a functioning market. Domestically and internationally, economically sophisticated government officials are often instrumental in the smooth functioning of the system and create an environment conducive to healthy growth. Collaboration between officialdom and the business community is the norm in East Asia, and the pervasive interaction between polity and economy is a defining characteristic of its political economy. The authority of the government to adjudicate economic matters may take different forms—direct management (Singapore), active leadership (South Korea), informed guidance (Japan), passive interference (Taiwan), or positive noninterference (Hong Kong)—but a governmental presence in important economic decisions is these days not only expected but desired by the business community as well as the general public.

Despite the universal applicability of democratic polity, East Asia's transformation of western democratic ideas strongly suggests that democratization as a process is not necessarily incompatible with bureaucratic meritocracy, educational elitism, and particularistic social networking. The western democratic experience itself has been significantly shaped by distinct cultural traditions of pragmatism, empiricism, skepticism, and gradualism in England; anticlericalism, rationalism, culturalism, and the revolutionary spirit in France; romanticism, nationalism, and ethnic pride in Germany; and the continuous presence of a strong civil society in America. The Confucian faith in the commitment to the family as the fundamental societal unit and to family ethics as the foundation of social stability, trust in the intrinsic value of moral education, self-reliance, the work ethic, mutual aid, and a sense of an organic unity within an ever-expanding network of relationships provides rich cultural resources for East Asian democracies to develop their own distinctive features.

It is true that Confucian rhetoric may be used to criticize the indiscriminate imposition of western ideas on the rest of the world. The new agenda of broadening human rights from an exclusive emphasis on political and civil rights to economic, social, and cultural rights may well be perceived as a strategic maneuver engineered by Asian leaders to divert attention from blatant violations of human rights by their own authoritarian regimes. This is to be expected. East Asian societies under Confucian influence must free themselves from nepotism, authoritarianism, and male chauvinism. However, democracy with Confucian characteristics is not only imaginable but also practicable.

East Asian intellectuals are actively probing the Confucian tradition for economic development, nation building, social stability, and cultural identity. But the echoes of the iconoclastic attacks on "Confucius and Sons" made in the early 1900s still reverberate through the halls of academia and the corridors of government in Japan and the "four mini-dragons." The Confucian ideals of personality (the authentic person, the worthy, or the sage) can be realized more fully in a liberal democratic society than in either a traditional imperial dictatorship or a modern authoritarian regime. Before East Asian Confucian ethics can effectively criticize the excessive individualism, pernicious competitiveness, and vicious litigiousness of the modern west, it must creatively transform itself in light of Enlightenment values.

Confucian intellectuals have been devoted students of western learning for more than a century. As they became seasoned in the "universal" discourses exclusively informed by the mentality of the modern western Enlightenment, they drew on their indigenous spiritual traditions to raise challenging questions. The transvaluation of Confucian values as a creative response to the hegemonic discourses of Enlightenment nations seems a natural outcome of this cross-cultural exchange. Part of the impetus came from a critical awareness among Chinese intellectuals that China is no longer an agrarian society with most of its population wedded to the land, but one of the most dynamic migrant communities in the world. With more than 36 million ethnic Chinese overseas, it is impossible to relegate China's enduring and dominant ethical system to the background—to the "feudal past" or the "agrarian present." China encompasses not only the largest farming population but also one of the most enterprising merchant groups in the emerging global community. If we assume that culture is important, that people act according to the values they hold, that what motivates people influences their economic ethics, and that the way society views life itself will influence its economic and political behavior, then whether or not our current ethical thinking can provide a strong enough moral basis for the global stewardship essential to world peace becomes vitally important.

The question was immensely complicated by the decision of the People's Republic of China, through the "reform and open" policy of the 1980s and early 1990s, to join the restless march toward modernity as narrowly defined by wealth and power. Already, an internal migration of more than 100 million people has occurred within the People's Republic, with most moving from the countryside to the cities, especially along the southeastern coast, where economic development has been most vibrant. As the tidal waves of commercialization begin to overwhelm the Chinese interior, the pressure of migration will be greatly increased.

A second migration in "cultural China," as contrasted with the nineteenth-century migration of millions of Chinese from Guangdong and Fujian provinces to Southeast Asia, is now under way. Chinese with substantial financial resources in Southeast Asia have, in the past two decades, begun to emigrate to Australia, Canada, and the United States for political security, economic opportunity, cultural expression, or education for their children. The number will be greatly increased as residents of Hong Kong and Taiwan join the process. In the United States, ethnic Chinese from South Vietnam and students from the People's Republic of China have altered the landscapes of Chinatowns and university communities in recent years, with a steady flow of return emigration of highly qualified scientific and engineering professionals to industrial East Asia. If we include industrial and socialist East Asia, the presence of Japanese, Korean, and Vietnamese communities throughout the world intensifies the need to understand Confucian ethics.

I would like to interject here a paragraph from Edwin Reischauer's prophetic statement, made in 1973 and subsequently published as "The Sinic World in Perspective" in *Foreign Affairs*:

> The peoples in East Asia . . . share certain key traits, such as group solidarity, an emphasis on the political unit, great organizational skills, a strong work ethic, and a tremendous drive for education. It is because of such traits that the Japanese could rise with unprecedented speed from being a small underdeveloped nation in the mid-nineteenth century to being a major imperial power in the early twentieth—and an economic superpower today. . . . And now her record is being paralleled by all the other East Asian units that are unencumbered by war or the economically blighting pall of communism—namely, South Korea, Taiwan, Hong Kong and Singapore, which, like Hong Kong, is essentially a Chinese city-state. Throughout the non-East Asian countries of Southeast Asia, Chinese minorities remain so economically and educationally dominant as to cause serious political and social problems. One cannot but wonder what economic growth might be in store for Vietnam, if peace is ever achieved there, and for China and North Korea if their policies change enough to afford room for the economic drive of which their people are undoubtedly capable.

If we maintain that Confucian ethics is an underlying East Asian value, two propositions must be conceded. First, the implicit designation of East Asia as "Confucian" in the ethical-religious sense is comparable to the validity and limitation of using "Christian," "Islamic," "Hindu," and "Buddhist" to identify geopolitical regions such as Europe, the Middle East, India, or Southeast Asia. The matter is confounded by the religious pluralism of "Confucian" in East Asia. However, it is not at all difficult to imagine that Shinto or Buddhist Japan, shamanist, Buddhist, or Christian Korea, and Daoist or Buddhist China are all constituents of the East Asian spiritual landscape. Second, Confucian ethics so conceived is not a simple representation of traditional Confucian teaching. Rather, it is a way of conceptualizing the form of life, the habits of the heart, or the social praxis of societies that have been under the influence of Confucian education for centuries.

As we confront a new world order to take the place of the exclusive dichotomy imposed by the capitalist and socialist superpowers, it is tempting to come up with facile generalizations: "the end of history," "the clash of civilizations," "the Pacific century." A more difficult and more significant line of inquiry is to address truly fundamental global issues: Are we isolated individuals, or do we each live as a center of relationships? Is moral self-knowledge necessary for personal growth? Can any society endure or prosper without a basic sense of duty and responsibility to its members? Should a pluralistic society deliberately cultivate shared values and a common ground for human understanding? As we become acutely aware of our planet's vulnerability and grow increasingly wary of social disintegration, what are the critical spiritual questions to ask?

Since the Opium War, China has endured many holocausts. Before 1949, imperialism was the main culprit, but since the founding of the People's Republic, China's own erratic leadership and faulty policies must share the blame. Although millions of Chinese died, the neighboring countries were not seriously affected and the outside world was largely oblivious of the tragedy. Since 1979, China has rapidly become an integral part of the global economic system. More than 30 percent of the Chinese economy is tied to international trade. Natural economic territories have emerged between Hong Kong and Quangzhou, Fujian and Taiwan, Shandong and South Korea. Japanese, European, and American as well as Hong Kong and Taiwanese investments are a part of virtually all Chinese provincial economies. The return of Hong Kong to the People's Republic, the conflict across the Taiwan Straits, the economic and cultural interchange among overseas Chinese communities and between them and the motherland, the intraregional communication in East Asia, the political and economic integration of the Association for Southeast Asian Nations, and the rise of the Asia-Pacific will all have a substantial impact on our shrinking global community.

The revitalization of the Confucian discourse can contribute to a much-needed communal self-criticism and self-analysis among East Asian intellectuals. We may well be at the very beginning of global history rather than witnessing its end. And, from a comparative cultural perspective, this new beginning must take as its point of departure a dialogue—not a clash—of civilizations. Our awareness of the danger of conflicts rooted in ethnicity, language, land, and religion makes the necessity of dialogue particularly compelling. An alternative model of sustainable development that emphasizes the ethical and spiritual dimensions of humanity must be sought.

It is time, and past time, to move beyond assumptions shaped by instrumental rationality and private interests. As the politics of domination fade, we witness the dawning of an age of communication, networking, negotiation, interaction, interfacing, and collaboration. Whether East Asian intellectuals, inspired by Confucian self-cultivation, family cohesiveness, social solidarity, benevolent governance, and universal peace, will articulate an ethic of responsibility as Chinese, Japanese, Koreans, and Vietnamese emigrate to other parts of the world is a profoundly meaningful question for global stewardship.

We can envision the Confucian perception of human flourishing as a series of concentric circles—self, family, community, society, nation, world, and cosmos. We begin with a quest for true personal identity, an open and transforming selfhood that, paradoxically, must be predicated on our ability to overcome selfishness and egoism. To cherish family cohesiveness we must move beyond nepotism. To fully embrace communal solidarity, we must transcend parochialism. To be enriched by social integration, we must overcome ethnocentrism and chauvinism. To achieve national unity and genuine patriotism, we must rise above aggressive nationalism. We are inspired by human flourishing, but we must endeavor not to be confined by anthropocentrism: the true meaning of humanity is not anthropocentric but anthropocosmic. On the occasion of the international symposium on Islamic-Confucian dialogue organized by the University of Malaya (March 1995), the deputy prime minister of Malaysia, Anwar Iberhim, quoted Huston Smith's *The World's Religions*. It very much captures the Confucian spirit of self-transcendence:

> In shifting the center of one's empathic concern from oneself to one's family one transcends selfishness. The move from family to community transcends nepotism. The move from community to nation transcends parochialism and the move to all humanity counters chauvinistic nationalism.

We can even add: the move toward the unity of heaven and humanity (*tianren heyi*) transcends secular humanism, a blatant form of anthropocentrism characteristic of the Enlightenment mentality.

It is in the anthropocosmic spirit that we find communication between self and community, harmony between humanity and nature, and mutuality between mankind and Heaven. An integrated comprehensive vision of learning to be human can serve as a point of departure for a new discourse on the global ethic.

See also Confucianism: Ethics; Confucianism: Rhetoric; Confucianism: Tradition; Marxism in China; Philosophy: Recent Trends in China since Mao; Scientism and Humanism.

Note: This article is a revised and condensed version of "Beyond the Enlightenment Mentality" in *Confucianism and Ecology: The Interrelation of Heaven, Earth, and Humans*, ed. Mary Evelyn Tucker and John Berthrong. Cambridge, Mass.: Harvard University Center for the Study of World Religions, 1998.

Bibliography

Tu, Weiming. "Confucianism and Civilization." *In Dialogue of Civilizations: A New Peace Agenda for a New Millennium*, ed. Magid Tehranian and David W. Chappell. London and New York: Tauris, 2002, pp. 83–89.

———. "The Ecologic Turn in New Confucian Humanism: Implications for China and the World." *Daedalus*, 130(4), fall 2001, pp. 243–264.

Confucianism: Japan

Mary Evelyn TUCKER

In its spread from China throughout East Asia, Confucianism has had a striking influence on the societies and cultures of Korea, Japan, and Vietnam. Although Japan was the last of these countries to be affected by Confucianism, its impact has nonetheless been significant. The particular forms that Confucianism took in Japan distinguish it from other East Asian countries, especially because of the absence of an enduring civil service examination system as a means of identifying suitable bureaucrats. Nonetheless, Japan was able to adopt and adapt certain Confucian ideas in political organization, social ethics, the educational curriculum, and ritual practice. Thus, although Confucianism may not have had the same institutional grounding that it did in the rest of East Asia where civil service exams and Confucian government bureaucracies were dominant, its influence was abundantly evident. This is true particularly in education and social ethics from the Tokugawa period through World War II, when Confucian values of self-cultivation, loyalty, respect, harmony, and consensus were considered important means of fostering social cooperation. This is not to suggest, however, that dissent and disharmony have not also been part of Japan's history from earliest times to the present. The continuing invocation of the opening line of Shotoku Taishi's *Seventeen Article Constitution*—"Harmony is to be valued and an avoidance of wanton opposition to be honored"—is only a reminder of how difficult this ideal precept was to actualize, socially or politically.

Stages and Characteristics of Japanese Confucianism

To trace the growth of the Confucian influence, I will outline the significant periods of Confucianism in Japan—its introduction, its medieval development, and its early modern phase. These periods can be identified in light of major movements in Chinese Confucianism. The first period, from the fifth century to the thirteenth, has been called the era of the Han and Tang commentators (*Kanto kunko jidai*); the second period, from the thirteenth century to the seventeenth, has been called the era of Song learning (*Sogaku jidai*); and the third period, from the seventeenth century to the middle of the nineteenth, has been known as the era of the learning of the Chinese scholars (*Kangakusha jidai*). Each of these periods reflects different issues of adoption and adaptation of Confucianism in the Japanese context. Confucianism was "naturalized" here in a less dogmatic or rigid manner than in Korea and in a less political manner than in China.

From the beginning, Confucianism was often blended with Shinto and Buddhism (as in Shotoku's *Seventeen Article Constitution*); in the medieval period it was used by the Zen (Chan) monks for its cultural and educational ideas; and in the early modern period it dominated the educational curriculum. Perhaps the most important means of indigenization of Confucianism in Japan has been through education, both in schools and in the family. This can be traced in textbooks and household codes used from the medieval period through the Tokugawa era and down to the present. The inculturation of social virtues and the high value of learning are outcomes of this Confucianization of Japan. This is not to suggest that harmony and consensus have dominated; it suggests merely that they are continually invoked, often with mixed results. Moreover, the process of adaptation of Confucianism into Japan involved numerous debates on the appropriateness of particular Chinese ideas, texts, rituals, or institutions for the Japanese context. Japanese Confucians debated, for example, the validity of the neo-Confucian synthesis as opposed to the exclusive use of the early classical Confucian texts. In contrast, Japanese nativists argued against Confucianism and for the priority of Shinto beliefs and practices as more suitable for Japan. In addition, there were heated debates regarding the use of Chinese Confucian rituals, especially funerary rites and sacrifices to ancestors. Even the use of rituals in daily life was contested, with regard to how they could be adapted to particular times, places, and circumstances in the Japanese context.

Thus, issues of selectivity, accommodation, and transformation of both foreign and native ideas and practices have continually arisen in Japan. Japan's particular ability to accommodate diverse views has resulted in what Watsuji Tetsuro has called the "stadial" character of Japanese thought and culture. The term is meant to imply that various cultural elements may coexist without definitive resolution, and that earlier cultural strata need to be displaced. Although exclusion of ideas has also occurred, the pattern of loose adaptation seems to dominate. With these qualifications in mind, let us briefly trace the influence of Confucianism in politics, ethics, and education in the three periods outlined above.

Early Development of Confucianism in Japan (404–1185)

Nearly 1,000 years after the time of Confucius his ideas were transmitted to Japan by way of Korea. It was during the Nara and Heian periods that Confucian political ideas of centralized imperial rule, supported by selected moral officials and legitimized by historical writing, were adopted. Clear evidence of the political influence of Confucianism can be seen in Shotoku Taishi's *Seventeen Article Constitution*, which was promulgated in 604, as well as in the Taika reforms of the mid-seventh century. The constitution promoted Confucian ideas of order, harmony, and consensus. While its tone was strongly Confucian, it also incorporated ideas from Buddhism and legalism. The Taika reforms helped establish a centralized bureaucratic state system in which the emperor ruled with Confucian moral exhortation, ritual propriety, and penal and administrative codes (*ritsuryo*) based on Chinese models. Humane government and moral rule were expected from the emperor and his officials, who were to be selected on merit.

Han and Tang Confucian ethical teachings were fostered by historical writing, through the system of correspondences, in educational institutions, and by the civil service examinations. The earliest Japanese histories, the *Kojikii* and the *Nihongi*, were compiled in the eighth century and promoted Confucian morality and statecraft. They blended Shinto myths of the divine origin of the emperor with views, based on Confucianism, of the moral authority of the imperial institution. The Han Confucian system of correspondences helped to reinforce imperial legitimacy as well as to spread Confucian ideas of the vast interconnections of microcosm and macrocosm. To help monitor these intricate relationships, a Bureau of Yin and Yang (*On'yoryo*) was established around 675 and incorporated into the Taiho Code of 701. Its main tasks were divination and prognostication of events, especially as they affected the government. To carry on this work, geomancy, astrology, and divination were applied to discern the elaborate interconnections between the planets, the elements, directions, the seasons, and the signs of the zodiac.

Confucianism was also promulgated through the establishment of a national university (*Daigakuryo*) and a provincial school system that served the civil service examination system. This system was based on traditional Chinese Confucian models of educating moral officials for government service. The national university was established under the ministry of ceremonials and observed spring and autumn rituals (*sekiten*) honoring Confucius. These rituals were a crucial religious ceremony of Confucianism in Japan and were still being performed at Confucian schools into the late nineteenth century. Two forms of examinations were implemented. The first kind were those in schools, which included end-of-term and annual tests. The second kind were examinations intended for entrance into the civil service and were administered by the ministry of ceremonials. This system, based on the Chinese model, lasted until the fourteenth century, although by the tenth century it had become so corrupt that the original intent of the examinations—to foster a meritocracy—was thoroughly undermined. Thus, heredity and nobility won over meritocracy as criteria for public service. Although the national university eventually went into decline and disappeared after several centuries, the Confucian-based curriculum of the provincial schools helped to maintain Confucian social ethics and political morality through much of the Heian period. Eventually, however, the locus of Confucian discourse passed into the Zen monasteries, where it flourished with the interest and encouragement of the Zen monks.

The Medieval Link to Buddhism (1185–1568)

It was during the Kamakura (1185–1333) and Muromachi (1333–1568) periods that Chinese neo-Confucian thought was introduced into Japan. In particular, it was studied intensively by Zen monks, who became at this time the principal means for the transmission of Chinese culture to Japan. Numerous monks visited China and brought back texts (both Buddhist and Confucian) and arts (such as the tea ceremony, painting, and calligraphy). As custodians of high culture from China they also became knowledgeable in political theory and the educational curriculum. Consequently, they were sought out as advisers to the shogun and local rulers. Moreover, the temples became important repositories of learning and centers for educating the young. Major libraries were collected, and texts were published. The temple schools (*terakoya*) adopted a mixed curriculum of Confucian texts and Buddhist precepts to educate children. Confucian morality spread not only through the schools and the copybooks (*oraimono*) that they used, but also through the publication of house codes (*kakun*) adopted by daimyo families, which lasted into the Tokugawa period. In addition, the Zen monks themselves were interested in Confucian ethical and religious teachings, especially with regard to self-cultivation. Confucian ideas on disciplining the mind and nourishing one's nature were incorporated into the Zen monks' practice.

This period thus reflects a remarkable coexistence of Buddhism and Confucianism, within and beyond the Zen monasteries. This was due in large measure to the intellectual and cultural exchange with China, which was at its peak, fostered by trade and diplomatic missions as well as by the journeys and scholarship of individual monks. A sign of this coexistence is the emergence of various Buddhist-Confucian monks (*juso*) who actively promoted such an interaction. For example, the monk Gido Shushin (1325–1388) helped to spread Confucian ideas among the aristocracy of Kyoto. He stressed the relevance of the *Analects* and *Mencius* as guides to humane government (*jinsei*). Another monk, Ben'en Enni, from Tofukuji monastery, was known for punctuating Zhu Xi's commentaries on the Four Books for easier reading by the Japanese. Moreover, the spread of Confucianism to the provinces was fostered by monks such as Keian Genju (1427–1508), who founded a Confucian school in Satsuma after the destruction of the Onin war; and Minamimura Baiken, who taught a syncretic Zen-Confucian concept in Tosa. In addition to the Buddhist-Confucian monks there were individuals who created a Shinto-Confucian synthesis, including Ichiro Kaneyoshi (1403–1481) and Yoshida Kanetomo (1434–1511).

One of the most striking examples of the syncretism of Buddhism and Confucianism during this period is the Ashikaga school, which was reestablished in 1439 on the site of an earlier provincial school in the present-day Tochigi prefecture. The intention was to revitalize provincial education in the region on the basis of the earlier model of the national university founded in Nara. The school blended Confucian and Buddhist rituals with a Confucian temple for seasonal sacrifices (*sekiten*) and a Buddhist hall enshrining a statue of Yakushi nyorai. The library contained Confucian, Daoist, and Buddhist manuscripts, in addition to texts on literature, history, medicine, and military science. Some of the central items of study were the *Yijing* (or *Yi jing, Book of Changes*) and *yin-yang* philosophy. Thus, elements of divination and geomancy were learned as a means of encouraging both personal cultivation and decision making, as well as auspicious military action and appropriate political ordering.

The Flourishing of Tokugawa Confucianism (1600–1868)

During the Tokugawa period, Confucianism flourished in distinctive ways, especially in politics, ethics, and education. This was a period when Japan was able to establish a lasting peace after several decades of internal wars. The country was closed off from trade and foreign influences, although some Chinese and western books were imported through Nagasaki harbor. It was in this setting that Confucianism was promoted, initially by the samurai class but later by other groups, including townspeople and merchants. Moving from out of the confines of the Zen monasteries, Confucianism began to have a direct influence in the society at large. This was due to the efforts of Confucian scholars, teachers, and political advisers who consciously and unconsciously assisted in the spread of Confucian ideas and texts. Confucianism took a variety of forms, and debates between schools and scholars were lively throughout the period. There were two main branches of neo-Confucianism: one based on the teachings of Zhu Xi and known as *shushigaku*, and the other based on the teachings of Wang Yangming and known as *yomeigaku*. The principal *shushi* scholars included Fujiwara Seika (1561–1619), Hayashi Razan (1583–1657), Yamazaki Ansai (1618–1682), Kaibara Ekken (1630–1714), and Muro Kyuso (1688–1734). The leading *yomei* scholars were Nakae Toju (1608–1648), Kumazawa Banzan (1619–1691), and later restoration scholars such as Sakuma Shozan (1811–1864) and Yoshida Shoin (1830–1859).

The principal avenues for the spread of Confucianism during the Tokugawa period were the schools and the writings and teachings of individual scholars. Tokugawa Japan presents important evidence for the inherent appeal of Confucian ideas across national and cultural boundaries. Although Confucianism was used along with Shinto and Buddhism to help formulate a loose Bakufu ideology for political legitimization, it clearly had an appeal to individual scholars as a broad humanistic system of thought, emphasizing self-cultivation and social participation. This dual effort toward transformation of self and society was considered an important means of establishing the grounds for human flourishing. For numerous samurai, merchants, townspeople, and even farmers, the ideas of Confucian virtue, ritual practice, and social consensus were compelling, especially after several decades of internal wars in Japan. This development was marked by a transition from the roles of *juso* to *jusha*—that is, from those who were considered to be both Buddhist monks and Confucian scholars in the late medieval period to those who saw themselves as Confucian scholars. This can be seen in the early seventeenth century, when Yamazaki Ansai, Nakae Toju, and others attacked Hayashi Razan's acceptance of a Buddhist clerical status in serving the Bakufu. The practice of shaving one's head, adopting Buddhist robes, or both was eventually discontinued by Confucian scholars. Nonetheless, on popular levels the syncretism of Confucianism and Buddhist ideas of self-cultivation occurred, for example, in the learning of the mind and heart (*shingaku*).

It was especially through the practice of *shingaku* that Confucian ideas regarding self-cultivation spread across East Asia. Indeed, one might say that it was this form of self-cultivation which became embedded in the cultural patterns and spiritual practices of the countries of East Asia. Certainly in Japan this became a principal means for the transmission of Confucianism. Throughout the Tokugawa period *shingaku* was taught in many venues from academies and schools to community halls and private homes.

It is instructive to note that this transmission transcended distinctions of class. We may take three case studies to illustrate the practice of the learning of the mind and heart among the samurai class and beyond (Kaibara Ekken, 1630–1714), among the merchant class (Ishida Baigan, 1685–1744), and among the peasant class (Ninomiya Sontoku, 1685–1744).

Kaibara Ekken. Ekken was one of the most versatile intellectuals of his day; his range of interests was both broad and practical. He engaged in sophisticated discussions of *li* (principle) and *qi* (material force) in Confucian philosophy, helped to promote more widespread understanding of Confucian moral teachings, and was deeply concerned about practical learning (*jitsugaku*) ranging from health care to agriculture, from astronomy to plant classification. Most significantly, Kaibara Ekken wished to spread Confucian moral and spiritual teaching not only among the samurai but among other classes as well. To this end he wrote moral treatises in a simplified Japanese for families, for women, and for children. His treatises were intended to popularize the learning of the mind and heart as a means of self-examination and moral improvement. One of his best-known treatises (*Precepts for Daily Life in Japan*) illustrates this process as a means of paying back one's debt to heaven and earth through extending one's knowledge and disciplining one's heart-mind. This discipline involves discernment, resolution, and balance between the Way, the mind, and the human mind. It calls for moral purification and emotional control. It suggests methods of practice, all of which lead to spiritual harmony and intellectual illumination. The fact that Ekken's treatises were republished throughout the Tokugawa period and even into the twentieth century is some indication of their persuasiveness and appeal. His *Onna daigaku* (*Learning for Women*) and *Yojokun* (*Precepts for Health Care*) were followed carefully up through World War II.

Ishida Baigan. Confucianism spread to the merchant class through the efforts of Ishida Baigan and his followers, as well as through schools like the Merchant Academy in Osaka (the Kaitokudo). Baigan's teachings, like Ekken's, consisted of the learning of the mind and heart (*shingaku*), which stressed purifying the mind and heart so as to be one with heaven and earth. Baigan was deeply influenced by Mencius in his optimistic view of human nature and its potential for self-transformation. He emphasized that knowing one's nature (*sei*) is the essence of learning (*gakumon*). This learning is a religious and ethical process and is the same as seeking the lost mind of which Mencius spoke. It could be done through reading texts, but it also could be attained even by illiterate people as part of their own self-cultivation. This process of *shingaku* involved meditation and quiet sitting (*seiza*), some forms of asceticism (frugality and simplicity), and dedication to one's duty in life. Each class in society had something to contribute to the welfare of the whole. In this way Baigan provided a rationale for the role of the merchants as contributing to a common good. He suggested that the merchants were deserving of their profits just as the samurai might justly receive a stipend for their public service. For Baigan the economic exchange of the merchants was the basis for a benevolent society that could assist those in need. *Shingaku*, then, was seen as an ethical religious means of self-cultivation which led to active participation in and contribution to the larger society.

Ninomiya Sontoku. Sontoku, frequently described as the "peasant sage" of Japan, revived the principles of self-cultivation and benevolent government as crucial to the indigenization of Confucianism in Japan. He preached discipline, frugality, and hard work to the peasants, along with the need for generous and constant care for the people by the rulers. At the heart of his teaching was the constant directive to give back what one had received from heaven and earth. Thus for Sontoku repayment of one's debt (*on*) for the sources of life was essential. This was known as *hotoku*, to return virtue and to pay back blessings. Those who were interested in serving society and giving thanks to heaven in this way formed the Hotokusha (Society for Returning Virtue). Eventually there were branches of this society all over Japan. Their purpose was to assist the poor, especially by uniting them in helping one another. There were two aspects of this: encouraging moral transformation and providing practical assistance in the form of such activities as reclaiming land and building irrigation systems or repairing roads and bridges. Society members contributed financial aid without interest and material assistance without expectation of reward. Sontoku's teachings have been described as being based on sincerity, energized by hard work and selfless service, and fortified by simplicity.

Scholars and Educators

In addition to the work of individual scholars, Confucianism was spread especially by the establishment of public schools in each of the provinces as well as by the growth of private schools and merchant academies.

The public schools included government schools (*kangakko*), prefectural schools (*hanko*), and local schools (*goko*). The private schools, known as *shijuku*, were set up by individual scholars and teachers. Temple schools (*terakoya*) also flourished during this period. In addition, in the capital, Edo, a national government school was set up under the direction of the Hayashi family, and a Confucian temple was established there. This school, known as the Yushima Seido or the Shoheiko, served as a model for the curriculum and the rituals of the provincial schools, whose teachers frequently were graduates of the national school. The curriculum in all of these schools was largely Confucian, based on reading the Four Books as well as the Five Classics. Although Shinto texts, Buddhist scriptures, and Japanese literature were also incorporated into the curriculum of various schools, the core of the curriculum was certainly Confucian.

Syncretism, Coexistence, and Difference

Confucianism did, however, form syncretic alliances with both Shinto and Buddhism during this period. Through the linkage to Shinto, Confucian scholars attempted to "naturalize" Confucianism. In so doing they hoped to demonstrate the similarity of their teachings by showing, for example, how Confucian virtues had counterparts in Shinto morality. Similarly, the syncretism with Buddhist moral and religious discipline, such as the learning of the mind and heart (*shingaku*), was seen as a path open to all people to recover one's original nature.

Although various forms of syncretism coexisted throughout the period, clearly distinct schools also arose in the late seventeenth and early eighteenth century. For example, the "national learning" school of Shinto (*kokugaku*) and the "ancient learning" school of Confucianism (*kogaku*) drew on earlier textual sources for inspiration. *Kokugaku* drew on distinctively Japanese texts, especially from history and literature. *Kogaku* harked back to the Five Classics as well as to the *Analects* and *Mencius*. The leading proponents of *kogaku* were Ito Jinsai (1627–1705), Ito Togai (1670–1736), and Ogyu Sorai (1666–1728). These thinkers questioned the authority of the Chinese neo-Confucians and stressed the reliability of the ancient Confucian classics. Sorai especially emphasized the importance of philology, the re-creation of rituals, and reverence for the sage kings.

Finally, there was a renewed interest in the connections between Shinto nationalism and Confucian historical writing in the Mito school. In the mid-seventeenth century Tokugawa Mitsukuni set in motion a project that would take more than two centuries to complete, the *History of Great Japan* (*Dai-Nihon-shi*). With the help of a Ming loyalist who had come to Japan, Zhu Shunshui, Mitsukuni launched a moral history that would support loyalty to the throne at all costs. This fervent nationalist school had a strong influence in formulating Japanese identity during the Meiji restoration and afterward. This particular mixture of Shinto nationalism and Confucian historicity eventually gave rise to militaristic nationalism of an extreme sort, as was evident in the ideology leading up to World War II.

From Meiji to World War II (1868–1945) and Beyond

The Meiji restoration saw two fundamental drives in Japan, one toward openness to the west and to modernization, the other toward a stronger Asian and nationalistic identity based variously on Shinto, Buddhism, or Confucianism. These were continually in an uneasy tension that is represented in three significant figures: Motoda Eifu (1818–1891), Ito Hirobumi (1841–1909), and Inoue Tetsujiro (1856–1944). Motoda, a Confucian tutor and adviser to the emperor, helped to formulate a national polity (*kokutai*). He also drafted two influential documents promulgating Confucian morals: *Fundamentals of Education for the Young* (1882) and *Imperial Rescript on Education* (1890). By contrast, Ito Hirobumi was a politician who encouraged the adoption of western science and technology in addition to western constitutional government. He helped to draft the Japanese constitution of 1889, which aimed at balancing citizens' rights with a centralized imperial government. Inoue Tetsujiro, on the other hand, was a public proponent of Confucianism and published extensively on the history of Confucian thought. A prominent philosopher at Tokyo University, he was critical of Christianity as being incompatible with Japanese culture and favored a Confucian revival as appropriate for Japan.

During the Taisho and Showa eras before World War II a national Confucian organization (Shibun) was formed that published a monthly periodical between 1918 and 1945. The Confucian temple (Seido) was revived in 1918, and the school was restored in 1926. Disillusionment with the west after World War I led to calls for a return to Confucian humaneness and benevolent government. Confucianism was not seen as incompatible with democracy, and responsibilities rather than individual rights were stressed. Moreover, Confucian moral education was invoked, and there was a revival of the study of the classics and of *kambun* courses which helped the Japanese read the Chinese texts directly.

Thus Confucianism, even into the twentieth century, was a means of evoking national identity and cultural pride. When it was mixed with Shinto exclusivism, however, the results could be highly problematic, as in the policies adopted by the military to justify their expansionist ambitions. Since World War II both Shinto and Confucianism in Japan have been somewhat eclipsed as fields of study or as ideologies per se. However, it is evident that the rise of Japan economically may be due, at least in part, to its Confucian heritage. As Tu Weiming has observed, modernization in East Asia has taken on its own distinctive forms with a Confucian base. Surely the case of Japan—as a society deeply imbued with certain Confucian values such as the importance of education and self-cultivation, valuing loyalty and duty to the group, capitalizing on practical learning, and investigating things—is worthy of further study. Moreover, the Confucian "habits of the heart" have been passed on in Japan through family structures and educational institutions. The struggle Japan faces at the present is how to balance the challenges of traditional heritage in the face of modernization from within and the continuing encroachment of westernization from without.

See also Confucianism: Korea; Confucianism: Tradition; Confucianism: Vietnam; Mencius; Wang Yangming; Zhu Xi.

Bibliography

Armstrong, Robert. *Just before Dawn: The Life and Work of Ninomiya Sontoku*. New York: Macmillan, 1912.

Bellah, Robert. *Tokugawa Religion: The Values of Pre-Industrial Japan*. Boston: Beacons, 1957.

Bito, Masahide. *Nihon hoken shisoshi kenkyu* (Studies in the History of Thought in Japanese Feudalism). Tokyo: Aoki shoten, 1961.

de Bary, William Theodore, and Irene Bloom, eds. *Principle and Practicality*. New York: Columbia University Press, 1979.

Dore, Ronald. *Education in Tokugawa Japan*. Berkeley: University of California Press, 1965.

Hongo, Takamori, and Kukaya Katsumi, eds. *Kinsei shisoron* (Discussions of Premodern Japanese Thought). Tokyo: Yukikaku, 1981.

Maruyama, Masao. *Studies in the Intellectual History of Tokugawa Japan*, trans. Mikiso Hane. Princeton, N.J., and Tokyo: Princeton University Press and University of Tokyo Press, 1974.

Minamoto, Ryoen. *Kinsei shoki jitsugaku shiso no kenkyu* (Studies in Practical Learning at the Beginning of the Premodern Era). Tokyo: Sobunsha, 1980.

Najita, Tetsuo. *Visions of Virtue in Tokugawa Japan: The Kaitokudo Merchant Academy of Osaka*. Chicago, Ill.: University of Chicago Press, 1987.

Najita, Tetsuo, and Irwin Scheiner, eds. *Japanese Thought in the Tokugawa Period 1600–1868: Methods and Metaphors*. Chicago, Ill.: University of Chicago Press, 1978.

Nosco, Peter. *Confucianism and Tokugawa Culture*. Princeton, N.J.: Princeton University Press, 1984.

Ooms, Herman. *Tokugawa Ideology: Early Constructs, 1570–1680*. Princeton, N.J.: Princeton University Press, 1985.

Sagara, Toru, et al. *Edo no shisokatachi* (Thinkers in the Edo Period). Tokyo: Kenkyusha, 1979.

Sawada, Janine. *Confucian Values and Popular Zen: Sekimon Shingaku in Eighteenth-Century Japan*. Honolulu: University of Hawaii Press, 1993.

Tucker, Mary Evelyn. *Moral and Spiritual Cultivation in Japanese Neo-Confucianism: The Life and Thought of Kaibara Ekken (1630–1714)*. Albany: State University of New York Press, 1989.

Confucianism: Korea

Young-chan Ro

Confucianism was the most influential intellectual and spiritual tradition in Korea: it provided the most common moral practice, the longest-sustained ideology, the most widely observed family ritual, and spiritual and moral self-cultivation. Korean Confucianism is characterized by the theoretical development and philosophical sophistication of the fundamental neo-Confucian ideas and concepts that determined the nature and the shape of Korean neo-Confucianism.

Korean neo-Confucianism took as its metaphysical base a discussion of the most fundamental neo-Confucian concepts such as "principle" (*i, li*) and "material force" (*ki, qi*) and the relationships between them. *I* and *ki* were fundamental to understanding the universe, nature, and human beings. They also became a foundation for understanding other paired concepts, such as the "moral mind" (*tosim, daoxin*) and the "human mind" (*insim, renxin*); and the "four beginnings" (*sadan, siduan*) and the "seven feelings" or "seven emotions" (*chilchong, qiqing*). The discussion of the moral mind and the human mind in turn became the foundation for an analysis of the moral aspects of the "mind-and-heart" (*sim, xin*); the controversy over the four beginnings and the seven feelings was considered in terms of the workings of human feelings and emotions (*chong, qing*). Thus the discussion of *i* and *ki* and their relationship to cosmology, ontology, and anthropology dominated Korean neo-Confucianism. Various schools of Korean Confucianism were defined by their understanding of the nature and function of *i* and *ki*.

Hwadam

Sŏ Kyŏng-dŏk (Hwadam, 1489–1546) dedicated himself to the study of Song neo-Confucianism and was the first Korean neo-Confucian to formulate a philosophy of *ki*. Following Zhang Zai (1020–1077), a Song neo-Confucian philosopher who had based his philosophy on the dynamic role of *ki*, Hwadam identified the "great vacuity" (*t'aeh, taixu*) with *ki*, the creative and transformative force of the universe. He considered *ki* unlimited. By contrast, *i* is inside *ki*: there is no "principle" outside "material force." For Hwadam, *i* has no ontological ground of its own and no creative or transformative power. Hwadam was a monist in developing his idea of *ki* as the original state of the universe, prior to the division into *ki* and *i*: for him, even after that division *i* exists in the form and activity of *ki*. Hwadam's emphasis on *ki* overshadowed *i*—this is what makes him a *ki* monist. Although he studied the "orthodox" Cheng-Zhu school of neo-Confucianism, he followed Zhang Zai's monistic approach in understanding *ki* as the origin and ultimate force of the universe.

Yi Ŏn-jŏk

Yi Ŏn-jŏk (Hoejae, 1491–1553), on the other hand, formulated a theory in which *i* was dominant; he is known as the first Korean neo-Confucian who emphasized *i* with respect to cosmology and morality. Although he followed Zhu Xi's theory of *i* and *ki*, he understood *i* as the basis of all activities of *ki*. For him, *i* was a cosmological, metaphysical, and ethical principle. He also understood *i* as "substance" (*ch'e, ti*), which is prior; and *ki* as "function" (*yong, yong*), which is posterior. Yi Ŏn-jŏk identified this *i* with the "great ultimate" (*t'aegŭk, taiji*), the principle of cosmic transformation and moral self-cultivation.

T'oegye

The most refined scholarship, and the maturation of Korean neo-Confucianism, was achieved by Yi Hwang (T'oegye, 1501–1570) and Yi I (Yulgok, 1536–1584). Arguably, T'oegye is the greatest Confucian scholar in Korean history; he is often described as the "Zhu Xi of Korea." T'oegye's thought also exerted a good deal of influence on the development of the *shushigaku* (Zhu Xi school) in Tokugawa Japan.

T'oegye was deeply influenced by the *Sŏngnidae-jŏn* or *Xing-li dazhun* (*Great Compendium of Human Nature and Principle*), a compilation of Song and Yuan neo-Confucian thinkers, and the *Simgyŏng* or *Xinjing* (*Classic for the Mind-and-Heart*), by Zhen Dexiu (1178–1235), a leading adherent of the Cheng-Zhu school in Song China. T'oegye served the government in many official positions, but he always intended to retire to his hometown to study and teach. In 1543, when he began to study the *Zhuzi daquan* (*Great Compendium of Master Zhu Xi*), he resolved to resign from public life. Before he retired from the government, he wrote two political treatises: the *Yukchŏ* (*Six-Article Memorial*) advising a young ruler (Sŏnjo) on fundamental matters of conduct and policy, and the *Sŏnghak-sipto* (*Ten Diagrams on the Learning of Sagehood*), a summary and synthesis of Cheng-Zhu metaphysics and ethics. Finally, he returned to the village of Tosan, where he died.

T'oegye wrote many significant works in his sixties. His intense involvement with Zhu Xi's letters is reflected in his first major work, a collection of them, *Chusŏchŏryo* (*The Essentials of Zhu Xi's Correspondence*). It is a selection of about one-third of the original corpus, emphasizing particularly Zhu's discussion of matters related to self-cultivation. By the end of his life T'oegye was already referred to as the "synthesizer" and "complete integrator" of the Cheng-Zhu school in Korea. Mature, integral appropriation of the Cheng-Zhu vision in both its intellectual and its spiritual dimensions began with T'oegye.

T'oegye had a tendency to divide *i* and *ki*, on the understanding that *i* was a primary agent over *ki*. For this reason, he was considered a champion of the school of "*i* primacy" (*churipa*). T'oegye's dualistic tendency became more apparent when he applied the concepts of *i* and *ki* to issues involved in "human nature" (*sŏng, xing*), "mind-heart" (*sim, xin*), and "feelings" (*chŏng, qing*). From T'oegye's point of view, although *i* and *ki* are interdependent, they are separable in terms of origin; thus it is possible to speak of *i* and *ki* in a temporal sense as, respectively, prior and posterior. This notion of a separate origin of *i* and *ki* has enormous significance for understanding T'oegye's idea of the dichotomy between the moral mind and the human mind, and between the four beginnings and the seven feelings. According to T'oegye, the reason for the duality of the mind—moral mind and human mind—has to do with the origins of *i* and *ki*:

the moral mind is due to *i* while the human mind is due to *ki*. The implication is that *i* and *ki* are the ontological grounds for these two minds; there is also a moral implication: *i* is morally pure and superior to *ki*.

T'oegye, then, clearly enhanced Zhu Xi's idea of *i* and *ki* as two separate entities, discarding the idea that they are not to be either divided or confused. T'oegye also related *i* and *ki* to human nature in terms of the "nature of original disposition" (*ponyŏnchisŏng, benranzhixing*), which he connected to *i*; and the "nature of physical disposition" (*kijilchisŏng, qichizhixing*), which he connected to *ki*.

As noted above, he also understood the four beginnings and the seven feelings in relation to *i* and *ki*. The Confucian term "four beginnings" (*sadan, siduan*) originally comes from the *Book of Mencius*:

> The mind-and-heart of commiseration is the beginning of benevolence; the mind-and-heart of shame and dislike is the beginning of righteousness; the mind-and-heart of courtesy is the beginning of propriety; and the mind-and-heart of right and wrong is the beginning of wisdom. All human beings have these Four Beginnings just as they have their four limbs. (2A.6)

According to Mencius, the feelings of "commiseration," "shame and dislike," "courtesy" (or "respect and reverence"), and "right and wrong" are present in all human beings and are the sign, and the beginning, of the goodness of human nature. The four beginnings are empirical evidence for the assertion that human nature is originally good.

The seven feelings (*chilchong, qiping*) are from the *Book of Rites* and the *Great Learning*. These feelings are pleasure, anger, sorrow, fear, love, hatred, and desire. According to T'oegye, they belong to the nature of physical disposition whereas the four beginnings belong to the nature of original disposition. T'oegye attributed the four beginnings to *i* and the seven feelings to *ki*.

Zhu Xi made no explicit statement about the relationship between the four beginnings and the seven feelings, though he did make a vague statement about origins—that the four beginnings are the manifestations of (or issuance from) *i* and the seven feelings are manifestations of (or issuance from) *ki*. He did not explore the ontological, moral, or ethical implications of that relationship, and the issue became the major theme for Korean neo-Confucianism. The crowning achievements of Korean neo-Confucian scholars, including—most notably—T'oegye and Yulgok, indicate the philosophical depth and theoretical sophistication involved in what was called the "four-seven" debate.

With regard to ontology, for T'oegye—once again—the four beginnings are associated with *i* and the seven feelings with *ki*. T'oegye noted explicitly that the four feelings issue from *i* and that *ki* follows thereafter, but the seven feelings issue from *ki* and *i* follows thereafter. Thus he understood the four and the seven in terms of mutual issuance. Although the four beginnings, since they were still "feelings," must have the aspect of *ki*, they were initiated by *i*, whereas the seven feelings were initiated by *ki*.

T'oegye's assertion became a problematic thesis with regard to the nature and the role of *i* and *ki*. The problem was twofold: the dualistic tendency to divide *i* and *ki* and the question whether or not *i* has the ability to "issue" or "move" as *ki* does. Although *i* and *ki* are different in terms of function, they are not two different ontological entities. Furthermore, *i* as a metaphysical principle does not have the power to move.

Kobong

For this reason, the brilliant young scholar Ki Taesŏng (Kobong, 1529–1592) raised serious questions about T'oegye's understanding of *i* and *ki* and the relationship between them. Kobong's challenge to T'oegye's thesis on *i* and *ki* and the four and the seven initiated a seven-year correspondence between them, from 1559 to 1566. In this debate, T'oegye formulated highly sophisticated theories and arguments on the mind, human nature, and feelings in relation to the neo-Confucian metaphysics of *i* and *ki*. Kobong's fundamental disagreement with T'oegye was that the four beginnings and the seven feelings were not divided in terms of *i* and *ki*; rather, the seven feelings represented the totality of all feelings.

Mencius had asserted that the four beginnings were the "good" side of the seven. In other words, the seven included the four and the four—not having an independent ontological foundation—did not exist outside the seven. Mencius mentioned the four especially in order to show that human nature is originally good. His understanding of the relationship between the four and the seven seems to correspond to Zhu Xi's two brief statements: "The seven feelings cannot be separated from the four beginnings" and "The four beginnings can be understood from the standpoint of the seven feelings."

Kobong argued that the four and the seven should not be understood in terms of a dualistic framework involving a dichotomy between *i* and *ki*; instead, the four should be understood as a subset of the seven. Kobong thought T'oegye's approach did not accord with the true essence of orthodox Cheng-Zhu teachings because T'oegye had been incorrect in seeing the origins of the four and the seven as due, respectively, to *i* and *ki*. Kobong held that the four beginnings were not "separate" feelings originating in *i* alone—they originated in *ki* as well.

Yulgok and Ugye

Yi I (Yulgok, 1536–1584) later took up Kobong's basic thesis and developed a clear, systematic theoretical formulation for the whole range of issues involved in the four-seven debate. He corresponded with Sŏng Hon (Ugye, 1536–1598), a scholar who had studied Cheng-Zhu thought primarily by reading T'oegye's work and respected T'oegye highly as the most prominent and most authoritative figure of the time. The debate between Yulgok and Ugye started when Ugye wrote to Yulgok asking for clarification of T'oegye's four-seven theory of "mutual (alternate) manifestation" of *i* and *ki* (*ikihobal, liqi hufa*). Ugye was simply representing T'oegye's view, so although Yulgok was writing to Ugye, his real debate was with T'oegye.

In defense of T'oegye, Ugye maintained that the four-seven could be spoken of in terms of *i* or *ki* and argued that it was logically correct to discuss the four and the seven in terms of the moral mind and the human mind respectively. The classical statement of the moral mind and the human mind is in the "Sixteen-Character Transmission of the Mind-and-Heart" from the *Book of History*: "The human mind is precarious; the moral mind is subtle. Remain refined and single-minded. Hold fast to the Mean" (Legge 1893, p. 61). This instruction, handed down from the sage-king Shun to his successor Yu, contrasted the precariousness of the human mind with the subtlety of the moral mind and involved cultivating the mind and maintaining equilibrium before the feelings are aroused. Zhu Xi and his followers took this instruction as the central theme for their intellectual investigation and their moral and spiritual practice.

According to Zhu Xi, the moral mind is the unaroused state of the mind in itself, which is pure and always good; the human mind is the aroused state of the mind mixed with desires that include both good and evil. As noted earlier, Zhu Xi did not explicitly discuss the moral mind and the human mind in relation to the four and the seven—it was T'oegye who inferred that relationship. Ugye, however, on the basis of his reading of T'oegye, thought that the mind might be dual because of the difference between its sources, *i* and *ki*. He thought that it was quite possible to conceive of the moral mind and the four beginnings as due to *i* while the human mind and the seven feelings were due to *ki*. Yulgok's response to Ugye was creative and original.

Yulgok, unlike many other scholars of the time, made a bold attempt to interpret the classical texts not literally but in light of authors' intent or spirit. However, he was keenly aware of the textual ambiguities at the heart of classics and the Cheng-Zhu writings, and so he emphasized careful reflection on the texts. Yulgok's interpretive (or hermeneutical) principle was an interactive dialogue between the text and the reader. He found the words and explanation of the sages and worthies clear in some cases and subtle in others. For this reason, he warned that one should not follow the texts blindly but should apply one's own experience and views to interpret them (*Yulgokchons, The Compendium of Yulgok*, 9.35b).

Taking this approach, Yulgok tackled the key issues of Korean neo-Confucianism. For Yulgok, T'oegye's theory of "alternate issuance" (*hobalsŏl*) regarding the four-seven was improper because it would imply that *i* and *ki* are two separate entities, one prior and one posterior in terms of their "issuance" and "followings." Yulgok was deeply concerned about the ontological division between *i* and *ki* and rejected Ugye's four-seven division in terms of the moral mind and the human mind. Yulgok emphasized, rather, the mind's interaction, interdependence, and ontological unity. According to Yulgok, ontologically the mind is one, but morally it does have two distinct aspects—the moral mind and the human mind. It is important not to confuse ontological unity and distinct moral phenomena.

Thus Yulgok was in agreement with T'oegye about the moral mind and the human mind, but he did not agree with T'oegye's view (originating with Zhu Xi) about the four beginnings and the seven feelings. Zhu Xi related the four beginnings (the feelings of commiseration, shame and dislike, respect and reverence, and right and wrong) in *Mencius* (6A.6) to the issuance of *i*, and the seven feelings (pleasure, anger, sorrow, fear, love, hate, and desire) in the *Book of Rites* to the issuance of *ki*. Yulgok's disagreement with this theory became a major conflict between his work and T'oegye's—and also with Zhu Xi's.

This issue, as mentioned above, originated in the debate between T'oegye and Kobong. To recapitulate, Kobong's main points of disagreement with T'oegye were:

1. That there are no four beginnings besides the seven feelings.
2. That the theory of the four as issuing from *i* and the seven as issuing from *ki* leads to dualism, dividing *i* and *ki* into two different things.
3. That if we fully divide *i* and *ki*, the seven will have no connection to *i* and the four will have no

connection to *ki*—an outcome T'oegye would be unwilling to accept.

Kobong insisted that while the moral mind and the human mind can be related to *i* and *ki*, respectively, the four and the seven cannot be viewed as belonging solely to *i* and *ki* respectively.

T'oegye had responded as follows:

1. Although *i* and *ki* are not separable, it is still possible to speak primarily in terms of *i* and *ki*.
2. The distinction between the four and the seven is merely the distinction drawn in human nature (*sŏng, xing*) between the "nature of original disposition" (*ponyŏnchisŏng, benranzhixing*) and the "nature of physical disposition" (*kijilchisŏng, qizhizhixing*), as these are identified primarily with *i* and *ki* respectively.
3. So, if we make this distinction between *i* and *ki* in human nature, why should we not make it with regard to feelings?

The debate with Kobong did not change T'oegye's position on the theory of mind, but it did lead him to make minor accommodations. He included the four in the seven in his *Diagram of the Mind Commanding Human Nature and Feelings* (*Simt'ongsŏngjŏngto, xin-tung xin-ching-tu*). While he said that the four are the issuances of *i*, he qualified this statement, adding, "*ki* follows thereafter" and noting that the seven are issuances of *ki*, and *i* rides thereupon. This theory—"*i* issues and *ki* rides thereupon"—later became a controversial issue and the basis, most importantly, of Yulgok's main criticism of T'oegye.

Yulgok assumed that there is neither a separate existence between the "moral mind" and the "human mind" nor a division between the four and the seven. Yulgok's understanding of the mind was, characteristically, nondualistic. Yulgok recognized that the moral mind and the human mind were qualitatively different, and that therefore the two could not exist concurrently. He reasoned that these concepts were contradistinctive. The relation between the moral mind and the human mind cannot be expressed by a static, rigid formula; it is, rather, a dynamic, changing process, because each aspect can be overcome by the other.

However, the relationship between the four and the seven involved not contradistinction but rather inclusiveness. The seven are the totality of human feelings while the four are purely the "good" side of the seven. Yulgok argued that the seven contained the four, but the four did not contain the seven. Yulgok did not think that the moral mind and the human mind were the sources of the four and the seven—the reverse was true: the four and the seven were the sources of the human and the moral mind. In other words, the moral mind and the human mind were not the origins but the *appearances* of the four and the seven.

The difference between T'oegye and Yulgok is due largely to their different assumptions about *i* and *ki*. T'oegye saw *i* and *ki* not only as cosmological and ontological principles but also as moral principles. For Yulgok, *i* and *ki* were the fundamental principles of the universe, yet they were not moral principles, although they might have moral implications. It was wrong to assume that they were the cause of the moral dichotomy between good and bad.

Another characteristic of Yulgok's understanding of *i* and *ki* was that "*i* is one yet *ki* is diverse" (*iilbunju*) and "*i* penetrates and *ki* limits" (*it'ongkiguk*). According to Yulgok, *i* was the one and all-encompassing principle, permeating all beings; *ki* made all beings diverse shapes and concrete forms.

The philosophical sophistication and intellectual elaboration of this four-seven debate, and subsequent discussions of the issue among many other neo-Confucian scholars in Chosŏn Korea, suggest the characteristics of Korean neo-Confucian scholarship. To Korean neo-Confucian scholars such as T'oegye and Yulgok, the works of Zhu Xi and the Cheng brothers were the most authoritative source. As Korean scholars worked to deepen their comprehension of the complex neo-Confucian synthesis, they had relatively little contact with—or respect for—Ming scholarship. When the new interpretations introduced by Wang Yangming (1472–1529) swept through China and even overshadowed the Cheng-Zhu school, Korea was already distant and intellectually independent and largely resisted them. The Koreans confidently pronounced themselves the sole guardians of the Cheng-Zhu school. The four-seven controversy was a significant philosophical and moral issue that established a distinctive intellectual agenda for many neo-Confucians and initiated a unique feature of Korean-Confucianism.

See also Cheng Hao; Cheng Yi; Mencius; *Qing*; Xin; Zhang Zai; Zhu Xi.

Bibliography

Chung, Edward Y. J. *The Korean Neo-Confucianism of Yi T'oegye and Yi Yulgok: A Reappraisal of the Four-Seven Thesis and Its Practical Implications for Self-Cultivation.* Albany: State University of New York Press, 1995.

de Bary, William Theodore, and Ja Hyun Kim Haboush, eds. *The Rise of Neo-Confucianism in Korea.* New York: Columbia University Press, 1985.

Hyun, Sang-yun. *Chosŏn yuhaksa* (A History of Korean Confucianism). Seoul: Hyamsa, 1948, 1982. (In Korean.)

Kalton, Michael C., trans. *To Become a Sage: The Ten Diagrams on Sage Learning by Yi T'oegye*. New York: Columbia University Press, 1988.

Kalton, Michael C., et al. *The Four-Seven Debate: Annotated Translation of the Most Famous Controversy in Korean Neo-Confucian Thought*. Albany: State University of New York Press, 1995.

Lau, D. C., trans. *Mencius*. New York: Penguin, 1970, pp. 82–83.

Lee, Peter H., et al. *Source Book of Korean Civilization*, Vol. 1. New York: Columbia University Press, 1993.

Legge, James, trans. *The Chinese Classics*, Vol. 3. Oxford: Clarendon, 1893.

Pae, Chong-ho. *Hanguk Yuhaksa* (A History of Korean Confucianism). Seoul: Yonsei University Press, 1973. (In Korean.)

Ro, Young-chan. *Korean Neo-Confucianism of Yi Yulgok*. Albany: State University of New York Press, 1989.

Confucianism: Ming

Thomas A. Wilson

The Ming dynasty (1368–1644) was a contradictory era, when the Confucian ministers' moral influence over the emperor had declined dramatically owing to the concentration of autocratic powers in the ruler's hands. Yet, with the establishment of "Cheng-Zhu learning" (that is, the school of Cheng Yi and Zhu Xi) as state orthodoxy, mastery of the Confucian classics could be translated into unprecedented political power and high social status by passing a civil service examination and obtaining a degree. Early Ming adherents of Cheng-Zhu learning were largely loyal to the philosophical teachings of the Song Dao School masters, although even in this group it is possible to detect evidence of the subjective turn that would dominate later Ming Confucianism. The trend toward conferring ever greater moral autonomy on the mind's capacity to make correct judgments is most succinctly articulated in Wang Yangming's doctrine of the extension of the mind's innate knowledge of the good, which became the basis of a systematic critique of Cheng-Zhu learning. Some of Wang's followers concluded that this innate goodness was drawn from a realm of absolute goodness that rendered correct all spontaneous acts of the mind, unfettered by moral doctrines. In response to what was regarded as the excesses of this position, some Confucians of the late Ming advocated a return to Cheng-Zhu teachings, whereas others mediated between this and Wang Yangming's school in an attempt to circumvent the shortcomings of both.

In 1368, after nearly two decades of widespread popular revolt against the Yuan dynasty (1234–1368), Zhu Yuanzhang's peasant army defeated the Mongols and established the Ming. As Emperor Ming Taizu (r. 1368–1398), Zhu Yuanzhang left intact much of the Yuan's government apparatus and continued many of its administrative practices, with the notable exception that Han Chinese were no longer discriminated against in upper-level bureaucratic appointments. Song Lian (1310–1381), a prominent Confucian thinker of the early Ming, was an important adviser to Ming Taizu, particularly on matters of court ritual, and was assigned such tasks as compiling the Ming calendar and the dynastic history of the recently defeated Yuan. Anticipating what might be termed the subjective turn of Ming thought, Song Lian emphasized the ability of mind in apprehending the *dao* by consciously imitating Confucius through direct understanding of the sage unhindered by layers of later commentary. "The good student," according to Song Lian, "will lay aside the commentaries and subcommentaries, embrace the bare classics, and internalize them. . . . Finally classics and mind become one, and he no longer knows whether his mind is the classics or the classics his mind."

For a brief time, it appeared that Confucian thinkers would regain the political influence they had enjoyed in earlier eras, at least in their collective historical memory. But in 1373 the emperor suspended the civil examinations (they would be resumed in 1384), putting the literati on notice that learned men enjoyed political power at the sovereign's pleasure. The status of Confucians at court and the power of the throne took a dramatic turn in 1380, when Taizu executed his prime minister Hu Weiyong for treason, killed an estimated 30,000 alleged co-conspirators and their kin, and abolished the position of prime minister, an institution that had long made possible the inculcation of Confucian values in the ruler's political thinking. Initially sentenced to death when his grandson was implicated in the Hu Weiyong affair, Song Lian was exiled to Sichuan, where he committed suicide.

John Dardess maintains that Confucians of the early Ming, like Song Lian and others from Jinhua, Zhejiang, and the founder of the Ming shared a profound faith that world salvation was possible through a moral transformation of the empire directed from the top by the emperor. Song Lian's young disciple Fang Xiaoru (1357–1402) was also convinced that he could assist an enlightened ruler in this moral transformation, a program he initiated as a high-ranking minister at the court of Taizu's successor, the Jianwen emperor (r. 1399–1402). After the Jianwen emperor's uncle led a bloody coup and established himself as the Yongle emperor (r. 1402–1425), he asked Fang Xiaoru to write the proclamation of the new enthronement. When Fang refused, the emperor had him executed by dismemberment outside Nanjing's southern gate.

Although Fang Xiaoru's martyrdom decisively undid the already uneasy relationship between Ming rulers and their Confucian advisers, the Yongle emperor soon ordered a series of large-scale scholarly projects intended to regain the waning support of the literati. The massive collection of earlier writings called *Great Canon of the Yongle Era* (*Yongle dadian*) consumed the energies of many scholars during the first several years of his reign, though it was so immense that it was never actually published. During the rest of the dynasty Confucians continued to answer the call to serve their lord, but their most significant contribution to virtuous rulership was proffered in the form of dissent rather than by the more positive means of political reform. The relationship between ruler and minister in Ming times was perhaps typified in 1524 when the Jiajing emperor (r. 1522–1567) had hundreds of ministers and officials imprisoned or publicly flogged (this led to the deaths of fifteen of them) because they had protested his decision to bestow imperial honors on his father, who was never emperor, rather than allow himself to be posthumously adopted into the line of his cousin, the previous emperor, who died without an heir. By the late sixteenth century, when palace eunuchs had usurped imperial power from the negligent Wanli emperor (r. 1573–1619) and waged a systematic assault on ministers in the capital, there was virtually no tradition in the Ming of cooperation between ruler and minister. The dissolution of this bond in Ming times accounts for the strident factionalism of court politics, whereby cliques, such as the one associated with the Donglin Academy, were pitted against one another as well as court eunuchs. The willingness of Confucian literati to serve an increasingly autocratic lord is clear evidence of the overriding importance in Confucianism of helping the monarch transform the world to enable all things to complete their nature as described in the *Doctrine of the Mean*. It also indicates their selective memory of Mencius's dictum that unless the ruler "honors virtue and delights in the Way . . . it is not worth getting involved" (2B.2). Benjamin Elman (1994) observes that "most Mandarins" in Ming times "were indispensable handmaidens in the wedding between 'Dao Learning' and state autocracy."

The Ming dynasty marks the official establishment of the Cheng-Zhu school's Dao Learning as state orthodoxy. Known also as the Dao School (*daoxue*), this was one of several schools associated with a Confucian "revival" in the eleventh century in response to a centuries-long period when Buddhism profoundly shaped the thought of the literati. Although Confucianism had not actually disappeared in that period—hence the problem with calling this a revival—in the eleventh century it began to assume a culturally dominant position generally. The idea of Song Confucianism as a revival is at least a partial legacy of the Cheng-Zhu sectarian notion of *daotong*, according to which the true *dao* of the ancient sages was lost after Mencius and was only apprehended again by Zhou Dunyi and Cheng Hao, who were claimed as progenitors of this school. Proponents of Cheng-Zhu contended that philologically inclined Confucians of the Han dynasty (202 B.C.E.–220 C.E.) and the Tang dynasty (618–907) failed to understand the *dao* because they missed the profound meaning of the sages by ignoring the underlying principles (*yili*) in the classics, whereas other Confucians who were secretly Buddhists (*yangru yinshi*) corrupted the *dao* by promoting Buddhist doctrines within the ostensibly Confucian framework of moral self-cultivation.

One of the most important institutions promulgating state orthodoxy in Ming society was the civil examination system, based on mastery of the Four Books and the Five Classics. Although Cheng-Zhu commentaries on the canon were favored since the Yuan, it was not until the compilation of the *Great Collection on the Five Classics and Four Books* (*Wujing sishu daquan*) under the Yongle emperor in 1415 that there existed an authoritative version of the canon to prescribe the exact content of Cheng-Zhu orthodoxy. Equally important in shaping the thinking of the literati was the *Great Collection on Nature and Principle* (*Xingli daquan*), an anthology of writings by Song-Yuan Confucians on a wide variety of topics that appeared on the civil examinations. Both of these sizable anthologies relied heavily on Yuan scholarship: the former consisted largely of Song commentaries collected in the Yuan and the latter was based on topical arrangements of the thirteenth-century anthology *Master Zhu [Xi]'s Categorized Conversations* (*Zhuzi yulei*). Among the more important items in the curriculum that the *Great Collection on Nature and Principle* shares with *Master Zhu's Categorized Conversations* are nature and principle (*xingli*), learning (*xue*), recent commentaries on the Confucian canon, and sectarian judgments on the claims made by Confucians and non-Confucians on the transmission of the *dao* (*daotong*). As official prescriptions of the knowledge necessary to pass the civil examinations, these two anthologies effectively integrated Cheng-Zhu learning into the ideological pedagogy that produced the Confucian gentry.

The precise means by which Ming scholars were to be examined on the Cheng-Zhu interpretation of the Confucian tradition was announced by Ming Taizu in June 1370: Ming examinations were to "follow the precedent of the Tang and Song," except that "examination questions would be taken exclusively from the Four Books and Five Classics." The "literary style would basically copy the Song's meaning of the classics," but the "voices of the sages and worthies" (*shengxian yuqi*) would be used as the basis of an essay's position. According to Gu Yanwu (1613–1682), it was not until 1487 that examiners began to observe the exacting formal prescriptions known as the eight-legged essay (*bagu wen*). The eight legs comprise a preliminary statement of the essay topic (*poti*) and an elaboration of the general theme (*chengti*), in which the examinee writes in his own voice; then an opening statement (*qijiang*) and a four-part section (*qigu, zhonggu, hougu, shugu*) in which the examinee comments in detail on the canonical passage that provides the substance of the examination topic by speaking with the voices of the sages and worthies, usually in the form of parallel prose; and finally a general conclusion (*dajie*). The throne periodically prescribed the number of sentences (and at times the number of characters) for each section. Although this literary template inculcated a logical form of argumentation and reasoning among educated men, it did not engender an attitude of contestation toward the canon, nor, no doubt, was it intended to do so.

Civil examinations ensured that the writings of Zhu Xi would have an enduring and immediate relevance to Confucian thought of the Ming. This is evident in the pervasive concern over the implications for moral praxis of Zhu Xi's explanation of mind and nature. Although he enunciated more than one position, Zhu Xi was remembered by Ming Confucians for the view that human nature (*xing*) was identical to principle (*li*)—the underlying pattern of the "myriad things" that constituted the unchanging source of their essential goodness—whereas the human mind (*renxin*) was identified with material force (*qi*) and was prone to err (*weiwei*). The innate goodness of human nature existed, according to Zhu Xi, in its pure and still (*jing*) state prior to its activation (*weifa*); thus it was difficult to apprehend (*weiwei*). The moral efficacy of the human mind, contrariwise, was precarious; it was particularly susceptible to material desires because of its constant interaction with, and affective responses to, the changes of the external world. Therefore, it was critical to rectify the mind (*zhengxin*) through a process that began, according to Zhu Xi, with an exhaustive investigation of the principles in things (*qiongli gewu*), primarily the Confucian classics, where the words and deeds of the ancient sages were thoroughly recorded. By understanding the goodness of the sages and following their example, the fallible mind could gradually follow the dictates of the innately good nature.

Historians generally agree that the first generation of Confucians born after the Ming was founded tended not to stray too far from the teachings of the Song Dao School. Wu Yubi (1397–1469) is said to have quit his preparations for the examinations after reading Zhu Xi's anthology of biographies of the Yi-Luo masters (i.e., Zhou Dunyi, the Cheng brothers, and their disciples), and determined to apprehend the *dao*, living out his days working in the fields and studying with his students. He resisted repeated attempts by at least three emperors to recruit him into government service. Wu's disciple Hu Juren (1434–1484) expressed his sentiments toward Cheng Yi and Zhu Xi in his statement, "Cheng and Zhu opened the gate to the courtyard of the Sage's learning. Taking reverence as the master and exhaustively investigating principle teaches students wherein to enter." Yet even Hu Juren represented a partial shift toward an interiorization of moral effort by arguing that the work of self-cultivation begins and ends with preserving and nourishing inner goodness while in quietude (*hanyang*). Evidently modifying Zhu Xi's approach to cultivation, which was divided into stages, Hu did not regard preserving and nourishing as a discrete phase in a larger process of cultivation; they had to be maintained constantly throughout the entire process:

> Before one can know [anything by investigating things], one must first preserve and nourish, only then can this mind extend knowledge. . . . After the extension of knowledge one must preserve and nourish [goodness] so that it will not be lost. The work of extending knowledge is periodic, but the effort of preserving and nourishing does not cease.

At the same time Hu staunchly protected the demarcation between Confucianism and what he regarded as heterodoxy:

> What Confucians cultivate is the truth [*daoli*], Buddhists and Daoists merely cultivate a spirit. Confucians cultivate the authentic *qi* of the self, thus nothing separates them from Heaven and Earth. Buddhists and Daoists cultivate the selfish *qi* of the self, thereby abrogating Heaven and principle.

Hu Juren was also critical of Confucians whom he regarded as secretly Buddhistic, such as Chen Xianzhang (or Baisha, 1428–1500), also Wu Yubi's disciple. According to Hu Juren, Chen Xianzhang's statement that "things are limited, whereas we are limitless" (*wu you jin er wo wu jin*)—a position that confers great moral autonomy on the self and indicates a limited capacity of things to yield up principle—is the Buddhist doctrine of apprehending the nature. Hu's overly rigid assessment notwithstanding, Chen Xianzhang was one of the first Ming thinkers to overtly criticize Cheng-Zhu learning. After years of a painstaking search for the truth in books, Chen Xianzhang concluded that the quest for external principles was insufficient to enable him to acquire the sages' learning as his own; he could never make the sages' words his words. Chen devised a method of quiet sitting (*jingzuo*) in order to "seek what was essential within himself." He said: "In time I was able to see the substance of my own mind reveal itself mysteriously. . . . Henceforth, in the daily round of social intercourse, everything followed my heart's desires, just like a horse guided by bit and bridle." Chen's approach to self-cultivation emphasized the mind's moral autonomy, which rejected the reliance on external sources of moral knowledge in Cheng-Zhu thought.

In certain respects Chen Xianzhang's attention to the mind as the ultimate ground and source of goodness anticipates the teachings of Wang Yangming (1472–1529), but Chen shared with the Cheng-Zhu school the assumption that pure goodness could be apprehended only in its quiet state before it was expressed. First, one needed to understand the substance of mind; then one's actions would naturally follow the goodness that came from it. Even in his early years, when his thinking was influenced by Cheng-Zhu learning, Wang Yangming began to have doubts about Zhu Xi's assertion that "all things possess certain principles which must be investigated" (*gewu*). The grip of Cheng-Zhu orthodoxy on Wang Yangming's mind—as well as on the minds of most educated men in his day—is suggested by a realization that evidently came very painfully to Wang during his exile in remote Guizhou in 1508. Wang came to understand that principles were immanently moral and could not possibly exist independently of the mind. Any investigation of principles, therefore, necessarily begins and ends with the principles in the mind; this, Wang concluded, was what Mencius (6A.4) meant in his criticism of Gaozi's doctrine of human nature as external to righteousness. Wang would later conclude that in fact there are "no things, affairs, principles, righteousness, or goodness outside the mind." When a student suggested that an investigation of things limited to the principles in the mind ignores such fundamental Confucian truths as filial piety, loyalty, trust among friends, and humane rule, Wang replied that one serves one's parents not "after finding an external principle called filial piety" but because this principle is already innate in the goodness of the mind. Wang soon thereafter summed up his enlightenment in a teaching called the unity of knowledge and action (*zhixing heyi*). Authentic understanding of principle, Wang maintained, perforce means that one practices it. Thus, those who profess to understand filial piety but do not practice it do not in fact understand the principle; that someone does not act in accordance with filial piety demonstrates that he has yet to understand it. Although this formulation was one of the clearest refutations of the gradualist approach to cultivation that proceeds through several stages, which Wang attributed to Zhu Xi, it did not precisely identify the source of the mind's innate goodness and also lacked the canonical sanction necessary to convince others.

It was not until late in his life that Wang identified this innate goodness as *liangzhi* spoken of by Mencius (7A.15). Wang further redefined two key terms of moral praxis inherited from Zhu Xi's exegesis of the *Great Learning*: *gewu* as investigation of principles in things and *zhizhi* as the extension of knowledge. So critical were these terms to the formulation of Zhu Xi's concept of learning that he resorted to altering the text of the *Great Learning*; his version became the standard version in the Four Books. In 1518 Wang Yangming published his own commentary on the ancient version of this text (*Daxue guben pangzhu*) found in the pre-Song version of the *Book of Rites*, in which he contested Zhu's changes of the original text to support the contention that the ancients believed moral cultivation began with an externally directed investigation of principles. In his commentary, Wang says that the key sentence on the extension of knowledge means "the extension of the innate knowledge of the good [*liangzhi*] in our mind" and *gewu* means to "rectify external things" with these innate principles. These external things, Wang elaborates, are "the function of intentions" (or thoughts, *yi*), which are themselves "issued by the mind." In other words, the source of external things is the mind, which Wang believed is inherently moral. These things are rectified by the extension of the innately good principles that exist in the mind.

Like virtually all great thinkers, Wang was thoroughly rebuked by his adversaries, and his teachings were vigorously debated by his disciples. The most significant debate among his disciples concerned four cryptic sentences which Wang Yangming enunciated in October 1427 at Tianquan bridge in an attempt to summarize his teachings. One rendering of these four sentences is:

> There is neither good nor evil in the mind's original substance. They arise in the activity of our intentions [or thoughts]. Original good knowing [*liangzhi*] distinguishes between good and evil. *Gewu* [which Wang Yangming defines as the rectification of things constituted by the mind's thoughts] does the good and rejects evil.

This descriptive moral metaphysics is ambiguous, for it does not specify whether this constitutes a sequence of discrete efforts, or whether it should be construed as a singular, but phenomenologically complex, instance of moral practice. Although the logic of these sentences suggests a sequential process, such an interpretation conflicts with Wang Yangming's doctrine of the unity of knowledge and action.

Wang Ji (1498–1583) argued that this could not be Wang Yangming's final position, for the "mind, intentions, knowledge, and things are nothing but one thing," beyond the distinction between good and evil. This doctrine, referred to as the "four nothingnesses" (*siwu*), is based on a claim that if intentions (or thoughts), knowledge, and things are the production of the mind, which is beyond good and evil, then they too must be beyond good and evil, thereby obviating the need to first investigate, then do the good. Insisting on the necessity of moral practice, Qian Dehong (1497–1574) replied that the "mind's substance is the heaven-conferred nature which is originally without good or evil." Moral effort is required to recover this original nature because, as Wang Yangming clearly states, evil appears in habitual thoughts of the mind. When Wang Ji and Qian Dehong presented their doubts to Wang Yangming for comment, he merely replied that the two interpretations were mutually reinforcing, and that "Wang Ji needs to use Qian Dehong's moral practice and Qian Dehong needs to penetrate Wang Ji's ontology."

Okada Takehiko characterizes Wang Ji's position as an existential conviction that moral perfection is not a result of the accumulation of conscious effort but an instantaneous apprehension of the ultimate being of the mind within moral action. This leaning among Wang Yangming's followers, usually associated with the Taizhou school, was based on an abiding faith in the inherent goodness and authenticity of the spontaneous intentions of the human mind. The Taizhou thinker Luo Rufang (1515–1588) likened this inner goodness to a "vast expanse without a shoreline" where moral praxis was like "releasing the boat; wherever the wind carried it, there would be nothing but goodness." Central to Luo Rufang's teachings was the notion that "without study or any other cogitation," by following the goodness of one's infant heart (*chizi zhi xin*) conferred upon everyone at birth, one would "naturally become a sage without any effort."

Though not a member of the Taizhou school, Li Zhi (1527–1602) was one of the more militant advocates of the position that whatever emanated from the mind was in itself immediately correct (*dangxia bianshi*) because unpremeditated acts amounted to an expression of the substance of the mind's innate goodness. Li Zhi sought to recover an original state of consciousness called the "child's mind" (*tongxin*), unclouded by moral teachings, which he regarded as the only "authentic mind." He said that the child's mind can be lost because the "beginning is lost after sounds and sights," which "enter through the ears and eyes," become "master of what is within." He continued:

> Once people's minds have been given over to received opinions and moral principles, what they have to say is all about these things, and not what would naturally come from their childlike minds. . . . What else can there be but phony men speaking phony words, doing phony things, writing phony writings? . . . Everything is phony, and everyone is pleased.

Such talk did not please sanctimonious officials like Zhang Wenda (*jinshi* 1583) who, in 1602, censured Li Zhi for "deluding the human mind . . . regarding Confucius's judgments as an inadequate basis to determine right and wrong," for "cavorting with bad elements, . . . entering nunneries on the pretext of discussing the *dharma* to seduce wives of the literati," and for a host of other crimes. Afterward Li's writings were burned and he was thrown into prison, where he committed suicide.

Clearly, preservation of the doctrinal purity of the Confucian tradition was not Zhang Wenda's sole concern in his censure of Li Zhi, but it was a significant part. Confucian orthodoxy of late imperial China differs from western orthodoxy in that the latter's monotheism could tolerate no competitors, whereas Ming Confucianism was part of a vast nexus of Buddhist, Daoist, and popular religious teachings and temple cults, most of which enjoyed varying degrees of official endorsement. Receptive to the value of other teachings in promoting the kingly Way, Ming Taizu espoused a syncretic approach to the "three teachings" (i.e., Confucianism, Buddhism, and Daoism). The syncretism prevalent in the sixteenth and seventeenth centuries entailed an integration of doctrines from these three traditions within a single framework that redefined the original teachings and legitimated the newly formed doctrinal framework on the basis of authority derived from all three traditions. According to Judith Berling (1980), Taizu regarded Confucianism as "the Way of *yang*, or manifest virtue," to be "relied upon for countless generations" as the basis of governing the empire, whereas Buddhism and Daoism were "*yin*, or hidden virtue, and [were] secret aids of the kingly Way." Both were needed to compose the totality of the Way of heaven. Although non-Confucian teachings were not persecuted, there is little question that Confucianism occupied the pinnacle of this hierarchy, and that by Ming times, political power was reserved largely for educated men who held an examination degree certifying mastery of the Confucian canon.

In the latter half of the sixteenth century and the early seventeenth century, many Taizhou scholars proselytized Wang Yangming's teachings to the common folk in lectures on learning (*jiangxue*) open to the general public. Wang's teaching that everyone possessed an innate knowledge of the good and that the attainment of sagehood did not require years of formal education had particular appeal to those sectors of society typically denied a Confucian education, such as urban merchants and artisans. According to some contemporary reports, these lectures drew large audiences—as large as a thousand people, including both literati and commoners. The lectures tended to focus on basic Confucian pedagogy—filial piety, family relations, and other civic duties—rather than explication of esoteric doctrinal disputes, though there were exceptions. More orthodox gentry were uneasy about these meetings because Taizhou lecturers tended to syncretically fuse Confucianism with Buddhism, Daoism, and popular beliefs—though this was an important factor in the popular success of the lectures. Some prominent Taizhou lecturers such as He Xinyin (1517–1579), moreover, were particularly adept at inciting audiences to act on righting social ills.

Another group that gained entrance to Confucian culture was women of literati families. In increasing numbers in the sixteenth century, these women received formal educations and were prolific composers and readers of poetry. Some Confucian thinkers, like Lü Kun (1536–1618), who was not a proponent of Wang Yangming, addressed themselves increasingly to women. Lü Kun wrote books on female virtue in the vernacular, one of which so pleased the emperor's consort that she wrote a preface for it and had it reprinted. It scandalized the court with its allegations of cliques, and Lü was urged to retire from his post in the capital earlier than originally planned. Popular conflation of the three teachings and other social changes, Kai-wing Chow (1994) points out, were important factors in the rise of a purist response in the early seventeenth century, a response that placed great emphasis on what were regarded as fundamental Confucian values, particularly as embodied in ritual.

One legacy of sectarian Confucian historiography is a tendency to locate the origins of Wang Yangming's learning in the teachings of Lu Xiangshan. Theodore de Bary (1970) observes that Wang was educated in Cheng-Zhu learning and that his concerns and doubts "arose naturally from an earnest commitment to the achievement of sagehood following Zhu Xi's method." Wang Yangming's formulation of the unity of knowledge and action and the extension of the mind's innate good knowledge was the result of a lifelong testing of the received wisdom of Cheng-Zhu learning, rather than a conscious effort to revive Lu Xiangshan's critique of Zhu Xi's allegedly fractured approach to cultivation. It is not entirely clear whether Wang read Lu's original writings before his precocious break with Zhu Xi. But his early training in the curriculum of nature and principle as defined in the imperial anthology the *Great Collection on Nature and Principle*—of which Zhu Xi's repudiation of Lu's teachings forms a significant part—must have made it difficult to sympathize with Lu's views. Around 1518, the year he finished his commentary on the ancient edition of the *Great Learning*, Wang put forth the argument that late in life Zhu Xi regretted his inadequate attention to inner cultivation in his early teachings, and that in the end Zhu Xi embraced Lu Xiangshan's views on cultivation. This version of Zhu Xi's intellectual biography was steadfastly rejected by Wang's contemporary Luo Qinshun, and repeatedly attacked by such stalwarts of Cheng-Zhu learning as Chen Jian (1497–1567), who argued that although Zhu Xi's early position brought him close to Lu Xiangshan, in his later years, Zhu repudiated Lu's learning as Buddhistic. Wang's contention that Zhu's final position was similar to Lu's became the basis of an agenda of mediation that shaped the attempts of Wang Yangming's proponents to establish their own doctrinal and sectarian legitimacy. This view of the convergence of Zhu's and Lu's thought was enunciated earlier by Cheng Minzheng (1445–c. 1499) in his anthology *The Way Is One* (*Daoyi pian*, 1490), but *Transmission of the Lineage of the Sage's Learning* (*Shengxue zongchuan*) by Zhou Rudeng (1547–c. 1629), completed in 1606, was one of the earliest attempts to write a history of the Confucian tradition based on Wang Yangming's claim that the doctrine of *liangzhi* represents "drops of blood and marrow transmitted from the ancient sages." Zhou Rudeng represents Zhu Xi and most other Confucians as enunciating a conception like Wang Yangming's of innate knowledge of the good. Within a few years, another anthology, *Orthodox Lineage of Dao Learning* (*Daoxue zhengzong*), was compiled, explicitly refuting Zhou's account of the Confucian tradition and separating Zhu Xi and the masters of the Dao School as the "orthodox lineage" (*zhengzong*) from thinkers like Wang Yangming, whose learning, according to this book's editors, was "mixed with heterodox Buddhism and Daoism."

Not all Ming proponents of Dao Learning were uncritical of their Song doctrinal ancestors, particularly beginning in the mid-Ming. One of the most significant philosophical trends within Dao Learning was a critique of Zhu Xi's account of the relationship between *li* (principle) and *qi* (material force). Zhu Xi describes *li* as the universal originating principle of the cosmos; it produces the material force that animates all things and is the means by which all things are what they are. Though never mixed with *qi*, principle never departs from it. Luo Qinshun, however, questioned whether *li* was in any sense prior to *qi*: "*Li* is simply the *li* of *qi*," Luo said. "It must be observed at the turning point of *qi* in its comings and goings. When [*qi*] goes, [*li*] cannot but go too; when it comes, so too must [*li*], and it is so regardless of whether we know it." Wang Tingxiang (1474–1544), a monistic thinker of the Dao School who sought to revive Zhang Zai's doctrine of primal *qi* (*yuanqi*), said that "principle is carried in material force. Confucians have said that principle can produce material force, but this is Laozi's teaching that the Dao produces Heaven and Earth." According to Wang Tingxiang, "Heaven and Earth, fire and water, and all things are productions of the movement of the primal material forces" *yin* and *yang*. *Li*, rather, is merely the orderly pattern (*tiaoli*) of the constant movement of *qi*. If *li* is not an eternal source of the "myriad things," then, Wang concludes, there is no singular, unchanging principle underlying human morality—a claim that had long been the authority for the Dao School's indictments of other competing Confucian doctrines for diverging from this eternal truth.

Sectarian disputes between thinkers who associated themselves with Cheng-Zhu or Wang Yangming often dominated Ming thought, but not all Ming schools were affiliated with either. A leader of the Donglin Academy, Gao Panlong (1562–1626), compiled several anthologies of Cheng-Zhu writings to promote a return to these Song teachings as an antidote to the excesses of Wang Yangming's teaching of innate knowledge of the good. Yet the founder of the Donglin Academy, Gu Xiancheng (1550–1612), recognized Lu Xiangshan as an authentic Confucian: "Master Zhu [Xi]'s words are Confucius's method of teaching; Master Lu [Xiangshan]'s words are Mencius's method of teaching." Gu criticized, however, the reckless confidence in Wang's contention that "there was neither good nor evil in the mind's substance," among Taizhou thinkers.

In his *Lineages of the Confucians* (*Rulin zongpai*), Wan Sitong (1638–1702) traces another significant master-disciple lineage through Zhan Ruoshui (1466–1560), Tang Shu (1497–1574), Xu Fuyuan (1530–1604), Feng Congwu (1556–c. 1627), Liu Zongzhou (1576–1645), and Huang Zongxi (1610–1695), Wan Sitong's mentor. Zhan Ruoshui was a close friend of Wang Yangming's who disagreed with Wang's conception of the investigation of things but whose teachings show signs of dialogue with Yangming over the innate goodness of the mind. To construe *gewu* as the rectification of thoughts, Zhan argued, was to confuse it with another critical phase delineated in the *Great Learning*: making the thoughts sincere (*chengyi*). According to Zhan Ruoshui, *gewu* referred to a personal encounter with heavenly principle that inhered in the "myriad things" from the mind, thoughts, and self to the family, state, and all under heaven. The continuum implicit in Zhan Ruoshui's teaching of "experiential realization of Heavenly principles wherever they are encountered" (*suichu tiren tianli*) bridges the chasm between an excessive reliance on the mind's presumed moral autonomy and the tendency to give priority to the acquisition of knowledge through learning over moral effort.

One recurring theme in the writings of Xu Fuyuan and Liu Zongzhou was an abiding disaffection for Wang Ji's doctrine of the four nothingnesses and a refocusing on the basics of moral practice, although they shared with Wang Yangming a conception of learning based on the authenticity of the mind's innate capacity to recognize the good. In a famous lecture called "Nine Queries" (*Jiudi*) on the Tianquan bridge dialogue of 1592, Xu Fuyuan scrutinized Wang Ji's doctrine of the four nothingnesses, saying that Wang Yangming's

> basic aim in learning was originally no different from that of the sages, thus he said the nature was nothing but the good. . . . His position is very clear. The expression "the mind's essence is without good or evil" refers to the unrestricted stillness of its pre-affective state [*weifa*]. . . . Those today who can describe the mind, intentions, knowledge, and things as lacking good and evil, are not [Wang Yangming's] true heirs.

Goodness (*shan*), Xu argued, has canonical sanction going back to the *Book of Change*, whereas the source of the doctrine of beyond good and evil is Gaozi, who was rebuked by Mencius (6A.1–4). Xu objected that Wang Ji advocated a sudden approach to apprehending goodness which lacked the necessary foundation for achieving moral perfection, conflicting with Confucius's dictum "Achieve greatness from fundamental learning" (*Analects*, 14.37).

In a retort titled "Nine Explanations" (*Jiujie*), Wang Ji's disciple Zhou Rudeng dismissed Xu's attribution of the four nothingnesses to Gaozi and maintained that Wang Ji was pointing to a realm of absolute good (*zhishan*), wherein, the *Great Learning* teaches, the ancient sages sought to abide. This absolute realm is not Gaozi's morally neutral human nature, but a goodness beyond the possibility of evil's ever arising; a goodness that cannot be understood in the contingent sense of a good that is opposed to evil.

In response to what he believed was an excessive faith among some of Wang Yangming's disciples in the untutored child's mind, Liu Zongzhou questioned the implication of the four-sentence formula that intentions or thoughts (*yi*) constitute the active function of the mind's substance. Wang Yangming said that "there is neither good nor evil in the mind's substance, they arise in the activity of our thoughts." Liu argued that the so-called thoughts (*yi*) spoken of in the *Great Learning* should be understood as the moral will that is the mind's master (*zhuzai*) and underlying substance. For Liu Zongzhou, the will to despise evil did not occur simply when the mind encountered a singular instance of evil; rather, as Chen Lai explains it, the will acts as a moral compass and amounts to an innate propensity to do what is right. Thus the principal task in Liu Zongzhou's conception of moral effort was making the will sincere (*chengyi*), one of the eight steps of cultivation outlined in the *Great Learning*. Unlike Zhu Xi and Wang Yangming, Liu maintained that as the innate master of the mind, the will could not be understood merely as the mind's affective response (*yifa*) to things, but also had an ontological status prior to the mind's activation (*weifa*). As something that could not be divided into two realms of pre- and post-activation, the will could be apprehended in a state that encompassed both, by being "watchful while in solitude" (*shendu*).

The correlation in Ming times among a Confucian education, high social status, and political power was unprecedented in Chinese history. This prestige did not always come at the cost of intellectual independence, though the adherence to Cheng-Zhu orthodoxy expected by the court's ideological apparatus created tension in Confucian thought throughout the dynasty. A dominant tendency of Ming Confucianism was a purist reading of the Confucian canon based largely on Zhu Xi's interpretation as represented in the Yongle imperial anthologies. Ming Confucianism also accommodated a syncretic inclination that, while not rewarded by the throne with high government appointments, undoubtedly enjoyed widespread support among literati outside officialdom and the gentry outside their official capacity.

The final years of the dynasty ended much as it began: the eunuch Wei Zhongxian (1568–1627) virtually ruled the empire—shrines honoring him were constructed throughout the realm—and terrorized his political opponents. His most eloquent critics died either by being executed as Huang Zunsu (1584–1626) was or by committing suicide like Gao Panlong—Huang and Gao were both prominent members of the Donglin Academy. Yet Ming Confucians remained ambivalent toward their autocratic lord to the bitter end. In an expression of profound loyalty to the emperor after the Manchus captured the last Ming emperor, Liu Zongzhou, a close friend to the martyred Donglin scholars, took his own life by starving himself to death.

See also Cheng Yi; Confucianism: Tradition; Huang Zongxi; Lu Xiangshan; Luo Qinshun; Wang Yangming; Wang Yangming: Rivals and Followers; Zhan Ruoshui; *Zhixing Heyi*; Zhu Xi.

Bibliography

Berling, Judith A. *The Syncretic Religion of Lin Chao-en*. New York: Columbia University Press, 1980.

Bloom, Irene. "On the 'Abstraction' of Ming Thought: Some Concrete Evidence from the Philosophy of Lo Ch'in-shun." In *Principle and Practicality*, ed. William Theodore de Bary and Irene Bloom. New York: Columbia University Press, 1979, pp. 69–125.

Chan, Wing-tsit. "The Ch'eng-Chu School of Early Ming." In *Self and Society in Ming Thought*, ed. William Theodore de Bary. New York: Columbia University Press, 1970, pp. 29–51.

Chen, Lai. *Song-Ming lixue* (Song-Ming Learning of Principle). Shenyang: Liaoning jiaoyu, 1991.

Ch'ien, Edward T. *Chiao Hung and the Restructuring of Neo-Confucianism in the Late Ming*. New York: Columbia University Press, 1986.

Chow, Kai-wing. *The Rise of Confucian Ritualism in Late Imperial China: Ethics, Classics, and Lineage Discourse*. Stanford, Calif.: Stanford University Press, 1994.

Cua, Antonio S. *The Unity of Knowledge and Action: A Study in Wang Yang-ming's Moral Psychology*. Honolulu: University of Hawaii Press, 1982.

Dardess, John W. *Confucianism and Autocracy: Professional Elites in the Founding of the Ming Dynasty*. Berkeley: University of California Press, 1983.

de Bary, William Theodore. "Individualism and Humanitarianism in Late Ming Thought." In *Self and Society in Ming*

Thought, ed. William Theodore de Bary. New York: Columbia University Press, 1970, pp. 145–247.

———. *The Message of the Mind in Neo-Confucianism*. New York: Columbia University Press, 1989.

———. *Neo-Confucian Orthodoxy and the Learning of the Mind-and-Heart*. New York: Columbia University Press, 1981.

Dimberg, Ronald G. *The Sage and Society: The Life and Thought of Ho Hsin-yin*. Honolulu: University of Hawaii Press, 1974.

Elman, Benjamin A. "Philosophy (*I-Li*) versus Philology (*K'ao-cheng*): The *Jen-hsin Tao-hsin* Debate." *T'oung Pao: Revue internationale de Sinologie*, 69(4–5), 1983, pp. 175–222.

———. "Political, Social, and Cultural Reproduction via Civil Service Examinations in Late Imperial China." *Journal of Asian Studies*, 50 (1), 1991, pp. 7–28.

———. "Where Is King Ch'eng? Civil Examinations and Confucian Ideology during the Early Ming, 1368–1415." *T'oung Pao: Revue internationale de Sinologie*, 79, 1994, pp. 23–68.

Gu, Qingmei. *Mingdai lixue lunwen ji* (Collected Essays on Ming Schools of Principle). Taipei: Da'an, 1990.

Handlin, Joanna. "Lü K'un's New Audience: The Influence of Women's Literacy on Sixteenth-Century Thought." In *Women in Chinese Society*, ed. Margery Wolf and Roxane Witke. Stanford, Calif.: Stanford University Press, 1975, pp. 13–38.

Hou, Wailu, et al. *Zhongguo sixiang tongshi* (Comprehensive History of Chinese Thought), Vol. 4, pt. 2. Beijing: Renmin, 1960.

Huang, Gongwei. *Song-Ming-Qing lixue tixi lun shi* (Historical Discussion of the Systems of the Schools of Principle in the Song, Ming, and Qing). Taipei: Youshi wenhua shiye, 1971.

Huang, Tsung-hsi (Huang Zongxi). *Mingru xue'an* (Cases of Ming Confucianism), ed. Shen Zhiying, 2 vols. Beijing: Zhonghua, 1985.

——— *The Records of the Ming Scholars*, ed. and trans. Julia Ching and Fang Chao-ying. Hawaii: University of Hawaii Press, 1987.

Hucker, Charles O. *The Ming Dynasty: Its Origins and Evolving Institutions*. Ann Arbor, Mich.: Center for Chinese Studies, 1978.

Ko, Dorothy. *Teachers of the Inner Chambers: Women and Culture in Seventeenth-Century China*. Stanford, Calif.: Stanford University Press, 1995.

Liu, Shuxian (Lin Shu-hsien). *Huang Zongxi xinxue de dingwei*. Taipei: Yunchen wenhua, 1986.

Mai, Zhonggui. *Wangmen zhuzi zhi liangzhi xue zhi fazhan* (Development of the Extension of the Innate Knowledge of the Good among Wang School Masters). Hong Kong: Chinese University of Hong Kong Press, 1973.

Okada, Takehiko. "Wang Chi and the Rise of Existentialism." In *Self and Society in Ming Thought*, ed. William Theodore de Bary. New York: Columbia University Press, 1970, pp. 121–144.

Rong, Zhaozu. *Mingdai sixiang shi* (History of Ming Thought). Taipei: Kaiming, 1962.

Tang, Junyi. *Zhongguo zhexue yuanlun: Yuanjiao pian* (Origins of Chinese Philosophy: On the Origins of Teaching). Taipei: Xuesheng, 1979.

Taylor, Rodney L. *The Cultivation of Sagehood as a Religious Goal in Neo-Confucianism: A Study of Selected Writings of Kao P'an-lung*. Missoula, Mont.: American Academy of Religion, 1978.

Wang, Daocheng. *Keju shihua* (Historical Discussions on the Civil Service Examinations). Beijing: Zhonghua, 1988.

Wilson, Thomas A. *Genealogy of the Way: The Construction and Uses of the Confucian Tradition in Late Imperial China*. Stanford, Calif.: Stanford University Press, 1995.

Confucianism: Qing (Ch'ing)

Ying-shih Yü

I

The best way to characterize Qing Confucianism—that is, Confucianism during the Qing dynasty—is to contrast it with what is called Song-Ming neo-Confucianism. Song-Ming neo-Confucians were primarily moral philosophers debating endlessly among themselves on metaphysical questions such as whether "moral principles" (*li*) are inherent in "human nature" (*xing*) or in "human mind" (*xin*). As a result, the Song-Ming period witnessed the emergence and development of a rivalry between two major philosophical systems represented, respectively, by the Cheng-Zhu and the Lu-Wang schools. By contrast, Qing Confucians were, first and foremost, scholars devoting themselves to painstaking philological explication of classical and historical texts. They took great pride in having reestablished the Confucian canon on the foundations of critical scholarship, aided by the newly sharpened tools of philology. This is precisely why "classical scholarship" (*jingxue*) has generally been identified by modern intellectual historians as the quintessence of Qing Confucianism, as opposed to the metaphysical speculation of Song-Ming neo-Confucianism.

This contrast makes it clear that whereas Song-Ming neo-Confucians and Qing Confucians studied the same body of sacred texts, they were guided by two entirely different paradigms. Therefore, it can be safely assumed that a paradigm shift must have taken place during the intellectual transition from the Ming to the Qing. An inquiry into why and how this epochal shift occurred will provide us with a convenient way to trace the origins of Qing Confucianism.

To begin with, the whole process of intellectual change that eventually led to the establishment of textual scholarship as the central task of Confucianism in the Qing period was initially triggered and propelled by forces generated from within the neo-Confucian philosophical development of the sixteenth century. Two striking examples may be cited from the two opposing sides of neo-Confucianism.

First, in 1518 Wang Yangming made a great effort to restore what he called the "old text" of the *Great Learning* with the explicit purpose of challenging the textual authority established by Zhu Xi in the twelfth century. Zhu had made some subtle rearrangements and emendations of the *Great Learning* in order to support his philosophical position, later accepted as the standard text. Wang Yangming needed the same text to support his philosophical views, which were the opposite of Zhu Xi's, and it was this need that impelled him into textual research. This is shown clearly in Wang's most important philosophical synopsis, *Inquiry on the Great Learning*, which is based wholly on his text of 1518.

Our second example is Luo Qinshun (1465–1547), a leading philosopher of the Cheng-Zhu school and a revered critic of Wang Yangming. Luo's philosophical debate with Wang over the years also contributed much to the rise of textual scholarship. In 1515 Wang made a selection of passages from several dozen of Zhu Xi's letters, which he published three years later under the title *Zhu Xi's Final Conclusions Arrived at Late in Life*. The purpose of this exercise, according to his preface, was to show that Zhu Xi in his later years had abandoned his earlier mistaken views and arrived at conclusions similar to those Wang now held. This work drew harsh criticism from Luo, who pointed out—rightly, as it seems—that many of the passages were from letters which could be easily dated from Zhu Xi's early years. In his reply Wang conceded that he had indeed failed to pay sufficient attention to the problem of dating. This exchange between Luo and Wang further testifies to the ever-growing importance of textual criticism in neo-Confucian controversies of the late Ming. What is even more significant is Luo's novel methodological suggestion regarding how the incessant metaphysical dispute in neo-Confucianism could ultimately be settled. Defending Zhu Xi's theory "the nature is principle" (*xing ji li*) against Wang's theory "the mind is principle" (*xin ji li*), Luo quoted extensively from a variety of classical texts in support of his case. He argued in conclusion, "If one carries on his studies without seeking evidence in the classics and is utterly arbitrary and opinionated it is inevitable that he will be misled. It is wrong to allow oneself to be misled, worse yet to mislead others." Here, the very notion of "seeking evidence in the classics" turned out to be prophetic with regard to where Confucianism was heading, for "evidential investigation" (*kaozheng*) constituted the central methodological principle of Qing classical scholarship.

To be sure, neither Wang nor Luo can be called a textual scholar. Nevertheless, by getting involved in textual entanglements—even to this limited degree, and rather unwittingly—both philosophers set an example for others to follow. As a result, the two rival neo-Confucian schools, Cheng-Zhu and Lu-Wang, moved their battlefield increasingly rapidly from philosophy to philology.

By consensus, Gu Yanwu (1613–1682) was the founding father of Qing classical scholarship; the new paradigm of research he established practically dominated the world of learning throughout the Qing period. It is also commonly held that he, more than anyone else, was responsible for turning Confucian scholars away from metaphysical speculation and opening up a field of classical study based on textual evidence. However, Gu by no means broke completely with neo-Confucianism. Contrary to a view that was established since Liang Qichao (1873–1929), Gu did not dismiss Song-Ming neo-Confucianism summarily or attack it indiscriminately. Of the two major neo-Confucian schools, he was clearly partial to Zhu Xi's tradition, and his sharp criticisms were all directed against Wang Yangming and Wang's followers. This is shown especially in Gu's enthusiastic endorsement of Luo Qinshun when Luo debated with Wang Yangming on the question of Zhu Xi's "final conclusions." Moreover, Gu's famous and influential statement that "the proper study of moral principles consists primarily in the study of the classics" can be read as his answer to Luo's clarion call "to seek evidence in the classics." It is true that Gu departed from the Ming neo-Confucian tradition by shunning metaphysics altogether. However, Gu also emphasized that the ultimate purpose of his advocacy of textual research on the classics was to bring the Confucian Way to light (*mingdao*), and in this respect he was carrying on the sacred mission of his neo-Confucian predecessors, though on an entirely different path.

This account suggests two closely related points of considerable historical importance regarding the transition from Ming neo-Confucianism to Qing Confucianism. First, the inner logic of neo-Confucian development—as exemplified, especially, in its endless metaphysical controversies—pushed itself to a point where reexamination of the original texts became absolutely necessary. This was true because neo-Confucian thinkers of all persuasions had to validate their claims to knowledge of the Confucian Way by citing the authority of these texts. Thus they initiated a movement which may be most appropriately described as "return to the sources"—and which took the Qing Confucian scholars more than a century to bring to completion.

Second, at the methodological level the intellectual transition from Ming to Qing can indeed be defined in terms of a shift from the philosophical to the philological approach. In this sense the transition may be viewed as more characteristically discontinuous than continuous. However, the discontinuity involved here is also a matter of degree. The philological turn had already begun with some of the philosophical followers of Wang Yangming in the late Ming, notably Jiao Hong (1540–1620), who, remarkably, opened up several areas of textual research that would be fully developed later, by early Qing scholars.

In view of these two closely related points, it would make little sense to take the beginning of Qing Confucianism as a sudden, negative reaction to Ming neo-Confucianism, as received wisdom suggests. Rather, it was not only largely continuous with but also necessitated by the internal development of Ming neo-Confucianism.

This continuity is nowhere more clearly shown than in the textual criticism developed in the early Qing. Two outstanding examples may be given. First, in 1654 Chen Que (1604–1677) wrote a famous essay on the text of the *Great Learning* that immediately created a stir in the academic community. Through textual analysis and terminological comparisons with other ancient sources, he came to the conclusion that the *Great Learning* is a document of much later date and therefore must be rejected as a sacred text directly linked to the teaching of Confucius. In Chen's view, Wang Yangming could have saved himself the trouble of restoring the "ancient text" had he known that the authenticity of the *Great Learning* as a Confucian text was questionable. But as a follower of Wang Yangming, Chen admitted that the main point he was making in this textual study was philosophical, intended to demolish the textual basis of Zhu Xi's theory about the relationship between "knowing" and "acting."

Second, from the 1670s on Yan Roju (1636–1704) became engaged in a long-term research project on the sixteen chapters in ancient script of the *Book of History*, whose authenticity had been suspect since the time of Zhu Xi. In the end, Yan was able to prove once and for all that they were indeed forgeries of the fourth century C.E. But significantly, in this purely philological study Yan made every effort to place himself squarely in the Zhu Xi tradition of neo-Confucianism. He not only specifically acknowledged his indebtedness to Zhu Xi for having led him to this project but also, and more importantly, professed to cling to Zhu's general intellectual position that Confucian moral principles must be grounded in a deep understanding of classical texts. Strikingly—and oddly—in this book Yan interspersed his textual analysis with harsh attacks on Lu Xiangshan and Wang Yangming. When Mao Qiling (1623–1716) read an early draft of Yan's study he was so furious that he immediately set out to write a refutation, also on evidential grounds. As a follower of Wang Yangming, Mao was keenly aware that Yan's work had negative philosophical implications for the Lu-Wang school as a whole, since one of the forged chapters contained a passage about "the mind of man versus the mind of *dao*" which he took to be a textual basis more crucial to the school of mind (*xinxue*) of his own day. From his letters to Yan it is clear that Mao's defense of the chapters in ancient script was actually a defense of his own philosophical position.

II

With the full flowering of classical studies in the second half of the eighteenth century, Qing Confucianism reached its peak. By this time various philological tools including, especially, etymology, phonology, paleography, and collation had been developed nearly to technical perfection. By applying these new techniques to the study of classical and historical texts in a systematic and sustained manner, mainstream Confucians in the mid-Qing period radically changed our understanding of the Confucian canon. In fact, Confucians in the mid-Qing were very much excited about their unique contribution the Confucian tradition and took great pride in it. Justifiably or not, they consistently believed that philology, not metaphysical speculation, could unlock the door to the classical world of ancient sages. This general sense of excitement and pride is expressed in a powerful statement made in 1765 by Dai Zhen (1724–1777):

> Alas, if the so-called moral principles of the sages can be obtained by sheer speculation apart from the Classics, then anyone is able to grasp them out of emptiness. If that is the case, what do we need classical scholarship for? It is

> precisely because free speculation cannot lead one to a proper understanding of the moral principles of the ancient sages that one has to seek it from the ancient Classics. Since messages contained in the surviving records have gradually fallen into oblivion due to the expanse of time between the past and the present, one therefore has to seek them through philological studies of the classical texts. Thus only if philology is clear, can the ancient Classics be understood; and only if the Classics are understood, can then the sages' moral principles be grasped.

This statement is an elaboration of Gu Yanwu's original proposal that "the proper study of moral principles consists primarily in the study of the classics." It makes Gu's deep distrust of metaphysical speculation more explicit and argues more cogently for the central importance of philology in classical scholarship. However, it may be noted that when Gu first changed the paradigm a century earlier, he had merely indicated in general terms, without going much further, that "the right way of reading the classics must begin with a thorough investigation of the language in which they are expressed." This difference between Gu and Dai testifies to the enormous growth of classical scholarship during the century that separated them. On the foundation of this accumulative scholarship Dai was able to give philological methodology a clear, precise formulation.

Qing Confucianism assumed its most distinctive shape during the Qianlong's reign (1736–1795), as the learned world in Qing China entered its most creative period. We must now consider that distinctive shape in its own terms with a view to determining more precisely the nature and place of Qing Confucianism in the history of Chinese thought.

To begin with, it is important to know how Qing Confucianism was perceived by its advocates. In this connection, Gong Zizhen (1792–1841) made a keen observation. Gong's credentials are impressive: he was personally trained in all kinds of classical philology by his maternal grandfather, Duan Yucai (1735–1815), the leading disciple of Dai Zhen, and later became a founder of the "new text" school. Thus what he had to say about Qing Confucianism deserves our serious attention. In 1817 he reflected on the state of Confucian learning in his day as follows:

> The Confucian Way consists of two main strands, namely, "honoring the moral nature" (*zundexing*) and "following the path of inquiry and study" (*daowenxue*). In its original conception these two strands are supposed not to contradict but rather lend support to each other. However, in actual practice it turns out that each of the two approaches to the Way tends to dominate the learned world in a given period. The expected harmonious unity between the two has never been realized. As a result the majority of Confucian scholars merely follow whichever approach happens to be dominant in their own times. With the founding of our dynasty the scope of Confucian studies has been enormously broadened. However, ours is an age dominated by the mode of intellectual inquiry. Thus since the beginning of the Qianlong era (1736–1795) "inquiry and study" has been established as the standard requirement which a Confucian must meet by definition.

Before we can explore the full implications of this important statement, some clarification is in order. The two key terms, *zundexing* and *daowenxue*, are taken from the *Doctrine of the Mean* and refer, respectively, to moral cultivation and intellectual inquiry. Generally speaking, in the neo-Confucian context both approaches are considered relevant to man's quest for *dao*. The moral approach consists primarily in awakening moral faith through meditation and metaphysical speculation. By contrast, the intellectual approach implies that every advance in our knowledge of the world brings us a step closer to the total understanding of *dao*, and only by "inquiry and study" can knowledge—whether knowledge of a classical text or of "a blade of grass"—be acquired. It was precisely the difference in emphasis of these two approaches that philosophically divided the Cheng-Zhu school and the Lu-Wang school. By and large the former took both as equally important for the attainment of *dao* whereas the latter gave the moral approach a central role and relegated intellectual inquiry to a place of insignificance.

When Gong used these two terms, he generally followed this neo-Confucian distinction between the moral approach and the intellectual approach. However, in suggesting that Qing Confucianism was dominated by "intellectual inquiry" he had in mind, specifically, the prevailing mode of classical scholarship of his own time. By the mid-eighteenth century at the latest there was a consensus among mainstream Confucian scholars that the original philosophical messages of ancient sages had been grossly misinterpreted by Song-Ming neo-Confucian thinkers who, under the influence of Buddhism, had relied too heavily on metaphysical speculation. The only reliable method to recapture the original meanings of ancient Confucianism, they insisted, was to subject every classical text to a most rigorous and critical examination based on the newly developed philology. What Gong meant by "intellectual inquiry" (*daowenxue*) in the passage above must be understood in this light.

We are now in a position to evaluate in more general terms the unique contribution of Qing Confucianism in the history of Chinese thought. In sharp contrast to the neo-Confucian metaphysical speculation on "moral nature" from Song to Ming, Confucianism in the Qing period took a decidedly intellectual turn. As a result, the study of the classics was fully justified as a Confucian calling. It has been widely held that since Qing Confucianism was concerned wholly with textual scholarship, it entailed little or no philosophical thinking by its practitioners. This view may well have been applicable to many individual classicists of the mid-Qing who carried on normal research within the philological paradigm. However, it fails to address Confucian intellectualism as a sustained learned movement throughout the Qing period that, viewed holistically, does reveal a central philosophical vision radically different from Song-Ming neo-Confucianism. This new vision is nowhere more clearly shown than in the redefinitions of Confucian tradition by Dai Zhen and Zhang Xuecheng (1739–1801), the two leading philosophical spokesmen of eighteenth-century China.

In his early years Dai was, philosophically, a close follower of Zhu Xi. As is shown in his essay of 1759 on moral cultivation versus intellectual inquiry, he defended Zhu Xi's pedagogical emphasis on intellectual inquiry and criticized the Lu-Wang school for giving exclusive attention to moral cultivation. With regard to the relative importance of "principle" (*li*) and "mind" (*xin*) in Confucian philosophy, he give *li* a more basic status. With the intellectual component in the Cheng-Zhu tradition as his starting point, he later developed a philosophy, uniquely characteristic of his own age, in which Confucian intellectualism reigned supreme. Here one or two examples will suffice.

First, Dai's final, definitive view of how moral nature stands in relation to intellectual inquiry and study merits attention. In his later philosophical writings he moved beyond the moral-intellectual duality of the Cheng-Zhu tradition and came to a position that may be described as intellectual monism. Consequently, he seriously questioned the distinction between moral knowledge and intellectual knowledge, a distinction central to all neo-Confucianists irrespective of sectarian differences. In this regard his analogy between man's physical body and his moral nature is highly illuminating. As he argues:

> Physical body begins with infancy and ends up with adulthood. So in the same manner man's moral nature begins with unenlightened ignorance and ends up with sagely intelligence. Physical body grows only because it feeds on the nutrition from drinking and eating. Similarly, moral nature also feeds itself on learning and inquiry in order to develop into sagely intelligence.

In this formulation moral nature is practically redefined as if it were an epiphenomenon of intellectual inquiry.

Second, Dai also took over the key concept of *li* (principles) from Zhu Xi and, again, intellectualized it to serve his own philosophical purposes. He rejected the orthodox neo-Confucian conception of *li* as a completely self-sufficient metaphysical entity that "man acquires from Heaven and holds in mind." Instead, on the basis of etymological evidence, he redefined *li* in terms of "internal texture of things." It follows that the only way to discover such "principles" is through intellectual inquiry. In Dai's words, "with regard to principles of things, they can be established only after things in question are analytically studied with utmost thoroughness." Thus Dai transformed *li* from a neo-Confucian idea of a priori moral principles, transcending and yet giving shape and meaning to things, to something like "laws" or "patterns" that are inherent in things and thereby constitute the very object of human knowledge. It may be further noted, however, that what Dai did to the concept of *li*, mutatis mutandis, applies to the idea of *dao* as well. He also refused to see *dao* as a metaphysical entity. Instead he took *dao* to be the way or ways in which the world—natural and human—ceaselessly evolves. How one seeks to understand *dao*, according to Dai, is also how one obtains knowledge about *li*, the "principles" of things. Hence his famous remark "The *dao* to be reached above is the *dao* to be learned below," which implies that *dao* can be known only by going through the normal intellectual process even though a higher level of synthesis and abstraction is involved.

There can be little doubt that the philosophical system Dai completed toward the end of his life is a radically intellectualistic one. To the extent that it identifies "intellect" as the most distinguishing characteristic of human nature and elevates "knowledge" to a pivotal position in Confucian learning, his philosophy marks the beginning of a new phase in the history of Confucianism. For the first time the centuries-old absolute presupposition that man's innate moral sense is the foundation of all intellectual creativities was seriously questioned. It is true that Dai still subscribed to the Mencian view of the moral seed in every human heart. Nevertheless, he argued forcefully that the moral seed will not grow to fruition unless and until it is planted in fertile intellectual soil. It is no exaggeration to say that Dai regarded morality as a product of knowledge.

Dai Zhen began his intellectualism from within the Cheng-Zhu tradition, but in the end he went far beyond the prescribed limits of that tradition. By contrast, Zhang Xuecheng came from the Lu-Wang background and made every effort to intellectualize its moralistic system. Highly sensitive to a rapidly changing climate of opinion in the eighteenth century, he embraced most of the intellectualistic assumptions of contemporary Confucian classicists. Like the majority of Qing Confucians, he believed that only original scholarship, not speculation, could lead to a true understanding of the *dao*. Zhang's version of intellectualism is nowhere more characteristically revealed than in his repeated attempts to reconstruct the two major neo-Confucian genealogies: Cheng-Zhu and Lu-Wang. Toward the end of his life he drew up two lists of names representing the lines of transmission of these two contending schools.

Several observations may be made about Zhang's genealogies. First, his explicitly stated criteria of selection are illuminating. According to Zhang, an intellectual heir to either Zhu Xi or Lu Xiangshan must meet two basic requirements. Positively, he must have a comprehensive knowledge of the classics and must respect tradition; negatively, he must not engage in "empty talk on moral nature." As a result, those included in the lists are mostly "scholars" rather than "philosophers."

Second, Zhang no longer saw the difference between Zhu and Lu as intellectual inquiry versus moral cultivation. Instead he saw it as inevitable expressions of two opposing tendencies in man's intellectual nature. Those who tend to grasp intuitively the significance of things and see things as large wholes would become followers of the Lu-Wang school, whereas those who tend to pursue knowledge of a vast number of subjects at various levels would become followers of the Cheng-Zhu school. What is referred to above as "intuitive grasp of the significance of things" is actually Zhang's redefinition of *zundexing* ("honoring moral nature"). It is indeed remarkable that he was able to turn such a central Confucian notion about moral nature into something purely intellectual without apparently feeling any deep psychological tension. Similarly, Zhang intellectualized Wang Yangming's idea of *liangzhi* ("innate knowledge of good"), reinterpreting it as a scholar's intuitive inclination toward a particular type of intellectual work—classics, history, or poetry.

Third and last, but not least, Zhang's famous thesis "the Six Classics are all history" was part and parcel of the rising Confucian intellectualism. According to his reconstructed genealogies, Qing classical scholars from Gu Yanwu to Dai Zhen were the true heirs of the Cheng-Zhu school whereas eastern Chekiang (Zhejiang) historians from Huang Zongxi (1610–1695) and Quan Zuwang (1705–1755) to Zhang himself developed the Lu-Wang tradition in a new direction. Instead of engaging in "empty talk" on such general principles as "human nature" and "destiny," Zhang says, eastern Chekiang historians always devoted themselves to historical scholarship in order to show how these principles actually operated in concrete human situations. It is important to point out that Zhang's famous thesis was formulated specifically to challenge the classicists' monopolistic claim to the Confucian *dao*. As shown earlier, a general assumption among Qing scholars under the new paradigm was that the *dao* discovered by sages of antiquity was all recorded in the classical texts and that the newly refined philological tools were capable of explicating the original meanings of these texts. Zhang considered this conception of *dao* fundamentally mistaken. To him *dao* is but the quintessence of the civilized way of life and as such constantly evolves in history. Ancient sages did not create the *dao*; they only discerned it in the everyday social activity of men and women. In his view, therefore, the Six Classics as historical texts of ancient sages can reveal the *dao* only as it had evolved up to the end of classical antiquity. They cannot possibly say anything about the *dao* as it continued to manifest itself in later events and changes. The real message behind Zhang's thesis is unmistakable: the classicist, if his specialization is confined to the texts of the Six Classics, is by definition incapable of seeing the *dao* fully. It is the historian with a comprehensive understanding of historical processes from the past to the present who is eminently qualified to grasp the *dao* in its essentials. In this way Zhang pushed intellectualism beyond the limit of the dominant paradigm of the classicists from Gu Yanwu to Dai Zhen. Critical inquiry and study as a methodological principle, he insisted, must extend to texts of all varieties, not merely the Six Classics, because historical and literary scholarship has a claim to the *dao* no less legitimate than that of classical scholarship. Thus he greatly broadened the intellectual base of Confucianism.

The extent to which Zhang intellectualized the Lu-Wang tradition may be most clearly shown by a brief contrast with its Song-Ming neo-Confucian version. For Lu Xiangshan and Wang Yangming *dao* or *li* (principles) and the mind (*xin*) are indistinguishable whether the concept of mind is understood in its cosmic or individual sense. They generally assumed that *dao* and the mind share the same spiritual substance of which the moral order as we find it in the cosmos or in the human world is constituted. This is precisely why neo-Confucians of the Lu-Wang persuasion always emphasized that in our quest of *dao* the moral approach must take precedence over the intellectual approach. The moral approach implied that the "original mind" (Lu) or "innate knowledge" (Wang) must be followed at all times, as our infallible guide. The intellectual approach, on the other hand, was at best peripheral and at worst misleading because *dao*, being internal to the mind, could not be studied from without as if it were an ordinary object of knowledge. In Zhang's intellectualized system, by contrast, "history" took the place of "mind" and, consequently, *dao* and history were viewed as the inside and the outside of each other. *Dao* in itself was indeed "above form" and therefore inaccessible to direct observation. However, we could instead grasp the invisible *dao* by tracing its historical process of objectivization. Thus to know *dao* was to know history, no more and no less. This explains why the moral approach is conspicuously absent from Zhang's theory of history. As a historian he apparently did not believe that there is an a priori shortcut to knowledge of the past.

Finally, Zhang's self-definition as a follower of the Lu-Wang tradition also made it necessary for him to assign the concept of mind (*xin*) a proper place in his system of thought. When he came to grips with this problem, it turned out that he was once more well served by his favorite strategy, intellectualization. The pivotal function of the mind is empasized in his discussions of how to reconstruct the past. As a genealogist of philosophical schools and a historian of ideas he often spoke as if the final goal of explicating a text was to transcend language in order to get at the thoughts of its author. His direct borrowing of the Chan Buddhist expression "transmission from mind to mind without a written text" (*fawai chuanxin*) testifies, in particular, to the influence of Lu Xiangshan, who advocated—more enthusiastically than any other neo-Confucian thinker—grasping the moral ideas of ancient sages directly, through a transhistorical meeting of minds. However, it can be demonstrated that the "mind" Zhang speaks of throughout his writings is a pure knowing mind without the built-in moral substance of what Lu called the "original mind."

In keeping with his redefinition of the rivalry between the two major neo-Confucian schools in terms of the opposing tendencies in man's intellectual temper, Zhang made another strategic move—he developed a methodology uniquely suited to the type of scholarship he was then advocating in order to counterbalance the radical philology so glorified by contemporary classicists. At first, he shared the classicists' enthusiasm about philology as a tool capable of bringing to light messages of the sages hidden in classical texts. However, as he developed his own distinct point of view about the Confucian tradition, he grew increasingly critical of the philological approach practiced in his day. His main complaint was that philology is effective only in getting to know the details through textual exegesis but quite inadequate to grasping a larger whole. He felt that this was true because more often than not the philologist fails to rise above the language of the text and penetrate the author's thought. To avoid getting lost in details in the search for *dao*, he proposed a new methodology with "grasping of the large whole" and "leaping into the minds of the ancients" as its two basic principles. These two principles had originally been formulated by Lu Xiangshan to serve the purpose of moral cultivation. The two key terms "large whole" (*dati*) and "mind" (*xin*), taken from Mencius, refer to man's moral nature and moral mind, respectively. Zhang retained the old terms but transferred them from the moral to the intellectual domain. He had to make this profound, though subtle, change because he was faced with a question wholly different from that of his predecessors. For Lu-Wang neo-Confucians the primary question was, "How to become a sage?" For Qing Confucian scholars, however, the first question was, "How can we be sure that we understand the ideas of ancient sages correctly?" Zhang's dissatisfaction with the classicists' answer to this question prompted him to offer his own methodological principles, with a distinctive Lu-Wang undertone. In this area his intellectualization of the Lu-Wang tradition consists of two interrelated moves. First, the original moral approach, with its emphasis on a transhistorical meeting of minds, was transformed into methods of interpretation and understanding allowing the possibility of grasping the author's intent in a given text through as well as beyond its language. Second, the notion that the search for *dao* must begin with a firm grasp of the "large whole" (*dati*) also provided a model for his methodology. In the radical philological point of view, mastery of every technical detail is prerequisite to an understanding of a given text as a whole; Zhang put forward the opposing principle that only a grasp of the whole can give meaning to scholarly research and determine the relevance of technical details to a chosen subject. In more general terms, Zhang may be characterized as a methodological holist particularly concerned with the relation of parts to the whole in interpretation. With the formulation of methodological holism his intellectualization of the Lu-Wang tradition became complete.

Dai Zhen and Zhang Xuecheng are the two most philosophically minded scholars who happened to live in the era when Confucian intellectualism reached its pinnacle. Dai was a philological classicist from the Cheng-Zhu background; Zhang was an intellectual historian who identified himself as a custodian of the Lu-Wang tradition. Together, their new and divergent conceptions regarding the Confucian tradition sum up the multifarious developments of mainstream Confucianism to the end of the eighteenth century. In this sense Dai and Zhang express not only their own views but also those of their predecessors, including Gu Yanwu,

Huang Zongxi, Chen Que (1604–1677), Wang Fuzhi (1619–1693), and Yan Yuan (1635–1704).

III

The main emphasis of mid-Qing Confucianism, and its main contribution, was classical and historical scholarship; but new developments in political and social thought also took place in the early and late Qing.

First, the Confucian idea of *jingshi* ("ordering the world") requires clarification. Broadly, the Confucian *dao* is always expected to function in two major categories corresponding to the classical "sageliness within" and "kingliness without." In Song-Ming neo-Confucianism the former refers to the cultivation of moral nature and the latter to "putting the world in order," that is, *jingshi*. Being worldly in nature, the Confucian *dao* is ultimately to seek full realization in the human world; it is not contented with salvation of the individual through moral cultivation. This is precisely why Zhu Xi's *Four Books* is headed by the *Great Learning*. As a general outline of the whole Confucian project this particular text states in no uncertain terms that the process of realizing *dao* begins with moral cultivation of the self but ends with "order of the state" and "peace of the world"—which are what *jingshi* is all about. Not surprisingly, then, *jingshi* was deeply rooted in the consciousness of many a devout Confucian whose irresistible impulse to put the world in order often broke out in times of adversity and chaos. Under such circumstances, almost as a rule, many Confucians would throw themselves into political and social action, promoting reforms, voicing protests, or both.

With this understanding of *jingshi* in the Confucian scheme of things, let us review the functional dimension of the Confucian *dao* in the Qing period. *Jingshi* seized the Confucians' consciousness twice during the Qing, first in the seventeenth century and later in the nineteenth, in response to a political and social crisis.

The first *jingshi* movement actually started in the late Ming but continued into the early Qing. The Manchu conquest in 1644 shocked the Confucians and deepened their consciousness of a political and social crisis. The first generation of Qing Confucians are an example. Divergent as their intellectual leanings were, Gu Yanwu, Huang Zongxi, and Wang Fuzhi all emphasized that the ultimate importance of *dao* was its wondrous power to set things right when the human world went terribly wrong. It was this Confucian impulse to "reorder the world" that initially prompted them to restudy the Six Classics, with the avowed purpose of clarifying the nature of *dao*. Gu Yanwu stated: "I decided not to do any writing unless it had a relation to the actual affairs of the contemporary world as indicated in the Six Classics." It was his firm belief that only a thoroughgoing study of the classics could bring *dao* to light and thus save the world from its current troubles. Huang Zongxi went a step further. He proposed to enlarge the core of Confucian learning by combining a study of the classics with a study of history, especially the history of the most recent past. Huang felt that whether the Confucian *dao* could function to improve the world would hinge on whether its practitioners could make creative use of historical experience to solve contemporary problems. Here, we see, he started an intellectual tradition in eastern Chekiang that culminated in the work of Zhang Xuecheng. A similar view was developed independently by Wang Fuzhi, who anticipated by a full century Zhang's definition of the aim of historical studies in terms of "setting the world in order" (*jingshi*).

Jingshi continued to be a pervasive trend well into the second generation, of which Li Yong (1627–1705) and Yan Yuan (1635–1704) may be considered the two outstanding representatives. Li was a neo-Confucian philosopher from Shensi who largely followed the teaching of Wang Yangming but also recognized the contributions of the Cheng-Zhu school. Throughout his life he never strayed from his Confucian idealism, centering on *jingshi*. Several of his early works have *jingshi* and "current affairs" in their titles. In 1656, in reply to a disciple, he made the categorical statement that "the central purpose of Confucian learning consists wholly in setting the world in order" as opposed to the Daoist "nonaction" and the Buddhist "nirvana." Yan Yuan agreed with this view when he learned of it in 1692. With his overwhelming emphasis on the importance of political and social practice he transformed late Ming neo-Confucian quietism into a radical form of activism. His sages are no longer "sitting" sages but men of action, and his *dao* is neither a metaphysical entity nor a linguistic construct but a driving force setting the human world in motion. Indeed, of all early Qing thinkers he alone may be said to have formulated a powerful philosophy with *jingshi* at its center.

This long-lasting commitment to the ideal of "setting the world in order" during the transition from Ming to Qing contributed significantly to a refocusing of Confucian political and social thought. As a result, a number of noticeably new attitudes and ideas emerged, only a few of which can be mentioned here.

Huang Zongxi's famous treatise *Waiting for the Dawn: A Plan for the Prince*, written in 1662, deserves special mention. This little classic offers not only a penetrating and devastating criticism of Chinese despotism, especially Ming despotism, and all the institutional malfunctions associated with it but also a comprehensive blueprint for restoring the Confucian world to order.

On the one hand, the treatise crystallized Huang's reflections of a lifetime on the deep-rooted troubles that eventually brought about the fall of Ming and the Manchu conquest; on the other hand, it consolidated his views about the functional dimension of *dao*, developed through his study of Confucian political principles in the classics in conjunction with a close reading of dynastic history beginning with the first unified empire. This work was received enthusiastically by its earliest readers, who generally hailed it as a set of reform proposals, which, if duly implemented, would "set the world right."

One of Huang's arguments against imperial autocracy is particularly indicative of where Confucian political and social thought was heading. It runs roughly as follows. Sovereigns in postclassical times such as the first emperor of Qin and the founding emperor of Han violated the terms of service originally expected of a universal king. Instead of advancing the interests of the people, they abused the enormous power vested in them by identifying their supreme private interests with the common good of the empire. They looked on the empire as if it were their private property, and as a result, the people did not even dare to think of their own interests.

This argument may be regarded as the sharpest expression of a general sense shared by many Confucians in the seventeenth century. Gu Yanwu also offered his view, as follows. It is in human nature that everyone should care for his own family and cherish his own children. Even if the son of heaven loves the people, he still cannot possibly do better than what they can do for themselves. Therefore the only way for common good to prevail in the world is that the son of heaven see to it that the people can all pursue their legitimate self-interests, each in his individual way. In Gu's words, "With all the individual self-interest (*si*) in the world combined, the common good (*gong*) is formed."

Both Huang and Gu revealed a keen sense of distrust of imperial power. They appear to have finally come to a realization that the centuries-old neo-Confucian project known as "bringing *dao* to the world with the blessing of the sovereign" (*dejun xingdao*) was an illusion. Consequently, in their efforts to establish a better social and ethical order, often at the local level, through a variety of educational, cultural, and philanthropic activities, they tended to seek support not so much from the state as from the local elite and the wealthy. It is significant that the focus of Confucian economic thinking was steadily shifting to how to protect the wealthy from the state. Huang Zongxi, Gu Yanwu, Wang Fuzhi, and Tang Zhen (1630–1714), to give only a few notable examples, all insisted that wealth must be kept in local communities in the care of those who created it so that in times of extreme adversity, such as famine, the poor could be given immediate assistance and relief. They also emphasized that if wealth was concentrated in the imperial treasury, the people would forever be deprived of access to it. Out of this deep skepticism about the function of the state grew a general notion that public enterprises should be entrusted to private entrepreneurs rather than state bureaucrats. As time went on, this notion became increasingly popular among Confucians and eventually was embodied in a system of "official supervision and merchant operation" at the end of the nineteenth century. In this regard, the interpenetration of the emerging business culture and Confucianism since the early Qing is unmistakable.

In social, economic, and ethical thought Qing Confucianism generally showed a tendency to relax moral absolutism. We have seen that Gu Yanwu and Huang Zongxi took the "common good" and "self-interest" as complementary, and this new reading was equally applicable to many other Confucian polarities, notably "righteousness versus profitableness," "frugality versus luxury," and above all "heavenly principle versus human desire." These polarities, which had been previously understood as mutually exclusive, were now redefined in relative terms. Of the early Qing Confucians, Chen Que did more than anyone else to give "human desire" a legitimate place in the Confucian scheme of things. His statement that "heavenly principle consists in the proper fulfillment of human desires" anticipated Dai Zhen's ethical theory by a century. This important revision, in particular, shows how Confucianism redirected itself toward the changing social and economic realities of the seventeenth century. This trend was closely linked to the Confucians' commitment to *jingshi*. As Dai Zhen repeatedly assured his readers, his redefinition of "principle versus desire" was prompted by the simple fact that, more often than not, those in power condemned the basic needs of the common people as "human desires" and summarily rejected their demands for fulfillment in the name of "heavenly principles."

IV

This account of Qing Confucianism would not be complete without a brief note on the nineteenth century. By the 1820s at the latest, mainstream Confucianism's focus on classical and historical scholarship had declined from its peak, although the tradition of research would continue well into the twentieth century.

The nineteenth century witnessed two major departures from mainstream Confucianism. The first one was a pervasive revival of *jingshi*, marked by the publication in 1827 of an enormous collection of Qing writings on practical matters of state and society: *Huangchao jingshi wenbian*, edited by Huo Changlin (1785–1848) and Wei Yuan (1794–1856). This was a revival because the title unmistakably suggests a direct borrowing of Chen Zilong's *Huang Ming jingshi wenbian*, compiled in 1638. Like the *jingshi* movement of the seventeenth century, this revival was a response to a political, social, and economic crisis—in this case, the crisis had been deepening since the beginning of Jiaqing's reign (1796–1820). However, unlike the earlier movement, the revived *jingshi* movement grew rapidly in influence, especially after the Opium War of 1839–1842. From Zeng Guofan (1811–1872) to Kang Youwei (1858–1927), *jingshi* was gradually established as one of the four major fields of Confucian studies, along with moral philosophy (*yili*), philology (*kaozheng*), and literary art (*cizhang*). Because history figured centrally in the *jingshi* studies, the revival was continuous with the original movement. But it is also important to note that by the end of the nineteenth century *jingshi* as category had already been expanded to include western learning, such as contemporary political history, institutions, commerce, science, military tactics, and even Christianity. Thus it was the idea of *jingshi* that gave Confucians of the late Qing a much-needed justification for seeking knowledge of practical relevance to China from the west. Hence the famous formula "Chinese learning for the fundamentals and western learning for practical use." It was natural for western learning, especially science and technology, to be accommodated in Confucianism: the Confucian idea of *jingshi*, being particularly attentive to all kinds of practical problems, had always emphasized the importance of technical expertise and innovation.

The second departure from mainstream Confucianism was the rise of the "new text" school. It began quietly with Zhuang Cunyu (1719–1788), an obscure scholar in the heyday of established classical scholarship. Classicists of the middle Qing often referred to their philological approach to classical texts as "Han learning," on the assumption that they generally followed the model of textual exegesis of the Han dynasty. However, in the course of his research Zhuang discovered that there was an early Han exegetical tradition which had been completely ignored by classical philologists of his day. This was the *gongyang* school (later known as the "new text"), with Dong Zhongshu (second century B.C.E.) as its outstanding representative. According to this tradition, Confucius was a prophet who wrote the *Spring-Autumn Annals* (*Chunqiu*) to convey his ideas as to how a future king of a unified China should establish his institutions. But these ideas were not explicitly expressed in writing. Instead, they were transmitted orally from generation to generation by the followers of the prophet. According to this view, therefore, the *Spring-Autumn Annals* was not a simple historical text to be read literally but rather a repository of the prophet's "esoteric words and great principles" whose meanings could be grasped through interpretation beyond the literal sense of the text.

Until Zhuang Cunyu appeared on the scene, this early "new text" tradition had remained virtually untouched by mainstream Confucians, simply because philology was wholly inadequate to the task. Thus Zhuang's excursion into "new text" studies may be understood as an anomaly in the "Han learning." As Ruan Yuan (1764–1849), the patron saint of Han learning, observed, Zhuang's work remained obscure during his lifetime because his approach was completely out of the mainstream of classical scholarship. It took half a century for the significance of his studies on the *gongyang* tradition to be generally recognized. This recognition was due, first, to the efforts of Liu Fenglu (1776–1829), his grandson, and Song Xiangfeng (1776–1860), his grandnephew, and then to the influential writings of Gong Zizhen and Wei Yuan.

In general, it may be suggested that nineteenth-century Confucianism took two turns: a practical turn in the revival of *jingshi* and an interpretive turn in the rediscovery of the *gongyang* tradition. We have seen that the revival of *jingshi* was a response to a political and social crisis. Was Zhuang Cunyu's interest in the "new text" school—as his biographer Gong Zizhen held—also motivated by a "secret desire to improve the world"? Not exactly. The evidence suggests that it began, first and foremost, as an internal revolt against mainstream classical scholarship. By the middle of the eighteenth century the majority of philologically trained classicists tended to be obsessed with technical details in their research. They typically failed to rise above the minute and disconnected to grasp the whole. This shreds-and-patches approach could not meet the spiritual needs of Confucians who were primarily interested in finding a broad vision in classical and historical texts. As a result, there was a subtle methodological shift: interpretation began to be at least as important as philological explication. In his search for the "great principles" in the *Spring-Autumn Annals* Zhuang Cunyu was undoubtedly a harbinger and an initiator of this new turn. Methodologically, he can be classed with Zhang Xuecheng and Dai Zhen even though their scholarly pursuits were worlds apart. Dai was also more interpretive than philological in his attempt to reconstruct a new Confucian philosophy—and he was severely criticized for this by many fellow philologists.

Despite their separate origins, these two new developments in Confucianism eventually converged, in the mid-nineteenth century, to form the powerful movement of reformism. On the one hand, "new text" Confucians like Gong Zizhen and Wei Yuan pushed for practical changes by expanding the notion of *jingshi* beyond its traditional limits. On the other hand, *jingshi* scholars unconnected to the *gongyang* tradition like Bao Shichen (1775–1855) also advocated fundamental institutional reforms. It was Kang Youwei who most successfully combined the two trends—the interpretive and the practical—into one well-integrated movement. In 1891 he formally introduced *jingshi* studies into the curriculum of his newly founded academy in Canton. At the same time he began to develop his most radical interpretation of "new text" Confucianism. In a study of the "forged classics" (*Xinxue weijing kao*, 1891) he made a heroic attempt to prove that many of the Confucian texts philologically explicated by mainstream Qing classicists were actually forged by what he called the "old text" school under the leadership of Liu Xin (d. 22 C.E.), in order to support the New Dynasty of Wang Mang (9–23 C.E.). Kang claimed that the true Confucian teachings could be found only in the sage's own writings—principally the *Spring-Autumn Annals*, since even the *Analects* had been falsified in the hands of Liu Xin and his colleagues. In another major work (*Kongzi gaizhi kao*, 1896) Kang presented Confucius as a prophet-reformer who had laid down plans for institutional reforms not only for his own age but for future generations. Following the *gongyang* interpretation, he believed that the *Annals* included a theory of a three-stage progress in human history: disorder, relative peace, and universal peace. In his view, therefore, the primary and real duty of every Confucian must by definition consist in carrying out reforms and initiating changes necessary for his own time as originally envisioned by Confucius. Thus the convergence of the practical turn and the interpretive turn culminated in Kang's version of Confucian reformism. However, as Kang had incorporated too many western ideas and values into his political philosophy, he also brought Qing Confucianism to an end.

See also Chen Que; Cheng Yi; Dai Zhen; Gu Yanwu; Huang Zongxi; Kang Youwei; Luo Qinshun; Wang Fuzhi; Wang Yangming; Yan Yuan; Zhang Xuecheng; Zhu Xi.

Bibliography

Bloom, Irene. *Knowledge Painfully Acquired: The K'un-chih chi by Lo Ch'in-shun*. New York: Columbia University Press, 1987.

Chin, Ann-ping, and Mansfield Freeman. *Tai Chen on Mencius: Explorations in Words and Meanings*. New Haven, Conn., and London: Yale University Press, 1990.

de Bary, William Theodore, ed. *The Unfolding of Neo-Confucianism*. New York and London: Columbia University Press, 1975.

———. *Waiting for the Dawn: A Plan for the Prince, Huang Tsung-hsi's Ming-i-tai-fang lu*. New York: Columbia University Press, 1993.

Elman, Benjamin A. *Classicism, Politics, and Kinship: The Ch'ang-chou School of New Text Confucianism in Late Imperial China*. Berkeley and Los Angeles: University of California Press, 1990.

———. *From Philology to Philosophy: Intellectual and Social Aspects of Changes in Late Imperial China*. Cambridge, Mass.: Council on East Asian Studies, Harvard University, 1984.

Huang, Chin-shing. *Philosophy, Philology, and Politics in Eighteenth-Century China: Li Fu and the Lu-Wang School under the Ch'ing*. Cambridge and New York: Cambridge University Press, 1995.

Levenson, Joseph R. *Confucian China and Its Modern Fate: The Problem of Intellectual Continuity*. Berkeley and Los Angeles: University of California Press, 1958.

Liang, Ch'i-ch'ao. *Intellectual Trends in the Ch'ing Period*, trans. Immanuel C. Y. Hsü. Cambridge, Mass.: Harvard University Press, 1959.

Nivison, David S. *The Life and Thought of Chang Hsüeh-ch'eng (1738–1801)*. Stanford, Calif.: Stanford University Press, 1966.

Peterson, Willard. *Bitter Gourd: Fang I-chih and the Impetus for Intellectual Change*. New Haven, Conn.: Yale University Press, 1979.

Qian, Mu. *Zhungguo jin sanbainian xueshu shi* (Chinese Intellectual History of the Past Three Hundred Years). Shanghai: Commercial Press, 1937.

Yu, Ying-shih. *Lun Dai Zhen yu Zhang Xuecheng* (Dai Zhen and Zhang Xuecheng). Beijing: Sanlian Bookstore, 2000.

———. "Some Preliminary Observations on the Rise of Ch'ing Confucian Intellectualism." *Tsing Hua Journal of Chinese Studies*, New Series, 11(1–2), December 1975, pp. 105–144.

———. "Tai Chen's Choice between Philosophy and Philology." *Asia Major*, Third Series, 2(1), 1989, pp. 79–108.

———. "Zhang Xuecheng versus Dai Zhen: A Study in Intellectual Challenge and Response in Eighteenth-Century of China." In *Chinese Language, Thought, and Culture: Nivison and His Critics*. Chicago and La Salle, Ill.: Open Court, 1996.

Confucianism: Rhetoric

A. S. Cua

In recent times, western scholars of rhetorical theory have shown interest in studying east-west comparative philosophical rhetoric. In August 1988 the National Endowment of the Humanities sponsored a symposium called "Rhetoric: East and West" at the East-West Center in Honolulu, Hawaii. In her instructive paper "Ethical Values in Classic Eastern Texts" (1988), Helen North, an established classicist in Greek philosophy of rhetoric, raises a central question for comparative east-west rhetorical studies:

> The topic of *arete* and the use of *ethos* as a mode of persuasion constitute the principal debts that classical Western rhetoric owes to ethics. Is there anything comparable to be found in Eastern classical texts? Specifically, what ethical qualities seem important for the purpose of persuasion, and how are they applied in Eastern classical texts?

Any attempt to deal with such a question must pay heed to the earlier work of another participant, Robert Oliver, especially to his pioneering work on the rhetoric of ancient India and China. Comparative east-west rhetoric is complicated by the acceptance of Oliver's thesis of cultural relativism: "The kinds of ideas that interest or move people and the reasons why they accept or reject are not universals, they are particular attributes of specific cultures" (1971, 7); moreover, the priority of topical considerations is determined by a value judgment relative to a holistic cultural system (9–10). With such a thesis, the focus would be on divergence rather than convergence of rhetorical concerns. The concluding chapter of Oliver's book presents some general but crucial contrasts between the rhetoric of the east and the west.

Nevertheless, Oliver's work provides a guide to comparative east-west rhetoric. Philosophical students of classical Chinese thought will certainly profit from reading his book whenever they attend to questions of rhetorical theory. Especially noteworthy are Oliver's discussion of the elements of rhetoric in the *Analects* and in the *Mencius*. However, from a philosophical point of view, any approach to comparative east-west rhetoric must deal with a more fundamental question concerning the nature of textual interpretation. Concern with this question does not vitiate the insightful contributions of North and Oliver.

Let us begin with the observation that in ancient China and India—unlike the west—there is virtually no work "explicitly devoted to rhetoric." Oliver explains this fact by pointing to the inseparability of philosophy and rhetoric in these cultures, and in the east in general. In his words:

> The reason for this difference is greatly significant. In the West, rhetoric has been of such high importance that it has received very considerable attention as a separate field of inquiry. In the East, rhetoric has been of such even higher consequence that it never has been separated from philosophy but has received continuous attention as an essential and integral part of generalized philosophical speculation. (260)

This explanation assumes that the absence of independent rhetorical treatises in both ancient China and India must not be construed as an absence of rhetorical concerns. Given this assumption, the task left to scholars may be conceived as the constructive interpretation of texts important to rhetoric as an academic discipline. The explanation is also consistent with the assumption that rhetorical theory is implicit in these texts and thus the task is reconstructive interpretation. In either case, what is involved is a sort of creative hermeneutics or plausible explication of notions or ideas that contribute to the development of a rhetorical theory.

Such a form of philosophical interpretive inquiry is a constructive interpretation. In the case of legal practice, it is "a matter of imposing purpose on an object or practice in order to make of it the best possible example of the form or genre to which it is taken to belong" (Dworkin 1986, 52). More perspicuously, the aim of constructive interpretation is to present, in the best light, a coherent explanation and justification of the practice. Insofar as epistemology is conceived as an inquiry into the coherent explanation *cum* justification of any human practice, Dworkin's work may be described as legal epistemology. Similar epistemological concern with moral practice is exemplified in my study of Confucian ethical argumentation (Cua 1985a).

North's paper provides an occasion for a preliminary exploration of the possibility of developing a Confucian theory of rhetoric. This exploration is an attempt to interpret the rhetorical import of Confucian ethical thought. Although North's question on the use of *ethos* and *arete* as a mode of persuasive discourse will have a central role in this inquiry, I shall not approach the question by comparing or contrasting classical Greek and Chinese texts. In what follows, I am mainly concerned with laying out part of the groundwork for such a comparative study.

In the first section, adopting the framework of Aristotle's *Rhetoric* with some modification and drawing from my study of Xunzi's conception of ethical argumentation, I discuss the role of *ethos* and *arete*, or more generally, the style of performance, that is, the desirable qualities of participants in argumentation. Special emphasis is placed on *ren* (benevolence), *li* (propriety), and *yi* (rightness, righteousness).

The second section deals at length with some issues of *logos* or reasoning in Confucian argumentation. After assessing the adequacy of the deductivist approach, as suggested by Aristotle's notion of *enthymeme*, I propose two types of reasoning as distinctive of Confucian argumentation: one akin to Aristotle's argument from example (rhetorical induction), and another, coordinative reasoning—that is, reasoning which uses a number of logically independent factors or premises, cooperatively, to produce a conclusion which is not logically compelling yet is reasoned.

In the third section, I respond to North's comparative remarks, especially on Mencius and Han Fei in relation to *basilikos logos*. I suggest that Xunzi's essays on the ways (*dao*) of the ruler and ministers provide a good case study, and conclude with some brief remarks on the divergent conceptions of *pathos* implicit in the works of Xunzi and Mencius, and on difficulties of examining classical Chinese texts for comparative rhetorical inquiry.

Concept and Conceptions of Rhetoric

Let me begin by reflecting on Xunzi's distinction between generic (*gongming*) and specific terms (*bieming*). For elucidation we may use the recent, functionally analogous distinction between concept and conception (e.g., Rawls 1971, 5–9). A generic term is a formal, general, abstract term amenable to specification by other terms in different discursive contexts. These terms, used in practical or theoretical contexts, may be said to be specific in the sense that they specify the significance of the use of a generic term adapted to a current purpose of discourse. Alternatively, we may say that there are various levels of abstraction or specification of the use of general terms. Thus a specific term in one context may function as a generic term in another context, whenever a current purpose requires such further specification. In the language of concept and conception, a generic term designates a "concept" that can be used in developing various "conceptions" (Cua 1985a).

While the distinction between concept and conception is quite different from the familiar distinction between meaning and extension of terms (Dworkin 1986, 71), the semantic distinction between generic and specific terms is properly between the wider and the narrower scope of application of a term. The crucial motivation for the distinction lies in the purposes at hand. Specification has to do primarily with the significant use of a concept, which may well represent, so to speak, a crystallized conception. Consider *dao*; were it to be viewed exclusively as a Confucian concept or generic term of Confucian discourses, it would be a crystallized conception of classical and neo-Confucian thought. But for the Daoists, *dao* would represent an altogether different concept or crystallized conception of their discourses, as preeminently exemplified in *Laozi* and *Zhuangzi*. This suggests that we may quite properly speak of *dao* as representing two different concepts, each of which is a product of a crystallized conception. And in both cases, *dao* can be viewed as a generic term. In the case of Confucianism, *dao* is a generic term subject to specification by way of such general and interdependent notions of virtue (henceforth, aretaic notions) as *ren* (benevolence), *li* (propriety), and *yi* (righteousness), and each of these in turn may be significantly specified further, as the occasion arises, by way of particular aretaic notions, for example, filiality (*xiao*), loyalty (*zhong*), trustworthiness (*xin*), consideration (*shu*), and courage (*yong*).

In light of the foregoing, we may distinguish the concept of rhetoric from various conceptions of rhetoric. With Aristotle, we may say that the concept of rhetoric pertains to the study or discovery of the means of persuasion "coming as near such success as the circumstances of each particular case allow" (1355a). A rhetorical theory, I suggest, is a systematic conception of rhetoric. The possibility of a Confucian rhetorical theory thus concerns the systematic development of a conception of rhetoric. One rhetorical theorist remarks: "Rhetoric proper starts with Aristotle. All rhetoric is in some way—more or less—derived from Aristotle" (Winterowd 1968, 18). While this claim may be questioned from the standpoint of the history of rhetoric, for a moral philosopher it is unproblematic if it is a claim to Aristotle as a guide for exploring the relation between ethics and rhetoric, a claim that seems to be attested to by Aristotle's remark that "rhetoric is an offshoot of dialectic and also of ethical studies" (1355a). Moreover, it is to Aristotle that we are indebted for a plausible philosophical framework for any rhetorical theory informed by ethical theory. For a Confucian ethical theorist, especially, Aristotle's framework of *ethos*, *logos*, and *pathos* offers an illuminating way of interpreting the rhetorical import of Confucian ethics. In Aristotle's own words:

> Rhetorical study, in its strict sense, is concerned with the modes of persuasion. Of the modes of persuasion furnished by the spoken word there are three kinds: The first kind depends on the personal character of the speaker; the second on putting the audience into a certain frame of mind; the third on the proof, or apparent proof, provided by the words of the speech itself. (1356a)

In view of Perelman's works on rhetoric as a general theory of argumentation and some recent contributions to informal logic (e.g., Perelman 1982; Taylor 1961; Toulmin 1958), I shall not follow Aristotle in assigning rhetorical deduction or enthymeme a central place. If rhetorical theory is conceived, as Perelman conceives it, as a systematic theory of argumentation, a general deductivist approach does not seem adequate (as we shall see below). In general, argumentation is a dialectical rather than a demonstrative activity or a deduction. As Perelman points out:

> The aim of argumentation is not to deduce consequences from given premises; it is rather to elicit or increase the adherence of the members of an audience to theses that are presented for their consent. Such adherence never comes out of thin air; it presupposes a meeting of minds between speaker and audience. (1982, 9–10)

In *Ethical Argumentation*, much along the same lines, though paying no heed to its rhetorical aspect per se, I viewed Confucian argumentation as a reasoned persuasive discourse, a cooperative enterprise aiming at a solution to a problem of common concern among participants. Presupposed in this conception is an operative ethical tradition as a background for explanation and/or justification of normative claims or value judgments. A profile of argumentation is presented, consisting of a characterization of the desirable qualities or *ethos* of participants, standards of competence, phases of discourse embracing both explanatory and justificatory activities, diagnosis of erroneous beliefs, as well as ethical reasoning and uses of definition in overcoming difficulties in communication. In what follows, adopting Aristotle's tripartite scheme of *ethos*, *logos*, and *pathos*, I shall sketch a Confucian conception of rhetoric by developing certain aspects of Confucian argumentation. At the outset, it must be noted that the conception proffered is only one possible way of interpreting Confucian moral thought and practice. Given that morality is a concept amenable to competing theoretical employment, it is an essentially contested concept (Gallie 1964, ch. 8).

Style of performance. Confucian argumentation is a cooperative activity of reasonable persuasion addressed to a particular rather than a universal audience (Perelman and Olbrechts-Tyteca 1969, 31f.). Apart from the requirement of satisfying certain standards of competence such as conceptual clarity, consistency, coherence, respect for linguistic practices, and accord with reason and experience, it is expected that participants possess and display certain qualities of character conducive to the proceeding. Ideally, these are the qualities of a *junzi* (an ethically superior person) or paradigmatic individual who governs his or her life by *dao*, the ideal of the good human life as a whole. The *dao* of the *junzi* is the *dao* of humanity embodying *ren*, *li*, and *i*. Says Xunzi:

> The superior man is not called a worthy because he can do all that men of ability can do. The superior man is not called wise because he knows all that the wise men know. The superior man (*junzi*) is not called a dialectician because he can dispute concerning all that the dialecticians dispute about. The superior man is not called an investigator because he can investigate everything investigators investigate into. He has his standard [*dao*]. (Dubs 1996, 96; *Ruxiao*, Li 1979, 131)

Because of the ethical responsibility involved, the *junzi* will refrain from engaging in contentious discourse (*Quanxue*, Li, 17). Contention is likely to transform argumentation into an adversarial proceeding and thus obstruct rather than promote the cooperative undertaking. Instead of addressing a problem of common concern, a contentious person is more often motivated by the desire to win an argument. Were such a desire intense, issues pertaining to right and wrong or to actual matters are bound to be ignored (*Xing'e*, Li, 557; Watson 1963, 70). Moreover, a contentious person will lack the patience to explain the reasoned support of his thesis (*Rungru*, Li, 57). Even if he offers explanations, they are likely to be hasty and inadequate to do full justice to the issues at hand. As Xunzi points out, "When one discourses on one's ideas, one should give a complete explanation of one's reasons" (*Zhengming*, Li, 521; Watson, 47). More important, as Chen Daqi remarks, contention is a sort of agitating passion that disturbs calmness of mind (Chen 1954, 91) and thus deprives the participant of the clarity of mind essential to the exercise of sound judgment. Xunzi compares the human mind to a pan of water:

> If you place the pan on a level and do not jar it, then the heavy sediment will settle to the bottom and the clear water

> will collect on top, so that you can see your beard and eyebrows in it and examine the lines in your face. But if a faint wind passes over the top of the water, the heavy sediment will be stirred up from the bottom and the clear water will become mingled with it, so that you can no longer get a clear reflection of even a large object. The mind is the same way. If you guide it with reason [*li*], nourish it with clarity, and do not allow external objects to unbalance it, then it will be capable of determining right and wrong and of resolving doubts. But if you allow petty external objects to pull it about, so that its proper form becomes altered and its inner balance is upset, then it will not be capable of making even gross distinctions. (*Jiebi*, Li, 490; Watson, 131–132)

Along with composure and clarity of mind, a *junzi* will engage in discourse with dignity, seriousness, and sincerity (Li, 88). As a person imbued with a *ren*-mind, an active and affectionate concern for the well-being of his fellows, he will be circumspect in explaining his ideas to others, while guarding against the possibility of injuring others' sense of self-respect (Li, 86). "The humane man (*renzhe*) loves others, hence he hates what injures others" (Dubs, 198; Li, 328). In general, "words of praise give more warmth than clothing and silk; words of injury are more piercing than a spear or two-pronged lance" (Li, 55). Whether or not he desires association or dissociation, the man of *ren* must respect others. However, not all expressions of respect are prompted by the same feeling. In the case of the worthy, he will respect and value their association. In the case of the unworthy, he will also respect them but with apprehension. In confronting the worthy, he will show his respect and try to be intimate. In confronting the unworthy, he will still show respect but keep them at a distance. "The outward expression of respect is the same, but one's inner feeling is different" (*Chendao*, Li, 298).

Characteristically, the *junzi* is magnanimous (*kuan*). He practices the art of accommodation, *jianshu* (Li, 86). Respect for both the worthy and the unworthy exemplifies such a practice, in accord with rules of civility or proper conduct (*li*). Observance of these rules is a matter of decency. As an appropriate requirement of discourse, the *li* provide a way of promoting argumentation as a cooperative enterprise, ensuring an open and orderly forum for airing differences of opinion. The *li* are, so to speak, diplomatic protocols facilitating the expression and consideration of competing views proffered as solutions to a problem of common concern. They provide acceptable channels for satisfying the desires of the participants. Much like our law of contracts and law of wills, they enable us to carry out our wishes effectively (Cua 1998, Essay 13).

Apart from the concern with *ren* and *li*, a *junzi* is a man of *yi*, who desires to arrive at a sound and reasonable judgment in response to changing circumstances of human life, *yiyi bianying* (Li, 43, 306). An exercise of *yi* requires an attitude of *gong* (impartiality). *Gong* is opposed to partiality (*pian*) in two different ways. As an expression of fairmindedness, a *junzi* will discount his own personal interest or preference (*siyu*) in favor of what he deems to be right and reasonable from an impersonal standpoint (Li, 36). This attitude also involves patience or receptivity (*xuexin*) in listening to competing opinions before arriving at a reasoned judgment. Argumentation, as we have seen, is not a prudential discourse engaged in for the purpose of personal gain. Preoccupation with personal interest, in another way, will also lead to obsession with aspects, while *dao* is, by contrast, a holistic and unifying perspective for dealing with problems of human life (Li, 472). Partiality in this way may lead to a clouding of the mind (*bi*) in dealing with exigent situations; thus it obstructs argumentation as a cooperative enterprise (Cua 1985a, ch. 4). In sum, a *junzi* is a man of integrity (*dechao*) who cherishes purity (*cui*) and completeness (*quan*). Given his dedication to *dao* and to *ren, li*, and *yi*, he will not allow his ethical will to be subverted by power or profit, or by the sway of the masses (Li, 19; Watson, 3). For him, discourse is an avenue for expressing concisely and coherently his ethical commitments, with due attention to relevant facts (Li, 525; Watson, 149). Unlike the sage, he has no comprehensive knowledge of the rationales (*li*) of facts or events that affect human well-being. He can only rely on his deliberation and planning, informed by extensive learning (Li, 89).

The foregoing discussion of the desirable qualities of *junzi* pertains, so to speak, to the style of performance of participants in argumentation. As Oliver has noted, echoing Buffon, if style is the man himself, "there must be as many different styles as there are speakers or writers. . . . Style is everywhere highly individualistic" (271). As an individual expression of ethical commitment, of the exercise of the virtues of *ren, li*, and *yi*, it is a unique ethical expression. The style of a man, as Schopenhauer put it, may be said to be an expression of "the physiognomy of the soul." As Danto (1981) insightfully remarks, the style represents the qualities of the man himself, "seen from the outside, physiognomically." There are no rules for self-representation in ethical discourse. Following Aristotle, Danto reminds us that the exercise of virtues is not rule-governed:

> To be kind is to be creative, to be able in novel situations to do what everyone will recognize as a kind thing. A

> moral person is an intuitive person, able to make the right judgments and perform the appropriate actions in situations in which he or she has perhaps never been before. (203–208)

In argumentation, apart from the possibility of misunderstanding, a *junzi*, because of his open-mindedness, is willing to run the risks involved in lending a receptive ear to others (*xuexin*). As Johnston put it:

> In making himself available to arguments, man transcends the horizons of his own perceptions, emotions, and instincts. . . . Knowledge and morality are possible only to the open-minded person who has transcended the horizons of immediate experience by taking the risks implicit in argument. (Johnston and Natanson 1965, 3)

The Problem of Moral Reasoning

The problem of reasoning in Confucian ethics is basically a problem of philosophical reconstruction aiming at an ideal, plausible explication of the nature of Confucian discourse. Confucian discourse is a form of reasoned discourse engaged in for the exposition and defense of moral claims or normative proposals. Independently of our interest in Confucian rhetoric, there are at least two underlying motivations for this theoretical inquiry in moral philosophy. An examination of the various uses of *li* in Xunzi or Wang Yangming, for example, may profit by regarding *li* as functionally equivalent to reason. Given the predominant ethical concern of the Confucians, it is plausible to maintain that their principal uses of *li* in normative contexts pertain to the reasoned justification of any value claim that is proffered in ethical argumentation (Cua 1985a, 20–30; 1997). A conceptual analysis of the notion of *yi* also discloses a principal use that pertains to "reasoned or correct judgment on what is right and appropriate" (Cua 1998, Essay 13). These notions of *li* (reason) and *yi* (reasoned judgment) suggest that an inquiry into the problem of moral reasoning is a proper concern for Confucian moral philosophers. At the outset, I shall assume that the notion of morality is applicable to Confucian ethics, when this notion is broadly construed as embracing the concern with character and conduct in the light of *dao*, the Confucian ideal of the good human life as a whole. Also, this ideal of *dao* is explicable in terms of the basic, interdependent, aretaic notions: *ren, li* (ritual rules), and *yi*. Given these assumptions, the problem of moral reasoning is a problem of assessing reasons proffered in support of Confucian moral judgments. In what follows, I offer some observations on this problem by commenting on two different approaches.

Deductivism. Since reasoning may be properly characterized as an inferential activity, the problem of moral reasoning may be viewed as a problem of determining the validity of moral arguments. In other words, the problem is essentially one of formal analysis and evaluation of Confucian reasoning in accordance with the canons of deductive logic. I shall call this approach "deductivism." The task here, more especially, lies in the reconstruction of Confucian reasoning, namely, appropriate arguments, and a subsequent determination of whether these arguments are instances of proper substitution of valid argument forms. It has been claimed that in Confucian discourses, e.g., the *Analects* and *Mencius*, certain arguments do possess the forms of *modus ponens* and *modus tollens* (Cheng 1987). While this claim seems uncontroversial, it is difficult to see how it throws light on the distinction between good and poor reasons. The notion of deductive validity does not enable us to distinguish acceptable from unacceptable premises.

Consider this famous argument on the importance of the right use of terms (*zhengming*) in the *Analects*:

> If terms are not correctly used, what is said will not sound reasonable; when what is said does not sound reasonable, undertaking will not culminate in success; when undertaking does not culminate in success, then *li* (ritual propriety) and music will not flourish. When *li* and music do not flourish, punishments will not fit the crimes; when punishments do not fit the crimes, the common people will not know where to put hand and foot. (13.3)

By making explicit the conclusion ("If terms are not correctly used, the common people will not know where to put hand and foot") and reformulating the argument in propositional logic, we have a valid chain argument. But what we want to know is why these premises are considered acceptable. For example, consider the nature of the connection between the antecedent and the consequent in the first premise. While the argument, when formally reconstructed, is logically impeccable, the deductive analysis provides us with no guide to assess the acceptability of the premises.

There are additional grounds for doubting the plausibility of the deductivist approach. In the first place, Confucian reasoning, in general, is highly inexplicit in its use of plausible presumptions (Rescher 1977, 38), i.e., appeal to shared knowledge, belief, or experience, as well as to the established or operative standards of argumentative competence (Cua 1985a). Making explicit and intelligible the relevant plausible presumptions is an extremely difficult task. Consider the widespread use of what may be called "historical appeal," i.e., the ethical use of the distinction between the past (*gu*) and the present (*jin*), of historical characters, situations, and events. The argumentative value of such an appeal does not seem to depend on conformity to rules of inference. Instead of regarding this as a form of argument, it is more illuminating to view it as a reasoned instrument performing a variety of legitimate functions in different contexts of discourse, e.g., pedagogical, rhetorical, explanatory, and justificatory functions. This thesis appears to be well supported by a study of Xunzi's recurrent use of the historical appeal (Cua 1985b). Deductivism offers us no guide to the study of the Confucian use of plausible presumptions. Because plausible presumptions, when articulated as premises of arguments, function as prima facie rather than conclusive reasons, they are essentially defeasible. It is not obvious that deductivism can help us in formulating the proper criteria of defeasibility for plausible presumptions. Moreover, it is doubtful whether such an effort is consistent with the Confucian notion of *yi* as reasoned judgment in a concrete situation of moral perplexity.

Another reason for rejecting deductivism rests on a plausible, though debatable, claim that one prominent type of reasoning in Confucian ethics, like a common form of legal reasoning, is case-by-case reasoning. This distinctive, nonformal type of reasoning was first noted by I. A. Richards in his *Mencius on the Mind* (1932), and can be shown to be a correct characterization of the Confucian use of argument from example, reminiscent of Aristotle's rhetorical induction. The principal ground for this ascription lies in the Confucian distinction between *jing* and *quan*, between normal and exigent situations (Cua 1978, chs. 4 and 5). For reasoning in normal situations, a deductivist characterization is quite in order. For example, if a situation is considered normal (*jing*), it can be viewed unproblematically as an instance of the application of an appropriate ritual rule (*li*). But in an exigent situation, what is required is an exercise of *quan* (discretion) in accord with reasoned judgment (*yi*). The reasoning here may, in part, be characterized as case-by-case reasoning rather than a deductive subsumption of all moral situations as instances of application of established rules or principles. Reasoning in exigent situations is underdetermined by application of ritual rules, although in normal situations these ritual rules may function as premises of deductive arguments. The problem of Confucian reasoning, in this light, is more a problem of articulating the Confucian conception of reasoned discourse rather than a problem of logical analysis and evaluation.

Schematic representation of coordinative reasoning. Nevertheless, the deductivist approach, in its insistence on the need for formal characterization, is valuable in calling attention to the importance of schematic representation of reasoning in nonnormal or exigent situations. Such a representation, although abstract, provides an illuminating way of clarifying the nature of such situations. Let us, by reflecting on an example, distinguish two different though complementary points of view in an exigent situation. Consider Shun's decision to marry the emperor's two daughters without first informing his parents (*Mencius*, 5A.2). Suppose we regard his decision as based on a reasoned judgment. The *li* (ritual rule) in question requires Shun to inform his parents first before marriage. To go against this established rule, he must *think* that his situation is exigent rather than normal. But what makes this situation exigent is its unprecedented character. Of course, Shun wants to do the right thing, yet the only guide he has is his sense of rightness or *liangzhi*, his ability to distinguish right from wrong actions. Wang Yangming comments:

> As for Shun's marrying without first telling his parents, was there someone before him who did the same thing and served as an example for him, which he could find out by looking into certain records and asking certain people, after which he did as he did? Or did he search into his *liangzhi* in an instant of thought and weigh all factors as to what was proper, after which he could not help doing what he did? (Chan 1963, 109–110)

For Shun, there are no previous cases of paradigmatic agents' decisions to guide his decision, nor is there any existing rule, say a priority rule or principle that determines a right decision over conflicting claims of filiality and marital relations. All he can do is rely on his *liangzhi*, his sense of what is right and good, weigh a variety of factors (*quan*), and arrive at a judgment based on relevant factors. We may note also that just as there are no rules of inference, there are no rules of relevance. Suppose Shun arrives at the following relevant considerations: (1) the emperor's wish, (2) the primacy of the relationship between husband and wife over that between parents and son, (3) the desire to marry someone with respectable social standing with the promise of acquiring political power and authority, and (4) the desire to contribute to the promotion of a *ren*-state. All these factors, for Shun, have weight as reasons supporting his judgment. To depict his reasoning, retrospectively, we might construct a diagram showing how different lines, representing considerations of presumably equal weight, are coordinated and converge upon a single conclusion. We have here a sort of coordinative reasoning. We may say with Wisdom (1957) that here:

> The process of argument is not a *chain* of demonstrative reasoning. It is presenting and representing those features of the case which severally *cooperate* in favor of the conclusion, in favor of saying what the reasoner wishes said, in favor of calling the situation by the name by which he

> wishes to call it. The reasons are like the legs of a chair, not the links of a chain. (Cua 1985a, 92–95; Wisdom, 157)

We find the same sort of coordinative reasoning in Xunzi, when he justifies his thesis on the necessity of regulative functions of ritual rules (*li*). When such factors as scarcity of resources to satisfy everyone's needs and desires, partiality or limited benevolence, limited foresight, and vulnerability are invoked together, they provide a sufficient warrant for accepting his thesis; yet each factor, viewed independently, is quite weak in supporting his thesis (Cua 1978).

For present purposes, we can thus regard reasoning in an exigent situation, as in Shun's case, retrospectively, as a coordinative form of reasoning. If we suppose that another person is in a similar situation and uses Shun's case as a paradigm for judgment, we can then say that its prospective significance can be represented as a form of case-by-case reasoning (Cua 1985a, 95–101). In short, reasoning in an exigent situation may be characterized as either coordinative or case by case, retrospectively or prospectively. Such diagrammatic representation, in my view, does help us to appreciate the nondeductive character of some types of reasoning (Cua 1998, Essay 7). Of course, there remains the question of assessing reasons in support of ethical judgment.

The *Junzi* as a Counselor to the Ruler

Before turning to the element of *pathos* in Confucian argumentation and to North's comparative remarks on Confucius and Aristotle, let me first supplement her discussion of the role of a Confucianist as a counselor to the ruler. Again, I base my discussion on that of *Xunzi*, especially the essays on the ways of ruler and ministers (*jundao pian* and *chendao pian*). At the outset, let me note that in classical Confucianism, there is an important distinction between a sage (*shengren*) and an ethically superior man or paradigmatic individual (*junzi*), a distinction presupposed in the first section of this essay. Although this distinction, perhaps, has no import in dealing with neo-Confucian literature, it is implicit in Confucius's remark that he could not hope ever to meet a sage (*shengren*); he could hope only to meet a *junzi* (*Analects*, 7.26). It is plausible to conjecture that for Confucius, the ideal of sagehood is an abstract ideal of a perfect moral character or personality rather than a practical objective of the moral life. Thus in his teachings he made use of the notion of *junzi* more often than sagehood.

In Xunzi, the distinction between *shengren* and *junzi* is explicit, though at times he seems to collapse it. Consider the following:

> In the discourse of a *shengren* (sage) there is no prior deliberation or planning. His utterances are fitting, refined, and in complete accord with his insight into the interconnection of different kinds of things (*lei*). Whether staying on one point or moving to another, he can respond to all changing circumstances. In the discourse of a scholar or *junzi*, there is prior deliberation and planning. In any occasion, his utterances are worthy to be listened to, refined and yet in accord with facts. (Li, 89)

In order to appreciate the role of a Confucian (*Ru*) as a ruler's counselor, it is better to focus on *junzi* than on *shengren*. It is indeed a common faith of classical Confucians and neo-Confucians that all humans are innately capable of attaining sagehood. As Xunzi reminds his readers, everyone is capable of becoming a sage, for everyone has the ability to learn and discern the rationales of *ren, yi*, and other standards of conduct and put them into practice. So long as we apply ourselves to study in seeking *dao* with single-mindedness and resolute will, examine things carefully and thoughtfully, persist in these efforts over a long period of time, and accumulate good acts without cessation, "we can achieve a godlike insight (*shenming*) into all things and form a triad with Heaven and Earth" (Li, 554; Watson, 167). But in reality, sagehood is not actually possible (*neng*) for everyone because of lack of will to engage in the pursuit. And, we may add, it is doubtful that humans, no matter how intelligent, can have the sage's insight to respond to all changing circumstances of human life without a need to engage in informed deliberation (*zhilü*). Perplexities over right and wrong conduct cannot be resolved without deliberation (Li, 284).

Even for a *junzi*, there are difficulties to be overcome in persuasion. Generally, one cannot accomplish one's goals by being direct or straightforward, for there is a risk in avoiding factual errors and platitudes, and there is also a possibility of injuring the listener's sense of self-respect. The appeal to historical events of the distant past, for example, unless carefully substantiated by evidence, is bound to be unreliable. The appeal to events near the present, unless their relevance or significance is demonstrated, risks becoming platitudinous. A *junzi* will thus adapt himself to the time and circumstances, will express his view fully after attending to all sides, and will not injure others' sense of self-respect. As a paradigmatic individual, he regulates his conduct by the standards of *ren, li*, and *yi*, and guides others accordingly (Li, 86).

Suppose a *junzi* assumes the position of the minister; there are then additional difficulties involved in relation to the ruler. As a person of integrity, the *junzi* will follow *dao* rather than comply with his ruler's arbitrary wishes (*congdao bu congjun*). How he conducts himself depends on the kind of ruler he serves. Naturally, he should prove himself worthy of trust and gain the ruler's confidence, assuming that the ruler is a sage or enlightened (*mingjun*)—that is, an exemplar of virtue, who, apart from self-cultivation, loves his people and enlists only the worthy for service. In this case, the *junzi*'s position is relatively easy. So long as the ruler's concern for *dao* is successfully expressed in policies and laws and is carried out in promoting order, there is only listening and obedience but no remonstration. "This is the way," Xunzi notes, "to serve the sage-king: be respectful, reverent and modest, swift in carrying out orders and not daring to make decisions nor give or receive things for the sake of self-interest, and consider obedience as one's will" (Li, 294). To be in such a fortunate position, of course, involves understanding the significance of laws and policies, not merely a mastery of their complexities. Unlike a muddleheaded ruler (*anjun*), who aims merely at acquiring power without regard to *dao* or to human welfare, the enlightened ruler is a model to his people. In Xunzi's words, "the enlightened ruler is like a sundial, and the people are like the shadows; when the sundial is set properly, the shadows will reflect accordingly" (Li, 270). For a *junzi*, serving an enlightened ruler is both a pleasure and a privilege, for in such a ruler he sees a marvelous exemplification of the actuating import of *dao* in human life.

Realistically, however, a *junzi* is more likely to serve under a ruler who is less than enlightened. While Xunzi, like Confucius and Mencius, believed in a golden age—the time of the sage kings Yao, Shun, and especially Yu and Tang—he would be quite content with seeing a *ba* (hegemonist) ruling the world, for a *ba* at least relies on laws and cares for his people (Li, 342).

If a *ba* is an average ruler (*zhongjun*), a *junzi* may engage in remonstration but not flattery. The *junzi* will be loyal and trustworthy, but refrain from self-depreciation; he will remonstrate and try to gain acceptance of his advice, but refrain from flattery; he will be firm and courageous in upholding his views with the sole intention of expressing what is correct and upright but will not allow his mind to be moved by extraneous considerations (Li, 294–295). The most difficult situation arises when the *junzi* is compelled to serve a cruel ruler (*baojun*) in a time of disorder. While he will be extremely cautious so as to preserve his life, he will maintain his integrity. He will refrain from overt remonstration and rectification of the ruler's misconduct but will attempt to transform the cruel ruler in a gentle and agreeable manner, with the hope that his words will gain the ruler's inner assent. For Xunzi, a cruel ruler is like a horse that needs to be tamed or an infant that needs to be nourished. The process will be slow and will require the utmost care and patience. The *junzi* will "adapt himself to different situations in a flexible and circuitous fashion in the course of transforming the cruel ruler's temperament" (Li, 295).

Pathos. The foregoing indicates Xunzi's attitude in persuading a particular audience. In general, any means of persuasion that does not violate the standards of *ren*, *li*, and *yi* will be endorsed. Were the participants in argumentation all actuated by these concerns, discourse would be facile in transforming disagreement into agreement. If, for analytical purposes, we distinguish the speaker from his or her audience and concentrate on the idea of a persuasive speaker, and further assume that the speaker is a *junzi*, we can explore the appropriate emotions of the audience to be aroused in speech. The topic of emotions in Confucian ethics is unexplored. My brief remarks here center on the divergent conceptions of Xunzi and Mencius. This divergence reflects contrasting views of human nature.

As North points out, Mencius's aim in persuading the king is to show him how he could "gallop on to goodness" and to demonstrate this by appealing to the king's original nature. For Mencius, all humans possess four beginnings or *xin* (heart-mind):

> The heart of compassion is the germ of benevolence (*ren*); the heart of shame, of dutifulness (*yi*); the heart of courtesy and modesty, of the observance of rites (*li*); the heart of right and wrong, of wisdom. (2A.6; Cua 2002)

Notably, the speaker's aim is to guide the listener by awakening his innately good nature, to encourage its development, for the virtues of *ren, li, yi*, and wisdom are the flowering of the four beginnings. It is unclear in Mencius what other sentiments are relevant objects of persuasion.

Xunzi, on the contrary, believes that human nature is originally bad, in the sense that it presents problems for regulation, particularly by *li* (ritual rules). Moods such as joy and sorrow; emotions such as love, hate, anger, and envy; and bodily feelings such as pleasure, pain, hunger, and thirst make up the basic human motivational structure. In themselves, these feelings (*qing*) are morally neutral. But coupled with man's natural self-seeking propensity to satisfy the desires aroused by these emotions, expressions of these feelings are likely to conflict, especially if there is a scarcity of goods to satisfy them. Given this view, all feelings and desires are materials for moral transformation (*hua*) in accord with *ren, li*, and *yi*. Persuading the listeners, in light of the speaker's *ethos*, amounts to transforming these desires into reflective desires, i.e., desires mediated by reason. Although they diverge in their conceptions of human nature, Mencius and Xunzi agree about the ultimate aim of persuasion. From the point of view of ethical theory, they are one in espousing the Confucian *dao*, although Mencius is more inclined to emphasize *ren* and *yi* than *li* and *yi*. This difference in emphasis does not constitute a difference in ethical intention. The role of *pathos* in Confucian rhetoric deserves exploration, as it has a key role to play in developing a Confucian moral psychology.

Conclusion

This essay has presented a sketch of the elements of a Confucian theory of rhetoric. It is difficult to say how much it contributes to comparative east-west rhetorical studies. Along with Max Hamberger, North has noted, throughout her paper, some analogies and contrasts, particularly in comparing Confucius and Aristotle. The theoretical significance of such efforts is difficult to assess, not because they are uninstructive, particularly for rectifying ethnocentrism, but because problems beset the inquirer when he or she focuses on the basic concepts of different ethical outlooks. *Ren*, for example, is functionally equivalent to benevolence. But Hamberger's comparison of *li* to *epeikeia* (reasonableness) is doubtful. In my view, the latter has some affinity to *yi*, which is functionally equivalent to *phronesis*. *Zhong*, often rendered as "the mean," does not correspond exactly to Aristotle's notion of the mean, nor is it unattainable by a *junzi*. Although *zhong* does consist in "not being inclined to either side" (*Analects*, 6.27), it is better rendered as "centrality" or "equilibrium," as Legge did, though not in his translation of the classic *Zhongyong*. According to one interpretation based on Wang Yangming, the distinction between *zhong* and *he* (harmony) does not constitute a dichotomy. *Zhong* may be viewed as an achieved state of mind, a result of the *he* of emotions; and *he* as an achieved state of mind is a result of the activation of the incipient tendency toward *zhong*. We may note with Hamberger, however, an interesting affinity between *junzi* and Aristotle's *spoudaios*. Functional equivalence of concepts is important in comparative inquiry, in exhibiting parallels of different conceptual schemes. Whether this sort of endeavor is helpful for constructing or developing a Confucian theory remains an open question. In my view, such an effort has value in pointing to the possibility of interaction of different conceptual schemes, thus providing an important resource for developing a rhetorical theory in Confucian moral philosophy.

See also Confucianism: Ethics; Confucianism: Tradition; *Junzi; Quan*; Reason and Principle.

Bibliography

Aristotle, *Rhetoric*, trans. W. Rhys Roberts. In *The Works of Aristotle*, ed. W. D. Ross, Vol. 11. Oxford: Clarendon, 1952.

Chan, W. T., trans. *Instructions for Practical Living and Other Neo-Confucian Writings by Wang Yang-ming*. New York: Columbia University Press, 1963.

Chen, Daqi. *Xunzi xueshuo*. Taipei: Zhonghua wenhuashe, 1954.

Cheng, Hsueh-li. "Reasoning in Confucian Ethics." Presented at the International Symposium on Confucianism and the Modern World. Taipei, Taiwan, 12–17 November, 1987.

Cua, A. S. *Ethical Argumentation: A Study in Hsün Tzu's Moral Epistemology*. Honolulu: University of Hawaii Press, 1985a.

———. "Ethical Uses of History in Early Confucianism: The Case of Hsün Tzu." *Philosophy East and West*, 35(2), 1985b, pp. 133–156. (Reprinted in *Virtue, Nature, and Moral Agency in the Xunzi*, ed. T. C. Kline and Philip J. Ivanhoe. Indianapolis, Ind., and Cambridge: Hackett, 2000.)

———. *Moral Vision and Tradition: Essays in Chinese Ethics*. Washington, D.C.: Catholic University of America Press, 1998.

———. "The Quasi-Empirical Aspect of Hsün Tzu's Philosophy of Human Nature." *Philosophy East and West*, 28(1), 1978, pp. 3–19.

———. "Reason and Principle in Chinese Philosophy." In *A Companion to World Philosophies*, ed. Eliot Deutsch and Ron Bontekoe. Oxford: Blackwell, 1997.

———. "*Xin* and Moral Failure: Notes on an Aspect of Mencius' Moral Psychology." In *Mencius: Contexts and Interpretation,* ed. Alan K. L. Chan. Honolulu: University of Hawaii Press, 2002.

Danto, Arthur C. *The Transfiguration of the Commonplace*. Cambridge, Mass.: Harvard University Press, 1981.

Dubs, H. H., trans. *The Works of Hsüntze*. Taipei: Ch'eng-wen, 1966.

Dworkin, Ronald. *Law's Empire*. Cambridge, Mass.: Harvard University Press, 1986.

Fogelin, Robert H. *Understanding Arguments: An Introduction to Informal Logic*. New York: Harcourt, Brace Jovanovich, 1978.

Gallie, W. B. *Philosophy and Historical Understanding*. London: Chatto and Windus, 1964.

Hamberger, Max. "Aristotle and Confucius: A Study in Comparative Philosophy." *Philosophy*, 31, 1956.

Johnston, Henry, and Maurice Natanson, eds. *Philosophy, Rhetoric, and Argumentation*. University Park: Pennsylvania State University Press, 1965.

Knoblock, John. *Xunzi: A Translation and Study of the Complete Works*, 3 vols. Stanford, Calif.: Stanford University Press, 1988–1994.

Li, Disheng. *Xunzi jishi*. Taipei: Xuesheng, 1979. (Citations of the original text of *Xunzi* refer to this book.)

North, Helen. "Ethical Values in Classic Eastern Texts." Presented at the symposium "Rhetoric: East and West," East-West Center. Honolulu, Hawaii, 12–18 June 1988.

Oliver, Robert T. *Communication and Culture in Ancient India and China*. Syracuse, N.Y.: Syracuse University Press, 1971.

Perelman, Chaim. *The New Rhetoric and the Humanities*. Dordrecht: Reidel, 1979.

———. *The Realm of Rhetoric*. Notre Dame, Ind.: University of Notre Dame Press, 1982.

Perelman, Chaim, and Anna Olbrechts-Tyteca. *The New Rhetoric: A Treatise in Argumentation*. Notre Dame, Ind.: University of Notre Dame Press, 1969.

Rawls, John. *A Theory of Justice*. Cambridge, Mass.: Harvard University Press, 1971.

Rescher, Nicholas. *Dialectics*. Albany: State University of New York Press, 1977.
Richards, I. A. *Mencius on the Mind*. London: Kegan Paul, 1932.
Taylor, Paul. *Normative Discourse*. Englewood Cliffs, N.J.: Prentice-Hall, 1961.
Thomas, Stephen Naylor. *Reasoning in Natural Language*, 3rd ed. Englewood Cliffs, N.J.: Prentice-Hall, 1986.
Toulmin, Stephen. *The Uses of Argument*. Cambridge: Cambridge University Press, 1958.
Watson, Burton, trans. *Hsün Tzu: Basic Writings*. New York: Columbia University Press, 1963.
Wisdom, John. *Philosophy and Psychoanalysis*. Oxford: Blackwell, 1957.
Winterowd, W. Ross. *Rhetoric: A Synthesis*. New York: Holt, Rinehart, and Winston, 1968.

Confucianism: Song (Sung)

Tzi-ki Hon

Neo-Confucianism of the Song dynasty (960–1276) was a philosophical movement with a dual nature: it was a creative response to the Buddhist and Daoist challenge on the one hand and an imaginative reappropriation of classical Confucianism on the other. As a response to the challenge of Buddhism and Daoism, neo-Confucianism had to come to terms with the sociopolitical situation in Song China. Since the disastrous fall of the Han dynasty in 221, the classical Confucian vision of a benevolent government ruling with the mandate of heaven had been discredited. For seven centuries, Chinese philosophy had been dominated by either the Buddhists' concern with attaining personal liberation from suffering or the Daoists' concern with transcending anthropocentrism. But the equally disastrous fall of the Tang in 906 and the subsequent foreign invasions in the Song brought the Confucian vision of a benevolent government back to the center of philosophical debate. Having witnessed the decay of the polity and the loss of northern China to the Jurchens and the Mongols, the Song neo-Confucians revived Confucian doctrine as the guiding principle of their personal ethics, social practices, and political philosophy. They wanted to establish a long-lasting sociopolitical structure in China so that the country would be free from warlords, political partisans, and foreign invaders.

Thus, the rise of neo-Confucianism was a response to the present as much as to the past. Confucianism in the Song is called neo-Confucianism because it clearly contained elements different from classical Confucianism founded by Confucius (551–479 B.C.E.) and Mencius (331–289 B.C.E.). A key difference was the redefinition of the Confucian canon. Neo-Confucians replaced the Five Classics of classical Confucianism (*Book of Changes, Book of Songs, Book of Documents, Book of Rites*, and *Spring and Autumn Annals*) with their own Four Books: the *Great Learning*, the *Analects*, the *Mencius*, and the *Doctrine of the Mean*. Furthermore, many terms in classical Confucianism, such as *ren* (humanity), received new meanings in the hands of the neo-Confucians. With these changes, the neo-Confucians creatively reappropriated classical Confucianism for their own purposes. They avoided the mistake of classical Confucians in focusing primarily on human relationships. They also made efforts to tailor their doctrine to an audience steeped in Buddhism and Daoism. In the end, they reinvented Confucianism so that it contained both the sociopolitical vision of classical Confucianism and the metaphysical sophistication of Buddhism and Daoism.

Neo-Confucians often traced their movement back to Han Yu (786–824). On the surface, Han Yu seems to be an odd choice. An accomplished literary stylist in the mid-Tang, Han Yu was neither a cool-minded philosopher nor an original thinker. His writings often give an impression of being more rhetorical than philosophical. But regardless of his limitations, the neo-Confucians honored him for his unyielding opposition to Buddhism and Daoism. They remembered him as a lone voice in a "decadent age" defending Confucian principles.

Among Han Yu's writings, his essay "An Inquiry on the Way" (*Yuan dao*) received widespread acclaim from the neo-Confucians. In this essay, Han Yu first distinguished the true Way of Confucianism from the false ways of Buddhism and Daoism. He called the true Way of Confucianism "the teachings of our ancient kings"—a universal love of humanity based on the proper regulation of the five cardinal human relationships (ruler and minister; father and son; husband and wife; elder and younger brother; friend and friend). Then he lamented the eclipse of Confucianism since the death of Mencius. At the end of the essay, he exhorted the reader to revive Confucianism by fighting against Buddhism and Daoism.

As a call to arms against Buddhism and Daoism, Han Yu's essay helped to define the nature of the neo-Confucian movement. First, neo-Confucianism was understood as a revival of classical Confucianism after its long eclipse. Despite the fact that there were "pseudo-Confucians" in the Han and the Tang, the neo-Confucians regarded themselves as the true Confucians, restoring what had been missing for thirteen hundred years. They believed that they were the first in history to put the Confucian sociopolitical vision into practice. Second, Han Yu proposed that to overcome Buddhism and Daoism, the neo-Confucians had to reemphasize the Confucian belief in the transformative function of human community. They had to argue that not all human bonds contributed to craving, suffering, and separation from nature as the Buddhists and the Daoists had suggested. Instead, human relationships based on "humanity" (*ren*) were personally fulfilling and spiritually uplifting. Properly regulated and earnestly practiced, human relationships were a fruitful ground for spiritual transcendence.

In the Song (which included the Northern and Southern Song), there were seven major neo-Confucians. Five of them lived in the Northern Song (960–1127), when the Song court was located in Kaifeng and the Song territory covered the valleys of the Yellow River and the Yangzi (Chang) River. These "five masters of the Northern Song" were Zhou Dunyi (1017–1073), Shao Yong (1011–1077), Zhang Zai (1020–1077), Cheng Hao (1032–1085), and Cheng Yi (1033–1107). In various ways, they helped to define the basic premise of neo-Confucianism: what is humanly is transcendental.

The other two neo-Confucians lived in the Southern Song (1127–1279), when the Song court was relocated to Hangzhou and the Song territory was confined primarily to the Yangzi River valley. The two Southern Song neo-Confucians were Zhu Xi (1130–1200) and Lu Xiangshan (1139–1193); their main concern was to develop a method that would help learners reach spiritual transcendence in mundane life. Their views on learning and their methods of self-cultivation were so radically different that they paved the way for the emergence of the "principle school" (*lixue*) and the "mind-and-heart school" (*xinxue*) of neo-Confucianism.

Among the five Northern Song masters, Zhou Dunyi and Shao Yong were the most Daoist in inclination. For instance, Zhou Dunyi's magnum opus, *An Explanation of the Diagram of the Great Ultimate* (*Taiji tushuo*), was based on a Daoist diagram for obtaining an elixir. Likewise, Shao Yong spent the later part of his life as a recluse in Loyang, and he is said to have learned his numerology from the Daoist Chen Tuan (c. 906–989). To complicate the matter, the writings of Zhou and Shao appeared in both the neo-Confucian anthologies and the Daoist canon (*Daozang*). Because of their ambiguous identity, many scholars are still debating whether it is more appropriate to consider them Daoists rather than neo-Confucians.

Despite their Daoist leanings, Zhou Dunyi and Shao Yong were unequivocally neo-Confucian in one regard: they both argued that humankind is organically related to the cosmos as a part to the whole. By arguing for a part-whole copartnership between humankind and the cosmos, Zhou and Shao questioned the basic premise of neo-Daoism. Beginning with Wang Bi (226–249), the neo-Daoists argued that the essence of the "myriad things" or "ten thousand things" lay not in the things themselves but in the overall principle which unified them. To illustrate the precedence of the whole over a part, the neo-Daoists often cited Laozi's example "thirty spokes, share one hub" (*Laozi*, ch. 15). They equated the thirty spokes with the myriad things and the hub with the overall principle. Just as the spokes depended on the hub in turning the wheel of a cart, the myriad things attained their functions because of the overall principle.

Zhou Dunyi and Shao Yong did not accept the neo-Daoist perspective. Building on the bipolar complementarity of *yin* and *yang* in the *Book of Changes*, they argued that there was as much part in whole as whole in part. If indeed the *Book of Changes* was right in depicting the universe as an organic entity continually renewing itself, part and whole are dependent on each other. Although the universe is never complete without the existence of the myriad things, the mission of the myriad things is to partake in the universe's self-renewal.

This codependence of part and whole was graphically represented in Zhou Dunyi's *An Explanation of the Diagram of the Great Ultimate*. Modifying a Daoist diagram, Zhou used five circles to depict the sequence by which the universe came into being. First he traced the creation of the myriad things back to the primordial and undifferentiated origin of the universe, the "supreme ultimate" (*taiji*). Then, turning from cosmology to ethics, he argued that as members of the cosmic family of beings, humans would contribute to the unfolding of the universe by doing what they are good at—acting morally. In simple terms, he elucidated the cosmological root of human morality.

In the same vein, Shao Yong discussed the codependence of part and whole in numerology. By rearranging the sixty-four hexagrams of the *Book of Changes* into a circle and dividing them into a series of multiples of four, he demonstrated how the myriad things were related to a gigantic cosmic system of ebb and flow, growth and decay. In his *Supreme Principles Governing the World* (*Huangji jingshi shu*), he offered an impressive chronological chart depicting how the universe had evolved over time. With this chart, he located human history in the *longue durée* of the universe's self-renewal. In relating human time to cosmic time, Shao Yong—like Zhou Dunyi—intended to demonstrate the codependence of humankind and the universe. Although the universe is infinitely larger and more diverse than the human community, they need each other; like sound and echo, shape and shadow, they exist for each other. For this reason, Shao Yong admonished the reader not to underestimate the transforming power of humankind.

In opposing neo-Daoism, Zhou Dunyi and Shao Yong had clarified the cosmological root of human morality, but it was Zhang Zai who first made a systematic argument about the metaphysical nature of human morality, or "moral metaphysics." In his essay "Western Inscription" (*Ximing*), Zhang Zai went beyond Zhou and Shao by abandoning cosmology. Instead of offering an account of the development of the universe, he picked up where Zhou and Shao had left off, discussing morality as human bonding with all beings in the universe. In the first few lines of "Western Inscription," he spelled out lucidly the neo-Confucian moral metaphysics:

> Heaven is my father and Earth is my mother, and even such a small creature as I finds an intimate place in their midst. Therefore that which fills the universe I regard as my body and that which directs the universe I consider as my nature. All people are my brothers and sisters, and all things are my companions. (Chan 1963, 497; *Song Yuan xuean*, 17.3a)

For Zhang, ethical deeds were not just good deeds in the interest of human society but also good deeds in the interest of the universe as a whole. For instance, to be a filial son involved not just a son's duty to his parents but also his duty to the cosmos. Similarly, to be a faithful minister was to be faithful not just to the emperor but to the universe as a whole. In short, what is moral is also metaphysical.

In the same vein, Cheng Hao emphasized the intimate connection of ethics and metaphysics by reinventing the Confucian concept of *ren*, "humanity." In classical Confucianism, *ren* was understood primarily as the ethical ground of human relationships. Etymologically, the Chinese character *ren* consists of two graphs: one symbolizes humankind and the other signifies the number two. This had led many classical Confucian scholars to argue that the root meaning of *ren* was the relationship of two persons.

Going beyond the classical rendition of *ren*, Cheng Hao defined it as the relationship between humankind and the cosmos. In his short essay "On Understanding the Nature of *Ren*" (*Shi ren pian*), Cheng Hao described *ren* as "forming one body with all things without any differentiation." To be humane, it was not enough to love just one's parents, kinsmen, and fellow countrymen; one had to love all things on earth. To be fully human, one had to recognize one's dual status as both a citizen of human community and a citizen of the cosmic family of beings. Certainly, given the multiplicity of beings on this earth, one might need to first cultivate relationships with those nearby before reaching out to those far away. Yet one should always remember that the goal of cultivating relationships with those nearby was to achieve the ideal of "forming one body with all things without any differentiation." Cheng Hao argued that a person who realized the cosmic meaning of an ethical act would know that what is human is cosmic and what is mundane is transcendental, and would see daily, humdrum life as sacred.

Much as Zhou Dunyi and Shao Yong were semi-Daoists in order to counter neo-Daoism, Zhang Zai and Cheng Hao were semi-Buddhists in order to counter Zen (Chan) Buddhism. The key argument in the moral metaphysics of Zhang Zai and Cheng Hao is that the human mind is fully equipped with the potential for spiritual transcendence. To be enlightened, human beings do not need to seek anything from without; they need to undertake an inward search to activate the innate potential of the human mind. For this reason, both Zhang Zai and Cheng Hao emphasized the simplicity and ease of the human quest for enlightenment. For Zhang Zai, enlightenment would come when, suddenly, one comprehended that "all people are my brothers and sisters, and all things are my companions." Likewise, for Cheng Hao, there was no need for an exhaustive search for enlightenment, because "if one preserves *ren* long enough, it will automatically dawn on him."

Zhang Zai's and Cheng Hao's emphasis on simplicity and ease in moral cultivation paralleled the Zen Buddhist teaching on the Buddha-mind. Believing that everyone was endowed with the Buddha-nature, the Zen Buddhists argued that the true substance of one's mind, or the Buddha-mind, was the storehouse of the Buddha-nature. By "pointing directly to the human mind" and "transmitting from one mind to another mind," the Zen Buddhists focused on the cultivation of the Buddha-mind as the direct way of activating one's innate Buddha-nature. Everything else, be it monastic rituals, *sutras* reading, and religious practices, was secondary.

Despite their similarity, Zhang Zai and Cheng Hao were different from the Zen Buddhists in their ultimate concern. For Zhang Zai and Cheng Hao, the universe was real and life on earth was joyful. Their ultimate concern was not to reach Nirvana by awakening to the emptiness of the universe, but to "preserve humanity" by enabling human beings to become fully human in light of the Confucian vision of *ren*. Their goal of cultivating the human mind entailed not leaving this world but being more deeply rooted in it. They wanted their fellow human beings to see their indispensable roles in the universe's self-renewal, and to feel their importance as members of the cosmic family of beings.

Still, Zhang Zai and Cheng Hao had so much in common with the Zen Buddhists that they caused alarm among some neo-Confucians. Cheng Yi, Cheng Hao's younger brother, was among the first to attempt to steer neo-Confucianism away from Zen Buddhism. To balance the idealistic bent of Zhang Zai and Cheng Hao, Cheng Yi argued that one could not rectify one's mind with intuition alone; intuition had to be actualized in daily practices. For Cheng Yi, the path to enlightenment consisted of intuition and learning: intuition informed learning and learning made intuition concrete.

To explain the codependence of intuition and learning, Cheng Yi invoked the example of Yan Hui, Confucius's favorite student. In his essay "A Treatise on What Yanzi Loved to Learn," Cheng Yi argued that Yan Hui's strength was less his intellectual acuteness than his earnestness in rectifying his mistakes—he was so conscientious in this regard that he earned a reputation for not committing the same mistake twice. His thought and his deeds were so mutually reinforcing that he did not see, listen, speak, or move contrary to propriety.

To highlight the codependence of intuition and learning, Cheng Yi coined the saying "Self-cultivation requires seriousness; the pursuit of learning depends on the extension of knowledge." The first half of this sentence—"self-cultivation requires seriousness"—represents Cheng Yi's summary of Zhang Zai's and Cheng Hao's position: the importance of cultivating the human mind. The second half—"the pursuit of learning depends on the extension of knowledge"—was his attempt to balance intuition with learning and thought with deed. The key point in the second half was the term "extension of knowledge" (*zhizhi*), originally one part of the "eightfold cultivation" in the *Great Learning*. Cheng Yi used "extension of knowledge" to highlight the importance of practicing one's thought in daily life. For him, the purpose of the "extension of knowledge" was not to lock oneself into an aimless daily routine. Instead, it was a way of cultivating the mind so that it would accept things as they are in themselves. In the final analysis, he did not see intuition and learning, thought and deed, as two separate realms; he saw them as mutually reinforcing.

In many ways, the idea that "self-cultivation requires seriousness; the pursuit of learning depends on the extension of knowledge" helps to elucidate a heated debate between the two Southern Song neo-Confucian masters, Lu Xiangshan and Zhu Xi. As philosophical rivals, Lu and Zhu often wrote to each other to argue about issues of cosmology, moral cultivation, and textual exegesis, and they once had a face-to-face encounter at the Goose Lake Temple in present-day Jiangxi province.

Taking the position of Zhang Zai and Cheng Hao, Lu Xiangshan stressed "self-cultivation requires seriousness." He had a tendency to go directly to fundamentals, and he considered the perfect truth as always a unity. Regardless of how vast and diverse the universe may be, he believed that its principle was one and was the same as the principle endowed in the human mind. On the basis of his theory of the unity of mind and principle (*xin ji li*), he argued that the cultivation of the mind is the direct method for achieving the neo-Confucian moral metaphysics. To search for the cosmic principle, he suggested, one did not need to seek from without; one needed to cultivate one's mind from within.

Taking Cheng Yi's position of balancing intuition with learning, Zhu Xi stressed "the pursuit of learning depends on the extension of knowledge." Zhu did not dispute Lu on the idea of the ultimate unity of mind and principle; nevertheless, he was keenly aware of the gap between what is given as potential and what is fully actualized. Even if the human mind was endowed with the cosmic principle, a potential that was not fully actualized remained an unused resource. So for him, a genuine theory of moral cultivation had to address the technical problems and the human anxiety in actualizing the innately endowed potential in the human mind. For this reason, he believed that the human mind had two distinct elements. He called the part of the human mind that had fully actualized its potential as the storehouse of the cosmic principle the "mind of the Way" (*daoxin*). He called the other part of the human mind, which had not actualized its potential, the "mind of man" (*renxin*). To deal with the gap between the potential and the actualized, he created a series of dichotomies: principle (*li*) versus material force (*qi*), the "shape above" (*xing er shang*) versus the "shape within" (*xing er xia*), the principle of heaven (*tianli*) versus human desire (*renyu*), and the mind (*xin*) versus the nature (*xing*). For him, the goal of moral cultivation was to actualize fully what is potentially available to human beings.

In his renowned work *A History of Chinese Philosophy*, Fung Yu-lan makes an insightful observation about the philosophical difference between Lu Xiangshan and Zhu Xi (1953, 1:587). He characterizes their difference as pertaining to how reality is conceived. Emphasizing the unity of mind (*xin*) and principle (*li*), Lu sees reality as comprising "only a single realm, wholly confined to time and space; hence it and our own mind constitute an undifferentiated unity." By contrast, Zhu sees reality as comprising "two distinct realms, the one lying within the limits of time and space, the other transcending these limits." For this reason, Lu is often considered a monist and a subjectivist and Zhu a dualist and an objectivist.

The debate between Lu Xiangshan and Zhu Xi was a landmark in the development of neo-Confucianism, and it encapsulated the fundamental difference between the two main schools of neo-Confucianism: "mind-and-heart" (*xinxue*) and "principle" (*lixue*). Arguing for the unity of the human mind and the cosmic principle, Lu paved the way for the "mind-and-heart" school, which stressed the cultivation of the human mind as the only way to achieve spiritual transcendence. Zhu, arguing for a balance between intuition and learning, became the founder of the "principle" school, which took a cautious attitude toward bridging the gap between what is potentially available and what is fully actualized.

In many ways, the ebb and flow of the two neo-Confucian schools indicated the development of Chinese thought in the last centuries of imperial China. After the demise of the Song, the "pinciple" school was quickly adopted by the Yuan court (1271–1368) and the Ming court (1368–1644) as the ruling doctrine. From 1313 on, Zhu Xi's writings were part of the civil service examinations. The "mind-and-heart" school, after having been inactive for a few centuries, came to dominate the Chinese philosophical scene under Wang Yangming (1472–1529) and remained dominant in the early part of the Qing (1644–1911).

See also Cheng Hao; Cheng Yi; Confucianism: Constructs of Classical Thought; Han Yu; *Li*: Principle, Pattern, Reason; Lu Xiangshan; Reason and Principle; Shao Yong; Wang Yangming; Zhang Zai; Zhou Dunyi; Zhu Xi.

Bibliography

Birdwhistell, Anne D. *Transition to Neo-Confucianism: Shao Yung on Knowledge and Symbols of Reality*. Stanford, Calif.: Stanford University Press, 1989.

Chan, Wing-tsit. *Chu Hsi: New Studies*. Honolulu: University of Hawaii Press, 1989.

———, trans. *A Source Book in Chinese Philosophy*. Princeton, N.J.: Princeton University Press, 1963.

Chang, Carsun. *The Development of Neo-Confucian Thought*, 2 vols. New York: Bookman, 1962.

Cua, A. S. "Reason and Principle in Chinese Philosophy." In *A Companion to World Philosophies*, ed. Eliot Deutsch and Ron Bontekoe. Oxford: Blackwell, 1997.

de Bary, William Theodore, ed. *The Unfolding of Neo-Confucianism*. New York: Columbia University Press, 1975.

Fung, Yu-lan. *A History of Chinese Philosophy*, 2 vols. Princeton, N.J.: Princeton University Press, 1953.

Gardner, Daniel K. *Chu Hsi and the Ta-Hsüeh: Neo-Confucian Reflection on the Confucian Canon*. Cambridge, Mass.: Harvard University Press, 1986.

Graham, A. C. *Two Chinese Philosophers: The Metaphysics of the Brothers Ch'eng*. La Salle, Ill.: Open Court, 1992.

Huang, Zongxi. *Song Yuan xue'an*. Taipei: Taiwan Zhonghua shuju. (Reprint.)

Liu, James T. C. *China Turning Inward: Intellectual-Political Changes in the Early Twelfth Century*. Cambridge, Mass.: Council on East Asian Studies, Harvard University Press, 1988.

Liu, Shu-hsien. *Understanding Confucian Philosophy: Classical and Sung-Ming*. Westport, Conn.: Praeger, 1998.

Mou, Zongsan. *Xinti yu xingti* (The Substance of the Mind and the Substance of Human Nature), Vol. 2. Taipei: Zhengzhong shuju, 1969.

Tillman, Hoyt Cleveland. *Confucian Discourse and Chu Hsi's Ascendency*. Honolulu: University of Hawaii Press, 1992.

Tu, Weiming. *Centrality and Commonality: An Essay on Confucian Religiousness*. Albany: State University of New York Press, 1989.

———. *Humanity and Self-Cultivation: Essays in Confucian Thought*. Berkeley, Calif.: Asian Humanities, 1979.

Wyatt, Don J. *The Recluse of Loyang: Shao Yung and the Moral Evolution of Early Sung Thought*. Honolulu: University of Hawaii Press, 1996.

Confucianism: Tang (T'ang)

David McMullen

The Confucian tradition of the Tang (or T'ang) period (618–907) demonstrates historically important continuities but also profound changes. As an ideology the main concerns of which were social, and as a system of thought without a tradition of rigorous inductive procedures, Confucianism both kept its commitment to its ancient canonical texts and responded throughout this period to changing political and social conditions. It also remained a rationalistic ideology, the property of an educated elite dedicated to the ideal of official service. This elite ensured that Confucianism retained its paternalistic ethic, its belief in political hierarchy, and its prejudice against women, non-Chinese, and merchants. Although philosophically one of its main concerns was with man's relation to the cosmic process (*tianren zhi ji*), Confucian scholars remained indifferent to the systematic empirical investigation of phenomena.

Dynastic government in the first half of the Tang, especially in the reigns of Gaozu (618–626) and Taizong (618–649), the foundation period, and then under Xuanzong in the High Tang (712–755), was, by the standards of premodern empires, effective, and developments within the Confucian tradition reflected this success. The period after An Lushan's rebellion of 755 saw both a drastic deterioration in political conditions and an increase in cultural sophistication, and Confucians reacted creatively to these developments.

Throughout these three phases of the dynasty, however, the state promoted the Confucian tradition as the ideology of imperial government in all its operations. Striking continuities are provided by recurrent measures to encourage Confucian teaching, and by the constant place Confucian texts had in education and in the examination system. Throughout the dynasty, there were scholars who knew the canonical texts as well as any of their successors in the late imperial period. But the Tang scholarly world, smaller and more centralized than it was to become in the late imperial period, was, interestingly, not bound by any rigid sense of doctrinal orthodoxy. Nor were the well-known militant anti-Buddhism and the revival of interest in Confucian interior ideas shown by Han Yu (768–824) and Li Ao (c. 772–836) the only developments of interest in the Confucianism of the second half of the dynasty. The same period saw substantial achievements in Confucian-focused political philosophy. These reflected the moral and intellectual concerns of the administrators of the most sophisticated bureaucracy that China had seen.

In Tang China, Confucianism was, alongside Buddhism and Daoism, one of the "three teachings" (*san jiao*). As an official of the early eighth century put it, Confucianism treated "the concerns of the immediate age" (*ji shi zhi wu*), whereas the rival teachings, Buddhism and Daoism, provided answers for questions of ultimate value. Confucianism was the "outer teaching" whereas Buddhism was the "inner teaching," and Daoism, like Buddhism, was concerned with the supramundane. Belief in the distinct character of the three teachings is indicated in each phase of the dynasty by the practice of staging court debates, mainly for entertainment, between representatives of each. But especially in religion, eclectic outlooks drawing on all three teachings were prevalent. It is important not to underrate the religious function of Confucianism; however, precisely because it concerned the secular world to an extent that Buddhism and Daoism did not, it was largely able to resist explicit intrusion from them and to remain a discrete body of texts and tradition of knowledge and practice.

This combination of conservatism and evolution in Tang Confucianism may be described in a number of ways. From being a teaching largely promoted through state-directed institutional measures, Confucianism became, with the generation of Han Yu and Li Ao, a body of thought that a small number of individuals, on the margins of central government, reexamined for answers to questions about how to live. An approach to canonical texts dominated by officially commissioned, compendious exercises in exposition came to coexist with a problem-centered outlook capable of radically reinterpreting canonical authority. In terms of the eightfold progression formulated in the *Great Learning* (*Daxue*), the motivation behind early Tang Confucianism was "peace in the world" (*tian xia ping*). In both the foundation period and the High Tang the ideology gained enduring strength from its identification with administrative stability, with the institutional, political, and ritual successes of Tang rule. But by the early ninth century a minority of intellectuals, responding to a much deteriorated situation, recaptured an original emphasis within the tradition on the cultivation of the self (*xiushen*), on spiritual fulfilment in Confucian terms. This historically momentous development has been called the start of an "interiorization" that was to culminate in the neo-Confucianism of Lu Xiangshan (1139–1193) and Wang Yangming (1473–1529). It has been seen as a "separation of morality and culture," or a realization that the individual should rediscover and reinterpret the Confucian moral way for himself, rather than locate it in inherited cultural norms. At the start of the Tang, although there were Confucian scholars, there were virtually no "Confucianists" in the sense of people for whom the teachings of Confucius were a creed setting them apart from others. By the ninth century, however, a small minority of scholars had identified in the Confucian tradition a resource for confronting not only social and political problems but also the ultimate meaning of life.

Confucianism in the Foundation of the Tang

The reunification of China under the founder of the Tang, the emperor Gaozu, in 618, followed by effective internal peace under the second emperor, Taizong, by 630, gave the scholars who advised the first Tang emperors a chance to promote Confucian ideals in government. The immediate concerns of high ministers like Fang Xuanling (578–648) and Wei Zheng (580–643) were predominantly practical and institutional. They believed that the well-being of the Confucian tradition should mean the successful running of the central and provincial school system, the state academy (*guozi jian*), and the temple and ritual cult of Confucius and his disciples honored there. They expanded the school system, amplified the cult of Confucius, and ennobled Kong Delun, his direct descendant. They held that the state was the guardian of the definitive text of the Confucian canon, and they took pains to preserve what remained of early stone engravings of the texts.

Ideologically, Wei Zheng, Fang Xuanling, and other scholars believed that the Confucian canon supported the state and provided norms for contemporary legal, administrative, literary, and scholarly traditions. They therefore upheld Confucian values in a number of discrete governmental and scholarly operations. This was imperial Confucianism, promoted by fiat of high officials. It was not intellectually original; rather, it involved reemphasizing ideas on the integration of early Confucianism and dynastic government developed over the period of disunion that preceded the Tang. Most of the scholars who formulated these Confucian norms served in state academic institutions and wrote from an official viewpoint. In contrast to the second half of the dynasty, very little private writing relating to traditional Confucian concerns survives from this period.

Thus in the seventh century, the main approach to the Confucian canon, the body of ancient texts that provided the authority for the tradition, was commentary. Official scholars drew up a definitive explication of the canonical texts in series, glossing terms and commenting on points of controversy. Reflecting the predominantly practical milieu, they were particularly concerned with providing an authentic understanding of the canonical ritual program of the dynasty. In 631, a first step was taken to establish the text of the canons when Yan Shigu (581–645), who claimed descent from Yan Hui, Confucius's favorite disciple, determined a correct version of the Five Classics (*Zhou yi, Shang shu, Mao shi, Li ji*, and *Chunqiu*, with the *Zuo zhuan*). But it was in drafting an exhaustive subcommentary series, the famous *True Meaning of the Five Classics* (*Wu jing zhengyi*), that the early Tang state achieved its greatest Confucian monument. Kong Yingda (574–648), a man of wide learning, "also skilled at mathematics and the calendar," who claimed descent from Confucius, was the director of a commission charged with an exhaustive review of the entire commentarial tradition. The commission's approach was to treat a chosen commentary as orthodox and use it to gloss the canonical text, paragraph by paragraph, refuting interpretations inconsistent with the selected commentary. It was assumed that all inconsistencies in the text could be explained, and that a specific meaning could be drawn even from obscure passages. The approach is said to have derived from expository or "oral-dialogic" practices in the official schools. The project, completed after Kong Yingda's death, in 653, has historical depth and thoroughness. About this time, the emperor also commissioned subcommentaries to the *Zhou li*, the *Yi li*, and the *Guliang zhuan*.

In contrast to the Former Han, this Tang subcommentary series endorsed the "old text" (*guwen*) rather than the "new text" (*jinwen*) versions of canonical texts. The reasons lie at the heart of the Tang commitment to the Confucian ideology, the concern for a stable political hierarchy. Kong Yingda's series therefore condemned the idea promoted by "new text" scholars that Confucius was an "uncrowned king" (*suwang*), worship of whom might threaten the position of the emperor. The series attempted to restrict the appeal of divination and prognostication, for these too potentially threatened the dynasty. It dismissed the apocryphal and divinatory texts that were developed under the influence of the "new text" scholars. Yet its attitude toward correlative cosmology, the belief that correspondences functioned between the political and social order and the physical universe and that irregular occurrences in nature derived from human, and specifically imperial, conduct was not radical. The original canonical texts, after all, provided numerous records of such occurrences, and these were authoritative in the eyes of the series editors. This cautious approach is evident in other state-initiated writings produced at the start of the dynasty. Lu Cai's officially commissioned *Book of Yin and Yang* (*Yin yang shu*, 641) attempted to extend state control over geomancy, divination, and fate prediction. It included an examination of records of burial in the canonical *Chunqiu*. Lu Cai concluded that there was no correlation between burial dates chosen through prognostication and the subsequent fortune of the families concerned.

In terms of metaphysics, Kong Yingda's series was undoubtedly influenced by the neo-Daoism of the southern dynasties. It defined the *dao* as "without form" (*wu xing*). The original oneness that preceded the phenomenal world was "void" (*kong*). Nonetheless, and importantly for the long-term identity of the Confucian tradition, it explicitly distinguished its position from Buddhism, though it did not undertake a systematic refutation of Buddhist concepts.

Because the series aimed to provide a survey of problems in the canonical tradition that had already been identified, it did not produce new philosophical ideas. Its "moderate skepticism" is apparent in its outlook on cosmology. Glossing a passage in the *Book of Documents* in which Shun was said to have used instruments to "regulate the Seven Directors" (the sun, moon, and five planets), the commentary stated: "The form of the heavens on high cannot be known. This is the one single instance of the activity of fathoming the heavens appearing in the [Confucian] canon." It then outlined, quoting postcanonical sources, the three theories of the shape of the universe—*huntian, gaitian*, and *xuanye*—and stated that historically the *huntian* theory was recognized as the best and had the support of recent scholars. The search for more precise knowledge of the shape of the cosmos and of terrestrial distances, another activity upheld by the canon, and the refinement of the calendar were in Tang times a court monopoly, dominated by men with Daoist or Buddhist loyalties. From the Confucian point of view, such activities were justified only as an aspect of the moral task of providing an even more accurate calendar. Confucian commentators like Kong Yingda implicitly warned against taking an interest in "the form of the heavens." There is little suggestion that they valued the accumulation of empirical knowledge about the cosmos for its own sake.

Kong Yingda's great commentary on the canon was symbolically central to the imperial Confucianism of the early Tang. For the Confucian canon was, from the start of the dynasty, the means to literacy itself. Knowledge of the canon was essential to success in the examination system, which developed from the Sui dynasty on and which served to identify the intellectual elite in public service. Confucian ideals also informed assessment of performance and promotion within the civil service. Confucian-inclined officials quoted canonical and historical precedents in policy recommendations—for example, to urge a policy of noninvolvement with the barbarians beyond China's traditional frontiers. Confucian ideals informed the unusually frank discussions on political morality between emperor and officials that the open atmosphere of Taizong's court encouraged. These exchanges, anthologized in the early eighth century as *Essentials of the Good Government of the Zhenguan Period* (*Zhenguan zheng yao*), remained influential for the remainder of the dynastic period.

Confucian social categories and moral ideals shaped the dynasty's criminal code. The extent to which the criminal law was ideologically Confucian is evident from the code itself and its commentary and from its memorial of submission. The Tang saw the climax of the "Confucianization of the law," the process that gave China a penal code many of the provisions of which were determined with great precision by social categories originating in the Confucian canon.

Confucian moral priorities also greatly influenced early Tang pronouncements on the literary scene. Early Tang officials considered literature an index of the condition of the state and an instrument for improving the mores of society. They condemned what they considered the sybaritic court literature of the late southern dynasties. The ideal that poetry expressed an individual's moral purpose may be traced back through the immensely influential "Great Preface of the Book of Songs" (*Maoshi daxu*) to the pre-Qin period and ultimately to the earliest stratum of the *Analects*. Early Tang scholars promoted it to require sobriety and decorum from the court literary circles that set the tone for the entire literary world.

Early Tang scholars saw recent and remote history as a working out of Confucian values in imperial government. They believed that "the mirror of the Yin [dynasty] is not far distant" (*Yin jian bu yuan*), by which they meant that unchanging principles of government demonstrated in remote canonical antiquity had been exemplified by recent events. It was their solemn responsibility to record these events accurately and to assess them in terms of Confucian morality. In the ongoing process of compiling and reviewing historical writing, they stressed the ideal, upheld by the Confucian canon and by the *Chunqiu* commentarial tradition, that the individual historian was morally independent of imperial power. Even though official historians worked for the state in the history office (*shi guan*), this ideal remained for most of the dynasty a way in which Confucianism expressed the idea that the tradition laid an absolute moral charge on the individual scholar-official.

The early Tang Confucian-inspired review of scholarship, literature, and history, doubtless because it was intended for the emperor, stressed the grand, cosmic role of the imperial state. Largely absent from it, therefore, was any sense that Confucian ideas were the private concern of individuals. Similarly, there was no expectation that Confucianism would provide answers to questions of ultimate value. Confucian canonical texts were not understood as emphasizing a process of introspection or as prescribing for self-cultivation. Although the term "exhausting principles and fully realizing the nature" (*qiongli jin xing*), from the *Zhou yi*, was used with reference to Confucius in this period, questions relating to contemplation and self-cultivation were, in effect, ceded to the rival traditions of Buddhism and Daoism. Buddhism was still, in the age of the great pilgrim monk Xuanzang (596–664), in contact with its Indian roots, and it was entering one of its most creative phases on Chinese soil, while the claim of the members of the imperial house that they were descended from Laozi meant that Daoism also enjoyed imperial favor. Confucian teaching, on the other hand, owed its standing to the fact that it was, in Taizong's words, as essential to good administration "as wings to birds or water to fish."

The Confucian Tradition in the High Tang

The first 130 years of Tang rule were largely a period of internal peace. Though there was instability in dynastic politics, though natural disasters occurred, and though foreign invasion was only narrowly averted, Tang society experienced a rise in wealth and Tang government increased in sophistication. In the reign of Xuanzong, the High Tang, these trends began to bring about important political and social changes. These changes were gradual before the An Lushan rebellion of 755, but they were ultimately to have far-reaching effects on the outlook of the Confucian-inclined elite.

High Tang attitudes to the Confucian tradition were again predominantly practical. The Confucian cult and the school system were expanded, so that by the late 730s they had become larger than ever before. Despite the great labor invested in the series, the state had never envisaged that Kong Yingda's *True Meaning of the Five Classics* (*Wujing zhengyi*) would provide a tight orthodoxy. At the level of the primary commentary, two commentaries for any one classic were allowed to circulate. Xuanzong particularly appears to have enjoyed listening to scholars disputing on proper interpretations of the canon. Just as Buddhist and Daoist clerics competed for imperial favor, so Confucian scholars at court vied for the sovereign's ear. The main context in which controversies arose was state ritual. Here the defining concern of Tang Confucianism for an authentically drafted ritual program for use is most clearly demonstrated. Performance of the major rituals occasioned frequent debates, and redrafting of directives was common. The empress Wu, China's first and only woman emperor, manipulated the ritual tradition to justify her own rule (690–705). Enormous energy and knowledge of canonical and historical precedent were invested in preparing for the major ritual projects, such as the Cosmic Hall (Mingtang), constructed for the first time by the empress in 688, and the Feng and Shan rites, performed first by Gaozong on Mount Tai in 666, then on Mount Song by the empress Wu in 695, and finally by Xuanzong on Mount Tai in 725.

In the High Tang period, scholars produced their own commentaries on Confucian canonical texts, and many titles of commentaries survive. Numbers of such independently produced works were taken into the imperial library (*bishu sheng*), indicating that the state did not disapprove of such activity. The freedom of individual scholars is exemplified by the famous historian and critic Liu Zhiji (661–721). His approach to the Confucian canon was shaped by his enthusiasm for detailed historical narrative. He valued the extended accounts of the *Zuozhuan* over the laconic *Chunqiu*.

In his *Generalities on History* (*Shitong*) of 710, Liu even criticized Confucius for encoding cryptic messages in the *Chunqiu*. He was also a "moderate skeptic" in the Tang tradition who believed in the primacy of human agency and who disapproved of explaining historical episodes in terms of correlative cosmology. Liu was ultimately banished, not for unacceptable views on the Confucian canon but because he intervened when one of his sons was accused of a crime. Indeed the Tang generally tolerated scholarly and intellectual diversity, and factional politics were far more divisive than differing scholarly views.

Liu Zhiji was one of several court scholars who, in the first three decades of the eighth century, debated the merits of different subcommentaries to Confucian and Daoist canonical texts. The arguments of the scholars demonstrate the sophistication of Tang concepts of textual authenticity and show that the two classic grounds for rejecting a text—the perceived unreliability of its content and evidence that its transmission was not fully or consistently documented—were carefully considered. The court-centered nature of their world is emphasized by Xuanzong's intervention in scholarly debates. The emperor himself also compiled a commentary to the *Canon of Filial Piety* (*Xiao jing*), and in 745 this was engraved in stone and displayed at the capital.

Some notable Confucian-oriented compilations were completed in the High Tang, and they symbolize the imperial Confucianism of the period. The Kaiyuan ritual code (*Da Tang Kaiyuan li*) of 732, the third ritual codification of the dynasty and the first complete ritual code to have survived in China, is outstanding for its detailed directives for the program of Confucian rituals to which the emperor and officials were committed. It followed a traditional division into five categories: "auspicious rituals" (*ji*), "rituals for guests" (*bin*), "army rituals" (*jun*), "felicitation rituals" (*jia*), and "rituals for ill omen" (*xiong*). There had been controversy for decades over many of the individual rites, but the code limited itself strictly to directives. The period was one of reaction to the reign of the empress Wu, and the code reduced the role of women in state ritual. Despite the religious eclecticism of the time, it rigidly restricted itself to Confucian rituals, the overwhelming majority of which originated in the Confucian canon. Another compilation, similarly normative, was the *Sixfold Compendium of Government of the Tang* (*Da Tang liudian*), an account of the institutions of government. The autocratic chief minister Li Linfu (d. 752) provided it with a commentary that traced the roots of all Tang administrative provisions back to the Confucian canon. Again, this document, much quoted in the second half of the dynasty, incorporated minimal entries in its institutional account of Buddhism and Daoism. Confucianism, it implies, remained the ideology that justified the dynastic state. Confucian moral priorities informed the state's internal procedures and its recruitment operations.

The middle period of Xuanzong's reign saw one of the most sophisticated attempts at empirical verification of cosmological and terrestrial measurements of the first millennium. This was an implementation of an enquiry that had been proposed in the pre-Tang period by the Confucian canonical scholar Liu Zhuo (544–612) of the Sui dynasty. In 725, a commission directed by two court astronomers, Ixing (683–727) and Nangong Yue (fl. c. 705–733), measured the solstitial shadows and polar altitudes on a chain of stations on a meridian line. Their aim was to refine the value of a single *li* (a unit of measurement) by expressing it in terms of a degree of difference between the shadow angles at successive points on the chain of stations, and to find the number of *li* corresponding to one degree of change in the altitude of the polestar. Their observations are recorded in detail in official documentation. But the Confucian-inclined historian who included them downplayed this spectacular series of observations and calculations, arguing that its true purpose should be not to prove the correctness of one or another theory of the "form of the heavens," the *huntian* or the *gaitian* model, but to address the moral task of predicting more accurately the cosmic process and the seasons. The Confucian outlook on natural science, and on a project very possibly given rigor by Indian calculation methods, remained primarily ethical. It diminished the value of empirical enquiry or the accumulation for its own sake of knowledge about the world.

In the final years of the High Tang, Xuanzong promoted Daoism both as a personal commitment and as a support for government. Daoist schools, a Daoist educational syllabus, and Daoist examinations were instituted. In 744, the emperor ordered the installation of statues of Tianzun (the highest Daoist deity), Buddha, and himself in all Buddhist and Daoist temples. His own statue, according to a later tradition, was dressed in a Daoist cap, Buddhist robes, and the shoes of a Confucian scholar. These measures symbolize the eclectic spirit at the end of the High Tang. After Xuanzong's death, his interest in Daoism met with disapproval from Confucian-inclined scholars, and neither the Daoist schools nor the Daoist examination were to be permanent.

The Middle and Late Tang: The Beginnings of Revival

The growing numbers of scholars denied access to the court in the mid-eighth century, combined with the drastic loss of political and social stability that followed the An Lushan rebellion, had profound effects on Tang Confucianism. In this third phase of the dynasty, the court now no longer functioned as the focus for scholarship, and the central school system deteriorated and lost prestige. The most creative intellectual activities took place either in the provinces or among lower-ranking metropolitan officials. The state, however, still acknowledged the responsibilities toward the tradition that it had identified at the start of the dynasty. It continued to honor the lineal descendants of Confucius. It made attempts to reform the school system and to promote canonical learning and expertise in state ritual. Individual examiners tried to make the *jinshi* and *mingqing* examinations better tests of candidates' knowledge of the Confucian canon.

The ideal of a text engraved in stone, inherited from the Han period, still carried weight. Successive attempts were made to redetermine the correct text of the canon. These resulted in the writing of versions on wood in the state academy. Finally, in 837 a full-scale stone engraving was completed and displayed there, to be known as the *Canon of the Kaich'eng Period Engraved in Stone* (*Kaicheng shijing*). Its purpose was to make permanently accessible to all scholars definitive answers to textual problems. The learned world, however, did not accept that the process of refining the text of the canon was over, and controversy inevitably followed.

In ritual, official scholars reacted against the religious eclecticism of the final period of Xuanzong's reign and continued to endorse the idea of a Confucian program of rites unmodified by intrusions from rival teachings. The detailed directives for the death rites of the emperor Daizong in 779 drafted by Yan Zhenqing (709–784), the *Directives for the Yuanling Mausoleum* (*Yuanling yizhhu*), indicate how the scholarly world still insisted on demarcation between the three traditions. Daizong, far from being the exclusive Confucian that the directives, read in isolation, might suggest, had been an ardent patron of Buddhism and was surrounded by kin who supported both Daoism and Buddhism. Yan Zhenqing himself seems likely, privately, to have had Daoist loyalties. But his funeral directives for the emperor are purely Confucian, in essence an adaptation of prescriptions from the Confucian canon, an imperial version of the directives for the funerals of officials contained in the Kaiyuan ritual code. This concern for authentically Confucian ritual directives also informed a later compilation that reviewed the Tang history of a number of state rites, the *Record of Suburban and Sacrificial Offerings in the Tang* (*Da Tang jiaosi lu*) by Wang Jing, who held office as a doctor of the court of sacrifices (*tai chang si*) over a long period into the ninth century. Several supplements were also compiled for the exclusively Confucian Kaiyuan ritual code.

Despite strong eclectic pressures from Buddhism and Daoism, the Confucian textual tradition therefore remained distinct. But such traditional state measures intended to promote Confucian scholarship and ritual were enacted after a time when individual scholars developed very different concerns. The experience of the collapse of a world of unprecedented political success led scholars to reexamine the Confucian texts that they had known since infancy. They now taxed the Confucian canon for ideas that would both help the state to recover and provide them with values by which to live. In this milieu, the compendious approach to the Confucian canon of the seventh century had little appeal. The tradition became focused on problems rather than texts. The flagrant administrative abuses surrounding the Buddhist church and imperial patronage of Buddhism, combined with cultural xenophobia, meant that some scholars increasingly resented Buddhism.

In this more devolved climate, commentaries were still written for the private teaching in which intellectuals of the period engaged. But some scholars now taught in an altogether freer spirit and without the aim of having their exegesis officially recognized. They also focused on particular texts rather than on the canon in series, as their seventh-century forebears had tended to do. The best-known example is the *Chunqiu* school of the southeast. The three scholars concerned—Dan Zhu (d. 770), Zhao Kuang (fl. c. 770), and Lu Chun (d. 805)—rejected the successive layers of exegesis that had been integral to Kong Yingda's exposition of the *Chunqiu*. They discarded the traditional Tang preference for the *Zuozhuan* among the "three traditions," and drew eclectically from all three. They also restored to the text of the *Chuncqiu* the authority that Liu Zhiji had questioned, maintaining that Confucius had encoded in it profound messages of direct relevance to the contemporary world. They emphasized the doctrine of "expedient action" (*quan*), referred to by Confucius in the *Analects* as being particularly difficult. In a time of political instability, expedient action justified political change and departure from precedent. It was probably no coincidence that at about this time the influential scholar official Lu Xuangong (754–805) expounded the concept of *quan* to the emperor Dezong.

The commentaries of the *Chunqiu* school, more interpretative than the seventh-century subcommentaries, were presented to the emperor Dezong probably at the turn of the eighth century. But there is no record of any ensuing discussion at court. Some members of the school were involved in the reform movement that held the political stage during the brief reign of Dezong's successor, Shunzong (805). After the movement's political defeat, the scholarship of the school again became unofficial. The famous skeptical scholar Liu Zongyuan was its most vigorous proponent, like earlier members of the school. He believed that texts had been subject to a process of corruption, but he appears to have been concerned with preserving the authority of Confucius as teacher and exemplar. In short essays, Liu applied the school's radical approach to a number of pre-Qin texts, but his only systematic work of textual exposition was a critique of the noncanonical *Discourses of the States* (*Guoyu*).

Liu Zongyuan's wide-ranging intellect and eclectic spirit led him to address many of the problems that preoccupied the Tang elite. Some of his ideas develop those in the political philosophy of his early contemporary Du You (735–812), compiler of a major work on government, the *Comprehensive Compendium* (*Tongdian*). Du You was an eclectic, who drew from the pre-Qin legalist tradition of statecraft as well as from the Confucian canon. He believed in the value of the state ritual program but also held the moderate skeptical belief that man and the cosmic process were separate. Liu Zongyuan was also eclectic, but his view of man's relation to the cosmos was more sharply skeptical than that of Du You. In a celebrated essay, he fiercely attacked the correlative cosmology that was integral to the "Monthly Commands" (*Yueling*), a chapter of the *Li ji* (*Liji*). This text had been compiled from a noncanonical source, the *Spring and Autumn Annals of Mr Lu* (*Lu shi Chunqiu*) and therefore had a marginal place in the canon. But it had been a source for much of the state's ritual program, and successive Tang emperors had shown it deference. Liu dismissed the *Yueling*'s assumption that climatic irregularities, plagues, or earthquakes were caused by imperial dereliction, and he maintained that the human and natural worlds were separate. He argued that the benefits of the imperial ritual program were social and moral and that "it was not necessary to take a supernatural view" of ritual. Much of Liu's skepticism has this public, political reference. Nor was he always consistent in his public attitudes. But like others of this generation, he also brought his skepticism to bear on popular attitudes on the supernatural and on the Daoist-inspired search for longevity that was so prevalent among the elite.

Liu's fellow political exile Liu Yuxi (772–842), a former political aide to Du You, was also opposed to traditional correlative cosmology and believed that the roles of heaven and man were separate. But Liu Yuxi, who debated this topic in essays exchanged with Liu Zongyuan, advocated a numerical understanding of the cosmic and human processes that had its origins in the *Zhou yi* exegesis of the court astronomer Yixing.

Liu Zongyuan thus took further than his contemporaries the "moderate skepticism" that had been official policy from the seventh century on. At its most philosophical, his argument was that human agency and cosmic processes were separate, and that heaven represented an unconscious, amoral, and spontaneous force. Events in the human and natural worlds that correlative cosmology and much conventional Tang political rhetoric claimed were linked were therefore spuriously connected. Belief in supernatural agency was also baseless. Ultimately, this outlook derived its authority from collective administrative experience in a large, rationalized bureaucratic structure. At the administrative level it may be seen in the suppression by many Confucian-inclined officials of local unauthorized religious cults. But this skepticism, though certainly rational in spirit and concerned with evidence, had limitations. It was motivated by pragmatic and political considerations. Both Liu Zongyuan and Liu Yuxi characterized natural processes only in general terms and never advocated systematic investigation of natural phenomena. Indeed Liu Yuxi, like Kong Yingda before him, dissociated himself from any interest in theories concerning the shape of the universe. If the classical Greek requirement for proof and the willingness to explore new ideas were encouraged by the law courts and market disputes of ancient Athens, Tang skepticism drew its inspiration from the experience of paternalistic administrators serving successive, varied tenures in a large, coherently organized government, from concern to restrain the credulousness of successive sovereigns, and from traditional Confucian reluctance to speculate on the supernatural.

Du You and Liu Zongyuan brought their minds to bear on a political structure that had, since the start of the dynasty, acquired enormous prestige and, from the seventh and early eighth centuries on, had earned a record of demonstrable success. The collapse that followed the An Lushan rebellion, on the other hand, suggested the perishability of institutions and the need to identify the permanently underlying principles of political philosophy. Liu and others promoted the ideal that the whole polity should be governed by the "public interest" (*gong*). This concept was supported by a well-known sentence in the canonical *Li ji*, "The world should be for the public interest" (*Tianxia wei gong*). In political rhetoric in their essays and other writings, Du You, Liu Zongyuan, and others applied it to the entire administrative structure, arguing that the general interest should govern the ruling house, the choice of imperial successors, and all operations of government. Han Yu, however, argued against Liu's position, maintaining that transmission of the throne to the eldest son resulted in less disruption than the exercise of choice on the basis of merit. Other scholars argued that the private (*si*), which could be identified with the domestic, was also in certain contexts positive. In this, they anticipated the position of a much later political philosopher, Gu Yanwu (1613–1682), who was to stress the value of the private. A feature of the problem-centered approach to canonical authority that now developed was a fresh readiness to identify corruption in the text of the Confucian canon. A fashion developed for altering the original text in favor of new wording, often a graphic variant that would permit a different interpretation. Some of these proposed changes appear fanciful today, but they indicate how unrestrained by traditional commentary scholars of the early ninth century could be. This freedom to alter the text may be seen as analogous to the liberty ninth-century intellectuals claimed to define the original intention of the sages.

In this period, historically the most significant development for the Confucian tradition was a renewed focus on the individual, on self-cultivation. A few scholars now recaptured something of the spirit of Confucius's original teaching, a sense of alienation from the political system, even while they supported many of its elements. There was much writing about the need to promote the *dao*. A number of scholars made the *dao* central to their concept of literature or literary culture (*wen*). One effect of the An Lushan rebellion was to accelerate a trend toward a less court-centered or state-centered literary world. To scholars of the late eighth century and the early ninth century, *wen* in the sense of literary practice included an enormous range of writing, from solemn pronouncements in the name of the emperor to romans à clef intended to amuse small groups of friends and to the prodigious quantities of verse, much of it intimate rather than public, written in the Tang. The great breadth of literature invited polemical comment. Officials experiencing political exile and young men trying to attract the attention of sponsors were expected to produce highly moralistic writing for potential patrons. Men in these situations tried explicitly to reinfuse literature with moral and political urgency. Liu Zongyuan during his political exile was again a leading example of a trend that had already gathered momentum by Xianzong's reign (815–820). Many intellectuals of this period wrote polemically about their own or their friends' literary experience and emphasized, in Confucian language, its political and moral function.

A distinct submovement within this general trend toward exploiting the Confucian canonical and literary tradition for self-analysis confronted the question whether exclusively Confucian religious fulfillment was possible. Here the contrast with the state-sponsored Confucianism of the seventh century was particularly sharp. The rival "inner teaching" of Buddhism promoted spiritually fulfilling prescriptions for religious attainment in life and sophisticated explanations of the afterlife. State-sponsored Tang Confucianism, on the other hand, focusing on "the concerns of the immediate age," provided a view of death that had changed little since the Han. The directives for death rites in the Kaiyuan ritual code of 732 and Yan Zhenqing's funeral directives for the emperor Daizong in 779 are based mainly on the *Yi li* and cannot have satisfied the concerns of Tang Chinese for the afterlife. The educated elite shared a commitment to Confucianism for their public and official roles; but religious belief was an individual matter, and there could be striking variety. Many intellectuals, often influenced by family tradition or by a domestic ambience that was strongly Buddhist, were friendly to Buddhism. Others might be agnostic. A few, however, incensed by the profligacy of successive emperors in expending large amounts of state money on Buddhism, were hostile toward it. Their criticisms were given an edge by the same complex of factors as those that had led officials to intervene against unofficial local religious cults.

This kind of attitude now gave impetus to the reformulation of Confucian interior concepts. In the late eighth century a number of writers showed interest in the *Zhou yi* ideal of the "complete development of their natures" (*jinxing*) and in the concept of "sincerity and enlightenment" (*chengming*) from the *Doctrine of the Mean* (*Zhong yong*). In the early stages of the movement most involved were content to relate these contemplative ideals to their Buddhist and Daoist equivalents. Interest in Mencius (Mengzi), the pre-Qin exponent of Confucian ideas who treated interior ideas most thoroughly, also increased. The examination system even registered this fashion. One of the earliest mentions of the *Daxue* and *Zhong yong* as supporting interior ideas occurs in an examination question of 805, set by Quan Deyu (759–818), an influential intellectual and patron of the period.

In the final decades of the eighth century this movement gathered force. Like the *Chunqiu* school, it had a southeastern dimension. Again, the number of intellectuals involved was small. The two scholars whose writings achieved lasting historical importance, Han Yu and Li Ao, had different temperaments and took different approaches to the issues involved. Both, however, were indebted to the southeastern milieu in which a tolerant eclecticism had been the characteristic religious outlook. Each turned his back on accommodation, became emphatically anti-Buddhist, and promoted an exclusive Confucianism. Li Ao, a subtler and more introspective thinker than Han Yu, wrote a lengthy analysis of the concept of the nature (*xing*) using Confucian canonical terminology. In this famous document, "Essay on Returning to the Nature"(*Fu xing shu*), he argued that the emotions (*qing*) tended to obscure the true nature and that they should be refined away by introspection. In this way, a state of "sincerity and enlightenment" could be realized. Li interpreted the "extension of knowledge" (*zhi zhi*), the process of self-cultivation at the internal pole of the eightfold progression of the *Daxue*, as meaning that the enlightened mind "lets external objects come to it" (*gewu*), for the mind "distinguishes things without responding to them." Li also adopted the Mencian idea that the nature possessed a propensity to good, and the Mencian universalist belief that any man could become a sage. He thus offered a version of a process of recovering goodness by self-cultivation that was later to become central to neo-Confucianism. But although his express purpose was to present an uncontaminated doctrine of Confucian nature in terms that Confucius himself would have approved, in fact he used concepts that were common to all three of the religious teachings. Even the idea of "'returning to the nature" seems likely to have been borrowed from Daoist commentary, and the same terminology had been used in Buddhist contexts by older members of Li Ao's circle.

Li Ao's friend and mentor in literature, Han Yu, was, by contrast, disinclined to consider contemplative goals. He was impatient with the idea of quiescence, which features centrally in Li Ao's analysis and which Kong Yingda, influenced by the neo-Daoism of the southern dynasties, had earlier promoted. Similarly, Han was unwilling to take a negative view of the feelings. He appears to have been politically conservative and to have rejected the striking universalism of Li Ao's thought. His ultimate aim in self-cultivation was "to make the intentions true" (*chengyi*), as the *Daxue* enjoined, to realize "sincerity." He advocated the idea, based on the *Analects* (*Lunyu*), that men were born with a nature in one of three categories, and that the feelings were categorized in the same way. Society was therefore hierarchical, and there is no echo in his writing of Li Ao's insistence that every man had the potential for sagehood. Han charged that concepts of the *dao* and of the nature had been corrupted by Buddhism and Daoism. He called for a return to a fundamental Confucianism that would revive the social morality of the original teaching. He was not happy dealing with Buddhism either by offering Li Ao's religious alternative or by analytical refutation. Instead, he preferred to attack it at the level of social or administrative action, or to recall past episodes in which Confucianism had prevailed over Buddhism or Daoism.

Li Ao and Han Yu both emphasized the idea that the transmission of true Confucian understanding had been broken after Mencius. Both claimed to have recovered a true Confucian doctrine. Their freedom to reinterpret had much in common with that of the southeastern *Chunqiu* school and with the freedom to alter the text of the canon evident in this period. Their break with the immediate past and their willingness to locate true understanding in themselves rather than in accumulated textual authority mark a fundamental change in the intellectual climate. In turn, Song neo-Confucians were to claim, even more emphatically, that they were able to recover lost truth.

The efforts of Li Ao and Han Yu to redefine the Confucian tradition have therefore been recognized as a turning point in Chinese intellectual history. Song and post-Song Chinese were readily able to identify with the straightforwardness of Han Yu's anti-Buddhist polemics and with his eloquent style of writing. He was accorded a landmark status in the tradition. His belief that many Buddhist practices were demeaning and his refusal to analyze the philosophy behind them were to be perpetuated by Sima Guang (1019–1086) and Zhu Xi (1130–1200). Li Ao's position was more complicated: since much of his terminology was common to Confucianism, Daoism, and Buddhism, the resemblance to Buddhist and Daoist doctrine of some of his thinking has meant that he has never enjoyed Han's secure esteem among later Confucians.

Li Ao, Han Yu, and a small number of their followers were exceptional for their commitment to an exclusive Confucianism and their hostility to Buddhism. The majority of their contemporaries, such as Quan Deyu, Liu Zongyuan, and Du You, and most scholars of the later ninth century continued to be eclectic in general intellectual orientation and especially in religion. Only a few scholars continued Han Yu's anti-Buddhism and his admiration for Mencius. Nonetheless, like earlier Tang scholars, most scholars in the ninth century remained committed to a Confucian education, Confucian priorities for the state, and a Confucian view of history, literature, and administration. As eclectics, they continued to focus on problems rather than texts. Their many essays and notes cover a wide range of topics in literature, religion, statecraft, and history.

Conclusion

During the Tang, the Confucian tradition engaged the commitment of a succession of learned members of the Tang elite. Confucian teaching kept its place as the principal support for the imperial state. Confucian values lay behind the recruitment provisions of the immensely prestigious civil bureaucracy. They permeated the rhetoric of the functioning political system and determined the ideals by which society was to be administered. When political conditions deteriorated, the Confucian tradition provided the resources both for redefining underlying principles of statecraft and for identifying a more meaningful introspective philosophy. Over the course of the dynasty, therefore, Confucian-inclined scholars developed both extremes in the eightfold progression of the *Daxue*: the "ordering of the state" and the self-cultivation of the individual. In recent scholarship there has been a tendency to see the antecedents of neo-Confucianism mainly in terms of the intellectual positions of writers of the late eighth century and the early ninth, particularly Li Ao and Han Yu and their immediate precursors. But this downplays the effect on the ongoing tradition of the success of the imperial Confucianism of the foundation period and of the High Tang. Tang Confucianism, with the exception of the ideas of Li Ao, Han Yu, and Liu Zongyuan, may appear philosophically uninteresting compared with the neo-Confucian tradition. Indeed, Song neo-Confucians were to dismiss almost all the Confucian writing of the Tang as lacking in doctrinal insight. But it can also be argued that the reassertion of the imperial, governmental, and ritual role of the Confucian ideology during one of China's most successful periods contributed greatly to the strength of the tradition. It was implicitly the cultural memory of the success—institutional, political, and ritual—of the first two phases of the dynasty, as well as the explicit formulation of new doctrinal positions in the third phase, that inspired later thinkers to reexplore all aspects of the Confucian tradition.

See also Han Yu; Li Ao; Philosophy of Human Nature; *Quan*.

Bibliography

Barrett, T. H. *Li Ao: Buddhist,Taoist or Neo-Confucian?* Oxford: Oxford University Press, 1988.

Beer, A., Ho Ping-yu, Lu Gwei-Djen, J. Needham, E. G. Pulleyblank, and G. I. Thompson. "An Eighth-Century Meridian Line: I-hsing's Chain of Gnomons and the Pre-History of the Metric System. *Vistas in Astronomy*, 4, 1961, pp. 3–28.

Bol, Peter K. *This Culture of Ours: Intellectual Transitions in T'ang and Sung China*. Stanford, Calif.: Stanford University Press, 1992.

Chen, Jo-shui. *Liu Tsung-yüan and Intellectual Change in T'ang China, 773–819*. Cambridge: Cambridge Unversity Press, 1992.

Hartman, Charles. *Han Yü and the T'ang Search for Unity*. Princeton, N.J.: Princeton University Press, 1985.

Hung, William. "A Bibliographical Controversy at the T'ang Court, A.D. 719." *Harvard Journal of Asiatic Studies*, 20, 1957, pp. 74–134.

Johnson, Wallace. *The T'ang Code*, Vol. 1, *General Principles*. Princeton, N.J.: Princeton University Press, 1979.

Kramers, R. P. "Conservatism and the Transmission of the T'ang Canon: A T'ang Scholar's Complaint." *Journal of Oriental Studies*, 2(1), 1955, pp. 119–312.

Lamont, H. G. "An Early Ninth Century Debate on Heaven." Part 1: *Asia Major*, New Series, 18, 1973, pp. 181–208. Part 2: *Asia Major*, New Series, 19, 1974, pp. 37–85.

McMullen, David. "Han Yu: An Alternative Picture." *Harvard Journal of Asiatic Studies*, 49, 1989, pp. 603–657.

———. "Li Chou: A Forgotten Agnostic of the Late Eighth Century." *Asia Major*, Third Series, 8(2), 1995, pp. 57–105.

———. *State and Scholars in T'ang China*. Cambridge: Cambridge University Press, 1988.

Pulleyblank, E. G. "Neo-Confucianism and Neo-Legalism in T'ang Intellectual Life." In *The Confucian Persuasion*, ed. Arthur F. Wright. Stanford, Calif.: Stanford University Press, 1960.

Twitchett, D. C. *The Writing of Official History under the T'ang*. Cambridge: Cambridge University Press, 1992.

Van Zoeren, Stephen. *Poetry and Personality: Reading, Exegesis, and Hermeneutics in Traditional China*. Stanford, Calif.: Stanford University Press, 1991, ch. 5, pp. 116–150.

Wechsler, Howard J. *Offerings of Jade and Silk*. New Haven, Conn.: Yale University Press, 1985.

Confucianism: Texts in Guodian (Kuo-tien) Bamboo Slips

Xiaogan Liu

Guodian bamboo slips (*Guodian zhujian*) are newly discovered pre-Qin texts written on 730 bamboo slips with about 10,000 Chinese characters. The bamboo slips were excavated from a Chu tomb (Chu was an important southern state in the Warring States era) in the village of Guodian near Jingmen City, Hubei Province, China, in October 1993. The nature and period of the archaeological culture to which the Guodian tomb belongs are clear: the tomb lies in a cemetery at Ying, the capital of the Chu. The archaeological sequence for Chu tombs in this area is relatively well known, allowing the tomb to be dated from not later than 278 B.C.E., and perhaps even before 300 B.C.E. Of course, the various bamboo slips would have been inscribed somewhat earlier, and the composition of the works themselves would have been earlier still.

The bamboo slips were sequenced and categorized into texts by archaeologists and paleographers responsible for their preliminary transcriptions and annotations during five years of painstaking work. All the texts, with actual-size photographs of the slips, were officially published as *Guodian Chumu zhujian* (*Guodian Chu Tomb Bamboo Slips*) in 1998. That is the source of the present essay, which will focus on some primary and substantial information on the texts. The essay will not take up the various suggestions and suppositions derived from animated discussions on the sequencing, naming, and attribution of some texts, but some hypotheses and analyses of the bamboo slips are listed in the bibliography. The slip texts are damaged, incomplete, and complex works that cannot be transcribed and organized into a perfectly established edition in a short period; however, the officially published volume is a convenient and relatively reliable foundation for further research.

According to their length, shape, handwriting, and content, the slips were arranged into sixteen texts—two Daoist and fourteen Confucian. Surprisingly, fourteen of the sixteen texts could not be identified in the Han bibliography, and thirteen of them were previously entirely unknown. The Daoist part consists of three partial *Laozi* or *Daodejing*, together constituting about two-fifths of the received versions, and one new text that the editors titled *Taiyi sheng shui* (*The Ultimate Generating Water*). Of the fourteen Confucian texts, only two were previously known: *Ziyi* (*Black Gown*), a section (*pian*) of the *Liji* (*Record of Rites* or *Book of Rites*), and *Wuxing* (*Five Moral Principles*), discovered at Mawangdui in 1973. The twelve others are *Lu Mu Gong wen Zisi* (*Duke Mu of Lu Asking Zisi*), *Qiongda yi shi* (*Adversity and Success by Fortune*), *Tang Yu zhi dao* (*The Way of Tang Yao and Yu Shun*), *Zhongxin zhi dao* (*The Way of Loyalty and Trustworthiness*), *Chengzhi wenzhi* (*Completing and Hearing*, about which there is a serious controversy concerning its reconstruction and title), *Zun deyi* (*Revering Virtue and Righteousness*), *Xing zi mingchu* (*Human Nature from Destiny*), *Liude* (*Six Virtues*), and four separate *Yu cong* (*Collection of Sayings*). Some doctrines of the Confucian texts will be briefly introduced later.

The magnitude of the discovery of the Guodian bamboo slips has been compared to that of the Dead Sea Scrolls. The corpus of Confucian texts suffered huge losses in wars and the Qin book-burning, but the number of Confucian works recorded in the bibliography of the *History of Han* (*Hanshu yiwenzhi*) is still quite large. Unfortunately, there have been further losses since that time, and the great majority of the texts listed there have not been transmitted. The period between Confucius and Mencius, in particular, appeared to be a blank, leading to a proliferation of conjectures and suppositions. Because the Confucian texts of the Guodian bamboo slips, including the text of *Zisi* and *Duke Mu of Lu*, could be dated from the period after Confucius and before the composition of *Mencius*, a complete history of early Confucianism is possible. The text of *Lu Mu Gong wen Zisi*, the only available text stating the story and doctrine of Zisi after the loss of the *Zisi*, confirms the existence of Zisi and the work bearing his name and proves the authenticity of the teacher-student relationship between Zisi and Duke Mu of Lu (r. 407–377 B.C.E.) in pre-Qin texts and Han histories. Zisi (c. 483–402 B.C.E.), named Kong Ji, according to the Confucian biography in *Shi Ji* (*Records of History*), was the grandson of Confucius and the author of *Zhongyong* (*The Doctrine of the Mean*), as well as the teacher of Mencius. The book *Zisi* (twenty-three sections, *pian*, in the Han bibliography) or *Zisizi* (seven volumes, *juan*, in the Sui bibliography *Suishu Jingjizhi*) was often cited before the Song dynasty. The ancient quotations from *Zisi* were collected and are useful in identifying the bamboo-slip texts. With the Guodian bamboo slips, the historical figure Zisi and his doctrines have emerged from clouds of skepticism.

Not only were books lost over the course of history, but in the early twentieth century the tendency to doubt antiquity (*yigu*) resulted in suspicion being cast on the few remaining texts, with the result that many historical records and texts were easily dismissed, or their dating was changed to a later time. For example, scholars did not believe there was a person Zisi or works by Zisi, and they considered the *Liji* an unreliable work of the Han dynasty. Once more, the Guodian bamboo-slip texts, along with bamboo slips in the Shanghai Museum and other archaeological discoveries, reveal a simple truth: historians in Han China saw more texts and records of their past than we can hope to imagine, and the histories and bibliographies from Han times have proved sounder than subsequent speculations and inferences.

It is noteworthy that Confucian and Daoist texts were unearthed from the same tomb. Not only does this fail to support the opposition between Daoism and Confucianism with which we are familiar from a later time; in some important passages we find a sharing of ideas by the Daoist and Confucian schools. For example, in a bamboo-slip Confucian text *Chengzhi wenzhi* (*Completing and Hearing*) the author contends, "In a boat race, it is better to be behind than ahead; in a dispute, it is better to give in than to win." Obviously, these ideas are akin to the phrase "not daring to be ahead of the world" in the *Laozi* (67). Likewise, we see the Daoist principle of softness in *Wuxing* (*Five

Moral Principles): "Softness is the method of *ren* (humanity)." We find Daoist-sounding ideas, such as following destiny, nurturing physical life, and withdrawing from office, in *Tang Yu zhi dao* (*The Way of Tang Yao and Yu Shun*). In addition, in *Xing zi mingchu* (*Human Nature from Destiny*), we recognize themes and patterns of language and thought familiar from the *Laozi*. The mixture of Daoist ideas and style in Confucian texts is readily understandable: the terms "Confucianism" and "Daoism" were later labels attached to certain texts; the texts obviously could not have been written to accord with these later definitions, and such labels could not have guided ancient writers. If we are to understand pre-Qin intellectual history more comprehensively and objectively, we must rethink the relationship between pre-Qin Daoism and Confucianism in light of the new material from the Guodian tomb.

Lu Mu gong wen Zisi (*Duke Mu of Lu Asking Zisi*) is the opening phrase of an essay of 150 characters and is used as the title by the transcribers and annotators, following an ancient textual convention. In the text, we are told:

> Duke Mu once asked Zisi, "What kind of behavior certifies a loyal minister?" "That one constantly criticizes the mistakes of his ruler certifies a loyal minister," answered Zisi. Duke Mu was not pleased and related the discourse to Chengsun Yi for clarification. "What a good point it is," Chengsun said, and continued, "There have been people who sacrifice their lives for a ruler, but not a person who constantly criticizes the mistakes of his ruler. This is because life-sacrificing may be rewarded with noble rank and salary, but constant criticism keeps them away. Except for Zisi, I hear this from no one."

This essay reveals new aspects of early Confucianism—independence, subjectivity, and political criticism—which were neglected by later Confucian scholars, though such features were embodied in the *Mencius*.

Ziyi (*Black Gown*) is a significant discovery among Confucian texts, which is easily identified with the section (*pian*) bearing the same title in the received *Liji* (*Records of Rites*). According to historical records and ancient quotations, *Ziyi* and three other sections in the received *Liji* are originally from the book *Zisi*. The discovery of *Ziyi* together with *Duke Mu of Lu Asking Zisi* suggests the probability that the *Ziyi* belongs to Zisi's doctrine, and some sections of the *Liji* originally existed in the middle Warring States period. The bamboo-slip *Ziyi* starts with the second chapter (*zhang* or subsection), which mentions the *Ziyi* in the first sentence; thus, the title is well explained. Although there are some divergencies between the bamboo and the received versions in sequence, wording, and citations of *Shijing* (*Book of Songs*) and *Shangshu* (*Book of Documents*), the general style and themes are identical. The essay consistently stresses the crucial importance of rulers' behavioral propriety and their preferences and dislikes, as well as the important function of following models. The theme resonates with *Chengzhi wenzhi*, which asserts:

> What a ruler advocates, people seldom will not follow. A ruler should search for successful leadership in his heart/mind and behavior, which is the foundation (*ben*) of good government. If he searches for success in externals and the people, which represent the trivial (*mo*), he could not gain it.

Another essay, *Zun deyi* (*Revering Virtue and Righteousness*), also echoes this thesis: "Subjects work for the ruler by following his behavior, not his orders. If the ruler loves something, subjects will do further more." These doctrines explain why Confucianism attaches so much importance to self-cultivation by the ruler and to the imitation of models.

Wuxing (*Five Moral Principles*) indicates *ren* (humanity), *yi* (righteousness), *li* (rites), *zhi* (wisdom), and *sheng* (sageliness), though the term is literally the same as the term for the five forces or elements (metal, wood, water, fire, and earth). The difference between the two kinds of *wuxing* was not confirmed until the discovery of the silk essay of *Wuxing* in 1973, which had been unknown before that. The essay clarified the meaning of *wuxing* in Xunzi's criticism of Zisi and suggested his authorship of the essay. The bamboo-slip *Wuxing* has only the original text (*jing*); the silk version also has the commentary (*shuo*), which was perhaps appended by later authors. The essay advocates that the five moral principles should be rooted internally and harmoniously: this is called virtue (*de*); their external expression and the harmony of the four are called goodness (*shan*). Virtue is the way of heaven and goodness is the way of humans. The author also emphasizes that a gentleman should have internal presentiments; otherwise, he would have no internal wisdom, and in return, he would have no internal gladness, no easiness, no happiness, and finally no virtue. The theory bases virtue on presentiments, and features the role of personal feelings as the content and condition of virtue. This is a new aspect of ancient Confucianism that we never knew about.

Xing zi ming chu (*Human Nature from Destiny*) is another previously unknown essay that may be attributed to Zisi's doctrine on the basis of a comparison with ancient quotations from the *Zisi*. The essay emphasizes the commonality of *xing* or human nature:

> People within the four seas share the same nature. Each one's mind-heart varies because of teachings. *Xing* indi-

> cates personal emotions such as likes and dislikes, and feelings such as happiness, anger, sorrow, and melancholy. *Xing* or human nature is internal, and it openly expresses itself when it is attracted by external things.

Here human nature has nothing to do with good or evil as disputed by Xunzi and Mencius. The author claims: "Human nature (*xing*) originates from destiny (*ming*), and destiny comes down from heaven. The way (*dao*) starts from feelings (*qing*), and feelings have their roots in nature." This statement is similar to the first sentences of the *Doctrine of Mean*: "What heaven imparts to man is called human nature. To follow our nature is called the way." However, the essay explicitly claims that emotions and feelings are the essential content of human nature; this is common in the bamboo-slip texts but differs from the received Confucian classics.

Liude (*Six Virtues*) promotes and analyzes the six virtues in three groups: *sheng* (sageliness) and *zhi* (wisdom) for father and husband, respectively; *ren* (humanity) and *yi* (righteousness) for son and ruler, respectively; and *zhong* (loyalty) and *xin* (trustworthiness) for minister and wife, respectively. Here, "father" takes the highest of the six virtues, sageliness, and "husband" takes the second, wisdom. The author also claims that humanity (*ren*) is internal and righteousness (*yi*) is external, as does Gaozi's doctrine cited in the *Mencius*. Thus, the ruler with his virtue (righteousness), the minister with his virture (loyalty), and the wife with her virtue (faithfulness) are classified as external, whereas the father (with sageliness), the son (with humanity), and the husband (with wisdom) are classified as internal. The family relationship is prior to political and social order; but the author also takes as a general feature of Confucianism the fact that political and social government is an enlargement of family life. The unique and hitherto unknown statement is: "One can break off with his ruler because of his father, but not break off with his father because of his ruler." Obviously, the position is different from the fixation on central government in later Confucian ideology.

Meanwhile, *Zhongxin zhi dao* (*The Way of Loyalty and Trustworthiness*) specifically stresses the significance of loyalty and trustworthiness from a different perspective. It says: "loyalty (*zhong*) is the essence of humanity (*ren*), and trustworthiness (*xin*) is the result of righteousness (*yi*)." These doctrines update our knowledge of the richness and diversity of early Confucianism.

Tang Yu zhi dao (*The Way of Tang Yao and Yu Shun*) argues for the moral function of the historical system of abdicating the throne and handing over the crown to the worthy, which was practiced by Yao, who gave the throne to Shun. Yao and Shun were said to embody the principle of loving family and revering the worthy. One who loves his family practices filial piety and one who reveres the worthy may abdicate. Filial piety is the ultimate expression of humanity and abdication is the supreme expression of righteousness.

Qiongda yi shi (*Adversity and Success by Fortune*) asserts that many figures won merit because they met the right persons, who appreciated and promoted them, as the crown was bestowed on Shun. Other figures met with adversity because they encountered evil persons. One's fortune is decided by heaven, not by oneself. One should consistently hold to virtuous behavior and should not worry about the practical result, since worrying is useless.

The final four bundles of slips, called the *Yu cong* (*Collection of Sayings*), are a mixture of sayings from the Confucians and other schools. They were probably used for teaching purposes.

It is still too early to evaluate the Guodian bamboo-slip texts comprehensively and appropriately. However, it is definitely necessary to modify or rewrite the history of early Confucianism in the light of new doctrines presented in the texts, such as universal human nature, the importance of personal emotion and feelings, individual independence and subjectivity, and political criticism. They will exert an influence on the dominant view of ancient Chinese intellectual history and philosophy. They suggest that perhaps there was no strong tension or distinction between Confucianism and Daoism in pre-Qin China, that the nature of Confucianism and other schools was probably more complex than has hitherto been thought, and that the pre-Qin speculations may have been much more philosophical than we believed. Furthermore, the Guodian bamboo texts, along with other archaeological discoveries, show that the histories and the Han bibliography are sounder and more reliable than we thought. We may need to reevaluate the information and messages in the historical literature and reflect on our methods in dating ancient texts under the influence of the trend called "doubting antiquity."

See also Daoism: Texts in Guodian Bamboo Slips.

Bibliography

Allan, Sarah, and Crispin Williams, eds. *The Guodian Laozi: Proceedings of the International Conference, Dartmouth College, May 1998.* Early China Special Monograph Series, No. 5. Berkeley, Calif.: Society for the Study of Early China and Institute of East Asian Studies, University of California Berkeley, 2000.

Chen, Guying, ed. *Daojia Wenhua Yanjiu* (Studies of Daoist Culture). Special issue: Studies of Guodian Bamboo Slips, No. 17. Beijing: Sanlian, 1999.

Defoort, Carine, and Xing Wen, eds. "Guodian, Part 1." *Contemporary Chinese Thought*, 32(1), fall 2000. "Guodian, Part 2." *Contemporary Chinese Thought*, 32(2), winter 2000–2001. (Special issues. New York: Sharpe.)

Guo, Qiyong, Chen Wei, and Xu Shaohua, eds. *Guodian Chujian guoji xueshu yantaohui lunwenji* (Proceedings of the International Conference on Guodian Bamboo Slips). Wuhan, Hubei: Hubei renmin, 2000. (Special issue of *Renwen Luncong*.)

Henricks, Robert G. *Lao Tzu Tao Te Ching: A Translation of the Startling New Documents Found at Guodian*. New York: Columbia University Press, 2000.

Jiang, Guanghui, and Xin Wen, eds. *Guodian Chujian yanjiu* (Studies on Bamboo Slips of Chu State from Guodian). Shenyang: Liaoning jwiaoyu, 1999. (Special issue of *Zhongguo zhexue*, No. 20.)

Jingmenshi Bowuguan (Museum of Jingmen City). *Guodian chumu zhujian* (Guodian Chu Tomb Bamboo Slips). Beijing: Wenwu, 1998.

Liao, Mingchun, ed. *Tsinghua Research on Bamboo and Silk Documents*, Vol. 1, August 2000.

Liu, Xiaogan: "Foreword to the Reprint Edition." In Donald Munro. *The Concept of Man in Early China*, Ann Arbor: Michigan University Press, 2001, pp. i–xv.

Shen, Andrea. "Ancient Script Rewrites History: This is Like the Discovery of the Dead Sea Scrolls." *Harvard University Gazette*, 22 January 2001.

Tomohisa, Ikeda, ed. *Kakuken Sokan no sisohiteki kenkyu* (Studies of Guodian Bamboo Slips in the Perspective of Intellectual History), Vols. 1–4. Tokyo: Society of Studies on Guodian Bamboo Slips, Tokyo University, 1999–2000.

Wen, Xin, ed. *Guoji jianbo yanjiu* (Newsletter: International Research on Bamboo and Silk Documents), Nos. 1–4. Beijing: International Center for Research on Bamboo and Silk Documents, 2000.

Confucianism: Tradition—*Daotong* (*Tao-t'ung*)

A. S. Cua

Like other enduring ethical or religious traditions with a long history—for example, Buddhism or Christianity—the Confucian tradition, as embodied in the notion of *daotong*, is often a target of contemporary critique. Consider this familiar appraisal: The *Ru* tradition is out of tune with our times. Like any cherished cultural artifact, it is best revered as a relic of the past. Moreover, many adherents of the Confucian tradition are dogmatic. They are unwilling to accept reasonable proposals for change or modification of some components of the tradition.

Replying to this charge, a Confucian thinker or scholar might point out that, to a certain extent, the critique is reasonable. Throughout the long history of Confucianism, there has been a recurrent tendency for many of its adherents to institute orthodoxy and uphold their perceived values as the true values of the tradition, indifferent to the distinction between perceived and real values. A personal ascription of value to an object cannot be logically equated with the value inherent in the object. Also, understanding a living tradition requires an appreciation of the distinction between the actual past and the perceived past and the distinction between a living, robust tradition and a dying, decaying tradition. Jaroslav Pelikan has said, "Tradition is the living faith of the dead, traditionalism is the dead faith of the living" (1984, 65).

This essay comprises three sections. The first section presents a general characterization of a living ethical tradition. Special emphasis is given to the role of interpretation in the community of adherents. The second section builds on this discussion to explicate Zhu Xi's conception of *daotong* (transmission of *dao*). The third section addresses a special problem in Zhu Xi's conception with respect to change and modification of the Confucian tradition. This problem can in part be resolved by attending to the connection between *daotong* and *quan* (weighing of circumstances). The concluding remarks briefly consider the role of argumentation in the evaluation of judgments based on the exercise of *quan* and suggest, as a project for further inquiry, the contrast between the Confucian cooperative model and the agonistic model of ethical argumentation.

The Concept of Tradition

In Edward Shils's *Tradition* (1981), the concept is presented as a cluster of salient features. Four features appear central to any conception or theory of tradition:

1. Tradition as *traditum* has a certain duration of existence.
2. Every tradition has custodians or exemplars.
3. Tradition is always an object of interpretation and thus is subject to change or modification.
4. The way in which the stock of a tradition is possessed, for example, its texts, is selective, and typically a subject for specialized inquiries.

As regards (1), tradition as *traditum* consists of all sorts of things handed down from the past to the present. They include things such as institutions, moral practices, cultural artifacts preserved in museums, and all sorts of beliefs. The scholar's main access to tradition is through collected texts and commentaries. To distinguish tradition from the prevailing fashion of a particular time, which has merely a temporary significance, we might expect a tradition to persist for at least three generations.

With regard to (2), every tradition has its custodians or exemplars. For our purposes, custodians and exemplars may be more broadly construed as representative adherents and paradigmatic individuals. For Confucians reared in the tradition of the *Analects*, Confucius's recurrent emphasis on *junzi*—paragons—has an enduring significance in their lives. It is important to note that the *junzi* are not mere conservers of the tradition but exemplary persons whose life and conduct embody the ethical ideal of the tradition at its best. Arguably, Confucius's concept of *junzi* expresses a notion of paradigmatic individuals as exemplary embodiments of the spirit and vitality of the tradition. Besides their role in moral education, they also serve as living exemplars of the transformative significance of the ideal of the tradition, thus investing the tradition with renewed vigor. Even more important, for those committed to tradition as a robust tradition, paradigmatic individuals serve as a focal point, as a standard, and as a source of inspiration (Cua 1978, chs. 3 and 5).

With regard to (3), perhaps the most salient feature of a living tradition is that the things transmitted do not always retain their original character or significance; during transmission they undergo changes or modification. Thus, tradition may be said to be an interpretive concept. As such, however, tradition is intelligible only if we suppose that the adherents constitute a community rather than a mere collection of individuals. Tradition as an interpretive concept implies that members of the community would acknowledge the possibility of conflicting judgments concerning the present significance of the tradition. Josiah Royce characterizes the community as a community of interpretation. Obviously, a community consists of members who are separate, distinct individuals. At any given time the individual interprets his experience and future anticipation, as it were saying to himself, "That past deed or future event belongs to my life." Especially in the ethical sense, personal identity at any moment is constituted by the individual's interpretation of its retrospective grounding and its prospective significance. This community is one of memory and of hope. A community of memory is especially evident on occasions commemorating men and women who have sacrificed their personal interests and even their lives for the sake of the community. A community of hope projects its ideal expectations of the future of the community and its members (Royce 1969, Lectures 9 and 10).

Implicit in the community of memory is an ideal of coherence, a shared ethical vision that makes sense of interpretation of both the individual and the common life. In the Confucian tradition, it is the ideal of *dao* that provides unity or a unifying perspective on the diversity of interpretations within the tradition. When the ideal is articulated in the form of a vision of the good life as a whole and becomes the focus of a common venture among the members of the community, it acquires an actuating significance for present cooperative endeavor.

A tradition of ethical thought and conduct inevitably faces the problem of coherence. Even if there is implicit agreement on an ideal, unifying perspective, intelligent adherents of the tradition must use the tradition to confront external and internal challenges. As Zhu Xi points out, the wisdom derived from tradition is a depository of insights always available for appropriation to deal with present and future problems and perplexities of human life.

Let us turn briefly to (4), that is, tradition's stock and possession. For our purposes, we focus on texts. The possession of texts is highly selective. Selective judgments and decisions determine the designation of certain texts as canonical, that is, as providing an authoritative point of reference for established standards of conduct. In different cultural and ethical traditions, these texts are a core of historical scholarship, and the emergence of certain texts as authoritative may be a culmination of a process of disagreement and eventual acceptance.

In the Confucian tradition, the canonical status of the Four Books (*Analects*, *Mencius*, the *Great Learning*, and the *Doctrine of the Mean*) is due to Zhu Xi's scholarly efforts, representing his selective decisions.

Perhaps even more important, interpretation of these texts at a particular time and place also involves selective decision and judgment.

Present needs and exigent situations are probably among the crucial factors in the process of selection. In any case, one would expect the adherents of tradition to engage in argumentation to resolve their different or conflicting perceptions of their current circumstances as well as their aspirations.

The Tradition of *Dao* (*Daotong*)

In light of our discussion of the concept of tradition, we have a way to explicate Zhu Xi's conception of *daotong* as an instance of its application. The explication, partly indebted to recent scholarship, is mainly intended as a proposal for reshaping *daotong*, serving as a point of departure for the critical development of Confucian moral philosophy. In explicating *daotong*, we focus on feature (3)—tradition as an interpretive concept—along with the assumption that features (1) and (4) are present in any notion of a Confucian tradition. The claim to a persistent *traditum*, for Mencius and Zhu Xi, is consistent with an acknowledgment of periods of interruption and discontinuity. As de Bary (1981, 99) points out, "Chu Tzu [Zhuzi] emphasized the discontinuities in the tradition almost more than the continuities, and underscored the contributions of inspired individuals who rediscovered or 'clarified' the Way in the new forms." This emphasis on "inspired individuals" also recalls feature (2), the indispensable role of exemplary adherents who are custodians or paradigmatic individuals of the tradition.

As a conjecture, Zhu Xi's hardly credible claim of a line of succession in the Confucian tradition may be an expression of his concern with preserving the recognition of certain exemplary or paradigmatic individuals in its history. Thus Confucius (551–479 B.C.E.) and Mencius (c. 371–298 B.C.E.), Zhou Dunyi (1017–1073 C.E.), Cheng Hao (1032–1085), and Cheng Yi (1033–1107) figure in the line of the transmitters of the Confucian tradition.

As for feature (4), the selective possession of the stock of tradition, as noted earlier, Zhu Xi's selective study of ancient texts, a lifelong preoccupation, shows his selective decision and concern with the recovery and revitalization of an ancient tradition.

According to Wing-tsit Chan, Zhu Xi coined the term *daotong*. For assessing Zhu Xi's conception, Chan directs our attention to the distinction between Zhu Xi's philosophical interpretation and his arbitrary historical claim about a single line of succession (1989, 321). The idea of *daotong* as a doctrine of an orthodox line of transmission is probably Zhu Xi's fanciful speculation, a bit surprising in view of the pragmatic-scientific spirit of some of his works. For Liu Shu-hsien, "the crux of the matter actually lies in one's existential decision over one's ultimate commitment or philosophical faith." The question lies in the "Confucian message," which is to be traced back to Confucius, not in the acceptance of a historical legend" (Chan 1986, 442–443).

Let me supplement Liu's contribution by focusing on a crucial and familiar aspect of Zhu Xi's conception of learning. In commenting on the expression "The perfection of knowledge depends on the investigation of things (*gewu*)" in the *Great Learning* (*Daxue*), Zhu Xi emphasizes the importance of *qiongli*, i.e., the exhaustive investigation of principles or rationales for the existence of things. Zhu Xi (1980, 6) writes:

> The first step in the education of the adult is to instruct the learner, in regard to all things in the world, to proceed from what knowledge he has of their principles [*li*], and investigate further until he reaches the limit. After exerting himself in this way for a long time, he will one day achieve a wide and far-reaching penetration [*guantong*].

Zhu Xi's use of the expression *guantong* is reminiscent of Xunzi's use of *guan* and *tong*. Zhu Xi's conception of *daotong* implicitly involves a conception of *guantong zhixue*, i.e., learning in order to acquire comprehensive insights. His conception of *dao* in *daotong* provides a unifying perspective for understanding the coherence of the ideals in sagely understanding that Liu emphasized in his instructive paper.

Regardless of the classical source of Zhu Xi's conception of moral learning, its ultimate objective is comprehensive understanding. The learning, *guantong zhixue*, is a form of integrated learning. I suggest, as a matter of constructive interpretation, that the *dao* in Zhu Xi's *daotong*, like Xunzi's *dao* in *daoquan*, be construed as the ideal unifying perspective or *telos* that provides the integration or the coherence of the Confucian tradition (Cua 1985). *Daotong* as the tradition of *dao* may thus be construed as the Confucian tradition of coherent sagely understanding of *dao*, exemplified preeminently in the life of Confucius, which Liu justly regards as constitutive of the "Confucian message." The interpretation of the Confucian texts from the personal point of view is self-interpretation. As Yü Ying-shih has shown, for Zhu Xi, interpretation of the classics is a process that culminates at a stage where the reader "can bring the text to life," that is, "what is interpreted is transformed into an organic part, so to speak, of the interpreter's spiritual life" (Chan 1986, 233). While interpretation must comply with objective rules of analysis, it ultimately involves the person as a whole and as a member of a community of interpretation. For adherents, the Confucian tradition is an object of affection and reverence, largely because it is perceived as an embodiment of wisdom (*zhi*). As stated earlier, for Zhu Xi, tradition is a repository of insights available for personal and interpersonal appropriation, for coping with present problems and with changing circumstances. *Daotong*, the tradition of *dao*, is thus a continuing object of interpretation and of change and modification.

A notable corollary of *daotong*, often overlooked by the critics of the Confucian tradition, is the "conservative" character of the *dao* perspective. In classical Confucianism, the tradition is represented by *li* (rites, rules of proper conduct). For the adherents of the tradition, the *li* comprise a coherent understanding of social practices or normative requirements, embracing customs, conventions, and acknowledged permissible forms of conduct. The *dao* perspective is conservative in the sense that it is inclined toward a critical conservation of the values of a living ethical tradition, informed by historical knowledge, as a common culture embodied in the Confucian classics. Also, the perspective is conservative in that *dao*, specified in *li*, conserves those natural feelings and dispositions that are deemed conducive to the acquisition and the promotion of the virtues (*de*). Both these senses of "conservative" are present in the use of *fang* in the *Liji* (*Book of Li*). Confucius is said to have compared *dao* to dikes (*fang*) for the sake of providing guidance in rectifying the deficiency of the customary standards of conduct followed by ordinary people. For this reason, "the superior person (*junzi*) uses the *li* as a dike to conserve virtues (*fangde*), punishment as a dike against licentiousness, and prescriptions as a dike against evil desires" (*fangji*).

Transformation of the Confucian Tradition

If the interpretation of classical Confucian texts is ultimately a matter of self-interpretation or self-transformation, its significance for dealing with changing circumstances in personal and social life remains a matter of individual judgment. The question of the relation of such a judgment to that of one's fellows in the community of interpretation naturally arises. More important, a deeper, more general and fundamental question concerns the possibility of change or modification of *daotong* as expressing the idea of the Confucian tradition.

Conceptually, a plausible answer lies in the explication of the Confucian framework, comprising three basic and interdependent notions: *ren* (humanity), *li* (propriety), and *yi* (rightness, righteousness). These basic notions represent the general specification of the concrete significance of *dao* as a generic term for a holistic vision of the good life or a unifying perspective in the Confucian community of interpretation. To put this differently, the Confucian conceptual scheme consists of *dao* as a generic term, *gongming*, and *ren*, *li*, and *yi* as specific terms, *bieming* (Cua 1998, Essay 13). This conceptual scheme may also be attributed to Zhu Xi, although important qualifications have to be noted. First, the framework is interpreted and elaborated by using the vocabulary of Song Confucian moral metaphysics, e.g., *liqi* (reason or principle, and vital force), *taiji* (the great ultimate), and *tiandi zhi xin* (the mind of heaven and earth). Second, Zhu Xi sometimes uses *ren*, as in *A Treatise on Ren*, both as a generic and as a specific term. For example, *ren* is said to embrace the four moral qualities in the mind of man, that is, *ren*, *yi*, li, and wisdom. *Ren* in the generic sense is said to be constitutive of *dao*, "which consists of the fact that the mind of Heaven and Earth to produce things is present in everything" (Chan 1963, 594). This remark suggests that *ren* as a generic term is functionally equivalent to *dao*. At any rate, with respect to *dao* as a generic term for the holistic ideal or unifying perspective, we may appeal to a couple of terse remarks in *Zhuzi yulei* (*Classified Conversations of Zhuzi*, ch. 37): (1) "*Dao* is a unifying term (*tongming*), *li* (reason-principle) is [a term referring to its] detail items." (2) "*Dao* is a holistic word (*dao zi hongda*), *li* is a word for details (*li zi jingmi*)."

These remarks suggest that *dao* is a holistic, generic term subject to a description of its significance using such specific terms as *ren*, *yi*, *li*, and *zhi* (wisdom). Note that *ren* can also be used as a generic term embracing these four, and each in turn may need to be specified for its significance in a particular context of discourse. In addition, the specification must be governed by *li* (reason-principle), that is, a *reasoned* rather than a subjective, arbitrary specification. In this sense, the *li* refer to those detailed reasons in support of one's claim to the adequacy of specification, presumably based on an assessment of the merits of a particular issue.

Our focus on the conceptual framework of Confucian tradition brings out only the synchronic aspect of the tradition of *dao*. A fuller discussion of the possibility of transformation of the Confucian tradition must also attend to the diachronic aspect of *dao*. In Xunzi's words, "*Dao* embodies constancy and embraces all changes" (*Xunzi*, Book 21). Zhu Xi's contribution to our question about the possibility of transformation of the Confucian tradition of *dao* is perhaps better approached by attending to his discussion of the distinction and connection between *jing* and *quan*. This distinction reflects a similar concern with *chang* (the constant) and *bian* (the changing). The latter is indispensable to elucidating the former. As Zhu Xi put it (*Zhuzi yulei*, ch. 6.1a), "*Jing* pertains to the constant aspect of *dao* (*jing zhe dao zhi chang ye*), and *quan* to the changing aspect of *dao* (*quan zhe dao zhi bian ye*)."

Distinction between jing and quan. The relevant meaning of *jing* is "an invariable rule or a standard of conduct; the constant or the recurring." The basic sense of *quan* is "steelyard or balance," and as a verb, "to weigh," "to estimate," or "to consider." It is used not only in the sense of measuring the weight of a thing as on a balance or scale, but also in the metaphorical sense of "weighing the importance or unimportance of things or events." A passage in *Mencius* (1A.7) is clear on these uses:

> It is by weighing [*quan*] a thing that its weight [lightness or heaviness] can be known and by measuring it that its length can be ascertained. It is so with all things, but particularly so with the heart.

In this sense, *quan* pertains to a value judgment that aims at achieving the mean (*zhong*) or balance of various competing considerations. Each of these considerations must be weighed, as on a balance. Significantly, for Zhu Xi and the neo-Confucians, as well as for Xunzi, the judgment must be based on *li* (reason, principle) or what we would call a principled or reasoned judgment (Cua 1997).

The situation in which *quan* is exercised is one in which *jing*, the normal or standard applications of basic Confucian notions, do not provide sufficient guidance. A careful examination of Zhu Xi's remarks on *quan* in *Zhuzi yulei* leads to this conclusion. The exercise of *quan* is quite properly an exercise of moral discretion in the sense of the power of the individual to act according to his or her judgment in dealing with uncertain, exigent situations, or "hard cases." As contrasted with the "soft cases" or normal problems in human life, the hard cases are rule-indeterminate; thus the established standards of conduct (*jing*) offer no clear guidance. Even if such standards are deemed appropriate, there may be a problem of application that calls for interpretive judgment and discretion. The problem cannot be resolved by mechanical or deductive procedures.

Six salient features of *quan* are the following:

1. As a metaphorical extension of the basic sense of a steelyard for measuring weight, *quan* pertains to assessment of the importance of moral considerations to a current matter of concern. In other words, the exercise of *quan* consists of a judgment of the comparative importance of competing options answering to a current problematic situation.
2. The situation is such that it presents a hard case, that is, a case falling outside the scope of operation of *jing*. Thus normal standards of conduct provide insufficient guidance.
3. *Quan* is an exercise of moral discretion and must conform to the requirement of *yi* (rightness, righteousness).
4. The judgment must accord with *li*, that is, be a principled or reasoned judgment.
5. The immediate objective of *quan* is to attain timely equilibrium (*shizhong*), that is, to do the right thing (*yi*) appropriate to the demands of the current situation.
6. The ultimate objective of *quan* is to further the realization of *dao* as the holistic ideal of the good life. Moreover, the proper exercise of *quan* presupposes that the agent has an open mind. As Mencius reminds the Confucian agent, he must not hold on to any one particular moral doctrine even if it represents a moderate position between extremes (*Mencius*, 7A.26).

Connection between jing and quan. According to Wei Cheng-t'ung (Wei Zhong tong), Zhu Xi is especially concerned with reconciling Cheng Yi's view that "*quan* is [nothing other than] *jing*" and the Han scholars' view that *quan* is "that which is at variance with the standard (*jing*) but in accord with the Way (*dao*)" (Chan 1986, 255). The irony, of course, is that Cheng Yi proposed his view in opposition to that of the Han scholars. Wei's essay provides a valuable discussion of Zhu Xi's attempt and some of the problems that arise out of Zhu Xi's application of his own view. In light of our interest in the possibility of transformation, we focus primarily on Zhu Xi's insight into the connection between *jing* and *quan* and its bearing on the tradition of *dao* (*daotong*). Zhu Xi is clear that Cheng Yi's seemingly reductionist thesis is unacceptable, for it collapses an important distinction. The fundamental issue is the *jing-quan* connection. It is *dao* that provides the unifying connection. According to Zhu Xi:

> *Jing* pertains to the constant aspect (*chang*) of *dao*, *quan* to the changing aspect (*bian*). *Dao* is a unifying substance (*tongti*) that penetrates through *jing* and *quan*. (*Zhuzi yulei*, ch. 37)

In the context of this remark, we are given no further explanation. When we turn to some other recorded remarks of Zhu Xi, we find three different interpretations. Below I cite the passages in which his interpretations are given (*Zhuzi yulei*, ch. 37), before proposing a reconstruction.

- Passage (a): *Jing* (the constant, normal) is the *quan* (discretion) already determined (*jing shi yit-*

ing zhi quan); *quan* is *jing* prior to determination (*quan shi weiding zhi jing*).

- Passage (b): *Yi* (rightness, righteousness) can be considered to embrace both *jing* and *quan*. One should not use it only in regard to *quan*. When *yi* requires us to abide by *jing*, we should do so. When *yi* requires us to use *quan*, we should do so. This is what is meant by saying that *yi* can embrace both *jing* and *quan*.
- Passage (c): *Jing* is an outline; *quan* pertains to the delicate twists and turns (of human affairs). For example, the ruler should be benevolent and the minister loyal; the father should be compassionate and the son filial. These are normal, constant requirements of *dao* (*jingchang zhi dao*). How can they be disturbed? In their midst there must be something inexhaustible. Thus, it is necessary to exercise *quan*. *Quan* pertains to fine and delicate details. Unless one sees the *li* (reason, principle, rationale) in terms of its important sections and details, one cannot understand it [*quan*].

Passage (a) may be used to elucidate Zhu Xi's general thesis: "*Dao* is the unifying substance (*tongti*) that penetrates through *jing* and *quan*." This passage suggests that the connection lies in their dynamic interplay. *Jing*, comprising the normal standards of conduct, is a product of settled or determinate *quan*. Presumably, the exercise of *quan* in exigent situations may become accepted as constitutive of *jing* or conventional wisdom, perhaps in the sense of paradigms of applications for given standards. *Quan*, on the other hand, may be regarded as *jing* prior to the determination of its significance in actual, particular situations. In other words, *jing*, the established standards of conduct, depend on *quan* in the sense that their application is undetermined prior to actual circumstances. When such a determination is made, *quan* would become part of *jing*, given the assumption that the judgments are accepted by the Confucian community of interpretation. In short, *jing* is the determinate *quan* and *quan* is the indeterminate *jing*. Of course, both represent the constant (*chang*) and the changing (*bian*) aspects of *dao*. If this interpretation is acceptable, the distinction between *jing* and *quan* is explainable in terms of their dynamic, flexible connection. Any attempt to collapse or dichotomize the distinction must on this interpretation be rejected.

Passage (b) focuses on the central role of *yi* (rightness, righteousness) in both *jing* and *quan*. Right judgment is necessary not only in exigent situations requiring the exercise of *quan*, but also in normal situations where the intelligent agent of the tradition confronts the problem of interpretation and application. In both sorts of situation, the agent has the same moral objective, that is, to do the right thing. This is, perhaps, the point of Zhu Xi's saying that *quan* is unavoidably exercised in changing situations that fall outside the scope of the regular practice of *daoli* (moral norm, principle). "When *quan* attains equilibrium (*zhong*), it does not differ from *jing*," that is, they have achieved the same moral objective. As passage (b) indicates, they are both governed by the exercise of *yi* or one's sense of rightness. This passage thus renders explicit the respect in which *yi* is presupposed in both normal and exigent situations. It also provides a way of understanding Zhu Xi's general thesis that the "*dao* penetrates (*guan*) through *jing* and *quan*." *Yi* constitutes the *guan*, the thread that runs though *jing* and *quan*.

Passage (c) advocates a different thesis, which appears to be inconsistent with passage (a). On the face of it, the connection between *jing* and *quan* consists in the subordination of *jing* to *quan*, in that *jing* requires the exercise of *quan* in specifying the details that govern the application of the normal requirements of *dao*. On this reading, however, the exercise of *quan* has no particular relation to exigent situations that fall outside the scope of application of *jing*, the normal standards of conduct. Rather, *quan* is always relevant to determining the concrete significance of *jing* in those cases where the entrenched, established interpretations of standards of conduct do not provide proper guidance, or as Zhu Xi put it, in the unexhausted region of *jing*. While this is consistent with the notion of *quan* as involving judgment of equity, Zhu Xi also maintains that the exercise of *quan* centrally requires a comprehensive knowledge of all the *li*, the delicate details of all possible circumstances. This reflects Zhu Xi's view that only a sage could exercise *quan*. As Chen Chun, Zhu Xi's eminent disciple, put it, "Only a sage, who understands moral principles very clearly, can use it [*quan*] without error" (1986, 130). If this is the case, ordinary, intelligent adherents of the Confucian tradition are not entitled to exercise *quan*. This view is contrary to passage (a) and to Mencius's notion of *quan*—a view Zhu Xi also accepts. The political implications of this view are no more acceptable to Confucians today than they were to Zhu Xi's critics. Consider Chen Chun's interpretation:

> *Quan* can be exercised only by people in a high position. Unless one understands moral principles [*yi*, righteousness] clearly, one will be mistaken and will fail to see even when expedience [*quan*] comes into play where the standard way fails to accomplish, it is not really opposed to the standard [*jing*]. When the standard has been exhausted, expediency must be used to remove the impasse. (173)

How can one be assured that such people have the requisite knowledge of *li* (reason, principle) in all possible human situations? If they claim to have such knowledge, one would want to know their credentials or justifications, which are subject to discursive evaluation. Recall Mencius's case of the drowning sister-in-law, which involved a *li* or ritual requirement (that men and women are not to touch hands in giving or receiving anything). Mencius is emphatic that such a case is not one that especially concerns people who occupy political positions (Cua 1978, ch. 5; *Mencius*, 4A.17). The exercise of *quan* is recommended for quite ordinary persons encountering exigent situations, regardless of the fear of the political authority. The liability to error in the exercise of *quan* is a common human failing whatever one's position in society or government. Becoming a sage with comprehensive knowledge is an ideal, but as Xunzi points out, it can sensibly be regarded only as theoretically possible, not actually possible, for human beings (*Xunzi*, Book 23). Recall Confucius's remark: "I have no hope of meeting a sage. I would be content to meet an ethically superior individual" (*Analects*, 7.26).

Consider another reading of passage (c) that may be consistent with passage (a). Zhu Xi's thesis here may be construed as a conceptual thesis concerning the function of generic terms such as those that express the requirements of benevolence, loyalty, compassion, and filiality in Zhu Xi's example. As noted earlier, generic terms are subject to specification of their concrete significance, that is, their relevance to situations. In the Confucian community of interpretation, there are always entrenched, established interpretations comprising *jing*, the normal or constant practice of *dao*. These interpretations are paradigms learned in the course of moral education and followed unquestioningly by ordinary members of the community. However, the paradigms cannot be said to exhaust the significance of *dao* in all possible worlds. Because of a lack of clear and determinate guidance in some situations in moral life, ordinary agents committed to the ideal of *dao* may wonder about the right thing to do. Unavoidably, *quan* is exercised in such cases. One's sense of rightness (*yi*) remains no less involved. *Quan* here is not something distinct from *yi*; that is, *quan* is functionally equivalent to *yi*, rather than being a notion contrasted with *jing*, as in our earlier discussion of the distinction between *jing* and *quan*. Passage (c) also points to the ideal of comprehensive understanding in the study of the classics (*guantong zhi xue*), which involves a total understanding of the minute details in an unerring exercise of the reason (*li*). On this reading, we do not need to revise our earlier reconstruction of the distinction and connection between *jing* and *quan*. I suggest that we adopt this reading of passage (c), as it furnishes a plausible, coherent interpretation of Zhu Xi's conception.

The foregoing discussion on the distinction and connection between *jing* and *quan* affords us an answer to the question about the possibility of change or modification of the Confucian tradition of *dao*. Intelligent adherents of the Confucian tradition can apply some skepticism without fear of corrupting the tradition. The dynamic interplay of *jing* and *quan* in relation to constancy (*chang*) and change (*bian*) shows that the distinction is not fixed or absolute. As Dai Zhen (1723–1777) points out, what is deemed important or unimportant in our assessment will vary in different times and places. To put this another way, the substantive content of the tradition of *dao* cannot be considered settled without prejudging the merits of particular circumstances. The exercise of *quan* in any situation requires a careful examination and analysis of all the factors. For a Confucian philosopher, further elaboration of the tradition of *dao* must consider the constructive interpretation of the basic conceptual framework, the critical development of tradition, and the possibility of reconciling the competing interpretive judgments of adherents of the tradition, especially judgments derived from the exercise of *quan* or moral discretion (Cua 1998, Essays 12–14). The urgent issue today is the adjudication of intercultural ethical conflicts. The task is to develop a cooperative model of ethical argumentation and to explore how such a model can accommodate the dominant agonistic and disputatious model of western philosophy.

See also Confucianism: Ethics; Confucianism: Rhetoric; Confucianism: Vision; *Dao*; *Junzi*; *Li*: Rights or Propriety; *Quan*; *Ren*; Xunzi; *Yi* and *Li*; Zhu Xi.

Bibliography

Chan, Wing-tsit, ed. *Chu Hsi and Neo-Conficianism*. Honolulu: University of Hawaii Press, 1986.

———. *Chu Hsi: New Studies*. Honolulu: University of Hawaii Press, 1989.

———, trans. *A Source Book in Chinese Philosophy*. Princeton, N.J.: Princeton University Press, 1963.

Ch'en, Ch'un. *Neo-Confucian Terms Explained*, trans. Wing-tsit Chan. New York: Columbia University Press, 1986.

Cua, A. S. "Competence, Concern, and the Role of Paradigmatic Individuals (*Chün-tzu*) in Moral Education," *Philosophy East and West*, 42, 1992, pp. 49–68.

———. *Dimensions of Moral Creativity: Paradigms, Principles, and Ideals*. University Park: Pennsylvania State University Press, 1978.

———. *Ethical Argumentation: A Study in Hsün Tzu's Moral Epistemology*. Honolulu: University of Hawaii Press, 1985.

———. *Moral Vision and Tradition: Essays on Chinese Ethics*. Washington, D.C.: Catholic University of America Press, 1998.

———. "Reason and Principle in Chinese Philosophy." In *A Companion to World Philosophies*, ed. Eliot Deutsch and Ron Bontekoe. Oxford: Blackwell, 1997, pp. 201–213.
de Bary, William Theodore. *Neo-Confucian Orthodoxy and the Learning of the Mind-and-Heart*. New York: Columbia University Press, 1981.
Lau, D. C., trans. *Mencius*. New York: Penguin, 1970.
Li, Disheng. *Xunzi jishi*. Taipei: Xuesheng, 1979.
Liu, Shu-hsien. "The Problem of Orthodoxy in Chu Hsu's Philosophy." In *Chu Hsi and Neo-Conficianism*, ed. Wing-tsit Chan. Honolulu: University of Hawaii Press, 1986.
Pelikan, Jaraslov. *The Vindication of Tradition*. New Haven, Conn.: Yale University Press, 1984.
Royce, Josiah. *Problem of Christianity*. Chicago, Ill.: University of Chicago Press, 1969.
Shils, Edward. *Tradition*. Chicago, Ill.: University of Chicago Press, 1981.
Wei, Cheng-t'ung. "Chu Hsi on the Standard [*Jing*] and the Expedient [*Quan*]." In *Chu Hsi and Neo-Conficianism*, ed. Wing-tsit Chan. Honolulu: University of Hawaii Press, 1986.
Yü, Ying-shih. "Morality and Knowledge in Chu Hsi's Philosophical System." In *Chu Hsi and Neo-Confucianism*, ed. Wing-tsit Chan. Honolulu: University of Hawaii Press, 1986.
Zhu, Xi. *Sishu jizhu*. Hong Kong: Tai-p'ing, 1980.

Confucianism: Twentieth Century

Chung-ying CHENG

After having flourished as a ruling ideology for 2,000 years of Chinese history, Confucianism suffered a fateful breakdown in the early twentieth century. Lingering in a state of self-assertion and self-transformation, it confronted a series of powerful, unprecedented challenges throughout the century. At the end of the century, although Confucianism had been relegated to the ashes of history as a political institution, it had, eventually, found its own peace and its own place in the world as a philosophy.

Despite its defeat, there was no concession or surrender by twentieth-century Confucianism; in fact, it has itself represented a challenge for those who rejected it. Levenson (1959) may not have been correct in saying that Liang Qichao, one of the last Confucian intellectuals at the turn of the century, had an intellectual commitment to value but an emotional attachment to tradition. By values, Levenson implied modernity and the west, whereas tradition implied the past and Confucianism. But the matter was not so simple, and the case is not closed. For a Confucian intellectual like Liang, the issue was not just a dualistic contrast, contradiction, or struggle between emotional and intellectual choices.

In Confucianism there has always been a system of values that is well understood and incorporated in practice. One has to be a Confucian with one's body and soul. Thus the sense of loss and perplexity experienced by Confucian intellectuals would be both intellectual and emotional. It involved self-doubt, produced by a collapse of a faith and a series of unbelievable events; a search for identity; and engagement in a profound critique. What is important to note is that a series of challenges may not cohere with each other and thus may have multiple impacts and conflicting effects. Such challenges are not merely political or economic or intellectual—they are all three. In the twentieth century, their force made itself felt in a relatively short period of time. Confucianism, as a symbol of Chinese culture and civilization and of the Chinese people, faced western civilization—an encounter for which it was unprepared and to which it brought both strengths and weaknesses. With little exaggeration, that encounter can be described as a duel to the death.

Confucianism as an Organic System of Substance and Function

How can we now understand and evaluate twentieth-century Confucianism? One advantage of considering the fate of Confucianism in the twentieth century from the standpoint of the twenty-first century is that we can see the whole story: Confucianism in decline; Confucianism enduring, undergoing transformation, and feeling the stirrings of a new life and a new identity. Another advantage is that we can see it more objectively, from a safe distance, in light of new hopes and new comparisons.

Many scholars have tried to understand the modern predicament of Confucianism from a specific political, social, or historical viewpoint, but there is no single perspective from which we can get an overview of Confucianism as a whole system, an organic structure, or a life form in a larger world of systems, structures, and life forms. We need to consider Confucianism as a fully established, entrenched cultural system, structure, or organic process in which political, economic, educational, moral, intellectual, and philosophical aspects are integrated and implemented. In short, we must see this system as a living organism with layers, levels, and shells. I will use the image of shells in order to stress the organic wholeness and solidarity of the Confucian system.

The outermost shell of this structure is political and economic; it represents the exercise of political power—control of actions, projects, and production, and the formation of substantive policies. This is a shell that we may identify as institutional; it has to do with the government, the official system of social organization and social control. Underneath the institutional shell are shells that we can call the moral and the social. The moral shell consists of standards of right and wrong or good and bad, and a model of an ideal person; society is formed and ordered in terms of these standards and ideals. The social shell has to do with the individual and community relationships and interconnections that make up the common life and common history of a people. The social shell sustains the community's morality or ethics and produces lifestyles, creativity, and patterns of thought, perception, and evaluation. We can see, in the social shell, how tradition and history nourish, encourage, and support the activities of life—and how those activities preserve the memory of cultural sources and maintain the sense of history.

Although I began with the "outer" shell, it is difficult to say which shell actually comes first, second, and so on. In terms of ontogeny, there is no doubt that a people or a community must have a social life before it can become fully aware of a need for normative moral standards to maintain order, and for ethical ideals to enable individuals and the group to aspire to something higher. One can also argue, though, that a community—a common culture and common values—can be generated and evolve only when a spirit of morality and an ethics of value and virtue have developed. However, the question of priority need not worry us here, because we easily see the shells as so closely interrelated in the course of historical evolution and development that it is not possible to order them, or even to separate them. For practical purposes, it is clear that a society has a communal life, and that morality and ethics, as an underlying system of values, support this community. Hence—as in the case of the actual exercise of political power, control, and direction through organizational and institutional structures and norms—social life is conducted through a normative morality, ideals, and values.

The distinction between surface activities (form) and underlying structures (content) exemplifies the paradigm of "substance and function" (*ti-yong*) in the metaphysical aspect of Confucianism. The surface activities are "function," suggesting action, operations, the application of a method, or the achievement of a purpose. The underlying institutions and standards are "substance," giving rise to the surface activities and supporting and sustaining them. Thus in the processes of life, substance is realized in function and function in substance.

To put our understanding in focus, we can see that political and economic activities are functions of the institutions and productive forces of a society, which are the substance of these activities. Similarly, on the moral and social level or shell, the relationship between the social and the moral is one of substance and function.

There is, then, a core or kernel in the whole structure or complex of culture, society, and government: the philosophy and the spirit or religion of the people. Here, we can understand philosophy as comprising basic views of reality, truth, and life that shape the character of our existence and culture—our thinking about order, our will and choices, and our values. And we can understand religion or spirit as the basic beliefs and norms we acquire in our interactions with reality—with nature and with ourselves as members of a people or community. We embody our settled understanding of reality in living and implement it in our actions.

With this analysis, we can see that we cannot really separate philosophy as a way of thinking and knowing from religion as a way of believing and acting. In theory, these are two aspects of the same process of living, or of the human being as body, mind, and spirit. It is illuminating to apply the paradigm of substance and function here. Philosophy can be both substance and function relative to religion, just as religion can be both substance and function relative to philosophy. Like the "shells" I have just proposed, they are so closely related that, in the process of living, they are inseparable. Also, the human being is substance in function and function in substance, so that the paradigm of substance and function is a metaphor for the person. Indeed, it is the human being that fully illustrates and clarifies the paradigm. (It is interesting to contrast this organic paradigm or metaphor with its nonorganic counterpart in Greek and modern European philosophy: the paradigm or metaphor of a separation of soul and body, or mind and body, that is referred to as a dualistic theory or a problem of dichotomy.)

With regard to philosophy and religion as I have defined them, we see that philosophy is substance relative to religion because knowledge and thinking define human consciousness and self-consciousness, which give rise to human identity (in terms of which we believe and act). Hence religion becomes the function of a philosophy. On the other hand, religion is the substance of philosophy because we position ourselves to think and to know in terms of our experience of actions and our habitual beliefs. To think, we must use our preconscious or unconscious beliefs; to know, we need to take "preknowledge" actions, because these provide a context for knowing—that is, knowing directed toward action or toward transformations of our own being. We can regard philosophy as a function of religion just as we can regard thinking as a function of believing and knowing as a function of action.

These arguments support the idea that philosophy is inseparable from the system of beliefs related to action that we call (in a broad sense) religion. We can, then, conclude that their aspects of substance and function are inseparable on the moral and social level or shell, or at the core of the human structure. In a deeper sense, there is always an ontohermeneutical "circle" in the substance and function relationship, so that substance gives rise to functions and functions enhance and substantiate substance; and, by the same token, functions substantiate substance so that substance can be activated as functions, thereby strengthening and enriching the functions. Our system of thinking and knowing and our system of believing and action have such a relationship: they interact; each is the foundation for the other; each nourishes the other; and they constitute an endless, unbroken process of initiation and return.

There is a similar relationship between morality and ethics on the one hand and society and community on the other. Morality substantiates society and community; society and community substantiate morality. Moreover, there is a substance-function relationship between the exercise of political power (control and direction) and social institutions or social organization. With regard to activities and enduring bodies, however, there is a greater distance between substance and function.

We can now consider substance and function with regard to Confucianism as an organic structure. As we have seen, political control and governmental institutions form a substance-function relationship with society and morality; and morality and society form a substance-function relationship with philosophy and religion. Perhaps we can, analogously, see society and morality as substance, relative to politics and government as function (this is implied in Mencius's philosophy of rulership and the people). In each case, the one draws its life force or vitality from the other. However, in light of the mutuality of substance and function, we can reverse this argument. In a well-founded society, the relationship of substance and function is an organic whole in which substance and the function are fused or are part of a dynamic circle, so that they cannot be separated or even distinguished.

All this suggests that a living culture or civilization has a three-level structure: individual, social entity, and society. Such a view can explain the nature of Confucianism as an organic complex consisting of the Confucian state, the Confucian society, and Confucian morality, philosophy, and religion. It can show how they are related, how they function and substantiate, and how, in a conflict with another system, they could suffer setbacks or even break down and disintegrate.

We will, then, regard Confucianism as a living organic structure—a complex of culture, society, and government. It has a core with two main "shells" that have a substance-function relationship, and each shell and the core also have internal substance-function relationships. The breakdown of Confucianism in the twentieth century started with the breakdown of its political and governmental shell; this was followed by a loss of faith in the social and moral shell; the process ended with challenges to the central core of Confucianism as a way of thinking, knowing, believing, and acting. In what follows, I shall discuss major events that symbolize what happened in each shell and the core.

Stages of Challenges: Return to and Discovery of the Core

After the Opium War of 1842, China struggled to renew itself, but this proved to be a tortuous and difficult process. It took some time before a self-critical spirit and efforts at self-strengthening had any effect, and in some respects inertia and systematic and personal obstacles were too formidable to overcome. In addition, although setbacks and defeats could create a sense of crisis and be an impetus for reform, in reality they tended to lead toward benighted conservationism. The defeat of China by Japan in 1894 was a crucial event for a few enlightened Confucian scholars, who intensified their attempts to institute reforms in the Confucian spirit of self-reformation and self-renewal. That is how the "reform of a hundred days" came about in 1898, by the order of Emperor Guangxu.

This reform was initiated, promoted, and headed by Kang Youwei (1858–1927), a devoted Confucian who developed his philosophy in the reformist spirit of what was known as *gongyang* Confucianism. According to this theory, the time had arrived for China to enter a new era of better order and better government—an evolutionary point of view based on the *Gongyang Commentary* on *Chunqiu* (*Spring and Autumn Annals*) and *Yijing* (*Book of Changes*), combined with Darwinism from the west. Much of the significance of the reform had to do with Kang's activities in its behalf. It symbolized not only that Confucianism was a living force but that it could change in the face of hardship. Its motivation came from the internal life of Confucianism, and its ideal or goal was defined in terms of the political philosophy of the *Chunqiu*. This was the first time a movement had arisen within Confucianism to speak out for reform and organize as political power.

However, the reform ended in total failure because conservatism fought back in the person of the dowager empress and because Kang exiled himself. The failure was as historically significant as the movement itself: Confucianism as a leading political force had faded, collapsed, and been drained of its vitality. In a deeper sense the failure signified that Confucianism as a political philosophy had lost its strength and relevance. This was because it was identified with political institutions that had been incapable of self-renewal and therefore had been unable to deal with threats and invasions by foreign powers. After 1842, China had continued to suffer inglorious defeats. Even though it had overcome the Taiping rebellion in the name of protecting the Confucian culture of *li* (propriety) and *dao*, it had not rallied itself quickly and decisively enough to adopt reform measures or to implement reforms efficiently—unlike Meiji Japan. There were personal factors in this failure, but the historical lesson to be drawn was that Confucianism as a political philosophy had not brought about a viable Confucian institution, government, ruler, or rule. On this basis, political revolution was considerd not only justified but necessary. The old regime was dealt a last blow by the Boxer Rebellion and the consequent invasion of the "eight nations" in 1899, which ended Confucianism as a political entity in China.

The revolution of 1911 by Sun Yat-sen was the start of a new political system. Although this system had some Confucian elements, it was clear that Confucianism as a traditional political paradigm had been forsaken. The question whether explicit democratic principles could be derived from the political philosophy of Confucianism remained an abstract issue. As a matter of historical practice Confucianism as a political entity had not gone beyond feudalistic despotism. It can be concluded that by 1920 the political level or "shell" of Confucianism as an organic political-social-moral complex or institution had dissolved both in form and in content, even though for decades afterward there was a residue of political Confucianism which from time to time managed or tried to reappear and insinuate itself in the name of democracy and law. This leads us to the dissolution of the social and moral shells of Confucianism.

China was on the winning side in World War I, but in 1919 it received the insult of losing its sovereign rights over its own territory to imperialist Japan. This led to the May Fourth movement, which was a combination of a patriotic campaign against Japan and the imperial powers of Europe and a deep critique of China's cultural values and mentality. It implied that Confucianism as a culture and a system of social and intellectual values displayed weaknesses and failings in comparison with western counterparts and was inadequate to protect the dignity of a people and a nation. This self-critique emphasized the failure of Confucianism to provide a modern democratic system of government that would educate the people to participate in controlling their own affairs, and its failure to develop science and technology because it had refused to seek knowledge of nature or to cultivate material benefits. In the critique we can see the birth of a new social and moral paradigm: implement democracy and practice science. "Mr. Science" and "Mr. Democracy"—these names were actually used—were called on to prevail over the outmoded Confucian morality and social ethics.

In the May Fourth movement of 1919 no special category was given to the spiritual and moral values of the west. The focus was on national strength, the ability to cope with a critical international situation, and the ability to protect basic dignity, equality, independence, and rights. Liang Qichao, as a Confucian scholar, wrote eloquently about the need to introduce and establish a new morality so that the Chinese would be a new people (*xinmin*). What he advocated with regard to morality and virtues was not really incompatible with Confucian morality. It was institutions of inequality, such as the Three Canons (*sankang*), that were repudiated. On the same grounds, Hu Shi as an anti-Confucian liberal and Chen Tuxiu and Li Dazhao as anti-Confucian socialists advocated and promoted a new morality and new social ethics. Presumably, Hu thought that a new morality would lead to democracy and technocracy, as in America, whereas Chen and Li thought that a new morality would lead to a socialist revolution which would wipe out all vestiges of feudalism and establish a truly free and equalitarian socialist state.

The struggle between these two implicit political ideologies would continue for many years. But the point here is that during the May Fourth movement and the subsequent debates (over materialist historicism, metaphysics, and science), with regard to founding a new morality Confucianism had lost its appeal for progressive intellectuals and the younger generation.

A result of the developing dialectics and ideological debates was that Confucianism broke down as a social and moral philosophy and as a system of social and moral values. This breakdown can also be understood as a consequence of the failure of political efforts after the revolution of 1911 to find a viable substitute for the old paradigm of the Confucian kingdom. Later, it coincided with a period of social instability (or chaos) and the invasion by Japan in 1938. The puppet regime under Japan was a strong indication of a betrayal of Confucian morality and the Confucian ethical code.

The period from the May Fourth movement of 1919 to the founding of the People's Republic of China in 1950 was characterized by the slow demise of Confucian ethics and Confucian society. Again, this is not to say that there were no pockets of resistance, but as a social force and a moral persuasion Confucianism no longer held sway or exercised authority. Thus the moral and social shells of Confucianism were divested of vitality. The Confucian institution as a political-social-moral entity was reduced to its core of intellectual thinking, a thin thread of philosophical statements and articles of faith. If we could still speak of the Confucian institution as a living force, that force was to be found only in its core—Confucianism as a philosophy and a religious faith.

Here, it will be useful to recall how Confucianism as a philosophy and a religion is to be understood. As a philosophy, Confucianism transcends political and social reality and history and has lost its influence on them. It goes back to the philosophical teachings of Confucius and other Confucians and exists as a philosophy of life and of ultimate reality, as faith in human nature, and as an approach to basic human relationships. The loss of political and social relevance is said to heighten the meaningfulness of Confucian wisdom—which is to define what humans should be and how they can become what they should be. In this sense Confucianism has returned or has been restored to its pristine state of intellectual and moral understanding. It is as this understanding that Confucianism is to compete with other forms of wisdom and philosophical paradigms. And perhaps it is as a quest for wisdom and for the essential values of life that Confucianism has received new life and new significance. To hold to this moral and intellectual understanding requires faith and conviction, which must be reflected in making decisions and taking action. This is the respect in which Confucianism as a philosophy of life involves Confucianism as an ultimate faith and a religion.

However, Confucianism as a philosophy and as a faith was originally at the core of the Confucian organism, and it was adopted by and incorporated into an existing political power, the Western Han, for its usefulness and meaningfulness. Confucianism was made a political ideology—and acquired what I have called its "outer" political shell—because it served the purpose of the state. And a political power could adopt a philosophy in this way because the core philosophy had existed long enough to become a social and moral force.

This seemed to happen to Confucianism as a body of philosophical doctrines after the death of Confucius. During his lifetime, Confucian thought had already become a distinct learning (*xianxue*), and this *xianxue* continued to flourish and to be spread by generations of Confucian disciples. With Mencius, Confucianism as a set of philosophical doctrines was brought to a second culmination. After Mencius, Xunzi took the teaching of Confucius in a different direction, which was essential for the combination and union of Confucianism and legalism. Thus Xunzi paved the way for the rise of Confucianism as an ideology, which in plain language meant the strategic incorporation of Confucianism into a political system.

The important point here is that when Confucianism was reduced or restored to its original state, it had in a sense recovered its original, primordial strength and vision. It was no longer hampered by political self-interest or historical social conventions. It became a pure, ideal system of thoughts that could become a subject of argumentation and an inspiration, and could rise to a position that commanded attention. It showed that it could appeal directly to humans and that they could respond to it as humans.

Rise of Contemporary Neo-Confucianism as a Metaphysical Philosophy

In contending with other systems of ideas, Confucianism as a philosophy and as a faith can develop by absorbing what is best from others and by enriching others. It has to stand on its own ground, not on political, social, or even conventional moral grounds. It has to survive and grow in terms of its own potential creativity based on a deep understanding of the human being and a reflection of the aspirations of humans and human society.

It was in this sense that the core of Confucianism as a philosophy and as a faith became prominent and spoke out as a new force in the 1930s, as exemplified in the formulations of Xiong Shili, Liang Shuming, and others. This was the rise of "new Confucianism" in modern and contemporary China. Without an understanding of the background—the collapse of Confucianism as a political and social force—we could not appreciate the source of its inspiration and strength. And without an understanding of its roots in classical Confucianism and Song-Ming neo-Confucianism we could not appreciate its creative strength and vision.

In retrospect, the rise of contemporary neo-Confucianism as a philosophy was not a historical accident. It was, rather, the way Confucian philosophy, deprived of political and social backing, responded to a challenging situation. This way of understanding contemporary neo-Confucianism helps us see how it was related to basic cultural, ethical, and metaphysical concepts in classical Confucianism and Song-Ming neo-Confucianism. The crucial question is how Xiong Shili (1885–1968) and Liang Shuming (1893–1988) came to formulate the Confucian philosophy and the Confucian faith against the historical background of the 1920s and 1930s after the May Fourth movement.

One factor we need to take into account is that no western philosopher known at the time—neither Darwin, Huxley, Bergson, Russell, nor Dewey—had provided ethics or metaphysics that could satisfy the minds of Chinese Confucian intellectuals, who tended to look for deeper truths in Chinese Buddhism. That both Xiong and Liang studied Buddhism before they turned back and formulated their philosophies of Confucianism shows that they searched for spiritual truth beyond political and social reality. Nevertheless, their return to Confucian philosophy needs an explanation. They were concerned with the actual state of society and the practical issues of cultural life, as they had demonstrated in their early engagement in social, political, and cultural matters. Hence, it was natural for them to go back to Confucian philosophy, and in this regard they were typical of many others.

Of these two, Liang, who was younger than Xiong, represents a retrieval of the Confucian faith. He identified three types of cultural spirit: the western, which took at its principle simply moving forward; the Indian, which took looking backward as its guiding principle; and the Chinese, whose guiding principle was harmony and a centralized balance. This theory provided a justification of Chinese culture but also suggested a way for the necessary development of the culture. What accounted for these types of culture? For an answer, we must look into human nature and the human mind. Liang held that our desires made us seek external material satisfaction, our moral intuition (*liangzhi*) made us feel a need to act morally toward others, and our intellectual wisdom or intuition enabled us to see into life and recognize the ultimate truth—which was to be achieved only through Buddhist learning. In this sense Liang came to regard Confucian philosophy as a stepping-stone to an ultimate understanding of reality.

In contrast, Xiong's approach directly confronted the original human mind or human nature and the ultimate reality of the universe. Xiong sought the metaphysical meanings of fundamental Confucian concepts and recognized what they stood for in terms of his own reflection and thinking. He spoke of the original substance (*benti*) of life and nature and argued for their unity in his insightful understanding of own his mind and self. Like Wang Yangming, Xiong saw the oneness of personal life, the universe, and things in the universe and spoke of how the profound sense of care and concern (*renxin*) in our own nature would enable us to realize that nature as well as the nature of others and things. This was how we would discover morality in the reality of human mind and nature and how morality would enable us to fulfill and complete our understanding of the ultimate reality of the world. Xiong cited the *Zhou Yi* (or *Yijing, Book of Changes*) to explain the ceaseless creativity of ultimate reality (*benti*) as experienced in one mind and the world, and he expounded the inseparability of substance and function (*tiyong bu'er*).

In an important sense, Xiong reconstructed the metaphysics of change in terms of his theory of *tiyong*: change was possible because of the closing (*xi* or *yin*) and opening (*pi* or *yang*) functions of ultimate reality, which is presented or disclosed by these functions in turn. Equally important was his explicit insistence that the oneness of ultimate reality could be found in all its functions: *qi* (vital force), *li* (principle, pattern, reason), *zhi* (knowledge), *xing* (nature), etc. He held that this ultimate oneness could be realized in a single original mind, that we could disclose our original mind (*benxin*) if we could remove our selfish desires and ignorance, and that we could thereby renovate our world. He believed in the absolute creativity of the original mind as the ultimate reality. He stressed the efforts (*gongfu*) involved in reflecting on one *benxin*, which entailed both thinking and cultivation, both deepening awareness and transcending consciousness. To reach this *benxin* as the ultimate reality was to have evidence and confirmation of the one original mind. In reaching the *benxin* one dissolved concepts and achieved enlightenment transcending knowledge and language. This state was the state of unity of heaven and the human being—a state that had both moral and ontological significance—and hence could be described as the unity of the *dao* and the *de* (power).

We can see that Xiong started by developing Confucianism as an ontology and cosmology of ultimate reality which had its unity in ontology and cosmology, but he ended by describing the state of discovery of the *benxin* as the ultimate reality in oneself. In this sense he formulated a Confucian philosophy that reflected his own deep faith in the truth of Confucianism, and he was not opposed to treating Confucianism as a living faith. Thus in certain ways he was even more deeply imbued with the Confucian faith than Liang was.

Both Liang and Xiong developed Confucianism as a philosophy and a faith, giving it new life. However, there was a difference between them. For Liang, Confucianism as a philosophy could be transcended but could also be enriched; therefore, we could absorb science and democracy from the west. But for Xiong, Confucianism as an ontology and cosmology was self-sufficient; we needed to reach ultimate reality in ourselves so that we could develop science and democracy. For Liang, Confucianism needed to be related to cultural matters and practical actions of the community; for Xiong, Confucian philosophy could be directly manifested in life when it was cultivated in seeking oneness with all things in the *dao*.

The Second Generation: A Cultural-Spiritual Declaration

After the rise of Marxism in the 1930s, Confucianism, whether as a philosophy or a faith, had to confront it. Marxist ideology had become the core of a new political and social structure in China after 1950. Its paradigms—historical materialism and dialectical materialism—became dominant politically, socially, and philosophically. Mao Zedong (1893–1976) represented and led the Marxist critique of and movement against Confucianism, which were both ideological and practical and culminated in the Anti-Confucius Campaign of 1972, during the height of the Great Cultural Revolution. It is noteworthy that although both Liang and Xiong were adversely affected by this campaign, they maintained their integrity and independence of mind, providing inspiration for the promotion and development of Confucianism in the postreform period after 1978.

We may regard Liang and Xiong as having established two prototypes of contemporary neo-Confucianism as it developed later, particularly among the second generation of neo-Confucians who lived in Hong Kong and Taiwan. Liang represented Confucianism as a practical and cultural philosophy ("practical-cultural" Confucianism); Xiong represented Confucianism as a moral and metaphysical philosophy ("moral-metaphysical" Confucianism). In the second generation of contemporary neo-Confucianism, Xu Fuguan (1903–1982) belonged to practical-cultural Confucianism and Mou Zongsan (1909–1995) to moral-metaphysical Confucianism. Tang Junyi (1909–1978) combined the two types, though in his later works he inclined toward the latter. Notably, all three acknowledged the influence of Xiong and regarded him as their personal teacher.

Xu started by affirming cultural values as the center of human life. He saw the human being as a cultural entity who fulfilled cultural values—including art, morality, and religion—in conjunction with seeking scientific knowledge. But fulfilling one's cultural values was more important. In the modern world, Xu held, people had lost their understanding of their nature and their visions of value by seeking modernization and scientific knowledge. This distinction also explained the difference between Chinese and western culture. The future of the world depended on the organic integration of these two cultures, which were complementary and needed each other. With regard to the modernization of Chinese culture Xu advocated reflection on and renovation of the Chinese tradition; Confucius had provided the moral standards and ideal values of culture for such reflection and renovation. Xu described Chinese culture as embodying reverence for virtues (*jingde*) derived from the ancient worship of heaven.

Xu saw Confucius as representing a crucial point in the transformation of ancient religious reverence into human reverence for culture and morality. In this sense Confucianism could be called oral humanism of the *dao*, where the *dao* suggested the self-awakening of humanity as derived from heaven. It was Confucius who had paved the way for Chinese cultural development in terms of human practice of the virtues, and it was in practicing the virtues that humans could develop and become settled in life. Xu also stressed the importance of the Cheng brothers and Zhu Xi, regarding them as having provided two different ways of fulfilling or perfecting the human world, the horizontal and the vertical. For Xu, Chinese culture and humanism had two main modes of expression: morality and art. The mode of morality was developed primarily by Confucianism and the mode of art by philosophical Daoism. Both drew on human nature and the human mind; they represented, respectively, how human values could be realized by realizing the creativity of human nature and the human mind. Xu was opposed to seeking metaphysical foundation or support for the Chinese humanistic spirit, because such an effort would not be stable and would have no practical uses in realizing moral and artistic values.

In contrast with Xu Fuguan's moral humanism is Mou Zongsan's moral metaphysics. Mou sought to build an ontological world of ultimate reality based on moral understanding and moral practice. In a sense, he inherited Xiong Shili's metaphysical spirit and developed it more extensively and more systematically. He could do this because he found a model in Kant, whom he saw as the apex of western philosophy and from whom he drew inspiration for a philosophical critique of Chinese tradition. At the same time, Mou wanted to show how Chinese philosophy could be said to differ from Kant's in transcending the Kantian system. For this purpose, he needed to conduct a systematic reexamination of Chinese philosophy in its historical development so that he could bring out its distinctive way of understanding and realizing the ultimate reality of the self and the world.

Mou attempted to evaluate later Confucian philosophers in light of the Confucian paradigm of unity of the internal and the external, heaven and man, and theory and practice. In this regard he saw Mencius as representing subjectivity or subjective intuition and Xunzi as representing objective reason. Both have importance for an understanding of Confucianism. But when he came to distinctions in neo-Confucianism he disparaged Zhu Xi, because he regarded Zhu Xi and Cheng Yi as deviating from the mainstream of Confucianism represented by Lu Xiangshan and Wang Yangming, and because Cheng Yi and Zhu Xi failed to recognize dynamism and activity in *li* (principle, pattern, reason) separately from *qi* (vital force)

Mou identified three periods in the development of Confucianism from classical times to Song-Ming, and then on to the future. The possibility of such a future stage depended on whether we would be able to create a better philosophy of history and culture, which would inspire people to embrace Confucianism. This is indubitably a Confucian insight—for what is culturally possible always requires the creative development of our nature (*xing*) and our mind (*xin*). If we have not attained our values, it is up to us to continue our efforts.

In developing his moral metaphysics Mou distinguished two levels of ontology: the ontology free from clinging (*wuzhi*) and the ontology of clinging (*zhi*). This distinction was based on Kant's distinction between noumenon and phenomenon. Kant insisted that humans were finite and thus incapable of seeing ultimate reality. But for Mou, humans can open their minds to the infinite so that they can realize and intuit the *dao*, the infinite and ultimate reality. For him it was important to integrate Kantian and Chinese (neo-Confucian) insights in order to reach a great substance (*ti*) of the philosophy of great function. Mou clearly believed that the essential value of Confucianism was that it offered a possibility of intellectual intuition leading from moral practice to ontological understanding.

Chinese philosophy provided metaphysics free from obstructions or clinging so that we could see ultimate reality, but it could not produce science, because it could not see things as objects of investigation. In order to develop science, Mou held, the infinite mind with its moral and intellectual intuition had to "abnegate" (*kanxian*) itself so that it could develop objective knowledge and scientific understanding. In this abnegation of the absolute self, reason would come into being and science would become a result of objective inquiry. In this regard we can see the ontology of *wuzhi* as the substance of the ontology of *zhi*, which is the ontology of function to the ontology of substance in *wu* (emptiness). With this understanding Confucian philosophy would reach its highest form of development.

Mou tried to meet the challenge of introducing science and democracy into China. He suggested an abnegation of moral reasoning in favor of theoretical reasoning so that we could realize the objective and value-neutral mentality of science and democracy, making science and democracy tools designed by theoretical reason. But the question remained how science and democracy, so produced, could sustain themselves once theoretical reason was transformed back into moral reason. Mou spoke of developing a tradition of learning (*xuetong*) to complement the tradition of the *dao* (*daotong*) and of developing standards of government to complement the skills of rulership. In this way he developed a comprehensive Confucian philosophy as an ideal system of metaphysical truth, moral goodness, and scientific reason in terms of which human society could embody both sageliness within and kingliness without (*neisheng waiwang*).

In contrast with Xu and Mou, Tang developed a basic philosophy of moral reasoning and moral self that had elements of both practical-cultural and moral-metaphysical Confucianism. Tang took the human mind as the original reality from which various systems of philosophy could be built. In this sense he regarded the human mind as having an absolute spirit (in both a Hegelian sense and the sense of Lu-Wang philosophy of mind) which was capable of presenting three modes of reality: objective, subjective, and trans-subjective-and-objective. These three modes multiplied to form nine realms or horizons (*jiujing*) of reality, which could be considered the functions of the mind as substance and thus could be unified in one "thought moment" (*nian*) of the mind. These nine realms of reality exhausted all the positions of human knowledge and beliefs, including science and religion, with Confucian ethics and metaphysics as the highest realm in the sense of achieving perfect harmony. This can be regarded as a variation of Hegel's *Phenomenology of Spirit* presented in a *Yijing*-Daoistic dialectic of differentiation, unification, and transcendence.

With Tang's phenomenology of "mind-substance" (which he formed later in life) we can see that almost all his earlier positions regarding epistemology, moral philosophy, theory of religion, philosophy of life, and political philosophy are easily explained. In his epistemology he uses his notion of mind-substance to transform knowledge into wisdom and transform wisdom into virtue or moral reason. This would then justify the theses of unity of mind and body, unity of object and subject, and unity of knowledge and action. In essence Tang argued on the basis of Kant and Lu-Wang. Similarly, on the basis of the autonomy and freedom of moral reason he argued for the realization of the moral self in the actual life of a person and thus supported the Mencian theory of the goodness of human nature and the Confucian and neo-Confucian theory of virtues and distinctions between right and utility, principle and desires, regard for others and self-interest. This is his moral philosophy.

Tang also formulated a philosophy of life based on the mind-substance that consisted of describing and explaining the meaning of life and death and the meaning of happiness, love, and hardship. He specifically discussed the Confucian approach to life's issues and how the cultivation of one's life and mind was important for resolving these issues. With regard to religion, he took the human desire to be liberated from life as the starting point of all major religions. In this regard he considered Confucianism higher than Christianity and Buddhism because it affirmed the value of life without any escape. He spoke of developing a Confucian religion as a basis for harmonizing all the world's religions.

Finally, in his political philosophy Tang held to the ideal of a Confucian moral government characterized by virtue and care for the people, regarding this as compatible with western democracy.

Although Tang's philosophy is highly spiritualistic, his main concern was to see how an idealistic mind-substance could be realized in human culture and human morality. In fact, he wanted to develop a comparative theory of Chinese and western cultures. He rejected the westernization of Chinese culture and tried to argue for the high spiritual values of Chinese culture and tradition. But he was no conservative. He saw a fusion and integration of Chinese and western culture as the most creative path for the future development of Chinese culture.

We may call Tang's philosophy spiritual humanism or moral humanism. His notion of moral reason is no doubt the mind of benevolence (*renxin*) in Confucian philosophy. But he also interpreted this moral mind as a spiritual metaphysical entity by transcending the classical Confucian framework in order to provide a base for all human cultural activities and give them a moral meaning. It is in this sense that Tang combined practical-cultural Confucianism with moral-metaphysical Confucianism.

We have considered in some detail how the second generation of neo-Confucians built large systems or discourses around Confucianism as a philosophy and a spiritual faith. In 1957 Tang Junyi visited the United States, and in coordination with Chang Chunmai (Carson Chang, 1887–1965), Mou Zongsan, and Xu Fuguan drafted, signed, and made public a "Declaration on Chinese Culture to People in the World." This was a momentous declaration of the Confucian faith in Chinese culture, and it indicates that Confucianism had by then regained momentum and aspirations.

Other Developments

The philosophical and speculative development of Confucianism by the neo-Confucian philosophers can also be found in other well-known Chinese philosophers of the same period. Notable figures on the Chinese mainland include Feng Youlan (Fung Yu-lan, 1895–1990), who developed a new neo-Confucian system in *New Learning of Li* (*Xin Lixue*), which reconstructed Zhu Xi's notion of *li* in terms of contemporary western realism with analytic and logical methods. Feng's philosophy of *li* was applicable to all areas of life, including knowledge, society, and politics. This is the Confucian spirit at work—no philosophical notion is devoid of practical meaning.

He Lin (1902–1992) was a neo-Confucian philosopher who interpreted the Lu-Wang philosophy of "heart-mind" (*xin*) by way of Hegelian idealism. The logician-metaphysician Jin Yuelin (1895–1990) took a logical-constructive approach to the problem of knowledge and reality that also reveals neo-Confucian thinking apart from Daoism.

In Taiwan, besides Xu Fuguan (discussed above) there was Fang Dongmei (Thomé H. Fang, 1899–1977), the best-known philosopher of the 1950s and 1960s. Fang interpreted Confucianism in a highly metaphysical and spiritual way. He spoke of formulating primordial Confucian philosophy (*yuanshi Rujia*) together with primordial Daoist philosophy (*yuanshi Daojia*) in terms of the Confucian understanding of life, the cosmos, and ultimate reality, and the formation of the human mind and nature. He described the discovery and realization of a sense of beauty (*meigan*). In his *Chinese View of Life* (1962) Fang argued that a genuine understanding of Chinese philosophy (including Confucianism) would lead to insights on ideal government and an ideal society.

It must be noted that all major contemporary neo-Confucian philosophical systems were developed outside mainland China from 1950 to 1980. They may be regarded as a response and a challenge to the prevailing Marxism in communist China, and they indicate that although Confucianism as a cultural organism lost its political and social shells, its spiritual core as a philosophy and faith was able to stay alive, prosper, and grow in Chinese communities where there were no doctrinaire and ideological restraints or official restrictions and where traditional Chinese culture still thrived. Hence Taiwan and Hong Kong became the natural places for second-generation contemporary Chinese philosophy and contemporary neo-Confucianism. Philosophers such as Fang Dongmei, Xu Fuguan, Mou Zongsan, and Tang Junyi were scholars who taught philosophy at universities or at institutes they founded after the victory of the Chinese Communist Party in China in 1949. In this way they were able to transmit and spread their words, ideas, and visions, sowing seeds in young minds of the next generation and going far beyond the traditional domain of Chinese culture. Thus when we come to the mid-century we see a transplanting of Chinese philosophy and Confucianism to the "land of the new continent," the United States—where Confucianism and other branches of Chinese philosophy took root and and started to grow overseas amid mainstream contemporary western philosophy.

The overseas development of Confucianism and other Chinese philosophies might be said to be linked to the convening of the East-West Philosophers' Conferences at the University of Hawaii (at Manoa in Honolulu) in 1965 and 1971. In those conferences and other, small conferences during the 1970s, Chinese scholars from Taiwan and Hong Kong such as Fang Dongmei, Xie Youwei (1901–1976), Tang Junyi, and Mou Zongsan presented their mature views on different aspects of Chinese philosophy and Confucianism and shared panel discussions with philosophers from the west and India. Confucianism as a philosophy and a cultural tradition was stressed. At the East-West conferences Chinese philosophers from Taiwan and Hong Kong were able, for the first time, to meet the few Chinese scholars who were then teaching Chinese philosophy in the United States. The meetings also inspired younger Chinese to organize in order to develop Chinese philosophy and Confucianism as a philosophy.

Wing-tsit Chan (1901–1995) played an important role in cofounding the East-West conference and in promoting Confucian thought in his public lectures. Chan immigrated to Hawaii in 1936 and taught Chinese philosophy at the University of Hawaii until 1942, when he moved to Dartmouth College.

Chung-ying Cheng (the present author) was born in China in 1935, graduated from college in Taiwan, and got his Ph.D. in philosophy at Harvard in 1972. He analytically reconstructs Chinese philosophy, including Confucianism and neo-Confucianism, and has contributed to the development of Confucian philosophy in the west. As a young faculty member in the department of philosophy at the University of Hawaii (Manoa) he founded and edited the English quarterly *Journal of Chinese Philosophy* with its publishers in the Netherlands. Later, he was able to get the journal printed in Taiwan; eventually it was published and printed in Boston and London by Blackwell. It had dawned on him that without a publishing forum in the west it would be difficult to establish the concept of Chinese philosophy as a living tradition there. Although Chinese philosophy including Confucianism had been studied in the west since the early modern era, it was treated initially as an exotic learning and later as a museum piece—something to be analyzed and assessed from an archaeological point of view. Cheng wanted to correct this image and bring Chinese philosophy into the mainstream of western philosophy. Also, influenced by his teacher Fang Dongmei and contemporary neo-Confucians such as Xiong Shili and Liang Shuming, he was convinced that Chinese philosophy could be developed creatively and could contribute to a genuine world philosophy and world culture. Hence the founding of the *Journal of Chinese Philosophy*—a milestone in the development of Chinese philosophy and Confucianism in the west following the second-generation philosophers living in Taiwan and Hong Kong. As of this writing the journal had been issued for twenty-seven years and had published more than 300 essays on every aspect of Confucianism.

In 1973, to further much the same goals as the journal, Chung-ying Cheng founded the International Society for Chinese Philosophy (originally the Society for Chinese Philosophy; at the suggestion of Lik Kuen Tong, its name was officially changed in 1975). This society planned to convene an international conference every two years in different parts of the world, and to meet annually and offer panels and papers in affiliation with annual meetings of the American Philosophical Association. In its first twenty-five years it held twelve international conferences in eleven places (Fairfield,

Charleston, New York, San Diego, Hawaii, Toronto, Munich, Beijing, Boston, Seoul, and Taipei).

The development of Chinese philosophy and Confucianism as a philosophy and a faith overseas, and perhaps especially in the west, has been a significant phenomenon from the 1960s to the present. Indeed, it is reasonable to regard this as the most significant aspect of the development of Confucianism in the late twentieth century. Besides the present author, many other Chinese scholars came to take Confucianism and neo-Confucianism seriously. Here, it will suffice to mention just a few.

Shu-hsien Liu (b. 1935), formerly at Southern Illinois University and at this writing a professor emeritus, was trained in both Taiwan and the United States. He became deeply involved with Mou Zongsan's moral metaphysics and advocated, basically, a neo-Confucian point of view. Antonio S. Cua (Ke Xiongwen, b. 1932, the editor of this encyclopedia), at this writing a professor emeritus at the Catholic University of America, came from the Philippines, received a Ph.D. from the University of California at Berkeley with a concentration in ethics, took a great interest in developing the Confucian ethical theory of paradigmatic individuals and Xunzi's theory of ethical argumentation, and has served as a coeditor of the *Journal of Chinese Philosophy*. Tu Weiming (b. 1940), as of this writing at Harvard University, graduated from Donghai University in Taiwan and came to Harvard to study in the department of Far East languages and civilizations; he dedicated himself to promoting Confucianism as a religious tradition and became the scholar perhaps best-known in the east and west. Julia Ching (1935–2001), who was a professor emeritus at the University of Toronto, first studied and wrote on a religious comparison of Confucianism and Christianity.

The development of Confucianism overseas was by no means an attempt by only a handful of Chinese scholars. Several westerners also took part in developing and articulating Confucian philosophy as a historical tradition with contemporary significance. Once again, just a few examples will be noted.

The late Benjamin Schwartz of Harvard University showed an appreciation of Confucian views in his works. William Theodore de Bary, a professor emeritus at Columbia University (his and the following affiliations are as of this writing), studied the work of Huang Zongxi and promoted Song-Ming neo-Confucianism; he also ventured into topics such as Confucianism and human rights. Herbert Fingarette, a professor emeritus at the University of California at Santa Barbara, published a brief but influential book, *Confucius: The Sacred as the Secular*. Roger Ames at the University of Hawaii (Manoa) and David Hall at the University of Texas (El Peso) collaborated on, and published, stimulating studies of Confucius and Han culture from a postmodern point of view. Robert Neville at Boston University began as a Daoist-minded theologician-philosopher and then came to appreciate the ritualistic (*lijiao*) tradition of Confucius and Xunzi. Neville promoted what he called the "Boston school" of Confucianism on the basis of his work with Weiming Tu and Chung-ying Cheng.

In mainland China itself, since the early 1980s there has been great interest among scholars in Confucianism as a historical tradition and as a philosophy. In 1981 a conference on Song-Ming neo-Confucianism was held in Hangzhou—the first such conference since the beginning of the period of openness and reform in 1978. In 1985 the International Conference on Xiong Shili, convened by Peking University and Wuhan University, was held in Hubei Province. This—and a conference on Confucius held in 1986 in Shandong Province—signified a "defreezing" of the study of contemporary neo-Confucianism.

In 1987 Chung-ying Cheng proposed to the authorities in Beijing that an international federation of Confucian studies be founded there, to promote and coordinate Confucian studies worldwide. The proposal was not responded to until October 1989, when the International Conference in Commemoration of the 2,545th Birthday of Confucius was held in Beijing. It took five years before Cheng's proposed federation was officially founded, with the blessing of the Chinese government. It is now called the International Confucian Association (in English)—Guoji Ruxue Lianhehui in Chinese. In addition to Chung-ying Cheng, Weiming Tu and other overseas Chinese and non-Chinese scholars of Confucianism (including representatives from Taiwan, Singapore, and Hong Kong) played important roles in the formation of this association.

It should be noted that the founding of this association indicated a return to Confucianism not as a political-social entity but as an academic-cultural institution in China. It was a recognition that Confucianism as a philosophy and a living faith had retained and regained a place in China, and it suggested that the intellectual, philosophical, moral, and spiritual aspects of Confucianism could develop independently of the "shells" of government and society. Through the efforts of many Confucians and neo-Confucians, the disembodied Confucian philosophy, together with its metaphysics and ethics, purified itself to express the free spirit of humanity in seeking truth and meaning

Conclusion

After its decline as a political and social institution and organism in the first half of the twentieth century,

Confucianism as a philosophy and a spiritual faith rose like the phoenix. We must be careful not to see it as having renewed its shells of government and society: the time when it dominated government and society was gone. But the development of Confucianism as a philosophy and a spiritual faith does not depend on the political or the social. Its vitality and force come from human self-understanding and the pursuit of value and truth, and its ultimate meaning lies in human reason and the human sentiments of love and justice. Confucianism originated with a human being, Confucius, seeking the realization of human potential. Confucianism as a philosophy has its own substance and function, which are inseparable from humanity and the diverse activities of human life.

The new birth and growth of Confucianism as a philosophy and a faith in the twentieth century were nourished by the development of Confucian metaphysics. This metaphysical system was not abstract and was not detached from life or from human spirit. Rather, it extended the human spirit to obtain an overview of life and reality, and so it demanded application and practice. Without such developments, Confucianism would not have been enriched and would not have had the freedom to respond to the changes of the past and present.

Confucian metaphysics must be true to the paradigm of the unity of substance and function. The development of metaphysics ("above form," *xingshang xue*) is substance, but its application to life and society is function ("within form," *xinxia xue*)—which must interact with substance in order to have vitality and take on new meanings. In this sense what is most metaphysical is also most practical, and metaphysics functions like knowledge, giving depth and scope to human actions and practices.

In the development of Confucian metaphysics in the twentieth century, resources from other traditions in the Confucian framework were assimilated. This was useful—indeed, necessary—because any development must be sustained by incentives and lessons from outside it. Neo-Confucianism of the Song-Ming, for example, integrated insights from Daoism and Buddhism. In the formation of contemporary neo-Confucianism, Xiong Shili, Liang Shuming, Mou Zongsan, and Tang Junyi used Buddhist insights and pronouncements. And as they encountered new views from western philosophy, they were often able to integrate and absorb these, further enriching their own systems.

In the future, this kind of integration must continue, as Confucian thinking faces new situations and newly developed philosophies and religious ideas from the west and elsewhere. Dialogue between the Confucian tradition and the other traditions and between Confucian philosophers and other philosophers is likely to be the most important channel for the sustainable development of Confucian philosophy.

In this regard, it is has often been asked how Confucian philosophy could adopt science and democracy, since it was regarded as antidemocratic and antiscientific, or at best indifferent. In the twentieth century, eminent neo-Confucians tried to resolve this issue. Mou Zongsan, for instance, proposed his famous theory of the abnegation of moral reason (the *kanxian* thesis). Such efforts made it clear that a creative development of Confucian metaphysics and philosophical anthropology or Confucian ethics had to take science and democracy into account, and there is no real reason why Confucian philosophy cannot be strongly prodemocratic and proscientific. A Confucian or neo-Confucian can explore the moral limitations of the paradigms of science and democracy without regarding them as isolated or dominating paradigms of individual and community development. Science and democracy must be seen as requisites for the moral development of human beings and the human community, just as moral reasoning and moral understanding are required for the sound intellectual growth of science and democracy.

With today's pervasive globalization, it is becoming increasingly clear that Confucianism as a philosophy may be essential to a sustainable ecology and to a global community—human and interspecies—and thus to the possibility that humanity will be able to endure, prosper, and live in dignity and peace. One task for Confucianism is to develop as a global ethics and as an anthropological-ecological philosophy of the human being, the community, and nature. Another task is to learn how to nourish and cultivate a meaningful human life in a scientific-technological world and how to make humanity fully relevant to everything we do. For both tasks, the experience of Confucianism in the twentieth century offers encouraging lessons.

See also Fang Dongmei; Hu Shi; Kang Youwei; Liang Qichao; Liang Shuming; Mao Zedong; Mou Zongsan; Philosophy: Recent Trends in China since Mao; Philosophy: Recent Trends Overseas; Tang Junyi; Xiong Shili; Xu Fuguan.

Bibliography

Berthrong, John H. *All under Heaven: Transforming Paradigms in Confucian-Christian Dialogue*. New York, 1994.

Cai, Zhongde, ed. *Study of Feng Youlan*. Beijing, 1997. (In Chinese.)

Chan, Wing-tsit, trans. *A Source Book in Chinese Philosophy*. Princeton, N.J.: Princeton University Press, 1963.

Chen, Weiping, "Theory of Wisdom and Wisdom in Chinese Philosophy: Feng Qi's Study of History of Chinese Philosophy." In *Lilun fangfa he dexing,* 1996. (In Chinese.)

Chen, Xiaolong. *Knowledge and Wisdom: On Jin Yuelin*. Beijing, 1997. (In Chinese.)

Cheng, Chung-ying. *New Dimensions of Confucian/Neo-Confucian Philosophy*. Albany: State University of New York Press, 1991.

Cheng, Chung-ying, and Nick Bunnin, eds. *Contemporary Chinese Philosophy*. Boston, Mass., and Oxford, 2002.

Ching, Julia. *Confucianism and Christianity*. Tokyo and New York, 1977.

Chou, Min-chih. *Hu Shi and Intellectual Choice in Modern China*. Ann Arbor, Mich., 1984.

Cua, Antonio S. *Dimensions of Moral Creativity: Paradigms, Principles, and Ideals*. University Park, Penn., 1978.

———. *Moral Vision and Tradition: Essays in Chinese Ethics*. Washington, D.C., 1998.

———. "Problems of Chinese Moral Philosophy." *Journal of Chinese Philosophy*, 27(3), 2000, pp. 269–285.

Fang, Dongmei (Thomé H. Fang). *Ideal of Life and Cultural Types: Selected Works of Fang Dongmei on Neo-Confucianism*. Beijing, 1992. (In Chinese.)

Fang, Keli, and Wang Qishui, eds. *Twentieth-Century Chinese Philosophy*. 2 vols. Beijing: Huaxia, 1995. (In Chinese.)

Feng, Qi. *The Collected Works of Feng Qi*. Shanghai, 1996–1998. (In Chinese.)

Feng, Youlan. *The Complete Works from Three-Pine Hall*. Beijing, 1986. (In Chinese.)

Guo, Qiyong. *The Philosophy of Liang Shuming*. Wuhan, 1996. (In Chinese.)

———. *A Study of the Thought of Xiong Shili*. Tianjin, 1993. (In Chinese.)

Guoji Ruxue Yanjiu (International Confucian Studies), 1995, 1996, 1997. (Annual publication of International Confucian Association.)

Hall, David, and Roger Ames. *Thinking through Confucius*. Albany: State University of New York Press, 1987

Hansen, Chad. *A Daoist Theory of Chinese Thought: A Philosophical Interpretation*. New York, 1992.

He, Lin. *New Unfolding of Confucian Thought: Key Writings of He Lin on Neo-Confucianism*. Beijing, 1995. (In Chinese.)

Hu, Shi. *Collected Essays of Hu Shi*, 4 collections. Shanghai and Taipei, 1921–1953. (In Chinese.)

———. *Collected Writings of Hu Shi*, Vols. 1–7. Beijing. (In Chinese.)

International Symposium on Fang Dongmei's Philosophy, ed. by Philosophy of Fang Dongmei Committee, 1989.

Jin, Yuelin. *Collected Works of Jin Yuelin*. Lanzhou, 1995. (In Chinese.)

Journal of Chinese Philosophy, 1973–2002. (Quarterly, 27 vols.)

Liang, Qichao. *Complete Works of Liang Qichao*. Beijing, 1999. (In Chinese.)

Liang, Shuming. *The Complete Works of Liang Shuming*. Jinan, 1989–1993. (In Chinese.)

Levenson, Joseph R. *Liang Ch'i-ch'ao and the Mind of Modern China*. Cambridge, Mass., 1959.

Li, Zehou. "Interview with Mr. Li Zehou." *Tianya*, 2, 1999.

———. *Philosophical Works of Li Zehou*. Hefei, 1999. (In Chinese.)

Liu, Shu-hsien. *Understanding Confucian Philosophy: Classical and Sung-Ming*. Westport, Conn., 1998.

Mou, Zongsan. *Mind-Substance and Nature-Substance*, 3 vols. Taipei, 1968–1969. (In Chinese.)

Philosophy Department of Peking University, ed. *Interpretation and Development of Chinese Philosophy: Essays in Honor of Mr. Zhang Dainian's Ninetieth Birthday*. Beijing, 1999. (In Chinese.)

Proceedings of the International Symposium on Xu Fuguan at Donghai University: Essays. Taizhong, 1992.

Rickett, Adele A. *Wang Kuo-wei's Jen-chien Tzu-Hua: A Study in Chinese Literary Criticism*. Hong Kong, 1977.

Song, Zhiming. *A Study of He Lin's Neo-Confucianism*. Tianjin, 1998. (In Chinese.)

Song, Zhongfu, Zhao Jihui, and Fei Dayang, eds. *Ruxue Zai Xiandai Zhongguo* (Confucianism in Modern China). Chengzhou: Zhongzhou Ancient Texts, 1991.

Tang Junyi (Tang Chün-i). *Life Existence and the Nine Realms of Heart-Mind*. Taipei, 1997. (In Chinese.)

Tong, Lik Kuen. "Confucian Ren and Platonic Eros: A Comparative Study." *Chinese Culture*, 14(3), 1973, 1–8.

Tu, Weiming. *Centrality and Commonality: An Essay on Chung-yung*. Honolulu, Hawaii, 1976.

Vittinghoff, Helmolt, ed. "Recent Bibliography in Classical Chinese Philosophy." *Journal of Chinese Philosophy*, 28(1–2), 2001, pp. 1–208.

Wang, Guowei. *Collected Works of Wang Guowei*. Beijing, 1997. (In Chinese.)

Wu, Kuang-ming. *On Chinese Body Thinking: A Cultural Hermeneutic*. Leiden, 1997.

Xiong, Shili. *Collected Works of Xiong Shili*. Wuhan, 2001. (In Chinese.)

Xu, Fuguan. *Exposition of Chinese Humanist Spirit: Selected Works of Xu Fuguan on Neo-Confucianism*. Beijing, 1996. (In Chinese.)

Zhang, Dainian. *Self-Selected Academic Works of Zhang Dainian*. Beijing, 1993.

Zhang, Dongsun. *Epistemology*. Shanghai, 1934. (In Chinese.)

Zhang, Xianghao. *Study of Tang Junyi's Thought*. Tianjin, 1994.

Zhang, Yaonan. *A Study of Zhang Dongsun's Theory of Knowledge*. Taipei, 1995.

Confucianism: Vietnam

Van Doan TRAN

Confucianism came to Vietnam with the Han army in the second century B.C.E., and its existence was inseparable from the force of occupation from the north. Following Dong Zhongshu's political philosophy, and especially legalism, Han administrators applied Confucian morals primarily as a means of governing Vietnam. They prescribed the model of a Confucian state to the Viet and forced them to obey. This meant that the arts of administration, control, and education were molded by Confucian morals. Confucian rites (*li*) as well as rules were de facto the law. The education promulgated by the first Han governors duplicated the contents of the Confucian classics, combined with an interpretation by Dong Zhongshu and the rigor of Han Feizi. Also, the introduction of the Chinese language to the Viet was simply an aspect of governance, not part of a program of civilization. In brief, Confucianism and the Chinese language were instruments for ruling and subjugating non-Han peoples.

Because Confucianism was inseparable from the oppressors, it was misunderstood and rejected by the Viet. Despite the exercise of absolute power in politics and education, it could not establish a firm footing in the soil of Vietnam, even after almost a thousand years. Buddhism and even Daoism held a better place in the hearts of Viet; these later ideologies left their imprint everywhere—in ways of thinking, in the way of life of Viet society, in the arts, and especially in philosophy.

One has to wait until the eleventh century C.E. to witness some success on the part of Confucianism: in 1070 the Ly dynasty built the Literati Temple (Van Mieu) for the worship of Zhou Gong and Confucius. In the sixteenth century Confucianism achieved a total triumph in education, politics, and social organization. However, this triumph did not last indefinitely. It began to erode at the end of the nineteenth century and collapsed in the early twentieth century, in the hands of the westernizers.

Confucianism has been reactivated only relatively recently, and without attaining the dominance or displaying the arrogance of the past. Its renaissance has been motivated not by nostalgia for its days of glory but by the needs of politicians and cultural thinkers and, especially, by a demand for "Viet consciousness." An even more important factor in this rebirth was the deep-seated psyche of the Viet. After twenty centuries, in spite of their resistance to Confucianism, they had incorporated its values deeply and intimately. Confucianism had become a part of Viet philosophy, and its moral values have had a decisive impact on the Vietnamese mind and Vietnamese life.

First Phase: Han Confucianism as an Instrument of Domination

The Han army invaded Au Lac (the original Vietnam, in the region of present-day Canton) c. 201–103 B.C.E. However, the first governors of the Han dynasty had their own agenda: they wanted to found an independent state. One of the most influential, Si Nhiep (second century C.E.), adopted a policy of separatism, relying on the Aborigines to cement his state. He considered Confucianism and the Han written language the most effective tools to "educate" his subordinates to follow him. Like Tich Quang and Nham Dien, Si Nhiep followed Dong Zhongshu's's strategy, taking Confucian morals and education as the most effective means of governing the Viet people. Dong's main doctrines were actually a rationalization and formalization of Confucian doctrines as well as a synthesis of different worldviews of the time. His practical philosophy was mixed with mythological elements, and his metaphysics was blended with popular beliefs and with Daoism. Thus Dong's main metaphysics—"union between heaven and man"—was certainly not purely Confucian. It transformed Confucianism into an ideology that was less rigid with regard to content but more closed-minded and dogmatic with regard to form. Precisely because of its syncretic nature, Dong's Confucianism attracted the attention of the Viet; and because it was so efficacious as a means of governance, it caught the attention of the rulers.

During this period, Vietnam produced some Confucians of its own, such as Khuong Cong Phu (who had earned a *chin-shi*, or doctoral, degree and held an important post in the royal court of Tang), Ly Cam, and Li Tien. Interestingly, though, although Si Nhiep came from the north, he was respected as the *Nam giao hoc to*, or "pioneer of Vietology." Si Nhiep transformed Confucianism into a kind of instrumental reason to serve the state, and even to keep a distance from the north. Similarly, he modified Dong's metaphysical principles of the harmony and union of man and nature to suit the taste of the Viet, blending in a Buddhist and a Daoist flavor.

Second Phase: The First Fusion

As we have seen, since Confucianism was often associated with external force and represented the ideology of the ruling class, it was not adopted or well received by the Viet people until the Ly dynasty. In 1070, for the first time, Zhou Gong and Confucius were officially enshrined and widely worshiped by the people. Confucian schools were established to assume the responsibility of nurturing talent that would then serve the state. This favorable tendency was most probably due to a rediscovery of Confucian ethics as an instrument of governance. The rulers, regardless of race, have always benefited from such an ideology.

It should be noted that after almost a thousand years under the yoke of the north, the south (Nam Viet) finally defeated the northern army and attained independence and freedom. However, this had a heavy cost. The superior military force of the larger north cannot be ignored; the north still menaced the south, whose best strategy was therefore flexible and nonconfrontational—follow the northerners' main politics and acquire their knowledge and techniques.

In this context, it is not surprising that Vietnamese Confucians strictly followed the ideology of the north. This means that they they embraced neo-Confucianism, the so-called *lixue* or school of *li* ("principle," "reason"), in the Song dynasty. The philosophy of the Cheng brothers (Cheng Hao and Cheng Yi) was adopted as the main subject of teaching in Vietnam. Wang Yangming's philosophy was also adopted, but almost all Vietnamese Confucians had to learn more from the Cheng brothers than from anyone else. Indeed, the Cheng's influence was so broad that their philosophy was often described as the mainstream of Confucianism. The phrase *Cua Khong san trinh* ("gate to Kong and the garden of the Chengs") was used to refer to Confucianism, reflecting not only a very peculiar understanding of Confucianism in general but also an official ideology adopted by Vietnamese rulers. However, this ideology differed somewhat from the Cheng brothers' philosophy. Although it was influenced by the Chengs, Viet Confucianism was not a strict copy of the Song and Ming (*lixue*). In other words, Vietnamese Confucians did not take up the philosophy of the Chengs or Wang Yangming or Zhu Xi in toto. They extracted elements of these philosophers' doctrines—*khi*, *qi* (energy), *nhan*, *ren* (benevolence), *ly*, *li* (principle, pattern), *thien ly*, *tianli* (heavenly principle)—and rites to construct a practical philosophy for dealing with the people and with their enemies. This is evident in Nguyen Trai and later Quang Trung, who mixed rationalist and pragmatic elements from Wang Yangming, Zhu Xi, and the Cheng brothers with Buddhist and Daoist doctrines of inner peace to produce a very individual form of Viet Nho (Viet Confucianism). They espoused the doctrine *Tam giao dong nguyen, sanchiao Dong yüan* ("All three religions come from the same root"), which was actually derived from Chinese thought (*sanjiao tongyuan*). This doctrine in Vietnam had an immense influence not only on ordinary people (as seen in China) but also on the Confucians themselves. In the works of Chu Van An, Nguyen Trai, Mac Dinh Chi (1272–1346), Nguyen Truc (1417–1474), Luong The Vinh (b. 1441), and Nguyen Binh Khiem (1491–1585) it had a double aspect: the practical side of Confucianism and the metaphysical side of Daoism and Buddhism.

Third Phase: The Second Fusion—Confucianism as the Main Current and Its Transformation in Viet Nho

Yet the first fusion could satisfy neither the Confucians nor the rulers. Orthodox Confucians objected to any syncretic form because they thought that syncretism might lead to doctrinal self-contradiction. Since the Tang dynasty Confucianism had in fact lost its purity by incorporating some Buddhist elements. The antipathy to such a fusion was rooted in a struggle for power. Confucians found that a fusion weakened their power—they had to share it with Buddhists and Daoists, whom they then considered superstitious and ignorant. Under Ly's rule, Buddhism had absolute power, and the Confucians had been relegated to the periphery; this still haunted them.

On their part, the rulers were well aware that most of the revolts came not from Confucians but from Buddhists. The overthrow of the Trinh-Mac, for instance, was carried out by Nguyen Hue and Nguyen Nhac, who were not educated in Confucianism. Similarly, the Nguyen dynasty was established by Nguyen Anh, who had betrayed the Confucian principle of self-reliance by relying on the power of France. There seemed to be no doubt that Confucians were the best, most loyal, and most obedient servants of the emperor and the state. For these reasons, Confucianism was taken up, glorified, and monopolized by the rulers. But by the same token, once those reasons were no longer considered persuasive, Confucianism was discarded.

One can say that the third phase of Viet Nho began gloriously in the late sixteenth century and ended disgracefully with the last Confucian examination in 1919. In this golden period, Viet Nho produced a second fusion, with a more encompassing system based on Confucian morals. Vietnamese Confucians attempted to incorporate Confucian morals into the stream of their cultural life. The Viet *ethos*, which included facing hardships and dealing pragmatically with actual problems, was blended with the Confucian virtues of benevolence, loyalty, and filial piety and formalized in civil laws, moral codes, social organization, the educational system, and family structure. Furthermore, the metaphysical elements of Buddhism and Daoism were not negated but were dialectically sublimated into the principle of the union of *tian* (heaven) and human beings, nature and man, etc. *Tian* no longer signified a natural body but came very close to the idea of a personal god.

This fusion transformed Confucianism into a form of religion (Nho Giao), which was taken for granted not only by the ordinary people but by the Confucians themselves. Confucius was worshiped as a god, like Buddha and Laozi; and Viet Nho assumes the name Nho Dao (Ru-dao), "Confucian religion." In this case Dao refers to a certain form of religion, not exactly to the *dao* as in Daoism. In this period, Le Quy Don (1726–1784), Nguyen Cong Tru (1778–1858), and Nguyen Truong To (1830–1871) are widely regarded as the representatives of Viet Nho.

The encyclopedist Le Quy Don tried to introduce empirical observation and historical experiences in order to develop a Viet Nho with practical aims. His realism was shaped by several generations of Viet Nho, beginning with Vu Cong Dao (1629–1714), but mostly by a synthesis of Ming-Qing's rationalism and the Viet *ethos*.

Similarly, Nguyen Cong Tru produced a more systematic synthesis. He took a threefold approach. First, he attempted to interpret Confucian values in terms of pragmatic, utilitarian understanding, adopting only those morals that would generate practical values, i.e., those that could solve the problems of the Viet. Second, like Le Quy Don, he was a realist in the sense that his philosophy was constructed in the context of a rural society; therefore, its metaphysical foundation was not an abstraction but a concrete harmony between nature and man, man and society. Third, he did not take Confucianism in toto; he took only the doctrines he considered relevant to the Viet. This way of viewing Confucianism is exemplified in his philosophy of engagement (*chap sinh*), his theory of the unity of knowledge and practice, his emphasis on the inseparability of sensibility and rationality, his cosmological view of the mutuality and reciprocity of the dynamic and passive forces, and his political philosophy, which was based on Wang Yangming's concept of "sageliness within and kingliness without." Such views were well known in Confucianism, but it was Nguyen Cong Tru who blended them into the Viet world. With some justice, it can be said that he achieved the second fusion.

Following the same approach, Nguyen Truong To extended this synthesis to a broader world. In the nineteenth century, Viet society was violently forced to open itself to the western, non-Confucian world. Consequently, the monolithic life of the Viet faced a crisis leading toward self-destruction. The Viet world became broader, more complex, and more problematic. In order to deal with new, emerging problems and avoid self-destruction, Viet Nho was urged to broaden its own vision, and to enrich itself with new scientific knowledge and methods. As a man of encyclopedic education, Nguyen Truong To saw an urgent need for a reformation; in fact, he foresaw a revolution, which—reluctantly and with anxiety—he prescribed to the rulers. On the one hand, he embraced the idea of "Confucian substance and western use," like neo-Confucians such as Tan Sitong, Liang Qichao, and Kang Youwei. On the other hand, he went farther in advocating a radical restructuring of the economy, as well as a kind of British politics. He readily abandoned the ideological elements of Confucianism while zealously keeping its moral dimension.

In these three thinkers we can see some common characteristics of the second fusion. First, they all adopted the same method of dialectical transcendence; second, they are more pragmatic than ideological; third, they based their metaphysics not on abstract idea or principle but on the needs of their country and their people. This is the reason why Kim Dinh (1915–1997) proudly claimed that Viet Nho reflected the original Ru—of which Confucianism was only a part.

Fourth Phase: The Decline of Confucianism

The collapse of Confucianism happened in a short span of time. There were various reasons for it, but the most decisive was the self-destruction of Confucian political power and its structure.

First, the inability of Confucians to appreciate the changes taking place in their world and their lack of scientific knowledge made them powerless in facing the challenge of western civilization and culture. Unlike Japan of the Meiji period, which pursued Ito's program of modernization, the Vietnamese rulers simply dismissed Nguyen Truong To's proposal for modernization, considering it fanciful. Blinded by their own power and their own ignorance, the Nguyen rulers faithfully followed the conservative course prescribed by the Qing dynasty. Thus, when the collapse of the Qing was imminent, the Vietnamese Confucians simply gave up hope and surrendered their power as well. Only a few Confucians like Nguyen Truong To and

Nguyen Lo Trach (b. 1853) were conscious of having a new role in the modern world.

Second, once colonialism put its mark on Vietnam, the Confucians could not adapt to the situation. They had been educated to be passive and obedient, and they were paralyzed. Their focus on morals rather than practical life made them resentful. In this period, pessimism and resentment pushed them toward Daoism or toward the Buddhist escape from the real world. In their poems, the affirmative character of Confucian engagement disappeared, to be replaced by resentment, nihilism, and passivity. Tran Te Xuong and Nguyen Khac Hieu best represented this feeling, which was shared by the majority of Confucians at the end of nineteenth century and the beginning of the twentieth. Only a few still engaged in a desperate battle for power, fighting the colonial force on the one hand, and on the other hand attempting—misguidedly—to destroy non-Confucian western ideology or religion (Catholicism). The nineteenth-century *phong trao van than* ("movement of literates") is a case in point.

In the early twentieth century, however, we can find something of a renaissance of Confucianism, due to the efforts of Phan Boi Chau and Phan Chu Trinh in the north and the Confucians in Gia Dinh in the south. They transformed Confucianism into a form of patriotism and nationalism by fusing western technology and science with Confucian ethics. Their main aim was the modernization of Vietnam, as well as the liberation of Vietnam from France.

Fifth Phase: The Renaissance of Confucianism

Confucianism, stripped of its protected power, became sterile. However, it was not stagnant; it was, rather, dormant, awaiting its opportune time. The naive belief of some western intellectuals that Confucianism had died was certainly unfounded. Within only forty years after the last Confucian examination (1919), Confucianism once again stirred immense interest, this time among educated westerners, especially Catholic intellectuals. In the 1960s, there was a revival of Viet Nho in South Vietnam, motivated partly by political purposes and partly by a search for self-identity. To the Catholic church and Catholic thinkers, Confucianism served as *preambula fidei* and as a bridge reconciling faith with patriotism. A synthesis of Confucian rites and moral teachings with Catholic doctrines might accelerate the process of assimilation, and it would be useful to absolve Catholic intellectuals of being the product of an "external" and "colonial" force. To the nationalists, Confucianism became a weapon against Marxism and communism. To western intellectuals who were dissatisfied with their own civilization and culture, Confucianism might offer a more reasonable approach to the Vietnamese world. In this context, Confucians could assume different roles: politician (Phan Boi Chau, Phan Chu Trinh, Tran Trong Kim), educator (Buu Duong, Kim Dinh), theologian (Vu Dinh Trac, Nguyen Van Thich), ideologist, and culturologist (Nguyen Dang Thuc, Gian Chi). Their valuable contribution to the building of their nation could no longer be denied, even by those who bitterly attacked them.

In North Vietnam, Confucianism was revived —somewhat later—owing to a new policy of *doi moi* (renovation) declared by the Communist Party in the late 1980s. In the north, Confucianism has been almost entirely neglected, partly because of the dominant role of Marxism-Leninism and partly because of the merciless anti-Confucian movement carried on by Maoists in the Cultural Revolution, which indirectly affected Vietnamese intellectuals. As a result, Confucianism disappeared or went underground. The generation of Phan Chu Trinh, Phan Boi Chau, and Tran Trong Kim has rarely if ever been mentioned. But Confucianism has survived; and in the 1990s a significant, though modest, number of new works on Confucianism appeared. One even finds a kind of neo-Confucianism synthesizing Confucianism and patriotism; for instance, in 1997–1998 conferences on Confucianism were held in Hanoi and Saigon. Many Marxist-inclined Confucians see Ho Chi Minh as having achieved this kind of synthesis.

A certain synthesis of Confucian morals and Vietnamese mores has been undertaken by some thinkers concerned with the origin and characteristics of Vietnamese culture. Kim Dinh and his followers claimed that Viet Nho had the quintessential elements of the original Ru, which comprised Confucianism; they indicate how Vietnamese Confucians are attempting to build their own version of Confucianism. Similarly, the discovery of a bronze drum in Dong Son in the early 1930s led to speculation about a relatively independent and highly advanced Viet civilization and Viet culture in Southeast Asia. That in turn suggests the idea of a Viet Nho which, though introduced from the north, developed into a particular form of Viet Confucianism. With Kim Dinh and his school, Viet Nho flourished and regained some of the prestige it had lost at the hands of the anti-Confucians.

See also Cheng Hao; Cheng Yi; Confucianism: Han; *Li*: Principle, Pattern, Reason; *Tian*; Wang Yangming.

Bibliography

Kim Dinh. *Cua Khong* (The Gate to Confucianism). Saigon: Ra Khoi, 1966.

———. *Su Diep Trong Dong* (The Message of Bronze-Drum). San Jose, Calif.: An Viet Foundation, 1984.

Le Sy Thang, ed. *Nho Giao Xua va Nay* (Confucianism in the Past and in the Present). Hanoi: Center of Social Science Press, 1998.

Nguyen Dang Thuc. *Lich Su Tu Tuong Vietnam* (History of Vietnamese Thought), 6 vols. Saigon, 1992.

Nguyen Tai Thu, ed. *Lich Su Tu Tuong Vietnam* (History of Vietnamese Thought), Vol. 2. Hanoi: Center of Social Science Press, 1993.

———. *Nho Hoc va Nho o Vietnam* (Confucianism and Confucianism in Vietnam). Hanoi: Center of Social Science Press, 1997.

Phan Boi Chau. *Khong Hoc Dang* (The Lamp of Confucian Learning). Hue: Thuan Hoa, 1990.

Phan Boi Chau and Tran Van Doan, eds. *Kim Dinh: Life and Works*. Los Angeles, Calif.: University Press of Vietnam, 2000.

Tran Trong Kim. *Nho Giao* (Confucianism), 2 vols. Hanoi: Tan Viet, 1998.

Tran Van Doan. *Viet Triet Luan Tap* (Essays on Viet Philosophy). Los Angeles, Calif.: University Press of Vietnam, 1999.

Vu Dinh Trac. *Triet Kly Chap Sinh Nguyen Cong Tru* (The Existential Philosophy of Nguyen Cong Tru). Orange: Hoi Huu, 1988.

———. *Triet Ly Nhan Ban cua Nguyen Du* (The Humanism of *Nguyen Du*). Orange: Hoi Huu, 1992.

Vu Khieu, ed. *Nho Giao Xua va Nay* (Confucianism in the Past and in the Present). Hanoi: Center of Social Science Press, 1990.

Confucianism: Vision

A. S. Cua

The conception of the unity and harmony of man and nature (*tianren heyi*) has been a pervasive feature in the history of Chinese philosophy. Of special interest to the inquiry concerning the relation between the individual and the community is the Confucian preoccupation with the problem of realizing this vision within human society. It is a concern with the possibility of transforming an existing social order, which has already established a cultural tradition, into an order invested with the ethical ideal of *ren* or humanity. In more concrete terms, *ren* is an ideal of the good life on the whole that is deemed capable of realization in varying human relationships within the setting of institutional practice and social structure as consisting of roles and statuses (*li*, ritual or propriety). In the teachings of Confucius, the task of "*ren* realization" has two aspects. The first aspect is a transformation of the social structure and the functional institutions into an order of *li*—into a condition of civility—wherein individuals pay heed to each other's integrity through compliance with formal requirements for proper behavior. The second aspect is a transformation of all social relationships into personal relationships. The latter task is both a necessary step to and constitutive of the former, for lying at the center of *li*-performance, ideally, is the exemplification of moral virtues or qualities which are a product of self-cultivation and actual engagement in promoting *ren* as a form of diffusive affection (Cua 1978).

Confucius once remarked that to be a man of *ren* is to "love all men" (*Analects*, 12.22; Chan 1963). It is, in effect, an affectionate concern for the well-being of all humans regardless of their abilities and circumstances. But this condition is an outcome of gradually extending the ambience of direct personal relations between individuals. More particularly, it is an extension of familial relationships, e.g., between parents and children, husband and wife, brothers and sisters. The task of creating a human community, in the words of Liang Chi-chao (Liang Chiqiao), is "to cultivate and to foster the commonest feelings of affection among men in order to extend them to build up a society based on *ren*" (Liang 1968). An ideal human community, apart from having a unity of a social structure, is also a community of extensive mutual concern and care among its members. This essay focuses on the nature and possibility of extensive concern in human relationships.

Let us first attend to *ren* as a moral ideal, that is, as an ideal of the good human life as a whole. Basically, it is a conception of equality of human beings, not in the sense that they possess the same empirical characteristics, but in the sense that they share the same status of being human. The ideal of *ren* is what confers this common status of humanity. In this light, we can endorse Mencius's saying that "*ren* is man. When we speak of the two together the result is the Way," or *dao* (*Mencius*, 7B.16). To be a man of *ren* is to be truly human, i.e., to live in a way inspired by *ren*. However, descriptively, humans have a variety of similarities and differences. The problem of *ren*-realization in human life is in part a problem of focusing on those similarities that can serve as a basis for extensive concern. The common characteristic of sociality may serve as this basis, since the point of having the ideal is to enable men to live together in unity and harmony.

In the words of Confucius, a *junzi* or morally superior man cultivates himself "so as to give people security and peace" (*Analects*, 14.45); "he is sociable but not a partisan" (15.21). Taking sociality as a point of departure, one can by reflection be gradually led to appreciate human intercourse as displaying a network of relationships. Every viable human society imposes a set of constraints, duties, and obligations, regulating interactions between people in various contexts. *Ren* signifies an ideal relation between two men. Notably, every society has evolved its own rules of behavior and classification of status. *Li*, for the Confucian, in part pertains to the established tradition governing various human relationships. The problem of *ren*-realization is thus a problem of *equalizing* the status of humanity without obliterating existing social distinctions. More specifically, it is a problem of focusing on the "root-possibility" of *ren*-realization.

What impresses Confucius and subsequent Confucian thinkers is the natural relationship between parents and their offspring. This natural relationship is considered both paradigmatic and normative, for in the family, the behavior of parents and children is characteristically one of care and affectionate concern. The family is the home and the natural setting in which care and concern have a vital role in its preservation. It is the locus in which members learn to see one another as a being actuated by needs and desires and see that their satisfaction depends on paying due regard to appropriate constraints, coupled with an appreciation of the importance of mutual aid and development for ensuring the unity and harmony and well-being of the family. One of Confucius's disciples notes:

> A superior man is devoted to the fundamentals [the root]. When the root is firmly established, the Way [of life inspired by *ren*] will develop. Filial piety and brotherly respect are the root of *ren*. (*Analects*, 1.2)

Filial piety and brotherly respect offer the root-possibility for *ren*-realization. They may be said to be the basis for extensive moral concern, i.e., as a sort of basis for what may be called an activity of "analogical projection" (Cua 1985). Analogy here does not purport to be an inference or an argument. It is an activity that aims at extending the orbit of one's moral concern. *Ren* as an ethical ideal indicates a culminating state of such an extension. What is the analogizing activity here? To answer this question, we need to attend to what is normatively implied in the notions of filiality (*xiao*) and brotherly respect (*di*). Both these notions imply an acknowledgment of mutual regard and respect for activities that significantly affect the lives of the members of the family in carrying out expectations that are embedded in direct personal relationships.

A father, for example, has the duty to care for his children by providing resources for the satisfaction of their needs and education; and his children have the duty to care for their father when he is sick or disabled in old age. Moreover, these reciprocal obligations are to be performed with an attitude of reverence or respect (*jing*) styled with an expression of affectionate concern. It is this caring attitude that lies at the heart of *ren* as an ideal of extensive moral concern. Other human beings, not in the status of being one's parent or brother, can also be cared for as one's parent or brother. This is possible because of the analogizing of one's affection and thought. The similarity of other people in terms of being members of families is crucially the basis for one's analogizing activity. In other words, the similarity of status serves as a basis for extensive moral concern. We can thus speak of extensive moral concern as essentially a form of analogical projection of familiar relationship.

This kind of analogical projection, through thought and feelings, is preeminently a display of one's reflective capacity to recognize other human beings as enjoying similar family status. And in light of *ren*, a recognition of such a status makes possible the extension of one's own moral concern, ultimately embracing all human beings, as envisioned by Zhang Zai, Cheng Hao, and Wang Yangming. It is in effect an expansive horizon for viewing all human beings as eligible for personal relations. However, each analogizing extension carries its own quality or style of personal relationship (Cua 1978, ch. 7). The relations between persons, in this sense, have their own distinctive features, by virtue of the style or qualities of performance of the persons involved. Moreover, how one ought to act in a particular relationship cannot be dictated by a set of determinate formulas or principles that may serve, so to speak, as premises of practical syllogisms. The analogizing of status has nothing to do with universalization, for it is an activity that occurs within the setting of an actual relationship between persons.

Apart from the prescriptions of *li* or conventional rules of proper behavior, there are, for the Confucian, no additional universal principles that can serve as a basis of conduct or, in other words, guide action. This is not to say that individuals have no moral commitments in terms of principles (Cua 1998, Essay 14), for any such a commitment is always subject to reconsideration in terms of the agent's actual encounter in particular circumstances which requires *yi* or an exercise of judgment. There are exigent situations in human life that have to be dealt with by an occasional judgment of the right thing to do (*yi*). Thus for Confucius "a superior man (*junzi*) in dealing with the world is not for anything or against anything. He follows what is right (*yi*)" (*Analects*, 4.10). This involves a sense of appropriateness. His occasional judgment may be guided by his personal rules of conduct, but such rules are not to be used for the purpose of universalization, for they are more like signposts that suggest directions of where one wants to travel and not a priori prescriptions for proper behavior. The conventional rules of conduct encapsulated in *li* are likewise subject to the determination by judgment of their relevance to particular cases. In this way, "the superior man (*junzi*) is broad-minded but not partisan" (*Analects*, 2.14). He is not to be an implement, i.e., "not [to] be like an implement which is intended only for a narrow and specific purpose." Rather, "he should have broad vision, wide interest, and sufficient ability to do many things" (*Analects*, 2.12; Chan 1963).

A question arises: What is the role of moral reflection with respect to the analogizing of status? Moral reflection is a form of thinking addressed to a particular situation that concerns the matters at hand. A disciple of Confucius put it this way: "To study extensively, to be steadfast in one's purpose, to inquire earnestly, and to reflect on what is at hand—*ren* consists in these" (*Analects*, 16.6). Cheng Yi, the Song neo-Confucian, points out that to reflect on things at hand (*jinsi*) is "to extend on the basis of similarity in kind." On this conception, Zhu Xi remarked:

> This is well said. We must not skip over steps and aim too far. We must only proceed from what we understand in what is near to us and move from there. For instance, if one is thoroughly familiar with doing one thing, he can, on the basis of this extend his skill to doing another. It is the same with knowledge. . . . For instance, if one understands how to be affectionate to his parents, he will extend this feeling, on the basis of similarity in kind, to being humane (*ren*) to all people, for being humane to people and being affectionate to parents are similar in kind. When he understands how to be humane to people, he will extend this feeling, on the basis of similarity in kind, to loving all things, for being humane to people and loving all things are similar in kind. (Chan 1967, 94)

Thus given a commitment to *ren*, the agent engages in this sort of moral reflection in extending his thoughts and feelings on the basis of similarity of status in an occurrent situation (Cua 1982, ch. 3). Here, the agent is not deducing consequences from a moral rule or principle but deciding whether or not such a rule or principle is relevant in the light of the ideal of *ren*. What one ought to do is a matter of one's appreciation of the concrete import of *ren*. And in any case, one can err or fail to realize *ren* in a particular situation. To put this another way, my analogizing of status may fail to realize *ren*, that is, in giving rise to undesirable consequences. And this failure may be experienced as shame (an emotion), but significantly, such an experience is an occasion or opportunity to reexamine one's decision and conduct in the light of *ren* (Cua 2003). In this way, the agent can and must rectify himself. As is said in *The Doctrine of the Mean*, "In archery we have something resembling the way of the superior man. When the archer misses the center of the target, he turns around and seeks for the cause of failure within himself" (Chan 1963, 102). Moreover, reflection on things at hand does not preclude consideration of long-range consequences of one's contemplated actions. As Confucius reminds his pupils, "If a man neglects to consider what is distant, he will find troubles with what is near at hand" (*Analects*, 15.11). The important thing to attend to is the current problem to be settled with a view to realizing *ren*. Consideration of distant consequences is a component of moral reflection, but such a consideration should not be regarded as a decisive solution to all future problematic situations. Every situation or human affair has, as it were, an integrity of its own, to be met as a distinct or individual situation, though this does not exclude an attention to its similarity with other situations, particularly the similarity of personal status which is the basis of our analogizing activity in moral reflection.

A focus on the particular occasion and judgment in moral reflection, however, is not without any methodical guide whatsoever. For Confucius, there is a "method" for realizing *ren* expressed in *zhong* and *shu*, which can be rendered as conscientiousness and regard for others, reminiscent of the Christian "golden rule" (*Analects*, 4.15). *Zhong* expresses loyalty to and conscientious regard for the moral standard or the ideal of *ren*, i.e., an attitude of sincerity and seriousness in one's commitment to *ren*; *shu* more especially pertains to other-regarding conduct. A commitment to *ren* is a commitment to realizing *ren* in the personal relations between oneself and another. In a word, it is an adoption of an attitude of moral regard. *Shu* may be said to be the golden rule that governs the exemplification of the *ren* attitude, i.e., "What I do not want others to do to me, I do not want to do to them" (*Analects*, 5.11). Alternatively: "What I do not desire, I ought not to do it to another" (12.2). In both formulations, what is crucial is the notion of *yu* or desire. It is misleading to say that *shu* concerns the nature of desire in the ordinary sense, for it has more to do with the manner of satisfaction than with the nature of occurrent desires. A plausible explication of *shu* thus requires a distinction between first-order and second-order desires, which may be explained in this way: "Someone has a desire of the second-order either when he wants simply to have a certain desire or when he wants a certain desire to be his will." This presupposes a capacity for reflective self-evaluation (Frankfurt 1971, 10).

In this sense, *shu* has to do primarily with second-order rather than first-order desires. *Zhong* and *shu* may be said to be a method of reflection on first-order desires, for an assessment of their appropriateness in the context of human relations. To pay heed to *shu* is to deal earnestly with the question: Do I want my present desire to be satisfied as I want analogous desires of others to be satisfied in a way that comports with *ren*? The wanting here is a second-order desire. Thus, a reflection on the character of one's first-order desires has consequences for the moral character of one's acts. *Shu* as moral regard has a practical import only when it becomes a moral desire of the second-order, i.e., a desire to pay heed to others' desires in light of one's second-order desire to realize *ren*.

It must be admitted that *shu* can also be construed as a concern for others in terms of personal standards. Following Marcus Singer, one may regard *shu* as functionally equivalent to the golden rule. It can be expressed negatively as "Do not do to others as you would not expect them to do to you," or positively as "Do unto others as you would have them do unto you" (Singer 1977, 122). Our interpretation of *shu* as pertaining to second-order desire is compatible with this general formulation of the golden rule. At issue is the question of one's willingness or desire to be treated in a certain way rather than the content of first-order desires. The issue has to do with the standard governing the satisfaction of one's first-order desires. What I morally want to do is to subject my present desires to assessment by the standard that I adopt as a matter of commitment. For a Confucian, to be a man of *ren* is to engage in reflection which brings the ideal of *ren* to bear in actual conduct, and this obviously implies a desire or willingness to make others' desires a relevant consideration in light of *ren*.

To pay heed to *shu* is to have an other-regarding attitude. Coupled with *zhong* or one's own sincere commitment to *ren*, such an other-regarding attitude is an aspect of self-regard, i.e., a regard for one's own character and moral condition. According to Confucius:

> A man of *ren* desiring to establish his own character, also establishes the character of others, and desiring to be prominent himself, also helps others to be prominent. To be able to judge others by what is near to ourselves may be called the method of realizing *ren*. (*Analects*, 6.28; Chan, modified)

In this way, the moral agent's own conduct serves as a measure or standard for others. But this is possible because his own character is achieved by way of embracing others as an integral component of his own moral development. *Shu* as extensive concern for others is thus a component of one's preoccupation with moral attainment or moral condition on the whole. My extensive concern for others is a concern for their moral being or condition on the whole. Whether or not another person accepts this concern is not a relevant issue, nor is the reciprocal regard of another person important to my own moral development. In Confucian language, the acceptance and reciprocation of others are matters of fate (*ming*). So long as my other-regarding desire and conduct are exemplified in my own life, I have preserved my moral integrity. In establishing or developing my own moral character in light of *ren*, I am also engaged in establishing or developing others' moral character, not in the sense of directly urging others to do so or of asserting myself to be a moral paradigm, but in the sense that my own case serves as an embodiment of the possibility and actuating import of *ren*-realization. In this way I indirectly contribute to the development of others' moral character. When *zhong* and *shu* are construed as a practical rule of conduct, it is a procedural rather than a substantive guide to *ren*-realization.

Given a commitment to *ren* and the procedural guide of *zhong* and *shu*, extensive concern for others as rooted in the analogizing of status is an extension of direct personal relationships. A direct personal relationship consists of two features: (1) an acknowledgment of reciprocal duties or obligations and (2) a display of those obligations in conduct imbued with affection (MacMurray 1961). What makes a relationship personal rather than impersonal is the presence of the affective component. In Confucian ethics, particularly in the Mencian tradition, emphasis on the role of *xin* brings out more clearly this aspect of extending moral concern. *Xin* can be rendered as mind and heart, i.e., as embracing both the cognitive and affective components of personal relationship. And since such a relationship can be sustained only by the desire and effort of the persons involved in conduct that displays mutual care and concern, the conative component is also present. The notion of *xin* is thus important in depicting, in the ideal sense, what it is to be a moral agent or a man of *ren* (Cua 2002). Notably, in terms of *shu*, extending personal relationship is extending *xin* in terms of the second-order desire to share one's moral outlook and affection. The character *shu* does suggest this view (Liang 1968, 39). It is composed of two characters, *ru* (similar) and *xin* (mind and heart). This suggests that extending a personal relationship involves, crucially, sharing a similar mind and heart. Imagination in the place of another who is affected by one's conduct is naturally involved, but such a sympathetic imagination assumes that the other, who is outside the ambit of one's personal relation, can share the same commitment and value the affection that sustains such a commitment.

Extending one's personal relationship is a *valuing* process in the sense of extending shared concern with the intrinsic value of the ideal of *ren* and the affection which this ideal entails. This is not merely an intellectual task but also a continuing practical task. A morally concerned and responsible agent in his dealing with others may not succeed in extending his personal relationships. Apart from failure in reciprocal acknowledgment and conduct, one may also experience dislike of others' defective character and misconduct. In this way, disliking people can be seen to be compatible with extensive concern for their moral well-being. In the words of Confucius, "only a man of *ren* is capable of liking and disliking people" in the sense of liking their good and disliking their bad conduct. However, "if a person has the will (or firm determination) to become a man of *ren*, to that extent, he can be free from dislike on account of his misconduct" (*Analects,* 4.3). To the extent that another person falls outside the moral agent's personal relationships, he can be an eligible partner in such a relationship. Even in cases of failure, extensive concern for others remains a concern for their moral condition and development. A personal relationship in this way, though self-contained within its ambit, is always *open* to anyone who has the desire and the will to enter such a relation. Ideally, the human community is a community of personal relationships. The task of realizing *ren* is the task of creating such a community. Whether or not such a vision of the unity and harmony of persons in a community can be realized is a question that addresses a more detailed consideration of the complex factors involved in the extensive moral concern and its implications for dealing with recurrent problems in human intercourse. From the agent's point of view, the important factors are these: (1) a proper conception of the current situation or matter, (2) the current capacity of the agent in actualizing the vision of *ren*, (3) acknowledgment and acceptance of others regarding one's own extensive concern, (4) liability to erroneous judgment and the decision to respond appropriately to what the situation requires, (5) freedom from the "paralysis" or weakness of will, (6) the relevance of conventional moral requirements, (7) the needs and desires of other people as affected by one's own moral decision, (8) the possibility of conflict between moral requirements, (9) the element of *ming* ("fate"—i.e., the situation may be such that it is beyond one's ability to change, even if one tries), and, last, (10) willingness to assume the burden of response to the challenge of reasonable justification of one's decision and actions (Cua 1985). All such factors require a plausible construction of a Confucian theory of moral psychology (Cua 1982, 2002, 2003). From the interpersonal point of view, a just treatment of relevant factors inevitably involves an excursion to social philosophy which goes beyond the scope of the present essay. But we can get a picture of such a community from the Confucian classic *Liji* (*Book of Rites*):

> When the great *Dao* (Way) prevails, all the people of the world will work in the light of public spirit (*gong*). The men of talents, virtues, and ability will be selected, and faithfulness will be the constant practice and harmony the constant objective of self-cultivation. Consequently, mankind will not only have their parents and care only for their children. All the elderly will be provided for and all the young will be employed in work. Commiseration will be expressed toward the widows and the widowers, the orphans and the children, the disabled and the sick in such ways that all are properly cared for. Men have their work and women their homes. . . . In this way, selfish scheming will be repressed and find no room for expansion, and thievery and disorder will not appear. Therefore, the gates of the houses are never closed. This state is called *datong* (the Grand Unity and Harmony). (adapted from Legge 1966)

This vision of human community as extensive moral concern has its primary locus or focal point in personal relationships which project an expansive horizon for embracing the whole of humanity. This vision of the human community, I believe, is a fair representation of the concrete possibility and significance of the Confucian ideal of *ren*. However, Confucians today will want to modify the vision to embrace a recognition of the equality of men and women, in terms both of ability and opportunity to achieve their aspirations, consequently, a recognition of the integrity of individual styles of life as harmonious polymorphous actualization of the vision of *ren* as an ideal of human community. Ultimately, the question of *ren*-realization depends on the committed agent's effort and performance in expanding personal relationships. We do not know whether all human beings are willing and capable of lending a hand in actualizing the vision, but a Confucian remains firm in his faith in the vision. As

Confucius once said: "It is man that can make the Way (*dao*) great, and not the Way that can make man great" (*Analects*, 15.28).

See also Confucianism: Confucius; Confucianism: Ethics; Confucianism: Tradition; *Junzi*; *Li*: Rites or Propriety; *Ren*; Wang Yangming; *Xiao*; *Yi* and *Li*; Zhang Zai; *Zhong* and *Shu*; *Zhong* and *Xin*.

Bibliography

Chan, Wing-tsit, trans. *Reflections on Things at Hand: The Neo-Confucian Anthology Compiled by Chu Hsi and Lü Tsu-ch'ien*. New York: Columbia University Press, 1967.

———, trans. *A Source Book in Chinese Philosophy*. Princeton, N.J.: Princeton University Press, 1963. (Citations refer to Chan's translation of the *Analects*, sometimes modified.)

Cheng, Chung-ying. "Harmony and Conflict in Chinese Philosophy." *Journal of Chinese Philosophy*, 4(3), 1977.

Cua, A. S. *Dimensions of Moral Creativity: Paradigms, Principles and Ideals*. University Park: Pennsylvania State University Press, 1978. (See especially chs. 4 and 5.)

———. *Ethical Argumentation: A Study in Hsün Tzu's Moral Epistemology*. Honolulu: University of Hawaii Press, 1985.

———. "Ethical Significance of Shame: Insights of Aristotle and Xunzi." *Philosophy East and West*, 53, April 2003.

———. "*Li* and Moral Justification: A Study in the *Li Chi*." *Philosophy East and West*, 33(1), 1983, pp. 1–16.

———. *Moral Vision and Tradition: Essays in Chinese Ethics*. Washington, D.C.: Catholic University of America Press, 1998.

———. *The Unity of Knowledge and Action: A Study in Wang Yang-ming's Moral Psychology*. Honolulu: University of Hawaii Press, 1982.

———. "*Xin* and Moral Failure: Notes on an Aspect of Mencius's Moral Psychology." In *Mencius: Contexts and Interpretations*, ed. Alan K. L. Chan. Honolulu: University of Hawaii Press, 2002.

Fingarette, Herbert. *Confucius—The Secular as Sacred*. New York: Harper Torchbooks, 1972.

Frankfurt, Harry. "Freedom of the Will and the Concept of a Person." *Journal of Philosophy*, 68(1), 1971.

Lau, D. C., trans. *Mencius*. Baltimore, Md.: Penguin, 1970.

Legge, James, trans. *The Li Ki or Collection of Treatises on the Rules of Propriety or Ceremonial Usages*. Sacred Books of the East Series, ed. Max Müller. Delhi: Moltilal Barnasidass, 1966.

Liang, Chi-chao. *History of Chinese Political Thought*. Taipei: Ch'eng-wen, 1968.

Macmurray, John. *Persons in Relation*. London: Farber and Farber, 1961.

Singer, Marcus. "Defense of the Golden Rule." In *Morals and Values*, ed. Marcus Singer. New York: Scribner, 1977.

Tu, Weiming. "The Creative Tension between *Ren* and *Li*." *Philosophy East and West*, 18, 1968.

———. "*Li* as a Process of Humanization." *Philosophy East and West*, 22, 1972.

Confucianism: Yuan (Yüan)

David GEDALECIA

North China, before the Mongol conquest of that region in 1234 and the subsequent conquest of the south and reunification of the country in 1279, was ruled by the Jurchen Jin, which had split the Song dynasty asunder in 1127. Confucian traditions were continued by the Jin rulers, who supported Confucian studies and the school system and especially the neo-Confucianism that had been introduced from the Southern Song in the late twelfth century. Scholars such as Li Qunfu (1185–1231), Wang Ruoxu (1174–1243), and Zhao Bingwen (1159–1232) established a context for neo-Confucianism that allowed it to develop and thrive, though the link between these three scholars and early Yuan Confucians is tenuous. Zhao Bingwen, for example, supported the Confucian moral approach through his literary work, complementing the Confucian political influence of Su Shi (1036–1101), whose teachings were prominent among Jin thinkers.

The premier member of the literati in Jin times, the poet Yuan Haowen (1190–1257), while not a classical scholar or thinker, refused to serve the Mongols when they captured the north. Nevertheless, he introduced his followers to the sinicized Khitan statesman Yehlü Chucai (1189–1243), who enjoined them to serve, as Yehlü did, the Mongol regime. This group, which included people such as Yang Huan (1186–1255), who was later recruited by Khubilai (Kublai Khan, r. 1260–1294), and Yehlü himself, while not deeply philosophical, supported Confucian social and political ideals and tried to promote Chinese cultural values among the Mongols. This practical emphasis on Confucian statecraft stood in contrast to the more purely philosophical strains in Song thought that were prominent in the south.

Highlighting this contrast was Wang Yun (1227–1304), whose family had achieved prominence after the Jin conquest of the north and who was associated with Jin scholar-officials who had retired from public service when the Mongols conquered the Jin. As part of the Jin-Yuan transitional generation, Wang exerted a civilizing influence in serving Khubilai (before and after he ascended the throne) and his successor Temür (r. 1294–1307). Wang was a proponent of the Dongping school of statecraft, and, while familiar with the works of Zhu Xi (1130–1200), he followed the traditions of Jin literati, whose Confucian commitment focused on politico-cultural values. For Wang, this meant an emphasis on Tang models of imperial rule, rather than neo-Confucian metaphysics. Eventually, the two traditions, which one might associate in the Song with Su Shi and Zhu Xi, respectively, merged after north and south were united.

About forty years before the south was conquered, in 1235, and after they had extinguished the Jin, the Mongols attacked the Southern Song and overran Hubei Province. Yang Weizhong (1205 or 1206–1260), a Chinese military commander who was in the employ of the Mongols and whose family had served the Jin, was assigned the task of recruiting scribes and scholars from among those who had been captured in the onslaught. Yang and the Confucian scholar Yao Shu (1203–1280) thus came to serve as catalysts in a developing Sino-Mongolian interaction by collecting classical and historical works and recruiting the distinguished scholars and teachers Zhao Fu (fl. 1235–1257) and Wang Pan (1202–1293) to serve at the Mongol court in Yanjing (Dadu), modern-day Beijing. In this way, Zhao became the most popular teacher of the Cheng-Zhu school of neo-Confucianism in the north.

Zhao Fu and Yao Shu influenced Yang Weizhong to broaden his support of neo-Confucian studies in the north, and together they established around 1240 the Academy of the Supreme Ultimate in Yanjing to honor the Song thinker Zhou Dunyi and to house the collection of neo-Confucian materials they had amassed. The texts that were printed under the auspices of Yang and Yao were the basis for the dissemination of neo-Confucian ideas during the early years of Mongol rule in the north.

Especially notable at the academy was the printing of the Four Books, along with Zhu Xi's commentaries on them. In his *Diagram of the Transmission of the Way*, Zhao traced the Confucian line of transmission, the *daotong*, from the sage emperors Yao and Shun, and down through Confucius and Mencius to Zhou Dunyi (1017–1073), the Cheng brothers (Cheng Hao, 1032–1085, and Cheng Yi, 1033–1107), and Zhu Xi, placing himself among those disciples of Zhu Xi in recent times. Zhao also introduced the basic ideas of the Cheng-Zhu school in his other writings.

Yao Shu's other associates, Dou Mo (1196–1280) and Yang Gongyi (1225–1294), openly expressed their sense of revelation when they were first introduced to Zhu Xi's philosophy through the commentaries on the Four Books introduced by Zhao Fu. One must conclude that Yao Shu's academy had a dramatic impact on intellectual life in northern China, as Cheng-Zhu neo-Confucianism came to supplant the dominance of the Dongping school through Yao's endeavors.

When Yao Shu went into retirement in 1241 to live at Sumen Mountain in Henan, the reputation of his academy as the repository of extensive neo-Confucian source materials attracted the budding younger northern scholars Xu Heng (1209–1281), Liu Yin (1249–1293), and Hao Jing (1223–1275), who came to Sumen to copy the Cheng-Zhu commentaries. Thus after more than a century of indirect intellectual contact between north and south, the reawakening of neo-Confucian learning in north China among those who frequented Yao's academy proved vital in reestablishing the tradition of Confucian discipleship.

Besides being one of the great educators of his generation, Xu Heng also became the most important transmitter of the basic ideas of Cheng Yi and Zhu Xi in the north among the younger generation at Sumen. Though a student of Dou Mo, he was actually the true successor to Zhao Fu, yet he was almost forty years old before he became active in bringing the neo-Confucian teachings to the Mongol court. He assisted Khubilai in recruiting scholar-officials in the 1250s, and though he was not a champion of the examination system, which had been suspended by the Mongols, Xu did support universal schooling, prompting Khubilai to reestablish the Imperial College. Xu eventually became chancellor of education in 1267. Along with Khubilai's Confucian-minded minister Liu Bingzhong (1216–1274), Xu became an adviser on the organization of the bureaucracy, and he took seriously the task of educating his Mongol sovereign in the Confucian values on which humane governance was based. By the same token, Khubilai was tolerant enough of Xu's counsel to use his skills judiciously.

In his educational curriculum, Xu emphasized Zhu Xi's *Lesser Learning* as the source for self-realization and Zhu's commentaries on the Four Books, writing his own simplified commentaries on the latter. In 1315, when the Four Books became the standard curriculum as the examination system was revived, it was clear that Xu had played a primary role in defining a course of study that continued for almost 600 years. Thus, although Xu was accused by his contemporary Liu Yin of serving the Mongols too willingly, he himself felt that he was helping to perpetuate Chinese culture and was loyal to a larger Confucian educational vision.

Xu Heng accepted basic Neo-Confucian ideas on self-cultivation and the development of one's mind, but he approached these ideas on a practical level, from the standpoint of human relations. In areas involving metaphysical speculation, such as the supreme ultimate (*taiji*), Xu made few contributions. But he felt that the path to Confucian virtue lay in careful attention to the *Lesser Learning*—such as his own *General Meanings of the Lesser Learning*. Eventually, one could cultivate a sense of reverence, *jing*, which would result in self-understanding.

Xu sincerely believed that the aim of rectifying one's mind was the development of a consciousness of public morality and impartiality. This was the fundamental lesson he imparted to his Mongol sovereign. In this emphasis on the moral sensitivity of the mind and the exhortation to moral rule through self-cultivation, Xu came close to some of the fundamental ideas of Zhen Dexiu (1178–1235), whose *Extended Meaning of the Great Learning* was popularized in north China during the late Song (in the 1320s, it was translated into Mongolian and taught at the Mongol court).

Xu's younger contemporary Liu Yin studied under the scholar Yan Mijian (1212–1289) and also Yao Shu at Sumen, and before he was twenty he had become well acquainted with the writings of the Song neo-Confucians. After his death, he was often praised by southerners who felt that he exemplified a pure understanding of Song learning in the north. Indeed, Liu believed that one could become a man of sagelike character only by investigating principle (*li*), as taught in the Cheng-Zhu vein.

Liu took an uncompromising stand on service to the Mongols. He retreated into eremitism and openly criticized Xu Heng's willingness to serve. Liu based his own refusal to take office on ethical and spiritual considerations, out of self-respect or personal dignity, and as a protest against what he regarded as an impure political order that stood in the way of self-cultivation. In so doing, he was not merely following a Confucian principle of loyalty to a fallen regime; rather, he was expressing a deeper dedication to the true way of government.

In the south during the Yuan there were more direct philosophical lines going back to Zhu Xi and his disciples in the late Song. Both in Jinhua prefecture (Wuzhou circuit in the Yuan), in present-day Zhejiang Province, and in Jiangxi, Zhu Xi's son-in-law and star pupil, Huang Gan (1152–1221), spawned significant lines of intellectual development. In Jinhua, Huang's teachings were transmitted to the Song thinkers He Ji (1188–1268) and Wang Po (1197–1274), and in the Yuan to Jin Lüxiang (1232–1303) and Xu Qian (1270–1337). Jinhua was known especially for its unique contributions to Confucian political thought. By elevating the scholar-official to a level of ethical perfection and administrative excellence, the Jinhua thinkers united Song moral philosophy with the utilitarian political thought associated with the eastern Zhejiang school, represented by Song thinkers such as Chen Liang (1143–1194), Tang Zhongyou (*chin-shih* 1151), Ni Pu (fl. 1150s), and Ye Shi (1150–1223; the most notable representative of the Yongjia branch), and, by association, Lü Zuqian (1137–1181). The Jinhua thinkers during the Yuan continued their predecessors' emphasis on statecraft, with special emphasis on history and economics. They were inclined to deemphasize the Cheng-Zhu penchant for moral cultivation. For example, Jin Lüxiang, who was a witness to the Mongol invasion of the south but refused to serve the Yuan, imbued his pupil Xu Qian with a sense of practical activism: while adhering to the transformational power of ethical example, Xu gave increased emphasis to the political necessity of laws and punishments.

In late Yuan times, Liu Guan (1270–1342) and Wu Lai (1297–1340), from the Pujiang district of Jinhua, expressed a great deal of interest in the codification of laws under the Yuan, though no formal code was ever established. They both made detailed studies of the *Tang Code*. Liu argued that responsible government officials should also be legal experts, and he placed legal codes on a par with the Confucian canon. Wu Lai even claimed that the lack of professional legal experts had resulted in too much reliance on penal law and that the Qin dynasty laws had perverted the ideal legal tradition of the ancient sage-kings. In this, he foreshadowed the arguments of Huang Zongxi (1610–1695) in the Qing era. Both the Qin and the Sui dynasties had failed to employ scholar-officials who knew how to apply the law in humane ways, and this was in part remedied in the Han and Tang dynasties. For Wu, legal and moral studies were essentially complementary.

Much later in the Yuan, in the 1340s and 1350s, members of the Confucian elite in Zhejiang, such as Wang Yi (1303–1354) and Zhao Jie (fl. 1271), applied Confucian doctrines of magnanimity and impartiality to the practical task of local fiscal reform. Interestingly, Zhao Jie was an avid follower of Yang Jian (1141–1226), the disciple of the Song idealistic thinker Lu Xiangshan (1139–1193), and he arrived at his notion of impartiality on the basis of a mystic visionary experience.

An important part of the Confucian enterprise in the Yuan was the writing of history. On an official level, the Yuan court sponsored the historiographical compilation of the dynastic histories of the Song, Liao, and Jin dynasties, which were eventually completed between 1343 and 1345. Interested initially in establishing the position of the Yuan in the legitimate line of dynastic succession, the *zhengtong*, the Mongol emperors perpetuated the Confucian-based historiographical tradition by commissioning scholar-historians to compile the histories of the dynasties they had conquered.

In the 1240s, the former Jin official Wang O and Liu Bingzhong urged Khubilai to establish a historical bureau and recruited Yang Huan and Yuan Haowen to staff it. Wang had been invited to lecture on the classics at Karakorum some fifteen years before Khubilai's enthronement in 1260, and Liu, who was a Buddho-Daoist adept, saw the bureau as a way to Confucianize Mongol rule. Wang, who was also a proponent of the reinstatement of the examination system, suggested that the chronicles of the early Mongol rulers be compiled as a way to make the overall project more attractive to those in power. After the conquest of Southern Song, the project was expanded to include Song history.

Political complications and the issue of dynastic legitimacy delayed the three histories project, but it was finally completed under Toghon Temür (r. 1333–1367), the last Mongol emperor. Thus, despite the historical opinions of Yang Weizhen (1296–1370), who questioned the legitimacy of Mongol rule in certain respects, Toghon, who directed the historical project, legitimized the Liao, Jin, and Song equally, and thus he also legitimized the Yuan as the successor to all three. This compromise solution to a Confucian-based historiographical issue was important in perpetuating the dynastic historical tradition.

In terms of individual historical writing, Ma Duanlin (1254–1324 or 1325), from Jiangxi, the author of the encyclopedic institutional history *Comprehensive Survey of Literary Remains*, exemplifies the Confucian approach to this endeavor in the Yuan. Declining to serve in government, Ma devoted his life to preserving the rich Confucian institutional tradition. His survey covers the period from ancient times into the Southern Song. Ma felt that the illumination of the past would provide a comprehensive model for statecraft in the present: the *dao*, the way, of the sages would be revealed through studying the evolution of institutions, laws, and statutes. In his methodology, Ma wished to downplay the didactic "praise and blame" approach to writing history associated with the *Spring and Autumn Annals*, as well as the mystical cosmological theories used by Han historians to analyze human affairs.

In tracing evolution and change in Chinese history, Ma Duanlin demonstrated how imperial power had become more and more concentrated from Qin to Song, with the aim of showing that Confucian moral leadership was necessary to preserve the welfare of the people. While Ma was conversant with the Cheng-Zhu moral teachings, his emphasis on promoting public welfare and limiting private interests represented a more practical approach to basic Confucian goals and so was in some ways similar to the legal-minded thinkers from Jinhua.

Another important development in Yuan Confucianism occurred in the south and was also derived from Zhu Xi through Huang Gan, whose teachings on *daotong*, the orthodox transmission of the way from the ancient sage kings down to Zhu Xi, as well as his emphasis on Zhu's commentaries on the *Great Learning* and the Four Books, became especially influential among neo-Confucian thinkers in Jiangxi. The most notable of these thinkers was Wu Cheng (1249–1333), who was arguably the most distinguished scholar in either north or south China during the Yuan, and whose lineage went back to Huang Gan through the late Song thinkers Rao Lu (fl. 1256) and Cheng Ruoyong (fl. 1260). Wu served only sporadically under Mongol rule, owing to the urging of scholars like Cheng Jufu (1249–1318), who recommended him to Khubilai in 1286, yet by the time he was forty he had written significant commentaries on a half-dozen of the thirteen Confucian classics.

When he did serve in Dadu, c. 1310, he was unhappy with the state of classical learning there and attempted to institute a comprehensive curriculum that challenged the educational establishment in the capital and eventually put him at odds with those who reestablished the examination system in 1315. He retired into private teaching and classical studies for the next decade, but he served again as chancellor of the Hanlin Academy between 1323 and 1325. During that time he supervised the editing of the *Veritable Record of the Yingzong Emperor* (r. 1311–1324), and this led to his being recommended to head the ongoing three histories project. He also opened the Classics Mat, or *jingyan*, a hall where the emperors and heirs apparent listened to lectures on Confucian themes.

Wu displayed creative independence in classical scholarship by using all three commentaries on the *Spring and Autumn Annals* to explicate that classic, in reconstructing the disorganized ritual classics, and in casting the most thorough doubt to date on the so-called ancient text, or *guwen*, chapters of the *Book of History*. In these endeavors, he maintained a critical attitude toward the Confucian classical tradition, and his work on the *Book of History* became important for textual critics in the Qing era.

Huang Gan did not expound at length on one of the fundamental ideas in neo-Confucianism, the supreme ultimate (*taiji*), but his followers in Jiangxi—Rao Lu, Cheng Ruoyong, and Wu Cheng—did elaborate on this concept, which was central in the philosophy of the Northern Song master Zhou Dunyi and which had been studied at length by Zhu Xi. Wu Cheng equated the supreme ultimate with the *dao*, and, like Cheng Ruoyong, he also identified it with the activity of the mind. As for analogies between the supreme ultimate and the crossbow trigger, which were advanced by Zhu Xi, Wu pointed out the inherent limitations of likening the dynamism of the universal process to something mechanical.

As a thinker, Wu Cheng stands out for his attempts to synthesize the teachings of Zhu Xi and his sometime rival Lu Xiangshan. As indicated above, Wu was trained in the Cheng-Zhu tradition by Cheng Ruoyong, but he was also exposed to the synthetic philosophical approach of Cheng Shaokai (d. 1280), who had also taught in Jiangxi and who had inherited a preference for uniting the Zhu and Lu teachings through the late Song thinker Tang Zhong.

In practical terms, Wu used Lu's emphasis on the mind to give priority to the cultivation of the moral nature. He felt that Zhu Xi's followers had mortgaged internal spiritual development to bookish pursuits. It was his task to enliven the Zhu Xi tradition with a dose of Lu's ideas on self-awakening, the illumination of one's spiritual potential. Wu had a large following among the students in Jiangxi and at Dadu, and he played a dominant role in the intellectual life of the south, as attested to by his pupil Yu Ji (1272–1348). In terms of philosophical significance, however, Wu's influence extended far beyond the Yuan era. Wu was recognized by thinkers in the Ming dynasty, such as Chen Xianzhang (1428–1500), Zhan Ruoshui (1466–1560), Cheng Minzheng (1445–1499), and especially Wang Yangming (1472–1529), for his contributions to the ongoing development of the philosophy of mind, *xinxue*.

Even though there were direct followers of the Lu school during the Yuan who emphasized the centrality of the mind, such as Chen Yuan (1256–1330) in Jiangxi and Zhao Jie in Zhejiang, Wu's synthetic approach, which parallels a similar one devised by his younger contemporary Zheng Yu (1298–1358), seems to have been the most important for later thinkers. In Wu's case, his emphasis on mental illumination as the root of the search for principle, or truth, *li*, adumbrated more thoroughgoing developments in Ming times.

In the late Yuan, Confucianism was also important as a doctrine for practical action, beyond the usual philosophical connections, as elite communities of scholars promoted fiscal and military reform. In this sense, such activist Confucian "professionals" were not necessarily following neo-Confucian traditions, and those involved included not only Chinese but also Mongols and Central Asians. One of these individuals, Liu Ji (1311–1375), realizing that the Mongol court would not challenge local elements that opposed reform measures, deserted the Yuan and eventually played a role in the founding of the Ming.

The history of Confucianism in the Yuan period may be studied as a five-part saga:

1. The introduction and nurturing of Song thought in north China on a foundation laid by thinkers of the Jin dynasty during a century of sporadic contact with southern intellectual trends.
2. The perfecting in the south of a practical tradition of Confucian statecraft which had been inherited from the Song but which was directed at Confucianizing the Mongol leadership.
3. The perpetuation of a historiographical tradition that kept alive the Confucian belief in kingship through morality.
4. The unique preservation of the ideas of both Zhu Xi and Lu Xiangshan, which led to a dramatic philosophical shift toward moral illumination that influenced Ming and Qing thinkers.
5. The cultivation of Confucian professionalism, which ultimately contributed to the rise of the new Ming order.

In these ways, Confucianism in the Yuan kept Chinese traditions alive under alien rule and created uniquely new directions for those traditions to take.

See also Lu Xiangshan; Zhu Xi.

Bibliography

Abe, Takeo. "Gendai chishikijin to kakyo." *Shirin*, 42, 1959, pp. 136–145.

Chan, Hok-lam, and William Theodore de Bary, eds. *Yüan Thought: Chinese Thought and Religion under the Mongols*. New York: Columbia University Press, 1982.

de Bary, William Theodore. *Neo-Confucian Orthodoxy and the Learning of the Mind-and-Heart*. New York: Columbia University Press, 1981.

Gedalecia, David. *The Philosophy of Wu Ch'eng: A Neo-Confucian of the Yüan Dynasty*. Bloomington: Indiana University, 1999.

———. *A Solitary Crane in a Spring Grove: The Confucian Scholar Wu Ch'eng in Mongol China*. Wiesbaden: Harrassowitz, 2000.

Huang, Zongxi, Quan Zuwang, et al. *Song Yuan xue'an*, Sibu beiyao (SPPY), ed.
Ke, Shaomin. *Xin Yuanshi*, 1930 ed.
Langlois, John D., ed. *China under Mongol Rule*. Princeton, N.J.: Princeton University Press, 1981.
Lao, Yan-shuan. "The *Chung-t'ang shih-chi* of Wang Yün: An Annotated Translation with an Introduction." Ph.D. dissertation, Harvard University, 1962.
Li, Zutao, ed. *Jin Yuan Ming badajia wenxuan*. 1845 ed.
Rachewiltz, Igor de, et al. *In the Service of the Khan: Eminent Personalities of the Early Mongol-Yüan Period (1200–1300)*. Wiesbaden: Harrassowitz, 1993.
Rossabi, Morris. *Khubilai Khan: His Life and Times*. Berkeley: University of California Press, 1988.
Shao, Yuanping. *Yuanshi leibian*. Taipei, 1968.
Song, Lian. *Yuanshi*. Bona ed.
Sun, Kekuan. *Yuanchu ruxue*. Taipei, 1953.
Tillman, Hoyt, and Stephen West, eds. *China under Jurchen Rule: Essays on Chin Intellectual and Cultural History*. Albany: State University of New York Press, 1995.
Wang, Deyi. *Yuanren chuanji ziliao suoyin*, 6 vols. Taipei: 1977.
Zhou, Zumo. "Songwang houshi Yuan zhi ruxue jiaoshou." *Furen xuezhi*, 14, 1946, pp. 191–214.

Cosmology

John B. Henderson

The word "cosmology" in modern usage generally denotes a science devoted to articulating the large-scale properties of the astronomical and physical universe. As such, cosmology in our own time is primarily in the domain of astronomers and astrophysicists. The cosmologies of premodern civilizations were by contrast somewhat more "cosmic" in scope and appeal: they referred not so much to a special science as to a more general view of the ways in which the components of the world were arranged and ordered. These components included not just the objects of physics and astronomy, but items of almost every scale and realm of being, from the architectural to the zoological. Behind most premodern cosmologies, moreover, there lay an assumption that the world was harmonious and proportionate. While the looseness and inconsistencies in many premodern cosmologies may seem to contravene this assumption, this situation may reflect the wide scope of cosmologists' ambitions rather than any lack of commitment to the ideal of a well-ordered universe.

What type of order did these premodern cosmologists conceive (or perceive) in the universe, if not one of scientific laws and mathematical relationships? For Chinese cosmologists, as well as their counterparts in other premodern cultures, the key to understanding order in the universe was correlative thinking. In general, correlative thinking draws systematic correspondences among various orders of reality or realms of the cosmos, such as the human body, the body politic, and the heavenly bodies. It assumes that these related orders are homologous, that they correspond with one another in number, in structure, in kind, or in some other basic respect. Correlative thinking may assume diverse forms and expressions, such as totemism (in primitive cultures), allegory (in medieval cultures), and to some extent even scientific models (in modern cultures). It also lies in the background of other kinds of thought, including analogical inferences and even analytical thinking, as A. C. Graham (1986) has pointed out. But it is most fully explicit in the correlative cosmology that first flourished in Han China (202 B.C.E.–220 C.E) and the Hellenistic west, developed further in both eastern and western civilizations in medieval times, and came under serious challenge in both China and the west during the seventeenth century. In the wake of the scientific revolution, correlative cosmology in its explicit and full-bodied form was confined increasingly to occultism.

Cosmological conceptions of the correlative type do not necessarily exhaust the field of Chinese cosmology. For example, both the cosmogonic myths that appear fragmentarily in early Chinese texts and the neo-Confucian philosophical speculation on the relationships between *li* (pattern or principle) and *qi* (vital force) are significant historically, yet not necessarily grounded in correlative thought. But none of these other cosmological themes was nearly so pervasive or influential in Chinese thought or culture through the ages as were forms of correlative cosmology.

The cosmological correspondences drawn by correlative thinkers vary widely in complexity and cohesiveness, as well as in type. Some are rather clear and simple, such as the homology between the structure of the human body and that of the body politic. Others are not only multidimensional but also of great numerological complexity. It is possible, however, to classify Chinese correlative cosmologies into a few basic types, beginning with those that are more universal in premodern cultures in general and then proceeding to those that are more peculiarly Chinese. But even with the latter, it is hard to detect the existence of the "cosmological gulf" that a few recent authorities have argued exists between Chinese and western cosmologies. On closer inspection, this cosmological gulf turns out to be not between two civilizations but rather between a mechanistic Newtonian worldview on the one hand and premodern cosmologies of both east and west on the other. As Graham (1986) has remarked, to treat correlative thinking as specifically Chinese "is in effect to contrast the correlative stratum of thinking which is more fully exposed in China with the analytical upper layer which is thicker and denser in the [modern] West, confusing different levels."

Correspondences between Macrocosm and Microcosm

Perhaps the most universal mode of correlative thinking to appear in early China was that based on correspondences between man and the cosmos, microcosm and macrocosm. Statements of this type of correspondence appear in texts from such diverse times and places as Vedic India, Elizabethan England, and pre-Columbian Mexico. Even the mythologies of preliterate peoples contain numerous anticipations of this mode of correlative thought, particularly in the form of anthropomorphic interpretations of natural phenomena.

Classical Chinese texts, ranging from the *Songs Classic* to the Confucian *Analects*, also relate correspondences between aspects of the human and natural worlds, as when Confucius likens the virtuous ruler to a polestar. But such correlative statements in the Confucian classics are not very systematic. They contain no explicit account of a general homology between the realm of man and that of the cosmos at large.

Detailed accounts of correspondences between man and aspects of the natural order do, however, appear in such compendiums of the Han era as the *Huainanzi* (c. 139 B.C.E.), the *Chunqiu fanlu* (*Luxuriant Dew of the Spring and Autumn [Annals]*) attributed to Dong Zhongshu (c. 179–104 B.C.E.), the *Baihu tongyi* (*Comprehensive Discussions in White Tiger Hall*, 79 C.E.), and the *Huangdi neijing suwen* (*Plain Questions of the Yellow Sovereign's Inner Classic*). The *Huainanzi*, for example, pairs the four seasons, five phases, nine sections, and 366 days of "heaven" with the four limbs, five viscera, nine orifices, and 366 joints of man. Proceeding to a nonnumerological plane, the same text likens the eyes and ears to sun and moon, blood and pneuma to wind and rain, and cold and heat to joy and anger. For the premier Han cosmologist, Dong Zhongshu, the closeness of the correspondences —numerological, anatomical, and even psychological—between heaven and man indicate man's superior position over other inhabitants of the earth, whose resemblance to heaven is more distant. Some Later Han versions of this type of correlative cosmology used such correspondences more politically and programmatically to justify various human rules and institutions. The *Bohu tongyi*, for example, explains that the ruler may take nine wives, one for each of the nine classical provinces in the realm. In sum, although the "man as microcosm" type of correlative cosmology is not peculiarly Chinese, Chinese cosmologists, especially those of the Han era, developed it to great lengths with a literalism that led even some of their contemporaries to question the validity of the enterprise.

A second type of correlative cosmology that also existed in most premodern high civilizations but was developed most extensively in Han China is what Joseph Needham (1956) has called the "state analogy." Whereas the "man as microcosm" mode of correlative cosmology pairs aspects of man with those of the cosmos at large, the state analogy is based on correspondences between state and cosmos. In other words, this mode of correlative thought takes the imperial state and bureaucracy, rather than man, as microcosm.

Like the idea of man as microcosm, the state analogy mode of correlative cosmology had classical antecedents going back to the Shang era (c. 1700–1045 B.C.E.), particularly in the patterning of the Shang afterworld after the structure of its earthly protobureaucracy. But the state analogy type of correlative thought was not fully formed or widely articulated until the Han era. Cosmological correlations of this type were particularly useful in legitimizing the structure and functions of the newly established imperial bureaucracy of the Han dynasty in the second century B.C.E. A text dating from that century, the *Huainanzi*, pairs particular offices of that bureaucracy with the five directions of space, as the *Chunqiu fanlu* does with calendrical periods, thus anchoring these human institutions in the deep structure of space and time. Perhaps the most famous Han source for the state analogy mode of correlative cosmology is the "Treatise on the Celestial Offices" (*Tianguanshu*) in the *Records of the His-*

torian (*Shiji*) of Sima Qian, which identifies certain constellations of the heavens by the names of posts at the imperial court.

The state analogy mode of correlative cosmology, as articulated in Han texts, not only helped to legitimize the structure of the newly established imperial state but also prescribed the ways in which it should function. The *Bohu tongyi*, for example, proposes a cosmic model for the proper relationship between ruler and minister, remarking that just as "the sun moves slowly and the moon moves quickly," so "the lord takes his ease while the vassal toils."

An important variation or extension of the state analogy type of correlative cosmology, which also crystallized in Han China, was the "field allocation" (*fenye*) astrological system. This schema, which is sometimes referred to as "disastrous geography," paired the classical nine or twelve provinces of China with their corresponding heavenly "fields." An untoward event in one of the latter, such as a comet, portended a disastrous occurrence in its corresponding earthly territory. Although the early forms of *fenye* simply paired heavenly fields with earthly territories, Han cosmologists later developed it into quite a complex and intricate system of correspondence which included such diverse sets as the eight trigrams and sixty-four hexagrams of the *Classic of Changes*, the five phases, the sixty days of the sexagenary calendrical cycle, the twenty-eight lunar lodges, and so forth. Throughout much of Chinese history, *fenye* prognostications based on this system were the special responsibility of the imperial bureau of astronomy.

Later Chinese cosmologists correlated earthly territories not only with fields of the heavens, but also with units of the heavenly bureaucracy. By the Ming period (1368–1644), almost every city or district in China had its own city god whose place in the celestial bureaucracy corresponded exactly to that of the city's earthly magistrate in the terrestrial. These city gods were not just objects of an official cult but prominent in Chinese popular religion as well.

While man and the state were the principal microcosms with which Chinese cosmologists correlated aspects of the larger natural order or macrocosm, they were not the only such entities. Chinese cosmologists presented artifacts ranging from the Chinese zither (*qin*) to alchemical furnaces as miniature universes that replicated larger cosmic processes through their structural and functional similarities to the macrocosm. Moreover, Chinese cosmologists correlated these various microcosms not only with the macrocosm but also with each other. Chinese medical texts, for example, likened the structure and functions of the human body to those of the state, arguing that the same kinds of cultivation and discipline produced normality and prosperity in both.

Cosmological Resonance

Although ideas of correspondences between macrocosm and microcosm are not unique to China, Chinese cosmologists developed them more intricately (and perhaps implausibly) than did their counterparts in most other premodern civilizations. The elaboration of this and other forms of correlative thought was the main subject of many if not most of the major philosophical texts of the early Han era. These texts, moreover—unlike many of their western counterparts—seldom presented the macrocosm as the locus of a superior state of being that controlled lower levels of the cosmic hierarchy. In Han cosmologists' conception, macrocosm and microcosm were more inclined to resonate with one another or move in mutual sympathy (*ganying*), as opposed to being governed by a single controller.

However, not all correlative sets were presented as resonant in Chinese cosmological texts. The *Huainanzi*, for example, does not assert that each of the four seasons, five phases, nine sections, and 366 days of "heaven" interacts with its correspondents among the four limbs, five viscera, nine orifices, and 366 joints of man. This particular system of correspondence, in other words, is primarily a numerological one with no action at a distance. Further, it is difficult to see how the idea of cosmic resonance could have first arisen between these rather static numerological sets.

This idea that corresponding entities in separate realms interact with each other on the principle that "like responds to like" first emerged where its empirical demonstration was most evident and striking—in music. As several late-classical and Han texts point out, the striking of a note on a lute string will evoke a sympathetic response from the corresponding string of another properly tuned lute placed nearby. This "experiment" seemed to establish a resonant interaction between corresponding entities in separate realms, as well as to justify the efforts expended in formulating cosmological systems of corespondence: if Archimedes needed a place to stand in order to move the world, Chinese cosmologists required only a lute to strum.

Since music and musical instruments furnished the primary illustration of and verification for the existence of resonant interaction between corresponding sets, it is small wonder that musical entities figured prominently in Chinese systems of correspondence, perhaps more so than in any other premodern civilization. In fact, the prominence of the numbers five, eight, and twelve in Chinese cosmological numerology may be partly attributed to the existence of musical correspondents in the form of the five tones, eight voices, and twelve pitchpipes, as Kenneth DeWoskin (1982) has pointed out. Having established numerological correlations between these musical entities and other sets, Han cosmologists proceeded to apply them to realms as distinct as meteorology and medicine. For example, they maintained that sounding each of the twelve pitchpipes in its appropriate month would facilitate the normal waxing and waning of *yin* and *yang* through the course of the year. A later Han text correlates the five tones of the pentatonic scale with the five major internal organs of the body, noting that sounding each of the five tones will ensure the good health of the corresponding organ. In the post-Han era, magicians applied these skills in manipulating musical resonance to such varied enterprises as exorcising demons and making birds dance.

Whatever the role of music may have been in inspiring the formulation of ideas of cosmological resonance, its primary field of application in imperial China was statecraft. Particularly prevalent was the idea that aspects of the natural order, ranging from stars and planets to winds and rains to birds and insects, would respond favorably to good government and unfavorably to misgovernment. But before disaster came crashing down on an unworthy ruler or his hapless subjects, heaven would generally see fit to issue portents of the calamity that would ensue unless the guilty parties mended their ways. In some cases, one might determine the specific character of the ruling party's faults according to the type of meteorological (or astronomical) mishap that presented itself. According to the "Great Plan," a chapter in the canonical *Classic Documents*, wildness brings on constant rain, incorrectness constant sunshine (or drought), and so forth. Naturally, those who were charged with reading and interpreting such portents could acquire considerable political leverage.

The earliest Chinese accounts of instances of cosmological resonance do not explain how this resonant interaction between corresponding sets takes place. While they implicitly posit the existence of some form of action at a distance, they give no indication of the particular mechanism by which this action (or reaction) occurs. Like the children of four and five years of age studied by the psychologist Jean Piaget (1972), Chinese protocosmologists seem to have believed that physical events may be caused by related objects acting on one another from a distance, while showing a remarkable lack of interest in how this is brought about. However, Chinese cosmologists, again like Piaget's children, later reached the stage of explaining apparent action at a distance by the reaction of the surrounding medium. In the earliest Chinese cosmological texts that offer this kind of explanation for resonant effects, the medium is rather crude and anthropomorphic, such as the noxious odors that revealed to the powers on high the people's lack of virtue, as related in the chapter "Punishments of Lü" in the *Classic Documents*. By the second century B.C.E., however, such odors were subsumed into a colorless, odorless, tasteless *qi*, which served as the primary medium for resonant interactions.

The term *qi* is as ubiquitous in Chinese cosmological texts from the Han era onward as the *qi* itself was supposed to be in the cosmos, as DeWoskin has indicated. But the meaning of this term is often as elusive as the forms of fogs and mists swirling about mountain peaks. Indeed, as Nathan Sivin (1969) has pointed out, the earliest appearances of the term tend to refer to "the mists, the fogs, and moving forms of clouds that are what we see of the atmosphere," but also to extrusions into that atmosphere such as breath, smoke, aromas, and even ghosts. Cosmologists of the third and second centuries B.C.E. used the term more abstractly to refer to the conveyor of resonant influences between corresponding entities in different realms. But later cosmologists also used *qi* to denote the primordial substance of the universe that congeals to form hard solids and disperses to make up the fogs and mists that were its original etymological as well as cosmological form. This *qi*, moreover, might differentiate itself into distinctive varieties, such as *yin* and *yang* or one of the five phases (*wuxing*). Thus action at a distance between two resonating entities might be facilitated not only by vibrations emitted through the medium of the *qi* connecting them, but also because they are composed of the same general type of *qi*, as John Major (1993) has remarked.

The cosmological career of the *qi* did not end even here. As Major has pointed out, the term also referred to temperament and mood, as well as to a kind of animating force or vital energy that could be nourished through various medical regimens and yogic practices. And Sivin has remarked that *qi* could be both the material basis of an activity and the activity itself. It might subsume both matter and energy or some combination thereof. But to trace all the multifarious manifestations of *qi* through Chinese cosmological and philosophical texts of the last 2,500 years would require a far more luminous form of *qi* than is cultivated by most modern scholars, including myself. Perhaps the subject might be made more manageable by taking up some of the different forms of this universal pneuma.

Yin and *Yang* and the Five Phases

As mentioned above, Chinese cosmologists of the Han era and later classified different types of *qi* by the *yin*-

yang and five-phase (*wuxing*) rubrics. But these two conceptions were not mere subsidiaries to a *qi* cosmology. They were both major cosmological ideas in their own right that served as bases for distinct types of systems of correspondence. In fact, so important, even dominant, were these ideas that present-day commentators sometimes use "*yin-yang–wuxing*" synecdochically to denote Chinese cosmology in general.

Like the *qi, yin-yang* and *wuxing* acquired their cosmological vitality only gradually through the course of the late-classical and Han eras. Down to the fourth century B.C.E., *yang* and *yin* meant "sunshine" and "shade," respectively, particularly the sunny and shady sides of a slope. Cosmologists of the late-classical and Han eras transformed this pair into a complementary duality that signified the active and latent phases of a process, such as the waxing and waning of the seasons of the year. Even at the height of the *yang* there exists the germ of *yin*, and vice versa. *Yin* and *yang*, moreover, are not absolutes but relational ideas: an old man may be *yang* with respect to a woman but is *yin* with respect to a young man.

The *yin-yang* duality, having been established, became the basis of a binary classification system which seemed to be reinforced with each new application, as Sivin has noted. With the *yang* were correlated light, heat, dryness, hardness, heaven, roundness, sun, south, incipience, activity, etc.; their complementary opposites were associated with the *yin*. Later cosmologists fit almost anything that could be conceived as a duality, from philosophical ideas to social relationships to medical remedies, into the *yin-yang* paradigm. But this paradigm was not simply a classificatory arrangement; it was used primarily to explain such dynamic processes as seasonal change, the human life cycle, and the rise and fall of dynasties. Cosmologists in residence at the Han imperial court also used the idea of *yin* and *yang* to establish instances of cosmological resonance, often with a political point. According to the "Treatise on the Five Phases" in the *Han History*, the political domination of the *yin* element at court (women) brings about an overabundance in the corresponding *yin* element in the natural world (floods).

So thoroughly did the *yin-yang* paradigm dominate the discourse of duality in postclassical China that it has obscured earlier expressions of dualism in China. Strong indications of a protodualistic cosmology in China may be traced as far back as the Shang era. As Richard Smith (1991) has noted, they appear in the form of the divinatory inscriptions on Shang oracle bones, as well as in the physical and conceptual symmetry of Shang art. But this evidence of dualism in Shang China may reflect a universal inclination to think in binary terms more than it does an early stage of *yin-yang* cosmology. For the *yin-yang* dualism that emerged in late-classical China was a dualism of a peculiar character, and not a mere expression of symmetry. It was complementary and relational, not conflicting or absolute. Moreover, it was used to describe and explain dynamic processes, not just as a static classificatory schema.

Chinese cosmologists of the Han era and later classified *qi* into five phases, as well as dualistically. In fact, from the perspective of later Chinese cosmologists, the five phases were simply a finer way of describing and explaining the processes of change in the world, particularly in that they divided such processes into five aspects instead of just two. Han cosmologists frequently arrayed the phases into several different sequences in order to support a particular theory of cosmic change (which often had political implications). According to the "mutual production" sequence, for example, wood produced fire, fire produced earth, earth produced metal, metal produced water, and water produced wood. In the "mutual conquest" series, on the other hand, wood conquered earth, metal conquered wood, fire conquered metal, water conquered fire, and earth conquered water. In these five-phase sequences, each of the phases was identified not so much with a particular material element or substance as with a quality or type of activity. For example, "wood" referred not so much to the material or texture of wood as it did to the phase of flexing and growing within a larger process of change, as Sivin has remarked.

Like the *yin-yang* duality, five-phase (*wuxing*) sequences were correlated with corresponding sets in other realms, such as the five colors, smells, tastes, tones, directions, seasons, planets, winds, animals, grains, mountains, reservoirs, sage-rulers, social classes, viscera, and emotions. The associations between corresponding entities in some of these sets seem to be less natural or commonsensical than is the case with most of the *yin-yang* correspondences outlined above. For example, while matching the color green with wood might make sense, what about pairing the emotion of anger with wood? The quest for cosmic completeness, however, obliged correlative cosmologists to extend their systems ever farther from their natural bases into increasingly unknown territory. Correlative cosmologists, like Aristotle's nature, abhorred a vacuum.

These cosmologists frequently found it necessary to force-fit some of the sets they counted off in fives in order to mesh them into the quinary framework. Thus, the convention that there were only four seasons required a bit of numerological juggling to synchronize the seasons with the phases. The inventiveness shown by Han cosmologists in resolving this numerological disjunction indicates the extent of their commitment to the five-phases paradigm.

Like the *yin-yang* correlations, the five-phase correspondences were not, however, simply a classificatory schema but a system for predicting and even guiding change in various cosmic realms. For example, a knowledge of the correct five-phase correlate of the Han dynasty would enable one to determine the appropriate rituals and policies that the dynasty ought to follow in order to deal with the temper of the times. And an understanding of the phase correlate of a particular disease in a patient would suggest the appropriate medical remedy according to the mutual conquest series of the five phases. Thus, a febrile disease might be neutralized by a "cooling" drug associated with water, which "conquered" fire. But while most cosmological practitioners might accept this general paradigm of five-phase correlations, there could be considerable disagreement, even passionate debate, over just what were the proper correlates of a given entity. As a result of these debates, the imperial Han dynasty changed its patron phase no less than four times. On two of these occasions, the dynasty adopted a different color of ritual paraphernalia, including court vestments of a different color, and a calendar beginning in a different month, both of which had to correspond to the newly inaugurated phase.

Like the *yin-yang* duality, the five phases took a while to reach their correlative cosmological stride in the Han era. Even though quinary categories appear in China as early as the Shang period, throughout most of the subsequent Chou era (c. 1045–256 B.C.E.) quinary sets were by no means dominant over competing numerological series, particularly those based on six. In their earliest classical appearances, moreover, fives were more often conceived as material substances or powers than as phases of cosmic change or forms of the universal *qi*. But the development and application of five-phase correlative systems by cosmologists of the third and second centuries B.C.E. to explain and legitimize dynastic change apparently made this system very attractive to the rulers of the newly established Han dynasty and helped to ensure its eventual triumph. Thus John Major's translation of *wuxing* as "five phases" is appropriate for most of the later occurrences of this term in Chinese cosmological texts in that they generally refer to phases of change in an ordered pattern.

The *Classic of Changes* and Correlative Cosmology

Han cosmologists not only developed the five-phase correlative system to explain changes in such varied dimensions as the political, the meteorological, and the medical but also syncretized it with the *yin-yang* system, despite the numerological disjunction between the two. But the *yin-yang* and five phases were not the only correlative systems with which Han cosmologists conjured. While it is impossible to cover all Chinese correlative schemas in this article, mention at least should be made of those based on the *Classic of Changes* (or *Book of Changes*, *Yijing*, or *I Ching*) and its canonical appendixes. As Smith has written, "The *I-ching* occupied a central position in the development of Han correlative thinking—not to mention the later evolution of science and medicine in China."

Although the text of the *Yijing* does not outline systems of correspondence, the canonical appendixes, compiled during the late-classical and early Han eras, offer more grist for the correlative cosmologist's mill. The canonical "Great Commentary" presents the *Yijing* itself as a sort of microcosm: its "broadness and greatness match that of heaven and earth and its flux and continuities match those of the four seasons." The sixty-four hexagrams of the *Yijing* (each of which consists of a set of six parallel lines that may be either broken or unbroken), moreover, supposedly furnished the patterns on which the sage kings modeled the artifacts and inventions of civilization, such as agricultural implements, burial customs, and even writing. A natural correlation thus existed between the hexagrams of the *Yijing* and the principal features of human culture.

Systems of correspondence devised by later cosmologists based on the *Yijing* grew to be as complex as those founded on *yin-yang* and the five phases. In fact, they sometimes incorporated the latter to produce veritable monuments of cosmological syncretism. One example of a correlative system based on the *Yijing* is the *najia*, which correlated the lines of the hexagrams with the twelve months of the year, the twenty-four solar periods, the twenty-eight lunar lodges, the twelve pitchpipes, the phases of the moon, and the five phases, as well as with the ten heavenly stems and twelve earthly branches, two enumerative orders used for counting days. The idea of numerological correspondence between the figures of the *Yijing* and those of the heavens furnished a cosmological basis for the science of mathematical astronomy in the Han era. Han cosmologists "deduced" from the manipulation of the figures in the *Yijing* not only various calendrical periods, such as the number of days in a year, but also the lengths of various astronomical concordance cycles.

Ramifications of Correlative Cosmology

Astronomy was not the only branch of learning or area of culture into which correlative cosmology ramified in postclassical China. Even though the invention and elaboration of primary correlative schemata were no longer the main concerns of most Chinese philosophers after the Han era, correlative thought continued to provide "the organizing concepts of proto-sciences such as astronomy, medicine, music, divination, and in later centuries alchemy and geomancy," as Graham has written. So extensive are the ramifications of correlative cosmology into all these fields that to explore thoroughly its influence on any one of them would require a major study, like Manfred Porkert's work (1974) on systems of correspondence in traditional Chinese medicine. Since a few examples of the influence of correlative thought in medicine and music have already been presented in this article, I will go on to offer illustrations from a couple of the more esoteric "protosciences" listed above, alchemy and geomancy.

The theory of Chinese alchemy was generally based on ideas of correspondence between macrocosm and microcosm. Alchemists regarded their materials, equipment, and even procedures, including the chemicals, the furnace, the reaction vessel, and the control of time and temperature, as in some sense microcosmic. An eighth-century illustration of an alchemical furnace described by Sivin depicts "three tiers, which correspond to sky and earth and man centered between them. The central tier has twelve doors, which correspond to hours in the day and months in the year." In such ways did alchemists seek to "be sure that what went on in their reaction vessels was identical with the work of nature." Even the language of alchemical texts was in a sense correlative, or perhaps polyphonic; it might be read on a number of different levels, as a description of laboratory operations, of cosmological processes, of sexual or yogic disciplines, and of spiritual cultivation or religious redemption.

Of the various divinatory protosciences in which correlative cosmology figured prominently, geomancy, the art of determining auspicious sites for buildings and burials, was among the most widely practiced in late-traditional China. Indeed, this art served as one of the principal conduits through which correlative thought was channeled from Chinese high culture to that of the folk. As in Chinese alchemy, the idea of man as microcosm loomed large in geomantic theory, as illustrated in a passage from the *Yellow Sovereign's Site Classic* (*Huangdi zhaijing*), translated by Steven Bennett (1978): "The forms and configurations [of the landscape] are considered to be the body; water and underground springs are the blood and veins; the earth is the skin; foliage is the hair; dwellings are the clothes; door and gate are the hat and belt."

But other modes of correlative cosmology besides that of man as microcosm also influenced geomantic theory. The geomancer's compass, which incorporated as many as thirty-eight circles of symbol sets—including the trigrams and hexagrams of the *Yijing*, the ten heavenly stems and twelve earthly branches, the five phases, *yin* and *yang*, the twenty-eight lunar lodges, the twenty-four solar periods, and the four seasons and directions—is a good emblem of the cosmological comprehensiveness of geomancy.

Correlative cosmology pervaded not only the protosciences in premodern China but also the protohumanities. The classic work of Chinese literary criticism, *The Literary Mind and the Carving of Dragons* (*Wenxin diaolong*) by Liu Xie (Liu Hsieh, c. 465–523), posits that if literary creation is to take place, inner and outer realities, mind and cosmos, and language and existence must correspond. As Pauline Yu (1980) has pointed out, "the notion of correspondences pervades Liu Hsieh's entire work."

Works of literature, as well as literary criticism, touched bases in correlative cosmology. As Andrew Plaks (1976) has shown, the structure of the classic Chinese novel *Dream of the Red Chamber* may be described in terms of the five phases and *yin* and *yang*. Another classic novel, *Journey to the West*, presents its main characters as personifications of five-phase and alchemical terms. DeWoskin has pointed to the existence of "extraordinary examples of highly correlative literary works in early China" as well: "For example, Chang Heng's *Rhyme-Prose about Meditations on the Mystery* makes use of images that correlate to the hexagrams and commentaries of the . . . *Change*." Not only the *wen* (civil or literary) but also the *wu* (military) aspect of Chinese culture betrayed the influence of correlative thought. For example, the *Six Strategies*, a manual of military tactics, asserts that by knowing the enemy's posture with respect to the five phases, one can "select an attacking phase that will conquer him."

Finally, correlative cosmology informed not just the waking world but also the world of dreams, as illustrated in the *Yellow Sovereign's Inner Classic*: "When *yin* is flourishing then there occur dreams, as if one had to wade through great waters, which cause bad fears; when *yang* is flourishing there occur dreams of great fires which burn and cauterize." But the entry of correlative cosmology into the field of dreams should not particularly surprise us, since correlative thinking continues to inform modern interpretations of dreams from Freud and Jung to the present.

Whereas forms of correlative thought dominated the intellectual scene from about 200 B.C.E. to 1600 C.E. in both Chinese and western civilizations, it came under attack thereafter in both areas, though more abruptly in Europe than in China. However, even after the scientific revolution and the "shift from correlative to causal explanation," correlative thinking in its various modes continued to dominate much of ordinary practical life, as Graham has remarked. Survivals of divination and occultism in modern cultures are only the most obvious and flagrant examples of contemporary correlative thinking. Not only does it appear prominently in the psychology of everyday life, but it is manifested in high culture as well, in such artifacts as symbolist poetry, program music, Gestalt psychology, and structuralist anthropology, and indeed in most forms of scientific reductionism as well as in model transference in the sciences. However remote or exotic the ideas of *yin-yang*, the five phases, and "man as microcosm" may seem from the perspective of our modern culture, the general mode of thinking that they represent is by no means peculiarly Chinese or medieval.

See also *Qi*; *Wuxing*; *Yin* and *Yang*.

Bibliography

Allan, Sarah. *The Shape of the Turtle: Myth, Art, and Cosmos in Early China*. Albany: State University of NewYork Press, 1991.

Bennett, Steven J. "Patterns of the Sky and Earth: A Chinese System of Applied Cosmology." *Chinese Science*, 3, March 1978, pp. 1–12.

Bodde, Derk. *Chinese Thought, Society, and Science: The Intellectual and Social Background of Science and Technology in Pre-Modern China*. Honolulu: University of Hawaii Press, 1991.

DeWoskin, Kenneth J. *A Song for One or Two: Music and the Concept of Art in Early China*. Michigan Papers in Chinese Studies, No. 42. Ann Arbor: Center for Chinese Studies, University of Michigan, 1982.

Eberhard, Wolfram. "Beiträge zur kosmologischen Spekulation in China in der Han Zeit." *Baessler-Archiv*, 16(1), 1933, pp. 1–100.

Graham, A. C. *Yin-Yang and the Nature of Correlative Thinking*. IEAP Occasional Paper and Monograph Series, No. 6. Singapore: Institute of East Asian Philosophies, 1986.

Granet, Marcel. *La pensée chinoise*. Paris: Éditions Albin Michel, 1950.

Henderson, John B. *The Development and Decline of Chinese Cosmology*. New York: Columbia University Press, 1984.

Karlgren, Bernhard, trans. *The Book of Documents*. Göteborg: Elanders Boktryckeri Artiebolog, 1950. (Reprinted from *Bulletin of the Museum of Far Eastern Antiquities*, No. 22.)

Lau, D. C., trans. *The Analects (Lun-yü)*. Harmondsworth, England: Penguin, 1979.

Major, John S. *Heaven and Earth in Early Han Thought: Chapters Three, Four, and Five of the Huainanzi*. Albany: State University of New York Press, 1993.

Needham, Joseph. *Science and Civilisation in China*, Vol. 2, *History of Scientific Thought*. Cambridge: Cambridge University Press, 1956.

Piaget, Jean. *The Child's Conception of Physical Causality*, trans. Marjorie Gabain. Totowa, N.J.: Littlefield, Adams, 1972.

Plaks, Andrew H. *Archetype and Allegory in the Dream of the Red Chamber*. Princeton, N.J.: Princeton University Press, 1976.

Porkert, Manfred. *The Theoretical Foundations of Chinese Medicine: Systems of Correspondence*. East Asian Science Series, Vol. 3. Cambridge, Mass.: MIT Press, 1974.

Rosemont, Henry, ed. *Explorations in Early Chinese Cosmology*. Chico, Calif.: Scholars, 1984.

Schwartz, Benjamin I. *The World of Thought in Ancient China*. Cambridge, Mass.: Belknap Press of Harvard University Press, 1985.

Sivin, Nathan. "Chinese Alchemy and the Manipulation of Time." In *Science and Technology in East Asia*, ed. Nathan Sivin. New York: Science History Publications, 1977, pp. 108–122.

———. "Cosmos and Computation in Early Chinese Mathematical Astronomy." *T'oung Pao*, New Series, 55, 1969, pp. 1–73.

———. *Traditional Medicine in Contemporary China*. Science, Medicine, and Technology in East Asia, No. 2. Ann Arbor: Center for Chinese Studies, University of Michigan, 1987.

Smith, Richard J. *China's Cultural Heritage: The Ch'ing Dynasty 1644–1912*. Boulder, Colo.: Westview, 1983.

———. *Fortune-Tellers and Philosophers: Divination in Traditional Chinese Society*. Boulder, Colo.: Westview, 1991.

Tjan, Tjoe Som, trans. *Po Hu T'ung: The Comprehensive Discussions in White Tiger Hall*. Sinica Leidensia, Vol. 6. Leiden: Brill, 1949. (Reprinted, Westport, Conn.: Hyperion, 1973.)

Unschuld, Paul U. *Medicine in China: A History of Ideas*. Berkeley: University of California Press, 1985.

Veith, Ilza, trans. *Huang Ti Nei Ching Su Wen: The Yellow Emperor's Classic of Internal Medicine*. Berkeley: University of California Press, 1972.

Xu, Fuguan. *Liang Han sixiang shi*, Vol. 2. Hong Kong: Zhongwen daxue, 1975.

Yu, Anthony C., trans. and ed. *The Journey to the West*. Vol. 1. Chicago: University of Chicago Press, 1977.

Yu, Pauline. *The Poetry of Wang Wei: New Translations and Commentary*. Bloomington: Indiana University Press, 1980.

D

Dai Zhen (Tai Chen)

Chung-ying CHENG

Dai Zhen (Dai Dongyuan, 1723–1777) was perhaps the most important critical-minded neo-Confucianist of the Qing era. He stood out as a critic of Song-Ming neo-Confucianism and made original contributions to a critical exposition of the classical Confucian philosophy of Mencius. Although he was not known as a philosopher during his own time, his neo-Confucian critique and exposition have been much discussed and quoted since Hu Shi wrote about him in the 1930s. Dai imbued his critique with a modern spirit of humanistic rationalism and naturalistic morality, which offered a new, modern perspective for understanding and evaluating classical and Song-Ming Confucianism. To understand him, we need to appreciate his textual, critical, and philological background as well as his methodology.

Dai Zhen was born in the Huizhou area of Anhui Province, in a place called Longfu (Tunxi City), which was part of Xiuling County, during a time of prosperity. Huizhou was a mercantile center, perhaps because it was so hilly and so densely populated that its people had to make a living in commerce and cross-provincial trade. It was also known as an academic center, excelling in textual criticism and philology, with well-known scholars who were Dai's contemporaries or near contemporaries. This may explain why Dai himself became a noted scholar, even though he came from a poor family with no academic tradition and received no good formal schooling; his success was derived from his dedication to independent study.

According to Duan Yucai's *Bibliography of Dai Dongyan Xiansheng*, from quite early in his life until age seventeen Dai studied basic works of Chinese philology, such as *Shuowen jiezi* (*Thirteen Classics: Commentaries*) and *Shisanjing zhusu* (*Commentaries on Commentaries*). From age eighteen to age twenty-two he continued his studies, learning much from the famous philologist-arithmetician Jiang Yun. He made progress in astronomical arithmetic and phonology, and he started to publish works in calender arithmetic and trigometry and philological annotations of *Kaogongji, Erya, Shijing*, and *Odes of Quyuan* from ages twenty-four to thirty-three.

What happened next was crucial in Dai's shift from philology alone to a critique of neo-Confucian philosophy. When he was thirty-three he became involved in a lawsuit concerning a transgression of his ancestral tomb site by someone in a powerful position. He lost the suit and thus came to realize how political and social forces could twist justice, ostensibly in the name of justice, citing the ideology of *li* (principle), the central notion of the Song-Ming neo-Confucianism. Whether Dai began to write his first philosophical work—*Yuanshan* (*Inquiry into Goodness*)—that year is not known, but it is reasonable to believe that he finished the first draft between then and age forty-one, as indicated in Duan's *Bibiliography*.

Dai Zhen's philological work on the classics led him to ponder certain issues of philosophy, notably the laws of nature as revealed in ancient documents such as *Shangshu* and *Yijing* and the nature of humanity as discussed in the *Xici of the Yi* and *Mengzi*. For example, he had earlier composed an astronomical and calendrical study of *Yuanxiang* (*Inquiry into Solar Movements and Seasons*, based on *Zhoubi* and other sources); and he followed this with an essay on the laws of nature (*Faxiang*), which became part of the first section of *Yuanshan*. The other part of the first section was his essay on the *Xici*, which established an inner link between the nature of heaven and earth and the nature of the human being. During the latter part of this period, Dai must have continued to develop his study of human nature, which led him to concentrate on Mencius. His essay on Mencius on human nature essentially constitutes the second section of *Yuanshan*. Finally, he discussed how a person could cultivate his nature in order to seek goodness and become a sage; this is the third section of *Yuanshan*.

Taking *Yuanshan* as a basis, Dai Zhen introduced quotations from the classics to support his philosophical points, and these together with *Yuanshan* became his *Xuyan* (*Prefatory Words*). After further consolidation and further concentration on Mencius he sorted out and expanded *Xuyan* into a philosophical commentary on Mencius's key notions. He called this work *Mengzi ziyi suzheng* (*Commentaries and Annotations on Concepts and Words from Mencius*); I will cite it simply as *Mengzi ziyi*. This was the last work he presented to his colleagues, when he was forty-four years old.

From then until his death at age fifty-five, Dai frequently referred to this work. He considered it his most important work because it was intended to rectify people's minds so that they would not mistake their own opinions (*yijian*) for objective principles of *li* and thus harm others. In fact, before his death he said that this was the reason why he had to write the work—a comment that shows how deeply he felt toward it and also reminds us that he himself had suffered from abuse and misunderstanding of *li*. His remark suggests as well that the work was not simply theoretical but a moral critique written from a profound sense of conscience.

For our own understanding of Dai's philosophy, however, we should recognize that its central principles had already been laid down in *Yuanshan*. Dai Zhen then worked for many years on *Mengzi ziyi*, providing concise explanations, relevant quotations from classical Confucian texts, and, finally, straightforward and revealing questions and answers. *Yuanshan* and *Mengzi ziyi* are equally important and must be read with equal attentiveness.

Methodology of Textual Critique and Hermeneutical Understanding

The rise of textual criticism in the Qing was not accidental; it can be explained through insights into the academic trends and political atmosphere of the time. Undeniably, with the downfall of the Ming the Lu-Wang school lost its appeal, particularly relative to the Chan tendencies of the later Wang school. Another factor was that the Qing rulers harbored suspicions regarding the liberating, individualistic leanings of popular followers of Wang. Hence Zhu Xi's doctrine of *lixue* made a comeback, with the implicit and explicit endorsement of officialdom. The Zhu Xi school—whose impact would continue to be felt throughout the Ming era—had a double effect. On the one hand, the doctrine of *gewu xiongli* (investigating things and exhausting the *li*) required a person to obey reason and principle rather than personal interest or the authority of the powerful. On the other hand, those in power could invoke the name of reason to guard and defend their own interests.

Although Dai Zhen objected strongly to the abstract use of principles (*li*), he did not deny the importance of reason when it was applied correctly in concrete situations. The question was how one came to acquire an understanding of reason and principle. The answer was twofold: one reached this understanding through a correct reading of the classical texts on which doctrines of moral reason were based, and through lucid reflection on what reason and principle would signify in reality. This meant that we would have to examine the classical texts in order to read them correctly and then, in light of our reading, interpret them correctly according to our best understanding. As a prerequisite, we would need to ascertain the authenticity of the classical texts and be assured of their semantic and philological clarity. If the texts were not authentic or not linguistically clear, how could we read and interpret them correctly? In this sense, textual criticism could be highly relevant to our understanding of the principles and reasoning of the classical philosophers such as Confucius and Mencius and works such as the *Yijing*.

This acknowledgment of the general usefulness of textual criticism, however, does not explain Qing textual criticism, since most of the well-known textual critics were not necessarily interested in discovering or rediscovering the principles and reasoning of the classical texts. Rather, they were interested in textual criticism as a science involving clarifying and sorting out difficulties with regard to textual authenticity and relationships between texts. This reason for the development of textual criticism may have conformed to the expectations of the early Qing rulers and may indeed have received official encouragement, for the sake of intellectual control. But Dai Zhen was obviously interested not just in authenticity but also in valid readings and interpretations for the sake of understanding of principles and reasons. In this regard he was unique among the textual scholars of the Qing era.

It is interesting to note that for Dai Zhen textual criticism was essential—not merely useful—to the discovery of principles and reasons:

> The ultimate idea of the classics is the *dao*. That which we use to understand the *dao* is the discourse (*ci*). That which we use to form discourse is nothing but the "linguistic study of texts and language" (*xiaoxue wenzi*). From such study we come to understand the speech [of the authors]; from the speech of the authors we will be able to understand the *xin* or heart-mind and the intention of the ancient sages. (*Gujing diaochen xu*)

Thus for Dai Zhen, to engage in textual criticism of a classic is to retrieve the original speech (not just the language) of the text from history so that one will discern the intended meaning of the original authors. For the purpose of understanding the reasons, truth, and principles behind the texts, one must appeal to textual criticism as the first step.

However, this is not to say that Dai Zhen was searching for "original meanings" (*yuanyi*). As a philosopher, he would have known that this is not really possible. We do not know how to verify a claimed "original meaning," nor can we necessarily come to know the true intentions of the ancient authors. Therefore, once a text has been made clear by textual criticism, we must discover and define a reasonable interpretation, which, conceivably, would conform to the intended meaning and at the same time present the truth of the matter. We might regard Dai Zhen as the first modern Chinese scholar to formulate and articulate a textual hermeneutics combining historical linguistics with philosophical reflections for the reading of classical texts. Considering that he lived in the eighteenth century, we might even regard him as the world's first practitioner of philosophical hermeneutics in the best sense of the term.

Apart from textual hermeneutics, the second concern in understanding the correct reading of a text is how to determine the meanings of terms and ideas in reference to one's own reflections on reality and life. For Dai Zhen, again, these reflections must not be groundless; they must, in fact, be grounded in the coherence of the Six Classics. One might object, here, that Dai Zhen was begging the question, for how can one determine the meaning of a term by appeal to a text whose meanings need to be determined in the first place? Dai Zhen's response would be that a standard reading of the Six Classics can be arrived at through contemplating these texts alone: "The *dao* of the Sage is in the Six Classics; [we may read the texts] by first analyzing the terms, clarifying the language, and finally illuminating the *dao*" (*Shen xuezi wenjisu*).

In taking the Six Classics for granted, Dai Zhen would agree with Cui Shu—who came after him—and in this regard both Dai and Cui were conservatives who refused to assert independent philosophical thinking as Zhu Xi or Wang Yangming did. What is more important for Dai's reading of *Yizhuan* and *Mengzi* is rather his own reflections on the reasonableness of using the ideas and terms in actual human situations. He argued for the importance of improving one's perceptiveness and judgment so that one might order the affairs of the people. He in fact introduced a projected element of understanding in terms of one's own observations of nature and human institutions as well as one's own experiences of life and social relations—despite his appeal to the Six Classics.

From Philosophy of Nature to Philosophy of Human Nature

The most important contribution of Dai Zhen's philosophy was his objection to the separation of human reason from human feelings and desires in Song-Ming Confucianism; he felt, rather, that reason was to be used in terms of feelings and desires. His position came from a deep appreciation of the naturalistic ontocosmology of the *Yijing*, in which he found the source of human nature and human reason. From his study of the *Xici*, he came to consider "productivity of life" (*shengsheng*) as the most basic fact of reality. It was owing to the purpose of *shengsheng*, he explained, that the matching and exchange of *yin* and *yang* (*yiyin yiyang*) was called the *dao*. *Yiyin yiyang* speaks to the unceasing transformation of life in heaven and earth. Hence for Dai Zhen *yiyin yiyang* is a matter of the productivity of life, from which necessarily follows the ordering of things (*tiaoli*) in heaven and earth. It is important to note that both *shengsheng* and *tiaoli* are key concepts in Dai's understanding of the larger nature, and they are derived from his reading of *yiyin yiyang*.

It is also clear that his reading of *yiyin yiyang* leads him to speak of the *dao* as the flow of *qi* and even of the five powers which come from the interaction of *yin* and *yang*. Nature (*xing*) and limitation of nature (*ming*) are simply results of inherent interactions of *yin* and *yang* and hence are the creative works of the *qi*. Dai Zhen likes to speak of the separation (*fen*) and integration (*he*) of the *qi* of fundamental forms of things such as the sun and moon. Thus by the differentiation and integration of *qi* we would have water and fire. He says:

> The interaction of sun and moon constantly gives rise to integration of *qi* and differentiation of *qi*. . . . The water arises by integration whereas the fire arises by differentiation; similarly for metal and wood. (*Faxiang lun*)

However, he gives no definition or explanation of the differentiation and integration of *qi*.

On the basis of his understanding of *shengsheng* and *tiaoli*, Dai Zhen sees the virtues of benevolence (*ren*), propriety (*li*), and righteousness (*yi*) as their inherent qualities. Productivity of life is a matter of benevolence; the ordering of things is a matter of propriety; and the clarity of such ordering is a matter of righteousness. In considering these three qualities of the *dao* of change one sees the paragon of supreme goodness. The conclusion is that the nature of heaven and earth, and hence reality, is inherently good. Here, Dai deduces values and virtues from the very fact of the productivity of life in nature. From the standpoint of western philosophy, he may seem to be confusing fact and value, but this is not necessarily true; what Dai does is to apply his insight about using human morality to interpret nature so that nature by itself can provide a basis for objectve morality. It is interesting to note that moral virtues can indeed be embedded in nature, because they can be given an ontocosmological meaning. What we see is an attempt to integrate morality and cosmology in an insightful hermeneutical or ontohermeneutical understanding of reality. One may therefore speak of the nature of the *dao*, which lies in a process of creating the world of things imbued with values and imprinted by nature with inherent virtues. One might say that to give life is to have nature and to have nature is to have virtues.

From the supreme goodness of reality of *shengsheng*, it follows that human life is endowed with a nature which is good in the sense of reflecting the larger nature. We say that human nature is good because humans are able to be benevolent and protective of life in general, think in an orderly way, use reason to organize things, and distinguish right from wrong—realizing that the right leads to life, creativity, order, and propriety whereas the wrong destroys them. In this sense Dai thinks that the human being has inherited the goodness of heaven or the *dao*; thus he provides a totally different argument for human goodness, a cosmological argument derived from the *Yizhuan*.

The consanguinity of heaven's nature and human nature, in their goodness, is extended to and realized in the desires, which are vehicles of this goodness. Dai Zhen simply affirms that "desires (*yu*) are the matters of nature." Similarly, "feelings (*jue*) are abilities of nature." Thus human nature—like the nature of all things—is constituted of inherent desires and feelings. As such it would also follow the natural virtues, and we can speak of the five powers of desires, the *yin* and *yang* of feelings, and the creativity of one's nature. Notice that we can speak of the larger nature in terms of morality, and we can also speak of human nature in terms of cosmology. For Dai, there is always an underlying or inner link between the two.

According to Dai, *li* (reason, principle) comes if these desires and feelings of one's nature conform to the virtues of heaven and earth—benevolence, propriety, and righteousness. *Li*, then, is simply the virtue of nature, inherent in the desires and feelings of nature. Hence *li* is not separate from or outside human nature; it must be realized in the harmony and unity of human desires and feelings with the larger nature. This implies a natural realization that is a matter of conformity, neither arbitrary nor unrestrained. The naturalistic principle of *li* applies to all things. All things that are different have different natures because they are produced by the *dao* in different life-forms, so their inherent *li* is also different; but this does not affect the fact that they are all part and parcel of the ontocosmology of nature and can all exhibit the *li* of the heaven and earth. This is actually how Dai Zhen interprets the statement in *Yizhuan* that "to succeed from the *dao* is to acquire goodness, and to accomplish a life-form is to have a nature."

We can see that Dai Zhen's philosophy of nature is predicated on his understanding of both the *Xici* and the nature of reality. His philosophy of human nature is similarly founded. His argument is surprisingly cogent: he is able to weave together the meanings of the relevant terms and justify them in terms of his sense of reason and his insights into life. With his interpretation of the ontocosmology of the *Yizhuan*, we have a full theory of human nature together with a full theory of the development of human virtues; we are also able to understand the common ground of values and virtues among all things, which would be a basis for self-cultivation and rational evaluation.

Analysis of Human Nature and the Human Heart and Mind

Dai Zhen's position on human nature can be described as moral realism in which reality has moral significance and morality has ontological significance. Hence we may speak of a kind of ontological morality or ontomorality based on his philosophy of the inner unity of nature and human nature. Again, this link can be explained by his notion of the integration and differentiation of the *qi*. He quotes *Dadai liji* to support his point: "To be differentiated from the *dao* is the *ming* (delimitation); to be unified in oneness is called *xing* (nature)." But human nature is formed from, or substantiated from, the *qi*, which is the *yin* and *yang* and the five powers.

In this substantiation—in giving rise to the entities it represents—the *qi* has limitations as well as strengths. Dai Zhen says: "*Yin-yang* and five powers are the substance of the *dao*; the blood-breath-heart-mind is the substance of the nature" (*Mengzi ziyi*, section on *Tiandao*). This means that the transformation of the *dao* or cosmic *qi* into the substance of human nature requires the creative power of differentiation and integration of the *qi*. This is inherent in the *dao* and is why we can speak of the *dao* as life-productive—*shengsheng*.

With this background, how do we understand the details of human nature? For Dai Zhen, human nature, composed of blood-breath-heart-mind, is utterly a matter of abilities (*neng*) and capacities (*cai*) and has no separate endowment from heaven. In other words, there is no dualism of any kind between mind and body as there is Platonism or Cartesianism—or even in Zhu Xi's philosophy, where *li* and *qi* are linked but unmixed and where a distinction is drawn between the nature of temperament and the nature of reason. But this does not mean that Dai draws no distinction between mind and body, or between a gifted person and a dullard. The quantity and the quality of the *qi* and its combination, separation, and configuration make a difference to what a person is—his bodily shape, complexion, talents, capacities, and inclinations. But a person may still change by making efforts to achieve values and express his inherent virtues. The point is that any person can have "heart-mind" just as he can have "blood-breath," which defines his body. The heart-mind can work to remove difficulties and attain refinements.

Here Dai Zhen has made an important point about how one may improve and refine one's body as well as one's heart-mind. His insight is that one should not separate oneself from heaven and earth in the pursuit of life's activities: "Therefore one lives if one's *qi* does not separate from heaven and earth, and one becomes a sage if one's way does not separate from heaven and earth" (*Yuanshanzhong*). This is also a matter of nourishment (*yang*). One has to nourish one's form and *qi* by observing the natural course of growth and development and not yielding to selfishness or obscuration. This implies that one should find the right measure of satisfying one's desires and fulfilling one's emotions. In this regard Dai Zhen is more explicit than Mencius in asserting the significance of desires and feelings for *xing* (nature) even though they have a strong component of *ming* (limitation). But he agrees with Mencius that it is better to nourish one's heart-mind than one's "form-body," so that one will not only develop one's abilities and capacities of heart-mind by interacting with the creative powers of heaven and earth but will also establish a limit or a norm for desires and emotions, thus gaining genuine satisfaction and fulfillment.

Since both mind and body are based on *qi*, Dai Zhen conceives of them as a continuum. Body may have all kinds of desires, and heart may have all kinds of emotions, as determined by heaven and earth within its nature and limitations. Mind, however, can have knowledge and extend itself to attain a spiritual understanding of heaven and nature and can even come to perceive the heavenly virtues of heaven and earth. Dai Zhen made some useful suggestions about how to conceive of the heart-mind. First, he regards the functions of life as having several qualities or aspects: *hun* (active soul) and *bo* (inactive soul), reflecting the functions of heaven and earth, activity and rest; *hun* and *bo* in turn gives rise to subtle perception and penetration (*shen*) and subtle reception and absorption (*ling*). These qualities are the basis for becoming more clear-minded and insightful as the mind interacts with heaven and earth to acquire the central principles of *dao*.

We can, then, speak of knowledge of heavenly virtues (*tiande zhi zhi*) and develop the action of heaven and earth, which is benevolence. In other words, the human mind can function like heaven and earth in terms of their virtues and influences, and this means that a person will act like a sage and fulfill the inherent virtue of benevolence. That the human mind can itself reach benevolence is due to its having been nourished with knowledge of this heavenly virtue. Once the mind becomes aware of benevolence it also becomes aware of its own benevolence, and this awareness will, consequently, influence all bodily desires so that they will be enacted benevolently.

Another function of mind is the ability to discern patterns of nature that Dai Zhen calls "differentiated order" (*fenli*). Moreover, the mind can also come to perceive larger interrelationships that he calls "regularized patterns" (*tiaoli*). We may perhaps call *fenli* the microscopic order and *tiaoli* the macroscopic order of things. It is a function of mind to see both, and—for Dai—both are examples of *li*. Thus *li* is what the mind recognizes or understands in things, and in this understanding one sees the cognitive powers of the mind. We may call the *li* of nature the natural principles, and the *li* of recognition or cognition the principles of mind and intellect. Another category of *li* governs the human rather than the natural order: it is the common human feelings and emotions. One may discover these universal and reciprocal feelings by oneself, through reflection and self-examination. Therefore, this *li* can be described as the human principle of the heart.

With human principles, as with natural principles, we can discern microscopic and macroscopic aspects. It is in reference to the microscopic aspects of human principles that the name *tianli* (heavenly principles) is applied. In making this distinction, Dai Zhen holds that we can establish moral principles by reflection on people's common likes and dislikes, and thus when we speak of moral principles we are speaking not of a priori or abstract ideas but of something everyone can verify by reflection and can come to know through his own desires and sentiments.

In this way, Dai Zhen redefines human nature itself as a concrete reality, not an abstraction. He identifies four levels of human nature: (1) blood and (2) breath configure the organism; and (3) heart and (4) mind configure a unique entity of feeling, desiring, knowing, and acting. It is important to see these levels as intimately and inseparably connected because they are rooted in *yin-ying* and the five powers. This indicates that the human being, as a complex entity, can interact with the larger nature on any of its existential levels of *qi*; it also explains why any action or movement on one level can affect the other levels. Accordingly, Dai Zhen is able to argue that we should nourish our minds to become aware of the heavenly virtue of benevolence as inhering in heaven and earth, so that we can act from the level of heart and mind and prevent our desires and feelings from becoming uncontrolled. But this is not to say that we should not pay attention to desires and feelings—on the contrary, desires and feelings are essential for life. But their satisfaction or fulfillment must be framed in the whole structure of human nature so that they will not thrwart or overturn it. In essence, Dai Zhen argues for a unity of desire, feelings, human reason, and knowledge.

Fulfillment of Talents (*Cai*) and the Logic of Self-Cultivation

From Dai Zhen's theory of *qi* with regard to human nature, we can conclude that he objected to the Song-Ming view of human nature in terms of a duality of *li* and *qi*. The question remains, though, whether a naturalistic theory of human beings can rise to morality and explain how to become a sage. I consider this feasible, on the basis of moral reality or ontomorality, but the specific analysis needs to be worked out. One would need to ask what problems and pitfalls might prevent human nature from transforming into moral reason so that the human being could become a moral person.

When we consider the earlier theories of classical Confucianism and neo-Confucianism, we find that Dai Zhen draws more inspiration from Xunzi and Zhu Xi than from Mencius or the Lu-Wang school. Since he is focusing on the concrete nature of a person, he regards the fulfillment of one's nature (*jinxing*) as the fulfillment of one's talents (*jincai*). That is, *jinxing* is not a matter of knowing principles, extinguishing desires, intuiting global transcendent truth, and then contemplating that truth. It is a matter of seeking to put all one's talents to use—which implies using one's mind and heart as well. To do so, one must beware of selfishness (*si*) and mental obscuration (*bi*). This is where Xunzi comes in.

Dai Zhen considers selfishness and obscuration common troubles that originate in the heart-mind and result in actions. He calls mental selfishness "self-indulgence" (*ni*), suggesting that one is engrossed with a single desire, neglecting all other desires and functions of the mind. Self-indulgence will lead to partisanship, deception, irrationality, and secretiveness. The desire is kept in the dark and cannot face openness, the public, heaven, or earth. Dai says that obscuration starts as mental confusion or obsession (*huo*), suggesting that one is ignorant of things and situations but takes one's own bias or partial view as if it were a norm of truth and knowledge. Obscuration will lead to partiality, absurd conduct, stubbornness, and stupidity. In a vicious circle, selfishness and obscuration create moral errors and character flaws that in turn worsen selfishness and obscuration, and so on until one's character is degraded and one's nature is eroded—perhaps to the point of no return

Dai Zhen defines the Mencian idea of self-violation as "stupidity under selfishness" and the Mencian idea of self-abandonment as "stupidity under obscuration." This means that when a person has lost the understanding of his nature as a whole and is obsessed with a single desire or a partial view, he can regress slowly into depravity or evil. It is not that the person lacks the talent to do good; it is simply that he lacks the desire to do good, or the correct view of doing good, because his eyes have been clouded and his mind has been overwhelmed by his obsession. This is in essence what Mencius says about the "crime of talents." The ultimate cause of the crime is that one has not applied one's heart-mind, has lost his view of his nature, and has become incapable of controlling oneself.

How does one recover from selfishness and obscuration? The answer is that to overcome selfishness one should "strengthen one's caring for others" (*qiangshu*), and to overcome obscuration one should devote oneself to learning (*xue*). How can one start to care for others and love learning? Dai Zhen's answer is rather different from what is suggested in the *Analects*. He suggests acting on the basis of integrity (*zhong*) and truthfulness (*xin*) and thus becoming illuminated —learning in what goodness consists—instead of practicing filial piety and brotherly love. But I believe that Dai Zhen intends much the same thing as the *Analects*: to treat others caringly and fairly and to be considerate of their feelings. By acting with integrity and truthfulness one reaches benevolence (*ren*). Integrity means doing one's best to be good; truthfulness means practicing what one is clear about. *Shu* also means fair-mindedness, however; and according to Dai Zhen, it enables a person to attain propriety (*li*). This is somewhat odd—we would expect *shu* to be closer to *ren* than to *zhong*, which Dai considers as approaching *ren*. There is of course no difficulty in seeing that truthfulness is close to righteousness. Perhaps Dai Zhen considered *zhong* in terms of its direct appeal to self-awareness.

As noted earlier, Dai Zhen describes supreme goodness as consisting of three virtues: benevolence, righteousness, and propriety. It would appear that benevolence has to do with the heart, righteousness with the mind, and propriety with actions. These are the "accomplished virtues." Other virtues—like integrity, truthfulness, and care for others—are personal feelings that can be cultivated into accomplished virtues. Their cultivation involves removing selfishness and indulgence and means that still other virtues can ensue. For example, if a person is *zhong* and *xin* without deception, he is sincere. If he is *zhong*, he is close to easiness (*yi*). If he is *shu*, he is close to simplicity (*jian*). And *yi* and *jian* can be derived from *xin* in combination with other traits of the heart. This shows us that all the virtues are linked. One entails another; if we have one virtue, we have the next, and we eventually rise to moral constancy. By the same token, lack of one virtue entails lacking another, so that we eventually lapse into wrongdoing. This organic theory of virtues in practice is important in showing that they are not simple or isolated and that creative understanding allows us to apply the whole heart-mind to achieve the supreme goodness of our nature.

In light of this organic nature of virtues, Dai Zhen is able also to delineate the virtue of moral wisdom (*zhi*) as truthfulness and considerateness (*shu*)—again, this is not a simple matter; it requires the ability to perceive and apply all other virtues. With moral wisdom, then, a person will be able to enjoy obeying the *li*, the principles of righteousness. *Li* itself is a matter of moral consciousness and common human feelings, but to enjoy obeying it, by controlling one's selfish desires, requires being thoroughly inculcated with the virtues, and this is not possible without developing a comprehensive understanding of them and a flexible, practical ability to apply them. Hence we might regard moral wisdom as a combination of moral perspicuity and moral dexterity: the highest use of one's talents and hence a sign that one has fulfilled them. The result is that one can do the right thing, attain goodness untinged by selfishness or obscuration, and effortlessly manage one's genuine desire to fulfill one's true nature. Therefore, we can speak of moral spontaneity arising from one's nature.

In his last work, *Mengzi ziyi*, Dai Zhen says that selfishness is born from the error of desire and obscuration is born from the error of knowing. We have seen how he proposed to deal with the error of desire. With regard to how he would deal with the error of knowing, he does not elaborate on learning as a cure; but the importance of learning seems clear, and the process of learning also seems fairly understandable, from classical sources such as the *Analects* and the *Great Learning*. To learn is to learn reasons and principles so that one may respond to things and events and act correctly. This assumes that the human mind has the ability to recognize reasons and principles.

As noted above, reasons and principles are in things, not in the mind, but we do have the ability to recognize them and respond to them if we guard against the intrusion of private feelings and desires, subjective guesses, prejudices, and self-interest. Dai Zhen says: "That which would respond to things is the mind, but if the mind is beclouded (*bi*), then it would not be able to respond to them . . . [or] acquire reasons and principles of things" (*Mengzi ziyi*, section on *Li*, answer to question 9). But even if we are sure that we are open-minded and unprejudiced, we may be mistaken in thinking that we have knowledge; how, then, do we respond to things correctly, and how do we acquire reasons and principles?

In *Mengzi ziyi*, Dai Zhen dinstinguishes between *li* (reasons and principles of things) and *yijian* (opinions). *Li* must be a result of objective observation and careful analysis of concrete things and situations, whereas *yijian* is simply what one takes to be the case without critical self-examination. Dai Zhen describes *yijian* as sometimes being held so serious-mindedly and with such self-confidence that a person forgets that no matter how strong one's opinions are, they may still be wrong and partial. Epistemologically, this is indeed an unsolvable issue: how do I know that what I know may not be only my private idea? Dai Zhen suggests that one should "know all the affairs of the world" (*tong tianxia zhishi*). This view, combined with the requirement that one must not be clouded by ignorance and prejudice but must maintain clarity of mind, could provide a criterion for distinguishing *li* from *yijian*.

What Dai Zhen is getting to is his critique of the Song-Ming neo-Confucian view of *li*, which had persisted in his time and had led to disasters. The Song-Ming masters held that one does have *li* if the mind is not blinded or clouded (*bi*) by desires. Dai Zhen points out that they are sure their minds are not clouded if their thoughts are not derived from desires, and consequently they are sure their thoughts represent *li*. This logic would enable the Song-Ming masters to believe that their opinions or thoughts were *li* insofar they were not derived from desires. But this is questionable. Dai Zhen's clarification of the meaning of *li* and his theory of finding *fenli* and *tiaoli* in concrete things would set a standard whereby one could not take one's thoughts or opinions as *li* simply because they were without desire.

In this sense *yijian* are just as bad as selfish desires, for they are made the basis of judgments and actions that can have have the consequence of harming people and society. In fact, acting on opinions is even worse than acting on selfish desires, because if one acts on opinions one believes that one is doing the right thing—when in fact it is the wrong thing. Acting on opinions as if they were based on *li* gives a person in power an excuse to inflict calamity and injury with formal justification and therefore lends legitimacy to his wrongdoing. Sometimes people do this knowingly, but they are protected by the name of *li*. Sometimes, ironically, people do it unknowingly and feel that what they are doing is praiseworthy. In either case, Dai Zhen says, this is "to use *li* to kill people" (*yili sharen*). He concludes:

> For those who think that *li* lives in their minds and believe that judgments are either based on desires or based on *li*, oftentimes they may or may not realize that they have used their thoughts and self-opinions as *li* to bring disasters to the world. (*Mengzi ziyi*, entry on *Quan* preface)

This is indeed a sagacious critique of the neo-Confucian philosophy of *li*, but it is, even more, an incisive condemnation of those who abuse power by confusing their opinions with objective reasons and principles—or substituting their opinions for reasons and principles—and hence obscuring truth and reality.

See also *Li*: Principle, Pattern, Reason; Mencius; *Qi*; Reason and Principle; Wang Yangming: Rivals and Followers; Xunzi; *Yin* and *Yang*; Zhu Xi.

Bibliography

Cheng, Chung-ying, trans. *Tai Chen: Inquiry into Goodness*. Honolulu: East-West Center, 1968. (Translation of and introduction to *Yuanshan*.)

Ching, Ann-ping, and Mansfield Freeman. *Tai Chen on Mencius: Explorations in Words and Meaning: A Translation of the Meng Tzu tzu-I shu-cheng*. New Haven, Conn.: Yale University Press, 1990. (With a critical introduction.)

Dai Dongyuan quanji (Complete Works of Dai Dongyuan).

Mengzi ziyi suzheng quanyi (Complete Modern Language Translation of *Mengzi ziyi suzheng*), trans. Mao Huaixin. Bashu Publishing, 1992.

Dao (*Tao*): The Way

Chung-ying CHENG

The word from eastern philosophy that is perhaps best-known in the west is *dao*—the way, or the Way. It has an ancient history in Chinese civilization, a broad scope in Chinese philosophy, and an extraordinary depth of meaning. It is in fact the most basic term in Chinese philosophy, designating ultimate reality, truth, method, and the essence of all things. Why, then, is its literal meaning "way"? The answer is that the way things move and events take place cause or determine what they are or what they become. There is also a human aspect to the meaning of the way—the road that humans create by walking. Zhuangzi says that "the Way is what walking makes and things are what sayings represent."

Both objective and subjective meanings are essential to our understanding of the *dao*, and it must be recognized that the *dao* integrates both as well as transcends both. In this sense it is both the most metaphysical and the most commonplace concept, because it can refer simultaneously to the invisible and the visible, the transcendent and the immanent, the internal and the external, the changing and the unchanging (the constant, *chang*), the large and the small, the near and the far. That *dao* can comprehend all these, and can be shown to comprehend them all, is precisely why the term has been so enduringly attractive. The concept of *dao* has been put to creative use, and the reality of *dao* has been invoked to attain creative power. This is the core philosophy of the *dao*, developed in the Daoism of Laozi and Zhuangzi; germinated in, and informing, the ancients' experience of the world as recorded in the *Yijing* (*Book of Change*); and articulated and explicated in the *Yizhuan* (*Commentaries of Change*). Before we discuss these traditions, it will be helpful to summarize or characterize the concept of the *dao*, as follows:

1. *Dao* is the whole of nature and the whole universe, as shown in our experiences of natural things. *Dao* envelops nature as a whole and produces nature as a whole.
2. *Dao* is thus the process in which the whole of nature manifests itself and the process in which and by which things are created or procreated and nature is manifested. The process is the way, and the way is the process.
3. *Dao* is the origin and source of the process of change and the creation of things. This origin and source is regarded as infinite, and its generative power as inexhaustible. Hence *dao* is a creative power that creates by sustaining and sustains by creating.
4. Because the *dao* embodies the way things are created and the way events change, it can represent laws, limitations, or destiny—which things must obey and follow.
5. Although it transcends time and place, the *dao* remains a concrete presence in things as a whole. It is as dynamic as any actual event or object. And things and events—in order to function as things and events—must not be separate from the *dao*.

This characterization suggests that the *dao* has both ontological and cosmological qualities, and that these qualities interpenetrate each other. In other words, the list above indicates an ontocosmological philosophy or, simply, ontocosmology of the *dao*. In tracing this ontocosmology, we must recognize the equal contributions of the *Yijing* from antiquity and the *Daodejing* of Laozi.

To begin, we can see how the *Yijing* (*Book of Change*) comes to take change (*yi*) as the essence of nature and things in nature and formulates this comprehensive observation by using solid and broken lines to symbolize the forces of change in various pairs of opposites: strength and weakness, firmness and softness, brightness and darkness. In this formulation, change finally comes to suggest an interchange of creativeness and receptiveness. On the basis of these two modes of change, the symbolism in the *Yijing* presents orderly but dynamic patterns of change in terms of the unity and polarity of complementary opposites; thus transformation is manifested as, say, ups and downs, or compensation and return. It further suggests that in the process of producing things and generating life, change is unbounded and unending.

In the *Xici* commentary on the *Yijing*, which was formed in the early Warring States period, the *dao* of *yi* is explicitly described as the "alternation and exchange of *yin* and *yang*" (*yi yin yi yang zhiwei dao*); and *yin* and *yang* are characterized in various places as rest and motion, softness and firmness, darkness and brightness, closing (*xi*) and opening (*pi*). As the process of change is seen as a creative process of formation and transformation of things, the alternation and exchange of *yin* and *yang* would be creative actions in reality. What, then, is this reality? The *Xici* suggests the concept of *taiji* (the "great ultimate") as representing the source of creative change, for it is the *taiji* that gives rise to *yin* and *yang*. It seems natural to conclude that *taiji* is the *dao* as a source of reality, and the *dao* is *taiji* as the process of reality. Both aspects of the *dao*—source and process—are developed in the *Xici*. Exactly what is the reality that would have these aspects remains unanswered. But perhaps the question can be addressed in terms of the *dao* of *yi*: "The spiritual has no location and the change has no substance." This means that reality is simply experienced as a process of change, and there is nothing which is ultimately identifiable as the substance of change.

But when we come to *Daodejing* in the fifth century B.C.E., we come to a view based on the "change of the *dao*" (*dao zhi yi*), distinguishable from the view in the *Yijing* based on the "*dao* of the change" (*yi zhi dao*). The *Daodejing* focuses, for the first time, on *dao* as the substance of a philosophical discourse. A mark of this turnabout is consciousness of the indefinability and ineffability of the *dao* as an object of thinking even though *dao* as a term can be meaningful. No characterization can fully capture *dao*: the *dao* would immediately transcend any characterization, so that it would not be identified with any thing or any aspect of things in the world. In this sense *dao* is simply no-thing, beyond our conceptualization or delimitation.

In this analysis, the apparent paradox "The *dao* that can be spoken is not the constant *dao*," from the *Daodejing*, is not really paradoxical: it simply points out a fact or logical inference about our power to conceptualize and our resulting linguistic formulations. Our language and mental concepts are not able to represent or grasp the essence and source of reality, because referential or conceptual thinking is based on demarcation and delimitation, which are in turn based on reification or on objects and exclude wholeness and self-reflection. That is a built-in feature of our thinking, and hence a constant feature of self-reference. But the intended meaning of *dao* must appeal to, and integrate, the whole of reality and cannot exclude the self in language or thought. This is not to say that *dao* does not include things we can think and speak about. In fact, the *dao* which is unspeakable includes the *dao* which we can speak because it includes our language—and our language does make references and becomes meaningful precisely because of the presence of the unspeakable *dao* as an "unconditional condition."

In the *Daodejing* we see how in Laozi's ontocosmology the *dao* is the very beginning of the beginning of heaven, earth, and the things of the world. As *dao* eludes language, it precedes heaven and the totality of actualities as oneness. Laozi uses the word "void" (*wu*) to describe the transcending but yielding and ever-creative force of the *dao*. But this does not mean that *dao* is nothingness in the sense of recession or regression. "Void" is better conceived as suggesting infinite and infinitely various creativity, which Zhuangzi later elaborates.

Another important contribution of the *Daodejing* is that it introduces a dialectic of the *dao* in terms of which we see how things originate from *dao*, thrive in *dao*, and then return to *dao*. Here, the Daoist principles of nonaction and receptivity and return are not only made explicit but also applied to individual persons and states, for a better conducting of human life and a better governing of communities. In other words, we find a formulation of the ethics and politics of the *dao* apart from an aesthetics of the *dao*.

Although we can identify differences between the *Daodejing* and the *Yijing* and *Yizhuan*, they appear to share the dialectics of *yin* and *yang*. Whereas the *Yijing* incorporates *yin-yang* into its ontocosmology of change, the *Daodejing* seems to apply this idea to individual things, particularly human beings.

When we come to Zhuangzi, the *dao* becomes more individuated and individualized. Perhaps in Zhuangzi's time the concept of *dao* had become too abstract or remote and people had lost their understanding of it as an intimate principle, an embodiment, and a practice—as the original *Dedaojing* suggests. (The "Mawangdui silk manuscripts" of Laozi, 1973, show that the *Dejing* precedes the *Daojing*; hence the notion of a *Dedaojing* distinct from the received *Daodejing* derived from the Heshanggong text in the early Han period.) Zhuangzi focuses on the *dao* as the nature in processes and things in transition. He speaks of the *dao* in concrete, mundane things like sand and dung. His point is simply that there is nothing that is not the *dao*, because *dao* is both the one and the many at the same time.

The interpenetration of the *dao* among things (*dao tongyu yi*) enables him to speak of "knowing the happiness of the fish" in his famous conversation with the logician Hui Shi in *Qiwulun*. Because of this interpenetrative aspect of the *dao*, the human mind not only can know the feelings of things in nature but is able to see things from the viewpoint of the *dao* and act in the world in the spirit of the *dao*. In order to do this, one has to transcend the tendency to conceptualize things and free from oneself from bias, emotions, logic, and argument. Bias and emotions confine us to a narrow range of understanding and interests; logic and argument entangle us in regression and contradictions. True knowledge comes from transcending our emotions and our knowledge. In this sense Zhuangzi initiates a state of mind that would be described by the Chan Buddhists of a later period as "enlightenment" or "awakening" (*wu*).

This means that one has to become a "true person" (*zhenren*) before one has true knowledge (*zhenzhi*). Zhuangzi's concepts of "resolution of the ultimate" (*di zhi xuanjie*) and "by-illumination" (*yiming*) are very close to and indeed may have inspired the Chan Buddhist notion of "sudden enlightenment." If we can achieve awakening, we will be liberated from emotion and knowledge and thus attain an internal spiritual freedom of the mind, identified with the *dao*. In this sense a human being may realize the creative power of self-transformation and transformations of things without being disturbed by death or harm. This approach no doubt makes the philosophy of the *dao* more practical for human life because it brings the *dao* closer to our experience of nature and ourselves.

Finally, we may point out that in Zhuangzi the philosophy of the *dao* comes close to a philosophy of *qi*. In many places Zhuangzi suggests images of breathing, of earth, of floods to reach an understanding the natural state of the *dao*. This leads one to expect Zhuangzi to speak explicitly of the *dao* as the way of change of the *qi*. He does not, but the reader cannot help feeling that there is no better illustration of *dao* than the movements of *qi*.

Lest we think that *dao* is exclusively a Daoist concept, we must also consider Confucian and neo-Confucian thought. In general, whereas the Daoists concentrate on the external and transcendent aspects of *dao*, the Confucians and neo-Confucian concentrate on its internal and immanent aspects. For a Confucian or neo-Confucian philosopher, *dao* is a humanist concept that represents the human approach to reality and truth as well as the humanist ideal of perfection, virtue, and the well-being of a society or state. To quote from the *Doctrine of the Mean* (*Zhongyong* or *Zhong Yong*): "The *dao* is such that [a human being] cannot be separated from it for a single moment. If [a person] can be separated from it, it is not the *dao*." It is clear that humanity is seen as embodying *dao*, and the ultimate purpose of life as fulfilling *dao*. Thus Confucius says: "It is the human person who can glorify the *dao*, it is not the *dao* which can glorify the person" (*Analects*, 15.28).

The point of this statement is that since a human embodies *dao*, we fulfill ourselves as humans when we glorify *dao*; otherwise, what is the point of being human? For Confucius, *dao* is no less than the "*dao* of the human person" (*ren zhi dao*), distinct from simply the "*dao* of heaven" (*tian zhi dao*) that engages the Daoists. Thus although Confucius and Laozi both use *dao* independently as a single term, their references are very different.

In the *Analects* Confucius, further, speaks of *dao* as threaded with unity. What is the Confucian way or the *dao* of the human being? How does it possess unity? In the first place, a human being must live by striving for moral perfection; this involves cultivating virtue (*de*). Without this cultivation of virtue we would not be able to fulfill our humanity, and our world would suffer a loss of community, social order, and harmony. What is called virtue is the power or ability to bring well-being and dignity to oneself and one's community. More specifically, the virtue of humanity consists in loving people and treating them with considerateness and compassion. Confucius calls such a virtue *ren* and defines it as "not to do others what you would not want others to do to you."

On the basis of *ren* (variously translated as "human goodness," "common humanity," etc.), a person would do the right thing, act gracefully, and relate to others in a correct manner and with propriety and respect. *Ren* is the source of all social virtues that characterize amicable, trustworthy human relationships. But no social virtue is possible unless one first reflects on oneself, knows how to empathize with others, and can restrain one's feelings and desires. Other aspects of *ren* are manifested in efforts to establish harmony between people through the proprieties (*li*), and to help others develop into virtuous persons. These too are essential to a full understanding of the virtue of *ren* and consequently of the way of humanity.

It must be pointed out that for Confucius the human way is still related to the way of heaven—for without the provisions and mandate of heaven (*tianming*), how could a person practice moral cultivation or aspire to moral perfection? However, the inner link between the way of heaven and the way of man is a profound relationship, not easily understood. One must realize that to fulfill the human way is precisely to fulfill the way of heaven, because humans are destined to carry out the enterprise of being human as endowed by heaven. The *Doctrine of the Mean* makes this amply clear: "What heaven ordains is the nature [of the human]; to follow one's nature through is the way [of the human]." Therefore, to know oneself is to know one's nature, which is to know human destiny and the mandate of heaven, which in turn is to know the way of heaven. In acting out one's nature, one fulfills the human way and at the same time the way of heaven. This is how Mencius comes to speak of human nature (*xing*) as the basis of human destiny.

Mencius concludes that to know one's nature (*zhixing*) is to know heaven (*zhitian*). How does one know one's nature? One cannot know it unless one engages in self-reflection so as to know the heart-mind (*xin*) and act it out according to one's nature. One's nature, since it comes from heaven, contains the seeds of moral goodness—the seeds of the virtues necesssary for self-fulfillment and familial and social harmony.

Mencius argues strongly for the goodness of human nature—not just (as some people believe) for a natural inclination toward moral actions. If human nature were not good in some fundamental sense, humans would not act morally or do good deeds for society or humanity as a whole. This is a vivid and practical understanding of the way of humanity as a continuous process of self-cultivation of human nature in order to understand the way of heaven, which consists in the fulfillment of the way of humanity. The *Great Learning* defines a complete program for self-cultivation aimed at fulfillment of the human way, beginning with acquiring knowledge and motivating the human will and going on to pacifying and harmonizing the whole world. In the same spirit, Mencius has laid down a plan for the achievement of a good society by a sage-king who knows the human way.

A question may arise regarding the nature of heaven in the classical Confucian texts. Without going into detail, we can say that for Confucius heaven has some of the features of a personal God. But when we move to *Zhongyong* and *Daxue*, heaven has become less personal; it is the larger nature of the cosmos. In fact, heaven becomes simply the way of change (*yi*) through the influence of the later Confucius and his grandson Zisi, as is revealed in the "bamboo manuscripts" of Guodian. Mencius simply identifies it with human destiny (*ming*), which is a delimitation of human life within the overall reality of nature. In Xunzi heaven is fully nature, so that he can challenge us to know and control heaven by way of knowledge and rational investigation. For neo-Confucianism of the Song-Ming period, heaven becomes "principle of heaven" or "reason of heaven" (*tianli*). Eventually, it comes to be identified with *li* (principle, reason) alone in Cheng Yi and Zhu Xi, or with human heart-mind (*xin*) in Lu Xiangshan and Wang Yangming. Hence the *dao* of the human being is finally realized in the human understanding of principles and reasons of things and minds.

We may conclude that the notion of *dao* is different in the Daoist and Confucian approaches. But despite the obvious differences between them, they share an ontocosmology of the *dao* influenced by the philosophy of the *Yijing*. Whereas Daoists want to transcend humanity by contemplating and imitating the *dao*, Confucians insist on transforming humanity by knowing it, and following on toward the *dao*. In either perspective, we may note, *dao* is profoundly different from the orthodox Christian concept of God or even from common usage of the term "God" in the west. It is interesting to see how these two fundamental concepts may interact in defining the human being and ultimate reality in today's philosophical dialogues between the Chinese and the west.

See also Confucianism: Confucius; Confucianism: Texts in Guodian Bamboo Slips; Daoism: Texts in Guodian Bamboo Slips; Laozi; Mencius; Philosophy of Change; *Qi*; *Ren*; Zhuangzi.

Bibliography

Yijing, Daodejing, Zhuangzi, Lunyu, Daxue, Zhongyong, Mengzi, and *Xunzi*. (Classical texts.)

Ames, Roger. "Tao and the Nature of Nature." *Environmental Ethics*, 8, 1986, pp. 317–350.

Berling, Judith A. "Taoism, or the Way." *Focus on Asian Studies*, 2(1), 1982, pp. 9–11.

Chan, Wing-tsit. *A Source Book in Chinese Philosophy*. Princeton, N.J.: Princeton University Press, 1963.

Cheng, Chung-ying. "Metaphysics of Tao and Dialectics of Fa: An Evaluation of HTSC in Relation to Lao Tzu and Han Fei and an Analytical Study of Interrelationships of Tao, Fa, Hsing, Ming, and Li." *Journal of Chinese Philosophy*, 10(3), 1983, pp. 251–285.

Creel, Herrlee G. *Confucius and the Chinese Way*. New York, 1960.

Danto, Arthur C. "Language and the Tao: Some Reflections on Ineffability." *Journal of Chinese Philosophy*, 1(1), pp. 45–55.

Fu, Charles Wei-hsun. "Lao-tzu's Conception of Tao." *Inquiry*, 16, 1973, pp. 367–394.

Fung, Yu-lan. *A Short History of Chinese Philosophy*, trans. Derk Bodde, Vol. 1. 1948.

Granet, Marcel. *La pensée chinoise*. Paris, 1950. (Reprint of 1934 ed.)

Hansen, Chad D. *A Daoist Theory of Chinese Thought: A Philosophical Interpretation*. New York, 1992.

"Special Issue on Dao and God." *Journal of Chinese Philosophy*, 29(1), 2002.

Wang, Bi. "Annotations on Laozi daodejing," "Annotations on Zhouyi." In *Wang Pi Ji Xiao Yi*, 2 vols., annot. Lou Yulie. Beijing, 1980.

Wilhelm, Richard. "On the Sources of Chinese Taoism." *Journal of the North China Branch of the Royal Asiatic Society*, 45, 1914, pp. 1–9.

Yates, Robin D. S. *Five Lost Classics: Tao, Huang-Lao, and Yin-Yang in Han China*. New York, 1997.

Daoism (Taoism): Classical (*Dao Jia, Tao Chia*)

Vincent SHEN

By "classical Daoism" we understand the thought that was first founded by Laozi (sixth century B.C.E.) and further developed by Zhuangzi (c. 375–300 B.C.E.) in pre-Qin China. It is distinguished from the syncretic Daoism of Huainanzi (d. 122 B.C.E.) and the neo-Daoism developed in the Wei-Jin dynasties. Concerning Liezi, who appeared (probably) in the fifth century B.C.E., it should be said that the works which carried his name were completed much later, probably in the fourth century C.E. For that reason, we will deal only with Laozi and Zhuangzi, who, responding to the social and cultural problems of their times, proposed their systems of thought as mature fruits of speculative philosophy.

It should be noted that these two thinkers envisaged different "interlocutors," emphasized different philosophical problems, and wrote in different philosophical styles. Laozi, who preferred spiritual solitude and wrote in the style of a monologue, took Confucianism as his implicit interlocutor. Zhuangzi, by contrast, took the school of names, especially Hui Shi, as his interlocutor, emphasized the philosophy of language, and proposed a discourse enriched by metaphors, parables, and historical and fictional narratives in addition to rigorous argumentation. Yet they had a common interest in the ultimate reality, the *dao*—its natural unfolding in cosmic processes and in human life.

Laozi, His Times, and His Interlocutor

Over its history, Laozi has given Chinese culture its most profoundly speculative philosophical thought. Although his ideas are expressed succinctly, in a text of only slightly more than 5,000 Chinese characters, their penetrating wisdom offers all readers, from east to west, an understanding of the Chinese way of thinking and Chinese culture in general.

Laozi's concept of *dao* was proposed as a solution to a sociopolitical and spiritual crisis. Through his criticism, developed from a profound "life praxis" (a term that will be discussed below), he established a paradigm for social and ideological critiques. His writing on the *dao* and the *de* (virtue), the *Daodejing*, reveals to us, when we give it a careful hermeneutic reading, an image of a society undergoing radical change. On one hand, we find a disintegration of the ancient Chinese social order constituted by *Zhouli*, that is, the social institutions and political-religious rites of the Zhou dynasty. On the other hand, new social dynamics were emerging, but these had not been stabilized as a new social order and thus did not offer a way out. It was in response to the society of his time and the ethics of Confucianism that Laozi's classical Daoism emerged as a meditative practice, and hence a fundamental trait of Chinese thinking and of the Chinese attitude toward life and society.

To Laozi's eyes, society was in a state of disorder:

> The people suffer because their rulers eat up too much in taxes. That is why they starve. The people become difficult to govern, because those in authority have too many projects of action. That is why they are difficult to govern. The people take death lightly, because their rulers have too many desires. (ch. 75)

It seems that, for Laozi, social problems were produced by rulers' political domination rather than by a disproportion between desired values and means of realization. He saw *Zhouli*, the most important cultural institution in ancient China, as nothing but a form of domination, hindering and distorting man's communication with nature, with other men, and, most important, with the *dao*. Laozi's writings suggest that the social disorder of his time was a result of this distortion of free, natural communication by various forms of domination.

In Laozi's texts are shown, also, the vehment interstate conflicts that led to military actions and unceasing wars. He said, "When the *dao* does not prevail in the world, warhorses have to breed on the border" (ch. 46). He also said, "Wherever armies are stationed, briers and thorns become rampant. Great wars are inevitably followed by famines" (ch. 30). And:

> The weapons of war are instruments of evil and they are detested by people. . . . War should be regarded as a mournful occasion. When multitudes of people are slaughtered, it should be an occasion for the expression of bitter grief. Even when a victory is scored, the occasion should be observed with funeral ceremonies. (ch. 31)

In this social disintegration, seductive new elements tended to emerge, influencing many a man's intellectual activities and desires. As the clan laws (*zongfa*) and "well-field" (*jingtian*) institutions gradually disappeared, there arose a semicommercial society. To escape the calamities of war, people left the land and devoted themselves to commerce, and this intensified their desire for goods and their lust for material success. Laozi discerned the new signs of the time: "There may be gold and jade to fill a hall, but there is none who keeps them. To be overbearing when one has honor and wealth is to bring calamity upon oneself" (ch. 9). "Do not exalt the worthy, so that people shall not compete. Do not display objects of desire, so that people's hearts shall not be disturbed" (ch. 3).

Laozi's texts show us a world in which social mobility had developed to a point where people of low origin could become high-ranking officials. People struggled for fame and position. Intellectuals rendered services to political power and became instruments of political domination. People sacrificed their spiritual freedom for their lustful desires and instrumental rationality.

Laozi was not only a social critic but also a critic of ideology, especially Confucian ethics. This is what I mean by saying that Confucianism was Laozi's implicit interlocutor. Confucianism, of course, is a main current of Chinese philosophy; it offers many insights and should not be treated as a mere ideology. Yet it could have an ideological function when it was applied to maintain social order and serve political purposes. Confucius himself had tried to revitalize the ancient social order instituted by *Zhouli*, by translating its ideal meaning into the concept of *ren* (benevolence, goodness). *Ren* represents an intimate, sensitive connection between man's inner self and nature, other men, and heaven. *Ren* manifests human subjectivity and responsibility in and through moral awareness. From the concept of *ren*, Confucius derived the ethical significance of *yi*, which represented for him moral rightness or fittingness; duties, as well as the consciousness of duties; and the virtue of acting according to duty. From *yi* Confucius derived the ethical significance of *li*, which represented codes of behavior, religious and political ceremonies, and social institutions. In this way, Confucius sought to reconstitute the ethical and social order once realized in *Zhouli*.

In Laozi's criticism, the *li*, as a code of behavior and social institutions, represented merely formalistic constraints devoid of any positive meaning. Laozi considered such codes and institutions means of social domination from which man needed to be emancipated in order to regain his free existence. He said:

> It is only when the *dao* is lost that the *de* (virtue, power) arises. When the *de* is lost, only then does *ren* arise. When *ren* is lost, only then does *yi* arise. When *yi* is lost, only then does *li* arise. *Li* is the superficial expression of loyalty and faithfulness, and the beginning of disorder. (ch. 38)

Laozi criticized all means of domination: to him, they resulted from losing the deep sense of the link between all men with the *dao*, and they immobilized the spontaneous virtue of each individual. Thus the Confucian *ren*, *yi*, and *li* were merely alienated forms of spontaneous human virtue and its ontological origin, the *dao*. To Laozi, Confucian ethics as a solution to the problems of the time presented the following difficulties:

1. Confucian ethics emphasized deliberate human action taken with anthropocentric self-consciousness. Thus Confucians were inclined to neglect human spontaneity and its roots in the *dao*. Laozi proposed, as the real solution, a mindless spontaneous creativity springing from the *dao* itself. Any course of action that separated human life from the *dao* lost its source of creativity and tended to be artificial.
2. Without the creative support of the *dao* and the spontaneous unfolding of the *de*, the transcendental base of Confucian ethics, which grounded *li* in *yi* and *yi* in *ren*, tended toward degeneration. *Ren* would degenerate into *yi* and *yi* into *li*. *Li*, separated thereby from its ontological and transcendental foundations, even when supported by instrumental rationality, could still be determined by lustful desire and therefore cause social conflict.
3. The social disorder and the commercial civilization created by lustful desire and calculative intellect would not be improved by the Confucian revitalization of *Zhouli*, because the hearts of people, according to Laozi, inclined toward freedom and creativity and wanted to be emancipated from any constraints.

For these reasons, Confucian ethics, in Laozi's eyes, could not be an adequate solution to the problems of his times. In fact, these sociopolitical crises—and Confucian ideology itself—were a consequence of having forgotten the *dao*. People needed a way out; for Laozi, an authentic way out consisted in returning to and following the *dao*. Confucianism could not offer that. Its ideological tendency had to be counteracted by ultimately referring to each being's spontaneity—the *de*—and the source of all creativity, the *dao*.

Laozi's cultural critique led him to think of a way out for a society in crisis. His critique of Confucian ethics led him to deny Confucianism as an adequate way out or solution, and to replace its conceptual framework of *ren-yi-li* with the emancipating philosophy of *dao-de*. His main argument consisted in pointing out that the human heart by nature tended toward liberation. Hence, any adequate solution must be capable of leading people back to their spontaneous creativity, *de*; and their ontological origin, *dao*.

The concept of *dao* is central to classical Daoism. This Daoist concept was original in Chinese intellectual history in the sense that it replaced the traditional—and especially Confucian—concept *tian* (heaven) as the ultimate principle of reality. *Tian* was the core concept representing ultimate reality, either as a personal God or as the highest principle, in the tradition of the *Shijing*, the *Shangshu*, and other classics of primordial Confucianism. As such, it was the foundation of the conceptual system of *ren-yi-li*. But in a troubled age like Laozi's, it was difficult for people to believe naively in either an impartial personal "God" or a highest moral principle that could render justice or alleviate their unending suffering. Therefore, Laozi came to interpret *tian* as "nature," as the locus where all things appear (as in the case of *tiandi*), and as the law of nature (as in the case of *tiandao*). Laozi saw all these as derivative manifestations of the *dao*, which alone was the ultimate reality. Human beings, together with all other things in heaven and earth, were but manifestations of the *dao* and had to return to the *dao*. The relation between the *dao* and man replaced the traditional anthropocentric, humanistic relation between *tian* and man. This implies a fundamental change in the metaphysics and philosophy of man in ancient China.

By the same token, Laozi's concept of *de* replaced the Confucian concept of *xing* (human nature), which he never used in his texts. Accordingly, for Laozi any idea of human nature was to be integrated into a global concept of the spontaneous nature of all beings. *De* represented the spontaneous virtue of every being begotten by the *dao* in a self-differentiating process. *De* remained in the innermost constitution of every being after it was differentiated into the "myriad things" and remained there as spontaneous virtue. This affirmation replaced the Confucian formula stated in *The Doctrine of the Mean*: "What Heaven imparts to man is called human nature" (*xing*). Laozi would say, rather, that what the *dao* imparted to all beings was their virtue, *de*. In form, these two statements are similar, but their emphases are quite different. The Confucian formula was anthropocentric and humanistic, although it recognized *tian* as the ontological foundation of man. In the Daoist formula, there was nothing anthropocentric or humanistic. It took the spontaneous virtue of all beings as the necessary mediator between the *dao* and man. Thus man had to recognize his link to, or unity with, all things. Laozi said, "The *dao* produces them. The *de* fosters them. Matter gives them physical form. Circumstances and tendencies achieve them" (ch. 51). Man and all things, then, shared the same metaphysical structure and the same destiny. Man should not dominate or exploit other beings as means or as objects or servants. Instead, he should treat them as mediators between him and *dao*.

Daoist virtue was therefore very different from the Confucian moral virtues such as *ren*, *yi*, and *li*. For Laozi, the sage had to achieve the spontaneous virtue imparted by the *dao* to all beings. Laozi called this achieved authentic virtue "profound virtue," "eternal virtue," "superior virtue," or "great virtue."

Zhuangzi and His Interlocutor

Zhuangzi was the second most important figure in classical Daoism. From the account of his life by Sima Qian (c. 145–89 B.C.E.) in *Records of the Historian,* three things seem certain. First, although we do not know the precise dates of his birth and death, Zhuangzi, named Zhou, lived at the time of King Hui (370–319 B.C.E.) of Liang and King Xuan (320–302 B.C.E.) of Qi. Second, he once served as low official in a lacquer garden. Third, he inherited the basic philosophy of Laozi, had very broad learning, and was said to have written works amounting to some 100,000 words. These works were divided, when Guo Xiang (d. 312 C.E.) compiled them, into three parts: seven "inner chapters," fifteen "outer chapters," and eleven "miscellaneous chapters." Only the seven inner chapters could be considered authentic, and even in these the origin of some paragraphs remains dubious.

Zhuangzi's philosophical position can be understood in contrast to the philosophy of Hui Shi and the school of names in general. As I have noted, if Confucianism was Laozi's implicit interlocutor, then Zhuangzi's was Hui Shi or the school of names. Hui Shi, although older than Zhuangzi, was a very good friend, and Zhuangzi considered him a worthy counterpart. According to legend, Zhuangzi grieved very much when Hui Shi died, even to the point of deciding henceforth to hold his tongue. Zhuangzi once said, "Since the death of Master Hui Shi, I have no counterpart for discussion. There has been nobody to talk with" (*xu wu gui*). Zhuangzi and Hui Shi debated about life and death, about relations among things, about whether it is necessary for ideas to have any practical use, about knowing or not knowing what a fish enjoyed. In these debates, Zhuangzi used metaphors, parables, historical or fictional narratives, and arguments to criticize Hui Shi and to convey his own philosophy. He shared with Hui Shi an interest in the philosophy of language; this may explain why, despite his presumption of the negative function of language, he wrote so much—more than twenty times as much as Laozi.

In criticizing Hui Shi, Zhuangzi reveals his own position. First, Zhuangzi criticized Hui Shi for seeking empirical data and causal explanations, and for using formal logic and semantics in arguments. Zhuangzi considered these devices superficial if they were used without tracing human experience back to the point where it met the *dao*, the origin of all origins. Zhuangzi preferred to enlarge the realm of human experience by appealing to the function of the imagination and to the metaphorical use of language.

Second, Zhuangzi criticized Hui Shi for "self-misunderstanding" in his preoccupation with the external world and in his forgetting to turn back to the *dao*. Zhuangzi urged a return to self-understanding through praxis, the processes of life. Praxis is, as the term implies, practical; it is a process in time. Thus Zhuangzi would appeal to the hermeneutic function of reason; through a creative interpretation of traditional texts, words, and deeds of a paradigmatic individual (Cua 1978, ch. 3), the human mind could be awakened to self-understanding.

Third, Zhuangzi criticized Hui Shi for indulging in "instrumental rationality," which clung to political power and impeded self-awareness and self-understanding. Zhuangzi wanted the human mind to be disengaged from all the dangers of instrumental rationality; he wanted to deconstruct all human achievement for the sake of the infinite *dao*. He would appeal to the negative or deconstructive function of human discourse in order to liberate the human mind from all instrumental rationality and finite achievements.

To free the human mind from its imprisonment in empirical and logical levels of meaning, Zhuangzi used fables—a kind of metaphorical discourse—to wake the human mind to the realm of possibilities and to sever it from all realistic attachments. To transcend the unending inquiry in the external world leading to self-misunderstanding, he used a dialogical, interpretive discourse. Such a discourse would lead to self-understanding through a fusion of new horizons with the tradition constituted of the texts, deeds, and words of the elders. To disengage the mind from instrumental rationality, he used a negative or deconstructive discourse; this would detach the mind from all situated accomplishments and finite systems, letting it open itself to the infinite creativity of *dao*.

Laozi's and Zhuangzi's Conceptions of *Dao* and Cosmogony

The *dao* in Laozi's and Zhuangzi's thought is equally unfathomable and unnameable. Nevertheless, both Laozi and Zhuangzi tried to attribute some characteristcis to the *dao* so as to help people understand it.

For Laozi, the *dao*, as the ultimate reality, was an undifferentiated whole, inaudible, invisible, independent of all beings, self-subsisting, boundless, great, far off but turning back, in a circular cosmic process. For Zhuangzi, the *dao* was, negatively speaking, invisible, inaudible, without action, without form, and incapable of being appropriated. Positively speaking, the *dao* was real, credible, self-dependent, prior in existence, the ultimate cause of all things, infinite in space and time, pervading all existent things. In this regard the most important difference between them had to do with infinity. For Laozi, the *dao*, though boundless in space, was yet asymmetrically finite and infinite; that is, the future was infinite but the past was somehow finite—there must be some beginning in time. For Zhuangzi, the *dao* was infinite in both space and time, so that it could unfold infinitely rich possibilities. (Zhuangzi's concept that both space and time were infinite can be considered a real philosophical advance.) It should be always kept in mind, however, that Laozi and Zhuangzi described these attributes reluctantly, as merely instrumental for human understanding.

The *dao*, as the original, self-manifesting ultimate reality, must have a tendency to manifest itself. According to Laozi, the *dao* manifested itself through two ontological "moments": the *you* and the *wu*. *You*, as being, signified the moment of manifestation, realization, actuality, fulfillment, and bodies. *Wu*, as nonbeing, did not represent sheer nothingness; it signified, rather, the moment of dissimulation, possibility, potentiality, transcendence, and functionality. According to Laozi, the *dao* manifested itself first as possibilities, as nothingness; then, among all possibilities, some were realized, and to be realized was to be embodied. At this moment, the *dao* was engendered into a realm of being. Therefore we can say that the possible is infinitely richer than the real, and nonbeing is infinitely vaster than being. In terms of ontology, there is what might be called a scarcity of being relative to nonbeing. In other words, nonbeing—the possible—is rich, whereas being, the real, is scant. Laozi then expounded cosmogony as a process of complex self-differentiation, and the *dao* as manifesting itself into opposites: being and nonbeing, *yin* and *yang*, movement and rest, and so forth. From the dialectical interaction of these opposites, all things were produced. This process is expressed in the following text:

> The *dao* gave birth to the One, the One gave birth to the two, and the two gave birth to the three, and the three gave birth to ten thousand things. Ten thousand things carry the *yin* and embrace the *yang*, and through the blending of *qi*, they achieve harmony. (ch. 42)

Zhuangzi recognized this cosmogony in principle, but through his philosophical reflections on language he set some limit on it. Since the human capacity to talk about cosmogony was intimately related to the capacity for language, the issue of cosmic origins was to be treated with the origin of language. He says in *On Making All Things Equal*:

> Since all things are one, how can there be anything to say? Since I said all things are one, how can there be nothing said? One and saying make two, two and one make three. Going on in this way, even the cleverest mathematicians couldn't get it, how much less an ordinary person. Therefore, if from nonbeing to being we proceed to three, how much farther shall we reach when we proceed from being to beings?

This text can be read as Zhuangzi's interpretation of Laozi's cosmogony (in ch. 42) through the origin of language, which implies that our capacity to talk about cosmogony is limited by our linguistic capacity. This idea is developed further in the chapter *Zi yang*:

> That there is some first cause (of the universe), or that no first cause would make it, these are the ultimate presuppositions our doubt could arrive at. When I look for its origin, the past is without limit; when I look for its end, the future is without end. Without limit and end, it is the absence of words, because words share the same principle as things. That there is some first cause (of the universe), or that no first cause would make it, these speculations were based on words, which begin and end with things. *Dao* as a name is borrowed as an expedient. To presuppose either a first cause or no first cause is but one limited corner of things; what do they have to do with the great *dao*?

Here, we can see, Zhuangzi proposed an antinomy: a theory of the first cause (of the universe) and a theory of no first cause. He solved it by arguing as follows: the *dao* is infinite, and it transcends all things; our language can express and discuss only things, not the *dao*; theories about the *dao* as first cause or no first cause are limited and biased by our language.

Laozi's and Zhuangzi's Conceptions of the Perfect Man

Concerning philosophical anthropology, both Laozi and Zhuangzi set up the idea of a perfect man or individual, a paradigm. For Laozi this paradigm is the sage (*shengren*). For Zhuangzi it is the supreme man (*zhiren*), the marvelous man (*shenren*), the sage (*shengren*), and especially the authentic man (*zhenren*)—the man who preserves his intrinsic nature. For both of them, the perfect man was the incarnation of the *dao*.

For Laozi, the sage was someone who had fully unfolded his own virtue or, in other words, had attained the highest virtue. Laozi understood this highest virtue as achieving a total union with the *dao* and sharing its spontaneous creativity. He characterized this virtue as all-embracing, innocent, simple, original, generous, and self-forgetful. Laozi held that the *dao* incarnated itself and was concretely manifested in the person of a sage. Though a human being among human beings, the sage had transcended all human weaknesses and selfishness, becoming one with the *dao* and thus realizing the highest virtue in spontaneous freedom and undefiled infinitude. The sage knew how to gain a world of love and reverence by giving himself generously for the sake of the world. Laozi said, "The sage has no fancy to accumulate. Having lived for the benefit of others, he is even richer in worth. Having given all he has to other men, he is more plentiful in being" (ch. 81). Also: "The sage has no fixed mind of his own; he immerses his own mind in the mind of all people" (ch. 49). Therefore:

> The sage is always skillful and wholehearted in the deliverance of men so that there is no deserted man; he is always skillful and wholehearted in the rescue of things so that there is no abandoned thing. (ch. 27)

The sage thus represents not only ethical and moral achievement, like the Confucian sage, but also, so to speak, an incarnation of the *dao* and the *de*. By incarnating *dao* and *de* he becomes the deliverer of things and persons, the one who restores them to their primordial union with the *dao*.

Whereas the Confucians had an image of the sage as a great personality, Laozi proposed the image of an infant as best representing the Daoist paradigmatic individual. This was because an infant realized, effortlessly, the characteristics of the highest virtue: all-embracing spontaneity, innocence, simplicity, originality, generosity, and self-forgetfulness:

> He who possesses virtue in abundance may be compared to an infant. Poisonous insects will not sting him. Fierce beasts will not seize him. Birds of prey will not strike him. His bones are weak, his sinews tender; but his grasp is firm. He does not yet know the union of male and female, but his organ is aroused. This means that his essence is at its height. He may cry all day without becoming hoarse. This means that his harmony is perfect. (ch. 55)

Here, the infant is a metaphor for, not the reality of, the Daoist paradigmatic individual. A sage behaves "as if" he were an infant, but of course he is not; and an infant, without any spiritual achievement, could of course not be called a sage.

To Zhuangzi, the perfect man, the ideal or best human being, was more diverse. Such a being could be called, for instance, *zhiren* (supreme person), *shenren* (marvelous person), *shengren* (sagely person), and *zhenren* (authentic person). Three of these terms are defined negatively: *zhiren* with respect to self, *shenren* with respect to particular achievements, *shengren* with respect to name. They refer to paradigmatic individuals defined negatively relative to those of Confucianism, Mohism, and the school of names. But *zhenren*—the authentic person—is defined positively as a paradigmatic individual.

Zhuangzi described an authentic person's spiritual achievement in terms of both social behavior and self-cultivation:

> The authentic man of old did not override the weak, did not attain their ends by brute strength, and did not gather around them counselors. Thus failing had no cause for regret; succeeding, no cause for self-satisfaction. And thus they could soar to heights without trembling, enter water without becoming wet, and go through fire without feeling hot. This is the kind of knowledge which reaches to the depth of *dao*.

Zhuangzi also described the authentic person's self-control, attained through the praxis of breathing. Self-control reduced desire even to the point of being able to master it in a state of unconsciousness, and to the extent of not manifesting it through the act of eating or even in dreams. An authentic person transcended all constraints of life and death and followed the natural rhythm of birth and death in absolute spiritual freedom.

However, in classical Daoism, even if the *dao* is manifested by the sage (as Laozi held) or the authentic person (as Zhuangzi held), neither the sage nor the authentic person is actually identified with the *dao*. In contemporary neo-Confucian interpretations, such as the "metaphysics of the spiritual horizon" of Mou Tsung-san (Mou Zongsan), the *dao* is but the "spiritual horizon" of the sage or the authentic person. By contrast, both Laozi and Zhuangzi affirm that the *dao* transcends any human being, even a perfect human being. This view rejects any anthropocentric interpretation of the *dao* and thus avoids enclosing the *dao* in self-inflating human subjectivity.

"Life Praxis" in Classical Daoism

Both Laozi and Zhuangzi proposed a concept of "life praxis" instead of the Confucian idea of moral praxis. Actually, Laozi initiated the idea of life praxis and Zhuangzi developed it.

According to Zhuangzi, life praxis begins with unifying bodily functions and the spiritual functions of the soul in meditation. Then, by natural breath, the spirit is purified to a point where it clarifies the consciousness, which in turn then reaches the point of becoming a metaphysical looking glass, so that an intuition of the essence of all things is attained by letting them be. Then, finally, through a kind of mystical passivity, one returns to a union with the *dao* itself.

Zhuangzi connects the Daoist life praxis to our ultimate concern with matters such as life and death. The perspective for understanding that concern is the cosmic process of realization of the *dao* in the body. On the one hand, to live means to take the form of a living body. According to Zhuangzi, this is the effect of an organic accumulation of cosmic energy. On the other hand, to die is the effect of a dispersion of cosmic energy. To live—the fact of being able to take the form of a living body—is in itself a joyful aspect of existence; but this does not mean that to die is lamentable. It was for this reason that Zhuangzi said in *The Great Master*:

> The Great Clod (that is, the earth) burdens me with the form of body, pummels me with tiresome life, eases me in old ages, and rests me in death. So if it makes my life good, it must for the same reason make my death good.

In this way one is liberated from the worrisome concern of life and death. Such freedom is essential for a life of sanity. Zhuangzi said:

> I received life because the time had come; I will lose it because the order of things passes on. Be content with this time and dwell in this order and then neither sorrow nor joy can touch you.

The openness of mind leading to ultimate harmony is not limited to this liberation from attachment to the differentiation of life and death. For Zhuangzi, human beings should follow the rhythm of cosmic creativity instead of imposing themselves on specific forms of existence. In other words, in the process of cosmic creativity one should not impose one's subjective will in discriminating between the human body and other kinds of bodies. The relative rarity of the human body does not mean that it is superior; Zhuangzi sees an ontological equality among all living bodies.

Accordingly, Zhuangzi makes no distinction between the noble and the mean, the true and the false, the rational and the sensible. He would assent even to becoming a rat's liver or a bug's leg. Nevertheless, in the depth of his soul, he had a beautiful dream. It was to become a butterfly, for him the most beautiful and freest being, wandering and playing in nature:

> Once Zhuang Zhou [Zhuangzi] dreamt he was a butterfly, a butterfly flitting and fluttering around, happy with himself and doing as he pleased. He didn't know he was Zhuang Zhou. Suddenly he woke up and there he was, solid and unmistakable Zhuang Zhou. But he didn't know if he was Zhuang Zhou who had dreamt he was a butterfly, or a butterfly dreaming he was Zhuang Zhou. Between Zhuang Zhou and a butterfly there must be some distinction. And this is called the transformation of things. (*On Making All Things Equal*, in Watson 1968, 49)

Becoming a butterfly, being free and graceful, wandering and playing in nature—this symbolized a golden age in which human beings would be united with nature. Thus instead of becoming a rat or a bug, Zhuangzi would prefer to be a butterfly. With regard to ontology, there is no distinction between Zhuang Zhou and the butterfly, although ontically there must be a difference between the two. The free, gracefully beautiful style of existence surpasses all differentiation and returns to the original union with the *dao*, the Way. This is achieved through a profound life praxis. According to Zhuangzi, as we have seen, it begins with a spontaneous control of breathing to minimize unconscious desire and its unconscious expression in dreams:

> The True Human of ancient times slept without dreaming and woke without care. . . . The True Human breathes with his heels; the mass of men breathe with their throat. Crushed and bound down, they gasp out their words as though they were retching. Deep in their passions and desires, they are shallow in the sensitivity to Heaven's working. (Watson, 77–78)

It is interesting, here, to compare Zhuangzi and Freud. For Freud, dreaming is a disguised expression of unconscious desires. For Zhuangzi, being deeply immersed in passions and desires makes us shallow with regard to our sensitivity to heaven's work. The way out is, to repeat, by way of breathing—breathing as deeply as if with one's heels. By this means we can minimize desire and so sleep without dreaming and wake without daily cares.

An even deeper life praxis is symbolized in a narrative concerning Butcher Ding, who, cutting up an ox, behaved in such a marvelous way that he slid the knife along artistically, with a rhythm like that in music and dance: "All was in perfect rhythm, as though he were performing the dance of the Mulberry Grove or keeping time to the Jingsou music."

An ox is a living being constituted in a very complicated way, and so it signifies the complexity of life, individual as well as social, constituted by all kinds of relations. With a life praxis that is capable of grasping this complexity, one can eventually follow natural rhythms and attain the way of freedom. As the narrative of the butcher runs:

> And now—now I go at it by spirit and don't look with my eyes. Perception and understanding have come to a stop and spirit moves where it wants. I go along with the natural makeup, strike in the big hollows guide, the knife through the big openings, and follow things as they are. . . . There are spaces between the joints, and the blade of the knife has really no thickness. If you insert what has no thickness into such spaces, then there's plenty of room—more than enough for the blade to play about it.

This story shows that, on the one hand, human life praxis is situated in an ontology of relation, in which all are complexly related one to another; for this reason one should act according to one's natural makeup and follow things as they are. But on the other hand, there are still possibilities for freedom—the "spaces between the joints," in which there is "plenty of room—more than enough for the blade to play about it." The ultimate fact of being-in-relation does not mean total determinism and does not deprive humans of their freedom. On the contrary, the possibility of human freedom is not freedom in isolation and does not lead to chaos. There is freedom-in-relation, and there is relation-in-freedom. In other words, the relation we have is a relation imbued with freedom, and the freedom we have is a kind of relational freedom. Zhuangzi's story of Butcher Ding conveys exactly the contrasting situations of relation and freedom, the dialectical interplay and mutual immersion of difference and complementarity, continuity and discontinuity.

The praxis of life, as illustrated by the narrative of the butcher, progresses from the technical level to that of the *dao* and thereby becomes art—an art that realizes itself in the dynamism and movement of the body. The body is therefore the locus of this praxis and the incarnation of the art. The rarity of the body is only one reason why human beings should regard and preserve the body in such a way as not to get lost in the vicissitude of events. The possibility of attaining a fresh, free way of life, the fulfillment of a life of harmony, lies in concentrating oneself and in following the natural way of life. The message of classical Daoism is a conception of harmony within the context of *dao*, nature, and man as the ultimate truth.

See also Confucianism: Constructs of Classical Thought; Confucianism: Ethics; Daoism: Neo-Daoism; Hui Shi; *Junzi*; Laozi; Liezi; *Sheng*: Sage; *Zhenren*; Zhuangzi.

Bibliography

Chan, Wing-tsit, trans. *A Source Book in Chinese Philosophy*. Princeton, N.J.: Princeton University Press, 1963.

———. *The Way of Lao Tzu: A Translation and Study of the Tao-te Ching*. New York: Bobbs-Merrill, 1963.

Cua, A. S. *Dimensions of Moral Creativity: Paradigms, Principles, and Ideals*. University Park: Pennsylvania State University Press, 1978.

———. "Forgetting Morality: Reflections on a Theme in *Chuang Tzu*." *Journal of Chinese Philosophy*, 4(4), 1977, pp. 305–328.

Fang, Thomé. *Chinese Philosophy: Its Spirit and Its Development*. Taipei: Linking, 1981.

———. *Yuanshi rujia daojia zhexue* (Philosophies of Primordial Confucianism and Taoism). Taipei: Li-ming, 1983.

Graham, A. C. *Chuang Tzu: The Inner Chapters*. London: Allen and Unwin, 1981.

Jingmen City Museum, ed. *Guodian chumu zhujian* (Guodian Chu Tomb's Bamboo Slips). Beijing: Wenwu chubanshe, 1998.

Laozi. *Lao-Tzu's Tao Te Ching: A New Translation of the Startling New Documents Found at Guodian*, trans. Robert C. Henricks. New York: Columbia University Press, 2000.

———. *Lao-Tzu: Te-tao Ching—A New Translation Based on the Recently Discovered Ma-wan-tui Texts*, trans. with intro. and commentary Robert C. Henricks. New York: Ballantine, 1989.

———. *Mawangdui hanmu boshu* (The Silk Manuscript of the *Laozi* Discovered at Mawangdui). Beijing: Wenwu chubanshe, 1976.

———. *Tao Te Ching: The Book of the Way and Its Virtue*, trans. J. J. L. Duyvendak. London: Murray, 1954.

———. *The Way and Its Power*, trans. Arthur Waley. London: Allen and Unwin, 1935.

Lau, D. C., trans. *Lao Tzu: Tao Te Ching*. Baltimore, Md.: Penguin, 1963.

Lin, Yutang. *The Wisdom of Laotze*. New York: Modern Library, 1948.

Maspero, Henri. *Le Taoïsme et les religions chinoise*. Paris: Gallimard, 1971.

Schipper, Kristofer. *Le corps taoïst*. Paris: Arthème Fayard, 1982.

Shen, Vincent. "Annäherung an das taoistische Verständnis von Wissenschaft: Die Epistemologie des Lao Tses und Tschuang Tses." In *Grenzziehungen zum Konstruktiven Realismus*, ed. F. Wallner, J. Schimmer, and M. Costazza. Vienna: WUV Universitätsverlag, 1993.

———. *Confucianism, Taoism, and Constructive Realism*. Vienna: Vienna University Press, 1994. (In English.)

———. "L'idée de la création dans la pensée taoïst." In *Création et événement: Autour de Jean Ladrière*. Louvain-Paris: Édition Peeters, 1996.

———. "Laozi di renxing lun chutan (A Preliminary Inquiry into Lao Tzu's Theory of Human Nature)." In *Zhongguo renxing lun* (Chinese Theories of Human Nature). Taipei: Dong da, 1990, pp. 3–18.

———. "Laozi di xingshang sixiang (Lao Tzu's Metaphysics)." *Zhexue yu wenhua*, 15(12), 1988, pp. 814–822.

———. "Laozi di zhishi lun (Lao Tzu's Epistemology)." *Zhexue yu wenhua*, 20(1), 1993, pp. 98–107.

———. "Tao and Cosmology in the Guodian Texts of Lao Tzu—In Comparison with Other Related Texts." *Zhexue yu wenhua*, 26(4), 1999, pp. 298–316.

———. "Zhuangzi di daolun—Dui dangdai xingshang kunhuo di yige jieda (Zhuangzi's Dao-Discourse—Answers to Contemporary Metaphysical Questions)." *National Chengchi University Philosophical Journal*, 1, 1994, pp. 19–34.

———. *Zhuangzi di renguang* (Chuang Tzu's Concept of Man)." *Zhexue yu wenhua*, 14(6), 1987, pp. 13–23.

Watson, Burton, trans. *The Complete Works of Chuang Tzu*. New York: Columbia University Press, 1968.

Zhuangzi. *Zhuangzi jishi*, ed. Guo Qingfan. Taipei: Shijie, 1985. (12th reprint.)

Daoism (Taoism): Neo-Daoism (*Xuanxue, Hsüan-hsüeh*)

Alan K. L. Chan

"Neo-Daoism" refers to a revival of Daoist philosophy that came into prominence during the third century C.E. and dominated the Chinese intellectual scene well into the sixth century. Like any convenient label, the term must be treated with care. It signifies a broad philosophical front united in attempting to discern the "true" meaning of the *dao*; it does not name a homogeneous, sectarian Daoist school. Alarmed by what they saw as the decline of the *dao*, leading intellectuals of the day initiated a radical reinterpretation of the classical heritage. Fresh insights emerged from a dynamic encounter with tradition, which occasioned intense debates and set new directions for the development of Chinese philosophy.

Chinese sources label the movement *xuanxue*, often translated "mysterious learning," "dark learning," or "profound learning." The word *xuan* depicts literally a shade of dark red. In the *Laozi* (*Daodejing*), it is used to describe the sublime mystery of the *dao*. As a type of learning or discourse aimed at explicating the meaning of *dao, xuanxue* may be best rendered as "learning of the mysterious *dao*" or "profound learning." There is nothing "mysterious" about it, except to critics who judge it obfuscating and detrimental to the flourishing of the Way. Innovative, abstract in some respects, and critical of the dominant Confucian orthodoxy, *xuanxue* is nonetheless committed to bringing to light what may otherwise seem "dark" or inaccessible to understanding.

Neo-Daoism has often been approached from a historical perspective. Toward the end of the Han period, a major protest movement known as *qingyi*, or "pure criticism"—i.e., pure in motivation and aimed at purifying corrupt practices—shook the Chinese political world. Led by eminent scholar-officials and students of the imperial academy, it was directed especially against the abuses of powerful eunuchs. The movement, however, was harshly suppressed. Consequently, many literati seem to have become disillusioned with the political process. This not only marked a turning point in Han politics but had a strong impact on the course of culture and philosophy.

The Wei dynasty formally ended the rule of Han in 220 C.E. Politics remained extremely volatile. Externally, two rival regimes challenged the claim of the Wei to supremacy; internally, power struggles among factions of the ruling elite rendered life at court doubly treacherous. In this context, we find the rise of an influential upper-class cultural phenomenon known as "pure conversation" (*qingtan*): men of letters gathered for pleasure and devoted their intellectual and creative energy to music, poetry, philosophy, and other forms of cultured discourse. *Xuanxue* formed a major topic of "pure conversation."

In view of the turbulent political background, some scholars have concluded that neo-Daoism contained a strong element of escapism. According to this interpretation, while *qingyi* centered on political criticism, its successor *qingtan* was self-consciously nonpolitical. Fearing for their safety, and disheartened by the apparent futility of political engagement in effecting meaningful change, the literati turned their attention to "purer" pursuits. Though not without merit, this does not give the whole picture. Certainly, to some people politics was so corrupt as to make a mockery of any sense of honor and moral integrity; but many continued to harbor hope of revitalizing the rule of *dao*. Richly complex, neo-Daoism encompasses a wide range of responses to the brave new world that was post-Han China.

When the Wei dynasty came to power, attempts were made to reform government. A first wave of neo-Daoist philosophers represented chiefly by He Yan (c. 190–249) and Wang Bi (226–249) sought new grounds for restoring unity and harmony. The Confucian orthodoxy established since the Han dynasty could no longer satisfy the demands of a new age. Indeed, it was deemed part of the problem that led to the demise of the Han empire.

The critique of Han Confucianism does not amount to rejecting the thought of Confucius. Virtually everyone agreed that Confucius was the highest sage. The problem, rather, has to do with the perceived misunderstanding and misappropriation of Confucian teachings. Scholarship had become an avenue for emolument, and as a result self-interest outweighed concern for the truth. This in part explains the emphasis on "purity" in neo-Daoism. Moreover, Confucian orthodoxy exacted compliance, which set limits to thought. The classics were restricted to a particular mode of interpretation, and noncanonical literature, including Daoist works, was often viewed with suspicion or dismissed outright. In the interest of unity, orthodoxy prescribed closure; but in an age of disunity, the quest for order demanded freedom from outmoded and debilitating constraints.

Methodologically, framed in a kind of "chapter and verse" (*zhangju*) format, Han commentaries emphasize detailed explanation of individual words and phrases in the classics. The attention to detail was at times so overwhelming, as the historian Ban Gu (32–92) observes, that a discussion of a text of five words could take up to 20,000 or 30,000 words. This necessitated heavy specialization, which heightened virtuosity but also opened the door for vain scholastic display and fragmentation of learning. One of the most important debates in "profound learning" confronts directly the question of interpretation, which brought hermeneutics for the first time to the forefront of Chinese philosophy.

The debate on "words and meaning," as it is called, has its roots in the *Yijing*, where Confucius is made to ask whether words can fully disclose meaning. This goes beyond the interpretation of any one work, probing the nature of understanding itself. Words, as common experience seems to suggest, often fail to express intense emotions or complex ideas. A minority, represented by the late third-century thinker Ou-yang Jian, defended the thesis that meaning is completely exhausted by words (*yan jin yi*). The majority of "pure conversationists," however, regarded words as necessary but not sufficient to understanding.

A spokesman for the view that "words cannot fully express meaning" (*yan bu jin yi*) was Xun Can (c. 212–240), who gained considerable fame for his claim that the classics are but the "chaff" of the sages' profound learning. The conclusion is inescapable, according to Xun, for meaning transcends the limiting confines of language. Wang Bi supplies a more complete and nuanced argument. Although meaning is mediated by words and other communicative instruments, the means of interpretation must not be confused with the end itself. Citing the *Zhuangzi*, Wang maintains that the words and images making up a text must be "forgotten" before meaning can be understood. To understand a poem, for example, it is not enough to assemble an exhaustive list of definitions. The words are "forgotten" or left behind in the sense that understanding reaches into the underlying world of ideas where a deeper meaning resides. Guo Xiang (d. 312), a second pillar of neo-Daoist philosophy, next to Wang Bi, also makes it clear that although ideas issue from words, they cannot be reduced to the literal, surface meaning of the words themselves.

This diverges sharply from the Han hermeneutical model, which typically assumes that meaning is defined by external referents. In particular, given the dominance of *yin-yang* theories, the classics were seen as referring to diverse cosmological phenomena. For example, Han commentators commonly took the word "one" to mean the polestar. In contrast, neo-Daoist writings show little interest in cosmological speculation. This does not mean that the authors had abandoned the *yin-yang* cosmology; rather, they believed, the classics were concerned with issues more profound than naming the various components of the cosmos. A poem may depict actual objects or events; but sense is not limited to reference, and the meaning of the whole transcends the identity of its parts. From a new hermeneutical perspective, proponents of "profound learning" thus endeavor to reverse an "outward"-bound interpretive course to return to the "roots," that is to say, to recapture the core teaching of the sages.

Understanding may depend on direct intuition. Nevertheless, to Wang Bi, Guo Xiang, and other major neo-Daoists, all of whom excelled in the art of argumentation, there is no substitute for careful philosophical analysis. The ancient sages shared a profound understanding of the *dao*. On this view, Confucius, Laozi, and other worthies were all "Daoists," in the nonsectarian sense of the term. The *Yijing*, *Laozi*, and *Zhuangzi* especially afford a wealth of insights into nature and the human condition. Most neo-Daoists concentrated on these texts, which were then collectively known as the "three profound treatises" (*san xuan*). Wang Bi, for example, is best-known for his commentaries on the *Yijing* and the *Laozi*; and Guo Xiang is arguably the most important commentator on the *Zhuangzi* in Chinese history. It should not be overlooked, however, that both Wang and Guo, and He Yan, too, had commented on the *Analects*. Convinced of the unity of the classics, each provided an integral account of the one "Daoist" tradition.

Critics, past and present, are adamant that neo-Daoists had distorted the teaching of Confucius, or worse, misused the authority of Confucius to give credence to their own agenda. Partisan disputes notwithstanding, the view presented here is that *xuanxue* scholars set forth the truth of *dao* in a philosophical synthesis. But this is not to say that they had understood the wisdom of the sages in the same way.

A keen interest in ontology furnishes a common point of departure. As a general claim, there is no disagreement that all beings are rooted in the *dao*. The question is, What does this mean? Should the *dao* be identified with a creator "heaven" or an original "vital energy" (*qi*), which according to Han scholars gave birth to the cosmos? He Yan and Wang Bi offer an alternative to understanding the origin of being. Although He Yan's writings survive largely in fragments, according to tradition he was adept in explaining the *Laozi* and the *Yijing*, and together with Wang Bi inaugurated the neo-Daoist movement on their view that being originates from "nonbeing" (*wu*).

Cosmological interpretations are unhelpful because they fail to resolve the problem of infinite regress. If the chain of beings were to be traced to a specific agent or entity, then the origin of the latter must itself be questioned. The concept of nonbeing, taken from the *Laozi*, is designed to bring out the transcendence of the *dao*. Nameless and without form, the *dao* as such can only be described negatively as *wu*, or literally "not having" any characteristics of things. Put simply, what gives rise to the category of being cannot itself be a being. To understand the *dao* and its creative power, reflection must venture beyond an ontology of substance to discern the logic of creation.

Not all neo-Daoists subscribed to the doctrine of nonbeing. Toward the end of the third century, the scholar Pei Wei of the Jin dynasty composed a treatise provocatively titled "Extolling (the Virtue of) Being" (*Chongyou lun*), to counter the widespread influence of He Yan and Wang Bi. Nevertheless, it was Guo Xiang who articulated the most important critique of nonbeing.

The logic of transcendence may seem appealing, according to Guo, but it does not explain the origin of being at all. This is because nonbeing is entirely conceptual, an abstraction, and as such cannot create anything. If nonbeing cannot bring forth being, and if the idea of a creator remains problematic, then the only alternative would be to regard the created order as having come into existence spontaneously. This implies that being is eternal. Particular beings can of course be traced to contingent causes, but ultimately, Guo concludes, the origin of being can be understood only in terms of a process of "self-transformation."

Chinese sources are fond of contrasting Wang Bi's "valuing nonbeing" (*guiwu*) with Guo Xiang's "exaltation of being" (*chongyou*). This gives an indication of the kind of vibrant debate that energizes neo-Daoist thought. Still, *xuanxue* is not only about ontology. For both camps, the ontological analysis lays the foundation of a *dao*-centered ethics and political philosophy.

If the *dao* is by definition what being is not, how is it related to the world? The concept of *li* ("principle") plays an important role in bridging the gap between transcendence and immanence. In his commentary on the *Yijing*, Wang Bi stresses that phenomena conform to fundamental principles, such as the laws of nature, which in turn can be traced to a logically necessary unity. Contrary to Han accounts, the *Yijing* has little to do with cosmological inventory or numerological manipulation but lays bare the philosophical basis of change. The sages of old recognized that the many stem from "one"—or "One"—and they devised the hexagrams to give systematic expression to the transformation of nature.

The concept of "one" does not suggest one particular agent or substance giving rise to the manifold processes of change. What it indicates is that conceptually, multiplicity and diversity presuppose unity. Temporal priority, in other words, is not the issue. "One comes before two," in this context, means rather that the latter is inconceivable without the former. Thus, Wang Bi specifically stipulates that although "one" makes possible all numbers, it is itself *not* a number. Dialectically understood, it complements nonbeing. Whereas nonbeing affirms the *dao* as the ground of being, the concept of "one" highlights the principle of unity that governs the Daoist universe.

If the *dao* as principle permeates nature, its presence can also be detected in the sociopolitical realm. Just as the mind commands the body, the family and the state should ideally be minded by a single sovereign. The hierarchical structure of sociopolitical relations is thus seen to have a basis in the natural order of things. In this way, traditional Confucian concerns merge with Daoist insights. With regard to politics, this means that the restoration of order and harmony hinges on a strong monarchical government.

Strength cannot be measured by brute force, however. In the Daoist sense, true strength is found in what the mundane world might regard as "weakness," in following the yielding ways of nature without artificial interference or aggressive control. Far from advocating any kind of strong-arm tactics, Wang Bi and his colleagues sought order in naturalness and spontaneity (*ziran*).

Specifically, naturalness suggests government by "nonaction" (*wuwei*), a concept enunciated in both the *Laozi* and the *Analects*, and attributed to no less a personage than the sage-king Shun. This may be contrasted with "legalist" policies that emphasize stiff punishment and political domination. In theory, *wuwei* aims at preserving the natural order so that the "myriad things" and affairs can flourish and attain their proper end in accordance with constant principles. Practically, it involves the elimination of willful intervention and a return to "emptiness and quiescence"—that is, a life of guileless simplicity and freedom from the dictates of desire. Firmly rooted in nonbeing, this is the one teaching that unites the ancient sages. Confucius may not have spoken of nonbeing explicitly, but as Wang Bi declares, his every word and action nonetheless embodies the truth of naturalness and nonaction.

Whereas Wang Bi celebrates the "one," Guo Xiang focuses on the many. It is true that natural and social phenomena testify to the operation of constant principles. But this does not warrant nullifying individuality in the name of a higher metaphysical unity. Individuals are born with different talents and character traits. The principle of nature dictates that everyone is endowed with a particular "share" of vital energy, the creative power of the *dao* that determines one's physical, intellectual, and moral capacity. Extending a naturalistic reading to an old religious concept, this is in Guo's estimation what is meant by the "mandate of heaven" (*tianming*).

Individual differences ought to be accepted, but they do not give cause for prejudice or discrimination. Each individual, the gifted as well as the disadvantaged, is in principle complete in his or her own way and constitutes an indispensable part in a larger whole. Daoist ethics, in this framework, thus consists in being true to oneself and nourishing one's nature. This is the practical significance of naturalness. The sage, as Guo Xiang points out in his commentary on *Zhuangzi*, precisely recognizes the principle of *ziran*, cultivates his inborn capacity, and in so doing fulfills his destiny.

In following nature, the sage abides by nonaction. Not to be confused with total inaction, *wuwei* signifies a mode of being that makes full use of one's natural endowment. Guided by inherent moral principles, the Daoist way of life has no place for artificiality or self-deception. Clearly, ethical purity does not entail renunciation. The sage need not avoid politics or other forms of worldly involvement. Though he finds himself in the corridors of power, the sage safeguards his nature and remains empty of desire. In government, the sage ruler naturally reduces arbitrary restrictions, adjusts policies to suit changing needs, identifies the right people for office, and generally creates a conducive environment in which all under heaven can dwell in peace and realize their potential.

The sage can accomplish all this because he is blessed with an exceptionally rich endowment. There is no point, however, in trying to imitate the sages. Any attempt to do so would in fact violate the spirit of naturalness. This brings into view a key difference between Guo Xiang and Wang Bi, and an important debate in neo-Daoist philosophy concerning the nature of the sage.

Historically, He Yan is credited with having established the view that sages are without feelings or emotions (*qing*). Although the exact arguments can no longer be reconstructed, He Yan's theory was widely accepted, as traditional sources relate that Zhong Hui, a contemporary and rival of Wang Bi, and others had elaborated on it. Guo Xiang seems to have shared the same view. The sage's extraordinary constitution translates into a purity of being that excludes emotional disturbances. For this reason, his action accords completely with principle. In being true to himself, the sage can therefore rule the world without being corrupted or enslaved by it.

Wang Bi was decidedly of a different opinion. If there is a fundamental unity to all beings, it cannot be maintained that some are nevertheless exempted from the rule. Further, if sages are born a species apart, they cannot serve as a source of motivation and inspiration. It would then be impossible to become a sage, which seems to contradict both classical Daoist and Confucian teachings. The sage is not without emotions but differs from ordinary beings in spirituality and understanding. Even Confucius could not help being pleased when he met Yan Hui, his favorite disciple, or being saddened by Yan's untimely death. With feelings, the sage is able to respond to things, but because of his clear understanding he is never burdened by them. It is logically invalid, as Wang astutely observes, to conclude from the absence of attachment an absence of emotions.

Sharing the same philosophical vocabulary and reacting to a common heritage, adherents of *xuanxue* nonetheless exercised remarkable independence and critical acumen. It is worth mentioning that politically Wang Bi benefited from He Yan's patronage, but certainly he did not submit to the latter in "profound learning." A generation later, Guo Xiang did not hesitate to reopen cases that many had considered settled. In this crisscrossing of ideas, neo-Daoism prospered.

He Yan died, a victim of political intrigue, at the close of the Zhengshi reign (240–249) of the Wei dynasty. Wang Bi died later in the same year, reportedly of a sudden illness. Historians thus refer to "Zhengshi *xuanxue*" to mark the first phase of neo-Daoism. From that point on, political power was controlled by the Sima family, who eventually founded the Jin dynasty in 265 C.E. During the Wei-Jin transition, a group of intellectuals, remembered fondly in Chinese sources as the "seven worthies of the bamboo grove," came to represent the voice of "profound learning." Although the term "bamboo grove" appears in Buddhist sources, it probably refers to a place (in modern Henan Province) where the group and other associates met to take pleasure in their friendship. Of the seven, Xi Kang (223–262), Ruan Ji (210–263), and Xiang Xiu (c. 227–280) are of particular interest to students of philosophy.

Xi Kang and Ruan Ji, the undisputed leaders of the group, exemplify the kind of free and critical spirit to which men of letters were increasingly drawn at that time. Xi Kang refused to serve the Sima regime and died for his beliefs. Ruan Ji was spared a violent end, but only because he took refuge in the forgiving oblivion of intoxicated stupor. Both were uncompromising in their attack on hypocrisy and the tussle for power and wealth. Extremely talented in music and poetry, daringly unconventional in thought and behavior, they both looked to naturalness to provide a basis for renewal.

Unlike Wang Bi and He Yan, Ruan Ji did not see nonbeing as the one thread running through the classics. Rather, it is the plenitude of nature that constitutes the starting point for philosophical reflection. The diverse phenomena, however, function in harmony. In his essay on the *Zhuangzi*, Ruan Ji traces this to the transformation of the one vital *qi*-energy that pervades the universe. In his essay on the *Laozi*, he states in no uncertain terms that this is what the *Yijing* means by the "great ultimate" (*taiji*); in the *Spring and Autumn Annals*, this is called the "origin" (*yuan*), and in the *Laozi*, the *dao*.

At the ethical level, the concept of *ziran* affirms that "fullness" can be realized only in "emptiness." Devoid of self-interest, the "great man" finds fulfillment in quietude and nonaction. In his famous essay "Biography of Master Great Man" (*Daren xiansheng zhuan*), Ruan speaks eloquently of the Daoist sage as one who rides above the servitude of mundane life in complete freedom and transcendence. But the most startling revelation arises from a philosophy of history, in which Ruan describes the world as having fallen from a pristine state of natural order where there were neither rulers nor ministers.

Anarchism, a doctrine rarely entertained in the whole of Chinese philosophy, thus made a notable appearance in neo-Daoism. In the fourth century, Bao Jingyan took up the same theme in his *Treatise on Not Having Rulers* (*Wu jun lun*). Little is known about Bao, whose views have been preserved in part by Ke Hong (c. 283–363) in his *Baopuzi* (*The Master Who Embraces Simplicity*); but the main thesis here is clearly that rulership is but a form of domination that violates naturalness. In comparison, the majority of neo-Daoists may be said to have espoused fairly "conservative" political ideals. He Yan, Wang Bi, and Guo Xiang had little difficulty justifying absolute monarchical rule, provided that it coincided with nonaction. Even Xi Kang, who is often depicted as a radical iconoclast, admits that rulership has a place in the natural order.

Xi Kang did not comment on the "three profound treatises." As "pure conversation" developed, essays, criticisms, and replies to criticisms grew in popularity as a more direct medium of philosophical discourse. In his essays, Xi Kang addresses some of the most controversial debates in "profound learning." On the relationship between words and meaning, it is clear that he sides with Wang Bi. In the interpretation of naturalness, Xi parts company with many of his contemporaries in recognizing a religious dimension to Daoist teachings.

The principle of *ziran* is to be understood concretely in terms of vital energy. Like Guo Xiang, Xi Kang believes that individuals receive an endowment of energy of varying abundance and richness which defines their nature and capacity. On this account, the sage must be considered a superior being, informed by the purest form of *qi*-energy. For the same reason, Xi Kang argues for the existence of "immortals," a popular ideal in religious Daoism. So defined, neither sagehood nor immortality can be achieved through effort or learning.

Immortality may be beyond reach, but as Xi Kang explains in his essay "On Nourishing Life" (*Yangsheng lun*), self-cultivation can substantially enhance one's physical and spiritual well-being. Specifically, breathing exercises, dietary control, and the use of drugs can help maximize the limits of one's natural endowment and bring about rejuvenation and long life. Drugs, incidentally, were widespread among the literati; He Yan, for example, is known to have championed a certain drug for its ability to "lift one's spirit." Useful as such practices may be, Xi Kang is careful to add, the task of self-cultivation will nevertheless be in vain if desires are allowed to dominate.

Desires are harmful to both body and mind. Purity of being, conversely, entails the absence of desire or any form of emotional disturbance. Does this mean that all desires are unnatural? The question was already raised in the debate on the nature of the sage. In this instance, Xi's essay led to a critique by Xiang Xiu, for whom desires arise naturally from the heart-mind. As such, they cannot be eradicated; rather, affects and appetites can be regulated only by means of ritual action and rules of propriety.

Other philosophers, as we shall see, were to add to this debate. In reply, Xi Kang points out that although anger and joy, and the desire for fame and beauty, may stem from the self, like a tumor they do not serve the interest of personal well-being. Basic needs are of course not to be denied, but desires are shaped by objects and reflect cognitive distortions that blind and consume the self. To quench one's thirst, one does not desire to drink a whole river. This is fundamentally different from the desire for power and wealth, which allows no rest. Further, the suppression of desire by artificial means may remove certain symptoms, but it does not cure the disease. It is only by recognizing the harmful influences of desire that one begins to seek calmness and emptiness of mind. Ultimately, nourishing life is not only a matter of health and longevity; it sets it sights on a higher—and to Xi Kang, more authentic—mode of being, characterized by dispassion.

In this connection, Xi Kang's famous thesis that emotions are foreign to music—or literally, that "sounds do not have (in them) sorrow or joy" (*sheng wu ai le*)—becomes readily understandable. If emotions and desires are not intrinsic to nature, and since sounds are naturally produced, it cannot be the case that music embodies sorrow or joy, as traditional Chinese musical theory generally assumed. Subjective and cognitive reactions, in other words, should be distinguished from what is natural and objective; otherwise, Xi argues, one can hardly account for the fact that the same piece of music may evoke different responses in different audiences.

If Xi Kang and Ruan Ji sharpened the Daoist sense of naturalness, Xiang Xiu provided a passage from Wang Bi's "valuing nonbeing" to Guo Xiang's "exaltation of being." Xiang was a brilliant interpreter of the *Zhuangzi*. Indeed, for a long time it was held that Guo Xiang had plagiarized Xiang Xiu's work. Guo's own contribution should not be underestimated, as modern scholarship rightly recognizes, but there is little question that he had benefited from Xiang's version of "profound learning."

Xiang Xiu's commentary on *Zhuangzi* is no longer extant, except for some 200 quotations preserved in various sources. It was Xiang who introduced the terms "self-production" (*zi sheng*) and "self-transformation" (*zi hua*); but he seems more concerned with the idea that "only that which is not produced and not transformed can be the root of production and transformation." This implies either nonbeing or an uncaused first cause, neither of which would be acceptable to Guo Xiang. "Self-transformation," in Guo's formulation, does not explain "how" being came into existence; instead, it offers a logical alternative, which bypasses the philosophical problems associated with both a pure negation and the positing of a particular causal agent.

As regards ethics, especially with respect to the interpretation of Daoist freedom, Guo seems to have followed Xiang Xiu's view more closely. Although the myriad creatures differ in infinite ways, according to Xiang, they are one in that they attain freedom and authenticity by following their nature. It is true that they cannot compare with the sage, who alone is not dependent on anything and is one with the universal flux; but even the most insignificant creature can find supreme happiness in complete self-realization. In the fourth century, the Buddhist monk Zhi Dun challenged the "Xiang-Guo" interpretation without differentiating between the two, arguing that only the enlightened sage can truly experience transcendental freedom.

From He Yan and Wang Bi to the "seven worthies" and Guo Xiang, the main features of neo-Daoism become fully distinguishable. From a broader, thematic perspective, given the dissatisfaction with Han Confucianism, many of the debates in "profound learning" revolve around the relationship between "orthodox teachings" (*mingjiao*) and *ziran*. Does the former, constituted by doctrines of propriety and government, oppose the order of nature and thwart all aspiration to transcendence and freedom from mundane concerns? Two main approaches can be discerned, whose impact far exceeds the quiet preserves of the philosophers' ivory tower or "bamboo grove," to spark new trends in both politics and culture.

For Wang Bi, it is clear that government and society should ideally conform to nature. Guo Xiang argues, even more specifically, that the norms and rites which define civilization are not foreign to nature but in principle flow spontaneously from it. The natural bond between mother and child, for example, attests to the inherent harmony of *mingjiao* and *ziran*. Inasmuch as Confucianism pays special attention to propriety and government, while classical Daoism focuses on naturalness, Wang Bi and Guo Xiang can be said to have synthesized the two traditions. The same is true for Xiang Xiu. As the famous poet Xie Lingyun (385–433) puts it, "Xiang Xiu treats Confucianism and Daoism as one."

To those who regard *mingjiao* and *ziran* as complementary, the question of talent or capacity (*cai*) and its relationship with human nature (*xing*) takes on particular significance. While most would agree that there are innate moral sensibilities, it is not clear if talent or capacity is also inborn. This is important because the right talent must be identified to serve political ends. If capacity is measured by *qi*-endowment, in principle it can be gauged from a person's appearance. A number of *xuanxue* scholars are especially known for their ability to identify talent; many neo-Daoists in fact subscribe to the then popular theory that to know a person, it is enough to look into his or her eyes.

A late second-century or early third-century work by Liu Shao, the *Renwu zhi* (translated into English as *The Study of Human Abilities*), has already mapped out different types of talent and the signs by which they might be recognized. In "profound learning," this developed further into a major debate on which Zhong Hui (225–264) is said to have compiled a treatise.

Zhong's scholastic labor has not survived; but it is widely reported that four distinct positions had been proposed—that talent and nature are (1) identical (*tong*); (2) different (*yi*); (3) convergent (*he*); and (4) divergent (*li*). This relates closely to the debate on the nature of the sage: whether through effort, one can acquire greatness and enlightenment. It is worth noting that whereas those who argued for identity or convergence bowed to the Sima regime, the chief proponents of the other two views staunchly defended the Wei rulers. Cao Cao, the founder of the Wei dynasty, had himself indicated that talent and nature do not always coincide. Capable men, he said, even if they lacked "benevolence and filial piety," should not be left out of office. Zhong Hui, representing the opposite camp, envisages an intrinsic harmony between talent and nature. Zhong rose to a high position in government after the Sima clan seized control in 249 C.E. According to historical sources, it was at his instigation that Xi Kang was put to death.

Both Xi Kang and Ruan Ji are evidently convinced that *mingjiao* impinge on nature. They reject the claim—supported, for example, by Guo Xiang (who, incidentally, enjoyed a successful political career) —that one could maintain inner purity and transcendence in the midst of worldly involvement. Genuine freedom is possible only if one goes beyond orthodox teachings and aligns oneself completely with naturalness. This not only invites philosophical debate but gives impetus to an avant-garde counterculture, which adds a tinge of romanticism to neo-Daoism.

Central to this debate is the place of emotion in naturalness. Leaving aside whether the sage experiences sorrow and joy, there is the question of human affection in the ethical life. Xi Kang's defense of dispassion notwithstanding, and despite Xiang Xiu's call to put passion under the rule of ritual, many had come to appreciate strong emotion as a sign of authenticity. Thus, Wang Rong (234–305), one of the "seven worthies of the bamboo grove," did not try to control his grief in accordance with ritual when his son died. The sage may be able to leave behind all traces of emotion, he explains, but "in people such as ourselves, this is where feelings find their deepest or most intense expression." Whether Wang had actually uttered these words is not the issue (some sources ascribe them to his cousin, another famous intellectual, Wang Yan); the more important point is that naked feelings had come to be cherished as a neo-Daoist ideal. In the same spirit, Xun Can was devastated by the death of his wife. In reply to criticism that he had surrendered himself to the dictates of the heart, Xun simply laments that it would be difficult to find again a woman of true beauty. His grief was so great, we read in his biography, that he died shortly afterward, at the age of twenty-nine.

The unaffected display of emotion often came into conflict with the norms and behavior sanctioned by orthodox teachings. Ruan Ji, for example, was criticized for having contravened the rules of propriety in sending his sister-in-law off on a journey. In reply, Ruan states bluntly that such rules were never meant for him. When Ruan Ji's mother died, he was found on various occasions drunk, taking meat, and generally acting in a manner so unconventional as to attract a call for his banishment from the realm. Nevertheless, traditional sources also relate that Ruan was by nature filial; his grief at his mother's death was so intense that he spat blood and "wasted away" for a long time. These accounts, more than providing a record of events, serve to dramatize the vast divide that separates naturalness from the artificial and often hypocritical observance of orthodox customs.

Once unconventional behavior is seen as expressing naturalness and authenticity, it is perhaps inevitable that more radical gestures would come to create a colorful but nonetheless extremely slippery slope. Ruan Ji, for example, frequented a neighbor's place for wine and the company of the neighbor's beautiful wife. When Ruan got drunk, he would innocently sleep next to her. Another neighbor had a talented and beautiful young daughter. When she died, the fact that Ruan Ji did not know the family did not prevent him from going to her funeral and crying with abandon. Liu Ling, a member of the "seven worthies of the bamboo grove," is well known for his fondness for wine and was never without a bottle in hand when traveling. On his travels, also, Liu would ask an attendant to carry a spade so that should he die, he could be buried on the spot. Liu took to nudity to express his naturalness and individuality. Answering his critics, who once found him naked, drinking in his house, Liu said, "I take heaven and earth as my dwelling, and my rooms are my coats and pants; so what are you gentlemen doing in my pants?"

As "pure conversation" gained currency, many literati were quick to imitate such behavior. It was fashionable to give free rein to one's impulses, to be outrageous; and many hoped to establish a reputation by opposing orthodox teachings. Whether this represents a deterioration of neo-Daoism need not concern us. The point to note is that serious practical implications follow from a philosophy of *ziran*. There are, of course, neo-Daoists who would defend the primacy of orthodox teachings. Yue Guang (252–304), for example, was obviously unimpressed by the extent to which many of his contemporaries had gone to seek a fulfilling life. "In *mingjiao* itself there is a blissful abode," he asks, "so why go to such extremes?"

In the early fourth century, the Jin dynasty was forced to flee its capital and rebuild in southern China. As the literati settled in a new land, they looked back to the time of He Yan and Wang Bi, to the "voice of Zhengshi," as the golden age of "profound learning." Although "pure conversation" continued with undiminished rigor, it did not introduce many new ideas. In the southern court, we are told, the senior statesman Wang Dao (276–339) would talk only about "nourishing life," "words and meaning," and Xi Kang's theory of music. Throughout the Jin period and beyond, as another early source relates, whether "sounds do not have sorrow or joy" and the "four views on talent and nature" remained the stuff of philosophical discussion.

As neo-Daoism entered its last phase, another Daoist work, the *Liezi*, came to rival the "three profound treatises." Zhang Zhan (c. 330–400) wrote an important commentary on the work—indeed, some would argue that Zhang had a hand in the formation of the *Liezi* itself—in which he recapitulates many of the ideas that span the spectrum of neo-Daoist philosophy. What is of particular interest is that Zhang explicitly introduced Buddhist ideas into "profound learning."

Buddhism had of course entered China long before the Jin period. Given the similarity between "nonbeing" and the Buddhist concept of "emptiness," there is some suggestion that neo-Daoism was influenced by Buddhist philosophy from the start. Though this is possible, there is so far no strong evidence linking He Yan, Wang Bi, and other early neo-Daoists to Buddhism. On the contrary, it is clear that "profound learning" had exerted considerable influence on the development of Chinese Buddhism. From the fourth century onward, Buddhist masters frequently engaged in "pure conversation" and challenged *xuanxue* scholars at their own game.

The Jin dynasty came to an end in 420 C.E. and was followed by a series of short-lived dynasties in the south as well as the north. While "pure conversation" survived, and *xuanxue* was in fact made a part of the official curriculum, it was Buddhism and religious Daoism that captured the philosophical and cultural imagination. Later still, with the rise of neo-Confucianism, many scholars rose up to condemn "dark learning" for having deviated from the teachings of Confucius.

Occupying a key place in the history of Chinese thought, neo-Daoism merits attention for its contribution to metaphysics, ethics, aesthetics, and other areas of philosophical concern. Most important, it should be remembered that the philosophy of naturalness does not give rise to pessimism or renunciation. Even Xi Kang and Ruan Ji did not abandon the promise of renewal. Although many had found in the ancient recluse a source of inspiration, and despite the fact that it was common for the literati to refuse office, there is an optimistic sense that naturalness and nonaction would in the end bring about harmony and peace. By redefining tradition in a Daoist light, a deeper understanding would help remove the obstacles that stand in the way of the unfolding of Daoist order.

See also Guo Xiang; Ruan Ji; Wang Bi; Xi Kang.

Bibliography

Balazs, Etienne. *Chinese Civilization and Bureaucracy: Variations on a Theme*. trans. H. M. Wright. New Haven, Conn.: Yale University Press, 1964.

Bauer, Wolfgang. *China and the Search for Happiness: Recurring Themes in Four Thousand Years of Chinese Cultural History*, trans. Michael Shaw. New York: Seabury, 1976.

Cambridge History of China, Vol. 1, *The Ch'in and Han Empires, 221 B.C.—A.D. 220*, ed. Denis Twitchett and Michael Loewe, ch. 16, "Philosophy and Religion from Han to Sui." Cambridge: Cambridge University Press, 1986, pp. 808–878.

Chan, Alan K. L. *Two Visions of the Way: A Study of the Wang Pi and Ho-shang Kung Commentaries on the Lao-tzu*. Albany: State University of New York Press, 1991.

Chan, Wing-tsit. *A Source Book in Chinese Philosophy*. Princeton, N.J.: Princeton University Press, 1963.

Dien, Albert E., ed. *State and Society in Early Medieval China*. Stanford, Calif.: Stanford University Press, 1990.

Fung, Yu-lan (Feng Youlan). *A History of Chinese Philosophy*, trans. Derk Bodde, Vol. 2. Princeton, N.J.: Princeton University Press, 1983.

Graham, A. C. *The Book of Lieh-tzu*. London: Murray, 1960.

Henricks, Robert G., trans. *Philosophy and Argumentation in Third-Century China: The Essays of Hsi K'ang*. Princeton, N.J.: Princeton University Press, 1983.

Holcombe, Charles. *In the Shadow of the Han: Literati Thought and Society at the Beginning of the Southern Dynasties*. Honolulu: University of Hawaii Press, 1994.

Holzman, Donald. "La poésie de Ji Kang." *Journal Asiatique*, 248(1–2), 1980, pp. 107–177; (3–4), 1980, pp. 323–378.

(Reprinted in Holzman, *Immortals, Festivals, and Poetry in Medieval China*. Aldershot: Ashgate Variorum, 1998.)
———. *Poetry and Politics: The Life and Works of Juan Chi, A.D. 210–263*. Cambridge: Cambridge University Press, 1976.
———. "Les sept sages de la forêt des bambous et la société de leur temps." *T'oung Pao*, 44, 1956, pp. 317–346.
———. *La vie et la pensée de Hi K'ang (223–262 Ap. J.C.)*. Leiden: Brill, 1957.
Kohn, Livia. *Early Chinese Mysticism: Philosophy and Soteriology in the Taoist Tradition*. Princeton, N.J.: Princeton University Press, 1992.
Lin, Paul J., trans. *A Translation of Lao-tzu's Tao-te ching and Wang Pi's Commentary*. Ann Arbor: Center for Chinese Studies, University of Michigan, 1977.
Lynn, Richard J., trans. *The Classic of Changes: A New Translation of the I Ching as Interpreted by Wang Bi*. New York: Columbia University Press, 1994.
———, trans. *The Classic of the Way and Virtue: A New Translation of the Tao-te ching of Laozi as Interpreted by Wang Bi*. New York: Columbia University Press, 1999.
Mather, Richard B. "The Controversy over Conformity and Naturalness during the Six Dynasties." *History of Religions*, 9(2–3), 1969–1970, pp. 160–180.
———, trans. *Shih-shuo Hsin-yü: A New Account of Tales of the World by Liu I-ch'ing with Commentary by Liu Chün*. Minneapolis: University of Minnesota Press, 1976.
Sailey, Jay. *The Master Who Embraces Simplicity: A Study of the Philosopher Ko Hung, A.D. 283–343*. San Francisco, Calif.: Chinese Materials Center, 1978.
Shih, Vincent Y. C., trans. *The Literary Mind and the Carving of Dragons by Liu Hsieh: A Study of Thought and Pattern in Chinese Literature*. New York: Columbia University Press, 1959.
Shyrock, J. K., trans. *The Study of Human Abilities: The Jen Wu Chih of Liu Shao*. New Haven, Conn.: American Oriental Society, 1937. (Reprinted, New York: Paragon, 1966.)
Wagner, Rudolf G. *The Craft of a Chinese Commentator: Wang Bi on the Laozi*. Albany: State University of New York Press, 2000.
Yü Ying-shih. "Individualism and the Neo-Taoist Movement in Wei-Chin China." *Individualism and Holism: Studies in Confucian and Taoist Values*, ed. Donald Munro. Ann Arbor: Center for Chinese Studies, University of Michigan, 1985, pp. 121–155.

Daoism (Taoism): Religious

Livia Kohn

Religious Daoism is the higher indigenous religion of China that developed first in the Later Han dynasty through a combination of ancient Daoist thought; the belief in immortality; various physical, medical, and meditative practices; and the millenarian belief in the beginning of a new age of "great peace," *taiping*. It is first apparent in various popular movements around the beginning of the Common Era and finds its initial formal organization in two groups, known as the Great Peace (Taiping) and the Celestial Masters (Tianshi). Both their systems of organization and their goals were very similar. Inspired by revelations from the deified Laozi, they practiced a stringent moral code, the public confession of sins, meditative recitation of the *Daodejing* and purification rituals in preparation of the new age to come, the Taiping even rising in rebellion to hasten its arrival.

Further revelations as well as the increasingly active presence of Buddhism in China led, over the following centuries, to the reorganization of the Celestial Masters into a universal religion and to the formation of further organized schools. The most important of these are Highest Purity (Shangqing) and Numinous Treasure (Lingbao), which both began in the fourth century and came to flourish in the fifth and sixth centuries. They differed from the Celestial Masters in that Highest Purity was a more upper-class phenomenon that placed foremost emphasis on individual realization of the *dao* through ecstatic visions, while Numinous Treasure was most strongly inspired by Buddhism and strove for universal salvation.

Around the beginning of the Tang dynasty, Daoism was organized into one integrated structure under the leadership of Highest Purity and became the dominant form of Chinese religion, bringing forth a number of inspiring leaders and scholastic thinkers. In the Song dynasty, with the collapse of earlier structures, a number of new schools emerged, the most important of which was Complete Perfection (Quanzhen), a monastic order patterned after Chan Buddhism. It focused on individual realization through both physical and spiritual practices, combined into a system known as inner alchemy (*neidan*), the dominant form of Daoist thought ever since. In the following centuries, this merged with Confucian, Buddhist, and popular ideas in a "harmony of the three teachings," re-creating the teaching in a new syncretism.

Religious Daoism as a whole is best divided into three types or stages: an early or classical stage from the ancient philosophers to the Han dynasty (500 B.C.E.–100 B.C.E.); a medieval or organized stage that begins with the Celestial Masters and ends with the Tang dynasty (100–900 B.C.E.); and a modern or new stage from Song times onward (900 to the present). Within this framework, its philosophy (with the exclusion of the ancient texts *Laozi* and *Zhuangzi*) can be described under six headings that are both typological in nature and chronological in arrangement: (1) early political visions; (2) medieval cosmology; (3) Buddho-Daoist thought; (4) speculation and systematizations; (5) inner alchemy; (6) the new syncretism. The following will present them one by one.

Early Political Visions

The religious Daoist movements of the second century were strongly eschatological, aiming to prepare a new age of *taiping* ("great peace"). This was originally a mainstream Chinese ideal, understood as the complete harmony of all cosmic, natural, and social forces in a state that had existed in the remote past and could be restored through perfect government. In the Former Han dynasty, it was taken up by the Huang-Lao school of Daoism, so called after the two senior representatives of its ideas, the Yellow Emperor (Huangdi) and the ancient philosopher Laozi. As documented in the philosophical text *Huainanzi*, Heshang Gong's commentary on the *Daodejing*, and in silk manuscripts found in tombs, the teaching of Huang-Lao was syncretic, combining the statecraft of legalism, classical Daoism, and *yin-yang* cosmology.

Huang-Lao Daoism sees the *dao* as the highest and most fundamental force of creation, which underlies all existence and orders both the human world and the universe at large. The *dao* pervades all, with the effect that there is no significant qualitative difference between the different levels of cosmos, nature, state, and the human body. Cultivation of one plane consequently must take into account not only the reverberations on all others but also how it influences the entire system. The cosmos is seen as an integrated unity, in which the government of the state, the personal cultivation of the self, and the observation of natural and celestial cycles are different aspects of one and the same system. In its ideal functioning, this overarching harmony constitutes *taiping*, a state of universal interaction in utmost harmony and openness.

Whereas both Confucian and Huang-Lao thinkers saw the realization of *taiping* mainly through the ruler's perfect government, early religious Daoists, facing an increasingly catastrophic situation both environmentally and politically, took its development into their own hands. Inspired by visions of the deity of the *dao*, they constituted communities to prepare the new age and, as in the case of the Great Peace movement, instigated insurrections to achieve their goal. The latter's vision in particular is documented in the *Taiping jing* (*Scripture of Great Peace*), an early text that was lost after the Yellow Turban rebellion of 184 (which it had inspired) and reconstituted in the sixth century.

According to this, *taiping* in antiquity was realized not so much through the government of the ruler as through the hidden (*wuwei*) activity of the sages, who stayed behind the scenes and made sure both nature and society functioned at their best. As time went on, culture declined, eventually leading to a period of utter decadence which in its turn, after a period of destruction and chaos, would make room for a renewed age of *taiping*. The renewal of the age begins with a recovery of the original energy (*qi*) within the individual through moral abstention from sin, a meditation known as "guarding the one" (*shouyi*), and other practices associated with immortality. Establishing perfect harmony within the person is thus the first step toward achieving a harmony of the entire cosmos.

Once the individual has found his own inner harmony, he will recognize himself as one of nine possible beings, ranging from slaves through commoners and wise men to divine immortals. Established in proper order, the main task of these beings is to maintain an open exchange and circulation of energy, allowing the cosmos to unfold without obstruction. This, in turn, will provide the necessary framework for the perfect harmony of *taiping*.

Medieval Cosmology

The organized schools of the fourth and fifth centuries inherited this vision and expanded it to include a complex cosmology and mythology. The Celestial Masters, reformed under the leadership of Lu Xiujing (406–477), developed it to include an active role of the deified Laozi as creator and savior. Like earlier Daoists they, too, felt the need for an open and harmonious cosmos, in which the three forces heaven, earth, and humanity joined together in smooth interaction. They similarly deplored the corrupt state of affairs of the present age, obvious particularly in the performance of blood sacrifices and other depraved practices.

In their new vision, however, the *dao* actively comes to the rescue. As described in the *Santian neijie jing* (*Inner Explanation of the Three Heavens*), the *dao* as underlying creative power of the world transforms into three basic energies (*qi*)—mysterious, primordial, and beginning—at the dawn of time. The energies, in turn, intermingle in chaos (*hundun*) and bring forth the Jade Maiden of Mystery and Wonder (*Xuanmiao yunü*), who then gives birth to Laozi, the personification of the *dao*, through her left armpit. Under Laozi's guidance, the planet earth and the world of humanity come into existence: mysterious energy rises up to form heaven, beginning energy sinks down and becomes earth, primordial energy flows everywhere and turns into water—thus giving shape to the three basic realms of the Celestial Masters' universe.

Next, Laozi establishes nine countries on earth, in which he places nine people each (three men and six women) and to whom he gives an appropriate religion: Daoism to China, Buddhism to the western barbarians, and the way of *yin* and *yang* to the southern countries. To ensure the proper prosperity especially of the Middle Kingdom, Laozi then appears as the teacher of dynasties to guide the government of the mythical rulers down to the late Shang dynasty. After that, he is born in human form to become the ancient philosopher, and as such leaves China to convert the western barbarians to Buddhism, now thought of as an inferior form of Daoism. Returning to China, he reveals the *Taiping jing* and the way of the Celestial Masters, forever ready to help the age and save humanity from its plight. Expanding the vision of Great Peace through the mythology of Laozi and a more complex cosmology, the Celestial Masters in the fifth century thus developed Daoism toward a more universal religion.

A similar tendency was also true in Highest Purity Daoism, whose scriptures were first revealed to the medium Yang Xi in 364–370 and codified by Tao Hongjing (456–536) in his major work *Zhengao* (*Declarations of the Perfected*). Its system greatly expands the cosmology and pantheon of the Han dynasty, yet still sees the *dao* as the one force at the center of all existence. The *dao* creates the two forces *yin* and *yang*, which develop the three and the five: the three vertical levels of heaven, earth, and humanity; and the five horizontal agents (*wuxing*) of wood, fire, earth, metal, and water, linked with the four cardinal directions and the center.

The center, in particular, is represented by the Northern Dipper in the sky and Mount Kunlun on earth, which both regulate the heavens, adjust *yin* and *yang*, and serve as the home of immortals and gods, who live there in magnificent palaces with golden terraces and jade towers. The south is the region of everlasting life, the place of purification and rebirth. Known as the Southern or Red Palace, it is a paradise where successful aspirants to immortality are registered and come to reside. The north, on the contrary, houses the underworld. Called Fengdu, it serves as a place of judgment and is staffed by a demon administration, among whose ranks many mythical heroes of old have found a place. They labor here for a period of time to eventually rise in rank and attain immortality in the Southern Palace.

The system contains a total number of thirty-six heavens, with Highest Purity at the top, where senior traditional deities reside, such as the Queen Mother of the West (Xiwang mu), the Ruler of Fates (Siming), and the Jade Emperor (Yuhuang). It is further complicated by the veneration of eight nodal points in time and space, of the twenty-four stars of the zodiac, and of nine major constellations in the sky. In addition, the entire cosmology is replicated in the human body, where the three vertical levels are the cinnabar fields (*dantian*) in the head, chest, and abdomen; the five agents are the five inner organs; the twenty-four zodiac stars are radiant divinities; and the nine major constellations are nine palaces in the head.

The system is activated in practice through visualizations of the energy centers, palaces, and gods in the body, as well as through ecstatic excursions both horizontally to the far ends of the world and vertically into the heavens of the immortals. Joining their consciousness with the celestial powers, adepts become heavenly beings, at one with the *dao* and in constant interaction with the world at large. Whereas the Celestial Masters find the openness of *taiping* in a communal organization, it is here realized individually through personal transformation to a cosmic level.

Buddhist-Daoist Thought

Buddhist influence shapes the third major school of medieval Daoism, Numinous Treasure. Transforming the vision of Great Peace into the ideal of universal salvation and expanding traditional cosmology, it borrows Buddhist technical terms, scriptural patterns, cosmological structures, ethical rules, and major doctrines, including most prominently that of karma and retribution (*yinguo*).

Numinous Treasure has thirty-two horizontal heavens, each created from a sacred *dharani* spell of eight characters that is translated from a sacred tongue called Brahma-language. Its cosmology centers on the number ten, so that it has ten directions, ten good deeds, ten stages to immortality (*bhìmi*), ten major precepts (*shijie*), and so on. Its highest god is the Heavenly Worthy of Primordial Beginning (Yuanshi tianzun), an adaptation of Buddha, and its scriptures follow the standard pattern of Mahayana sutras. Thus, in a typical scripture, as for example the *Zuigen pin* (*The Roots of Sin*), the deity resides in great splendor among a celestial assembly and teaches the "divine law" to his primary assistant and savior bodhisattva, the Highest Lord of the Dao (Taishang daojun).

The world, moreover, develops in a series of declining ages or *kalpas*. First, during Dragon Han (Longhan), people are pure and lead a simple life, helped by the Heavenly Worthy to live without sin and in perfect peace with the *dao*. Second, in Red Radiance (Chiming), there is a trace of impurity and evil among living beings, and karma and retribution first begin. Third, during Opening Sovereign (Kaihuang), people still live simply, but there are the beginnings of culture and civilization. Fourth and finally, in Highest Sovereign (Shanghuang), culture develops fully and the world declines toward jealousy and strife, hatred and war. All the Heavenly Worthy can do is hand down precepts and rules and accept the bodhisattva vow of the Lord of the Dao to ensure the salvation of as many as possible.

The Numinous Treasure universe is governed by the law of karma and retribution. Deluded by the six passions (*liuqing*), the excesses of the five senses and the mind, people engage in sinful acts and accumulate bad karma. Precepts attempt to contain the activity of the passions, and scriptures specify the rewards and punishments one is to expect, such as better or worse forms of rebirth, the delights of heaven, or the tortures in the various hells. The key practice of the school is ritual and prayer, aimed to expiate sins, enhance goodness on earth, and foster a striving for universal salvation (*dushi*). Overall, Numinous Treasure Daoism can be described as the most indigenous adaptation of Buddhism in China.

A different form of Buddhist-Daoist thought is apparent in works of the northern Celestial Masters who, in the fifth century, established a major religious center at Louguan in the Chung-nan mountains. Centering on the revelation of Laozi's *Daodejing* and its accompanying oral instructions, these works, as, for example, the *Xisheng jing* (*Scripture of Western Ascension*), merge Buddhist concepts with the classical Daoist worldview and cosmology. They link the four Indian elements with the four seasons, describe the three karmic causes (*sanye*, *trividhadvara*) of body, speech, and mind as originally part of the *dao*, and connect the doctrines of causation and rebirth with the indigenous concept of fate.

More specifically, the word *se* in these writings refers to both visual stimulation and matter (*rupa*); *fan* indicates both *klesa* and general troubles and afflictions; *shen* is the self as cultivated in the Confucian and Daoist traditions as well as the *atman* denied in Buddhist doctrine. "No-self" (*wushen*, *anatman*) is interpreted as the state before one was born, again giving a native tinge to a foreign concept, while "unknowing" (*wuzhi*), the ultimate state of mind, is seen in the light of both *Zhuangzi* and Chinese Buddhism. The tendency of joining Buddhist concepts with traditional Daoist ideas is very similar to contemporaneous Buddhist writings, as, for example, those of Sengzhao. Typical for this kind of Daoist thinking, it continues in a more scholastic and sophisticated manner well into the Tang dynasty.

Speculation and Systematization

Whereas pre-Tang Daoists strove to establish a basic set of canonical scriptures, an ordination hierarchy with a working ethical code, and an overarching cosmology, Daoist thinkers of the Tang developed the already integrated, complex religious system toward higher sophistication. They turned to logical speculation, asked more subtle theoretical questions, gave new interpretations to the scriptures, and provided various systematizations to the Daoist teaching.

In the seventh century, Daoist logic emerges as based on the Madhyamika theory of the two truths. Formulated in China by Jizang (549–623), they describe realization in three stages: first, through a passage from worldly truth to the absolute truth of emptiness; second, from emptiness, now understood as another form of worldly truth, to the new absolute truth of complete nonduality, neither being nor nonbeing; third, from duality and nonduality to neither duality nor nonduality.

This model was adapted in Daoism under the name of Twofold Mystery (Chongxuan), an expression that goes back to the line "mysterious and again mysterious" in the first chapter of the *Daodejing*. In the Tang, the word "mysterious" appears as a verb in the sense of "to make mysterious," so that the phrase "mysterious and again mysterious" is parallel to "decrease and again decrease" (*Daodejing*, 48). The idea is that one discards all desires in two steps; it also implies a theoretical approach to the *dao* in the twofold movement of making mysterious and decreasing ever more.

Twofold Mystery finds its main expressions in commentaries that give new vision to ancient scriptures. Most important among them are Cheng Xuanying's exegesis of the *Daodejing* and the *Zhuangzi*, and Li Rong's commentaries on the *Daodejing* and the *Xishengjing*. The school's thinking is also dominant in newly compiled, highly philosophical scriptures, the most famous of which are the *Benjijing* (*Scripture of the Genesis Point*) and the *Haikong jing* (*Scripture of Master Haikong*), both placed in the mouth of the Heavenly Worthy preaching from a lotus throne in the heavenly realm.

Two major systematizations of Daoist thought date from the late seventh century. There is first Wang Xuanhe's *Sandong zhunang* (*A Bag of Pearls from the Three Caverns*), in ten scrolls and forty sections, which covers the major areas of ideal Daoist lives, forms of physical and meditative practice, ritual activities, and the cosmology of gods and heavens. It follows in both pattern and outlook—with a rather low-key Buddhist influence—the earlier encyclopedia *Wushang biyao* (*Esoteric Essentials of the Most High*), a state-sponsored work of the year 574.

The other systematic work of the seventh century is Meng Anpai's *Daojiao yishu* (*The Pivotal Meaning of the Daoist Teaching*), written in response to Buddhist criticism. In ten scrolls and thirty-seven sections, it outlines the basic doctrines and path of the religion, covering the "*dao* and the virtue," the organization of the scriptures, the psychology of karma and retribution, and major meditative methods, as well as supernatural powers and ultimate attainments. In each case, there is strong Buddhist influence, and the work shows an enormous scholastic effort at systematizing the various Daoist teachings in a complex integrated vision.

Systematization continued along different lines in the eighth century, with three masters writing treatises to make the Daoist teaching more accessible to interested literati. The three are the physician-cum-alchemist Sun Simiao (601–693), the Highest Purity patriarch Sima Chengzhen (647–735), and the Daoist poet Wu Yun (d. 778). Prolific writers, they all strove to simplify the complex constructions and logical convolutions of their forebears in favor of straightforward outlines of the path.

According to them, the key purpose of Daoism is the transformation from ordinary to immortal life, which takes place on the levels of body, emotions, and conscious thinking. The aim is first to develop the personal body (*shen*), an individual entity, into a cosmic body (*xing*), a sense of physical self as part of a larger framework of nature. This is achieved with the help of longevity practices (*yangsheng*), such as breathing exercises, diets, and gymnastics. Next, the conscious mind (*xin*) with its thoughts and desires, through a variety of meditations such as concentration (*ding*), observation (*guan*), and sitting in oblivion (*zuowang*), is trained to see and feel a distance between the underlying perfection of the *dao* and the surface waves of feeling and consciousness. Worldly tasks and pursuits are found shallow and considered hindrances to the goal, while the ordinary understanding of the world is reevaluated as "foolish imaginings" and eventually given up altogether. Through this transformation, the individual with a set personality is lost in favor of a wider sense of self in immortal oneness with the *dao*.

Continuing this synthesis, Du Guangting (850–933), a court Daoist who served as editor of imperial memoranda and commissioner of Daoist ritual, wrote various works, including mirabilia, saints' biographies, liturgies, and commentaries, with the goal to rescue the *dao* in an age of civil war and cultural decline. His philosophical contribution is found most explicitly in his commentaries, the largest of which is the *Daode zhenjing guangsheng yi* (*Wide Sage Meaning of the Perfect Scripture of the Dao and Virtue*) in fifty scrolls, a masterpiece of *Daodejing* systematization and integrative interpretation. Going back to ancient philosophical concepts, Du's vision of Laozi and his teachings continues an age-old philosophical tradition, while his understanding of the gods reflects the pantheon of the Celestial Masters, his ritual concepts are influenced by Numinous Treasure, and his ideals of Daoist practice reflect Highest Purity. His work is thus representative of the doctrinal integration and high scholastic standards of Daoism in the Tang.

Inner Alchemy

After the Tang-Song transition and the decline of traditional religious forms, inner alchemy (*neidan*) became the dominant form of Daoist thought and practice, and it has remained so ever since. It newly integrates the various strands of the tradition, making use of ancient physical and meditative practices and going beyond them in placing a heavy emphasis on the trigrams and hexagrams (*gua*) of the *Yijing* (*Book of Changes*) and identifying the inner meditative development of the adept with the process of concocting elixirs in operative alchemy. In other words, Daoist attainment in inner alchemy is understood as a sequence of internal quasi-chemical reactions that, when applied properly, lead people out of the limitations of this world and into the celestial sphere.

The inner alchemical process takes place in three transformative stages: from essence (*jing*) to energy (*qi*), from energy to spirit (*shen*), and from spirit to emptiness (*xü*) or the *dao*. The first stage begins with essence, a gross, materially visible form of energy that is identified as semen in men and as menstrual blood in women. It is originally transformed from primordial energy, which in men resides in the "ocean of energy" in the abdomen and in women is found in the "cavity of energy" in the breast area. The aim of the practice at this stage is to restore essence that has already been formed from energy back to its original form and to prevent future disintegration of energy into more essence, as which it could be discharged, thus giving the life force away. Massages and exercises together with a meditative reversion of the downward movement of energy accomplish this goal.

The second stage sees the emergence of a pearl of pure energy in the newly replenished store of energy and its transformation into an immortal embryo through the union of the adept's internal *yin* and *yang* forces. *Yang* then is identified as the heart, the agent fire, the trigram *li*, pure lead, and the dragon; *yin* is linked with the kidneys, the agent water, the trigram *kan*, pure mercury, and the tiger. In a strictly regulated rhythm, the two types of energy revolve through the front and back of the torso and the head in the so-called microcosmic orbit to eventually mate and produce the immortal embryo. The embryo is then nurtured for ten months with a method called "embryo respiration" (*taixi*), a form of inner meditative breathing.

Once the embryo is complete, its still semimaterial body is transformed into a pure spirit body of immortality, which is a body of pure *yang* and pure life (higher forms, not counterparts of *yin* or death). It then develops in four phases: first, it is born as an independent entity, yet still within the adept's body; next, it is carefully fed for three years and taught to exit the body through the Heavenly Gate at the top of the head; third, over nine years of meditation, it learns to blend its existence with emptiness and dissolve into the pure *dao* itself; and finally, already a spirit of pure *yang*, it merges completely with the cosmic force of the *dao*.

Based on *Yijing* exegesis and traditional alchemical texts, such as the *Cantong qi* (*Tally to the Book of Changes*), inner alchemical thinking is first apparent in the eighth century. It merges technical *Yijing* interpretation with ecstatic visions of Highest Purity. In the ninth century, the earliest inner alchemical works are the *Huanjin shu* (*The Art of Reverting Gold*) and the *Ruyao jing* (*Mirror of Entering the Divine Drug*).

During the Song dynasty, inner alchemy develops in distinct northern and southern schools. The northern school, closely associated with Complete Perfection Daoism, goes back to the legendary patriarchs Zhongli Quan and Lü Dongbin and is accordingly also known as the Zhong-Lü school. Documented, among others, in the *Lingbao bifa* (*Ultimate Methods of Numinous Treasure*) and the *Zhong-Lü chuandao ji* (*Record of Zhong and Lü's Transmission of the Dao*), the teaching of this school is strictly ascetic, eschewing sexual practices and favoring poverty in a primarily monastic setting. It places foremost emphasis on meditative and psychological transformation, favoring the cultivation of *xing*, inner nature, over that of *ming*, physical life or destiny.

The southern school shows a contrary emphasis and does not demand a strictly monastic discipline. Its most famous representatives are Zhang Boduan (984–1082), Liu Cao (c. 1134–1229), Bai Yuchan (c. 1209–1224), Chen Nan (d. 1213), and Li Daochun (c. 1290). Major works include the *Wuzhen pian* (*Awakening to Perfection*) and the *Zhonghe ji* (*Collection of Central Harmony*). In the fourteenth century, the two schools undergo a process of integration, documented most clearly in the works of Chen Chixu (c. 1330), better known as Shangyangzi, such as his *Jindan dayao* (Great Principles of the Golden Elixir, 1067). In this form, inner alchemy has remained dominant in Daoist thought to the present day, unfolding in new variants and influencing both literati and popular practice.

The New Syncretism

During the Ming and Qing dynasties, religious Daoist thought merged variously with Confucianism, Chinese popular culture, and Buddhism. First, inner alchemy made its way into the neo-Confucian elite of the late Ming, influencing the practice and teachings of important thinkers, such as Wang Yangming (1472–1529) and his disciple Wang Ji (1498–1583). Practicing friendly interaction with Daoist monks and priests, these thinkers actively learned Daoist techniques, followed exercises and diet regimens, and even attained oneness with the *dao*. This practice influenced their idea of meditation, understood as the pondering of things in a state of unperturbed mind, and their vision of the ideal mind or "innate knowledge" (*liangzhi*), which was then defined along the lines of the three inner-alchemical agents as spirit (*shen*) in its function, energy (*qi*) in its pervasion, and essence (*jing*) in its condensation. Although they acknowledged the inherent oneness of the three teachings and wrote books that were, like Zhu Dezhi's *Xiaolian xia* (*A Sheathed Sword for Nocturnal Practice*), classified as Daoist cultivation manuals, they did yet not pursue the traditional aim of immortality but used Daoist theory and practice to give greater illumination to reverence and righteousness.

Both literati and the general populace were further influenced by Daoist thought in a growing movement of keeping ledgers of merit and demerit (*gongguo*) that would allow one to judge one's standing in the otherworldly registers. The movement goes back to a short text of the Song dynasty, the *Ganying pian* (*Tract on Action and Response*). First published around 1164, it was put together by Li Zhiji (d. 1182), a Confucian official from Sichuan, who used originally Daoist notions in his vision of moralizing the masses. The book outlines heaven's blessings, exhorts people to be socially conscious and do good, and details the punishments in store for evildoers. It gave rise to numerous editions and similar treatises, of Confucian, Buddhist, and Daoist origin, on the karmic importance of merits and demerits.

A close interaction of Daoism with Buddhism is further observed in the Qing literature of "precious scrolls" (*baozhuan*), which contain revealed popular teachings that center on the eternal mother goddess and specify the karmic rewards and punishments for actions on earth. Merging popular beliefs with Daoist cosmology and Buddhist doctrine, they have dominated the religious scene of China in the past several centuries, continuing ancient forms of thought in a mode that is both syncretistic and highly popular.

Within Daoism, moreover, there was a revival of the ancient classics of Laozi and Zhuangzi, not unlike the dominant tendency in neo-Confucianism, and many masters and scholars wrote commentaries to them. Most notable among the later ones is the work of Liu Yiming of the early Qing, who edited both the *Yijing* and the *Daodejing* and also wrote inner-alchemical treatises of his own. In addition, formerly lost texts were being reconstituted, as for example the philosophical work of Guanyinzi, an ancient thinker who was identified with Yin Xi, the first recipient of the *Daodejing*. His work of the same name was reedited, if not actually rewritten, in the Yuan dynasty, and appears in the Daoist canon with various commentaries (*Wenshi zhenjing*, or *Perfect Scripture of Master Wenshi*).

Inner alchemy, finally, developed several specific strands of its own. A number of new texts appeared, by both Daoist monks and lay practitioners, which reformulated the traditional threefold transformation in more spiritual or more medical terms. An example here is *the Secret of the Golden Flower of Great Unity* (*Taiyi jinhua zongzhi*) translated variously into English. In a different vein, there were, from about 1600 onward, specialist works on inner alchemy for women that described the process of refining menstrual blood into pure energy ("decapitating the red dragon") and the creation of an immortal embryo not in the abdomen but in the chest.

In the mid-twentieth century, inner alchemy was transformed in the popular movement of *qigong* (energy exercises), a medical application of traditional techniques that left out the ecstatic visions and embryo ascension and instead concentrated on the health benefits of the practice. *Qigong* was suppressed during the Cultural Revolution but was later widely performed all over China in the 1980s and 1990s, with new forms and models appearing almost monthly. It also became an accredited field at schools of traditional Chinese medicine and grew in popularity among alternative health practitioners in the west. After its controversy with the more religious *falun gong* in 1999, the Chinese government prohibited many *qigong* practices, persecuting and often torturing adherents. *Qigong* is still undertaken, but publications and medical accreditation are on the decline. *Qigong* thought, for the most part highly medical and predominantly focused on practice, recovers much of traditional inner alchemy and, in its mythical origins, is often linked with ancient masters, naming Sun Simiao, Laozi, Zhuangzi, and the Yellow Emperor among its patriarchs.

In all cases, the various Daoist ideas and practices, be they physical (*yangsheng*), cosmological (*kunlun*), or spiritual (*jing, qi, shen*), are united in their common goal to guide people to the underlying universal oneness of the *dao*. Although formulated in highly divergent views of philosophy, mythology, and physiology, they yet have the inherent power of the creative force as their central focus, elucidating its manifestations and the divergent ways in which human beings can activate and realize it in an ever-ongoing search for perfection.

See also Buddhism in China; Buddhism: Zen (Chan); Daoism: Neo-Daoism; Jizang; Sengzhao.

Bibliography

Baldrian-Hussein, Farzeen. *Procédés secrets du joyau magique*. Paris: Deux Océans, 1984.

Bokenkamp, Stephen R. *Early Daoist Scriptures*. Berkeley: University of California Press, 1997. (With a contribution by Peter Nickerson.)

———. "Stages of Transcendence: The *Bhumi* Concept in Daoist Scripture." In *Chinese Buddhist Apocrypha*, ed. Robert E. Buswell. Honolulu: University of Hawaii Press, 1990, pp. 119–146.

Boltz, Judith M. *A Survey of Daoist Literature: Tenth to Seventeenth Centuries*. China Research Monograph, No. 32. Berkeley: University of California, 1987.

Brokaw, Cynthia. *The Ledgers of Merit and Demerit: Social Change and Moral Order in Late Imperial China*. Princeton, N.J.: Princeton University Press, 1991.

Cahill, Suzanne. *Transcendence and Divine Passion: The Queen Mother of the West in Medieval China*. Stanford, Calif.: Stanford University Press, 1993.

Cantoung qi (Tally to the Book of Changes). TT 999. Schipper Concordance.

Chan, Alan. *Two Visions of the Way: A Study of the Wang Pi and the Ho-shang-kung Commentaries on the Laozi*. Albany: State University of New York Press, 1991.

Chen, Chixu (Shangyangzi). *Jindan dayao* (Great Principles of the Golden Elixir). TT 1067.

Cleary, Thomas. *The Daoist I jing*. Boston, Mass.: Shambhala, 1986.

———. *Vitality Energy Spirit: A Daoist Sourcebook*. Boston, Mass.: Shambhala, 1991.

Du, Guanting. *Daode zhenjing guangsheng yi* (Wide Sage Meaning of the Perfect Scripture of Dao and Virtue). TT 725.

Haikong jing (Scripture of Master Haikong). TT 9.

Huanjin shu (The Art of Reverting Gold). TT 922.

Kaltenmark, Max. "The Ideology of the *Taiping-ching*." In *Facets of Daoism*, ed. Holmes Welch and Anna Seidel. New Haven, Conn.: Yale University Press, 1979, pp. 19–52.

Kobayashi, Masayoshi. *Rikuchodokyoshi kenkyu*. Tokyo: Sobunsha, 1990.

Kohn, Livia, ed. *Daoism Handbook*. Leiden: Brill, 2000.

———. *The Daoist Experience: An Anthology*. Albany: State University of New York Press, 1993.

———. *Daoist Mystical Philosophy: The Scripture of Western Ascension*. Albany: State University of New York Press, 1991.

———. *Early Chinese Mysticism: Philosophy and Soteriology in the Daoist Tradition*. Princeton, N.J.: Princeton University Press, 1992.

———. *Seven Steps to the Dao: Sima Chengzhen's Zuowanglun*. Monumenta Serica Monograph No. 20. St. Augustin/Nettetal, 1987.

Li, Zhiji. *Ganying pian* (Tract on Action and Response). TT 1167.

Lingbao bifa (Ultimate Methods of Numinous Treasure). TT 1191.

Liu Ts'un-yan. *Buddhist and Daoist Influences on Chinese Novels*. Wiesbaden: Harrassowitz, 1962.

———. "Daoist Self-Cultivation in Ming Thought." In *Self and Society in Ming Thought*, ed. William Theodore De Bary. New York: Columbia University Press, 1970, pp. 291–331.

Major, John S. *Heaven and Earth in Early Han Thought: Chapters Three, Four, and Five of the Huainanzi*. Albany: State University of New York Press, 1993.

Meng, Anpai. *Daojiao yishu* (The Pivotal Meaning of the Daoist Teaching). TT 1129.

Peerenboom, R. P. *Law and Morality in Ancient China: The Silk Manuscripts of Huang-Lao*. Albany: State University of New York Press, 1991.

Reiter, Florian C. *Grundelemente des religiösen Daoismus: Das Spannungsverhältnis von Integration und Individualität in seiner Geschichte zur Chin-, Yüan- und frühen Ming- Zeit*. Stuttgart: Franz Steiner Verlag. (Also Ostasiatische Studien, No. 48. Munich, 1988.)

———. *Der Perlenbeutel aus den drei Höhlen: Arbeitsmaterialien zum Daoismus der frühen Tang-Zeit. Asiatische Forschungen*, Vol. 12. Wiesbaden: Otto Harrassowitz, 1990.

Robinet, Isabelle. *Les commentaires du Dao to king jusqu'au VIIe siècle*. Mémoires de l'Institut des Hautes Études Chinoises, No. 5. Paris, 1977.

———. *Histoire du Daoisme: Des origins au XIVe siècle*. Paris: Éditions Cerf, 1991.

———. *Introduction à l'alchimie intérieure daoiste: De l'unité et de la multiplicité*. Paris: Éditions Cerf, 1995.

———. "Original Contributions of *Neidan* to Daoism and Chinese Thought." In *Daoist Meditation and Longevity Techniques*, ed. Livia Kohn. Ann Arbor: University of Michigan, Center for Chinese Studies Publications, 1989.

———. *La révélation du Shangqing dans l'histoire du Daoisme*, 2 vols. Paris: École Française d'Extrême-Orient, 1984.

Ruyao jing (Mirror of Entering the Divine Drug). TT 263, 21.1a.

Santian neijie jing (Inner Explanation of the Three Heavens). TT1205.

Seidel, Anna. "The Image of the Perfect Ruler in Early Daoist Messianism." *History of Religions*, 9, 1969, pp. 216–247.

Sivin, Nathan. *Chinese Alchemy: Preliminary Studies*. Cambridge, Mass.: Harvard University Press, 1968.

Tao, Hongjing. *Zhengao* (Declarations of the Perfected). TT 1016.

Verellen, Franciscus. *Du Guangting (850–933): Daoiste de cour à la fin de la Chine médiévale*. Mémoires de l'Institut des Hautes Études Chinoises, No. 30. Paris: Collège du France, 1989.

Wang, Xuanhe. *Sandong zhunang* (A Bag of Pearls from the Three Caverns). TT 1139.

Wenshi zhenjing (Perfect Scripture of Master Wenshi). TT 667, 727, 728.

Wile, Douglas. *Art of the Bedchamber: The Chinese Sexology Classics Including Women's Solo Meditation Texts*. Albany: State University of New York Press, 1992.

Wushang biyao (Esoteric Essentials of the Most High). TT 1138.

Wuzhen pian (Awakening to Perfection). TT 263, 27.1a.

Xisheng jing (Scripture of Western Ascension). TT 726.

Zhongheji (Collection of Central Harmony). TT 249.

Zhong-Lü chuan-dao ji (Record of Zhong and Lü's Transmission of the Dao). TT 1017, 39–41.

Zuigen pin (The Roots of Sin). TT 457.

Zürcher, Erik. "Buddhist Influence on Early Daoism." *T'oung-pao*, 66, 1980, pp. 84–147.

Daoism: Texts in Guodian (Kuo-tien) Bamboo Slips

Xiaogan Liu

Among the Guodian bamboo slips (*Guodian zhujian*), three different bundles, distinguished by their size, shape, and handwriting style, are identified as Daoist texts. Group 1, with the longest slips, labeled "Laozi A," is the largest of the three bundles, containing paragraphs or sections corresponding to chapters 2, 5, 9, 15, 16, 19, 25, 30, 32, 37, 40, 44, 46, 55, 56, 57, 63, 64a, 64b, and 66 in the traditional eighty-one-chapter versions of the *Laozi*. Group 2, with slightly shorter slips, labeled "Laozi B," includes counterparts of chapters 13, 20, 41, 45, 48, 52, 54, and 59 in the traditional versions. Group 3, with the shortest slips, is divided into two parts according to its content. The first part, "Laozi C," comprises sections from chapters 17, 18, 31, 35, and 64. Thus, the slips of the *Laozi* contain a total of thirty-three chapters or passages corresponding to thirty-one chapters in the received traditional versions. The second part of Group 3 was a previously unknown text. It was given the title *Taiyi sheng shui* (*The Ultimate Generating Water*), from its first sentence.

Opinions about the date of the *Laozi* and its author can be roughly classified into three theories: "Laozi and Confucian," "before Zhuangzi," and "after Zhuangzi." The "Laozi and Confucian" theory, based on traditional literature and new investigations, proposes that the essential part or the core of the *Laozi* reflected the concepts of Laozi, a senior contemporary of Confucius. After reexamination and encouraged by recent archaeological discoveries, some leading scholars have returned to this theory. According to the "after Zhuangzi" theory, the *Laozi* came later than the *Zhuangzi*, or later than its inner chapters. According to the "before Zhuangzi" theory, the text was composed in the middle of the Warring States period before the time of the *Zhuangzi*. This seems to be a compromise between the other two positions. The new discovery of the *Laozi* from Guodian seems not to have resolved the conflict: all the theorists have found in the slips certain reasons to defend their own hypotheses and to reject other theories.

The various standpoints are supported by different evaluations of the slips of the *Laozi*. The first assumption is that the Guodian versions were the three excerpts of the earlier and relatively complete text of the *Laozi*. This is maintained by the "Laozi and Confucian" theory. The evidence for this position is that in both bundle A and bundle C there is a section easily seen as identical to Chapter 64 in the received versions, except for different wording. This suggests that they were inscribed from the two different earlier editions of the texts, and their common ancestral edition must be still earlier. The ancestral edition is likely to be the text called the *Laozi*. One advantage of this theory is that it is in accordance with and supported by historical literature about Lao Dan, the supposed author of the *Laozi*. Some scholars argue that the chapters or passages of the *Laozi* in each of the three groups of slips seem to be classified according to their themes. The only difficulty with this theory is how to explain the fact that there are no counterparts of chapters 67 to 81, the last fifteen chapters, in the slips. However, it seems plausible in light of the explanation that the excerptors selected the slip chapters which suited their needs and preference—that is, their use of the *Laozi* in their own time.

The second assumption is that the three bundles consisted of the earliest and complete text of the *Laozi*. However, the difficulty with this assumption is how to explain the two different versions of Chapter 64 in Laozi A and and Laozi C.

The third assumption is that the slip versions represent the middle phase of the composition of the text by compilers and editors over a long period.

The second and third assumptions support the "before Zhuangzi" theory or the "after Zhuangzi" theory. The evidence for these two claims is the fact that only sixteen of the thirty-one chapters found on these slips are complete. This may suggest that later compilers and editors added other sayings. The disadvantage of these assumptions is that they have to abandon all historical literature and records and rely only on inferences from and speculation about the isolated texts. They have to imagine a story to explain why the short, coherent text took many people a long time to compose, and why all pre-Qin texts attributed the doctrines found in the received versions of the *Laozi* to a Lao Dan, who some skeptics say never existed. These theories have to suppose that theoretical reasoning based on an isolated text is more reliable than historical literature. However, archaeological discoveries often reveal the opposite, in basic facts if not in all details.

It is noteworthy that the discovery of the slips was a coincidence, and so there must be many similar and different ancient texts we will never see. Furthermore, people in ancient times were free to excerpt texts to reflect their personal preferences and intentions. Therefore, the discovery of the bamboo slips may suggest only the possibility that the *Laozi* existed earlier than had been supposed; we cannot rely merely on the slip versions of the *Laozi* to build up a new theory about the formation and composition of the texts.

Concepts in traditional versions of the *Laozi* are broadly reflected in the three sections of slips. Most important Daoist concepts—such as *dao, ziran*, and *wuwei*—can be found in the sections. The term *dao* appears twenty-two times in fourteen chapters, as compared with seventy-six appearances in thirty-six chapters in the received versions. *Wuwei* (nonaction) appears seven times in six chapters (compared with twelve times in nine chapters in the received versions). *Ziran* (naturalness) is used three times in three chapters (five times in five chapters in the received versions). The unique Daoist proposition "When there is no doing, there is nothing left undone" (*wuwei er wu bu wei*), which was absent from the silk versions, is also found in the slips. Sayings and thought are easily identified with the traditional versions, though there are different wordings and sequences of chapters. Generally speaking, the slip versions cover most themes of the received editions—for example, the description of the *dao*, self-cultivation (*xiushen*), and the management of societies (*zhiguo*) with the principles of *wuwei* and *ziran*.

There are some significant differences between the slips and the traditional versions. For example, the first sentence of Chapter 25 in Laozi A is "There is a *form*, formed from murk" (*you zhuang hun cheng*), instead of "There is a *thing*, formed from murk" (*you wu hun cheng*). So the slip versions of the *Laozi* tell us that *dao* is not a *wu* (thing), but it has a *zhuang* (form). Thus the slips make the difference between *dao* and *wu* more apparent and support the suggestion in the received versions that *dao* is conceived as "without shape and yet having an image" (*wu xing er you xiang*).

The most important distinctions in the slip versions are found in Chapter 19. Two sentences in the received versions—"Abandon humanity (*ren*) and discard righteousness (*yi*)" and "Abandon sageliness (*shen*) and discard intelligence (*zhi*)"—are replaced in the slips with "Abandon pretension (*wei*) and discard cunning (*zha*)" and "Abandon intelligence (*zhi*) and discard dispute (*bian*)." This critical difference suggests that the earlier version of the *Laozi* did not attack Confucianism as the received versions did, and this helps us correct our stereotype of the conflict between Daoism and Confucianism in the Warring States period.

The text *Taiyi sheng shui* (*The Ultimate Generating Water*) is a new discovery and has generated great excitement in academic circles. It consists of two or three sections of related slips of texts, according to a tentative order in the current published versions of the new text. One feature of this text is that it emphasizes the importance of water in the generation and development of the universe, in comparison with the traditional concept of *qi* (material force, element). A Daoist proposition, "The way of heaven values softness" (*Tiandao gui rou*), is presented; this was unknown before, although the idea was revealed in the *Laozi*. The key term *taiyi* is often used in the Chinese tradition and had various meanings in ancient China, such as an ultimate, a supreme spirit, an astral body, and the *dao*. In this text, *taiyi* generates (in the following order) water; heaven and earth; *shen* (mysteriousness, or perhaps the sun) and *ming* (brightness or perhaps the moon); *yang* (masculinity) and *yin* (femininity); spring and summer; autumn and winter; heat and cold; dry and wet; and finally the year. All these derivatives assist *taiyi* in return, and the opposites in each pair assist each other. This procedure is generally understood to be the earliest known Chinese cosmogony, though it may be interpreted mainly as having to do with the formation of the year and time rather than the universe.

See also Confucianism: Texts in Guodian Bamboo Slips; Laozi.

Bibliography

Allan, Sarah, and Crispin Williams, eds. *The Guodian Laozi: Proceedings of the International Conference, Dartmouth College, May 1998*. Early China Special Monograph Series, No. 5. Berkeley: Society for the Study of Early China and Institute of East Asian Studies, University of California, 2000.

Chen, Guying, ed. "Daojia wenhua yanjiu." *Studies of Daoist Culture*, No. 17. Beijing: Sanlian, 1999. (Special issue on studies of the Guodian bamboo slips.)

Defoort, Carine, and Xing Wen, eds. "Guodian, Part 1." *Contemporary Chinese Thought*, 32(1), Fall 2000. "Guodian, Part 2." *Contemporary Chinese Thought*, 32(2), Winter 2000–2001. (Special issues, New York: Sharpe.)

Guo, Qiyong, Chen Wei, and Xu Shaohua, eds. *Guodian Chujian Guoji Xueshu Yantaohui Lunwenji* (Proceedings of the International Conference on Guodian Bamboo Slips). Wuhan, Hubei: Hubei Renmin, 2000. (Special issues of *Renwen Luncong*.)

Henricks, Robert G. *Lao Tzu Tao Te Ching: A Translation of the Startling New Documents Found at Guodian*. New York: Columbia University Press, 2000.

Ikeda, Tomohisa, ed. *Kakuken Sokan no sisoshiteki kenkyo* (Studies of Guodian Bamboo Slips in the Perspective of Intellectual History), Vols. 1–4. Tokyo: Society of Studies on Guodian Bamboo Slips, Tokyo University, 1999–2000.

Jiang, Guanghui, and Xin Wen, eds. *Guodian chujian yanjiu* (Studies on Bamboo Slips of Chu State from Guodian). Shenyang: Liaoning Jiaoyu, 1999. (Special issue of *Zhongguo zhexue*, No. 20.)

Jingmenshi Bowuguan (Museum of Jingmen City). *Guodian Chumu Zhujian* (Guodian Chu Tomb Bamboo Slips). Beijing: Wenwu, 1998.

Liao, Mingchun, ed. *Tsinghua's Research on Bamboo and Silk Documents*, Vol. 1. August 2000.

Liu, Xiaogan. Foreword. In Donald Munro, *The Concept of Man in Early China*. Ann Arbor: University of Michigan Press, 2001, pp. i–xv. (Reprint ed.)

———. *Laozi niadai xinkao yu sixiang xinquan* (*Laozi*: A New Investigation of Its Date and New Interpretation of Its Thought). Taipei: Grand East, 1997.

Shen, Andrea. "Ancient Script Rewrites History: This Is Like the Discovery of the Dead Sea Scrolls." *Harvard University Gazette*, 22 January 2001.

Xin Wen, ed. *Guoji Jianbo Yanjiu* (Newsletter: International Research on Bamboo and Silk Documents), Nos. 1–4, 2000. (Published by International Center for Research on Bamboo and Silk Documents.)

Daxue (Ta Hsüeh): The Great Learning

Yanming An

Daxue is one of the most important classics in the Confucian tradition. Originally, it was a relatively obscure chapter (ch. 42) in *Liji* (*Record of Rituals*). Zheng Xuan (127–200) in the later Han dynasty (25–188) wrote the first commentary on the text. Later, in the Tang dynasty (618–896), Han Yu (768–824) stressed its importance for students wishing to enter the gate of the Confucian school. Nevertheless, scholars before the Song dynasty (960–1279) had never seriously investigated the issue of its authorship.

In Song times, the neo-Confucian philosophers, especially the Cheng brothers (Cheng Hao, 1032–1085; and Cheng Yi, 1033–1107), claimed, "*Daxue* is a book transmitted by the Confucian school." Along the same lines, Zhu Xi (1130–1200) exhaustively studied and thoroughly reshaped the text. First, he divided *Daxue* into two major components: the classic (*jing*) part and explanations (*zhuan*). It was his opinion that the former was Confucius's actual words, handed down by his disciple Zengzi. The latter was Zengzi's sayings recorded by his own disciples. Second, Zhu restructured the whole text, even creating a new passage to supply a chapter (ch. 5) which, he believed, had been lost in the process of historical transmission. Third, he contributed a highly consistent commentary on the text. Thereafter, the text of *Daxue* and Zhu Xi's own philosophical insights became a unity, in which the two parts explained and illuminated each other. Traditionally, the text on which Zheng Xuan commented was called "*Daxue* in the ancient version"; the text after his work was called "*Daxue* in the modern version." In addition, Zhu Xi selected *Daxue* as one of the "Four Books," along with *Lunyu* (*Analects*), *Mengzi* (*Mencius*), and *Zhong Yong* (*Doctrine of the Mean*).

Because of its academic strength, as well as imperial support, Zhu Xi's version and commentary became a key to relevant questions asked in the national civil service examinations from 1313 until 1905. The *Daxue* that greatly influenced Chinese intellectual and social life was the one structured and interpreted by Zhu Xi. Despite all kinds of criticism, including criticism from the Wang Yangming (1472–1529) school, it retained its prestige. Today, scholars generally agree that the composition of *Daxue* may belong to the period from the late Warring States to the early Han (around the third century B.C.E.); thus Zhu Xi's account of its authorship seems unacceptable. But, interestingly, most of them continue to conduct their research, explanation, and translation of *Daxue* within the framework that Zhu Xi constructed. Thus Zhu Xi is still a dominant figure in scholarship on the *Daxue*.

According to Zhu Xi, *Daxue* contains eight "items": "investigation of things, extension of knowledge, sincerity of willing, rectification of mind, cultivation of person, regulation of family, ordering of state, and peace throughout the world." In this list, each successive item stands as a necessary condition for the next. Together, the items represent eight phases that a *junzi* (gentleman, nobleman, paradigmatic person) must go through one by one. Also, they designate eight virtues that the *junzi* exhibits when he exerts himself to pass through the phases. In sequence, the items start from a person's inner self and proceed to his external successes, moving from things at hand to those in remote corners of the world.

There are three "principles" in *Daxue*. The first principle, "manifesting illustrious virtue," refers to a moral effort whose content is concretely expressed by the first five items. The second principle, "loving people," underscores the substance of external success elucidated by the last three items. The third principle, "abiding in the highest good," expresses an ideal realm that the paradigmatic individual attains after passing through all the eight phases, as well as a moral imperative to hold to the eight virtues firmly and constantly.

Daxue stresses the "root" (*ben*) and "branches" (*mo*) of personal cultivation. This metaphor conveys a fundamental idea. In a plant, the branches grow naturally and automatically from the roots; and a person's external achievements, like branches, necessarily originate in his internal actions, the roots. In other words, humans "from the son of Heaven down to the common people" all must cultivate their personal life, because this is the only way to realize the highest good or ideal—the good life as a whole.

Of the internal actions, the first one, "sincerity of will," is the most crucial. According to *Daxue*, "What is meant by 'making the will sincere' is allowing no self-deception, as when we hate a bad smell or love a beautiful color." This definition presupposes an evaluating mind that stands behind moral judgments—or, to use another image, is their foundation—and provides criteria for such judgments. When we smell certain things, we know intuitively that they are offensive. When we see certain things, we know intuitively that they are beautiful. Here no reflection or discursive reasoning is involved. Similarly, because of the evaluating mind, we are immediately aware of our transgressions as soon as we behave immorally. Any attempt to deny one's awareness of immorality falls into the category of "self-deception." "Sincerity of will" requires that a gentleman keep his evaluating mind sharp, be cautious of his own inner self, and reject self-deception of any kind. *Daxue* insists that there is a close correlation between inner sincerity and the physical life: "What is true in a man's heart will be shown in his outward appearance." A man free from self-deception enjoys not only a peaceful mind but also physical health: "His mind is broad, and his body is at ease."

When dealing with other people in a society, a morally cultivated person should always put into effect the "principle of the measuring square" (*xiejue zhi dao*). This principle is stated in *Daxue* as follows:

> What a man dislikes in his superiors, let him not show it in dealing with his inferiors; what he dislikes in those in front of him, let him not show it in preceding those who are behind. What he dislikes in those behind him, let him not show it in following those in front of him.

This is an echo of Confucius's idea of "reciprocity" (*shu*): "Not to do to others as you would not wish done to yourself" (*Analects*, 12.2). The key word in both is *tui*, "to extend." An individual is asked to extend consideration of his own wants and desires to those of others. A good ruler is one who consistently applies this principle to regulate his conduct: "He likes what the people like and dislikes what the people dislike." At the same time, *Daxue* implies that all people share an innate tendency to follow a good moral model, as long as there is one. Therefore:

> When the ruler treats the elders with respect, then the people will be aroused toward filial piety. When the ruler treats the aged with respect, then the people will be aroused toward brotherly respect. When the ruler treats compassionately the young and the helpless, then the people will not follow the opposite course.

Thanks to the ruler's application of the principle and the people's tendency toward goodness, it becomes possible to realize peace and tranquillity in the world—the loftiest goal of the Confucians.

In *Daxue*, tranquillity means, primarily, a situation in which people all spontaneously manifest their own "illustrious virtue" and therefore voluntarily regulate their families and put their affairs in order. By the same token, the key to the realization of tranquillity is not sophisticated statecraft or governmental manipulation, but a morally perfect exemplar that people can and will follow. "The ruler will first be watchful over his own virtue" so as to be such an exemplar. His example will then motivate and encourage the people to accomplish their own moral cultivation. Only when everybody in the world cares about his own virtue can the ideal of tranquillity become a social reality. According to *Daxue*:

> If the ruler has virtue, he will have the people with him. If he has the people with him, he will have the territory. If he has the territory, he will have wealth. And if he has wealth, he will have its use.

By this reasoning, the ruler's moral cultivation is not only a moral imperative but also the most efficient way to govern. In premodern China, many intellectuals and officials accepted this idea.

See also Self-Deception; Zhu Xi.

Bibliography

Cua, A. S. "A Confucian Perspective on Self-Deception." In *Self and Deception*, ed. Roger T. Ames and Wimal Dissanayake. Albany: State University of New York Press, 1996), pp. 177–199. (Reprinted in *Moral Vision and Tradition: Essays in Chinese Ethics*. Washington, D.C.: Catholic University of America Press, 1998.)

Gardner, Daniel K. *Chu Hsi and the Ta-hsüeh: Neo-Confucian Reflection on the Confucian Canon*. Cambridge, Mass.: Harvard University Press, 1985.

Wang, Fuzhi. *Du sishu daquan shuo*. Beijing: Zhonghua shuju, 1975.

Wang, Yangming. *Chuan xi lu*. Taipei: Liming Wenhua Shiye Gongsi, 1986. (See also Wing-tsit Chan, trans. *Instructions for Practical Living and Other Neo-Confucian Writings*. New York: Columbia University Press, 1962.)

Zhao Shunsun. *Daxue zhuanshu*. Shanghai: Huadong shifan daxue chuban she, 1992.

Zheng, Xuan, and Kong Yingda. *Liji zhushu*. In *Shisan jing zhushu*. Beijing: Zhonghua shuju, 1986.

Zhu, Xi. *Daxue zhangju*. In *Sishu jizhu*. Beijing: Zhonghua shuju, 1986. (See also Wing-tsit Chan, trans. "The Great Learning." In *A Source Book in Chinese Philosophy*. Princeton, N.J.: Princeton University Press, 1969. James Legge, trans. "The Great Learning." In *Confucius: Confucian Analects, the Great Learning, and the Doctrine of the Mean*. New York: Dover, 1972.)

———. *Zhu Zi yulei*. Beijing: Zhonghua shuju, 1986.

De (Te): Virtue or Power

David S. Nivison

De has a variety of meanings and uses in Chinese philosophy and in ancient Chinese ordinary language. In modern Chinese it is the second syllable of the word *daode* "(moral) virtue"; and *de* appears to have a similar meaning in ancient moral philosophy sufficiently often to have led translators usually to render it as "virtue." But this translation is often obviously inaccurate, and much debate has ensued. It is a very old word, identifiable as early as the Shang oracle inscriptions of about 1200 B.C.E.; and in different senses it is a key term in ancient moral philosophy (perhaps "virtue"), political thought (the prestige of an important person or the staying power of a dynasty), and even metaphysics (the specific efficacious character, good or bad, of a person, class, or type of thing). In much ancient ordinary language the graph seems to represent a word meaning "a favor," "generosity," or "to be generous" toward someone, or "to regard (some benefactor) as generous."

Still, the consensus is that *de* is one word, not two or more unrelated words that happened to be homophones and so got written the same way. One wants an analysis that identifies a basic meaning and offers a semantic history which explains all the meanings, yielding a deeper understanding of ancient Chinese ethics. There are two problems: What have the Chinese conceived *de* to be? And how can these conceptions be analyzed in such a way as to explain why the Chinese came to think what they thought?

An ancestral graph is found in the oracle inscriptions of the era of King Wu Ding (c. 1200 B.C.E.) of the Shang dynasty that for most of a century was misread as representing a word meaning "go and inspect." This error was refuted by Jao Tsung-i (1976) followed by Nivison (1979; the present author), both pointing out that the Shang word occurred in phrases also found in early Zhou literature: phrases such as *de xing* ("fragrance of virtue"), *ruode* ("virtue approved" by the spirits), *jingde* ("to revere virtue"), and *yuande* ("preeminent virtue" or efficacious prestige of the king). Such phrases indicate that the word already had an incipient moral philosophical meaning. Two other uses are found in this material: (1) as a verb, in military inscriptions, e.g., "the king will *de fa*" ("go on a *de* campaign"), or "the king will *de fang*" ("*de* the border enemies"); and (2) (apparently) in the phrase "A has *de* with B," i.e., A has earned B's gratitude.

The second use is a standard idiom in old Chinese (see below). The first use had prompted the "go and inspect" error; but the meaning seems to be "make a display of force without actually using it." An example of this idea is found in the *Zuo zhuan* for 656 B.C.E., Xi Gong 4.4 (Legge 1872, 5:4.3, p. 141): Duke Huan of Qi and his allies are confronting the forces of Chu, and there is a parley, the Qi ruler demanding that Chu make ritual submission to the Zhou king. The Chu envoy replies that if battle is joined, Chu is well able to defend itself; but "if your lordship by his virtue seek the tranquillity of the states, who will dare not to submit to you?" There is then an accommodation, without bloodshed.

Putting these examples together has suggested (to Nivison) that the primary meaning was "generosity-gratitude" (be generous–recognize as generous). There has always been in China (and in Japan) an especially strong social-psychological compulsion to respond (*bao*) positively to a gift or favor, sacrifice, or show of deference (Yang, 1957). Thus, *Shi jing*, Ode 256.6–8:

> Every word finds its answer; every (*de*) generous act has its response. . . . When one throws me a peach, I return to him a plum. (Legge, 4:514–515, adapted)

The word *de* is used of the generous act, and also of the converse recognition of the act as generous, together with a compulsion to respond. The converse sense explains one person's "having *de* with (or from)" another: The compulsion to respond favorably is felt by the recipient as a psychic force emanating from the giver, that force being the giver's *de*.

De in this sense is generated by generosity (giving of what is one's own, or of oneself) in every way—gifts, kindness, forbearance (including forbearing to use military force or penal sanctions), humility and respect toward others, listening to advice, self-sacrifice, and (toward the spirits) performance of sacrifices and other religious obligations. Therefore, *de* is a force generated by characteristic moral behavior; so *de* comes to be thought of as moral character. It will be squandered if one is unrestrained, harsh, or cruel. This seems to be a consistent extension of the view of Marcel Granet (1950), applying the anthropological analysis of gifts of Marcel Mauss (1967). The psychic force, as force of character of a ruler, imprints itself on the people, so that a reign of good order seems to emanate from the person of a "virtuous" king, who himself in a sense does nothing. Thus Confucius (*Analects*, 2.1): "He who rules with *de* is like the polestar, which rests in its place while all the other stars bow to it."

An alternative view, that of Donald Munro (1969, 96–112, 185–197), is that *de* simply as moral character is the primary concept; that it is acquired by a self-disciplined subjective appropriation of the norms of behavior willed by heaven and the spirits; and that such behavior and perceived character naturally elicit admiration, a favorable response, and imitation. These natural responses are a sufficient explanation for the texts that seem to describe *de* as a psychic force.

Both analyses face the difficulty that *de* can be bad as well as good (a major obstacle also to the translation "virtue" in the moral sense). Munro would explain that a person who is a model of "virtue" can focus attention on the "heavenly norms" and reject them, thus becoming a person of bad virtue and bad influence. The "anthropological" view—sometimes characterized, e.g., by Boodberg (1952, 323–326), as seeing *de* as a kind of *mana*—must suppose that the notion of *de* as psychic force takes on a life of its own (even if originally it was the felt "force" of gratitude), if *de* is to have the extended meanings it soon acquires; but the same must be said of the analysis that takes moral character as the basic sense. For example, a young woman's sexual attractiveness is her *de* (*Zuo zhuan*, Xi Gong 24.2) and sometimes also a man's (*Zhuangzi* 5, "Signs of Virtue Complete"). But this specifically sexual sense is rare. Heaven (perhaps blindly) endows us with our *de*-character; so thought Confucius (*Analects*, 7.23): "Heaven produced the *de* in me." This endowment of *de* can be either "fortunate" (*ji*) or "disastrous" (*xiong*, as in *Shang shu*, 16, "Pan Keng" 38), defined in moral terms: "filial and reverential, loyal and honest," or "thieving and villainous, secretive and traitorous" (*Zuo zhuan*, Wen Gong, 18.9).

The notion of *de* as involving man's relation to heaven is a fundamental one in early (and enduring) Chinese political philosophy. Heaven, having given its endowment, surveys humankind to see how we are cultivating our "virtue" (such as it may be), granting to each of us long or short life (*Shang shu*, 18, "Gaozong's *Yong*-day"). So also the beginning, flourishing, and ending of a dynastic line of kings or emperors, the concept of the "dynastic cycle": the founder is picked out by heaven as worthiest to hold its "mandate" to rule. "Now this King Wen, Di (God = Heaven) measured his heart. Quiet was the sound of his Virtue; his Virtue could shine . . .; he could preside, could rule, being king over this great country (Zhou)" (*Shi jing*, Ode 241.4). "Di said to King Wen, I esteem your shining Virtue; it is not merely displayed because of your great repute, nor altered because of your prominence" (*Shi jing*, 241.7). An adviser to King Cheng (grandson of King Wen) stresses that preceding dynasties, though founded by rulers of superior virtue, came to an end "because their rulers did not reverently cultivate their virtue" (*Shang shu*, 32, "Shao Gao"). Thus a king's *de*, though a part of himself and good, is something he is given; he cannot take pride in it but has a responsibility to preserve it.

King Cheng is quoted in an inscription (*He zun*, perhaps dated 1031 B.C.E.) as asking his hearers, a group of young nobles, to "help me, your king, to uphold my Virtue, so that Heaven will instruct me when I am negligent" (Nivison 1996). The tone of humility points to a paradox: the mark of a good, i.e., "virtuous," king is that he is open to instruction, the very instruction that would make him virtuous, whereas his opposite is not. Worse, it is only a good king who will attract and employ wise men to serve and advise him; a bad king, lacking virtue and so really needing help, drives good men away and chooses as advisers only men who are like himself (*Shang shu*, 32, "Shao Gao," and 39, "Li Zheng," passim).

How, then, can virtue be taught, if to be taught to be virtuous, one must be virtuous already? This "paradox of virtue"(Nivison 1996) leads in time to Mencius's doctrine (fourth century B.C.E.) of the goodness of human nature. Mencius says that we all have, already, the beginnings of virtues: benevolence (*ren*), a dislike of what is dishonorable (*yi*), an incipient sense of propriety (*li*), and a sense of right and wrong (*zhi*); we can learn to notice these "beginnings" and develop them (2.A6, 6.A6).

According to the *Bamboo Annals*, King Cheng formally "emplaced the cauldrons of Shang" in the newly constructed capital at Loyang in the eighteenth year of his reign. These bronze objects, tradition has held, were cast by the founders of the Xia dynasty, were taken by the Shang when the Xia was overthrown, and in turn were captured by the Zhou. They were supposed to symbolize the legitimacy of these dynastic lines and therefore now embodied the "virtue" of the Zhou. Thus *de* comes to be an abiding power that is no longer an aspect of a single person. The *Zuo zhuan* (Xuan Gong, 3.5, i.e., 606 B.C.E.) tells the story that the lord of Chu, visiting the Zhou king (this monarchy had held no real power for almost two centuries) asked about the size and weight of the cauldrons. The receiving officer rejected the inquiry, saying that the weight of the cauldrons depended on the virtue of the dynasty; and "although the Virtue of Zhou is in decline, Heaven's Mandate has not yet changed; so the weight of the cauldrons may not be inquired about."

Angus Graham (1989, 13) has written that the term *de* is used "of the power, whether benign or baleful, to move others without exerting physical force." Two developments are hardly surprising: (1) One can speak of the *de* of kinds of persons, meaning not necessarily their power to affect others but their characteristic way of interacting with others. Thus Confucius: "The *de* of the gentleman is wind; the *de* of the ordinary man is grass. Let the wind pass over the grass and it is bound to bend" (*Analects*, 12.19). (2) One can speak of the *de* of something other than a human being. Thus Zhuangzi: The kind of dog that is merely motivated to catch prey "has the *de* of a wildcat" (*Zhuangzi*, 24, "Xu Wugui"). And Confucius: "A *ji* (a horse that can run 1,000 *li* a day) is not praised for its strength, but for its *de*" (*Analects*, 14.33). The concept is extended still farther in the metaphysical thought of the third century B.C.E. In the broadest sense, a causal tendency of a category of things in the world, or of a historical epoch, is its *de*; there are five, otherwise called the "five phases" (*wuxing*, metaphorically earth, fire, wood, metal, water); in the third century, e.g., by Zou Yan, these are called the "five powers" (*wude*).

And in a particular sense, in thought associated with the "Jixia" scholars in Qi around 300 B.C.E., each individual thing has its *de*, which makes it what it is and enables it to function as it ideally should. This *de* it "gets" (*de*) from the *dao* ("Way"), now thought of by the metaphysicians as the ground of all being:

> *Te* [*de*] is the dwelling place of *Tao* [*Dao*]. Things obtain it (from *Tao*) so as to be produced. Living things obtain it so as to function; it is the essence of *Tao*. Therefore *Te* is an obtaining [*de*]. This means that it is that through obtaining which a thing is what it is. That which is Doing Nothing (*wu wei*) is called *Tao*. The dwelling place of this is *Te*. Therefore there is no separation between *Tao* and *Te*. And therefore those who speak about them make no discrimination." (*Guanzi*, 13.36 "Xin Shu part 1," quoted in Fung, 1952, 180)

The assumption here that the verb *de* is a paronym of *de* is a common idea in the etymological metaphysics of late antiquity (and may be valid, though not in the sense intended in the *Guanzi*: to give a gift is to cause someone to get it). In chapters in *Zhuangzi* written later than this (8, 13, 15, 20, 23), the expression *daode* is found, meaning either *dao* or *de* or both, not in the modern sense "moral virtue" but in the *Guanzi's* non-"discriminating" sense of effective natural character, and some (notably the "primitivist" chapters 8–10) actually call for the suppression of morality and of moral philosophers in favor of premoral naturalness, idealizing a supposed anarchic stage of human innocence before the corruptions of civilization.

There is also the title of the often translated short Daoist book of verses and epigrams supposedly by a sixth-century sage called Laozi, *Daodejing*, "classic of *dao* and *de*"—or, perhaps, "of *daode*." Section 1 is about *dao*, and section 38, apparently beginning a second half of the book, begins with statements about *de* (this part is even sometimes called the *De jing* or *Dejing*, "classic of *de*"; but in its early form in the third century B.C.E. the two halves were in reverse order, simply titled *Laozi*, and so the whole book may have been conceived as a text on *de*.

Perhaps not the work of a single author but an editorial organizing of an accumulation of varied dicta, much of it idealizes a primitive stage of society and nongovernment presided over by a sage ruler who "does nothing" (like the *dao*) and is but a "shadowy presence" to a populace living in a state of innocent (and ignorant) bliss. (The book is often quoted in the "primitivist" *Zhuangzi* chapters, much later than Zhuangzi himself.) *De* in this book is a quality of a "sage" who is preternaturally effective because he is noncontriving, nonassertive, the antithesis of forceful. (This sage is often likened to an infant.) The partly moral *de* of the pre-Confucian good king, who rules by the effect of his character on the people without needing to use punishments or compulsion, is the background of this idea, but it has evolved far. The evolution may be (partly) by way of a military concept. Mencius several times maintains that a king who rules with "humaneness," *ren*—for Mencius (1.A7) the primary kind of *de*—will be unopposed (1.A5, 7.B4); the thought also is found in *Mozi* (19, "Against Attacking," 3). The *Zuo zhuan* (Xi Kong, 28.5) quotes a similar aphorism from a lost military treatise: "One who has *de* cannot be opposed." This invites the paradox that *de* as the antithesis of force (compare the *ji* horse), and so in itself weakness, is stronger than physical strength and can overcome it. The *Laozi* embraces this paradox and abounds in formally similar paradoxes: ignorance is wiser than knowledge, softness more resistant than hardness, silence more understanding than speech.

And the ultimate paradox (with which section 38 begins), explicitly concerning "virtue" itself:

> The highest virtue isn't virtuous (doesn't seek to be, and be known as, virtuous); therefore it has virtue; lower virtue never misses a chance to be "virtuous," therefore it lacks virtue.

Paradoxes are not necessarily false: virtue—whether it be moral prestige or the effortless efficacy resulting from utter naturalness—cannot be sought, because seeking is inconsistent with it and negates it. So, desirable though it is, one can get it only by rejecting it. The paradox is dramatized in stories historians of the Han savor. Memorable examples are recounted in Sima Qian's biography (*Shiji*, 77) of the Wei prince Wuji, Lord Xinling, famous for his deference to the thousands of "worthy" but humble "guests" in his establishment, who for their part battle with him for *de*, sometimes even by sacrificing, for his benefit, their own reputation for worth. In one incident, the king of the neighboring Zhao state, which the prince has saved from destruction by Qin, wants to shed the burden of gratitude by giving him five cities, and Wuji is about to accept. One of his "guests" protests:

> There are things that cannot be forgotten, and sometimes there are things that must be forgotten. If someone else "has *de* with" you (i.e., you owe him a debt of gratitude), you must not forget it. But if you "have *de* with" someone else, I beg you to forget it!

At the ensuing reception in his honor, the prince behaves so humbly that the Zhao king cannot bring himself to offer the cities, thus sparing the prince the necessity of refusing, which would have been to seek *de*, thereby losing it.

Chinese philosophical literature yields numerical lists of *de* in the sense of either "virtue" or "tendency": three (e.g., *Zhongyong*), four (*Mencius*, *Yi jing*), five (as in *Zou Yan*), six (*Shang shu*), eight (*Zhuangzi*), nine (*Shang shu*). The "three *de*," for example, are the three moral virtues wisdom (*zhi*), benevolence (*ren*), and courage (*yong*) in the *Zhongyong*—or the tendencies of heaven, earth, and man in the *Liji* (*Li ji*) of the elder Dai. And later there are various Buddhist lists of three, e.g., (adapting Samkhya metaphysics) *sattva* (goodness), *rajas* (passion), and *tamas* (illusion).

In the ninth century, the Tang writer Han Yu, in his famous essay "On the *Dao*," defends the Confucian virtues benevolence and rightness but says that the terms *dao* and *de* are "empty": the Confucians and the Daoists have their own concepts; and (in another sense) the *de* of a person can be "fortunate" (*ji*) or "disastrous" (*xiong*); in general *de* is "what you have in yourself, not depending on what is outside," a definition that fits either sense—"virtue" or "tendency." Liu Xie (fifth–sixth centuries), with a didactic ideal of writing, speaks of the *de* of literary art (*wen*) as its capacity to express the (both moral and marvelous) *dao*. But for Zhang Xuecheng in the eighteenth century, *wende* refers to a moral ideal for the writer, that he must both "respect" (*jing*) the creative process in himself and be other-regarding (*shu*) in criticism, putting himself in the other's place; similarly, Zhang writes of "virtue" in a historian (*shide*), as being cautious lest one's bias infect one's narrative. Thus Zhang's concept is moral, and true to the classical motif of *de* as self-restraint; but his focus is that of his time, the objectivity of the scholar. Any full account of the shifts in application and sense of the word *de* in later thought would have to be a complete history of postclassical philosophy.

See also Zhang Xuecheng.

Bibliography

Bamboo Annals (*Jinben*) *Zhushu jinian*. (Reproduced and translated in Legge, Vol. 3, "Prolegomena.")

Boodberg, Peter A. "The Semasiology of Some Primary Confucian Concepts." *Philosophy East and West*, 2(2), 1952, pp. 317–332.

Fung, Yu-lan. *A History of Chinese Philosophy*, Vol. 1, *The Period of the Philosophers*, trans. Derk Bodde. Princeton, N.J.: Princeton University Press, 1952.

Graham, Angus C. *Disputers of the Tao: Philosophical Argument in Ancient China*. La Salle, Ill.: Open Court, 1989.

———. "How Much of *Chuang Tzu* Did Chuang Tzu Write?" *Journal of the American Academy of Religion, Thematic Issue*, 47(3S), 1979, pp. 459–501.

Granet, Marcel. *Chinese Civilization*. London: Routledge and Kegan Paul, 1950.

Jao, Tsung-i. "The Character *Te* in Bronze Inscriptions." In *Proceedings of a Symposium on Scientific Methods of Research in the Study of Ancient Chinese Bronzes and Southeast Asian Metal and Other Archaeological Artifacts, October 6–10, 1975*, ed. Noel Barnard. Melbourne, Australia: National Gallery of Victoria, 1976.

Karlgen, Bernhard. "Grammata serica recensa." *Museum of Far Eastern Antiquities* (Stockholm) *Bulletin*, No. 29, 1957. (Reprinted by Elanders Boktrykeri Actiebolag, Kungsbacka, 1972. Abbreviated GSR.)

Legge, James. *The Chinese Classics*, 7 vols. (Vol. 3, *Shang-shu*; Vol. 4, *Shih-ching*; Vol. 5, *Ch'un-ch'iu* and *Tso-chuan*.) London: Henry Frowde, 1872.

Mauss, Marcel. *The Gift*, trans. Ian Cunnison. New York: Norton, 1967. (Translation of *Essai sur le don: Forme archaïque de l'échange*.)

Munro, Donald J. *The Concept of Man in Early China*. Stanford, Calif.: Stanford University Press, 1969.

Nivison, David S. "Royal 'Virtue' in Shang Oracle Inscriptions." *Early China*, 4, 1978–1979, pp. 52–55.

———. " 'Virtue' in Bone and Bronze" and "The Paradox of Virtue" (1980). In D. S. Nivison, *The Ways of Confucianism: Investigations in Chinese Philosophy*, ed. Bryan Van Norden. La Salle, Ill.: Open Court, 1996.

Yang, Lien-sheng. "The Concept of *Pao* as a Basis for Social Relations in China." In *Chinese Thought and Institutions*, ed. John K. Fairbank. Chicago: University of Chicago Press, 1957, pp. 291–309.

Dong Zhongshu (Tung Chung-shu)

Roger T. Ames

Dong Zhongshu (c. 195–105 B.C.E.; traditionally 179–104 B.C.E.) is generally regarded not only as an early champion of Confucianism during the Han dynasty but as the prime mover in establishing Confucianism as a state ideology—an ideology that would endure through the two millennia of imperial China until its end with the fall of the Qing dynasty in 1911. Perhaps his most remarkable contribution was to provide imperial authority with a cosmic context, locating the ruler as *axis mundi* between the social and political worlds of the human being and the divinely driven processes of cosmic change. He has traditionally been regarded as the author of the *Chunqiu fanlu* (*Luxuriant Dew of the Spring and Autumn Annals*), although current scholarship has brought this attribution into question. What is not in question is that he was one of the foremost interpreters of the *Gongyang Commentary* to the *Spring and Autumn Annals*, so that he was empowered intellectually as a direct transmitter of Confucian wisdom.

The Warring States period (403–221 B.C.E.) was not only an era of intense political struggle, as the name would suggest, but also a formative intellectual period in which the "hundred schools" of contending scholars sought adherents for their ideas. The political unification under the state of Qin in 221 B.C.E. brought the wide diversity in ways of thinking and living that defined preimperial China under one rule, and a program was initiated by the central court to reinforce this unity at every level. The unification of the many state walls into the Great Wall became an enduring symbol of an accelerating search for a shared cultural identity. Standardization of currency, weights and measures, axle widths, the written language, and so on, was the order of the day. The diverse populations of China, while retaining their local identities, were lifted into a political federation in which the richness of competing diversity became the substance of one continuous polity.

Intellectually, a similar story was unfolding. As the Han dynasty dawned, eclectic compendiums of existing knowledge were compiled, rites were standardized and codified, canonical texts and commentaries were established, comprehensive histories were edited out of the archives of the now unified central states, and even competing cosmologies and mythologies were rationalized into coherent linear accounts.

Perhaps two Confucian scholars—Xunzi and Dong Zhongshu—can be identified as the most powerful representatives of this drive toward intellectual syncretism, which established porousness and creative reinterpretation as distinctive features of "Han thinking." The importance of Xunzi in the Han is largely understated. He is pivotal as a philosopher who won ascendancy for Confucianism by effectively co-opting the vocabularies and the substance of rival thinkers—the Mohists, the school of names, the militarists, the legalists, the Daoists—and then revising their insights to conform to Confucian sensibilities. One example will suffice. A careful reading of Xunzi's chapter "Attuning Names" reveals that he has appropriated the disputative vocabulary of the later Mohist canons but has abandoned notions such as "necessity" (*bi*) and "a priori" (*xian*) as anathema to the historicist commitment of classical Confucianism.

Dong Zhongshu, the second major force in promoting Confucianism, held Xunzi in high esteem, writing a letter (referred to in Liu Xiang's preface) in praise of his precursor. Recent scholarship, recounted and extended by Sarah Queen (1996), has brought the traditional attribution of the *Luxuriant Dew of the Spring and Autumn Annals* to Dong Zhongshu into question, with the consensus being that this text is a composite work compiled over an extended period of time, with many lacunae and much corruption. Any close reading of the text certainly reveals both stylistic and philosophical inconsistencies.

Although it would be a stretch to describe Dong Zhongshu as a systematic thinker, there are several respects in which he qualifies as a transmitter of classical Confucian precepts. The *Analects* centers economic policy on the notion of equal distribution of goods, with the well-being of the people as a consequence of limited taxation and fiscal responsibility on the part of those who would rule over them. Importantly, economic security is seen as a precondition for moral edification. This policy is summarized in *Analects* 13.9:

> Ran You drove the Master's carriage on a trip to Wei. The Master remarked, "What a teeming population!" Ran You asked, "When the people are already so numerous, what

> more can be done for them?" The Master said, "Make them prosperous." "When the people are already prosperous," asked Ran You, "what more can be done for them?" "Teach them." replied the Master.

Similarly, Dong Zhongshu advocates an agriculturally based economy with limited taxation and strategies for redistributing accumulated wealth, all as a precondition for the ruler's primary responsibility: moral education.

A second Confucian theme that is picked up and further developed by Dong Zhongshu is the attunement of names (*zhengming*); Dong lifts this notion to a cosmological level. There are paronomastic echoes in the way the sages have taught us to use language that reflect a correspondence between the purposes of *tian* and the appropriate conduct of the human being. The exemplary person or ruler (*jun*) is the source (*yuan*) and the model around whom the people gather (*qun*); the people (*min*) without proper moral instruction are benighted (*ming*); to be right (*yi*) is to be appropriate (*yi*); the scholar-official (*shi*) is to serve (*shi*); the king (*wang*) is the august one (*huang*) to whom the people repair (*wang*); and so on. Careful attention to the use of language is integral to the project of self-cultivation because invested in the language are the insights of those moral exemplars who have come before us. Language, like a ritual discourse, enables us to locate and maintain our appropriate place in society, and to further refine our personal contribution to the social, natural, and cultural order.

A third related precept that Dong inherits from early Confucianism is a variation on the Mencian theme that a ruler is deserving of popular allegiance only if he carries out the duties of rulership and secures the well-being of the people. Although one of Dong Zhongshu's central themes is a celebration of the ruler as the intermediary between the divine and the human, as we will see, there is much in his philosophy that is an attempt to set real constraints on the power of the emperor.

Dong Zhongshu also enters the debate between Mencius and Xunzi over human nature, taking the middle position that human beings have both positive (*yang*) and negative (*yin*) proclivities as natural conditions. He sides with Xunzi against Mencius in insisting that only with moral education can the inchoate conditions of human nature be transformed into something worthwhile, but he disagrees with Xunzi's claim that these original conditions are themselves entirely negative. Still, these initial conditions make the kind of Confucian education available in a ritualized community under the guidance of exemplary persons essential to proper human development. Where Dong goes beyond this early Confucian debate is by giving this definition of the human capacity a cosmological dimension, making the process of moral education a significant factor in cosmic harmony.

In fact, this cosmological extension of early Confucianism, hinted at in the more mystical side of Mencius and by Xunzi's ritualized natural forces, represents the distinctive contribution of Dong Zhongshu. Where Xunzi had rejected the notion that human beings should attempt to penetrate the mysteries of *tian* (conventionally translated "heaven"), Dong Zhongshu developed this curiosity into a science. For Dong, there is a natural triad, where the ruler stands between a personified *tian* and a fecund earth. These three realms are symbiotic: each is an immediate factor in the harmony or disorder of the others. This mutual influence between the natural and moral orders—captured in the expression "mutual resonance (*ganying*)"—means that moral order in the human realm is not only divinely sanctioned but naturally enforced.

There is much in the writings of Dong Zhongshu that gives the human being a special place in the cosmic order, distinguishing humanity from all other forms of life by virtue of its intimate relationship with *tian*. The human being is the child of a divinely inspired nature to the extent that the human body and its various functions are a microcosm of the natural processes and regularity. Since the human being is produced by *tian* and is defined by correspondences with nature, it follows that the proper model for human development is *tian* itself. And the patterns and purposes of *tian* are revealed immediately in the world around us. It is thus incumbent on the ruler to organize the human world—its defining values and institutions—on the basis of what can be understood about the natural world.

But the role of the human being is more than just to be a compliant creature of *tian*. The human being, by living in harmony with and contributing to nature, becomes a cocreator of the cosmic order. Where nature leaves off, humanity begins. Not only is human efficacy determined largely through concerted effort within the realm of human affairs; it is further the responsibility of the efficacious human being, led by the virtuous ruler, to bring the possibilities of the natural world to fruition.

The processes of natural and human interaction had become systematized in the "*yinyang* five phases theory" (*yinyang wuxing*) before Dong Zhongshu, but he certainly had a role in popularizing these ideas as the center of Han dynasty cosmology. Dong Zhongshu developed a theory for decoding irregularities in the natural order as a way of reading the intentions of *tian*. Of course, this science of omenology empowered the court ministers to criticize the conduct of a less than successful ruler, and on one occasion nearly cost the imprudent Dong Zhongshu his life.

The political context of the early Han is important for understanding the development of Dong Zhongshu's thought. The process of political centralization, begun long before the Warring States period, had continued unabated into the Han, coming to its climax precisely during Dong Zhongshu's mature years. Liu Bang, the founder of the Han, initially exercised direct control over the fourteen western commands, with nominal power over the ten eastern "countries" (*guo*) that were ruled by vassal kings. His first move was to quickly replace the vassals with imperial relatives and then to implement a conscious strategy of reducing the size and strength of these kingdoms. He and his successors took advantage of any and all reasons available to the court to first divide these kingdoms into smaller territories and then, through various machinations, redefine them into imperial commands. Dynastic power became increasingly focused in the person of the emperor.

A lesson having been learned from the despotism of the Qin dynasty, the major problem of the age became how the court bureaucracy could set boundaries on the increasingly absolute authority invested in the imperial throne. The answer to this problem was for the court officials to exploit the theory of the "mandate of *tian*" (*tianming*) by persuading the emperor that he ruled at the pleasure of a divine power. They could then claim authority for themselves as the legitimate interpreters of nature's language, restraining imperial power by soliciting and interpreting reports of calamities, prodigies, and heavenly portents.

Perhaps Dong Zhongshu's most remarkable contribution, beyond his role in the canonization of the Confucian classics and the perpetuation of Confucian values, was his attempt to direct the imperial court away from the excesses and abuses of the Qin dynasty. His practical influence on reforming the Qin statutes, on revising the defining ritual practices of the court, and on recasting the role of the sovereign, all within the first century of imperial China, had repercussions that resonated throughout its long career.

See also Confucianism: Han.

Bibliography

Arbuckle, Gary. "Restoring Dong Zhongshu (195–115 B.C.E.): An Experiment in Historical and Philosophical Reconstruction." Ph.D. dissertation, University of British Columbia, 1991.

Dong Zhongshu. *Chunqiufanlu*. Taipei: Taiwan Zhonghua shuju, 1982. (Sibu beiyao edition.)

Hsiao Kung-chuan. *A History of Chinese Political Thought*, trans. F. W. Mote. Princeton, N.J.: Princeton University Press, 1979.

Lai Qinghong. *Dong Zhongshu zhengzhi sixiang zhi yanjiu*. Taipei: Wenshizhe chubanshe, 1981.

Lau, D. C., and Chen Fong Ching. *A Concordance to the Chunqiu fanlu*. ICS Ancient Chinese Texts Concordance Series. Hong Kong: Commercial Press, 1994.

Li, Weixiong. *Dong Zhongshu yu Xi Han xueshu*. Taipei: Wenshizhe chubanshe, 1978.

Li, Zehou. *Zhongguo gudai sixiang shilun*. Peking: Renmin chubanshe, 1985.

Pokora, Timoteus. "Notes on New Studies on Tung Chung-shu [Dong Zhongshu]." *Archiv Orientalni*, 33, 1965, pp. 256–271.

Queen, Sarah A. *From Chronicle to Canon: The Hermeneutics of the Spring and Autumn, According to Tung Chung-shu [Dong Zhongshu]*. Cambridge: Cambridge University Press, 1996.

Zhang, Dainian, ed. *Dong Zhongshu: Da Ru liezhuan*. Guilin: Guilin wenshi chubanshe, 1997.

Zhou, Guidian. *Dongxue tanwei*. Peking: Shifan daxue chubanshe, 1989.

中國哲學

E

Egoism in Chinese Ethics

Kim Chong CHONG

The term "egoism," *wei wo,* in Chinese ethics is usually associated with Yang Zhu, but it encompasses issues much wider than the narrow and overriding conception of self-interest attributed to him by Mencius (Mengzi): "Even if he could benefit the Empire by pulling one hair he would not do it" (*Mencius*, 7A26). These include questions about the possibility of universal love, the extension of benevolence, human nature, the ultimate motivation for behavior, self-cultivation, the value of spontaneity, and the conflict between particularistic concern—i.e., concern for one's kin—and nonparticularistic concern. These related issues surround classical figures like Mozi, Yang Zhu, Gaozi, Mencius, and, beyond them, the neo-Confucians.

Before describing these issues, we should first mention egoism in western ethics, where it has often been discussed in terms of ethical egoism and psychological egoism. This will enable us to make comparisons at certain points, so as to highlight the features of egoism in Chinese ethics. Ethical egoism is the principle that everyone ought to pursue his or her own self-interest; psychological egoism is the theory that, ultimately, self-interest motivates people's actions.

The main issues concerning ethical egoism are whether it is rational and whether it can be called a moral or ethical principle at all. In this regard, ethical egoism has served as a testing ground for theories of morality that stipulate criteria of rationality such as universalization and the maximization of self-interest. Ethical egoism is therefore largely a heuristic device of the twentieth century, although the two criteria just mentioned had precursors in Hobbes and Kant.

A. C. Graham (1989) recounts a dialogue in the *Mozi* between Wumazi and Mozi, which can illustrate the issue of universalization, although we shall have to qualify this later. Wumazi claims to be incapable of concern for everyone; he says that although he is concerned for the people of his own neighborhood, he is by degrees more concerned for his family than for his neighbors, for his parents than for other members of his family, and ultimately for himself than for his parents. The issue for Mozi is whether this is a morality that can be prescribed: "Are you going to hide your morality, or tell others about it?" To Wumazi's response that he will tell others, Mozi argues that Wumazi will harm himself by doing so. Wumazi's egoistic doctrine benefits no one, since it cannot be prescribed. In that case, "If as beneficial to no one you refuse to say it, you might as well not have a mouth." In contemporary western terms, Wumazi logically cannot espouse a morality of righteousness (in Chinese, *yi*) that is self-contradictory, although some have disputed the sense in which the egoist needs to prescribe or espouse his morality, what "universalization" really amounts to, and whether it is a necessary criterion of morality.

Although Chinese ethics has not been directly concerned with these issues, Mozi's doctrine of universal love poses a challenge to the particularistic concern of the Confucians and raises the question how it may be extended. This question arises, for example, in *Mencius* (1A7) when Mencius tries to persuade King Xuan of Qi to *tui* or extend his compassion for a sacrificial ox to his people. It also arises (3A5) when the Mohist Yi Zhi argues that the Confucians cannot say there should be gradations in love, given their endorsement of the ancient sage kings who cared for the people, "as if they were tending a newborn babe." It may be tempting to see this and the dialogue between Mozi and Wumazi as an issue of logical inference and consistency or, in Kantian terms, of universal principle. A. S. Cua (1985), however, has pointed out that what is applicable here might not be universalization but rather *tui lei*, "analogical projection": "to project or extend on the basis of analogy between kinds of things." In this respect, ethical reasons are always contextual, concrete, and particular, and they appeal to shared conceptions of reasonableness and the ideal of a *dao*, instead of universal reason.

Psychological egoism in western ethics has a longer and more varied history. It is espoused by certain speakers in the works of Plato, by Hobbes, and by twentieth-century psychologists such as Sigmund Freud and B. F. Skinner and, more recently, sociobiologists like E. O. Wilson and R. Dawkins. They have sought, in various ways, to establish the ultimately self-seeking or self-preserving nature of human drives. In Book 2 of Plato's *Republic*, Glaucon describes the nature and origin of justice as a compromise between suffering from the injuries others inflict on us and being able to injure others with impunity. He tells the story of Gyges's ring to demonstrate that anyone with the power to do as he liked would have a natural tendency to trespass, steal, seduce, murder, etc. Not everyone in the western traditions shares this bleak picture of human nature. There are more enlightened notions of self-interest that accommodate love for, or solidarity with, others as part of a natural and healthy human constitution. For example, Plato responds to the challenge raised by the story of Gyges's ring (how to show that it pays to be just or moral) by presenting a theory of the three parts of the soul—reason, spirit, and desires—and their harmonious interaction through the governance of reason, the highest part. Aristotle, in *Nichomachean Ethics,* holds that *eudaimonia* is the ultimate good and end of human life. Although roughly translatable as "happiness," *eudaimonia* is an enlightened and contemplative sense of happiness that is far removed from hedonism. For Aristotle, the cultivation of friendship based on admirable moral qualities is part of this ultimate good.

This conception of friendship is also important to Confucius (Kongzi) and Mencius, as part of the process of self-cultivation. For them, even though self-cultivation is not described in terms of an ultimate good, it is nonetheless either related to communal goals or crucial to the maintenance and development of human nature. Thus, for Confucius, self-cultivation is intimately linked to establishing oneself on the *li* or the rites, as well as being committed to and identifying oneself with others in terms of the ideal of *ren* or benevolence. For Mencius, self-cultivation is nourishing and developing the ethical predispositions of compassion, shame, courtesy or modesty, and (a sense of) right and wrong into the virtues of benevolence, righteousness, propriety, and wisdom. The ability to relate to others depends on the development of these virtues; the person who "fails to develop them . . . will not be able even to serve his parents" (*Mencius*, 2A6). Several times, Mencius laments that, ironically, although people know how to tend to various external things (a tree, domestic animals) and the "smaller" parts of themselves (such as the mouth and belly), they seem to neglect the "greater"—their *xin* or heart-mind, which is the seat of the ethical predispositions (6A11–12, 14). In other words, ethical failure is a failure to act according to self-interest under a certain conception of human nature.

It should be evident by now that in both the western context and the Chinese context, self-interest is not to be equated with selfishness, and also that it is a much wider concept than, say, benefit or profit. Mencius, for example, strongly opposes speaking of benefit or profit (*li*) in contrast to *ren* and *yi* (benevolence and righteousness). If those who hold public office, for instance, think in terms of benefit or profit, "then those above and those below will be trying to profit at the expense of one another and the state will be imperiled" (1A1).

Both Plato and Aristotle have an enlightened sense of self-interest in which friendship and solidarity play an important naturalistic role in the life of the individual, but in recent western philosophy the model of social relations as a compulsion or imposition has been more influential. This model depicts morality as a bargaining process leading to a social contract between individuals that is an uneasy compromise—at worst, one avoids being harmed; at best, one maximizes self-interest. On the other hand, the basis of discussions of egoism in Chinese ethics has not been the problem of a social contract. Instead, the family has been assumed to be the basis of society, and filial piety is said to lead to obedience to a hierarchical order, and also to be the root of *ren* or benevolence, as stated in the *Analects*

(1.2). But again, this raises the problem of how benevolence can be extended beyond the family. This will be discussed later.

The idea that moral behavior is based not on natural, spontaneous dispositions but on the conscious imposition of rules is found in the *Xunzi*. Xunzi holds that besides the appetitive desires, humans are born with feelings of envy and hatred, aggressive and greedy tendencies, love of profit, etc. Social disorder is the consequence if they are not transformed by the influence of a teacher and model, and guided by ritual. We are asked to imagine what would happen in the absence of authority, ritual rules, and penal laws:

> The strong would inflict harm on the weak and rob them; the many would tyrannize the few and wrest their possessions from them; and the perversity and rebelliousness of the whole world would quickly ensure their mutual destruction. (Knoblock 1994, 23.3a)

This is reminiscent of the motivations cited in the *Republic* and the "war of every man against every man" in Hobbes's *Leviathan*. But it should be noted that for Xunzi, human nature is not evil in a deep or permanent sense, something to be restrained by law and ritual. Just as clay can be molded, human nature can be morally transformed through education, including aesthetics—cultivation of music and the rites. Cua has, notably, referred to this function of the rites as "ennobling" (1998, Essay 13). There is no discussion here of two matters commonly addressed in western social and political philosophy: the possibility of being a free rider while pretending to uphold the social contract, and the rationality of either maintaining the contract or opting out. For Xunzi, the rites are not only regulative but morally and aesthetically transformative. The rules and functions of the rites come about not as a result of a bargaining process but through the accumulated wisdom of the sages.

In holding that human nature is evil, Xunzi was disagreeing with Mencius. According to Xunzi, the virtues are learned through a process of *wei*, conscious effort or acquired ability. Something that belongs to nature, like the appetitive desires and senses, cannot be learned. Mencius himself was reacting against Yang Zhu and Mozi; he said that the teachings of these two philosophers "filled the empire," and he had no alternative but to oppose them (3B9). Graham (1986) has described Yang Zhu as being among certain "individualists who first urge the advantages of private against public life, and refuse to sacrifice a hair of their bodies for power, possessions or any other external benefit which involves the risk of injury to health and life." This is due to their doctrine of nature (*xing*) as the process of life (*sheng*), and its nurturance. This doctrine encompasses a belief in the spontaneous enjoyment of sensual pleasures, although not without awareness of the danger of overindulgence. At the same time, however, its sense of self-interest need not necessarily exclude a concern for others. Consider, for instance, the story of King Dan Fu, whose state was invaded by the people of Di, as described in the Yangist chapter "Giving Away a Throne" in the *Zhuangzi*. (Graham identifies certain chapters in the *Zhuangzi* as "Yangist." Other works describing the Yangist philosophy are *Lüshi chunqiu* and *Huainanzi*.) After failing to entice the invaders to leave, Dan Fu decides to leave the state himself, to preserve his subjects' lives and his own life. He feels that there is no difference whether he or the Di are the rulers, citing the principle that "one must not injure that which he is nourishing for the sake of that by which he nourishes it." In other words, one should not confuse attachment to material things with life itself. Thus, although the cost of pulling out one hair seems trivial, this example is a way of emphasizing that the risks of holding office during the a time of social and political disorder outweigh the benefits. On the other hand, there may be circumstances where refusing to take office or to do one's duty could result in dire consequences for the empire as a whole. One can therefore imagine Mencius's chagrin about the implications of Yangism, if it was widely adopted.

In other Yangist chapters of the *Zhuangzi*, such as "Robber Zhi" and "The Old Fisherman," there are criticisms of the rituals of the Confucians, who are seen as imposing artificial morality, thereby inhibiting or cramping natural, spontaneous behavior. Mencius's response is to argue for the spontaneity of moral behavior in terms of the *duan* or "sprouts" of the *xin* (heart-mind), referred to earlier as ethical predispositions. This is in fact the strategy he adopts against Gaozi, who asserts that there is nothing more to human nature than the life process typified by the desire for food and sex. As he says, "Appetite for food and sex is nature" (*Mencius*, 6A4). In his debate with Mencius, he likens the construction of morality from the nature of human beings to making cups and bowls from willow.

Unlike Yang Zhu or Gaozi, Mozi cannot be said to be an egoist in any sense, but his insistence that it is possible to love others as oneself, their parents and friends as one's own, their cities and states as one's own, etc., gives rise to skepticism as to how all this is possible. This is the doctrine of *jian ai*, variously translated as "universal love" (Watson 1963), "indiscriminate concern" (Shun 1997), "concern for everyone" (Graham 1989), and "impartial caring" (Nivison 1999). Mozi traced the disorder of his time to the partiality of particularistic relationships. Partiality leads to conflict, war, and injustice. The remedy is to reject partiality and adopt an attitude of equal regard for everyone. Thus universal love amounts to a rejection of particularistic concern.

It is possible to interpret Mozi as holding the egalitarian idea that in the moral scheme of things, each is to count as one. However, although Mozi does take as his measure of right action the utilitarian criterion of whether a course of action benefits everyone, he constantly harps on the possibility of loving others as oneself, others' friends and parents as one's own, etc. The question how this is possible is raised several times but is not answered convincingly. Thus, in response to the point that trying to adopt universal love would be like picking up a mountain and leaping over a river with it—i.e., that it is practically impossible—Mozi denies the relevance of the analogy by claiming that the ancient sage kings practiced universal love. However, it is doubtful that the beneficent rule of the sage kings actually took the form of universal love as advocated by Mozi. We may also doubt Mozi's charge that partiality is inconsistent because a partial-minded man would go off to war and leave his family under the care of a universal-minded man. In reality, given the choice of leaving his family in the hands of someone who would treat them just like anyone else, i.e., impartially, or leaving them with someone—a friend or a relative—who would treat them partially, the partial-minded man would be unlikely to opt for the former.

Mozi seems to realize that his replies are none too convincing and so is ultimately forced to appeal to the concept of benefit (*li*). For example, a filial son wants to ensure his parents' welfare. One way to do this is "to make it a point to love and benefit other men's parents, so that they in return will love and benefit my parents." Mozi cites a passage from the Book of Odes—"There are no words that are not answered, no kindness that is not requited. Throw me a peach, I'll requite you a plum"—and comments: "The meaning is that one who loves will be loved by others, and one who hates will be hated by others. So I cannot understand how the men of the world can hear about this doctrine of universality and still criticize it!" Thus we may say that in the final analysis, the motivation for universal love is reduced to an egoistic investment to ensure benefits for oneself and particular others. When Mencius preferred to talk about righteousness and benevolence instead of benefit or profit (1A1), he may well have had Mozi in mind.

It is illuminating to see how Mencius's account of human nature is a response to Yang Zhu, Gaozi, and Mozi. Consider the famous example of the child about to fall into a well:

> No man is devoid of a heart sensitive to the suffering of others. . . . My reason . . . is this. Suppose a man were, all of a sudden, to see a young child on the verge of falling into a well. He would certainly be moved to compassion, not because he wanted to get in the good graces of the parents, nor because he wished to win the praise of his fellow villagers or friends, nor yet because he disliked the cry of the child. (*Mencius*, 2A6)

Hardheaded empiricists will refuse to accept this as an empirical theory, since it is unfalsifiable. Indeed, if someone failed to come to the rescue of the child, Mencius himself would explain this as a loss of the "original heart."

However, instead of seeing Mencius as espousing an empirical claim or theory, we may see him as clarifying the conceptual grounds of altruism and other direct social and moral responses by using this and other hypothetical examples (e.g., 3A5). Note that Mencius carefully distinguishes compassion from certain motives. In a sense, "nothing" motivates the concern for the child. In other words, concern is direct, and it is different from these motivations. The idea that this concern is direct may be reinforced by seeing that the perception of the child on the verge of falling into a well is not pure cognition. Compassion is not a concomitant part of this cognition, but it may be said to constitute the mode in which the situation is registered or perceived. Clearly, concern for the child's welfare is unlike the desire to attain pleasurable states and escape unpleasurable states. Those desires are directed inward and seem to require consummation. Compassion for the child, on the other hand, is directed outward. (Compare this with Bishop Butler's critique of psychological egoism, "That all particular appetites and passions are towards external things themselves, distinct from the pleasure arising from them," in sermon 11 of his *Fifteen Sermons*.)

This example may explain the possibility of a direct, nonparticularistic concern, independent of whether the object of concern is related to one. However, Mencius would still insist that, other things being equal, one would (and should) give preference to one's kin, especially one's parents (3A5). There is a tension here between the two kinds of concern. Mozi would argue that particularistic concern is opposed and also harmful to nonparticularistic concern. Certainly, with its emphasis on particularistic relationships and on giving priority to one's kin, Confucianism faces the problem of how to extend this concern to nonparticular others—a problem that has cropped up repeatedly. If it is unable to meet this challenge, Confucianism is actually committed to egoism regarding the family or kinship group, despite its avowal of concern for others in terms of a harmonious social and political order.

One answer Mencius seems to offer is that although priority is to be given to one's parents, ethical predispositions are themselves neutral between particularistic and nonparticularistic concern. These predispositions need to be developed into the virtues if one is to flourish as a human being. For Mencius, a human being is defined not just by possession of the four sprouts of the heart-mind (*xin*) but also by an ability to relate to others in terms of the corresponding virtues of benevolence, righteousness, observance of the rites, and wisdom. In general, this means that concern—particularistic and nonparticularistic—is a function of the development of these virtues, which both define and shape human relationships. As mentioned earlier, Mencius holds that without the overall development of these virtues, one cannot be in a position even to tend to one's parents, let alone have regard for others (2A6). Thus the parent-child relationship is important not just for the special love it involves but also as a basis for the development of love and concern for others. Nonparticularistic love begins with the feelings and the virtues that one develops in a particularistic relationship. Wong (1989) discusses this in relation to psychological theories of child development.

This does not deny the possibility of conflict between the two forms of concern, and Mencius could also agree that there are circumstances in which a particularistic concern may unrighteously triumph over nonparticularistic concern. But, contrary to Mozi, there is nothing inherently wrong with particularistic relationships or the partiality inherent in them. Instead of taking particularistic concern as simply a hindrance to nonparticularistic concern, one would have to evaluate the situations and contexts in which partiality may or may not be appropriate. Furthermore, partiality is constrained by the role one occupies. Here is an example: Mencius is asked by someone called Tao Ying to consider what the sage emperor Shun would have done if his father had killed someone. Mencius's reply is "The only thing to do was to apprehend him." Mencius is then asked whether Shun would not have tried to stop his father's arrest. He replies, "How could Shun stop it? Gao Yao (the judge) had authority for what he did." Pressed to say what Shun would have done, Mencius says:

> Shun looked upon casting aside the Empire as no more than discarding a worn shoe. He would have secretly carried the old man on his back and fled to the edge of the Sea and lived there happily, never giving a thought to the Empire. (7A35)

In this case, the conflict between particularistic and a nonparticularistic concern is resolved by referring to one's roles and what, given these roles, it would be appropriate or inappropriate to do. In his role as emperor, Shun would be morally powerless to prevent the arrest of his father; the duty attached to this role would override his duty as a son. Shun, however, could decide that the empire was not as important to him as his filial duty, relinquish his post, and perform the filial duty. This example is but one illustration of an allowance for the exercise of *quan*—discretion—in Confucianism (*Mencius*, 4A17; *Analects*, 5.30), amounting to the exercise of autonomous judgment in deciding about an exigent situation (Cua, 1998, Essay 12).

A doubt could be raised about the example just discussed: Is this actually a case of conflict between the two kinds of concern? Should it not be described, instead, as a conflict between two duties—to the state and to one's father? This leads us to the realization that no conflict between the two kinds of concern can be resolved simply by weighing one against the other. In other words, in determining the rightness of an action, motivation alone is inadequate; roles, duties, proprieties, responsibilities, etc., must also be considered. Nice questions can arise here about whether Shun was taking his duties as emperor too lightly or being irresponsible. To make a proper judgment, one would have to determine specific factors, such as how important it was that Shun remain as emperor, what the social and political circumstances were, whether there were any able successors, and so on. But it is interesting that Mencius describes Shun's attitude toward his position as emperor in terms that a Yangist could appreciate: "Shun looked upon casting aside the Empire as no more than discarding a worn shoe." This reminds us of the attitude of King Dan Fu, who was prepared to relinquish his state. In the same chapter where this example appears, it is commented of another character:

> The Empire is the weightiest thing of all, but he would not harm his life for the sake of it, and how much less for any other thing! Only the man who cares nothing for the Empire deserves to be entrusted with the Empire.

Perhaps we can say that because Shun was concerned about his (particularistic) duty as a son, he manifested an admirable virtue and was therefore worthy to be an emperor. In this capacity, he was able to do much for (nonparticular) others. Similarly, the Yangist who cherishes his life above material possessions and office has gone beyond the desire for riches and power, with its associated intrigues; he would be able to devote himself to the (nonparticularistic) tasks of public service.

These examples illustrate the close link between character and action. For the Confucians in general—and this is something shared by the classical trio of Confucius, Mencius, and Xunzi—what is *yi* or right cannot be totally divorced from the person who is *yi* or righteous. Not everyone will be disposed to act righteously or even to see what is right. (*Yi* can be analyzed as a second-order "aretaic" notion, referring to the conscientious and committed agent who is concerned with performing the right action; Cua 1998, Essay 13.) We have already seen how Mencius laments the fact that some people fail to look after their best interests. For Confucius, there is self-deception if a man says that he does not have the strength to act (*Analects*, 6.12); and for Xunzi, although the agent may be able to do something, he cannot be made to do it. In addition, although it may be possible for someone to do something, in fact he may not be capable of doing it (Knoblock, 23.5a, b).

Finally, we should note that the neo-Confucians have taken the problem of extending benevolence seriously and given it a metaphysical solution. Cheng Yi and Zhu Xi have described benevolence or *ren* as a metaphysical reality (*ti*) that is different from love as a function (*yong*). As a pair, "reality" and "function" are technical terms in the neo-Confucian lexicon, which among other things encapsulates the attempt by Cheng-Zhu and others to give a metaphysical explanation for the simultaneity of universal love and love with distinctions. Their predecessor Zhang Zai took love to be universally applied to all things as well as people; he also supplied the theory that "the Principle is one but its function is differentiated into the many" (*li yi fen shu*). This paved the way for Cheng-Zhu to harmonize universal love and love with distinctions (Chan, 1955).

See also Mencius; Mohism: The Founder, Mozi; *Ren*; Xunzi; Yang Zhu.

Bibliography

Chan, W. T. "The Evolution of the Confucian Concept *Jên*." *Philosophy East and West*, 4, 1955.

Chong, K. C. *Moral Agoraphobia: The Challenge of Egoism*. New York: Peter Lang, 1996.

Cua, A. S. *Ethical Argumentation: A Study in Hsün Tzu's Moral Epistemology*. Honolulu: University of Hawaii Press, 1985.

———. *Moral Vision and Tradition: Essays in Chinese Ethics*. Washington, D.C.: Catholic University of America Press, 1998.

Dawkins, R. *The Selfish Gene*. Oxford: Oxford University Press, 1976.

Freud, S. *Beyond the Pleasure Principle*. London: Hogarth, 1922.

Graham, A. C. "The Background of the Mencian Theory of Human Nature." In *Studies in Chinese Philosophy and Philosophical Literature*. Singapore: Institute of East Asian Philosophies, 1986.

———. *Disputers of the Tao*. La Salle, Ill.: Open Court, 1989.

Knoblock, John. *Xunzi: A Translation and Study of the Complete Works*, Vol. 3. Stanford, Calif.: Stanford University Press, 1994. (See Book 23, "Man's Nature Is Evil.")

Lau, D. C. *Confucius: The Analects*. Harmondswoth: Penguin, 1979.

———. *Mencius*, Vols. 1 and 2. Hong Kong: Chinese University Press, 1984.

Lee, Desmond. *Plato: The Republic*. Harmondsworth: Penguin, 1955.

Matthews, W. R. *Butler's Sermons*. London: Bell, 1969.

Nivison, David. "The Classical Philosophical Writings." In *The Cambridge History of Ancient China: From the Origins of Civilization to 221* B.C., ed. Loewe and Shaughnessy. Cambridge: Cambridge University Press, 1999.

Oakeshott, Michael. *Thomas Hobbes: Leviathan*. Oxford: Blackwell, 1955.

Paton, H. J. *Immanuel Kant: Groundwork of the Metaphysic of Morals*. New York: Harper and Row, 1964.

Shun, Kwong-loi. *Mencius and Early Chinese Thought*. Stanford, Calif.: Stanford University Press, 1997.

Skinner, B. F. *Beyond Freedom and Dignity*. London: Cape, 1972.

Thomson, J. A. K. *The Ethics of Aristotle: The Nichomachean Ethics*. Harmondsworth: Penguin, 1976.

Watson, Burton, trans. *The Complete Works of Chuang Tzu*. New York: Columbia University Press, 1968. (See the chapters "Giving Away a Throne," "Robber Chih," and "The Old Fisherman," all classified by Graham as "Yangist.")

———. *Mo Tzu: Basic Writings*. New York: Columbia University Press, 1963. (See the chapter "Universal Love.")

Wilson, E. O. *Sociobiology: The New Synthesis*. Cambridge, Mass.: Harvard University Press, 1975.

Wong, David. "Universalism Versus Love with Distinctions: An Ancient Debate Revived." *Journal of Chinese Philosophy*, 16, 1989.

中國哲學

F

Fa: Model, Law, Doctrine

Roger T. Ames

The basic meaning of *fa* is "to emulate" (in the sense of imitate, rather than surpass) or "standard." In the *Daodejing* (25) we read: "The human being emulates (*fa*) earth, earth emulates the heavens, the heavens emulate *dao* and *tao* emulates what is so-of-itself."

It was only in the Warring States period (403–221 B.C.E.) that *fa* became a technical philosophical term meaning penal law, associated as it was with a lineage of legal theorists who post hoc have been labeled with this same name, *fajia*: the legalists. This name would seem to be appropriate because a survey of the early corpus reveals that this particular group of philosophers appropriated the term *fa* and invested it with the new meaning. Before the emergence of *fa* as "law," the term *xing* was used primarily for punishment and, by extension, penal law.

Probably the first legalist philosopher to use the term *fa* extensively was Shang Yang (d. 338 B.C.E.), to whom tradition attributes the work *The Book of Lord Shang*. Although his actual authorship is much debated, most scholars agree that this work is a fair summary of Shang Yang's political precepts.

For Shang Yang, who became prime minister in the state of Qin, the appropriate use of *fa* serves the ruler, securing order in his state. History had taught the rulers of the Warring States period that the intercourse between states was what we would now call a zero-sum game, and that to lose was to lose utterly. Failure meant political extinction. His question, then, became what was the best means of survival amid the political chaos around him. And his answer was to turn the state into a military camp through the judicious application of reward and punishment to take advantage of the natural fear and the greed of the people.

His vision of law had several characteristics. First, laws must be clear and simple, and must be promulgated so that everyone is properly informed. Second, the law must always be equitable, absolutely objective in its application, and strictly enforced. Severe punishments must be meted out for the least infringements of these laws as a way of "using punishment to prevent punishment."

Shang Yang went beyond simple theory to advocate the establishment of legal institutions to put his ideas into practice. Further, under Duke Xiao of Qin, Shang Yang had the opportunity to translate his philosophical program for political dominance into historical fact. His regime was so effective in dislodging the landed aristocracy from power, and implementing a program of rewards and punishments driven by an indoctrinated bureaucracy, that an extension of this same strategy ultimately brought political unity to China in 221 B.C.E.

Han Fei (Han Feizi, d. 233 B.C.E.) is perhaps the most prominent representative of the legalist lineage, building his philosophical system on penal law as the foundation of political order. Adopting in its entirety Shang Yang's understanding of the effective application of law, Han Fei added additional "techniques of rulership" (*shu*) and "political purchase" (*shi*) as reinforcements that would make even a mediocre ruler secure in his position.

In the dominant Confucian culture, social order was pursued through the observance of ritualized roles and relationships (*li*), and appeal to law was seen as an admission of communal failure. A representative passage in the *Analects* draws a comparison between a state ordered by ritual propriety and one ordered by penal law:

> The Master said, "Lead the people with administrative injunctions and keep them orderly with penal law (*xing*), and they will avoid punishments but will be without a sense of shame. Lead them with excellence and keep them orderly through observing ritual propriety (*li*) and they will develop a sense of shame, and moreover, will order themselves."

This does not mean that the Confucians were hostile to the notion of penal law; in fact, even Confucius saw law as a sometimes necessary evil for setting a boundary on the community and excising what could not be corrected by some better means. For the legalists, too, the ruler could not engineer social order without relying on its ritualized horizontal and vertical structure.

The contrast between the legalists and the Confucians tends to be drawn too sharply as "government by law" versus "government by man." In fact, the legalists were more Machiavellian pragmatists than political philosophers. They did not dispute the effectiveness of the Confucian alternative or claim that their recipe for social order was for all times. Rather, they claimed simply that the unrelenting chaos of their present historical moment required extraordinary measures—different solutions for different problems.

Although the harshness of the legalist program for social and political order was much reviled in the subsequent Confucian-dominated tradition, its impact on the structure and function of the Chinese imperial institutions was initially enormous, and was persistent. When Buddhism entered China in the second century C.E., the term *fa* was appropriated as a translation for the key Sanskrit term *dharma*, which means "reality," "true teachings," and "moral duty." Perhaps the most important distinction that separates this Buddhist understanding from what was indigenously Chinese is the introduction of a distinction between "reality" and "appearance." For the Buddhists, one required a religious regimen to escape from a common delusory way of seeing oneself in the world. In overcoming the assumed substantiality of the ego (self) and the tendency toward acquisition that is entailed by such a belief, one comes to see phenomena as they really are. The experience of phenomena as they really are (*fa*) is ultimate achievement of Buddhist teachings (*fa*) and leads the adept through meditative practice to the moral life (*fa*).

See also Han Feizi; Legalism; Shang Yang.

Bibliography

Ames, Roger T. *The Art of Rulership: A Study of Ancient Chinese Political Thought*. Albany: State University of New York Press, 1993.

Hansen, Chad. "*Fa* (Standards: Laws) and Meaning Changes in Chinese Philosophy." *Philosophy East and West*, 44(3), 1994, pp. 433–488.

Hsiao, Kung-chuan. *A History of Chinese Political Thought*, trans. F. W. Mote. Princeton, N.J.: Princeton University Press, 1979.

Peerenboom, R. P. *Law and Morality in Ancient China: The Silk Manuscripts of Huang-Lao*. Albany: State University of New York Press, 1993.

Fang Dongmei (Thomé H. Fang)

Vincent SHEN

Thomé H. Fang (1899–1977), also known as Fang Dongmei, was one of the most creative contemporary Chinese philosopers. In synthesizing western and Chinese philosophy from the metaphysical point of view, he created an organicist system that emphasized "comprehensive harmony." Fang characterized Chinese philosophy as a transcendent-immanent metaphysics and brought to his creative synthesis ideas of western philosophy that he found pertinent to understanding cosmic process and human nature. For Fang, Chinese philosophy had three common constituents: (1) a vision of pervasive unity or comprehensive harmony, (2) a doctrine of the *dao*, and (3) a raising of the human being into ever higher realms of existence.

Because of his openness to life, his creativity, and his sense of beauty, Fang never confined his inquiry to the narrow focus of the philosophy of subjectivity we find among some of his contemporaries, such as Mou Zongsan (Mou Tsung-san) and Tang Junyi (T'ang Chün-i). Fang's philosophy could thus withstand the challenge of postmodernism.

Life and Works

Thomé H. Fang was born in 1899 into a famous learned family in Tongcheng County of An Hui Province. The family was proud of its prominent members, such as Fang Bao and Fang Yizhi, and Thomé Fang grew up in an atmosphere of Chinese learning. Because of the family tradition and his own early talent, he began to learn the Chinese classics when he was quite young. In 1917, the year when John Dewey came to China, Fang entered the department of philosophy at Jinlin University in Nanjing. When Dewey came to Nanjing to teach, it was Fang who, representing the students, delivered the welcoming address in English. He also took Dewey's course on the history of ancient western philosophy. As a student, Fang had already published his first book-length translation—a translation of D. L. Murray's work on pragmatism, *Shiyan zhuyi* (*Pragmatism*); the publisher was Zhong Hua.

In 1921 Fang went to the United States to study philosophy at the University of Wisconsin, Madison. There he learned French and German and began to read texts by western philosophers: Kant, Hegel, Goethe, Nietzsche, Bergson, William James, Bertrand Russell, and others. His master's thesis was "A Critical Exposition of the Bergsonian Philosophy of Life." He then studied Hegel at Ohio University for one year. In 1924, he came back to the University of Wisconsin and presented his doctoral thesis, "A Comparative Study of British and American Realism," but he was obliged to return to China before he could publish it as required.

After he returned to China, he taught first at Wuhan High Normal School (which later became Wuhan University). Then, in 1925, he moved to Dongnan University in Nanjing (later National Central University). At this time, his main philosophical interest was comparative philosophy and the philosophy of life. Regarding the latter, he wrote *Science, Philosophy, and Life* (*Kexue zhexue yu rensheng*, published in 1937), a book in which he articulated his creative vision of life with a sense of tragedy as well as beauty. Just before the war against Japan, he broadcast to the youth of China a series of lectures, "Chinese Ancient Philosophers' Philosophy of Life" (*Zhongguo xianzhe di rensheng zhexue*), later published as a book.

Fang's essay "Three Traditions of Philosophical Wisdom" (*Zhexue sanhui*), first presented at the Third Annual Conference of the Chinese Philosophical Association in 1937, though brief, is a very important work of this time, stating his vision of comparative philosophy and culture. The three traditions were ancient Greece, modern Europe, and China. To Fang, ancient Greek philosophy represented realistic wisdom that developed into a culture of *logos*; modern European philosophy represented pragmatic wisdom that developed into a culture of power; and Chinese philosophy represented egalitarian wisdom that developed into a culture of "marvelous nature" emphasizing comprehensive harmony, equality among all things, and responsive interconnectedness.

In 1948, one year before China became a communist regime, Fang moved to Taiwan, where he became the first chairman of the department of philosophy at National Taiwan University. Because of his concern for the destiny of Chinese culture, his philosophical interest began to turn back to Chinese philosophy itself, as he tried to synthesize his interpretations of western philosophy. At the invitation of Chiang Kai-shek, he began lectures titled "The Historical Background and Present Difficulties of Hegelian Philosophy," which were later published (1956). In this work, he analyzed and compared the philosophy of Hegel and its relationship to Kant, Fichte, and Leibniz, before tracing it back to the philosophies of Plato and Aristotle. His main concern here, besides synthesizing his evaluative interpretations of western philosophy, was to develop a conceptual framework or image of an organic cosmos permeated with comprehensive harmony, in which different layers of existence and harmonious relationships were articulated and elaborated.

During this period, Fang was much inspired by the Indian philosopher S. Radhakrishnan, who advised him to write in English so that the western world might understand the true Chinese philosophy. Accordingly, Fang wrote *The Chinese View of Life* (1957), in which he developed his concept of comprehensive harmony as articulated in Chinese philosophy—cosmology, the theory of human nature, the "spirit of life," morality, aesthetics, and political thought.

In 1959 Fang began various international academic activities. He was a visiting professor at South Dakota University and then at University of Missouri. Also, he was an invited speaker at the fourth Conference of East-West Philosophers in 1964 and the fifth in 1969. These activities not only made him famous but also convinced him of the necessity of showing the western world the true spirit of Chinese philosophy. Therefore, after returning to Taiwan in 1966, he no longer gave courses in western philosophy but concentrated instead on teaching and writing about Chinese philosophy. During this period he taught a series of courses called "Chinese Philosophy: Its Spirit and Its Development." That later became the title of his magnum opus in Chinese philosophy, written in English and finished in 1976.

Fang taught at National Taiwan University until his retirement in 1973. He was then invited to teach at the graduate school of philosophy of Fu Jen Catholic University. His lectures there were recorded by his students and, together with some recordings made earlier at National Taiwan University, were transcribed after his death in 1977. Two of his major works in English were published posthumously: *Creativity in Man and Nature* (1980) and *Chinese Philosophy: Its Spirit and Its Development* (1981). In addition, two collections of his essays and conferences and one volume of his poems were later published in Taipei. The transcribed recordings became the basis of a series of books on different periods and schools of thought in Chinese philosophy, published beginning in 1980; these include *Primordial Confucianism and Taoism, Chinese Mahayana Buddhism, The Philosophy of Huayan School*, and *Eighteen Lectures on Neo-Confucianism*.

A Philosophy of Comprehensive Harmony

Thomé Fang's philosophy can be characterized as organicism or comprehensive harmony. He emphasizes the ultimate value of life, beauty, and creativity in philosophy and culture. His affirmation of creativity as the ultimate reality, self-manifesting in the interplay between human beings and nature, places the human in the natural. He cherishes the aesthetic dimension of human experience and in this regard complements twentieth-century ethical theory, which tends to neglect the aesthetic dimension.

Perhaps the most important idea in Fang's philosophy is "creative creativity" (*shengsheng*), a concept that can be traced back to the *Book of Changes*. It represents the ultimate reality of the cosmic process as whole and is similar to Whitehead's concept of "creative advancement" and Henri Bergson's *évolution créatrice*. The concept begins with the creative movement of life, achieves a system of comprehensive harmony, and ultimately returns to the freedom of the creative force itself.

The point of departure for Fang's philosophy is aesthetic experience, through which an affective, free, creative mode of life develops. Affectivity and structural intelligibility are characteristics of the sense of beauty, and it is through this sense of beauty that cosmic processes and human life can be understood as a complex synthesis of feelings and reason. By means of language—especially language that is poetic or otherwise expresses a sense of beauty—feelings and reason are articulated as comprehensive harmony. Artworks in general and poetry in particular, although they are based on a finite material realization, are themselves infinite in their creative intention and imaginative function. Space, not simply the totality of all beings, is the milieu of creativity. Time, not simply a mechanical or continuous succession of instants, is the cumulative process of reason and the emergence of novelty. Fang had fully grasped these aesthetic aspects of Chinese culture, and he saw in them a contrast with Greek civilization and modern western civilization. Fang himself was both a philosopher and a poet. Many readers enjoy his work particularly because of its pervasive elegance and sense of beauty and even experience catharsis through it. Thus for many thoughtful people, Fang is more profound and more inspiring than other contemporary western or Chinese philosophers, especially those who focus on abstract argumentation.

In sum, aesthetic experience forms the core of Thomé Fang's philosophy of life. He stresses the unending creativity that finds and reflects a common denominator among all sorts of differentiated realms, and even in the unfathomable. Thus Fang's philosophy incorporates western and Chinese elements to develop a new system of thought. The two pillars of Fang's philosophical system are the theory of being and the theory of human nature, which interact in a comprehensive harmony.

Being and Human Nature

In the domain of being, Fang affirms the multifaceted nature of existence, including the physical, biological, psychological, aesthetic, moral, and religious, as well as the unfathomable—which, inspired by Nicolas of Cusa, he calls *deus absconditus*. These levels of existence form a hierarchical order going upward from the physical to the unfathomable and downward from *deus absconditus* to the physical. Fang never asks why and or whence come the lower and the higher levels and their hierarchical structure; he seems to take the hierarchy for granted. He is more interested in arguing that beings can evolve and develop from a basic, fundamental level to higher levels ("turning upward"), and that beings on higher levels can pour their creative forces back into, and thereby fortify, those on the lower levels ("turning downward"). "Turning upward" and "turning downward" represent two cosmic processes that ceaselessly infuse each other. In this sense, we can say that for Fang, God, the transcendent unfathomable, is still in all things and all things are also in God. To express this idea, Fang uses the term "panentheism" rather than the traditional "pantheism."

In the domain of human nature, Fang, like the Confucians, maintains that there is an innate dynamism in human nature, which is good itself and tends toward the fuller development of goodness. He sets up an ideal model of man in Chinese philosophy as a compound, "prophet-poet-sage," thereby including Confucian, Daoist, and Buddhist models. Regarding the structure and dynamism of human beings, he argues—drawing on his understanding of Chinese philosophy, German idealism, and other modern philosophies—that a human being undergoes levels of development. One can advance from *Homo faber* to *Homo creator, Homo sapiens* (a person of knowledge), *Homo symbolicus, Homo honaestatis* (moral man), and finally *Homo religiosus*. These terms represent different types of human existence and different horizons that humans can, through their efforts, attain. Human nature can either develop from a lower to a higher level or move down from a higher level and become firmly settled on a lower one, thus realizing within itself both turning upward and turning downward.

With these two theoretical points as a framework, Fang's philosophy emphasizes specifically the creativity, reasonableness, and interconnectedness of thinking and existence. The order of being and the order of man, with their responsive processes of turning upward and turning downward, interact and interconnect—and thus create the comprehensive harmony.

Comprehensive harmony is, for Fang, the ideal system. Each individual constituent is respected, but together the constituents all harmonize optimally. Using this ideal model, Fang could evaluate any system of philosophy, Chinese or western, and could bring it to a perfect architectonic whole capable of directing the development of a culture.

But if the point of Fang's philosophy is to elaborate an ideal architectonic world system supported by a theory of human nature and a theory of being, his heart nevertheless turned back—after the laborious construction of this ideal—to a concept of ultimate freedom. Just before he died, he wrote:

> From emptiness I came.
> To emptiness I return.
> Emptying the emptiness without possessing any being
> It is in no where that my heart will dwell.

Fang's last words suggest that, although the system of comprehensive harmony was the culmination of his philosophy, he still thought that any system, once constructed, should submit itself to deconstruction, so as to give space—emptiness—for new creative possibilities. But we should not form an attachment even to emptiness, nor should we consider emptiness a finality or a fixed foundation. Emptiness itself should be deconstructed to motivate new movements of creativity.

The Significance of Thomé Fang's Philosophy

Fang's philosophy is especially significant when we compare it with contemporary western and Chinese philosophy. Under the serious critiques of Heideggerian phenomenology, structuralism, critical theory, and postmodernism, the philosophy of subjectivity—essential to modern western philosophy and modernity in general—has been deconstructed. But this does not mean that the human being or the self is unimportant. The question now is how to situate human beings and the formation of the self in the context of cosmic processes. In this sense, other contemporary Chinese philosophers, the new Confucians such as Mou Zongsan and Tang Junyi, may have overemphasized subjectivity (Mou, for example, inflated human subjectivity to "infinite free mind") and thus may not be able to survive the challenge of deconstruction. On the other hand, Fang's philosophy, which already puts human beings in the context of cosmic processes, will itself present a challenge for future philosophical exploration.

The culture of representation is also under vehement attack by contemporary thinkers. Although today's technology of information is leading from a culture of representation to a culture of simulacra, that may be no improvement; the human mind is as unsatisfied with simulacra as with mere representations and now seems to be moving toward investigations of reality or, better, of life itself. Fang, who inherited the insights of Nietzsche (the hero of postmodernism), Bergson, and Whitehead, transforms these by means of a Chinese philosophy of life that emphasizes the ultimate value of life and creativity. With his elegantly beautiful Chinese style of writing, he will, one hopes, attract more attention than philosophies constructed on conceptual representations and abstract arguments.

With regard to ontology, twentieth-century philosophy moved from the ontology of substance to that of events, which in turn is now giving way to an ontology of dynamic relations—something that all schools of Chinese philosophy articulate in one way or another. The philosophy of Thomé Fang, a philosophy of organicism and comprehensive harmony, is the best expression of an ontology of dynamic relations. His affirmation of creativity as the ultimate reality, demonstrating in itself in the interplay between human beings and nature, articulates a creative and dynamic ontology of relations that is likely to inspire philosophical thought in the twenty-first century.

See also Mou Zongsan; Philosophy: Recent Trends in China since Mao; Philosophy: Recent Trends in Taiwan; Philosophy: Recent Trends Overseas; Tang Junyi.

Bibliography

Executive Committee of ICPTF, ed. *Fang Dongmei xiansheng di zhexue* (Philosophy of Mr. Fang Dong-mei). Taipei: Youshi, 1989.

Fang, Thomé. *Chinese Philosophy: Its Spirit and Its Development.* Taipei: Linking, 1981.

———. *The Chinese View of Life*. Hong Kong: Union Press, 1956.

———. *Creativity in Man and Nature*. Taipei: Linking, 1980.

———. *Fang Dongmei yanjiang ji* (Collected Conferences of Thomé Fang). Taipei: Li-ming, 1978.

———. *Huayanzong zhexue* (Philosophy of the Hua-yen School), Vols. 1 and 2. Taipei: Li-ming, 1981.

———. *Jianbai jingshe shiji* (Poetic Works of Thomé Fang). Taipei: Li-ming, 1978.

———. *Kexue zhexue yu rensheng* (Science, Philosophy and Life). Shanghai: Commercial Press,1937. (Reprinted, Taipei: Rainbow, 1959. Reedited, Taipei: Li-ming, 1980.)

———. *Shengsheng zhi de* (The Virtue of Creative Creativity). Taipei: Li-ming, 1979.

———. *Xin rujia zhexue shiba jiang* (Eighteen Lectures on Neo-Confucianism). Taipei: Li-ming, 1983.

———. *Yuanshi rujia daojia zhexue* (Philosophies of Primordial Confucianism and Daoism). Taipei: Li-ming, 1983.

———. *Zhongguo Dasheng Foxue* (Chinese Mahayana Buddhism). Taipei: Li-ming, 1984.

———. *Zhongguo rensheng zhexue* (Chinese Philosophy of Life). Taipei: Li-ming, 1980.

Shen, Vincent, ed.. *Shengming meigan yu chuangzhao* (Life, Aesthetics, and Creativity). Taipei: Wunan, 2001.

Fazang (Fa-tsang)

Ming-wood Liu

Fazang (643–712) was the foremost systematizer of Huayan thought and, in the view of some historians of Chinese Buddhism, the actual founder of the Huayan school. The Huayan school of thought, as its name signifies, takes as its mission the elaboration and propagation of the teaching of the *Huayan jing* (*Garland Sutra*, henceforth cited as *Garland*), a voluminous mid-Mahayana text first translated into Chinese in its entirety by Buddhabhadra (359–429) in the early fifth century.

The *Garland Sutra* opens with a majestic scene of the Buddha sitting under the bodhi tree, worshiped by a huge assembly of bodhisattvas, devas, and human beings, and so is commonly regarded as the record of the first words of the Buddha after his enlightenment. The main body of the scripture is made up of detailed analyses of the Buddha's path to enlightenment, as well as some of the most divine, awesome portrayals of his enlightenment experience in Buddhist literature. A famous passage depicts Hinayana saints such as Sariputra, Maudgalyayana, and Mahakasyapa as totally oblivious of the Buddha's display of supernatural power, which is generally taken as indicating that the unadulterated truth propounded in the *Garland* is comprehensible only to Buddhist practitioners of the highest intelligence. The main objective of Fazang teaching is to highlight the religious significance and draw out the philosophical implications of the unadulterated truth embodied in the *Garland*, and the majority of Fazang's writings, including his two masterpieces, the *Wujiao Zhang* (*Treatise on the Five Teachings*, henceforth cited as *Treatise*) and the *Huayan Jing Tanxuan Ji* (*Inquiry into the Profound Meaning of the Garland Sutra*), were composed with this purpose in mind.

When the *Garland* was introduced into China, it was immediately recognized as a major Buddhist scripture. It was very popular in the sixth and seventh centuries among the Dilun masters and the Shelun masters, whose teachings represented the initial Chinese reception of the teaching of the Indian Yogacara school. A common feature of Dilun and Shelun teachings is their idea of intrinsic pure mind, which they often refer to as the *tathagatagarbha*. According to the *Dasheng Qixin Lun* (*Awakening of Faith in the Mahayana*, henceforth cited as *Awakening of Faith*), a text closely connected with the Dilun tradition, every sentient being is endowed with the *tathagatagarbha*, which is originally immaculate and which possesses all the qualities of the Buddha. Sentient beings become involved in the tumult of samsaric existence and suffer the pains of incessant rebirths when their *tathagatagarbha* comes under the influence of ignorance, just as ocean water assumes the appearance of waves on being stirred by the wind. And just as when the wind ceases, the waves will vanish and the ocean water will resume its calm appearance, so when ignorance is destroyed, sentient beings' involvement in samsaric activities will come to an end and their inborn pure essence will reveal itself. In this way, the *Awakening of Faith* represents enlightenment not as the coming into being of a new spiritual state (as in Yogacara thought), but as the return to a preexistent pure condition. Some Dilun and Shelun masters, including Fazang's mentor, Zhiyan (602–668), applied this concept of enlightenment to the interpretation of the picture of enlightenment given in the *Garland*. Fazang was an expert on the *Awakening of Faith*, and his commentary on it, *Dasheng Qixinlun Yiji* (*Exposition of the Meaning of the Awakening of Faith in the Mahayana*), is generally recognized as one of the most authoritative works of its category. In Fazang's writings, the practice of integrating the teaching of *tathagatagarbha* of the *Awakening of Faith* with the teaching of enlightenment of the *Garland* reached a new height.

To see the Huayan teaching that Fazang propounds in the right perspective, some knowledge of his theory of *panjiao* (classification of teachings) is necessary. *Panjiao* is basically the practice of distinguishing and integrating various trends of Buddhist thought, various systems of Buddhist praxis, and various kinds of Buddhist texts, with a view to pointing up their special characteristics and reconciling their apparent disparities. Different Chinese Buddhist schools, each with its particular understanding of the essential meaning of Buddha's message, considered the significance of the heterogeneous elements of the Buddhist heritage differently, and so there came to be a variety of *panjiao* schemes, each identified with a Buddhist school.

The *panjiao* scheme most commonly identified with the Huayan school is the "five teachings" (*wujiao*):

1. Hinayana teaching. This is the most elementary form of Buddhist teaching, dealing with phenomenal existence only. Fazang describes it as the "teaching of the existence of dharmas and the inexistence of the self," as its main interest is to demonstrate the emptiness of the phenomenal self by reducing it to its constituent elements. This teaching is found in Hinayana sutras and sastras.
2. Preliminary teaching of the Mahayana. This is superior to the Hinayana teaching in maintaining the emptiness of not only the self but also the constituent elements, all of which it regards as originating from a basic consciousness known as the *alaya*. However, as its knowledge of reality is still confined to the phenomenal realm, and as it affirms the existence of sentient beings incapable of enlightenment, it is deemed "preliminary." This is the form of teaching found in the works of the Yogacara and the Madhyamaka schools.
3. Final teaching of the Mahayana. This excels the second teaching in averring the presence in every sentient being of an intrinsic pure mind, the *tathagatagarbha*. This pure mind has two aspects, the noumenal and the phenomenal. In the noumenal aspect, it is unborn, imperishable, and undifferentiated. It takes on a phenomenal aspect when it is soiled by ignorance. The entire samsaric realm and its objects, including the dharmas and the *alaya* considered as ontologically primary in the Hinayana teaching and the preliminary teaching, respectively, are all merely creations of the phenomenal aspect of the pure mind, and so are all empty in essence. In affirming the existence of the mind with a noumenal aspect that is of the nature of enlightenment, and in attributing this mind to all sentient beings, this teaching provides a theoretical underpinning for the Mahayana ideal of universal buddhahood, and so is given the epithet "final." It is the form of Buddhist teaching found in works having the *tathagatagarbha* as the main theme, such as the Mahayana *Niepan Jing* (*Nir-*

vana Sutra), the *Lengjia Jing* (*Lankavatara Sutra*), and the *Awakening of Faith*.

4. Sudden teaching. This focuses attention on the noumenal aspect of the pure mind, highlighting its ineffable and inapprehensible nature. It can be found in the *Lengjia Jing* and the *Weimo Jing* (*Vimalakirti Sutra*).
5. Perfect teaching. This is the Buddhist teaching par excellence. Its main concern is to enunciate the supreme vision of reality revealed in the *Garland*, in which the noumenal and the phenomenal levels of existence, as well as the innumerable elements constituting the phenomenal level, are seen as interpenetrating and mutually determining; in which each being is perceived as an inalienable part of the totality of existence, each contributing to the nature of the totality as well as obtaining its nature from the totality; and in which each event is viewed as a mirror of the entire universe, reflecting every event past, present, and future, and vice versa ad infinitum.

This scheme of five teachings shows that among the three major Mahayana doctrinal traditions—the Madhyamaka, Yogacara, and *tathagatagarbha*—Fazang affirms the superiority of the third in classifying its teaching as "final," in contradistinction to the first two, which he lumps together as "preliminary." While he places above the final teaching the "sudden teaching," his representation of it shows that it is largely an expansion of a particular aspect of the concept of *tathagatagarbha*. As for the supreme "perfect teaching," we shall soon see that Fazang often falls back on the *tathagatagarbha* in elaborating its significance. All in all, Fazang's *panjiao* doctrine of five teachings points to his allegiance to the *tathagatagarbha* tradition.

Fazang's lifework was devoted to elucidating the perfect teaching that the *Garland* exemplifies. He also calls this the "distinct teaching of the one vehicle" in order to underline its distinctive character and to differentiate it from the kind of superior teaching (referred to as one-vehicle teaching) found in the *Fahua Jing* (*Lotus Sutra*), which he calls "common teaching of the one vehicle" to indicate that it has features in common with inferior Buddhist teachings (referred to as three-vehicle teachings). Fazang spends an entire chapter of the *Treatise* explaining the significance of the distinct teaching of the one vehicle. This chapter, which contains the most systematic doctrinal statement in Fazang's entire corpus of writings, is generally accepted as the most important source for the study of Fazang's philosophy.

Fazang opens the chapter with a radical reinterpretation of the Yogacara theory of "three natures" (*sanxing*): "discriminate nature" (*fenbie xing*), "dependent nature" (*yita xing*), and "true nature" (*zhenshi xing*). The theory was first brought up in early Yogacara writings to explain the central Mahayana teaching of universal emptiness.

Yogacara discussions about the three natures usually begin with "dependent nature," which is given out to indicate the conditioned nature of all entities of the phenomenal realm. In conformity with its theory of "ideation only," the Yogacara attributes the dependent nature of phenomenal entities to their being mental constructs arising from the activities of the consciousnesses, the possession of which is considered in Buddhism as the most basic characteristic of sentient existence. The nonenlightened, not being able to see the conditioned nature of phenomenal entities, ascribe to them the character of independent existence; and this constitutes "discriminate nature." The enlightened recognize the absence of independent existence in things, and this constitutes the "true nature."

Fazang, however, starts his account of the three natures with the "true nature," which he represents as denoting the *tathagatagarbha* and as comprising the two aspects of "being immutable" (*bubian*) and "responding to conditions" (*suiyuan*), the former indicating the noumenal aspect of the *tathagatagarbha* that is eternal, and the latter indicating the phenomenal aspect assumed by the *tathagatagarbha* on being influenced by ignorance. The functioning of the phenomenal aspect of the *tathagatagarbha* gives rise to the phenomenal world; and "dependent nature," according to Fazang, denotes the nature of the entities of the phenomenal world. This nature also comprises two aspects: first, "without self-nature" (*wuxing*), indicating the dependence of phenomenal entities on the *tathagatagarbha* for their existence; second, "semblance of existence" (*shiyou*), indicating the appearance of existence that all phenomenal entities have. Ordinary sentient beings, not realizing the dependent nature of phenomenal entities, look on them as existing independently; and "discriminate nature," according to Fazang, denotes the nature of independent existence sentient beings imagine into phenomenal entities. This nature likewise comprises two aspects: first, "being inexistent in reality" (*liwu*), as it is the false creation of discrimination; second, "appearing to be existent to the senses" (*qingyou*), as it is the object of discrimination of the senses.

We can see that whereas the ideas of "dependent nature" and "discriminate nature" serve in Fazang's interpretation (as in the Yogacara) the function of drawing attention to the empty nature of phenomenal existence, Fazang's interpretation of "true nature" as denoting the *tathagatagarbha* adds an ontological dimension to the three-nature doctrine as a whole; and in Fazang's hands, the three-nature teaching is turned into a vehicle for demonstrating the unobstructed interfusion of the *tathagatagarbha* and the phenomenal realm originating from it.

This fact is especially evident in Fazang's exposition of the two aspects of the three natures. Thus, with respect to "true nature," Fazang points out that its noumenal aspect, "being immutable," forms the ontological ground of its phenomenal aspect, "responding to conditions"; that its phenomenal aspect, "responding to conditions," shows up its noumenal aspect, "being immutable"; and that these two aspects, in Fazang's words, "completely encompass one another, forming one, not two natures." With respect to the relation between the three natures, Fazang asserts that as true nature, dependent nature, and discriminate nature have, respectively, the aspects of "being immutable," "without self-nature," and "inexistence in reality," it can be seen that affirming the eternal existence of the noumenal "base" (*ben*) does not entail negating the phenomenal existence of the "derivatives" (*mo*). He further asserts that as true nature, dependent nature, and discriminate nature have, respectively, the other aspects of "responding to conditions," "having semblance of existence," and "appearing to have existence to the senses," it can be seen that the continuous arising of the derivative phenomenal order does not conflict with the presence of an immovable noumenal base. Fazang concludes that the "true origin" (*zhenyuan*) which is the *tathagatagarbha* and the "false derivatives" (*wangmo*) constituting the phenomenal realm interfuse perfectly, pervading one another without obstruction.

Having demonstrated the perfect interfusion of the phenomenal "derivatives" and the noumenal "base," Fazang continues his exposition of the "distinct teaching of one vehicle" in the *Treatise* with extensive analyses of the perfect interfusion of various entities constituting the phenomenal "derivatives," and these analyses are generally taken to be Fazang's most important contribution as a Buddhist thinker. In accordance with common Buddhist practice, Fazang represents entities of the phenomenal realm as "causes" (*yin*). Following the suggestion of Yogacara texts, he maintains that all causes, and so all phenomenal entities, have six features:

1. Being instantaneous.
2. Being simultaneous with their effects.
3. Being dependent on conditions.
4. Being fixed in nature.
5. Giving rise to effects of their own kind.
6. Continuously evolving.

Contemplating the meaning of these features shows that, depending on which feature is under consideration, a cause can be seen correspondingly as:

1. Being empty, having power, not dependent on conditions.
2. Being empty, having power, dependent on conditions.
3. Being empty, not having power, dependent on conditions.
4. Having being, having power, not dependent on conditions.
5. Having being, having power, dependent on conditions.
6. Having being, not having power, dependent on conditions.

In this way, Fazang arrives at three pairs of concepts: "being empty" and "having being"; "having power" and "not having power"; and "dependent on conditions" and "not dependent on conditions." With the help of these concepts he illustrates the harmonious interfusion of phenomenal entities, a state that he refers to time and again as *fajie yuanqi*.

So Fazang explains that phenomenal entities can be viewed either as "dependent on conditions" or as "not dependent on conditions." In the first case, they are regarded as different beings dependent on each other for their existence and nature, a state that Fazang refers to as "separate essence" (*yiti*). In the second case, they are regarded as individual beings each contributing to the existence and nature of the totality of phenomenal existence, a state that Fazang refers to as "common essence" (*tongti*). Fazang maintains that whichever state one considers, phenomenal entities can be seen as mutually "nonobstructive" (*wu'ai*).

To explain the mutual nonobstruction of phenomenal entities viewed as of "separate essence," Fazang brings in the other two pairs of concepts: "being empty" and "having being," and "having power" and "not having power." He asserts that if phenomenal entities are considered dependent on each other, then when one entity is perceived as "having being," the other entities would be perceived as "being empty," for the other entities derive their existence and nature from this one entity. On the other hand, if one entity is perceived as "being empty," the other entities would be perceived as "having being," for this one entity derives its existence and nature from the other entities.

Fazang calls this interdependence of phenomenal entities "mutual determination" (*xiangji*). According to Fazang, it can be conceived as an active interplay of forces permeating each other. In that case, it would be perceived that when one entity "has power," the other entities would "not have power"; and that when one entity "does not have power," the other entities would "have power." Fazang calls this relation of reciprocal assimilation of phenomenal entities "interpenetration" (*xiangru*). He goes on to apply the ideas of "mutual determination" and "interpenetration" so obtained to describe the mutual nonobstruction of phenomenal entities viewed as of "common essence." In this connection, he asserts that the existence and the nature of each phenomenal entity determines, and is determined by, the existence and the nature of the sum of phenomenal existence, a condition which he sums up as "one is many, many is one" (*yi ji duo, duo ji yi*). He also asserts that the existence and the nature of each phenomenal entity penetrates, and is penetrated by, the existence and the nature of the sum of phenomenal existence, a condition which he sums up as "one in many, many in one" (*yi zhong duo, duo zhong yi*).

To explicate fully the signifance and implications of the mutual nonobstruction of phenomenal entities, Fazang brings in a detailed analysis comprising ten points, which he calls "ten profound principles" (*shi xuanmen*). As given in the *Treatise*, the ten profound principles are as follows:

1. Simultaneous, complete correlation: In the phenomenal world appearing in the supreme vision of the Buddha, all entities correlate perfectly with each other, each embodying all the rest without the distinction of the prior and the subsequent, the first and the last.
2. Mutual inclusion of one and many in difference: Each phenomenal entity, while remaining distinct, takes in all other phenomenal entities, and vice versa.
3. Mutual determination of all dharmas in freedom: Phenomenal entities, while existing in perfect freedom, determine the existence and nature of each other.
4. Realm of Indra's net: Phenomenal entities are comparable to the jewels forming the net of the god Indra. Each jewel of Indra's net reflects and is reflected by all the other jewels. Furthermore, each jewel reflects all the other jewels' reflections of itself as well as its reflections of all the other jewels, and so on ad infinitum. In the same way, each phenomenal entity determines and penetrates, and is being determined and penetrated by, all other phenomenal entities. Furthermore, each phenomenal entity determines and penetrates all the other phenomenal entities' determination and penetration of itself, as well as its determination and penetration of other phenomenal entities; and so on ad infinitum.
5. Mutual inclusion and establishment of the minute (and the totality): The most minute and subtle phenomenal entity, such as a moment of thought or a speck of dust, contains and contributes to the existence of the totality of phenomenal existence, and vice versa.
6. Simultaneous formation of the "hidden" and the "manifested": Every phenomenal entity can be simultaneously considered "hidden" or "manifested," depending on whether we perceive it as determining and penetrating, or as being determined and being penetrated, by other phenomenal entities of the totality.
7. Miscellaneous storehouses having the characteristics of both being "pure" and being "mixed": Phenomenal existence can be considered as at once "pure" and "mixed." When phenomenal entities are viewed *each in turn as being itself*, determining and penetrating miscellaneous other phenomenal entities, they would be seen as "pure." When miscellaneous phenomenal entities are viewed *together as involving each other*, determining and penetrating the being of each other, they would be seen as "mixed."
8. Dharmas existing separately in the ten periods and yet contributing to the formation of each other: Past, present and future are known as "three periods" in Buddhism. When each of the three periods is again divided into past, present, and future, we get "nine periods." When the truths of mutual determination and interpenetration are applied to the perception of the nine periods, there come to be "ten periods." The ten periods, as well as phenomenal entities pertaining to them, perfectly interfuse, so that any phenomenal entity of any period embodies all the phenomenal entities of all the ten periods.
9. Wondrous formations of the evolution of "mind-only": All phenomenal entities are nothing but the transformation of the *tathagatagarbha*, the originally pure mind.
10. Each phenomenon as revealing all dharmas and begetting true understanding: In each phenomenal entity, all other phenomenal entities are revealed. By observing one phenomenal entity, one can obtain the true knowledge of the perfect nonobstruction of all forms and all levels of existence.

Fazang's teaching of the ten profound principles may be too repetitive and schematic for modern tastes, but traditional Buddhist scholarship has always considered it a cornerstone of Fazang's thought. There is no gainsaying that the ten profound principles together afford a clear view of the supreme vision of reality made out by Fazang as the leitmotiv of the *Garland*. It is a vision of perfect harmony, in which all forms and levels of phenomenal beings, understood as formations of the *tathagatagarbha* (9), are perceived as existing in perfect accord (1), penetrating (2) and determining (3) each other irrespective of size (5) and temporal distinctions (8). Each phenomenal entity is like each jewel in the net of Indra (4), penetrating and determining all other phenomenal entities as well as being penetrated and determined by them (6), appearing at once as the center of the entire phenomenal realm and as one of its elements (7). Even the most minute phenomenal entity appears as containing the whole universe (5) and as exemplifying the ideal state of total nonobstruction (10).

Fazang closes his exposition of the "distinct teaching of one vehicle" in the *Treatise* with a detailed exposition of the "six characteristics" (*liuxiang*):

1. Universality. It indicates the totality of phenomenal existence. In discussing this characteristic, Fazang emphasizes the mutual dependence of the totality and its constituents, asserting that each constituent is indispensable to the existence of the totality, and vice versa. He further emphasizes the mutual dependence of the constituents themselves, asserting that each constituent is indispensable to the existence of each other constituent.
2. Specialty. The totality and its constituents are distinct despite their mutual dependence, and precisely because they are distinct they can contribute to one another's existence.
3. Sameness. The constituents combine to form the same totality, and there is no conflict among them.
4. Difference. The constituents are different from each other, each having its special appearance and existing apart from the rest.
5. Formation. The totality and its constituents, owing to their mutual dependence, conduce to one another's formation.
6. Disintegration. The constituents, in coming together to form the totality, retain their individuality and have not given up their separate identity.

It is obvious that the three characteristics "universality," "sameness," and "formation" highlight the aspect of oneness of phenomenal existence, whereas the three characteristics "specialty," "difference," and "disintegration" underscore the aspect of diversity. According to Fazang, the teaching of six characteristics, in demonstrating the union of these two aspects in phenomenal existence, illustrates perfectly the truth of nonobstruction.

Over the centuries, Huayan thought has often been referred to as the "true way of nature-origination" (*xingqi famen*), and an introduction to Fazang's teaching would not be complete without some comments on this idea. The term "nature-origination" appears in the title of Chapter 32 of Buddhabhadra's translation of the *Garland*, where "nature" refers to the nature of the *tathagata*, i.e., Buddha-nature. According to Fazang, nature-origination can be viewed from the perspective of "cause" or of "fruit."

When it is viewed from the perspective of "cause," "nature" indicates the nature of the Buddha innate to all sentient beings, i.e., the *tathagatagarbha*. This nature is at present covered with adventitious defilements, and its manifestation on the removal of all impurities constitutes "nature-origination." Fazang's exposition of the idea of three natures is, to a large extent, an attempt to elucidate this aspect of nature-origination.

When nature-origination is viewed from the perspective of "fruit," "nature" indicates the nature of the Buddha realized on the attainment of buddhahood. This nature comprises innumerable excellent qualities and wonderful powers, and the functioning of these qualities and powers constitutes nature-origination. Fazang's exposition of "separate essence," "common essence," "ten mysteries," and "six characteristics" is largely an attempt to explicate this aspect of nature-origination, highlighting the vision of perfect harmony that Fazang considers the prime feature of buddhahood.

The ideas of unity in multiplicity and universal interrelatedness, commonly considered as Fazang's most significant contributions to Buddhist philosophy, also appear in the writings of a number of prominent western thinkers; and their growing popularity has contributed to a steady rise in interest in Huayan Buddhism in the west in recent decades. In his seminal work *Process Metaphysics and Hua-yen Buddhism*, Steve Odin (1982) draws attention to a number of important parallels between the Huayan teaching of Fazang on the one hand, and Whiteheadian process philosophy, Husserlian descriptive phenomenology, Jungian depth psychology, etc., on the other hand; and convincingly demonstrates the fruitfulness of applying western hermeneutical systems to Huayan thought. It is to Odin's credit that he warns against unqualified identification of Huayan Buddhism with the western doctrinal systems just mentioned, and in this connection takes notice of the difference between Fazang's and Whitehead's concepts of causation. Both Fazang and Whitehead conceive each phenomenal entity or event as conditioned by every other phenomenal entity or event. But whereas Whitehead articulates a notion of "asymmetrical" causation, in which past events condition present events, not vice versa, Fazang, as can be seen from his exposition of the first and the eighth of the ten mysteries, entertains a "symmetrical" notion of causation, in which past and present phenomenal entities are seen as conditioning each other. Odin calls Whitehead's notion of causation "cumulative penetration" to distinguish it from Fazang's idea of "interpenetration" and argues that the latter, if taken literally as indicating the structure of reality, would entail strict determinism, since each phenomenal entity would be "exhaustively factored or reductively analyzed into its causal relation and supportive conditions without remainder" (1982, 78). As a consequence, there would be no novelty or freedom, and the cardinal Buddhist teaching of *karma* would be rendered meaningless. A way out, which Odin has indicated and which finds support in the *Garland* and the writings of praxis-minded Huayan thinkers, is to look on the teaching of interpenetration as aiming at providing a conceptual framework for the understanding and the achievement of enlightenment. This interpretation could certainly save the idea, but only at the expense of its ontological relevance.

See also Buddhism in China.

Bibliography

Chang, Garma C. C. *The Buddhist Teaching of Totality*. University Park and London: Pennsylvania State University Press, 1971.

Cleary, Thomas. *Entry into the Inconceivable*. Honolulu: University of Hawaii Press, 1983.

Cook, Francis. "Fa-tsang's *Treatise on the Five Doctrines*: An Annotated Translation." Ph.D. dissertation, University of Wisconsin, 1970.

———. *Hua-yen Buddhism*. University Park and London: Pennsylvania State University Press, 1977.

Fang, Dongmei. *Huayanzhong Zhexue* (The Philosophy of the Huayan School). Taipei: Liming wenhua, 1981.

Fang, Litian. *Fazang*. Taipei: Dongda, 1991.

Gimello, Robert M. "Chih-yen (602–668) and the Foundations of Hua-yen Buddhism." Ph.D. dissertation, Columbia University, 1976.

Gimello, Robert M., and Peter N. Gregory, eds. *Studies in Ch'an and Hua-yen*. Honolulu: University of Hawaii Press, 1983.

Gregory, Peter N. *Tsung-mi and the Sinification of Buddhism*. Princeton, N.J.: Princeton University Press, 1991.

Ishii, Kosei. *Kegon shiso no kenkyu* (A Study of Huayan Thought). Tokyo: Shunjusha, 1996.

Kagimeshi, Ryokei, and Kiyotaka Kimura. *Hozo* (Fazang). Tokyo: Daizo shuppan, 1991.

Kamata, Shigeo. *Chugoku kegon shisoshi no kenkyu* (A Study of the History of Chinese Huayan Thought). Tokyo: Tokyo daigaku toyo bunka kenkyujo, 1965.

———. *Kegon gokyo sho* (A Treatise on the Five Teachings). Tokyo: Daizo shuppan, 1979.

———. *Kegongaku kenkyu shiryo shusei* (A Bibliography on Works in Huayan Study). Tokyo: Daizo shuppan, 1983.

Kimura, Kiyotaka. *Chugoku kegon shiso shi* (A History of Chinese Huayan Thought). Kyoto: Heirakuju shoten, 1992.

———. *Shoki chugoku kegon shiso kenkyu* (A Study of Early Chinese Huayan Thought). Tokyo: Shunjusha, 1977.

Liu, Ming-Wood. "The Teaching of Fa-tsang: An Examination of Buddhist Metaphysics." Ph.D. dissertation, University of California, 1979.

Mou, Zongsan. *Foxing yu bore* (Buddha-Nature and *Prajna*). Taipei: Student Bookstore, 1977.

Odin, Steve. *Process Metaphysics and Hua-yen Buddhism*. Albany: State University of New York Press, 1982.

Takamine, Ryoshu. *Kegon shiso shi* (A History of Huayan Thought). Tokyo: Kyak-kaen, 1963.

Yoshizu, Yoshihide. *Kegon ichijo shiso no kenkyu* (A Study of the Teaching of One Vehicle in Huayan Buddhism). Tokyo: Daito shuppan, 1991.

———. *Kegon-Zen no shisoshi no kenkyu* (A Study of the History of the Thought of Huayan Chan). Tokyo: Daito shuppan, 1985.

Feng Youlan (Fung Yu-lan)

Lujun YIN

Feng Youlan (Fung Yu-lan, 1889–1990) was a Chinese philosopher and a renowned historian of Chinese philosophy. A graduate of National Peking University, Feng held a doctoral degree in philosophy from Columbia University, where he studied under John Dewey and Frederick Woodbridge in the early 1920s. His two-volume *History of Chinese Philosophy* (1932) has remained the standard work on this subject in the west since its first appearance. Feng's works on Chinese philosophy were translated into French, German, Russian, Japanese, and seven other languages.

The highlight of Feng's philosophical career was his creation of a new philosophical system, *xin lixue* ("new theory of *li*"—that is, of principle, reason, form), during the Sino-Japanese War. Between late 1937 and 1946, Feng wrote six nationally acclaimed books, which he called a "series written at a time of national rebirth," representing six aspects of his new philosophical system. The first and most influential book, *Xin lixue*, elaborates the metaphysical basis of his philosophy and incorporates pragmatism, neorealism, and logical positivism into the neo-Confucian tradition. His other important philosophical works include *Xin shilun* (*A New Treatise on Human Affairs*), *Xin shixun* (*A New Way of Life*), *Xin yuanren* (*A New Treatise on the Nature of Man*), *Xin yuandao* (*A New Treatise on the Nature of the Way*), and *Xin zhiyan* (*A Treatise on the New Methodology of Epistemology*).

Feng's metaphysics is built on four basic concepts: *zhenji* (the realm of reality), *li* (principle or form), *qi* (matter), and *dao* or *daquan* (totality). Feng stated that *zhenji* contains *li*, which gives a type of things its common quality. If there is a square thing, for instance, the *li* of square, which belongs to the realm of reality, is what makes the square thing square. However, the realm of reality is neither *li* in itself nor equivalent to the "world of *li*" (*li shijie*). This is because the realm of reality includes all that subsists and all that actually exists, while *li* is what makes a type of thing what it actually is. For Feng, the notion of *li* refers both to principles of things, or, in a platonic sense, "forms" of things, and to eternal moral principles. The world of *li*, which includes all principles or forms, is the world of "universals" (*gongxiang*), and this stands in contrast to the world of "particulars" (*shuxiang*). The world of *li* is a transcendent world (*xing er shang*) above the world of particular individual things (*xing er xia*), and it exists eternally because it is independent of time and space. Prior to the existence of a kind of thing, the *li* of this kind exists potentially (that is, it subsists). Once this kind of thing comes into existence, its *li* constitutes the "nature" (*xing*) of the thing.

In the realm of actuality, every individual thing has two aspects: what makes it exist, and what it actually is. What actualizes a thing is *qi*, or, as Feng sometimes called it, "matter." Feng argued that *qi* is a purely logical concept. It refers neither to any concrete thing nor to *li*. *Qi* in itself does not follow any kind of *li*; therefore, *qi* is capable of following any *li* and actualizing anything in accordance with its *li*.

To distinguish his own use of *qi* from the notion of *qi* in traditional Chinese philosophy, Feng gave his *qi* the name *zhenyuan zhi qi* (original *qi*), a phrase he borrowed from the works of Cheng Yi. Original *qi* has the following characteristics: (1) it is potentially and existentially capable of actualizing each and every individual thing in accordance with its *li*; (2) like *li*, it stands outside time and space; (3) it is undifferentiated (*wuji*); and (4) like the concept of *li*, it is perceivable only by abstract thinking and logical inference. In Feng's metaphysical system, *dao* refers to all the processes in which *qi* (vital force) is in limitless ways realizing or actualizing the totality of *li*. *Dao* thus includes both the realm of reality and the realm of actuality. In this sense, *dao* is like the notion of the *daquan*, "universe," in Feng's metaphysics. However, although *dao* and *daquan* refer to the same universe, *dao* presents an "active universe" (*dongdi yuzhou*) from the perspective of the universe as an endless process, from *wuji* (nonultimate) to *daji* (great ultimate). *Daquan*, on the other hand, refers to the infinite existence of the "static universe" (*jingdi yuzhou*).

These four concepts fall into the "category of formal concepts" and "have no positive content," because they all are deduced from logical propositions. Those propositions are based on the analytic statement "something exists," in which the concept of the predicate merely asserts a characteristic already contained in the subject. Feng thus claimed that his metaphysical system is constructed entirely on the basis of logical necessity because the denial of an analytic judgment involves a contradiction.

Feng asserted that his metaphysical system does not increase our positive knowledge of the realm of actuality, nor can it provide us with scientific or empirical knowledge of what things really are. This is because metaphysics, according to Feng, is a special learning that enables people to lift themselves above the realm of actuality to see the perfect world of *li* and thus enter spiritually the highest sphere of living. The subject of philosophy, Feng insisted, is to understand the totality of the universe, the realm of universals, and the spiritual and moral sphere of living.

Accordingly, Feng developed his moral philosophy and formulated a set of new doctrines: (1) the distinction between the nonmoral, immoral, moral, and transcendental realms of human life; (2) moral life as a rational choice of self-enlightenment; (3) the four spheres of moral consciousness; (4) human nature as both good and morally necessary; and (5) the path of cultivation to moral perfection.

In *Xin shilun*, Feng developed a theory of the three different realms of human life:

1. Activities that accord with the moral principles necessary to all societies. These activities are always moral in any society.

2. Activities that accord with the moral principles necessary to a given society. These activities are moral merely in a certain type of society.
3. Activities that neither accord with nor are in opposition to types 1 and 2. These activities are neutral, standing outside the demands of morality, and are thus nonmoral.

Feng made use of neo-Confucian moral values but reconstructed them on a radically different basis. Like the neo-Confucians, Feng insists that the basic Confucian values—benevolence, righteousness, ritual propriety, wisdom, and trustworthiness—remain unchanged in all societies at all times. However, he based his justification of the eternal moral values on a logical distinction between moral principles necessary to all types of societies and moral principles necessary only to a given type of society. The unchangeable nature of these moral values arises from the eternal *li* of all types of societies. Unlike the neo-Confucians, Feng regarded some fundamental moral virtues of the Confucian tradition, e.g., filial piety and loyalty, as moral principles necessary only to a feudal society that had a family-centered mode of production. He charged that the neo-Confucians failed to see the distinction between these types of moral principles and thus mistakenly understood the moral principles of a given society as being indispensable to all societies.

On the basis of his distinction between moral and nonmoral human activities, Feng developed (1) methods that apply to activities that ought to accord with moral principles, (2) methods that apply to activities independent of moral principles, and (3) methods necessary to both realms of activity. Among the first type of methods there are two subdivisions: methods that lead one to be a moral person and methods that lead one to be a morally perfect sage.

To respect *lixing*, Feng proposed, is the principal method or way of being human. It is applicable to both divisions of human activity. By the term *lixing*, Feng meant the capacity for moral reason and the ability to make rational judgments. Feng argued that reason should be respectfully followed if one is to lead a life that is both morally good and nonmorally healthy. The fact that everyone possesses *lixing* makes everyone capable of being moral. The method whereby a person respects or follows *lixing* makes the person actually moral.

In Feng's philosophy of morals, the four spheres of living are the four stages of the development of the "self." In the first stage, the natural sphere of living, humans are not conscious of their self; they blindly follow the natural instincts that drive them to seek pleasure and avoid pain. In the second stage, the utilitarian sphere of living, humans are conscious of their self and selfishly pursue their own interests. Only in the third stage, the moral sphere of living, do humans discover their "real self" by coming to understand their own nature and then consciously following its demands. By understanding the relation of the real self to the wholeness of the universe, one enters the highest stage of spiritual development—the "transcendent sphere of living" or the "sphere of heaven and earth" in which one finally fulfills the perfect goodness of one's own nature. In this sphere, actions are neither moral nor nonmoral but "transcendent"—a term that refers to, on the one hand, the highest value, and on the other, the absolute goodness that transcends the distinction between moral and immoral (which is applied in the moral and utilitarian spheres of living). Feng also calls the transcendent sphere the "sphere of philosophy," for it cannot be achieved unless one acquires an understanding of the totality of the universe through philosophy and reason.

For Feng, as for the neo-Confucians, sagehood is the highest spiritual perfection that human beings can achieve. The sage in the transcendent sphere of living in Feng's philosophy of morals, however, is radically different from the sages depicted by the neo-Confucians. The neo-Confucian image of the sage is marked by three main characteristics: (1) the sage identifies himself with the wholeness of the universe, and he acts, speaks, and thinks on behalf of Heaven (*tian*); (2) the sage has penetrating knowledge of everything; and (3) the sage's action is not only morally perfect and spiritually enlightened but, at the same time, effortless. The neo-Confucian concept of the sage, Feng charged, involves the belief that the sage's enlightenment gives him a thorough knowledge of the *li* and the *shi* (human affairs). It follows that, in the neo-Confucian tradition, the sage is thought to understand heaven and, at the same time, to know everything and possess all kinds of skills. This misconception arises from the fact that the neo-Confucians perceive the enlightenment of the sage as an achievement of both the highest human wisdom and an all-embracing knowledge of the actual world. As for knowledge of the actual world, Feng contended that the sage might know even less about daily affairs than common people do. The sage is not different from any other person except in having an enlightened understanding of the realm of reality.

Feng is credited with making original contributions to the study of the history of Chinese philosophy. He revealed the differences between the school of "identifying similarity with difference" (*he tongyi*) and the school of "separating hardness from whiteness" (*li jianbai*) among ancient Chinese "dialecticians" (*mingjia*). The basic distinction between the schools is that the former concerns itself more with the relativity of difference among various things, while the latter places more stress on the absolute existence of universality independent of particular things. In addition, Feng's discovery of the essential difference between the Cheng brothers led him to point out that Cheng Yi is the forerunner of *lixue* (the school of *li*) and Cheng Hao of *xinxue* (the school of mind-heart)—the two major schools in neo-Confucianism.

In contemporary China, Feng is a controversial figure. Some believe Feng's philosophy to be a new development of the rationalist school in neo-Confucianism because it continues the Confucian pursuit of the union of man and the universe and at the same time modernizes Confucian philosophy with western logic and rational analysis. According to this view, Feng's philosophy represents a part of the contemporary Confucian revival. In the opinion of others, Feng, in both his *History* and his own philosophical system, produced a distorted interpretation of both neo-Confucianism and the entire Chinese philosophical tradition in terms of certain western philosophical movements, particularly Platonism and neorealism.

See also *Li*: Principle, Pattern, Reason; Philosophy: Recent Trends in China since Mao.

Bibliography

Briere, Octave. *Fifty Years of Chinese Philosophy: 1898–1950*, trans. Lawrence C. Thompson. London: Allen and Unwin, 1956.

Cai, Yuanpei. "Wushi nian lai zhongguo zhi zhexue," 1923 (Fifty Years of Philosophy in China). In *Xiandai zhongguo zhexue* (Contemporary Chinese Philosophy). Shanghai: Shangwu yinshu guan, 1940, pp. 27–58.

Chan, Wing-tsit. "Fung Yu-lan." In *Encyclopaedia Britannica*, Vol. 9. Chicago: Encyclopaedia Britannica, 1968, p. 1030.

———. "Fung Yu-lan: A Short History of Chinese Philosophy." *Philosophy East and West*, 1(1), 1951, pp. 74–76.

de Bary, William Theodore, ed. *Proceedings of the Heyman Center for the Humanities*. New York: Columbia University Press, 1982.

Feng, Yu-lan. *A Comparative Study of Ideals of Life*. Shanghai: Commercial Press, 1924.

———. *Sansong tong quanji* (The Complete Works of Feng Yu-lan), Vol. 1. Chengzhou: Henan renmin chupan she, 1985, p. 149.

———. *Sansong tong zixu* (Memoir). Peking: Sanlian chupan she, 1984, p.1.

———. *A Short History of Chinese Philosophy*, ed. Derk Bodde. New York: Free Press, 1948.

———. *Xin li xue* (A New Philosophy of *Li*). Shanghai: Shangwu yinshu guan, 1939.

———. *Xin shi xun* (A New Treatise on the Way of Life). Kunming: Kaiming shudian, 1940.

———. *Xin yuan dao* (A New Treatise on the Way). Chongqing: Shangwu yinshu guan, 1945.

———. *Xin yuan ren* (A New Treatise on the Nature of Man). Chongqing: Shangwu yinshu guan, 1943.

———. *Xin zhi yan* (A Treatise on the New Methodology of Epistemology). Shanghai: Shangwu yinshu guan, 1946.

———. *Zhongguo zhexue shi* (A History of Chinese Philosophy). Shanghai: Shengguang shuju, 1934.

———. *Zhongguo zhexue shi xinbian* (The New Version of the History of Chinese Philosophy). Peking: Renmin chubanshe, 1962

Fu, Weixun. "Feng Youlan de kanke xinli lucheng" (Feng-Yu-lan's Rocky Intellectual Journey). *Dangdai* (Contemporary), No. 13, 1 May 1987, pp. 113–117.

He, Lin. *Dangdai zhongguo zhexue* (Contemporary Chinese Philosophy). Shanghai: Shengli shuju, 1947.

Masson, Michel C. *Philosophy and Tradition: The Interpretation of China's Philosophic Past—Fung Yu-lan (1939–1949)*. Paris: Ricci Institute, 1985.

Feng Youlan (Fung Yu-lan): Works on the History of Chinese Philosophy

Nicholas Standaert
Bie Giever

Feng Youlan (1895–1990) started his academic career with an article on the history of Chinese philosophy (1922). A few months before he died, he finished the seventh volume of his *New Version of the History of Chinese Philosophy*. In the seven decades between these two publications, Feng Youlan produced extensive writings on the history of Chinese philosophy.

The core of this writing is his *History of Chinese Philosophy*, which is at present still the best-known and most extensive introduction to Chinese philosophy in any western language. It has been made known through a translation by Derk Bodde of a two-volume work originally written in Chinese in the early 1930s. Immediately after its publication, Feng started to write complements and revisions; a seven-volume new version was published during the 1980s.

Feng Youlan, however, considered himself more a philosopher than a historian. One constant element in his various definitions of philosophy is that it is "reflective and systematic thinking." In this sense Feng treated the history of Chinese philosophy as a philosophical topic. For an understanding of Feng's thought on this subject, two kinds of writings should be considered: works on (1) the history and (2) the historiography of Chinese philosophy

Given the extent of Feng's writings and the duration of his academic career, a comparative method can be adopted to elucidate the evolution of his thought.

Works on the History of Chinese Philosophy

Feng Youlan's works on the history of Chinese philosophy can be divided into three stages.

Stage 1. The first version of *Zhongguo zhexue shi* (*History of Chinese Philosophy*), in two volumes, was published when Feng was a professor of philosophy at Qinghua University in Beijing (from 1927 on). Volume 1 (1931) describes Chinese thought from the beginnings to c. 100 B.C.E. Volume 2 (1934) covers the period from the second century B.C.E. to the twentieth century.

Stage 2. The next version, *Zhongguo zhexue shi xinbian* (*New Version of the History of Chinese Philosophy*), was published in 1962–1964, on the eve of the Cultural Revolution. Four volumes had been planned, but only two were actually published. Volume 1 covers the same period as the original first volume; Volume 2 covers the subsequent period until the Sui dynasty. According to Feng, this new version was written "with Marxism, Leninism, and the ideas of Mao Zedong as guide."

Several works published in the thirty years between the original version and the new version illustrate the evolution of Feng's thought during that period.

Zhongguo zhexue shi bu (*Supplement to the History of Chinese Philosophy*), published in 1936, only two years after the second volume of the *Zhongguo zhexue shi*, included reprints of a number of articles that had appeared mainly in the early 1930s.

Another work of this period is the English translation of *A History of Chinese Philosophy* by Derk Bodde (first volume, 1937, revised in 1952; second volume, 1953). Feng himself read and checked the translation and made major revisions in comparison with the Chinese version. Especially for the translation of the second volume, Feng also rewrote several chapters in Chinese.

More significant, however, is A *Short History of Chinese Philosophy*, originally written in English, while Feng was a visiting professor at the University of Pennsylvania in 1947, and translated into Chinese in 1985. This work was not a translation of a much shorter *Zhongguo zhexue xiaoshi* (*Short History of Chinese Philosophy*) that had already been published in 1934. The new *Short History* was written with the western reader specifically in mind. But it also embodied a number of conclusions and points of emphasis that Feng had arrived at after the publication of his original *History* in 1934. Moreover, the final chapter is devoted to Feng's own philosophical ideas, which were first expressed in a series of creative philosophical books that he wrote during the war years.

Stage 3. The second new version of the larger history, *Zhongguo zhexue shi xinbian* (*New Version of the History of Chinese Philosophy*), was published during 1980–1990. Most of the volumes were actually written during this ten-year span, although Feng had begun the rewriting of the first two volumes as early as the mid-1970s. The work therefore represents developments in his thought at this time. In the preface to the first volume, Feng is still explicitly doctrinaire and rather rigid, whereas in the prefaces to the later volumes he looks back on the earlier works and expresses himself with more emotion. This work divides the history of Chinese philosophy in seven periods corresponding to seven central philosophical issues: Pre-Qin philosophers (Vols. 1 and 2); the Han text school (Vol. 3); Wei-Jin neo-Daoism and Sui-Tang Buddhism (Vol. 4); Song-Ming neo-Confucianism (Vol. 5); political reform in the modern period (Vol. 6); contemporary revolutionary thought (Vol. 7). The last volume was initially not published in mainland China. It was edited as a separate volume by Zhonghua shuju in Hong Kong in 1992, under the title *Zhongguo xiandai zhexue shi*, and later included in the seven-volume reprint by Landeng wenhua in Taipei in 1993. A mainland edition did not appear until 2000.

Significant characteristics of the new version. A comparison of the table of contents of Volume 2 with corresponding chapters in the earlier versions shows significant differences with regard to (1) names of philosophers, (2) names of schools, and (3) the order of the chapters. These differences illustrate characteristics of the *New Version.*

Names of the philosophers. The philosophers are no longer called "masters" (Mengzi, Zhuangzi, Xunzi) but instead are referred to by their proper names (Meng

Ke, Zhuang Zhou, Xun Kuang). This change may seem minor, but the "rectification of names" is nonetheless important.

In the first place, the change reflects a "secularization" that had taken place since the Cultural Revolution and the anti-Confucius campaign. The first new version, published just before the Cultural Revolution, still referred to each philosopher as "master." At that time, despite his critical attitude, Feng held the ancient philosophers in respect. He also offered praise for the "new philosophers." For example, following the title page of the first new version, there was a poem by Feng (dated June 1962) comparing Mao Zedong with Confucius and comparing himself with Confucius's favorite pupil Yan Hui, who had said that the master was so lofty that the more Yan looked up to him, the higher the master seemed to be (*Analects*, 9.10).

The historical circumstances seem insufficient to explain the change in the latest version. For instance, another well-known collection on the history of Chinese philosophy, *Zhongguo zhexue fazhan shi* (*The History of the Development of Chinese Philosophy*), edited by Ren Jiyu beginning in 1983, continued to call the philosophers "masters." An additional explanation is that Feng's *New Version* distinguishes more clearly between a philosopher as a historical figure and a work that bears his name but was not necessarily completely written or composed by him. In Volume 2, for example, Feng distinguishes clearly between Zhuang Zhou and the *Zhuangzi*. In any case, the change reflected historical-critical studies of Chinese texts in the past forty years.

Names of the schools. In the earliest version, Feng Youlan used what might be called static descriptions: school of Mencius (*Mengxue*), school of Lao (*Laoxue*), Mohists (*Mojia*), legalists (*fajia*). In the latest new version, he fully integrated dynamic descriptions that had already appeared in the first new version: "the development of Confucian thought in the direction of idealism" (Meng Ke); "the further development of Daoist philosophy in the direction of idealism" (Zhuang Zhou); "the development of the later Mohist in the direction of materialism" (the Mohist dialecticians).

This suggests a change from a static to a dynamic concept of the history of philosophy and is characteristic of the second new version. We can analyze this change as follows. In the *History of Chinese Philosophy*, even if there was a concept of the progress of history, Feng Youlan wanted primarily to discover relations between a particular historical period and the thought produced in that period. History was conceived as a succession of times and periods. In the new version, Feng has a new definition of the history of philosophy: "History of philosophy is the history of the development of philosophy." The important word here is "development" (*fazhan*).

Although most of these elements were present in the 1930s, Feng Youlan had undoubtedly developed his new concept of the history of philosophy more fully as a result of his extensive readings in Marxism in the 1950s–1960s. In one article in the *Supplement to the History of Chinese Philosophy*, Feng had already revealed his "materialistic" interpretation of history. By "materialism" Feng meant at that time "objective laws of social evolution." In his view, historical evolution happens according to "nonspiritual forces" and the role of the human being is limited. Different systems appear in the course of history, each one having its own logic. History does not make mistakes, and its development is dialectical, as far as it is both circular and progressive, and so on.

In Feng's eyes, the development of thought follows its own rule: when a certain idea arises, it will necessarily be pushed forward to its logical conclusion. In this respect, the thought of later philosophers of any school is broader and more profound than that of their predecessors. That is the reason why, in the second new version, Feng Youlan divides systems (*tixi*) of thought into an earlier and a later period.

Several other concepts are associated with the sense of a development from an earlier to a later period: "further progress" (*jinyibu*), "contribution" (*gongxian*), "for the first time" (*diyici*) and "basis" (*jichu*). These concepts suggest a linear view: the history starts with an idea that appears "for the first time" and then becomes a "basis" constituting a major "contribution" to philosophy. Through "further progress," this idea pushes forward to its logical conclusion. But in his theoretical exposition of this view of history, Feng also explains that the history of human thought is very complex and that it progresses with "knots" (*xiansuo*) and "links" (*huanjie*). Finally, we should note the term "stages" (*jieduan*): Feng uses this less frequently, and it seems to be restricted mainly to changes within a particular system of thought.

Order of the chapters. There are different reasons for changes in the order of chapters. Sometimes, such changes result from rearrangement according to chronological order; in other instances they result because new historical or philosophical significance is given to a certain philosopher or school. For example, the *Laozi*, previously ascribed to one philosopher, was now considered to be a compilation over a longer period.

The *Laozi* is not the only "collected writing" (*zongji*). In the first *History of Chinese Philosophy*, the Mohist canon (*Mojing*) was already identified as writings used by later Mohists in discussions with other philosophers. The new version considers the *Zhuangzi, Han Feizi, Xunzi, Guanzi*, and *Yanzi chunqiu* to be collected writings.

Feng's concept of collected writings represents considerable progress in comparison with the earlier versions. Still, such a concept supposes very precise hermeneutic criteria for identifying earlier and later parts of specific writings. Moreover, once these sections are identified, a historical analysis is required to establish the link between them and the times during which they were written or compiled. Feng Youlan was not really successful in this regard.

Works on Historiography

Besides writing and rewriting the *History of Chinese Philosophy*, Feng Youlan also thought and wrote about this process of writing and rewriting itself. He developed his thoughts on this process mostly in various articles and in his introductions and complements to his historical works.

Addressing the question "How to write a history of Chinese philosophy?" Feng Youlan focused on five themes: (1) What is philosophy? (2) What is Chinese philosophy? (3) What is history? (4) What is the writing of history (of philosophy)? (5) Specific problems in the history of Chinese philosophy.

1. What is philosophy? In his definitions of philosophy Feng investigates what the object, method, limits, characteristics, and goals of philosophy are and how philosophy relates to science, religion, common sense, and art. Two main points in his definition are the object and characteristics of philosophy.

During the 1930s and 1940s Feng identified human life as the object of philosophical thinking. He subdivided this into thought on the universe (*yuzhou*), on human life (*rensheng*), and on knowledge (*zhishi*). During the 1950s he stated that the main object of philosophical thinking was the "fundamental opposition in all things," with idealism and materialism as the two approaches to it. During the 1980s he defined philosophy as reflective thinking "on the human mind," i.e., on action (theoretical thinking) and products (philosophy, science, culture). He subdivided this into thought on nature (*ziran*), society (*shehui*), and individual human things (*geren de renshi*).

The main characteristic of philosophy is its consistency. Feng Youlan identifies "formal" and "substantial" consistency. He says that formal consistency—which Chinese philosophy often lacks—is not a necessary condition of philosophy, but substantial consistency is.

2. What is Chinese philosophy? In the 1930s Feng confirmed the different inclination or focus of Chinese philosophy relative to western philosophy and explained it as a difference in their "starting points"—their different views of the "happiness" that can be pursued through philosophy. In the 1980s he insisted that the content of philosophical thinking was the same in China as in other cultures but pointed out differences of expression, attributable partly to specific characteristics of the Chinese languages.

3. What is history? The main direction of historical development is "progress." This central idea remains unchanged in Feng's works, although in his later writings he stressed that progress is not linear but complex and diverse.

Feng affirms the "objective" existence of the historical past independent of human knowledge and also, after the 1950s, the logical structure inherent in historical development. However, in the 1980s he emphasized that history is a complex "living thing," which cannot be captured in a simplified structure.

4. What is the writing of history, or of philosophy? The goal of written history is correspondence with "original history" (*benlai de lishi*). Except in the 1950s–1960s, Feng Youlan noted the impossibility of such a complete correspondence. He concluded that a historian could only do his utmost and that there was no end to the rewriting of history.

In the 1930s Feng defined the task of a historian of Chinese philosophy as finding substantial consistency in works without formal consistency. During the 1960s he emphasized that the vision of a historian was always biased and therefore that "objective historiography" was impossible. In the 1980s he defined the two necessary qualities of a historian of philosophy as the capability to "understand" (*liaojie*) and "experience" (*tihui*) former philosophies. This corresponds to his later emphasis on the "living aspect," rather than the "rational aspect," of philosophy.

5. Specific problems in the history of Chinese philosophy. As Feng wrote his *History of Chinese Philosophy* and read his critics' comments, he was confronted with certain specific problems, such as the origin of the different schools, the dating of historical works, the evaluation of the position of philosophers and the general meaning of a philosophy, the division of historical periods, the continuation of the philosophical heritage, the use of original sources, and the relevance of a philosopher's social background.

Feng Youlan's works on history of philosophy are not so much a product of his need to elaborate on the problems of historiography as an explanation offered to his critics. The articles he wrote during the 1950s and 1960s, especially, are a mixture of self-defense and self-criticism. All these writings are a result more of an external debate with others than of his own meditation about his work.

See also Feng Youlan; Philosophy in China: Historiography.

Bibliography

Cua, Antonio S. "Emergence of the History of Chinese Philosophy." *International Philosophical Quarterly*, 40(4), December 2000, pp. 441–464.

Feng, Youlan. *A History of Chinese Philosophy*, trans. Derk Bodde. Princeton, N.J.: Princeton University Press, 1953.

———. "More on Some Problems Relating to Research in History of Chinese Philosophy." *Selections from Mainland China Magazines*, 541, 1966.

———. *A Short History of Chinese Philosophy*. New York: Macmillan, 1948.

———. "Why China Has No Science: An Interpretation of the History and Consequences of Chinese Philosophy." *International Journal of Ethics*, 32, 1922, p. 3.

———. "Zhongguo xiandai zhexue shi yanjiu bixu he xiandai lishi xiang lianxi" (Research in the History of Modern Chinese Philosophy Should Stay in Contact with Modern History). In *Zhongguo xiandai zhexue yu wenhua sichao*, ed. Ji Yongfu, Beijing: Qiushi, 1989.

———. *Zhongguo zhexue shi* (The History of Chinese Philosophy), 2 vols. Shanghai: Commercial Press, 1934.

———. *Zhongguo zhexue shi bu* (Supplement to *The History of Chinese Philosophy*). Shanghai: Commercial Press, 1936.

———. *Zhongguo zhexue shi lunwen erji* (A Second Collection of Articles on the History of Chinese Philosophy). Shanghai: People's Press, 1962.

———. *Zhongguo zhexue shi lunwenji* (A Collection of Articles on the History of Chinese Philosophy). Shanghai: People's Press, 1958.

———. *Zhongguo zhexue xiaoshi* (Short History of Chinese Philosophy). Shanghai: Commercial Press, 1933.

———. *Zhongguo zhexue shi xinbian* (New Version of the *History of Chinese Philosophy*), 2 vols. Beijing: People's Press, 1962–1964.

———. *Zhongguo zhexue shi xinbian* (New Version of the *History of Chinese Philosophy*), 6 vols. Beijing: People's Press, 1982–1989.

———. *Zhongguo zhexue shi xinbian* (New Version of the *History of Chinese Philosophy*), 7 vols., Taipei: Landeng wenhua, 1991.

中國哲學

G

Gewu (*Ke-wu*) and *Zhizhi* (*Chih-chih*): Investigation of Things and Extension of Knowledge

Kwong-loi SHUN

Gewu (or *ke-wu*, investigation of things) and *zhizhi* (or *chih-chih*, extension of knowledge) are two of the four steps in self-cultivation described in the *Daxue* (*Great Learning*): *gewu, zhizhi*, *chengyi*, and *zhengxin*. *Chengyi* refers to making one's thoughts and inclinations fully directed toward ethics; *zhengxin* refers to the process of making correct (the activities of) the heart or mind.

Although, as above, *gewu* and *zhizhi* are often translated as "investigation of things" and "extension of knowledge," their interpretation has been a matter of controversy among Confucian thinkers. *Ge* can mean "correct" or "arrive at," *wu* means "things"; *zhi* can mean "extend" in the sense of expanding (as in "extend one's territories") or letting something reach out (as in "extend one's arm"); and the second *zhi* means "knowing" or "understanding." This variety of meanings makes possible different interpretations of *gewu* and *zhizhi*. Those by Zhu Xi (1130–1200) and Wang Yangming (1472–1529) are particularly important because of the influence of these two thinkers. Their disagreement involves the nature of the text itself: Wang opposed Zhu's reorganization and emendation of the text as well as Zhu's addition of an explanation of *gewu* and *zhizhi*.

The *Daxue* was originally a chapter of the *Liji* (*Record of Rites*), which was probably compiled in the early Han and on which Zheng Xuan (127–200) wrote a well-known commentary. It gained importance for Confucian thinkers before the Song dynasty (960–1279). Li Ao (eighth to ninth century), for example, drew on ideas in the *Daxue* in developing his thinking. In his "Essay on Restoring Nature" (*Fuxingshu*), he proposed interpreting *gewu* and *zhizhi* to mean that when things (*wu*) arrive at (*ge*) the heart—that is, come into contact with the heart—the heart's understanding (*zhi*) will reach out to (*zhi*) such things. The *Daxue* was probably circulated as an independent text in the early Song, and its significance was particularly highlighted by the brothers Cheng Hao (1032–1085) and Cheng Yi (1033–1107), who proposed a reorganization of parts of the text and also certain emendations. Zhu Xi, whose thinking was often influenced by Cheng Yi, reordered parts of the *Daxue* and divided it into a main text and ten chapters of commentaries, as well as emending one character and deleting four. More significantly, noticing that there was no explanation of *gewu* and *zhizhi*, he added such an explanation to one of the chapters of commentary, drawing on ideas of Cheng Yi. Later, some people objected to Zhu Xi's alteration of the text, and Wang Yangming advocated going back to the earlier version found in Zheng Xuan's commentary. Wang proposed an interpretation of *gewu* and *zhizhi* that differs radically from Zhu's, and this difference reflects fundamental differences in their thinking.

A key concept in Zhu Xi's thinking is *li* (pattern, principle), which is the pattern or order underlying everything and explaining why things operate as they do, as well as that to which the operation of things should conform. For example, it is *li* that trees flourish in the spring and fade in the autumn, that fire is hot and water cold, or that a boat travels on water and not on land. In the human realm, *li* includes all the norms of human conduct; for example, it is *li* that parents are compassionate to children and children filial to parents, or that human beings do not cut down trees unnecessarily. According to Zhu Xi, everything is composed of *li*, which is abstract, as well as *qi* (material force), which is concrete. *Qi* is the material of which things are composed; it is fluid and always moving, and it can have different degrees of density and purity. *Li* in human beings comprises the norms of human conduct. In its original state, the heart has perfect insight into or knowledge of *li*, an insight that Zhu often describes with metaphors related to perception—the mind is said to "see" or to "illuminate" *li*. Such insight guides one's responses to situations, and Zhu compares the way knowledge guides action to the way the eyes guide the legs in walking. In the original and ideal state, then, one has perfect insight into *li* and one's responses to situations are fully ethical. However, because the endowment of *qi* can be impure, the insight into *li* can be obscured, and this accounts for people's failure to be fully ethical. Zhu referred to the obscuring factors that stem from impure *qi* as selfish desires and sometimes as human desires; certain basic desires such as the desire for food are not problematic, but other desires—such as the desire for power—are problematic and hence are selfish.

For Zhu, the task of self-cultivation is to restore the heart's original insight, and *gewu* and *zhizhi* are ways of restoring it. Following Cheng Yi, he interpreted *ge* as meaning "arrive at" and *wu* as referring to things and affairs or, rather, the *li* that pertains to things and affairs. Therefore, *gewu* is a matter of arriving at the *li* in things and affairs, and this involves examining daily affairs such as the way parents and children interact, as well as studying classics and historical records. *Zhizhi* is a matter of expanding (*zhi*) one's knowledge (*zhi*) of *li*, until one penetrates into the pattern that underlies everything, thereby restoring one's original insight. *Gewu* and *zhizhi* are different aspects of the same process, with *gewu* emphasizing one's arrival at the *li* in affairs and *zhizhi* emphasizing an expansion of the mind's knowledge of *li*.

The process of *gewu* and *zhizhi* exhibits two characteristics. First, with regard to a particular affair, such as the relationship between parent and child, it is not enough to know about the *li* pertaining to that affair, in this case filial piety. One has to act on it in order to realize, personally, that this is genuinely *li*. By analogy, only when one attempts to push a boat on land does one personally realize that it is indeed *li* for boats to travel not on land but on water. By acting, one attains a clearer, firmer knowledge of *li*, until one is entirely at ease with acting in this way and indeed cannot act otherwise: one acts without the slightest hesitation, takes joy in so acting, and regards going against *li* like plunging a hand into boiling water. Only then does one have real knowledge of the *li* pertaining to an affair.

Second, in addition to acting on the *li* that one discerns in particular affairs, it is also important to examine different things and affairs in order to unravel their *li*. The *li* in each individual thing or affair is part of a larger pattern that runs through everything, and by repeatedly examining different things and affairs, one uncovers this underlying pattern. The process is not induction or empirical generalization but more like penetration or insight into what lies behind observable things and affairs—an insight that is made possible by extensive examination of affairs and by constant practice. For this reason, Zhu advocated extensive study of classics and historical records, which for him included writing commentaries on such texts.

The way Wang Yangming's interpretation of *gewu* and *zhizhi* differs from Zhu Xi's reflects a different understanding of what the heart is like in its original state. According to Wang, in its original state the heart has a disposition to respond to particular situations in appropriate ways, but without guidance from an insight into *li*. The responses may be accompanied by thoughts about what is proper, but such thoughts do not explain a person's responses or actions. An analogy is the taste for food: while one's taste may move one to respond favorably to certain kinds of food, and while such responses may be accompanied by the thought that such food is delicious, the thought is part of the response and does not guide it. There is a "unity of knowledge and action" (*zhixing heyi*)—a well-known slogan of Wang's—in that proper conduct and thoughts about what is proper are, in the ideal state, inseparable parts of one's response to a situation but do not guide it. This contrasts with Zhu Xi's view that knowledge guides action as the eyes guide the legs. Wang referred to the heart's disposition to respond appropriately as "innate knowledge" (*liangzhi*), a term he borrowed from Mencius's thought. He was opposed to Zhu's description of the relation between the heart and *li* as one of insight or perception guiding responses. Instead, *li* resides in the responses of the heart, just as what constitutes delicious food resides in the way the human taste for food is structured. Wang put this by saying that "heart is *li*" (*xinzhili*), and he criticized Zhu for separating the heart and *li* by making *li* the object of the heart's insight.

Like Zhu Xi, Wang believed that this state of the heart can be obscured by selfish desires, and that the task of self-cultivation is to restore the heart's original state. But he put less emphasis on learning directed at gaining knowledge of *li*. Instead, he favored attending directly to the heart, in self-cultivation: one should constantly watch out for and get rid of selfish desires when they arise, in the way that a cat watches out for and catches mice when they emerge from their hole. Thus, in conversing with his pupils, he often warned them to be aware of and suppress tendencies such as showing off, criticizing others, feeling happy when praised, and feeling dejected when criticized.

For Wang Yangming, *gewu* and *zhizhi* are different aspects of this process of suppressing selfish desires. *Ge* means "to correct," and *wu* refers to the things and affairs to which the heart's activities are directed; *gewu* is the process of correcting the activities of the heart by overcoming selfish desires. *Zhizhi*, on the other hand, is the extension of knowledge in the sense of letting one's innate knowledge (*zhi*) reach out (*zhi*). *Gewu* and *zhizhi* are intimately related, since one suppresses selfish desires by letting innate knowledge reach out to the activities of the heart, and by suppressing selfish desires one also enables innate knowledge to reach out to one's affairs. Consider, for example, someone who is reluctant to share his enjoyment of certain goods with others. His innate knowledge enables him to recognize this inclination as a selfish desire and to suppress it; having suppressed it, he will share his enjoyment with others, and this sharing is itself a reaching out of his innate knowledge.

Because Wang Yangming regarded *li* as residing in the heart—not learned from the outside—he opposed the extensive studies that Zhu Xi advocated. Wang regarded extensive commentaries on and analysis of classics as a misdirection of attention, a kind of fragmentary study that directs the heart away from what is really important in self-cultivation. However, their disagreement is not so much total opposition as a difference in emphasis, and both considered other aspects of self-cultivation. Zhu also talked about directly suppressing selfish desires when they arise, and he advocated nourishing the self through *jing* (seriousness, reverence), which involves attentiveness, concentration, being in possession of oneself, and freeing oneself from distractions. *Jing* and *gewu* are complementary in that nourishing the self with *jing* makes one better situated to investigate the *li* in affairs, and gaining a clearer perception of *li* through *gewu* makes the heart better able to concentrate. Wang also advocated *jing*, understood as a kind of quiet sitting that involves concentrating the heart and avoiding distractions. While *gewu* is what one does after selfish desires have arisen, *jing* is what one does before selfish desires arise—both to prevent them from arising and to prepare oneself for catching and suppressing them if they do appear. And, although he opposed the extensive study and analysis of classics, he did allow room for reading basic classics so as to stimulate the heart, and he acknowledged the need to learn such things as music, rites, and the institutions of government.

See also *Li*: Principle, Pattern, Reason; Reason and Principle; Wang Yangming; *Zhixing Heyi*; Zhu Xi.

Bibliography

Daxue (Great Learning). See James Legge, trans. *Confucius: Confucian Analects, the Great Learning, and the Doctrine of the Mean*, 2nd ed. Oxford: Clarendon, 1893.

Li, Ao. *Li wengong ji*. (*Siku chuanshu* Series.)

Wang, Yangming. *Quanxilu*. In *Yangming Chuanshu*. (*Sibu beiyao* Series.). See also Wing-tsit Chan, trans., *Instructions for Practical Living and Other Neo-Confucian Writings by Wang Yang-ming*. New York: Columbia University Press, 1963.

Zhu, Xi. *Daxue Zhangju* (Commentary on the *Daxue*).

———. *Zhuzi Yulei*. Beijing: Zhonghua shuju, 1986. (See also Wing-tsit Chan, trans. and comp. *A Source Book in Chinese Philosophy*. Princeton, N.J.: Princeton University Press, 1963, ch. 34.)

Gongsun Long (Kung-sun Lung)

Whalen Lai

Gongsun Long (b. 380 B.C.E.) is considered a member of the school of names. A logician or sophist, he is best-known for a theoretical essay called "Pointing and Thing" and for his thesis "white horse is not horse." Xunzi (fl. 298–238) accused him of abusing names to the extent of creating havoc: since a horse with the color white is very much a horse, Gongsun was twisting words and flying in the face of what is obvious when he said that it is not. A number of modern scholars, however, have come to Gongsun Long's defense.

Feng Youlan (Fung Yu-lan) compared Gongsun to a European realist who would consider "white" and "horse" two real universals. As the embodiment of two universals, "white horse" is necessarily more than just "horse." But there is no evidence that Chinese thinkers ever subscribed to a realist theory of universals. Furthermore, Gongsun Long himself said that any horse by itself, with no color, was unreal.

A. C. Graham initially held that Gongsun was confusing classification (horse is of the horse-shaped kind) with identification (horse is the animal horse). Later, Graham took a somewhat different approach, comparing "white horse is not horse" with synecdoche, as in the English statement "sword is not blade." In synecdoche, a figure of speech, blade may stand for sword as whole, but this is poetic license—in reality, blade denotes only the cutting edge and is not equal to sword, which is hilt plus blade. Analogously, "white horse is not horse" is true, because the whole, "white plus horse," is more than the part, which is just "horse." Graham's analysis avoids the pitfalls of Feng Youlan's criticism, though it is not clear that the Chinese ever used "horse" as a synecdoche.

Graham said he took over this argument, which is based on the logic of part and whole, from Chad Hansen. Hansen connected the problem of "white horse not horse" to a semiotic quirk in the Chinese language. This language does not require the noun *ma* for "horse" or "horses" to be preceded by an article or a numeral—unlike, say, English, in which we expect "horse" or "horses" to be preceded by "a," "the," "one," "two," or the like. Hansen characterizes *ma* as a "mass noun," similar to something like "sand" in English, whereas the English word "horse" is a "count noun." Hansen then maintains that the case for "white horse not horse" is like the Mohist argument for "ox-horse not horse." "Ox-horse" is the Chinese binominal *niuma* for cattle; it denotes a mixed herd. Because ox and horse remain separate and distinct, Hansen calls the compound ox-horse a "mass sum," distinguishing it from a compound like hard-white, which is a "mass product." Hard-white describes a blending of two elements in a "vessel object"; the elements are inseparably one, as when every inch of a piece of marble is simultaneously hard and white. But ox-horse is a sum of (an unspecified count of) ox and horse. Similarly, Hansen argues, "white horse" is a sum of "horse mass" and "white stuff." In both cases, the mass sum is more than a part thereof, so "white horse" is more than just "horse." An example of an English mass noun is "sand," and we can argue that "white sand is not sand." Sand is the mass or stuff: sand spread on a beach can be variously colored, and a patch of white sand is not equal to the whole spread of sandy stuff.

This application of part-whole logic and the concept of mass nouns may be problematic, though. It runs up against a basic dictum in Gongsun Long's "Pointing and Thing": that all things can be pointed out except "thing" itself. Gongsun reasoned as follows. To point out a thing *X*, we must have at least one non-*X* to exclude. If there is no non-*X*, we cannot point to *X*. Since the word "thing" covers everything there is, it leaves nothing to exclude, and so there is no way to isolate it from its surroundings. This rule is based on the law of the excluded middle. If "a thing is either *X* or non-*X*," it follows that *X* can be pinpointed when every non-*X* has been excluded. But if, as all the evidence suggests, Gongsun Long was observing this "either-or" rule, he cannot possibly have subscribed to "both-and" logic—which is essentially what is involved in a part-whole argument. And if that is true, then Gongsun Long would not have condoned a synecdoche either, because when, say, blade is allowed to denote both the cutting edge and the whole sword, that amounts to having a single word "blade" mean both *X* and not-*X*.

The rule of the excluded middle, though stated negatively, informs Gongsun Long's thesis "white horse not horse." The Buddhist logician Dignaga avoided ever saying *X* is *X*, because that would seduce the speaker—be he Greek or Hindu—into assuming that there was an essence or *atman* to *X*. By the same token, Gongsun Long would concede that *X* is best defined not positively as *X* but negatively as what *X* is not. In other words, *X* is not non-X. As a negative remainder, *X* is whatever is left over when each non-*X* is systematically excluded. Therefore, "white horse," which excludes both non-white and non-horse, does not equal "horse," which excludes only non-horse. Pragmatically, or linguistically, this means that to locate white horse, we do not rely on an ontological (*atman*-like) reference; this is comparable to Frege's (real) sign pointing to (real) thing. Instead, we rely entirely on (*anatman*-like) sense, which is comparable to Ferge's sign networking with other signs to yield sense. We find *X* by purely logical means; thus first we exclude from among the barnyard animals all shapes other than the horse-shape, and second we exclude from the remainder all colors except white. Whatever is left over after both exclusions is white horse. This is why Gongsun Long says, "Excluding some colors is not the same as excluding no colors, therefore white horse is not horse." The remainder after a double exclusion is white horse; this is not the same as the remainder after a single exclusion, horse. Mathematically, he is right, since the number of items omitted by two exclusions is larger than the number omitted by one exclusion. "White horse not horse" is therefore sound; it is what Buddhist logic would recognize.

Gongsun Long was aware of the irony in this thesis, in which sense (classification) is made to yield reference (identification). It is a roundabout procedure, but the result is flawless. In "Pointing and Thing" he goes through four apparently circular steps:

1. *Name as reference points to thing*. The name "horse" seems to point to the animal.
2. *It does not*. Why? Because pointing understood as sense—sign networking with other signs to yield logic—would imply that "horse" is a category describing (classifying by shape) things of the horse-shaped kind.
3. *Pointing as sense does not point*. Why? Because to point to *X* (the horse shape), we actually point away from *X* to non-*X* (non-horse shapes). *X* is the negative remainder.
4. *But then it is not that pointing does not point*. It does. How so? Because precisely by pointing to and then excluding all the non-horse shapes (cow shape, etc.), we arrive at what is left over: the target, *X*.

Step 4 takes us back back to step 1. Sense yields reference. Classification coughs up identification.

In classical China, logical debates on name and reality were also ethical debates. Logic aside, Gongsun Long has a moral agenda. Coming after Yang Zhu and Mozi, he sided more with Yang and less with Mozi. He safeguards the sanctity of the self by showing how each of us (as *X*) is distinct and valuable by virtue of not being like any other (any non-*X*). He doubts the reality of the Mohist "whole"; we cannot point to the whole. Thus we find him preaching "nonaggression" (against any party), but not "universal love" (for all). The reason is that to love *X* and benefit *X*, one must not love and not benefit a non-*X*. Since loving all leaves none not to love, loving all amounts to benefiting none. In this, Gongsun Long was the reverse of Hui Shi, the other logician, who sided with the whole and extended Mohist love to its maximum, to loving all things generously.

See also Feng Youlan; Hui Shi; Names, School of.

Bibliography

Fung, Yu-lan (Feng Youlan). *A History of Chinese Philosophy*, 2 vols., trans. Derk Bodde. Princeton, N.J.: Princeton University Press, 1952–1953.

Graham, A. C. *Disputers of the Tao: Philosophical Argument in Ancient China*. La Salle, Ill.: Open Court, 1989.

———. "Three Studies on Gongsun Lung." In *Studies in Chinese Philosophy and Philosophical Literature*. Albany: State University of New York Press, 1990.

Hansen, Chad. *Language and Thought in Ancient China*. Ann Arbor: University of Michigan Press, 1983.

Lai, Whalen. "White Horse Not Horse: Making Sense of a Negative Logic." *Asian Philosophy*, 5(1), 1994, pp. 59–74.

Gu Yanwu (Ku Yen-wu)

Thomas Bartlett

From the time of China's modern intellectual revolution in the 1920s, Gu Yanwu (Tinglin, 1613–1682) has been best known to most educated Chinese through Liang Qichao's description of him. Liang presents Gu as the founding genius of the dominant intellectual trend since the mid-seventeenth century, commonly known as "evidential learning" (*kaozhengxue*). In this regard, Liang's view of Gu continues the tradition of commentators of the Qing period such as Jiang Fan (1761–1830). But Liang also reflects the spirit of his own age by imputing to Gu's distinctive mode of learning the essential character of modern scientific method, by which Liang means the use of induction to derive conclusions based on objective evidence. For this reason, Liang, who had previously favored preserving a reformed monarchy, speaks of the Qing period as a "renaissance" of Chinese thought following the presumably benighted Song and Ming eras, which were dominated by neo-Confucian metaphysical abstractions.

But a generation before "science" became a watchword of the May Fourth movement, Gu Yanwu's intellectual legacy had been judged very differently by the radical nationalist and revolutionary Zhang Binglin (Taiyan). Zhang saw in Gu a kindred spirit and praised Gu above all for his uncompromising rejection of the claim of the alien Qing dynasty to imperial legitimacy. This dimension of Gu's thought fundamentally informs his "statecraft learning" (*jingshixue*). A prominent aspect of Gu's *jingshixue* is moral revival through the humane Confucian values implicit in the doctrine of *fengjian*, or decentralized administration. Open discussion of Gu's view of statecraft was not officially condoned until signs of dynastic decline became evident in the 1830s, 150 years after Gu's death. Nevertheless, one may surely say that, even throughout the high tide of imperially sponsored evidential learning during the reigns of Qianlong and Jiaqing (1736–1820), the specter of Gu Yanwu's concerns about statecraft had haunted establishment scholars, such as Zhao Yi (1727–1814), who conspicuously refuted one of Gu's best-known conclusions regarding evidence for decentralized rule in Han times.

In recent years Gu Yanwu, Huang Zongxi, and Wang Fuzhi have often been cited as the three great thinkers of the late Ming–early Qing era. Gu's reputation as an early nationalist is a point of similarity to Wang, and Gu's criticism of despotic government in Ming times led him to make proposals for political decentralization that were, by his own testimony, largely in accord with the spirit of Huang Zongxi's famous *Mingyi daifanglu* (*Plan for a Prince*). But Gu's typical mode of expression on these politically sensitive subjects was less explicitly elaborated than Wang's or Huang's, a fact which may be a consequence of Gu's more embattled personal circumstances.

Gu was born into an old and distinguished Jiangnan clan; as a child he was named Gu Jiang. Prefigured by a family tradition of official service and intellectual realism, Gu's own thought assumed its distinctive character in direct response to a dynastic crisis during the Chongzhen period (1628–1644) of the late Ming and reached maturity during the first two decades of the long, decisive reign of Kangxi (1662–1722) in the early Qing. Gu himself summarized the elements of his lifelong commitment to substantial, practically directed learning by reference to two aphorisms in Confucius's *Analects*: "In your conduct let there be some things that you are ashamed to do. In your studies make use of the widest range of sources." Accordingly, by no means the least influential aspect of Gu's didactic legacy has been the ethical example of his personal loyalty to the Ming dynasty, a commitment so thoroughgoing that he threatened to commit suicide if he was forced to participate in a politically motivated project of the Qing court—the compilation of an official history of the previous dynasty.

Gu's radical attitude toward learning was profoundly at odds with a dominant intellectual trend since the early Ming period, which typically caused aspirants to the official *cursus honorum* to devote their youth, and in some cases even their early middle age, to mastering the rhetorical devices used to write the highly formalistic *bagu* ("eight-legged") essays required for the civil service examinations. In addition to his disgust at the constraining artificiality imposed on the literary mode cultivated by candidates for civil office, Gu also opposed, as a matter of principle, the arbitrary limitation of scholars' concerns to a narrow range of abstract moral issues restrictively defined by neo-Confucian orthodoxy. Gu's fundamental aversion to the intellectual fashions of his age is indicated by his numerous failed attempts at the provincial examination.

Gu was also keenly contemptuous of another contemporary philosophical trend. This was the fashion for academic lectures on neo-Confucian topics, a practice with Song antecedents that had taken on new vigor since the mid-sixteenth century. In the first phase of its revival in the mid-Ming, lecturing was promoted by scholars such as Wang Yangming, in reaction to the stultifying conformity required by the official curriculum. Later, as developed under epigones of the Wang school—which emphasized a subjectivistic interpretation of Zhu Xi's understanding of the classical doctrine of "investigation of things" (*gewu*)—such scholarly gatherings degenerated into facile conversations on metaphysical topics, in which partial, intuitively derived insights might suffice to justify highly iconoclastic conclusions. Gu Yanwu excoriated Wang Yangming for the socially and politically destabilizing effects that flowed from this school of unrestrained philosophy. Gu likened Wang Yangming's doctrine of *liangzhi* (innate knowledge of the good) to the socially irresponsible *qingtan* thought of Wang Yan (256–311), which flourished among escapist literati against a background of foreign invasions during an era of medieval disunity. Indeed, Gu's evaluation of neo-Confucian thought was generally negative. Gu explicitly rejected the influence of the Cheng brothers, holding that their teachings were little more than a disguised form of Chan (Zen) Buddhism, which emphasized spontaneous enlightenment over the study of classical sutras. Accordingly, Gu derided the influence of Chan Buddhism on the recent fashion for compiling "recorded sayings" of neo-Confucian masters; Zhu Xi's compilation was a prominent example. Gu respected Zhu Xi only to the extent that Zhu's scholarship did not depart from the example of Confucius, especially as regards the master's emphasis on broadly based study. As to Zhu's famous and influential "philosophy of rational principle" (*lixue*), Gu wrote:

> From ancient until modern times, how could there be a separate entity called the "philosophy of rational principle"? Classical learning is itself a study of rational principle. Ever since men started to discuss the philosophy of rational principle apart from classical learning, heterodoxy has arisen.

Gu's opposition to neo-Confucian thought made him liable to partisan accusations of favoring utilitarian (*gongli*, i.e., implicitly "amoral") solutions to institutional issues. Indeed, conspicuous in Gu's writings are favorable references to Southern Song opponents of Zhu Xi, so-called utilitarians like Cheng Liang and Ye Shi. Scholars who favored Gu's approach to scholarship customarily called it *shixue* or *puxue* ("substantial learning"); these terms became synonyms for the new style of seventeenth-century thought that spread from China to Korea and Japan.

The rise of neo-Confucian philosophy has been associated with heightened political autocracy since Song times. This issue is implicit in Gu's essay *Junxian lun* ("On Centralized Administration"), which should be read with the famous contrary essay by Liu Zongyan (733–819)—*Fengjian lun* ("On Decentralized Administration")—in mind. Gu argues that the political and social crisis of his time is the final stage of a long process in which ever-greater restrictions were imposed on local officials by central governments anxious to curtail local power. The effect, says Gu, has been to inhibit responsible district magistrates from taking necessary initiatives to ensure even minimal well-being for their constituencies, leading to social instability and weakened local defense against external invasion. Contrary to the long-standing practice by which magistrates were required to avoid serving in areas near their homes, Gu recommends that descendants of an outstanding magistrate be granted hereditary appointment in one locale. In this way, says Gu, a magistrate's natural inclination toward preservation of himself and his descendants, summarized by the term *si* (concern for private interest), will motivate him to provide actively for the stability and security of the area with which he is personally affiliated, thus fulfilling the state's legitimate needs. Whereas neo-Confucian education would indoctrinate scholar-officials to suppress *si* in favor of *gong* (concern for public good), Gu argues that only one man, the emperor, need be motivated by *gong*, since it is his proper role to balance the myriad privately motivated concerns of his subjects to attain the general good of all. In this brief reference to the emperor's proper state of ethical cultivation, Gu implies a trenchant criticism of Ming imperial history since the Yongle emperor's usurpation, an event which Gu blames, in large part, for the subsequent degradation of Ming politics. Gu's justification of *si* anticipated the later development of this issue by Qing scholars, most notably Dai Zhen (1724–1777).

Despite Gu's prescriptions for reform, modern historiography of China finds a high degree of continuity between the institutions of the Ming and Qing dynasties. Clearly, Gu did not have the advantage of hindsight from a twentieth-century or even a mid-eighteenth-century perspective, so he may be excused for not having anticipated the extraordinary and unprecedented achievements of the sixty-one-year Kangxi era (1662–1722), the longest formal reign in all of Chinese history. The best resource available to Gu for understanding the implications of the Manchu conquest was the flagrantly negative example of the chaotically fratricidal Mongol Yuan dynasty. In that case, not even the relatively enlightened rule of Khubilai Khan (Kublai Khan, c. 1214–1294), who revived the civil service examinations, could suggest what Kangxi would achieve by providently suppressing Manchu nobles hostile to Chinese civilization, by skillfully provoking into rebellion and then defeating the last vestiges of decentralized authority, and by subtly coopting a decisive portion of the Chinese elite. Still, Gu did note a condition that gave the Manchus a distinct advantage over the Mongols. That is, he warned that when foreign powers gained intimate knowledge of Chinese civilization, they might pose an even greater danger to native Chinese rule; in this regard he cited the disruptive effect in the Six Dynasties caused by Xiongnu tribes allowed to settle in China during the Eastern Han.

Beginning in the late 1630s, when Gu was a member of the Revival Society (Fu She), and for more than twenty years thereafter, his scholarship was largely directed at preserving the Ming and supporting resistance to the Qing. In particular, during these years Gu collected copious quantities of geographical writings, derived mainly from gazetteers and dynastic histories, which he compiled under the titles *Tianxia junguo libing shu* and *Zhao yu zhi*. The prefaces to these two rather loosely organized compilations indicate that he ceased his efforts on them in or around 1662, the year when the last Ming pretender died. An original manuscript edition of *Tianxia junguo libing shu* was published in the early republican period and is a rich source of materials on economic and social conditions of various localities. These two works also remain of interest not least because they reflect a geographical definition of China predating the large territorial expansion that occurred under the Qing.

Gu wrote that from his fiftieth year on, he turned to study of the classics, by which he meant a reappropriation of fundamental principles for thought and action. Apparently having abandoned hope of early overthrow of the Manchus, Gu painstakingly prepared a digest of reading notes on a wide range of subjects that he believed would be of concern to anyone who wanted to restore native Chinese rule in the future. This digest, *Rizhi lu* (*Record of Knowledge Gained Daily*), is one of Gu's two works published during his lifetime and is commonly taken to represent the substance of his thought on Confucian statecraft. Its anti-Manchu implications had to be carefully disguised, so controversy has arisen over whether it is to be valued more for its statecraft motivations or for the refinement of its philological method. An apparently expurgated version was included in the imperial library during the Qianlong period, but with an editor's comment pointedly devaluing the statecraft component in the work.

Shortly after a revival of discussions on statecraft was officially sanctioned in the 1830s, Huang Rucheng compiled a new edition of *Rizhi lu* incorporating numerous previously unpublished commentaries. As late as 1833, at a time marked by new threats from a nascent eastern power allied with Manchu remnants, another previously unknown version of Gu's masterwork, identified as an "original manuscript copy" (*yuan chaoben*) and containing strongly antiforeign entries not found in other editions, is said to have been found in a book market in Beijing.

Huang Rucheng's edition of *Rizhi lu* (1834) is divided into thirty-two *juan*, generally falling into the following categories: 1–7, Confucian classics; 8–12, administrative institutions; 13–15, mores and customs; 16–17, the examination system; 18–20, historiography; 21, literature; 22, geography; 23–25, nomenclature and forms of address; 26, standard histories; 27, classical commentaries; 28, ceremonial and vestimentary proprieties; 29, military and foreign topics; 30, astronomy; 31, geography; 32, foreign topics and miscellany.

The name Yanwu, which Gu adopted in his mature years, is understood to mean "fervent militancy" or "Chinese militancy" and bespeaks his zealous devotion to defending the homeland against alien invaders. The traditional story that Gu was involved during his thirties in military activities opposing the Manchus appears credible. Even more grievous than the destructiveness and brutality of foreign invasion, in Gu's view, was the consequent exacerbation of social divisions among the Chinese. Gu participated in drowning a disloyal hereditary bondservant who had opportunistically colluded with a predatory neighbor to accuse Gu of seditious acts against the new regime; for this Gu was punished only by a beating, after influential friends interceded on his behalf. Later, the neighbor hired an assassin who made a nearly successful attempt on Gu's life.

From the perspective of the early twenty-first century, Gu Yanwu's experience and overall intellectual outlook show salient points of comparison to the situation of cultural fundamentalists in other civilizations. Gu suffered devastating personal loss as a direct result of a swift and brutal foreign conquest, which, Gu believed, threatened the continued existence of his ancestral way of life. Thus he distinguished between the mere fall of a dynastic state (*guojia wang*), which was of concern only to the members and adherents of its ruling clan, and the full-scale demise of civilized practices that defined the Chinese ecumene (*tianxia wang*), for which even the humblest committed participant bore a share of responsibility (*pifu you ze*). Faced with a sudden outbreak of fearsome threats, as it were, from almost every quarter, Gu was driven to call into question what things, under such circumstances, could be reliably believed. His response to this crisis was a sophisticated Confucian call for going "back to basics." Gu's intellectual project was devoted to a radical review and reorganization of China's cultural heritage, in order to strengthen China. At the same time, some of the means he adopted to advance this purpose were evidently of recent foreign origin, whether he knew that or not.

Apart from *Rizhi lu*, Gu's only other major work published in his lifetime was *Yinxue wushu* (*Five Treatises on Phonology*), a project on which he labored for more than thirty years. Phonology is the branch of traditional Chinese learning devoted to recovery of lost ancient poetic rhymes, particularly those of the Confucian classic *Odes*. As early as the Six Dynasties, readers of poetry were aware of an uncomfortable gap between contemporary and ancient pronunciations of many characters, rendering many classic verses awkwardly unrhymable. For Gu Yanwu, this historic change amounted to nothing less than loss of direct access to the poetic voice of the ancients. Gu noted that the earliest poetic criticism used the word *yin* ("meaningful sound," "voice") to indicate spontaneous utterances arising from a poet's mental state. In this vein, Gu also observed that the earliest dictionaries defined the pronunciation of characters by citing only one other whole character, known technically as the *yin* or "homophone" of the character in question. Gu regretted that, after a new, more powerfully analytic concept of a partial sound, called *yun* or "rhyme," came into common use from the time when Lu Ji (fl. fourth century) wrote the influential *Wenfu* (*Rhyme-Prose on Literature*), the integrity of the ancient poetic voice (*yin*) became fragmented and obscured. Gu observed further that the later introduction of the foreign *fanqie* system of phonetic analysis was instrumental in consolidating this historical change, so that pronunciations of many characters were incorrectly defined in several major dictionaries, compiled from the Sui through the Song, which organized characters by assigning them to categories of rhyme. In Song times, the Confucian revival spread interest in phonology to a wider readership, but Gu deplored the fact that some careless or ignorant scholars simply changed texts which no longer rhymed, corrupting the original meaning. To reverse the effects of this progressive decline, Gu says, he cited pre-Song medieval sources to correct the errors of Song scholars, some of which had become enshrined in neo-Confucian orthodoxy, and he also corrected the errors of the medieval sources, by citing Han and pre-Qin sources.

Gu's early phonological study is commemorated in a preface of 1643 written for *Shi benyin* (*Original Rhymes of "Odes"*), one of the five titles included in the published *Treatises* of Gu's late years. This preface names Chen Di (1541–1617) as a major influence on Gu's phonology. Fang Chaoying has written, "In [phonological] methodology, . . . Chen first demonstrated the effective application of inductive reasoning" (Goodrich and Fang, 1976, 183). Fang also supposes that Chen, who lived for ten years (from 1604) in Nanjing, where he was a close associate of the eminent scholar-official Jiao Hong (1541–1620), was influenced by Matteo Ricci's explanations of European phonetic spelling. Fang says that Gu developed and "popularized" Chen's method, which became indispensable for the full development of Qing philological and historical research (Hummel 1970, 424).

The scholar Zhou Zumo of the late twentieth century found three major limitations in Gu's phonological scholarship:

1. Crudity of the rhyme categories. As the eighteenth-century philologist Jiang Yong put it, Gu's work showed "much success in drawing evidence from ancient texts, but limited achievement in analysis of distinctions between sounds." Nevertheless, Zhou notes that the design of Gu's rhyme categories remained the basis for progressive refinements by scholars into the twentieth century.
2. Limited application of historical method. Confucians traditionally believed that the decline of ideal ancient institutions and culture became conspicuous from the Spring and Autumn period on. Accordingly, Gu supposed that the pronunciations of the Western Zhou period and earlier high antiquity had been entirely uniform across the fifteen states of the ancient Yellow River valley heartland and during the more than one millennium since the start of the legendary Xia dynasty.
3. Incomplete treatment of historical phonetics. Gu considered finals only and failed to place individual characters within a comprehensive phonetic system (see also Shen 1994, 295).

But Gu did not justify his scholarship as only for the sake of knowledge in itself. Rather, he dedicated his phonology to a fundamental purpose of statecraft. Having lived in both northern and southeastern China, Gu was well aware that differences of dialect contributed to psychological and political alienation between regions. Gu's writings contain numerous expressions of dismay that esprit de corps among scholars was inhibited by their speaking mutually unintelligible dialects. Gu considered it shameful that some educated Chinese supported the Qing consolidation. It is known that appointments of Chinese to high positions under the early Qing regime showed a clear regional preference for northerners, corresponding roughly to the linguistic fault line between northern and southern dialect areas. Gu's assumption that there had once been a uniform ancient pronunciation, ancestral to the modern regional dialects, was determined by his faith in the Confucian vision of an ancient era when the fraternal spirit of *fengjian* institutions held sway. Gu aspired to revive, among the educated elite at least, awareness of this culturally authoritative mode of speech, believing implicitly that modern scholars' minds would thereby be brought to resonate harmonically with a lively awareness of their common identity as Confucian Chinese.

Gu's vision of the import of his phonological study was thought quaintly amusing, at best, by his contemporaries. If Gu may be said to have adumbrated implicitly the need for a common spoken Chinese language, at any rate his response to this need was very different from that advanced by twentieth-century proponents of the "national language" movement. This movement took shape at a time when the criteria of Confucian faith had largely given way to those of "science" and "democracy," so modern standard Chinese has been defined by a less austerely authoritative standard than Gu proposed.

Regarding the source of his vision of cultural renewal through a purified spoken language, Gu cites a brief passage in the Confucian classic *Li Ji* (*Liji*), which refers to ancient ceremonies that periodically brought regional musical tones and pronunciations into conformity with a common sagely standard. Beyond this Chinese precedent, however, there remains the intriguing possibility of an indirect Jesuit influence on Gu. Given Ricci's explicit efforts to make the techniques of phonetic spelling known to his hosts, it seems likely that some literati of the late Ming also came to understand the implications of the fact that the Jesuits could actually *speak* Latin, as the primary mode of their daily communication. That is, Jiao Hong and his colleagues, living at the time of the Donglin revival in the late Ming, may have recognized in the Jesuits a living example of how speaking an ancient and authoritative language both expressed and reinforced the highly self-conscious corporate unity of this polyglot cultural elite, and also substantively defined their spiritual ties to a common tradition, of which they were the energetic agents for contemporary renewal in the face of unprecedented challenges.

See also Confucianism: Qing; Dai Zhen; Liang Qichao.

Bibliography

Bartlett, Thomas. "Ku Yen-wu's Response to 'The Demise of Human Society.'" Ann Arbor, Mich.: University Microfilms International, 1985.

Goodrich, L. Carrington, and Chaoying Fang, eds. *Dictionary of Ming Biography, 1368–1644*, 2 vols. New York: Columbia University Press, 1976.

Hagman, Jan. *Bibliographical Notes on Ku Yen-wu*. Stockholm: Föreningen för Orientaliska Studier, 1973.

Huang, Rucheng, annot. *Rizhi lu jishi*. Taipei: Shih-chieh shuchu, 1974.

Hummel, Arthur H. *Eminent Chinese of the Ch'ing Period*. Taipei: Ch'eng-wen, 1970.

Gu Yanwu. *Gu Tinglin shiwen ji*. Beijing: Zhonghua shuju, 1959.

———, comp. *Tianxia junkuo lipingshu*. Shanghai: Shangwu yinshu guan, 1935–1936.

———. *Yinxue wushu*. Beijing: Zhonghua shuju, 1982.

Liang, Ch'i-ch'ao (Liang Qichao). *Intellectual Trends in the Ch'ing Period*, trans. Immanuel C. Y. Hsu. Cambridge, Mass.: Harvard University Press, 1958.

Peterson, Willard. "The Life of Ku Yen-wu (1613–1682)." *Harvard Journal of Asiatic Studies*, 28, 1968.

Shen, Jiarong. *Gu Yanwu lunkao*. Nanjing: Jiangsu renmin chubanshe, 1994.

Guanzi (*Kuan Tzu*): The Book of Master Guan

W. Allyn Rickett

The *Guanzi* (*Book of Master Guan*), which bears the name of a famous minister of the state of Qi, Guan Zhong (d. 645 B.C.E.), is a large collection of early Chinese materials put together from various sources by Liu Xiang (77–6 B.C.E.) about 26 B.C.E. All of our present editions list eighty-six titled chapters (*pian*), grouped into twenty-four books (*juan*). Ten of the eighty-six chapters have been lost; two chapters—8 and 9—are duplicates except for a rearrangement of their subsections; and two or three others appear to be later substitutes for chapters that had been lost. Some chapters are made up of short fragments of varying origin or different versions of the same material, and four of the surviving seventy-six chapters consist of *jie* or line-by-line explanations of other chapters. The text is also divided into eight named sections, beginning with *Jing yan* ("Canonical Statements") and ending with *Qing zhong* ("Light and Heavy"), which deals primarily with economic theory. The origin and true significance of this grouping into sections is not known, but it may be related to the way the material entered the collection. *Jing yan* is generally considered to represent the earliest portion of the text; however, that is doubtful in the case of some chapters, especially 8 and 9.

Although the *Guanzi* has been traditionally attributed to Guan Zhong, linguistic and stylistic evidence as well as numerous historical anachronisms make it clear that the work as a whole could not have come from his time. In fact, although some Chinese scholars believe that a number of chapters, especially those in *Jing yan* (1–9), represent the thought of Guan Zhong himself as transmitted by a "Guanzi school" of political philosophy centered in the state of Qi, none of the existing chapters would appear to predate the end of the fifth century B.C.E. What appears to be the earliest reference to the *Guanzi* occurs in the *Han feizi* (Liao, 2:290), whose reputed author died in 233 B.C.E.

The most widely accepted theory concerning the origin of the text is that there was a proto-*Guanzi*, which took shape about 250 B.C.E. and which consisted of essays by men associated with the Jixia Academy in Linzi, the capital of the Qi and the intellectual center of China under the three Qi kings, Wei, Xuan, and Min (357–284 B.C.E.). Guan Zhong's name probably became attached to the text because he was a hero of the Qi, being considered an exemplar of the wise minister and largely responsible for its rise as a political and economic power. During its heyday, the Jixia Academy attracted scholars representing various schools of thought from all over China. Thus this proto-*Guanzi* that formed the core of our present collection was already very diverse in content, and in the present text only a half dozen or so chapters clearly share their authorship with others. During the Qin and Han periods the number and variety of works associated with the proto-*Guanzi* continued to grow until the collection was stabilized by Liu Xiang's editing. Why these later works came to be associated with the proto-*Guanzi* collection remains a mystery, except that a number of them are written in the form of dialogues between Guan Zhong and his ruler, Duke Huan (r. 685–643 B.C.E.).

Because the content of the *Guanzi* is so diversified, Chinese catalogers have had difficulty classifying it. In the *Qian Han shu* (*History of the Former Han Dynasty*) it is listed as a Daoist work; later catalogs generally list it as legalist. This ambiguity, plus the fact that the text is often corrupt and extremely difficult to read, has meant that until recently it did not receive the attention it deserves.

The *Guanzi* is primarily a work devoted to political economy and statecraft, and in spite of its diversified content, with the exception of Chapters 68–84, its general point of view is physiocratic and reflects a benign feudalism best summed up in Chapter 1, *Mu min* ("On Shepherding the People"):

> All those who possess territory and shepherd the people must pay heed to the four seasons and watch over the granaries. If the state has an abundance of wealth, people will come from afar; if the land has been opened for cultivation, they will settle down. When the granaries are full, they will know propriety and moderation; when their clothing and food are adequate, they will know the distinction between honor and shame. If those on high exercise proper measure in dress and expenditure, the six relationships will be secure. If the four cardinal virtues (propriety, righteousness, integrity, and a sense of shame) prevail, the prince's orders will be carried out. Therefore, the essential compo-

> nent in reducing punishments is to prohibit luxury and artfulness. The primary measure for preserving the state is to promote the four cardinal virtues. The basic precepts for achieving obedience among the people are to honor the spirits, respect the mountain and river gods, revere the ancestral temples, and venerate ancestors and great men of the past.

The so-called *Qing zhong* chapters (68–84), which appear to date from Han times, are much less moralistic and more commercial. Here the primary concern is how to increase the wealth and power of the state and its ruler by manipulating the supply of money and the price of goods. The government is urged to establish monopolistic controls over the market so that it can buy commodities such as grain when they are plentiful and cheap and sell them when they become scarce and expensive. It also urges placing taxes on indispensable commodities such as salt and iron that the people will be unable to avoid. These *Qing zhong* chapters are perhaps most famous for presenting what may be among the world's first discussions of the quantity theory of money.

A number of chapters dealing with statecraft have a strong legalist bias, especially Chapter 16, *Fa fa* ("On Conforming to the Law"), which stresses the primacy of law. Even the ruler must adhere to it; otherwise, "government affairs will lack a constant standard." And "legal statutes, regulations, and procedures must be patterned on the way of good government; orders must be publicized and made clear; and rewards and punishments must be made reliable and absolute." However, even this chapter sounds a warning for rulers who are too demanding:

> No one has ever been able to seek too much and gain it all, prohibit too much and have all that is prohibited stopped, or issue too many orders and have them all carried out. Therefore, it is said: "If the sovereign is too demanding, his subjects will not be obedient." If subjects, being disobedient, are forced to conform by means of punishments, the masses will scheme against him.

He must also exercise restraint in his personal expenditures:

> The enlightened prince builds his ancestral temple just adequate enough to provide for guests at sacrificial feasts, but does not strive for lavish beauty. He erects palaces and pavilions just adequate enough to avoid dryness and dampness, cold and heat, but does not strive for grandiosity.

As the text states: "Frugality is the way."

It should be noted that the legalism of the *Guanzi*, except for Chapters 45 and 46, differs from that of Shang Yang and Han Fei, who stressed positive law. In *Guanzi*, most of the chapters dealing with statecraft, even the more legalistic ones, tend to stress natural law and the relationship between heaven and man. The governing principle of order in this relationship and throughout the universe is the *dao*, or Way. (In a lesser context *dao* is also used to refer to a moral way or the way of good government.) The result is often a combination of Daoism and legalism mixed with traditional Confucian social values that has generally come to be known as Huang-Lao thought. The Daoist component of Huang-Lao thought in the *Guanzi* also tends to differ from the Daoism of the *Zhuangzi* and *Laozi*. The Way becomes much more naturalistic and less mystical. It remains a first principle, but it is no longer entirely nameless. It tends to be treated as a natural law of the universe, but at the same time tends to lose its position as something beyond heaven and earth. In fact, at times it appears to be merely a creative force existing between heaven and earth. Emphasis is placed on the relationship between names (*ming*) and forms (*xing*) or realities (*shi*); timeliness instead of timelessness; law (*fa*), which is rooted in the Way; and political methods (*shu*) as a means of establishing good order. The ideal ruler becomes a Daoist sage, ruling through nonassertiveness (*wuwei*) and practicing various quietist techniques, while the work of administration is performed by his ministers and bureaucracy. Confucian virtues, especially *ren* (human goodness or benevolence), *yi* (righteousness or sense of duty), and *li* (ritualistic principles or propriety) are valued.

The theoretical foundation of this Daoism is presented in Chapter 49, *Nei ye* ("Inner Workings"), one of the earliest of surviving Daoist works, probably dating from the beginning of the fourth century B.C.E. According to the *Nei ye*, the source of all living things is a seminal or vital essence (*jing*) whose kinetic form is a vital force, *qi*. This *qi* can never be restrained by physical strength or force, but it may be brought to rest by the mystical or spiritual power (*de*), the manifestation of the *dao* or spirit (*shen*) within the individual. Only when the mind is quiescent (*jing*) and the vital force is well managed can the *dao* be "made to stay." The text goes on:

> When our minds are well regulated, our sense organs are also well regulated. When our minds are at ease, our sense organs are also at ease. What regulates them is the mind; what sets them at ease is the mind. The mind therefore contains an inner mind. That is to say, within the mind there is another mind. In that mind's mind, the power of awareness (*yi*) comes before sound. After awareness come forms. After forms come names. After names comes putting the mind to use. After putting the mind to use comes its regulation.

The *Nei ye* itself has little to say about statecraft. Its primary practical concern is the prolongation of life through the exercise of mental quiescence, breath control, and dietary restraint.

The development of the Daoistic sage ruler appears in five other chapters closely associated with the *Nei ye* but of a later date: *Zhou he* (11), *Shu yen* (12), *Xin shu shang* (36), *Xin shu xia* (37), and *Bai xin* (38), all of which are extremely important in the study of early Huang-Lao thought. Perhaps the most complete expression of Huang-Lao thought in its later manifestations appears in the *Chi mi* chapter (35), which probably dates from the early Han. The overriding message throughout this very long and difficult chapter is the need for flexibility in dealing with changing political and economic conditions: "Change is the ultimate truth of heaven and earth." This requires not only being in accord with the fluctuations of *yin* and *yang* and the five phases (*wuxing*) but also adopting unusual techniques and methods, such as the encouragement of extravagant spending on the part of the rich in order to stimulate the economy. At the same time, the writer lashes out at Daoist, Mencian, and other idealistic approaches to government:

> A poorly organized government cannot rule a country. Talk of yielding and quiescence cannot express the way of good government. Being timely in government means going along with changing times. Such escapist doctrines as taking non-activity as a way of good government and the equality of all things as a guiding principle are unacceptable.

Of the four major chapters dealing with the art of war, Chapter 6, *Qi fa* ("Seven Standards") is primarily legalist and is quite similar to Chapter 10, *Zhan fa* ("Methods of Warfare"), in the *Shang jun shu* in stressing a strong government and an efficient administrative system at home as the basis for success in military affairs. The other three, *You guan* (8), *Bing fa* ("Methods of Warfare," 17), and *Can huan* ("Evil Consequences," 28), tend to adopt an early Huang-Lao approach, stressing the *dao*, flexibility, acting in accord with the seasons and the terrain, and the use of various techniques and stratagems. According to the *You guan*:

> Rear your people in accordance with the Way (*dao*); nurture them with the power (*de*). If reared in accordance with the Way, the people may be harmonized. If nurtured with the power, the people may be united. Since they are harmonious and united, they can live on intimate terms. Since they live on intimate terms, they can cooperate. Since they live in complete cooperation and on such intimate terms, no one can harm them.

Moreover, whereas the legalists tend to view war in very positive terms as a means of expanding one's power, the *You guan* plainly considers it a last resort—"It is best to have no battles at all: next best is to have only one of them."

The core of the *You guan* is a political-agricultural calendar outlining the fluctuating natural phenomena of the seasons and the activities in which men should be engaged. A number of such calendars from the Warring States period have survived, some of them apparently as early as the fourth century. Perhaps the most famous is the *Shi ji* ("Seasonal Record") from the *Lüshi Chunqiu* (also known as the *Yue ling*, "Monthly Ordinances," as it appears in the *Liji*), which adopted an arrangement based on the five phases. By the end of the Warring States period, concepts related to the five phases (*wuxing*) had come to dominate Chinese thinking, and the *You guan* calendar—like the *Shi ji*—lists five seasons corresponding to the five phases (wood-spring, fire-summer, earth-center, metal-autumn, and water-winter). How to handle this extra center season posed a difficult problem for calendar makers. No actual time is assigned to the center summer season in the *Shi ji* or the *You guan*, but a later calendar appearing in the *Huainanzi* assigns the third month of summer to it.

In the *You guan* and its duplicate, *You guan tu* (9), the text of the calendar has been supplemented by an essay on political and military strategy that has been cut up and rearranged under the five seasonal divisions. When the different divisions, having been correlated with the four directions (spring-east, etc.) and the center, are laid out geographically on paper, they then form the pattern of a so-called *He tu* or "Yellow River chart" mentioned in the *Yi jing*. This *yin-yang* and five-phases numerology chart is based on the magic square of nine sections with the number five dominating the center.

Although the term *wuxing* (five phases) itself does not appear in the *Guanzi* except in the title of Chapter 41, thought based on *yin-yang* and the five phases plays an important role in many of the later chapters, such as *Chi mi* (35, discussed above). However, the five phases receive their most detailed expression in the *You guan* and three other calendar chapters: *Si shi* ("Four Seasons," 40), *Wu xing* ("Five Phases," 41), and *Qing zhong ji* ("Light and Heavy," part F, 85).

They are also mentioned in Chapter 39, *Shui di* ("Water and Earth"), along with their correlated tastes and colors, but the primary topic is water, both in terms of its natural physical properties and in terms of its being a supernatural force, even a divine spirit. In the standard "five phases" text, all five—wood, fire, earth, metal, and water—are treated as being of equal importance, although each, along with its correlates, has its time of dominance in a cycle. Here, "water is complete in its virtue," and "the source of all life," qualities unrestricted by cyclical changes. Thus the ideas expressed here seem to represent an independent line of thought, more in tune with medical texts such as *Huang di nei jing su wen* and *Huang di nei jing ling shu* than with the primarily political writing in "five phases" texts such as the *Yue ling*. In general, the chapter calls to mind the theory of humors propounded by the early Greek philosopher Empedocles (484–424 B.C.E.), and it is especially interesting for its information about early Chinese folklore and its surprisingly modern understanding of the development of the human fetus. The chapter also contains one of the earliest references to the circulation of blood and oxygen in the body, antedating by some two thousand years the discoveries of William Harvey.

See also Daoism: Neo-Daoism; Han Feizi; Laozi; Legalism; Shang Yang; *Wuxing*; Zhuangzi.

Bibliography

Haloun, Gustav. "Legalist Fragments: Part I; *Kuan-tsï* 55 and Related Texts." *Asia Major*, New Series 2, part 1, April 1951, pp. 85–120.

Kanaya, Osamu. "Taoist Thought in the Kuan-tzu." In *From Benares to Beijing: Essays on Buddhism and Chinese Religion*, ed. Koichi Shinohara and Gregory Schopen. Oakville, N.Y.: Mosaic, 1991.

Liao, W. K. *The Complete Works of Han Fei Tzu*.

Maverick, Lewis, "T'an Po-fu, and Wen Kung-wen." In *Economic Dialogues in Ancient China: Selections from the Kuan-tzu*. Carbondale, Ill.: Maverick, 1954.

Rickett, W. Allyn. *Guanzi: Political, Economic, and Philosophical Essays from Early China*, Vol. 1. Princeton, N.J.: Princeton University Press, 1985. (See also revised ed. Boston: Cheng and Tsui, 2001.)

———. *Guanzi: Political, Economic, and Philosophical Essays from Early China*, Vol. 2. Princeton, N.J.: Princeton University Press, 1998.

———. *Kuan-tzu, a Repository of Early Chinese Thought*. Hong Kong: Hong Kong University Press, 1965.

Roth, Harold David. "Psychology and Self-Cultivation in Early Taoistic Thought." *Harvard Journal of Asiatic Studies*, 51(2), December 1992, pp. 599–650.

———. "Redaction, Criticism and the Early History of Taoism." *Early China*, 19, 1994, pp. 1–46.

Guo Xiang (Kuo Hsiang)

Alan K. L. Chan

Guo Xiang (Kuo Hsiang (c. 252–312) was a champion of "the learning of the mysterious *dao*" (*xuanxue*), a neo-Daoist movement that came into prominence during the third century C.E. Guo Xiang, styled Zixuan, is by far the most important interpreter of the *Zhuangzi* in Chinese history. Through him, the *Zhuangzi* has come down to us in its present form, divided into thirty-three chapters. His reading of this Daoist classic has been hailed as a greater achievement than even the original. Ironically, Guo Xiang has also been accused of no less a crime than plagiarism.

As early as the fifth century, the charge was made that Guo had plagiarized the work of another famous neo-Daoist, Xiang Xiu. Although Guo was undoubtedly influenced by Xiang, recent scholarship generally agrees that he had nevertheless drawn his own conclusions. In his commentary on *Zhuangzi*, seeking harmony in the midst of turmoil, Guo fuses ontological and ethical insights and offers to reconcile the yearning for freedom and transcendence with sociopolitical engagement. It is worth mentioning that despite the extremely unstable political conditions that plagued the early Jin dynasty (265–420), and despite the fact that he came from a humble background, Guo enjoyed a long and distinguished public career. Adept in philosophical debates and other forms of cultured discourse, Guo was fondly regarded by his contemporaries as being second only to Wang Bi, the bright star of *xuanxue* a generation earlier. Besides the *Zhuangzi*, Guo also wrote on the *Analects* and the *Laozi*. These works, however, have not survived, except for a few quotations preserved by later scholars.

Like Wang Bi, Guo Xiang was dissatisfied with the orthodox mode of classical learning, established since the Han dynasty, which emphasized philological and cosmological interpretations. To understand the classics, Guo was convinced, one must look beyond the surface meaning of the words to discern the underlying ideas. Words are important tools, but they must not be taken uncritically at face value. This is especially important to understanding the *Zhuangzi*, which uses a large number of parables and metaphors, often involving spiritual figures or supernatural exploits. Taken literally, they verge on the fantastic; properly understood, they intimate the wonder of the *dao* and the greatness of the Daoist sage. Putting the *Zhuangzi* under fresh philosophical scrutiny, Guo challenges not only the established views of Han Confucian scholars but also those of Wang Bi and other neo-Daoist philosophers.

The main disagreement lies in ontology. Guo recognizes the ontological import of Daoist philosophy—that all beings are rooted in the *dao*. But, unlike Wang Bi and others, he rejects the claim that all beings originate from nonbeing.

The concept of nonbeing—which was a major innovation in the history of Chinese philosophy—discloses a metaphysical view of the origin of being. If infinite regress cannot be admitted, the logic of creation seems to demand a "first cause." For this reason, Han scholars were eager to identify the "great ultimate," be it in terms of an anthropomorphic heaven or an original vital energy, which initiated the process of creation at the "beginning."

The idea of a creator or original substance, however, is untenable, for it begs the question of the cause of its own being. The *dao*, as both the *Laozi* and *Zhuangzi* stipulate, is nameless and without form; it cannot be reduced to any particular entity or agent. As such, it can be described only as nonbeing, a negative concept that captures the transcendence and absolute "otherness" of *dao*. In the light of nonbeing, the *dao* signifies not a godlike being or substance but the transcendental unity on which the multiplicity and diversity of phenomena are logically based. The chain of being, linked by contingent causes, requires a necessary ontological foundation. The concept of nonbeing thus establishes the *dao* as the metaphysical ground of being, and in this sense the "beginning" of heaven, earth, and all beings.

Attractive as it may seem, according to Guo Xiang, this view nevertheless fails to account for the origin of being. Nonbeing remains an imaginary construct, a pure abstraction, and as such cannot bring about creation. So defined, nonbeing and being are mutually exclusive; consequently, as Guo states, "nonbeing cannot change into being" (*Zhuangzi* commentary, ch. 22). The appeal to a divine creator should indeed be rejected, but that does not entail a nihilistic absence. Having disposed of these options, what does Guo Xiang have to offer in their place? He writes:

> Since nonbeing is nonbeing, it cannot produce being. Before being itself is produced, it cannot produce other beings. Then by whom are things produced? They spontaneously produce themselves, that is all. (*Zhuangzi* commentary, ch. 2, trans. Wing-tsit Chan)

This introduces Guo's famous concept of "self-transformation" (*zihua* or *duhua*). Whereas Wang Pi values nonbeing, as Chinese sources generally distinguish the two positions, Guo Xiang favors being. The claim of being does not posit an objectified, transcendent *dao*. Guo's point is rather that since the other alternatives are clearly unacceptable, self-transformation proves to be the only logical explanation. At the most basic ontological level, prior to the birth of the "ten thousand things," being is "so of itself" or "naturally so." In this way, Guo thus finds a deeper meaning in the well-known Daoist concept of "naturalness" or "spontaneity" (*ziran*).

This implies that being exists eternally. In Guo's words:

> We may know the causes of certain things and affairs near to us. But tracing their origin to the ultimate end, we find that without any cause, they of themselves come to be what they are. Being so of themselves, we can no longer question the reason or cause of their being, but should accept them as they are. (*Zhuangzi* commentary, ch. 14; cf. Fung, 1983, 2:209–210)

At the epistemological level, a further implication is that ultimately self-transformation remains a mystery. Far from being a source of perplexities, for Guo Xiang, this frees the mind and redirects it to realize the nature of *dao* and the ethical implications of Daoist naturalness.

The doctrine of self-transformation affirms that the *dao* is everywhere and in all things. The logic of immanence takes full effect once nonbeing is removed from view. Even in the most lowly and base, as the *Zhuangzi* emphasizes (ch. 22), the presence of *dao* can be detected. Redeploying an old cosmological concept, Guo explains that the *dao* is manifest in nature as vital energy (*qi*). Subtle and without determinate form, it pervades and gives form to the created order. All beings are endowed with a "share" or "allotment" (*fen*) of the inexhaustible life-giving power of *dao*. The myriad creatures thus embody what the classics call the "virtue" of *dao*, or in Guo's rendition, the fullness of nature.

The way of *ziran* depicts not a state of random disorder but an organized regime in which all parts have a role to play. With respect to human beings, in perfect harmony the body functions as a unified whole in accordance with specific "principles" (*li*). Further, without undermining the interdependence of the multitude of organs, there is a hierarchical structure to the workings of the body, where the mind assumes sovereign control. Central to Guo's reformulation of Daoist philosophy, the concept of *li* renders explicit the inherent order of nature.

Li (principle) extends beyond physical laws. It also defines one's natural "share" or endowment as a fund of essential characteristics, such as capacity, life span, and temperament. According to Guo Xiang, this is precisely what is meant by human "nature" (*xing*), a term common to all schools of Chinese thought but here interpreted in terms of *li*. Significantly, nature includes innate moral sensibilities: "benevolence and rightness are [a part of] human nature" (*Zhuangzi* commentary, ch. 14). These basic insights set the direction for ethics and political philosophy.

The emphasis on interdependence eliminates any suspicion of solipsism. Just as the body forms an integral whole, natural and social phenomena find themselves inextricably bound in a network of relationships. Natural processes flourish in a delicate ecological balance; dysfunctionality or disharmony at any level could create serious ripple effects that would threaten the survival of the environment. Human relationships are also governed by constant principles; individuals, like different parts of the body, have their proper place in the social and political assembly. From this perspective, as opposed to conventional arrangements that can be changed or discarded at will, both the family and the state should be understood as expressions of *ziran*.

In view of the hierarchical order of nature, Guo does not hesitate to say that the father should be the head of the family, and that the country should be ruled by the king. Inasmuch as benevolence (*ren*) and rightness (*yi*) stem directly from nature, social and political institutions ought to reflect a strong moral base. From self-transformation to society, Guo thus provides a comprehensive guide to the Daoist universe.

Given that individuals enjoy a particular "share" of the *dao*, differences in natural endowment should be recognized. For example, owing to the different allotment of vital energy, some people are born more intelligent or gifted in other ways. Because everything is what it is—"so of itself" (*ziran*)—Guo can say that "what one is born with is not something undue or vain" (*Zhuangzi* commentary, ch. 5). Because one's nature is determined by exact principles, one can also speak of "destiny" (*ming*) in this connection. Is Guo, then, committed to a kind of thoroughgoing fatalism? Does this entail a rigid system in which individuals merely conform to prescribed roles?

Many scholars favor such an interpretation. It is a matter of "destiny" or "fate" that one is born of sagely character, of average capacity, or disadvantaged. In all cases, Guo maintains that one ought to accept one's natural endowment. Yet he is also concerned to distinguish *ming* as "fact" from "value," and to make room for change and development in human flourishing.

Fundamentally, differences based on endowment, including gender, appearance, talents, and so on, do not constitute any basis for value judgments. Rather, as the *Zhuangzi* repeatedly urges, what needs to be recognized is the "equality of things."

Equality is not to be confused with sameness. In this context, equality suggests that all beings are partners in the larger architecture of *dao*. Being gifted does not necessarily make one "better"; even a physically or mentally handicapped person is "complete" in his or her own way. Differences among individuals are undeniable, but they do not legitimize prejudice or discrimination.

At the social level, the basic values of family and state should certainly be guarded. Anarchy amounts to a violation of the norms of nature. On the other hand, although the hierarchical structure of society no doubt indicates a gradation of authority, this does not absolve any form of authoritarian government that oppresses the people. The father may be the authoritative figure in the family, but he would not be in that position if not for his children. As "children" of the *dao*, all individuals are indispensable and occupy equally important stations in the order of nature.

Unlike Wang Bi, who stresses the "one" over the many, Guo Xiang thus takes into view the richness and diversity of being. Individuality is not sacrificed for political interests or dissolved in a sea of metaphysical oneness. On the contrary, as Guo forcefully argues, there is no greater calamity than the loss of individuality and authenticity, of one's identity as defined by nature (*Zhuangzi* commentary, ch. 10). Conversely, the Daoist goal can be defined as the realization of one's nature, and in particular the optimization of one's inborn capacity. As nature blossoms, "destiny" is fulfilled.

While he may not be able to avoid the charge of fatalism altogether, Guo does aim to introduce a dynamic view of nature and destiny. The world of *ziran* is never static; it changes and renews itself constantly. A mountain or an ocean may appear unchanging, but it is perpetually in flux. This is mirrored in human existence, where individuals grow with the passage of time (*Zhuangzi* commentary, ch. 6). Limits notwithstanding, one's potential should not be underestimated. Whether in terms of physical strength, courage, love, or simply a knack for certain things, deep reserves may be hidden until they are propelled into the open in moments of truth. Although constituted and regulated by principles, human beings and societies need not be viewed as fixed assets with no possibility of change or development.

Indeed, while the order of nature must be respected, the person of *dao* recognizes the inevitability of change. The sage, whom the *Zhuangzi* calls the "perfect man" and describes figuratively as a "spiritual being," nourishes his nature and adapts constantly to changes in the environment and society. This, as Guo Xiang sees it, brings out the real meaning of "nonaction" (*wu-wei* or *wuwei*).

Nonaction "does not mean folding one's arms and keeping quiet" (*Zhuangzi* commentary, ch. 11). Nor is it a technical skill requiring special effort or training. In neo-Daoist terms, nonaction stems from a profound discernment of the way of *ziran*, which translates into a mode of being and a spirit of action, according to which one performs all functions.

There are two aspects to Guo's understanding of nonaction. First, as things and affairs are informed by principles, there is a natural way of action and interaction. Just as the fabulous cook (or butcher) Ding could cut up an ox without having to rely on sensory perception or mental calculation (*Zhuangzi*, ch. 3), and just as a spontaneous affection characterizes the parent-child relationship, the sage accomplishes all tasks by simply following the "grain" or nature of phenomena.

Furthermore, in light of the equality of things, nonaction ideally leads to a sense of freedom and equanimity. Instead of chasing after false ideals, trying to be like someone else, and ending up a prisoner of restless striving and deceit, one stays true to oneself and develops one's nature. If self-sufficiency is assumed, there is no point imitating others, even the sages. This is important, for nonaction cannot be divorced from naturalness or reserved for the sage alone. What is required of self-fulfillment has already been given; to clamor after what is foreign to one's genuine "share" is not only futile but self-negating.

Against helplessness and passive resignation, Guo Xiang calls for a constructive celebration of individuality and the plenitude of the Daoist world. Free from the tyranny of desires and the ceaseless undulation of discontent, one reaps an inner calm and comes to be at ease with the outside world. Even death loses its fearsomeness, for one realizes that life and death are but moments of the transformation of nature.

The Daoist sage need not live as a recluse or shun politics. Any deliberate disavowal of communal life, in fact, violates the spirit of naturalness. The important point is that "although the sage finds himself in the halls of ritual and government, his mind is not different from when he is surrounded by mountains and trees" (*Zhuangzi* commentary, ch. 1). Beyond the sway of emotions, the sage roams the world without being moved or enslaved by it. This, to Guo Xiang, truly captures the essence of "free and easy wandering," a theme central to the *Zhuangzi* and now shown to bear directly on mundane activities.

Politically, the ruler should also abide by naturalness and nonaction. This means, besides self-cultivation, allowing and encouraging the people to develop their nature and potential. Thus, artificial restrictions and interference should be minimized. Official appointments, moreover, must be made on the basis of talent and capacity, not on the basis of family background, as was commonly the case in Guo's China. In return, as Guo confidently predicts, ministers and subjects will naturally fulfill their duties, and all under heaven will share peace and contentment. As needs and circumstances change, social and political practice should not be fossilized. Timely adjustments ensure renewal and harmony in a dynamic realm.

In this way, Guo Xiang tries to reconcile "orthodox teachings" (*mingjiao*) with *ziran*. Whereas *mingjiao* refers to doctrines of propriety and government, which sustain order in society, *ziran* aspires to transcendence and freedom from mundane concerns. Conflict arises when orthodox teachings are seen to impinge on nature, or when transcendence is equated with renunciation. For Guo Xiang, however, since social and natural phenomena are governed by the same set of principles, *mingjiao* and *ziran* coincide and merge into one.

Naturalness does not seek to escape from but embraces society. It signifies an inner transcendence that is the mark of authenticity. The norms and rites that define civilization are not foreign to nature; in principle, they flow spontaneously from it. This attempt to mediate between order and spontaneity broke new ground in the history of Daoist thought, and made possible a mutually enriching dialogue between Daoist and Chinese Buddhist philosophy. Inasmuch as neo-Daoism had a strong impact on the development of Chinese aesthetics and literary theory, Guo Xiang's contribution in these areas should also be recognized.

See also Daoism: Neo-Daoism; Zhuangzi.

Bibliography

Chan, Wing-tsit. *A Source Book in Chinese Philosophy*. Princeton, N.J.: Princeton University Press, 1963.

Fung, Yu-lan (Feng Youlan), trans. *Chuang Tzu: A New Selected Translation with an Exposition of the Philosophy of Kuo Hsiang*. Shanghai: Commercial Press, 1933. (Reprint, New York: Gordon, 1975.)

———. *A History of Chinese Philosophy*, Vol. 2, trans. Derk Bodde. Princeton, N.J.: Princeton University Press, 1983.

Holzman, Donald. "Les sept sages de la forêt des bambous et la société de leur temps." *T'oung Pao*, 44, 1956, pp. 317–346.

Kohn, Livia. *Early Chinese Mysticism: Philosophy and Soteriology in the Taoist Tradition*. Princeton, N.J.: Princeton University Press, 1992.

———. "Kuo Hsiang and the *Chuang-tzu*." *Journal of Chinese Philosophy*, 12, 1985, pp. 429–447.

Mather, Richard B. "The Controversy over Conformity and Naturalness during the Six Dynasties." *History of Religions*, 9(2–3), 1969–1970, pp. 160–180.

———, trans. *Shih-shuo Hsin-yü: A New Account of Tales of the World by Liu I-ch'ing with Commentary by Liu Chün*. Minneapolis: University of Minnesota Press, 1976.

Robinet, Isabelle. "Kouo Siang ou le monde comme absolu." *T'oung Pao*, 69, 1983, pp. 73–107.

Yü, Ying-shih. "Individualism and the Neo-Taoist Movement in Wei-Chin China." In *Individualism and Holism: Studies in Confucian and Taoist Values*, ed. Donald Munro. Ann Arbor: Center for Chinese Studies, University of Michigan, 1985, pp. 121–155.

Ziporyn, Brook. "The Self-So and Its Traces in the Thought of Guo Xiang." *Philosophy East and West*, 43, 1993, pp. 511–539.

中國哲學

H

Han Feizi (Han Fei Tzu)

Yuk Wong

Chen Qiyou and Zhang Jue's *Guided Readings in Han Feizi* has two appendixes of Chinese and Japanese references on Han Feizi (Han Fei Tzu, 281–233 B.C.E.). For English translations, we have W. K. Liao's *Complete Works of Han Fei Tzu* and Burton Watson's selected essays. Yan Lingfeng edited the *Collected Works Concerning Han Fei*. Chen Qitian, Liang Qiqiao, Rong Zhaozu, Wang Xiaobo, and Zhang Suzhen are also among the established scholars of Han Fei's philosophy.

Han Fei, a proponent of legalism, came from a noble family of the Han state. He had a speech handicap but was a talented writer; Li Si—who, like Han Fei, was a student of Xunzi's—admitted that he was Han's inferior. When Han Fei's native state, under attack by the Qin, suffered repeated defeats, Han on several occasions advised his ruler to adopt legalism. He did not succeed and, bitterly disappointed, he wrote more than 100,000 words to defend his political ideas. The first Qin emperor, after reading Han's essays "Solitary Indignation" and "Five Vermin," exclaimed that if he could see and befriend the author, he would die without regret. Learning from the premier, Li Si, who the author was, the emperor commanded the Qin army to attack the Han state and capture Han Fei; in consequence, the Han king reluctantly sent Han Fei to Qin as an envoy.

At the Qin court, Han Fei admonished the emperor for invading the state of Han and attacking the Zhao and Qi. He also warned the emperor not to employ Yao Jia, revealing unsavory facts about Yao's past. Han Fei had already aroused the jealousy of Li Si and now incurred the hatred of Yao Jia; these two slandered him, accusing him of being a spy for his own country. The Qin ruler went along with Li and Yao and imprisoned Han, who had no chance to vindicate himself. Han died a victim of Li's poison.

Han's disciples compiled the book *Han Feizi*. The first essay, "First Interview in Qin," for Emperor Zhao of Qin, condemned his ministers' stupid strategies. Some scholars suspected that the real author was Cai Ze of the "eloquence school" or Lü Buwei, who might have been the father of the first emperor. Moreover, the latter half of the essay "Enquiring about Fields" came from the writings of Han's disciples; they had also modified the essay "Minimizing Decrees" of the *Shangjun shu* to compose a new essay, "Revising Decrees."

Sima Qian wrote biographies of two Daoists (Laozi and Zhuangzi) and two legalists (Shen Buhai and Han Fei), covering them in a single essay because he thought that Han Fei had assimilated Daoist metaphysical naturalism, although he interpreted all the Daoist "mindless actions" as intentional tactics. According to Lao-Zhuang, *dao* is the eternal metaphysical substance, which is the origin of the complementary material forces *yin* and *yang*, natural laws, ethics, politics, and craftsmanship. Han Fei, strongly influenced by his chief mentor, Xunzi, weakened this sense of *dao* (objective idealism) but retained the Daoists' stress on nonaction, nonassertiveness, and nonintervention. Without creating anything, Han Fei's *dao* is simply natural law governing the universe, time, and space.

As the category second to *dao, de* is the internal cause of everything, or individual shares of the all-inclusive, all-pervasive *dao*. Like Laozi, Han Fei regarded *de* as accumulating *jing* (vital force or harmonious energy). Extending this Daoist concept, Han Fei used *de* to stand for family wealth, the national population, and even favor or awards.

The third category, *li*, has the same status as *de*. But while *de* is the material ground of everything, *li* is specific properties and principles.

In sum, Han Fei removed all elements of transcendental mysticism from Daoist metaphysics, as the earlier *jixia* school had done. Hence, Han Fei rejected Confucian moral fatalism and Daoist passive determinism and promulgated active nonmoral or amoral indeterminism and atheism. He urged people to follow *dao* and *li* and abide by laws. Laozi's terms "vacuity" and "quietude" implicitly exclude passion and empirical knowledge, but Han Fei used these terms to mean freedom from restriction, indulgence, and subjective arbitrariness. By nonaction (*wuwei*), Han Fei meant refraining from irrational actions and thus acquiring the benefits to be derived from rational projects. By contrast, Zhuangzi would not even advocate planning, let alone projects. But, influenced by Han Fei's definition of nonaction, the *Huainanzi* defines *wuwei* as an activity.

Han Fei emphasized that the deliberate pursuit of nonaction and nonthought—vacuity and quietude—would lead to spiritual self-control. However, his emphasis on diminishing thinking and cognition seems faulty because it neglects the necessity for active mental training. Xunzi avoided this mistake, and Han Fei elaborated on Xunzi's concept of *yinguo*, a term that originally referred to an instrument for straightening crooked wood but later came to mean artificial modification in general. As a result of this legalist doctrine, the neo-Daoist Guo Xiang adapted Zhuangzi's naturalism to affirm the Confucian idea of domesticating animals, especially oxen and horses.

Like the Mohists, Han Fei valued practicality, or utility. He gave no significance to impractical or spiritual achievements in religion, philosophy, or art. To Han Fei, Mozi had wasted his energy inventing a wooden kite that could fly for three days: Mozi might better have produced some more useful wooden gadgets. Ironically, Han's quasi-utilitarianism was combined with a narrow intellectualism that discouraged the Chinese from developing the natural sciences, either experimental or theoretical. Nevertheless, he enriched and illustrated Daoist dialectics, in addition to coining the term "contradiction."

Han Fei—in sharp contrast to Mencius—endorsed Xunzi's view of human nature. Probing into the depths of human mind, he observed that relations between sovereign and minister, husband and wife, and even father and son were based on profit. For humans, it is instinctive to seek safety and benefits and avoid danger and harm. Han Fei understood the Confucian virtues of benevolence and righteousness as entailing moral autonomy rather than heteronomy; i.e., sages never perform good deeds for the sake of reward. Still, most people cannot be morally autonomous. Dissatisfied with Xunzi's doctrine of rule by ritual propriety, Han Fei advocated government by laws, which must be followed by kings and ministers as well as the people. Lao-Zhuang belittled proprieties and laws, and the Huang-Lao school believed that all laws were produced by *dao*. For Han Fei, the king himself should make all laws, lest ministers or elites take advantage of him.

Addressing the Daoist view of social devolution, Han Fei suggested that societies evolve: if people exalt ancient sage kings, modern sages will deride them. He drew an analogy with a farmer of the Song who laid aside his plow to watch beside a stump that a hare had run into and broken its neck. Ancient peoples, having sufficient material resources, had rarely quarreled; but later the population increased (geometrically, although Han did not know this mathematical concept), resources became inadequate, people were driven to fight, and chaos ensued. Long before Hong Liangji in the Qing dynasty and Malthus in England, Han Fei paid attention to the problem of overpopulation.

In *Shi ben*, Han Fei claimed that Yao and Shun did not abdicate and relinquish the rule of the world. On the contrary, they usurped the throne. In "Five Vermin," Yao and Shun were said to have relinquished the throne because it offered only slight advantages, rather than from more lofty sentiments. King Wen of the early Chou practiced benevolence and righteousness to become a global ruler, whereas King Yen of Xu did the same but ruined his state. Men of the golden age of antiquity had striven for virtue; men of the in-between period had sought wise schemes; men of the present vied with strength and spirit. Han counseled the king to discard benevolence, righteousness, eloquence, and wisdom. In any critical age, adopting the ways of a generous, lenient government is like riding a wild horse without whip or reins. When parental love cannot prevent children from becoming unruly, how can Confucian benevolence and Mohist universal love bring people to order? Although Confucius had been benevolent and righteous, only seventy men had studied under him. (Han was wrong about this; Confucius had some three thousand disciples.)

According to Han, the five vermin were (1) Confucian scholars, (2) the "eloquence" school, (3) chivalrous swordsmen, (4) deserters from military service, and (5) merchants and craftsmen. In his mind, Confucian education was superfluous, because laws and regulations served as teachings; and people need not memorize a sage king's sayings and lessons, because officials served as superb mentors. Traders and craftsmen might violate laws or undermine husbandry and warfare. (From the standpoint of modern economics, Han underestimated the function of people engaged in trade and crafts.) Han was overly prone to negate the value of anything that was not beneficial to the king, whose happiness, rather than people's welfare, sometimes seemed to be his ultimate concern.

On the whole, however, legalists concerned themselves with national welfare, sometimes at the cost of their own lives. Shang Yang in "Six Lice," and Han Fei as well in "Five Vermin," blamed those who pursued private but not public happiness. Han, applying the Chinese character *si*, "private," created by Chang Jie, interpreted it as the opposite of *gong*, "public": giving up the selfish habit of embracing oneself. In his essay "Prominent Learning," Han attempted to prevent the king from patronizing useless worthies (scholars and cavaliers) while despising useful soldiers who beheaded their enemies in battle. "Useful," to Han Fei, meant merely industrious in farming, weaving, and killing antagonists. "Sages" devoted themselves to law instead of virtue. "Enlightened rulers" allotted little time to extol the ancients. To counsel rulers, the legalists lauded only those measures that would bring order today. To Han, it was unnecessary for an emperor to win the people's hearts, since people were mostly childish and unreliable. Otherwise, good government would need no one like Yi Yin or Guan Zhong. It was not overly stern for a king to press farmers to till more land.

Han discerned that stupid rulers accepted both Confucian piety and extravagance (mainly in funerals) and Mohist impiety and frugality, just as they honored both the broad-minded, forgiving Song Yong and the upright but violent Confucian Qidiao. The existence of contradictory schools of thought worried Han Fei, who felt that it implied a lack of stable policies for gentlemen to follow. Radical legalists prohibit heterodoxies. This objection of Han to multicultural contention among the "hundred philosophers" denigrated civilian wisdom and obstructed the development of Chinese thought.

In his political philosophy, Han synthesized three themes: Shen Dao's stress on power or prestige, Shen Buhai's emphasis on statecraft, and Shang Yang's reliance on law. Han's essay "Discourse on Power" gave too much importance to the necessity of political status, overlooking the spiritual cultivation that might induce a people to overthrow tyranny, as Tang of Shang rebelled against Jie of Xia. Probably influenced by Zhuangzi's chapter "Abdicating Thrones," Han wrote that Tang had abdicated his throne to Wu Guang hypocritically, for fear of incurring an accusation of avarice, and Emperor Wu of Zhou did the same with regard to Boyi and Suqi. Han's ideal was that sages would establish global order by exerting power; by contrast, villains who exerted power caused global disorder. Although Han believed in destiny, he counseled the king to enjoy life and even mysticism after mastering two "handles"—chastisement and commendation. A "motivationalist" would forgive transgressors if they were moved by goodwill; a "consequentialist" would forgive transgressors who achieve desirable results. Not so Han Fei. Han applauded the marquis of Han for executing the keeper of his crown, who had put clothes on the sleeping marquis when the weather suddenly turned cold (the marquis also punished his wardrobe keeper). When ministers and officials do not exceed their authority or go beyond the bounds of their posts, they can concentrate on their own duties, and the whole will state benefit from their leadership.

Whereas the Daoists described worthies, Han identified eight treacheries that a ruler needed to guard himself against: (1) wives or lovers; (2) staff members who were close to the ruler's person, such as dwarfs; (3) father and brothers; (4) ministers who built grand palaces and adorned their children or pets to please the king ("rearing disaster"); (5) people whose loyalty to the king could be subverted by a minister's generosity; (6) sophists who prostituted their private, subtle words for the sake of feudal lords; (7) ministers who enlisted swordsmen and fugitives to expand their power; and (8) ministers who increased taxes, spent national wealth, and weakened their state to serve a larger nation. Han's "Eight Treacheries" ends with promoting the capable and awarding the meritorious. Succeeding Confucius's rectification of names, Han's statecraft included a correspondence between titles and salaries on the one hand and ability and merit on the other. Regrettably, Han's model emperor attracted and trained ministers who were foolishly loyal and incapable of admonition. Liberalists might attack authoritarian governments; but for Han Fei, the emperor must be the unique legislator, in absolute control of his court.

Besides Confucian critics like Xiong Shili and his disciple Xu Fuguan, Fang Yizhi in the late Ming and early Qing denounced Han Fei as a tragic example of a thinker who had condemned and undervalued humanity and righteousness in order to flatter the first emperor of Qin—and had then evoked the fatal jealousy of Li Si, the first unifier of Chinese regulations.

See also Laozi; Legalism; Shang Yang; Shen Buhai; Shen Dao; Xunzi; Zhuangzi.

Bibliography

Chen, Qitian. *Zhengding Han Feizi jiaoshi* (Revised Collations and Interpretations of Han Feizi). Taipei: Commercial Press, 1969.

Chen, Qiyou. *Han Feizi jishi* (Collected Commentaries on Han Fei Tzu). Beijing: Zhonghua, 1958; Taipei: Shijie, 1963; Shanghai: Renmin, 1974.

Chen, Qiyou, and Zhang, Jue. *Han Feizi daodu* (Guided Readings in *Han Feizi*). Chendu: Bashu, 1990.

Feng, Qi. *Zhongguo gudai zhexue de luoji fazhan* (The Logical Development of Ancient Chinese Philosophy). Shanghai: Jen-min, 1983.

Fong, Ssu-yi. *Han-fei-tzu ssu-hsiang san-lün* (Brief Articles on the Thoughts of Han Fei Tzu). Taipei: Commercial Press, 1975.

Hall, David, and Roger Ames. *Self, Truth, and Transcendence in China and Western Culture*. Albany: State University of New York Press, 1998.

Liao, W. K. *The Complete Works of Han Fei Tzu: A Classic of Chinese Political Science*. London: Arthur Probsthain, 1959.

Liu, Ruizhong. *Han Feizi zhengzhi sixiang xintan* (New Inquiries in the Political Thoughts of Han Feizi). Taipei: Author, 1989.

Liu, Wenying, and Xu Xiaojin. *Han Fei pingjuan* (A Critical Biography of Han Fei). Xi'an: Shenxi renmin, 1976.

Shao, Zenghun. *Han Feizi xinzhu xinyi* (Modern Commentaries and Translations of Han Fei Tzu). Taipei: Commercial Press, 1982.

Sun, Shiming. *Han Fei sixiang xintan* (New Inquiries in Han Fei's Thought). Wuhan: Hubei renmin, 1990.

Wang, Dezhao. "Machiavelli yu Han Fei zhi yitong" (Similarities and Differences between Machiavelli and Han Fei). *New Asia College Academic Annals*, No. 9, 1967.

Wang, Zhanyuan. *Han Fei yu Machiavelli bijiao yanjiu* (Comparative Studies of Machiavelli and Han Fei). Taipei: Yushi Monthly, 1972.

Watson, Burton. *Basic Writings of Mo Tzu, Hsün Tzu, and Han Fei Tzu*. New York and London: Columbia University, 1961.

Wei, Zhengtong. *Xian Qin qi da zhexue jia* (Seven Great Pre-Qin Philosophers). Taipei: Mu-tong, 1979.

Wong, Yuk. "Legalism from Kuan Chung to Shang Yang." *Chinese Culture* (Taipei), 40(2), June 1999.

———. *Zhongxi zhexue lunwen ji* (Collected Papers in Chinese and Western Philosophy). Taipei: Buffalo, 1995.

Xiong, Shili. *Haniizi pinglun* (Criticisms on Han Feizi). Taipei: Xuesheng, 1978.

Xu, Hanchang. *Han Fei de faxue yu wenxue* (Jurisprudence and Literature of Han Fei).

Yan, Lingfeng. *Wuqiubei za Han Feizi jicheng* (Collected Works Concerning Han Fei Tzu in the Study Entitled "No Demand of Readiness"). Taipei: Cheng-wen, 1980.

Zhang, Jun, and Wang Xiaobo. *Han-fei sixiang duo lishi yanjiu* (Historical Studies of Han Fei's Thought). Beijing: Zhonghua, 1986.

Zhang, Suzhen. *Guojia de jixu: Han Feizi* (National Orderliness: Han Fei Tzu). Taipei: Shibao, 1981.

———. *Han Feizi nanpian yanjiu* (A Study of the Four Chapters "Refutations" in Han Feizi). Taipei: Xuesheng, 1987.

———. *Han Feizi pingjuan* (A Critical Biography of Han Fei). Nanjing: Nanjing University Press. (Forthcoming.)

———. *Han Feizi sixiang tixi* (The Thought System of Han Fei Tzu). Taipei: Liming, 1974.

Zheng, Liangshu. *Han Feizi zhi zhu shu ji ssu-hsiang* (Works and Thoughts of Han Fei Tzu). Taipei: Xuesheng, 1993.

Zhou, Zhongling. *Han Feizi duo luoji* (The Logic of Han Feizi). Peking: Renmin, 1958.

Zhou, Xunchu. *Han Feizi zaji* (Notes on Han Fei Tzu). Nanjing: Jiangsu renmin, 1958.

Zhu, Shouliang. *Han Feizi shiping* (Explanations and Comments on Han Feizi). Taipei: Wunan, 1992.

Han Yu (Han Yü)

Jo-shui CHEN

It is often hard to decide whether a premodern Chinese thinker can be properly called a "philosopher." With Han Yu (Han Yü, 768–824) the case is clear-cut: few modern scholars would consider him a philosopher, because he consistently neglected to support his ideas with systematic arguments. Nevertheless, it is also hard to think of another "nonphilosopher" whose impact on the history of Chinese philosophy was as great as Han's.

Han was born into an old but second-rate aristocratic clan in what is now central Henan. By the time of his birth, his family had been settled for some time in Heyang, on the northern bank of the Yellow River just across from Luoyang, about 150 kilometers from the place where the Han clan had originated. Han Yu had a difficult childhood. Both his parents died before he was two, and he was raised by his eldest brother Hui and Hui's wife (née Zheng). In 777, when Han Yu was nine years old, his brother Hui was exiled to Shaozhou, in modern northern Guangdong. Yu went with him. Around 780, his brother died too, and his sister-in-law took him back to the north. Two years later, internal warfare in the north forced her to bring her family to the south again. This time, they went to Xuancheng, in today's southern Anhui. Yu stayed there until 786, when he went to Chang'an to prepare for the *jinshi* examination. Regarding Han's family background, one matter deserves special mention. Two members of the family—his uncle Yunching and his brother Hui—took part in the burgeoning trend of *guwen* (ancient prose). This background probably contributed to Han Yu's lifelong devotion to the goals of the *guwen* movement: the reform of prose style and the promotion of the Confucian *dao*.

Han received the *jinshi* degree, after three attempts, in 792. Afterward, he failed three times to pass the prestigious *boxue hongci* examination, given by the ministry of personnel, which would take a successful candidate directly to the position of a ranked official. As a result, Han started his official career as a staff member for several regional military governors. Han was appointed an instructor in the imperial university in 802, becoming a courtier for the first time. From then until 819, he served mainly in the central government, stationed either in Luoyang or in Chang'an, except for a period of more than two years that he spent in exile, for mysterious reasons. In early 819, Han presented a memorandum to Emperor Xianzong, in which he severely criticized the emperor's conduct in greeting a relic said to be a fingerbone of Buddha. This was to become one of the best-known anti-Buddhist documents in Chinese history, and it greatly incensed Xianzong. As a result, Han was banished to Chaozhou in modern Guangdong. After he had served in another local position, the court recalled him in 820, and he was appointed chancellor of the imperial university. Thereafter, his career took an upward turn. Before his death in 824, he served as minister of war (twice), minister of personnel (twice), and governor of Chang'an.

For most of his life, whether his career was prospering or being frustrated, Han remained a central figure of his time. From the late 790s on, he was an eminent leader of the literary community and the greatest champion of a Confucian revival. In his last years, he became increasingly active in politics. Han's creative achievements parallel his intellectual activism. He was a great writer—an innovative poet and essayist. Indeed, he is one of the pivotal figures in Chinese cultural history.

Han's most important contribution as a thinker is his idea that Confucianism was the sole legitimate teaching for human conduct, to the exclusion of Buddhism and Daoism. This was an extreme position in his own time, but it exerted profound influence throughout later Chinese history. Han presented this view most comprehensively and forcefully in his famous essay "Essentials of the Moral Way" (*Yuan dao*).

In this essay, Han asserts that the only *dao* is the one based on everyday life, which is the Confucian way (or Way), discovered and developed by ancient sage kings. What are the teachings of these sages? Han declares:

> To love universally, which is called humanity; to apply this in the proper manner, which is called righteousness; to act according to these, which is called the Way; to [follow the Way and] become self-sufficient without seeking anything outside, which is called virtue. The *Book of Poetry*, the *Book of History*, the *Book of Changes*, and the *Spring and Autumn Annals* are their writings; rites and music, punishments and government, their methods. Their people were the four classes of scholar-officials, farmers, artisans, and merchants; their relationships were those of sovereign and subject, father and son, teacher and friend, guest and host, elder and younger brother, and husband and wife. Their clothing was hemp and silk; their dwellings halls and houses; their food grain and rice, fruit and vegetables, fish and meat.

One crucial point in this statement is Han's emphasis on the self-sufficiency of the Confucian way; this signifies that neither Buddhism nor Daoism had a claim to the *dao*. Moreover, by going as far as to describe the food the people of the sage kings ate, he dramatically highlights the "secular" nature of the Confucian way.

In his essay, Han not only rejects all moral or religious teachings attempting to find the meaning of life outside or beyond the social order prescribed by Confucian sages but also makes the claim that Confucianism values spiritual life as well. However, the Confucian mode of self-cultivation is intrinsically linked to mundane life; spiritual purification should be a basis for bettering, not transcending, the world. Hence, Han says:

> When the ancients spoke of rectifying the heart and being sincere in their thoughts, they had in mind the purpose of getting something done. But now people [he is referring to Daoists and Buddhists] seek to govern their hearts by escaping from the world, the state and the family. They violate the heavenly law.

In short, Han completely denied the legitimacy of all otherworldly pursuits, and thus the goals of Buddhism and Daoism. He granted man's need for spirituality but insisted that a rightful kind of inner life must be an integral part of a worldly existence regulated by Confucian ethics.

It is evident that the chief target of Han's cultural criticism was Buddhism. He is both famous and notorious for this. He held that Buddhism was a barbarian teaching and even claimed that, historically, Buddhist beliefs had shortened the lives of imperial rulers. However, much of Han's reasoning had nothing to do with Buddhist doctrine itself: he maintained that donations to Buddhist activities deprived society of its economic resources and that Buddhist monks and nuns—who consumed but did not produce—deprived society of its human resources.

These were all familiar attacks, which had been leveled against Buddhism before Han's time. Yet this is not to say that, except for its remarkably poignant style and intense passion, his critique of Buddhism was a repetition of long-standing bigotry and utilitarian reasoning. Han expressed a more general view: that Buddhism was wrong in trying to seek what it considered an emancipation from suffering by abandoning the very foundation, both material and ethical, of human existence. This point may have been implied in the conventional criticism of Buddhism as violating men's fundamental obligations as members of a family and subjects of a sovereign, but Han was nearly unique in medieval China in making it explicit and vocal.

Although Han is better known for his hostility toward Buddhism, the true significance of his thought is clearer in his criticism of Daoism, both philosophical and religious. Han categorically disagreed with the primitivist, anticivilization attitude of the *Laozi* and the *Zhuangzi*. He held that ancient sage kings did nothing but good in constructing what we now call the Confucian order: they saved humankind from chaos and savagery. The Daoists' calls for a return to an innocent primeval age were absurd. Han also accused religious Daoists, who sought seclusion in life and immortality afterward, of abandoning their inviolable duties as members of the human community. His renowned poem "Xie Ziran"—the name of a poor girl who was said to have become an immortal—vividly illustrates this idea.

Had Han been opposed only to Buddhism, he would have been just one of many anti-Buddhist figures in medieval China, albeit one who left some memorable expressions of his critique. But he was against Buddhism, religious Daoism, and philosophical Daoism alike, on the basis of his conviction that human society in toto must be built on Confucian principles. Han was challenging the view, predominant in China's intellectual world since the rise of the *xuanxue* ("dark learning") philosophy in the early third century C.E., that Confucianism had failed to give satisfactory guidance on questions concerning the essence of the world and the spirituality of individuals, and that this gap was to be filled by Daoist philosophy, religious Daoism, or Buddhism. Han may not have been the first person during the Tang to oppose this view, but he was the first to repudiate it articulately and strongly.

Aside from a new intellectual direction, Han offered some concrete ideas that later became highly influential. Two of them—the succession of the way (or Way) and the concept of the teacher—are closely related to the history of Confucian thought.

The "succession of the way" (*daotong*) is not actually a term that Han himself used. But in his "Essentials of the Moral Way" and another essay, Han claimed that the ancient sage king Yao had taught the way to Shun, and then it had passed from "Shun to Yu, Yu to Tang, and Tang to kings Wen and Wu and the Duke of Zhou. These men taught it to Confucius and Confucius to Mencius, but when Mencius died, it was no longer handed down." One important implication of this statement is that there was an original "way" of the civilized world and it enjoyed an unbroken transmission in ancient times. This way had been lost after Mencius, but Han was trying to resuscitate it. Apparently, this idea was taken directly from the Buddhist notion of the transmission of *dharma* from one patriarch to another, though in Han's depiction some of the carriers of the Confucian way were separated from each other by hundreds of years. The "succession of the way" gave Confucian-minded literati during the Tang-Song transition (c. ninth–eleventh centuries) a strong sense of mission and identity, which no doubt contributed to the ongoing, and growing, Confucian revival.

Another influential project of Han's had to do with the concept of the "teacher" (*shi*). He affirmed that a Confucian must find and follow a teacher, because such a teacher embodied the way. Han both elevated and redefined the status of the teacher. A person who merely gave instruction in textual knowledge, he held, did not deserve the name of teacher. A true teacher gave guidance in the way—the Confucian spirit and Confucian principles. Han's notion of the teacher also originated in Buddhist and Daoist ideas, in this case, the concept of the religious mentor. It eventually had the effect of raising the teacher's status in the Chinese mind to one equal to heaven, earth, the sovereign, and parents.

Han tried also to say something about Confucian spirituality, but this effort was not very successful. He left us with a few works on questions of human nature and self-cultivation. They contain mostly fragmentary ideas, and they failed to attract the imagination of later thinkers. It was said that Han wrote a commentary on Confucius's *Analects*, which may have included some discussion of issues concerning self-cultivation. Fragments of this exegesis seem to have survived in *LunYu bijie* (*Random Notes on the Analects*), a book attributed to Han Yu and Li Ao (c. 774–836), but the authorship of this text as a whole remains very doubtful.

In sum, Han is an original and influential thinker who challenged a fundamental intellectual premise of medieval China. His ideas were untypical during the middle and late Tang, but they opened up a path for the formation of the "learning of principle" (*lixue*), or neo-Confucian philosophy. His main contribution lies not in a working out of specific theories but rather in a changed worldview.

See also Confucianism: Qing; Confucianism: Tradition.

Bibliography

Chen, Yinke. "Lun Han Yü." *Lishi yanjiu*, 2, 1954, pp. 105–114.
Chien Jibo. *Han Yu zhi*. Taipei: Heluo tushu chubanshe, 1975. (Reprint of rev. ed., 1957.)
de Bary, William Theodore, Wing-tsit Chan, and Burton Watson, eds. *Sources of Chinese Tradition*, Vol. 1. New York: Columbia University Press, 1960, pp. 371–382.
Hartman, Charles. *Han Yü and the T'ang Search for Unity*. Princeton, N.J.: Princeton University Press, 1986.
Liu, Guoying. *Han Yu pingzhuan*. Beijing: Beijing shifan xueyuan chubanshe, 1991.
Luo, Liantian. *Han Yu yanjiu*. Taipei: Xuesheng shuju, 1977.
McMullen, David. "Han Yu: An Alternative Picture." *Harvard Journal of Asiatic Studies*, 49(2), December 1989, pp. 603–657.
Owen, Stephen. *The Poetry of Meng Chiao and Han Yu*. New Haven, Conn.: Yale University Press, 1975.
Pulleyblank, Edwin G. "Neo-Confucianism and Neo-Legalism in T'ang Intellectual Life, 755–805." In *The Confucian Persuasion*, ed. Arthur F. Wright. Stanford, Calif.: Stanford University Press, 1960, pp. 77–144.
Qian, Mu. "Zalun Tangdai guwen yundong." *Xinya xuebao*, 3, 1957, pp. 123–168.
South, Margaret T. "Han Yu: Guide, Philosopher, and Friend." *Journal of the Oriental Society* of Australia, 5(1, 2), December 1967, pp. 158–175.
Zach, Erwin von, trans. *Han Yü's poetische Werke*. Harvard-Yenching Institute Studies, No. 7. Cambridge, Mass.: Harvard University Press, 1952.

The *Heguanzi* (*Ho Kuan Tzu*) Treatise

Carine Defoort

The *Heguanzi* is a treatise of nineteen chapters—seven dialogue chapters and twelve essay chapters—attributed to the otherwise unknown "Pheasant Cap Master." Although the treatise has long been rejected as a forgery, the general agreement is now that the core of the *Heguanzi* was probably written in the southern state of Chu during the late third century B.C.E., shortly before the establishment of the Han empire in 206 B.C.E.

Since the beginning of the twentieth century, treatises attributed to masters (*zi*) or entered under this category in traditional bibliographies have generally been labeled "philosophy" (*zhexue*), in an attempt to bring into agreement ancient Chinese and western bibliographical or intellectual categories. In the case of the *Heguanzi* one could certainly question the appropriateness of this label, without, however, thereby rejecting its philosophical significance. Aside from a challenging confrontation with one's own concept of "philosophy" involved in this very question, the *Heguanzi*'s relevance to Chinese thought can be approached from two different angles: as a treatise within the Chinese category "masters," subcategory "Daoism" (*daojia*), or as an object of contemporary (western) philosophical interest.

Heguanzi as a Daoist Master

The *Heguanzi* was first recorded in the bibliographical treatise of the *History of the Han Dynasty* under the category "masters," which the imperial librarian described as consisting of political advice for rulers of the turbulent Warring States period (453–221 B.C.E). The crucial question for these authors was to find, not the "truth" as such, but the "way" (*dao*) toward stability and order in the state as well as in "all under heaven." The imperial librarian considered the strength of the Daoist treatises to be their passive and yet effective approach to political matters. The *Heguanzi* suits these minimal characterizations well. Its content is mainly political, expressing a deep concern with order, stability, and unification beyond the borders of the central states of China. The ideal is of one family joining Chinese and barbarian people, and presided over by a loving though stern paternalistic ruler. As a loving parent, he protects the people from harm and respects their feelings and wishes; as a stern paterfamilias, he promulgates objective laws and judges all according to the same standards.

The political context is so dominant in the *Heguanzi* that many other fields of knowledge, such as ethics, depend heavily on it. Most of the virtues promoted in the *Heguanzi* are traditionally associated with the Confucian heritage: humaneness (*ren*), rightness (*yi*), propriety (*li*), reliability (*xin*), integrity (*cheng*), loyalty (*zhong*), insight (*zhi*), incorruptibility (*lian*), bravery (*yong*), and so forth. The author discusses them in the context of personnel administration, which he considers a key to political success. He therefore provides the reader—ideally the ruler of his home state—with advice concerning the division of governmental functions, the criteria for selecting officials, and the evaluation of these officials' performance. Two more general virtues often stressed in the *Heguanzi* are worthiness (*xian*) and capability (*neng*), reflecting the meritocratic tendencies of the late Zhou dynasty. The ruler's reliance on worthy and capable assistants instead of family members or powerful nobility demands a specific virtue, in the *Heguanzi* mainly reserved for the "one man" (*yiren* [*yi ren*]): to be unbiased or public-minded (*gong*) instead of biased or family-minded (*si*). This attitude makes the ruler clearheaded and insightful (*ming*) concerning the presence of talented men within and beyond the borders of his realm. In order to attract such assistants, the ruler needs a second virtue: loving care and respect. The author once even explicitly states that the lord does not necessarily need to be worthy, if only he is able to take advice respectfully from scholars (*shi*) or gentlemen (*junzi*) who are in the possession of the crucial political skills (ch. 11). The virtue of sagacity (*sheng*), finally, is preserved either for ideal rulers from the past—before the installation of hereditary rule—or for the ruler's main assistant: the sage.

None of the virtues promoted in the *Heguanzi* is attributed to or demanded from all men alike, as one would expect in a general theory of moral philosophy. The virtues constitute practical suggestions and concrete insights in the domain of governmental and administrative matters.

What counts for the author's approach to ethics also holds for other branches of philosophy, such as theories of language, psychology, and views on nature. For instance, the concern for language (*ming*) in *Heguanzi* does not share the neo-Mohist disinterested pursuit of its functions but always relates to the performative power and political use of words: orders, titles, job descriptions, and promises in diplomacy.

In a similar manner, the author's views on the human disposition bypass the once heated discussion on "human nature" (*ren xing*) concerning whether it is good or bad, variable or unchanging. Whenever man's inherent disposition is brought up, it is in terms of personnel management, political use, or manipulation, depending on the context. At worst, man—as a member of the masses—is described as naturally attracted by profit and deterred by punishments; at best, as a potential sage, man is a source of political and even cosmic order. The power that the "Pheasant Cap Master" attributes to this person is exceptional in the corpus of pre-Han texts, to the extent that the sage is said to generate the way (*dao*) and its standards (*fa*): "The sage generates the way; the way generates standards" (ch. 14).

As one can expect from a treatise categorized in the Daoist section, the *Heguanzi* exhibits a predominant concern with nature and its mysterious source. But this interest also has deep political significance. The reliability of the sequence of seasons, the order of the stellar movements, and—most important—the uniquely powerful position of the central axis all make heaven (*tian*) a model par excellence for the ruler. The "one man" is often identified with *tian* and particularly with its pole or *tai yi* ("supreme one"). While the central position is vacuous, the circumpolar field abounds with orderly motions. Using this image, Heguanzi argues that the ruler should not be knowledgeable about any concrete governmental affair (*zhishi* [*zhi shi*]) but should only find the right men (*zhiren* [*zhi ren*]) to handle it successfully. The nonactivity of the "one man" at the center allows others to lay out the most efficient tracks or "ways" to proceed. "The vacuous is what is meant by 'one'; nothing being incomplete is what is meant by 'way'" (ch. 5). The ultimate importance of the "one," often in contrast with the way, is a remarkable feature of the *Heguanzi*.

The energetic stuff (*qi*) that fills the universe is most tenuous at the amorphous or vacuous center. This is where reality begins to take shape, ideally according to the ruler's plans. To shape reality and respond effectively to changes, one needs to see through the situation, undertake as little action as possible, and handle problems even before they have visibly taken shape. According to the author, contemporary rulers need an assistant to fulfill this task: the sage, who "proceeds by night" (ch. 3). While ordinary men do not notice or acknowledge his healing influence, they all walk in his tracks and thus follow his "way." Through this line of argument, even the mystical passages in the *He-*

guanzi, strongly reminiscent of the *Laozi*, amount to practical politics.

In a similar vein, war is depicted as ideally a matter of perspicacity and psychological insight. On the battlefield, the general imitates the heavenly pole and, as the unique source of military orders, presides over the army. Aside from personnel administration, military proficiency—an exercise in appropriateness and subtlety—is the most important aspect of political action in the *Heguanzi*. Five chapters of the extant treatise are predominantly military (chs. 7, 12, 14, 17, and 19), and there are occasional remarks concerning warfare in the other chapters. It is therefore not surprising that the *Heguanzi* derives its name from a military context. The snow pheasant (*he*) was a symbol of courage and martial valor because it would fight its opponent until death. A cap (*guan*) was decorated with two of its feathers to distinguish military officers: first in the state of Zhao, and from the Qin dynasty (221–209 B.C.E.) onward throughout the whole empire.

This wide variety of topics and approaches—Confucian values, legalist policies, Daoist attitudes, militarist concerns—has sometimes cast doubt on the authenticity of the *Heguanzi*. A recent reevaluation of the typical syncretist tendencies during the late Zhou and early Han dynasties has, to a certain extent, dispelled these doubts. Many scholars have characterized the syncretism of the *Heguanzi* as "Huang-Lao," a hitherto vague and much debated intellectual category. In this combination, Lao stands for Laozi, said to be the founder of the Daoist lineage, and Huang stands for the "Yellow Emperor" (Huang Di), a symbol of warfare, centralized bureaucracy, and rulership. Thus the term refers to a down-to-earth Daoism fashionable during the third and second centuries B.C.E.

The *Heguanzi* as an Object of Philosophical Interest

An alternative approach to the *Heguanzi*, distinguished from discussions within the frame of the Chinese "masters," is to read it with particular (western) philosophical questions in mind. Although the treatise has long been neglected by scholars of Chinese philosophy, there is one debate in which it has attracted particular attention: the question whether Chinese masters thought of order in terms of "laws of nature." Joseph Needham was the first to call attention to the *Heguanzi* in this respect. He claimed that the ancient Chinese never thought in terms of such laws, because their tradition had no idea of a body of laws laid down by a transcendent God, but he nevertheless suggested that the *Heguanzi* might contain counterexamples (1956, 547). According to the *Heguanzi*, heaven and the "one" are undeniably important models for the ruler to follow in political action such as warfare, personnel administration, and legislation. But the question remains whether *fa* (standard, model, law)—or any other character, for that matter—can justifiably be translated as "law," either in the positive scientific sense, as in "laws of nature," or in the political and juridical sense, as in "natural law" founded on the impersonal natural order. Because the question involves one's understanding of these terms and their role in western philosophy as much as one's views on the Chinese text, they have triggered ongoing discussions reaching far beyond the limits of the *Heguanzi*. The different positions in this controversy depend on different interpretations of the treatise and, in turn, determine one's answer to other philosophical questions, such as the author's views on reality, knowledge, law, and language.

Heguanzi's view of language or "names" (*ming*), for instance, has recently drawn attention, again as a possible counterexample, in the controversy about the ascription of nominalist or realist concepts of language to ancient Chinese authors. One much debated passage in the *Heguanzi* has called into question Angus Graham's claim that the nominalist position is always either assumed or asserted in ancient China (1989, 82). According to Graham, the authors all implicitly or explicitly saw language as depending on users, not as reflecting previously given universals or "ideas," which realists considered more real than actual things. The ambiguous passage in the *Heguanzi* states that "names," through "intentions" and "plans," come from "energetic stuff," which ultimately emerges from the "one" (ch. 5). As with the discussion of transcendent "laws of nature," the controversy amounts to whether or not we understand the "one" as a source of order (including language) in the *Heguanzi*: either as an unnegotiable and natural given or as a unique ruling force that determines reality by naming it. The reticence of the *Heguanzi* in this regard—it does not clearly defend or reject familiar philosophical positions in these debates—does not necessarily raise doubts about its philosophical viability, but constitutes a challenge for reflection, on the treatise as well as our approach to it.

The *Heguanzi* has received little or no attention in western philosophy. This is partly because western philosophers tend to consider the Chinese masters too fragmented, rhetorical, and mundane to count as genuine "philosophy." Even within Chinese philosophy, the *Heguanzi* has long been neglected because of its questionable authenticity, its textual complexities, and its unclear intellectual affiliation. But during the past few decades the situation has begun to change. A self-reflective movement characteristic of contemporary philosophy, together with a growing interest in so-called

Huang-Lao thought, has created the conditions for an adequate appreciation of the *Heguanzi*, and for research that leads far beyond the limits of this particular treatise.

See also Confucianism: Ethics.

Bibliography

Defoort, Carine. *The Pheasant Cap Master: A Rhetorical Reading*. Albany: State University of New York Press, 1997.

Graham, Angus C. *Disputers of the Tao: Philosophical Argument in Ancient China*. La Salle, Ill.: Open Court, 1989.

———. "A Neglected Pre-Han Philosophical Text: *Ho-kuan-tzu*." *Bulletin of the School of Oriental and African Studies*, 52(3), 1989, pp. 497–532.

Hosokawa, Kazutoshi. "Kakkanshi to Hansho Koro shiso to no kankei to sono igi (The Relation of the *Heguanzi* to Early Han Huang Lao Thought and Its Significance)." *Bungei Ronso*, 14(2), 1979, pp. 1–14.

Needham, Joseph. *Science and Civilization in China*, Vol. 2. Cambridge: Cambridge University Press, 1956.

Neugebauer, Klaus K. *Hoh-kuan tsi: Eine Untersuchung der dialogischen Kapitel (mit Ubersetzung und Annotationen)*. Frankfurt: Peter Lang, 1986.

Ogata, Toru. "Kakkanshi—Fukyu no kokka o genso shita inja no hon (*Heguanzi*—The Book of a Hermit Who Fantasized an Imperishable State)." *Tohoshukyo*, 59, 1982, pp. 43–65.

Peerenboom, Randall, "Heguanzi and Huang lao Thought." *Early China*, 16, 1991, pp. 169–186.

Rand, Christopher, "Chinese Military Thought and Philosophical Taoism." *Monumenta Serica*, 34, 1979–1980, pp. 171–218.

Williams, Bruce. "*Ho-kuan-tzu*: Authenticity, Textual History, and Analysis, Together with an Annotated Translation of Chapters 1 through 4." M.A. thesis, University of California at Berkeley, 1987. (Unpublished.)

Wu, Kuang. *Huang Lao zhi xue tonglun* (General Survey of the Huang-Lao School). Hangzhou: Zhejiang renmin, 1985.

Hu Hong (Hu Hung)

Conrad Schirokauer

Hu Hong (Renzhong, Wufeng xiansheng, 1105–1161) was a first-generation neo-Confucian of the Southern Song. Through his father, Hu Anguo (1074–1138), he received an official rank, but he never served in government, although he did send a memorandum to the emperor urging political reform and the reconquest of the north. His revanchism put him at odds with the government dominated by Qin Gui (1090–1155), but Hu Hong continued to decline office even after Qin's death. He preferred to remain in the remote Mount Heng area of Hunan, where he and his father were associated with several academies; however, Hong did not realize his aspiration to head the Yueluo Academy (Changsha). Later he came to be regarded as the founder of what is known as the Hu-Xiang, i.e., Hunan, school of thought.

Like his father, the author of a very influential commentary on the *Spring and Autumn Annals*, Hu Hong was deeply interested in history, a concern also shared by his brother by adoption and cousin, Hu Yin (1098–1156). All three men are identified with the political, moral, and intellectual teachings of the Cheng brothers (Cheng Hao and Cheng Yi) and were adamant critics of the Northern Song reformer Wang Anshi. Hong and Hu Yin also shared an antagonism toward Buddhism, unusual for their time.

Hu Hong's most extensive work, *The Great Records of Emperors and Kings* (*Huangwang daji*, in eighty chapters), is an account of the world from the primordial differentiation that first set history in motion down to the end of the Zhou dynasty (249 B.C.E.). Confident that he could help set the record right, he explained that classics and histories complement each other like veins and arteries, or like the trunk and limbs. His best-known work, *Understanding Words* (*Zhiyan*, in five chapters)—a compilation of statements, many quite short, on a variety of topics—was more influential than *Great Records* and is of greater philosophical interest. In addition, his *Collected Writings* (*Wenji*) preserves letters, prefaces, records (*ji*), poems, and other material usually found in such compendiums.

Hu Hong had an unusually strong sense of the unity of all things and the universality of cosmic process, which he saw as permeated by the same forces and rhythms:

> Observing the waxing and waning of sun and moon we understand the fluctuations of *yin* and *yang*. Observing the

> fluctuations of *yin* and *yang*, we understand the advancing and withdrawing of the sages.

People occupy an important role in this world. They are the essence of heaven and earth, and they complete heaven and earth. Animals, too, can distinguish forms and sounds, but only humans can combine and distinguish sense perceptions, while it takes a sage to go on to "see shapes and colors and understand the nature of a thing, to hear sounds and penetrate to their meaning, to reach beneath the surface of what he sees and hears and beyond the shape of concrete objects."

Hu Hong is well within his tradition in depicting the sage as attaining an understanding so complete that he will "follow his heart's desire and not transgress what is right"—just as Confucius did at seventy, when, according to Hu, "Heaven became Confucius; Confucius became heaven." Going beyond what Confucius himself had claimed, Hong states that even death is comprehensible: after investigating principles to the utmost, we are able to link them into one. After you understand life, you can understand death.

An emphasis on understanding is also suggested by the very title of Hu Hong's collection *Understanding Words*, derived from Mencius, whom Hu Hong championed. Among the key words used by Hu himself are *dao* (the way or Way), *xing* (nature, human nature), and *xin* (mind-heart—something that can be and was transmitted by sages). All three concepts express his sense of cosmic unity. Living at a time when the loss of the northern heartland suggested that the world had gone awry, Hu was all too aware that crucial processes were not functioning as they should, but this did not diminish his reliance on these concepts as links between humans and the cosmos. (These key concepts are sometimes capitalized in transliteration and translation, though with the exception of "Way," that is not done here.)

The *dao* is essential for human life. Just as fish can live only in water and plants depend on land, humans live in and need the *dao*. The *dao* here comprises the moral rules necessary for human order; as characterized in another statement, *dao* is the general term for substance and function, with "humaneness" (*ren*) as substance and "dutifulness" (*yi*) as function. Hu Hong also discusses the "*dao* of heaven," which has always existed, the *dao* coextensive with time, the *dao* devoid of number or form:

> What is shaped by shape is called things, what is not shaped by shape is called the Way. Things are limited by number and have an end. The Way penetrates the transformations and is infinite.

The Way is not limited as things are, but at the same time the Way and things are as inseparable as wind and motion, or as water and current.

Hu's sense of the unity of humans and the cosmos also pervades his discussion of *xing* and *xin*, central concepts that loom even larger than the *dao* in his own writings as well as in traditional and contemporary discussions of his thought. Hu Hong was not a rigorous systematizer, but in a remarkable passage he subsumed "the nature" and "mind-heart" (hereafter called mind) to the *dao*:

> Heaven and earth are the parents of the sage; the sage is the son of heaven and earth. There are the parents and consequently there is the son; there is the son, and consequently there are the parents. This is why the myriad creatures become manifest and why the Way is named. It is not that the sages are able to name the Way; but there is this Way and consequently there is this name. Designating its substance, the sages called it "nature"; designating its function, they called it "mind." The nature cannot but be active. Active, it is mind. The sages transmitted the mind taught the world by humaneness (*ren*).

Nature and mind link humans directly to the cosmos. Like the *dao*, the nature is inseparable from things. When Hu says, "There is no thing outside the nature, and no nature apart from things," he might as well be talking about the *dao*. Though all things have it, Hu's focus is on people. *Understanding Words* begins by quoting the opening words of *The Doctrine of the Mean* (*Zhong Yong*), "What heaven imparts to humans is called the nature," and continues, "The nature is the great foundation of all under Heaven." Later in the same work Hu indicates that *qi* (breath of life, material force, vital force) flows from the nature just as water endlessly streams from a spring or trees are ever-growing from roots. It is the "root of *qi*."

As the "innermost mystery of heaven and earth and the spiritual forces," the nature is beyond good and evil. Citing his father, Hu maintains that Mencius's assertion that the nature is good was intended not to delimit it but to express admiration. The nature exists on a level where the distinction between good and bad does not apply. Another (though different) glimpse of an entity beyond ordinary notions of right and wrong is provided by a remark that may reflect Hu's study of history:

> There is right and wrong in human affairs, but the mandate of heaven is not restricted to right and wrong. It transcends right and wrong and after that is able to bring peace to the world.

The nature and the mandate are more than good. It takes mind to understand all this, and like the *dao* and the nature "the mind is everywhere." Consistent with the idea that mind is function to the substance that is the nature, Hu holds that it "completes" (*cheng*) the nature. At the same time, however, it rules the operations of the nature. Although the original mind is inherent in all from birth, and although the mind has been transmitted by the sages, the mind*s* of ordinary people are likely to go astray. Even sense perceptions are unreliable—otherwise, why would the garment that feels light in winter feel unbearably heavy in summer? It is wrong for people to rely on their feelings when making moral judgments.

To the question "When someone dies, where is the mind?" Hu answered, "You already know of its death, and yet you ask where it is?" The dialogue continued:

> "What do you mean?" Hong replied, "It is only because it is not dead that you know it. What is the problem?" Again the disciple did not understand. Hu laughed and said, "Your obtuseness is really too much! If you would consider mind not in terms of mind, you would understand it."

The point of this passage is clearer when we distinguish the mind that suffers a hundred ills and dies—the perishable and fallible mind of the individual—from the mind that endures. But this clarity is obtained at the cost of doing violence to Hu's vision of unity.

Like others in his tradition, Hu Hong is nothing if not a moralist, but he was no puritan: "People despise the way of husband and wife because they consider it lascivious desire, but the sages are at ease with it because they take preservation of harmony as its meaning." Human desires are not only legitimate but the same in substance as the moral principles of heaven, from which they differ only in function. Both desires and moral principles are manifestations of the nature, just as billows and waves are manifestations of water.

Hu emphasized and gave much thought to self-cultivation. In contrast to advocates of quiet sitting, Hu advocated perceiving the goodness of the original mind in the midst of action. A disciple asked, "The reason why a person is not humane is that he has lost his original mind. Can the lost mind be used to seek the [true] mind?" Hu answered by citing the king of Qi, who, according to Mencius, could not bear the sight of an ox being led off to slaughter. Once perceived, the original mind must be nourished with the utmost seriousness.

Referring again to the *Doctrine of the Mean*, Hu holds that centrality (*zhong*, "centeredness") is the way of the nature, and *ren* the way of the mind. It is the highest virtue, and, as we have seen, the substance of the *dao*. With the classics as veins and arteries and the histories as trunks and limbs, it is *ren* that makes all live. It is the creative force in the world even as it is the ultimate object of self-cultivation:

> What joins with heaven and earth and penetrates spirits and deities? I say it is humaneness. If a person be humane, he can ride the movement of heaven, control the six energies [*yin*, *yang*, wind, rain, darkness, light], assist in nature's transforming process, produce the myriad things, "form a trinity with heaven and earth," and be a human in the true sense of the word.

Appropriately, this passage occurs in Hu's record of the establishment of a school.

Although Hu was sensitive to the extreme difficulty of attaining humaneness and living according to the *dao*, he did not have much to say on the nature and origin of evil. In this connection it is worth recalling the widespread acceptance of the equation of the natural and the good not only in the Chinese tradition but also in the modern west before John Stuart Mill.

It is important to bear in mind that any summary of the topics Hu discussed almost inevitably focuses on his consistency and may thus present him as unduly systematic. Asked about Wang Tong's giving contradictory answers to two of his disciples, Hu Hong answered, "If you are humane you will understand that Tong's answers were one and the same; if you are not humane, you will consider them different." His scattered and largely undated pronouncements on key concepts were and are open to various interpretations. By the same token, they invite reflection and debate.

Hu's most famous disciple, Zhang Shi (1133–1180), became a close friend of Zhu Xi, who was stimulated by Hu Hong's ideas to develop his own theory of self-cultivation. Zhu Xi then went on to criticize Hu, and Zhu's more comprehensive and systematic philosophy soon overshadowed that of the Hunan thinkers. Between the twelfth and twentieth centuries, only Liu Zongzhou (1578–1645) is considered as thinking along similar lines. However, Hu Hong's pithy sayings and original formulations remained a resource for thinkers seeking alternatives to Zhu Xi, a resource used most notably in our own time by Mou Zongsan (1909–1995) as he sought to reclaim and rechannel Song philosophy.

See also Mou Zongsan; Zhu Xi.

Bibliography

Cai Renhou, *Song-Ming lixue: Nan Song Pian*. Taipei: Student Book Company, 1980.

Hu Hong. *Chi*. Beijing: Zhonghua shuju, 1987.

——. *Huang wang daji*. (SKCS Second Series.)

Levey, Mathew. "The Clan and the Tree: Inconsistent Images of Human Nature in Chu Hsi's Settled Discourse." *Journal of Sung-Yuan Studies*, 24, 1994, pp. 101–144.

Okada, Takahiko. "Ko Go-*hō*." *Tōyōbunka*, 10, 1965, pp. 23–33.

Schirokauer, Conrad. "Chu Hsi and Hu Hung." In *Chu Hsi and Neo-Confucianism*, ed. Wing-tsit Chan. Honolulu: University of Hawaii Press, 1986.

Tillman, Hoyt C. *Confucian Discourse and Chu Hsi's Ascendancy*. Honolulu: University of Hawaii Press, 1992, pp. 29–36.
Takahata, Tsunenobu. *Sōdai Konangaku no kenkyā*. Toyko: Akiyama shoten, 1997.
Wang, Kaifu. *Hu Wufeng de xinxue*. Taipei: Student Book Company, 1978.
Wang, Lixin. *Hu Hong*. Taipei: Dadong tushu gogsi, 1996.
Zhu, Hanmin. *Hu-Xiang xue yü Yue luo Shu yuan*. Beijing: Jiao yu kexue chupanshe, 1991.

Hu Shi (Hu Shih)

Min-chih CHOU

Hu Shi (Hu Shih, 1891–1962), also known by his *zi* or other name as Shizhi, was the most important exponent of John Dewey's pragmatic philosophy and experimental logic and was among the most influential intellectual leaders in China in the first half of the twentieth century.

Hu Shi was born in Jixi, Anhui. He was a precocious child. Recognizing his son's unusual intelligence, his father began classical lessons for him when he was a young boy. When Hu went to Shanghai, he continued the classical education and also began a modern curriculum, studying English, the sciences, and mathematics. Hu left China in 1910 to enroll at Cornell University, as a student first of agriculture and later of philosophy, a subject he pursued further at Columbia University from 1915 to 1917. Hu Shi returned to China in 1917 to teach at Beijing University, with which he was associated for the next three decades. In the late 1930s and 1940s, he was under considerable pressure to enter politics. From 1938 to 1942, he served as China's ambassador to the United States. In 1946 he was elected to the national assembly. He resisted other temptations, turning down opportunities to become a presidential candidate and to serve as prime minister or foreign minister. In the spring of 1949, when the communists' victory in mainland China was imminent, Hu left for the United States, where he stayed until 1958. He returned to Taiwan to become president of the Academia Sinica. He died in February 1962.

Hu left behind voluminous material for researchers. A few of his writings reveal his general views of philosophy. In 1919 he published "Experimentalism," a long essay in Chinese providing an introduction to the philosophies of Charles Peirce, William James, and John Dewey. This essay also gives a statement of his own position. Several other essays in Chinese—"Introducing My Thought," "Chinese Literature of the Past Fifty Years, "World Philosophy of the Past Fifty Years," and "Our Attitude toward Modern Western Civilization"—are representative works. All are collected in *Hu Shi wencun*. His dissertation, "Development of the Logical Method in Ancient China" (1922), and *Zhongguo zhexueshi dagang* (1918, in Chinese) cover the same period of Chinese philosophy, but they are different in approach and content. Hu's Haskell Lectures, delivered at the University of Chicago in 1933 and published as *The Chinese Renaissance*, offer broad views on China's cultural and intellectual heritage. Among his numerous English-language essays, the most notable are the following: "The Literary Revolution in China" (1922), "Buddhist Influence on Chinese Religious Life" (1925), "The Renaissance in China" (1926), "Civilization of the East and West" (1928), "Conflict of Cultures" (1929), "The Establishment of Confucianism as a State Religion during the Han Dynasty" (1929), "Religion and Philosophy in Chinese History" (1931), "The Scientific Spirit and Method in Chinese Philosophy" (1959), "The Chinese Tradition and the Future" (1960), and "Social Changes and Science" (1961). All these pieces are conveniently gathered in *Collection of Hu Shih's English Writings*. Some of these English essays are liberal translations of Hu's Chinese essays, while others offer different perspectives on the same issues.

Assumptions and Concerns

Hu Shi's philosophy was aimed at freeing the mind of China from outmoded traditions and conventions. This required a thorough redirection of the nation's outlook and values. Hu's intellectual maturity coincided with an age of iconoclasm in modern China, and he was deeply influenced by the mood of that age. Even in his youth, the direction of his intellectual development was clear. He showed an obvious affinity for the empirical and agnostic principles of the rational neo-Confucian thinkers Cheng Yi (1033–1108) and Zhu Xi (1130–1200). This background, coupled with his readings of Sima Guang (1019–1086) and others, provided Hu with the first weapon he needed to question the existence of gods and spirits and reject the moral concept of causality. During the six years he spent in Shanghai (1904 to 1910) his secular, pragmatic, and iconoclastic tendencies continued to develop. At that time, western ideas were his main source of inspiration, coming to him from Yan Fu (1853–1921) and Liang Qichao (1873–1929), two of the most influential intellectual leaders in China in the early years of the twentieth century. Hu read Yan's renditions of Huxley's *Evolution and Ethics* and John Stuart Mill's *On Liberty*, and as a result became aware of some major issues in western thought. According to Hu, Liang was an even greater influence, raising his consciousness on many issues and introducing him to the concepts of progress, political participation, activism, liberty, public spirit, and profit.

Shortly after he came to America, Hu embraced the pragmatic, positivistic, scientific traditions of the west. He was particularly receptive to the ideas of John Dewey (1859–1952), Charles Darwin (1809–1882), and Thomas Huxley (1825–1895). He later said that the influence of Huxley and Dewey was indelible. From Huxley, he learned skepticism—doubting everything that cannot be proved with adequate evidence. From Dewey, he learned to think critically, to treat all theories as hypotheses awaiting proof, to keep current issues in mind, and to be conscious of the potential consequences of one's ideas. Huxley and Dewey taught him the nature and function of the scientific method.

Dewey's philosophy, which deals more directly with social and intellectual issues, was even more important for Hu than Huxley's, providing him with a tool of analysis and a direction. During the summer of 1915, he read all of Dewey's writings; and at this time he left Cornell for Columbia, where he would study with Dewey for two years.

Hu chose the term "experimentalism" (rather than "instrumentalism") to suggest the spirit of the philosophy of pragmatism. Experimentalism, Hu said, denotes two qualities, both of which are products of modern science: the "laboratory attitude" and the genetic method. The phrase "laboratory attitude" indicates that in science and philosophy there are no absolutely certain, indubitable truths; what we call scientific laws are merely the most suitable hypotheses at a given moment, and over time they are continually replaced by more refined hypotheses. An inquiry is a self-correcting, unending process; it may be criticized, corrected, or rejected on the basis of subsequent inquiries and experiences.

The genetic method is a philosophical derivation of Darwin's theory of evolution. Much as species evolve as a result of their responses to the environment, so morals and values—all the truths in the human world—are also instruments by means of which humans adjust their responses to the challenge of their environment. As such, morals and values are concrete, not abstract, and are particular to specific situations. It was obvious, then, that Darwin's theory of evolution by natural selection, as manifested in the philosophy of experimentalism, had the potential to emancipate human beings from the bondage of the past.

Hu states his own conviction by quoting Dewey's *Reconstruction in Philosophy*:

> We do not merely have to repeat the past, or wait for accidents to force change upon us. *We use* our past experiences to construct new and better ones in the future. The very fact of experience thus includes the process by which it directs itself in its own betterment.

Hu valued this view as an agent of action rather than passive observer or subject, and as a creator rather than a recorder of individual incidents. Experience becomes an activator, able to predict and connect humans with their future. All meaningful experiences and ideas now have the potential to produce practical and relevant results.

This was a position with which Hu Shi felt very comfortable. Important as Dewey and other western thinkers were in helping him formulate his philosophy, Hu's encounter with them did not so much give him a new philosophy as affirm and reinforce a position he had already formed. Before he came to America in 1910, he had already written a number of essays on the challenges China faced. They unequivocally indicate the rational, practical, and secular strains in his thought. It is not surprising, then, that soon after he came to America, Hu enthusiastically accepted the pragmatic and scientific philosophy of Dewey and Huxley and sought to study with Dewey. Still, even if Dewey's ideas did not give Hu a new philosophy, they did more than merely validate his opinions; they added a new dimension to his outlook and enhanced his ability to articulate his convictions. In other words, Dewey's philosophy gave Hu Shi a theoretical touch and a sophistication he might not otherwise have acquired.

Over the years, Hu turned to a variety of sources other than Dewey to support specific cases and for specific situations, but he never departed from pragmatism. When Hu's prestige was at its height, from the late 1910s to the late 1930s, he played an important role in popularizing and furthering pragmatic, iconoclastic, and scientific approaches in China. His critical, pragmatist views of his nation's past had a profound impact on Chinese social, cultural, and intellectual life and helped shape opinions in the liberal sector of the educated elite.

Evaluation of China's Literary, Historical, and Philosophical Traditions

Hu Shi first established a reputation in January 1917, with his proposals to modernize China's language and literature. Literature, he felt, as an integral part of the human experience, reflects the reality of its age, and how we read it reflects the concerns of our own age. The subjects of literature, along with their mediums of expression—language and genre—change as reality changes. Literature becomes stale and dies when it can no longer express current, relevant themes. Hu was delighted with the imagists' "aim for the real, the natural." The imagists' work was a protest against the artificial in life as well as in poetry. They strove to "use the language of common speech, but to employ always the *exact* word; . . . to create new rhythms, . . . not to copy old rhythms, which merely echo old moods; . . . to allow absolute freedom in the choice of the subject . . .; render particulars exactly and not deal in vague generalities." Hu urged Chinese writers not to use clichés or allusions and not merely to imitate masters of the distant past; instead, they were to write in the colloquial language (though with correct grammar) about subjects reflecting genuine feelings and real concerns.

Hu was keenly aware of the potential of literature as a means for social and intellectual change. He believed that the right kind of literature would help China modernize. Only "living" or colloquial Chinese had the power to convey new ideas, develop fresh themes, and disseminate them among the citizens. If writers stopped using stereotyped expressions and blindly imitating past masters, they would emancipate themselves from the bondage of outdated values, obsolete conventions, and antiquated concepts. He advocated realist literature to depict contemporary Chinese society. He urged authors to write about hard-pressed laborers, the disintegration of the Chinese family, the oppressiveness of arranged marriages, social injustice, and corrupt politics. René Wellek wrote that in realist literature, "didacticism is implied or concealed." A mere depiction of contemporary social reality "implied a lesson of human pity, of social reformism and criticism, and often of rejection and revulsion against society." The realist believes that writers ought to describe society not only as it is but also as it should be. Often, the realist makes no clear distinction between description and prescription, truth and instruction. Similarly, realist literature, in Hu Shi's mind, would be a means of criticizing the past and helping to produce a better society for the future.

Hu Shi was also one of the most important leaders of the modern historical scholarship of his time. He considered all aspects of China's past proper for historical inquiry and advocated that they be studied and interpreted in a "scientific" manner, relying only on sound scholarship. Of course, being scientific does not mean being neutral, and Hu was by no means interested in the kind of history that is entirely factual and devoid of judgment—as advocated, for instance, by the nineteenth-century German historian Leopold von Ranke (1794–1886). Hu wanted historians to cultivate a critical attitude and an independent spirit. They should never be credulous, never simply accept conventional views, never treat long-held historical myths with veneration; rather, they should be skeptical and ready to question and reexamine established interpretations. For Hu the new historical scholarship had a broad scope and included all aspects of human experience; it was modern in its perspective and receptive to different explanations. It should have no preconceived judgment and accept no conclusions without convincing evidence. These views were influential, and Hu was in no small measure responsible for the emergence of modern historical scholarship in China.

Hu Shi's interest in Chinese philosophy was more than academic; he felt that philosophy could act as China's guide in its quest for a new destiny. The "genetic method" enabled Hu to trace Chinese philosophy to its various historical origins. The application of Darwin's thought and social Darwinism (which was not Darwin's thought) is evident: every school of philosophy is a response to concrete challenges, not an exercise of abstract ideas for its own sake. Hu's endeavor was to "find a congenial stock" with which the Chinese might "organically link the thought-systems of modern Europe and America." This link would enable China to build its "own science and philosophy on the new foundation of an internal assimilation of the old and the new." To accomplish this, the Chinese should criticize the "precursory theories and methods" of logic that China had to offer centuries ago, "in the light of the more modern and more complete developments." This in turn would enable the Chinese to "understand wherefore the ancient Chinese antecedents have failed to achieve the great results which their modern counterparts have achieved," to see "wherefore the theories of natural and social evolution in ancient China have failed to accomplish the revolutionary effect which the Darwinian theory has produced on modern thought."

Hu's assessments of the schools of philosophy in ancient China reveal his positions on significant issues. He liked Laozi's idea that nature is neither benevolent nor teleological, but amoral and without designs. This naturalistic view, according to Hu, resembles that of Herbert Spencer. Zhuangzi (third century B.C.E.) carried this a step further by repudiating attempts to prove a "first cause." This was an important point for Hu, because it meant that evolution is entirely natural, without a god or moral purposes. He would evoke this naturalistic view when he stated his agnostic position or challenged the neo-Confucian concept that *li* (reason, principle) is the ultimate moral principle. Hu's assessment of the school of Confucius was positive, but he lamented that Confucius's followers turned his ideas into a set of rigid moralistic and rationalistic doctrines. Hu was fond of the philosophy of Mozi (fifth century B.C.E.), which he said had much in common with utilitarianism and pragmatism. He held neo-Mohism in even higher esteem, saying that it continued the pragmatic tradition of Mozi, had developed an experimental method, and was the only school of Chinese thought to have developed a scientific logic with inductive and deductive methods. Of the schools of philosophy of the Song period (960–1279) and the Ming (1368–1644), Hu preferred the rationalistic, concrete approach of the Cheng-Zhu neo-Confucianism to the idealistic, speculative Lu-Wang neo-Confucianism. Among the thinkers of the Qing period (1644–1911), Hu praised the reasonable and realistic view of human nature held by Dai Zhen (1723–1777), who considered that all natural human feelings, as long as they were properly expressed, were within reason.

The foregoing summary does not include all the issues Hu discussed, but it should provide a glimpse of his major concerns.

Science and Democracy

Hu Shi advocated a new culture for China, to be founded on the complementary principles of science and democracy. Largely as a result of his advocacy, "science" and "democracy" became the most appealing concepts in China in the 1910s and 1920s. Hu understood correctly that the spirit of science lies in its method, and he was attracted to Huxley and Dewey because of their expositions of the scientific method. Huxley identified four important steps in the scientific method: (1) empirical investigation of facts; (2) general propositions based on factual observation, comparison, and classification; (3) deduction from those general propositions; and finally (4) verification. Dewey thought of science as a state of mind, a critical spirit—a pursuit, "not a coming into possession of the immutable." Thus, the experimental method is important in determining the universality of results.

Hu Shi's understanding of the scientific method was in general based on Huxley and Dewey's concept of science. It consists of two steps: "boldness in hypotheses, to be verified by solicitous evidence" (*dadan de jiashe, xiaoxin de qiuzheng*). This statement implies a number of assumptions. For Hu, as for Dewey, the scientific method is above all a state of mind and a critical spirit, characterized by its universality, and applicable to all areas of human activity. However, in one crucial area Hu was unwittingly influenced by the Chinese mode of thinking and departed from Dewey and Huxley. While Dewey and Huxley emphasized the public and objective conditions affecting scientific research and the importance of improving those conditions, Hu stressed personal qualities of the individual—a critical attitude, judgment, and an objective state of mind in the pursuit of the truth—that Chinese thinkers, particularly neo-Confucians, underscored. There is little emphasis in Hu's writing on the public and objective aspects of science. The boldness involved in suggesting hypotheses meant, to him, an objective attitude and a critical spirit, a willingness to discard prejudicial views from the past in favor of new ideas and knowledge. Both Dewey and Hu Shi believed that the scientific method not only can but should be applied to things that improve human life. But here again, there is a significant difference in their thinking. While Dewey emphasized making life better by improving social and economic conditions, Hu focused on the quality of an independent spirit and on tolerance toward those who dissent.

On the basis of what he considered the latest scientific knowledge, Hu arrived at a "naturalistic conception of life and the universe" or "scientific philosophy of life" in 1923. It consisted of ten claims:

1. The universe is infinite in space.
2. It extends infinitely in time.
3. It follows the natural laws of movement and change (there is therefore no need for the concept of a supernatural ruler or creator).
4. The struggle for survival is so brutal that the hypothesis of a benevolent ruler is untenable.
5. Humans are only one species in the animal kingdom and differ from other species only in degree, not in kind.
6. Anthropology, sociology, and the biological sciences allow us to understand the history and evolution of living organisms and human society.
7. All psychological phenomena are causally explainable.

8. Morality and religion are subject to change, the causes of which can be studied scientifically.
9. Matter is full of motion, not static.
10. The individual self is subject to death, but the sum total of individual achievement lives on in the "larger self," which is immortal. The highest religion, therefore, is to strive for the welfare of the larger self; the desire of the individual to go to heaven is selfish.

From Hu Shi's point of view, these were bold hypotheses backed up by solid scientific evidence. We find here the imprint of Dewey's philosophy and, to a lesser extent, Huxley's. Dewey took issue with the old view of the universe as closed, with definite boundaries. Modern science, said Dewey, presents a universe that is infinite in space and time, having no limits. Instead of holding men's minds captive, such a universe is associated "with boundless power, with a capacity for expansion that knows no end, with a delight in progress that has no external limit." Science also imbued Hu Shi with a tremendous sense of optimism and enormous hope for the future. He maintained that infinite space enhances our "aesthetic appreciation of the universe," and infinite time makes us more aware of the hardships our forebears endured for millennia and therefore makes us appreciate efforts to overcome difficulties. Most important, understanding the regularity of movement and change in the universe provides us with the key to our "dominion over nature." The universe, then, offers us an expanded vision and inexhaustible opportunities. Hu welcomed the concept of "agnosticism" in Huxley's sense, as a way of refuting the argument for an omnipotent god—whose existence, Hu argued, would imply an uncaused cause. But Hu was far less interested in the first cause as a philosophical issue than in its practical implications.

Indeed, Hu's "scientific philosophy of life" is founded on his supreme confidence, rather than on sound logic. Scientific statements are value-free and factual. They can and often do help us make daily decisions, but they do not necessarily have the same practical implications for different people in varying circumstances. There is, therefore, no intrinsic or logically necessary relationship between scientific statements and value judgments. Hu, an optimist, found the infinity of the universe exhilarating, whereas a pessimist might find only futility in human efforts in the face of the overwhelming vastness of space and time. A philosophy of life is a personal belief that may or may not be based on any "scientific" facts.

The logical relationship—or nonrelationship—between scientific statements and value judgments escaped Hu completely, but it would not have troubled him anyway. Science gave him such confidence that he deemed anything "unscientific" undesirable. Religion was one of those undesirables. He saw religion at best as a reflection of man's lack of confidence in himself, and at worst as sheer ignorance. In either case, it was an obstacle to progress. For Hu, Chinese history could be seen largely as a struggle between the forces of enlightenment and those of religion. The native Chinese religion and popularized Buddhism were in essence a set of superstitions. The concept of moral retribution, deeply ingrained in their teachings, was philosophically untenable. Culturally, it inculcated an attitude of resignation and abetted indolence, ignorance, and dependency. It is the law of causality, not any principle of retribution, Hu pointed out, that explains the effects of our behavior. The individual should not seek comfort in a supernatural creator but rather should exercise what Dewey called "creative intelligence," which alone determined well-being. Hu maintained that specific moral standards and religious precepts were spatially and temporally qualified and were subject to change as external circumstances changed.

Hu's position was a resounding criticism of the neo-Confucians. The Cheng-Zhu school of neo-Confucianism considered *li* (principle, reason) as a self-evident universal truth and the source of all good. Inherent in *li* was a standard for differentiating right from wrong and an imperative to do good. By cultivating our innate moral quality, we could eliminate our selfish desires and realize the "principle of nature" (*tianli*). The Lu-Wang school of neo-Confucianism, on the other hand, declared that the mind (*xin*) was the principle of the universe and was endowed with an innate knowledge of good and an innate ability to do good (*liangzhi*).

Taking a very different position from either school, Hu interpreted *li* as the rational basis of being, denoting the natural course of evolution of the universe; it was amoral and had no design or purpose. As a young man, Hu had tried to refute the Mencian position that human nature is innately good by following the reasoning of Mencius's contemporary Gaozi. According to Gaozi, human nature, like water, is indifferent to good or bad; it turns to whichever direction it flows. Later in life, Hu took the realistic position that humans have selfish desires and that human behavior is not always dictated by moral principles but rather is often calculation and aimed at personal profit. Thus Hu Shi favored the social Darwinians' tough-minded, agnostic, independent perspective rather than the neo-Confucian view of the virtues as manifestations of the immutable *li*. He considered the introspective, moralistic philosophy of the Lu-Wang school detrimental to the development of an outlook conducive to the demands of a modern age. Cultivation of the right attitude was important to Hu.

Here again we see the influence of a mode of Chinese thinking on Hu, though he does not seem to have been aware of it. Like the neo-Confucians, whose views he opposed, he believed that personal qualities—the right frame of mind and self-discipline—enable the individual to overcome obstacles and create new possibilities. Indeed, Hu's assertions that the struggle for existence is brutal, that man is only one species in the animal kingdom, and that science teaches us the history of evolution carry unmistakable messages. Human beings are different from other animals not by nature but as a result of the creative use of their intelligence. And only by degree, the history of evolution and the brutal nature of our struggle for survival combine to strengthen our will to improve our lot.

From the outset, it was clear that the emancipation of the individual was not Hu's only concern. His scientific credo was meant to benefit the nation and society—the "greater self" or "larger self"—more than the individual, the "small self." When Hu spoke of Darwin's survival of the fittest, he had in mind mainly the survival of the group. An ideal society was composed of citizens strong in resolve, modern in outlook, and independent in judgment, but always with society's interests in mind. In 1920, concerned that some Chinese might become absorbed in a self-indulgent individualistic lifestyle at the expense of societal wellbeing, Hu proposed an outlook based on nonindividualistic values (*feigeren zhuyi de xinshenghuo*). In his later years, he placed greater emphasis on tolerance (*rong ren*) than on freedom.

Herein lies a contradiction that Hu was not able to resolve. He took freedom and democracy to be the most precious human values and the highest achievements of western civilization, concurring with Immanuel Kant's imperative: to treat humanity as an end in itself, not a means. In China, Hu was an ardent champion of civil rights. But in the harsh reality of Chinese society and politics, Hu had difficulty reconciling his abstract belief with concrete situations. The individualism he advocated was a form of protest against outdated values, political oppression, and blind obedience to conventions—a plea for the cultivation of individuality and an independent vision. Hu showed less interest in the central tenet of modern liberalism: that the individual has the right to think and do whatever he chooses without governmental interference.

Dewey believed that science gives birth to the concept of democracy. Modern science asserted that the same laws held everywhere and that there was a "homogeneity of material and process everywhere throughout nature." The result of this discovery was "the substitution of a democracy of individual facts equal in rank over the feudal system of an ordered gradation of general classes of unequal rank." Hu Shi, on the other hand, thought of democracy as a state of mind—an acceptance of divergent ways of thinking and behavior, the confidence that even ordinary citizens have the ability to manage a multitude of affairs, and a sense of self-discipline that entailed never resorting to force to settle disputes. How these qualities of mind came about always intrigued Hu. His intimate knowledge of western culture convinced him that through a combination of factors—education, a liberal atmosphere, and the practice of democracy itself—a democratic lifestyle would emerge naturally. This led him to conclude that even though the Chinese were not fully prepared, China should adopt democracy because it would be invaluable training for the citizens and would foster tolerance and a spirit of independence. Citizens with such an attitude would not only achieve their own emancipation but also respect the dignity and freedom of others and contribute to the collective good of society.

According to Hu Shi, then, the success of democracy and the attainment of freedom depended more on individual self-restraint, a rational state of mind, and a spirit of goodwill toward one's fellow citizens than on the existence of political institutions. This idea, of course, puts an enormous demand on individuals, who can rely only on their own wisdom and efforts. When there are conflicts, should individual freedom be acknowledged as more important than the demands of society or the state? Hu Shi did not provide a clear answer to this question.

See also Liang Qichao; Philosophy in China: Historiography; Reason and Principle.

Bibliography

Chou, Min-chih. *Hu Shih and Intellectual Choice in Modern China*. Ann Arbor: University of Michigan Press, 1984.

Chow, Tse-tsung. *The May Fourth Movement: Intellectual Revolution in Modern China*. Cambridge, Mass.: Harvard University Press, 1960.

Cua, A. S. "Emergence of the History of Chinese Philosophy." *International Philosophical Quarterly*, 40(4), December 2000, pp. 441–464.

———. "Reason and Principle in Chinese Philosophy." In *A Companion to World Philosophies*, ed. Eliot Deutsch and Ron Bontekoe. Oxford: Blackwell, 1997, pp. 201–213.

Eber, Irene. "Hu Shih and Chinese History: The Problem of *Cheng-li kuo-ku*." *Monumenta Serica*, 27, 1968, pp. 169–207.

Geng, Yunzhi, *Hu Shi nianpu*. Chengdu: Sichuan renmin, 1989.

Grieder, Jerome B. *Hu Shih and the Chinese Renaissance: Liberalism in the Chinese Revolution, 1917–1937*. Cambridge, Mass.: Harvard University Press, 1970.

Hu, Shi. "Autobiographical Account at Forty," trans. William A. Wycoff. In *Two Self-Portraits: Liang Ch'i-ch'ao and Hu Shih*, ed. Li Yu-ning. New York: Outer Sky, 1992.

———. *Chinese Renaissance: The Haskell Lectures 1933*. Chicago: University of Chicago Press, 1934.

———. *Collection of Hu Shih's English Writings*, 3 vols., comp. Chou Chih-p'ing. Taipei: Yuanliu, 1995.

———. *Dai Dongyuan de zhexue*. Taipei: Commercial Press, 1967.

———. *Development of the Logical Method in Ancient China*. Shanghai: Oriental, 1922.

———. *Hu Shi liuxue riji*, 4 vols. Taipei: Commercial Press, 1973.

———. *Hu Shi wencun*, 4 vols. Taipei: Far East, 1971.

———. *Hu Shi yigao ji micang shuxin*, 42 vols., ed. Geng Yunzhi. Hofei: Huangshan shushe, 1994.

———. *Hu Shi zaonian wencun*, comp. Zhou Zhiping (Chou Chih-p'ing). Taipei: Yuanliu, 1995.

———. *Sishi zishu*. Taipei: Far East, 1974.

———. *Zhongguo zhexueshi dagang*. Shanghai: Commercial Press, 1919.

———. *Zhongguo zhonggu sixiangshi changbian*. Taipei: Hu Shi Memorial Library, 1971.

Hu, Shi, and T. K. Tong. "Reminiscences of Dr. Hu Shih." In *Two-Self-Portraits: Liang Ch'i-ch'ao and Hu Shih*, ed. Li Yu-ning. New York: Outer Sky, 1992.

Hu, Songping. *Hu Shi xiansheng nianpu changbian chugao*, 10 vols., Taipei: Linking, 1984.

Huang, Jiande, et al. *Xifang zhexue dongjianshi*. Wuhan: Wuhan chubanshe, 1991.

Kwok, D. W. Y. *Scientism in Chinese Thought, 1900–1950*. New Haven, Conn.: Yale University Press, 1965.

Li, Youning, ed. *Hu Shi yu tade pengyou*, 2 vols. New York: Tianwai, 1990–1991.

Lien, Chan. "Chinese Communism versus Pragmatism: The Criticism of Hu Shih's Philosophy." *Journal of Asian Studies*, 27(3), 1968, pp. 551–570.

Lin, Yu-sheng. *The Crisis of Chinese Consciousness: Radical Antitraditionalism in the May Fourth Era*. Madison: University of Wisconsin Press, 1979.

———. "Jindai Zhongxi wenhua jiechu zhi shi de hanyi." In *Zhengzhi zhixu yu duoyuan shehui*. Taipei: Linking, 1990, 75–91.

Schwartz, Benjamin I., ed. *Reflections on the May Fourth Movement: A Symposium*. Cambridge, Mass.: Harvard University Press, 1972.

Yang, Zhende. "Hu Shi kexue fangfakuan lunxi." *Zhongguo wenzhe yanjiusuo jikan*, No. 5, 1994, pp. 1–151.

Yü, Ying-shih. "The Radicalization of China in the Twentieth Century." *Daedalus*, spring 1993, pp. 125–150.

———. *Zhongguo jindai sixiangshi shang de Hu Shi*. Taipei: Linking, 1984.

The *Huainanzi* (*Huai-nan Tzu*) Text

Griet VANKEERBERGHEN

The *Huainanzi* is a text in twenty-one chapters, written by a group of scholars at the court of Liu An, the king of Huainan (r. 164–122 B.C.E.). The text has clear political intent: it was meant to show Liu An's command of knowledge indispensable to a sage king and to demonstrate his worthiness as a ruler. The *Huainanzi* was written at a time when the Han emperors were putting more pressure on the kings, descendants of the founder of the Han, by reducing both the size of the kings' territories and the scope of their authority. The fact that in 139 B.C.E., during a visit to the court, Liu An offered the *Huainanzi* to his cousin, Emperor Wu (r. 141–87 B.C.E.), may be seen as an attempt on Liu An's part to reverse the tide of history and advertise his own suitability as an adviser to the young emperor. Emperor Wu gave Liu An's book a positive reception at first but then grew eager to concentrate all power in his own hands. In 122 B.C.E. a hard-fought legal campaign against Liu An (involving accusations of plotting revolt) ended in the king's death by suicide. The events of 122 B.C.E. involving Liu An are important: they signaled the end of a period in which authorship of a text could entitle one to political power and intellectual authority could be gained independently of the political center. The *Huainanzi* may well be regarded as the last book of its kind.

The *Huainanzi* is a typical product of the early Han dynasty. Just as the fledgling Han dynasty sought to unite under its rule regions that had since long developed separate political, religious, ritual, and artistic traditions, the *Huainanzi* claimed to present in its twenty-one chapters a grand synthesis of all there was to know, insofar as knowledge bore on rulership. The *Huainanzi* was an attempt to come to terms with the enormous intellectual legacy of the Spring and Autumn period (771–403 B.C.E.) and the Warring States period (403–221 B.C.E.). The text is inclusive, intending to absorb within itself as many of these pre-Han traditions as possible. It also seeks to digest all the insights handed down from the past and present them in a compelling new synthesis, meant to serve as a plan for the dynasty. By the time of Liu An's death in 122 B.C.E., however, the open climate so characteristic of the early Han dynasty had changed drastically. Politics of exclusion were now favored, and the *Huainanzi* was left in the imperial archives as an awkward reminder of earlier times.

The attempt in the *Huainanzi* to present a grand synthesis of pre-Han traditions resulted, first, in an unusual breadth of topics covered and, second, in massive borrowing from earlier sources. The text contains treatises on the fundamental characteristics of the *dao* (the way, or Way, ch. 1), on cosmogony (ch. 2), on astronomy and astrology (ch. 3), on geography (ch. 4), on calendrical science (ch. 5), on the resonance between things of the same kind (*ganying*, ch. 6), on physiology and psychology (ch. 7), on history (ch. 8), on rulership proper (ch. 9), on the art of communication (ch. 10), on Chinese and non-Chinese ritual systems (ch. 11), on the military (ch. 15), on the causes of failure and success (ch. 18), on the importance of human effort (ch. 19), and on the interactions between the human world and the cosmos at large (ch. 20). One treatise is an exegesis of passages from the *Laozi* or *Zhuangzi* (ch. 12); two other treatises provide behavioral guidelines for the sage ruler (chs. 13–14); two more are lists of *topoi* useful in persuasion (chs. 16–17). On almost all these topics the *Huainanzi* presents what may be regarded as a mature early Han synthesis. The same can be said for themes and concepts that occur throughout the chapters of the text: the classification of things in the dual scheme of *yin* and *yang*, or according to the five phases (*wuxing*); or the assertion that everything is made of *qi*. The *Huainanzi* also provides innovative discussions of concepts such as *qing* (sensitivity), *quan* (adjusting the scale), *shi* (political purchase), *li* (ritual), and *wuwei* (non-action).

Charles Le Blanc (1986) estimates that one-third of the text derives directly from more than twenty pre-Han works. These works include such texts as the *Laozi* or *Zhuangzi*, the Five Classics (as they were canonized during the Han), the *Mengzi*, the *Lunyu*, and the *Lüshi chunqiu*. The challenge for the modern scholar in working with the *Huainanzi* is to acknowledge its indebtedness to earlier sources while also allowing for its creative adaptation of those sources to its own message. Many scholars, past and present, have tried to come to terms with the bewildering variety of sources on which the text draws by claiming that the *Huainanzi* gives preferential treatment to certain pre-Han texts, specifically the *Laozi* and the *Zhuangzi*. While, together with the *Lüshi chunqiu*, these two texts are indeed referred to most frequently, this by no means proves that the *Huainanzi* can be classified as a Daoist text. Rather than seeking to defend one particular intellectual tradition against another, the *Huainanzi* wanted most of all to present itself as a text that could be put to positive, practical use. This is clearly stated in its postface (ch. 21), which claims that the *Huainanzi* is heir to specific texts of the past; it furthermore shows how the named texts have all been effective in historical crises. The postface also demonstrates the intricate organization of the twenty chapters that precede it and insists that no part can be omitted without harming the integrity of the whole. The *Huainanzi* sees itself as an original creation, and this is also how it should be studied.

The *Huainanzi*'s main purpose was to lay out the methods by which a ruler can perfect his craft, thus becoming a sage ruler. Since the ruler is regarded as the guardian of a delicate cosmological balance, it is important for him to grasp the basic operational principles of nature and the cosmos. Therefore, the text engages in a study of nature and its phenomena not for its own sake, but for the education of the ruler. The *Huainanzi* posits various cosmogonic schemes involving a progression from an undifferentiated void, over the creation of space and time and the separation of heaven and earth, to the multifarious phenomena of the known world; often these incorporate the myth of the cosmic struggle between Gong Gong and Zhuan Xu, which would have caused heaven to tilt to the northwest. The *Huainanzi*'s cosmological model is a square earth topped by a round heaven. The celestial equator is organized around the polestar and subdivided into various celestial fields. Whereas a great deal of observation and intricate calculations went into constructing this model, it also allotted a place to the many celestial deities that were thought to inhabit the sphere of heaven. The *Huainanzi* sees the earth as divided into nine continents. One of these is inhabited and itself divided into nine subcontinents. The known world is one of these subcontinents: it is thought to be surrounded by lands inhabited by strange and monstrous creatures and is encircled by magical mountains (the pillars of heaven) and crisscrossed by mythological rivers. The taxonomy of earth's living creatures—mythological or other—is set up according to schemes of *yin* and *yang*, or in fives. The calendar that makes up Chapter 5 of the *Huainanzi* illustrates how all knowledge is geared toward the ruler: organized around the twelve lunar months, the calendar indicates how the ruler should ritually respond to the astronomical, meteorological, and theological characteristics of each month. A failure to do so properly would upset the balance of the cosmos.

In the perspective of the *Huainanzi*, the ruler should do more than meticulously follow the ritual calendar. He should also effect a thorough inner transformation, a process that is described in various forms throughout the text. It always involves discarding selfish desires, which arise through excessive bondage to things, and connecting with something larger than the self: the *dao* (Way), *yi* (what is right), *shan* (what is good), *xing* (human nature), etc. Humans, like everything else, are thought to be made up of *qi*. *Qi*, which by its very nature is always in motion, is found throughout the universe in various degrees of purity and density. What humans ought to do is to either preserve the finite pool of quintessential (*jing*) *qi* within themselves or transform their earthly, impure *qi* into something more akin to heaven and the gods (*shen*). The heart (*xin*) is often singled out as the organ that has to take charge of this process of physiological and psychological purification. A person who has thus cultivated himself is described, depending on the source from which the *Huainanzi* draws, as a sage (*shengren*), a true man (*zhenren*), or a superior person (*junzi*). Self-cultivation gives a person control not only over his own desires and emotions but also over other humans. Everything a well-cultivated person does is genuine, and this quality of genuineness is perceived by others, who are compelled to put trust in such a person and obey him. The sage is the master of communication from heart to heart. The sage ruler, who is regarded as a bridge between heaven and earth, also exerts a soothing influence on his environment at large, causing the advent of all kinds of auspicious phenomena. This process is thought of mechanistically; no benevolent god has to interfere.

A person with a properly cultivated heart finds inner guidance for all his actions. He contains within himself the standard for right and wrong. One may therefore wonder what attitude the *Huainanzi* takes toward systems of law, ritual, or virtue that put forward rules for action. The *Huainanzi* never simply rejects such systems but always expresses concern lest they become goals in themselves: laws, rituals, and virtues should be honored only insofar as they correspond to the dictates the sage finds within himself. The *Huainanzi* does not seek to abolish laws or political institutions, but it does express concern that such laws or institutions could be abused by those who seek to enhance their own power, refusing to take the well-being of the people to heart. An ideal society, in the *Huainanzi*, is one that allows everyone to develop to the fullest possible degree the particular talents he or she may possess. The *Huainanzi* stresses that the main purpose of ritual is to express emotions; once that emotional basis is no longer present, ritual becomes an empty shell. The *Huainanzi* also shows a remarkable awareness of how rituals have shifted over time and even acknowledges the customs and rituals of the non-Chinese groups living at the edges of the Han empire. Rather than arbitrarily endorsing the ritual system of one particular geographical location or historical era, the text sees all of them as potentially valuable. Similarly, the *Huainanzi* neither rejects nor fully supports the Chinese repertoire of virtues: wary of the possibility that virtues will be observed solely to establish a person's reputation, the text stresses that the sage does not excel in one particular virtue but commands the entire gamut: depending on the circumstances, he is alternately benevolent, righteous, filial, respectful, or courageous. The same point is made when the *Huainanzi* posits the centrality of the concept of *quan* (adjusting the scale): rather than being a blind follower of rules, the sage is someone who understands when rules need to be bent. Whenever the sage ruler decides not to follow a rule, he need not proclaim his intentions in public. The *Huainanzi* recognizes that authoritative action and public discourse do not necessarily coincide.

Since the sage in the *Huainanzi* is one who understands the intricate relationship between all things in the world, he may, therefore, also be expected to fully foresee the implications of his own actions. The sage, in short, should be able to always achieve success and avoid failure. Indeed, at times in the *Huainanzi*, failure or success in particular historical circumstances is taken as an indicator of a person's worth. In other passages, however, the text suggests that certain factors in life are not up to the agent but are decreed for him by fate (*ming*). According to the latter passages, the sage should not seek to achieve success in the world; rather, his efforts at self-cultivation will result in deep inner contentment at being in tune with the Way and make him indifferent to possible failures.

The received text of the *Huainanzi* is believed to be very close to the text that was deposited in the imperial archives during or shortly after Liu An's court visit of 139 B.C.E. Possibly also a second copy of the text, one confiscated when Liu An's kingdom was dismantled in 122 B.C.E., remained in circulation. Several commentaries to the *Huainanzi* were composed during the second and third centuries C.E. The commentaries of Gao You (c. 168–212) and Xu Shen (c. 55–149) are the only ones that have survived; at some point in time they were merged into one. A printed edition from the Northern Song is regarded as ancestral to all editions now known. The Daozang edition of 1445 corrects mistakes in the Northern Song edition on the basis of other, now lost, early editions.

See also Confucianism: Han; Laozi; Mencius; Zhuangzi.

Bibliography

Ames, Roger T. *The Art of Rulership: A Study of Ancient Chinese Political Thought*. Honolulu: University of Hawaii Press, 1983; Albany: State University of New York Press, 1994. (Translation and study of ch. 9.)

Ames, Roger T., and D. C. Lau. *Yuan Dao: Tracing the Dao to Its Source*. New York: Ballantine, 1998.

Chen, Guangzhong. *Huainanzi yizhu*. Changchun: Jilin wenshi, 1990. (Translation of all 21 chapters.)

Kraft, Eva. "Zum Huai-nan-tzu: Einfürung, Übersetzung (Kapitel I und II), und Interpretation," *Monumenta Serica*, 16, 1957, pp. 191–286. (Translation and study of chs. 1 and 2.)

Larre, Claude, Isabelle Robinet, and Elisabeth Rochat de la Vallee. *Les grands traités du Huainan zi*. Paris: Éditions du Cerf, 1993. (Translation of chs. 1, 7, 11, 13, 18.)

Lau, D. C., and Fong Ching Chen, eds. *A Concordance to the Huainanzi*. ICS Series. Hong Kong: Commercial Press, 1992.

Le Blanc, Charles. *Huai-nan Tzu: Philosophical Synthesis in Early Han Thought. The Idea of Resonance (Kan-Ying), with a Translation and Analysis of Chapter Six*. Hong Kong University Press, 1986. (Translation and study of ch. 6.)

Major, John S. *Heaven and Earth in Early Han Thought: Chapters Three, Four, and Five of the Huainanzi*. Albany: State University of New York Press, 1993. (Translation and study of chs. 3, 4, and 5.)

Roth, Harold D. *The Textual History of the Huai-nan Tzu*. Association for Asian Studies Monograph Series. Ann Arbor, Mich.: Association for Asian Studies, 1992.

Vankeerberghen, Griet. *The Huainanzi and Liu An's Claim to Moral Authority*. Albany: State University of New York Press, 2001.

Wallacker, B. *The Huai-nan-tzu, Book Eleven: Behavior, Culture, and the Cosmos*. New Haven, Conn.: American Oriental Society, 1962. (Translation of ch. 11.)

Xiong, Lihui, and Hou Naihui. *Xin yi Huainanzi*. Taipei: Sanmin, 1997. (Translation of all 21 chapters.)

Zhang Shuangdi. *Huainanzi jiaoshi*, 2 vols. Beijing: Beijing daxue, 1997.

Huang Zongxi (Huang Tsung-hsi)

Lynn STRUVE

Huang Zongxi (also known as Huang Lizhou, 1605–1695) was a vastly learned man whose scholarly accomplishments stand out even in a century notable for intellectual giants in China. He left to us broadly informed, incisive writings in almost every field that was of major interest to scholars in his day—history (especially the history of Confucian learning), classicism, governance, (historical) geography, literary appreciation, (mathematical) astronomy, and calendrics. It was indeed unfortunate that his life from young adulthood to middle age coincided with the terrible events and nationwide disruptions that attended the fall of the Ming dynasty and the establishment of the Qing. But it was fortunate, in a backhanded way, that the effect of those troubles on Huang was to steel his dedication to certain modes of thought and inquiry, and to ensure that he would spend his maturity using those modes in extraordinary scholarly productivity, rather than in a bureaucratic career.

The foundation of Huang's outlook on life was the leadership of his father, Huang Zunsu, a prominent Ming official, in the Donglin partisan opposition to the arrogation of imperial power by eunuchs in the early 1620s. That Zongxi thus received early initiation to the trench warfare of reform politics, and that his father was put to death in prison for persistently struggling against the eunuch faction, dictated that he would remain strongly, bitterly concerned about politics for the rest of his life. This concern soon took the form of active participation in the Fushe reform movement, which succeeded the decimated Donglin. Then, with the Manchu-Qing invasion of 1644, Huang wholeheartedly joined the Ming loyalists' struggle in Zhejiang Province and its offshore islands and did not give up overt or covert resistance to the Qing until the middle 1650s. Thereafter Huang evaded recurrent pressure to enter Qing officialdom, and, while his attitude toward the new dynasty seems to have softened with time, he cooperated with the Qing government, through private channels, only in matters concerning the compilation of the standard history of the Ming dynasty. Far from being eremitic after the Qing conquest, however, Huang was repeatedly engaged to lecture at various sites in Zhejiang, was invited to use the libraries of famous bibliophiles, and was consulted personally and through correspondence by other leading intellectuals of his day. He was keenly attentive to relations between politics and academics, especially the competition among different schools of thought from the late Ming for favor with the early Qing court. Most of Huang's major writings can be seen as attempts to dissuade scholars and scholar-officials from accepting as orthodox ideas and interpretations that he had come to reject as a young adult during the Ming, but which he saw gaining ground in his later years under Qing rule.

Another fateful factor in Huang's life course as a scholar was the fact that his father, when facing probable execution, placed Huang's schooling in the hands of a close compatriot in the Donglin movement, the renowned teacher Liu Zongzhou, an outstanding expositor of the school of Confucian thought that in Ming-Qing times was called the "learning of mind" (*xinxue*). Huang Zongxi thus became one of Liu's most devoted disciples, studying with him for almost twenty years, from 1626 until Liu's martyrdom by suicide in 1645. After a decade-long hiatus, during which Huang learned mainly from adversity, in the middle 1650s he began to deepen his understanding of Liu's philosophy through a careful study of his deceased mentor's writings. From 1665 through 1670 Huang produced several works illuminating Liu Zongzhou's life and thought, and he lectured on Liu's teachings for study societies in Ningbo and especially at the Zhengren Academy in Shaoxing, which was established in memory of Liu. Furthermore, in 1676 Huang completed the peerless *Mingru xue'an* (Cases in Ming Confucianism), which give Liu the seat of honor at a veritable banquet of rich Confucian learning from the Ming period.

Huang was somewhat supercilious in claiming to be the only surviving student who truly understood Liu Zongzhou's teachings, and—exemplifying a much-changed generation of intellectuals—he did not replicate Master Liu in his general scholarly profile. This has led some commentators to cast aspersions on Huang's status as Liu's successor in Confucian philosophy. However, careful analysis in recent studies has shown that Huang indeed intimately understood even Liu's most esoteric points and articulated them faithfully. Differences in Huang's teachings are mainly a matter of emphasis; they arose because Huang's identification of the current main challenge to valid Confucian learning differed from Liu's identification in his day. We can see both Huang's fidelity to Liu Zongzhou's philosophy and those significant shifts in emphasis principally in Huang's disagreements with certain of Liu's other surviving pupils, in the *Mengzi shishuo* (My Teacher's Teachings on the Mencius) and in the *Mingru xue'an*.

Among Liu's close disciples had been his son, Liu Shao, who in 1653 initiated collaborative efforts to edit and publish his father's collected works. Huang Zongxi refused to go along with Liu Shao's desire to expurgate passages in which his father had directly disagreed with founding figures of the Cheng-Zhu school. Later, in 1669, Huang declined to write a preface for a synopsis of Liu Zongzhou's teachings prepared by another of Liu's principal disciples, Yun Richu, apparently because Yun obscured the very matter that Huang thought not only distinguished Liu most clearly from Zhu Xi but also made him a crucially reconstructive critic of Wang Shouren (Wang Yangming): the reality of primary will (*yi*) as the cardinal capacity in the heart-mind (*xin*), and the reflective and reflexive functioning of human nature (*xing*). More extensively documented are Huang's objections to the ideas of a scholar who had studied only briefly with Liu, but who wrote a record of Liu's oral teachings (partly from materials previously supplied by one of the master's longtime disciples, who had since died), and who credited Liu with setting him on the path of Confucian moral-ethical learning—Chen Que. To cite just one telling point, in works on the human nature and on the *Daxue* (Greater Learning, or Great Learning), Chen argued that the goodness of inborn human nature is developmental, that it can be known to us and brought to full fruition only through the exercise of our talents and intelligence in learning and in carrying out just, humane acts. Huang Zongxi countered that Chen wrongly gave priority to outward efforts while slighting the effort that must, as a prerequisite to true good action, be applied in realizing the source of goodwill, the always fully good operation of human nature as heart-mind (*xin*). If the source of inner strength in heart-mind and the role of primary will as the self-guide and self-control (*zhuzai*) of heart-mind is not directly apprehended, Huang wrote, then one might as well say that from our bad behavior we know our human nature to be bad.

In the *Mengzi shishuo*, Huang takes advantage of the relative congeniality of the *Mencius* toward the "school of mind" classical interpretation to repeatedly batter Zhu Xi. Zhu is taken to task for splitting the properly unitary principle *li* (principle, pattern) and *qi* (ether, material force), creating a dichotomy between human nature and its *xin* function, and devaluing *qi* and *xin* in ways that led to misconstructions of moral and spiritual effort (*gongfu*). In this work, Huang purported to set forth Liu Zongzhou's teachings based on the *Mencius* because Liu himself, though he wrote treatises on all the other Four Books, had never done so for the *Mencius*, whose interpretation so readily reveals differences between the Cheng-Zhu and Yangming philosophies. Indeed, Liu had never stressed his differences with the Cheng-Zhu school, having been more concerned to correct crucial problems within the Yangming tradition.

In the *Mingru xue'an*, also, can be seen Huang's concern to remove his mentor farther from Cheng-Zhu teachings than Liu Zongzhou had cared to do for himself, as well as a tendency to portray adherents of Cheng-Zhu whom he respected (such as Gao Panlong and Gu Xiancheng) as having really belonged to the Yangming camp. The work as a whole is unique in the long history of Chinese sectarian "genealogies" for its keenly discerning, capacious examination of different points of view among thinkers and its presentation of itself as a resource for readers in making up their own minds on philosophical issues. Nevertheless, it also unmistakably advances Huang's own vision of Ming Confucianism as having lived for and through Yangming learning and having reached its perfection in Liu Zongzhou. Admiration of the *Mingru xue'an*, especially in the twentieth century, has been such that present-day scholars cannot easily envision Ming Confucian thought in other ways.

Huang was moved to adopt a more trenchant attitude toward Cheng-Zhu learning because the healthy revitalization of that tradition, which Liu Zongzhou had seen in his time, had by the 1660s and 1670s turned into aggressive dogmatism. Huang observed that this dogmatism, vehemently inimical to the school of mind, was gaining imperial favor through the influence of such highly placed officials as Xiong Cili and was growing among scholars at large through the influence of such well-known essayists as his erstwhile friend Lü Liuliang. Huang's response was not only to point out, ever more vigorously, flaws in Zhu Xi's ontology, epistemology, and ethics, but also to rescue from obscurity Liu Zongzhou's focus on primary will in the good functioning of *xin*, because he regarded that as the key corrective to problems which had been weakening the Yangming position.

Also broadly evident in Huang Zongxi's writings is a general emphasis on the ontological priority of *qi* as the stuff of all phenomena, and the importance of the most refined activity of *qi*, the *xin* function of the human nature, as the medium in which regularity (*li*, pattern or principle) appears. In this, Huang does not depart from Liu Zongzhou, but he presents with more distinctness than we usually see in Liu (who was more concerned with moral self-cultivation than moral ontology) differences from the Cheng-Zhu tradition, which gives priority to a reified *li* and identifies that with a separate, fixed *xing* (human nature). Huang's tendency to underscore the primacy of *qi* and *xin* is related, of course, to his opposition to the dogmatism of Zhu Xi's followers. But his emphasis on *qi* as the stuff of the universe and his tendency to refer to *xin* in general terms, without probing its finer workings, also evinces the marked outward thrust of Huang's inquisitiveness, compared with the intense interiority of Liu Zongzhou's contemplative style of exerting conscientious effort. Quintessential here are the leading statements in Huang's original preface to the *Mingru xue'an*:

> Only *qi* fills heaven and earth. Its transformations are unfathomable; it cannot but take myriad forms. *Xin* (heart-mind) has no substance-in-itself (*benti*); the extent of its effort (*gongfu*) *is* its fundamental being (*benti*). So, to exhaust [our understanding of] *li* (principle, pattern) is to exhaust the myriad manifestations of *xin*, not the diverse manifestations of myriad things.

Where Liu's effort had been mainly to realize the glow of primary will within, Huang's effort is distinctly to test the resonance of *xin* with the endless permutations of *qi* in the world.

Having given the *qi* of *xin* such a range of inquiry in which to get lost, Huang naturally found essential Liu Zongzhou's teaching about *zhuzai*, the capacity of *xin* for self-control and self-guidance. Liu had used *zhuzai* (reminiscent of Xunzi's concept of *xin*) to reinforce his own concept of the absolutely subjective self-reliance of primary will, independent of ordinary experiences and volition. Huang understood that, but he tended to use the sense of *zhuzai* to advocate having a *zongzhi*, a main idea or aim, in all forms of inquiry. Since a valid *zongzhi* could be developed only by opening one's mind completely, Huang regarded it as the true antithesis of bias, which is born of ignorance and self-interest. In this way Huang adapted a philosophy of ethical autonomy to a need for conceptual and modal control in empirical study.

By practicing what he preached, Huang became noted for his ability to penetrate complex issues with lucidity and to mine mountains of material for gems of insight. In all his major works, his *zongzhi* is clear. For instance, in the *Mingyi daifang lu* (De Bary, trans., *Waiting for the Dawn: A Plan for the Prince*), Huang's most widely read work in the twentieth century, he draws on the best and boldest ideas of the Donglin and Fushe movements of his youth to formulate the most compelling critique of autocratic governance that appeared in the later imperial era—at a time when the Manchu-Qing conquest state was adding yet another tier to the usual Chinese hierarchy of dictatorial political power. In his enormous anthologies of Ming prose literature—the *Ming wen'an*; the *Ming wenhai*; and a distillation from the latter, the *Mingwen shoudu*—as well as in a great deal of literary criticism, Huang promoted the expressive theories characteristic of the late-Ming Gongan school of writing, which can been seen as an extension of Yangming thought into literary activity. This was at a time when archaism, with its emphasis on imitating past models, was regaining dominance. And Huang's very important but little-studied *Yixue xiangshu lun* (On Image and Number in Studies of the Classic of "Changes") offered a devastating critique of various common numerological and associational theories about meanings in the *Yijing* that he felt were not firmly grounded in the text as a document of ancient life and thought, rational mathematics, or empirical knowledge. He attacked with special vigor the abstract numerical and symbolic systems of the Song scholar Shao Yong, which had become part of *Yijing* orthodoxy through the auspices of Zhu Xi. Again, Huang's work was written just as the young Kangxi emperor was being inculcated with Zhu Xi's approach to the *Classic of Changes*.

Although Huang's enterprise to uphold the persuasiveness of Yangming learning ultimately failed in the early Qing period, he succeeded eminently in adapting certain strengths of the school of mind—the immanent monism of *qi*, the emphasis on the power and range of *qi* as *xin*, and faith in the power of *xin* for self-regulation—to the needs of a more pragmatic generation and the interests of an age that valued broad learning and textual-empirical research.

See also Confucianism: Ming; Liu Zongzhou.

Bibliography

Deng, Liguang. *Chen Qianchu yanjiu*. Taipei: Wenjing chubanshe, 1992, ch. 8.

Gu, Qingmei. *Mingdai lixue lunwen ji*. Taipei: Daan chubanshe, 1990. (See especially pp. 299–394.)

Huang, Zongxi. *Huang Zongxi quanji*. 12 vols., ed. Shen Shanhong and Wu Guang. Hangzhou: Zhejiang guji chubanshe, 1985–1994. (Numerous biographical materials of the Qing period are appended to Vol. 12.)

——. *Mingru xue'an* (Cases in Ming Confucianism). Selected translations in *The Records of Ming Scholars,* ed. Julia Ching. Honolulu: University of Hawaii Press, 1987.

——. *Mingyi daifang lu. Waiting for the Dawn: A Plan for the Prince*. Trans. and intro. by William T. de Bary. New York: Columbia University Press, 1993.

Hummel, Arthur W., ed. *Eminent Chinese of the Ch'ing Period*. 2 vols. Washington, D.C.: U.S. Government Printing Office, 1943–1944, Vol. 1, pp. 351–354.

Li, Jixiang. "Qingchu Zhedong Liumen de fenhua ji Liuxue de jieshi quan zhi zheng." In *Dierjie guoji Huaxue yanjiu huiyi lunwen ji*. Taipei: Zhongguo wenhua daxue wenxueyuan, 1992, pp. 703–728.

Liu, Shuxian. *Huang Zongxi xinxue de dingwei*. Taipei: Asian Culture, 1986.

Ono, Kazuko. *Ko Sogi*. Tokyo: Jimbutsu oraisha, 1968.

Struve, Lynn A. "Enigma Variations: Huang Zongxi's Expectation of a New Age." *Ming Studies*, 40, Fall 1998, pp. 72–85.

——. "Not 'Conversant'? William James and Huang Zongxi on Being and Knowing." *Philosophy East and West*, 42(1), January 1992, pp. 139–161.

Wilson, Thomas A. *Genealogy of the Way: The Construction and Uses of the Confucian Tradition in Late Imperial China*. Stanford, Calif.: Stanford University Press, 1995. (See especially pp. 184–196.)

Xu, Dingbao, comp. *Huang Zongxi nianpu*. Shanghai: Huadong shihfan daxue chubanshe, 1995.

Hui Shi (Hui Shih)

Whalen Lai

Hui Shi (380–305 B.C.E.), one of the two major logicians of the school of names, was the chief minister to King Hui of Wei. Ideologically, Hui was the reverse of the logician Gongsun Long but was a like-minded friend of Zhuangzi, who mourned when Hui died.

Whereas Gongsun Long was known for "separating hard and white," Hui Shi was remembered for "equalizing semblance and dissemblance." Gongsun had uncovered very clear, logical differences (*X* is not like non-*X*); Hui Shi would reverse or erase them. As scholars of names (*ming*), they had both rejected the correspondence theory of language, which assumes that the name "horse" describes the animal horse (i.e., is a sign serving as a direct reference); instead, they chose to explore a sign pointing to or networking with other signs (intralinguistic sense). But Gongsun Long came up with a good logic of sense, while Hui Shi exposed that as the "non-sense" of logic.

In "separating hardness and white," Gongsun Long was reducing reality to its logically discrete constituents. He observed a strictly negative logic, rejecting "a horse is a horse" and endorsing instead, as horse (*X*), "whatever is left over when every non-horse shape (every non-*X*) has been eliminated." He assumed that categories like *X* and non-*X* are clear and distinct, that they are "separable." Discovering an inherent difference between signifier and signified, Hui Shi came up with the opposite thesis: nothing in the world is ever clearly one thing or the other, *X* or not *X*. Little of Hui Shi's original argument has been preserved, but one clue to it may be this recorded exchange with his patron. An exasperated King Hui of Wei wished that his chief minister would speak plainly and not go around in circles. To that, Hui Shi replied:

> "Let us suppose that there is a man who does not know what *tan* is and he asks what its characteristics are like, and you say, 'Like *tan*.' Would that communicate anything?" The king said no. "But if you say *tan* is like a bow but with a string made of bamboo instead, would he then know?" The king admitted he would. "So it is inherent in explanation that we always use what a person knows to make him understand what he has yet to know. To deny the use of analogies as your majesty would wish me to would therefore not do."

For Hui Shi, the extension of knowledge is never exact; induction is always approximate. Human communication being inherently metaphoric, it is always—as Aristotle says of metaphor—calling one thing by the name of another.

Xunzi (fl. 298–238 B.C.E.) would later accuse Hui Shi of abusing names to create havoc, because Hui said things like "marshes are as high as the hills" when linguistic convention had established marshes as low and hills as high. But if language is inherently "calling *A* by the name of *B*," then such confusion of names would be only natural. Xunzi trusted reference and assumed that the name "horse" does describe (can reach) the animal horse. Hui Shi, considering the pitfalls of intralinguistic sense, seriously doubted that. When we read them in context, it is most likely that Hui Shi (not Gongsun Long, as is sometimes supposed) was the one who argued for the thesis that "the pointing never reaches (the object); things never end." To put it differently, the signifier "horse" never meets up with the animal horse that is being signified. And since no two horses in the world are exactly alike, even the common noun "horse" used to describe them is suspect. Moreover, if the distinction of every individual thing has to be properly registered, then the process of specification (subclassifications) would be endless. It would be like continually "halving a bamboo." We would end up with as many names as there are things—that is, if we could ever exhaust the count of things.

Like Zeno, whose paradoxes (Achilles and the tortoise, etc.) resemble Hui Shi's, Hui injected into the discussion something new, something seen in no previous thinker: an awareness of infinity. This new element jeopardized the strategy of Gongsun Long, whose negative search for "horse" (finding *X* by eliminating every non-*X*, i.e., every "non-horse" shape) assumes that there is only a finite number of barnyard animal shapes to eliminate. Any possibility of an infinite regress would defeat the exercise and would show that "pointing does not reach (the target); thing does not end." That this is what Hui Shi had in mind can be inferred from his paradox "a dog is a horse." The shape of a horse and the shape of a pig are fairly distinct and therefore separable, but the silhouette of a large greyhound seen from a distance may easily be confused with the shape of a small, lean horse. If so, the search for "horse" by reliance on "shape" may fail. By undercutting Gongsun Long's assumption of semblance and dissemblance among various classes of things, Hui Shi could make a mockery of names and turn good logical sense into utter logical nonsense.

The culmination of this destruction of sense is a list of ten paradoxes attributed to Hui Shi:

1. The largest has no "outer"; it is the maximal unit. The smallest has no "inner"; it is the minimal unit.
2. That dimensionless thing [a point] has no volume, but [moving] it can cover a thousand miles.
3. Heaven is as low as earth; mountain is as level as marshes.
4. The sun at its height is setting; as we are born, we die.
5. General (overall) semblance with (only) minor dissemblance constitutes the "lesser same-yet-different"; ultimate semblance with ultimate dissemblance constitutes the "greater difference-yet-same."
6. The south has no limit, and yet it has a limit.
7. Going to Yue (in the south) today is arriving there yesterday.
8. Joint rings can be separated.
9. The center of the earth is north of Yan (in the north) and south of Yue.
10. Love all things generously; heaven and earth are of one body.

Many readings of these ten paradoxes have been offered by thinkers from traditional commentators and Feng Youlan to A. C. Graham and Chad Hansen. Of the ten, however, the fifth and the tenth deserve our special attention, for they hold the key to appreciating the deeper levels of their complexity.

The simplest reading of the paradoxes is to see names as inherently subjective and relative. What is large to some people in one context is small to others in a different context. If so, big and small may be said to be equal. But this reading addresses only subjective relativity. Although it may account for the call to "equalize dissemblance," it cannot explain why Hui Shi called for "equalizing *both* semblance and dissemblance." A better and truer reading would shift attention away from the ontological to the epistemic, from reference to sense, and to seeing a flaw in the naming process itself. If naming is always by way of analogy, then we are dependent on Wittgenstein's "family resemblance." Family resemblance gives us an idea what *tan* is like; it does not tell us exactly what *tan* is. Furthermore, "family resemblance" is inherently flawed, for wherever semblance is involved, it by definition falls short of total identity, so that dissemblance is already implied. No two peas in the world are alike; we call peas "peas" only by virtue of their general similarity—not their identity. This comes under Hui Shi's fifth paradox, within the category of "general semblance with minor dissemblance constituting the lesser same-yet-different." That does not as yet explain "ultimate semblance and ultimate dissemblance making up the greater different-yet-same." The latter involves moving beyond the relative scale of part-whole logic into the absolute measure of the infinite. Only in infinity would a part, which normally is different from (less than) the whole, be equal to the whole. That is because any part of an infinity is itself infinite. This is the "greater different-yet-same," hinted at in the fifth paradox. It is what informs the tenth and final paradox: "Love all things generously [because] heaven and earth are of one body."

Since the debate over name and reality is tied to a debate over ethics, Hui Shi's logic shows itself to be a moral logic. Whereas Gongsun Long (following the egoist Yang Chu) defends the sanctity of the self, Hui Shi here extends the imperative of the "all" (following Mozi's call to universal love). But Mozi stays at or with the materialistic and gauges love by actual benefits, with the result that he would never love horses—*jian'ai* by definition is a love of members of one's own species, of beings that hold humanity in common (*jian*); Mozi simply needs horses as "gifts" to benefit man. Hui Shi, by contrast, would boldly "love all things." He loves them indiscriminately, horses no less than men, in a genuine sense of being "one with all things" (*ai wanwu*), their seeming dissemblances notwithstanding—and with no concern for measuring material benefits. Hui Shi was the first thinker to openly love all things; he would pass that dictum (*ai wanwu*) to Zhuangzi and Mencius in the next generation, and it would become a staple of Chinese moral metaphysics from then on.

Meanwhile, as Gongsun Long had pushed the logic of the self to one extreme, ending up with a "loveless self" (*X* being naturally opposed to non-*X*), Hui Shi pushed the logic of the whole to the other extreme, advocating a "selfless love" (*X* being blended into all other things). That created a problem for the Mohists, who came back with a defense of universal love as a love of both *ti* (part) and *jian* (whole), and specifically "real" (positive, not Gongsun Long's negative) self and "real" (finite, not Hui Shi's infinite) whole. Mencius and Zhuangzi would tackle that same problem more subtly by speaking of the greater and the lesser self (within) and the larger and smaller universe (without).

See also Gongsun Long; Language and Logic; Names, School of; Philosophy of Language.

Bibliography

Cua, A. S. *Ethical Argumentation: A Study in Hsün Tzu's Moral Epistemology*. Honolulu: University of Hawaii Press, 1985.

Fung, Yu-lan (Feng Youlan). *A History of Chinese Philosophy*, 2 vols., trans. Derk Bodde. Princeton, N.J.: Princeton University Press, 1952–1953.

Graham, A. C. *Disputers of the Tao: Philosophical Argument in Ancient China*. La Salle, Ill.: Open Court, 1989.

Hansen, Chad. *Language and Thought in Ancient China*. Ann Arbor: University of Michigan Press, 1983.

Huineng (Hui-neng): The Sixth Patriarch

Hsueh-li Cheng

Huineng (Hui-neng, 638–713), the sixth patriarch, is the best-known master of Chinese Chan Buddhism, or simply Chan, popularly known in the west as Zen. He was born into a poor family at Canton. It is said that he received no formal education and hence could neither read nor write. Yet Huineng presented the most brilliant teaching of Chan and has been considered the real founder of its southern school.

When Huineng was a child, he sold firewood to support his mother. One day on his way to deliver wood to a customer's home, he encountered a man reciting the *Diamond Sutra*. As the story goes, the moment he heard the text, his mind was enlightened. He was advised to study Buddhism with Hongren (601–674), the fifth patriarch, then living at Yellow Plum in Qinzhou.

The master asked him where he came from and what he wanted. Huineng replied, "I am a commoner from Xinzhou of Canton. I have traveled far to pay you respect and ask for nothing but buddhahood." The master rejected him, saying, "You are a native of Canton, a barbarian? How can you expect to be a buddha?" Huineng answered, "Although there are northern men and southern men, north and south make no difference as to their buddha-nature. A barbarian is different from Your Holiness physically, but there is no difference in our buddha-nature." The fifth patriarch was impressed by the boy's statement and let him stay at the monastery. However, Huineng was accepted not as an actual disciple but merely as a worker to pound rice in the barn.

Huineng first became famous because he had composed an insightful poem. At that time, Master Hongren wanted to appoint a successor and asked his disciples to write a poem to display their understanding of Chan. Shenxiu (d. 762), the most outstanding disciple in the monastery, wrote the following poem on a wall in the temple hall:

> The body is the Bodhi tree,
> The mind is like a clear mirror stand.
> Take care to wipe it all the time,
> Allow no speck of dust to cling.

Master Hongren praised the poem in public and ordered all the disciples to memorize it. But in private he told Shenxiu to write another one, since the original verse expressed Hinayana *vinaya*, gradual moral discipline, rather than the Mahayana philosophy of emptiness. Huineng, although he was an uneducated man, seemed to be the only one who could identify the flaw in Shenxiu's verse. He composed his own poem and asked a temple boy to write it on the wall:

> There is no Bodhi-tree,
> Nor is there a stand with a bright mirror.
> All things are originally empty.
> Where can the dust alight?

Huineng's poem is an excellent expression of Mahayana philosophy; it teaches that all things—including meditation, religious discipline, enlightenment, good, and evil—are empty.

Chan is indeed the practice of *sunyata*, emptiness. Publicly, Master Hongren said that Huineng's poem was not good, but privately he called Huineng to his side and appointed him the successor. Then, following an order from the master, Huineng fled south to avoid the other disciples' jealousy and persecution.

According to Huineng, meditation and other religious disciplines are good, but enlightenment depends on human nature; it is an opening of the flower that is one's inner mind. Huineng advises us to seek neither good nor evil; rather, we should show our original nature as it was before birth.

For Huineng, Chan is the practice of the Buddhist teachings of the middle way and the twofold truth. After the Buddha's enlightenment, the first sermon he gave pertained to the doctrine of the middle way. He advised five mendicants not to live a pessimistic, ascetic life or a hedonistic, worldly life, but to find a life between these two extremes. Huineng followed this doctrine of the middle way and extended it beyond the concept of ways of life to address extremes in philosophical and religious positions. For Huineng, the middle way is the way to avoid all conceptual and dualistic thinking by eschewing "is" and "is not." For example, people may describe the universe as in reality permanent or impermanent, going or coming, internal or external, appearing or disappearing. But Chan masters dismiss all these conceptual and verbal expressions as extreme views. Huineng repudiated such dualistic thought and stated:

> The true nature of an event is marked by
> No permanence, no impermanence;
> No arrival, no departure;
> No exterior, no interior;
> No origination, no extinction.

Chan negation is not merely these eight negations but a general negation of all views. Truth, for Chan, is not a new view but an absence of views. Huineng taught that right is "that which is without any view" and wrong is "that which is with some view."

Huineng conveyed his teachings by means of the "twofold truth," a term that conveniently expresses the standpoints of worldly truth and ultimate truths. The twofold truth reflects a difference in the way one may perceive things. Worldly truth involves emotional and intellectual attachment to what one perceives, whereas ultimate truth discards all attachments. In light of this teaching, many paradoxes in Chan do not seem so illogical or absurd as one might at first suppose. For example, the sixth patriarch beat his brilliant disciple Shenhui with a stick and asked, "Do you feel pain?" Shenhui replied, "I am both pained and painless." From an ordinary standpoint, we would suppose that anyone must feel pain when he is beaten. However, from the higher point of view all things, including pain, are empty. Shenhui expressed the twofold truth by stating, "I am both pained and painless."

Truth, including religious truth, is often considered something that can be spoken and written. The Buddhist scriptures are believed to be the words of Buddha and are the ultimate source of Buddhism. Accordingly, a nun named Wujinzang diligently studied the *Mahaparinirvana sutra* for a long time. But she could not understand its message, and so she came to see Huineng. The master told her, "I am illiterate. But if you wish to know the purport of this work, please ask." The nun asked, "How can you grasp the meaning of the text when you do not even know the words?" The master replied, "The wonderful teachings of the Buddha have nothing to do with words and letters."

According to Huineng, the Buddhist *dharma* cannot be grasped by literal recitation or exposition of scriptures. Nor can it be found by a conceptual analysis of the texts. The key to truth is the mind. A monk named Fada is said to have read the *Saddharmapundarika sutra* (*Lotus of the Good Law Sutra*) three thousand times. Yet he still could not understand *dharma*. Huineng told him, "Fada, the *dharma* is quite clear; it is only your mind that is not clear. . . . Whether *sutra*-reciting will enlighten you or not, or benefit you or not, all depends on yourself. . . . If the mind is deluded, the lotus turns you round; if the mind is enlightened, you turn round the lotus."

Chan *dharma*, according to Huineng, is transmitted not so much through rational understanding as through personal encounters, mind-to-mind communication. In appointing Huineng the sixth patriarch, the master Hongren is said to have taught: "When the patriarch Bodhidharma first came to this country, most people had no confidence in him, and so this robe was handed down as a testimony from one patriarch to another. As to the *dharma*, this is transmitted from mind to mind."

Although truth should not be identified with scriptural propositions, scriptures are not useless. Scriptures can serve as a witness to truth and provide an occasion for learning the truth. As we have seen, Huineng himself became interested in Buddhism and was enlightened because of the *Diamond Sutra*.

So although language can sometimes damage the "eyes of wisdom," it can also serve to open them. Thus Huineng said, "You men should know that it is serious offense to speak ill of the scriptures." He often encouraged people to recite the *Diamond Sutra* in order to see into their nature and thereby attain buddhahood.

Religious experience in Chan Buddhism, according to Huineng, is rich and complex. In Chan, liberation means a complete transformation that involves the entire person and affects all aspects of life—mental, physical, intellectual, moral, and social. Chan discipline consists of *dhyana* (meditation), *prajna* (wisdom), and *sila* (morality). Meditation, wisdom, and ethics are seen as interrelated and inseparable. Being, knowing, and acting are synonymous. One is and becomes as one knows and as one behaves.

In Huineng's teaching, Chan meditation is not merely illumination or wisdom but also the practice of ethics. For Huineng, *dao* is right action, and seeing into "the nature" is *gongde*, meritorious virtue. For one whose tongue is ready with good words but whose heart is impure, *ding* (*dhyana*) and *hui* (*prajna*) are useless. If one's outward appearance and one's inner feelings are in harmony, then *ding* and *hui* become one, and thereby *wu* (enlightenment) is truly achieved.

An enlightened person will not ignore evil and suffering. He will care for others and respect the social order. As Huineng expresses this, Chan enlightenment "means that our mind is free from all impediments. We constantly look into our self-nature with wisdom and refrain from doing all kinds of evil. Although we do all kinds of good deeds, we are not attached to them. We are respectful toward our superiors, considerate of our inferiors, and sympathetic to the destitute and the poor."

Meditation, for Huineng, is a moral act; it causes one to abstain from causing harm and nourishes positive moral attitudes such as compassion for others. Morality comes from within, not from outside. It is not merely an emotional expression; it also has a cognitive element. Compassionate, egoless virtue is the natural manifestation and practice of wisdom, of the understanding that all things are causally dependent on each other and are devoid of selfhood or their own being.

The master Shenxiu taught gradual enlightenment, and his teaching was popular in northern China. According to Huineng, an important difference between his teachings and those of Shenxiu's northern Chan school concerned the essence of, and relationship between, *sila*, *dhyana*, and *prajna*. Shenxiu held that these were three different things. To avoid evil is *sila*. To do good is *prajna*. To purify the mind is *dhyana*. But for Huineng, although they appear to be different, all three are actually interrelated and depend on one's motives. Once the heart is purified, one will be illuminated and will not do evil. Whatever an enlightened person does will be good.

Huineng promoted the Chan *dharma* of abrupt or sudden enlightenment in the south. Eventually, he was recognized as the sixth patriarch and his teachings became the orthodox message of Chinese Chan Buddhism. The *Sutra Spoken by the Sixth Patriarch from the High Seat of the Treasure of the Law* is the only Chinese Buddhist writing that has been called *sutra*, scripture.

See also Buddhism: Zen (Chan).

Bibliography

Abe, Masao. *Zen and Western Thought*. Honolulu: University of Hawaii Press, 1985.

Chen, Nanyan. *Huineng Dashi Zhuan* (The Biography of the Great Master Huineng). Taipei: Foguang, 1996.

Cheng, Hsueh-li. *Empty Logic: Madhyamika Buddhism from Chinese Sources*. Delhi: Motilal Banarsidass, 1991.

———. *Exploring Zen*. New York: Peter Lang, 1996.

Cua, A. S. "Uses of Dialogues and Moral Understanding." *Journal of Chinese Philosophy*, 2(2), 1975, pp. 131–148.

Dumoulin, Heinrich. *Zen Buddhism: A History*, Vol. 1, *India and China*. New York: Macmillan, 1988.

McRae, John R. *The Northern School and the Formation of Early Chan Buddhism*. Honolulu: University of Hawaii Press, 1986.

Suzuki, D. T. *Essays in Zen Buddhism*. New York: Grove, 1949.

———. *Manual of Zen Buddhism*. New York: Grove, 1978.

———. *Zen Buddhism*. Garden City, N.Y.: Doubleday, 1956.

Wong, Mou-lan, ed. *Sutra Spoken by the Sixth Patriarch on the High Seat of the Treasure of the Law*. Hong Kong: Hong Kong Buddhist Book Distributor, 1952.

Yampolsky, Philip B., trans. *The Platform Sutra of the Sixth Patriarch*. New York: Columbia University Press, 1967.

Yinshun (Shi Yinshun). *Zhongguo chanzong shi* (History of Chinese Chan Buddhism). Taipei: Cheng-wen, 1988.

Zhang, Mantao, ed. *Chanzong dianji yanjiu* (Studies in Chan Documents). Taipei: Dacheng wenhua, 1977.

中國哲學

Intercultural Hermeneutics

Robert E. ALLINSON

The short definition of intercultural hermeneutics is that it is the proper study, and thereby understanding, of any message passed between cultures and what happens in the course of that transmission. The "proper study" includes comprehensive and philosophical study of the essence, process, problems, limits, and criteria of what counts as successful intercultural communication; desiderata of intercultural communication; products of intercultural communication; the final stage of understanding itself; the understanding of that understanding and the understanding of the understanding of understanding; the practice of that understanding; and the occurrence of that understanding whether or not self-concious. This is the short definition.

The long definition of intercultural hermeneutics cannot be encapsulated in a single sentence or paragraph. One must begin one's long definition with a reminder that intercultural hermeneutics is a label for an academic subdiscipline or branch of study which attempts to describe problems and methods in inquiring into the intellectual products of a culture which is external to the culture of the inquirer with educational background and professional training, and relatedly, the formation of the inquirer's intellectual categories and evaluative criteria. The word "intercultural" refers to the exchange which takes place between two or more cultures, that is, an exchange which is *between* cultures external to each other. Cultures external to each other can and often do coexist within a wider "common" culture. For example, within the Judeo-Christian culture, one is confronted with intercultural problems of communication. One need only think of the fact that in the Hebrew language there is no single word which can be translated by the English word "sin."

The word "hermeneutics" in the phrase "intercultural hermeneutics" refers to the fact that the type of interaction or exchange taking place is one of attempted understanding through the reception of a message or the attempted transmission of a message to be understood. All attempts at intercultural understanding require that a message or a communication from one culture is passed to another culture. The root of the word is the Greek word *hermeios*, which referred to the priest at the Delphic oracle. The verb *hermeneuein* and the noun *hermeneia* refer to the god Hermes (now also known by his Roman name, Mercury), who was charged with carrying messages from one goddess or god to another goddess or god and also with carrying messages from the goddesses or gods to men and women. Richard Palmer, in his book *Hermeneutics*, raises the question whether the words *hermeneuin* and *hermeneia* are derived from Hermes or vice versa. It would not seem to matter to the issue at hand, since in either case the words are associated with the function of carrying messages from one realm of discourse to another, and with the degree of interpretation and understanding entailed. Symbolically, and most importantly for our present purposes, hermeneutics would stand for the task and the process of transmuting what is beyond human or common understanding into a form which human or common understanding can grasp.

The concept of culture can even be extended to one's own changing culture within one's own self. Even within the very same self, one must interpret when one attempts to comprehend one's previous statements. It works the other way around as well. The point is well put in a story Oscar Wilde tells on himself. When he fails to recognize a friend on the street, he says, "I'm sorry I did not recognize you. You see, *I've* changed."

Intercultural hermeneutics in general involves a specially refined kind of understanding in that initially one must understand another culture's understanding through the categories of one's own understanding. Since every communication may be either intended or understood in a number of different ways, every act of understanding a communication requires an interpretation and hence an interpreter. When one attempts to understand the intellectual products of one culture with the intellectual presuppositions and tools of another culture, the interpreter carries the additional burden of understanding both cultures and successfully interpreting each culture for the other. Today's Hermes—generally a role taken up by comparative philosophers, cultural anthropologists, intercultural communication scholars, and scholars of area studies—is faced with the task of carrying messages from one culture to another and the attendant charge of *interpreting* the messages of one culture so that these messages can be understood by the extrinsic culture.

The actual use of the word "hermeneutics" can be traced back to the seventeenth century, with reference to biblical interpretation. One can date the actual practice of hermeneutics from the writings making up the Talmud, examples of explicit commentaries that make intensive and extended use of hermeneutics. An example of talmudic hermeneutics would be the *Pirketh Abot*, one of the treatises of the Talmud. One could trace hermeneutics back even further to the writings making up the Torah, since portions of the Torah are commentaries on other portions. Later examples of hermeneutic practice would include comments on the Upanishads by Indian philosophers such as Sankara and Gaudapada.

The proper understanding of the project of the task of intercultural hermeneutics and the capacity to carry it out requires four separate acts of understanding:

- Firstly, one must be capable of understanding the categories of understanding of one's own culture. This requires the ability to transcend the categories of one's own culture so as to be able to become aware of the proper limits of their application.
- Secondly, one must be able to understand the categories of understanding of the culture one intends to understand. This requires the capacity both to understand and to transcend the categories of the culture to be understood as well, in order to become aware of the limits of their application. Thus, fluency in at least two cultures and a capacity to transcend the limitations of each culture is a prerequisite.
- Thirdly, one must carefully consider what constitutes a successful act of intercultural hermeneutics. Since one cannot by definition understand the intellectual products of one culture by reference to the criteria of understanding of the intellectual products of a disparate culture (if the two cultures are the same or similar, then the task of hermeneutics is less demanding, though it still exists), it is critical that the end product of an act of intercultural hermeneutics be an intellectual product which is different from its existence as an intellectual product in its original culture or its existence as an intellectual product viewed as the product of a foreign culture from the standpoint of the original culture. In other words, if there is to be understanding of one culture by another culture, the final result of such an understanding cannot be found as already existent in either culture. The act of intercultural hermeneutics must result in the creation of a hybrid product.
- Fourthly, the final product of the act of intercultural hermeneutics can be taken as a standpoint from which to look back and understand the two cultural standpoints from which it has emerged. As a result, the product of intercultural hermeneutics can bring with it a greater understanding of one's original culture as well as a greater understanding of the culture one intends or intended to understand.

The long definition of intercultural hermeneutics may now be applied specifically to the attempt to understand Chinese philosophy through the eyes of western philosophy. The four parts that have been outlined can now be analyzed with application to the project of attempting to understand Chinese culture, specifically Chinese philosophy, with the categories of western European culture, specifically Anglo-American philosophy.

The first requirement is the capacity to understand the starting point of the particular hermeneuticist at work, in this case, western culture and western philosophy. Understanding of one's own starting point has already been defined as the capacity both to understand and to transcend the limits of the criteria of understanding of one's own starting point, in this case, western philosophy.

At this juncture, a question may well arise, and in fact should arise, as to how to eliminate or at least take into account the entire issue of cultural prejudice or cultural bias. Specifically, for example, the western philosopher may well begin to attempt to understand Chinese philosophy from the standpoint that Chinese philosophy is an inferior product. This has been a historical encumbrance, the most famous example of which is Hegel's treatment of eastern philosophy. The origin of the attitude that in general eastern philosophy is inferior to western philosophy may have been inspired by the concept that eastern philosophy in general or Chinese philosophy in particular, in order to be considered philosophy, would have to meet certain standards which must be met by certain traditions within western philosophy. The adoption of such an attitude would appear to be an avoidance of intercultural hermeneutics as it is being defined here. If one wished to approach Chinese philosophy with less *hubris* and with an attempt to discover a more sinocentric axis, it would be necessary to be willing to take the view that western philosophy itself had limits, and to attempt not to impose the standards of western philosophy on Chinese philosophy. The concept of limits to western philosophy would entail an understanding that western criteria of truth or rigor were themselves open to question. If one approached Chinese philosophy from the standpoint that western philosophy did have certain limits, then one could take these to be a willingness to tolerate some degree of logical ambiguity, an ability to achieve some level of intellectual satisfaction without requiring every unintelligible matter or every unanswered question to be sorted out, and a willingness to accept that the final product which is understood may not be understood until or unless one's criteria for understanding were abandoned, and that therefore the intellectual product to be understood is not to be understood as a lesser intellectual product.

For example, it may be said that the criterion of what is acceptable as western rationality is provided by the philosophy of Kant, which attempts to set out and prove the necessity of certain categories of understanding. Likewise, it may be said that the western philosophical intellect is satisfied by the array of proofs for the existence of the deity that may be found in the history of western philosophy. No such array of proofs for the existence of categories of understanding or a deity can be found in Chinese philosophy. Is it therefore appropriate to conclude either that western philosophy is more rigorous than Chinese philosophy or that it has demanded or has achieved more (theoretically) than Chinese philosophy? Such a conclusion and muted versions of such a conclusion—e.g., the western mind is more theoretical (and hence more thoughtful and therefore more intelligent or intellectual) than the Chinese mind—are common. Such conclusions do not result in a genuine understanding of Chinese philosophy, because they are based upon an acceptance of the goals or achievements of western philosophy without an attempt to transcend the project of accepting such goals or attempting to satisfy them. If one accepts the definition of self-understanding ex hypothesi, then the goals of possessing certain categories of understanding or proofs for the existence of a deity will no longer appear as rational intellectual demands. They will appear as intellectual cultural quirks, products of various cultural forces of determination, but not as prerequisites for or evidence of rationality itself. In order to be able to truly understand an interpreted culture, one must be able to truly transcend the criteria of rationality of the culture of interpretation. If one no longer sees the construction of logical proofs of any kind either as necessary or as evidence of the ingenuity of one's own culture, one will therefore not judge another culture as irrational or less theoretical. Such categories of judgment will disappear. Then and only then is one in a position to begin to attempt to understand the other culture.

Second, in order to understand the products of the culture to be interpreted, one must also be able to transcend the criteria of understanding of the culture to be understood. For example, in the effort to understand Chinese philosophy, one must be able to transcend the tradition of appealing to authority as a final solution to philosophical issues. A thorough understanding of Chinese philosophy is not to be gleaned from staying entirely within the existing, established Chinese traditions, whether or not this is the Chinese way. One may have to transcend *argumentum ad authoritatum* in order to understand the Chinese tradition.

For example, a traditional or historically traditional means of understanding the Chinese philosophy of Confucius's negative formulation of the golden rule has been to perceive it as inferior to the Christian affirmative formulation (affirmative in terms of sentential structure, not positive in terms of evaluative content). However, if one transcends this traditional position of understanding, one may perceive Confucius's negatively formulated rule as superior to the most common variant of the western formulation. Wing-tsit Chan agrees with Liu Baonan (1791–1895), who commented in his *Lunyu zhengyi* (*Correct Meanings of the Analects*) that while it is linguistically negatively formulated, Confucius's version of the golden rule was intended to be taken as a proactive injunction rather than a prohibition of action and asserts that "the followers of Confucius have never understood it (the Golden Rule) to be negative. . . . Commentators on the *Analects* in the last eighteen centuries have never understood the Golden Rule to be negative" (1963). But eighteen centuries of traditional Chinese commentators may well have misinterpreted Confucius's meaning. Thus the proper understanding of another culture may require the abandoning of the typical or traditional means that culture may have evolved for understanding itself. It may well be the case that the golden rule is more properly and better understood if it is understood and formulated in a negative sentential form. And such a negative formulation may be far more congruent with the rest of Confucius's moral philosophy. Most important, it *is* negatively formulated in its original language, and such a formulation should not be circumscribed by and construed to fall under or to be equivalent to a western affirmative formulation in an effort not to be perceived as inferior to the western formulation.

To take another example, it has become historically and thus traditionally acceptable to interpret the argument of Zhuangzi as that of a relativist and his famous "butterfly dream" as a classic statement of relativism. However, one may obtain a deeper and arguably truer understanding of Zhuangzi's brilliance as a philosopher by abandoning these traditional and historically bound interpretations and understanding Zhuangzi to be exploring the grounds for certain knowledge in a more sophisticated version of such an inquiry than one can find even in Descartes. One can find in Zhuangzi's "great sage" dream a formulation of a dream argument that is more precise, comprehensive, and subtle than its famous Cartesian counterpart—which it preceded by two millennia.

One can discover more of value and more to value in Chinese philosophy and Chinese philosophers than one can find if one remains strictly within historically grounded and therefore traditionally accepted interpretations. One can understand another culture more fully if one can transcend the criteria of understanding of the culture to be understood.

Third, one must accept that the final product to be understood is a hybrid product which did not exist before the attempted act of understanding. If one considers that one can understand the products of one culture through the eyes of another culture, one remains tied to the view that understanding requires no change of assumptions either about one's own culture or about the culture to be understood. But such an act of attempted understanding is doomed to failure. If one remains rooted in one's own assumptions and attempts to interpret a culture that by definition is grounded on a different set of assumptions, one cannot understand the second culture (or the first) without prejudice. What would such an attempted act of understanding amount to? For example, what can be understood from the typical acts of understanding attempted by western scholars who make only superficial attempts to alter their own categories of understanding and attempt in all goodness to change the products to be understood as little as possible? The products of the other culture will in the end be unintelligible and thus not understood. For example, the western scholar who would not wish to alter the frameworks from which she or he is interpreting Chinese texts may wish to interpret *dao* as a divine creation with purpose and possible ethical intentions. But such an interpretation, as intriguing as it might be, may be of little assistance in reaching a genuine understanding of the categories of another culture.

On the other hand, the western scholar who goes to the opposite extreme and wishes to leave the Chinese categories untouched by interpretation may as a result leave them unintelligible and hence do them equal injustice. Any understanding of understanding that leaves both sides intact conceives of the understanding of understanding as the construction of an intellectual museum or intellectual zoo in which the observer leaves the perusal with his or her assumptions intact and in the mind's repository now has an "understanding" of another alien and primitive culture. It is alien and primitive precisely because it has not been understood.

All understanding requires an alteration of one's starting points and an alteration of the data to be understood. Gadamer has referred to such an alteration as "fusion of horizons" (1975). There is no such thing as understanding that leaves the subject and the object of understanding intact. If the subject and object of understanding remain the same after the act of understanding, what has been achieved is some kind of "toleration," not understanding. Toleration always entails not real understanding but only tolerance of a "primitive" or lesser datum by a superior mind. This is intellectual imperialism, not understanding.

One caveat. This is not to say that when an operation of understanding is completed, one may arrive at any interpretation at all, regardless of the data to be interpreted. That position is postmodernism, not intercultural hermeneutics. What is being said here is, rather, that data to be understood cannot be understood as raw data. They must be assimilated and understood by living minds. Living minds, likewise, cannot operate from frozen categories. Such minds are by definition not living; they are imprisoned by categories from the past.

On the other hand, this is not to say that in the world of understanding "anything goes." It is to say that understanding requires true intelligibility: what is to be understood must truly make sense to the inquirer. It cannot be merely "tolerated" as some kind of "intellectual datum." Toleration is not understanding; it is an admission of ignorance.

In order to make sense truly, one does not make up meaning out of the whole cloth or destroy meaning altogether, as with the whim of deconstructionism or postmodernism. It is not that every word can mean anything one wishes. That is a project not of understanding but of misunderstanding. Or, to put the matter another way, postmodernist "interpretation" is creation, not understanding.

From the standpoint of the enterprise and discipline of hermeneutics, there is a meaning that one is attempting to decipher. The meaning can be deciphered only if one is willing and able to abandon preconceived criteria of understanding that belong either to the interpreting or the interpreted culture. This is not the same as abandoning any meaningful input from either culture. Flexible criteria are not the same as no criteria. When one is interpreting Xunzi, one is, after all, attempting to interpret an ethicist. One is not attempting to interpret a mathematician. If any word can mean anything at all—if this is the thesis of postmodernism—then intercultural hermeneutics is not postmodernist. It is simply an attempt at the genuine understanding of one culture by another culture, and in this attempt it acknowledges that one must not remain fixed in either standpoint. It is not saying that understanding is impossible; it is saying that understanding is possible only if one is willing to free oneself from being ruled by a preexistent standpoint.

Finally, after one has achieved the hybrid product of understanding, one can utilize it to further understand both the culture one has been attempting to understand and the culture from which one has attempted the understanding. Intercultural hermeneutics can also be a means of understanding the limitations of previous attempts at understanding—both limitations arising from the prejudices with which one has attempted to understand another culture and those arising from the prejudices which have accompanied attempts or a lack of attempts of one culture to understand itself. Intercultural hermeneutics thus also serves the task of understanding previous acts or attempted acts or omission of such acts of understanding, and assists one in understanding the limits of previous attempts of understanding. One can, after the task of intercultural hermeneutics completes itself, understand oneself better than one could have understood oneself before the attempted act of understanding.

At the beginning of its formally named and self-conscious career, hermeneutics was a project that essentially arose within the intellectual tradition of western thought attempting to understand products of western thought. For the purposes of this essay, however, it was appropriate to concentrate on the project of western thought attempting to understand eastern thought, or more specifically, western thought attempting to understand the products of Chinese thought. While it would be fascinating to discuss the project of eastern thought attempting to understand western thought, such a consideration would venture beyond the purposes of this essay.

What happens after the work of intercultural hermeneutics has been carried out? Presumably, one has arrived at understanding, which is the central goal of hermeneutics. Understanding, as has been argued, always involves assimilation. In the assimilation, one tradition must willy-nilly interpret the products of the other tradition. But it is equally important to emphasize that in order to interpret, one must first assimilate and be assimilated by the other tradition, and understanding can take place only when one becomes the other tradition, or, in short, assimilates and is assimilated by it. One can stand back after one has (and has been) assimilated and consider any contrasting residue, but one cannot meaningfully stand back until one has first identified or become one with the other tradition. Identification with the other is the first step in the process of hermeneutics. In the popular injunction "Do not criticize another until you have walked in his (or her) shoes," one is being told that one must identify with the other before one can criticize or evaluate or even make sense of another tradition. The first step in hermeneutics is becoming one with the other or identifying with the other so that there no longer is an alien other. There is only one. In the second step, one may distance oneself from the other and point out meaningful contrasts. In the third and most meaningful step, one chooses the best from both traditions and forges a new meaning that is a hybrid of both traditions and did not exist beforehand in either tradition. One may see in this description of hermeneutics an analogy with Hegel's concept of *Aufheben*, in which one compares thesis and antithesis in such a way that in one's synthesis one captures elements of both thesis and antithesis but produces an understanding that goes beyond both. (The similarity with Hegel is very close; the only difference is that one must first identify closely with each tradition separately, a step which Hegel perhaps does not emphasize strongly enough.) The third step is the real point of hermeneutics and is its ultimate desideratum. In the fourth step, one may utilize such theoretical understanding of the process of hermeneutics to understand other traditions or to discuss the enterprise of hermeneutics itself, as in the present essay. But the understanding of, and thus the correct discussion of, hermeneutics is not possible unless one has sucessfully completed the first three steps.

It must be mentioned that hermeneutics and hermeneutic development are not to be conflated with history and historical development. One need only recall Hegel's chronological twisting of history in his *Phänomenologie des Geistes*: he describes Greek philosophy as beginning with stoicism and developing into skepticism, when chronologically it was the reverse. This is not because Hegel was ignorant of history but because philosophically (in Hegelian dialectics), skepticism may be perceived as a logical development from stoicism even though historically it emerged as a psychological and philosophical result of a perceived failure of platonism.

In Chinese thought, one can go a step further and use later philosophical developments to understand earlier developments. Such a hermeneutics, while it has been applied in the analysis of Chinese philosophy, has (with the arguable exceptions of Aristotle, Hegel, Kierkegaard, Nietzsche, and possibly Heidegger) yet to be successfully applied to the history of western philosophy. In the project of using the later to understand the earlier, one must be careful not to do violence to the real meaning of the earlier and impose an unintended meaning of the later on the earlier. Only when it is evident that the later truly reveals and perhaps even expands on the meaning of the earlier can one properly say that one is using the child to understand the parent, as in Wordsworth's phrase "the Child is Father to the Man." In this sense, the later can be said to be saying what the earlier was attempting to say but, as Aristotle put it, could say only lispingly. It is not to be inferred from this that every later philosophy states what an earlier philosophy was attempting to state but could not. This would be to conflate historical development with philosophical development, which would be to equate the empirical with the theoretical. Historical development has only empirical connections and lacks theoretical necessity. This discussion of hermeneutics may itself be taken to be a hermeneutics of hermeneutics (hermeneutics by itself is an effort to achieve understanding), and so it can be said that what has been achieved is an understanding, an understanding of understanding, and an understanding of the understanding of understanding.

See also Confuciansim: Tradition.

Bibliography

Allinson, Robert E. *Chuang Tzu for Spiritual Transformation: An Analysis of the Inner Chapters*. Albany: State University of New York Press, 1989, 1996.

——. "The Negative Formulation of the Golden Rule in Confucius." *Journal of Chinese Philosophy*, 12(3), 1985, pp. 305–315.

——. "An Overview of the Chinese Mind." *In Understanding the Chinese Mind: The Philosophical Roots*, ed. Robert E. Allinson. Hong Kong: Oxford University Press, 2000. (10th impression.)

——. "Taoism in the Light of Zen: An Exercise in Intercultural Hermeneutics." *Zen Buddhism Today*, Vol. 6. Kyoto: November, 1988, pp. 23–38.

Chan, Wing-tsit, trans. *A Source Book in Chinese Philosophy*. Princeton, N.J.: Princeton University Press, 1963.

Gadamer, Hans Georg. *Truth and Method*. New York: Continuum, 1975.

Palmer, Richard E. *Hermeneutics*. Evanston, Ill.: Northwestern University Press, 1969.

中國哲學

Jia Yi (Chia I)

Mark Csikszentmihalyi

Jia Yi (Chia I, 200–168 B.C.E.) was a classical scholar, philosopher, and poet who served in the office of erudite (*boshi*) and then palace grandee (*taizhong daifu*) beginning in 179 B.C.E. under Emperor Wen of the Han dynasty. After being slandered at court, Jia was sent away from the capital to serve as grand tutor (*taifu*) to the prince of Changsha. A few years later, Jia was rehabilitated and served briefly as grand tutor to the prince of Liang before dying at age thirty-three. Despite Jia's early death, his memorandums, poems, and essays preserved in the standard histories, taken with the fifty-eight chapters of the *New Writings* (*Xinshu*) attributed to him, constitute an exceptionally large body of work—from which we can reconstruct his highly original efforts to integrate Confucian moral psychology with political philosophy.

Jia Yi's writings reveal the influence of both Mencius (371–289 B.C.E.) and Xunzi (d. 244 B.C.E.) and synthesize their opposing perspectives on human nature to portray a malleable nature with a negligible disposition toward good or evil. Jia's conscious adaptation of earlier Confucian ethical thinkers, coupled with his emphasis on the classics and his record of service in government office, earned him the reputation of an exemplary Confucian official as early as Liu Xin (d. 23 C.E). However, Jia's metaphysical and poetical writings reveal a strong influence from Daoist texts such as *Laozi* and *Zhuangzi*. This underscores the important fact that Jia Yi was the last major philosopher writing before the establishment, in 136 B.C.E., of the Confucian classics as the material for the official examination. Consequently, his writings represent the apogee of the syncretic and synthetic tendencies of the early decades of the Han dynasty.

Jia's memorandums to Emperor Wen, preserved in the *Standard History of the Han* (*Hanshu*) by Ban Gu (32–92 B.C.E.), develop a pragmatic political philosophy grounded in a novel conception of human nature. Among the governmental measures Jia recommended were a reduction in the power of the feudal kings, the establishment of a government monopoly on the minting of coins, the reestablishment of traditional social ranks and customs, calendrical and ritual reforms, and the abolition of mutilation as a punishment for high officials.

The basis of Jia Yi's political philosophy was his belief in the importance of nurture over nature. To show this he outlined a thought experiment similar to one in the *Mencius* (3B6). Take the case of two people born in regions separated by a vast distance. As infants they have identical basic tastes and desires, as we can see from the fact that their cries sound the same when they are exposed to something unpleasant or deprived of something they need. Despite this initial similarity, when they are grown, they will be completely unable to communicate with each other. Jia used this example to show the importance of education and habituation, which may also guide a person toward good or evil. He argued that Hu Hai (d. 207 B.C.E.), the corrupt second emperor of the Qin, was corrupt not because of an innately evil nature but because "those who taught and guided him did not adhere to principle." This picture of human nature as malleable implies that a ruler can depend on neither kinship nor loyalty to keep his vassals in line. A feudal lord's rebelliousness is directly proportional to the size of that lord's power base, Jia argues, "because it is a case not simply of people having different dispositions, but of the nature of their circumstances." Thus, the malleability of human nature implies that the ruler must make policy under the assumption that the dependability of both allies and enemies is determined by circumstances.

The political emphasis of Jia Yi's writing was novel in its time, and it signaled a shift toward a more instrumental use of Confucian moral psychology. Thinkers of the pre-Qin period such as Mencius and Xunzi concentrated on innate moral dispositions. The deterministic cast of Jia's picture of human nature recalls statements about the effect of environment such as the parable of Ox Mountain in *Mencius* (6A8), but in the end Jia rejected the Mencian notion that humans have "sprouts" of morality—he favored a model of continuous moral learning closer to that of Xunzi.

For Jia Yi, education and ritual training should play a pivotal role in government. His is the fullest development of early educational theory aside from the first chapter of the *Xunzi*, with which it has many similarities. The education of the crown prince begins with fetal education (*taijiao*): a pregnant empress is to be exposed only to ritually correct music and is to eat only food that has been correctly prepared. As a youth, the prince is to be surrounded only by correct officials as he completes his ritual training in the five studies (*xue*), each dedicated to inculcating a specific moral virtue and a means of acting toward a particular sector of society. For example, in the "eastern study" the prince learns the importance of benevolence (*ren*) as a process of extending his kindness (*en*). Ritual training does not cease when the prince ascends the imperial throne. In the *New Writings*, Jia sets forth strict ritual prescriptions regarding the ruler's deportment and countenance, at one point describing a series of twenty-seven ritual behaviors. His analysis implies a porous boundary between the outward expression of a moral quality through symbolic ritual action and its interior existence. For Jia, the ethical dimension of ritual action concerned actual ritual observances more than the intrinsic moral significance of these rites.

Once one moves beyond the political prescriptions outlined in Jia Yi's memorandums and considers the more eclectic *New Writings*, the philosophical picture grows much more complex. Opinions concerning the authenticity of the text vary, and although several sets of chapters might be later interpolations, the core of the *New Writings* contains the same set of memorandums as the *Standard History*, although worded differently and presented in a different order. Additionally, there are in the *New Writings* chapters based on classical exegesis, chapters devoted to history and foreign policy, and three chapters that reflect a strain of thought known as Huang-Lao—the theories of the Yellow Emperor and Laozi. These chapters prompted one authority, Cai Tingji (1984), to argue that Jia uses Laozi's metaphysical framework as a basis for his version of Confucianism. While it is true that these chapters do develop the concepts of *dao, de*, and *xu* found in the *Laozi*, they also rely on a nuanced idea of *li*, translated as "principle" in accord with its use by Song Confucians. Considered as a whole, the *New Writings* represent an attempt to compose an original philosophical picture from the available philosophical sources—much the same synthetic approach as that found in Jia's literary efforts.

Jia Yi is known at least as well for his literary accomplishments as for his political and philosophical writings. He is famous for three works in particular, all included in the most influential literary collection in early imperial China, the *Wenxuan*. All three of them show the same divergent influences that may be found in Jia's philosophical writing.

The first of these works, the best-known of Jia's prose writings, is the essay "Discussion of the Faults of the Qin" (*Guo Qin lun*), excerpted in the *Historical Record* (*Shiji*) and reproduced in the *Standard History of the Han*, the *New Writings*, and a number of later prose collections. This essay attributes the fall of the Qin to many factors, in particular its lack of benevolence and lack of propriety. The Song scholar Hu Jie described this essay as the one Jia's other writings revolve around.

The other two works are found in the poetical writings attributed to Jia Yi. They are two prose-rhyme pieces, "The Owl" (*Fu'niao fu*) and "Lament for Qu Yuan" (*Diao Qu Yuan*). "The Owl"—which the sinologist Herbert Giles called a Chinese equivalent of Poe's "The Raven" because it is framed by a portentous discussion with a bird—borrows extensively from the *Zhuangzi* and *Laozi*. Jia puts words from the *Laozi* in the mouth of the visiting owl when it observes, "Who understands [destiny's] limit?" "Lament for Qu Yuan" is a mildly reproachful panegyric dedicated to an earlier poet who had been slandered at court; Jia reflects that in troubled times a gentleman's destiny might be to "observe the danger inherent in petty virtue, and soar aloft to distance himself from it," like the mythical *peng* bird from the *Zhuangzi*. Thus both poems stress destiny and the importance of understanding and adapting to it. The singular importance of destiny in Jia Yi's poetry reflects the influence of texts associated with Daoism.

Taken together with the writing of his contemporary Lu Jia, Jia Yi's literary works and memorandums foreshadow several major changes that Chinese philosophy was to undergo during the four centuries of the Han dynasty. While it is tempting to consider Jia Yi with regard to the long-standing debate on human nature in pre-Qin China, the question of innate dispositions is somewhat tangential to the main thrust of his work. One phrase he used—"holding to the path (*dao*) as if it were one's nature (*zhuangdao ruo xing*)"—reveals that human nature was not his central concern but was rather a metaphor for adherence to the correct path. In part, this change was an effect of the historical context of the early Han. Legalism, the dominant philosophy of the Qin, ignored or minimized the effect of innate disposition and focused instead on appetites or drives, which can be considered external controls. Following in the tradition of more teleological ethical systems such as Mohism, and influenced by the axiomatic ethics of Daoist thinkers, the legalists subordinated the discussion of personal ethical decisions to goods defined at the level of the state. In a way that was characteristic of writers during the immediately post-Qin period, Jia reflected legalist and Daoist influences by magnifying the importance of environmental factors to a point where concerns about moral disposition became somewhat irrelevant. The ultimate expression of this concern with destiny and the evolution of Confucian ethics toward a more naturalistic model during the Han would await the writings of Dong Zhongshu. While Jia Yi's thought does not fit neatly into the category "Confucian" as the term is generally used, its systematic and syncretic nature is characteristic of the dominant trend of humanistic philosophy during the early Han.

See also Confucianism: Han; Dong Zhongshu; Lu Jia.

Bibliography

Cai, Tingji. *Jia Yi yan-jiu*. Taipei: Wenshi zhe, 1984.

Hsiao, Kung-chuan. *A History of Chinese Political Thought*, trans. F. W. Mote, Vol. 1. Princeton, N.J.: Princeton University Press, 1979, ch. 9, pp. 469–548.

Jia, Yi. "The Faults of Ch'in (*Guo Qin lun*)." In *Sources of Chinese Tradition*, ed. William T. DeBary. New York: Columbia University Press, 1960, pp. 166–169. (Translation.)

———. "The Owl," trans. J. R. Hightower. "Lament for Ch'ü Yüan," trans. Burton Watson. In *Anthology of Chinese Literature from Early Times to the Fourteenth Century*, ed. Cyril Birch. New York: Grove, 1965, pp. 138–141.

Kanaya, Osamu. "Ka Gi no fu ni tsuite." *Chugoku Bungaku Ho*, 8, 1958, pp. 1–25.

Qi, Yuzhhang. *Jia Yi tanwei*. Taipei: San-min, 1969.

Zhu, Jui-k'ai. *Liang-Han sixiang shi*. Shanghai: Ku-chi, 1989, ch. 4, pp. 58–70.

Jizang (Chi-tsang)

Hsueh-li CHENG

I

Jizang (c. 549–623 C.E.) was the greatest master of Sanlun Madhyamika Buddhism in China. His ancestors had migrated from Parthia to southern China and then to Nanjing. His father, a Parthian, grew up in Nanjing and married a Chinese woman. Jizang himself looked more Parthian than Chinese; however, his upbringing and education were mainly Chinese.

Not long after Jizang was born, his father became a Buddhist monk; and in 555, when Jizang was seven years old, he, too, left household life and joined a Buddhist monastery—his father took him to become a disciple of Falang (506–581), the great promoter of Sanlun Madhymika Buddhism at the Xinghuang Temple at Sheshan. From then on, Jizang was a devoted follower of this school.

Under the influence of his father and Falang, Jizang devoted his early life to the study of Mahayana Buddhism, especially Madhyamika thought. He was exceptionally intelligent. At age nineteen, he was said to have mastered everything given by the teacher. Having established himself as a good student of Sanlun Madhyamika Buddhism, Jizang was ordained a monk at age twenty-one. In 590, when he was forty-two, he moved to Zhejiang Province; there, he lived in the Jiaxiang Temple on Kuaiji Mountain for seven or eight years, propagated Buddhism, and earned the name Jiaxiang Dashi, "great master of Jiaxiang."

Madhyamika Buddhism had been founded in the second century by Nagarjuna (c. 100–200) and developed by Aryadeva (c. 163–263). In China, Korea, and Japan this Mahayana school is called the Sanlun Zong ("three treatises" school) because it is based on three main texts: (1) Nagarjuna's *Middle Treatise* with commentary by Qingmu (Pingala) in 445 verses; (2) his *Twelve Gate Treatise*, with his own commentary; and (3) Aryadeva's *Hundred Treatise*, with commentary by Vasu.

Madhyamika was introduced to China from India chiefly by Kumarajiva (344–413), who became a well-known Buddhist scholar in Kucha, Xinjiang. He was captured by a Chinese army and brought to the court of the Later Liang about 383. After the Later Liang was conquered by the Later Chin, Kumarajiva was taken to Chang'an in 401. With the support of the king of Chin, he translated Madhyamika and other Buddhist scriptures from Sanskrit into Chinese. Thousands of Chinese monks became his disciples, and although most of them were not intellectuals, some, such as Huiyuan (334–416), Sengrui (352–446), and Sengzhao (374–414), were fine Sanlun scholars.

Sanlun logic, metaphysics, and epistemology were well received and well expounded by Chinese intellectuals during the Six Dynasties. This was largely due to their promotion by Sanlun masters such as Senglang (494–512), Sengquan (d. 528), and Falang. But Jizang provided the best exposition of Sanlun Madhyamika thought. Because of his fame as a great *dharma* master, he was invited by Emperor Yang of the Sui dynasty to the Huiri Temple in Yangzhou in 599 and to the Riyan Temple in Changan, where he stayed for nineteen years. During this period he wrote commentaries on the three treatises of the Madhyamika school and composed the well-known books *Sanlun Xuanyi* (*The Profound Meaning of Three Treatises*) and *Erdiyi* (*The Meaning of the Twofold Truth*).

Jizang also had an affinity for many other Mahayana teachings and was skilled at expounding them. In addition to his writings on Sanlun thought, he wrote a great number of commentaries on Mahayana scriptures such as the *Lotus Sutra, Nirvana Sutra, Pure Land Sutra, Vimalakirti, Suvarnaprabhasa*, and the *Prajna* sutras. Among these, he was drawn most to the philosophy of the *Lotus Sutra*, particularly as he grew older. It is said that while he taught the three treatises of Sanlun Buddhism more than a hundred times, he lectured on the *Lotus Sutra* more than three hundred times. Jizang systematized and established Sanlun philosophy, but he was also known as a great master of the *Lotus*. The Sanlun doctrine of emptiness teaches that all things are empty. This teaching appears to be negative, even nihilistic. But Jizang seemed to suggest that the Sanlun eightfold negation really empties and opens the mind so that one can apprehend the beauty of cosmology in the *Lotus Sutra*.

Besides writing and teaching, Jizang engaged in service to others. Just as the Chan master Tanxian was noted for his humanitarian activities, Jizang was said to have been solicitous for Tanxian's welfare. He was also interested in the arts. During the Sui and Tang dynasties, he helped make twenty-five statues of bodhisattvas at the Riyan Temple. Jizang not only produced the fine conceptual analyses we find in his writings but he also practiced the dialectical thinking of the Sanlun School in his daily life. He was also a fine debater. In 609 he debated with Sengcan (529–613) and others for several days. It is said that there were more than thirty participants, who argued back and forth more than sixty times.

Buddhist monks, particularly *dharma* masters, are supposed to follow the *vinaya*—the rules of the monastic order—and strictly observe moral precepts. Jizang, however, was flexible in his behavior. In fact, his lifestyle can be viewed as the practice of his philosophy of emptiness. For him, good and evil, or right and wrong, had no intrinsic value and hence were empty; he felt that one should not be enslaved by conventional values and traditional morality. Some of his actions would appear to have been careless and unacceptable from the conventional standpoint; he was criticized, for instance, for consorting with women. However, Jizang also taught that ordinary people should follow the ordinary moral code.

II

Perhaps more than any other Chinese philosophy, the Sanlun school showed a fondness for logical argument, and its practitioners analyzed logical issues systematically and critically. Jizang examined, brilliantly, the nature and function of logic and its apparatus, such as negation, affirmation, and the concepts of true and false, right and wrong. He carefully investigated various logical propositions and the meaning and use of thesis, antithesis, and synthesis in conceptual disputes and theories.

According to Jizang, the Sanlun doctrine of emptiness was intended to show that logic is illogical. All conceptual schemes are conventional. They may have practical value, but they have no absolute a priori validity. Logical principles may be useful in daily life. They can be good, expedient guides in conceptual thinking and linguistic expression. But logic cannot and should not be viewed as a pinnacle of reality and rationality. One should not be bound by any conceptual tools in spiritual life. Nirvana itself is understood as liberation from the enslavement of conventional logic.

Philosophers and religious people as well have often accepted the absolute validity of logical assertions and have become attached to rationality. Jizang thought that this attitude was caused mainly by a failure to see the emptiness of negation and affirmation. Many misunderstandings and mispresentations of the Buddha's *dharma* have come from an inappropriate intepretation of the function of negation and affirmation in Buddha's statements and Buddhist scriptures. Usually, people assume that whenever someone makes a judgment, it must be either true or false, valid or invalid, right or wrong. If a viewpoint or thesis is false, its antithesis must be true. And if both thesis and antithesis are wrong, then some synthesis must be right. In general, negation entails affirmation. Logically, if a proposition *P* is false, non-*P* must be true; and if non-*P* is wrong, *P* must be right. In ordinary logic, negation is really a premise for affirmation.

Jizang contended that, unfortunately, most people follow this way of thinking, but in fact Buddha's use of negation is different. It is not a negation of affirmation. Non-*P* does not imply something other than *P*; it merely means the absence of *P*. The view that a certain thesis is wrong does not necessarily entail that some other theory or antithesis is right. According to Jizang, to have a proper understanding of the place of logic in Buddhism, one should know *poxie xianzheng*—the refutation of erroneous views as the illumination of right views. For him, *poxie xianzheng* is the key message of Sanlun treatises.

Poxie (refutation of erroneous views) and *xianzhheng* (illumination of right views), according to Jizang, are not two separate acts but the same act. The Madhyamikas critically investigated all views and repudiated them all. Their refutation was not intended to establish any particular view but was merely a declaration that metaphysical views are erroneous. In the strict sense, a right declaration is not a view in itself but rather the absence of views. If a "right" view is held in place of an erroneous view, this "right" view itself will become one-sided and require refutation. *P* is wrong not because non-*P* is right. If non-*P* is held as a view, it, too, is subject to refutation. Like one contemporary critique of metaphysics, the refutations of *P* and non-*P* in Sanlun writings proclaim that all metaphysical views are erroneous and ought to be refuted. To refute them, one does not have to present another metaphysical viewpoint; one merely needs to set aside metaphysical speculation.

Metaphysical speculation, for Jizang, is a disease (*bing*). It causes people to become attached to illusions. The Buddhist doctrine of emptiness is a medicine (*yao*) for this sickness, ridding the mind of illusions. Thus a Buddhist scripture may repudiate the viewpoint that a *dharma* is real (*you*). This negation does not mean that a *dharma* is unreal (*wu*). Metaphysical speculation about nonbeing, according to Jizang, is as untenable as speculation about being. Buddha did use terms such as *wu*—unreality or nonbeing—but Jizang contended:

> Tthe idea of *wu* is brought out primarily to handle the disease of the concept of *you*. If that disease disappears, the useless medicine is also discarded.

A Sanlun critique of metaphysical statements does not imply that the Sanlun philosophers assume the validity of ordinary language. For Jizang, no linguistic terms have intrinsic validity. In a careful analysis of conceptual structures, Sanlun Madhyamikas point out that all logical and linguistic expressions consist of two basic units: subject and predicate. Yet a relationship between two cannot be rationally established, and hence predication itself, as used in ordinary language, is really no more intelligible than metaphysical assertion.

They ask, Is the subject the same as or different from the predicate? If the subject of a sentence is identical with the predicate, the statement will be tautological and thus of dubious value. It would certainly say nothing about the world, and therefore there would be no functional predication. If the subject and the predicate are different, they ask, how can two different linguistic forms make up the same sentence and express the same state of affairs? In this case predication would be inconsistent and contradictory. Yet if the absence of inconsistency and contradiction is a basic requirement of rationality, then our logical statement would be irrational.

Jizang did not develop his own logic. He simply applied the logic of others to show the absurdity of all logical reasoning. When he was engaged in an argument, he did not set the standard of reasoning. He merely followed the logical norms of his opponents to reveal the irrational nature of their reasoning and so repudiate their viewpoints. Finally, when all erroneous views were eliminated, no such thing as negation and affirmation would be needed. The term "right" is used to put an end to wrong, but actually what we call "right" is as empty as the wrong view. It is truly called right only when there is neither affirmation nor negation. For Jizang, the Buddha's *dharma* teaches that originally there is nothing to affirm, and now there is not anything to negate.

Sanlun logic is a kind of empty logic. It does not assume any particular logical principles, nor does it aim to establish a standard of reasoning. Conventional logic, according to Jizang, makes people attached to certain particular reasoning and particular viewpoints. Their intellectual and spiritual life becomes confined to conventional rules and extreme viewpoints; it may look rational, but in essence it is irrational. For Jizang, the empty logic of the Sanlun school is primarily therapeutic, eradicating intellectual and emotional attachments. It is also liberating, freeing us from conceptual illusions. Once attachments and illusions are gone, even empty logic is no longer needed and can be abandoned.

The apprehension and practice of emptiness can be called *nirvana*. According to Jizang, *nirvana* is not a state ontologically different from *samsara*, the world of life and death as we know it. *Nirvana* is not something remote; it can occur on this earth, in this life. Whenever one lives without views or attachments, one abides in *nirvana*.

III

The Buddha's *dharma*, according to Jizang and other Madhyamikas, is conveyed by means of the twofold truth (*erdi*). Those who do not know the twofold truth cannot really understand the teachings of Buddha. "Twofold truth" refers to conventional or relative truth (*sudi, samvrtisatya*) and ultimate or absolute truth (*zhendi, paramarthasatya*).

Buddhist twofold truth has often been seen as standing for two fixed sets of truths. The meaning or truth-value of each set is said to lie in the reality or objects it denotes. If a true statement does not correspond to an empirical fact, it must point to something transcendental. Therefore, worldly truth is seen as a true assertion about empirical reality, while ultimate truth is seen as a true claim about transcendental reality.

Jizang wrote the *Meaning of the Twofold Truth* (*Erdi yi*) to correct this mistaken theory. For him, words and names are empty—they have no meaning by themselves; rather, they acquire their meaning in use. The meaning of a word is not the same as the object for which it stands; instead, meaning lies in context, or how the word is used in life. If the context changes, the meaning of the word will change and may even disappear. Even the word *nirvana* has no meaning by itself. It is as empty as any other word we may use to describe the world. We should not seek an extralinguistic reality and give a special ontic status to *nirvana*.

According to Jizang, language is *xilun*, a conceptual game. All words, rules, propositions, and logical assertions are conventional. None has a fixed, intrinsic essence or value. All true and false statements are devoid of a definite truth-value. It is a mistake to believe, or to search for, the validity of any conceptual expression. For Jizang, the search for a priori intrinsic value in linguistic proclamations is a delusion. This delusion often makes people "sick," in the sense that it commits them to an unrewarding search for a fixed truth.

However, according to the Sanlun school, a linguistic expression has practical value. Language can serve as a fish trap (*quan*), a convenient device to attract people to the Buddha's *dharma*. Buddha, according to Sanlun masters, was a skillful teacher. He might conform to worldly linguistic usage and use conceptual statements to explain his *dharma*. But he used words without attributing any reality or intrinsic value to them. His discursive exposition was designed to lead sentient beings to know the empty nature of words so as to help them to discard reliance on language. For Sanlun masters, only when language is forgotten as a signifier of ultimate truth can one realize the true *dharma*.

For the Sanlun school, the concept of truth is devoid of reference. Since the concept of meaning as a relation between words and objects is untenable, truth cannot merely be a copy or right presentation of extralinguistic reality. So the Sanlun teaching of the twofold truth is also given to repudiate the idea that ultimate truth is something absolute, fixed, or eternal. Metaphysical visions of reality, apart from their practical bearings, are absurd because the meaning of words lies in useful contexts and circumstances. Claims to truth should have practical consequences.

Sanlun masters reminded people that Buddha was a pragmatic teacher. He rarely discussed any purely theoretical issues. His simile of the poisonous arrow illustrates the pragmatic character of his truth. Those who adhere to a fixed concept of truth would be like a foolish man wounded by a poisonous arrow. Instead of removing the arrow or looking for medical treatment, he engages in speculation about the origin, essence, and source of the arrow.

Buddha's twofold truth, according to Jizang, is not a pure theory of knowledge. It stands neither for two definite, extralinguistic realities nor for two fixed sets of truths; it is a convenient tactical device. For Sanlun masters, this practical device reflects a difference in the way one perceives things, or one's viewpoint on the world. So-called worldly or relative truth involves emotional and intellectual attachment; hence, objects of knowledge are considered extralinguistic and self-existing. This outlook assumes the intrinsic reality of things and the intrinsic validity of logic; it is as if the true state of affairs can be described by language, and conceptual expressions can be vindicated by logic. This "attached" standpoint is called *sudi, samvrtisatya*.

But one could see the very same things in a different way, without emotional or intellectual attachments. In this "unattached" way of judging the phenomenal world, what one perceives is empty of a fixed, determinate, or self-existing nature. Taking this standpoint, one is liberated from conceptualization. One is committed neither to ontological entities nor to linguistic terms. The meaning of words is no longer seen as extralinguistic, and one awakes to the insight that no reality is really real and no truth is truly true. Discursive knowledge is a human projection. This enlightened standpoint is termed *zhendi, paramarthasatya.*

Alternatively, the aspiring mind could also be a victim of the illusion that ultimate truth can be seen as something eternal. If this occurs, the so-called *zhendi* would become another extreme view, *sudi*, and would deserve to be repudiated. For Jizang, the very rejection is the illumination of a right standpoint. Once all attachments are eliminated, the ultimate truth is illuminated.

In a sense, ultimate truth is higher and finer than worldly truth, but these two truths do not exhaust all truths. If one clings to something absolute as a higher truth or reality, it would become a lower or worldly truth. The discipline of negation needs to be implemented until all such attachments are removed. Ultimately, all truths are empty. They are essentially pragmatic in character, and whether they are true or not depends on whether they lead to attachment. Their "truth-value" lies in their effectiveness as a means to salvation.

According to the Sanlun school, the twofold truth, like empty logic, is therapeutic. In order to reject the nihilist position, Buddha may have taught that existence was real; and for the sake of repudiating the eternalist position he may have said that existence was unreal. As long as Buddha's teachings effectively help remove attachment, they can be considered true.

For Jizang, the twofold truth is also a good exegetical technique. It is presented to explain contradictions in Buddhism and make Buddha's teachings all true. It seems that there are certain ambiguities and contradictions in the sutras. Sometimes the scriptures teach that all things are causally produced and impermanent, but elsewhere they state that cause and effect, and impermanence, cannot be established. Buddhist texts contrast enlightenment with ignorance, yet claim that one should not think like a dualist. According to Jizang, one should know that all Buddhist messages are given as the twofold truth. Different messages were delivered from different standpoints, and each can be apprehended from its appropriate standpoint. From the standpoint of worldly truth, the sutras say that things are causally produced and impermanent, and distinguish enlightenment from ignorance. Those teachings are true in terms of worldly truth, but all things are empty from the higher standpoint. The scripture may examine the same issue from this higher perspective and claim that causality and impermanence cannot be established, and that one should give up dualistic thinking. If one understands that Buddha's teachings were given by means of a twofold truth, one will not find contradictions.

IV

Ultimately, all truths are empty, and one should not cling to any of them. For Jizang, even the term "empty" or "emptiness" is empty. It has no definite meaning by itself but acquires a meaning in the process of salvation. The Sanlun doctrine of emptiness is not metaphysics, nor does it convey discursive knowledge. It is essentially a device for salvation and has various meanings in different contexts.

Kong (empty or emptiness) in Sanlun Buddhism is often used as a verb rather than a noun. It refers to an action—emptying one's mind. According to Jizang, the chief function of emptiness is the refutation of erroneous views as the illumination of right views. This refutation helps sentient beings remove attachment and give up worldly things. Because "clinging" itself is the source of evil and suffering, emptiness implies emptying life of evil and suffering. To practice emptiness is to live a nirvanic life and practice the way of salvation.

According to Sanlun masters, Buddhist salvation is a liberation and transformation of the entire person; it touches on all aspects of human life—emotional, intellectual, volitional, physical. Psychologically, craving or desire is the chief cause of suffering. Emptiness as a device for salvation signifies detachment. Jizang called emptiness *shui* (water), whose chief function is to extinguish the burning fire of desires. If one fails to see this function of emptiness and regards it as a metaphysical concept, the water will not perform its proper function. Jizang asked, How then can we extinguish the fire?

The term "emptiness" is also used by Sanlun masters to devalue and discredit conventional values and worldly views. When a Buddhist says that life is empty, he means, in part, that life is sorrowful and human existence is like a dream. It is not as delightful or as valuable as ordinarily believed. Many people tend to think that there is a permanent self or soul which persists through physical and mental changes and exists before birth and after death, and that the most important thing is to take care of this eternal soul. But Buddha teaches that *wo kong*: I, self, ego, or soul is empty. According to Sanlun masters, the so-called immortal self is not an intelligible concept, and searching for the immortality of the soul is as senseless as looking for fire after the fuel has run out. In this context "emptiness" connotes the absurdity of many concepts.

The Sanlun process of mental purification has not merely emotional and volitional but also cognitive aspects. Its discipline is logical and dialectical. This dialectical way of emptiness has been called the middle way (*zhongdao*) or more properly the middle way of the twofold truth (*erdi zhongdao*). The Sanlun Buddhists critically examine all possible intellectual illusions and attachments.

On the first possible level, ordinary people naively hold that what appears to the senses is the true nature of things. This is worldly truth, a view of being. But more knowledgeable persons may reject this commonsense view, and this approach is described as "ultimate truth." However, the latter approach could become metaphysical. Then "ultimate truth" would involve a metaphysical assertion of nonbeing and would be another extreme position. One has to repudiate it from a higher standpoint.

The second possible level reveals that both the worldly and the "ultimate truth" of the first level belong to the sphere of worldly truth. A denial of both being and nonbeing would be the actual ultimate truth. This nondualistic thinking appears more tenable than dualistic thinking.

However, when examined from a still higher perspective, both duality and nonduality are considered worldly truth—neither is ultimate truth. This third level, according to Jizang, explains that saints will abandon all conceptualizations.

The advance from one level to another is the process of salvation, according to the Sanlun school. This dialectical process is not limited to three levels but is to be followed progressively to infinite levels until all attachments are eliminated. Epistemologically, "emptiness" means an unattached apprehension that all truths are provisional. This makes one open-minded and undogmatic. In this way, one can think freely and can live leisurely in this world.

V

Jizang was a skillful teacher, but he did poorly at organizing his followers and securing the transmission of the Sanlun school. After his death Sanlun Buddhism as a sectarian school declined rapidly. This decline could also have been due to the fact that Jizang's philosophy was too advanced to be understood and appreciated by ordinary people.

However, the essentials of Sanlun philosophy continued to exert a great influence on the development of Buddhist schools in China, Korea, and Japan. The Sanlun philosophies of emptiness, the middle way, the twofold truth, and the refutation of erroneous views as the illumination of right views were absorbed into the teachings and practices of later Chinese Buddhist schools, such as Tiantai, Huayan, Chan (Zen), and Pure Land Buddhism. The Sanlun philosophy of emptiness seems to have opened the way for the popularity of the cosmology of Tiantai and Huayan metaphysics. It teaches that all things are empty. It implies a philosophy that all is one and one is all. The Sanlun doctrines of the middle way and the twofold truth later inspired Chinese Chan (Zen) masters to convey seemingly illogical teachings and take unorthodox actions. For example, Chan masters might say that all, including a dog, have Buddha-nature from the conventional standpoint. Yet from the higher standpoint, they may proclaim that nothing has Buddha-nature.

Chan appears to be illogical and irrational but actually is not. Its teachings are conveyed by means of the twofold truth. If Chan is apprehended in this way, one sees that its messages and actions are all *dharma*. Like Jizang, Chan masters taught that a right view is not a view but the absence of views. In many ways, Chan and other Chinese Mahayana ideas are practical applications of Sanlun philosophy. Thus, philosophically speaking, one cannot properly understand the development of Chinese Buddhism without an adequate apprehension of Sanlun thought.

See also Buddhism in China; Buddhism: Zen (Chan).

Bibliography

Cheng, Hsueh-li. "Chi-tsang's Treatment of Metaphysical Issues." *Journal of Chinese Philosophy*, 8, September 1981, pp. 371–389.

——. *Empty Logic: Madhyamika Buddhism from Chinese Sources*. New York: Philosophical Library, 1984.

——. *Nagarjuna's Twelve Gate Treatise*. Boston: Reidel, 1982.

——. "Truth and Logic in Sanlun Madhyamika Buddhism." *International Philosophical Quarterly*, 21, September 1981, pp. 260–276.

Robinson, Richard, H. *Early Madhyamika in India and China*. Madison: University of Wisconsin Press, 1967.

Yang, Huinan. *Jizang*. Taipei: Dongda, 1989.

Zhang, Mantao, ed. *Sanlun dianji yanjiu* (Studies in Sanlun Documents). Taipei: Dacheng Wenhua, 1979.

——. *Sanlunzong zhi fazhan jiqi sixiang* (The Development of Sanlun School and Its Thought). Taipei: Dacheng Wenhua, 1978.

——. *Zhongguan sixiang lunji* (Collection of Essays on Sanlun Thoughts). Taipei: Dacheng Wenhua, 1978.

Junzi (*Chün-tzu*): The Moral Person

A. S. Cua

The *Analects* of Confucius provides an ample vocabulary for virtues or excellencies of ethical character. The frequent recurrence of certain terms such as *ren* (benevolence, humanity), *li* (rites), and *yi* (rightness, righteousness) suggests Confucius's ongoing concern with the cultivation of fundamental virtues. Confucius's remark that one thread runs through his teachings may be cited as partial support for ascribing a holistic quality to his thought (*Analects*, 14.15). However, we do not find a systematic scheme for conduct in the *Analects*. There is a lack of an explicit and coherent ordering of moral ideas. Also, throughout the history of Chinese thought and contemporary Chinese and western writings on Confucianism, we find a great variance of interpretation of fundamental concepts such as *ren* (Chan 1955, 1975).

The unsystematic character of Confucius's ethical thought in part reflects his emphasis on the concrete and the particular. In this sense the ethics of Confucius is an ethics of flexibility. This aspect of Confucian ethics is perhaps best understood by way of understanding Confucius's notion of *junzi* as an ideal ethical exemplar for practical morality. This essay is an inquiry into the plausibility and significance of this notion as an underlying theme of Confucian ethics.

Although Confucius believed that only a sage (*shengren*), divinely inspired and intuitively wise, can envision and establish a harmonious social order, he did not regard the ideal of sagehood as practically attainable by ordinary moral agents. He once remarks that he cannot hope to meet a sage but can only hope to meet a *junzi* (7.25). The ideal of sagehood, in his mind, functions more like a supreme but abstract ideal of a perfect moral personality (Cua 1978). Mencius and Xunzi, as well as neo-Confucians in Song and Ming periods of Chinese history, aspire to greater heights. For them, common people, if they follow the prescriptions for self-cultivation and persist in their efforts, can all become sages (*sheng*). More realistic is Confucius's insight into the practical possibility of attaining human excellence. To him every ordinary human, with unwavering effort in self-cultivation, even in adversity or in the best of changing circumstances, can become a *junzi*. Sagehood is an object of wishing, not a feasible objective of ethical pursuit.

Interpretations of *Junzi* in the *Analects*

The different translations and notes on the *Analects* indicate the difficulty of settling on a definitive or adequate English translation of *junzi*. This difficulty is also evident in some translations and notes since the nineteenth century. Here is a short list of translations of *junzi*: "superior man" (Legge, Chan, Bodde, Dubs), "gentleman" (Waley, Lau, Watson), "noble man or person" (Giles, Fingarette, Schwartz). In some explicitly interpretive studies, we also find "paradigmatic individuals" (Cua 1969, 1971; see 1978, chs. 3 and 5), "model of emulation" (Munro 1969), and "exemplary persons" (Hall and Ames 1987). In *The Doctrine of the Mean* (*Zhongyong*), we also find "profound person" (Tu 1976). Since there is no English equivalent, *junzi* is best left untranslated. This view does not deny the necessity of choice in translation in the service of readability and consistency. But whatever English term is chosen, the writer must offer some explanation and justification for this choice. Let us consider some examples.

James Legge, the pioneering translator of the *Analects* in the late nineteenth century, used "superior man" for translating most occurrences of the ethical uses of *junzi*. In two exceptional cases (1.2 and 1.14), we find "man of complete virtue." The first exception and also the first occurrence is 1.1, where the master says: "Is he not a man of complete virtue [*junzi*], who feels no discomposure though men may take no note of him?" (1960, 1:137). Legge gives a terse comment on *junzi*:

> Literarily, it is a "princely man." . . . It is a technical term in Chinese moral writers, for which there is no exact correspondency in English, and which cannot be rendered always in the same way.

The second case is 1.14, where the master says:

> He who aims to be a man of complete virtue [*junzi*] in his food does not seek to gratify his appetite, nor in his dwelling place does he seek the appliances of ease; he is earnest in what he is doing, and careful in his speech; he frequents the company of men of principle that he may be rectified: such a person may be said indeed to love to learn.

Legge gives no explanation for using "man of complete virtue" in these remarks. The translation also collapses the distinction between *junzi* and sage (*sheng*), for "a man of complete virtue" conveys the idea of morally perfected state or highest degree of moral attainment, sagehood, rather than a *junzi*, who, as we shall see later, is an imperfect being—a being who has reached a high or superior degree of excellence as compared with ordinary people who have lesser or no distinguishing ethical achievement. This sense of *junzi* provides an explanatory justification for Legge's preference for "superior man" for the other occurrences of *junzi* in passages of the *Analects* having to do with ethics.

Lionel Giles (1907), while agreeing with Legge that *junzi* literarily means "princely man," thinks that "superior man" is a misleading translation. For *Analects* 1.2, Giles has, "The Master said: Is he not a princely man [*junzi*]—he who is never vexed that others know him not?" A long note follows Giles's translation:

> This is the much discussed *chün tzu* [*junzi*], an expression of which the stereotyped English equivalent is "the superior man." But in this there is, unhappily, a tinge of blended superciliousness and irony absolutely foreign to the native phrase, which in my opinion makes it unsuitable. "Princely man" is as nearly as possible in literal translation, and sometimes, as we shall see, it actually means "prince." But in the majority of cases the connotation of rank or authority is certainly not explicit, and as a general rendering I have preferred "the higher type of man," "the nobler sort of man," or sometimes more simply as "the good man." Perhaps the nearest approximation in any European language is to be found in the Greek *ho kalos kagathos*, because that implies high mental and moral qualities combined with all the outward bearing of a gentleman. Compare also with Aristotle's *ho spoudaious* who is however more abstract and ideal. (52n)

In defense of Legge we may say that Giles's remark actually echoes Legge's reminder that there is no exact English correspondence or equivalent for *junzi*. The difference in translation lies in the explanatory addendum, which provides the rationale. Considered as a descriptive term for a moral ideal today, "superior man" does not have the connotation of "a tinge of blended superciliousness and irony," though we would prefer a gender-neutral term, "individual" or "person." As we pointed earlier, the *junzi* is "superior" to other people because of his superior ethical character and achievement. Giles's preference for "the higher type of man," or "the nobler sort of man," is no less misleading, for it may suggest that a *junzi* belongs to a special class of persons with "higher mental and moral qualities"—an idea that Confucius would reject. For Confucius, humans are born pretty much alike; it is practice that sets them so far apart from one another (17.2). For the Confucians Mencius and Xunzi, since all ordinary people can become *junzi* or sages, their achieved moral status does not mark them as members of a special type of humanity. As Xunzi put it:

> With respect to inborn nature and endowment, intelligence and ability, the *junzi* and small-minded persons are one and the same. In desiring honor and averting shame, the *junzi* and small-minded persons are the same. However, if we focus on the Way they pursue these matters, we would find them to be diametrically opposite. (*Xunzi*, Book 4)

Giles's allusion to the Greek ideal of *kalos kagathos* and Aristotle's notion of *spoudaious* as somewhat akin to *junzi* offers valuable hints for comparative ethical study. Later, when we focus on the *junzi*'s concern for *li* (rites), particularly in the observance of *wen* (cultural refinement), it is illuminating to compare *junzi* with *kalos kagathos*, especially if we construe *junzi* in *Xunzi* as a refined Confucian (*ya Ru*). A similar remark may be made about the now popular translation of *junzi* as "gentleman." More interesting and significant is Giles's halfhearted reference to *spoudaious*, for the interpretation of *junzi* as ethical, paradigmatic individuals may in part be elucidated by recalling Aristotle's conception of *spoudaious* (Cua 1978, ch. 3B).

Let us turn to the familiar translation of *junzi* as "gentleman," also suggested by Giles. It is interesting to note the different rationales for this translation given by Arthur Waley and D. C. Lau. Says Waley:

> As regards the translation of the term *chün-tzu* [*junzi*], I see no alternative but to use "gentleman," though the effect is occasionally somewhat *absurd* in English. One needs a word which primarily signifies *superiority of birth*, but also implies moral superiority. Neither Legge's "superior man," nor Soothill's various equivalents ("man of the higher type," "wise man") fulfil this condition. (1938, 37)

Contrast this view with Lau's, where "superiority of birth" is, rightly, deemphasized:

> In the *Analects*, . . . *chün-tzu*, *junzi* and *hsiao-ren* [*xiaoren*] (small man) are essentially moral terms. The *chün-tzu* is the man with a cultivated moral character, while the *hsiao-ren* is the opposite. It is worth noting that the two usages indicating the social and moral status are not exclusive, and, in individual cases, it is difficult to be sure whether, besides their moral connotations, these terms may not also carry their usual social connotations as well. (1979, 14)

For Confucius, as well as Mencius and Xunzi, *junzi* expresses an ideal of a cultivated, ethical character. Although more explanation is needed to avoid misleading interpertations, the various translations of *junzi* may be viewed as valuable attempts to bring forth the translator's own appraisal of the salient features of this ideal of ethical character in a way that will be intelligible to English readers. In this light, we may regard *junzi* as a sort of emphatic term that, in context, serves to point up certain ethically desirable and commendable qualities of the ideal person—in short, ethical excellencies. In Hume's term, these excellencies are "personal merits" that deserve emphasis especially in moral education (1952). In the case of Xunzi, the classical Confucian philosopher, we have insightful essays on learning and self-cultivation (books 1–2). We find forceful statements of the practice of *li* (ritual propriety, rules of proper conduct) and *ren* (humaneness, benevolence) and the importance of learning the classics, guidance of moral teachers, self-examination and reflection, and accumulation of good deeds as crucial elements in the process of becoming a sage. For attaining the ideal of *junzi*, Xunzi insists on integrity (*quan*) and purity (*cui*) or incorruptibility. Along with this emphatic function, the *junzi* also serves as an exemplar of how the fundamental Confucian ethical concerns—i.e., *ren, li*, and *yi*—have concrete significance; that is, they are practically attainable in varying degrees by ordinary moral agents.

Qualities of a *Junzi*

In general *junzi* is a notion of a morally excellent person, a paradigmatic individual who sets the tone and quality of life for ordinary moral agents. A *junzi* is a man who embodies *ren* (humanity, benevolence) and *li* (ritual propriety). Every man can strive to be a *junzi* in the sense of a guiding paradigmatic individual, rather than a *xiaoren* (small-minded person). There are of course degrees of personal ethical achievement, depending on the situation, character, ability, and opportunity of moral agents.

Legge's translation of *junzi* as "superior man" brings out the *junzi* as a person who has a superior moral character and aptitude. The translation of *junzi* as "true gentlemen" or "gentleman" focuses on the *junzi's* relation with the cultural setting of his actions, his ability to satisfy, so to speak, the stylistic requirements of a form of life (Cua 1978, ch. 7). A *junzi*, in this sense, is an embodiment of a cultural lifestyle. Some of the qualities of *junzi* resemble those of the ideal of gentleman as articulated by Douglas McGee:

> The gentleman as defined by tradition aspired to nothing less than becoming a concrete universal. Guided and sustained by his limitation, he took as his moral ideal the cultivation of humanity. . . . His conduct was judged by its appropriateness, a measure that took account of particular circumstances, but always in conformity to the human ideal. Conduct regulated by this form felt congruous and fitting, hence purposeful. In the widest sense of "manners," the manners of the gentleman were textures of his life, a texture isomorphic with the structure of his class. (1966, 222).

Let us turn to a general constructive interpretation of *junzi*. Confucius's varying remarks on *junzi* in the *Analects* may be regarded as setting forth the different requirements or qualities for a life of moral excellence. A *junzi* is, first of all, a man of moral virtues pervaded by a concern for *ren*, that is, an affectionate concern for the well-being of humanity, as well as concern for *li* and *yi* (rightness, righteousness).

Concern for ren (humaneness). Some of Confucius's remarks portray the *junzi* as a man who possesses various virtues pervaded by the ideal of *ren* (humanity, benevolence). Confucius said:

> Wealth and honor are what all human beings desire. But if they were not obtained in accord with proper way (*dao*), I would not be at home with them. If a *junzi* disavows and gives up his commitment to *ren*, how can he be worthy of that name? The *junzi* does not, even for a single meal, act contrary to *ren*. Whether he confronts an urgent or difficult situation, he abides by *ren*. (4.5)

A person genuinely committed to the practice of *ren* would even sacrifice his or her life for its sake (15.8). *Ren*, in the broad sense, is Confucius's *dao*, that is, an ideal of an inclusive end that embraces the whole of humanity as well as the interdependence or relatedness of particular moral dispositions or virtues. On one occasion, responding to an inquiry about *ren*, Confucius said that a man of *ren* practices five things: "respectfulness, generous-mindedness, trustworthiness, adroitness, and kindness." His reasoning consists in a series of hypothetical propositions:

> If you are respectful, you will not be treated with disrespect. If you are generous-minded, you will win the people. If you are reliable, people will entrust responsibility in you. If you are adroit, you will accomplish much. If you are kind, you will be in an adequate position to employ the services of others. (17.6)

The consequents in these hypothetical propositions appear to be rooted in the notion of reflective desirability or undesirability, in this case, avoidance of undesirable states of affairs. If this interpretation is correct, particular moral virtues cited, with others such as knowledge and courage (15.17), are recognized as having moral value insofar as they promote the realization of a life of *ren*. They are virtues in the sense that their absence would lead to undesirable consequences that would hamper the pursuit of *ren*. This appeal to the reflective desirability of ethical commitment is an important aspect of Confucian argumentation (Cua 1985; 1998, Essay 1). For our present purpose, it is sufficient to note that a *junzi* cultivates particular virtues for the purpose of attaining to a life of *ren*, and this task presupposes knowledge of the reflective desirability of actions and human affairs. More formally, *ren*, like *yi* and *li*, is a fundamental concept that provides ethical significance of various, particular, dependent notions of virtues such as respectfulness and trustworthiness. These dependent notions, so to speak, are specifications of the concrete significance of the abstract, basic, Confucian concepts of virtue that define the *dao*, the ideal life of human excellence.

Concern for li (propriety) and yi (righteousness). *Li* and *yi* are also fundamental moral virtues. Because of the Confucian stress on tradition and civility, and the need for independent ethical judgment of committed individual moral agents, *yi* and *li* deserve special attention in Confucian ethics. Our discussion of *ren* and particular virtues pertains, so to speak, to the internal aspect of *ren*-morality. The focus is on self-cultivation rather than the external or outward form of conduct. In times of moral failure, the *junzi*—unlike a small-minded person—seeks the cause within himself rather than others (15.21). One who is committed to the Confucian d*ao* or *ren* must examine himself for the cause of failure. As an eminent disciple, Zengzi, reminds his pupils:

> Every day I examine myself on three counts. In what I have undertaken on another's behalf, have I done my best? In my dealings with my friends, have I failed to be trustworthy in what I said? Have I passed on to others what I have not tried out myself? (1.4; Lau 1979, p. 59)

Among others, one contribution of Mencius to the development of Confucian ethics is his emphasis on the function of *xin* (mind-heart) in connection with moral failure (Cua, 2001). Xunzi also offers insight on how an ethically informed human mind may be obscured by concern with immediate satisfaction of desires without regard to distant consequences (Cua, 1985, ch. 4).

Confucius said, "If a *junzi* studies extensively and conducts himself in accord with the *li*, he is not likely to do wrong" (6.25). For elaboration, we may cite Xunzi's remark: "If the *junzi* engages in extensive learning and examines himself daily, his moral understanding will become perspicuous and his conduct free from fault" (*Xunzi*, book 1). This and many other remarks of Confucius suggest that the *li* is a set of rules delimiting the ethical domain of proper conduct. And for the most part, *li* is considered by Confucius and his followers as a set of established customs or conventions, presumably of the Confucian community, to define the form and possibility of moral actions. In this sense, the *li* may be said to delineate the conventionally accepted style of actions, that is, the form and possibility of moral achievement within a culture or cultural lifestyle. *Li*, unlike *ren*, does not define the nature of morality; it defines only the limiting form of execution of moral performance. In a more contemporary idiom, we may express this idea in terms of the tie or contact between an individual agent's actions and the cultural form of life that gives them the locus of identification and the possibility of moral achievement.

More fundamentally, an appropriate action conforming to a ritual requirement of *li* has its ethical significance because such an action is performed in the light of a concern for *ren*. However, without a persistent regard for *ren*, ritual observances would amount to mere formal gestures with no moral substance. Notably, in addition to imposing restraint on human behavior, as Xunzi (book 19) points out, the *li* also support the satisfaction of desires within the limits of proper conduct. And when a *junzi*'s compliance with *li* is informed by the spirit of *ren, li* has also an ennobling function, exemplifying the *junzi*'s respect for *li* as an ideal, *ren*—embedded in tradition (Cua 1989). This attitude toward *li* also signifies respect for the reality of a situation, the background and possibilities that furnish the context for successful moral performance. This emphasis on *li* is one justification for the Confucian homage to the concrete. Every action, in this view, has a conventional aspect from which its normative meaning and import can be understood. Whether or not we accept this stress on *li*, some sort of convention for identifying the normative import of action must be an element of any moral theory. Granted the importance of ethical convention or tradition, attention to the aesthetic and religious dimensions of *li* will also lead us to an appreciation of valuable facets of human life in different cultures and civilizations (Cua 2003).

The other aspect of action relates to the importance Confucius assigned to the role of the concept *yi* (rightness, righteousness). Confucius once remarked that the *junzi* considers *yi* of supreme value (17.25). *Yi* is contrasted with self-serving concerns or profit (4.16). This contrast brings out the Confucian distinction between morality and egoism. The notion of *yi*, not clearly elucidated in the *Analects* or in later Confucian classics, is difficult. In the *Doctrine of the Mean*, *yi* is defined by its homophone, meaning "appropriateness" or "fitness" (sec. 20). The focus is on right conduct, that is, conduct appropriate to or fitting in a situation, and one who regularly aims at such an action may be said to have the virtue of righteousness. Aspiring to be a perfect person (*chengren*), a *junzi*, informed by the spirit of *ren*, would give up his life for the sake of *yi* rather than yield to a desire for personal gain (14.13). Even a less committed scholar, in opportune moments where profit is imminent, would think of right conduct (*yi*) as the primary consideration (19.1). Insofar as *yi* is opposed to exclusive concern with self-interest without regard to other people's interests, it may be regarded as representing the Confucian moral point of view. *Yi*, like courage, knowledge, and other virtues, would also seem to be a particular virtue (i.e., righteousness) that results from correct moral performance. If *li* defines an aspect of right act in *ren*-morality, it is an emphasis on the tie between actions and the cultural lifestyle. *Yi*, on the other hand, gives us a sense of rightness as relating to the concrete, problematic situation that calls for action inspired by *ren*. *Yi* may also be construed as the "oughtness" of a situation (Fung 1950, 42). However, this "oughtness," though a characteristic of obligatory actions, focuses mainly on the right act as appropriate to the particular situation that a moral agent confronts. Doing what is right in a situation is not just a matter of conformity to moral and ritual rules (*li*), but also conformity to a judgment of relevance in actual situations. *Yi* is another Confucian focus on an aspect of the concrete. If *li* is the emphasis on the contact between *ren* and the ethical tradition or cultural lifestyle, *yi* is a bridge between *ren* and *li* as a cultural lifestyle—in effect the contact between *ren* and actual situations. Thus, the judgment of what is to be done, informed by reflection, is reserved to the moral agent. In this sense, Confucius remarked:

> The *junzi* considers *yi* to be the basic stuff of conduct. In the light of *yi*, he observes the rules of proper conduct (*li*), expresses [the significance of *yi*] in humility, and completes it in trustworthiness. (15.17)

We may sum up the significance of these requirements as follows. A *junzi* regards *li* and *yi* as fundamental considerations in ethical judgment and conduct. However, *ren*, the Confucian ideal of human excellence, provides the ultimate concern that renders *yi* and *li* worthy of pursuit. Thus the concern with *ren* pervades the life of a *junzi*. This is the focal point of his pedagogical function as a standard of aspiration for many ordinary moral agents. In this sense, the *junzi*, for ordinary persons, is a "model of emulation" (Cua 1998, Essay 8; Munro 1969)—that is, emulation in the sense of imitating or following, rather than surpassing. More profound is the function of *junzi* as a paradigmatic individual, for *ren* may also be construed as an ideal theme, rather than an ideal norm, that is, as a standard of inspiration, which provides a "beacon of light" more than a norm or principle or rule of conduct (Cua 1978, ch. 8). The habitat of *ren*, the ethical ideal of humanity, is a moral, cultural tradition; in Confucian language, it is a ritual context of action (*li*) in which human transactions occur with interests and motives of varying import. *Li* gives the moral action a locale of normative identification and an orbit of restraining conditions for the proper achievement of the moral ideal. More important, *li* also provides enabling and ennobling conditions for the possibility of fulfillment of desires of the individuals within its regulative limits (Cua 1989). Generally, actions that conform to *li*-requirements may be said to be in contact with the cultural lifestyle—the Confucian form of life. If *li* focuses on the tie of individual actions to culture, the freedom of a moral agent is radically limited in terms of what he can do and accomplish. However, the restraining function of *li* defines only the form but not the content of this freedom. The emphasis on *yi* as a requirement of being a *junzi* preserves a great deal of latitude in action. Just as *ren* cannot be practiced without *li*, the ethical, cultural setting, so *ren* cannot be realized without *yi* or judgment of the relevance of *ren* and *li* to concrete situations of human life. Our next two sets of descriptions of *junzi*, together with the present account, explain in large part this flexible and adaptable feature of Confucian ethics.

Catholicity and neutrality. For Confucius, the *junzi* is not an implement (2.12), which is fit for a specific, narrow purpose. Instead, "he should have broad vision, wide interests, and sufficient ability to do many things" (Chan 1963, 24). He is broad-minded and nonpartisan (2.14, 7.30), and aspires to higher and more valuable things in life (14.23).

These remarks on the aptitude and broad-mindedness of the *junzi* are natural, in view of Confucius's emphasis on *ren, li*, and *yi*. If *ren* consists in being affectionately concerned for the well-being of humanity, the possibility of attaining *ren* presupposes that the moral agent has the ability to "know other humans" (*zhiren*) and sympathize with the predicament of moral agency. However, the ability to execute one's moral intentions within ritual contexts is also important. If *yi* is required to give import to *ren* and *li*, then the *junzi* must exercise the "secret art" that makes his moral nature efficacious as an exemplar for other agents. This theme of "contagion" of the *junzi*'s conduct in Confucius's thinking is perhaps best expressed in the *Zhongyong*:

> The way which the superior man (*junzi*) pursues, reaches wide and far, and yet is secret. . . . The way of the superior man may be found, in its simple elements, in the intercourse of common men and women; but in its utmost reaches, it shines brightly through heaven and earth. (Legge 1892, sec. 12)

Also, "The superior man can find himself in no situation in which he is not himself" (Legge, sec. 14). Although the *junzi*'s way is secret and capable of expansive influence in the lives of other moral agents, he is not a mere spectator of human behavior, for he wishes both to establish his own and his fellows' ethical character. And this wish also involves an effort to actualize their ethically good rather than bad dispositions (12.16).

This "secret way" or art of the *junzi* is not a mere matter of actions intellectually determined by moral and ritual rules. If a *junzi* has a natural preference for *ren*-morality, this preference does not commit him to specific courses of action before a confrontation with an actual moral situation. Thus Confucius said of himself, "I have no prejudgment about acceptable or unacceptable conduct or states of affairs" (18.8). Moral actions in concrete contexts are not a straightforward deduction from given moral rules. The mere intellectual determination of the morality of action does not suffice in the assessment of moral performance. For the relevance of moral and ritual rules has to be assessed in concrete situations. This flexible and varying function of *yi* accounts for the neutrality of the *junzi*'s attitude or his lack of commitment to specific courses of action. The actual assessment of moral and ritual rules is at the same time a way of vindicating their importance in human life. This act of assessment requires a neutral attitude.

It is also this neutral attitude of the *junzi* that gives scope to the exercise of *yi* in novel and exigent situations. Thus a *junzi* "in dealing with people and affairs of the world, has neither prepossession or prejudice; he follows what is right" (4.10). He is "composed and satisfied" (7.36) and free from anxiety, fear, and perplexities. "Being a man of *ren*, he is free from anxiety about acting contrary to morality; being a man of courage, he is free from fear; being a man with knowledge of human affairs, he is free from perplexities" (14.30). His easeful life is a matter of his attitude and his confidence in his ability to deal with difficult and varying situations rather than a matter of infallible judgment or authority.

This aspect of the notion of *junzi* poses a problem in Confucian ethics. How can a man of virtue (*ren*) and moral integrity be indifferent to specific courses of action that follow from his espoused moral principles and rules? If a moral agent is to serve as a paradigm for actual conduct, it seems reasonable and proper to expect from him specific commitments to what he will do in accordance with moral rules. In Confucian ethics, moral rules and expected types of obligatory actions are by and large a matter of social roles within a cultural lifestyle (*li*). If the *junzi* is a man of *li*, it seems reasonable to expect from him at least a commitment to the application of these moral rules in concrete situations. In concluding this essay, I will say something on this complex problem.

Correspondence of words and deeds (*yanxing heyi*). The neutral attitude of a *junzi* is related to Confucius's emphasis on the harmony of words and deeds. If morality deals with the relations between men, as the character *ren* suggests, living in accordance with *ren*-morality requires a knowledge of men. However, without knowledge of the force of words, we would have no reliable way of knowing and judging people's moral character (20.3).

This doctrine of words and deeds, to borrow an observation from J. L. Austin, may be said to be a case of suiting the action to the word (1962, 81–82). Accomplishing this sort of action, in real life, is a formidable task, not only because it requires a strength of character but also because human situations are dynamic and highly diverse in their normative import. To preserve the *junzi*'s freedom to adapt to changing and varying circumstances, Confucius laid more stress on suiting one's words to one's action. Thus Confucius remarked that a *junzi* "acts before he speaks, and afterward speaks according to his action" (2.13). "He is slow in speech but swift in his action" (14.2). In general, one should feel ashamed to make immoderate claims that cannot be sustained by action (14.20). Ideally a morally correct speech corresponds to morally correct performance. A *junzi*, therefore, does not engage in moral discourse for its own sake. He attempts to suit his words to actions performed. Conversely, his actions must, in other cases, conform to his words. This is particularly true of evaluative labels that others bestow on him. He must live up to being called a *junzi* (4.5). Our present discussion is intimately related to the famous Confucian doctrine of rectification of names (*zhengming*), for words of honor and morality have normative import. The names or titles of persons and roles in society pragmatically imply certain obligatory actions befitting those names. To rectify names (*ming*) or moral words is to conform in action to the normative implications of these names (13.3). Later in the Ming dynasty, Confucius's emphasis on the harmony of words and deeds is developed more perspicuously in Wang Yangming's doctrine of the unity of moral knowledge and action (Cua 1982).

The notion of correct speech and action is important in Confucian ethics, not only for conduct in accordance with *ren*-morality but also for the successful execution of moral intentions within a cultural lifestyle (*li*). Moral words and actions are embedded in ritual contexts. The significance of this performative aspect has been emphasized by Herbert Fingarette (1972). In stressing this aspect of *li*, he brings the Confucian view closer to Austin's insight on the significance of the forces of "speech acts." It is the *junzi*, as we have seen, who is aware of the forces of speech. And from the standpoint of Confucian morality, the *junzi* provides a moral exemplar in both his words and his deeds. Suiting one's words to actions, of course, presupposes the satisfaction of the requirements of *ren*-morality.

In sum, the *junzi* is Confucius's ideal of a paradigmatic individual who functions as a guide for practical conduct. In Confucius's view ordinary moral agents may not attain sagehood (*sheng*). However, they can look to a *junzi* for guidance and may become *junzi* themselves. The *junzi*, though an exemplar for practical conduct, is an ideal not of a perfect man but of an ethically superior person who embodies the various qualities we have discussed. More important, construed as a paradigmatic individual, the *junzi* provides a standard of inspiration, rather than aspiration—that is, he funtions more like a beacon of light than a norm of conduct. For this reason, the ideal of the *junzi* does not imply any given set of principles or rules. His freedom of judgment lies in his exercise of discretion (*quan*), especially in exigent situations. However, *quan* must be exercised with caution and circumspection and must be informed by knowledge, experience, and reflection. The judgment so reached is defeasible, and the moral agent must vindicate himself by engaging in ethical argumentation (Cua, 1985).

See also Confucianism: Confucius; Confucianism: Ethics; Confucianism: Rhetoric; Confucianism: Tradition; Quan; *Ren*; *Yi* and *Li*; Zhengming; *Zhixing Heyi*.

Bibliography

Austin, J. L. *How to Do Things with Words*. Cambridge, Mass.: Harvard University Press, 1962.

Chan, Wing-tsit. "Chinese and Western Interpretations of *Jen*." *Journal of Chinese Philosophy,* 2(2), 1975, pp. 107–129.

———. "The Evolution of Confucian Concept *Jen*." *Philosophy East and West,* 4, 1955, pp. 295–319.

———. *A Source Book in Chinese Philosophy*. Princeton, N.J.: Princeton University Press, 1963.

Cua, A. S. "The Concept of *Li* in Confucian Moral Theory." In *Understanding the Chinese Mind: The Philosophical Roots*, ed. Robert Allinson. Hong Kong: Oxford University Press, 1989.

———. "The Concept of Paradigmatic Individuals in the Ethics of Confucius." *Inquiry*, 14, 1971, pp. 41–55. (See also A. S. Cua, *Dimensions of Moral Creativity: Paradigms, Principles, and Ideals*. University Park: Pennsylvania State University Press, 1978, ch. 5.)

———. *Dimensions of Moral Creativity: Paradigms, Principles, and Ideals*. University Park: Pennsylvania State University Press, 1978.

———. "The Ethical and Religious Dimensions of *Li*." In *Confucian Spirituality*, ed. Tu Wei-ming and Mary Evelyn Tucker. New York: Crossroad, 2003.

———. *Ethical Argumentation: A Study in Hsün Tzu's Moral Epistemology*. Honolulu: University of Hawaii Press, 1985.

———. "The Logic of Confucian Dialogues." In *Studies in Philosophy and the History of Philosophy*, Vol. 4, ed. John K. Ryan. Washington, D.C.: Catholic University of America Press, 1969.

———. *Moral Vision and Tradition: Essays in Chinese Ethics*. Washington, D.C.: Catholic University of America Press, 1998.

———. "Morality and Paradigmatic Individuals." *American Philosophical Quarterly*, 6(4), 1969. (See also A. S. Cua, *Dimensions of Moral Creativity: Paradigms, Principles, and Ideals*. University Park: Pennsylvania State University Press, 1978, ch. 3.)

———. *The Unity of Knowledge and Action: A Study in Wang Yang-ming's Moral Psychology*. Honolulu: University of Hawaii Press, 1982.

———. "*Xin* and Moral Failure: Notes on an Aspect of Mencius's Moral Psychology." In *Mencius: Contexts and Interpretations*, ed. Alan Chan. Honolulu: University of Hawaii Press, 2002.

Dubs, Homer H. *Hsüntze: The Moulder of Ancient Confucianism*. London: Arthur Probsthain, 1927.

———. *The Works of Hsüntze*. London: Arthur Probsthain, 1929.

Fingarette, Herbert. *Confucius: The Secular as Sacred*. New York: Harper and Row, 1972.

Fung, Yu-lan. *History of Chinese Philosophy*, Vol. 1, trans. Derk Bodde. Princeton, N.J.: Princeton University Press, 1952.

———. *A Short History of Chinese Philosophy*. New York: Macmillan, 1950.

Giles, Lionel. *Sayings of Confucius*. London: John Murray, 1907.

Hall, David L., and Roger T. Ames. *Thinking through Confucius*. Albany: State University of New York Press, 1987.

Hume, David. *An Inquiry Concerning the Principles of Morals*. Indianapolis, Ind.: Library of Liberal Arts, 1957.

Ku, Hung-ming. *English Translation of the Analects*. Taipei: Taipei City Government, 1984.

Lau, D. C. *Confucius: The Analects*. New York: Penguin, 1979.

Legge, James. *The Chinese Classics*, Vol. I. Hong Kong: University of Hong Kong reprint from Oxford University Press, 1960. (Preface dated 1892.)

Li, Ti-sheng. *Xunzi jishi*. Taipei: Hsüeh-sheng, 1979.

McGee, Douglas. *The Recovery of Meaning*. New York: Random House, 1966.

Munro, Donald. *The Concept of Man in Ancient China*. Stanford, Calif.: Stanford University Press, 1969.

Tu, Wei-ming. *Centrality and Commonality: An Essay on Chung Yung*. Society for Asian and Comparative Philosophy Monograph No. 3. Honolulu: University of Hawaii Press, 1976.

Schwartz, Benjamin. *The World of Thought in Ancient China*. Cambridge, Mass.: Harvard University Press, 1985.

Waley, Arthur, trans. *The Analects of Confucius*. New York: Modern Library, 1938.

Watson, Burton, trans. *Hsün Tzu: Basic Writings*. New York: Columbia University Press, 1963.

中國哲學

K

Kang Youwei (K'ang Yu-wei)

Lauren PFISTER

Kang Youwei (K'ang Yu-wei, 1858–1927), a critical thinker and controversial Confucian philosopher of the "new text" school, is unusual among modern Chinese philosophers because of his rise to political prominence in 1898 as the reformist adviser to the Guangxu emperor. Kang wrote under the literary title "gentleman" or "sage from Nanhai," referring to the place of his birth in Guangdong Province, and in his position as the leading figure among Confucianist reformers, his charisma was enhanced by his stylish calligraphy and fluent poetry as well as his adventurous political reformism and utopian teachings. His prolific output over nearly five decades includes significant developments in his multidimensional philosophical outlook and reveals some major changes in his political and intellectual positions. After the Chinese revolution of 1911 Kang seemed to be an anachronism, as he continued to advocate government by constitutional monarchy and the legalization of a Confucian state religion. Continual failures in these political areas disrupted his philosophical strategies, and so led him late in life into eclectic metaphysical musings.

Kang had been trained from childhood on in the traditional Confucian classics, but he did not succeed in the traditional civil examinations. By his early twenties he had changed teachers and expanded his reading to include a wide range of translated western literature in the natural sciences, politics, history, and religion. During this time of his life he intermittently spent prolonged periods in isolation or at mountain retreats, studying Daoist and Buddhist texts and practicing esoteric arts. Convinced that through his meditative disciplines he had achieved enlightenment, Kang determined to use his intellectual gifts to relieve the sufferings of the world. This religious dimension remained a major motivation in his tumultuous career as a philosophical and political reformer and colored his interpretation of Confucius's life and works.

An initial form of Kang's shift toward a nontraditional Confucian way of thinking appears as early as the mid–1880s. His *Kangzi neiwai pian* (*The Esoteric and Exoteric Essays of Master Kang*) displays at the outset some admiration for scientific methods and supports a hedonistic ethic. Nevertheless Kang also asserts a traditional emphasis on the five constant relationships and supports monarchical government. Further reflections tend toward pessimism in the face of human suffering and the inability of the masses to learn and grow out of their misery.

A significant stylistic and philosophical departure appears in *Shili gongfa* (*Substantial Truths and General Laws*). Here Kang was experimenting with a Cartesian-like set of axioms, "substantial truths," and moral principles that would guide a seeker to discover the general laws of related social institutions. Believing that argumentation paralleling deductions from geometric axioms could be applied in ethical and social realms, Kang was exploring the status of some basic human rights such as self-determination, legal and institutional consistency, and democratic policy making. The twelve sections that constitute the main portion of the essay after the initial list of axioms present general laws deduced from these axioms as self-evident principles. Below the presentation of these general laws is appended a further group of less perfect public principles approximating the substantial truths. Kang's pragmatic prudence dictated that he recognize other degrees of social principles, but his justifications are intended to support the higher and more general laws. In the end Kang fails to convince most readers that these general laws are self-evidently valid, but this early exploration does end up identifying values which would become central to his later reformist policies.

An important element in these arguments, which reappears in his utopian work *Datong shu* (*The Book on the Great Unity*), is the flexible nature of the "general," *gong*. By this term Kang refers to a wide range of phenomena, from the public to the more general, extending in other contexts to embrace what is global and even universal. In this earlier period there are only faint hints of the global and universal realms, categories that would dominate Kang's utopian vision of the "great unity."

The direction of Kang's mature philosophy was intimately bound up with a critical alternative to the orthodox interpretive traditions in Confucianism. The "new text" school (*jinwen pai*) grew out of disenchantment with the philosophical rationalism and cultural conservatism of the Cheng-Zhu school, relying heavily on doubts about the authenticity of the main scriptures of the Confucian tradition. Certain of these texts—the "old texts" (*guwen*)—had been preserved in an ancient style of calligraphy, while others, called the "new texts," appeared in a more modern style of writing. Having debated which canonical texts were actually written by Confucius, in the end Kang wrote at great length to argue for a controversial position: the best and most authentic texts were those of the "new text" tradition, and only one set of these texts, the *Spring and Autumn Annals* and its *Gongyang* commentary, were genuinely the work of the preeminent sage himself. From this critique of the redaction of the Confucian canon, Kang built up his own reformist Confucian philosophy.

After 1888 there was a watershed in Kang's Confucian studies, resulting from his support of the "new text" school. In his controversial book *Xinxue weijing kao* (*A Study of the Forged Classics of the Xin Period*), Kang sought to justify the claim that a particular Han scholar, Liu Xin (d. 23 B.C.E.), had distorted most of the traditional Confucian classics by—as Kang's title implies—inserting forged entries. This led Kang to refocus his attention on the *Spring and Autumn Annals* and the *Gongyang* commentary as a basis for the true understanding of Confucius's philosophy and way of life. Rather than portray the master as "a transmitter and not an innovator," Kang applied a deconstructive strategy to open the door for presenting him as a reformer.

In *Kongzi gaizhi kao* (*Confucius as a Reformer*, 1897), Kang argues from a skeptical standpoint to support a reformist and religious interpretation of Confucius's life. Denying that the accounts of the time of the ancient sage kings were historical fact, Kang insists that the master consciously created these images to portray different ideal levels of benevolent government. In essence, Kang's skepticism denied the earliest authoritative texts any objective historical legitimacy but also set the stage for allowing for other accounts of Confucius's activities. Convinced that the master had acted for the good of the people, Kang presents a picture of the Chinese sage as an uncrowned king, one who creates images of a benevolent world that would guide people to truly virtuous forms of life. In addition, Kang opts for myths and stories that raised Confucius up as a spiritual leader, the founder of a Confucian religion. This was necessary to reaffirm, not only because of historical precedents in the oral traditions of the Han dynasty but also because of Kang's concern about China's cultural crisis and a threatened loss of national identity at the end of the nineteenth century. Buddhism and Christianity had achieved high spiritual levels, but Kang insisted that the most suitable religion for the Chinese people in his own day would be a Confucian religion. These arguments scandalized conservative Confucianists and alienated others who were willing to support political reforms but not to challenge the ancient traditions.

Backing up this reconstructed image of Confucius was a special philosophy of history called the "three eras" theory. It was culled from a variety of advocates of the "new texts," especially certain writings of the Han scholar Dong Zhongshu (179–104 B.C.E.) and from a chapter of the *Book of Rites*, "The Evolution of the Rites" (*Liyun*). Essentially the theory describes the movement of Chinese history in two stages: (1) a descent from an ancient period of "supreme peace" (*taiping*) through lesser ages, ending in political chaos, and (2) a countermovement ascending from chaos through more peaceful periods into a new and progressive form of *taiping*. Kang did not fully reveal the dynamics of this theory in his writings of this period, but he did identify institutions of the Qing dynasty as part of a chaotic system that needed to be transcended through reform, producing as a consequence a period of "lesser peace." Much of Kang's ethics and politics is grounded in an attempt to adjust his practical principles to the current stage of history. It provided reasons for restraint in political activism but also restricted political options.

In the mid-1880s, convinced that the Manchurian despotism was embedded in a chaotic period requiring transformation, Kang established study groups to strengthen the political cause of reform and gain support for a new government, a constitutional monarchy. Some of his propaganda followed patterns used by Protestant missionaries in China, and so Kang was simultaneously viewed as being innovative in his ideas and strange in his methods. When, in 1888, the politically weak Guangxu emperor invited Kang to initiate reform with imperial approval, Kang attempted to reorganize the pervasive imperial bureaucracy while promoting numerous other institutional reforms. This political practice reflected his reformist philosophy and his belief in the general laws of humane life, but it provoked bitter antagonism from officials in entrenched positions of power. Considered ideologically controversial and politically destabilizing, Kang's policies had little chance to convince the opposition that gathered around the powerful dowager empress Cixi. A hundred days after his elevation, Kang and a few others were forewarned of disaster and fled the capital to save their lives, while most of the rest of the reformist leadership, including Kang's only brother and the philosopher Tan Sitong (1865–1898), were brutally subdued.

For sixteen years Kang remained in exile, traveling to various countries to rally support for his political causes. His persistent call for reforms ultimately estranged even his brilliant student and closest supporter, Liang Qiqiao. Meanwhile, revolutionary forces were gradually being consolidated. In the aftermath of the demise of the "hundred days' reform," Kang also continued his Confucian philosophical writing, bringing together and elaborating his "new text" position in a more systematic manner. Some have argued that Kang reversed his political position at this time, becoming a more conservative and pragmatic thinker. His philosophical writings also are claimed to havc taken on an orthodox hue. Both of these observations need to be carefully qualified.

Returning to the certain fundamental texts of orthodox Confucian teachings, Kang in 1901 and 1902 published commentaries to the Four Books and added to them a commentary to the chapter "Evolution of the Rites" in the *Book of Rites*. All these commentaries were written along the lines of interpretations by the "new text" school, illustrating and promoting the benevolent reformist attitudes of Confucius while criticizing the legalistic influences of Xunzi (c. 298–238 B.C.E.) throughout subsequent Confucian traditions, and particularly attacking the narrow restrictiveness of the highly influential commentaries written by Zhu Xi (1130–1200). In addition, Kang elaborated his theory of the "three eras," claiming that within each of the three fundamental periods there were also progressive subdivisions. So, for example, a period of chaos should have its own movement toward lesser peace and unification before being transformed into the next major era of "lesser peace" (*xiaokang*). Kang's historicism added a veneer of rational precision and geometric progression to what was becoming an unwieldy doctrine.

The full implications of the publication of these commentaries need to be precisely understood. Having doubted the historical reliability and authenticity of most of the older classics, the Six Classics, Kang reaffirmed the importance of the later classics—the *Analects*, the *Mencius*, the *Great Learning*, and the *Doctrine of the Mean*. All these had been written after the time of Confucius and so were not directly susceptible to criticism by the "new text" school. The addition of the commentary on the "Evolution of the Rites" was more radical, raising this chapter to the canon—a status it had never before received. In doing this, Kang was following the precedent of previous influential Confucianists: Zhu Xi himself had raised two other chapters of the *Book of Rites* into the Confucian canon as the *Great Learning* and the *Doctrine of the Mean*. However, nothing like this had been done for centuries afterward.

Why was "Evolution of the Rites" so significant to Kang? In this chapter, Confucius presented in his own words descriptions of the ancient golden age, the "great unity," encapsulated in the phrase *Tianxia weigong*, "a public spirit ruling all under the heavens." This was contrasted with a more restrictive era, a period of lesser peace, in which "a family spirit ruled all under the heavens" (*tianxia weijia*). Although the rest of the chapter was a pastiche of other doctrines, some long criticized as Daoist interpolations, Kang rendered these passages liberally in order to forecast an age of humane pleasure under a globally extended peace. In essence, Kang was claiming that Confucius had conceived of the "great unity" in his own heart and mind, and that Kang himself was seeking only to fulfill the sage's vision.

The comprehensive vision of this globally extended great unity was written down in its first form in 1902 but was not made fully public until several years after Kang's death. Liang Qichao verifies that he saw a manuscript presenting the basic tenets of Kang's utopian system at that time, but it is manifest that Kang also added to its details and length after years of traveling in Europe and North America. This *Book of the*

Great Unity is a pseudo-scientific vision of a perfect world, one full of pleasures made possible by humane advances in all areas of social and personal life.

Four major philosophical streams flow together in Kang's justifications and practical recommendations for his utopian world: (1) the extendable realm of public and global values (*gong*), (2) historical progression in "three ages" (*sanshi*), (3) the implementation of unity and harmony (*tong* and *he*), and (4) an ethics of utilitarian happiness (*le*). Whereas his other works dealt with philosophical concerns more closely related to the specific cultural and historical problems of traditional China, in this book Kang extends his vision into a future world otherwise inconceivable in his own age.

Advocating the ultimate elimination of all state and national identities under a global democratic system, Kang describes how social, economic, educational, religious, and governmental institutions must be transformed over time to reach this stage of preparedness for entering the "age of extreme peace." The formal basis of this new age was the achievement of a comprehensive uniformity in human status. Without any knowledge of genetics, Kang imagines something like eugenics—techniques to eliminate all racial and individual differences, producing a global set of identical males and females. Once this basic stage of development is achieved, individual freedoms are expressed politically through a globally extensive democratic system, linked by a technological network. Self-determination also reaches new heights because of the elimination of traditional family structures. Marriages are only temporary contracts developed for the sake of shared personal pleasure and procreation. This form of individual hedonism is not left without restrictions, because Kang's utilitarianism requires seeing the social group and its activities as more valuable and more pleasurable than any solitary individual. Censorship of literature, music, and sexual activities is imposed to preserve social peace and prevent harm, especially harm to growing children. It becomes evident that certain purely pragmatic measures may be allowed in the approach to the era of supreme peace, but they will no longer be permitted once that era has been attained. The contrast between this hedonism and Kang's depiction of education institutions in the "great unity" reflects more of his own experience as a teacher. Admitting that children need supervision in every aspect of their lives before they become self-directed, Kang advocates progressive learning, which starts with more playful forms of interaction and leads to training in social rites and public laws. Envisioning a completely literate populace—a radical vision in his day—Kang permits specialized training, structured according to the desires and abilities of individual students, only at the university level. Once again a more formal unity leads to later diversification. Kang believed that this diversity in education was the key to strengthening the creative potential and dynamic progressiveness of the "great unity."

Kang's hopes for a global realization of this era of supreme peace revolved around actual events in his own day. After the peace conference of 1898 in Russia, he envisioned that the great unity would necessarily materialize as a consequence of similar international events and their institutionalization within the following 200 to 300 years. More personally, Kang's utopian vision asserts that the basic goals of human life are comprehended in an ever-progressive relief from all forms of suffering and a fuller participation in the advance of scientific forms of knowledge and technologically produced forms of pleasure. The final stages of personal attainment are cast by Kang in terms similar to a radical humanism and end in a transcendent Buddhist-like liberation.

Although the full utopian vision of the great unity was never published during Kang's lifetime, the institutional reforms leading up to it did appear as a series of articles after the Chinese revolution, in 1913–1914. Under the new conditions of a republican China, Kang returned to his homeland and lobbied to establish a Chinese state religion, *Kongjiao*, "Confucian teaching," following ritual patterns of Christian traditions he had seen firsthand in Europe and North America. Ironically, in this period Kang began to support once more the cultural values of the same Confucian traditions he had previously cast doubt on in his more skeptical writings. Nevertheless, when these religious and institutional suggestions failed to receive republican sponsorship, Kang placed his political support once more behind a constitutional monarchy under the new emperor. Here again he and those who backed his policies failed to achieve any positive political impact.

Kang was castigated as an anachronistic statesman and eclectic philosopher, and his final philosophical writings were cosmic musings, *Lectures on the Heavens* (*Zhutian jiang*), reflecting a modern but already dated picture of the solar system and other astronomical phenomena. Here Kang describes the magnificence of the universe, its grand complexity, and the subtle nature of human and divine existence. In this work Kang was influenced to some degree by the vision of a progressive deity described in the metaphysics of Henri Bergson (1859–1941).

Never precisely articulate in their scientific discussions, persistently eclectic in their philosophical principles, and generally syncretistic in their religious worldview, Kang's philosophical works summarized the skeptical and dynamic Confucian tradition of the "new text" school, promoted a religious and reformist image of Confucius, and produced a unique Chinese utopian literature. Kang's attempts to practice the philosophical principles he drew from these diverse sources produced a remarkable political surge that weakened the traditional Chinese cultural and political system. Undoubtedly, his activities did hasten some reforms later institutionalized by the imperial bureaucracy, but they came too late to save the imperial dynasty. Even Kang's "new text" style of Confucian philosophy did not endure as a major trend among twentieth-century Chinese philosophies, but the world has advanced along a number of directions anticipated in inchoate form within his utopian vision.

See also Dong Zhongshu; Liang Qichao; Tan Sitong; Xunzi; Zhu Xi.

Bibliography

Chan, Wing-tsit. *A Source Book in Chinese Philosophy*. Princeton, N.J.: Princeton University Press, 1963.

Chang, Hao. *Chinese Intellectuals in Crisis: Search for Order and Meaning (1890–1911)*. Berkeley: University of California Press, 1987.

Fang, Delin. *Ruxue di weiji yu shanpian—Kang Youwei yu jindai Ruxue* (Crisis and Transmutation of Confucian Studies—Kang Youwei and Modern Confucian Studies). Taipei: Wen-chin, 1992.

Feng, Youlan. *Zhongguo zhexue shi xinpian: Di liuci* (The New Edition of a History of Chinese Philosophy: Vol. 6). Beijing: People's Press, 1989.

He, Zhaowu, et al. *An Intellectual History of China*, rev. and trans. He Zhaowu. Beijing: Foreign Languages Press, 1991.

Henderson, John B. *The Construction of Orthodoxy and Heresy: Neo-Confucian, Islamic, Jewish, and Early Christian Patterns*. Albany: State University of New York Press, 1998.

———. *Scripture, Canon, and Commentary: A Comparison of Confucian and Western Exegesis*. Princeton, N.J.: Princeton University Press, 1991.

Hsiao, Kung-ch'üan. *A Modern China and a New World: Kang Yu-wei, Reformer and Utopian*. Seattle: University of Washington Press, 1975.

Kang, Youwei. *Kang Youwei daquan*. Shenyang: Liaoning People's Press, 1988.

———. *Kang Yuwei quanji* (The Complete Works of Kang Yuwei), ed. Jiang Yihua and Wu Gengliang. Shanghai: People's Press, 1987–1995.

———. *Kang Youwei zhenglun ji* (Collected Political Essays of Kang Yuwei). Beijing: Zhonghua, 1981.

———. *Ta T'ung Shu: The One World Philosophy of Kang Yuwei*, trans. Lawrence G. Thompson. London: Allen and Unwin, 1958.

———. *Wanmu caotang yigao* (Unpublished Manuscripts from the Thatched Hut among Myriad Trees), ed. Kang Tongbi. Beijing, 1960.

———. *Wanmu-caotang yigao waipian* (Additions to Unpublished Manuscripts from the Thatched Hut among Ten Thousand Trees), ed. Jiang Kuilin. Taipei: Chengwen, 1978.

Li, Zehou. *Zhongguo jindai sixiangshi lun* (Historical Essays on Modern Chinese Philosophical Thought). Beijing: People's Press, 1979, 1986.

Liang Ch'i-ch'ao. *Intellectual Trends in the Ch'ing Period*, trans. Immanuel C. Y. Hsu. Cambridge, Mass.: Harvard University Press, 1959.

Lo, Jung-pang, ed. *K'ang Yu-wei: A Biography and a Symposium*. Tucson: University of Arizona Press, 1967.

Pfister, Lauren F. "A Study in Comparative Utopias—K'ang Yu-wei and Plato." *Journal of Chinese Philosophy*, 16, 1989, pp. 59–117.

Wong, Young-tzu. "Revisionism Reconsidered: Kang Youwei and the Reform Movement of 1898." *Journal of Asian Studies*, 51, August 1992, pp. 513–544.

Zhao, Jihui, et al. *Zhongguo Ruxue shi* (A History of the Chinese Confucianism). Zhengzhou: Zhongzhou guji, 1991.

中國哲學

L

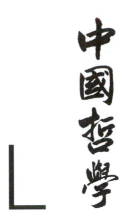

Language and Logic

Chung-ying CHENG

Two Aspects of Language in Early Chinese Philosophy

Classical Chinese philosophers from the sixth to the third centuries B.C.E. were as a rule concerned with problems of names (*ming*). To them names were not simple units of language but representations of substantive things and objects. It was not until Xunzi that names were classified into a hierarchy of categories or types and a theory of the origin and nature of names was offered. Names in general were considered identification labels that were intended to apply to and correspond with reality (*shi*). As conceived, this correspondence between names and reality was such that things in nature could be given names, and the names had to identify or distinguish reality. The idea was that names were the products of naming (*ming*), and naming was intended to give a label to a thing, a relation, or a state of affairs in nature, in society, or in a system of values.

This general assumption that all things can be named was perhaps the earliest belief held by Chinese philosophers and was not questioned until the rise of the Daoists in the fifth century B.C.E. The Chinese term *ming* as a verb is logically prior to its sense as a noun, for until the action of naming takes place, there are no names. To name is to identify and distinguish individual things, relations, and states of affairs, or types of these. Thus *ming* is primarily explained as "naming oneself" (*ziming ye*) in Xu Shen's *Shuowen* (*Discourse on Language*), and as a "process of illuminating" in Liu Xi's *Shiming* (*Interpretation of Names*) in order to distinguish between names and actuality. It is clear, then, why names as the outcome of naming provide a picture of the furniture of the world: they record the common results of our powers of discrimination. That is, they are claimed or held to illuminate things as experienced by humans.

But when some thinkers pondered the idea of the genuine or ultimate reality, they thought that this reality need not be nameable or need not actually be named, and that not all names need correspond to, capture, or represent reality. Consequently, various theories of the relationship between names and actuality (*shi*) have been proposed, and various explanations of names and of language characterized by names have been offered—explanations that find them of limited usefulness or potentially misleading. At the same time, other theories propose to defend the validity of names. It might even be suggested that various ontological and logical theories in classical Chinese philosophy are responses to questions about the nature and validity of naming and the nameability of reality.

Although *ming* as a verb and a noun occupies a crucial position in philosophical issues, the classical notion of *ming* does not lead to a definition of language in terms of *ming*. Instead, language is defined in terms of speech or "saying" (*yan*), which is considered the natural unit of expression of meaning—which in turn is identified with the intention of the speaker. Naming, names, and expressions of names occur, but even though names might serve some useful purpose, there would be no real need to introduce them if there were no need to "say." In this sense, saying seems to be more basic to language than names. However, although naming and names were sources of philosophical issues and disputes in classical Chinese philosophy, saying and/or statements (the results of saying) generally were not.

The reason for this is not difficult to find. Naming and names relate to and contrast with the actuality of which they are made, but saying relates to speakers and their intent. In order to make a statement, one needs to introduce names to refer to or characterize the things and affairs of the world. Thus, strictly, naming and names depend on the context of saying in order to be introduced, whereas saying depends on our actual and possible ability to name (to identify, reidentify, or characterize by using labels) for the purpose of explaining intent or meaning. In general, early Chinese philosophers always recognized this contextual principle of saying and were never seriously interested in an atomistic analysis of language in terms of names as such. Thus it is said in the *Rites of Great Tai* (*Da Tai liji*), "To express one's intent (*zhi*) leads to saying; to speak language (i.e., to make statements) leads to names." The Song neo-Confucian Shao Yong, in his *Huangji jingshi guanwu neipian*, says: "For the ancient people names arise from speech" (*fayan wei ming*).

To summarize, the difference between *ming* and *yan* is as follows: (1) *Ming* must be true to reality and therefore must have ontological significance, whereas *yan* must be true to the intent of the speaker and therefore must have intentional significance. (2) *Ming* must be established on the basis of human knowledge or understanding of perception, whereas *yan* must serve some practical purpose of life and action, for its truth need not always be a matter of correspondence or verification. Also, *yan* is often conceived as a matter of practical or pragmatic fulfillment of expectations. (3) The institution of *ming* or even the possibility of its institution requires some presuppositions regarding what there is, whereas *yan* requires no such presuppositions. What *yan* is about need not be some distinctive object or state of affairs, and it is logically possible that some intended objects or states of affairs may not have names.

The last point about *yan* is very important, for, as we shall see, in Chinese philosophy it is generally held that unless names are specifically used to refer to things or objects, one cannot depend on *yan* for making a specific nameable reference. Often it is suggested that one can intend something without using even *yan*, let alone *ming*. In the context of *yan* a reference need not be mentioned by name at all. In the present writer's view, this is due to an ontological consideration—a deep structure—as well as considerations having to do with the complexity and sophistication of intent and purport in *yan*.

In the basic classical writings of various philosophical schools, it is clear that *yan* is most frequently judged on the basis of conduct (*xing*). This is particularly true of the Confucian school. The reason is that *yan* embodies someone's intent and thus is borne out in conduct, which carries out such intent. *Yan*, then, has a pragmatic dimension. Confucius says: "In saying something, what one says must be true to one's conduct." He also says: "In ancient times, people did not say something if they had misgivings about being able to practice it in person." And: "The superior man wants to be slow in saying and quick in action" (*Lunyu*, 4.24).

Confucius does not neglect to indicate a link between *yan* and *ming*. In his doctrine of "rectifying names" (*zhengming*), he suggests that in order for saying (use of language) to be "fit" (*shun*), names must be rectified (*zheng*). Without elaborating at this point on what Confucius intends by rectification of names, we can note that he has made one thing clear: correct names must be assumed for fit speech, where fit speech means clarity, pertinence in a situation, and being true to one's intent. He says: "Names must be sayable, and saying must be practicable" (*Lunyu*, 13.3). This suggests that no name can be considered rectified if it cannot be used in saying. Insofar as language remains a practicable human activity, names must also be created to serve human and practical purposes.

Mencius also conceived of *yan* as directed toward fulfillment in conduct. But Mencius makes it clearer than Confucius that *yan* is closely related to the mind—the basis of one's intent. He says (criticitzing Gaozi): "It is permissible to say that if one is not satisfied with the mind (*xin*), one should not seek reasons in vital feelings (*qi*). But it is not permissible to say that if one is not satisfied with *yan*, one shouldn't seek reasons in the mind" (*Mencius*, 2A2). That is, one must find the source of merits or demerits of *yan* in mind, for it is mind which gives meaning to *yan* through its intent and purposefulness. In this sense Mencius asserts that he "knows *yan*" (*zhiyan*) because he knows its practical consequences and theoretical limits in relation to the good of the community and political goals.

Our purpose in distinguishing between *ming* and *yan* in Chinese philosophers' concept of language is to see that, in a way, these philosophers recognize two dimensions of language—a referential or characterizing dimension and an intentional or practical dimension. The former can be conveniently identified with the informational content of reference and predication in a proposition; the latter can be identified, as Austin (1962) identifies it, with the performative or illocutionary functions of speech. The important point here is that in early Chinese philosophy, language (which literally may be called "name-speech," *ming-yan*) is always a unity with an objective and a subjective side—naming reality and expressing intent. It may be suggested that the ideal form of language consists in expressing intent by using correct names or using names correctly. This implies that using names is an integral part of expressing intent, but not vice versa. The focus is obviously on language as communication, developed to consolidate a community or preserve order in it; and in such a context naming is necessary and meaningful. Thus the distinction between *ming* and *yan* is significant and leads to a distinction between modes of usage; to a large extent, it underlies later Chinese philosophical disputes.

Although it is recognized that *ming* is introduced in the context of *yan*, one can ask whether some *yan* could be developed for the purpose of *ming*, and some *ming* for the purpose of *yan*. Apparently Confucius, in his doctrine of rectifying names, thought only the latter—that *ming* could be developed for the purpose of *yan*. But he and his school could not prevent the assertion of the former. We shall see that in neo-Mohist logic, *yan* is purified of its intentional aspect and is held, primarily, to refer to and characterize things in the world. The reasoning is that naming things in the world is warranted, and the most significant use of *yan* should be to identify, name, and describe such things. On the other hand, it is also possible to hold that names are central to our understanding of reality and that *yan* should be totally subject to an understanding of the nature of naming and the relation of names to actuality. This leads to the doctrine of Gongsun Long, who formulates an objectified system of *yan* based on an abstract ontology of names. The difference between Gongsun Long and the neo-Mohists is that Gongsun explains names by concentrating on the process of naming and the origin of using names, whereas the neo-Mohists explain names by concentrating on the recognition of actuality (*shi*). In this regard, Xunzi, of the school of Confucianism, sides with the neo-Mohists.

Finally, it may be suggested that neither *ming* nor *yan* reveals anything objective or actual; that neither serves any pragmatic purpose; that both *ming* and *yan* are irrelevant to ultimate ontological understanding, which must be founded on what we know or experience about the origin or background of naming and saying; and that both can create mental agitation and confusion and obstruct our perception of reality. In this view, language is at most convenient—an expedient invented for a very limited human purpose—and carries no ontological significance at all. This is the Daoist position of "no names" (*wuming*) and "no speech" (*buyan*); the Daoists deny that either aspect of language has any ontological import. Nevertheless, language can be considered capable, if only obliquely, of suggesting or pointing to ontological understanding. The Daoists and Chan Buddhists both attempt to exploit the oblique uses of language (*ming* and *yan*) for the ultimate ontological insight that they call illumination (*ming*) or enlightenment (*wu*).

Five Doctrines on Language and Logic in Chinese Philosophy

Against the background of concepts of language as *yan* and *ming*, Chinese philosophers in the classical period developed five basic competing doctrines:

1. Rectification of names
2. "No names no saying"
3. Nominalism
4. Platonism
5. Empirical or scientific realism.

The first doctrine was developed and maintained by the Confucians and the second by the Daoists. Historically, these two doctrines precede the others, but it is difficult to say which of the two is earlier.

Apparently, doctrines 1 and 2 both presuppose the existence of *ming* (names, terms) and can be correctly said to have developed in response to unsatisfactory uses and actual abuses of names at the time. For the Confucians, the primary function of names was to serve the purpose of well-regulated *yan* (saying, speech, language), which was taken as the basis of institutionalized social order and political stability. Since *yan* was conceived as focused on goals, society and government therefore provided the ultimate context, basis, and rationale for the rectification of names and language. Because sociopolitical considerations and the practical significance of *yan* and *ming* have been constant concerns of Chinese thinkers from very ancient times on, we might conclude that the Confucian doctrine was historically prior to any other theory.

With regard to the Daoist doctrine of *wuming* ("no names no saying") and *wangyan* ("forgetting *yan*"), it seems that the Daoists focused on the nature of reality more than on human affairs. But this concern about ontology may be more apparent than real, for the Daoists can also be said to have searched for a rule for solving current problems of social and political order and stability. They thought that ontological insight would lead to the solution of these problems. What they held is that only when we "discard" names, not rectify them, can social and political order be secured or restored. Of course, they might have first found their nonlogocentric ontology of the *dao* and then tried to apply it to life and society; or they might have noticed the disruptive and destructive nature of names and formed their ontological theory in consequence. A plausible suggestion is that they wanted to solve the problem of social order and political stability and found a solution when they conceived the true nature of the *dao*. From this perspective, the Daoists are as practical-minded as the Confucians. They pay equal attention to *yan* and *ming*, and Zhuangzi's doctrine of *wangyan* and Confucius's doctrine of *wuyan* are interdependent.

The proponent of nominalism (doctrine 3) was Yinwenzi, and the proponent of Platonism (doctrine 4) was Gongsun Long; both are remembered in Chinese philosophy as logicians from the school of names. Nominalism and Platonism may both seem far removed from practical considerations. But although their doctrines appear to be focused on the logical analysis of the origins of nature and references of *ming*, there is evidence that both were nevertheless concerned with practical problems, such as the rectification of names (*zhengming*). Possibly their doctrines were motivated by practical considerations (as was true of the Confucians) but, once formulated, became more a matter of logical and ontological theory. To put this another way, their doctrine of *ming* could have first been intended to relate to the practical-minded doctrine of *yan*.

Thus only the doctrine of *ming* and *yan* devoid of overt practical considerations is the version of empirical realism (doctrine 5) advanced by the neo-Mohists. Although the neo-Mohists were disciples or members of a practical-minded school founded by Mozi, their research on language, logic, and science provided self-sufficient, self-contained results comparable to the products of Aristotle. Their writings are known as *Jing* (*Canons*), *Jingshuo* (*Discourse on Canons*), *Daju* (*The Greater Taking*), and *Xiaoju* (*The Smaller Taking*). These are brilliant works of rigorous, organized research. Discussions of them by Needham, A. C. Graham, Chmielewski, Chung-ying Cheng, and Chad Hansen have made it amply clear that rather than being guided by fixed preoccupations or vague goals, the neo-Mohists were logically and scientifically disciplined thinkers who intended to establish a logical, scientific philosophy and methodology for answering questions of value and norms (Cheng 1971). From this standpoint, one can regard their work as reflecting a scientific, methodological spirit. They developed both a logical theory of names and a logical theory of speech (*yan*).

The Confucian Doctrine of Rectifying Names: *Zhengming*

As we have noted, the Confucians regarded language as a matter of *yan* instituted for the practical purpose of stabilizing society and ordering government. Therefore, those in a position to ensure conformity of usage and correspondence between names (*ming*) and the things named must do so, for the sake of communication and social control. *Ming*, specifically, must be incorporated into *yan* so that they will identify and characterize things correctly. This is the general basis for the Confucian doctrine of rectifying names. The principles of the doctrine are as follows:

- Language is for social communication and social control, and so it must be correctly instituted and used for this purpose. Confucius says: "If a person does not know language, he will not know people" (*Lunyu*, 20.3).
- Names are for *yan*; and *yan*, ultimately, is to serve the purpose of social order. Thus names must be correctly regulated and understood and not abused, lest disorder and confusion result.
- All things are nameable. To name a thing is to identify it by its true characteristics. Thus names provide us with knowledge of things in the world. In speaking of the merits of learning poetry, Confucius says that one should "know the names of grass, wood, birds, and beasts" (*Lunyu*, 17.9).
- Human relations, as well as human goals and values, can also be named. As names, they must match their counterparts in reality.
- To use names correctly is to rectify names. A precondition is a correct understanding of reality. Since the reality of human relations, goals, and values is to be understood in terms of our experiences and our vision of human nature and its relation to heaven, names resulting from that understanding involve a correct recognition of that reality. To name correctly is to see correctly and understand correctly the norms and standard goals of human behavior and their relation to society and government.
- Once the names of things and values are established, they should be correctly used to refer to the things they are intended to represent. Otherwise, communication and social control will be impeded and confusion will arise about what is referred to; this will lead to a breakdown of social norms and values, which in turn will lead to confused think-

ing and reasoning, inevitably eventuating in political instability or even chaos. Therefore, to rectify names one must not only have names that correspond to reality but also take precautions to prevent confusion and the abuse of names.

The practical goal of rectifying names and the main tasks of rectification are suggested in Confucius's own remark:

> If names are not rectified, saying will not serve its purpose. If saying does not serve its purpose, then rites and music will not flourish. If rites and music do not flourish, then codes of punishment (laws) will not function well. If codes of punishment do not function well, then people will not know how to behave. Thus, being a superior man, a ruler must make sure that names must be sayable and saying must be practical. A superior man must be very serious and cautious with regard to his saying. (*Lunyu*, 13.3)

Although Confucius does not distinguish explicitly between facts and values, it seems clear that he identifies two kinds of names: natural names, which are governed by facts and things; and names of values or norms, which govern human behavior. It might be suggested that natural names must correspond to reality, but with regard to human values reality must correspond to names. Concerning values, man makes his own reality; he conforms to a social standard or value so that he can be a certain kind of social entity and so that larger societal goals can be achieved. This view seems to be suggested in Confucius's remark: "The ruler acts as a ruler; the minister as a minister; the father as a father; the son as a son" (*Lunyu*, 12.11). The rule of rectifying is therefore twofold: natural names must conform to natural objects; value names must make humans conform to them.

It is clear that Confucius's doctrine of rectifying names develops around the latter principle. Confucius does not actually suggest how to avoid confusion in the use of names once names have been made to represent reality correctly, yet in his various discourses we can see that he adopts two basic rules for applying names. First, one name should apply to one type of thing. Second, a thing or a person may have many names, depending on its relation to other things or other persons.

Xunzi elaborates and develops Confucius's doctrine. Xunzi's essay on *zhengming* (book 21) makes it clear that language is a human social institution and therefore always has human and social significance. He points out that a ruler, being responsible for social order, must regulate language as a means to that end; this will contribute to peace and the well-being of the people and eliminate confusion and disorder. More than Confucius, Xunzi recognizes two aspects of language besides its practical and social aspect: that it is empirically based and conventional. Xunzi is committed to demonstrating all three aspects of language by inquiring into (1) how names are introduced (*suowei you-ming*), (2) how similarities and differences in names originate (*suoyuan yi tongyi*), and (3) how names are instituted or formulated as they are used (*zhi-ming-zhi-shu-yao*). Let us briefly consider his responses to these three questions.

Question 1. Xunzi points out that if there are no fixed names, we cannot clearly express our ideas of things, and so we are likely to become confused about what objects we want to refer to. Consequently, differences and similarities cannot be distinguished—for instance, we cannot distinguish the noble from the lowly—and so communication and social action will be difficult or impossible. To prevent this, the sage decides to institute names to refer to different things. These names imply that we can distinguish between the different values we attach to things and that we can classify and record things according to their similarities and differences. The result will be ethically desirable social communication and interaction.

Question 2. The basis for instituting names for similarity and difference, according to Xunzi, is our natural senses. Our senses share common impressions of things. Consequently, we can adopt the same names to refer to the same things and different names to refer to different things. Xunzi's approach to what names stand for, therefore, is realistic and empirical. He recognizes the different qualities of sight, sound, taste, smell, touch, and feelings (desires and emotions). He recognizes that the human mind (*xin*) has the power to reason and organize. He concludes, therefore, that names correspond to things in the world because of our ability to know things through the senses and mind. Xunzi conceives of names in language as representing objects in the empirical world; language, therefore, has empirical origins and empirical referents.

Question 3. Things that are different must have different names, and things that are the same must have the same name. This is the principle of correspondence. Regarding difference and similarity, correspondence seems to imply that things can be recognized as a hierarchy of classes. Things are the same because they belong to the same class or different because they belong to different classes. Class, then, is the implicit criterion for similarity and difference. By recognizing the names of various classes, Xunzi, together with the neo-Mohists, introduced the notion of *lei* (sort, kind, class) into the Chinese logical vocabulary. The purpose of naming is to identify similarities among things belonging to the same class and differences among things belonging to different classes. A specific name (*bieming*) will thus distinguish one thing from all other things; a generic name (*gongming*) will distinguish one class from other classes. The highest general name (*da gong-ming*) will encompass all things in the same class.

Although Xunzi is basically realistic with regard to the institution of class names, he introduces the principle of convention by saying:

> A name has no intrinsic quality which necessitates its correspondence to a particular object. We stipulate the correspondence between one name and one object by convention (command). Once the convention is agreed on and usage established, we will say that the name is proper. If a name is introduced or used in disagreement with another according to convention, we will say this is improper. (*Xunzi*, book 22)

Conventions for names, of course, are the conventions involved in the initial choice of names for certain purposes. What names correspond to does not affect the nature of correspondence itself, nor does it affect the nature of whatever the names correspond to. Xunzi's theory does not allow us to infer that we can, so to speak, legislate reality through our conventions for names. His view of language is, as noted above, realistic and empirical. He gives the following principle for individuation: Things are to be individuated by their location and forms. When one thing changes form but does not change its nature and location, it is still regarded as the same thing. But if two things occupy two different locations, even if they have the same form, they are to be regarded as two things.

On the basis of his theses concerning the origin, purpose, and nature of language, Xunzi is able to identify certain errors or fallacies:

> "Saying" based on using names that are confused with other names, without regard for their intended meaning and purpose.
>
> Saying based on using objects (*shi*) that are confused with names, without regard to the origin of names (perceived similarities and differences).
>
> Saying based on using names that are confused with reality, disregarding the goals for which names, specifically class names, are intended.

Two more observations can be made about Xunzi's theory of rectifying names. First, Xunzi recognizes that names are necessary for human life in general and social life in particular, because human communication and society are based on human desires, which are ineradicable. Thus language can be introduced to satisfy human needs. To avoid confusion within language and confusion resulting from language, one needs to know the truth with one's mind (by reasoning, for example), but one need not rid oneself of desire as the doctrine "no names and no language" (*wuming wuyan*) would imply.

Second, at the beginning of his essay on rectifying names, Xunzi mentions common values, such as life (*sheng*), nature (*xing*), feeling (*qing*), deliberating (*lü*), human doing (*wei*), business (*shi*), virtuous deeds (*xing*), cognition (*zhi*), knowledge (*zhi*), natural capacity (*neng*), developed talent (*neng*), illness (*ping*), and accident (*ming*). If these are presented as examples of his three theses about names, then clearly he would recognize that the reality to which names correspond is not simply a matter of perceptual experience but also of being subject to rational understanding by the mind. Thus, correct naming implies the mind's correct understanding of the world. A presupposed ontology determines what names are to be introduced, and the names introduced will reflect what ontology has been presupposed. It is interesting to note that the *Xunzi* provides ample materials for reconstructing a Confucian theory of ethical reasoning (Cua 1985).

The Daoist Doctrine of No Names and No Logic

The doctrine of no names (*wuming*) appears in Laozi's work and that of "forgetting" (*wang*) language in Zhuangzi's. The rationale for the namelessness of the *dao* in Laozi is that the *dao* as the ultimate reality is whole and indeterminate, and we cannot characterize it without losing sight of its totality, of its unlimited nature, and of its nature as a source. Names are names of being (*you*). *Dao* is not exactly being in the ordinary sense and therefore essentially cannot have a name to identify or characterize it. That is why Laozi calls it "void" (*wu*). In fact, because everything has a hidden side, the side of *yin* or *wu*, nothing can be exactly identified and characterized by a name—nothing can be conceived as completely determinate. For Laozi, this is the true nature of things, and that is why he considers language superfluous and dispensable. Although language may help us identify and characterize things in useful ways, language can be misleading and can generate illusions simply because it can prevent us from seeing the true nature of things and the totality of reality.

Laozi's implicit theory or argument is that things and the *dao* could remain nameless if we could diminish or eliminate our need to name them. In other words, Laozi's doctrine of the namelessness of *dao* goes hand in hand with his doctrines of "no desires" (*wuyu*) and "no action" (*wuwei*), or effortlessness. He holds that if we are devoid of desires (*yu*), we are able to see the true nature of the *dao*; when we have desires, we see the beginning of things. Thus the true nature of reality is related to perception in a state of no desires, whereas the reality of differentiated things is related to perception in the state of having desires. What are desires? Although Laozi does not discuss this question in detail, his discourse gives us some indication.

Desires are egocentric and selfish claims to possession and thus products of the self in opposition to the world. They therefore exclude the viewpoints of other things. They give rise to so-called knowledge that serves private interests. They lead to actions that blind us to the true nature of things. Laozi is not opposed to natural desires, or desires that occur spontaneously, as he suggests in his image of water and an uncarved block. But desires cultivated by cunning and promoted by intelligence are unnatural. They distort the nature of man and cannot show the true nature of the *dao*. Having a desire is wanting to do something specific (*youwei*), to possess things, control things, and divide things. Having no desires is letting things happen spontaneously and letting one's creativity develop in harmony with reality without forcing or imposing anything on reality. Having no desires means creating without possessiveness, acting without arrogance, and leading without dominating.

Laozi points out that when the *dao* does not do anything specific, everything is done. This means that the cosmos, with its variety of life-forms, involves spontaneity precisely because there is no convention or goal for the *dao*. In this sense the *dao* can be said to have no desires and to make no effort toward a designated goal. Man should be guided by the image of the *dao*. To achieve creativity, man should remain (in Laozi's sense of these terms) desireless and effortless.

This means that man should retain or cultivate a spontaneous life and a selfless attitude. To do nothing and to have no desires is, therefore, to have no desires and to do nothing from the point of view of oneself. It is to abandon the self (*wuwo*), though not to abandon life or creativity. In this sense man will not only come to perceive or understand the *dao* but will be like the *dao*. In this sense, too, language becomes superfluous and dispensable, because it is a medium for expressing desires and knowledge and a guide for actions—when desires, knowledge, and guides to action are no longer needed, there is no further reason for language to exist. Of course, this does not mean that man will not act or know and will have no life. It means that when man comes to live in harmony with other men and nature, language, like weapons, will perform no useful function. Its use will not create difficulty and commotion as the use of weapons does.

Laozi's vision is that in a spontaneous state of nature, people need little commerce with one another, do not make war, and thus have no need for transportation or weapons (*Daodejing*, ch. 80). Similarly, when there is no need for communication by language, language should be laid to rest and names need not be used. The true nature of things and the totality of the *dao* will be shown precisely because they are nameless. This is the second reason why Laozi rejects names and language. He says: "The primal simplicity (the uncarved block) which is nameless (*wuming*) will alone do away with desires (*wuyu*)" (ch. 37).

The Daoist doctrine of no names is the antipode to the Confucian doctrine of rectifying names. Whereas the Confucians wish to develop language as a human institution and regulate it to serve human goals, the Daoists wish to abolish language because it is a human invention, ontologically biased and having ill effects. Whereas Laozi sees desirelessness as a reason for namelessness, Xunzi holds that desires cannot be dispensed with, and that names and language must be founded on experience and reason so as to guide and satisfy desires.

The Doctrine of Nominalism in Yinwenzi

Chinese thinking takes place in a framework of naturalistic concepts and concrete terms. This does not mean that Chinese language or Chinese philosophy does not permit or does not involve abstract theoretical thinking (Cheng, 1973). But a characteristic of Chinese thinking in general is that the abstract and the theoretical are inseparable from the concrete and the particular. They illuminate, illustrate, and symbolize each other and are related ontologically. To encounter ontological nominalism in Chinese philosophy is, therefore, less surprising than encountering ontological Platonism.

Ontology pulls more strongly toward concrete particulars than toward abstract universals. Even in Zhu Xi's neo-Confucian philosophy, principles (*li*) cannot be ontologically prior to the power of material generation (*qi*), nor are they transcendently separable from *qi*.

Regarding the ontology of names, then, we can expect to find philosophers and logicians, such as Yinwenzi (350–270 B.C.E), who argue that names are essentially intended to represent things on the basis of their material and observable forms (*xing*). In fact, Yinwenzi is typical of the nominalistic theory or doctrine of names and language in ancient Chinese philosophy. In the surviving essays attributed to Yinwenzi, we find the following important assertions:

> The great *dao* has no forms, but to refer to concrete things (*qi*) we need names. Names are what correctly represent (*zheng*) shapes (or forms). Since shapes (forms) are to

> be correctly represented by names, names must not be inaccurate. (*Yinwenzi*, 1)
> The great *dao* cannot be named. All shapes, on the other hand, must have names. It is because of its unnameability that there is the *dao*. Because of the nameless *dao*, all shapes have their peculiarities (squareness, roundness). As names are born out of the peculiarities (squareness and roundness) of shapes, all names have their respective referents. (2)

Although Yinwenzi affirms the Daoist premise that the great *dao* has no names, he would not draw the Daoist conclusion that we should abolish names and forget language. On the contrary, he holds that names serve an important purpose: they represent reality as it is diversified into things. This diversification happens by way of a differentiation of shapes, and so names must be faithful to these shapes in order that things can be identified or characterized.

In the following two passages, Yinwenzi formulates the nominalistic requirement for the institution of names or language:

> Names are to name shapes. Shapes are in answer to names. If shapes were not to give rise to correct names, or to identify correct shapes, then shapes and names would remain irrelevant to each other. Though names should not be confused with shapes, they are not independent of each other either. (8)

> In having no names, the great *dao* cannot be said. Having names, we use names to correctly represent shapes. Now ten thousand things exist at the same time; if we do not apply names to represent them (identify them), we will have confusion of knowledge. Ten thousand names exist at the same time; if we do not resort to shapes to answer them, we will have difficulties of thought. Therefore, shapes and names cannot but be made to correctly represent each other. (5)

The nominalistic principle here is that names must answer to shapes, just as shapes must answer to names. If shapes are concrete criteria for the existence of things, then names are ontologically meaningful if and only if they correspond to concrete features of things, such as shapes. Names that do not name shapes or things having shape (concrete particulars) must be in error, or they must have some other justification for their existence. Yinwenzi seems to favor the requirement that names are not ontologically significant if there are no concrete objects corresponding to them. Yet he also allows that names without reference to shapes can be useful for human purposes and therefore justifiable in pragmatic terms:

> All things which have shapes must have names. But we could have names which need not have shapes. Shapes that are not names do not necessarily lose the reality of their being square or round, white or black. In the case of names which do not have shapes referred to them, we must identify these names and investigate why they are different. Thus then we could use names to find out of which shapes they are true. Shapes determine names. Names determine certain states of affairs (*shi*). States of affairs will control names. When we investigate why certain names refer to shapes and certain other names do not, then we shall see that no reason is hidden from us in regard to the relation between shapes and names on the one hand and between states of affairs and things on the other. (8, 5)

Although Yinwenzi does not specify how to justify and construe names without representing shapes, he lets it be understood that some reason must be found other than the existence of shapeless things. In his essay, which has been reconstructed by scholars such as Sun Yirang, he moves quickly to a Confucian-like doctrine of rectifying names, suggesting the introduction of names as the basis for distinguishing values and in the context of achieving practical social and governmental goals. This may suggest (if rather remotely) a possibility of construing nonshape names in the context of practical language and thus confining ontology to names that correctly represent the shapes of things. It should be noted that *xing*, "shapes," can be interpreted to mean not just literal shapes such as squareness and roundness but any quality of things perceptible by the senses. Thus qualities such as white and black can be the basis for names of things.

The Doctrine of Platonism in Gongsun Long

Although Chinese languages may appear to preclude it, Platonistic ontology appears in the work of Gongsun Long—demonstrating that ordinary or natural language does not determine our ontological picture of the world. In fact, Gongsun Long's philosophy shows that language is subject to different local and ontological interpretations and there is no necessity to adopt one interpretation rather than another. Gongsun's ultimate goal may be to clarify the relationship between names and reality, for social and political purposes. But his discourse and basic thesis leave no doubt that language is focused on names and should have ontological significance independent of and prior to its social or political applications (Cheng 1997).

Gongsun presented the celebrated thesis "white horse is not horse" (*baima fei ma*), and it was in arguing for this thesis that he developed a Platonic theory of reality. He formulates two main arguments.

First, he argues that since "horse" is a name for shape and "white" is a name for color, and since the name for color is not the name for shape, therefore "white horse" is not "horse." This is a peculiar argument because its premises do not immediately require the conclusion. Apparently one can draw only the conclusion that what the name "white" stands for is not what the name "horse" stands for, but this is presupposed in the premises. To conclude that white horse is not horse, one has to inquire into what the names "white" and "horse" stand for. Apparently, for Gongsun Long "white" designates the color white and "horse" designates a horse shape. As this color and this shape are not particulars, they can be alternatively construed as universals, attributes, classes, or concepts, and how we construe them seems to make a real difference to the argument. For instance, let us see what happens if we assume that they are universals and then that they are classes.

If "white" and "horse" are universals, then to say that "white" is not "horse" is to say (x) $[(x \text{ is white}) \neq (x \text{ is horse})]$. Since $(x \text{ is horse} = x \text{ is horse})$, it follows that (x) $(x \text{ is white. } x \text{ is horse} \neq x \text{ is horse. } x \text{ is horse})$. Therefore: (x) $(x \text{ is white horse} \neq x \text{ is horse})$. This conclusion is that saying anything is a white horse is not equivalent to saying anything is a horse, because the "truth conditions" of the two statements are different. From this we can derive Gongsun's thesis.

If "white" and "horse" are classes—a class of white things (w) and a class of horse-form things (h)—we have the following:

Premise: $w \neq h$
But $h = h$
Therefore $w.\ h \neq h.\ h$ and $w.\ h \neq h$

Here we are saying that the class of things which are white and horse is not the same as the class of horse things. On this interpretation of "white" and "horse" Gongsun's argument can again be derived.

To prove Gongsun's thesis under either interpretation, it is essential to recognize the nonequivalence of propositions or nonidentity of two classes. This creates a paradox, because normally we would say that white horse is horse because the class "white horse" is a subclass of "horse"; in other words, saying that anything is a white horse implies that it is a horse. Gongsun's thesis may appear simply to deny the relationship of class inclusion and sentential implication. But in fact it denies equivalence and class identity. The question is whether this denial is correct. The answer is that because he uses the Chinese negation word *fei* ("is not") in "white horse *fei* horse," Gongsun is justified in denying identity and negating equivalence. Actually, he argues merely for the admissibility (*keyi*) of such an interpretation, not its necessity, as he makes clear at the outset of his essay:

> Q: To say that white horse is horse, is it admissible?
> A: Yes, it is admissible.

Thus Gongsun's first argument does not rule out a concrete ontology. It merely indicates the possibility and acceptability of an abstract ontology because our language is capable of being construed in terms of an abstract ontology of universals or classes.

Gongsun's second major argument for his thesis is that if one asks for "horse," horses of different colors will meet this requirement. But if one asks for "white horse," only a white horse meets the requirement. This may appear to be an obvious pragmatic argument. What makes it pragmatically valid, according to Gongsun, is some ontological fact about the qualities of white horse and horse. He would argue that we refer to horse, as such, as a single quality which may combine with other qualities to produce white horse, yellow horse, black horse, etc. Thus to ask for "horse" is to ask for a thing identifiable by a single quality, but to ask for "white horse" is to ask for a thing identifiable by a conjunction of two qualities. Since the conditions for identifying the two objects are different, the objects themselves are different.

Gongsun's second argument assumes the independence of different qualities and thus their separability. He holds that all names are names of independent qualities. There are two kinds of names: single names for single simple qualities, such as white; and compound names for compounds or conjunctions of single simple qualities, such as white horse. Gongsun's inferential logic involves identity; according to this logic, no simple name is equal to a compound name, or what a single name stands for is not identical to what a compound name stands for. Gongsun says:

> "Horse," which does not specify a color, is different from "white horse," which does specify a color. Therefore white horse is not a horse. (*Gongsun Longzi, Baima* ch.)

It is clear that Gongsun's thesis "white horse is not horse" leads to or presupposes an abstract ontology of qualities or universals. Once this abstract ontology is accepted, a question arises as to how we understand concrete things. Are concrete things of a different order of existence from abstract qualities, or can they be analyzed as or reduced to abstract qualities? In *Zhiwu lun*, Gongsun develops the ontology suggested in *Baima lun* into a full theory that recognizes no concrete things. But before turning to that theory, and to Gongsun's reductive theory, let us consider another argument for the separability and independence of individual qualities. This appears in his essay *Jianbai lun*, on hardness and whiteness.

In *Jianbai lun*, Gongsun argues that our different sense organs, respectively, independently identify different qualities; for instance, we identify the hardness of a stone by touch and the whiteness of a stone by sight. If we observe only by sight, we don't perceive hardness, and thus relative to sight there is no hardness. If we observe only by touch, we do not perceive whiteness, and thus relative to touch there is no whiteness. Gongsun concludes that whiteness and hardness are external to each other and are therefore independent qualities. He denies the relevance of our concept of a stone that possesses both qualities. Since what we see and what we touch are not stone, Gongsun Long tends to rule out the actual existence of stone. Therefore, he denies that there are three things—stone, white, and hardness. His argument is therefore used to establish both the separability of independent qualities and the nonexistence of things such as stone.

The separability and independence of qualities such as white and hard are also based on an appeal to verification. When we verify whiteness by sight, hardness is hidden; when we verify hardness by touch, whiteness is hidden. What is hidden does not exist in the same sense as what is perceptible.

That Gongsun Long considered whiteness and hardness separate universal qualities in a Platonic sense is indicated in the following statements:

> Things have white color, but white is not fixed and confined (*ding*) to a specific white thing. Things have hardness, but hardness is not fixed and confined to a specific hard thing. What is not fixed and confined to a specific thing can characterize all things. Then how can we say that hardness and whiteness belong to a stone? (*Gongsun Longzi, Jianbai* ch.)

> Hardness, even when not yet conjoined with stone, is hard. It is hard even when it is not confined to other things. Hardness itself possesses the quality to make nonhard things hard. Thus it is hard in stone and in other things. If we find no independent hardness in the world, it is because it is hidden. If whiteness cannot make itself white, how could it make a stone and other things white? If whiteness possesses by itself the quality which makes itself white, then it can remain white even when it is not making things white. By the same token, yellow and black are the same. (*Gongsun Longzi, Jianbei* ch.)

Gongsun draws the Platonic conclusion "All things (qualities) have independent and separate existence. Things (qualities) of independent and separate existence are normal states of being in the world."

To complete his abstract ontology, Gongsun eventually maintains the Platonic reduction thesis that all things in the world are conjunctions of qualities and thus that there are no concrete things per se. Concrete things are, rather, qualities manifested (*wei*) in space and time. When qualities are not manifested in space and time, they are hidden from us and are not identifiable by our senses. But this does not mean that they do not exist or subsist. Like Platonic forms, these qualities not only are separate from each other but are absent from the world if they do not make themselves available to characterize things in the world.

When qualities in the world are identified by names, they are called *zhi* (objects of reference). In *Zhiwu lun*, Gongsun Long holds that nothing in the world is not *zhi* and *zhi* is not *zhi*. Again, there are many possible interpretations of this paradox. But in light of his Platonistic tendencies, we may focus on just two:

1. Since all things in the world (space and time) are identifiable in terms of qualities, they are therefore compounds or conjunctions of identifiable qualities. But identifiable qualities need not themselves be identifiable in the things of the world, for they themselves may not exist in the world. Thus they are not identifiable qualities (apart from things). This interpretation makes it clear that qualities can be hidden and can be manifested and that things are manifested qualities which become referents of names, whereas qualities per se are not manifested (are hidden) and thus do not become referents. The abstract ontology of qualities is not only abstract but transcendent.
2. All things are describable in terms of their qualities, and there is nothing else in things aside from their qualities. But qualities per se are not to be further described or characterized by qualities, at least not by qualities of the same order. Since qualities are essentially simple and separate (independent), neither are they to be described by second-order qualities, for there would be no second-order qualities. Therefore it is misleading and wrong to say that qualities or identifiable *zhi* are things identifiable by qualities. This is a logical interpretation of the nature of qualities. The outcome of this interpretation is not only that the abstract ontology of qualities is abstract but that it cannot be described or characterized at all. We come to know qualities only through names applicable to things for purposes of identification. Thus one may see language (names) as a means of knowing the abstract ontology of qualities.

The moral of Gongsun Long's Platonism is that, given a certain logic, a language can generate an ontology different from the ontology which is normally presupposed or assumed. This means that ontology is a product of language, under a certain interpretation or construction satisfying certain inferential arguments.

The Doctrine of Empirical and Scientific Realism in Neo-Mohism

We come now to the fifth doctrine of names in classical Chinese philosophy. It was developed above all by logical-minded and scientific-minded followers of the Mohist school, who are referred to as neo-Mohists. In developing their views of logic and language, they may have been motivated by a wish to prove their social, ethical, and religious beliefs and disprove those of their rivals. But in their rigorous collective works on logic and empirical science, such as optics and mechanics, they achieved an objective methodology and a neutral attitude toward investigation that one does not find in other schools. Thus it is in neo-Mohist works that objective scientific language is developed and the concept of language as a means of expressing scientific and logical truth is established. Language is not used for persuasion or social control. It is used to indicate and formulate truths as discovered by observation of reality and by clear thinking.

The neo-Mohists see language as having three important aspects, each with specific objectives: names, propositions, and inferences. They say in the *Xiao qu*:

> We use names to mention realities (things in reality, *yinning jushi*). We use propositions (judgments) to express intention and meanings (*yici shuyi*). We use discourse or inference (agreement) to reach reasons (explanations) of things (*yishuo chugu*).

Thus the neo-Mohists pay equal attention to *ming* and *yan* in language and link both to a context of inference and reasoning in which their roles can be understood and their contributions recognized. *Ming* and *yan* are equally necessary for reasoning, for reaching truth about the world, for settling doubts, and even for producing reasons for our actions. The neo-Mohists also explicitly recognize class as a basis for inference:

> We should illustrate our knowledge from taking examples from the same class of things; we should infer to unknown things by examining examples from the same class of things (*yileiju, yileiyu*). (*Xiao qu*)

Class plays an important role in neo-Mohist logic. There is no space here to elaborate on this concept, but it will suffice to say that the neo-Mohists developed a extensional logic of concrete things, in opposition to Gongsun Long's intensional logic of abstract qualities. On the basis of this extensional logic, they advanced their scientific, realistic understanding of the world. To say that the neo-Mohists' view of ontology and language is realistic is to say that they are neither nominalists like Yinwenzi nor Platonists like Gongsun. To say that their views are empirical or scientific is to say that these views are neither dominated by practicality (like those of the Confucians) nor determined a priori by a total approach (like those of the Daoists). The neo-Mohists understand language as somehow capable of presenting the true nature of the world. But this true nature of the world is subject to empirical investigations and logical clarification. Thus language can be used to define and describe reality through a process of logical analysis and clarification. Also, reality can be used to refine and reform language through scientific observation and experimentation.

This interchange and interaction of language and reality enable the neo-Mohists to produce an image of the world and language not far from what modern scientific philosophers or logical philosophers have striven to achieve. What the neo-Mohists want to establish is the objectivity of truth, which is their criterion for ontological understanding. They believe that language can be used to establish objective truth and that the way to do this is to follow logic and argue according to logical principles:

> Language is to make representation of reality possible. . . . Since names are used to represent reality, *yan* is to use names to represent things for achieving objective truth by saying something about things named. Thus *yan* is to say something about names. (Mozi, *Mojing*, Canon 1.32)

The importance of reasoning and argument lies in the need to establish objective truth. The neo-Mohists believe that in an argument the goal for both sides is objective truth and only the side that reaches it can be said to win.

> Argument: The purpose of it is to compete for the truth (*bi*).
> When an argument is won, it is because truth has been reached. (1.74)

Of course it is possible that both sides in an argument can be wrong. But it is not possible that both sides are right. The neo-Mohists are strongly opposed to the skeptics' rejection of all statements or "saying" about reality as false. The Daoists are believed to take such a position, and the neo-Mohists hold that it is logically absurd:

> To regard all sayings (*yan*) as false (self-contradictory) is self-contradictory. The explanation consists in the nature of the saying formulating this position. (2.5)

The neo-Mohists have advanced many theses and views in subjects bearing on problems of language and ontology. To discuss all of them would require a separate treatise; here, we can simply note several highlights.

First, the neo-Mohists have constructed definitions of basic terms (or categories and concepts) for purposes of classification. These definitions are also a basis for reasoning and scientific investigation. The terms, therefore, refer to the fundamental nature of things. For example, the neo-Mohists have defined metalinguistic terms referring to kinds of names and "saying," methodological terms of identity and difference that they distinguish, life, time, space, and important ethical terms.

Second, the neo-Mohists have conducted empirical experiments on optical and mechanical phenomena in order to describe them and explain them correctly. In Canon 2 we find interesting experiments on the refraction and reflection of light. This indicates that the neo-Mohists permit a construction of knowledge on the basis of empirical observation and scientific hypotheses. In this sense, they permit our understanding of the world and our formulation of our understanding in language to be guided by objective inquiry and an objective conception of reality. Therefore, they do not favor a nominalistic approach to the description of reality.

Third, the neo-Mohists firmly reject Gongsun Long's Platonistic theses. In this case their rejection amounts to holding that Gongsun does not have an explicit notion of class, does not know how to classify things, and therefore does not know how things are similar and different. For example, cow, horse, and sheep belong to the same class (genus); they should not be treated as thoroughly different things, as Gongsun tends to treat them (Canon 2.65). Without a correct notion of class, one will have a false representation of things (*kuangju*).

Regarding Gongsun's thesis "white horse is not a horse," the neo-Mohists have this to say. First, in the case of two things (or qualities), one should distinguish a disjunction (union) from a Cartesian product or conjunction. Two things *A* and *B* are disjunctively *A* or *B*, but conjunctively they are neither *A* nor *B*. On the basis of this distinction and the two associated principles of inference, one can infer that

> Cow and horse disjunctively are cow and horse.
> Cow and horse conjunctively are neither cow nor horse. (2.66)

By the same token one can say:

> White horse disjunctively is white or horse.
> White horse conjunctively [is] neither white nor horse. (2.13)

In this light, Gongsun's thesis can be said to be misleading and not totally right, if not totally wrong. Inference depends on a clear analysis of concepts in our language. Gongsun's Platonism therefore can be regarded as resulting from confused reasoning or a lack of reasoning.

Fourth, the neo-Mohists also repudiate Gongsun's thesis that hard and white are separate, independent qualities. According to the neo-Mohists, the error here arises from not understanding or not having a proper concept of space and time as individuating principles for an individual thing such as a stone. Although we can perceive hard and white successively in time and through different sense organs, what we have perceived resides in one location (space) and belongs to one interval (time). Insofar as location is one and time is one, the separate impressions of white and hard cohere into one thing. Therefore they are not separate from each other but rather fill each other (*xiangyin*) in the same time and in the same space:

> If one separates hard from white, the explanation is that one lacks a concept of intervals of time and location. Hard and white are one, the explanation being that they originally belong to the same location and the same time interval.

Fifth, the neo-Mohists also discuss the notion of *zhi*. They differ from Gongsun Long in that they regard *zhi* as basically acts of reference rather than objects of reference or indefinable qualities and things. They hold that we can know that something exists without being able to identify it by describing or pointing to identifiable qualities. For example, we know that spring has come and gone without being able to point to it; we know that a person has disappeared or hidden without being able to point to that person; we know that a neighbor's dog is around without knowing the dog's name; and we know that something is beyond reasonable doubt, even in the presence of *zhi* as ways of characterization or identification or as simple names. The neo-Mohists' point here is to reject Gongsun Long's doctrine that no things are not *zhi* and *zhi* is not *zhi*.

Conclusion

We have discussed the concept and ontological import of language in various perspectives developed in classical Chinese philosophy. Also, we have distinguished names (*ming*) from "saying" (*yan*)—two aspects of Chinese language—and distinguished ontology in and of language from ontology independent of or without language. For the Confucians, the ontological consideration of names is subject to the practical, normative consideration of *yan*. For the Daoists, both *ming* and *yan* are to be abolished; their reasons are ontological, normative, and practical, and they offer an ontology without language. For Yinwenzi and Gongsun Long, the ontological import of names dominates the practical, normative ends of *yan*. Finally, for the neo-Mohists ontological considerations are to be regulated by logical and methodological considerations, and language is to be developed and refined, through logic and scientific discovery, into a tool for expressing objective truth and objective knowledge.

See also Gongsun Long; Names, School of; Xunzi.

Bibliography

Austin, J. L. *How to Do Things with Words*. Oxford: Oxford University Press, 1962.

Cheng, Chung-ying. "Aspects of Chinese Logic." *International Philosophical Quarterly*, 15, 1971, pp. 213–235.

———. "A Generative Unity: Chinese Language and Chinese Philosophy." *Tsing Hua Journal of Chinese Studies*, New Series, 10(1), 1973, pp. 90–105.

———. "Philosophical Significance of Gongsun Long: A New Interpretation of *Zhi* as Meaning and Reference." *Journal of Chinese Philosophy*, 24(2), 1997, pp. 139–177.

Cua, A. S. *Ethical Argumentation: A Study in Hsün Tzu's Moral Epistemology*. Honolulu: University of Hawaii Press, 1985.

Graham, Angus. *Later Mohist Logic, Ethics, and Science*. Hong Kong and London: Chinese University Press, 1978.

Hansen, Chad. *Language and Logic in Ancient China*. Ann Arbor: University of Michigan Press, 1983.

Wang, Dianji. *Zhongguo louji sixiang fengxi* (Analysis of Chinese Logical Thought). Beijing, 1961.

Laozi (Lao Tzu)

Vincent Shen

Laozi (Lao Tzu, c. sixth century B.C.E.) seems to be the Chinese philosopher best known to the western world, through his short treatise the *Laozi* or *Daodejing*, consisting of some 5,000 Chinese characters. Beginning with its Sanskrit translation in 661 C.E., it has been the most frequently translated Chinese book; indeed, it may be the second most frequently translated of all books, after the Bible. In a very limited space, and in very profound and appealing words, similar to but more systematic than the pre-Socratic fragments, the *Laozi* or *Daodejing* offers the best summing-up of a deep-layered way of thinking in traditional Chinese culture. As Wing-tsit Chan has put it:

> No one can hope to understand Chinese philosophy, religion, government, art, medicine—or even cooking—without a real appreciation of the profound philosophy taught in this little book. (1963b, 136)

In fact, the name Laozi refers to one or a few questionable historical figures and a group of texts. First, as a historical figure, Laozi was the founder of Daoism, although much about him remains unknown, and the historical accounts we have are not very certain about his identity and life. According to Sima Qian's *Records of the Historian*, Laozi was a curator in the royal archive in the capital of Zhou, and Confucius once visited him to ask about problems of *li* (rites). Sima Qian also narrates the legend that after retirement, Laozi, on the demand of the barrier keeper Yin Si (Guan Yin), wrote a work of more than 5,000 words. This story might have been told by the school of Guan Yin, which interpreted Laozi. In any case, Sima Qian writes quite hesitantly and mentions other related figures, such as "Lao Lai Zi" and "Taishi Dan," without seeming very sure of their identity.

Yet even in the absence of any complete historical reconstruction of the author and his life (or the authors and their lives), the texts attributed to Laozi show the reader their own philosophical meaning. Therefore, for the purposes of philosophy, it is more important to consider "Laozi" as referring to a group of texts. In this respect, we have traditional texts in the commentaries by Yan Zun (53–24 B.C.E.), Wang Bi (226–249 C.E.), and Heshang Gong (probably third–fourth century C.E.), and Fu Yi's version from the Tang dynasty. Apart from all these, we have texts of *Laozi* discovered recently, including the silk texts found at Mawangdui in 1973, whose transcription might date from a bit before the Han dynasty (version A) or during the early Han (version B), and the three Guodian bamboo slip texts discovered in 1993. The Guodian texts were transcribed before 300 B.C.E.—this is the latest possible date of their burial, and the transcription must have been earlier than the burial itself. Because of the discovery of the Guodian texts, it could be assumed that Laozi's texts must be earlier than works bearing the names of Zhuangzi, Mencius, and Xunzi, contrary to the claim of some scholars, such as Qian Mu, that Laozi came later than Zhuangzi. It should also be mentioned that version C of the Guodian bamboo slips includes a text, *The Great One Gave Birth to Water*

(*Taiyi sheng shui*), that had never been included in any of the traditional texts.

In the Guodian versions, Laozi's texts were read together with Confucian texts; this suggests that Daoism and Confucianism were not then considered antagonistic schools of thought. In particular, the vehemently critical words referring to basic Confucian concepts such as *ren* (humanness) and *yi* (righteousness)—for example, in Chapters 19 and 20 of the traditional versions—are minimized in the Guodian version. It could be said that the Mawangdui silk texts show an intermingling of Daoist and legalist thought, especially in the case of *Huanglao boshu*, whereas the Guodian texts show a certain intermingling, or at least a peaceful coexistence, of Daoist and Confucian thought.

In the two Mawangdui silk versions of the *Laozi*, both version A and version B consist of a first part on *de* (virtue) and a second part on the *dao*, an order that is just the reverse of existing versions such as Wang Bi's, Heshang Gong's, and Fu Yi's. This fact has led to many historical hypotheses and arguments. But in the earlier Guodian *Laozi*, there is no order of this kind. It does not have divisions into chapters, and sometimes even the order of sentences is quite different from either the silk *Laozi* or other traditional versions.

Dao, Its Attributes, and the Great Categories

Laozi posits *dao* as the most important concept in his system of thought, replacing heaven in ancient Chinese thought as representing the ultimate reality. Etymologically, the Chinese word *dao* means a way on which one could work out a direction and a way out. It could also mean "to say," "to speak," or "to discourse," though this aspect is generally denied by Laozi, for whom the function of discourse is always taken in its negative sense.

Philosophically, the following meanings of *dao* are the most important:

- First, *dao* as laws of becoming or laws of nature, especially when combined with heaven or heaven and earth, as in *tian dao* (heavenly *dao*) or *tiandi zhi dao* (the *dao* of heaven and earth).
- Second, *dao* as the origin that gives birth to all things, as in Laozi's saying, "The *dao* gave birth to one. One gave birth to two. Two gave birth to three. Three gave birth to all things."
- Third, the *dao* as the always self-manifesting ultimate reality. The self-manifesting *dao* is "reality itself," whereas all we say about the *dao* is but "constructed reality," which is not and never could it be reality itself. This is as shown by Laozi's saying "The *dao* that could be said is not the constant *dao*," which can be found in all the texts except the Guodian bamboo slips.

In *Laozi*, the *dao*, as the ultimate reality, is said to be an undifferentiated whole, either as a "state of undifferentiated whole" (*you zhuang hun cheng*) in Guodian text A, or as a "thing of undifferentiated whole" (*you wu hun cheng*) in Chapter 25 of all the other texts. Since the *dao* is that which makes all things as beings, and that which makes all things as beings is not itself a thing, the Guodian text seems to be better in this sense. In any case, the *dao* is seen as the undifferentiated whole existing before heaven and earth. It is very much like the Heideggerian *Il y a*.

In Chapter 25 of all versions and its corresponding part in the Guodian text, the *dao* is said to be inaudible, invisible, independent of all beings, and self-subsisting. The Guodian text uses "boundless," which is a better term than the traditional "changeless" because it avoids a possible contradiction between the *dao* as changeless and the *dao* as the original dynamism pushing all things into an unending process of change. Also, the Guodian text corresponds better with the following passage: "If I am forced to name it, then, reluctantly I will call it 'the great.' 'Great' means departing from all boundaries, which means being far off; and being far off means turning back." Here we have other attributes of *dao*, such as "great," "departing from all boundaries," "far off," and "turning back," indicating a circular cosmic process quite different from the linear cosmic process in modern western science. Laozi made it clear that these were not ostensive or real attributes, but rather fictitious or figurative attributes constructed for the understanding of human beings.

Concerning the "great categories" of existence, we find an interesting consensus among all versions in Chapter 25, the text that reads: "Man models himself upon earth. Earth models itself upon heaven. Heaven models itself upon *dao*. *Dao* models itself upon what is of itself." Apart from its decentralizing progression from man to earth, and then from earth to heaven, and then from heaven to the *dao* itself, we can see an ontological categorization into four realms: man, earth, heaven, and the *dao*. In these four interrelated categories, man models himself on the earth, say, the environment; and earth, the environment, should follow the laws of nature or the cosmic process. And the whole cosmic process, being itself produced by the *dao*, should model itself on the dynamism of the *dao*, which has no other model than that coming from itself.

Since these sentences are the same in all versions, we can take the categories for granted and check related texts thereby. In all versions except Fu Yi's, we read:

> Heaven is great, earth is great, the *dao* is great, and the king is also great. There exist four great categories in the kingdom, the king is one among them.

But the king, even if he is the greatest political power within one kingdom, is not as great as humankind and should not be treated as one of the four great categories of existence. In making the king one of the four categories of existence, the text has committed an error, misplacing a category and politicizing ontological thinking. Also, how can one put the *dao*, earth, heaven, and humankind into the realm of a kingdom and change the status of these categories of existence into categories of the political? Here we can see a human-centered way of thinking and a politicization of ontology. Only Fu Yi's version reads more reasonably:

> Heaven is great, earth is great, the way is great, and man is also great. There are four great categories in beings; the king is the noblest among one.

Here we have the four great categories of existence—man, earth, heaven, and the *dao*—which correspond exactly to the consensus. Also, the king is seen here merely as the noblest in one category, that is, humankind; and there is no mistaking of the ontological category as a political category to which the political framework of the kingdom belongs. We can see from this how valuable Fu Yi's version is.

The Cosmic Process: "Giving Birth" and "Returning"

Laozi conceives the cosmic process as constituted of, first, the process of giving birth to all things by the *dao* and, then, the process of all things returning to the *dao*. Nonbeing (*wu*) and being (*you*) can be seen as the two ontological moments through which the *dao* manifests itself. The *dao* first manifests itself into nonbeing, as the realm of possibilities. When compared with actuality, these are nonbeing, but in themselves they are marvelous possibilities. From this realm of nonbeing some possibilities are realized in the realm of being, and to become being is to take the form of body. That is why the realm of being is rare and the realm of nonbeing is much richer. One important insight of Laozi's is that human beings should cherish what they have as actuality but always be open to the unfathomable possibilities.

After the realm of being is realized, all beings are structurally constituted of opposites such as *you* and *wu, yin* and *yang*, movement and rest. Dynamically, when one state of affairs is fully realized to the degree of being exhausted, it goes to the opposite state of affairs. Notice that here the opposites include "disaster and fortune," "correct and deviant," "good and evil" (ch. 58); "beauty and ugliness," "good and not good," "being and nonbeing," "difficult and easy," "long and short," "high and low," "front and back" (ch. 2); "the twisted and the upright," "the hollow and the full," "the worn out and the renewed," "little and much" (ch. 22); "heavy and light," "tranquillity and agitation" (ch. 26).

You and *wu*, the most important concepts besides the *dao* and the *de*, can be analyzed on three levels of meaning. First, ontologically, *you* means being, the real, the actual; *wu* means nonbeing, the possible, the potential. Second, spiritually, *you* means fulfillment and constraint, whereas *wu* means transcendence and freedom. Third, ontically, *you* means full, presence, whereas *wu* means void, absence.

In Chapter 42 of Wang Bi's version, the Mawangdui silk version, and other traditional texts, the cosmic process of giving birth to all things is expressed in this way:

> The *dao* gave birth to the one, the one gave birth to the two, and the two gave birth to the three, and the three gave birth to ten thousand things. Ten thousand things carry the *yin* and embrace the *yang*, and through the blending of *qi* (vital force), they achieve harmony.

Here "the one" (or "the One") should be understood minimally as the beginning of being, and not necessarily as the *qi* as some scholars have suggested, since in the Guodian version "the great one gave birth to water," where water, as an archaic mediating material, is more original than the *qi*. "The two," not necessarily limited to the *yin* and the *yang*, are better understood as different pairs of opposites such as being and nonbeing, *yin* and *yang*, movement and rest. "The three" can be understood as their interactive and dialectic interplay.

But in the Guodian texts, version C, this is replaced by a text later given the title *The Great One Gave Birth to Water*:

> The great one gave birth to water. Water returned to assist the great one, so as to form heaven. Heaven returned to assist the great one so as to form earth. Heaven and earth (again assisted one another) so as to form divinities. Divinities assisted one another so as to form *yin* and *yang*. *Yin* and *yang* again assisted one another so as to form four seasons. Four seasons assisted one another so as to form cold and heat. Cold and heat assisted one another so as to form damp and dry. Damp and dry assisted mutually so as to complete the year and there halted.

This text shows the great one giving birth to two opposing yet interacting elements such as heaven and earth and *yin* and *yang*, through a mediator, water. Also, it is remarkable that divine intellects intervened after the formation of heaven and earth, to further the formation of *yin* and *yang*, cold and heat, damp and dry, etc. In short, this text makes concrete the process of cosmogenesis explained in the Chapter 42 of all the other versions, but with the specific aim of explaining the emergence of physical and temporal order.

The Great One Gave Birth to Water in version C of the Guodian *Laozi* is unique in the sense that it is not found in other versions of *Laozi* or any Daoist texts. The concept of the great one can be found in the chapter "Under Heaven" of the *Zhuangzi*, which mentions that the barrier keeper Yin (Guan Yin) and Lao Dan "headed their doctrine with the concept of the great one." It could therefore be said that the doctrine of the great one belongs to the school of Guan Yin and his interpretation of Laozi; in the school of Guan Yin, the great one represents the *dao*. In *The Great One Gave Birth to Water*, the great one gives birth to all things through step-by-step materialization and ordering. In pre-Socratic philosophy, Thales took water to be the *arché* of all things; similarly, in the Guodian *Laozi*, water—which is different from the water of wet and damp material that comes into being much later, after cold and heat—should be considered the primary material medium, with all Daoist characteristics: it is tender and soft, penetrates everything, is beneficial and good to all things.

Ontologically and cosmologically, therefore, water is much higher even than *qi*, a concept which becomes more important in the work of Zhuangzi, for whom all things are penetrated by one *qi*. In the Guodian text, *qi* appears later with heaven, whereas water comes into being before heaven, and therefore before *qi*, to serve as the medium favorable to the productivity of all things, although water is not itself among the productive causes such as the great one, heaven and earth, divinities, and *yin* and *yang*. Water seems to be only a mediating material principle with all the favorable qualities of productivity.

We should notice that in all versions of *Laozi*, divinities came on the scene much later. In the Guodian texts, divine intellects come to be after the formation of heaven and earth and before that of *yin* and *yang*. And in Wang Bi's version and the Mawangdui version, the *dao* "seems to have preceded the supreme deity," *di* (ch. 4). The supreme deity was produced by the ever-creative self-manifesting *dao*, which is nonsubstantial in itself. In this way, Laozi seems to avoid the ontological, theological metaphysics that we find in western philosophy.

Concerning the cosmic process of returning to the *dao*, we read:

> Reversal (return) is the movement of *dao*, weakness is the function of *dao*, all things under heaven are produced from being, and (being) from nonbeing. (ch. 40)

The term "reversal," meaning both "opposition" and "return" in all other versions, gives a more complete vision of cosmogenesis and the finality of cosmic process. In the Guodian text, read as "return," it emphasizes merely the process of returning to the *dao*. When interpreted as "opposition" (*xiangfan*), it would mean that the *dao* manifests itself and moves itself through the interactions of pairs of opposites such as being and nonbeing, *yin* and *yang*, movement and rest. When interpreted as return—and this is the transcription of the Guodian texts—the whole process of becoming of all beings leads finally back to the *dao*, that is, to return to the *dao* itself.

When read together with "*dao* gave birth to one, one gave birth to two, two gave birth to three, and three gave birth to all things," where we see a process of differentiation and increasing complexity, these texts reveal a cosmological vision in which the origin of existence is also the finality of becoming. We may say that this process is brought about by the *de* (virtue), inherent in all things after their coming into being. *De* could be seen as the *dao* inside all things after their being created. It begins to function when the thing in question is in a state of weakness. This is the meaning of the saying, "Weakness is the function of the *dao*." In *Laozi*, both weakness and strength are to be interpreted with reference to subjectivity or enclosure within empirical individuality. Weakness means passivity in following the way of *dao* rather than subjectivity, letting things be themselves rather than seeking domination over things. Thus the *dao* begins to function in all things and bring them back to *dao* itself. This returning, as led by the *dao* in each and every thing, can therefore be seen as an operation of virtue, *de*.

The Concept of *De*: Virtue

The concept of *de* in Laozi replaces the Confucian concept of *xing*, meaning the nature of each and every thing, including human beings. In Confucianism, there is a tendency to humanize nature, or to use the concept "nature" (*xing*) for human nature. But in all the versions of Laozi, we cannot find a single instance of *xing*. Instead we find the concept of *de* (virtue, power). In Laozi, unlike Confucianism, *de* has no ethical connotation of moral virtue. Rather, *de* means the spontaneous creative capacity inside all things after they were produced by the *dao* and leading everything to return to the *dao* in their process of becoming. The *dao* gives birth to all things in the process of differentiation and increasing complexity; after that, it remains in everything, serving as spontaneous creativity. The *de* is therefore that which both human and natural beings inherit from the *dao*, or the presence of the *dao* in everything, not as a cause is present in its effect but rather as the whole is present in its parts. Everything—including every human being—has its own *de*. Therefore Laozi's concept of *de* deconstructs the Confucian view of humans as the center of the universe. Because everything has its own center, Laozi does not need a doctrine of anthropocentrism.

Any human being, through effort and praxis in the *dao*, can attain the highest levels of virtue, expressed in terms such as *xuande* (supreme virtue), *changde* (constant virtue), *shangde* (upper virtue), *kongde* (large virtue), *guangde* (expansive virtue), *jiande* (firm virtue), and *zhide* (authentic virtue). Yet in the Guodian texts, we find only those virtues that human beings can attain through "life praxis," and so the concept of virtue (*de*) loses its ontological and cosmological meaning. For example, "supreme virtue is like a valley" means that the sage, after industrious praxis, attains supreme virtue—as if he had climbed the highest mountain—but still comports himself humbly. Then, "expansive virtue seems to be insufficient, firm virtue is like being indolent, and authentic virtue is like being whimsical or capricious." All these *de* become human virtue, though still keeping the sense of Daoist dialectics, and therefore differ from Confucian virtues, which are merely moral and ethical achievements.

A Problem of Methodology: The Retracing Regard, *Guan*

For Laozi, knowledge is a mode of being, and his method of knowing is a kind of praxis—that is, practical. Generally speaking, the "retracing regard" (*guan*) is the most important method of knowing and can be applied to all things, including nature and human affairs. *Guan* can be seen as a method similar to intuition of essence in phenomenology—not in the form of Husserl's phenomenological reduction, which presumes a transcendental ego grasping the essence of things, but rather more like Heidegger's *Seinslassen*, letting things be themselves. The "tracing regard" or *guan* is an intuition of essences of things in letting things be themselves. In all the texts of *Laozi* except the Guodian, this method is applicable to both natural phenomena and human affairs.

But the term *guan* as found in the corresponding passages of all other versions disappears from the following Guodian text:

> Reaching the supreme emptiness, keeping to the firm vacuity, ten thousand things start to emerge, and exist in a way so as to return. Heaven's way is circular; each thing returns to its root.

This text says that supreme emptiness and firm vacuity are the original state of the *dao*, whence all things emerge. And all things, after having emerged, are waiting to return to it. Here, waiting is not a passive kind of existence; rather, all things exist positively as waiting for a return to the *dao*. "Ten thousand things start to emerge, and exist in a way so as to return" is purely cosmological. It is quite different from all the other versions, which read, "Ten thousand things start to emerge, and I grasp their return by a retracing regard." The other texts posit a retracing regard (*guan*) as a method for intuiting the essence of all things. The Guodian text, lacking the word *guan*, transforms a passage with both cosmological and methodological meaning into a purely cosmological passage.

We also find the term *guan* in Chapter 54:

> Regard body (or self) in letting body (or self) (be) as it is. Regard the household in letting the household (be) as it is. Regard the community in letting the community (be) as it is. Regard the state in letting the state (be) as it is. Regard the all under heaven in letting all under heaven (be) as they are.

Here we can see that the method of *guan* was used at all levels of human affairs from the body to social organizations. The sentence "regard body (self) in letting body (self) (be) as it is" can be found in all versions except the Guodian text. The entire passage means that we can have an intuition of the essence of all things, including the human body and all levels of human social groupings—such as family, community, state, and all under heaven—by letting them be themselves: we have the an intuition of the essence of body by letting body be body; we can have an intuition of the essence of family in letting family be family; and so on. But in the Guodian texts this sentence has been dropped, and the method of *guan* is not applicable to the human body; it applies only to human social organizations.

Political Philosophy

Laozi's political philosophy concerns mostly the art of governing, which, for him, should refer to the *dao*, follow the *dao*, and unfold the *de* of all people and all things. An ideal state is, negatively, a state with no political domination and, positively, a place where people and things can spontaneously unfold their own virtue. The unfolding of the creative abilities or spontaneous virtues of the people is therefore the greatest wealth of a state. In order to attain this, the ruler should adopt a politics of nonaction (*wuwei*). This does not mean ruling without any action; rather, it means ruling according to the *dao*—that is, no particular action or no action of particular interest but universal action, acting for all things; no artificial action but spontaneous action. The politics of nonaction is a politics of nonintervention, of letting everyone be himself or herself. This kind of politics, not necessarily limited to a small country, embodies an ideal unit of political construction, exemplified in the famous Chapter 80:

> Let there be a small country with few people. Let there be ten times and a hundred times as many *powerful* utensils. But let them not be used. Let the people value their lives highly and not migrate far. Even if there are ships and carriages, none will ride in them. Even if there are armor and weapons, none will display them. Let the people again knot cords and use them in place of writing. Let them relish their food, beautify their clothing, be content with their homes, and delight in their customs. Though neighboring communities overlook one another and the crowing of cocks and barking of dogs can be heard, yet the people there may grow old and die without ever *interacting* one with another.

Many scholars maintain that, for Laozi, a small country with few people constitutes the best social and political environment. This view is based on an isolated reading of the chapter. Some even say that Laozi's position is very similar to what E. F. Schumacher calls "small is beautiful." Yet under scrutiny terms like "small" and "few" mean nothing quantitative. Laozi does not have any intention. On the contrary, a contextualist reading renders implausible the idea of returning to an ancient tribal society. Laozi has talked much about the art of governing a large state. Consider the following:

> Ruling a big country is like cooking a small fish. If the *dao* is employed to rule the empire, . . . not only will the supernatural power not harm people, the sage also will not harm people . . . , and virtue will be accumulated. (ch. 60)

> A big country may be compared to the lower part of a river. It is the converging point of the world. (ch. 61)

From these texts, it is clear that Laozi does not exclude the possibility of governing a large state. The question for him is whether one can apply the *dao* to rule the empire and both supernatural beings and the sage so as not to harm the spontaneous creativity of the people but let the country become a place for accumulating *de*.

Therefore the most important question for Laozi is how one can establish a social political order by referring to the *dao* and the spontaneous virtue of people. Chapter 59 answers this most clearly:

> In ruling the people and in serving heaven it is best to be sparing. It is because one is sparing, that one may be said to follow the way from the start. Following the way from the start he may be said to accumulate an abundance of virtue. Accumulating an abundance of virtue, there is nothing he cannot overcome. When there is nothing he cannot overcome, no one knows the limit of his capacity. When no one knows the limit of his capacity, he is fit to rule a state. He who possesses the mother (*dao*) of the state will last long.

Moreover, Laozi has taught many lessons about attaining the large from the small and overcoming the difficult from the easier:

> Make the small big and the few many, . . . prepare for the difficult while it is still easy. Deal with the big while it is still small. Difficult undertakings have always started with what is easy. And great undertakings have always started with what is small. (ch. 63)

> Deal with things before they appear. Put things in order before disorder arises. A tree as big as a man's embrace grows from a tiny shoot. A tower of nine stories begins with a heap of earth. The journey of a thousand *li* starts from where one stands. (ch. 64)

It is possible, then, for Laozi, to govern a large state if we begin by building up ideal political units.

Laozi considers the *dao*, virtue, and wisdom the three preconditions of establishing an ideal social and political order. Only when there are virtues and wisdom corresponding to the levels of body (self), family, community, country, and world, resulting from an authentic conversion to the *dao*, can a social and political order with intense spiritual communication be established. An ideal social and political order must begin with the self and progress through family, community, and larger units to the establishment of a large-scale political environment. For Laozi, political praxis is based on the praxis of virtue and wisdom, and the praxis of virtue and wisdom is based on the praxis of conversion to the *dao*.

What Laozi envisages is therefore an ideal social and political environment emancipated from all political domination. In this ideal state, men can communicate freely and are responsible for one another. But this cannot be realized without acquiring virtue and wisdom by communicating with the *dao*.

Conclusion

Since the discovery of the Guodian texts we have been able to assume, with a great degree of certainty, that Laozi came much earlier than Zhuangzi. Laozi, then, was the real founder of Daoism, which, together with Confucianism and Buddhism, is one of the most important schools in Chinese philosophy. Laozi is also seen as the divine founder of religious Daoism, which appeared in the Han dynasty. Philosophically, both Confucianism and Buddhism, in the long history of their development, have been influenced by Daoism. Today,

Laozi's philosophy is significant especially in that it considers human beings in relation to their environment, to the cosmos, and to *dao* itself and considers the meaning of human life in the context of nature. We need to resituate the human in the natural and reestablish an optimal harmony with it. This is a lesson that we can continue to learn from Laozi's philosophy.

See also Confucianism: Ethics; Daoism: Classical; Daoism: Neo-Daoism; Daoism: Texts in Guodian Bamboo Slips.

Bibliography

Chan, Wing-tsit, trans. *A Source Book in Chinese Philosophy*. Princeton, N.J.: Princeton University Press, 1963a.

Chan, Wing-tsit. *The Way of Lao Tzu: A Translation and Study of the Tao-te Ching*. New York: Bobbs-Merrill, 1963b.

Duyvendak, J. J. L., trans. *Tao Te Ching: The Book of the Way and Its Virtue*. London: John Murray, 1954.

Henricks, Robert, trans. *Lao-Tzu: Te-tao Ching—A New Translation Based on the Recently Discovered Ma-wan-tui Texts*. New York: Ballantine, 1989.

———, trans. *Lao-Tzu's Tao Te Ching: A New Translation of the Startling New Documents Found at Guodian*. New York: Columbia University Press, 2000.

Jingmen City Museum, ed. *Guodian Chumu zhujian* (Guodian Chu Tomb's Bamboo Slips). Beijing: Wenwu chubanshe, 1998.

Laozi. *Mawangdui hanmu boshu* (The Silk Manuscript of the Laozi Discovered at Mawangdui). Beijing: Wenwu chubanshe, 1976.

Lin, Yutang. *The Wisdom of Laotze*. New York: Modern Library, 1948.

Shen, Vincent. "The Concept of *dao* in Wenzi and Its Comparison with Laotzu." *Zhexue Yu Wenhua*, 23(8), 1996, pp. 1857–1870. (In Chinese.)

———. *Confucianism, Taoism, and Constructive Realism*. Vienna: Vienna University Press, 1994.

———. "L'idée de la création dans la pensée taoïst." In *Création et événement: Autour de Jean Ladrière*. Louvain-Paris: Édition Peeters, 1996.

———. "Laozi di renxing lun chutan (A Preliminary Inquiry into Laozi's Theory of Human Nature)." In *Zhongguo renxing lun* (Chinese Theories of Human Nature). Taipei: Tung-ta, 1990.

———. "Laozi di xingshang sixiang (Laozi's Metaphysics)." *Zhexue Yu Wenhua*, 15(12), 1988, pp. 814–822.

———. "Laozi di zhishi lun (Lao Tzu's Epistemology)." *Zhexue Yu Wenhua*, 20(1), 1993, pp. 98–107.

———. "Tao and Communication: Lao Tzu versus J. Habermas." In *China and Europe Yearbook 86*. Leuven: Leuven University Press, 1986, pp. 191–208.

———. "Tao and Cosmology in the Kuodian Texts of Lao Tzu—In Comparison with Other Related Texts." *Zhexue Yu Wehua*, 26(4), 1999, pp. 298–316.

Waley, Arthur, trans. *The Way and Its Power*. London: Allen and Unwin, 1935.

Legalism

Yuk Wong

The term "legalist school" (*fa jia*) first appeared in 90 B.C.E., in Sima Qian's *Records of the Historian*. This school includes eight chief figures, whose common conviction was that law rather than morality was the most reliable and useful instrument for ruling a state.

Despite his emphasis on propriety, righteousness, incorruptibility, and the sense of shame, Guan Zhong (d. 645 B.C.E.), premier of the state of Qi, deserves the title "father of legalism." The book *Guanzi*, compiled in the period of the Warring States and the early Han dynasty, included at least seven legalist chapters: *Quan xiu* ("On the Cultivation of Political Power"), *Fa jin* ("On Laws and Prohibitions"), *Zhong ling* ("On the Importance of Orders"), *Fa fa* ("On Conforming to the Law"), *Ren fa* ("Reliance on Law"), *Ming fa* ("On Making the Law Clear"), and *Zheng shi* ("Rectifying the Age"). According to these chapters, law and prestige are more precious than pearls or even people, and prestige and power are more important than rank or salary. If rewards and punishments are reliable and yet orders are not carried out, it is because the ruler does not set an example by obeying them himself; that is, prohibitions take precedence over the king. The enlightened king controls six "handles": letting people live, executing them, enriching them, impoverishing them, honoring them, and humiliating them. In other words, rulership resides in four things: civil power, military power, the power to punish, and the power to be benevolent. Guanzi considered the law to possess six characteristics: supremacy, compulsion, objectivity, normalization, unity, and permanence. He inspired many statesmen and generals, such as Bai Zhongxi.

The second legalist figure, Zi Chan, inflicted heavy penalties on criminals.

Li Kui (c. 453–395 B.C.E.), the third legalist, was both the premier and the mentor of Marquis Wen in the state of Wei. Unfortunately, he was usually erroneously identified with Li Ke, who should be Confucian, according to *Lüshi chunqiu* and *Hanshu* (*History of Han*). Li Kui concentrated on education and the development of agriculture.

The fourth important legalist, Wu Qi of Wei, studied under Confucius's disciple Zeng Shen. Wu swore to his mother that he would come home when and only when he became premier and, having learned the appropriate strategies in Chu, he did climb to the premiership. But he offended all the Chu noblemen, who conspired to murder him with arrows or by using five horses to tear him apart. Wu lacked filial piety, though he shared food, clothes, and labor with his inferiors. Pan Gu used the phrase "capture enemies to triumph immediately" to describe four legalistic militarists: Sun Wu, Sun Bin, Wu Qi, and Shang Yang. Wu, by contrast, took pride in three civil achievements: improving customs, promoting righteousness between kings and ministers, and establishing moral order between father and son. Although Wu failed to keep his promise to his mother, he considered keeping promises the chief principle of statecraft. He did not believe in an immortal soul, but in moments of frustration he still turned to fatalism and mysticism. Indifferent to Wu's metaphysics, Sima Qian criticized him as harsh, violent, and not benevolent.

The fifth important legalist, Shang Yang (Wei Yang, c. 390–338 B.C.E.), was born in Wei; his original surname was Gongsun. Shang served Duke Xiao of Qin and managed to enlighten him in the "way of the lord protector." Ignoring the people's disgust at his severe laws, Shang persisted on punishing the tutor of the crown prince when the latter refused to comply. Wu Qi's reforms failed utterly, but Shang's succeeded, especially with regard to reducing the power of aristocratic families. Consequently, the people enjoyed social order and material wealth without being menaced by bandits and thieves. However, as soon as Duke Xiao died, the crown prince accused Shang, falsely, of planning a revolt. Because of Shang's own law making it a capital crime to aid criminals, no one dared rent him a room where he could hide, and so he was executed, torn apart by five horses—an example of the Confucian warning that whoever makes severe laws will become their victim. In Shang's opinion, the Confucian classics and virtues were simply a nuisance, like vermin. Three chapters of the *Shang jun shu* identify two sets of "vermin": one set consisting of peasants, merchants, and officials; the other set consisting of the *Book of Odes*, the *Book of History*, propriety and music, humanity, righteousness, honesty, trustworthiness, fidelity, incorruptibility, filial piety, and the denial of absolute priority to warfare or the reluctance to fight.

Shen Buhai, the sixth legalist figure, seemed to have benefited from Laozi's doctrine of tenderness and weakness. In *Shenzi* the term *dao* appeared nine times, and the Daoist concept of nonassertiveness also appeared several times. Like *Zhuangzi*, this book used the mirror and balance as metaphors.

The American sinologist H. G. Creel conjectured that Shen Buhai enlightened Laozi and Zhuangzi, but *Zhuangzi* mentions the seventh legalist figure, Shen Dao, instead of Shen Buhai. Whereas Shen Buhai focused on prestige and power, Shen Dao focused on statecraft. During the reign of Emperor Wu of Han, people confused Shen Buhai and Shang Yang, although Shang modified *Laozi* without adopting Lao's term "nonassertiveness."

The emperors Wen, Jing, Wu, and Wu's great-grandson Xuan liked reading Shen Buhai and the eighth legalist, Han Feizi (Han Fei Tzu). Sima Qian grouped Laozi, Zhuangzi, Shen Buhai, and Han Fei together in writing *Shiji*. According to Sima, Han Fei, the supreme legalist, based his doctrines on the Huang-Lao school.

There are at least six contrasts between Confucianism and legalism:

1. In ethics, Confucianism appeals to moral autonomy, whereas legalism appeals to heteronomy.
2. Turning to their historical and political heritage, most Confucians advocate ancient kings as models. The legalists, like Xunzi, advocate later or recent kings as models.
3. Regarding the political system, Confucians prefer feudalism as stabilized in the Zhou dynasty; Shang Yang, during the period of the Warring States, stressed the utter necessity of dividing the state into counties (analogous to British shires).
4. According to the *Zuozhuan*, the Confucian official hierarchy depends on kinship; but in the state of Qin, Shang Yang's reform replaced the kinship system with a system based on military merit, and particularly on the number of enemies beheaded. In legalism, it is illegal to inherit a parent's rank, title, or salary.
5. Concerning the economy, Confucians adhere to the "well-field" system, which began to collapse in the reign of King Li of the late Western Zhou dynasty. Shang Yang abolished that system, opening fields to division and free purchase.
6. Regarding penal law, the chapter *Qu li* in the *Book of Rites* maintained that proprieties must not apply downward to ordinary people, and penalties for

ordinary people should not apply upward to officials. *The Book of History* recorded that noblemen could redeem themselves by paying gold and thus avoid harsher penalties. When Zichan (Gongsun Qiao) of the Zheng state promulgated *The Canons of Penalty* in 536 B.C.E., Shuxiang, a nobleman of the state of Chin, wrote a letter denouncing him. Twenty-three years afterward, Confucius objected passionately to *The Book of Penalty*, written by Fan Xuanzi of the state of Jin and inscribed in an iron tripod. By contrast, legalists judge everything according to law and regulation, irrespective of kinship and status. Except for sovereigns, all people are equal before the law. Legalism completely denied privilege to noblemen and officials.

The great achievement of legalism was the first unification of China after the Spring and Autumn period and the Warring States period, for five centuries. The first emperor of Qin established an authoritarian political institution with a pyramidlike structure of ministers and officials. Xunzi's disciple Li Si assisted the king in unifying Chinese rules and characters and then in strengthening communication between the central government and the districts.

In the early Han a bitter, and epochal, controversy broke out between Confucianism and legalism. The Confucian Huan Kuan's compilation *Yan tie lun* (*Discourses on Salt and Iron*) included Confucius's and Mencius's distinction between righteousness (sense of duty) and profit. Sang Hongyang, as the representative of profit-minded ministers, propounded new economic policies in order to secure material resources and cope with the tremendous expenses entailed by famines and warfare. On the opposite side, literati and worthies representing civilians emphasized the Confucian spirit of treasuring righteousness and husbandry over profit and commerce. In accord with Dong Zhongshu's radical sense of duty, the literati and worthies believed that profit-minded ministers who had risen from the merchant class would worsen customs and widen an already large gap between the wealthy and the underprivileged. Although Han Fei considered merchants vermin, Sang cherished commerce rather than forming a broader economic foundation. Ostensibly Confucian but essentially legalist, the Han policies were focused on profit. Since Xunzi blended Confucianism with legalism, and early Han scholars like Lu Jia and Chia Yi synthesized Confucianism and Daoism, this controversy might also be regarded as a spiritual combat between Daoistic Confucianism and Confucian legalism. Like Wu Qi and Shang Yang, Chao Chuo proposed some policies undermining noblemen's profit and thus incurred a tragic death.

In the period of the Three Kingdoms, Juge Liang, as the premier of Shu, managed to synchronize Confucianism, Daoism, and legalism. Shedding tears, he executed his stupid general Ma Su. Cao Cao of Wei resembled a legalist only in valuing talent and merit over morality, except for loyalty. During the Eastern Jin dynasty, Ge Hong, who called himself Baopuzi, modified primitive religious Daoism to assimilate Confucianism and legalism without absorbing Buddhism. In the Northern Song, under the impact of legalism, Li Gou and his disciple Wang Anshi emphasized the vital importance of seeking profit for the people. In the Southern Song the utilitarian school of East Zhejiang revealed a formidable tendency toward profit. Chen Liang propounded the equal necessity of righteousness and profit. The famous controversy between Chen Liang and Zhu Xi was really a conflict between legalistic utilitarianism and neo-Confucian deontology. As a result of Wang Anshi's influence, the Ming premier Zhang Juzheng behaved like a legalist. In the late Qing, Tan Sitong opined that two thousand years of Chinese politics had arisen from the learning of Xunzi; actually, he intended "Xun" to refer to Han Fei. For Tan all legalist emperors were bandits, robbing people of their lives and property. After the American psychologist J. B. Watson introduced the term "behaviorism" in 1913, some intellectual historians detected traces of behaviorism in legalism. During the anti-intellectual Cultural Revolution in mainland China in 1966–1976, certain leftists wrongly ascribed legalism to Qu Yuan, Xunzi, Wu Zetian, Li Ji, and Liu Zongyuan. Marshal Lin Biao playfully broke down the term "legalists" into its homonyms "experts in punishment" without acknowledging any contribution of legalism to Chinese culture.

See also *Guanzi*: The Book of Master Guan; Han Feizi; Shang Yang; Shen Buhai; Shen Dao.

Bibliography

Chen, Qitian. *Zhongguo fajia gailun* (Introduction to Chinese Legalists). Taipei: Zhonghua, 1970.

Chen, Xianghun. *Juge Liang xingxiang shi yanjiu* (A Study of the History of Juge Liang's Image). Hangzhou: Zhejiang Classic, 1990.

Jiang, Lihong. *Shangjun shu zhuizhi* (Sharp Commentaries on *Shang Chün Shu*). Beijing: Chung-hua, 1986.

Feng, Youlan. *Zhongguo zhexue shi xinpian* (A New Compilation of the History of Chinese Philosophy), Vol. 1. Peking: Jen-min, 1962.

Hansen, Chad. *A Daoist Theory of Chinese Thought*. New York and Oxford: Oxford University Press, 1992.

Li, Yuanqing, and Anbang Sun, eds. *Sanjin yibai mingren pingjuan* (Critical Biographies of One Hundred Famous People of the Three Jins). Taiyuan: Ren-min, 1992.

Liu, Zehua, ed. *Zhongguo chüangtong zhengzhi siwei* (Political Thought in the Chinese Tradition). Changqun: Jilin renmin, 1991.

———, ed. *Zhongguo gudai zhengzhi sixiang shi* (History of Political Thought in Ancient China). Tianzhen: Nankai University, 1992.

Rickett, W. Allyn. *Guanzi: Political, Economic, and Philosophical Essays from Early China: A Study and Translation.* Princeton, N.J: Princeton University Press, Vol. 1, 1985; Vol. 2, 1998.

Wong, Yuk. *Zhongguo xueshu sixiang lunqiong* (Book Reviews Concerning Chinese Academic Thought). Taipei: Mingwen, 1994.

Yü, Ying-shih. *Zhongguo sixiang chuantong de xiandai quanshi* (A Modern Interpretation of the Tradition of Chinese Thought). Taipei: Linking, 1987; Nanjing: Jiangsu Jenmin, 1995.

Yü, Yonggen. *Rujia fa sixiang tonglun* (General Discourses on Confucian Ideas of Law). Nanning: Guangxi Renmin, 1992.

Zhao, Shoucheng. *Guanzi tongjie* (Penetrating Commentaries on Guanzi). Beijing: Beijing College of Economics, 1989.

Zhao, Shoucheng, and Te-min Wang, eds. *Guanzi yanjiu* (Studies on Guan Tzu), Vol. 1. Chi-nan: Shan-tung Jen-min, 1987.

Zhu, Dongrun. *Zhang Juzheng dajuan* (A Grand Biography of Zhang Juzheng). Wuhan: Renmin, 1957.

Li: Principle, Pattern, Reason

Shu-hsien Liu

Li—principle, pattern, or reason—developed into perhaps the most important concept in Chinese philosophy beginning in the Northern Song period. In fact, posterity has called Song-Ming neo-Confucianism "Song Ming *lixue*": the study of *li*. In ancient Chinese philosophy, *li* was not a prominent idea, but it acquired richer and richer meanings throughout its later history. In the Tang dynasty, Huayan Buddhism elevated it to a philosophical concept. In the Song dynasty, neo-Confucian philosophers transformed it into a Confucian idea.

It seems impossible to offer a neat definition of this concept, but as noted above, *li* can be loosely understood as principle, pattern, and reason. Tang Junyi (T'ang Chün-i) studied the evolution of the idea and identified six different but interrelated meanings (1968, 1–69):

1. *Wenli*—principle in cultural activities.
2. *Mingli*—principle in logical reasoning and philosophical speculation.
3. *Kongli*—principle of *sunyata* (emptiness).
4. *Xingli*—principle of nature.
5. *Shili*—principle of events or affairs.
6. *Wuli*—principle of physics or empirical sciences.

Wenli

Tang Junyi pointed out that the concept of *wenli* was rediscovered by Qing scholars such as Dai Zhen (Dongyuan, 1723–1777) who were opposed to the dominance of Song-Ming *lixue*. They felt that the concept of *li* as taught by Song-Ming neo-Confucian philosophers was too transcendent to conform to the teachings of ancient Confucian philosophers, even though the neo-Confucians claimed to be the true heirs of Confucius and Mencius. Dai Zhen studied the text of the *Mencius* from a philological point of view. According to him, in ancient times *li* referred to something concrete. His followers pointed out that originally *li* referred to patterns in a piece of jade. Such an interpretation appeared to have a certain merit, as *dao* was the term that referred to something comprehensive while *li* was used to refer to something specific. But Tang found the account unsatisfactory, because this interpretation of *wenli* assumed that its proper use had to do with patterns inherent in a physical object, when in fact *li* was closely related to human activities. Granted that originally the term may have had something to do with jade, the emphasis was nevertheless on the human activity involved in working on jade, because *li* was also a verb referring to the carving that transforms a piece of crude jade into a refined cultural object. Tang felt that this use of the term indicated a basic characteristic of ancient Chinese thought, elaborated in Xunzi's writings.

According to Tang, *li* was not a prominent idea in ancient Chinese philosophy. Confucianists like Mencius barely mentioned the term, and when they did use it, it was associated with *yi* (righteousness) and was clearly related to morality. The Mohists used the term in logical reasoning to correlate names with reality. Both approaches took *li* as something closely related to human activities. But Daoists like Zhuangzi tried a rather different approach. Zhuangzi talked about *li* of heaven and earth, or *li* of the "myriad things," and took *li* to be something transcendent and metaphysical. Still, in the Daoist tradition, the idea of *li* was regarded as far less important than the idea of *dao*. The Confucianist Xunzi discussed both the subjective and the objective aspects of *li*: it was seen not only as closely related to human activities but also as pointing to the traits of things. Xunzi's understanding of *li* had a profound influence on the subsequent development of Chinese thought. Legalists like Han Feizi (Han Fei Tzu) studied under Xunzi. Han Feizi wrote a commentary on *Laozi* and stated that *li* is used to refer to specific details among things. This was exactly the line of thought followed by Qing scholars. But such an understanding of *li* merely emphasized the static aspect of things, unrelated to human activities. Also, the Qing Confucians failed to notice that Xunzi's conception of *li* has systematic import, as is evident in his use of the term *dali* ("large" or comprehensive reason) to indicate a systematic order of things. Xunzi placed special emphasis on cultural activities such as rites and music, which formed a comprehensive hierarchical order. Xunzi's thought influenced later Confucian scholars who composed chapters of the *Book of Rites*. For example, the chapter on music took *li* (rites) to be manifestations of *li* (principle, pattern, and reason).

In sum, even though different conceptions of *li* were already present in ancient Chinese thought, only *wenli* was sufficiently developed and extensively discussed by Xunzi. It alone can be said to represent the understanding of *li* achieved in ancient Chinese thought.

Mingli

The concept of *mingli* was not fully developed until the Wei-Jin period but can be traced back to ancient Chinese philosophy. Confucius advocated *zhengming* (rectification of names): "Let the ruler be a ruler, the minister be a minister, the father be a father, and the son be a son" (*Analects*, 12.11). The idea is that there must be correlation between name and reality; otherwise, there will be dire consequences. The Daoists urged that names must be transcended. We find this saying in the first chapter of *Daodejing*: "The name that can be named is not the eternal name." During the Warring States period there was a "school of names," *ming jia*. Among its prominent exponents were Hui Shi (c. 380–305 B.C.E.) and Gongsun Long (b. 380 B.C.E.). Wing-tsit Chan has called them "logicians" (1963, 232), but that label seems somewhat misleading, as the Chinese have never developed a system of formal logic. Hui Shi and Gongsun Long were more like Greek sophists, masters of dialectics who excelled in debate. A typical example was Gongsun Long's thesis "white horse is not horse," because if someone ordered a white horse, it would not do to deliver just a horse. While Gongsun Long emphasized difference, Hui Shi emphasized unity, arguing, "Heaven is as low as the earth; mountains and marshes are on the same level," and urging us: "Love all things extensively. Heaven and earth form one body."

Hui Shi was said to have been a friend of the Daoist Zhuangzi (between 399 and 295 B.C.E.), who was also a master of dialectics, even though he looked beyond dialectics. There were certainly interactions between the Daoists and the dialecticians. The Daoist philosophers like Laozi did not much care to pursue mundane careers; they sought to realize the metaphysical depth that transcends being (*you*) and merges into nonbeing (*wu*). They were said to open up the metaphysical realm of *xuanli*. *Xuan*—"black," "darkness"—symbolizes depth or profound wisdom. Living in a turbulent period full of uncertainties, most Wei-Jin intellectuals were disillusioned with Confucianism. They loved metaphysical discussions and were most interested in the "three *xuan*": *Laozi*, *Zhuangzi*, and *Yijing* (or *Yi jing*, *Book of Changes*). *Xuanli*, reason transcending worldy reason, may be a somewhat paradoxical concept, but in any case, according to Tang Junyi, *mingli* was a further development of it. In ancient Chinese thought, names were considered to refer to reality. Han intellectuals developed comprehensive systems of cosmology, but their thoughts always tended toward something real, whether existing in the present or in the remote heavens. Wei-Jin intellectuals wanted to go further, to seek spiritual freedom and probe metaphysical depths. They loved to play on names, roamed in the realms of being and nonbeing, and constructed worlds of meanings beyond the world of actualities. Nevertheless, there is also an implicit emphasis on reason in their philosophical speculation—hence the term *mingli*. Mou Zongsan (Mou Tsung-san) was of the opinion that the Wei-Jin intellectuals developed something closest to philosophy in the western sense.

Kongli

Buddhism was imported into China from India in the late Han period. As some Buddhist ideas were similar to Daoist ideas, Wei-Jin intellectuals used the latter to interpret the former—hence the practice of *geyi* (matching concepts). But Buddhist thought was in a way even more radical than that of the Daoists. The Daoist *wu* (nonbeing) was understood as a mystical *xuan*, something "dark" or "profound," a substantial metaphysical principle; but the Buddhists seemed to want to get rid of the concept of substance altogether. The Chinese translated the Buddhist *sunyata* as *kong*, "emptiness." But Buddhism should not be misunderstood as nihilistic. As taught by Jizang of the "three treatises" school, Nagarjuna's doctrines were said to have steered a middle course, on the one hand rejecting a substantial metaphysics and on the other hand refusing to accept a nihilistic philosophy. Up to a point, Nagarjuna's critique of the concept of substance and causality is very much like Hume's. But Hume ended up a skeptic, whereas Nagarjuna took his own critique as a point of departure, in order to find enlightenment that would free humans from bondage to life and the world. From the Buddhist point of view, nothing substantial exists, because there is unceasing change; there is no constancy. Yet things do appear as one thing leading to another, and they must not be reduced to nothing in the absolute sense. So long as we do not cling to a substance metaphysics or nihilistic philosophy, we can find the middle course between these two extremes. Xuangzang of the "consciousness-only" school took a different approach. Things lack substantiality, in his view, because they result from the transformation of eight "consciousnesses." Only through discipline and enlightenment can thusness or suchness (*tathata*) be realized.

The Indian emphasis on logical or cosmological analysis, however, was somewhat alien to the Chinese tradition. Henceforth the well-rounded teachings of Huayan and Tiantai were developed by Chinese Buddhist thinkers. Chan (Zen) Buddhism went even further to teach sudden enlightenment. These three Chinese schools of Buddhism—Huayan, Tiantai, Chan—favored the ideal in the Mahayana ("great vehicle") of universal salvation and took a worldly attitude in contrast to the Indians' otherworldly attitude. Huayan painted a bright picture of life and the world: *li* (principles) and *shi* (events) interpenetrate one another without obstruction. Surely the Huayan understanding of *li* should never be taken in a substantial sense. Such principles are revealed only through discipline and enlightenment; thus we have the term *kongli*, principle of *sunyata* or emptiness.

Xingli

Facing challenges from neo-Daoism and Buddhism, Song Confucian philosophers revived the moral insights of Confucius and Mencius. They developed new moral metaphysics and a cosmology, inaugurating a second golden age of philosophy in Chinese thought—the first having been the late Zhou period, when a hundred schools of thought were said to contend with one another. Song Confucianism was different from Han Confucianism in emphasizing spiritual enlightenment rather than Confucian classics or political indoctrination. It was called *daoxue* because its followers were devoted to the manifestation of the Way (or way, *dao*). Some western scholars simply labeled it "neo-Confucianism," a term that was later also adopted by Chinese scholars. Philosophically, however, the term *lixue* seems to characterize this trend of thought best, and so the commonly accepted term is Song-Ming *lixue*.

As we have seen, *li* in a philosophical sense may be traced to Huayan Buddhism, but the spirit underlying neo-Confucianism was certainly different. It was a conscious effort on the part of Confucian thinkers to develop a philosophy to counter the influence of Daoism and Buddhism. They had profound faith in the ultimate ontological principle of creativity, a *li* that works incessantly in the universe. For them, the cultural achievements of man are real—not illusory, as the Daoists and Buddhists intimated. In other words, *li* is real (*shi*); it must not be taken as empty (*xu*) or as originating in *wu* (nonbeing) or *kong* (emptiness).

The *li* that neo-Confucian philosophers talked about was, rather, *xingli*, as contrasted with the Taoist *xuanli* or the Buddhist *kongli*. Such principles are intrinsic in our lives. The opening of *The Doctrine of the Mean* includes these statements: "What Heaven (*tian*) imparts to man is called human nature (*xing*). To follow our nature is called the Way (*dao*). Cultivating the way is called education." Neo-Confucian philosophers understood Heaven as the ultimate ontological principle, working incessantly in the universe. The *Commentaries* of *Yijing* (*Book of Changes*) gave more details of the operation of the creative way of Heaven: "The successive movement of *yin* and *yang* constitutes the Way. What issues from the Way is good, and that which realizes it is the individual nature." On the basis of the insights they obtained from such Confucian classics, Song-Ming neo-Confucian philosophers further developed *xingli zhi xue* (studies of principle of nature).

A related concept, *qi* (material force), was also developed; it was considered inseparable from *li*. As Cheng Yi (1033–1107) said:

> It would be incomplete to talk about the nature (*xing*) of man and things without including material force (*qi*) and unintelligible to talk about material force without including nature.

Neo-Confucian philosophers followed Mencius in maintaining that human nature is good. But they made an important distinction between moral nature and physical nature. For them, only moral nature is good without any qualification, since it is composed of *li*; physical nature can be good or evil, as it is composed of *qi*. Through the discipline of *xin* (mind-heart) we can always hope to manifest *li* inherent in our nature, follow the examples of sages and worthies, and transform our temperament in overcoming the limitations due to our physical makeup. The concepts of *li* and *qi* were also used to explain cosmological evolution. Whether *li* and *qi* are one or two became a controversial issue among Song-Ming neo-Confucian philosophers. But all shared the belief that our nature comes from Heaven and that there is union between Heaven and man, so that a correlation can be found between microcosm and macrocosm.

Shili

Song-Ming philosophers loved reflection and speculation. In the late Ming period, however, some of the followers of Wang Yangming (1472–1529) developed trends of thought that were considered to have harmful consequences. Wang taught that every human has *liangzhi* (innate knowledge) within the self. Unquestionably, such thought can be traced to Mencius; unfortunately, however, it somehow merged with a corrupted form of Chan Buddhist "sudden enlightenment" and spread widely among the populace. Adherents were convinced that no study of the classics or moral discipline was necessary, and that sages were walking along every street. They were accused of empty talk and unruly behavior, which led to the downfall of the Ming dynasty.

Thinkers like Wang Fuzhi (Chuanshan, 1619–1692) urged scholars to find *li* (principles) within *shi* (events or affairs). He studied history and indeed was devoted to the study of the operation of principles in real historical contexts with the hope of drawing lessons from them. Most early Qing scholars were engaged in practical learning. They turned away from metaphysical speculation about transcendence and considered discussions of metaphysical problems empty. Their primary concern was to manage worldly affairs; accordingly, the kind of *li* they were interested in was also *shili*, i.e., principles inherent in events or affairs. However, under alien rule in the Qing dynasty they were not allowed to take an active part in national affairs. Henceforth they were driven to evidential studies of classics. This was a new direction in the development of Confucian thought. It was under such circumstances that Dai Zhen proposed to study Mencius from a philological point of view and claimed that in ancient times *li* was understood as *wenli*, like the patterns in a piece of jade. Dai's disciples were not interested in his philosophical reflections but devoted their scholarly efforts to philological investigations, which, ironically, had hardly any relevance to practical affairs.

Wuli

In the early Qing period, China cut off its relationship with the west. After the industrial revolution in the west, China suddenly found itself lagging far behind in science and technology; moreover, the imperialist west repeatedly humiliated the Qing regime. Finally a revolution broke out, and the republic of China was established in 1911. In 1949, after World War II, the People's Republic of China was established on the mainland. In the modern period, the main problem for the Chinese has been to catch up with western progress. The west excels in studies of *wuli*, "principles of things." *Wuli* has been translated narrowly as the English word "physics" and more broadly as studies of nature, including practically all branches of science. Some Chinese scholars denounced their own tradition and called for wholesale westernization; others believed that China should preserve the good parts of its tradition and eliminate the bad parts. But all agreed that China had to learn science and technology from the west in order to strengthen itself and survive in the world. The emphasis on *wuli* became a vogue after the turn of the twentieth century.

Tang Junyi's evolutionary approach sheds light on the concept of *li* in the history of Chinese thought. But Mou Zongsan felt that the idea of *wenli* was not very clear and that the evolutionary approach should be balanced by a systematic approach, so he replaced *wenli* with *xuanli* and rearranged the six meanings of *li* in the following order:

1. *Mingli*
2. *Wuli*
3. *Xuanli*
4. *Kongli*
5. *Xingli*
6. *Shili*.

Mou's thought was somewhat influenced by his understanding of western philosophy. His rearrangement of the six meanings of *li* was an effort to place Chinese philosophy among world philosophies. According to the logical positivists, only formal sciences, i.e., logic and mathematics, and factual or empirical sciences have cognitive meaning. Mou would concede that China lagged behind the west in both areas and urgently needed to learn from western science and technology. The traditional concept of *mingli* needed to be expanded to cover logic and mathematics (the formal sciences), and the traditional concept of *wuli* needed to be expanded to cover the empirical sciences. But Mou affirmed that the three great traditions (*sanjiao*) in China, i.e, Daoism, Buddhism, and Confucianism, had developed the concepts of *xuanli*, *kongli*, and *xingli*, respectively; and that such concepts had no equivalents in the western tradition. All three asserted the function of *zhi de zhijue* (intellectual intuition), whereas Kant, for example, under the influence of the Christian tradition, denied that human beings could ever have intellectual intuition, as all their knowledge had to come through the senses; as a consequence, humans could have only sensible intuition, not intellectual intuition. Mou held that Kant could develop only a metaphysics of morals and a moral theology—never a moral metaphysics, which happened to be the mainstream of Song-Ming neo-Confucianism. Mou further argued that the kind of metaphysics developed by the Chinese was not the *shiyu xingshang xue* (substance metaphysics) developed by the Greeks, which could not stand against Kant's critique. The ultimate metaphysical principle—such as the Daoist *wu*, the Buddhist *kong,* or the Confucian Way—was never regarded as eternal or as transcending all changes. On the contrary, these principles were considered to be realizable amid change. Mou's choice of the term *zhi de zhijue* may cause unnecessary misunderstanding or disputation, but his intended meaning was clear enough. In traditional Chinese thought, whether Daoist, Buddhist, or Confucian, there was no dichotomy between substance and function, noumenon and phenomenon, transcendence and immanence. The Way (*dao*), the ultimate metaphysical principle, permeated everything; the Chinese loved to use a metaphor of the ocean and waves to illustrate this. They also used a metaphor of light: so long as artificial obstructions are removed, the Way shines through our daily lives.

Along with their tendency to reject all sorts of dualism, the Chinese also showed a strong syncretic tendency. In the late Ming period, the three traditions were said to have come from the same family—like red lotus flowers, green lotus leaves, and white lotus roots, which all have the same origin. Chinese Buddhists were much more worldly than Indian Buddhists. They came to terms with the Confucian moral order and were much concerned about worldly affairs; hence their increasing emphasis on *shili*. Insights could be derived from the study of history and the handling of affairs. These insights were not reducible to those derived from either metaphysics or empirical sciences but might be said to belong to the realm of historical and practical wisdom, which provides a guide to grasping *li* inherent in events or human affairs. Mou's scheme is useful not only in helping us to appreciate the achievements and limitations of traditional Chinese philosophy but also in offering a ground for possible future synthesis between east and west.

Among the three traditions—Confucianism, Daoism, and Buddhism—there is little doubt that Confucianism still occupied the central position; Buddhism was after all an import from India, and Daoism had always been kept in the background as a complement to Confucianism. As has been mentioned, the concept of *xingli* was highly developed in Song-Ming neo-Confucianism. For this reason *xingli* deserves special attention. Even though virtually all neo-Confucian philosophers committed themselves to the Way of *neisheng waiwang* (sageliness within and kingliness without), there were many variations under the same cap. The term "Song-Ming *lixue*" is used in its broader sense to refer to a general trend covering the whole neo-Confucian movement.

At least two major schools of thought can be identified within the movement: Cheng-Zhu *lixue* and Lu-Wang *xinxue*. The kind of *lixue* (study of principle) propounded by Cheng Yi (Yichuan, 1033–1197) and Zhu Xi (Yuanhui, 1130–1200) was understood in its narrower sense. The other school—*xinxue* (study of mind-heart)—was represented by Zhu Xi's rivals, Lu Xiangshan (Jiuyuan, 1139–1193) and Wang Yangming (Shouren, 1472–1529).

The difference between the two schools should not be misunderstood as one putting exclusive emphasis on *li* and the other on *xin*. Both took *li* to be the ultimate metaphysical principle and *xin* to be the agent for transforming human life and society, according to principles inherent in the mind and heart. But Lu-Wang maintained that *xin* is identical with *li*. Here *xin* refers not to the empirical mind but rather to *benxin*, i.e., the original mind, which is the same as principle. Following Mencius, Lu-Wang believed that once our "lost mind" was recovered, all our actions would be conducted according to principles. Here we find a union between heaven and man because there is a correlation between the microcosm and the macrocosm. Cheng-Zhu, however, could say only that the mind comprises principle or principles. Zhu Xi developed a dualistic metaphysics of *li* and *qi* (material force): *li* is static, eternal, universal, and transcendent; *qi* is dynamic, transient, particular, and immanent. The relation between the two is that they must neither be mixed up with each other nor separated from each other. *Li* must inhere in *qi* in order to find manifestation in the world, and *xin* is made of the subtlest kind of *qi* that has the ability to regulate our behavior so that we can act according to principles inherent in the mind. Zhu Xi's thought may be characterized as a combination of constitutional dualism and functional monism. But Lu-Wang rejected his thought and taught monism. The Lu-Wang school believed that *li* is immanent in *qi*, which does not have a separate origin other than *li*. While Zhu Xi interpreted *gewu zhizhi* in *The Great Learning* as investigation of things and extension of knowledge, a young Wang Yangming raised the question, How can an investigation of a bamboo in a courtyard help us extend our moral knowledge? Wang interpreted *gewu zhizhi* as our effort to rectify things, in order to extend our innate moral knowledge (*liangzhi*) to events or affairs. It seems that one school emphasized "following the path of study and inquiry" while the other school emphasized "honoring the moral nature." For the former, *li* means principles found both in man and in nature; for the latter, *li* means the ultimate metaphysical principle realized by our *liangzhi*, which has nothing to do with the empirical study of nature. According to Mou Zongsan, for Zhu Xi *li* has being but not action, whereas for Lu-Wang *li* is a creative ontological principle working incessantly in the universe. Although Zhu Xi established the orthodoxy of the Way, Mou thought that he had deviated from Mencius's insight into the creative Way, which was inherited by Lu-Wang.

Today, this is a controversial issue in the study of Song-Ming *lixue*. But both schools maintained the transcendent character of *li*, whereas Qing Confucian scholars such as Dai Zhen, as we have seen, maintained that *li* was immanent, like patterns of a piece of jade. Throughout the Qing dynasty scholars were no longer interested in metaphysical problems. The significance of the insights of Song-Ming *lixue* was reemphasized by contemporary neo-Confucian scholars such as Tang Junyi and Mou Zongzan. Through their efforts, scholars today realize that although Confucian philosophy contains secular ethics, it also has religious import.

Another important question is the relation between *li* (rites) and *li* (principle). *Li* as rites was already an important concept in ancient Confucianism. It is generally agreed that Confucius saw the inner spirit within the self as the foundation for the practice of rites inherited from the past, since the early Zhou dynasty. Song-Ming neo-Confucian philosophers related *li* as rites to *li* as principle. Rites for them were not just something artificially designed by humans to maintain the social and political order; rather, rites were based on *tianli*, the heavenly principle inherent in human nature. Therefore, they firmly believed in a correlation between microcosm and macrocosm; humans were creative agents who could act according to *tianli* through self-discipline in compliance with the rules of propriety. But early Qing scholars such as Dai Zhen lost sight of the transcendent character of Heaven. *Li* for them became patterns found in human behavior. It was assumed that human desires would regulate themselves. Hence, followers of Dai Zhen such as Ling Tingkan suggested that *li* as principle had to be replaced by *li* as rites. Ironically, although the original intention was to see human desires affirmatively, a system of rites with no foundation in human nature became something totally external that could have the effect of suppressing human desire. At any rate, during the cultural movement of 1919, Chinese intellectuals influenced by the west were uncompromising in calling for the abolition of what they called the "man-eating system" of traditional rites. At one time, wholesale westernization became the vogue. But as the twentieth century ended—after two world wars and the Vietnamese war, among others—the progressive west was found to have its own problems in the postmodern era.

Today, with the world becoming a global village, new reflection on tradition and modernity is urgently needed. In these circumstances contemporary neo-Confucian thinkers say that certain insights implicit in traditional ideas, such as *liyi fenshu* (principle is one while manifestations are many), deserve to be reexamined and reformulated, as the world seeks all possible resources to form a new order so that different peoples and cultures can live together harmoniously in the future.

See also *Li*: Rites or Propriety; *Liyi fenshu*: Principle and Manifestations; Mou Zongsan; Reason and Principle; Tang Junyi.

Bibliography

Chan, Wings-tsit. *Chu Hsi: Life and Thought*. Hong Kong: Chinese University Press, 1987.

——, trans. and comp. *A Source Book in Chinese Philosophy*. Princeton, N.J.: Princeton University Press, 1963.

Chang, Carsun. *The Development of Neo-Confucian Thought*, 2 vols. New York: Bookman, 1957, 1962.

Cua, A. S. *Ethical Argumentation: A Study in Hsün Tzu's Moral Epistemology*. Honolulu: University of Hawaii Press, 1985.

——. "Reason and Principle in Chinese Philosophy." In *A Companion to World Philosophies*, ed. Eliot Deutsch and Ron Bontekoe. Oxford: Blackwell, 1997.

——. *The Unity of Knowledge and Action: A Study in Wang Yang-ming's Moral Psychology*. Honolulu: University of Hawaii Press, 1982.

Fung, Yu-lan. *A History of Chinese Philosophy*, trans. Derk Bodde, 2 vols. Princeton, N.J.: Princeton University Press, 1952–1953.

Liu, Shu-hsien. *Huang Zongxi xinxue ti dingwei* (A Study of Huang Zongxi's Philosophy of Mind). Taipei: Asian Culture, 1986.

——. "On Chu Hsi's Understanding of *Hsing* (Nature)." *Tsing-hua Journal of Chinese Studies*, New Series, 17(1, 2), December 1985, pp. 127–148.

——. "Postwar Neo-Confucian Philosophy: Its Development and Issues." In *Religious Issues and Interreligious Dia-*

logues, ed. Charles Wei-hsun Fu and Gerhard E. Spiegler. New York: Greenwood, 1989.
———. "The Problem of Orthodoxy in Chu Hsi's Philosophy." In *Chu Hsi and Neo-Confucianism*, ed. Wing-tsit Chan. Honolulu: University of Hawaii Press, 1986.
———. "Some Reflections on the Sung-Ming Understanding of Mind, Nature, and Reason." *Journal of Chinese Studies of the Chinese University of Hong Kong*, 21, 1990, 331–344.
———. *Zhuzi zhexue sixiang ti fazhang yu wancheng* (The Development and Completion of Master Chu's Philosophical Thought). Taipei: Xuesheng, 1982.
Mou, Zongsan (Mou Tsung-san). *Cong Lu Xiangshan dao Liu Jishan* (From Lu Xiangshan to Liu Qishan). Taipei: Xuesheng, 1979.
———. *Xianxiang yu wu zisheng* (Phenomenon and the Thing-in-Itself). Taipei: Xuesheng, 1975.
———. *Xinti yu xingti* (The Metaphysical Principle of the Mind and Nature), 3 vols. Taipei: Zhengzhong, 1968–1969.
———. *Zhengdao yu zhidao* (The Way of Politics and the Way of Government), rev. ed. Taipei: Xuesheng, 1980.
———. *Zhi de zhijue yu zhongguo zhexue* (Intellectual Intuition and Chinese Philosophy). Taipei: Commercial Press, 1971.
———. *Zhongguo zhexue de tezhi* (Special Characteristics of Chinese Philosophy). Hong Kong: Young Son, 1963. (See also new ed., Taipei: Xuesheng, 1963.)
———. *Zhongguo zhexue shijiu jiang* (Nineteen Lectures on Chinese Philosophy). Taipei: Xuesheng, 1983.
Tang, Junyi (T'ang, Chün-i). *Tang Junyii quanji* (Collected Works of Tang Junyi), Vols. 12–17. Taipei: Xuesheng, 1986–1990. (New ed. of *Zhongguo zhexue yuanlun*.)
———. *Zhongguo wenhua zhi jingshen jiazhi* (The Spiritual Values of Chinese Culture). Taipei: Zhengzhong, 1953. (See also new ed., *Tang Junyi quanji*, Vol. 4. Taipei: Xuesheng, 1991.)
———. *Zhongguo zhexue yuanlun* (The Development of Ideas in Chinese Philosophy), Vol. 1, Hong Kong: Young Son, 1966. Vols. 2–6, Hong Kong: New Asia Research Institute, 1968–1975.

Li: Rites or Propriety

A. S. CUA

This essay presents a Confucian perspective on *li*—rites, propriety, or rules of proper conduct. The main question concerns the transition from the ethical to the religious dimension of *li*. The first section provides an analysis of the scope, evolution, and functions of *li*. The second section deals with the inner aspect of the foundation of conduct, the motivational aspect of *li*-performance. The third section discusses the outer aspect of the foundation of *li*, focusing on Xunzi's vision of the triad of *tian*, earth, and humanity (*can tianti*), an interpretation of his use of *tian*, *shen*, and *shenming* as expressing a respect for established linguistic, religious practices without endorsing associated popular religious beliefs. This interpretation leaves open the question of the validity of reasoned religious beliefs, while presuming that the religious dimension of *li* is an extension of Confucian ethics (Cua 1998, Essay 13). The fourth section centers on the ethical significance of the *li* of mourning and sacrifice and concludes with some remarks on the transformative significance of the religious dimension of *li*.

An Analysis of *Li*

For more than two millennia, traditional Chinese moral life and thought have been much occupied with *li* as a means for the realization of the Confucian ideal of *dao* (way or Way) or human excellence (*shan*). Implicit in this notion of *li* is an idea of rule-governed conduct. A rough indication of its scope may be gathered from a list of possible translations. Depending on the context of Confucian discourse, *li* can be translated as "religious rites, ceremony, deportment, decorum, propriety, formality, politeness, courtesy, etiquette, good form, good behavior, [or] good manners" (Dubs 1927, 113n). For convenience of reference it is sometimes desirable to use such terms as "propriety," "rules of propriety," or "rules of proper conduct" (Dubs; Legge, 1893). As the pervasive feature of the members of this list, one might propose such terms as "rites," "rituals," "ritual propriety," or "ritual rules," especially if we think of "rites" in the broad sense as including any established practice or set of guides to action stressing formal procedures for proper behavior. But without explicit explanation, this usage is likely to be misleading, particularly in view of the different connotations of the term. For this reason, I retain the transliteration *li* and adopt Xunzi's distinction between generic terms (*gongming*) and specific terms (*bieming*). A generic term is a formal, general, abstract term amenable to specification by other terms in different contexts of discourse. These terms, used in practical or theoretical contexts, may be said to be specific terms in the sense that they specify the significance of the use of a generic term adapted to a current purpose of discourse. *Li* will be used as a generic notion subject to specification in context by such locutions as "the *li* of *x*," where *x* may mean "mourning," "sacrifices," "marriage," "manners," etc. (Cua 1985a, 6 et passim). In this sense, law, morality, religion, and other social institutions, insofar as they require compliance with formal procedures, may be said to be concerned with ritual propriety. However, as a term for a compendious description of the scope of *li*, "ritual propriety" or the like presupposes some understanding of the connection of *li* with other cardinal notions of Confucian ethics. Although I occasionally refer to the dependence of the ethical significance of *li* on *ren* (benevolence, humanity), and *yi* (rightness, righteousness), for present purposes, I assume their conceptual connection without elaboration (Cua 1998, Essay 13).

Here, the explication of *li* is based mainly on the works of Xunzi and *Liji* (*Record of Li*). The *Liji* is one of the three extant ancient texts on *li*, the other two being *Zhouli* and *Yili*. *Zhouli* deals with Zhou organization and institutions, *Yili* with codes of social conduct. The *Liji* mainly "deals with the meaning and significance of organization and institutions as well as with rules of social life and certain related academic matters" (Kao 1986, 313). The extensive scope of *li* is indicated by the title of Legge's translation: *Collection of Treatises on the Rules of Propriety or Ceremonial Usages*.

Scope and evolution of li. In the *Liji*, we find a wide scope of *li*, ranging from the *li* governing special occasions, such as mourning, sacrifices, marriage, and communal festivities, to the more ordinary occasions relating to conduct toward ruler, parents, elders, teachers, and guests. Different classifications are possible. Zhu Xi points to five different sorts of concerns exemplified in the *li*: family, communities, study, states, and dynasties. More modern but misleading classifications can be offered in terms of law, religion, military matters, politics, and ethics (Kato 1963).

To elucidate the concept *li*, let us briefly consider its conceptual evolution. Following Hu Shi (1891–1962), we may view the wide-ranging scope as exemplifying three different strata in the conceptual evolution of *li* (Hu Shi, 1947, 134–143). The basic meaning of *li* lies in the idea of rule. (In this sense, Dubs's rendering of *li* as "rules of proper conduct" is perhaps the best.) The evolution of *li* refers to its increasing extension. The earliest use, as far as scholars are able to ascertain, pertains to religious rites. The etymology of *li* suggests its connection with sacrifices to spirits. *Shuowen*, an ancient dictionary, notes that *li* is "compliance [with rules] for serving spirits (*shen*) and obtaining blessings" (Duan 1980, 1.2B).

In the second stage, *li* becomes a comprehensive notion embracing all social habits and customs acknowledged and accepted as a set of rules to guide action. In this sense, the scope of *li* is coextensive with that of tradition comprising established conventions, that is, customs and usages considered a coherent set of precedents. *Li* is what distinguishes human beings from animals (*Quli*, Legge, 1:64–65).

The third stage in the evolution of *li* is connected with the notions of right (*yi*) and reason (the homophone). In this sense, any rule that is right and reasonable can be accepted as an exemplary rule of conduct. Rules can be constructed or revised and thus are not exclusively determined by old customs and usages (Hu Shi, 137–138). As one writer remarked: "The *li* are [the prescriptions of] reason. . . . The superior man (*junzi*) makes no movement without [a ground of] reason" (*Zhongni yanqu*, Legge, 2:275). Another emphatic passage maintains:

> [The rules of] *li* are the embodied expression of what is right (*yi*). If an observance stands the test of being judged by the standard of what is right (*yi*), although it may not have been among the usages of the ancient kings, it may be adopted on the ground of its being right. (*Liji*, Legge, 1:390)

It is quite evident that the *Liji*, like *Xunzi*, was concerned with the problem of ethical justification. As Waley reminds us:

> The task of the ritual theorists in the third century B.C. was to detrivialize ritual, to arrest its lapse into a domain of mere etiquette or good manners by reintegrating it into the current system of thought. (1938, 59)

The task consists in part in defending specific rules of propriety and in part in offering reasoned justification for the existence of an established normative system. This concern of ancient Confucians is shown in their occasional tendency to associate *li* with its homophone *li* (reason or rationale) and *yi* (rightness or fittingness; Mao 1977, 185–187). The notion of *yi*, in part, is an attempt to provide a rationale for the acceptance of *li*. *Yi* focuses principally on what is right or fitting. Since what is right and reasonable depends primarily on judgment, *yi* may be understood as reasoned judgment concerning the right thing to do, more especially in particular exigencies. In two respects, acceptability of *li* depends on *yi*: (1) *yi* determines whether specific rules of *li* are the right sort of rules to regulate different types of conduct, and (2) the application of *li* requires *yi*, in the sense of reasoned judgment for their application to particular cases. Thus any established system of *li* is subject to an evaluation of *yi*, given the conceptual connection of *li* and *yi* (Cua 1998, 277–287).

To explicate the rationale of *li*, we attend to overlapping questions concerning its significance and foundation of *li* (Chen 1957).

Significance of li *(lizhiyi)*. In his essay on *li*, Xunzi points out that the rationale of the homophone *li* (*lizhili*) is truly profound (*Lilun*, Li, 1979, 428; Watson, 1963a, 93). One must not confuse questions concerning the plurality or numerousness of *li* (*lizhishu*) and their underlying significance (*lizhiyi*). The *li* or rules of proper conduct provide models without explanation (*Quanxue*, L14, W20). For a *junzi* (the paradigmatic individual), moral learning must culminate in the state of integrity or "completeness and purity" (*quancui*). And the achievement of integrity depends on efforts to attain *guantong*, that is, to gain a comprehensive understanding of the meaning and practical import of the texts (Cua 1993; *Quanxue*, Li 19; Watson 22). We find similar emphasis on the significance of *li* in the *Liji*. In the chapter on border sacrifices, the writer stated:

> What is esteemed in the *li*-performance is its [underlying] significance. When this is missed, the number of things and observances may [still] be exhibited. (*Jiaode xing*, Legge, 1:439, modified)

To appreciate the significance of *li* (*lizhiyi*), it is instructive to consider its principal functions by looking at Xunzi's remark on the origin of *li*:

> What is the origin of *li*? I answer that men are born with desires. If their desires are not satisfied, they cannot but seek means for satisfaction. If there are no limits or measures to govern their pursuit, contention will inevitably result. From contention comes disorder and from disorder comes poverty. The ancient Kings hated such disorder, and hence they established *li* (rules of proper conduct) and inculcated *yi* (sense of rightness) in order to make distinctions (*fen*) and boundaries of responsibility for regulating men's pursuit, to educate and nourish (*yang*) men's desires, to provide opportunity for their satisfaction (*keren zhi qiu*). They saw to it that desires did not overextend the means of satisfaction, and material goods did not fall short of what was desired. Thus, both desires and goods mutually support each other. This is the origin of *li*. (*Lilun*, L417, Watson 1963, 88, modified)

Delimiting function. The main objective of *li* or its primary function is to prevent the social disorder that, for Xunzi, is an inevitable result of humans' conflicting pursuit of things to satisfy their desires. Elsewhere he reminds his readers that the scarcity of resources to satisfy everyone's desires inevitably leads to contention (*zheng*) or conflict. Notably as a set of rules for proper conduct, *li* has a delimiting function, that is, defining the limits of individual pursuit of self-interest as well as boundaries of ethical responsibility. In this respect, the rules of *li* are functionally analogous to those of negative moral injunctions against killing, lying, stealing, etc. We must also note that for Xunzi, there is a complementary positive objective in *li*-regulation, that is, the rules of *li* are necessary to human life in society and community. For this reason, cooperation through division of labor and observance of social or class distinctions (*fen*) is required for an orderly, harmonious social life.

For Xunzi, the most important social distinctions are the eminent and the mean, the elder and the younger, rich and poor, important and unimportant members of society. These distinctions represent different sorts of responsibilities. From the sociological point of view, the *li* are concerned with the maintenance of social structure as a harmonious pattern of roles and statuses. Much in the spirit of Xunzi, one writer in the *Liji* remarks:

> It is by the *li* that what is doubtful is displayed, and what is minute is distinguished, that they may serve as dykes for the people. Thus it is that there are grades of the noble and the mean, the distinctions of dress, the different places at court; and so the people [are taught to] give place to one another. (*Fangji*, Legge, 2:285; also 1:63)

Again, "it is by the universal application of the *li* that the lot and duty [of different classes] are fixed" (*Liyun*, Legge, 1:378). For the ruler, the *li* are an important instrument of social and political control, but notably, the social distinctions are valued not only because of their traditional backing but also because of their display of personal moral merits. The significance of *li* as a tradition thus lies in its implicit critical moral acceptance.

Supportive function. The idea of the *li* as dikes for conserving virtues provides us a way to appreciate the supportive function, i.e., the rules of *li* also provide satisfaction of desires within the boundary of proper conduct. Within this boundary of proper conduct, expression of feelings and desires must be recognized. In Xunzi's words, the *li* must provide for opportunity for their satisfaction (*geiren zhi qiu*). Thus, in addition to the delimiting function, the *li* have a supportive function, that is, they provide conditions or opportunities for satisfaction of desires within the prescribed limits of action. With respect to their nature (*xing*) and capacities (*cai*) for acquiring knowledge and action, the *junzi*, the ethically paradigmatic individuals, are the same as the small-minded persons:

> When hungry, they desire food; when cold, they desire to be warm; when exhausted from toil, they desire rest; and they all desire benefit and hate harm. Such are the nature

> that men are born possessing. They do not have to await development before they become so. (*Rongru*, Li, 64; Knoblock 1988–1994, 1:191)

In an important sense, the supportive function of *li* acknowledges the integrity of our natural desires. So long as they are satisfied within the bounds of propriety, we accept them for what they are, whether reasonable or unreasonable, wise or foolish, good or bad. The main supportive function of *li* is the redirection of individual self-seeking activities, not the suppression of motivating desires. This is the sublimating function of *li*. Just as the delimiting function of *li* is functionally analogous to that of negative moral injunctions or criminal law, their supportive function may be compared with that of procedural law, which contains rules that enable us to carry out our wishes and desires, for example, the law of wills and contracts. Like these procedural rules, the *li* contribute to the fulfillment of desires without pronouncing value judgments. More important, the *li* also have an educational and nourishing function (*yang*) in encouraging learning and cultivation of personal character, the subjects of the first two essays in the *Xunzi*. To be a human being, in the ethical rather than the biological sense, is to aspire to become an ethically responsible scholar or official (*shi*), a paradigmatic ethical person (*junzi*), or a sage (*sheng*).

More generally, in ordinary human intercourse, we can appreciate the supportive function of *li* by pondering the significance of the *li* of civility. Many of the *li* of civility facilitate human intercourse, especially among strangers. The *li* of civility are especially important in discursive or argumentative context, for their supportive function reminds the parties in a conflict that there must be agreeable procedures for resolving it before they deal with substantive matters at issue (Cua 1985a, ch. 1). A Confucian philosopher, while aware of the possibility of mere observance of *li* without appropriate regard for *ren* and *yi*, will not altogether reject their ethical value, because conformity to the *li* of manners and civility is an example of regard for the necessity of *li* as having an enabling function in promoting the conditions for easy, effortless, smooth human interaction.

Ennobling function. The focus on the ennobling function of *li* is a distinctive feature of Confucian ethics and traditional Chinese culture. The keynote of the ennobling function is "cultural refinement," the education and nourishment (*yang*) of emotions or their transformation in accord with the spirit of *ren* and *yi*. The characteristic concern with the form of proper behavior is still present. However, the form stressed is not just a matter of fitting into an established social structure or set of distinctions, nor is it a matter of methodical procedure that facilitates the satisfaction of the agent's desires and wishes; rather, it involves the elegant form (*wen*) for the expression of ethical character. A *li*-performance is not just an exhibition of an empty form, for the *junzi* complies with *li* in order "to give proper and elegant expression to his feelings" (Legge, 1:331). In other words, the ennobling function of *li* is directed primarily to the development of commendable or beautiful virtues (*meide*). The "beauty" (*mei*) of the expression of an ethical character lies in the balance between emotions and form. What is deemed admirable in the virtuous conduct of an ethically superior person (*junzi*) is the harmonious fusion of elegant form and feelings (*Lilun*, Li, 430; Watson, 96). In the ideal case, a *li*-performance may be said to have an aesthetic dimension. In two different and related ways, a *li*-performance may be said to be an object of delight. In the first place, the elegant form is something that delights our senses. It can be contemplated with delight quite apart from the expressed emotional quality. In the second place, when we attend to the emotion or emotional quality expressed by the action, which we perceive as a sign of an ethical virtue or character, our mind is delighted and exalted, presuming of course that we are also agents interested in the promotion of ethical virtues in general.

Notably for Xunzi, the desired transformation of man's original, problematic nature (*xing*) is not just an outcome of a process of inculcation of moral virtues, principally directed to resolving conflicts, but also a beautification of man's original nature. As Xunzi put it:

> Human nature (*xing*) is the basis and raw material, and constructive human effort (*wei*) is responsible for the glorification and flourishing of elegant form and orderly expression. If there were no human nature, there would be nothing for constructive human effort to work upon; and if there were no constructive human effort, human nature would have no way to beautify itself (*zimei*). Only when human nature and constructive human effort become one does a true sage merge and perform the task of unifying the world. (*Lilun*, Li, 439; 103, Watson, 102–103, modified)

In this light the *li*-performance culminates in the experience of joy. In Xunzi's words: "All rites (*li*) begin in simplicity, are brought to fulfillment in elegant form (*wen*), and end in joy (*Lilun*, Li, 427; Watson, 94).

With the ennobling function of *li* in mind, we can appreciate the preference of some scholars (Giles, Fingarette, Schwartz) for "noble person" as a translation of *junzi*. Divested of its aristocratic connotation, a noble person is an ethically superior person or paradigmatic individual whose life and conduct exemplify *meide* or virtues in a very high degree, embodying particularly the concern for *ren* and *yi*. As we shall see below, respect for the traditional *li* or rites of mourning and sacrifices is in part an expression for the concern with *ren* and *yi*, because such practices exemplify the Confucian *dao* or ideal of humanity.

Foundation of *Li* (*Lizhiben*): Inner Aspect

For a contemporary Confucian moral philosopher, there are questions concerning the foundation of a person's commitment to the practice of *li*. Of course, lying in the background is an implicit commitment to the ennobling function of *li*, i.e., to *ren* and *yi*. Our question of foundation (*ben*) inquires, so to speak, into the supporting edifice that provides the actuating force to the commitment to the practice of *li*. We may approach this question by distinguishing the inner (*nei*) and outer (*wai*) aspects of the foundation of *li* deemed as the anchorage of the agent's serious commitment to the Confucian *dao* or ideal of human excellence (*shan*). In the language of *Daxue* (*The Great Learning*), such a person has attained *cheng* (sincerity) and is free from self-deception, that is, he or she has attained, in Zhu Xi's words, the state of "truthfulness, genuineness, and freedom from falsity (*zhenshi wuwang*)" (1980, 19). Whereas the inner aspect of the *li*-performance pertains to *cheng* (sincerity) embracing a variety of moral attitudes, dispositions, and emotions, the outer aspect to the underlying Confucian vision of the unity and harmony of humanity and *tian* (heaven, nature) and its implication for concern for the well-being of all things in the universe (Cua 1998, Essays 2 and 7). In other words, the inner aspect pertains to the psychology of *li*-performance, the outer aspect to the committed person's ultimate concern, to his or her understanding of the *dao* as a moral vision with cosmic significance. As we shall see later, the outer aspect of the foundation of *li* provides a transition to Confucian spirituality or the religious dimension of *li*.

Let us first consider the inner aspect of a *li*-performance conformable, say, to a *li* of civility, manners, or deportment. The *li* of manners and deportment are formal prescriptions governing ordinary incidents of life, e.g., greetings, bowing, handshakes, smiling on appropriate occasions, and decency in speech and appearance. In this context, respectfulness (*gong*) and reverence (*jing*) are essential to the *li*-performance. More generally, the person must express *cheng* (sincerity). In one striking passage in the *Xunzi*, reminiscent of *Zhongyong* (*Doctrine of the Mean*), we find the following: "For nourishing (*yang*) the mind of *junzi* (paradigmatic individual), there is nothing better than sincerity (*cheng*). For attaining sincerity there is no other concern than to abide by *ren* and to practice *yi*" (*Bugou*, Li, 47; cf. Knoblock 1:177). Recall Mencius's saying, "Benevolence (*ren*) is man's peaceful abode and rightness (*yi*) his proper path" (4A.10).

Thus the *cheng* (sincerity) of a *li*-performance presupposes a concern with *ren* and *yi*. In light of *ren*, the agent, apart from attention to *wen* or cultural refinement, must also have an affectionate concern for the well-being of his fellows. And this concern involves *zhong* and *shu*—doing one's best to realize one's ethical commitment to the practice of *ren* (*Analects*, 4.15; Lau 1979), and consideration of others' desires and thought (*Analects*, 15.24). Presupposed is *yi* as the ethical standard for the evaluation of conduct in an appropriate context of action (Cua 1984). Confucius's idea of *shu*, i.e., "Do not impose on others what you yourself do not desire" (*Analects*, 15.24), may be construed as a counsel of humility and modesty. While humility is compatible with just pride, it is a desirable moral attitude, because one's claim to knowledge about what is good for oneself and another must be proportional to accessible information and experience. While such knowledge may provide grounds for a claim for its significance for future conduct, reasonable persons would avow their sense of fallibility or humility. Sagacious or judicious judgments will also be informed by a sense of timeliness (*shi*), that is, an adaptation to the current situation in order to achieve equilibrium and an adjustment to varying, changing circumstances through the exercise of one's sense of rightness (*yi*).

Also, for the *ren*-person, humility is a desirable ethical attribute, because no human possesses the knowledge of all possible, appropriate specifications of the significance of the good for individual human life. As a result, one's understanding and concrete specification of the ideal of the good human life will be always made from a limited and partial perspective. When *shu* is positively construed, while it is compatible with just pride in ethical attainment, it is best construed as a counsel of modesty, which stresses the importance of making reasonable or moderate claims on others. One ordinary sense of "reasonable" indicates that a reasonable person will refrain from making excessive or extravagant demands on others (Cua 1982a). More fundamentally, in the light of Confucian *dao* or *ren* as an ideal theme of the good (*shan*), one must be modest in imposing wishes and desires on others. A person committed to *ren* and *yi*, actuated by modesty or moderation, will be concerned with the mean (*zhong*) between excess and deficiency. Such a concern, however, presupposes that the agent exercises moral discretion (*quan*). As Mencius reminds us:

> Holding on to the middle [*zhong*] is closer to being right, but to do this without moral discretion [*quan*] is no differ-

> ent from holding to one extreme. The reason for disliking those who hold to one extreme is that they cripple the Way. One thing is singled out to the neglect of a hundred others. (Lau 1970, 7A.26, modified)

Expression of concern for *ren* and *yi* requires, to borrow Hume's words, delicacy of taste, sensitivity not only to *wen*, the elegant form of conduct, but also to others' "prosperity and adversity, obligations and injuries" (1963, 4). Again, recall Mencius's notion of commiseration as a beginning or seed of *ren* and a *ren*-person as one who has a *xin* (heart-mind) that is sensitive to the suffering of others (*Mencius*, 2A.6) and a sense of shame as a seed of the virtue of *yi*. On the latter, Xunzi would add that just as it is important to distinguish between intrinsic honor or honor justly deserved (*yirong*) and extrinsic honor or honor derived from a person's circumstances (*shirong*), one must also distinguish shame justly deserved (*yiru*) and shame derived from a person's circumstances (*shiru*). Honor and shame justly deserved are conditions of character for which one is ethically responsible. Shame justly deserved is thus the agent's responsibility, because the person has deliberately engaged in ethically wrong conduct, e.g., conduct that is wayward and abandoned, reckless, arrogant and cruel, oppressive and rapacious (*Zhenglun*, Li, 410–411; Knoblock, 3:46). There is no assurance that intrinsic and extrinsic honor will coincide in practice. Abiding by benevolence (*ren*) and acting in accord with one's sense of what is right (*yi*), and virtuous acts (*de*) are ordinarily reliable ways of managing one's life; however, it is possible that they may bring about dangerous (or unwanted) consequences (*Rongru*, Li, 60; Knoblock, 1:189). Yet it cannot be doubted that the honor and shame one morally deserves are products of one's own intentional acts and thus properly reflect one's virtues and vices (*Quanxue*, Li, 5; Watson, 17). Implicit in both Mencius's and Xunzi's conceptions of shame is something like the distinction between social and ethical standards (Shun, 1997, 58–63). Like Aristotle, classical Confucians were concerned with the noble and the base in light of moral virtues and vices. Xunzi, in particular, would exalt a man of *li*, not just because his outward appearance and actions conform to *li* but also because such a display makes manifest and glorious (*long*) his moral attainment (Cua 2003).

Before turning to the outer aspect of the foundation of *li*, let us briefly note that attitudes, dispositions, and emotions involved in the inner aspect are complex and are often associated with the names of virtues. The *Analects* provides an ample vocabulary of ordinary ethical virtues amenable to interpretation and reinterpretation of their significance. One thinks of such generic terms designating particular virtues as filiality, courage, loyalty, fidelity, yielding to elders or superior, uprightness, circumspection, and accommodation. Different times and circumstances of the Confucian agents would yield different interpretations. Moreover, these terms refer to dependent virtues, for their ethical significance depends on concern for the cardinal virtues such as *ren* and *yi*. Positive attitudes toward these cardinal and dependent virtues are considered praiseworthy, just as negative attitudes toward the same virtues are disapproved by the Confucians. Expression of emotions such as joy and sorrow, anger and resentment, as well as desires and aversions must observe the relevant *li* with due regard to *ren* and *yi*. Ethical attitudes, dispositions, and emotions are for the most part an outcome of education. The *junzi* or paradigmatic individuals, persons whose lives exemplify a high degree of ethical attainment, play an important role in ethical education (Cua 1998, Essay 8).

Perhaps a bit stringent for people today, a Confucian would agree with Xunzi that such learning never ceases until death (Book 1). Nevertheless, while moral learning is a heavy burden (*Analects*, 7.7), it is not a process devoid of joy. Confucius once said of himself that his life is "so full of joy that he forgets his worries" (*Analects*, 7.19). On another occasion, perhaps in a lighthearted mood, Confucius said that a *ren*-person would find joy in mountains and have a long life. The *ren*-person, inspired by the ideal of *ren*, finds joy in mountains because his or her life is distinguished by an inspiration derived from the commitment to *ren*, as the highest ideal of the good human life as a whole (*shan*). In this sense, symbolically we may compare the value of *ren* to the height of a mountain. And a person's *ren*-achievement, because of unwavering commitment and integrity, may be said to be as still and firm as a mountain. But the idea that the *ren*-person is long-lived cannot be taken literarily, for Confucius says that a paradigmatic individual (*junzi*), if the situation demands, "would sacrifice his life for the sake of *ren*" (*Analects*, 15.9). "Long life" should be construed as "lifelong" commitment to the ethical vision and the enduring character of *ren*-achievement. Perhaps for this reason, an eminent Confucian scholar, Qian Mu (1992, 2:165), points out that this dialogue implicitly appeals to the Confucian ideal of *tianren heyi* (the unity and harmony of humans and heaven). When we turn to the outer aspect of the foundation of *li*, the relevance of this Confucian vision will become manifest.

Foundation of *Li* (*Lizhiben*): Outer Aspect

One way to approach the religious dimension of *li* is to attend to the outer aspect of the foundation of *li*, which is intrinsically connected with the inner aspect. Because of the complexity of scholarship on the religious or spiritual aspect of classical Confucianism, it is difficult for a Confucian moral philosopher to present an indubitable interpretation of the outer aspect of the foundation of *li*. Perhaps the reason lies in the essentially contestable and vague concepts such as "religion" and "spirituality" in contemporary Confucian and comparative Chinese and western philosophy. If we think of such terms as somewhat descriptive of a person's "ultimate commitment," then for a Confucian, particularly a neo-Confucian like Cheng Hao or Wang Yangming, commitment to *ren* may be so characterized, because the Confucian *ren*, by virtue of the indefinite and inexhaustible extension of affectionate concern for all things, envisages the attainment of an exulted state in which one would "form one body with all things without differentiation" (Cua 1998, Essay 7). Chinese scholars commonly call this Confucian vision *tianren heyi*, the ideal of the unity and harmony of humanity and heaven (*tian*). More commonly in the classical texts, we find the notion of *can tiante*, humans "forming a triad with heaven and earth."

Because of this vision, Xunzi exalts (*long*) the *li* as "joining heaven and earth in harmony" (*Lilun*, Li, 427; Watson 94). He is emphatic, however, that the profound rationale of *li* (*lizhili*) cannot be captured by the practitioners of the school of names (*Mingjia*), arguing over such topics as "hardness and whiteness," "similarity and difference"; or by "uncouth and inane theories of the system-makers"; or by the "violent and arrogant ways of those who despise customs and consider themselves to be above other men" (*Lilun*, Li, 429; Watson 94–95). Xunzi continues:

> He who dwells in *li* and can ponder it well may be said to know how to think; he who dwells in *li* and does not change his ways may be said to be steadfast, and in addition has a true love for *li*—he is a sage. Heaven is the acme of loftiness, earth the acme of depth, the boundless the acme of breadth, and the sage the acme of the Way. Therefore, the scholar studies to become a sage; he does not merely study to become one of the people without direction. (Watson, 94–95, modified)

As a preliminary to understanding Xunzi's ideal of *can tianti*, let us briefly consider the different conceptions of the relation of *tian* and *ren* (humanity). In ancient China we find three different conceptions, embodying different ideals of the good human life: first, the idea of *tianren ganying*, the vision of mutual interplay of *tian* and humans exemplified in *Mozi*; second, the Daoist vision of *yinren ziran* embodied in *Laozi* and *Zhuangzi*, the vision of humans' harmony with the natural order of events, oblivious of human desires and ethical concerns; and third, the more influential Confucian (Mencian) vision of *tianren hede* in the *Mengzi*, the vision of achieving unity and harmony of *tian* and humans through the perfection of ethical character and virtues. A fourth vision is exemplified in Xunzi's *tiansheng rencheng*, the vision that *tian* provides materials for humans to complete their proper tasks, through the exercise of their native capacities (Cua 1998, Essays 2–5 and 9; Yang 1981).

Tian as nature. At the outset of Xunzi's essay on *tian*, we find a sharp distinction between *tian* and humans (*tianren zhi fen*). *Tian* is the domain of *chang*, constancy or regularities of natural occurrences. For the most part, human fortune or misfortune depends on human efforts. As long as one single-mindedly follows the *dao*, *tian* cannot bring misfortune. Says Xunzi:

> To bring completion without acting, to obtain without seeking—this is the work of *tian*. Thus, although the sage has deep understanding, he does not attempt to exercise it upon the work of *tian*; though he has great talent, he does not attempt to apply it to the work of *tian*; though he has keen perception, he does not attempt to use it on the work of *tian*. Hence, he does not compete against *tian*'s work. *Tian* has its seasons, earth has its riches, man has his government. Hence man may form a triad (*can*) with the other two. But if he sets aside that which allows him to form a triad with the other two and longs for what they have, then he is deluded. (*Tianlun*, Li, 362)

The passage above is Watson's translation (79–80), except that I have substituted *tian* for "heaven," a common rendering of *tian* (Watson, 79–80). One may question the adequacy of this translation in the *Xunzi*, for unlike Confucius and Mencius, *tian* in most of Xunzi's uses, especially in our citation, is best rendered as "Nature" or "nature" in the sense of *tian* as "the objective, abstract operation of certain processes and principles of Nature" (Knoblock 3:7). On the other hand, rendering *tian* as "Nature" or "nature" often leads to implausible interpretive theses ascribed to Xunzi (Machle 1993). While we cannot settle the interpretive issues here, "nature" seems a useful term for capturing Xunzi's conception of *tian*. For *tian*, like *dao*, in Chinese philosophy, is a generic term (*gongming*) adaptable to different uses by different schools of thought. For rendering *tian* as "nature" or "natural," some explanatory notes are in order.

First, *tian* as nature is *chang*, the domain of regularities, i.e., our normal, usual, or customary experience of events or states of affairs. In practical planning and deliberation, we rely on such experience in expecting occurrence or recurrence of events and states of affairs. For Xunzi, this domain of natural phenomena must not be confused with that of *wei*, that is, events and phenomena occurring as a result of constructive human efforts. This distinction is explicit in Xunzi's essay on *xing* (human nature), where he maintains that it is a mistake to attribute goodness to inborn human nature (*xing*), for human goodness or excellence (*shan*) is a product of *wei*. Attainment of *shan* is an outcome of *wei* or constructive human activity in molding *xing*, the basic, problematic, motivational structure of humans, into an ethically acceptable and beautiful nature. Of course, when a cultivated person achieves goodness, the virtues of integrity (*quan*) and purity (*cui*) will become second nature. Human nature is a raw material much like a potter's clay or a carpenter's wood for making pots and utensils (*Xing'e*, Li, 550; Watson, 164).

Second, *tian*, as the domain of *chang* or natural regularities, does not preclude apparent anomalies such as falling stars and eclipses, which ordinary people see as terrifying events or phenomena (*kong*), as objects of fear and anxiety, because of their superstitious belief that these occurrences portend misfortune. For Xunzi, these strange, abnormal, and uncanny occurrences are proper objects of wonder or awe rather than fear.

> The sun and moon are subject to eclipses, wind and rain do not always come at the proper season, and strange stars occasionally appear. There has never been an age that was without such occurrences. If the ruler is enlightened and his government just, then there is no harm done even if they occur at the same time. But if the ruler is benighted and his government ill-run, then it will be no benefit to him even if they never occur at all. (*Tianlun*, Li, 373; Watson, 83–84)

The proper objects of fear are such human portents as a poor harvest, evil government that loses the support of the people, neglect of the fields, and starvation. These are calamities due to human actions rather than natural causes (Watson 84–85).

While Xunzi clearly rejects superstitious beliefs concerning apparent anomalies of *tian* as objects of fear, it is difficult to interpret with confidence his view that they are proper objects of wonder or awe. Perhaps his view is that these are marvelous events requiring no explanation, because they have no relevance to human well-being. It is also possible that Xunzi has a special regard for the belief that the anomalies exemplify "the uncanny and the supernatural" as awesome events, for he does not deny significance to all omens. "He makes a clear distinction between those which presage human misfortune, and hence are to be held in awe, and those which do not, and may only be deemed weird (*guai*)" (Machle 1993, 117).

Notably, some seemingly unusual or rare occurrences are often viewed by common people as miraculous and as having potential beneficial or harmful effects. For people who believe in the efficacy of magical practices, certain humans possess extraordinary power. While Xunzi considered the belief superstitious, on par with belief in physiognomy (*Feixiang*, Li, 73–91; Knoblock 1:196–211), he did not condemn these practices.

> Suppose you perform a sacrifice for rain and it rains. Why? For no particular reason, I say. It is just as though you had not prayed for rain and it rained anyway. When the sun or moon are eclipsed, you try to save them; a drought occurs and you pray for rain; you consult the art of divination before making a decision on some important matter. But it is not as though you could hope to accomplish anything by such ceremonies. They are done merely for the sake of *wen*. The ethically superior person (*junzi*) regards them as matters of *wen*, but the common people regard them as matters of *shen*. He who considers them matters of *wen* is fortunate; he who considers them matters of *shen* is unfortunate. (*Tianlun*, Li, 376; Watson; 85, modified)

Recall that *wen*, the beauty or elegant form of behavior, pertains to matters of cultural refinement. In this passage, the belief that *shen* (spirits, gods) are responsible for rain is considered unworthy of acceptance, yet Xunzi does not condemn the rain sacrifice. Why? Perhaps when we turn to Xunzi's remark on the three bases (*ben*) for the practice of *li*, another expression of *can tianti*, a plausible explanation is available.

> The *Li* have three bases: *Tian* and earth are the basis of life, the ancestors are the basis of the family, and rulers and teachers are the basis of order. If there were no *tian* or earth, how could men be born? If there were no ancestors, how would the family come into being? If there were no rulers or teachers, how would order be brought about? If even one of these were lacking, there would be no peace and security for people (*an*). Hence, *li* serves Heaven (*tian*) above and earth below, honors the ancestors, and exalts (*long*) rulers and teachers. These are the three bases of *li*. (*Lilun*, Li, 421–422; Watson, 91, modified)

This passage suggests that peace and security (*an*) are a primary consideration in the enforcement of the *li*, regardless of their reasoned explanation and justification. This concern with people's peace and security reflects the commitment to *ren*, an affectionate concern for the well-being of one's fellows in the community (Cua, 1978). Says Xunzi, "a *ren* person loves others. He loves others and thus hates what injures others" (*Yibing*, Li, 328; Watson, 69, modified). But a *ren*-person must respect others regardless of their capabilities or his own desire for association (*Chendao*, Li, 298; Knoblock, 2:202). To ensure peace and security, the ruler and the well-informed Confucian elites must not interfere with people's religious beliefs, regardless of their reasonableness. For Xunzi the mind (*xin*) has a volitional function that may counteract its intellectual function. Given its autonomy, it can act on its own will without regard to reason. And without the guidance of reason, it is bound to lead to delusion (Cua, 1985, ch. 4). Yet regarding the efficacy of rules of proper conduct (*li*), government cannot ignore or legislate against ordinary people's religious beliefs, even if they are deemed unreasonable. It is not the business of those in government or ethical persons of the community to ensure that ordinary people hold reasonable religious beliefs. To borrow William James's term, respect for people's "will to believe" is essential to the preservation of a harmonious social and political order. Perhaps this concern with the efficacy of the enforcement of the *li* is implied in the following passage:

> The [efficacy of] *li* relies on conformity to human *xin* (mind) as foundation. Hence, even if there were no *li* in the *Classic of Li*, so long as they accord with *xin*, they may be considered as part of *li*. (*Dalue*, Li, 605; Knoblock, 3:211)

Moreover, recall our earlier discussion of *shu* as embracing modesty and humility. Having no infallible knowledge of the good (*shan*), the *junzi* or ethically superior persons, without compromising their integrity, would refrain from condemning religious beliefs that they consider ill-founded or superstitious. For example, they would adhere to their conviction that the rain sacrifice is a matter of *wen*, a cultural embellishment. The associated popular belief in magic has no positive ethical significance, since it does not contribute to the realization of the Confucian vision of the unity of *tian*, earth, and humanity (*can tianti*). Unless superstitious beliefs are detrimental to the ethical order of the community, they may be condoned without endorsement. Perhaps Xunzi's attitude may be characterized by Berkeley's epigram: "We ought think with the learned, and speak with the vulgar" (1949, paragraph 51). Admittedly some of Xunzi's uses of *shen* indicate approval of some religious beliefs, though we cannot be certain of his definitive views. Let us consider passages using *shen* and the *shenming* (which, on the analogy of mathematics or biology, I will call a "binomial").

Shen and shenming. Xunzi gives two explanations of the meaning of *shen*. We find the first and primary definition in his essay on *tian*. For convenience, let us call this definition D1. This passage involving *shen* pertains to natural regularities of *tian*, the transformative process of *yin* and *yang*:

> Although we do not see the process, we can observe the results. All people understand that the process has reached completion, but none understands the formless or unobservable factors underlying the process. For this reason, it is properly called the accomplishment of *tian*. Only the sage does not seek to understand *tian*. (*Tianlun pian*, Li, 65; Machle 1993, 93; Watson, 80, modified)

In this passage, *shen* pertains to the unobservable and inexplicable thing that underlies the process. This use of *shen* recalls the succinct remark in the *Yijing*: "The unfathomable *yinyang* process is what is meant by *shen*" (Nan and Xu 1976, 372). This use of *shen* seems to imply the existence of a supernatural or transcendental entity at the base of natural processes. Thus *shen* is often translated as "spirit" or "god," as this is a common use of in ancient literature. This use is exemplified in our earlier citation of the passage on the rain sacrifice. Here, our question concerns not the propriety of translation but the interpretation of *shen* as referring to a special superhuman being. For Xunzi, the question concerning the existence and nature of such a being has no special relevance to resolving human problems; thus the person who aspires to sagehood will not seek knowledge of *tian*. Because of his pragmatic attitude toward metaphysical or ontological discourse, Xunzi discourages inquiry into the inexplicable factors that underlie natural processes, though, as we have seen earlier, he appreciates wonder or awe as a fitting response to strange and uncanny phenomena.

A secondary definition of *shen* (D2) pertains to ascription of ethical excellence or goodness to ideal persons. "To be wholly good and fully self-disciplined is called *shen*" (*Ruxiao pian*, Li, 141). In both D1 and D2 Xunzi makes use of the quasi-definitional locution *zhiwei* in two different ways. D1, where *zhiwei* is a component of *fushi zhiwei*, provides both the necessary and sufficient conditions for the proper use of *shen*. D2, on the other hand, provides only the necessary condition (Cua, 1985a, ch. 3). Divested of ontological interpretation, anything that satisfies D1 must be considered mysterious and incomprehensible. I suspect that Xunzi is offering a demythologized conception of *shen* that echoes the one given in the *Yijing*. D2, however, seems to be an explanation of the use of *shen* as a metaphor, while conveying the sense of the mysterious and the inexplicable. The context in which *shen* occurs in D2 is concerned with characterizing the sage as one whose way of life and thought proceeds from "oneness," i.e., as a person who resolutely holds fast to *shen*. This use of *shen* is plausibly a metaphor implying an analogy with *shen* in the sense of D1, as in the expression *rushen*, which occurs in three passages that deal with good and well-ordered government.

Let us look at one passage involving *rushen*. In this instance, the discussion pertains to how an enlightened ruler (*mingjun*) unifies and guides the people by the Way (*dao*), making clear the ethical teachings and the use of punishment to forbid evils. Thus, says Xunzi, "His people are transformed by the Way as though his actions were those of a *shen*." Here *shen* can be properly rendered as "spirit" or "god." In effect, Xunzi is saying that what an enlightened ruler accomplishes through *dao* is much like (*ru*) a *shen*. As in the *yinyang* process, there is something mysterious and inexplicable, as indicated by Xunzi's remark that precedes his discussion: "It is easy to unify the people by means of the Way, though the ruler could not make them understand all the reasons for things" (Dubs 1927, 289, modified). This remark recalls Confucius's: "The common people can be made to follow a path but not to understand it" (*Analects*, 8.9; Lau 1979).

First, let us note that the use of *shen* according to D2 implies a positive normative judgment, expressing both approval and commendation. If we consider this use metaphorical, then, as in the case of D1, ontological interpretation is irrelevant. At the heart of this use is an analogy between one thing and another. For instance, the expression "He is a *shen*" is essentially a collapsed simile, "He is like a *shen*." Here *shen* is a metaphor in that it is a term applying to something to which it is not literally applicable in order to suggest a resemblance to *shen* in the primary sense of D1, a metaphorical extension of D1.

To deal with Xunzi's conception of *shenming*, let us look at an interesting passage where we find a connection between *cheng* (sincerity), *ming* (insight, clarity), and *shen*:

> For nourishing (*yang*) the mind of *junzi* (paradigmatic individual), there is nothing better than sincerity (*cheng*). For attaining sincerity there is no other concern than to abide by *ren* and to practice *yi*. When his mind (*xin*) has attained *cheng* and abided by *ren*, his *cheng* will become manifest. In this way, he becomes a *shen* and is capable of transforming things (*hua*). When his mind is sincere (*cheng*) and he acts according to his sense of rightness (*yi*), he becomes reasonable (the homophone *li*). When his mind is reasonable, it is in the state of *ming*. Consequently, he [can adapt himself] to changing circumstances. (*Bugou pian*, Li, 47; Knoblock, 1:177–178)

In this passage, construing *shen* as a metaphor, an ellipsis of *rushen*, we can render it as "godlike." Remarkably, the passage recalls a similar idea of the connection of *cheng* and *ming* and the vision of the triad of *tian*, earth, and humanity (*can tianti*) in the *Doctrine of the Mean* (*Zhongyong*), where we find the view that truly sincere (*cheng*) persons who possess *ming* can develop themselves as well as others and "can then assist in the transforming and nourishing processes of Heaven (*tian*) and Earth, [and] can thus form a trinity with Heaven and Earth" (*can tianti*; Chan 1963, 107–108). More important, as Xunzi goes on to point out, although the sages are wise, without *cheng* they cannot transform the multitude (*Bugou pian*, Li, 47). Implicit is the notion of the sage (*shengren*) as one who embodies the confluence of *cheng* and *ming*.

Let us turn to a passage involving *shenming* in the context of Xunzi's claim that all ordinary persons are capable of becoming sages—a view shared by Mencius and Song-Ming Confucians. According to Xunzi, all ordinary persons have a native capability to understand the rationales (homophone *li*) of *ren*, *yi*, and rules and regulations. If they devote themselves single-mindedly to moral learning; contemplate the significance of *ren*, *yi*, and rules and regulations; and persevere over a long period of time, then, through unceasing effort to accumulate good deeds,

> they can acquire a comprehensive *shenming* (*tong yu shenming*) into the inner significance of things and form a triad with *tian* and earth (*can tianti*). Thus the sage is one who has attained the highest state through the accumulation of good deeds. (*Xing'e*, Li, 552; Watson, 167, modified)

After we consider another use of the binomial *shenming*, I will comment on this use.

In the essay on dispelling *bi* (obscuration, blindness of the mind), Xunzi maintains that unless the mind is in the state of *ming* (clarity), it is likely to suffer from *bi*. Earlier we referred to this passage for Xunzi's conception of the autonomy of human mind without considering the full context involving the use of *shenming*. The passage runs: "The mind (*xin*) is the ruler of the body and *shenming zhi zhu*" (*Jiebi pian*, Li, 488). We find different English translations for "*shenming zhi zhu*," e.g., "master of godlike intelligence" (Watson, 139), "master of the daemonic-and-clear-seeing" (Graham 1989, 252), "master of spiritual intelligence" (Knoblock, 3:105), and "host to such a divine manifestation" (Machle 1992, 383). It is difficult to resolve the issue here. I propose, as a minimal interpretation, perhaps acceptable to these translators, that we regard *shenming* here in light of the connection between *shen* and *ming*. Interpreting *shen* as "godlike" and *ming* as "insight" gives us a reading of *shenming* as a special characteristic of the sage, an interpretation closer to Graham and Knoblock, with an additional appreciation of Machle's rendering of *zhu* as "host." Construing *shen* in *shenming* as "godlike," we have the sense of insight (*ming*) that befits a god or spirit (*shen*), a rare and extraordinary human achievement. In this light, it is also acceptable to render *shenming* as "spiritual insight," which suggests an affinity to Descartes's notion of *intuitus* (Joachim, 1957, 25ff.), although for Xunzi *shenming* is more a form of wisdom or perspicacity—a product of cultivation, accumulation of goodness, and evidential learning (*chengzhi*)—than an a priori intuition or way of knowledge. In the essay on encouraging learning, Xunzi remarks that "if a *junzi* engages in extensive learning and daily examines himself, his wisdom will become *ming* and conduct be without fault" (*Quanxue*, Li, 2; Watson, 15, modified).

However, more accomplished is the sage who possesses an understanding (*zhi*) of the holistic character of *dao*. A doctrine of the *dao* based on a limited perspective, raising for attention "one corner" of *dao*, is insufficient to capture its intrinsic holistic nature (*Jiebi*, Li, 478; *Tianlun*, Li, 381; Watson, 87, 126). Because of this understanding of the "thread of *dao*" (*daoguan*), without deliberation or planning, the sage can respond appropriately to changes as they come (Cua 1985a, 31–35, 61–65). The understanding (*zhi*) is an insight into the interconnection of things rather than factual knowledge. Unlike a claim of truth, the sage's insight is akin to keen appreciation or perception of the significance of the interconnection of facts that sheds light on human problems (Cua 1998, 95–99). In brief, a sage has a "keen insight which never fails" (*Xiushen*, Li, 33; Watson, 30).

If these remarks on *shenming* are considered adequate for understanding Xunzi's use of the term, we can also appreciate Machle's translation of *chu* as "host," rather than the common translation "master," thus rendering the phrase on the mind (*xin*) as "the host of *shenming*." For insight (*ming*) arrived at through a long process of learning and self-cultivation, including constant self-examination, is something that one acquires, not as a result of thinking or inference, but as a consummation and reward of a lifelong effort in pursuing *daoquan* or a holistic understanding of *dao* and *liguan*, the "thread that runs through the rationales of things." The sage is a recipient of *shenming*. Something echoing this interpretation of *shenming* may be found in Zhu Xi's conception of *qiongli* (exhaustive investigation of the rationales [the homophone *li*] of things). Zhu Xi writes:

> The first step in the education of the adult is to instruct the learner, in regard to all things in the world, to proceed from what knowledge he has of their rationales (*li*), and investigate further until he reaches the limit. After exerting himself in this way for a long time, he will one day achieve a wide and far-reaching penetration [*quantong*]. (Chan 1963, 89, modified)

Understanding the living significance of classical texts is an occurrence, something that happens independently of one's efforts, though efforts are a prerequisite for this experience. Recall our earlier emphasis on efforts to attain *guantong* as essential to the *junzi*'s attainment of moral integrity, i.e., to gain a comprehensive understanding of the meaning and practical import of the classical texts.

As regards Xunzi's uses of *shen* and *shenming*, whatever translation one adopts, e.g., "spirit," "god," "godlike," "godliness," absent our knowledge of his view on the nature and existence of *shen* and *shenming*, I sometimes wonder whether Xunzi's attitude of wonder or awe toward *shen* as the unfathomable that underlies the *yinyang* process reflects the attitude of a conservative linguistic revisionist as suggested in his essay on "rectifying terms or names" (*zhengming*). There he points out that it is the task of a sage king to preserve old terms and create new ones as needed. To do so, he would have to consider these questions: "Why are terms needed? What is the basis for distinguishing similarities and differences between things, and the essential standard in regulation?" (*Zhengming*, Li, 510; Watson, 141, modified). The essential standard governing the uses of terms lies in abiding by appropriate conventions, for "terms have no intrinsic appropriateness. It is agreement that determines their actuality or concrete application (*shi*)" (Cua 1985a, ch. 3; *Zhengming*, Li, 616; Watson, 144, modified).

Moreover, for Xunzi, respect for linguistic practices is an important criterion of successful communication. Would Xunzi similarly regard his own use of *shen* and *shenming* as an example of respect for the linguistic practice of his time? An affirmative answer to this question would ascribe to Xunzi the thesis that the established usages of *shen* and *shenming* are acceptable independent of their associated religious beliefs, superstitions as well as doctrines concerning their metaphysical or ontological status. Of course, this established linguistic practice provides a language for honoring and glorifying *shen* and *shenming*, indirectly exemplifying our pivotal ethical concerns in the light of *dao*. This interpretation has partial support in Xunzi's uses of *long* (magnifying, glorifying, exalting) in connection with *ren, li*, and *yi*. In this regard we find an interesting analogue in Hobbes's view on the language of Christianity, that the use of "the Spirit of God" does not imply an understanding of

> *what he is*, but only that *he is*; and therefore the Attributes we give him, [that he is omnipotent, benevolent, and wise] are not to tell one another, *what he is*, but on *that he is* nor to signifie our opinion of his Nature, but our desire to honour him with such names as we conceive most honorable amongst ourselves. (1952, 304)

I also wonder whether Xunzi would endorse Hobbes's saying: "Words are wise men's counters; they do reckon by them; but they are the money of fools" (29; Turbayne 1962, 101).

The Religious Dimension of *Li*

For Xunzi, the practice of religious rites of his times, the *li* of mourning and sacrifice, has a profound significance for a good life, not because of any association with specific religious beliefs, say, concerning the existence of the spirits of the dead, but because of ordinary, human yearning for a long life and reverence for the dead, especially the beloved dead. His attitude echoes Confucius's and an earlier view of immortality (*shi er buxiu*), that immortality pertains to "establishing virtues (*lide*), establishing accomplishments (*ligong*), and establishing words (*liyan*)" (Chan 1963, 13). However, the fact of human mortality is a proper concern of *li*. While the wish for continued existence after death cannot be fulfilled, the beginning and the end can be properly honored. All human beings encounter the beginning of life and death as boundaries. The religious rites for mourning and sacrifice provide occasions for honoring our roots, a symbolic expression of our reverence for human life. These rites deal with our conception of our own boundaries—birth, marriage, and death.

Austin once remarks that "a word never—well, hardly ever—shakes off its etymology and its formation. In spite of all changes in and extensions of and additions to its meaning, and indeed rather pervading and governing these, there will persist the old idea" (1961, 149). As noted above, the etymology of *li* suggests its connection with sacrifices to spirits. The common translation of *li* as "rites" or "ritual" thus recalls the early pre-Confucian use of *li* in a religious context. We have occasionally noted, especially in connection with *shen* and *shenming*, the associated beliefs in the existence of gods and their influence in human life. This feature is also prominent in some essays in the *Liji*. Xunzi's view somewhat echoes Confucius's. Confucius seems to have an insouciant attitude toward the existence of spirits and the relevance of belief in an afterlife, though sometimes he appealed to heaven (*tian*) as a quasi-purposive, spiritual being. We find, for instance the following:

> The Master said, "There is no one who understands me." Tzu-kung said, "How is it that there is no one who understands you?" The Master said, "I do not complain against heaven (*tian*), nor do I blame men. In my studies, I start from below and get through to what is up above. If I am understood at all, it is, perhaps, by heaven (*tian*)." (*Analects*, 14.3; Lau 1979)

But at another time, when he was asked about wisdom (*zhi*), Confucius said that one must serve the people with a sense of what is right and appropriate (*yi*), and respect the ghosts and spirits (*guishen*), but keep them at a distance (*Analects*, 6.22). Confucius approved of the *li* of mourning and sacrifices largely because of his adoption of the Zhou tradition as an ethical guide to communal intercourse, not because of the specific associated religious beliefs about the existence of ghosts and spirits.

Confucius seems to have an "as if" attitude toward the dead as objects of sacrifice (3.12), and he stresses the importance of reverence in sacrifice and sorrow in mourning (19.1). In the *Liji*, it is said that King Wen "in sacrificing, served the dead as if he were serving the living" (*Jiyi*, 2.608, Legge, 2:212). We find similar attitude in Xunzi: "The funeral rites have no other purpose than to clarify the rationales (*li*) of life and death, to send the dead person away with grief and reverence, and to lay him at the ground" (*Lilun*, Li, 441; Watson, 105, modified). In sacrificial rites, "one serves the dead as though they were living, the departed as though present, giving body to the bodiless and thus fulfill the proper form of *li*" (*Lilun*, Li, 451; Watson, 111, modified). Moreover, appropriate expression of emotions is essential. Says Xunzi:

> The sacrificial rites originate in the emotions of remembrance and longing for the dead. Everyone is at times visited by sudden feelings of depression and melancholy longing. . . . [These rites] express the highest degree of loyalty, love and reverence, and embody what is finest in ritual conduct and formal bearing. (*Lilun*, Li, 450–451; Watson, 109–111)

For Xunzi, it is especially important for participants in a *li*-performance to aim at the "middle state," i.e., between excessive emphasis on formality and the inordinate expression of emotions (*Lilun*, Li, 430; Watson, 96).

Rites of mourning and sacrifices have a profound significance for Xunzi, not as a statement of religious beliefs but as a profound expression of our attitude toward human life as a whole. The beginning and the end of our life may be depicted as extreme points of a line. These rites are especially important in *li*-performance, for they bespeak the spirit of human life in the intermediate regions. When we think of a person's life along a succession of stages from childhood, adolescence, and adulthood to old age, the beginning and the end occasionally cry out for attention. We mark their importance as rites of passage. The *li* of mourning is an acknowledgment of the terminus of a person's life, accomplishments, failures, fortunes, and misfortunes. It is a life worthy of respect and reverence. Thus, the rites are to be performed with sincere generosity and reverent formality. The dead have significance for the living. We honor them in rites as if they were present in order to ornament our grief and make sacrifices to them to ornament our reverence. These rites are an expression of our reverence and reasonable concern for *wen*, cultural refinement. As Xunzi remarks, "cherishing our roots (*ben*) is called *wen*, and familiarity with practical usage (*chinyong*) is called *li* (reason, reasonableness)" (*Lilun*, Li, 424; Watson, 92). The rites have a purely symbolic meaning. They are performed for the sake of unifying and honoring the beginning and the end. In these ritual performances, we consciously engage in a pretense without self-deception, in order to express our moral emotions of respect and reverence in a proper setting.

Focusing on the *wen* or "ornamenting" of emotions of grief, melancholy, and the longing for our loved ones, the religious rites represent more an extension of the moral and the aesthetic rather than an autonomous domain of *li*-experience. It is an extension of a horizon for viewing life as a whole in terms of *ren*, the ideal of humanity; and *yi*, the right and fitting concern for the dead. The *li* of mourning and sacrifice are important for appreciating the value of human life, because they are an articulation, in a concrete setting, of the practical and actuating force of a commitment to *dao* or *ren* as an ideal theme, a standard of inspiration for Confucian agents (Cua, 1978a, ch. 8). In this light, honoring the dead with reverence is a way of celebrating our humanity. Our *li*-performances here attain their distinctive character, transcending our animality. Our care for the dead is in effect a care for the living human as a being invested with an ideal import. The ideal of *ren* or humanity has in this way acquired a quasi-natural habitat. Whatever virtues unfold in this habitat may thus be seen as a partial realization of the Confucian ideal of human excellence (*shan*).

If we consider the moral, aesthetic, and religious dimensions of *li* together, the notion of *li* has an amphibious character. On the one hand, it expresses what the living humans regard as morally and aesthetically valuable. On the other hand, it points to the world in which humans anchor on a form of life that must, for each person, come to an end. Between the beginning and the end, we live our lives. To be mindful of the significance of religious rites as another dimension of *li* is to have an additional, special regard for our past and future. The past, in light of *li*, is no longer something fossilized and gone; we recall it, and in doing so in religious rites of mourning and sacrifice, we may be said to experience its significance in memory. It lives in our thought and action, as our beginning is a long tradition incarnate—the tradition in which human life anchors. This feature of *li* is brought out by Fingarette. The powerful image of sacrificial vessels of jade

> in the *Analects* may in this way be viewed as the transformation of the secular into the sacred. It is sacred not because it is useful or handsome but because it is a constitutive element in the ceremony. (1972, 75)

And when the contemplation of the end of life is seen as having prospective as well as retrospective significance, to honor the dead is to be mindful also of the continuing responsibility of the living. While we cannot separate ourselves from the anchorage, we cannot ignore the recurrence of problems. It is the here and now that must occupy the living. When the rites are properly performed, we take our leave and go on with our usual occupations. The symbolic significance of these rites must be taken seriously for our own sake. Notably, Xunzi's conception of rituals is acknowledged as an insightful precursor of an influential anthropological view that rituals have a social and symbolic function, independent of magical beliefs (Radcliffe-Brown 1965, 119).

The instruments deployed in the rites, costumes, and varying bodily motions, to a sensitive Confucian, inspired awe and reverence just as they serve to express the emotions of the participants in the *li* of mourning. Sorrow and depressing grief are not just painful but can be experienced as emotions that express gladness at being alive. When they are directed toward the cosmos, they may even commemorate the Confucian vision of *can tianti*, the grand harmony of man and his world. In one passage, Hsün Tzu exalts the *li*:

> Through *li*, heaven and earth are joined in harmony; the sun and the moon shine, the four seasons proceed in order, the stars and constellations march, the rivers and streams flow, and all things flourish. Through the *li*, men's likes and dislikes are regulated and their joy and anger are expressed in proper occasions. Those below are obedient, those above are enlightened (*ming*). All things change without creating disorder. Only those who turn back against the *li* will be destroyed. Indeed, we have no greater expression of the perfection of the *li*! Establish and exalt (*long*) the *li* to its utmost, no one in the world can add or subtract [from their significance]. Through the *li*, the root and the branches are put in proper order; beginning and end are made consonant; the most elegant forms embody all distinctions; the most penetrating insight explains all things. (*Lilun*, Li, 427; Watson, 94, modified)

Here we have an example of Xunzi's exaltation of *li*, reflecting his vision of *can tianti* or *dao*, a vision of the good life. In this exaltation of *li*, moral values occupy their preeminent place in social and personal intercourse, aesthetic values mark their pervasive quality, and religious values celebrate the grand unity or harmony of man and the natural order. One finds neither independent normative ethics, nor normative aesthetics, nor a philosophy of religion. Rather, with the moral alongside aesthetic and religious values, one finds an interesting and challenging view in axiological ethics. If the foregoing discussion of this conception is deemed plausible, it is owing to the inspiration of Xunzi in offering us a distinctive, complex notion of *li*, providing an occasion for reflecting on an important problem of the interconnection between different types of values.

Conclusion

For a contemporary Confucian philosopher, an appreciation of the religious dimension of *li*, the *li* of mourning and sacrifices, does not depend on inquiry into their metaphysical or ontological significance. Tang Junyi points out that the significance of sacrifices to spiritual beings (*guishen*) depends not on any ontological view of their independent and external existence, but on our *ren*-capacity to *guantong*, that is, to permeate or penetrate through all existent things (Tang 1978, 141). Spiritual beings may be said to exist only insofar as they are the objects of this penetrating process—they "exist" as objects of our emotions or thought, expressive of our moral attitudes. In the ontological sense, they need not exist, for we have no knowledge of their nature independent of our emotions or thought. In the spirit of Xunzi, we may regard these entities as our own creations (*wei*); they exist as supervenient qualities of our reflective ethical experience, the resultant attributes of the expression of our ethical emotions or thought in the context of religious observances (Ross 1930, ch. 2). In this sense, the religious dimension of *li*, like its aesthetic dimension, is an extension of its primary ethical dimension, and may properly be considered as a constitutive feature of the Confucian ethical life. Ideally, in the growth of the ethical experience of a committed Confucian agent, religious quality may become a salient feature of life. Xunzi's endorsement of the uses of *shen* and *shenming* in his own thought, aside from his respect for established linguistic practices, possibly reflects his appreciation of the transformative character of religious beliefs, insofar as they are consistent with *ren*, *yi*, and *li*.

In light of the Confucian vision of the unity and harmony of *tian* and humanity, especially in Cheng Hao and Wang Yangming, this ideal of the good human life encompasses all living and nonliving things. Although this ideal is a wish rather than an object of reasoned deliberation, it may be considered a religious ideal, for a person seriously committed to *ren* will regard all things as "one body." In the words of Wang Yangming:

> The great man regards Heaven, Earth, and the myriad things as one body (*yi-ti*). He sees (*shi*) the world as one family and the country as one person. . . . Forming one body with Heaven, Earth, and the myriad things is true not only of the great man. Even the mind (*xin*) of the small man is no different. Only he makes it small. Therefore, when he sees a child about to fall into a well, he cannot help a feeling of alarm and commiseration. This shows that his humanity (*ren*) forms one body with the child. Again, when he observes the pitiful cries and frightened appearance of the birds and animals about to be slaughtered, he cannot help feeling an "inability to bear" their suffering. This shows that his humanity forms one body with birds and animals. (Wang 1963, 273)

Wang goes on to point out that a man of *ren* also forms "one body" with plants, stones, tiles, mountains, and rivers. In this version of the Confucian vision of *can tianti*, the unity and harmony of humanity and all things becomes an ethical ideal that provides a cosmic perspective. In Tu Weiming's words, it is an "anthropocosmic" vision, where the human "self" is the center of all human and nonhuman relationships (1989). If the primary function of the language of religious beliefs is to express religious commitment or the "will to belief," this Confucian vision may properly be regarded as a religious vision, presupposing the Confucian ethical ideal of the good life as a whole, variously termed *dao, ren, tianren heyi*, or *can tianti*. For a committed agent, this vision may provide a motivating force in self-transformation, since the vision answers to vital personal perplexities that resist problematic formulation (Cua 1978a, ch. 8). In this way, we can have an open, ethical vista that embraces and preserves the integrity of religious beliefs without prejudging their reasoned justification, thus leaving open a serious inquiry into the possibility of Confucian philosophy of religion and comparative religion.

See also Confucianism: Ethics; Confucianism: Tradition; *Junzi; Ren*; *Yi* and *Li*.

Bibliography

Allinson, Robert E. "The Confucian Golden Rule: A Negative Formulation." *Journal of Chinese Philosophy*, 12(3), 1985, pp. 305–315.

Austin, J. L. "A Plea for Excuses." In *Philosophical Papers*. Oxford: Clarendon, 1961.

Berkeley, George. *A Treatise Concerning the Principles of Human Knowledge*. In *The Works of George Berkeley*, Vol. 2, ed. T. E. Jessop. London: Thomas Nelson, 1949.

Chan, Wing-tsit, ed. *Chu Hsi and Neo-Confucianism*. Honolulu: University of Hawaii Press, 1986.

———, trans. *A Source Book in Chinese Philosophy*. Princeton, N.J.: Princeton University Press, 1963.

Chen, Daqi. *Chen Bainian xiansheng wenji*, Vol. 3. Taipei: Shangwu, 1994.

———. *Kongzi xueshuo*. Taipei: Zhengzhong, 1977.

———. *Mingli luncong*. Taipei: Zhengzhong, 1957.

———. *Xunzi xueshuo*. Taipei: Zhonghua Wenhua Publication Committee, 1954.

A Concordance to Hsün Tzu, 5/82270. (Extensive occurrence of *long* in connection with *li* or *li* and *yi*.)

Cua, A. S. "The Concept of *Li* in Confucian Moral Theory." In *Understanding the Chinese Mind: The Philosophical Roots*, ed. Robert E. Allinson. Hong Kong: Oxford University Press, 1989.

———. "Confucian Vision and the Human Community." *Journal of Chinese Philosophy*, 11(3), 1984, pp. 226–238.

———. "Dimensions of *Li* (Propriety): Reflections on an Aspect of Hsün Tzu's Ethics." *Philosophy East and West*, 29(4), 1979, pp. 373–394.

———. *Dimensions of Moral Creativity: Paradigms, Principles, and Ideals*. University Park: Pennsylvania State University Press, 1978a.

———. *Ethical Argumentation: A Study in Hsün Tzu's Moral Epistemology*. Honolulu: University of Hawaii Press, 1985a.

———. "Ethical Uses of History in Early Confucianism: The Case of Hsün Tzu." *Philosophy East and West*, 35(2), 1985b, pp. 133–156.

———. "Feature Review: John Knoblock, *Xunzi—A Translation and Study of the Complete Works*, Volume 1, Books 1–6." *Philosophy East and West*, 41(2), 1991, pp. 215–227.

———. *Moral Vision and Tradition: Essays on Confucian Ethics*. Washington, D.C.: Catholic University of America Press, 1998.

———. "The Possibility of Ethical Knowledge: Reflections on a Theme in the *Hsün Tzu*." In *Epistemological Issues in Ancient Chinese Philosophy*, ed. Hans Lenk and Gregor Paul. Albany: State University of New York Press, 1993.

———. "The Quasi-Empirical Aspect of Hsün Tzu's Philosophy of Human Nature." *Philosophy East and West*, 28(1), 1978b, pp. 3–19.

———. "Reason and Principle in Chinese Philosophy." In *A Companion to World Philosophies*, ed. Eliot Deutsch and Ron Bontekoe. Oxford: Blackwell, 1997.

———. "Reasonable Persons and the Good: Reflections on an Aspect of Weiss's Ethical Thought." In *Philosophy of Paul Weiss*, ed. Lewis E. Hahn. Library of Living Philosophers. La Salle, Ill.: Open Court, 1995.

———. "Reflections on the Structure of Confucian Ethics." *Philosophy East and West*, 21(2), 1971, pp. 125–140. (See also A. S. Cua. *Dimensions of Moral Creativity: Paradigms, Principles, and Ideals*. University Park: Pennsylvania State University Press, 1978a, ch. 4.)

———. *The Unity of Knowledge and Action: A Study in Wang Yang-ming's Moral Psychology*. Honolulu: University of Hawaii Press, 1982.

Duan, Yucai. *Shuowen jiezi zhu*. Shanghai: Shanghai guji, 1980.

Dubs, Homer H. *Hsüntze: The Moulder of Ancient Confucianism*. London: Arthur Probsthain, 1927.

Fingarette, Herbert. *Confucius: The Secular as Sacred*. New York: Harper and Row, 1972.

———. "Following the 'One Thread' of the *Analects*." *Journal of the American Academy of Religion*, Thematic Issue 47(3S), 1979, pp. 373–406.

Fogelin, Robert J. *Understanding Arguments: An Introduction to Informal Logic*. New York: Harcourt Brace Jovanovich, 1978.

Gao, Ming (Kao Ming). *Lixue xintan*. Taipei: Xuesheng, 1980.

Giles, Lionel. *The Sayings of Confucius*. London: Murray, reprinted by Charles Tuttle, 1993. (Reprint of 1907 ed.)

Graham, A. C. *Disputers of the Tao: Philosophical Argument in Ancient China*. La Salle, Ill.: Open Court, 1989.

Hobbes, Thomas. *Leviathan*. Oxford: Clarendon, 1952.

Hu, Shi. *Zhongguo zhexue shi dagang*, Part 1. Taipei: Commercial Press, 1947. (Reprint of 1918 ed.)

Hume, David. *An Inquiry Concerning the Principles of Morals*. Indianapolis, Ind.: Bobbs-Merrill, 1957.

———. "Of the Delicacy of Taste and Passion." In *Essays: Moral, Political, and Literary*. Oxford: Oxford University Press, 1963.

Joachim, Harold H. *Descartes's Rules for the Direction of the Mind*. London: Allen and Unwin, 1957.

Kao, Ming (Gao Ming). "Chu Hsi and the Discipline of Propriety." In *Chu Hsi and Neo-Confucianism*, ed. Wing-tsit Chan. Honolulu: University of Hawaii Press, 1986.

———. *Sanli yanjiu*. Taipei: Liming, 1981.

Kato, Joken. "The Meaning of *Li*." *Philosophical Studies of Japan*, 4, 1963.

Knoblock, John. *Xunzi: A Translation and Study of the Complete Works*, 3 vols. Stanford, Calif.: Stanford University Press, 1988–1994.

Nan, Huaijin, and Xu Qinting. *Zhouyi jinzhu jinyi*. Taipei: Shangwu, 1978.

Lau, D. C., trans. *Confucius: The Analects (Lun yü), Translated with an Introduction*. London: Penguin, 1979.

———, trans. *Mencius*. London: Penguin, 1970.

Legge, James, trans. *Chinese Classics*, Vol. 1. Oxford: Clarendon, 1893.

———. *The Li Ki or Collection of Treatises on the Rules of Propriety or Ceremonial Usages* 1885, 2 vols. In *The Sacred Books of the East*, ed. Max Müller. Delhi: Motilal Banarsidass, 1966.

Li, Disheng. *Xunzi jishi*. Taipei: Xuesheng, 1979.

Machle, Edward J. "Hsün Tzu as a Religious Philosopher." *Philosophy East and West*, 16, 1976, pp. 443–461.

———. "The Mind and the *Shen-ming* in *Xunzi*." *Journal of Chinese Philosophy*, 19, 1992, pp. 361–386.

———. *Nature and Heaven in the Xunzi: A Study of the Tian Lun*. Albany: State University of New York Press, 1993.

Mao, Zishui. *Lunyu jinzhu jinyi*. Taipei: Commercial Press, 1975.

Mou, Zongsan. *Mingjia yu Xunzi*. Taipei: Xuesheng, 1979.

Munro, Donald J. *The Concept of Man in Ancient China*. Stanford, Calif.: Stanford University Press, 1969.

Qian, Mu. *Sishu duben*, 2 vols. Taipei: Liming, 1992.

Radcliffe-Brown, A. R. "Taboo." In *A Reader in Comparative Religion*, ed. W. A. Lassa and E. Z. Vogt. New York: Harper and Row, 1965.

Ross, W. D. *The Right and the Good*. Oxford: Oxford University Press, 1930.

Ryle, Gilbert. "Systematically Misleading Expressions." In *Logic and Language*, First Series, ed. A. G. N. Flew. Oxford: Blackwell, 1951.

Schwartz, Benjamin. *The World of Thought in Ancient China*. Cambridge, Mass.: Harvard University Press, 1985.

Shun, Kwong-loi. *Mencius and Early Chinese Thought*. Stanford, Calif.: Stanford University Press, 1997.

Tang, Junyi. *Zhongguo zhexue yuanlun: Yuandao Qian*, Vol. 1. Taipei: Xuesheng, 1978.

Tu, Wei-ming. *Centrality and Commonality: An Essay on Confucian Religiosity*. Albany: State University of New York Press, 1989.

Turbayne, Colin Murray. *The Myth of Metaphor*. New Haven, Conn.: Yale University Press, 1962.

Turner, Victor. *Dramas, Fields, and Metaphors*. Ithaca, N.Y.: Cornell University Press, 1974.

Urmson, J. O. *The Emotive Theory of Ethics*. London: Hutchinson University Library, 1968.

Waley, Arthur. *The Analects of Confucius*. New York: Random House, 1938.

Walsh, Vivian Charles. *Scarcity and Evil*. Englewood Cliffs, N.J.: Prentice-Hall, 1961.
Wang, Yang-ming. *Instructions of Practical Living and Other Neo-Confucian Writings*, trans. and ed. Wing-tsit Chan. New York: Columbia Unviersity Press, 1963.
Watson, Burton, trans. *Hsün Tzu: Basic Writings*. New York: Columbia University Press, 1963a.
———, trans. *Mo Tzu: Basic Writings*. New York: Columbia University Press, 1963b.
Wheelwright, Philip. *The Burning Fountain: A Study of Language and Symbolism*. New and rev. ed. Bloomington: Indiana University Press, 1968.
Wittgenstein, Ludwig. *Philosophical Investigations*. Oxford and New York: Macmillan, 1968.
Xiong, Gongzhe Xunzi. *Jinzhu jinyi*. Taipei: Shangwu, 1975.
Yang, Huijie. *Tianren guanxi lun*. Taipei: Ta-lin, 1981.
Zhu, Xi. *Sishu jizhu* (An Annotated Edition of the Four Books). Hong Kong: Taiping, 1980.

Li Ao

Jo-shui CHEN

Li Ao (style name Xizhi, c. 774–836) is the Tang thinker, apart from Han Yu, who contributed most to a new version of Confucian philosophy that addressed issues of human nature and spiritual cultivation. Li was born into an old aristocratic family that had orginated in what is now Gansu Province; his recent ancestors settled in the Kaifeng area of modern Henan, which became his real hometown. During his early years, he concentrated on passing the *jinshi* examination, which valued the art of writing and was the most prestigious way of entering officialdom during most of the Tang era. He received the *jinshi* degree in 798, after several failed attempts, and entered the civil service shortly afterward. Li had a rocky early career but rose quite steadily within the bureaucracy later in life. He mainly served on the staff of various regional military governors until 821, when, at age forty-seven, he was first appointed a middle-level official in the ministry of personnel and then the prefect of Langzhou (in modern Hunan). Thereafter, he received a succession of substantial appointments. In 831, he became for the first time a military governor. He was appointed minister of justice in 834, and in the next year obtained the important assignment of military governor of the Jingzhou and Xiangyang regions (in modern southern Henan and northern Hubei). He died in that position a year later. Throughout his adult life, Li was known in the community of literati as a leading essayist, but his historical importance rests primarily on his philosophical works.

Li Ao's contribution as a thinker comes almost entirely from a treatise he wrote just before the age of thirty: *Fuxing shu* (*Writings on Returning to One's True Nature*). This is a monumental work in the history of Chinese philosophy. It is arguably the first post-Han text that gave a systematic treatment of human nature and spiritual cultivation from a Confucian stance. It is clearly the first important work of Confucian philosophy taking into consideration Buddhist and Daoist ideas. (The latter include both religious Daoism and *xuanxue* thought, or "dark learning.")

The *Fuxing shu* is divided into three parts. Part 1 outlines Li's general view on the theme of the work: how to become a sage, the Confucian ideal of personality. Li holds that a sage is a person who has realized his "nature" (*xing*), the character of which can be described as "sincerity" or "honesty" (*cheng*). The nature of human beings is bestowed on them by heaven, and all people share the same nature. The reason why most people fail to become sages is that their "emotions" or "feelings" (*qing*) obscure their true nature. Yet ordinary people do not understand this, and make no effort toward the illumination of their nature. Li wrote:

> Nature is the decree of heaven: the sage is he who obtains it and is not deluded. The emotions are the movements of nature: common folk are those who drown in them and are unable to know their basis. . . . Therefore the sage is he who is the first of men to be awakened.

Part 2 of this treatise considers the method of becoming a sage, and the discussion largely takes the form of an interpretative essay on the *Zhongyong* (*The Doctrine of the Mean*), which was written around the third or the second century B.C.E. and which Zhu Xi (1130–1200) would designate as one of the Four Books. In this part, Li contends that if one quiets down and thus clarifies one's emotions, one's nature will be revealed and will direct one's life. One can then naturally act in a proper manner, that is, in accord with Confucian norms for behavior. The central point this part makes is that men's true nature exists only in a state of tranquillity. While the character of one's nature is "sincerity," "sincerity is fixity, not moving." Yet Li emphasizes that the tranquillity of one's nature is not equivalent to a suspension of emotions, because emotions will inevitably shift to a state of movement. Men, he suggests, should learn to respond to the world directly with their true nature. The nature that is at the same time tranquil and able to have full control of one's life exists beyond the level of emotions. Li also asserts that it is not possible for one to achieve sagehood overnight; constant cultivation is necessary.

Part 3 principally contains Li's personal comments on the goal of achieving sagehood. He says that life is short, and if one does not act on the matter that draws a distinction between men and other living beings—the possible perfection of morality—then what will human life mean?

In relation to Li's thought expressed in the *Fuxing shu*, several issues deserve further discussion. The first concerns the subject of this treatise. The search for sagehood through self-cultivation is a significant notion in classical Confucian thought, but Li also states that, after the Qin dynasty (221–207 B.C.E.), Confucianism ceased to probe the questions of human nature and destiny. People have mistakenly believed that these are the sole concerns of Daoism and Buddhism. What Li says is an exaggeration, but it can apply very well to the situation during the Six Dynasties and the Tang, that is, from the third century to his own age. To be more precise, it was owing to Buddhism that the perfection of human existence through spiritual cultivation became a major issue in medieval Chinese thought. Li's revival of a dormant Confucian subject is in itself an indication that the *Fuxing shu* represents a Confucian response to the centuries-old dominance of Buddhism and Daoism in metaphysical and spiritual philosophy. Li's project anticipates the endeavor of neo-Confucianism in Song times (960–1126).

Medieval Daoism and Buddhism not only gave birth to the theme of Li's treatise but also substantially affected its ideas. The sharp contrast between "nature" and "emotions" is a case in point. This distinction had roots in Confucian thought. For example, it had already appeared in the seminal Han work *Chunqiu fanlu*, attributed to the Confucian thinker Dong Zhongshu (c. 179–104 B.C.E.). However, generally speaking, early Confucians did not consider "nature" and "emotions" to be diametrically opposed. Even for those believing that moral values were rooted in the essence of human beings and that human nature was primarily good, goodness did not just exist in one's nature. It was more important to realize men's moral potential in their actual lives, filled with all kinds of emotions. Simply put, in ancient and Han Confucianism, there was no notion that a return to one's nature, defined as the original state of human existence, represented the perfection of human life. This idea, which is at the core of Li's theory, owed its origins principally to classical and religious Daoism. It also resembles the Huayan and Chan conceptions of Buddha-nature. Yet it seems that the most crucial formative force behind this idea was the fundamental Daoist belief that the ideal state of life lies in its reunion with its "roots" (*gen*), its "basis" (*ben*)—indeed with the "primordial breath" (*yuanqi*).

Another element in Li's treatise also shows a strong Daoist influence. This is Li's central claim that an important feature of men's true nature is *jing*—tranquillity, stillness, or quietude. In its genesis, the notion that the origins of the cosmos and human lives are tranquil came from ancient Daoism. For instance, Chapter 16 of the *Laozi* states: I do my utmost to attain emptiness (*xu*)"; "I hold firmly to stillness (*jing*). . . . Returning to one's roots is known as stillness. This is what is meant by returning to one's destiny." This idea figures prominently as well in medieval *xuanxue* thought. Religious Daoism used the notion of *jing* primarily to designate a method of self-cultivation—the "quieting down" of one's body and mind. Yet in at least one case, the *Discourse on Sitting in Oblivion* (*Zuowang lun*) by the Tang Daoist Sima Chengzhen (647–735), the notion of tranquillity was used to counter the Buddhist idea of "emptiness" (*sunyata*). Tranquillity, Sima explains, is a state of mind in which one comes into contact with the fundamental source of human life (and of the cosmos) to which Daoists sought to return. The Daoist truth thus uncovered was essentially different from the Buddhist perception of the world as nothing but illusory. It should be pointed out that in the Tang, the notion of tranquillity was also a commonplace in discourses related to Buddhism. It was closely related to a basic Buddhist way of religious training: *dhyana*. In sum, an examination of some central ideas in the *Fuxing shu* seems to suggest that the theme of this work was formed very much under Buddhist influence, but the substantial ideas Li used to construct his philosophy of spirituality drew mostly from the Daoist tradition.

The sources of the originality of the *Fuxing shu* as a work of Confucian philosophy are a complex and controversial problem. The difficulty arises in part from the fact that in this treatise Li cites Confucian texts only. Yet it seems quite certain that Li's thought is largely a product of the intellectual environment of his own time. His ideas had more to do with medieval theories of spiritual cultivation, which were overwhelmingly Buddhist and Daoist in thier inclinations, than with the ancient Confucian passages that he quoted. Even medieval commentaries on the Confucian classics, in regard to issues of human nature and moral cultivation, were heavily influenced by *xuanxue* thought, which had strong Daoist tendencies.

One point needs to be made about the relationship between Li and Buddhism. A number of Buddhist sources claim that Li was a disciple of the Chan (Zen) master Yaoshan Weiyan (751–834) and had connections with other Chan monks, implying that the philosophy of the *Fuxing shu* was based on the Chan doctrine. Modern scholars have proved convincingly that the story about Li and Weiyan was forged by Chan Buddhists, apparently to show their superiority to Li, whose thought seemed to pose a challenge to Buddhism. Personal associations aside, Li's intellectual relationship with Chan Buddhism was not particularly strong.

In what sense, then, can one say that Li's philosophy is Confucian in nature? The answer lies chiefly in the purpose of his treatise: to provide a theoretical framework for a Confucian way of self-cultivation. To achieve this aim, Li cannot end with the assertion that men's true nature is tranquil. He emphasizes that "sincerity" is a characteristic of this nature as well. He does not explain why this nature may be considered so, except for invoking the authority of the *Zhongyong*. Li does say, following the *Zhongyong* again, that one's nature in its unmoved, unclouded state will enable one to see things clearly, and that correct knowledge and actions will issue from it. In short, in his attempt to construct a credible theory of human psychology and self-cultivation, Li borrows heavily from religious ideas current in his time. Yet at the crucial points of his treatise, he brings in Confucian ideas, especially those from the *Zhongyong* and the *Daxue* (*The Great Learning*), making his theory fundamentally divergent from Daoism or Buddhism. One may say that Li uses a great deal of Buddhist and Daoist material to build a Confucian house.

Owing to the scarcity of information, it is difficult to know exactly what motivated Li to develop a Confucian philosophy of spiritual cultivation. Li himself states in the *Fuxing shu* that he had become interested in the Confucian "Way" only about four years earlier. He happened to meet Han Yu and was attracted by his ideas about six years before the writing of this treatise, so it is quite possible that his interest was aroused by his association with Han. Li remained in the circle of Han's friends and disciples until Han's death. It is noteworthy that, shortly before the appearance of Li's *Fuxing shu*, a few Confucian-minded literary men showed their interest in the spiritual implications of the Confucian teaching, but no one went as far as Li to conduct a systematic exploration into this topic.

Li's extant writings other than the *Fuxing shu* do not shed much light on his philosophy. They can confirm that the thought expressed in this treatise was his consistent belief. These works also disclose that Li's views on Confucianism were fairly close to those of Han Yu, an unusual case in the early ninth century. Li was in general of the opinion that Buddhism was not compatible with Confucianism and that a Confucian theory of self-cultivation should be based on its family and social values. Yet he seems to be tolerant of Daoism, either philosophical or religious. This indicates that his opposition to the medieval intellectual tradition was much milder than Han's.

Li probably cannot be considered a great philosopher. He wrote too little, and the ideas in his only major philosophic work are too terse. The historical impact of his thought is also limited, mainly because his line of thinking (describing nature as tranquil) was repudiated by such dominant neo-Confucian philosophers as Cheng Yi (1033–1107) and Zhu Xi. Yet he was one of the rare individuals in the history of ideas to really make a breakthrough.

See also Han Yu; Confucianism: Tang; Daoism: Neo-Daoism.

Bibliography

Barrett, T. H. "Buddhism, Daoism, and Confucianism in the Thought of Li Ao." Ph.D. dissertation, Yale University, 1978.

———. *Li Ao: Buddhist, Taoist, or Neo-Confucian*. New York: Oxford University Press, 1992.

Chen, Jo-shui. " 'Fuxing shu-sixiang yuanyuan zaitan: Han Tang xinxing guannian shi zhi yizhang." *Zhongyang Yanjiuyuan Lishi Yuyan Yanjiusuo Jikan*, 69(3), 1998, pp. 423–482.

Emmerich, Reinhard. *Li Ao (c. 772–841): Ein chinesisches Gelehrtenleben*. Wiesbaden, 1987.

Kunugim, Tadashi. *Ri Ko no kenkyu: Shiryohen*. Tokyo: Hakuteisha, 1987.

Fung, Yu-lan. *A History of Chinese Philosophy*, trans. D. Bodde, Vol. 2. Princeton, N.J.: Princeton University Press, 1953, pp. 413–422.

Liu, Guoying. "Li Ao he guwen yundong." In *Tangdai guwen yudong lungao*. Xian: Shanxi renmin chubanshe, 1984.

Luo, Liantian. "Li Ao yanjiu." *Kuoli Bianyiguan Guankan*, 2(3), 1973, pp. 55–89.

Oishi, Harutaka. "Fukuseisho ni tsuite." *Kaitoku*, 38, October 1967, pp. 52–73.

Liang Qichao (Liang Ch'i-ch'ao)

Min-chih Chou

Liang Qichao (Liang Ch'i-ch'ao, 1873–1929), scholar, reformer, and journalist, is also known by other names: Zhuoru, Renfu, and Rengong. His views on China's modernization occupy a place of central importance in modern Chinese history. His essays and scholarly monographs are contained in his collected work, *Yin binshi heji*, published in 1936; a biography, chronologically arranged, *Liang Qichao nianpu changpian*, is exceptionally valuable because of its extensive use of the otherwise unavailable correspondence to and from Liang. Of the major studies of Liang Qichao, those by Chang Hao and Xiao Gongquan (Gongquan) offer particularly useful discussions of Liang's views on various subjects.

Liang was born in Xinhui, Guangdong and received a classical education at an early age. In 1887, he enrolled at the famous Xuehaitang, a private academy founded by Ruan Yuan (1764–1849), where he studied philology and textual criticism of the classics and their commentary. From 1890 to 1894, Liang was first a student and then an associate of Kang Youwei (1858–1927), a scholar and reformer who exerted a strong influence on Liang's early intellectual development. Following China's defeat by Japan in 1895, Liang busied himself in bringing about reform to rejuvenate China; he played a major role in the reform movement of 1898. After the republican revolution of 1911, he briefly held positions under several governments, serving as minister of justice in 1913 and minister of finance in 1917. From 1918 until his death, he devoted himself to cultural and educational affairs, teaching at universities and writing about Chinese history and culture.

Liang is not interested in philosophy for its own sake; he is a pragmatic thinker deeply concerned about China's well-being and survival in an age of imperialism, and as such he centers all his ideas on that issue. This is a characteristic he shares with traditional Confucian thinkers. The central concern of Chinese philosophy is not to acquire abstract knowledge but rather to perfect a set of rules to govern human behavior, social relations, and political affairs. That attitude helps explain why Liang readily embraces the Confucian ideal of *jingshi*, practical statesmanship. *Jingshi*, as the dominant concept among Chinese scholars in the latter part of the Qing dynasty (1644–1911), signifies an involvement in current affairs, a political commitment to public service, and a realization of the need for a reform of political institutions and practices. But Liang is a *jingshi* scholar only in terms of the direction of his thinking. The content of his thought and that of his predecessors is far apart. Not only is Liang much less concerned with moral perfection and the preservation of traditional polity than Confucian thinkers of the past, but the sources of many of his ideas in the spirit of *jingshi* come from the west.

Liang Qichao is one of the most important and influential Chinese thinkers in the past hundred years. He, along with Yan Fu (1854–1921), is among the most articulate critics of Chinese tradition and perspicacious observers of western culture up to their time, expressing his thoughts in a powerful and passionate style. His views helped erode the Chinese value system considerably and anticipate most of the radical antitraditional ideas of the May Fourth era of the 1910s and 1920s.

Qun

One of the central concepts in Liang's philosophy is *qun*, around which many of his ideas regarding society and politics revolve. *Qun* means "group" as a noun and "to group" or "to form groups" as a verb. The word has a cosmological meaning in Liang's thinking. He tells us that it is the one common characteristic which the "myriad things" in the universe share. Because all things are composed of individual parts, their survival depends on their ability to hold these constituent parts together. This principle explains why all things have a tendency to integrate themselves into groups for the continuous development of their lives. The survival rate of a species is in direct proportion to its ability to form groups.

This concept of *qun* has little in common with traditional Chinese notions of group harmony, moral solidarity, association by means of scholarship, or the fostering of gregarious dispositions; nor is it, in spirit or content, similar to Xunzi's ideal of kinship. Rather, Liang's concept is western in origin and shows the influence of social Darwinism. One of his sources is *Evolution and Ethics*, by Thomas Henry Huxley (1825–1895), which he read in the Chinese translation by Yan Fu. The concept of *qun*, in Liang's mind, will be an important instrument to promote group consciousness and cultivate a sense of national community among the Chinese. Nearly all the things he ever discussed, from religion, particularly Buddhism, and fiction to political integration, popular participation, and the nation-state, can be traced back to his conviction of the importance of group survival.

Ethos of a New Citizenry

Liang is the first person to offer a set of ideals for modern citizenship in China. He distinguishes two kinds of virtue—that which promotes public well-being (*gongde*) and that which governs personal conduct (*side*). Only when both are present can one expect a strong and healthy society.

Liang maintains that Chinese tradition is strong in the area of personal virtue, whereas western philosophy yields insight into the desired qualities in the realm of civic virtue. The qualities in the latter category, combined with traditional Chinese virtues, will be able to produce a "new citizenry" (*xinmin*) for China. Liang urges the Chinese to develop a national consciousness; cultivate the habit of taking initiatives and risks in their thinking; foster an assertive, independent, missionary personality; instill in themselves a spirit of cooperation and concern for public well-being; commit themselves to the concept of rights and freedom; embrace the idea of progress; and accept the value of profit-making and utility.

We see a strong imprint of social Darwinism in the personality traits that Liang treasures. In the following, we shall discuss only the qualities mentioned above whose implied meanings are not immediately apparent. By national consciousness, Liang intends a consciousness which elevates the importance of the nation above that of the individual; a constant awareness of foreign threats; and an understanding of China's political evolution from dynasty to nation. Moreover, he wants his compatriots to replace their commitment to the ideal of a universal community (*tianxia*) with a sense of loyalty to the nation-state. The nation thus becomes a "terminal community" in Liang's thinking. This point is important enough to warrant further analysis later. Although he treasures harmony in personal and familial relations, Liang underscores the value of the spirit of struggle when he discusses national development. History is a record of human progress, he says, and "struggle is the source of progress." Such an attitude is precisely the opposite of the Chinese notion that the golden age is in the past. But China's lack of progress, Liang tells us, is more than a result of its conservative disposition. There are other factors: the state of China as a unified empire over the centuries inhibited competition, authoritarian rule drained the people's energy, and a lack of diversity in China's intellectual tradition since the Qin dynasty (221–207 B.C.E.) weakened the Chinese people's spirit.

Liang believes in the intrinsic value of freedom (*ziyou*). After that general observation, however, he quickly moves to the concrete, making it clear that he is interested not in personal freedom but in group freedom. It is with China's collective interests in mind that Liang particularly cherishes freedom. The concept, he believes, will be an effective antidote to the meek and overly complying personality of the Chinese and help them free themselves from control by others. Freedom, he says, is the "antithesis of slavery," and the concept of freedom has been a driving force in human history in the past several centuries. But Liang immediately reminds his "new citizenry" that the sense of freedom has to be tempered with self-restraint and obedience to the law. At issue is China's collective freedom. Because the Chinese government lacks effective means of control, he observes, the Chinese individually always have a great deal of freedom. The freedom the Chinese enjoy, however, is mere license because it lacks discipline. This would not be tolerated in a society of laws.

Only a sense of self-discipline and obedience to the law can make true freedom possible and meaningful. Without them, freedom sooner or later becomes chaos, and strong men, eager for law and order, will emerge and take away all freedom. This position indicates that while Liang is in general attracted to the liberal ideals of Jean-Jacques Rousseau (1712–1778), he rejects the theory of a social contract. To Liang, Rousseau's passionately expressed liberal ideals appeal powerfully to the emotions and can be effective in arousing the Chinese people's desire to fight for national liberation. But Liang loses his enthusiasm when Rousseau becomes more specific. Rousseau insists that the institution of any genuine political community cannot be anything other than the result of an association of intelligent human beings who choose by their free will to form the kind of community to which they will owe allegiance. This, in his view, is the only valid basis for a community that wishes to live in accordance with the demands of human freedom. Liang, however, has profound misgivings about this central tenet of Rousseau's *Social Contract* and his concept of natural rights.

Invoking the authority of the Swiss-German political theorist Johann Kaspar Bluntschli (1808–1881), Liang rejects Rousseau's position that citizens are free to form political communities or to renounce their own countries. Liang does not want to see freedom become an obstacle to China's quest for modernity.

Liang's understanding of rights (*quanli*) is essentially in the context of the social Darwinist concept of might as right (*qiangquan*). Thus, in his mind the concept of rights is synonymous with that of struggle. He laments that China has no strong tradition of the concepts of freedom and rights—indispensable elements in obtaining human dignity and independence. He blames not only Daoism but also the entire Confucian tradition for this. The Chinese, by placing so much emphasis on benevolence and humanity (*ren*), are overly attentive to harmony with others, at the expense of righteousness (*yi*), underscored by the west. We are here to fight not just for our own rights, Liang maintains, but also for those of our group. He concludes that the first order of action for China's new citizenry is to gradually to perfect the legislation which will help improve group cohesiveness internally and resist foreign encroachment.

The overriding concern with the purity of motives and moral perfection in Confucian philosophy produces a mentality that looks down on profit-making and on obvious utilitarianism. This constitutes an idealistic strain in Chinese thinking, which otherwise is pragmatic. Above all, Confucian thinkers value economic stability and frugality. Liang, however, argues that China's new citizenry must seek to increase wealth and social utility in order to create a better future for China. Knowledge of "political economy," a term that Liang uses in English, is the source of wealth and power in the western world, and the *Wealth of Nations* by Adam Smith (1723–1790) was singularly important in the rise of the west. It is clear that Liang's concern is entirely practical. Similarly, he values the utilitarian philosophy of Jeremy Bentham (1748–1832), concurring that the desire for profit is inherent in human nature. Liang points out that Thomas Hobbes (1588–1679) and Xunzi share the view that human nature is innately bad. Significantly, Liang agrees with Hobbes that all human beings have selfish ends.

Nationalism

For all his enthusiasm about Smith, Hobbes, and Bentham, however, Liang has misgivings about their laissez-faire thinking and their emphasis on benefiting the individual. Liang disagrees with Smith that the general welfare is served by allowing each individual to pursue his own interests. Smith's laissez-faire was, after all, meant to correct the shortcomings of mercantilism prevalent at the time. But unlike Europe in the eighteenth century, Liang feels, twentieth-century China needs the protection of a strong government. Smith's prescription for Europe therefore will not be suitable for China. According to Liang, personal interests and the public interest converge in Bentham's utilitarianism because Bentham presumes the greatest happiness for the greatest number as an ultimate moral principle. Liang points out, however, that the two kinds of interest not only do not always converge but often conflict. The public interest, therefore, should take precedence over personal interests because it is society that provides the necessary environment in which the individual will be able to fulfill his desires. But of all the above, Liang singles out one view in Hobbes's philosophy for praise. According to Hobbes, Liang says, human beings eventually turn their selfish desires into constructive forces by organizing themselves into larger communities for the benefit of the group. This is the result of people's reasoning that when everyone seeks to gratify his own desires at the expense of others, his interests will be likewise harmed by others. The purpose, therefore, of forming organizations with rules and regulations is to ensure that the interests of all will be protected.

The new citizenry, Liang thinks, also possesses private virtues to complement his civic ethics. In the area of personal conduct, Liang in general does not take issue with the ideals emphasized by Chinese culture. He believes in such virtues as filial piety, loyalty, rectitude, moral cultivation, disciplined character, and family harmony. Because Liang was born and raised in a society that emphasized these virtues and gave them a central place, when he speaks of these qualities, he does so with a feeling of personal affinity.

But at the same time Liang's departures from traditional Chinese culture are quite pronounced. First, whereas Confucianists are moral absolutists, Liang's attitude is relativistic: personal virtues, he believes, form but a part of the larger moral system he has in mind. Moral values in the realms of both personal and public virtues frequently change as circumstances change; the intention of Liang's larger system is to further the interests of the Chinese as a group. Second, since his ultimate ideal is no longer the fulfillment of a moral life, Liang's interest in the Confucian moral system often only touches on its form. Chang Hao observes that Liang is mainly interested in the "precepts of the techniques of personality cultivation" of neo-Confucian moral philosophy and that the idea of setting goals holds greater appeal for him than the specific life goal found in Confucian philosophy. Significantly, not only do Confucian moral values have a less exalted status in Liang's writings, but the nature of these values has also changed.

One of the most important phenomena in China in the second half of the nineteenth century was the abandonment of culturalism and acceptance of nationalism. Liang Qichao played no small role in the emergence and heightening of the Chinese national consciousness.

The traditional Chinese view of world order is dominated by the utopian vision of a universal moral community in which the world exists as one family. The last of the "three ages" in the Kung yang (Gongyang) tradition is the "age of universal peace" (*taiping shi*). The Confucian concept of "all under heaven" (*tianxia*) and Mozi's "universal love" (*jian'ai*), according to Liang, can be interpreted as espousals of a universal community. This universal vision, on the practical level, has a sinocentric element because in such a scheme, China perceives itself to be the most sophisticated of all, surrounded by less cultured peoples. In Liang's own time, the yearning for a universal community continues. Among his contemporaries, Kang Youwei's "universal harmony" (*datong*) and Tan Sitong's philosophy of "benevolence" (*ren*) are two prominent expressions of this ideal. It is also at this time, however, that China's sense of superiority disappears. In its place is a national consciousness grown out of an awareness of the existence of other competing nations and an acute feeling of insecurity. Liang now sees China the nation as, in Rupert Emerson's words, "a 'terminal community' with the implication that it is for present purposes the effective end of the road for man as a social animal, the end point of working solidarity between men." On the other hand, on the abstract level, Liang does not reject a utopian vision. He remains convinced that the human race should strive for an international community of peace and harmony. However, such a community, he says, will no longer be built on Confucian moral principles, or dominated by one morally benevolent and culturally superior member. It is, above all, in Liang's thinking before the revolution of 1911, a utopia for the distant future. For the time being, he encourages his fellow Chinese to develop a sense of national identity, reminding them that, because of the atmosphere in the world, the time for such an international community will not come for many years.

According to Liang's analysis, China faces some serious problems. The Chinese are either too mindful of their own interests or are only vaguely aware of the rest of the world, a consequence of having been the dominant country in their own region for too long. As a result, they are not conscious enough of China as a nation-state. Within their own boundaries, Liang continues, the Chinese have a sense of loyalty to the imperial house, but not to China as a political entity. Nationalism therefore will be indispensable if China is ever to attain independence and respect. In his reading, he is greatly attracted to Bluntschli's theory of the state. Bluntschli perceives the state as a "moral and spiritual organism." The body of the state, its constitutional organization, is—like a physical body—subject to the law of growth, decay, and death; and its soul, the national spirit, is manifested in the common language, customs, and outlook of the people. Liang is convinced that China must become an organic unit in order to have a clear sense of order for the future. With China's survival and well-being in mind, he embraces Bluntschli's view that the "proper and direct end" of the state is "the development of the national capacities, the perfecting of the national life, and, finally, its completion." Indeed, it is reassuring to Liang that he finds in the writings of Bluntschli, Gustav Bornhak, Jean Bodin, Hobbes, and others theories which help him justify his contention that the collective interests of the Chinese nation-state should be the ultimate concern of the Chinese.

At this juncture, it is important to note some of the characteristics of Liang's understanding of nationalism. It is, Liang says, the most upright and morally the purest belief in the world. It is based on the premise that no country should suffer the humiliation of being violated and that no country has the right to violate others. Nationalism fervently acknowledges that each people has aspirations for its country. Indeed, we find no element of self-aggrandizement in Liang's nationalistic thinking; it is, rather, primarily a defensive response to the threat of what he calls the "national imperialism" of powerful countries. The Darwinian law of survival of the fittest is ruthless, and the only way to counter the relentless expansion of western powers, Liang insists, is to develop Chinese nationalism. In his opinion, only nationalism can serve as a rallying force to unite his fellow Chinese and involve them in nation building. He does not entertain the idea that nationalism will be a means to enable China to restore its past glory or expand its influence. Because of his overriding concern about the danger of imperialism, Liang does not have in mind the ethnically different Manchu rulers when he speaks of Chinese nationalism. Indeed, we find little evidence that he ever shares the strong anti-Manchu sentiment of the revolutionists. In fact, he draws the conclusion, based on his reading of western political theories, that a state does not have to be composed of a single nation, and he takes pains to point out that the future Chinese state must be multinational to reflect the multiethnic characteristic of the Chinese people.

While he is very much occupied by the theme of nationalism, Liang's interest in the utopian ideal is rekindled after the republican revolution in 1911. The founding of the republic makes nationalism less of an issue. In fact, promoting nationalism may no longer be a prudent move now that the republic, which contains a number of ethnic groups within its boundaries, has to deal with the lively issue of ethnic equality and representation in government. Following World War I, Liang's belief in the desirability of an international community is once again confirmed. In 1918, traveling in Europe and observing postwar conditions there, he becomes convinced that contentious and divisive nationalism is responsible for the destruction and suffering in Europe. Disillusioned with nationalism, he returns to Chinese culture and rediscovers the vision of utopia. Over the centuries, he says, the Chinese have been more aware of the ideal of universal harmony than the notion of nationalism, regarding all human beings as equals and being indifferent to racial and ethnic differences. This attitude explains, he observes, why China has assimilated many ethnic groups throughout its history, sometimes without regard to its own interests. Liang urges the Chinese to make a contribution to world culture by working toward the realization of a common world community whose focus will no longer be the narrow interests of individual nations. Liang's change of position suggests that he no longer feels that a cultivation of nationalism need be China's first priority. Deeply struck by the destruction and pessimistic mood in Europe, Liang with a fresh eye and renewed confidence now looks at the possibility of a world community built on aspirations and interests shared by all. This change of mood is coupled with a change of circumstances. While he is still concerned about China's interests, he feels less threatened by developments in the international scene now that Europe is preoccupied with its own affairs.

Joseph Levenson (1967) suggests that Liang finds some psychological satisfaction in seeing Europe's hardship and in identifying a potentially unique contribution China may be able to make. If Liang indeed dwells "lovingly on European confusion and pessimism" and takes delight in the possible "bankruptcy" of European civilization, then he is expressing his nationalistic sentiment under the guise of internationalism. In that case, his defense of Chinese culture and his criticism of the west are really defense mechanisms prompted by his psychological need to conceal his feeling of insecurity.

Levenson's interpretation points out a less tangible aspect of the "mind of modern China." The tension between an "emotional commitment" to China's past and an "intellectual commitment" to the west is a real burden to some Chinese. The observation, however, describes less reflective Chinese better than it describes Liang. Levenson derives his conclusions from a liberal reading of Liang's writings and an imaginative interpretation of Liang's psychology. Liang certainly is not immune from the psychological tension that Levenson skillfully analyzes, but we would suggest that he feels more secure than Levenson supposes and that his position is far from being completely dictated by his subconscious psychological urges.

We can be fairly certain that Liang feels threatened, particularly in the early years of his reform activity, by the pervasiveness of western ideas in the Chinese consciousness. While he himself is alienated from some of the Chinese cultural values and is responsible for introducing many western ideas into China, Liang sometimes goes out of his way to stress the validity of Chinese culture in China's quest for modernity and to find an affinity between Chinese and western cultural elements. While he is seeking self-assurance, however, Liang may also be motivated by a desire to soften the conservative opposition to the introduction of western ideas by pointing out their similarity to Chinese ideas. More important, Liang is among the first to detect the profound cultural crisis China faces and to seek ways to avert it. As early as 1896, he expresses his concern that the Chinese are losing their balance under the relentless onslaught of the west. He asks those who hold the west in awe not to be obsequious; and he takes pains to point out to those who defend Chinese culture emotionally that no artificial lines of demarcation should be drawn between Chinese and western ideas. Liang has a fine understanding of the importance of a nation's sense of identity. He calls that identity "national character" (*guoxing*). All human faces are alike, says he, yet no two are carbon copies of one another; similarly, while all peoples and nations share certain traits, no nation will have a sense of self-worth if it does not have something distinctive and unique of its own. For all his criticism of Chinese culture, Liang does not entirely reject it. In fact, he favors most of the ideas and ideals governing personal morality over those in western culture; he and his generation still live comfortably and even deeply within the old culture. Therefore, while we detect in him some psychological tension, we see Liang's position on Chinese culture as a genuine attempt to address an identity crisis in China. If some of Liang's ideas regarding Chinese culture have a "nationalistic" element, it is neither elitist nor adversarial: in order to create a sense of identity and a feeling of strong self-worth, this nationalism underscores China's "differentness."

Monarchism, Democracy, Freedom

This discussion should have given us some insight into Liang Qichao's thinking on various political systems. Hsiao Kung-chuan observes that Liang is a moderate civil libertarian. Beyond this general conclusion, however, we should note that Liang holds different positions on different issues at different times, always influenced by political realities in China. Thus his conviction regarding civil liberties, while sincere and fundamental, is always counterpoised and sometimes overshadowed by his concern with the larger issue—China's survival and future as a nation.

Liang no longer has confidence in traditional Chinese monarchism. Benevolent rule, he points out, is only an ideal. The reality is very different. When one person holds all the political power, he often abuses it, like many Chinese emperors throughout Chinese history. Liang laments that Chinese sages sing the praises of benevolent rule too often while paying little attention to devising ways to curb the absolute power of despots. Further, monarchy is bad because it invariably suppresses freedom. The authority of a government has to have limits so that the governed will have their freedom. Liang stresses that the relationship between government and the governed is a matter of balance, observing that, in the words of John Stuart Mill (1806–1873), if a person "merely acts according to his own inclination and judgment in things which concern himself . . . he should be allowed . . . to carry his opinions into practice at his own cost," and that only when "any part of a person's conduct affects prejudicially the interests of others, society has jurisdiction over it." At one point, Liang even goes so far as to give democracy and freedom an unconditional endorsement, praising them as eternal human institutions.

When Liang speaks of individual freedom as a result of national independence, he apparently does not believe that a person will experience inner liberation simply because his country is free. Ultimate freedom of the individual, he says, comes only when one is completely at peace with himself through self-mastery. Self-mastery helps us eliminate the forms of bondage that enslave us—the authority of ancient sages, the weight of conventions and fashions, the constraints imposed by our environment, and the burdens created by our desires and passions. The four types of bondage resemble the "idols" described by Francis Bacon (1561–1626). The approach, however, is reminiscent of the Confucian and Daoist position. In fact, Liang's appeal to one's self-mastery may be considered a modern version of the Confucian and Daoist teaching that one may rely on one's inner resources to overcome undesirable thoughts and achieve self-perfection. This approach places no demand on society and needs no institutional apparatus as a prerequisite. Instead, Liang and the Confucian and Daoist thinkers put the entire burden on the individual, asking the individual to have such self-discipline and cultivate such strong individuality as to become immune to the influence of the outside world. This is an introverted individualism that has little to do with liberalism. Liberalism is in essence a political concept; its central spirit is the protection of the liberties of the individual under all circumstances.

This unqualified endorsement of democracy and freedom, however, does not reflect Liang's constant position. It is more accurate to say that Liang is far more committed to democracy than to freedom. The reason is to be sought in the collectivist bent in his thinking. Democracy is an ultimate goal for him, but only in the abstract sense; when he speaks of democracy in the concrete sense, he perceives it chiefly as a means. Democracy presupposes popular sovereignty and political participation, which in his opinion are effective instruments to foster a sense of community and national unity. Echoing Yan Fu's thinking, Liang believes that opportunity to participate means bringing out individuals' collective wisdom and energy, which in turn contribute to nation building. The freedom he has in mind, then, has little to do with the individual. Generally speaking, there are two kinds of freedom involving individuals. In the negative sense, a person has "freedom from" when he is free of being coerced or constrained by another. John Stuart Mill's "On Liberty" is one of the better-known expositions of this kind of freedom. Freedom in its positive sense means that a person can choose for himself and act on his own initiative. While he is interested in both, what really concerns Liang is something more concrete and urgent—the relation between freedom and power in the broadest sense. Within a society, the more powerful are often able to determine within a fairly narrow range the alternatives between which their fellow citizens can choose, thus effectively limiting the freedom the latter may enjoy. A corollary of this phenomenon frightens Liang deeply. In the international community in his time, powerful nations deprived the weak nations of their freedom and dignity with impunity. Of all the aspects of the question of freedom, this is clearly the most relevant to him. The many species of freedom in the abstract as a class—freedom of thought and speech, freedom of assembly, freedom of movement, freedom of worship, freedom in the choice of one's occupation, and so on—do not occupy a central place in his mind. As Liang sees it, citizens will have no freedom when their country is under the yoke of another. There is no mistake about the priority here. Political participation, he thinks, will be a countermeasure to help China regain its freedom and independence by arousing the national consciousness of the Chinese people and mobilizing them. Since national freedom is a prerequisite for individual freedom, too much individual freedom or individual freedom too soon in the course of China's nation building effort will be likely to impede the realization of that ultimate goal. He reminds his compatriots that the people who enjoy the most freedom are also those who willingly obey the most laws and rules imposed by society. Those laws and rules are there to ensure that one person's freedom does not infringe on another's. Freedom and discipline, therefore, always go hand in hand. Otherwise, society will have no order and cannot survive. Liang's emphasis, on the other hand, is philosophical in nature. In his world of thinking, overcoming the self is all-important.

With the ultimate goal of national freedom and independence in mind, Liang is flexible regarding the political systems of the future China, entertaining the possibilities of democracy, enlightened despotism, and constitutional monarchy. But all these are subsumed under the interests of the Chinese nation-state. Rousseau believes that sovereignty of a state is founded on the general will of the people; Jean Bodin (1530–1596), who, like Rousseau, was a French philosopher, maintains that sovereignty rests with the ruler. Liang disagrees with both, concurring with Bluntschli instead that sovereignty resides in the organic body of the state. Therefore, the survival and well-being of a state should be the paramount consideration. Any means which serves that end is justified. Following the republican revolution in 1911, Liang writes a long article discussing the future polity of China. He takes pains to try to convince his readers that the American style of federalism will not be suitable, because of China's political tradition and contemporary condition, and that a constitutional monarchy should be preferred for China. But, he continues, the Manchu monarchy is so corrupt and inept that it cannot assume the important function of a constitutional monarchy in the new China. Liang concludes his essay by asking his fellow Chinese to ponder the great question of the specific form of government on which the future welfare of China rests. Hsiao Kung-chuan observes that while ostensibly arguing for a constitutional monarchy, Liang has in fact tacitly acknowledged the legitimacy of the republican government. In his discussion in 1912 of the importance of the national character for the life and development of a nation, Liang declares that monarchy is not a cornerstone of the Chinese national character. Beyond the issue of polity is a strong central government, which Liang yearns for more than anything else. As a realistic man, Liang is convinced that to challenge the newly established republic will only create more chaos. He wants by all means to give it a chance to succeed. If a strong government emerges in China, then it will have fulfilled all his dreams.

See also Kang Youwei; Tan Sitong.

Bibliography

Chang, Hao. *Liang Ch'i-ch'ao and Intellectual Transition in China, 1890–1907*. Cambridge, Mass.: Harvard University Press, 1971.

Ding, Wenjiang, and Zhao Fengtian, comps. *Liang Qichao nianpu changbian*. Shanghai: Renmin, 1983.

Goldman, Merle, and Leo Ou-fan Lee, eds. *An Intellectual History of Modern China*. Cambridge: Cambridge University Press, 2002.

Huang, Kewu. Yige beifang qui de xuanze: Liang Quichao tiaoshi sixiang zhi yangiu (Rejected Path: a study of Liang Qichao's eclectic thought). Taipei: Institute of Modern History, Academia Sinica, 1994.

Huang, Philip C. *Liang Ch'i-ch'ao and Modern Chinese Nationalism*. Seattle: University of Washington Press, 1972.

Levenson, Joseph R. *Liang Ch'i-ch'iao and the Mind of Modern China*. Berkeley: University of California Press, 1967.

Liang, Ch'i-ch'ao. *Intellectual Trends in the Ch'ing Period* (*Ch'ing-tai hsueh-shu kai-lun*), trans. with introduction and notes Immanuel C. Y. Hsu. Cambridge, Mass.: Harvard University Press, 1959.

———. "My Autobiographical Account at Thirty," trans. with notes Li Yu-ning. In *Two Self-Portraits: Liang Ch'i-ch'ao and Hu Shih*, ed. Li Yu-ning. New York: Outer Sky, 1992, pp. 1–31.

———. *Yinbinshi hechi*, 12 vols. Beijing: Chunghua, 1994.

Nathan, Andrew J. "Liang Qichao and the Chinese Democratic Tradition." In *Chinese Democracy*. Berkeley: University of California Press, 1985, pp. 45–66.

Pusey, James Reeve. *China and Charles Darwin*. Cambridge, Mass.: Harvard University Press, 1983.

Xiao, Gongzhuan (Hsiao Kung-chuan). *Zhongguo zhengzhi sixiang shi*, 2 vols. Taipei: Linking, 1982.

Yi, Xinding. *Liang Qichao he Zhongguo xneshu shixiang she* (Liang Qichao and the intellectual history of China). Zhongzhou, Honan: Zhongzhou guji.

Zhang, Pengyuan. *Liang Qichao yu Qingji geming*. Taipei: Institute of Modern History, Academia Sinica, 1964.

———. *Lixian bai yu xinhai geming*. Taipei: Institute of Modern History, Academia Sinica, 1983.

———. *Liang Qichao yu Minguo zhon zhi*. Taipei: Hansheng, 1992.

Liang Shuming (Liang Shu-ming)

Guy Alitto

Liang Shuming (Liang Shu-ming, Huanding; 1893–1988) was one of the founders of "new Confucianism" (Xin Rujia). He was perhaps unique among twentieth-century Chinese philosophers because he was a man of action whose philosophical thought was the basis for his own social and political programs. He was a leading figure in the nationwide rural reconstruction movement and its only philosopher. Early in the war with Japan, Liang founded the liberal democratic "third force" in Chinese politics. He is generally regarded as someone who exemplified the ideals of Confucianism in his life as well as in his writings, and who maintained his own integrity in the face of all odds. In the early 1950s, alone among the intellectuals in China, he defied Mao Zedong publicly.

Liang's philosophical thought was a modern development of the Wang Yangming (1472–1529) school of philosophy. Like the early master, Liang was not a cloistered academic but a man of action who emphasized the unity of knowledge and action (*zhixin heyi*). Liang's fundamental philosophical thought is a unifying strand that runs through a great variety of cultural, political, educational, religious, and psychological theories. His ideas are close to some of Wang's followers of the Taizhou school, especially Wang Gen (1483–1541) and He Xinyin (1517–1579). Liang's rural and educational movements were a "modernized" version of those mass-based reform enterprises of Wang and He.

Although Liang was born and raised in Beijing in the family of a minor metropolitan official, he was not classically educated. Instead, his iconoclast father, Liang Ji, sent him to various local schools that emphasized western learning. He graduated from Xuntian Middle School in 1911 (in the same class as future philosophical thinkers Zhang Songnian and Tang Yongtong) and, as a member of the Revolutionary Alliance (Tongmenghui) underground, participated in revolutionary terrorist activities in the Beijing area. In 1912 Liang was paralyzed by a spiritual crisis that led him to two suicide attempts and a period of solitary study of Weishi Buddhism ("consciousness only"—Vijnaptimatra or Yogacara) and deep reflection on the meaning of human life. The fundamentals of his later philosophical thought emerged during this period of intense contemplation.

Liang's first publication of his philosophical ideas appeared in *Eastern Miscellany* (*Dongfang zazhi*) in 1916. In this piece, "On Ontological Inquiry and the Perplexities of Life" (*Jiuyuan jueyi lun*), Liang argued that the metaphysics of Weishi Buddhism, Henri Bergson, and Arthur Schopenhauer shared the ontological assumption of a "live" universe—a great cosmic élan vital—in continuous flux and evolution. He also systematically compared aspects of contemporary western philosophical thought (such as Bergson's) with eastern thought (such as Buddhism). The fundamental cosmology that was adumbrated in this article, and which he would from time to time elaborate on throughout his life, was an eclectic blend of neo-Confucian idealism and Yogacara Buddhism with elements of European vitalism. "Ultimate reality" (*benti*), the "life force," and the Confucian supreme virtue (*ren*) were identical. Their basic nature, eternal and continuous, is in a process of continual transformation, yet maintains its inner identity.

This venture into comparative philosophies so impressed the newly installed chancellor of Beijing University, Cai Yuanpei, that he immediately appointed Liang as a professor of Indian philosophy. So Liang, who had never attended a university himself or formally studied philosophy, was now a faculty member at China's most important university. It was as a specialist in Buddhist thought and as part of the early twentieth-century Chinese Buddhist intellectual revival that Liang first became known to the public.

In 1918, Liang's father committed suicide, proclaiming that he died for the ideals of Chinese culture. This event perhaps ensured what was to follow in the next year, when Liang publicly "abandoned Buddhism for Confucianism" and began his most famous book, *Eastern and Western Cultures and Their Philosophies* (*Dong Xi wenhua ji qi zhexue*, 1921). The work catapulted him into national prominence. This book contains the fundamentals of his lifelong philosophical thought. It also marks the formal commencement of an ongoing public debate on Chinese culture that has continued until the present.

The philosophical starting point of Liang's book is a concept of a live monist universe in eternal flux, which he identified as common to the thought of Schopenhauer, Nietzsche, Bergson, and Weishi Buddhism.

The life process is a continuous sequence of problems presented to individual expressions of a Schopenhauerian "will." It has no inherent meaning, and at the outset human beings are just another expression of the will, no different from animals or plants. Culture is the means by which humanity resolves the contradictions between the will's demands and the obstacles presented by environment. Liang posited three ideal cultural types, which are expressions of three distinct directions the will may take and should succeed each other in a historical continuum. These phases are portrayed by western, Chinese, and Indian cultures.

In the first phase, represented by the west, basic problems of physical survival are not yet solved. The "will" goes forward to conquer the environment and satisfy primal desires. In the second phase, represented by China, the will moves sideways to adjust and harmonize itself with the environment, thus gaining inner contentment and joie de vivre. In the third phase, represented by India, the will turns backward onto itself, seeking self-negation. By way of illustration, the archetypal westerner would resolve the contradiction between the will's demand for shelter and the obstacle of a dilapidated house by demolishing the house and building a new one; the Chinese would repair the old house; and the Indian would attempt to extinguish the desire for housing.

As the nature-mastering equipment of western culture had solved its primal needs, humanity would now turn from an epoch of material want to one of spiritual unrest, which only Chinese culture could solve. The heart of Chinese culture was Confucianism, and the heart of Confucianism was the virtue *ren* (perfect humanness). Strongly influenced by Henri Bergson, Liang virtually equated intuition and instinct with *ren*.

Liang's book began a twentieth-century reconstruction of the Confucian tradition. It provided a Confucian philosophy relevant to a democratic age of nation-states and nationalism and also provided a blueprint for action.

By the late 1920s Liang had settled on rural reconstruction as the vehicle by which he would revive Chinese culture for the Chinese nation and for humanity as a whole. He was the philosophical theorist of the movement as well as the administrator of Zouping, an experimental self-governing county in Shantung Province.

With the Japanese invasion in 1937, the rural reconstruction movement and the Zouping experiment came to an end, and Liang shifted his attention to politics. In a trip behind Japanese lines, he discovered that Nationalist and communist guerrilla troops were fighting each other as much as they were fighting the Japanese. Fearing outright civil war, Liang organized the small liberal democratic parties into one political union in order to preserve national unity by serving as a mediating third force in Chinese politics. This party, renamed the Democratic League in 1945, attempted to avoid a civil war after the Japanese had surrendered. After a year of frustrating work at mediation between the communists and Nationalists as general secretary of the Democratic League, Liang retired from politics at the end of 1946 and, settling in western China, planned to devote the rest of his life to education and writing.

Between 1930 and 1949, Liang formulated an expanded philosophy of culture that was more complex, intricate, and detailed than what he had written in *Eastern and Western Cultures* but was in essence an amplification of the same message, with a shift in approach from philosophy to sociology and history. Like the first theory, it is based on a grand cosmological evolutionary plan. The material universe was evolving upward into more complex and higher forms. Inherent in them is a tendency toward "reason" (*lixing*), which runs through and directs this ongoing advance. With *Homo sapiens*, intellect (*lizhi*) appeared, and although this faculty distinguishes people from animals, there is still a gulf between the animal with intellect and the true human, who achieves *lixing* and so can reach a "sphere of disinterestedness" transcending biological instinct or self-interest. The essence of humanity and the ultimate product of the evolution of the the cosmic vital force is precisely *lixing*. This term became the functional equivalent of *ren* and intuition, in this second version of Liang's theory. The word is certainly not translatable by the usual English equivalent "reason," except as Samuel Coleridge distinguished it from "rationality." To Liang, it was the heart of Confucianism and Chinese culture and so "what makes humankind human." This second version of the theory was summed up in the book *The Essence of Chinese Culture* (*Zhongguo wenhua yaoyi*, 1949).

In January 1950, Mao Zedong (with whom Liang had a long personal friendship) brought Liang back to Peking to participate in the newly established government of the People's Republic of China. Liang refused to take a major office but agreed to serve on a standing committee of the People's Political Consultative Conference, the representative body of the central government. In that capacity, Liang criticized the Communist Party's general line at a meeting in 1953. Mao lost his temper and violently execrated Liang several times over the course of the meetings. Criticism campaigns against Liang were subsequently launched in the national press and Liang could no longer publish. In 1966, at the outset of the Cultural Revolution, Red

Guards attacked him and his wife, burned his personal library, and drove him from his house. From 1966 to 1979, he and his wife lived in extremely difficult circumstances, but he continued to write.

In 1979, with the more relaxed political atmosphere of the Deng Xiaoping's reforms, Liang's living conditions improved greatly. He published his last book, *The Human Heart-Mind and Human Life* (*Renxin yu rensheng*) in 1984, and so developed the fundamental theory adumbrated in 1916 into a third and final version. In this book, Liang exhibits the same eclectic tendencies that characterize all his work. To his vitalist-Buddhist-Confucian mixture he adds Marxist terminology, and he even borrows terms from Mao. "Culture" as a category recedes from prominence, but the elements of vitalism remain conspicuous. *Xin* (mind-heart) replaces "reason" (*lixing*) as it had replaced *ren* and intuition in the second formulation. The unfolding of the cosmic élan vital Liang now described as the mind-heart's pursuit of freedom and autonomy and the expression of conscious dynamism. All that has life partakes of *xin*. Yet the essentials of this third theory are the same as his earlier work.

When asked in 1980 if in retrospect he thought that his philosophical theories and ideas were in error, Liang reflected for several moments and replied that his understanding of instinct (which he had almost equated with intuition and *ren*) had been wrong. He would not allow that anything else had been proved mistaken.

Liang died in 1988 at age ninety-six. By that time, he had become the focus of much scholarly attention, both within China and abroad. A definitive edition of his large output was issued in eight thick volumes on his centennial in 1993. By then he had become an important historical figure, the focus of academic conferences and the subject of a dozen biographies.

See also *Li*: Principle, Pattern, Reason; Reason and Principle; *Zhixing Heyi*.

Bibliography

Alitto, Guy. *The Last Confucian: Liang Shuming and the Chinese Dilemma of Modernity*, 2nd ed. Berkeley: University of California Press, 1986.

Guo, Qiyong, and Pang Jianping. *Liang Shuming zhexue sixiang* (Liang Shuming's Philosophical Thought). Wuhan: Hubei, 1996.

Jing, Haifeng. *Liang Shuming pingzhuan* (Critical Biography of Liang Shuming). Nanchang: Baihua zhou, 1995.

Li, Yuanting. *Liang Shuming xiansheng nianpu* (Chronological Biography of Liang Shuming). Guilin: Guangxi Shifan, 1991.

Liang, Shuming. *Liang Shuming quanji* (Collected Works of Liang Shuming), ed. Academic Committee of the Institute of Chinese Culture (Zhongguo wenhua shuyuan xueshu weiyuanhui), 8 vols. Jinan, Shandong: Shandong, 1989–1993.

Ma, Yong. *Liang Shuming wenhua lilun yanjiu* (Liang Shuming's Theories of Culture). Shanghai: Renmin, 1991.

Shan, Feng. *Liang Shuming shehui gaizao gouxiang yanjiu*. (A Study of Liang Shuming's Concepts of Social Reform). Jinan: Shandong daxue, 1996.

Wang, Donglin. *Liang Shuming yu Mao Zedong* (Liang Shuming and Mao Zedong). Changchun: Jilin, 1989.

Wang, Zongyu. *Liang Shuming* (Biography of Liang Shuming). Taipei: Dongda, 1992.

Zheng, Dahua. *Liang Shuming yu Hu Shi* (Liang Shuming and Hu Shi). Beijing: Zhonghua. 1994.

———. *Liang Shuming yu xiandai xin ruxue* (Liang Shuming and Modern New Confucianism). Taipei: Wenjing, 1993.

Liezi (Lieh Tzu)

T. H. Barrett

Liezi (Lieh Tzu), the name of an ancient Daoist sage already mentioned in *Zhuangzi*, is also used as the title of a work in eight chapters that has traditionally been ascribed to the sage and classified next to the *Daodejing* as the second Daoist masterwork of early China. But this Liezi, even if he existed, is otherwise known only as he appears in sources too brief or too self-serving to allow a reconstruction of his thought. Since the Tang dynasty, moreover, doubts have been expressed as to the authenticity of the text under Liezi's name, and these doubts have increased in more recent times as modern techniques of textual scholarship, such as linguistic analysis, have been brought to bear on the question of authorship. The results for the study of the philosophy contained in the current *Liezi* have been unfortunate, in that researchers have tended either to debate the narrow question of authenticity or to confine themselves to broad generalizations about the "worldview" of the work. As a consequence of this comparative neglect, this survey aims not so much to give a full treatment of all the philosophical issues raised by the *Liezi* as to suggest how the two approaches adopted be brought together in a manner at present exemplified only in the unpublished work of June Won Seo.

Thus, while this is not the place to enter into a detailed discussion of the text of the *Liezi*, any reader should bear in mind that the first we hear of the body of writing currently passing under the name of Liezi is in the late fourth century C.E., when a scholar named Zhang Zhan introduced the text, together with a commentary of his own composition, to the Chinese world of learning. Modern research has established to the satisfaction of most experts that the *Liezi* was probably composed—albeit in part so as to incorporate genuinely ancient texts, including some now no longer available elsewhere—by either Zhang's father Zhang Kuang or his grandfather Zhang Yi. Zhang's own commentary, while evidently extremely well informed about the text, shows one or two lapses of understanding that rule him out as an author.

But there had at one time been another work under Liezi's name, which is said to have circulated during the early Han and which was described by the imperial bibliographer Liu Xiang (79–8 B.C.E.) in 14 B.C.E.. Liu's report on this *Liezi* still circulated until Tang times as part of his now lost general account of the imperial library (it is currently found only as appended to the *Liezi* text), and so Zhang senior would have been obliged in his own work to follow the description of this long-vanished first *Liezi* given by Liu. This source appears to offer information on four of the eight chapters Liu saw, though Seo advances reasons for doubting its reliability.

Liu describes the chapters "King Mu" and "Questions of Tang" as extravagantly fanciful and not the words of a gentleman (*junzi*)—a turn of phrase implying that the materials he saw included overtly mythological elements of the sort which Confucians, like Liu himself, preferred to exclude from the literary tradition.

The chapters "Effort and Destiny" (*Liming*) and "Yang Zhu" are described by Liu as flatly contradictory, the former emphasizing one's allotted fate, the latter esteeming untrammeled behavior. In addition, the chapter "Confucius" as listed in Liu's overall bibliography seems to have carried the alternative title "The Extreme Limit of Knowledge" (*Zhizhi*), giving a good indication here also as to what its contents might have covered. Liu's comparisons of this "Book of Liezi" with the work of Zhuangzi also imply (though they do not state) that miscellaneous material might be found attached to a more homogeneous core, as in Zhuangzi's case, and this may have suggested the somewhat disparate nature of the final chapter of the eight. Liu in fact uses the phrase *waishu*, "outer books" (a term applied to Zhuangzi's more miscellaneous material), with reference to *Liezi*, but apparently meaning portions of the text in private hands.

It follows that the first two chapters, named in the full version of Liu's bibliography but not described in his account, perhaps gave the author of our *Liezi* his greatest freedom in addressing his own concerns, though he still had to take care to include ancient material in order to give verisimilitude to his work (by suggesting that these ancient sources were in fact quoting a genuine and even earlier work by Liezi himself, and to present his ideas primarily through the medium of "parables (*yuyan*), since Liu explicitly links the use of such stories by Liezi to the similar practice of Zhuangzi. Chapter 1, "Heaven's Gifts" (*Tianrui*), uses as its title a Han term referring to omens. But whatever it may have meant in the text allegedly seen by Liu Xiang, in the text that we have, it introduces through the medium of a number of self-contained stories a discussion of human mortality, which is seen as an inevitable outcome to which we should be reconciled with complete equanimity. Individual existing things are but eddies in the endless flux of the world we live in, nor can we hope to arrive at a just appreciation of death from the limited and temporary standpoint of life. The chapter "The Yellow Emperor" discusses in like style the ability of the undisturbed mind to survive the most threatening external events because of its unwavering nature, even in cases where the reasons for such mental tranquillity are actually misplaced.

The following three chapters—"King Mu of Zhou," "Confucius," and "The Questions of Tang"—all deal in different ways with the relativity of knowledge. The first of them concentrates on the problematic nature of the division between dream and reality; the second contrasts the limited ways of knowing mastered by Confucius with the unreflective complete awareness of the Daoist sage; the third questions the limitations of common sense in coping with the vastness of time and space, or even the infinite variety of human experience.

The chapter "Effort and Destiny" promotes a thoroughgoing fatalism as the key to abandoning the tension involved in choice for the freedom of simply following the Way. "Yang Zhu" casts the ancient rival of Mencius as the spokesman of a hedonism completely unconcerned with social convention. So flatly opposed are these two chapters that A. C. Graham (1960, 1990), chief proponent of the case for seeing a member of the Zhang family as author, found it difficult to accept them as the work of the same man and was forced to suggest that the hedonist chapter drew on writing from an earlier phase in the thinking of Zhang senior, though here as elsewhere genuine early accounts of Yang Zhu are interspersed with Zhang's material.

Finally, "Explaining Matching" (*Shuofu*—again a title which in Han times would have related to omens), for all its diversity, in fact seems unified by a concern over the "matching" of actions and circumstances.

All the questions addressed in the *Liezi* are, in keeping with themes first mentioned in authentic ancient texts like the writings of Zhuangzi, with the possible exception of the chapter "Yang Zhu," which patently understands "untrammeled" behavior very much in the fashion of the famous libertines of the late third century C.E.. Yet throughout the rest of the work also, though less overtly, the general approach, and indeed the reading of the ancient texts assembled under Liezi's name, both arguably reflect what is very much a fourth-century point of view.

By then the Han dynasty, which had made rule by an educated imperial bureaucracy a reality, had been brought low by religiously inspired uprisings. The reverberations of this unprecedented and highly disturbing disaster for China's educated elite may be traced throughout succeeding centuries not simply in the opprobrium they heaped on the rebels themselves, but in their broader insecurity also. For the more we learn of the type of religion involved, the more we see it as possessed of a certitude, specifically about existence after death, which gave its adherents a dangerous fanaticism. From the third century onward, the trend in interpretation by the elite of those early texts closest to this religious milieu—*Laozi, Zhuangzi*, and the *Yi jing* (or *Yijing*)—is firmly away from anything that might promote religious enthusiasm: Laozi himself, a messianic figure to some rebels, is reduced to purely human stature, for example. The *Liezi* (which almost completely ignores Laozi) fits extremely comfortably into this trend, especially in its opening chapters. The first chapter, despite its antecedents in Zhuangzi, could be read as a sustained critique of the religious mentality, the second as an explanation of the apparent power of even misguided religious commitment.

The middle chapters, by contrast, while likewise drawing on Zhuangzi's perceptions on the relativity of knowledge, seem informed by a sense of the rich variety within the wider inhabited world (and indeed the larger cosmos), and so of the cultural relativity of knowledge. This would seem to point to an awareness of the world beyond China present only to a lesser degree in genuinely ancient texts. Such an awareness was fostered in particular in the fourth century C.E. by the incipient popularity of Buddhism, which to judge from its impact on the early scriptures of the Daoist religion dramatically enlarged Chinese conceptions of the dimensions both of the real world and of the cosmos beyond human observation. Zhang Zhan himself comments in his preface on the occasional Buddhist overtones of our *Liezi*, and one story about an automaton in the "Questions of Tang," which has a clear Buddhist source, reveals that the real author of the work now under Liezi's name must have been to some degree familiar with Buddhist lore. Even so, many of the wonders drawn on by our author to construct his picture of a world in which, for example, cannibalism is remarked on as socially acceptable in some societies may spring, if not from his imagination, then from earlier Chinese mythology, but mythology divorced from its religious context and redeployed to satisfy an educated taste for marvels, such as is catered for in the work of late third-century figures like Zhang Hua (232–300).

Hence, although A. C. Graham asserts that the *Liezi* is "by far the most easily intelligible of the classics of Taoism" (Daoism), one fears that as a guide to earlier literature it may prove something of a false friend. Its compiler must have possessed an enviable library of authentic ancient materials (Zhang Zhan tells us his family were keen bibliophiles), and after his fashion he appears to have remained true to the tradition into which he sought to insinuate his work. But his view of the tradition is colored by his own situation, especially by his need to reread the traditional texts so as to exclude attitudes that made him uneasy. Thus the problematic closeness of some of the genuinely early literature to the world of mythology and religion is replaced here by a much more detached stance, and certainly the *Liezi* never attracted successive religious interpretations in the same way that the *Zhuangzi* sometimes and the *Daodejing* always did from religious groups.

On this understanding the worldview of the *Liezi* remains worthy of comment precisely because it would appear to date from a period when the horizons of the educated elite were expanding rapidly, yet at the same time there were elements within Chinese culture from which some of them now preferred to avert their gaze.

See also Laozi; Zhuangzi.

Bibliography

Barrett, T. H. "Lieh tzu." In *Early Chinese Texts: A Bibliographical Guide*, ed. Michael Loewe. Berkeley: Society for the Study of Early China and Institute of East Asian Studies, University of California, 1993, pp. 298–308.

Graham, A. C. *The Book of Lieh-tzu*. London: John Murray, 1960.

———. "The Date and Composition of *Lieh-tzu*." In *Studles in Chlnese Philosophy and Philosophical Literature*. Albany: State University of New York Press, 1990, pp. 216–282.

Seo, June Won. "The Liezi: The Vision of the World Interpreted by a Forged Text." Doctoral dissertation, School of Oriental and African Studies, University of London, 2000.

Yang, Bojun. *Liezi jishi*. Beijing: Zhonghua shuju, 1979.

Zurcher, E. "Buddhist Influence on Early Taoism." *T'oung Pao*, 66(1–3), 1980, pp. 84–147.

Lin Yutang

Dian Li

Lin Yutang (1895–1976) is one of the few literary giants coming out of early modern China, when an air of soul-searching and cultural reconstruction encouraged the making of generalists rather than specialists. Versatile and adventuresome, Lin Yutang has left a huge body of works that cut across many disciplines of the humanities. Without doubt, Lin Yutang is at his best when he compares the cultures of China and the west—a comparison that never lost its currency in the twentieth century and has continued to challenge interested scholars all over the world. Lin Yutang's authority on this topic comes not only from his well-informed arguments but also from his total immersion in both cultures. Even so, Lin Yutang may not be called a "philosopher" in the conventional sense of the word. For one thing, he has not produced many philosophical writings that can withstand the microscope of the discipline—even his best-known works, *My Country and My People* and *The Importance of Living*, will fall far short. Also, he is not that original a thinker, a fact he himself cheerfully acknowledged on many occasions. Where Lin Yutang triumphs is in his style and language, which enabled him to find a new mass western audience for ancient Chinese philosophy. Simply put, he has done more than any other person of his day to popularize Chinese philosophy and to turn it into an applicable guide to the chaotic life of modern times. To understand how Lin Yutang accomplished this, one must consider his life and writing in their entirety and read them as expressions of Chinese wisdom.

No other man of letters in modern China can match Lin Yutang's aptitude at adapting western culture, and he is a very successful example of writing in one's second language. In his long career as an essayist, translator, editor, scholar, novelist, and lexicographer in China and the United States, Lin Yutang left a literary legacy that balances two modes of thought, the eastern and the western. Writing in his native language, Lin Yutang first established his name in China as one of the most influential advocates of western ideas in the ongoing transformation of Chinese culture, particularly in popularizing humorist prose as a worthy literary genre. Later, in his voluntary exile of more than thirty years in the United States, Lin Yutang produced an incredible amount of nonfiction and fiction in English with the purpose of bringing Chinese wisdom to western readers. The best of Lin Yutang's works not only changed westerners' perception of China for the better but also in many ways became a permanent part of the American mind.

Lin Yutang's initial contact with the west came from his own family, which was Christian, and particularly from his father, a progressive Chinese Presbyterian minister, who borrowed money to send the young Lin Yutang to St. John's College in Shanghai so that he could have the best possible education in English and other western subjects available in China at the time. But Lin Yutang lost interest in theological studies even before he graduated from St. John's College. In 1919, after being a professor of English at Tsinghua University for a few years, Lin Yutang journeyed to Harvard University to study comparative literature, and then to Paris to take up the job of teaching Chinese laborers who had been sent to France during World War I. He finally earned his doctorate in 1923 from the University of Leipzig, with a thesis on old Chinese phonetics.

Lin Yutang returned to China in the same year. He then held various teaching and editorial posts in universities and publishing houses, where his liberalism often ran afoul of the establishment. Meanwhile, he became known as the author of a best-selling English grammar book and the editor of several successful literary magazines. Lin Yutang's concerns about modern China, which was riddled with political corruption and social instability, matched those of most reform-minded intellectuals. Lin Yutang wrote many poignant essays honestly and frankly criticizing China's ills, and he even had a brief stint as a secretary for the short-lived Wuhan revolutionary government. But Lin Yutang was no revolutionary. His humanism led him to oppose a cultural radicalism that increasingly became the tune of the times. By 1935, Lin Yutang's continuous advocation of humor and character building had alienated him from the dominant left-leaning writers led by Lu Xun; and his literary magazines, owing to internal disputes, ran into financial troubles. When the American writer Pearl Buck invited him to write a book about China for western readers, Lin Yutang jumped at the opportunity.

My Country and My People, published in 1935, was a runaway best-seller and made him known as an interpreter of the spirit and mind of China to the west. In the same year, Lin Yutang moved his family to the United States at the urging of Pearl Buck. Two years later, Lin Yutang published his most widely read book, *The Importance of Living*. These and a series of "wisdom books" that followed made Lin Yutang almost a household name in the English-speaking world. The books filled a vacuum left by the unapproachable works of traditional sinologists and by missionaries' overwhelmingly negative depictions of Chinese society, which had formed the western perception of China since the nineteenth century. From the Confucian concept of humanity blended with the Laozian passivity, Lin Yutang extracts a philosophy of self-content that is supposed to govern the Chinese way of living. Often critical of certain aspects of the Chinese national character, Lin Yutang nevertheless holds a set of values, such as detachment and high-mindedness, which can guarantee intense joy in living, as essentially distinct from the western philosophy of life. Writing in a lively and witty style aided by a mastery of idiomatic English, Lin Yutang reveals a sense of humor that is both endearing and persuasive to his western readers.

Lin Yutang also tried his hand at fiction. All his novels were written in English; but when they were translated into Chinese—in many cases without his permission—he acquired a greater name as a novelist with the Chinese readers than English-speaking readers. Although Lin Yutang was less successful as a writer of fiction, his fictional works provided a medium for him to reconcile the conflict between an "idealized China" ("the China of blue porcelain bowls and exquisite silk scrolls") and a "real China"—the China of chaos and misery in the twentieth century. The best of his novels, such as those in the *Lin Yutang Trilogy*, demonstrate the triumph of Daoist wisdom over adversity and turmoil in war-torn China.

Over the years, as a result of his diligent writing and to some degree his conscious self-promotion, Lin Yutang came to be known in the west as the very personification of the Chinese wisdom he wrote about. In 1948, he became head of the arts and letters division of UNESCO, but he resigned in less than a year because of his disdain for bureaucracy. In 1954, on the occasion of his appointment as chancellor of the New Nanyang University in Singapore, an editorial in the *New York Times* described him as a "witty and wise writer, speaker, and philosopher," and proudly claimed him as "one of our very own."

But in 1966 Lin Yutang suddenly ended his sojourner's life and settled down in Taiwan. He began to write in Chinese again, after having written in English for thirty years, and his Chinese readers received him warmly. Lin Yutang's fame reached international proportions with the translation of his works into many languages, including Chinese. In the 1960s, Lin Yutang made several world tours in which he continued to expound on the wisdom of the east. In 1975, he was elected vice president of PEN International and was nominated for the Nobel Prize in literature.

Lin Yutang's last significant work is his widely acclaimed *Chinese-English Dictionary of Modern Usage*. He spent the final decade of his life completing this project, a goal that had originated in his early training as a linguist. The dictionary was an entirely appropriate conclusion to the remarkable career of this bilingual writer. Lin Yutang died in Hong Kong in 1976.

In his lifework of promoting a "lyrical philosophy," Lin Yutang does not claim to be objective or exact. In fact, he takes great pride in giving his western readers a highly personal and individual outlook on the arts of living. The authority of his outlook, however, rests on the fact that he was a Chinese living in a self-imposed exile in the United States, and on the assumption that he possesses all the wisdom afforded by the splendid and long-standing Chinese civilization. To cultivate this image, Lin Yutang is compelled to produce a narrative of the Chinese philosophy of life, however subjective and sketchy it might be. In a grand stroke, he calls this narrative "Chinese humanism," by which he means a mixture of Confucianism, Daoism, and Buddhism. Chinese humanism, in a nutshell, implies both a conception of the ends of human life and the means to attain these ends. Confucianism provides an ideological basis, Daoism a variety of possibilities, and Buddhism a spiritual compromise between the two. But Lin Yutang's narrative quickly shifts its focus from Confucianism to Daoism, because Daoist values such as simplicity, contentment, and ease fit better in his construction of a Chinese sage living in modern times. Buddhism also soon disappears from the scheme, because it is too logical and metaphysical, too interested in the afterlife. In his typically lively, witty fashion, Lin Yutang tells us that every Chinese is a good Confucian when he is successful but a Daoist when he is in trouble or frustrated and beset by difficulties and failures. As men fail more often than they succeed, and even those who apparently succeed have secret doubts of their own in the middle of the night, the Daoist influence is at work more often than the Confucian.

It is, therefore, no surprise that Lin Yutang's mapping of the Chinese character and mind has strong echoes of Daoism. Terms such as "mellowness," "pacifism," "femininity," and "patience" are new translations of age-old Daoist concepts. In passages where nuanced analysis and interested criticism are required, Lin Yutang provides episodic examples and humorous gossip, often taken from marginal Chinese texts.

There is no doubt that Lin Yutang's oversimplification of the Chinese character and mind made him vulnerable to all sorts of faultfinding. Critics may be right to point out a strong strain of "orientalism" in Lin Yutang's image of China, but one should keep in mind that simplicity is a value he holds dear, a value that governs all other values and stands at the center of his "lyrical philosophy," as he has elucidated repeatedly:

> Now it must be taken for granted that simplicity of life and thought is the highest and sanest ideal for civilization and culture, that when a civilization loses simplicity and the sophisticated do not return to unsophistication, civilization becomes increasingly full of troubles and degenerates.

Although this "degenerated" civilization would include modern China, the main thrust of the passage is clearly directed at the west, a culture in which Lin Yutang is both a spectator and a participant. The west, according to Lin Yutang, is overburdened with the pursuit of logic, progress, and materialism—all illnesses of the age of mechanical reproduction. Therefore, a Chinese philosophy for living that is devoid of these illnesses is presented as an alternative, and as an ideal that the ancient Chinese sage has in fact lived many times over. It matters very little to Lin Yutang's western readers who embraced his vision enthusiastically that this vision is riddled with contradictions, was built on a shifting philosophical ground, and came under increasing scrutiny in his native land. Questions of legitimacy and authenticity may have been of little interest to Lin Yutang, who was working in a different historical context; still, in glossing over these problems, he shows both the advantage and the perils of cross-culturalism.

See also Buddhism in China: A Historical Survey; Confucianism: Twentieth Century; Daoism: Classical.

Bibliography

Fu, Yi-jin. "Lin Yutang: A Bundle of Contrasts." *Fu Jen Studies: Literature and Linguistics*, 21, 1988.

Lin, Yutang. *Bashi zixu* (Memories of an Octogenarian). Beijing: Paowentang shudian, 1990.

———. *The Importance of Living*. New York: Reynal and Hitchcock, 1938.

———. *My Country and My People*. New York: Reynal and Hitchcock, 1935.

———. *On the Wisdom of America*. New York: John Day, 1950.

———, ed. *The Wisdom of China and India*. New York: Random House, 1942.

———, trans. *The Wisdom of Confucius*. New York: Modern Library, 1938.

———, trans. *The Wisdom of Laotze*. New York: Modern Library, 1948.

Shi, Jian-wei. *Lin Yutang yanjiu lunji* (A Study of Lin Yutang). Shanghai: Tongji daxue chubanshe, 1977.

Sohigian, Diran John. *The Life and Times of Lin Yutang*. 1992.

Wan, Ping-jin. *Lin Yutang lun* (On Lin Yutang). Xi'an: Shannxi renmin chubanshe, 1987.

Ling Ting-kan (Ling T'ing-k'an)

Kai-wing CHOW

Ling Ting-kan (Ling T'ing-k'an, 1757–1809) was the most eloquent exponent of the ritualist ethics of the "Han learning" classicists in the high Qing. However, his ethical philosophy has not received the attention it deserves, owing to the strong aversion to theorizing prevalent among these classicists. Hu Shi called Ling's ethical teachings a "philosophy of ritual" (*li*) but regarded them as more exceptional than representative of high Qing Confucianism.

In Ling's time—the second half of the eighteenth century—students of the classics accorded the highest honor to the Han exegetes and dismissed Song scholarship as inferior in credibility. But Ling did not believe that the term *Hanxue* (Han learning) was an accurate characterization of eighteenth-century classical studies. He had misgivings about the increasingly fragmented textualism that had obscured the purist goal of seeking the original Confucian teachings.

Confucian purism had been a dominant force in shaping intellectual change since the early Qing. Scholars like Chen Que (1604–1677), Gu Yanwu (1613–1682), and Yan Yuan (1635–1704) had made strong, even strident, attempts to purge heterodox elements from the Confucian canon. Ling's ethical view cannot be thoroughly understood without reference to his purist hermeneutics. Ling condemned all versions of *Daoxue* Confucianism since the Song as Chan Buddhism. What distinguishes Ling from preceding purists is the rigor with which he applied purist hermeneutics to his philological studies. He felt that the attempts to purify Confucian teachings by scholars like Gu Yanwu, Mao Qiling (1623–1716), and Dai Zhen (1724–1777) left something to be desired.

For Ling, even Dai Zhen could not completely wean himself from Buddhist influence. Ling found vestiges of Buddhist ideas in Dai's major critique of *Daoxue* Confucianism, *Verification of the Literal Meanings of Mencius* (*Mengzi ziyi shuzheng*). Dai began his treatise with an exposition of the meaning of the term *li*, "principle." He even discussed "elementary learning" (*xiaoxue*) in terms of "substance-function" (*tiyong*), a concept widely applied in the works of Song *Daoxue* Confucians. According to Ling's study, *tiyong* was essentially a Buddhist concept of dualism. In the *Analects*, the word *yong* (function) was used by itself, not in conjunction with the character *ti* (substance). The two characters were used as a term in *Daoxue* Confucian writings and applied liberally in Song *Daoxue* exegesis of the Confucian classics. What the *Daoxue* Confucians had been expounding, Ling argued, was nothing but Chan Buddhism.

In Ling's view, it was a deviation from Confucianism to speak of human nature independently of ritual propriety. In 1802, he put forth a more coherent monistic conception of human nature in his famous treatise *On Returning to Ritual Propriety* (*Fuli lun*). This treatise represented a purist effort to formulate a cogent reinterpretation of Confucian ethics. Contrary to the *Daoxue* Confucian notion, Ling maintained that human nature was anything but principle, *li*. In fact, he had deep disdain for the term *li*: The *Daoxue* Confucians had appropriated it for their discussion of human nature, substituting a Buddhist notion for Confucian teachings. To Ling, principles were abstract and elusive and could hardly be verified. They were of no avail in moral cultivation, because people would mistake their own personal opinions for principles that were presumed to be absolute truths. Ling understood human nature essentially in terms of physical endowment. The human being was constituted of "material force" (*qi*) and "five elements" (*wuxing*). These comprised the bodily senses and faculties and were in perfect balance (*zhihzhong*) before feelings, emotions, and desires arose. In Dai Zhen's favorite term, they were *xueqi*, "blood forces" or "physiological force." Human desires were neither to be denigrated as essentially evil nor conceived as the opposite of true nature. They were necessary for the nourishment of the body and needed only to be controlled rather than extirpated. When the external world was presented to the senses, likes and dislikes emerged. As feelings developed out of physiological reactions, they were unreasoned and tended either to run to excess or emanate insufficiently; as a result, the balance of nature was disturbed. To "restore" (*fu*) the balance, ritual propriety was required—this would keep the expression of feelings and desires at an appropriate level. Since "nature" was not "principle" embedded in the mind, it could not be "discovered" by introspection. In theory, the balance before the emergence of feelings and desires was irrelevant, because feelings and desires arise continuously in response to internal impulses as well as external stimuli. What mattered was the balance achieved during their expression. When feelings and desires were expressed and satisfied in accord with ritual propriety, nature was restored to its harmonious state.

For Ling, the Confucian method of self-cultivation was not a personal undertaking that could be done in isolation. It was a far cry from the Buddhist or Daoist method that aimed to achieve spiritual liberation or physical immortality. Nor were the introspective exercises practiced by *Daoxue* scholars Confucian in origin. On the contrary, moral qualities must be acquired in the context of human relationships. In this context, rituals reinforced Confucian social ethics such as filial piety, loyalty, and the notion of social hierarchy and governed the conduct of people of all stations. What Ling is arguing is that there is no morality if no other persons are involved in one's action. Morality cannot be simply contemplated as an abstraction. This means that meditation or otherworldly introspection will not be ethical, even though it may involve action.

The authoritarianism of Ling's ethics is unmistakable. His strong disdain of abstract principles and his belief in a closed ethical system encoded in ancient rituals tend to undermine people's autonomy in making decisions in social interactions. His authoritarian bent is revealed clearly when he explains why people should be taught to abide by proper rules of behavior rather than seek to understand "principles." If people were not taught how to conduct themselves by developing habits of proper behavior, they would have to use their own judgment in social interaction, and this impromptu decision making would always result in improper conduct. Ling's argument parallels that of Dai Zhen in its stress on developing proper habits by observing clearly defined patterns of behavior.

Ling went a step further than Dai Zhen in more systematically applying the hermeneutical rules of linguistic purism against *Daoxue* Confucian works. While Dai Zhen still spoke of ritual propriety in terms of *li* in the sense of "pattern" or "order" (*tiaoli*), Ling simply jettisoned the term *li* and designated optimal rules as ritual propriety. According to his study, the *Analects* that preserved Confucius's sayings never used the word *li* (principle) but made numerous references to the character for "ritual propriety."

In spite of his commitment to philological methods, Ling's interpretation of classical ideas was sometimes based more on ideology than philology. Dai Zhen's critique showed that the term *li* (principle) was used in other classics, but Ling's abhorrence of the term and his preoccupation with ritual propriety led him to disregard this evidence.

Ling sought to reevaluate the purity of the teachings of preceding Confucians in terms of ritualist ethics. For him, Xunzi surpassed Mencius in knowledge of ancient ritual rules. Xunzi's teachings had long been discredited because of his theory of "evil nature" (*xing'e*)—*Daoxue* Confucians shared with their predecessors a strong disapproval of that view. Ling's perspective on Xunzi, however, undercut the *Daoxue* Confucian exaltation of Mencius, and his reinterpretation of Xunzi was clearly an attempt to appraise anew the overall doctrine of Confucianism.

In light of his ritualist ethics, the Four Books took on different meanings as Ling reexamined some critical passages and concepts. The *Doctrine of the Mean* and the *Great Learning* had been important sources of *Daoxue* Confucian ethics and metaphysics. But for Ling, they were no more than expository writings on ritual propriety. Since the rise of Song *Daoxue* Confucianism, the doctrine of *shendu*, "vigilance in solitude," had been understood as a method of spiritual cultivation in association with the Buddhist and Daoist practice of "quiet sitting." Ling argued that *Daoxue* Confucians who practiced quiet sitting and introspection had read Buddhist and Daoist ideas into the text. He agreed that the term *shendu* involved introspection but contended that it referred to ritual propriety as used in the *Doctrine of Mean* and the *Great Learning*: in solitude one should be vigilant about whether one's conduct was properly cultivated according to ritual propriety. Ling's view of "vigil in solitude" was reminiscent of Liu Zongzhou's teaching in his *Manual for Humankind* (*Renpu*).

The term *gewu*, "investigation of things," had elicited much debate between the followers of the Cheng-Zhu tradition and the Wang Yangming tradition. To Ling, however, the explanations of both schools were mere speculation. He argued that *wu* (things) could not be anything other than ritual propriety, reasoning that if the term did mean things in general, not even a lifetime could permit the investigation of them. Therefore, *wu* must mean ritual propriety, and *gewu* is *geli*, "investigation of ritual propriety." Moreover, not just the investigation of things but also "sincerity in intention" (*chengyi*), "rectification of the mind" (*zhengxin*), and "self-cultivation" (*xiushen*) all required ritual propriety. Hence to speak of the way (*dao*) as separated from ritual propriety was both elusive and unreliable.

As all *kaozheng* scholars would argue, Ling regarded the classics as the repository of absolute ritual propriety. It is not surprising that he considered the *Yili* (whose title can be translated as *Book of Etiquette and Decorum*) paramount among the classics. He spent thirty years trying to exhaust the rules he believed to be the absolute moral truth encoded in the ritual and institutions of high antiquity. In 1792, he finished the first draft of a systematic analysis of the *Yili*. It was an attempt to enumerate the general rules of ceremonies underlying all the rituals recorded in that classic. This work remains one of the great achievements in ritual studies.

See also Dai Zhen; *Daxue; Li*: Principle, Pattern, Reason; *Li*: Rites or Propriety; Mencius; Xunzi.

Bibilography

Chow, Kai-wing. *The Rise of Confucian Ritualism in Late Imperial China: Ethics, Classics, and Lineage Discourse*. Stanford, Calif.: Stanford University Press, 1994.

Elman, Benjamin A. *From Philosophy to Philology: Intellectual and Social Aspects of Change in Late Imperial China*. Cambridge, Mass.: Harvard University Press, 1984.

Hu, Shih. *Dai Dongyuan de zhexue* (The Philosophy of Dai Zhen). Taipei: Shangwu yinshuguan, 1971.

Ling, Tingkan. *Jiaoli tang wenji* (Collected Writings from the Studio for Studying Rituals). In *Ling Zhongzi yishu, Anhui congshu*, Series 4. Anhui, 1935.

Qian, Mu. *Zhongguo jin sanbai nian xueshu shi* (History of Chinese Scholarship during the Past Three Centuries). Taipei: Shangwu yinshuguan, 1957.

Yu, Ying-shih. "Some Preliminary Observations on the Rise of Ch'ing Intellectualism." *Qinghua Xuebao*, 11(1–2), 1975, pp. 105–129.

Zhang, Shou'an. *Yi li dai li: Ling Tingkan yu Qing zhongye ruxue sixiang zhi zhuanbian* (Substituting Principle for Ritual: Ling Tingkan and Change in Confucianism in the High Qing). Taipei: Institute of Modern History, Academia Sinica, 1994.

Liu Zongzhou (Liu Tsung-chou)

Lynn Struve

Liu Zongzhou (Liu Tsung-chou, Liu Xianzhang, Liu Jishan; 1578–1645) began life in the midst of family hardship, grew to maturity during a time of social and political turmoil, and in death epitomized a national tragedy. Faced with unremitting spiritual and ethical challenges, he developed and lived by the most demanding philosophy of moral will to emerge in neo-Confucian learning.

Because Liu's father died before Liu was born, leaving the paternal line in penury, Liu was reared, very strictly, by his widowed mother and maternal grandfather. They both were assiduous about Liu's schooling and his progress in the civil service examinations. He achieved the coveted status of *jinshi* in 1601, at only twenty-four years of age.

Liu's grandfather imparted to him a lifelong interest in the interpretation of the *Yijing* (*Classic of Changes*). Apart from this, Liu's earliest education was in a conservative Cheng-Zhu neo-Confucian mold. Throughout his middle years, Liu was daringly active in the political reform movement identified with the Donglin Academy in the Yangtze delta region, whose founders, Gao Panlong and Gu Xiancheng, were Zhu Xi restorationists. Nevertheless, Liu formed his own philosophy mainly in the academic environment of the eastern Zhejiang (Zhedong) region south of Hangzhou Bay. This was the native soil of Wang Shouren (Wang Yangming), whose family was from the Yaojiang area west of Ningbo but resided principally in Liu's home prefecture, Shaoxing. It was one of the two regions of China where Yangming learning retained its most dedicated following. Thus Liu's thought naturally became imbued—through stages of relative acceptance and doubt—with concepts and ideas of the "Yaojiang school."

Some scholars stress Liu's independence as a thinker and characterize him as having been an outside critic of (Chan) Buddhism, the Cheng-Zhu "learning of principle" (*lixue*), and the Yangming "learning of mind" (*xinxue*) as well. But the predominant view is that Liu stood within the bounds of Yangming learning, broadly conceived, and dedicated himself to correcting key errors in the formulation and transmission of that learning. Whether Liu's contribution is seen as having supplied something that was missing in Wang's philosophy of *liangzhi* ("good knowing," "conscientious consciousness"), as having perfected something that had been imperfectly articulated by Wang, or as having merely made explicit something that already was implicit in Wang's teaching—in other words, regardless of the degree to which he is seen as having headed a new school or as having reformed the Yaojiang school—Liu's efforts brought to a culmination the intense investigation of the "moral mind" that was a hallmark of intellectual endeavors in the Ming period.

In Liu's philosophical anthropology, human nature (*renxing*) is the objective state of being human, which is determined by the cosmological "good force" of heaven (*tian*). This state and its source constitute the fundamental reality (substance) of our nature (*xingti*). Since human nature is of heaven, it naturally also functions (*yong*) as heaven does in its Way (or way, *dao*)—with constancy, fecundity, and regularity (as in, for instance, the constancy, fecundity, and regularity of the four seasons). However, distinct from the many other natures (such as those of plants or animals) that are determined by heaven and function in accord with its Way, the functioning of the specifically human nature has a subjective aspect: *xin* (heart-mind), which is capable of self-reflection, instantiated in each living person. Uniquely human *xin* is greater than mere sentience not only in its self-consciousness but also in that it exhibits awareness—through cognition and feeling—of both what is and what ought to be, what is rightly so. Moreover, this uniquely human faculty of knowing the good or right is also a will (*yi*) or disposition to do or promote it. These special qualities are the fundamental reality (substance) of the heart-mind (*xinti*). They ensure that human consciousness is not arbitrary, wholly prompted by externals, or value-neutral; rather, it exhibits a reliable, regular pattern (*li*, principle), is self-controlling (*zhu*), and ceaselessly inclines to the good (*shan*).

Precisely because human nature can manifest itself through and function as *xin* to reflect on and respond with moral-ethical appropriateness to all things, including inward phenomena such as private thoughts and emotions, so the good force of heaven, in which human nature partakes, can be realized in the world. It is the *xin* function, often characterized as a radiation (*zhao*) that subjectively glows of itself and objectively illuminates other phenomena, which enables humans not only to know their own nature but also to positively impel the good force of heaven in the sphere of actuality. Therefore, unlike passive beings that lack self-consciousness, we can fulfill our collective role as necessary assistants to heaven and earth in bringing to fruition their life-sustaining, creatively transformational activities. In sum, one can say that in Liu's view, human nature and its heart-mind function are cosmologically dictated, ontologically inseparable, and ethically essential.

An important aspect—some would say the centerpiece—of Liu's philosophy, pertaining to the goal and practice of self-cultivation, is his explanation of the respective meanings and the relation between *chengyi* (authentic will) and *shendu* (ultimate solitariness), two terms that occur most saliently in the *Daxue* (*Greater Learning*) and the *Zhongyong* (*Doctrine of the Mean*). In Liu's conception, *chengyi* refers to the objective truth that human nature is at base a "good-willing" state; complementarily, *shendu* refers to the absolute subjectivity of that willing in the operation of heart-mind—subjectivity in the sense of dynamic self-sustenance and nondependence on the contingencies of ordinary experience. By concentrating on the true, heaven-derived existence and transcendent condition of primary will, we can heighten awareness of the unfailing operation of heart-mind and disencumber its inherently powerful, luminously "good-knowing," "good-feeling," "good-willing" capacities. In practice this is to be done principally by "quiet sitting" in an attitude of self-respect, to maximize the self-illumination of the heart-mind. Disencumbering requires the identification and removal of the residual effects (*yuqi*) of habitual thoughts and acts, to which Liu attributes the chronic clogging up of properly "free-flowing" *xin*.

Clearly this set of ideas is at odds with Buddhism in emphasizing the centrality of ethical valuation to our nature and heart-mind. It is at odds, also, with the Cheng-Zhu school of neo-Confucianism in not according primacy to principle (much less recognizing any a priori "fixed principles"). Rather, the regularity and rationality of principle are seen as inherent qualities of the unity *xin-xing* (mind-nature), along with the intuitiveness of feeling, which Cheng-Zhu learning tended to distrust as a continual source of alienation between the nature and the mind, seen as dual. The most original elements in Liu Zongzhou's philosophy, however, were not directly intended to confound either Buddhism or the school of principle. Standing well within the tradition of the Ming neo-Confucian "school of mind," Liu sought to reform certain teachings which had exposed that tradition to criticism, especially from adherents of Cheng-Zhu thought, for being too Chan-Buddhistic and thereby losing ethical and epistemological control and causing—or at least greatly exacerbating—the perceived deterioration of social and political standards of conduct and authority in the late Ming.

The chief perpetrators of the erroneous teachings were considered, by Liu and others, to have been leaders of the Jiangyou and Taizhou schools of Yangming learning, epitomized by Wang Ji and Wang Gen, respectively. Wang Ji regarded *liangzhi* (intuitive goodness) as a transparently "pure-knowing," serenely reflective, voidlike entity, beyond and forming no attachment with the good and bad of ordinary experience. Indeed, Liu considered Wang Ji to have been the real author of the well-known—at that time increasingly infamous—"Four-Sentence Teaching of Wang Yangming," which begins with the statement, "Heart-mind (*xin*) is neither good nor bad." This Liu looked on as overemphasizing the transcendent reality (*ti*, substance) of heart-mind and neglecting its crucial role (*yong*, function) in realizing the good force of heaven in the world. Taizhou thinkers, on the other hand, characteristically identified *liangzhi* with the natural, spontaneous practice of morality in everyday life—hence their dictum, "Every man a sage." Judgments of good and bad, appropriate and inappropriate thus became subject to the ebb and flow of quotidian circumstances among ordinary, perhaps naive, self-deluding, or self-serving people. This Liu regarded as seeing only the heart-mind's activity in the world (*yong*) and ignoring *what it is* that is active (*ti*): the self-controlling, good-impelling, principled will of heaven-in-humankind. Liu's strong emphasis on the unity of human nature as an objective state (*ti*) and heart-mind as its subjective functioning (*yong*) was an attempt to redress the blind sides of one or the other in these two schools.

That such errors could arise among Wang Yangming's latter-day followers Liu attributed to a fateful oversight or ambiguity in Wang's conception of *liangzhi*. Wang had taught that *liangzhi* is simultaneously active and quiescent and that, while never losing quiescence, it acts by responding to ambient movements of the empirical mind, such as likes and dislikes (*hao, yu*) and ordinary people willing (*nian*) to do good or bad things. The right and wrong in those movements are recognized and corrected to maintain and reduce departures from an overall good course. It is unclear whether *liangzhi* stands independently and impassively as a good-knowing, reflectorlike judge of empirical ideas and ordinary volitions, or whether it is the homeostatic, self-correctional capacity within those movements themselves. The former view led to the overly detached moral relativity of Jiangyou, the latter to the overly engaged moral relativity of Taizhou. Also, Wang had stressed the "good-knowing" feeling of *liangzhi*, not its absolute "good-willing," which left the will liable to identification solely with volitional will. Hence, there was slippage into the Jiangyou denial that will is a quality of vacuous heart-mind, on one hand, and into the Taizhou faith in common willfulness, on the other.

Liu Zongzhou cogently addressed these problems by insisting that:

1. Absolute good-willing (*yi*), rather than good-knowing, is the most important faculty of heart-mind.
2. This primary will must be clearly distinguished from ordinary volition.
3. Good-willing heart-mind, though transcendent, is *not* "beyond" good and bad; rather, it is unceasingly engaged in promoting the former and dispelling the latter.
4. The force of moral will, radiating outward from the subjective heart-mind into the world of affairs, is the link between our infinite and finite selves and therefore must be made central to the theory and practice of self-cultivation.

Besides being dissatisfied with the state of Yangming learning, Liu also was troubled by the growing popularity in his day of moral self-improvement manuals (*gongguo ge*). These were guides by which people kept careful records of their differential values and disvalues, and good and bad deeds, often under the watchful eyes of spirits and for purposes of worldly advancement—for instance, to pass the civil service examinations, gain an official appointment, or bear male heirs. One example of that genre was the *Liming pian* (*Determining Your Own Fate*), formulated jointly in the previous generation by a Chan master, Yungu, and a scholar-official from northern Zhejiang, Yuan Huang. Liu criticized this work directly because it had been the chief vector in Confucian intellectual circles of what Liu saw as a vulgar, heterodox practice. Liu and other leading Confucians regarded as anathema the pursuit of morality for selfish gain, the arithmetical dissection of goodness according to a point system, and the idea, clearly rejected by Mencius, that righteousness was something external which could be "put on" like an article of clothing. Liu also joined others in worrying that practitioners of *gongguo* calculation would become prideful over their merits, take the matter of watchfulness over themselves too mechanically, or be led out into the "twigs" of moral life caricatured in the lists of good and bad deeds, away from the "root" of their true moral being within. Liu went beyond others, however, to compose a homeopathic antidote, the *Renpu (Manual for Humankind)*. This work does not set out any good deeds for spiritually misleading, psychologically seductive pursuit, nor does it attempt to quantify morality. Rather, it prescribes a regimen for exercising primary will in the continual task of recognizing and correcting transgressions of the volition. Those transgressions are laid out in a six-level scheme (derived from the stages of moral effort in the *Great Learning*), with universally condemned social sins at one end and the most subtle movements of private thought and emotion at the other.

It would be difficult to overstate the stringency of the ethical demands that Liu placed on himself and others—especially others in positions of authority. Like any serious Confucian, he held in high regard the principle of service in government, but his periods in office tended to be brief and conflict-ridden. His high moral standards clashed with the realities of trenchant political factionalism in the late Ming. And his classical idealism regarding rulership and statecraft was not pragmatically attuned to the numerous exigencies faced by the Ming dynasty, beset with fiscal ills, military dysfunction, large-scale domestic rebellions, and encroachments by a Manchu-led coalition of peoples from the Liaodong region. In the course of forty-five years, Liu was appointed to ten successively higher positions, culminating in censor-in-chief, and he left a large body of memorandums that testify to his concern for governance. Yet he actually served in office a cumulative span of only four years.

The call of filial duties, resignations out of disgust at the degeneracy of official culture, and dismissals for persistent stridency and refusal to compromise ensured that Liu would practice his Confucian calling mainly as a teacher. Although Liu occasionally lectured in such relatively open forums as the Zhengren Society, which he founded in Shanyin, he taught and wrote principally in private quarters at Ji Hill (Jishan) near his birthplace. As was typical in Song-Ming Confucian "learned discussion" (*jiangxue*), Liu put forth his views—often in a very convoluted style—largely by explicating various terms and passages in the Four Books (*Sishu*) and the *Yijing* commentaries (*Yi zhuan*). Consequently, although he was one of the most sought-out teachers of his day, only a small percentage of his many pupils came to understand his philosophy of *xin* (heart-mind) thoroughly, in the round. But he was widely respected by his students and peers for his scholarly integrity, staunch character, and political incorruptibility.

When the Manchu-Qing armies seized the Ming southern capital, Nanjing, and invaded the lower Yangtze region in the summer of 1645, Liu gave his final demonstration of the firmness of his Confucian ethical will: he committed suicide by fasting for twenty-three days. His suicide profoundly affected the intellectual, social, and political leaders of Zhejiang and inspired many of them, also, to die out of loyalty to the Ming. Among the few true disciples of Liu Zongzhou to survive the Qing conquest, Huang Zongxi was the most accomplished and has exerted the strongest influence on later generations' understanding of Liu's thought.

See also Huang Zongxi; Wang Yangming; *Xin*.

Bibliography

Brokaw, Cynthia. *The Ledgers of Merit and Demerit: Social Change and Moral Order in Late Imperial China*. Princeton, N.J.: Princeton University Press, 1991, pp. 121–138.

Dai, Lianzheng, Wu Guang, and Zhong Caijun, eds. *Liu Zongzhou quanji*, 5 vols. Taipei: Zhongyang yanjiuyuan Zhongguo wenzhe yanjiusuo, 1996.

Gu, Qingmei. *Mingdai lixue lunwen ji*. Taipei: Daan chubanshe, 1990. (See especially pp. 209–297.)

Huang Zongxi. *Mingru xue'an*, 2 vols. Beijing: Zhonghua shuju, 1985. (See especially the introductory *Shishuo* and the concluding ch. 62, *Jishan xuean*. See also selected translations in *The Record of Ming Scholars*, ed. Julia Ching. Honolulu: University of Hawaii Press, 1987, especially Part 2, sections 3 and 4.17.)

Hummel, Arthur W., ed. *Eminent Chinese of the Ch'ing Period*, 2 vols. Washington, D.C.: U.S. Government Printing Office, 1943–1944, Vol. 1, pp. 532–533.

Mou, Zongsan. *Cong Lu Xiangshan dao Liu Jishan*. Taipei: Xuesheng shuju, 1979, ch. 6.

Okada, Takehiko. "Ryu Nentai no shogai to shiso." In *Ryushi zensho oyobi ihen*, 2 vols. Kyoto: Chubun shuppansha, 1981.

T'ang, Chün-i. "Liu Zongzhou's Doctrine of Moral Mind and Practice and His Critique of Wang Yangming." In *The Unfolding of Neo-Confucianism*, ed. Willliam Theodore de Bary. New York: Columbia University Press, 1975, pp. 305–331. (See also *Zhongguo zhexue yuanlun, Yuanjiao pian—Song-Ming ruxue sixiang zhi fazhan*, ch. 18 in *Tang Junyi xiansheng quanji*, No. 19. Taipei: Xuesheng shuju, 1984.)

Tu, Wei-ming. "Subjectivity in Liu Zongzhou's Philosophical Anthropology." In *Individualism and Holism: Studies in Confucian and Taoist Values*, ed. Donald Munro. Ann Arbor: Center for Chinese Studies, University of Michigan, 1985, pp. 215–235.

Wu, Guang, comp. and annot. *Huang Zongxi quanji*, Vols. 7–8. Hangzhou: Zhejiang guji chubanshe, 1992.

Yao, Mingda, comp. *Liu Jishan xiansheng nianpu*. Shanghai: Commercial Press, 1934.

Zeng, Jinkun. "Liu Jishan sixiang yanjiu." *Guowen yanjiusuo jikan* (National Taiwan Normal University), 28, 1984, pp. 539–643.

Zhong, Caijun, ed. *Liu Jishan xueshu sixiang lunji*. Taipei: Zhongyang yanjiuyuan Zhongguo wenzhe yanjiusuo, 1998.

Liyi fenshu (Li-i fen-shu): Principle and Manifestations

Shu-hsien Liu

When Zhu Xi (1130–1200) first studied under Li Tong (1093–1163), the master offered his advice: "There is no need to worry about principle being one; what is difficult lies in manifestations being different." From the time of Cheng Yi (1033–1107), the dictum *liyi fenshu*—"principle is one but its manifestations are many"—was transmitted from one generation to another, and it was used to give instructions to disciples of the Song-Ming neo-Confucian philosophers.

The phrase was first coined by Cheng Yi in an answer to a question by Yang Shi (1053–1135) about a famous essay, "Western Inscription," by Zhang Zai (1020–1077), which Cheng Yi considered the most powerful declaration of Confucian ethics since the time of Mencius. The essay begins with this passage:

> Heaven is my father and earth is my mother, and even such a small creature as I finds an intimate place in their midst. Therefore that which fills the universe I regard as my body and that which directs the universe I consider as my nature. All people are my brothers and sisters, and all things are my companions.

Yang Shi realized that the primary purpose of the essay was to urge students to seek *ren* (humanity). He thought that Zhang's doctrine could be traced back to Mencius (7A.45), but Zhang extended *ren* not only to living beings but to the whole universe. The outcome is his doctrine of "forming one body with the universe"—an all-important doctrine throughout neo-Confucianism. However, Yang Shi was still dissatisfied, as he felt that the essay dealt only with the substance, not the function of *ren*, and that it taught universal love without distinctions, apparently a Mohist doctrine rather than a Confucian doctrine; the Confucians would teach graded love. Cheng Yi took pains to explain to Yang Shi that this was not the case. It is precisely in harmonizing substance and function that the essay is of great significance to Confucian ethics.

According to Cheng, underlying "Western Inscription" is Zhang's idea of *liyi fenshu*, although Zhang himself had never used such an expression. The Confucian doctrine differs radically from the Mohist teaching of universal love, which implies *er ben wu fen*, "two foundations without distinctions." Cheng's answer to Yang Shi was based on Mencius's criticism of the practice of his contemporary, the Mohist Yi Zhi. Yi Zhi had buried his parents in an elaborate manner. When he was queried about his behavior, he answered:

> According to the way of the learned, the ancients treated their people as though they were embracing and protecting an infant. To me the saying means that love makes no distinctions, but that its application must begin with one's parents.

When Mencius heard of this explanation, he pointed out that Yi Zhi would have two foundations (*Mencius*, 3A.5). From the Confucian position, loving the parents and the children and then extending this love to others would entail the same principle, whereas being a father or a son, a husband or a wife, involves different roles calling for the performance of different duties—the implication of *fenshu*. By extending love to all, a Confucian has no difficulty in seeing that all men are brothers "within the four seas" (*Analects*, 12.5). But the Mohist Yi Zhi separates theory (universal love) from practice (beginning with one's parents); hence he has two foundations and fails to make the necessary distinction between one's own parents and strangers in the street.

Yang Shi took Cheng Yi's instruction to heart; he later said:

> As we know, the principle is one, and that is why there is love. The functions are many, and that is why there is righteousness. . . . Since functions are different, the application [of *ren*] cannot be without distinctions.

Thereafter, the idea of *liyi fenshu*, as we have noted, was passed on from one generation to another. Zhu Xi further discussed its implications as follows:

> There is nothing in the entire realm of creatures that does not regard heaven as the father and earth as the mother. This means that the principle is one. . . . Each regards his parents as his own parents and his son as his own son. This being the case, how can principle not be manifested as many? . . . When the intense affection for parents is extended to broaden the impartiality that knows no ego, and absolute sincerity in serving one's parents leads to the understanding of the way to serve heaven, then everywhere there is the operation that "the principle is one but its manifestations are many."

As neo-Confucians see it, there is a vast difference between Zhang's doctrine and that of the Mohists, who recognize no distinctions and therefore fail to understand function. In the understanding of Zhu Xi and other neo-Confucians, "Western Inscription," in thus preserving the harmony of substance (*ti*) and function (*yong*) of *ren* and putting it on a metaphysical basis, carries the doctrine of *ren* to a level higher than before. Zhu Xi liked to use the metaphor "the moon reflecting itself in ten thousand streams" to illustrate this idea. Therefore, for Zhu Xi, loosely speaking, there are principles, but in the final analysis there is only one principle. Zhu Xi's famous essay on *ren* was guided by this idea:

> The mind of heaven and earth is to produce things. In the production of man and things, they receive the mind of heaven and earth as their mind. Therefore, with reference to the character of the mind, although it embraces and penetrates all and leaves nothing to be desired, nevertheless, one word will cover all of it, namely, *ren* (humanity). . . . The qualities of the mind of heaven and earth are four: origination, flourishing, advantage, and firmness. And the principle of origination unites and controls them all. In their operation they constitute the course of the four seasons, and the vital force of spring permeates them all. Therefore in the mind of man there are also four moral qualities—namely, *ren*, righteousness, propriety, and wisdom—and *ren* embraces them all. In their emanation and function, they constitute the feeling of love, respect, being right, and discrimination between right and wrong—and the feeling of commiseration pervades them all.

Thus, according to Zhu Xi, there is a unity between heaven and man, the creativity (*sheng*) of heaven embodied in man becomes humanity (*ren*), the principle remains one, and manifestations of it can be seen in various heavenly and moral virtues as specified in the passage above. Zhu Xi's understanding of *li* (principle) was dominant for a long time, until the days of the dynasties were over.

The "new" neo-Confucians (*xin Ru xue*) of the second half of the twentieth century made attempts to work out further implications of *liyi fenshu*. Zhu Xi's interpretation of the idea may have been good for his time, but it implied a medieval worldview that was outdated from the perspective of modern science. Therefore, it was felt that Zhu Xi's cosmology needed something analogous to the demythologizing of certain aspects of medieval theology that had been urged by contemporary Protestant theologians in the west. In other words, the Confucian message of creativity and humanity needed to be extricated from Zhu Xi's elaborate formulation of the idea some seven hundred years ago. The spirit and the principle underlying Confucian expressions of creativity and humanity remain the same, but their manifestations differ from time to time, and some manifestations become dated and cannot be applied to a later age. Hence, the idea of *liyi fenshu* came to have the additional meaning that principle is one, while manifestations are different at different times, and every age must seek its own manifestations of the same principle.

The "new" neo-Confucians believe that the principle of creativity and humanity transcends not only time but space as well, so that its manifestations can be different in various countries and cultures, even though the spirit underlying such pluralistic expressions remains the same. This idea is not something that has been vigorously promoted only by the "new" neo-Confucians. In 1993 the Parliament of the World's Religions, which met in Chicago from 28 August to 4 September, worked out a "Declaration toward a Global Ethic." Representatives of very different religions, including Bahai, Brahma Kumaris, Buddhism, Christianity, native religions, Hinduism, Jainism, Judaism, Islam, neo-Paganism, Sikhism, Daoism, Theosophy, and Zoroastrianism, endorsed this declaration. It was pointed out:

> There is a principle which is found and has persisted in many religious and ethical traditions of humankind for thousands of years: "What you do not wish done to yourself, do not do to others." Or in positive terms: "What you wish done to yourself, do to others!"

Indeed, we find the negative and positive versions of the golden rule in *The Analects* (12.2, 4.15). A global ethic seeks to work out what is already common to the religions of the world despite all their differences regarding human conduct, moral values, and basic moral convictions. As the world becomes a global village, and if we want to live peacefully together, the idea of *liyi fenshu* must have profound contemporary significance, and we would expect to find still further new expressions of it in the future.

See also *Li*: Principle, Pattern, Reason.

Bibliography

Chan, Wing-tsit, comp. and trans. *A Source Book in Chinese Philosophy*. Princeton, N.J.: Princeton University Press, 1963.

Chu, Hsi, and Lu Tsu-ch'ien, comps. *Reflections on Things at Hand: The Neo-Confucian Anthology*, trans. Wing-tsit Chan. New York: Columbia University Press, 1967.

Liu, Shu-hsien. "Liyi fenshu de xiandai jieshi" (A Modern Interpretation of *Li-i-fen-shu*). In *Xianshiyu lixiang de jiujie* (On the Complexity of Interaction between Ideals and the Real World). Taipei: Xuesheng, 1993, pp. 157–188.

———. *Understanding Confucian-Philosophy: Classical and Sung-Ming*. Westport, Conn., and London: Greenwood, 1998.

Swidler, Leonard, ed. *For All Life: Toward a Universal Declaration of a Global Ethic—An Interreligious Dialogue*. Ashland, Ore.: White Cloud, 1999.

Lu Jia (Lu Chia)

Mark Csikszentmihalyi

Lu Jia (d. 178 B.C.E.) was an influential Chinese scholar-official during the first decades of the Han dynasty. Lu was most notable for his attempts to integrate concepts such as *wuwei* and *yinyang* into the Confucian mainstream, thereby setting the stage for the synthetic approaches of thinkers such as Jia Yi and Dong Zhongshu in the following century. Lu developed a theory of a mechanistic heaven first presented in Xunzi's *Discourse on Heaven* (*Tianlun*) into a naturalistic description of Confucian ethics.

Lu Jia was born in the late third century B.C.E. in the state of Zhu in southern China. His early association with Liu Bang (d. 195 B.C.E.) proved to be the basis of a long official career as Liu assumed the titles of prince of the state of Han in 206 B.C.E and then for Emperor Gao in 202 B.C.E. Lu served Emperor Gao in various capacities, most notably as an envoy to the independent kingdom of Nan Yue in 196 B.C.E. For securing the friendship and vassalage of the prince of Nan Yue, Lu was promoted to the post of palace grandee (*taizhong daifu*). Following the death of his patron, during the reign of Emperor Hui (r. 195–188 B.C.E.) and the subsequent de facto rule of Dowager Empress Lü (c. 188–180 B.C.E.), Lu Jia retired and held no government position. Lu lived to see the fall of the Lü clan which he had helped engineer and again served as palace grandee under Emperor Wen (r. 180–157 B.C.E.).

According to Sima Qian's *Shiji*, Emperor Gao was not very fond of the scholar-officials of his age, and remarked to Lu Jia that since he had unified the empire on horseback, he had little need for the classics of poetry and history. In response, Lu Jia argued that while an empire may be conquered on horseback, its maintenance required the study of the successes and failures of past rulers. Persuaded by this argument, Emperor Gao commissioned Lu Jia to submit a series of memorandums on the signs of success and failure in government. The resulting twelve essays were given the name *New Discussions* (*Xinyu*). Lu Jia's writings in other areas were also influential during the Han dynasty. His lost prose-rhyme (*fu*) compositions were one of four "schools" of this genre defined by Liu Xin (d. 23 C.E.). Although only fragments of Lu Jia's *Spring and Autumn Annals of Chu and Han* (*Chu Han chunqiu*) remain, they were one of the sources used by Sima Qian in his historical writing.

Whether or not the story about the composition of *New Discussions* is apocryphal, a twelve-fascicle text of the same name is attributed to Lu Jia and remarked on with approval by Sima Qian. Modern scholars are divided over whether the transmitted twelve-fascicle text called *New Discussions* is the same as the one seen by the author of the *Shiji*, but recent research into Han thought supports the conclusion that several sections of the received text are authentic. Modern studies of the thought of Lu Jia uniformly rely on *New Discussions*, a text that contains original attempts to relate Confucian theories of government to the interpretation of portents, Confucian epistemology to the search for the principles of nature, and Confucian ethics to *yin* and *yang*.

In both title and content, *New Discussions* harks back to the *Analects* (*Lunyu*) of Confucius. While the text is not a formal imitation of the *Analects*, it often quotes Confucius, and it develops a theory of governance based on the virtuous example of the ruler first seen in the *Analects*. Lu Jia's reading of Confucius, however, differs significantly from interpretations of Confucius dating from the Warring States period.

Lu Jia finds authority for the transformative power of the ruler's virtue in texts that were attributed to Confucius during the Han dynasty. Lu quotes the *Analects* (12.19) when he describes the influence of the virtuous ruler as being "like the wind which sweeps over the grass." He explains the need to use this influence to transform the people by citing Confucius's hope of being able to change habits and alter customs, and it is through the sage's "emphasis on virtue and stress on the Way that he is able to make the people of the world follow" (*Xiaojing*, or *Classic of Filial Piety*, chs. 12 and 1). The transformative power of sagely virtue is more powerful than penal law, a lesson which was neglected by the hegemonic first emperor of the Qin but which Lu traced back to the didactic lessons in *Spring and Autumn Annals*. Lu Jia's reliance on the authority of Confucius is characteristic of early Confucian writers.

Lu Jia's analysis diverges from earlier interpretations of Confucius in the way he explains the mechanism by which the virtuous ruler's example transforms the people. His reconstruction of a Confucian theory of governance makes use of several aspects of the Han view of the universe as governed by a set of correlative schemata dependent on the idea of mutual resonance. Whereas earlier Confucian thinkers like Mencius explained the influence of the ruler in more psychological terms (*Mencius*, 3A2), Lu Jia's analysis hinges on the Han belief in the mutual influence between things of the same category (*lei*). He writes that just as mountains produce clouds and hills produce thin veils of mist, so the great ruler transforms (*hua*) the people to a greater extent, and the lesser ruler to a lesser extent. The effect of a ruler's virtue on the people is a natural process like mountains producing mist.

The phenomenon of good government is integrated into the natural world and therefore obeys the same laws of resonance as other natural phenomena. This resonance is made possible by the influence of the ruler's virtuous acts on *qi* (vital force)—the influence which courses through the living body and serves as the medium between heaven and earth. Because of this movement of the *qi*, various terrestrial and celestial phenomena may be interpreted as signs of good or bad government. Lu Jia appeals to this system to show how bad government results in natural disasters:

> Bad government produces bad *qi* and bad *qi* produces calamities and prodigies. It is as a result of [bad] *qi* that things in the category of locusts and insects are produced, and it is as a result of [bad] government that rainbows and their reflections are produced.

By contrast, sagely government can reverse the course of such events:

> Sagely government benefits even the swarming insects and moistens the grasses and trees. It is created upon the heavenly *qi* and moved according to the heat or cold. People crane their necks to gaze upon such government, and turn their ears to listen and be transformed (*hua*) by it.

The sageliness of a good ruler is demonstrated by signs that are open to all to interpret. Lu's theory of portents places him at the beginning of a trend that became increasingly popular over the next several centuries. Sima Qian singles out the "signs" (*zheng*) of the successes and failures of former rulers as the guiding concern of Lu's *New Discussions*, and the same term, "signs," is used to describe the interpretive proofs used in various Han divination practices. Characteristically, Lu did not see this as diverging in any way from the Confucian tradition. According to him, the sage king Tang and Emperor Wen were also students of portents.

Inherent in this shift toward a more naturalistic justification of Confucius's political theories is a change in the understanding of the roots of moral knowledge. Lu Jia echoes the legalist critique of appeals to tradition as a justification for moral action. Instead, he argues that virtue is timeless and therefore the practices of antiquity should not necessarily be considered superior to contemporary policies. Neither the widespread acceptance of a policy nor practice is considered an argument in its favor. The good rulers of the past, such as the sage king Tang and Emperor Wu, considered only whether a policy was in harmony with the natural cycles. They enforced punishment according to the seasons of heaven and took action according to the mutual change of *yin* and *yang*. The origin of moral knowledge, for Lu Jia, is the recognition of natural patterns.

In this area, also, Lu Jia situated himself within the orthodox Confucian tradition. The first section of *New Discussions* details the creation of the world and begins by echoing Xunzi: "Heaven gave birth to the myriad things, earth nourished them, and the sages brought them to completion." The natural creation of the world, according to the cycles of *yin* and *yang*, the cycles of the seasons and the five phases, was the prototype for the creation of human institutions by the sage kings. The ancient sage kings "looked up at the patterns of heaven, looked below to the principles of earth, diagrammed the essential hexagrams, and thereby determined the human way." It has been pointed out by scholars such as Hu Shi that the emphasis on observation of externals is close to the position articulated by Xunzi, who wrote that all knowledge must be verified by observation. Specifically, the idea of a heaven which orders by way of natural principles is similar to the picture presented in Xunzi's essay "Discourse on Heaven." However, Xunzi argues that such observation is important to confirm the principles learned through a Confucian education, whereas Lu Jia makes a stronger claim that to a large extent such observation itself must be the core of the Confucian education. In terms of the search for the origins of moral knowledge, Lu Jia might be better read as looking ahead to certain neo-Confucian thinkers than as looking back to previous models from the Warring States period.

Lu Jia's ethical stance is strongly influenced by his understanding of the origins of moral knowledge. For him, the most important Confucian virtues are benevolence (*ren*) and righteousness (*yi*). Unlike previous writers, however, Lu at times associates these two virtues with *yang* and *yin*, respectively. For example, it is these physicalized virtues which govern the twenty-four solar divisions of the year. Lu is not as interested in the content of these virtues as in removing impediments to their natural application. Virtue is therefore best realized by the ruler through the theory of *wuwei*, "not acting." One reason why such virtues lead to better government than rule by law is that harsh punishment troubles the ruler's mind, clouding his judgment. The ruler who uses virtue as his standard, however, is as peaceful as if he had no tasks, and as silent as if he had no voice. The ruler must eschew material possessions, concentrating instead on his own development of the virtues. These practices speak to a conception of the virtues that grows out of a concern with cultivating clarity of mind and display a Daoist-influenced attitude toward governing.

Despite obvious similarities to the work of Confucians of the Zhou dynasty like Confucius himself and Mencius, *New Discussions* incorporates philosophical developments of the third century B.C.E. to augment the views of Lu's predecessors. Every major aspect of Lu Jia's philosophy is rooted in Confucianism, but he used strategies and explanations from legalism, *yin-yang* theory, and the Huang-Lao Daoism of his time to explain and justify these Confucian tenets. This inclusive perspective has caused several noted commentators to argue that *New Discussions* was a forgery. In light of the new understanding of the syncretic nature of early Han thought, it is precisely on this basis that the text appears so reliable.

See also Confucianism: Han.

Bibliography

Gabain, Annemarie von. "Ein Fürstenspiegel: Das Sin-yü des Lu Kia." *Mitteilungen des Seminar für Orientalische Sprachen*, 33(1), 1930, pp. 1–82.

Ku, Mei-kao. *An Introduction to the Study of the Hsin-yü of Lu Chia*. Singapore: Island Society, 1990.

Loewe, Michael. "Hsin yü." In *Early Chinese Texts: A Bibliographical Guide*, ed. Michael Loewe. Berkeley, Calif.: Society for the Study of Early China, Early China Special Monographs Series, No. 2, 1993, pp. 171–177.

Lu, Jia. *A Chinese Mirror for Magistrates*, ed. Ku Mei-kao. Canberra: Australia National University Faculty of Asian Studies, Faculty of Asian Studies Mongraphs, New Series 11, 1988.

Wang, Liqi. "Qianyan (Foreword)." In *Xinyü jiaozhu*, ed. Wang Liqi. Peking: Zhonghua, 1986.

Lu Xiangshan (Lu Hsiang-shan)

Joanne D. Birdwhistell

Best-known for his learning of the heart-and-mind (*xinxue*), Lu Jiuyuan (Xiangshan, 1139–1193) was an important thinker of the Southern Song (1127–1279) whose thought has traditionally been viewed as a neo-Confucian alternative to that of his eminent contemporary Zhu Xi (1130–1200). Lu was a passionate teacher, impatient with book learning not accompanied by action, and later part of a philosophical alliance with Wang Yangming (1472–1529) that opposed the orthodox school of Cheng Yi (1033–1108) and Zhu Xi. Lu's personal name was Jiuyuan, his style Zijing, and his honorific name Xiangshan after the mountain (which he renamed) where he located his retreat, and he was posthumously called Wen'an. Interested in social, political, and moral problems, Lu focused most on issues concerning order in society and the necessity for taking personal responsibility for social-moral action. The concepts of *li* (pattern, order, principle) and *xin* (heart-mind) were central to his thinking.

Although Lu wrote many letters and a variety of short pieces, he produced no major philosophical work—a fact that reflects his emphasis on practical affairs. *[Lu] Xiangshan [xiansheng] quanji* (*The Complete Works of Lu Xiangshan*), in thirty-six *juan* (chapters), contains all his writings: letters (especially important for presenting his philosophical ideas), memorandums, special accounts, compositions for departing friends, essays, lectures, poems, epitaphs, and some miscellaneous pieces. This collection also preserves his recorded sayings and several biographies, including a chronological biography.

Lu came from a large multigenerational family that lived in Jinqi County, Fuzhou Prefecture, Jiangxi Province. His family had lived there since moving south in the tenth century during the post-Tang (618–906) period of dynastic upheaval. There were more than one hundred family members during his lifetime, and he was the youngest of six brothers. Belonging to the local elite, the Lu family had diverse interests that included farming, local military defense, a medicinal drug shop, social welfare projects, and Confucian education. Lu and two of his brothers, Jiushao (Suoshan) and Jiuling (Fuzhai), were especially active in continuing a family tradition of Confucian learning.

Lu Jiuyuan and Jiuling were known as the two Lus, a designation alluding to the Cheng brothers, Cheng Hao (1032–1085) and Cheng Yi, influential philosophers of the Northern Song (960–1126).

Lu attained the *jinshi* degree in his early thirties and served in several official posts late in life. Although his tenure in official life was brief, he was a vigorous and active official, and he was known for his efforts to improve the conditions of the people. Politically, Lu was especially interested in local affairs, in contrast to national or court matters. The last years of his life were spent teaching at his retreat on Elephant Mountain (Xiangshan), where he attracted several thousand followers and had a well-earned reputation as an unusually inspiring teacher.

Although in his teachings Lu promoted the importance of teachers, he himself apparently did not have one, outside of his family. Lu's thought reflects the family's emphasis on, and a common Song claim to, "real" or practical learning, which stressed ritual action and morality, in contrast to (in Lu's case) examinations, speculative thought, and the writing of commentaries. Emphasizing the social, moral, and political focus of classical Confucianism, Lu saw himself as "the" successor to Mencius (371–c. 289 B.C.E.). Lu gave little attention to metaphysics, epistemology, literary subjects, or commentary, although there was much contemporary interest in these areas. Later trends and developments in thought led to disagreements over interpreting of Lu's ideas, and thus it is important to recognize the philosophical context of Lu's position. The Cheng-Zhu thinkers engaged in metaphysics and commentary, and although Lu rejected these interests, he still used much of the same terminology. The shared vocabulary led others, then and later, to interpret Lu's thought as if Lu accepted the same theoretical framework and had the same concerns as the Cheng-Zhu position. Forced into the Cheng-Zhu perspective, Lu's views were mistakenly considered a simple, or lesser, counterpart to Zhu Xi's and were often criticized as Chanist. Only a few scholars have studied them in light of the views of other contemporaries.

Lu's philosophy drew a great deal from Confucius, Xunzi, and particularly Mencius. Lu also looked to the *Book of Change* (*Yijing*) and, to some extent, the *Record of Rites* (*Liji*), both works from the Han (206 B.C.E.–220 C.E.). From the latter, Lu favored the chapters called "Great Learning" (*Daxue*) and "Doctrine of the Mean" (*Zhongyong*) and was critical of the chapter "Record of Music" (*Yueji*). Although Lu expressed antagonism to certain speculative and "empty" aspects of Buddhism, especially in the popular Chan form, Buddhist ideas and terminology are found in his thought. Buddhist ideas and phrases were common to Chinese culture by the twelfth century, however, and Lu was no different from others in this respect. Lu was critical of the ancient Daoists, Zhuangzi and Laozi, as well as the "Record of Music," insofar as he believed them to be responsible for the metaphysical and moral dualism that he adamantly rejected. In addition, Lu built on ideas from Shao Yong (1012–1077) and Cheng Hao, prominent thinkers of the Northern Song who both developed ideas about the heart-mind (*xin*).

The term *xinxue*—the learning of the heart-and-mind—does not reflect the scope of Lu's vision, for he offered a comprehensive view of the world that unified everything into a single system. Like other Song thinkers, Lu addressed ontological issues, or issues concerned with the nature of "being," but his ontological perspective was based on relationships, not on metaphysical substances, as Zhu Xi's metaphysical distinction between *li* and *qi* (energetic configurations, matter-energy) ostensibly was. Lu held that the existence of the world and everything in it entailed both constant, patterned change and patterned, enduring order. As his interest in patterns of order and change reveals, Lu thus thought in terms of social rather than metaphysical ontology.

To summarize briefly, the Cheng-Zhu metaphysical position that Lu rejected placed *li* and *qi* in a discourse concerned with basic substances and considered *li* and *qi* two different substances. As such, *li* and *qi* became two different roots or sources of activity in the world. *Li* was identified with ultimate, unchanging moral values, with heaven, with *dao* (the way or Way), with human nature, and with goodness. *Qi* was associated with evil, human actions, human desires, and all the various failings of human beings and this world. Although not inert as matter was in western metaphysics, *qi* (like matter) was the "physical" substance and described as "within forms" (*xing er xia*). While not the "spark" as the soul or mind was in western thought, *li* (like soul or mind) was the "nonphysical" substance and characterized as "before forms" or "above forms" (*xing er shang*). *Li* was the hidden order, pattern, or principle "behind" the manifest world of ever-changing *qi*. *Li* and *qi* required each other but were ontologically distinct.

Lu, in contrast, regarded social relationships, or patterns of order, as fundamental. In this sense, Lu's thought may perhaps be closer to the Mencian social-political position than to Song metaphysical ideas. Lu's ontology consisted of such things as the five relations (ruler-minister, father-son, husband-wife, older brother-younger brother, friend-friend); Mencius's four "sprouts" of the good mind (sense of compassion, sense of shame, sense of modesty, sense of right and wrong); the differing social-political levels of world, state, family, person; and the three ultimates of heaven, earth, and humanity. For Lu, a major problem with the Cheng-Zhu type of dualism was that it separated the pattern, or principle, of activity from the entity that acted. This separation in turn implied that *li* was "empty" (*xu*) and hidden while *qi* was "real" (*shi*) and manifest—a view he considered absolutely unacceptable. For Lu, *li* was the heaven-derived, given pattern of activity that constituted order in the world. All the "constant" relationships (such as those noted above) were *li*, and both *li* and relationships were real. *Li*, in one sense, even produced the world, for without order the world as known would not exist. *Li* was thus opposed to turmoil or disorder (*luan*).

Focusing on the concepts of pattern and heart-mind, Lu's learning posited a highly ordered world, characterized by multiple levels of social integration. Beginning with the "highest" level (and continuing ideas found in the *Book of Change*), Lu assumed that the world consisted of the three ultimates (*sanji* or *sancai*) of heaven, earth, and humanity. (These separate but correlated realms were each represented by lines in the trigrams and hexagrams.) Each realm had its own characteristic activities, events, and entities, but each participated in the same pattern or patterns of order. Thus, the three realms were correlated with each other. Given that the world was characterized by continuous, but ordered, change, the most fundamental rhythm of change was a dichotomous pulse. In reference to heaven this dichotomous pattern (*li*) was termed *yin* and *yang* (dark and light); in reference to earth it was termed soft-yielding and hard-firm (*rou* and *gang*); and in reference to humanity it was termed benevolence and rightness (*ren* and *yi*). This order (*li*) further entailed reciprocal relationships whose parts were mutually interacting and influencing.

Yijing cosmological thought contributed further aspects to Lu's concept of *li*. The supreme ultimate (*taiji*) gave rise to the two forces (movement and stillness), and then a doubling process occurred, eventually producing all the things in the world—from the four images (*yin* and *yang, rou* and *gang*), to the eight trigrams, and so on to the sixty-four hexagrams and all the "myriad things." From a social perspective, this pattern (*li*) made the world what it was. This pattern was a natural and intrinsic aspect of the world, and its existence did not depend on human perception. Without it, the world and all things would not exist, for there would be no order making it possible to distinguish separate events (both activities and entities). All things, no matter in which of the three realms, in some way participated in this one pattern.

Lu seldom discussed good versus evil; but as the order of all life, *li* was the good, and as goodness (*ren*), its opposite was disorder, or evil. Lu emphasized that *li* was real, for it belonged to this world of human experience. That is, the patterns or "rules" of events helped to constitute those events, and there was no invisible order separate from what was manifest in human experience. Since Lu was talking about the social world, the world of human experience, the lack of (moral) order led to destruction and death, while order entailed life and goodness (*ren*). (Mencius and Xunzi would have agreed.) The Cheng-Zhu pairing of *li* with *qi* from a metaphysical perspective was simply not relevant here, nor was the Buddhist metaphysical conception of *li* as pure, empty "principle" opposed to physical "things" (*shi*).

There also was only one *li*, one ultimate standard of activity. This claim meant that all things belonged to a single, unified order and that the three realms did not have different and unrelated patterns of activity. Mandated by heaven, *li* could not be changed by human beings. Even the social and moral standards of human behavior, such as the distinction of superior and inferior, were part of the universal order. The notion of only one *li* further meant that *li* had reference to the public (*gong*) context, for instance, the people (*min*) as opposed to separate bodily selves (*shen*). To put this another way, the idea of *li* as public emphasized that *li* referred to a social context, rather than, say, a psychological or physiological personal context.

In sum, Lu described *li* as the correct (*zheng*), the real, the constant (*chang*), and the public order or pattern of all the world. "Rooted in the bodily self, evidenced in the people, and recorded in the actions of the ancient sage kings," this pattern was "established in heaven and earth" and "witnessed by the ghosts and spirits." There was only one *li*, not two or more. *Li* was *dao*, the heart-mind, and human nature (*xing*). Lu represented his position in such pithy claims as "the heart-mind is *li*" and "my heart-mind is the universe and the universe is my heart-mind."

Of the three realms, humanity most concerned Lu. Earth received little attention, while heaven was important mainly in its sense of *li*. The term "heaven" had several referents, including the sky of nature paired with earth, as well as the ultimate source of values. According to this latter sense, heaven and humans followed the same *dao* (Way). Heaven was conceived as a ruler, somewhat as a root rules by regulating the plant and by being the source of its developmental capability. Lu used terms like "heaven" (*tian*) and "patterns of heaven" (*tianli*) interchangeably with *li*.

This flexibility of language was a point made by Lu to reinforce his social perspective and distinguish it from a metaphysical view. Lu acknowledged that one term could have different referents depending on the context, and different terms could refer to one and the same thing, although from different perspectives. The existence of different terms did not necessarily imply separate entities. For instance, in refusing to make an ultimate distinction between terms like human nature (*xing*) and heart-mind (*xin*), Lu claimed that apparent differences were a matter of how the words were used—human nature in relation to heaven and heart-mind in relation to humanity.

Although Lu focused on humanity from a social perspective, this characterization did not imply that he denied the individuality of particular persons. On the contrary, Lu was known for extolling the worth of individual human beings–even if they could not read a single character. Lu was not thinking of individuality or human rights in a modern sense, however. Rather, he emphasized the integration of all levels of existence—the person, the state, the world—into one system, and he recognized that the basis of all moral order lay in the actions of specific persons while the authority of such order lay in people's natural capacities. The source and authority of morality did not lie in written records, for these were cultural products derived from actual human experience.

Like other Confucian thinkers, Lu placed more value on the higher levels or entities of social organization. Although some variation existed in the terms used and in the significance of particular groupings, generally, from higher to lower, these levels included the world (*tianxia*, "all under heaven"), states, families, persons in society, and individual persons as bodily selves. In addition, there was the source of universal order within and inseparable from all things, variously called the root-mind (original mind), heart-mind, pattern, *dao*, root, source, host, and ruler. Similar to the level of the state, the people also constituted a particular concern to Lu, and here individual persons as bodily selves were contrasted with the people as the social body. Conflict between these two entities was a primary source of disorder and, Lu assumed, could not be stopped completely. The existence of individual persons was fundamental, but the pursuit of private interests alone led to conflict with the interests of the people as a whole. This view of the world further assumed the broader context of the cosmos (*yuzhou*, space and time) and the natural world (heaven and earth).

Along with the concept of pattern (*li*), heart-mind (*xin*) occupied the most important place in Lu's thought. Lu acknowledged the ordinary activities of people, such as thinking, examining, reflecting, making distinctions, feeling, desiring, deciding, willing, and setting goals—all activities for which the heart-mind was considered responsible. These activities in themselves were not Lu's concern, although they became a concern for him when they involved social-moral matters. Although it was the source of all these activities, the heart-mind was also much more.

Like Shao Yong, Lu regarded human beings as the most *ling* (luminous, spiritual, profound, intellectual) of all beings—as possessing an ultimate radiating, spiritual, mysterious power—and this luminosity (*ling*) was associated with the heart-mind. Humans were human because they had this heart-mind. Following Mencius's perspective and terminology, this heart-mind was a person's greater part, as opposed to the lesser parts. The heart-mind was responsible not only for the kinds of actions noted above but for all social and moral behavior. The lesser parts, in contrast, were responsible for seeing, hearing, tasting, and smelling. When Lu spoke of the heart-mind in its greater sense, he was claiming its equivalence to Mencius's root-mind, or good mind (*liangxin*).

Lu used the term *xin* (heart-mind) interchangeably with such terms as root-mind (*benxin*), *li, dao*, and human nature (*xing*). For Lu, the heart-mind was the Mencian originally good mind, the seat of the four "sprouts" of goodness—the senses of commiseration, shame, modesty, and yielding, and knowing right and wrong. The development of these natural capacities and abilities led to the four recognized social-moral virtues of benevolence, ritual action or proper behavior, rightness, and wisdom. All people have an inherent knowledge of and capability for social-moral behavior. This source of morality only had to be developed. Learning could aid in its development, but moral knowledge and capability did not have to be completely learned and were not imposed from without.

Lu stressed that the genuine follower of Confucianism (*ruxue*) was a morally responsible person who had a critical role in society—to act on behalf of others. He contrasted this role with the self-centered behavior of most people. Lu used a variety of terms to clarify the distinction between the two kinds of behavior, including the people as opposed to the self, public as opposed to private, rightness as opposed to selfish profit, and the superior person as opposed to the petty person; and he maintained that to achieve an orderly moral society and benevolent government, one had to act for the whole, not the part. One had to learn in order to be a genuine person, and that entailed fulfilling the "way of humanity" (*rendao*).

In discussing personal action, Lu was concerned with persons as members of society, not as physiological or psychological entities. The relevant context of Lu's ideas consisted of other people and human relationships, not one's own particular and private characteristics. His goal was for people (as members of society) to choose to act so that their behavior would be as much as possible in harmony with *li* or *dao*. They would then be contributing to the maintenance of social-political life, its health, and the good. While he instructed people on how to behave, their personal behavior was not for the sake of satisfying their individual physiological and psychological needs and desires. Thus, for instance, in the context of a parent-child relationship, behaving in a filial manner was encouraged because it contributed to social-moral order. How such behavior affected one in a private sense was not the issue.

Lu taught that people must understand, preserve, and develop their root-mind, their moral-social potential. If they do develop it, they will act in accord with the patterns of social order that constitute the world. The originally good mind was to be preserved by realizing its sprouts, by making one's natural, moral capacities a manifest reality in society. It was not done by "quiet sitting" or meditating for long periods while seeking for one's "original substance," a charge that others often wrongly made with regard to Lu's position. One need not force understanding and action; success would occur by letting one's efforts proceed simply, easily, and naturally.

Self-development and its resulting moral-social action began with taking a critical attitude toward oneself. One should have an attitude of doubt and questioning in examining one's thoughts and actions; read both broadly and in depth, while keeping in mind what is important and what is not; recognize one's own illnesses (faults) and constantly correct oneself; seek help from teachers and friends, even more so than from reading; and proceed from what is easier and nearby to what is more difficult and advanced. One must "honor one's virtuous nature" before following the path of "inquiry and study," that is, first understand the essential values and then make them the guide by which one pursues learning.

Lu stressed that people ought to have great aims, for one's aims lead to one's practices and desires. Emphasizing the conative aspect of human beings, Lu claimed that a person must first establish his or her aim. This intentional effort entailed first distinguishing between rightness and selfish benefit. Rightness is a matter of public interest, impartiality, heavenly pattern, or simply *li*, and so it is a social matter. Rightness implies certain kinds of relationships, the ordering of action in specific ways (ultimately derived from heaven). In contrast, selfish benefit is a matter of private interest and selfish individuality, and so it pertains to personal human desires (*renyu*). Human desires are specifically desires of particular persons in reference to their own physiological or psychological contexts. The term "human desires" must not be used for desires that focus on the people or society as a whole. Selfishness implies action and thought for the sake of the individual person as a bodily entity, not as a social entity. Since selfish actions are not done for the sake of society, they harm society by disrupting its patterns of moral order.

Establishing the moral aim for oneself and critically examining oneself are required if one is to remove the faults (illnesses) or "obscurations"—Lu used both metaphors—from one's heart-mind. If successful, the heart-mind becomes luminous (*ling*) and *li* becomes bright (*ming*). The obscurations or faults of common persons result from excessive desires, while those of the educated result from biased and faulty views. Obscurations or faults of the originally good heart-mind lead to evil, rather than good, actions. Since Lu was not speaking from a metaphysical context, evil was not an entity opposed to goodness but was the extent to which one's thoughts and actions did not conform with moral order.

In emphasizing actual affairs over books as the authoritative source of moral knowledge and action, Lu was urging people not to substitute indirect knowledge, gained from books, for knowledge gained directly by oneself. The former was the wrong approach to self-cultivation. Since all people in the world possessed the root-mind, one only had to develop the moral capacities and potential that one naturally had. Lu thus emphasized one's inner, natural capacities over outer, textual knowledge, and action in society over reading. These efforts were "establishing one's greater part" and involved a kind of knowing that reached completion only through moral-social action. Lu said that in contrast to the ease and simplicity of his own approach, Zhu Xi's approach was complicated and hard. Lu claimed that Zhu Xi wrongly put textual study before moral reflection, divided the one heart-mind into two—the *dao* heart-mind and the human heart-mind—separated heart-mind and human nature, and proposed a *wuji* ("without ultimate") cosmological state before *taiji* (supreme ultimate).

Like many Song thinkers, Lu drew on pre-Qin (221–207 B.C.E.) Confucian thought and certain legalist ideas of Han Feizi in his political thought. Lu held that the ruler should rule on behalf of the people, not himself, and his responsibility, and that of the government, was ultimately to nourish and teach the people and to maintain their welfare. The people cannot exist without a ruler, because their natural crowding together leads them to fight and stir up disorder, actions that then lead to their destruction. The ruler thus must regulate and order the people in order to preserve their lives and well-being. The ideal ruler will implement a benevolent government and bring peace to the world.

Thinking of contemporary problems as well as perennial issues, Lu emphasized that the relationship between the ruler and ministers ought to place ultimate authority in morality, not in official title or position. Whereas Confucius had urged the convergence of morality and official position with his advocacy of the rectification of names, Mencius and Xunzi had stressed the minister's responsibility of teaching (morality). Lu continued these lines of thought, regarding moral officials as necessary. He criticized officials who acted for their own self-interest, not for the people's. Appealing to a common social situation, Lu emphasized that *li* or *dao* (here, morality) is the host, and position and title (officials) are the guests.

Like others, Lu mixed the Confucian view of employing the wise and using the capable in government with the ideas (originally legalist) of rewarding accomplishments and punishing crimes. In regard to an important contemporary topic, reform, Lu generally supported the much-disputed political reforms of Wang Anshi (1021–1086) but believed that the reformers and their opponents (the conservatives) both were responsible for the lack of success. Lu particularly emphasized that reforms must begin by establishing the root-mind of everyone and proposals must be adapted to the changing conditions of the times.

Although many twentieth-century scholars interpreted Lu's thought as a form of monism or idealism (or subjective idealism), these western labels are misleading because Lu was not concerned with the metaphysical and epistemological kinds of questions such labels represent. Lu did not ask questions about fundamental metaphysical substances, or distinguish between "objective" and "subjective" reality, or claim that the mind (or reality) was consciousness, or assume the unreliability of sensory knowledge. Although some of Lu's statements, such as "my heart-mind is the world; the world is my heart-mind," seem to suggest an idealistic position similar to that of George Berkeley (1685–1753), Lu made his statements from a different set of assumptions. Taking a social perspective, Lu was concerned with order (especially moral order) in the world, and his claim was that all things have or follow the same patterns of order. Berkeley, however, addressed metaphysical and epistemological questions. He was concerned with what exists, what we know and can know, and how we know it. Concluding that we cannot know for sure whether there is any reality "out there" unless it is perceived, Berkeley denied the existence of matter as a metaphysical substance paired with the metaphysical substance of the soul.

Lu's philosophical position has occupied an important place in Chinese philosophy or learning (*xue*) despite having had a relatively low profile historically. Some of the outstanding thinkers from the Song to the Qing sympathized with his position, but after his immediate followers and disciples, there were no influential thinkers who established a long-term "transmission" of his thought. There was no institutional support for Lu's thought, as the official examination system was for Zhu Xi's. Lu was often (unjustly) criticized as a Chanist, in large part because of his emphasis on the heart-mind, his rejection of a preoccupation with texts, and his advocacy of a simple and easy method of self-cultivation. Ironically, he even became identified in the late Ming (1368–1644) with "empty" speculative thought and meditative practices.

What makes Lu important philosophically is his stress on the role of Confucians in society, that is, their mission to take responsibility for all arenas, social, moral, political, and cultural; his stress on this world and action in it; his rejection of scholasticism, of metaphysical and speculative thought, and of (excessive) quiet sitting and meditation, all of which he believed undermined the necessary focus on the social context; and his stress on and development of such classical Confucian themes as a common humanity, that everyone has the moral potential within, that government should be benevolent, the importance of self-initiative and self-responsibility, and the welfare of the group over that of the individual person. By stressing that the heart-mind not only was private and internal but extended outside oneself to the whole world, Lu conceived of human nature truly as a social nature. He also greatly appreciated the aesthetic dimension of human beings.

Although the eminent Ming philosopher Wang Yangming must be given credit for rekindling widespread interest in Lu, Wang's success would probably not have been possible had not both Wang and Lu been addressing issues that were historically central to Chinese culture itself and to the Confucian conception of philosophy (learning). Lu's philosophy was not the kind that was a matter of studying books, forming new concepts, or establishing elaborate systems of thought. It was the kind that expected others to be like Lu himself—the "hero" who taught people to pay attention to their own development, rather than attack others.

The lack of sophisticated metaphysical, epistemological, or logical ideas in Lu's thought has generally led scholars to emphasize Lu's own emphasis on the easy and simple. Perhaps, however, the most critical human issues, those of concern to Lu, are so much a part of what we know and who we are as human beings—even without our knowing that we know what we know—that such issues are the most difficult to examine in critical, analytic ways. These especially include issues of behaving morally, contributing to the health of society, and understanding the many contexts of the self. Lu's thought stands for a "lived" conception of philosophy, as opposed to a linguistic, a logical, or another more specialized type, and thus the issues raised in his thought offer relevant perspectives for comparisons with philosophy in the modern world.

See also Cheng Hao; Cheng Yi; *Li*: Principle, Pattern, Reason; *Qi*; Reason and Principle; *Xin*; Wang Yangming; Zhu Xi.

Bibliography

Akizuki, Kazutsugu. *Riku O kenkyu* (Studies on Lu and Wang). Tokyo: Shobasha, 1935. (In Japanese.)

Birdwhistell, Anne D. "Dichotomies in Social Experience in the Thought of Lu Jiuyuan (1139–1193)." *Journal of Sung-Yuan Studies*, 27, 1997, pp. 1–26.

———. "Lu Xiangshan." In *Routledge International Encyclopedia of Philosophy*, rev. ed. New York: Routledge, 1998.

———. "Social Reality and Lu Jiuyuan (1139–1193)." *Philosophy East and West*, 47(1), January 1997, pp. 47–65.

Cady, Lyman Van Law. "The Philosophy of Lu Hsiang-shan, a Neo-Confucian Monistic Idealist." Ph.D. dissertation, Union Theological Seminary, 1939.

Chan, Wing-tsit. *Chu Hsi: New Studies*. Honolulu: University of Hawaii Press, 1989.

———, trans. and comp. *A Source Book in Chinese Philosophy*. Princeton, N.J.: Princeton University Press, 1963.

Chang, Carsun. *The Development of Neo-Confucian Thought*, Vol. 1. New York: Bookman, 1957.

Chang, Li-wen. *Song-Ming lixue loji jiegou di yenhua* (The Evoluation of the Logical Structure of Song-Ming Learning of Pattern-Principle). Taipei: Wanxiang lou/Sanmin,1993. (In Chinese.)

———. *Zouxiang xinxue zhi lu—Lu Xiangshan sixang de zuji* (On the Road of the Learning of the Heart-and-Mind—The Traces of Lu Xiangshan's Thought). Beijing: Zhonghua shuju, 1992. (In Chinese.)

Ching, Julia. "The Goose Lake Monastery Debate (1175)." *Journal of Chinese Philosophy*, 1, 1974, pp. 161–178.

Chu, Ping-tzu. "Tradition Building and Cultural Competition in Southern Song China." Ph.D. dissertation, Harvard University, 1998.

Foster, Robert Wallace. "Differentiating Rightness from Profit: The Life and Thought of Lu Jiuyuan (1139–1193)." Ph. D. dissertation, Harvard University, 1997.

Fukuda, Shigeru. *Riku Shozan Bunshu* (Collected Works of Lu Xiangshan). Tokyo: Meitoku Shuppansha, 1972. (In Japanese.)

Fung, Yu-lan. *History of Chinese Philosophy*, Vol. 2, trans. Derk Bodde. Princeton, N.J.: Princeton University Press, 1953.

Gao, Zhuanxi. *Li xin zhijian: Zhu Xi he Lu Jiuyuan de lixue* (Between Principle and Mind-Heart: The Learning of Principle of Zhu Xi and Lu Jiuyuan). Beijing: Shenghuo tushu xin zhi sanlian shudian, 1992. (In Chinese.)

Huang, Chin-hsing. "Chu Hsi versus Lu Hsiang-shan: A Philosophical Interpretation." *Journal of Chinese Philosophy*, 14(2), June 1987, pp. 179–208.

Huang, Siu-chi. *Lu Hsiang-shan: A Twelfth-Century Chinese Idealist Philosopher*. New Haven, Conn.: American Oriental Society, 1944.

Huang, Zongxi, and Quan Zuwang. *Song-Yuan xue'an* (Scholarly Records of Song and Yuan Scholars), Vols. 57–58, ed. *Sibu beiyao*. (In Chinese.)

Hou, Wailu. *Zhongguo sixiang tongshi* (Comprehensive History of Chinese Thought), Vol. 4, part 2. Beijing: Renmin chubanshe, 1960. (In Chinese.)

Hymes, Robert P. "Lu Chiu-yuan, Academies, and the Problem of the Local Community." In *Neo-Confucian Education: The Formative Stage*, ed. William Theodore de Bary and John W. Chaffee. Berkeley: University of California Press, 1989, pp. 432–456.

———. *Statesmen and Gentlemen: The Elite of Fu-chou, Chiang-hsi, in Northern and Southern Song*. Cambridge: Cambridge University Press, 1986.

Kim, Oaksook Chun. "Chu Hsi and Lu Hsiang-shan: A Study of Philosophical Achievements and Controversy in Neo-Confucianism." Ph.D. dissertation, University of Iowa, 1980.

Kusumoto, Masatsugu. *Chugoku tetsugaku kenkyu* (Studies in Chinese Philosophy). Tokyo: Kokushikan daigaku toshokan, 1975. (In Japanese.)

Li, Zhijian. *Lu Jiuyuan zhexue sixiang yanjiu* (A Study of the Philosophical Thought of Lu Jiuyuan). Henan: Renmin chuban she, 1985. (In Chinese.)

Lin, Jiping. *Lu Xiangshan yenjiu* (A Study of Lu Hsiang-shan). Taipei: Shangwu, 1973. (In Chinese.)

Liu, Shu-hsien. "The Universal Mind in Lu Jiuyuan." In *Sources of Chinese Tradition*, 2nd ed., Vol. 1, comp. William Theodore de Bary and Irene Bloom. New York: Columbia University Press, 1999, pp. 714–719.

Liu, Zongxian. *Lu Wang xinxue yanjiu* (A Study of the Learning of the Mind-Heart of Lu and Wang). Jinan: Shandong renmin chubanshe, 1997. (In Chinese.)

Lu, Jiuyuan (Xiangshan). [*Lu*] *Xiangshan* [*xiansheng*] *quanji* (The Collected Works of Lu Jiuyuan [Xiangshan]), thirty-six *juan*. (First published 1212 in twenty-eight books. In Chinese.)

———. *Recorded Sayings*. (First published 1237. Combined ed. published 1521 by Wang Yangming in thirty-six *juan*. Republished in 1559 by Wang Zongmu in thirty-six *juan*.)

Mahony, Robert Joseph. "Lu Hsiang-shan and the Importance of Oral Communication in Confucian Education." Ph.D. dissertation, Columbia University, 1986.

Mou Zongsan (Mou, Tsung-san). *Cong Lu Xiangshan dao Liu Jishan* (From Lu Hsiang-shan to Liu Chi-shan). Taipei: Xuesheng, 1980. (In Chinese.)

Pease, Jonathan O. "Lin-ch'uan and Fen-ning: Kiangsi Locales and Kiangsi Writers during the Sung." *Asia Major*, 3rd Series, 4(1), 1991, pp. 39–85.

Qian, Mu. *Zhuzi xin xue'an* (A New Scholarly Record of Zhu Xi), 5 vols. Taipei: San-min, 1971. (In Chinese.)

T'ang, Chun-i. *Zhongguo zhexue yuanlun: Yuanxing pian* (Fundamental Discussions on Chinese Philosophy: On the

Original Nature). Hong Kong: New Asia Institute, 1968. (In Chinese.)

Tillman, Hoyt C. *Confucian Discourse and Chu Hsi's Ascendancy*. Honolulu: University of Hawaii Press, 1992.

Xu, Fuguan. *Zhongguo sixiangshih lunji* (Collected Essays on the History of Chinese Thought). Taipei: Xuesheng, 1983. (In Chinese.)

Zeng, Chunhai. *Lu Xiangshan*. Taipei: Dongda tushu, 1988. (In Chinese.)

Luo Qinshun (Lo Ch'in-shun)

William Yau-nang NG

Luo Qinshun (Lo Ch'in-shun, 1465–1547), a famous neo-Confucian scholar in the Ming dynasty (1368–1644), came from Taihe in Jiangxi. Luo had a successful career. In 1492, he ranked first in the provincial examination. In the following year, he placed third in the metropolitan examination and was appointed a compiler at the Hanlin Academy. Eventually he was promoted to the position of a lecturer at the Imperial University in Nanjing, where he served under the newly appointed chancellor, Zhang Mou (1436–1521). They worked together to improve the standards of the university. As a lecturer, Luo devoted himself to studying the Four Books, the Five Classics, and the writings of the neo-Confucian scholars in the Song period. He concluded that Cheng Hao (1032–1085), Cheng Yi (1033–1107), Zhang Zai (1020–1077), and Zhu Xi (1130–1200) had all studied Buddhism. However, once they understood Confucianism thoroughly, they came to know the errors of Buddhism and began to make serious attempts to refute it. Luo also agreed with Zhu Xi's criticism of Lu Xiangshan (Jiuyuan, 1139–1192), the founder of the "school of mind," and this sheds light upon his disagreement with Wang Yangming (1472–1529).

In 1504, Luo returned home to take care of his father. Later that year, he requested an extension of his leave. Even though it was not granted, he decided to stay at home and send the authorities another request. He met with the anger of the notorious and powerful eunuch Liu Jin (d. 1510) and was thus deprived of both rank and office.

Before long, however, Liu Jin was executed and Luo was restored to his previous position. Then he was promoted repeatedly, ending as minister of personnel in Nanjing in 1522. He observed mourning for his father in 1523. After that, he was recalled to office first as minister of rites and then as minister of personnel. However, he declined the offer and, on his request, he was granted retirement in 1527. He then spent the rest of his life studying, writing, and reflecting. These activities led to the completion of his major work, *Kunzhi ji*. In 1547, Luo died peacefully at age eighty-two. He was awarded the title of grand guardian of the heir apparent and given the posthumous name Wenzhuang. In 1724 his tablet was placed in the Confucian Temple. Luo's works include *Zhengan cunkao* and *Kunzhi ji*; the latter is his most important philosophical work.

In Luo's philosophy, particularly noteworthy are his views on the relation between *li* (principle) and *qi* (material force) and between *xin* (mind) and *xing* (nature), and his criticism of Chan Buddhism and the "school of mind" in neo-Confucianism. To understand these views, it is important to grasp the central theme of Luo's philosophy—achieving or returning to "unity." This unity is based on his metaphysical conception of reality. All reality is *qi*, which, in Luo's words, is "originally one." However, following "an endless cycle of movement and tranquillity, going and coming, resting and falling," the "myriad things" come into being. Such a metaphysical conception is antithetical to Zhu Xi's dualistic position of *li* and *qi*. Unlike Zhu Xi, who viewed *li* as a determinative force that is prior to and distinct from *qi*, Luo interpreted *li* as the pattern or order that could be discovered in *qi*. In fact, *li*, according to Luo, is essentially naturalistic. Luo also disagreed with Zhu Xi's idea of *li* and *qi* as two separate entities and pointed out that this thesis was a result of a wrong conception shaped by Zhou Dunyi's *Taijitu shuo*. According to Luo, *li* and *qi* are not separable, and they always come into existence in unity.

In Zhu Xi's system, the metaphysical dualism of *li* and *qi* was paralleled by the ethical dualism of *xin* (mind-heart) and *xing* (nature). For Luo *xin* was a subjective function whereas *xing* was an objective reality.

On the basis of this understanding of *xin* and *xing*, Luo criticized the Buddhist notion of "clarifying the mind and perceiving the nature." He disagreed with the Buddhists' unbalanced emphasis on the mind alone, for they overlooked the "perfect subtlety and absolute unity" of the nature (*xing*).

Nonetheless, Luo and Zhu Xi shared some views. Regarding spiritual cultivation, Zhu Xi's dual emphasis on "quiet sitting" and reading books was accepted by Luo and many other Confucian scholars. Realizing the limitations of "quiet sitting," Luo also devoted himself to textual study. In fact, textual studies occupied the most important place in Luo's own understanding and practice of personal cultivation.

Despite the similarity of some of Luo's and Zhu Xi's views, however, Wu Kang, in his work on neo-Confucianism, seems too hasty in describing Luo as a follower of Zhu Xi just because Luo objected to the philosophy of Wang Yangming, the most important thinker of the school of mind in the Ming dynasty. While it is true that Luo and Wang did not come to a consensus on certain points, it does not follow that Luo should be put into the school of Cheng-Zhu, the "school of principle." It is ahistorical to arbitrarily divide all neo-Confucian philosophers into the school of mind and the school of principle.

Luo's polemic against Wang Yangming is essential to understanding his thought. He argued that Wang's views, affected by Chan Buddhism, actually contradicted the Confucian classics. Besides, he rejected Wang's interpretation of *gewu* as directly contradictory to Zhu Xi's ideas. The term *gewu* came from the *Book of Great Learning* (*Daxue*), one of the Four Books, and occupied a central place in the controversy among neo-Confucian scholars. To put it simply, Zhu Xi interpreted *gewu* as "investigation of things" whereas Wang Yangming reinterpreted it as the rectification of one's mind. Luo believed that Wang had misconstrued this classical text, because Wang's interpretation concentrated on the mind alone while neglecting the external world; actually, Luo held, *gewu* is a very important means by which the moral agent relates himself to the outside world. The two philosophers exchanged frank letters on various issues. Unfortunately, Wang died before Luo's second letter was sent.

As mentioned, Luo also criticized Buddhism. In his early years, Luo learned about Chan (Zen) Buddhism and felt that he had benefited from the *gong'an* (in Japanese, *koan*) and the *Chanzong zhengdaoge* (songs testifying to the truth in the Chan sect). It is clear that Luo read quite a lot of Buddhist texts. In his *Kunzhi ji*, many Buddhist scriptures, including the *Diamond Sutra, Platform Sutra*, and *Garland Sutra*, are mentioned, along with other Buddhist texts. However, after he became a lecturer at the imperial university in Nanjing, he took a Confucian attitude and criticized Buddhism for taking *jue*, the capacity for enlightenment, as our nature. In his opinion, humans are born with both *li* and a capacity for *jue*. In overlooking *li*, the Buddhists, according to Luo, also failed to see the importance of *ren* (humanity, benevolence). Luo also criticized the Buddhist notion of emptying the mind by eliminating opinions and thoughts. Luo held that the Confucian practice of *gewu* is an important method of moral and spiritual cultivation. In such an endeavor, *xin* (mind-heart) should never be vacuous; it should be filled with sincerity in the course of self-cultivation.

It is not easy to evaluate Luo properly in the history of Chinese philosophy. Modern Chinese scholars inspired by Marxism often call Luo's philosophy materialistic; in fact, Luo and Wang Tingxiang (1474–1544) have been called the two most important materialist philosophers of the Ming dynasty, representing a progressive challenge against the "subjective idealism" of the Cheng-Zhu school and the "objective idealism" of the Lu-Wang school. However, this evaluation is far from satisfactory. What is certain is that Luo's thought faced the rise of Wang Yangming's philosophy, and thus Luo no longer attracted many followers after his death. However, his *Kunzhi ji* spread to Korea and Japan and received considerable attention there. Yamanoi Yu in his *Ki no Shiso* notes the development of the philosophy of *qi* from Zhang Zai onward in neo-Confucianism, placing Luo at the beginning of this line of development in the Ming period. Luo's philosophy of *qi* gives him a special place in the intellectual history of the Ming because his position represents not just a move away from the then prevailing school of principle but also a challenge to the rising school of mind.

See also Confucianism: Ming; *Gewu* and *Zhizhi*.

Bibliography

Bloom, Irene, trans. and intro. *Knowledge Painfully Acquired: The K'un-Chih Chi by Lo Ch'in-shun*. New York: Columbia University Press, 1987. (This is the only authoritative English translation of Luo's work.)

———. "On the Abstraction of Ming Thought: Some Concrete Evidence from the Philosophy of Lo Ch'in-shun." In *Principle and Practicality: Essays in Neo-Confucianism and Practical Learning*, ed. William Theodore de Bary and Irene Bloom. New York: Columbia University Press, 1979, pp. 69–125.

Ching, Julia. *To Acquire Wisdom: The Way of Wang Yangming*. New York and London: Columbia University Press, 1976.

Ching, Julia, ed., with Chaoying Fang. *The Records of Ming Scholars*. Honolulu: University of Hawaii Press, 1987, pp. 213–218.

Cleary, J. C., trans. and ed. *Worldly Wisdom: Confucian Teachings of the Ming Dynasty*. Boston and London: Shambhala, 1991, pp. 159–162.

Cua, A. S. *The Unity of Knowledge and Action: A Study in Wang Yang-ming's Moral Psychology*. Honolulu: University of Hawaii Press, 1982.

Luo, Qinshun. *Kunzhi Ji* (Knowledge Painfully Acquired). Beijing: Zhonghua, 1990.

———. *Luo Zhengan Xiansheng cunkao* (Occasional Writings of Luo Qinshun). Siku quanshu zhenben, Series 4. Taipei: Commercial Press, 1973.

Onozawa, Seiichi, Fukunaga Mitsuji, and Yamanoi Yu, eds. *Ki no shiso* (The Philosophy of *Qi*). Tokyo: Tokyo Daigaku shuppan-kai, 1978.

Rong, Zhaozu. *Mingdai sixiang shi* (History of Thought in the Ming Dynsaty). Shanghai: Kaiming shudian, 1933.

Tu, Ching-i. "Lo Ch'in-shun." In *Dictionary of Ming Biography*, ed. L. Carrington Goodrich and Chaoying Fang. New York and London: Columbia University Press, 1976.

Wu, Kang. *Song Ming Lixue* (Song-Ming Neo-Confucianism). Taipei: Huaguo chubanshe, 1973. (Reprint of 1950 ed.)

Yamanoi, Yu. *Min Shin shiso shi no Kenkyu* (Studies on the History of Ming and Ch'ing Thought). Tokyo: Tokyo aigaku shupan-kai, 1980.

中國哲學

M

Mao Zedong (Mao Tse-tung)

Stuart R. SCHRAM

In the course of a long and eventful life, Mao Zedong (1893–1976) was shaped by various influences, both Chinese and western. The primary purpose of this article is not to lay out in detail his intellectual itinerary, but to assess his overall contribution as a philosopher. In so doing, it is not, however, appropriate to treat "Mao Zedong's thought" as though it were some kind of timeless essence that could be reconstructed on the basis of evidence selected arbitrarily from the whole corpus of his writings. In a China undergoing constant revolutionary upheaval, Mao's ideas often changed significantly from one decade to the next, and any serious assessment must take these changes into account. I will therefore review the main phases in Mao's development, before offering some generalizations by way of conclusion.

The ideas Mao entertained in his youth provide a useful prelude to the thought of his mature years. The young Mao was in many respects a typical representative of the May Fourth generation, but his first known writing dates from June 1912, before he had felt the impact of the "new tide of thought." In a middle-school essay in praise of Shang Yang, the eighteen-year-old Mao asserted: "Shang Yang's laws were good laws. If you have a look today at the four-thousand-odd years for which our country's history has been recorded, and the great political leaders who have pursued the welfare of the country and the happiness of the people, is not Shang Yang one of the very first on the list?" The fact that the people of Qin did not trust this great reformer he explained by the assumption that "at the beginning of anything out of the ordinary, the mass of the people always dislike it." The Chinese people's "ignorance and darkness during the past several millennia" had, he added, "brought our country to the brink of destruction" (Schram 1992, 1:5–6).

During his years at the Changsha First Normal School in 1913–1918, Mao's view of the relations between the ruler and the ruled underwent a radical transformation, in large part as a result of his exposure to western ideas. A landmark in this respect was his study, during the winter of 1917–1918, of Paulsen's *System of Ethics*. Among the authors to whom Mao was thus introduced were (in alphabetical order) Aristotle, Bentham, Fichte, Goethe, Hobbes, Kant, Leibniz, Mill, Nietzsche, Plato, Schopenhauer, Spencer, and Spinoza. As can be seen from this list, the western influences to which Mao was exposed at this time cannot be characterized simply as the "liberal tradition." Nonetheless, the role of the individual, and the importance of the freedom of the will, is the most prominent single theme in Mao's annotations to the Chinese translation of Paulsen (Schram 1992, 1:175–313).

"The value of the individual," Mao wrote, "is greater than that of the universe. Thus there is no greater crime than to suppress the individual or to violate particularity." And again, "The group in itself has no meaning, it has meaning only as a collectivity of individuals." And finally, "The only goal of human beings is to realize the self. Self-realization means to develop fully both our physical and our spiritual capacities to the highest." Building on this position, Mao formulated his conception of the hero: "The truly great person develops the . . . best, the greatest of the capacities of his original nature. . . . Everything that comes from outside his original nature, such as restraints and restrictions, is cast aside." Despite a passing reference to Mencius, who spoke of nourishing his "vast, flowing passion-nature," Mao's view of the hero plainly owed more to Nietzsche. At the same time, if the young Mao attached high priority to understanding and assimilating western ideas, this should perhaps be seen as reflecting not simply a critical attitude toward China's own traditions but impatience with tradition as such. His attention was drawn to a passage in which Paulsen cites Nietzsche as a protagonist of the trend toward calling into question established ideas and customs. "All our nation's two thousand years of scholarship may be said to be unthinking learning," Mao remarked.

Mao's ideas during the actual May Fourth period are best summed up in his article "The Great Union of the Popular Masses" (Schram 1992, 1:368–389). The key points include a shift from "superior men" to "the popular masses" as the main artisans of historical change, and a call for "revolution," in order to achieve "liberation" from "oppression," and thereby to remedy "the decadence of the state, the sufferings of humanity, and the darkness of society." Although the liberation of heroic energies was now to take place in the collective context of the various "unions" that were springing up, Mao stressed that a new climate could be created in China only by the exercise of freedom of thought and freedom of speech, which were "mankind's most precious, most joyous thing." Thus "Mr. Democracy" came to the fore.

Noting, in March 1920, that world civilization "can be divided into two currents, eastern and western," and adding, characteristically, "Eastern civilization can be said to be Chinese civilization," Mao gave it as his goal to form a "lucid concept" of all the various ideologies and doctrines at large in the world. He planned to do so by "distilling the essence of theories, Chinese and foreign, ancient and modern" (Schram 1992, 1:368–389). Increasingly, however, he tended to regard world culture as one. In July 1919, Mao had referred to the Renaissance and the Reformation as decisive events in a world history that he plainly saw as relevant to China and to himself. In 1920, he praised the example of Li Shizeng and others in sending students to France to learn "cosmopolitanism" (*shijie zhuyi*). "With cosmopolitanism," he wrote, "there is no place that one does not feel at ease. . . ." But as a Chinese patriot, he also added: "World-wide brotherhood needs to be built upon the foundation of national self-determination" (501).

In January 1921, Mao at last drew the explicit conclusion that Russia's proletarian dictatorship represented the model which China must apply (Schram 1994, 2:35–36). Earlier, Mao had expressed the view that despite the "antiquated" and otherwise undesirable traits of the Chinese mentality, Fukuzawa Yukichi's position regarding the lack of correspondence between "Oriental thought" and "the reality of life" was too one-sided. "In my opinion," he declared, "Western thought is not necessarily all correct either; very many parts of it should be transformed at the same time as Oriental thought" (127–133, passim). In a sense, this sentence sums up the problem Mao sought to resolve throughout his whole career: how could China become "civilized," rich, and powerful, while remaining Chinese? As noted above, Mao's exposure to westernizing influences was not limited to Marxism, and other currents of European thought played a significant role in his development. Whether he was dealing with liberalism or Leninism, however, Mao tenaciously sought to adapt and transform these ideologies, even as he espoused them and learned from them.

After Mao proclaimed his adherence to Leninism, there followed a decade and a half of revolutionary activity and armed struggle, during which he produced a large number of writings. Although most of these deal concretely with Chinese and international politics, and with military affairs, some of them, although not of an explicitly philosophical character, unquestionably have broader implications. Two themes are particularly prominent and significant. In September 1926, he argued, in his introduction to a collection of pamphlets on the peasant problem, that since "the feudal class in the countryside constitutes the only solid basis for the ruling class at home and for imperialism abroad," the peasants are in a better position than the workers to overthrow this reactionary power. "The Chinese revolution," he remarked, "has only this form and no other" (Schram 1994, 2:387–392). This statement should not be taken as a definitive characterization of Mao's revolutionary road, but it does represent an important dimension of his thinking for the remaining half century of his life.

In a letter of January 1930 to Lin Biao, Mao raised another issue central to his vision of revolution: the power of the human will. Lin, he wrote, was unduly pessimistic about the prospects for victory, because he had committed the error of "underestimating subjective forces and overestimating objective forces" (Schram 1995, 3:237). As Benjamin Schwartz has written:

> Many of us have stressed the degree to which Mao has . . . emphasized the power of the human will and de-emphasized the "objective forces" of history. None of this has been incompatible with a kind of deeper general faith that history (as a kind of general cosmic force) has been supportive of his efforts, or with the faith that history (as a series of events) will inevitably lead to Communism. It was the October Revolution which kindled this faith. (1977, 22)

During the period of the Jiangxi Soviet Republic, in 1931–1934, Mao wrote little of any relevance to broad general issues. Following the Long March, in the relatively peaceful and secure surroundings of Yan'an, he produced in the space of just over a year three works that still figure among the most significant expositions of his philosophy.

The first of these was a series of lectures on dialectical materialism, delivered in July and August 1937, of which the concluding sections in revised form later appeared in the *Selected Works* as "On Practice" and "On Contradiction." The second, *On Protracted War*, consisting of lectures given in May and June 1938, may not appear on the face of it to address philosophical issues but is in fact regarded by Chinese philosophers as one of his most important works. The third, *On the New Stage*, Mao's report to the Sixth Plenum of the Chinese Communist Party Central Committee in October 1938, is remarkable above all because it was there that he first put forward the sinification of Marxism (*Makesizhuyi de zhongguohua*) as a slogan.

Before Mao could talk about sinifying Marxism, it was necessary to assert himself as a Marxist philosopher. Before 1937, Mao had acquired some knowledge of Marxism from translations and secondary sources but had not had the leisure to study Marxist theory systematically. Beginning in November 1936, he read and annotated in considerable detail translations of two Soviet works on dialectical materialism, before producing his own lectures on the same subject (Mao, 1988, 5–189; extracts trans. in Knight 1990, 267–280).

Not surprisingly, there was a substantial measure of correspondence between the views Mao put forward in the summer of 1937 and the orthodox Soviet interpretation of Marxism that he had just been studying. There were also significant differences, which I will note below in discussing the definitive versions of "On Practice" and "On Contradiction," as revised for the *Selected Works* in the early 1950s. In 1937, however, Mao treated Marxist philosophy as defined in Moscow with a veneration that found expression in the following passage of his lecture notes:

> Because of the backwardness of the evolution of Chinese society, the philosophical current of dialectical materialism developing in China today has resulted not from taking over and reforming our own philosophical heritage, but from the study of Marxism-Leninism. Nevertheless, if we wish to make the dialectical materialist current of thought penetrate deeply and continue to develop in China, give firm direction to the Chinese revolution, and lead it onto the road of complete victory, then we must struggle with all the outworn philosophical theories presently existing in China, raise the flag of criticism on the ideological front throughout the whole country, and thereby liquidate (*qingsuan*) the philosophical heritage of ancient China. Only thus can we attain our goal. (Takeuchi 1984, 5:196)

Half a year later, in May and June 1938, Mao delivered his lectures *On Protracted War*. Broadly speaking, this work is regarded as important in China because it is perceived as a model application of Marxist dialectics to the military domain, which was of such decisive importance in Mao's career and in the history of the Chinese revolution. Two themes are regarded as particularly relevant: the argument, which runs through the whole work, that China's weakness can be turned into strength, while Japan's strength can be turned into weakness; and Mao's emphasis on the importance of "conscious activity" (*zijue de nengdongxing*) and of subjective factors in shaping the course of events. Mao links these two dimensions by arguing that the possibility of turning weakness into strength depends on "correct subjective direction." "Conscious activity," writes Mao, "is a distinctive characteristic of man, especially of man at war. . . . The stage of action for commanders in a war must be built upon objective conditions, but on this stage they can direct the performance of many living dramas, full of sound and color, of power and grandeur . . ." (Schram 1989, 55).

In October 1938, barely a year after calling for the liquidation of the Chinese tradition, Mao launched the famous slogan about the sinification of Marxism, declaring: "There is no such thing as abstract Marxism, but only concrete Marxism . . . , that is, Marxism applied to the concrete struggle in the concrete conditions prevailing in China." In the context of this process of sinification, the assimilation of the legacy of the Chinese past, from Confucius to Sun Yat-sen, "itself becomes a method that aids considerably in guiding the present great movement" (Schram 1989, 70). Thus, not only must Chinese revolutionaries apply creatively the ideology of western origin called Marxism, but they could also make use of another, distinctive framework of analysis, drawn from their own country's history and tradition.

Unquestionably, Mao regarded himself, and would continue to regard himself, as a Marxist. Nevertheless, in thus placing Marxism and the Chinese heritage side by side he raised by implication the question whether in the last analysis he was bent on the sinification of Marxism or on the Marxification of Chinese thought. In editing this text for republication in the early 1950s, Mao was clearly aware of this ambiguity, and sought to dispel it by deleting with his own brush the sentence characterizing the assimilation of the Chinese past as a "method" (letter to the author from Gong Yuzhi and Pang Xianzhi, 21 March 1988), but the problem continued to hover over his thought for the rest of his life.

During the Yan'an period, Mao produced no detailed assessment of which aspects of traditional Chinese thought could and should be assimilated, but indications regarding his views can be found in letters of 1939 discussing drafts of articles by Chen Boda on Confucius and Mozi, which were subsequently published in the authoritative organ *Jiefang*. "Confucius's system," wrote Mao, "was idealist, but as partial truth it is correct. . . . Not only Confucius, but we too, are engaged in 'rectifying names.' " The difference, he added was that "Confucius gave primacy to the names, while we give primacy to reality." Not surprisingly, in view of the importance he attached to the conscious participation of human beings in shaping history, noted above, Mao added, "A strong point of idealist philosophy is its emphasis on conscious activity. . . . We should mention Confucius's strong point in this respect" (Mao 1983, 144–152).

Commenting on Chen's article "The Philosophical Thought of Mozi," Mao began by stating, "It is a great contribution of yours to have identified a Chinese Heraclitus." Since Heraclitus had been called by Lenin "one of the founders of dialectics," Mao suggested that the article should be retitled "The Philosphical Ideas of Mozi: An Ancient Materialist Philosopher." Regarding the doctrine of the mean, Mao asserted—in light of Mozi's call for "maintaining a balance between the two without veering to one side" and the exhortation in the *Doctrine of the Mean*, "stand erect in the middle and do not incline to either side"—that "the two schools, Confucian and Mohist, mean the same thing although they use different words. The Mohists made no special advance." He went on, however, to criticize Chen Boda's gloss on Mozi's formulation as showing that "Mozi saw that one particular substantive disposition contains two different sides and not veering to either one side or the other is the only correct way" as "rather inappropriate, because it makes the Mohist school out to be eclectic." Mao summed up his own view as follows:

> A substantive disposition does have two sides, but in the course of a single process only one is the principal side, and it is relatively stable, so there must necessarily be some inclination, a veering towards this side. . . . Therefore, what Mozi means by "without veering to either side" is to avoid deviation to the right or the left, or veering towards a different substantive disposition, and not to avoid deviation towards one of the two sides of a particular substantive disposition (actually this would not be deviation, but rather, precisely, correctness). This is the explanation that should be made if the Moist school is, indeed, dialectical materialist. (1983, 140–143)

It is evident from these extracts that during the Yan'an period, Mao automatically approached every topic, including ancient Chinese philosophy, in terms of Marxist categories. But it seems equally obvious that he retained strong ties to the world of traditional Chinese thought and welcomed the opportunity to engage in a discussion of it.

In the early 1940s, an important new dimension began to appear in Mao Zedong's thinking about the dynamics of the historical process. He had long been concerned with the interaction between the leaders and the people, and with the relationship between China and the west. He had also referred in passing, in the original version (1937) of his discussion of contradictions, to the contradiction between the productive forces and the relations of production, but in rather vague and abstract terms (Knight 1990, 177, 185). Now, as a result of his experience in governing the communist-controlled border region, he began to take a more concrete interest in economic development as a factor in social change.

The details of economic and financial policy, to which Mao devoted a book-length report in December 1942 (Watson 1980), are not relevant here. More to the point is the following statement of May 1944:

> If we want to strengthen and guarantee China's national independence, we must industrialize. . . . Economic work, particularly in industry, . . . is the thing that determines all the others; it decides military, political, cultural, intellectual, moral, and religious matters, and it determines the changes in a society. (Takeuchi 1971, 9, 97–98)

This formulation might be seen as defining the main thrust of Mao's conception of building socialism in the early 1950s. It can be argued that this is, in a broad sense, a philosophical issue. In China, however, what is called Mao Zedong's philosophical thought is defined more narrowly, essentially as epistemology and Marxist dialectics, though these topics are given a certain concreteness by stressing Mao's emphasis on investigating and learning from Chinese reality, and applying dialectics to China, as important dimensions of knowing and changing the world (Knight 1992, passim).

To shed light on these issues, let us briefly discuss Mao's two major philosophical writings, "On Practice" and "On Contradiction," in their final published form. These are still considered, in many respects, the key to understanding Mao Zedong as a philosopher. Mao made relatively few changes in "On Practice" before it appeared in Volume 1 of the *Selected Works* in 1951. Nick Knight holds that there is an irreconcilable contradiction in Mao's epistemology as presented in this text between a rationalist and an empiricist approach. On the one hand, truth is derived from practice; but on the other hand, Mao postulates the existence of "essences," and of objective laws providing criteria of truth. Knight suggests that the rationalist element is more marked in the original text of 1937, though the differences are in fact not very great (1990, 24–30). In any case, Knight agrees with Chinese philosophers who argue that Mao's epistemology is greatly superior to Stalin's, because it postulates that knowledge originates in practice, not simply in the relationship between matter and spirit (1992, 38–40, 233–246).

The situation regarding "On Contradiction" is more complex. Despite significant rewriting in 1951, this essay was not, as some western scholars argued in the 1960s, a forgery concocted after 1949 to establish Mao's credentials as a Marxist philosopher. Chapter 3 of *Lecture Notes on Dialectical Materialism* of 1937 did contain much of the substance of the text published in 1952 in *Selected Works*, including the insistence on the importance of the "principal contradiction" and the "principal aspect of the contradiction," and the argument that the superstructure, and subjective factors, could play a leading and decisive role in the process of social change (Knight 1990, 154–229; Schram 1989, 61–69).

At the same time, it should be noted that Chapter 3 of *Lecture Notes on Dialectical Materialism*, "Materialist Dialectics," was never completed. In the introduction to this chapter, Mao invoked the three basic laws making up the materialist theory of dialectics, as defined by Engels—unity of contradictions, transformation of quality into quantity and vice versa, and negation of the negation—and stated that he would take up each in turn (Knight 1990, 121–127). In 1937, because his attention was occupied by other matters following the outbreak of the Sino-Japanese war, Mao completed only Part 1 of this chapter, dealing with the law of the unity and struggle of contradictions, and in revising the work for publication after 1949, he did not go on to write the two missing parts.

In fact, Mao did not find it easy to recast this text to his own satisfaction. In May 1951, he informed the editors of his *Selected Works* that he was still not happy with it, and it should be held over for publication in the second volume. In the end, among many other changes, he deleted Section 2 of the discussion of the law of contradictions, "The Law of Identity in Formal Logic and the Law of Contradiction in Dialectics." According to those in Beijing well informed about these matters, Mao did so because he had become convinced after reading Stalin's *Marxism and Questions of Linguistics* that the view he had put forward in 1937 was oversimplified (personal communication from Gong Yuzhi to the author, 1988). It should also be noted, however, that the long passage thus deleted contained the only references to the law of the negation of the negation in Chapter 3 of the lectures, which served as the basis for "On Contradiction." Formal logic, Mao had argued in 1937, cannot "acknowledge the importance of contradictoriness and the negation of the negation within things and concepts," so its partisans "advocate the rigid and inflexible law of identity" and the law of the excluded middle (Knight 1990, 159–163). Whether or not the elimination of this passage in 1951 was a conscious step on Mao's part toward his subsequent repudiation of the "negation of the negation," which will be discussed below, remains an open question.

Another distinctive aspect of Mao's approach to Marxist dialectics, the importance he attached to the "principal contradiction," can be linked directly to his subtle understanding of Chinese reality. A Marxist revolutionary in a society of the type analyzed by Marx himself, which was perceived as increasingly polarized into capitalists and proletarians, could be in no doubt as to which were the basic contradictions between classes, or between the productive forces and the mode of production. Moreover, this pattern was expected to remain more or less the same until the conflict was resolved by revolution. In China, on the other hand, where neither the internal situation nor relations with foreign powers were stable or predictable, it was not merely an intriguing intellectual problem but a pressing tactical necessity to determine which factor, or contradiction, was crucial or dominant at a given time. This context undoubtedly played an important role in shaping Mao's theory of contradictions.

While widely divergent assessments of the philosophical level of "On Practice" and "On Contradiction" have been put forward in recent years, both in China and abroad, there can be no doubt that in these works Mao used Marxist terminology and reasoned in Marxist terms. During the remaining quarter century of his life, he continued on the whole to do so. At the same time, because he was much more confident in his use of Marxist categories than he had been earlier, he felt able to incorporate a wide range of ideas and insights drawn from the Chinese tradition into that theoretical framework. One of the most striking expressions of Mao's self-assurance in this respect can be found in his talk of August 1956 to Chinese music workers, in which he asserted that China must and could take as its guide a theory imported from the west, while still remaining itself. Zhang Zhidong's formula "Chinese learning as the substance, western learning for practical use" was therefore wrong. Marxism was a "general truth which has universal application," and this "fundamental theory produced in the west" constituted the substance or *ti* of China's new revolutionary order (Schram 1974, 85–86). But within the framework defined by Chinese Marxism—in other words, by Mao Zedong's thought—everything precious in China's heritage could find a place.

During the three years from his proclamation of the "Hundred Flowers" policy in 1956 to the bitter clashes at Lushan in the aftermath of the "Great Leap Forward," Mao's numerous and important utterances were focused primarily on policy issues such as the treatment of the intellectuals, the political and economic advantages of agricultural collectivization, and the possibility of unprecedentedly rapid economic growth. In dealing with these matters, he did, however, raise some questions with philosophical implications. The crucial importance of "conscious action" on the part of the masses in carrying forward the revolution, and the need to guide and inspire the masses so as to release this great force, remained one of the most central themes. Not surprisingly, Mao linked this objective to the experience of the struggle for power. In a directive of early 1958, he wrote:

> Our revolution is like fighting a war. After winning one battle, we must immediately put forward new tasks. In this way, we can maintain the revolutionary enthusiasm of the cadres and the masses, and diminish their self-satisfaction, since they have no time to be satisfied with themselves even if they wanted to; new tasks keep pressing in, and everyone devotes his mind to the question of how to fulfil the new tasks. (Schram 1971, 227)

In a speech of January 1958, Mao said:

> Now our enthusiasm has been aroused. Ours is an ardent nation, now swept by a burning tide. There is a good metaphor for this: our nation is like an atom. . . . When this atom's nucleus is smashed the thermal energy released will have really tremendous power. We shall be able to do things which we could not do before. When our nation has this great energy we shall catch up with Britain in fifteen years. . . . (Schram 1974, 92–93)

In August 1958 at Beidaihe, during the high tide of the Great Leap, Mao asserted once again, "The spontaneity of the masses has always been an element inherent in communism" (MacFarquhar 1989, 430).

In 1960–1961, reflecting on the collapse of his hope that communism was already at hand, Mao returned to the consideration of basic questions of Marxist theory. Commenting on a Soviet textbook of political economy, he declared, "The book shows that its authors do not have a dialectical method. One has to think philosophically to write an economics text" (Roberts 1977, 109). "All revolutionary history shows," Mao asserted:

> that the full development of new productive forces is not the prerequisite for the transformation of backward production relations. Our revolution began with Marxist-Leninist propaganda, which served to create new public opinion in society, and thereby to push forward the revolution. . . . It is a general rule that you cannot solve the problem of ownership, and go on to develop the productive forces in a big way, until you have created public opinion and seized political power. (Schram 1989, 5)

This view that, while change could be triggered by an incremental development of the productive forces, fundamental changes could only follow political revolution, was in harmony with Mao's consistent stress on the importance of subjective forces, and of the superstructure. Criticizing Stalin's *Economic Problems of Socialism in the USSR*, Mao complained that it spoke "only of the production relations, not of the superstructure nor politics, nor the role of the people." And he added, "The conscious activity of the party and the masses is not sufficiently brought out" (Roberts 1977, 136).

Despite his continuing use of Marxist categories and modes of analysis, Mao sometimes espoused positions that raised doubts as to whether the substance of his thinking was Marxist or Chinese. Hints of this new trend can be discerned in his view regarding what has been called the "dialectics of backwardness." In his "Reading Notes" of 1960 on the Soviet manual of political economy, a section is devoted to the topic "Is revolution in backward countries more difficult?" Needless to say, Mao concluded that it was not. The poisons of the bourgeoisie were, he said, extremely virulent in the advanced countries of the west after two or three centuries of capitalism, and affected every stratum of society, including the working class. Consequently, "the more backward the economy, the easier, and not the more difficult, the transition from capitalism to socialism. The poorer people are, the more they want revolution" (Schram 1989, 192–193).

Such a passage clearly reflects the emphasis on the human and moral dimension of politics that is so much a part of Mao's thought, and of the Chinese tradition, but it does not constitute an explicit statement of a philosophical position. On 18 August 1964, Mao did say in a talk on philosophy with a small group of comrades: "You are foreign philosophers; I am a native philosopher (*Nimen shi yang zhexue, wo shi tu zhexue*)." In the course of this long conversation, he raised a number of important issues. Among those that have attracted the most attention is Mao's repudiation of two of the three basic laws of Marxist dialectics, which he had himself endorsed in his lectures of 1937 on dialectical materialism. Responding to a question from Kang Sheng as to whether the Chairman "could say something about the problem of the three categories," Mao declared:

> Engels talked about the three categories, but as for me I don't believe in two of those categories. . . . The juxtaposition, on the same level, of the transformation of quality and quantity into one another, the negation of the negation, and the law of the unity of opposites is "triplism," not monism. The most basic thing is the unity of opposites. The transformation of quality and quantity into one another is the unity of the opposites quality and quantity. There is no such thing as the negation of the negation. Affirmation, negation, affirmation, negation . . . in the development of things, every link in the chain of events is both affirmation and negation. Slave-holding society negated primitive society, but with reference to feudal society it constituted, in turn, the affirmation. Feudal society constituted the negation in relation to slave-holding society but it was in turn the affirmation with reference to capitalist society. Capitalist society was the negation in relation to feudal society, but it is, in turn, the affirmation in relation to socialist society. (Schram 1974, 225–226)

Although Lenin had stated that the law of the unity of opposites is the most basic law of dialectics, thereby placing it in some sense above the other two laws, and Mao had reiterated this view in "On Contradiction," it was nonetheless a notable step to deny Engels's other two formulations the status of distinct laws at all. This is the only full and explicit statement along these lines available to us, but its authenticity is difficult to impugn. Apart from the fact that the existing record of Mao's conversation was taken down by Gong Yuzhi, then a bright young specialist in the philosophy of science, and recently vice president of the Central Party School, the way the topic is introduced by Kang Sheng makes crystal-clear that Mao was known to have something to say about it, and Kang was simply giving him the opportunity.

If we take this statement at face value, "the unity of the opposites quality and quantity," though demoted to the status of a subsidiary law, is not called into question. As for the "negation of the negation," Mao appears to be calling simply for a change in terminology which he had first introduced in 1958 but had not consistently followed thereafter. In "Sixty Articles on Work Methods" of January 1958, Mao substituted "affirmation and negation" for "negation of the negation" as the name of the third law (Schram 1971, 228). Some Chinese scholars argue that this is a more accurate name, free of the idealism of the Hegelian triad (Xu in Knight 1992, 219–232). Yang Chao, who had been a member of Mao's small philosophical study group in Yan'an when he was preparing the lectures on dialectical materialism, declares that in Mao's view most of the previous phase was eliminated at each negation. Mao had therefore replaced the old formulation because he thought it implied that the end result of the whole process was a return to the *initial* affirmation (Yang Chao 1980, 199–217).

Zhou Yang, on the other hand, judged that Mao's misgivings about the old name reflected a tendency to exaggerate the absolutely antithetical and mutually exclusive nature of successive moments in the dialectical process, and to lose sight of the fact that "negation" meant the supersession of some elements of the thing negated, while retaining others and incorporating them into a new synthesis. In so doing, he concluded, Mao opened the door to the destructive excesses of the Cultural Revolution (Zhou Yang 1983, 4). It can also be argued that the replacement of the three laws of dialectics by the single "basic law" of the unity of opposites signaled a drift back toward the traditional Chinese dialectics of the *yin* and the *yang*, though whether or not a return to Daoism might have contributed to the chaos of the Cultural Revolution remains, of course, open to discussion (Schram 1989, 141).

The argument that Mao was returning to his roots, while not necessarily correct, is given some support by the fact that in 1965 he explicitly rejected the idea of a western or Marxist *ti* which he had endorsed a decade earlier:

> At the end of the Ch'ing [Qing] dynasty some people advocated "Chinese learning for the substance, Western learning for practical application." The substance was like our General Line, which cannot be changed. We cannot adopt Western learning as the substance, nor can we use the substance of the democratic republic. . . . We can only use Western technology. (Schram 1974, 234–235)

Once again, Mao repeated the statement, "You are foreign-style philosophers, I am a native-style philosopher" (239). This assertion could, of course, be taken to mean simply that he was a Marxist revolutionary whose thought had been thoroughly sinified. He did still speak of moving toward communism, but his vision of the future opened up far vaster horizons. In his talks of August 1964, recalling that Marx had characterized man as a toolmaker and a social animal, Mao observed:

> In reality, it is only after undergoing a million years [of evolution] that man developed a large brain and a pair of hands. In the future, animals will continue to develop. I

> don't believe that men alone are capable of having two hands. Can't horses, cows, sheep evolve? Can only monkeys evolve? . . .
>
> The life of dialectics is the continuous movement toward opposites. Mankind will also finally meet its doom. When the theologians talk about doomsday, they are pessimistic and terrify people. We say the end of mankind . . . will produce something more advanced than mankind. Mankind is still in its infancy. Engels spoke of moving from the realm of necessity to the realm of freedom, and said that freedom is the understanding of necessity. This sentence . . . only says one half and leaves the rest unsaid. Does merely understanding it make you free? Freedom is the understanding of necessity *and* the transformation of necessity—one has some work to do too. (Schram 1974, 220–221, 228)

Mao's concluding remark, "One has some work to do too," clearly reflects the perspective of the man who had been the ruler of China for a quarter of a century and saw it as his duty to set tasks for the Chinese people, one after the other. But it also continues the emphasis on "conscious activity" that had long characterized Mao's thought.

In his speech of December 1965, Mao reiterated the view that "there is only one basic law and that is the law of contradiction. Quality and quantity, positive and negative, external appearance and essence, content and form, necessity and freedom, possibility and reality, etc., are all cases of the unity of opposites" (Schram 1974, 240).

Was Mao, then, primarily and essentially a Marxist dialectician, or was he guided not by an "ism" but by a more loosely constructed and inclusive "thought"? In 1942, when the political and ideological primacy of Mao Zedong was being established in Yan'an, one of Mao's own secretaries wrote an article in praise of "Maoism" (*Mao Zedong zhuyi*; see Zhang 1942). The term was, however, soon dropped, at Mao's own request. His Marxist-Leninist thought, Mao declared in April 1943, still did not constitute a mature system and should not be played up too much, except for a few speeches during the "rectification" campaign. Moreover, Stalin himself had spoken only of "Leninism-Stalinism" and had not ventured to talk about "Stalinism," so he might be displeased if Mao laid claim to his own "ism" (Gao 2000, 607). In August 1948, the question was raised again, and Mao replied that at present there was "no such thing as Mao Zedongism," so it could not be discussed. Apart from the works of Marx, Engels, Lenin, and Stalin, the object of study should be the "experience of the Chinese revolution," as analyzed in the light of Marxist theory in the writings of "Chinese Communists (including Mao Zedong)" (Mao 1999, 5:123–124).

Two decades later, when the alliance with Moscow had given place to open hostility, and the cult of Mao had risen to unprecedented heights, the official terminology remained the same, though some Red Guard extremists tried to raise the banner of "Mao Zedongism." Thus, apart from Mao's evident concern in the 1940s about offending Stalin, it may well be that he saw his own intellectual contribution not solely in terms of a new stage in the development of Marxism-Leninism-Stalinism but in a broader context, as the reflections of a Chinese Marxist on China, the world, and life in general.

In his later years, Mao's musings, and his obsession with his own power, led him to a vision of the future that culminated in the disasters of the Great Leap Forward and the Cultural Revolution. The official judgment on the man is that, despite the terrible mistakes he made, he was a great revolutionary leader. This point does not concern us here, but what of his doctrine? An interesting clue to the Chinese assessment of Mao as a thinker is provided by the reemergence of the term "sinification of Marxism," which Mao himself had struck from the text of his report of 1938 when revising it in 1950, presumably to avoid offending Stalin. As recently as 1990 this expression was still viewed with suspicion, but in 1991 the full original text of Mao's report of October 1938 containing this passage was reprinted in an official publication of the Central Party School (*Zhonggong zhongyang wenjian xuanji*, 11:557–662). In 1994, a pioneering book on this topic appeared (Yang Kueisong 1994); and in 1998, on the 105th anniversary of Mao's birth, a full-scale symposium was held in Changsha, with the participation of many leading party officials and intellectuals (see *Mao Zedong Deng Xiaoping yu makesizhuyi zhongguohua*, 1999). The function of this term today is basically the same as it was in 1938. It indicates that Mao Zedong was a genuine Marxist, and therefore that the party he led to victory was a genuine communist party; but at the same time, it underscores the fact that he was thoroughly Chinese, and his thought should therefore speak also to noncommunist patriots. Time will tell how convincing this argument proves to be in enhancing the standing of Mao as a philosopher.

See also Marxism in China; Shang Yang.

Bibliography

Gao, Hua. *Hong taiyang shi zenyang shengqide: Yan'an zhengfeng yundong de lailong qumai*. Hong Kong: Zhongwen daxue chubanshe, 2000.

Gong, Yuzhi, Pang Xianzhi, and Shi Zhongquan. *Mao Zedong de dushu shenghuo*. Beijing: Sanlian shudian, 1986.

Knight, Nick. *Mao Zedong on Dialectical Materialism: Writings on Philosophy, 1937*. Armonk, N.Y.: Sharpe, 1990.
———, ed. *The Philosophical Thought of Mao Zedong: Studies from China, 1981–1989*. In *Chinese Studies in Philosophy*, 23(3–4). Armonk, N.Y.: Sharpe, 1992
MacFarquhar, Roderick, et al., eds. *The Secret Speeches of Chairman Mao: From the Hundred Flowers to the Great Leap Forward*. Cambridge, Mass.: Harvard University Press, 1989.
Mao, Zedong. *Jianguo yilai Mao Zedong wengao*, Vols. 1–13. Beijing: Zhongyang wenxian chubanshe, 1987–1998.
———. *Mao Zedong junshi wenji*, Vols. 1–6. Beijing: Junshi kexue chubanshe and Zhongyang wenxian chubanshe, 1993.
———. *Mao Zedong shuxin xuanji*. Beijing: Renmin chubanshe, 1983.
———. *Mao Zedong wenji*. Beijing: Renmin chubanshe. Vols. 1–2, 1993. Vols. 3–5, 1996. Vols. 6–8, 1999.
———. *Mao Zedong xuanji*. Beijing: Renmin chubanshe. Vols. 1–4, 1951–1960. Vol. 5, 1977.
———. *Mao Zedong zhexue pizhuji*. Beijing: Zhongyang wenxian chubanshe, 1988.
———. *Selected Works of Mao Tse-tung*. Beijing: Foreign Languages Press. Vols. 1–4, 1961–1965. Vol. 5, 1977.
Mao Zedong Deng Xiaoping yu makesizhuyi zhongguohua. Beijing: Zhongyang wenxian chubanshe, 1999.
Roberts, Moss. *A Critique of Soviet Economics by Mao Tse-tung*. New York: Monthly Review Press, 1977.
Schram, Stuart R., ed. *Mao's Road to Power: Revolutionary Writings, 1912–1949*. Armonk, N.Y.: Sharpe. Vol. 1, 1992. Vol. 2, 1994. Vol. 3, 1995. Vol. 4, 1997. Vol. 5, 1999. (Ten-volume work in progress. Vols. 6 and 7 were scheduled to appear in 2001.)
Schram, Stuart R. *Mao Tse-tung Unrehearsed*. Harmondsworth: Penguin, 1974. (See also U.S. ed., *Chairman Mao Talks to the People*, New York: Pantheon, 1974.)
———. "Mao Tse-tung and the Theory of the Permanent Revolution, 1958–1969." *China Quarterly*, No. 46, April–June 1971.
———. *The Thought of Mao Tse-tung*. Cambridge: Cambridge University Press, 1989.
Schwartz, Benjamin I. "The Philosopher." In *Mao Tse-tung in the Scales of History*, ed. Dick Wilson. Cambridge: Cambridge University Press, 1977, pp. 9–34.
Takeuchi, Minoru, ed. *Mao Zedong ji*, Vols. 1–10, 1st ed. Tokyo: Hokubosha, 1970–1972. (See also 2nd ed., Tokyo: Sososha, 1983.)
———, ed. *Mao Zedong ji: Bujuan*, Vols. 1–9 and unnumbered index vol. Tokyo: Sososha, 1983–1986.
Wakeman, Frederic. *History and Will: Philosophical Perspectives of Mao Tse-tung's Thought*. Berkeley: University of California Press, 1973.
Watson, Andrew, ed. and trans. *Mao Zedong and the Political Economy of the Border Region: A Translation of Mao's "Economic and Financial Problems."* Cambridge: Cambridge University Press, 1980.
Yang, Chao. *Mao Zedong sixiang de xin fazhan*. Chengdu: Sichuan Renmin chubanshe, 1985.
———. *Weiwulun bianzhengfa de ruogan lilun wenti*. Chengdu: Sichuan renmin chubanshe, 1980.
Yang, Chungui, and Li Huolin. *Zhexuejia Mao Zedong*. Beijing: Zhonggong zhongyang dangxiao chubanshe, 1994.
Yang, Kueisong. *Makesizhuyi zhongguohua de lishi jincheng*. Zhengzhou: Henan renmin chubanshe, 1994.
Zhang, Ruxin. "Xuexi he zhangwo Mao Zedong de lilun he celüe." *Jiefang ribao*, 18 and 19 February 1942.
Zhonggong zhongyang wenjian xuanji, Vol. 11. Beijing: Zhonggong zhongyang dangxiao chubanshe, 1991.
Zhou, Yang. "Guanyu Makesizhuyi de jige lilun wenti tantao." *Renmin ribao*, 16 March 1983.

Marxism in China

David Kelly

Chinese thought in the twentieth century was shaped by a series of western intellectual doctrines, including social Darwinism, idealism, pragmatism, anarchism, socialism, and liberalism. The most far-reaching in its influence was Marxism, a doctrine emphasizing class struggle in history, with the goal of a classless, communist society to be achieved through the revolutionary emancipation of the proletariat. Serving this goal, Marxist philosophy proclaims itself to be absolute truth, a scientific view of reality based on irrefutable axioms and methods. At the opening of the twenty-first century, the Peoples' Republic of China remained a bastion of Marxism, albeit in the distinctive Chinese form of Marxism–Leninism–Mao Zedong thought. While increasingly overshadowed by other modes of thought, it provides an essential background for modern Chinese intellectual history generally, and modern Chinese philosophy in particular.

The Chinese Communist Party (CCP) proclaims Marxism as its official ideology, holding it above challenge as absolute, scientific truth. On Taiwan and more widely abroad, Marxism, in general and in Chinese form, is rejected just as absolutely, especially since the collapse of communism in the former Soviet Union in

1989. In academic settings, many outside observers, and not a few Chinese citizens in private, massively discount the intellectual content of the doctrines of Mao Zedong and his close collaborators in the CCP. All the discussions of dialectics, principal and secondary contradictions, refutations of dogmatism and opportunism, and the like are on this view no more than a symbolic code without philosophical substance. The symbols and power over their correct or canonical adoption in the intellectual community are applied expressly to further the political interests of aspirants for supreme power within the CCP (Meissner 1990).

Other scholars find on the contrary a core philosophical vision which, while committed to practice as a touchstone of intellectual legitimacy, is robust in the face of changing political emphases and fortunes (Dirlik and Meisner 1989; Knight 1996). A modified form of that perspective is adopted here. Even if Chinese Marxism does act as a power-political code, this code has to make reference to some theoretical content if its target audience is to understand and act on it. The "code" perspective tends to treat unfairly the lived, historical experiences of Chinese philosophers and others who take this content seriously. Vast numbers of people in mainland China accepted that what they were experiencing was the direct expression of the philosophy of Marx and Engels, Lenin and Stalin, and indeed Mao.

Chinese Marxism started as a loose set of appropriations acquired on the run by radicals intent on gaining power and transforming their society. Beginning in the 1930s, Marxism was given a Chinese vernacular expression. By the mid–1950s it came to possess an elaborate doctrinal system propounded in textbooks and study guides. A massive apparatus of popular culture continues to transmit echoes of these abstractions through the press, in bookstores, on stages, and on television, to the point where it is often academic to define where the doctrine ends and contemporary secular culture begins.

As formal doctrine, Chinese Marxism is often expressed as a system of tightly interwoven ontological and epistemological concepts, such as dialectics, materialism, and reflection. These, however, cannot be understood in isolation from the wider context of Marxism as a vision of social development. This vision has three major aspects: the analysis of all societies in terms of the concept of class; a theory of history as a sequence of class struggles; and its "emancipatory normative" theory, i.e., a theory purporting to define human bondage, and thereby to enhance freedom (Wright 1993). Marxist philosophy, understood as intellectual discourse separate from general social, political, or economic theory, is often concerned with the third category: emancipatory normative theory. This theory was arguably central to the thinking of the philosophically trained Marx (Walicki 1995). But just as the three aspects form a tightly interlocking corpus of ideas, so the vast series of downstream discourses generated by each (including those belonging to philosophy) continue to resonate with logical or discursive implications of the others. For instance, aesthetics, one of the arguably open and pluralist branches of philosophy in Chinese Marxism, is typically developed within the "emancipatory normative" node. Leaving overt politicization aside, the region of possible debate in aesthetics is to a great extent framed by the rise and fall of views regarding class analysis and the theory of historical trajectory.

The evolution of the schema of formal doctrine in these terms can be divided into three historical phases or periods, each with its own dominant motif:

1. *Initial reception.* A strong pragmatic drive to acquire an ideological framework that might serve party political organization, military mobilization, and eventual national integration.
2. *Mao Zedong's ascendency.* An interest in legitimating the new ruling elite both within the international Communist movement and as against other local rivals.
3. *Post-Mao era.* A quest to reform or shore up the entire social order by strategically replacing elements of the now seemingly discredited, ossified, disabled, or otherwise defunct Maoist structure.

In the last of these periods, characterized by ideological decentralization and even fragmentation, different elements could be considered candidates for replacement, the choice reflecting one's position on the spectrum of positions running from "conservative" to "reformist." As a side effect, the 1980s became a golden age of independent Marxist philosophy, though, as we shall see, this was something of a twilight of the gods. An appreciable turning to "western Marxism" reflecting disillusionment with later accretions of Lenin, Stalin, and Mao and corresponding interest in the young Marx coincided with widely publicized rejection of Marx in toto.

Phase 1: Initial Reception

In 1920, following the Bolshevik revolution in Russia, Chinese communism was established by small groups of idealistic professors and their students. By 1927, the disciplined Chinese Communist Party had established its identity, and from the ashes of near destruction had begun its rise to total power over the mainland. The career of Chinese Marxism, while not totally identical with that of the CCP, was increasingly determined by the latter. After 1949 the already monistic ideological scheme was applied to society with the whole weight of the political apparatus, and the realm of critical thought narrowed to those few minute apertures unsuitable for determination in advance.

Before the 1920s, progressive intellectual circles had little understanding of Marxism. Anarchism and non-Marxian socialism were more familiar in radical circles, which typically were strata composed of students and other intellectuals, forming and re-forming with each school generation (Luk 1990, 17). Following hard on the May Fourth movement of 1919 and attendant disillusion with the new world order emerging from the peace talks at Versailles, leading figures of the New Culture movement, in particular Li Dazhao (1883–1927), began to study and publicize Marxism. Its application to Chinese politics was always shaped by factors extrinsic to the doctrine itself. One great advantage was its ability to create cellular networks of committed radicals, which evolved seamlessly into a mobilized mass party supporting professional revolutionaries (Dirlik 1978, 1989). Again, there was a fit between Marxist rhetoric and the "New Culture" intellectuals' rejection of the republican political sphere as hopelessly corrupt and divorced from social reality. Rather than emerging from actual class struggle (as had happened in Europe), Marxism was taken on as a package because it filled a void; a working-class movement that might fulfill its program was then to be supplied (Van de Ven 1991, 54).

Marxism in this period had recognized intellectual and literary leaders like Li Dazhao, Chen Duxiu (1879–1942), Qu Qiubai (1879–1942), and Guo Moruo (1894–1979). Possibly more influential, however, were exegetes and popularizers like Li Da (1889–1966), Ai Siqi (1910–1966), and Ye Qing (Ren Zhuoxuan, b. 1896). As the intellectual world increasingly polarized into right- and left-wing camps, and as Chinese society felt a growing sense of economic and political crisis, Marxism, promoted as truly democratic and progressive by such figureheads, gained broad support, from freethinkers like Lu Xun and the Nietzschean Li Shicen (Brière 1965) as well as from committed radicals.

Reconciling the complexities of Chinese history with Marxian class theory and teleology was far from straightforward. China was hardly capitalist, even though commercial capital, commercial relationships, and private property—including alienable rights in land—had existed in some form even in ancient times. The proletariat or working class was a tiny proportion of the whole population and very recent at that. Nor was China's long-transformed but still formative framework of classical feudalism strictly comparable with anything in the premodern west. Civil officialdom supported absolute monarchy. Still more ancient formations of slavery and bond servitude had risen and fallen, and existed in attenuated forms in the southwest and other marginal areas.

Trial and error ruled (Luk 1990, 144–153). Lenin had provided a lead in his theory of imperialism, and Li Dazhao extended the principle to argue that the Chinese nation was functionally equivalent to the proletariat. As late as 1927, the Provisional Politburo of the CCP, in a draft resolution on the agrarian question, referred with approval to Marx's and Lenin's theory of the "Asiatic mode of production," AMP (Hong 1991, 70).

However, these problems did not much dull the attractiveness of Marxism. The early republic, with its faith in constitutional democracy, was regarded as a failure. The classic liberalism of Liang Qichao and Yan Fu and, following their eventual return to more traditional political ideas, Hu Shi (1891–1962) and Zhang Junmai (1887–1969) lost credibility as formulas for strengthening the nation. China's major problems in this period included dependency on the colonial powers, the growing threat of Japan, and warlordism. All these demanded a strengthening of sovereignty and state power. Emancipation was seen principally in national rather than individual terms; whereas the Russian Bolsheviks appeared to have applied Marxism to building up the nation-state with great success, individualist doctrines in China appeared to invite only a further weakening.

Finally, for most of the period in question Marxist doctrine was supposed to bring about a willing change in those inculcated with it. Compliance with the party's guidance would otherwise be backed up with coercion, to be sure. But experiences of conversion were also widely testified to and produced a generation of sincere "true believers."

Phase 2: Mao Zedong's Ascendancy

As the Comintern was transformed into an instrument of Moscow in the late 1920s, so Chinese communism was bolshevized in successive waves, and Marxist doctrine narrowed accordingly. Well before Mao's ascendancy, the corpus of ideas much later associated with his thought had taken shape (Benton 1996; Luk 1990). Stalin, in the name of his own "five-stage" theory (primitive communism, slavery, feudalism, capitalism, communism), was already suppressing Lenin's theory of the Asiatic mode of production, a by-product of Marx and Engels's historical speculation which had seemed—falsely, as it turned out—to fit China like a glove (Brooks n.d.). Formal periodization by Guo Moruo, a scholar and writer with close ties to Mao, further forced the facts of Chinese history onto the procrustean bed of Stalinist orthodoxy.

By 1937, Mao, having defeated rivals trained in and politically loyal to Moscow, was chairman of the CCP. Although his military and political policies were strikingly original and independent, ideologically he upheld Stalinist orthodoxy. Indeed, he insisted on one narrow, polemical brand of it. Certain party leaders, figures as diverse as the erstwhile president of the People's Republic, Liu Shaoqi, and the "Gang of Four" who helped to overthrow and destroy him, were to make their own statements on Marxist theory at times over the years. But it was Mao Zedong (including his expanded persona of writing assistants including known official ghostwriters, secretaries, and nameless others) who above all controlled the interpretation of Marxist theory in this period. The contribution of other "establishment intellectuals" was limited to rationalizing and explicating the "line" of such authorities. In addition to masses of trained lay preachers, licensed only to present the truth as he saw it, Mao wanted a small number of philosophical brainstormers, popularizers like Ai Siqi and later orthodox ideologues like Zhou Yang (champion of the party line in literature who was to organize attacks on humanism in the early 1960s). In 1937 Ai arrived in Yan'an, where he joined in philosophy discussion classes organized by Mao himself. Certain Maoist classics—"On Practice," "On Contradictions," and "Dialectical Materialism"—owed much to Ai, who in turn was immersed in Soviet writings of the Mitin school (Fogel 1987; Knight 1990). These, together with the "Yan'an Talks on Literature and Art" and certain other writings, were to provide the textual core of doctrinal Maoism up to the 1980s and even later. The importance of the Mitin doctrine lies in its explicit, triumphant assertion that philosophy is a tool of the party. While not necessarily inconsistent with certain lines of thought in Marx, Engels, and Lenin (Knight 1996), the resulting orthodoxy relied increasingly on harsh administrative powers to restrict dissenting views.

A constant theme of Mao's view of class was that poor and lower-middle peasants should be seen as a driving force in Chinese history; not a source of feudal backwardness. Capitalists and compradors were of intermediate class identity. In the "new democratic" period before the takeover of the mainland there was clearly an interest in appealing to wider social constituencies; the petty bourgeoisie were even treated as revolutionary. In more radical periods, e.g., the Cultural Revolution of 1966–1976, when radical Maoism insisted that class struggle was the crucial link, these strata were treated as part of the enemy.

After coming to power on the mainland in 1949, Mao and the CCP, seeking to impose their ideology over huge areas previously beyond their direct influence, made active use of philosophy in three broad phases. In the first, between 1950 and 1957, strong efforts were made to break down the influence of earlier philosophical ideas. Campaigns against Hu Shih and Liang Shu-ming were prime examples that showcased the republished Maoist essays "On Practice" (1950) and "On Contradiction" (1952) against the still popular non-Marxist doctrines of pragmatism and idealism. By 1957, the orthodox schema had cleared the field of these vestiges. Debates became methodological "in the sense that theoreticians had begun to articulate their views on the basis of a consensus of the existence of the schema" (Hanafin 1987, 1:161). This period ended in 1966 when, with the Cultural Revolution, philosophy along with most other branches of cultural activity barely existed. The tragedy of this era is perhaps summed up in the persecution to death in 1966 of Li Da, an early key figure in the development of orthodox Marxist philosophy in China (Knight 1996, 24).

Mao's thought can hardly be exonerated from blame for this result (and it has been officially blamed in the People's Republic). After 1949, the Maoist theory of actually existing class had become simpler and more rigid in application; the population was fitted with rigid class labels that had immense implications for all social relationships. At the same time Mao's view of the overall historical trajectory, of where class development might lead, was gradually overhauled. Mao and his followers now inclined toward a "generative" theory of class, the notion that classes are dynamic and contingent processes. Thus a notionally revolutionary class might lose its "redness" as a result of incorrect policies (Brugger 1978, 20–27).

The end result was the development of the Cultural Revolution of the 1960s. In "On the Correct Handling of Contradictions among the People" (1986, 682, originally delivered as a speech in February 1957), Mao defined two broad categories: the "people" and the "enemy," who are subject to political and physical prejudice. The people are defined as all classes, strata, and social groups that favor, support, and work for the cause of social construction, and the enemy as all those who resist the socialist revolution and are hostile to or sabotage socialist construction.

Formal institutions of Marxist philosophy were quite few, beyond the Party School, some university departments, and the division of philosophy and social science within the Chinese Academy of Science

(CAS). All matters of doctrine were subject to the unaccountable and unquestionable "line" of the leadership. Nonetheless, the trend toward systematization went on steadily, if painfully, as can be seen in the dissemination of textbooks (*keben*) and other exegetical material. In the zones left untouched by Mao's politicization the Stalinist formula was largely taken for granted and mechanically reproduced.

Formal philosophy developed under the schema adapted from Mitin and Stalin. Certain other developments in the Soviet Union, including Zhdanov's (1947) reduction of philosophy to a struggle between dialectical materialism and idealism, were transferred to China with few adaptations. Dialectics, defined in opposition to both mechanistic materialism and formal or Aristotelian logic, was expounded as the sole discourse adequate to a changing material reality. Here, the true formulation of reality was conceived as the consummation of a struggle between rival deviations (right- or left-deviationism in politics; idealism and mechanical materialism in philosophy). Materialism was posed as the scientific answer to the "fundamental problem of philosophy"—is reality primarily material or mental? In epistemology, Mao, no doubt mindful of daunting material obstacles to his programs, supported an active role for consciousness, which in popular homilies translated into a full-blooded voluntarism ("The foolish old man who moved the mountains").

The dogmatic core of Chinese Marxism. By the 1960s Chinese Marxism had become a formalized dogma made up of borrowings from Soviet dialectical materialism, and Mao's formulas, which were more voluntarist. This "orthodox schema" was the complex result of efforts to identify and propound a Chinese Marxism distinct from its opponents, its local doctrinal variants, and false forms.

The orthodox schema is defined largely by its opposition to what it identifies as anti-Marxist thought on the one hand, and false Marxist thought on the other (Hanafin). Chinese Marxism insists that there is a "fundamental problem of philosophy"—should the material order be seen as more real or more fundamental than the ideal order? It answers this question in the affirmative. In expanding on this basic dogma, Chinese Marxism develops formal divisions. These divisions may be expressed as three sets of ontological concepts or principles, dealing respectively with materialism, dialectics, and social practice (Hanafin, 1:112). Each of these may be paired with a corresponding epistemological concept. Thus ontological materialism includes two postulates: (1) The material (also called "being") is primary in the relation of thinking and being. (2) Consciousness is a product, function, or property of highly developed matter organized in a particular form.

Two epistemological postulates correspond to these: (1) Thinking is a reflection of being (that is, of the material world as object) and is therefore secondary to it. (2) The material world is in essence knowable. Principles 1 and 2 are summed up in a third epistemological postulate: the identity of thinking and being.

As a component of Marxist ontology, dialectics is referred to as objective and encompasses three postulates: reality as (1) contradiction, as (2) interconnection, and as (3) motion, development, and change. These are once again mirrored in the epistemological dimension as subjective dialectics, where contradiction and interconnectedness are regarded as fundamental characteristics of the process of knowledge. Motion, development, and change characterize cerebral and neural materiality.

Social practice or general material activity similarly encompasses a series of terms in the ontological dimension: (1) the struggle for production, (2) class struggle, and (3) scientific experiment. The theory of knowledge corresponding to this is described as "dynamic, revolutionary reflection theory" (*nengdongxin de fanying lun*). "Reflection theory" in this sense asserts that all mental activity—including science, art, religion, and all other forms of experience—is, in the final analysis, a reflection of one kind or another of material reality. Crucially, such reflection is mediated by the conscious practical activity of human groups. The higher the level of this activity, the higher the grade of knowledge and the more adequate its correspondence to material reality. The self-emancipation of the proletariat is the highest form of practice, and its theoretical expression, Marxism, constitutes absolute truth.

Phase 3: The Post-Mao Era

Eclipsing Mao's successor Hua Guofeng as paramount leader in the late 1970s, the "pragmatist" leader Deng Xiaoping (1905–1997) recognized the need to return to stability and therefore to legitimize the status quo. Retreating from the utopian slogans of the Cultural Revolution, he declared the class struggle essentially resolved. Deng restored dignity to the intellectuals, a formerly despised social element. Hu Yaobang, Deng's initial choice as general secretary of the party, encouraged a new pluralism in intellectual circles.

This found practical expression when the former division of philosophy and social science of the Chinese Academy of Science (CAS) was detached and established as a new Chinese Academy of Social Science (CASS). The mission of CASS was to determine and apply formulas under which Marxism could appear unchanged in symbolic terms while undergoing radical overhaul as an operational ideology. Under successive presidents like Hu Qiaomu and Deng Liqun, CASS was to harbor a number of thinkers who, in striving to renovate the scaffolding of Maoist orthodoxy, increasingly went beyond and into open conflict with it. A counterestablishment amounting at times to a quasi-liberal elite emerged in CASS and other institutions.

The CCP's urgent policy concerns gave this counterelite crucial points of leverage. The switch from Mao's forays in utopian social transformation to pragmatic economic policies (restoration of market mechanisms; decentralization of control to productive enterprises, including peasant households; foreign investment) was justified by reference to new realities defining Chinese society (Ding 1994; Goldman 1994). This required a dramatic shift in an important element of Marxism, the theory of historical trajectory. The basis of such a shift, the theory of a "primary stage of socialism," was formulated in 1978–1979 by Su Shaozhi, then director of the Institute for Marxism-Leninism in CASS (Su 1993). Class struggle could be reduced to a low priority for the party-state, since a minimum standard of socialism had been constructed. However, movement to a higher stage called for a different set of priorities, above all economic reform.

Change in such a fundamental reference point, however, cannot be quarantined; it must affect the whole doctrinal framework. A renewed defense of humanism became the slogan of reform for such theoreticians as Wang Ruoshui, Li Honglin, Gao Ertai, Su Shaozhi, Feng Lanrui, and Li Zehou (b. 1930; Brugger and Kelly 1990; Ding 1994; Misra 1998). The de-Stalinization in eastern European countries in the 1950s and 1960s had evoked a similar movement around such figures as Kolakowski in Poland and the Lukacs school in Hungary. As a reform movement in Chinese Marxism, humanism attempted to recover the emancipatory normative theory or *telos* attributed to classical Marxism.

Among philosophers, Wang Ruoshui and Li Zehou were most influential. Wang had won the acclaim of Mao with an essay of 1964, "Philosophy of the Table," which supported Mao's thesis of the active role of consciousness. He also joined the attacks on Yang Xianzhen concerning "one dividing into two" versus "two combining into one" (Hamrin 1986). Part of a research group organized to support Zhou Yang's attack, in the early 1960s, on humanism and the theory of alienation under socialism stemming from eastern European adherents of the young Marx, Wang had undergone conversion to the "revisionist" doctrine under the rigors of the Cultural Revolution (Kelly 1987; Wang 1985).

Li won acclaim with his reassessment of Kant, and the Kant-derived view that aesthetics was determined by the ethical category of freedom. Li and Wang, both "true believers" in the sense of having been converts to Marxism in noncommunist areas of China before 1949, now read the western Marxism of Lukacs and the Frankfurt school, where Freud and Weber blended with the theories belatedly found in the young Marx's *1844 Economic Manuscripts*. Li was to conclude in 1980 that Chinese Marxism was a deformed ideological system. Both Wang and Li openly challenged major elements of the old schema, notably the reflection theory, which, as Lukacs had argued in the 1920s, led to a loss of the subjective dimension of social practice and emancipation. This critique drew strength from Marx's famous equation of the subjective with the core meaning of "practice" in the *Theses on Feuerbach* (Kelly 1992). (Li also distanced himself from socialist humanists like Lukacs, the Frankfurt school, and Wang Ruoshui. He regarded their ethical and cultural emphasis as unbalanced. Practice, he argued, must make more than token reference to the role of science, technology, and the economy.)

Despite their open challenges to orthodoxy, Su, Wang, and Li continued to hope for some redemptive movement within Chinese Marxism. By the mid-1980s, a younger generation had emerged for whom any such hope was now problematic. Many, like Jin Guantao (b. 1947) and Yan Jiaqi (b. 1942), emerged from the Cultural Revolution conversant with contemporary science and capable of relating it to political concerns. Jin initially worked within official doctrine, producing a new theory of dialectics that purported to bring it up to date with the *san lun* or "three-logies," which had become a fad in the 1980s: cybernetics, systems theory, and futurology. Between the lines, Jin was signaling a repudiation of dialectics itself as pseudoscientific. More openly, he elaborated a theory of China as culturally determined as a "superstable system," in which Marxism fitted the need for a centralized ideology isomorphic with classical Han Confucianism (Brugger and Kelly, 70–79).

Both the older humanists and the younger systems theorists made outward concessions to the maintenance of Marxism in a symbolic sense while transforming its contents. At many points the inward transformation went beyond what, for the traditional schema, represented the acceptable bounds of Chinese Marxism. In particular, Marx's distrust of bourgeois liberal doctrines of freedom as a standard in ethics and democracy in politics was clearly abandoned in several of the key works of these post-Mao theoreticians.

Post-Marxism. In 1981, Deng Xiaoping announced the "four cardinal principles," one of which was to uphold the distinctive Chinese form of Marxism–Leninism–Mao Zedong thought. This enabled him to maintain a coalition promoting economic reform, while persuading its conservative wing that their ideologically backed interests would not be sacrificed. Given the periodically renewed political control mechanisms based on the these principles, open dissent from Marxism has been a rarity in China. Freethinkers constructed a series of halfway houses where enough lip service was paid to the "correct" ideas to allow quite unorthodox agendas to be pursued with relative impunity. In the late 1980s, a number of these thinkers openly abandoned belief in Marxism. Most telling, perhaps, was the apostasy of Fang Lizhi, who was a former party member, a university vice president, and a physicist of international standing. He could point with little fear of contradiction to the weakness of Marxism as a guide (or predictor) for science (Fang 1990; Miller 1996). Liu Xiaobo spoke for the nontechnical or "cultural" intellectuals but was if anything more damaging in his range of philosophical references, including Locke, Hume, Nietzsche, and Sartre, and his emphasis on a central ethical value, freedom, as a yardstick of intellectual integrity (Chong 1993).

In the long run the survival and development of Chinese Marxism is bound up more deeply with problems of its class analysis and theory of historical trajectory than with abstractions of epistemology or ethics. The most severe challenge faced in the 1990s was from a variety of developmentalist social theories known as "new authoritarianism" and "new conservatism." These doctrines sought the support of "traditional Chinese values" in promoting modernization, and in the latter case referred to the CCP as the "traditional authority," which must also be maintained. However, the Marxist aims of a socialist (nonmarket) economy and classless society were quietly disengaged, if not explicitly dropped. So too was dialectical materialism, the ontological and epistemological heart of the old schema (Gu and Kelly 1994).

Confronted with serious erosion of faith in Marxism, erstwhile supporters of reform like Hu Qiaomu and Deng Liqun began as early as 1981 to campaign for the restoration of orthodoxy. They were hampered by the many gaps and much incoherence in the doctrine, but thanks to their efforts, modifications at the level of textbooks and the like have been relatively minor. Inculcation in the schema and its supporting historical and political tenets remains a fixture in contemporary Chinese education. Official Marxism remains in the hands of capable but unoriginal expositors like Xing Fensi (CASS philosophy, later president of the Central Party School; Xing 1996). Significantly, Xing was initially allied with the humanist reconstruction of the doctrine championed by Wang Ruoshui and others.

In the apparent absence of a young generation of true believers, however, the exuberance of Marxist debate in the 1980s increasingly seems to have been a short-lived phenomenon, a symptom of generational transition. In a computerized age it was difficult to argue that the capitalist world, whatever its other problems, had made fundamental epistemological mistakes about the nature of reality and cognition. The orthodox schema worked out by Li Da and Mao Zedong indeed has strong roots in the ideas of Marx and Engels. But its role as a tool of the CCP's self-legitimation has tended to undermine it, as society as a whole turns to other models of liberation and development.

See also Mao Zedong; Philosophy: Recent Trends in China since Mao; Scientism and Humanism.

Bibliography

Benton, Gregor. "Bolshevizing China: From Lenin to Mao, 1921–1944." *Journal of Communist Societies and Transition Politics*, 12(1), 1996, pp. 38–62.

Brière, O., S.J. *Fifty Years of Chinese Philosophy*, 1898–1948. New York: Praeger, 1965.

Brooks, Timothy. *The Asiatic Mode of Production*. Armonk, N.Y.: Sharpe, n.d.

Brugger, Bill. *China: The Impact of the Cultural Revolution*. London: Croom Helm, 1978.

Brugger, Bill, and David Kelly. *Chinese Marxism in the Post-Mao Era*. Stanford, Calif.: Stanford University Press, 1990.

Chong, Woei Lien. "The Tragic Duality of Man: Liu Xiaobo on Western Philosophy from Kant to Sartre." In *China's Modernization: Westernization and Acculturation*, ed. Kurt Werner Radtke and Tony Saich. Stuttgart: Steiner, 1993, pp. 111–162.

Ci, Jiwei. *Dialectic of the Chinese Revolution: From Utopianism to Hedonism*. Stanford, Calif.: Stanford University Press, 1994.

Ding, X. L. *The Decline of Communism in China: Legitimacy Crisis, 1977–1989*. Cambridge and New York: Cambridge University Press, 1994.

Dirlik, Arif. *The Origins of Chinese Communism*. New York: Oxford University Press, 1989.

———. *Revolution and History: The Origins of Marxist Historiography in China, 1919–1937*. Berkeley: University of California Press, 1978.

Dirlik, Arif, and Maurice Meisner, eds. *Marxism and the Chinese Experience: Issues in Contemporary Chinese Socialism*. Armonk, N.Y.: Sharpe, 1989.

Fang, Lizhi. *Bringing Down the Great Wall: Writings on Science, Culture, and Democracy in China*. New York: Knopf, 1990.

Fogel, Joshua A. *Ai Ssu-chi's Contribution to the Development of Chinese Marxism*. Cambridge, Mass.: Harvard University Press, 1987.

Goldman, Merle. *Sowing the Seeds of Democracy in China: Political Reform in the Deng Xiaoping Era*. Cambridge, Mass.: Harvard University Press, 1994.

Gu, Xin. *Hege'erzhuyi de youling yu Zhongguo zhishifenzi* (The Ghost of Hegel and Chinese Intellectuals). Taipei: Fengyun shidai chubanshe, 1994.

———. *Zhongguo fanchuantongzhuyi de pinkun* (The Poverty of China's Anti-Traditionalism). Taipei: Fengyun shidai chubanshe, 1993.

Gu, Xin, and David Kelly. "New Conservatism: Ideological Program of a New Elite." In *China's Quiet Revolution: New Interactions between State and Society*, ed. David S. G. Goodman and Beverley Hooper. New York: St. Martin's, 1994.

Hamrin, Carol. "Yang Xianzhen: Upholding Orthodox Leninist Theory." In *China's Establishment Intellectuals*, ed. Carol Hamrin and Timothy Cheek. Armonk, N.Y.: Sharpe, 1986, pp. 51–91.

Hanafin, John. "Chinese Marxism as Philosophy: The Ontological, Epistemological, Methodological, and Axiological Dimension of Chinese Marxist Philosophical Discourse." Ph.D. dissertation, Griffith University, Brisbane, 1987.

Hong, Lijian. "Chinese Marxist Historiography and the Question of the Asiatic Mode of Production." Ph.D. dissertation, Research School of Social Sciences, Australian National University, Canberra, 1991.

Jin, Guantao. "Fazhan de zhexue (Philosophy of Development)." In Jin Guantao and Liu Qingfeng, *Lun Lishi yanjiu zhong de zhengti fangfa: Fazhan de zhexue*. 1986, pp. 89–148.

Kelly, David. "Chinese Marxism since Tiananmen: Between Evaporation and Dismemberment." In *China in the Nineties: Crisis Management and Beyond*, ed. David S. G. Goodman and Gerald Segal. Oxford: Clarendon, 1991.

———. "The Emergence of Humanism: Wang Ruoshui and the Critique of Socialist Alienation." In *Chinese Intellectuals and the State: In Search of a New Relationship*, ed. Merle Goldman, Carol Lee Hamrin, and Timothy Cheek. Cambridge, Mass.: Harvard University Press, 1987.

———. "Philosophers Revisited." *China News Analysis*, No. 1453, 1 February 1992, pp. 1–9.

Knight, Nick, ed. *Li Da and Marxist Philosophy in China*. Boulder, Colo.: Westview, 1996.

———. *Mao Zedong on Dialectical Materialism: Writings on Philosophy, 1937*. Armonk, N.Y.: Sharpe, 1990.

Ladany, Lazlo. *The Communist Party of China and Marxism, 1921–1985: A Self-Portrait*. London: Hurst, 1988.

Luk, Michael Y. L. *The Origins of Chinese Bolshevism: An Ideology in the Making, 1920–1928*. Hong Kong: Oxford University Press, 1990.

Mao, Zedong. "Guanyu zhengque chuli renmin neibu maodun de wenti." In *Mao Zedong zhuzuo xuandu*, Vol. 2. 1957, 1986.

Meissner, Werner. *Philosophy and Politics in China: The Controversy over Dialectical Materialism in the 1930s*, trans. Richard Mann. Stanford, Calif.: Stanford University Press, 1990.

Miller, Lyman. *Science as Dissent in Post-Mao China: The Politics of Knowledge*. Seattle: University of Washington Press, 1996.

Misra, Kalpana. *From Post-Maoism to Post-Marxism: The Erosion of Official Ideology in Deng's China*. London: Routledge, 1998.

Schoenhals, Michael. "The 1978 Truth Criterion Controversy." *China Quarterly*, No. 126, June 1991, pp. 243–268.

Schram, Stuart R. *The Thought of Mao Zedong*. Cambridge and New York: Cambridge University Press, 1989.

Su, Shaozhi. *Marxism in China*. Nottingham: Spokesman, 1993.

Van de Ven, Hans. *From Friend to Comrade: The Founding of the Chinese Communist Party, 1920–1927*. Berkeley: University of California Press, 1991.

Walicki, Andrzej. *Marxism and the Leap into the Kingdom of Freedom*. Stanford, Calif.: Stanford University Press, 1995.

Wang, Ruoshui. "Writings of Wang Ruoshui on Philosophy, Humanism, and Alienation," ed. D. A. Kelly. *Chinese Studies in Philosophy*, 16(3), spring 1985, pp. 1–120.

Wright, Eric Olin. "Class Analysis, History, and Emancipation." *New Left Review*, 202, November–December 1993, pp. 15–37.

Xing, Fensi. "Jianchi Makesizhuyi bu dongya: Huaqing Makesizhuyi yu fan Makesizhuyi de jiexian (Sticking Unshakably to Marxism: Draw a Clear Distinction between Marxism and Anti-Marxism)." *People's Daily*, 6 June 1996.

Yan, Sun. *The Chinese Reassessment of Socialism, 1976–1992*. Princeton, N.J.: Princeton University Press, 1995.

Zhang, Wei-wei. *Ideology and Economic Reform under Deng Xiaoping, 1978–1993*. London and New York: Kegan Paul, 1996.

Mazu Daoyi (Ma-tsu Tao-i)

Whalen Lai

Mazu—or "Patriarch Ma"—Daoyi (709–788) heads the Hongzhou school of Chan Buddhism. Traditionally listed as the *dharma* heir to Huineng (638–713), the sixth patriarch of the southern school, Mazu was tutored by one of Huineng's ten great disciples, Nanyue Huairang (677–744). The truth could be that Mazu came out of the Baotang school in Sichuan (Szechwan), but his spiritual lineage was rewritten to accord with the universal recognition then given to Huineng. Huairang's encounter with Huineng and Mazu's encounter with Huairang were fictional accounts of personalized teachings. Capping all this mythmaking is a legend told in the legitimization text of the Hongzhou school, the *Baolinzhuan*, or *Record of the Baolin Temple* (801). At the Baolin temple, in Canton, Huineng once taught, rewrote, and expanded on the "transmission verses" of the *Platform Sutra* and related a prophecy of the twenty-seventh Indian patriarch (teacher to Bodhidharma) that one day a "horse" (Ma) would trample (dominate) the world. And indeed Mazu was the vital eighth Chinese patriarch, who headed the eventual Linji line and also affected the Caotong line. Mazu has the distinction of being the last of the patriarchs, *zu*; after him, Chan teachers are called only "masters." He is also the only one to be so known by his secular family name, Ma.

The four lines frequently cited to summarize the essence of Chan Buddhism have been attributed to Huineng and even to Bodhidharma:

> No reliance on words.
> Transmission outside the scriptures.
> Point directly at the mind of men.
> See your nature and be enlightened.

Actually, however, these lines appeared only after Mazu and should best be seen as describing the style of teaching perfected by him. Known for teaching the principle of Buddha-mind ("mind is Buddha"), Mazu was not bound even by that formula. He is just as well known for teaching, later, "neither mind nor Buddha." And in case anyone should think for a moment that the later formula is more clever or more profound, we have the testimony of Damei, a student of Mazu's: on hearing that Mazu had recently changed the older formula to the newer one, Damei exclaimed, "That old rascal! He fools people to no end." Mazu, for his part, honored Damei by remarking that the "Great Plum" (*damei*) had indeed ripened.

This freedom from words, or nonreliance on words, naturally supported modes of nonverbal "mind to mind" transmission of the *dharma* ("truth"). Despite earlier attempts to link Chan to particular *sutra* teachings, from the start it had never followed any one particular scripture. Wisdom being ultimately beyond words, all verbal teachings were considered just means, like a finger pointing to the moon. This was nothing new. The Mahayana tradition had always admitted it, and had conceived of "teaching the *dharma* in accordance with the capacity of the audience." But Mazu finally made the teaching relative and the opportunity for enlightenment, *ji*, absolute. *Ji* can be described as the moment of ripeness or, to use another image, the moment when the Buddha-mind is triggered, releasing a sudden self-awakening. Mazu is said to have perfected the use of the Chan "trigger." With no set scripture to rely on, his disciples took to keeping alive the memory of those moments by recalling his life and deeds, and especially those sparkling mind-to-mind encounters. The result was the first known collection of the Chan *Yulu* (*Recorded Sayings*). They replaced the Sanskrit sutras, and their selective but well-chosen excerpts anticipated the rise of a later genre, the *gong'an* (Japanese *koan*).

True to form, Mazu—who did not have to depend on words—was one of the first to use the shout and the kick to trigger enlightenment in his students. The monk Suiliao could not stop laughing over the day when Mazu had kicked him, head over heels, into awakening. The *Baolinzhuan* considered such physical demonstrations, even the wink of an eye, indicative of the Buddha-nature in action, or "Buddha essence-in-function."

Mazu is also known for the formula "The everyday (*pingchang*) mind is the *dao*"—by which he meant not the contrived or the conspiring mind, but the mind with the least ado, at peace (*ping*) with itself and forever constant (*chang*). This suggests Mazu's able use of everyday language, puns, metaphors, and ordinary circumstances to instruct. From an apocryphal source (not included even in the comprehensive *Basho no Goroku* compiled by Iriya), we learn that Mazu once told his uncle, who had been pestering him for the *dharma*, to "get it from the well." This is like saying in English, "Go jump in the lake." Since a Chan master is a living buddha, his word is law. The uncle did not actually jump into the well, but he did spend the next few months sitting by it, asking it for the truth. One wintry morning, Mazu saw that the moment (*ji*) was ripe. Picking up a pail of water that had been left in the courtyard the night before and was thoroughly chilled, he dumped its contents over the old man. The moment the cold penetrated his bones, the uncle was enlightened. This is a classic example of an exercise of Chan *ji*: no words, no scripture, but the perfect timing, using whatever is at hand to illuminate—to remind the uncle that if you ask the well for *dharma*, all you will get is water. Ask not, and it will be given unto you. The truth is not without; it is within you and was within you before you were born.

Such encounters in the extant Mazu *Yulu*—the compilation may be late, but the material seems primitive enough—often have a hidden but decipherable structure. In this they are unlike the later *huatou* ("heading words") abbreviated from the *gong'an*, which are utterly unstructured. Consider this encounter. A certain learned scholar presumed that he knew what Mazu "the Lion" (a symbol of Buddha) was up to. He responded well to Mazu's antics but was floored when Mazu asked him, "What then is the lion that is neither inside nor outside the den?" Unable to come up with an answer, he beat a shamefaced retreat. Mazu called after him as he was leaving, hoping that the man would see the light. The implication is that the man was then at the door, being therefore "neither inside nor outside (the den)"—which means that he was the "lion," a buddha no less than Mazu. But the man missed the cue. And Mazu, regretfully, judged him a fool. Mazu's point—an ingenious use of circumstances—was also lost on later commentators. However, the point may have been well known at the time, perhaps even too well known, so that it had to be hidden by breaking up the original "encounter dialogue" and changing it into an enigmatic *gong'an*.

By seeing that essence is function, that knowledge acts, that the sacred is the everyday, in every moment and every person, Mazu helped to usher in what has been called the golden age of Chan, a century and more of colorful personalities, each one unique and inimitable, all teaching the same truth in very different styles. Modern textual criticism, being suspicious of all pious teleology, has deflated that picture somewhat, but one hopes not so much as to miss seeing the truth of the obvious.

See also Buddhism, Zen (Chan); Huineng: The Sixth Patriarch.

Bibliography

Bavo, Levens. *The Recorded Sayings of Ma-tsu*, trans. (from Dutch) Julian Pas. New York: Mellon, 1987.

Cheng Chien, Bhiksu. *Sun Face Buddha: The Teachings of Mazu.* Fremont, Calif.: Asian Humanities, 1992.

Iriya, Yoshitaka. *Basho no Goroku* (The Recorded Sayings of Mazu). Kyoto: Zenbunka kenkyusho, 1984.

Lai, Whalen. "Ma-tsu Tao-i and the Unfolding of Southern Zen." *Japanese Journal of Religious Studies*, 12(4), 1985, pp. 172–192.

———. "The Transmission Verses of the Ch'an Patriarchs." *Chinese Studies*, 1(2), 1984, pp. 593–624.

Mencius (Mengzi, Meng Tzu)

Chung-ying CHENG

Sima Qian's *Historical Records* did not mention the dates for Mencius (371–289 B.C.E). But we can arrive at his dates on the basis of Ming and Yuan sources as well as by calculating the years when he was active in the state of Liang. Sima Qian did mention that Mencius was born in the state of Zhou and studied under a disciple of Zisi who was the grandson of Confucius. This perhaps gave Mencius his reason for saying that he was a follower of Confucius, by means of private self-instruction, nearly 200 years after Confucius's death. Mencius also said that he had taken Confucius as his role model and examplar. And indeed throughout his life Mencius devoted himself to promoting and defending Confucian idealism—that is, to rectifying human hearts and dismissing "heresies" so that the sagely wisdom of King Wen, Duke Zhou, and Confucius could be continued. One may say that Mencius was the first Confucian to advance a view on transmitting a tradition which Han Yu in the Tang identifies as the "heritage and transmission of the *dao*" (*daotong*). Here the *dao* is to be conceived primarily as a way of achieving peace and harmony in the world. Confucius came to see the *dao* as loving people with benevolence (*ren*) derived from cultivation of one's own virtues (*de*). For Mencius, the *dao* is articulated with accentuation of both *ren* and *yi* (righteousness), and consequently social practice and institutional reform are stressed.

Like Confucius, Mencius spent much of his life seeking an audience with rulers and promoting his idealistic approach—*yi*—to good government. He saw King Xuan of Qi, who did not use him. He saw King Hui of Liang, who appointed him an adviser but did not want to implement his ideas about the "way of kings" (as opposed to the "way of hegemony") or about benevolent government. In Mencius's time, most states were competing for power and wealth; if the long-term purpose was to achieve unity, or unification, the immediate goal was to survive and be competitive. Like Confucius, Mencius spoke about government from the point of view of a sovereign who had already achieved unity, such as King Wu or Duke Zhou, but achieving unity could be a difficult challenge. Besides, there was a gap between society and state, and between morality and politics, and how to bridge it or fill it was another difficult challenge. The Confucian-Mencian approach was to build a state and government on the basis of individual and social ethics. As a practical matter, Mencius was unable to do this, and so he retired, turning instead to teaching his disciples—using the Confucian classics—and to writing his own views, which led to the seven chapters of the *Mencius*.

It is said that Confucius seldom spoke of the "way of heaven" (*tiandao*), human nature (*xing*), or human destiny (*ming*). But Mencius could not avoid addressing these issues explicitly, because he had to confront fundamental questions relevant to the clarification of concepts, the justification of theories, and systematic persuasion. He also had to deal with notions such as the way (*dao*), heart-mind (*xin*), principle-reason (*li*), and vital force (*qi*). This meant that he had to find an understanding of, and penetrating insights into, these fundamental notions of reality and life. Also, it indicated that Confucianism had reached a point in its development where basic notions needed to be organized into coherent discourse. It should not be forgotten that Confucianism after Confucius—that is, in Mencius's time—had become one of the "illustrious schools," and the preceding three generations of Confucian learning must have produced a large corpus of commentaries on classic poetry (*shi*), ancient history (*shu*), and rituals and social rules (*li*) in which these notions had to be included. Hence, the theoretical understanding of these concepts was epochal, advancing Confucianism to a higher stage of development in which its metaphysical aspects would be expressly stated.

Human Nature and the Goodness of Human Nature

I shall begin by discussing human nature (*xing*). First of all, Mencius wanted to see human nature in a broad sense and a narrow sense. Broadly, human nature included both rationality and animal desires such as food and sex; narrowly, however, "human nature" distinguished the human being from animals in terms of moral feelings, moral choices, and moral actions.

Second, human nature should not be conceived as a quality that predetermined our character or actions, or restricted our free will. On the contrary, human nature should be conceived as what made free will possible, insofar as free will represented the dignity and worth of human existence. The question can be raised whether a person can exercise free will to choose something against human nature, or against free will itself. The logical conclusion is that generally, under natural conditions, free will is expressed in the spontaneity of active tendencies of human feelings. This was a crucial point for Mencius, for he believed that one could retain or restore one's nature after having been forced to forsake or abandon it. To restore one's nature was to go back to a state of spontaneity and freedom from external and internal pressures.

Third, for Mencius human nature was a creative ability, self-motivating and given as a part of human existence. In the free exercise of this creative ability, humans could transform themselves through their actions, participate in external changes (events), and hence participate in making reality or making the world: "Whatever he works on transforms, whatever he preserves flows." Because of this creative ability, humans could practice self-cultivation and reach a state of maximum clarity and tranquillity of mind, a state in which they could follow the heart's dictates without transgressing the bounds of rightness described by Confucius.

Fourth, human nature was innate, not imposed from outside. This point is very important, as it is related to *Zhong yong*, the "doctrine of the mean": "What is endowed by heaven is nature." Mencius himself quoted the *Book of Poetry* in asserting the heaven-born virtue of human beings. Here, we need not identify heaven with a personal god; nor need we identify it simply with physical nature, as in Xunzi. Heaven, for Mencius, was the ultimate reality; it had an internal order and structure that were to be realized in creative activities—in the formation and transformation of things and people. Hence Mencius spoke of *tianming, tiandao*, and *tianxing* to indicate that heaven was to be seen and understood in terms of how things take place, how things act as they do, and how things are conditioned. In this sense Mencius was suggesting a certain rational order that he referred to as the "pattern of things" (*tiaoli*). Thus to say that human nature is inborn was to suggest that it was neither arbitrarily formed nor externally imported or imposed; rather, it came from a source and developed into what it was through a process of ordering and organization. Human nature, like life itself, had organic wholeness; it existed in the form of proclivities and dispositions and was expressed in feelings and emotions and in the will—the capacity for making choices and determinations.

Fifth, human nature for Mencius was good in the sense that it was the source and resource for anyone's cultivation and transformation of himself into a person who was moral, trustworthy, "appreciable," even great, sagely, or divine. The qualities of morality, trustworthiness, appreciation, greatness, sageliness, and divinity were both subjective and intersubjective perceptions to which Mencius gave special connotations and which formed an intrinsic hierarchical order. Thus, for example, goodness (*shan*) was defined as desirability (*keyu*). This definition suggested that good was something one could desire and yet be an object of intersubjective valuation. Furthermore, this object of valuation should be the basis for communal trust, indicated by the notion of trustworthiness.

What qualified as good had to be rooted in one's own experience, intersubjectively appreciated and valued, and finally made a basis for communal trust that could lead to an even higher level of understanding. To say that human nature is good, then, was to say that it was the beginning and the reservoir of something valued and appreciated by a given person and community. The community was not limited or confined; potentially, it could encompass all of humankind; in other words, human nature was to be realized with regard to an increasing circle of communities. Before it was actually realized in this way, it was experienced as feelings, as described above. When these feelings were acted on and incorporated into one's habitual behavior, they were then understood as the virtues of *ren* (benevolence), *yi* (righteousness), *li* (propriety), and *zhi* (wisdom). For Mencius, the sense of integrity or trustworthiness and that of belief or faith (all these stand for *xin*) was an expression of the virtuous self or the self as a subject of these virtues. *Xin* could be regarded as a virtue based on the other four virtues. I shall return to Mencius's specific arguments for the goodness of human nature below.

One salient point is that for Mencius a human person always had an active power of personal choice and self-determination and could have a transforming influence on the world. This active power was an expression of a will toward harmony and life itself. We might call it the moral nature of man or simply human nature, which was to be considered active, not static or fixed. In this sense human nature was also human feeling, the human mind, and hence heart-mind (*xin*). Mencius called it the "original mind" of man or the "mind of a newborn child" (*chizi zhixin*). He implied that human nature was something to be felt and experienced by a person as his or her own nature: it was something concrete and individual, apart from being universal and intersubjective.

Mencius listed four basic human feelings: (1) sympathy-empathy, (2) shame, (3) reverence, and (4) the distinction between right and wrong. These feelings were both concrete expressions and individual experiences of one's own nature. In Mencius, we can find for each of these feelings a particular example with reference to a concrete situation. Perhaps the most vivid is his observation that one would rush to help a child who was about to fall into a well. As all can empathize and sympathize, these reactions are both particular and universal, both abstract and concrete; the same was true of the other feelings. In fact, Mencius used the word *xin* (heart-mind) for the feelings, perhaps implying a conscious awareness of them.

Heart-mind was significant as the basis for knowing one's nature (*zhixing*) and knowing heaven (*zhitian*). Mencius said: "By fulfilling one's heart-mind (*jinxin*), one comes to know one's nature; by knowing one's nature, one comes to know heaven." One fulfilled the heart-mind only by thoroughly reflecting on one's feelings, experiences, and intentions. In doing so, one would come to realize that there was a nature in and behind the heart-mind which made its activities possible. But human nature need not be considered separable from the heart-mind as in Mencius's account; one may consider the heart-mind an emergent creation of human nature, just as human nature can be considered an emergent creation of heaven.

We can see how Mencius inspired the views of Lu Xiang-shan and Wang Yang-ming in the Southern Song and Ming; they maintained that the heart-mind was principle (*xinjili*), since human nature was principle. Mencius, then, can be said to be the originator of this neo-Confucian school of heart-mind. By reflecting further on human nature, one would come to realize the nature of heaven, for by tracing nature to heaven one could see that the creativity and rationality of human nature were based on and derived from an even deeper source of reality—heaven. Here we see that a significant feature of Confucian philosophy was developed by Mencius: the idea of mind, humanity, and cosmic reality are integrated into a unity of emergent levels.

Human Destiny and Cultivation of the Heart-Mind

According to Mencius, human destiny (*ming*) and human nature formed two aspects of human existence as a person reflected on himself. In fact, what was called the self could be regarded simply as composed of these two aspects, which were related and derived from the same source, heaven. However, in contrast to human nature, human destiny was imposed from without and appeared to be a restriction of individual activity. One's individual situation could be explored for its advantages to oneself; nevertheless, it was an objective condition that one had to accept and could not change. In light of *ming*, one cannot simply do as one wishes; one must work in accordance with what it determines. However, this is not to say that a person is fully determined by *ming*.

Ming, like *xing*, is both particular and general. For example, that every human will die is a general condition of human destiny, but when and where each person dies is an individual matter, reflecting particular conditions of destiny. In this sense, Mencius would say that one must know one's own conditions of destiny and work out one's life accordingly. One had to be aware that these conditions could be self-imposed—that is, created by one's active decisions as well as one's social situation—and that it was important to observe them, since a violation could lead to more severe restrictions. This meant that one could act against certain conditions and thereby incur a risk.

Our point in clarifying Mencius's notion of *ming* is to see how complex and yet how flexible it was. Mencius's point, with regard to understanding one's *ming*, was to take a correct attitude toward it and become adjusted to it; one could then use one's active nature to achieve the life goals that had been adjusted in light of one's *ming*. We must remember that even though a person might or might not have the *ming* to reach an ultimate value or truth, there was no theoretical reason for being unable to reach it: the ability to achieve it belonged to human nature, in the absence of contingencies of life. Thus it was possible for everyone to become a sage, because everyone could practice self-cultivation to become sagely and virtuous. It was also possible for anyone to practice self-cultivation in order to experience and understand the unity of heaven and humanity, or to do things that could be understood as exhibiting this unity. Whether a person could overcome certain habits or transcend certain contingencies was up to the person himself—his efforts, theoretically, were within his control and were part of his free will.

The *ming* of a person was, again, derived from heaven, and thus the "mandate of heaven" (*tianming*) was beyond human control. However, this notion is somewhat ambiguous: is *tianming* what one perceives as beyond one's control, or is it what one actually encounters as an obstruction? Mencius defined heaven as that which is beyond one's control, but this does not preclude the idea that one must plan one's life by knowing *tianming*. One must know heaven and, consequently, one's own nature; in knowing one's limitations, one comes to know one's destiny. Perhaps, then, there is a narrow region of indeterminacy between nature and destiny.

Mencius's notion of the duality of human nature and human destiny in the unity of heaven is illustrated in his contrast between sensory or bodily desires and the virtues of the heart-mind such as *ren, yi, li*, and *zhi*. Each of our senses has its objects of satisfaction, and this is both nature and destiny; but in our efforts to cultivate moral virtues we must not indulge in sensual desires simply because we can regard them as based on our nature. Instead, we must be aware of them as conditions of living and be alert to how they might affect or obstruct our pursuit of virtues. By the same token, in our cultivation of virtues we can also see nature and destiny; but a morally superior person (*junzi*) will not simply accept the difficulties imposed by destiny but will do his utmost to overcome them. Indeed, this is the difference between a small person and a superior person: the superior person pursues his active nature to its utmost and guards against letting desires create impediments, whereas the small person pursues his desires to the utmost and is stopped by any impediment to cultivating his virtues.

Mencius said that a *junzi* "followed heaven and knew destiny." The *junzi* did his best to follow his nature in achieving his life goals but was aware of limitations and cultivated his active nature in order to overcome obstructions and avoid causing contingent difficulties. Once this was done, *ming* was simply something beyond one's knowledge or control. Mencius urged everyone to understand this and, on that understanding, to cultivate the moral virtues, whose seeds were a natural part of our existence. Mencius used this duality of human existence to explain many historical examples of imperfections, such as why a good person like Confucius could not become a king or why the son of a sage king like Yao or Shun could turn out to be a rascal. More important, Mencius endorsed a program of self-cultivation and self-transformation in order to live up to one's potential as a human being.

How was a person to practice such self-cultivation? Simply, one needed to conform to the *ming* he knew and do his best to develop and fulfill his nature, which he would also come to know in the process of natural growth. Mencius specified a threefold process: (1) rectification of one's *ming* (to know one's destiny and adjust to it), (2) cultivation of one's nature, and (3) fulfillment of one's talents.

To cultivate one's nature, one had to "fulfill one's mind." For Mencius, this entailed a conscientious effort to discipline one's feelings and hold steadfast to one's will, because human nature was manifest in feelings and the will as well as in reason. In developing one's nature it was crucial to safeguard one's moral sentiments and not let desires and bad feelings obstruct and obscure self-understanding or daunt the spontaneous sense of morality. In this regard, Mencius specified four aspects or requirements of self-cultivation.

1. Bu dongxin. The first requirement was "being not moved in heart" (*bu dongxin*). This meant holding to the beginnings and principles of the good that emerged from the heart-mind so as not to be carried away by external temptations and forces. Mencius believed that being "settled" in the heart-mind was crucial; only then could one act. In his critique of Gaozi's description of "being not moved in heart," Mencius agreed that "if one does not get settled (*de*) in heart-mind, don't try to seek [truth or meaning] from the *qi*." However, as we will see later, he did not agree with Gaozi that "if one does not get [truth or meaning] from the language of reason (*yan*), one would not seek out from the heart-mind."

To be "settled" in the heart-mind was to have both knowledge and conviction so that one would know what to act on and would never wander from or waver in one's attitude toward life. This amounts to being determined to fulfill one's nature, knowing what one can and cannot do, and holding to one's goals in light of one's limitations. Confucius spoke of not having doubts at age forty, and this accords with his notion of *bu dongxin* at that age. Perhaps in his own self-cultivation Mencius followed Confucius, although he does not actually mention achievements at age fifty and later.

As the source of understanding and conviction, the heart-mind should always be safeguarded and consulted. Mencius clearly indicated that one should seek in the heart-mind whatever truth and understanding one did not obtain from language and learning. It is interesting to note that for Mencius the heart-mind contained everything in the world: "All things are complete in me" (*Mencius* 7A4).

This suggests that it would be possible for the human mind to know the principles of all things and for the human heart to feel everything. But it may also recall the ontocosmology of the *Book of Changes* (*Zhouyi*), in which everything is said to derive from the same source, the *taiji* or the *dao*. In this sense all things have a common origin and the existence of human mind requires or presupposes the existence of all things in the world. By thinking deeply about this, one would experience the affinity of all things in oneself and realize in oneself the "feeling and response" (*kanying*).

For Mencius, profound thinking and profound experiencing were always necessary: "If one reflects on oneself and realizes [by experiencing] (*cheng*) the unity and affinity of all things, there is no greater joy than this" (7A4). *Cheng* as realization in experiencing the ultimate reality is also discussed in the *Doctrine of the Mean* (*Zhongyong* or *Zhong yong*), in greater detail.

Finally, we can also see that feeling the unity and affinity of things is the basis for taking benevolent love (*ren*) seriously. It was Mencius who spoke of *ren* as "being close to one's parents, being benevolent to people and loving all things." This was part of the inspiration of the "idealistic wing" of neo-Confucianism about a thousand years later.

2. Zhi. The second requirement was holding steadfast to one's will in pursuing righteousness. Whereas *bu dongxin* indicated resistance to undesirable outside influences, holding steadfast to one's will (*zhi*) meant developing perseverance in advancing moral virtues in one's character. Here we again see the threefold structure of heart-mind as conceived by Mencius: the function and activity of (1) thinking (*si*), (2) will (*zhi*), and (3) vital force—which is more directly related to the human body than the first two functions. *Zhi*, however, is ambiguous: it could mean a specific aspiration or goal, or it could mean the general function of the will.

In the western tradition, classically, "will" represents free agency: making decisions and commitments among possible choices and, hence, an independent cause of actions. We can understand *zhi* in this sense, for it is the medium of freely chosen pursuits and goals of life, and it no doubt is the efficacious, initiating, or motivating force for action. Those who deny that there is a notion of will in Chinese ethics have failed to notice this meaning of *zhi*. Moreover, *zhi* needs to be held steadfast, and the ability to do this is, again, a matter of will—or will in a generalized sense. We should note that Mencius recognized the possible weakness of will: without making conscientious efforts to "hold steadfast," one might succumb to influences from outside or to desires from inside oneself. Thus determination and perseverance in following one's choice and commitment (*zhi*) were most important.

Mencius specifically discussed the moral choice between life and righteousness. In a normal situation, a person could desire and have both. But in an exigent situation where he could have only one, how was he to choose? Mencius thought it was obvious that a choice had to be made and that how one chose would depend on understanding the significance of the choice and also on free will. A "choice" that was not one's own could not be considered a choice, even if it was the correct choice.

A morally commendable choice, then, had to be both freely made and correct, and this no doubt presupposed correct understanding and free will as the basis of reasoned evaluation, independent of any considerations of profit or advantage. But when the will recognized the righteousness of a choice and committed itself to that choice, it could not be said to be determined by the choice. In fact, the commitment constituted a determination of the rightness of the choice and the resulting action. In this sense, Mencius discovered the moral will, which wills righteousness (*yi*), long before Kant. Moreover, Mencius recognized a broader ground of moral choice than Kant: not just righteousness but benevolent love (*ren*) should constitute the will. In other words, in its free exercise, the will wills nothing other than *ren* or *yi*. Therefore, one might choose righteousness over life in some situations, and that choice would be a manifestation of the purity, goodness, and strength of the will.

The question then arises whether a person may choose life over righteousness. How do we characterize this choice? The will, or the good will, has not prevailed but has yielded to temptation and to considerations of wrong or unrighteous advantages. Such a choice might be made because the fear of death and the desire for life obscured and weakened the good will. It could therefore be described as moral weakness or weakness of the will, but it would more correctly be called domination by desire and habit. Because this domination was possible, Mencius strongly advocated cultivating the right vital force (*qi*), the source of moral courage and the power to overcome desires for advantage (*li*), and the will for righteousness (*yi*). This is known as the thesis on the distinction between *yi* and personal advantage.

Mencius specifically linked *zhi* to the vital force of one's mind and body. He recognized that if *zhi* of the mind is concentrated, it can influence the *qi* of the body; and if *qi* of the body is concentrated, it can influence the *zhi* of the mind: "If *zhi* is concentrated it will move the *qi*, and if *qi* is concentrated it will move the *zhi*. Thus if a person walking trips, it is a matter of *qi* and yet it rebounds to affect his mind." Hence if heart-mind was not to be affected by *qi*, one had to hold to one's willed goal. This of course presupposed a specific goal as an object of the will; otherwise, there would be nothing for the mind to hold to. The specific goal stabilized the mind and separated itself from the flowing *qi* of the body. When one had the right goal and the right view in mind, then one could work up one's *qi* so as to act on that goal and view. But when one had not reached a right goal or had not formed a right view, one should not be rash in provoking the *qi* or taking action. (In this respect, Mencius agreed with Gaozi.)

3. Yangqi. The third requirement was to nourish one's vital force, *yangqi*. This would provide a strong supporting base for moral courage and moral vision and thus for exercising free will so as to make correct moral choices. But the vital force one sought to nourish had to be the the correct one—the one that would encourage dedication to moral truth and moral action. For Mencius no *qi* was more correct than the *qi* that filled, generated, and sustained the cosmos. (Here Mencius seems to reveal how deeply he had absorbed the cosmology of heaven-earth-man derived from the tradition of the *Zhouyi* and manifested in *Yizhuan* and *Zhongyong*.) Mencius called it the "great flood of the vital force" (*haoran zhiqu*). He described it as matching both righteousness and the *dao* and said that it could even be considered as coming from the accumulation of righteousness. This last point implied that the cosmic *qi* was from the very beginning a matter of righteousness, not something to be absorbed into our conception of righteousness. In other words, Mencius wanted to maintain that the cosmic and the morally good or righteous were internal to each other and hence that the moral life was the cosmically natural life. When one had this cosmic *qi*, one was not intimated in making any moral choice and would lead a moral life rooted in the ultimate reality of the cosmos.

4. Zhiyan. The fourth and final requirement was to seek and value knowledge as formulated in the language of reason. Mencius described it as "knowing language" (*zhiyan*). This is the dimension of cultivation that one would identify with the thinking ability of the heart-mind. For Mencius, language was an expression of the thinking mind and was therefore internal, not external, to thinking. Gaozi held that if one did not get truth or meaning in language, one need not seek it in the mind. Mencius rejected that reasoning: on the contrary, he held, if we did not receive truth and meaning from language, we should look into the mind to try to clarify our thinking and work through our puzzles and problems. The mind produced language, and no language could not be traced to the thinking of the mind. Besides, for Mencius the heart-mind contained profound truths about the world and the self, and so it was necessary to look into the heart-mind to recognize and know these truths.

There is another sense of "knowing the language": in a given passage of language, one needs to be able to assess its intended meaning and its value. Is it sophistry? Is it an overstatement? Is it a vicious attack? Is it a clever pretext? To assess language correctly, one needs to know the standards of speech and the right ways of expressing thoughts. For Mencius, a bad passage of language reflected bad thinking and ill-will. Through experience, one would also be able to see the limitations of such language and not be misled by it.

From these four requirements of self-cultivation, we can conclude that a moral person had to take morality very seriously, and this entailed strengthening the heart and refining the mind. In particular, the moral person had to be able to engage in profound self-reflection, for it was in his own mind that he would discover profound truths and a profound source of strength.

Methods of Thinking and Arguments

With regard to "knowing the language," Mencius was dedicated to "rectifying names" and advancing arguments for his moral convictions. But the basis for such intellectual efforts is to be found in his insightful observations of natural human feelings. He discerned the beginnings of these feelings, traced them to the goodness of human nature, and argued that every person should preserve and develop them.

Because Mencius's arguments for the goodness of human nature were based on his observations rather than on philosophical argumentation, the arguments he presented in his debates with Gaozi and his chapter on Gaozi are instructive and illuminating with regard to Mencius as a philosopher. Overall, Mencius's arguments were formulated so as to reject Gaozi's Daoist view of human nature as originally neither good nor bad. Mencius wanted to establish his thesis that human nature was innately good, and that therefore one needed to cultivate it so that moral virtues could flourish.

There are four arguments. In the first argument, Gaozi speaks of an uncarved block of wood and argues that it differs from the utensil to be made from it. He uses this analogy to show the difference between the natural state of human nature and what results from changing it—cultivated morality. Mencius responds by pointing out that one does not destroy the uncarved wood to make a utensil; one must, rather, follow the nature of the wood. Similarly, one does not destroy human nature to create morality but instead follows human nature to develop morality. Here we can see that Gaozi and Mencius are exploring different aspects of the analogy. For Gaozi, human skill does destroy the nature of the wood; for Mencius, the wood must be capable of being so treated. If we push the analogy further, we will see that the making of the utensil is more an external human imposition than the internal development of the piece of the wood.

If Mencius accepted this analogy, he would have to concede that strong human efforts are needed for moral transformation. But Mencius's own position is that the natural tendencies of man are good and the active capacities of human beings accomplish moral actions. By contrast, a piece of wood has no natural tendency to become a utensil. We can conclude that Gaozi has made his point, but his analogy is not appropriate for the point Mencius has made.

In the second argument—over the nature of water—it is both true that water can go eastward and westward and that water will flow naturally downward rather than upward. Clearly, the nature of water is to flow downward rather than upward, but it is neutral regarding the direction of its flow. The downward flow does not determine whether it goes eastward or westward. Hence Mencius's argument that human nature has a tendency to do good does not change the fact that human nature can be cultivated to become good or bad. What matters is the cultivation, not the natural tendencies—so Gaozi would conclude. Again the belief in the goodness of human nature is based on empirical observations and theoretical understanding, and there is reason to doubt that for Mencius self-cultivation in terms of this description is crucial for the development of human nature into moral nature.

In the third argument, the question revolves around the relation of life to nature and hence human life to human nature. Gaozi treats life (*sheng*) as what gives a species or a living thing a nature. Mencius inserts the question of universal features of things. There are many things that are white, and so white can be considered a universal. Is human nature a universal? Of course not. It is a universal for the human species but not for the other animals. But this does not negate the fact that white is a universal for white things. Hence the suggestion that *sheng* is called nature should be understood not as a matter of universals but as describing the different natures of living things. Each living thing has its specific nature; to deny this leads to the position not that human nature must be good but only that it is specific to human life.

In the fourth argument, Gaozi proposes that our respect for old people depends on their presence and hence is a matter of exterior existence. Mencius looks at respect as an inward feeling in a person who encounters an external respected object. Apparently, with regard to respect for others, no distinction is made between the objective reference and the subjective feeling. Gaozi and Mencius are each looking at one aspect of the relation of respect without paying attention to the other side; hence we can simply conclude that they are talking about separate issues. This leads to other problems of identifying the exteriority or interiority of personal activities or actions: thus a question could be raised as to whether drinking hot soup in winter and drinking water in summer are a matter of external existence or internal existence. In fact the correct answer is that they are both because the relation results from both a thing outside and a human mind inside.

We can see from this analysis that Mencius was not much of a logical philosopher or a cogent arguer. His strength lay in his insightful discernment of the beginnings of things and his experiences of the unity of things in their ultimate reality. He was a macroscopic, not a microscopic, philosopher. This conclusion is borne out not only by his profound and penetrating reflections on human nature but also by his ability to define concepts of relevant ideals and values. Thus, he was able to offer the following visions and definition of values:

> What is desirable is called the good; when one holds something as his own, it is called faith (*xin*); to have a sense of fulfillment is called the beautiful. To have a sense of

> fulfillment and feel radiant is called greatness; what is great, and yet capable of transforming, is called sageliness. Being sagely and capable of being known is called divineness.

Mencius's precise definitions of *liu* (flow), *lian* (link), *huang* (waste), and *wang* (ruined) also show his insight into the various social conditions under a tyrant. His redefinition of a ruler as killed by the people is refreshing and reflects his deep feelings of disgust for oppressive tyrants.

Theory of Benevolent Government and the Rights of Revolution

In his time Mencius witnessed many wars for territory and wealth and a prevalent pursuit of hegemony by states. Despite their common social origins, Mencius came to make a fundamental distinction between action involving pursuit of self-profit (*li*) and action involving benevolence (*ren*) and righteousness (*yi*). Obviously, he did not deny the importance of benefiting the people, but he objected to pursuing profit for the sake of expanding one's power of domination, or for self-glorification. He argued strenuously that to seek profit for oneself was wrong, that as a universal principle it was self-defeating, and that a ruler should not seek profit and glory at the expense of the people's well-being. In his famous encounter with King Liang Hui, Mencius stressed that if everyone from the king to the lowest rank sought only his own profit, there would be killing among the ranks, social disorder, and political instability. Hence self-profit could not be a principle for strengthening a nation—or a family. He also described how the warring states had brought chaos and destruction to the people, whose lives could be dramatically contrasted with the rulers' life of richness and luxury. This was certainly not the correct way of governing, and such rule would not last long.

From these observations Mencius came to his ideas on how a good government was to be conducted. This is his theory of benevolent government.

In the first place, although (like Confucius) Mencius did not speak of the origin of government, he had moved away from the position one finds in the classics that the power and the right to rule derived from the mandate of heaven. Instead, he took the position that this right should be conceived as ultimately coming from the people. He said: "People are most valuable, land and grain are next valuable, and the ruler is least valuable." This observation rested on what Mencius saw as a simple fact: only when a ruler had gained the confidence and support of the people at large did he have the power to reign.

Important questions in this connection are how a ruler would get his support from the people and how people would express their support. Before we deal with this, however, it is important to notice Mencius's placement of people over land and grains, which is expressed by the term *sheji*. People are more important than land and grain because without people land and grain hold no meaning for the existence of a state. No doubt Mencius was thinking of "people" as a collectivity rather than as individuals, but his concern for people still signifies a beginning of the appreciation of the persons who constitute "a people," and it is their well-being that would justify the need for establishing a state.

Mencius did not deny the relevance of the mandate of heaven, but for him it had to be expressed as the mandate of the people. Heaven did not speak, and so its intentions had to be shown in actions and reality. People were part of heaven, and their likes and dislikes should exhibit in a natural way what heaven intended. One might even say that in this sense heaven was people and people were heaven. Hence Mencius quoted the Shangshu statement: "Heaven sees through the seeing of the people and heaven hears through the hearing of the people." This makes clear the humanism that would give content to his theory of benevolent government. It also meant that the legitimacy of government was based on the general sentiments of the people, whose minimal goal of life was freedom from oppression and persecution and whose general desire in life was satisfaction of basic needs and comforts in old age.

Hence the Confucian doctrine of benevolent love was not to be considered simply a matter of feeling for the people; it entailed bringing substantial well-being to the people. Still, feeling for the people was a starting point, for only from attentiveness to sympathetic and empathetic understanding of the conditions of the life of the people was the ruler able to design and implement a system of institutions and policies for actually benefiting them.

There were two policies that a benevolent government could follow: "Do not get used to killing people" and "Let people share the same joys the ruler has." Apparently, these two rules reflected what was lacking in Mencius's time. To practice them, for Mencius, was the beginning of benevolent government.

The two rules would also draw people to the benevolent ruler as if to a magnet, and hence the world would be unified under him. When he was asked by King Liang Xiang how the world would be settled in peace, Mencius replied, "settled in oneness." What was this unifying oneness? Mencius replied: "Those who do not love to kill people are capable of unifying the world." All people would aspire to such a state, where they would have freedom from persecution and oppression; they would—to use another image—flow to the benevolent ruler as water flows downward. We may note here that Mencius was applying the history of the expansion of the Western Zhou to the present state. One difficulty, however, was that the people of his time had less freedom of choice than the people of the Western Zhou; another difficulty was that the benevolent state had to be strong enough to withstand invasion.

As to the ruler's sharing his joys with the people, it was also necessary not to tax people heavily to pay for the ruler's exclusive luxuries. But Mencius was advocating this rule on the basis of the Confucian principle of reciprocity: if a ruler enjoys the joys of the people, people will also enjoy the joys of the ruler; if a ruler worries about the troubles of the people, people will also worry about the troubles of the ruler. Hence the people would form a unity with the ruler, and there was no reason why the benevolent ruler might not unify the world. The Confucian principle of reciprocity could also be extended to all circumstances, so that benevolent feelings and benevolent policies would apply in all circumstances, which would lead to defining the "way of a virtuous king" (*wangdao*). *Wangdao* is simply the way of government and a way of living in which nothing is not geared toward mutuality of feelings and support.

It is on the basis of *wangdao* that the killing of a king (regicide) becomes inconceivable. Thus for Mencius, the killing of Zou (or Zhu), the last king of the Shang, was not a killing of a king at all, for Zou had not behaved like a king and had exhibited no benevolence toward his people. The people had risen to remove Zou as their sovereign in favor of a ruler who would give them their basic needs. Hence he says: "I have heard that one tyrant by name of Zou was killed and there is no hearing on regicide." Does this formulate a "right of revolutionary removal of a ruler"? The answer is both yes and no. Mencius did not advocate the killing of a cruel and vicious king as a general principle; he merely cited the killing of Zou as an instance of removing a tyrant. Yet there is no denying that this instance of removing a tyrant has been given a moral justification and represents a timely reminder of the necessity to maintain a society free from persecution and oppression.

In general, however, Mencius did not indicate how people should express their sentiments for the formation or transformation of a government. That is, he did not formulate a rational theory for the people's exercise of their concern or their right and power to form a government of their choice. In this sense, Mencius may not have articulated a formal theory of democracy or rule by the people. Instead, he simply argued for the rule for the people. On the other hand, one could imagine that Mencius would endorse a democratic government by the people if he could imagine that people knew the art of rulership. For him, "people" was still a collective term and lacked the sense of being able to select or elect individuals from this collectivity for the purpose of ruling. Hence Mencius's "rule of the people" could be best achieved through the person of a sage king. Whether he was elected or not would not be essential to benevolent rule.

Mencius went on to outline, in some detail, how a sage king would care for the people. He included protecting their natural resources, economic and material sufficiency, moral interests, and social harmony. According to his social plan for protecting the property of the people (*zhimin zhizhan*), each person and each family would have a means of support and would at the same time contribute to public collective welfare of the community. One may still question the practicality and efficacy of his system, in light of the radically changed circumstances of population and social organization in his time.

See also Confucianism: Confucius; Confucianism: Constructs of Classical Thought.

Bibliography

Bosley, Richard. "Do Mencius and Hume Make the Same Ethical Mistake?" *Philosophy East and West*, 38(1), 1988, pp. 3–18.

Chan, Alan, ed. *Mencius: Contexts and Interpretations*. Honolulu: University of Hawaii Press, 2002.

Cheng, Chung-ying. "Mencius." In *Chinese Thought: An Introduction*, ed. Donald H. Bishop. New York: 1994, pp. 110–149.

———. "Warring States Confucianism and the Thought of Mencius and Its Development." *Academia Sinica Chinese Studies in Philosophy*, 8(3), 1977, pp. 4–66. (Translation of *Mengzidesixiang jiqifazhan*.)

Ivanhoe, Philip J. *Ethics in the Confucian Tradition: The Thought of Mencius and Wang Yangming*. Atlanta, Ga.: Scholars, 1990.

Lau, D. C. *Mencius*. New York: Penguin, 1970.

Nivison, David S. "Problems in the Mengzi: 6A3–5" and "Problems in the Mengzi: 7A17." In *The Ways of Confucianism: Investigations in Chinese Philosophy*, ed. Bryan W. Van Norden. Chicago and La Salle, Ill.: Open Court, 1996.

Ryan, James A. "Moral Philosophy and Moral Psychology in Mencius." *Asian Philosophy*, 8(1), 1998, pp. 47–64.

Shun, Kwong-loi. *Mencius and Early Chinese Thought*. Stanford, Calif.: Stanford University Press, 1994.

Tang, Junyi. *Zhongguo zhexue yuanlun* (On the Origins of Chinese Philosophy), 3 vols. Taipei: Xuesheng, 1966, 1968, 1973.

Yearley, Lee H. *Mencius and Aquinas: Theories of Virtue and Conceptions of Courage*. Albany: State University of New York Press, 1990.

Zhao, Qi. *Mengzi zhu*.

Zhu, Xi. *Sishu jizhu*. Hong Kong: Taiping, 1980.

Metaphysics

Vincent SHEN

The term *xing er shang xue* or simply *xingshangxue*, which now serves as a translation of the western word "metaphysics," is connected to a long tradition of Chinese philosophy. This term comes from the *Great Appendix I* of the *Book of Changes* (*Yijing*), where we read: "Therefore that which is above *xing* (material form) is the *dao*; that which is under *xing* is *qi* (implements or ontic things)."

The term *dao* is a common denominator for "ultimate reality" in all schools of Chinese philosophy, such as Confucianism, Daoism, and Buddhism. All discourses on the *dao* in Chinese philosophy can be seen as belonging to *xing er shang xue*, that is, to metaphysics. Since appealing to a doctrine of the *dao* so as to expound a vision of the ultimate reality is common to all schools of Chinese philosophy, we can also say that there really is some metaphysics in Chinese philosophy. On this point, we can also compare metaphysics in Chinese philosophy with metaphysics in western philosophy.

Comparing Metaphysics in Western and Chinese Philosophy

In western philosophy, "metaphysics" came from *ta-meta-ta-physica*, a term given by Andronicus of Rhodes to a group of Aristotelian manuscripts arranged after those of *Physics*. It has different meanings, stemming from two metaphysical traditions.

First, in the Aristotelian tradition the prefix "meta-"means "after," and metaphysics means a science that is to be learned after physics. The term therefore had to do with the order of learning. On the basis of his epistemological theory of three levels of abstraction—physical (of the material and kinetic aspect of being), mathematical (of forms and quantity), and metaphysical (of being as such)—Aristotle defined metaphysics as "a science which investigates being qua being and the attributes which belong to this in virtue of its own nature" (*Metaphysics*, 1003a, 21–22).

Second, in the Platonic tradition the prefix "meta-" means "trans-" or "above," and metaphysics is the study of "true beings"—that is, the "ideas" or "forms" which exist in a higher way than the physical world and of which all physical things are but copies. This sense has to do more with the ontological status of the object under study than with an order of learning.

In Chinese philosophy, we find this statement in the *Book of Changes*: "That which is above *xing* (material form) is the *dao*; that which is below *xing* is *qi* (ontic things)." Thus, we discern three levels of things: *qi*, *xing*, and *dao*, which correspond more or less to the physical, the mathematical, and the metaphysical in Aristotle. But for Aristotle the three levels pertain to the classification of sciences, a hierarchy of abstraction, and an order of learning, whereas in Chinese philosophy *qi*, *xing*, and *dao* are derived from a distinction that applies to the totality of existence and is not limited to science and knowledge.

Qi

Qi refers to anything definite and concrete, either natural or artificial. In others words, it concerns things existing in nature and the human world. Sometimes *qi* means, abstractly, the characteristic of being definite, or being constrained or limited. For example, Confucius's saying *junzi bu qi* means that a *junzi* (noble man) should not set limits on himself (regarding any definite achievement). *Qi* is the first level of things. Generally, the term *qi* is connected to the term *xing*, so as to constitute a definite and concrete thing.

Xing

Xing, "material form"—which is understood as "form," "paradigm," or "model"—refers to that which renders a concrete being its ideal yet definite form. The *Book of Changes* says: "The construction of implements should emphasize its emblematic figures." And: "To appear is always to appear with an emblematic figure; when it receives its complete form, we call it a definite thing." *Xing* is the second level of things.

It should be noticed that in Chinese thinking, which attaches itself more than western thought to the concrete world of life, the abstract forms have no independent existence and their development is not considered in terms of logic. For this reason, "form" in Chinese philosophy is not the kind of abstract forms that are part of mathematics and logic. Rather, it is always made concrete as a definite form in the shaping of natural things or artificial implements; we might describe it as a concrete universal.

Although mathematics was developed to a very advanced stage in the history of Chinese science and technology, it was always used pragmatically, that is, in measurement and calculation. Mathematics and logic were used in Chinese thought to describe or discuss empirical data—not, as in modern western science, to construct theories. Also, we can say that traditional Chinese science, which involved advanced mathematics, was opposed to any pure, abstract concept of form. However, it is true that the character of formal combination after the *Book of Changes* foreshadowed a certain development toward abstract form, from the traditional emphasis on concrete forms.

Dao

In traditional Chinese thought, *xing* and *qi* unite in a concrete world of existence; and human beings, living in this unceasingly changing world, comprehend—especially in their moral and artistic actions—the existence of "creative creativity," a continuous creative act above the human world and the natural environment. This idea brought Chinese philosophers to the concept of *dao*, "that which is above *xing*," i.e., above material form. *Dao* is the third level of things.

The meaning of dao. We can analyze *dao* as having several layers of meaning.

First, etymologically, the Chinese word *dao* is composed of two elements, the head and the act of walking along a way. Together, they mean a "way" on which one can work out a direction and a way out. This image of a way is very suggestive, and it is important to understanding *dao*—which can be a way of life, a way of civilization, the way of a people, and so on, although *dao* is never limited to the idea of a physical way. As Heidegger says, it is actually improper to represent *dao* as a physical way, as the distance between two points. However, *dao* might be "the Way which puts everything on the ways."

Second, *dao* means "to say," "to speak," or "to discourse." This is the sense of the second word *dao* in Laozi's saying, "The *dao* that could be said (*daoed*) is not the eternal *dao*." In Chinese philosophy, especially Daoism and Buddhism, the function of discourse is always taken in its negative sense. Discourse, once said, must be hushed; words, once written, must be erased. The ultimate reality is never to be pronounced by any human language. This is quite different from western philosophy, which from the outset has emphasized the function of language, of *logos*, in expressing reality, sometimes even to the point of taking language as the only reality.

Third, *dao* means "law of becoming" or "law of nature." In Chinese cosmology, *dao*, especially *tiandao* (heavenly *dao*), always has this meaning, which in turn has two aspects. One aspect is that according to structural law, all things are constituted of elements which are different yet complementary, such as being and nonbeing, *yin* and *yang*, movement and rest, or weak and strong. The second aspect is that according to dynamic law, once a state of affairs is developed to an extreme limit in the process of change, then it will naturally move to the opposite state of affairs.

Fourth, *dao* means "the origin," which gives birth to all things. If the law of nature reigns over all things, there must be an origin that gives birth to all things, so as to constitute the cosmic law. Normally, the process by which the origin gives birth to all things is seen as its self-manifestation through differentiation and progressive complexity. Laozi says: "The *dao* gave birth to one. One gave birth to two. Two gave birth to three. Three gave birth to all things." Different Chinese philosophical schools formulated various doctrines about this cosmogonic process, but they cannot be covered in this brief essay.

Fifth, as we have seen, *dao* also represents the "ultimate reality." In Confucianism, this could be the heavenly *dao* or the *ren dao*. In Buddhism, the ultimate reality could be emptiness—or, so as not to attach oneself to emptiness, the "emptying of emptiness." In Daoism, the *dao* is the ever self-manifesting "act of existence."

The Daoist concept is perhaps most interesting with regard to understanding *dao* as the ultimate reality. If there is an origin giving birth to all things, then there must be a self-manifesting act of existence before it becomes the origin for all things, which is defined in relation to all things. The self-manifesting act of existence is "reality itself." All that we say about the *dao* is but a "constructed reality," and constructed reality is not and never can be "reality itself." There is something of a paradox here: one should say *dao* in order to express it; but once said, it becomes a constructed reality, not reality itself. Thus in order to keep the human mind open to reality itself, all human constructions are subject to deconstruction.

Dao in metaphysics. The "discourse of *dao*" as metaphysics in Chinese philosophy generally refers to the third, fourth, and fifth meanings of *dao*:

- *Dao* as laws of nature, generally called the heavenly *dao*, which represent the cosmological aspect of Chinese philosophy.
- *Dao* as the origin giving birth to all things, which represents the process of transition from ontology to cosmology.
- *Dao* as reality itself, which represents the ontological aspect.

However, we should be aware that usually these three meanings or levels are closely related to one another, so much so that they were often mixed up in traditional Chinese philosophical discourse, and texts seldom distinguished among them. Therefore, analyzing them as clearly distinct yet forming a well-connected whole is a task of today's Chinese philosophers.

Somehow, the *dao* is above all empirical beings and all formal beings. In this sense, the "meta-" of Chinese metaphysics is closer to that of Platonic metaphysics. But in Chinese metaphysics—unlike Plato's metaphysics—there is no dualism of ideal world and physical world, sensation and reason. In Chinese philosophy, the *dao*, even though as origin it transcends all things, is still present in all things. And all things, even when born from the *dao*, are still in the *dao* and return to it through their internal dynamism. This is best illustrated in the chapter "Knowledge Wandering North" in the *Zhuangzi*:

> Dong Guozi asked Zhuangzi, "Where does it exist, the so-called *dao*?"
> Zhuangzi said, "There is no place in which it doesn't exist."
> "Please specify so that I can catch your idea."
> "It is in the ant."
> "As low as that?"
> "It is in the grass."
> "How can it be lower?"
> "It is in the tiles and shards."
> "How can it be lower still?"
> "It is in piss and shit."
> Thereupon Dong Guozi refused to respond.

In this metaphysics, constituted of the interplay between transcendence and immanence, not only is everything imbued inherently with the *dao*, but also the meaning of the existence of everything is to manifest the *dao*, to be a concrete manifestation of it. We can understand, then, why Wang Fuzhi maintains that events cannot be separated from *li* (principles, patterns) and *li* cannot be separated from events: the *dao* cannot be separated from *qi* (vital force), and *qi* cannot be separated from the *dao*. In his commentary on the proposition "That which is above *xing* (material form) is *dao*; that which is under *xing* is *qi* (ontic things)," Wang Fuzhi wrote:

> "That which is under *xing*" pertains to those material forms which are concretized into things, and thereby become visible and traceable, in which the *dao* which is above the *xing* becomes implicit. There must be material forms so that its precedent formative power could become explicit, and the functional effectiveness of that which is in consequent use could be determined. That is why we call it "above *xing*" but never "separated from *xing*"; *dao* and *qi* will never be separated each from other.

We can see, therefore, that in Chinese metaphysics, the *dao* should always manifest itself through *qi*, through the relationship between one *qi* and another *qi*, and through human efforts—moral, artistic, and historical creativity. Also, all natural phenomena, all cultural values, and all social and historical processes are simply occasions for the manifestation of the *dao*; their meaning consists always in manifesting the *dao* and marching toward the *dao*. The task of the metaphysician is to experience and grasp the *dao* in all its manifestations: natural phenomena, human thought, artistic creation, moral acts, historical process. This is the special characteristic of all Chinese metaphysics.

Moral Metaphysics

In contemporary Chinese philosophy, we find the term "moral metaphysics," proposed by Mou Zongsan (Mou Tsung-san), a famous figure in neo-Confucianism. Mou distinguishes between "moral metaphysics," understood as a kind of metaphysics proper to Confucian moral praxis, and "metaphysics of morals," which for Mou is a metaphysical study of morality, and therefore a kind of moral philosophy rather than metaphysics. In fact, what is called moral metaphysics represents an effort to underline the role of Confucianism and moral actions in Chinese metaphysical thinking.

Mou distinguishes between the moral metaphysics (*daode di xingshangxue*) of Confucianism and the liberation metaphysics (*jietuo di xingshangxue*) of Daoism and Buddhism. He assumes that all three schools of Chinese philosophy consider the human mind capable of "intellectual intuition," *zhi di zhijue*. (That term is borrowed from Kant, who made a distinction between intellectual intuition and sense intuition; however, Kant believed that God alone was capable of intellectual intuition and humans were capable only of sense intution.) But despite this assumption, Mou would prefer the Confucian way of attaining the ultimate reality through moral actions and moral self-awareness.

According to Mou, the human being, in his moral actions, can actualize his own intellectual intuition through the dynamism of moral awareness, the reality of *jen* (*jenti*), which, transcending all subject-object dualism, represents for him the ultimate reality or the "thing in itself." Sometimes Mou names this: for instance, as the "free infinite mind-heart" or the "true self." The free infinite mind, possessing in itself the characteristics of universality, infinity, and creativity, is for Mou the ultimate reality in the metaphysical sense, or the world of noumena, which, through a process of self-negation similar to Fichte's "I" positing a "non-I," can unfold itself into a world of phenomena. Human intellectual intuition comes out as an act of self-awareness of the free infinite mind-heart. Therefore, Mou has no need to posit a personal God.

We should note that, in making Confucianism a kind of metaphysics, Mou of necessity neglects the methods of Confucian moral praxis—which becomes an instrument for attaining the ultimate reality. In this regard, Mou's moral metaphysics shows a certain weakness relative to western philosophy, with its grand metaphysical systems. Also, in positing such a moral metaphysics exclusively, Mou disregarded other "metaphysical experiences," such as those to be found in encounters with nature, artistic creativity, religious piety, and historical process—all of which, in traditional Chinese culture, have rich metaphysical implications. Moreover, Mou's absolute idealism blurred the distinction between reality itself (the *dao*) and constructed reality, such as that posited by human moral actions and moral self-awareness.

Conclusion

Although philosophical metaphysics is historically best developed in western philosophy, we can nevertheless say that Chinese philosophy has its own metaphysical way of thinking, as expressed in its discourses on the *dao*, its cosmology, and its theories of human nature. Still, without systematical development, Chinese philosophy presents only what might be described as "implicit metaphysics," in contrast to the "explicit metaphysics" of western philosophy.

Mou Zongsan's moral metaphysics can be seen as a modern effort to articulate and construct a systematic metaphysics by bringing Confucianism to confront the challenge of certain German idealists, such as Kant, Fichte, and Hegel. But in making his moral metaphysics an absolute idealism, he seems to lead Chinese philosophy into the dead end of self-enclosed humanism.

We might conclude, therefore, that Chinese philosophy is still in need of a more open way of doing metaphysical thinking. A task for the future is to make explicit and systematic a Chinese metaphysics, based on the rich cultural experiences and philosophical depth of the Chinese tradition, but avoiding the logical-ontotheological constitution of western metaphysics.

See also *Dao*; Mou Zongsan; Wang Fuzhi; Zhuangzi.

Bibliography

Chan, Wing-tsit, trans. *A Source Book in Chinese Philosophy*. Princeton, N.J.: Princeton University Press, 1963.

——. *The Way of Laozi: A Translation and Study of the Tao-te Ching*. New York: Bobbs-Merrill, 1963.

Fang, Thomé. *Chinese Philosophy: Its Spirit and Its Development*. Taipei: Linking, 1981.

Fung, Yu-lan. *A History of Chinese Philosophy*, trans. Derk Bodde, 2 vols. Princeton, N.J.: Princeton University Press, 1952–1953.

I Ching or Book of Changes, trans. Cary F. Baynes, 2 vols. New York: Pantheon, 1950. (Translated from the German version of Richard Wilhelm.)

Mou, Zongsan. *Xinti yu xingti* (The Substance of Mind and the Substance of Nature). Taipei: Zheng-zhung, 1978.

——. *Yuanshan lun* (On Supreme Good). Taipei: Student Bookstore, 1985.

——. *Zhi di zhixue yu Zhongguo zhexue* (Intellectual Intuition and Chinese Philosophy). Taipei: Commercial Press, 1971.

Shen, Vincent. *After Physics—The Development of Metaphysics*. Taipei: Newton, 1987. (In Chinese.)

——. "Dao and Cosmology in the Kuodian Texts of Laozi—In Comparison with Other Related Texts." *Zhexue Yu Wenhua*, 26(4), 1999, pp. 298–316.

——. "Laozi di xingshang sixiang (Laozi's Metaphysics)." *Zhexue Yu Wenhua* 15(12), 1988, pp. 814–822.

——. "Zhuangzi di-daolun dui dangdai xingshang kunhuo di yige jieda (Zhuangzi's Dao-Discourse—Answers to Contemporary Metaphysical Questions)." *National Chengchi University Philosophical Journal*, No. 1, 1994, pp. 19–34.

Tang, Junyi. *Zhongguo zhexue yuanlun—Yuandao pian* (Inquiry on Chinese Philosophy: Inquiry on the Dao), 3 vols. Hong Kong: New Asia Institute, 1973.

Wang, Fuzhi. "Zhouyi waizhuan (Outer Commentary on the Book of Changes)," Book 5. In *Quanshan Yi xue* (Quanshan's Studies on the Book of Changes), Vol. 2. Taipei: Kuang-wen Bookstore, 1974, pp. 915–965.

Watson, Burton. *The Complete Works of Chuang Tzu*. New York: Columbia University Press, 1968.

Mohism: The Founder, Mozi (Mo Tzu)

David B. Wong

Very little is known about Mozi (Mo Tzu, fl. 470–391 B.C.E.; his personal name was Di). However, the fact that he frequently uses analogies from the crafts, such as carpenter's squares, compasses, and plumb lines, suggests that he came from the artisan class. He studied Confucianism but came to vehemently oppose it for what he saw as its aristocratic elitism, preoccupation with ritual, overelaborate musical performances, and advocacy of partiality instead of equal concern for all. The text *Mozi* appears to be the product of a common oral tradition, given the extremely repetitive structure of the argumentation and the fact that different versions of the same essay sometimes have very close but never identical phrasing. The ten essays propound ten central doctrines. The three versions of each essay (some of them missing) may correspond to three different sects of Mohism (Graham 1978, 35–36). Taken together, however, the chapters provide a reasonably consistent portrait of Mozi's philosophy.

Mohism became the major rival to Confucianism for a good part of the ancient era up to the beginning of the Han dynasty (206 B.C.E.–220 C.E.) but afterward lost virtually all its following. A possible historical factor in its downfall was the development of the highly centralized bureaucratic state that subordinated the interests of the artisan class (Hansen 1992, 99) and could not tolerate an organized political and social movement existing outside the confines of the established political order (Schwartz 1985, 169). Another factor is that Mohism was incompatible with the deep-rooted features of the Chinese elite culture; this also helps to explain why Mozi is often taken lightly in the post-ancient philosophical tradition.

Dispassionate Intellect and Utilitarianism in Mozi

Confucianism is a virtue ethics that focuses on traits and attitudes of ideal persons such as the *junzi* (the superior person), in whom right feeling and wise intellect fuse (Cua 1978, ch. 4). Mozi, by contrast, emphasizes the need for detachment from emotions such as pleasure, anger, joy, sadness, and love as unreasoned attachment (*Mozi*, ch. 47). The dispassionate intellect alone is necessary and sufficient for discovering the truth. The *Mozi* provides the first textual evidence of reasoned argument in the classical period and even the beginnings of a methodology of argument. Just as Mozi was said to have made himself an expert in the tactics of siege warfare in order to defend smaller states from larger states, he conceived of the search for truth as a war between conflicting views. In Chapter 35, Mozi presents three standards or gnomons (*biao*, but in other places he uses *fa*) of argument: in verifying a proposition, one first consults the actions of the sage kings; second, one relies on the consensus of humankind based on their experience; third, one relies on the beneficial or harmful consequences of a given belief. It is in his third standard, the utilitarian evaluation of belief, that Mozi distinguishes himself from the Confucians. In fact, the first standard arguably receives its warrant from the third in Mozi: it is because the sage kings produced prosperity and harmony that we see their superior wisdom.

Mozi applies dispassionate intellect analytically to identify the causes of things, especially the causes of human conflict. He sees one characteristic unifying all the causes: partiality. To his credit, he observes that partiality does not simply take the form of egoism. Heads of families, he says, know only to love their own families. They consequently mobilize their families to usurp others. Feudal lords know only to love their own states and consequently mobilize their own to attack others (*Mozi*, ch. 16). Such partiality causes a Hobbesian war of all against all, where the warring entities are families and states as well as individuals. Since the war harms everyone, in terms of self-regarding interests and interests in families and states, the proper conclusion is to override one's own tendency to partiality and to practice *jian ai*, traditionally translated as "universal love." In accordance with Mozi's emphasis on the dispassionate intellect, love in this context means neither *eros* nor *agape* but something closer to "impartial reasoned concern" (Schwartz, 149). It is only through such concern, Mozi argues, that one can advance one's own welfare and the welfare of those to whom one is partial.

Mozi's doctrine of universal love, combined with his emphasis on evaluating beliefs according to consequences in terms of benefit and harm (*li-hai*), makes him the singular representative of utilitarianism in Chinese thought. His is, however, a materialistic utilitarianism rather than the hedonistic variety most commonly represented in the western tradition. In accordance with his deemphasis of feeling and his desire for objective standards, Mozi's conception of benefit and harm refers to no psychological goods and harms such as pleasure and pain but rather exclusively to material goods and harms such as enriching the poor, increasing the population, and bringing about order (*Mozi*, ch. 25). In its focus on *yi* (what is proper or right) and the determination of what is *yi* according to beneficial and harmful consequences, Mozi's ethic is wholly outer-directed (Schwartz, 147) and contrasts with the inner-directedness one finds in Confucianism, which focuses at least partly (though certainly not exclusively) on developing oneself and ensuring that one has the right motives for acting correctly.

Mozi's Critique of Confucian Traditions

The dispassionate intellect does not rely on tradition. That a practice is old does not in itself mean that it is valid (*Mozi*, ch. 25). After all, the ancient practices the Confucians endorsed were once new (ch. 39). Mozi's critical reflection on tradition is not completely unprecedented. Confucius (*Analects*, 9.3) endorses a contemporary ceremonial practice over traditional practice on the ground that the contemporary practice is more frugal. While *li* (rules of ritual ceremony, propriety) is obviously a central value for Confucius, so is *ren* (humanity, benevolence), and *ren* seems not simply reducible to *li* (Shun 1993). Moreover, some scholars have argued that *yi* in Confucius provides grounds for departing from *li* and even that *yi* can provide a perspective justifying observance of *li* (Cheng 1991, 233–237; Cua 1984, 230; Tu 1979, 22, 30). Mozi's new contribution, however, was to explicitly emphasize the importance of the distinction between the traditional and the right in order to mount a broad attack on tradition.

For example, Mozi argued that elaborate funerals and the lengthy mourning periods advocated by Confucians simply bury wealth, keep the people poor, and take up time that could have been used productively (*Mozi*, ch. 20). Similarly, he condemned the musical performances that Confucius prized so highly because of the expenditures rulers lavished on staging them (ch. 32). He did not deny music some aesthetic value, but clearly he did not see in it the power of moral transformation that Confucius saw, nor does Mozi's materialistic conception of benefit and harm allow much importance to the psychological and expressive satisfactions of music. Rather, a sense of urgency runs throughout his criticisms of various traditions: the people live in poverty without adequate shelter, warm clothes, and nourishing food; elaborate funerals, mourning rites, and musical performances are luxuries of the aristocracy bought at the expense of the vast majority.

Mozi is best-known for criticism of the traditional acceptance of partiality, which may be defined as a tendency to favor someone's interests over others because of that person's relation to oneself. Although Mozi criticizes partiality on the basis of a contestable reading of the sage kings, his most compelling criticism is the utilitarian argument that it is ultimately bad for everyone and especially bad for those without power and wealth. Mozi was aware, of course, that Confucians rejected his utilitarian standard. But in a series of interesting arguments in Chapter 16, he claims that even the advocate of partiality must in practice be "universal-minded" if he is to achieve his goals.

If people were to choose a ruler, Mozi argues, they would be well advised to choose the universal-minded ruler over the partial ruler, who, being partial to himself, would not feed, clothe, care for, or bury the people. Similarly, a man setting out to war would entrust the care of his family to a universal-minded man rather than a partial man. The filial son who is concerned to benefit and love his parents will make it a point to love and benefit other parents so that they in turn will love and benefit his parents. The person who loves himself will love others because they will love him in return. Hansen (112) takes the thrust of such arguments to be that the Confucian *dao* (way, or Way) is a self-defeating *dao*—i.e., complying correctly with this *dao* commits one to advocating that people should heed a rival *dao*. However, there are problems with this strategy of argument that raise questions about the nature of Mozi's utilitarian standard of universal love and about the way he contrasts his standard with the rival Confucian doctrine of love with distinctions.

The Contested Meanings of Love with Distinctions and Universal Love

The first problem with Mozi's argument is that it works best as an argument against a kind of partiality the Confucians never endorsed. Partiality, as Mozi conceives it for the purposes of his argument, seems to be an absolute preference for those standing in an appropriate relationship to oneself, where "absolute" means that no weight is given at all to others outside the relationship. By assuming that this is what partiality means, Mozi is able to argue that the partial ruler will not care for his people at all and that it would be folly to turn the care of one's family over to a partial man. However, Confucians do not prescribe such absolute preference. They do not hold that one owes everything to those with whom one has a special relationship and owes nothing to strangers. Love with distinctions has a universalistic element. In the *Analects* 6.30, 14.42, and 5.16, for example, the ruler's duties include ensuring peace and security for his people. Love with distinctions thus in principle includes everyone within its scope, but even though certain things are owed to everyone, one owes more to certain people because one stands in certain relationships to them. Natural love and felt obligations that obtain between family members form the core of the Confucian way to live, but this core is not the entire Confucian *dao*. While the proper Confucian ruler might do things for his family that he would not do for other subjects, he would certainly strive to feed, clothe, care for, and bury his subjects as necessary, unlike the partial-minded ruler of Mozi's argument.

Still, one can defend Mozi by arguing that in the case of going off to war, one would prefer to turn the care of one's family over to a universal-minded man rather than a Confucian *junzi*. The reason is that the *junzi* would give greater weight to the interests of his own family even as he gave some weight to the interests of one's own family. But if this is the argument, another problem arises. Does Mozi really mean to prescribe that one give equal weight to *everyone's* interests in deciding how to distribute one's time, energy, and resources? If so, then it might be foolish to turn the care of one's family over to the universal-minded man, since such a man would be spreading himself too thin in attempting to tend to the needy. The universal-minded man might decide to exhaust his resources and to give some bare minimum for survival to as many of the needy as he could, in which case the benefit to one's family might be greatly inferior to what the Confucian *junzi* would provide. One is hard-pressed to find a way to save Mozi's argument. Mozi is free, of course, to insist on the rightness of addressing the urgent needs of the greatest number in as egalitarian a fashion as he can, just as the contemporary utilitarian Peter Singer (1972) argues that the relatively affluent have a duty to contribute their resources to famine relief until the point where their own welfare begins to be worse than the welfare of those they are aiding. There is much that is admirable in this position, but it cannot support the argument that the Confucian *dao* is self-defeating.

The preceding discussion gives rise to a more fundamental question about Mozi's utilitarianism: in what sense did he mean that we must give equal weight to the interests of all? One possibility is that he meant this quite literally: on each and every occasion of acting, one must give equal weight to the interests of all with no regard to one's relationship to them. This is an act-utilitarian conception of universal love. But the fact that Mozi seems to interpret, or misinterpret, Confucian love with distinctions as requiring an absolute preference for one's own makes possible a second way in which he could have opposed that doctrine. If he interprets Confucianism as advocating that one give no weight at all to the needs of strangers, his doctrine would differ from love with distinctions if it merely required one to address the interests of everyone while allowing greater attention to the interests of some. Mozi could have held such a doctrine if he held, like some contemporary utilitarians, that one promotes the interests of everyone in the long run if one adheres to a general rule or practice of giving greater weight to people standing in relationships to the self such as family, but that such a rule or practice is strictly justified by its conduciveness to the welfare of everyone in the long run. More important, such a rule or practice is limited by the requirement that everyone's good be promoted in the long run. Such a position would amount to a kind of rule or practice utilitarianism (for the distinction between act and rule utilitarianism, see Smart 1956).

In rule or practice utilitarianism, one judges not individual acts by their consequences, but general rules or practices. One reason given for such a procedure is that deciding each individual action by its consequences is an overwhelming task, which human beings, with their very limited rationality and information, are not well equipped to handle. Hence the task of individual agents is to go by general rules or practices, which are themselves judged according to their conduciveness to utility over the long run. With this principle in mind, one might argue that people's interests are best satisfied by those who know them best and who are naturally disposed to have affection for them. Family members arguably fit this description. This would be a utilitarian basis for a general rule or practice permitting and even requiring agents to give greater attention to those closest to them. Forms of acceptable partiality on a rule-utilitarian basis might include having direct and full responsibility for the welfare of one's elderly parents, where one has no similar responsibility for the elderly parents of others.

However, since the ultimate justification of the practice of partiality toward one's own family would be its conduciveness to the general utility, there would have to be limits on what constituted permissible partiality. One possible limit is suggested by the famous case in the *Analects* (13.18) in which a son testifies against his father for stealing a sheep. In his part of the country, Confucius says, right-thinking family members cover up for each other. Where any acceptable form of partiality is defined by its conduciveness to the general good in the long run, a rule-utilitarian case could be made for disallowing Confucius's partiality. Therefore, even though the rule-utilitarian interpretation of universal love would permit a certain amount of partiality in action, a strict limit on such partiality would be prescribed, based on the ultimate Mohist value of promoting the good of all equally.

No textual evidence exists to settle decisively the issue between the act-utilitarian and rule-utilitarian interpretations of Mozi's universal love, even if it sometimes appears that Mozi had in mind the act-utilitarian interpretation. For example, he argues in Chapter 16 that a filial son who wants to benefit his parents will benefit other parents so that they will in turn benefit his parents. However, one could act on Mozi's advice and provide other parents benefits that were less than what one provided to one's own parents. Sometimes Mozi characterizes the universal-minded man as "treating others the same as myself" (ch. 16). But one could interpret this phrase in two ways: one could be treating others the same as oneself if one promotes the interests of all equally in each and every action (the act interpretation); or one could treat others the same as oneself if one accepts only rules and practices that are justified by their utility to everyone in the long run (the rule interpretation).

Both Mohist universal love and Confucian love with distinctions, therefore, are more complex in their meaning and application than either Mozi or his Confucian opponents made them out to be. Confucian criticisms of Mohism assume something like an act-utilitarian interpretation of universal love and neglect the possible rule-utilitarian interpretation that allows people to treat their family members differently from others. Mohists incorrectly interpret love with distinctions as requiring absolute preference for one's own and neglect the fact that the doctrine requires some degree of concern for everyone even if that concern is not equal to the concern one ought to have for one's family. Such omissions and errors in understanding undermine the force of many arguments each side brings against the other. Are there better arguments available to both sides?

The Argument That Confucian Love with Distinctions Leads to Destructive Partiality

The fact that Mohism would prescribe a strict limit on acceptable partiality, on either the act or the rule interpretation, suggests a better argument against Confucianism: love with distinctions gives no guidance as to when the interests of one's own do and do not override the interests of others. It fails to set clear limits on our tendency to favor our own, and therefore potentially legitimates every kind of favoritism. The universalist element in Confucianism is at continual risk of being subordinated to partiality. After all, if Confucius requires the son to cover up for the father's theft of a sheep, why not steal or kill for the father? This criticism of Confucian love with distinctions is directed at the way the doctrine is likely to be practiced, given the vagueness with which the universalist and partialist elements are balanced. In effect, it strikes at the heart of a central feature of Confucian ethics: its contextuality. Confucianism is not a principle-based ethic, though principles such as *shu* (altruism) and rules such as the *li* (rules of propriety) are used to identify considerations and guidelines that should be taken into account. In the end, it all rests on the judgment and wisdom of the *junzi*, who very much responds to the situation at hand and decides whether the *li* do or do not apply to it. The rest of us take guidance from the *junzi* among us. But the question is how the *junzi* decides conflicts between universal concern and partiality. Given no guidance from the doctrine of love with distinctions, Mohists could argue, people are likely to act on their partiality with no real limits.

Though the contextualism of Confucian ethics has such liabilities, Confucians could retort that these are liabilities of the moral life. From their perspective, clear and definite limits on acceptable partiality would be possible only if Mohist utility were the one and only supreme value. But one's relationships to others matter morally, and in a way not reducible to the idea of the greatest good for the greatest number. Having clear guidelines for behavior may be desirable, but such guidelines are useless if they ignore the complexities of moral life. Furthermore, it is not even obvious that the utility standard yields clear, measurable, definitive guidelines. The precise utility of actions and practices with long-term ramifications is extremely difficult to determine. It is difficult partly because of the limited ability of human beings to gather reliable information about long-term consequences that affect many people, and partly because utility itself—benefit or harm—is not as easy to measure as Mozi assumed.

Arguments from Human Nature: The Possibility of Following Universal Love

The radical nature of Mozi's ethics forced a turn to the discussion of human nature, and in this respect he permanently influenced the course of Chinese philosophy. Universal love seemed to differ so much from people's actual practice that one natural argument against Mozi is that the nature of human beings makes it impossible for them to act on universal love. He responds to such an impossibility argument in Chapter 16, where "men of the world" claim that one could no more put universal love in practice than to pick up Mount T'ai and leap over a river with it. Mozi gives three kinds of response to such an argument: first, that the sage kings proved the possibility of universal love by acting on it; second, that the command of a ruler can motivate people to do even very difficult things; and third, that acting on universal love is not even difficult, because doing so is in one's rational interests.

The first response, fatally, relies on the caricature of love with distinctions as requiring absolute preference for one's own. The sage kings' actions in caring for the people seem to be as much in accord with the universal element in love with distinctions as with universal love. The second response certainly has some weight, but it presumes that rulers themselves can be motivated to command universal love. Furthermore, the power of rulers to influence the behavior of their subjects is not unlimited, so the real question is where the limits lie. The third response relies on three assumptions that are controversial at best and baldly implausible at worst: that people whom one benefits will reliably return those benefits in such proportion that one will have improved one's own position by giving; that heaven (*tian*) will reliably reward conformity and punish nonconformity to universal love; and that people can reliably act on what they know to be in their rational self-interest, regardless of their affective and behavioral dispositions (see Nivison 1980 for a discussion of the problems with this last assumption).

The inadequacy of Mozi's responses, however, does not guarantee a victory for the argument of impossibility. For one thing, that argument loses considerable force under the rule interpretation of universal love. Under such an interpretation, people are indeed permitted and even required to devote more concern to their own. But what they are also required to do is limit that concern when it is harmful to the good of all, and it is not at all clear that this is impossible. Confucians may retort that natural inclinations toward partiality make it impossible for human beings to conform even to this less stringent version of universal love. However, such a retort is double-edged because it can be used to undermine the possibility that human beings can conform to the universalistic element in love with distinctions. That is, if human nature makes it impossible to limit natural partiality for the sake of the general good, wouldn't human nature make it equally impossible to limit natural partiality in favor of the duties to all that Confucians do recognize?

Even under the act interpretation of universal love, which requires people to depart more radically from their current practices of partiality, the argument from impossibility does not clearly succeed. Universal love is not necessarily faulty simply because it is unlikely that everyone will live up to it. It could inspire many people to try to live up to it and, as a consequence, move them to do more good than they would otherwise. Perhaps they will do more good trying to live up to the ideal than they would in trying to live up to a less demanding ideal. Moreover, it is not even clear that the act-utilitarian ideal of universal love is impossible for any human being to follow. Some people in history have shown in their actions an admirable impartial concern for all, even if it is not clear whether the sage kings acted on such a concern. The fact that ordinary people do not often show such concern is not proof of a human impossibility.

The Mencian Response: An Appeal to the Independent Moral Value of Special Relationships

Mencius sometimes appears to be making the impossibility argument against Mohism. For example, in 3A.5, he criticizes the Mohist Yizi (Yi Zhi; Yi Chih) by asking, "Does Yi Zhi seriously believe that a man loves his brother's son no more than his neighbor's newborn son?" Mencius is saying that partiality in some sense is inevitable, that it is going against human nature to strive to be completely impartial. However, it is likely that Mencius was not making a simple impossibility argument. In this context, one must recall the nature of Mencius's "four beginnings" (*duan*, sprouts) of morality. They are not simply behavioral tendencies or blind, unthinking feelings. Mencius's "beginnings" are in part intuitive normative judgments.

In support of his charge against Yizi, Mencius tells a story about ancient times when people did not bury their parents but instead threw the bodies into gullies. After they saw their parents' bodies eaten by animals and insects, a sweat broke out on their brows and they could not bear to look. This sweating, says Mencius, was an "outward expression of their innermost heart." It is significant that Mencius concludes this story with the judgment that it was right for them to bury their parents, suggesting that their "innermost heart" had revealed this rightness to them. Indeed, a feeling of shame is suggested by their breaking out into a sweat and not being able to look at the bodies. Therefore, Mencius's response to Mohism is not simply that it is impossible for human beings to be impartial. It is, rather, that human beings, because of their nature, inevitably judge that one owes the most love to one's own.

This is why *Mengzi* 3A.5 begins with the charge that the Mohist Yizi has been inconsistent with what he advocates in showing partiality toward his own parents by giving them a lavish burial. Emphasizing the idea that innate moral tendencies are constituted not simply of tendencies to act and to feel, but also of tendencies to judge, helps us to understand better why Mencius thinks he has replied to Yizi. If Mencius's point were simply that people tend to be partial toward their own, he would not be meeting Yizi's challenge. Pointing out what people have a tendency to do is not showing that it is right. He is arguing that as a matter of fact, we all do make normative judgments requiring partiality. Even Yizi does, when he is not advocating his universalist theory and when he is faced with burying his parents.

To put this in other terms, Mencius has defended the independent justification for the duties of special relationships. Mozi recognizes only one sort of moral value at the most fundamental level of moral deliberation: promoting the good of all, where such a good amounts to the sum total welfare to which each person's welfare contributes equally. The rule interpretation of universal love allows differential treatment of people's interests according to relationships to oneself, but only if such treatment promotes the sum total welfare in the long run. By contrast, Confucians recognize at least two sorts of value. For them, the moral duties of family relationships do not merely derive from promoting the good of all. Rather, the duties of these relationships have a justification independent of any consequentialist deliberation. If there is a basic justification for Confucian duties of relationship, it seems to rest on the nature of the relevant relationship.

In some of the most important relationships, the basis of duty is the idea that one must reciprocate a great good that is received. For example, In the *Analects* (27.21), Confucius responds to a student's proposal that the traditional three-year mourning period for parents be cut short by asking the student whether he hadn't been given three years worth of love by his parents. As pointed out above, Confucians do recognize the value of promoting the good of all, but they differ from Mohists in holding to an independent justification for the duties of special relationships; moreover, they hold that in at least some cases of conflict between such duties and duties of more general concern, the particularist duties take priority. This seems to be the lesson of the *Analects* 13.18, where Confucius endorses a son's covering up for his father's theft of a sheep.

The debate between Mencius and the Mohists resonates across time and culture (Wong 1989). Some contemporary western moral philosophers argue that the duties pertaining to special relationships can be justified only by reference to some impartial principle such as utilitarianism (Railton 1984). Others argue that these duties have an independent justification (MacIntyre 1984). It is difficult to deny that the basis of duties to, say, one's children is something other than one's duty to consider the good of every person. The basis probably has something to do with the fact that one has created them or (in the case of adopted children) taken them in and that in doing so one has assumed a special responsibility with respect to their vulnerabilities and their capacities to thrive. Moreover, it is difficult to deny that other things being equal, children owe their parents much because it is their parents who gave life and made possible their capacity to work and to love. The basis of such a special duty may be as Confucius conceived it: reciprocity, returning good for great good received. On the other hand, one reason why moral life is difficult is that one can take the impersonal perspective from which one recognizes the urgent needs of those not standing in a special relationship to oneself. When one takes the perspective that, morally, no one person is more important than another, one sees as unjustifiable many of the mundane acts of care and devotion one directs to particular others. The unjustifiability emerges in comparing what is at stake for one's own and what is at stake for millions of people elsewhere in the world: life itself, and some small measure of human dignity in the face of brutality and degradation. When one takes this perspective, one can be very sympathetic toward Mozi's radical criticism of love with distinctions.

Perhaps Mencius and the Mohists represent two sides of an enduring human dilemma. It is true that one owes one's own parents and children special love, as the Confucians say. But it is also true that one must recognize the equal importance of all human beings, as Mozi says. It often seems impossible to do equal justice to both moral insights, both of them equally fundamental. This is the sense in which Confucianism and Mohism are each at once right and wrong, as the Daoist Zhuangzi claimed, and he may be correct in arguing that neither Confucian nor Mohist theories can do justice to the complex reality of the human, ethical dilemma. Perhaps the most one can say is that one has a duty to try to reconcile as much as possible the demands of special relationships and the demands of universal concern.

Fate, Heaven, and Political Theory in Mozi's Philosophy

Mozi excoriates the Confucians for what he interprets as their belief in fate and its governance of length of life, wealth or poverty, order and disorder, and safety and danger (ch. 48, 277). Schwartz (138–139) contrasts Mozi's activist attitude with Confucius's belief that the only area he can ultimately claim to control is his own self-cultivation and his capacity to influence his disciples. Furthermore, the Confucians with whom Mozi came into contact might have become outright skeptical about the existence of ancestral spirits and even the interest of heaven (*tian*) in human affairs. Mozi sees such Confucian beliefs as encouraging passivity: under his thoroughgoing utilitarianism, there is little value in self-cultivation if it does not lead to benefits for all. In opposition to Confucian beliefs, he portrays heaven as actively concerned with human welfare, and indeed as rewarding and punishing each individual act of conformity to or violation of righteousness (*yi*). Heaven designed the world so that human beings might satisfy their needs; it sends down punishment for killing an innocent man (*Mozi*, ch. 26).

Besides guaranteeing a motive for conforming to universal love, Mozi's heaven provides an ultimate justification for it. In Chapter 26, Mozi declares that "the Son of Heaven cannot decide for himself what is right. There is Heaven to decide that for him" (Watson 1963, 80). The argument that heaven wills universal love is based on the actions of the sage kings toward heaven and various citations of historical incidents in which the wicked are punished. Mozi does nothing to counter the obvious reply that by common observation the wicked are not always punished, nor does he explain why heaven had not elevated a sage king in his own time. The argument here is embarrassingly weak and surely provided fodder for Zhuangzi's assertion that ultimate standards cannot be justified in a noncircular manner (*Zhuangzi*, ch. 2). Perhaps a more charitable interpretation of Mozi would see the third standard of utility lurking in the background. Mozi thought that disorder is the inevitable result of disbelief in a heaven that rewards righteousness and punishes wickedness. In presenting arguments for heaven's existence and will, Mozi is more like a lawyer presenting his side of the case, in the belief that whatever the arguments on the other side, his side must win.

The charitable interpretation raises two possibilities: one is that Mozi knew that the truth of heaven's existence or its will to righteousness was not as clear as he publicly asserted; the other is that Mozi really did think the truth about heaven was evident because he held a pragmatic conception of truth—that whatever beliefs have the best results are necessarily true. The text underdetermines the choice between these two possibilities. In Chapter 31, on ghosts, Mozi clearly argues for the necessity of believing in ghosts, on the basis of the utility of doing so, but whether he really believes in ghosts is not clear. Perhaps Mozi, if confronted with the two possibilities of interpreting him, would have rejected the question as irrelevant and distracting us from the all-important project of promoting human benefit. After all, both possibilities imply the necessity of believing in heaven, in its providence, and in the helping role of ghosts in rewarding the righteous and punishing the wicked.

Hansen (116) offers a more radical interpretation of Mozi as a pragmatic antirealist who is focused not on sentences and their truth but on the application of names to their objects and the consequences of doing so. On this interpretation, Mozi holds that what name applies to a thing simply depends on human practical purposes. It is true that Mozi, like many thinkers in the classical tradition, focuses on names and objects rather than on sentences and facts or states of affairs, and it is difficult to find a word he uses that is the clear equivalent of the English "true" as it is applied to sentences and propositions. However, one can speak of a name that is truly applied to an object just as well as one can speak of a sentence being true, and there are ways in which Mozi talks about the correct application of names that can be spelled out in this way. Furthermore, it is difficult to make good sense of much of his criticism of Confucianism without interpreting him as holding that it is "not true to" or does not see the truth about the way the world is, particularly the distribution of benefit and harm that results from partiality. It is extremely awkward, to say the least, to try to resolve the truth of this issue by reference to a pragmatic conception of truth.

In Chapter 11, Mozi locates the origin of laws and government in the need to control conflict caused by differences in people's views of what is right (*yi*). In "Identifying with the Superior" (*Mozi*, ch. 13, 46), it is said that "the world" chose the wisest man to unify different ideas of the right (*yi*). The idea of human beings' choosing the ruler is something like the social contract (Schwartz, 144). Mozi does not receive enough credit for telling a story that anticipates Hobbes (though not necessarily with Hobbes's assumption that human motivation is purely self-interested) and that turns up in expanded form in the Confucian Xunzi.

Another characteristic of Mozi's political theory is reflected in the idea that disorder makes necessary a supreme ruler. However much Mozi was concerned for the nonelite, his idea of political organization was extremely hierarchical. He pairs an emphasis on hierarchy with an emphasis on the necessity of selecting only meritorious men to occupy the highest ruling positions. This vigorous advocacy of meritocracy might have had a significant influence on Mencius. Confucius qualified his advocacy of meritocracy by accepting a hereditary principle for rulers, perhaps out of loyalty to the house of Chou (Schwartz, 161), whereas Mencius is much less ambivalent about the need for meritocracy. Mozi also might have influenced Mencius to place comparatively greater emphasis than Confucius on the material needs of the many. Mozi's vehement appeal for universal love responds to the desperate situation of most people in his time, and it would not be surprising if a discerning opponent such as Mencius would see a great deal of justice in this appeal.

Later Mohism

Later Mohism, as reflected in six chapters of the *Mozi*, goes considerably beyond Mozi's urgently practical philosophy in propounding a rather sophisticated theory of knowledge and of names and their relation to objects, and in addressing logical puzzles, geometry, optics, mechanics, and economics. Unlike Mozi, later Mohism expends a great deal of effort in defining the basic terms of utilitarianism. The benevolent and the right are defined as what will be desired on behalf of humankind by the sage, who "consistently weighs benefits and harms on the principle of preferring the total to the unit" (Graham 1989, 146). The role of the sage in this definition strikingly anticipates the role of the "ideal spectator" in western utilitarian theories. The function of the sage and the ideal spectator is the same: to address the problem that what one desires for oneself or others is not necessarily an objective benefit for oneself or others. One's desires must be informed by knowledge. Of further interest is the striking absence of any reference to heaven as the ultimate standard by which universal love is justified. The problems with such an ultimate justification must have been recognized.

Graham (1978, 1989) has reconstructed the remains in Chapters 41 and 42 of later Mohists' explanations of the founder's doctrines. One such explanation takes a position on the question of the act or rule interpretation of universal love:

> Doing more or less for those for whom it is right to do more or less is what is meant by "grading." Creditors, ruler, superiors, the aged, one's elders, near and far kin, are all among those for whom one does more. (*Mozi*, ch. 42, trans. Graham 1989, 158)

Nevertheless, doing more for some than for others is not the same as having unequal concern: "Concern is as much for another's parents as for one's own" (ch. 42). The resulting position seems to be a rule or practice utilitarianism. Practices justifying an unequal doing for others can be justified by the basic principle of promoting a total utility calculated on the basis of an equal concern for all.

Some confirmation of the later Mohists' adoption of the rule interpretation appears in the *Mengzi* (3A.5). In response to Mencius's questioning of Yizi's elaborate burial of his parents, Yizi replies that the Confucians praised the ancient rulers for acting "as if they were tending a newborn babe." This means, says Yizi, that "there should be no gradations in love, though the practice of it begins with one's parents." Yizi's meaning is not transparent, but one possible meaning is that the principle of universal love is compatible with the practice of treating one's parents differently from others. It could be compatible if the principle of universal love requires that everyone's interests be treated equally not on the level of everyday practice but on the level of evaluating the validity of everyday practice for the results it produces in the long run.

Mozi's Place in the Chinese Tradition

Mozi introduced reasoned, discursive argument into the Chinese tradition of philosophical thought. His use of argument against the Confucians provoked argument in response. His radical challenge to the accepted practices of partiality made human nature a central topic after Confucius and must have been one of the provocations for Mencius's theory of the innate basis of moral judgments. Further, the Daoists recognized the importance of his provocation in citing the Mohist-Confucianist debate as the paradigm of the futility of reasoned argument. His naturalistic, social-contract version of the origin of government and laws presaged Xunzi's naturalistic conception of morality.

Mozi's faith in the power of the dispassionate intellect, his conception of the discovery of truth as contest to be decided by the best arguments, his emphasis on articulated standards and principles rather than the cultivated and contextualized wisdom of the Confucian *junzi*, or for that matter the Daoist sage, are all more typical of the western tradition. The eclipse of Mohism in the Chinese tradition indicates the difference between the two kinds of tradition. If a serious liability of Confucianism is its lack of clear and forceful constraints on the tendency to favor one's own, or at least a lack of awareness of the moral liabilities of love with distinctions, then it is unfortunate that Mohism was defeated so completely. Chinese philosophy would have benefited from a more enduring dialogue between the two schools of the kind that took place between Confucianism, Daoism, and Buddhism.

See also Confucianism: Ethics; Confucianism: Tradition; Mencius; Mohism: Later.

Bibliography

Cheng, Chung-ying. *New Dimensions of Confucian and Neo-Confucian Philosophy*. Albany: State University of New York Press, 1991.

Confucius. *Lunyu* (*Analects*). In *The Chinese Classics*, trans. James L. Legge. Hong Kong: Hong Kong University Press, 1989.

Cua, Antonio S. "Confucian Vision and Human Community." *Journal of Chinese Philosophy*, 11, 1984, pp. 227–238.

———. *Dimensions of Moral Creativity: Paradigms, Principles, and Ideals*. University Park: Pennsylvania State University Press, 1978.

Forke, Alfred. *Me Ti des Sozialethikers und seiner Schuler philosophische Werke*. Berlin: Kommissionsverlag der Vereinigung Wissenschaftlicher Verlager, 1922. (German translation of the complete text.)

Fung, Yu-Lan. *A History of Chinese Philosophy*, trans. Derk Bodde, Vol. 1. Princeton, N.J.: Princeton University Press, 1953. (See ch. 5.)

Graham, Angus C. *Disputers of the Tao: Philosophical Argumentation in Ancient China*. La Salle, Ill.: Open Court, 1989.

———. *Later Mohist Logic, Ethics, and Science*. Hong Kong: Chinese University Press, 1978.

Hansen, Chad. *A Daoist Theory of Chinese Thought: A Philosophical Interpretation*. New York: Oxford University Press, 1992.

MacIntyre, Alasdair. "Is Patriotism a Virtue?" *The Lindley Lectures*. University of Kansas, 1984.

Mei, Y. P. *Ethical and Political Works of Motse*. London: Probsthain, 1929. (English translation of chapters that most credibly reveal the views of Mozi.)

———. *Motse: The Neglected Rival of Confucius*. London: Probsthain, 1934.

Mencius. *Meng Tzu*. In *The Chinese Classics*, trans. James L. Legge. Hong Kong. Hong Kong University Press, 1964.

Mozi. *Harvard-Yenching Institute Sinological Index Series*. Taipei: Chinese Materials and Service Center, 1973.

Nivison, David S. "Two Roots or One?" *Proceedings and Addresses of the American Philosophical Association*, 53, 1980, pp. 739–761.

Railton, Peter. "Alienation, Consequentialism, and Morality." *Philosophy and Public Affairs*, 13, 1984, pp. 134–171.

Schwartz, Benjamin. *The World of Thought in Ancient China*. Cambridge, Mass.: Belknap, 1985.

Shun, Kwong-loi. "*Jen* and *Li* in the *Analects*." *Philosophy East and West*, 43, 1993, pp. 457–479.

Singer, Peter. "Famine, Affluence, and Morality." *Philosophy and Public Affairs*, 1, 1972, pp. 229–243.

Smart, J. J. C. "Extreme and Restricted Utilitarianism." *Philosophical Quarterly*, 6, 1956, pp. 344–354.

Tu, Wei-ming. *Humanity and Self-Cultivation: Essays in Confucian Thought*. Berkeley, Calif.: Asian Humanities, 1979.

Watson, Burton, trans. *Mo Tzu: Basic Writings*. New York: Columbia University Press, 1963. (Best-known English translation of chapters related directly to Mozi's views.)

Wong, David. "Universal Love versus Love with Distinctions: An Ancient Debate Revived." *Journal of Chinese Philosophy*, 16, 1989, pp. 251–272.

Zhuangzi. *Zhuangzi jishi*. Peking: Zhonghua, 1961. (See especially ch. 33.)

Mohism: Later (*Mo Jia, Mo Chia*)

Chad Hansen

We use "later Mohists" to refer to the wing of the school of Mozi whose central work is known as the *Mohist Canon*. This and two later writings make up Chapters 40–45 of the *Mozi*. Some accounts also refer to these thinkers as neo-Mohists or dialectical Mohists. They focused on theory of language, though their writings also contain fragments on ethics and embryonic scientific reflections on economics, geometry, and optics. Traditional scholars sometimes include them in a pseudo school called the "school of names"—a cluster of thinkers who analyzed names (*ming*) in conflicting ways. Their reconstructed motivations reflect three differing trends in social political thought: Confucianism, Mohism, and Daoism. The usual additional members of this school included Gongsun Long and Hui Shi.

The later *Mohist Canon* was continuously extant in library collections. However, a freak textual accident rendered it virtually unintelligible, and traditional Confucian orthodoxy effectively lost all access to its content. Its importance came to light only in comparatively modern times. Rescuing the text rekindled a long-lost interest in Chinese theories of language and revealed hitherto unappreciated links with the thought of Xunzi, Laozi, and Zhuangzi. Confucian orthodoxy, however, still tends to treat their sophisticated linguistic theories as "un-Chinese."

Textual Rediscovery

Before discussing the later Mohists in detail, let us glance at the textual explanation of the loss and recovery of the *Mohist Canon*. According to the currently accepted theory, the Mohists wrote two "canons" (I and II), each consisting of some 80 short maxims. Since these were short, the Mohists economized by writing the first half of each canon vertically across the top of a standard-size book of bamboo strips.They wrote the second half along the bottom; a key phrase at the end instructs us to read this text "in rows." The editors indexed the terse theorems of these canons to another bamboo book, called *Canon Explanations*, which contained longer passages including explanatory formulas, examples, and arguments for the maxims. They indexed the *Canon Explanations* by writing the first character of the relevant canon to the side of the explanatory string.

We suppose that later scribes, with no understanding of either the organization or the philosophical thrust, copied straight through each strip, ignoring the "rows." Effectively, they shuffled the material like a deck of cards. Since classical Chinese had no punctuation or grammatical inflection, this textual disaster (1) obscured the slogans, (2) jumbled the order, and (3) shrouded the indexing principle. The scribes also shifted the indexing characters into the flow of the text of the orphaned explications. Having lost the ordered link between canon and explanation, the tradition then treated the whole corpus as incoherent essays. Other common sources of textual corruption, including displaced strips of characters, mistakes in copying, emendations by scribes, and so forth, further complicated the textual puzzle.

Given the philosophical sophistication and difficulty of the text, the school's obliteration at the beginning of China's philosophical "dark age" (roughly 200 B.C.E.), and the central position of the most vociferous anti-Confucian classical text, medieval Confucian orthodoxy did not tackle the puzzle, and it was not taken up until the textual studies movement of the late Qing (1644–1911). Sun Yirang (1848–1908) eventually saw the essential clue to reordering and analyzing the content—the instruction to "read these horizontally." Various Chinese scholars proposed reconstructions. Angus Graham's *Later Mohist Logic, Ethics, and Science* provided western sinologists with a well-argued version of the reconstructed text in 1972. Many problems and obscurities remain, but Graham's reconstruction was enough to reveal a reflective, coherent, and reasonably sophisticated theory of language.

The maxims do deal with central philosophical concepts and, like Chinese dictionaries, frequently consist of lists of substitution characters or a range of examples. Some slogans are metaphors on which the *Canon Explanations* expand. Others are helpful ways of rethinking and reflecting on a familiar concept. In addition to a theory of language, intelligible sections of the canon present, as noted above, fragments of ethics, epistemology, geometry, optics, and economics.

Ethics

Graham speculated that the scattered fragments of one of the remaining sections (traditionally known as *The Greater Pick*) might have included a more formal treatment of Mozi's ethical utilitarianism. The fragments gave it in the form of axioms: morality is utility, and utility is what satisfies you when you get it (as opposed to what you desire). Later Mohists gave a "weighting" account of the original standard of benefit versus harm—one prefers the lesser harm or the greater benefit. They differentiated between "thick" and "thin" concerns. This may be a way to address the supposed conflict between utilitarian universalism and our special care for those closest to us. Just as self-care is an efficient means to general well-being, so is the care of our relatives and neighbors. Since I know my own father's preferences and we enjoy each other's company, my caring for him—like your caring for your father—achieves the good more efficiently than if I cared for a stranger. Thus appropriate caring for yourself and your "thick" relations is consistent with a "thin" moral concern for everyone's well-being.

The later Mohists probably were the first to abandon the authority of *tian* (nature) and both reference to and reliance on *xin* (heart-mind). They viewed these as terms used in theories to avoid normative accountability. Unlike Mozi, they treated *ren* (humanity) as a kind of Confucian partial love. Their realism presupposed that carving the world "at the joints" promoted utility. One obvious rationale was that objective standards of language yield an operational or a measurementlike interpretation, which facilitates widespread linguistic agreement and promotes coordinated judgment and action.

They worked out an alternative to rectifying names that was consistent with objective or neutral standards for word reference. They proposed to rectify guiding phrases instead of "names." While thieves are human, the act of killing thieves (execution) is not the act of killing humans (murder). Making this ethical point led the Mohists to skeptical conclusions about linguistic "stability."

Epistemology

The Mohists did not separate epistemology from their more general theory of language. They were "analyzing" terms like *zhi* ("to know"). This analysis did not contrast *zhi* with believing. Rather, they distinguished (1) know-how or skill from (2) knowledge by acquaintance and (3) a rare (perhaps idiosyncratic) use of *zhi* ("know") that strikes us now as a substitute for consciousness (for which there was no rival term). This use also replaced (for the Mohists) *xin* (heart-mind) as the "locus of knowing." One important form of skill or knowledge is the ability to "discourse" on a topic. This arguably sweeps propositional knowledge into the category "skill."

The main topics related to *zhi* (know) describe a process: we learn names (words) and objects, then how to "combine" them, and finally how to *wei* (act). The *Mohist Canon* stands out among classical texts for its emphasis on checking linguistic knowledge against reality. The later Mohists left the form of that verification vague, however. The thrust appears, again, to be drawing a contrast with rectifying names. The standard of correct use of terms should be, not mere convention or authority, but actual similarities and differences among things. This arguably gives a theory of language as an anchor for Mozi's anticonventional attack on Confucian ethics.

Mozi used an example that can help us fix on the later Mohists' concept of "knowing." Blind people, he argued, can know how to produce utterances like "black as coal" or "white as snow" but cannot distinguish things that are placed in front of them. They know names, but not "stuff" and not how to "combine" names. Thus they cannot use language to guide their actions.

The Mohists, as we noted above, used no propositional "belief" analysis and paid scant attention to other sentential contexts. "Knowing how to combine" meant competently assigning terms to things in actual contexts. The Mohists accepted that knowing names was conventional knowledge. They stressed, however, that we apply conventions to an external reality, known independently of language. The goal of knowledge remained practical guidance, not representation or picturing.

Theory of Language

Realism: The base analysis. The most comprehensive discussion in the collection of later Mohist writings deals with questions about language. The texts give us a plausible general Chinese theory of how words work. A term "picks out" part of reality. When we use a name to pick something out, we commit ourselves to using that name to pick out similar things and "stopping" with the dissimilar. Thus, for each term we learn the skill of judging *shi* (is this) and *fei* (is not this). *Fei* generates an opposite for each name and marks the point of distinction or discrimination from the other stuff of the world.

Once we conventionally attach a term to some reality, inherent similarities and differences determine its subsequent application. Conventions presuppose a "world-guided" way to mark distinctions. Mohists view relationships between names and objects using a "mereological" model, that is, by talking about distinctions and boundaries. A name applies to a (scattered) reality having some kind of *tong* (similarity).

The Mohists' pragmatic substitutes for "reference"—*ju* (pick out) and *qu* (choose)—had a nonabstract, practical tone. A name picks out stuff from its background. Convention determines which similarities and differences mark the boundary between *shi* (is this, i.e., what a name picks out) and *fei* (is not this, i.e., what it excludes). In using a name, we commit ourselves to go to some real limit and then stop.

The Mohists argued against "one name, one reality"—the theme implicit in the doctrine of rectifying names. Some terms are more general than others, and several might pick out the same object. Names, the Mohists argued, could be very general (like "thing" itself), or based on similar classes (such as "horse"), or applied to only one thing (such as "John"). They had no objection in principle to overlapping "scopes" or two names for the same thing.

Their analysis sees disagreements as stemming from different ways of making the distinctions that give rise to contraries. Translators thus render the word *bian* as either "distinction" or "dispute." In Mohist use, it came to stand particularly for philosophical dispute—including disputes in ethics. The Mohists argued that in a "distinction dispute," one party will always be right. For any term, the thing in question will either be *shi* (is this) or *fei* (is not this).

The central term of assessment in the Mohists' study was *ke*, "assertable," not any counterpart of "truth." They used *ke* in several related ways. We can say that an expression is "assertable" of some object. One phrase may be assertable of whatever another phrase "picks out." "Assertable" thus became a way of exploring semantic relations between terms. Mohists asked whether we can sometimes, always, or never describe things picked out by term *X* as *Y*.

The analysis, although it used assertability rather than truth, yielded a familiar and important conclusion against certain forms of relativism. The Mohists argued that in any dispute involving "distinctions," there would be a "winner." If one disputant claimed that something was "ox" and the other that it was "not ox," only one could be correct. When one disputant claimed that the object was ox and the other claimed that it was horse, this would not count as a "distinction dispute." This was merely a formal result, but the Mohists took it as confirming that the world, not conventions, determined the right designation. The winner was the one whose description hit the target.

Semantic paradoxes. The Mohists, as noted above, had the most realistic theory about the relation of language and the world. Real-world similarities and differences should guide our use of words. They "Quined" the apparently common "mystical" claim that language distorts the *dao*. To say anything along these lines was to treat all language as "not acceptable" or "perverse." Regarding all language as perverse, they noted, was itself perverse. They similarly rebutted claims that we should abandon distinctions. To reject distinctions is to *fei fei* (not-this "not-this"). To *fei fei* is also perverse ("Quining" again that the person who rejects it does it). Finally, they similarly dispatched "learning not to learn."

These results are distant cousins of "All sentences are false." Unlike the classic liar paradox, the universal form sentence does have a consistent truth-value, i.e., false. The Mohists' conceptual tools, however, lacked both the concepts that seem to be crucial for the classic paradox: "sentence" and "truth." They had a separate, self-condemning analysis of each mistake and explained all mistakes as resulting from self-reference ("one's own language"). They suggested that the poser of such absurdities try harder to find acceptable words. These results undermined the popular antilanguage intuitionism in Chinese thought—notably that of Mencius and Laozi. They invalidated any claim that language distorts the *dao* (guidance).

Compound terms. The Mohists, however, uncovered grounds for skepticism in their own system. They argued that the way terms combined was not "world-guided," at least not as a straightforward extension of the way the terms themselves worked. Here is a striking case for postulating a contrasting Chinese conceptual structure. The analysis of compound terms makes most sense if we suppose that the theorizing was going on against a background assumption of a part-whole or mereological metaphysics. This also explains both the assimilation of common nouns to adjectives and the tendency to describe all terms as *ming* (names).

Paradigmatic or straightforward compounds, in the Mohist view, pick out the sum of two things. Classical Chinese lacked pluralization, and compounds such as *niu-ma* (ox-horse) worked like "cats and dogs." Classical Chinese was rich in similar compounds, e.g., sky-earth = world, boy-girl = child, mountain-water = scenery. Modification compounds, such as *bai-ma* (white horse), worked like similar structures in English. The Mohists took the former model to pick out "compound stuff"—the sum of the range of the two component terms (e.g., draft animals). They called the unit a *jian* (whole) and its parts *ti* (substantive parts). Their analysis of such compounds made them analogous to generalization.

The Mohists asked what was assertable of the things picked out by compound terms. In the case of "ox-horse," the Mohists observed that "not-ox" is assertable of "ox-horse" on the same grounds that "ox" is. The explanation was that part of ox-horse is non-ox, so "non-ox" is assertable. We can understand the idea by reflecting on another example. We may ask someone how many children he has by asking about his "boys and girls." Suppose the answer is "three." Now we may ask how many are boys. The answer may be "none." This is a case in which we could say, "His boy-girls are not boys."

However, the Mohists seem to have something stronger in mind. Even if he said "two girls and a boy," the Mohists would argue that it would be right to say (some of) his boy-girls were non-boy. Thus, the Mohists conclude that, although we cannot say ox is non-ox or horse is non-horse, we can say intelligibly that ox-horse is non-ox-non-horse.

The paradigm contrast is "hard-white." This is also a compound term, but its component stuffs "blend" and so are inseparable when combined. Wherever you go in the hard-white, the Mohists say, you get both. This reflects the more familiar (to the west) semantics of modification: an intersection compound. The scope of combined term is where the scopes of the two components intersect. Ox-horse, by contrast, is a sum compound. The scope of the combined term is the union of the scopes of the two component terms. The Mohists used "ox-horse" as a general description of the sum paradigm and "hard-white" for the "product" or "intersection" model.

The Mohists described "ox-horse combining" as combining in which there was no "interpenetrating": the two components remained separate in the compound. In "hard-white penetration," by contrast, the two things "exhaust" each other. They called ox-horse compounds separable compounds, as opposed to inseparable hard-white compounds. They never used the term *ti*, "substantive part," for the components of the latter.

The Mohists do not give us any rule for distinguishing intersection from union compounds beyond the metaphysical interpretation as "penetrating" or "excluding." They do not explicitly use the language of scope. These results arise partly from their treating both nouns and adjectives as "names"—terms with a range of application. They share the pragmatic function of "picking out" or "distinguishing" one part of reality from the rest. Without a focus on the grammatical distinction between noun and adjective, the Mohists have this choice. Either the way names form compounds is simply arbitrary or it is explained mainly metaphysically, i.e., by whether or not its "stuffs" or "realities" can "penetrate."

A question lurked behind this treatment. In what sense is a compound really two things? The system acknowledged the flexibility of language and seemed to let the matter rest there. We could view almost anything either as a compound of more basic stuffs or as a part of some greater compound.

Problems. The Mohists' realism failed to give any adequate account of what similarities and differences should count in making a distinction. They neither offered a causal criterion nor used a concept of axiomatic science to ground their selection of relevant similarities. Graham argued that their propositions resembled a deductive scheme of Euclidean definitions. However, the most common "definitions" were partial synonyms—apparently thought of as terms that we might substitute for the head term in some contexts. This (along with an etymology) seems to be the technique of most early Chinese dictionaries, too. The Mohist text points to a semantics without "meaning."

They noticed many senses in which things can be the "same" or "different." Some reality might differ only in that we use alternative names. "Being two" was necessarily different even though we use one name. Realities could also be "same" in the sense of being included in some compound object. Conversely, things could be different in not being included in some "substantial part." They could differ or be alike in location. Finally, they could be similar in belonging to the same "kind" (*lei*).

The Mohists analyzed "kind" loosely, however. Having that with which to "same" was the criterion of being "same kind." Not having "same" was the criterion of "not being of a kind." Although they might initially have intended to limit "kind" to natural kinds, the account generalized it to almost any similarity-based grouping of stuffs. Thus the Mohists could refer to oxen and horses as the same "kind." The only clear examples of "not of a kind" are things so unlike that they are not comparable. "Which is longer, wood or night?" The Mohists suggest that this question is unintelligible because it attempts to compare two different "kinds."

The Mohists rejected "wild pickings out" but did not give any way of identifying them. The examples were of using unconventional similarities or distinctions. The looseness of this account of classifying, together with the indeterminacy of the result of compounding, buttressed the skeptical position. Hui Shi and Zhuangzi, as we shall discuss below, took the result to be that the world offered no reliable basis for linguistic distinctions.

Gongsun Long and the white-horse paradox. Against the Mohist background, we can now make some sense of the writings of Gongsun Long, which are so often considered obscure. The text that bears his name consists of several apparent dialogues between a "sophist" and an "objector." The sophist typically starts each dialogue with a counterintuitive paradox. The objector dissents, and the sophist defends his thesis. Graham argued that later writers forged at least two of these dialogues using misunderstood fragments of Mohist semantics. They apparently copied the phrases after copyists had shuffled the *Mohist Canon* and mixed the indexing characters into the text.

We will discuss two of the remaining dialogues: "White Horse" and "Referring and Things." They pose difficult puzzles for which various scholars have offered speculative, controversial, and mutually inconsistent interpretations. The varied readings flow partly from different standards for choosing "translation manuals." I discuss two interpretations here, both to illustrate that point and to allow us to locate a range of alternative views of Gongsun Long's *dao*.

In the (possibly apocryphal) preface to the dialogues, Gongsun gives a Confucian motivation for his theorizing. Confucius rectified names; Gongsun asserts that he is defending the master's linguistic *dao*. Most Confucians would reject the affiliation, but it does make sense on formal grounds. If Confucians intended rectifying to remove ambiguity from a guiding *dao*, then it was necessary that exactly one name from the guiding discourse should refer to the object in the action situation. I regard the male before me either as "father" or as "ruler" or as "person." He may be in one sense all three, but if I am to extract guidance from a code, I must decide which rule to use here and now. That requires deciding which term is relevant to this situation. The Mohists rejected the principle of "one name, one thing" and argued that we should rectify phrases instead. So thieves are people, but killing thieves is not killing people. (See below.)

The Mohists' account of compounding also had negative implications for the Confucian maxim. Separable or sum compounds, such as "ox-horse," technically conform to "one name, one thing." The combination of names picks out a sum of the two. Hard-white compounding, by contrast, violates the principle of strict clarity and consistency in naming. When we compound terms, we change each term's scope of reference. The terms thus pick out different "things" when compounded.

Other sources confirm that Gongsun Long defended two further theses: "separating the inseparable" and "separating hard-white." However, Graham's identification of the spurious source of the dialogue on

"Hard-White" remains convincing. That Gongsun had defended the thesis gave the forger an invitation. Accordingly, we cannot rely on the dialogue to explain the slogan. Still, we can plausibly deal with both slogans together, since "hard-white" is the Mohist example of an "inseparable" or "interpenetrating" compound. To "separate" would be to regard them as "excluding each other" and hence to treat the compound as a sum. Gongsun could consistently have objected to the Mohist's hard-white model.

Gongsun's example, "white horse," takes one term from each type of compound. The "White Horse" dialogue begins with a question in the canonical analytic form: "Is 'white horse not horse' assertable?" The answer, "assertable" (yes), follows. The sophist's first defense of the paradox is that "white" names a color and "horse" names a shape. Shape and color are different, so a combination of shape and color is not merely a shape.

The sophist's other most frequently cited argument is this: "If you ask for a horse, both a black horse and a yellow horse can answer. If you ask for a white horse, a black horse or yellow horse will not answer." This illustrates one of the sophist's fallbacks. "*X* is not *Y*" follows from "*X* is different from or distinguishable from *Y*." The linking theme of the two arguments is that white horse is a combination of two things. This requires that "white horse not horse" be assertable. The objector gives the plausible Mohist response that "asking for a white horse" is indeed different from "asking for a horse," but a white horse is still a horse.

So one line of interpretation links the paradox to Mohist semantics and takes *ma* as "naming" its scope. If its scope changes, it is a different name. The other line of interpretation takes the paradox as flowing from what, in Chinese, was a novel and technically inexpressible Platonic insight. It takes the term *ma* (horse) to refer to an abstract or semantic object—horseness. *Bai ma* (white horse) similarly refers to white-horseness. The opening sentence thus expresses the true proposition that the two abstract entities are distinct. Since the connected terms are logically singular, *fei* (is not) represents "nonidentity."

The principle of charity motivates this abstract line of interpretation. (The principle of humanity undermines it.) Humanity makes Gongsun Long's paradoxical thesis accessible from the philosophical context, but wrong as an account of semantics. The abstract analysis makes the paradox true but leaves unexplained how the sophist would have had access to the concepts involved. It also lacks consistency. The abstract reading cannot work in the supporting arguments—all of which make more sense with *ma* referring to a concrete horse or horses.

The first interpretation, where *ma* refers holistically to horse-stuff, can still motivate the line of argument "distinct, hence different" and yet consistently interpret the concrete references in the rest of the dialogue. If we similarly regard white as the mass-substantive (white stuff rather than abstract whiteness), we can draw a parallel with the Mohist theory of compound names. Gongsun Long regards "intersection" or "interpenetrating" compounds as contrary to "one name, one thing." If white horse consists of two names, each should consistently name (scattered) things. When these names are used in combination, the "naming" ought to remain consistent. Thus, they should name the sum of the two stuffs and, as in the case of "ox-horse," "not-horse" would be assertable of it.

Alternatively, we may deny either that "white horse" consists of two names or that they are the same names as when used separately. We must think of "white horse" as having no essential relation to "horse." It must be a sui generis term for a new stuff. We could then say "white horse is horse" is not necessarily true. Its truth is an accident of usage that might have been otherwise. Thus "white horse not horse" is assertable.

Gongsun Long's argument perhaps consists of a dilemma. Either we regard "white-horse" as a sum-compound term (in which case the result "ox-horse" follows) or we regard it as a sui generis noncompound name (in which case the conventions for its use could tie it to anything at all). It need not necessarily be horse. The assumption must be that a name is the same only if it has identical scope (names the same mereological thing). Since "horse" in "white horse" does not have that scope, it is a different name. Its use in a compound requires treating it as a distinct name from the same character used alone.

Gongsun Long's other dialogue poses, if possible, even more daunting barriers to interpretation. The first sentence seems to be an explicit contradiction—everything under heaven is *zhi* (pointing) and yet pointing is not pointing. The rest of the dialogue is content-thin and teeters repeatedly on the brink of syntactic contradiction. The only content words are the puzzling "pointing" along with "thing-kind" and "the world."

Most interpreters take the issue to be the meaning of *zhi* (pointing). Most treat it as semantic reference or meaning. It is literally a finger and is the most plausible candidate for a counterpart of "referring." The later Mohists, recall, used the terms *ju* (picking out) and *qu* (choosing) instead. There are reasons to worry about the second interpretation, since we saw no evidence of any intensional account of "meaning." Using "meaning," however, makes this dialogue support the abstract interpretation of the "White Horse" paradox.

As in western conceptualism, the abstract object may serve as the semantic "content." Otherwise, we would have no sign of a distinction between sense and reference or any indication that we "point to" individual objects rather than mereological wholes or types.

Graham's speculative interpretation uses the "reference" reading. Although far from proved, it is philosophically interesting and relevant to issues that emerge in theory of language and metaphysics. Graham treats the crucial first phrase as saying that although you can refer to things, you cannot refer to everything. In talking about everything, you fail to talk about your own act of referring. Zhuangzi later makes a similar argument against assertions of absolute monism—to say "everything is one" is to have the one and the saying, which makes two! Tempting as it is, it has little theoretical connection to the white-horse thesis. Graham treats them as exhibiting the principle that the whole is different from the part. The maxim needs both careful formulation and plausible motivation. There are no other very persuasive interpretive theories.

Phrase matching. Although the Mohists proposed a realist account of "picking out," they embedded it in the theory that language guides action. Thus the final object of knowing is knowing how to "deem act." They treat guiding action as the real point of combining names. Thus words pick out stuff, while strings or "phrases" convey intentions. In "Name and Object" (*Smaller Pick*), this led them to analyze compounds that pick out actions. In the intact long section of their text, the Mohists pursued a new analysis—one that took a superficially logical form.

> Premise: *X* is *Y* (white horse is horse).
> Conclusion: *KX* is *KY* (ride white horse is ride horse).

They called this linguistic algebra "matching phrases" and argued that it was not "reliable." We take for granted that we know the appropriate or assertable form of each phrase. A successful outcome would be this: whenever the assertable form with simple terms was positive (a *shi*, "is this," phrase), then the parallel with compound terms should also be positive (a "so" phrase). Conversely, a negative base (*X* is not *Y*, a "not this" phrase) should yield a negative result (*KX* is not *KY*—a "not so" phrase).

The Mohists argue for the instability of this ideal of phrase matching by listing several different kinds of breakdown:

> Sometimes an "is this" yields a "not-so."
> Sometimes a "not this" yields a "so."
> Sometimes a reference is comprehensive and sometimes not.
> Sometimes one reference is "is this" and another one is "not this."

The body of the essay consists of examples that illustrate the respective outcomes.

Graham, drawing on his part-of-speech analysis of "is this" (subject) and "so" (verb), treated the chapter as evidence that the Mohists had discovered the subject-predicate sentence. He translated the procedure as "matching sentences" and treated it as a discussion of logical form. The first two models do rely on syntactic complexes (*X* is *Y*) that resemble syllogistic premises, but the latter two do not.

A technical note on grammar is in order here. Classical Chinese uses no articles and has no "is" connective. Expressions ending with the particle *yeh* (assertion marker) mark descriptive uses of noun phrases (predicate nominative). *Yeh* signals that one is applying a descriptive term to a contextually selected object—not using the word to identify the topic. Translators typically render such structures in English as "(*X*) is *Y*." In Chinese topic-comment structure, the topic term (*X*) is optional. The comment may stand alone if the context supplies a topic. In other words, we should think of the assertion marker not as linking two terms but as tying a predicate to some reality.

The "this-so" analysis given by the Mohist does fit the examples in a way consistent with the topic-comment analysis. If, on the other hand, we focus on the examples as sentences and treat the pattern as a form of inference, then the Mohist's analysis will resemble a kind of algebraic logic. I so regarded it in my own earlier study. However, consistent with a topic-comment structure, I now regard it as extending the analysis of the conventional semantic effects of combining "names" to form "phrases."

That the analysis focuses on conventional semantics of terms rather than the logic of sentences sheds new light on how the examples work. The Mohist does not use the model to correct conventional reasoning errors. He depends on "proper" use. What we would conventionally say determines whether a result is a "so" or a "not-so." The most thoroughly illustrated breakdowns are those where an "is this" base produces a "not-so." The examples are:

> Parents are people; serving one's parents is not serving the people.
> [Suppose] a younger brother is a handsome man; loving one's younger brother would not be loving a handsome man.
> A carriage is wood; riding in a carriage is not riding wood.
> A boat is wood; entering a boat is not entering wood.
> Robbers are people; abounding in robbers is not abounding in people; lacking robbers is not lacking people.

The Mohist expands on the last example in a way that signals both the ethical importance of the analysis and the nature of the alleged breakdown in parallelism.

> Disliking the abundance of robbers is not disliking the abundance of people.
> Desiring to be without robbers is not desiring to be without people.
> Everyone would agree with these so they should not object if we say, "Robbers are people but killing robbers is not killing people."

We suppose, following Graham, that the Mohists are defending their inherited doctrine of universal love by arguing that it is consistent with the (presumed) practice in Mohist communities of executing thieves.

What the denial amounts to is this: even if naming were objectively constant and reliable, the use of names in descriptions of actions or intentions does not reliably take us from an "is this" to a "so." An execution is not murder. Loving a brother is morally required; loving a handsome man is (presumably) shameful. Serving one's parents is one kind of duty and serving the people another; one does not fulfill the latter merely in doing the former.

What emerges is an alternative strategy for dealing with the problem that Confucius addressed by way of rectifying names. The Mohists resist the implication that in executing thieves we must deny that thieves are people. Instead, they deny that executing thieves is murdering. Rectifying takes place at the "phrase" or "so" level rather than at the "name" level.

The next set of examples illustrates the converse case—where we start with a "not this" base and get a "so" result.

> To read books is not books; to like reading books is to like books.
> Cockfights are not cocks; to like cockfights is to like cocks.
> About to fall into a well is not falling into a well. To stop one about to fall into a well is to stop one falling into a well.

The Mohist here expands on fatalism: "That there is fate is not fated; to deny that there is fate is to deny fate." It is harder to reconstruct an ethical problem that this analysis plausibly solves.

In illustrating the next two breakdowns in parallelism, the Mohists abandon the algebraic form. The first is "part comprehensive; part not."

> "Loving people" depends on comprehensively loving people. "Not loving people" does not. "Rides horses" does not depend on comprehensively riding horses. To have ridden on horses is enough to count as riding horses.

These examples highlight the holistic pattern in reasoning about reference. In one phrase the term-reference is implicitly comprehensive, in the other it is not.

Finally, we come to the examples of "one 'is this' and one 'not this.' "

> Fruit of a peach is a peach; fruit of a bramble is not a bramble.
> Asking about a person's illness is asking about the person. Disliking the person's illness is not disliking the person.
> A person's ghost is not the person. Your brother's ghost is your brother. Offering to a ghost is not offering to a person. Offering to your brother's ghost is offering to your brother.
> If the indicated horse's eyes are blind, then we call the horse blind. The horse's eyes are large, yet we do not call the horse large.
> If the indicated oxen's hairs are brown, then we call the oxen brown. The indicated oxen's hairs are many, yet we do not call the oxen many.
> One horse is horse; two horses are horse. Saying "horses are four-footed things" is a case of one horse and four feet, not a pair of horses and four feet. Saying "horses are partly white" is two horses and some white, not one horse and partly white.

There is no further analysis or summing up. The moral, we assume, is a negative one. Had we treated the first algebraic model as a kind of logic, the Mohists' argument by example still would show that it was invalid. It is not a reliable form in the sense that a true premise formally guarantees a true conclusion. However, I now argue that it is not about sentences and truth at all. It concerns whether we can draw reliable parallels from terms to longer (guiding) phrases. The implicit answer is no. The Mohists offer no constant or reliable principles guiding the construction of longer phrases out of terms, even when we consistently apply the words to external realities. They offer no systematic way to rationalize the conventional patterns of use. They retreat implicitly from Mozi's goal of replacing convention with a constant guide. If there is such a way or guide, then it is not a product of any simple projection from linguistic reference. Moral guidance cannot derive from knowledge of natural kinds. It requires conventional, creative human social activity. Dialectically, the negative result gives ammunition to the Daoists who argue that no constant "guide" exists.

See also Gongsun Long; Hui Shi; Laozi; Mencius; Mohism: The Founder, Mozi; Names, School of; Philosophy of Language; *Zhengming*; Zhuangzi.

Bibliography

Fung, Yu-lan. *History of Chinese Philosophy*, trans. Derk Bodde, 2 vols. Princeton, N.J.: Princeton University Press, 1952. (A classic account that highlights the abstract interpretation of the "white horse" dialogue. Good for general purposes.)

Graham, Angus. *Disputers of the Tao: Philosophical Argument in Ancient China*. La Salle, Ill.: Open Court, 1989. (Easier but less detailed treatment than Graham 1978, in the context of his account of ancient Chinese thought.)

———. *Later Mohist Logic, Ethics, and Science*. Hong Kong: Chinese University of Hong Kong Press, 1978. (Only source in English for the later Mohist text. Difficult—understanding Graham virtually requires knowledge of classical Chinese.)

Hansen, Chad. *A Daoist Theory of Chinese Thought*. New York: Oxford University Press, 1992. (Easier and more extended treatment than Hansen 1983, in an account of ancient Chinese philosophy that emphasizes language.)

———. *Language and Logic in Ancient China*. Ann Arbor: University of Michigan Press, 1983. (Difficult—based on Graham's reconstruction. A philosophical argument for a radically different interpretation of the linguistic doctrines.)

Moral Philosophy

Kwong-loi SHUN

Suppose we characterize an ethical concern as a concern with the question how one should live, where the scope of "one" is supposed to extend considerably beyond the person raising the question. Chinese thinkers do share an ethical concern in this sense, although the scope of the individuals to whom their conceptions of the ethical life are supposed to be applicable is a subject for scholarly investigation. We can say that these conceptions of the ethical life are applicable to all human beings, where "human beings" is a translation of the character *ren*, but then the scope of *ren* has itself undergone changes and is subject to different interpretations. Probably, *ren* was used in early times to refer to members of certain aristocratic clans and carried the connotation of someone with accomplishments, as when it is used in the combination *chengren* (complete person) to refer to such a person. By the sixth to the third centuries B.C.E., the period during which various movements of thought emerged and flourished, its scope had broadened to include the so-called barbarian tribes as well as infants, and *ren* was viewed as a kind that is contrasted with lower animals (*qinshou*). How *ren* as a kind is specified, however, differs for different schools of thought; for example, whereas the Yangists emphasize biological tendencies, the Confucians emphasize social capacities. Xunzi, a Confucian thinker of the third century B.C.E., explicitly states that what makes a *ren* a *ren* is not biological or physiological characteristics, such as being a featherless biped, but the capacity to draw and abide by social distinctions and norms.

Although different schools of thought vary in the ways they characterize the kind to which *ren* belongs, they more or less agree on the scope of the individuals to which *ren* is applicable. For this reason, their different conceptions of the ethical life may be regarded as competing conceptions. While there are significant differences between these competing conceptions, there are also important similarities underlying them that distinguish Chinese ethical thought from western ethical traditions. The following discussion will examine such differences and similarities by considering the concerns in response to which Chinese ethical thought emerged, the different conceptions of the ethical life characteristic of different schools of thought, and the different ways the schools defend these conceptions.

During the sixth to third centuries B.C.E., China was divided into states waging wars against each other and seeking to usurp the power of the central Chou (Zhou) government. Families within the states also struggled for power, and there was pervasive corruption in government. Different schools of thought, retrospectively classified as Confucian, Daoist, Yangist, Mohist, and so forth, emerged during this period, addressing the questions how to restore order and how an individual should conduct himself or herself given the problems of the times. They gave different diagnoses of the problems and proposed different remedies, but they agreed in viewing their answers to the two questions as intimately linked and in seeing a convergence between what is in the public interest and what is in an individual's real interest.

For example, the Mohist movement, originating with Mozi (fifth century B.C.E.), diagnoses the disorder of the times as resulting because each individual, family, and state is working for its own interest at the expense of others' interests; the Mohists therefore propose as a remedy an indiscriminate concern (*jian'ai*) for each individual, family, and state. In response to a common objection that human beings lack the ability (*neng*) to practice indiscriminate concern because they are more concerned for themselves and those more closely related to them, Mozi argues that the practice of indiscriminate concern is actually to the interest of oneself and those to whom one stands in special relations—others will have concern for and will benefit me and my parents if I have concern for and benefit others and their parents. People do have the ability to practice indiscriminate concern and will practice it once they realize that it is in their own interest. So, according to Mozi, private and public interests converge in that the former is promoted by actively pursuing the latter.

The Yangist movement—one representative of which is Yangzhu (fifth to fourth centuries B.C.E.)—advocates nourishing one's own nature (*xing*) or life (*sheng*), understood primarily in terms of health and longevity, and idealizes individuals who shun political involvement to avoid the associated dangers. The Yangists have often been interpreted as concerned primarily with their own interests, but there is evidence that they also demonstrated a concern for others and for the political order. They do not advocate nourishing one's own nature at the expense of harming others; instead, they describe government as serving the purpose of preserving people's nature. They observe that those in power often seek external possessions, including political power, at the expense of harming their own and their subjects' nature, and regard those who shun political involvement as individuals who are ideally suited to rule. Probably, they diagnose the ills of the times as stemming from a preoccupation with external possessions among those in power, and propose as the remedy that each person, especially each person in office, should attend to his or her own nature and become indifferent to external possessions. Like the Mohists, they see private and public interests as converging, though the public interest is promoted by having everyone attend to private interests.

The Confucians and Daoists, whose conceptions of the ethical life will be considered in greater detail later, likewise regard the two kinds of interests as converging. However, they work with concepts of what is in one's real interest that differ from the ordinary concept of self-interest. The Confucians diagnose the ills of the times as a result of the disintegration of the traditional social structure, including various norms and values within the family and state, and propose as a remedy the restoration of such norms and values. Shaping oneself in accordance with such norms and values is also in one's interest. Xunzi (third century B.C.E.) regards human beings as moved in the natural state by self-regarding desires whose unregulated pursuit leads to conflict and disorder; the social structure serves as a means of promoting order and increasing resources through cooperative enterprises, thereby allowing each individual's desires to be satisfied. Mencius (fourth century B.C.E.), on the other hand, thinks that human beings in the natural state already share inclinations that are realized by shaping oneself in accordance with traditional norms and values, so that upholding the traditional social structure is in one's real interest as well as for the public good.

The Daoists diagnose the ills of the times as a result of people's preoccupation with worldly goods and with ethical doctrines (*yan*) of the kind that the Confucians and Mohists advocate. Such preoccupation leads to anxiety and exhaustion within the individual, as well as to strife and disputation between individuals, and the remedy is to relax one's concern with such worldly goods and doctrines. It is difficult to extract from Daoist writings a clear picture of how individuals should ideally relate to the family and state, and Daoist thought has sometimes been interpreted as opposed to ordinary social participation. Whatever their attitude toward ordinary social participation may be, the Daoists probably regard the kind of relaxed concern they advocate as something that frees the individual from anxiety and exhaustion as well as eliminating the pervasive conflict and disorder of the times. Again, what is in one's real interest coincides with the public interest.

That the different schools of thought all view the two kinds of interests as converging can be explained, in part, in terms of the kind of audiences they are addressing. While their audiences share a concern with the disorder of the times, a concern with one's own interest is also a fact about human motivations that is difficult to alter. The presence of the second kind of concern explains why, although the Confucians and Mohists emphasize social participation and devotion to the public good, they also make an effort to show how such a life links up with one's real interest. On the other hand, the presence of the first kind of concern explains why the hypothetical figure of the egoist who is totally indifferent to the public good never plays a role in the ethical discussions of Chinese thinkers of that period. These thinkers are addressing concrete audiences who, though no doubt also concerned with their own interests, are acutely aware of and concerned with the social and political ills of the times. Even the Yangists, who propose that one should attend primarily to one's own life, regard such a proposal as itself instrumental to restoring order.

Turning to the content of the conceptions of the ethical life that these movements advocate, we will focus on Confucianism and Daoism, the two movements from the early period that still continue to influence Chinese thought. Three concepts which are distinctive in Confucian thought and to which the Daoists are opposed are *li* (rites, observance of rites), *ren* (humanity, benevolence), and *yi* (propriety, righteousness).

Li originally refers to rites of sacrifice, and subsequently broadens in scope to include rules governing ceremonial behavior in various social contexts, such as marriage and burial, as well as ways of presenting gifts, receiving guests, asking after the health of parents, or having an audience with a prince. Subsequently, its scope broadens further to include rules governing behavior appropriate to one's social position, such as supporting one's parents in their old age. The nonceremonial aspect of *li* is sometimes emphasized in early texts, as when the *Zuozhuan* contrasts *li* with proper forms; *li* deals with conduct between people in different social positions while proper forms deal with procedures in ceremonial behavior. But *li* often retains the connotation of ceremonial behavior and concerns minute details of such behavior. The *Xunzi*, for example, while sometimes using *li* interchangeably with *liyi* (rites and propriety) to refer to various social norms, more often uses *li* in connection with ceremonial practices and their details. Whether the ceremonial or the nonceremonial is emphasized, *li* includes only rules that are part of an ongoing cultural tradition and pertain to relations between people in different social positions or in recurring social contexts; behavior such as saving a drowning person, though proper, is not a matter of *li*.

Confucian thinkers emphasize the spirit behind the observance of *li*, which Mencius describes in terms of *gong* (respectfulness), *jing* (reverence, seriousness), *ci* (politely declining), and *rang* (yielding to others). *Jing* is a reverential attitude directed initially to the spirits, and subsequently also to other human beings as well as to one's responsibilities and other affairs to which one should be devoted; it involves an attitude of caution, seriousness, attention, and devotion. *Gong* involves being attentive to the manner in which one deals with others, including one's appearance, posture, speech, and attire. *Ci* involves politely declining something good or an honor. *Rang* involves letting others have the good or honor; for example, one should politely decline addressing certain questions put to one by an older person, since one would otherwise be presumptuous in presenting oneself as more knowledgeable. What is common to these ways of viewing others is described in the *Liji* (*Record of Rites*) as the attitude of "lowering oneself and elevating others," akin to the attitude one has toward the spirits in sacrifices. This attitude is not based on a mistaken assessment of how one compares with others in worth and ability, nor does it involve an insincere display that does not correspond to one's actual assessment of others. Rather, it reflects a heightened awareness of one's own limitations and others' merits, whether by virtue of experience, ability, ethical character, or actual accomplishments, as well as an awareness of the fact that one is no more significant or deserving of certain goods and honors than others.

The Confucian emphasis on *li*, which embodies the cultural heritage of the past, has been interpreted by some western scholars as a failure to distinguish between the moral and the traditional, a charge reinforced by the fact that *li* encompasses what contemporary western ethical discussions regard as nonmoral as well as moral matters. Putting aside for now a discussion of the distinction between the moral and the nonmoral, we may note, in response to this charge, that the Confucian attitude toward *li* is not entirely conservative. Although the *Lunyu* contains only one passage that apparently endorses on economic grounds a deviation from an existing *li* practice, the *Mengzi* is more explicit in saying that *li* can be overridden by other considerations in exigencies. The *Xunzi* discusses the importance of adapting *li* to the changing circumstances of life, and later Confucian thinkers such as Wang Yangming (1472–1529) also observe that what is of importance is to preserve the spirit behind *li* rather than to adhere to its minutiae.

Furthermore, while *li* encompasses rules of conduct that may appear oblivious of the contemporary western distinction between the moral and the nonmoral, these rules exhibit a unity both in the attitude that they are supposed to reflect and in the social functions they perform. A serious and reverential attitude toward others underlies both the observance of the responsibilities one has in virtue of one's social position and the observance of rules governing ceremonial behavior; a breach of *li* even in ceremonial contexts, such as improper dress when receiving a guest, demonstrates a lack of the proper attitude and constitutes a serious offense. And, just as the rules governing conduct between individuals in different social positions serve to promote order and minimize conflict, the rules governing ceremonial behavior serve to promote harmony and to properly channel as well as beautify one's emotions in areas of life associated with strong feelings, such as funerals and mourning, or marriage ceremonies during which individuals from different families become united as one family. The common attitude underlying the various rules of *li* and their common social functions shows that their being grouped together as part of a network of *li* is not based on a failure to distinguish between categorically different areas of life.

The Confucian understanding of *yi* (propriety, righteousness) and *ren* (humanity, benevolence) emphasizes respectively strictness with oneself in doing what is proper and affective concern for others. *Yi* has the earlier meaning of a proper regard for oneself or a sense of honor, involving not brooking an insult, and lack of *yi* is often linked to disgrace (*ru*) in early texts. It is subsequently used to refer to what is fitting or proper to a situation and is linked to *chi*, a character often translated as "shame." *Chi* is a reaction to an occurrence or situation that one regards as beneath oneself and potentially lowering one's standing, and it is like shame in presupposing standards to which one is seriously committed. However, it is unlike shame in that it can be directed not just to past occurrences that fall below such standards but also to the prospect of future occurrences. Although *chi* can be directed to the way one is treated in public, it is not typically associated with the thought of being seen or heard, and the typical reaction associated with it is not hiding or disappearing. Rather, it is associated with the thought of being tainted by a certain occurrence, and the typical reaction associated with it is to "wash off" the taint by distancing oneself from or remedying the situation. Even when directed to the past, it does not carry the connotation of dwelling on the past occurrence; instead, it emphasizes a firm resolve to remedy the situation. It is more like the attitude of regarding something as contemptible or beneath oneself, and it is linked to ideas such as disdain (*buxie*) or a refusal to do certain things (*buwei*). *Yi*, for Confucian thinkers, has to do with a firm commitment to certain ethical standards, involving disdaining and regarding as beneath oneself anything that falls short of such standards. These standards include not being treated in a disgraceful manner as measured by certain public standards, and so one common example of *yi* behavior is a refusal to accept treatment in violation of *li*. But the standards also include other things that go beyond what is honorable or disgraceful by public standards, and so can provide a basis for departing from a rule of *li*.

The character *ren* (humanity, benevolence) is probably connate with *ren* (human beings), and in its earlier use it refers either to kindness, especially from a ruler to his subjects, or to the qualities distinctive of members of certain aristocratic clans. It is sometimes used by Confucian thinkers in a broader sense to encompass all the ideal attributes of human beings, and sometimes it refers to an ideal attribute that emphasizes affective concern for others. Even for early Confucians such as Mencius, such affective concern should extend not just to human beings but also to animals. For later Confucians of the Song-Ming period, it includes a concern for everything, including plants as well as what we would describe as inanimate objects. They put this point by saying that the "ten thousand things" form one body with oneself—being indifferent to harm done to such things is compared to being unfeeling (*buren*) toward an injury to part of one's own body. For both early and later Confucians, *ren* involves a gradation. One should have a special concern for parents and family members that one does not have for other people, not just in the sense of a more intense affection but also in the sense of observing certain special obligations as defined by *li*. One's relation to other human beings also differ from one's relation to other animals and objects; for example, in the case of animals bred for food, *ren* toward them is primarily a matter of one's being sparing in their use, involving not using them in excess and not abusing them.

The Confucians' emphasis on *ren, yi*, and *li* reflects the significance they attach to the traditional social structure. Confucius explicitly describes himself as not an innovator but just someone upholding the cultural heritage of early Zhou, and Mozi subsequently criticizes the Confucians for confusing what is proper (*yi*) with what is customary. Later, Mencius and Xunzi both defend the Confucian ideal by reference to their respective conceptions of the basic human constitution that exists before social influence. Mencius believes that the human constitution contains certain shared inclinations which are realized in the Confucian ideal. Xunzi emphasizes the self-regarding desires that human beings share and regards the traditional social arrangements as a means of promoting order and increasing resources, thereby enabling satisfaction of such desires.

By contrast, the Daoists regard the Confucian emphasis on *ren, yi*, and *li* as at odds with the basic human constitution, just like a preoccupation with worldly goods such as external possessions and political power. The *Zhuangzi* and the *Laozi* use different starting points in arriving at this conclusion. *Zhuangzi* appeals to how reflection on the use of language reveals that apparently opposed judgments about what is desirable or proper are often made from different perspectives between which there is no neutral adjudication. *Laozi* appeals to how reflection on the operation of the natural order reveals that aiming at ordinary objects of pursuit, such as strength and reputation, leads to their opposites, and that by dwelling in weak and obscure positions one becomes truly strong and renowned. Through a heightened awareness of the true nature of language or the way things operate, one can come to relax one's concern with ordinary objects of pursuit.

A similar point applies to ethical teachings. According to the *Zhuangzi*, there is no neutral adjudication between the competing doctrines of the Confucians and the Mohists; thus Confucian teachings are themselves judgments made from a perspective to which there are equally viable alternatives. Accordingly, it is misguided to attach the kind of significance that the Confucians do to what they uphold. According to the *Laozi*, Confucian teachings emerge only because human beings have already deviated from a way of life more in tune with the basic human constitution, so that a preoccupation with *ren*, *yi*, and *li* already falls short of the ideal. It is difficult to extract from Daoist writings a clear conception of how, ideally, one should relate to ordinary social activities—whether one should live a life of withdrawal or continue ordinary social participation. Given their opposition to ethical doctrines, it would go against the spirit of the Daoists' writings to give an explicit statement of what the ideal way of life involves. Still, whatever the Daoists' attitude toward ordinary social participation may be, it is clear that they believe one should not attach to such participation the kind of significance that the Confucians do.

Despite this disagreement between the Daoists and the Confucians, they share some characteristics that distinguish them from certain western ethical traditions. Both regard the main ethical task as reshaping the self and both thus involve self-cultivation. The Confucians emphasize embodying the attributes *ren, yi,* and *li* in such a way that one is fully directed toward ethics, a state of existence characterized in terms of *cheng* (sincerity, wholeness). *Cheng* refers to a state in which there is not a single thought or inclination that could lead to the slightest hesitation or reluctance in doing good. The term is sometimes translated as "sincerity," and there is a similarity to sincerity if that is understood not just in the sense of a correspondence between one's outward representation of oneself and one's state of mind, but in the sense of purity or singleness of mind. The Daoists also emphasize a total reshaping of the self, but understood as freeing one's mind from the kind of preoccupation that they regard as at odds with the basic human constitution. This state of mind is characterized in terms of *xu* (vacuity), in which the mind is not guided by any specific aims or goals; instead, one responds spontaneously to the situations one confronts without guidance from preconceptions about how one should respond. For both the Confucians and the Daoists, this reshaping of the self also affects the body; it alters one's outward appearance and so is also perceptible by others. Furthermore, this reshaping of the self has a transforming and attracting effect on others, and both the Confucians and the Daoists regard this effect as the ideal basis for order.

Another common characteristic is that they both regard this reshaping of the self as continuous with the way human beings are in the natural state. Mencius sees it as a full development of ethical inclinations that human beings already share, while Xunzi sees it as a way to enable human beings to satisfy the desires that they have in the natural state. For Xunzi, just as agriculture is a human activity that gives completion to the resources bestowed by *tian* (heaven, nature), self-cultivation is a human activity that gives completion to the desires and capacities human beings have received from *tian*. The *Zhuangzi* and the *Laozi* also view the process of self-cultivation as continuous with human nature. The process involves freeing human beings from the preconceptions that separate them from their natural state of existence, and so serves to restore natural human functioning.

Our discussion shows that, despite the differences between these schools of thought in China, they share certain characteristics distinctive of Chinese ethical thought. These movements are responses to concrete practical concerns of the times, and their representative thinkers are concerned to bring about actual changes in concrete audiences. They share the view that public interest and self-interest coincide, though some schools of thought work with a conception of what is in one's real interest that differs from ordinary conceptions of self-interest. Confucianism and Daoism, the two most influential movements from the early period, both entail self-cultivation. They share the view that the ethical life is continuous with the basic human constitution, though they spell out the relation between the two in different ways. To conclude the discussion, let us consider the question whether Chinese schools of thought may be described as moral thought.

The question admits a straightforward affirmative or negative answer if the notion of morality is construed in certain ways. Earlier, we characterized the ethical in terms of a concern with the question how one should live; an answer to such a question can take different forms and need not be tied to other-regarding concerns or to upholding the social order. Accordingly, even proposals that one should look after one's own interest or that one should live a life of withdrawal would count as conceptions of the ethical life. The notion of morality, if understood as identical with the notion of the ethical, would clearly apply to Chinese schools of thought. On the other hand, the notion of morality has sometimes been described in recent philosophical discussions as carrying connotations specific to certain western ethical traditions, such as the Kantian tradition and its associated notions of rationality and autonomy, or as a peculiar and objectionable development of contemporary ethical thinking that has Kantian roots. When so understood, the notion of morality clearly has no application to Chinese ethical thought.

In between these two extremes are other ways of understanding the notion of morality that characterize it in terms of certain specific ideas. For example, the literature sometimes refers to a "moral point of view" that is characterized by some kind of impartiality or impersonality, suggesting that taking up the moral viewpoint involves going beyond oneself or one's perspective. One way this can occur has to do with an independence from previous motivations; that is, moral thinking involves deliberating in terms of certain practically relevant considerations whose relevance can be appreciated independently of prior motivations. This independence from prior motivations is, on one interpretation, distinctive of Kantian ethics. Alternatively, moral thinking may go beyond oneself in exhibiting an agent-neutrality; that is, it may involve deliberating in terms of practically relevant considerations that can be stated without essential reference to the person who is deliberating in terms of such considerations, so that such deliberation is oblivious of any special relation between the agent and the parties affected. Such considerations are highlighted in utilitarian theories.

It is unlikely that there are important aspects of Chinese ethical thought that are captured by the idea of independence from prior motivation or agent-neutrality. There is little evidence of a concern with considerations whose practical relevance can be appreciated independently of the concerns of the individuals to whom they are addressed. Instead, as we have seen, Chinese thinkers direct their conceptions of the ethical life and their defense to concrete audiences; in doing so, they seek to link their proposals to concerns that the audiences already share. As for agent-neutrality, understood in terms of considerations that are oblivious of the agent's special relations to others, the Mohist teaching of indiscriminate concern may appear to emphasize such considerations; indeed, Mohist teachings have often been compared to utilitarian thought, which highlights agent-neutrality. However, unlike contemporary utilitarian thought, the Mohists do not work with a conception of goods that pertain to particular individuals on the basis of which one can determine the optimal state of affairs. Instead, the kind of benefits they emphasize are what may be described as "social goods," including restoring order, increasing the population, and enriching the poor. Furthermore, whether the Mohists do indeed advocate a kind of deliberation that is oblivious of the special relations between oneself and others is not entirely clear; for example, the actual attitude of the Mohists toward the family still awaits scholarly investigation.

In addition to independence from prior motivations and agent-neutrality, at least three other ways of characterizing the notion of morality can be found in western philosophical discussions. The first characterizes it in terms of its content; it regards morality as having to do with human well-being and how one relates to fellow human beings. The second characterizes it in terms of its purpose; it regards morality as comprising norms that serve primarily to control and redirect potentially destructive desires that could lead to interpersonal conflict, thereby making possible orderly social life. The third characterizes it in terms of the attitude people have toward certain areas of life; it regards morality as comprising norms governing matters that human beings regard as of importance, as reflected in the way they react to a violation of such norms—for instance, with repugnance, shame, and remorse. These three ways of characterizing morality are related; for example, if morality serves the purpose described in the second characterization, it will probably have the content described in the first and be associated with the kind of attitude described in the third. On the other hand, the three characterizations can diverge; for example, certain practices (such as burial practices) may not serve the purpose described in the second characterization and yet be associated with the attitude described in the third. These characterizations allow room for distinguishing between the moral and the nonmoral within the broader notion of the ethical; for example, someone who regards the ethical life as one of withdrawal and serenity would not exhibit a concern with morality as understood in these three characterizations.

If morality is characterized in these ways, there might be room to emphasize the distinction between the moral and the nonmoral for certain purposes in discussing Chinese thought. However, an unqualified application of the distinction to Chinese schools of thought might still incur the risk of oversimplifying the nature of such movements. Consider, for example, the characterization of the moral in terms of a concern for the well-being of others. One might say that a contrast between Confucianism and Mohism on the one hand, and Yangism and Daoism on the other, is that the former but not the latter advocate a moral concern in this sense. This captures the fact that the Yangists and the Daoists do not advocate that individuals should actively seek to promote others' well-being. However, it will be misleading if we make the plain assertion that the Yangists and Daoists are not concerned with morality; as we have seen, they are probably also concerned with the public good, though unlike the Confucians and the Mohists, they do not regard an active concern with the public good as a means of promoting it.

An unqualified application of the distinction between the moral and the nonmoral can also be misleading when we are discussing a particular movement to which the notion of morality appears applicable, as the distinction might not capture anything of significance to that movement. Consider, for example, the characterization of morality in terms of the importance one attaches to a certain area of life, as reflected in such reactions as repugnance, shame, and remorse. Putting aside the differences between *chi* and shame considered earlier, let us assume that *chi* captures a kind of reaction characteristic of morality so construed. This allows us to say that the Confucians, who emphasize the importance of *chi*, are concerned with morality in this sense. However, for the Confucians, any ethical deficiency, including such things as being vulnerable to anxiety, is an object of *chi*, since the deficiency reflects a shortcoming in self-cultivation. So while the notion of morality may appear applicable, the distinction between the moral and the nonmoral does not actually capture anything of significance to the Confucians themselves.

See also Confucianism: Ethics; Confucianism: Tradition; Daoism: Classical; *Li*: Rites or Propriety; *Yi* and *Li*.

Bibliography

Chan, Wing-tsit, trans. and comp. *A Source Book in Chinese Philosophy*. Princeton, N.J.: Princeton University Press, 1963.

Laozi. See D. C. Lau, trans. *Lao Tzu: Tao Te Ching*. London: Penguin, 1963.

Liji. See James Legge, trans. *The Li Ki or Collection of Treatises on the Rules of Propriety or Ceremonial Usages* [*1885*], 2 vols. In *The Sacred Books of the East*, ed. Max Müller. Delhi: Motilal Banarsidass, 1966.

Lunyu (*Analects*). See D. C. Lau, trans. *Confucius: The Analects*. London: Penguin, 1979.

Lushi chunqiu. See Xu Weiyu. *Lushi chunqiu jishi*. Beijing: Shangwu Yinshuguan, 1955. (Chs. 1.2, 1.3, 2.2, 2.3, 21.4.)

Mengzi (*Mencius*). See D. C. Lau, trans. *Mencius*. London: Penguin, 1970.

Mozi. See Burton Watson, trans. *Mo Tzu: Basic Writings*. New York: Columbia University Press, 1963.

Xunzi. See John Knoblock, trans. *Xunzi: A Translation and Study of the Complete Works*, 3 vols. Stanford, Calif.: Stanford University Press, 1988–1994.

Zhozhuan. See James Legge, trans. *The Chunqiu with the Zuo Chuan*, rev. ed. Taipei: Wenshiche chubanshe, 1972.

Zhuangzi. See A. C. Graham, trans. *Chuang-tzu: The Seven Inner Chapters and Other Writings from the Book Chuang-tzu*. London: Allen and Unwin, 1981.

Moral Psychology

Kwong-loi SHUN

A discussion of how human beings are viewed in Chinese thought requires an examination, first, of how aspects of the person are distinguished and, second, of how different Chinese ethical consider these aspects to be related.

The term *ti*, often translated as "body," is used to refer to the body of a person. It is used sometimes to refer to the four limbs and occasionally to refer to other parts of the body; for example, Mencius in one passage refers to both the heart (*xin*) and the sense organs as *ti*, describing the former as the greater and the latter as the lesser *ti*. In addition, there are other terms referring to parts of the body such as the sense organs and the four limbs. The different parts of the body have their own characteristic capacities, such as the eye's capacity of sight, as well as certain characteristic tendencies. For example, the four limbs are drawn toward rest, while the senses are drawn toward such ideal objects as beautiful colors or pleasurable tastes.

These tendencies are referred to as *yu*, a term often translated as "desire" and paired with the opposite term *wu*, often translated as "aversion." *Yu* can be used to describe tendencies of the person as a whole, suc as the desire of human beings for life and honor; correspondingly, human beings have an aversion (*wu*) to death and disgrace. But, unlike the western terms "want" and "desire," *yu* can also be used to describe how parts of the body, such as the sense organs and the four limbs, are drawn toward certain ideal objects.

That human beings are draw toward life and honor, and various parts of the body toward their ideal objects, are regarded as facts—pervasive and difficult to alter. Facts of this kind are referred to as the *qing* of human beings and of the respective parts of the body. *Qing* has the general meaning of facts; in this context, it has the meaning of certain facts about human beings and about parts of the body that reveal what they are genuinely like. Subsequently, at least by the third century B.C.E., *qing* comes to refer to what we would describe as emotions, including joy, sorrow, and anger. As with *yu* (tendencies) of the kind described earlier, the fact that human beings have *qing* (emotions) is also regarded as part of their basic constitution.

The emotions are often related to *qi*, a term for which it is difficult to find a close western equivalent. *Qi* is viewed as a kind of energy or force that fills the body, flowing freely in and giving life to the person. It is responsible for the operation of the senses; for example, *qi* is supposed to generate speech in the mouth and sight in the eyes. It can also be affected by what happens to the senses; for example, *qi* can grow when the mouth takes in tastes and the ear takes in sounds. It explains the operation of the emotions, and a proper balance of *qi* is regarded as necessary for a person's physical and psychological well-being. For example, both illness and such emotional disturbances as fear are explained in terms of an imbalance of *qi*. When used to refer to the forces or energies flowing freely in a body, *qi* may be translated as "life forces" or "vital energies."

Of the various parts of the body, *xin*, the organ of the heart, is particularly important for Chinese thinkers because it is viewed as the site of what we would describe as cognitive and affective activities. *Xin* (the heart) can have *yu* (tendencies) in that it can be drawn toward certain things; it also has *qing* (emotions) and can take pleasure in or feel displeasure at certain things. It can deliberate (*lü*) about a situation, direct attention to and reflect on (*si*) certain things, or keep certain things in mind (*nian*). One capacity of *xin* that is particularly important for Chinese thinkers is setting directions that guide one's daily activities as well as one's life as a whole. One important disagreement between different schools of thought is whether one should let one's life be guided by the directions set by the heart.

These directions of the heart are referred to as *zhi*, a term sometimes translated as "will" and sometimes as "intention." *Zhi* can refer to specific intentions such as the intention to stay or leave a certain place, or general aims in life such as the goal of learning to be a sage. It is something that can be set up, nourished, and attained; it can also be altered by oneself or swayed by the influence of others, and it can be lost through insufficient persistence or a preoccupation with other things. Early texts sometimes compare setting one's *zhi* in certain directions to aiming at a target in archery, and *zhi* is sometimes used interchangeably with another character that means recording something or bearing something in mind. Probably, *zhi* has to do with the heart's focusing itself on and constantly bearing in mind certain courses of action or goals in life, in such a way that *zhi* will guide one's actions or one's life as a whole unless it is changed (by oneself or under the influence of others) or unless one is led to deviate from it by other distractions.

Zhi differs from *yu* (tendencies) in that, while *zhi* pertains specifically to the heart, *yu* can pertain to the heart or to other parts of the body such as the sense organs or the four limbs. Furthermore, while *zhi* involves focusing the heart in a way that guides one's actions or one's life in general, *yu* involves tendencies that one may choose to resist rather than act on.

There is another term, *yi*, often translated as "thought" or "will," that refers to tendencies differing from both *zhi* and *yu*. The term can refer to one's thoughts or opinions, or the meaning of what one says. It can also refer to one's inclinations, involving wanting to see certain things happen or thinking of bringing about certain things. Unlike *yu*, which can involve tendencies (such as the senses' being drawn toward their ideal objects) that just happen to obtain without one's having a reflective awareness of wanting certain things, *yi* is something one is aware of as part of one's thoughts, which pertain to the heart. On the other hand, *yi* is in a less focused or directed state than *zhi* in that, while *yi* can be just a thought in favor of something without one's actually having decided to act in that direction, *zhi* involves actually forming an intention or aim to so act.

The way the different aspects of a person are related is a matter of controversy among different schools of thought. One main issue concerns the role of the heart (*xin*) in relation to other aspects of the person. This disagreement can be illustrated by considering the different views of the relation between the heart (*xin*) and the life forces (*qi*) from the late fourth century to the early third century B.C.E. Certain schools of thought advocate quieting the heart to let the life forces respond to situations on their own, free from its guidance. For example, the chapters *Neiye* and *Xinshuxia* in the *Guanzi* advocate not letting emotions disturb the heart, and not letting things disturb the senses and thereby disturb the heart. Quieting the heart allows the life forces to attain their proper balance. Similarly, the *Zhuangzi* advocates not letting the heart give direction to one's life, a point it puts by describing how someone truly good at archery can hit the mark without aiming. The point is that one should free oneself from the guidance of *zhi*—the directions of the heart that are often compared to aiming in archery in early texts—and instead respond spontaneously to situations one confronts.

By contrast, other movements of the period advocate letting the heart guide and give shape to the life forces. Consider, for example, Gaozi, a contemporary adversary of Mencius's who is reported in the *Mengzi* to have debated with Mencius. On one interpretation of his position, Gaozi believes that the heart should obtain a conception of what is proper (*yi*) from ethical doctrines (*yan*), and should then use that conception to guide the life forces. Mencius disagrees with the first part of Gaozi's view about deriving guidance from ethical doctrines but agrees with the second part, concerning how the heart should guide the life forces. In elaborating on the second part of Gaozi's view, Mencius describes the heart's directions (*zhi*) as the commander over the life forces (*qi*), conveying the point that such directions should guide and give shape to the life forces that fill the body.

Among the texts just considered, the *Mengzi* is classified retrospectively as a Confucian text and the *Zhuangzi* as a Daoist text. However, the distinction between these two views of the relation between the heart and the life forces need not coincide with the distinction between the two schools of thought. For example, the school of thought represented in the chapters *Neiye* and *Xinshuxia* in the *Guanzi* maintains various Confucian values although it also advocates quieting the heart and not letting it guide the life forces. And while Gaozi believes that the heart should guide the life forces, there is no clear evidence that he endorses Confucian values. Still, as a matter of fact, the early Confucian texts that were subsequently more influential do emphasize the guiding role of the heart, while the more influential Daoist texts advocate freeing the person from such guidance.

In the classical Chinese language, there are two characters with the meaning "oneself"; one (*ji*) emphasizes one's relation to oneself whereas the other (*zi*) emphasizes oneself as contrasted with others. In addition, another character (*shen*) can also be used to refer to oneself or one's own person when prefixed with the appropriate possessive pronoun. These characters are often used in early Confucian texts to talk about examining oneself and cultivating oneself on the basis of that self-examination; the capacity for self-cultivation is ascribed to the heart. For example, although Mencius and Xunzi disagree on the basic constitution of the human heart—Mencius believes while Xunzi denies that it has, independent of social influence, certain inclinations bearing an affinity to the Confucian ideal—they both emphasize the importance of the heart in self-cultivation. Mencius emphasizes the heart's capacity to *si* (reflect), which involves directing attention to, reflecting on, and seeking what is proper (*yi*); Xunzi emphasizes its capacity to understand (*zhi*) the rationale (*li*) behind the Confucian way, or Way. Once this capacity has been exercised and an understanding of what is proper or of the rationale behind the Confucian Way has been acquired, that understanding should guide one's whole life; this involves not just regulating one's behavior but also reshaping one's person as a whole. Mencius emphasizes this guiding role of the heart by comparing its directions (*zhi*) to the commander of an army (the life forces); while Xunzi does so by comparing the heart to a ruler who presides over officials (the senses).

Another characteristic of the heart is that it is not subject to further control by any other factors. The *Lunyu* (*Analects*), which records Confucius's teachings and which also compares the heart to the commander of an army, emphasizes the following dissimilarity: while an army can be deprived of its commander, even a common fellow cannot be deprived of his heart's directions (*zhi*). The *Xunzi* also observes that, like the ruler, the heart issues orders but does not take orders from anything; and while the mouth can be forced to keep silent, the heart cannot be made to alter its thoughts (*yi*) under threat, but draws its own distinction between what is acceptable and what is not.

In addition to its guiding role and its independence from external control, early Confucian texts also emphasize the heart's reflectivity—its capacity to constantly step back and reflect on its own activities. This is highlighted, for example, in the idea of constantly watching over *du* (solitude, privacy) found in the *Xunzi, Daxue* (*Great Learning*), and *Zhongyong* (*Centrality and Commonality*). The elaboration on the idea in the *Daxue* and *Zhongyong* suggests that *du* probably refers to the subtle activities of the heart which first emerge when the heart comes into contact with and responds to a situation; such activities are not yet manifested on the outside and are thus known to oneself alone (*du*). These activities are hidden and minute, though they will eventually become manifested outwardly. The idea of watching over *du* highlights the heart's self-reflectivity: for any of its own activities, however subtle and minute, it has the capacity to reflect on and reshape them to ensure their inclination in an ethical direction.

Early Daoist texts emphasize instead that the heart should not play a guiding role in one's life. The *Zhuangzi* considers how, for any judgment about what is desirable or proper, one can make an opposing judgment from a different perspective and there is no neutral standpoint from which we can adjudicate between the competing judgments. This shows that, in attaching weight to the judgments one makes from one's own particular perspective, one is giving them undue significance. This realization leads to a loosening of one's attachment to such judgments, so that one is no longer preoccupied with ordinary objects of pursuit (such as life and honor) or with judgments about what is proper (such as Confucian or Mohist teachings). Ideally, the heart should be vacuous (*xu*) in that it does not guide one's activities with any preconceptions about how one should act; instead, one just responds spontaneously to the situations one encounters, just as a clear mirror or still water reflects accurately any object that is brought up to it. The *Laozi* takes a different starting point but arrives at similar conclusions. By directing the audience to the way the natural order operates, it seeks to instill an awareness that the ideal human life involves not being guided by any conception of what is desirable or by ethical doctrines; such a state of existence it also describes in terms of vacuity (*xu*) as well as in terms of nonaction (*wuwei*).

As we have seen, unlike Mencius, who advocates that the heart's directions (*zhi*) should guide the life forces (*qi*), Zhuangzi advocates that the life forces should respond free from the guidance of such directions. For Mencius, wisdom (*zhi*) is a capacity to properly set the directions of the heart, a capacity that requires flexibility in adjusting such directions to circumstances. For Zhuangzi, it is a matter of freeing the heart from such directions, and this involves illumination (*ming*) in the sense of the kind of understanding and relaxation of concern described earlier. Mencius is opposed to Gaozi's view that one acquires a conception of what is proper from words or doctrines (*yan*), because he believes that the heart already shares certain ethical inclinations that give ethical directions. However, he is not opposed to expressing in words the ethical directions one derives from the heart. By contrast, Zhuangzi regards anything expressible in words as potentially misleading, since it will itself be an ethical teaching purporting to perform the guiding role to which Zhuangzi is opposed. While words (*yan*) may help guide one to the kind of realization that constitutes illumination (*ming*), they are something to be dispensed with once one has attained illumination; hence, the *Zhuangzi* refers to its own teaching as the teaching that cannot be expressed in words.

Despite these differences, there are important points of similarity in how Confucians and Daoists view the heart. First, they both ascribe to the heart the capacity to reflect on and reshape the person as a whole. Although the Daoists oppose guiding one's life under the heart's directions and trace the source of human problems primarily to the problematic inclinations of the heart, the capacity to understand the inappropriateness of such guidance and the problematic nature of such inclinations is itself ascribed to the heart. This understanding enables one to be free from such problematic inclinations, and so attaining illumination is itself an activity of the heart. This capacity of the heart to transcend and reshape itself is expressed in the chapter *Neiye* of the *Guanzi* in terms of a heart within the heart. Although *Neiye* speaks of stilling (*jing*) the heart and not allowing it to be disturbed by external things or the senses, it also emphasizes that the heart gives order to itself and the senses, as if there is a heart within the heart.

Second, Confucian and Daoist thinkers agree that in its ideal state the heart should exhibit tranquillity and effortlessness, although they develop this idea in different ways. In Daoist writings, the notions of vacuity (*xu*), stillness (*jing*), and nonaction (*wuwei*) are used to convey the point that the heart should ideally not be perturbed by any preconceptions about its own responses, responding spontaneously and effortlessly to situations free from guidance by such preconceptions. The *Xunzi* also uses the notion of nonaction (*wuwei*) to describe the effortlessness of the sage's responses, and it uses the notions of vacuity (*xu*) and stillness (*jing*), as well as the analogy of still water found in the *Zhuangzi*, to describe the ideal state of the heart. It differs from Daoist writings in that it regards this ideal state of the heart as enabling the heart to be receptive to the rationale (*li*) behind the Confucian Way. Although the *Mengzi* does not use similar notions, it describes the heart as unmoved or unperturbed in the ideal state, because one has cultivated the life forces (*qi*) to give full support to the heart's directions (*zhi*), enabling one's responses to be free from fear, temptation, or uncertainty. The idea of *cheng* (wholeness, sincerity) in the *Xunzi, Zhongyong*, and *Daxue* also emphasizes a completely ethical direction of the heart that enables it to respond ethically without effort. Later Confucians also use the notion of nonaction (*wuwei*) to describe this effortlessness of *cheng*, and the notion of vacuity (*xu*) to describe the undisturbed state of the heart that makes possible such effortless responses.

Third, working within a tradition of thought that regards *de* (virtue, power) as having a transforming effect on one's whole person as well as on others, both Confucian and Daoist thinkers ascribe such an effect to the heart in its ideal condition. Confucians often emphasize that the condition of the heart affects the person as a whole, including the life forces (*qi*) as well as the body. Mencius describes the heart's condition as manifested in the whole person—not just in action and speech but in the face, the look of the eyes, the four limbs, and one's physical bearing in general. Similarly, Xunzi describes the heart's role in cultivating the heart's directions (*zhi*) and thoughts (*yi*) as well as in giving order to the life forces (*qi*), and describes how *cheng* (wholeness, sincerity), the completely ethical inclination of the heart, will inevitably be manifested outwardly. The effect of the ethical inclination of the heart extends to others, on whom a person of good character has a transforming and attracting effect; in government, the person will also ensure that everything is properly nourished and attains its proper place. Thus, the *Xunzi* describes *cheng* as having a transforming and nourishing effect on the "ten thousand things"; the *Zhongyong* presents *cheng* as the basis of the social and political order by virtue of its transforming and nourishing effect.

In Daoist texts such as the *Zhuangzi*, the significance of physical appearance is deemphasized; to point out the insignificance of physical appearance relative to the heart's condition, people with *de* (virtue, power) are often depicted as having physical deformities. However, *de* is still supposed to be manifested outwardly and to have its transforming, attracting effect on others. For example, in one story in the *Zhuangzi* a physically ugly person with *de* attracts all those who come into contact with him; the point is that people are drawn by what is within a person, not by physical appearance. The *Laozi* also describes the transforming, nourishing effect of the sage, who has this effect without effort. So, like the Confucians, the Daoists regard the condition of the heart as intimately related to its effect on others.

Our discussion shows that both Confucian and Daoist thinkers emphasize a distinction between the heart and other aspects of the person. For the Confucians, the heart has the distinctive capacity of reflecting on these other aspects as well as on its own activities, and it can form a conception of what is proper and should ideally use this conception to regulate and shape both itself and the other aspects of the person. For the Daoists, human problems have their source primarily in the problematic inclinations of the heart, in its attaching itself to certain objects of pursuit or ethical teachings. Still, the remedy is itself performed by the heart, showing that even Daoist thinkers presuppose that the heart has the capacity to reflect on and reshape its own activities. This capacity for self-reflection that both Confucians and Daoists ascribe to the heart justifies our using the notion of self in discussing these thinkers, and the notion of self-cultivation to refer to the process of reflecting on oneself and bringing about changes in oneself on the basis of such self-reflection.

Although these thinkers do emphasize the distinction between the heart and other aspects of the person, they focus on the distinctive capacities and modes of operation of the heart, rather than on the heart's being a distinctive kind of entity that occupies a "mental" as opposed to a "physical" realm. The character *xin*, which we have translated as "heart," refers to the organ of the heart within the body, and Chinese thinkers emphasize the distinctive capacities and modes of operation of this organ, as opposed to, for example, the sense organs. This does not mean that the heart is itself something merely "physical"; rather, the point is that a distinction between two realms, one physical and one mental, is not useful in discussing the contrast between the heart and other parts of the person. Furthermore, while emphasizing the distinctive modes of operation of the heart, Chinese thinkers also emphasize its intimate relation to other aspects of the person. The heart is not a "private" entity that eludes observation by others; instead, its condition affects other aspects of the person and is something that will inevitably be manifested outwardly and be discernible by others. This last point shows that, if we use the notions of self and self-cultivation in discussing Chinese ethical thought, the notion of self should be construed so as to refer not just to the heart but to the person as a whole, since the whole person is affected in the process of self-cultivation.

See also *Cheng*; *Qing*; Reason and Principle; Self-Deception; *Ti* and *Yong*; *Wuwei*; *Xin*; *Xu*.

Bibliography

Note: All references to *Zhongyong* (*Centrality and Commonality*, or *Doctrine of the Mean*) and *Daxue* (*Great Learning*) are by chapter numbers (following Zhu Xi's division of the text) in James Legge's translation.

Chan, Wing-tsit, trans. and comp. *A Source Book in Chinese Philosophy*. Princeton, N.J.: Princeton University Press, 1963.

Cua, Antonio S. *Ethical Argumentation: A Study in Hsün Tzu's Moral Epistemology*. Honolulu: University of Hawaii Press, 1985.

———. "Reason and Principle in Chinese Philosophy." In *A Companion to World Philosophies*, ed. Eliot Deutsch and Ron Bontekoe. Oxford: Blackwell, 1997.

Graham, A. C., trans. *Chuang-tzu: The Seven Inner Chapters and Other Writings from the Book Chuang-tzu*. London: Allen and Unwin, 1981.

Lau, D. C., trans. *Confucius: The Analects*. London: Penguin, 1979.

———, trans. *Lao Tzu: Tao Te Ching*. London: Penguin, 1963.

———, trans. *Mencius*. London: Penguin, 1970.

Legge, James, trans. *Confucius: Confucian Analects, The Great Learning, and the Doctrine of the Mean*, 2nd ed. Oxford: Clarendon, 1893.

Knoblock, John, trans. *Xunzi: A Translation and Study of the Complete Works*, 3 vols. Stanford, Calif.: Stanford University Press, 1988–1994.

Rickett, W. Allyn. *Guanzi: A Study and Translation*, Vol. 1. Princeton, N.J.: Princeton University Press, 1985, pp. 376–386.

———, trans. *Kuan-tzu*, Vol. 1. Hong Kong: Hong Kong University Press, 1965, pp. 151–172.

Mou Zongsan (Mou Tsung-san)

Shu-hsien Liu

Mou Zongsan (1909–1995) has been considered the most original and probably the most influential thinker in the second generation of contemporary neo-Confucianism (*Xin Ruxue*). He was raised as a farm boy, with his roots deep in the soil. He was a graduate of Peking (Beijing) University, but he was not impressed by the trend of liberalism, positivism, and pragmatism promoted by Hu Shi (1891–1962) and did not go along with the tide. On the contrary, he was attracted by Xiong Shili (1885–1968), who was then an obscure teacher but would later be honored as the founder of the contemporary neo-Confucian philosophical movement.

In addition to Mou, Xiong's disciples included Tang Junyi (T'ang Chün-i, 1909–1978), and Xu Fuguan (Hsü Fu-kuan, 1903–1982). Although Xiong chose to remain in mainland China after the communist takeover in 1949, Mou, Tang, and Xu fled to Hong Kong and Taiwan. Along with Carsun Chang (1887–1969), they issued the famous *Manifesto for a Reappraisal of Sinology and Reconstruction of Chinese Culture* on New Year's Day 1958. They condemned communist China for destroying traditional culture, and they urged the reconstruction of tradition by reviving the spirit of Chinese philosophy, especially Confucianism, while absorbing insights from the west.

During the Cultural Revolution, Confucianism became a dirty word in mainland China. Ironically, however, after the Cultural Revolution, contemporary neo-Confucianism was designated a concentrated study area on the national level beginning in 1986. Hundreds of articles and a number of books were published on the subject, and an academic conference on Mou's thought was held in Shandong Province, the native place of Confucius, Mencius, and Mou. Even though neo-Confucian thought is still considered incorrect according to the official ideology, it has attracted a great deal of attention and has produced important scholarship and stimulating formulations, combating national nihilism on the one hand and rejecting wholesale westernization on the other. It has provided many useful insights as China faces both its own tradition and the west in the process of modernization.

Mou's teaching career may be divided into three periods:

1. Before 1949 he taught at various universities on the mainland.
2. From 1949 to 1960 he taught in Taiwan. He taught first at Normal University and then, in 1955, joined Xu Fuguan to teach at Donghai (Tunghai) University, forming a second center of contemporary neo-Confucianism besides New Asia College, established by Qian Mu (Ch'ien Mu, 1895–1990) and Tang Junyi in Hong Kong in 1949.
3. From 1960 to 1974, he taught in Hong Kong, first at the University of Hong Kong and then—from 1968 until his retirement in 1974—at New Asia College, Chinese University of Hong Kong. Thereafter, until his death in 1995, he continued to teach at New Asia Research Institute (which later became a private institute) and had various visiting appointments in Taiwan.

In this essay, I shall discuss in some detail Mou's ideas at different times in his life. The development of his thought may be divided into five stages:

- Stage 1. As a college student, he was primarily interested in cosmology. His only publication during this stage was his study of Han cosmology through the commentaries on the *Yijing* (*Book of Changes*).
- Stage 2. Mou's interest next turned to logic and epistemology. He studied Russell and Whitehead's *Principia Mathematica* and Wittgenstein's *Tractatus Logico-Philosophicus*. To gain a deeper understanding of the function of reason, he found that he had to return to Kant. His work during this period culminated in the book *Renshixin zhi pipan* (*A Critique of the Cognitive Mind*, 1956–1957).
- Stage 3. Owing to the changes brought about by the communist revolution in 1949, it was impossible for Mou to engage only in purely theoretical research. He devoted himself to reflections on the strengths and limitations of traditional Chinese culture and tried to find a way for the future. His books published during this period included *Philosophy of History* (1955) and *The Way of Politics and the Way of Government* (1961).
- Stage 4. Mou then returned to the study of Chinese philosophy, trying to recover the great insights implicit in the three traditions: Daoism, Confucianism, and Buddhism. During this period he published important scholarly works, including *Physical Nature and Speculative Reason* (1963),

The Substance of Mind and the Substance of Nature (3 vols., 1968–1969), *From Lu Xiangshan to Liu Qishan* (1979), and *The Buddha-Nature and Prajna* (2 vols., 1977).

- Stage 5. Mou now gave expression to his own thought, in *Intellectual Intuition and Chinese Philosophy* (1971), *Phenomenon and the Thing-in-Itself* (1975), and *On Summum Bonum* (1985). He also gave several series of lectures and translated into Chinese Kant's *Critique of Pure Reason* (a part), *Critique of Practical Reason*, and *Critique of Judgment*. He said he was following Xuancang's example in translating Buddhist scriptures. Interestingly, Mou has often been compared to Kant: it is said that a student of western philosophy must work hard to go beyond Kant but can never bypass Kant, and the same may be said of Mou with regard to students of Chinese philosophy.

Early Interests

In this section, I lump together Mou's first two stages. As a college student Mou was fascinated by Whitehead's cosmology and was inspired to study the implications of philosophy of nature in *Yijing*. But soon his interest turned inward, and he was attracted by the rigorous rules of mathematical logic.

After he mastered the operational aspect of symbolic logic, however, he was driven to reflect on the philosophical foundation of logic and mathematics, and he found that he was not satisfied by current theories such as Russell's theory of logical atomism. He felt that formalism, positivism, realism, and pragmatism could not provide an adequate explanation for logic. There had to be something a priori presupposed by these theories. But it was wrong to look for a transcendent world of "ideas" as suggested by Plato. Thus Mou went back to Kant.

Mou felt that many of Kant's insights were insufficiently appreciated by our contemporaries. Our age had seemed to move away from reason, and Mou urged us to revive our faith in it. True, today our understanding of reason was no longer the same as what had been understood during the Enlightenment. Different logical systems, such as propositional, modal, and many-valued logic, had been developed. Aristotle's laws of thought—identity, contradiction, the excluded middle—did not seem as sacred as before. But Mou urged that we should not be misled by appearances. Even though it is impossible for us to formulate a law of contradiction that would apply to all logical systems, no logical system can be allowed to contradict itself. Thus Mou pointed out that noncontradiction is a transcendental, a priori regulative idea behind all formulated logical systems and should not be confused with a formulated law of contradiction within a certain logical system. Therefore, for Mou, the regulative principle must not be confused with the constitutive principle. Even though there are many logical systems, they still come from the same source—which is none other than reason. The function of reason is manifest in its schemata. One schema is *yingu* (ground-consequence), which is closely related to *yinguo* (cause-effect). There is an isomorphism between thought and nature; otherwise, we would have no reasonable explanation for the application of mathematics to physics. And reason tends to express itself in a dualistic structure, through the *eryong* (dual-function) schema of affirmation and negation. It is here that we can find the origin of the so-called law of identity and law of contradiction. Mou firmly believed that we should commit ourselves to understanding the function of reason in thought and in nature. Once the root is found, the construction of a cosmology is a distinct possibility.

Existential Reflections on Chinese Culture

In the early stages Mou was immersed in the abstract world of ideas. But no one living in his time was allowed to philosophize in an armchair for long. China not only went through World War II but also was embroiled in its own civil war; finally, the communists took over the mainland in 1949, and the Nationalists retreated to Taiwan.

Mou was among the few intellectuals who were not persuaded by communist propaganda and were firmly against communism and Mao Zedong's thought on philosophical grounds. He reflected on Chinese culture in terms of his own deep existential concern and was convinced that the communists were choosing the wrong way to change Chinese tradition. He became a refugee scholar, wrote a number of essays criticizing communist ideology, and thought profoundly about Chinese roots in order to lay bare the mistakes of his contemporaries who followed the communists in destroying the traditional culture. These articles were later published as a book, *Moral Idealism* (1982), whose title suggested exactly what was lacking in an age that Mou characterized as *wuti, wuli, wuli*: no substance, no principle, no strength. Mou also wrote essays criticizing communist theories as represented by Mao Zedong's articles "On Contradiction" and "On Practice"; in addition, he criticized Sartre's view that there is no human nature.

For his own part, he formulated a doctrine of three traditions.

1. Assertion of *daotong* (the tradition of the Way): We must assert the value of morality and religion, jealously guarding the fountainhead of the universe and human life as realized by Confucius and Mencius.
2. Development of *xuetong* (the tradition of learning): We must expand our cultural life and further develop the knowing subject to absorb the western tradition of science, so that learning will gain its independent status.
3. Continuation of *zhengtong* (the tradition of politics): We must recognize the necessity of adopting the democratic system of government to fulfill truly the political ideals of the sages and worthies of the past. This doctrine provided a ground for a synthesis of east and west.

Of Mou's writings, *Philosophy of History* (1962) is probably the most Hegelian. Mou used a philosophical scheme to analyze Chinese history until the end of the Han dynasty, reviewing the past in order to look toward the future. He used two pairs of concepts to analyze significant historical events in the past: analytic and synthetic, and *li* (principle) and *qi* (material or vital force). He pointed out that traditional Chinese culture had a highly developed "synthetic spirit of realizing *li*," as represented by Confucius, and also a "synthetic spirit of realizing *qi*," as represented by Liu Bang, a commoner who founded the Han dynasty and whom Mou regarded as a genius. But the Chinese had failed to develop an "analytic spirit of realizing *li*," as represented by Kant, whom Mou regarded as embodying the spirit of western culture. We have to appreciate the strengths of the western tradition in order to absorb them into our own culture. In short, the Chinese tradition had made great achievements in the moral and artistic worlds but had contributed little to abstract thinking and had not been able to develop a democratic form of government.

The Way of Politics and the Way of Government (1980) is devoted to a critique of the traditional political culture. According to Mou, the Chinese tradition had developed only *zhidao* (the way of government); it had never developed *zhengdao* (the way of politics). He meant that the Chinese tradition had produced a number of able administrators who could take care of the welfare of the people and could solve problems pragmatically, but it had never produced a democratic western-type constitution. This was because traditional Chinese culture excelled in "operational" and "intensional" representations of reason but was deficient in the "structural" and "extensional" representations that found full expression in western science and democracy. The Chinese idea of *neisheng waiwang* (inward sageliness and outward kingliness) treats politics as an extension of ethics. If sages and worthies were always at the helm, as in the legends of the Three Dynasties, then codified law and constitutional government might not be necessary. However, in actual politics there were many more evil and mediocre kings than good and able ones, and so laws and constitutions were necessary to provide protections. Mou concluded, rather ironically, that the traditional Chinese *zhiguan* (straightforward) way, which treats politics as an extension of ethics, may appear superior while in actual practice common people living under dynastic rules were often deprived of their welfare and rights. Realization of the ideal—a government of *ren* (humanity), i.e., a government for the people—might need to come by a different route: the *judong* (roundabout) way, as developed and practiced in the west. The personal cultivation of the moral subject is important but is not enough; it has to be balanced by the establishment of a constitutional government on an objective basis.

Scholarly Studies of Traditional Chinese Philosophy

After the days of the "hundred contending schools" in the late Zhou period, Confucianism was honored as orthodoxy during the Han dynasty, and it was complemented by Daoism—just as *yin* and *yang* are mutually complementary. After Buddhism was imported to China, Chinese thought was dominated by the *sanjiao* (three traditions) of Confucianism, Daoism, and Buddhism. Anyone who is interested in Chinese thought must go back to the roots of these three traditions. When the Korean War broke out, it appeared that the communist regime in mainland China and the Nationalist regime in Taiwan would coexist for a long time, and Mou returned to scholarly studies of traditional Chinese philosophy in order to provide a foundation for his urgent calls for cultural reform at a time of crisis.

While teaching at Donghai (Tunghai) University, he published *Physical Nature and Speculative Reason* (1963), a solid scholarly work examining in depth neo-Daoist thought during the Wei and Jin period. It is interesting to note that even though Mou was ultimately committed to Confucianism, he chose to work first on neo-Daoism. He showed a penetrating understanding of the two trends of thought he identified in the period: one emphasizing the physical nature of man, the other focusing on transcendent metaphysical speculation. Mou elaborated on the idea of *mingli* (principle in logical reasoning and philosophical speculation). The term *ming* literally means names. Confucius first developed the concept of *zhengming* (rectification of names), which demanded a correlation between name and reality. The Daoists, on the other hand, urged that names must be transcended because *dao* (the way, or Way) cannot be expressed in language. During the Warring States period there was a *mingjia*, "school of names." Gongsun Long (b. 380 B.C.E), a representative of the school, was greatly skilled in dialectics, arguing, for example, that "white horse is not horse," because if a white horse is ordered, it will not do to deliver just a horse. Wei-Jin thought attempted to blend the thinking of Confucianism, Daoism, and the school of names. The Wei-Jin philosophers followed the Han tradition of probing into the physical nature of man, they were master dialecticians, and they wanted to transcend the mundane world in order to carry on metaphysical speculation. There was *li* (reason, principle) in such an approach—hence the combined term *mingli*. Mou felt that this approach was probably closest to the western approach of logical argumentation and philosophical speculation, though not as fully developed.

When Mou left Taiwan to teach at Chinese University of Hong Kong, he felt quite isolated, as he did not speak Cantonese and had very little communication with local people. As a result, he concentrated on his study of Song-Ming neo-Confucianism, which culminated in the three volumes of *The Substance of Mind and the Substance of Nature* (1968–1969). Ten years later he published *From Lu Xiangshan to Liu Qishan* (1979), which could be regarded as the fourth volume. Today no one who wants to study this subject can afford to bypass these works.

In contrast to the Wei-Jin philosophers, who emphasized the physical nature of man, Song-Ming philosophers emphasized man's moral nature. They rejected determinism, believing that because everyone was endowed with the same moral nature, temperament could be transformed through personal cultivation. Song-Ming philosophers fought against the moral decadence of their time and formulated sophisticated theories of human nature and the universe to counter the influence of Buddhism and Daoism, which dominated the minds of intellectuals. They were committed to reviving the spirit of Confucius and Mencius. In the introductory part of *The Substance of Mind and the Substance of Nature*, Mou took a comparative approach in order to capture the unique characteristics of the Chinese philosophy of mind and nature, distinguishing it from western philosophies such as those of Plato, Aristotle, and Kant. To the Song-Ming philosophers, *li* means none other than *tianli* (heavenly principle); that is, the transcendent metaphysical principles originate in Heaven but are inherent in man and must not be understood as something external like Platonic "ideas," Aristotelian "forms," or principles reached through empirical generalization. Mou felt that only in Kant's *Critiques* could we find a bridge to connect the insights of Chinese and western philosophy. But even Kant, limited by his own tradition, was able to establish only a metaphysics of morals or a moral theology; he was not able to develop a moral metaphysics—which happened to be the main concern of Song-Ming neo-Confucian philosophers.

Mou, using his own theoretical framework, studied nine thinkers in depth: Zhou Dunyi (1017–1073), Zhang Zai (1020–1077), Cheng Hao (1032–1085), Cheng Yi (1033–1107), Hu Hong (1110–1155), Zhu Xi (1130–1200), Lu Xiangshan (1139–1193), Wang Yangming (1472–1529), and Liu Qishan (1578–1645).

Zhou and Zhang were usually regarded as early cosmological thinkers in the Northern Song period, but Mou pointed out that it was Zhou who had first built a bridge between *The Doctrine of the Mean* and the *Commentaries of the Book of Changes*. Zhou took *cheng* (sincerity) as the characteristic of the Way of Heaven, the creative ontological principle working incessantly in the universe; he saw trying to achieve *cheng* as characteristic of the Way of man. Even though Zhang Zai had been greatly interested in cosmological speculation, we should not forget that he was the first to distinguish between knowledge through seeing and hearing (empirical knowledge) and moral knowledge, and between physical nature and moral nature (nature of heaven and earth).

The Cheng brothers had made neo-Confucian philosophy the dominant trend in their own time. Cheng Hao testified that he had been enlightened about *tianli* (heavenly principle) through personal realization and only then had returned to the Confucian Way, after wandering for nearly ten years in Buddhism and Daoism. After Cheng Hao died, Cheng Yi continued to spread their teachings; indeed, he became the greatest teacher of these doctrines and exerted a profound influence on the next generation of scholars. The two brothers were temperamentally very different, but philosophically they seemed to be in basic agreement, since many of their recorded conversations were blended with no identification of who was speaking about what. Mou's contribution regarding the Chengs was his finding that they actually had rather different ideas, and he established definite criteria to sort out their respective sayings. Mou believed that Cheng Hao's thought was monistic: for him *li* (principle) both exists and acts. Cheng Yi's thought was dualistic: *li* (principle) exists, but for action it has to depend on material force.

What Zhu Xi inherited and further developed was Cheng Yi's thought; therefore, what is called the

Cheng-Zhu school should refer only to Cheng Yi, not Cheng Hao. Furthermore, Mou believed that Cheng-Zhu's thought had deviated from Mencius's thought as inherited by Zhou, Zhang, and Cheng Hao. Posterity honored the Cheng-Zhu school as representing the orthodox line of Confucian philosophy, and so a strange phenomenon occurred: as Mou argued, if Mencius was accepted as representing the orthodox line of Confucian philosophy, then it was a "side branch" that took up the position of orthodoxy.

Mou's own sympathies were more with Lu Xiangshan and Wang Yangming. But he recognized that there were also shortcomings in Lu's and Wang's approach, because the assertion that everyone has *liangzhi* (innate knowledge of what is morally good) could be misinterpreted to mean that "there are sages all over the streets," as in the Ming period. Therefore, Liu Qishan emphasized "sincerity of the will" and directed attention from the obvious to the subtle. Mou found that Liu's thought had characteristics similar to that of Hu Hong, an important member of the Hunan school, which was almost extinguished as a result of severe criticism by Zhu Xi in the Southern Song period. Therefore, Mou suggested that instead of talking about only two trends of Song-Ming thought—i.e., Cheng-Zhu and Lu-Wang—we should add another trend: Hu-Liu. This would give a more complete picture of Song-Ming neo-Confucian philosophy, which had revived some of the thoughts of Zhou, Zhang, and Cheng Hao in the Northern Song period.

Many of Mou's ideas are controversial, but he takes us to a new stage in the study of Song-Ming Ming philosophy. Even though one may disagree with some of his ideas, his views cannot be ignored.

After joining New Asia College at the Chinese University of Hong Kong, Mou completed two thick volumes, *The Buddha-Nature and Prajna* (1977), representing many years of reflection on the Buddhist tradition. Mou did not endorse his teacher Xiong Shili's critique of "consciousness-only" Buddhism; he felt the critique had been based on a misunderstanding of that philosophy. According to Mou, *prajna*—the wisdom to realize *sunyata* (emptiness)—is common to all Buddhist sects; what differentiates the sects is their various understandings of how to achieve buddhahood. The Chinese favored Mahayana (the great vehicle) over Hinayana (the small vehicle), which was considered the more elementary teaching of Buddhism. Also, they believed that only in his later years had Sakyamuni delivered his mature views or "rounded teachings" as presented in Huayan and Tiantai Buddhism. Most scholars thought that the Huayan school set forth the perfect teachings of Buddha in the most mature fashion, but Mou preferred Tiantai. Huayan must renounce the nine lower worlds in favor of the world of *li* (principle), whereas Tiantai, paradoxically, announces that the *dharma* nature is none other than *avidya* (ignorance) and hence gives expression to the truly rounded teaching of Buddha. Not everyone would agree with Mou's assessment, but his interpretation is undeniably original and sheds light on the Tiantai teachings, which had been overlooked by scholars for hundreds of years. Mou, of course, was not a Buddhist, but he took pride in the fact that even Buddhists would have to consult his works for a deeper understanding of Buddhist philosophy.

Philosophical Synthesis from a Comparative Perspective

Although Mou dug deep into his own tradition, his thought never lacked a comparative perspective. This became prominent in his late thought. Somewhat by chance, he read Heidegger's book on Kant, which prompted him to write his own last three books. He felt that Heidegger could develop only a phenomenological ontology, of a kind which Mou called inner metaphysics and which lost sight of the truly transcendent. Therefore, we must go back to Kant. Kant's theoretical framework could help us understand the implications of Confucian moral insights.

Contrary to current views of Confucianism as authoritarian, Mou argued, convincingly, that moral autonomy was implicit in Confucian philosophy. But even Kant was insufficient in this regard. Limited by his Christian background, Kant could treat free will only as a postulate of practical reason, the other two postulates being the immortality of the soul and the existence of God. Hence he could establish only a metaphysics of morals, at best a moral theology, but never a moral metaphysics. Mou felt that the Chinese tradition went further than Kant in this respect. For the Chinese, there was no need to postulate either the immortality of the soul or the existence of God. Mou entirely agreed with his teacher, Xiong Shili, who rejected Feng Youlan's view to take *liangzhi* (innate knowledge of the good) as a postulate. For Mencius, the mind-heart that cannot bear to see the suffering of man is a presence. Kant, whose starting point was pure reason in the western tradition, had to take a roundabout way to speak about the postulates of practical reason. But the Confucian philosophers started with *xin* (mind-heart) and *xing* (nature) as an endowment from Heaven; thus we need only develop to the full what is already in us. The presence of *benxin* (original mind) should never be taken as sympathy, an empirical psychological state. That human nature is good can never be established in terms of empirical observation or generalization. Only Kant realized that morality was not the subject matter of anthropological studies.

Thus Mou chose Kant as his point of departure. For Kant, all human knowledge must depend on sensible intuition; only God has intellectual intuition. Hence (to repeat) it is impossible for Kant to establish a moral metaphysics; he can only appeal to the demands of practical reason to formulate a moral theology. But for the major Chinese traditions, humans—even though they are admittedly finite—have been endowed with the ability to grasp the Way as both transcendent and immanent, regardless of whether the Way is understood as Daoist, Buddhist, or Confucian. Since the Chinese believe they have the ability to penetrate reality, there is no longer a wide gap between phenomenon and noumenon. In this sense Mou insisted that intellectual intuition understood as personal realization of the Way must not be denied to humans. It is here that he found the special characteristics of Chinese philosophy.

In *Phenomenon and the Thing-in-Itself* (1975) Mou went a step further. By way of a comparative study of Heidegger and Kant, Mou distinguished between what he called "ontology without adherence" and "ontology with adherence." Ontology without adherence had been highly developed in Asian traditions, which emphasize a liberation from adherence so as to enhance the meaning of our existence. Ontology with adherence had been elaborately formulated in the western traditions, which emphasize the pursuit of knowledge and the establishment of institutions. Mou firmly believed in a link between the finite mind and the infinite mind. To manifest itself, the infinite mind must go through a process of *ganxian* (falling on objectivization) in which it restricts itself. In this way the duality of knowing and the known is formed, as a result of a dialectical process. If we can get to the bottom of things, the adherence of the knowing mind and the realization of the infinite mind have the same origin. It is here we find the foundation for the unity of perspectives.

Mou's last work was *On Summum Bonum* (1985). Here again, he used Kant as a point for departure to explicate meanings implicit in Chinese philosophies—Confucian, Daoist, and Buddhist. Kant saw this world as imperfect; summum bonum (the highest good) could be realized only in the kingdom of God. But the Chinese tradition is thoroughly this-worldly; there is no need to escape to another world. Kant's problem was not really solved in Chinese philosophy, as only an omnipotent God can bring about the unity of happiness and goodness. The Chinese know only too well that in real life, happiness and the good rarely go together. But the Chinese do not need to look forward to an otherworldly kingdom of God. No matter what happens in our lives and no matter how imperfect the earthly world is, we can always find fulfillment in this world. I need not go into the details of Mou's reflection on the subject; it will suffice to mention just one example. Mou characterized the rounded teachings of Tiantai as paradoxical because the realization of *dharma* nature is not apart from *avidya* (ignorance). Thus enlightenment and adherence are really two sides of the same coin. Consequently, we can always find fulfillment in nonfulfillment; summum bonum is realized here and now; and there is no need to look for a kingdom of God in the other world.

Conclusion

Mou was certainly the most original thinker of his generation. He was inspired by his teacher Xiong Shili but independently developed his own system of philosophy. He was the first to apply conceptual analysis successfully to the highly elusive ideas and insights of traditional Chinese philosophy. Partly because he lived longer than most other second-generation contemporary neo-Confucian scholars, he exerted a more profound influence on the next generation. However, even though his achievements were unparalleled, there are still considerable limitations in his thought. As he worked to counter what he saw as the degenerative tendency of his time, he may have overemphasized *liyi* (one principle) at the expense of *fenshu* (many manifestations). But his intention was to honor all insights, whether they came from China, India, or the west. Future attempts to carry his work further would probably take the direction of giving more emphasis to *fenshu*. Pluralism is characteristic of our time; what we need is to avoid the extreme of relativism without subscribing to the other extreme, absolutism. We should still follow the guiding principle of the middle way implicit in the idea of *liyi fenshu*.

See also Confucianism: Twentieth Century; *Liyi fenshu*; Philosophy: Recent Trends Overseas.

Bibliography

Chan, Wing-tsit, trans. and comp. *A Source Book in Chinese Philosophy*. Princeton, N.J.: Princeton University Press, 1963.

Chang, Carsun. *The Development of Neo-Confucian Thought*, 2 vols. New York: Bookman, 1957–1962.

Furth, Charlotte, ed. *The Limits of Change: Essays on Conservative Alternatives in Republican China*. Cambridge, Mass.: Harvard University Press, 1976.

Liu, Shu-hsien. "Confucian Ideals and the Real World: A Critical Review of Contemporary Neo-Confucian Thought." In *Confucian Traditions in East Asian Modernity*, ed. Tu Wei-ming. Cambridge, Mass.: Harvard University Press, 1996.

———. "The Contemporary Development of a Neo-Confucian Epistemology." *Inquiry*, 14, 1971, pp. 19–41. (Republished as the second chapter in *Invitation to Chinese Philosophy*, ed. Arne Naess and Alastair Hannay. Oslo, Bergen, and Trömso: Universitetsforlaget, 1972, pp. 19–40.)
———. "On New Frontiers of Contemporary Neo-Confucian Philosophy." *Journal of Chinese Philosophy*, 23(1), 1996, pp. 39–58.
———. "Postwar Neo-Confucian Philosophy: Its Development and Issues." In *Religious Issues and Interreligious Dialogues*, ed. Wei-hsün Fu and Gerhard E. Spiegler. New York: Greenwood, 1989, pp. 277–302.
———. "The Religious Import of Confucian Philosophy: Its Traditional Outlook and Contemporary Significance." *Philosophy East and West*, 21(2), April 1971, pp. 157–175.
———. "A Review of Mou Tsung-san: *Hsin-t'i yü hsing-t'i*." *Philosophy East and West*, 20(4), October 1970, pp. 419–422.
———. "A Review of Mou Tsung-san: Intellectual Intuition and Chinese Philosophy." *Philosophy East and West*, 23(1–2), January and April 1973, pp. 255–256.
———. *Xianshi yu lixiang de jiujie* (On the Complexity of Interaction between Ideals and the Real World). Taipei: Xuesheng, 1993.
———. *Zhongguo zhexue yu xiandaihua* (Chinese Philosophy and China's Modernization). Taipei: China Times, 1980.
Mou, Zongsan. *Cong Lu Xiangshan dao Liu Qishan* (From Lu Xiangshan to Liu Qishan). Taipei: Xuesheng, 1979.
———. *Daode de lixiangjuyi* (Moral Idealism), rev. ed. Taipei: Xuesheng, 1982.
———. *Fuxing yu panro* (The Buddha-Nature and Prajna), 2 vols. Taipei: Xuesheng, 1977.
———. *Lishi zhexue* (Philosophy of History). Hong Kong: Young Son, 1962.
———. *Renshixin zhi pipan* (A Critique of the Cognitive Mind), 2 vols. Hong Kong: Union, 1956–1957.
———. *Shengming de xuewen* (The Learning of Life). Taipei: Sanmin, 1970.
———. *Xianxiang yu wuzesheng* (Phenomenon and the Thing-in-Itself). Taipei: Xuesheng, 1975.
———. *Xinti yu xingti* (The Substance of Mind and the Substance of Nature), 3 vols. Taipei: Zheng-zhong, 1968–1969.
———. *Yuanshanlu* (On Summum Bonum). Taipei: Xuesheng, 1985.
———. *Zaixing yu xuanli* (Physical Nature and Speculative Reason). Hong Kong: Young Son, 1963.
———. *Zhengdao yu zhidao* (The Way of Politics and the Way of Government), rev. ed. Taipei: Xuesheng, 1980.
———. *Zhi de zhijiao yu zhongguo zhexue* (Intellectual Intuition and Chinese Philosophy). Taipei: Commercial Press, 1971.
———. *Zhongguo zhexue de tezhi* (Special Characteristics of Chinese Philosophy). Hong Kong: Young Son, 1963.
———. *Zhongguo zhexue shijiujian* (Nineteen Lectures on Chinese Philosophy). Taipei: Xuesheng, 1983.
Yan, Pinggang. *Zhenghe yu chongzhu* (Integration and Reconstruction: Study of the Great Contemporary Confucian: Mou Tsung-san's Thought). Taipei: Xuesheng, 1995.
Zai, Renhou (Tsai Jen-hou), et al. *Mou Zongsan xiansheng de zhexue yu zhuzuo* (Master Mou Tsung-san's Philosophy and Writings). Taipei: Xuesheng, 1978.

Mythology and Early Chinese Thought

Whalen Lai

Before there is philosophy, says Comte, there was religion. To the extent that myth was once the collective representation of how the world appeared to early men, early Chinese myth could well contain the seeds of later philosophical reflection. Without going into a long justification for choosing them, I offer here a few examples of how myths might have anticipated philosophy.

Rulership

In an early myth involving the seventh ruler of the Xia dynasty, King Kongjia brought home a child newly born to a peasant family. Some prophesied that the child was destined for greatness while others foresaw only harm, but in any case the king gave the child the security of the palace. Several years later, when the child had become a young man, a storm toppled a tent and an ax flew up and crippled him. Kongjia regretted that this crippled man could rise no higher in rank than a palace guard.

When we look more closely, we see that this is a reverse of the myth of Oedipus. Kongjia did the opposite of what Laius did. By being willing to bring up someone who could become great—that is, could challenge his claim to the throne—he defused a potential threat. The Chinese myth is, however, not about a father-son conflict. It is about whether the royal succession should remain within a bloodline or not. Since Kongjia adopted someone who was not his kin, the implication is that he allowed the possibility of a nondynastic succession. If so, perhaps the moral imagination that created this myth postulated what is usually considered the Zhou ideology: that the mandate of heaven may change, and rule can be given to a man of proven virtue. This myth may be an early example of what Sarah Allan (1981) sees as tension between the sage and the heir.

However, Kongjia is remembered as the ruler whose reign marked the beginning of the decline of the Xia. And whatever wisdom he demonstrated by adopting the child—a story that registers not so much virtue as fate—the death of Kongjia has all the markings of royal folly. Heaven supposedly sent this king a pair of dragons when he ascended the throne. Not knowing how to feed or rear them, he had to rely on a dragon trainer. According to one story, when one dragon died, it was made into a meal for the king. Later, when Kongjia inquired about the pair, the trainer either fled or was exiled. Soon afterward, the king died, in his carriage as he was returning from an autumnal sacrifice and witnessing a heavenly fire. What could this myth be saying when it is properly demythologized? Probably this.

The Xia dynasty was descended from the sage king Yu, who could well have been a dragon, and so it was not unnatural for heaven to bless the new reign of Kongjia with a gift of two dragons; the problem is with the king's inability to rear and feed them. The Chinese verb for "to feed" is the same as the word for "to eat." So it appears that not only was Kongjia unable to nurture the dragons; he also violated them by eating one. The fault could be the dragon trainer's. In one story, though, the king did not heed the trainer's advice. The story that the trainer "fled" or was "exiled" is ambiguous, since the verb here is the same word used to describe the "dance" or "flight" of a shaman. It could simply mean that the trainer deserted the king and flew away, as an immortal could, leaving the king to an early death.

In myths, kings often represented the noblest of men; therefore, this story can be translated into a universal Mencian parable about human nature. All men are given at birth the seed of goodness, the "dragon essence," which must be nurtured. He who nurtures it to fruition can become a sage—or an immortal. He who violates it, like Kongjia, will court his own downfall. This myth probably predates Mencius; thus what it sees as heaven's gift to a king, dragons, may be what Mencius would see later as the goodness of human nature mandated by heaven.

Myths Reinscribed as Philosophy

Of all the classical thinkers, Zhuangzi is thought to have made the most of ancient myths, retelling them as his own philosophical parables. From the story of two friends who in gratitude drilled seven openings into their host, the shapeless *Hundun* (Chaos), Zhuangzi would derive his philosophy of nature. Likewise, Chapter 5 of the *Zhuangzi* gives a litany of sage cripples and monstrous savants, the point being that those who are physically handicapped (or "incomplete") are precisely the "tallies of virtue (*de*) replete."

This litany of cripples can be traced back to a basic motif of lunar myths. As the sun is known for being constant, the moon is known for being ever-changing, or fickle. The moon is, however, more potent (*de*) because it is seldom full. This is the point behind the lines in "Questions to Heaven" in *Songs of the South* that ask: "What virtue the moon/the bright of night/that lives as it dies?" (that is, waxes and wanes). Zhuangzi turned this lunar mystique into his parade of sage cripples who could accept all the changes in life by somehow abiding with a changeless core. Zhuangzi called such roving with the universe "free and easy wandering." His Chapter 1 is itself built on the myth of a seasonal metamorphosis: the giant *kun* fish hibernates through the winter in the depths of the northern sea (later known as the "dark warrior of the north"), awakes in spring, and changes into a giant *peng* bird that flies south to the Lake of Heaven (now known to us as the "vermilion bird of the south"). These are but two of the seasonal forms of the dragon, which, as the *Shouwen* dictionary, says "rises skyward during the spring equinox" (as the phoenix) only to "dive into the deep during the fall" (as the giant fish or turtle). Here too is a philosophy of the great, endless changes (*dahua*) of nature.

Cosmological Theories

We can find in the early myths of China what seems to be knowledge of the movements of the sun, moon, and stars. The *yin-yang* and "five processes" (*wuxing*) philosophy was systematized as a school, rather late, by Zou Yan. But its rudiments were used very early on by people involved in medicine and in making calendars.

The layout of the royal Shang tombs at Anyang from the time of King Wuding, in which every one is about 11 degrees off due north, shows the depth of cosmographical and astrological knowledge of the Shang. Porter's analysis (1996) of the myth of a flood involving the sage king Yu and his father Gun (isomorphic with *kun*, above) suggests that it could well be based on a very exact knowledge of the displacement of the Corona Australis in the night sky—i.e., its sinking beneath the horizon as a result of the precession of the equinoxes. The precession is a combined effect of lunar, solar, and planetary movements: the rotation of these spinning bodies causes a slightly earlier occurrence of the equinoxes each year; the complete to-and-fro movement would take 25,800 terrestrial years.

That knowledge, kept alive by the myths, may offer clues to one of the lingering mysteries in Chinese metaphysics: the rationale behind the "mutual conquest" of the five elements, phases, or processes. The rationale for the "mutual birth" series is fairly straightforward; it follows the succession of the seasons or the daily path of the sun (east, south, west, north, with an interruption in the southwest). The "conquest series" is more puzzling; it zigzags through the four seasons or directions (with the interruption in the northeast).

Birth series
Wood Spring
Fire Summer
[Earth Center]
Metal Fall
Water Winter

Conquest series
Spring Wood
Fall Metal
Summer Fire
Winter Water
[Earth Center]

The Chinese traditionally memorize the "conquest series" in reverse—i.e., as "water, fire, metal, wood, earth"—because as water follows fire, it conquers or overtakes fire. The rationale for those conquests, however, cannot be accounted for by a liberal use of analogies, i.e., by noting how water can put out fire or metal (an ax) can cut up wood. That is an ex post facto justification, and you can always find an analogy for any sequence. There has to be, besides the numerological explanation involving the "river diagram" and "river writing," a geological-astrological reason behind it. And all that could well be tied to the tilt of the earth's axis and its effect on the perceived movement of the sun and the moon.

In myths, the tilt of heaven above and the incline of earth below have been attributed to the rage of the giant Gonggong. During a battle with the god of fire, Gonggong toppled the mountain, Mount Buzhou, holding up heaven in the northwestern corner. This caused heaven to fall down in that direction. As a result, the heavenly bodies all slid down. And as earth was also jacked up in that corner, the rivers of China all pour downward from it. (Basically, the subterranean water is seen as surging up and washing the submerged southeastern shore.) Over that backdrop of a tilt of the earth's axis, the movements of the sun and the moon were mapped and their different paths and rotations were described in myths.

For example, a myth about the sun's daily journey appears in a legend of the sage king Shun involving two attempts on his life. In the first attempt, Shun's father, the Blind Man, sent Shun up into a barn and then set the barn on fire; but Shun escaped by flying down to safety, using his bamboo hat as wings. In the second attempt, his evil stepbrother Xiang ("Elephant") tricked Shun into going down a well and then rolled stones over the opening to block his exit; but Shun escaped by finding a secret passageway out. When all this is deciphered, it is about the daily (or yearly) circuit of the sun. The Blind Man stands for the dark of night; the "bright and beautiful" Shun, whose eyes have "double pupils," stands for the brilliance of day. Night chasing day is the Blind Man (north) compelling Shun, the morning sun (east), to climb up the "world tree" (the barn). Reaching, by noon, the zenith (south), Shun—the midday sun—incinerates the sky. After that, the afternoon sun, or Shun, is a winged sunbird alighting among the hills (west). Sinking below the horizon (i.e., going underground) at night, Shun reaches (via the well) the subterranean ocean (north) and swims back (east) to appear aboveground the next day.

This myth tells of the triumph of Shun (*yang*, day) over his evil father (*yin*, night). Its clockwise movement—east, south, west, north; spring, summer, fall, winter—informs the "birth series" of the five processes. Earth interrupts the series at midyear or in the southeast. The "mutual conquest" series should be a reversal of this but actually zigzags through the four directions, going north, south, west, east and allowing earth to interrupt the series in the northwest. (In early China, the southwest was regarded as the most vital and auspicious corner; northwest was the gate of death and most inauspicious.) The zigzag is ultimately due to the northwest-southeast tilt supposedly caused by Gonggong; it is due to the precession of earth, moon, and sun.

For a simple lunar myth, in which the moon simply follows the path of the sun—east, south, west, north—we have the story of Guafu. From the *Shanhaijing*:

> Guafu was chasing after the sun when he came too close to it. He became very thirsty. Thereupon he drank from the Yellow River and the Wei River, but there was not enough water in them (to quench his thirst). So he turned north, intending to drink from the Daizhe (Great Pool), but he died of thirst before reaching there.

Gua can mean "to cut," "to diminish" as well as to "to expand," "to boast"; *fu* means "man," "adult." The name Guafu then designates a lunar titan, a moon that waxes (expands) and wanes (diminishes). In chasing the sun, Guafu followed the path of the sun: starting at the delta of the Yellow River (east) and going upstream (south) until he reached the river bend (west), at which point he turned toward the Great Pool (north). He died before reaching this large body of subterranean water, and that would place his death ideally in the northwest, i.e., at Mount Buzhou, which Gunn supposedly butted against and toppled. Buzhou, which can denote the "immovable" point under the North Star, can also be read as the "incomplete round"; that would describe the moon's inability to complete the full round by remaining intact. Waning fast, it died or disappeared from the night sky in the north.

The story does not end there. Another record tells us that before his death, Guafu threw away his walking stick, which, fed by his decomposing body, later turned into a peach orchard. Since a walking stick is basically a dead branch and an orchard consists of live trees, this story notes how even as the old sliver of a moon dies in the northwest, three (moonless) nights later a new crescent rises in the northeast. Indeed, in the northeast is another mountain, a tiny hillock called the Inauspicious Ox—inauspicious because the new moon is small and bovine (a cow). This myth tells of the failure of the moon (*yin*) to conquer or overcome the sun (*yang*) because, foolishly, it travels on the clockwise path of the sun instead of devising a different lunar path of its own.

For a myth involving a lunar or counterclockwise circuit and also having very complicated *yin-yang* elements, we turn to the story of Jingwei. She was the third (*yang*) daughter (*yin*) of the Fiery Emperor (*yang*), was drowned at sea (*yin*), and came back to life (*yang*) as a black (*yin*) sunbird (*yang*) vowing to battle the waves (*yin*) forever. From the *Shanhaijing*:

> Two hundred leagues north [of central China] was a mountain [in a secondary range] called the Fajiu Hill. On its summit grew many *zhe*-thorn trees [a kind of mulberry]. Among them lived a bird that looked like a crow. It had a colorful head, a white bill, and red claws. Its call sounded just like its name: Jingwei. The bird was once Nuwa, the youngest [third] daughter of Yandi [the Fire or Fiery Emperor]. She drowned [or sank] while frolicking on the Eastern Sea and never returned [or resurfaced]. She had turned into this bird Jingwei that would forever carry these bits of twigs and pebbles in her beak all the way from the Western Hill to the Eastern Sea—in the hope of filling it up.

To understand this myth, the following scheme—standardized since the Han era—is helpful:

vermilion
bird
summer
south
green   white
dragon   tiger
spring   fall
east   west
north
winter
turtle
black

In light of this scheme, the myth of Jingwei can be broken down into several phases of a phoenixlike metamorphosis. This daughter of the Fiery Emperor is identified as Nuwa. The script for *wa* is easily changed into the *wa* script for "frog." Hence we are dealing with a frog princess. Since the frog is amphibious, Nuwa could not have literally drowned at sea. This frog princess only changed her habitat. She "sank" (died) only to "return" (be reborn) as a bird.

Implied (though not told) in this account are other changes in the interim. She waded into the sea (east) as a frog but sank deep into the Great Pool (north) as the turtle. From there she swam further (west) and reappeared on land as the tiger on the hill, which would provide her with rocks and twigs for damming the sea. This is a variant of the flood myth. Leaping from the hills (land) into the sky (air), she changed finally into the bird Jingwei, which, as a "sun crow," would fly overhead (south) back to the sea (as a sea swallow) to do battle with the sea. In her role as the "earth diver," Jingwei travels defiantly, going counterclockwise—east, north, west, south—refusing to be conquered or defeated. But her circuit is still not yet the zigzag path that makes up the "conquest series."

The resolution of the tension beteen *yin* and *yang* is, I believe, buried in the Qian hexagram in the *Book of Changes* (*Yijing*). In the explanation appended to those six *yang* lines (six dragons), we read:

1. Hidden dragon [in the deep].
Do not use.
2. Dragon appearing in the field.
It furthers one to see the great man.
3. All day long the superior man is creatively active.
At night his mind is beset by worries.
Danger. No blame.
4. Wavering flight over the abyss [separating earth and sky].
No blame.
5. Flying dragon in the sky.
It furthers one to see the gentleman.
6. Arrogant dragon [overshoots].
Will have cause to regret. (Wilhelm 1950)

Overall, the six lines read: "A band of (six) dragons with no head or leader—auspicious." The reference to there being no leader is about the six mutations completing a loop, a cycle: a perfect circle has neither beginning nor end. It has no head (and no tail).

Behind these cryptic lines lies a forgotten mythic narrative. It concerns a seasonal transformation of the dragon in six steps making up a perfect loop:

1. The dragon in the deep is the turtle (north).
2. The dragon coming onto the rice fields or marshes is the frog (east).
3. The dragon toils hard all day making a trip (east to west).
4. The dragon in hesitant flight is the tiger (west) leaping into the air.
5. The dragon in confident flight is the bird high above (south).
6. The dragon that overshoots its target falls straight down (south to north: top to bottom), reverting into the dragon in the deep.

Without going into all the reasons why, we can simply note that this path of the six Qian dragons runs (in terms of directions) north, east, west, south, north. Translated into the elements, it is water, wood, metal, fire. This is the core of the "mutual conquest of the five phases"; the fifth element, earth, can be inserted later (in the northeast).

The "conquest series" is based primarily on reversing the values on the east-west and north-south axis. Normally, *yang* should lead and *yin* should follow. But in the conquest series, the *yin* elements that follow (metal and water) overtake the *yang* elements that lead (wood and fire). The axial "conquests" are the key; the rest is there to complete the loop. That is because the combined vector of the two axial conquests (imagine them as two arrows, one pointing south and the other pointing east) would yield one force, an arrow pointing southeast, the reverse of the northwestern collapse of the heavens. Mathematically, the heavenly bodies pouring down the northwest translate into the "birth series" (a simple adjustment of sunrise and sunset into an east-south-west-north circuit). The inverse, the flow of water from the hills down toward the South China Sea, is equal to the "conquest series": a somewhat complicated loop that translates back into the two axes of north overtaking south and west overtaking east. To see that, perhaps readers can try tracing the journey of the Qian dragons through the four directions on a piece of paper. They would come up with a helix like an angular figure eight. That figure eight combines in one continuous loop both the clockwise (*yang*) and the counterclockwise (*yin*) movement. It is the inspiration hidden behind what is now the well-known *yin-yang* circle. (The two-dimensional S figure is a truncated fully looping figure eight.)

See also Zhuangzi.

Bibliography

Allen, Sarah. *The Heir and the Sage: Dynastic Legend in Early China.* San Francisco: Chinese Material Center, 1981

———. *The Shape of the Turtle: Myth, Art and Cosmos in Early China.* Albany: State University of New York Press, 1991.

Girardot, Norman. *Myth and Meaning in Early Taoism.* Berkeley: University of California Press, 1983.

Lai, Whalen. "Oedipus at Anyang: Unmasking the Filial Sage-King Shun." *History of Religions*, 34, 1995.

———. "Symbolism of Evil in China: The K'ung-chia Myth Analyzed." *History of Religions*, 23, 1984, pp. 316–343.

Porter, Deborah Lynn. *From Deluge to Discourse: Myth, History, and the Generation of Chinese Fiction.* Albany: State University of New York Press, 1996.

N 中國哲學

Names, School of (*Ming Jia, Ming Chia*)

John MAKEHAM

The members of the *ming jia* (*mingjia*), or "school of names"—like the ancient Greek sophists after whom they are sometimes called (they are also, variously, called dialecticians, nominalists, and logicians)—were not an actual school of thinkers bound by a common philosophy or having a common founder. Rather, they were individual thinkers who have been retrospectively identified as a school by virtue of a perceived common eristic approach to disputation or discrimination (*bian*).

It was for their skills in disputation that in pre-Qin times they were sometimes known as *bian zhe*, "those who argue out alternatives." The Mohist *Summa* explains proper disputation in the following terms:

> One calling it "ox" and one calling it "not ox"; this is to contend over "that." This being the case, they are not both appropriate. Since they are not both appropriate, one is necessarily appropriate. (Explanation A.74)

Unlike Greek dialectics, in which further development remains an open possibility, in disputation there must be a winner. In stipulating that something must be either *X* nor not-*X*, there is no room for shades of gray because once a standard has been established, an object either does or does not conform to it. Like the Mohists, the thinkers of the school of names excelled in the art of disputation; but for the school of names, unlike the Mohists, disputation was an opportunity to shock and disconcert by arguing for propositions that defied common sense. It was their perceived frivolous attitude to disputation—in which victory was valued above real understanding—rather than any lack of argumentative skill, that led many contemporary and later critics to hold them in disdain.

The intellectual creativity of the school of names flourished in the late fourth and third centuries B.C.E., a period of diverse and rapidly changing social, political, and intellectual values that challenged thinkers to question the assumptions behind traditional and commonsense beliefs about their perception of the world and their ability to articulate that perception. The question of the relationship between names or words (*ming*) and the actuality (*shi*) they denoted became an important topic of philosophical interpretation. Daoist thinkers, such as Zhuangzi (fourth century B.C.E., criticized words as limited and limiting, arbitrary and conventional, for in imposing artificial boundaries they were seen as distorting, as imposing a straitjacket, and in the process creating pseudo actualities. The later Mohists, by contrast, saw names as of primary importance because names represented distinctions that were then embodied in definitions, which in turn functioned as standards. To this end they developed rigorous and logically consistent sets of arguments. The thinkers of the school of names, stimulated by both attitudes, delighted in the newfound power of manipulating language, by using ad hoc and circumscribed senses of words, paradoxes, and specious logic to make distinctions and thereby prescribe actualities. As opponents in disputation, the school of names not only benefited from the Mohists' rigor and conciseness but, in turn, also sharpened the focus of debate and set new challenges for the Mohists. One striking example of this is the "white horse" argument, which will be discussed below. Like the Mohists, the school of names had little influence on subsequent Chinese thought, although the forged parts of *Gongsun Long, Yin Wenzi*, and possibly also *Deng Xi* do provide evidence that from the third to the seventh centuries C.E. there was intermittent interest in their ideas.

Discussion of the Essentials of the Six Schools (*Shiji, juan* 130) by Sima Tan (d. c. 110 B.C.E.) is the earliest extant writing to use the term *ming jia*, "school of names"; as noted above, this was a retrospective classification. Sima's accounts of the six schools, to varying degrees, reflect the syncretism that prevailed in early Han thought, and this may explain why he uses such legalist formulas as "bringing in names to check actualities" and "checks and matches" (*can wu*) to characterize the thought of this school. Nevertheless, before this, *ming jia* thinkers who applied concepts that also featured prominently in legalist writings had been associated with *ming jia* thinkers for whom this was not the case. Xunzi, for example, associates Hui Shi (fourth century B.C.E.) and Deng Xi (late sixth century to early fifth century B.C.E) on several occasions (*Xunzi, Bugou*; *Fei shi'erzi*; *Ruxiao*). Deng Xi, who had served as a senior official in the state of Zheng, is reputed to have drawn up a code of penal laws. As he was also associated with litigation, it is plausible that his original writings did include examples of hair-splitting debate in connection with the interpretation of laws, legal principles, and definitions (see, for example, *Lü shi chun qiu, Nanwei*). This, however, is not a feature of the book which survives under his name but which dates from a much later period. This book may also be distinguished in part, at least, from a book of the same name cited by Liu Xiang (79–8 B.C.E.) in which Deng is said to have argued for the admissibility of contradictory propositions (Yang Liang's ninth-century commentary on *Xunzi, Buguo*, 2.1B).

Nevertheless, one concept that is a feature both in this book and in the one cited by Liu Xiang (although how it was used in the latter cannot now be known) is *xingming*, which in the former book is to be understood as a method of administrative accountability designed to ensure that the "shape" or outcome of a functionary's words matches the evidence of his deeds. *Xingming* was introduced by Shen Buhai (d. c. 400 B.C.E.) into the corpus of writings that from Han times on was known as *fa jia* (*fajia*), or "school of law," "models," "legalists." Curiously, *xingming* was also a term used to refer to thinkers who were later associated with the school of names. The earliest extant example of this application of *xingming* is recorded in *Zhanguo ce*:

> Su Qin said to the King of Qin, "Exponents of *xingming* all say that a white horse is not a horse." (3.63A)

As will be discussed later, in his "white horse" sophism, Gongsun Long argued that the name "white" refers to color and the name "horse" to shape. Thus if there is any connection with the legalist concept of *xingming* it would surely be only at the most general level: just as the legalists were concerned with the relationship between word and the "shape" or outcome of a functionary's deed—which, as Han Fei (c. 280–233 B.C.E.) confirms, is a specific expression of the more general concept of *ming shi*, "names and actualities"—so too was the school of names concerned with the relationship between names and the actualities they denoted. Thus *xingming*, as used by the school of names and the pre-Qin writers who used it to refer to *ming jia* thinking, should be distinguished from its use by thinkers such as Shen Buhai or Han Fei.

Ban Gu (32–92 C.E.) wrote a "Treatise on Bibliography" in *Han shu*, which is based on the earlier bibliographies of Liu Xiang and Liu Xin (46 B.C.E.–23 C.E.); this puts us on a firmer footing in being able to identify which pre-Qin writings (some) Han scholars classified as representative of the school of names. Seven books are listed:

1. *Deng Xi*, of which it is suspected that only Liu Xiang's preface to the original *Deng Xi* survives in the extant *Deng Xizi*.
2. *Yin Wen*, attributed to Gongsun Long's teacher, Yin Wen (fourth and third centuries B.C.E.). The received text is considered a forgery of c. 200 C.E. (Daor 1974, 1–39).
3. *Gongsun Longzi*, attributed to Gongsun Long, a client of the lord of Pingyuan in Zhao (d. 251 B.C.E.), of which the received text preserves at least two genuine essays from the school of names—*Bai ma* and *Zhi wu*—and possibly also the dialogue "Left and Right" at the beginning of *pian* 4. The material contained in *pian* 1 may also be drawn from pre-Qin sources (Graham 1957).
4. *Cheng Gongsheng*, attributed to Cheng Gong sheng (fl. late third century B.C.E.), is no longer extant.
5. *Huang Gong*, attributed to Huang Gong (fl. late third century B.C.E.), is no longer extant.
6. *Mao Gong*, attributed to Mao Kung, a contemporary of Gongsun Long and fellow client at the court of the lord of Pingyuan, is no longer extant.

7. *Hui Zi*, attributed to Hui Shi, who served as chief minister of King Hui of Wei c. 340–320 C.E., is no longer extant. A number of sophisms associated with his name are preserved in extant sources, and he is also featured commonly in dialogues with his friend Zhuangzi in *Zhuangzi*.

In addition to the individuals associated with these writings, the names of a few other thinkers who also engaged in sophistic disputation may be gleaned from pre-Qin and early Han sources.

Because almost half the books known by these titles were not transmitted after the Han dynasty, the ideas of this school came to be represented principally by the books and fragments attributed to Deng Xi, Hui Shi, Gongsun Long, and Yin Wen. On textual grounds, modern scholarship has focused principally on the writings and fragments attributed to Hui Shi and Gongsun Long. While there is little controversy that the propositions attributed to Hui Shi in extant writings such as *Zhuangzi* and *Xunzi* were, in some form or other, expounded by him, A. C. Graham's cogent thesis (1957) that a substantial portion of *Gongsun Longzi* dates from 300 to 600 C.E. has been influential only among western scholars—a fact which underscores both a generally poor acquaintance with (and possibly a low regard for) western sinology among scholars in China and Japan, and the even poorer efforts made by western sinologists to present their work in Chinese and Japanese.

What we do know about Hui Shi as a thinker of the school of names is largely limited to the ten propositions listed in the *pian Tianxia* of *Zhuangzi* and the six listed in the *pian Bugou* of *Xunzi*. Another twenty-one propositions listed in *Tianxia* are said to have been used by "disputers" (*bian zhe*) in debate with Hui Shi. As some of those in *Bugou* are also included either in the list of ten or the list of twenty-one in *Tianxia*, and as the six in *Bugou* are attributed both to Hui Shi and to Deng Xi, it would seem reasonable to infer that any given proposition may have had several exponents who may or may not have given it the same interpretation. A further complication in identifying Hui's thought is that all the propositions are presented without proofs or explanations. Later commentators have generally understood the list of ten propositions to trade on the variable perspectives of place, size, and time, although some commentators have tried to show how they related to political issues of Hui Shi's day (Asano 1976, 16–30; Reding 1985, 350–377). Given Gongsun Long's close acquaintance with Zhuangzi, the "perspectivist" approach seems more fruitful.

A tentative interpretation of the ten propositions listed in *Tianxia* is as follows:

1. "So great that it has nothing outside it; call this 'making the one great.' So small that it has nothing inside; call this 'making the one small.' " A unity can be viewed both as encompassing all and as encompassing nothing but itself and still be a unity.
2. "That which is without thickness cannot be piled up, yet it can be as large as 1,000 *li*." A geometric plane has no thickness, yet can extend in two dimensions to any length whatever. (Compare this with Cook Ding's point about the edge of his cleaver being dimensionless in *Zhuangzi, Yangsheng zhu*.)
3. "Heaven is as low as earth, and mountains and marshes are level." When viewed on the horizon heaven and earth "meet"; hence, heaven may be said to be as low as earth. When mountains and marshes are viewed from the perspective of heaven, then they will be equally level.
4. "At the same time as the sun is in the middle of the sky it is declining; at the same time as something is living it is dying." Like the glass of water that is both half full and half empty, depending on one's perspective, so, too, may the midday sun be said to be both at the end of its ascent and at the beginning of its decline, or a creature be said to be both living and dying.
5. "While, on the one hand, there is similarity on a large scale, yet, on the other hand, it is different from similarity on a minor scale—this is called similarity and difference on a minor scale. The 'myriad things' are completely similar and completely different—this is called similarity and difference on a large scale." Oxen and horses, understood collectively as livestock, or as things, are similar; yet when oxen and horses are understood as separate categories, the oxen will be similar to other oxen, but not to horses. In respect of their similarities (that is, their being *wu*, "things," which the Mohists call an "unrestricted name" and Xunzi calls "the most general name"), all things are similar; and in respect of their differences, all things are different.
6. "The south has no limit yet has a limit." Given that the south is defined relative to the other cardinal directions, it does have a limit; but having no beginning or end, it has no limit.
7. "To go to Yue today yet to arrive yesterday." Tomorrow, today will be yesterday, just as yesterday was then today.
8. "Interlinked rings can be disconnected." If either one of the rings is positioned so as not to touch any part of the other ring, it can be rotated endlessly and hence said to be disconnected.

9. "I know where the center of the world is: it is north of Yan and south of Yue." (Yan and Yue lay in the northern and southern parts of China, respectively.) Just as the south is without limit, so are the other three cardinal directions; thus the world must be infinite, and so its center is everywhere.
10. "Spread a loving concern to the myriad things; heaven and earth are one body." This has more the sense of a conclusion than a proposition. If the preceding nine propositions do have a general sense, it is that different perspectives generate different but equally assertible propositions. Hence, instead of rejecting those who hold a perspective that differs from one's own, one should extend a loving concern to all people and in doing so share in their perspectives.

Only Gongsun Long's extant writings provide us with an account of how the thinkers of the school of names argued their propositions. Central to his arguments is the ambiguous notion of "compounding." The ambiguity of compounding arises from whether a particular combination of two parts results in an aggregation in which each component part retains its individuation or whether the two parts combine to form an interpenetrating whole. Chad Hansen, who calls these two antithetical conceptions "union compounding" and "intersection compounding," respectively, describes the different effects that each type of compounding has on the range of objects the compound picks out. The former "sums across the two ranges. It picks out the union of the stuff picked out by the compound terms. The other compound intersects the two ranges. It refers to the interpenetration of the component terms" (Hansen 1992, 258).

Gongsun Long's dialogue "Left and Right" neatly illustrates the difference between these two notions of compounding. The counting sticks that Gongsun used to demonstrate his argument may be represented diagrammatically with Roman numerals:

I + I (union compound)
II (intersection compound)

The gist of his argument is that when the two units of I combine as II, their individuality gives way to interpenetration; hence, "there is no I in II." The assumption behind the argument is that I + I is different from II because I + I (1 + 1) is a whole in which its two parts remain distinct (a union compound), while II (2) is a whole in which its two parts have become as one (intersection compound).

Gongsun Long's reputation as a disputer lay in being able to argue successfully for propositions that flew in the face of common sense. His skill lay in relentlessly arguing his case from premises that implicitly assumed either a "union" or an "intersection" understanding of compounding. An example of each will be selected for analysis, beginning with the *jian bai* sophism as an example of the former.

References in the early literature frequently describe Gongsun Long as an exponent of *jian bai*, "the separation of hard and white." Some modern commentators, such as Graham, maintain that *jian bai* referred only to a theme in disputation, not a sophism, but there is good circumstantial evidence that the *pian Bei li* of *Lü shi chun qiu* (c. 239 B.C.E.) does, in fact, preserve an account of *jian bai* being used as a sophism. (It is also plausible that *jian bai* was perhaps used in more than one sense in a number of sophisms.) The relevant passage records a dispute between a sword expert and a nameless opponent about the tempering of swords. Although Gongsun Long is not specifically identified as the opponent, there was an early tradition linking the term *jian bai* and Gongsun Long with the tempering of swords: *Jingdian shiwen* (26.8B) quotes Sima Biao (d. c. 306 C.E.) and Cui Jian (d. 290 C.E.). Furthermore, in his commentary to *Shiji* (74.2349), Sima Zhen (eighth century C.E.) cites a passage from *Jin taikang diji* (*Record of the Topography of the Jin Dynasty Tai Kang Period*)—i.e., 280–289—that records a corrupt version of the sophism in which a specific association is made between the story about sword tempering and *jian bai* being used as a sophism.

The passage in *Lü shi chun qiu* (25.4A–B) is as follows:

> A sword expert said, "White is that which is used to make the blade hard (*jian*); yellow is that which is used to make it flexible. If yellow and white (*bai*) are fused, then the result will be both hard and flexible—a good sword!"
>
> The objector said, "White is that which is used to make the blade not flexible; yellow is that which is used to make it not hard. If yellow and white are mixed, then the result will be neither hard nor flexible. Further, if too soft, it will bend and break. If a sword breaks and bends, how can it be considered a fine sword?"

"Yellow" and "white" are references to copper and tin, respectively. When the two metals are fused, a higher proportion of copper or tin results in a higher degree of flexibility or hardness, respectively. The sophism involves a debate between the sword expert, who advances the commonsense proposition that hardness and flexibility can be maintained as distinct properties in a state of interpenetration (that is, when copper and tin are fused as an alloy), and the objector, who, by refusing to acknowledge the existence of a metallic compound (bronze), argues that the properties of flexibility and hardness are not interpenetrable. Thus while the sword expert (correctly) regards the alloy as being an intersection compound, the objector is able to advance his argument by assuming that tin and copper combine as a union compound. And as long as his premise remains unchallenged, his argument can be established.

In this example, (presumably) Gongsun Long assumes that $X + Y$ is a union compound to argue that "$X + Y$ are neither X nor Y." By contrast, in the white horse sophism he assumes that $X + Y$ is a intersection compound to argue that "$X + Y$ is not Y." The proposition "a white horse is not a horse" is Gongsun's most celebrated sophism; he himself was even being quoted as saying that this particular discourse had made him famous (*Gongsun Longzi*, 1.1A). Graham (1986, 94) argues that its close parallel with the "oxen-horses" sophism, which the later Mohists took particular trouble to deconstruct in *Canon* B.67, "strongly suggests that it was in current use in arguments unacceptable to the Mohists." It would seem, however, that insofar as Gongsun successfully defends the proposition that the whole is not one of its parts by treating white horse as an intersection compound rather than as a union compound, it is more appropriate to see this as a dialectical response to the later Mohists' arguments. An analysis of both sets of arguments shows this to be the case. The Mohists' argument is as follows:

> *Canon*: There are the same grounds for regarding the proposition "oxen and horses are not oxen" as inadmissible as there are for regarding it as admissible. The explanation is compounding (*jian*).
>
> *Explanation*: If, since part is non-oxen, it is admissible [that "oxen and horses] are not oxen," then—since part is non-oxen and part is oxen—it is admissible that ["oxen and horses] are oxen." Thus, if it is inadmissible to say either that "oxen and horses are not oxen" or that "oxen and horse are oxen," then—since a proposition is either admissible or inadmissible—it would also be inadmissible to say that " 'oxen and horses are horses' is inadmissible."
>
> If, however, oxen are not regarded in two ways and horses are not regarded in two ways, but oxen and horses are regarded in two ways, then while oxen will not be the coordinate of non-oxen, nor horses be the coordinate of non-horses, yet there will be no difficulty in accepting that "oxen-and-horses is neither horses nor oxen."

Already in the opening sentence of the explanation the Mohist succeeds in demonstrating the thesis he states in the canon: given that the admissibility of the proposition, "Oxen and horses are not oxen," is premised on part of the whole that is oxen and horses being non-oxen, then given also the entailment that the other part must be oxen, the converse proposition, "Oxen and horses are oxen," would, on the same line of reasoning, be equally assertible. (Given Liu Xin's statement that Deng Xi argued for the admissibility of contradictory propositions, it is possible that he also developed arguments along these lines.) It is, of course, self-evident that the whole is not one of its parts. As long as oxen and horses are understood as a union compound, then part of the whole being non-oxen does not prove that oxen and horses are both not oxen; it proves only that part of oxen and horses is not oxen. It is not, however, the Mohist's immediate concern to criticize the non sequitur; rather, he wants to show how its assumption results in a contradiction.

The Mohist next proceeds to apply the principle of contradiction to show that the proposition "Oxen and horses are not oxen," being both admissible and inadmissible, is illicit because it fails to satisfy the criterion of being either admissible or inadmissible. He then concludes the first paragraph of the explanation with the further observation that it would be just as illicit to assert only that " 'oxen and horses are horses' is inadmissible" because the grounds for its validity are the same for its converse, " 'oxen and horses are horses' is admissible." Proper disputation obliges one to choose between two alternatives: "Someone says it is this and someone says it is not and the one whose claim is appropriate wins" (*Mohist Summa*, Explanation B.35). Because arguments that take the form of either "$X + Y$ are not X" or "$X + Y$ are X" cannot produce a conclusive winner, they are not examples of genuine disputation.

In the second paragraph of the explanation, the Mohist sets out his own position, arguing that if we stop treating "oxen" and "non-horses" as interchangeable equivalents (and the same with "horses" and "non-oxen"), this would disallow the whole, "oxen and horses," to be treated as a combination of a non-oxen part and an oxen part (and hence avoid the contradiction he identifies in the first paragraph of the explanation). And unlike Gongsun Long in the "hard and white" sophism, who treats copper and tin as a union compound that is neither hard nor flexible, the Mohist instead treats oxen-and-horses as an intersection compound that is either made up of both an oxen part and a horse part or made up of both a non-oxen part and a non-horse part. He is thus able to conclude that oxen-and-horses is neither horses alone nor oxen alone. We might thus conclude that for the Mohist, "oxen-and-horses," understood as an intersection compound, means something like "livestock."

The Mohist's explanation thus comprises a deconstructive thesis and a constructive thesis. The deconstructive thesis demonstrates that so long as $X + Y$ is understood as a union compound, propositions of the type "$X + Y$ are not X" have no more claim to validity than converse propositions of the type "$X + Y$ are X."

The constructive thesis then proceeds to demonstrate that only if $X + Y$ is understood as an intersection compound can propositions of the type "$X + Y$ is not X" or "$X + Y$ is not Y" be asserted without entailing a contradiction should they be asserted simultaneously.

In modern times, the two most popular approaches to interpreting the white horse argument have been variations of either a member-class analysis or a universal-particular analysis, where "white horse" is understood to function as a particular or member of the universal or class "horse." (Of the many versions, see, for example, Ch'eng 1983; Chmielewski 1962; Fung 1952, 203–205; Kaji 1983, 170–191; Luan 1982, 13–27; Lucas 1993; Pang 1990, 7–12; Xiao 1984, 47–49; and Xu 1986, 104–111.)

An alternative approach has been to analyze the argument in terms of part or whole. The first commentator to take approach was Chad Hansen (1983), who argued that "horse" and "white" function like mass nouns rather than count nouns. According to this hypothesis, horse and white are "stuffs" or substances scattered throughout space and time, and "white horse" is a whole that combines a horse-stuff part and a white-stuff part. Christoph Harbsmeier's criticism (1991) of Hansen's hypothesis on the ground that classical Chinese nouns do not generally function as mass nouns (including "horse," which he shows can function as a count noun) removed the theoretical underpinning from Hansen's stimulating interpretation. Graham's version of the whole-part analysis, developing Hansen's insight, but making no appeal to the "mass noun" hypothesis, is, to date, the most coherent interpretation of the white horse argument.

Gongsun Long's white horse argument can be seen not only as avoiding the deconstructive part of the Mohist's argument but even as turning the constructive thesis to his own advantage. The sophism takes the form of a series of dialectical exchanges between Gongsun and a nameless objector. Gongsun treats "white horse" as a whole consisting of a white part and a horse part while the objector assumes the commonsense interpretation that "horse" is in its own right a whole, of which "white" happens to be a part. A translation and full analysis would be too long to undertake here, but the argument may be summarized as follows.

Gongsun Long's principal argument for his proposition that "A white horse is not a horse" is already made explicit in the opening exchange: "white horse" is a compound of a white part that names the color and a horse part that names the shape. What ensues is a series of criticisms and defenses of this proposition. Reconstructing part of the following exchange on the basis of an old commentary, Gongsun is seen to use the objector's point, that there are no colorless horses in the world, to his own advantage, arguing that "a white horse is horse and white combined," that is, horses always exist in combination with color; hence the whole cannot be called by one of its parts.

In the next exchange the objector protests that Gongsun is treating the combination "white + horse" (a union compound) as equivalent to "white horse" (an intersection compound). The gist of Gongsun's response is that as a union compound, the white part does not fix anything as white, nor does the horse part fix any one color to the exclusion of other colors: "one may answer it with either a yellow or a black." As an intersection compound, however, the white part fixes only horse as white and the horse part fixes only white and no other colors; therefore, "white horse" is not equivalent to the sum of "white" and "horse."

In the next exchange the different premises from which Gongsun and the objector are operating are made particularly apparent. The objector—operating from the premise that horse is a whole, not a part—argues that "having a white horse is deemed having a horse," so why is a white horse deemed not to be a horse? Gongsun—operating from the premise that both horse and white are parts—replies that this cannot be the case because to suppose that a white horse is a horse is to treat them as identical (by denying that the white adds anything to the horse), which would open the way for treating a black horse or a yellow horse as being identical to "horse." And if this were the case, then the objector would be committed to accepting the contradiction that having a white horse is having a black horse.

In the final exchange, the objector first concedes that in deeming a white horse to be a horse what he is really doing is disregarding the color white to focus on the horse component: "The reason why it is deemed having a horse is the horse alone." In then proceeding to claim that "having a white horse is having a horse" is admissible, while "having a horse is deemed having a yellow horse" is not admissible, Gongsun concludes the dialogue by rightly accusing him of inconsistency because in unwittingly accepting Gongsun's premise that "horse" refers only to shape, the objector has removed the grounds for being able to distinguish between a yellow horse and a white horse.

There are two grounds for suspecting that Gongsun formulated this argument as a response to the Mohist's "oxen-horses" argument. First, in understanding "white horse" as an intersection compound, he avoids the contradiction exposed by the Mohist, thus opening the way for his argument that precisely because part of the whole, $X + Y$, is Y, therefore the whole cannot be the part. (If "white horse" is understood as a union compound, all that can be demonstrated is that part of $X + Y$ is Y.) Second, not only does he adopt the same position as the Mohist in understanding $X + Y$ to be an intersection compound; he furthermore uses it to defend a proposition of the very type that the Mohist has criticized: "$X + Y$ is not Y." It is not difficult to imagine that few prospects would have been so enticing to a thinker of the school of names as the opportunity to use one of the Mohist's own arguments against him.

See also Confucianism: Rhetoric; Gongsun Long; Hui Shi; Mohism: The Founder, Mozi; Mohism: Later; Xunzi.

Bibliography

Asano, Yûchi. "Kei Shi zô no zaikôei-Bensha to Gi shô to no setten." *Nippon Chûoku Gakkaihô*, 28, 1976, pp. 16–30.

Chan Guo ce. Si bu bei yao Edition.

Chan, Wing-tsit. *A Sourcebook of Chinese Philosophy*. Princeton, N.J.: Princeton University Press, 1963. (For *pian* 2–6.)

Ch'eng, Chung-ying. "Kung-sun Lung: White Horse and Other Issues." *Philosophy East and West*, 33(4), 1983, pp. 341–354.

Chmielewski, Janusz. "Notes on Early Chinese Logic (Part 1)." *Rocznik Orientalistyczny*, 26(1), 1962, pp. 7–22.

Cua, A. S. *Ethical Argumentation: A Study in Hsü Tzu's Moral Epistemology*. Honolulu: University of Hawaii Press, 1985.

Daor, Dan. "The Yin Wenzi and the Renaissance of Philosophy in Wei-Jin China." Thesis, University of London, 1974.

Elvin, Mark. "The Logic of Logic." *Papers on Far Eastern History*, 42, 1990, pp. 131–134.

Fung, Yu-lan. *A History of Chinese Philosophy*, Vol. 1. Princeton, N.J.: Princeton University Press, 1952.

Gongsun Longzi. Si bu bei yao Edition. (Passages from the dialogue "Left and Right" and the sophism "white horse" are based on A. C. Graham's reconstructed Chinese texts as reproduced in his *Studies in Chinese Philosophy and Philosophical Literature*. Singapore: Institute of East Asian Philosophies, National University of Singapore, 1986, pp. 194–195; 201–206.)

Graham, A. C. "The Composition of Gongsuen Long Tzyy." *Asia Major*, New Series, 5(2), 1957, pp. 147–183.

———. *Disputers of the Tao: Philosophical Argument in Ancient China*. La Salle, Ill.: Open Court, 1989.

———. "Gongsun Long's Discourse Reread as Argument about Whole and Part." *Philosophy East and West*, 36(2), 1986, pp. 89–106.

———. *Mohist Logic, Ethics, and Science*. Hong Kong: Chinese University Press, 1978.

Hansen, Chad. *A Daoist Theory of Chinese Thought: A Philosophical Interpretation*. New York: Oxford University Press, 1992.

———. *Language and Logic in Ancient China*. Ann Arbor: University of Michigan Press, 1983.

Harbsmeier, Christoph. "The Mass Noun Hypothesis and the Part-Whole Analysis of the White Horse Dialogue." In *Chinese Texts and Philosophical Contexts: Essays Dedicated to Angus C. Graham*, ed. Henry Rosemont, Jr. La Salle, Ill.: Open Court, 1991.

Jing dian shi wen. Shanghai: Shanghai guji chubanshe, 1985.

Kaji, Nobuyuki. *Chûoku ronrigaku shi kenkyû*. Tokyo: Kembun shuppan, 1983.

Lü shi chun qiu, Lü shi chun qiu jishi, comp. Xu Weiyu. Beijing: Wenxue guji kanxingshe, 1955.

Luan, Xing. *Gongsun Long Zi chanjian*. Henan: Zhungchou shuhuashe, 1982.

Lucas, Thierry. "Hui Shih and Kung Sun Lung: An Approach from Contemporary Logic." *Journal of Chinese Philosophy*, 20, 1993, pp. 211–255.

Makeham, John. "The *Chien-pai* Sophism—Alive and Well." *Philosophy East and West*, 39(1), 1989, pp. 75–81.

Mei, Y. P. "The Kung-sun Lung-tzu." *Harvard Journal of Asiatic Studies*, 16, 1953, pp. 404–437.

Pang, Pu. *Gongsun Long Zi jinyi*. Chengdu: Ba-Shu shushe, 1990.

Perleberg, Max, trans. *The Works of Kung-sun Lung tzu*. Hong Kong: n.p., 1952.

Reding, Jean-Paul. *Les fondements philosophiques de la rhétorique chez les sophistes grecs et chez les sophistes chinois*. Bern: Peter Lang, 1985.

Shi ji. Beijing: Zhonghua shuju, 1983.

Tan, Jiefu. *Gongsun Long Zi xing ming fawei*. Beijing: Zhonghua shuju, 1987.

Xiao, Dengfu. *Gongsun Long Zi yü Ming jia*. Taipei: Wenjin chubanshe, 1984.

Xu, Kangsheng. *Xian Qian Ming chia yanjiu*. Changsha: Hunan remin chubanshe, 1986.

Xunzi. *Sibu beiyao* Edition.

中國哲學

P

Philosophy in China: Historiography

A. S. Cua

The translation of western philosophical concepts and doctrines provides an impetus for the development of Chinese philosophical discourse. In perusing a Chinese dictionary of philosophy, first published in 1925 (*Zhexue cidian*), we find a few Chinese translations of philosophical subjects and terms still in current use, e.g., ethics, logic, ontology, essence, accident, substance, attributes, and reason. In fact "logic" appears as a transliteration that becomes part of modern Chinese. It is instructive to reflect how some translations represent an effort to find functional equivalents in Chinese. Consider the word "philosophy." An ingenious Japanese scholar's translation of "philosophy" as *zhexue* is a good example. In Chinese the first character or graph *zhe* means wisdom. An alternative term for wisdom is *zhi*, often used interchangeably with its homophone, meaning "knowledge" or "capacity to acquire knowledge" (or both). Given their primarily practical focus, ancient Chinese thinkers were, for the most part, preoccupied with ethical questions about right conduct and the best conception of human life. The good human life is commonly envisaged by the Confucians as a life of *ren*, an affectionate concern for the well-being of one's fellows in a society or state governed by a wise and virtuous ruler. *Xue* is learning. "Philosophy" translated as *zhexue* means in Chinese "learning to become a wise and knowledgeable person." As learning and practice can be a delightful experience, the student may come to love the subject.

Of course, philosophy construed as the love of wisdom is likely to be understood in the Confucian way. One can recall Confucius's remark at the beginning of the *Analects*: "Is it not a pleasure, having learned something, to try it out at due intervals?" (1.1). For the Confucian, learning is important because of its relevance to resolving problems of human life. It is the acquisition of practical, not theoretical, knowledge. This translation of "philosophy" as *zhexue* seems to be a very good attempt to find a functional equivalent in the Chinese language before the careful study of western philosophy. Indeed, the translation of "philosophy" from the Greek, on one interpretation, is closer to the ancient Chinese conception. John Passmore (1967) remarks:

> The Greek word *sophia* is ordinarily translated into English as "wisdom," and the compound *philosophia*, from which "philosophy" derives, is translated as "the love of wisdom." But *sophia* has a much wider range of application than the modern English "wisdom." Wherever intelligence can be exercised—in practical affairs, in the mechanical arts, in business—there is room for *sophia*.

Passmore goes on to discuss different conceptions of philosophy—a topic familiar to philosophy majors today. The Chinese translation, though an interpretive adaptation, at least captures part of the meaning of *philosophia*. *Zhexue* is now a standard Chinese term.

However, if we think of philosophy as the construction of grand systems of thought as exemplified in Aristotle, Aquinas, Hobbes, Kant, or Hegel, we may find the idea of Chinese philosophy problematic. Arguably, the works of Zhu Xi may be considered an embodiment of a grand system. Setting aside this essentially contestable issue and focusing on ethics as a basic or even the basic subject of philosophical inquiry, the history of Chinese thought is replete with examples. Since translation is an interpretive task, the Chinese translation of "ethics" as *lunli xue* perhaps illustrates best the concern of the Confucian tradition. Read independently of its being a translated term, *lunli xue* may be explained as an inquiry concerning the rationales of human relationships—a principal concern of Confucian ethics. Those impressed with the recent western emphasis on personal relationships will find an ancient Confucian predecessor for their ethical or political theory.

Since a translation is an interpretive adaptation of an idea in a foreign language, it should not be surprising that a western philosophy student or scholar would have difficulties with the existing translations of some Chinese texts. Wing-tsit Chan's *A Source Book in Chinese Philosophy* is not a very helpful introduction for many western philosophers. While it is an impressive contribution to sinological scholarship, his use of English words for key Chinese concepts is not always clear to western philosophers, in spite of his painstaking efforts to explain them. For example, when *li*, *yili*, and *tianli* are rendered as "principle," "moral principle," and "principle of nature," one can be puzzled about what these English terms mean. Without an explanation of the uses of *li*, the translation of *li* as "principle" unavoidably gives rise to such misleading questions as: "What are the principles of Chinese or Confucian ethics?" "If such principles exist, do they serve as premises for deriving moral rules?" "Are Confucian principles universal or relative?" The selected texts do not provide clear answers to the question "How does one go about formulating the so-called principle?" (Cua 1982, 26–50; 1985, 20–29).

Moreover, though perhaps unavoidable, the use of such labels as "idealistic," "naturalistic," and "rationalistic" for certain tendencies of Chinese thought may be misleading: readers may think of these tendencies—inaccurately—as Chinese counterparts of those in western philosophy. Unless they are carefully defined, even in western philosophy today, these labels are useful largely as convenient pedagogical or mnemonic devices. Note that, to a certain degree, a philosophical bilingual would face similar difficulties in reading Chan's book, while admiring his marvelous achievement.

This essay deals with the question of the positive influence—or more accurately, some examples of the constructive challenge—of western philosophy. I will focus on the development of the history of Chinese philosophy as exemplified in three brilliant works that appeared from 1919 to 1982. These works have been selected not only to illustrate the different western philosophical assumptions and backgrounds of their Chinese writers, but also for their importance in Chinese philosophical education and discourse.

Ancient History of Chinese Thought

While the idea of the history of Chinese philosophy is a western import, the significance of critical exposition of prevailing "winds of doctrine" is recognized in some works in ancient Chinese thought. Somewhat reminiscent of Book Alpha of Aristotle's *Metaphysics,* Chapter 33 of the *Zhuangzi* gives a critical account of Zhuangzi's contemporaries or predecessors (Mei 1964). While acknowledging that there are many thoughtful persons in the world concerned with *dao* (way, or Way), it asks:

> Where do we find what the ancients called the arts of *dao*, i.e., the arts for pursuing *dao* [the ideal of the good human life]? I say that *dao* pervades everything that exists in the universe.

In this essay we find an extant critical account of ancient Confucians, Mozi, Shen Dao, and Hui Shi, a famous proponent of such logical paradoxes as "I set off for Yue today and came there yesterday," "The southern region has no limit and yet has a limit," and "Fire is not hot." This chapter in the *Zhuangzi* praises Laozi and Zhuang Zhou, showing the author's ethical commitment. Notably, Zhuangzi has a holistic moral vision of the unity of humans and nonhumans in the universe: "Heaven and earth were born at the same time as I was, and the ten thousand things are one with me" (Watson 1963, 43). In Chapter 2, Zhuangzi offers a brilliant critique of the Mohists and the Confucians. Among other things, Zhuangzi maintains that there are no fixed meanings of words or neutral, external standards for deciding whether their claims are right or wrong, true or false. The best course is to transcend the dispute and maintain clarity of mind (*ming*). Says Zhuangzi: "The torch of chaos and doubt—this is what the sage steers by. So he does not use things but relegates all to the constant. This is what it means to use clarity" (42).

In much the same holistic spirit, although he is hardly skeptical about the value of argumentative discourse, Xunzi gives an insightful critique of influential thinkers in his time from the Confucian perspective. Also, echoing Zhuangzi, Xunzi acknowledges the merits of the doctrines of various Confucian and non-Confucian thinkers, for their doctrines were plausible, i.e., they had good reasons for espousing their doctrines. Regrettably, they grasp only "one corner" of *dao* and mistake it as characteristic of the whole. For example, Mozi exaggerated the importance of benefits or utility without appreciating the beauties of form or cultural refinement in human life. Zhuangzi was too preoccupied with the thought of heaven and paid hardly any attention to the needs of humanity. Says Xunzi: "*Dao* embodies the constant, yet exhausts all changes. One corner is insufficient to characterize it" (Watson 1963, 125). These thinkers were victims of *bi* (obscuration, blindness); that is, their minds were so dominated by one persistent idea that, as a consequence, they could not see the other equally important aspects of *dao*. Like Zhuangzi, Xunzi emphasizes clarity of mind. But for Xunzi, clarity of mind is a mental state free from cognitive blindness or obsession with doctrines, a preparation for the acquisition of knowledge and sagely wisdom—not a characteristic of attained sageliness.

It is remarkable that apart from defending the Confucian tradition against external challenges, Xunzi is also an internal critic of the Confucian thought and practice of his time. He reminds the learned Confucians that they must not confuse different sorts of Confucians (*Ru*): the great and sagacious, the refined, and the vulgar (Li 1979, Book 8). The value and integrity of Confucian teachings should not be identified with common practices.

The Confucian doctrine of rectifying the uses of names or terms (*zhengming*) is meant partly to ensure that names and titles are assumed by persons who carry out their tasks in accordance with the responsibility implicit in those names and titles. Hu Shi (or Hu Shih, 1963) states that for Confucius, rectification of names is not a task for the grammarian or lexicographer, because it primarily involves intellectual reorganization:

> Its object is, first, to make the names stand for what they ought to stand for, and then to so reorganize the social and political relations and institutions as to make them what their names indicate they ought to be. The rectification of names thus consists in making real relationships and duties and institutions conform as far as possible to the *ideal* meanings, which, however obscured and neglected they may now become, can still be re-discovered and re-established by proper study and, literally "judicious" use of the names. (26)

Influenced especially by later Mohist logic, Xunzi expands the scope of the doctrine of rectifying names to embrace more extensive linguistic, conceptual, and pragmatic concerns (Cua 1985, chs. 3–4).

The Confucian task of intellectual reorganization may also be ascribed to the concern of Zhu Xi (1130–1200) with the idea of Confucian tradition (*daotong*) as a way of meeting the internal and external challenges of non-Confucian thought, such as Buddhism and Daoism (Cua 1992).

History of Chinese Philosophy

In the twentieth century, the challenge for rewriting the history of Chinese thought came from western philosophy. Some western-trained scholars of "Han learning" or Chinese studies must have experienced what Alasdair MacIntyre calls an "epistemological crisis"—a realization that Chinese thought had for some time been stagnant. To them, the issues in discourse must have appeared sterile, as they could no longer be resolved by applying current internal standards of reasoned discourse. MacIntyre says, "The solution to a genuine epistemological crisis requires the invention or discovery of new concepts and the framing of some new type or types of theory" (1988, 362). In the older spirit of the Confucian doctrine of rectifying names, the epistemological crisis calls for "intellectual reorganization." The challenge of western philosophy involves nothing less than a wholesale reconsideration of the philosophical significance of the history of Chinese thought. On the one hand, the task involves adapting alien western philosophical concepts and doctrines to interpret the significance of Chinese classics. On the other hand, especially for those who espouse Confucianism as a living tradition amenable to philosophical transformation, the task also involves preserving the integrity of the classics. More generally, adopting Ronald Dworkin's term, the task may be characterized as "constructive interpretation." The aim of constructive interpretation, as a species of the enterprise of creative interpretation, is to present in the best light a coherent explanation of an object or an existing practice, and more significantly a sound or adequate justification of the practice (Dworkin 1986, 52). The key issues involved in constructive interpretation remain a continuing concern of Chinese philosophers today. Below, I consider some of these issues in three outstanding works of Hu Shi, Feng Youlan (Fung Yu-lan), and Lao Sze-kwang (Lao Siguang) on the history of Chinese philosophy.

Hu Shi (1891–1962). Plausibly, writing the history of Chinese philosophy requires an extensive training in western philosophy. Indeed, as a subject, the history of Chinese philosophy is a philosophical transformation of the history of Chinese thought or Chinese intellectual history. To my knowledge, the pioneering work is Hu Shi's *An Outline of the History of Chinese Philosophy*, Part 1 (in Chinese), published in 1919, two years after he submitted his brilliant doctoral dissertation to Columbia University. Hu did not complete this three-part project; the last two parts were intended to be an account of "medieval" and contemporary Chinese philosophy. While Hu's work pretends to be no more than an outline, in some respects it is still a useful reference. One finds an insightful discussion of the evolution of the Confucian concept of *li* (rules of proper conduct) as well as logical-conceptual issues involved in interpreting, say, Xunzi's conception of empirical knowledge (Cua 1989).

It is significant to note Cai Yuanbei's Foreword, dated 3 August 1918. Cai mentions four special qualities of this book: (1) Hu's use of the methods of evidence; (2) his skill in distinguishing the "pure" elements of philosophical thought from those of mythology and political history; (3) his ability to evaluate, impartially and discerningly, the merits and demerits of different philosophies; and (4) the systematic character of his inquiry. Cai reminds the reader that Hu is among the very few scholars trained in western philosophy who have also mastered "Han learning."

Hu's own long introductory chapter explains his aims, methodology, and aspirations. At the outset, Hu points out that there is no fixed definition of "philosophy." He proposes a tentative broad definition:

> Any kind of study and research that deals with the most important questions of human life from the standpoint of fundamental questions and solutions may be called "philosophy."

An example would be questions concerning the goodness or badness of human conduct.

Hu goes on to outline six different sorts of philosophical inquiry, familiar to students of western philosophy: cosmology, epistemology, ethics, philosophy of education, political philosophy, and philosophy of religion:

> These kinds of inquiry, from the ancient times until the present, have passed through many philosophers' investigations. Continually, since the inception of the formulation of a question, different interpretations and methods of solution have been proposed and contested in argumentation. Sometimes, one question, after a few thousand years, still has received no definitive method of resolution.

Hu cites as an example the ancient Chinese dispute concerning human nature (*xing*) in the doctrines of Gaozi, Mencius, and Xunzi, and in subsequent views.

Hu focuses on three objectives of a history of philosophy: (1) understanding changes or transformations in a particular school of thought, (2) seeking the reasons and causes for such transformations, and (3) objective, critical evaluation.

Hu pays a great deal of attention to the method for evaluating sources, modeled after the western method of writing history. Perhaps, as Lao Sze-kwang complained later, Hu spends too much time on the problem of distinguishing genuine materials from forgeries. Hu briefly discusses five kinds of evidence: (1) historical events, (2) linguistic usages of the time, (3) literary styles, (4) the coherent or systematic character of thought, and (5) secondary collaborative evidence. In the last section of his introduction, Hu stresses a deeper level of the method of *guantong*, the orderly, sequential presentation of development of a school of thought. In the bibliographic notes for the introductory chapter, Hu lists mostly western sources such as *A History of Western Philosophy*, by the German Wilhelm Windelband (1848–1915), translated into English by J. H. Tufts and published in 1893.

This sketch of Hu's concerns is familiar to teachers of western philosophy. Noteworthy is Hu's use of the notions of syllogism, proposition, and judgment in his discussion of later Mohist logic.

In 1919, eight years after the founding of the republic of China, a Chinese scholar or university student of "Han learning" would have found Hu's book important, as it presented a new perspective on the history of Chinese thought. In the 1920s, a fellow Chinese with a graduate education in western philosophy would have found it an inspiring and enlightening work of Chinese scholarship.

Philosophers interested in the informal, pragmatic, logical aspect of ancient Chinese thought will find another pioneering study in Hu's *The Development of the Logical Method in Ancient China* (1963). Influenced by Dewey's "experimental logic," Hu critically expounds the logical aspects of the *Analects of Confucius*, Mozi and his school, and Xunzi's works. The impressive attempt at a comprehensive, reconstructive study of the later Mohists' fragmentary, discursive texts appeared almost a half century after Hu's doctoral dissertation (Graham 1978).

This work on logical method also expresses Hu's attitude toward the history of Chinese thought, his solution, so to speak, to the "epistemological crisis." Hu writes: "How can we [Chinese] best assimilate modern civilization in such a manner as to make it congenial and congruous and continuous with the civilization of our own making?" The more specific problem is to find "a congenial stock with which we may organically link with the thought-systems of modern Europe and America, so that we may further build up our own science and philosophy on the new foundation of an internal assimilation of the old and the new." Hu is critical of Song-Ming Confucianism, or what is commonly known in the west as neo-Confucianism, as represented by major works of Zhu Xi and Wang Yangming. Hu says that these thinkers "rejuvenated the long-dead Confucianism by reading into it two logical methods which never belonged to it," that is:

> the theory of investigating into the reason in everything for the purpose of extending one's knowledge to the utmost, which is the method of Song School; and the theory of intuitive knowledge, which is the method of the School of Wang Yangming.

While appreciative of Wang's merits, Hu feels that the method is "wholly incompatible with the method of science." As to the Song method of the investigation of things, it is fruitless in three ways:

> (1) by the lack of an experimental procedure, (2) by its failure to recognize the active and directing role played by the mind in the investigation of things, and (3) most unfortunate of all, by its construction of "thing" to mean "affairs."

Hu has no doubt that the future of Chinese philosophy depends on "emancipation from the moralistic and rationalistic fetters of Confucianism" (1963, 7–9).

Hu's view raises important issues concerning his reading of Song-Ming Confucianism. One wonders, also, whether he has neglected a principal concern with ethical methodology in the works of Cheng Yi, Zhu Xi, and Wang Yangming. Significantly, their different conceptions of ethical methodology apply to the Confucian classic *The Great Learning* (*Daxue*), which emphasizes self-cultivation as the root of or basis for attaining the Confucian ideal of human excellence. This emphasis on self-cultivation crucially involves not only the development of moral character but also empirical inquiry, for example, Zhu Xi's interpretation of "investigation of things" as exhausting the *li* (rationales) for their existence and our normative conception of what they ought to be. More important, does it make sense to "build up our own science and philosophy on the new foundation of an internal assimilation of the old and the new" without a constructive, philosophical interpretation of Song-Ming Confucianism?

Feng Youlan (*Fung Yu-lan, 1895–1990*). The first volume of Feng's *A History of Chinese Philosophy* (in Chinese) was published in 1931, and the second volume in 1934. Derk Bodde's English translation is an outstanding achievement, particularly in introducing Feng's work to English speakers. The coverage of the first volume, from the beginnings to about 100 B.C.E., is more extensive than Hu Shi's *Outline of the History of Chinese Philosophy*. All the major thinkers and schools discussed by Hu reappear in Feng's first volume. Since Hu and Feng received a similar western training at Columbia University, it is not surprising that they made the same judgment about the philosophical significance of the literature of ancient Chinese thought. However, the difference in time between their works marks a difference in influence. Hu's work was influenced by Dewey in the 1910s, Feng's by William P. Montague in the 1920s.

Feng points out in his Introduction (which is reminiscent of but more explicit than Hu's) that "philosophy" is originally a western term. According to Feng, one main task of "the history of Chinese philosophy" consists in selecting those works of scholarship in that history which lend themselves to philosophical treatment. This task presupposes some understanding of the term "western philosophy." Feng remarks:

> In the west, the use of "philosophy" has a long history. Different philosophers have their own definitions of "philosophy." However, for purposes of convenience, let us attend to the content. If we know the content of philosophy, we can know what sort of thing philosophy is. We need not take up, as a separate topic, the "official" definition of philosophy." (1)

Much in the spirit of Hu, Feng proceeds to mention the Greeks' threefold division of philosophy into physics, ethics, and logic or, alternatively, a "theory of world," a "theory of life," and a "theory of knowledge." Feng maintains that philosophy is a product of reason:

> . . . if philosophers want to establish the reasoned foundation of their theses, they must provide arguments, proofs or demonstrations. This is the purport of Xunzi's saying, "They [the thinkers criticized] have reasons for supporting their views and thus their words appear plausible" [*Xunzi*, 93–97] and Mencius's saying, "Do I love to argue? I have no other alternative" [*Mencius*, 3B.9].

Possibly addressing western-trained Chinese thinkers who have no special interest in the philosophical study of Chinese thought, or those skeptical about the intelligibility of talking about Chinese philosophy, Feng remarks:

> There are three questions that most often occur to all persons interested in the history of Chinese thought. First, what is the nature of Chinese philosophy, and what contribution has it to make to the world? Secondly, is it true, as is often said, that Chinese philosophy lacks system? And thirdly, is it true that there is no such thing as development of Chinese philosophy? (1952, 1:1)

With regard to the first question, Feng points out that we do find ethical and metaphysical concerns, but very little attention to logic or methodology and epistemology. For the most part Chinese philosophers do not think that knowledge has intrinsic value. Even in the case of practical knowledge, Chinese philosophers would stress its application to actual conduct rather than engage in empty discussions. The lack of any Chinese contribution to epistemology can be explained partly in terms of the widely shared ideal of "inner sageliness and outer kingliness" (*neisheng waiwang*) and partly by the fact that they had no clear "distinction between the individual and the universe"—to put this another way, they did not have the western concept of the "ego." As to methodology, given their ideal of "inner sageliness and outer kingliness," the Chinese thinkers emphasized methods of self-cultivation. In this regard, China has "a great contribution to offer."

This suggests a partial answer to the second question, "Is it true, as is often said, that Chinese philosophy lacks system?" Feng maintains that we must distinguish "formal" from "real" systems:

> It may be admitted that Chinese philosophy lacks formal system; but if one were to say that it therefore lacks any real system, meaning that there is no organic unity of ideas to be found in Chinese philosophy, it would be equivalent to saying that Chinese philosophy is not philosophy, and that China has no philosophy. The earlier Greek philosophy also lacked formal system. Thus Socrates wrote no books himself, Plato used the dialogue form in his writings, and it was not until Aristotle that a clear and ordered exposition was given on every problem. Hence if we judge from the point of view of formal system, Aristotle's philosophy is comparatively systematic, yet insofar as the actual content of the philosophy is concerned, Plato's philosophy is equally systematic. . . . Although Chinese philosophy, formally speaking, is less systematic than that of the west, in its actual content it has as much system as does western philosophy. This being so, the important duty of the historian of philosophy is to find within a philosophy that lacks *formal* system, its underlying *real* system. (1952, 4)

Perhaps Feng's distinction between formal and real systems is more plausibly rendered as a distinction between explicit, articulate systems and implicit, inchoate systems of philosophy. The idea of a formal system of philosophy sometimes has as its paradigm a logical, deductive, or quasideductive system as exemplified in Spinoza and Kant. Feng's use of "organic unity" suggests his adoption of Hegelian terminology.

If one accepts Feng's thesis that Chinese thought has "real" systems although it lacks "formal systems," this thesis must be qualified by saying that so-called real systems are products of philosophical reconstruction or constructive interpretation. In the untranslated section "The Unity of Philosophy," Feng cites Confucius's remark, "There is one thread that runs through my teachings" (*Analects*, 4.15). More informatively, Feng cites Xunzi's critique of different influential thinkers (noted earlier): that in their preoccupation with one thing, such as utility, they completely ignored the importance of other things (aspects of *dao; Xunzi*, Book 4). Feng also reminds his readers of William James's view in *A Pluralistic Universe* (1971, 125–126): "If one aspect of the universe attracts the special attention of a philosopher, he would hold to it as if it were characteristic of the whole."

A similar view is expressed in a succinct remark of Wittgenstein's, reminiscent of Xunzi's view of philosophers as victims of *bi* (obscuration or blindness) or aspect-obsession: "A main cause of philosophical disease—a one-sided diet: one nourishes one's thinking with only one kind of example" (1958, no. 595). This sort of preoccupation leads to neglect of other examples that may be even more important in formulating an adequate view of things. Like ordinary people, great thinkers of the east and west tend to exaggerate the significance of their insights as embodying "the whole truth and nothing but the truth." They tend to regard their partial views as representing the whole, assuming that they have the best understanding of the subject. They are prompt to overstate the scope of their insights, "forgetful" of the limits of our intellectual capacity. This seems to be a lesson we can learn from Zhuangzi's view of "forgetting" morality and other earthly concerns (Cua 1977).

Let us turn to the third question, "Is it true that there is no such thing as progressive growth in Chinese philosophy?" Feng answers:

> The problems and scope of Chinese philosophy from the Han dynasty onward are not so numerous and comprehensive as those of the philosophy that preceded it, and yet the later philosophy is certainly more clearly expounded than the earlier one. (1952, 1:5)

(This judgment seems implicit in Hu Shi's critique of Song-Ming Confucianism.) Invoking Aristotle's distinction between potentiality and actuality, Feng maintains, in his introduction to the first volume, that "movement from such potentiality to actuality constitutes progress."

However, as is evident in Feng's division of the history of Chinese philosophy into two periods presented in two separate volumes, progress does not mean advancement or development of new philosophical perspectives in the modern western sense. The two periods are the "period of the philosophers" (*zhexue shidai*), from Confucius (551–479 B.C.E.) to Huainanzi (d. 122 B.C.E, and the "period of classical learning" (*jingxue shidai*), from Dong Zhongshu (c. 179–104 B.C.E.) to Kang Youwei (1858–1927).

The period of philosophers is characterized by a "simultaneous flourishing of many schools." It is a period when many original thinkers confronted each other in a free arena of argumentative discourse. This explains the scope of Feng's first volume, covering "only some four-hundred-odd years." Indeed, for any philosophy student today, that is the most exciting period of Chinese thought. Perhaps for this reason, today many philosophical scholars and historians of Chinese thought devote their time and energy to ancient literature.

The period of classical learning, on the other hand, is for the most part a period of Confucian classicism or "scholasticism." According to Feng, if one follows the usual division of western philosophy into ancient, medieval, and modern, "it may be said that China has actually had only an ancient and a medieval philosophy but still lacks a modern philosophy." Feng said in 1934:

> China, until very recent times, regardless of how we view it, has remained essentially medieval, with the result that in many respects it has failed to keep pace with the west. A modern age, indeed, has been lacking in Chinese history, and philosophy is but one particular aspect of this general situation. (1952, 2:1–5)

Feng's view raises an important issue regarding the "development of Chinese philosophy" or, alternatively, the evolution of the history of Chinese thought into a history of philosophy.

When Feng published his work in the early 1930s, Chinese philosophy and its history must have been an established subject of study. His long introduction could have in mind a particular audience of philosophy students and perhaps skeptics. Feng's work was the first full-scale effort to present a history of Chinese philosophy; Derk Bodde's is still the only English translation. Before he died (in 1990, at age ninety-five), Feng completed a new, comprehensive seven-volume history of Chinese philosophy, written from a single-minded Marxist point of view. His earlier work, presented here, though more limited in scope, is informed by a spirit of liberty absent from much of Chinese Marxist history of Chinese philosophy today, and thus is open to a more liberal philosophical interpretation of Chinese thought (Standaert 1995).

Lao Sze-kwang (*Lao Siguang*). The third and final volume of Lao's *History of Chinese Philosophy* (in Chinese) was completed and published in 1982. It has a narrower scope than Feng's history; the last chapter deals with Dai Zhen (1723–1777). As any recent western-trained Chinese philosopher would expect, Lao must provide some justification for his own attempt to write a history of Chinese philosophy, given the widespread familiarity with Feng's. Lao's work, then, is philosophically more sophisticated and is addressed to an audience knowledgeable about works of western philosophy published since the 1930s.

It is worth noting here that after World War II, many Chinese studied philosophy in the United States and Europe; given their background in Chinese philosophical education, they were familiar with writings in Chinese on both western and Chinese philosophy. For philosophers and scholars in Taiwan, Hong Kong, and elsewhere in the Chinese diaspora, Chinese philosophy was and is a subject worthy of serious scholarly and philosophical attention. Except for the occasional encounter with western skeptics ignorant of the extensive works in Chinese philosophy since the 1960s, a Chinese philosopher or historian of philosophy is no longer bothered with the question of whether Chinese philosophy exists. Of course, what is presumed is a contemporary Chinese philosophical audience—and this is Lao's implicit audience in his preface in the first volume and his postscript in the third.

In his preface, Lao points out that the course "History of Chinese Philosophy" had been an established offering in Chinese universities before Hu Shi's lectures (at the University of Peking in the late 1910s). Lao claims that until he completed his first volume in 1967, there had been no "acceptable" work on the history of Chinese philosophy conforming to "proper [western] standards." Lao assumes that there are general standards of competence for western philosophical writings. He remarks that there are philosophy textbooks in Chinese, arbitrarily and conveniently composed by instructors for lecture purposes. With the exception of Feng Youlan's *History of Chinese Philosophy*, there are no competently written works on the history of Chinese philosophy.

Hu Shi's incomplete *Outline of the History of Chinese Philosophy* is said to be an object of ridicule, presumably by Lao's audience of colleagues and graduate students in Chinese universities. For Lao, the defect of Hu's *Outline* is not that it is incomplete but that it lacks "philosophical" elements. To Lao, a history of philosophy must be a "philosophy" and a "history." The historian of philosophy must not only present a narrative account of actual thought and related events but also have an "explanatory theory." The narrative is the task of historians; the explanation requires a "theoretical foundation and analytical method." If these two requirements are not satisfied, what is written can be considered only "history," not "history of philosophy." While Hu's history is a pioneering work, "strictly speaking, it can only be viewed as an unsuccessful experiment." Hu spends too much time with questions of the dating and authenticity of texts. Although these questions may be considered part of the task of a historian of philosophy, they are not the most important part. Moreover, Hu Shi's use of *changshi* (common sense or common knowledge) as a basis of explanation is problematic. Lao says, "In any case, using *changshi* to interpret philosophy cannot make any contact with the real questions" (1981–1984, 1: 1–2).

As regards Feng Youlan's *History*, Lao considers it definitely superior to Hu's work. But according to Lao, although Feng's is a history of philosophy, it is still not a successful piece of work. Feng shows little depth in his command of western philosophical literature; his use of concepts and theories is limited to Plato's early theory and "new realism." Feng hardly shows a firm grasp of western philosophical theories. Moreover, he lacks understanding of the special characteristics of Chinese philosophy. He could handle simple theories:

> But as soon as he confronts Song-Ming *lixue* [neo-Confucianism], he displays his weaknesses. From the very beginning, he could not deal with the concept of moral subjectivity. Though it may seem improbable, he was unaware of his lack of understanding of [the concept of] subjectivity itself. Consequently, he could only give an account, in a forced manner, of the Confucian doctrine of perfect virtue (*chengde zhi xue*) as a mere metaphysical theory and failed to understand its essential aspects. (1:3)

Lao goes on to claim that because Feng's work is informed only by Plato's early works and new realism, there is a "great distance" between Feng's later *Xin lixue* (*A New Doctrine of Li*) and Song-Ming *lixue*.

Lao expounds at greater length his own conception of the history of philosophy, stressing the importance of methodology. Four methods of inquiry are discussed: (1) systematic, (2) developmental, and (3) analytic inquiry, and (4) inquiry into fundamental philosophical questions.

The systematic method must also pay attention to the original contexts of theoretical thought. However, because of the writer's own philosophical interest, frequently he or she is likely to focus on philosophical questions and neglect the actual contexts of discourse. While the method of systematic inquiry has its pitfalls, from the holistic point of view it has merits when it is used with care.

The developmental method raises complex questions. If systematic inquiry tends to err on the subjective side, the developmental method often results in a partial grasp of segments of actuality with no appreciation of the holistic character (*chuanti*) of theory. As a result, what we get is a narrative of fragments. (Recall Xunzi's doctrine of aspect-obsession.) For Lao, from the philosophical point of view, this is a serious defect, because it is contrary to the basic objectives of philosophy.

Regarding the analytical method of inquiry, Lao stresses the importance of "philosophical analysis," which gives rise to "syntactical analysis" and "semantics." Particularly worthy of attention and also influential is the emergence of the theory of "meaning criteria" and the use of this kind of theory in the critique of traditional philosophy. While it is not expected of a historian of philosophy, training in the skills of philosophical analysis can be useful in carrying out these tasks. Nevertheless, philosophical analysis cannot be a substitute for the historian's task of synthesis, for it can deal only with existing materials and cannot propose new materials—in particular, it cannot offer an overall judgment of the history of philosophy as a whole. In sum, the three conditions for a history of philosophy are truth, a system, and unity. The first requires that the narrative be faithful to the actual texts and circumstances; the second requires a systematic exposition of theory; the third requires a unifying judgment of the whole history of philosophy.

How is it possible for a historian to satisfy these requirements? Lao proposes his fourth method, embracing the other three methods. Lao says he has devoted a great deal of thought and energy to this question for some time and has arrived at the conclusion that, comparatively speaking, the fourth method is a good method. There are three steps in this method of inquiry into fundamental questions of philosophy. The first step consists in having a good understanding of the foundation of Chinese thought. Every individual thinker or school has, as its basis, an ideal theory for resolving certain fundamental problems. Although explanation is central to this task, one must also deal with the question of textual analysis. As regards the second step, after having a grasp of fundamental questions, we can then proceed to an explication of the relevant theory. In the process, secondary questions may emerge. Each of these questions has its own answer, forming a section of the theory. Third and finally, we organize all levels of the theory, thus completing the task of explicating an individual theory. In doing so, we satisfy the first two conditions: truth and a system.

The last step, corresponding to the third requirement of unity, entails coherently organizing the materials into a series of the fundamental questions of different historical periods before rendering a holistic theoretical judgment. However, one must acknowledge certain "presuppositions" (*shezhun*), reflecting the writer's "own knowledge and experience (*shijian*) as well as his philosophic wisdom." Finally, the method of inquiring into fundamental questions must be consonant with the writer's presuppositions.

In the concluding section of Lao's "Prefatory Remarks," he takes up some distinctive problems of the history of Chinese philosophy. The first problem, as Hu and Feng noted, lies in managing the extant ancient textual materials. As an excuse for not engaging in argumentation, many pre-Qin thinkers were fond of appealing to the past. Also problematic is the tendency of some post-Qin and post-Han writers to forge documents. Second, hitherto Chinese philosophy has paid no attention to analysis. It has neither logic nor epistemology. Lao says: "We must admit that what China lacks is analytical skills. Naturally, we have to adopt most of these skills derived from western achievements." Third, the fundamental questions of Chinese philosophy differ from those of western philosophy. In the course of exposition, it is inevitable that the writer will apply his theoretical presuppositions, hoping to encompass both Chinese and western philosophy. In a somewhat modest tone, Lao reminds his reader that his *History of Chinese Philosophy* is but one attempt to use the method of probing fundamental philosophical questions. He expresses the hope that when the draft for the whole project is completed, others may write a more successful history of Chinese philosophy. (The third and last volume of Lao's *History* was published in 1982.)

Lao's critique of Hu and Feng may be viewed as an unfair commentary. Granted, Lao's own work is a philosophical, analytic reconstruction of the history of Chinese thought, distinguished by its conceptual analysis, emphasis on arguments, and reasoned justification of interpretation, and by a much greater command of western philosophy and the recent Confucianism that flourished in Hong Kong and Taiwan. However, his critique of Hu and Feng makes no allowance for the nature of a particular audience (Perelman and Olbrechts-Tyteca 1969). Like many philosophers and writers of other philosophical persuasions—indeed, most western philosophers since Plato—Lao seems to regard his audience as universal. Lao, like many philosophers of our age, has a penchant for objectivity or "the view from nowhere"; he is a child of those western philosophers beset by a fear of relativism and subjectivism. He does not seem to be worried by problems such as those recently presented by Richard Rorty, Derrida, and Derrida's fellow deconstructionists. In this regard it is worth noting that the late distinguished sinologist and philosopher Angus Graham, in his book on ancient Chinese philosophy (1989), proposed a novel deconstructionist interpretation of Laozi; that Graham's philosophical history of ancient Chinese thought is based largely on his philological research in classical Chinese and the works of Benjamin Whorf and Gilbert Ryle; and that in Graham's book we find hardly any use of the insights derived from the works of John Wisdom and J. L. Austin.

Were Hu Shi alive today, he would probably respond pragmatically to Lao's or Graham's work by appealing to the middle and later works of Dewey, such as *Experience and Nature* (1925; 2nd ed., 1929), *Art as Experience* (1934), and *Logic: The Theory of Inquiry* (1938), or perhaps to the more recent methodological pragmatism of Nicholas Rescher (1977). Perhaps out of courtesy, Lao acknowledges Hu's *Outline* as a pioneering work, but he pays no attention to Hu's introductory chapter, especially those sections in which Hu articulated his concept of the subject. While there is a terminological difference, would Lao disagree with Hu's three objectives: understanding the changes or transformations of a particular school of thought, the reasons and causes for such transformations, and objective critical evaluation? As to Lao's complaint that Hu's is not a "philosophical" book, presumably because Hu spent too much time on textual analysis, it must be noted that when Hu wrote his book, in 1918, ancient Chinese texts—as Lao is well aware—were in a state of confusion. Although textual scholarship has no essential connection with philosophy, it is still important for a philosophical historian to use the state of the art as a point of departure for determining the development of a school of thought. Textual scholarship was more advanced when Lao wrote his first volume. However, there is still much uncertainty about the background, current circumstances, climates of opinion, and contexts of discourse (Knoblock 1988–1995, 3:xi).

Instead of a sweeping rejection of Hu's book as nonphilosophical, Lao should have offered an examination of Hu's objectives and shown how Hu failed to accomplish them. We must agree that Hu's remarks about methodology are, in light of Lao's or any later writer's philosophical training and commitment, much too biased toward Dewey's instrumentalism. For instance, Hu's unqualified condemnation of Song-Ming Confucianism was based on an implausible assumption that Zhu Xi and Wang Yangming were concerned with the application of inductive, deductive, or intuitive scientific method to human affairs. Even a cursory reading of some of Zhu's and Wang's works would lead to an appreciation of the different ways they tried to preserve what they considered the "Confucian tradition" and their concern with how that tradition was misinterpreted, abused, and misused, particularly in the hands of irresponsible scholars and officials. A living tradition, as distinct from traditionalism or blind adherence to tradition, is amenable to quite different constructions, especially as to its concrete, temporal significance (Cua 1992). In passing, we can note that a contemporary Confucian appreciative of the insights of Zhu Xi and Wang Yangming might even welcome Dewey's version of pragmatism, as a supplement to explicating the nature of Confucian ethics, since it provides a fairly effective way of clarifying the practical focus of that ethical system.

Consider that two salient features of Confucian ethics are the primacy of practice and the legitimate use of plausible presumptions. The former admits of a pragmatic interpretation, because of the Confucian preoccupation with problematic situations and their ethical solutions. Although Confucians do not explicitly reject the doctrine of "fixed" or absolute ends, their emphasis on *yi* (rightness) suggests that ethically acceptable conduct in problematic situations must in some way be based on reasoned judgment appropriate to the case at hand. In Xunzi's words, in coping with difficult and exigent situations of human life, one must use *yi* or one's sense of rightness or discretion (*yiyi bianying*). In a way that is reminiscent of Dewey's conception of deliberation in *Human Conduct*, Xunzi insists on clarity of mind as a prerequisite to wise and informed deliberation in dealing with problematic situations of human life. Xunzi would have agreed with Dewey that, in the final analysis, the important matter pertains to the resolution of problematic situations through the use of means derived from past experience. The propensity to rely on common knowledge of the day without regard to the relevance of past experience or the wisdom of tradition is a ubiquitous human failing. An appeal to the wisdom of the past should not be rejected outright, because the past is considered a repository of insights and plausible presumptions. Moreover, in their insistence on the unity of moral knowledge and action, thought, and words the Confucians have an affinity with Dewey's thesis on the intrinsic connection between theory and practice (Cua 1982).

Lao's critique of Feng is especially revealing of his own conception of philosophy and the history of philosophy. Lao is not satisfied with Feng's limited knowledge and use of western philosophy. He cites Feng's inability to appreciate the character of Song-Ming Confucianism because Feng has no conception of "moral metaphysics." It is true that Lao has a more extensive knowledge of western philosophy. But his appeal to "moral metaphysics" is an anachronism—"moral metaphysics" is a Chinese-English term coined in the 1960s by Mou Zongsan, who was then a senior colleague of Lao's at the Chinese University of Hong Kong. Some words of explanation are in order here.

Mou, an encyclopedic and original Chinese philosopher, expounds his thesis against the background of Kant's conception of a "metaphysics of morals." For a student of western philosophy with no knowledge of Chinese philosophy, "moral metaphysics" is an unfamiliar term. As used by Mou, it is a technical term distinguishing his Confucian metaphysical theory from Kant's metaphysics of morals. The term "moral metaphysics" is valuable in suggesting an important enterprise for Chinese moral philosophy. According to Mou, Kant has only a metaphysics of morals but no moral metaphysics; Kant's conception is no more than a "metaphysical exposition of morals" or a "metaphysical deduction of morals." Metaphysics of morals takes morality as its subject matter. It borrows from the fruits of metaphysical inquiry in order to discover and establish the fundamental principles of morality. Moral metaphysics (including ontology and cosmology) takes metaphysics as its subject matter and approaches that subject through human moral nature. In other words, for Mou (1973, 1:156ff), moral practice, in the sense of authentic attainment of Confucian sagehood, is the basis for conferring metaphysical significance on all things.

Whether or not Mou is right about Kant or about mainstream Confucianism, the distinction between moral metaphysics and metaphysics of morals is useful in discussing Song-Ming Confucianism. This distinction raises an important question about the interpretation of Chinese Confucian ethics as normative ethics, metaethics, or metaphysical ethics. I wonder whether Lao's use of Mou's interpretive thesis and such terms as *zhuti* (subjectivity) in criticizing Feng's work is an example of a fallacious "appeal to authority." If we regard moral theory as a relatively autonomous discipline, we can appropriate Mou's distinction for delineating an important aspect of philosophical inquiry without depreciating Feng's history.

Underlying Lao's dissatisfactions with Hu's and Feng's work are his philosophical presuppositions, informed by his greater knowledge of recent western and Chinese philosophy. It is not surprising that Hu's and Feng's presuppositions were informed by philosophical movements that prevailed in their own times. Philosophical presuppositions in a history of Chinese philosopy, or of western philosophy, reflect the influence of current philosophical concerns, as is evident in Chinese—and western—graduate education. Hu was influenced by John Dewey but perhaps was not sensitive to the Hegelian elements in Dewey's philosophy. Feng was influenced by his studies of early Plato, James, and neorealism. How could Hu and Feng be faulted for not knowing about analytic philosophy or Mou Zongsan? Feng seemed to be familiar with some works of the "Vienna circle." He said of his *Xin lixue*, one target of Lao's critique: "The work of New *Lixue* is to *re-establish* metaphysics by going through the empiricism of the Vienna Circle" (Wang 1994). But he could not be expected to know Wittgenstein's *Philosophical Investigation.*

Nevertheless, Lao's effort in writing a philosophical history of Chinese thought merits approval, for a mastery of the literature of the history of Chinese thought and analytical method is a gigantic undertaking. Most Chinese and western scholars of Chinese thought are specialists in a historical period or in specific works of individual thinkers. Many of them do not have extensive philosophical training. Lao's emphasis on philosophical and argumentative analysis, as contrasted with Hu's emphasis on textual analysis, is a valuable contribution. From the standpoint of philosophical analysis, Lao's history is superior to Feng's. For philosophical readers of Chinese classics, Lao's *History* provides an excellent guide to the rich sources of philosophical thought, even though these readers may not accept Lao's rash judgment about the worth of the works of Hu and Feng. Setting aside questions of textual fidelity and the acceptability of his philosophical interpretations, Lao has performed a great service in providing a most useful resource for the development of the history of Chinese philosophy. While Lao's requirements for writing a history of Chinese philosophy may appear too exacting, a western-trained Chinese philosopher or a sinicized western philosopher would find Lao's *History* an invaluable guide to research.

Although textual scholarship is an important enterprise, philosophical interpretation of Chinese thought has an integrity of its own, independent of its contribution to textual scholarship. Apart from philosophical interpretation, there are also legitimate philological, intellectual, religious, and political interpretations. Admittedly, the history of Chinese thought may be interpreted in these different, and possibly complementary, ways. Confusing these interpretative approaches, however, will impede not only efforts at any broad philosophical transformation of the history of Chinese thought but also the development of Chinese philosophy.

If Lao's requirements for writing the history of Chinese philosophy may appear too exacting, he is right in saying that a historian of Chinese philosophy must to some extent be a philosopher. Ideally, an understanding of basic philosophical questions in different branches of philosophy is a prerequisite to any serious philosophical inquiry into the thought of a historical period or of a major philosopher. A coherent statement of presuppositions in writing a history of philosophy, as Lao insists, would give the reader a unifying perspective on the writer's philosophical convictions. Nevertheless, in the "Postscript" to the third volume, Lao expresses his belief that Chinese philosophy has "universal significance" if we distinguish between "open and closed concepts" of philosophy. The terminology is reminiscent of Karl Popper's *Open Society and Its Enemies.* In a later article (in English), Lao explains that an "open concept" of philosophy would "enable people of different philosophical traditions to communicate with each other." In this conception, philosophy is a reflective enterprise. Understanding Chinese philosophy rests on appreciating its primary "focused" or "directed" character—that is, Chinese philosophy "intends to effect some change in the self or in the world." Alternative terms are "self-transformation" and "transformation of the world." Such a philosophy would give a statement of purpose, justification, and pragmatic maxims. Lao cites Zhuangzi and Mencius as examples. It is noteworthy that Lao shows concern with intercultural communication. Presumably he would also agree that this concern must be followed by an endeavor to provide some guidelines for resolving intercultural conflict (Cua 1998, Essay 14).

In this account of the works of Hu Shi, Feng Youlan (Fung Yu-lan), and Lao Sze-kwang I have presented illustrative examples of the positive influence of western philosophy in the development of the history of Chinese philosophy. There are also other works, such as Lo Guang's extensive *History of Chinese Philosophical Thought.* The seventh and last volume, published in 1986, deals with the period since the founding of the republic of China in 1911. Separate chapters are devoted to major nonhistorical philosophical works of Hu Shi and Feng Youlan as well as important contributions of the recent past—e.g., works of Xiong Shili, Tang Junyi, and Thomé H. Fang (Fang Dongmei)—and Lo Guang's own philosophy of life. Today, philosophical writings in Chinese are quite extensive, covering topics in western, Chinese, Indian, Buddhist, and comparative east-west philosophy. Philosophy journals in Taiwan, for example, are pretty much modeled after those in English. Unfortunately, except for some works of Thomé H. Fang, many original works of such influential philosophers as Mou Tsung-san and T'ang Chün-i are not available in English. Perhaps when English translations of their principal writings are available, there will be a beginning of a creative and fruitful Chinese-western philosophical dialogue on the history of philosophy, east or west.

See also Confucianism: Tradition; Fang Dongmei; Feng Youlan: Works on the History of Chinese Philosophy; Mou Zongsan; Philosophy of History; Tang Junyi; Translation and Its Problems, Xiong Shili; *Zhixing Heyi.*

Bibliography

Chan, Wing-tsit, trans. *A Source Book in Chinese Philosophy*. Princeton, N.J.: Princeton University Press, 1963.

Cua, A. S. "The Concept of *Li* in Confucian Moral Theory." In *Understanding the Chinese Thought*, ed. Robert E. Allinson. Hong Kong: Oxford University Press, 1989.

———. *Ethical Argumentation: A Study of Hsün Tzu's Moral Epistemology*. Honolulu: University of Hawaii Press, 1985.

———. "Forgetting Morality: Reflections on a Theme in *Chuang Tzu*." *Journal of Chinese Philosophy*, 4(4), 1977.

———. "The Idea of Confucian Tradition." *Review of Metaphysics*, 45, 1992, pp. 803–840.

———. *Moral Vision and Tradition: Essays in Chinese Ethics*. Washington, D.C.: Catholic University of America Press, 1998.

———. "The Possibility of Ethical Knowledge: Reflections on a Theme in *Hsün Tzu*." In *Epistemological Issues in Classical Chinese Philosophy*, ed. Hans Lenk and Gregor Paul. Albany: State University of New York Press, 1993.

———. *Unity of Knowledge and Action: A Study in Wang Yangming's Moral Psychology*. Honolulu: University of Hawaii Press, 1982.

Dewey, John. *Essays in Experimental Logic*. Chicago, Ill.: University of Chicago Press, 1916.

Fang, Thomé H. (Fang Dongmei). *Chinese Philosophy: Its Spirit and Its Development*. Taipei: Linking, 1981.

———. *The Chinese View of Life: The Philosophy of Comprehensive Harmony*. Taipei: Linking, 1980.

Feng, Youlan (Fung Yu-lan). *A History of Chinese Philosophy*, 2 vols., trans. Derk Bodde. Princeton, N.J.: Princeton University Press, 1952.

———. *Zhongguo zhexue shi, fubu pian*. Hong Kong: Taipingyang, 1975. (lst ed., 1931.)

Graham, A. C. *Disputers of the Tao: Philosophical Argument in Ancient China*. La Salle, Ill.: Open Court, 1989.

———. *Later Mohist Logic, Ethics, and Science*. Hong Kong: Chinese University of Hong Kong Press, 1978.

Hu, Shi. *The Development of the Logical Method in Ancient China*. New York: Paragon, 1963.

———. *Zhongguo zhexue shi dagang*, 4th ed. Peking: Commercial Press, 1947. (1st ed., 1919.)

James, William. *Essays in Radical Empiricism and a Pluralistic Universe*. New York: Dutton, 1971.

Knoblock, John. *Xunzi: A Translation and Study of the Complete Works*, 3 vols. Stanford, Calif.: Stanford University Press, 1988–1995.

Lao, D. C., trans. *Confucius: The Analects*. London: Penguin, 1979.

———, trans. *Mencius*. Baltimore, Md.: Penguin, 1970.

Lao, Sze-kwang. "On Understanding Chinese Philosophy: An Inquiry and a Proposal." In *Understanding the Chinese Thought: The Philosophical Roots*, ed. Robert E. Allinson. Hong Kong: Oxford University Press, 1989.

———. *Xinbian Zhongguo zhexue shi*, 3 vols., 1st rev. ed. Taipei: Sanmin, 1981–1984. (Postcript in Vol. 1 dated 1967; in Vol. 3 dated 1980.)

Li, Disheng. *Xunzi jishi*. Taipei: Xuesheng, 1979.

Lin, Tongqi, Henry Rosemont, Jr., and Roger T. Ames. "Chinese Philosophy: A Philosophical Essay on the State-of-the-Art." *Journal of Asian Studies*, 54(3), 1995, pp. 727–758.

Lo, Guang. *Zhongguo zhexue sixiang shi*, 7 vols. Taipei: Xuesheng, 1986.

MacIntyre, Alasdair. *Whose Justice? Which Rationality?* Notre Dame, Ind.: University of Notre Dame Press, 1988.

Mei, Y. P. "Ancient Chinese Philosophy According to the *Chuang Tzu*, Chapter 33, 'The World of Thought,' with an English Translation of the Chapter." *Tsing Hua Journal of Chinese Studies*, New Series, 4(2), 1964.

Mou, Zongsan. *Xinti yu xingti*, 3 vols. Taipei: Zhengzhong, 1973.

Passmore, John. "Philosophy." In *Encyclopedia of Philosophy*, Vol. 6, ed. Paul Edwards. New York: Macmillan and Free Press, 1967.

Perelman, Chaim, and Anna Olbrechts-Tyteca. *The New Rhetoric: A Treatise on Argumentation*. Notre Dame, Ind.: University of Notre Dame Press, 1969.

Rescher, Nicholas. *Methodological Pragmatism*. New York: New York University Press, 1977.

Standaert, Nicolas. "The Discovery of the Center through the Periphery: A Preliminary Study of Feng Youlan's *History of Chinese Philosophy* (New Version)." *Philosophy East and West*, 45(4), 1995, pp. 569–590.

Tang, Junyi. *Zhongguo zhexue yuanlun*, 7 vols. Taipei: Xuesheng, 1978.

Watson, Burton, trans. *The Complete Works of Chuang Tzu*. New York: Columbia University Press, 1968.

———, trans. *Hsün Tzu: Basic Writings*. New York: Columbia University Press, 1963.

Wittgenstein, Ludwig. *Philosophical Investigation*, 3rd ed., trans. G. E. M. Anscombe. New York: Macmillan, 1958.

Zhexue cidian, 4th ed. Taipei: Commercial Press, 1976.

Zhong, Shaohua. "Qingmo zhongguo ren tuiyi zhexue de zhuichiu." *Newsletter of the Institute of Chinese Literature and Philosophy*, 2(2), 1992. (Taipei: Academia Sinica. See especially pp. 162–167.)

Philosophy of Art

Stanley MURASHIGE

As in the west, the arts in China have maintained a distinction between the high arts and the arts of craftsmanship. Traditionally, the supreme forms of artistic expression were calligraphy and painting; and within painting, by the tenth and eleventh centuries, landscape painting, literally "mountain and water" painting (*shanshui hua*), emerged as the most important subject. The other arts, such as sculpture, jade carving, ceramics, lacquerware, silk embroidery and weaving, cloisonné, bamboo, ivory, and wood carving, though highly admired by connoisseurs, were not of the same stature as either calligraphy or painting. The appreciation of sculpture is an interesting and little explored phenomenon. Extant large-scale sculpture in stone, clay, or bronze is principally Buddhist, funerary, heraldic, or protective; and much early sculpture, primarily earthenware figurines, was made exclusively for interment within tombs. Generally speaking, sculpture, particularly Buddhist sculpture, whether large or small, was of less interest to the traditional connoisseur. With these considerations in mind, this article will concern itself primarily with the philosophy of painting.

The earliest extant writings specifically addressing the art of painting date from the fourth, fifth, and sixth centuries; and these writings survive only in editions from the Ming dynasty (1368–1644) or as quotations in Zhang Yanyuan's (c. 815–after 875) *Lidai minghua ji* (*Record of Famous Painters through the Dynasties*) of c. 847, itself known only in editions from the Ming. Three of the most important early texts—*Hua shanshui xu* (*Introduction to the Painting of Landscape*) by Zong Bing (375–443), *Lunhua* (*Discussing Painting*) by Gu Kaizhi (c. 345–406), and *Xuhua* (*Discussing Painting*) by Wang Wei (415–443)—are quoted in *Lidai minghua ji*, a rich compilation of mythical origins, biographies, essays on connoisseurship, critical judgments, and recorded observations.

Perhaps the most important period in the literature on the aesthetics of painting after the Northern and Southern dynasties (420–589) and the Tang dynasty (618–906) was the Song dynasty (960–1279). Much important aesthetic literature was written by charismatic members of the scholar-official elites. Significant surviving statements on the art of painting come, for example, from Su Shi (1037–1101) and Huang Tingjian (1045–1105), both important government officials and talented painters, poets, and calligraphers. Mi Fu (1052–1107), an important painter, calligrapher, connoisseur, and scholar, compiled a rich document of his observations, thoughts, and criticism in a text called *Huashi* (*A History of Painting*). A substantial compilation of teachings on mountain and water painting, by the eleventh-century imperial court painter Guo Xi (after 1000–c. 1090), the *Linquan gaozhi* (*The Lofty Truth of Forests and Streams*), survives in an early twelfth-century compilation by Guo Xi's son Guo Si (d. after 1123). Other important surviving texts are: *Tuhua jianwen zhi* (*Record of Things Seen and Heard with Regard to Painting*, c. 1080) by Guo Ruoxu (active in the first half of the eleventh century); *Shanshui Chunquan ji* (*Chunquan's Collected Notes on Landscape*) by Han Zhuo (active c. 1095–1125); *Huaji* (*On Painting*, c. 1167) by Deng Chun (twelfth century); and *Hua shanshui jue* (*The Secrets of Painting Landscapes*) by Li Chengsou (c. 1150–after 1221). Another important text, usually discussed in the context of writings from the Song dynasty, is *Bifaji* (*Note on the Art of the Brush*) by Jing Hao (c. 870–c. 930).

Much of the literature on painting from the ensuing dynasties—the Yuan (1279–1368), Ming (1368–1644), and Qing (1644–1911)—furthers ideas that emerged during Song times. Perhaps two of the major later contributions to the Chinese discourse on the aesthetics of painting are the writings of Dong Qichang (1555–1636) and Shitao (1642–c. 1707; also identified in modern studies as Dao Ji or Yuan Ji). Dong Qichang's writings have principally contributed to subsequent art historical writing, and his writings have had influence well into our era. Shitao's major written work specifically addresses issues in the practice, theory, and philosophy of Chinese painting. The major work is the *Hua yulu* (*Enlightening Remarks on Painting*), which expresses his theories and views on painters' approaches and methods.

The surviving early literature suggests that the aesthetics of Chinese painting was first articulated during the fourth through the sixth centuries. But these early writings are difficult to interpret. They are brief, are removed from their historical contexts, included textual corruptions and errors of transmission, and are not what a western philosophical tradition would regard as analytical discourses on clearly defined aesthetic positions. Indeed, any study of the philosophy or aesthetics of Chinese painting must sift through writing that is often a complex mixture of connoisseurship, commentary, general discussions of technique and method, anecdotes, chronological records, and statements of general principles. When philosophical issues are discussed, they usually appear as restatements or reaffirmations of generally accepted truths. The philosopher trained in western methods will be hard put to find the long analytical arguments and rigorously formulated definitions familiar in western discourse on aesthetics. Chinese aesthetic discourse shares the open-textured character of its counterpart in philosophy. Aesthetic terms respond to the exigencies of context and obtain meaning only within a particular context. Chinese aesthetic terminology and rhetoric occasions interpretation and demands implementation. In this sense, Chinese aesthetic writing is also about practice. Texts, such as Guo Xi's *Linquan gaozhi* or Shitao's *Hua yulu*, though often read as theoretical treatises, are also manuals on the practice of painting. As in Chinese philosophy, performance lies at the heart of Chinese aesthetics.

Beauty is notably not an important issue in the literature on painting, and when it does arise, it appears as "outward beauty," superficial and unworthy of good painting. Instead, much of the literature, whether explicitly or implicitly, asserts the power of painting to embody, convey, or transmit a special reality. Gu Kaizhi's *Lunhua* uses the expression *zhuanshen*, "transmit the spirit," suggesting that figure painting, if successful, could and should convey the singular character of its subject. Zong Bing's *Hua shanshui xu*, from a Buddhist point of view, outlines the power of painting to embody the karmic efficacy of mountains and streams, that is, of nature. Guo Xi in the eleventh century claims that one may experience the reality of mountains while at home by viewing a great painting. The scholar-official aesthetic that emerges in the Song dynasty and will come to dominate later aesthetics claims that painting, as well as calligraphy, may effectively communicate the moral character of the practitioner. So powerful were painting and calligraphy in this regard that one could base critical judgments on the character of the artist.

One may trace this faith in the efficacy of images at least as far back as the Shang dynasty (c. 1700–1045 B.C.E.), when theriomorphic forms, some recognizable—bovine animals, birds, elephants, etc.—and some not, bestow power on bronze ceremonial vessels and their contents of food and millet wine. Much of the imagery of art in the Han dynasty (206 B.C.E.–220 C.E.) would seem possessed of a talismanic power to protect, guide, nurture, or entertain the dead. Moreover, like rites and ceremonies, images had the power to forge, affirm, and reaffirm kinship ties among the living, as well as between the living and their ancestral spirits. By the ninth century, Zhang Yanyuan, in the *Lidai minghua ji*, proclaims the power of painting to foster and promote appropriate social relations and values. Zhang restates the mythic origins of writing and painting, observing how each played its important role in the founding and cultivation of human society.

The urge to bring the power of images into the world of human activity finds its clearest expression in the aesthetics of the Song dynasty, particularly in the writings of the educated elites who served as officials in the government bureaucracies. The writings of Su Shi (1037–1101), Huang Tingjian (1045–1105), Mi Fu (1052–1107), and many others, as well as the writings of less prominent figures, such as Guo Ruoxu (active in the last half of the eleventh century), and of painters, such as Guo Xi (after 1000–c. 1090), attest to the rising importance of painting in the social, ethical, political, and philosophical discourse of Song culture. It is in Song writings on the arts that the human being assumes his place as the principal agent in the efficacy of imagery. Along with calligraphy, painting becomes one of the supreme arts, particularly suited to the expression of the artist's character and moral constitution. Susan Bush and Hsih-hsio Yen (1985) have noted that the supreme power of art, identified in earlier times as *qiyun*, is in Guo Ruoxu's *Tuhua jianwen zhi* identified with the painter. The talismanic efficacy of the image is now more clearly and specifically situated in the charismatic and moral quality of the artist. As the literature often proclaims, painting derives its potency from the insightful performance of the well-educated artist and becomes a spontaneous play of personal expression. This idea of painting comes to dominate art writing during the next centuries and into the modern era; and one may see the continuing history of painting aesthetics as a restatement or inflection of this central theme. In the Song dynasty and especially in the Yuan dynasty, the aesthetic formula incorporates the power of tradition, as the painter-literatus begins, consciously, to comprehend a classical past within the person of the artist. At this point, painterly expression assumes the power to express and re-create both the past and the present, as revealed in the individuality of the artist.

Perhaps the most important principle in the aesthetics of Chinese painting was *qiyun*, variously translated as "spirit consonance," "rhythmic vitality," "sympathetic responsiveness of the vital spirit," "vitality," and "harmonious manner." The life of things in a successful painting was called *qi* or *qiyun*. Both terms appear in art writing in Northern and Southern dynasties and remain important throughout the history of traditional aesthetics of painting to the present day. Lending themselves to diverse interpretations, the terms are impossible to translate adequately: they are multiple in connotation and meaning, and their significance shifts incessantly with context and history.

Perhaps the most widely discussed and studied adumbration of *qiyun* is in *Six Principles*, or *Liufa*, by Xie He (fl. c. 500–535). Scholars of Chinese art (Acker, Cahill, Fong, Soper, and others) have struggled to define the meaning of the term as articulated in *Six Principles*; recently, some, like Martin Powers (1991), have tried to place this early usage of the term in its historical context. Xie He does not discuss, analyze, or interpret these laws or principles but merely enumerates them.

Qiyun appears in the first and most important of the following principles. The first (principle) is *qiyun shengdong shi ye*, the consonance of vital rhythm within engendering movement. The other five principles would enumerate the means by which a painter may effect *qiyun shengdong* in his or her painting. Meant in part to be a critical as well as an aesthetic principle, *qiyun shengdong* denotes the animating power inherent in nature, in all things, and in a painting (if the painting is successful). *Qi* means "breath," "vapor," "spirit," or "vital force"; *yun* denotes "resonance," "rhyme," "harmony," or "consonance." *Qi* suggests something in motion, barely tangible, perceived and sensed in shifting relationships of form and appearance. *Yun* suggests a condition of harmony and confluence among these moving, changing relationships. Power lives in motion. Indeed, some later (Qing dynasty) writings substitute the character *yun*, meaning "motion" or "rotation," for the earlier *yun*, meaning "resonance" and "consonance."

The expression *shengdong* suggests that the life of anything is manifest both in movement and in the engendering of something by another. *Sheng* means "life," "to live," "to give birth," "to engender" and thus names the creative and transformative character of existence. *Dong* means "motion," "movement," "to move" and denotes the gestures of form and the interaction and exchange among forms. *Shengdong* addresses the formal or phenomenal character of existence and defines existence as gesture, movement, and metamorphosis; it identifies the formal or phenomenal character of *qiyun* in operation.

Xie He's first principle, *qiyun shengdong*, constitutes an ever-changing cosmos of correlations, correspondences, and consonances among rhythmic patterns of motion—qualities evident in the linearity and shifting points of view in Chinese painting, and in Chinese art in general. The value bestowed on the brush and ink in Chinese aesthetics reflects the importance of linearity and rhythmic patterns in Chinese art.

Xie He's second principle concerns the handling of the brush: *gufa yongbi*, literally "bone method," "use the brush." James Cahill (1961) translates this as "use the brush [with] the bone method"; William B. Acker (1954, 1974) translates it as "bone method, which is [a way of] using the brush." The specific meaning of this principle remains open to interpretation, although generally it is thought to recommend some structural principle in the handling of the brush. Much of the critical writing from the period of the Northern and Southern dynasties into the modern era addresses the importance of brushwork, either directly or implicitly. Zhang Yenyuan in the *Lidai minghua ji* considers brushwork in his discussion of important painters of the Tang dynasty. Jing Hao, in his *Bifaji*, identifies four "forces" or "kinetic dispositions," *shi*, in brushwork and characterizes them in the context of achieving *qi* and *yun* in painting nature. Shitao's *Huayulu* is in effect a treatise on the cosmological efficacy of the *yihua* or "singular brush stroke."

In Chinese painting, the fluctuation of line and pattern embodies the meaning and character of the subject, whether the human figure or nature. The world appears as vital rhythms, gestures, actions, and responses signaled by the polyphonic movement of brush strokes and by the temporal play among the forms and objects within an image. Time, and relationships changing in time, impart vitality to the image and reveal the animating power inherent in things. Rhythm is always relational; it consists of a complex of responses that happens in an exchange among relations: *qiyun* lives in the reflections of things within one another, and in the harmonious responses of different points of view with respect to each other. *Qiyun* is itself the harmonious rhythm of response. A painter who grasps this principle participates in the vitality of this unfolding rhythm.

In nature, *qiyun* is the consonance of response—of statement and rejoinder—that plays itself out among the myriad relations constituting the natural world. Vitality is the rhythm of response, or the gestures of motion that happen spontaneously, as the infinite modes or perspectives of nature shift in relation to each other. What defines existence or a thing in nature is thus not its circumscribable "objecthood" but its active relations. Things do not live as self-enclosing, limiting, delimiting essences, bound in and of themselves; rather, they live as inflection and exchange among shifting points of view. Perspectives that encounter each other engender response, and exchange, and mutual inflection. *Qiyun* may be passive, as the potential or propensity for response, or active, as the actual response. A dialogue ensues in which one response engenders another in a cycle of infinite alternation and permutation; and within this dialogue, the interlocutors see themselves both mirrored in the gestures of exchange and as themselves—the very gestures of the exchange. The identity of each perspective plays itself out in the exchange of responses, as nothing other than those very responses. Life and vitality reside in the gestures of performance as performance itself. Whether one speaks of one or the other, one is merely articulating the same singular exchange, the same identity, from different points of view. *Qiyun* is the rhythmic pulse of such exchanges.

One may see *qiyun* as simultaneously form and content. As content, *qiyun* is constancy, formative power, cause, and possibility; it bestows on all form or matter the propensity for action and response. In nature, *qiyun* lives as the disposition or inclination of things to respond to given conditions in certain ways: water flows downward, mountains rise upward; water is yielding, mountains are unyielding; the clash of warm humid air and cold air produces thunderstorms; birds fly, fish swim; large animals often prey on smaller ones. In human society, *qiyun* happens in kinship ties and the performance of social roles. *Qiyun* imparts the urge and potential to form social bonds, from the biological bonds of family to the more general bonds of community. *Qiyun* structures identity and individuality by bestowing an urge for interaction and communication.

As form, *qiyun* appears as particular responses to the unique character of given situations. A particular mountain derives its special character from the way it "responds" to its geography and climate. A mountain is endowed with its own propensities and inclinations—height, breadth, solidity, etc.—played out in its particular geography, geology, and climatic conditions.

Given its disposition, the mountain responds to its given conditions; it grows and achieves its own particular shape. But the mountain's circumstances in turn determine its peculiar geological and geographic character, further shaping its disposition, its propensity to respond. The mountain's identity is thus an endless cycle of exchange between potential responses and a history of particular responses. The mountain in a sense "makes itself" in the character of its responses, but it is also "made" in that it must respond to given, changing situations. Its identity is a tautology that plays itself out in the rhythm of this exchange. One is befuddled if one searches for either origins or ends, or for borders or boundaries that define or circumscribe the identity of the thing. In *qiyun*, the identity of the mountain, or of anything, dwells in the rhythm of exchange, simultaneously as form and content, origin and end.

If it represents anything at all, a painting represents the *qiyun* of its subject, that is, the subject's particular pattern of rhythm and response. The painter strives to render the rhythm of the exchange, to embody it in the image. Thus a painting entails layers of exchange in infinite complexity: exchange among forms within the subject, between the painter and the subject, between the painter and the world at large, between the subject and the world at large, between the painter and the painting, between the subject and the painting, between the painting and the viewer, between the viewer and the world at large, between the viewer and the subject, and so on and on. The identity of a painting expands and contracts in concentric circles of mutual influence, so that it no longer seems to work at all as a representation of something beyond itself. The identity of anything in *qiyun* is like a bending mirror whose endlessly shifting reflections turn with one's shifting point of view. Whether we address *qiyun* or its phenomenal presence, *shengdong*, depends only on our point of view, not on any inherent differences in the ontology of either.

The interactive, relational character of *qiyun* shapes the meaning of another important term in art writing of the Northern and Southern dynasties. The expression *lei*, "likeness or semblance of kind," is an important concept in logical discourse. As A. S. Cua (1985) points out, in Confucian ethics *lei* is particularly important for explanation and justification in ethical discourse. In art historical discourse *lei* has often been taken to mean likeness of form and has thus been linked with the expression *xingsi*, which more clearly denotes likeness of appearance or form. The term *lei* is of particular importance in Zong Bing's *Hua shanshui xu*. In his study of Zong Bing's text, Kiyohiko Munakata (1983) has argued against a formalist reading of *lei* and suggests that *lei* may have roots in ritual categories of correspondence. He argues that the use of the term *lei* in the *Hua shanshui xu* may denote a kind of karma of sympathetic response. What constitutes likeness is less a matter of resemblances of form, *xingsi*, than either ritual or, in a Buddhist context, karmic correspondences.

Claims that mimesis or formal likeness (*si* or *xingsi*) is relatively unimportant abound in the literature on painting. Alhough formal resemblance is never denied its proper place, it must satisfy the efficacy of *qi* and *qiyun*. *Qiyun* remains the painter's ideal, but it is difficult to achieve. Formal resemblance, on the other hand, is all too easy to achieve. The painter's fault lies in his or her inability to achieve the appropriate relationship between these two qualities. Art writing of the literati in the Song dynasty makes clear the writers' distaste for painting that gives too much significance to formal semblance or to a show of beauty. These lines from a poem by Su Shi (1037–1101), here translated by Susan Bush, are often cited as evidence of this attitude in the Song dynasty:

> If anyone discusses painting in terms of formal likeness,
> His understanding is nearly that of a child.

Ouyang Jiong (896–971), in a discussion of the painter Huang Quan quoted in the *Yizhou minghua lu* (*Record of Famous Painters of Yizhou*), notes the importance of achieving a balance of *qiyun* and formal likeness, *xingsi*. In a translation by Susan Bush and Hsio-yen Shih, the passage reads:

> Within the Six Elements (*liu fa*) [of painting], only two, formal likeness (*xingsi*) and spirit resonance (*qiyun*) are of the first importance. If a painting has spirit resonance, but not formal likeness, then its substance (*zhi*) will dominate over its pattern (*wen*), if it has formal likeness, but not spirit resonance, then it will be beautiful (*hua*), but not substantial.

A similar kind of balance is advocated by Jing Hao in the Five Dynasties period. Painting is not merely about *hua*, beauty or outward appearance; it is also about *hua*, or "measuring," in Kiyohiko Munakata's translation. The painter (again in Munakata's translation, 1974):

> examines the objects and grasps their reality (*zhen*). He must grasp the outward appearance (*hua*) from the outward appearance of the object, and the inner reality (*shi*) from the inner reality of the object. He must not take the outward appearance and call it the inner reality. If you do not know this method [of understanding truth], you may get lifelikeness but never achieve reality in painting.

The reality or inner reality referred to here is both its *qi* and its phenomenal substance, *zhi*. *Qi* is inseparable from particular phenomena and in this sense is never an abstractable essence. In painting, inner reality and outward appearance must be balanced, because they are mutually dependent. Each defines the existence of the other, and each is the measure of the other. *Hua* as measuring thus addresses the efforts of the painter to realize this balance. The painter in a sense "measures" the proper balance in the exchange of outward appearance, *hua*, and inner reality, *shi*. If successful, the painting will reveal the harmonious, and most appropriate, play of responses: the rhythm of exchange that defines the life of things.

Confusion results when one reads "inner reality" and "outward appearance" as a mutually exclusive duality, an absolute and insurmountable difference. The Song critique of formal likeness is not a denial of either its reality or its ontological value. One must not mistake the Song critique for a modernist critique of form. From the modernist perspective, outward form is but a medium or conveyance for some invisible, incorporeal content. Form merely serves content and must never be taken for content itself. A dynamic tension, a dialectic, lives between the two, but it remains a tension premised on a relationship of opposition and separation. Paradoxically or perhaps tragically, meaning, or identity, must define itself by something perpetually other than itself.

Here one might suggest a different reading of *lei* and a different role for *xingsi* within the workings of *qiyun*. Building on Munakata's argument, one might define *lei* as the structure of correspondences and correlations among things within particular contexts or circumstances. *Lei* thus identifies the specific relationships of form or structure by which interactions play themselves out in given situations: if nature is a rich complex of rhythmic exchange, then it plays itself out in the metamorphosis of the four seasons. Nature is *lei* with respect to the seasons; and the seasons are *lei* with respect to nature. Moreover, the seasons are *lei* with respect to each other, and within each season certain phenomena are *lei* with respect to that particular season as well as with respect to each other: snow and winter are *lei*; and heat and shady trees are *lei* with respect to summer. Mountains are *lei* with great height, ascending movement, and the solidity of rock; water is *lei* with descending motion, fluid intangibility, and the growth of flora; mountains are *lei* with respect to water—hence the term *shanshui*, "mountains and water," for landscape. In Guo Xi's *Linquan gaozhi*, the emperor and the great mountain may be said to be *lei* with respect to each other, although Guo Xi does not actually use the term *lei*. Kuo Hsi (1959) finds a particularly close correspondence between the world of human society and that of the mountain. Indeed, this social character of the relationship between humankind and nature becomes the dominant focus of *qiyun* from the Song dynasty on.

Given its ethical significance, categories of *lei* operate within human interaction. In human discourse, *lei* resides in social roles, hierarchies, and kinship ties: father and son may be said to be *lei* with respect to each other; husband and wife are *lei*. Particular social gestures, clothing, and speech are *lei* with respect to each other within the contexts of given social situations and social roles: in the contemporary west, one might say that black tie, patent leather shoes, and a cummerbund are *lei* with respect to each other on formal social occasions, but they are not *lei* with respect to casual gatherings. *Lei* may indeed connote a likeness of form and appearance, but this likeness is above all measured by the nature of the interaction and exchange and is only coincidentally iconic. Resemblances among forms may or may not reflect correspondences of *lei*.

One might define *lei* as correspondences and correlations at work within an ever-changing, self-defining body of ritual, social, cultural, or aesthetic conventions. Related to *li*—rites, ceremonies, decorum—*lei* addresses correspondences among the elements of *li*. And like *li, lei* may specify particular correlations (or likenesses) or may refer to such correspondences or likenesses in general. *Lei* is thus both particular and general in meaning and connotation.

Lei in its particular mode defines and prescribes specific correspondences among artistic media, subject matter, motifs, combinations of motifs, use of color, rhetoric of brush and ink, compositional relationships, format, figural types, etc. Sometimes misleadingly, historians refer to particular modes of such conventions as "styles." *Lei* in its general mode names the principle of correspondence itself and denotes the "likeness" among diverse points of view, or modes at work within any given condition or situation.

Lei in either its general or its specific mode is rarely if ever spelled out in the literature of the Northern and Southern dynasties, and although the term itself is of little importance in writing on painting after this period, its structure resonates in later texts, such as Jing Hao's *Bifaji*, Guo Xi's *Linquan gaozhi*, and Han Zhuo's *Shanshui Chunquan ji*. Although these texts do not address the term *lei* or its possible meanings, they do identify and enumerate both general and specific structures of correspondence in nature and in the process and materials of painting.

Whereas *qi* lives as the harmonious rhythm, *yun*, that oscillates between mutually reflecting points of view, *lei* names the structures of correspondence that inhere within *qiyun*, that are engendered by *qiyun*, and that are the means by which *qiyun* obtains phenomenal manifestation. If *qiyun* is the rhythmic play that is in and of itself vitality, then *lei* is the harmonious and phenomenal structure through which this vitality plays itself out. *Lei* is then but another aspect or mode of *qiyun*, and the categories, conventions, gestures, and rhetoric constituted as *lei* share the tautological character of *qiyun*. Though social, *lei* does not arise from an assumed dichotomy between nature and culture, and thus it should not be considered either artificial or synthetic.

The conventions of painting, and the correspondences of things as depicted in painting, ultimately derive from the interaction of certain charismatic personae with nature. Brief, often repeated accounts of the origins of painting and writing (see, for example, the opening chapter of Zhang Yanyuan's *Lidai minghua ji*) recount these fertile exchanges. Cang Jie, the legendary semihistorical figure who gave form to writing and painting by gazing up at the constellations and observing the tracks of birds in the soil, did not "invent" writing and painting but rather established some kind of principle, some kind of graphic formula that carried within it the basic rhythm of his encounter with nature. Neither Cang Jie's invention nor something bestowed on him by nature, this principle or formula embodies the structure of question and answer, response and rejoinder, that happened in the encounter between Cang Jie and nature. The principle thus circumscribes both Cang Jie and nature and constitutes them as commutable and self-reflecting modes of the same existence. Identity is here neither one nor the other but the singular exchange itself, and the phenomenal and social character of *lei* emerges as the natural instantiation of that identity.

While much of modern scholarship recognizes and addresses the profound difficulties of Chinese art theory and aesthetics, many students of Chinese aesthetics at least implicitly assume a dichotomy between representational and nonrepresentational approaches, between naturalistic and expressionistic, between objective and subjective attitudes toward making art. This assumption persists in the current discourse on Chinese aesthetics and on the art of the literati or scholar-officials. One continues to see this in the scholarly literature on the Song dynasty and the literati's critique of *xingsi*, formal likeness. But the assumption may obscure other ways of reading the formulation of identity and meaning as they emerge in Chinese aesthetics.

See also Aesthetics; Calligraphy; *Li*: Rites or Propriety; *Sheng*; *Shenming*.

Bibliography

Acker, William. *Some T'ang and Pre-T'ang Texts on Chinese Painting*. Leiden: Brill, 1954 and 1974.

Bush, Susan. *The Chinese Literati on Painting: Su Shih (1037–1101) to Tung Ch'i-ch'ang (1555–1636)*. Harvard-Yenching Institute Studies, Vol. 27. Cambridge, Mass.: Harvard University Press, 1971.

———. "Tsung Ping's Essay on Painting Landscape and the 'Landscape Buddhism' of Mount Lu." In *Theories of the Arts in China*, ed. Susan Bush and Christian Murck. Princeton, N.J.: Princeton University Press, 1983, pp. 132–163.

Bush, Susan, and Hsio-yen Shih, eds. *Early Chinese Texts on Painting*. Cambridge, Mass.: Harvard University Press, 1985.

Cahill, James. "The Six Laws and How to Read Them." *Ars Orientalis*, 4, 1961, pp. 372–381.

Chou, Ju-hsi. *The Hua-yü-lu and Tao-chi's Theory of Painting*. Arizona State University Center for Asian Studies Occasional Papers, Vol. 9. Tempe: Arizona State University, 1977.

Cua, A. S. *Ethical Argumentation: A Study in Hsün Tzu's Moral Epistemology*. Honolulu: University of Hawaii Press, 1985.

Fong, Wen. "Ch'i-Yün-Sheng-Tung: Vitality, Harmonious Manner, and Aliveness." *Oriental Art*, 12(3), 1966, pp. 159–164.

Hay, John. "Values and History in Chinese Painting, I." *Res*, 6, autumn 1983, pp. 72–111.

———. "Values and History in Chinese Painting, II." *Res*, 7–8, spring–autumn 1984, pp. 102–136.

Hurvitz, Leon. "Tsung Ping's Comments on Landscape Painting." *Artibus Asiae*, 32, 1970, pp. 146–156.

Kuo, Hsi (Guo Xi). *Lin-ch'üan kao-chih: An Essay on Landscape Painting*, trans. Shio Sakanishi. London: Murray, 1959.

Lin, Yutang. *The Chinese Theory of Art: Translations from the Masters of Chinese Art*. New York: Putnam, 1967.

Maeda, Robert J. *Two Twelfth-Century Texts on Chinese Painting*. Michigan Papers in Chinese Studies, Vol. 8. Ann Arbor: University of Michigan Press, 1973.

Munakata, Kiyohiko. *Ching Hao's Pi-fa Chi: A Note on the Art of the Brush*. Ascona: Artibus Asiae, 1974.

———. "Concepts of Lei and Kan-lei in Early Chinese Art Theory." In *Theories of the Arts in China*, ed. Susan Bush and Christian Murck. Princeton, N.J.: Princeton University Press, 1983, pp. 105–131.

Powers, Martin J. "Character (*Ch'i*) and Gesture (*Shih*) in Early Chinese Art and Criticism." In *Proceedings: Painting and Calligraphy*, Part 2. International Colloquium on Chinese Art History. Taipei, Taiwan: National Palace Museum, 1991, pp. 909–931.

Sakanishi, Shio. *The Spirit of the Brush*, 4th ed. London: Murray, 1957.

Shih-t'ao (Shitao). *Enlightening Remarks on Painting*, ed. and trans. Richard E. Strassberg. Pacific Asia Museum Monographs, Vol. 1. Pasadena, Calif.: Pacific Asia Museum, 1989.

Sirén, Osvald. *The Chinese on the Art of Painting*. New York: Schocken, 1963.

Soper, Alexander C. "The First Two Laws of Hsieh Ho." *Far Eastern Quarterly*, 8(4), August 1949, pp. 412–423.

———. *Kuo Jo-hsü's [Guo Ruoxu's] Experiences in Painting (T'u-hua chien-wen chih): An Eleventh Century History of Chinese Painting*. Washington, D.C.: American Council of Learned Societies, 1951.

Zhongguo hualun leibian (Chinese Texts on Painting Arranged According to Category), ed. Yu Jianhua. Beijing: Zhongguo gudian Yishu chuban she, 1957. (Reprint, 1997.)

Philosophy of Change

Chung-ying CHENG

The book known as *I Ching* or *Yijing* (*Book of Changes*) has, since the Han dynasty, been acknowledged as the leading work among the Confucian classics (variously known as the Six Classics or Five Classics). The present version of the *Yijing* is said to have been composed or edited by King Wen of Zhou (around the early twelfth century B.C.E.), and so it is also known as the Zhou *Yi*, to be distinguished from the *Yi* of Shang and the *Yi* of Xia, whose names are recorded in the *Liji*. In light of recent textual research and archaeological findings, the antiquity of *Yijing* is not to be doubted. The pertinent question is how early the book can be said to have first been developed.

Before that question can be answered, one must understand how the book is organized. There is in the first place a system of sixty-four symbols (*zhonggua*, hexagrams) that can be analyzed as combinations of 8 × 8 subsymbols (*gua*, trigrams), each of which has a name describing or indicating what it stands for. These symbols can be considered icons or indexes. Each symbol is attached to or associated with a judgment, prognosis, or evaluation of a given situation to which the symbol applies, in the sense of divination. Each line of a hexagram symbol is also numbered and gives an individual prognosis and evaluation implying action. These forms in the original text of the *Yijing* are known as the *jing*. Comments on and explanations of either a whole symbol or lines of the symbol are called "commentaries" (*zhuan*). The commentaries are traditionally known as the *Ten Wings* (*Yizhuan*); they include the "*Duan* Commentaries" (two parts), the "*Xiang* Commentaries" (two parts), the "*Wenyan* Commentary," *Xici*, the "*Shuo* Commentary," the "*Xu* Commentary," and the "*Zha* Commentary."

Given this complex organization, we may see the book as a result of a process of evolution. Such a process would begin with using cosmic symbols to understand and participate in natural processes and would culminate in an abstract (and abstruse) formulation of a comprehensive system of cosmology, culture, and ethics, in a later era when the philosophical mind and reflective reason are especially active. Specifically, we can perhaps date the book according to five stages of development.

1. 6000–2000 B.C.E., from the late Neolithic period to the founding of the first dynasty, the Xia: Observation of the cosmos and formation of basic cosmic symbols known as the eight trigrams.
2. 2000–1200 B.C.E., from the beginning of the Xia to the beginning of the Zhou: Divination using the cosmic map as a reference manual, producing judgments such as those recorded in oracle bones.
3. 1200–1100 B.C.E., at the beginning of the Zhou: Elaboration and systematization of the cosmic symbols and a sorting out of the divination judgments in correlation with the cosmic symbols, producing sixty-four hexagrams and correlating names and judgments with them.
4. Sixth century–fourth century B.C.E.: Interpretation of the symbols and judgments from a philosophical perspective, consistent with the underlying cosmic picture or image, producing the *Ten Commentaries* or *Ten Wings* (*Yizhuan*).
5. Second century–first century B.C.E., at the beginning of the Han dynasty: Standardization of texts and elaboration of symbolic and numerological meanings.

I shall discuss five topics corresponding to these five stages: (1) observational origins of the cosmology of changes; (2) philosophical implications and justification of divination; (3) the *Yijing* as a symbolic system of interpretation; (4) creativity, individuation, and decision making in the *Yijing*; (5) Confucius and the *Yijing* in Confucianism. I shall also consider how the philosophy of changes relates to Daoism, Buddhism, folklore, and modern science.

Observational Origins of the *Yijing* and Cosmography

Regarding the first stage in the development of the *Yijing*, a legendary culture hero named Fuxi is said to have invented the system of *gua* or *yi* symbols on the basis of his observations of nature and things in nature. There is some question whether or not Fuxi actually existed. However, there is no doubt that the eight basic symbols known as *bagua* signify the most notable natural phenomena a human being would normally come across and observe: heaven and earth, fire and water, lake and hill, wind and thunder. Humans would further observe that these natural phenomena are powers and processes of change and transformation which would account for the creation and destruction of things and life-forms. These natural phenomena can then be seen as forming a framework in which all things are to be located and all changes are to take place. Finally, humans would observe that things and life-forms found in nature are in some sense governed and participate in certain basic natural processes. Hence all things far and near, including cultural and technological inventions and human activities, could be related to these basic processes and powers—in so far as we experience correlations between them.

Clearly, it would take a long time to make such observations, which are assumed to be comprehensive in scope and profoundly insightful. Once made, however, the observations would lead to an understanding of the world characterized by unity of vision, totality of scope, a network of linkages and relations, and a multitude of concrete references and identifications. That indeed would be the goal of comprehending the world as it is given to us. This observational process is called *guan* (comprehensive and contemplative observation) in the *Xici*, and the resulting vision of the world is a cosmography of related powers and processes, a dynamic picture of the natural world in which things are to be situated.

Questions arise about the nature of *guan* in relation to the formation of the early symbolic system of cosmography in the *Yijing*. It is safe to say that *guan* was both a process and a method of observation intended to provide a total, holistic, relational, perspectival understanding of nature. *Guan* involves an attitude of detachment and what can be described as tranquillity and receptivity. It is a sense of seeking understanding and learning things without forcing any prior theoretical model onto nature and without being impeded by emotions and desires. It is not quite phenomenology in the sense of Husserl's conscious "bracketing-off," nor is it an objectivist methodology of attempting to capture the essences of objects exclusive of the feeling, perceiving mind. *Guan* can perhaps be described as seeing the natural world in terms of large and minute changes and relationships, on the basis of our general experiences of nature. Thus the resulting cosmic image, view, or vision—also known as *guan* (outlook or view)—is global, dynamic, individual, and rich in meaning; also, it is open to possible correlations and analogies with other observations of things, including human and cultural matters. We may call *guan* phenomenological observation or a natural phenomenological method as opposed to either rational scientific methodology or the phenomenology of rationality.

Historically, *guan* as a method was cultivated in both the Confucian and the Daoist tradition. It was also adopted by Chinese Buddhists, who merged the meanings of comprehensive observation and inner meditation, as is conveyed by the term *dyana* or *samadhi*. But *guan* as a way of reaching a deep and complete understanding of reality originates in the *Yijing*. In the text of the *Yijing*, we can identify and name the twenty-first hexagram of wind above and earth below as a special symbol for *guan*. As an icon and index this symbol suggests that one must maintain an upright, central position in order to observe the world. We may easily see how the system of symbols as a cosmography is based on comprehensive observation, by an observer who does not suffer from preconceptions or biases.

Logic of Divination and the Ethical Foundation of the Practical

The fashionable view today is that the *Yijing* began as a book of divination and should be seen essentially as something to consult for its divinations, judgments, and symbolism. Undeniably, the Zhou *Yi* was used in this way, as is alluded to in the divinatory practices recorded in *Zuozhuan*. In this sense, Zhu Xi is correct in saying that the book was formed from the practice of divination. However, we must ask how it could be used for divination if there were no underlying cosmic map to which diviners could refer for constituting or deriving meanings. Zhu Xi himself recognized that before King Wen there was "Fuxi," who must have observed the universe in order to provide insights that Wen could follow in making divinations. In this sense, we need to recognize that divination must presuppose the development of a cosmic map: this is necessary for the *Yijing* to be meaningful and fruitful as a guidebook for making practical decisions and acting so as to achieve benefits and avoid harm.

Divination is one use to which the Zhou *Yi* is put, but the Zhou *Yi* cannot be seen merely as a book of divination. Its rich, subtle cosmological significance enables it to be rediscovered and reconstrued metaphysically in the *Yizhuan*, and to be used for other purposes in other areas of life, such as medicine and military strategy. This explains why, by the time of Confucius and Xunzi, someone who is not engaged in divination can still can make moral or practical judgments—ordinary and extraordinary—based on an understanding of the Zhou *Yi*. The *Yijing* is, henceforth, read and interpreted as a book of profound wisdom and cosmic and ethical insights.

Divination was certainly practiced from the Shang on and was common until the late Spring-Autumn period. In this regard, then, the question is not simply whether one divines but why one divines and how one understands or interprets the results of divination. In general the reason why divination is practiced is that people are worried about the future, do not know what it holds for them, and therefore cannot determine what action to take. Specifically, we want to assess the possibilities of certain future events that concern us because they have to do with serious goals we want to attain or serious ills we want to avoid. Hence arise the "values" of future events, "beneficial" (*ji*) or "harmful" (*xiong*), and our sense that they may depend on our own actions. Divination becomes important because (albeit randomly) it refers a given concern to actuality and history and offers an occasion for articulating insights into the situation.

Divination relies on a method that guarantees randomness; it also uses certain meaningful rules. This entails that the result of divination must be related to a given situation or a given purpose (or both) if it is to yield an understanding of the present situation and the future event. This is why interpretation of the resulting *gua* is required, and the interpretation in turn requires experience and expertise. In short, divination can be seen as a method of "anchoring" the future in the present so that one can see alternatives, assess the "values" of their consequences, and take the appropriate actions.

With this analysis of divination, we can appreciate both its significance and its limitations and understand why the practice would wither when the philosophical understanding represented by the *gua* system arose. We can also understand that the logic and process of divination would, in a way, contribute to the elaboration and application of this hidden cosmology.

Divination is not a philosophy, but it has an underlying philosophy or logic. The underying logic is that divination should be seen as indicating both the limitations of the human condition and its freedom of decision and action. On the one hand, a human being is limited by his situation and even by his own purposes, and the future is not dictated by his wishes. On the other hand, he can seek knowledge of the future or a way of understanding its possibilities and can make his own decisions. Divination provides at once a way to reveal limitations in one's life and a way to change one's situation by acting appropriately.

On the basis of oracle inscriptions and the twenty-two recorded cases of divination using the Zhou *Yi*, one can identify certain criteria for divination:

1. One divines when one has a momentous or urgent problem at hand—not otherwise.
2. One divines when one has exhausted all one's knowledge and still cannot decide what to do.
3. One divines in order to relate a historical precedent to the present situation, or to identify one's position in the scheme of things.
4. A reasonable interpretation has to be given for the recommended action or actions.

5. One must choose or decide in the light of acceptable interpretations.

Hence divination does not imply determinism or fatalism; rather, it presupposes that a human being is a codeterminant of the future which is significant for him. We may call this understanding of divination "codeterminism by human interpretation and human choice."

One issue which pertains to the relevance of divination for the Zhou *Yi* is the discovery of "numerical hexagrams" (*xuzi gua*) recorded on bones, pottery, and bronze objects: the odd numbers 1, 5, 7, 9 and the even numbers 6 and 8 in the shape of ancient Chinese numerals. This seems to indicate that the Zhou *Yi* was developed as a matter of sorting out "numerical hexagrams." But, logically, the understanding of the *gua* as relevant in a given situation still requires reference to the "map of reality" that I suggested above—the cosmography conveyed in the *bagua* system. Furthermore, the evolution of the "number hexagrams" would converge on the representation of the *gua*, composed of *yin-yang* lines that, surprisingly, correspond to the numbers 1 and 8. This suggests that numbers are no substitute for the lines of the hexagrams which convey the images of the odd and even numbers.

Yijing as a Symbolic System of Interpretation

As we have seen, divination creates a need for interpretation, and interpretation of a symbol requires an appeal to a cosmic map or cosmography. There is no reason why the practical need for divination would prompt a theoretical or contemplative consideration of reality (or "world-reality"), which in turn would satisfy a practical need. We may ask which is primary, the practical or the theoretical; but in fact the two are interdependent and inseparable. With regard to the development of the system of *gua* as symbols for the interpretation of reality, we should realize that from the outset it presented reality by way of "comprehensive observation," so that each symbol could be interpreted adequately in divination.

Methodologically, there are four factors in the transformation or historical evolution of the *Yijing* texts into a philosophical treatise in the form of the commentaries.

First, one has to reflect on the system of the symbols as a whole in order to see how it captures reality as a field of changes and transformations. As noted earlier, this system of symbols can be seen as arising from precisely the effort to understand reality in the first place. To comprehend the texts philosophically is to rediscover or disclose the underlying cosmography by way of *guan*. To realize this is also to discover a method of understanding reality as it is presented to us.

Hence the second factor in this philosophical transformation is directly confronting the reality of natural phenomena and natural processes so that one can grasp the possibilities for understanding and action. The *Xici* says:

> Consequently, the superior man at rest observes the (natural) images and contemplates the judgments attached to the symbols for these images, whereas in action he observes their changes and contemplates the divination processes.

Even a superior man cannot read a *gua* without reference to an actual image of the world for which the *gua* stands. When we reflect on the whole system of symbols and understand how each part of it stands for the reality of changes, we attain profound insights into the representation, reformation, and theoretical elaboration of the cosmography within it.

The third factor is more hermeneutical than ontohermeneutical; nevertheless, it depends on the ontohermeneutical interpretation that has just been offered. Here we are concerned with reconciling the symbolic meanings of the hexagrams and the meanings of the original judgments (*ci*) attached to them. In a sense, the judgments are the first or original individual interpretations of the symbols (or images of the symbols), apart from the meanings they derive from the underlying cosmography. That these judgments are attached is basically a matter of contingency, even though we must acknowledge the sorting out and correlation that took place when the system was first formulated as a whole by an early thinker such as King Wen. Because of this contingent correlation, there is tension between the symbols and the judgments. To resolve that tension, various interpretative philosophies of the *Yijing* arose as the discourses were developed. Generally, two schools of interpretation are identified: (1) "image-number" (*xiangshu*), with the two subschools "image" and "number"; and (2) "meaning-principle" (*yili*), with the two subschools "meaning" and "principle." We should note that no school focuses on just one of these four dimensions (image, number, meaning, principle) to the exclusion of the others. In fact, the schools are reductionist rather than exclusionist in their interpretation of the symbols and judgments: each school would establish principles of interpretation on the basis of one dimension and then interpret the other dimensions by reducing them to it.

As a historical note, I might mention that in the early Han the image-number (*xiangshu*) school arose with scholars like Meng Xi and Jing Fang; it flourished throughout the Han era until Wang Bi of the Jing.

Wang Bi undertook a Daoist metaphysical critique of the image-number school and gave rise to the *yili* (meaning-principle) school. For Wang Bi himself the principle of the *dao* dominated the meanings of the language, and this no doubt led to the emergence of the meaning-and-principle interpretation of and commentary on the *Yijing* by Cheng Yi, one of the founders of neo-Confucianism in Northern Song. It is not until Zhu Xi that we see a synthetic approach to the interpretation of the *Yijing* which includes *xiangshu*. After Zhu Xi we see two tendencies—either to turn to the *xiangshu* considerations, as many *Yijing* scholars in the Qing dynasty did; or to transcend *xiangshu*, as Wang Yangming and Jiao Xun did. In recent times there appear to have been many meaning-focused studies, particularly in light of the discovery, in 1973, of the "Mawangdui silk manuscripts" of the Zhou *Yi*. There also seems to have been a contemporary revival of *xiangshu* in both China and Taiwan, stressing practical uses for individual purposes. The problem of how to resolve the tension between *xiangshu* and *yili* remains, however, since it reflects what actually exists in the original texts of the *Yijing*; these interpretations need to be integrated into a holistic understanding of reality and its representation in a system of symbols. Chung-ying Cheng (the present author) has stressed such a balanced and unified approach in his work on *Yijing* and its underlying methodology of ontohermeneutics. The approach would integrate image-number and meaning-principle as four dimensions of the *Yijing*'s philosophy of reality: perceptive experience, rational organization, the language of understanding, and the ontocosmology of reality.

Yijing as a Basis for Decision Making and Action

We now come to the fourth factor in the philosophical interpretation of the *Yijing*: human decisions and action. In this regard, the need for interpretation is practical; interpretation is to relate the present situation to a given symbolism—with primary meanings and associated meanings established by experience—so that we can make relevant decisions about action. The impetus for decision making is that we need or want to act in a particular situation; thus we may also say that the situation calls for a decision and action. This need reflects the ontology of our situated state of being, which is in turn a matter of changes in and transformations of the world. Our action is part of these changes and transformations, and they are required if we are to attain the goals that will expand our being and avoid the harmful or disastrous outcomes that would diminish our being. To make the correct decisions, we need to have understanding—that is, we need to place ourselves in a picture of the world in which our actions and choices are rhetorically, if not rationally, justified.

In this kind of practical interpretation, there are two considerations: (1) understanding the situation relative to one's problem so as to acquire a reason for acting one way or another; (2) assessing the quality and consequences of one's actions. The second consideration has no significance without the first; thus interpretation of the situation is a prerequisite for decision making and action.

Regarding the validity of interpretation of a given situation in the *Yijing*, there is the obvious problem of identifying its nature, either by divination or by knowledge. In the absence of knowledge, divination is a substitute; but when knowledge can be established, there is no need for divination. Note that what gives us the knowledge we need is an interpretation of the situation in light of a relevant worldview or cosmology—or finding a tacit interpretation which applies. In the *Yijing* texts, this tacit interpretation becomes explicit in the *Yizhuan*. Once knowledge is established, one can make a choice and decide what to do.

Apart from knowledge of a situation, but going along with such knowledge, there is a valuation of the situation. There are several categories of valuation: "auspicious" (*ji*), "small error" (*ling*), "regret" (*jiu*), "perilous" (*li*), "misfortune" (*xiong*). Of course, we can also note the absence of any of these features in a situation. These categories identify the nature of a known situation for the purpose of decision making and action. One has to make a decision about a proper action in order to compensate for the evil of a situation or to take advantage of the goodness of a situation. Here we see a duality between the situation as necessary or given and human action as a positive power of balance and transformation. One is position (*wei*); the other is movement (*dong*), as represented by the line (*yao*).

The crucial principle for decision and action is to achieve the maximum unity or harmony between position and movement, or situation and action. Although the *Yijing* texts normally indicate that one should try to reach unity and harmony, one also has the freedom not to seek that goal but instead to act on one's own wishes and take the consequences. In this sense the categories of valuation are not moral values, although they coincide with a moral life if one persists in attempting to maximize unity and harmony. However, one would have to see harmony as an overall norm or a general goal of life but tolerate disharmonious and yet morally right actions on certain occasions. This requirement reflects a cosmic worldview; thus morality has an ultimate cosmological significance—it is what would contribute to the ultimate goodness of the universe. This is precisely what is meant by "acting morally," which is, literally, acting according to the way (*dao*) of heaven and earth or acting so that one will "cherish and embrace primal harmony" (*baohe taihe*). Here again, there is no denial of free will, because free will is nothing but the independent power to act and transform according to an internal decision made in the light of knowledge. Free will is creativity with a consciousness of choice as rooted in the cosmic source, the *dao*.

One must recognize the realism of axiology together with the realism of human existence in the philosophy of the *Yijing*. There is also a sense of the link between the universe and the human being, reflected in the sense of a link between the creative changes of the universe and creative human actions. The purpose of interpreting the *gua* is enlightened understanding of such a link and enlightened action or inclination in light of it, so that both the universe and the person will maintain sufficient creative advances and transformations. Morality as free human action toward a vision or understanding of a situation is an aspect of this onto-cosmological process.

Confucius and the *Yijing* in Confucianism

One important question is how values such as benefits and harms to a person can be transformed into moral values: good and bad, right and wrong. The answer is to be found in the Confucian understanding of humans and human society. Confucius (551–479 B.C.E.) undertook the step of explicitly transforming cosmological thinking into moral consciousness and moral reasoning in an effort to define and develop the human being. First of all, Confucius recognized the universality of humanity, which he calls the virtue of *ren* (benevolent love) and which he attributes to every human being. He further recognized a necessary social ordering and harmonizing principle, which he calls *li* (proprieties, rites) and which has been instituted for the maintenance of humanity and the creation of civilization. We can detect two avenues by which Confucius developed his insights: (1) general observation and reflection on humanity and (2) historical understanding of human society. It was at the beginning of the Zhou that sources for these insights, if not the insights themselves, were formulated in the basic texts of the Zhou *Yi* and Zhou *Li* (which consist of the Zhou *Kuan* and *Yili*); therefore, we may say that Confucius inherited both insights and then made them explicit in his dialogues with his disciples.

Ren and *li* were the foundation or fountainhead of Confucius's thinking as he tried to reform and transform the society and individuals of his time. Perhaps a lack of such insights in the general populace made him acutely aware of a need to articulate and emphasize them. This would explain why Confucius devoted more than forty years to teaching after he became disillusioned with the politics of the Lu. More significantly, it would also explain the profound unity in his philosophy of man and society. When Confucius says, "To overcome oneself and restore the practice of proprieties is benevolent love" (*keji fuli wei ren*), he is fusing two notions—*li* and *ren*—into a unity with two distinct aspects.

The Confucian *Analects* may appear to be simply a collection of diverse dialogues and conversations between Confucius and his disciples. But the unifying thread in Confucius's thinking, and in his vision of humanity, is *xin* (heart-mind, feelings) and *ren*. His basic ideas of *ren* and *li* in unity lead to other ideas of polar contrasts and polar complementarity, as in various notions of virtues and human relationships. Eventually, there emerges an intense interest in thinking about the way of heaven (*tian*), which is rooted in the way of change and constancy in the *Yijing*. Confucius says in the *Analects* that "heaven does not speak" but simply lets the four seasons rotate and all things grow. This numinous feeling of heaven as a silent power underscores the creativity of the *taiji* or the *dao* in the *Yizhuan* (*Ten Wings*). It is also linked to Confucius's (perhaps earlier) notion of *tian* as a power capable of endowing him with innate virtue and also capable of sustaining human culture. With regard to the latter, one may argue that *tian* is a source for the rise of *ren* and *li*. Hence this *tian* is not the Daoist *dao*, which manifests itself more in nature than in man, but the *dao* of the *Yizhuan* from which human values and human cultures arise and flourish.

Confucius saw age fifty as a time of critical self-understanding in man, and this self-understanding was derived from knowledge of the mandate of heaven (*tianming*), which can be described as knowing in oneself the limitations of human life as well as the potentialities of human nature. To fulfill oneself by doing one's best to realize one's potentialities, within one's limitations, is to fulfill *tianming* for oneself. This suggests that one comes to know both the natural tendency of things, which is the way of heaven (*tiandao*), and one's own moral disposition, which is the way of man (*rendao*). One also comes to know that one should model oneself after the way of heaven, which is continuously creative and productive.

It might be suggested that this understanding came to Confucius because he devoted himself to the study of the *Yijing* after reaching age fifty. He makes a famous statement in the *Analects*: "Give me more years, and if I started to study the *Yi* by the age of fifty, I would then be free from big mistakes." This was the object of a philological critique by Ouyang Xiu in the Song period, but the critique seems unfounded, because the statement makes sense in the context of the *tianming*, Confucius's interest in studying the *Yi*, and his actual study of it. This leads to a useful suggestion that the *Analects* is based on Confucius's responses to and reflections on humanity dating from before he reached age fifty, whereas after age fifty, and particularly during a later period of his life, Confucius may have been intensely engaged in studying, reflecting on, and teaching the *Yi*. This could explain why a relatively large body of statements on items in the *Yi* were listed as direct quotations from Confucius in various parts of the *Xici* and other sources. Recent findings in the Mawangdui *Yijing* silk texts make it amply clear that in his later years Confucius engaged in enthusiastic discussions of the *Yijing*, seeking individual as well as general understanding that would lead to interpretations of diverse *gua*. On the basis of this understanding, Sima Qian's statement that Confucius completed the commentaries on the *Yijing* is not totally groundless. Historically, though, it is more likely that several disciples and their own disciples actually composed and edited commentaries which were originally inspired by Confucius.

Once we see how this implicit reference to the *Yi* cosmology of creativity and timely moral action in the *Analects* became conceptualized and developed in the formation of the *Yizhuan*, we are able to see how an explicit philosophy of the creative *tiandao* and the self-cultivating *rendao* became established in other, later Confucian writings after Confucius's own time. I mean specifically *Zhongyong* (*The Doctrine of the Mean*) and the *Mengzi* (*Mencius*). There one sees specifically how an ontocosmological unity of man and heaven could be transformed into a socially and politically meaningful unity of the way of man and the way of heaven. From this, one can easily come to see how the philosophical aspects of *Yijing* became involved with and part of the development of Confucianism. Ever since the time in the Former Han when Confucianism was established as a mainstream ideology and philosophy, the *Yijing* was known more as a source of cosmic wisdom than as a book for divination.

The rise of neo-Confucianism with *Yijing* as its guiding principle in the Song period was no accident. The challenges of Buddhism and Daoism as metaphysics, practical philosophy, and religion made *Yijing* a significant, even an outstanding, alternative. The focus is now on understanding the categories of being and nonbeing not just as as *wuji* and *taiji* but as principles constituting rationality (*li*) and the creative movement of something experienced as real—the vital force (*qi*). This understanding makes it possible to apply the philosophy of the *Yijing* to moral self-cultivation and to the political regulation of society. We can see that the tradition of *Yijing* is not only an origin of Chinese philosophy but the very ground of Confucianism and neo-Confucianism. In contemporary neo-Confucianism, this ontocosmological thinking seems to be treated from outside, yet in a deeper sense it still serves as an inspiration for absorbing, harmonizing, and integrating new challenges from modern science and western philosophical thought.

Yijing and Daoism and Modern Science

Since *Yijing* is a primary origin and source of Chinese philosophy, its relevance for Daoism should not be forgotten. The notion of the *dao* could have emerged in a relatively early period from a comprehensive observation of the cosmos and nature at large, and then have been written down in a later period. This could suggest why we find two philosophical positions regarding the notion of the *dao*: the Daoist concept of the *dao* as unspeakable and the *Yizhuan* (and essentially the Confucian–neo-Confucian) concept—"Alternation of one *yin* and one *yang* is called the *dao*." Perhaps the *Yizhuan* concept is a later response to the Daoist concept. But this may simply imply that the Daoist Laozi responded to a notion of the *dao* articulated by even earlier philosophers. If we contemplate the world of things and things in the world, do we come to some notion of the way things form and transform, interrelate and interact?

Both Laozi and the *Yizhuan* recognize the nature of the *dao* as a source; but with regard to how to describe the workings and the true identity of the *dao*, it seems clear that nothing can be articulated in language. Language develops primarily to refer to individual things and fixed categories, and so it cannot illuminate the *dao*. One can use language to allude to things beyond language, but not to describe them. In this respect there is really no contradiction between the *Laozi* and the *Yizhuan*. The real difference between the Daoist and Confucian concepts has to do with how the ontocosmology of the *dao* is to be applied to human life and action. The *Duan* and *Xiang* commentaries are no doubt Confucian-minded, urging participation and action on the part of the human being, in contrast with the Daoist idea of withdrawal and inaction. It is indeed possible to write a Daoist commentary on the *Yijing* texts of symbolism and judgments, as was done in the Ming era. The point here is that it is also possible for the *Yijing* to inspire the Daoist view of the source of things in the world. Actually, the *Yijing* can then be seen as providing all the basic elements of a naturalistic cosmology or even a naturalistic ethics. It might be said that *Yijing* has inspired and enriched the Daoist views of the world and continues to do so.

If the relation of the *Yinjing*'s philosophy to Confucianism and Daoism is internal and historical, its relation to modern science is external and theoretical. How and why the *Yijing* applies to modern science has to do with the abstract mathematical structure of the symbolism in the *Yijing* and the abstract theoretical nature of modern science. One can easily see how the primary interpretation of the *Yijing*'s symbolism as a system of *yin-yang* forces might operate in various scientific systems, which could then be seen as systems of *yi* symbolism on different levels of reality. Leibniz, for instance, was surprised to find his system of binary numbers confirmed in the "diagram of hexagrams" in the Fu Xi order. The natural system of DNA in modern biology could be expressed by the sixty-four *zhonggua*. In modern elementary physics, perhaps one could eventually formulate a system of quarks or even subquarks based on the binary system of *yi* symbolism. Such remarks suggest that a link between the scientific system and the underlying philosophy of the *Yijing* and its symbolic forms might be a subject of research based on experience, experimentation, identification, and interpretation. However, serious studies of that kind have yet to be initiated.

See also Confucianism: Confucius; Confucianism: Ethics; *Dao*; Laozi; *Li*: Rites or Propriety; *Qi; Ren; Tian; Yi* and *Li*; Zhu Xi.

Bibliography

Cheng, Chung-ying. *C Lilun: Yijing guanli zhexue* (C Theory: Yijing Management Philosophy). Taipei: Sanmin, 1995.

———. "Chanpu de quanshi yu hen zhi wuyi: Lun yichan yuanzhu sixiang de zhexue yansheng (Interpretation of Divination and Five Meanings of *Zhen*: On the Philosophical Extension of the Primary Idea of Divination in the *Yi Jing*)." *Zhongguo Wenhua*, Issue 9, February 1994, pp. 29–36.

———. "*Li* and *Ch'i* in the *I Ching*: A Reconsideration of Being and Non-Being in Chinese Philosophy." *Journal of Chinese Philosophy*, 14(1), 1987.

———. "On the Origin and the Futurity of the Yi Philosophy." In *Da Yi Collected Papers*, ed. Liu Dajun. Jinan, 1991.

———. "On the Same Substance and Common Origin of *Xiang (Image), Shu (Number), Yi (Meaning), Li (Principle)* in the Philosphy of the Yijing." *Zhou Yi Studies*, No. 1, 1990, pp. 1–14.

———. "On Timeliness (*Shih-Chung*) in the *Analects* and the I-Ching: An Inquiry into the Philosophical Relationship between Confucius and the I Ching." *International Sinological Conference Proceedings*, 1982.

———. "On Transformation as Harmony: Paradigms from the Philosophy of the *I Ching*, Part I." In *Philosophy of Harmony and Strife*, ed. Shu-hsien Liu and Robert Allinson. Hong Kong: Chinese University Press of Hong Kong, 1986.

———. "Philosophical Significances of *Guan* (Comprehensive and Contemplative Observation)." *International Studies of I Ching Theory* (Beijing), No. 1, 1995, pp. 156–203.

———. "Zhouyi and Philosophy of Wei (Positions)." *Extreme-Orient, Extreme-Occident*, No. 18, 1996, pp. 149–176.

Cheng, Chung-ying, and Elton Johnson, eds. "A Bibliography of the *I Ching* in the Western Languages." *Journal of Chinese Philosophy*, 14(1), 1987, pp. 73–90.

Fleming, Jesse. "Categories and Meta-Categories in the *I Ching*." *Journal of Chinese Philosophy*, 20(4), 1993, pp. 425–434.

Goldenberg, Daniel S. "The Algebra of the I Ching and Its Philosophical Implications." *Journal of Chinese Philosophy*, 2(2), 1975, pp. 149–180.

Kunst, Richard. *The Original "Yijing," A Text, Phonetic Transcription, Translation, and Indexes, with Sample Glosses*. Ann Arbor: University Microfilms International, 1985.

Legge, James, trans. *The Book of Changes*. New York: Dover, 1964. (Reprint.)

Liu, Dajun, ed. *Studies in Zhou Yi (1988–1991)*. Jinan, 1993.

Lynn, Richard John, trans. *The Classic of Changes*. New York: Columbia University Press, 1994.

Peterson, Willard. "Making Connections: Commentary on the Attached Verbalizations of the *Book of Changes*." *Harvard Journal of Asiatic Studies*, 42, 1982, pp. 67–116.

Rutt, Richard. *The Book of Changes*. Richmond, England: Curzon, 1996.

Shaughenessy, Edward. *Yi Qing: The Classic of Change*. New York: Ballantine, 1997. (English translation of the "Mawangdui silk manuscript" of the *Yijing*.)

Smith, Kidder, Peter K. Bol, Joseph A. Adler, and Don J. Wyatt. *Sung Dynasty Uses of the I Ching*. Princeton, N.J.: Princeton University Press, 1990.

Smith, Richard. "The Place of the *Yijing* in the World Culture: Some Historical and Contemporary Perspectives." *Journal of Chinese Philosophy*, 25(4), 1998, pp. 391–422.

Tong, Lik-Kuen. "The Appropriation of Significance: The Concept of *Kang-T'ung* in the *I Ching*." *Journal of Chinese Philosophy*, 17(3), 1990, pp. 315–344.

Wilhelm, Richard, trans. *The I Ching or the Book of Changes*. Princeton, N.J.: Princeton University Press, 1968.

Zhu, Bogun. *Zhuyi Zhexue Shi* (History of Philosophy of *Zhou Yi*), 4 vols. Taipei, 1991.

Philosophy of Culture

Robert C. Neville

"Philosophy of culture" is a western category that has no exact Chinese counterpart. Chinese philosophical traditions, often far finer than western ones, discriminate among kinds and conditions of cultural elements, including the development of the virtues such as humanity, righteousness, propriety, and wisdom (see, for instance, *Mencius* 2A.6); the cultivation of the "five relations" (between parents and children, ruler and minister, husband and wife, older and younger, and friends; see, for instance, *Mencius* 3A.4); the elaboration of the arts and philosophical life; the honing of skills such as calligraphy, sewing, sericulture, archery, cooking, music, and dance; the maintenance of economic practices such as agriculture, pottery, and trade; and practices of public life from the village to the empire. How do all these things, and others, add up to culture as such? With what is culture to be contrasted? What are the particularly Chinese philosophies about this?

The standard western anthropological notion is that culture is what has to be learned from other people and can be passed on. It contrasts with nature and what comes naturally to people. The contrast is complex because most natural human dispositions need also to be specified and shaped by culture, as the disposition to eat is culturally shaped by specific ways of finding and preparing food, or the disposition to procreate is culturally shaped by social habits of family life. Most elements of culture not only need to be learned but should be learned well, that is, cultivated: good cuisine, healthy and nurturing families. So most elements of culture can be assessed as to their appropriateness and their degree of excellent development. Societies acknowledge not only distinctions between high and low culture but also distinctions between degrees of appropriate acculturation. All these elements are present in the Chinese appreciation of culture.

The specific elementary Chinese approach to philosophy of culture, however, is reflected in the trinity of heaven, earth, and the human. The classic *Doctrine of the Mean* said:

> Only those who are absolutely sincere can fully develop their nature. If they can fully develop their nature, they can then fully develop the nature of others. If they can fully develop the nature of others, they can then fully develop the nature of things. If they can fully develop the nature of things, they can then assist in the transforming and nourishing process of heaven and earth. If they can assist in the transforming and nourishing process of heaven and earth, they can thus form a trinity with heaven and earth. (ch. 22)

The Chinese philosophy of culture has to do with the human contribution over and above what is given by heaven and earth, a contribution that fulfills heaven and earth but is not reducible to their natural principles and processes. The *Doctrine of the Mean* cites the development of the nature of the self, other people, and things as the content of the human contribution. Chinese philosophers differ widely in their interpretations of these elements and in the attitudes they advocate toward their development.

Two Chinese words are especially associated with the idea of culture, although that idea is too complex to be matched with any single word. The most common association is with *wen*, which usually means high culture, refinement, the arts, especially language and literary arts; its roots go back to the idea of pattern. The other is *li*, which is translated variously as ritual, ritual propriety, manners of civility, or rules of proper conduct; its basic root meaning, however, is learned, conventional, semiotically shaped behavior (see Neville 1995, ch. 7). In this broad sense of symbolic behavior, ritual encompasses artistic culture and language, and is the locus for a discussion of Chinese philosophy of culture.

The Chinese philosophy of culture can be analyzed under the following heads: (1) an elementary theory of culture relative to nature in Xunzi; (2) a schematic contrast of Confucian, Daoist, legalist, Mohist, and Chinese Buddhist approaches to culture; (3) ancient Confucianism in Confucius, Mencius, and Xunzi; and (4) the enduring contribution of Chinese philosophy of culture to the contemporary world philosophical situation. This discussion, except in its final section, restricts itself to ancient sources; the motifs there were elaborated in extremely diverse ways for two millennia.

An Elementary Theory of Culture and Nature: Xunzi

Xunzi (Hsün Tzu, c. 310–210 B.C.E.) was an extraordinarily careful and responsible thinker who explicitly defended Confucianism in relation to Daoism, Mohism, and incipient legalism. But in his essay *Tian lun* (Chan 1963, pp. 116–124; Knoblock 1998–1994, Vol. 3, Book 17; Machle 1993, ch. 7), he analyzed the relation of the human sphere to heaven and earth in a way that articulated what the other schools pretty much presupposed. Even the other Confucians, however, did not agree with all the conclusions Xunzi drew from this analysis. His elementary analysis, if we suspend judgment about the conclusions, is a good introduction to the Chinese philosophy of culture.

For Xunzi and his predecessors "nature" was a binary, not a single, notion. On the one hand are the natural processes of things, extensive in time and space, the "stuff" of nature ranging from gross material processes to spiritual impulses and historical forces; these were called "earth," and in various ways were identified with *qi* (material force, energy, vital force). On the other hand are the principles that order or harmonize the natural processes, that define regularity and integration, that are the source of goodness in contrast to chaos, and that in some spheres can fail to be fully actualized, in which cases there is disaster, failure, or, for human beings, an obligation to make the principles effective; these principles were called "heaven" and in deep antiquity were personalized in the form of a high God, though by the time of Confucius and especially Xunzi they were not personalized. Frequently heaven and earth were spoken of together as a rough equivalent to the western range of meanings for "nature." Heaven was often paired with the human sphere in discussing obligation, especially the self-cultivation of what is the best in human beings. Heaven and earth were subsequently given extensive metaphysical interpretations as "principle" (*li*) and "material force" (*qi*) by the neo-Confucians.

Xunzi, in the *Tian lun* (Machle, pp. 95ff), pointed out that human beings are born with four kinds of natural endowments—heavenly orderings of biological processes. One is *feelings* such as desire, aversion, delight, anger, grief, and joy. Another is *sensibilities* such as the ear, eye, nose, mouth, and body, each of which has an appropriate object such that the objects should not be interchanged. A third natural endowment, which Xunzi calls the "ruler," is the *mind* that can order the five sensibilities and that can use things other than mind to nurture its own intrinsic fulfillment; that is, the mind can use nonmental things as instruments for ordering human activity. The fourth natural endowment is *government*, the capacity to harmonize with the things that fulfill the human sphere, which is a blessed capacity. To be at odds with what is fulfilling is human disaster. Government, in Xunzi's conception, refers to personal and familial as well as social governance.

"Fulfillment," in these remarks, refers to the supposition in Xunzi and elsewhere that each thing has its own *dao*, an intrinsic way of playing itself out with excellence. *Dao* has some connotations of unfolding, although not in the Aristotelian sense of actualizing potentialities given at the beginning or in early stages; a thing's *dao* needs to relate to and harmonize with other things and is not a function of the thing's essence. *Dao* also has some connotations of achieving an end, of purposive behavior in humans and other higher animals, although again not in the Aristotelian sense of an end or purpose defined in the thing; rather, the end of the *dao* has to do with the appropriate contribution the thing might make to a larger harmony. The daos of natural things are intricately interrelated, and also dependent on the *dao* of heaven and the *dao* of earth; they relate as well to more cosmic conceptions of the universal *dao*.

Human feelings, sensibility, mind, and government are all natural, biologically based capacities. But, unlike most if not all other natural things, those human endowments cannot fulfill themselves by nature alone, nor by any combination of heaven and earth. The human *dao* requires culture in order for feelings, sensibility, mind, and government to exercise their daos and fulfill themselves. That we have capacities for desire, aversion, delight, anger, grief, and joy does not mean we direct them at the right things. We need culture to define their direction, and then those cultural elements themselves are appropriate objects of desire, aversion, and so forth. Moreover, high culture gives us extraordinarily excellent things to desire, and extraordinary evils to avoid, far beyond what nature might provide without culture. The sensibilities have their objects, but their responses cannot be integrated without culture; and with their integrating culture, such as dance, more complicated and excellent harmonies of sensibilities are possible. The mind has the natural capacity to act instrumentally, but it needs cultural knowledge of what to do to accomplish its ends, i.e., the fulfillment of the human *dao*; especially, it needs to know that the *dao* is. Government, which at the natural level is the capacity to control the self and others relative to the fulfillment of the daos involved, needs culture to give it shape so that the exercise of control does not destroy the fulfillment but nourishes it to flourishing.

What then is culture? It is the sum of the conventions that shape the natural endowments so that they can be fulfilled and together fulfill the human. The body can move in countless different ways, but it needs a culture to teach it a way of moving for walking, for eating, for making eye contact, for gesturing and expressing meaning through body language. The body can make sounds of many sorts, but it needs a culture to teach it ways of communicating and speaking through systems of verbal symbols. People can interact in a great many ways, but every interaction, to be understood so that people assume roles within it, must have some ritualized conditions, such as greeting and feasting rituals. With minimal conventions people can copulate and reproduce, but only with the rituals of high civilization can there be family life with love and nurturing. With minimal conventions people can cooperate in the hunt and economic production, but only with the rituals of high civilization can there be public life and effective, just government. With minimal rituals people can be colleagues, but only with the rituals of high civilization can people become genuine friends. The problem with the barbarians, the ancient Chinese thought, is not that they have the wrong customs but that they have customs and conventions inadequate to the actual exercise of high civilization. All the rituals of high civilization need to be coordinated with each other and with the larger environment. Seasonal rituals of family and public life, up to the imperial court, are intended to set the rhythms and choreograph the dance of social interaction and of human interaction with heaven and earth. For Xunzi and the other early Confucians, all these learned conventions, from styles of movement to court rituals, were encompassed under the notion of ritual propriety (*li*). All of them, with extraordinarily complex connections, constitute culture, that which the human sphere adds to the original endowments of heaven and earth to bring those biological and other natural daos to their fulfillment. Something like this complicated sense of culture was understood by all the early schools, although they took different stances toward it (on the ways this was expressed in Chinese language, see Hansen 1983).

A Schematic Contrast: Confucian, Daoist, Legalist, Mohist, and Chinese Buddhist Perspectives on Culture

Xunzi himself represented the generally positive Confucian approach to culture. The Confucians affirmed the assertion quoted above from the *Doctrine of the Mean* that the cultural human sphere fulfills heaven and earth and adds a positive ontological reality. The ancient Confucians differed among themselves as to how to attain high culture and avoid the obstacles to its realization, a point addressed in the next section.

The Daoists, by contrast, emphasized the fact that culture is artificial and therefore can interfere with the natural daos of nature. They saw high culture as an ambiguous good, if not a plain evil, and advocated the deconstruction of ritual behavior and cultivation of more naive, spontaneous behavior (on primitiveness in Daoism, see Girardot 1983). It is hard to know just how serious they were in their advocacy of going "back to nature," because they lived in a highly ritualized and cultured society, even when the culture was in trouble. Consider *Daodejing* Chapter 80 (Chan, 175):

> Let there be a small country with few people.
> Let there be ten times and a hundred times as many utensils
> But let them not be used.
> Let the people value their lives highly and not migrate far.
> Even if there are ships and carriages, none will ride in them.
> Even if there are armor and weapons, none will display them.
> Let the people again knot cords and use them (in place of writing).
> Let them relish their food, beautify their clothing, be content with their homes, and delight in their customs.
> Though neighboring communities overlook one another and the crowing of cocks and barking of dogs can be heard,
> Yet the people there may grow old and die without ever visiting one another.

Some themes in *Daodejing* and *Zhuangzi* are about government and social administration. But at the very least, the classical Daoist attitude toward culture, especially high culture, was suspicion.

The Daoists and Confucians shared an image of human life as a kind of hierarchy of organized functions. Toward the bottom are physiological processes, such as heartbeat and metabolism, which have a natural rhythm and are deeply embedded in the surrounding natural rhythms—say, of the ecosystem. Moving up, these physiological processes are organized into behaviors such as moving, working, eating, and primitive cooperation; the forms for such organization are learned and are the rudiments of culture. Then the processes are organized into speech, family life, and political cooperation; and then into the arts of high civilization. The most harmonious and sophisticated civilized flourishing of the *dao* requires beating hearts and a food system; but we understand it mainly in terms of the cultural levels of organization shaping the natural processes. The Confucians were convinced that the higher levels of cultural organization are necessary for the flourishing of the lower levels and the merely natural processes; without those higher levels, the lower levels will not be able to fulfill their human *dao* and might even be self-destructive. The Daoists, by contrast, even though they admitted the higher levels, and excelled at the most sophisticated virtues, were fearful that the higher levels would distort and pervert the rhythms of the lower levels; if the higher levels cannot be seen as natural and spontaneous outgrowths of the lower, they are to be distrusted. Moreover, as Zhuangzi so often argued, the higher levels are ambiguous with regard to how they build on the lower—language is deceptive about intentions, and even the discrimination of waking and sleeping is ambiguous about simply being.

Another element in the Daoist approach to culture is its peculiar focus on cultivated insight. Like the Confucians, the ancient Daoists advocated meditation and the cultivation of subtle perception. But whereas the Confucians focused on the human sphere and the setting of the human within the cosmic, the Daoists focused more on the cosmic first, on what western philosophy would call the metaphysical or ontological. The *Daodejing* opens with a reflection on the *dao* that cannot be named. Zhuangzi speculates about reality and appearance. Perhaps the most metaphysical of the philosophical Daoists was Wang Bi, who wrote at length about being and nonbeing and developed the distinction between substance and function, influenced by Buddhism. Processes of meditation and philosophical speculation are as much part of culture as institutions of family life and government; for many, especially in the west, the Daoist sage of contemplation rather than the Confucian sage of human action is the epitome of Chinese culture (Hansen 1992).

The legalist philosophy of Han Feizi focused on a different aspect of culture as ritual. The Confucians had argued that moral and holy behavior to a large extent consists in shaping life by the conventions of high culture and believed that when people widely practiced or exercised these conventions, proper justice, deference, and distribution would happen as a matter of course. The authority for the rituals of high culture was attributed to the ancient sage kings by the Confucians, but they thought the merits of high civilization were apparent on their own. The legalists observed that however good and just the conventions of high culture might be, people do not take to them naturally. The authority of the sage kings is irrelevant and not easily knowable. Moreover, many of the policies of good governments take the form not of general habitual behavior but rather of making specific changes. Therefore the legalists were emphatic that laws and policies should be explicit and that people do good when they are shaped, perhaps even coerced, to do so by a clear regimen of rewards and punishments. The legalists rejected the efficacy of the rather aesthetic appeal of both Confucian cultural practices and Daoist spontaneous naturalism, and said that high culture should be built by the clear statement of laws and their strict enforcement by rewards and punishments. Concomitant with the demystifying of the aesthetic and antiquarian authority of social convention and ritual, legalism had the effect of promoting social equality and also a pragmatic rationalization of culture (Graham 1989, 267–292). Although the legalists were influential in the authoritarian Qin dynasty (221–206 B.C.E.), they were rejected as deeply insensitive to high civilization for some of their policies such as book burning.

The Mohists took an even more utilitarian approach to the conventions of high culture. They developed a rather straightforward conception of social benefit and universal respect or love, and judged conventions by the extent to which they promoted social benefits. In this they did not deem the fairly esoteric matters of ritual practice of high civilization, accessible only to the elite, to be beneficial, and thus attacked elaborate funerals and mourning customs, displays of music, and the like. Whereas the Confucians saw mourning customs, for instance, as part of the very reality of respect for persons, and the performance of music and dance as the very stuff of what makes life worth living, the Mohists saw such things as probable impediments to economic progress and fair distribution. Wing-tsit Chan speculates that whereas the Confucians aimed to draw people from all walks of life to take on an elite life of ritual propriety, the Mohists represented peasants for whom "high civilization" meant little (1963, 212).

Early Buddhism in China did not develop a distinctive attitude toward culture as such except to see it as having only instrumental value for the liberation or enlightenment of sentient beings. (For a study of the historical diversity of Buddhism in China, see Ch'en 1964.) The Buddhists did not see much importance in completing the trinity of heaven, earth, and the human when the real human task is enlightenment. Nevertheless, an enlightened person still lives in the world, dealing with issues of *samsara*, and in that capacity can contribute as much as anyone to the building of a high civilization. The Buddhist contributions to Chinese art are of extraordinary importance. Although there have been many forms of Buddhism in China, beginning in the first century or earlier, in practice they share a middle path between the Confucian pressure to create ever more sophisticated and elite conventions and the Daoist pressure to deconstruct these in favor of natural immediacy with the *dao*. It should be noted that by the time Buddhism came to China, Daoism had evolved, even in its mystical forms, into a ritualized religion with temples and a priesthood (Kohn 1991; Lagerwey 1987).

This schematic survey of Chinese attitudes toward culture is of course too selective and broadly generalized. The ancient Confucian movement will be investigated here in more detail.

The Confucianism of Confucius, Mencius, and Xunzi

Although the historical figure of Confucius has been overdetermined by the legendary roles to which subsequent interpreters have subjected him, it is clear that by his activities and the force of his personality he formed a school (perhaps also a model for a widely imitated type of school) for the cultivation of ritual competence (Eno 1990). His recorded sayings (*The Analects*) express the suppositions, motivations, and goals of his movement. Three points are important with respect to Confucius's philosophy of culture.

First and probably most important was his interpretation of the social situation. He lived in the declining years of the Spring and Autumn period as it was degenerating into the worse political chaos of the period of the Warring States. The imperial government had relatively little power, the various states warred against one another, and none kept the peace very well. Groups were desperate to enhance their own power, and the quality of life declined, at least according to their way of thinking. This is the kind of social chaos Thomas Hobbes described, in discussing the English revolution, when he called the quality of human life "solitary, poor, nasty, brutish, and short." But whereas Hobbes thought the problem was a lack of governmental power to enforce civil order (a point to which the legalists would have been sympathetic), Confucius's analysis was quite different. The evils of his day consisted in the operative failure of rituals and conventional forms of social behavior to keep the peace automatically, to distribute goods fairly, and to facilitate the fulfillment of people of varying stations and conditions. Instead of good family life, political competence, and friendship, there was barely more than procreation, strongman politics, and exploitation. Even if there were a powerful enough government to bring a cessation of violence by authorized force (Hobbes's solution), without civilized ritual according to which people could behave the government would have nothing to do with lasting good. And with civilized ritual, the need for governmental force would be minimal. So Confucius argued that the key to social life is the inculcation of properly ritualized habits of life, beginning with the students in his school.

Confucius argued that the rituals he advocated were a recovery of the high civilization of the legendary sage kings, and he claimed that he himself was no innovator, only passing on what he had learned. A logical problem lies behind this stance: if humanizing conventions are in addition to heaven and earth, where do they come from and with what authority? A past golden age answers that question, at least on the surface. Because of Confucius's denial of originality, he has often been regarded merely as a reformer. But in fact he was a radical revolutionary, radical in the sense of going to the root of the trouble—lack of operative civilizing rituals—and revolutionary in the sense of calling for a total transformation of his society and a reversal of the direction in which it was moving with regard to power politics. The genre of western literature which the *Analects* is most like is that of the Hebrew prophets, especially Jeremiah—professions of highly purified ideals are juxtaposed with bitter complaints about the current state of affairs, with strident calls to amend our ways before it is too late.

The second element of Confucius's philosophy of culture is the conception of high civilization to be made possible by ritual. Fundamentally, civilization is to enable people to live harmoniously with themselves, their fellows, and the cosmos. The rituals and conventional social habits are to incline or direct people so that the daos of nature, social institutions, and themselves are caused to flourish in harmony. Moreover, all the personal and social activities that exist in their exercise are themselves players in the harmony, so that harmonization is recursive. The rituals that incline us harmoniously are themselves the object of harmonious inclination. The result is an extraordinarily rich conception of the texture of things that should be brought into harmonious balance, and things are understood in terms of the correlations and connections that highlight issues of harmony and balance (Hall and Ames 1987, 1995). Confucius did not have as exalted or as metaphysically expressed a notion of the cosmic *dao* as was prevalent in Daoism, but he saw that the human project requires harmony with the cosmos. He did not have (or was not recorded as having) as detailed a conception of ritual as Xunzi, or as elaborate a theory of pedagogy as Mencius. But he knew and taught about those things and was extraordinarily effective as a teacher. The rest of the Confucian tradition can be understood as a development and elaboration of Confucius's ideals for civilization as made possible through ritualized conventions.

The third element of Confucius's philosophy of culture was his conception of the *junzi* (superior, noble, paradigmatic individual), or the sage. The most obvious element in the *junzi* is competence at ritual and the habits of practicing it in all circumstances. Less obvious but perhaps as important was Confucius's requirement of humanness (*ren* or *jen*). Scholars such as Cua (1971, 1978) and Fingarette (1972) have shown that ritual (*li*) and humaneness (*ren*) are intimately bound up with each other. Humaneness for Confucius seemed to have three aspects: toward objects, toward personal constitution, and toward practical effects. Regarding objects, the sage should be properly deferential, acknowledging and prizing each thing for what it is and comporting himself or herself appropriately. Rituals provide the forms for deferential comportment, but they also can be practiced without real deference in the heart. Regarding personal constitution, the ethical paradigm, *junzi*, should be pure in the sense of clarity of heart through activities and dispositions; he (or she) should not be muddied by selfish desires but should be able to perceive the nature and worth of things without distortion and respond appropriately to changing circumstances. Regarding practical effects, the *junzi* should not only live a moral and politically beneficial life but should do so in such a way that others are inspired to conform as well. Force is not so important in government, Confucius thought, because the exemplary power of *junzi*, especially a sage emperor, moves people's hearts so as to bring them into humaneness and civilized ritual practice. The ritual practice by itself might not be powerfully commanding, but the humane heart of *junzi* is hard to resist. The love between parents and children is the seed from which humaneness grows (Tu 1979).

Culture, for Confucius, is thus not merely the rituals and conventions superimposed on nature, but the way of life that connects the human heart in resonance and harmony with all the things in the universe, including the rituals, symbols, and institutions that facilitate this harmony. All these themes have been stressed in one way or another by subsequent Confucians.

Mencius focused primarily on humaneness and emphasized how natural it is to human beings; this is epitomized in the slogan that human nature is good. Western philosophers have often seen a sharp distinction between the natural and conventional; under the influence of substance philosophies, western thinkers have sometimes represented the natural as one kind of thing and the conventional as another. For the Confucians, it is the *dao* innate in human beings that itself develops the conventions of civilized life. The *Doctrine of the Mean* begins:

> What heaven (*Tian*, Nature) imparts to man is called human nature. To follow our nature is called the Way (*Dao*). Cultivating the Way is called education. The Way cannot be separated from us for a moment. What can be separated from us is not the Way. (Chan, 98)

Mencius elaborated this point with his theory of the "four beginnings" (2A.6), which are the innate feelings of commiseration, shame and dislike, deference and compliance, and right and wrong. Illustrated in the famous parable of the instant feeling of alarm people feel when they see a child about to fall into a well, these four beginnings are incipient sensitivities, ready to respond spontaneously to appropriate things. When cultivated through civilized education, they lead to the sophisticated virtues of humanity, righteousness, propriety (ritual observance), and wisdom (Chan, 65).

If the development of these civilized virtues springs from natural endowment, how does Mencius conceive that we ever go wrong? Like any Confucian, he was convinced that children need to be surrounded by an educational environment to shape their growth, beginning with the family and including communal ritual (3A.3; Chan, 66–67). Sometimes that might be lacking. But he was more troubled by the destructive forces of society that would teach selfishness, bad habits, and barbaric conventions. Somewhat like the Daoists, therefore, but with no diminution of the Confucian stress on effort, he thought that the larger social task is to remove destructive social elements and get out of the way of the natural exfoliation of the virtues, especially humanity. Because of this, he did not stress as much as some others the importance of ritual learning: ritual can be learned without humanity, and it can be bad ritual in the first place. But no matter how misguided and depraved a person might become, the root of virtue remains and is ready to sprout, given half a chance.

Mencius had much to say about the social conditions that allow humanity to flourish naturally. They include a commanding humanity on the part of the emperor, and a just and cooperative local social structure in which people bear one another's burdens and make sure everyone has enough to eat and good work to do. When the emperor lacks virtue, his authority is lost and the people have the right of rebellion. Mencius's emphases on personal virtue and social justice have been major themes of the Confucian tradition ever since.

Xunzi was less impressed with the readiness of human nature to flower into virtue than he was with the fact that without fairly explicit social cultivation, people would not grow into the explicitly human *dao* at all. Human beings start out selfish, and from this he concluded that human nature is bad. Virtue comes not from a given nature but from activity that develops this nature (Chan, 128–135; Knoblock, 3:150–162; *Xunzi*, ch. 23). Xunzi thus stressed the importance of culture that elicits humane activity:

> In antiquity the sage kings took man's nature to be evil, to be inclined to prejudice and prone to error, to be perverse and rebellious, and not to be upright or orderly. For this reason they invented ritual principles and precepts of moral duty. They instituted the regulations that are contained in laws and standards. Through these actions they intended to "straighten out" and develop man's essential nature and to set his inborn nature aright. They sought to tame and

> transform his essential nature and to guide his inborn nature with the Way. They caused both his essential and inborn natures to develop with good order and be consistent with the true Way . . . It is the environment that is critical! It is the environment that is critical! (Knoblock, 3:151–152, 162)

Like nearly all good philosophers, Xunzi developed his position by a subtle criticism of neighboring conceptions.

The main line of the Confucian tradition, especially in the neo-Confucians and down to our own time in the work of Mou Zongsan and Tu Weiming, has followed Mencius rather than Xunzi in stressing the continuity of innate human nature with the development of civilized forms. But the difference between them has been overstressed. If one considers a situation in which social forms are actually degenerate and helpful ritual is lacking, the result will be the development of greedy and power-seeking people, as Xunzi said. However ready human nature might be to learn right action in the presence of civilizing conditions, a matter Xunzi would not dispute, when those conditions are absent people will not develop any way except defensively and selfishly. Xunzi is perhaps closer than Mencius to Confucius's concern about what to do with degenerate social conditions, although his rhetoric runs counter to that of classics such as the *Doctrine of the Mean*. (For a discussion of the culture of virtue and courage that places the ancient Confucians in relation to western thinking, see Yearley 1990.)

The subsequent developments of Confucianism and neo-Confucianism are extremely various and not to be summarized here. During the neo-Confucian period the personal cultivation of sagehood became a dominant theme, though never without a political concern. The school of Zhu Xi in the Southern Sung was explicit about its political involvement in foreign policy and with respect to the education of persons for the literati class and the government bureaucracy. Others, such as Wang Anshi, who are not customarily thought of as philosophers, were deeply involved in the shaping of Song culture.

The explicit emphasis on ritual dropped back from prominence in neo-Confucian discourse in favor of an emphasis on personal cultivation and humanity. This was not because the neo-Confucians did not share the logical point of the ancients about the ritual constitution of civilization, but because Confucianism had largely won. From the Han through the Song, China had become a highly ritualized society and the point that ritual was important no longer had to be made. The concern was rather with the cultivation of genuine sagehood and the performance of the proper rituals (Zhu Xi).

The advent of western thought in China in the nineteenth century, especially Marxism more recently, was devastating to the authentic appreciation of the ritualized aspects of culture, however much many of the rituals have been carried on. The utilitarianism of the western influence has been a delegitimating force in the Chinese philosophy of culture as much as it has in the pretechnological aspects of that culture itself. Even John Dewey, whose own theory of the social construction of culture as part of human nature is remarkably similar to many ancient Confucian themes, strained that down to a crass scientism in his lectures in China in 1919–1920 (Dewey 1973). Perhaps before the genius of the ancient Chinese philosophy of culture can be appreciated in China today, its contribution to world philosophy needs to be made manifest. In contrast to the effort to revitalize the Chinese philosophical tradition characteristic of the previous generation of Chinese philosophers, the contemporary generation focuses its effort on reconstructing Chinese philosophy, especially Chinese philosophy of culture, for the world conversation. Among the most important thinkers in this movement are John Berthrong, Cheng Chung-ying, Julia Ching, Antonio Cua, William Theodore de Bary, Liu Shu-hsien, and Tu Weiming.

The Enduring Contributions of Chinese Philosophy of Culture in the Contemporary World

At least four distinctive contributions from the ancient Chinese philosophy of culture are important for contemporary world philosophy. They can be called the semiotics of ethics, the aesthetics of culture, the personal competence of civilization, and the irony of convention.

The contemporary expression of much of what the ancient Chinese meant by ritual is in semiotics, the study of signs and conventionally meaningful behavior, as in, say, the semiotics of pragmatism (Neville 1995, chs. 6–7). A pragmatic semiotical reconstruction of Chinese ritual theory gives the Chinese tradition "thick" access to the western philosophies leading to semiotics. But the Chinese tradition has shown how rituals make possible all layers of civilization in ways far more subtle than western semiotics, which has tended to identify sign systems with mere languages, not with the institutions and behaviors whose exercise constitutes civilization. This vastly enriches the discussion of signs. Moreover, it contributes even more to contemporary ethics. Western ethical traditions generally have focused on actions, decisions, and goals or values, missing the Confucian point that social activities are not possible without the significant ritualized behaviors whose exercise constitutes their existence; how can one decide to be good or do right if there is no behavioral vocabulary for good and bad, right and wrong, behavior? The Chinese philosophy of culture allows for the critical examination of the social habits and rituals of a society, and for the invention of good ones where they are lacking, a topic almost entirely obscured by the western preoccupation with decisions, actions, and goals. The specific ancient rituals of China might be entirely inappropriate for egalitarian and meritocratic societies; but something like them needs to be developed for the civilizing of societies formed by the technologies and economies of late modernity.

The aesthetics of culture to be gleaned from the Chinese tradition, both Daoist and Confucian, stands to supplement and correct the modern western preoccupation with the instrumentalities of culture. The western Enlightenment focused on the development of cultural elements that foster progress, and great progress has been made in matters of health, security, farming, economic production, and social justice. (For the ancient Chinese conception of social justice, see Lee 1995.) But as the demand to "die with dignity" shows, for instance, progress can be dehumanizing. The aesthetic contribution of Chinese culture is not an arty or appreciative contrast to instrumentalism but rather a reconceiving of the problem of instrumentalism itself. The Chinese contribution is to insist that the purpose of culture is to harmonize human life with the *dao* in the cosmos, in society, and in other people; moreover, because of its recursive quality, the institutions of civilization have daos of their own with which everything else should be brought into harmony. Progress itself should be conceived as the enhancement of harmony, properly understood according to the causal connections among natural and conventionally constituted processes. The Chinese aesthetics of culture need not depreciate technology and the western impulse to progress; it need only put them in an appropriate context of harmonization.

The personal competence of civilization is a definition of the human project which recognizes that people are neither born civilized nor born into civilizations. They need to undertake to become civilized by appropriating their culture's civilizing forms. Personal life has the task of becoming civilized. This ideal stands in some contrast with the western emphasis on the fitness of the ordinary and the glorification of popular culture. But it also stands in contrast with heroic ideals requiring extraordinary effort and open only to a few: sagehood is open to everyone, both Confucians and Daoists would agree. This theme is not absent from western culture; it was in fact a centerpiece of Dewey's philosophy. But it has often been associated with the aristocracy. The Chinese can bring the theme into the world discussion without the associations of aristocracy (though modern Confucianism often had that association). The theme resonates with Christian ideals of holiness.

The irony of convention is a consciousness that comes from China's long preoccupation with ritual and its obvious temptations to abuse. Crudely put, Daoist humor punctures Confucian pomposities when ritual is glorified without humaneness. Of course the situation is more complicated than this crude statement; religious Daoism is highly ritualistic, and Confucians long appreciated the need to make ritual humane. But the Chinese tradition with these checks and balances has been able to recognize from very early on that conventions are conventions, not natural processes or singularly authoritative like natural law, and yet very important indeed for civilization. It does not matter in the Chinese tradition what conventions a society has, so long as they serve to make possible the practice of high civilization. The west has tended to vacillate between taking its conventions to be singularly and exclusively normative or treating them as merely relative and therefore not important, perhaps even unnatural. The Chinese contribution of the irony of convention is particularly important in a situation where the great world civilizations are in commerce, if not conflict, with one another.

The contributions of Chinese philosophy of culture to the contemporary situation therefore are potent for ethics, philosophy of technology, personal cultivation, and the encounter of civilizations.

See also Confucianism: Tradition; Daoism: Religious; *Junzi*; *Li*: Rites or Propriety.

Bibliography

Berthrong, John H. *All under Heaven*. Albany: State University of New York Press, 1994.

Chan, Wing-tsit, trans. *A Source Book in Chinese Philosophy*. Princeton, N.J.: Princeton University Press, 1963.

Ch'en, Kenneth. *Buddhism in China: A Historical Survey*. Princeton, N.J.: Princeton University Press, 1964.

Cheng, Chung-ying. *New Dimensions of Confucian and Neo-Confucian Philosophy*. Albany: State University of New York Press, 1991.

Ching, Julia. *To Acquire Wisdom: The Way of Wang Yang-ming*. New York: Columbia University Press, 1976.

——. *Probing China's Soul: Religion, Politics, and Protest in the People's Republic*. San Francisco, Calif.: Harper and Row, 1990.

Chu, Hsi. *Chu Hsi's Family Rituals: A Twelfth-Century Chinese Manual for the Performance of Cappings, Weddings, Funerals, and Ancestral Rites*, trans. and ed. Patricia Buckley Ebrey. Princeton, N.J.: Princeton University Press, 1991.

Cua, Antonio S. "The Concept of *Li* in Confucian Moral Theory." In *Understanding the Chinese Mind: The Philosophi-*

cal Roots, ed. Robert E. Allinson. Hong Kong: Oxford University Press, 1989.

———. "The Concept of Paradigmatic Individuals in the Ethics of Confucius." *Inquiry*, 14, 1971. (Also published in A. Naess and A. Hannay, eds. *Invitation to Chinese Philosophy: Eight Studies*. Oslo: Universitetforlaget, 1972, pp. 41–55.)

———. "Dimensions of *Li* (Propriety): Reflections on a Theme in Hsün Tzu's Ethics." *Philosophy East and West*, 29(4), 1979, pp. 373–389.

———. *Dimensions of Moral Creativity: Paradigms, Principles, and Ideals*. University Park: Pennsylvania State University Press, 1978.

———. *Ethical Argumentation: A Study of Hsün Tzu's Moral Epistemology*. Honolulu: University of Hawaii Press, 1985.

———. "*Li* and Moral Justification: A Study in the *Li Chi*." *Philosophy East and West*, 33(1), 1983, pp. 1–16.

———. *Moral Vision and Tradition: Essays in Chinese Ethics*. Washington, D.C.: Catholic University of America Press, 1998.

———. *The Unity of Knowledge and Action: A Study of Wang Yang-ming's Moral Psychology*. Honolulu: University of Hawaii Press, 1982.

De Bary, William Theodore. *Learning for Oneself: Essays on the Individual in Neo-Confucian Thought*. New York: Columbia University Press, 1991.

———. *The Liberal Tradition in China*. New York: Columbia University Press, 1983.

———. *The Message of the Mind in Neo-Confucianism*. New York: Columbia University Press, 1989.

———. *The Trouble with Confucianism*. Cambridge, Mass.: Harvard University Press, 1991.

Dewey, John. *Freedom and Culture*. New York: Capricorn, 1963.

———. *Lectures in China, 1919–1920*, ed. and trans. (from the Chinese) Robert W. Clopton and Tsuin-Chen Ou. Honolulu: University of Hawaii Press, 1973.

Eno, Robert. *The Confucian Creation of Heaven: Philosophy and the Defense of Ritual Mastery*. Albany: State University of New York Press, 1990.

Fingarette, Herbert. *Confucius: The Secular as Sacred*. New York: Harper, 1972.

Girardot, N. J. *Myth and Meaning in Early Taoism: The Theme of Chaos (Hun-tun)*. Berkeley: University of California Press, 1983.

Graham, A. C. *Disputers of the Tao: Philosophical Argument in Ancient China*. La Salle, Ill.: Open Court, 1989.

Hall, David L., and Roger T. Ames. *Anticipating China: Thinking through the Narratives of Chinese and Western Culture*. Albany: State University of New York Press, 1995.

———. *Thinking through Confucius*. Albany: State University of New York Press, 1987.

Hansen, Chad. *A Daoist Theory of Chinese Thought: A Philosophical Interpretation*. Oxford: Oxford University Press, 1992.

———. *Language and Logic in Ancient China*. Ann Arbor: University of Michigan Press, 1983.

Knoblock, John. *Xunzi: A Translation and Study of the Complete Works*, Vols. 1–3. Stanford, Calif.: Stanford University Press, 1988, 1990, 1994.

Kohn, Livia. *Taoist Mystical Philosophy: The Scripture of Western Ascension*. Albany: State University of New York Press, 1991.

Lagerwey, John. *Taoist Ritual in Chinese Society and History*. New York: Macmillan, 1987.

Lee, Thomas H. C. "The Idea of Social Justice in Ancient China." In *Social Justice in the Ancient World*, ed. K. D. Irani and Morris Silver. Westport, Conn.: Greenwood, 1995.

Liu, Shu-hsien. "Postwar Neo-Confucian Philosophy: Its Development and Issues." In *Religious Issues and Interreligious Dialogues*, ed. Charles Wei-hsun Fu and Gerhard E. Spiegler. Westport, Conn.: Greenwood, 1989.

Liu, Shu-hsien, and Robert E. Allinson, eds. *Harmony and Strife: Contemporary Perspectives Easy and West*. Hong Kong: Chinese University Press, 1988.

Machle, Edward F. *Nature and Heaven in the Xunzi: A Study of the Tian Lun*. Albany: State University of New York Press, 1993.

Neville, Robert Cummings. *Normative Cultures*. Albany: State University of New York Press, 1995.

Tu, Weiming. *Centrality and Commonality: An Essay on Confucian Religiousness*. Albany: State University of New York Press, 1993. (Rev. enlarged ed. of *Centrality and Commonality: An Essay on Chung-yung*.)

———. *Confucian Thought: Selfhood as Creative Transformation*. Albany: State University of New York Press, 1985.

———. *Humanity and Self-Cultivation*. Berkeley, Calif.: Asian Humanities Press, 1979.

———. *Way, Learning, and Politics: Essays on the Confucian Intellectual*. Albany: State University of New York Press, 1993.

Wang, Pi. *Commentary on the Lao Tzu*, trans. Ariane Rump in collaboration with Wing-tsit Chan. Society for Asian and Comparative Philosophy, Monograph No. 6. Honolulu: University Press of Hawaii, 1979.

Yearley, Lee H. *Facing Our Frailty: Comparative Religious Ethics and the Confucian Death Rituals*. Gross Memorial Lecture for 1995. Valparaiso, Ind.: Valparaiso University Press, 1995.

———. *Mencius and Aquinas: Theories of Virtue and Conceptions of Courage*. Albany: State University of New York Press, 1990.

Philosophy of Governance

Stephen ANGLE

Classical Chinese philosophy of governance revolved around three sets of questions: (1) How should a state be organized and governed? In particular, who or what should the people be expected to take as authoritative? (2) What are the proper goals of governance? Which goals are most fundamental? (3) How are the answers to the previous questions justified? What renders the means and ends of governance legitimate? The following sections will examine the range of answers to these questions found in the philosophical classics of the Warring States period (479–221 B.C.E.) in China.

A small amount of historical context will be useful before we begin. The Warring States era received its name from the incessant warfare conducted between the realms that had established themselves as independent powers after the effective demise of the Zhou dynasty. Not only was warfare common in this period; it was also increasingly vast in scope, as the chariot armies of the elite made way for much larger conscript-based armies. This change was in turn related to the increasing abilities of states to raise, organize, and feed such large armies. Larger populations and more complex governmental structures lay behind these developments (Lewis 1990). All these interrelated developments, in turn, both drove and were shaped by the philosophers of governance.

Since the schools of thought we now read into the Warring States were largely an invention of later (Han dynasty) historians, the best approach is to take individual texts, and sometimes individual chapters, as our basic unit of analysis. I proceed in approximately chronological order.

Guanzi: Carrot and Stick

The earliest chapters of the *Guanzi*, which were composed in Qi and date from the mid-fourth century B.C.E., are among the first theoretical writings on governance. In a famous passage from "Shepherding the People," we find that "Success in government lies in following the hearts of the people." Success is not defined as making the people happy—we learn elsewhere that success for the ruler is having a strong state that endures through the ages—but following the people's wishes turns out to be a necessary condition for success. Thus: "When the granaries are full, the people will know propriety and moderation; when their clothing and food are adequate, they will know the distinction between honor and shame." Similarly, "If the ruler can ensure the people their existence and provide them with security, they will be willing to endure danger and disaster for him."

This is not to say that the people should be given free rein. If they are well fed and put to work at tasks well suited to them, they are likely to accord with propriety and moderation, but the author adds that rulers must "Make clear the road to certain death," by which he means "having severe punishments" for those who go astray. In another chapter of the text (ch. 3), possibly by the same author, we find: "Those who shepherd the people desire them to be controllable. Since they desire them to be controllable, they must pay serious attention to standards (*fa*)." These "standards" are then enumerated; they include honoring ranks and ceremonial dress, giving salaries and rewards to the deserving, granting offices, and applying punishments. The *Guanzi* thus presents us with versions of the two techniques of governance that will run throughout the texts of the Warring States: nurturing the people and setting standards for them.

Mozi: Theological or Utilitarian Justification?

Roughly contemporary with the *Guanzi* was the *Mozi*, one chapter of which begins:

> In ancient times, when people were first born and before there were any punishments or government, in their languages each had a different notion of rightness (*yi*). One man had one notion, two men had two. . . . Thus those with good doctrines (*liangdao*) would keep them secret and refuse to teach them. (ch. 11)

This of course led to chaos and suffering, the cause of which was the absence of "a leader to govern." A ruler was therefore selected, declared the "son of heaven," and provided with a staff of ministers to aid him. The ruler then established the single idea of rightness that all would heed. The text describes a comprehensive hierarchy according to which each individual would heed his or her superior's judgment as to what was "good" (*shan*), ultimately leading up to the ruler, who would base his judgment on heaven.

"Heaven" (*tian*) is a difficult term. It once clearly referred to a religious entity but eventually comes to be understood in more naturalistic terms. Which it means in this chapter is a matter of scholarly disagreement. For the most part, philosophers of governance during the Warring States period do not appeal to supernatural standards to justify their claims. Even in the *Mozi*, if one takes evidence from other chapters into account, the interpretive dispute over *tian* remains. These other chapters record that just as carpenters can use a compass to determine what is circular, so an understanding of the "will of heaven" leads one to reliably judge what is right. The striking thing about a compass is that no special knowledge is needed to use it: it is a public, objective standard for circles. If the "will of heaven" is to be analogous, then there must be a public, objective standard for right. Mysterious knowledge of the will of a deity does not sound like a good candidate for such a public, objective standard. The text offers an alternative, though: it regularly speaks of maximally "benefiting" (*li*) the people as a standard. A neat way of resolving all these loose ends, then, is to conclude that the "will of heaven" is a metaphorical reference to the standard of "benefit." Proper Mohist governance thus would ultimately be a matter of utilitarian judgment.

Analects (*Lunyu*) and *Mencius*

The *Analects* is ostensibly a collection of sayings by Confucius and his students, but much if not all of it was composed after Confucius's death, and its various chapters express the teachings of individuals who identified themselves with his legacy. The earliest chapters in the text (mid-fifth to mid-fourth century B.C.E., chs. 3–9) may well be the earliest written philosophical reflection in China, but they show little direct concern with governance. In one of the most dramatic shifts in the text, governance takes center stage in a set of chapters (12, 13, 2) which may date from the last quarter of the fourth century B.C.E. (Brooks 1998). The theory of this segment of the *Analects* has much in common with the *Guanzi*. Asked about government, "Confucius" is made to say: "Enough food; enough weapons; the people having confidence in the ruler" (12.7). Of these, "confidence" (*xin*) is most important. Confidence here means that one identifies with the state, symbolized by the ruler, doing so because the state manifestly seeks what is good for one. This kind of identification was crucial to the success of states in an era of increasingly large and conscript-filled armies (see also 13.29–30).

The text's understanding of governance is permeated by the dynamics of people identifying with and modeling themselves on the ruler. Asked whether a ruler should kill those who fail to follow the way (*dao*), Confucius responds:

> You are there to govern; what use have you for killing? If you desire the good, the people will be good. The virtue of the gentleman is the wind; the virtue of the little people is the grass. The wind on the grass will surely bend it. (12.19; see also 2.1)

Unlike the emphasis put on "punishments" as one kind of "standard" (*fa*) in the *Guanzi*, the *Analects* here minimizes the importance of killing. This point is reinforced in perhaps the most famous saying in the text about governance:

> Lead them with government and regulate them by punishments, and the people will evade them with no sense of shame. Lead them with virtue and regulate them by ritual, and they will acquire a sense of shame—and moreover, they will be orderly. (2.3)

There are only a few passages that stress the continued need for punishments in a good society, and they all come quite late in the text: 13.3 is an obvious interpolation, and like the similar 20.2, it probably dates from the mid-third century B.C.E.

In a variety of ways the *Mencius* picks up where *Analects* 12, 13, and 2 left off; indeed, it is possible that Mencius (Meng Ke) was involved in the formulation of some of this material in the *Analects*. One innovation of the *Mencius* is to give a name to its preferred mode of governance: "humane government" (*renzheng*). This means that one should rule by loving the people like a parent: providing for them, educating them, giving them a role model. The text stresses that while this policy is beneficial to all involved, one must pursue it out of humane concern rather than out of cold calculation. Because of the ruler's ability to transform others through his example, if he acts on the basis of "benefit" (*li*) alone, his subjects will do so as well, each from his or her own narrow perspective. The result will be chaos and suffering, rather than the order, harmony, and mutual benefit that arise from genuinely humane governance (1A.1).

The *Mencius* emphasizes *renzheng* as well as the distinction between *yi* (rightness) and mere concern with benefit, rejecting utilitarian calculation without regard to *yi*. It also opposes coercive authority, recognizing that even modeling and imitating a role work indirectly:

> You can never win the allegiance of men by trying to dominate them with goodness; but if you use goodness to nurture them, then you will win the allegiance of the whole world. (4B.16; see also 7A.14)

From other places in the text we can tell that Mencius (or his followers) knew and disapproved of the Mohists; this passage criticizes the Mohist practice of directly enforcing a standard of goodness through hierarchy. The *Mencius* contains numerous hierarchical ideas (see especially 3A.4), but it has considerable faith in the people's ability to do good if they are provided for, and not otherwise (see 1A7, 3A3).

Both the *Mozi* and the *Guanzi*, as will many subsequent texts, stress the need for objective standards (*fa*). In this context *Analects* 12, 13, and 2 and *Mencius* stand out as not taking *fa* seriously. Even when we come upon the metaphor of a tool in *Mencius* (4A.1), it is applied to the idea of "humane government" rather than to specific standards that can be institutionalized. This is not to say that the *Analects* and *Mencius* were devoid of any notion of "standard." Their standard, though, is resolutely particular, rather than objective and general: the model set by the ethical ruler. The later *Analects* (e.g., 13.3, a late interpolation) and the *Xunzi* (see below) recognize a role for coercion, but authority in the earlier "Confucian" texts is noncoercive. People follow willingly, initially because the good ruler provides for them, and increasingly because they come to love him as a father: they are transformed from individuals into members of a single national family.

Daodejing: Nature and Nonaction (*Wuwei*)

A recently discovered version of the *Daodejing* begins:

> Cut off knowledge, abandon argumentation, and the people will benefit a hundredfold. Cut off cleverness, abandon "benefit," and there will be no more thieves or bandits. Cut off activity and abandon purposefulness, and the people will again be filial. . . . Exhibit the unadorned and embrace the simple. Have little thought of self and few desires. (Guodian *Daodejing A*; cf. ch. 19 of the received version)

In several respects the attitude expressed here echoes that of the *Mencius*: explicit discussion of "benefit" is rejected, though the indirect goal of benefiting the people is endorsed; argumentation—whether referring to litigation or logical disputation—is rejected; a simple life with "few desires" (cf. *Mencius* 7B.35) is favored. On at least the first two counts, Mohism seems the specific target (as it is in the *Mencius* as well).

Despite these resonances, though, there are also important differences between the *Daodejing* and *Mencius*. Most important are the differences in their respective positive accounts of what rulers should do. In the *Mencius*, as we have seen, rulers are enjoined to follow the way of the ancient kings and establish a humane government. The *Daodejing* is much more reticent about articulating any specific human standard; indeed, in the received version of the text, the line that reads "Cut off activity and abandon purposefulness" in the Guodian version has been updated to "Cut off 'benevolence' and abandon 'rightness,' " thus extending to followers of Confucius the treatment initially reserved only for Mohists.

The best communities, as far as the *Daodejing* is concerned, are those that form and flourish naturally, with little guidance from above. Later chapters will add that the community is best if small and isolated (ch. 80), as well as providing theoretical justifications for the success of such communities, as for instance ch. 51: "The way is revered and virtue is honored not because this is decreed by any authority but because it is natural for them to be treated so." Rulers succeed by allowing nature to take its course: by "not acting" (*wuwei*).

Zhuangzi: Rejecting Governance

Unlike the *Daodejing*, with which it is often lumped as a fellow "Daoist" text, it is difficult to read the *Zhuangzi* as concerned with governance or aimed at rulers. This is not to say that the text advocates anarchism; like all texts from the Warring States, it seems to take for granted that states will have rulers. To a greater extent than any other text, though, it is uninterested in the problems rulers faced and even seems disinclined to grant rulers any special authority. It is certainly at odds with those thinkers who believe that people must come to identify with their states. One gloss for the attitude of the text toward issues of governance, in fact, might be: avoid commitment, accept what comes.

At the heart of the text is a radical linguistic and epistemological argument against accepting any one perspective as ultimately, eternally correct. "Clarity" (*ming*) comes when one realizes the perspectival nature of all affirmations and denials. Once one has attained this kind of clarity, it makes no sense to put oneself on the line for any single set of evaluations, like "our state must triumph" or even "it is better for humans to flourish than plants." In the context of the harsh realities of the Warring States, these doctrines may well have appealed to many.

Shangjun shu: Benefit through Order

The *Shangjun shu* builds on two themes that we have already encountered. First (in ch. 7), it argues that "the greatest benefit to the people is order" (*zhi*). This is to implicitly accept that "benefit" (*li*) is the standard by which theories of governance are judged, but it also places particular stress on the collective character of "benefit." In a war-torn world, we are told, only when the state is strong can its inhabitants flourish. Those who act for their own interests rather than for the "benefit of the state," therefore, are to be punished (ch. 14). The text is no friend of those who like to debate and push their own agendas; it prefers a people devoted to agriculture who are "simple (*pu*) and easy to direct" (ch. 3). We can see here, in short, that one result of the fuzziness surrounding the idea of "benefiting the people" is that if clearer criteria can plausibly be seen as necessary conditions for benefiting the people, they take center stage. A prime example is "order." Disorder, it is natural to assume, is incompatible with the people's well-being, so rulers could concentrate on order and allow benefit to follow in its wake. Especially when combined with the idea that the people tend to be selfish and not understand what is really good for them, though, a focus on order can rapidly lead to tyranny.

Another idea we have seen already is that governance demands objective standards. This is a central theme of the *Shangjun shu*. It repeatedly stresses the importance of public, impartial standards (*fa*) for the application of punishment and reward. *Fa* is often translated "law," but its uses here and elsewhere are clearly broader than mere penal law. One kind of standard, to be sure, is the penal statute (*xian*), but standards take many other forms. The fact that rewards and punishments are regularly attached to standards makes it clear that these are normative expectations, not just ideals. In another way the *fa* are more than ideals: they are institutionalized. This aspect no doubt explains part of the appeal of translating *fa* as "law," since we often think of laws as norms that are subject to some kind of enforcement, unlike ethical ideals.

Finally, the text also insists that there be no debate over what the standards are or about when they have been fulfilled: the ruler alone fixes the standard, basing it on his assessment of the needs of the age. He should neither imitate antiquity nor follow current standards. What is crucial is that his standards set out the distinct roles (*fen*) expected of people, as well as the rewards and penalties that will enforce these roles. The text adds that the intelligent ruler will not fail to carry out his own role, on pain of "harming the standards."

Shen Buhai: Bureaucratic "Nonaction"

Shen became chancellor of the state of Han in 354 B.C.E. and died in 337 B.C.E. Early bibliographies list a text bearing his name, but nothing remains of it except quotations in other works; the original has been lost. It is thus difficult to date this material.

Shen's central insight seems to have been that government should be based not on feudal principles but on a bureaucratic system. Creel observes that Shen favored "a system of administration by means of professional functionaries, whose functions are more or less definitely prescribed" (1974, 55). Rulers should not find good men and give them responsibility, but instead find the right man for each role in the system. The role of the ruler in such a theory is simple: define the needed functions and select men to perform them, then "do nothing" (*wuwei*). Doing nothing does not mean literally abstaining from action, but the ruler does nothing more than keep the system running smoothly. Shen compares the ruler to a scale: ". . . which merely establishes equilibrium, itself doing nothing; yet the mere fact that it remains in balance causes lightness and heaviness to discover themselves" (Creel, 352). Unlike the *Daodejing*, which seems to trust nature more than man, Shen Buhai trusts human-made institutions more than individuals' decision-making powers.

Xunzi: Transforming the People

Chapter 19 of the *Xunzi* contains one of the most famous origin stories from the Warring States era:

> What is the origin of ritual (*li*)? I reply: man is born with desires. If his desires are not satisfied, he cannot but seek some means to satisfy them. If there are no limits and degrees to his seeking, then he will inevitably fall to wrangling with other men. From wrangling comes disorder and from disorder comes poverty. The ancient kings hated such disorder, and therefore they established ritual in order to establish distinctions, to nurture men's desires, and to provide for their satisfaction.

Ritual (*li*—a different character from that for "benefit") was important in many chapters of the *Analects*, but it takes on an even more central role here. While people (unlike animals) have the ability to notice and pay heed to distinctions (*fen*), they will not do so naturally. Their desires have to be shaped through ongoing education in ritual in order for society to be harmonious and for people to flourish. The text explicitly links ritual with the idea of "standard" (*fa*): "To reject ritual is to be without standards," and "a man without standards is lost and guideless" (ch. 2). That is, whereas the *Shangjun shu* presents the explicit regulations for when punishments and rewards are deserved, the *Xunzi* takes standards as coming through having been taught ritual by an expert teacher—by one's immediate teacher, by one's ruler, and by the sage kings, who originally established the proper set of rituals. Both texts seek to exploit features of human psychology to establish order, both in the name of benefiting the people. The central difference, which harks back to *Analects* 2.3, is that the *Shangjun shu* relies directly on people's desire for benefit and hatred of harm while the *Xunzi* relies on people's ability to care about "distinctions" in order to transform them. Once this transformation has taken place, ritual propriety and shame, rather than direct concern with benefit, will guide them.

Han feizi: Pragmatic Justification of Practical Policies

Like several earlier texts, the *Han feizi* (or *Han Fei Zi*) puts considerable stress on objective criteria for governance. Rulers are to compare "names" (*ming*)—that is, explicit statements of the duties of a position—with results and bestow awards or inflict punishments based on how the two correspond. We also read: "A truly enlightened ruler uses standards (*fa*) to select men for him; he does not choose them himself" (ch. 49). While the ruler does not choose ministers according to his own judgment or whim, he still must establish standards in the first place; he cannot simply rely on tradition or precedent. "The sage does not try to practice the ways of antiquity or to abide by a fixed standard, but examines the affairs of the age and takes what precautions are necessary." This contrasts with strands in several earlier texts that advocated conforming with past tradition. In some of these texts, the recorded or imagined practices of earlier ages are thought to have epistemological significance: to be evidence of the insights of the sages. Others, more skeptical about naturalistic justifications, imply that observing tradition is our only means of agreeing on a single set of standards, and without such agreement, disorder looms.

More common than a desire to conform to old practices, though, is the notion that times change and the good ruler must be prepared to change with them. New standards are needed for a new age. This is even endorsed by some of the texts that ground ultimate justification in the natural order: the underlying patterns of nature may not change, but their specific applications can, as human society grows and changes. Other justifications of change are more pragmatic, though, and the *Han feizi* is perhaps the most explicit. Here we read that rulers are enjoined to measure the gains that come from enacting new standards against the losses that ensue; ". . . if one finds gain will exceed losses, one goes ahead with them" (ch. 47).

The *Han feizi* also gives us a clearer idea than any earlier text of why rule by standards was to be preferred to rule by the wise and virtuous. Chapter 40 puts readers through the following dialectic. We begin with the idea, attributed to Shen Dao, that virtue and wisdom are unnecessary for good governance; everything depends on "political purchase" (*shi*) and "status" (*wei*). To this a critic responds that "talent" (*cai*) is also necessary: give power to the unworthy, and the result will be chaos. The author then replies that when rulers are so good or bad that nothing will change them, he will call it *shi*-by-nature and grant the critic's point. The author is interested in the average ruler, for whom *shi* is crucial. So in the end we come back to Shen Dao's position as the only tenable one for the vast majority of rulers—and for all the rulers for whom the author's advice is going to make any difference.

Another theme of the text is the conflict between individuals and impartial, state interests. We are shown that even for the virtuous, family loyalties regularly trump state loyalties, and thus:

> Since the interests of superior and inferior are as disparate as all this, it is hopeless for the ruler to praise the actions of the private individual and at the same time try to insure blessing on the state's altars of the soil and grain. (ch. 49)

The author analyzes this as a conflict between "partial" (*si*) and "impartial" (*gong*) perspectives and argues that the two are mutually irreconcilable.

The ruler, in particular, must heed the distinction between *gong* and *si*. For instance, "For his part the ruler must never make selfish (*si*) use of his wise ministers or able men, so the people are never tempted to go beyond their communities to form friendships." The clear suggestion is that the ruler can be blamed if people conspire against him. We also read, in Chapter 10, that "To fail to heed your loyal ministers when you are at fault, insisting on having your own way, . . . will in time destroy your good reputation and make you a laughingstock to others." While there are certainly some sections of the text that paint the relationship between rulers and ministers as conflictive—since the latter tend to look only to their personal concerns, at the expense of the state's more general well-being—this chapter, at least, urges a more constructive relationship between them.

Huang-Lao Boshu (Silk Manuscripts): Natural Law?

We have long known, on the basis of histories compiled in the Han dynasty, that an intellectual movement known as Huang-Lao (from "Yellow Emperor" and "Laozi") was an important player in the early Han and perhaps the late Warring States. Little has been known about Huang-Lao until recently, though, because none of the texts associated with this trend of thought was known to have survived. In 1973 four texts that have been identified as exemplifying Huang-Lao ideas were discovered, and scholars have been working since then to interpret them and reinterpret the intellectual era of the Warring States, Qin, and Han in their light. While each of the individual texts has a title, it is not known if they together constituted a single work; for convenience, I will follow Peerenboom (1993) in referring to the group as the *Boshu* ("silk manuscripts").

In many ways the *Boshu* resemble texts that we have already discussed. They put great stress on standards (*fa*); they advocate a centralized, bureaucratic state in which each person has a clearly assigned place and role, with failure to fulfill said role resulting in certain punishment. The goal of the state is to bring benefit to all: "To bring it about that the masses share equally in the benefit and all rely on one is what is meant by rightness (*yi*)."

In certain places, though, emphases distinct to the *Boshu* emerge. Unlike some of the harsher chapters in the *Shangjun shu*, the *Boshu* do not contemplate using severe punishments to deter minor offenses; punishment must fit the crime. We also read that the ruler should exercise moderation so that the masses prosper, since: "When the masses prosper, they have a sense of shame. When they have a sense of shame, edicts and orders become customs, and penal laws and penalties are not violated." The idea that the ruler's standards can be transformed into the people's customs is not unique to this text; it also appears in Chapter 11 of the *Shangjun shu*. Still, the invocation of a "sense of shame" certainly echoes the *Analects*.

The greatest difference between the *Boshu* and texts like the *Analects* or the *Shangjun shu*, though, lies in what Peerenboom calls its "foundational naturalism." The first of the texts begins this way:

> The way (*dao*) produces standards (*fa*). Standards are what draw the line between gain and loss, and make clear the curved and the straight. He who grasps the way, therefore, produces standards and does not dare to transgress them.

The *dao* is the natural order in which our human standards are grounded. There is a right way and a wrong way to produce standards—and once one has done it correctly, one does not dare to transgress them.

Many of the texts discussed to this point appeal to natural appropriateness. They vary in the degree to which human intervention or invention is required. The *Daodejing* deplores putting human standards between us and nature. The *Mencius* has considerable faith in the natural inclinations of people, though it requires that they be nurtured so that their ethical dispositions develop properly. The *Xunzi*, on the other hand, believes that only the sages were able to understand the patterns of nature well enough to set up a ritual system which would properly train us to live harmoniously within the limits nature imposes. The *Boshu* goes a step beyond that, arguing that the standards all rulers must heed are themselves natural—something very like the western conception of natural law.

Conclusion: The Next Two Millennia

The ideas raised during the Warring States era were revised, synthesized, rejected, and raised again countless times over the following 2,000 years of Chinese history. Despite the fact that thinkers and texts labeled by historians of the Han era (202 B.C.E.—220 C.E.) as belonging to the "school of standards" (*fajia*; also translated as "legalists") were widely rejected, governmental institutions continued to implement many of their ideas. "Confucian" thinkers regularly brought up the issue of standards; perhaps the most famous of these thinkers was Huang Zongxi, who wrote in the seventeenth century C.E. that a "rule of men" could succeed only if it was established on the back of a "rule of standards" (*fazhi*). Huang seemed to mean primarily the establishment of institutions to transform people—closest perhaps to Xunzi, of those here examined—but twentieth-century reformers have also looked to this as a recognition from within Confucianism of the need for law. The debate that surfaced throughout the later imperial era over whether civil servants should be chosen primarily through examination (i.e., *fa*) or through recommendation (i.e., human judgment) is another example of this ongoing tension.

The roles and responsibilities of both ministers and rulers continued to be at the center of the philosophy of governance. Attempts to articulate reasons for limiting the ruler's power continued, most notably with the neo-Confucian idea of "pattern" (*li*), which, like the Huang-Lao idea of "standard" examined above, shares something with the western idea of natural law (Wood 1995). On the other hand, part of the explanation for the extreme violence certain rulers showered on their ministers stems from the selfless devotion that one version of Confucianism taught these rulers to expect from those who served them (Dardess 1983).

The vocabulary and concerns of Chinese philosophy of governance began to change at a much faster rate in the late nineteenth century, as Chinese thinkers began to take seriously various European and American theories of politics. The discourse over governance in the past hundred years has continued to include many themes from earlier eras, including the importance of benefiting the people, of identifying with the state (or nation), and of order. Alongside these have developed concerns for rights (*quanli*) of various kinds, equality (*pingdeng*), and a variety of understandings of democracy (*minzhu*) (Angle 2002). The past hundred years, in fact, have seen a flourishing of perspectives on the philosophy of governance unparalleled in China since the Warring States.

See also *Fa; Li*: Principle, Pattern, Reason; *Quanli*; *Yi* and *Li*.

Bibliography

Ames, Roger T. *The Art of Rulership: A Study in Ancient Chinese Political Thought*. Honolulu: University of Hawaii Press, 1983.

Angle, Stephen C. *Human Rights and Chinese Thought: A Cross-Cultural Inquiry*. New York: Cambridge University Press, 2002.

Brooks, E. Bruce, and A. Taeko, trans and eds. *The Original Analects: Sayings of Confucius and His Successors*. New York: Columbia University Press, 1998.

Creel, Herrlee G. *Shen Pu-hai: A Chinese Political Philosopher of the Fourth Century B.C.* Chicago, Ill.: University of Chicago Press, 1974.

"*Daode jing A*." In *Bamboo Slips from the Chu Tomb at Guodian*, ed. Jingmen City Museum. Beijing: Wenwu, 1998.

Dardess, John W. *Confucianism and Autocracy: Professional Elites in the Founding of the Ming Dynasty*. Berkeley: University of California Press, 1983.

de Bary, William Theodore. *The Trouble with Confucianism*. Cambridge, Mass.: Harvard University Press, 1991.

Hsiao, Kung-chuan. *A History of Chinese Political Thought*, trans. F. W. Mote. Princeton, N.J.: Princeton University Press, 1979.

Lewis, Mark Edward. *Sanctioned Violence in Early China*. Albany, N.Y.: State University of New York Press, 1990.

Metzger, Thomas A. *Escape from Predicament: Neo-Confucianism and China's Evolving Political Culture*. New York: Columbia University Press, 1977.

Mizoguchi, Yuzo. "The Development of the Concepts of 'General' and 'Personal' Found in China." *Shiso*, No. 669, 1980. (In Japanese.)

Nathan, Andrew J. *Chinese Democracy*. Berkeley: University of California Press, 1985.

Peerenboom, Randall P. *Law and Morality in Ancient China: The Silk Manuscripts of Huang-Lao*. Albany: State University of New York Press, 1993.

Rickett, W. Allyn, trans. *Guanzi*. Princeton, N.J.: Princeton University Press, 1985, 1998.

Schwartz, Benjamin. *In Search of Wealth and Power: Yen Fu and the West*. Cambridge, Mass.: Harvard University Press, 1964.

Turner, Karen. "War, Punishment, and the Law of Nature in Early Chinese Concepts of the State." *Harvard Journal of Asiatic Studies*, December 1993.

Wakeman, Frederic, Jr. "The Price of Autonomy: Intellectuals in Ming and Qing Politics." *Daedalus*, March 1972.

Wood, Alan T. *Limits to Autocracy: From Sung Neo-Confucianism to a Doctrine of Political Rights*. Honolulu: University of Hawaii Press, 1995.

Yates, Robin D. S., trans. *Five Lost Classics: Dao, Huang-Lao, and Yin-Yang in Han China*. New York: Ballantine, 1997.

Zarrow, Peter. *Anarchism and Chinese Political Culture*. New York: Columbia University Press, 1990.

Philosophy of History

David S. Nivison

Our word "history" can mean either what has happened in the past or what is thought or written about what has happened in the past. Accordingly, in "philosophy of history" a distinction is commonly made between philosophizing about the meaning or patterns in what has happened over past time (perhaps extending to what supposedly will happen in the future); and philosophical analysis and criticism of how historians think or ought to think (and write).

In recent American and European philosophy, "philosophy of history" of the latter kind, sometimes called "critical," has been driven by the problem of the unity of the sciences, and specifically by the question whether there are special kinds of reasoning and explaining proper for historians; and in the background is always the problem of induction. These problems can't be found in Chinese philosophy before the twentieth century (or in the west before the nineteenth century, or possibly the eighteenth). But questioning about what the pattern of the past is, and where we all are in it, is conspicuous in Chinese philosophy from its beginning. Eventually one begins to see the Chinese attending also to questions we will have to call "critical" ones.

There is one very important point to make first: The Chinese have always been extraordinarily interested in their own history, and over centuries have written vast amounts about it. The history section of any traditional Chinese library was enormous, with texts dating back as far as the eleventh century B.C.E. (India was utterly different. Most of what we know about early Indian history we learn from the accounts of the

Greeks, or of Chinese Buddhist pilgrims.) It has been conjectured that this interest in history grew out of a basic root, ancestor worship, in the earliest Chinese religion. Ancestor spirits were maintained by sacrifices made by their present descendants, who in turn depended on their ancestors' support. The cult therefore required regular reports to the ancestors, and also seeking their guidance and assent through divination. For example, certain oracle inscriptions (*Bingbian* 83, 1–2) appear to indicate that the Shang king Wu Ding (late thirteenth century) thought that an affliction he suffered was due to his having failed to report a military order to the ancestral shrines. And this (it is argued) led in time to the keeping of chronicles by important lineages and so, later, by the states that were the extensions of a lineage's authority. The living had to justify what they were doing, and so had to know what they were doing. (See Pines 1997, 80–81.)

So, the basic questions: What has been going on? And where are we? How these questions are answered will depend on when they are asked. Reaching back as far as I can, I look back at what in later times the Chinese have called the Three Dynasties. This was a long period of about twelve centuries, when northern China was made up of many small "states" (I will call them), three of them being dominant in turn for four or five centuries at a stretch. Their names are Xia, Shang (or Yin), and Zhou. At the time of this writing, a vast research project was going on in China, involving scores of scholars and backed by the government in Beijing, trying to discover the exact or approximate dates of reigns and major events during these dynasties—the earliest heretofore recognized date being 841 B.C.E., when Li, the tenth king of the Zhou dynasty, was driven into exile and a regent, Gong He, took over for fourteen years. Adding spice to this development is the fact that probably more than half of the community of scholars believes that the "Xia dynasty" is a myth.

The question at this stage of Chinese history has to be, What justifies a dynasty? What gives it the right to "rule" (or dominate) the world (China was the world—"all under heaven"—for the Chinese at this time, and for long after); and when and why would this right ever end? The earliest evidence for an answer is astronomical, suggesting that astrology played a role. A conjunction of the planets in February 1953 B.C.E. has been linked with the beginning of Xia. Another quasiconjunction, in November–December 1576 B.C.E., was seen as heralding the rise of Shang. And a conjunction in May 1059 B.C.E. was regarded as heralding the rise of Zhou. Implicit in this is the idea that each of these dynasties enjoyed the approval of what the Chinese came to call *tian*, "heaven." There had to be a reason for heaven's favor—expressed as heaven's "mandate" (*ming*) to rule. It came to be thought that the founder of a dynasty was seen by heaven as the worthiest man in the world to govern and care for the people. The concept was that he was endowed, more than anyone else, with a quality called *de*, usually translated "virtue," giving him awe-inspiring prestige and disposing him to moderation and the inclination to heed good advice, and to piety in sacrifices to spirits. The "virtue" of the founder was the virtue of his dynasty, continuing from generation to generation, but in time ebbing away. It came to be thought that somewhere in the middle of the dynasty's run, or later, there was a revival (*chongxing*), guided by wise ministers; but this would be followed by more decay, until in a final time of troubles the virtue of the dynasty had run out, in the reign of a last ruler who was either a hopeless weakling or a tyrant who squandered the remaining virtue in an outburst of vicious government and personal license. Heaven would then discover a new paragon of virtue, who would receive the "mandate of heaven" to found a new dynasty, and the cycle would be repeated.

When did these ideas take shape? The earliest texts are early Zhou; we have no direct information on what the Shang thought of the Xia, or of themselves. And during the Zhou the ideas were still forming. A speech that pretends to be (and may be) of the late eleventh century B.C.E., probably by the duke of Zhou as chief tutor for the junior King Cheng, delivers a salutary warning to the victorious Zhou people and their young king:

> We cannot fail to mirror ourselves in the Xia; also we cannot fail to mirror ourselves in the Yin [Shang]. We must not presume to suppose that Xia had the Mandate of Heaven for a fixed period of years; we must not presume to suppose that it was not going to continue. It was because they did not reverently care for their virtue that they then early let their mandate fall. (Nivison 1995, 181)

Thus although heaven decrees changes of dynasty, these changes are not fated; they follow on human failings (which seem, nonetheless, always to occur, in the long run). How does heaven act? Not by issuing verbal commands, of course. Heaven's will, explains Mengzi (Mencius)—a philosopher of the fourth century B.C.E. who was a supporter of Confucius—is revealed by the way human beings act (5A5): if they accept a new ruler, this shows that it is heaven's will that he be the ruler. (See also Bokenkamp 1994, 61–63.)

This way of thinking was firmly in place by the time of the classical philosophers, starting with Confucius (Kongzi) in the early fifth century. In the earliest books of the *Analects* (*Lunyu*), likely to contain genuine remarks of the master, he complains that there is not enough present evidence for him to discuss the institutions of Xia and of Shang (3.9), though it is possible to make some inferences from later eras to earlier ones (2.23); nonetheless Zhou was able to draw on the experience of the two earlier dynasties and had an excellent culture, which he, Confucius, prefers (3.14). We see in this three points: the "three dynasties" are now the standard picture of the historical past; it was assumed there was progress from one to the next; and one must look to the past for models of excellence, but to the relatively recent past, both because it was better and, perhaps, because one can know it better.

Confucius was talking about Zhou in its strength, what we call the Western Zhou, before the king was driven east to Loyang in 770, becoming virtually powerless in a world of interstate anarchy. Confucius is represented as lamenting this situation in a later book (16.2): when things are going well—"when all-under-heaven has the Way"—then "rites and music" (institutional standards) and military campaigns are authorized by the "son of heaven," i.e., by the king; when the Way is lacking, these things are written by the regional lords; and when this happens, seldom do they fail to lose this authority within ten generations, controls passing to their great officers; and when this happens, one can expect that these officers will lose control in five generations; and so on. We see in this a point of view that becomes entrenched: good times were in the past; and good times were times when authority was firmly in the hands of the "one man" (as the king called himself) at the political center of the world.

Within two generations after Confucius we can see these ideas undergoing a cosmic transformation. This takes the form of a basic alteration in the "three dynasties" picture of the historical past. The growing anarchy, and the multiplication of local lords' courts where an adviser with a message could get a hearing, led to more persons who, like Confucius, gathered a group of students and preached recipes for the betterment of the world, or of individual life. These new "ways" appealed to the past for justification, and the past was improved to fill the need. On the one hand, the dynastic concept seems to have been sharpened. The last rulers of Western Zhou and of Shang became archetypes of evil, while the founders were mythicized as paragons of benevolence; thus the Zhou conquest of Shang, actually a bloody affair, was claimed to have been carried off by the sheer power of the "virtue" of King Wu. The last ruler of the Xia, actually a nobody, was upstaged by an invented frightful "bad last ruler" named Jie.

The emerging "philosophers" went on to ask what happened before dynasties began. Their answer was to dress up two perhaps imaginary predynastic utterly perfect rulers named Yao and Shun. Yao reigned for 100 years, and in his seventieth year sought out the worthiest man in the world, Shun, to be his successor, giving Shun his two daughters in marriage. Shun in his turn selected Yu, who became the first king of Xia. (Thus Yao and Shun could be, and for a long time were, thought of as the opening chapter of the story of Xia.) When Yu approached death, he too selected a successor; but after he died, his people chose to acknowledge his son as his heir. This was a step down, morally: best was the practice of passing on the royal authority to a man chosen for his excellence, not by the accident of birth. This Yao-Shun myth was thus a reproach to existing lords and kings.

But the fertility of the Chinese historical imagination was only getting started. More ancient and yet better archaic "emperors" were discovered. Several steps farther back, Huang Di, the "Yellow Emperor," seems to have entered Chinese historical and political consciousness in the late fifth century. Lists of yet earlier emperors vary; one of these, Shen Nong, the "Divine Farmer," had devotees whom Mencius had to argue with in the mid-fourth century. The followers of Shen Nong believed that he had presided over a world of peaceful anarchy, in which rulers (if one could call anyone that) never exploited their subjects in any way: no taxes, no salaries to idle dignitaries. The ruler himself grew his own food, working in the fields as a farmer like everyone else. Mencius (3A4) gently tried to get across to these people the beautiful concept of the division of labor. He concluded crisply: Some work with their minds; some work with their muscles. Those who work with their minds govern others; those who work with their muscles are governed by others. Those who govern others are fed by others; those who are governed by others feed others. That's just the way it is.

Mencius was something of an antinomian himself. He was an earnest pacifist, and insisted to his royal patrons that a ruler had no need for warfare; if he desired to expand his domains, all he need do was govern with benevolence, and the people of the whole world would want to be his subjects. And no other ruler, trusting in arms, would dare face him. Consistently with this stance, Mencius was insistent that the Zhou conqueror Wu Wang had achieved his victory without bloodshed. One of the texts that became a chapter in the classic the *Book of History* (*Shangshu*), the "Completion of the War" (*Wu cheng*, perhaps now lost) gave a bloody description of the battle. Mencius is rather famous for his comment (7B3):

> If one believed everything in the *Book of History*, it would have been better for the book not to have existed at all. In the "Wu Cheng" chapter I accept only two or three strips. A benevolent man has no match in the world. How could it be that "the blood spilled was enough to carry staves along with it," when the most benevolent waged war against the most cruel? (Lau 1970, 194, adapted)

Should we call this (as some do) an instance of critical courage, in being ready to question even a revered classic? ("Critical" philosophy of history here?) Perhaps better, an instance of myth in the making. Mencius wants to admire King Wu, and is applying a "principle of charity," assuming the best (from Mencius's viewpoint) of him. Or is it wishful thinking? And is there a difference? Mencius can be found smoothing out the developing legend of Shun in much the same way (e.g., 5A4).

Philosophical appeals to a perfect (if unreal) past could be carried farther than the followers of Shen Nong took them. The most basic norms of morality and of society could be questioned, as having developed by dialectical stages, only after humankind departed from primal innocence. So in the *Laozi* (a collection of sayings and verses that grew by accretion in the fourth and third centuries), one reads that "when the Way was lost there was virtue; when virtue was lost there was benevolence; when benevolence was lost there was rectitude; when rectitude was lost there were the rites"—the "Way" being the state of humanity in which all doing was unself-conscious and unscheming. Primitivist flights of this kind were challenges to an increasingly harsh political and social world, as out of the anarchy that followed the Western Zhou there gradually developed a picture of fewer and larger and more tightly organized "warring states" in the century or more before the Qin conquest that established the first empire. All viewpoints felt the effect. Besides primitivist and anarchist reactions, there were apologists of a more conservative stamp, who at the same time were radical, in trying to see man's present condition in time in total terms. Followers of Mozi (Mo Di, c. 400 B.C.E.) argued that warfare would stop if all would adopt an attitude of concern for one another's welfare—hardly a realistic hope unless it were guaranteed that all would do so.

Accordingly, this school of thought offered a historical analysis and justification of law-governed political order. In the beginning of things, each person had his own concept of the right, which was what satisfied his own interest; and there was a "war of all against all." To remedy this, a king created government, appointing the highest officers, who appointed those below themselves, and so on, down to heads of villages. Then each of the officers at the bottom of the structure ordered his people to accept the dictates of the next officer up, who in turn ordered those under him to follow the orders and accept the judgments of right and wrong of his own superior, and so on, up to the king, who ordered all the people of the world to accept the will of heaven—which was, naturally, that all adopt an attitude of concern for one another's welfare. All very logical. Except that one wonders how it was all supposed to get started, by the choosing and recognition of a king. The same kind of question can be asked about western "contractarian" justifications of social and moral order.

Mozi created a tight sectarian movement around himself, his followers heaping scorn on Confucius and his adherents, who not surprisingly reciprocated. Not least was Xunzi, the most prominent Confucian voice during the 200s B.C.E., in the generation after Mencius, and the decades preceding the creation (by conquest) of the first "empire" under Qin. Xunzi also contended against Mencius, deploring Mencius's invitation (as Xunzi saw the matter) to moral and philosophical chaos. Mencius (6A7) had held that the "sages"—founders of moral order—had merely "anticipated" and first articulated moral sentiments that we all have access to in our own "hearts." Not so, said Xunzi: The sages created morality, or more exactly, discovered by the exercise of their superior intelligence the political and moral order that alone could make an acceptable human life possible. Xunzi's statement at the beginning of his treatise on "the rites"—metaphorically the whole body of rules, standards, and laws we live by—puts the matter clearly:

> What is the origin of ritual? I reply: man is born with desires. If his desires are not satisfied for him, he cannot but seek some means to satisfy them himself. If there are no limits and degrees to his seeking, then he will inevitably fall to wrangling with other men. From wrangling comes disorder, and from disorder comes exhaustion. The ancient kings hated such disorder, and therefore they established rites and norms in order to curb it, to train men's desires and to provide for their satisfaction. (Watson 1963, 89, adapted)

Xunzi, the authoritarian Confucian, is not unlike the Mozi he criticizes: there is the same concept of social order as deliverance from an intolerable state of nature; and there is the same difficulty, that the beginning of it all is not really explained, because we don't in the end know where kings came from.

For Xunzi, at least, "morality," though invented, was still morality. Some of his contemporaries had a brutally naturalistic view of the matter. One stripe of thinker—Han Feizi, said to have been a sometime student of Xunzi, is notable—argued frankly that the means a state must use to control a population need be restrained by no "moral" or historical scruples. A book of the third century B.C.E. bearing the name of the fourth-century Qin high officer Shang Yang sees a dialectical process of development of standards and laws:

> During the time when heaven and earth were established, and the people were produced, people knew their mothers but not their fathers. Their way was to love their relatives and to be fond of what was their own. This led to discrimination and insecurity. Therefore as peoples increased in number they fell into disorder, . . . subjecting each other by force, leading to quarrels and disputes. . . . So men of talent established equity and justice and instituted unselfishness, and the people began to delight in moral virtue. At that time the idea of loving one's relatives began to disappear and that of honoring talent arose.
>
> Now . . . the way of talented men is to try to outdo one another. As people further increased, without restraint long trying to outdo one another, there was again disorder. So a sage, having been given direction of things, made divisions of land and property, and distinctions between men and women; it was then necessary to have restraining measures, so he established interdicts. It was then necessary to have those who could enforce them, so he established officials. This having been done, it was necessary to have someone to unify them; so he set up a ruler. Once this had been done, the idea of honoring talent disappeared and that of prizing noble rank arose. Thus in the highest antiquity people loved their relatives and were fond of what was their own; in middle antiquity they honored talent and delighted in moral virtue; and in later days they prized noble rank and respected office. . . . As conditions in the world change, different principles are practiced. (Duyvendak 1928, 225–227, adapted)

As a historical anthropology of morals, this is messy. But the point is that by now some thinkers could take a completely cold view of morals as simply a historical phenomenon, each successive age generating its own standards.

Both Shang Yang (in the book) and Han Feizi had a strikingly "social scientific" conception of history. Its moving force is the inevitably increasing stress of population growth. An apparently benevolent near anarchy was possible in early ages, Han Feizi writes, but no longer:

> The generosity with resources in ancient times was not benevolence, it was because resources were ample. The competition and robbery of today is not dishonesty, it is because resources are sparse. (ch. 19.49 Graham 1989, 273)

Like Xunzi, these men object to those who would take the very remote past as a model for the present; but the reason differs: times change, and one must keep one's eye on present conditions. Change is a stage-by-stage movement away from primitive simplicity; but (unlike the Daoists) they do not see this as deterioration; different times are simply different, neither better nor worse. What is called for now is severity.

All of these—Mozi, Xunzi, Shang Yang, Han Feizi—can be seen as justifying the increasingly severe measures of control necessary in the relatively new centrally organized states of the Warring States era (c. 403–221 B.C.E.). All of these take it for granted that if other people pay attention to the past at all, they will be looking to the past for guidance in present decision making: but the former are moralists, still looking themselves to the wisdom of the past; the latter are starkly amoral, brutally realistic, warning against letting past ways hobble present expediency. One more step, and we find the idea—looking toward a new imperial world order—that the present, or the imminent future, is or will be better than the past, even the idea that history, if one takes a really long view, is progressive. This tendency takes various forms.

In the second half of the fourth century B.C.E. the rulers of the leading states claimed the title *wang*, "king." The background concept was that there could be only one legitimate king in the world. So these new "kings" were doing two things. First, they were declaring war on each other (and had therefore to agree by treaty, pro tem, to recognize one another's claims). And second, they were saying out loud what all by this time thought: that the nominal Zhou dynasty was over, and that there would soon be a new one; and the advent of a new dynasty was (by the dynastic concept) supposed to usher in an age when whatever was wrong with the world would be righted. Philosophers were eager to explain to these kinglets how to do it.

Mencius was notable in this regard. Having been a guest of the king of Qi for several years, without having his advice accepted, he left sometime after 314 B.C.E. and reflected:

> Every five hundred years a true king should arise. . . . From (the beginning of) Zhou to the present it is over seven hundred years. The five hundred mark is passed; the time seems ripe. It must be that Heaven does not yet wish to bring peace to the world. . . . (2B13; see also 7B38)

So dynasties were supposed to last five hundred years; and the Xia and the Shang had done so, approximately. History by the numbers, in the popular mind, exact numbers.

The number 700 was in the air. According to the *Zuo Commentary* (written in the late 300s B.C.E.), in 606 the lord of Chu after a victory received congratulations from an envoy of King Ding of Zhou, and asked him the weight of the royal tripods (made by Xia, acquired by Shang, then by Zhou), thought to represent the royal "virtue." The envoy replied that the virtue of

Zhou, though attenuated, was not exhausted, and the weight might not be asked; the second king, Zheng, had divined that Zhou would last thirty generations and 700 years (*Zuo*, "Duke Xuan" 3.4.) (King Xian, in the thirtieth generation, reigned from 368 to 321; the Zhou began in 1040—I think; the date is still disputed.) The *Bamboo Annals* records that the tripods were placed in Loyang in 1027, and lost in the Si River in 327; this book was a chronicle of the Wei state, carefully constructed to glorify its kings. The royal reign of the first Wei "king" announced his claim in 335; the *Annals* dates the Zhou king's appointment of the ancestral first lord of Jin (succeeded by Wei) to 1035. The astute student of Chinese history of this time will notice much more of this sort of thing.

In the next century, and on into Qin and Han, one sees another motif, very characteristic of this very credulous and imaginative age. Xunzi had insisted that the basic principles of society and government are the same from age to age, though most clearly revealed in later history. But he also had conceived of "rites and principles" as formulated by the "sages" as necessary for human civilized life, and therefore as in effect a continuation in the human world of the order of nature, which was Xunzi's concept of heaven. When combined with the concept of successive dynasties, this idea naturally suggests (though Xunzi would have rejected this) that in different dynasties different ordering principles are in effect. And this in turn leads to the idea that a series of characteristics will manifest itself in successive dynasties in an unending cycle. It is now that the idea of the "five elements" or "five phases" (*wuxing*), or "five powers" (*wude*) appears in popular thinking.

An elder contemporary of Xunzi named Zou Yan is noteworthy for popularizing this concept. (Zou was also a moral philosopher of a Confucian persuasion.) He was feted by local kings, and wrote an enormous volume of stuff, none of which survives. Zou's term was "five virtues" or "powers" (*wude*); for him they were—to judge from an account in the philosophical encyclopedia *Lüshi chunqiu* of the mid-third century, which is thought to express his ideas—earth, wood, metal, fire, and water, correlated with Huang Di (and following reigns), Xia (probably including Yao and Shun preceding), Shang, Zhou, and—? What next? The question was to excite much discussion. A complicating factor is that there are other orders of the elements or "powers"; the foregoing is the order of nonovercoming (e.g., fire cannot overcome water); but another ordering is the order of production (which I will leave to the imagination). For these assignments to have any meaning, one must think of broad categories of things, actions, attitudes, etc., as falling under the heading of this or that element. For instance, colors were correlated with the "elements," also tastes, emotions, seasons of the year (with one element to spare). Metal belonged to autumn, and cruelty; so autumn was the time for executing criminals. This correlational type of pseudoscience captured the Chinese imagination permanently.

The early Han dynasty, succeeding the short-lived empire established by the Qin conquest, went wild with it. Noteworthy is an official and scholar of the second century B.C.E. named Dong Zhongshu (c. 179–104), followed by a commentator named He Xiu (129–182) in the second Han era; and I will sketch only a small part of their exuberant speculations. Dong was not satisfied with just five categories succeeding each other dynastywise through time. He perceived also a cycle of three, and a cycle of two. The three were colors, white, red and black, in that order: Zhou was red. The two were refinement (*wen*) and simplicity (*zhi*). For example, Shang's principle was simplicity, Zhou's was refinement. There are two important correlates of these cyclical concepts: One is that the characteristic of an age is determined by heaven, but also commanded by heaven, who will show the dynastic founder by some telling portent what this age is to be; and if the human world does not act accordingly, natural calamities will ensue. The second is that the shift in motif from one age to the next is correctional: thus an excess of "refinement" must be followed by a return to "simplicity." These ideas too had a long future, reappearing in other guises.

This brings me to a decisive point in Chinese history, the formation of a universal empire in the Chinese world. Summing up so far: First, I noted the emergence, during the Three Dynasties, of the concept of a dynasty as enjoying the mandate of heaven and as being succeeded by another when it fails to deserve that mandate. Next, in the decades following the reduction of the Western Zhou state and its disintegration into warring entities, there was an increasing tendency to look back to a past which was better than the present, and when there was a respected central power. Following that, there was an exaggeration of this idea, in perfect times in a remote past variously conceived, under earlier and earlier mythical "emperors," as protest against present-day harsh government and warfare. Then, there were philosophical justifications of the regimes of control (as new states develop and grow stronger), set in historical terms, that try to explain why and how political and social order arose in the first place. And last, there were expectations of a new unification of the world, typically seen as decreed by heaven, playing on the old idea of the dynastic cycle, with new metaphysical coloration.

The ideas of Dong, as elaborated by He Xiu, for which he was best-known in his own time were his ideas about a book—a history—that Confucius himself was said to have written, called the *Chunqiu* or *Springs and Autumns*. But to put this in place I must say something about the development of historical writing. One kind of historical text was recorded documents, especially speeches by royal officers and edicts of rulers. Some of these were often quoted by philosophers, and by the third century some of them had been gathered together into a book, part of which survives as the *Shangshu*, one of the so-called Chinese classics. And as opposed to records of words, there were records of actions, in the form (at first) simply of official chronicles. According to another "classic" there were two recorders, a "right" and a "left," who were charged with recording the words and the actions, respectively, of the sovereign (*Liji* 13, *Yu Zao*). A generic name for such chronicles was *chunqiu*, "springs and autumns," i.e., years. One may note the state-centered character of early historical writings; "private" histories followed later. The Zhou court had its *chunqiu*, and all of the regional courts had theirs (sometimes named differently).

The *Chunqiu*, which became one of the "classics," was, or was derived from, the *chunqiu* of the state of Lu, Confucius's native state. These chronicles were apparently available for public inspection. After its conquest of the other states, the Qin decreed that all chronicles other than its own were to be destroyed; for each chronicle naturally gave precedence to its own state. Another indication that they were public is a story of an episode in the history of the eastern state called Qi (recorded under year 558 in the *Zuo, Xiang* 25): A high officer in Qi named Cui Zhu arranged the assassination of Duke Zhuang, in retaliation for the duke's affair with Cui's wife. The chief recorder then entered in the record, "Cui Zhu murdered his ruler." Cui had him put to death. The recorder's two brothers in turn did the same, and they too suffered death. A fourth brother then entered the damning line in the record, and Cui let it stand. A recorder in the south, hearing that the chief recorder had been executed for doing his duty, set out for the capital with his writing instruments, but turned back when he heard that the event had finally been recorded. Perhaps this is myth, but it has remained famous as a dramatization of the ideal of the historian's "recording the truth" (*zhibi*). Unfortunately Cui Zhu's example of the savagery of power was to prove just as effective. An especially horrible incident occurred in 450 C.E. The Northern Wei emperor ordered the minister of instruction Cui Hao to write a history of the regimes of the royal ancestors, urging him to make it a "true record." Cui naively took him literally, and a bloodbath ensued: Cui and his entire staff of 128 persons were executed; Cui himself suffered the extreme punishment of having his entire clan and the clans of his wives extirpated.

The point here is that if these chronicles were intended to be seen, it is likely that Confucius and his students had access to the *Chunqiu* of Lu, and could have copied it or abstracted it, as tradition says they did; and this is also attested to by the fact that the *Chunqiu* of Lu does survive, in part, the part being the record of the twelve reigns terminating with the fourteenth year (481) of Duke Ai (494–468), in whose reign Confucius died (in 479). The cult of the *Springs and Autumns*, as being a book that the master actually wrote, has been fantastic, and has had a great influence on later Chinese historiography. It is a very spare chronicle. Confucius is said to have expressed his moral judgments ("praise and blame," *baobian*) on men and events recorded in it, not explicitly, but in what he chose to record or omit (*bixue*), and by subtle choices of words (*weiyan*). As the basis of instruction in moral philosophy, this bare chronicle was useless without elaborate explanation. In time three long commentaries materialized, keyed to every line, two of them (*Gongyang* and *Guliang*) explaining the imagined subtleties of the wording, and a third (*Zuo*) filling in, at great length, the missing historical details, or fancied details.

When ambitious and extensive historical works began to be written in the Han era, setting the models for later compilations, Confucius's example, in avoiding explanatory digressions, can be seen at once. In the first of these large works, the *Shiji*, finished around 90 B.C.E. by Sima Qian, the author adds a final chapter in which he explains how and why he came to write, and there he quotes Confucius: "If I were to put what I want to say in abstract statements" (literally, in "empty words"), "it would not be as penetrating and clear as it would be if I showed it in doings and events." This idea has two possible discordant implications, both evident in later historiography. One is that it is the historian's proper job to see to it, by selection and wording, that the "doings and events" do convey ("penetratingly") the lessons they are supposed to convey. The other is that the "doings and events" will have a clear meaning if you just put them down plainly, letting the facts speak for themselves, as we would put it. Either way, we have a paradox. For all their obsession with history and their great industry in writing it up, the Chinese in their historical writings eschew explanations. Broad theorizing about the course of history is found in the essays of philosophers, or if in a history is confined (sparingly) to prefaces or terminal comments. Narrative is one detail after another, without intermediate-type generalization in the text itself, that would point out to us the threads of near-term causal connections. It is all supposed to be "penetrating and clear"; but to the modern eye, a great Chinese history is likely to look like a vast encyclopedia of historical data.

The cult of the *Chunqiu* in the Han led to some strange theories. Another idea of Dong Zhongshu and his school (claiming the *Gongyang* commentary as its basis) was that Confucius had a grand ulterior historical vision, hidden in the text. There were twelve ducal reigns covered. The last three were the times of Confucius's own experience. The preceding four were times he heard about from people who had experienced them. The first five he knew about only by transmitted information. Therefore, his attitude—we can say, his affection—differed. Toward the most remote era it was least: for him, at that time, only the Lu state was "we," "inside"; all else was "outside." As for the middle era, all the Chinese states—the *zhu Xia*—were "inside," and only the non-Chinese, ethnically alien peoples in localities within China and those on the peripheries, were "outside." And in the most recent times all humanity was "inside." Thus viewed, the entire chronicle could be seen allegorically as a vision of a time of "great peace" in the future, when the whole of mankind would be a "great unity"—of course, in the Han. (See also Kaltenmark 1979, 21–24.)

So the master had a vision of history as progress. This idea was to have a strange future. Dong's concept was only one of the ways in which the backward-idealizing habit of thought was reversed in the Han. In the first century C.E., in the second half of the Han era, a philosopher named Wang Chong, too, insisted that the Han owed no apologies to the golden past of such as Yao and Shun. And He Xiu, elaborating the "*Gongyang*" interpretation of the *Chunqiu*, described Confucius's supposed "three ages" as a progress from "disorder" through "approaching peace" to "great peace." One glimpses another conception, of the history of civilization as technological progress, in the "Great Appendix" to the *Yijing* ("first" among the "classics," but actually the last to be included; this "Appendix" was attributed to Confucius but is probably an early Han text). First a sage invented the symbols of the *yi*; then sages in turn derived from these symbols the ideas of nets for hunting and fishing, of ploughs for farming, markets for trading, boats and carts for traveling, etc. And, of course, writing: "In the highest antiquity, government was carried on by means of knotted cords; in later times the sages substituted for these written characters."

Another quite different Han thinker deserves mention in any review of historical thought. In the middle of the dynasty, and during the regime of the usurping Wang Mang, there was Liu Xin (c. 46 B.C.E.–23 C.E.), who with his father Liu Xiang before him had been court librarian. Both father and son were polymaths: both were deeply interested in astronomy (and of course astrology). As court librarians, they cataloged the Han imperial library; and the catalog survives in large part, having been incorporated into the *Hanshu*, second of the great series of works known as the "Standard Histories." By Liu's time, it was possible to think of other things besides the acts of governments and rulers as the subject matter of history. Living in a world of books, Liu addressed the problem of the origin and development of the kinds of knowledge and teaching the books represent, especially the exuberant intellectual scene of the last three centuries before the unification of China under the Qin state, the age of the so-called "hundred schools." There had been earlier attempts simply to classify the main "schools," but Liu went farther, and in his catalog speculated about their origin. His idea was that each developed out of the knowledge and expertise maintained and developed by hereditary officers in this or that department of the government of the ancient Zhou court, before its decline and disintegration after 771 B.C.E. For example, the school called the *Ru*, who honored Confucius, originated in the ministry of education, which (Liu thought) preserved and expounded the texts that later were collected together as the "classics." The Daoists—he is thinking of Laozi—derived from the department of the official chroniclers; hence their sensitivity to time, change, and impermanence. The "legalists" (illustrated by my quotation from *The Book of Lord Shang*) came from the ministry of justice; and speculators about "*yin* and *yang*" represented a tradition that developed among official astronomers (and astrologers).

Liu's idea was that in the ancient state all teaching and all writing, by official specialists, were public, functional, and anonymous; and only after the breakup of the Zhou state did private authorship and the "private" teachings of "philosophers" arise. The whole idea seems strange at first. A striking feature is its state-centeredness—that's very Chinese. But the insight that human knowledge must at first have been functional within society, and anonymous, and only later became the teachings of nameable individuals, is probably right. We could almost call Liu Xin the first intellectual historian. His ideas will reappear later.

Liu Xin's astronomy included schemes for calculating the positions of the planets in the zodiac for any time in the past, and he used it as the basis for constructing (from his point of view) a scientific calendar, which took as a base first year the year 143,127 years before his contemporary base year, which was

104 B.C.E.—i.e., 143,231 B.C.E. In the Han dynasty, the Chinese were thinking big about past time. Liu was also a historian, and he used his computational astronomy to date events associated with sidereal phenomena described in astrological texts. He got it all wrong, because his astronomy was faulty, and he relied on records that were actually invented. But his sheer audacity is astonishing; he was probably the first historian in the world to attempt this.

More big thinking about past time—which we can fairly call a kind of speculative philosophy of history—was a basic part of the worldview of Buddhism, which began to come into China in the middle of the Han era. Most varieties of Buddhism, from about the beginning of the Christian era in the west, saw the present situation of humanity in time as being in the last stages of an unimaginably long "world-period," from an original creation to a soon-to-come final destruction. (Furthermore, the present world-period was but one in an endless series of world-periods before and after.) Earlier in a world-period a Buddha appears, preaching the "law" of conduct and cultivation leading to salvation and release (life being conceived as essentially suffering). At first humanity is vigorous enough so that individual adepts can follow the law by their own efforts. But in the last stages (*mofa*), where we are now, general spiritual decay has gone so far that one can no longer save oneself by one's own efforts, and must rely on faith in the saving power of a virtual divine being, conceived as a (timeless) Buddha, or a bodhisattva, i.e., a saint who has reached the brink of salvation but holds back, vowing first to save all "sentient creatures," and acquiring the power to do this by his own act of infinite self-sacrifice. (Similar religious ideas were spreading over the European and Asian world at this time.)

From the third to the ninth centuries China was almost entirely a Buddhist country. But during the Tang dynasty—the first long-lasting state to unify the whole country since the end of the Han in 220—a strong central government had created institutions that tended to reinvigorate Confucianism, and by the ninth century there were signs of revival, which accelerated in the following Song era. One of the early Song Confucian philosophers, Shao Yong (1011–1077), picked up the idea of the "world-period." Shao developed a metaphysics that expanded the sixty-four hexagrams of the *Yijing* (the classic of divination) into a kind of chain-of-being account of everything. He also used this scheme to account for the world in time, and this gave him a world-period of a mere 129,600 years. But such expansive conceits could not have an impact on actual historical writing. (See also Birdwhistell and Schirokauer 1997.)

The preceding Tang era (618–906) saw a prodigious development of official historiography, and the Tang system with variations continued down to the twentieth century. There were official recorders who kept a day-to-day account of the "actions and repose" of the sovereign (*qi zhuzhu*). From this at the end of a reign other official historians compiled a still very detailed "true record" (*shilu*). Another historical office was responsible for compiling from time to time an ongoing "state history" (*guoshi*) covering several reigns and including biographies of important persons. These texts were secret, and almost none survived from the Tang, Song, or Yuan (there is only one text from the Tang; see Solomon 1955). The Ming *shilu* exists, and from the Manchu (Qing) era both the *shilu* and the *qi zhuzhu*. In the Tang and later there were also official compendiums of basic statutes and edicts, called *huidian*, and these were public. From the Tang on, it became the regular practice at the beginning of a dynasty for an official history to be compiled for the preceding dynasty—a practice that at once conferred legitimacy on the new order and consigned its predecessor safely to the past. These, like their models, the *Shiji* and *Hanshu* of the Han era, had a complex structure: annals of the court; tables of occupants of official positions, etc.; monographs on problems of state such as taxation, or the official hierarchy; and always a long final section of biographical sketches of prominent persons in a multitude of categories (Beasley and Pulleybank 1961, especially 45–46).

In the Tang, in the early 700s, one of the historian officials was a man named Liu Zhiji (661–721). To relieve his impatience with the incompetent supervision and rule-making of the officials in charge, Liu wrote a book titled *Shitong* (*General Principles of Historiography*). It is probably the first such book in the world. It contains invaluable detailed chapters on the history of historical writing in the past seven centuries, and a passionate defense of the role of the historian in preserving a record of deeds and misdeeds as models and warnings for the present and future. Liu accepts the idea of a dynasty as formally controlling, to the extent of recommending that chapters on bibliography should cover only writings of the dynasty being described (a recommendation ignored, fortunately, by later historians). He also thought that there should be special sections in an official history on cities, and on clans and families.

In the next century we find Liu Zongyuan (773–819), famous as an essayist and remembered especially for one fine "Essay on Feudalism" (*Fengjian lun*), analyzing perceptively the loose distribution of power in ancient times before the rise of centralized bureaucratic states, and opposing proposals to reintroduce "feudal"-tending institutions in his own time, as invitations to anarchy. Another sometime laborer in the office of history (with whom Liu corresponded) was a man much better known as a poet and essayist, Han Yu (768–824). His prose style has been highly esteemed for its supple beauty and sensitivity. Perhaps his best-known and most influential essay is "The Origin of the Way" (*Yuan dao*), defending Confucian ethics and social norms against the Buddhists and Daoists. Near the close, tracing the line of succession of those who embodied the ancient "Way" from Yao down to Mencius (where he thinks it breaks off), he says, "Earlier than the duke of Zhou, these men were rulers, hence their actions went forward; after the duke of Zhou, they were subjects, hence their teachings were enduring."

In the eleventh century another almost equally esteemed writer, Ouyang Xiu (1007–1072), collaborated on a *History of the Tang* (an official history had already been done), and in his preface to one of the sections for which he was responsible he expresses another sentiment on cultural history:

> During the Three Dynasties and earlier, government had one source, and rites and music were spread through the the world; after the Three Dynasties, government had two sources, and "rites and music" became an empty term.

Of course he had to explain himself. His meaning was that in ancient times classic social norms and customs were the living structure of the people's ordinary lives, functioning naturally both as governing rules and as moral instruction; government and instruction were thus combined in the "rites." In later times—specifically, after the arbitrary changes introduced by the Qin—"government" became a matter of record-keeping, prisons and trials, military service, etc., while "rites" became performances managed by officials on special occasions, which are not understood by the persons involved in them, and which ordinary people often never witness in their whole lives. In the next century the philosopher Zhu Xi (1130–1200) wrote a well-known essay on what Ouyang Xiu had said, extending his idea to writing and cultural refinement generally: the "Way" had to be a living part of the life of a writer if his work was to be other than artificial and false. In both, we see the idea that in antiquity human culture had been whole and alive; later it became split into uninspired functioning and mere artifice. The "golden bowl" had been shattered.

Another famous nonofficial historian, contemporary with Ouyang Xiu in the eleventh century, was Sima Guang (1019–1086), whose masterwork is the enormous *Zizhi tongjian*, or *Comprehensive Mirror for Aid in Government* (the title was bestowed on it by the Song emperor, who gave support to the project midway). Sima Guang and his staff undertook to rewrite history from the Warring States (conceived as beginning in 403 B.C.E.) down to but not including his own dynasty (Song, 960–1280), using a "chronological" (*piannian*) structure rather than the "annal-biographical" (*jizhuan*) form of the "standard" official dynastic histories. There was actually a gain, in this, in explanatory lucidity, e.g., in the concurrent treatment of the northern and southern polities of the Six Dynasties (third to seventh centuries). There is also liberal use of flashback episodes and of speeches, which tend toward explanation. Most noteworthy is Sima's conscientiousness as scholar. We have a long letter from him to his chief collaborator Fan Zuyu, detailing procedures—the method was, without apology, "scissors and paste," but with the most careful effort to include everything relevant in a "long compilation," then to weed out material that could not withstand critical scrutiny. Variant accounts of points in dispute were covered in a final volume, *Kao yi*, or *Examination of Discrepancies*.

What happens when one combines Han Yu's thought with Ouyang Xiu's—and with Liu Xin's? Liu had seen an archaic world in which there was an uncomplicated amalgam of learning and teaching with the functioning of government. Apply this to Han Yu, and you have the thought that in high antiquity "sages" were rulers; wisdom and social creative action were combined. Then somehow they separated: government went one way, in the hands of mundane rulers; and the preservation of wisdom, the "Way," went another, in the hands of sages like Confucius who had no "position" and so could merely "transmit" the wisdom of the past.

Add Ouyang Xiu, and you have something like the concept of alienation: a sickness in the human condition that once didn't exist, and that ought to be overcome. We can see something like this idea of overcoming a culture-damaging duality in words addressed to the Kang Xi emperor in the early Qing by a high official close to him, Li Guangdi (1642–1718). Eulogizing the emperor as a modern sage-ruler, Li said, "In your servant's view, the relation between the Way (*dao*) and government is this: in ancient times they proceeded from one single source, but in later times they proceeded from two separate sources." The greatest of the ancient sages appeared at 500-year intervals; down to King Wen, the founder of the Zhou, they were rulers, and accordingly until the end of the Western Zhou "centralized unity was continued." But:

> . . . when Confucius appeared during the Eastern Zhou, and when Zhu Xi appeared during the Southern Song,

> Heaven found it expedient to entrust them with the true Way, but their times rejected them, and thus the Way and government proceeded from two separate sources. From Zhu Xi to our present sovereign has also been a period of 500 years; our sovereign has fulfilled the expectations of a true ruler, and has personally displayed the learning of sages and worthy men. Surely Heaven is about to recommence the succession, and the authoritative lines of the Way and of government will again be united. (Nivison, in Wright 1953, 133)

There is more in this than just another instance of pairing *dao* and government. An old problem in Chinese historical thought was keeping straight the "authoritative line" or "correct succession" (*zhengtong*) of dynasties. (The matching of dynasties with "elements" was an early form of it.) The classic case was the Three Kingdoms (San Guo) period, the forty-five years following the end of the Eastern Han in 220 C.E. These three "kingdoms" were Wei, which the Western Jin claimed to be replacing in 265; Han, set up in Shu (Sichuan or Szechwan) by a claimant to kinship with the imperial line of the defunct Han dynasty; and Wu, in the south. Some historians (e.g., Chen Shou, author of the *Sanguo zhi*; and Sima Guang) recognized the primacy of Wei; others (e.g., Zhu Xi in his *Zizhi tongjian gangmu*, revising Sima Guang's work) accorded the torch to (Shu) Han. The *zhengtong* problem (Rao 1977) is forced on the Chinese historian by the background assumption, which seemed obvious to the ordinary person even down to the eighteenth century, that China was the center of the world, and at any time there must be just one sovereign authority, effective or not. Sima Guang does not belabor the idea, but language has its rules: in his writing about the northern and southern courts, the ruler of Northern Wei is the *Wei zhu*; the (puny) southern head of state is the *di*—the emperor.

Closer attention is given by philosophers, including Ouyang Xiu (author of a three-part essay on *zhengtong*) and Zhu Xi, and also Fang Xiaoru (1357–1402) in the early Ming, and the recluse Wang Fuzhi (1619–1692) in the early Qing. They begin to notice that the word *tong* has two senses, signifying either continuity (*tongxu*) or unity (*yitong*). The latter sense required limiting *zhengtong* to dynasties that really did unify the "world"; and these were not continuous. This line of thought leads the early Qing philosopher Wang Fuzhi, in the concluding essays of his *Du Tongjian lun* (*Essays on Reading the Tongjian*, i.e., of Sima Guang) to put the concept aside as useless, and to substitute his own analysis of history. Wang sees the ideal of world unity, but not the fact, evident in the regional distribution of power under a nominal single "emperor" in early antiquity. A long second stage of history follows, in which periods of division (Warring States, Six Dynasties, Five Dynasties) alternate with periods of unity (e.g., Han, Tang). Then comes a third stage, with periods of unity alternating with chaos. (The implication is that he would so characterize ages of "barbarian" dominance such as his own time.) The explanation of it all? Simply "heaven." Wang's writings of this kind remained unpublished for two centuries, and would otherwise probably have been proscribed.

But if one takes the commonsense view of *tong* as continuity, it must seem unproblematic that some power always had the valid "succession." And if one thinks of it as "unity," the restoration of unified government after a period of disunity is no conceptual problem. The extension of the concept of *tong* to moral philosophy in the concept of *daotong*—implicit in Han Yu, and explicit in Li Guangdi and many writers—was quite another matter. Here there was not just the problem of identifying the torch-bearer, but more, the problem of what to make of a gap of fourteen centuries. Did the torch just stay lit when no one was running with it? Let it not be objected that I misuse my own metaphor, for it is not my own. It is found among the Buddhists, in the concept of the "transmission of the lamp" (*chuandeng*) from one Chan Buddhist "patriarch" to the next. There the flame always burns, but also it is never out of hand (or mind). The Buddhist embraces the implication: transmission of insight is direct, from mind to mind, unmediated by lifeless words and meanings (*fawai chuanxin*).

But why, then, boggle at a temporal gap? Why cannot Zhu Xi, or I, now, in a leap of intuition, make direct contact with the minds and thoughts of the ancient philosophers? (Mencius could even be thought to have said something like this, in talking about "looking for friends in history"—*shang you*, 5B8—not just reciting verses and reading books, but apprehending the writers in their existential wholeness as human beings.) This seems to be just what was sometimes claimed, and it became an underlying issue between some conservative moralists and no-nonsense hard-nosed philologists of the Qing era, with their ideal of "seeking for the truth in actual facts" (*shishi qiushi*). Thus Gu Yanwu (1613–1682) and others find occasion to sneer at those who claim they have authority for their speculations by virtue of a "mental transmission from the Two Emperors" Yao and Shun (Nivison 1966, 187–188 and n. 64, 309).

Chang Xuecheng (1738–1801; see below; Nivison 1966, pp. 186–190), acute philosopher of history in the next century, is tempted in this direction, e.g., in characterizing the true historian, as contrasted with the mere cataloger of facts, as one with insight, able to grasp the larger picture (*quanti*) of the past; and what emerges for him (as it must for anyone) is the vexing puzzle: to understand details of past history rightly, one must grasp the gestalt of the whole; but to do that, one must first have command of details. If one looks closely at another aspect of the problem, not in what an understanding of ancient thought would consist, but in how it is passed on, one sees that at every historical moment of transmission something is likely to be missed or added; and one must wonder (as Zhang did, briefly) whether we can understand past thought at all. Thinking in this way, Zhang approaches Collingwood's problem of the rethinking of past thought—which must be both mental activity, time-and-context-bound, and idea, timeless.

If the foregoing is the problem of how we can understand the world of the past, intimately related is the question how we should read past writings—most notably, the classical texts. A student of the moralist Wang Yangming in the early 1500s asked about the apparent difference between the *Chunqiu*—obviously a history—and the other classics, which one supposes to present the Way. Wang answered, "If you're considering events, you call them histories; if you're considering the Way, you call them Classics. But events are the Way, and the Way is events. Thus the *Chunqiu* is also a Classic, while the other five Classics are also histories." He goes on to comment on other classics (*Chuanxi lu* 13; cf. Chan, 23). The thought applies Wang's "unity of knowledge and action": an act is informed with intention; and one "knows" something only if one's knowing is or in appropriate circumstances would be incipient act. Of course, what informs the acts of the sages must be the Way. But also, Wang is always insisting that in the midst of involvement in anything our mind has the capacity, if we will let ourselves use it, of just seeing the distinction between what is right and what isn't. Even in reading a past statement of "the Way," we are appraising an act; and it is our intuitive judgment of the statement as act that constitutes our grasp of "the Way."

Chang Xuecheng, writing in the 1780s, begins his philosophical essay collection *Wenshitongyi* with the gnomic statement "The Six Classics are all histories." He explains: this as follows. The Way cannot be formulated, so the classics cannot be seen as sacred books that tell us what it is. They show us what the Way is by being what they are, which is documentary residues of the government—i.e., the acts—of the ancient kings. And they can do this precisely because in the ancient times they come from, government and the Way were one—or as Zhang puts it, "governing and teaching (*zhijiao*) were united." Or as he also puts it (echoing Han Feizi), "Officials were teachers." Obviously he is thinking of Ouyang Xiu, whose writings he admired.

He gives a much more nuanced picture in his monographic essay, obviously an expansion of and response to Han Yu, *The Origin of the Way* (*Yuan dao*), which he wrote in 1789. He starts at the very beginning: Man "had his *dao* in himself but was not aware of it"; by which he means that humankind had the potential for social organization. Zhang is (without mentioning him) getting into the problem Xunzi addressed and fumbled: how did man create a moral order that we must recognize as the moral order? We cannot simply say that there were wise men in authority who set it all up for us, because then we have no account of how they got there or could have done it. The answer is that it all happened gradually, beginning with "a household of three persons" (i.e., a man, a woman and a child), going on to ever-increasing social complexity, each step a response to immediate need, so gradually that even the "sages"—the persons who through superior ability rose to the top of the evolving structure of society—did not see themselves as sages and did not realize what they were doing, beyond solving each problem as it arose, over many generations. The whole process was the Way "taking shape" in human life. But this means that no concrete detail of civilization, not even the basic moral rules governing social intercourse, can be identified as "the Way" in itself. We are to think of the Way as like a wheel, and everything that is done, with the entire historical accumulation of moral norms and institutions, as so to speak the "track" of the wheel. It is right that we all look up to and learn from our betters, and they from their betters, and ultimately from the "sages" (Xunzi would applaud); but from whom then did the sages themselves learn? They learned from the unself-conscious behavior (*bu zhi qi ran er ran*) of the common people, who could never understand the "why" (*suoyi ran*) of things but could understand only the "what" or "ought" (*dangran*); in this manner the sages gained an intuitive insight into the Way.

In the fullness of time the cumulative development of civilization became perfect. (But by what standard does one measure the perfection of all standards?) The fullness of time turns out to be the Western Zhou. After that—only heaven knew why—perfection fell apart. The Way ceased to be embodied in a seamless social-political whole; "government" and "teaching" separated; and from then on—Zhang is interested in intellectual history, not political history—a cyclical pattern can be discerned. As humanity ceased to be able to collectively grasp the whole of the Way at once, first one aspect, then another, became emphasized in intellectual life. First came an age of philosophy, a focus on principles (*li*)—Zhang is thinking of the "hundred schools" era of the Eastern Chou and Warring States. Then came an age of scholarship and philology, in the Han. And then came an age of literary art (*wen*), in Six Dynasties and Tang. And then, again, came philosophy (Song-Yuan-Ming). And now in the Qing, again comes philology. At the end of each stage, excess leads inevitably to change. This triad of motifs is not just basic to history itself; it is an aspect of historical writing (rooted in forms of human thought), which must exhibit qualities in any good historian: literary skill (*cai*), command of material (*xue*), and insight (*shi*).

Notice that while Zhang is fully aware of the common concept of history as a sequence of dynasties, the dynastic concept does not structure his picture of history at all. On the contrary, one major emphasis in his writing on historiography is the importance of "comprehensiveness," *tong*. (Here we have philosophy of history of the "critical" kind.) A "comprehensive" history will cut through artificial dynastic divisions, as recommended (and, Zhang thought, practiced) by the Song historian Zheng Qiao (1104–1160), whom Zhang esteemed, battling with contemporaries like Dai Zhen (1724–1777) over this preference. (Zhang was thinking of Zheng's "summary"—*lue*—chapters on selected topics.) Zheng is famous, or infamous, for attacking the integrity and competence of Ban Gu (first century C.E.), in his preface to his compendium the *Tong zhi*, charging Ban with having put historiography on a wrong course in compiling the first history of a single dynasty (Western Han).

But what of Zhang himself as historian? His works were all "local histories" (*difang zhi*) or "family histories" (*jia shi*). The comprehensiveness came in with his conception of where these forms fitted in the whole historical scheme: there should be histories of individuals, of families, of localities, of provinces, all made available to keepers and compilers of the history of the whole. (He thought that such works could not be final, but must be redone from time to time.) Zhang did, with his friend Shao Jinhan (1743–1796), plan to do a new history of the Song era. Would this, if they had lived to do it, have been materially different from previous works? I doubt it. Zhang esteemed the words ascribed to Confucius by Sima Qian: you must let doings and events display their own meaning, without intruding your own views in "empty words." This could only mean a history like others, any originality taking the form of novel categories of material to include, and novel ways of arranging one's categories.

The story of Chinese philosophies of history continues with a quite different turn in the last years of the Manchu (Qing) dynasty. Pressure from the west had forced thoughtful Chinese to ask why China was weak and always defeated. There were things China needed from the west to strengthen itself, not just guns but also ideas. But adopting ideas, if it were not to be capitulation, must be to find in Chinese traditions western-like elements to emphasize. A misperception born perhaps of the conspicuousness of missionary activity was that one source of strength for the west was its religious faith. (Whereas we can see clearly that a major source of its strength was the capacity of the captains of its gunboats to forget their religious scruples.)

One aspect of the philological fashion of middle Qing scholarship had been its shifting of attention and respect back from the Buddhized Confucianism of the Song to the scholars of the Han. Perhaps inevitably, there were those who moved farther, seriously taking up again the ideas of Han figures like Dong Zhongshu. This interest increased in the nineteenth century, and at the end of the century Chinese intellectual reformers like Kang Youwei (1858–1927) seized on Dong's kind of thinking as providing just what was needed. Dong and his like had seen Confucius not as a mere transmitter of ancient knowledge but as a divinely inspired innovator with a progressive vision of the future, in the "three ages" concept supposedly embedded in the *Chunqiu*. And in the Han, Confucius had been the object of an official religious cult. Kang and the people around him thus were able to persuade themselves that Confucianism was a religion, and that its founder Confucius had been a sage who grasped a concept of historical progress. The "three ages"—disorder, approaching peace, and universal peace—really describe the course of history for the whole of humanity. Chang Xuecheng had been largely forgotten for most of a century; but now he began to be noticed again, in a way that would have disturbed him. Zhang had seen historical progress reach its peak in the age before Confucius, followed by a decline into limited understanding, so that his Confucius had to be only a "transmitter," not a "creator"; and he had framed this scheme explicitly on his understanding of Liu Xin's hypothesis about the origins of different schools of learning and writing. Kang turned on Liu Xin with a vengeance, seeing him as having corrupted the Confucian vision by actually forging classical texts wholesale. Kang's influence on scholarship lasted for decades into the twentieth century.

Perhaps it should be said that after that any specifically Chinese philosophy of history can no longer be discovered. This is not quite true, because the Marxist theories of history have taken a distinctive form in China, for Chinese reasons. What one might call vulgar Marxism had taken a simplified analysis of European history and applied it to the world. There were four ages, of different "modes of production": slave society, feudal society, bourgeois-capitalist, and communist. Actually Marx had spoken of a distinctive "Asiatic" mode, changeless, based on water control, as was in evidence outside Europe (he had India in mind, rather than China). The Chinese would have none of that (one would not wish to see China as stuck fast in the backwaters of history). So the four ages had to be adapted to China.

This has led communist historians to strain for ways to see ancient China as a "slave society"; and to see the long expanse of the successive imperial dynasties with their elaborate bureaucratic government structures as in some sense a "feudal" (*fengjian*) era—which would have astonished Liu Zongyuan, as much as it annoys non-Marxists who are uneasy even with applying the European concept "feudalism" to the hierarchic regional distribution of power in the early Zhou. (The Marxist focus is on the impact of the power structure, of whatever kind, on the actual producers, the peasants.) Confucius is praised or damned, depending on how the current "line" divides slave society from feudal society. He defended "feudal" values. Therefore, if his times were "feudal," he was a "reactionary," and he has been condemned as such in orchestrated campaigns of denunciation. But if he lived in a "slave society," then he was a "progressive," and he receives honorable attention—as seems to be happening now.

It is obvious that whatever their politics or philosophy, modern Chinese have felt their history to be a problem they must confront. In the middle nineteenth century the idea was that western technology could be safely adopted as "function" (*yong*) as long as Chinese historical culture was honored as "essence" (*ti*). Later—one sees it in Kang Youwei, but also in many others, even now—western ideas could be adopted and adapted, so long as some anticipation of them could be discovered in China's own past. The Chinese communist form of accommodation has been different, but still accommodation. Here the fear has been not that the present would betray the past, but that the past would subvert the present, since what was always does enter into the process of becoming what is; so, make the process deliberate: freedom is the recognition of necessity. Mao Zedong counseled communists to review the Chinese past and draw from it what is found to be useful. Confucius could be honored but must first be tamed. Even intimate elements of Confucian ethics—its self-cultivationist moral philosophy—were consciously adapted, into the programs of "study" aimed at perfecting the "party-viewpoint" (*dangxing*) of a true communist. This too, perhaps, is philosophy of history.

See also Confucianism: Tradition; *De; Li*: Rites or Propriety; Philosophy in China: Historiography; Zhang Xuecheng.

Bibliography

Note: The concept of a dynasty is inevitably the concept of a temporally finite entity; dynasties are mortal. Predictions using the concept of dynastic mortality, or predictions of the advent of a new world order, are therefore subversive. Material of this sort should be of great interest in the study of Chinese philosophies of history, but space has not permitted its inclusion here. Such material includes the *chan* and *wei* texts of the Han (now mostly lost), the doctrinal texts of Daoist mass rebellions of the later Han, the Maitreya cults of the Six Dynasties and later, and in more recent times the doctrinal texts of popular rebellions in the Qing era—e.g., White Lotus, Eight Trigrams, and Taiping. This bibliography includes some material that can be explored on these subjects.

Beasley, W. G., and E. G. Pulleyblank, eds. *Historians of China and Japan*. London: Oxford University Press, 1961.

Bingbian, ed. Zhang Bingquan. See *Xiao-tun di er ben: Yin-xu wenzi: bingbian*. Taipei: Institute of History and Philology, Academia Sinica, 1957–1972.

Birdwhistell, Anne D., and Conrad Schirokauer. "Two Song Thinkers Engage History: Shao Young and Hu Hong." Nassau: Song Historiography Workshop, 1997. (Unpublished paper.)

Bokenkamp, Stephen R. "Time after Time: Taoist Apocalyptic History and the Founding of the T'ang Dynasty." *Asia Major*, 3rd series, 7(part 1), 1994, pp. 59–88.

Chan, W. T., trans. *Instructions for Practical Living and Other Neo-Confucian Writings by Wang Yang-ming*. New York: Columbia University Press, 1963.

Duyvendak, J. J. L. *The Book of Lord Shang*. London: Probsthain, 1928.

Fung, Yu-lan (Feng Youlan). *A History of Chinese Philosophy*, 2 vols., trans. Derk Bodde. Princeton, N.J.: Princeton University Press, 1952–1953.

Gardner, Charles S. *Chinese Traditional Historiography*. Cambridge, Mass.: Harvard University Press, 1938.

Graham, A. C. *Disputers of the Tao*. La Salle: Open Court, 1989.

Ivanhoe, P. J. "Chinese Philosophy of History." In *International Encyclopedia of Philosophy*. London: Routledge.

Jin, Yufu. *Zhongguo shixue shi* (History of Chinese Historiography), 2nd ed. Shanghai: Commercial Press, 1946 (n.d.).

Kaltenmark, Max. "The Ideology of the T'ai-p'ing ching." In *Facets of Taoism: Essays in Chinese Religion*, ed. Holmes Welch and Anna Seidel. New Haven, Conn.: Yale University Press, 1979, pp. 19–52.

Knoblock, J. *Xunzi: A Translation and Study of the Complete Works*, 3 vols., Stanford, Calif.: Stanford University Press, 1988–1994.

Lau, D. C., trans. *Mencius*. Harmondsworth: Penguin, 1970.

Levenson, Joseph R. *Confucian China and Its Modern Fate*, Vol. 2, *The Problem of Monarchical Decay*. Berkeley, Calif.: University of California Press, 1964.

Loewe, Michael, ed. *The Cambridge History of China*, Vol. 1, *The Ch'in and Han Empires, 221 B.C.–A.D. 220*. Cambridge: Cambridge University Press, 1986.

Louie, Kam. *Critiques of Confucius in Contemporary China*. New York: St. Martin's, 1980.

Naito, Torajiro. *Shina Shigaku Shi* (History of Chinese Historiography). Tokyo: Kobundo, 1949.

Naquin, Susan. *Millenarian Rebellion in China: The Eight Trigrams Uprising of 1813*. New Haven, Conn.: Yale University Press, 1976.

Nivison, D. S. "Communist Ethics and Chinese Tradition." *Journal of Asian Studies*, 16, 1956, pp. 51–74.

———."An Interpretation of the *Shao Gao*." *Early China*, 20, 1995.

———. *The Life and Thought of Chang Hsueh-ch'eng (1738–1801)*. Stanford, Calif.: Stanford University Press, 1966.

———. "The Problem of Knowledge and Action in Chinese Thought since Wang Yang-ming." In *Studies in Chinese Thought*, ed. A. F. Wright. Chicago, Ill.: University of Chicago Press, 1953, pp. 112–145.

Overmyer, Daniel L. "Folk-Buddhist Religion: Creation and Eschatology in Medieval China." *History of Religion*, 12(1), 1972, pp. 42–69.

———. *Folk Buddhist Religion: Dissenting Sects in Late Traditional China*. Cambridge, Mass.: Harvard University Press, 1976.

Pines, Yuri. "Intellectual Chang in the Chunqiu Period: The Reliability of the Speeches in the *Zuo zhuan* as Sources of Chunqiu Intellectual History." *Early China*, 22, 1997, pp. 77–132.

Puett, Michael. "Nature and Artifice: Debates in Late Warring States China Concerning the Creation of Culture." *Harvard Journal of Asiatic Studies*, 57(2), December 1997, pp. 471–518.

Rao, Zongyi. *Zhongguo shixsue shang zhi zhengtong lun* (*Zhengtong* Theories in Chinese Historiography). Hong Kong: Longmen Shudian, 1977.

Schwartz, B. I. "A Marxist Controversy Concerning China." *Far Eastern Quarterly*, 13(2), February 1954, pp. 143–154.

Sivin, Nathan. *Cosmos and Computation in Early Chinese Mathematical Astronomy*. Leiden: Brill, 1969. (Reprinted from *T'oung Pao*, 55, 1–3.)

Solomon, Bernard S. *The Veritable Record of the T'ang Emperor Shun-tsung* (28 February 805–31 August 805: Han Yu's *Shun-tsung shih-lu*). Cambridge, Mass.: Harvard University Press, 1955.

Teng, Ssu-yu. "Chu Yuan-chang." In *Dictionary of Ming Biography, 1368–1644*, ed. L. Carrington Goodrich and Chaoying Fang, pp. 381–392.

Von Falkenhausen, Lothar. "Issues in Western Zhou Studies: A Review Article." *Early China*, 18, 1993, pp. 138–226.

Watson, B., trans. *Hsun Tzu: Basic Writings*. New York: Columbia University Press, 1963.

Welch, Holmes, and Anna Seidel, eds. *Facets of Taoism: Essays in Chinese Religion*. New Haven, Conn.: Yale University Press, 1979.

Wilhelm, Hellmut. "The Problem of Within and Without: A Confucian Attempt in Syncretism." *Journal of the History of Ideas*, 12, 1951, pp. 48–60.

Wright, A. F., ed. *Studies in Chinese Thought*. Chicago, Ill.: University of Chicago Press, 1953.

Wright, Mary C. *The Last Stand of Chinese Conservatism: The T'ung-chih Restoration, 1862–1874*. Stanford, Calif.: Stanford University Press, 1957.

Wu, Kang. *Les trois theories politiques du Tch'ouen Ts'ieou*. Paris: Leroux, 1932.

Yang, C. K. *Religion in Chinese Society*. Berkeley: University of California Press, 1967.

Philosophy of Human Nature

Kwong-loi SHUN

Suppose we call an account of human nature an account of what the basic human constitution is like before learning and social influence; an interest in human nature understood in this sense has always been an important part of Chinese ethical thought. This interest stems in part from the concern of Chinese thinkers to understand the basic human constitution and its relation to their proposed ethical and political ideals, especially the way an account of human nature fits in with their defense of such ideals and explains the capacity of human beings to live up to them. It also stems in part from their concern to understand the way human beings relate to the cosmic order: what constitution human beings have in virtue of their being part of the cosmic order, and what they can and should do to that constitution.

The Chinese character often translated as "nature" is *xing*, derived from *sheng*, meaning "life" or "growth," and eventually acquiring the meaning of livelihood, tendencies characteristic of things of a kind, and tendencies with which a thing is born. The character usually translated as "human beings" is *ren*, whose earlier use was probably restricted to members of certain clans or social classes, but which came to be used to refer to human beings generally, sometimes even to members of the so-called barbarian tribes. While it has become standard for Chinese thinkers to use *renxing*, or just *xing*, to discuss human nature, views of human nature can also be expressed through other concepts or distinctions, such as *sheng* (life) in the chapter *Jie* of the *Guanzi*, the reference in the *Mozi* to what people were like in ancient times when they were first born and when government had not yet been instituted, or the contrast in the *Zhuangzi* between what is due to heaven (*tian*) and what is due to human beings (*ren*). Views of human nature are implicit in these texts, even though the character *xing* does not occur or does not play a prominent role in them.

At least five different views of the content of human nature can be discerned in the history of Chinese thought. First, certain thinkers view human nature primarily in biological terms. For example, the Yangist movement, one representative of which is Yang Zhu (fifth to fourth centuries B.C.E.), views human nature primarily in terms of health and longevity, and often uses *sheng* (life) interchangeably with *xing* (nature). Gaozi, a contemporary of Mencius (fourth century B.C.E.), explicates *xing* in terms of *sheng*, probably viewing human nature in terms of what gives life to human beings. For him, human nature comprises eating and having sex, the former being that which continues life in an individual and the latter that which continues life across generations. The chapter *Jie* in the *Guanzi* describes *sheng* (life) in terms of the senses, bodily movements, and the emotions, probably viewing *sheng* in terms of the life forces at work within a person. This way of understanding *xing* and *sheng* is also related to a common tendency in early times to view them in terms of the biological desires and needs of human beings, a tendency that can be discerned in the historical texts *Zuozhuan* and *Guoyu*. A biological conception of human nature can be developed in different directions; for example, while the Yangists advocate nourishing human nature (understood primarily in terms of health and longevity) and not letting any other activities do harm to it, Gaozi and *Jie* in *Guanzi* advocate imposing propriety (*yi*) on human nature, which does not itself have an ethical direction.

Second, certain thinkers view human nature primarily in terms of the self-regarding desires of human beings. For example, when discussing the basic human constitution, Mozi (fifth century B.C.E.) often refers to self-regarding desires, such as the desire for life and that for wealth and honor; when describing what human beings are like after heaven (*tian*) has given birth to them, he presents them as not having affection for others, even for immediate family members. This shows that, although *xing* is not a prominent term in the *Mozi*, Mozi probably views human beings in their natural state as being motivated primarily by self-regarding desires. Similarly, Xunzi (third century B.C.E.) also emphasizes the self-regarding desires of human beings in his explication of *xing*, although he sometimes also acknowledges that human beings are attached to beings of their own kind in the natural state. While the two defend ethical ideals that involve having and acting out of an active concern for others, they also regard living up to that ideal as instrumental in satisfying one's self-regarding desires. This way of viewing human nature differs from the first in that the self-regarding desires that form part of the basic human constitution may involve desires, such as those for wealth and honor, that are not biological in any ordinary sense.

Third, certain thinkers view human nature primarily in terms of ethical inclinations that human beings share. For example, Mencius opposes Gaozi's biological conception of human nature, and argues that the human heart (*xin*) has a sense of propriety (*yi*) and that human beings give precedence to propriety over such tendencies as eating and having sex. He also opposes any conception of human nature which emphasizes benefit (*li*), whether it is the Yangist proposal that one should engage in activities beneficial to one's life and avoid harmful activities, or the Mohist proposal that one should have concern for and benefit others and as a result, benefit oneself. Instead, Mencius advocates explicating human nature in terms of certain ethical inclinations that he believes human beings share; by developing these, one attains the ethical ideal. Mencius is like the Yangists and unlike Gaozi and Xunzi in regarding human nature as something that should be nourished and developed rather than radically reshaped, but he differs from the Yangists in his opposition to a biological conception.

Fourth, texts like the *Zhuangzi* leave the content of human nature unspecified but advocate that human beings should respond spontaneously to situations and not let anything, whether it be preoccupation with worldly goods or subscription to ethical doctrines such as those of the Mohists and the Confucians, interfere with their natural responses. Thc heart should be vacuous (*xu*) in that it responds to situations without preconceptions, just as a clear mirror or still water reflects what is brought up to it without distortion. Thus, the *Zhuangzi* regards the ethical ideal as basically a restoration of the natural state of human beings, although because of its opposition to ethical doctrines the text leaves unspecified the relation between the ideal and social participation—whether it involves withdrawal from ordinary social activities or is compatible with such activities though with a lessened attachment. The commentary by Guo Xiang (d. 312) on the *Zhuangzi* adopts the latter interpretation. According to Guo, different individuals have different natures and are suited to occupy different social positions in accordance with their respective natures.

Fifth, Song-Ming Confucians such as Zhu Xi (1130–1200) and Wang Yangming (1472–1529), have a view of human nature that draws on the third and fourth of the positions just described. Being professed Mencians, they regard the heart (*xin*) as sharing certain ethical inclinations. However, unlike Mencius, who regards such inclinations as requiring nourishment to develop into the ideal ethical attributes, they regard the ethical attributes as already present, full-blown, in the heart. Certain distorting factors, including what they call selfish desires and personal opinions, can prevent the ethical attributes from fully manifesting themselves, and the ethical task is to restore the original state of the heart, thereby allowing full manifestation of the ethical attributes. Thus, like the *Zhuangzi*, they regard the ethical ideal as basically a restoration of the natural state of human beings. They even use analogies and concepts found in the *Zhuangzi*, such as the analogy of the clear mirror or still water and the concept of vacuity (*xu*), to describe the ideal state of the heart in which it is free from distorting influences. But for them (unlike the *Zhuangzi*), vacuity of the heart does not mean that the heart has no ethical direction; instead, it involves only the absence of distorting influences that prevent the full manifestation of the ethical attributes already present in the heart.

Other views of human nature can be found in the history of Chinese thought. For example, aware of Mencius's and Xunzi's respective views that human nature is good and that it is evil, Han thinkers engage in extensive debates about whether human nature is good or evil. Dong Zhongshu (c. 179–104 B.C.E.) believes that, just as *tian* (heaven) operates through the *yang* and *yin* forces, subordinating the *yin* to the *yang*, human beings have both good and evil elements in their nature and should subordinate the evil to the good elements. Yang Xiong (53 B.C.E.–18 C.E.) states explicitly that human nature is mixed, and Wang Chong (first century C.E.) argues that different human beings have different natures and that the views of Mencius, Xunzi, and Yang Xiong describe different kinds of human beings. The idea of different grades of human nature is further highlighted by the Tang Confucian thinker Han Yu (768–824) who, drawing on a remark of Confucius's, proposes that there are people of the superior or inferior kind who are respectively unchangeably good or unchangeably evil; on the other hand, Mencius's, Xunzi's, and Yang Xiong's views describe different individuals belonging to the medium grade. This attempt to accommodate different views of human nature can also be found among the Sung Confucians; for example, invoking the cosmological view that everything is composed of pattern (*li*) and material force (*qi*), Cheng Yi (1033–1107) proposes that Mencius's view of nature as good applies to nature construed in terms of pattern, while other views such as those of Confucius, Gaozi, Yang Xiong, and Han Yu are all about nature construed in terms of both pattern and material force.

Though not exhaustive, the above survey of different views of human nature suffices for the purpose of illustrating how such views relate to the ethical and political ideals and cosmological views of Chinese thinkers. The way a proposed ethical ideal relates to an account of human nature may take at least three forms: the ideal may be viewed (1) as involving a radical transformation of natural human tendencies, (2) as a development of such tendencies, or (3) as a restoration of the natural state of human beings. The first position is illustrated by Mozi's advocacy of indiscriminate concern (*jianai*) despite viewing human beings as primarily self-seeking in the natural state, and by Xunzi's view that the self-regarding desires of human beings should be reshaped and transformed by the Confucian Way. The second is illustrated by the Yangist view that the ideal human life involves nurturing the natural biological tendencies of human beings, and by Mencius's view that it involves a full development of the ethical inclinations human beings share in the natural state. The third is illustrated by the *Zhuangzi*, which advocates freeing the heart from preoccupation with worldly goods and ethical doctrines to allow it to respond freely to situations, and by the Song-Ming Confucians' view that the ideal ethical attributes are already part of human nature.

These different positions are illustrated by the use of different analogies. Mozi compares ethical development to dyeing silk and Xunzi to straightening a crooked piece of wood, thereby emphasizing that human nature needs to be reshaped and transformed to attain the ethical ideal. Mencius compares it to the growth of a sprout into a full-grown plant, thereby emphasizing that the ethical ideal is a development of one's natural ethical inclinations. The *Zhuangzi* and the Song-Ming Confucians compare what self-cultivation does to the heart to keeping a mirror clear or water still, thereby emphasizing that the ethical ideal involves freeing the heart from distorting influences. Despite such differences, all these positions see a continuity between the ethical ideal and human nature. This is true not just for the last two positions, but also for the first. For Mozi and Xunzi, living up to the ethical ideal promotes satisfaction of the self-regarding desires that human beings have in their natural state, even though it also involves reshaping them; according to Xunzi, the reshaping of such desires is what human beings do to bring to completion what they have received from heaven.

Chinese views of human nature play a role not just in defending certain proposed ethical ideals, but also in explaining the human capacity to live up to them. Mozi's opponents often criticize his doctrine of indiscriminate concern on the ground that human beings cannot practice it because it is at odds with their emotional makeup; for example, Wumazi argues that he cannot practice indiscriminate concern because he has more concern for himself and for those closer to him. Mozi's response is that human beings can practice indiscriminate concern because it is in the interest of themselves and those close to them, thereby retaining a link to their natural tendencies. Mencius, on the other hand, argues that human nature already contains ethical inclinations pointing in the direction of the Confucian Way, and therefore humans do have the ability (*neng*) to practice the Way. In an objection to Mencius, Xunzi draws a distinction between ability (*neng*) and capacity (*keyi*). Human beings in their natural state do not have the ability to practice the Confucian Way because they lack the appropriate emotional disposition. But they have the capacity to acquire the ability (*keyi*)—that is, the capacity to acquire the emotional dispositions in virtue of which they have the ability—and they will exercise this capacity when they understand the rationale behind the Way. Thus, the attempts by these thinkers to explain how human beings can live up to their proposed ethical ideals all appeal to their respective conceptions of the content of human nature.

Chinese views of human nature also have implications for certain proposed political programs. For example, while Xunzi believes that human beings have the capacity to understand the rationale of the Confucian Way and to have their natural tendencies transformed accordingly, he also believes that they need guidance from teachers and rulers to acquire the proper understanding. Accordingly, he emphasizes the role of rulers in educating and guiding the people and, given his view that human beings in the natural state are driven primarily by self-regarding desires, he also allows room for the use of punishment to regulate people's behavior prior to their being properly educated and transformed. Han Feizi (or Hanfiezi, third century B.C.E.), his student, who is retrospectively classified as a legalist, believes that the self-interested nature of human beings cannot be transformed, and so regards the use of punishment as indispensable for regulating people's behavior. Later, Dong Zhongshu, who holds the view that human nature contains both good and bad elements, regards the good elements as the beginnings of goodness that need to be awakened by the ruler before one can become fully good. Accordingly, he emphasizes the ruler's role as a teacher who awakens the people; Dong also advocates the use of punishment to regulate the bad elements in human beings.

Finally, the Chinese thinkers' views of human nature are also intimately related to their cosmological views. Early thinkers regard human nature as due to *tian* (heaven, nature), and the way they view the content of human nature is linked to their views on *tian*. For example, Mencius regards *tian* as a purposive being whom human beings should serve, and believes that the nature human beings have received from *tian* has an ethical direction; by realizing this direction, one serves *tian*. On the other hand, Xunzi emphasizes *tian* as the source of the resources and regularities that can be found in the natural order; the task of human beings is to give order to such resources—for example, by nourishing crops through agriculture—and thereby complete the work of *tian*. In regard to human nature, human beings complete the work of *tian* by instituting and maintaining the appropriate social arrangements, thereby giving order to and making possible the satisfaction of the desires they receive from *tian*. Later, the Han thinker Dong Zhongshu regards human nature as comprising a good and an evil component, just as *tian* operates through the *yang* and *yin* forces; in both cases, the latter component or force should be subordinated to the former. Still later, Sung Confucians like Cheng Yi and Zhu Xi worked with the cosmological picture of pattern (*li*) and material force (*qi*), explaining human nature in terms of the pattern and the endowment of material force that human beings receive at birth. Human nature is good if construed in terms of pattern, but it can take on different ethical qualities if construed in terms of the combination of pattern and material force, because the endowment of material force can differ in quality in different human beings. These examples illustrate how Chinese views of human nature are informed by the way they understand the nature and operation of the cosmic order.

See also Han Yu; Mencius; Wang Chong; Wang Yangming; Xunzi; Yang Xiong; Zhu Xi.

Bibliography

Chan, Wing-tsit, trans. and comp. *A Source Book in Chinese Philosophy*. Princeton, N.J.: Princeton University Press, 1963.

Cheng, Yi. *Ercheng Chuanshu. Sibu Beiyao* Series.

Dong, Zhongshu. *Chunqiu Fanlu. Sibu Beiyao* Series.

Guo, Xiang. *Zhuangzizhu. Sibu Beiyao* Series.

Han, Feizi (Hanfiezi). *Han Fei Tzu: Basic Writings*, trans. Burton Watson. New York: Columbia University Press, 1963.

Han, Yu. *Han Changli Chuanji. Sibu Beiyao* Series.

Mengzi (Mencius), trans. D. C. Lau. London: Penguin, 1970.
Mozi. *Mo Tzu: Basic Writings*, trans. Burton Watson. New York: Columbia University Press, 1963.
Rickett, W. Allyn, trans. *Guanzi: A Study and Translation*, Vol. 1. Princeton, N.J.: Princeton University Press, 1985, pp. 376–386.
———, trans. *Kuan-tzu*, Vol. 1. Hong Kong: Hong Kong University Press, 1965, pp. 151–172.
Wang, Chong. *Lunheng. Sibu Beiyao* Series.
Wang, Yangming. *Instructions for Practical Living and Other Neo-Confucian Writings by Wang Yang-ming*, trans. Wing-tsit Chan. New York: Columbia University Press, 1963.
———. *Quanshilu*. In *Yangming chuanshu. Sibu Beiyao* Series.
Xu, Weiyu. *Lushi Chunqiu Jishi*. Beijing: Shangwu Yinshuguan, 1955. (See chs. 1.2, 1.3, 2.2, 2.3, 21.4.)
Xunzi. *Xunzi: A Translation and Study of the Complete Works*, trans. John Knoblock, 3 vols. Stanford, Calif.: Stanford University Press, 1988–1994.
Yang, Xiong. *Fayan. Sibu Beiyao* Series.
Zhozhuan. *The Ch'un Ts'ew with the Tso Chuen*, rev. ed., trans. James Legge. Taipei: Wenshije chubanshe, 1972.

Philosophy of Knowledge

Chung-ying CHENG

To understand the Chinese theory of knowledge—its nature and its significance in a modern context—we must first discuss its western counterpart. Some discussions of the Chinese notion of knowledge have tended to assume too many western epistemological concepts and thus have failed to bring out the true character of Chinese epistemology—or, perhaps, the fact that there is no Chinese "epistemology" in precisely the western sense.

Background: Western Epistemology

In western philosophy, epistemology—theory of knowledge—was developed in response to and as a critique of a tradition of skepticism that had questioned the possibility of knowledge and the validity of claims to truth. Epistemology was thus intended as a rational construction and reconstruction of knowledge. Three stages can be discerned in this development.

Stage 1. In the first stage, knowledge is identified with truth, and truth is identified with reality. It is recognized that knowledge comes from our experience of reality; therefore, knowledge must correspond to reality, if not embody reality in some way, and what would implicitly justify or explain knowledge is a theory of reality: metaphysics. Interestingly, Plato offers a theory of reality first, in his *Republic*, before taking up the nature of knowledge in his *Theatetus*; Aristotle takes up metaphysics last, as a justification of knowledge of physics and ethics. Socrates did not deal with knowledge in general, but he can be said to have first raised the question of what constitutes a concept or definition of knowledge of specific things, such as the self and virtues; his questioning led to the Platonic theory of the human soul and its virtues.

Evidently, the seeds of skepticism are sowed when what we experience as real is said not to be real. This is precisely what happened when Parmenides (c. 515–445 B.C.E.), in his poems, distinguished between the "way of truth," which was a matter of recognizing reality as an undivided and immutable unity; and the "way of opinion," which was merely a matter of deceptive experience of differentiation and changes in things of the world. This led to a division between reality and appearance in western philosophy that has lasted to the present day. Pyrrho of Elis (360–272 B.C.E.) developed a skepticism that denies rational knowledge of reality (presumably because it would be a mystic experience) and suspends judgment or opinion, *epoché* (because no sufficient reason can be given for it), in order to achieve peace of mind (*ataraxia*).

Plato's and Aristotle's efforts might be described as attempts to meet the challenge of skepticism, attempts that led them to construct or reconstruct a theory of reality in order to explain how our knowledge of reality is possible. At this stage and in this context, theory of knowledge is implicit in a theory of reality and is not an autonomous discipline.

Stage 2. The second stage of western epistemology starts with Descartes (1596–1650) and culminates in Kant (1724–1804). In this period traditional theory of reality and the human soul had lost its authority, and scientific methods for knowing the empirical world were being proposed and practiced, requiring a new worldview. Descartes experimented with the method of doubt in order to find a solid foundation for our knowledge of the external world, the internal self, and a transcendent God. He was able to formulate a method of analysis complete with principles and criteria for identifying basic truths of reality and judging the validity of our concepts of things. His constructive and reconstructive approach is called the Cartesian project or enterprise and is considered the model of epistemological "foundationism." Descartes's search for a conceptual and methodological basis or framework for modern analytical epistemology did not, however, silence the skeptics. In fact, modern skepticism was revitalized by Hume (1711–1776), who asked, in effect, whether we really know the world, the self, or God—a question that pushes reason to its limits and demands critical self-examination.

In taking up this challenge, Kant eventually formulated a critical theory of knowledge in which the question "How is knowledge possible?" is posed, a full logical-conceptual analysis is conducted, and deductions are made about our knowledge of things in time and space and their causality. In Kantian theory, knowledge is understood in terms of given phenomena, experience, and the structure of the human mind. Kant provided a basis for analyzing scientific knowledge as a paradigm of knowledge in general. But in establishing the discipline of what we know and how knowledge is possible, Kant also undermined the approach to knowledge by way of a theory of reality, or metaphysics. We can use critical analysis only to uncover what knowledge consists of. This critical analysis shows knowledge to be internal to a transcendental mind that constructs knowledge according to its own rules and categories and perhaps to serve its own puposes. What is ultimately real is something we do not know and cannot hope to know because our critical, theoretical reason is limited to our own experience of the world and hence to our exposition and explication of that experience. With Kant, then, we have what Putnam called "internal realism."

Stage 3. The third stage of western epistemology came with the highly successful development of science and technology in the twentieth century. Although post-Kantian philosophers, one after another, built systems of reality in order to provide new, alternative foundations for knowledge, a scientific view of the world was gradually formed from modern scientific inquiry. If Kantian epistemology provided a philosophical and methodological justification for Newtonian physics, that justification was challenged by relativity theory and quantum mechanics, which demanded, at the least, a new formulation. Philosophically, Einstein's theory of relativity showed that we can approach the same body of empirical evidence from different theoretical perspectives and hence explain it by two or more incompatible theoretical views. This recognition led Quine (1992) to his thesis of the indeterminacy of meaning of theoretical terms and the "underdetermination" of scientific theory.

This idea that there is no unique, universal, or necessary foundation for a body of scientific knowledge has profound significance. It implies that knowledge is merely tentative, temporary hypotheses which can help us explain our experiences and predict future experiences. The existence of an external world is not denied in science; indeed, it must be assumed in order to give rise to our sensory experience of the world—the evidence for our theoretical explanations. But this reality is not fixed once and for all, nor is it to be known by us as a result of any finite process of inquiry. At this point, we must say that we cannot predicate a knowledge of reality or deduce reality from our knowledge. We have to to reconstruct or reconfigure our understanding of reality in an open-ended, indefinite process of collective inquiry. In this sense there is no theory of knowledge apart from what we have actually come to know through scientific inquiry. What Quine calls the "naturalization of epistemology" abolishes both "modern traditional" epistemology as a unique, closed theory of reality and modern epistemology as a critical analysis of our conceptual presuppositions of knowledge.

Thus Cartesian-Kantian foundationism and Kant's internal realism or phenomenalism lost their appeal. Instead, we can now speak of a "nonfoundational" approach to knowledge, or at least to scientific knowledge—an approach that has many criteria of validity other than simple correspondence and coherence. These additional criteria include simplicity, collectivity (or the possibility of collaboration), falsifiability, and even aesthetics. But there is no insistence on a universal logic; according to Quine, we may have to reformulate our deterministic two-valued logic in light of quantum physics and quantum phenomena. We might characterize this epistemological development as a combination of "nonfoundationism" and "noninternalism" or even "externalism." Whatever we call it, we can see that it dissolves traditional theories of knowledge. We see also that in such a context, no issue involving knowledge is free from problems of theoretical interpretation, empirical verification, and practical application. There is no special theory of knowledge apart from a theory of scientific knowledge or of scientific inquiry and explanation.

Characteristics of Chinese Epistemology

With regard to these stages of western epistemology, we can make certain observations that are relevant to our understanding of Chinese theory or philosophy of knowledge. First, despite its focus on deconstruction, stage 3 is derived from and contains the past—it could not have been developed without stages 1 and 2. Thus although we do not know in what subtle ways the philosophical theory of knowledge stimulates or enhances theoretical and empirical science, or vice versa, we can find a clear correlation between epistemology and the development of science in the west. Second, at each stage western epistemology has been primarily directed toward the factual world of external objects. Third, one important feature of contemporary epistemology as represented by Quine is the holistic character of knowledge: knowledge is not a single item existing by itself but a system of interrelated, interlocking concepts, theories, and experiences. Hence we come to know not simple entities in the world but processes and processes of processes. Unraveling their order, structure, meanings, and implications requires observation, reflection, and analysis. Such a holistic theory of reality seems to be presupposed or presented by analyses of the ontogeny and functioning of language.

We may now examine what "theory of knowledge" means and how it functions in Chinese philosophy, beginning with a seven-point summary.

1. Because Chinese philosophy has a strong sense of reality and a deep-rooted theory of reality, it has no strong inclination toward skepticism. Doubts about knowledge and language are occasionally raised; however, they are used not to reject the validity of ordinary knowledge or common sense but rather to express higher forms of knowledge and wisdom.

2. In China, unlike the modern west, theory of knowledge has never been separated from a theory of reality and a theory of practice. We can speak of three Chinese theses regarding knowledge: unity of substance and function, unity of experience and insight, and unity of theory and practice. The first thesis actually represents a unity of reality as substance and knowledge as function. This does not mean that Chinese philosophy has no epistemology at all; what it does mean is that Chinese epistemology is to be understood, illustrated, and appreciated in the context of these theses. Because Chinese epistemology is always part of a theory of reality, we might better describe it as "ontoepistemology."

3. Chinese epistemology develops along with metaphysics, ontology, and morals. That is why Chinese philosophy has not produced the kind of epistemology represented by Kant and certain post-Kantian analytical philosophers. Nevertheless, it is possible—and interesting—to critically analyze, reconstruct, and interpret the Chinese theory of knowledge. Similarly, we can also see how Chinese epistemology or ontoepistemology might respond critically to traditional and contemporary western epistemology.

4. The Chinese notion of knowledge shares at least one feature with contemporary western theory of knowledge: the concept of knowledge as holistic, in the sense of involving a system of relations.

5. Chinese philosophy does not confine the notion of knowledge to things and facts in nature; it extends the notion to values, virtues, and ultimate reality. In fact, its most important concern is the "ultimate reality" that would justify our claims to knowledge.

6. Chinese theory of knowledge is not directly related to the development of science and technology and cannot be regarded as an effort to justify current science (unlike Kantian epistemology) or as an extension of current science (unlike Quine's epistemology). Throughout its long history, China has developed excellent empirical science and technology, but their impact on the Chinese philosophy of knowledge is not material in comparison with the effect of western science and technology on western philosophy. This might even be a reason for suggesting that philosophy of knowledge is relatively unimportant in the scheme of Chinese philosophical thinking as a whole.

7. Although Chinese philosophy has not formulated or theorized about rigid procedures or a methodology of knowing, there do exist in the humanities and sciences various macroscopic and microscopic ways of verifying empirical knowledge of things (as in lexicography) and of classifying information (as in Chinese medicine).

In light of these seven points, we can examine how Chinese philosophers view knowledge, how their views function in various philosophical texts and contexts, and how they affect the development of science and rationality.

A Primary Model of Ontoepistemology: *Zhouyi*

In the symbolic texts of the *Zhou Yi*, or *Zhouyi* (*Book of Changes from the Zhou*, c. 1200 B.C.E.), with their "commentaries" (*zhuan*), we can glimpse the early formation of Chinese epistemology. It is based on a comprehensive experience of and reflection on reality, which includes the large universe and the small human world. Its purpose is to ascertain and present our understanding of reality so that we may act rightly. To act rightly, one must know both the macroscopic and the microscopic aspects of reality, both nature and human beings, in a related and holistic manner; decisions about actions are made in light of this knowledge. The process of knowing is "comprehensive observation" (*guan*); the result of *guan* is a "clear overview" or "insight" (*ming*). To know (*zhi*) is, then, a matter of reaching a clear insight and overview of things by way of comprehensive observation. Among the sixty-four hexagrams of the *Zhouyi*, the twentieth, on *guan*, may be said to formulate a model of Chinese knowledge in terms of comprehensive observation.

What is comprehensive observation? As explained in the "Great Appendix" (*Xici*), it involves seeing things in nature—large and small, up and down, far and close, and over a long period of time—so that we will be clear about how things stand in relation to each other in an overall system of representation of reality. It is assumed that in the process of *guan* the true nature of things will be manifested to our senses, so that we will receive a direct understanding of things and the world. Thus we come to know the process of change, things undergoing change, their relationship to us, and their impact on us. We can speak of knowing, seeing the truth, or seeing the true states of the "ten thousand things" by observing various features of things, as asserted by the *Duanzhuan* ("*Duan* Commentaries") on the hexagrams *heng*, *cui*, and *xian*. The *Duanzhuan* for the hexagram *fu* suggests that in the return of the seasons, we can see the "heart-mind of the heaven and earth." In the hexagram *kui* we find a mode of attention and "seeing things in difference" or "seeing the differences of things." In the *Duanzhuan* for the hexagrams *pi* and *daxu* the modes of careful observation (*cha*) and recognition by language and conduct are also mentioned. All these forms of knowing are forms of observation, which requires concentrated vision and mental clarity. There is no single suggestion that we have any reason to doubt our knowledge of things and the world.

Not until later, in Xunzi's essay *Jiebe*, do we find a mention of many (up to eleven) forms of *bi* (shadings or cloudings) of the mind; we need to remove these *bi* before we can be sure that the mind is in a state of "great pure illumination" (*da qingming*), complete with the functions of vacuity, unity, and stillness (*xuyi er jing*), which are required for understanding the patterns of things and the ways of nature.

It might be suggested that all forms of observing (*guan*) things are possible because the mind is by nature a "great pure illumination." Knowledge of reality in small and large details is possible because of the mind's intrinsic, ontological vacuity, unity, and stillness. This suggests further that the mind is originally endowed with cognitive power; it is able to organize sensory experiences into an understanding of things, and from this understanding concepts and naming of things become possible. We shall return to the nature of mind later, when we discuss Xunzi.

How can we be sure that we have correct knowledge of the world? To answer this question, we may formulate two fundamental principles. First, we can see whether our knowledge is correct or incorrect through our actions and practices. Knowledge is sought only in order to act; correct knowledge leads to correct actions, and incorrect knowledge must be corrected in light of the results of incorrect actions. Also, correctness of knowledge or action is defined in terms of correspondence with, or the attainment of, an expected utility. Second, it is assumed as an ontocosmological fact that things present themselves to us and make themselves known (or clear) to us, and there is a natural interaction (perhaps due to the nature of vital mediating force, *qi*) between things and the human body and mind.

This second principle leads us to feeling and response (*gan* and *ying*) as a correlative principle of knowing. As formulated in the *Duanzhuan* of the thirty-first hexagram, *xian* (feeling), the principle is: "Two vital forces (i.e., *yin* and *yang*) feel and respond to each other so that they participate in each other." Unlike *guan, xian* focuses on direct, intimate, interactive understanding. It is also the source of our knowledge of values and what to do. Combining feeling and observation, we can observe what we feel and feel what we observe; this would then constitute a method of reflection on both what we feel and what we observe. It also becomes the source of self-reflection, which gives us knowledge of our nature and mind or self. One important mark of correct or true knowledge is the clarity one sees in things and in the mind.

Clarity (*ming*) is regarded as fundamental; we may say that it shines forth from things and illuminates the mind. But it is perhaps mainly a matter of rationality, because we can use it to achieve knowledge of the world and ourselves. The term *yiming* suggests that *ming* is an instrumental function, the power of clarification, which we can use to pursue the ultimate truth of being and becoming. This is what Zhuangzi means when he speaks of knowing the *dao*. This notion of *yiming* may be the prototype of Xunzi's notion of *da qingming* ("great clarity") of mind.

In this ontoepistemological model, knowing is a direct, intimate experience of things and nature—without, however, reducing our knowledge of things to sensory experiences. Knowledge is never elevated to abstractions or mere concepts, as often happens in western epistemology. We must see the "knowing act" and the "knowing event" as rich, lively, concrete, actualizing experiences in a real world, for our knowing is part of the real world. Reality (or "world-reality") and being are inseparable, comprehensive, holistic, and interrelated (whether harmoniously or in conflict).

Our knowledge is vulnerable to "darkening" by bias and error but also open to "brightening" when we clear away bias and error, to further exploration, and to different configurations and interpretations.

Knowledge is, furthermore, part and parcel of our life and living, incorporating moral conduct and daily actions. Therefore, to be valid, the "knowing event" must be subject to tests of consistency, coherence, and cogency relative to prevailing knowledge. It must be continually "tried" to see if it usefully guides, regulates, and informs our actions and our goals. When illusions and errors occur, one can quickly notice incoherence, weakness, dullness, or unfruitfulness as the illusion or error comes up against "knowing events" as a whole and knowledge as a living unity. In this sense, knowledge is an organic "web of beliefs" (to use Quine's words), a "network of connected feelings and responses."

This theory of knowledge combines the merits of commonsense or intuitive realism, "new realism," critical realism, and pragmatism (in American philosophy) and thus may be called "ontoepistemic" realism. The unit of knowing is not a simple item but a whole field and a whole context. As a result, the arguments against new realism that are based on illusion and error lose their force.

In the *Xici* we find frequent use of the term "know" (*zhi* as a verb), apart from the single use of *zhi* (also as a verb) in the *Xiangzhuan* ("*Xiang* Commentaries") for the third line of the hexagram *kun*. The "creative" (*qian*) is characterized as "knowing the great beginning" by which reality was influenced and from which great deeds are achieved. Knowing is conceived as an enduring, powerful creative activity; it emerges to rule or lead in relation to the power of the receptive (*kun*), which assures us of "spaciousness" for our activities. All the patterns and principles of things are exhibited, and all things find their positions in this process or reality of knowing, leading, and action as pervasive, unceasing ontological functions. Through this understanding of the formation of reality, a comprehensive and sustained observation of things becomes the way a human being realizes himself.

If we see the *Zhouyi* as symbolically embodying such an ontoepistemic reality, we can say that its scope is as wide as the way of heaven and earth. The person who achieves an understanding of the *yi* as the way of heaven and earth will be able to know profound causes, reasons, and counterreasons by observation, reflection, and reasoning. He might even come to know the divine and the spirits by knowing the changes of fine vital forces (*jingqi*). A person who has attained such an understanding or vision can be said to have a comprehensive knowledge of all things and thus to have an insight into the Way—an insight that will benefit "all under heaven."

We can make several comments about this description of knowing and knowledge. First, it meets the challenge of capturing reality or directly confronting reality and is therefore "simple and easy," as the author of *Xici* suggested. To say that knowing is simple and easy is to say that in this ontoepistemic sense it is creative and generative. For this reason, it is comprehensive and penetrating and can be called an ontocosmological process.

Second, such knowing is comprehensive not only in scope but in functions and capabilities: it presents reality as creative change and leads to an understanding of the potential and limitations of things, as well as to the moral vision and virtues that enable a person to participate in creative change. Thus it is capable of "cultivating benevolence" (*tunhu ren*) and giving love. Knowing, then, is a matter not only of reflecting reality but of enhancing and enriching reality.

Knowing can be described as a pure activity of change and as a part of change. Whether as unified noetic consciousness or an ecstatic experience, it is intertwined with things and cannot be conceived as above or over them. It cannot be extracted from its interaction with things; if we attempted to isolate knowing in this way, it would become a pale abstraction and its referents would be left dangling in a void.

Third, knowing leads to practical valuation of things in the world and to a creative reflection on what to do and what to achieve as a moral agent. Knowledge is linked to values and to practice. It prompts us to act because it is linked to our creative impulse of continuing, amplifying, and refining life. In this sense it integrates life, from the individual level to the community and society. Our nature is to know, and through knowledge to do good and to achieve integrity and universal love. Therefore, not only knowledge of reality but also kowledge of ethics and aesthetics is possible and indeed necessary.

In terms of contemporary analytical epistemology, this ontoepistemology is a form of "reliabilism" that consists in following a reinforced verifiable pattern of experience in the community over a period of time. It is also a synthesis of the principles of internalism and externalism, combining the internal feeling of certitude and truthfulness with external observation of things in the world to produce a judgment or decision about the presumed trustworthiness of one's beliefs. As a theory of truth, ontoepistemology requires both correspondence with reality and coherence within a set of beliefs in light of actual, vivid experience.

Confucian Epistemology of Mind and Nature

Given the *Zhouyi*'s model of ontoepistemology, it is much easier to understand the epistemological ideas in the writings of Confucius, Mencius, and the *Liji* on the one hand and Laozi and Zhuangzi on the other. By the time of Confucius (551–479 B.C.E.) the world of reality is conceived as heaven and earth, human beings, the "myriad things," their changes, and their interactions. It is essential to this concept that things have the potential for change and that change has regular patterns. The human being can initiate change, can actively cultivate a response to the world, and can thus contribute to the well-being and harmony of a community or society as a model, a sage, or a man of virtue and wisdom. It is in this context that Confucius speaks of knowledge and knowing: "knowing other people" (*zhiren*), "knowing the mandate of heaven" (*zhi tianming*), "knowing rites" (*zhili*), "knowing benevolence" (*zhiren*), "[someone] knowing myself" (*zhiwo*), "knowing life and death" (*zhisheng, zhisi*), and "knowing speech" (*zhiyan*).

What Confucius says about knowing concerns concrete things—persons, social customs and norms, ideals and rules of conduct—as well as the profound nature of or the reasons for life and reality. To know such things is to recognize certain patterns and understand certain underlying forces or tendencies so that we can deal with them, acting correctly to avoid undesirable consequences and achieve desirable goals. We know about them and know of them as well as experiencing them directly, so that we can actively interact with or participate in them for the purpose of producing a better world and a better self (in whatever sense we mean "better").

Confucius does speak of knowing speech or language, but with regard to relating oneself to others and expressing what is known in social relationships—not for the purpose of articulating ideas or formulating propositions. In order to understand what Confucius means by knowing, we need to be aware of his philosophy of human nature and human society and how he construed the meaning of ethics and the role of language and rhetoric. In other words, understanding his theory of knowledge is a matter of identifying his views on reality and the human being, not simply of finding out how knowledge of the world is possible.

In the ontoepistemology of the Confucian *Analects*, learning (*xue*) occupies a central position. Learning consists in recognizing affairs and things and observing and investigating the nature of things. Learning is aimed primarily at human affairs and social-political matters and involves practical intentions for correct action and self-cultivation. Essentially, it is a process of self-development or self-perfection. Both observation and action are important, and knowing always has moral and historical significance. Knowing and knowledge involve not the cognition of objects independent of us, but people and affairs or history—which are related to us and with which we can interact. "Object" is, in effect, not a reference or a target of investigation. This concept continues the ontoepistemology of the *Zhouyi* and develops it into a moral ontocosmology. It may presuppose a "moral nature" of virtues and a moral mind capable of making correct judgments and, therefore, a theory or understanding of moral virtues and the morality of the human mind. Confucian ontoepistemology in fact gave rise to a theory of moral nature or the moral mind (or both) in Mencius.

The question has been raised whether Confucius is referring to a transcendent heaven when he speaks of heaven (*tian*) or the mandate of heaven (*tianming*). *Tian*, like the *dao* or *ren*, may not be very far from the human being; thus Confucius does not imply that *tian* is above all things or that it operates on a different and higher level of being or power. How we define its level of being or power is significant. Certainly, Confucius's thought about reality involves no Platonic or Cartesian dualism; however, we cannot assume that the notion of transcendence is confined to the Judeo-Christian meaning or model—that is, a transcendent God. To speak of the mandate of heaven and to speak of human nature as mandated by heaven, as in the *Zhongyong*, suggests a higher level of reality, transcending sensory experience and providing the source of life, human nature, and values. The Daoists call this source the *dao* and say that it defies articulation in language. Neo-Confucians such as Zhou Dunyi (1017–1073) speak of a "great ultimate" (*taiji*), which is both transcendent and immanent. Such a model of transcendence cannot be ruled out by stipulating a narrower definition.

Another question is whether the Confucian program of rectifying names presupposes any external theory of reality of things and people. In this regard it seems clear from a close logical analysis that there is no way to replace a realist sense of rectification (*zheng*) with a pragmatist sense of ordering, as some sinologists have proposed. One reason is that actual people are not constructs but living things to be coped with. Nor are values and virtues arbitrary constructs, even when they refer to systems of organizations and patterns of behavior. To "rectify names" (*zhengming*) in Confucian philosophy is to criticize our use of language in the light of actuality (whether social and natural), practical virtues based on human nature and human understanding, and their desirable correlation and cohesion. Rectifying names reflects a moral will and a moral vision based on the Confucian understanding of humanity and the ideals of human social and political order. This rectification presupposes an ontoepistemology and an axioepistemology—as becomes even more obvious in Mencius (371–289 B.C.E.). One may interpret the development of Mencian philosophy as a natural extension of Confucian philosophy.

With regard to the theory of reality in Mencius, we can make at least three specific comments that are relevant to his notion of knowing. First, Mencius advanced a theory of human nature as exhibiting moral goodness. For Mencius, the nature of a person cannot be decreased or increased by his actions, because it is endowed by heaven (following the Zisu thought that human nature comes from heaven; see the *Book of Mencius*, 7A21). However, it takes conscientious efforts to activate one's nature and realize it in one's ethical life. One must thoroughly examine and reflect on one's mind in order to know the moral potential of one's nature. Once one knows one's nature, one would then know heaven, which is the source of one's moral nature. To say that one knows one's nature is to say that one comes to experience it not only existentially but consciously; the will—not simply a tendency to act from one's nature—is involved. One then comes to know heaven, in the sense of a deeper reality, and thus gains a deeper knowledge of reality. Knowing heaven is also both existential and a matter of consciously transforming, participating, and realizing. This is not "knowing" in the sense of making an objective reference or identification for the sake of explanation. Still, one could explain "knowing heaven," and for that matter "knowing one's nature," in terms of a hypothesis with a definite or indefinite reference.

Second, a neglected aspect of Mencius lends itself to both ontocosmological and epistemological functions: his notion of vital force (*qi*). Although he does not specify the exact nature of *qi*, it can be regarded as energy filling the human body and heart-mind, and also as the vital and creative force from heaven and earth. The human mind, human nature, and the body are manifestations of *qi*, although on different levels. When Mencius speaks of *haoran zhiqu* (vital force as a vast flood), he may be revealing his belief in a living universe, in which what is most elemental is most creative and is also endowed with moral qualities, because it is matched with righteousness and the moral way. *Qi* is, then, both the vital and the moral nature of the ultimate reality. This explains how or why human nature and the human mind are also formed from *qi*, have its inherent moral quality, and should be cultivated in order to maintain its strength, its resilience, and its endless capacity to refresh itself. There is common ontocosmological ground between one's own mind, the minds of others, and the mind of heaven; and so there is a level on which our knowing and our being and the being of the universe are interchangeable. On that level, the harmony and unity between man and heaven and among men will be established, marking out our knowledge of heaven and our identification with heaven.

Admittedly, Mencius's idea of heaven is ambiguous or ambivalent; it has many shadings and dimensions. Heaven is the power of creating life, the speechless source of human nature and morality, a conscious divine mind, an unpredictable will or destiny, the ultimate power beyond human power, the urge to live, moral reason, a tendency to do what is natural, a mandate to cultivate and enlighten. To understand heaven, one must think, reflect, observe, read history, reason, and philosophize. To reach a knowledge of heaven, one must follow multiple channels and use one's mind to intuit their unity. That knowledge is a sagely insight into a profound reality with many manifestations.

Mencius says (7B25): "That which is powerful and transforms is the sagely (*sheng*), and the sagely which is incapable of being known is divinity (*shen*)." For "sagely" we could substitute "heavenly." As a reality transcending our ordinary language and reason, heaven cannot be known; but it can be known as a reality that, perhaps, we come to experience existentially. In this regard, Mencius approaches the Daoist position concerning knowledge of the *dao*.

The third point we can make about Mencian epistemology has to do with Mencius's concept of "knowing speech" (*zhiyan*). "Knowing speech" is the ability to detect weaknesses in one's understanding and insincerity in the intentions behind one's speech. This implies that knowledge of speech is a matter not of literal or even metaphorical meaning but of the mind as revealed in speech. Apparently, one has to assume that knowing involves understanding the context of speech as well as feeling and experiencing the style and mood of language, as a clue to the mind of the speaker. Knowledge is then an insight based, possibly, on experience and analysis. This is another example of epistemic "reliabilism" and a synthesis of internalism and externalism.

Xunzi (fl. 298–238 B.C.E.) takes the Chinese or at least the Confucian theory of knowledge in an unmistakably critical-rational direction. For this reason, Xunzi's contribution, and his significance, should never be underestimated. His critical-rational approach has several aspects. First, heaven, as a reality, is considered an independent natural object with regularities or laws governing its functioning. It is not something that would by its nature confer good or bad fortune on human society—humans themselves must govern a state well and plan for the welfare of the people. Heaven acts independently of human intentions and human wishes, following its own patterns or regularities, which include how life evolves and how things are generated. In this regard Xunzi inherited the natural cosmology of the *Zhouyi*.

The "naturalism" of heaven applies to human organisms and societies, which also have natural functions and normal regularities of functioning and growth. It takes a sage "not to know heaven" (*buqiu zhitian*), in the Mencian metaphysical sense of knowing heaven, but to discover these regularities and their underlying principles in order to preserve or promote the functioning and growth of individual persons and societies. This involves knowing the ways of the change of seasons and the behavior of natural forces called *yin* and *yang*. There should be no link between human action and heaven; on the contrary, one should see the realm of nature and the realm of human action as separate. Xunzi made the famous statement:

> Instead of glorifying heaven in one's thinking, why not treat it as an object or as an animal and control it? Instead of praising heaven and following it blindly, why not manipulate the mandate of heaven and make use of it? Instead of waiting for a time of good fortune, why not respond positively to any time and make it work for us? (*Tianlun*)

Xunzi is not suggesting simply a neutral attitude toward heaven. He is suggesting a positive, critical, rational approach to nature that would consist in finding the objective features of things and designing methods to control things for one's political and social purposes or make use of them on the basis of this objective knowledge. He calls this "knowing the *dao*" (*zhidao*). Not only does the *dao* become an object of knowing; knowing as a process of observation and discovery becomes a rational activity that reflects a critical-rational mind capable of removing bias and error and establishing theories and systems of objective knowledge.

Xunzi's critical rationalization of knowledge consists in showing how the human mind is capable of observing and experiencing the world of objects and at the same time is capable of using its own reason to organize and establish a system of language for social living and political order. It also consists in showing how the human mind is capable of removing its own biases, errors, illusions, hallucinations, and misconceptions and reaching out for rational knowledge based on thoroughgoing clarity. We see this in Xunzi's essays on *zhengming* (rectification of names) and *jie bi* (removing obscuration). Without going into details, we can note the following salient points. First, by identifying the reasons and purposes behind naming, Xunzi demonstrates that the human mind knows things and defines concepts for the purpose of description and identification. This is not an arbitrary or an a priori process, but a process tied up with our actual experiences of things in the world and our ability to organize or classify experiences and make distinctions. Although one may argue for conventional elements in naming and defining, these cannot be divorced from observation of reality.

Xunzi regards naming or creating a language as a matter of sorting out what gives rise to names on principles of similarity and dissimilarity and combining it with principles governing uses of names or language. He therefore presupposes a theory of a reality that becomes a world of objects or properties of objects, in humans and in nature. The purpose of naming is to designate actualities (*zhishi*) so that one can accurately grasp states of affairs and make correct judgments about values and ranks of things and positions. Naming in its turn presupposes knowing, and knowing is a process of applying one's senses to feel out different properties of things. It takes one's mind to know things on the basis of sensory evidence. The mind has this capability because it can sort out different classes of experiences and make objective references. This is called "knowing by evidence" (*zhenzhi*).

The mind is able to know by evidence because it can eliminate inconsistency, preserve coherence, and establish an order of reference. This leads to the invention of common names (*gongming*) and discriminating names (*bieming*) on different levels with different scopes of reference for the purpose of distinction and identification. Xunzi concludes by saying that "names have no unique and fixed reference and are a matter of convention by agreement" (*Zhengming*). This does not make Xunzi a "conventionist," because he is speaking of conventionally naming an object by a linguistic term. But the fact remains that many things are identified in our process of knowing, these things need to be identified by names, and the names we choose are a matter of convention.

This is not to say that knowing a thing is a convention or is determined by convention. Once a name is chosen for a known thing, its reference is fixed unless our knowing produces a different content for a given name. Xunzi says: "Names have fixed appropriateness, and if it is easy to understand what a name signifies, it is then called a good name" (*Zhengming*). A good name is a well-defined name that allows us to identify or describe an object or a situation. The conventions of naming do not preclude a process of knowing and conceptualizing before we commit ourselves to names or to language, even though in practice knowing, naming, and using language conventionally may occur at the same time.

Xunzi cannot be described as an epistemological internalist or pragmatist. However, his explanation or ideal of how new systems of language and new names are established has both internalist and pragmatist elements—and even social and political elements. Actually, Xunzi has gone a long way toward developing an empirical theory of knowing and naming and has abandoned the notion of knowledge as rooted in reality or as part of a living reality. That is, he has at least to some degree turned away from a theory of reality to a theory of knowledge and language based on an examination of our sensory experience and our reasoning. As a realist, though, Xunzi insists that we should not confuse names with actualities, actualities with names, or names with names. Each kind of confusion leads us to misconstrue our knowledge of things or misuse our language, or both.

We should also note that Xunzi's examination of the mind and reason in his essay on *jie bi* does not make him a Kantian philosopher. His appeal to removing "obscurations" from the human mind in order to reveal reason makes him more a realist than a phenomenalist. We cannot look in detail at his theorizing about such obscurations, but we can briefly consider how he criticized doctrines of government and morality prevalent in his time. He asserts that often one's mind is obscured by or obsessed with one idea or one view to the point where it loses sight of large truths. This can also mean that a theory or view tends to lose sight of the whole truth. Knowing the whole truth is not forming a theory but, rather, disclosing and removing all the differing views and theories that obscure the truth even while they claim to possess it. Xunzi enumerates eleven kinds of obscurations, citing historical examples and the works of earlier philosophers to show how each kind can be harmful; Confucius, however (Xunzi says), suffered from no obscurations because he remained open in his views, as a result of his benevolence. Xunzi argues that there must be a balanced view, founded on a central standard (*heng*). For Xunzi, such a standard is named the *dao*.

Apparently, the *dao* is assumed to be a state of reality that allows a correct understanding of things and a correct formulation of values and precludes prejudice and error. It can also be regarded as a fundamental principle applicable to all things and giving each thing a proper place in a system of knowledge. On either interpretation of the *dao*, we can say that for Xunzi knowledge of truth and reality still requires an affirmation. The question is how we come to know this truth or reality. Xunzi asserts that the mind cannot help knowing the *dao*. It would seem that he means this is true once the mind has made itself "void, one, and tranquil" (*xuyi er jing*) and so has become a "great clear illuminator"; but he does not really explain the process of knowing the *dao*—perhaps because some of his text is missing and some is garbled.

In this regard we may recall the method of "comprehensive observation" in the ontoepistemology of the *Zhouyi*. Perhaps when the mind becomes a clear illuminator, it is able to reach a correct, unbiased understanding of all things and their changes and thus will be able to form a conception of the ultimate reality—that is, the *dao*. The mind that is "void, one, and tranquil" allows one to observe things without prejudice, makes one less susceptible to being misled by unstable and deceptive conditions, and therefore makes one less prone to mistakes.

Xunzi advocates a process of cultivating and nourishing the mind in this state of being "void, one, and tranquil"; this suggests that to know the *dao* requires a process of observation, absorption, self-reflection, and self-correction. Once one has reached a knowledge of the *dao*, one may be able to achieve knowledge of individual things in reference to the principle or system of the *dao*. Again, this does not preclude an empirical but realistic understanding of things or a method or procedure of self-examining, self-criticism, and self-correction.

From Confucius to Mencius to Xunzi we see 300 years of development of classical Confucianism. During this time, the chapters of *Liji* (*Records of Rites*) were formed that represent the ideas of the first and second generations after Confucius. *Daxue* (*Great Learning*) and *Zhongyong* (*Doctrine of the Mean*)—two remarkable essays from the *Liji*—fit in with our project of understanding Confucian epistemology. *Daxue* opens the way toward a critical-rational attitude for reconstruing or reconstructing knowledge and language in terms of an investigation of things. The program of self-cultivation begins with the requirement of *kewu zhizhi* (investigating things and extending knowledge); this suggests a bold new direction that was only implicit in the Confucian notion of learning (*xue*).

To reach knowledge by investigating things also suggests that knowledge is a serious matter of rational inquiry and requires a mentality inclined toward external things and affairs of the world. This is "externalism," and it leads to a theory of reality as independent of the mind that knows reality. But knowledge is not considered to be derived exclusively from inquiry; at the beginning of *Daxue* there is a suggestion of "illuminating the bright virtue" (*ming mingde*) of a person. This means that knowledge of things needs both an external and an internal base; knowing implies a connection between the knower, or the knower's mind, and things in the world. Truth has to be experienced in an open, interactive process of "feeling and response" (*kanying*) in which the faculty of reason is manifested, or active, at the same time as patterns and principles of things are presented. Propositions in language can be considered secondary; hence, knowing is not simply establishing a truthful correspondence between sentences and facts but building an interactive, trustworthy relation of interpenetration. Only in view of this understanding of knowing by investigation of things can knowing can be said to be intimately related to efforts, sincere intentions (*chengyi*), and rectifying the mind (*zhengxin*).

The impact of external knowledge on the heart-mind leads to an internal response—the heart-mind seeks further truth and focuses on specifics. External knowing, then, is internally centered; the external and the internal have formed a relationship of "feeling and response"; consequently, there is no barrier between responsive desires and the impact of specific knowledge. The organic nature of knowledge makes possible an organic response in the form of sincere intentions and corrections of errors; this will lead to correct actions relating to various norms on different levels. Such an interpretation shows how external knowing leads to internal sincerity and suggests that knowledge is and should always be a synthesis of internalism and externalism, practice and theory.

Daxue also formulates a six-step methodology of rational inquiry: (1) have a goal or vision (*zhi*), (2) concentrate on the idea or ideal (*ding*), (3) remain tranquil in preparing to think (*jing*), (4) settle on issues (*an*), (5) think hard (*lue*), and finally (6) gain insights (*de*). This method seems to pave the way for Xunzi's epistemology, which is based on critical rationalism and led him to develop his idea of the mind as requiring purification and tranquillity in order to know.

Zhongyong (*Doctrine of the Mean*), by contrast, moves in an ontocosmological direction: from the human sense of reality and the human feeling of sincerity to the ultimate reality. Knowing reality is a matter of embodying and realizing the potential of reality. This is not accidental; at the outset, *Zhongyong* posits the homogeneity and consanguinity of heaven and human nature, asserting that human nature is endowed directly by heaven. It asserts further that what flows and follows from human nature is the *dao*—the way, or Way. The *dao* is a manifestation of the inner necessity of heaven. This is a significant departure from *Yijing*. The *Zhongyong* stresses the inner feelings and an inner ability to know reality and ascertain truth, whereas the *Yijing*, although it does not exclude self-reflection, stresses observation of things in the world. Thus *Zhongyong* enables a Confucian to justify human culture and morality in the philosophy of *li* (rites) and *ren* (benevolence). It also provides a basis for Mencius to hold that human nature is good, even in a metaphysical sense.

Zhongyong goes a step further, holding that human nature has an ontocosmological source and status. It thus provides a foundation for knowing heaven and presenting the Way, as well as for realizing oneself in a creative process that reaches toward the ultimate—heaven—as human knowing appropriates heaven's power and creativity. The necessary link in the ontocosmology of heaven and humanity is a powerful, unlimited source of creative energy and moral goodness, insofar as what follows or flows from nature and heaven is good. Thus a person can speak of realizing himself, realizing others, and realizing all things under heaven. "Realization" here means the "utter fulfillment" (*jing*) of the moral potential of people and things. Moral potential, in turn, stands for the nature of things and has a normative meaning: it is the potential for realization that would contribute to a harmonious, mutual enhancement of good among the totality of realizations of the moral nature of people and things. *Zhongyong* calls this state the "fulfillment of centrality and harmony" (*zhi zhonghe*); in it, heaven and earth are well positioned and all things are well nourished.

In this ontocosmological context, knowing the *dao* or heaven is not simply consciousness or an intellectual, explanatory understanding of things in the world; it is deep insight, creativity, and momentum toward actions and activities seen as meaningful and as realizing the *dao*. To say that this is "embodied knowledge" (*tizhi*) is not enough; it is also a motivational, creative knowledge leading to creative activities which are described in the *Zhongyong* as "supporting the transformations of heaven and earth."

Zhongyong presents a thoroughly epistemological position of internally inclined and internally rooted "foundationalism." That is, knowledge is a matter of unfolding a prior, conceived, or experienced reality as described in an ontocosmology. Hence "to know" is a part of the cosmic drama and serves a cosmic function—fulfilling the *dao*. This internalism, however, is not idealism, for it is not a Hegelian or even a Kantian theory of constructing reality. Nor is it a Berkeleyan idealism based on a God who causes ideas to be present in the human mind. It is still realistic, insofar as it affirms a reality that we otherwise could identify by learning and observation; this is unquestionably a Confucian methodology and is still given in the *Zhongyong*. We can describe the epistemology of the *Zhongyong* as a metaphysical realism based on an internalism of human nature and human feelings. Knowing and knowledge are given an ontocosmological significance that one does not find in the epistemology of critical reason of the *Daxue* and the *Xunzi*.

Zhongyong does not speak specifically of mind; it refers almost exclusively to the feeling of sincerity (*cheng*). *Zhongyong* in effect gives sincerity the function of knowing and realizing the ultimate reality of heaven: "Sincerity is the way of heaven, and to sincerely fulfill the way of heaven is the way of man." Sincerity is regarded as a characteristic of truth and reality, which is manifested in the nature of the sage, and as a moral or conscientious intention and a mental inclination toward the good. Sincerity implies or brings out knowledge or enlightenment (*ming*). A sincere person will pursue and reach for enlightenment and knowledge of reality; by the same token, an enlightened person will demonstrate sincerity in continuing to pursue a creative realization of himself and other people and things. *Zhongyong* comes to speak of "accomplishing oneself" as a matter of benevolence and of "accomplishing things" as a matter of "knowledge" (*chengwu, zhiye*), in the sense of knowledge embodying motivation and realizing creativity in a holistic or overall understanding of things and people.

What needs to be specifically brought out from an analytical, epistemological point of view is the internalistic "foundationalism" in *Zhongyong*. When *Zhongyong* speaks of sincerity, it implies certainty, a direct feeling. To be sincere in oneself is to be sure of one's sincerity; otherwise one cannot be said to be sincere. To be utterly sincere (*zhicheng*) is to be utterly certain about one's feeling of sincerity and the consequent motivating power of creative action. We can conclude that *Zhongyong* brings to the development of knowledge of the world an inner foundation and an inner source. This is possible because a theory of reality has overtaken and become part of a theory of knowledge. We may describe the epistemology of *Zhongyong* as "internalistic foundationalist realism" or an ontoepistemology of internalistic foundationalism. This contrasts with the externalistic nonfoundational approach in the critical rationalism of the *Xunzi* and even perhaps of the *Daxue*.

We can also detect the ontoepistemology of Daoism in the context of ontophenomenology. We can, further, detect the rationalistic epistemology of Mohism and neo-Mohism, and the nominalistic epistemology of Gongsun Long. For neo-Confucianism in the Song and Ming, we may cite the epistemology of Zhu Xi and Wang Yangming, which reflects a broad ontoepistemology of reason (principle), nature, and mind.

Conclusion

Throughout the history of Chinese philosophy we can see a development of Chinese epistemology from a model of observational ontoepistemology in the *Zhouyi* to an epistemology of virtues in Confucianism and an epistemology of the ontocosmological *dao* in Daoism. With regard to meta-epistemology, we can see that Chinese epistemology is dominated by an ontoepistemology with a universal, shared experience and faith in a reality that precludes skepticism. But in the classical period there also develops a scientific epistemology of reason in later Mohism and even in Xunzi, which takes a rationalistic, linguistic turn. Knowledge becomes more a construction than an embodiment or profound experience of reality. By analyzing language, Gongsun Long presents a new interpretation of what we can say we know and to what ontology we might commit ourselves. This is a reversal of the earlier model of ontoepistemology that treats epistemology as a reconstruction or retrieval of a theory of reality based on experience.

In the neo-Confucian tradition, epistemology once again becomes ontoepistemology, basically following the earlier model of ontoepistemology and ontocosmology in the *Zhouyi*. But there is a difference: in neo-Confucianism, unlike the *Zhouyi*, the theory of reality and the methodology for knowing reality are equally emphasized. Both Zhu Xi and Wang Yangming demonstrate tension and partiality between an ontological commitment to objective reason and nature and an ontological commitment to subjective feeling and mind. Zhu and Wang are complementary. Zhu Xi presents a model of knowledge as knowing the *li* (principle, reason), whereas Wang Yangming argues for a model of knowing the mind or knowing as action issuing from mind. In contemporary China, epistemology follows a direction of ontoepistemology much like that of neo-Confucianism. The problem of balancing a theory of reality and a theory of methodology remains to be resolved.

In comparison with western epistemology, the mutual relativity of theory of reality and theory of knowledge in Chinese philosophy is an important contribution to the general problem of understanding human knowledge. In the west, skepticism, although it destroyed a comprehensive theory of reality, was an impetus for a more carefully phrased theory of methods of knowing and perhaps, indirectly, for the development of modern science. Admittedly, however, this same skeptical tradition often leads to dualism between the mind and the world and, in terms of beliefs and knowledge, opens a gap between the physical world of science and the world of humanity or the self. Furthermore, there is notable separation of knowledge from practice, whether individual or social. If we are to construct and integrate a comprehensive theory of knowledge that can achieve unity of reality and reason, unity of knowledge and action, and unity of knowledge and valuation—which are intrinsically and extrinsically important—there is much we can learn from the epistemological tradition and the various models of knowing in Chinese philosophy.

See also Philosophy of Change; Xunzi.

Bibliography

Cheng, Chung-ying, and Nick Bunnin, eds. *Contemporary Chinese Philosophy*. Oxford and Boston, Mass.: Blackwell, 2002.

Crumley, Jack S. *An Introduction to Epistemology*. Mountain View: Mayfield, 1999.

Dancy, Jonathan, and Ernest Sosa, eds. *A Companion to Epistemology*. Boston, Mass., and London: Blackwell, 1994.

Gongsun, Longzi. *Gongsun Longzi* (Works of Gongsun Longzi).

Greco, John, and Ernest Sosa, eds. *Blackwell Guide to Epistemology*. Boston, Mass., and London: Blackwell, 1998.

Laozi. *Daodejing* (Book of *Dao* and *De*).

Lenk, Hans, and Gregor Paul, eds. *Epistemological Issues in Classical Chinese Philosophy*. Albany: State University of New York Press, 1993.

Lunyu (The Analects).

Mencius. *Mengzi* (The Book of Mencius).

Moser, Paul K., Dwayne H. Mulder, and J. D. Trout. *The Theory of Knowledge: A Thematic Introduction*. New York and Oxford: Oxford University Press, 1998.

Mozi. *Mozi* (Works of Mozi). (Includes the *Mobian*.)

Quine, W. V. O. *From Stimulus to Science*. Cambridge, Mass.: Harvard University, 1995.

———. *Pursuit of Truth*. Cambridge: Harvard University Press, 1992.

Xunzi. *Xunzi* (Works of Xunzi).

Zhu, Xi. *Sishu jizhu* (Commentaries on the Four Books).

———. *Zhouyi benyi* (Original Meanings of Zhouyi).

———. *Zhuzi quanji* (Complete Works of Zhu Xi).

———. *Zhuzi yulei* (Conversations of Zhu Xi).

Zhuangzi. *Zhuangzi* (Works of Zhuangzi).

Wang, Yangming. *Zhuanxi lu* (Instructions for Practical Living).

Philosophy of Language

Chad Hansen

Theory of language is a key part of classical Chinese thought. It provided the crucial insights that informed the original, indigenous philosophy of China. It shaped discussions of metaphysics, moral psychology, normative and applied ethics, and political theory. Classical debates about language produced progressively more tenable theories whose surprising distinctiveness reflects features of Chinese language.

Partly because these pre-Han theories of language represent a high-water mark and the most rigorously developed thought, this article will focus only on them. Comparatively crude linguistic theory characterized the philosophical "dark age" that followed. The break in the transmission of reflective analysis accompanied a substitution of superstitious and manipulative religious cosmology for philosophy. A countervailing trend produced a scholastic Confucianism that dominated Chinese thinking until early modern times.

Buddhism imported its peculiar version of the familiar Indo-European theory of language and mind (sententials, concept theory, private mind idealism). How well it was understood and how influential it was in China are both controversial questions. Buddhism, in turn, influenced the neo-Confucian revival, but it failed to develop an independent theory of language. Neo-Confucianism reflected some of the antilinguistic posture of Buddhism, but with little sustained consideration either of language itself or of the problems that classical philosophers exposed in antilinguistic positions.

The original Chinese theories have many interesting background assumptions about language. First, they seldom remarked on the use of written characters, probably regarding these as a normal way of writing. Their use did not incline writers to draw strong distinctions between writing and speaking. Key terms like *ming* (names) and *yan* (language, words) seem to function much as our English translations do, i.e., referring to abstract types of which both written or spoken items are tokens. Modern Chinese distinguishes between *wen* (literature) and *hua* (speech).

Despite the pictographic derivation of written Chinese, all classical thinkers tended to treat reference as a matter of historical convention. Ideally, we conform to the practice of the hypothetical coiners of names (sage kings). Oddly, no philosopher seems even to have formulated a representational picture of how language operates, although a representational theory would seem natural, given a pictographic view of writing. However, would dealing with written symbols, rather than idealized mental images tempt them less to propose a pictographic semantics?

Two things might suggest so: (1) Anyone who learned to write would appreciate that it required conformity to conventional form; not any picture, however accurate, would do. (2) The conventional symbols do not resemble their objects in ways that allow direct interpretation without learning the conventions.

Chinese theory also differs from western sentential "picture theory." The theorists did not understand sentences as true when they pictured analogously structured metaphysical facts. Chinese linguistic thought focused on names, not sentences. We can easily understand this preoccupation. The vivid, graphic writing focuses attention on the character units. More important, characters were not modified as parts of speech. Chinese writers did not notice the functional parts that point to sentential composition. Further, in their topic-comment structure, subjects were optional and comparatively rare in written texts. The familiar western idea of a sentence "frame" that speakers "fill in" with functional units would not be as inviting for Chinese linguistic thinkers.

Those features explain adequately the focus on words rather than sentential units, but not the companion treatment of all words as *ming* (names). Again, this is an assumption made more natural by a feature of Chinese languages: not only are common nouns unmarked for singular and plural, but also, like proper nouns (and mass nouns), they stand alone as noun phrases. Although grammatically dividing reference, the use of common nouns was developing a reliance on counting "sortals" (measures or classifiers). Such sortal counting had become standard by the Han dynasty.

The ideograph translated most commonly in metaphysical formulations as "thing" (*wu*) yields more plausible claims when translated as "thing-kind." The implicit metaphysics is a part-whole, mereological structure. Thinkers associate "names" with ways of making distinctions rather than with reference to particulars.

This explains the anomaly of treating all *terms* as "names" but fails to explain the similar treatment of adjectives and verbs. Lack of function marking is again part of a possible explanation. Adjectives used in the nominal position did not undergo abstract inflection, so theorists treated "red" and "gold" as analogous. They could associate descriptive adjectives, like mass nouns, with a range or extension and view adjectival "names" as distinguishing one range from others. The ranges distinguished by different "names" can overlap. In such cases, compound "names" would be used. Distinguishing between the ways adjectives and nouns worked in compounds produced puzzles for pre-Han theorists.

One-place verbs and verbs with ergative transformations were enough like adjectives to yield to analogous treatment. A pattern of using both nouns and adjectives as two-place verbs further reduced any "felt" differences between transitive verbs and substantives. This use replaced belief-contexts. "*X* believes *S* is *P*" could be expressed as "*X P-s S*" or as "*X*, using *S*, deems it *P*." The natural way of construing the former verb is as a "quote verb." People use the name of the contextually identified stuff; and classify or distinguish it into the category of *P*-stuff.

We should note that we can now identify grammatical distinctions (word order, admissible combinations with other words and particles, etc.) between common and proper nouns, between terms and adjectives, and verbs. My argument is that the implicit ancient Chinese analysis is understandable (not blatantly naive) but not that it is correct.

Another shared assumption is harder to explain. The only explanation is that the view is intuitively as plausible as the contrary assumption which drives much of western theory of language. Chinese thinkers view language pragmatically. They emphasize the social role guiding and coordinating group behavior over the descriptive, fact-stating role. This view also fits the background goal of conforming to the intentions of the sage kings. They were moral exemplars and social engineers as well as "inventors" of lanuage. They formulated the ritual code of behavior (*li*). This assumption also reflects the most important known prehistoric use of writing in China, guidance by divination. Archaeologists unearthed the earliest forms of Chinese characters known on oracle bones. Chinese priests used these in divination and then "stored" them to accumulate *dao* (guidance).

Confucius: Rectifying Names

We notice this last feature of Chinese theory of language first in Confucius's "rectifying names." Confucius studied and taught a historical discourse that he attributed to the sage kings. Central among the ancient documents that formed the curriculum of his school was the *Book of Ritual* (*Li*)—the traditionalist Confucian conception of ethics. Confucius addressed mainly problems in practical interpretation with his students. Studying with Confucius meant learning to do the rites correctly, e.g., wear the right hat at the right time in the right ceremony. His theory reflected the pragmatic relation between language and objects. For traditional discourse to guide us, we must correctly put its "names" on the world "stuff." Confucius assumed that we learn this ability to discriminate by imitation. Teacher-actors model the use of names for us in the process of performing rituals. We extrapolate from these examples in following the code as it applies to us. Confucius called this "rectifying names" and treated it as the key to good government:

> Zilu said, the ruler of Wei awaits your taking on administration. What would be master's priority? The master replied, Certainly—rectifying names! . . . If names are not rectified then language will not flow. If language does not flow, then affairs cannot be completed. If affairs are not completed, ritual and music will not flourish. If ritual and music do not flourish, punishments and penalties will miss their mark. When punishments and penalties miss their mark, people lack the wherewithal to control hand and foot. Hence, a gentleman's words must be acceptable to vocalize and his language must be acceptable as action. A gentleman's language lacks anything that misses—period. (*Analects*, 13.3)

Confucius here focused on the relation between language and action, not that between language and objects. His strategy of setting examples threatens a vicious regress in two ways. First, someone in the chain of models (supposedly the sage king) must know *in some other way* what example to set. Second, the example itself requires interpretation in extrapolating it to new states of affairs. Confucian intuitionism was the main way of blocking these regresses. Confucius seemed to regard a mysterious quality, *ren* (humanity), as the key to correct practical interpretation of the ritual. Humanity is a moral insight that guides the attribution of terms in specific circumstances—guides us in rectifying names.

Notice the absence of definitions in his account. Chinese accounts of language are unswervingly extensional. They rarely invoke any concept such as "meaning," "idea," or "concept." The relationship between language and the world relation is a political matter. Social authorities tag things for the purpose of guiding discourse. Accordingly, two rival Confucian theories of tagging emerge: one relies on tradition and the other on innate moral intuition.

We see traces of grammatical topic-comment structure in Confucius's doctrine. In the place of sentences, describing states of affairs, literary Chinese attaches "names" to relevant stuff (comments on topics). The topics are typically contextual, and Chinese thinkers are sensitive to the context-dependence of language. They rarely reflect on freestanding utterances detached from a social moral context. Chinese linguistic theory focused on what terms to assign to things rather than on what propositional units are true or accurate pictures of reality.

Mozi: Language Utilitarianism

The natural development of this model (arguably its source, since the dating of the passage on "rectifying names" is controversial) comes in the work of Confucius's first critic, the utilitarian philosopher Mozi. His early work (and the subsequent elaboration in later Mohism) focuses on *bian* (distinctions). The use of a term involves a way to *shi* (is this–right) and to *fei* (is not this—wrong) in using it. To learn the term is thus to learn to *shi-fei* appropriately with it. Mozi argued that society should use the preconventional or natural "will" toward benefit (and against harm) to guide its *shi-fei* practice for the words used in social discourse. This initial interpretive proposal turned into a proposal to order the words in guiding discourse differently, i.e., to change Confucius's traditional *dao* (guide).

Mozi's arguments about spirits and fate clarify how this works. General utility, he argued, favors a social discourse with the string *wu-ming* (lack fate) and *you-shen* (have spirits). He represents this conclusion about strings as an example of knowing the *dao* of *you-wu* (have-lack). That means making a *shi-fei* (is this—is not this) distinction for the *you-wu* using the benefit-harm distinction as our guide. We use *you* (have) or *wu* (lack) of things when doing so will lead to general utility.

The implication of Mozi's line of analysis was initially antirealistic. Mozi advocated three standards of language use. The first acknowledged the historical, conventional aspect of language. Our discourse should conform to the guiding intentions of the ancient sage kings. Second, language standards should be appropriate for use by ordinary people using their "eyes and ears." One hypothesis is that this means that standards of correct use should be objectively accessible, like standards of measurement. Mozi's illustrations include a plumb line, a compass, a square, and stakes for plotting where the sun rises and sets. Finally, we should use words in ways that maximize general utility.

Mozi probably supposed that these standards pull in essentially the same direction. He assumed that the people's well-being motivated the sage kings and clear standards promoted general utility. The utility criterion itself was an example of an objective standard. First, it was the "will of nature," not the product of a particular conventional history, and it was measurement-like.

These standards govern the content and practice of discourse, regulations, injunctions, maxims, and slogans. Including any string in the proposed ideal social guiding discourse was "making it constant." The ideal of a constant discourse *dao* was one that could guide society consistently (reliably) and correctly (objectively). Mozi identified this *dao* as the one that resulted in the greatest utility for the country and its people. Thus, assignment of names was a handmaiden to ethics.

To count as the constant *dao*, Mozi's benefit-harm standard must itself be constant. It should be a reliable, unambiguous, objectively correct, unchanging distinction. He alleged that since it came from *tian* (nature) rather than from society, convention, or contingent history, it was all of these.

Mozi's attack on conventional guiding discourse led Mencius to defend Confucianism by postulating an innate moral intuition that carried antilinguistic implications. Mencius argued that language should not manipulate or guide human action. Guidance should come only from the innate patterns or dispositions in the heart-mind. These include an innate ability to *shi-fei* ("is this—is not this") in situations involving choice of actions. The *xin* (heart-mind) selects the appropriate assignment and thus the appropriate behavior. Social language should not distort or reshape those natural moral inclinations. Mencius's argument presupposed that, left to itself, everyone's heart-mind would innately select the *correct* action for him or her.

The *Laozi* also took a negative view of language, but its pragmatic analysis of the effects of language undermined Mencius's optimism about innate moral psychology. Laozi agrees that we should resist the conventional socialization that comes with language. Learning names means learning one arbitrary way of making distinctions. We also learn to guide our action by making these distinctions. Laozi interprets this as acquiring or changing our desires. Thus acquiring a language constrains our natural spontaneity and creates new, disruptive, and usually competitive desires.

Laozi implicitly portrayed natural (prelinguistic) behavior as much more "primitive" than Mencius did. Few of our desires are instinctual. Most are learned. Learning names involves training in how to make distinctions and how to "desire" with them. The names, distinctions, desires, and conventional actions are linked distortions of natural spontaneity. Without linguistic embellishment, the natural desires would sustain social concerns that extend no farther than the local agrarian village.

The *Laozi*, more than Mencius, highlights the antilinguistic aspect of intuitive guidance. It suggests that Mencius's idea (that the Confucian moral values in particular were natural) was a result of confusing the unconscious outcome of learning a guiding language with native intuition. The conventional patterning of distinctions and desires is arbitrary. Laozi makes this point in arguing that we can reverse most conventional values. His conclusion is his opening line—no guiding discourse is constant.

Later Mohist Realism

Followers of the school of Mozi emphasized theory of language and formulated the most realistic and sophisticated theory of language of the period. Here I mainly summarize their conclusions.

They taught that although language could itself be a source of information, it works only when it shadows objective similarities and differences in reality. They failed to produce a satisfactory account of how objective features guided language distinctions. They did, however, note differences in scope between particular names ("John"), species terms ("horse"), and very general terms ("thing") and distinguished several types of similarity.

Like their founder, Mozi, the later Mohists targeted problems in the Confucian posture as name "rectifiers." They thought of their study broadly as *bian* (distinctions) and assumed that philosophical and ethical disagreements reduced to our having different ways of using language to cluster and label things. A "world-guided" approach, they believed, would give us an objective basis for settling such disagreements.

They rejected an implicit assumption of rectifying names—that each thing should have only one name appropriate to use in guiding our action toward it. They noted that many things have more than one "name" (my horse, Dobbin, is a thing). Confucian rectification of names addressed the problem of conflicting rules by restricting which name was relevant to action here-now. Mohists argued that we should restrict not the descriptive scope of names but the scope of compound action descriptions. For example, a thief is human, but killing a thief (execution) is not (morally) killing a human (murder).

Their most successful result was a series of propositions targeting antilinguistic and antidistinctions sentiments. They showed that statements such as "all language is perverse" and "make no distinctions" are self-condemning. They also argued that in any dispute revolving around distinctions, one party must be right and one wrong. If we disagree about the thing over there, one saying it is an ox and the other that it is not an ox, then one will be right. If we are not disputing about a distinction, e.g., when one holds it is ox-stuff and the other that it is dog-stuff, then both could be wrong.

Later Mohism also struggled with a rudimentary theory of composition, focusing mainly on an analysis of compound terms. Given the grammar of ancient written Chinese, such compounding seemed the salient feature of language. They distinguished between two results of compounding terms that suggested a vague metaphysical distinction. The paradigms were "ox-horse" and "hard-white." They held the former to be more inclusive (it embraced two things that did not mix) while the latter was more particular (everywhere you go, you get both).

The School of Names: Gongsun Long and Hui Shi

The analysis of compounds led to a famous debate with one of the figures traditionally identified as belonging to something called the "school of names." There probably was no school as such. The two thinkers usually included, Gongsun Long and Hui Shi, seem to have held radically different theories and to represent, respectively, a Confucian and a Daoist analysis of language. Both were likely targeting some aspect of the later Mohist theory.

Gongsun Long is best-known for his defense of the paradoxical claim "White horse is not horse." "White horse" drew obviously from both later Mohist compounds, ox-horse and hard-white. Gongsun Long seemed to want to reduce the two to a single analysis.

The interpretation of the paradox is still wildly controversial. The traditional view is that his analysis is broadly Platonic. It holds that Gongsun Long postulated abstractions, and so the paradox should read "White-horseness is not horseness." The alternative, concrete interpretation draws on the mass-like character of Chinese nouns. It holds that Gongsun Long was arguing for a concrete "one name, one thing" analysis; thus "White-horse-stuff is not horse-stuff."

The other traditional figure from the school of names, Hui Shi, was a "debating" companion (possibly the teacher) of the Daoist Zhuangzi. Hui concentrated on comparatives and other terms with obviously relativized reference. So, for example, "tall" does not have any fixed range. "Tall" for a giraffe is not "tall" for a horse. Generalizing this feature of relativism in language, Hui apparently concluded that no distinctions or differences rest on external reality. All are projections of different perspectives. The appropriate conclusion, he thought, was to treat the world as an absolute "one," to treat all things as evaluatively equal.

Zhuangzi: Skeptical Relativism

The rediscovery of the later Mohist analysis confirmed that Zhuangzi, usually considered a Daoist mystic, was deeply influenced by these various reflections on language. He seems to have appreciated Laozi's insight that language shapes the patterns of distinctions and valuation which we normally regard as "natural" or "obvious." He probably combined Laozi's view with Hui Shi's critique of the perspectival character of linguistic reference, but without the illegitimate perspective-free claim that all is one.

This combination led him to a nuanced pluralism that he reflected in his philosophical style, making most philosophical discussion take place in dialogues between paradigms of radically different perspectives (including nonhuman ones). One advantage of this posture was that it did not commit him to any self-condemning antilinguistic conclusion. At the same time, he could incorporate Daoist skepticism toward conventional wisdom and toward the pretensions of sages to authoritarian insights into the *dao*.

His analysis highlighted the role of indexicals in language—particularly "this" and "that." They do refer, but what they refer to changes in each instance of use. Anything can be a "this" in some context and anything can be a "not this." Thus, while agreeing with the Mohists that objective features influence what terms of a language pick out, he notes that they do it in many ways. There seems no limit to the number of ways we might assign terms in choosing things.

Drawing on Hui Shi's argument, Zhuangzi's analysis suggests that we apply even "same" and "different" perspectivally. What counts as "the same" from one point of view or purpose would be "different" from another. He generalized this notion of perspective to include all the implicit standards fueling the bitter dispute between Mohists and Confucians about which *dao* was correct. They say *shi* ("this–right") and *fei* ("not this–wrong") from different perspectives and different starting points, and so the dispute looks irresolvable. Merely persuading someone or getting someone to agree with your side in such a dispute is not enough to show that you have made the right *bian* (distinction).

Exactly what substantive position Zhuangzi offers is open to interpretive dispute. However, classifying him as a Daoist together with accepting a conventional view of Daoism as a version of mystical or intuitive monism creates a problem. Zhuangzi marshals powerful arguments against both intuitionism and monism. He shows many signs of a pragmatic analysis (perhaps drawn from Mohism) of certain kinds of language (including abiding by ordinary convention).

Especially in view of his detached, fantasy-like dialogue style of writing philosophy, the safest conclusion may be that he is a skeptic, and most likely one who accepts an implicit realist background. There may be a right way to attach names to things, but we cannot neutrally determine what it is. Further, we can never decisively rule out the possibility of a better way of doing this.

Xunzi: Confucian Conventionalism

The final chapter in Chinese language theory comes in the chapter "Rectifying Names" of the *Xunzi*. Xunzi focuses on language because he wants to reassert that ritual (*li*) is the only standard of correct behavior. He rejected Mencian intuitionism and gleaned insights from Zhuangzi and the dialecticians. The apparent moral he drew was this: since reality cannot be a standard of correctness in language, the default standard must be convention.

Appeal to the usage of the sage kings determines correct use of names. The correct account of that usage is a historical tradition (interpreted, Xunzi insists, by the judgment of *junzi*, Confucian scholar-gentlemen). Thus, he sees Confucianism as vindicated by the weakness Mozi exposed in launching the philosophical dialectic. Xunzi goes on to construct an overtly conventionalist theory of language that carried political implications.

Xunzi introduced an important clarification. He distinguished between two kinds of distinctions: noble-base and same-different. The former correspond roughly to value distinctions and the latter to empirical or descriptive distinctions. The descriptive distinctions enable us to interact with other cultures. A king may alter these "miscellaneous" terms. Even a king, however, should not change conventional evaluative distinctions: ranks, titles, punishments, or anything in the *li* (ritual). For these we rely on the inherited guide of the sage kings (by way of the scholar-gentlemen's interpretation). Xunzi regards moral terms as conventional "artifice" arising from thought, not from nature.

Political authorities rectify names for the traditional Confucian purposes (order and obedience). Xunzi treats the positions and paradoxes of the dialecticians exclusively in these political terms. Philosophy of language causes social instability by undermining the public guiding language. Philosophers confuse the conventional relations of names and make *shi-fei* (is this–not this) unclear. The ruler must prohibit this wordplay. We should have only one standard terminology. The king, not disputing philosophers and warring schools, should govern the introduction of new descriptive terms.

The king should keep three things in mind as he creates names:

1. The reason for having names: The reason for having names is coordinating social behavior and achieving social order. Hence, value terms govern how we assign descriptive terms.
2. The basis of classifying as similar and different: We classify by taking the distinctions delivered by sense organs and using them according to the dictates of a heart imbued with the correct evaluative distinctions.
3. The essentials of regulating names: The basis of regulating names is social order and the preservation of a stable, traditional scheme of language.

Xunzi's account of classifying similar and different takes a markedly empirical (epistemological) turn. Unlike the Mohists, Xunzi did not rely on claims that reality presented objective similarities and differences. Zhuangzi had argued that human standards of *shi-fei* (is this–not this) were no more natural than the rival standards of other animals. Taking Zhuangzi's hint, Xunzi focused on human sense reactions to reality. Indeed, he suggests, we have no neutral interspecies ways of distinguishing things as similar and different. The senses of one species may work differently from those of another; however, within any one species we find similar distinctions. In humans, these ground moral conventions.

All humans sense and respond to approximately the same range of natural distinctions. The eyes of humans distinguish the same range and bands of colors, the mouth distinguishes the same range of taste, the ears distinguish the same range and discriminations of pitch, etc. The shared nature of interspecies distinctions underwrites the possibility of community and language. Thus, we abandon appeal to cosmic nature and rely on what is pragmatically possible for humans in achieving natural human goals.

Our languages conventionally cluster some sensible differences and ignore others. Historical, conventional standards dictate how they do this. Mastering the inherited sage kings' scheme of values transmits these norms into the cultured gentleman's heart. The heart rules the sense organs (as it did for Mencius). It determines what range of sensible discriminants should count as a category for moral purposes. Thus, categories mesh with the moral system of the sage kings and ideally match the clustering they originated.

Clearly, Xunzi absorbed a good deal of his contemporary theory of language. It is less clear if he understood the arguments and motivation. He dispatches the problem of compound terms by ignoring it. "If a single term is sufficient to convey the intent, then use that and otherwise use a compound term." The intent, presumably, is the conventionally understood intent. He does accept the Mohists' view of names with varying scopes and disowns the idea of "one name, one thing." The only important kind of clarity or consistency is the constancy of convention.

Xunzi treats a number of related problems about names in a sensitive way. He saw that spatial separation was a basis of describing two things of the same kind as two "stuffs" (individuation). Then he defines "change" as occurring when a thing's spatial position does not change (exhibits characteristic continuity) but its type does. We then treat it as the same thing, which has changed something. This discussion of metamorphosis is the closest approximation to the classical western problem of change.

Whether or not Xunzi understood the theories behind the paradoxes he criticizes, he clearly did not respect their motivation. He exhibits no philosophical fascination with solving conceptual puzzles for their own sake or using them to drive linguistic theory. He criticizes paradoxical statements on essentially political grounds—the deleterious social effects of asserting their conclusions. Each of them upsets conventional ways of using terms. His solution is political, not intellectual—ban such talk!

Xunzi classifies the paradoxes into three groups in a way that vaguely suggests the line of thought leading to each. Each paradox, he argues, violates one of the three insights into names. The reason for naming is coordinating behavior, so paradoxes which "use names to confuse names" include the Mohists' conclusion that "Killing thieves is not killing men." This claim relies on a theory of names to yield a conclusion that conflicts with unconventional judgments. Therefore, we forbid saying such things.

The second set is "use reality to confuse names," and the central examples are Hui Shi's paradoxes of relativity. They ignore the shared human empirical basis for assigning similarity and difference and use the insight that having different perspectives on reality might lead us to say unconventional things about size and shape. Again, the king should forbid saying such things.

The final group uses names to confuse reality and includes "White horse is not horse." Xunzi's analysis does little to resolve the interprctive puzzles about Gongsun Long's line of reasoning, since it addresses only the pragmatic consequences of allowing such theorizing. His solution, once again, is for the king to avoid and prevent such distracting sophistry.

The Aftermath: Death of Philosophy

Han Feizi (Han Fei), one of Xunzi's students, was a minor royal in one of the warring states. He became a central figure of a school called legalists. He had learned a bit of Xunzi's theory of language. He wildly exaggerated the threat of interpretative anarchy to further buttress Xunzi's case for entirely repressing creative philosophy of language.

Han Fei absorbed Xunzi's argument that the ruler should enforce uniformity in language but rejected using scholarly tradition as the norm. He based his theory of regulation and punishment on a crude argument about shape and name (*xing-ming*). It takes us back to the unexplained Confucian notion that names by themselves guide action. An official post is a capsule description of function (duties) the holder should perform. Han Fei never says how. In the light of recent discoveries, this doctrine appears to be an application of the doctrine of a cult of ruler worship (Huang-Lao). It taught that the *dao* (guide) was in nature and names were embedded in natural shapes.

Legalism became the official doctrine of the repressive Qin empire that brought the classical period of Chinese philosophy to an abrupt halt. In the aftermath, the insights of Chinese theory of language slipped into obscurity. Huang-Lao became the dominant theory surviving during China's philosophical dark age until the importation of Buddhist theory. The early medieval Daoist interpreters argued that we can have names only for things we see. Suppression had worked its magic.

See also Confucianism: Rhetoric; Language and Logic; Laozi; Mohism: The Founder, Mozi; Mohism: Later; Philosophy of Mind; *Wuwei*; Xunzi; Zhuangzi; Zhuangzi: Schools.

Bibliography

Bao, Zhiming. "Language and World View in Ancient China." *Philosophy East and West*, 2, 1990, pp. 195–210.

Chao, Y. R. "Notes on Chinese Grammar and Logic." *Philosophy East and West*, 5, 1955, pp. 31–41.

Cua, A. S. *Ethical Argumentation: A Study of Xunzi Moral Epistemology*. Honolulu: University of Hawaii Press, 1985.

Graham, Angus. *Later Mohist Logic, Ethics, and Science*. Hong Kong and London: Chinese University Press, 1978.

Hansen, Chad. "Chinese Ideographs and Western Ideas." *Journal of Asian Studies*, 52, 1993, pp. 373–399.

———. "Chinese Language, Chinese Philosophy, and 'Truth.' " *Journal of Asian Studies*, 44, 1985, pp. 491–519.

———. *A Daoist Theory of Chinese Thought*. New York: Oxford University Press, 1992.

———. *Language and Logic in Ancient China*. Ann Arbor: University of Michigan Press, 1983.

Philosophy of Literature

Dian Li

In China, as in many civilizations, literature started with poetry. What is unique about Chinese poetry is its supremacy over other literary forms, as well as how long that supremacy has been maintained. For centuries, poetry has been at the top of the hierarchy of genres and the center of Chinese literary life, rarely challenged by other genres, such as drama and fiction. Although each of these genres had its own golden age within the history of Chinese literature, none could match the expanse and continuity of poetry or its influence on Chinese culture. Poetry is, to put it simply, the epitome of Chinese literature and the crown jewel of Chinese civilization. It is no wonder, therefore, that writing about Chinese literature—particularly in early China, when ideas were formulated and entered the canon rapidly—starts and ends with poetry. In effect, the philosophy of poetry has become the philosophy of literature as a whole. References to other genres will be made when relevant, but this essay is mainly concerned with the philosophy of poetry. The time line is from antiquity to the end of the nineteenth century, when Chinese literature underwent a drastic reform in the presence of western intervention. The term "philosophy of Chinese literature" might need clarification. Although "philosophy of Chinese literature" is appropriate as an entry in this encyclopedia of Chinese philosophy, more commonly known terms are "criticism" and "theories of Chinese literature." I will use all of them interchangeably throughout this essay.

The earliest writings about literature are found in philosophical works before the Qin (221–207 B.C.E.); those of Daoism and Confucianism are the most prominent among them. Both Laozi (c. sixth century B.C.E.) and Zhuangzi (369–286 B.C.E.) contributed substantially to the understanding of literature as a form of self-expression and to a theory of language that would henceforth figure in the Chinese poet's consciousness. In particular, Zhuangzi's creative writing and writings about literature exemplify both an imaginative power and a metaphorical ingenuity that have exerted a strong influence on later writers. However, it is Confucius (551–479 B.C.E.) who has left the most indelible mark on the history of Chinese literature. In *Lunyu* (*The Analects*) literature is mentioned no more than a dozen times, but these instances were enough to project a tremendous normative power over later critics as Confucianism quickly acquired the status of a state ideology. Owing to their compact nature and their early entry into the canon, these few quotations, much like the rest of *The Analects,* have been subjects of requotation, exegesis, commentary, and misinterpretation, all familiar practices that give room for reformulating old ideas and for generating new theories. The interplay between Confucian and Daoist understandings of literature is also a fertile ground for constantly reexamining literature.

The period from the first century to the sixth century C.E., crossing the Late Han (25–220) and the Northern and Southern dynasties (420–589), was a golden age—many believe the peak—of Chinese criticism. One sees not only a numerical explosion of critical works in contrast with the sporadic attention of earlier times, but also a trend toward critical writing as a distinctive and worthy pursuit, which is evidenced by the fact that quite a few writers were confident enough to devote themselves solely to criticism. China had never had a professional critic as the concept was understood in the west, and this is as close as it would get until the twentieth century. Representative writings on the philosophy of literature from this period include Wang Chong (c. 27–97), *Lunheng* (*On Constancy*); Anonymous (Han dynasty), *Maoshi xu* (*Great Preface*); Cao Pi (187–226), *Dianlun lunwen* (*On Literature*); Lu Ji (261–303), *Wenfu* (*Discourse on Literature*); Zhi Yü (d. 311), *Wenzhang liubie lun* (*On Genre*); Liu Xie (c. 465–521), *Wenxin diaolong* (*The Literary Mind: Elaborations*); Shen Yüe (441–513), *Songshu Xie Lingyun chuanlun* (*Life of Xie Lingyun in the "Song History"*); Zhong Rong (c. 468–518), *Shipin* (*Poets Graded*); and Xiao Tong (501–531), *Zhaoming wenxuan* (*The Zhaoming Anthology of Literature*). In response to the fecundity of literature in this period, these critical works took on a variety of forms, from book, preface, and letter to essay, entry, and poem, and offered a nuanced understanding of some fundamental questions about literature, such as the nature and function of literature, the creative process, the cultivation of aesthetic connoisseurship, and the techniques of writing. The authors' shared attention to the problem of genre and their efforts to apply form-based genre theories to anthologizing literature helped highlight as well as reinforce Chinese poetry as an elaborately regulated type of writing for centuries to come.

Writings on the philosophy of literature multiplied after the Southern dynasty. Theoretical innovation thrived and fell in ensuing dynasties, not necessarily corresponding with the cycles of creative writing. In terms of the number of titles and critics, the Song dynasty (960–1279) and the Qing (1611–1911) are two of the most prolific periods, but the intervening dynasties also offered some memorable entries in the history of Chinese criticism. Tour-de-force works such as Liu Xie's *The Literary Mind: Elaborations* are rare; the typical work of criticism is a dedicated writing on specific aspects of literature, most of which are in self-standing books. As the body of the poetic canon increased steadily in size and quality, the Chinese critic faced a different challenge from that of Liu Xie's time, when the construction of a grand and complete theory about literature was paramount. The new challenge was less a demand for alternative literary theories, although those were attempted from time to time; the pressing need was to account for the omnipresence of poetry in China's intellectual life and to ensure the continuity of this glorious cultural practice. In China, as well as elsewhere, it is the critic's role and duty to offer commentary on a tradition in order to keep that tradition alive, for a tradition cannot last without commentary by succeeding generations. The Chinese critic's answer to this duty is to write *shihua*, continuously and inexhaustibly.

Shihua or "poetic talk" as a form of criticism may be traced to Zhong Rong's *Shipin*, but the term was first used by Ouyang Xiu (1007–1072) in the Northern Song (960–1125). Ouyang Xiu's work was originally titled simply *Shihua*, with a later compiler adding *liuyi* (Six-One, the author's style name) to distinguish it from the innumerable imitations that followed. This journal-like work was Ouyang's last writing before he died, and he intended it as "a resource for casual talk" (part of the book's subtitle). In twenty-eight entries, Ouyang offered his observations on dozens of poets and their poems, disguising his serious purpose in a lighthearted tone and embellishing his critical insights with off-the-record information about the subjects. This vantage point of both an "expert" and an "insider" was characteristic, although not unique, to Ouyang Xiu, who was a politician, poet, essayist, scholar, and historian all at the same time. Ouyang's *Shihua* is of tremendous value to later poets and readers, who read it to learn the craft of writing and the art of reading.

After Ouyang Xiu, *shihua* as a form of critical writing prospered and became the most lasting legacy in the history of Chinese criticism. Writers of *shihua* had all shades of reputation, and the length of *shihua* varied from a short article to multiple volumes. *Shihua* also spawned other genre-based criticism, such as *cihua* (talk on *ci* poetry), *pingdian* (commentary on fiction), and *quhua* (talk on drama). But all *shihua* and its variants are true to the spirit of Ouyang Xiu, which is, as one of his contemporaries put it, to serve the functions of "studying the language, chronicling history, registering virtues, recording strange events, and correcting mistakes." Not to mention the flexibility of the *shihua*, which afforded writers a way to comment on existing philosophies of literature and present their own theories, no matter how impulsive and fragmented. The best-known works of *shihua* include Ye Mengde (1077–1148), *Shilin shihua*; Yan Yu (c. 1195–1264), *Canglang shihua*; Yüan Mei (1761–1797), *Suiyüan shihua*; Chen Yan-chao (1853–1892), *Baiyuhai shihua* (all of the above titles have the style or studio names of the authors preceding *shihua*); and Wang Guowei (1877–1927), *Renjian cihua* (*Poetic Talks in the World of Men*).

While poetry dominated the literary scene uninterrupted throughout all dynasties, other genres of literature sprouted forth and developed slowly but steadily, not so much to challenge the supremacy of poetry as to satisfy different needs. In the case of drama, which had its golden age in the Yuan dynasty (1234–1368), and the novel, which had its in the Ming (1368–1644) and the Qing, the needs were the common folk's demand for popular entertainment, an area on which poetry had very little impact. The popularity of these two genres then gave rise to their own dedicated critical writings, which became an important part of the Chinese critical tradition. Some of the most influential titles in the field of drama criticism are He Liangchun (1506–1573), *Qulun* (*On Drama*); Li Zhi (1527–1552), *Piping Pipaji* (*A Critique of "The Story of Pipa"*); Li Yü (1611–1679), *Xian Qingou ji* (*A Casual Record of Idle Feelings*); Li Diaoyüan (1734–1803), *Yuchun quhua* (*Talk on Drama*); and Jiao Xün (1763–1820), *Qushuo* (*On Drama*). In criticism of the novel they are Jin Shengtan (1608–1661), *Pingdian Shuihuchuan* (*Commentaries on "Water Margins"*); Mao Zonggang (c. early Qing dynasty), *Sanguo yanyi pingdian* (*Commentaries on "The Three Kingdoms"*) and Wang Guowei, *Hongloumeng pinglun* (*On "The Dreams of the Red Chamber"*). These critical works largely dwell on specific issues of the genre in question, but when they venture to generalize about literature, they tend to rely heavily on terminology borrowed from criticism focused on poetry, and poetry is upheld both as a literary measuring stick and as a means of legitimization of the respective genres.

This survey of Chinese critical writings shows that the philosophy of literature is an expansive and varied tradition. To trace that tradition in a summary manner, as is typical of encyclopedic entries, will have a few seeming difficulties, one of which is the difficulty of terminology. Terminology is a challenge even for scholars of classical Chinese literature in China, and the challenge becomes more acute when one writes about the subject in a foreign language. Unlike western critics who value analytical and logical arguments, Chinese critics rely on impressionistic and intuitive uses of terms. One memorable critical term, in many cases, is all a critic has to offer. Problems of interpretation arise when one term is used by different critics or, in some cases, by the same critic to express many different concepts. Related to the plurality of terminology is the Chinese critic's practice of using literary language to talk about literature, aiming to express not so much intellectual concepts as intuitions. This is perhaps where western criticism and Chinese criticism differ the most: a good work of western criticism is one that discovers a philosophical truth through the power of discursive analysis; a good work of Chinese criticism is one that reaffirms the truth through a new set of terms. The use of synonymous and parallel terms on the part of the Chinese critic is not evidence of a lack of creativity but a self-conscious strategy to rejuvenate an old tradition in ever-changing historical contexts.

But there are certain essential questions that all philosophies of literature must answer. To start, they must say what literature is and why literature is important. In China, just as in the western literary tradition, these answers are embedded in early philosophy. Confucius is quick to recognize the power of literature, for poetry can serve the functions of *xing* (inspired expression), *guan* (observation), *qun* (association), and *yuan* (protest). Therefore, unlike Plato, who wants to banish the poet from his ideal kingdom, Confucius would like poetry to be part of his moral universe; he lists it as one of the three methods—the others being ritual and music—of personal cultivation and perfect government. Such an elevation of poetry actually brings its downgrading, for poetry is thus considered subordinate and secondary, in the service of achieving *de* (virtue) and *ren* (benevolence), which are two manifestations of *dao*. This functionalistic view of literature would permeate later critical writings and become an orthodoxy well protected by the privileged status of Confucianism. New expressions were invented at different times to constantly reaffirm its truth, such as *wen yi mingdao* (literature for illuminating the *dao*), *wen yi zaidao* (literature for carrying the *dao*), *wen yi guandao* (literature for implementing the *dao*), and *wenbi yu daoju* (literature must have the *dao*). Literature for Confucianism is primarily informative and didactic, serving a social and moral purpose.

An important contribution of the Confucian view of literature is that it opened a very lively discourse on the relationship between the poet and his poetry. Since poetry is to positively describe the *dao*, the content of the poet's character matters a great deal. In other words, the virtue of the poet precedes that of his poem, as a person preexists his mirror image. Well-known expressions such as *wen ru qiren* (writing is like the person) or *jianqishi ru jianqiren* (seeing his poetry is like seeing the person) reflect this widely held belief. This explains the Chinese critic's strong interest in studying a poet's life, which is unreservedly used to interpret his poetry and his styles, a practice that is frequently used to help place or displace the poet in question in the ranks of the poetic canon. It is also interesting to note that the assumption of individualism at work here is not readily detectable in the orthodox Confucian view of literature: a poet's experiences and styles are both uniquely determined—in Liu Xie's scheme—by his talent, temperament, learning, and habits. This is just one of the many areas in which Chinese criticism breaks away from orthodox Confucianism and works according its own logic.

No discussion of *dao* and literature, however, would be complete without the participation of Daoism, for *dao* is foremost a Daoist term. Although there are no irreconcilable contradictions between the Daoist and Confucian understanding of *dao*—both take it as the totality of all things and all beings—they differ in emphasis in applying the concept to theorizing about literature. Where Confucianism makes *dao* concrete, giving it a morally and socially specific interpretation, Daoism sanctifies *dao* in the realm of nature. Even though Daoism agrees with Confucianism that literature must express *dao*, they disagree on how that goal should be achieved. By enshrouding *dao* in paradoxical and mystical language—*dao* is nothing and everything—and thus emptying it of its social and political implications, Daoism promotes writing as an echo of the inner world, an exhibition of subjective emotions, and a means to attaining harmony with nature. An appearance of such Daoist views in critical theories is the expression *shi yuan qing* (poetry traces emotions), first articulated by Lu Ji (261–303) to counter the Confucian idea *shi yan zhi* (poetry expresses intent). Whether or not these two expressions are mutually exclusive in theory and in practice is a matter of contention. While some Chinese critics combine these perspectives, many have adhered to one view and opposed the other, vigorously debating the merits of their position down through the history of Chinese criticism.

Another important contribution to the philosophy of literature from Daoism is its concept of language. Language for Zhuangzi is merely a functional instrument and an imperfect instrument at best. This instrument is used to capture meaning, which according to

Zhuangzi is none other than the *dao*. The way language captures meaning could be compared to the way one uses a trap to catch fish and a snare to catch a hare. But unlike the trap or the snare, language is inadequate for its purpose, for language can never fully describe the *dao*. One uses language to talk about the *dao* because one has no other choice, yet the "*dao*" described in language is not the true *dao* but merely a surrogate image. This Daoist view of language can be summarized in Zhuangzi's two famous phrases: *yan bu jinyi* (language cannot fully convey meaning) and *deyi wangyan* (one forgets language once meaning is obtained). Zhuangzi's understanding of language as an arbitrary system of signs and its use as fundamentally self-referential corresponds remarkably with modern theories of language articulated by many western philosophers and critics such as Ferdinand de Saussure, Jacques Derrida, and E. D. Hirsch.

If what Zhuangzi engages in is largely a philosophical discourse, how then has it been transformed into a literary discourse? First, Zhuangzi has raised the Chinese critic's awareness of the problem of language. Poetry, after all, is a language art. The only way to deal with the inadequacy of language is to fully explore the suggestive power of language—that is, capture meanings by insinuation rather than by plain explication. Zhuangzi demonstrates this convincingly in his own writing by a glittering display of metaphor, simile, allegory, parable, and mythical narrative. Thus Zhuangzi uses literature to write about philosophy and subsequently turns philosophy into literature. In Chinese poetics, Zhuangzi's mode of writing is directly responsible for the emergence of what has been generally referred to as the "aesthetics of indirection," which informs most of Chinese poetry, particularly in the late Tang and Song periods. The aesthetics of indirection, simply put, is an aesthetics of "speaking in other words." In practice, it means to achieve the effects of suggestion, symbolism, plurality, and opaqueness through the use of reinforcing metaphors, synonymous expressions, analogous references, and parallel imagery.

Second, Zhuangzi's separation of *dao* and language foreshadows the Chinese critic's strong interest in the creative process. What makes a poem a poem and a poet a poet? How does a poet's mind work? What is behind the process of turning raw language into a finished poem? These questions, as one can expect, defy clarity and are ultimately unanswerable, but that does not deter the Chinese critic from trying. Attention quickly shifts from the problem of the creative process to the larger issue of the relationship between the poet, his poetry, and the world. The various answers are more prescriptive than descriptive, and thus become guidelines for both writing and reading poetry. Focus and terminology differ from critic to critic, but there emerges a consensus about recognizing *yan* (language), *yi* (meaning, intention), *qing* (emotion), and *jing* (the material world or scene) as the most important components in a poem. Although one can generally understand these four categories as they are used in the western critical tradition, one should pay close attention to the Chinese context in each of them. For example, *yan* recalls the problem of linguistic inadequacy, *yi* the Confucian connotation of moral and social purposes, *qing* the correspondence between nature and the inner self, and *jing* the subjective nature of the material world both without and within the poem.

Chinese critics debate about the meanings of some categories and their relationships. Concerning *yan* the debate is between embellishment and simplicity, imitation and innovation; concerning *yi* it is between Confucian engagement and Daoist escapism. Furthermore, does *yi* govern *qing* or vice versa? Does *qing* affect *jing* or *jing* stimulate *qing*? But many agree that a unified presence of both *qing* and *jing* is the prerequisite of a good poem, assuming that its *yan* and *yi* are properly positioned. This aesthetic principle is fortified in expressions such as *qingjing jiaorong* (emotion and scene melt together) or *qingjing heyi* (emotion and scene become one). This idea of a fusion of emotion and scene informs much of Chinese critical writing about poetry as well as drama and fiction. In many cases, *qingjing heyi*, or its variant expressions, is the ultimate compliment that a poet, playwright, or story writer receives from a Chinese critic.

Qingjing jiaorong as a critical position has exerted a strong influence in Chinese aesthetics. It assumes the ontology of the individual and yet affirms the value of the individual's existence in the phenomenal world—the poem is the product of their interdependence. The poet, or any individual for that matter, lives in emotions, but his emotion, be it anxiety, sadness, nostalgia, or melancholy, would be weightless and indistinguishable without contextualization. It is imperative, therefore, for the poet to externalize his emotions through his own unique choice of natural objects and metaphors, so that his emotions can be individualized and consequently universally appreciated. In the process, he brings himself closer to nature by simultaneously objectifying himself and personifying nature. In this sense, writing is the poet's experience with nature at the highest level, and the poem is a testimony to his success or failure.

Does the fusion of emotion and scene have different shades and shapes? How should one describe the different ways in which Chinese poets have attempted to write about their experiences with nature? The

Chinese critic's response is the concept of *jing*, also known as *jingjie*. This *jing* is a homophone of the *jing* that means the material world or scene; in what follows here, *jing* alone or *jingjie* means the homophone as opposed to *jing* (material world), and their association is *jing jing*.

Jingjie was the invention of the critic Wang Guowie of the late Qing, but *jing* as a critical concept was first used by a number of critics during the Tang (618–907), the most famous of whom is Sikong Tu (837–908). *Jing* for Sikong Tu is a complete poetic context in which ideas are produced and appreciated, and he pioneered the principle of *siyu jing xie* (the unity of ideas and *jing*). Following the tradition of poetic commentary, he composed twenty-four poems to describe possible poetic moods (*shipin*), which are the epitome of Chinese intuitive criticism. The currency of *jing* in Chinese poetics since Sikong Tu is evidenced by how frequently it is invoked in the works of many important critics, such as Su Shi (1037–1101), Jiang Kui (c. 1155–1221), Wang Fuzhi (1619–1692), and Yao Nai (1731–1815), to name just a few. Some innovative and influential critical theories in later dynasties are also informed by the concept, for example, the theory of "intuitive awakening" (*miaowu*) by Yan Yu, "divine resonance" (*shenyun*) by Wang Shizhen (1634–1590), and "inspired sensibility" (*xingling*) by Yüan Mei (1716–1798). Wang Guowei was the last significant scholar of classical Chinese literature and a harbinger of modern criticism; his contribution was to use some ideas borrowed from western philosophy—from Schopenhauer and Nietzsche in particular—to explain the concept of *jingjie*. Notably, his examples are exclusively from the Chinese poetic canon, the same kinds of examples that have inspired many Chinese critics before him. After Wang Guowei, the notion of *jingjie* has, no doubt, become more accessible to those well versed in both western philosophical and Chinese literary traditions.

Like many Chinese critical terms, *jing* or *jingjie* is simply untranslatable. The usual rendering of the term in English as "world" or "realm" cannot possibly convey its far-reaching implications in Chinese poetics. Literally, this *jing* means "spectacle," "vista," or a number of synonyms that describe a piece of reality under the human eye, but in criticism it refers primarily to the metaphysical relationship between the observer (the poetic persona) and the observed (the reconstructed reality). A good place to start is to look at the term's relationship with the four basic poetic building blocks: *yan* (language), *yi* (meaning, intention), *qing* (emotion), and *jing* (material world). Except for *yan*, which as the medium of poetry is already embedded in all critical concepts, each of the other poetic building blocks has its own association with *jing*, such as *yi jing*, *qing jing*, and *jing jing*, yet these *jing* exist only for the purpose of creating the *jing* of the whole poem. Consequently, *jing* requires that different components and devices within a poem are not merely self-referential but evocative of a metaphysical connotation or context. In the Chinese critic's expression, this is articulated as the pursuit of "language beyond language" (*yanwai zhi yan*), "image beyond image" (*xiangwai zhi xiang*), and "scene beyond scene" (*jingwai zhijing*).

Evidently, the idea of *jing* aims at the problem of interpretation or, more accurately, it offers a way of interpreting Chinese poetry—how poetry reflects the self and the world and how one should read that reflection. In short, *jing* unifies the signifying process and its end result in writing as well as in reading. It is a very fluid but powerful word that tries to mean both the signifier and the signified, materiality and essence, text and textuality, the poet's intention, and the effect of reading of the poem. In this connection, *jing* reflects a philosophical position about self and nature as much as a metaphysical view of literature, and makes the reading of poetry almost a religious experience, which it is, no doubt, primarily under the auspices of Chan (Zen) Buddhism. That is why the locus classicus of the concept of *jing* in the Tang corresponded with the rise of Chan Buddhism and the subsequent critical writings informed by it were mostly enshrouded in Chan Buddhist terms.

See also Calligraphy; Confucianism: Confucius; Laozi; Philosophy of Art; Wang Fuzhi; Wang Guowei; Zhuangzi.

Bibliography

Barnstone, Tony, and Chou Ping, eds. *The Art of Writing: Teaching of the Chinese Masters*. Boston, Mass.: Shambhala, 1996.

Denton, Kirk A., ed. *Modern Chinese Literary Thought: Writings on Literature 1893–1945*. Stanford, Calif.: Stanford University Press, 1996.

Guo, Shaoyu. *Zhongguo gudian wenxue lilun pi ping shi* (A History of Chinese Literary Criticism). Beijing: Renmin wenxue, 1959.

He, Wenhuan, ed. *Lidai shihua* (Poetic Talks from All Dynasties). Zhonghua shuju, 1981. (Reprint.)

———, ed. *Lidai shihua xubian* (Supplement to Poetic Talks from All Dynasties). Zhonghua shuju, 1983. (Reprint.)

Huang, Haichang. *Zhongguo wenxue piping jianshi* (A Brief History of Chinese Literary Criticism). Guangdong renmin, 1981.

Liu, James J. Y. *The Art of Chinese Poetry*. Chicago: University of Chicago Press, 1962.

———. *Chinese Theories of Literature*. Chicago: University of Chicago Press, 1975.

Liu, Wu-chi. *An Introduction to Chinese Literature*. Bloomington: Indiana University Press, 1966.

Marshall, Donald G. (ed.). *Literature as Philosophy, Philosophy as Literature*. Iowa City: University of Iowa Press, 1987.

Owen, Stephen. *The End of the Chinese "Middle Ages": Essays in Mid-Tang Literary Culture*. Stanford, Calif.: Stanford University Press, 1996.

———. *Traditional Chinese Poetry and Poetics: Omen of the World*. Madison: University of Wisconsin Press, 1985.

———, ed. *Readings in Classical Chinese Literary Thought*. Cambridge, Mass.: Harvard University Press, 1992.

Rickett, Adele. *Chinese Approaches to Literature from Confucius to Liang-Ch'i-ch'ao*. Princeton, N.J.: Princeton University Press, 1992.

Tokei, Ferenc. *Genre Theory in China in the Third–Sixth Centuries: Liu Hsieh's Theory on Poetic Genres*. Budapest: Akademiai Kiado, 1971.

Wang, John Chingyu. *Ch'in Sheng-t'an*. New York: Twayne, 1972.

Watson, Burton. *Chinese Lyricism: Shih Poetry from the Second to the Twelfth Century*. New York: Columbia University Press, 1971.

Wong, Siu-kit, ed. *Early Chinese Literary Criticism*. Hong Kong: Joint Publishing, 1983.

Wu, Wenzhi, ed. *Zhongguo gudai wenxue lilun mingzhu tijian* (Annotations on the Famous Works of Classical Chinese Literary Criticism). Hehui: Huangshan shushe, 1987.

Yu, Pauline. *The Reading of Imagery in the Chinese Poetic Tradition*. Princeton, N.J.: Princeton University Press, 1987.

———. "Ssu-k'ung T'u's *Shih-p'in:* Poetic Theory in Poetic Form." In *Studies in Chinese Poetry and Poetics*, Vol. 1, ed. Ronald C. Miao. San Francisco, Calif.: Chinese Materials Center, 1978.

Zhang, Longxi. *The Tao and the Logos: Literary Hermeneutics, East and West*. Durham, N.C., and London: Duke University Press, 1992.

Zhao, Shende, ed. *Zhongguo gudai wenxue lilun mingchu tansuo* (Writings on Famous Works of Classical Chinese Literary Criticism). Guilin: Guangxi shifan daxue, 1989.

Philosophy of Mind

Chad HANSEN

Classical Chinese theory of mind is similar to western "folk psychology" in that each mirrors its respective background view of language. They differ in ways that fit those folk theories of language. The core Chinese concept is *xin* (the heart-mind). As the translation suggests, Chinese folk psychology lacked a contrast between cognitive states (representative ideas, cognition, reason, beliefs) and affective states (desires, motives, emotions, feelings). The *xin* guides action, but not through beliefs and desires. It takes input from the world and guides action in light of that input. Most thinkers share those core beliefs.

Herbert Fingarette (1972) argued that the Chinese (Confucius at least) had no psychological theory. They did not use beliefs and desires to explain action, and they did not use psychology (inner mental representation) to explain language (meaning). We find neither a focus on an inner world populated with mental objects nor any preoccupation with questions of the correspondence between the subjective and objective worlds. Fingarette explained this as reflecting an appreciation of the deep conventional nature of both linguistic and moral meaning. He saw this reflected in the Confucian focus on *li* (ritual) and its emphasis on sociology and history rather than psychology. The meaning, the very existence, of a handshake depends on a historical convention. It rests on no mental acts such as sincerity and intent. Such mental acts may accompany the conventional act and give it a kind of aesthetic grace, but they do not explain it.

Fingarette states the point in misleading terms. Confucianism may not be psychologistic in its linguistic or moral theory, but it still presupposes a psychology, albeit not the familiar individualist, mental, or cognitive psychology. Its account of human function in conventional, historical society presupposes some behavioral and dispositional traits. Most Chinese thinkers indeed appear to presuppose that humans are social, not egoistic or individualistic. The *xin* coordinates our behavior with that of others. Thinkers differed in their attitude toward this natural social faculty. Some thought we should reform this tendency and try harder to become egoists, but most approved of it as the basic "goodness" of people. Most also assumed that social discourse influenced how the heart-mind guides our cooperation. If discourse programs the heart-mind, it must have a dispositional capacity to internalize the programming.

Humans accumulate and transmit conventional *dao* (guiding discourses, ways). We teach them to our children and address them to each other. The heart-mind then executes the guidance in any *dao* it learns when triggered (e.g., by the sense organs). Again, thinkers differed in their attitude toward this shared outlook. Some thought we should minimize or eliminate the controlling effect of such conventions on human behavior. Others focused on how we should reform the social discourse that we use collectively in programming each other's *xin*. Typically, thinkers in the former group had some theory of the innateness (or what we might now call the hard-wired programming) of the *xin*. Some in the latter camp had either a "blank page" image or a negative view of the heart-mind's innate patterns of response.

According to some thinkers, the sense organs delivered a processed input to the heart-mind as a distinction: salty and sour, sweet and bitter, red or black or white or green, and so forth. Most had thin theories, at best, of how the senses contributed to guidance. It is tempting to suppose that they assumed the input was an amorphous flow of "qualia" that the heart-mind sorted into categories (relevant either to its innate or to its social programming). However, given the lack of analysis of the content of the sensory input, we should probably conservatively assume they took the naive realist view that the senses simply make distinctions in the world. We can be sure only that the *xin* did trigger reactions to stimuli that were relevant to discourse.

Reflecting the theory of *xin*, the implicit theory of language made no distinction between describing and prescribing. Chinese thinkers assumed that the core function of language is guiding behavior. Representational features served that prescriptive goal. In executing guidance, we have to identify relevant "things" in context. If the discourse describes some behavior toward one's elder, one needs a way to identify correctly both the elder and what counts as the prescribed behavior. Correct action according to a conventional *dao* must also take into account other descriptions of the situation such as "urgent" and "normal." These issues lay behind Confucian theories of "rectifying names."

The psychological theory (like the linguistic) did not take on a sentential form. Classical Chinese language had no "belief-grammar," i.e., no forms such as "*X* believes that *P*" (where *P* is a proposition). The closest grammatical counterpart focuses on the term, not the sentence, and points to the different function of *xin*. Where westerners would say "He believes (that) it is good" classical Chinese would use either "He goods it" or "He, *yi* (with regard to) it, *wei* (deems, regards) good." Similarly, *zhi* (to know) takes noun phrases, not sentences, as its object. The closest counterpart to propositional knowledge would be "He knows its being (deemed as) good." The *xin* guides action in the world in virtue of the categories it assigns to things, but it does not house mental or linguistic "pictures" of facts.

Technically, the attitude was what philosophers call *de re*. The "subject" was in the world, not in the mind. The context of use picked out the intended item. The attitude consisted of projecting the mental category or concept onto the actual thing. We distinguish this functional role best by talking about a disposition rather than a belief. It is a disposition to assign some reality to a category. The requisite faculty of the heart-mind (or the senses) is the ability to discriminate or distinguish *T* from not-*T*, e.g., good from bad, human being from thief. Alternatively, we might think of Chinese "belief" and "knowledge" as predicate attitudes rather than propositional attitudes.

Predicate attitudes are the function of the heart-mind. A basic judgment is, thus, neither a picture nor a representation of some metaphysically complex fact. Its essence is picking out what counts as *X* in the situation (where *X* is a term in the guiding discourse). The context fixes the object and the heart-mind assigns it to a relevant category.

Hence, Chinese folk theory gives the central place to the (learned or innate) ability to make distinctions correctly in following a *dao*—unlike western folk psychology, which puts ideas in the central place. The Chinese theorists implicitly understood correctness as conformity to the social-historical norm. One project of some Chinese philosophers was trying to provide a natural or objective ground of *dao*.

Western "ideas" are analogous to mental pictographs in a language of thought. The composite pictures formed out of these mental images (beliefs) were the mental counterparts of facts. Truth was "correspondence" between the picture and the fact. Pictures play a role in Chinese folk theory of language but not of mind. The Chinese understood their written characters as having evolved from pictographs. They had scant reason to think of grammatical strings of characters as "pictures" of anything.

Chinese folk linguistics recognized that history and community usage determined the reference of the characters. They did not appeal to the pictographic quality or any associated mental image individuals might have. Language and conventions are valuable because they store inherited guidance. The social-historical tradition, not individual psychology, grounds meaning. Some thinkers became skeptical of claims about the sages and the "constancy" of their guidance, but they did not abandon the assumption that public language guides us. Typically, they advocated either reforming the guiding discourse (*dao*) or reverting to "natural," prelinguistic behavior patterns. Language rested neither on cognition nor on private, individual subjectivity. The role of philosophy of mind in Chinese theory of language was mainly application (execution of instructions).

Chinese theory of language centered on counterparts of reference or denotation. To have mastered a term was for the *xin* and senses working together to be able to distinguish or divide realities "correctly." "Correctly" was the rub, because the standard of correctness was discourse. It threatened a regress—we need a discourse to guide our practical interpretation of discourse. Philosophy of mind played a role in various attempted solutions. Chinese philosophers (except for innatists) mostly agreed that actual distinguishing would be relative to past training, experience, assumptions, and situation. However, they did not regard experience as a mental concept in the classic western sense of subjective or private content.

An important concept in philosophy of mind was, therefore, *de* (virtuosity). One classic formulation identified *de* as embodied, inner *dao*. *De*, though "inner," was more a set of dispositions than mental content. The link seemed to be that when we learn a *dao*'s content, it produces *de*. Good *de* comes from successful teaching of a *dao*. When you follow *dao*, you need not have the discourse "playing" internally. We best view it as the behavioral ability to conform to the intended pattern of action—the path (performance *dao*). It would be "second nature." We may think of *de*, accordingly, as both learned and natural.

We can distinguish Chinese thought from Indo-European thought, then, not only in its blending affective and cognitive functions but also in its avoiding the nuts and bolts of western mind-body analysis. "Inner" and "outer" did distinguish the psychological from the social, but this did not mean that "inner" was mental content. The *xin* has a physical and temporal location and consists of dispositions to make distinctions in guiding action. It is not a set of inherently representational "ideas" (mental pictograms).

Similarly, we find no clear counterpart to the Indo-European conception of the faculty of reason. Euclidean method in geometry and the formulation of the syllogism in logic informed this Indo-European concept. Without this apparatus, Chinese thinkers characterized the heart-mind as properly or improperly trained, virtuous, skilled, reliable, etc. Prima facie, however, these were social standards that threatened circularity. The heart-mind required some kind of mastery of a body of practical knowledge. Chinese thinkers explored norm realism mainly through an "innatist" strategy. Innatists sought to picture the heart-mind's distinctions as matching "norms" or "moral patterns" implicit in the natural stasis or harmony of the world.

Historical Developments: The Classical Period

Confucius indirectly addressed philosophy of mind in his theory of education. He shaped the moral debate in a way that fundamentally influenced the classical conception of *xin* (heart-mind). Confucius's discourse on *dao* was the classical syllabus, including most notably history, poetry, and ritual. On one hand, we can think of these as "training" the *xin* in proper performance. On the other, the question of how to translate the texts into action seemed to require a prior interpretive capacity of *xin*. Confucius appealed to a tantalizingly vague intuitive ability that he called *ren* (humanity). A person with *ren* can translate guiding discourse into performance correctly—i.e., can execute or follow a *dao*. Confucius left open whether *ren* was innate or acquired in study, though the latter seems more likely to have been his position.

It was, in any case, the position of China's first philosophical critic, the anti-Confucian Mozi. Again, concern with philosophy of mind was subordinate to Mozi's normative concerns. He saw moral character as plastic. It was shaped by natural human communion (especially our tendency to "emulate superiors," i.e., in the sense of imitate rather than surpass). Thus we could cultivate utilitarian behavioral tendencies by having social models enunciate and act on a utilitarian social discourse. The influence of social models would also determine the interpretation of the discourse. Interpretation takes the form of indexical pro and con reactions—*shi* (this, right, assent) and *fei* (not this, wrong, dissent). The attitudes when associated with terms pick out the reality (object, action, etc.) relevant to the discourse. We thus train the heart-mind to make distinctions that guide its choices and thereby our behavior—specifically in following a utilitarian symbolic guide. Utilitarian standards should also guide practical interpretation (execution or performance) of the discourse.

At this point in Chinese thought, the heart-mind became the focus of more systematic theorizing—much of it in reaction to Mozi's issues. The moral issue and the threat of a relativist regress in the picture led to a nativist reaction. On the one hand, thinkers wanted to imagine ways to free themselves from the implicit social determinism. On the other, moralists want a more absolute basis for ethical distinctions and actions.

Several thinkers may have joined a trend of interest in cultivating the heart-mind. Mencius's theory is the best-known within the moralist trend. He analyzed the heart-mind as consisting of four natural moral inclinations. These normally mature just as seeds grows into plants. Therefore, the resulting virtues ("benevolence," "morality," "ritual," and "knowledge") were natural. Mencius thus avoided having to treat the *ren* intuition as a learned product, a social *dao*. It is a *de* that signals a natural *dao*. This view allowed Mencius to defend Confucian ritual indirectly against Mozi's accusation that it relied on an optional and thus changeable tradition.

Mencius's strategy, however, presupposed that a linguistic *dao* could either distort or reinforce the heart-mind's innate program. In principle, we should not need to prop up moral virtue educationally. Linguistic shaping, other than countering linguistic distortion, therefore, ran an unnecessary risk. It endangered the natural growth of the moral dispositions. The dispositions *shi* (this, right, assent) and *fei* (not this, wrong, dissent) necessary for sage-like moral behavior should develop "naturally." Mencius's theory implied not that we know moral theory at birth but that it develops or matures along with the physical body and in response to ordinary moral situations. The heart-mind functions by issuing *shi-fei* (this–not this) directives that are right in the concrete situations in which we find ourselves. It does not need or generate ethical theory or hypothetical choices. The *xin*'s intuitions are situational and implicitly harmonious with nature.

A well-known advocate of natural spontaneity or freedom as motivation was the Daoist Laozi. He analyzed the psychology of socialization at a different level. Learning names was training us to make distinctions and to have desires of what society considered the appropriate sort. Both the distinctions and the desires were "right" only according to the conventions of the language community. Learning language meant not only losing one's natural spontaneity but also subjecting oneself to control by a social-historical perspective. We allowed society to control our desires. Laozi's famous slogan, *wuwei* (or *wu-wei*), enjoined us to avoid actions motivated by such socialized desires. We achieve that negative by forgetting socially instilled distinctions—by forgetting language!

Laozi's implicit ideal had some affinities with that of Mencius except that Laozi's conception of the "natural" realm of psychological dispositions was considerably less ambitious in moral terms. Interpreters usually suppose that he assumed there would be a range of natural desires left even if socialized desires were "subtracted." These would be enough to sustain small, nonaggressive, agrarian villages. In them, people would lack the curiosity even to visit neighboring villages. This "primitivism" still requires a natural level of harmonious impulses to action, but not nearly enough to sustain Mencius's unified moral empire.

The later Mohists became skeptical about the neutral status of these allegedly "natural" heart-mind states. They noted that even a thief may claim that his behavior was natural. They watered down the conventionalism of Mozi by appealing to objectively accessible similarities and differences in nature. Our language ought to reflect these clusters of similarity. They seldom reflected on the epistemology of the senses. Still, supposedly, like Mozi, they would have appealed to testimony from ordinary people relying on their "eyes and ears."

Others, like Zhuangzi, insisted that any apparent patterns of similarity and difference were always perspectival and relative to some prior purpose, standards, values, or attitude. Linguistics did shape attitudes of the heart-mind but did not carve the world into its real parts either reliably or accurately.

The later Mohists had given a cluster of definitions of *zhi* (to know). One of these seemed close to consciousness—or rather to point to a lack of any such concept. *Zhi* was the capacity to know. In dreaming the *zhi* did not *zhi*, and we took (something) as so. They analyzed the key function of the heart-mind as the capacity to discern linguistic intention.

The *Zhuangzi* takes a step beyond Laozi in his theory of emotions. Zhuangzi discusses the passions and emotions that were raw, presocial inputs from reality. He suggested a pragmatic attitude toward them—we cannot know what purpose they have, but without them, there would be no reference for the "I." Without the "I," there would be neither choosing nor objects of choice. Like Hume, he argued that although we have these inputs and feel there must be some organizing "true ruler," we get no input (*qing*) from any such ruler. We simply have the inputs themselves (happiness, anger, sorrow, joy, fear). We cannot suppose that the physical heart is such a ruler, because it is no less natural than the other organs and joints of the body. Training and history condition a heart's judgments. Ultimately, even Mencius's *shi-fei* (this–not this) are input to the *xin*. Our experience introduces them relative to our position and past assumptions. They are not objective or neutral judgments.

Xunzi also concentrated on issues related to philosophy of mind, though in the context of moral and linguistic issues. He initiated some important and historically influential developments in the classical theory. His most famous (and textually suspect) doctrine is "Human nature is evil." While he clearly wanted to distance himself from Mencius, the slogan at best obscures the deep affinity between their respective views of human nature and mind.

Xunzi seems to have drawn both from the tradition advocating cultivating heart-mind and from the focused theory of language. This produced a tense hybrid theory that filled out the original Confucian picture on how conventions and language program the heart-mind. Xunzi made the naturalism explicit. Human guiding discourse takes place in the context of a three-tier universe—*tian* (heaven-nature), *di* (earth-sustenance), and *ren* (the social realm). He gave humans a special place in the "chain of nature," but not on the basis of reason. Animals shared the capacity for *zhi* (knowledge). What distinguishes humans is their *yi* (morality), which is grounded on the ability to *bian* (distinguish).

Presumably, distinguishing is unique among animals with knowledge, since it is shorthand for the ability to construct and abide by conventions—conventional distinctions or language. The *Xunzi*'s naturalistic justifications for Confucian conventional rituals includes one based on economics. Ritual distinctions guide people's desires so that society can manage scarcity. Only those with high status learn to seek scarce goods. Xunzi's departure from Mencius thus seems to lie in seeing human morality as informed or "filled out" by historical conventional distinctions. These are the products of reflection and artifice, not nature.

However, in other ways Xunzi seems to edge closer to Mencius. He also presents ritual as part of the structure of the world—implicit in the natural context of heaven and earth. One natural line of explanation is this: while thought creates the correct conventions, nature sets the concrete conditions of scarcity and the human traits that determine what conventions will be best for human flourishing.

Historical Developments: Han Cosmology

The onset of the philosophical dark age, brought on by repression in the Qin dynasty followed by politics in the Han dynasty, resulted in a bureaucratic, obscurantist Confucian orthodoxy. The Qin buried the technical ideas informing philosophy of mind along with the active thinkers who understood them. The eclectic scholasticism that emerged had an essentially religious and superstitious ontology. It was, still, overtly materialist (assuming that *qi*—ether, matter—is material). So the implicit philosophy of mind of the few philosophically inclined thinkers during the period tended toward a vague materialism.

The Han further developed the five-element (five-phase) version of materialism. They postulated a correlation based on fives linking virtually every system of classification that occurred to them. The scheme included the organs of the body and the virtues. Interpretation and analysis of "correlative" reasoning is a controversial subject. From here, the mental correlations look more like a frequency selection from the psychological lexicon than a product of philosophical reflection, observation, or causal theory.

The *yin-yang* analysis also had mental correlates. Following Xunzi, orthodox Han Confucians tended to treat *qing* (reality, desires) as *yin* (typically negative). The *yang* (value positive) counterpart was *xing* (human moral nature).

An important development in the period was a compromise that emerged in the Confucian view of the role of mind in morality, which eventually informed and dominated scholastic neo-Confucianism from the Sung dynasty to the Qing. A small book known as the *Doctrine of the Mean* gave the canonical formulation of this notion of mind. Heart-mind is an input-output device that preserves homeostasis. It begins in a state of tranquillity. The brief account leaves open whether this initial state results from ideally structured moral input, resolution of inner conflicts, or the absence of (distorting) content. Xunzi's view of the empty, unified, and still mind seems the proximate ancestor of the last of these. The vagueness, conveniently, makes Mencius's doctrines fit it as well.

The input is a perturbation from the outer world requiring action. The output, the heart-mind's action-guiding response, restores harmony to the world and the inner heart-mind returns to a state of tranquillity. However, if the inner state before the input is not tranquil, the response will not restore harmony to the situation.

Han Confucianism filled out this cosmic "black box" view of the interaction between heart-mind and world harmony with the concept of *qi* as "life-material." *Qi* is a blend of energy and matter rather than pure matter—translations such as "life force" bring out an essential connection with vitality. This makes it appropriate in a cosmology that links the active heart-mind with the changing world. *Qi* was the underlying and constituting element of spirits and ghosts as well as ordinary things.

Wang Chong's skeptical, reductive application of *qi* theory focused on *shen* (spirit-energy). He did not view its consequences for heart-mind as particularly iconoclastic. It still lacked a notion of "consciousness" independent of *zhi* (know). Our *zhi*, he argued, stops when we are asleep and so almost certainly it does when we are dead. His argument that nature had no intentions or purposes illustrated his reductive behaviorism—if it has neither eyes nor ears, then it cannot have *zhi* (purposes or intentions). This argument would hardly make sense if he had the familiar western concept of consciousness. Similarly, he argues that the five virtues are in the five organs; so when the organs are dead and gone, the virtues disappear with them.

Historical Developments: The Introduction of Buddhist Philosophy of Mind

The next developments stem from the introduction of Buddhist mental concepts into China. Most accounts credit a movement dubbed neo-Daoism with paving the way for this radical change in philosophy of mind. Wang Bi's neo-Daoist system was explicitly a cosmology more than a theory of mind, but interpretations tend to read it epistemically.

Wang Bi addressed the metaphysical puzzle of the relation of being and nonbeing (*you-wu*). He postulated that nonbeing was the "basic substance." Nonbeing produced being. He called their obscure relationship "substance and function." Interpretations often use an analogy to Kant's noumenon and phenomenon. As we have noted, Wang Bi had few epistemological interests, but the analysis did have implications for heart-mind theory. He applied the metaphysical scheme to his Confucian slogan—"sage within, king without." The mind was empty "within" while behaviors were in perfect conformity with the Confucian ritual *dao*. This tilts the Daoist tradition toward the "emptiness" reading of the "black box" analysis of heart-mind.

Wang Bi also placed *li* (principle) in a more central explanatory position than it had been classically. This paved the way for using it to translate the sentence or law-like *dharma* of Buddhism. *Li* played roles in both Buddhist epistemology and theory of mind. In sparse pre-Han usage, *li* was objective tendencies in thing-kinds. (Intuitionists and naturalists took *li* to be the valid norm for that kind, i.e., species-relative bits of *dao*.) Wang Bi gave *li* a more essentialist reading in the context of the *Book of Changes*. He postulated a *li* guiding the mixtures and transformations of *yin* and *yang*. One should be able to bypass the complexity of the system by isolating and understanding its essential *li*.

Buddhism introduced revolutionary changes into the Chinese conceptual scheme of the heart-mind. The original Indo-European religion probably began the familiar western phenomenalism (consciousness, experience-based mentalism). Indian philosophy came complete with the familiar western sentential analyses, mental content, and cognitive emphasis (belief and knowing-that). It even mimicked Aristotle's subject-predicate syllogism and the familiar epistemic and metaphysical dualism between the subjective and the objective. It introduced a semantic (eternal) truth predicate into Chinese thought along with a representational view of the function of both mind and language. Reason-intellect and emotion-desire formed a basic opposition in Buddhist psychological analysis. An inner "idea-world" parallels (or replaces) the ordinary world of objects. Soul and mind are roughly interchangeable, and familiar arguments for immortality suggest both metaphysical dualism and mental transcendence or superiority over the physical. Reality (knowledge, reason) is conceptually linked to permanence, and appearance (illusion, experience) to change. A universal chain of causation was a central explanatory device and a mark of dependence and impermanence.

Two caveats are in order, however. First, although Buddhism introduced a dualist conceptual scheme, many schools (arguably) denied the dualism so formulated and rejected any transcendent "self." Second, it is unclear how well the philosophy of mind was generally understood and whether much of it actually took hold in China. One of the early and notoriously unsuccessful schools was "consciousness only" (translated as "only heart-mind"), which interpreted the idealism of Yogacara Buddhism. The Yogacara analysis was Hume-like in denying that anything linked the infinitesimal "moments of awareness" into a real self. Scholars tend to blame its demise, however, as much on its objectionable moral features (its alleged Hinayana or elitist failure to guarantee universal salvation) as on its conceptual innovations.

The most successful schools were those that seemed to eschew theory of any kind—like Chan (Ch'an, Zen) or Pure Land Buddhism—or those that opted for intuitive, mystical simplicity (Tiantai and Hua Yen). The most important conceptual legacy of Buddhism, therefore, seems to be the changed role and importance of the character *li* (principle). In Buddhism it served a wide range of important sentential and mental functions. It facilitated the translation of "law," "truth," and "reason." Neo-Confucianism would take it over (with notoriously controversial implications) as a key concept in its philosophy of mind.

Neo-Confucianism is a western name for a cluster of medieval schools. Philosophy of mind played a central role in their views. Scholars (somewhat controversially) present these schools as motivated by an antiforeign attitude that sought to resurrect indigenous classical systems. These had lain quasi-dormant for six-hundred-odd years when the freshness of Buddhism started to attract the attention of China's better intellectuals. Resurrecting Confucianism required providing it with an alternative to Buddhist metaphysics. For this, the intellectuals drew on *qi* metaphysics, the "black-box" "homeostasis-preserving" analysis of heart-mind, the *li* of Wang Bi and Buddhism, and Mencius's classical theory of the inherent goodness of heart-mind.

The neo-Confucian systems are too intricate to analyze in detail here. The earliest versions focused on the notion of *qi* as a link between the heart-mind and the world influenced by our action. They characterized the tranquil state of the "black box" as void. The school of *li* criticized that analysis as too Zen-like. (This was a typical and damning charge to participants in this movement, although going through a period of Zen during one's development of thought was a common pattern among neo-Confucians.)

The *li* school insisted that any adequate account of heart-mind had to include original moral content. It did this by postulating an interdependent and inseparable dualism of *li* and *qi*. The *li* permeates the heart and all of reality, which is composed of *qi*. The most tempting (and common) elaboration uses the Platonic distinction between form and content, but that analysis teeters on the edge of incoherence. The school fell back on dividing the human mind from some transcendental or metaphysical *dao*-mind. This made it dubious as a theory of mind at all—in the ordinary sense. It essentially became a metaphysics in which heart-mind was a cosmic force.

One way of understanding the motivation that drove the otherwise puzzling metaphysical gymnastics links philosophy of mind and ethics. Neo-Confucians were searching for a metaphysical system such that anyone so viewing the cosmos and one's place in it would reliably do what was right. The goal was having the metaphysical outlook of the sage. The criterion of right and wrong was that the sage's mind would so judge it. If we could replicate the outlook, we would be sage-like in our attitudes, including both beliefs and motivations. The effect on motivation and behavior was more important than the theoretical coherence of the system. The complexity of moral choice and human motivation required bringing so many perturbations into their account of the proposed system that it became an almost infinitely flexible rationalization for intuitionism.

Mencian optimism about innate heart-mind dispositions proved an uncomfortable legacy. If human nature and the heart-mind are innately and spontaneously moral, it was unclear why we require such mental gymnastics to cultivate and condition the dispositions. Mencians portrayed the *li* as inherently good in all things, but somehow humans, alone in all of nature, might fail to conform to its own natural norms. The attempt to explain this through the dualism of *li-qi* flounders on the metaphysical principle that the dualism pervades all things. Despite this well-known (and intractable) Confucian problem of evil, the school again became the medieval orthodoxy. Officeholders were required to show their moral character by parroting the view in detail.

The school of heart-mind was a rebellion against that orthodoxy. We can best understand this rival as a species of normative, objective idealism. It saw the actual heart-mind as *li* and therefore inherently good. The *xin* projects that *li* onto the world in the act of categorizing and dividing it into types. Thus our normative, (phenomenal) world is good, but its good is a function of the mind. Moral categorization and action are simultaneous and inseparable responses of the heart-mind to the perturbations or the disharmonies we encounter. The analysis of mind is functional—there is no goodness of the mind separate from the goodness of its categorizing and acting. Knowing is acting.

The school of heart-mind somewhat gingerly accepted the implication of the Mencian heritage. There is no evil. I say "gingerly" because whether one should formulate or teach this conclusion or not is itself a choice that the mind must assess for its contextual value. In itself, as it were, the heart-mind is beyond good and evil. Others, hence, criticized the school of heart-mind for its Zen-like implications. Any moderately clever student could figure out that whatever he chose to do was right (see Zhuangzi's initial criticism of Mencian idealism). They, in turn, criticized the Buddhist character of their rivals' assumptions that some kind of state of mind (enlightenment, realization) would magically result in sagehood.

The moralistic name-calling of this debate among Confucians sapped further development of theory of mind. That coupled with its irrational optimism in the face of growing awareness of the vulnerability of China and its inability to resist western and Japanese military and political power resulted first in mildly more materialistic and utilitarian systems. Eventually intellectuals developed a wholesale interest in the next invasion of Indo-European thought, which took the form of Marxism. Maoist theory of mind was an unstable mixture of Marxist economic and materialist reductionism and traditional Chinese optimism. The right political attitude (typically that of the party member) would give good communists spectacular moral power and infallible situational intuitions about how to solve social problems.

Again, the obvious failure in the face of irrational theoretical optimism has produced a general antipathy to idealizations. One can guess that the next phase, like the Buddhist phase, will involve borrowing and blending. However, the current skepticism about the general outlines of folk psychology in the west and its essentially alien character probably will keep Chinese theory of heart-mind distinctively Chinese.

See also *Dao*: The Way; *De*.

Bibliography

Chan, Wing-tsit, trans. *Neo-Confucian Terms Explained (The Pei-hsi tzu-i) by Ch'en Ch'un*. New York: Columbia University Press, 1986.

Fingarette, Herbert. *Confucius: The Secular as Sacred*. New York: Harper and Row, 1972.
Graham, Angus. "The Background of the Mencian Theory of Human Nature." *Tsing Hua Journal of Chinese Studies*, 6(1, 2), 1967, pp. 215–274.
———. *Disputers of the Tao: Philosophical Argument in Ancient China*. La Salle, Ill.: Open Court, 1989.
———. "The Place of Reason in the Chinese Philosophical Tradition." In *The Legacy of China*, ed. Raymond Dawson. Oxford: Clarendon, 1964.
Hansen, Chad. *A Daoist Theory of Chinese Thought*. New York: Oxford University Press, 1992.
———. "Qing (Emotions) in Pre-Buddhist Chinese Thought." In *Emotions in Asian Thought*, ed. Joel Marks and Roger T. Ames. Albany: State University of New York Press, 1995.
———. "Should the Ancient Masters Value Reason?" In *Chinese Texts and Philosophical Contexts: Essays Dedicated to A. C. Graham*, ed. Henry Rosemont. La Salle, Ill.: Open Court, 1991.
———. "Term Belief in Action." In *Epistemological Issues in Chinese Philosophy*, ed. Hans Lenk and Gregor Paul. Albany: State University of New York Press, 1993.
Munro, Donald J. *The Concept of Man in Contemporary China*. Ann Arbor: University of Michigan Press, 1977.
———. *The Concept of Man in Early China*. Stanford, Calif.: Stanford University Press, 1969.
———. *Images of Human Nature: A Sung Portrait*. Princeton, N.J.: Princeton University Press, 1988.
———, ed. *Individualism and Holism: Studies in Confucian and Taoist Values*. Ann Arbor: University of Michigan Press, 1977.
Schwartz, Benjamin. *The World of Thought in Ancient China*. Cambridge, Mass.: Harvard University Press, 1985.

Philosophy: Recent Trends in China since Mao

Tongqi Lin

The year 1978, two years after Mao Zedong died, marked the beginning of a new period in modern Chinese history, known as a time of reform and opening. In that period, however, as was the case in traditional China, philosophical exploration is entwined with intellectual inquiry in general. Instead of purely philosophical trends, we can only speak of intellectual-philosophical trends or simply currents of thought. For the sake of convenience, in this article, "philosophical" is not used in its strict sense and is mostly used interchangeably with "intellectual."

Broadly speaking, the intellectual-philosophical trends of the period can be described in terms of three contending but interwoven strands. First, there is the self-transformation of Maoist Marxism prompted mainly by the new economic and social reforms of that era. Second, there is a renewed effort to reinterpret the Chinese philosophical heritage, especially Confucianism. It is an attempt to tap the indigenous intellectual resources as a response to but also a critique of ideas coming from the west. Third, there is an unprecedented importation and eager borrowing of western ideas. It serves both as a means to critique Maoist Marxism and Chinese traditional thinking and as a search for solutions to newly arising social and political problems. These three stands are characterized by what I call a "triadic tension" in the basic fabrics of a new intellectual discourse that started in 1978 and has grown steadily since then. This article will first introduce briefly the major trends in terms of these three strands, with their representative exponents. Then it will describe the major developments of the new intellectual discourse in which these trends are situated.

Trends and Authors

The first strand—the self-transformation of Marxism—started soon after 1978, the year that marked the end of the Mao Zedong era. Although this development has been neglected by western academia, it has engaged the attention of a great number of mainland scholars, including some of the most brilliant ones.

The two best-known early innovators in this endeavor are Wang Roushui (1926–2002) and Su Shaozhi (b. 1923). Wang, a former deputy editor-in-chief of the *People's Daily*, the organ of the Chinese Communist Party, was the standard-bearer of the trend known as "Marxist humanism" in the early 1980s. Su, a former director of the Research Institute of Marxism-Leninism-Mao Zedong Thought of the China Academy of Social Sciences (CASS), initiated the important theory of "staged development of socialism." This theory provided a broad theoretical basis for the reform policies of the Chinese Communist Party throughout the 1980s. The efforts to "develop" Marxism, however, went far beyond these two pioneers. The presence of Marxism in the post-Mao intellectual discourse is far more pervasive than might first appear to western observers, especially in the 1980s. What has actually emerged is a broad spectrum of gradual departure from Maoist orthodoxy, ranging from minor revisions in epistemology to a major shift in ontology. This is best exemplified by the protracted discussions and variegated development of "praxis materialism" as distinct from the orthodox Marxist theory of "natural materialism."

Many scholars claim in one way or another to be advocates of "praxis materialism," a term they invest with quite different meanings. Among them the two most prominent and original are Li Zehou (b. 1940) and Feng Qi (1915–1995). Li, who settled in the United States and taught at Colorado College, was undoubtedly the most influential and original thinker throughout the 1980s. He calls his thinking "Chinese post-Marxism." He severely criticizes the dialectical materialism and "natural ontology" of routine Marxism but holds firmly to the basic tenets of Marx's historical materialism. He calls the philosophical system he laboriously constructs "anthropological ontology," using the formal structure of Kant's three *Critiques* but "turning it upside down," so to speak, to suit his materialist approach. Li also incorporates into his system a singular aesthetics of his own construction, to which, he believes, Confucianism, supplemented by Daoism, can make a special contribution. Feng, a professor of the Normal University of Eastern China, Shanghai, departs from orthodox Marxism less drastically than Li but is equally innovative. He focused his lifelong effort on the time-honored problem of how to "transform knowledge into wisdom" and tried to solve it by constructing what he calls "epistemology in a broad sense." He tries to graft part of the epistemology of Kant and of Russell's logical positivism onto the dialectical materialism and historical materialism of Marx and Engels and interpret them with the Chinese traditional thinking on "human nature" (*xing*) and "heaven's way" (*tiandao*). Despite its apparently "conservative" stance, the originality of Feng's thinking should not be underestimated.

Besides Li and Feng, intellectual historians like Xiao (Hsiao) Jefu (b. 1924) and Zhang Dainian (b. 1909) are also well-known scholar-thinkers in the self-transformation of Marxism. Zhang, a venerated senior professor at Beijing University, tried as early as the 1930s to enunciate the basic tenets of Marx's materialism and dialectics using Chinese philosophical categories and the method of logical analysis he learned from "new realism." Xiao, leader of a group of scholars with Wuhan University as their center, argues forcefully for the emergence of a "Chinese Enlightenment" in the Ming-Qing period (i.e., in the seventeenth century). Xiao's intention is to tap the indigenous resources of Chinese culture for the western Enlightenment spirit and bring them to bear on the modernization process in post-Mao China. Zhang Liwen (b. 1935), a professor at the People's University, Beijing, and a scholar of neo-Confucianism, tries to formulate a philosophical system, which he calls a "theory of harmony and integration" (*hehe xue*). The theory emphasizes dynamic equilibrium and progressive integration as the defining characteristics and also the most valuable part of Chinese philosophy. If these Marxist thinkers represent an attempt to achieve their self-transformation by constructing new theories and systems synchronically, Wang Yuanhua (b. 1920) can be seen as embodying the transformation process diachronically. As a veteran communist with a strong intellectual commitment, Wang has engaged in relentless self-reflection in the past two decades. The result is a tortuous intellectual "metamorphosis" that brought him from being a sincere Marxist to being an adamant advocate of western Enlightenment and finally to being a scholar who is also deeply sympathetic to certain core values of traditional Chinese culture. The trajectory of Wang's intellectual evolution tells much of the agony and resilience of the best Marxist minds in the post-Mao period. It is noteworthy that the self-transformation of Marxism finds its advocators among younger scholars. Yang Guorong (b. 1957), who had published ten books and over a hundred articles, discusses topics ranging from classical Confucianism and neo-Confucianism to issues such as thinking, being, and ethics. He draws inspiration from his mentor Feng Qi and Li Zhehou but has a wider access to western philosophical thinking. His pondering on fundamental issues could prove to be a prelude to the construction of a modern version of transformed Marxism different from the social and cultural critique of the Frankfurt School.

The second strand—the modern interpretation of traditional Chinese philosophy—is largely involved with Confucianism but has also spread to Daoism. The modern interpretation of Confucian tradition started as early as the 1920s and has already engaged the efforts of four generations. It was initially a response to the western challenge that, since the mid-nineteenth century, had threatened China's survival both as a nation-state and as a civilization. It was, however, also a reaction to the mainstream of the well-known May Fourth movement (1915–1923), which advocated vigorous antitraditionalism and a drastic westernization of Chinese culture. Since the 1950s, this school of thought has been known as the new Confucians or contemporary new Confucians (*xinrujia*), a term of unsettled meaning and contested reference. The key figure of the first generation of new Confucianism was Xiong Shili (1885–1968) and that of the second Mou Zongsan (1909–1995). It is interesting to note that the initial impetus for a modern interpretation of Confucianism in the mainland came from the third generation of new Confucians who live abroad. Among them the most influential are Tu Weiming (b. 1940), a professor at Harvard University; Cheng Chung-ying (b. 1935), a professor at the University of Hawaii-Manoa; and Liu Shu-hsien (b. 1934), an emeritus professor at Hong Kong Chinese University. Yü Ying-shih (b. 1930), a professor at Princeton University, and probably the best-known Chinese intellectual historian today, is sometimes also included in this school of thought, although he does not consider himself part of it. Most of these scholars live in the United States, but they have been so actively engaged in intellectual dialogue with their colleagues in mainland China that they have become an integral and indeed an important part of the mainland discourse.

Tu Weiming has developed what he calls an "anthropocosmic (or inclusive) Confucian humanism." The central piece of the theory is a well-developed "ethics of Confucian humanism" with its Confucian core values productively reinterpreted to meet the challenges from the west and also challenge the west. It adds a virtually new dimension to the "moral metaphysics" constructed by Tu's mentor, Mou Zongsan. Tu has also been instrumental in developing a Confucian discourse both in mainland China and internationally. Cheng Chung-ying has developed what he calls "ontohermeneutics," an integration of Chinese metaphysics with Gadamerian hermeneutics. Cheng, Tu, and Li Zehou (who also identified himself later as a "new Confucian" thinker) can be seen as representing the three typical approaches in modern interpretation of Confucianism. While Tu stresses inner good (ethics) and hence the human faculty of will as the core and point of departure of Confucianism, Li chooses to make beauty (aesthetics) and hence human feelings the essence and the highest achievement of Confucianism. Cheng, on the other hand, gives the highest priority to truth (epistemology) and hence intellect in his reconstruction of Confucianism.

Some other Chinese-American scholars, although not considered new Confucians, also show a deep interest in the modern transformation of Confucianism. Among them are Antonio S. Cua (Ke Xiongwen, b. 1932), Chang Hao (b. 1937), Charles Fu Wei-hsun (1933–1997), and Lin Yusheng (b. 1934). Like their new Confucian colleagues in the United States, they have had a considerable impact on discourse in mainland China. Lin is a disciple of F. Hayek and Yin Haiguang (1919–1969), the guiding spirit of liberalism in Taiwan in the 1960s and 1970s. While retaining his liberal stance, Lin argues forcefully for what he calls a "creative transformation" of the Confucian cultural heritage. Chang, who has a genuine sympathy for Confucian spirituality, seeks to combine sympathetic interpretation with acute criticism in his reevaluation of Confucianism. Fu, a comparative religionist with a strong interest in Buddhism, adopts an attitude similar to Chang's. Cua, a moral philosopher specializing in western ethical theory, has engaged in an extensive conceptual reconstruction of Confucian ethics. In the past two decades, Cua has devoted much effort to developing Confucian ethics as an ethics of virtue against the background of what he envisages as the living Confucian tradition. Topics of concern are the conceptual framework of Confucian ethics and the role of ethical principles in dealing with problems that arise out of intercultural conflict (Cua 2000). Cua has also written illuminating books on Xunzi and Wang Yangming, bringing a reinterpreted Confucian moral thinking into the mainland discourse (1982, 1985).

In mainland China, some scholars have begun to identify themselves openly as new Confucians. Renowned scholars like Tang Yijie, president of the Academy of Chinese Culture (based in Beijing), and Peng Pu (b. 1928), a senior researcher at China Academy of Social Sciences (CASS), have ideas that resonate strongly with those of the new Confucians. Interestingly, new Confucianism owes much of its spread in the mainland to a government-sponsored ten-year research project (1986–1996), which was originally intended to "subject new Confucianism to a critical scrutiny." Guided by Fang Keli, dean of the graduate school of CASS, the project contributed significantly to bringing into focus the newborn Confucian discourse and to the training of competent scholars in this field. Today, a group of burgeoning scholars of new Confucianism have appeared in the mainland, including Chen Lai of Beijing University, Guo Qiyung of Wuhan University, and Zheng Jiadong (b. 1956) of CASS. Their fruitful efforts have aroused the interest and attention of participants in the Confucian discourse.

The revival of the study of Daoism and its modern interpretation occurred much later than the new wave of Confucian study. It did not attract much attention until 1992, when the journal *Daojia wenhua yanjiu* (*Study of Daoist Culture*) was founded. Chen Guying, who taught both at Beijing University and in Taiwan, has had a central role in the Daoist revival. Now a "new Daoism" has appeared on the horizon. Relative to the new Confucians, it serves as both a competing and a complementary philosophical trend. Lin Xiaogang (b. 1947), apart from exegetical study of Daoist literature, has written extensively on the modern implications of Daoism, including issues like ecology, global ethics, feminism, and meditation in the modern world.

The third strand—the borrowing of western ideas—started in the early 1980s as a thin thread but soon widened and now is enriching almost all areas of academic study. This powerful source of ideas has produced two strands in China: "classic modernity" and "postmodernity."

Classic modernity, which remains the mainstay of western civilization today, is represented and understood in China chiefly as Enlightenment thinking that can be traced back to eighteenth-century Europe. Its core values include secularity, progress, positivistic objectivity, instrumental rationality, scientific method, and autonomy of the individual, which in turn inform the market economy, the democratic polity, the rule of law, and the crucial role of science and technology in modern society. Works of Kant, Max Weber, and Habermas have aroused great interest and have exerted an unabated influence on the intellectuals ever since their introduction (or reintroduction) into China in the early 1980s. However, it was the technoscientific trend represented by systems theory, cybernetics, and information theory—then newly developed, and known as the "three theories" among mainland scholars—that created a sensation in the early 1980s. The most influential figure in this trend was Jin Guantao (b. 1947), who had been a chemistry student at Beijing University during the Cultural Revolution of 1966–1976. He calls his theory the "philosophy of holistic evolution." In fact, Jin's theory is, as he himself has admitted, "only a more accurate, scientific, and updated" version of what he believes to be the three basic principles or tenets of Marxism: objectivity, development, and knowing the world through changing it. Partly owing to his efforts, exploring scientific methods and their application in historical and social studies became a fashion for several years. Jin's strong scientistic inclination, however, set a limit to his influence in the humanities, and the fashion gradually faded, especially in the 1990s. Chen Kuide (b. 1946), a Ph.D. in philosophy at Fudan University and in exile in the United States since 1989, is typical of the audacity of the younger scholars of the time. On the basis of a study of Kant and the philosophy of science, he and a few of his peers had the courage to challenge the long-entrenched doctrine of routine dialectical materialism as early as 1983. Starting in the mid-1980s, Christianity as an intellectual pursuit began to find its way into the academic world, largely owing to the effort of Liu Xiaofeng (b. 1956), another graduate of Beijing University (at the time, he had just received his master's degree). With the rapid spread of Christian gospel in China in the past two decades, there has been an increasing interest in the study of Christianity.

The second imported western trend, postmodernity, in contrast with classic modernity, was almost exclusively humanistic. It was brought about through ambitious translation projects undertaken by younger scholars, e.g., the works of Nietzsche, Freud, Sartre, Heidegger, Gadamer, Derrida, and Foucault. The projects were further accelerated in the 1990s. The impact they produced on post-Mao thinking can hardly be exaggerated. Among the organizers in the 1980s, Gan Yang, who obtained his master's degree in philosophy from Beijing University (he was a doctoral candidate at the University of Chicago in 2000), was probably the most important.

Throughout 1980s, these western-inspired scholars and seekers of truth, aided by various versions of Marxism, launched a sustained attack on those who tried to tap the resources of Chinese cultural tradition, especially the Confucian tradition. An antitraditionalist tide quickly rose and swept across the intellectual world, reaching its climax in 1988, and then fed into the Tiananmen student protest movement of 1989.

However, as the discourse moved into the 1990s, for various reasons, the antitraditionalist tide ebbed. A reverse tide set in: neotraditionalism. Meanwhile, two new currents of thought, both borrowed from the west, appeared: postmodernism and postcolonialism. However, the two most important new trends that emerged in the 1990s were liberalism (in its classic and neoclassic sense), and the "new left." Liberalism has a long but frustrated history in China. It was first introduced at the turn of the nineteenth century and then became a major part of the legacy of the May Fourth Movement of 1919. Following the communist takeover in 1949, it was relentlessly suppressed for three decades and was hardly tolerated even in the post-Mao era. Therefore, when in the late 1990s a group of scholars openly declared themselves proponents of liberalism, the event was truly noteworthy. These scholars believed that to give the development of constitutional democracy in China a solid theoretical grounding, it was imperative to make a serious, although belated, effort to grasp the real spirit of liberalism in the west. This return of liberalism was, however, based on a realization of the differences between two types of liberalism: the relatively moderate Anglo-American liberalism, which advocates evolutionary reformism; and the more radical French version, which advocates drastic revolutionary means for social changes. John Locke, Adam Smith, John Stuart Mill, Alexis de Tocqueville, Edmund Burke, F. A. Hayek, and Isaiah Berlin are the masters to be carefully studied, while Jean-Jacques Rousseau is a target of critique. Lin Yusheng has played a noticeable role in the spread of liberalism in post-Mao China. Rule of law, checks and balances, and civil rights are the major topics for discussion. Individual liberty is set as the highest priority in theory construction, and the protection of private property is seen as the foremost prerequisite. The apparatus of government is considered the greatest threat to individual liberty and its monopoly of political and economic power the primary source of all forms of oppression. Cultural pluralism is vigorously argued for and its guarantee by law is forcefully upheld. Li Shenzhi, a veteran communist once labeled a "rightist" in the political campaign of the 1950s, is acknowledged by many as the major proponent of the trend.

The "new left" represents, loosely, a group of scholars who mostly trace their intellectual pedigree back to Marxism, neo-Marxism, or western Marxism, and some third world postcolonialist theorists. They give Mao Zedong's legacy a more lenient assessment than that which prevailed in the 1980s and was upheld by liberals in the 1990s. Its most influential figure is Wang Hui, a researcher at CASS. Wang criticizes dominant theories of modernization in the west as a grand narrative that covers up the conflicts and injustice accompanying the rise of capitalism both in the west and within China as a nation-state. He proposes a new paradigm that can better explain both the ongoing globalization process and Chinese intellectual history in the past century. Meanwhile, he also makes a sweeping critique of almost all the trends that have so far appeared since 1978, labeling them essentially different kinds of "ideologies of modernization." Wang's efforts are highly praised by some of his peers. His thinking could turn out to be an influential current in the mainland in the twenty-first century.

The New Intellectual Discourse

It is important to note that the intellectual trends mentioned above, divergent as they are, also converge to form a new coherent intellectual discourse. Without an understanding of the new discourse, the various trends would appear to be isolated, unrelated intellectual endeavors, and their significance could hardly be fully appreciated.

The new intellectual discourse started in 1978 and took shape in the mid–1980s. Ever since its birth it has vigorously challenged the old discourse sponsored by officialdom and dominating China's intellectual stage since the communist takeover in 1949. Although locked together, the two discourses have quite different central concerns, debated issues, and tacit theoretical assumptions. The central concern of the old or orthodox discourse, particularly before 1978, was and has been the justification of the shifting political needs of the Chinese Communist Party, especially its general lines and basic policies. The theoretical assumptions shared by, or imposed on, its participants are based on Maoist Marxism and formulated by the party's theoreticians. They are known as *tifa* (propositions). They are theoretical norms that have been worked out by authoritative figures and endorsed by the party. As a body of rules, they serve as unifying guidelines for theoretical discussions, reaching their tentacles into almost every corner of the discourse, leaving little room for independent thinking. As a result, the issues debated are mostly insignificant or even unintelligible to outsiders, turning the discourse into an isolated domain, impervious to outside influences. The situation has changed visibly since 1978, but the major defining characteristics remain largely intact.

In contrast, the new discourse was basically initiated by the intellectuals themselves in the late 1970s. The discourse has survived wave after wave of government suppression and grown into an essentially independent sphere of intellectual activities. The central concern of the discourse is China's modernization as variously understood by its participants. Its shared assumption is what I call a "humanist quest." It sets its own agenda, selects its own issues for debate, and even has certain linguistic features of its own. The discourse, which has spanned a period of two decades, can be divided into two phases with the student protest movement of May–June 1989 as the line of division.

Phase 1 (1978–1989): The humanist quest, the triadic tension, and the new Enlightenment. In the first phase of the discourse, two themes quickly developed and loomed large: self and culture. How to "modernize" self as an individual and how to modernize culture with its system of ideas and values became the two central concerns of the discourse. Both concerns were reactions to what had happened during the preceding period, especially during the Cultural Revolution (1966–1976), later denounced as the "disastrous ten years." The deep concern with the individual was a reaction to the "dissolution" of self in the ocean of the masses on the one hand and its submission to the will of a man-made god, Mao Zedong, on the other. The intense interest in culture was a reaction to the long reign of economic determinism and cultural vandalism in the same period. The discovery of self or individuality spearheaded the emerging discourse; but the individual finally returned to culture for intellectual and spiritual nourishment. The deep longing for self-realization thus merged with the quest for cultural identity. Together they formed a persistent effort on the part of Chinese intellectuals that foreshadowed a long search for China's soul.

This intense concern for individuality and culture shows that philosophy in the post-Mao period, despite its yearning for modernity, still retains much of its traditional character for Chinese intellectuals. Philosophy is understood as an endeavor to find a proper form of life, accompanied by watchfulness for the destiny of Chinese culture, i.e., the survival and flourishing of the people and the nation. Philosophy in this sense is (unlike most philosophical inquiry in the west) primarily a search for a meaningful way of life rather than an acquisition of objective truth. In the social and historical context of the post-Mao era, the search manifested itself in what might be called a "humanist quest." This quest provides the vision and driving force of the new discourse and makes it possible.

The "humanist quest" reflects a perennial human concern, a constant topic for human reflection and exploration. From the practical point of view, it is an audacious attempt to deal with a problem that has no ultimate solution. Any attempt at a solution would automatically become part of an ongoing open-ended dialogue—an endless process of critique and countercritique. However, the concrete manifestation of the dialogue is always culturally specific and historically constrained. For example, it was the nearly total suppression of the quest during the Mao era that in the first place made its reemergence such a historically significant and conspicuous event. Quoting Clifford Geertz, Benjamin I. Schwartz remarks, "The problems being existential are universal; their solutions being human are diverse."

Throughout the two decades of the post-Mao era, the humanist quest unfolded in a series of sharp intellectual encounters, resulting in the publication of hundreds of articles and often lasting more than two or three years. In the first decade, we find three overlapping and interconnected phases.

In the first phase, the quest focused on a search for the independent existence of the individual self, with its inherent value, dignity, and rights. People sought to assert themselves as human beings, both individually and collectively, or to "rediscover *ren*," that is, the human being. (The Chinese character *ren* in Chinese contexts always refers to human beings, both individually and collectively, male and female, and it carries a moral and spiritual weight that cannot really be rendered in English.) Broadly speaking, the rediscovery of *ren* could be described as going though two steps. The first step was achieved in a debate known as "Discussions on the Criteria of Truth" (1978). The discussions were politically motivated and yielded practically nothing of theoretical value. But this debate had a wide impact on the discourse because it marked, as one participant put it, the "moment of sudden awakening—the awakening of *reason*" after a long slumber. "Dare to know! Be guided by your own understanding," as Kant put it. The second step was accomplished in an event known as the "Discussions on Humanism and Alienation" (1980–1984). In the debate *ren* finally emerges as a full-fledged independent person with not only the faculty of reasoning but also that of feeling and willing. Wang Roshui wrote: "A specter stalks the earth of China. Who are you? I am *ren*."

The second phase of the quest focused on the nature and characteristic features of *ren*. With the newly discovered creature, *ren*, standing before the inquirer, the question naturally arose: what is this *ren*? As a result, the humanist quest shifted its focus to a search for the distinguishing features and inner structure of *ren*, its essence and strength. This was a "reexploration of *ren*," a quest in which people, after asserting themselves, sought to know themselves. It constitutes the content of the discussions centering on the "subjectivity of *ren*," a powerful trend initiated by Li Zehou in 1980 that spanned the whole decade up to 1989.

The third phase of the quest came when it probed into the proper structure of valuation one should adopt in one's daily life and the ultimate meaning of human existence. In times of need, culture as a system of values, or a web of meanings woven by humans themselves, is always the repository to which people turn for moral and spiritual guidance. This was what happened in the "cultural fever" or the "great debate on culture" (1984–1989). The many intellectual trends that had been building up in recent years now found an opportunity to express themselves. More than 1,500 articles and a large number of books were published. More than a dozen centers for cultural studies sprang up. However, the bulk of the debate focused on an exploration of the moral, aesthetic, and spiritual resources in Chinese and western cultures that supply the ideas and values needed for the fulfillment of the newfound individual. The quest therefore became a "rebuilding of *ren*" in which people sought to realize themselves.

This persistent humanist quest—the rediscovery, reexploration, and rebuilding of *ren*—or rather a faith in the value of the quest constitutes the shared assumption, the common ground for the many contending trends in the discourse and gives coherence and continuity to an otherwise disconnected series of intellectual episodes.

It is worth noting again that the strife and contention between the various trends in the discourse result in the pattern I call "triadic tension." This is the tension between the three contending intellectual strands mentioned earlier: (1) the self-transformation of Marxism, (2) the modern interpretation of Chinese cultural cum philosophical heritage, and (3) the introduction of western philosophical thinking. As strands rather than fixed directions or static structures, they allow for the initiative of individuals who think and act. Therefore, they can also be seen as three operating cultural, intellectual forces that attract and repel each other, turning the intellectual arena into a sort of magnetic field, though with triple poles. On the individual level, these forces work through the mind and heart of each participant and influence and shape the actual position each individual chooses in the intellectual arena. Indeed, few of the innovative minds in the Chinese mainland during this period could completely escape the tug-of-war between these forces. The concept of "triadic tension," therefore, serves not only to describe broadly the intellectual landscape but also to analyze the thinking of each individual in the discourse.

Retrospectively, the triadic tension in the first decade of the discourse can be described mainly as "new Enlightenment" thinking, for two reasons. First, the thinking is considered a direct heir to the May Fourth Movement of 1919, which is often referred to as the "Chinese Enlightenment." This movement also had a similar dominant motif in the "discovery of *ren*." More important, it represents an attempt to break through the theoretical boundary set by Marxism and seek inspiration directly from the sources of western modernity—the Enlightenment of eighteenth-century Europe, with its faith in the use of reason, its questioning of traditional doctrines and values, its tendency toward individualism, its emphasis on universal human progress and its empirical method in science. The new Enlightenment subsumes under its vague umbrella a variety of thought ranging from Confucian humanism to Marxist humanism. Its mainstream is represented by a quest for modernity as depicted by Max Weber and further specified by Talcott Parsons. The hard core of the new Enlightenment is the humanist quest described above.

Like the Chinese Enlightenment of the May Fourth Movement, the mainstream of the new Enlightenment also called for a reevaluation of tradition and advocated a westernization of Chinese culture. A tide of antitraditionalism soon swept across the intellectual community. Aided by the Marxists, it succeeded in containing the spread of new Confucianism, which had barely made its "landing" on the mainland. New Confucianism was criticized as an outmoded "feudal ideology" and hence a roadblock to be cleared away in China's march toward modernity. Indeed, the new Enlightenment ethos not only prevailed in the academic world but also captured the imagination of the general public. The trend reached its climax in August 1988 in the broadcast of *River Elegy*, a television series advocating a total westernization of Chinese culture. It created an enormous sensation. Then, the trend faded rapidly but quietly into the political activism of the student movement of May–June 1989.

Phase 2 (1989 on): The rise of neotraditionalism and the confrontation between liberalism and the new left. The crackdown on the student movement and its tragic ending brought the first phase of the discourse to an abrupt end. For two years or so the voice of the discourse was silenced. A cooling spell set in. It provided a chance for the participants to stand back and reflect on the hectic years that had just passed—the ideas and visions that had inspired the discourse. In 1992, China's leader and strongman, Deng Xiaoping, known as the architect of the country's "reform and opening" policy, made a famous whirlwind tour to south China. It sparked a spectacular expansion of the market economy, bringing about a political climate conducive to intellectual activities. The discourse soon revived and steadily flourished. But it underwent a series of important changes in its second phase. First, thanks to the policy of reform and opening, the goals of modernization had been partially achieved and the benefits it brought were many and substantial. But the problems it created were just as many, and as obvious. Reality seems to have pushed the discourse to take a practical and empirical turn. The focus of attention shifted from the inner world of the individual to the outer environment, from systems of ideas and values to social, economic, and political institutions. Second, several new trends appeared and interacted with the old ones. Voices, instead of coming from a few "centers" or groups of scholars as in the 1980s, were further split and became, as one scholar puts it, "cacophonous." The discourse became much more diversified. Third, the exchange of visiting scholars, students, and ideas with western academia began to show effects. Chinese scholars with graduate degrees had a much better chance than ever before to understand the western world of thought through direct contact and personal experience. Almost every major trend in western academia would soon be echoed among mainland scholars. Some of them even entered into direct personal alliances with like-minded colleagues in the west. The discourse, in other words, was further internationalized or "globalized." Fourth, among the participants in the discourse there was a widely shared drive for "professionalism," which lent a distinct hallmark of academic scholarship that had been absent from the discourse in the 1980s.

Like the first phase of the discourse, the second phase was punctuated by heated debates. The following are the four major debates.

1. "Scholarship" versus "thinking." This debate began in 1991 with the publication of a symposium whose eleven contributors sought to revitalize the study of the "Chinese history of scholarly research and learning." Their impetus came from a critical reflection on the intellectual activities of the 1980s, now found, to be too "trendy and flamboyant," excessively "vague and empty," and "based merely on common sense," showing a lack of academic training and discipline. There was an acute awareness of the importance of substantial hard work (or rather hard homework) in theoretical exploration along with a strong demand for the reestablishment of professional standards or norms modeled on those of western academia. This, however, drew the objection that undue stress on scholarship was detrimental to the flowering of creative thinking, believed to be an admirable feature of the 1980s. It would lead, the opponents warned, to a "phasing out of the thinker" and would bring only the scholar to the foreground. The contrast of thinkers with scholars was intended to highlight the difference between a committed public intellectual and a completely disinterested professional scholar. The debate ended in a broad consensus that what was needed was "scholarship imbued with thinking or thinking supported by scholarship." This consensus suggests that Chinese intellectuals, in the face of the relentless push toward rationalization and professionalism, are determined to continue their quest for humanist values by striking a balance between public responsibilities and purely academic obligations.

2. "National studies fever": *guoxue re*. This debate began silently in 1992 with the establishment of the Center for the Studies of Chinese Learning at Beijing University. It was the first important sign of a revival of the intellectual discourse cut short in 1989 and was immediately reported by the *People's Daily*, the organ of the Chinese Communist Party. Although calling it a "fever" was an exaggeration, it did restore and boost the study of the Chinese cultural heritage. It also set off the publication of a large number of articles and dozens of monographs. However, it was immediately denounced by some routine Marxists as a possible attempt to downplay the leading role the new socialist culture will play in the reconstruction of Chinese culture by stressing the importance of "national studies." The denunciation created some pressure on intellectuals to "ideologize" or politicize the discourse. But for various reasons, the "fever" managed to survive the pressure. In fact, it signaled the advent of a new tide of "neotraditionalism."

The tide of neotraditionalism mainly consisted of three streams: the study of (1) Confucianism, (2) Daoism, and (3) the history of scholarship and learning of the past century. The study of Confucianism received special attention. The outcome of the research is truly impressive. It covers the whole range from pre-Confucian thought to classic Confucianism, neo-Confucianism, Qing Confucianism, and New Confucianism. The long-neglected study of Confucian classics was revitalized. The topics of study became more microscopic, the scholarship more solid, and the methods increasingly interdisciplinary. Many studies were comparative, with "global consciousness." The study of Daoism also witnessed a revival. Scholars who felt uneasy with the authoritarian and moralist bias of Confucianism turned to Daoism, which espoused individual freedom and had a naturalistic vision of the universe. An in-depth study of the history of scholarly research and learning of the past century was believed to be particularly helpful in rectifying the "unscholarly" aberrations of the 1980s described earlier. But it was also prompted by a strong desire for the independence of academic research and freedom of thought. Certain eminent scholars of the first half of the twentieth century who were independent thinkers, well-versed in both Chinese and western learning, and known for their erudition and the art of exegesis were held up as models to emulate. The rise of neotraditionalism seemed to indicate that the study of Chinese philosophy, after being marginalized for almost a century, was entering a stage of steady growth.

3. The "humanist spirit." This debate began in 1993 with the publication of "Steer Clear of Being Noble," an article by Wang Meng, a famous writer and former minister of cultural affairs. Wang defended Wang Shuo, an emerging popular writer who had been accused of spreading "hoodlum literature" with demoralizing "hoodlum values" because the characters in his novels were often cynical and antisocial, indulging in hedonism, fraud, crime, and seduction. Wang Meng argued that it was not Wang Shuo who was spreading demoralizing values and cynicism; rather, the repeated political campaigns in Mao's era had turned everything noble into a joke. If Wang Shuo is not a serious writer, Wang Meng contends, at least he is honest, and his works could be an effective antidote to much of the hypocritical literature produced in the name of serving the people. Wang's contention drew immediate attacks accusing him of sponsoring the degradation of moral and artistic standards and betraying the time-honored tradition that invests Chinese intellectuals with the responsibilities of cultural guardians. Wang's critics also held that the essence of literature is human beings in pursuit of the dignity of *ren* and their aspiration to truth, beauty, and goodness, and that literature should primarily aim at enhancing human sensitivity to these high values and help create a better and more ideal world. They lamented the "loss of humanist spirit," a dire consequence which some of them attributed to the corruption and commercialization caused by the fast-growing market economy. The discussions soon moved to a contrast between "serious literature" and mass or popular literature, the standard by which literature is to be judged, the social role of intellectuals, and what constitutes their proper worldview. The debate lasted for almost four years and is regarded by many as the most important (if not especially fruitful) event since the "cultural fever" of the 1980s.

In this debate some cultural critics, self-styled postmodernists, joined Wang Meng to attack the humanists. Postmodernity in the Chinese context refers vaguely to a wide spectrum of ideas and values that challenge the standard western modern thought of the seventeenth and the eighteenth centuries. The range of postmodern thought may be seen as having its beginning in Freud, Marx, and Nietzsche; its transition in Heidegger and Gadamer; and its latest expression in thinkers like Derrida, Foucault, and Lyotard. The trend was introduced to China in the 1980s, first by Fredric Jameson, whose lectures at Beijing University in 1982 had aroused great interest. But its circulation was then limited to some avant-garde literary circles. The rapid expansion of the market economy and the emergence of a consumer society in the 1990s caused conspicuous changes in almost every aspect of social and cultural life. Situated in a strange milieu in which postmodernity coexists with modernity, some Chinese intellectuals found in postmodernism a relevance and significance it hardly possessed in the 1980s. They are convinced that the consumerism of mass culture, as exemplified by Wang Shuo, is part of a universal postmodernist phenomenon. By declaring the end of modernity, they announce the dawn of a "new epoch" in China that would embrace a progressively secularized society as distinct from the idealistic, utopian society painted by the nostalgic humanists. For intellectuals espousing postmodernism, it is ridiculous to lament a "loss of humanist spirit," for that only suggests anachronism.

This postmodernist critique found its natural ally in postcolonialism. Like postmodernism, postcolonialism in China, inspired by Edward Said's arguments against "orientalism," exposes the modernist strategies of domination and containment directed at the cross-cultural "other." The very concept of western modernity is denounced for its cultural hegemony, its myth of universalism, and its repression of third world identities. By taking western modernity for granted, China has forfeited the autonomy of its national culture. The new Enlightenment of the 1980s is held to be nothing but a flawed replica of western modernity, a new form of colonial domination. With a strong nationalistic sentiment, postcolonialist critics announce: "It is time to replace modernity with Chineseness."

It is not difficult to see that the whole debate over the humanist spirit revolves on the axis of the humanist quest initiated in the 1980s. It was in fact a counterattack staged by the humanists of the new Enlightenment when the raison d'etre of the humanist quest was jeopardized first by Wang Shuo and then by the postmodernists. While the humanists were committed to the noble ideals of the quest, the postmodernists found satisfaction in more secular and even hedonistic pursuits. However, on the whole it was the humanists who were on the offensive. Joined by Marxists, they seem to have carried the day. If we suppose that the humanist quest had averted excessive professionalism in the debate on scholarship and thinking, and that it had withstood the pressure of politicalization in the debate on national studies, then we may say that it had resisted the temptation of commercialization in the controversy over the humanist spirit.

4. Liberalism and the new left. This debate, or confrontation, began in late 1997. It could prove to be the most important event in the second phase of the discourse, with far-reaching implications. The debate involved a wide range of fundamental issues, both historical and theoretical. They include, for example, the implications for and the impact on China of the ongoing globalization process; the nature of Chinese society as it stood in the 1990s; the role of the state in social changes in general and in the historical rise of capitalism in the west and the sociopolitical transformation of today's China in particular; the priority of liberty versus equality and justice and of political freedom versus economic democracy; the relationship between market economy and democracy; the assessment of Mao's legacy and that of the new Enlightenment of the 1980s; and the validity of modernization theories and even the very concept of modernity. Indeed, the two sides are of totally different epistemic genealogies. While the liberals draw their inspiration from the mainstream of western academia, the new leftists rely heavily on, although are not limited to, its marginal or rebellious discourses, such as Marxism, neo-Marxism, or western Marxism (such as the Frankfurt school), third world theories, and also postmodernism and postcolonialism. Probably more important, the two sides claim to represent the interests of different social strata. While the liberals bet on the emergence of the bourgeoisie in China, some new leftists openly announce that they stand on the side of the exploited and oppressed.

The appearance of the new left seems to indicate that the triadic tension still persists in the discourse. Contrary to the expectation of many observers in China and abroad, the influence of Marxism has proved to be deep-seated and is likely to retain its presence in the near future. It is also significant that the humanist quest, instead of withering away, only withdrew from the center of the stage and continued to be a potent "hidden presence," so to speak. As Xu Youyu, an outspoken liberal, puts it:

> Liberalism in the 1990s is a continuation of the humanism and Enlightenment thinking of the 1980s. It simply transforms the affirmation of the value of humanity on the philosophical level to the level of institutional arrangements.

Wang Xi, the most influential figure in the new left, stressing the need for Chinese intellectuals to search for a new self-identity, remarks:

> A new faith and new self-identity need new social institutions that can provide conditions for their social practice.

While Xu understands the humanist quest basically in terms of values embraced by the new Enlightenment, Wang chooses to interpret it in terms of the historical and cultural context that makes it possible, avoiding any universalist or essentialist reading. But both seem to acknowledge that it is the unsolved and probably unsolvable humanist quest that underlies the institutional shift of focus in the 1990s. In this sense, it seems reasonable to assume that so long as Chinese scholars remain personally committed to their social responsibility and cultural mission, the humanist quest will persist, although with different contents, in different forms, and to different degrees.

See also Mao Zedong; Scientism and Humanism.

Bibliography

Barmer, Germie, and Jaivin Linda. *New Ghosts, Old Dreams*. New York: Times Books, 1992.

Brugger, Bill, and David Kelly. *Chinese Marxism in the Post-Mao Era*. Stanford, Calif.: Stanford University Press, 1990.

Chen, Guying. *Lao-Zhuang xinlun*. Shanghai: Guji, 1992.

Chen, Kuide, ed. *Zhongguo dalu dangtai wenhua bianqian*. Taibei: Kueiguan, 1991.

Chen, Lai. *Yu-wu zhijing: Wang Yangming zhexue de jingshen*. Peking: Renmin, 1991.

Cheng, Chung-ying. *Lun zhongxi zhexue jingshen*. Shanghai: Dongfang, 1991.

———. *New Dimensions of Confucianism and Neo-Confucian Philosophy*. New York: Albany: State University of New York Press, 1991.

Cheng, Jiadong. *Xiandai xin ruxue gailun*. Nanning: Guanghsi renmin, 1990.

Cua, Antonio S. (Ke Xiongwen). *Dimensions of Moral Creativity: Paradigms, Principles, and Ideals*. University Park: Pennsylvania State University Press, 1978.

———. *Moral Vision and Tradition: Essays in Chinese Ethics*. Washington, D.C.: Catholic University of America Press, 1998.

———. "Problems of Chinese Moral Philosophy." *Journal of Chinese Philosophy*, 27(3), 2000.

Feng, Qi. *Feng Qi wenji*, Vols. 1–3. Shanghai: Huadong sifan daxue, 1996

Gan, Yang. *Zhongguo dangtai zhi wenhua yishi*. Hong Kong: Sanlian, 1989.

Hua, Shiping. *Scientism and Humanism: Two Cultures in Post-Mao China (1978–1989)*. Albany: State University of New York, 1995.

Jin, Guandao. *Wo de zhexue tanshuo*. Shanghai: Renmin, 1988.

Li, Zehou. *Huaxia meixue*. Peking: Zhongwai wenhua, 1989.

———. *Pipan zhexue de pipan: Kangde shuping*. Biejing: Renmin chuban she, 1979.

Lin, Tongqi, Henry Rosement, and Roger T. Ames. "Chinese Philosophy: A Philosophical Essay on the State of the Art." *Journal of Asian Studies*, 54(3), 1995, pp. 727–758.

Lin, Yusheng. *Zhongguo zhuandong de chuanzao xing zhuanhua*. Beijing: Sanlian, 1988.

Liu, Xiao-feng. *Zhengro jui xiaoyao*. Taibei: Fengyun, 1990.

Pang, Pu. *Yi fenwei san: Zhongguo zhuantong sixiang kaoshi*. Shenzhen: Haitian, 1995.

Ren-min chu-pan shehui bienji bu, ed. *Ren shih Makesi zhuyi de chufadian*. Peking: Renmin, 1981.

Tu, Wei-ming. *Centrality and Commonality: An Essay on Confucian Religiousness*. Albany: State University of New York Press, 1989.

———. *Confucian Thought: Selfhood as Creative Transformation*. Albany: State University of New York Press, 1985.

Wang, Hsi. "Dangdai Zhongguo de sixiang chuangkuang yu xiandai xing wenti." *Tianya* (Beijing), 5, 1997.

———. "Kexue zhuyi yu shehui lilun de jige wenti." *Tianya* (Beijing), 6, 1998.

Wang, Yuanhua. *Wenxue chensi lu*. Shanghai: Shanghai Wenyi chubanshe, 1983.

Xiao, Jefu. *Chuisha ji*. Chengdu: Bashu Shudian, Vol. 1, 1991; Vol 2, 1999.

Xu, Yuyu. "Ziyu yu zhuyi yu dangdai zhongguo." *Gaifeng shidai*, 5 and 6, 1999.

Yang, Guorong. *Lunli yu cunzai*. Shanghai: Renmin, 2002.

———. *Qingyuan jinsi lu*. Beijing: Zhongquo shehui kexue, 1998.

Yu, Yingshi. *Neizai chaoyue jilu: Yu Yingshi xin ruxue lunju jiyao*. Beijing: Zhongguo guangbo tianshi chubanshe, 1992.

Zhang, Dainian. *Wenhua yu zhexue*. Beijing: Jiaoyu, 1988.

Zhang, Liwen. *Dai Zhen*. Taibei: Dongda, 1991.

Zhang, Xudong. *Chinese Modernism in the Era of Reform: Cultural Fever, Advance Guard Fiction, and New Chinese Cinema*. Durham, N.C.: Duke University, 1997.

Zhongguo shehui kexue ya zhexue yanjiu suo, ed. *Zhongguo zhexue nianjian*. (1982–). Beijing: *Zhexue yanjiu zaji*, 1983–.

Philosophy: Recent Trends Overseas

Chung-ying CHENG

One cannot understand and appreciate the activities and fruits of recent Chinese philosophy without understanding something of how Chinese philosophy was studied in the west.

Chinese philosophy has been known to the west since the seventeenth century, when Jesuits went to China and communicated with intellectuals and scholars there. The Jesuits wished to convert Chinese intellectuals to Christianity, but they also gained a knowledge of Chinese philosophy, specifically Confucianism. They discussed what they had learned about the Confucian classics with their own people and also with other scholars in Europe. In the mid-seventeenth century *Confucius the Philosopher* was published; this book aroused intense interest in Chinese learning among European scholars. Notably, Leibniz mentioned this book and also came to correspond with the Jesuit Father Buvet in China; and through him Leibniz came to know the hexagrams of the *Yijing* (*Book of Changes*) and the binary system of numbers in the *Yijing*. Throughout the next century many European philosophers in Germany, France, and England commented on Chinese philosophy.

This smooth exchange of ideas between Chinese scholars and Jesuits who acted as a cultural and intellectual bridge came to an abrupt end by the beginning of eighteenth century as a result of the "rites controversy," in which the pope restrained Jesuits in China from condoning the Confucian rituals of filial piety. The Jesuits' training and scholarship in classical Greek and medieval philosophy had equipped them to debate Confucian doctrines as well as spread their own teachings, and the termination of this exchange meant that the west lost an opportunity to learn about Chinese cultural and philosophical traditions and introduce the western tradition to China.

For the next two centuries, Chinese philosophy was probably known only to a small circle of scholars and missionaries in Europe, and its true nature and significance were very often misunderstood. Although Confucianism had some influence throughout Europe in the seventeenth and eighteenth centuries, philosophers of the Enlightenment such as Kant, Hegel, and Rousseau all came to debase Chinese philosophy as a result of such misunderstandings. There were no new texts to be read in Chinese philosophy, and it had no exponents. There were no scholars who knew Chinese philosophy well and none who could discuss issues in both Chinese and western contexts or evaluate western philosophy adequately from a Chinese point of view. The situation did not change until two well-known western philosophers, Bertrand Russell and John Dewey, came to China in 1923 and 1924, four years after the May Fourth Movement of 1919.

Before Russell and Dewey arrived, a group of Chinese intellectuals at Peking University (later Beijing University) had invited other western philosophers, such as Bergson and Eucken, to lecture, so that China might learn what the best philosophers of the west could offer. However, no Chinese philosophers cared to have a dialogue or conversation on philosophical issues with Bergson or Euken from a Chinese philosophical point of view—not surprisingly, since at the time Chinese tradition was not very well regarded by Chinese intellectuals, and in any case there were very few Chinese who could argue about philosophy in the language that prevailed in philosophical discourse in the west. Hu Shi, Feng Youlan, and Jin Yuelin were active, but they seemed to want to promote western philosophy, not argue for Chinese philosophy. Nor were philosophers like Xiong Shili and Liang Shuming ready to confront the west in person; they were going through a period of philosophical transformation from tradition to modernity.

In the west from the end of nineteenth century to the middle of twentieth, Chinese philosophy was studied in a frozen and fossilized form—texts translated from Chinese by writers whose field was ancient Chinese culture in general. These writers were not trained in philosophy; in fact, they were often Christian Protestant missionaries who had gone to China when China opened its doors, to a degree, after the Opium War of 1842. Like their Jesuit predecessors, these missionaries turned themselves into translators of Chinese texts; they became known as sinologists. The two who were best-known were James Legge, who translated all the major works of classical Confucianism into English; and Richard Wilhelm, who translated the *Yijing* and *Daodejing* into German. They did a great service in introducing Chinese philosophy to the modern west. But, as noted, they were not philosophers; their comments often revealed their Christian background, and their discussions made no attempt to relate to the living tradition or to current issues of western philosophy. Also, Chinese philosophy remained limited to a circle of "China specialists" or sinologists who worked at research universities in Europe and America. Chinese philosophy became a museum piece, to be studied as a historical record of a past tradition. It became known as "Chinese thought" or "Chinese intellectual history" and was studied in departments of Asian studies or departments of history.

This attitude was reinforced by a persistent myth—the notion that Chinese philosophy was no philosophy, because it did not have the same form or format as western philosophy, which was systematic, argumentative, logically presented, and discussed in terms of sharply defined and hotly debated issues. In the west, also, there were diverse and novel positions, argued freely from logical and metaphysical perspectives; and there was a close relationship among philosophy, religion, and science, although these different areas were clearly demarcated. By contrast, in Chinese philosophy these properties were not well articulated or distinguished.

However, all this does not mean that there were no logical discourses or clearly stated theses in Chinese philosophy. In China, although arguments may be conducted in fewer paragraphs than in the west, debates may be conducted over wide expanses of space and long periods of time—even hundreds of years. Moreover, Chinese languages are not the same as western languages; in China, persuasion and often meanings and references are hidden. That is just a style of expression; it does not imply a lack of reasoned positions, novelty, critiques, or methods. Even today, there are still some western philosophers who argue, on the basis of very limited knowledge, that Chinese philosophy has no concepts of morality or truth. This is a parochial attitude caused by ignorance, bias, and misunderstanding, which in turn are caused by an absence of dialogue; and it belittles eastern and western philosophy alike.

After the May Fourth movement, Chinese philosophers trained themselves, in detail, to speak the universal language of argument and discourse; they learned western philosophy and methods of analysis, and they began to focus on issues and positions and, in one way or another, to reconstrue or reconstruct the Chinese philosophical tradition. In my own studies I have found that since the beginning of twentieth century, the learning of western philosophy in China proceeded at a much faster pace than the learning of Chinese philosophy in the west. For example, Kang Youwei, Liang Qichao, and Wang Guowei tried to catch up with current trends in western philosophy; and numerous works of Bergson and Dewey not only were translated into Chinese but became elements in the formation of new Chinese philosophy and in new constructions of traditional philosophical systems. Xiong Shili and Liang Shuming often referred to Bergson and others. In fact, not until Fang Dongmei (Thomé Fang), Mou Zongsan, and Tang Junyi (Tang Chün-i) do we find a critical attitude toward specific western philosophers.

The western philosophical works that were studied in modern China transformed the language of Chinese philosophy and helped bring into the open certain of its insights. Eventually, Chinese philosophers were able to hold a lively conversation with western philosophers as colleagues and partners. This took place as early as 1935 at the University of Hawaii at Manoa, where the founding chairperson of the department of philosophy, Charles Moore, and his Chinese colleague Wing-tsit Chan (a historian of Chinese philosophy and a translator) felt a need to bring eastern and western philosophers together to discuss fundamental issues of the major cultural traditions of the east and west. Chinese philosophy, as one such major tradition, was for the first time articulated, discussed, and debated by philosophers meeting in person. Fang Dongmei, Mou Zongsan, Tang Junyi, and Wing-tsit Chan, from the older generation; and Chung-ying Cheng (Cheng Zhongying, the present author) and Shu-hsien Liu, from the younger generation, participated in discussions and debates in subsequent east-west philosophers' conferences in 1965 and 1970.

The recent development of Chinese philosophy "overseas" (meaning mainly in the west, and in the west mainly in the United States) can be traced to the founding of the *Journal of Chinese Philosophy* (*JCP*) in 1972 and the International Society for Chinese Philosophy (ISCP) in 1965, both by Chung-ying Cheng at the University of Hawaii at Manoa. In this regard I should perhaps sketch Cheng's background (that is, mine, although I will continue to use the third person).

After graduating from National Taiwan University, Cheng came to the United States and obtained his Ph.D. in philosophy from Harvard University. As a young professor of philosophy at the University of Hawaii at Manoa, who taught both western analytical philosophy and classical Chinese philosophy, Cheng felt it was necessary to organize Chinese and western philosophers in order to promote the the study of Chinese philosophy, for at least two reasons. First, Chinese philosophical wisdom offered significant resources that needed to be periodically and systematically presented; second, an east-west dialogue in Chinese philosophy would enable it to become a vital force, enrich world civilization, and contribute to the development of human society. Cheng, having taught contemporary western philosophy and classical and neo-Confucian philosophy, wanted Chinese philosophy to be recognized in the west as a living tradition. He was pained by the treatment of Chinese philosophy (mentioned above) as "Chinese thought" or "Chinese intellectual history" and wanted to restore it to its proper place in the world of living philosophy, not simply presenting or repeating the tradition. It was largely through *JCP* and ISCP that Chinese philosophy came to be recognized among western philosophers and, gradually, was absorbed into the regular philosophy curriculum of western (American) universities.

As of this writing, *JCP* (issued quarterly by Blackwell in Boston and London) had published twenty-seven volumes in twenty-seven years and was the leading journal for Chinese philosophy in the world. From 1975 to the present writing, ISCP had held twelve international conferences on various topics in Chinese philosophy in many places, including universities in the United States, Europe, and Asia (such as Munich, Beijing, Boston, Seoul, and Taipei). *JCP* and ISCP have been very influential internationally and at the turn of the twenty-first century were continuing to grow, testifying to the potential of the Chinese philosophy as a vigorous living tradition. At least partly because of their influence, the United States became the place where "overseas" Chinese philosophy mainly developed throughout the 1970s to the end of the twentieth century.

In addition to such institutional developments, no description of recent Chinese philosophy overseas would be complete without some mention of individuals—Chinese scholars who have taught in western departments of religion or Asian studies, and non-Chinese who came to the study of Chinese philosophy under the influence of overseas practitioners. The individuals discussed below—Wing-tsit Chan, Antonio S. Cua (Ke Xiongwen), Liu Shuxian, Fu Wexiun, Lik-kuen Tong, Julia Ching (Qin Jiayi), and Tu Weiming—have made significant contributions in the past three decades. I have also included myself (Chung-ying Cheng) in this discussion and in fact will describe my own work in some detail.

Wing-tsit Chan

Wing-tsit Chan (Chen Rongjie, 1901–1994) came to study in the United States in 1924 and obtained his Ph.D. in Chinese studies in 1929 at Harvard. After spending a few years in China, he came back to the United States; he started to teach at the University of Hawaii at Manoa in 1936 and stayed for six years. Then he went to Dartmouth as a professor of Chinese culture and philosophy; he remained there until his retirement.

Chan was a distinguished translator of Chinese philosophical sources. His translations of Chinese texts were published in *A Source Book in Chinese Philosophy* (1963), which covers selected major sources from the ancient period to the time of Xiong Shili; this book has been widely used at universities in the United States. Later in his career, Chan translated the *Chuan silu* of Wang Yangming, under the title *Instructions for Practical Living*. As this title suggests, there is a strong practical strain in the method of understanding and transforming the self in the neo-Confucian tradition. Chan also translated Zhu Xi's *Jinsilu* into English with annotations, under the title *Reflections on Things at Hand*; this title is close to the original Chinese title and indicates a more mature style of translation. Both these translations are important for introducing neo-Confucian thought to the west; Chan hoped that through them the study of Confucianism in the west would grow into a study of neo-Confucianism. No similar types of translations are yet available for other major texts in Chinese philosophy. Chan's unique influence in promoting the study of Chinese philosophy must be acknowledged.

Chan describes the special features of Chinese philosophy as basically humanist and Chinese metaphysics as simple and unsystematic. According to Chan, the difference between Chinese and western philosophy is that western philosophy moves from metaphysics to social and moral philosophy whereas Chinese philosophy developed in the reverse direction. Although this observation may not be entirely accurate, it gave him a reason to think that western logic and science had to be introduced in order to consolidate Chinese metaphysics. However, what he means by "Chinese metaphysics" remains unclear.

Chan wrote a very useful paper (1955) on the meaning of the Confucian concept *ren* (or *jen*, benevolence), tracing its development from Confucius to the 1950s. He identified several meanings: *ren* as the soul of Confucianism; as "whole virtue" in Confucius; as love; as universal love; as nature and principle; as forming one body with heaven, earth, and all things; as creative vitality; as virtue of the heart-mind; and as the principle of love. Chan wrote another such historical synopsis of the meanings of *li* (principle, pattern, reason) in neo-Confucian philosophy (1964).

Chan devoted considerable study to Song-Ming neo-Confucianism. He especially respected Zhu Xi, considering Zhu the most influential Chinese philosopher after Confucius. Chan described Zhu as the founder of the tradition of the Confucian *dao*, who opened up a new direction of learning in the investigation of things. He also saw Zhu as having integrated philosophy, religion, and ethics into a unified system; however, Chan does not show how this integration actually took place.

Chan himself should perhaps not be considered a philosopher. He did not develop any new insight into the Confucian *ren* or the neo-Confucian *li*. Unlike some later figures, he had no background in western philosophy and had not made a systematic comparative study of Chinese and western philosophy.

Chung-ying Cheng

Chung-ying Cheng (Cheng Zhongying, b. 1935 in China) went to Taiwan in 1949, graduated from National Taiwan University in 1956, and received his Ph.D. in philosophy from Harvard University in 1964. His analytical dissertation, *Peirce and Lewis's Theories of Induction*, was published in 1966. He has been a professor of philosophy at the University of Hawaii at Manoa since 1972 and has also taught at National Taiwan University and Yale University. In recent years he has lectured at universities in China, Japan, Germany, and England. He was awarded an honoary doctorate by the Institute of Far Eastern Studies of the Russian Academy of Sciences in 1995 for his own work in Chinese philosophy and for his efforts to advance the study of Chinese philosophy across cultures and traditions.

In addition to founding the *Journal of Chinese Philosophy* and the International Society for Chinese Philosophy, he founded the International Society for the *Yijing* and the Far Eastern Institutes of Advanced Studies, both in 1985; the latter led to the formation of the International East-West University in 1995.

Although Cheng was trained in contemporary analytical philosophy of language and science, he also had a background in Chinese philosophy and thus has been able to do work in Chinese philosophy in a contemporary context with analytical methods. He is interested in the application of philosophy and has, accordingly, also ventured into communication and management studies. As a result of his concern with the future and the creative development of Chinese philosophy and Chinese cultural tradition, he has kept in close contact with philosophers in China since 1985.

Cheng addresses the modernization and globalization of Chinese philosophy. His central concern is an analytical reconstruction for the purpose of theoretical and practical integration of Chinese philosophy with western philosophy in ontology, epistemology, and ethics. His philosophical work has five important aspects, as follows.

1. The nature of western philosophy. In his book *On the Philosophical Spirit of China and the West* (in Chinese, 1986, 1996), Cheng defines several problems of western philosophy in historical order:

- The axiological problem of the distinction between appearance and reality and the transcendence or incorporation of ideals and values (the Platonic problem).
- The metaphysical problem of dualism between the subject (self) and the object (world), and the foundation of knowledge (Descartes's problem).
- The epistemological problem of transcendental reconstruction of reason and science and its relevance for moral subjectivity (the Kantian problem).
- The dialectical problem concerning how the nature of reality and the creativity of change bear on humanity and human culture (the Hegelian problem).
- The dialectical problem of understanding and interpreting meaning and truth in the humanities and in the use of language (Gadamer's problem).

To deal with these problems, modern western philosophy has gone through a process of differentiation of schools and perspectives as well as a process of revolution in methods and theories. Cheng identifies, basically, ten schools in recent times; in these schools, one also sees a differentiation of rationality. There are genuine disagreements among them in ideas and approaches, and hence debates and disputes. Cheng sees these debates and disputes as coming from tension between theory and method, and between experience and theory. Classical and modern western philosophy have both tended to exhibit philosophical "turns" in which method overcomes theory or vice versa. Whether the new developments in philosophical hermeneutics or in analytical philosophy can resolve this inherent tension remains to be seen. Cheng thinks that we can learn a lesson from the history of western philosophy and from its contemporary disputes; this lesson has to do with rational differentiation and analytical reconstruction and critique and entails conceiving philosophy as an intellectual quest for meaning, knowledge, and truth. We can use the lesson to reflect on the nature of Chinese philosophy and see how it differs significantly from but also complements western philosophy.

2. Origins of Chinese philosophy. On the basis of his understanding of western philosophy, Cheng—in "Origins of Chinese Philosophy," "On *Guan* as Onto-Hermeneutics," and other articles—takes an analytical approach to reconstructing and reinterpreting Chinese philosophy from methodology to ontology. He wants first to seek the beginning of Chinese philosophy, which in his view has not been clearly explained or identified in earlier studies. He speaks of this beginning as the "primordial experience of change" (*yi*), which integrates our experience of the unity of many qualities in one substance, the unity of opposites, and the interpenetration of wholes and parts in nature and in human life (such as unity of intention and goal, and unity of theory and practice). The dominant feature of this experience is comprehensiveness and wholeness including every aspect of micro- and macrochanges, such as generation, formation, transformation, disintegration, and dissolution. Cheng sees this as resulting from the natural use of a method called "comprehensive observation" (*guan*). Reflections on this experience lead to a paradigmatic notion of the "way of change" or simply the way, or Way (the *dao*), which finds its expression in the symbolism of the *Yijing* and its divinatory judgments.

In its symbolism *Yijing* presents an implicit system of images or representations of things by dialectical "analysis in synthesis" and creative "synthesis in analysis" of the experience and observation of the *yi*. In this paradigm of "symbolic realism," as Cheng calls it, one sees the remote but also immediate base for the development of all the classical schools of philosophy, specifically Confucianism and Daoism. This explains the complementarity of Confucianism and Daoism in the primordial experience of the *dao*. This symbolic realism functions as the theoretical basis for the development of a harmonic dialectics of unity of heaven and the human and ontocosmology of the *dao*; historically, it is also a fountainhead of new philosophical thinking and rethinking. Cheng argues, specifically, that on the basis of this paradigm of the *yi*, modern Chinese philosophy could and should develop a creative ontocosmology, preserving the source and insights of original Chinese philosophy while integrating the western philosophy of reason and analysis.

Cheng was the first to propose an "analytical reconstruction" of Chinese philosophy—i.e., a theoretical explanation and interpretation (*quanshi*) of a given thesis or view based on a conceptual analysis of the original text and one's discovery of new meaning and new truth or a new aspect of reality through reflection and integration. He distinguishes three kinds of philosophical reconstruction or interpretation: ontological, epistemological, and conceptual-semiotic (language-focused). The reconstruction of Chinese philosophy must use western philosophy as a mirror, not for imitation, but for learning its strengths and overcoming its weaknesses.

3. The place of Confucianism and neo-Confucianism. Cheng has written many articles in connection with classical Confucianism and neo-Confucianism. His book *New Dimensions of Confucian and Neo-Confucian Philosophy* (1995) covered considerable new ground. Is Cheng a contemporary neo-Confucian? In one interview, he answered that his main concern is to reconstruct an ontocosmology of reality and an ontoethics of human nature and the human mind integrating the essence of Confucianism and neo-Confucianism, and he therefore is in sympathy with Xiong Shiyi and Mou Zongsan. But he also sees a need to go beyond the contemporary neo-Confucian systems they advanced. He feels that a philosophy based on self-reflection must be founded with elements which can best be interpreted in terms of the Confucian notions of human nature, mind, and will. He has advocated the moral philosophy (ethics) of virtues, which is based on love (*ren*) and justice (*yi*), and on a certain understanding of the formation of human nature and human mind. He developed an integrative ethics in which duties, utilities, and rights are founded on the concept of virtues. He insists on the Confucian spirit as rooting ethics in an ontological or ontocosmological understanding. He has expounded and analytically reconstructed this Confucian morality in his articles on Confucian ontohermeneutics and Confucian ontoethics. He has integrated the classical Confucian positions of the *Four Books* (*Sishu*) into a system of moral metaphysics and ontological ethics or ontoethics.

Cheng has also attempted to interpret Zhu Xi, Wang Yangming, and other Song-Ming neo-Confucians from a modern philosophical point of view. He is aware of the problem of differentiating between Cheng-Zhu and Lu-Wang and has proposed integrating them in an ontocosmological and ontoethical system of understanding the self, the universe, and the ultimate being. He has applied ontohermeneutical insights to the study and reconstruction of neo-Confucianism in order to make it meaningful even in a modern context of philosophical understanding. He differs from Mou Zongsan in treating Zhu Xi not as a branch but as a mainstream development of the spirit of Xunzi, and as an attempt to synthesize Xunzi and Mencius. He also differs from Mou in speaking of ontoethics instead of moral metaphysics; he sees a circular onto-moral-hermeneutical process in the practice and understanding of Confucian and neo-Confucian philosophy. Finally, although Cheng agrees with Mou about transcending Kant, he does not see Mou as having succeeded in presenting a method of understanding that justifies the claim of having developed a moral metaphysics. Cheng's own ontocosmology, ontohermeneutics, and ontoethics are intended to pave the way toward a higher order of synthesis that would come closer to this goal.

4. Ontohermeneutics. Cheng develops a philosophical hermeneutics independent of the tradition of the west; his version is rooted in the *Yijing* tradition of ontocosmology and the neo-Confucian tradition of self-cultivation. Cheng's philosophical hermeneutics or ontohermeneutics, which he describes in *On the Spirit of Chinese and Western Philosophies*, is more holistic and integrative than Gadamer's "philosophical hermeneutics," which has a unique background—the criticism of Romanticism—and departs from a Heideggerian *Dasein* metaphysics. Cheng's ontohermeneutics stresses the importance of overall integrative understanding that combines immanence and transcendence, observation and reflection, and avoids relativism based on the historicity and linguistic nature of understanding alone. Three major considerations distinguish Cheng's ontohermeneutics:

- Cheng speaks of an "ontohermeneutic circle" and wants interpretation to be realized and justified in a system that always has ontological reference or meaning.
- Cheng wants to incorporate the tradition of Chinese philosophical interpretation in Confucian, Daoist, and Buddhist texts into his theory of interpretation and therefore enlarge its scope to a cross-cultural context which is not limited to the western tradition.
- Cheng wants to incorporate the analytical epistemology of Quine and a philosophy of science into his ontohermeneutics, as the analytics of his system has to do with building a creative and dynamic understanding of science and nature.

In an essay on ontohermeneutics, Cheng discusses four principles of interpretation from the point of view of Betti and Hirsch and supplements them with six more principles of his own. In retrospect, this was an attempt to develop a practical methodology of interpretation from western philosophical hermeneutics in light of the debates of Gadamer with Betti and others such as Habermas and Derrida. In 2000 the first volume of his book series *Ontology and Interpretation* (*Benti yu quanshi*) was published in Beijing.

5. Integration of ethics and principles of management. Cheng has given thought to the practical rationality of the Confucian and non-Confucian philosophy. He finds Confucian philosophy, specifically Confucian ethics, useful not only in individual and community life but in the modern world of corporations and institutions. In groups, Confucian ethics becomes principles of organization, decision making, and leadership or management. Thus management and ethics are interdependent: one is directed inward and deals with individual and internal issues; the other is directed outward and deals with the group and organization or external issues.

The trouble with Confucian ethics in the past is that it was used to deal with both internal and external problems, with no realization that it should, functionally, give rise to other considerations and thus other principles provided by other schools of thought. Having simply "Confucian management" would be a limitation. Although Confucianism was used in government in the past, Cheng argues that it would be best to develop an integrative theory of management and ethics based on all the major schools of classical Chinese philosophy; these would complement one another, each adding to the other's strengths and canceling out the other's weaknesses—if we found the right areas of application for each school. Cheng would include seven schools of Chinese thought: (1) the *Yijing*, (2) Confucianism, (3) Daoism, (4) Mohism, (5) military strategy, (6) legalism, and even (7) the insights of Chinese Chan Buddhism as a post-Confucian and post-Daoist principle of transcendence, deconstruction, and reconstitution. He has worked out his theory and applied it to business with some success. This theory is presented in his book *C Theory: Philosophy of Management from the Yijing*.

Antonio S. Cua

Antonio S. Cua (Ke Xiongwen, b. 1932 in the Philippines) is the editor of the present volume and a past president of Society for Asian and Comparative Philosophy and the International Society of Chinese Philosophy. He kept his Chinese cultural tradition when he came to the United States for graduate studies. He received his Ph.D. in 1958 from the University of California at Berkeley, having done his dissertation on Richard Price's ethical theory. A revised version of his doctoral dissertation, under the title *Reason and Virtue: A Study of the Ethics of Richard Price*, was published in 1966.

Cua's interest in ethical analysis and ethical theory has persisted throughout his career. His early articles focused on the ethics of moral agents and led to his book *Dimensions of Moral Creativity* (1978), which proposes "an ethics of moral agents." In this work—as is characteristic of much Cua's writings these past three decades—one finds an example of the internal-reconstructive approach. It adopts an internal point of view of morality, i.e., a view from the position of a reflective moral agent seeking an understanding of the nature of his moral practice or tradition. The central theme of *Dimensions of Moral Creativity* revolves around the problem of moral creativity: the possible contributions of a moral agent to his moral tradition or practice. For Cua, the main problem of moral creativity is actuating moral commitments—bridging the gap between moral knowledge of a tradition and conduct. It is not a spectator's problem of moral motivation. Cua discusses three dimensions of ethical practice in which a moral agent can make creative contributions: exemplary, reconstitutive, and ideal. The first pertains to the contributions of paradigmatic individuals to existing moral traditions, the second to the problems of rules and rulings, and the third to the ideals of the moral life. A distinctive feature of this book is Cua's inclusion of two chapters on Confucian ethics as an example of an ethics of paradigmatic individuals, an ethics of character that contrasts with the ethics of principle. His conception of *junzi* as paradigmatic individuals focuses not on their function as models but on their function as providing standards of inspiration.

During the same period Cua also explored the significance of Wang Yangming's doctrine of the unity of knowledge and action as a case study of moral psychology (1982), and various aspects of Xunzi's philosophy: human nature; ethical uses of history; the ethical, aesthetic, and religious dimensions of *li* (rites); the ethical insights of Laozi and Zhuangzi; and so on. His interest in the dialogical and argumentative aspects of Confucian ethics leads to a constructive Confucian theory of ethical argumentation based on the *Xunzi* as exemplified in his pioneering work *Ethical Argumentation: A Study in Hsün Tzu's* [*Xunzi's*] *Moral Epistemology* (1985). This study of the development of Confucian moral epistemology ranges over desirable qualities of participants, standards of competence, the nature of moral language and justification, and diagnosis of erroneous ethical beliefs.

In 1998 Cua published a collection of essays, *Moral Vision and Tradition*, dealing with various problems that arise in a philosophical explication of the nature of Chinese ethical thought. The essays focus principally on what Cua considers salient features of Confucian ethics. For the most part, his approach is analytical, attending mainly to the conceptual and dialectical aspects of Confucian ethics. This is a work on conceptual analysis for the development of Chinese moral philosophy from many angles. What is noteworthy is Cua's effort to formulate a Confucian virtue ethics. But here Cua raises more significant questions than providing a system of ethics. He asks what role the tradition plays in formulating a satisfactory theory of Confucian ethics and how a conceptual framework can be developed that would accommodate certain basic Confucian notions such as the *dao, ren, yi, and li* (rites), and how we could develop them in order to meet demands of normative regulation in evolving modern life. These questions touch on the problem of formulating intercultural ethics for an increasingly globalized world. Cua has proposed certain ground rules for resolving intercultural conflicts (such as nonprescriptivity, cultural integrity, mutuality, procedural justice, rectification, and reconsideration), which appear to be useful but need further development, as well as further discussion of their applicability.

In light of the need to formulate a Confucian ethics of virtues, Cua has also raised the important question whether an appeal to history or tradition is an essential component of ethical argumentation. But it is interesting to note that after the May Fourth movement of 1919 very few contemporary Confucian or neo-Confucian philosophers used an appeal to history or tradition as a ground for defending Confucian ethics. Most defenses appealed, rather, to human nature, and some offered insights into how humans should act. Confucian philosophers such as Mencius, Zhu Xi, and Wang Yangming were often cited as examples in theoretical—not historical—justifications. Based on his study of Xunzi's uses, Cua's essay "Ethical Uses of History in Early Confucianism" (1985, 2000) is an important attempt to assess the legitimacy and plausibility of the Confucian appeal to history in ethical theory.

Shu-hsien Liu

Shu-hsien Liu (Liu Shuxian, b. 1934), who is a contributor to the present volume, belongs to the same generation as Chung-ying Cheng and Charles Fu Weixun. Like Cheng and Fu, Liu graduated from National Taiwan University and studied at its Graduate Institute of Philosophy. Liu graduated from this institute in 1958 and in 1964 went to the University of Southern Illinois, where he received his doctorate in philosophy in 1966 and remained to teach. Liu visited Chinese University of Hong Kong (CUHK) on several occasions beginning in 1971 and, as a professor, became the chair of its department of philosophy in 1981. He officially retired from CUHK as a professor emeritus in 1995 and moved to Taiwan to become a researcher at the Institute of Literature and Philosophy at Academia Sinica in Taipei. Like Cheng, Cua, and Tong, Liu is a past president of the International Society for the Chinese Philosophy.

Liu has summarized his own philosophical development as falling into three periods; during each period he made contributions based on his interests at the time. In the period from 1955 to 1964 he published a book on literary appreciation and a book on semantics and truth and translated Cassirer's *An Essay on Man* and a book by Oswald Spengler on the origin and decline of civilizations. He explored western philosophy and culture and attempted a comparison between Chinese and western views on methods. In the period from 1964 to 1978, he completed his Ph.D. dissertation—a critical study of Paul Tillich—under the direction of Henry N. Wieman at Southern Illinois University. This is where he found his future direction of development. He started to publish a few essays in *Philosophy East and West* and *Journal of Chinese Philosophy*. It is apparent that his interests centered on exposition and studies of Confucian and neo-Confucian philosophy of religion. He also wrote critical essays on a few western philosophers and published two collections of essays written in this period. In the third period, from 1978 to 1992, he felt a deeper concern for the future of Chinese culture and came to reflect on the problem of modernizing China; this led to his book *Chinese Philosophy and Modernization* (in Chinese).

A culmination of his work seems to have been his Chinese book *Development and Completion of Zhu Xi's Philosphical Ideas* (1982), which coincided with the first International Conference on Zhu Xi at the University of Hawaii at Manoa, Honolulu. Liu participated in this conference when his book was still in press. In 1986 Liu went to do research at the Far East Institute of Philosophy in Singapore and published his study on Huang Zongxi. These works show how Liu developed as a contemporary neo-Confucian sharing many insights with Xiong Shili and Mou Zongsan.

Although Liu has spent most of his time in Hong Kong and Taipei and has published his major writings in Chinese, he is especially well known for his early activities in Chinese philosophical circles in the United States during the second period of his academic life; he is also known for his contributions to the philosophical study of Confucianism and neo-Confucianism and is considered a representative of the third generation of contemporary neo-Confucians.

Fu Weixun

Fu Weixun (Charles Fu, 1933–1996) graduated from National Taiwan University and received his Ph.D. in philosophy from Ohio State University. He taught at National Taiwan University before he went to Temple University to teach in the department of religion in the early 1970s. From then until his retirement, Fu devoted himself to the teaching and study of Chinese Buddhism and Chinese religions. He has published some edited works on Chinese religions and many essays on various subjects ranging over Marxist ethics, Chan (Zen) Buddhism, and what he calls "creative hermeneutics" in both English and Chinese. Fu's concept of "creative hermeneutics" is important: he conceived the meaning of a text as determinable and open to various levels of creative interpretation. Fu died (in 1996) before he had been able to develop his views into a full system. Shortly before his death he initiated the study of death as a subject for philosophical and religious thinking; this aroused great interest among the Chinese Buddhists in Mount Foguang in Taiwan.

Lik Kuen Tong

Lik Kuen Tong (Tang Liquan, b. 1935 in Hong Kong) came to the United States to study economics at New York University. But he did not take a degree in economics; he switched to studying philosophy at the New School for Social Research. He received his degree in philosophy in 1969 and started to teach philosophy at Fairfield University in Connecticut. He has been a president and an executive director of the International Society for Chinese Philosophy.

Tong's main work is *Between Zhouyi and Whitehead—Introduction to the Philosophy of Field-Being*. In this book Tong uses basic concepts of the *Zhouyi* to integrate Whitehead's metaphysics and Heidegger's philosophy of life. Tong's central idea is that being depends on fields and exists in fields. This notion of "being-in-field" or simply "field-being" is not the same thing as the substance or any substantive entity in traditional western philosophy; it is something inherent in the interrelatedness of things. It is therefore the relevance and relativity of things, but being in this sense also has its potency and activity. It is called the power and capacity (*quanneng*) of things. Tong stresses the unity of activity and being, from which enfolds the panorama of things in a process of change in which they are opposite and complementary. Here we have the usual idea of the *dao* and the *taiji* (the "great ultimate"). Tang holds that all things are field-being and there is nothing outside field-being. In his theory, one cannot see the universe and life from outside the field; one must see them from inside the field. How one sees the world depends on how one positions oneself in one's being. This position is metaphysical and can be described as a basic attitude toward life—from which a philosopher could develop his view of life.

Tong has a novel explanation of the statement, "The change (*yi*) has its great ultimate (*taiji*)." For him the *taiji* points to the upright walking body of the human being whereas the *yi* means our body, capable of reflexes and various ways of movement. Thus one sees how two norms and eight trigrams can be described as related to bodily movement. What Tong called the study of forms of the "root body" seems to reflect and capture someone's experience in doing the *taiji quan* exercise.

For Tong, the human being contains two opposed forces: moral nature and natural talent. How a person combines or develops the two determines behavior.

The opposition and the combining of the two forces also conditions how human cultures differ and develop. This would explain the differences between Chinese and western cultures. For Tong, the purpose of field-being studies is to establish a theory of human nature in which moral nature and natural talent would play equal parts so that there would be no partiality in human behavior. On this ground, science and democracy could take root. It is interesting to see how Tong's basic terms and basic views are related to traditional Chinese philosophy on the one hand and to Whitehead and Heidegger on the other.

Julia Ching

Among recent scholars of neo-Confucianism, Qin Jiayi (1935–2001), better known in the west as Julia Ching, is one of the few who made early studies of Wang Yangming; she promoted a wave of interest in the tradition of Song-Ming Confucianism. She was trained in theology and history, but her interests also included neo-Confucianism and Chinese culture. In 1971 she obtained her Ph.D. in Asian studies from Australian National University; her dissertation was "To Acquire Wisdom: The Way of Wang Yang-ming." In 1979, after teaching at Columbia University and Yale University for a few years, Qin became a professor in the departments of Asian studies and religion at Victoria College of the University of Toronto. Her strengths are shown particularly in her comparative studies of Chinese religions and Christianity. In 1977 she published *Confucianism and Christianity*, in which she urged dialogues among world religions. Qin wanted to advance the exchange of ideas between cultures so that each party could learn something from the other. She also stressed critiques of traditions: without such critiques, there would be no progress. As a Catholic she was nevertheless critical of established Catholicism, and as an East Asian she was critical of East Asia's traditions.

Qin had a concept of a critical or moral subject with moral independence and a conscience. On the basis of this concept she promoted a pluralism of religions in which each religion would be respectful and open to the others. Specifically, Qin treats Confucianism as a religion, making the point that it is humanistic but it is open to the transcendent spirit of God. She even held that Confucianism was originally a religion of prophets with belief in a personal God. She suggested that the unity of heaven and man was derived from the ancient belief in the unity of man and God. She also interpreted the neo-Confucian tradition as being full of religious significance. This is a challenging view.

Tu Weiming

Tu Weiming (Weiming Tu, b. 1940 in China) graduated from Donghai University in Taiwan. He went to the United States in 1963 to study Chinese intellectual history at Harvard University and received his Ph.D. in its department of Far Eastern languages and civilizations in 1968. Afterward he taught at Princeton and the University of California at Berkeley, and then returned to Harvard as a professor of Chinese history and Chinese philosophy. He became a member of the American Academy of Humanities, Arts, and Sciences in 1989. In recent years he has headed the Harvard-Yenching Institute at Harvard University and has been much engaged in developing academic exchanges between China and the United States.

The central concern of Tu's thinking is the modernization of Confucianism. On the basis of his exposure to various social and psychological theories in modern social sciences, Tu seems to approach Confucianism from different angles. Essentially, he sees his work as having to do with Confucianism as a living religious tradition. He speaks of a need for a living spiritual testimony and opposes studying or reconstructing Confucianism as a system of philosophy. He stresses the importance of preserving Confucianism in practice and points out that Confucian thought is never separable from an internal experience of the Confucian spirit. In this regard he speaks of the "living embodiment" of knowing the Confucian spirit. But he is not explicit about what he regards as Confucian testimony or as an embodiment of knowing of the Confucian spirit. His work on interpreting the *Zhongyong* (*Doctrine of the Mean*) is an attempt to show how the living Confucian spirit can be understood in this important Confucian classic. But Tu seems to worry about or to oppose philosophical study of Confucianism with modern methodology. As suggested above, he wants to defend Confucianism as a religion rather than as a philosophy. One can see that as a religion Confucianism can be studied religiously, but it also seems true that as a philosophy Confucianism can be studied philosophically. One has simply to decide whether Confucianism is more a religion (and in what sense of "religion") or more a philosophy (and in what sense of "philosophy"). If Confucianism is neither philosophy nor religion, then we need to find out what it is. If it is both philosophy and religion, we can study it both as a theory and as a spiritual practice. There seems to be no reason to pitch one method against the other except for polemic purposes.

A challenge for Tu as a spokesman of Confucianism is how one comes to understand Confucianism in light of the works and experiences of two generations of contemporary neo-Confucians and how he himself manages to testify to it in his own conduct and speeches. In his studies of the early life of Wang Yangming, Tu was inspired by psychology of religion as an approach to great religious figures such as Martin Luther. In his recent endeavors he wishes to retrieve the faith or the spirituality in the deep understanding of life and reality of the great figures of Confucianism. But it is not clear whether his writing or practice provides such testimonials. It is even less clear how an ideal Confucian person would live in a modern society, how Confucianism could transform modern society, and what a form of modern life on the societal level would be in Confucian terms. In practical terms it is not clear that Confucianism in a projected third wave of revival constitutes a revival of Chinese culture, cultural vitality, or creativity. Without a clear statement of the Confucian philosophy such a projection tends to become vague.

As a Confucian activist Tu has engaged in dialogues with many specialists and edited a few books on Confucianism. But his most important contribution is to present Confucianism as a spiritual tradition and as a philosophical issue.

Conclusion

I have described and to some extent discussed the contributions of recent Chinese philosophy overseas up to 2001. My aim has not been to give a complete picture and critique. It is important to realize that Chinese philosophy overseas is a field in the making. Its vitality has been increased not only by an accumulation of efforts of those who have taught and done research and written on Chinese philosophy in the past three decades, but also by the increasing frequency and momentum of the interaction of Chinese philosophers overseas and in mainland Chiana, Hong Kong, and Taiwan since the opening of China in the 1980s. In the past three International Conferences on Chinese Philosophy organized by the International Society for Chinese Philosophy in 1995, 1997, 1999, one saw a growing number of dialogues and exchanges among Chinese philosophers from home and abroad. One finds intermingling at such international conferences and through the wide use of interactive communication. Also, there are Internet home pages and electronic publications in philosophy that promote interchange and interaction—a process crucial to growth and development. The impact on the growth of Chinese philosophy overseas deserves attention from students and scholars.

To understand the richness and dynamic nature of overseas Chinese philosophy, one must also recognize the contributions made by scholars and thinkers who are not themselves Chinese philosophers. Since the late 1970s many capable western scholars have written about and taught Chinese philosophy after receiving training or learning through reading and discussion. Well-known figures include the late Benjamin Schwartz at Harvard University; the emeritus professors Friedrich Mote at Princeton University, Derk Bodde at the University of Pennsylvania, William Theodore de Bary at Columbia University, and Donald Munro at the University of Michigan; and Chad Hansen (a contributor to this volume) at the University of Hong Kong. Robert Cummings Neville at Boston University (who is also a contributor to this volume) is an example of a religious philosopher who came to appreciate Chinese philosophy; he has been active in the International Society for Chinese Philosophy since the 1970s, was elected its president in 1993, and organized the Ninth International Conference on Chinese Philosophy at Boston University in 1995. Roger T. Ames (another contributor) and David L. Hall have taken a great interest in interpreting Confucius and Chinese culture from a postmodern point of view. In the past two decades many younger Chinese philosophers have emerged from departments of philosophy in the United States and sinological institutes in Europe. In the United States, for instance, Kwong-loi Shun (another of our contributors) has made a detailed analytical study of Mencius. Recently, an American Chinese Philosophers Association was formed by a group of young scholars.

The future of Chinese philosophy overseas seems bright. We can expect its development to quicken with the globalization of the world and the incorporation of China and the west in a world system. We might also expect to see an increasing interaction between Chinese philosophy and western philosophy overseas, giving rise to more detailed studies of individual philosophers from the Chinese tradition and more theoretical and comparative works of Chinese and western philosophy.

See also Confucianism: Ethics; Confucianism: Rhetoric; Confucianism: Tradition; Confucianism: Twentieth Century; Fang Dongmei; Hu Shi; Kang Youwei; Liang Qichao; Liang Shuming; Mou Zongsan; Philosophy in China: Historiography; Philosophy: Recent Trends in China since Mao; Philosophy: Recent Trends in Taiwan; Tang Junyi; Wang Guowei; Xiong Shili.

Bibliography

Chan, Wing-tsit. "Chinese and Western Interpretations of *Jen*." *Journal of Chinese Philosophy*, 2(2), 1975, pp 107–129.

———. *Chu Hsi: New Studies*. Honolulu: University of Hawaii Press, 1989.

———. "The Evolution of the Confucian Concept *Jen*." *Philosophy East and West*, 4, 1955, pp. 295–319.

———. "The Evolution of the Neo-Confucian Concept *Li* as Principle." *Tsing Hua Journal of Chinese Studies*, New Series, 4(2), 1964, pp. 123–149.

———, ed. *Chu Hsi and Neo-Confucianism*. Honolulu: University of Hawaii Press, 1986.

———, trans. *A Source Book in Chinese Philosophy*. Princeton, N.J.: Princeton University Press, 1963.

Cheng, Chung-ying. *New Dimensions of Confucian/Neo-Confucian Philosophy*. Albany: State University of New York Press, 1991.

Cheng, Chung-ying, and Nick Bunnin, eds. *Contemporary Chinese Philosophy*. Boston, Mass., and Oxford: Blackwell, 2002.

Ching, Julia. *Confucianism and Christianity*. Tokyo and New York: Kodansha, 1977.

———. *To Acquire Wisdom: The Way of Wang Yang-ming*. New York: Columbia University Press, 1976.

Cua, Antonio S. *Dimensions of Moral Creativity: Paradigms, Principles, and Ideals*. University Park: Pennsylvania State University Press, 1978.

———. "Emergence of the History of Chinese Philosophy." *International Philosophical Quarterly*, 40(4), 2000, pp. 441–464.

———. *Ethical Argumentation: A Study in Hsün Tzu's Moral Epistemology*. Honolulu: University of Hawaii Press, 1985.

———. "Ethical Uses of History in Early Confucianism: The Case of Hsün Tzu." *Philosophy East and West*, 35(2), 1985, pp. 133–156. (For a pinyin version of this essay, see *Virtue, Nature, and Moral Agency in the Xunzi*, ed. T. C. Kline and Philip J. Ivanhoe. Indianapolis, Ind., and Cambridge, Mass.: Hackett, 2000.)

———. *Moral Vision and Tradition: Essays in Chinese Ethics*. Washington: Catholic University of America Press, 1998.

———. "Problems of Chinese Moral Philosophy." *Journal of Chinese Philosophy*, 27(3), 2000, pp. 269–285.

———. *The Unity of Knowledge and Action: A Study in Wang Yang-ming's Moral Psychology*. Honolulu: University of Hawaii Press, 1982.

Hall, L. David, and Roger Ames. *Thinking through Confucius*. Albany: State University of New York Press, 1987.

Hansen, Chad. *A Daoist Theory of Chinese Thought: A Philosophical Interpretation*. New York: Oxford University Press, 1992.

Liu, Shu-hsien. *Understanding Confucian Philosophy: Classical and Sung-Ming*. Westport, Conn.: Greenwood, 1998.

Tong, Lik kuen. "Confucian Ren and Platonic Eros: A Comparative Study." *Chinese Culture*, 14(3), 1973, pp. 1–8.

Tu, Weiming. *Centrality and Commonality: An Essay on Chung-yung*. Honolulu: University of Hawaii Press, 1976.

———. *Humanity and Self-Cultivation: Essays in Confucian Philosophy*. Berkeley, Calif.: Asian Humanities, 1979.

Vittinghoff, Helmolt, ed. "Recent Bibliography in Classical Chinese Philosophy." *Journal of Chinese Philosophy*, 28(1–2), 2001, pp. vi, 1–208.

Wu, Kuang-ming. *On Chinese Body Thinking: A Cultural Hermeneutic*. Leiden: Brill, 1997.

Philosophy: Recent Trends in Taiwan

Vincent SHEN

By "recent philosophical trends in Taiwan" I mean the development of Chinese philosophy in Taiwan since 1949, the year when the government of the republic of China moved to the island of Taiwan after having lost mainland China to the communists. In Taiwan, Chinese philosophy developed in an ambiguous, or ambivalent, situation. On the one hand, philosophical research in Taiwan, though it was not totally free from all ideological constraints, had more academic freedom than research in mainland China under the communists. On the other hand, Taiwan was a utilitarian society in which success was measured by economic and political criteria; philosophical research was marginalized and received much less support from public resources, having to depend more on individual and private initiatives.

In this setting, despite its ambivalence, Chinese philosophy experienced a new period of development. Research on western philosophy became more sophisticated and refined. Researchers were no longer content with mere translation and introductory studies, as had been the case in China from the 1920s to the 1940s. Also, scholars of traditional Chinese philosophy made themselves more familiar with western philosophical concepts and incorporated these concepts into their studies, creating more eclectic Chinese philosophical systems.

The main characteristic of Chinese philosophical activity in Taiwan since 1949 is evident in a conscious effort to effect a meeting of Chinese and western philosophies so as to produce a new way of doing Chinese philosophy. This attempt has been fruitful; indeed, it has been even more fruitful than similar attempts in other human and social sciences. However, whether it is relevant to actual life (or to what I call the "life-world," a concept I will explain below) is still open to discussion.

Generally speaking, there are three approaches to a synthesis of Chinese philosophy and western philosophies in Taiwan: (1) an organicist or comprehensive synthesis, (2) a contemporary new Confucian synthesis, and (3) a Chinese neoscholastic synthesis.

Organicist or Comprehensive Synthesis

The organicist synthesis is represented by Fang Dongmei (Thomé Fang, 1899–1977) and his followers. For Fang, the essence of Chinese philosophy is a unique transcendent-immanent metaphysics. The Fang school appropriates philosophical ideas, whether Chinese or western, that offer pertinent insights into human nature and cosmic existence. Fang characterizes his own philosophy as organicism or "comprehensive harmony"; this, he believes, is the spirit of Chinese philosophy. Here "organicism" is defined as a comprehensive, creative, interrelated way of thinking in contradistinction to western dualistic, mechanical, abstract thought. Fang has said:

> Chinese philosophical ideas are centered [on] the integrative whole explicable in terms of organicism, which, as a form of thought, may be bilaterally characterized. Negatively, it denounces the possibilities (1) of taking things and persons [as] absolutely isolated systems, (2) of reducing the plenitude of reality into an impoverished mechanical order of merely juxtaposed constituents, and (3) of squeezing the dynamic universe into a tightly closed [completely developed] system . . . , devoid of continual creativity. Positively, it is an endeavor to encompass the integral universe in all aspects of its richness and plenitude without any indulgence in the most abstract form of an underlying unity which is never unearthed. (1980, 30)

Fang identifies three common features in the different systems of Chinese thought: (1) The doctrine of pervasive unity taken in multifarious significations. (2) The doctrine of the *dao*—a common idiom that imbues the systems with richly different meanings. (3) An exaltation of the individual into ever higher realms of existence, variously conceived.

The two pillars of Fang's own philosophical system are a theory of being and a theory of human nature. With regard to being, he affirms the multifaceted nature of existence, including the physical, biological, psychological, aesthetic, moral, religious, and unfathomable. He argues that beings can evolve from a basic level to a higher level (he calls this "turning upward"), and that beings at higher levels can pour their creative forces back into, and thereby fortify, those on lower levels ("turning downward").

Regarding human nature, Fang argues that a person can advance from *Homo faber* to *Homo creator* and then to *Homo sapiens* (a person of knowledge), *Homo symbolicus, Homo honaestates* (a moral person), and finally *Homo religiosus*. Human nature can either develop from a lower to a higher level or come down from a higher level to become firmly settled on a lower one; thus it realizes within itself both turning upward and turning downward.

Taking these two theoretical points as a framework for his philosophical system, Fang specifically emphasizes the creativity, rationality, and interconnectedness of thinking and existence.

Aesthetic experience is the core of Fang's philosophy of life. It stresses the unending creativity that finds a common denominator between all sorts of differentiated realms and the unfathomable, and combines them. In this way he incorporates elements of both western and Chinese philosophy into a new system of thought.

Fang was very open-minded and never wanted his followers to form a philosophical clique. A few of his students, such as Charles Fu, Liu Shu-hsien (Liu Shuxian), Chung-ying Cheng (Cheng Zhongying), Peter Woo, Fu Pei-jung (Fu Peirong), and the present author, Vincent Shen (Tsing-song Shen), have become influential in Chinese philosophy, in Taiwan or elsewhere.

Synthesis of Contemporary New Confucianism

The synthesis of contemporary new Confucianism is represented by Tang Junyi (T'ang Chün-i, 1909–1978), Mou Zongsan (Mou Tsung-san, 1909–1995), and their followers. Contemporary new Confucianism emerged as a transcendentalist movement against what had been a trend toward positivism since the Qian Jia school. It seeks transcendence in human subjectivity as a foundation for science and democracy—Chinese intellectuals since the May Fourth Movement have considered these essential. In accordance with this philosophy of subjectivity, contemporary new Confucians have also tried to find a way out of the cultural crisis of modern China since the advent of the Communist regime. They emphasize a synthesis of Chinese and western philosophies; they also emphasize idealistic Confucianism, especially that of Mencius, Lu Xiangshan, and Wang Yangming. In their teaching, they attempt to appropriate and accommodate German idealism, in particular Kant's transcendental philosophy and Hegel's phenomenology.

Briefly, moral experience is the source of Tang Junyi's philosophy. Its end is to construct an image of the perfect human being. Tang explores the structure and dynamism of subjective experience in much the same way as Hegel did in his *Phenomenology of Spirit* and schematizes the structure of this subjective experience as what he calls "nine horizons of human mind." Respectively, the first three horizons ascertain the status and content of "individual," "concept," and "principle" to work out a transcendental foundation for science. The second three horizons explore "perception," "language," and "morality" to constitute a world of meaning, thus laying a transcendental foundation for the humanities. The last three horizons treat God, *dharma*, and "heavenly virtue" and thereby reconstruct monotheism, Buddhism, and Confucianism. In this way, Tang gives religion a transcendental base and adds a religious dimension to Confucianism.

Mou Zongsan, on the other hand, takes human cognitive activity as the point of departure for his philosophical reflections. His aim is to synthesize Confucianism with the philosophy of Kant, so as to clarify the transcendental capacity as well as the legitimacy of human subjectivity in order to lay a transcendental foundation for both science and democracy. His book *Fourteen Lectures on the Encounter and Synthesis of Chinese and Western Philosophy* (1990) takes up the synthesis of Chinese and western philosophy as its main concern. Mou Zongan's philosophy may be summarized as follows:

1. Using a Kantian critical approach, Mou traces the transcendental foundation of the sciences, especially formal logic, in order to save them from the trap of positivism.
2. He tries to overcome Kant's limitations and affirms the necessity of intellectual intuition—the existence of which is proved by Confucianism, Daoism, and Buddhism.
3. He reinterprets on an ontological level the Kantian concept of free will; this results in an affirmation of the free, unlimited human mind.
4. Through a process of *zi wo kan xian* (self-negation) and a "twofold unfolding of the unlimited free mind" (conceived through Mou's interpretation of the *Mahayana-sraddhotpadsastra*), the free and infinite mind can be developed into both modern science and democracy.
5. Mou proposes coordination rather than subordination as the basic principle of modernization.

We can say that Mou's philosophy is a reaction against positivism, with the help of Kant's transcendental philosophy; and a reaction against westernization, with the help of a reinterpretation of Chinese philosophy, especially idealistic Confucianism. His concept of a free and unlimited mind replaces the Christian God, thus giving contemporary new Confucianism a religious overtone.

Among the students of Mou, Liu Shu-hsien is perhaps most balanced, taking Mou's philosophy as a "creative inheritance" while also reflecting critically on it. Liu has a broad knowledge of western philosophy, especially that of Ernst Cassirer, and has worked on Confucianism, philosophy of culture, and the modernization of Chinese philosophy; he has written monographs on Zhu Xi and Huang Zongxi. With regard to methodology, he proposes to reinterpret the concept of *liyi fenshu* (one principle, many manifestations) using Cassirer's notion of functional unity. With regard to metaphysics, Liu proposes to renovate Mou's moral metaphysics so as to avoid either a one-sided anthropocentric interpretation or one-sided cosmological speculation. With regard to praxeology, he proposes to recombine theory and praxis through the principle of *liyi fenshu* and the lived experience of "letting be" (*liang xing*).

After Mou died, younger contemporary neo-Confucians took up two lines of scholarship. Those in one line are more apologetic, following Mou's thought as a way to legitimize their own works, sometimes appealing to new resources in western philosophy, such as Heidegger and Habermas. Those in the other line focus more on critical reflection, emphasizing the relevance of neo-Confucianism to real life and to the philosophical challenge of postmodernism.

Chinese Neoscholastic Synthesis

The Chinese neoscholastic synthesis is represented by Wu Jingxiong (Wu Ching-hsiung), Lo Guang (Lo Kuang), and other Catholic philosophers. This school mainly continues the legacy of Matteo Ricci and his followers, based on the Aristotelian-Thomist tradition, which it systematically combines with Chinese philosophy. In its incorporation of Chinese philosophy, it places particular stress on the classical Confucianism of the pre-Qin period.

Wu Jingxiong's main contribution is in legal philosophy. In books such as *Fountain of Justice* and *Cases on Jurisprudence*, and in articles such as "Mencius's Theory of Human Nature and Natural Law," "My Philosophy of Law—Natural Law in Evolution," and "Comparative Studies in the Philosophy of Natural Law," Wu combines Confucius's and Mencius's thought with Thomist philosophy. He argues that a Confucian *dao* consists of a set of ethical principles, comparable to the "natural laws" of scholastic philosophy. Such Confucian concepts as the mandate of heaven (*tianming*), human nature (x*ing*), and "educative formation" (*jiao*) refer to different aspects of Confucianism while still remaining closely interconnected. According to Wu's interpretation, they are quite similar to the conceptual scheme constituted by "eternal law," "natural law," and "positive law" in Thomist philosophy—which are also distinct yet related concepts.

Lo Guang proposes to link the ontology of scholastic philosophy with the doctrine of change in Chinese philosophy, so as to lay a foundation for a philosophy of life encompassing both the ethical and the religious. He uses the concept of a personal God to interpret the "great ultimate" (*taiji*) in Chinese philosophy. He argues that the great ultimate is the heavenly God, the uncreated "being itself," the source of life, the creator of the ceaselessly changing universe. The main concept of the philosophy of life is humanity, or *ren*. Through *ren*, the human being is capable of endless development, because *ren* itself is a dynamic aspect of existence relating all human beings and all things. This development includes the Confucian ideal of taking the welfare of others into consideration in everything one does, so as to achieve a great world commonwealth of love, harmony, and peace. It proceeds to a realization of the unity of all things—even the union of heaven (*tian*) and humanity. But although humanity can be in union with heaven, humanity is not itself heaven. For this reason, one must examine one's errors and try to eradicate one's "small self," in order to find the way to a loving communion with the heavenly God.

Other Catholic philosophers, such as Gabriel Ly and Thaddeus Hang, continue this line of thought. Thaddeus Hang, under the influence of Carl Jung and Martin Heidegger, tries to elaborate a balanced philosophy combining existential subjectivity with the universal function of reason, the multiple layers of life, the individual, Chinese culture, and Christianity. Two of his scholarly achievements deserve particular mention. First, he develops a comprehensive philosophy of life, most interestingly, in his *Philosophy of Man*, emphasizing individuality, interconnection, and the capacity for development as three essential characteristics of life. Second, in *Ways of Chinese Philosophy* he proposes a four-step methodology for Chinese philosophy: (1) retracing historical resources, (2) fusing horizons through hermeneutics, (3) conducting logical and semantic analysis, and (4) drawing pertinent comparisons with western philosophies. As a Catholic philosopher, Hang has done some comparative studies concerning the concepts of heaven, *ren* (humanity), *wu* (nonbeing), and *xin* (mind-heart).

Gabriel Ly focuses on two sets of basic philosophical problems: (1) immanence and transcendence and (2) being and nothingness. Taking immanence as his point of departure, he affirms the inner dynamism of human nature, which allows it to go beyond itself and achieve transcendence, seen as the fulfillment of human nature. The "self-enclosure" of immanence will lead to atheism, studied by Gabriel Ly in a five-volume book, *Man and God*. Ly studies being and nothingness in his *Basic Problems of Philosophy*; he seems to see a perfect being, or the fullness of being—God rather than nothingness—as the foundation of all beings. He takes inner dynamism (an inclination toward others) and the fullness of being as the foundation of creativity; he tends to emphasize unselfish love and generosity as the most essential ethical principle.

In short, Chinese scholastic philosophers posit a personal God as the creative source of all forms of life and the communion of love as the ultimate attainment in human life. Such insights are closely linked to these philosophers' own religious experience.

New Developments

Chen Daqi (1887–1983) is a somewhat special figure in Taiwan. He was a scholar of logic and comparative logic in mainland China before 1949 and published works on logic and Indian logic. After he moved to Taiwan with the Nationalist government, he began to study Confucianism. His achievement in this field is quite remarkable, since he combined logical analysis with Confucian studies and thus established a conceptual framework for the study of Confucianism. According to Antonio S. Cua (Ke Xiongwen, 1985, 1998), a Chinese-American scholar who follows the same line of research, Chen Daqi's *Kongzi xueshuo* is the pioneering study of the conceptual aspect of Confucian ethics. This is an important observation; other scholars of logic and the analytic school in Taiwan had not done this sort of work—nor had they even considered it necessary to turn back to their own traditional resources, such as Confucianism.

Absorbing and evaluating western philosophy has been from the outset a major task of contemporary Chinese philosophers. Analytic philosophy, phenomenology, existentialism, structuralism, hermeneutics, critical theory, postmodernism, etc., have all been introduced and given close study. These may someday become components of a new synthesis.

For example, existentialism enjoyed a period of popularity in Taiwan in the 1960s, and the works of Sartre, Kafka, Camus, Heidegger, and others were translated into Chinese and widely studied. Existentialist thinking satisfied the intellectual and emotional needs of Taiwan's dejected, apprehensive youth as the country underwent industrialization; it also accorded with the traditional concern of Chinese philosophy for the meaning and value of life. Existentialism was particularly compatible with Chan (Zen) Buddhism.

Phenomenology was introduced in Peter Woo's monograph *Husserl's Concept of Epoqué*, and its study was continued in works by Zhang Kejun, Vincent Shen, and others. Phenomenology emphasizes intentionality and subjective meaning and so is quite near to traditional Chinese philosophical thinking. Structuralism as a philosophy was introduced to Taiwan by Albert Zhao; later, it was applied to analyze classical Chinese literature and mass culture. Hermeneutics, introduced to Taiwan by Vincent Shen, has opened the door to a new way of understanding and reinterpreting Chinese philosophical texts. Studies on critical theory in Taiwan are mainly motivated by a need for improvements in political communication and a critique of ideology. Tran Van Toan (Van Doan Tran)—who was born in Vietnam, is well-versed in German idealism and recent western philosophies, and at the time of this writing was teaching in Taiwan—has been the main figure in directing research toward "critical theory" and related social philosophy.

Philosophies of science and technology have also begun to receive considerable attention in Taiwan: inquiries into the relationship between science, technology, society, and culture have been raised to the level of philosophical reflection. This begins, perhaps, with Vincent Shen's *Disenchantment of the World* (1984, 1998), a philosophical study on the cultural impact of science and technology in the context of a meeting of western and Chinese values and philosophies.

In general, Chinese philosophers in Taiwan can use their study of western philosophy for at least three purposes: first, western philosophical languages can be conceptual instruments for translating Chinese philosophical ideas and identifying themes; second, different philosophical languages can reveal and express different cultural experiences; third, western philosophical languages can be appropriated to express philosophical ideas emerging from new contexts in the real world.

Recent philosophical developments in Taiwan have caught up with trends elsewhere in the world and will surely contribute to a new outlook for Chinese philosophy in the years to come. Most important, perhaps, Taiwanese philosophers now see Chinese philosophy in the context of world philosophies. The present author, Vincent Shen, is an example.

Since 1980 Shen has worked out a philosophy of contrast with methodological, historical, and ontological significance. He defines contrast as a dialectical interplay between difference and complementarity, continuity and discontinuity, which manifests itself in the structure and dynamism of experience, history, and being. Shen explores the epistemological strategy for interdisciplinary research, first by expanding the concept of rationality so as to integrate scientific rationality and hermeneutic reasonableness. He is convinced that science is culture-bound and tries to make explicit the concept of science implicit in Confucianism and Daoism. In cooperation with the New Vienna School of Constructive Realism, Shen has added a dimension called "life-world" to mediate between "reality itself" and "constructed reality" and has proposed, in reinterpreting the Confucian concepts of *ren* and *shu* (reciprocity), the idea of "appropriation of languages" and a strategy called "strangification." The latter concept—"strangification"—was proposed by Fritz Wallner, though only for interdisciplinary studies. It is a process of going out of oneself and going to the other, the stranger, either by translating one's discourse into languages understandable to others or by recontextualizing one's social-cultural commitment; and it could therefore be applicable in intercultural interaction as well as interdisciplinary research.

Conclusion

Synthesizing what are presumably the best parts of western and Chinese philosophies in order to find a better way of conducting Chinese philosophy is essential to contemporary Taiwanese philosophers; however, the idea of synthesis must be critically examined. The most crucial problem it faces is what might be called "incommensurability." Different Chinese and western philosophical perspectives, such as Confucianism, German idealism, and scholasticism, might be mutually incommensurable because of their internal structures or their external relationships. Still, this would not preclude any possibility of mutual understanding. Such understanding requires that we either appropriate the philosophical languages of others or translate our own philosophy into their languages. Thus synthesis may be seen as a process of appropriation of languages and what I have called strangification.

In this process, it is not enough to consider synthesis as merely something to be done on the level of philosophical ideas. "Appropriation of languages" and "strangification" are continuous and broader, and lead to new creations. The synthesis of Chinese and western philosophies is, then, not just a synthesis of systems of ideas, but rather a process of enriching one's philosophical languages and of making oneself known, philosophically, to others in order to open new possibilities for creativity in an ever-changing "life-world." In short, it should be considered within a context of contrast, enrichment, and dynamism; and its end is to have Chinese philosophy stand among the other philosophies in the world.

See also Chen Daqi; Fang Dongmei; Lu Xiangshan; Mou Zongsan; Wang Yangming.

Bibliography

Cua, A. S. *Ethical Argumentation: A Study in Hsün Tzu's Moral Epistemology*. Honolulu: University of Hawaii Press, 1985.

———. *Moral Vision and Tradition: Essays in Chinese Ethics*. Washington, D.C.: Catholic University of America Press, 1998.

Fang, Thomé (Fang Dongmei). *Chinese Philosophy: Its Spirit and Its Development*. Taipei: Linking, 1981.

———. *The Chinese View of Life*. Hong Kong: Union Press, 1956.

———. *Creativity in Man and Nature*. Taipei: Linking, 1980.

———. *Fang Dongmei yanjiang ji* (Collected Conferences of Thomé Fang). Taipei: Liming, 1978.

———. *Shengsheng zhi de* (The Virtue of Creative Creativity). Taipei: Liming, 1979.

Fu, Pei-jung. *Rujia zhexue xinlun* (New Treatise on Confucian Philosophy). Taipei: Yeqiang, 1993.

Liu, Shu-hsien. *Dangdai zhongguo zhexue lun: Wenti pian* (On Contemporary Chinese Philosophy: Its Problems). Hong Kong: Pafang Cultural Enterprise, 1996.

———. *Understanding Confucian Philosophy: Classical and Sung-Ming*. Westport, Conn.: Praeger, 1998.

———. *Zhongxi zhexue lunwen ji* (Essays on Chinese and Western Philosophies). Taipei: Students Bookstore, 1987.

Lo, Guang (Lo Kuang). *Rensheng zhexue* (*Philosophy of Life*). Taipei: Students Bookstore, 1981.

———. *Rujia zhexue tixi* (The System of Confucian Philosophy), 2 vols. Taipei: Students Bookstore, 1983, 1989.

———. *Zhongguo zhexue di zhanwang* (*The Prospect of Chinese Philosophy*). Taipei: Students Bookstore, 1985.

———. *Zhongguo zhexue sixiang shi* (History of Chinese Philosophical Thought), 7 vols. Taipei: Students Bookstore, 1976–1986.

Mou, Zongsan (Mou Tsung-san). *Daode di lixiang zhuyi* (Moral Idealism), rev. 4th ed. Taipei: Students Bookstore, 1980.

———. *Fourteen Lectures on the Encounter and Synthesis of Chinese and Western Philosophy* (in Chinese), Taipei: Students Bookstore, 1990.

———. *Rensheng xing zhi pipan* (Critique of Cognitive Mind). Hong Kong: Union, 1955.

———. *Xinti yu xingti* (The Substance of Mind and the Substance of Nature). Taipei: Zhengzhong, 1978.

———. *Yuanshan lun*. (On Supreme Good). Taipei: Students Bookstore, 1985.

———. *Zhiti zhexue yu zhongguo zhexue* (Intellectual Intuition and Chinese Philosophy). Taipei: Commercial Press, 1971.

Shen, Vincent Tsing-song. *Chuantong di zaisheng* (Rebirth of Tradition). Taipei: Yeqiang, 1991.

———. *Confucianism, Taoism, and Constructive Realism*. Vienna: Vienna University Press, 1994.

———. *Jiechu shijie mozhou* (Disenchantment of the World). Taipei: Times, 1984. (Rev. 2nd ed., Taipei: Commercial Press, 1998.)

———. *Xiandai zhexue lunheng* (Essays on Modern Philosophy). Taipei: Liming, 1985.

Tang, Junyi (T'ang Chün-i). *Shengming cunzai yu xingling jingjie* (The Existence of Life and the Horizons of Spirit). Taipei: Students Bookstore 1977.

———. *Zhongguo zhexue yuanlun: Yuandao pian* (Inquiry on Chinese Philosophy: Inquiry on the *Dao*), 3 vols. Hong Kong: New Asia Institute, 1973.

———. *Zhongguo zhexue yuanlun: Yuanjiao pian* (Inquiry on Chinese Philosophy: Inquiry on Cultivation), 2 vols. Hong Kong: New Asia Institute, 1975.

———. *Zhongguo zhexue yuanlun: Yuanxing pian* (Inquiry on Chinese Philosophy: Inquiry on Xing). Hong Kong: New Asia Institute, 1968.

Wu, Jingxiong (Ching-hsiung). *Neixin yuele zhi quanyuan* (The Spiritual Sources of Joy). Taipei: Dongda, 1981.

———. *Zhexue yu wenhua* (Philosophy and Culture). Taipei: Sanmin, 1971.

中國哲學

Q

Qi (Ch'i): Vital Force

Chung-ying CHENG

What is *qi*? Etymologically, the Chinese character for *qi*, in the form found in Zhou oracle inscriptions, symbolizes the cloudy vapors one observes in the air. Hence we can speak of *yuanqi* (cloud-vapor) or *yueqi* (cloudy vapor around the moon) in reference to observed phenomena of nature. In the present ideogram, *qi* suggests vapors rising from rice paddies, and hence a term dating from the agricultural period of early China. The commonly used term *kongqi* (air in empty space) is perhaps more recent, suggesting an understanding that in what seems to be empty space, invisible air is present. This suggests that *qi* can be invisible, even though it must in some way be experienced as physically real. *Huoqi* (fire-vapor) could refer to something other than the visible wave of heat when something is burning: that is, to the sensation of heat (*reqi*) and the underlying cause, which is described as a *qi* "of the fire type." In this sense *qi* is no longer observable but is still a potent agent, causing the combustion of wood and the emission of heat. The human body receives evidence of *huoqi* as a physical sensation, experiencing a change when heat is conveyed to it.

When we think of *qi* as an organic state internalized in the human body, the concept has been made more abstract and more general, an underlying cause of change and transformation. Eventually, the concept of *qi* acquires the meaning of both energy or force and vitality and thus becomes "vital energy" or "vital force," but it has not lost its naturalistic or even its materialistic reference or meaning. In fact, what we have observed about the visible natural *qi* is extended to the invisible internal *qi* of the organism. It is even extended to the atmosphere—which is invisible but can be experienced—resulting from harmonious human interactions or a lack of such interactions; hence the terms *heqi* (harmonious relationship) and *shenqi* (radiation of lively energy, or being angry).

There is one more step. We come to see evidence and signs of vital life in the breathing in and breathing out of air and the consequent circulation of blood in the body, and so *qi* comes to suggest an internal life force. That force can produce consciousness, knowledge, and wisdom; we may even conceive of *qi* as an unpredictable power of creative change. *Qi* is then elevated, becoming a cosmic and even a cosmological creative power of production, reproduction, formation, transformation, penetration, and efficacious participation and presence, transcending even the system of visible or invisible *qi*. It becomes a philosophical term—specifically, a metaphysical term. As *qi* underwent this philosophical development, it also acquired the meaning of a force for all living things.

In the case of human beings, *qi* has to do with physical and physiological phenomena—such as the activities and functions of the organs, seminal fluid, and blood—and also with invisible neural-electronic currents, which are explored in the Chinese arts of acupuncture and psychosomatic exercises. Most subtly, it becomes the human spirit, *jingshen*. When the *jingshen* develops, it may become a power of creation and fulfillment. It is then said to be divine (*shen*) and transcendently efficacious (*ling*).

Clearly, *qi* is one of the most fundamental categories of reality and understanding in Chinese philosophy—as in common sense—and this has been so since very early antiquity.

A conceptualization of *qi* in a discourse occurs in the *Zhouyu* portion of *Guoyu* (*Records of States*, c. 500 B.C.E.), where the "grand historian" mentions an "explosion of *tuqi*" (*qi* of earth) and an "evaporation of *yangqi*" (the masculine *qi*), apparently referring to an earthquake. Boyangfu is recorded as having said: "The masculine [*qi*] was suppressed and cannot get out, while the feminine [*qi*] oppresses and cannot evaporate; therefore there is an earthquake." *Qi* seems to be regarded as having two modes or two forms: the *yang* mode is masculine, firm, a force rising upward; the *yin* mode is feminine, soft, a force pressing downward. Their combination in things would explain how things move. An earthquake is just one example of how a natural event could be explained in terms of the dynamics of *qi*. Boyangfu also speaks of the *qi* of heaven and earth and its orderly circulation, attributing disorder among people to disorder in the *qi* of heaven and earth.

In *Zuozhuan* a certain Yi He speaks of six *qi* of nature—(1) *yin*, (2) *yang*, (3) wind, (4) rain, (5) clouds, and (6) light—which give rise to four seasons and five "periods" (*qujie*). It is not clear whether the five periods have anything to do with the five powers described in the chapter *Hongfan* in the *Book of Documents* (*Shangshu*): metal, wood, water, fire, earth. But it is clear that by the sixth century B.C.E., *qi* is seen as the cause of basically all natural events, not just as a term describing these events. Along the lines of this categorization of *qi*, the descriptive theory of *wuxing* (five powers) is gradually developed into a causal theory. We can distinguish several versions of the theory of *qi*, including a theory of its five powers.

Guanzi's theory of jingqi (*quintessential qi*). In the chapter *Shuyan* of *Guanzi*, Guanzi holds that things live because they have *qi*; when they lose *qi*, they die. Here *qi* causes and sustains life and, by extension, causes and sustains the cosmos (*tiandi*). In the famous chapter *Neiye*, Guanzi speaks of the quintessence of *qi* that gives rise to all life, and of how it flows between heaven and earth as spirits and resides in the minds of sages (hence it is called the *mingqi*, "*qi* of reputation"). This implies that *qi* can be very refined and also coarse.

In effect, Xunzi elaborates on the *Guanzi* in his chapter *Wangzhi*. There, changes take place and things arise because of the interaction of *yin* and *yang* (modes of *qi*). Xunzi maintains that water and fire have *qi* and yet no life, but a human being can have *qi*, life, knowledge, and morality. In identifying a certain *qi* as the basis of morality, Xunzi appears to have followed Mencius.

Mencius's theory of yangqi (*nourishing qi*). Mencius speaks of *qi* primarily as a life force pervading the whole person. He also sees the human heart-mind as a refined *qi* on a higher level (which we may call the heart-mind-force). If one does not learn something in one's heart-mind, one should not seek it out in the *qi*, because one can act only in light of one's understanding of the principles of righteousness. However, if one does not learn anything from a given discourse (*yan*), one should always consult one's mind for understanding. This shows that Mencius considers the heart-mind a center of knowing and reflection as well as a center of willing. He conceives the heart-mind as the leader of the *qi* of the body and also as the creative matrix for generating a sense of righteousness and moral transformation from nourishing the *haoran zhiqi* (oceanic overflooding force) of the cosmos. The *haoran zhiqi* is a felt "life-world" of righteousness and vitality, resulting when a person cultivates interactions between his nature and the nature or life force of the cosmos. The *haoran zhiqi* must be cultivated and nourished carefully and conscientiously. Significantly, *qi* can acquire a moral quality, and hence can become a moral force, through the cultivation of the heart-mind and an understanding of the way of heaven and earth.

Zhou Yan's theory of five powers. The distinctive feature of Zhou Yan's theory of *qi* is not only that there are five basic kinds of *qi*, each distinguished by its own virtuous power, but that they can be related in mutual conquest (*xiangke*) and mutual generation (*xiangsheng*). Thus earth generates metal, metal water, water wood, wood fire, and fire earth; and earth conquers water, water fire, fire metal, metal wood, and wood earth. Zhou Yan uses his theory to explain changes in the natural world, and to explain and predict political relationships and dynastic changes. Apparently, he bases these explanations on his understanding of *qi* as a pervasive but differentiated power controlling both natural and sociopolitical events.

Theory of cosmic qi in Huainanzi. Beginning in the Han dynasty, the theory of *qi* expanded to encompass everything in reality, including life. Specifically, *qi* is considered the origin of the universe and is described as having an inexhaustible power of change and transformation. Moreover, the theory undergoes an ontogenetic process of development from *yinyang* polarity to the five powers and to all things in the universe. In *Huainanzi*, it is proposed that all things in nature are simply the materialization of a fundamental *qi*, and all changes are due to changes in the inherent *qi*. Wang Chong, accordingly, calls the cosmic *qi* the "original *qi*" (*yuanqi*). This cosmogonic idea of *qi* was actually first formulated in the *Commentaries* of the *Zhouyi*, especially the "*Xici* Commentary." It is also found in Laozi's *Daodejing* and *Zhuangzi*. But in the *Yizhuan* formulation, the emphasis is on the process of change of the *taiji* and the *yin-yang* forces, without any explicit focus on the nature of *qi*. Laozi refers to *qi* implicitly as a cosmic force and explicitly as an mental experience, whereas Zhuangzi describes the world of events as a profuse paradigm of *qi* in his *Qiwulun*.

Theory of bodily qi in Neijing (*Inner Classic*). In the later Warring States period, Chinese medicine took a step toward a systematic understanding of the human body, seeing it as essentially organized by *qi*. In this context, *qi* refers to blood, other fluids, and breath and to invisible currents of vital energy. As a living organism the human being is organized by *qi* on many levels and with many aspects; one may say that any mark of living and consciousness is explained by *qi*. But *qi* is not just an explanatory concept; it has a richer, though not readily describable, content. Chinese accupuncture testifies to a belief in the existence of bodily *qi*: it was devised to stir up "points of inflection" of *qi* in the human body.

On the basis of these primarily naturalistic theories of *qi*, Chinese philosophy can be regarded as mainly a philosophical tradition of *qi*—particularly if we follow Mencius and Xunzi in conceiving of *qi* as equally manifested in human morality and moral consciousness and thus making it the foundation of principles of both nature and humanity. The philosophy of *qi* on all levels was eventually fully developed in the writings of Zhang Zai in the Northern Song. The philosophy of *qi* was continued by Luo Qinshun in the Ming and by Wang Fuzhi in the late Ming. In recent times in China, naturalistic or materialistic philosophical views are called *qi* philosophy to contrast them with the *li* (rationalistic) philosophy of the Zhu Xi tradition.

See also Luo Qinshun; Wang Fuzhi; *Wuxing*; Zhang Zai.

Bibliography

Note: For classical texts, see *Guanzi, Guoyu, Huananzi, Laozi, Mengzi, Neijing, Xunzi, Yijing*, and *Zuozhuan. Sibu beiyao* Series.

Cheng, Chung-ying. "*Li* and *Ch'i* in the *I Ching*: A Reconsideration of Being and Non-Being in Chinese Philosophy." *Journal of Chinese Philosophy*, 14(1), 1987, pp. 1–38.

———. "On the Environmental Ethics of the Tao and the Ch'i (Qi)." In *The World and I*. 1986, pp. 577–594.

Engels, Friedrich. *Dialectics of Nature*. New York, 1935, 1941.

Friedrich, Michael, and Michael Lackner. "Once Again: The Concept of *Wu-hsing*." *Early China*, 9–10, 1983–1985, pp. 218–219.

Govinda, Lama Anagarka. *Foundations of Tibetan Mysticism*. New York, 1974.

Kono, Sawaseiichi, Fukunaga Koshi, and Yamae Yu, eds. *The Thought of Qi*. Tokyo: Tokyo University Press, 1978. (In Japanese.)

Needham, Joseph. *Science and Civilization in China*, Vols. 1 and 2. Cambridge: Cambridge University Press, 1956.

Pang, Pu. "Origins of the Yin-Yang and Five Elements Concepts." *Social Sciences in China*, 6(1), 1985, pp. 91–131.

Rubin, Vitaly A. " The Concept of Wu-hsing and Yin-yang." *Journal of Chinese Philosophy*, 9(2), 1982, pp. 131–158.

Zhang, Zai. *Zhengmeng* (Rectifying Obscurations). In *Zhang Zai ji*. Beijing: Zhonghua, 1978.

Zhu, Xi. *Zhuzi yulei* (Classified Conversations of Zhuzi), Parts 1–2. Taipei: Cheng-chung, 1962.

Qian Mu (Ch'ien Mu)

Kirill O. Thompson

Qian Mu (1895–1991), a master of the classical Chinese humanities, was a prodigious scholar, author, and teacher and a living embodiment of traditional Chinese thought and culture. Although he grew up in an age when many distinguished scholars and activists were absorbed in mastering western disciplines and challenging traditional Chinese thought and culture, Qian devoted himself to pure traditional learning. He saw in the ample, subtle five-thousand-year tapestry of recorded Chinese experience resources needed for contemporary nation-building as well as "society-building" and "person-building." He thus devoted himself to a life of studying, recording, and expounding on this tapestry, almost in spite of the incursions of the twentieth century. Qian's influence in republican China, Taiwan, and Hong Kong has been deep and far-reaching: he wrote numerous texts and sourcebooks covering nearly every period of Chinese thought and history, and he taught generations of students from the 1920s through the 1980s. Even though he bore some of the markings of an eccentric autodidact, Qian rose to eminence by virtue of his clear mind, prodigious memory, scholarly productivity, and steadfast devotion to his ideals.

Qian Mu was born in 1895 in Qifang Qiao (Seven Mansions) village, Wuxi County, Jiangsu Province, and died in 1991 in Taipei, Taiwan. He thus witnessed a century of upheaval and change in all aspects of national life. Through it all, he remained enamored of the unutterable beauty and quaint delights of traditional Chinese culture. He kept his faith that this precious culture itself contained the resources necessary for revitalizing China and its people, that there was no need to draw wholesale on western models. He remained confident that, by cultivating a sympathetic appreciation of traditional history, thought, literature, and art, Chinese people could still realize themselves in a rich and meaningful way. Despite the inroads of social Darwinian among the intelligentsia, together with the rise of modern politics and economics in society, Qian still saw a material basis for preserving the humane traditional culture in the Chinese home, community, and school.

Interestingly, Qian recommended seven books as essential testaments of the tradition that people who identify with Chinese culture should read. They included four ancient texts: Confucius's *Analects, Mencius, Laozi*, and *Zhuangzi*. They also included three medieval texts: *The Platform Sutra of the Sixth Patriarch,* Zhu Xi's anthology *Reflections on Things at Hand*, and Wang Yangming's *Instructions for Practical Living*. (These books are all available in English translation.)

During an age when most distinguished scholars have sought to apply "standard" modern western analytic modes of definition and analysis to ancient Chinese philosophy texts, Qian insisted on the priority of carefully reading the original texts and commentaries with unblinkered eyes. Through his own careful reading of ancient texts, he stressed the insight that, rather than offering real definitions of concepts, Chinese thinkers usually assumed a working understanding of the terms and gave practical accounts of terms according to the needs of the audience at hand. Thus, for example, Confucius offered a variety of terse, practical accounts of his "cardinal" virtue, *ren* (benevolence, human-heartedness), to different disciples—which modern interpreters have been misguided in generalizing into a "general theory" of *ren*. Thus, too, Wang Yangming could offer a "four-sentence teaching" on mind and moral value to one disciple, and then accept its denial by a more advanced disciple—on the understanding that different formulations were required for students with different needs and levels of attainment. What "worked" at a lower level could be false at a higher level. Qian showed that Chinese thought did not proceed along the linear deductive lines required by western-trained interpreters. Thus, unlike most western-trained interpreters, Qian argued that Zhu Xi's notion of *li* (pattern) was not identifiable as a platonic "form" or even a generic western "principle." Using Zhu's own words, Qian showed that *li* represented the inner patterning which structures and relates all phenomena, that *li* made up the warp and woof of the world. As Zhu said, the *li* are like textures of grains in wood, lines in jade, and veins in leaves. Zhu's conception of *li* thus presents an order that is aesthetic and organic, not linear and logical. Qian's rectification of twentieth-century interpretations of *li* ranks as a major contribution to Chinese philosophy and as a testament to his method of meticulous reading of ancient texts.

Moreover, Qian liked to show that the Chinese schools of thought did not present an antagonistic Hegelian dialectic of conflicting "theses" and "antitheses." Rather, he insisted, they absorbed and adapted each other's concepts, usually in view of practical applicability, rather than simply offering denials and refutations. He illustrated this pattern in his depiction of intellectual development from Confucianism to Mohism, the "school of names," and Daoism (Taosim). Thus he also sought to show that the neo-Confucian term *qi* (fluid vapor) had been adopted from Daoist texts and that Zhu Xi's notion of reality as an organic composition of *li* and *qi* had been inspired by the Huayen Buddhist theory of *li* (reality) and *shi* (phenomena).

Qian insisted that Chinese thought also differs from "logocentric" western philosophy and modes of analysis by virtue of its inherently historical, contextual, and practical character. Ironically, western philosophy is beginning to notice its own historicity, its contextuality, and the limits of logocentrism; thus more nuanced methods of analysis are appearing in the west that might be tailored to the study of ancient Chinese texts. Qian in this regard displayed great prescience and insight, although he did not attempt to prescribe an efficient methodological program apart from painstaking, meticulous study.

Qian wrote several influential books on Chinese intellectual history and the history of Chinese thought. In each book, he sought to rectify misconceptions that had arisen among contemporary scholars by marshaling extensive textual evidence. His first scholarly book, *Chronological Studies of the Pre-Qin Philosophers* (*Xian-Qin zhuzi yinian*), appeared in the late 1920s and brought him instant recognition and acceptance by the scholarly community. Because of the errors punctuating popular studies of the pre-Qin thinkers of the day, in this work Qian attempted to establish the relative time frames of those thinkers and their ideas in order to present the actual stages of intellectual development in ancient China clearly and accurately.

History of Chinese Thought of the Last Three Hundred Years (*Zhongguo jinsanbainian xueshushi*, 1977) is arguably Qian's most famous scholarly book. Scholars of the early twentieth century generally spoke in support of the textual research of the Qing and against the speculative learning of the Song, yet none of them displayed a clear, accurate overview of Qing scholarship. In their minds, the textual research school itself constituted the sum of Qing learning. Accordingly, in this book Qian sought to trace the Song roots of Qing learning, and then to describe each of the Qing schools and major figures in detail. This book was an invaluable contribution to scholarship and is still regarded as an essential sourcebook today.

In *Assessment of the Han Old and New Text Controversy* (*Liang-Han jingxue jinguwen pingyi*, 1958), Qian sought to uncover and examine the original disputes and evidence involved in the Han controversy over old and new texts, which had been completely obscured by the factionalized Qing reenactment of the controversy. This book is divided into four sections: a chronicle of the lives of the Han scholars Liu Xiang and Liu Xin (father and son), an examination of the Han methods of textual exegesis, a consideration of Confucius's authorship of the *Annals of the Spring and Autumn Period*, and an inquiry into the authenticity of the *Rites of Zhou*. Qian's critical analyses of these issues, always supported by careful objective research, have been generally regarded as broadly definitive and as having laid to rest disputes that had preoccupied leading Chinese scholars for two centuries.

In *Case Studies of the Qing Literati* (*Qingru xue'an*, 1938), Qian focused on the Qing neo-Confucians—long neglected by twentieth-century scholars—who had continued Song learning and focused on the concepts of mind, human nature, righteousness, and pattern (*xin*, *xing*, *yi*, *li*). Qian was intrigued that, whereas the Song neo-Confucians had inherited these concepts from the identifiable passages in the *Book of Change*, with "Appendixes," and the *Four Books* (*Analects, Mencius, The Doctrine of the Mean*, and *The Great Learning*), the Qing neo-Confucians drew on a wider variety of sources, often difficult to trace. Contrary to the prevailing view, Qian emphasized that these discourses on quintessential neo-Confucian concepts expressed the spirit of Qing scholarship in a way that textual exegesis never could. This book inaugurated a new wave of interest in neo-Confucianism from the Song to the Qing that has persisted to the present day.

Qian's crowning achievement was his five-volume work *New Anthology and Critical Inquiry into Zhu Xi* (*Zhuzi xinxue'an*, 1971). Again, in this work Qian set out to rectify errors of interpretation regarding Zhu's thought perpetuated in twentieth-century scholarship as well as to present Zhu, not as a narrow-minded neo-Confucian moral thinker, but as a "Renaissance man," a scholar of breadth and depth who had made significant contributions in many of the traditional disciplines. In countering interpreters armed with western models and methods who considered Zhu a dualist, Qian marshaled textual evidence showing the organic unity and integrity of Zhu's fundamental concepts. In countering idealist critics of Zhu's objective notion of "investigating things," Qian offered evidence showing its practical value. To subjectivist believers in moral intuition who regarded "investigating things" as taking responsive moral action, Qian defended Zhu's view that life in society is so complex that, even though we might be endowed with moral intuition, we still have to inquire into the objective nexus of human affairs. Even if we have the right impulses, we still must be well-informed if we are to express them appropriately. Qian further showed that Zhu effectively applied his notion of "investigating things" in textual research as well as in observing natural phenomena, and attributed to him several major scientific discoveries.

In addition, by tracing Zhu's intellectual development in rich detail, Qian showed that Zhu had created a genuine neo-Confucian synthesis, not just an unwieldy eclectic arrangement of ideas. Qian also showed that Zhu's historical, literary, and textual research was subtle and sophisticated, and not blinkered by his neo-Confucianism. Thus, in a time when major scholars were showing a bias toward Zhu's more narrowly focused rivals, Lu Xiangshan (Jiuyuan) and Wang Yangming (Shouren), Qian reestablished the intellectual preeminence of Zhu Xi and inaugurated a renaissance of Zhu Xi studies that continues to the present.

Qian also wrote several influential histories of Chinese thought, including *History of Chinese Thought* (*Zhongguo sixiang shi*, 1952); *Introduction to Song-Ming Neo-Confucianism* (*Song-Ming lixue kaishu*, 1953); and *Essays in the History of Chinese Thought* (*Zhongguo xueshu sixiangshi luncong*, 8 vols., 1977–1980). Again, these works are distinguished by Qian's interest in tracing the deep historical roots of ideas, showing the interconnections among schools, and bringing historical and cultural background to bear. Qian always infused his discussions with a wealth of knowledge and insight derived from his wide reading and deep reflection.

Qian Mu emerged as a towering figure in the kaleidoscopic world of the Chinese humanities in the twentieth century. His observations on many subjects are noteworthy and frequently surprising, for he invariably attempted to speak for the old tradition: he always sought to demonstrate its continued vitality and relevance. His chief scholarly works, especially *History of Chinese Thought of the Last Three Hundred Years* and *New Anthology and Critical Inquiry into Zhu Xi*, have advanced knowledge in the field immeasurably and continue to inspire new inquiries, as was Qian's ultimate purpose.

See also *Li*: Principle, Pattern, Reason; Philosophy: Recent Trends in Taiwan; *Qi*; Zhu Xi.

Bibliography

Dennerline, Jerry. *Qian Mu and the World of Seven Mansions*. New Haven, Conn., and London, 1988.

Lin, Mumiao. *Qian Mu jiaoshou zhuanlu* (A Biographical Sketch of Professor Qian Mu). Taipei: Yangzhi, 1995.

Qian, Mu. *Bashi yi shuangqin; Shiyu zayi hogan* (Recollections of My Parents at Age Eighty; Reminiscences of Teachers and Friends). Taipei: Dongda, 1983. (Combined publication.)

———. *Xiandai Zhongguo xüeshu lunheng* (Assessment of Contempory Chinese Academic Learning). Taipei: Dongda, 1984.

———. *Zhongguo sixiang shi* (History of Chinese Thought). Taipei: Xuesheng, 1977.

———. *Zhuzixüe tigang* (Overview of Zhu Xi's Learning). Taipei: Dongda, 1971.

———. *Zong Zhongguo lishi lai kan Zhongguo minzuxing ji Zhongguo wenhua* (Chinese Ethnicity and Chinese Culture from the Perspective of Chinese History). Taipei: Lianjing, 1979.

Qing (*Ch'ing*): Reality or Feeling

Chad HANSEN

Standard dictionary entries give two puzzling equivalents for *qing*: (1) affections, feelings, emotions; and (2) facts, circumstances, reality. Both contribute to a large number of compound phrases. We find the emotion-linked "love letter" and "sentiments" alongside the fact-linked "truth" and "reason." The character consists of a heart radical and a phonetic *qing* (color of living nature—green-blue—hence young, growing, etc.). We find the phonetic in other complex characters with the sense of "pure," "clean," and "clear." Classically, it was linked phonetically with "request," "please!" which uses a language radical with the same *qing* phonetic.

I will develop the hypothesis that in early China, the character referred to input from the world that is relevant to following a guide (a *dao*). The writers implicitly contrasted *qing* with conventions, the complement of guidance. Thus, we can explain two uses—"reality" and "sentiment"—as both emerging from the conception of the presocial inputs we use to direct our behavior according to social guides.

Confucius's *Analects* used the character only twice in contexts that suggest a contrast with and complementary relation to ritual morality. "If those above favor reliability, then the no one will fail to use *qing*" (*Analects*, 13.4). Mozi developed a political role for the concept and emphasized the contrast between natural or self-nurtured *qing* and conventions or ritual. According with the *qing* of those below marks a well-ordered society (government). The ideal type of harmony is that between the heart *qing* (from below) and the language *qing* (from above). Requests for guidance harmonize with the people's natural reactions in the real world. When guidance precisely maps onto the *qing* of those below, they will desire things like benevolence and morality.

Because Mozi formulated a utilitarian moral theory, interpreters took his *qing* to be a subjective measure of utility—pleasure or happiness. Generally, however, Mozi explained utility in real, material terms—actual well-being. That he did link moral utilitarianism with *qing* suggests that the sense of the character was still mainly objective reality. For Mozi, it was important to distinguish between *qing* and *wei* (artifice).

Mozi's best-known theoretical use of *qing* was in his theory of language. He argued that among the measures of correct use of language was "its according with the *qing* of the people's eyes and ears." He spells out this accord in two key arguments—whether people say "have" or "lack" of spirits and fate. The other tests of language are a use test (pragmatic) and a historical test (conventions). Mozi assumes that all three tests favor utilitarian grounds for guiding language use. He does not explore the possibility that the standards might pull in other directions.

Mencius's intuitive moral theory postulates a natural, presocial guidance scheme. He does not use *qing* to refer to this moral content, though his later interpreters did. He preferred using *xing*, which also attaches a heart radical to a *sheng* (life) phonetic. Presumably, he wants to distinguish a growing, maturing, systematic moral sensibility from the piecemeal natural inputs into the heart. *Qing* itself continues to serve Mencius as a concept of reality that is relevant to guidance.

Laozi's *Daodejing*, conversely, totally forgoes *qing* in favor of *yu* (desire)—a term with which *qing* was later frequently combined. Perhaps his motive was to suggest that desires are products of socialization while *qing* are not. In the process of learning language itself, this analysis suggests, we learn distinctions and acquire new desires guided by those distinctions. This socialization pulls us unconsciously away from our spontaneous nature. Like Mencius, supposedly, Laozi regards spontaneous nature as good. His strategy for avoiding this socially guided departure from natural behavior was "forgetting" language and socialization.

Though Laozi did not use *qing* in developing his position, it was assumed in subsequent developments. Other philosophers took up and developed the insight that learning a language instills a kind of unnatural prejudice in our attitudes and, consequently, in our behavior. The most famous and sophisticated of these was Zhuangzi. He accepted the later Mohists' proof that we could not coherently conclude that we should abandon language. Instead, Zhuangzi emphasized a kind of pluralism. He encouraged us to recognize that different languages, conventions, lives, and even various species produce divergent guiding views. All base their guidance on conflicting standards of justification and interpretation.

Zhuangzi's usage was important in forcing interpreters to notice the "reality" implications of the character. In many passages Zhuangzi uses it where it can hardly be intelligible as feelings. Still, *qing* clearly retains a prescriptive role in the *Zhuangzi*. At one point, the text gives the conventional list of what we have come to regard as *qing*—happiness, anger, sorrow, pleasure, fear, and regret. Zhuangzi does not call them *qing* but goes on to wonder, as Hume did, if we have any *qing* of something (a self?) that links them all together. Without them, he notes, there would be no "I" and neither choosing nor objects to be chosen. However, when I seek for a "true ruler" of them, I do not find its *qing*.

Zhuangzi most famously pairs *qing* with *xing* (shape). Both are givens for purposes of guidance, but the content of *qing* is comparatively amorphous. In a well-known (and interpretively controversial) passage, Zhuangzi debates with Hui Shi about *qing*. Zhuangzi's conclusion (on one parsing) is that *qing* inputs are pro-con judgments (*shi-fei*), and his advice to lack *qing* amounts to his saying, "Do not let such judgments harm yourself or multiply excessively." Our shape is given in life, but our "self" is a product of judgments. However, we should each monitor the development of these, not surrender them to the manipulation of social authority. Presocial *qing* are positive elements for Zhuangzi.

The strongest early negative views on *qing* emerged in the writing of Xunzi. There is tension in Xunzi's use of *qing*. In general philosophy, he seems to assume that *li* (ritual) can shape and control *qing*. (This is consistent with Laozi's theory of *yu*, desires.) The novel point is Xunzi's argument from political economy that we should welcome such social control. He suggests that use of *li* (ritual) to control desires is how society can achieve "equal" fulfillment in conditions of material scarcity. Ideally, the lower classes will have tastes and desires for things that are plentiful, and only high officials will cultivate tastes for things that are relatively rare—and not for coarse and common things. In these contexts, his attitude toward *qing* reflects a view of their malleability.

However, in other sections the text treats *qing* as a more purely negative source of disorder. *Qing* is the ground for Xunzi's famous argument that human nature is evil. He vociferously attacks the philosopher Song Xing for his view that *qing* desires are few. On its face, however, Song Xing's theory resembles that of Laozi. Most desires are socialized; reality-based presocial (or natural) desires are few. This could be the basis for an attack on Xunzi's position since it suggests that conventions like *li* (ritual) create unnecessary desires. They thus generate competition and strife. Xunzi would want to insist that *li* (ritual) is essential for order, not the cause of disorder.

In these sections, Xunzi specifies that *qing* and desires are initially limitless in their range and content.

We cannot control desire itself, but we can control our "seeking" behavior. This analysis is at odds with the political-economy argument because it implies that in any well-ordered society, we will not satisfy most of our natural desires. Citizens will be "repressed" by conventions so that they do not act on their desires. Xunzi, here, assigns the name *qing* to the classical list of emotions—like, dislike, happiness, anger, sorrow, and pleasure.

Xunzi bequeathed his attitude toward *qing* to the emerging Confucian orthodoxy in the Han. Dong Zhongshu linked *qing* to the classical dualism of *yin* and *yang*. The *qing* were classed as the "evil" *yin* (female), and *xing* (moral nature) was the good *yang* (male). *Qing* became a generalized reference to the mechanism of human evil. This analysis underwrote the negative view of *qing* that helped it mesh with Buddhism. That implication dominated the residual "reality" component in post-Buddhist Confucianism.

Buddhism introduced into the Chinese intellectual world a western "folk psychology" complete with the contrast of beliefs and desires. Moreover, at the initial or introductory level, Buddhism used desire to explain evil or suffering. Salvation or enlightenment consists in overcoming desire. The Buddhist goal is individualized in comparison with the social-political stance of the classical Chinese thinkers, and the notion of *qing* was almost exclusively linked to individual psychological states. The esoteric or advanced teachings often take back this initial simple, dualistic stance, but Buddhism cemented the subjectivist component of *qing* firmly in Chinese consciousness.

Some of the dual nature reemerges in orthodox neo-Confucianism. *Qing* themselves, as long as they are not one's own but a reflection or accurate view of the *qing* of things themselves, may be orderly. So the orthodox versions of the theory often modify *qing* by "human" or "things." They do speak of Mencius's responses of the heart as *qing*, and insist that the heart's *qing* are metaphysically in accord with the moral structure of the cosmos. They contrast this with "human *qing*" or "selfish *qing*."

The distinction, in general, between a "human" and a *dao* heart-mind is one target of the attack by the "school of mind" on Chu Hsi's orthodoxy. Wang Yangming, the dominant theorist of the school of mind, denied that even natural, subjective *qing* were inherently evil. He analyzed them as functions of innate knowledge (inherently good) and thus prior to good and evil. They still explain evil, for example, when they are "attached" to things (have a "thing-content") because in that case they become "grasping" or "selfish." If we recognize and "realize" their source in innate good knowledge, we class them as orderly and good. If our *qing* are spontaneous responses, without calculation, that arise from our contact with the world, then our responses should be good ones. This direction of neo-Confucian thought led to an incipient utilitarianism immediately preceding and during China's modern contact with the west.

See also Buddhism in China; Dong Zhongshu; Laozi; Mencius; Mohism: The Founder, Mozi; Wang Yangming; Xunzi; Zhuangzi.

Bibliography

Chan, Wing-tsit. *Neo-Confucian Terms Explained.* New York: Columbia University Press, 1986, pp. xi–277.

———. *A Source Book in Chinese Philosophy.* Princeton, N.J.: Princeton University Press, 1963.

Cua, A. S. *Ethical Argumentation: A Study in Hsunzi's Moral Epistemology.* Honolulu: University of Hawaii Press, 1985.

Graham, Angus. *Disputers of the Tao: Philosophical Argument in Ancient China.* La Salle, Ill.: Open Court, 1989.

Hansen, Chad. *A Daoist Theory of Chinese Thought.* New York: Oxford University Press, 1992, pp. xv–448.

———. "Qing (Emotions) in Pre-Buddhist Chinese Thought." In *Emotions in Asian Thought*, ed. Joel Marks and Roger T. Ames. Albany: State University of New York Press, 1995.

Munro, Donald J. *The Concept of Man in Early China.* Stanford, Calif.: Stanford University Press, 1969.

Wu, Yi. *Chinese Philosophical Terms.* Lanham, Md.: University Press of America, 1986.

Qiongli (*Ch'iung-li*): Exhaustive Inquiry into Principles

Chung-ying CHENG

To understand the doctrine of *qiongli*, "thorough realization of *li*," we need to know something about *li*, "pattern," "order," "reason," "principle." Etymologically, *li* stands for natural patterning in a piece of jade; as a verb, it means carving a pattern on jade. This idea of *li* can, in theory, be traced to the late Neolithic, when Chinese people began to use fine stone tools, including jade. We find jade used as a sacred symbol with cosmic meaning in the Neolithic Longshan culture of about 6000 B.C.E. The natural patterning (*li*) of jade provided a paradigm for understanding reality by making it possible to conceive of natural patterns within or underlying all things in the universe. The word *li* does not actually occur in the original texts of the *Yijing*, which may date from 4000 B.C.E.; nevertheless, the concept of *li* seems to have become philosophically relevant for understanding the universe, nature, human life, and society during the period between 6000 and 4000 B.C.E.

The major texts in which the concept *li* explicitly appears are the *Commentaries of the Yi* (*Yizhuan*), and it is in the "Discourse Commentary" (*Shuogua*) that the term *qiongli*—full realization of the *li*—occurs. The version of the *Yizhuan* that we know was formed in the later years of Confucius, under his influence. This suggests that the formation of the concept of *li* as order and *qiongli* as realizing an underlying order and principle of reality had to do with reflections by the Confucian school on the nature of life and the universe. In Confucian philosophy from Confucius to Mencius and Xunzi, the idea emerges that everything has its underlying reason and cause, and that the reasons and causes of all things are interrelated in an organic order, pattern, unity, and oneness.

We may say that this is the reason why Confucius speaks of his way, or Way, as having a thread of unity. In later time, Mencius speaks of the *li* and *yi* as something the mind "likes" and says that eventually nature and mind are to be conceived in terms of the *li*.

Mencius expresses the insight that *li* and the mind are closely related. The underlying order of reality must be revealed by the ordering activity of the mind or heart-mind. To bring out the order of reality or *li* fully not only will enable us to understand the world better, so that we can act correctly and rightly, but will bring the capacity of mind to its fullest development—in other words, "realize" the mind to its full extent. Zhu Xi uses the term *lijie* (understanding order) to describe understanding the world in terms of the *li* or the order of reality. When *li* is brought to the fullest extent in the activity of *lijie*, that can be said to be *qiongli*. The purpose of *qiongli* is not just to understand order but to fulfill the functions and potential of the mind; Mencius calls this *jingxin*: fulfillment of the mind or heart-mind.

There are two complementary ways of articulating *qiongli*.

1. In the "Discourse Commentary" we read that one must engage in "*qiongli* and fulfillment of the nature (*xing*) so that one will reach destiny (*ming*)." This means that by way of *qiongli* we also fulfill our human nature and consequently reach an understanding of our ultimate reality. Here *xing* is not just our bodily nature but the nature of our spirit and mind; together, body and mind are endowed by heaven, as the *Zhongyong* maintained. That is, heaven endows a person with his nature—with what makes him human and constitutes human potential. This endowment is also a reflection of heaven, which has both finitude and a large cosmic purpose that may be infinite. Hence there is unity between a person's nature and his destiny, just as there is unity between his internal and external aspects. To start with *qiongli* is to reach external order from the internal mind; then, to fulfill nature is to bring an internal order to external practice and growth. In this sense, one reaches fate from nature and also fulfills *ming*, thus fulfilling the human being as a person. *Qiongli* is the start of this fulfillment.

2. In the *Mencius*, although *qiongli* is not explicitly mentioned, fulfilling the mind is a matter of fulfilling the *li* in the mind. This is because mind is closely linked with the *li* and is capable of understanding things through *li*. Mencius has actually reached a very subtle understanding of the concept of *qiongli*—that is, *qiongli* in terms of *jingxin*. When we understand *jingxin* in this way, we can see how it would bring about the fulfillment of nature and, consequently, the fulfillment of heaven. Mencius does not use the terms *jingxing* and *zhiming* (knowing destiny), however; instead, he speaks of knowing nature (*zhixing*) and knowing heaven (*zhitian*). *Zhi*, in classical usage, means or suggests an intimate experience and embodiment of what is known. To know *xing*, heaven, the human being, *li*, or speech as mentioned in the *Analects* already carries the meaning of knowing not just "what" (consciousness, knowing about something externally) but also "how"—and knowing something "as it is" (which would be a link to oneself as a person) or "as it should be." This kind of knowledge requires practice, immersion, and embodiment; hence it can be called immersed or embodied knowledge as contrasted with externalized or objective knowledge. This is why knowing nature and heaven is also fulfilling nature and heaven, or reaching nature from the mind and reaching heaven from one's nature. Heaven brings to the human being both finitude and infinity. To know heaven is to know one's destiny in an understanding of the total reality of heaven.

This Mencian interpretation of *qiongli* does not differ essentially from the interpretation in the "Discourse Commentary." However, we should note that because of his insight into *jingxin*, Mencius can be considered the founder of the "school of mind" (*xinxue*) in Song-Ming neo-Confucianism, whereas the "Discourse Commentary" can be considered as having initiated the "school of principles" (*lixue*).

With regard to the neo-Confucian *lixue*, we may explain Zhu Xi's doctrine of *qiongli* in terms of his proposed commentary on the methodology of *gewu* (investigation of things) and *zhizhi* (reaching knowledge) in the *Daxue* (*Great Learning*). Since the original explanation of *gewu* and *zhizhi* was presumably missing from the *Daxue*, Zhu Xi felt that he should undertake the task of providing the required commentary. His commentary runs:

> To say that *zhizhi* resides in *gewu* is to say that if one wishes to reach one's knowledge, one must thoroughly realize the *li* (*qiong qi li*). All human minds have the ability to know, and all things have their *li*. But as the *li* of a thing (or things) is not thoroughly realized (in mind), the mind cannot be said to exhaust its knowledge. Hence in developing my learning I must use what my mind already knows to pursue more knowledge so that it may push my knowledge to the fullest. Once one has exercised oneself long enough in this direction, one could reach a stage or state where there is a "sudden opening up and breaking through" (*huoran guangtong*). It is a stage or state in which the inside and outside, the fine parts and coarse parts of things will be covered in one's knowledge and the great function of my mind will be illuminated. (From Zhu Xi's *Sishu jichu*)

This description of *qiongli* suggests an organic, comprehensive learning of *li*, implying that one may use what one already knows to reach a full, whole system of knowledge of things. We should not expect Zhu Xi to offer this as a final system of scientific knowledge in the modern sense; clearly, for Zhu Xi and other neo-Confucian philosophers, the knowledge involved has to do with principles of reality in reference to things or with knowing things in reality in terms of their principles. To achieve this, one must see that all things are related through principles and that all principles are related, so that knowing one principle will illuminate other principles. One must also assume that the mind's internal knowing has the power to bring a full clarity of consciousness or awareness, illuminating and understanding all things and all principles. This implies a link between the mind and the principles of things; it also implies that the mind and principles form an organic unity. Thus when all the principles become known and all aspects of things, small or large, are presented, the mind will have become illuminated and clear. The result is a unity of knowledge of principles, knowledge of things, knowledge of principles of things, and the self-knowledge of the mind. We can call this the thorough realization of all *li: qiongli*.

In this theory of *qiongli*, the mind is assumed to grow as it knows things, to be inclined to know, and to have the capacity to know. For Zhu Xi, this is so because human nature is endowed with the capacity of knowing, which realizes itself in mind. Nature (*xing*) is itself a matter of *li*, which ontologically forms a unity with ultimate reality. This is not to say that the mind will never make mistakes; it can be mistaken if the capacity of knowing is insufficiently exercised or is obscured by prejudice and desires. For Zhu Xi, the mind needs a source and supporting foundation for its activity; thus the function of nature is necessary for the exercise of mind. Mind can reach toward nature just as it can reach toward principles, for both share an underlying reality. In the process of *qiongli*, the mind is externally directed toward things and what underlies things and internally directed toward itself so that it can provide insight and intuition into the order and unity of all principles. This explains how mind can reach a state of thorough integration and interpenetration of principles in a process of inquiring into the *li* of things. Preexisting knowledge and new knowledge are brought together to form a unity and to reveal an underlying order.

Zhu Xi—unlike Plato or Kant—does not need to assume that the mind is equipped with a priori innate ideas. Mind simply grows as it obtains knowledge from experience and from its interaction with its own underlying nature, which implicitly contains all the *li*. Hence *xing* is *li*, and it takes mind to reach a knowledge of *li*. To know (*zhi*) the *li* of things is to form an understanding of things in *li* and *li* in things (*lijie*). Understanding is always a system of knowledge to be achieved in a process of interaction between mind and things.

Zhu Xi does not separate *li* from mind, because there is the mediation of *xing*. Hence the duality of *li* and mind (or *qi*, because mind is conceived as a matter of activity of *qi*) does not imply a dichotomy between subject and object as in western epistemology, nor does it lead to a domination of mind over *li* as in the school of mind of Lu Xiangshan and Wang Yangming. When Lu Xiangshan and Wang Yangming speak of the mind as being the *li*, they are thinking of a full realization of the mind's potential, and hence of nature. In this sense, mind is indeed the *li* because it is already nature. This is not to dismiss the notion of *xing*; it is simply a way to understand nature better. As Mencius says, once one has fully realized the mind one would know nature. We can say, then, that there is really no disagreement between Mencius and Zhu Xi; they share a vision of how to achieve the *li* to the fullest extent so that mind is realized, nature is clarified, and the ultimate reality of heaven and destiny is revealed as the culmination of one's full self-understanding of mind and nature and one's full knowledge of the world —principle and destiny or heaven.

It may be objected that we cannot have the truly complete knowledge and understanding that is implied by *qiong*, "thorough." But it can be answered that *qiongli* must be conceived as a creative process, and the system of understanding must be conceived as open. Once we achieve such a system through such a process, we are able to maintain self-correction, an attitude of harmonization, and an interactive application of knowledge to things.

According to Zhu Xi, one's intention can be made sincere through *qiongli*, and one's mind can be rectified with regard to planning or thinking about goals. To be sincere in one's intentions is a concrete activity requiring direction and references to reality. Without a sense of knowing reality, one cannot develop goals and values. Sincerity is part of the self and so is always present, but when it is needed for application to the world, it must develop an understanding of things and principles. A thorough understanding of things and principles will provide a framework of reference and a motivation, so that sincerity will become relevant, well-placed, productive, and a source of values. Once again, we see the extreme importance of *qiongli* as explained by Zhu Xi.

See also *Li*: Principle, Pattern, Reason; Mencius; Reason and Principle; Zhu Xi.

Bibliography

Mencius.
Yizhuan (Commentaries on the Book of Changes).
Zhu, Xi. *Sishu jichu*.

Quan (Ch'üan): Weighing Circumstances

A. S. CUA

The important Confucian concept *quan* may be rendered as "weighing of circumstances," "exigency," or "moral discretion." Understanding *quan* depends on its contrast with *jing* (the normal or standard). The possibility of transformation of the Confucian tradition of *dao* (*daotong*) depends on our understanding of the distinction between *jing* and *quan*. This distinction reflects a similar Confucian concern with *chang* (the constant) and *bian* (the changing). Indeed, the latter is indispensable to elucidating the former. As Zhu Xi put it, "*Jing* pertains to the constant aspect of *dao*, and *quan* to the changing aspect of *dao*" (*Zhuzi yulei*, 6.1A).

Translating *quan* as "expediency" would be misleading if it were to suggest the agent's concern for self-serving purposes rather than a concern for what is appropriate or proper under the circumstances. Expediency in the first sense is contrary to the Confucian concern with *yi* (rightness, righteousness). In the second sense, however, it is functionally equivalent to the other renderings, that is, weighing (the importance or unimportance) of circumstances and discretion. D. C. Lau's "moral discretion" is perhaps the best rendering of *quan* in a perplexing passage in the *Analects* (9.30). Reflection on the nature of moral discretion may give us a systematic way of dealing with Zhu Xi's preoccupation with the distinction between *jing* and *quan*. In fact, as Wei Cheng-t'ung points out (1986, 255), Zhu Xi's concern was in part motivated by his students' repeated query on the notion of *quan* in that passage.

> The Master said, "A man good enough as a partner in one's studies need not be good enough as a partner in the pursuit of the Way [*dao*]; a man good enough as a partner in the pursuit of the Way need not be good enough as a partner in a common stand; a man good enough as a partner in a common stand need not be good enough as a partner in the exercise of moral discretion [*quan*]."

The exercise of *quan* is quite properly an exercise of discretion in the sense of the power of the individual to act according to his or her judgment in dealing with uncertain, exigent situations, or "hard cases." As contrasted with the "soft cases" or normal problems in human life, the hard cases are rule-indeterminate; thus the established standards of conduct (*jing*) offer no clear guidance. Even if such standards are deemed appropriate, there may be a problem of application that calls for interpretive judgment and discretion. The problem cannot be resolved by some mechanical or deductive procedures.

Most moral and legal traditions thus allow for the exercise of discretion, though such an exercise is always subject to constraints. In the Confucian context, the constraints involve the *li*, the operative ritual rules or formal prescriptions of proper conduct. Arguably, Confucius has a recurrent interest in discretion as an indispensable means for coping with the hard cases of moral life. Recall his autobiographical remark: "I have no preconceptions about the permissible or impermissible"; and the student's description of his character: "There were four things the master refused to have anything to do with—he refused to entertain conjectures or insist on certainty, he refused to be inflexible or to be egotistical" (*Analects*, 18.8, 9.4).

A study of Confucius's conception of *junzi* or paradigmatic individuals also discloses his concern with the need for flexibility in conjunction with *ren* (humanity), *li* (ritual rules), and *yi* (rightness).

In two ways, the focus on *yi* (rightness) especially brings out the moral aspect of *quan* or discretion. First, *yi* is contrasted with personal gain or self-serving interests. Second, *yi* focuses on doing the right thing as determined by a judgment of the relevance of moral rules to particular circumstances. More important, the exercise of *yi* is required in dealing with changing, exigent situations of human life (Cua 1978, ch. 4). Xunzi's emphasis on the use of *yi* in varying one's response to changing circumstances (*yiyi bianying*) echoes this concern (Cua 1985, 23–24). We would expect an adequate account of the distinction between *jing* and *quan* distinction to give a pivotal role to *yi*, since the exercise of *quan* or discretion is fundamentally an exercise of *yi*.

The need for discretion in the interpretation of *li* or ethical rules can in part be accounted for by the open texture of natural languages. That is, there is always a possibility of vagueness in the empirical and practical application of words in relation to the natural and the human world (Waismann 1952). More fundamentally, the need for discretion arises out of two deficiencies of humanity: "relative ignorance of facts" and "indeterminacy of aim" (Hart 1961, ch. 7, sec. 1). In formulating rules of conduct, we rely on our tradition and experience. We cannot always foresee the consequences of the enforcement of established rules or anticipate without error our future situations, especially those that are exigent, demanding immediate attention and action. In these cases, discretion is necessary, given the human predicament. Thus Aristotle (1962, 1094B) considers the subject matter of ethics as one that cannot be treated with exactitude and holds that "the truth" can be indicated only "with a rough and general sketch." In the case of legal justice, equity or reasonableness (*epieikeia*) is needed as a supplement or a corrective.

As indicated by his preference for voluntary arbitration or mediation over adjudication in settling disputes within the community, and by his recurrent emphasis on the importance of being a *junzi* or paradigmatic individual, Confucius would concur with Aristotle on the role of equity or reasonableness in human affairs. The preference for arbitration is evident in his remark: "In hearing litigation, I am no different from any other men. But if you insist on a difference, it is, perhaps, that I try to get the parties not to resort to litigation in the first place" (*Analects*, 12.13).

The exercise of *quan*, moral discretion, is also necessary in the light of the Confucian *dao* as a holistic ideal. This ideal of the good human life as a whole is more of a theme than a norm (Cua 1978, ch. 8). However, this ideal is a topic of communal discourse somewhat analogous to a theme in literary or musical composition, not only always recurring, in ever-different ways, but even permeating the piece in its palpable absence, amenable to varying interpretations, calling for the diverse exercise of disciplined imagination. Discretion is essential in specifying practical objectives to be pursued in the hard cases of the moral life. This "indeterminacy of aims" in conjunction with human fallibility or "ignorance of facts" renders such moral discretion (*quan*) unavoidable.

Hence, if the Confucian agent is to cope with exigent, changing circumstances in the course of pursuing *dao*, he or she must be disposed to exercise *quan*. This is perhaps the force of Zhu Xi's saying, *Zhe daoti haohao wu qiongchong*, "This substance of *dao* is vast and inexhaustible" (*Zhuzi yulei*, ch. 8.1a); and of Wang Yangming's remark, *Dao wu chongqiong*, "*Dao* cannot be exhausted with finality" (Chan 1963, 46), that is, the concrete significance of *dao* cannot be specified with any claim to finality. Any attempt to do so must be informed by a sense of timeliness (*shih*) to attain the mean or equilibrium (*zhong*), aiming at doing the right thing in accord with the agent's judgment of what a particular situation demands. Perhaps this is the basis for Mencius's remark that Confucius was "the sage whose actions were timely" (*Mencius*, 5B.1, 2A.2). The specification of the concrete significance of *dao* must be reasoned or principled. The exercise of *quan* or moral discretion is thus constrained by the exercise of practical reason (Cua 1998).

In the proper exercise of *quan* or moral discretion, as in the study of the classics, an open mind is required. While the objective is to achieve timely equilibrium (*shizhong*), the Confucian tradition must not favor any one doctrine of interpretation, even if it happens to be a moderate position between extremes. As Mencius says:

> Holding on to the middle [*zhong*] is closer to being right, but to do this without moral discretion [*zhizhong wu-quan*] is no different from holding to one extreme. The reason for disliking those who hold to one extreme is that they cripple the Way [*dao*]. One thing is singled out to the neglect of a hundred other. (*Mencius*, 7A.26, emended)

Moreover, Xunzi would advise the Confucian agent to consider carefully all the salient features of a situation before pronouncing judgment on his current desires and aversions. In Xunzi's words:

> When one sees something desirable, he must carefully consider (*lü*) whether or not it will lead to detestable consequences. When he sees something beneficial, he must carefully consider (*lü*) whether or not it will lead to harmful consequences. All these consequences must be weighed together (*jianquan*) in any mature plan before one determines which desire or aversion, choice or rejection, is to be preferred. (Li 1979, 52)

In sum: (1) *Quan* essentially pertains to assessment of the importance of moral considerations to a current matter of concern. In other words, the exercise of *quan* consists in judging the comparative importance of competing options answering to a current problematic situation. (2) The situation is such that it presents a hard case, that is to say, a case falling outside the normal scope of the operation of standards of conduct. (3) *Quan* is an exercise of moral discretion and as such must conform to the requirement of *yi* (rightness). (4) The judgment must in accord with *li* (principle, reason), that is, be a principled or reasoned judgment.

See also Confucianism: Tradition; *Junzi*; Reason and Principle; Time and Timeliness.

Bibliography

Aristotle. *Nicomachean Ethics*, trans. Martin Ostwald. Indianapolis, Ind.: Bobbs-Merrill, 1962.

Chan, Wing-tsit, trans. *Instructions of Practical Living and Other Neo-Confucian Writings by Wang Yang-ming*. New York: Columbia University Press, 1963.

Cua, A. S. *Dimensions of Moral Creativity: Paradigms, Principles, and Ideals*. University Park: Pennsylvania State University Press, 1978.

———. *Ethical Argumentation: A Study in Hsün Tzu's Moral Epistemology*. Honolulu: University of Hawaii Press, 1985.

———. *Moral Vision and Tradition: Essays in Chinese Ethics*. Washington: Catholic University of America Press, 1998.

Hart, H. L. A. *The Concept of Law*. Oxford: Clarendon, 1961.

Lau, D. C., trans. *Confucius: The Analects*. New York: Penguin, 1979.

———. *Mencius*. Baltimore, Md.: Penguin, 1970.

Li, Disheng. *Xunzi jishi*. Taipei: Xuesheng, 1979.

Waismann, F. "Verifiability." In *Essays on Logic and Language*, First Series, ed. Antony Flew. Oxford: Blackwell, 1952.

Wei, Cheng-t'ung. "Chu Hsi on the Standard and the Expedient." In *Chu Hsi and Neo-Confucianism*, ed. Wing-tsit Chan. Honolulu: University of Hawaii Press, 1986.

Zhu, Xi. *Chu Tzu yulei*, Vol.1, ed. Li Jingde. Taipei: Zhengzhong, 1962.

Quanli (*Ch'üan-li*): Rights

Stephen ANGLE

Until the mid-nineteenth century, there was no single term in Chinese that corresponded to the English term "rights" or its cognates in other European languages. This disparity was not accidental: classical and postclassical Chinese discourses on politics, ethics, and law were configured differently from their European counterparts, so the concerns that led to discussion of rights in Europe were handled differently in China. In the nineteenth and, especially, the twentieth centuries, though, a substantial discussion of rights took place in China, albeit one that in many ways still reflected cultural, political, and philosophical differences between China and the various western nations.

Rights and Chinese Thought

There have been many conceptions of "rights," and the word is by no means univocal even today. According to Hohfeld's well-known analysis, for instance, "right" is often used for things as diverse as privileges, powers, and immunities, though he argues that its strict sense refers only to those claims one can make which correlate directly to duties others bear. In general the western tradition has taken rights to be claims on or protections of individual interests—often interests that are identified as essential to being respected as a person, rather than being treated as a mere means to someone else's end. In most cases these rights are sharply distinguished from other, more mundane interests. As Dworkin puts it, "a right is a claim that it would be wrong for the government to deny an individual even though it would be in the general interest to do so" (1977, 269).

While there is ample discussion of privileges and powers in classical and postclassical Chinese thought, we find rights in none of these more particular senses: no explicit claims correlative to duties; no protected claims essential to individual personhood; no antimajoritarian concerns overriding the general interest. Admittedly, some of these are rather new ideas in the west, but their roots run deep, and the very different philosophical terrain one finds in China goes a long way toward explaining why these western ideas may not flourish in China even today. In each case, the three conceptions of rights take it for granted that the human world is made up of independent individuals whose duties or personhood can be independently assessed. Classical Confucianism, along with most other Chinese schools of thought, denies that the basic unit of ethical or political assessment is the individual. Instead, theorizing begins with relationships and roles in relationships. Confucian thinkers stress reciprocal responsibilities rather than correlated rights and duties. Consider, for instance, *Mencius* 1B,4, which reads in part: "To condemn those in authority because one is not given a share is wrong. But for one in authority over the people not to share his enjoyment with the people is equally wrong." The responsibilities of a subject include not condemning authorities. To do so is to fail as a subject, whether or not the relevant authority has failed in his responsibilities. There is room in the *Mencius* for asserting one's interests when the authority structure has failed, but here, too, one is not claiming something as a right (see 1B.8).

A New Word?

The earliest use of the two characters *quan li* occurs in the Confucian classic *Xunzi* (c. 220 B.C.E). The author says that when one has perfected one's learning and self-cultivation, "*quan li* cannot move one" to do wrong. In commentaries, the standard interpretation of this sentence renders *quan li* as "power and profit" (*quanshi lilü*). The negative connotation that Xunzi attaches to *quan li*, which is of course related to the repeated admonitions against *li* (profit) in the *Mencius* (e.g., 1A.1), derives from his Confucian belief that one should attend to ritual or ethical propriety rather than any sort of utility. The two characters are used together many times in classical writings and writings of the imperial era, typically with this negative judgment, though on occasion they seem to be merely neutral.

In his translation (1864) of Henry Wheaton's *Elements of International Law*, however, the missionary W. A. P. Martin used *quanli* as a compound term to translate "rights." Though other terms were subsequently tried as alternative translations by writers in both Japan and China, *quanli* has, since the beginning of the twentieth century, been the standard equivalent for "rights." Many scholars have been puzzled by Martin's choice of *quanli*, some even suggesting that it was a bad translation. The difficulty with this suggestion is its implication that the only process at work in the origins of discourse on *quanli* was a (failed) attempt to mirror and adopt western concepts and standards. Whatever Martin's personal goal, though, given the way that the concept *quanli* was used in the late nineteenth and early twentieth centuries, the word *quanli* is actually a very apt formulation. There can be no doubt that the new meaning was a departure from the original. For one thing, the negative connotation was clearly gone. *Quanli* had now become one's proper powers and interests—powers and interests that one merited by performing one's responsibilities. Thinkers like Liang Qichao (1873–1929) and Liu Shipei (1884–1919) used *quanli* as part of an effort to rethink the Confucian ethical and political heritage, drawing on some strands of the tradition much more than others.

Although it is important that discourse about *quanli* be understood as a Chinese discourse, developing from Chinese concerns and in dialogue with the Chinese tradition, this is not to deny that western texts and terminology played important roles. Authors like Rousseau, Mill, Jhering, Hobbes, and Locke were all known and discussed, to varying degrees, by advocates of *quanli*. Numerous essays in the first years of the twentieth century asserted that the French, Germans, and English all had different understandings of *quanli*, and usually defended one or another of these conceptions. These essays mention a whole range of freedoms and rights, regularly including freedom of thought, speech, and publication. It should be clear from this list that even in its earliest years, the discourse on *quanli* challenged conservative aspects of traditional Chinese thought and institutions and was not restricted to concern with "welfare" or "positive" rights, as some have recently claimed.

The Discourse on *Quanli* to 1949

In the years before the outbreak of war with Japan, the significance of *quanli* was a central topic of progressive political and ethical theorizing. These were years in which western philosophies were interpreted and adopted with increasing sophistication, as numerous young people studied in and then returned from western countries, and important American and European thinkers visited and lectured in China. In such a context, *quanli* of course underwent important developments. It lost most of its previous explicit connections to the Confucian tradition, which itself came under sharp, though often simplistic, attack. The other aspect of this increased distance from Confucian vocabulary and sources of authority was an increasingly direct and complete engagement of numerous Chinese writers with themes from the contemporary western discourse on rights. If the Confucian source of discourse on *quanli* and the western stimulus to that discourse were of approximately equal importance from 1895 to 1915, those dynamics changed after 1915. Western writings were no longer merely a stimulus but became full-fledged participants in the debates over *quanli*.

Some of the major players in these debates were Chen Duxiu (1879–1942), Gao Yihan (1884–1968), Sun Yat-sen (1866–1925), Hu Shi (1891–1962), and Luo Longji (1898–1965). There were of course many important differences between these writers' approaches to *quanli*, but certain themes can be seen in most of them. First, while rights are of great, perhaps even essential importance, they are rarely an end in themselves. The most common end that *quanli* enabled one to attain was a flourishing, independent "personality" (*renge*), a term that was applied equally to individuals and to groups (like the nation). That many writers took developing one's "personality" or "being a person" (*zuoren*) as the ultimate political and ethical goal suggests both the continued resonance of Confucian ideals of character cultivation and, perhaps more important, the influence of Hegelian ideas, often filtered through English and American sources like Dewey, Hobhouse, and Laski. A second theme has to do with the specific *quanli* that were claimed: the right to free expression was regularly demanded, but so was the right to subsistence. Both negative and positive rights—in today's parlance—were seen as required for the achievement of larger goals like personality development and communal well-being. A third theme, finally, was the often implicit sense that a harmony of interests between individual and collective was attainable and desirable: individual *quanli* and personality contributed directly to the group's *quanli* and personality, and vice versa. One thinker who addressed this explicitly, Gao Yihan, is particularly noteworthy for having begun to question this assumption—pervasive in Chinese political thinking—in his writings of the 1920s and especially in his *Outline of Political Science* (*Zhengzhixue gangyao*, 1930).

Recent Developments

Abstract Marxist theory and actual Chinese Marxists have not been very friendly to rights, especially not to "human rights." In "On the Jewish Question," Marx saw the doctrine of human rights as a prop for political, bourgeois society and thus as an obstacle to the genuine realization of our "species being." Chinese Marxists have tended, until recently, to reject the idea that all humans have innate, equal rights as both false—because ignoring the class nature of humankind—and pernicious, for reasons similar to Marx's.

The 1990s saw some dramatic changes in the Chinese discourse on rights, however. First it must be noted that throughout the twentieth century, Chinese constitutions included major statements of the *quanli* of citizens. Rights have thus not been completely absent even from official communist documents. In 1991, though, the official *White Paper on Human Rights* went several steps beyond this, declaring that China was committed to the international recognition of human rights, albeit human rights as "circumscribed by the historical, social, economic, and cultural conditions of various nations," and as involving a "process of historical development." In 1993, China was an active participant in the Regional Meeting for the Asia-Pacific in preparation for the United Nations World Conference on Human Rights, and played a role in shaping the document that emerged from this meeting, called the Bangkok Declaration. Here again the signatories professed support for the general goals of the international human rights movement but insisted that human rights differed in different cultural, historical contexts. Both of these documents also sounded a second theme: the importance of economic rights, especially the right to subsistence.

Alongside these official pronouncements, Chinese academic writing on rights has blossomed again. Scholars like Li Buyun, Luo Mengda, He Hangzhou, Xia Yong, Liang Huixing, and others have begun exploring a whole range of issues, from the difference (if any) between interests and rights to the relation between duties and rights to the possibility that various societal interests may be unavoidably plural. Dissidents, both in China and abroad, are also contributing to the discourse both through evidence of Chinese abuses of individuals' political rights and through theoretical writings. Foreign academics have joined the fray, some urging that the Confucian tradition be mined for insights that can be used to construct a distinctively Chinese understanding of rights—from which, some have gone on to argue, people in the west can also learn.

See also Hu Shi; Liang Qichao; Sun Yat-sen; Xunzi.

Bibliography

Angle, Stephen C. *Human Rights and Chinese Thought: A Cross-Cultural Inquiry*. Cambridge: Cambridge University Press, 2002.

Angle, Stephen C., and Marina Svensson, trans. and eds. *The Chinese Human Rights Reader*. Armonk, N.Y.: Sharpe, 2001.

Bauer, Joanne R., and Daniel A. Bell, eds. *The East Asian Challenge for Human Rights*. Cambridge: Cambridge University Press, 1999.

Cua, A. S. "*Li* and Moral Justification: A Study in the *Li Chi*." *Philosophy East and West*, 33(1), 1983, pp. 1–16.

DeBary, Willaim Theodore, and Tu Wei-ming, eds. *Confucianism and Human Rights*. New York: Columbia University Press, 1998.

Dworkin, Ronald. *Taking Rights Seriously*. Cambridge, Mass.: Harvard University Press, 1977.

Edwards, R. Randle, Louis Henkin, and Andrew J. Nathan, eds. *Human Rights in Contemporary China*. New York: Columbia University Press, 1986.

Hohfeld, Wesley Newcomb. *Fundamental Legal Conceptions*. New Haven, Conn.: Yale University Press, 1919.

Kent, Ann. *China, the United Nations, and Human Rights—The Limits of Compliance*. Philadelphia: University of Pennsylvania Press, 1999.

Munro, Robin. *Punishment Season: Human Rights in China after Martial Law*. New York: Asia Watch, 1990.

Peerenboom, Randall P. "What's Wrong with Chinese Rights? Toward a Theory of Rights with Chinese Characteristics." *Harvard Human Rights Journal*, 6, 1993, pp. 29–57.

Rosemont, Henry, Jr. "Why Take Rights Seriously? A Confucian Critique." In *Human Rights and the World's Religions*, ed. Leroy S. Rouner. Notre Dame, Ind.: University of Notre Dame Press; 1988.

Santoro, Michael A. *Profits and Principles: Global Capitalism and Human Rights in China*. Ithaca, N.Y.: Cornell University Press, 2000.

Svensson, Marina. *Debating Human Rights in China, 1899–1999: A Conceptual and Political History*. Lanham, Md.: Rowman and Littlefield, 2002.

Weatherley, Robert. *The Discourse of Human Rights in China: Historical and Ideological Perspectives*. London: Macmillan, 1999.

Tang, James T. H., ed. *Human Rights and International Relations in the Asia-Pacific Region*. London: Pinter, 1995.

Xia, Yong et al., eds. *Zouxiang quanli de shidai* (Toward an Age of Rights), 2nd ed. Beijing: Chinese Political University Press, 1999.

Zhongguo shehui kexue yuan faxue yanjiu suo (Chinese Academy of Social Sciences, Legal Research Institute), ed. *Dangdai renquan* (Contemporary Human Rights). Beijing: Chinese Academy of Social Sciences Press, 1992.

中國哲學

R

Reason and Principle

A. S. CUA

Perhaps the best approach to the Chinese conception of reason is to focus on the concept *li*, commonly translated as "principle," "pattern," or sometimes "reason." While these translations in context are perhaps the best, an explication of the uses of *li* is desirable and instructive for understanding some main problems of Chinese philosophy. Because there is no literary English equivalent, one cannot assume that *li* has a single, easily comprehensible use in Chinese discourse. This assumption is especially problematic in appreciating the basic concerns of Confucian ethics. A closer examination of the uses of *li* and "principle" reveals a complexity that cannot be captured by a simple formula. Apart from the question whether *li* and "principle" are functionally equivalent, one may also ask whether *li* in Confucian ethics can be properly considered a context-independent notion in the way that "principle" can. For a contemporary Confucian moral philosopher, Confucian ethics is more plausibly viewed as a form of virtue ethics (Cua 1992a). Without an explanation of the uses of *li*, the translation of *li* as "principle" unavoidably leads to such misleading questions as these: What are the principles of Chinese or Confucian ethics? If such principles exist, do they serve as premises for derivation of moral rules? Are Confucian principles universal or relative? While these questions are fundamental in western moral theory, their importance for Confucian ethics depends on a prior consideration of the status of principles in Confucian ethics (Cua 1989b).

Difficulties also arise with the translation of *li* as "pattern." Again we need to have some clear answers to certain questions: What sort of pattern? Are these patterns natural or artificial—that is, products of human invention? If they are natural, how do we go about finding them? More important, even if we regard "principle" or "pattern" as an acceptable rendering of *li*, we still need to explore its role in ethical argumentation (Cua 1985). Such an inquiry presupposes that we have some understanding of the uses of *li* in Chinese ethical discourse.

This essay is a tentative, highly selective treatment of *li*. It is an attempt to provide an ideal explication or constructive interpretation of *li* from the perspective of Confucian moral philosophy. The first section deals with the basic uses of *li* as a generic term. The second section discusses the function of *li* "binomials" (a term borrowed from mathematics and biology) and the significance of principled interpretation of some basic notions of Confucianism.

Basic Uses of *Li*

In pursuing the study of *li*, Tang Junyi's pioneering study (1978) is a valuable guide, particularly to the place of *li* in the history of Chinese thought. Also instructive is Wing-tsit Chan's essay (1964) on the conceptual evolution of the neo-Confucian notion of *li*. As a preliminary, following Xunzi (Li 1979, book 22), let us distinguish between *li* as a single term, that is, a single Chinese character or graph (*tanming*), and *li* as a constituent element of a compound term (*qianming*)—say, a "binomial" term such as *wenli*. For resolving problems of ambiguity and vagueness in single terms, it is a common practice of modern Chinese and western sinologists to appeal to relevant "binomials." This method of interpretation is widely used by modern Chinese translators and annotators of classical Chinese texts. In the second section of this essay, I will say more about that procedure.

Among pre-Qin classical Confucian texts, only in *Xunzi* do we find extensive use of *li* as a single term or graph. In this text, we find about eight-five occurrences of *li* with different uses. The descriptive use of *li* in the sense of pattern or orderly arrangement may be shown by using the "binomial" *wenli*, as Xunzi sometimes does. Since *wen* pertains to (cultural) "refinement," *wenli* can properly be rendered as "cultural pattern." Often, this descriptive use of *li* has normative import; that is, *wenli* has not only de facto but also de jure status. Chan points out that there are also uses of *li* in ancient literature in the sense of "to put in order or distinguish" (1964, 125).

Since the descriptive use of *li* frequently has an explanatory function, its occurrence is sometimes associated with *gu*, which can be rendered as "reason" or "cause." While the explanatory use of *li* sometimes has normative import, the distinction between its descriptive or explanatory and normative uses remains philosophically and practically significant. This distinction seems implicit in Zhu Xi's explanation of the meaning of *li*:

> Regarding things in the world, if they exist, then (*zhe*) we may say that each must have a reason or cause (*gu*) which accounts for its being what it is (*soyiran zhigu*). Also, each must have a standard (*zhe*) for [determining] what it ought to be (*dangran zhizhe*). This is what is meant by *li*. (Wei 1983, 481; my translation)

The first remark suggests that *li* has an explanatory use and that the reason for or cause of a thing's being what it is (*soyiran zhigu*), in some sense, is derived from observation or experience. This seems implicit in the first occurrence of *zhe* as a conclusion-indicator. In neo-Confucianism of the Song and Ming dynasties, however, we do not find any interest in natural causation akin to that of western philosophy. Xunzi, perhaps the most "rationalistic" among Chinese philosophers, does acknowledge that participants in ethical argumentation must "exhaust the *gu* of things." The *gu* here pertains to reasons for supporting one's practical thesis, say, as a policy of action (Cua 1985). Instead of a theoretical conception of causal explanation, we are more likely to find the notion of *kanying*, functionally equivalent to that of stimulus and response (Cua 1975).

In Song Confucian metaphysics, every entity consists of *li* and *qi* (ether, energy, material or vital force). *Li* and *qi* are inseparable. The former is static, the latter dynamic. Thus the preferred explanation of the interaction between things makes use of the notion of *kanying* or "stimulus and response." As A. C. Graham points out, these concepts of *kan* and *ying*:

> occupy the same place in Song philosophy as causation in the West. . . . If it is assumed that things consist of inert matter, it is natural to think in terms of "effect" which passively allow themselves to be pushed by "causes." But if inert matter is only the essentially active ether [*qi*] in an impure state, this kind of action will only be of minor importance; in the purer ether, when *A* acts on *B*, *B* will not only be moved by it, but will respond actively. (1958, 38)

With the notion of *kanying* in mind, if we render *gu* in Zhu Xi's first remark as "cause," we must use the notion of practical rather than theoretical causation (Collingwood 1962). From the Confucian perspective, *kanying* conveys the idea of human sensitivity to natural things and events as having a decisive impact (*kan*) on human life. Humans must respond (*ying*) to these things and events by acting in a way that ultimately accords with the Confucian ethical vision or ideal of the unity and harmony of humanity and nature (*tianren heyi*). In other words, things and events in nature are challenges to human ingenuity in coping with problems in their lives (Cua 1975).

Zhu Xi's second remark, that "each must have a standard (*zhe*) for [determining] what it ought to be (*dangran zhizhe*)," stresses the normative sense of *li*. *Zhe* can also be rendered as "rule" or "law." However, since we do not find any notion of "natural law" comparable to that of western philosophy, *zhe* is better construed as the standard that determines things as they should be (Chan 1986). One can try to conform to standards (unlike rules) according to one's conception of the best thing to do. There are, so to speak, degrees of perfection in individual efforts at attaining the ideal of the good human life.

While the *zhe* of each thing is said to be inherent, it has ontological import. Nevertheless, if we are right that *zhe* in Zhu Xi's first remark is a conclusion-indicator, understanding the *zhe* of a thing is an outcome of study and reflection. For elucidation we may consider Zhu Xi's comment on the phrase "extension of knowledge" in the *Great Learning* (*Daxue*):

> If we wish to extend our knowledge to the utmost, we must investigate exhaustively the *li* of things. . . . It is only because we have not exhausted the *li* of all things that our

> knowledge is still incomplete. In the education of the adult, the first step is to instruct the learner, about all things in the world, to proceed from what knowledge he has of *li* [of things], and investigate further until he reaches the limit. After exerting himself in this way for a long time, he will one day achieve a wide and far-reaching penetration [*guantong*]. Consequently, he can apprehend the qualities of things, whether internal or external, the refined or the coarse. (Chan 1963, 89, emended)

Guantong, rendered by Chan as "wide and far-reaching penetration," is an attainment of comprehensive understanding of things through *qiongli*—the exhaustive investigation of the *li* of things. More important, as a metaphor, *guantong*, the "thread that runs through things," intimates the idea that understanding consists in having an insight into the interconnection of all things. This idea of *guantong* echoes Xunzi's notion of *liguan* or *li* as the thread that runs through things, events, and human affairs. Implicit in the idea of *guantong* is a holistic ideal or unifying perspective (Cua 1993). Cheng Yi's famous apothegm *liyi er fenshu*, "*li* is one with diverse manifestations"—an idea he attributed to Zhang Zai's "Western Inscription"—is perhaps a good way of characterizing this Confucian ideal of the good human life (Chan 1963, 550). As a component of *liyi er fenshu, li* is used as a generic term. On the other hand, the *li* in our citation from Zhu Xi is a specific term. This use of *li* as a specific term is clear in Zhu Xi's contrast between *dao* (the holistic, unifying ideal) and *li* in a couple of terse sayings (*Zhuzi yulei*, ch. 6A): (1) "*Dao* is a unifying term (*tongming*), *li* is [a term referring to its] details." (2) "*Dao* is a holistic word (*daozi hongda*); *li* is a word for details (*lizi jingmi*)." As a specific term, *li* has various uses that may be further specified in a particular discursive context. Furthermore, Zhu Xi's remarks suggest that *li* is a generic term functionally equivalent to "reason," which can be contextually specified either as a descriptive-explanatory term or as a normative term. This suggestion has partial support in the modern Chinese notion of *liyou*, meaning "reason," "ground," or "rationale."

Before we go further, a caveat is necessary. Because of their fundamental ethical inclination, for the most part Confucian thinkers, with Xunzi as a possible exception, do not clearly distinguish descriptive, explanatory, and normative uses of terms. Terms such as "father" and "son" are commonly used with implicit normative force. That is, factual statements made in ethical contexts are generally regarded as invested with moral import. Being a father or a son already implies certain obligations. In the classical Confucian language of rectification of names, when a son does not live up to his obligations, the "name" (*ming*) of being a son requires ethical correction. Ideally, correction of misconduct must be accompanied by a transformation of the person's character. In this sense, rectifying names (*zhengming*) is a procedure for rectifying misconduct. This Confucian view has some affinity with that of Arthur Murphy:

> The term "brother," in the statement of a ground of obligation, is not a practically noncommittal term. To be a brother is not just to be a male sibling—it is a privilege, a burden and, whether we like it or not, a commitment. (1965, 109–110)

While the doctrine of the exclusive disjunction of facts and values is questioned, the legitimacy of the distinction in appropriate contexts is acknowledged. In cases where a reasonable Confucian agent is unhappy with the connection of facts and values, he or she may appeal to the distinction. If, say, a father makes an unethical demand, the filial son, who is expected to obey his father's wishes, may in this case quite properly disobey. The virtue of filial piety does not require unconditional obedience. Xunzi points out that there are circumstances in which a son should follow *yi* (rightness), his own sense of what is right, rather than his father's commands—for example, when obedience to the parent's wishes may harm or disgrace the family or require bestial behavior. Accordingly, the Confucian may invoke the distinction between fact and value without adopting the doctrine of a dichotomy between facts and values. At issue is the problematic connection between fact and value. Doubt about the connection may result in divesting the factual content implied in one's moral attitude. The task of a Confucian moral philosopher is not to legislate on the connection between fact and value. The task is to elucidate the contexts in which questions about the connection may appositely arise for moral agents, and to map out possible answers that are consistent with an intelligent adherence to the Confucian ethical tradition.

If *li* is functionally equivalent to "reason," in relevant contexts, we may regard the common Confucian expression of the form "*X zhi li*"—roughly, "the *li* of *X*"—as subject to specification in terms either of "reasons for belief" or "reasons for action." Zhu Xi's remarks on the two basic uses of *li* are amenable to this procedure of explication. "The reason that a thing is what it is" (*soyiran zhi gu*) may be paraphrased as "the reason for believing that such and such a thing exists" and "the norm for what a thing ought to be" (*dangran zhi zhe*) as "the reason for acting in accord with the norm or standard of action." In both cases, we are concerned with the rationale for accepting factual beliefs and norms for conduct, although, as stated earlier, we must not assume the exclusive disjunction of facts and values.

From the Confucian point of view, concern with facts is important because they have implications for conduct. *Dangran zhi zhe* may thus be rendered as rationales for accepting norms or standards of action. Such rationales presuppose an understanding of the idea of Confucian tradition (*daotong*). This living ethical tradition, to borrow Josiah Royce's term, is a "community of interpretation" (Cua 1992b). Its members are united by a sense of common good or well-being informed by knowledge of its cultural history, and they recognize its relevance for dealing with present and future problems. Moreover, like any ethical tradition today (for example, Daoist, Buddhist, Jewish, Christian, or Muslim), the tradition undergoes changes because of reasonable internal and external challenges (Cua 1991).

Since the two basic uses of *li* represent the exercise of reason in the generic sense—that is, as a distinctive capacity of the human mind exemplified in such mental acts as thinking, deliberating, inferring, and judging—rendering *li* as a functional equivalent of "reason" is plausible. A Confucian moral philosopher emphasizes the practical, not the theoretical, exercise of reason. However, this emphasis does not depreciate the importance of theoretical inquiry, especially in contexts where empirical knowledge is needed as a ground for ethical judgment. In *Xunzi*, for example, "accord with evidence" (*fuyan*), along with conceptual clarity and consistency, is an important requirement for participants in ethical argumentation. An ideal of rational coherence (*tonglei*) is presupposed as the basis for ethical justification (Cua 1985, 61–65).

In one passage, Xunzi points out that human mind can either fail (*shili*) or succeed (*zhongli*) in the exercise of reason (Li 1979, book 22, 527). The main obstacle lies in *bi* (mental obscuration, mental blindness). A *bi* is any sort of factor that obstructs the mind's cognitive task. According to Xunzi, whenever we make distinctions among things, our minds are likely to be obscured or blinded (*bi*) by our tendency to attend to one thing rather than another. This is a common human tendency. All distinctions owe their origin to comparisons and analogies among different kinds of things. They are made according to our current purposes and thus are relative to particular contexts of thought and discourse. Distinctions, while useful, are not dichotomies. In *bi*, a person attends exclusively to the significance of one item and disregards that of another. Both common people and philosophers are prone to exaggerate the significance of their favored views of things. For example, Mozi is beset by *bi* in his exclusive attention to utility and neglects the importance of culture (*wen*); Zhuangzi is beset by *bi* in his preoccupation with heaven (*tian*) and his disregard of the importance of human beings and affairs. For Xunzi, the common sources of *bi* are desire and aversion (*yuwu*), distance and proximity (*yuanjin*), breadth and shallowness of knowledge (*bojian*), and past and present (*gujin*).

Since the state of *bi* is contrary to reason (*li*), it is unreasonable to attend to the significance of one thing at the expense of another. Well aware of the distinction between desire and aversion, a person may pursue a current desire without thinking about its possible unwanted or harmful consequences. That person's mind may be said to be beset by *bi*. More generally, humans suffer because of their concern for acquiring benefits and avoiding harm. When they see something beneficial, they often do not consider carefully whether it may lead to harmful consequences. Moreover, when they do consider consequences, they may concentrate only on immediate consequences (*jin*) and fail to attend to distant consequences (*yuan*) —even if they are well aware that distant consequences may be influential and relevant. Or they may be preoccupied with distant consequences and fail to attend to immediate consequences that might be disastrous.

When the mind is in the state of *bi*, reason is not functioning properly. The opposite of *bi* is clarity of mind (*ming*). Xunzi says:

> If a person guides his or her mind with *li* (reason), nourishes it with the view of attaining clarity (*ming*), and does not allow things to upset mental composure, then that person is adequately prepared to resolve perplexities concerning right and wrong. (Cua 1985, ch. 4; Li 1979, book 21, 490)

Li "Binomials" and Principled Interpretation

The previous section provides a guide to understanding the generic sense of *li*, but exploring its concrete significance in particular contexts of discourse is also important. A useful line of inquiry is to ponder some uses of *li* as a component of what can be called "binomials." Since this is largely uncharted territory, the hypothesis concerning the function of *li* binomials is proffered as simply a recommendation.

Formally, the hypothesis may be stated by way of Xunzi's distinction between generic (*gongming*) and specific or differentiating terms (*bieming*): *li* binomials are specific terms for *li* as a single, generic term (Li 1979, book 22, 515–516). A generic term is a formal, general, abstract term amenable to specification by other terms in different discursive contexts. These terms, used in practical or theoretical contexts, may be said to be specific terms in the sense that they specify the significance of the use of a generic term adapted to a current purpose of discourse.

Alternatively, a generic term may have various levels of abstraction differentiated by the use of specific terms. A specific term, in turn, may function as a generic term in a particular discursive context when the current purpose requires such further specification. In the language of concept and conception, a generic term designates a concept that can be used in developing various conceptions. To avoid misunderstanding, the hypothesis about binomials is not intended to cover all the specific terms for *li* as a generic term. The generic sense of *li* can have many specific terms (*bieming*), say, as instantiations of the schema "*X zhi li*" (the *li* of *X*). For example, one can talk about the *li* of love (*ai zhi li*), the *li* of filiality (*xiao zhi li*), the *li* of rites (*li zhi li*), or the *li* of tables or chairs. In all these cases, we are talking about rationales for our factual or normative beliefs about *X*.

In his study of the history of the idea of *li* in Chinese thought, Tang Junyi (1978) uses six binomials. This study, though brilliant, is intricate, and difficult to appreciate if one does not have Tang's encyclopedic knowledge of the texts; but for philosophical scholars who have some knowledge of Chinese thought, it will be an exciting challenge.

Tang proposes that there are six different meanings of *li*, expressed in such binomials as *wenli, mingli, kongli, xingli, shili*, and *wuli*, exemplified in Chinese thought from the pre-Qin to Qing times. Roughly, these pertain to highly articulated conceptions of *li* in different periods of Chinese thought. *Wenli* focuses on the ethical significance of cultural patterns inclusive of social and political orders in the pre-Qin period; *mingli* on the use of "names" or language in quasi-theoretical speculations in the Wei-Jin period, often associated with "dark" or "profound" speculations (*xuanxue*); *kongli* on the Buddhistic notion of *sunyata* or emptiness; *xingli* on nature and human nature in the Song-Ming periods; and *shili* on human affairs in the Qing period.

Instead of stating his methodology, Tang stresses the pivotal role of *li* in Song, Ming, and Qing Confucianism. Equally important is his reminder about the renewed attention to the significance of *li* after the introduction of western philosophy and scientific thought in the late nineteenth century and the early twentieth. He cites various examples of the use of *li* in the Chinese translation of different western concepts. In each case, he uses a binomial. For instance, "reason" was translated as *lixing*, "axiom" as *gongli*, "theorem" as *dingli*, and, notably, "principle" as *yuanli*. More examples are familiar to educated Chinese today. Given that *xue* as a familiar Chinese expression for an academic discipline, "physics" is translated as *wuli xue*, "psychology" as *xinli xue*, and "ethics" as *lunli xue*. Significantly, although "logic" used to be translated by some scholars as *lizhe xue*, this is now rejected by Chinese philosophers. The familiar Chinese term for "logic" today is a transliteration, *luoji*.

Since Tang gives no guide to the basis of his interpretative study of *li*, his use of binomials is possibly influenced by his knowledge of western philosophy and modern science. The use of *li* in the translation of "physics" may be a native linguistic adaptation of *wuli* (the *li* of things), a familiar term in neo-Confucianism (or Song and Ming Confucianism). Especially significant is Tang's example of *yuanli* as a translation of "principle." Among Chinese philosophers today, the use of *lizhe* as "principle" is also quite common.

A Confucian philosopher would ask about the *li* or rationales for Tang's examples. What is the rationale for using *li* in such translation of English terms? If "principle" is translated as *yuanli*, what does *yuanli* mean for an educated Chinese who does not know that *yuanli* is originally a translation of "principle?" Additionally, it is significant to note that "principle" is also commonly translated as *yuanzhe*. Recall our earlier discussion of the use of *zhe* as a conclusion-indicator or a standard for determining what a thing "ought to be," in Zhu Xi's explanation of the meaning of *li*. The translation of "principle" as *yuanzhe* probably results from the influence of the western preoccupation with "laws of nature," "natural law," and "rules for conduct." As a conjecture, these Chinese translations of key terms in western philosophical discourse reflect the influence of western philosophical education. One also wonders whether the acceptance of the translation of *li* as "principle" is an unconscious reading by western sinologists of *li* as *yuanzhe*, which is a standard Chinese translation of "principle."

To avoid misunderstanding, we must note that the hypothesis about binomials does not prejudge the issue of the proper reading of Chinese philosophical texts. Implicit in the hypothesis is that the binomials express distinct notions, although they are specific terms (*bieming*) that distinguish the concrete significance of *li* as a generic term (*gongming*). An alternative hypothesis is to regard these binomials as simply conjunctions of single terms or graphs. Our hypothesis here does not reject this alternative, especially as an approach to the study of ancient Chinese philosophical texts. Since there is no punctuation system, the scholar has to use his or her linguistic intuition in resolving queries about the reading of texts and arriving at a reasoned decision. In *Xunzi*, this alternative approach is plausible in cases of co-occurrence of *li* (rites) and *yi* (rightness). If one views this co-occurrence as a binomial, *liyi*, expressing a single concept, the punctuation problem is resolved. This interpretative method of translation is sometimes used by Burton Watson, who construes the co-occurrence of *li* (rites) and *yi* (rightness) as the bionomial "ritual principles" (Li 1979, book 23; Watson 1963 160). Arguably, a more plausible answer to the problem of co-occurrence of *li* and *yi* in the *Xunzi* is to view it as a conjunction of single graphs (e.g., Chan 1963 130). Many crucial passages are hardly intelligible if we read the co-occurrence of *li* and *yi* as *liyi* (Cua 1989a).

Perhaps the best way to deal with the plausibility of a principled interpretation of *li* is to consider some common binomials in Song-Ming Confucianism. In Wang Yangming's case, we find four: *tianli, daoli, yili*, and *tiaoli*. These are challenging to interpret. They are unintelligible when construed as different sorts of principles (Cua 1982, ch. 2). As compound terms (*jianming*), they function more like focal notions, expressing distinct ideas associated with *li* in different contexts of discourse. *Tianli* is often used to convey the neo-Confucian notion of *ren*, the ideal of the universe as a moral community; *daoli* conveys the dynamic indeterminacy of the ideal *dao* (often used interchangeably with *tianli*); *yili* conveys the rightness or appropriateness of reason to a situation that requires independent judgment or discretion; *tiaoli* conveys an occasional achievement of a temporal, practical order (Cua 1982, ch. 2).

Suppose we adopt the translation of *tianli* as "principle of nature," and *yili* and *daoli* as "moral principle" (Chan 1963). Apart from the questions raised at the beginning of this article, we may ask for a clear statement of the sort of principle, say, implied in *tianli. Tianli* is often used in Song-Ming Confucianism as something (an ethical ideal) obscured (*bi*) by human desires. We do not find any statement comparable to Kant's "principle of the law of nature." To Cheng Hao and Wang Yangming, as an ethical ideal, *tianli* is a matter of personal realization, not a principle to be used for deriving moral rules or standards. Similar remarks apply to the translation of *daoli* and *yili* as "moral principle," which suggests that the Confucians have a principle analogous to Kant's "principle of humanity." The Confucians do have an ideal of dignity or respect for persons, but this pertains to a recognition of meritorious performance rather than a respect for person *qua* person independent of actual conduct (Cua 1978, ch. 7). Translating *yili* as "moral principle" is especially questionable. In Wang Yangming's major works, this focal notion emphasizes reasoned judgment in a problematic, exigent situation—that is, a situation in which no guidance is available from established standards of conduct. In other words, in hard cases of the moral life, we must attend to the merits of particular situations independent of our favored doctrines or beliefs about the proper application of established norms of conduct.

Ideally, disagreement or dispute concerning the current import of the Confucian tradition is subject to criticism. Thus, the notion of *li* has a crucial role in ethical argumentation conceived as a cooperative enterprise in which participants attempt to arrive at an agreeable solution to a problem of common concern. In such a discourse, *li* has both explanatory and justificatory uses in proffering and evaluating normative claims (Cua 1985). Thus the translation of *li* as "reason" or "rationale," in light of its argumentative functions, is more plausible and philosophically significant. Accordingly, we can ask questions amenable to reasoned answers, though these answers are matters of philosophical reconstruction. However, such scholarly efforts in reconstruction also contribute to the development of Confucianism. For example, with respect to *tianli*, we can now ask what the *li* or rationale is for espousing the notion of *tianli*. If *tianli* is alleged to be opposed to the pursuit of human desires as in Song-Ming Confucianism, then one must have some reason for accepting that thesis. This was a momentous issue for Qing Confucianists.

Also, questions can be raised about the *li* of *yili*, or of *daoli*. Even if both binomials convey change and the indeterminacy of natural events and human affairs, one can still ask about the *li* or rationale for characterizing such matters in particular situations falling outside the scope of the application of normal, established standards of conduct. Regardimg *tiaoli*, which clearly expresses an idea of pattern or order, questions about the translation of *li* as "pattern" may be asked, as was suggested at the beginning of this essay. Our questions, say, concerning the nature of pattern or order are best formulated as questions about the *li* or rationales for taking a certain order as normative rather than as merely descriptive.

Although the translation of *li* as "principle" is misleading, the question concerning the role of principles in Confucian ethics or Chinese philosophy is important. Presumably, concern with this question underlies the principled interpretation of *li*. Three different yet complementary ways of exploring answers to this question must be considered. First, one may acknowledge that the occasional use of the concept of principle in contemporary Chinese philosophy or ethics is significant. "Principle" has a role in articulating preceptive principles, that is, "first-personal precepts adopted by particular persons and dependent for their authority entirely upon such persons' loyalty to them" (Aiken 1969, 113). In this sense, principles represent the agent's understanding of the preceptive guidance of Confucian ethics. Second, as statements of belief or theses in argumentative discourse, principles can function as means for internal or external critiques of the established Confucian tradition. These principles are not mere instruments of criticism, but proposals for reconstituting the tradition. As argumentative topics, they are not fixed rules for ethical deliberation. Third, and perhaps most important, the use of the language of principle, in the light of wide intercultural contact today, is an attempt to reformulate the relevance of some basic Confucian concepts of virtue in order to set forth certain ground rules or procedures as preconditions of adjudicating intercultural ethical conflict. (This function of principle is perhaps the point of translating "principle" as *yuanzhe*, since *zhe* can be used as a Chinese translation of "rule" or "procedure" and *yuan* can be used to translate "fundamental" or "essential.") The presumption, though defeasible, is that external challenges to a particular tradition are reasonable only from the internal point of view of the tradition (Cua 1991; 1998, Essay 14).

The preceding uses of the language of principle may be adopted in Confucian discourse and dialogue with other ethical traditions. Notably, the use of "principle" contextually implies that the claims at issue are in some sense fundamental, the *principia*, the originating sources of ethical discourse. (Perhaps this is the motivation for writers who adopt the translation of "principle" as *yuanli*, as *yuan* may be considered a functional equivalent of *principium*.) In other words, the claims formulated in the language of principles express convictions about the foundation or the core of ethical beliefs deemed to be inherent in the ethical tradition. Arguably, tradition is an interpretative concept (Cua 1992a, b; 1998, Essay 12). Principles, as claims about the *principia* of ethical discourse, are defeasible and therefore cannot be considered final or absolute norms. As a focus on *principium*, one can appreciate the translation of "principle" as *yuanli*, for this suggests that the ethical foundation of the tradition provides the point of departure for intellectual discourse.

Conclusion

This essay has presented some aspects of the Chinese conception of reason. As a single generic term, *li* is functionally equivalent to "reason" in the sense of our capacity for thinking, imagining, or reasoning. Obviously, one may ask, with respect to Confucianism, familiar philosophical questions concerning the relationship between reason and experience, reason and passion, and reason and insight. An exploration of these questions will undoubtedly contribute to further understanding and more accurate evaluation of certain pivotal aspects of Chinese philosophy. In another sense, the essay has dealt with the Chinese, Confucian conception of rationality, provided that rationality is not so narrowly conceived as to be exclusive of reasonableness as an intelligent way to cope with exigent, rule-indeterminate situations of human life (Cua 1982, ch. 4). It is hoped that the essay has provide some useful guides for further study.

See also Confucianism: Vision, *Li*: Principle, Pattern, Reason; *Li*: Rites or Propriety; *Liyi fenshu*.

Bibliography

Aiken, Henry D. "On the Concept of a Moral Principle." In *Isenberg Memorial Lecture Series, 1965–1966*. East Lansing: Michigan State University Press, 1969.

Chan, Wing-tsit, "The Evolution of the Neo-Confucian *Li* as Principle." *Tsing Hua Journal of Chinese Studies*, New Series, 4, 1964, pp. 123–149.

———. "Li." In *Zhongkuo zhexue cidian daquan* (Comprehensive Dictionary of Chinese Philosophy), ed. Wei Cheng-t'ung. Taipei: Shuiniu, 1983.

———, trans. *Neo-Confucian Terms Explained: (The Pei-hsi tzu-i) by Ch'en Ch'un, 1159–1223*. New York: Columbia University Press, 1986.

———, trans. *Reflections on Things at Hand: The Neo-Confucian Anthology Compiled by Chu Hsi and Lü Tsu-ch'ien*. New York: Columbia University Press, 1967.

———. trans. *A Source Book in Chinese Philosophy*. Princeton, N.J.: Princeton University Press, 1963.

Collingwood, R. G. *An Essay on Metaphysics*. Oxford: Clarendon, 1962.

Cua, A. S. "Confucian Ethics." In *Encyclopedia of Ethics*, Vol. 1, ed. Laurence Becker. New York: Garland, 1992a: 194–202.

———. *Dimensions of Moral Creativity: Paradigms, Principles, and Ideals*. University Park: Pennsylvania State University Press, 1978.

———. *Ethical Argumentation: A Study in Hsün Tzu's Moral Epistemology*. Honolulu: University of Hawaii Press, 1985.

———. "The Idea of Confucian Tradition." *Review of Metaphysics*, 45, 1992b, pp. 803–840.

———. *Moral Vision and Tradition: Essays in Chinese Ethics*. Washington: Catholic University of America Press, 1998.

———. "The Possibility of Ethical Knowledge: Reflections on a Theme in the *Hsün Tzu*." In *Epistemological Issues in Classical Chinese Philosophy*, ed. Hans Lenk and Gregor Paul. Albany: State University of New York Press, 1993, pp. 159–180.

———. "Practical Causation and Confucian Ethics." *Philosophy East and West*, 25, 1975, pp. 1–10.

———. "The Problem of Conceptual Unity in Hsün Tzu and Li Kou's Solution." *Philosophy East and West*, 39, 1989a, pp. 115–134.

———. "Reasonable Challenges and Preconditions of Adjudication." In *Tradition and Modernity: East-West Philosophic Perspectives*, ed. Eliot Deutsch. Honolulu: University of Hawaii Press, 1991, pp. 279–298.

———. "The Status of Principles in Confucian Ethics." *Journal of Chinese Philosophy*, 16, 1989b, pp. 273–296.
———. *The Unity of Knowledge and Action: A Study in Wang Yang-ming's Moral Psychology*. Honolulu: University of Hawaii Press, 1982.
Fu, Charles, and Wing-tsit Chan, eds. *Guide to Chinese Philosophy*. Boston, Mass.: Hall, 1978.
Fung, Yu-lan. *History of Chinese Philosophy*, 2 vols., trans. Derk Bodde. Princeton, N.J.: Princeton University Press, 1953.
———. *The Spirit of Chinese Philosophy*, trans. E. R. Hughes. London: Routledge and Kegan Paul, 1947.
Graham, A. C. *Disputers of the Tao: Philosophical Argument in Ancient China*. La Salle, Ill.: Open Court, 1989.
———. *Later Mohist Logic, Ethics, and Science*. Hong Kong: Chinese University of Hong Kong Press, 1978.
———. *Two Chinese Philosophers: Ch'eng Ming-tao and Ch'eng Yi-ch'uan*. London: Lund Humphries, 1958.
Kennedy, George, trans. *Aristotle on Rhetoric: A Theory of Civic Discourse—Newly Translated with Introduction, Notes, and Appendixes*. New York: Oxford University Press, 1991.
Knoblock, John. *Xunzi: A Translation and Study of the Complete Works*, Vols. 1–3. Stanford, Calif.: Stanford University Press, 1988, 1990, 1994.
Li, Disheng. *Xunzi jishi* (An Annotated Edition of *Hsün Tzu*). Taipei: Xuesheng, 1979.
Munro, Donald J. *The Concept of Man in Early China*. Stanford, Calif.: Stanford University Press, 1969.
Murphy, Arthur Edward. *The Theory of Practical Reason*. La Salle, Ill.: Open Court, 1965.
Rescher, Nicholas. *Dialectic*. Albany: State University of New York Press, 1977.
Royce, Josiah. *The Problem of Christianity*. Chicago, Ill.: University of Chicago Press, 1969.
Tang, Junyi. *Zhongguo zhexue yuanlun, daolun pian* (Foundations of Chinese Philosophy: Introductory Volume). Taipei: Xuesheng, 1978.
Watson, Burton, trans. *Hsün Tzu: Basic Writings*. New York: Columbia University Press, 1963.
Wei, Zhengtong. *Zhongguo zhexue cidian* (Dictionary of Philosophy). Taipei: Talin, 1981.
Wittenborn, Allen, trans. *Further Reflections on Things at Hand: A Chu Hsi Reader*. Lanham, Md.: University Press of America, 1991.
Zhang, Liwen. *Li*. Taipei: Hanxing, 1994. (Anthology, in Chinese.)
Zhu, Xi. *Learning to Be a Sage*, trans. Daniel K. Gardner. Berkeley: University of California Press, 1990.
———. *Sishu jizhu* (Collected Commentaries on the Four Books). Hong Kong: T'ai-ping, 1980.
———. *Zhuzi yulei* (Classified Conversations of Master Chu), ed. Li Qingde. Taipei: Zhengzhong, 1962.

Religions

Pei-jung Fu

This essay provides a brief introduction to materials for the study of Chinese religions, focusing mainly on the contributions of Confucianism, Daoism, and Buddhism. The idea that Confucianism, Daoism, and Buddhism represent the three major religions of China is widely accepted. However, it was not until the Han dynasty that they gradually emerged as institutionalized religions, and before then—that is, during the fifteen centuries from the Shang to the Han—religious beliefs and practices were no less prevalent in the life and world of the Chinese people.

Religion before the Han

Religious activities of the Chinese people up to the time of the Shang dynasty are believed to have had features similar to those of other primitive societies; for example, traces are found of various beliefs such as fetishism, totemism, and worship of nature gods and the spirits of the dead. Shamanism and divination were also present and influential.

The Shang dynasty (c. 1600–1054 B.C.E.) unified the people both tribally and politically and facilitated the institutionalization of official religious functions. The Shang people had three kinds of deities: Di (god) or Shangdi (God on High), nature gods, and ancestors. Shamanism and divination provided technical functions in sacrificial rituals for these deities. These two "religious arts" continued in later generations. The Shang people had legends and myths describing the creation of the world and the mysterious birth of their rulers, although the significance of these stories has not been easy to grasp, because available sources are limited.

The Shang people regarded sacrificial rituals as a crucial part of life. One relatively recent study found that eighteen different kinds of offerings were made in a single year. The performance of all these rites occupied 110 days out of each year. In the rites, offerings were most frequently made to ancestors. For the Shang, ancestors died but never passed into oblivion. Their spirits survived physical death and maintained the same status, authority, feelings, and pleasures as when they were alive. Moreover, after physical death they acquired a mysterious power that enabled them to bless or curse their descendants. If we inquire into the origin of such a power, one answer directs our attention to Di or Shangdi. Di was thought to be the ultimate foundation of Shang theocracy. Ancestral spirits, after their physical death, would go to heaven and serve Di at his celestial palace. They could also mediate between Di and a ruler in the human world. Since there is a blood relationship between ancestors and their posterity, an ancestor was expected to acknowledge the claims and welfare of descendants. Later, this belief in ancestors' power, fostered by the Confucian emphasis on filial piety as a foundation for the ideal of *ren*, or benevolence (*Analects*, 1.2), became the prominent characteristic of Chinese religion.

After the Zhou dynasty (1045–256 B.C.E.) replaced the Shang, *tian* (heaven) rather than *di* referred to the supreme deity. In a few passages in *Shujing* (*Book of Documents*) and bronze inscriptions, *tian* and *di* seem interchangeable, but the scope and implications of *tian* became distinct from those of *di*. For the Zhou people, heaven, *tian*, was the ruler of both the natural world and the human world. Heaven performed various functions: it was a being that produced and sustained the "myriad things" (*wanwu*) and also a judge that revealed standards of good and evil, decided accordingly, and practiced virtues. A ruler on earth was supposed to exemplify these functions of heaven in addition to human ethical virtues before he could claim the title "son of heaven" (*tianzi*). If a "son of heaven" was virtuous, he deserved recognition as one who had received the "mandate of heaven" (*tianming*), i.e., a command to govern the terrestrial world. If he failed to exercise ethical virtues, the mandate of heaven would be withdrawn, and as a consquence his kingdom would perish.

This idea, prevalent among the Zhou people, led to the development of magnificent rituals devoted to *tian*, and presiding over these rituals was one of the exclusive prerogatives of the "son of heaven." There were three sacrificial rituals in the worship of heaven:

1. *Jiaoji* were held at a suburban site. This sacrifice was performed twice a year, in spring and autumn. The objective was to petition heaven for successful agriculture and good yearly harvests.
2. *Miaoji* were held at a temple. In the course of worshiping ancestral spirits, the "son of heaven" offered a sacrifice to heaven, acknowledging it as as the origin of the "myriad things" on earth.
3. *Fengshan* was an inauguration ritual performed by the "son of heaven." After coming to the throne, the ruler went to Mount Tai and set up a special altar to perform a sacrifice to heaven. This ritual was supposed to be a public announcement that he had received the mandate of heaven.

The Zhou dynasty established highly integrated administrative institutions. *Li* (rites, rules of proper conduct) is a key to understanding Zhou culture and its religion. According to *Shuowen jiezi*, a lexicon of the Eastern Han, the graph *li* means "practice." It was by this practice that men served the gods and attained good fortune. This suggests that *li* originally meant religious affairs, pertaining to human beings' expression of reverence toward and deference to the spirits. Later, the use of *li* was extended to political, social, and ethical matters and became a basic concept of the Chinese Confucian tradition.

The Zhou dynasty constructed the Mingtang ("bright hall"), where Zhou kings offered sacrifices, read political reports, and issued imperial decrees. This practice suggests the theocratic nature of Zhou politics and exerted a strong effect on the attitude of the Chinese people toward religious matters. Down to the Spring and Autumn period (770–476 B.C.E.), it was still widely recognized that the most important state events—even more important than military operations—were sacrificial rituals. Confucius (who lived during the Spring and Autumn period; his dates are 551–479 B.C.E.) took a similar view, as is indicated by his cautious attitude toward three things: "fasting, war, and sickness" (*Analects*, 7.13); "fasting" clearly denotes preparation for offering sacrifices.

Confucius is the important figure who transmitted the old tradition and enlightened later generations. His role as a mediator is confirmed by his attitude toward religious matters. To clarify this point, we will consider three concepts: the mandate of heaven (*tianming*), spirits (*shen*), and *li*.

Mandate of heaven. Originally, the only recipient of the mandate of heaven was the "son of heaven," but later the concept went beyond this narrow political sense: the mandate of heaven became the object of knowledge or fear of a *junzi* (superior man, gentleman) like Confucius. Those who wanted to become *junzi* had to know and fear the "mandate of heaven," and then fulfill their endowed mission by attaining personal perfection and enhancing social harmony. Here, Confucius's notion of the mandate of heaven appears to have no idealistic implications, because whenever he faced such unusual situations as being misunderstood by others, disillusioned by political and social reality, or being in danger of being killed, he never failed to pray to heaven. This suggests that he saw his conduct as conforming to the mandate of heaven and may explain why he "worked toward a goal the realization of which he knew to be hopeless" (*Analects*, 14.38).

Spirits. Confucius is often suspected of having been an agnostic, but this is not plausible for the following reasons. First, Confucius never denied the existence of spirits and ghosts. He praised the "great Yu" because Yu "made offerings to ancestral spirits and gods with the utmost devotion proper to a descendant" (*Analects*, 8.21). Confucius argued that attendants at a sacrificial ritual should be sincere, though not obsequious. Second, we must consider the relevance of *Analects* 6.22, where, when Fan Chi asked about wisdom, Confucius replied: "One must work for what common people justly deserve, and revere the gods and spirits while keeping them at a distance." This may sound like the remark of an agnostic, but on a more persuasive interpretation it is simply an appropriate and reasonable reminder that a ruler, *junzi*, or ordinary persons should not pass their responsibilities on to spiritual beings—practical wisdom depends on assuming one's own responsibilities. In fact, Confucius always expressed sincerity and respect on occasions involving religious rites. His concern was to combine religious faith with educational purposes, that is, to make religion a factor in improving human moral life.

Li: Ritual, rules of proper conduct. In transmitting the tradition of the *li*, Confucius emphasized *ren*, with the intention of awakening people's inner moral self-awareness. Mencius elaborated the concept of *ren* more fully, focusing on the moral sensibility of the human mind and heart (*xin*). Later, the *Doctrine of the Mean* proposed the concept of *cheng* (sincerity), as a realizable ideal that could enable virtuous, enlightened persons to assist in the transformation of heaven, earth, and the "myriad things." Xunzi had a different perspective: he gave the primordial meaning of *li* a humanistic, naturalistic interpretation. In a discussion of sacrifices and rituals, Xunzi maintained that gentlemen (*junzi*) consider rituals an expression of humane and cultural attitudes, while the common people regarded them as having to do with spirits. This view had a strong influence on later intellectuals.

Before the end of the Zhou dynasty, there were another three strands of thought relevant to the later development of Chinese religion: Mohism (philosophical), Daoism, and the *yin-yang* school.

- *Philosophical Mohism.* The Mohists advocated, as human duties, obeying the will of heaven, practicing universal love, and promoting mutual benefit. The religious teachings of Mohism, by contrast with its philosophical aspects, are often regarded as undeserving of serious attention because the Mohists, on the basis of superstitious stories, described ghosts and spirits as affecting the human world; however, religious Mohism always had some believers among the people.
- *Daoism*: The naturalism of the founder of Daoism, Laozi (Lao-tzu), suggests something of pantheism, and in connection with Zhuangzi's ideal of an emancipated human spirit we find many ancient mythical stories. Later, religious Daoists worshiped Laozi and Zhuangzi as their spiritual inspiration. What attracted the later Daoists was an intimation of mysticism, more than the aspect of enlightened wisdom.
- *Yin-yang school*: These thinkers espoused correlations among all things. In the Han dynasty, we find an enormous theological system designed to explain all phenomena and all beings.

Religion since the Han

Beginning with the Han dynasty, there were advocates of three major religions (*sanjiao*) in Chinese religious history. Following is a brief discussion.

1. Confucianism as the state religion. Confucianism acquired the status of an official religion in the Western Han dynasty. During the reign of Emperor Wu (140–87 B.C.E.), Dong Zhongshu strongly urged the official adoption of Confucianism and set aside the "hundred schools" (of thought). This recommendation was approved by Emperor Wu, and subsequently all political and educational operations were organized on the basis of Confucian teachings. Actually, however, the social atmosphere was still dominated by a mechanistic concept of the universe that originated with the *yin-yang* school: the "correspondence between heaven and human beings." According to this view, human beings were capable of fortune-telling and could predict disasters by perceiving signs that appeared in the natural world; even the virtuous or vicious deeds of a ruler and the rise and fall of a state were determined and could be detected before they occurred.

The institutionalization of Confucianism had some adverse effects on it as a body of thought. Vivid philosophical ideas and substantive religious implications degenerated into formalities such as the formulaic expression "three ethical principles and five permanent norms." When Confucianism became a state cult, its functions were confined to the maintenance and regulation of rituals and norms intended to promote social stability. In the Eastern Han period, when books about the occult, omens, or prophetic signs (*chenwei zhi xue*) obtained the enthusiastic support of officials and scholars, Confucius was exolled as the "king without a worldly crown." As a result, he was seen as the head of the state cult and entered the pantheon of deities who received sacrifices authorized by imperial decree. Fabrications, myths, and legends about Confucius's miraculous powers followed.

However, this historical development also had some positive effects: the doctrine of Confucianism, after its being established as the state cult, functioned as a counterbalance limiting excessive imperial power. This is a Chinese version of the concept of "checking" the exercise of political power by imposing ethical standards.

Confucianism, on the basis of its political support, had a great effect not only on Chinese society but also on other religions. Not until the end of the imperial system in the early twentieth century would Confucianism lose its place as the state cult, and some of its religious trappings.

2. Buddhism. Buddhism was introduced to China during the reign of Emperor Ming (57–75 C.E.) of the Eastern Han. By that time, Buddhism had existed for seven centuries in India and had developed into a comprehensive system of doctrines, rituals, precepts, monastic organizations, and canonical texts with explications and discussions of their metaphysical foundation. At least four factors affected the spread of Buddhism in China.

First, the Chinese had their own idea of retribution and regarded the family as the basic unit of "practical causation." For example, the *Yi Zhuan* (or *Yizhuan*, the *Ten Commentaries* on or *Ten Wings* of the *Yijing*) says: "A family that accumulates virtuous deeds will obtain fortune; a family that accumulates vicious deeds will meet disaster." That idea, because it holds the family rather than the individual responsible for the wrongdoing, does not accord with the western individualistic principle of justice. Nor did it accord with Buddhism, in which the individual is the recipient of rewards and punishments: the individual himself is responsible for the *karma* in this life and will receive its retribution in the next life. This factor might have militated against Buddhism; on the other hand, the concept of individual responsibility could also have considerable appeal.

Second, in the Spring and Autumn period, the Chinese already had an idea of the world of the dead, which could be construed as divided into heaven and hell, both essentially extensions of and analogous to the real world. However, it was not clear how rewards for good conduct and punishments for bad conduct were meted out in the other world. Buddhism offered a more systematic explanation, which replaced the original Chinese version.

Third, after its introduction to China, Buddhism used *keyi zhi xue* or "matching concepts" as a means of clarifying ideas. One well-known example is a comparison between the Buddhist concept of *sunyata* (emptiness) and the Daoist concept of *wu* (absence, nonbeing). Ontologically and functionally, these two concepts seemed equivalent, and they offered similar clues about attaining spiritual enlightenment.

Fourth, Buddhism encountered and adjusted itself to the strong Confucian ideas of self-cultivation and participation in social activities, and to the insistence of Confucians such as Mencius and Xunzi that every person could become a sage. In response, Buddhism proposed that all human beings had the virtue of buddhahood, so that all could reach the same enlightenment as Buddha himself. Another way in which Buddhism adjusted to Confucian ideas was by expressing a high valuation of filial piety. For example, the character *xiao* (filial piety) was chosen for naming some Buddhist temples, such as the Guangxiao (Enlarging Filial Piety) Temple.

Buddhism flourished increasingly in Chinese society, eventually establishing the "Ten Sects." Indeed, the term Mahayana Buddhism represents a special achievement of Chinese culture. The widespread influence of Buddhism persuaded many Chinese intellectuals to consider it one of the major Chinese religions.

3. Religious Daoism. Religious Daoism is an indigenous religion of China that appeared during the late Eastern Han dynasty. The fundamental text of its early stage was the *Taiping jing* (*Book of the Grand Peace*). The origin of religious Daoism can be traced back to Confucianism and Mohism, and to pre-Qin Daoistic texts. In the course of its development, Daoism adapted itself to the political aspirations of peasants as well as the popular worship of deities and came to win the broad support of the people.

During the reign of Emperor Shun (126–144 C.E.) of the Eastern Han, Zhang Ling, who had mastered the "Way" at Mount Heming in Sichuan (Szechwan) Province, established Wudoumi *dao*, also called Tianshi *dao*, the sect of the Heavenly Masters. By the introduction of shamanistic arts and rituals, Tianshi *dao* was, evidently, imbued with various religious traditions of minorities in southwestern China. The doctrinal foundation of religious Daoism can also be discerned in the practice, or art, of prophetic signs and in *shenxian fangshu*, magical arts for becoming an immortal, prevalent in the Han dynasty. Tianshi *dao* was merged with Taiping (Grand Peace) *dao* by Kou Qienzhi (365–448) during the Northern Wei dynasty

(386–533), forming a single sect. Through Kou's efforts at integration, the doctrines, canon, and organization of religious Daoism reached maturity.

From its beginning, religious Daoism was characterized by pragmatic and eclectic tendencies. With regard to pragmatism, the three techniques of Daoism—*yao* (cinnabar), *fu* (talisman), and *qi* (vital breath)—were designed to facilitate health and longevity; they were also used to drive away vicious spirits and invoke auspicious deities so as to avert all disasters. Also, in addition to the principal deities, there were other kinds of deities that seem to have arisen from the need to solve problems in daily life.

With regard to eclecticism, we find that Daoism highly esteemed Laozi and Zhuangzi, imported ethical values from Confucianism, and learned the concpet of reincarnation and the other world from Buddhism. The Chuanzhen *dao* (True Purity) sect, which flourished during the Yuan dynasty (1279–1368), proposed a doctrine called "integration of three teachings"—that is, Daoism, Confucianism, and Buddhism. Adherents of the Chuanzhen *dao* were required to learn the *Diamond Sutra* (in Chinese, *Jingang jing*), *Xiaojing* (*Book of Filial Piety*), and *Daodejing*. Religious Daoists also stressed cultivating purity of mind and nourishing the vital breath (*qi*), and they did not neglect the claims of morality.

Conclusion

This survey, focusing on the evolution of Confucianism, Buddhism, and Daoism, has offered an introduction to understanding the general attitude of the Chinese toward religious matters. One may also ask about the rare occurrences of religious conflicts in Chinese history. A plausible explanation might appeal to three considerations. First, no specific religion ever successfully organized nationwide activities for resisting authoritarianism. When faced with the pressure of political authority, religious groups could respond only sporadically. This response helped keep a balance between political authorities and religious groups and helped prevent large-scale conflicts among different religious groups. Second, there are many examples of mutual learning among the major religions. We find similarities in doctrines, rituals, precepts, organizations, myths, and shamanistic arts. In particular, we can find a similar emphasis on Confucian ethical values and a strong leaning toward participation in social life and the community—characteristics that were facilitated by the Confucian education. Third, religious Chinese tend to have a generous, eclectic attitude toward beliefs. The Chinese have rarely taken much interest in the differences among monotheism, polytheism, and pantheism. Generally, they respect age-old religious practices, such as ritual sacrifices to ancestors and deities. However, it is also true that many Chinese believe in the existence of a powerful, supreme ruler, a fair judge of human conduct dispensing rewards for good deeds and punishments for bad deeds.

In addition to the three major religions in China, there are various popular faiths. These popular religious groups have their own distinctive concerns but have generally shared the Confucian focus on ethics and social participation. Originally, Confucianism had the status not so much of a religion as of a philosophy, but it had an immense effect on the formation of religious faith as well as on Chinese ethics. This has contributed to the significance of Chinese religion in world cultural history.

See also Buddhism in China; Confucianism: Classical; Daoism: Classical; Daoism: Neo-Daoism; Daoism: Religious; *Li*: Rites or Propriety.

Bibliography

Ching, Julia. *Confucianism and Christianity*. Tokyo: Koudansha International, 1977.

Fu, Pei-jung. *Rudao tianlun fawei* (An Explication of the Concept of Tian in Early Confucianism and Daoism). Taipei: Xuesheng, 1985.

Wang, Zhixin. *Zhongguo zhongjiao sixiang shi dagang* (An Outline of Chinese Religious Thought). Shanghai: Zhonghua, 1933.

Yang, C. K. "The Functional Relationship between Confucian Thought and Chinese Religion." In *Chinese Thought and Institution*, ed. John K. Fairbank. Chicago, Ill.: University of Chicago Press, 1957.

Yü, Ying-shih. *Zhongguo sixiang de xiantai quanshi* (A Modern Interpretation of the Tradition of Chinese Thought). Taipei: Linking, 1987.

Zhu, Tianshun. *Zhongguo kutai zhongjiao jutan* (A Study of Ancient Chinese Religions). Shanghai: Renmin, 1982.

Ren (Jen): Humanity

Vincent SHEN

Ren (or *jen*, humanity or humaneness) is a fundamental concept of Confucianism and of Confucian sociopolitical ethics. In proposing this concept, Confucius seems to have been responding to conditions of social turmoil. His aim was to revitalize the ancient social order of the *Zhouli* by investing it with a transcendental meaning. *Ren* can be construed as an ethical virtue, as the summation of all ethical virtues, and as a universalizing capacity within human nature—a realization of goodness. The concept of *ren* underwent notable changes in the course of the development of Confucianism throughout Chinese history.

Laying the Transcendental Foundation of Social Order

In pre-Confucian China, social order was instituted by the *Zhouli*, which encompassed both the ideal and the actual aspects of religious, ethical, and political life. *Zhouli* has three essential components: (1) sacrificial ceremonies, (2) social and political institutions, and (3) a code of daily behavior. It represented an ideal image of the cultural tradition as an order imbued with a sense of beauty or harmony. For Confucius, the *Zhouli* exemplified a comprehensive ideal of human life in general, analogous to the concept of *paideia* in ancient Greece.

Confucius's era, the Spring and Autumn period, was a time of political turmoil leading to social disorder; Confucius described it as "without order." In this situation, the *Zhouli* began to lose its meaning as a cultural ideal; and although it retained its its realistic meaning as a code of behavior, compliance with the ceremonial rules governing social, political, and religious life was often just a formality, and the rules themselves presented conflicting requirements. Confucius wanted to restore *Zhouli* by tracing it back to its origins and then basing its ideal meaning on the concept of *ren*.

Confucius believed that social and cultural order, represented by *li* (rites) and *yue* (music), must have a deeper ethical foundation. He once said, "It's *li* they say. It's *li* they say. Are gems and silk all that were meant by *li*? It's *yue* they say. It's *yue* they say. Are bells and drums all that were meant by music?" The *li* and *yue*, as instituted by the duke of Zhou, did not consist merely of an outer, formalistic code of behavior such as the donation and exchange of gems and silk and performances on bells and drums. There seemed to be something more original in human nature from which *li* and *yue* were derived and which they expressed. The original capacity from which *li* could be derived transcendentally was *ren*. That is why Confucius said, "If a human being is deprived of *ren*, how could *li* have anything to do with him? If a human being is deprived of *ren*, how could *yue* have anything to do with him?"

To Confucius, *ren* signified the sensitive interconnection of the inner self, other human beings, nature, and even heaven (*tian*). *Ren* was a manifestation of human subjectivity and "responsibility"—in the basic sense of the ability to respond in and through sincere moral awareness. It also meant the intersubjectivity that supported all social and ethical life. Accordingly, Confucius said that *ren* was not remote from human beings and was not difficult for them to realize. However, *ren* was present in the self only when an individual willed its actualization. With this concept of *ren*, Confucius offered a transcendental foundation for human beings' interaction with nature, society, and heaven.

Confucius did not say much about connecting *ren* with *yi* (rightness, righteousness), although what he did say about *yi* was very significant for Confucian ethics and metaphysics:

> A wise and good man makes *yi* the substance of his being; he carries it out with the ritual order (*li*). He speaks of it with modesty and attains it with sincerity—such a man is a really good and wise man!

Here, *li* is what a wise, good man uses to carry out *yi*, the substance of his own being. *Yi* is also the criterion for distinguishing a good person from a bad or base person. *Yi* is the basis of all moral norms, all moral obligations, our consciousness of them, and the virtue of always acting according to them.

When we come to Mencius, we gain a better appreciation of the connection between *ren* and *yi*. The recently discovered texts in Guodian bamboo slips, probably dating from earlier than 300 B.C.E.—before Mencius's works—may be seen as showing the transition from Confucius to Mencius. In these texts, we find a distinction between *ren* as interior and *yi* as exterior, a distinction similar to that of Gaozi, against which Mencius fought. The bamboo slips texts read:

> Among the hundred things the heaven gives birth to, human beings are the most noble. The way of man either comes out from the interior or enters into him through the exterior. Coming from the interior are humanity (*ren*), royalty, and fidelity; coming from the exterior are knowledge, righteousness (*yi*), and sagehood. Humanity is born from within human beings, whereas righteousness is born from the Way. They were born either from within or from without.

In opposition to the distinction between the *ren* as interior and *yi* as exterior, Mencius proposed his famous theory that both *ren* and *yi* are immanent in human nature and come out of the same dynamics. This was the context of Mencius's theory of the "four beginnings": both *ren* and *yi* come from the inner beginnings of the human mind-heart (*xin*), an inner tendency toward excellence and virtue.

Synthesizing and reorganizing all this, we can conclude that Confucianism derived *yi* (rightness)—a concept representing respect for and proper actions toward others—from *ren*, humanity, which represented interconnections with and responsiveness to others. (For this reason, the present author interprets *ren* as the original "communicative competence" of human beings.) Then, from *yi*, Confucianism would derive the concept of *li* (ritual, rites, proprieties), which represented both ideal harmonious order and actual codes of behavior, political institutions, and religious ceremonies. *Li*, as an overall cultural ideal, meant a graceful order leading to harmony, or harmony imbued with a sense of beauty.

Through this procedure of transcendental derivation, Confucianism did reconstitute and revitalize the ethical and social order and the meaning of human exisitence implied in the *Zhouli*. It should be noted that "transcendental derivation" is not a kind of logical deduction; we do not deduce *yi* from *ren* as we deduce one logical proposition from another. Neither is this derivation the Kantian transcendental deduction through which a cognitive object is constituted. Rather, the "transcendental derivation" of *li* means tracing back and showing forth the possibility of *li* in the original capacity within human subjectivity and intersubjectivity. It is, therefore, an unceasing interplay between manifestation and foundation. On the one hand, there is an order of manifestation, in which we derive or manifest *yi* from *ren* and *li* from *yi*. On the other hand, there is an order of grounding, in which we trace back and thereby ground *li* in *yi*, and *yi* in *ren*. The Confucian model involves interaction back and forth between the order of manifestation and the order of grounding.

Ren as a Virtue and a Universalizing Ability

In Confucianism, an ideal life of harmony has to be realized as a life of virtue. Confucian ethics is an ethics of virtue, not an ethics of obligation as some contemporary neo-Confucians such as Mou Zongsan (Mou Tsung-san) would think. We can discern that Confucian virtue consists of two things: the "excellence of human abilities" and the harmonization of human relationships. Because virtue is given such a high priority, Confucian ethics could certainly accept some considerations of an ethics of obligation and even of utilitarian ethics. But the most important principle is that a life of harmony can be achieved only through exercising one's ability to harmonize human relationship—or, to put this the other way around, by harmonizing human relationships in order to accomplish one's abilities. In addition to *ren* (humaneness), Confucius cherished virtues such as *zhi* (wisdom) and *yong* (bravery). We can interpret *ren* as the excellence of human feeling, *zhi* as the excellence of human intellect, and *yong* as the excellence of the human will.

Virtue, as excellence of human abilities, is never confined within the individual; it always refers to relations with others. When Zizhang asked about a life of *ren*, Confucius answered:

> A man who can carry out five virtues leads a life of *ren*. . . . They are earnestness, considerations for others, trustworthiness, diligence, and generosity. If you are earnest, you will never meet with want of respect. If you are considerate to others, you will win the heart of the people. If you are diligent, you will be successful in your undertakings. If you are generous, you will find plenty of men who are willing to serve you.

It is clear that all these virtues are relational: they refer to others and to reactions from others and are ways of harmonizing human relationships. Notice also that although *ren* includes other virtues—earnestness, consideration for others, trustworthiness, diligence, and generosity—it is not any of them individually. *Ren* is the summation of all other virtues.

Mencius saw *ren, yi, li, zhi*, and *sheng* (sageliness) as the most important virtues. These can be found as early as the Guodian bamboo slips, in the texts *On Five Virtues*:

> *Ren* when formed within is called "virtuous action"; when not formed within is called "action." *Yi* when formed within is called "virtuous action"; when not formed within is called "action." *Li* when formed within is called "virtuous action"; when not formed within is called "action." *Zhi* when formed within is called "virtuous action"; when not formed within is called "action." *Sheng* when formed within is called "virtuous action"; when not formed within is also called "virtuous action." All together there are five

> virtuous actions. When there is a synthesis of all five virtuous actions, it is called virtue. When there is a synthesis of four virtuous actions, it is called excellence. To be excellent is the way of the human, whereas to be virtuous is the way of heaven.

Sheng (sageliness) seems to be higher than *ren* in this text, which distinguishes between virtuous action and mere action, excellence and virtue, the human way and the heavenly way. It appeals to formation and expression from within as the criterion distinguishing virtuous action from mere action, as regards *ren, yi, li,* and *zhi*. By contrast, *sheng* is on the highest level, where that which is within and that which is without are already in harmony. The harmonization of *ren, yi, li*, and *zhi* is called excellence; when these four are synthesized with *sheng*, the harmonization of all five is called virtue. To achieve excellence with *ren, yi, li*, and *zhi* is the human way; to be virtuous in terms of all five virtues, including *sheng*, is the heavenly way.

How virtue is to be formed and expressed from within was made clear in Mencius's theory of the beginnings of human goodness and their ultimate unfolding. Human nature possesses four "beginnings," which are certain senses: (1) sympathizing, (2) yielding to or respecting others, (3) distinguishing right from wrong, (4) shame about doing wrong. These senses can be seen as four natural capacities inclining humans toward goodness. Virtues such as *ren, yi, li*, and *zhi* are to be seen as a fulfillment of these four beginnings. From this perspective, virtue always precedes moral obligation. For example, *yi* as a virtue always precedes *yi* as obedience to moral obligation.

The harmonization of relationships is a process of enlargement from reciprocity to universality. In Confucianism, reciprocity is essential for human relationships. For instance, consider the matter of funeral rites. Zai Wo proposed two arguments against them, one based on the necessity of maintaining social order, the other on a circle of natural processes. But Confucius said that in this matter Zai Wo was without *ren*. Confucius argued as follows. In early childhood we were taken care of by our parents, and it is in response to their love for us that we observe their funeral rites. The form of these ritual practices could be changed according to the demands of the time, but the essence remains: responsiveness or reciprocity in human relationships. *Ren* is this sense of responsiveness or reciprocity within human nature.

However, human relationships are completely fulfilled when they expand from reciprocity to universality, and *ren* is also the human capacity for universalization. When Zi Lu asked how a *junzi*—a paradigmatic individual—behaves, Confucius answered: first, by self-cultivation for the sake of one's dignity; then by self-cultivation for the happiness of others; and finally by self-cultivation for the happiness of all. In other words, he proceeds from responsiveness to universalizability. This means that humankind should behave so as to go beyond the limits of particular relations, toward the level of universality. At the universal level, one treats others with *ren*—regardless of their family, profession, community, race, or country—simply because they are members of humankind. *Ren*, the universalizing capacity within the human being, has been realized as universal love.

Later Development of the Concept of *Ren*

The concept of *ren* was subjected to historical changes in later periods, although we can say that all these changes were merely different versions or interpretations of the original core concept. For the most part, Xunzi focused on the narrow sense of *ren* as benevolence. In the Tang dynasty, Han Yu (768–824) interpreted *ren* as universal love—that is, a concept including love and universality. In the early Song dynasty, Zhou Dunyi (1017–1073) emphasized the aspect of universality in the "way of sagehood." Slightly later, Zhang Zai (1020–1077) returned to *ren* as universal innerconnectedness. He considered *qian* (heaven) as the common father and *kun* (earth) as the common mother of all things; for that reason, we should regard others as our brothers and sisters and regard all things as participating in the same nature with us. Zhang Zai thus gave *ren* a cosmological interpretation.

Zhang had considerable influence on Cheng Hao (1032–1085), who saw all things as penetrated with one *ren*, which gave them their sense of liveliness. In learning, the beginner should first become aware, or self-aware, of the ethical significance of *ren*, so that he can feel his own self sharing the same essence of life with all things. Cheng Hao thought that love belonged to the order of emotions or affections, whereas *ren* belonged to the order of nature, and so he did not agree with Han Yu's interpretation of *ren* as universal love.

For Zhu Xi (1130–1200), *ren* was the "virtue of *xin* or heart-mind" (*xinzhide*) and the "rationale or principle of love" (*aizhili*). As the virtue of *xin, ren* was a sense of vividness, the inner force of living beings, serving as the *xin* of the whole cosmos. Each human being should take this cosmic *xin* as his own *xin* and express it through the four virtues of *ren, yi, li*, and *zhi*. As the principle of love, *ren* was the essence of all loving acts, just as sweetness is the essence of sugar and acidity is the essence of vinegar. But these two aspects were not different from each other. Zhu Xi felt that *ren* integrated both the virtue of *xin* and the principle of love.

In the Ming dynasty, Wang Yangming (1472–1529) interpreted *ren* as the essence of all things, the universal sensibility with which the "great man" could feel as one body with children, animals, plants, and stones. Toward the end of the Qing dynasty, Kang Youwei (1858–1927) interpreted *ren* as a love for all beings resembling oneself, as an attractive force, as "ether," as electricity, and as feeling one with all things. Kang's disciple Tan Sitong (1865–1898) interpreted *ren* as communicability or responsiveness; "ether," electricity, and mental powers were but instruments through which one became responsive to or communicative with others. In responsiveness, all things became equal to one another. Equality was therefore an expression of *ren*, and everything constraining or limiting to it should be broken and destroyed.

Conclusion

From this short historical review, we can say that *ren*, as the founding and core concept of the Confucian system of philosophy, can be interpreted as a sensitive interconnectedness of inner human nature with all other beings, as one virtue among others, as the summation of all virtues, and finally as the universalizing power in human nature and even in all things. Historical developments give us only different interpretations or versions of one or another aspect of the three most important meanings of *ren*.

See also Cheng Hao; Confucianism: Confucius; Confucianism: Ethics; Mencius; Wang Yangming; Zhou Dunyi; Zhu Xi.

Bibliography

Chan, Wing-tsit. "The Evolution of Confucian Concept *Jen*." *Philosophy East and West*, 4, 1955, pp. 295–319.

———, trans. *A Source Book in Chinese Philosophy*. Princeton, N.J.: Princeton University Press, 1963.

Chen, Daqi. *Kongzi xueshuo* (Confucius's Doctrines). Taipei: Zhengzhong, 1964.

Cua, Antonio S. *Dimensions of Moral Creativity: Paradigms, Principles, and Ideals*. University Park: Pennsylvania State University Press, 1978.

———. *Moral Vision and Tradition—Essays in Chinese Ethics*. Washington, D.C.: Catholic University of America Press, 1998.

Fu, Pei-jung. *Rujia zhexue xinlun* (New Treatise on Confucian Philosophy). Taipei: Yeqiang Book Store, 1993.

Hang, Thaddeus. *Das kosmische Ren—Die Begegung von Christentum une Konfuzianismus*. Frankfurt: IKO-Verlag für Interkulturelle Kommunikation, 1993.

Jingmen City Museum, ed. *Guodian chumu zhujian* (Bamboo Slips of the Guodian Chu Tomb). Peking: Wenwu chuban she, 1998.

Liao, Mingchun. "Jingmen Guodian Bamboo Slips and Pre-Chin Confucianism." In *Zhongguo Zhexue* (Chinese Philosophy), 20, 1999, pp. 36–74. (Special Issue on Guodian Bamboo Slips. Liauning: Liauning Education Press. In Chinese.)

Shen, Vincent Tsing-song. *Chuantong di zaisheng* (Rebirth of Tradition). Taipei: Yeqiang, 1991.

———. "A Modern Interpretation of Confucian Hierarchy of Value." In *Chinese Concept of Value—The Humanist Viewpoint*, ed. Vincent Shen. Taipei: Guiguan, 1993. (In Chinese.)

———. "Virtue Ethics and Today's Meaning of Confucian Ethics." *Zhexue Yu Wenhua*, 22(11), pp. 975–992. (In Chinese.)

Tang, Junyi. "Kongzi zhi rendao (The Way of Ren according to Confucius)." In *Zhongguo zhexue yuanlun: Yuandao pian* (Inquiry on Chinese Philosophy: Inquiry on the Tao), Vol. 1. Hong Kong: New Asia Institute, 1973.

Ritualism

Kai-wing CHOW

An entry for "ritualism" in an English-language encyclopedia of Chinese philosophy requires an explanation, because one can hardly find that term in dictionaries or encyclopedias of European philosophy. When the term is used at all in other disciplines, it often refers to a mental disposition: being "ritualistic" as opposed to rational and reflective. Despite this caveat, the term is chosen to represent and translate a Confucian approach to ethics. "Ritualism" in its semantic scope, excluding its negative connotation, overlaps to some degree with this Confucian ethics. This essay will attempt to reinvent the meaning of "ritualism" in the light of Chinese ethics. By ritualism in Chinese thought, two philosophical positions are meant: ritualist ethics (*lijiao*) and a ritualist approach to government (*lizhi*). These two approaches were closely related in Chinese philosophical discourse throughout the long period of Chinese history down to the Qing era (1644–1911).

The Chinese term *li* defies translation. The English word "ritual" is inadequate to suggest its semantic range but does echo the emphasis in *li* on the regulative nature of structured forms of behavior. In the scholarly traditions of modern Europe, "ritual" is often considered an important concept in religion, anthropology, ethnography, sociology, and psychology, but it is also often treated in the same categories as religion, magic, and myth, all of which deal with the nonrational, deep structure of the mind and culture. With few exceptions, e.g., the works of A. S. Cua and Herbert Fingarette, it is seldom a central topic in philosophical treatises on ethics. But in the case of China, *li* has been an extremely important topic in philosophical discourse. *Li* bears on ethics, politics, philosophy, and cosmology.

Li initially began as a term for sacrifices to ancestors and deities. Its meanings expanded later to include the institutionalized, stylized behavior of the nobility, ranging from political institutions such as the "feudal system" (*fengjian*), ceremonies, and rites pertaining to the life cycle to etiquette, decorum, and social demeanor. *Li* has come to mean all patterns of behavior, both stylized and nonstylized, and their symbolism. By extension it also means the dispositions, inclinations, and emotions that were essential for the appreciation and performance of *li*.

The concept and practice of *li* is deeply rooted in religion in ancient China. The character *li* in oracle bones refers to sacrifice. Sacrifices are made to honor ancestors and to seek their help, their advice, and their approval of planned actions. As a method of communicating with ancestors and deities, *li* is central to our understanding of the Chinese notion of the relationship between the human world and the other world. Benjamin Schwartz has remarked that "the orientation to ancestor worship" is omnipresent and "central to the entire development of Chinese civilization." From the Shang dynasty on, ancestor worship was been an important way of legitimizing political authority. Schwartz suggests that "ancestor worship may indeed have contributed to the powerful conception of political order in China." It gave kinship groups a major means for achieving solidarity and organizing lineages.

Although *li* was important to religious Daoism and Buddhism, and Confucianism was not the only intellectual force that shaped the discourse on and the practice of ritual in imperial China, *li* is often associated with Confucianism. There is no doubt that ritual continued to play an important role in the culture of the Eastern Zhou period (722–256 B.C.E). It was Confucius (551–479 B.C.E.), however, who made "ritual and music" (*liyue*) the central approach to moral cultivation and social order.

Confucius

In the Spring and Autumn period (722–481 B.C.E.), a general breakdown of authority and the feudal hierarchy made it all the more important to stress the ordering function of *li*. In Confucius's thinking, one major function of *li* was the "rectification of names" (*zhengming*). To observe *li* was to conduct oneself in accordance with the "name" of one's social station. *Li* not only encodes a hierarchy of social relations but also conveys religious, moral, and aesthetic meanings to the participants. Social order depends on the observance of the rules of behavior by members of society. But for Confucius, these rules were humanized and internalized so that—unlike codified law—they were not regarded as arbitrary or coercive. When all members of society participated in ritual practice, their very presence and participation legitimized the authority and hierarchy embedded in *li*. The acceptance of *li*, and with it authority and hierarchy, resulted from a long process of participation and learning the proper manner of human interaction in the family and community. As Benajmin Schwartz has observed, obedience to public authority has to be learned in the family.

Given Confucius's concern with the breakdown of authority in his time, we can see why, with regard to government, he often stressed the ritualist approach. Given his elitist disposition, Confucius assumed ignorance on the part of a ruler's subjects. These people were not intellectually equipped to learn from historical experience, and hence they were incapable of deliberating on the symbolic meaning and propriety of rituals. For Confucius, the general approach to good government concerned teaching *li* to the subjects. Ritual was crucial to "standardizing" (*qi zhi yi li*) their behavior and cultivating a sense of shame.

Ritualism is only one of the two prongs of Confucius's approach to ethics. Despite its importance, it was subsumed under the higher commitment to love for humanity (*ren*). The apparently conservative and rigid patterns of behavior cultivated through ritual practice are subject to change and criticism from nobles with higher achievements in learning and moral cultivation. Confucius himself argued that the Zhou court owed its ritual institutions to preceding dynasties—the Shang and Xia—clearly indicating his understanding of the need to change the formal aspects of ritual. And the love for humanity is the measure of propriety and the justification for changing traditional practices.

Confucius felt that all members of society should participate in ethical life. But the nobles were expected to serve as exemplars. Confucius set the goal of moral perfection—humanity (*ren*)—so high that he rarely found an example among his contemporaries. The apparently unbridgeable gap between the ideal person of *ren* and the common experience of failing to bring every act in line with ritual propriety created constant tension between the real person and the ideal moral person. It was the effort to align one's conduct with ritual propriety that provided a sure ground for reaching the goal of moral perfection (*ren*). Often Confucius had to clarify the meanings of *ren* in terms of observance of *li*. He said: "To subdue oneself and return to propriety is perfect virtue" (*keji fuli*). It was *li* that set the perimeter for the elusive virtues. Attempts to understand Confucius's idea about "perfect virtue" only from the process and consequence of ritual practice have resulted in some misconceptions about the role of ritual in Confucius's ethics.

The eventual success in "following ritual propriety" (*fuli*) marks a decline in the importance of the role of conscious intellectual effort in making choices for the same daily or recurrent situations. The initial choice became a routine, a habit. Hegel and Max Weber saw this objectified, routinized stage of ethical practice as inferior to European ethics. Confucian ethics was characterized as lacking critical consciousness, or "reflection" in Hegel's term, and hence tension in Weber's analysis. Some scholars of Chinese philosophy reiterate this view, though they cast it in a different light. Some scholars, e.g., Herbert Fingarette, Roger Ames, and David Hall, have noted the importance of ritual in Confucian thought. They view the centrality of ritual as a distinctively Confucian approach to ethics: ethical life without a demand for ethical reflection. In Fingarette's formulation, ritual in Confucian ethics has something like magical power. One takes part in ethical life without effort. But in Confucius's ethics, effortless and even seemingly unconscious compliance is not the beginning of ethical life. It originated in an awareness and an intellectual choice about the good. Confucius's awareness of these two stages of ethical practice is clear in the remark quoted above: "To subdue oneself and return to propriety is perfect virtue" (*keji fuli*). "To subdue" one's desires and misconduct was a subjective, voluntary act of choice, a result of reflection. It involved, first, awareness and acceptance of the judgment regarding the "impropriety" of one's behavior. The desire to change one's behavior in order to conform to the norm was at odds with the person's habitual conduct and disposition. Overcoming one's own desires and habits was extremely difficult. To be able to do so was to take control over oneself, the consequence of having made a moral choice.

Although the will or desire to observe *li* began as an ethical choice of action, through repeated practice and overcoming resistance, a person's behavior would be routinized and dispositions would be cultivated accordingly. As resistance gave way to routinized conformity, one's ethical life required no new effort in making choices. But as Confucius conceded, he himself did not reach the stage where no struggle was required until his last years. Therefore, for Confucius, morality begins as a conscious effort to correct one's conduct through observing ritual propriety. There is always an inner struggle between the person's desire to align himself with ritual propriety and resistance to changing his improper behavior. For Confucius, *li* actually requires both reflection and an ethical life.

The ability to make a good ethical choice depends on one's learning, not on reverential acceptance of tradition. In Confucius's thought, the nobles (*junzi*) were expected to learn ritual broadly and practice it. They were expected to know why they performed a ritual. They could question the specific way a *li* was instituted and performed, as is evidenced by Confucius's decision to use silk instead of hemp for his headgear. But Confucius did not expect subjects to question the *li* taught to them by the moral leaders of a government. The subjects were expected to have an ethical life and the capacity to learn to distinguish right from wrong, but they were not expected to deliberate on the rationales for the existence of and compliance with *li*.

When the good of a specific *li* was no longer understood and appreciated, it would degenerate into formalism and traditionalism. When formalism reigned, there would be only ethical life, without ethical consciousness. This is the situation in which Confucius voiced his objection: "Ritual, ritual! Does it mean no more than presents of jade and silk? Music, music! Does it mean no more than bells and drums?" When ritual was practiced perfunctorily and its moral significance was forgotten, it was perpetuated only as custom, and traditionalism would result. To be sure, this criticism was directed against the nobles, not the subjects.

Xunzi

The ritualist strand of Confucius's ethical thought was further elaborated in the teachings of Xunzi. Of the two major interpreters of the teachings of Confucius—Mencius and Xunzi—Xunzi has been known for his emphasis on the regulative function of *li* in his approach to the sociopolitical order. Whereas Mencius confessed that he knew little about ancient rituals,

Xunzi was esteemed for his knowledge of the theoretical and technical aspects of ancient rites. It is believed that the writings of Xunzi were the major source of the ritual knowledge and classical learning of scholars in the Han dynasty (206 B.C.E.–220 C.E.).

According to Xunzi, *li* is what distinguishes human society. It is the greatest of all rules (*fa*) and the organizing principles of peoples. It regulates one's daily life and interaction with others, channels emotions properly, distinguishes civilized patterns of behavior, and ultimately maintains the political order.

The centrality of ritual in Xunzi's thought rests on two premises derived from his view of the general conditions of human existence. First, the inferior natural ability of humans to survive as solitary individuals in the wild necessitates the formation of groups (*qun*). Only as a group can humans subdue other animals and survive adversities in nature. But human beings are naturally "bad" in the sense of being selfish. They are driven primarily by an inborn urge to seek unrestrained satisfaction of their needs and desires, and this results in conflict and struggle over limited resources. As a group, human beings must cooperate in order to obtain resources for their daily needs. Limited resources necessitate parceling out shares. The allotment or distribution of resources requires compliance with established rules. The allotment of each individual is called *fen* (station), and *fen* are structured in accordance with principles such as kinship, seniority, and sociopolitical status.

A fundamental function of *li* is to distinguish and structure the *fen* of members of society so that all will receive their appropriate amount of resources to fulfill their needs. The distribution of resources or wealth should be based on the degree of importance of the social responsibilities the person assumed toward the maintenance of order. For Xunzi, no disaster was greater than human disorder (*luan*). Those who were able to provide leadership in creating and maintaining order were entitled to larger shares of resources. Thus nobles with responsibilities of government were allotted more and were distinguished from subjects. Only persons with either "abilities" (*neng*) or "virtue" (*de*) would be given official positions and higher status (*guei*). Ritual therefore functioned to regulate both compensation and the hierarchy of social distinctions. For example, while all nobles were expected to make sacrifice to their ancestors, the amount of sacrificial goods and the number of ancestors one could worship varied with rank or status. Those occupying lower positions with less resources were expected and required to spend less on ritual. Ritual was what distinguished the nobles (*junzi*) from commoners (*xiaoren*). The sons and grandsons of the political elite would have to be classified with the commoners if they did not observe ritual requirements. Ritual rules were designed to justify and humanize the allotment by transforming the "bad" nature through human efforts (*huaxing qiwei*). Ritual was the most important means of cultivating virtues such as respect for parents and elders, submission to the authority of the nobles, and compliance with rules and norms of society.

Xunzi defined humanity in terms of humans' ability to organize themselves into differentiated social stations, and their interest in doing so. One meaning of *ming* (name) in Confucius's notion of *zhengming* is what Xunzi called "station." In this sense, *ming* is simply the "name" of the "station." Therefore, in common usage, *mingfen* is often used as a term to denote social station. The teachings about social stations, the crux of Confucian social ethics, are called either *mingjiao* (doctrine of names) or *lijiao* (doctrine of ritual propriety). While *mingjiao* refers to the sum total of social ethics, *lijiao* can be used both in the sense of *mingjiao*, the content of the teachings, and in the sense of an approach, or a teaching method that inculcated the ethical values of Confucianism. We must note, however, that Xunzi's doctrine of *zhengming* is quite complex, as it involves semantic, conceptual, and pragmatic functions.

Political Radicalism of "New Text" Ritualism in the Han Dynasty

The radical dimension and the conservative dimension of ritual for order were both borne out in the development of Confucian thought in the Western and Eastern Han. Xunzi's ethical and political thought was one influential strand in the Western Han. When Xunzi's ritualist approach to sociopolitical order was combined with the "five elements" (*wuxing*) theory of dynastic change in "new text" classicism, the radicalism of the transformative function of ritual became unequivocal.

The demand for change in *li* as a comprehensive restructuring of the Han government was high on the agenda of Confucians in this period. Most traditional commentary on the classics in the Western Han belong to the "new text" school. In the view of one of the most influential Confucians, Dong Zhongshu (c. 179–104 B.C.E.), existing *li*, including institutions, rites, and ceremonies, needed to be changed in order to synchronize and complete the change of dynastic regimes with the cycle of "five elements." The "five elements" overcome one another (*wuxing xiangke*), symbolizing the rise of new dynasties. As a response to the change in the cosmic pattern on which human forms of organization were based, the ruler of a new dynasty was obliged to change his pattern of government accordingly. This political theory called for the abolition of Qin institutions based primarily on legalist principles.

The subversive claims of the "new text" Confucians disappeared in the Eastern Han when Confucianism evolved into the "old text" scholastic tradition, devoted to meticulous study of philology and ancient rituals. Political criticism became muted, and Confucianism was co-opted by the Han government. The classical scholarship of Cheng Xuan (127–200) was representative of this new trend. A formidable scholar of ancient rituals and classcial philology, Cheng developed a new mode of ritualism, which was scholastically and philologically inclined.

Song Neo-Confucian Ritualism and Anti-Buddhism

Rituals continued to be important markers of aristocracy during the period from the Wei-Jin (220–419) through the Tang (618–907). There was, however, no intellectual movement making ritual a cardinal topic of philosophical discourse until the rise of the *daoxue* movement in the early Song. Recent studies have found that ritual had an important role in the theory of self-cultivation and social order. The *daoxue* leaders wrote profusely to relate ritual to their philosophical issues. Cheng Yi (1033–1107) and Zhang Zai (1020–1077) in the Northern Song and Zhu Xi (1130–1200) in the Southern Song wrote about a wide range of rituals pertaining to funerals, burials, mourning, and ancestor worship. The ritualist strand in *daoxue* Confucianism evolved as an intellectual response to a perceived threat from Buddhism and to a weakening of the privileged status of the *daoxue* Confucians in the imperial court as a result of a challenge from new elites entering the bureaucracy through the civil service examination.

Among the *daoxue* leaders in the Northern Song, Zhang Zai was particularly noteworthy for the coherence of his philosophy. He formulated a theory of moral cultivation that put a very high value on ritual. This ritualist ethics informed his much-studied cosmology and ontology. What distinguished Zhang Zai was his strong emphasis on moral education through ritual practice. His view is epitomized in his pedagogical method of "teaching morality through ritual" (*yi li wei jiao*).

To understand Zhang Zai's ethical thought, we need to examine his conception of the relationship between the cosmos and human nature, which form an inseparable and coherent system. According to him, all things are the same in terms of the constituent *qi* (material force) and the incessant process of condensation and dispersion they undergo. But things in the universe do not flow freely and chaotically; they all have their proper positions and sequence of coming into being. Zhang said: "Heaven creates things in an orderly manner, and, after taking shape, things come to have a hierarchical order."

In Zhang's view, human beings are identical with everything else in terms of their cosmic origin and the material that constitutes their bodily form. When they shape as individuals, while retaining the cosmic connection, they differ as a result of their inevitable "imbalance" of "physical constitution" (*qizhi zhi xing*). This partial rupture between man and the cosmos is central to Zhang's moral and social philosophy. It functions as the essential bridge between his seeming egalitarianism derived from cosmology and his defense of social hierarchy. Zhang's main concern was how to explain the myriad differences of the human species in terms of their varying physical constitution, and hence the social hierarchy in terms of the variations in human intelligence and innate abilities. The notion of physical nature is crucial to the *daoxue* Confucians' response to the Buddhist idea that there is no distinction in the cosmic genesis of being. This notion of physical nature made it possible for the *daoxue* Confucians to reconcile ontological egalitarianism and the Confucian doctrine of social hierarchy based on the family.

Human nature instantiated in individual beings was a far cry from its cosmic perfection. Zhang's teaching about the transformation of nature presupposes a belief in the presence of patterns of improper conduct or evil (*e*) in a given person. According to Zhang, man's unbalanced constitution is a necessary but not sufficient condition for the generation of evil because different social environments can prevent or facilitate its development. Under the proper tutelage and government of ancient sages, deviations from the mean were rare. With the disappearance of the sage kings of the golden age, human society had suffered from the loss of their teachings, and hence people failed to conduct themselves properly, succumbing to all sorts of vices. In Zhang's view, therefore, the process by which man acquired a bad character was originally historical. While humans' unbalanced constitution was the necessary precondition, the social environment was the precipitating cause. The beginning of morality in most cases therefore involved the eradication of bad patterns or habits of behavior. The transformation of character by developing good habits would always help humans to act properly, as heaven (*tian*) always acts. Zhang in fact regarded rituals as grounded in heaven's spontaneous, natural course (*li ben tian zhi ziran*). For Zhang, ritual practice was the most effective way to cultivate proper behavior.

Cheng Yi has been credited with contributing the notion of "heavenly principle" (*tianli*), which helped the *daoxue* Confucians counteract the Buddhist teaching of ontological nihilism. Like Zhang Zai, he grounded ritual and the social hierarchy embedded in it in the cosmic order. Cheng Yi often refers to ritual institutions such as the *fengjian* ("feudal") and the *zongfa* (descent-line) systems as grounded in heavenly principles. He wrote extensively on rituals pertaining to the family and lineage, and his views had a great influence on Zhu Xi, whose ritual scholarship was to overshadow Cheng's and Zhang's in the Ming-Qing period.

In neo-Confucian studies, the role of ritual in Zhu Xi's moral philosophy has received the least attention. Its centrality in his moral and social thought is revealed in his remark: "Ritual is the particular manifestation of heavenly principle" (*li zhe tianli zhi jiewen*). Chu interpreted the *ji* (oneself) in the phrase *keji fuli* to mean selfish desires (*siyu*), and *fuli* (return to ritual) to mean realignment with heavenly principles. Since rituals embody heavenly principles (*li ji li*), the phrase simply means "eradicating all selfish desires and returning completely to heavenly principles" (*kejin renyu, fujin tianli*). For Zhu Xi, in order to "discover heavenly principles," one has to pursue learning. The ritualist approach to moral cultivation and its implications for intellectual pursuits became more prominent in Zhu Xi's philosophy in his later years. Not only did he write on rituals for familial practice in the *Family Ritual by Master Zhu*; in his last years he began a comprehensive work of ritual called *Yili jingzhuan tongjie* (*General Exposition of the Book of Etiquette and Decorum and Its Commentaries*). In these and his other writings, Zhu Xi expressed his views on ancient ritual as well as on previous scholarship pertaining to rituals.

Subjectivist Ethics in Late Ming Thought

Confucian ritual in the form of social custom and religious and familial practices continued to have a strong hold on the Chinese. But in philosophical discourse throughout most of the Ming period, ritual was insignificant. Qiu Jun (1420–1495), Huang Zuo (1490–1566), and Lü Kun (1536–1618) were the among the few who found it worthwhile to write about ritual. The rise of WangYangming's philosophy and the various intellectual trends he spawned marked a further decline in interest in ritual as an object of discourse in the latter half of the Ming period. This lack of interest in ritual in philosophical discourse coincided with the growing fluidity of late Ming society and with many attempts to redefine ethics more along the lines of mutual love and care. The ethical life promoted by the ritual of Cheng-Zhu orthodoxy became too rigid and was considered inappropriate for the more fluid social relations of the late Ming. It was no longer possible to live in accordance with social conventions regarding proper behavior. Individuals needed to make decisions and adjustments to changing social conditions as the conventional moral code became inapplicable.

Ethical thought in the late Ming dwelled on the dynamic nature of the mind, underscoring the role of making choices in a person's ethical life. This emphasis on the immediacy and spontaneity of moral experience resulted in radical attempts to reinterpret Confucian ethics. The strong subjectivism inherent in Wang Yangming's teachings was regarded with increasing suspicion and was seen as eroding conventional morality. Gu Xiancheng (1550–1612) and Gao Panlong (1562–1626), leaders of the Donglin Academy, began to restore the important role of ritual in their theory of moral cultivation. They argued that to dwell on the essence of the mind (*benti*) was nothing but empty talk. Discourse about human nature itself did not constitute morality. Ethical consciousness has to be actualized in conduct through moral effort (*gongfu*), and rituals provided the most concrete and reliable ways to cultivate an ethical life. The conquest of China by the Manchu was to propel this ritualist ethics into the main current of thought throughout the early and high Qing period.

Classical Studies, Lineage, and Ritualist Ethics of the Qing Period

A number of factors contributed to the rise of ritualist ethics in the Qing. Most important of all, perhaps, was the profound identity crisis created by the Manchu conquest. For those who refused to serve in the Manchu court, rituals, especially those proscribed by the Ming government, took on cultural and political symbolism. To perform ritual was to retain a sense of self-identity and to repudiate the Manchu regime. And for those who served the Manchus, ritual served to attenuate their sense of guilt, allowing them to compensate for political desertion by displaying cultural allegiance. The *Family Ritual by Master Zhu*, the basis of many Ming official rituals, became a popular work for both scholarly and practical reasons.

As scholars searched for an internal explanation for the collapse of the Ming and the inability of the gentry to mobilize popular support in resisting the Manchu invasion, they began to identify a host of problems: ineffective local government due to overcentralization of power, and demoralization of the gentry by skewed Confucian doctrine as well as by the materialism of urban life. In their efforts to resolve these problems, they converged on ritualism as a fundamental solution. There was a consensus that the dereliction of duties by, and the demoralization of, the gentry were major factors in popular uprisings. Many thinkers maintained that the proponents of syncretism were responsible for eroding the Confucian commitment to social and political values. As a consequence, many scholars reemphasized the boundary between Confucianism and "heterodoxies" such as Buddhism and Daoism. The hostility toward Buddhism and its hybrid form—syncretism—contributed to a rise of purism both in classical scholarship and in ritual studies.

Scholars rejected abstract discussion of human nature for fear of succumbing to the pitfalls of late Ming scholars, who embraced Buddhism and Daoism through ontology. There was a commonly felt need to re-create a distinctive Confucian ethics stressing the cultivation of moral conduct through ritual practice. Ritualism emerged in the Kangxi period as an integral part of the revival of Cheng-Zhu orthodoxy. Many returned to Zhu Xi and Zhang Zai for their ideas about moral cultivation through ritual practice. The rise of ritualism in the Qing was clearly revealed in attempts at reinterpreting Song *daoxue* Confucianism, especially those of Zhang Zai and Zhu Xi from a ritualist perspective. Zhu Xi's ritual scholarship was extensively studied and admired. The *Family Ritual of Master Zhu* and the *Yili jingzhuan tongjie* were in most cases the point of departure for many grand projects on ritual studies undertaken during the reigns of Kangxi and Qianlong.

Ritualist ethics was further strengthened by a strong interest in building lineages. Scholars like Gu Yanwu and Lu Shiyi advocated strengthening kinship bonds as a basic social institution so as to deal with local problems such as urban riots and peasant uprisings. Through their leadership and control over strong lineages, the gentry hoped to reestablish their hegemonic position in local society. They were interested in all the ritual issues pertaining to ancestor worship for the entire lineage. The models of lineages were closely related to ancient rites of ancestor worship, the structure of ancestral halls, and methods of compiling genealogy, which were crucial to delimiting a lineage.

The quest for pure Confucian doctrine and ritual gave rise to a series of attempts to purge non-Confucian elements, textual and conceptual, from the Confucian canon. Confucian purism drove some scholars like Yan Yuan and Li Gong to reject the ritual scholarship of Song *daoxue* Confucians as uncanonical, because of the Buddhist and Daoist influences in these works. Increasingly, scholars came to condemn the ritual and classical scholarship of Song *daoxue* represented by the great synthesis of Zhu Xi. Many argued that the uncontaminated doctrines and rituals could be retrieved only by studying the commentaries of Han scholars such as Cheng Xuan and Xu Shen, which provided philological knowledge of the archaic Chinese in which the classics were written. This belief in the reliability of Han scholarship regarding the classics was to polarize rituals and classical scholarship into two camps—Han versus Song—in the last quarter of the eighteenth century.

"Han learning" classicists continued to study the classics in search of authentic Confucian rituals. Their intellectual endeavor in phonology and philology was motivated by the same commitment to ritualist ethics. Prominent classicists like Dai Zhen and Ruan Yuan were no less committed to a ritualist approach to ethics. Their ritualist ethics was best spelled out in Ling Tingkan's treatises on rituals. This ritualism of the "Han learning" scholars continued to shape Qing thought until the early nineteenth century, when changes in political and social conditions compelled many to seek new solutions outside the ritualist approach.

See also Confucianism: Ethics; *Li*: Rites or Propriety; *Ren*.

Bibliography

Chow, Kai-wing. *The Rise of Confucian Ritualism in Late Imperial China: Ethics, Classics, and Lineage Discourse*. Stanford, Calif.: Stanford University Press, 1994.

———."Ritual, Cosmology, and Ontology: Zhang Zai's (1020–1077) Moral Philosophy and Neo-Confucian Ethics." *Philosophy East and West*, 43(2), 1993, pp. 201–228.

de Bary, William Theodore. "Individualism and Humanitarianism." In *Self and Society in Ming Thought*. New York: Columbia University Press, 1970.

———.*The Message of the Mind in Neo-Confucianism*. New York: Columbia University Press, 1990.

Cua, A. S. "The Concept of *Li* in Confucian Moral Theory." In *Understanding the Chinese Thought: The Philosophical Roots*, ed. Robert E. Allinson. Hong Kong: Oxford University Press, 1989.

———."Dimensions of *Li* (Propriety): Reflections on an Aspect of Hsün Tzu's Ethics." *Philosophy East and West*, 29(4), 1979, pp. 373–394.

———."The Ethical and the Religious Dimensions of *Li*." In *Confucian Spirituality*, ed. Tu Weiming and Mary Evelyn Tucker. New York: Crossroads, 2002.

———. *Ethical Argumentation: A Study in Hsün Tzu's Moral Epistemology*. Honolulu: University of Hawaii Press, 1985. (See chs. 3 and 4.)

———. "*Li* and Moral Justification: A Study in the *Li Chi*." *Philosophy East and West*, 33(1) , 33(1), 1983, pp. 1–16.

Ebrey, Patricia. *Confucianism and Family Rituals in Imperial China: A Social History of Writing about Rites*. Princeton, N.J.: Princeton University Press, 1991.

Elman, Benjamin A. *From Philosophy to Philology: Intellectual and Social Aspects of Change in Late Imperial China*. Cambridge, Mass.: Harvard University Press, 1984.

Fingarette, Herbert. *Confucius: The Secular as Sacred*. New York: Harper Torch, 1972.
Graham, A. C. *Disputers of the Tao: Philosophical Argument in Ancient China*. Lasalle, Ill.: Open Court, 1989.
Hall, David, and Roger Ames. *Thinking through Confucius*. New York: State University of New York Press, 1987.
Qian, Mu. *Zhongguo jin sanbai nian xueshu shi* (History of Chinese Scholarship during the Past Three Centuries). Taipei: Shangwu yinshuguan, 1957.
Roetz, Heiner. *Confucian Ethics of the Axial Age: A Reconstruction under the Aspect of the Breakthrough toward Postconventional Thinking*. New York: State University of New York Press, 1993.
Schwartz, Benjamin. *The World of Thought in Ancient China*. Cambridge, Mass.: Harvard University Press, 1985.
Weber, Max. *The Religion of China*, trans. and ed. Hans H. Gerth. New York: Free Press, 1951.

Ruan Ji (Juan Chi)

Alan K. L. Chan

Ruan Ji (Juan Chi, 210–263 C.E), styled Sizong, claims his place in Chinese history as an outstanding poet and essayist, an expert musician, and above all a chief spokesman for neo-Daoist philosophy during the Wei-Jin era. He is also remembered for his daring defiance of the Confucian orthodoxy at a time when deviation from the norms of tradition could easily be deemed seditious. Together with Xi Kang, he stood at the center of a group of intellectuals—the "seven worthies of the bamboo grove"—who openly rejected conformity in their passionate embrace of Daoist freedom.

To his admirers, Ruan Ji was a tragic hero. Well-versed in both Confucian and Daoist learning, he was evidently a man of principle who took seriously the calling of the literati to bring peace and harmony to the world. He came from a distinguished family and was in a strong position to make a difference in public affairs. The unforgiving realities of third-century Chinese politics, however, soon took their toll on Ruan, who found himself trapped in a world of violence and duplicity.

The year 249 C.E. marked a turning point in the history of the Wei dynasty, when General Sima Yi overpowered his opponents and seized control of the government. Scores of eminent literati were killed at this time and in subsequent purges. Ruan was commissioned under the Sima regime—cherished, in fact, at the highest level for his talents and influence. Unlike his friend Xi Kang, whose refusal to submit to the new government cost him his life, Ruan reluctantly took his place in the halls of power and avoided a violent end. This does not mean that he had betrayed his ideals out of fear, or that survival did not come at a price. Proud and uncompromising, never a consenting partner in the intercourse of power, Ruan had to endure repeated slanders and escaped censure only by finding refuge in an almost constant intoxicated stupor.

Drinking was an important aspect of literati culture. In Ruan's case, wine became a means of self-expression as well as a lifeline for preserving his integrity. According to his biography, he avoided a marriage proposal from the Sima house itself by staying drunk for sixty days. Whether this actually happened, or whether he was an alcoholic, is not the issue; what emerges from this report and others is a portrait of a frustrated but sensitive and ardent thinker, whose outrage at an immoral world finds precise expression in "outrageous" opinions and behavior challenging the legitimacy of established practice. Even at his mother's funeral, Ruan did not stop drinking, an act which patently disregarded the requirements of the ritual and resulted in a call for his banishment from the realm. The full significance of this story comes to light when we learn that Ruan was in fact famous for his filial piety. When his mother died, his grief was so intense that he vomited blood and "wasted away" for a long time.

Although he was unable to escape from the world of power, Ruan took every opportunity to assert his free and indomitable spirit. Rituals and convention were not meant for him, as he announced boldly in response to a charge that he had contravened the rules of propriety in seeing his sister-in-law off on a journey. Disgusted with and disdainful of the shallow men of high society, Ruan would literally "eye" his visitors in different ways—gleaming with pleasure when they were to his taste, or rolling his eyes superciliously when the company was foul. This certainly did not earn him many friends at court. But despite his unyielding distaste for hypocrisy, Ruan never allowed himself to criticize individuals openly by name; this reticence no doubt helped save his neck and earned the admiration of Xi Kang, whose more fiery temperament proved less amenable to the wise counsel of silence.

Ruan Ji left behind a large number of poems and several essays. In an early work, "Discourse on Music" (*Yuelun*), he discusses along Confucian lines the function of music in bringing about harmony. Like most neo-Daoists, Ruan believed that the teachings of Confucius had been distorted by orthodox scholars who, under the banner of Confucianism, sought merely to further their own interests.

From the neo-Daoist perspective, Confucius, like all ancient sages, was concerned only with the *dao*. The classics bring to light but one Daoist truth. Among the classics, the *Yijing, Laozi*, and *Zhuangzi* were seen as offering the best approach to the *dao*, and they came to be known collectively in neo-Daoist circles as the "Three Profound Treatises." Ruan devoted an essay to each of them. The essay on the *Yijing* (*Tong yi lun*) probably dates from his youth, and that on the *Laozi* (*Tong Lao lun*) survives only in fragments, but the *Da zhuang lun* ("Discourse Reaching Fully the *Zhuangzi*") reflects his mature thinking. Equally important is his famous poetic essay, "Biography of Master Great Man" (*Daren xiansheng zhuan*), in which Ruan takes aims at the corrupt ways of the world and evokes an image of Daoist transcendence, a biting contrast that is rendered all the more powerful in light of his own predicament.

Like Xi Kang, Ruan Ji focuses on the concept of naturalness (*ziran*) in his reformulation of Daoist philosophy. Commenting on the *Laozi*, Ruan affirms that the *dao* models itself after *ziran* and gives rise to the transformation of things. Whether it is described as the "great ultimate" (*taiji*) as in the *Yijing*, the "origin" (*yuan*) as in the *Spring and Autumn Annals* (traditionally ascribed to Confucius), or the *dao* as in the *Laozi*, there is no disagreement among the classics that the created order derives ultimately from *ziran*.

Literally meaning what is "of itself so," *ziran* points to a process of self-transformation at the ontological level. "The ten thousand things are born of heaven and earth," as Ruan writes in his essay on the *Zhuangzi*, and "heaven and earth are born of *ziran*." This means that the origins of being need not be traced metaphysically beyond the natural world, as some neo-Daoists have done; indeed, there is nothing beyond it. Rather, the theory of naturalness suggests that the created order originates from the one "vital energy" (*qi*) that pervades the universe. All natural phenomena are constituted by *qi*; thus, according to Ruan, Zhuangzi is surely right when he declares that "the ten thousand things are but one body or substance."

The plenitude of nature reflects the inexhaustible resourcefulness of the *dao*. The diverse phenomena, moreover, conform to constant principles and function in harmony. In his essay on *Zhuangzi*, Ruan details in traditional cosmological terms how the "original *qi*" differentiates into *yin* and *yang*, the two basic forms of vital energy that not only shape but continue to govern the phenomenal world. Male and female, hot and cold, light and darkness, and other *yin-yang* correlates underpin the structural order of the Daoist universe. The movement of the sun and the moon, the regularity of the seasons, the operation of wind and rain, and other natural processes disclose further a dynamic regime of self-regulating change and renewal. In this way, an inherent harmony is found at the heart of *ziran*. This has important ethical implications.

The ideal sage—the person of ultimate attainment (*zhiren*)—embodies naturalness in his or her entire being. This presupposes a profound understanding of what the *Zhuangzi* calls the "equality of things," now explained in terms of the oneness of *qi*. Life and death, fortune and misfortune, and other seemingly unbridgeable divides form but moments in the same continuum of natural transformation. The sage, accordingly, regards them as one. Distinctions, in the sense of discrimination of values, can thus no longer be maintained. Whether this entails a mystical union with nature remains a question. Ruan's poetic eloquence, especially in "Biography of Master Great Man," often appears to rise to mystical heights. Nevertheless, the more important point seems to be that the "great man" recognizes the centrality of tranquillity and emptiness in a life of *ziran*.

Devoid of self-interest, unmoved by riches and power, completely at ease with his own nature and the natural order at large, the sage attains freedom and in this sense transcendence. In contrast, in "Biography of Master Great Man" the learned "gentlemen" of polite society are no better than the lice that dwell in one's pants. Hiding deep in the recesses of tradition, they dare not move against ritual and dread any threat to the status quo. When hungry, they feast parasitically on the people. There is little question that Ruan Ji regarded the teachings of orthodox tradition—the normative "naming" that determines standards and values (*mingjiao*)—as deficient and impinging on naturalness.

More precisely, Ruan's theory of *ziran* envisages an inner spirituality that must be protected against the corrupting influence of power and desire. There is a wholesome sincerity and innocence to natural feelings. When desire for gain is allowed to dominate, however, what is spontaneous mutates into hidden designs and false appearances. For this reason, complete openness ranks high on Ruan's ethical agenda. In a world dominated by small-minded "gentlemen," when sincerity is judged a threat to the establishment, an ethics of naturalness inevitably finds itself engaged in a struggle for freedom.

Later neo-Daoists took great pleasure in recounting how, despite venomous opposition, Ruan Ji persisted in his unorthodox ways. For example, we are told that he frequented a neighbor's place for wine and the company of the neighbor's beautiful wife. When he got drunk, he would fall asleep next to her. Understandably suspicious at first, the husband nonetheless found Ruan completely innocent, honorable, and above reproach in both intention and act. In this, we see how moral character is traced directly to naturalness. Another neighbor had a talented and beautiful daughter who unfortunately died young. Although Ruan did not know the family, he went all the same to her funeral and cried with total abandon. In these and other accounts, the point is always that whereas rituals and taboos stifle the authentic self, naturalness promises liberation and atonement—i.e, being at one with the *dao*—by following *ziran*.

Does not the open display of emotion contradict the emphasis on "emptiness?" An important neo-Daoist doctrine in fact holds that sages do not have feelings. One way of resolving this difficulty is to regard the sages as rare, exceptional beings—ontologically distinct from the rest of humanity and akin to the "immortals" of religious Daoism—whereas mere mortals can aspire only to stay true to their natural feelings.

Not all neo-Daoists, however, subscribed to this view, which implies that sagehood is an inborn quality and not to be reached through self-cultivation. "Emptiness" need not suggest the absence of feeling; rather, it suggests a realized mode of being that is not blinded by emotional and other attachments. Since feeling gives voice to authenticity, and since the sage is described as a man of "ultimate attainment," Ruan Ji may have sided more with this position. Genuine feeling should not be confused with irrational desire; it does not imply selfish pursuits or a lack of Daoist understanding. There is no reason to believe that the sage, responding spontaneously to the nature of things, would behave any differently.

If nature yielded an originally pristine order, how did it come to be infested with an army of "lice?" Ruan Ji could hardly have avoided this issue. In the *Daren xiansheng zhuan*, Ruan provides a radical solution.

At the "beginning," when *yin* and *yang* naturally ran their course, when domination and deceit were yet unknown, all under heaven indeed lived in perfect harmony. There were neither rulers nor ministers, and yet order prevailed of its own accord. When rulership was established, Ruan goes on to say, domination arose; when ministers were appointed, conflict and deceit also came into the world. It is not entirely clear why or how rulership came to be established, but one surmises from the *Da Zhuang lun* that much of the blame lies with subjective discrimination. When natural distinctions (e.g., differences in size) become value markers (big is "better" than small), in other words, desire and domination have already begun to cloud the true picture.

In elevating naturalness above all political institutions, Ruan Ji thus found a place for anarchism in neo-Daoist philosophy. This is not to say that Ruan actively plotted to overthrow the monarchy. On the contrary, most scholars seem to believe that Ruan yearned for a life of splendid isolation that would free him from the pain of worldly involvement. According to this view, whereas in his early writings Ruan accorded a positive place to ritual and music as the work of ancient sages to maintain harmony in the world, in his later years he had become totally disillusioned and thus turned toward escapism. Although this view is not without merit, it does not seem to do full justice to the perceived redemptive significance of *ziran*.

The logic of naturalness recognizes the possibility of renewal; it has little to do with renunciation. From this perspective, the sages of old were all concerned with diminishing the power of desire, so as to enable the people to dwell in quietude and simplicity. The Daoist recluse furnishes a powerful symbol because he abides by *ziran*, not simply because he refuses to have anything to do with the world. Similarly, the "great man" does not aspire to a life of freedom to realize his own ambition; rather, he wants to initiate a process of healing that would revitalize the rule of the *dao*. This would leave little room for escapism in neo-Daoist ethics, if naturalness had any restorative power at all. In this regard, Ruan Ji can indeed be seen as a heroic figure, precisely because he did not resign in defeat.

See also Daoism: Neo-Daoism; Daoism: Religious; Xi Kang.

Bibliography

Balazs, Etienne. "Nihilistic Revolt or Mystical Escapism: Currents of Thought in China during the Third Century A.D." In *Chinese Civilization and Bureaucray*, ed. H. M. Wright.

New Haven, Conn., and London: Yale University Press, 1964, pp. 226–254.

Bauer, Wolfgang. "The Hidden Hero: Creation and Disintegration of the Ideal of Eremitism." In *Individualism and Holism: Studies in Confucian and Taoist Values*, ed. Donald Munro. Ann Arbor: Center for Chinese Studies, University of Michigan, 1985, pp. 157–197.

Chen, Bojun. *Ruan Ji ji jiao-zhu* (Critical Edition of Ruan Ji's Collected Works). Peking: Zhonghua shuju, 1987.

Hartill, Graham, and Wu Fusheng, trans. *Songs of My Heart: The Chinese Lyric Poetry of Ruan Ji*. London: Wellsweep, 1988.

Holzman, David. "Les sept sages de la forêt des bambous et la société de leur temps." *T'oung Pao*, 44, 1956, pp. 317–346.

———. *Poetry and Politics: The Life and Works of Juan Chi (A.D. 210–263)*. Cambridge: Cambridge University Press, 1976.

Mather, Richard. "The Controversy over Conformity and Naturalness during the Six Dynasties." *History of Religions*, 9, 1969–1970, pp. 160–180.

———, trans. *Shih-shuo Hsin-yü: A New Account of Tales of the World*. Minneapolis: University of Minnesota Press, 1976.

Yü, Ying-shih. "Individualism and the Neo-Daoist Movement in Wei-Chin China." In *Individualism and Holism: Studies in Confucian and Taoist Values*, ed. Donald Munro. Ann Arbor: Center for Chinese Studies, University of Michigan, 1985, pp. 121–155.

Science and Technology

Robin D. S. Yates

The definition and the cultural implications of the term "science" have posed serious problems for resolving debates as to whether the Chinese ever had the capability of practicing "science" or the reasons why the Chinese, although apparently more advanced in the traditional sciences and in technology than western peoples for centuries, were not, like their western counterparts, able to make the breakthrough to modern science in the seventeenth century. This latter question was made famous by the late eminent historian of Chinese science and technology Joseph Needham (Jin, Fan, and Liu 1996). Clearly, it was not the Chinese who developed modern science in which mathematical hypotheses about the natural world are tested using a systematic, empirical, and experimental method with the aim of generating theories or discovering general laws. Indeed, the term "science" has a rich intellectual history in the western tradition that cannot be matched in China: there was no word for science in the Chinese classical literary language, and the current word used nowadays, *kexue*, is a neologism. Nathan Sivin (1995) is certainly correct in suggesting that the Chinese had many and various sciences but no overarching science.

As a working definition, it has been proposed that science is a systematic, coherent, ideally abstract and objective discourse about natural phenomena. Yet even this definition, useful as it is as a preliminary guide, has problems when applied to the Chinese scientific tradition. Bodde (1991) notes that there were at least seven different approaches in premodern China to "nature," from the "antagonistic-indifferent" to the "wholly receptive," none of them particularly conducive, in his opinion, to the development of modern science. This makes one wonder how the Chinese were able to achieve any advances at all. Although there was among some, especially Daoist, circles the notion of a "maker of the phenomenal world" (*zaowuzhe*), the Chinese tradition was never characterized by the idea that the phenomenal world was created ex nihilo by a creator deity at the beginning of time and that therefore one goal of scientists was to understand the workings of the cosmos so created in order to gain a better comprehension of that deity. Furthermore, the Chinese never gave human beings a privileged position as being created in the deity's image and as possessing the right or duty to name and therefore control and exploit the rest of creation. Nor was there any idea comparable to Plato's "forms of the ideal" or a radical division between the mind or soul and the body. The *dao* was certainly the origin of all things (*wanwu*), but the *qi* in its multifarious forms, that issued out of the nonbeing of the *dao*, was the constituent of all things—whether the most refined and pure, like the stars in the heavens, or the most turbid and polluted, like man, shards, or fecal matter. Thus "natural phenomena" were for the Chinese not of a different kind from man himself; and as all things partook of the ultimately incomprehensible *dao*, there was a sense that ultimately it was not possible to comprehend the workings of the *dao* completely. There would always be some things that humans, with their limited rational faculties, simply could not understand.

Nor did the Chinese always engage in a thoroughly objective and abstract analysis of phenomena in a systematic or coherent way. Many texts of great scientific and technological interest were composed in the form of jottings (*biji*) and contained little systematic argument; records of ghosts and similar phenomena were set down next to more scientific observations, with the author apparently accepting the validity of both. Even mathematical treatises often have a pronounced practical focus:

> A Chinese mathematician was in the first place a technologist, who was able to solve a variety of practical problems in the fields of chronology and astronomy (if he studied in the Board of Astronomy), or in the fields of financial affairs, taxation, architecture, military problems, and so forth; and this determined his social role. (Libbrecht 1973)

Finally, there is still a lack of analysis concerning how scientific discourses in the Chinese tradition were framed textually and rhetorically. Most efforts to date have gone into excavating the content of scientific and technological texts rather than considering how they structured their arguments and made claims for the scientific truthfulness of their discoveries (but see Martzloff 1997 for modes of reasoning in mathematical treatises).

Categories of Chinese Science

Needham, in his great multivolume opus *Science and Civilisation in China* (1954–), tried to force the Chinese scientific tradition into western scientific categories of the early twentieth century, such as chemistry, botany, and zoology. This interpretation has largely been rejected as an anachronistic and culturally inappropriate model; nevertheless, the model has enabled Needham and his associates to reveal the immense riches of the scientific and technological tradition that still have not been adequately incorporated into general histories of China, whether intellectual, sociological, or cultural. Needham also refuted the "orientalist" assumption that science had been practiced only in the intellectually more advanced Europe and that there was an unbroken chain of scientific evolution from ancient Greece to the contemporary world with little influence from the traditions of other cultures.

To remedy the weaknesses of Needham's categories, over the years Sivin has suggested various lists of self-conscious traditional Chinese sciences. Perhaps the most satisfactory of these is the following:

1. Mathematics (*suan*)
2. Mathematical harmonics (*lü*)
3. Mathematical astronomy (*li, lifa*) and astrology (*tianwen*)
4. Medicine (*yi*) and materia medica (*bencao*)
5. Alchemy, external and internal (*waidan and neidan*)
6. Geomancy or siting (*fengshui*)
7. Physical studies (*wuli*)

Sivin identifies the middle of the Han dynasty (c. first century B.C.E. to second century C.E.) as the period when the basic Chinese sciences were established, the result of an amalgamation of the traditions of various specialists—*yinyang* and five-phase (*wuxing*) or five elements; and *shushu*, "numbers and techniques" —with ideas drawn from Ruist (Confucian) thinkers and the *Book of Change* (*Yijing*). This was the period when the correspondence between heaven, earth, and man came to be accepted as a paradigmatic representation of the natural order of the cosmos, and cosmological discourse became the primary vector of scientific inquiry among the elite.

Some of the sciences recognized at that time were based on an original founding text or canon (*jing*, "classic"), although recent archaeological discoveries have revealed that these texts were derived from previous written sources that were subsequently lost (Harper 1998). Later masters, Sivin and Lloyd (1996) argue, could create their own texts and their own lineages; but there is little evidence that disciples criticized their masters or debated with other experts to advance knowledge, enhance their own prestige, and debunk competing ideas, as in ancient Greece.

The canons were often attributed to a revelation from a deity or a culture hero, such as the "Yellow Thearch" (Huangdi, or Yellow Emperor) in the case of the medicine of systematic correspondence (Porkert 1974; Unschuld), a primarily male elite science; or the "Divine Agriculturalist" (Shen Nong) in the case of pharmacopeia (*bencao*), a tradition that was not really theorized about until the Song, Yuan, and Jin masters. In the case of mathematics, one of the six arts (*liuyi*) in the curriculum taught by Confucius—the text that became the "classic of classics," as Martzloff (1997) puts it—was the *Jiuzhang suanshu* (*Computational Canon in Nine Chapters*), even though other texts of comparable antiquity from the mid-Han dynasty, such as the *Zhou bisuan jing* (*Zhou Dynasty Canon of Gnomonic Computations*; Cullen 1993, 1996) had been compiled by that time.

Inner alchemy traces its descent from two texts attributed to Wei Boyang of the second century C.E., the *Cantong qi* (*Tally to the Yijing*) and the *Guwen longhu jing* (*Old Text Dragon and Tiger Scripture*). Robinet (1995) characterizes texts belonging to this discipline as having:

> (1) a concern for training the mind as much as the body, with the mental aspect usually predominant; (2) a tendency to synthesize various Taoist [Daoist] currents, certain Buddhist speculations, and specific Confucian lines of thought; (3) references to the *Yijing*; and (4) references to chemical procedures.

External alchemy, on the other hand, which was inclined toward producing the elixir from various mineral, vegetable, and animal raw materials that could perpetuate the human life span (achieve immortality), had its origins in the efforts of the "masters of recipes" in the Qin and Han dynasties to create longevity drugs. The earliest text that has survived in this genre is *Baopuzi*, or *The Master Who Embraces Simplicity*, by the southern aristocrat and Daoist Ge Hong (Ware 1966). Ge records that his library contained many earlier texts of this tradition, but they have not survived.

Institutional Setting of Scientific Inquiries

Huff (1993) and others have noted differences between Chinese and European and Arabic scientific traditions with respect to institutional settings of scientific inquiry. Astronomy and judicial astrology were primarily located in the central government administration from Han times on, in the bureau of astronomy. The emperor was responsible for maintaining harmony between the heavens and the terrestrial world; and untoward events—the appearance of comets, retrogression of the planets, solar eclipses, and so on—were interpreted as omens of future calamities, reflecting morally inappropriate behavior by the ruler, his palace entourage, or his high officials. Therefore, specially trained bureaucrats had the obligation to monitor all celestial events carefully, record them, and duly report them to the throne (Schafer 1977; Sun and Kistemaker 1997). This practice resulted in the survival, in Chinese historical sources, of the longest continuous and most complete astronomical records in the world, valuable even today for historians of astronomy trying to determine, for example, the periodicities of comets or the appearance of supernovas in the past.

It was also the responsibility of the emperor to promulgate the lunar-solar calendar, and the acceptance of the emperor's version was tantamount to an acceptance of his legitimacy as the holder of political and ritual power. Circulation of alternative calendars was viewed as a direct threat to the throne and was strictly proscribed. Since the phenomenon of precession led over time to increasing discrepancies between the authorized calendar and actual celestial events, there were many occasions when reforms were attempted, often engendering intense political and ideological conflicts at the court and among amateur astronomers in the population at large (Cullen 1993). Nevertheless, the emperors were not at all averse to calling in and appointing foreign experts, such as Indians or Muslims, who were in possession of more advanced computational techniques than native scholars. The conflict between the Jesuits in the seventeenth century and their traditionalist Confucian rivals was only the last of a long series of debates between expert astronomers at court (Hashimoto 1988).

The *Zhouli* (*Rites of the Zhou*) or *Zhouguan* (*Offices of the Zhou*), one of the three Confucian canons of ritual, suggests that in preimperial times official doctors and shamans were appointed to look after the ruler and members of his palace. It is unclear whether the *Zhouli* records actual practice or represents a later ideal. Probably, some of the medical texts recorded as being held in the Han imperial library were used by members of the palace entourage, but whether they were produced specifically for the members of the court is unknown. In 610, during the Sui dynasty, Chao Yuanfang and others, on the orders of Emperor Yang, compiled the massive fifty-chapter *Zhubing yuanhou fang* (*On the Cause and Course of All Illnesses*), which, as its title indicates, was about the etiology of known diseases; it initiated a practice of imperial sponsorship of medical compendia. Under the Song, as Needham has pointed out, special examinations were held to test physicians on their knowledge, and the state even went so far as to establish pharmacies to issue drugs to the population at large, especially during epidemics. These efforts at state intervention petered out in the Ming, being replaced by private entrepreneurs or benefactors, as Leung (1987) has demonstrated, so that most of the ten thousand or so surviving medical works, including the voluminous case histories (*yi'an*), were produced by individuals in their private capacity.

From Song and Yuan times on, many doctors either were born into families of physicians or took up medical practice to administer to the needs of their parents, relatives, or close friends as an expression of filial piety and moral rectitude when they were prevented by political circumstances from serving as bureaucrats (Hymes 1987). These elite doctors chose to serve their clients out of compassion and benevolence and did not charge for their services, for that would have laid them open to accusations of working for profit. Perhaps they acted in this way because they were in competition with a wide array of lower-class purveyors of medical assistance, including the abhorred six types of "old ladies" (*liupo*), shamans, and others who plied their trade even in the houses of the rich and scholarly elite (Furth 1999).

Generally speaking, however, the sciences in China were not subordinated to a dominant theology, as they were in the European and Islamic worlds (as Sivin and others have shown). Most other sciences, too, were not based at court, nor were they taught at the imperial university or in the private and public academies that flourished from Song times on—again, this was unlike the situation in the west. External alchemy was generally practiced at the margins of society, although some experts, such the great patriarch of Shangqing Daoism, Tao Hongjing (452–536), were sponsored and protected by the throne (Strickmann 1979).

Practitioners of another traditional science, geomancy or siting (*fengshui*), encountered stiff opposition from Confucian scholars, especially in the Song when they were seen as preventing the proper burial of the deceased according to Confucian ritual prescriptions, such as those of Zhu Xi. The state tried to regulate geomantic practices by issuing officially sponsored siting manuals, but fierce competition persisted between those offering services related to when and where to inter the dead; these practitioners included geomancers, Buddhist and Daoist priests, and Confucian scholars, and it cannot be said that the Confucians were ultimately successful in vanquishing their rivals (Ebrey 1991). Bringing in a *fengshui* master to properly align a structure with the *qi* flowing in the environment remained *de rigueur* throughout the later imperial period whether the building was for the living or the dead.

Chinese Attitudes toward Technology

Generally speaking, Chinese literati were encouraged to be generalists and to cultivate themselves morally for the task of administering "all under heaven" on behalf of the emperor (the son of heaven) and to avoid technical specialization and concern with how things actually worked. Still, they were considered responsible for the welfare of the people in their area of jurisdiction, and, as a consequence, many officials promoted agricultural innovations or were obliged to manage projects that required specialized technical knowledge (Bray 1997; Elvin 1973).

Furthermore, the financial health of the empire depended on the payment of agricultural taxes in the form of grain (produced by men) and cloth (produced by women), at least up until the Song dynasty (Bray 1997), and occasionally other manufactured products, such as iron (Hartwell 1962; Wagner 1993) and salt (Yoshida 1993). As a consequence, over the centuries scholars produced a wealth of technical manuals describing actual or recommended agricultural and manufacturing processes, either for the direct benefit of the people or to assist their fellow officials in managing the facilities for production for which they were responsible, or to help the literate elite understand how the objects they used in daily life were actually created (Sung 1996).

The last section of the *Zhouli* now contains the *Records of the Artisans* (*Kaogong ji*), an independent work possibly originating in the state of Qi in northeast China in approximately the fifth century B.C.E. This work has been studied intensively by the Japanese scholar Yosida Mitsukuni (1979) among many others. He argues that the text reveals a notion that the materials needed for human subsistence are five in number (*wucai*). These five—wood, fire, earth, metal, and water—are produced by heaven and they later developed into the concept of the "five phases" (*wuxing*). The text also states:

> Men of wisdom (*zhizhe*) create things and skilful men (*qiaozhe*) inherit and preserve them. This act is generally called *gong* (handicrafts). Therefore we owe the hundred types of handicrafts to sages.

Thus the text proclaims that sages (intellectuals) have the intelligence to create new devices which craftsmen merely reproduce and pass down to later generations. This attitude became characteristic of premodern China. As Sivin observes, there was very little communication between low-class artisans and their social superiors, the literati scholar-bureaucrats; this was unlike the situation in the Royal Society in seventeenth-century England, where scientists rubbed elbows and cooperated with craftsmen who were able to create the instruments the scientists needed to test their hypotheses. Nor were the sciences the basis for professions in China, and there was an unbridgeable gulf between the theoretical discourse of philosophers and intellectuals and those who could test their ideas in practical experiments.

"Heaven has its seasons; Earth has its *qi*; materials have their aesthetic qualities; and craftsmen have their skill" (*Zhouli*). The right timing of or harmonizing with the changing seasons to carry out technical activities was considered essential because different times were conceived to have different qualities. Within the dominant system of correlative cosmology, the five phases were correlated with time (the four seasons) as well as space (the five directions) and numerous other sets of five. In the practical application of this system the sciences and technologies were largely no different from other popular practices that were based on a wide variety of religious proscriptions, involving powerful astral and other deities and hemerological observations (Poo 1998). Raising the central beam in a house or providing acupuncture or moxa therapy on an inappropriate day was thought to be inauspicious and to lead to injury or death.

Technologists and craftsmen also recognized implicitly the fundamental scientific notion that all material objects and phenomena were composed of *qi* (energy, material substance). Thus it was essential to manipulate *qi* in order to build things, each according to its own particular material composition that enabled its inherent aesthetic qualities to be brought out by the skill of the maker. Note, however, that in usual Confucian discourse "skill" was not necessarily a quality that was favored or that a scholar was encouraged to possess. Rather, the term *qiao* (skill) had the pejorative connotation of "craftiness," something not entirely morally upright. Thus skill in handicrafts was by implication opposed to the ethical and moral principles espoused by the intellectual elite.

The attitudes toward technology in the *Records of the Artisans* became embedded in traditional Chinese thinking. The invention of quite a large number of machines was attributed to the ancient sages who were supposed to have ruled China as emperors at the very beginning of time. In addition, there was also a tendency to attribute devices that were developed by anonymous artisans to the scholar-officials who brought the new inventions to the attention of the emperor. For example, the eunuch Cai Lun, after his promotion to take charge of the office responsible for manufacturing instruments and weapons (Shangfang si) in the second century C.E., was said to have invented paper. Paper was invented at least one hundred years or more earlier, as fragments of early paper have been discovered in the forts in the Gobi desert dating from the Western Han. What Cai may have done is to present a better-quality paper made of new materials—tree bark, fragments of hemp, cloth rags, and fishing nets (Tsien 1985). Needless to say, this invention, together with the Tang invention of printing, has had an immense impact on the reproduction and survival of Chinese culture, and may even have had a significant impact on the way humans who adopted the technology think (Goody 1968; Street 1984).

Second, it was relatively common for inventors of machines or introducers of new technologies to be worshiped later on as gods. For instance, Lu Ban, an engineer of the Warring States period who invented a type of siege ladder called a "ladder that flies to the clouds" (*yunti*), became the patron god of carpenters (Ruitenbeek 1993). The possibly legendary Hua Tuo of the Eastern Han dynasty, who is said to have been the first Chinese to perform surgery, became a god of medicine. In the late thirteenth century, a commoner woman, Huang Daopo (Mistress Huang), introduced into the lower Yangtze (Chang jang) valley area from the south a cotton gin for removing seeds, a technique of bowing to untangle the cotton fiber and fluff it up, and the multiple-spindle treadle-operated wheel for spinning thread so that it could be more easily woven into cotton textiles. These innovations helped create an enormously important industry. As a result of her gifts to the population, she was worshipped as a spiritually effective goddess, and many shrines were erected in her honor (Bray 1997).

Needham makes the point, regarding examples such as these, that the Chinese did not just have a cyclical notion of time, which has been the usual interpretation, but they also possessed a notion of technical progress.

It is equally important to dispel the myth that, because the Chinese had a huge population, they had no interest in developing new technologies. The idea is that they could always conscript large numbers of people for, say, construction projects, and so they had no need to develop any labor-saving machines. This is also not true. China was vast in extent, embracing many different ecological zones and microclimates, so in many cases technological progress took the form of devices or techniques that were invented in one small region and then transported and adapted elsewhere. Such transmission was often sponsored by the government; because the emperor and the government were responsible for the people's welfare, because of the extent of bureaucratic control, and because officials were promoted for increasing tax receipts and improving conditions in their local areas. The downside of this process was, of course, that in times of dynastic collapse, "balkanization," or fragmentation of the empire, these technologies ceased to flow from one region to another. On the other hand, dynastic collapse also not infrequently resulted in significant migration, whether forced or free, during which the technologies that people were accustomed to in one region were introduced into another.

Finally, as a result of the notion of links and correlations between the three realms of heaven, earth, and man, the Chinese believed that what happened in one realm of activity could be reproduced in another. Thus, alchemists could reproduce in reaction vessels, modeled on their conceptions of the cosmos, changes in natural substances that took place over long periods of time inside the earth (Needham; Sivin). Nevertheless, alchemists, whether they practiced external or internal alchemy, were not protochemists, as Sivin argues; rather they were seeking personal spiritual transformation.

It will take many more years of research to determine exactly how the sciences and technologies were viewed by the practitioners themselves, their relations to philosophical speculation and religious doctrine, and how they were actually embedded in the ever-changing patterns of Chinese cultural and social practice.

See also *Dao*; *Qi*; *Wuxing*.

Bibliography

Bates, Don, ed. *Knowledge and the Scholarly Medical Traditions*. Cambridge: Cambridge University Press, 1995.

Benedict, Carol. *Bubonic Plague in Nineteenth-Century China*. Stanford, Calif.: Stanford University Press, 1996.

Bennett, Steven J. "Patterns of the Sky and Earth: A Chinese Science of Applied Cosmology." *Chinese Science*, 3, 1978, pp. 1–26.

Bodde, Derk. *Chinese Thought, Science, and Society: The Intellectual and Social Background of Science and Technology in Pre-Modern China*. Honolulu: University of Hawaii Press, 1991.

Bray, Francesca. *Technology and Gender: Fabrics of Power in Late Imperial China*. Berkeley: University of California Press, 1997.

Cullen, Christopher. *Astronomy and Mathematics in Ancient China: The Zhou Bi Suan Jing*. Needham Research Institute Studies, 1. Cambridge: Cambridge University Press, 1996.

———. "Motivations for Scientific Change in Ancient China: Emperor Wu and the Grand Inception Astronomical Reforms of 104 B.C." *Journal of the History of Astronomy*, 24, 1993, pp. 185–203.

Ebrey, Patricia Buckley. *Confucianism and Family Rituals in Imperial China: A Social History of Writing about Rites*. Princeton, N.J.: Princeton University Press, 1991.

Elvin, Mark. *The Pattern of the Chinese Past*. Stanford, Calif.: Stanford University Press, 1973.

Farquhar, Judith. *Knowing Practice: The Clinical Encounter of Chinese Medicine*. Boulder, Colo.: Westview, 1994.

Feuchtwang, Stephan D. R. *An Anthropological Analysis of Chinese Geomancy*. Vientiane, Laos: Vithnaga, 1974.

Furth, Charlotte. *A Flourishing Yin: Gender in China's Medical History, 960–1665*. Berkeley: University of California Press, 1999.

Goody, Jack, ed. *Literacy in Traditional Societies*. Cambridge: Cambridge University Press, 1968.

Graham, A. C. *Later Mohist Logic, Ethics, and Science*. Hong Kong: Chinese University Press; London: School of Oriental and African Studies, 1978.

Harley, J. Brian, and David Woodward. *The History of Cartography*, Vol. 2, Book 2, *Cartography in the Traditional East and Southeast Asian Societies*. Chicago, III.: University of Chicago Press, 1994.

Harper, Donald. *Early Chinese Medical Literature: The Mawangdui Manuscripts*. London and New York: Kegan Paul International, 1998.

Hartwell, Robert M. "A Revolution in the Chinese Iron and Coal Industries during the Northern Song," *Journal of Asian Studies*, 21(2), 1962, pp. 153–162.

Hashimoto, Keizo. *Hsü Kuang-ch'i and Astronomical Reform: The Process of the Chinese Acceptance of Western Astronomy 1629–1635*. Osaka: Kansai University Press, 1988.

Ho, Peng Yoke. *Li, Qi, and Shu: An Introduction to Science and Civilization in China*. Hong Kong: Hong Kong University Press, 1985.

Ho, P. Y., and F. P. Lisowski. *A Brief History of Chinese Medicine*. Singapore: World Scientific, 1997.

Hsu, Elisabeth. *The Transmission of Chinese Medicine*. Cambridge: Cambridge University Press, 1999.

Huff, Toby E. *The Rise of Early Modern Science: Islam, China, and the West*. Cambridge: Cambridge University Press, 1993.

Hymes, Robert P. "Not Quite Gentlemen? Doctors in Sung and Yuan." *Chinese Science*, 8, 1987, pp. 9–76.

Institute of the History of Natural Sciences, Chinese Academy of Sciences, ed. *Ancient China's Technology and Science*. Beijing: Foreign Languages Press, 1983.

Jin, Guantao, Fan Hongye, and Liu Qingfeng. "The Structure of Science and Technology in History: On the Factors Delaying the Development of Science and Technology in China in Comparison with the West since the Seventeenth Century." In *Chinese Studies in the History and Philosophy of Science and Technology*, ed. Fan Dainian and Robert S. Cohen. Dordrecht: Kluwer Academic, 1996. (See Part 1; Part 2: "A Commentary.")

Kalinowski, Marc. *Cosmologie et divination dans la Chine ancienne: Le compendium des cinq agents (Wuxing dayi, VIe siècle)*. Paris: École Française d'Extrême-Orient, 1991.

Kuriyama, Shigehisa. *The Expressiveness of the Body and the Divergence of Greek and Chinese Medicine*. New York: Zone, 1999.

Leung, Angela Ki Che. "Organized Medicine in Ming-Qing China: State and Private Medical Institutions in the Lower Yangzi Region." *Late Imperial China*, 8(1), 1987, pp. 134–166.

Li, Guohao et al., eds. *Explorations in the History of Science and Technology in China*. Shanghai: Shanghai Classics, 1982.

Li, Yan, and Du Shiran. *Chinese Mathematics: A Concise History*, trans. J. N. Crossley and A. W.-C. Lun. Oxford: Clarendon, 1987.

Libbrecht, Ulrich. *Chinese Mathematics in the Thirteenth Century: The Shu-shu Chiu-chang of Ch'in Chiu-shao*. Cambridge: Massachusetts Institute of Technology (MIT) Press, 1973.

Lloyd, G. E. R. *Adversaries and Authorities: Investigations into Ancient Greek and Chinese Science*. Cambridge: Cambridge University Press, 1996.

Lu, Gwei-Djen, and Joseph Needham. *Celestial Lancets: A History and Rationale of Acupuncture and Moxa*. Cambridge: Cambridge University Press, 1980.

Martzloff, Jean-Claude. *A History of Chinese Mathematics*. Berlin: Springer Verlag, 1997.

Nakayama, Shigeru, and Nathan Sivin, eds. *Chinese Science: Explorations of an Ancient Tradition*. Cambridge: Massachusetts Institute of Technology (MIT) Press, 1973.

Needham, Joseph. *Science in Traditional China*. Cambridge, Mass.: Harvard University Press, 1981.

Needham, Joseph et al. *Science and Civilisation in China*. Cambridge: Cambridge University Press, 1954–.

Ni, Maoshing. *The Yellow Emperor's Classic of Medicine: A New Translation of the Neijing Suwen with Commentary*. Boston, Mass., and London: Shambala, 1995.

Poo, Mu-chou. *In Search of Personal Welfare: A View of Ancient Chinese Religion*. Albany: State University of New York Press, 1998.

Porkert, Manfred. *The Theoretical Foundations of Chinese Medicine*. Cambridge: Massachusetts Institute of Technology (MIT) Press, 1974.

Robinet, Isabelle. *Introduction à l'alchimie intérieure taoiste: De l'unité et de la multiplicité*. Paris: Le Cerf, 1995.

———. "Original Contributions of *Neidan* to Taoism and Chinese Thought." In *Taoist Meditation and Longevity Techniques*, ed. Livia Kohn. Ann Arbor: Center for Chinese Studies, University of Michigan, 1989, pp. 297–330.

Ruitenbeek, Klass. *Carpentry and Building in Late Imperial China: A Study of the Fifteenth-Century Carpenter's Manual Lu Ban Jing*. Leiden: Brill, 1993.

Schafer, Edward H. *Pacing the Void: T'ang Approaches to the Stars*. Berkeley: University of California Press, 1977.

Sivin, Nathan. *Chinese Alchemy: Preliminary Studies*. Cambridge, Mass.: Harvard University Press, 1968.

———. *Medicine, Philosophy, and Religion in Ancient China: Researches and Reflections*. Aldershot: Variorum, 1995.

———. "Science and Medicine in Imperial China—The State of the Field." *Journal of Asian Studies*, 47, 1988, pp. 41–90.

———. *Science in Ancient China: Researches and Reflections*. Aldershot: Variorum, 1995.

———. *Traditional Medicine in Contemporary China*. Ann Arbor: University of Michigan Press, 1988.

Street, Brian. *Literacy in Theory and Practice*. Cambridge: Cambridge University Press, 1984.

Strickmann, Michel. "On the Alchemy of T'ao Hung-ching." In *Facets of Taoism: Essays in Chinese Religion*, ed. Holmes Welch and Anna Seidel. New Haven, Conn.: Yale University Press, 1979, 123–192.

Sun, Xiaochun, and Jacob Kistemaker. *The Chinese Sky during the Han: Constellating Stars and Society*. Leiden: Brill, 1997.

Sung, Ying-hsing (Song Yingxing). *T'ien-kung k'ai-wu: Chinese Technology in the Seventeenth Century*, trans. E-tu Zen Sun and Shiou-Chuan Sun. University Park: Pennsylvania State University Press, 1966.

Tsien, Tsuen-hsuin. *Science and Civilisation in China*, Vol. 5, *Chemistry and Chemical Technology*. Part 1, "Paper and Printing." Cambridge: Cambridge University Press, 1985.

Unschuld, Paul U. *Chinese Medicine*, trans. Nigel Wiseman. Brookline, Mass.: Paradigm, 1998.

———. *Medical Ethics in Imperial China: A Study in Historical Anthropology*. Berkeley: University of California Press, 1979.

———. *Medicine in China: Historical Artifacts and Images*. Munich, London, and New York, 2000.

———. *Medicine in China: A History of Ideas*. Berkeley: University of California Press, 1985.

———. *Medicine in China: A History of Pharmaceutics*. Berkeley: University of California Press, 1986.

———, trans. *Nan-Ching: The Classic of Difficult Issues*. Berkeley: University of California Press, 1986.

Wagner, Donald B. *Iron and Steel in Ancient China*. Leiden: Brill, 1993.

Wardy, Robert. *Aristotle in China: Language, Categories, and Translation*. Needham Research Institute Studies, 2. Cambridge: Cambridge University Press, 2000.

Ware, James, trans. *Alchemy, Medicine, and Religion in the China of* A.D. *320: The Nei P'ien of Ko Hung (Pao-p'u tzu)*. Cambridge: Massachusetts Institute of Technology (MIT) Press, 1966.

Yoshida, Tora. *Salt Production Techniques in Ancient China: The Aobo Tu*, trans. and rev. Hans Ulrich Vogel. Leiden: Brill, 1993.

Yosida, Mitsukuni. "The Chinese Concept of Technology: A Historical Approach." *Acta Asiatica*, 36, 1979, pp. 49–66.

Scientism and Humanism

Shiping Hua

One way of characterizing philosophical starting points is the distinction between two perspectives: the nonhumanistic (sometimes misleadingly called "scientific") and the humanistic. In ancient Greece, Plato (c. 427–347 B.C.E.) may be said to have advocated a "nonscientific" approach by relying on cultivation of proper behavior by philosopher-kings, whereas Aristotle (384–322 B.C.E.) advocated law instead of relying on the goodness of human nature. In modern times, John Locke (1632–1704) tried to introduce principles of physical science into social science, whereas Jean-Jacques Rousseau (1712–1778) inspired romanticism by emphasizing sentiments and emotions.

Tension between the "scientific" and the "humanistic" also exists within individuals. Max Weber (1864–1920) discerns a fundamental tension between scientific "instrumental rationality" and humanistic "value rationality." There is also a "scientific" and a "humanistic" Karl Marx (1818–1883); those who see Marx as scientific and those who see him as humanistic both find support in his writings. Similarly, Immanuel Kant (1724–1804) is regarded as a highly influential figure in the western humanistic tradition and also as one of the main sources of modern positivism.

Scientism: China and the West

At the turn of the twenty-first century few philosophers or scientists were confident that they had a deep knowledge of the nature of science. Although natural and social scientists presumably apply some principles or methods of science, the limitations of these approaches are widely acknowledged. Therefore, the term "scientism" has to be construed very broadly, in the sense that the objective world is to be understood by way of "science," however defined, which provides the best method for resolving all human problems. This attitude toward the use of science may be found in many places in the world; in China, it assumes forms that differ from their western counterparts—a situation that has significant intellectual and political implications.

Western scholars tend to regard scientism as an exaggeration of Baconian science, i.e., empirical scientism, but Chinese forms of scientism are broader. In addition to empirical scientism, we find Marxist scientism, an economic reductionist interpretation by Friedrich Engels (1820–1895) and the Russian Marxists, and a version of technological determinism.

Marxist scientism, a type of materialistic scientism, belongs to metaphysical discourse because it emphasizes matter and neglects ideas. Metaphysics is an attempt to characterize existence or reality as a whole, instead of characterizing parts or aspects as in the natural sciences. Materialism and idealism are examples of metaphysics in this sense. Since metaphysics was excluded from western social sciences at the turn of the twentieth century, "materialism" has lost its tie with science. Therefore, there has been little materialistic scientism in western academic discussions.

Such is not the case in China. Although China has its own tradition of science, modern science is by and large an imported idea. With regard to philosophy of science, the Baconian spirit has never occupied the center of China's intellectual arena as happened in the west, although Chinese natural scientists have always resorted to it when doing experiments. In contrast, materialism, which is often elevated to the level of science, has had a strong voice throughout China's modern and contemporary history. Marxist scientism is the major version of this materialistic scientism. Although Marxist scientism is said to depart from metaphysics in the sense that it is dialectical, they are similar in the sense that both focus on matter and ideas in argumentation. Therefore, materialistic scientism not only was a main version of scientism during the first half of the twentieth century but is still part of the Chinese "enlightenment" today.

Empirical scientism, as inspired by Bacon and modern science, pays hardly any attention to ontological questions. It is largely modeled on the experimental tradition in western physical science. However, there seems to be a political connection between empirical scientism and political liberalism or pluralism. This may partly explain the lack of enthusiasm for empirical scientism in China as compared with materialistic scientism. First, the point of departure of empirical scientism is not monistic as materialistic scientism is, because it does not care about the ultimate reality of the universe. Consequently, it is more flexible. This view, accordingly, seems "democratic" and "pluralistic." Second, while Marxist scientism is presumably deductive, empirical scientism is more cautious, relying on rigorous testing. Historically, Chinese intellectuals who believed in empirical scientism were likely to be liberals. (The majority of western mainstream social scientists are also liberals, partly because their research methods are more often than not in the Baconian tradition.)

According to Marxist scientism, all events are manifestations of the fundamental nature of matter, and one fundamental science can grasp the nature of the material world and therefore can explain all these manifestations. This view is not in the Baconian experimental tradition. Specifically, it has two origins in western philosophy: (1) dialectics in methodology, which emphasizes the changing nature of the world and the concept of contradiction; (2) the materialistic tradition in ontology, which claims that the ultimate origin of the world is objective rather than spiritual or subjective (human).

There is an intellectual link between Marxist scientism and state socialism. Materialism can be described as axiomatic and monistic. That fits state socialism, in which only one source of power is needed. Materialistic scientism lacks the pluralism and fallibility that are embodied in empirical scientism. In addition, some crucial theories in Marxist scientism—e.g., theses on the demise of capitalism and the success of communism—do not admit of proof. Such theses are largely deduced from monistic materialistic assumptions. In addition, Marxist dialectics stresses contradiction, which can provide intellectual support for the political concept of class struggle.

The Chinese version of scientism or technological determinism is largely generic. Compared with empirical scientism and Marxist scientism, it is less consistent theoretically. This technological determinism often involves a misconception, equating matter with technology in the way that ideas are equated with human initiatives. Usually it starts from a materialistic premise but reaches a technologically deterministic conclusion that is not logically connected with the philosophical starting point. This version of scientism is identified as a Chinese version because it coincides with some key characteristics of the Chinese scientific tradition.

China's scientific development in ancient times was characterized by (1) politicization, (2) an emphasis on technology, and (3) neglect of comprehensive theories. "Politicization" refers to the fact that science was very much influenced by politics. For instance, the development of astrology in ancient China was politically influenced because the formation and movements of the stars were believed to explain the mandate of the emperor. As a result, the development of Chinese science followed a zigzag path rather than a linear progression.

The consequent technological attitude toward science in ancient China is exemplified in its focus on aspects of technology that were considered useful for the maintenance and advancement of the political system. China's four important scientific discoveries—paper, the compass, typographic printing, and gunpowder—are examples. All four were closely connected with the desire of the central government to control the vast land; none of them was inspired by a concern for the people's welfare. Another characteristic of China's scientific tradition is not valuing the pursuit of knowledge for its own sake; the acquisition of knowledge is encouraged because it can provide practical solutions to problems of daily human life.

Humanism: China and the West

Humanism, like modern science, emerged from the western Enlightenment tradition. Although most thinkers in the Enlightenment were concerned with the problem of liberty, they looked at it from different perspectives: some were more "scientific," others more humanistic.

Three types of humanism in western thought had a major impact on the Chinese "enlightenment" in the twentieth century. The first type relies on human intuitions as a means for discovering truth; this type is represented in the works of Rudolf Eucken (1846–1926) and Henri Bergson (1859–1941). This approach has some similarities with traditional Chinese thought as embodied in the works of Mencius and Wang Yangming. Chinese "intuitionism" could also provide philosophical support to religion, such as Christianity.

The second type of western humanism relies on analysis of human language to discover truths about human beings; this type is represented by postmodernists such as Jacques Derrida (b. 1930). Postmodernism was mainly developed in the twentieth century and has no traditional Chinese counterpart. It denies that positivism is the only legitimate approach to truth, and it is quite pessimistic about human understanding of the world, or even self-understanding.

The third type is Marxism. Although Marxism has both scientific and humanistic aspects, people read Marx differently. One reading is economic reductionism; the other is more flexible regarding the relations of base and superstructure and recognizes many ideas in the writings of the young Marx. Through Mark's earlier works, "humanism" and "alienation" became new paradigms for western Marxists, replacing the old slogans: "revolution," "class struggle," and "dictatorship of the proletariat." The wide range of figures who interpreted Marx in a humanistic light include Antonio Gramsci (1891–1937), the members of the Frankfurt school, and Louis Althusser (1918–1990). This flexible approach has political implications primarily for the question whether the worldwide collapse of capitalism and the realization of communism are inevitable.

Confucianism, with its numerous modern modifications, is an indigenous Chinese humanism. It may be contrasted with Chinese scientism, the technological determinism that focuses on developing productive forces. Confucianism is noted for its humane ethical concerns and for relying on experience and practice to understand the world. A relatively recent example is Liang Shuming's thesis that nature, including mountains and rivers, has a life of its own, like human beings.

Probably, a humanistic approach emerges when the "scientific" approach is seen as failing to answer important questions or failing to address human concerns; but humanism that disregards the utility of science and technology in resolving human problems is equally one-sided. Therefore, some thinkers endorse both approaches and, as a result, are likely to feel the tension noted earlier. The Chinese philosopher Wang Guowei (1877–1927) summarized this tension as follows: things that can be loved cannot be believed (humanistic), and things that can be believed cannot be loved (scientific).

Development of Chinese Scientism and Humanism in the Twentieth Century

Although China's first contact with modern science came as early as the seventeenth century, its intense enthusiasm for modern science began after its defeat by the British in the Opium War of 1840, when Chinese intellectuals saw that modern western weaponry was superior to Chinese swords and spears. At this stage, enthusiasm for western science was largely confined to its contribution to technology. China imported a great deal of modern weaponry and, using western technology, built many modern plants to make advanced guns and munitions.

A second stage in China's endorsement of science followed another humiliating defeat: in 1895, the Chinese Beiyang Fleet, even though it was modeled on western navies, was destroyed in Bohai Bay by a smaller Japanese fleet. This exposed a connection between the weakness of the Chinese navy and the corruption of the Qing dynasty, and Chinese intellectuals realized that modern technology alone could not save China—modernization could not be accomplished without "scientific" changes in the political system. Intellectuals like Kang Youwei, Liang Qichao, and Tan Sitong began to urge Emperor Guang Xu to reform.

Nevertheless, the "hundred days" reform of 1898 failed, although the reformers were supported by Emperor Guang Xu and had adopted some measures derived from western countries and Japan. This brought a new realization that the Chinese political system could not be changed without a change in people's consciousness—a realization that led directly to broad attacks on Confucianism and to a new worship of science. The empress dowager and conservatives succeeded in suppressing the reformers, but the trend toward enlightenment continued. The collapse of the Qing dynasty in 1911 paved the way for a new period of enlightenment characterized by iconoclasm and scientism.

Enthusiasm for science does not necessarily equal understanding of it; often, such enthusiasm is more accurately described as an uncritical endorsement of scientism. That was true in China, where the intellectuals who advocated science had no real understanding of the nature of the scientific enterprise. Three kinds of scientism can be identified during this period: empirical scientism, represented by Hu Shi (Hu Shih, 1891–1962); Marxist scientism, the major materialistic scientism, represented by Chen Duxiu (1897–1942); and the technological determinism propounded by Wu Qihui.

To be sure, opposition to these developments occurred as early as in the first stage and were always based on some "humanistic" ground. In the first stage, opponents of reform relied largely on the Confucian classics, however interpreted. The conservatives believed that only people of loyalty and sincerity could subdue foreigners and only people of propriety and righteousness could strengthen themselves.

During the second and the third stages, opponents of the introduction of western science as an ideology not only continued to rely on Confucianism but also began to borrow western ideas. During the debate over science in 1923 and throughout the 1920s, the "metaphysicians"—a term applied to those who were against science as represented by Carsun Chang—borrowed from Bergson and Eucken.

It is important to note the link between materialistic scientism and metaphysics. For instance, although the debate on science in the 1920s was called *kexuan zhizheng*, a polemic between science and metaphysics, materialistic scientism actually belonged to metaphysics as well as to science. Therefore, the term *xuan xue gui*, "metaphysicians," should be considered a sort of nickname rather than a strict academic term. Otherwise, metaphysicians would also include some figures who advocated science—materialistic scientists such as Chen Duxiu.

In any case, the advocates of science won this debate, and thereafter nobody dared challenge "science." During a debate concerning the nature of Chinese society that started in the late 1920s and lasted well into the late 1930s, the application of Marxist scientism or historical materialism was almost completely accepted. Although the two sides in that debate disagreed about whether China was then more feudal or more capitalist, both were actually functioning within the same Marxist discourse, historical materialism. Some intellectuals who considered China feudalistic urged the Chinese people to reject both feudalism and imperialism; representatives of this view, associated with the leftist magazine *New Trends* (*Xinsichao*), included Wang Xuewen, Pan Tongzhou, and Wu Liping. Those who argued that China was capitalist, and that efforts should therefore be made against capitalism, were represented by the magazine *New Life* (*Xinshengming*) and included Tao Xisheng, Yen Lingfeng, and Ren Shu.

In the debate over science in the 1920s, Chen Duxiu took historical materialism as the best worldview, but he had few followers among his own generation. Actually, most of those who favored science were anti-Marxist. In the debate of the 1930s concerning Chinese history, however, Marxist scientism predominated; and from then on Marxist scientism became the dominant ideology in China, replacing not only traditional Confucianism and metaphysical theories but also empirical scientism. Henceforth, "science" in China was equated with Marxist scientism, which compelled everyone's allegiance. (In the west, by contrast, Marxism was typically regarded as only one school of thought among many, serving no greater purpose than to provide some insights about a complex world.)

This was not a victory of science but a victory of ideology. Marxist historical materialism succeeded because it provided a rationale for real-world politics.

It told people in what direction Chinese society should move. The ivory tower scholarship of Hu Shi's "bold hypothesis and careful verification" seemed far-fetched to Chinese intellectuals, who were witnessing a fierce struggle between communists and nationalists and between the Chinese resistance and the Japanese occupation.

In the 1940s there was no explicit debate over science, but a debate concerning literature was connected with it. One side, represented by Hu Feng, was in favor of continuing the May Fourth movement by advocating "modern" and "international" arts and literature; the other side, represented by Xiang Linping, was in favor of the "traditional" and the "national."

From 1949 to the present, the dominant ideology in China has nominally been Marxist scientism: that is, historical and dialectical materialism. This is so in spite of the fact that the "great leap forward" of 1958 and the Cultural Revolution of 1966–1976 functioned on a completely different basis—voluntarism—and the post-Mao regime has not adhered to any single ideology. If the first surge of scientism came in the 1920s, the post-Mao era may be called the second surge. As in the late nineteenth century and the early twentieth, the development of scientism after Mao went through three stages:

1. The second surge of scientism began with a new worship of modern technology, beginning around 1977, just before Deng Xiaoping came to power in the early 1980s.
2. The Chinese bureaucracy proved to be ill-prepared to handle modern science and technology. Beginning in the early 1980s, this led to a realization that China could not become modernized without changing its political system along "scientific" lines.
3. Political reform met with great difficulty, and this situation led directly to a realization that the political system could not be changed without a change in people's consciousness. This accounts for the debate on cultures in the mid–1980s.

During the post-Mao era, the three kinds of scientism identified in the 1920s continued to exist. Although there were some important differences, Jin Guantao's theory was similar to Hu Shi's empirical scientism, Hu Qiaomu's theory was similar to Chen Duxiu's Marxist scientism, and Su Shaozhi's theory was similar to Wu Zhihui's technological determinism.

By contrast, the humanistic countertrends during the post-Mao period were definitely different from those of the 1920s. Although Confucian humanism is present in both periods, the post-Mao intellectuals who saw Confucianism in a positive light—represented by Li Zehou—were more sophisticated than the Confucianists of the republican era. Also, two western humanistic trends, i.e., Marxist humanism and postmodernism, which had not been introduced to China in the early republican era, had a strong impact on the Chinese cultural transformation of the 1980s. Marxist humanism, represented by Wang Ruoshui, was a major voice in 1983; and various forms of postmodernism, represented by Gan Yang, were still visible in China's intellectual arena in the early twenty-first century.

As intellectual-political trends, scientism and humanism are not only in opposition to but also complementary with each other; however, scientism seems to be dominant while humanism is marginalized. In most of the world today, those who profess to uphold science are themselves likely to be in a dominant position relative to the humanists; but in China, the dominance of scientific over humanistic perspectives may have different origins.

First, the two surges of scientism in China in the twentieth century were related to the Chinese cultural tradition. Scientism, which claims to be the only path to truth, is continuous with traditional Chinese holistic-monistic intellectual-political modes of thought. Second, because scientism appears objective, it can be understood as a response to the ethical purism that characterized not only the dynasties but also the Cultural Revolution. Third, scientism claimed to be a panacea for China's severe socioeconomic and political problems during these periods. Fourth, the "objective" image of scientism suited the Chinese political culture of the two periods, which was characterized by ideological confusion.

The various versions of humanism were not as fortunate as scientism. In the 1920s Marxist humanism was not a part of the debate over "science" and "metaphysics," because the several types of neo-Marxism had not been introduced into China from the west. During the post-Mao period, the gradual loss of influence of Marxist humanism after the mid-1980s was a result of governmental repression and accorded with a gradual erosion of Marxism in general.

With its tradition of "rule for the people," Chinese culture is perhaps more closely linked to humanistic concerns than to "neutral" scientism. Consequently, in the late nineteenth century and early twentieth century, Confucianism was easily viewed as responsible for the humiliations China had suffered, because the door had been forced open mainly by products of science: guns, munitions, ships. The communist regime combined elements of China's feudal tradition and Stalinism, and it was not easy for the new political culture of the post-Mao era to endorse Confucianism. This is so even if the regime may try to use authoritarian elements of the Chinese tradition to legitimize one-party rule and individual intellectuals may take advantage of the relaxed political atmosphere to revitalize Confucianism. Confucian humanism, although it perhaps retains a place in the hearts of most Chinese, is unlikely to emerge as an important voice in academic circles, because the iconoclastic May Fourth tradition has to some degree persisted.

The various schools of western humanism have never been a strong voice in China. In the debate about science in the 1920s, Chiang Kai-shek (Jiang Jieshi) and Ch'en Li-fu (Chen Lifu), who held political power, advocated the vitalist and antirationalist theories of Eucken and Bergson, and some versions of Confucianism. But versions of scientism triumphed. During the post-Mao period, versions of western humanism such as postmodernism were not as influential as scientism, partly because they did not even try to appeal to the general population. More important, it was not easy for a premodern society like China to endorse postmodernism.

Issues of Chinese Enlightenment

Notably, the thinkers with whom scientism is said to have originated may not actually support it. The idea that science can save us—science as a panacea—is not easy to find among seventeenth-century writers; nor is it found in Francis Bacon (1561–1626), Thomas Hobbes (1588–1679), or René Descartes (1596–1650), who did not believe that science was the only source of learning. Thus scientism as an intellectual phenomenon often has to be considered in light of socioeconomic and political situations.

Politics had a significant impact on the Chinese "enlightenment." In twentieth-century China, the endorsement of science was always accompanied by thoroughgoing attacks on Chinese tradition. Iconoclasm, whether directed against the Confucian or the Maoist tradition, can be said to have gone hand in hand with scientism. There may be a conceptual link between scientism and iconoclasm. Scholars have pointed out that iconoclasm has been a distinct phenomenon not only in China's intellectual history but also elsewhere in the world. Iconoclasm and scientism both have a holistic, monistic understanding of the universe, and such an understanding is characteristic of Chinese intellectual and political leanings. Iconoclasm is a precondition for a surge of scientism, and scientism is a by-product of iconoclasm.

A phenomenon that reveals the intimate relationship between the Chinese holistic-monistic cultural tradition and the modern endorsement of scientism was represented by two slogans of the May Fourth movement of 1919: "Mr. Democracy" (*de xiansheng*) and "Mr. Science" (*sai xiansheng*). "Mr. Science" has had a wonderful life. The Chinese obsession with science was disrupted only twice in the twentieth century, both times during the Mao era: one interruption was the "great leap forward," the other, the Cultural Revolution. "Mr. Democracy's" life has not been so easy. Democracy was not readily accepted; most of the time, modifiers had to be added to the term "democracy"—thus we have the "people's democratic dictatorship" and the "three principles of the people" (*sanmin zhuyi*), i.e., livelihood, nationalism, and democracy.

Another issue of the Chinese enlightenment is that although most Chinese thinkers have drawn strength from western intellectual trends, their own theorizing has drifted apart from its western provenance. This has happened either because the thinkers were not sophisticated enough, especially in the early part of the century, or because they wanted to use western theories to suit their own needs. Consequently, although scholars of Chinese intellectual history in the twentieth century had to categorize Chinese thinkers for convenience or for purposes of analysis, (as is done in this entry), such labels are somewhat misleading.

For instance, Hu Shi did not function strictly within the category of empirical scientism. He made many comments—not casually—that can be described as materialistic scientism. Wu Zhihui's emphasis on developing technology did not grow in any logical way from his materialistic scientism; in addition, he was sometimes idealistic but at other times shared the positivism of Auguste Comte (1798–1857). Therefore, Wu is not, as he is sometimes called, a "philosophical materialist." Similarly, Su Shaozhi's emphasis on developing productive forces was not logically derived from historical materialism. Both Wu and Su may be more properly put in the category of technological determinism. Wang Ruoshui's advocacy of liberalizing Chinese society certainly does not have to be based on Marxist humanism. Examples like these are abundant.

Situations in which intellectual debates were heavily influenced by real-world events, especially political events, became more marked in China in the late twentieth century. The debate over the transformation of Chinese consciousness during the post-Mao era was more politicized than the debate over science of 1923.

First, while those who upheld scientism in the early 1920s may have sincerely believed in the omnipotence of science, those who upheld it in the 1980s did not. In the 1920s the mechanistic, monistic concepts of Newtonian physics had already been challenged by Albert Einstein's theories of general and special relativity; but most people had not yet felt the impact of relativity. Thus Chen Duxiu, Hu Shi, and Wu Zhihui, for example, may have really believed that science was omnipotent in a Newtonian sense. In the 1980s, the situation was different. For most Chinese social scientists, science was not omnipotent. People were unlikely to endorse scientism on an abstract level, although they might still endorse it in the context of concrete studies.

Second, in 1923 the battle line was clearly drawn between scientism and humanism; but in the 1980s the line was not that clear. This was because real-world politics played a more important role in the post-Mao era, with the result that there was no genuine academic debate. For instance, Wang Ruoshui and the humanist school, although seemingly embracing something other than scientism, did not attack those who embraced scientism, such as Jin Guaotao and Su Shaozhi. Instead of attacking Hu Qiaomu's historical materialism, the Marxist humanist school aimed at a political target—political alienation; that is, the servants of the people have become the masters. Li Zehou focused on what he called a "less essential" aspect of ontology—the cultural-psychological aspect—but nevertheless encouraged the experiment of adopting systems theory in the study of Chinese history. Su Shaozhi, who concentrated on the issue of developing productive forces, attacked none of the various kinds of humanism. Jin Guantao saw too much irrationality in contemporary Chinese academic circles but never attacked any humanistic philosophers.

See also Confucianism: Tradition; Confucianism: Twentieth Century; Hu Shi; Kang Youwei; Liang Qichao; Philosophy: Recent Trends in China since Mao; Philosophy: Recent Trends Overseas; Tan Sitong; Wang Guowei.

Bibliography

Baum, Richard. *Scientism and Bureaucratism in Chinese Thought: Cultural Limits of the Four Modernizations*. Sweden: University of Lund, 1981.

Brugger, Bill, and David Kelly. *Chinese Marxism during the Post-Mao Era*. Stanford, Calif.: Stanford University Press, 1990.

Cheng, Chung-ying. *Zhongguo zhexue yu zhongguo wenhua* (Chinese Philosophy and Chinese Culture). Taipei: Sanmin, 1974.

Chih, Andrew. *Chinese Humanism: A Religion Beyond Religion*. Taipei: Fu Jen Catholic University Press, 1981.

Chow, Tse-Tsung. *The May Fourth Movement: Intellectual Revolution in Modern China*. Stanford, Calif.: Stanford University Press, 1960.

Collinicos, Alex. *Against Post-Modernism: A Realist Critique*. New York: St. Martin's, 1990.

Hall, David L., and Roger T. Ames. *Thinking through Confucius*. Albany: State University of New York Press, 1987.

Harvey, David. *The Condition of Post-Modernity*, Part 1. Oxford: Blackwell, 1989.

Hermann, E. *Eucken and Bergson: Their Significance For Christian Thought*. Boston, Mass.: Pilgrim, 1912.

Hu, Shih. *The Development of the Logical Method in Ancient China*. New York: Paragon, 1963.

Hua, Shiping. *Scientism and Humanism: Two Cultures in Post-Mao China*. Albany: State University of New York Press, 1995.

Hucker, Charles O. *China's Imperial Past: An Introduction to Chinese History and Culture*. Stanford, Calif.: Stanford University Press, 1975.

Kuhn, Thomas S. *The Structure of Scientific Revolutions*. Chicago, Ill.: University of Chicago Press, 1962.

Li, Zehou. *Zhongguo jindai sixiang shilun* (Modern Chinese Intellectual History). Taipei: Fengyun shidai chuban gongsi, 1991.

Lin, Yu-sheng. *The Crisis of Chinese Consciousness*. Madison: University of Wisconsin Press, 1979.

———. "The Origins and Implications of Modern Chinese Scientism in Early Republican China: A Case Study—The Debate on Science versus. Metaphysics in 1923." In *Proceedings of the Research Conference on the Early History of the Republic of China*. Taipei: Academia Sinica, 1984.

Liu, Qingfeng. "Ershi shiji zhongguo kexue de liangci xingqi (The Two Surges of Chinese Scientism in the Twentieth Century)." In *Ershi yi shiji*, 4th ed. Hong Kong, 1991.

———. *Rang kexue de guangmang zhaoliang ziji* (Let the Light of Science Shine over Ourselves). Chengdu: Sichuan renmin chubanshe, 1984.

Manicas, Peter. *A History and Philosophy of Social Sciences*. Oxford: Blackwell, 1987.

Marx, Karl. *The Economic and Philosophic Manuscripts of 1844*. New York: International Publishers, 1964.

Owen, R. G. *Scientism, Man, and Religion*. Philadelphia, Pa.: Westminster, 1952.

Schwarcz, Vera. *Chinese Enlightenment: Intellectuals and Legacy of the May Fourth Movement of 1919*. Berkeley: University of California Press, 1986.

Sorell, Tom. *Scientism: Philosophy and the Infatuation with Science*. London: Routledge, 1991.

Tu, Weiming. *Rujia ziwo yishi de fansi* (Self-Reflection on the Sense of Self-Awareness of Confucianism). Taipei: Lianjing chuban shiye gongsi, 1990.

Weber, Max. *The Theory of Social and Economic Organization*. New York: Oxford University Press, 1974.

Wellmuth, Hohn, S.J. *The Nature and Origins of Scientism*. Milwaukee: Marquette University Press, 1944.

Yang, Guorong. "Wang Guowei de neizai jinzhang: Kexue zuye yu renben zuyi de duizhi (Tension within Wang Kuo-wei: The Confrontation between Scientism and Humanism)." In *Ershi yi shiji*, 11th ed., Hong Kong, 1992.

Self-Deception

A. S. Cua

This essay is an inquiry into the possibility of a Confucian response to the problem of self-deception. The paucity of textual materials makes extensive reconstruction and interpretation necessary (Zhang 1991). The following investigation is based mainly on my studies of Xunzi's moral philosophy. Section I treats the classical Confucian concern with self-deception in *Daxue* (*Great Learning*). Section II deals with the diagnosis of self-deception in light of Xunzi's conception of *bi* (obscuration) and the problems that arise in discussing the Confucian notion of the self.

I

In the *Great Learning*, personal cultivation (*xiushen*) is considered the foundation of peace and order both in the world and in family life (Chan 1963, 87). Along with the investigation of things (*gewu*), extension of knowledge (*zhizhi*), and rectification of the mind or heart (*zhengxin*), *chengyi* is said to be an essential step in or component of personal cultivation. The "three principal items" (*sangang*) provide the objective of abiding in the highest good or excellence (*zhishan*) by manifesting clear character or virtue (*ming mingde*) and loving the people (*qinmin*). The concern with self-deception is explicit in Chapter 6, a gloss on what it means to make one's thought sincere (*cheng qi yi*). Before we attend to this text, something must be said about the notions of *cheng* and *yi*.

The notion of cheng. At the first occurrence of *cheng* in *Daxue*, Zhu Xi says, without further explanation, that *cheng* means *shi*. A longer gloss on *cheng* in *Zhongyong* (*The Doctrine of the Mean*) is more helpful. According to Zhu Xi (19), *cheng* means *zhenshi wuwang*. Roughly, *cheng* means "truthfulness" (*zhen*), "genuineness" (*shi*), and "freedom from falsity" (*wuwang*). I suggest that we regard *zhen, shi*, and *wuwang* as characteristics of *cheng* construed as an ideal, ethical condition of personhood. If a person possesses *cheng*, such characteristics would be expected to be present in his thought, belief, speech, and action. In Wang Yangming's understanding of the term, such a person would embody the unity of knowledge and action, *zhixing heyi* (Cua 1982).

If we render *chen* as "truthfulness," we may say that a "*cheng* person" (*chengzhe*) is one who is sincere in acknowledging his thoughts or beliefs to himself and to others. Presumed in this acknowledgment is a concern for the truth of the belief and for the explanation of factual claims and justification of normative claims. This presumption perhaps accounts for Xunzi's recurrent emphasis on *li* (reason, principle), *lei* (kinds, categories), and *fuyan* (accord with evidence) as standards of argumentative discourse (Cua 1985). However, for the Confucian, *chen* is more than a desirable epistemic attitude or disposition, since the agent must also express this "*chen* concern" with *gong* (respectfulness), *jing* (seriousness, reverence), and *jin* (caution, circumspection). *Gong* is a virtue of *li* (ritual). At issue here is whether *chen* is expressed in a respectful manner. Often this respect takes the form of deference to the opinions and wishes of others, particularly elders and more experienced persons in the community. *Jing* is seriousness in expressing one's convictions, especially those that affect the well-being of the family and the community. A related consideration is *jin* (caution, circumspection), since the expression of one's view must take account of the feelings of the audience. Xunzi says, "Words of praise for another are warmer than clothing of linen and silk. The wound caused by words is deeper than that of spears and halberds"; even more important is "to consider the long view of things and think of consequences" (Knoblock 1989, 1:186, 195). In sum, *chen* as truthfulness is more than just a matter of sincere avowal of one's beliefs and concern for their truth; it is directed toward the proper expression of these beliefs in the context governed by *li* or rules of proper conduct.

Shi can be rendered as "genuineness" or "reality" as opposed to "counterfeit." A genuine person, for example, is devoid of any hypocrisy or pretense with respect to the expression of his thoughts or feelings. In the case of ethical commitment, *shi* pertains to something concrete or substantial; that is, the committed person is disposed to discharge his obligation in the appropriate situation. In the case of the commitment to the ideal of the good human life as a whole, say, to *dao* or *ren* (humanity) in the broad sense, such a commitment must not be halfhearted, though it does not preclude inquiry to dispel doubt in the course of the agent's endeavor to specify its concrete significance. The commitment to *dao* or *ren* calls for a creative clarifying of what *ren* means in personal life. Zhu Xi's recurrent use of *shili*, commonly rendered as "concrete principle," displays a concern with the concrete significance of *dao* (Cua 1997). As a word having to do with achievement, however, *shi* stresses not only the genuineness of commitment but also its actualization. Thus Dai Zhen explains *cheng* in terms of *shi* in the sense of fulfillment (Chin and Freeman 1990, 159).

Finally, *wuwang* can be rendered as "freedom from falsity," but the emphasis lies not so much in abstention from making false statements, which may indicate a disregard for truth, as in the manner in which utterances are made. *Wang* is a characteristic of speech or action that is uttered or performed in a cunning or crafty fashion with the intention to mislead or deceive others; such deceit is not easily detectable, especially by trustful persons. Perhaps for this reason, Chen Chun, Zhu Xi's eminent disciple, remarks that "the word *cheng* is closely similar in meaning to *zhong* (loyalty, doing one's best) and *xin* (trustworthiness, faithfulness), but *zhong* must be distinguished from *cheng*" (Chan 1986, 97; Chen 1979, 116). *Wuwang* is perhaps best rendered as "freedom from deliberate and cunning deception." When we add that such an ascription to persons also involves *zhen* and *shi*, we have a Confucian conception of *cheng* as an ideal ethical condition of personhood.

It is interesting to note that the whole expression *zhenshi wuwang* has a modern Chinese use. One recent dictionary offers the following translation: "a really honest heart; genuinely honest without any guile" (Lee 1980, 317). If our exposition of *zhen, shi*, and *wuwang* is assumed as the basis for elaboration, this entry could be used as a convenient summary of our discussion of *cheng* thus far. But adopting this entry, however, leaves entirely open the question how the notion of honesty or self-honesty is to be analyzed.

The notion of yi. As Chen Chun (1979) observes, the basic sense of *yi* pertains to thinking and estimation or consideration (*siliang*) with respect to feelings. Their expression requires the direction of the mind, the master (*xin*). *Yi* can also be used concurrently to refer to will (*zhi*):

> Take for example that some thing is encountered. The master inside that controls is the mind [*xin*]. As it is activated to become joy or anger, that is feeling. That which is inside that can be activated is nature. To operate the mind and to consider to whom the joy or anger is to be directd is *yi*. When the mind is directed to the person who is the object of joy or anger, it is will [*zhi*].

In another use, *yi* refers to intention (*yisi*). As Chen Chun points out, "People often talk about intention [*yisi*]. *Si* is to think. Contemplation, consideration, etc., all belong to *yi*" (Chan 1985, 68). In sum, Chen Chun offers us a way of explaining *yi* in three possibly interconnected uses. In the basic sense, *yi* is thoughtful consideration of the proper expression of feelings, involving an appraisive judgment that furnishes the object of will, and it is often accompanied by the intention to carry it out in actual performance.

Before we turn to a discussion of *chengyi* and *ziqi* (self-deception), something must be said about the connection of *chengyi* to the Confucian ideal of ethical excellence (*zhishan*), which is the ultimate objective of *Daxue*. The question naturally arises, what is its subject matter? The formal answer must involve such familiar notions as *ren* (humanity, benevolence), *yi* (rightness, righteousness), and *li* (ritual, rules of proper conduct). Notably, these are generic notions. There is a need to draw attention to the concrete setting in which these notions function in the lives of committed persons. Dai Zhen points out that there are two complementary ways of speaking about *cheng* as an effort to realize the highest good: "Speaking plainly (*zhiyanzhi*), we mean human relationships, affairs and activities of everyday life. Speaking more accurately (*jingyanzhi*), we mean *ren, li*, and *yi*" (1975, 122). The former provide the concrete context, and the latter the objectives of our endeavor.

Chengyi and ziqi (self-deception). Presupposing our explication of *cheng* in terms of *zhen, shi, wuwang* (truthfulness, genuineness, and freedom from falsity), and *yi* in terms of *siliang* (thought), let me adopt for convenience of reference Legge's rendering of *chengyi* as "sincerity of thought" and attend to the commentary in *Daxue* enjoining avoidance of self-deception in making one's thought sincere (*cheng qiyi*). The analysis proceeds along the lines of Legge's division of Chapter 6 into four sections. The text runs:

> Section 1. What is meant by "making the thoughts sincere" [*cheng qiyi*]? One must not allow self-deception [*mu ziqi ye*], as when we detest a bad smell or as when we love a beautiful color. This is what is called *ziqian*. Therefore, the superior man [*junzi*] will always be watchful when alone.

The difficulty of interpreting this section lies in the character *qian* in the "binomial" *ziqian* (I have borrowed the term "binomial" from mathematics and biology). According to Zhu Xi, *qian* should be read in terms of *qie*, which means *zu* (satisfaction or contentment). Thus *ziqian* means "self-satisfaction." This interpretation is puzzling, for what is the connection between detesting a bad smell or loving a beautiful color and self-deception? While the passage implicitly refers to avowal of aversion, preference, or desire, such an avowal hardly constitutes self-satisfaction. An alternative reading without the substitution of *qian* is more plausible. In *Shuowen, qian* means *jing* (respect). Accordingly, the "binomial" *ziqian* can be rendered as "self-respect." In this sense, avowal of one's preference, desire, or aversion is a matter of self-respect. Whether such a preference can be satisfied remains a separate issue. Of course, its realization may well lead to self-contentment or self-satisfaction (*zizu*). The imperative "One must not allow self-deception," as Zhao points out (1972, 174), appertains to *zhen* (truthfulness) and *shi* (genuineness). If a person really detests a bad smell, he will not pretend otherwise to himself or others. Hence, the attitude of a self-respecting person is such that he will not deceive himself and others.

While Zhu Xi's substitution of *ziqi* for *ziqian* is arbitrary, his explanation of *ziqi* (self-deception) is informative. The self-deceiver is "one who knows that he must do good and avoid evil, but what emanates from his mind contains something that is not yet genuine" (*shi*). Recall that a person concerned with *shi* is a genuine person devoid of any hypocrisy or pretense. Zhu's explanation of *ziqi* thus suggests that the victim of self-deception may not be aware that he is in that state of mind: "The person who desires self-cultivation [*zixiu*] knows quite well that if he is to do good and avoid evil, he must exert effort in order to prevent self-deception" (1980, 6). Elsewhere Zhu remarks that self-deception may be explained in this way:

> A person knows well that he must realize excellence or goodness [*shanhao*], that he must do good. Yet within his heart and mind (*xin*) he thinks that there is no urgency in doing so. This is self-deception [*ziqi*], this is mere pretension, lacking genuine conviction [*xuwei bushi*]. (*Zhuzi yulei* 1986, vol. 3, ch. 16, 328)

In Zhu Xi's view the self-deceiver lacks genuine ethical conviction. He persuades himself, as it were, to believe that there is no urgency in doing good and avoiding evil, and he persuades himself precisely in order to evade his responsibility. There is an element of purposiveness (*yi*) involved (Fingarette 1969, 28–29), but the self-deceiver need not be aware of his state of mind (Johnston 1988). The lack of genuine conviction (*bushi*) is contrary to the requirement of *cheng*. As *cheng* involves *zhen* (truthfulness), the self-deceiver may also disregard relevant truth or evidence. When he thinks that there is no urgency for ethical performance, it is this *yi* (thought) that misleads him. Of course, Zhu is assuming that he is committed to doing good and avoiding evil. Zhu's account of self-deception suggests that it is a product of lack of discernment or insensitivity to the relevant context of action. As we shall see later, there is likely to be a hidden, operative motive such as selfish desires (*siyu*).

Because of the possibility of self-deception, the ethical exemplar (*junzi*) concerned with personal cultivation "will always be watchful when he is alone." For it is solitude that affords ample opportunity to examine his thoughts and feelings. As Zhu Xi says, "When a man is alone [*du*], he himself knows what others do not know. Hence he must be careful in examining his incipient tendencies [*ji*]." Since human relationships, as noted earlier, furnish the context of action, they are the principal topic of examination. Recall Zengzi's remark:

> Every day I examine myself on three counts. In what I have undertaken on another's behalf, have I failed to do my best? In my dealings with my friends have I failed to be trustworthy? Have I passed on to others anything that I have not tried out myself? (*Analects*, 1.4)

Ideally, the result of self-examination is freedom from self-reproach (*Analects*, 12.4). But this requires the person to engage in reflection detached from preoccupation with personal gain, especially when it is contrary to *yi* (rightness). As Confucius reminds his pupils, the *junzi* considers *yi* to be of the highest importance (*Analects*, 17.23, 4.16; Mao 1977, 281, 54). Moreover, as the *Yijing* put it:

> The right sort of self-examination . . . consists not in idle brooding over oneself but in examining the effects one produces. Only when these effects are good, and when one's influence on others is good, will the contemplation of one's own life bring the self-satisfaction of knowing oneself to be free of mistakes. (Wihlelm 1950, 1:90–91)

The aim of self-examination is self-knowledge. At a minimum, self-knowledge consists in acknowledging one's knowledge and ignorance. This is perhaps the force of Confucius's observation (*Analects*, 12.17): "To say you know when you know, and to say you do not when you do not, that is knowledge" (*zhi*). For Xunzi, the cultivated Confucian (*Ru*) will be concerned with knowledge in this sense so that "within they do not delude themselves [*wu*], and without they do not deceive others" (Knoblock, 2.80; Li 1979, 149). This means that they will be true to themselves (*zhen*) and avow their knowledge or ignorance to themselves and to others. Self-deception in this light may thus be characterized as a sort of "evasion of full self-acknowledgement of some truth or of what one would view as truth if one were to confront an issue squarely" (Martin 1986, 13). Self-deception and deception of others is a sort of concealment. Such concealment is unlikely to be successful in "the eyes of others." As the commentary continues:

> Sections 2–3. When the small man is alone and at leisure, there is no limit to which he does not go in his evil

> thoughts. Only when he sees a superior man [*junzi*] does he then disguise himself, concealing his evil thoughts and displaying his goodness. But what is the use? For other people see him as if they see his lungs and livers. This is what is meant by the saying that what is true in a man's heart will be shown in outward appearance. Therefore the superior man must be watchful when he is alone. Tseng Tzu [Zengzi] said, "What ten eyes are beholding and what ten hands are pointing to—isn't it frightening?"

The metaphor of sight is familiar in western philosophy (Butler 1850, 117, 124; Kant 1964, 92). But as Fingarette points out, in the *Analects*, the emphasis is on shame rather than guilt. Fingarette plausibly maintains that "there is developed in the *Analects* no notion of guilt and repentance as a moral response to one's wrongdoing" (Cua 2003; Fingarette 1972, 28ff). But his thesis on the absence of a developed notion of choice in the *Analects* cannot be generalized to apply to both classical Confucianism and neo-Confucianism, for the notion *quan* ("weighing of circumstances or alternatives") is explicit in Mencius and Xunzi, as well as Zhu Xi (Cua 1998, Essay 12). Thus the classical Confucian concern with shame (*chi, ru*) is not just a matter of disgrace, that is, the loss of honor in the "eyes of others." As Xunzi insists, there is a distinction between intrinsic or just shame (*yiru*) and circumstantial shame (*shiru*), and between intrinsic honor (*yirong*) and circumstantial honor (*shirong*). A *junzi* may have circumstantial shame, which is a matter of circumstances beyond one's power or control; but not intrinsic shame, which has its source within oneself (Li 1979, 410–411). At any rate, self-deception is analogous to "self-presentation." The deception cannot succeed, "for other people will see him as if they see his lungs and livers" and "this is what is meant by saying that what is true [*cheng*] in a man's heart [*xin*] will be shown in outward appearance." As we shall see later, concealing one's thoughts and conduct before oneself or others is an example of *bi* (obscuration, blindness).

The commentary continues:

> Section 4. Wealth makes a house shining and virtue [*de*] makes a person shining. The mind is broad and the body at ease. Therefore, the *junzi* always makes his thought or will sincere [*cheng qiyi*].

The analogy of *de* (virtue) with wealth is instructive, for *de* is a sort of power or force. Thus a *junzi* has the power or capacity to influence the course of human affairs. As Confucius remarked: "Virtue [*de*] never stands alone. It is bound to have neighbors." "The virtue of *junzi* is like the wind. . . . Let the wind blow over the grass and it is sure to bend" (*Analects*, 4.25, 12.19). So also, no matter how a person conceals his wealth before others, it is probably evident to them. It is possible for a self-deceiver concerned with personal cultivation, and in the course of time preoccupied with earnest self-examination, to experience self-disclosure and accordingly to disavow self-deception (Fingarette 1969, 110).

The preceding exposition of the commentary in *Daxue*, provides, I hope, a coherent Confucian perspective on self-deception. Self-deception must be avoided because it undermines personal cultivation (*xiushen*)—in particular, it undermines making one's thoughts sincere (*chengyi*). Our discussion provides a picture of a person of ethical integrity or self-respect (*ziqian*), who engages in constant self-examination in order to attain *cheng*, involving *zhen* (truthfulness), *shi* (genuineness), and *wuwang* (freedom from falsity). However, self-examination cannot be carried out without some understanding of the potential sources of self-deception.

II

Diagnosis of self-deception. Given its primarily ethical focus, the Confucian interest in self-deception lies in its use as an interpretive and diagnostic concept (Audie 1986, 19; Toulmin 1977, 291–317). Zhu Xi's explanation of the "binomial" *ziqi* (self-deception), for example, is a textual interpretation. Moreover, the interpretation is proffered in part as a diagnosis of failure to attain *chengyi*. For diagnosing the sources of self-deception I shall attend to Xunzi's conception of *bi*.

Let me briefly note the background of Xunzi's concern with *bi*. For Xunzi, *dao* is a holistic ideal of the good human life, comprising *li, yi*, and *ren* as basic interdependent foci of ethical interest. The failure to comprehend the *dao* is a result of *bi*—a common human liability. Philosophers are not excepted. They err not so much because of mistaken doctrines as because their doctrines represent only partial views: "Some of what they advocate has a rational basis enough to deceive [*qi*] and mislead [*huo*] the masses" (*Xunzi*, Book 6; Knoblock, 1:233ff). Yang Liang's gloss on *bi* is this: "The man beset by *bi* is one who is unable to see through things clearly. His view is impeded by one corner as if there were things that hindered his vision" (1976, ch. 15.1A).

A *bi*, literally, is a "screen," "shelter," or "cover." *Bi* is Xunzi's metaphor for an obscuration of the mind. In this condition the mind is obstructed in its proper functioning, e.g., thinking, remembering, imagining, and judging. In short, a *bi* is any sort of factor that obstructs the mind's cognitive task. When the mind is in the state of *bi*, reason is not operating properly. The opposite of *bi* is clarity of mind. Thus Xunzi says:

> If you guide it [the mind] with reason [*li*], nourish it with clarity, and do not allow external objects to unbalance it, then it will be capable of determining right and wrong and of resolving doubts. (Li, 495; Watson 1963, 134)

In this light, *bi* can also be rendered as "blindness." As Watson reminds us, Xunzi's use of *bi* (in Book 21) denotes "a clouding or darkening of the faculties or the understanding, and Xunzi plays on the image of light and darkness throughout the chapter" (Cua 1985, 138–145; Watson 1963, 121n). Humans beset by *bi* may be said to be in the state of *huo* (delusion). For example:

> A drunken man will try to leap a ditch a hundred paces wide as though it were a narrow gutter or stoop to go through a city gate as though it were a low doorway. This is because the wine has disordered his spirits. (Watson 1963, 134)

In *huo* a person's mind is misled or misguided in his belief or judgment. *Huo* is a condition in which the person is responsible for assenting to misleading guidance—a failure in the exercise of reasonable judgment in accord with his sense of *yi* (rightness). A person in *huo* is a self-deceiver. The potential sources of *bi* may thus be construed as sources of self-deception.

According to the *Xunzi*, whenever we make distinctions among things, our minds are likely to be obscured (*bi*) by these distinctions. "This is a common affliction [*gonghuan*] of our ways of thinking." For Xunzi, all distinctions owe their origin to comparisons of and analogies among different kinds of things. They are made in accordance with our purposes and thus are relative to the context of thought and discourse. Distinctions, while useful, are not dichotomies. In the case of *bi*, the person attends exclusively to the significance of one item without considering the significance of the other. Common people, as well as philosophers, are prone to exaggerate. For example, Mozi is beset by *bi* in his exclusive attention to utility without recognizing the importance of culture (*wen*); Zhuangzi is beset by *bi* in his preoccupation with heaven without recognizing the importance of human beings. For Xunzi, the common sources of *bi* are desire and aversion (*yuwu*), distance and nearness (*yuanjin*), breadth and shallowness of knowledge (*boqian*), past and present (*gujin*). I shall discuss these sources of *bi* in terms of desires and aversions, or positive and negative desires, proceeding on the assumption that in all cases of *bi*, desire is present as a motive.

Since *bi* is contrary to reason (*li*), it may be regarded as a state of irrational preoccupation with one side of a distinction at the expense of careful consideration of the other. Well aware of the distinction between desire and aversion, a person may pursue his current desire without attending to its possible unwanted consequences. That person's mind may be said to be in the state of *bi*. More generally, humans suffer because of their concern for acquiring benefit and avoiding harm. When they see something beneficial, they do not consider carefully whether it may lead to harmful consequences (*Xunzi*, Book 3; Knoblock, 1:180). However, even if consequences are considered, the person may fail to attend to distant consequences (*yuan*) and simply focus on near or immediate consequences (*jin*), well aware of the relevance of the distinction at issue. Conversely, a person may be preoccupied with distant consequences and not attend to immediate ones that may well bring disaster. Xunzi cites examples of ancient rulers preoccupied with their concubines and ancient subjects preoccupied with the acquisition of power. Thus "their minds became deluded [*huo*] and their actions were thrown into confusion" (Watson 1963, 122, modified; *Xunzi*, Book 21, 472). Similarly in matters of life and death, a person may be victim of *bi* because of his inordinate attention to one without regard to the other, so also in regard to the present and past, and the breadth and shallowness of knowledge.

Xunzi's discussion of *bi* does not provide any systematic scheme for diagnosis of self-deception. However, it does suggest that our desires are the main motives and that they cannot be reduced to just one factor such as selfish desires—a prominent view in neo-Confucianism. Wang Yangming, for instance, thinks that selfish desires alone are the obscuring factor (*bi*) which accounts for moral failure, but the mind may be obscured (*bi*) in many ways. We may expect that in the case of self-deception, such obscurations may be reflected in a variety of patterns such as willful ignorance, emotional detachment, pretentiousness, and rationalization (Martin 1986, 6–11). Regarding a remedy, Xunzi would recommend that the person concerned with self-cultivation engage in wise, informed deliberation (*zhilü*). In such deliberation, the person weighs all relevant considerations so as to arrive at a unified preference in the light of *dao* (Cua 1993).

The Confucian notion of the self. Recently, some scholars have proposed different conceptions of the self for Confucian ethics. I take these proposals as primarily constructive interpretations of an aspect of classics such as *The Analects* (*Lunyu*) and *The Doctrine of the Mean* (*Zhongyong*). Before expressing my critical appreciation of these efforts, I will consider the more general question whether there is a Confucian notion of the self in the classics.

Following Toulmin, we may distinguish three different uses of "self" in English: (1) as a prefix or suffix in everyday reflexive idioms, "self-" and "-self"; (2)

as the "name of a hypothetical entity, or intervening explanatory variable," in speculative psychology; and (3) as a diagnostic term in "clinical psychotherapy and comparable, non-medical modes of psychological description." Toulmin goes on to show how a careful extension of the reflexive use "provides grounding for, and in due course develops into, the fully-fledged terminology of the 'self,' as it figures in clinical theory, psychiatric diagnoses and/or psychoanalytic interpretation" (1977, 291f).

Toulmin provides a useful approach to the Confucian notion of the self. It is uncontroversial to note that one would search in vain for a theoretical use of "self" in Confucian ethics. Earlier I suggested that "binomial" *ziqi* (self-deception) is best construed as a diagnostic term. In light of Toulmin's essay, our question is perhaps best approached by examining reflexive "binomials" such as *zi*-locutions, then exploring the possibility of the diagnostic use of some of these locutions, not as a means for developing a philosophical, psychological, or clinical theory, but as a means of articulating an aspect of personal cultivation, especially in attaining the sincerity of thought (*chengyi*).

In *Lunyu* (*Analects*, 4.17, 5.27, 19.17), for example, we find *zixing* (examine oneself), *zisong* (reproach oneself), and *ziru* (disgrace oneself). In *Mengzi* (4A.10, 3A.2, 3A.4, 4B.14) we find *zibao* (do violence to oneself), *ziyang* (nourish oneself), and *zide* (realize, *dao*, in oneself). And in *Xunzi* (Book 2, 23; Book 4, 59), apart from *zixing*, we find *zicun*, "preserve (goodness) in oneself," and *zizhi*, "know oneself." In *Xunzi*, one passage on mind (*xin*) as "the ruler of the body" contains a series of six different *zi*-locutions: *zijin, zishi, ziduo, ziqu, zixing*, and *zizhi*, roughly "the mind itself issues its own prohibitions and commands, makes its own decision and choices, initiates its own action and omission" (Book 21, 488; Dubs 1966, 269, modified). Except for Xunzi's series of *zi*-locutions in one passage, all the other *zi*-locutions, even in modern Chinese, are part of the language of practical, reflexive conduct. In Section I, we have noted *ziqi* (self-deception) and the necessity of avoiding it in order to attain *ziqian* (self-respect). The earlier suggestion of *ziqi* as a diagnostic term perhaps can be applied to most of the other *zi*-locutions, with a primary focus on *zixing* (self-examination) as the general context for constructive interpretation. The singular exception is *zide*, but *zide*—"realize (*dao*) in oneself"—for some Chinese thinkers, such as Chen Baisha, has a special significance, influenced by Mencius and Cheng Hao. And quite apart from the use of *zide*, Wang Yangming's insistence on *ren* or *dao* as a matter of *tiren* (personal realization) also reflects these influences (Cua 1998, Essay 9; Tu 1976b).

As self-examination (*zixing*) is the keynote of the Confucian doctrine of personal cultivation (*xiushen*), the other *zi*-locutions may be construed as having primarily a diagnostic use; they call attention to the need of the learners of *dao* to preserve (*zicun*) and nourish (*ziyang*) their ethical dispositions against the onset of wayward tendencies or proclivities that impede the pursuit of *dao*, in particular, those that do violence (*zibao*) and bring disgrace to themselves (*ziru*). Of special importance in self-examination is a careful review of one's conduct in order to see whether one has done anything that merits self-reproach (*zisong*). As Mencius says, "A *junzi* differs from other men because he examines his heart [*xin*]. He examines his heart by means of *ren* and *li* (rites)." Suppose he is treated by someone in an outrageous manner. He will turn around and examine himself (*zifan*), and say to himself "I must be lacking in *ren* and *li*, or how could such a thing happen to me?" When such a self-examination discloses that he has done nothing contrary to *ren* and *li*, and yet the outrageous treatment continues, he will say to himself "I must have failed to do my best for him" (Lau 1979, modified; *Mengzi*, 4B.28). Yet the possibility of others' reproaches or concern with one's "face" (*mianzi*) is also a proper subject of self-examination (Hu 1944). For the Confucian, concern with one's "name" (*ming*) or reputation is always a just concern, except in adverse circumstances—that is, when one is placed in a situation of shame beyond one's control, *shiru* (Hume 1957, 96). In the end, if frequent self-examination is successful, one can claim to have a modicum of self-knowledge (*zizhi*). One hopes the process of self-examination in conjunction with the constant practice of *ren, li*, and *yi* will culminate in personal attainment or realization of *dao* (*zide*).

The foregoing suggestion on the possible connection between the reflexive and diagnostic uses of *zi*-locutions is not an adequate response to the question of the Confucian notion of the self. It is a legitimate question for a Confucian philosopher today whether he can find a use of "self" other than as a "name of a hypothetical entity" in the construction of psychological or philosophical theory. Moreover, the suggestion does not seem to accommodate the insights into the use of "self" in some writings of Ames, Fingarette, and Tu Wei-ming. This caveat, thus, is in order: my thesis is not intended as a solution to the philosophical problem of the self, say, as an alternative to the theses of an enduring self, no-self, and a constructed self (Kupperman 1991).

A Confucian today may proffer a nominal use of "self" by adapting Xunzi's distinction between generic (*gongming*) and specific terms (*bieming*). Suppose we regard "self" as a generic term (*gongming*). Such a term has a proper use in formal, abstract, theoretical discourse. The use of "self" as a generic term in the title of Fingarette's essay, "The Problem of the Self in the *Analects*" (1979) is quite intelligible. However, the question naturally arises, how is such a use to be rendered intelligible in expounding some passages in the *Analects* (*Lunyu*)? This question can be handled by using specific terms such as the *zi*-locutions we have considered. To put this differently, the generic term "self" has "cash value" in specific terms (*bieming*), which function as possible specifications of the concrete significance of "self" as a general term. To translate *zixing* in Zengzi's remark cited earlier as "I examine myself," is a mistake, for *zixing* is a "binomial," reflexive idiom, as Fingarette later came to realize in his response to Ames's critique. This acknowledgment focuses on the use of the reflexive idiom in translating *zixing* (Bookover 1991, 198–199). Of course, specific terms (*bieming*), such as *zisong* (self-reproach), also may need further specification—for example, in answer to the question "What is the object or content of self-reproach?" in practical discourse. We must note also that apart from *zi*-locutions, such specific terms as *shen* (in one's own person) or *ji* as contrasted with *ren* (distinguishing oneself from others) can also function as specific terms for "self" as a generic term. The variability and degree of specification of "self" as a generic term depend on the purpose and context of practical occasion.

Equipped with "self" as a generic term, we can appreciate Tu Wei-ming's claim that in Confucian ethics the conception of the self is a "center of relationships." In his essay on *Zhongyong*, Tu declares: "Since a person in the Confucian tradition is always conceived of as a center of relationships, the more one penetrates into one's *inner self*, the more one will be capable of realizing the true nature of one's human relatedness." Alternatively, "as the Confucians argue, it is more difficult to imagine ourselves as isolable individuals than as centers of relationships constantly interacting with one another in a dynamic network of human relatedness" (1976a, 27, 95). As noted earlier, human relationships (*lun*) are the concrete setting for conduct in accord with *ren, li*, and *yi*. Tu's metaphor of a dynamic network suggests the complex, indeterminate, or changing character of the interconnection of the various roles in an individual human life. The individual concerned with self-cultivation (*xiushen*) is, from his own standpoint, a center, the focal point around which interpersonal relationships revolve. As a metaphor, "center" may be misleading in suggesting self-centeredness or self-serving preoccupations, a potential source of *bi*. Moreover, Tu's use of "inner self" is best construed as a generic term subject to specification, for example, by the reflexive *zi*-locutions, rather than as a name of some sort of an abstract entity—a reification of concrete reflexive *zi*-locutions in practical Confucian discourse. But Tu (1989) seems to be aware of the possible misleading use of "self" when he shifts to the term "true self" as a convenient way of referring to "the Confucian *idea of the self* in terms such as self-cultivation [*xiushen* or *xiuji*], in contrast to the idea of the 'private ego' in such terms as self-centeredness [*si*]." But the retention of an idea of the self has force only if such an idea has implicit reference to reflexive *zi*-locutions; otherwise, the expression would be entirely freestanding without any concrete anchorage.

In his critique of Fingarette's essay on the self, Ames (1991) is implicitly committed to a view of the self as process, rather than the substantive view. Ames's view is reminiscent of Mead's thesis that "the self is not so much a substance as a process in which the conversation of gestures has been internalized within an organic form" (1934, 178). Indeed, Ames cites a passage from Mead on the relationship between "I" and "me" to elucidate his thesis that "the conception of self in Confucius is dynamic as a complex of social roles." Ames points out that Fingarette fails to make the distinction between "autonomous individual and unique individual," that is, the distinction between individual as a member of a class of human beings and as "one of a kind," like J. M. W. Turner's *Seastorm*. Ames maintains that *ren*, "a unique person-specific goal," can also be understood as denoting "self." For Ames:

> Given that *jen* [*ren*] is always a unique and particular achievement, it can only refer to a self. . . . "Self" as Confucius defines it is irreducibly interpersonal. It is not the case that *jen* refers to "other" in contradistinction to "self." (105–108)

Before attending to Ames's insights, we must note again that, like Tu and Fingarette, Ames pays no attention to the crucial role of reflexive *zi*-locutions in providing for his use of "self" as a generic term. Also, he gives no evidence for his claim that Confucius defines "self" as "irreducibly interpersonal," though it is a plausible, interpretive claim acceptable to modern Confucians. However, the plausibility of this claim presupposes that, for the Confucian, the habitat of interpersonal relationships (*lun*) is a community with a tradition such as *li* (ritual) that renders intelligible any individual claim for being a distinct, unique individual (Cua 1983). Ames maintains that *ren* is a "unique and particular achievement," since *ren* is more an ideal theme, a standard of inspiration, than an ideal norm. The realization of *ren* will thus be manifested in an individual's style or manner of performance, style of life, or both. As an ideal theme, *ren* is a quasi-aesthetic vision that provides a focal point. It is expected that the achievement of *ren* as an ideal theme will be a polymorphous exemplification, especially in the lives of paradigmatic individuals (Cua 1978, ch. 8). As for Ames's insightful suggestion on the relevance of Mead to the Confucian notion of the self, I think it is a worthwhile project for further inquiry by anyone interested in comparative Chinese and western ethics.

Conclusion

These reflections on the ethical aspect of self-deception have focused mainly on the Confucian idea of self-deception, its context and background, as well as the possibility of diagnosis and remedy. In the Confucian perspective, avoidance of self-deception is required in personal cultivation or character formation, especially in the task of attaining sincerity of thought (*chengyi*). Indispensable to the success of this task is constant engagement in self-examination, a process partially exemplified in the diagnostic use of reflexive *zi*-locutions. A tentative thesis on the notion of the self was offered as a topic for further inquiry. In this sketch of the Confucian response to the problem of self-deception, no attempt has been made to respond to specific issues in current discussions. My aim has been solely to present some materials for a comparative east-west dialogue.

See also Chen Xianzhang; *Cheng; Chengyi*; Confucianism: Ethics; *Daxue*; *Junzi, Quan; Xiushen*; Wang Yangming; *Zhongyong*.

Bibliography

Ames, Roger T. "Reflections on the Confucian Self: A Response to Fingarette." In *Rules, Rituals, and Responsibility: Essays Dedicated to Herbert Fingarette*, ed. Mary I. Bookover. La Salle, Ill.: Open Court, 1991.

Audie, Robert. "Self-Deception and Rationality." In Mike W. Martin. *Self-Deception and Morality*. Lawrence: University of Kansas Press, 1986.

Bookover, Mary I., ed. *Rules, Ritual, and Responsibility: Essays Dedicated to Herbert Fingarette*. La Salle, Ill.: Open Court, 1991.

Butler, Joseph. "Upon Self-Deceit." In *The Works of Joseph Butler*, ed. Samuel Halifax. Oxford: Oxford University Press, 1850.

Chan, Wing-tsit, trans. *Neo-Confucian Terms Explained* (*The Pei-hsi tzu-i*). New York: Columbia University Press, 1985.

———, trans. *A Source Book in Chinese Philosophy*. Princeton, N.J.: Princeton University Press, 1963.

Chen, Chun. *Beixi xiansheng ziyo xiangjiang*. Taipei: Guangwen, 1979.

Chin, Ann-ping, and Mansfield Freeman, trans. *Tai Chen* [*Dai Zhen*] *on Mencius: Explorations in Words and Meaning*. New Haven, Conn.: Yale University Press, 1990.

Cua, A. S. "Confucian Vision and the Human Community." *Journal of Chinese Philosophy*, 11(3), 1984, pp. 226–238.

———. *Dimensions of Moral Creativity: Paradigms, Principles, and Ideals*. University Park: Pennsylvania State University Press, 1978.

———. *Ethical Argumentation: A Study in Hsün Tzu's Moral Epistemology*. Honolulu: University of Hawaii Press, 1985.

———. "Ethical Significance of Shame: Insights of Aristotle and Xunzi." *Philosophy East and West*, 53 (April 2003).

———. *Moral Vision and Tradition: Essays in Chinese Ethics*. Washington, D. C.: Catholic University of America Press, 1998.

———. "The Possibility of Ethical Knowledge: Reflections on a Theme in the *Hsün Tzu*." In *Epistemological Issues in Ancient Chinese Philosophy*, ed. Hans Lenk and Gregor Paul. Albany: State University of New York Press, 1993.

———. "Reason and Principle in Chinese Philosophy." In *A Companion to World Philosophies*, ed. Eliot Deutsch and Ron Bontekoe. Oxford: Blackwell, 1997.

———. *The Unity of Knowledge and Action: A Study in Wang Yang-ming's Moral Psychology*. Honolulu: University of Hawaii Press, 1982.

Dai, Zhen. *Mengzi ziyi*. In *Dai Zhen wenji*. Taipei: Heluo, 1975.

Dubs, Homer H., trans. *The Works of Hsüntze*. Taipei: Chengwen, 1966.

Fingarette, Herbert. "Comment and Response." In *Rules, Ritual, and Responsibility: Essays Dedicated to Herbert Fingarette*, ed. Mary I. Bookover. La Salle, Ill.: Open Court, 1991.

———. *Confucius: The Secular as Sacred*. New York: Harper Torchbooks, 1972.

———. "The Problem of the Self in the *Analects*." *Philosophy East and West*, 29(2), 1979, pp. 129–240.

———. *Self-Deception*. London: Routledge and Kegan Paul, 1969.

Fung, Yu-lan (Feng Youlan). *A History of Chinese Philosophy*, Vol. 1, trans. Derk Bodde. Princeton, N.J.: Princeton University Press, 1952.

Gardner, Daniel K. *Chu Hsi and the Ta-hsüeh: Neo-Confucian Reflection on the Confucian Canon*. Cambridge, Mass.: Harvard University Press, 1985.

Hu, Hsien Chin. "The Chinese Concepts of Face." *American Anthropologist*, New Series, 46, 1944, pp. 45–64.

Hume, David. *An Inquiry Concerning the Principles of Morals*. Indianapolis, Ind.: Bobbs-Merrill, 1957.

Jiang, Paul Yung-ming. *The Search for Mind: Ch'en Pai-sha, Philosopher-Poet*. Singapore: Singapore University Press, 1980.

Johnston, Mark. "Self-Deception and the Nature of Mind." In *Perspectives on Self-Deception*, ed. Brian P. McLaughlin and Amélie Oksenberg Rorty. Berkeley: University of California Press, 1988.

Kant, Immanuel. *The Doctrine of Virtue*, trans. Mary J. Gregor. New York: Harper Torchbooks, 1964.

Knoblock, John. *Xunzi: A Translation and Study of the Complete Works*, Vol. 1, Books 1–6. Stanford, Calif.: Stanford University Press, 1989.

Kupperman, Joel. *Character*. New York: Oxford University Press, 1991.

Lau, D. C., trans. *The Analects of Confucius* [*Lunyu*]. New York: Penguin, 1979.

———, trans. *Mencius*. Middlesex: Penguin, 1970.

Lee, S. T., comp. *A New Complete Chinese-English Dictionary*. Hong Kong: China Publishers, 1980.
Li, Disheng. *Xunzi jishi*. Taipei: Xuesheng, 1979.
Mao, Zishui. *Lunyu jinzhu jinyi*. Taipei: Commercial Press, 1977.
Martin, Mike W. "Honesty with Oneself." In *Rules, Ritual, and Responsibility: Essays Dedicated to Herbert Fingarette*, ed. Mary I. Bookover. La Salle, Ill.: Open Court, 1991.
———. *Self-Deception and Morality*. Lawrence: University Press of Kansas, 1986.
Mead, George H. *Mind, Self, and Society*. Chicago, Ill.: University of Chicago Press, 1934.
Shi, Ciyun. *Mengzi jinzhu jinyi*. Taipei: Commercial Press, 1978.
Toulmin, Stephen. "Self-Knowledge and Knowledge of the Self." In *The Self: Psychological and Philosophical Issues*, ed. Theodore Mischel. Oxford: Blackwell, 1977.
Tu, Wei-ming. *Centrality and Commonality: An Essay on Chung Yung*. Honolulu: University of Hawaii Press, 1976a.
———. *Neo-Confucian Thought in Action: Wang Yang-ming's Youth (1472–1529)*. Berkeley: University of California Press, 1976b.
———. "On Confucian Religiousness." In *Centrality and Commonality: An Essay on Chung Yung*, 2nd ed. Albany: State University of New York Press, 1989.
Watson, Burton, trans. *The Complete Works of Chuang Tzu*. New York: Columbia University Press, 1968.
———, trans. *Hsün Tzu: Basic Writings*. New York: Columbia University Press, 1963.
Wilhelm, Richard. *I Ching or Book of Changes*, trans. Cary F. Baynes. New York: Pantheon, 1950. (Translated from the German version of Richard Wilhelm.)
Yang, Liang. *Xunzi*. Taipei: Zhonghua, 1976. (Sibu bi pi-yao Edition.)
Yang, Lianggkan. *Daxue jinzhu jinyi*. Taipei: Commercial Press, 1977.
Zhang, Zhongxing. "Ziqi zhiqi ti ji qi fangzhi." In *Tan ziqi qiren* (Colloquium on Self-Deception and Other-Deception). Taipei: Commercial Press, 1991.
Zhao, Zehou. *Daxue yanjiu*. Taipei: Zhonghua, 1972.
Zhu, Xi. *Sishu jizhu*. Hong Kong: Taiping, 1980.
———. *Zhuzi yulei*, Vol. 3, ed. Li Jingde. Taipei: Wenjin, 1986.

Sengzhao (Seng-chao)

Hsueh-li CHENG

Sengzhao (374–414) was the leading disciple of Kumarajiva (344–413), who was the greatest Buddhist translator of Kucha and had translated numerous Buddhist texts from Sanskrit into Chinese. Sengzhao was also the ablest philosopher of the early Sanlun Madhyamika Buddhist school.

Kumarajiva often complained that his Chinese disciples did not really understand his translations and teachings, although he had hundreds of followers in China. Sengzhao, it appears, was the first Chinese thinker who had a genuine comprehension of Indian Mahayana philosophy and knew how to use Chinese to express Indian Madhyamika thought authentically. Kumarajiva once praised Sengzhao's Chinese exposition of the Indian doctrine of emptiness by saying, "My understanding does not differ from yours, and in principle we might borrow from each other."

Seng was born in Chang'an and grew up in a poor family. He earned a living by working as a copyist. This work gave him an opportunity to read widely in Chinese literature. After reading the Buddhist scriptures such as the *Vimalakirti*, he was converted to the Buddhist *dharma* and became a monk. When Sengzhao reached manhood, he went to Kucha to become a follower of Kumarajiva. Then when Kumarajiva went to Chang'an in 401, Sengzhao helped with Kumarajiva's translation work on Buddhist scriptures.

After the translation of the *Pancavimsati*, Sengzhao wrote a famous essay, *Boruo wuzhi* ("*Prajna* without Knowledge"). He continued to show his brilliant understanding of Buddhist thought by writing such well-known essays as *Bu zhenkong* ("Emptiness of the Non-Absolute"), *Wu buqian* ("Things Do Not Shift"), and *Nianpan wuming* ("Nirvana without Name"). Sengzhao also wrote a commentary on the *Vimalakirti*.

Sengzhao's writings strengthened the epistemology, metaphysics, axiology, and philosophy of religion in Chinese thought and Chinese culture. Usually, people believe that when we know, we must do something, that is, there are objects to be known, if and only if there are knowers and acts of knowing. For Sengzhao, this is really a delusion and attachment. *Prajna* (wisdom) transcends this kind of knowing. It is an unattached insight which finds that the act of knowing, the knower, and the object to be known are all empty. Sengzhao wrote:

> Real *Prajna* is as pure as empty space, without knowing, without seeing, without acting and without objects. Thus knowledge is in itself without knowing, and does not depend on anything in order to be without knowledge.

So-called knowledge or truth, according to Sengzhao, is really a projection of the human mind. By contrast, Buddhists help people, not to acquire knowledge or obtain something, but rather to realize that "something" is empty, so as to empty themselves of all illusions and attachments, which are the sources of evil and suffering in life.

People ordinarily tend to assume that language represents reality. If we want to know the meaning of a word, we should look for an extralinguistic object for which the word stands. A word is considered meaningful only if it stands for an object. For Sengzhao, this view of language is erroneous. He contended that a word has no meaning by itself and that the meaning of a word is really not an extralinguistic object; instead, the meaning depends on the context or conditions. If the context changes, the meaning of the word would change and might even disappear.

According to Sengzhao, words have no essence of their own. Whatever they express is also without its own essence. In fact, words as well as objects are empty. Sengzhao stated:

> If you seek a thing through a name, in the thing there is no actuality that matches the name. If you seek a name through a thing, the name has no efficacy to obtain the thing. A thing without an actuality to match its name is not a thing. A name without efficacy to obtain a thing is not a real name. Therefore, names do not match actualities, and actualities do not match names.

The popular approach to knowing the reality of a thing is analysis. For example, time is examined and analyzed as something consisting of past, present, and future; and motion is analyzed as something shifting from the past through the present to the future. Sengzhao contended that if this analytical approach is the only way to know reality, motion would be impossible. When we examine motion, we reason that it must occur in what is gone, what is "being gone," or what is yet to be gone. But we cannot find motion in what is gone, because it is gone already. We cannot find motion in what is yet to be gone (the future), since it is not yet. Nor can we find motion in what is "being gone" (the present), since a thing is "being gone" if and only if it shifts from the past to the present or from the present to the future. But this is the very issue we are examining now. Therefore, motion cannot be established. Since motion is impossible, rest cannot be established either. So-called rest means a cessation of motion. If there is no motion, how can there be a cessation of motion? Therefore, one should not be attached to the analytical approach.

People also tend to have a dualistic way of thinking and describe things as real or unreal, existent or nonexistent. For Sengzhao, things can be neither real nor unreal. Objects cannot be real, because all things are causally dependent on each other and are devoid of their own nature or their own being. They cannot be unreal either, because the "myriad things" arise interdependently. Sengzhao said, "Things do not really exist, since in some ways they are nonexistent; they are not nonexistent, since in some ways they do exist." An enlightened person would avoid the concepts "is" and "is not." *Nirvana* is understood as a liberation from analytic, dualistic, and conceptual thought.

Kumarajiva died at Chang'an in 413. Sengzhao was distressed by the master's death and wrote *Nianpan wuming* ("Nirvana without Name") in memory of the great teacher. He combined this essay with three others—*Wu buqian* ("Things Do Not Shift"), *Bu zhenkong* ("Emptiness of the Non-Absolute"), and *Boruo wuzhi* ("*Prajna* without Knowledge")—and his letters to Liu Yimin (Li Yimin Shu) in a book, *Zhaolun* (*The Book of Zhao*). He then died in 414, at age forty-one.

Sengzhao's works were indeed an excellent exposition of Madhyamika philosophy, especially the doctrine of emptiness. They helped spread Sanlun Madhyamika thought in China and laid a foundation for the development of Mahayana Buddhism among intellectuals in China, Korea, and Japan. In many ways, especially in its rejection of analytic, dualistic, and conceptual thought, Chan (Zen) is the practice of Sengzhao's Sanlun Madhyamika philosophy.

See also Buddhism in China; Buddhism: Zen (Chan).

Bibliography

Cheng, Hsueh-li. *Empty Logic: Madhyamika Buddhism from Chinese Sources*. New York: Philosophical Library, 1984. (2nd ed., Delhi: Motilal Banarsidass, 1991.)

———. *Nagarjuna's Twelve Gate Treatise*. Boston, Mass.: Reidel, 1982.

Robinson, Richard H. *Early Madhyamika in India and China*. Madison: University of Wisconsin Press, 1967.

Sengzhao. *Zhaolun* (The Book of Zhao). Dazheng, 1858.
Shan, Peigen. *Zhaolun Jiangyi* (Treatise on the Book of Zhao). Taipei: Fangguang Culture Publishing, 1996.
Wencai. *Zhaolun Xinshi* (New Commentary on the Book of Zhao). Dazheng, 1860.
Yuankang. *Zhaolun Shi* (Commentary on the Book of Zhao). Dazheng, 1859.
Zhang, Mantao, ed. *Sanlun dianji yanjiu* (Studies in Sanlun Documents). Taipei: Dacheng Wenhua, 1979.
———. *Sanlunzong fazhan ji qi sixiang* (The Development of Sanlun School and Its Thought). Taipei: Dacheng Wenhua, 1978.
Zhang, Qiang. *Sengzhao Dashi Zhuan* (Biography of the Great Master Sengzhao). Taipei: Foguang, 1996.

Shang Yang

Chad HANSEN

Shang Yang (Gongsun Yang, d. 338 B.C.E.) was a controversial and influential statesman of the pre-Han period in China. Confucian orthodoxy presents him as a central—and extremely brutal—figure among legalist thinkers (whom, in general, they portray in very negative terms). Liberals and anti-Confucians portray him as a principled defender of the rule of law and a bulwark against authoritarianism.

Scholars doubt that the collection bearing Shang Yang's name contains any of his own writings, but—as with other thinkers in China—it probably grew out of his influence. His philosophical influence stems primarily from the *Hanfeizi*, which credits him with the theory of *dingfa* (fixing the standards) and *yimin* (treating the people as one). Much of the controversy is about the content of these notions and, in consequence, the moral significance of Shang Yang.

Shang Yang was a remote descendant of a once powerful family in the early Zhou period. Orthodox histories record that as a young man he studied law. He worked for a minister in the Wei kingdom (perhaps as a royal tutor). Then he went to the Qin, where his modernizing strategies initiated the growth of Qin power that eventually made its unification of China in 221 B.C.E. possible. The Qin formed the historical dynasty from which China gets it western name.

We can summarize Shang Yang's broad political strategy as substituting rationalized structures for the organic families and amorphous traditions that characterize Confucian feudalism. First, he exchanged the feudal division for a system of centrally chosen governors; then he set out to standardize local administration. This was the first step toward a unified system that combined localities into counties and counties into prefectures, all supervised by a central administration.

He enacted a series of measures to reduce the power of dominant families (e.g., by abolishing primogeniture). The eventual result was the first area in which the nuclear family was more dominant than the Confucian extended family. He argued that noble rank and privileges should attach only to those who measurably benefited the state. He particularly favored military merit and began to replace clan and extended family structures with military-style "groups of fives and tens." The groups inherited the family's political role, its responsibility for controlling its members' behavior, and its susceptibility to group punishment.

At the same time, he enacted measures to stimulate economic growth and immigration. These included restricting occupations so as to favor farming and military careers. He took measures to reward farmers who cultivated wasteland, opened game and fishing reserves for agricultural development, and recruited labor from other states. The entire social-political structure aimed at economic wealth, a large population, and—as a result—state power.

These organizational moves may have been as important to Shang Yang's legacy as any of his novel legal theories. The powerful families were probably also responsible for his cruel death when he fell out of favor—they tied him to chariots and tore him apart.

Han Feizi, as noted, credited Shang Yang with the doctrine of *dingfa* (fixing the standards). This philosophy of social organization combined the existing practice of formal penal codes with the Mohist idea of operational or measurement-like standards of interpretation for guiding behavior. Mohists and the writers of the *Guanzi* likened *fa* (standards) to craft-linked instruments like the compass eyes and ears, could get reliable guidance. Shang Yang's idea was to reform penal codes to give them that kind of objectivity, clarity, and accessibility.

Shang Yang did not invent or initiate legal codes themselves. The historical evidence shows that laws in various forms had existed well within the Spring and Autumn period (according to some sources as early as 513 B.C.E.). Scholars think the move away from feudal conventions and toward more formal mechanisms of rule marked the beginning of the Zhou's decline. Tradition records Dengxi as having composed a bamboo penal code and having engaged in litigation. Confucius claimed to be good at hearing litigation. Shang Yang, as we saw, reportedly studied penal codes as a youth. The scholar Qian Mu, in the 1930s, explained the point of the new institution by noting that when punishments and rewards were codified in statutes, they could be meted out to common people accordingly rather than depending on the whims of aristocrats; also, the common people now had a basis for challenging their treatment.

That the idea of penal codes was familiar at the dawn of the philosophical era is further confirmed by Confucius's famous argument against the rule of law and punishment:

> If you guide with the punishment institutions, people will do what is right, but they will not develop shame. If you guide them with conventional codes of behavior and order them with virtuosity, they will have a sense of shame and rule themselves. (*Analects*, 2.3)

Let us call this argument Confucius's psychological objection to penal codes. It rests on the assumption that institutions of law and punishment will "exercise" the human tendency to self-interest more than the equally natural human tendency to social conformity. It is an argument that legal punishment is, in the long term, a self-defeating strategy for achieving social order. Social order is more likely to come from a moral education that instills good character in people.

There is another line of Confucian argument against rule of law, however. This one we can call the interpretive objection. Its core is a suspicion of using fixed codes of conduct to guide behavior. The *Analects of Confucius* does not give this objection in its classical form, but it does record Confucius complaining about glib moralists and, while observing that he was "good at" litigation, expressing an antipathy to litigation. Confucians (especially those tending toward Mencius's analysis) celebrate their liberation from the constraints of principle in favor of a cultivated, finely honed intuition for the complexities of the moral situation. The point is that using any code to guide behavior requires interpretation. The Confucian faction, for partisan and theoretical reasons, argued for a monopoly on interpretation. They favored the traditional ritual code, rather than positive legal guides, since they could then insist that they were the competent interpreters. Early texts represent Confucius arguing that the use of legal codes, equally accessible to all, will result in the loss of the people's awe of those of noble rank. Ordinary people will be able to know the code and thus will not be subject to the judgment of people of rank. "As soon as people know the grounds on which to conduct disputation, they will reject the ritual and make their appeal to the written word."

Shang Yang's proposal targets the interpretive issue. He wants standards of behavior that are accessible, uncontroversial, and relatively objective. He sympathizes with the people's point of view and, in language reminiscent of Confucius's psychological argument, argues against the Confucian preference for cultivated moral intuitions. "The multitude of people all know what to avoid and what to strive for; they will avoid calamity and strive for happiness, and so govern themselves" (Hsiao 1979, 399). This sets publicity as a condition for guiding discourse in the interest of the people. This liberal line of argument distinguishes Shang Yang from legalist thinkers such as Han Feizi who argued only the ruler's point of view.

The important feature of Shang Yang's reforms was their emphasis on standardized, predictable, reliable guidance. His rule for military promotion was a famous example. Han Feizi cites the regulation that ties rank and salary increases specifically to the number of enemy heads cut off in battle. Two points about this frequently cited case deserve emphasis. First, it has a measurementlike objectivity: one rank per head. Second, it shows that the quest for measurementlike objectivity applied to rewards, promotions, and salary as well as to punishment. The important thing, thus, is changing all codes of guidance so they do not rely on intuitive, moral evaluation. Punishment and reward should attach to objective measurable performance, not to motive or character. Applying guidance correctly should not require cultivated (Confucian) moral intuition.

Shang Yang further instituted an elaborate system to spread knowledge of the law. He puts the liberal argument against Confucian authority, albeit without the concept of individual rights:

> Government officials and people who are desirous of knowing what the standards stipulate shall all address their inquiries to these officers, and they shall in all such cases clearly tell them about the standards and mandates about which they wish to inquire. Since the officials well know that the people have knowledge of *fa* and orders, . . . they dare not treat the people contrary to the *fa*.

Shang Yang's line of argument is aimed at officials, not the people. As in his other reforms, he uses explicit laws and public, objective standards to break the power of traditional authorities over the people. Standardization pacifies the people by giving them the means to avoid official coercion. In the hands of Han Feizi, this justification subtly shifts so that he makes the point solely from the ruler's point of view. His version of Shang Yang's technique limits the officials' scope of unpredictable authority over the people. If they have to abide by measurementlike standards in punishing and rewarding, they cannot arbitrarily reward loyalty and punish enemies. Objective standards governing punishment and reward limit the officials' scope of action and inhibit their ability to build grassroots power bases.

At the same time, of course, Shang Yang was prepared to execute the law's punishments (usually quite draconian) whenever there was a violation. Scattered passages give some sense of the retributive "appropriateness" of certain punishments. Mostly, however, he justifies punishments on utilitarian grounds. The appropriate punishment is whatever is necessary to inhibit a behavior. Death distressingly frequently plays this role.

He offered other reforms to increase efficiency in apprehending lawbreakers:

> Whoever did not denounce a culprit would be cut in two; whoever denounced a culprit would receive the same reward as he who decapitated an enemy; whoever concealed a culprit would receive the same punishment as he who surrendered to an enemy.

Other aspects of "retributive justice" emerge in the text. They include a kind of "equality before the law." Another core in the *Hanfeizi* seems to signal this value—*yimin* or treating the people as one. We should not adjust the law for high rank, even rank that was earned as a reward for earlier performance. High officials are subject to the same punishments as commoners. The ruler should guide himself by *fa* as he issues edicts, commands, and ordinances, which are in turn interpreted and implemented by *fa*. Some passages suggest that individuals cannot change the *fa* themselves.

The justifications of this mild form of application of law to the rulers are more pragmatic than a typical western counterpart would be. The ruler's consistency in conforming his own choices and behavior to *fa* makes him less subject to manipulation, flattery, etc., by officials. Instead of directing their actions toward his whims, biases, and preferences, the officials must concentrate on the objective standards of benefit to the state and society for their advancement and reward.

The mechanisms to prevent shading the administration of law to favor the advantaged severely constrained interpretation. The result was a negative one that best explains the eventual popular reaction against the legalist system. As in the west, ignorance of the law was no excuse. The standards were designed to be as simple and predictable as possible, but Chinese thinkers had no recourse to the concept of a faculty of reason. The predictability could not depend on rational application of a concept of justice. It had to be a rigid application of operational or measurement standards against actual effects of action. Intention, exceptional circumstances, and situational rule conflicts produced unacceptable juridical results. Theorists contextually had only the despised Confucian theory of cultivated moral intuition to go on. Given their theoretical opposition to this invitation to "rule of men," they probably felt they had no alternative to rigid application of the measurement-like standards. That way of construing the alternatives left the culture with a Hobson's choice and eventually doomed the fledgling "rule of law."

See also *Fa*; Han Feizi; Legalism; Shen Buhai; Shen Dao.

Bibliography

Chang, Leo S., and Wang Hsiao-po. *Han Fei's Political Theory*. Monographs of the Society for Asian and Comparative Philosophy, No. 7. Honolulu: University of Hawaii Press, 1986.

Creel, Hurlee G. *The Origins of Statecraft in China*. Chicago, Ill.: University of Chicago Press, 1970.

Duyvendak, J. J. L. *The Book of Lord Shang*. London: Arthur Probsthain, 1928.

Fung, Yu-lan (Feng Youlan). *History of Chinese Philosophy*, Vol. 1. Princeton, N.J.: Princeton University Press, 1952.

Hansen, Chad. "Meaning Change and Fa/Standards: Laws." *Philosophy East and West*, 44(3), 1993, pp. 435–488.

Hsiao, Kung chuan. *A History of Chinese Political Thought*, Vol. 1, *From the Beginnings to the Six Dynasties*. Princeton, N.J.: Princeton University Press, 1979.

Liang, Qichao. *History of Chinese Political Thought*. London: Kegan Paul Trench Trubner, 1930.

Rickett, W. Allyn. *Guanzi: Political, Economic, and Philosophical Essays from Early China*, Vol. 1. Princeton, N.J.: Princeton University Press, 1985.

Shao Yong (Shao Yung)

Joanne D. Birdwhistell

A major thinker of the Northern Song (960–1126), Shao Yong (1012–1077) is known as one of the five founders of neo-Confucianism. His style name was Yaofu, his honorific was Kangjie, and he was called Teacher Peace-and-Happiness (*Anle xiansheng*), after the name of his home in Luoyang. Shao Yong is most famous for his ideas on numerology and foreknowledge associated with the *Yijing* (*Book of Change*), but he was concerned with many other issues as well, including those relating to knowledge and experience. Unlike many philosophers, Shao was popular among both the elite and the masses. His widespread appeal may be explained in part by the scope and imagination of his thought, which addressed such topics as patterns of cosmic change, practices concerning prediction, standards for philosophical judgments, achieving sagely knowledge and unity with the cosmos, and delighting in the experiences of life.

His writings consist of the *Supreme Ultimate Ordering the World* (*Huangji jingshi*) and the *Yi River Teacher's Beating the Rang* (*Yichuan jirang ji*), a collection of poetry. Traditionally attributed to Shao, but of uncertain authorship, are two additional works, the *Biography of Master No Name* (*Wuming gong zhuan*), and the *Conversation between the Fisherman and the Woodcutter* (*Yuqiao wendui*). The *Conversation* contains passages and ideas drawn from *Huangji jingshi*, and the *Biography* is a thinly disguised intellectual biography of Shao modeled after the *Biography of Teacher Five Willows* by the poet Tao Qian (372–427).

Shao Yong belonged to a northern Chinese family that considered Fanyang (in modern Hebei) its ancestral home and traced its lineage to Duke Shao of the Zhou dynasty (1027–256 B.C.E.). Shao's great grandfather, who was responsible for the family's move to northern Henan, held a military post, but neither Shao's grandfather nor Shao's father became an official. The grandfather died young, and the father engaged in farming, village teaching, and classical scholarship. When Shao was young, his family moved to Gongcheng, where he met his future teacher, the magistrate Li Zhicai. Sharing intellectual interests with his son, Shao's father wrote a commentary (not extant) on the *Book of Change* (*Zhouyi*) and investigated correlative thought involving the sounds of language and music.

Shao originally set his sights on the state or civil service examination and consequently received a thorough education in the classics. He abandoned this aim by his early twenties, however, and although he was later recommended for an official post, he never accepted one. He traveled extensively in north China during his twenties, eventually returning to Baiyuan, near Gongcheng. There he studied with Li Zhicai, who taught him the images and numbers (*xiangshu xue*). In his late thirties, Shao moved to Luoyang, where he lived for the remainder of his life.

As a famous and cultured gentleman in Luoyang, Shao pursued philosophy and wrote poetry, and he became a highly respected, nationally known teacher. He associated with antireform statesmen and philosophers who bought a home and garden for him and supported him in other ways. He farmed a little, living quite modestly. Shao married in his mid-forties, and one son and two grandsons became officials. Continuing to travel intermittently until his late fifties, Shao composed numerous poems on the scenic wonders of his trips.

The date of completion of Shao's *Supreme Ultimate Ordering the World* is not known, but the bulk of it was probably written during the 1060s and 1070s. Its chapters are all called "Contemplating Things" (*Guanwu*). The "inner chapters" are by Shao and the "outer chapters" are attributed to his followers. Shao composed approximately 3,000, of which about half appear in his collection. These poems mostly date from the 1050s to the 1070s, when he lived in Luoyang. Despite the comment by Zhu Xi (1130–1200) that Shao's philosophical work represents the "bones and marrow" and his poetry represents the "flowers and grasses" of his thought, Shao's prose and poetry present complementary and often similar ideas. They both contribute to Shao's philosophical position.

Based on ancient traditions of thought that were merging by the time of the Han dynasty (206 B.C.E.–220 C.E.), Shao's philosophy gave central importance to three interrelated concerns: patterns of cosmic order, characteristics of human knowledge, and aims of human life. Shao was interested in how to understand and describe the patterns of change in the universe. He thought about change in reference to the natural world (heaven and earth) and the human world, both on the social level (political history) and on the level of personal experience. A second interest was knowledge itself, including how to define, attain, and communicate it. Shao offered a method of expressing qualitative judgments with numbers, and he described the particular kind of knowledge that enabled a person to become a sage. A third major interest was how human beings and their activities were linked to the activities of heaven and earth. Here, Shao was concerned with the heart-mind (*xin*), or spirit (*shen*), shared by humans and heaven and earth.

The range of his ideas has often been overlooked in modern scholarship, however, as scholars have focused primarily on the charts of his "prior to heaven" learning (*xiantian xue*). This learning was Shao's contribution to the learning of the images and numbers, which, along with the learning of moral principles (*yili xue*), dominated philosophy related to the *Yijing* philosophy during the Northern Song.

In his thought about the cosmos, Shao, like others, assumed that ceaseless change was inherent in heaven and earth and such change was characterized by regular and knowable patterns. The most fundamental pattern entailed a complementary relationship between the two inseparable aspects of *qi* (matter-energy), conceived in various terms, including *dong* (activity, motion) and *jing* (rest, stillness) or *yin* (the "structive," female, dark) and *yang* (the active, male, light). Shao viewed many kinds of activity in human society and in nature in terms of two-, four-, and eight-part patterns and their multiples. He accepted the widespread assumptions of correlative thinking, with its categories of classification and reliance on relationships between macrocosm and microcosm, resonance as an explanation of behavior, and the unity of the three spheres of heaven, earth, and humans.

Shao assumed, but did not stress, that everything in the cosmos is composed of *qi*, which includes the formless, infinite, and imperceptible as well as the phenomenal, finite, and perceptible. For Shao, the former type of *qi* was the unknowable spirit and origin of the universe, as well as the continuing (vital) substrate of the universe, and the latter was the sensory world of human experience. Shao used different terms to refer to that amorphous origin, including supreme ultimate (*taiji*), supreme one, Way (or way, *dao*), spirit, heaven, great mystery, mind or heart-mind (*xin*), center (*zhong*), *qi, li* (pattern, principle), and "prior to heaven (and earth)."

In Shao's learning of the images and numbers, the eight trigrams and sixty-four hexagrams of the *Yijing*, which are constructed of different combinations of *yin* (divided) and *yang* (solid) lines, constituted the basic set of symbols and were known as images (*xiang*). Numbers (*shu*) were an additional set of symbols, correlated and used with the images (trigrams and hexagrams). Beginning with the number one, odd numbers were associated with *yang* and even numbers with *yin*.

In addition to the commentaries on the trigrams and hexagrams, *Yijing* learning incorporated charts and diagrams that arranged the trigrams, hexagrams, and numbers in various sequences. Different arrangements of the images and numbers in the charts signified different aspects of and ideas about the world. Shao composed diagrams and charts, which were called the prior-to-heaven charts, or charts of Fu Xi (or Fuxi, a legendary figure) and were paired with posterior-to-heaven (*houtian*) charts, or charts of King Wen. It was believed that the images and numbers represented the world's activities in complex, mysterious ways, and that one could gain an understanding, even foreknowledge, of the activities by understanding these symbols and their commentaries and charts. Contributing to the appeal of the images and numbers as symbols was the philosophical assumption, associated especially with Zhuangzi and Laozi, that words are inherently arbitrary, incapable of fully communicating what they represent, and that symbols can better represent what cannot be said entirely in words.

Shao used both verbal statements and diagrams to express the view, from the *Great Commentary* to the *Yijing*, that *taiji* produces the two "forces" (*liangyi*), which produce the four images (*sixiang*), which produce the eight trigrams (*bagua*). The two forces consist of movement (*dong*) and stillness (*jing*), and here the four images consist of *yin* and *yang*, *gang* (strong, hard, firm), and *rou* (weak, soft, yielding). Through division into greater and lesser, *yin, yang, gang*, and *rou* expand to the eight trigrams. The eight trigrams expand to the sixty-four hexagrams, which represent (through a system of permutations) all possible situations in the world.

Using these fundamental ideas, Shao offered a system describing the order, or patterns of activity, of the universe in terms of correlated categories and levels of activity. He presented this system, which resembles that in the *Huainanzi*, in his "Chart of the Four Images of Heaven and Earth That Order the World." This system integrates six theoretical levels (or aspects) of experienced reality:

1. (Sensible) forms and activities (*tiyong*) of heaven and earth.
2. Changes and transformations (*bianhua*) of heaven and earth.
3. Movements and responses (*ganying*, resonance) of the "myriad things."
4. Consciousness (*ling*, or spirituality, vitality, intelligence) of human beings and other living things.

5. Ends and beginnings (*zhongshi*, cycles) of heaven-and-earth.
6. Affairs (here meaning obligations) and accomplishments (*shiye*) of the sages and worthies.

Each level in this chart consists of binary and quaternary groupings of images that clearly retain their original association with the natural world. Correlated with the eight trigrams, the images at each level represent categories of *qi*. Things in the world are assumed to interact according to their *qi* category. Although analytic itself, Shao's system describes a dynamic, unified universe with unceasing, but orderly, activity.

The forms (*ti*) and activities (*yong*) of heaven and earth refer both to the sensory level of experience with its perceived entities and to the extrasensory level of *qi* with its hypothesized categories of *qi*. Heaven is *yang qi*, arising in movement (*dong*), while earth is *yin qi*, arising in stillness (*jing*). On the extrasensory level of *qi*, the forms and activities of heaven consist of greater and lesser *yin* and *yang*, and their alternation, while the forms and activities of earth consist of greater and lesser *gang* and *rou* and their alternation. On the sensory level, the forms of heaven consist of sun, moon, stars, and planets, and the forms of earth consist of water, fire, earth, and stone. The activities of heaven and earth consist of the cycle of the four seasons (the year), which constitutes the way (*dao*) of heaven, and the completion of the four directions, which constitutes the pattern (*li*) of earth.

The interactions at this first level (of forms and activities of heaven and earth) produce the next level, the changes and transformations (*bianhua*) of heaven and earth. Correlated with all previously established images, the changes of heaven are heat, cold, day, and night; and the transformations of earth are rain, wind, dew, and thunder. Thus, in the sphere of heaven, for instance, sun changes into heat, and images of both the sun and heat belong to the category of greater-*yang* and the trigram *qian*, while in the sphere of earth, water transforms into rain, and the images of both water and rain correlate with the category of greater-*yin* and the trigram *kun*.

Drawing further on ancient traditions, Shao also used numbers and basic mathematical processes to symbolize the interactions of the different *yin* and *yang*, *gang* and *rou* categories of *qi*. For example, first assigning form numbers (*tishu*) and activity numbers (*yongshu*)—the number ten or twelve—to the eight categories of *qi*, Shao then multiplied the numbers to arrive at the change and transformation numbers. He further multiplied these numbers on the next theoretical level to produce the number associated with the myriad things. Shao used this multiplication process as a symbolic and more abstract way to conceptualize processes of change (on the extrasensory level). These processes were more commonly conceived in such metaphorical terms as rising and falling, expanding and contracting, flourishing and declining, waxing and waning, succeeding and failing.

The changes and transformations of heaven and earth produce the third level, the movements and responses (*ganying*, resonance) of the myriad things. Here the binary opposition focuses on the pairing of the four fundamental aspects of living things and the four kinds of living things. The four aspects correlate with heaven and consist of nature (*xing*), feelings (*qing*), form (*xing*), and body (*ti*). The four kinds correlate with earth and consist of walking, flying, grassy, and woody (animals, birds, grasses, trees). Since these eight images correlate with all other images, walking things (animals) correlate, for instance, with *kun*, greater *rou*, water, and rain. Through processes of resonance based on categories of *qi*, these eight categories give rise to all the things in the world. Shao conceived these processes in such terms as movement and response, leading and following, singing and harmonizing, and beginning and completion. Thus he emphasized the idea that the interaction of two or four things (such as the seasons) formed a new thing, or "whole" (a year), which in turn interacted within a binary or quaternary grouping to form a new whole. And thus the process continued.

The interactions of the myriad things according to patterns of resonance produce the fourth level, which concerns the special position of humans among the myriad things, a position based on the special *ling* (consciousness, spirituality, vitality, intelligence) of human beings. Humans are more *ling* than other living things. With the first four images associated with heaven and the latter four with earth, the eight images representing the notion of *ling* are eyes, ears, nose, and mouth, and appearance, sound, odor, and flavor. To explain the sensory abilities of humans, Shao used the idea of harmonious fit (*he*) between the *qi* categories (represented by the images) associated with heaven, or humans, and those associated with earth, or the sensory world. For example, humans can see because eyes correlate with appearances, eyes belong to the category of greater *yang* or *qian*, appearances belong to the category of lesser *gang* or sun, and *qian* and *sun* intermingle. In other words, the resonance among things of correlated categories makes sensory experiences possible.

While Shao and many thinkers believed that *qi* categories existed independently of human experience, Shao further proposed a conceptual level of reality that was a product of, and dependent on, human experience and the special *ling* of human beings. Shao expressed this idea in his concepts (perhaps Buddhist in origin) of *shan*, "to complete," and *shou*, "to receive." For instance, the functioning of the eye, or seeing, completes the appearances of things, and the functioning of the ear, or hearing, completes the sounds of things. And humans are conscious (*ling*) of the myriad things because their noses can receive the odors and their mouths can receive the flavors of the myriad things. Appearance, sound, odor, and flavor were concepts belonging to a social level of experience, a level of shared and mediated knowledge. Representing aspects of human awareness, these concepts were different forms of, and different ways of conceptualizing, human consciousness. Shao associated other ideas with the complex of ideas about consciousness, such as the beginning and completion and *ti* and *yong*. Thus, seeing was the functioning (*yong*) of the eye and began the process, while the appearance of a thing was the form (*ti*) and the completion of the process.

With humans as the ultimate kind of living things, the final two levels of Shao's system (expressed in both chart and verbal form) link the natural cycles of the universe with the patterns of human history. These two levels—the cycles of the universe (the ends and beginnings of heaven and earth) and the affairs and accomplishments of the sages and worthies—form a binary relationship. Internally, each sphere exhibits a quaternary division that Shao discussed especially in terms of number and the four treasuries (*sifu*). "August" heaven (*haotian*) is responsible for heaven and earth and the sage for human society, and thus each sphere has a "ruler" that follows the one *dao* of the universe.

The concept of *fu* (treasury, storehouse, orb) occurs not only in *Yijing* learning but in medical thought in the concept of orbs (*zangfu*, or simply *zang*, found in the Han classical medical text, *Basic Questions of the Inner Canon of the Yellow Sovereign*). The fact that three quaternary groupings of orbs became additional images in Shao's "Chart of the Four Images That Order the World" suggests that the *fu* (treasuries) and other images in Shao's system were conceived in a way similar to orbs. That is, like the orbs in medicine, the four treasuries were not in themselves the focus of thought and were not conceived as discrete entities standing alone with necessarily definable boundaries. Rather, Shao was emphasizing the system (of the functioning of the four treasuries), along with the idea that the four treasuries represent on the sensory level different *qi* concentrations on the extrasensory level. The fact that the four treasuries and other symbolic entities were given specific names (such as summer, *qian* in the *Yijing*) makes them appear to western (and perhaps some later Chinese) readers to be more ontologically distinct than they were originally conceived them to be.

On the level of heaven and earth, "august heaven" orders and completes things through its four treasuries, the four seasons. Comparably, in human society the sage (Confucius) orders the world through his four treasuries, the *Book of Change, Book of Documents, Book of Poetry*, and *Spring and Autumn Annals*. Correlated with the four treasuries of both spheres is the biological cycle of birth, growth, maturity (or harvest), and death (or hiding away). This cycle, in turn, correlates with numerous other characteristics, such as the four virtues of nature (originating growth, prosperous development, advantageous gain, and correct firmness, from the *Yijing*) and the four virtues of human society (benevolence, ritual, rightness, and wisdom, from Confucian thought).

The cycles of heaven and earth include cosmic and calendrical cycles, enabling Shao to link patterns of activity at all levels into one grand numerical system. The cosmic cycles are represented by the images of cycle (*yuan*), epoch (*hui*), revolution (*yun*), and generation (*shi*), and the calendrical cycles by the images of year (*sui*), month (*yue*), day (*ri*), and hour (*chen*). Twelve generations constitute one revolution, thirty revolutions one epoch, and twelve epochs one cycle; and twelve hours constitute one day, thirty days one month, and twelve months one year. The two cycles are connected in that thirty years constitute one generation. Performing mathematical operations with these numbers, Shao offered various numerical characteristics of the universe. For instance, one cycle equals 129,600 years ($30 \times 12 \times 30 \times 12$). Shao's calculations and later expansions of them became an important technique of prediction used by others.

Referred to as the affairs and accomplishments of the sages and worthies, the sixth level in Shao's system is the sociopolitical world of human society. It is represented by the images of sage (*huang*), emperor (*di*), king (*wang*), and hegemon (*ba*), correlated with heaven; and the *Change, Documents, Poetry*, and *Annals*, correlated with earth. The four classics, for instance, are correlated with the seasons, the biological cycle, kinds of rulers, and kinds of political conditions.

Defining the type of ruler by his method, Shao held that rulers' methods and values varied with the times, which followed the pattern of the four seasons. Using the idea of adaptive behavior (*quan*), Shao asserted that the method of the sage, or the ruler, followed the changes of "august heaven." Ruling in a period comparable to spring, a sage, for example, used nonaction to rule, whereas a hegemon, ruling in "winter," used cunning and strength. The waning and waxing of the seasons, or the times, resulted in bad and good fortune, while the following and changing (*yinge*) of the classics, or the rulers, resulted in harm and benefit (*sunyi*). These reciprocal and interrelated patterns of activity entailed four kinds of ruling mandates—the correct, the received, the changed, and the substituted—which varied in how many generations they endured. Shao recognized, of course, that later events did not always fit this pattern which ancient history was believed to have exhibited.

Shao held that the ultimate goal of learning was to become a sage, the highest form of a human being. In ranking kinds of knowledge from lowest to highest, Shao distinguished among knowledge in words, in actions, and in consciousness. Only the sage achieved the last kind of knowledge, a special knowing that in turn led to action described as completely natural, nondeliberate, and spontaneous.

Shao described the special capability of the sage in terms of his concept of *guan* (observe, perceive, contemplate, understand). The sage can use one mind, self, thing, and generation to perceive all minds, selves, things, and generations because he understands the patterns of things and knows that similar kinds of things have similar patterns. The sage perceives the universe and things not from his own particular limited perspective, but from the perspective of the whole, variously called heaven, "august heaven," or *dao*. Insofar as sagely achievement is equivalent to the sage's substituting himself for heaven, the sage becomes confluent with the universe. Reversing cosmological development from the one to the many, the sage achieves a unity epistemologically and, through his timely actions as a ruler, in a political, social, and moral sense as well.

Shao's concept of reflective perception (*fanguan*) suggests how the sage's knowledge is possible. Assuming that true knowledge is analogous to reflection and concerns the patterns of things (*wu*), Shao claimed that the sage does more than just reflect (*ming*) the appearances (*xing*) of things, like a mirror, or unite (*yi*, reflect even more clearly) the appearances of things, like still water. The sage unites, or reflects perfectly, the feelings of things. The sage not only perceives the patterns, nature, and destiny (*ming*) of all things by perceiving one thing but also perceives the feelings of all things by perceiving one thing—himself. Since all things in the universe form a unity by sharing the same patterns or spirit, the sage attains perfect knowledge by reflecting on himself (*fanguan*).

Although Shao discussed his conception of feelings (sentiments, responses, emotions) only briefly, they were important to his view of the ultimate goal in life. Using accepted ideas in aesthetics and distinguishing between the inner, private person and the outer world, Shao suggested a relationship between the world, the person, the feelings, and the creation of poetry and music. He said that what is called feelings within the heart-mind is called poetry when expressed in words. Feelings stir on the inside and take form in words, while sounds are called music only after being arranged in patterns. Taking an important position philosophically by stressing the experiential, relational, and communicative nature of the feelings, Shao defined feelings as the phenomena of a person's "embracing the times and responding to things." Feelings are particular responses of people to certain aspects of their environment. Words and sounds are manifestations of feelings, while poetry and music are the artistic patterning of words and sounds.

Shao noted two critical contexts for the statement of feelings—the self (*shen*) and the times (*shi*). Feelings of joy and sorrow are most important for the self, because people focus on wealth and poverty, high rank and low. Comparably, good and bad fortune are critical in regard to the times, as they flourish and decline, and exhibit order and disorder. Shao was critical of contemporaries who considered feelings to be bad—interpreting sorrow, for instance, as resentment and joy as debauchery.

Rejecting a contemporary view that feelings themselves are good or bad, Shao compared feelings to water's capability to hold a boat up or sink it. He claimed that feelings can drown a person even more than water, thus affirming the moral-spiritual dimension over the physical. He urged people to distinguish between the characteristics of something, such as water or feelings, and judgment of its effect on people. Judging something only in terms of its effect on something else ultimately harms that thing. Moreover, a person and his or her feeling are not separate.

Shao described the relationship of the individual person to the *dao* as analagous to a series of concentric circles, with the *dao* an ineffable reality at the center. "Enclosing" the *dao* is the nature (*xing*), then the heart-mind (*xin*), then the self (*shen*), and finally the sensible body (*wu*, thing). The nature is the embodiment of the *dao*, the heart-mind the city wall of the nature, the self the territory of the heart-mind, and the body the vehicle of the self. Harm done to an outer entity also results in harm to an inner entity. Thus, harm to the body results in harm to the self, harm to the self results in harm to the mind, and so on. To think in these terms is, however, to view the nature from the viewpoint of the *dao*, the mind from the viewpoint of the nature, the self from the viewpoint of the mind, and the body from the viewpoint of the self.

Shao acknowledged that order will prevail if the two aspects of each such pair are in harmony, but the question of harm still remains. Harm can be eliminated by judging and conceiving things in terms of themselves. Extending this position from the person to the times, Shao advocated viewing the family from the viewpoint of the family, the state from the state, the world from the world. He opposed viewing a person's feelings from the viewpoint of something else, because that practice distorts and consequently harms feelings. Shao was interested in feelings, moreover, because they promote joy and happiness, for himself and for everyone. Ultimate joy involved an aesthetic-mystical experience of oneness with the world achieved by expanding one's own joyful feelings to include the world, not by just focusing on oneself.

Historically, Shao was a transitional thinker, a bridge from classical to later contexts and traditions. Philosophically, he emphasized both analysis and synthesis. Some ideas that became important later in neo-Confucianism are found in Shao's thought, but many are not. The reverse is also true. Emphasizing the numbers and images, Shao's "prior to heaven" learning was based in ancient beliefs and practices associated with Laozi, Daoist religious sects, Daoist adepts, alchemy, naturalist thought, the *Yijing* and its apocryphal thought, astronomy, astrology, music, Han texts like the *Huainanzi*, and Huang-Lao thought. Shao thus assumed an unknowable, amorphous spiritlike origin of the universe, relationships of macrocosm and microcosm, and ideas of correlation and resonance.

He accepted Confucian concepts about morality, society, and government, the Confucian aim of harmonious order from the personal to the universal level, the importance of political participation, the Confucian classics, and the Confucian and Daoist goal of personal joy. He appropriated many ideas and issues associated with Zhuangzi, including those concerning the universe, the *dao*, the sage, knowledge, and words. Buddhist influence is also apparent, both in specific concepts and in Shao's general approach. Shao's focus on cosmic cycles, his goal of an ultimate personal merging with the whole of reality, his concern with the issue of knowledge, his use of certain vocabulary, and his general efforts to analyze and classify all suggest contact with Buddhism.

Although the different aspects of Shao's thought together formed a coherent system, later thinkers tended not to emphasize the full range of his position. In the Song, the numerological and predictive aspects received particular attention, as did his poetry. Shao's refusal to serve in office led Liu Yin early in the Yuan (1279–1368) to admire Shao's commitment to Confucian morality. In the Ming (1368–1644), Chen Xianzhang, an older contemporary of Wang Yangming and indirectly a predecessor of the Taizhou school, admired Shao as the ultimate of spontaneity, a genuine free spirit who emphasized the joy of learning and living.

In the early Qing (1644–1911), Huang Zongxi recognized, but criticized, Shao's spirit of spontaneity, while Wang Fuzhi depicted Shao's thought as mechanistic and deterministic. Wang claimed that Shao's systematic thought was obsessed with fate, distrustful of feelings, and representative of an incorrect understanding of the universe—particularly because Shao viewed *qi* as segmented and used a false principle of opposition (numerical doubling). Although not generally acknowledged, Wang's view has combined with western rationalist views of reality (as an underlying, independent, unchanging substance, not accessible to sense perception) to produce twentieth-century claims (highly questionable) that Shao advocated objectivity (in the sense of either western rationalism or modern science).

The wide range of interpretations of Shao is due not only to changing interests and perspectives of scholars but also to the theoretical sophistication of his thought. Shao was concerned with theoretical issues in a way that was unusual, although not unique, for Chinese philosophers. He offered ideas on such problems as theoretical levels of reality, movable observational viewpoints, kinds of knowledge, uses of symbols, patterns of regularity in the universe and in society, and the place of humans in the universe. His views kept Chinese thinkers intrigued with his thought and make it still inviting for comparative philosophy.

See also Confucianism: Song.

Bibliography

Berkowitz, Alan. "Scholarly Note: On Shao Yung's Dates (21 January 1012–27 July 1077)." *Chinese Literature: Essays, Articles, Reviews*, 5, 1983, pp. 91–94.

Birdwhistell, Joanne D. "From Cosmic to Personal: Shao Yong's Narratives on the Creative Source." In *Confucian Spirituality*, ed. Tu Weiming and Mary Evelyn Tucker. New York: Crossroad, 2002.

——. "The Numerically Patterned Universe in the Philosophy of Shao Yong." In *Sources of Chinese Tradition*, 2nd ed., Vol. 1, comp. William Theodore de Bary and Irene Bloom. New York: Columbia University Press, 1999, pp. 678–682.

——. "The Philosophical Concept of Foreknowledge in the Thought of Shao Yung." *Philosophy East and West*, 39(1), 1989, pp. 47–65.

——. "Shao Yong." In *Routledge International Encyclopedia of Philosophy*, rev. ed. London and New York: Routledge, 1998.

——. "Shao Yung and His Concept of Objective Observation (*Fan-kuan*)." *Journal of Chinese Philosophy*, 9(4), 1982, pp. 367–394.

———. *Transition to Neo-Confucianism: Shao Yung on Knowledge and Symbols of Reality*. Stanford, Calif.: Stanford University Press, 1989.

Black, Alison Harley. *Man and Nature in the Philosophical Thought of Wang Fu-chih*. Seattle: University of Washington Press, 1989.

Cai, Te'an. *Kangjie xiantian Yi xue pingyi* (An Analysis of K'ang-chieh's Prior-to-Heaven Yijing Learning). Taipei: Lung-ch'an ch'u-pan she, 1973. (In Chinese.)

Chan, Wing-tsit, trans. and comp. *A Source Book in Chinese Philosophy*. Princeton, N.J.: Princeton University Press, 1963.

Chang, Carsun. *The Development of Neo-Confucian Thought*, Vol. 1. New York: Bookman, 1957.

Chao, Ling-ling. *Shao K'ang-chieh "Kuan-wu nei-p'ien" te yen-chiu—T'ien-jen ho-i li-nien te t'an-suo* (Study of Shao K'ang-chieh's "Contemplating Things, Inner Chapters"—Inquiry into the Concept of the Unity of Heaven and Humans). Fu-jen ta-hsüeh che-hsüeh yen-chiu suo, 1970. (In Chinese.)

Chen Yüfu. *Shao Kangjie xueshu* (The Learning of Shao Kangjie). Taipei: Wenjin chupan she, 1977. (In Chinese.)

Freeman, Michael D. "From Adept to Worthy: The Philosophical Career of Shao Yung." *Journal of the American Oriental Society*, 102, 1982, pp. 477–491.

Fung, Yu-lan (Feng Youlan). *A History of Chinese Philosophy*, Vol. 2, trans. Derk Bodde. Princeton, N.J.: Princeton University Press, 1953.

Miura, Kunio. "Isen Gekijo shu no sekai (The World of the Yi River Teacher's Beating the Rang)." *Toho Gakuho*, 47, 1974, pp. 117–190. (In Japanese.)

Ryan, James A. "The Compatibilist Philosophy of Freedom of Shao Yung." *Journal of Chinese Philosophy*, 20(3), 1993, pp. 279–291.

Sattler, Gabriele. "Shao Yung." In *Sung Biographies*, ed. Herbert Franke. Wiesbaden: Franz Steiner Verlag, 1976. (In German.)

Shao, Yong. *Biography of the Gentleman with No Name* (*Wuming gong zhuan*), trans. James A. Ryan. In *The Columbia Anthology of Traditional Chinese Literature*, ed. Victor Mair. New York: Columbia University Press, 1994.

———. *Conversation between the Fisherman and the Woodcutter* (*Yuqiao wendui*). c. 11th–12th centuries. Edition: *Siku quanshu*. (In Chinese. See also Knud Lundbaek, trans. *Dialogue between a Fisherman and a Woodcutter* by Shao Yong. Hamburg: C. Bell Verlag, 1986.)

———. *Supreme Ultimate Ordering the World* (*Huangji jingshi shu*). 1060s–1070s. Editions: *Sibu beiyao, Siku quanshu, Daozang*. (In Chinese.)

———. *The Yi River Teacher's Beating the Rang* (*Yichuan jirang ji*). 1050s–1060s, Preface 1066. Editions: *Sibu congkan, Daozang*. (In Chinese.)

Smith, Kidder, Jr., Peter K. Bol, Joseph A. Adler, and Don J. Wyatt. *Sung Dynasty Uses of the Yijing*. Princeton, N.J.: Princeton University Press, 1990.

Ueno, Hideto, ed. and trans. *Isen gekijo shu* (Collection of the Yi River Teacher's Beating the Rang). Tokyo: Meitoku shuppansha, 1979. (In Japanese.)

Wei, Shaosheng, comp. *Huangji jingshishu (Book of the Supreme Ultimate Ordering the World) by Shao Yong*. Zhengzhou shi: Zhongzhou guji chubanshe, 1993. (In Chinese.)

Wieger, Leon, S.J. *Histoire des croyances religieuses et des opinions philosophiques en Chine* (History of Religious Beliefs and Philosophical Views in China). H. Maquet, S.J., 1917. (In French.)

Wu, Kang. *Shaozi Yi xue* (The Yijing Learning of Master Shao). Taipei: Shangwu, 1959. (In Chinese.)

Wyatt, Don J. "Chu Hsi's Critique of Shao Yung: One Instance of the Stand against Fatalism." *Harvard Journal of Asiatic Studies*, 45(2), 1985, pp. 649–666.

———. *The Recluse of Loyang: Shao Yung and the Moral Evolution of Early Sung Thought*. Honolulu: University of Hawaii Press, 1996.

———. "Shao Yung: Champion of Philosophical Syncretism in Early Sung China." Ph.D. dissertation, Harvard University, 1984.

Shen Buhai (Shen Pu-hai)

Chad Hansen

Shen Buhai (d. 337 B.C.E.) was one of the three sources Han Feizi (Han Fei Tzu, Han Fei) credited with developing the elements of legalist thought (*fajia*). Shen championed the concept of *shu* (method, art, technique). History records that he was a rather successful chief minister under Marquis Zhao of Han—successful in particular in that he appears to have died of natural causes, which was somewhat rare for the legalists. Tradition also credits him with writing a two-chapter book, the *Shenzi*, but scholars believe that it has not survived. Most of our information about Shen's theories, therefore, comes indirectly from doctrines attributed to him by others. Given Han Feizi's account, most scholars categorize Shen as a legalist. Other historical sources, however, say that he studied Huang-Lao—a religion blending Daoism and legalism. A great portion of the apocryphal book attributed to Shen was supposed to have patterned itself on the deliberate obscurity of Huang-Lao mysticism and to share significant concepts with that political-religious movement. We will, however, elaborate Shen's ideas as if they were primarily concepts of government.

Much of our discussion of the thought of Shen Buhai draws on a detailed study by Hurlee Creel (1974), who pieced together nearly every extant passage or idea attributed to Shen Buhai in an attempt to get an overall picture of his theory. Creel concluded that Shen's focus was on bureaucracy and that he had not been a legalist. This account will accept the former but depart from the latter, though the basis for this decision presumes the plausibility of a different view of the legalists.

Strategy: Control of Ministers

Scholars almost universally agree that Shen Buhai's *shu* (method) focused primarily on controlling the official bureaucracy—the ministers. Shen senses that the greatest danger to the ruler comes from within his own power structure:

> The reason why a ruler builds lofty inner walls and outer walls, and looks carefully to the barring of doors and gates, is to prepare against the coming of invaders and bandits. However, one who murders the ruler and takes his state does not necessarily force his way in by climbing over difficult walls and battering in barred doors and gates. He may be one of the ruler's own ministers, who gradually limits what the ruler is permitted to see and restricts what he is allowed to hear, until finally the minister seizes his government and monopolizes his power to command, possessing his people and taking his state.

At the same time, Shen Buhai apparently appreciated that a complex state can function only with a capable, responsible, powerful bureaucracy. The ruler has to find ways to employ and control his ministers without letting them usurp his central ruling position:

> The intelligent ruler is like the torso; the minister is like an arm. . . . The ruler controls the principles; the ministers carry them out in detail. The ruler holds the controls; the ministers carry on routine functions.

Another respect in which Shen Buhai appears like other legalists is in his serious worry about the vagueness of language and the dangers of verbal persuasion. The ruler must insist on having access to all channels of information, not merely ministers' reports. These he has to view as "objectively" as possible:

> One who sees things independently is called clear-eyed. One who hears things independently is called sharp-eared. He who can reach decisions independently is therefore able to be the ruler of the whole world.

At the same time, Shen condemns trying to master all the details. That is the business of the ministers. The ruler must have access to information, but mainly to prevent ministers from deceiving him about the situation or their accomplishments. The reverse, however, does not apply. The ruler is not to communicate clearly with his ministers, for fear they will get information about his personal views, desires, biases, etc., which they can use in manipulating, flattering, and ultimately controlling him.

Shu: Methods

The *shu* (method) thus concerned ways of controlling ministers in view of the vagaries of language. According to Han Feizi, the key was to focus on reality or accomplishment, not fame or reputation in appointment and dismissal. The ruler was to attend primarily to the abilities and accomplishments of his ministers, not to the details of their duties. The power over life and death had to remain firmly in the ruler's hands. Perhaps this meant that he could review, pardon, or reverse any juridical decision made by ministers as well as having the power to punish or execute them. The other techniques concerned ways the ruler prevents ministers from reversing the direction of control. One key, therefore, was that the ruler could not have a "favorite" or "controlling" minister, since such a person would replace the ruler in all but name.

Wuwei and Hidden Motives

The most famous method borrows a notoriously murky concept from Daoism—*wuwei* (nondeeming action). Let us view a range of linked interpretations of this notion in Shen Buhai and legalism. An explanatorily satisfactory interpretation is that acting with *wuwei* is acting in a way that does not reveal the ruler's motives. A twist on this explanation is that the ruler has no motives other than those of the state itself. In "hiding his motives and concealing his tracks" the ruler makes it hard for ministers to manipulate him (except by doing what is in the interest of the state). If the king has formulas, policies, or particularly valued virtues or goals, the ministers will try to accomplish these rather than giving open, unguarded, objective advice.

Another interpretation focuses on the issue of delegation, discussed more fully below. The ruler should not use his own knowledge or conception of the way of government. He should concentrate entirely on the *shu* (methods) that make his decisions "operational" or "mechanical." That way the ministers have no incentive to try to divine the ruler's heart-mind (*xin*). "The sage ruler depends on methods, not on his sagacity. He applies technique, not theory."

Moreover, the ruler does not compete with ministers or handle details. The ruler must have full access to information, yet he should not bother with details. It is dangerous for a ruler to try to master all the information needed for every decision. A quotation attributed to Shen Buhai makes this point, reminiscent of Laozi:

> Discard listening and do not use it to hear; then your hearing will be keen. Discard looking and do not use it to see; then your sight will be clear. Discard sagacity and do not use it to understand; then your knowledge will be all-embracing and your judgment impartial.

Nor should the ruler display his own insights and skills. Not only does this give ministers personal information to use in manipulating him; it also reveals his weaknesses. Trying to compete with his ministers in what they do best invites reciprocal competition—something the ruler does not want.

Numbers

Creel treats *shu* (method) as conceptually linked with its homophone, *shu* (numbers), and avers that the notion of technique implicitly has roots in something like statistical or categorizing methods. He observes that the management of financial resources, taxation, army logistics, etc., always requires keeping numerical records. Probably, he concludes, Shen carried this notion of numerical accuracy or objectivity into his concept of *shu* (method) as applied to controlling ministers.

This conceptual link suggests that the way the ruler gets information about ministers will be in terms of numerical measures of accomplishment rather than evaluative adjectives in recommendations. It gives the ruler the capacity to judge accomplishment in a more "objective" way.

This focus on operational, effective, or mechanical decision making links Shen Buhai with the notion of *fa* (measurement standards) that started with the Mohists. The Mohists thought of *fa* as publicly accessible standards for the application of language or words in general.

Mystical *Xinshu*

There is a more obscure and troubling interpretive possibility, however. The notion of *shu* (method) may be tied to the authoritarian doctrine of *xinshu* (heart-mind methods), Shen Buhai's link to the mystical governing school of Huang-Lao. The obscurity and vagueness of his writings suggest that this may be part of his notion. Presumably, the comparatively "mystical" side of authoritarianism comes when the followers of Shen Buhai claim to have cultivated—or to be able to cultivate—"supernatural" epistemic states that allow one to know everything or to be perfectly responsive to events. One does this by a mystical process that transcends language and gives one immediate access to the "right decision." We find this position most famously in *Mencius*; we also find it in some chapters of *Guanzi* that have recently become famous.

Such a skill could underwrite one's claim to a superior position over "ordinary" people, who are limited by their perspectives or by the doctrines they have learned. It also excuses persons in authority from accountability for their decisions. We could not expect those who cultivate this heart-mind *shu* (method) to put their grounds of action into words, nor could they expect the likes of us to comprehend them. So they can act quite arbitrarily in the comfortable knowledge that they are "transcendentally" right.

Shen Buhai does not seem to have been concerned with justifying the ruler's superior position and most commonly did not assume rulers were of higher intelligence or ability than others.

Xingming: Performance and Title

Secondary sources often credit Shen Buhai with the development of one of Han Feizi's important doctrines: *xingming*. Han Feizi's own account of Shen's *shu* (method) avoids these words but depicts it exactly and presents it as the essence of *shu*. However, as Creel notes, the term *xingming* itself does not occur in the extant fragments of Shen's writings.

The character *xing* seems linked to punishment (carving or marking) or shape (perhaps carved shapes). Creel says that it may also mean behavior or performance. The notion of *ming* (names) was central to philosophical developments of the period—especially the analysis that the legalists considered distressingly vague. It also, famously, could mean something like reputation or status and can be linked with the homophone *ming* (destiny or command). Creel understands the pair *xingming* as "performance and title." We can understand why Shen Buhai would be credited with the doctrine even if he did not use the words. Clearly, his account of the mechanical basis for appointment and dismissal is one that gives the "status" for the "performance" (as determined by "terms" whose reference is fixed by "objective" results).

Fa

As Creel notes, Shen Buhai does not talk about *fa* (laws, standards); in fact, Han Feizi criticizes him for ignoring it. This does not distinguish him from other members of *fajia* (legalism) other than verbally. Many translators agree that *fa* often must be rendered as "models" rather than "laws." It is not clear that the legalists change the use of the term at all. They advocate *fa* as an operational standard that removes ambiguity. The *fa* consist of objective, particularly measurement-like standards for fixing the referents of names. Shen Buhai's doctrine is broadly consonant with this view and with the emphasis on using *fa* to control ministers more than the people.

The important insight that Shang Yang, Han Feizi, and Shen Buhai share is their focus on objective measurement of results for any decision—appointment, promotion, reward, punishment, etc. They focus on names that are tied to explicit or objective categories, and on using these in recording and measuring situations and change. The rulers and ministers are or should be so controlled.

See also Confucianism: Ethics and Law; *Fa*; Han Feizi; Shang Yang; Legalism.

Bibliography

Chang, Leo S., and Wang Hsiao-po. *Han Fei's Political Theory*. Monographs of the Society for Asian and Comparative Philosophy, No. 7. Honolulu: University of Hawaii Press, 1986.

Creel, Hurlee G. *The Origins of Statescraft in China*. Chicago, Ill: University of Chicago Press, 1970.

———. *Shen Pu-hai*. Chicago, Ill.: University of Chicago Press. 1974.

Fung, Yu-lan (Feng Youlan). *History of Chinese Philosophy*, Vol. 1. Princeton, N.J.: Princeton University Press, 1952.

Hansen, Chad. "Meaning Change and Fa/Standards: Laws." *Philosophy East and West*, 44(3), 1993, pp. 435–488.

Hsiao, Kung-chuan. *A History of Chinese Political Thought*, Vol. 1, *From the Beginnings to the Six Dynasties*. Princeton, N.J.: Princeton University Press, 1979.

Liang, Ch'i-chao. *History of Chinese Political Thought*. London: Kegan Paul Trench Trubner 1930.

Shen Dao (Shen Tao)

Chad Hansen

Shen Dao (c. 350–275 B.C.E.) influenced both Daoism and legalism. He was a native of Zhao who served at the Jixia academy in Qi (an ancient center of philosophical debate). A Han history lists him, along with Tian Pian, as having studied Huang-Lao doctrines and *daode* (Laozi's *Daodejing*). The earliest Daoist history (*Zhuangzi*, ch. 33) lists him, along with Tian Pian and Peng Meng, as leading up to Laozi and Zhuangzi. Han Feizi credits him with originating the legalist theory of *shi* (circumstance, power, charisma). Shen Dao's own writings were presumably lost, so we know of him primarily through these indirect reports.

One Han source says that Shen Dao wrote a book of twelve chapters, and another lists a book with forty-two chapters under his name. These seem to have disappeared by the Song dynasty, when someone assembled an apparently spurious book of fragments. Most scholars are skeptical of its historical reliability, though others still debate the issue. We will rely only on the classical citations. These, in any case, give the views of Shen Dao that philosophers took as having influenced other developments in classical Chinese thought.

Issues of Text and Interpretation

How can one thinker belong to both an authoritarian legalist and an anarchist Daoist tradition? This interpretive puzzle reminds us that early thinkers made no such distinction. The Han historian who created the names of the two schools drew them from what he claimed were their respective core concepts—*dao* (ways, guides) and *fa* (standards). In fact, most philosophers from the classical period regularly used both terms. Han orthodoxy, however, viewed Daoists and legalists as having changed the meaning of their respective defining concepts. For Daoists, *dao* meant ultimate reality; for legalists, *fa* meant law. We must entertain the possibility, therefore, that the sharp distinction between them might be an entrenched interpretive error.

We have other indications of a uniform distribution of views across the range. Han Feizi, the paradigm legalist, wrote one of the earliest commentaries on the *Laozi* (purportedly the basic classic of Daoism). Recent work on Huang-Lao religion suggests that it also followed a more authoritarian reading of the *Laozi*. Many scholars now trace the attitudes and influence of Huang-Lao back well into the Warring States period. Han histories seem to identify Shen Dao as Huang-Lao. Working out a coherent interpretive theory for Shen Dao can be a way of exploring the shared background of these two directions of development.

For my purposes, therefore, I will concentrate on the account of Shen Dao in the *Zhuangzi* and try to show how Han Feizi's theory of political circumstance might have flowed from the metaphysical theory. Then I will look at the brief criticisms of Xunzi to see how they can be reconciled with the resulting picture.

Stoicism and the Great *Dao*

The account in the *Zhuangzi* characterizes Shen Dao and his associates, Tian Pian and Peng Meng, as "universal" rather than "partial" and as lacking selfishness. These attitudes justify positioning them as a link between Mohism and Daoism. It also separates Shen Dao from Yang Zhu, an ethical egoist who is said to have been a proto-Daoist. The rest of the moral description, however, makes them sound like ancient Roman Stoics. They merely "flowed" with events without calculating or choosing. The metaphysical description alleges that they united all things and avoided dividing them into two.

They called the absolute "one" the great *dao*—the way or Way. The Way embraced everything but had no distinctions within it. It included the acceptable and the unacceptable. One hypothesis is that Shen Dao's innovation in the moral thought of his time lay in denying the traditional view that nature was a moral force—sort of. He makes his point somewhat puckishly, like the libertine who claims that God intends him to do whatever he does. Shen Dao advocates following the actual *dao*—the actual course of world history. He adds (truly enough), "Even a clod of earth cannot miss the *dao*" (guide).

Shen Dao's slogan was "Abandon knowledge; discard the self." In the context of ancient Chinese philosophy, this was amoral advice. Knowledge would have implied knowledge of some *dao*, e.g., the traditional Confucian *dao* or the Mohist utilitarian *dao*. To describe it as "knowledge" was to imply that one had the correct *dao*, and an associated assumption was that one's own *dao* was correct because it was natural (*tian*).

Let us call the course of action that results from learning and applying a *dao* (guide) a "performance *dao*." Each classical school advocated that we execute (i.e., make actual) a different performance *dao*. Obviously, people disagreed about what was the correct way to perform a *dao*, just as they disagreed about the content of the instruction. Shen Dao, in effect, finessed both questions by prescribing the actual *dao*. Surely the actual *dao* is a natural one and any actual performance is a natural one, so he can safely dispense with any further moral reflection and theory.

How do we get the flavor of determinism from this stance? While there are many rival prescriptive future world histories, Shen notes there is only one actual past history and there will be exactly one future history. Of the many things you might do in the future, exactly one is what you will do. The one actual world history is the great *dao*. This invites us to conclude that the future is now fixed, but the argument is no stronger than the familiar tautology "what will be will be."

"Follow the *dao*" now has the required consequences. We do not need to study or learn, or make choices or distinctions. Whatever we do, it will count as following the *dao*—the course of nature. Thus, we can abandon even Yang Zhu's egoism. For all its shocking content, it too is a form of know-how—a prescriptive doctrine.

Therefore, the text tells us, Shen Dao:

> . . . flowed with what couldn't be changed and was indifferent to things.
>
> He said: "Know to not know (what to do)." He would have reduced know-how to something harmful. Naked and without responsibility, he laughed at the social world for elevating worthies. Dissolute and with no standards of conduct, he rejected the social world's great sages. Skillful and crafty, he responded to natural kinds. He lived together with *shi* ("this") and *fei* ("not"), mixed acceptable and avoidable. He did not treat knowing and deliberation as guides, did not know front from back. He was indifferent to everything. If he was pushed he went, if pulled he followed—like a leaf whirling in the stream, like a feather in a wind, like dust on a millstone. He was complete and distinguished (*fei*) nothing. In motion and rest he never went too far. He was without crime. How was this? Natural kinds that lack knowledge are free from the trouble of creating a self and from the entanglements of knowing what to do. In motion or rest, he did not miss the natural tendencies. For this reason, he had no high status. So he said, "Reach for being like things without knowledge of what to do. Do not use worthies and sages."

One notable difference from Roman Stoicism is that Shen Dao's doctrine does not enjoin us to approve of or accept what happens. Rather, it suggests that we should make no judgment about this at all. The Stoics, by contrast, because of their deterministic conception of reason, concluded that, rationally, we should approve of whatever happens. The concept of reason plays no counterpart role in Shen Dao's view.

Political implications. Assuming this interpretation, we can explain how Shen Dao's ideas could have motivated the political insight Han Feizi claimed to have derived from him. Shen Dao's system challenged the prephilosophical Confucian doctrine of the mandate of *tian* (sky, constant nature), which put nature on the side of moral virtue. Confucian legitimization required that the ruler hold his position by virtue of his superior moral character and wisdom. Shen Dao can be seen as rejecting the entrenched myth of the mandate of heaven with the simple observation that rulers become rulers because of circumstance, not because of their moral worth or desert. It just happens! The legalists, unlike Shen Dao, found it interesting to reflect more on what makes it happen.

Their study, however, is not of a moral *dao*; it is a study of the actual circumstances that result in one's becoming a ruler. The circumstances of power are subtler than sheer coercion. There is a natural social tendency (noticed by Mozi) to conform to those in higher position. The ruler relies on this tendency—whether he deserves conformity or not. The ruler is in his position because he relies on a hierarchy of authority, and on the natural charisma of whoever is on top, more than on moral qualities or even force.

As Han Feizi develops Shen Dao's theory, it includes techniques to enhance that natural charisma by elevating the throne; requiring ritual kneeling, kowtowing, and debasing forms of address; imposing severe punishment for looking directly into the ruler's face; and publicizing stories of the ruler's strength, accomplishments, and skill. Han Feizi also ties Shen's theory to Laozi's doctrine of taking "no deliberate action." The ruler maintains his situational authority by not expressing desires or decisions, by remaining aloof and mysterious as he observes the process of official decision making. How much of this elaboration stems from Shen Dao we can only speculate. The important component of the common contribution to Daoism and legalism is the portrayal of nature and natural process as amoral.

Xunzi criticizes Shen Dao in ways that suggest he used the concept of *fa* (standards), but Han Feizi's account attributes this concept to another source, Shang Yang. However, the concept itself was important to Mozi and could easily have been part of Shen Dao's system. Possibly, he advocated the use of clear, objective standards precisely because he doubted any moral reality. This would explain Xunzi's criticism that "his learning revered *fa* but he lacked *fa*" (Xunzi argued that the fundamental *fa* could be the judgment of only a cultured Confucian gentleman) and that "blinded by the *fa*, he lacked awareness of worthy human capacities." Xunzi's third criticism, that Shen Dao had insight into following but not leading, fits his stoicism but conflicts with the fact that Han Feizi credits him with a detailed theory of how to maintain leadership. Xunzi's criticism may be a way of disagreeing with the amoral theory of leadership. Claiming that he had no theory means he had no sound one. Alternatively, Han Feizi may have embellished Shen Dao's essentially negative theory with some positive content.

The blending of metaphysical and political-moral theory itself further recalls the Roman Stoics. Plausibly, Shen Dao and his group would have endorsed continuing to participate in government. If circumstances have so placed me, I will flow along. This classic Stoic attitude offers a way to harmonize moral alienation from a system seen as corrupt and the practical imperative to work within it. Traces of it can be seen in a later formulation by the school of Zhuangzi, "sage within; king without"—the famous ideal of *wuwei* (nondeeming action) action. One can respond to circumstances without thinking they are right.

Daoist influence and paradox. The account of Shen Dao in the *Zhuangzi*, despite its seeming Daoist inclination, is ultimately critical and dismissive. It declares that his *dao* is for the dead, not the living. His *dao* was not really a *dao*. We can easily interpret this censure in the language of Laozi (whom the presentation treats as the next step in the dialectic). This notion of the natural *dao* does not tell us to do anything at all. It is a *dao* that cannot *dao* (guide) us.

Another way to make the same point is to focus on the slogan "Abandon knowledge." The knowledge in question is not factual representation (to which, supposedly, Shen Dao would be favorable) but prescriptive guides. Thus the slogan amounts to the prescription "Do not follow prescriptive guides." This generates a prescriptive paradox. If you follow it, you disobey it. If you ignore it, you follow it. It is a *dao* that cannot *dao*.

We see here perhaps the beginnings of the Daoist interest in paradox. The *Zhuangzi* suggests that Laozi took something valuable from Shen Dao. Most plausibly, it is his antiknowledge, antisage attitude. In *The Laozi,* we get almost no hint of logical determinism. Laozi recommends abandoning knowledge on the quite different grounds that conforming to social systems of knowledge deprives us of natural freedom and spontaneity. He broadens his analysis of knowledge to include the knowledge implicit merely in the names and distinctions we use to construct guiding theories. This would have been the other route of influence from Shen Dao.

Zhuangzi also arguably draws some inspiration from Shen Dao, although he notes the incoherence of "all is one" metaphysics. The insight that an appeal to nature gives no guidance is crucial to Zhuangzi's mature Daoism.

See also Han Feizi; Legalism; Mohism: The Founder, Mozi; Xunzi; Yang Zhu; Zhuangzi.

Bibliography

Ames, Roger. *The Art of Rulership: A Study in Ancient Chinese Political Thought*. Honolulu: University of Hawaii Press, 1983.

Fung, Yu-lan (Feng Youlan). *History of Chinese Philosophy*, Vol. 1. Princeton, N.J.: Princeton University Press, 1952.
Graham, Angus. *Disputers of the Tao: Philosophical Argument in Ancient China*. La Salle, Ill.: Open Court, 1989.
Hansen, Chad. *A Daoist Theory of Chinese Thought*. New York: Oxford University Press, 1992.
Thompson, Paul, ed. *The Shen Tzu Fragments*. London: Oxford University Press, 1979.

Sheng: Life or Creativity

Shu-hsien Liu

The philosophy of creativity has had a long history in Chinese philosophy. The idea of creativity (*sheng*) can be traced back to Laozi (c. fourth or sixth century B.C.E.) and Confucius (551–479 B.C.E.); it was further developed into a major concept in Song-Ming neo-Confucianism. Even today, it is still a living idea in contemporary Confucian philosophies.

Laozi believed *dao* (the "way" or Way) is the creative source of all things. In Chapter 51 of the *Daodejing*, he said:

> *Dao* produced them (the "ten thousand things"). *De* (virtue) fosters them. . . . Therefore, the ten thousand things esteem *dao* and honor virtue. (*Dao*) produced them but does not take possession of them. It acts, but does not rely on its own ability.

Dao is seen as creative without being possessive, and humans must model themselves after *dao*:

> Therefore the sage manages affairs without action (*wuwei*) and spreads doctrines without words. All things arise, and he does not turn away from them. He produces them, but does not take possession of them. He acts, but does not rely on his own ability. He accomplishes his task, but does not claim credit for it. It is precisely because he does not claim credit that his accomplishment remains with him. (ch. 2)

Laozi thought that some of the so-called achievements of human civilizations actually run counter to the creative functioning of *dao*. He believed that it is better to have "small countries with few people" (ch. 80). And he gave the following advice:

> Abandon sageliness and discard wisdom; then the people will benefit a hundredfold. Abandon humanity and discard righteousness; then people will return to filial piety and deep love. Abandon skill and discard profit; then there will be no thieves or robbers. . . . Therefore let people hold on to these: Manifest plainness, embrace simplicity, reduce selfishness, have few desires. (ch.19)

In other words, one should follow the way of nature and not be led astray by the artificial ways of humans.

Laozi's words were apparently intended as a criticism of some values upheld by the Confucians. Interestingly, however, the Confucians had also shown a deep appreciation of the creative functioning of *dao* of Heaven, although their understanding of it was different. The following exchange was recorded in the *Analects*:

> Confucius said, "I do not wish to say anything." Zigong said, "If you do not say anything, what can we little disciples ever learn to pass on to others?" Confucius said, "Does heaven (*tian*) say anything! The four seasons run their course and all things are produced. Does heaven say anything?" (17.19)

Heaven seems to be the creative source of all things; it works incessantly in nature without showing any personal characteristics. Confucius said (2.4), "At fifty I knew the mandate of heaven" (*tianming*). Thus the Way of heaven is not cut off from the way of man. In effect, there is a two-way relationship between the Way and man. Confucius even went so far as to say, "It is man who can make the Way great, and not the Way that can make man great" (15.28). People are creative beings whose primary duty is to develop to the utmost extent their own potentiality as well as the potentiality of their fellow human beings. For Confucius, government is not necessarily something evil in itself; what is important is that government must be conducted in the proper way. The ideal ruler would be someone like the emperor-sage Shun, whom Confucius praised in these words: "To have taken no [unnatural] action and yet have the empire well governed, Shun was the man!" (15.4). From this quotation we find that Confucius also believed in the practice of *wuwei*, like Laozi, although they understood it in different ways. Confucius put great faith in people, whose creativity is manifested in human institutions—which should be understood not as an obstruction to the Way but rather as a necessary instrument for realizing it.

Mencius (c. 371–189 B.C.E.) further developed Confucius's ideas by declaring that human nature (*xing*) is good. His debates with Gaozi (c. 420–350 B.C.E.) are highly instructive. Gaozi believed that what is born (*sheng*) is nature (*xing*) and is neither good nor evil, a position he probably inherited from the ancient past, when the character *sheng* was used interchangeably with the character *xing*. Mencius rejected this view, as it failed to see a difference between humans and other animals. Mencius broke totally new ground, as he recognized only what is specifically human, i.e., *ren* (humanity) and *yi* (righteousness), as pertaining to human nature, which is good. Gaozi may be said to have held a naturalistic point of view whereas Mencius held an idealistic point of view. For Mencius, *sheng* is not the most precious thing; he said:

> I like life and I also like righteousness. If I cannot have both of them, I shall give up life and choose righteousness. . . . Therefore there is something men love more than life and there is something men hate more than death. It is not only the worthies alone who have this moral sense. All men have it, but only the worthies have been able to preserve it. (*Mencius*, 6A.10)

What Mencius said set the basic tone for the Confucian understanding of life and death. While one is alive, one's primary duty is to fully develop what is inherent in one's life. So long as one acts according to the Way, there will not be any regrets in facing death. Similar thoughts also found expression in other Confucian classics. The *Doctrine of the Mean* (*Zhongyong*) stated at the outset: "What Heaven (*tian*) imparts to humanity is called human nature. To follow our nature is called the Way (*Dao*). Cultivating the Way is called education." And the *Great Learning* started by giving its three principles as follows: "The Way of learning to be great (or adult education) consists of manifesting a clear character, loving the people, and abiding (*zhi*) in the highest good."

Through the *Commentaries* of the *Yijing* (*Book of Changes*), the idea of creativity was further developed into a major concept for the Confucian tradition. This classic was originally a book of divination. According to *Historical Records* by Sima Qian, Confucius loved it in his later years and actually wrote the *Commentaries*—the so-called *Ten Wings*—for it. This may be an exaggeration. But the recent discovery of a silk version of the *Yijing* in a Han tomb proved that Confucius indeed had something to do with the *Commentaries*, although we cannot be sure which sayings are by him and which are by his followers. At least it is safe to conclude that these were the work of the Confucian school and had incorporated insights from Daoism and the *yinyang* school. *Yijing* explicitly stated: "The great characteristics of Heaven and Earth is to create" (*sheng*). And, even more important: "Changes mean creative creativity" (*sheng sheng*). This expression is definitely not a rhetorical redundancy. A single *sheng* (life) indicates what is born as intimated by Gaozi. But *sheng sheng* means inexhaustible creativity, which is characteristic of heaven, the ultimate ontological principle working incessantly in the universe.

Creativity is manifested dialectically. "The successive movement of *yin* and *yang* constitutes the Way (*dao*). What issues from the Way is good, and that which realizes it is the individual nature." This is how we receive our nature, and by working out what is inherent in our nature, we can then join forces with the creativity of heaven and earth and form a trinity with them, as set forth in the *Doctrine of the Mean*. It is in creativity that we find the union between heaven and humanity and the goodness of our nature as taught by Mencius. Confucianism never denied that there could be dark moments in life and the world; its profound wisdom lay in its belief that at the high point one must always be concerned about what will come next, and at the low point there will always be room for creativity and hope for restoration. The creative process will never be at an end: the last of the sixty-four hexagrams, *wei chi*, means "not completed," and it is placed after the hexagram *chi chi*, meaning "already completed."

Neo-Confucians of the Song and Ming dynasties, including the great Zhu Xi (1130–1200), inherited the insights of pre-Qin Confucianism and went even further, identifying *sheng* (creativity) with *ren* (humanity). A neo-Confucian like Xiong Shili (1885–1968) still took the *Yijing* as his origin of inspiration and tried to give new expressions to the philosophy of creativity that he considered to be the core of traditional Chinese philosophy.

See also *Dao; Wuwei; Zhongyong*; Zhu Xi.

Bibliography

Chan, Wing-tsit, comp. and trans. *A Source Book in Chinese Philosophy*. Princeton, N.J.: Princeton University Press, 1963.

Fang, Thomé H. *Chinese Philosophy: Its Spirit and Its Development*. Taipei: Linking, 1981.

———. *The Chinese View of Life*. Hong Kong: Union, 1956; Taipei: Linking, 1981.
———. *Creativity in Man and Nature: Collected Philosophical Essays*. Taipei: Linking, 1980.
Liu, Shu-hsien. "On the Functional Unity of the Four Dimensions of Thought in the *Book of Changes*." *Synthesis Philosophica*, 7, January 1989, pp. 323–345. See also *Journal of Chinese Philosophy*, 17(3), September 1990, pp. 359–385.
———. "The Philosophy of Creativity and the Progress of Culture: A Chinese Perspective." *Ching Feng* (Hong Kong), 34(4), December 1991, pp. 1–14.

Sheng: Sage

Pei-jung Fu

The character *sheng* consists of two parts: *er*, denoting an ear; and *cheng*, a phonetic graph. The formation of *sheng* implies a connection with a sense organ, but in an ethical context it is a metaphor signifying comprehensive insight or wisdom. This point is well preserved in the description of the chapter *Hongfan* in the *Book of Documents*: "*si* (thinking), *rui* (intelligence), and *sheng*" in conjunction refer to "five psychological abilities." Thus, this character suggests a reference to the innate thinking ability of human beings, and this ability will, through strenuous efforts, be transformed into *sheng*, a state of comprehensive wisdom.

Confucius's use of *sheng* significantly transforms its meaning. First of all, Confucius's ideal of *ren* (benevolence) is the *summum bonum* of moral cultivation. *Ren* can be attained only after one has practiced virtue and fulfilled all one's moral obligations. Achieving *sheng* is implied to be greater than achieveing *ren*. Becoming a Confucian sage, as compared with a "*ren* person," presumes the most demanding, even marvelous effort, and the sage influences all people under heaven. Hence, *sheng*, in the Confucian tradition, became a privileged appellation applicable only to a few paradigmatic or exemplary individuals, such as Yao, Shun, and Confucius himself. This point reminds us of the unique relationship between the sage and heaven (*tian*). Ancient Chinese religious practice was based on this belief. Confucius pointed out that even Yao and Shun, ancient sages par excellence, would find themselves imperfect, because the requirements of being a sage include "bringing peace and security to the people" (*Analects*, 14.42) and giving extensive assistance for the welfare of the people (12.9). This suggests that Confucius saw the sage as one who transforms the human world into a utopia. This notion perhaps explains Confucius's saying that throughout his life, he had never met a sage, although he avowed his respect for the words of ancient sages. After Confucius's death, his disciples began to add the name of their master to the list of sages, but they firmly believed that no one since Confucius had attained sagehood. Actually, for his disciples, Confucius's sagehood surpassed even that of the ancient sage kings.

Mencius followed this trend while at the same time proposing a clearer image of the sage. His idea of "sagehood" consists of three elements:

- First, a sage is not necessarily a king or an emperor; there are in fact different types of sages who exemplify specific qualities such as "purity," "harmony," "responsibility," and "timeliness." This view substantiates a principle that an ordinary person can become a sage. Mencius's famous claim, "All people can become a Yao or a Shun," can be well understood in this context.
- Second, the possibility of becoming a sage is present in human nature, and its source is heaven (*tian*). In other words, human nature is endowed with the immanent orientation toward goodness. For Mencius, human nature is to be understood in terms of the human mind, which possesses "sprouts" or germs of goodness. Thus, for Mencius, sagehood is the outcome of a person's full realization of his human nature.
- Third, in Mencius's thought sagehood has a mutual relationship with heaven. This mutuality reveals two characteristics of his thought—its focus on transcendence and its mystic tone.

Xunzi, the third eminent figure of classical Confucianism, agreed with Mencius only on the first point stated above—that every human being is capable of becoming a sage. But for Xunzi the method of becoming a sage consists neither of the human mind (human nature) nor of the Way of heaven; rather, sagehood could be achieved only through the acquired knowledge and practice of goodness. If a person accumulates goodness and embodies it fully in his life, then he will deserve the name of a sage. When sagehood was mentioned in the context of discourse, Xunzi considered political achievements important. Not surprisingly, therefore, his disciple Han Feizi (the most prominent advocate of legalism) insisted that only the ruler deserved the name of a sage.

To understand the Daoist usage of *shengren* (sage), we have to rely on some relevant texts. In *Laozi*, the term "I" and the term "sage" are interchangeable, both being used in contrast with common people. This contrast invariably manifests Laozi's "sage" as a ruler. What makes this ruler completely different from ordinary political leaders is the strategy he follows. The sage "does the deeds of nonaction and practices the teachings of no-words" (ch. 2). His real master is the Way. At the same time, he regularly learns from heaven and earth, which represent the world in its original state. This effort enables him to transcend the relative values of the human world.

Another passage, "the sage avoids excess, extravagance, and arrogance" (ch. 29), suggests that the Way enables all things to recover the inborn natural state and to maintain perpetual harmony and tranquillity. Thus, the sage's "doing nothing" is actually "leaving nothing undone." However, this idea should not be considered a mere means of rulership; rather, it expresses the highest degree of wisdom after the sage has been enlightened by the Way.

The image of a sage in the *Zhuangzi* does not have this political implication. In describing the sage, Zhuangzi shifts the emphasis to the individual spirit, which reaches a realm of absolute freedom. If Zhuangzi had criticized the earlier image of the sage, it would have been because that image was explicitly fabricated from and polluted by worldly values. What he did was to remove the shield that obstructed communication between human beings and the Way.

Thus Zhuangzi could endorse his own image of sage with no reservations. He said, "The one who takes heaven as his master, virtue as his foundation, the Way as his doorway, and is able to handle all kinds of changes and transformations will be called the sage" (*Tianxia*). He also said, "The sage seeks out the beauties of heaven and earth and masters the principles of the myriad things" (*Zhibeiyu*). In these two passages, the wisdom and intelligence of the sage are prominent—so much so that the concept of sage recovers its primordial meaning. The virtuous acts of the sage, if any, are not taken into consideration. His spirit strolls freely, much as a great artist is guided by his boundless inspiration.

It is interesting to note that in the *Zhuangzi* we find the earliest use of the phrase "internal sagehood and external kingship" (*neisheng waiwang*), an idea later integrated into Confucianism. This idea provided Confucianism with a model for describing the relationship between the practice of virtue and its political implementation.

From the Han dynasty on, various meanings of *sheng* were intermingled and used interchangeably. In general, on the Confucian side, there were two kinds of interpretation. One viewed the sage from the perspective of political reality and recognized that the supreme dignity and authority of the emperor made him the only person qualified to be called a sage. The other interpretation adhered to the academic tradition, worshiped Confucius as the sage, and continued to affirm that all human beings are capable of attaining sagehood by cultivating their virtue. In the Daoist tradition, two inclinations can be seen: one was to follow Laozi's idea of "orderly governing by nondoing"; the other was to cherish Zhuangzi's idea of a "spiritual state of overall transcendence."

Buddhism, after its introduction into China, won the broad support of the Chinese people, and Buddhist ideas facilitated the development of Chinese thought. Buddhist influences can be noted in speculative metaphysics, which is an outcome of the encounter with the Buddhist idea of "emptiness" along with Daoist idea of "nothingness," and in "practice in one's life." Buddhism presented the idea that all human beings have the virtue of buddhahood so that they can reach the same enlightenment as Buddha himself. This idea corresponded well with the Confucian idea that all human beings are capable of becoming sages. Nevertheless, this similarity must be confined to what is described as the "highest stage" of human cultivation. That is to say, if we address their theories of human nature, we will find that Buddhism and Confucianism have little in common. Thus the concept of "sagehood" retains a unique significance in Chinese culture.

Neo-Confucianists in the Song-Ming periods scrutinized concrete methods for and steps to becoming a sage. They offered quite a few insights. For example, neo-Confucianists expected all persons to accomplish the ideal self by extending sincerity to the outer expression of sagehood.

See also Confucianism: Confucius; Mencius; Xunzi.

Bibliography

Cua, A. S. "The Concept of Paradigmatic Individuals in the Ethics of Confucius." *Inquiry*, 14, 1971, pp. 41–55.

Hall, David, and Roger Ames. *Thinking through Confucius*. Albany: State University of New York Press.

Schwartz, Benjamin. *The World of Thoughts in Ancient China*. Cambridge, Mass.: Harvard University Press, 1985.

Tu, Wei-ming. *Humanity and Self-Cultivation: Essays on Confucian Thought*. Berkeley, Calif.: Asian Humanities, 1979.

Shenhui (Shen-hui)

Hsueh-li CHENG

Shenhui (Shen-hui, 670–760) was the most brilliant disciple of the sixth Chan (Zen) patriarch, Huineng (638–713). Shenhui lived at Hezesi Monastery and was known as the founder of the Heze Chan school. He became famous in Chinese Buddhism primarily because he set up a great debate between the followers of Huineng and Shenxiu (605–706) and persuaded people to accept Huineng's teaching as the orthodox teaching of Chan.

According to Chan tradition, Bodhidharma (d. 532) brought a special message from India to China and founded Chan Buddhism. He is revered as the twenty-eighth Indian patriarch and the first patriarch of Chan in China. After the death of the fifth patriarch, Hongren (601–674), Chan split into the northern school of moral discipline and gradual enlightenment and the southern school of sudden or abrupt enlightenment and the wisdom of emptiness. Huineng belonged to the southern school and competed with the northerners for the title of sixth patriarch.

It was Shenhui who first raised the flag of the southern school and argued that Huineng, rather than Shenxiu of the northern school, was the rightful successor of the fifth patriarch. On 15 January 732, Shenhui arranged a great debate on *dharma* at the monastery of Dayunsi in Huatai, Henan. He delivered an opening address in which he attacked northern Chan. He also reviewed Bodhidharma's transmission of Chan from India to China and expounded on how Bodhidharma had passed the *dharma* seal and robe on to Huike of the Shaolinsi Monastery. He related how the *dharma* seal had been passed down in an unbroken line to Hongren and then to Huineng. He contended, therefore, that Huineng was the true sixth patriarch and that southern Chan, which possessed the robe, had inherited the true Chan *dharma*.

Shenhui began this campaign against northern Chan when he was in his sixties. During his youth he had studied Chinese culture, and he was well-versed in the Confucian classics and the works of Laozi and Zhuangzi. At age fourteen he became a Buddhist monk at Guochangsi Monastery. When he was in his early thirties, he studied Chan Buddhism under Shenxiu, from 699 to 701. At that time northern Chan was very popular, and Shenxiu was a very well-known Buddhist master. When Shenxiu was called away to the capital city, Shenhui went to study under Huineng in Caoxi, Canton.

When Shenhui first saw Huineng, the master was already sixty-four years old. Initially, Huineng beat Shenhui a number of times and then asked him, "Did you feel pain?" Shenhui famously replied, "I am both pained and painless." Shenhui also expressed his desire to be able to see into the Buddha-nature. Huineng then told him, "If your mind is deluded, you will not see and will ask for the way; if your mind is enlightened, you will see by yourself." He was referring to *wu*, enlightenment, as an opening of one's own mind. Soon Huineng and Shenhui got along very well. Shenhui spent a number of years in Caoxi. Then he traveled for two years, but he returned when Huineng was on his deathbed. He is said to have received the *dharma* seal from Huineng just before the master died.

When Shenhui was fifty-three, he lived at Longxingsi Monastery in Henan. He propagated the Chan teaching of the sixth patriarch for the first time in Luoyang, the capital.

According to Shenhui, Shenxiu and Huineng presented two different "ways" of Buddhism, although they had developed these ways from the same master, Hongren. Shenxiu promoted a path of gradual enlightenment whereas Huineng taught a way of sudden enlightenment. Shenxiu was a master of *guanjing* (observing purity) and sought the purification and pacification of the mind only. This is more limited than the actual teaching of Mahayana Buddhism. According to Shenhui, true enlightenment was not merely a gradual concentration of the mind but rather an abrupt breakthrough to a state of "no mind" (*wuxin*).

Shenhui believed that the essence of meditation was not the physical act of crossing one's legs and the mental act of controlling one's mind. Instead, *zuochan* (*zazen*, "sitting meditation") means "having no attachment and seeing into one's nature." While one practices meditation, one should be devoid of any attachment, even an attachment to the purity of the mind.

For Shenhui, only one person could receive the *dharma* seal. Therefore, if Huineng had inherited the right teaching, Shenxiu's version of Chan could not be authentic. As we have seen, Shenhui contended that the robe was the authentic evidence of the transmission of the *dharma* seal. Since southern Chan possessed the robe, only southern Chan represented the true *dharma* of Chan Buddhism.

The conflict between the northern and southern schools was not at all friendly; indeed, their attacks and accusations were sometimes ugly. Shenhui and his followers accused the northern Chan Buddhists of plotting to steal the patriarchal robe from the southern Chan temple, and of altering the inscription on Shenxiu's tomb. They also claimed that Puji (651–739), a chief disciple of Shenxiu, had called himself the seventh "leaf" (patriarch) and had built a monument to himself.

In order to make southern Chan more intelligible and acceptable, Shenhui may possibly have altered Huineng's message. According to some contemporary scholars, certain sayings in the Huineng's *Sutra of the Sixth Patriarch* are actually the work of Shenhui. In any case, Shenhui made a great contribution to the development and spread of southern Chan in China. Without him, the history of Chan Buddhism would surely have been very different. After the period of the debate, the northern school soon began to disappear, and Huineng was recognized and venerated as the sixth patriarch of Chan throughout China.

Shenhui died at Hezesi Monastery at age ninety-three. He had many able disciples, such as Faru, Fulin, and Guangbao. Chan Buddhism as propagated by his disciples was known as the Heze school.

See also Buddhism: Zen (Chan); Huineng: The Sixth Patriarch.

Bibliography

Chen, Nanyan. *Huineng dashi zhuan* (The Biography of the Great Master Huineng). Taipei: Foguang, 1996.

Cheng, Hsueh-li. *Empty Logic: Madhyamika Buddhism from Chinese Sources*. Delhi: Motilal Banarsidass, 1991.

———. *Exploring Zen*. New York: Peter Lang, 1996.

Dumoulin, Heinrich. *Zen Buddhism: A History*, Vol. 1, *India and China*. New York: Macmillan, 1988.

McRae, John R. *The Northern School and the Formation of Early Ch'an Buddhism*. Honolulu: University of Hawaii Press, 1986.

Suzuki, D. T. *Essays in Zen Buddhism*. New York: Grove, 1949.

———. *Manual of Zen Buddhism*. New York: Grove, 1978.

———. *Zen Buddhism*. Garden City, N.Y.: Doubleday, 1956.

Wong, Mou-lan, ed. *Sutra Spoken by the Sixth Patriarch on the High Seat of the Treasure of the Law*. Hong Kong: Hong Kong Buddhist Book Distributor, 1952.

Yampolsky, Philip B., trans. *The Platform Sutra of the Sixth Patriarch*. New York: Columbia University Press, 1967.

Yinshun (Shi Yinshun). *Zhongguo Chanzong shi* (History of Chinese Chan Buddhism). Taipei: Cheng-wen, 1988.

Zhang, Mantao, ed. *Chanzong dianji yanjiu* (Studies in Chan Documents). Taipei: Dacheng Wenhua, 1977.

Zeng, Puxin. *Zhongguo Chanzu shizhuan* (Biography of Chinese Chan Masters), 2 vols. Taipei: Foguangshan, 1990.

Shenming (*Shen-ming*): Gods or Godlike Intelligence

Edward MACHLE

Shenming is a term of various uses, made up of the graph for "spirit," "god," or "numinous" (*shen*) plus that for "shining," "intelligent," or "evident" (*ming*), elucidated by Graham (1989, 101–105), Knoblock (1988, 252–255), Machle (1992 and 1993, 159–163), and others. Examples of translations are "godlike intelligence," "gods," "superhuman knowledge," and "mental resources." Translators often render the term as a phrase, or fall back on giving the two words separate readings and then conjoining them, but *shenming* should probably always be treated as a single term, even though it has rich overtones that can require more than one word in translation. Although it still has a popular use, it appears in philosophically significant works mainly in ancient texts, infrequently and scattered through a variety of sources.

Except for six occurrences in *Xunzi*, two in *Xiaojing*, and a few in the *Liji* and the appendixes to the *Yijing*, it is scarcely found in Confucian contexts—it does not appear in the *Odes, Spring and Autumn Annals, Analects, Mencius, Doctrine of the Mean*, or *Great Learning*—but is found in such Daoist-leaning works as *Zhuangzi*, *Guanzi*, and *Huainanzi* (not, however, in *Daodejing* or *Lushi chunqiu*). It appears in a variety of uses whose interrelations are as yet unclear and are open to various readings depending on the context and the inclinations of the interpreter. At least six different uses can be discriminated, often overlapping and not always clearly distinguishable by context.

1. In what is probably the earliest and most common oral use, though infrequent in literary contexts, it refers to gods or spirits. In *Zuozhuan* (*Xiang* 14) and *Xunzi* (XVI) the people revere the good ruler "as [they do] *shenming*." In *Chu Ci*(*xishi*), the author admits that he would he would have liked to spend more time with the *shenming* of Kunlun Mountain. In *Zhuangzi* (ch. 2) we find "Heaven is honorable, Earth lowly—that is their ranking as *shenming*"; in the final essay (ch. 33) it occurs four times, in two of which (though hardly in the other two) it may be read as "the gods."

2. Close to this use is that referring to spirits or gods in their function of enforcing moral sanctions. Thus *Mozi* (85.48.31f) complains that no longer are the ghosts and spirits (*guishen*) considered to be *shenming* and to reward good and punish evil. In this connection, it seems relevant that the reverse combination *mingshen* is used in *Zuozhuan* of spirits appearing in order to punish evil—or, possibly, to reward good. In *Zuozhuan* they are engaged in observing, judging, punishing, and rewarding, just what *Mozi* predicates of ghosts and spirits as *shenming*. *Ming* ordinarily means "bright," but ritual utensils used in funerals are *ming*, which suggests some numinous quality. *Ming* in *mingshen* suggests that the spirits are "manifested"—Makra translates an occasion of *shenming* in *Xiaojing* XVI as "the spirits manifested themselves brilliantly" (1961, 35). *Xunzi* (III) sets *shen—ming* as a parallel to *ren—yi* and *hua—bian*, as if *ming* is the overt working out of the deeper and more mysterious *shen*. These uses suggest that *mingshen* may stress the spirits as manifesting themselves, while *shenming* stresses rather the manifestation.

3. As loci of the gods' manifestation, *shenming* is still used today to refer to the images of gods in temples of religious Daoism (*daojiao*) or of Buddhism (these images are not to be confused with ancestral tablets, or *shenzhu*). Images are not *shenming* until they have been ritually dedicated and placed for worship. Though evidence of archaic religious rituals involving images is insufficient, this seems to be an ancient usage, as in *Shiji* (12.29A.13 and 28.29A.3) we are told that the emperor Wu built an "elegant public building," which contained "on the south . . . a balcony for the *shenming*." If images were important in archaic Chinese popular religion—which is not much in evidence, but likely—then the usage of number 1 could understandably entail this meaning.

Shamanism, involving intercourse with spirits but also often identification with them, lay behind much in Chinese and neighboring cultures, especially in early times, continuing more notably in the states of Chu and Qi—*Guo Yu* (18) speaks of *mingshen* as appearing in shamans who sacrificed to *shen*; it may underlie the phrase *tongyu guishen*, "to have intercourse with ghosts and spirits" in *Shen Dao* fragment 16 (Thompson 1970, 518). The parallel *tongyu shenming* appears three times in *Xunzi*. Although the parallel would suggest "have intercourse with *shenming*," as in Makra's "[has] free commerce with the spirit world" (1961, 35) and Köster's "unmittelbaren Kontakt mit den Geistern und Göttern" (1967, 311), it has also been translated in other ways ranging from "become as wise as the gods" (Dubs 1966, 115) to "partakes of a godlike intelligence" (Watson 1963, 67). Makra's and Köster's reading presents us with a third use—a shamanlike involvement with the spirit world on the part of an appropriately developed human, while the latter readings give us a fourth, more important for subsequent philosophy.

4. Of more philosophical interest are the uses that deal, to one degree or another, with extraordinary spiritual virtues and powers as if separable from divine entities, and attribute to humans intellectual abilities derived from or appropriate to spirits. This represents no significant violation of categories, since Chinese thought assumes more continuity between the spiritual and the human than is typical in the west—something that encouraged Chinese critical thought to set aside identifiable deities and to diffuse the numinous into the cosmic structures. Philosophers manifested an increasing antipathy toward popular pieties (except for ancestor veneration—that was a part of *li*, ceremony, and *jing*, reverence, not of *ji shen*, worshiping spirits).

Thus, *shenming* is predicated of the sages; *Guanzi* (30) says the people followed the *shenming* virtue of the early kings, who were of course sages. Indeed, it would seem to be a prerequisite for sagehood. Li Disheng says the term "indicates practical wisdom beyond the ordinary, extending beyond what ordinary humans can fathom" (1979, 7). Knoblock expands this, as "a 'divine' or 'magical' clarity and sharpness of awareness, unmediated by conscious effort or thought, which enables those who possess it to discern subtle and minute distinctions that others miss" (1988, 255). It enabled the sages to be infallible without needing to be taught. *Xunzi* (XXI) speaks of one having such enlightenment as able to sit in his room and see the whole world, to comprehend every sort of thing, to identify the proper places of everything in the scheme of things, and to cause everything to function properly, as he knows the "warp and woof of heaven and earth," the *dali*, and his mind is never at odds with itself. The sage's *shenming* is part of his perfect harmony with, and his harmonizing of, heaven and earth.

Since the ultimate aim of the scholar was to become a sage, *shenming* is treated as the goal of mental development. This may be the result of quasi-mystical discipline: *Huainanzi* (1.7.7–8) says, "When the mind is freed from joy and from sorrow, from passion and desire, from ties to externals, *tong yu shenming* follows." Or the discipline may be primarily moral: *Xunzi* (I) says that if one piles up good acts to build up virtue, then *shenming* is attained spontaneously, and in essay VIII, "if one concentrates on unity without deviating, *tong yu shenming*, then one would form a triad with heaven and earth"—that is, be aligned with them as an equal, as a sage. Yet in essay XXI he speaks of the highest enlightenment as that of a mind which has become "empty, unified, and still." *Guanzi* (49) follows the requirement that the "body be corrected, the center serene," so that the *ren* of heaven and the *yi* of earth cooperate in the complete arrival of the ultimate *de* by which one can know the "myriad things," with the advice that "to control anger there is nothing like poetry, to banish anxiety nothing like music, to discipline joy nothing like ritual, to safeguard ritual nothing like reverence, to maintain reverence nothing like stillness." Just how Daoism and Confucianism intersect here is a problem. Graham (1989, 105) thinks their separation was incomplete at the time when *Guanzi*, or this part of it, was written. Other interpretations, even later glosses, are possible, since the textual history of the *Guanzi* is far from settled.

5. In *Zuozhuan* (*Zhao* 7) *shenming* is considered the final fruition of the human spirit (*hun*), which is added, under the influence of *yang*, shortly after the beginning of life, to the *yin* animal soul (*po*) present at conception. These souls make use of material things to grow toward maturity, with *shenming* as the ultimate goal. This acknowledged the potentiality of *shenming* as something within every human by nature (or at least within every male), and as something complementary to one's animal vitality. In several tractates of the *Guanzi*, the *hun* derives from the *qi* (material force) of heaven and needs to be developed by disciplines of silence, study, concentration, etc. This accords well with Mencius's claim in 2A.2 that his specialty was "cultivating my 'floodlike' *qi*," but not as well with the more rational Confucianism of Xunzi, who acknowledges *qi* but links ordering *qi* and training the mind together by following ritual, finding a good teacher, and focusing on one thing, putting emphasis on the mind rather than on the vital spirits. Thus, in XXI, he claims that the rulership of the mind (*xin*) over the body enables the mind to become host to *shenming*, with no mention of *qi* at all.

In *Huainanzi*, the highest result comes from the purification of *qi*, so that true keenness of vision, acuity of hearing, truthfulness of speech, and incisiveness of thought ensue when the very finest *qi* penetrates the appropriate organs. This strand of thought is expanded in (20.1A) as a continuity with heaven's regulation of the things of nature, including both the production and the death of living things.

6. In a very few instances, it is possible to read *shenming* as referring strictly to the human mind; in *Zhuangzi* (2) Watson translates *shenming* simply as "your brain" (1968, 41), though it would be entirely in accord with the exaggerations frequent in the style of the *Zhuangzi* to read *shenming* as having a much more elevated intention. However, centuries later, we have the observation of the rather skeptical Wang Chong, in *Lunheng* (24.71), "There are those who say that . . . the *qi* of Heaven and Earth reside within one's body; this is *shenming*," and the modern note of Li Disheng (1979, 488) on *Xunzi* (XXI) which elucidates *shenming* as "soul, consciousness" (*jingshen, yishi*).

The ambiguity in the Chinese religious background, that the numinous which punishes or blesses may present itself either in objective images and visitations or through shamanistic invasions of the body, allowed a dual development of the term *shenming*. On the popular side, an ancient use referring to images used in worship continued and is still present today. Among intellectuals—and hence in philosophic usage—the early connection with shamanistic spirit-possession evolved into a concept of supernormal sagely wisdom, which, viewed as the goal of disciplines of self-development, was construed to be a consequence of refinement of cosmic *qi*, something present in some form in every conscious human. In consequence, as philosophy became more and more detached from popular religion, the continuity between ordinary human life and attainable sagehood broadened the term so that it apparently can now be read, as Li reads it, as "consciousness." Thus what the term is intended to convey in any past literary use must be judged, sometimes precariously, on the basis of context.

See also *Guanzi*; The *Huainanzi* Text; Zhuangzi.

Bibliography

Cua, A. S. "The Ethical and the Religious Dimensions of *Li*." *Review of Metaphysics*, 65(3), March 2002.

Dubs, Homer H., trans. *The Works of Hsüntze*. Taipei: Ch'eng-wen, 1966.

Graham, A. C. *Disputers of the Tao*. La Salle, Ill.: Open Court, 1989.

Knoblock, John. *Xunzi: A Translation and Study of the Complete Works*, Vol. 1. Stanford, Calif.: Stanford University Press, 1988.

Köster, Herrmann. *Hsün-Tzu, ins Deutsch übertragen*. Germany: Kaldenkirchen, 1967.

Li, Disheng. *Xunzi jishi*. Taipei: Xuesheng, 1979.

Machle, Edward J. "The Mind and the *Shen-Ming* in Xunzi." *Journal of Chinese Philosophy*, 19, 1992.

———. *Nature and Heaven in the Xunzi*. Albany: State University of New York Press, 1993.

Makra, Mary Lelia, trans. *The Hsiao Ching*. New York: St. John's University Press, 1961.

Thompson, Paul M. "The Shen Tao Fragments." Ph.D. dissertation, University of Washington, 1970.

Vankeerberghen, Griet. "Emotions and the Actions of the Sage: Recommendations for an Orderly Heart in the Huainanzi." *Philosophy East and West*, 45(4), 1995.

Watson, Burton. *The Complete Works of Chuang Tzu*. New York: Columbia University Press, 1968.

———. *Hsün Tzu: Basic Writings*. New York: Columbia University Press, 1963.

Shifei (*Shih-fei*): This and Not, Right and Wrong

Chad HANSEN

In Chinese philosophy, *shifei* fills the space occupied in the west by the concept of "judgment." The differences illustrate some deep contrasts between the two traditions. The grammatical roles *shi* and *fei* have evolved dramatically in modern Chinese. A typical modern dictionary entry for *shi* might be: "yes, right; to be (verb)." (We use "to be" in far more grammatical contexts than modern Mandarin speakers use *shi*.) *Fei* would be "wrong, bad, non- or without" in a dictionary. In modern Chinese it functions more as "non" than as "is not." The modern compound *shifei* (gossip) is far removed from its classical meaning.

Classical grammar never used *shi* (or any other verb) as a link between subject and predicate. Subjects were optional, and a sentence might consist merely of a noun predicate followed by *ye* (an assertion marker) or a verbal predicate. Minimal strings would be "Horse *ye*" and "Runs." *Fei* negated only the noun predicates. *Bu* would normally negate verbal predicates (including adjectives). In classical use, *shi* was simply a demonstrative pronoun or modifier. It was very much like "this" except that, in verbal sentences, it could occur only before the main verb. It could act as the subject, the exposed topic, or the object of an "instrumental" preverbal preposition (usually *yi*, "with").

We can summarize this grammar of classical Chinese in the following three rules (S = sentence, T = term, P = predicate):

$$S\,(T) + (T) + P$$
$$P\,[(fei) + T + yeh\,(pu) + P' + (\text{speech act marker})]$$
$$P'\,[i + (T)] + P_n + T + (y\ddot{u} + T)$$

The *shi* may occur in any of the optional T positions before the main verb or as the predicate nominative. It was never the direct or indirect object of a verb and could not occur after *bu* (is not). Therefore, strictly speaking, *shi* did not mean "right." Pragmatically, of course, people could say "(it is) this" in all situations in which we would say "this one is right."

One interpretive controversy swirls around *shi* because Chinese translators disagree about the best way to translate the Indo-European concept of "being." Some favored the pair *youwu* (existence-nonexistence); others favored the pair *shifei*. The envisioned translation project (translating Aristotle) makes this dispute too specialized for our interest. Angus Graham, however, revisited the argument from the opposite perspective, asking what the option of two translations told us about differences in Chinese conceptual structure. He argued that they actually divided Aristotle's concept of being in two. Aristotle famously distinguished between what we now call the "existential" and "predicative" uses of "to be." (Note, for example, the difference between saying "God is" and "God is good.") Roughly, Graham suggested, *shifei* corresponds to the predicative concept and *youwu* to the existential.

Graham noted, however, that *shi* was never a copula in classical Chinese but an indexical pronoun ("this"), and that *shifei* did not fit together grammatically the way *youwu* did. It is not much of an exaggeration to say that the key philosophical dispute in ancient China is about *shi* and *fei*. However, this was more an ethical dispute than a metaphysical one. Given its centrality to classical thought, this analysis suggests that Chinese thinkers structured philosophical issues in a radically different way. Translators typically render *shifei* disputes as familiar-sounding disputes about what judgments are right or wrong. However, there are important differences. We can explain them best by pausing to analyze how a dispute about *dao* (which way to follow) involves disputes about *shifei*.

The most concrete sense of *dao* is "path." We follow a path to get somewhere. Sometimes two paths lead to the same place; sometimes they lead to different places. Disputes about which path to follow easily blur this distinction. We may think of ethics as a dispute about which path to follow. When we disagree about the end, we would say we have different moral theories. A dispute about which *dao* to follow is like a choice at a crossroads. I say *shi* (this) and you say *fei* (not).

In Confucius's *Analects*, the language of *shifei* was comparatively rare. (This may explain Fingarette's sense that Confucius envisioned a "way without a crossroads.") The *shifei* approach to analyzing philosophical issues appears to have originated with Mozi. Mencius's and Xunzi's version of Confucianism incorporated it, and tradition read original Confucian concerns through their later analysis.

The sense of *dao* in which we disagree on some path while agreeing on a goal informs many of Confucius's sayings. It also contributes a sense of *dao* as "discourse." The Confucian *dao* was initially a corpus of classical texts (the syllabus in Confucius's "school"), and the implicit moral conception was a quasi-religious traditionalism. The path and goal were set by "sage kings" and *tian* (heaven, nature). The path came to us in the form of texts, particularly texts on *li* (ritual). In early Confucian contexts, dispute was mainly interpretive. Does the text say we should do this or not (*shifei*)?

The *shi* can refer to an object or an action—the right object to use (the right cap to wear) or the right behavior (a proper bow). Within Confucianism, this kind of dispute motivated the doctrine of "rectifying names." The correct answer is correct interpretive performance of the ceremonies—this is the behavior prescribed in this situation. Modeling was the typical way to give an answer to such questions.

Mohism implicitly broadens the analysis to deal with questions of normative theory—what counts as *yi* (moral), *ren* (humane), or *de* (virtue). Mozi retains and emphasizes the use of *shi* for picking out particular actions. This feature shapes his utilitarianism. Formally, he proposes that we should govern our use of *shi* and *fei* by distinguishing between benefit and harm. His doctrine of agreement with the superior, however, emphasizes the utility to society of merely having agreement in *shi* and *fei*. Supposedly, Mozi would prefer that the agreement came from everyone's applying the standard of benefit and harm.

Mozi's utilitarianism thus represents a blend of overt normative theory and a theory of interpretation (reference). The right way to use moral terms like *yi* (moral) and *de* (virtue) is to use them of things that maximize benefit. However, this obviously depends on how the guiding discourse goes. Therefore, benefit can be a standard for changing the discourse as well as our application of it. Some of Mozi's arguments illustrate how the two sides can interact. We ought to *shi* saying "exists" of "spirits" and *fei* saying it of "fate." Thus which string society perpetuates in its guiding discourse (*dao*) is governed by the *shifei* assignment that maximizes benefit.

This duality of *shifei* in classical Chinese explains why thinkers intimately link ethical issues to the question of making distinctions. Essentially, getting *shifei* right is making distinctions in the right place—carving the world at its normative joints. Technically, *fei* is the key to making distinctions, and in Daoism it becomes a focus of a theory of language. We count as "knowing" a word in the language when we know that something does not count as the "thing in question" (*fei*). To know the word is more than simply knowing what counts as "it" (*shi*). Translators have no easy way to capture this analysis in English and mostly bury it behind idiomatic English. Sometimes they render *shi* as "this" (noun); sometimes they render it as "right" (adjective) or "approve" (verb). Some translators, following Graham, translate *fei* as "not this" in more analytical contexts, but most stick with "wrong" (adjective) or "disapprove" (verb).

The later Mohists built a more realistic semantic theory around *shifei*. A society hits on a conventional pattern of selecting things with names. Given that convention, our application of *shifei* with that word is thereafter guided by the world, i.e., by the actual distribution of similarity and difference in the structure of things. They championed the use of *fa* ("law") as a measurement-like or operational standard for the application of terms. Clear *fa* gives us even more objective, "world-guided," and determinate answers to questions of *shifei*. The concept of *fa* was taken over (in somewhat distorted form) by the legalists in ancient China.

Mencius, seeking to evade the Mohists' utilitarian conclusions, focused on the immediate action-guiding function of *shifei*. Knowing *shifei* was knowing specifically what to do here and now. He relied on an optimistic theory of moral psychology to replace *fa*. Humans have an action-guiding intuition that fits the moral structure of reality. It requires proper nurturing, but when it is fully matured it directly guides concrete *shi* and *fei* choices of actions.

Sagelike action, thus, requires no intermediate discourse *dao*. Implicitly, Confucius's intuition guiding us to interpret the ritual (rectifying names) presupposed that we could directly choose the right thing to do—*shi*. If so, then we needed no guidance from texts.

Mencius had a doctrine of "four fonts." The first was a kind of natural compassion. It leads to the elusive moral attitude Confucius called *ren* (benevolence). The fourth was a natural inclination to *shifei* that leads to *zhi* (wisdom). Presumably, "wisdom" here denotes the ability to do the right thing. Mencius does not suggest that theoretical wisdom is innate.

The other major classical figure who discussed *shifei* was Zhuangzi. His analysis exploited the grammatical and the interpretive complexity we have developed. (The interpretation of Zhuangzi motivated much of Graham's analysis.) In the first step, Zhuangzi contrasts *shi* with its indexical opposite *bi* (other) to emphasize their indexical character. Then he concludes that all *shifei* assignments (all judgments) reflect the position of the utterer rather than the nature of reality.

Judgments, in this tradition, were not propositions but indexical assignment of objects to social categories. The categories determined their role in action-guiding discourse. Therefore, Zhuangzi's position suggested semantic pluralism. There are many ways to assign terms from guiding discourse to objects in the world. Which assignment we use depends on our perspectives. A perspective is the position we arrive at following a history of commitments and training.

A commitment, as the later Mohists said, was a prior decision to use a term of some object. The processes of learning language in infancy and childhood and the inculcation of guiding attitudes, categories, and so forth shape our perspectives. Each of us can elaborate our pattern of assigning terms from a guiding discourse so as to guide their application to new cases. In doing so, we still rely on prior decisions and guidance. Our justifications of *shifei* judgments rely on other *shifei* judgments, and those on some our parents and their predecessors made.

Zhuangzi called the views that "accumulate" as we develop *cheng* (complete). He used the term with such ironic overtones that translators frequently render the word in Zhuangzi's writings as "prejudice" or "bias." Past traditions, experiences, conclusions are always changing our "achieved angle of view," yet it always seems to us "complete." Those who disagree seem to have missed something.

Zhuangzi's paradigm is the dispute of the Confucians and Mohists. Each has a different discourse *dao*. Accordingly, for key terms of moral discourse, they disagree on "what counts as "this" and "not-this" (*shi*-ing themselves and *fei*-ing their opponents). They disagree about the extension or scope of terms like *yi* (moral), *de* (virtue), and *ren* (humane).

Zhuangzi also argued against Mencius's allegedly perspective-free conception of intuitive *shifei* judgment. Any assignment of *shifei*, Zhuangzi argued, presupposes some discourse content and some acquired background or perspective. We cannot get a *shifei* out of the heart-mind (*xin*) unless it has been instilled there by *cheng*. Mencius had to reach outside the intuitions of the heart-mind to justify relying on the heart-mind. He relied on something other than the heart-mind to conclude that some heart-minds make sages and others make fools.

We may imagine undoing our learning to arrive at a state prior to all *shifei*. From there, any pattern of assignment would be possible. However, no pattern would be *shi*. The cosmos has no "point of view." Thus the appeal to nature or metaphysics cannot solve our disputes about what *dao* to follow. From this "axis" of *dao*, we would have nothing to say.

See also *Fa*; *Youwu*.

Bibliography

Bao, Zhiming. "Language and World View in Ancient China." *Philosophy East and West*, 40(2), 1990, pp. 195–210.

Fingarette, Herbert. *Confucius: The Secular as Sacred*. New York: Harper and Row, 1972.

Graham, Angus. "Chuang-tzu's Essay on Seeing Things as Equal." *History of Religions*, 9, 1969, pp. 137–159.

——. *Disputers of the Tao: Philosophical Argument in Ancient China*. La Salle, Ill.: Open Court, 1989.

——. *Later Mohist Logic, Ethics, and Science*. Hong Kong and London: Chinese University Press, 1978.

Hansen, Chad. *A Daoist Theory of Chinese Thought*. New York: Oxford University Press, 1992.

——. "Meaning Change and Fa Standards." *Philosophy East and West*, 43(3), 1994, pp. 435–488.

——. "Mozi: Language Utilitarianism—The Structure of Ethics in Classical China." *Journal of Chinese Philosophy*, 16, 1989, pp. 355–380.

——. "Term Belief in Action." In *Epistemological Issues in Chinese Philosophy*, ed. Hans Lenk and Gregor Paull. Albany: State University of New York Press, 1993.

Sun Yat-sen (Sun Yixian)

Ke-wen Wang

Sun Yat-sen (Sun Wen, Sun Zhongshan, 1866–1925) was the revolutionary leader and founder of the Chinese republic. The son of a peasant family in Guangdong Province, Sun emigrated to Hawaii at a young age and received most of his education in western-style schools. Upon graduation from the College of Medicine for Chinese in Hong Kong in 1892, he practiced medicine in Macao and Guangzhou, but he soon turned to his real ambition—politics. His brief association with the gentry reformers in Guangdong proved disappointing to him, and in 1894 Sun established his first anti-Manchu revolutionary organization, the Revive China Society (Xingzhonghui), in Honolulu. In 1895 the society's first attempt at armed revolt failed. Sun escaped to Japan. For the next sixteen years he was wanted by the Qing government and was unable to return to China. In 1896 a botched attempt by the Chinese embassy in London to kidnap Sun inadvertently brought him international fame as China's leading revolutionary.

Sun then moved his base of operations to Japan, where he received assistance from Japanese sympathizers. For a while after the aborted "hundred days" reform of 1898, Sun's revolutionary movement faced serious competition from the exiled monarchist reformers in attracting support from overseas Chinese. The Boxer Rebellion of 1900–1901, however, helped revitalize Sun's movement, as the Qing government was fatally discredited by the catastrophe. More and more Chinese students in Japan became Sun's followers. In 1905 Sun won the support of two other revolutionary groups in Japan—the China Arise Society (Huaxinghui) and the Restoration Society (Guangfuhui)—and formed the Revolutionary Alliance (Tongmenghui) in Tokyo. He was elected its chairman. Between 1906 and 1910, the Revolutionary Alliance organized a series of uprisings in China; none of them succeeded, but the revolutionary spirit was gathering momentum. Its alliance's organ in Tokyo, *People's Tribune* (*Minbao*), debated fiercely with monarchist publications on the issue of reform or revolution for China.

When the revolution began in 1911, it was launched by groups with no direct connection to Sun. Learning the news in the United States, Sun traveled back to China by way of Europe. He arrived in Shanghai at the end of 1911 and was elected by delegates of the independent provinces as provisional president of the revolutionary government in Nanjing. Months later, Sun yielded the presidency to the Qing premier Yuan Shikai in exchange for Yuan's support for the revolution. Sun then became director-general of the National People's Party, a parliamentary party he founded on the basis of the old Revolutionary Alliance. In 1913 Song Jiaoren, Sun's assistant and de facto leader of his party, was assassinated by Yuan's men. This led Sun to openly oppose Yuan's government and start the "second revolution," which was easily crushed by the government. Once again Sun escaped to Japan, where he reorganized the National People's Party into the Chinese Revolutionary Party and continued his opposition to Yuan.

In 1916 Yuan died in the midst of his aborted monarchist efforts. The country sank into warlordism. Sun returned to China and led a "constitutional protection" movement to defend the provisional constitution he had promulgated in 1912 and oppose the warlord-controlled government in Beijing. From 1917 to 1923, he made three attempts at establishing his own "national government" in Guangzhou. The first two attempts failed, owing to conflicts between Sun and the southern militarists he had to ally himself with. These militarists, such as Chen Jiongming, found Sun's aspiration for national leadership a hindrance to their regionalist schemes. In between these Guangzhou regimes, Sun strengthened his political following by once again reorganizing the Chinese Revolutionary Party, this time into the Chinese Nationalist Party (Guomindang). In 1923 he reached an agreement with the Soviet Union, accepting the Chinese communists into his new party in exchange for the Russians' military and financial assistance.

Following the founding of the third Guangzhou regime in 1923, Sun worked closely with his Soviet adviser Mikhail Borodin to reshape the Nationalists into a Leninist party. Meanwhile, he continued to form alliances with various warlord factions in the country in the hope of toppling the Beijing government. In late 1924, his warlord allies captured Beijing. At their invitation, Sun went to the capital for a conference on national reunification. He fell ill on the way and died shortly after arriving there, in March 1925.

Among political leaders in modern China, Sun was undoubtedly the most westernized. Educated overseas, fluent in English, and a Christian since childhood, he was greatly attracted to western ideas and institutions. Throughout his career Sun never hesitated to adopt foreign models and accept foreign aid in his effort to build a new China. Yet he was also influenced by Chinese tradition, great or small. His early revolutionary activities relied heavily on the support of secret societies, with which he maintained close ties. The five-power constitution he designed in 1906, later adopted by the Nationalist government, modified the western constitutional separation of power by adding to it two traditional Chinese governmental functions, i.e., examination and censorship. As Sun once claimed, his role models came from both east and west: "Tangwu (founder of the ancient Shang dynasty) of China and George Washington of America."

Sun's most important political formulation was his "three people's principles" (*sanmin zhuyi*): the principle of people's national consciousness (*minzu zhuyi*), or nationalism; the principle of people's rights (*minquan zhuyi*), or democracy; and the principle of people's livelihood (*minsheng zhuyi*), or socioeconomic well-being. Sun first constructed these doctrines during his brief stay in Europe in 1896–1897. After 1905 he and his followers further elaborated them in *People's Tribune*. In their original connotations, "people's national consciousness" emphasized anti-Manchuism, "people's rights" advocated American-style republicanism, and "people's livelihood" suggested moderate measures of the regulation of capital and the equalization of land rights. Combining these three efforts into one, according to Sun, would have brought about "political and social revolutions at one stroke" in China.

After the revolution of 1911, Sun abandoned his anti-Manchu stance and proposed instead the assimilation of the major ethnic groups in China—Han, Manchu, Mongols, Tibetans, and Muslims—into one "Chinese race" (*Zhonghua minzu*). The failure of the early republic also caused Sun to reformulate his other doctrines. As he turned to the Soviet Union for help and guidance in the early 1920s, Sun's three people's principles assumed new meanings. "People's national consciousness" stressed anti-imperialism, because the western powers were by then regarded as the major menace to China's independence; "people's rights," while still upholding democratic principles, now subjected individual freedom to freedom of the state; and "people's livelihood" came to be closely identified with socialism and communism.

The three people's principles never appeared in detailed written form. A series of lectures Sun delivered on the subject in Guangzhou, still unfinished at the time of his death, were taken by his followers as the final version of his doctrines. Yet these lectures were often vague in wording and colored by political considerations. Conflicting interpretations of Sun's doctrines, particularly the principle of people's livelihood, have since arisen. While Sun declared that this principle shared goals with communism, he frequently criticized Marx. The moving force behind human history, he argued, is not class struggle as Marx had suggested, but cooperation for the purpose of survival. Sun also believed that China's economic condition had not reached the level of disparity that warranted Marx's drastic prescriptions. Instead he proposed a set of preventive measured that would save the country from the pain of capitalist exploitation as well as a socialist revolution. Nevertheless, Sun envisioned a noncapitalist path of development for China. His blueprint for China's socioeconomic reconstruction may be described as a form of state socialism.

Sun's other major works included *Revolutionary Strategy* (1906), *Program of National Reconstruction* (1919), and *Fundamentals of National Reconstruction* (1924). The second work comprises three separate writings: *The Theory of Sun Wen, Beginning Steps of People's Rights*, and *An International Development of China*. In *The Theory of Sun Wen*, Sun challenges the neo-Confucian view of knowledge and action and introduces his own thesis that "to know is difficult, to act is easy" (*zhinan xingyi*). Presented as a universal cognitive theory, the thesis also reflected Sun's desire to refute the common perception of his revolutionary programs as "empty talk" and to encourage serious implementations of those programs. In both *Revolutionary Strategy* and *Fundamentals of National Reconstruction*, Sun proposes a three-stage approach to revolutionary reconstruction: military rule, political tutelage, and constitutional democracy. He considered the intermediate stage, political tutelage (*xunzheng*), critical in preparing the Chinese people for the full implementation of democracy. He initially described the stage in *Revolutionary Strategy* as a six-year "rule by provisional constitution"; but later, in *Fundamentals of National Reconstruction*, influenced apparently by the Russian model, he changed it into an unspecified period of party rule. This formula was to have a profound impact on Nationalist rule in the years to come.

A bold, and sometimes crude, mixture of various existing ideological formulations, the political doctrines of Sun Yat-sen have been accepted, after his death, by most political groups in China as an authoritative blueprint for the country's reconstruction. Today both Chinese regimes across the Taiwan Strait claim to be true adherents of his teachings.

See also *Zhixing Heyi*.

Bibliography

Bergere, Marie-Claire. *Sun Yat-Sen*, trans. Janet Lloyd. Stanford, Calif.: Stanford University Press, 2000.

Chang, Sidney H., and Leonard H. D. Gordon. *All Under Heaven: Sun Yat-sen and His Revolutionary Thought*. Stanford, Calif.: Hoover Institution Press, 1991.

Guangdong Academy of Philosophy and Social Sciences et al., eds. *Sun Zhongshan nianpu* (A Biographical Chronology of Sun Zhongshan). Beijing: Zhonghua Book Store, 1980.

Qin, Xiaoyi, ed., *Guofu quanji* (Complete Works of the Father of the Republic). Taipei: Jindai Zhongguo, 1989.

Sharman, Lyon. *Sun Yat-sen: His Life and Its Meaning*. Stanford, Calif.: Stanford University Press, 1968.

Schiffrin, Harold. *Sun Yat-sen and the Origins of the Chinese Revolution*. Berkeley: University of California Press, 1968.

Wilbur, C. Martin. *Sun Yat-sen: Frustrated Patriot*. New York: Columbia University Press, 1976.

Wu, Xiangxiang. *Sun Yixian xiansheng zhuan* (A Biography of Mr. Sun Yatsen). Taipei: Yuandong, 1982.

中國哲學

T

Tan Sitong (T'an Ssu-t'ung)

Lauren Pfister

An eclectic philosopher, Tan Sitong (1865–1898) sought to integrate selective religious, philosophical, scientific, and political themes into a coherent reformist philosophy. Tan was the son of a governor of Hubei Province. He was trained in traditional Confucian texts but was also influenced by Chinese Buddhist teachings, and he was later stimulated by exposure to a wide range of translated western texts. Convinced of the need for political reform in China, he became attached to Liang Qichao (1873–1929) and the teachings of Kang Youwei (1858–1927) in the mid-1890s, and worked actively to support their reformist platform. His single most important work, *Renxue* (*An Exposition of Benevolence*), completed in 1897, amalgamates all these various influences into an unusual monistic philosophy. In 1898, when Kang's policies received imperial support, Tan was called to Beijing and arrived just in time to be caught up in a reactionary military coup. After Tan was executed by the military leaders who deposed the reformers, his *Renxue* was published for the first time by Liang in 1899.

The complex structure and style of Tan's *Renxue* arise from his attempt at a critical synthesis of the traditional and modern, the mystical and scientific, and the ideal and practical. The work begins with twenty-seven axiomlike explanations; these are followed by fifty essays divided into two parts. No overall pattern of thought gives structure to the essays, though the explanations do anticipate many of their themes. The first part, consisting of thirty essays, focuses on a variety of metaphysical, religious, and ethical issues; the second part highlights the political need for reform, a special view of the historical unfolding of benevolence, and Tan's political and religious ideals. Although Tan advocates breaking out from all traditional "traps" —including pedantic writing styles—that hinder the realization of benevolence, he quotes extensively from the classics, using these quotations ironically and cleverly to support his own transvaluation of older ideas. To the quotations Tan adds discussions of modern non-Chinese political and cultural developments, intending by this rhetoric strategy to urge on Chinese reforms. What makes his *Renxue* decidedly different from previous Confucianist (or Ruist) treatises is that he integrates scientific concepts into his central thesis about benevolence.

Normally, the virtue *ren* expressed cultivated humaneness in ritual, moral, and political spheres. Influential medieval Confucianists or Ru scholars added a cosmological dimension to this virtue, presenting it as an embodiment of heavenly principle (*tianli*). This formulation tended to place "principle" (*li*) in opposition to the cosmic vital energy (*qi*) by which principle took on its phenomenal existence. Later scholars argued against this dualistic metaphysics. Tan in particular relied on an account by Wang Fuzhi (1619–1692), claiming, among other issues, that the heavenly principle was identical to human emotions. This overcame a significant dualism within traditional philosophical anthropology, since human emotions were regularly described as an expression of *qi* needing refinement through self-cultivation. Rejecting the relatively ascetic attitudes that this traditional Confucianist or Ruist anthropology supported, Tan mapped out arguments for an egalitarian ethics based on this new metaphysics.

Yet Tan's account of metaphysics goes beyond this criticism of past dualism. Deeply impressed by advances in scientific knowledge revealed in western studies, Tan argues that all things, even those not perceivable by human senses, must be transformations of some pervasive energy like *qi*. This energy he identifies with the European cosmological concept of ether (*yitai*). For Tan, ether is the material cause of phenomena like electricity and brain waves, and it is the universal material grounding of benevolence. Qualitative degrees between these different phenomena can be recognized by discerning heart-minds, according to Tan, but in essence all things are infused with and linked in a cosmological monism of *yitai*. Cosmologically, his system approximates a modernized version of the dynamic *qi* monism of Zhang Zai (1020–1077).

This corrective and replacement of earlier Confucianist or Ruist metaphysics is symptomatic of a broader critical philosophy that Tan had learned in part from Kang Youwei. Critical textual attitudes stemmed from Kang's support for the "new text" school. Its rejection of many standard readings of the classical Confucianist or Ruist canon, justified by historical studies of canonical forgeries, promoted in its place an image of Confucius (Kongzi, "Master Kong") as a religious founder and a political reformer open to the new truths revealed through the progressive embodiment of benevolence. In addition, Tan claimed that the philosophical trends after Mencius (Mengzi, "Master Meng") were polluted from the outset by strains of rationalized antibenevolence and legalism stemming from the influences of Xunzi ("Master Xun," c. 298–238 B.C.E.). From this viewpoint, philosophical terms used by Confucius were historically determined, manifesting Confucius's sensitivity to personal and epochal limitations of benevolence in his Chinese disciples and the broader contemporary audience. Tan and other reformers argued that the real goal of all major religious leaders like Confucius, including Buddha and Jesus, was a future world in which peace and egalitarian institutions pervaded a globally united political entity, the "great unity" (*datong*) or "great sameness" (*da yitong*). Their approach to this ideal varied, Tan's being distinguished by appeals to Daoist and Buddhist philosophical tenets.

If all things are an expression of ether (*qi*), then what is the actual status of different things in the world? Tan envisioned a dynamic interaction between the "one" and the many, worked out in a dialectic of historical movements. So, like the Daoist philosopher Zhuangzi ("Master Zhuang," c. 369–286 B.C.E.), Tan argues that all words and linguistic differences are merely conventional; if words and names are held to refer to independent entities in the world, they obstruct our awareness of the interconnection of all phenomena in the ether.

From a historical and cultural perspective, words and names reflect a particular stage in the unfolding of benevolence. For example, Tan believed that the five stages of self-cultivation in the *Great Learning* (*Daxue*) mirrored the five levels of consciousness in the Huayan Buddhist tradition, even though they were expressed in different Chinese cultural contexts. Similarly, Jesus' altruistic ethics paralleled the universal love of Mozi ("Master Mo"), even though they were historically and culturally distinct. These are all different functions of the transformative ether in various historical contexts, manifestations of benevolence in periods of relatively limited social development. Believing that these restrictions still existed in China, Tan appealed at the end of the first part for a Chinese "Martin Luther" to lead reforms, a historical parallel pointing to Kang Youwei. Yet at the end of *Renxue*, Tan relied on Buddhist imagery to project the incomplete task of saving all sentient beings, looking beyond reform to some greater ideal state.

The essence of ether transcends both naming and its particular functions. It is virtually indestructible because of its continuance in various creative and destructive transformations. So, while brain waves consist of electricity in a perceptible form, the soul is an expression of ether, a power that can grasp the interconnected wholeness of the cosmos through its imagination and its perception. Buddhists and Confucianists or Ruists would agree that the human soul is able to penetrate the cosmos with its understanding, but Tan adds that its sympathetic perceptive powers are among the most refined dimensions of ether, the highest functions of cosmic benevolence. Tan presents here a revised vision of the Buddhist form of "no self" (*wuwo*), a noneternal soul that can be transformed into other expressions of ether and has the refined powers to comprehend the interconnection of all phenomenal reality.

From this perspective on the benevolent soul and the expansive heart-mind, Tan supports a liberative form of ethics. He argues against the order of the five cardinal relationships in traditional Confucianist or Ruist ethics, insisting instead that the highest relational virtue is friendship. Anything resistant to egalitarian relationships, especially the traditional hierarchies in familial and social institutions, is a hindrance to the fuller development of cosmic benevolence. For this reason, in politics Tan is explicitly antagonistic to the existing Manchurian despotism, and in ethics he advocates more liberal heterosexual relationships, criticizing traditional Confucian restrictiveness.

In suggesting benevolent equality as a way to liberation, Tan consciously opposes the traps of conventional Chinese living in his own day. These traps include, for Tan, overemphasis on profit and prosperity, academic training in textual criticism and ornate literary essays, political monarchies, and restrictive moral obligations. Here the basis for his dialectical form of thought is grounded in political practice, for the goal of transcending these traps is to promote the future realization of the "great unity." While affirming a wide range of scientific discoveries and the value of the contributions of the three great religious figures, Tan believes that all these are stepping-stones to a globally united humanity no longer limited by national distinctions. Those issues and values, which serve their purpose at a certain time, can consequently be cast away in the historical movement toward a globally expressed egalitarian benevolence.

Tan's model for this unfolding of benevolence is drawn from the *Book of Changes* (*Yijing*). In Kang's philosophy it was called the theory of the "three ages," but Kang justifies it on the basis of other classical texts. Tan's own "three ages" theory is an interpretation of the line judgments in the first hexagram, *qian*, which represents heaven or the universe. The commentaries and judgments related to the six full lines of the hexagram indicate, in Tan's view, an unfolding of human histories in a seesaw movement. First there is a downward movement from an ancient golden age through periods of lesser peace, which ultimately lead to an epoch of political chaos. The reversal comes in an upward movement through chaos to new periods of lesser peace, all of these heading ultimately toward the full political embodiment of benevolence, the "great unity." By means of this historical projection and a kind of Buddhist dialectic, Tan urges the Chinese people, facing an age of chaos, to break through past traps in their approach to this egalitarian, benevolent new world. Although this utopian vision may appear to imply revolution, Tan meant it only to lend credence to reformist changes that would not annihilate past institutions but stimulate their transformation into more benevolent forms.

Following Buddhist precedents expressed in new ways through his ether metaphysics, Tan claims that the human powers of the heart-mind (*xin*) can bring about the full implementation of the interconnection of phenomenal reality. These idealistic trends follow the Buddhist "consciousness-only" teachings (*weishi lun*) but link them to social egalitarianism and political reform. Although Tan had studied both Buddhist and Daoist mysticism, he was not exclusively devoted to spiritual liberation or to an occultic vision that departed from the needs of the everyday social world. His implementation of benevolence through the refined powers of the heart-mind is consciously described as the primary agent of change in political reform. Since all forms of benevolence are ethically and phenomenally interconnected, he believed that self-sacrifice for the sake of greater benevolence would be a catalyst in advancing benevolence in wider ranges of society, citing examples from classical Chinese literature to support this claim. Compassion expressed by the active powers of the heart-mind could overcome the traps and fears of selfish existence—including the fear of death, loss of social status, and punishment in the netherworlds of traditional Buddhist cosmology. In Tan's mind such fearlessness would enhance the movement of benevolent beings toward the "great unity."

Tan's own willingness to die for the reform movement in 1898 may have been in accord with his egalitarian ethics and his cosmic understanding of benevolence; but some have argued that his martyrdom was actually meaningless, because his support for reform under the aegis of the Guangxu emperor was a complete failure. In addition, most of his philosophical claims remained in an inchoate form, inspired more by the rhetoric of reform than by a principled attempt at comprehensive philosophical expression. Nevertheless, his political idealism was expressed in a reformist practice consistent with his understanding of the historical unfolding of benevolence. His personal sacrifice has been interpreted by postrevolutionary Chinese intellectuals as an inadequate but inspiring foretaste of later Marxist movements.

See also Kang Youwei; Liang Qichao; Wang Fuzhi; Xunzi.

Bibliography

Chan, Sin-wai. *T'an Ssu-t'ung: An Annotated Bibliography*. Hong Kong: Chinese University Press, 1980.

Chan, Wing-tsit. *A Source Book in Chinese Philosophy*. Princeton, N.J.: Princeton University Press, 1963.

Chang, Hao. *Chinese Intellectuals in Crisis: Search for Order and Meaning (1890–1911)*. Berkeley: University of California Press, 1987.

——. *Lie shiqing shen yu pipan yishi: Tan Sitong sixiang de fenxi* (Martyr Spirit and Critical Consciousness: An Analysis of Tan Sitong's Philosophical Thought). Taipei: Lien-king, 1988.

Feng, Qi. *Zhongguo jindai zhexue de geming jincheng* (The Revolutionary Course of Modern Philosophy in China). Shanghai: Shanghai People's Press, 1999.

Feng Youlan (Fung Yu-lan). *Zhongguo zhexue shi xinbian: Di liu ce* (The New Edition of a History of Chinese Philosophy: Volume Six). Beijing: People's Press, 1989.

He, Zhaowu et al. *An Intellectual History of China*, rev. and trans. He Zhaowu. Beijing: Foreign Languages Press, 1991.

Kwong, Luke S. *Tan Ssu-Tung, 1865–1898: Life and Thought of a Reformer*. Boston: Brill USA, 1996.

Li, Zehou. *Zhongguo jindai sixiang shi lun* (Historical Essays on Modern Chinese Philosophical Thought). Beijing: People's Press, 1979, 1986.

Tan, Sitong. *An Exposition of Benevolence: The Jen-hsüeh of T'an Ssu-t'ung*, trans. Chan Sin-wai. Hong Kong: Chinese University Press, 1984.

——. *Tan Liuyang quanji wen* (The Collected Works of Tan Sitong). Taipei: Wenhai, 1962.

——. *Tan Sitong wenxuan zhu* (Annotations to Selected Works of Tan Sitong), ed. Zhou Zhenfu. Beijing: Zhonghua, 1981.

Wang, Yüeh. *Tan Sitong bianfa sixiang yanjiu* (Studies on Tan Sitong's Ideas on Political Reform). Taipei: Taiwan Student Press, 1990.

Zhao, Jihui, et al. *Zhongguo ruxue shi* (A History of Chinese Confucianism). Zhengzhou: Zhongzhou guji, 1991.

Tang Junyi (T'ang Chün-i)

Tu Li

Tang Junyi (T'ang Chün-i, 1909–1978), a renowned neo-Confucian, was born in Sichuan (Szechwan) Province and was educated under the new system of modern China. In 1932 he received his B.A. degree in philosophy from National Central University in Nanjing, the capital of the republic of China. After graduation, he returned home to teach part-time at several middle schools. In 1933 he was employed as a tutor in the department of philosophy of National Central University; in 1937 he was appointed a lecturer in philosophy at Western China University; in 1940 he became a lecturer in philosophy at National Central University; in 1941 he was promoted to associate professor; in 1943 he was promoted to full professor; in 1947 he was appointed dean of students at Jiangnan University in Zhejiang Province. In the spring of 1949 he accepted an appointment from Overseas Chinese University in Canton, Guangdong Province. But when he arrived in Canton, the whole city was shaken by the fear of "liberation" by the Chinese communist army. As he could not teach there, he went to Hong Kong, then a colony of Great Britain. Arriving in Hong Kong, he and some other scholars who had also escaped from mainland China—such as Qian Mu (Ch'ien Mu, 1895–1991), a renowned Chinese historian; and Chang Bejia, an economist—founded New Asia College, which was later a main member college of the Chinese University of Hong Kong. When Tang retired from Chinese University of Hong Kong, as a professor of philosophy and chair of the department, at age sixty-five, he concentrated on teaching and research at New Asia Institute of Advanced Chinese Study and Research, and he was also its director. He died in 1978 and was buried in Taipei, Taiwan.

At about age thirty—with his good traditional Chinese education, and influenced by western naturalistic and speculative philosophy—Tang wrote many philosophical articles discussing problems of philosophy and culture, such as the original spirit of Chinese culture, characteristics of Chinese naturalism, the basic idea of *tianren heyi* (the transcendental unity of heaven and humanity) in Chinese philosophy, relations between aesthetics and philosophy, relations between literature and philosophy, changes in the idea of substance in Chinese and western philosophy, moral foundations in Chinese and western philosophy, and the metaphysics of Zhuangzi and Hegel. These articles were collected and published as a book, *A Comparison of Chinese and Western Culture and Philosophy*.

Moral Idealism and Humanism

In his mid-thirties, Tang turned from a speculative naturalistic understanding of philosophy to a study of Confucianism, Kant, and German idealism. On the basis of this study, he wrote *On the Establishment of the Moral Self*, a book in which he attempted a convergence of his understanding of the problems of philosophy with the basic idea of a moral self. In this regard he focused on the following three topics.

1. An explanation of the meaning of moral life from moral consciousness and moral practice. Tang points out that humans have different ideas of the meaning of moral life, but he maintains that the moral life is characterized by self-arrangement, self-control, and self-discipline. It is not a life in accordance with changes in the physical world, and not a life that follows biological or psychological desires, but a life in which the desires of the physical body are controlled. The will that controls and arranges human physical or psychological desires cannot be outside the physical body, nor can it be a psychological activity of the mind. It should be something else, transcending the physical body and the psychological mind. This "something else" is what Tang considered the moral self. Moral life is the life of the moral self; thus humans have moral freedom, which is neither confined to natural circumstances nor limited to bodily desires or to human emotions and passions.

Tang did not deny that humans lead different kinds of lives. But he believed that the aim of human life was to accomplish the ideal of the moral life—to live in accordance with moral freedom, which originates from the moral self. Tang also said that in the activity of the moral life, a common character can be found. This common character is in all humans, but it also becomes transcendent in those who are living in accordance with their moral selves. Recognizing this character can help us understand more clearly how the moral life involves self-control, self-arrangement, and self-discipline and transcends the physical world. "Transcending the physical world" also conveys the idea of liberation from physical life. Tang sometimes calls the moral self the "metaphysical self," as well as the *benxin* (original human mind) and *benxing* (original human nature)—terms used by traditional Confucianists.

2. A confirmation of the moral mind from the world accepted as actual. What is the world? When Tang asked this question, it did not indicate an intention to explain the world from the point of view of scientific knowledge. Rather, the question arose from his observation that some philosophers and ordinary people regarded the world as cruel and illusory, an attitude that seemed to imply doubt about its reality. Tang did not want to discuss whether such a description was right or wrong; he was mainly concerned with the affirmation of the moral mind in this state of doubt. Tang believed that doubt originated in the moral mind rather than in the "intelligent mind" of Descartes's proposition "I think, therefore I am." The affirmation of the moral mind was based on a moral feeling—a feeling that indicated that humans could not bear a cruel, illusory world. This moral feeling was rooted in the moral mind, and the moral mind inspired the individual to pursue what goodness there was in the world.

Tang further maintained that the moral mind is eternal. He explained this thesis in terms of the relation of the moral mind to the body. The body, which is inhabited by the moral mind, is limited; the moral mind is unlimited. Both the physical world and the social world, which are presented to the moral mind, are precarious and perishable, but the moral mind in itself is stable and imperishable. The body exists for the sake of the activity of the moral mind. The body is passive; the moral mind is active.

3. The activity of the human spirit. Tang drew a disctinction between the external and internal understanding of man. In external understanding, what can be seen of man is his physical body, which is confined to space and time because the body must exist in a particular space and time. In internal understanding, what can be seen of man is his spirit, which transcends spatial and temporal limitations because it is not confined to any particular space or time, or to any actual events or facts.

Physical life is maintained by nutrition, from which comes physical things. But human activity can transcend the physical world, and so it does not arise out of the physical human body. For Tang, the real human nature was revealed by the activity of the spirit, not the body. He concluded that human nature was therefore originally good. The activity of the human spirit was not only for the sake of goodness but also for the sake of truth and beauty. As a result, the human spirit was not only good but also true and beautiful.

Regarding the problem of the origin of evil, Tang's answer was that it was a *xianni*, a deviation of the passions. Correcting such a deviation was good. Evil was something that should be overcome; good was something that should be practiced. As to the way to correct a deviation, Tang appealed to *xiuxin*, "self-cultivation," the traditional Confucian teaching.

Aspects of the Moral Self

To promulgate his idea of the moral self, Tang wrote two books: *Consciousness of Culture and Moral Reason* and *The Spirit of Value of Chinese Culture*. In the first of these, he said that the moral self could also be called the spiritual self or the "transcending" self. Human culture, he felt, was nothing but diverse "presentations"—or manifestations—of this self, and all human activities were based on it. We can identify eight aspects of the moral self, or of moral reason.

1. The family. To Aristotle, the family was only a means through which to complete political life. To Tang, the family was not just a means but an end; it had intrinsic value in human life. Like human culture in general, the family consisted of diverse presentations of the moral self. Tang explained that a family is formed by love between the male and the female, arising out of moral reason. The central idea of the family is love, and love indicates an end, not a means. Grandparents, parents, brothers, sisters, and children are all members of the family. Respect for grandparents and parents, concern about brothers and sisters, and taking care of children are all based on love.

2. *Economics*. Tang understood that economic activity—such as production, exchange, and consumption—can take place without concern for moral problems. However, all economic activities had to be based on the consciousness of moral reason, and not separated from it. These activities should not be regarded as simply the activities of natural human desires. With this understanding, Tang held that every economic activity had to correspond to moral reason and had to be based on moral reason.

3. *Politics*. Tang recognized the influence of the human will to power and the pursuit of natural desires in the realm of politics. But he did not think that these had to be the fundamental elements of politics. Rather, human society—including China—should be instituted on man's moral reason. Tang explained that countries instituted on moral reason would enjoy mutual respect and pursue international peace. Their ultimate expectation or aspiration would be to build an ideal "world family."

4. *Philosophy and science*. Tang saw the pursuit of pure knowledge as different from, and independent of, moral practice. However, the pursuit of specific kinds of knowledge, such as empirical science, formal science, applied science, and history, must not be contrary to moral reason. Tang also believed that in this pursuit, what was indicated as "justice" in the activity of the mind was a presentation of moral reason.

5. *Literature and fine arts*. Tang regarded literature and the fine arts as activities in pursuit of beauty. This pursuit was different from the pursuit of truth, indicating that the meaning of beauty was different from the meaning of truth. But the "activity" of beauty also revealed a way of realizing moral value. A just, unselfish moral mind was also revealed in the pursuit of beauty. That indicated an integrated presentation of beauty and moral reason—the highest presentation of beauty.

6. *Religion*. According to Tang, the human consciousness of religion was a pure demand of the transcendental self, which transcended the empirical self in terms of that demand. God is the transcendental self, which objectifies itself. God is an absolute existence transcending empirical life. The transcendent activity of man arises out of moral reason.

7. *Morality*. Moral life was a presentation of moral consciousness. Tang understood moral consciousness as self-conscious and subconscious. Its subconscious component was the foundation of all cultural activities; this component was both embraced and transcended by its self-conscious component.

8. *Physical education, army, law, general education*. Tang gave only a general discussion of these topics. He affirmed that each of them belonged to human cultural activities, and that all were intimately related to the activity of moral reason and were guided by it to carry out moral values.

Tang was once regarded as a moral idealist or transcendental idealist. He attempted to interpret traditional Chinese philosophy from the viewpoint of moral idealism, and indeed to reconstruct it as a kind of moral idealism. Eventually he abandoned moral idealism as a system of philosophy, but he retained it as a way of understanding philosophical problems and interpreting Chinese philosophy. In his moral idealism, he showed a broad understanding of traditional Chinese philosophy as well as western philosophy.

Humanism

In the mid-1950s, Tang and some of his friends, such as Mou Zongsan and Xu Fuguan, began to advocate humanism. This was closely connected with Tang's understanding of moral idealism. The articles he wrote on humanism—they took up traditional Chinese and western humanism and the ideal system of humanism—were collected and published as a book, *The Reestablishment of the Spirit of Humanism*. Tang then wrote another book, *On the Development of the Spirit of Chinese Humanism*, in which he devoted special attention to a historical discussion of traditional Chinese humanism of various schools and in different dynasties.

Thus Tang has also been regarded as a humanist. From this standpoint, he treated humanism as a philosophical truth by which to protest against dialectical materialism; he also tried to interpret traditional Chinese philosophy as humanism. He believed that traditional Chinese philosophy was antithetical to materialism, pan-scientism, or pan-naturalism. Since the implications of humanism are not different from those of his moral idealism, Tang once tried to reconstruct traditional Chinese philosophy as a kind of humanism. When he was dean of students at New Asia College, he adopted humanism as the college's educational theory, with the assent of Qian Mu, its president.

Nine-Level Aspectism

After spending about twenty years on moral idealism and humanism, Tang turned his attention to historical research in Chinese philosophy, with the intention of connecting his moral idealism more closely to traditional Chinese philosophy. He wrote four books on this topic: *An Introduction to the Original Discussion on Chinese Traditional Philosophy, An Original Discussion on Human Nature in Chinese Traditional Philosophy, An Original Discussion on Dao in Chinese Traditional Philosophy* (in three volumes), and *An Original Discussion on Education in Traditional Chinese Philosophy*.

When he began to write these books, Tang planned to strengthen what he had already expressed in his system of moral idealism. But in the process of his research—especially when he was writing the second book, on human nature—he found that the implications of the idea of human nature in traditional Chinese philosophy did not quite correspond to what he had presented in *On the Establishment of Moral Self*, and this discrepancy led him to rethink his early moral idealism. The main difference was that in traditional Chinese thought, human nature (*renxing*) cannot be considered simply the moral mind (*xin*), or Tang's moral self; rather, it is a combination of the moral mind (*xin*) and the natural life (*sheng*). Thus the activity of the moral mind cannot be separated from natural life. As Tang reflected on his "practical activity" of moral life in light of traditional Chinese philosophy, his understanding of moral problems, and indeed of the meaning of philosophy, changed. Notably, he now saw the basic idea on which philosophy was built not as the moral self but as human nature. On the basis of his understanding of human nature, he developed a new system of philosophy, a philosophy of human life. This can be described as a change from an abstract idea—the moral mind—to an idea of the totality of human activity, directed by moral disposition and inclination.

In his later years, Tang tried to build a new system of philosophy on this new understanding, to replace the old one. He realized his ambition in *Existing Life and Aspects of the Understanding of the Human Mind*. This book is quite different from his moral idealism. In it, he discusses the problems of philosophy in terms of "looking through" nine aspects of the activity of the human mind, which he regarded as an indication of human life. Tang's new philosophical system may be called, briefly, "nine-level aspectism." The meaning of "looking through" is that the mind reflects on problems of human life from different standpoints. Since philosophy cannot be dissociated from the reflections or activities of the human mind, the various problems of philosophy are presented as corresponding with the nine aspects of the mind. These aspects are subdivided into three standpoints: "looking through" (1) horizontally, (2) sequentially, and (3) vertically.

Accordingly, Tang systematically interpreted the problems of philosophy as related to three different aspects of the understaning of the human mind. (1) The "objective" aspect was subdivided into (a) the discrete existence of the "myriad things," (b) changes and transformations as related to different classes, and (c) functional and orderly operations. (2) The "subjective" aspect was subdivided into (a) interpenetration of perceptions, (b) abstract contemplation in the void, and (c) moral practice. (3) The "transcendence" of the subjective and objective aspects was subdivided into (a) conversion to the one God, (b) the void of myself and that of existent things, and (c) the real and the continuity of heaven and earth (*tiande*).

This division was related to the traditional difference between substance, form, and function; Tang regarded the subdivisions of each his three aspects as (a) understanding of substance, (b) understanding of form, and (c) understanding of function.

For Tang, the main problems of philosophy, whether in historical China, India, or the west, had to do with the three problems he discussed in *Existing Life and Aspects of the Understanding of the Human Mind*; this was also true of present-day philosophy and would be true of philosophy in the future.

Moreover, the problems should be divided into objective, subjective, and transcendental; and each should further be divided into three aspects, as involving an understanding of substance, form, or function. Problems concerning human beings should be regarded as different understandings of the different aspects of the human mind. The understanding of the objective aspect of the human mind is concerned with the physical world; the subjective aspect is concerned with the mental world; the transcendental aspect is concerned with the spiritual or religious world. To repeat, all these various understandings have to do with human beings, who live in this world and transcend it.

With regard to transcendence of this world, Tang was not limited to any specific religion, such as Buddhism, Christianity, or Confucianism. An expression of his religious spirit may be found in his observance of traditional Chinese religion. He set up a shrine to *tian*, *di*, *zu*, and *sheng* (heaven, earth, ancestors, and sages) in his home as the religious object of his admiration, respect, and worship.

The central idea of Tang's nine-level aspectism (by virtue of which he can be regarded as a "nine-level aspectist") is not the moral self but human nature. The new philosophical system that Tang wanted to build on this new central idea was not only a reconstruction of traditional Chinese philosophy but also a system for philosophy in general, encompassing the main traditional currents of Chinese, Indian, and western philosophy. He absorbed, as much as he could, the main materials of all these philosophies.

Tang as a Contemporary Neo-Confucian

Tang has also been regarded as a contemporary neo-Confucian, and recently this view has been emphasized by some Chinese scholars. As related to an understanding of contemporary Chinese philosophy, the rise of contemporary neo-Confucianism can be understood from five different but related points of view: (1) as disagreement with pan-scientism and pan-naturalism; (2) as a development of traditional Confucianism that makes it adaptable to modern Chinese society; (3) as incorporating insights of western philosophy into Confucianism and "Confucianizing" them, as was done with Buddhism in the past; (4) as a theoretical and systematic improvement of traditional Confucianism associated with a protest against dialectical materialism; (5) as applying the Confucian idea of human nature as the central idea in a new system of philosophy.

The prevalence of pan-scientism and pan-naturalism in Chinese academic and educated circles was a result of translations of Darwin's *Origin of Species* and *Descent of Man*, Thomas Huxley's *Evolution and Ethics*, and works of certain other English thinkers, as well as the propagation of John Dewey's pragmatism in the later nineteenth century and the early twentieth century, before the collapse of the Qing dynasty. Undeniably, the introduction of scientific knowledge to Chinese society was necessary and had positive effects; and the introduction of Dewey's philosophy was also acceptable to some Chinese scholars. But those who had been educated in Buddhism or Confucianism considered it unacceptable (even alarming) to advocate these views as pan-scientism or pan-naturalism, as Yan Fu or Hu Shi did—especially when pan-scientism or pan-naturalism was applied to problems of human life and morality. Two noted dissenters were Liang Shuming and Xiong Shili, who held that human life had to be understood in terms of the moral theory of Confucianism, which is based mainly on the concepts of *ren* (benevolence) and *yi* (justice).

Later dissenters included Feng Youlan, He Lin, Tang Junyi, and Mou Zongsan, who also appealed to Confucianism but described the limitations of pan-scientism and pan-naturalism more clearly. They pointed out that scientific knowledge and pragmatic understanding should be confined to the empirical world, and that moral problems could not be interpreted adequately from the point of view of science or pragmatism. They also argued that metaphysics, because it had transcendental meaning, could not be rejected from the empirical point of view. The problems of philosophy were not based only on scientific knowledge, as advocates of pan-scientism or pan-naturalism asserted.

These dissenters recognized the importance of scientific knowledge; in fact, they tried to absorb it into their philosophical understanding. But they focused mainly on issues of traditional Confucianism as a systematic philosophy. All of them intended to use traditional Confucian ideas of man and heavenly *dao* (*tiandao*) as the basis for constructing a new system of Confucianism. The significance of western philosophy and science was understood in light of this system.

Besides pan-scientism and pan-naturalism, they also dissented from dialectical materialism, which prevailed later in China and then became the official philosophy of the People's Republic of China. This dissent could not be openly expressed by those who lived in mainland China, under the communist regime, after 1950. But those who left mainland China and lived in Hong Kong or Taiwan did express their ideas; these thinkers included Tang Junyi and Mou Zongsan, a student of Xiong Shili's. Their new interpretation and reconstruction of traditional Confucianism is called contemporary neo-Confucianism (*xin Ruxue*).

The contemporary neo-Confucians differ among themselves in their understanding of the implications of Confucianism and their reconstructions of Confucianism as a system of philosophy. The various branches of contemporary neo-Confucianism are beyond the scope of this article. However, we can note that Tang Junyi is properly considered a contemporary neo-Confucian, mainly because of his later system—nine-level aspectism—although his early system of moral idealism can also be understood in this way.

See also Feng Youlan; Hu Shi; Liang Shuming; Mou Zongsan; Xiong Shili.

Bibliography

de Bary, William Theodore, ed. *The Unfolding of Neo-Confucianism*. New York: Columbia University Press, 1975. (This book, dedicated to Tang Junyi, includes Tang's English article "Liu Tsung-chou's Doctrine of Moral Mind and Practice and His Critique of Wang Yang-ming.")

Li, Tu. *The Philosophy of Tang Junyi*, 3rd. ed. Taipei: Xuesheng, 1982. (In Chinese.)

Metzger, Thomas A. *Escape from Predicament: Neo-Confucianism and China's Evolving Political Culture*. New York: Columbia University Press, 1977. (This book devotes one chapter to Tang Junyi's philosophy.)

Tang, Junyi. *Complete Works of Tang Junyi*, 30 vols. Taipei: Xuesheng, 1991. (In Chinese. Vol. 19 is a collection of Tang's eighteen English essays on Chinese philosophy.)

Ti: Body or Embodiment

Chung-ying CHENG

Ti is one of the earliest, most basic, and most essential concepts in Chinese philosophy. It derives its meaning from an intimate understanding of reality, self, and practice. On its most elementary level *ti* is the concrete, corporeal human body in terms of which human life is maintained and developed. But *ti* is not simply a matter of organization of physical components. It is a structure and system of organic functions and vital spirit in the vehicle of the physical body. By virtue of the form of the physical body, *ti* realizes its living spirit and vitality; and in virtue of the living spirit and vitality the physical body maintains its organic unity and organization. Thus the *Yijing* (*Book of Changes*) says that in following the principle of soft *kun*, "The superior man should understand order-and-principle within the softness of earth and reside in a correct position in his body (*ti*)."

The etymology of the word *ti* clearly shows its double aspect: the physical and the living or the spiritual. The bone radical of the word suggests the physical structure of the *ti* whereas the other side symbolizes the performance of the ritual of offering food to spirits. In common usage, the meaning of *ti* extends from an organic system to groups of people organized for a special purposes and even to concrete things in the world. By abstraction the word also applies to anything that has a definite form and style of organization, such as a writing style.

Ti also has verb senses that assume a fundamental position in Chinese philosophy of knowledge. As *ti* is our living body, one meaning of *ti* is to experience the body as living and as a whole. To experience something intimately and to be aware of this intimate experience is referred to as *tiyan* (coming to know by intimate, personal experience). An important point to note about *tiyan* is that there is no restriction on what we can intimately experience. Not only can we intimately experience our own life or some event or situation; we can intimately experience life and its meaning in general, as well as the *dao* and other properties or basic categories of reality. This is possible because, as humans, we have the ability to experience intimately both internal and external reality on many levels. However, to develop this ability—to make it active and productive—we need to cultivate ourselves.

Hence *tiyan* is, potentially, a way to reach reality and understand meanings that are sources of vision, faith, and values. This does not mean that we have no check on the validity of *tiyan*. *Tiyan* must begin with things at hand and must be congruent with our observations, our thinking, and our insights in order to form a system or body of understanding and knowledge. It is not something to be understood apart from a context of cognitive or moral understanding.

Ti as a verb also means "to embody." To intimately experience something is *tiyan*, but to embody it is to actually participate in and share it, so that one forms one body with a thing, a value, an idea, or an ideal. This meaning of *ti* captures the notion or an organic system. To embody something is to form a system with it, so that the thing can be said to be a part of a whole reality resulting from the embodiment—or that oneself becomes part of the resulting system. As we shall see, in terms of this embodiment the *Yizhuan* (*Ten Commentaries*) in the *Yijing* speaks of a superior man forming one body with heaven, earth, and the "ten thousand things." To form such a body is to experience intimately the ten thousand things and to establish a continuing organic, interactive, and mutually supportive relationship with them. It implies an affective attitude of care and regard as well as an actual understanding of interdependence in life and vitality as described in *Yijing Xici shang*. Today, when we speak of the ecological system in nature, we have reached the meaning of *ti* as an embodiment of an interdependent system. *Tiyan* might then suggest "embodied knowledge."

A third meaning of *ti* as a verb is "to practice and implement." This meaning is no doubt related to the second meaning of *ti*, as embodiment, for in this case *ti* is to embody something or make something happen in action and practice. A sagely person must do what he says he will do and cultivate his action in virtue, because virtue is a matter not of abstract understanding but of embodiment in life—in practice—and of forming one's personality and spirit. Knowledge can be said to be genuine only in terms of actual, bodily practice; that is how the thesis of unity of knowledge and practice derives its significance and value. In the "*Wenyan* Commentary" of the *Yizhuan* it is said, "When a superior man embodies *ren* (*tiren*), he will lead others." This means that to lead others, the superior man must not only experience *ren* deeply but also put *ren* into practice. In the "Great Appendix" it is said that a sage must understand and embody the creativity of heaven and earth (*ti tiandi zhi zhuan*). This must be the basis for human participation in the creative transformation of things as described in the *Zhongyong* (or *Zhong Yong*, *Doctrine of the Mean*).

In Chinese metaphysics, *ti* acquires a deeper meaning, as the subject and substance of a person or a thing; and it is a core concept. Thus we can speak of a person's subjective existence as *zhuti*, or the "host" substance or "ruling" substance; this suggests activity, autonomy, and a position from which to relate to the world of objects, which are referred as *keti*. *Keti* is objective existence, which becomes a "guest" substance relative to the subject substance and therefore something receptive—although it too is autonomous in some sense. Here, *ti* functions as something that is either subjective because we can relate to ourselves as living selves or objective because it can be seen as an object of the subject's action or cognition. In an abstract sense *ti* is something real to which we can refer in our experiences of ourselves or the world and hence something with a metaphysical status. This brings us to the most fundamental and most creative term in Chinese metaphysics: *benti* (original body, original substance, fundamental or essential reality).

What is *benti*? In general, it is the source of reality that gives rise to the cosmos, life, and all things in the world, forming and transforming them, ceaselessly sustaining and completing them; thus it presents itself as the ultimate reality of all things. But this does not mean that *benti* is a substance like the Indian *brahma* or the Hegelian "absolute spirit" that manifests all things. On the contrary, what is essential to the notion of *benti* is that it is an open process of creative formation and transformation. In this formation and transformation there is no domination or absolute control. *Benti* is like *dao* as described by Laozi in the *Daodejing*: "Create without dominating, grow without possessing, and do things without asserting itself."

The *dao* as described in Chapter 25 of *Daodejing* is, perhaps, one primary model of *benti* (the other model being *taiji* in the *Yizhuan*). Then *benti* is the *dao* and the *dao* is *benti*. But *benti* is more a general term, which is used in later Chinese philosophy, after Wang Bi's commentary on the *Laozi*. In Wang Bi we find what is perhaps the first use of the words *ben* and *ti* referring to what he regards as the ultimate reality of the world, the void, *wu* (*Daodejing zhu*, chs. 38 and 40). Thereafter *benti* becomes the unique general term for ultimate reality in all branches and all schools of Chinese philosophy. We find it used by contemporary neo-Confucianists such as Xiong Shili and Mou Zongsan; it is also used by analytical philosophers such as Jin Yuelin and the present author (Chung-ying Cheng), and by cultural philosophers such as Liang Shuming and Li Zehou.

Following are some important characteristics of *benti* as the ultimate category of reality.

1. Although the term *benti* did not appear in the *Yijing*, the words *ben* and *ti* occur separately in *Yizhuan* as crucial philosophical terms. In the *Xici* of the *Yizhuan* there is a notion of the "great ultimate" (*taiji*), the origin and source of all things in the universe. It is said in *Xicixia* that there is *taiji* in the change of all things, that *taiji* gives rise to the two norms of *yin* and *yang*, the two norms give rise to four forms, and the four forms give rise to eight trigrams. All things are based on or derived from the eight trigrams. *Taiji* is the *ben* (root and source) of things because all developments of things can be traced to it. The *Wenyan* says that what originates in (*benyou*) heaven is close to heaven and what originates in the earth is close to earth.

Xicixia also says that the firm and the soft establish the root of things. Hence when we speak of *benti*, we mean this ultimate source of reality, the "great ultimate." In this identification we can see that the concept of *ben* is dynamic: it gives rise to life and the world; it is a creative power, inexhaustibly forming and sustaining life and creating novelty and difference in the world. As the ultimate source of everything, including our human existence as moral and intelligent beings, *benti* is heaven (*tian*). If we can identify *ben* as the ultimate being and *ti* as the resulting reality of the universe and world, then *benti* is the combination of being, becoming, and actuality and is therefore a union of ontology and cosmology, or "ontocosmology" (Cheng 2001).

2. Benti is also the process of creative development and hence, as explained above, the *dao*. As the *dao* it comprehends all things in an interrelated, transforming network. It is both above forms and within forms; it is self-transcending and self-submerging; and it provides both the multiplicity and the unity of things. It is both the principle of creativity and the principle of comprehension; it is the principle of identity and unity; it is the principle of difference and multiplicity. When Confucius sees and comments on how fast a river flows, he can be said to be experiencing *benti* in the flow of the river. Also, in the *Analects* it is said that filial piety and brotherly respect are the root (*ben*) of benevolence (*ren*) and thus, "When the root is founded, the way will rise and grow" (*benli er daosheng*). It is clearly suggested, then, that the *dao* grows and develops from such a source.

3. Since *benti* is *ti* or reality (actuality), it explains the reality of this world. Since it is the source and sustenance of the world's indefinite development, it also explains the potentiality of all things. But *ti* is always an organic system of things and an activity that actualizes or realizes potentiality. Because we do intimately experience our bodily substance and are closely acquainted with it, to call the ultimate reality that is source, actuality, process, and world *benti* is to extend our understanding of *ti* to an existence beyond the limits of time and space. If there is *benti*, things and myself must be included in it; therefore, to experience my own bodily self is to experience *benti*. But we cannot simply identify ourselves or our bodies with *benti*, for *benti* transcends our finitude and sustains it. To realize *benti*, we need to transcend ourselves and understand, observe, and experience the whole world as one body.

We also need to reflect on ourselves and cultivate ourselves in order to experience and witness the way we grow morally and the way our minds function. The *Wenyan* says, "The great man (the sage) will unite himself with heaven and earth in virtue, unite with the sun and moon in brightness, unite with four seasons in ordering, and unite with the spirits in fortune and misfortunes." This statement reflects a high degree of understanding derived from deep experience of oneself, heaven and earth, sun and moon, the seasons, and spirits. Mencius is also relevant here: he asserts that "All the ten thousand things are complete within me." This amounts to saying that my mind has deeply felt all the "ten thousand things" in the universe, and this feeling has uplifted me to a point where I feel a union of myself with all things. In other words, as Mencius says, one has to fulfill one's mind (*jinxin*) in order to know one's nature (*zhixing*), and on the basis of knowing one's nature one comes to know heaven (*zhitian*). *Benti* is not unknowable, then, but is to be known through unifying and integrating deeply felt internal self-cultivation of the mind and comprehensive external observation and close experience of things.

Wang Yangming is thus able to say that the great learning of the sage consists in forming one body of oneself with heaven, earth, and the ten thousand things.

4. Because human beings have mind (*xin*) and nature (*xing*) and because the human mind and human nature are considered an endowment from heaven or the ultimate source, *benti* not only embodies the ultimate source but is capable of functioning as a principle of creativity, comprehension, and ordering, as one finds in the the *Yizhuan* and *Zhongyong*. It is the ideal goal of one's life, to be realized and fulfilled within one's capacity. The Song-Ming neo-Confucians consider the substance of nature, *xingti* (as in Zhu Xi), and the substance of mind, *xinti* (as in Wang Yangming), the ultimate substance or *benti*. Similarly, in light of the creative power of being sincere—*cheng* (as an ontological way of realizing reality) as mentioned in the *Zhongyong*—we can speak of the body of *cheng, chengti* (as in Liu Zongzhou). The ultimate, the actuality, and the activity (or potential) of our self-reflective mental experience, or our penetrating comprehensive experience of the world by observation, gives rise to the different degrees or different expressions of *benti*. Thus within contemporary neo-Confucianism we find the terms "life *benti*" (*shengming benti*), "cosmos *benti*" (*yuzhou benti*), and "value *benti*" (*jiazhi benti*). We also find *benti* as *benxin* (original mind) or *benxing* (original nature) in the Mencius-Lu Xiangshan-Wang Yangming school. And the moral substance (*daode benti*) must be approached with the "*benti* spirit" of self-cultivation, which is *gongfu* (efforts).

5. In the *Xici* of the *Yizhuan* it is said, "The divine has no directions and the change has no substance (*ti*)." Does this mean that the ultimate reality of change (*yi*) has no substance by itself? Many interpretations of this passage are possible. The most commonsensical interpretation is that the authors simply want to draw attention to the fact that the creative activity of the *benti* has no form or substance by itself: it is a pure creative power which, in exercising itself, brings about forms of things and the substantiality of the world. Since there is no break between the formless and the formed, the formed world is at the same time the formless *dao*. Change as the unformed, the unlimited, and the creative would continue to bring new forms into the world and sustain the process of formation and transformation. *Benti* can be considered the source of this creative activity from formless to formed, and from nonbeing to being. It can also bring the formed into the formless, or being into nonbeing, as a matter of return and balance.

However, there could be another interpretation: the absence of *ti* in change indicates an existence prior to *ti* or prior to *benti*, which is eventually described as *wuji* ("ultimateless") in the *Taiji tushuo* of Zhou Dunyi. As a negative concept, *wuji* should be conceived as *wuti* (no substance). But undeniably the internal principle of creativity in *wuji* gives rise to *taiji*, so that *taiji* is *benti*. As Zhou Dunyi makes clear in the *Taiji tushuo*, there is *wuji* and then there is *taiji* (*wuji er taiji*). But *taiji*, again, is *wuji* (*taiji er wuji*). Here we see the primary ontocosmological circle in Chinese philosophy, whether by way of Confucianism or by way of Daoism. The insubstaniality of change and the substantiality of things are inseparable, just as *taiji* and *wuji* are inseparable.

Conclusion

The term *benti* signifies a profound understanding of the boundless, ceaseless creative source and the creative, transforming process of reality. It gives a place to everything, including human beings. The idea of *benti* is not confined to things or even to the universe but includes the idea of ultimate human identity, unity, and reality or actuality. *Benti* becomes the ultimate universal notion of the ultimate reality in its creative transcendence and engagement with things, which in a grand synthesis integrates and fuses heaven, *dao, taiji*, and *wujie*. From this notion of the ultimate reality one can see the unlimited function and activity of *benti*, which is reflected in the Chinese philosophical thesis of the unity of substance and function (*tiyong heyi*).

See also *Ti* and *Yong*: Substance and Function; *Ti-Yong* Metaphysics; Wang Bi; Wang Yangming; Zhu Xi.

Bibliography

Note: For the classical texts, see *Daodejing, Daxue, Lunyu, Mengzi, Neijing, Xunzi, Yijing*, and *Zhongyong*, in the *Sibu beiyao* Edition.

Ames, Roger. "The Meaning of Body in Classical Chinese Philosophy." *International Philosophical Quarterly*, 24, 1984, pp. 39–54.

Cheng, Chung-ying. "Confucian Onto-Hermeneutics: Morality and Ontology." *Journal of Chinese Philosophy*, 27(1), 2000, pp. 33–68.

———. "The Nature-Being Principle: A Consideration from Chu Hsi." *Analecta Husserliana*, 21, 1986, pp. 159–163.

———. "On a Comprehensive Theory of *Xing* (Naturality) in Song-Ming Neo-Confucian Philosophy: A Critical and Integrative Development." *Philosophy East and West*, 47(1), 1997, pp. 33–46.

———. "Onto-Cosmological Visions and Analytical Discourse: Interpretation and Reconstruction in Chinese-Western Philosophy." In *Two Roads to Wisdom: Chinese and Analytical Philosophical Tradition*, ed. Bo Mou. La Salle, Ill.: Open Court, 2001.

———. "Reality and Divinity in Chinese Philosophy." In *Companion to World Philosophy*, ed. Eliot Deutsch and Ron Bontekoe. London: Blackwell, 1997.

———. "The Trinity of Cosmology, Ecology, and Ethics in the Confucian Personhood." In *Confucianism and Ecology*, ed. Mary Evelyn Tucker and John Berthrong, Cambridge, Mass.: Harvard University Center for the Study of World Religions, 1998.

———. "Zhouyi and Philosophy of Wei (Positions)." *Extreme-Orient Extreme-Occident* (Paris), No. 18, 1996, pp. 149–176.

Tu, Wei-ming. *Centrality and Commonlity: An Essay on Chung-Yung*. Honolulu: University of Hawaii Press, 1976.

———. "On the Mencian Perception of Moral Self-Development." *Monist*, 61(1), 1978, pp. 72–81.

Wang, Pi. *Commentary on Laozi Daodejing* and *Commentary on Zhouyi*. In *Collected Works of Wang Pi*, annot. Lou Yulie. Beijing, 1980. (In Chinese.)

Ti and *Yong* (*T'i* and *Yung*): Substance and Function

A. S. CUA

W. T. Chan's translation of *ti* and *yong* as "substance and function" in his *Source Book of Chinese Philosophy* (1963a) has been widely adopted in English-language writings on neo-Confucian thought. This translation is perhaps the best one, as it is a fairly accurate rendering. *Ti* literally means "body," and *yong* "utility," "function," or "operation." A. C. Graham observes:

> The word *ti* (literally "body") has a wide range of meanings, but it resembles the English word "substance" in being used both for a solid body and also, as in this pair of terms, for what is assumed to underlie the changing surface of a thing. . . . The *yong* of a thing is its activity, its response when stimulated. (1958, 39)

This use of *ti* seems implicit in Zhang Zai's remark (Graham, 39): "That which is never absent, that is, through all transformations is what is meant by substance (*ti*)." This notion would imply that the *ti* of a thing is its immutable substratum, somewhat akin to Kant's schema of substance as "permanence of the real in time, that is, the representation of the real as a substrate of empirical determination of time in general, and so as abiding while all else changes" (1953, B183). On the other hand, the *yong* of a thing is "its response when stimulated." So construed, the distinction between *ti* and *yong* seems fixed, or context-independent.

However, this distinction is used in varying ways, as Zhu Xi points out, indicating that it is actually relative, or context-dependent:

> Just as the distinction between what is prior and posterior is indeterminate, *ti-yong* distinction is indeterminate. Thus *yin* can be the *ti* of *yang*, and *yang* can be the *ti of yin*. . . . The *ti-yong* distinction is relative [to the context of] discourse. Yichuan [Cheng Yi] has said: *ti* and *yong* "come from the same source, and there is no gap between the manifest and the hidden." (Chan 1963b, 570)

"This saying is one we can flexibly use in the live context of discourse" (Qian 1972, 1:433). *Ti* is a metaphorical extension of its literal meaning (i.e., body), and the relative, dynamic nature of the distinction between it and *yong* is succinctly illustrated in another remark of Zhu Xi's. When someone asked about *dao* (the way, or Way) with respect to its *ti* and *yong*, Zhu Xi replied: "Let us suppose that the ear is *ti*, its *yong* is hearing. Likewise, if the eye is considered *ti*, its *yong* is seeing." To repeat, then, for Zhu Xi the distinction between *ti* and *yong* is relative to the context of discourse. The *ti* of one thing may be the *yong* of another thing. If we:

> consider our body as *ti*, seeing and hearing, as well as the movements of our hands and legs, are its *yong* (functions/operations). But if we consider our hand as *ti*, then the movement of the fingers is its *yong*. (Qian, 1:431)

Zhu Xi reminds his students that, in general:

> . . . one must adopt a dynamic, rather than a fixed, determinate, limiting attitude in understanding the meaning of words. [For example,] in one speech situation, in relation to *ren* (benevolence), *ren* is *ti* and knowledge (*zhi*) is *yong*. But in the speech situation when we are concerned with knowledge alone [independently of its relation to *ren*], knowledge may be said to have both *ti* and *yong*. (Qian 1:434–135)

Thus, the translation of *ti* as "substance" may be misleading from the western philosophical point of view. In western philosophy, there are competing concepts of substance, e.g., that which can exist by itself; the unchanging essence of a thing as contrasted with its attributes or accidents; and, in traditional logic, the subject of predication. None of these conceptions has a counterpart in Chinese philosophy, especially in Song-Ming Confucianism. Unlike, say, the distinction between substance and attribute, as noted earlier, the distinction between *ti* and *yong* is relative, or context-dependent. However, because of the wide acceptance and currency of "substance," it is important to remind non-Chinese readers that "substance" is better construed in the more ordinary nonphilosophical sense, as something that has concrete content and significance deemed essential to practical thinking in a particular situation. In nonpractical contexts, however, the *ti* of a thing cannot be understood apart from its *li* (rationales) in the explanatory sense, particularly in explaining the distinction between individuals.

Since the distinction between *ti* and *yong* is context-dependent, *ti* may also be used to refer to "bone-structure" and *yong* to its functions. The metaphorical extension of *ti* as "body" has extensive applications. For example, as a basic metaphor, the *ti* of a thing may be construed as the rationale (*li*) for any observed event that has its *yong* or utility or relevance to human affairs. The *ti* of a thing, for example, may require an earnest effort at comprehending the rationale (*li*) for its existence, or a standard for judging a thing in terms of an ideal character, or both. Thus the *yong*, function or utility, of a thing requires understanding the rationales of its existence and its significance to human life. Thus, Zhu Xi (1980, 6) comments on a passage in the *Great Learning* (*Daxue*) that the "extension of knowledge lies in the investigation of things": the required effort must "exhaust the rationales (*li*) of things. After a long period of persistence, the learner will one day attain a unifying, comprehensive understanding of the matter under investigation (*haoran guantong*)."

In addition to rendering *ti-yong* as "substance and function," there are other possibilities. In each case, the use of the distinction between *ti* and *yong* depends on its rationale in a particular context of discourse. First, consider *ti-yong* as the distinction between a thing's intrinsic nature and its expression, manifestation, or realization. In this sense, the *ti* of a thing pertains to its essential nature. As reflecting its fundamental ethical concern, this Confucian distinction seems to be similar to the distinction between intrinsic and extrinsic goods or values in ethics and value theory. A thing is an intrinsic good or value if it is good in itself or something that is desired for its own sake by virtue of its essential nature, as contrasted with a thing whose value is derived from external sources. This distinction is especially relevant to understanding ethical ideals of the good human life. G. E. Moore's *Principia Ethica*, for example, was concerned with goods in themselves or ideals in the sense that they are goods in themselves "in a high degree." Moore offers intrinsic values such as personal affection and aesthetic appreciation, because they are valuable even if they exist "absolutely by themselves." Moreover, these examples satisfy the "principle of organic unities"—the principle "that the intrinsic value of a whole is neither identical with nor proportional to the sum total of the values of its part" (1962, 184).

If we construe *ti* in Confucian ethics as an intrinsic value in Moore's sense and *dao* or *ren* (in the broad sense) as a holistic, ethical ideal of the good human life, then the *ti* of the good ethical life would be an intrinsic good. However, *dao* or *ren* is not something valuable because of its "absolute" existence, for as a holistic ideal of the good human life, its existence is necessarily connected with its concrete significance, that is, its function or possibility of realization in the actual world. The ideal *dao* or *ren* is cherished not because of its intrinsic nature but because of the possibility of realization within a cultural tradition of *li* or rules of proper conduct and the reasoned exercise of *yi* or sense of what is fitting and right in particular or changing circumstances. Discourse on *ren*, as Zhu Xi reminds us, must presuppose its connection with knowledge, since *ren* is the *ti* of knowledge—ethical knowledge of the connection of *ren* with *li* (propriety) and *yi*. Were this not the case in Confucian ethics, discourse about the ideal of *ren* would simply be devoid of ethical content. For this reason, anicipated by Zhu Xi, Wang Yangming stresses the unity of knowledge and action (*zhixing heyi*) and the inseparability of *ti* and *yong*:

> When we speak of *ti* [which Chan renders as "substance"], *yong* or function is already involved in it, and when we speak of function (*yong*), substance (*ti*) is already involved in it. This is what is called "substance and function coming from the same source." (Chan 1963a)

J. L. Austin once wrote:

> A word never—well, hardly ever—shakes off from its etymology and its formation. In spite of all changes in and extensions of and additions to its meaning, and indeed rather pervading and governing these, there will persist the old idea. (1961, 149)

Probably the root, primary meaning of *ti* is "[human] body; limb; embody; form, shape" (Karlgren 1966, No. 594); alternatively, it is a generic term for "the head, body, hands, and legs" (Duan 1981, 166). This meaning is still present in modern Chinese, for example, in *shenti* (health) and *tizao* (physical exercise). As *ti*, our living body exists because of the proper functions of our organs. As a metaphorical extension of the primary sense of *ti*, in the light of the ideal of *dao* or *ren*, human life, its bodily movements, and its behavior are the *yong* (functions or operations) in the sense that our body provides the basic locus for the realization of the Confucian ideal. For this reason, ritualized bodily movements in accord with *li* or rules of proper conduct are stressed. The indeterminate, concrete significance of the Confucian ideal of *dao* or *ren* reflects its nature as an ideal theme, rather than an ideal norm (Cua 1978, ch. 8). As an ideal theme, *ren* is a creative challenge to the committed person to delineate and develop the meaning of *ren*, and its connection with *li* and *yi*, in his or her own life. There are no a priori ways of defining the *yong* of *ren*, and there is no prefigured setting for its actualization, because the signficance of *ren* is indeterminate. Alternatively, as the *ti* of the ideal way of life, *dao* or *ren* has no determinate *yong* in human life. As Wang Yangming put it: "The Way (*dao*) has neither restrictions nor physical form, and cannot be pinned down to any particular" (Chan 1963a, sec. 66).

The distinction between *ti* and *yong* is perhaps best rendered as a distinction between the inner or inward and outer or outward—in familiar Confucian language, the distinction between *nei* and *wai*. In this sense, *ren* represents the *ti*, that is, the inward character, of ethical commitment. The *yong*, its outer or outward expression, depends on the committed person's endeavor to actualize the ideal. Since the concrete significance of *ren* depends on *li* (moral tradition) and *yi* (rightness), the *ti* or nature of the ethical life depends on one's efforts, successes, and failures in pursuing *ren*.

Another use of the distinction between *ti* and *yong* suggests its association with the Confucian distinction between the "latent" (*yin*) and the "manifest" (*xian*) in the *Zhongyong*, the *Doctrine of the Mean*. (Recall Cheng Yi's remark cited by Zhu Xi.) In the case of *ren*, the *ti* of the ethical life provides a rationale, a standard for judging a thing in terms of an ideal character, i.e., what the thing ought to be. Thus, as noted above, the *yong*, the function or utility, of a thing requires understanding the rationales of its existence and significance to human life.

Another line of exploration in appropriate contexts is to consider a western legal counterpart of the distinction between *ti* and *yong*: substantive and procedural law. A case at law that has an important impact on the life of the parties to the dispute requires the established *modus operandi* of legal practice. The notion of legal procedure is functionally equivalent to that of *li* (ritual propriety) in Confucian ethics. *Li* draws attention to the significance of the Confucian conception of rules of proper conduct as a way of defining the boundary of acceptable behavior, and in certain circumstances, like procedural law, *li* supports rather than suppresses a person's desires and concerns for self-interest. As Xunzi points out, apart from the delimiting function of *li*, there is also a supportive or enabling function that provides proper means and occasions for satisfying individual desires, without pronouncing judgment on their ethical merit or demerit.

See also *Li*: Principle, Pattern, Reason; *Li*: Rites or Propriety; Reason and Principle; *Ti*: Body or Embodiment; Wang Yangming; *Yi* and *Li*: Rightness and Rites; Zhu Xi.

Bibliography

Austin, J. L. "A Plea for Excuses." In *Philosophical Papers*. Oxford: Clarendon, 1961.

Chan, Wing-tsit, trans. *Instructions of Practical Living and Other Neo-Confucian Writings by Wang Yangming*. New York: Columbia University Press, 1963a.

———, trans. *A Source Book in Chinese Philosophy*. Princeton, N.J.: Princeton University Press, 1963b.

Cua, A. S. *Dimensions of Moral Creativity: Paradigms, Principles, and Ideals*. University Park: Pennsylvania State University Press, 1978.

———. *Moral Vision and Tradition: Essays in Chinese Ethics*. Washington: Catholic University of America Press, 1998.

———. "Reason and Principle in Confucian Ethics." In *Blackwell Companion to World Philosophy*, ed. Eliot Deutsch and Ron Bontekoe. Oxford: Blackwell, 1997.

———. *The Unity of Knowledge and Action: A Study in Wang Yang-ming's Moral Psychology*. Honolulu: University of Hawaii Press, 1982.

Duan, Yuzai. *Shuowen jiezhi zhu*. Shanghai: Guji, 1981.

Graham, A. C. *Two Chinese Philosophers: Ch'eng Ming-tao and Ch'eng Yi-ch'uan*. London: Lund Humphries, 1958.

Kant, Immanuel. *Critique of Pure Reason*, trans. Norman Kemp Smith. London: Macmillan, 1953.

Karlgren, Bernhard. *Gramata Serica: Script and Phonetics in Chinese and Sino-Japanese*. Taipei: Chengwen, 1966.

Moore, G. E. *Principia Ethica*. Cambridge: Cambridge University Press, 1962.

Qian, Mu. *Zhuzi xin xue'an*, 5 vols. Taipei: Sanmin, 1972.

Zhu, Xi. *Sishu jizhu*. Hong Kong: Tai-ping, 1980.

Ti-Yong (Tiyong, T'i-yung): Metaphysics

Chung-ying CHENG

Benti, viewed as the creative source and creative process giving rise to all the things in the universe, is a matter of ontocosmology, or "being" or "actuality." By itself, *benti* contains three meanings in one unity: source, process, and end result. Thus we must see *benti* by itself as highly active, highly functional, and highly efficacious. The *ti* of *benti* implies its functionality, and its functionality, must presuppose its being the source or a source—not a source traced or even untraceable to some "beginning of time," because there could be no such beginning, but a source that is always happening in the present and in the presence of all the things in the world. *Benti* is the *dao*, and *dao* is always to be conceived as a creative continuum and unity of substance and function, body and spirit, cause and effect, end and means.

The idea of *yong* (function, activity, use, application) is well presented in the text and commentaries of the *Yijing*. It may be the word most frequently used in the whole corpus of the *Yijing*; there are more than ninety occurrences. The typical use appears in the judgment on the "first nine" of the hexagram *qian* ("the creative"): "Being in a state of hidden dragon, do not act" (or do not apply oneself, *qianlong wuyong*). *Yong* is to act or to apply oneself in a situation to reach a goal. But *yong* as activity (*wei*) must be based on the *ti* of the *yong*. Here we see the base or ground as the "state of hidden dragon." This state is the substance and to act or not act is the function of the *ti*; that is, "not to act" is the *yong* or function of the *ti*, the hidden state of the dragon, because such a state would naturally imply nonaction. Hence nonaction by the person consulting the text is the function of the *ti* for that person.

In divinatory texts, there are many instances when nonaction is demanded, but there are also many occasions when action is recommended. For example, for the hexagram *qian* ("modesty"), the "first six" has the judgment *yongshe dachuan*, "act to cross the great river." There is also the paradigm *liyong*, "it is advantageous to act," which becomes a common usage. It is said that the sage will act to bring "thick" benefits to the life of people, *liyong housheng*.

Yong as action is based on a free choice, for a person can act contrary to the advice or judgment, bringing misfortune on himself. The *yong* of a situation is based on our understanding of its intrinsic nature or *ti* and also on our ability to choose the right course of action, as both action and nonaction can be regarded as the function of the *ti* of the situation. In understanding *ti* one sees the possibilities of development and causation. *Yong* is a function not just because it is rooted in *ti*, but because it is conducive to our purposes. In the example of the "hidden dragon," the reason for nonaction is that that is the best course to achieve good fortune and avoid misfortune. Similarly, when the advice is to act, action will lead to the attainment of our goals and the satisfaction of our desires. Therefore, for human beings the relationship between substance and function has to do with our understanding or knowledge and our freedom to make decisions relative to our knowledge and our goals in life. The *yong* or function of the *ti* of a situation is a means for reaching our goals, implying a free choice of action or nonaction.

In the *Yizhuan* (*Ten Commentaries*) of *Yijing*, however, the function of change (*yi*) is considered as flowing from the *ti* of the *yi*. If the *taiji* ("great ultimate"), the two norms, the four seasons, the eight trigrams, and so on are considered substance on different levels of reality and generality, one can see that each *yi* would have activity and nonactivity as its function. The two norms of *yin-yang* are the function of the *taiji*, just as the four seasons are the function of the *yin* and *yang*. Similarly, all things in the world are the functions of eight forms and sixty-four hexagrams, as they are creative results of these forms and hexagrams (as real situations) in action. The *taiji* (great ultimate) is the substance of all things on different levels, and all things are the actualized functions of the *taiji*. Here no choice is needed and no external purpose is required. This is because the great ultimate is considered the ontocosmological substance and source from which all things are created and evolve. This substance has the function of comprehensive creation and pervasive sustenance of things and life. Its substance is defined by its function, and its function is defined by its goal, whereas both the function and the goal are inherent within the substance of the *taiji*.

The *taiji* is the *dao* or the way of change, and the *dao* is the alternation of the *yin* and *yang*. The source entails the process, and the process entails creativity—exchange and the production of things. It is said in reference to the function of the way of change or the *dao*, "It manifests benevolence and hides all its functions" (*xian zhu ren, zang zhu yong*). The manifestion of benevolence is a matter of bringing out its potential power and bringing that power to bear on the creative activities which lead to life and the eternal continuation of life. Thus, "To be creatively creative is called the change (*yi*). To form forms is the creative and to follow up the formation is called the receptive" (*Xici shang*, 5). We may see this as a cosmic function relative to a cosmic substance. When we know that, we can divine the future and understand how things develop; and in cultivating this ability we realize that the cosmic substance "holds" functions which are important for our own life.

The substance-function relationship without mediation on the ontocosmological level is basic. But the substance-function relationship as mediated by our knowledge, choices, and goals is derivative; it must be based on the direct substance-function relationship of the ontocosmology of the great ultimate and the *dao* of the *yin* and *yang*. Accordingly, the *Xici* develops a theory of cultural and technical inventions for the development of human material and spiritual culture. It goes on to recommend knowing things in order to "reach" their use (*zhiyong*) so that life can be improved and more settled. When we "know" things in this way, we can enjoy their daily use without being conscious of knowing why or even being conscious of using them, because the use or function of a substance has been incorporated into the processes of life on a commonsense level.

Very early in Chinese philosophy, there is a recognition of substance (*ti*) that entails *yong* because it is inseparable from its function and use; there is also a recognition that any use or application of an idea, talent, or knowledge implies or presupposes an understanding of a situation or the substance in a situation. The unity and inseparability of substance and function are, therefore, implicit in the Chinese notion of reality. The human being needs to know how this unity can be applied in his life; he must come to know substance profoundly so that he can function naturally in accordance with the unity. He must put his knowledge into practice if the unity of substance and function is to be efficacious; then, what pertains to the good in life will ensue, under appropriate conditions. The unity of substance and function bears on the unity of theory or knowledge, and practice and action.

The unity of substance and function also bears on the unity of heaven and humanity. To know substance is to know the *dao* of origination, development, completion, and return; and to know this is to know how one's life and onself as a person originated and can be cultivated and completed—that is, to know human nature and its ontocosmological roots. This is also to know the values and goals of life and how to shape one's own life so as to participate in the activities of the world. This is what *Zhongyong* (*Doctrine of the Mean*) calls the fulfillment of one's nature and what Mencius calls the fulfillment of one's mind. It implies knowing and reaching one's destiny and settling on a course of life that will complete life and give it its full value. This is the unity of heaven and humanity—and it is to be realized by understanding and applying the unity of substance and function. To do so is to function as substance and to realize one's substance in action and nonaction of the function of that substance. Both the unity of knowledge and action (*zhixing heyi*) and the unity of heaven and humanity (*tianren heyi*) are a realization of the unity of substance and function (*ti yong*).

The principle of the unity of substance and function has been maintained and cherished throughout the history of Chinese philosophy, and it explains why Chinese philosophy sees no fundamental Cartesian dualism of mind and body, no Platonic dualism of reality and appearance, and no Kantian dualism of knowledge or understanding of objects and rational intuition of "things in themselves." From the Chinese point of view of the *tiyong heyi* or *tiyong bu'er*, mind and body are both functions of the deeper reality or substance of the human being, which is his nature, his principle of being, or his destiny (*ming*). Similarly, reality as noumena is the substance of appearances as phenomena; thus to know the appearance of things in a deeper way is to know things in themselves. If things are unknowable, that is not because of their nature but because of the way we approach them; we need to reach a knowledge of reality as an inseparable whole. This is not to say that there are no distinctions between knowledge of man and knowledge of heaven, or no purposeful distinctions between the human being and human nature as in the *Xunzi*. But even in *Xunzi* the human mind is said to be able to know the *dao*, and in knowing the *dao* a sage is able to construct a reasonable society with a humanized system of rules of propriety or *li*, and thus to realize the order and harmony preexisting in nature.

This view, once again, reflects the idea of the unity of substance and function. Substance is always the root (*ben*), the starting point, the source, the ground; function is always the branch (*mo*), the development, the result stemming from that root. Our intelligence, reason, and emotions are functions of our human existence and as such can be developed and fulfilled. When they are fulfilled, they realize the harmony and value of the great ultimate (*taiji*) and the *dao*: comprehensive creation and an uplifting and enriching of life, knowledge, and culture.

In neo-Confucianism we see the emergence of a metaphysics of *li* (principle) and *qi* (vital force). With regard to substance and function, there are several possible positions. Cheng Yi and Zhu Xi would take *li* as substance and *qi* as function. Since *li* and *qi* may not always meet in a human being, Cheng and Zhu would suppress and even eliminate desires, which are a matter of *qi*, in favor of cultivating *li*. But this position does not seem to reflect the actual cosmic unity of *li* and *qi*. In nature, there is no suppression of *qi* in favor of *li*; on the contrary, there is a dynamic interaction and harmony between *li* and *qi*, which are ontocosmologically inseparable. Zhang Zai would take *qi* as substance and hence treats *li* as function or as creation of "*qi* activity." If we apply Zhang's model to humanity, the logical consequence is to recognize human emotions and desires as natural constituents of life; they need to be cultivated, without being suppressed, so that a rational order and discipline will emerge from them. Another position is that mind or the "spirit of mind" is the unifying ground and hence the ultimate substance of both *li* and *qi*, which can be regarded as two functions or two manifestations of the powers of mind. But for Wang Yangming, such a mind is ontologically a matter of *qi* that has embodied *li*.

In Buddhism the ultimate substance is considered nothing positive but rather a state of emptiness and nothingness from which things arise and life begins as a matter of "pollution" (*ran*) and "coorigination" (*yuan*). Chinese philosophy has tended to reject this Buddhist conception of reality as alienated from life and as lacking an understanding of the function of ultimate reality. Possibly, the transformation of Indian Buddhism into Chinese Buddhism such as Tiantai, Huayan, and Chan incorporates the unity of substance and function and so brings back human life and the human world as useful functions for salvation or the transcendence of life. As substance, the ultimate reality of life is the individual's Buddha-nature. When the Buddha-nature is realized, life and the world function so as to embody reality in appearance; this functioning would exhibit or be seen as a state of nonobstruction of principles and things, among all the different things. Chinese Buddhists stress not only the unity of substance and function but the unity of substance, image (or forms of things), and activity. Bringing out the category of image (*xiang*) is important, because as a result function can be said to present images of things. But we should not be misled by images; we should see the unity and dynamism of substance and activity under the form of "cosmic things."

In the modern period, Xiong Shili is the foremost Chinese philosopher to address understanding *benti* or the ultimate reality or substance of the world. He concentrates on its functions and proposes that the great ultimate substance is none other than its functions (*tiyong bu'er*). He bases his position on the philosophy of the *Yijing* and starts with understanding the great ultimate as substance. But he also says that to be able to love belongs to ourselves as substance, and we can apply this knowledge of ourselves as substance to benefit others, as the cosmic *dao* or *benti* brings benefits. On the basis of the inseparability of substance and function, Xiong develops a cosmological ontology in which change is an alternation between the creative (*pi*) and the receptive (*xi*). Regarding human beings, he focuses on their active role as participants in the creativity and transformations of heaven and earth as stated in the *Zhongyong* (*Doctrine of the Mean*).

In order to modernize and open up Chinese culture, Chinese intellectuals introduced western learning and science. In the early twentieth century, Zhang Zhitong coined the famous slogan "Chinese culture as substance and western learning as function" (*zhongxue weiti xixue weiyong*). But this slogan does not show how the paradigm of unified, interflowing substance and function could be applied to the relationship between Confucian morality and western science or democracy. Under its influence, Mou Zongsan claimed that the Chinese could work out or develop science and democracy from traditional Chinese morality and despotism. In this regard it is equally difficult to see how western culture could be "substance" or Chinese culture could be "function." One has to go back to the ontocosmology of the unity of substance and function to understand how it can be incorporated into a situation and then interpreted and applied fruitfully.

See also *Li*: Principle, Pattern, Reason; Mou Zongsan; *Qi*; Reason and Principle; *Ti; Ti* and *Yong*; Xiong Shili.

Bibliography

Note: For the classic texts, see *Mengzi* and *Yijing, Sibu beiyao* Edition.

Chan, W. T., trans. *Reflections on Things on Hand: A Neo-Confucian Anthology*, comp. Chu Hsi and Lü Tsu-ch'ien. New York: Columbia University Press, 1967.

Cheng, Chung-ying. "Model of Causality in Chinese Philosophy: A Comparative Study." *Philosophy East and West*, 26(1), 1976, pp. 3–20.

———. "On the Creativity Principle in the Philosophy of Confucius." *Proceedings of International Confucian Studies Symposium* (Taipei), 1988.

———. "On Timeliness (*Shi-chung*) in the *Analects* and the *I Ching*: An Inquiry into the Philosophical Relationship between Confucius and the I-Ching." *Proceedings of International Sinological Conference* (Academia Sinica), 1982.

———. "Practical Learning (*Shih-hsueh*) in Chu Hsi and Wang Yang-ming." In *Principle and Practicality: Essays in Neo-Confucianism and Practical Learning*, ed. William Theodore de Bary and Irene Bloom. New York: Columbia University Press, 1979.

———. "Reason, Substance, and Human Desires in Seventeenth-Century Neo-Confucianism." In *The Unfolding of Neo-Confucianism*, ed. William Theodore de Bary. New York: Columbia University Press.

Cua, A. S. "The Nature of Confucian Ethical Tradition." *Journal of Chinese Philosophy*, 23(2), 1996, pp. 133–152.

Bodde, Derk. "Harmony and Conflict in Chinese Philosophy." In *Studies in Chinese Thought*, ed. Arthur Wright. Chicago, Ill.: University of Chicago Press, 1953.

Schwartz, Benjamin. "On the Absence of Reductionism in Chinese Thought." *Journal of Chinese Philosophy*, 1(1), 1973, pp. 27–44.

———. "Transcendence in Ancient China." *Daedalus*, 104(2), 1975, pp. 57–68.

Xiong, Shili. *Ti yong lun*. Taipei: Xuesheng, 1980.

———. *Xin weishi lun*. Taipei: Guangwen, 1973.

Tian (*T'ien*): Heaven

Pei-jung Fu

The origin of the character *tian*, "heaven," is detectable in the records and decrees of the early Western Zhou. Many scholars supposed *tian* to be functionally equivalent to Di of the Shang dynasty, who had been worshiped as "God on High." The first Zhou kings (King Wen, King Wu, and particularly the duke of Zhou) believed that their legitimacy as rulers was based on *tianming*, the "mandate of heaven." Thereafter, Zhou kings and emperors of later dynasties were called *tianzi*, "sons of heaven." The "son of heaven" was the only person entitled to preside over state rituals for serving *tian*. The predilection of Chinese emperors for the title of the "son of heaven" can be observed in the fact that imperial decrees were headed with the phrase "In observing the will of heaven and following the trend of fortune." A historical monument named Tian Tan ("altar for serving heaven") still stands today in Beijing (Peking). After the collapse of the Chinese imperial system, Chinese leaders could no longer appeal to *tian* for their official political legitimacy. However, the positive attitude of the Chinese people toward *tian* is still apparent in ordinary discourse.

The meaning of *tian* and its historical usages varied, so that the implications of the term became too intricate to be explained simply. This brief exposition of the meaning of *tian* consists of three sections: (1) a rough outline of the concept found in the Western Zhou documents, (2) the evolution of the concept in Confucianism and Daoism through the Spring and Autumn period and the Warring States period, and (3) new developments of the concept since the Han dynasty.

Tian in the Western Zhou Period

The theocratic aspect of the Western Zhou was no less dominant than that of the two preceding dynasties.

Tian was manifested as the "supreme god" who would govern both the human and the natural world. The lack of source materials makes it difficult to trace out all the early stages of the conceptual evolution of *tian*. Still, the usage of the term in *Shujing* (*The Book of Documents*) and *Shijing* (*The Book of Odes*) enables us to analyze what the ancient people believed about *tian* and what their expectations were. According to those texts, *tian* had five functions.

1. Dominator. *Tian*, as the "dominator" or "omnipotent ruler," governs all creatures. The function and role of this *tian* may be compared with God in the western religious tradition. Concerning the relationship between *tian* and the "myriad things," we may approach it from the perspectives of existence and value.

2. Creator. All beings originate from *tian*. Passages in the *Book of Document* and the *Book of Odes* such as "Heaven produced teeming people" and "Heaven made high mountains" reveal *tian* as the "creator." But this denotes "origin," not "creation from nothingness."

3. Sustainer. After creating the "myriad things," "*tian* does not leave them alone without its control and support." *Tian* works as the "sustainer." This aspect is observable in such phrases as "the sustaining task of heaven above" and "the ongoing of the four seasons (being related to the nonspeaking aspects of heaven)." Since the complexity of the human world is a product of human freedom, through which persons resolve questions of value and choice, *tian* as sustainer must also perform two other functions as discussed below.

4. Revealer. The function of *tian* is not confined to the appointment of a ruler (the son of heaven) to lead his people. *Tian* is also conceived as the "revealer," and this role is evident in the frequent use of divination and in appeals to the collective will of the people, and the prominent wisdom of a ruler. In this function, *tian* is expected to transmit the standards of goodness and evil, by which people are guided toward the performance of good conduct and abstention from evil. This function of *tian* presupposes concern for the welfare of the people.

5. Judge. *Tian* as the revealer is associated with another function—*tian* as "judge." *Tian* responds to human acts in various ways: the rise or fall of a state, the success or failure of a human life, and auspicious or inauspicious portents in the natural world.

This fivefold function of *tian*, in normal circumstances, is supposed to be manifested through the "son of heaven." Therefore, in his reign the "son of heaven" must follow the will of *tian* as the creator and the sustainer by exhibiting his virtue of *ren* (benevolence). He must also follow the model of *tian* as revealer and judge by realizing his own virtue of *yi* (rightness or justice).

Tian in Confucianism and Daoism

In the Spring and Autumn period, the concept of *tian* faced a serious challenge: a collapse of royal authority, which resulted from a presumption that the son of heaven had lost his virtue and was unable to embody benevolence and justice. The role of *tian* as ruler gradually receded into a shadowy background. The disorder of the world of that time was accompanied by an awakening of humanism. In this transitional period, *tian* as the "benevolent" being descended to "nature," and *tian* as the symbol of "justice" developed into "fate." From then on, these two new features of *tian* were always present as factors in the history of Chinese thought. Confucian and Daoist thinkers acknowledged the situation as a crisis and participated in a creative transformation of the concept of *tian*. Mohist philosophers, by contrast, were strongly conservative and held to the earlier formulation of the concept; thus, according to many modern scholars, the Mohist conception of *tian* does not have universal import.

Confucius highly valued "being mindful of the past, so as to acquire new knowledge" (*Analects*, 2.11). He appreciated both the primordial significance of *tian* and the conceptual predicament of his time. Obviously, Confucius considered *tian* the creator and the sustainer; otherwise he would not have asked, "Does heaven say anything?" (17.17). Confucius did not fail to regard *tian* as an object of "pious veneration," especially in certain critical situations—such as when he was misunderstood by one of his disciples, when he emphasized the moral rule that a person must not deceive others, when his thought was not appreciated by others, when he faced the danger of being killed, and when he lamented the untimely death of Yan Yuan, his favorite.

Confucius also endeavored to develop the concept of *tian*. He transformed the meaning of *tian* as "fate" (*ming*) into "mission." He claimed that at fifty, he knew the decrees of heaven (2.4). At this moment, the "mandate of *tian*" went beyond the framework of political authority. Afterward, the concept acquired a nonpolitical application extending to all humankind.

As advocated by Confucius, the "mandate of *tian*" had two dimensions. One was that every human possessed the capacity to practice goodness. The second was that all individuals had to embody this goodness in their daily lives, because they were invested with a mission from heaven. Mencius developed the first dimension. He combined the "mandate of *tian*" with the human mind, insisting that mind should realize its inherent value, which is transcendent as well as immanent. On the other hand, Xunzi seemed inclined to limit the concept of *tian* to the natural sphere. As a consequence, for Xunzi, *tian*, being "nature," had nothing to do with order or disorder in the human world. This is one reason for the common claim that Xunxi's concept of *tian* shows a Daoist influence.

Unlike Confucians, the Daoists, such as Laozi, did not place human values at the center of the world. Laozi takes two attitudes toward *tian*. First, he uses the term "heaven (*tian*) and earth (*di*)," a conjunction implying that significance of *tian* would be limited to the natural world. Second, his philosophical thought does not admit a "transcendent dimension" of *tian*. It is *dao*, rather than *tian* and *di*, that represents the concept of transcendence. An investigation into the function of *dao* in *Laozi* suggests that *dao* replaced *tian* as it was used originally in ancient times. For example, Laozi's *dao* functions as the origin of the "myriad things," maintaining their state of existence and providing human beings with the right attitude toward daily life; thus *dao* promotes the harmony of all things. Zhuangzi went further, using the term *zaowuzhe* ("creator") in representing *dao*. The significance of all these usages cannot be precisely recognized unless one grasps the traditional meaning of the term.

Tian after the Han Period

Since the Han dynasty, *tian* has been the object of sacrificial rites offered by the "son of heaven" and of worship by ordinary people. In the history of thought, the conceptual implications of *tian* have changed continuously, according to the comprehension of scholars in different eras. Four implications have been salient in the evolution of the concept: (1) supreme god or "God on High"; (2) the natural world, or its structuring and regulation; (3) destiny, chance, or mystery, i.e., events that do not admit of any reasonable explanation; and (4) the endowed moral human nature—for example, the idea that the human mind has an inborn ability to know moral goodness. Although it is possible for *tian* to be used in just one of these senses, it is more frequently used to denote combinations of two or more of them. For this reason the concept *tian* has been perceived by many Chinese as an intimate yet unfathomable, familiar yet remote idea. A proper appreciation of the various uses of *tian* is indispensable to understanding one of the basic characteristics of the Chinese mentality, as well as to understanding why the Chinese people have often been called "believers in heaven."

See also Confucianism: Constructs of Classical Thought.

Bibliography

Creel, H. G. *The Origin of Statecraft in China*. Chicago, Ill.: University of Chicago Press, 1970.

Fung, Yu. *Tian yu ren* (Heaven and Man). Taipei: Zhongqin, 1990.

Finazzo, Giancarlo. *The Principle of T'ien: Essays on Its Theoretical Relevancy in Early Confucian Philosophy*. Taipei: Mei-ya, 1967.

Fu, Pei-jung. *Ru dao tianlun fawei* (An Explication of the Concept of Tian in Early Confucianism and Daoism). Taipei: Xuesheng, 1985.

Schwartz, Benjamin. *The World of Thoughts in Ancient China*. Cambridge, Mass.: Harvard University Press, 1985.

Li, Tu. *Zhongxi zhexue sixiang zhong de tiandao yu shangdi* (Heaven, Dao, and God-on-High in Chinese and Western Philosophies). Taipei: Linking, 1978.

Time and Timeliness (*Shizhong, Shih-chung*)

Chung-ying CHENG

It is often suggested that Chinese ethics in the tradition of Confucianism is an ethics of situations, which means that perceptions of right and good, and consequent actions, are results of one's consideration of a given situation, with no unchanging principles involved. The ethics of situations is contrasted with ethics of principles, in which what is right or good is determined according to principles that are absolute commands to the individuals involved. Actually, the concept of Confucian ethics as situational and the contrast with ethics of principle are both mistaken, as can be seen from a close analysis of Confucian ethics in Chinese philosophy, and of the philosophical ground underlying Confucian ethics.

The key to Confucian ethics is stated by Confucius: "Do not do to others what you do not wish others do to you" (*Analects*, 15); this is sometimes called the "silver rule." In this rule, I use myself as a measure to determine what is undesirable for others and what I should not do to them. But the content of what I do not want others do to me has to be specified. To specify it, I must go by my own natural feelings and desires (my desire not to get hurt, for example); but more than that, I have to go by my understanding of a situation and what I particularly want to avoid in that situation. So the specification is twofold: something stable in people's common feelings, based on human nature; and something varying and changeable, based on the situation.

There is nothing absolutely arbitrary in reaching a moral judgment in a given situation, nor is there anything entirely relative in a situation. It is a mistake to think that a situation determines what one wants to avoid and what one desires and that individual subjectivity has no role to play. Morality always relies on individual subjectivity, which gives "value content" to a judgment or action. This subjectivity can be considered autonomous and yet universal; therefore, morality cannot be considered merely relativistic, even though it is related to situations.

Applying moral principles to situations is not simply a matter of mechanical procedures; it involves weighing (*quan*) complex considerations so as to understand and appraise the situation. A situation always has some element of indeterminacy and ambiguity, and so the perception and cognizance of a situations may be hypothetical. Also, situations are subject to change; thus the input from a situation to an agent fluctuates, at least theoretically. For these reasons, morality cannot be determined solely by situations; subjective elements having to do with the agents determine the meaning of moral judgments and moral actions.

We can now return to the question of what I wish others not to do to me. I know what I will not do to others, on the basis of my humanity. But this does not tell me what I should do to others in a situation. In this case, I cannot rely on considering what I want others to do to me, because what I want from others may not be what they want from me. The reason is that so many elements of a situation are indeterminate, even if we assume that human feelings and desires are normally essentially the same and universally shared. Jesus' golden rule seems to make that assumption; Confucius's silver rule makes a different point—it is a principle of "no harm," of some minimal protection of humanity. It also invites us to explore what is positively right and positively good for one person to do.

To determine what to do to others, Confucius suggests quite a few possibilities for practice. This is part of his positive theory of cultivating and practicing *ren* (benevolence). To cultivate and practice *ren*, I have to love others, or I have to discipline my desires for the purpose of practicing established proprieties (*li*), or I have to establish and help others (of course according to their legitimate wishes) so that I will establish and help myself. The whole point of the Confucian principle of *ren* is to hold a vision and develop a community and a common destiny in which others and myself can share and our actions not only conform to but enhance our interests. In the *Daxue* (*Great Learning*), the principle of reciprocity (*jieju zhi dao*) is suggested for positive moral action in the same Confucian spirit. Reciprocity is a principle of putting oneself into others' place in order to develop empathy, and genuine insights into what others want us to do. Mencius stresses this same principle, describing it as "to think of others in terms of others' feelings" (*nairuo qiqing*) and—vividly—in terms of his own "feelings of unbearability" (*buren ren zhixin*).

Confucius and Mencius emphasize many virtues as principles of moral action. For Confucius, *ren* is the core virtue; for Mencius, both *ren* and *yi* are at the center. As expounded by Confucius and Mencius, *yi* is at once righteousness, fairness, and justness. *Yi* makes the performance of *ren* and other virtues necessary and also constitutes a requirement: preserving the social dignity of man. For Mencius, sympathy and empathy are the beginning of *ren*, and feeling ashamed or unworthy of oneself is the beginning of *yi*. *Yi* is a principle of self-dignity and self-respect, which in turn are the basis for all legitimate human rights; thus it is a principle of respecting others, preserving and enhancing their well-being, and recognizing distinctions and differences in things as real and worthy of respect and consideration. If human beings have the potential for development, recognizing this potential and assisting in its realization would also be *yi*. In this regard *yi* would coincide with *ren*—showing that *ren* requires *yi* for its realization and rational justification, and *yi* requires *ren* for setting its purposes and for its holistic justification. Perhaps there is also such a complementary relationship between *ren* and *yi* on the one hand and other virtues (such as propriety, or *li*) on the other.

All of this tells us that Confucian ethics is not an ethics of situations only, or of principles only; it considers both situations and principles. For this reason, one should practice self-cultivation so as to develop not only into a moral person (*junzi*) but also into a sagely person, a person of comprehensive wisdom (*shengren*). These two aspects of self-cultivation bring us to the consideration of time in Confucian ethics, because both aspects involve time and a profound understanding of time.

Moral self-cultivation is a process that takes place over time; in fact, it should be maintained continuously throughout life. Confucius stresses the constant effort involved, and the sincere heart that this effort requires. This process is long, and the mission is a heavy burden, as his disciple Zengzi would say, but we have to undertake it no matter how difficult the circumstances may be, and we should feel naturally and morally bound not to give up. If we lost this sense of "self-duty," we would lapse into a life of what Mencius calls "self-violation" (*zibao*) and "self-abandonment" (*ziqi*). However, Mencius insists that we have the sense of self-duty by nature, and under normal circumstances it will always come back to us. Mencius calls this sense "innate knowledge of good" (*liangzhi*), a description that suggests pursuing what is good and right in one's life and thus cultivating one's nature.

If self-duty is identified with *liangzhi*, any virtuous act we perform has two aspects: the correct, moral treatment of others and the realization of our own moral nature. In Confucian ethics, unlike Kantian ethics, the performance of duty entails the growth of the moral person, so that moral duty becomes a matter of virtue; it might be called "virtue of duty," in contrast with Kant's "duty of virtue." Thus our performance of moral virtues always has historical and temporal significance: it demonstrates that we have developed over time—that is, grown morally—and that we have used time (specific events and occasions) to develop ourselves. More profoundly, self-cultivation is a manifestation in the human being of the ultimate reality—a manifestation in a self-sufficient individual of ontocosmological creativity, which is at the same time particular and universal. The moral performance of virtues and self-cultivation together bring out a hierarchical interaction of levels of time (Cheng 1994).

Confucius saw his life as a sequence of progressive efforts at, and results of, moral self-cultivation. He was dedicated to learning at age fifteen and became established in his community and society at age thirty. He reached a state of "firmness" and freedom from temptation in the heart at age forty. At fifty he came to know the mandate of heaven (*tianming*). When he was sixty his ears became "pliable" and he came to understand people and things in terms of their causes and reasons and knew how to respond to them. At seventy he became fully and truly morally free so that nothing he did naturally would transgress against righteousness and he could do whatever his heart dictated. This sequence represents a temporal process of moral maturation in which every stage is necessary and no stage can be skipped.

We may now move on to how we should respond morally in the situations where we find ourselves. Again, the answer involves gaining a profound understanding of time as a motivating force and as a rationale for moral action in such situations. This means that we have to understand things in the world in terms of their formation and transformation—which in turn must be understood in terms of change as time and time as change. We can call this an ontocosmological theory of time or a temporal theory of ontocosmology, as represented by the implicit and underlying philosophy of the *Yijing*. To say that time is ontocosmological is to say that it is rooted in the ontocosmology of the world; that we must see the ontocosmology of the world as a substantive embodiment of time; and that time presents itself in many stages, on many levels, and in a multiplicity of things. Dogen, the twelfth-century Japanese Zen master, said: "Dogs and tigers are times," and we may also say that times are dogs and tigers.

This brings us to the assertion that ontocosomology is temporal: based on time and derived from time. Time is the origin and source of all things; but time transcends itself and so is itself timeless. Timeless time is the same as temporal timelessness, so that time and the timeless represent two aspects of the same thing, which we may call the "great ultimate" (*taiji*) or the "way" (*dao*). In the great ultimate or the *dao*, time and the timeless are unified. Their unity is present in all the things time gives rise to. However, if we do not have this ontocosmological vision, we will be unable to see the unity of time and the timeless in things, and thus we will not be able to make our acts "timely." The *Yijing* (*Book of Changes*) contains an ontocosmology of time and a temporal theory of the "ontocosmos" (the whole of things with their ontological grounding), enabling us to interpret ontocosmos in terms of time and interpret time in terms of ontocosmos so that we may reach a dynamic identification of the two in a "hermeneutical fusion of horizons" (Cheng 1994).

Following are the salient points of an ontocosmology of time.

1. The *taiji* or the *dao* (as timeless time or timed timelessness) gives rise to all things in the world in orders of increasing differentiation and individuation, whereas things are transformed in terms of concentration and dissipation of the *qi*, which can be regarded as the substance of the *taiji* or the *dao*.

2. All things are natural combinations of natural forces, generally represented by the "five powers," eight trigrams, and *yinyang* in orders of increasing or decreasing dimensionality. They are embedded in transformations such as those represented by the sixty-four hexagrams, which form a progressive order of changes. The changes are creative manifestation of the timeless (*buyi*) in organic unity and interpenetrating cyclic changes (*bianyi*, on different levels) as well as "conic" changes (*jianyi*, ascent or descent through different levels). The distinctions among and the interrelation of *buyi*, *bianyi*, and *jianyi* can be diagrammed; the result can be regarded as the structure of timeless time or temporal timelessness, the "great ultimate" of reality and process.

3. In the *Yijing* system or framework, eight trigrams generally represent natural things and forces, and sixty-four hexagrams generally represent transformations or situations that are combinations of events or forces in change, in terms of which the true nature of things (involving the unity of past, present, and future) can be understood. Therefore each trigram or hexagram can be said to stand for a "form structure" or image (*xiang*) of things as well as for a "phase structure" of process or change (*yi* or *yaobian*) of things.

4. Each trigram or hexagram represents a microcosm of change, with its internal dynamics of opposition-unity, balance-imbalance, support-suppression, harmony-disharmony, creativity-anticreativity, etc. Each trigram or hexagram also has a place in the system of hexagrams, which can be described as the macrocosmos of interhexagram changes in terms of which the three "ecstasies" of time (history, present, and future) can be analyzed. We also find the dynamics of opposition-complementariness, unity-disunity, etc., on this interhexagram level. A third form of relations of change is found in at the level of codependency between levels of systems of forms or situations, such as between trigrams and hexagrams. It is clear from the very beginning that the *taiji* or the *dao* differentiates itself into things on different levels, and thus imparts to each thing an individual ontocosmological history. The *taiji* or the *dao* also sustains each thing and its transformation so that each thing will have its proper place among all things and all transformations at all times. This is why time is, ultimately, both ontological and cosmological. Cosmogenesis and ontogenesis are basically one, yet ontogenesis may transcend cosmogenensis through the human mind (Cheng 1983).

5. Sixty-four hexagrams are used specifically to represent human situations—that is, situations in which humans participate and are transformed, and through which these transformations can be understood. This understanding is a matter of relating a human being to a situation in terms of the impact of the situation on him and his response to it.

6. A human being can understand a situation in terms of the "time formation" and "time change" structure and system, as described by the ontocosmology of time. This understanding is an effective starting point for participating in the natural transformation of the situation and "changing the changes" through one's creativity. In general, understanding brings the possibility of self-transformation and transformation of situations external to the self. This understanding of a situation leads to self-reflection, self-transformation, and the ability to participate in the natural transformation of the situation and the creative initiation of changes in that natural transformation.

7. When a person deeply understands his situation, he can respond by acting in conformity with it—exercising self-control or "self-reduction" or even choosing nonaction. Nonaction—"acting with no action"—is a Daoist idea: one responds like the *dao* and thus lets the *dao* take care of the change through its innate or intrinsic creativity, which has the capacity to do everything (*wuwei er wubuwei*). Other Daoist virtues are thereby developed: desirelessness, knowledgelessness, thoughtlessness, will-lessness, humidity, quietude, innocence, simplicity.

8. A second mode of responding to a situation consists in mobilizing one's moral abilities for self-development in terms of acts of benevolence, righteousness, diligence, participation, cultivation of consonance and harmony, hard work, and prudence or cautiousness. These Confucian virtues are particularly relevant for situations involving other persons either individually or collectively. They are the basis of and resources for harmonization of changes as well as for inspiring consonant and synergic efforts toward the solution of problems and the management of crises.

9. In both Daoistic and Confucian responses to a situation, the "time energy" and "time changes" of the situation and the human participant are fully used. This may be described as using time to control or overcome time, or as using time to adjust time or harmonize with time as time individuates itself on many levels and in many periods. The principle and essence of human action is to respond to time in a timely fashion, with the ontocosmology of time as a foundation or ground. Moral action, whether Daoist or Confucian in focus, can be described as "time-minded," "time-fitting," "time-based, and "time-valued," and this is how the Confucian notion of the timeliness—*shizhong*—of a moral action is to be understood. All moral actions are and must be a matter of *shizhong*, for only in seeking *shizhong* can an action be considered moral.

Morality is by its deep nature a matter of ontocosmological creativity with both holistic and individual significance. When Confucius and Mencius seek out moral cultivation, it consists in understanding oneself and others, and in applying this understanding to achieve creative harmony by way of timely actions. Daoist virtues can be similarly explained—as, indeed, can all the major ethical theories in the modern west. We can use the concept of timeliness, based on an ontocosmology of time, to evaluate and even synthesize or integrate all the important western theories (such as virtue theory, duty theory, rights theory, and utility theory), gaining a more sophisticated understanding of moral decision making and moral evaluation.

10. The *Yijing* is an example of the ethics of timeliness. Although the original texts of the *Zhouyi* use evaluative words such as "fortune," "misfortune," "prosperity," "advantage," "firmness," "regret," and "mistake" to describe situations in which one may find oneself, these words have to be analyzed and understood in terms of the underlying ontocosmology of time so that we will not draw any simplistic conclusions regarding the nature of ethics in the *Yijing*. It is not an ethics of situations in the sense of making solely relativistic or purely utilitarian responses to situations. The responses prescribed by the texts to each *gua* (a symbolic form of a human situation) reflect time-ontocosmological principles as well as human transformations—greater self-realization, greater harmonization with others and the environment, and greater identification with nature and the *dao*. Thus the ethics involved is not an ethics of situations, as is commonly understood, but an ethics involving both principles and individual subjectivity through the power of understanding in time and of time. This may perhaps be called an "ethics of timeliness."

11. Admittedly, there have been vulgar uses of time-cosmology in Chinese society, even up to the present day. These uses belong to popular culture, traditional agriculture-based social ethics, social climatology, and popular astrology. In the popular "lunar calendar" (*yinli*), what is fit or not fit to do is described for every day of the year. What is fit to do and what is not fit to do are determined by the place, time, nature, and potential of the day as found in the complicated system of five powers and *yin-yang* cosmology developed for timely, productive farming. The twenty-four occasions of climatic change (*jieqi*) are based, objectively and empirically, on observations of time changes in connection with lunar movements. Even in this concrete case there is no ethics of situations but rather an "ethics of timeliness," although here time is not consciously understood within a philosophy of time, nor is human creativity with regard to time fully recognized and used.

We may now summarize the human response to a situation leading to an action of moral significance, according to the *Yijing*.

1. Identify the situation in which one finds oneself. Traditionally, and in popular folkways, people identified their situation by divination (*bu*). After the Confucian commentaries made the implicit philosophy of time in the *Yijing* explicit, divination was no longer needed: one could come to know one's situation by knowing the *dao* and what one actually encounters in life.

2. Apply the time ontocosmology of the *Yijing* to the given situation so that it can be seen as a phase structure of the *gua*.

3. Analyze and understand the interhexagram structure for a given situation in terms of the dynamics of time relations; further, see how the given hexagram is transformed into another hexagram or other hexagrams.

4. In terms of this understanding, see what "time-fitting" action is called for, in order to achieve the maximum harmony and transformation toward creativity.

5. Act with free will. This action will make a difference to both the human world and the world of nature from a temporal point of view.

We can now see how the philosophy of change in the *Yijing* argues for recognizing the "time meaning" and "time significance" of human action against a background of the ontocosmology of time, or the philosophy of *yi* (change). Elsewhere, I have discussed and elaborated on this time ontocosmology in terms of the *Xici* ("Great Appendix") in the *Yijing* (Cheng 1994). The *Xici* was evidently developed as a result of philosophical reflections on the original texts of the *Yijing* and its divinatory uses in the past. Apart from the *Xici*, the present *Duan* (*Tuan*) *Commentary* and other commentaries, such as *Wenyan*, *Xiang*, *Shuogua*, *Xuxu*, and *Zagua*, can be regarded as resulting from similar philosophical reflections. These philosophical reflections were possible because a point had been reached where an overall query on the meaning of change and transformation in the world—and thus a justification of divination—was called for. The query was no doubt set in motion by Confucius in his effort to lay a foundation for his humanistic ethics. Thus one may see the *Xici* and other commentaries (particularly *Duan* and *Wenyan*) as an explicit elucidation of the implicit philosophical ontocosmology and methodology of time in the original texts of the *Yijing*.

In virtue of the Confucian background, the *Xici*, *Duan*, and *Wenyan* have come to provide a moral application of the implicit philosophy time in the *Yijing* as made explicit in the *Xici*. Hence, there is a close link between the philosophy of time in the *Yijing* and the moral philosophy of Confucius. This link is historically justifiable because the *Yijing* system was originally intended for practical application, particularly with regard to human actions. The moral application of the philosophy of time in the *Yijing* would consist in applying time to the analysis and understanding of a situation and the associated human response. As a consequence, the *Yijing* and the related commentaries may be said to effect both a metaphysical and a moral transformation of the original texts of the *Yijing*. Hermeneutically, this twofold transformation is possible because the philosophy of time and its moral application to human action are implicitly presupposed in the original texts of the *Yijing*. The original texts of the *Yijing* can be seen as "applied ethics," and the practical judgments of the *guan* as normative ethical statements in this applied ethics.

In the *Duan* and *Wenyan* commentaries we find many indications of explication of the philosophy of time in the *Yijing* and its applications to an individual *gua* as a representation of a situation. Let us take the first and the primary *guan* (*qian* and *kun*) as examples. With regard to the *qian*, the *Duan* says:

> By understanding the beginning and ending of the creativity of the *dao*, one can see the six positionings (as represented by the six lines in the hexagram) as accomplished by time. It is in riding these six dragons in time (or in timeliness) that the sage practices the way of heaven.

This suggests how, ontologically, a situation is formed in time and of time and how, morally, man can apply knowledge of time and become creative in following the norms suggested in the six lines. Each of the six lines has a judgment advising us to act in a certain way (within the framework of the situation as provided by the six lines). To understand the moral meaning of the advisory statement one has to apply one's understanding of the philosophy of time in the *Yijing*.

For the first line, "The hidden dragon, do not use it," the message is that the right time has not arrived for acting on one's beliefs. For the second line, "Seeing the dragon in the field, it is good to see a great man," the message is that the right time has arrived for seeing an important person for advice. For the third line, "A gentleman works hard every day and takes precautions in the evenings. Danger but no blame," the *Wenyan* says that the gentleman needs time to cultivate his virtue and learning and takes precautions because of consideration of time (*yinqishi erti*), and thus there is no blame even if there is danger. For the fourth line, "(The dragon) sometimes jumps into deep water. No blame," the *Wenyan* suggests that in order to cultivate virtue and "advance deeds" the gentleman must strive and reach for time (*yuqishi*). For the fifth line, "The dragon flies in the sky, and there is advantage to seeing a great man," the *Wenyan* says that what originates from heaven is close to things above and what originates from earth is close to things below, for everything follows its own class. This expresses a full realization of time in changes of things; in following its own class, everything follows its own time and "time change." The "time change" in the sixth line, "High dragon has regrets," means that the gentleman has separated himself from people and friends and has come to regret this. This again means that time is running out for maintaining one's high position, and therefore it is time to retreat and step down.

The *Wenyan* uses two important phrases to indicate the component of time, and time as a motif, in human action: "to move with time" (*yushi jiexing*) and "to reach the limit with time" (*yushi jieji*). These two principles are applied in the explication of the sixth line of the *gua*. Terms like "arising from time" (*shifa*) and "moving from time" (*shixing*) are used to suggest that all *kun* actions, like the *qian* actions, are fundamentally based on time and considerations of time. Hence, the morality of an action can be seen as a matter of considering time in light of the philosophy of time in the *Yijing*.

Apart from the *qian* and the *kun*, many *guan* in the original texts of the *Yijing* have explicit statements or judgments concerning the meanings of actions or norms for actions in terms of considerations of time and the meaning of time. The following *guan* have *duan* respectively enunciating the "greatness of time" (*shiqida*) in the *gua*, the "greatness of the meaning of time" (*shiyi zhida*) in the *gua*, and the "greatness of the function of time" (*shiyong zhida*) in the *gua*:

- For the "greatness of time" in the *gua*, we have *daguo, yi, ge, jie*.
- For the "greatness of meaning of time" in the *gua*, we have *tun, ge, lu, yu, shui*.
- For the "greatness of the function of time" in the *gua*, we have *kui, qian* (obstruction).

Many other *guan* have *duan* referring to "having time" (*youshi*), "moving together with time," "not losing time" (*bushi shi*) or "losing time" (*shishi*), and "following time" (*suishi*) or "rising and resting together with time" (*yushi xiuxi*). The most significant statement seems to come from the *duan* of the *ken*: "When it is time to stop, then stop; when it is time to move, then move; moving and resting should not lose the time to do so. Consequently, one's way will be bright." This suggests both the "meaning" (*yi*) and the "function" (*yong*) of time. The *yi* of time refers to its substance and principle, whereas the *yong* of time refers to the interaction between a temporal situation and the person in that situation, which gives rise to an action as a consequence of the person's understanding of time in the situation and time in himself. One cannot understand the principle, substance, or function of time—and thus cannot understand time itself—unless one comes to grips with the philosophy of time in the *Yijing*. By the same token, one cannot achieve a moral action in a situation unless one applies the philosophy of time to oneself and to the situation in question.

We have discussed why and how time is essential in Chinese ethics as represented by the primary paradigms of classical Confucianism in Chinese history. The philosophy of time is also relevant, or essential, for determining human action and conduct in other systems of philosophy such as Daoism, neo-Daoism, neo-Confucianism, and even contemporary Chinese philosophy based on Chinese tradition. There is a common heritage of philosophy of time among all these philosophies, and an understanding of time is a basic requirement for understanding all of them.

See also Confucianism: Ethics; Confucianism: Tradition; *Junzi*; Philosophy of Change; *Quan*; Reason and Principle; *Sheng*: Life or Creativity; *Zhong* and *Shu*.

Bibliography

Note: For the classical texts, see *Daodejing, Lunyu, Mengzi, Zhuanhzi, Zhongyong*, and *Zhouyi*.

Cheng, Yi. *Yi chuan* (*Yizhuan*, Commentary on the *Zhouyi*).

Chung-ying, Cheng. "On the Hierarchical Theory of Time: with Reference to Chinese Philosophy." *Journal of Chinese Philosophy*, 10(4), 1983, pp. 357–384.

———. "On the Origin of Chinese Philosophy." In *Encyclopedia of Asian Philosophy*. London, 1995, pp. 324–349.

———. "On Timeliness (*Shi-chung*) in the *Analects* and the *I-Ching*: An Inquiry into the Philosophical Relationship between Confucius and the *I-Ching*." *Proceedings of International Sinological Conference*, 1982, pp. 277–338.

———. "A Theory of Confucian Selfhood: Self-Cultivation and Free Will in Confucian Philosophy." *Far Eastern Affairs*, 6, 1995, pp. 46–47.

———. "Time in Chinese Philosophy." In *Encyclopedia of Time*, ed. Samuel L. Macey. New York and London, 1994.

———. "Toward Constructing a Dialectic of Harmony." *Journal of Chinese Philosophy*, 4(3), 1977, pp. 209–246.

Cua, A. S. "Confucian Vision and the Human Community." *Journal of Chinese Philosophy*, 11(3), 1984, pp. 226–238.

Kupperman, Joel J. "Confucius and the Problem of Naturalness." *Philosophy East and* West, 18, 1968, pp. 275–285.

Yu, Jiyuan. "Virtue: Confucius and Aristotle." *Philosophy East and West*, 48(2), 1998, pp. 323–347.

Zhu, Xi. *Lunyu chi chu* (Collected Annotations on the *Lunyu*).

———. *Mengzi ji zhu* (Annotated Annotations on the *Mengzi*).

———. *Zhouyi benyi* (Original Meanings in the *Zhouyi*).

Translation and Its Problems

Lauren Pfister

From a hermeneutic point of view, translation is one of the most difficult tasks involved in interpreting texts—one specifically involving cross-cultural horizons entailing many differences in linguistic, aesthetic, axiomatic, logical, metaphysical, and political "pretexts" and practices. The problems involved in translating Chinese "teachings" (*jiao*) as "philosophy" can be concretely located within a number of specific historical cross-cultural encounters beginning in the seventeenth century with French Jesuits. Although previous translations of the scholarly canonical works were rendered into other languages as part of the Chinese political or cultural hegemony in Mongolian, Korean, Vietnamese, Japanese, and Manchurian cultures, we will focus here on the transmission of ancient "Confucian" (*Ru jiao*) source texts into modern English. Our discussion will rarely deal with specific terms or phrases except as they illustrate larger problems in the history of the English translations of these Chinese classics.

To understand more fully the problems inherent in translating ancient Chinese philosophical texts, it is proper to recall the historical context of translations, the background and motivation of translators, and the differences in the basic presuppositions bound to modern conceptions of "philosophy" and the changing attitudes toward the *jing* or "classical canon" in traditional and post-traditional China. Then there are additional questions about the choice of texts, their published formats, and other features affecting the meaning of these authoritative texts in translation. Finally there are some important questions about producing "proper" renderings for key Chinese philosophical concepts that continue to tax translators and interpreters of these traditions. Although we cannot comprehensively explore all these questions here, this approach will serve as an outline for the following discussion.

The first attempts at making English translations directly from Chinese originals were meager. Selective portions of the *Four Books* (*Sishu*) were prepared by two of the first generation of British Protestant missionaries, Robert Morrison (1785–1834) and Joshua Marshman (1768–1837), but their efforts were sharply criticized by the more sophisticated French sinologists. In fact, portions of all of the "Confucian" (*Ju* or *Ru*) canonical works were selectively translated throughout Morrison's pioneering Chinese-English dictionary. Still, these were neither systematic nor complete, and they were often translated inaccurately, especially in the case of the oldest authoritative texts.

Only in 1828 was a complete version of the *Four Books* finally produced from classical Chinese into modern English by David Collie (d. 1828), a British Protestant missionary and teacher in Malacca. This translation was flawed by some elementary linguistic mistakes, showed little contact with Chinese traditions of commentary, and was at times, in footnotes, aggressive in criticizing these ancient Chinese teachings from the perspective of Christian theology. Various portions of other canonical texts appeared as articles within the serialized *Chinese Repository* (1832–1851) published in Guangzhou (Canton) and edited by two American missionaries, Elijah Bridgman (1801–1861) and Samuel Wells Williams (1812–1884). Published as independent translations with small introductions, they were relatively free from comparative religious comments even though they were prepared by missionaries and Christian thinkers. During these same decades complete renderings of the *Shijing* (or *Book of Poetry*) and the *Shangshu* or *Shujing* (later called the *Book of Historical Documents*) were published, respectively, by a British gentleman, John Francis Davis (1795–1890), and the prolific English missionary, Walter Medhurst (1796–1857). These constituted the first phase of English sinological versions of the Chinese canonical literature.

This period of sporadic missionary scholasticism reached a new zenith in the monumental *Chinese Classics* (first edition, 1861–1872), produced in Hong Kong, and the six volumes of the *Sacred Books of China* produced in Oxford (1879–1891) by the Scottish master translator, commentator, and missionary-scholar, James Legge (1815–1897). Appearing soon after the end of the Second Opium War, Legge's *Chinese Classics*, consisting of five volumes in eight tomes, marked a watershed in English sinological studies of Confucianism. In it, Legge published translations of the *Four Books* and three of the *Five Classics* (*Shujing*; *Shijing*; and *Chunqiu* or the *Spring and Autumn Annals* along with its commentary, the *Zuozhuan*, in a bilingual format). The first four volumes of the *Sacred Books of China* consisted of some additional Confucian canonical texts: *Xiaojing* or the *Classic of Filial Piety*, *Yijing* or *Book of Changes*, and the extensive *Liji* or *Book of Rites*. No other non-Chinese person before or after Legge has produced an equivalent range of translations and commentaries of the Confucian classics, except for the German missionary and sinologist, Richard Wilhelm.

After Legge, some important developments occurred in the style and precision of translations as well as in the changing contexts and standards of their interpretations. Legge's translations were at times awkwardly wooden, often because he rendered terse Chinese passages into similarly brief English verse echoing the original. At other times his translation carried controversial interpretations of key concepts, especially when passages offered explicit references to "God" (*shangdi* and in some cases *di*) or "sin" (in some uses of *zui*). Nevertheless, these translations set the stage for a new level of critical philosophical research into these canonical Chinese texts. Two specific kinds of English translations developed under the shadow of Legge's vast legacy: those that were critical academic works, and those published by ethnic Chinese scholars.

Legge himself was a fulcrum figure at Oxford, stimulating critical and post-traditional translations within academic sinology. Other representatives of this group are the critic, Herbert Giles (1845–1935), and the translators, Arthur Waley (1889–1966) and Bernhard Karlgren (1889–1978); Waley and Karlgren each published new versions of some of the Confucian canon. While following Legge's standard of relying on Chinese commentaries, all these men approached their translations with a more independent spirit, regularly offering radically rationalized criticisms of textual traditions, often presenting the texts in non-traditional formats. Like Legge, they also had an international corpus of sinological translations and linguistic tools to use and compare, but theirs were more numerous and precise than the materials available to Legge. Giles and Waley brought to their works an interpretive freshness expressed in vividly modern English; Karlgren produced rigorously "scientific" renderings of "glosses" of the *Book of History* (*Shujing*), the *Book of Odes* (*Shijing*), the *Book of Rites* (*Liji*), and the *Zuozhuan*. Consequently, these critical academic translations offered greater sinological precision, but did not always tally with more traditional Chinese commentary or philosophical positions.

Among the first few ethnic Chinese translators of selective English versions of the Confucian canon were Ku Hung-ming (1856–1928) and Lin Yutang (1895–1976). Ku prepared his own renderings after having studied at Edinburgh University in the late nineteenth century, producing a popular English version more readable but less cautious or precise. Nevertheless his versions are significant in reflecting conservative trends in canonical interpretations during the revolutionary period before 1911. More influential among English speakers were the literary and fluent renderings of Lin, a polymath intellectual and respected translator. *The Wisdom of Confucius* appeared in 1938, followed a few years later by *The Wisdom of China*, which included full translations of smaller works and selective renderings of a broad range of canonical literature, all sparsely garnished with nontechnical explanatory footnotes. In Lin's efforts a more philosophical style predominates, his breadth of interests mirroring the range of literature covered by Legge's much earlier translations. What remains hidden are the interpretive nuances guiding his renderings, there being no accompanying commentary providing clues that might allow readers to weigh his translation choices.

Still, the fact that Lin referred to the whole as "wisdom" indicates an important shift in interpretive understanding and philosophical emphasis. By this time the traditional Chinese canon had been challenged by both critical Chinese scholarship and the political demise of the Qing empire. Afterward, European and North American "philosophy" had started to take a firm hold in Chinese educational systems during the early 1920s, when both John Dewey (1859–1952) and Bertrand Russell (1872–1970) made extensive lecture tours throughout republican China. In addition, German and Russian forms of Marxist philosophy furnished further intellectual and political ammunition to dislodge Chinese "Confucianism" from its monopolistic stronghold. The traditional situation having passed away, Lin's account of "Chinese wisdom" not only reflected the traditional Confucian standard, but also included translations of Daoist philosophical texts, noncanonical poetry, and other literature.

This philosophical and political context shifted once more during and after World War II. From the chair Legge had once held at Oxford, Ernest Richard Hughes (1883–1956) produced during the war new selective translations of the canon in his *Chinese Philosophy in Classical Times*, presenting after them lengthy renderings of other materials from the ancient pre-imperial period, some supporting and others opposing "Confucius" and his disciples. His nuanced reading of these traditions was overshadowed by the much more influential interpretations produced a decade later in the English translation of *A History of Chinese Philosophy*, the sweeping non-traditional intellectual summary of Chinese philosophical traditions by Feng Youlan (Fung Yu-lan, 1895–1990). At the same time in mainland China the communists' victory brought about an even more devastatingly thorough ideological critique of all "feudalistic" traditions, these trends being reflected also in the 1960s through the burgeoning movement of "Chinese studies" in North America.

Since the 1960s there has developed a hermeneutically more expansive rendering of classical Chinese philosophical traditions as well as a subtle but important shift in emphasis for what now counts as the Chinese philosophical canon. Typical of this development were the joint work published in 1960 entitled *Sources of Chinese Tradition* and then, in 1963, the monumental effort by Wing-tsit Chan (1901–1996), *A Source Book in Chinese Philosophy*. Both contain selective translations of representative Confucian, Daoist, and Buddhist works along with general interpretive introductions to each historical section, but the differences in content and emphasis reveal much that shaped the understanding of classical Chinese philosophy in the later decades of the twentieth century. Where the former volume includes historical, poetic, and literary selections, the latter almost completely excludes these while emphasizing ethical and political discourses as well as rational accounts of human nature and metaphysics. In Chan's *Source Book* a new set of categories are imposed on the traditional corpus, creating a Chinese philosophy more strictly in tune with European and North American philosophical tastes. These interests informed his selection of classical Confucian passages, narrowing the focus to a very modern alternative reading of these traditions.

While academic studies of the broader Chinese classical traditions in English continue to this day, Chinese philosophical studies in these areas have focused more on the *Four Books* and much less on the *Five Classics*. This emphasis has been manifest in the translations of D. C. (Dim-cheuk) Lau (b. 1910), whose very successful renderings and interpretations of the *Analects* (*Lunyu*) and *Mencius* (*Mengzi*) continue to have influence. Next to Chan's *Source Book*, Lau's versions are probably the most influential texts in this area, even though other, newer translations of the *Analects* have been issued. Very significantly, Lau never produced versions of the *Daxue* (*Great Learning*) or *Zhongyong* (*Doctrine of the Mean*), believing their texts to be too corrupted for any critical rendition to be offered.

Our wide-ranging historical overview of the contexts of these translations and varying kinds of translators illustrates that none of the renderings of classical Chinese philosophical texts are free from broader cultural preconceptions or innocent of more or less explicit intellectual interests. When a scarcity of basic interpretive tools further complicated the translators' task, as was the case during the missionary scholasticism of the first half of the nineteenth century, the resulting texts manifestly suffered from various degrees of misunderstanding and ignorance. Justifications for new translations generally appeal to these kinds of issues, and they constitute special clues regarding the shifting preconceptions and interests that have guided later renderings. In this light Legge's *Chinese Classics*, as noted above, constituted a watershed in the quality and standards of translations and so deserves special consideration.

Unlike previous translators, Legge printed his English renderings of the *Chinese Classics* underneath or following a modern critical version of the original Chinese texts, texts originally prepared under the patronage and intellectual leadership of Ruan Yuan (1764–1849). In addition, he provided systematic and extensive exegetical notes, often including quotations in Chinese from the diverse traditions of commentary he cited for the *Four Books* and the *Five Classics* (more than 300 Chinese scholars were cited by name). These followed Chinese precedents, but were hampered by the lack of internationally standardized Chinese transliterations. The text, translation, and commentary present on nearly every page offered readers more interpretive freedom than an isolated English translation. Legge paralleled precedents in Confucian exegetical literature where modern Chinese paraphrases stood in the place of his English translations. Legge's lengthy prolegomena to each volume underscore that he was an authentic foreign participant in the Qing scholarly world.

A good number of crucial philosophical terms —including "benevolence" (*ren*) and "propriety" or "decorum" (*li*)—were rendered by Legge and earlier sinologists with Latin classical literature and elitist philosophy self-consciously in mind, reflecting in part the philosophical influence of Cicero (106–43 B.C.E.). Conscious also of his own motivations as a missionary-scholar, Legge provided in the prolegomena incisive evaluations from philosophical and religious perspectives drawn mainly, but not exclusively, from the Scottish realist ("common sense") school and Dissenter Protestant theology. These cultural underpinnings especially influenced Legge's multiple offerings for the term *dao*, sometimes also reflecting other sinological precedents, including "principle," "truth," "reason," "path of duty" and "the way."

Although more could be stated about Legge's production of alternative popular translations during his later years, a more salient feature of the formal presentation of the texts should be considered. In the Qing imperial collection of the Complete Library of the Four Branches of Books (*Siku quanshu*) compiled in the late eighteenth century, the preferred order of the Confucian canon started with the *Book of Changes* (*Yijing*) and ended with the *Four Books*. Legge not only reversed the order of the imperial design (publishing his rendering of the "mysterious" *Book of Changes* only later in 1882) but also rearranged the order of the *Four Books* to reflect his abiding critical interest in the person and influences of Confucius. Practical interests for his English readership in the relatively accessible *Four Books* and the impact of his own religious calling clearly shaped Legge's overall presentation of the Confucian canon.

These preconceptions and interests prompted later sinologists and internationally educated Chinese to provide alternative translations, but it would be shortsighted not to notice their own implicit and explicit guiding principles. Although some presentations of texts and commentary on the Confucian canon as philosophical literature were relatively comprehensive—as in the cases of Lin Yutang, E. R. Hughes, and Wing-tsit Chan in translation and Fung Yu-lan (Feng Youlan) in exegesis—the majority of English translations of the Confucian philosophical texts emphasized the *Four Books* to the near exclusion of the other texts. One exception to this rule is the renewed interest in the *Book of Changes*, including, along with translations, other critical studies of its significance and alternative texts (Shaughnessy 1996). Some figures, such as Karlgren, elevated precision over fluidity in translation; others (such as Ku, Lin, and Lau) provided texts attuned to modern ears; and a few (such as Chan) pursued diachronic consistency in rendering key terms. The best of the later translators have always appealed to modern philosophical and textual research, in spite of the fact that most were not trained philosophers.

While current philosophical research and sinological studies do continue to offer new and nuanced readings of key terms in the *Four Books* and other canonical Chinese philosophical texts (as in Brooks and Shun), one technique of translation that continues to highlight the difficulty of precise renderings is the use of transliterations. Recognizing the diversity of meanings developed for single terms within the canon that were further extrapolated in alternative traditions of commentary, certain translators have opted to transliterate key words (*yi, xing, ren, dao, li qi, ti yong, yin yang* among others) rather than offer any particular translations. This requires more sensitivity to the general meanings of texts and presupposes an informed and sympathetic readership. While this technique will continue to be expressed in research, it is designed to frustrate the lucidity of translations.

Contrary to this trend are those who call for radical retranslations of all key terms and phrases in an attempt to free previous renderings of their "cultural biases" and "intellectual prejudices." Suspicion of the hidden agenda behind these calls for "purer" translations is hermeneutically justified. At least one historical example of a similarly radical claim related to the *Book of Changes* illustrates the inherent difficulties of this reaction: the philologist Terrien de Lacouperie (d. 1894) blasted Legge's rendering of the *Yijing* on the basis of new research philologically connecting Babylonian, Assyrian, and Chinese languages. When Legge justifiably challenged Lacouperie to offer his own full rendering of the text, his suspicions were confirmed when nothing appeared even after a full decade. Even if retranslations can be worked out and published along these radical lines, they will continue to be constrained by consensual concerns and critical reevaluations over time. Shifts in cultural preconceptions and intellectual interests, especially as informed by recognized advances in sinological and philosophical research, will regularly provide warrant for new translations and involve a philosophically conceivable multiformity. Such a shift also provides a justified challenge to purists by indicating that their translation projects are more constrained than they themselves realize.

On the basis of a hermeneutic approach to the diachronic renderings of classical philosophical texts of Confucian traditions, we have illustrated how the translations have varied in quality, style, and philosophical emphasis. Although they were initiated by missionaries, these translations have now become the bailiwick of sinological experts responsive to, but rarely trained in, philosophical research. This in itself is a cause for further reflection. Yet if translation is itself intimately bound up within the interpretive process, as I have argued here, we should look forward to new translations and other shifts in the locus of classical Chinese philosophical literature in the twenty-first century. The recent trend of publishing bilingual Chinese-English versions of these classical texts indicates that there are concrete justifications for these expectations.

See also Intercultural Hermeneutics.

Bibliography

Brooks, E. Bruce, and A. Taeko Brooks. *The Original Analects: Sayings of Confucius and His Successors*. New York: Columbia University Press, 1998.

Chan, Sin-wai, and David Pollard, eds. *An Encyclopaedia of Translation: Chinese-English, English-Chinese*. Hong Kong: Chinese University Press, 1995.

Chan, Wing-tsit, trans. *A Source Book in Chinese Philosophy*. Princeton, N.J.: Princeton University Press, 1963.

Collie, David. *The Chinese Classical Work Commonly Called the Four Books*. Malacca: Mission, 1828.

de Bary, William Theodore, Wing-tsit Chan, and Burton Watson, eds.. *Sources of Chinese Tradition*, Vol. 1. New York: Columbia University Press, 1960.

Durrant, Stephen. "Ching." In *The Indiana Companion to Traditional Chinese Literature*, ed. William H. Nienhauser, Jr. et al. Bloomington: Indiana University Press, 1986, pp. 309–316.

Feleppa, Robert. *Convention, Translation, and Understanding: Philosophical Problems in the Comparative Study of Culture*. Albany: State University of New York Press, 1988.

Fung, Yu-lan (Feng Youlan). *A History Of Chinese Philosophy*, Vol. 1, *The Period of the Philosophers (from the Beginnings to circa 100 B.C.)*, trans. Derk Bodde. Princeton, N.J.: Princeton University Press, 1952.

Giles, Herbert Allen. *Confucianism and Its Rivals*. London: William and Norgate, 1915.

Girardot, Norman J. *The Victorian Translation of China: James Legge's Oriental Pilgrimage*. Berkeley: University of California Press, 2002.

Hughes, Ernest Richard, trans. and ed. *Chinese Philosophy in Classical Times*. London: Dent, 1942.

Karlgren, Bernhard, trans. *The Book of Documents, the Shu King: A Word-for-Word Translation of All Authentic Chapters*. Göteborg: Elanders Boktryckeri Aktiebolag, 1950.

———, trans. *The Book of Odes*. Stockholm: Museum of Far Eastern Antiquities, 1950.

Ku, Hung-ming, trans. *The Conduct of Life or the Universal Order of Confucius*. Taipei: 1976 reprint.

———, trans. *The Discourse and Sayings of Confucius: A New Special Translation Illustrated with Quotations from Goethe and Other Writers*. Shanghai: Kelly and Walsh, 1898.

Lau, D. C. (Dim Cheuk), trans. *Confucius: The Analects*. Harmondsworth: Penguin, 1979.

———, trans. *Confucius: The Analects (Lun yü)*. Hong Kong: Chinese University Press, 1983.

———, trans. *The Mencius*. Harmondsworth: Penguin, 1983.

Legge, James. *The Chinese Classics with a Translation, Critical and Exegetical Notes, Prolegomena, and Copious Indexes*, 8 tomes in 5 volumes. Hong Kong: Anglo-Chinese Press, 1861–1872. (See also 2nd ed., 5 vols. Oxford: Clarendon, 1893–1895.)

———, trans., with Qin Ying and Qin Hui, eds. *Zhou yi* (The Zhou Dynasty Book of Changes). Changsha: Hunan, 1993.

———, trans. *Hanying Sishu* (The Four Books in Chinese and English), ed. Liu Chongde and Luo Zhiye. Changsha: Hunan, 1992.

Lin, Yutang, trans. and ed. *The Wisdom of China and India*. New York: Random House, 1942.

———. *The Wisdom of Confucius*. New York: Random House, 1938.

Liu, Jiahe, and Shao Dongfang. "Li Yage yingyi Shujing ju Zhushu jinian xilun" (A Critical Assessment of James Legge's English Translations of the *Book of Historical Documents* and the *Bamboo Annals*), in *Zhongyang yanjiu yuan Lishi yuyan yanjiu suo jikan (Bulletin of the History and Philology Institute of the Academia Sinica)* 71(3) September 2000, pp. 681–726, 737–744.

Liu, Jiahe, Shao Dongfang, and Fei Leren. "Li Yage shi yingyi Chunqiu Zuozhuan xilun" (A Critical Assessment of James Legge's Translation of the *Spring and Autumn Annals* and its *Zuo Commentary, Zhongguo jingxue yanjiu (Studies of Chinese Canonical Learning)* 8 (September 2000), pp. 100–130.

Loewe, Michael, ed. *Early Chinese Texts: A Bibliographical Guide*. Berkeley: Institute of East Asian Studies, University of California, 1993.

Lundbaek, Knud. "The Establishment of European Sinology, 1801–1815." In *Cultural Encounters: China, Japan, and the West*, ed. Soren Clausen et al. Aarhus: Aarhus University Press, 1995, pp. 15–54.

Marshman, Joshua, trans. *The Works of Confucius: Containing the Original Text . . . with a Translation . . .* [and] *Dissertation on the Chinese Language and Character*. Serampor: Mission, 1809.

Morrison, Robert. *Dictionary of the Chinese Language in Three Parts*. Macao: Printed at the Honorable East India Company's Press by P. P. Thomas, 1820.

Pfister, Lauren. "James Legge." In *An Encyclopaedia of Translation: Chinese-English, English-Chinese*, ed. Chan Sinwai and David Pollard. Hong Kong: Chinese University Press, 1995, pp. 401–422.

———. *Striving for "The Whole Duty of Man": James Legge and the Scottish Protestant Encounter with China*. Frankfurt am Main: Peter Lang, forthcoming.

Shaughnessy, Edward L., trans. *I Ching: The Classic of Changes*. New York: Ballantine, 1996.

Shun, Kwong-loi. *Mencius and Early Chinese Thought*. Stanford, Calif.: Stanford University Press, 1997.

Tu, Ch'ing-I, ed. *Classics and Interpretations: The Hermeneutic Traditions in Chinese Culture*. New Brunswick and London: Transaction Publishers, 2000.

Waley, Arthur, trans. *The Analects of Confucius*. New York: Vintage, 1938.

———, trans. *The Book of Songs*. London: Allen and Unwin, 1937.

中國哲學

W

Wang Bi (Wang Pi)

Alan K. L. CHAN

Best-known in the west as an important representative of neo-Daoism, Wang Bi (226–249) is remembered in traditional Chinese sources as a brilliant interpreter of the *Laozi* and the *Yijing*, whose radical reformulation of the *dao* in terms of "nonbeing" (*wu*) sparked not only a revival of Daoist philosophy but a new current of thought known as *xuanxue*, the "learning of the mysterious" or "profound learning." This does not mean, however, that Wang was a Daoist in the sectarian sense of the word, especially if it implies anti-Confucian sentiments.

Wang Bi, styled Fusi, arrived on the scene at a point of rupture, when China was still reeling from the collapse of the Han dynasty. As the Wei kingdom, under whose government Wang Bi served, struggled to overcome internal dissension and to unify the country against two rival regimes, the question of order and unity dominated the philosophical agenda. The turbulent political situation, no doubt, was reason enough for some to aspire to a "higher" order beyond "worldly" concerns. Wang Bi, however, remained committed to the ideal of establishing the true "Way" in government, an ideal that he saw as the one thread running through the entire classical tradition.

Although highly regarded by his contemporaries, Wang Bi died too young to have made an impact on politics. Despite his untimely death—reportedly of a "sudden illness," soon after a coup d'etat rocked the Wei government and sent many of his friends to a violent end—he left behind a considerable written legacy, including major commentaries and shorter writings on the *Yijing* and the *Laozi*, which set new standards for later scholars. There is also a work on the *Analects*, of which unfortunately only fragments now survive. Wang's extant writings have been collected and critically annotated by Lou Yu-lie (1980). English translations of his major works are also available.

As an interpreter of the classics, Wang Bi was convinced that the ancient "sages" had discerned the true meaning of *dao*, and that the fall of the Han empire had resulted in no small measure from a misunderstanding and misappropriation of their teachings. Confucius, Wang felt, must be regarded as the sage *par excellence* because in transmitting the wisdom of antiquity, he had arrived at a comprehensive vision of *dao* and so "broadened the Way" (*Analects*, 15.29). Similarly, the *Laozi* was important because it focused directly on the nature and ethical relevance of *dao*. Instead of trying to make clear the one "Daoist" message, however, Han scholars had turned to cosmological speculation and had become obsessed with details extraneous to the classics. This might give an impression of erudition, which scholars put to clever use to advance their careers; but to Wang Bi it only testified to the decline of learning, which seriously compounded the forces of fragmentation tearing the country asunder.

To confront the problem, Wang Bi not only put forward a new interpretation of the classics but probed the basis of interpretation itself. Taking the lead from the *Yijing*, in which Confucius is made to tackle the issue of whether "words can fully express meaning," Wang argues that although words are necessary, they are not sufficient and must be distinguished from the underlying ideas. Words can in fact become an obstacle to understanding, if they are made the focus of interpretation. Building on an insight first developed in the *Zhuangzi*, another important source of *xuanxue*, Wang concludes that the words and images lying on the surface must be "forgotten" before meaning can be understood.

The issues involved are complex, but the argument is directed against the mode of interpretation typical of Han scholarship, which reduces meaning to reference. For example, what does the *Yijing* mean when it declares that "the number of the great expansion is fifty, but use is made only of forty-nine"? As the noted Han commentator Ma Rong (79–166) explains, "fifty" refers to the "great ultimate" or the polestar, the "two forms" of *yin* and *yang*, the sun and the moon, the four seasons, the five elements or phases, the twelve months, and the twenty-four calendar periods. Since the polestar resides in the middle and does not move, it is therefore not "used."

Other Han accounts may enumerate different phenomena, but they share the same hermeneutical approach. Based on a kind of "correspondence" theory, they assume that words have fixed meanings defined by external referents. For Wang Bi, in contrast, sense is much more than reference. The Han approach is fundamentally wrong, he holds, because it fails to recognize the reality of ideas. The words of a text must be "forgotten" in the sense that understanding requires, as it were, reading between the lines to penetrate into the world of ideas, which endows words with meaning. As far as the *Yijing* is concerned, what the numbers stand for is clearly not the issue. Wang Bi writes:

> In the amplification of the numbers of heaven and earth, one is not used. Because it is not used, use of the others is made possible; because it is not a number, numbers are made complete. This indeed is the great ultimate of change. . . . As nonbeing cannot be made manifest by nonbeing itself, it must be mediated by beings. Thus, focus on the ultimate of things; then one will understand the root from which they spring.

Once the chains of reference are broken, Wang Bi is free to pursue the perceived deeper meaning of change. Once the hermeneutical perspective is altered, the chase after multiplicity gives way to a fresh search for the ground of multiplicity. Properly understood, the concept of "one" reaches the very basis of change and existence. At the most basic level where change finds expression in the transformation of beings, it points to "nonbeing" as the root of all beings. To Wang Bi, this not only is crucial to an understanding of the *Yijing* but captures the core teaching of the sages. Among the classics, it is the *Laozi* that brings out most fully the idea of *dao* as "nonbeing."

"The way that can be spoken of is not the constant Way." The *Laozi*, or *Daodejing*, opens with these famous words. According to Wang, this means that the transcendence of *dao* must be recognized. Without form and without limit, the *dao* cannot be objectified and named. Nevertheless, this does not render the *dao* totally inaccessible, for it is also the "beginning" and "mother" of all things. In different ways, these two images relate the "mystery" of Daoist creation and disclose the central insight that "all beings originate from nonbeing" (*Laozi* commentary, chs. 1, 40).

What does Wang Bi mean by "nonbeing"? Does it refer to an "original substance" or "energy," which brings forth all forms of life? "The Way gives birth to one," the *Laozi* announces, which produces "two," and the rest of creation (ch. 42). Whereas Han commentators unanimously identified the "one" with the vital energy (*qi*) that generated the *yin* and *yang* forces at the "beginning," Wang Bi broke new ground in offering a conceptual account of how the multiplicity and diversity of things could be traced ultimately to a single source.

The genesis of the cosmos certainly cannot be understood apart from *dao*, but it does not begin with any particular agent. "Beginning" is not a temporal reference; rather, it indicates logical priority. The *dao* constitutes the absolute "beginning" in that all beings have causes and conditions which derive logically from "one" (*Laozi* commentary, chs. 42, 51). But "one" remains a metaphysical concept; it returns to the fold of "nonbeing" and cannot be reduced to a first being or original substance. Indeed, although infinite regress cannot be admitted, the idea of a first being or substance seems self-defeating. Precisely in tracing the chain of beings from particular, contingent causes to a necessary foundation, Wang Bi is able to account for the unity of creation without having to resort to the language of time and beings. The logic of Daoist creation, in other words, points directly to *wu*, "nonbeing"—literally, "not being" or "not having" any determination. While students of Wang Bi have yet to reach a consensus, the suggestion here is that nonbeing is to be understood as a negative concept, which sets the *dao* categorically apart from the domain of beings.

On the one hand, clearly not a formless "something," nonbeing safeguards the transcendence of *dao* without undermining its creative power. This is why Wang Bi is careful to specify that "one" is not a number but that on which numbers and functions depend. In relation to beings, on the other hand, the concept of "one" brings out the order of creation without compromising the nonbeing of *dao*. Nonbeing, as we have also seen, cannot be otherwise than mediated by beings. Thus a dialectical reading emerges from Wang Bi's interpretation of Daoist philosophy.

Having established the ground of being, Wang proceeds to explain the way in which the *dao* is manifested in nature. Metaphorically described as the "mother" of all beings, the *dao* not only "created" the world—as the source of being, in the sense described above—but continues to "nourish" it. The "constancy" of *dao* translates into basic "principles" (*li*), which govern the universe. The regularity of the seasons, the plenitude of nature, and other expressions of "heaven and earth" all attest to the presence of *dao*. Human beings also conform to these principles, and so are "modeled" after heaven and earth, and ultimately after *dao*.

This analysis, however, is incomplete. The *dao*, complete and without antecedent, can be modeled only on itself; it is, as the *Laozi* puts it, "so of itself" or "naturally so" (*ziran*). The claim that human beings are patterned after *dao* does not entail an external standard. Human nature cannot be equated with any particular principle. In the light of *ziran*, which Wang explicitly describes as an "expression for the ultimate," human nature is also "one," which suggests fundamentally "what is true in human beings" (*Laozi* commenary, chs. 10, 25). This is also the meaning of "virtue." Not to be confused with specific moral values, it signifies what human beings have "obtained" from *dao* (ch. 51). The words may be different, but they convey the same idea. If the *dao* were a godlike "something," its image would presumably inform the nature of beings. If beings originate from nonbeing, then they cannot be modeled on any "thing" but are "naturally so," like an "uncarved block" (ch. 32), an integral whole at the fundamental level.

The concept of *ziran* is doubly important because it sets the direction of Daoist ethics and politics. In the language of ethical theory, what is the case also forms the basis for what ought to be the case. The "constancy" of *dao* constitutes a pristine order. Effortlessly and spontaneously, nature accomplishes its myriad tasks; impartial and unmoved by favors or rewards, it provides for all beings. In principle, the human world should reflect this same order; that is, it should be naturally simple, noncontentious, and self-sufficient. If present realities deviate from this order, as Wang Bi believes they do, it becomes imperative to recover what is "true," to redirect human thinking and action by realizing *ziran*, and in this sense to "return" to *dao*. This is essentially what Wang Bi understands by the key Daoist concept of "nonaction" (*wuwei*).

As an explanatory tool, nonaction helps pinpoint the practical meaning of naturalness. Found not only in the *Laozi* but also in the *Yijing* and the *Analects*, nonaction does not mean total inaction, or an esoteric "technique" to get things done. For Wang, it above all entails a mode of being characterized by "emptiness"; that is to say, nonaction stands in stark contrast to action ruled by desires. Put simply, desires corrupt one's nature. Conversely, if one could only lose, be empty of, the insatiable appetite for power, recognition, wealth, and other objects of desire, one would stand to gain the natural "fullness" of being. This, too, follows from the analysis of nonbeing. Genuine well-being can be measured only on a scale of freedom, by the extent to which one is not fettered by desires or does not engage in the kind of interest-seeking thought or action that invariably precipitates disorder. Nonaction acts constantly to diminish desires, and to diminish any false sense of self that engenders desires, until one reaches the tranquil depth of emptiness and quiescence. This defines not only the goal of self-cultivation but also that of government.

In politics, the ideal sage ruler naturally does not act willfully to violate the order of nature. The truth of *ziran* dictates that one does not try to artificially alter or "improve" nature. Surely, to borrow from the *Mencius*, no ruler would want to model himself after the fool who pulled up his young plants by force to help them grow. Instead, Wang Bi advises, government must aim constantly at "honoring the root and putting to rest the branches."

The people, first of all, must be supported. In the context of the early Wei period, this would mean allowing the people to work their fields and enjoy the fruits of their labor. Excessive taxation, heavy punishment, and war—measures that Wang Bi considers the bane of Chinese politics—only reflect the tyranny of desires and have no place in the order of *ziran*. Given the bounty or "virtue" of *dao*, the ruler—like a mindful farmer—needs only ensure that obstructions to human flourishing are removed. Desires must be "put to rest," so that the "root" may grow; in other words, the people will never find lasting peace and contentment if the "root" of all social and political problems is not eradicated.

Specific policies may be helpful, but they are not sufficient. Ultimately, it is the ruler himself who must embrace emptiness and nonaction so as to establish a model to transform the people: that is, to enable those under the spell of desires to reclaim their true nature.

Government by nonaction thus rests on the claim that the transforming power of *dao*, defined in terms of *ziran* and exemplified by the ideal sage ruler, would naturally permeate the mind and heart of the people. There is perhaps a degree of optimism in this view, but Wang Bi considers it well justified. This is because the all-encompassing order of nature extends to the sociopolitical level. The institution of family and state is not extrinsic to nature. The hierarchical structure of sociopolitical institutions is rooted in the principles governing the Daoist world. As Wang argues in his shorter work on the *Yijing*, "the many cannot govern the many" but rely on "one." This is also why the *Laozi* ranks the "king" as one of the "four great ones" after *dao*, heaven, and earth (ch. 25).

In this respect, Wang Bi the radical reformer thus turns out to be quite a "conservative." The sociopolitical framework as a whole must be carefully "conserved" because it forms an integral part of the natural order. While the king occupies a privileged position, it is also the case that the art of rulership can now be defined in terms of Daoist principles. Embodying these principles, the sage naturally serves as a model for all rulers. This raises an important question regarding the nature of the sage, which completes Wang Bi's reformulation of Daoist philosophy.

Without desires or any concern for selfish gain, the sage doubtless cannot be compared to ordinary human beings. In fact, the majority view, established since the Han dynasty, was that the sage is inherently without feelings and emotions. Endowed with an "energy" so rich and pure, the sage is "destined" (*ming*) to greatness and should be ranked properly among the gods. Wang Bi, however, argued otherwise. The sage is subject to the same ontological conditions as ordinary human beings. He is different only in terms of his profound "spirituality and enlightenment." Although the sage has the same basic feelings, he is not tied or burdened by them. In his humanity, the sage "cannot be without sorrow and pleasure to respond to things"; yet, Wang Bi adds, he is able to "embody emptiness and harmony, and become one with nonbeing." Responding to the needs of humanity but not bound by them, the sage consequently can effect sociopolitical change and bring about the reign of "great peace."

Wang Bi is consistent. In view of the philosophy of *ziran*, the ruler cannot "model" himself after the sage in an artificial manner. To revitalize the rule of *dao*, the ruler himself has to "embody emptiness and harmony." The possibility of becoming a sage, in other words, must be affirmed. Further, the way of the sage must be carefully delineated because it can be invoked in judgment of governments. The quest for "sagehood" is difficult; but, once the principles of naturalness and nonaction are understood, they offer an objective standard by which actual performance may be measured. On this account, for Wang, the classics are in complete agreement.

When compared with the established view of the sage, it is as if Wang Bi undertook to "demythologize" the hallowed tradition. The inspiration may have come from the *Zhuangzi* (ch. 23), but Wang Bi's critical spirit can hardly be underestimated. While standing within tradition, he came to understand it anew. Whether in hermeneutics, metaphysics, or the question of the sage, Wang Bi takes his place in the history of Chinese philosophy as a bold and innovative interpreter of the *dao*, who in the footsteps of Confucius and other sages, and in search of order and unity, endeavored to foster renewal. The philosophy of nonbeing made a strong impact on the development of Buddhist philosophy. The concept of *li* (principle) played a pivotal role in later neo-Confucian philosophy. In both instances, Wang Bi's contribution is substantial.

See also Daoism: Neo-Daoism.

Bibliography

Bergeron, Marie-Ina. *Wang Pi: Philosophie du non-avoir*. Taipei: Institut Ricci, 1986.

Chan, Alan K. L. *Two Visions of the Way: A Study of the Wang Pi and Ho-shang Kung Commentaries on the Lao-tzu*. New York: State University of New York Press, 1991.

Chan, Wing-tsit. *A Source Book in Chinese Philosophy*. Princeton, N.J.: Princeton University Press, 1963.

Chang, Chung-yue. "The Metaphysics of Wang Pi (226–249)." Ph.D. dissertation. University of Pennsylvania, 1979.

——. "Wang Pi on the Mind." *Journal of Chinese Philosophy*, 9(1), 1982, pp. 77–106.

Fung, Yu-lan (Feng Youlan). *A History of Chinese Philosophy*, trans. Derk Bodde, Vol. 2. Princeton, N.J.: Princeton University Press, 1983.

Kohn, Livia. *Early Chinese Mysticism: Philosophy and Soteriology in the Taoist Tradition*. Princeton, N.J.: Princeton University Press, 1992.

Lin, Paul J., trans. *A Translation of Lao-tzu's Tao-te ching and Wang Pi's Commentary*. Ann Arbor: Center for Chinese Studies, University of Michigan, 1977.

Lou, Yu-lie. *Wang Bi ji jiaoshi* (Critical Edition of Wang Bi's Collected Works), 2 vols. Peking: Zhonghua shuju, 1980.

Lynn, Richard J., trans. *The Classic of Changes: A New Translation of the I Ching as Interpreted by Wang Bi*. New York: Columbia University Press, 1994.

——, trans. *The Classic of the Way and Virtue: A New Translation of the Tao-te Ching of Laozi as Interpreted by Wang Bi*. New York: Columbia University Press, 1999.

Robinet, Isabelle. *Les Commentaires du Tao To King jusqu'au VIIe siècle*. Paris: Universitaires de France, 1977.

Rump, Ariane, and Wing-tsit Chan, trans. *Commentary on the Lao-tzu by Wang Pi*. Honolulu: University of Hawaii Press, 1979.

T'ang, Yung-t'ung (Tang Yongtong). "Wang Pi's New Interpretation of the *I Ching* and the *Lun-yü*," trans. Walter Liebenthal. *Harvard Journal of Asiatic Studies*, 10, 1947, pp. 124–161.

Wagner, Rudolf G. *The Craft of a Chinese Commentator: Wang Bi on the Laozi*. Albany: State University of New York Press, 2000.

———. "Wang Pi: 'The Structure of the Laozi's Pointers' (*Laozi weizhi lilüe*)." *T'oung Pao*, 72, 1986, pp. 92–129.

Wang Chong (Wang Ch'ung)

Michael NYLAN

In the twentieth century, most historians of philosophy, in both China and the west, regarded Wang Chong (27–97 C.E.), author of the *Lunheng* (*Discourses Weighed*), in eighty-five chapters (*pian*), as a materialist thinker of a skeptical turn and striking originality. Early biographical materials for Wang Chong, when correlated with the *Lunheng* text itself, show Wang instead to be the first of the *qingtan* ("pure talk") masters, a master rhetorician more intent on winning debates than constructing a coherent philosophy, even when winning required open appeals to contemporary superstitions. An embittered individual hungry for public recognition, Wang spent more time in the *Lunheng*, the product of his last years, justifying his failure as a career bureaucrat and laying the groundwork for future fame than setting forth novel ideas for the reader's consideration.

Wang's reputation as a skeptic derives largely from his surprising attacks on certain figures in Chinese history (e.g., Confucius, Mencius, and Mozi), his point-by-point refutations of accepted superstitions and legends (many of them mere expansions of earlier critiques by famous scholars working in the well-developed skeptical tradition of Han), and his frequent denunciations of a host of absurdities propounded as theory by the "vulgar" Ru (classical scholars) of his own time. Wang reserved his greatest scorn for the popular and scholarly excesses associated with the doctrine of "mutual sympathy between heaven and man" (*tianren ganying*), which implied that heaven was somehow subservient to man. But Wang's skeptical sections usually represent a pastiche of earlier views, with the result that they fall short of systematically revising either the core beliefs of earlier thinkers or the underlying tenets of Han orthodoxy. Instead, Wang in a series of dialogues deftly plays on the reader's preconceptions to build his own case. Essentially, Wang sees himself as a forgotten genius, a *tongren* (polymath) or "true" Ru willing to put his considerable talents in service to the throne and the current sociopolitical system. As Wang deemed the single most reliable test of a scholar to be his ability to defeat his opponents (imaginary or real) in written or spoken debate (ch. 80), each of the eighty-five chapters of the *Lunheng* should be read as a separate set piece designed to illustrate Wang's rhetorical skill and remarkable command of the facts on topics of general interest. As a result, arguments posed in different chapters of the *Lunheng* contradict one another with surprising frequency, although the "proofs" marshaled within each chapter are generally consistent with one another. Furthermore, anecdotes queried in one passage are likely to be cited as "evidence" to clinch later points.

Perhaps the clearest example of the foregoing assessment comes from the large blocks of chapters devoted to questions of fate, a topic that preoccupied many philosophers during the Han dynasty. In those chapters (chs. 1–7, 9–12, 20–21, 42–43, 53–55), Wang seeks to prove that most, if not all, aspects of human existence are determined (*ming*) at birth—not only the person's gender, relative strength, and physical conformation, as one might expect, but also the individual's innate character (*xing*), aptitude for goodness, lifespan, wealth, status, professional success, and likelihood of achieving fame. This is because each individual's original endowment of *qi* (vital force) is a specific blend of varying amounts and qualities of *qi*, which can be classified into two main types (ch. 4): the *qi* that determines what events and persons the individual will encounter in life (the external factors), and the *qi* that determines the physical and psychic makeup of the individual (the internal factors). In conjunction with cosmic time and timely opportunity (both signified by the term *shi*), this distinctive allotment of *qi* produces a series of outcomes in a person's life, unless they are countermanded by still more compelling cycles of *qi* operating to influence that life. For instance, a person destined to be long-lived may still die young if he resides in a state destined to be vanquished at that moment. The reader should thus imagine the individual's life entirely shaped by interlocking cycles of timely opportunity (*shi*) and *ming* (his own; that of his location, which is tied to the stars; that of the people with whom he chances to interact; and so on).

According to Wang, any expert trained in the technical arts of prediction can easily "read" a person's fate in his physiognomy or in concurrent omens produced from coincident *qi*. By this, Wang hopes to dispel the pious notion that virtuous conduct is invariably repaid with conventional success, a belief that ultimately reflects, however much it distorts, the standard Confucian and Mohist pronouncement on fate: that one's conduct is the chief determinant of the quality of each individual life. In his zeal, Wang comes perilously close to denying both the utility of moral action and the possibility of free will. There is little, if anything, that a person can do to improve his fate or that of his state. And conduct is fated, rather than chosen, as is shown by the "facts" that "rich merchants are bound to snatch away the property of poor families" (ch. 10), and sages are produced by "harmonious *qi*" (ch. 51).

This cohesive picture of original *qi* (*yuanqi*), however, is cast aside as soon as Wang turns to consider (in chs. 8 and 13) another major topic in Han philosophy: the effect of human nature upon moral learning (*xue*). Here, Wang draws on a number of hypotheses proposed by earlier thinkers, only to conclude rather lamely that while "human nature is sometimes good and sometimes bad" (ch. 8), the individual's decision to reform, his choice of a teacher, and force of habit play such a crucial role in the augmentation and refinement of *qi* that the character cultivated (*xiu*) by the individual may function for all intents and purposes like second nature—a conclusion that inadvertently undermines Wang's writings on predetermination imposed by the original endowment. Unique among the "myriad things," humans may transform their basic nature through their special ability to make value distinctions and forge artificial likenesses (in other words, through their ability to reason and to create). Given the proper exemplary moral guides (starting with Wang himself), all but the most recalcitrant of evildoers (i.e., the insane) may be brought to embrace the "way of goodness," loosely equated in Wang's terms with the pursuit of factual knowledge (ch. 38). This process of transformation, effected through rites, music, and book learning, then becomes a firm foundation for an improved sociopolitical order.

With regard to that order, Wang supplies a contradictory account mirroring the fundamental inconsistency of his views on fate and human endeavor. (Only Chapter 45 tries to reconcile the discrepancies, when it distinguishes calamities caused by government from those that occur spontaneously.) On the one hand, Wang writes that the political order is spawned by the same unconscious commingling of heavenly (*yang*) and earthly (*yin*) *qi* that produces human destiny, so that all human efforts to induce political change are pointless in the end. When good rule occurs, it is fated to occur; "it is not due to transformative influence of virtue." In consequence, bad government policies are not responsible for any dearth in the grain supply, nor should the imperial administration be blamed for other symptoms of disorder. Whether they live in an age of order or disorder, the most that humans may do, then, is to watch for the various signs (often interpreted by popular kinds of divination) that coincide with change, in order to gain sufficient insight into their present predicament to "ride" contemporary trends to relative safety (chs. 9, 53, 55, 71). On the other hand, Wang insists that the ruler's neglect of truly "worthy" scholars and reliance on law clerks is all that prevents the Han ruling house from realizing the idyllic peace and prosperity associated with the "great peace" (*taiping*) in canonical literature. Only "worthy" scholars (i.e., those who cannot be stymied in disputations) know how to use the rites to inculcate in the common people the necessary deference and loyalty to superiors that "preserves the state" and reduces crime (ch. 29), relegating the harsh methods advocated by some legalists (*fajia*) to a supplementary tool of government. Such arguments are followed by several other chapters (chs. 56–60) that alternately deny the possibility of human progress and declare the imperial order of Wang's own epoch to be the best of all possible worlds. Sadly, to Wang's mind, many scholars share the common people's preference for anything antique, preposterous, or exaggerated, so they ignore the unparalleled achievements of present-day masters like himself.

Wang's writings on predestination and on human nature make sense only if we understand them against the background provided by the more openly autobiographical chapters of the *Lunheng*. They then appear to offer a series of subtle "proofs," both negative and positive, attesting to Wang's own outstanding merit. His writings on *ming*, for example, show that Wang should not be considered inferior to those who have already won the usual plaudits, since fame and rank are absolutely determined by fate; that explains the somewhat startling opening lines of the *Lunheng*: "Even if one's conduct and principles exhibit consistent worth, one may fail to achieve consistent success when serving in office." Then the succeeding, rather commonplace, discussions on the importance of scholarship to both the cultivation of human nature and the improvement of public morals (especially ch. 80) implicitly attest to Wang's conservatism on issues of hierarchy, duty, and the need for social cohesion (as in chs. 29 and 61), demonstrating Wang's eminent suitability for office. Not surprisingly, Wang announces himself to be one of those "awaiting an opportunity to offer his services" to the throne (ch. 1), and there are dark hints that Wang feels himself the victim of slander and ill-use by his fellow officials (chs. 2–3). Finally, Wang's writings on government reveal Wang's moods, swinging between a desire to mollify, even flatter those in power, in particular the local elites in Kuaiji and Emperor Zhang, and an equally strong compulsion to tout his own superiority. (Such passages lend substance to charges in Wang's official biography that Wang, despite a phenomenal memory, lost his only post owing to his quarrelsome nature.)

No fewer than four consecutive chapters of the *Lunheng* (chs. 34–37) refute the "vulgar" assumption that classical scholars are useless in running a state; Wang argues instead that Ru of real erudition are too seldom well positioned to do what they do best: offer advice and remonstrance. With a modicum of practical experience, the finest of the Ru (defined as the most widely read men of literary and rhetorical skill) could combine the best qualities of the literate clerks (who are good enough at day-to-day administrative tasks) with those cognizant of the "great principles of the Five Classics of Confucianism," for they alone would then command truly comprehensive factual and moral knowledge. "That worthy Ru do not advance [in their careers] is due to a lack of insight on the part of generals, ministers, and chief officers," for knowledge, especially factual knowledge, when combined with sufficient rhetorical skill, invests its owner with real power (chs. 14, 37–38, 40, 58, 80).

Once Wang Chong's polemic is seen as a rather obvious plea for recognition, the *Lunheng* may be read either as guide to the Han rhetorical conventions in "aid of conversation" (*tanzhu*), as Wang's near contemporaries used it, or as sourcebook for an extraordinary range of Han beliefs (e.g., the self-perceptions of typical classical scholars at court; the nature of dreams; the interactions between body and soul; the source of heat, cold, rain, and thunder; and the movements of the heavenly bodies), enriched by frequent references to authoritative texts on similar subjects. A good number of Wang's arguments depend on the character of heaven itself. According to Wang, whether heaven is a physical body (*ti*) or dispersed *qi*, it must certainly act without intention, for if heaven were conscious, it would have arranged society more appropriately, so as to obviate the problems of evil, strife, and disorder (chs. 42, 54); an interventionist heaven would also have managed to send mankind unambiguous instructions regarding its wishes, in place of those vague signs liable to misinterpretation that are cited as "omens" by theorists at court (chs. 18, 50–51). Given the vital importance of man's original allotment of *qi*, heaven (sometimes shorthand for "heaven and earth") inevitably, if unthinkingly, affects human lives profoundly, although humans, occupying a place in the universe roughly analogous to that of lice within a suit of clothing (chs. 43, 71), can never expect to exert any countervailing influence on heaven, no matter how talented or highly placed they may be. So while it is true that men to some degree share the same *qi* as heaven, the widely accepted doctrine of mutual sympathy between heaven and man is patently a lie, the well-intentioned construct of court scholars who saw in it a way to frighten the ruler into adopting right conduct and sensible policies (ch. 42). Continuing the skeptical tradition of Warring States and the Han, Wang further argues that the dead are not conscious (ch. 62); that sacrifices and divination edify the living, not the dead (chs. 71, 76–77); that meticulous observance of taboos is futile; that illness and death are not the work of vengeful ghosts; and that no humans can attain immortality (chs. 24, 72, 77). With each such declaration, Wang aims to free humans from their fear of the unknown.

The careful reader of the *Lunheng* can also gain valuable insights into the form and content of early scholastic debates. As Wang's conceit is that the *Lunheng* eschews all rhetorical flourishes in the interest of ascertaining a unitary truth, the *Lunheng* uses few of the emphatic particles, exaggerated claims, and parallel passages that customarily embellish Han polemics. Nonetheless, Wang makes the usual appeals to classical authorities (especially to Confucius), to eyewitness accounts, and to deduction by analogy, the validity of each to be judged by the discerning mind in light of other available pieces of "evidence." Equally standard for his time, though likely to confuse the modern reader, is Wang's propensity to "argue from a lodging place" (i.e., to adopt his opponent's stance temporarily) in order to skewer the logical fallacy in a rival hypothesis. Some of Wang's most notable remarks, however, are those that touch, simply in passing, on larger epistemological problems, including the impossibility of finding the truth on the basis of partial evidence (e.g., in ch. 18), the criteria for distinguishing a good analogy from a bad one (chs. 14, 30, 42), and methods for untangling cause-and-effect relations from coincidental occurrences (e.g., in chs. 10, 43, and 55). Noteworthy remarks also include those that dispute the possibility of foreknowledge and omniscience (chs. 15, 28, 79) and those that try to determine the exact degree of affinity prevailing between heaven and man (e.g., in chs. 19 and 42). Still, Wang's real genius lay in his ability to adapt metaphors, analogies, and quotations to his own rhetorical uses. In one instance, Wang quotes Yang Xiong's famous maxim on fate, claiming its authority while subverting its meaning (ch. 3). In another, Wang takes a well-worn metaphor in a new direction: whereas previous texts had drawn a comparison between the upright official's remonstrances to the throne and strong medicine administered by a wise doctor to an ailing patient, Wang contends that even the wisest of doctors can effect a cure only if the "doctor happens to get a patient whose time has not yet come and whose disease is not yet fatal" (ch. 53).

For centuries, scholars have debated Wang's rightful place in philosophy. Wang is certainly no Daoist, although many would like to make him into one. His cosmological writings, which supposedly qualify as Daoist, claim Huang-Lao thought as their inspiration but seldom depart from those of the Han Confucian masters Yang Xiong and Huan Tan. In addition, Wang not only ridicules the main goal of religious Daoism, *xian* immortality, but also mocks the philosophical Daoist's assertion that personal failure in life is often attributable to an inability to accede to changing circumstances. By his own estimate, Wang is a Ru, since the Ru are the principal conservators of the social order (ch. 29, 35), but he is indisputably a "great Ru" (*hong Ru*) of "enlarged views"; he is the best sort of scholar, one trained in the past, like the fellow classicists of his own age (*shi Ru*), but with no undue reverence for the past or the Confucian classics (ch. 39). And while Wang delights in pricking the vanity of the professional academicians engaged in compiling cumbersome "commentaries by chapter and verse" (hence, Wang's assignment by traditional scholars to the "archaic script" school), he is not above lavishing praise on the "secret texts" (apocryphal writings) housed in the imperial library as repositories of the highest order of truth. Recent historians of Chinese philosophy seem content to label Wang, in company with most Han philosophers, an eclectic, whose debt to both the legalists (e.g., in ch. 49) and the Mohists (e.g., in ch. 67) is far greater than he cares to acknowledge. More intent on "asking questions and posing challenges" (ch. 28) than faithfully transmitting any one tradition, Wang asserts his right to seek the truth wherever he may find it, particularly in the philosophical works of the masters of the Warring States period.

See also Legalism; Mohism: The Founder, Mozi; Yang Xiong.

Bibliography

Fung, Yu-lan. *A History of Chinese Philosophy*, Vol. 2, trans. Derk Bodde. Princeton, N.J.: Princeton University Press, 1953. (The most judicious overview of Wang's philosophy in English.)

Wang, Ch'ung. *Lun-heng*, 2 vols., trans. Afred Forke. Chicago, Ill.: Paragon Book Gallery, 1962. (Reprint. Originally published in 1907. A new translation by Michael Nylan is in preparation for the Yale Civilization in China Series.)

Zhou, Guidian. *Wang Chong zhexue sixiang xintan* (New Research into Wang Chong's Philosophical Thought). Hebei renmin, 1984.

Wang Fuzhi (Wang Fu-chih)

JeeLoo Liu

Wang Fuzhi (Wang Chuanshan, 1619–1692) was born at the end of the Ming dynasty (1368–1644). His father was a scholar, so Wang grew up in a highly intellectual environment. At the age of seven, he had read all thirteen of the classics. When Wang was twenty-five, bandits kidnaped his father and demanded Wang's service in exchange for his father's life. Wang injured himself badly and had himself carried to the bandits, who then let both father and son go.

The following year the Manchus invaded China and established a new dynasty (the Qing, 1644–1911). The Ming royal family fled to the south and established a new government. Wang, reflecting on how neo-Confucianism in the Ming dynasty had brought about the dynasty's cultural as well as political downfall, began his writing career with an attempt to renew what he took to be the true spirit of Confucianism. The next few years saw constant struggles between the Ming government in the south and the powerful new Manchu government. Wang participated in the resistance movement but eventually concluded that it was futile. In 1661, the last Ming emperor was caught and the Manchus took control over the whole country. Wang refused to collaborate, and to avoid being constantly pressed to serve by local authorities he escaped to a remote mountainous region where he fled from one place to another. He eventually settled down in a hut at the foot of a barren mountain that he named Chuanshan ("Boat Mountain," after a huge boulder in the shape of a boat). Wang stayed here for the remainder of his life, taking up the name Chuanshan himself. He died at age seventy-four, having devoted more than forty years to writing and having completed more than a hundred books. Fourteen years after Wang's death, his son collected and organized the manuscripts, but not until 1842 were they put into print, and some of Wang's works were lost forever.

Philosophical Heritage

Wang Fuzhi saw that neo-Confucianism in the Ming dynasty was dominated by Lu-Wang, a school of thought influenced by the writings of Lu Xiangshan and Wang Yangming. In Wang Fuzhi's opinion, this school deviated from true Confucian teaching. Therefore, he dedicated his life to a study of the classics. His philosophical thinking can be traced back to *The Book of Changes* (*Yijing*), on which he completed five different commentaries that contain the roots of his cosmological view. He also wrote several commentaries on *The Book of History* (*Shujing*), *The Book of Odes* (*Shijing*), *Chungin*, *The Book of Rites* (*Liji*), and *The Four Books* (*Sishu*), all of which represent the origin of classical Confucianism.

Among neo-Confucians, Wang respected Zhang Zai (1020–1077) most highly. He believed that Zhang Zai's philosophy came closest to the essence of *Yijing*, and that his own philosophy was basically a continuation of Zhang's. Thus the two major sources of Wang Fuzhi's philosophy can be summed up as the *Book of Changes* and Zhang Zai. But Wang Fuzhi also drew from many other books and thinkers. In his earlier years, Wang praised Zhu Xi and the whole Cheng-Zhu school; and although he later rebutted many of Zhu Xi's interpretations of the Four Books, there can be no denying that he was greatly influenced by Zhu. Wang Fuzhi also drew philosophical as well as literary inspiration from *Laozi* and *Zhuangzi*, even though he strongly criticized the later Buddhist association of Daoism.

Cosmology

One prominent feature of Wang Fuzhi's cosmology is his materialistic monism. His view is not strictly materialism, since he does not deny the existence of principle (*li*). But Wang criticizes Zhu Xi's separating principle from material force (*qi*) and rendering principle transcendent. Even though Zhu often emphasizes the coexistence and inseparability of principle and material force, he does put them into different logical categories and considers them two different entities. When Zhu was pressed to trace the origin of principle and material force, he would put principle prior to material force. Wang Fuzhi considers this a mistake: in Zhu's metaphysics, principle is left dangling. Wang, instead, takes material force as the fundamental element (*arché*) of the universe. Principle is simply the "principle of material force"; it is the order inherent in *qi* itself. Therefore, principle has no transcendental status; it is also not logically prior to material force. Wang says, "Principle is simply the principle of material force. The way material force *ought to be* is principle itself. Principle is not prior and material force is not posterior" (*Du sishu daquan shuo*, Vol. 10).

In this respect Wang's view is very similar to that of Zhang Zai. However, for Zhang Zai material force itself is the substance (*ti*) of the cosmos. When it consolidates, it forms material objects; when it disintegrates, it is simply a massive, formless *qi* that he calls the "great vacuity" (*taixu*). Thus, material force for Zhang Zai remains an abstract entity divided into two levels of existence: its substance (*ti*), and its function (*yong*). Material objects are manifestations of material force, whose function is revealed in them. The great vacuity (*taixu*) is the substance of material force; it is invisible and formless. Wang Fuzhi, on the other hand, does not posit a separate substance (*ti*) independent of its function (*yong*). He carries Zhang Zai's monism one step further to argue that the universe is "one," not just in its constituents but also in its ontological order. Wang Fuzhi says, "When we talk about substance and function, we cannot separate the two" (*Du sishu daquan shuo*, Vol. 7). Therefore, Zhang Zai is mistaken in assuming that there is another state of being for material force separate from, and logically prior to, the existence of material objects. Also, Zhu Xi is mistaken in treating principle as "the substance" and material force as "the function." Wang Fuzhi thinks that principle and material force can serve as each other's substance or function. There is thus no substance that stands behind reality. Reality is nothing but material force and its function (concrete things).

The emphasis on material objects and concrete existence is another important aspect of Wang Fuzhi's cosmology. "Concrete existence" (*qi*) is a notion derived from the *Book of Changes*, which sees the Way (*dao*) as metaphysical (what is above shapes, *xing er shang*) and concrete existence (*qi*) as physical (what is within shapes, *xing er xia*). Confucianists generally see the Way on a transcendental level, treating it as something superior to concrete existence that prescribes how concrete things should be. Wang Fuzhi's theory is thus revolutionary in its rejection of a division between the two realms. He especially criticizes those who posit an ontological level above the physical world. Wang argues that the Way does not predetermine the world; rather, it is developed as the world evolves. He says:

> What exist in this world are nothing but concrete things. The Way (*dao*) is simply the Way of concrete things, while concrete things may not be called concrete things of the Way. . . . There is no Way of the father before there is a son; there is no Way of the elder brother before there is a younger brother. There are many Ways that could exist but are not yet existent. Therefore it is indeed true that without a concrete thing, there cannot be its Way. (*Zhouyi waizhuan*, 5:25)

The world as we experience it, the physical realm, is what Wang Fuzhi takes to be the only existence.

The notion of heaven (*tian*) is also divested of its metaphysical status. In contrast to Cheng Yi and Zhu Xi, who said "Heaven is nothing but *li*," Wang argues that heaven is nothing but material force. Wang says:

> Heaven has its principle, but heaven itself cannot be separated from material force. Only when we recognize the principle as the principle of material force can we define the principle of heaven. If we abandon talk of material force to discuss the principle, then we cannot even find the principle of heaven. (*Du sishu daquan shuo*, 719)

Furthermore, in Wang's view, heaven is simply the totality of nature: natural phenomena and natural objects. Natural phenomena and natural objects are made up of the two kinds of material force: *yin* and *yang*. The principle of heaven lies in the order of transmutation between *yin* and *yang*. There is no virtue—neither humanity (*ren*), creativity (*sheng*), impartiality (*gong*), sincerity (*cheng*), nor diligence (*jian*)—inherent in heaven itself. All such values are assigned by human beings; nature itself is value-free. In this respect Wang Fuzhi's cosmology can also be seen as naturalism.

Another feature of Wang Fuzhi's cosmology is his theory of being. He advocates realism, the theory that the world exists independently of the mind. In this respect his theory directly opposes Wang Yangming's idealism. Wang Fuzhi says, "The Way (*dao*) is real" (*Zhouyi waizhuan*, 5:44). He strongly criticizes the neo-Confucianists of the Lu-Wang school for mixing Confucianism with the Daoist teaching of nonbeing (*wu*) and the Buddhist teaching of emptiness (*kong*). To him, the universe is simply the totality of material objects. Individual objects may not exist eternally, but the totality has always been here. Being does not come from nonbeing, because there was never a nonbeing. Being simply is; in other words, it exists all the time. Nothing precedes reality. Wang says:

> People cannot see the beginning or the end of the universe, so they conclude that there was an initial beginning at the ancient past, and that there will be an end of everything in the far future. This is really stupid. (*Zhouyi waizhuan*, 4:35)

Wang thinks that talk of creation and annihilation results from the corrupting influence of Buddhism.

Wang also argues that the universe was not generated by the "great ultimate" (*taiji*) as Zhou Dunyi and Zhu Xi hold, nor was it preceded by the "great vacuity" as Zhang Zai holds. The universe has always been here, since material force has always been in existence. According to Zhou Dunyi, the *taiji* (great ultimate), through movement, generates *yang*, and through tranquillity generates *yin* (*Zhouzi quanshu*, 4). Wang argues that "*tai* means 'great,' *ji* means 'ultimate.' The term *taiji* is simply a description of the combination of *yin* and *yang*" (*Zhouyi neizhuan*, 517). Therefore, the great ultimate is not something over and above *yin* and *yang*, from which *yin* and *yang* are generated. Regarding Zhang Zai's notion of the great vacuity, Wang comments: "The so-called 'great vacuity'—I don't know what it can refer to. . . . The heaven is principle as well as the emanation of material force. It is not at all empty or unreal" (*Liji zhangju*, 42:21). The world consists of material force manifested in material objects. This is reality, and nothing can be more real than the totality of material objects.

In sum, Wang Fuzhi's cosmology, with its emphasis on the concrete existence of material objects, is revolutionary compared with the preceding theories. His monism leads him to reject any abstract, transcendental entity—nonbeing, principle, mind, the great vacuity, the great ultimate, or substance. Ultimately his interest lies in the real, living, full, visible, tangible world that surrounds us.

Philosophy of Human Nature

Neo-Confucianists, in the Cheng-Zhu school and the Lu-Wang school alike, treat human nature (*xing*) as that which heaven confers on man. Humans and other creatures derive their nature from the "heavenly principle" (*tianli*). The same heavenly principle makes possible the nature of different creatures. Therefore, humans and other creatures share the same nature. What makes humans different from other creatures is the endowment of material force (*qi*). The purity or impurity of the material force in each being is responsible for the good or evil in different lives.

Wang Fuzhi, however, rejects the theory of the sameness of nature. He argues that nature is determined by the matter from which a life is formed. Humans and animals are made of different matter and thus have different natures. The nature of vegetation includes growth and decay; the nature of animals includes perception and motion. Human nature, on the other hand, includes moral consciousness. Furthermore, human nature is not just "that which at birth is so," as most neo-Confucians take it to be. Wang Fuzhi thinks that nature is also what develops throughout one's life: "Nature is principle (*li*) at one's birth; it gets perfected daily from its daily renewal" (*Shangshu yinyi*, 3:6). Our nature is not determined at birth; the external environment and later cultivation help to make us the way we are. To Wang, there is no sharp division between nature and nurture. At any moment of our lives, we can change our nature for the better or for the worse. This view clearly opposes the theory of human nature advocated by Mencius and promoted by most neo-Confucians.

Wang Fuzhi also departs from neo-Confucianism in his confirmation of the value of human desires. Members of the Cheng-Zhu school emphasize that only through the extinction of human desires can we see the prevalence of the heavenly principle (*tianli*). Wang argues against setting up an antithesis between the heavenly principle and human desires. Basic human desires are nothing but culinary and sexual desires. Wang thinks that even the saints could not rid themselves of these desires. Desires are not evil; they do not stand in the way of our moral cultivation. On the contrary, to cultivate one's moral self, one has to appreciate the heavenly principle inherent in human desires. Wang says, "There cannot be heaven apart from the human; there cannot be principle apart from desires" (*Du sishu daquan shuo*, Vol. 8). This thought is derived from Zhang Zai's view on principle and desire. Zhang thinks that food and sex are nothing but nature, and Wang comments, "Principle lies within them" (*Zhengmeng zhu*, 274). Wang defines desire as our hearts' interaction with that which is desirable. He says: "Things like music, women, goods, wealth, power and success, anything that is desirable such that I desire it, is called desire" (*Du sishu daquan shuo*, 369).

As long as we are alive, we cannot avoid interacting with objects; once we interact with them, we cannot avoid the generation of desires. Therefore, "to expect one to completely rid oneself of human desires is an impossible demand" (*Du sishu daquan shuo*, 371). Wang criticizes the Cheng-Zhu school for treating indulgence in material possessions as the source of evil. He also rejects the Buddhists' denunciation of desirable material objects and the whole material world. He says:

> All desirable objects are the products of heaven and earth. To blame natural products of heaven and earth and not blame people is like blaming the owner for having too many treasures while acquitting the thieves. (*Du sishu daquan shuo*, 675)

Wang Fuzhi does not condone indulgence in material desires, however. He thinks that the basic rule is moderation. If one's desires are moderated, then they are in accord with principle (*li*). Wang's notion of moderation is paired with the notion of fairness (*gong*). He says, "Fairness lies in everyone's getting a share of his own" (*Zhengmeng zhu*, 141). In other words, if everyone's desires can be gratified, then there is nothing wrong with desires themselves. If the gratification of one's desires means the sacrifice of others' desires, then those desires are not one's entitlement. That is why one needs to modify one's selfish desires so that the gratification of everyone's desires is fair. "When everyone gets his desires met, there is a prevalence of heavenly principle" (*Du sishu daquan shuo*, 248). On the other hand, principle is nothing but the moderation and fairness of desires; it does not have a separate ontological status. Wang Fuzhi compares principle without desires to a pond without water—both are simply empty. The relationship between the two can be best summarized as follows: "Without principle, desires become excessive; without desires, principle gets abolished" (*Zhouyi neizhuan*, 212).

Basically, Wang Fuzhi believes that there is innate goodness in human nature. Human nature is not separable from the material force that makes up human existence, and "there is nothing that is not good in material force" (*Du sishu daquan shuo*, 10:2). Evil is a failure to moderate desires and a failure to consider others. Since Wang also argues that human nature is developed and perfected day by day, he does not think that evil is external to human nature. Individuals are thus responsible for being good or bad; their nature does not determine the way they are.

Theory of Knowledge

Theory of knowledge in neo-Confucianism involves mostly the meaning and the order of "investigation of things" (*gewu*) and "extension of knowledge" (*zhizhi*), from *The Great Learning* (*Daxue*). Wang Fuzhi's theory of knowledge opposes Wang Yangming's theory. According to Wang Yangming, "things" (*wu*) means the objects toward which the activity of the mind is directed. Extension of knowledge begins with investigation of things, and "investigation of things" consists in rectifying of one's thoughts. Therefore, knowledge is not to be sought from outside one's mind. One's mind is originally endowed with innate knowledge of the good, and thus one needs to examine one's own mind to gain this intuitive knowledge. To Wang Yangming, "extension of knowledge" turns out to mean "extension of mind," and he argues that principle and mind are "made one" in this way. Wang Yangming's theory of knowledge is thus a form of subjectivism or mentalism.

Wang Fuzhi criticizes this theory as being too close to the Buddhists' "emptiness" and the Daoists' "inactivity." Wang Fuzhi's own theory of knowledge is based on his realism. Since reality is not a product of our mental activities, the principle of reality is external to, and independent of, our minds. To investigate the objective principle of different objects, we need to study these objects themselves. This study is the first step toward knowledge of the external world.

To Wang Fuzhi, knowledge can be obtained only through practice and experience. One cannot acquire experience without activity; hence, one's activity or action (*xing*) precedes knowledge (*zhi*). Thus he also rejects Wang Yangming's doctrine of the "unity of knowledge and action" (*zhixing heyi*). Wang Fuzhi argues that the doctrine of the unity of knowledge and action actually replaces action with knowledge; it assumes that action lies within knowledge. But to Wang Fuzhi, action is the only way through which one can accrue knowledge:

> Knowledge has to rely on action to be complete; action does not have to rely on knowledge to be complete. Through acting one can gain the effect of knowing, but just through knowing one does not gain the effect of acting. (*Shangshu yinyi*, 3:25)

Therefore, action is the foundation, and the completion, of knowledge. Knowledge and action must be separated.

Wang Fuzhi divides knowledge into two stages: knowledge of the sense organs, which refers to "studying" (or observing) objects; and knowledge of the mind, which refers to thinking. He believes that Zhu Xi overemphasizes the latter and undervalues the former. Wang stresses that if we do not study objects, our thinking becomes futile. Therefore, knowledge of the mind begins with knowledge of the sense organs. Through the accumulation of our studies we can acquire knowledge of the external world. The learning process is progressive and never-ending. Wang Fuzhi also rejects the theory of "sudden enlightenment" that Zhu Xi seems to endorse. To him, there is no leap of understanding. The universe is renewed daily, and our knowledge must also be renewed daily.

Philosophy of History

Wang's philosophy of history is another major contribution. Wang takes a progressive modernistic view of history. He thinks that the universe continuously renews itself; within it, human civilization continues to advance. In opposition to those who praise ancient civilization and view later human history as a decline, Wang argues that in primitive society where rites and culture were not established, men were no different from beasts. If we see how human efforts have transformed human society for the better, we will have no need to exaggerate the merits of the ancients or to disparage modern civilization. This is clearly a modernist's view.

But even though Wang argues that history keeps progressing, he also sees it as cyclical: after prosperous times, chaotic times will come, and vice versa. He calls this pattern "one prosperous era followed by one chaotic era" (*yi zhi yi luan*), considers it a manifestation of alternations between *yin* and *yang*, and describes it as the principle (*li*) of human history. In other words, he claims that the unfolding of human history reflects the movement of *yin* and *yang*. When *yang* is manifested in human history, it results in prosperity and order. When *yin* is manifested in human history, it results in decline and chaos. Material force is forever dynamic, and thus the two forms of material force are always in motion and mutating. When one rises, the other declines. Therefore, human affairs never stay still. The transition from order to chaos or from chaos to prosperity in human history is inevitable:

> One prosperity and one chaos, such is heaven, just as the sun brings us day and night, the moon has its waxing and waning. Human subjects cannot use their virtues to determine the fate of heaven. (*Du tongjian lun*, 1108)

However, human history is not predetermined by principle, since principle does not precede historical development. This view is consistent with Wang's cosmological interpretation of the relationship between principle and material force. Principle is nothing but the order of material force, and it is realized only after material force has developed in a certain way. Wang argues that before there were rituals or musical instruments, there was no proper way (*dao*) governing rites and music; before there were bows and arrows, there was no proper way (*dao*) of archery. Principle comes to be defined as a result of the actual development of the human world. Furthermore, the principle or the proper way for an earlier dynasty, however ideal that dynasty was, is not necessarily the principle or the proper way for a later dynasty. There is no perfect *li* or *dao* for all times. Material force is dynamic, as are human affairs and states of affairs. People living in a historical context must therefore recognize it, identifying the different situations they face and reacting accordingly.

The tension between this inevitable cyclical pattern of human history and its freedom from predetermination is resolved through Wang's notion of *tendency* (*shi*). When events develop in a certain way, states of affairs naturally follow. This is called "tendency." As Wang defines it, "A tendency (*shi*) is what naturally follows with no forced alteration. High ground yields to low land, largeness incorporates smallness; the tendency is what one cannot defy" (*Du sishu daquan shuo*, 601). For instance, extreme wealth and prosperity breed negligence and corruption in a government, which, if unheeded, will eventually bring about the destruction of the government. On the other hand, when society is at its worst, there will be an outcry from the people, leading to regeneration. These natural developments of worldly affairs are tendencies.

The notion of tendency can also be explained in terms of the development of material force. Human deeds and states of affairs contribute to the ongoing development of *yin* or *yang*. *Yin* is manifested in the human world as turbulence and degradation; *yang* is manifested as order and peace. When a government and a society at large do not check their performance, a tendency toward their downfall emerges. When rulers and the people possess virtues such as diligence and honesty, a tendency toward advancement emerges. At the same time, the movement of material force is governed by a continuing competition between *yin* and *yang*. When *yin* rises, *yang* falls; when *yang* rises, *yin* falls. Each form of material force will, then, find an opportunity to regain its strength. Wang Fuzhi says, "All tendencies of the world are such that if one follows a tendency, it will grow to its extreme; once it reaches the extreme, the opposite will come" (*Chunqiu shilun*, 4:12). Hence, as noted above, we find the pattern of "one prosperous era followed by one chaotic era" (*yizhi yiluan*) in human history, and this pattern represents the principle (*li*) of human history.

The notion of principle and the notion of tendency are closely related. Wang Fuzhi says, "Following what is inevitable in tendencies, this is principle; being what is natural according to principle, this is heaven" (*Song lun*, 7:1). "What is natural according to principle or tendency is simply what is right for that time" (*Liji zhangju*, 10:5). Even though history is not determined before the human world has developed into a certain state, there is a dominant tendency present in each particular state. Human efforts can affect this tendency most of the time; thus it is crucial that historical figures recognize the tendencies of their time. However, when a tendency is fully matured, there is no stopping it. In his commentaries on historical dynasties, Wang Fuzhi often describes a "tendency of inevitable destruction." This is probably how he viewed the fate of the Ming dynasty; he gave it his lifelong loyalty but eventually abandoned his futile effort to resurrect it.

Political Philosophy

The basic political ideology of traditional Confucianists is that of feudal propriety: the emperor should act like an emperor; the subjects should act like subjects. Each has a proper place, and usurpation is morally unacceptable. But the true spirit of Confucian political philosophy is not simply to uphold blind loyalty to the ruler. The demand for loyalty from the subjects is matched by a demand for humanity from the ruler. Under the basic framework of feudal loyalty, there are different ways a Confucianist can justify people's right to revolution. Mencius, for example, denies the ruler's absolute legitimacy. Mencius argues that a ruler who is disrespectful of humanity and righteousness is not a legitimate ruler but should be regarded as a bandit. Murdering a ruler may be unacceptable; murdering a bandit is totally justified. In other words, if the emperor is not humane, the people have the right to revolt.

Wang Fuzhi's political thinking seems to be greatly influenced by Mencius. The emperors of China were called "sons of heaven" (*tianzi*), but Wang Fuzhi says, "What people's hearts share in common, principle is here, and heaven is here" (*Zhengmeng zhu*, 47). That is, the emperor is the son of what people desire in common. This remark seems to echo Mencius, who says that to win the empire is to win the people, and to win the people is to win their hearts. To win the people's hearts, Mencius further suggests, is nothing but to amass for them what they desire and to avoid doing what they resent (*Mencius*, 4A.9). Similarly, Wang thinks that what determines political success or failure is ultimately people's affection or resentment: "To appease a dangerous situation, the main thing to do is to win the people's hearts" (*Du tongjian lun*, 393). Wang Fuzhi also derives his view on the relationship between heaven and the people from the classic *Book of History* (*Shangshu*), which says, "Heaven sees and hears what the people see and hear; heaven manifests its power through the people's manifested power." Wang states that people's desire is where the will of heaven lies. What he calls the "tendency of inevitable destruction" is formed by an accumulation of a despot's cruelty, stinginess, injustice, and intemperance. Thus, in Wang's view, the emperor does not have a heavenly mandate to rule. If he does not do his job properly, eventually—inevitably—his rulership will be destroyed. This outcome, to Wang Fuzhi, reveals the natural development of principle (*li*).

We may say that Wang Fuzhi's political view is government for the people. He does not advocate government of the people or by the people, however. From historical observation, he concludes that one should use caution in following the people's hearts. The masses can be fickle and short-sighted. They can turn their back on those they loved a moment ago, or they can worship someone they once despised. Therefore, Wang Fuzhi does not think that the ruler should simply comply with whatever the people desire. What people's hearts share in common is not simply what the masses want as a fad or a vogue; it is rather what universal human nature would desire. Wang thinks that what humans desire in common begins with food and sex and expands to power and wealth. What the ruler should do is to put himself in his people's shoes and exercise empathy. Wang says, "The way of an enlightened ruler (*wang dao*) is based on human sentiment" (*Sishu xunyi*, 5243). Therefore, in the political ideal that Wang advocates, the ruler understands his people's desires and promotes the satisfaction of those desires. This is a political ideology that sets economic and social well-being as primary goals.

It would be a stretch to say that Wang Fuzhi's political view is comparable to the modern notion of democracy. It is not even clear that he would deem revolution justifiable. Ultimately Wang Fuzhi is a supporter of traditional monarchy. He says, "There can only be one king, just as there cannot be two fathers" (*Du tongjian lun*, 680). He thinks that an intellectual should select his sovereign in entering politics. If the sovereign is not suitable, then the proper thing for the intellectual to do is simply to quit politics. Wang himself has certainly lived up to his own standard. This attitude is not pessimistic, since Wang also believes in the existence of principle (*li*) in the human world. If the ruler defies the heavenly principle—which is nothing but what the people desire in common—then he has put himself into the "tendency" of inevitable destruction. We may conclude that Wang's support for traditional monarchy is certainly not support for despotism or tyranny. Wang Fuzhi thinks that if traditional monarchy could be continued in China for thousands of years, then it had withstood the test of "what the people's hearts have in common." At least in Wang's mind, his time is not yet the time for the abolishment of monarchy. As he remarks:

> What can be practiced for a thousand years without change represents what people want; it also represents heaven. . . . What are stealthily passed along as popular customs represent what people want, but they do not represent heaven. (*Du tongjian lun*, 626)

He thus defends monarchy on the basis of its endurance in Chinese history.

The Significance of Wang's Philosophy

Wang Fuzhi's philosophy can be seen as the real summation of neo-Confucianism of the Song-Ming era. Wang refused to participate in the endless debate between the Cheng-Zhu school and the Lu-Wang school on the issue of principle and mind. Instead, he redirected attention toward material force and concrete existence. He opened the door to the pragmatism prominent in the Qing dynasty. Yan Yuan (1635–1704) and Dai Zhen (1723–1777) continued this direction and gave both the school of principle and the school of mind a further critique. Later, in the nineteenth century and the twentieth century, philosophers such as Tan Sitong (1865–1898) and Tang Junyi were also greatly influenced by Wang.

See also Dai Zhen; Philosophy of History; Wang Yangming; Yan Yuan; Zhang Zai; Zhu Xi.

Bibliography

Chan, Wing-tsit. *A Source Book in Chinese Philosophy*, 4th ed. Princeton, N.J.: Princeton University Press, 1973.

Chang, Xitang. *The Chronological Study of Wang Chuanshan (Fuzhi)*. Taipei: Taiwan Shangwu, 1978. (In Chinese.)

Cua, A. S. *The Unity of Knowledge and Action: A Study in Wang Yang-ming's Moral Psychology*. Honolulu: University of Hawaii Press, 1982.

Fung, Yu-lan (Feng Youlan). *A History of Chinese Philosophy*, Vol. 2, trans. Derk Bodde. Princeton, N.J.: Princeton University Press, 1983.

Lao, Szekwang. *A History of Chinese Philosophy*. Hong Kong: Union, 1980. (In Chinese.)

Liu, Jee Loo. *A Treatise on the Problem of "Heavenly Principle As Manifested in Human History" in Wang Fuzhi's Philosophy*. Taipei: National Taiwan University, 1984. (In Chinese.)

Liu, Zhunjian. *The Chronology of Wang Fuzhi's Scholarship*. Henan: Zhungzhou guji, 1989. (In Chinese.)

Meng, Beiyuan. *The Development of the School of Li: From Zhu Xi to Wang Fuzhi and Dai Zhen*. Taipei: Wenjing, 1990. (In Chinese.)

Teng, S. Y. "Wang Fuzhi's Views on History and Historical Writing." *Journal of Asian Studies*, 28, 1979, pp. 111–123.

Wang, Fuzhi. *Commentary on Zhang Zai's Zhengmeng (Zhangzi Zhengmeng zhu)*. Post-1677.

———. *The Complete Collection of the Posthumous Works of Chuanshan* (*Chuanshan yishu quanji*, Vols. 1–22. Taipei: Chinese Chuanshan Association and Liberty Press, 1972.
———. *A Contemporary Interpretation of the Meaning of the Four Books* (*Sishu xunyi*), 1679.
———. *Discourse on Reading the Great Collection of Commentaries on the Four Books* (*Du sishu daquan shuo*), 1665.
———. *Extended Interpretation on Lao Zi* (*Laozi yan*), 1655.
———. *The Extended Meaning of the Book of History* (*Shangshu yinyi*), 1663.
———. *External Commentary on the Book of Changes* (*Zhouyi waizhuan*), 1655.
———. *A General Treatise on Chun Qiu* (*Chunqiu shilun*), 1668.
———. *Internal Commentary on the Book of Changes* (*Zhouyi neizhuan*), 1685.
———. *Interpretation on the Images of the Book of Changes* (*Zhouyi daxiang jie*), 1676.
———. *Interpretation on Zhuang Zi* (*Zhuangzi jie*), 1681.
———. *Record of Thoughts and Questions* (*Siwen lu*). After 1677.
———. *A Textual Annotation on the Book of Rites* (*Liji zhangju*), 1673–1677.
———. *A Treatise on Reading Tongjian* (*Du Tongjian lun*), 1687–1691.
———. *A Treatise on the Song Dynasty* (*Song lun*). 1691.
Xiao, Tianshi. *The Collected Study on Chuanshan's Thought*. Taipei: Chinese Chuanshan Association and Liberty Press, 1972. (In Chinese.)
Xu, Guanshan. *Wang Chuanshan's Theory of Knowledge*. Hong Kong: Chinese University Press, 1981. (In Chinese.)

Wang Guowei (Wang Kuo-wei)

Min-chih Chou

Wang Guowei (1877–1927), also known by the names Jing'an and Guantang, was a pioneer student of western philosophy and one of the seminal minds of twentieth-century China. His philosophical and scholarly writings are collected in twenty-five volumes, as *Wang Guowei xiansheng quanji*. Most of the correspondence to and from Wang is now available as *Wang Guowei quanji: Shuxin* and *Luo Zhenyu Wang Guowei wanglai shuxin*. Wang's early essays on philosophy are gathered in *Wang guowei zhexue meixue lunwen jiyi*. While there are many interpretive works on Wang's classical scholarship and literary criticism, there are relatively few on his philosophical ideas.

As a child and youth in Haining, Zhejiang, Wang received a solid classical education. In 1898, he left for Shanghai to begin his modern schooling. What interested him most was western philosophy, and because of his excellent English and Japanese, he was able to read widely in it. While his readings covered many important thinkers, he was particularly attracted to Arthur Schopenhauer (1788–1860), Friedrich Nietzsche (1844–1900), and Immanuel Kant (1724–1804). Wang made four attempts in four years to try to understand Kant's first critique. Between 1900 and 1907, Wang wrote a number of essays about some of the key issues in philosophy.

In 1907, realizing that he was not capable of becoming a philosopher, but unwilling to settle for being a historian of philosophy, Wang gave up philosophy. From 1908 to 1911, he devoted himself to writing poetry and literary criticism and studying traditional Chinese plays. When the republican revolution broke out in 1911, he fled to Japan as a loyal subject of the fallen Qing dynasty. Thereafter, he immersed himself in Chinese historical scholarship, establishing himself as one of the leading historians of his time. Intellectually, he became conservative. In 1924, the dethroned emperor appointed him an attendant in the imperial study. In June 1927, fearing that the approaching revolutionary army would humiliate him and the emperor, Wang drowned himself in the imperial lake in Beijing. After his death, the emperor bestowed on him the honorific title *zhongquegong* ("duke of loyalty and sincerity").

Wang's importance lies in his ability to treat philosophical issues at an abstract level without any concern for their pragmatic or contemporary significance. This quality of being interested in abstract ideas for their own sake is rarely found among Chinese thinkers, the majority of whom were steeped in pragmatic Confucian thought. The ability to conceptualize enables Wang to penetrate the superficial aspect of issues and discuss them in a refreshing manner. Drawing inspirations from Schopenhauer, Kant, and many other western thinkers, Wang analyzes human nature, reason, and freedom from perspectives different from those of all his Chinese predecessors.

The Status of Philosophy

Philosophy occupies a place of central importance in Wang's thought. In 1906, he proposed that it be given the status of an independent subject in the curriculum of Chinese higher education. For Wang, philosophy was the foundation of intellectual inquiry in the humanities and social sciences, a curriculum of philosophy should include all schools of thought, not just Confucianism. In particular, Wang had western philosophy in mind. He argued that knowledge of western philosophy was indispensable for a critical study of Chinese thought, because it would add a new dimension to the monolithic Chinese outlook and serve as a point of reference. He was convinced that in the future only those who were well-versed in both Chinese and western scholarship would be able to advance the understanding of China's past. This was an extraordinary insight, which few were able to appreciate at the time. It remained for Wang himself to break new ground in applying his knowledge of western philosophy to the interpretation of Chinese thought.

Human Nature

In 1904, departing from traditional Chinese interpretations, Wang wrote that innate human nature is unknowable. According to him, if we can establish apparently contradictory propositions based on the same set of assumptions, then we are dealing with an unknowable entity. The debate on human nature in ancient China was an example. Wang pointed out that there are two kinds of judgment: a priori and a posteriori. The former, independent of all experience, is universal and necessary. The latter, empirical and dependent on sensory impressions, only provides the basis for certain claims to knowledge—not for claims to absolute necessity or universal validity. An a priori judgment, being abstract, deals only with the form, not the material content, of knowledge. From these premises, Wang argued that when we analyze human nature, we have access only to its material content as an object of knowledge. Therefore, we really do not know innate human nature; we know only the human nature that has been shaped by heredity and the environment.

Wang's key ideas come from Kant and Schopenhauer. Wang's statement on contradictory proposals reminds us of Kant's discussion of antinomies in *The Critique of Pure Reason*. The antinomy is an unresolved conflict between assertions. Although none of the four opposing propositions that Kant discusses is specifically applicable to Wang's case, Wang nevertheless uses Kantian logic to support his argument. And his understanding of the a priori is based on Kant and Schopenhauer's analyses of the *noumenon*. Unlike the phenomenon, the *noumenon*, according to Kant and Schopenhauer, is an object we reach only by intellectual intuition, not through sense experience. As such, the *noumenon* is the "thing in itself" that Kant and Schopenhauer regard as unknowable except in its abstract form.

That Wang chooses human nature as a topic for detailed discussion underscores his recognition of its central place in Chinese philosophy. Wing-tsit Chan writes that the issue of human nature is "the most important one in Chinese metaphysics . . . and has engaged the attention of practically every Chinese philosopher worthy of the name." In his writing, Wang challenges all the traditional views. He identifies three positions in the Chinese interpretations of human nature.

First, according to Wang, Confucius (551–479 B.C.E.) and Gaozi, a contemporary of Mencius (c. 372–298 B.C.E.), take the stand that human nature is neither good nor bad but neutral. Confucius believes that human beings have many common characteristics at birth; it is culture and environment that make people different. Gaozi maintains that human nature, because it is neutral, is malleable by outside forces. Wang describes the opinions of Confucius and Gaozi as "transcendental monistic," because they transcend the dualism of good and evil. Their interpretations are plausible, he says, because they are based on empirical observation. However, no theses of human nature based on empirical observation, including these, advance our knowledge. Such theories merely remind us of the power of the environment in shaping our personalities; they do not offer additional insights for our understanding of innate human nature.

The second position, according to Wang, is the monism represented by Xunzi (fl. third century B.C.E.), who maintains that human nature is bad. For Wang, Xunzi's theory is highly implausible. Xunzi, deeply concerned about stability and order, argues that sages, mindful of the undesirable elements in humans, establish political institutions, enact laws, and set up rules to regulate conduct and moderate human desires. However, sages are human beings too. Therefore Wang offers a challenge: if human nature is bad, how does Xunzi account for the goodness and wisdom of the sages? Furthermore, Wang points out that Xunzi was apparently unable to account for the fact that some human beings do have compassion for those who suffer and that children do love their parents; Xunzi therefore had to compromise his theory by acknowledging that there are indeed good qualities in human nature. For Wang, these difficulties indicate fundamental inconsistencies in Xunzi's theory.

Mencius is the chief exponent of the third position. Wang observes that Mencius takes a dualistic view: Mencius distinguishes between innate human nature, which he believes is good, and human beings' worldly desires, many of which he thinks are bad. But this dichotomy, Wang maintains, is the source of a problem. If our nature is good, then where do our bad desires come from? If heaven (*tian*) endows us with all the good qualities, as Mencius argues, why are our senses—the ears and eyes, which can be the source of bad desires—not similarly endowed?

Apart from his critique of ancient Chinese theories of human nature, Wang also expresses dissatisfaction with some theses of his German mentors. Wang observes that while Kant believed that we apprehend the formal principle of morality as a categorical imperative, he also spoke of morally evil elements in our nature. According to Schopenhauer, all life is suffering because of our will and desires; will as willing is inexhaustible, and desires are endless. If that is the case, Wang asks, how do we explain the origin of our power to reject our will to live?

It is important to point out a crucial difference between Wang and other interpreters of human nature in Chinese history. Unlike his predecessors, Wang is not concerned with the moral, didactic, or pragmatic implications of the issue. He enjoys philosophizing, and his interest in the question of human nature comes from a burning desire to understand, kindled to a large extent by his knowledge of western philosophy.

Li as Reason

Wang observes that human nature and *li* are the two most important and most contested concepts in Chinese philosophy. According to Wing-tsit Chan, "The concept [of] *li* as principle has been the most important in Chinese thought in the last 800 years. The entire movement is called *Lixue* in Chinese, that is, the Philosophy of Principle, generally termed Neo-Confucianism in English." Wang takes exception to the neo-Confucian position, insisting that *li* should not be interpreted as principle or rendered in any other manner that would have a similar connotation. In a long essay written in 1904, Wang proposes to view *li* as "reason," not as "principle" (cf. Cua 1997).

Following Schopenhauer, Wang regards *li* as "ground" or "reason" (*Grund*) and as man's reasoning faculty (*Vernunft*). Wang concurs with Schopenhauer that the first meaning of *li* (*Grund*) pertains to the "principle of sufficient reason." This principle "is not . . . a *veritas aeterna*; in other words, it does not possess an unconditioned validity before, outside, and above the world, . . . but only a relative and conditioned one, valid only in the phenomena." In other words, it is "subjective" and not "objective." Wang appreciates Schopenhauer's distinction between the logical ground (reason) of knowledge and its general reason (cause). The principle of sufficient reason belongs to logic and is a fundamental principle of all knowledge. Schopenhauer formulates this principle as the claim that "nothing is without a ground or reason why it is" and considers it a general formulation of the principle of explanation. But the metaphysical notion of a "first cause" or the theological notion of a "god," according to him, is untenable because it is a "cause of itself."

Like the first, the second meaning of *li*, i.e., man's reasoning faculty, Wang says, is also subjective, not a priori or transcendental. Reason as *Vernunft*, Schopenhauer writes, "has absolutely no material, but only a formal, content which is the substance of logic." Thus, reason is not "a faculty of direct metaphysical knowledge or, to speak more plainly, of inspirations from above." If it were, Schopenhauer continues, then there would necessarily be among us just as much agreement on the subjects of metaphysics, religion, and morality as there is on the subject of mathematics. Wang is in complete agreement with Schopenhauer.

Wang's exposition of *li* is an unequivocal rejection of the interpretations of other Chinese thinkers, particularly the Song and Ming neo-Confucians. Wang observes that *li* began to acquire a metaphysical meaning in the Song period (960–1368). Many philosophers of the Song and later periods assume not only that there is a transcendental principle in the universe but also that we have an absolute ability to understand it. Zhu Xi (1130–1200) is a chief exponent of this doctrine. Zhu believes that the "supreme ultimate" (*taiji*) is none other than *li* (principle). According to Zhu, *li* manifests itself and exists in material forces. It has no physical form, because it is a priori and transcendental (*xing'ershang*); it precedes everything else in existence and is the source of whatever has physical form (*xing'erxia*). Wang Yangming (1472–1529) of the Ming period (1368–1644) is one of a few dissenters from this thinking: he considers *li* "subjective," insisting that our mind-heart is *li* (*xinjili*). Wang Guowei tells us that the moral significance of *li* is implicit in classical works such as *Li ji*, compiled during the formative age of Chinese thought. However, to repeat, it is in the Song period that *li* begins to acquire its metaphysical—and moral—meaning. For example, Xie Liangzuo (1050–1103), Cheng Yi (1033–1108), and Zhu Xi regard *li* and *yu* (desires) as opposites. They insist that *li* contains the ultimate moral principle which enables us to rein in our worldly desires.

Wang rejects this view and all the metaphysical and moral interpretations of other Song-Ming philosophers. He maintains that we should see *li* as denoting the principle of sufficient reason and as our reasoning faculty. The former indicates the universal form of our intellect; the latter manifests our ability to engage in logical thinking. Both these interpretations make *li* a subjective quality, not something a priori. Therefore, *li* may but does not necessarily lead us to a more moral life.

Wang's study of *li* is the first of its kind among Chinese scholars, preceding Tang Junyi's by half a century and Wing-tsit Chan's by sixty years. Unlike these eminent Chinese scholars, Wang does not offer us a comprehensive treatment of the evolution of the concept of *li* in Chinese philosophy. He is more concerned with deconstructing traditional Chinese modes of thought and with the philosophical transformation of Chinese thought. In his criticism of the neo-Confucian interpretations of *li*, he supposes that *li* is an abstract concept with no moral or social meaning. In contrast, cultural radicals of the May Fourth period of the 1910s and 1920s, examining *li* with China's modernization in mind, attacked the neo-Confucian thinkers as having been responsible for creating a set of oppressive rules, which these radicals believe impeded the development of a critical spirit among the Chinese. Deeply preoccupied with practical matters, the May Fourth radicals either were unaware of Wang's discourse on the subject or, failing to see its relevance, ignored it completely.

Freedom

Wang points out that freedom is one of the most important issues in western philosophy. However, it does not occupy nearly as an important place in Chinese thought. Wang observes that Chinese thinkers take autonomy and moral responsibility for granted; thus few of them feel a need to discuss the issue of freedom.

One focal point in the debate on freedom in western philosophy is whether there are uncaused causes. Wang notes that Kant's third antinomy concerns the existence of freedom. The thesis of this antinomy assumes causality through freedom, whereas its antithesis says that there is no freedom and that everything in the world takes place entirely in accordance with laws of nature. For Kant freedom is a postulate of pure practical reason. As "sensible" beings, we are part of the natural causal order; however, we can think of ourselves as "intelligible" beings, independent of the causal chain. In fact, he advocates, we must think that we are morally free, because we not only impose a moral law on ourselves but also can choose to obey or violate it. As phenomenon we are part of the causal order, but as *noumenon* we are free. Wang has difficulty with Kant's argument; he finds Schopenhauer's position more to his liking. Schopenhauer believes that we are part of the causal order and that we can never alter our nature; but with improved knowledge of ourselves, we may develop a feeling of "repentance" toward our past that helps us to some extent alter the direction of our future behavior. This opinion of Schopenhauer's convinces Wang that we do have a sense of moral responsibility, which does not require a theory of freedom for validation.

Freedom versus determinism is one of the most difficult issues in western philosophy. Wang has a good grasp of the issue and appreciates the enormous challenge it presents. In the end he, too, affirms our moral autonomy. While he does not make an original contribution to the discussion of free will, he nevertheless gains enormous insight and becomes more sensitive about the many facets of the issue than any of his Chinese predecessors.

Aesthetics and Literary Criticism

According to Wang, art and literature grow out of our impulse to playfulness, and originally have no utilitarian purposes. The most important element in aesthetic appreciation is a state of "disinterestedness." Here, by embracing the theories of Friedrich Schiller and Kant, Wang decidedly departs from the dominant Chinese thinking. James J. Y. Liu points out that the traditional Chinese concept of literature is predominantly pragmatic and didactic, perceiving literature as "a means to achieve political, social, moral, or educational purposes." This utilitarian view of literature, "sanctioned by Confucianism," becomes sacrosanct in Chinese thinking. Wang displays none of this pragmatic mentality. He maintains that we do not acquire our notions of beauty entirely from empirical observation, because part of our understanding of beauty is a priori. Imagination and creativity are important ingredients in art and literature.

Knowledge of western aesthetics enables Wang to appreciate the values of drama and fiction, two literary genres treated with some disdain in traditional Chinese culture. He is delighted that Schopenhauer esteems narrative literature highly. Drama of the Yuan period (1264–1368), Wang tells us, is incomparable literature, because of the beauty and simplicity of its language and the unpretentiousness in its expression. Yuan playwrights write only for pleasure; the absence of utilitarian purposes, Wang maintains, explains the exceptional quality of their art. He considers the novel *Dream of the Red Chamber* (*Honglou meng*) a great work. It belongs to the highest type of literary tragedy in Schopenhauer's scheme—the kind of tragedy that "shows us the greatest misfortune not as an exception, not as something brought about by rare circumstances or by monstrous characters, but as something that arises easily and spontaneously out of the actions and characters of men." The *Dream of the Red Chamber* evokes a sense of the sublime, Wang says. Kant and Schopenhauer tell us that we sense sublimity when faced with an overwhelmingly large and hostile force, a force that awes but does not frighten us; and this is the effect of a fine tragic work. Therefore, while we are incapable of resisting the stupendous force of a tragedy, we are in the end cleansed and remain in aesthetic contemplation. Here, Wang's understanding of catharsis comes not only from Kant and Schopenhauer but also from Aristotle's *Poetics*. What Wang means is that we in the audience achieve catharsis as a result of the sense of the sublime we derive from watching a tragedy.

Wang's achievement here is by no means slight. Of the numerous commentaries on *Dream of the Red Chamber* up to his time, not a single one had dealt with its literary quality. The novel was written in the middle of the eighteenth century. Wang's study, in 1904, was the first literary and philosophical analysis of the work and established it as an enduring masterpiece in Chinese literary criticism. C. T. Hsia notes that Wang's essay "is still consulted by scholars today for . . . [its] critical insights."

Finally, Wang's knowledge of the aesthetics of music sets him apart from his contemporaries. Regarding music, Wang concurs with Schopenhauer that it is a universal language of the highest degree, expressing the quintessence of life. The universality of music is never an empty abstraction; it is associated with thorough, unequivocal distinctness. However, music is not related to any particular feelings or to any concrete things or events. Therefore, instrumental music—music without words—is the most objective kind. Wang puts great emphasis on music education in the school curriculum, not because music should be a tool for moral instruction but because of its powerful effect on our innermost nature.

Conclusion

Wang Guowei was not only an erudite scholar of Chinese culture but also one of a handful of his generation with a good command of English and an appreciation of the western ideas. His ability to traverse the two worlds at ease proved to be most beneficial. His formidable knowledge of Chinese philosophy helped him understand and appreciate similar concerns in western philosophy. His knowledge of western philosophy in turn gave him an analytical tool that was lacking in the Chinese intellectual tradition; this knowledge also inspired him to revisit some of the key issues in Chinese philosophy from a different, new perspective.

The results are always refreshing and suggestive. Many of Wang's opinions were breakthroughs—radical departures from the long-standing Chinese views. They are, however, not "paradigms" in Thomas S. Kuhn's definition of the concept. Discoveries are paradigms when they are accepted by practitioners in the field as shared examples "for further articulation and specification under new or more stringent conditions." Wang's discoveries, however, had a different fate in China. Few of his contemporaries were aware of his work and still fewer were capable of appreciating it. In his own time, no one else pursued these philosophical issues either in agreement with his opinions or in opposition to them. Yü Ying-shih observed, from the vantage point of 1974, that Wang's study of *Dream of the Red Chamber* was a lone voice without followers. In 1923, when Hu Shi (1891–1962) offered a comprehensive assessment of the development of Chinese literature of the past half century, he did not even mention Wang's name. Wang's ideas simply did not have much influence in his own time, and none of his works in philosophy and aesthetics was taken as a paradigm. To point out how much he was neglected, however, is to pay Wang the ultimate compliment of recognizing his uniqueness in the world of Chinese thought.

See also Aesthetics; Philosophy of Human Nature; Reason and Principle.

Bibliography

Bonner, Joey. *Wang Kuo-wei: An Intellectual Biography*. Cambridge, Mass.: Harvard University Press, 1986.

Chan, Wing-tsit. "The Evolution of the Neo-Confucian Concept *Li* as Principle." *Tsing Hua Journal of Chinese Studies*, 1964, pp. 123–148.

Chen, Hungxiang. *Wang Guowei nianpu*. Ji'nan: Qilu shushe, 1991.

———. *Wang Guowei yu wenxue*. Xi'an, Shaanxi: Shaanxi renmin chubanshe, 1988.

Chou, Min-chih. "Hu Shi yu Wang Guowei de xueshu sixiang jiaoyi." In *Hu Shi yu tade pengyou*, 2 vols. New York: Outer Sky, 1990–1991, Vol. 2, pp. 1–57.

———. "Wang Guowei de jiaoyu sixiang." *Zhongyang Yanjiuyuan Jindaishi Yanjiuso Jikan*, No. 19, June 1990, pp. 109–134.

———. "You kaiming er baoshou: Xinhai zhengju dui Wang Guowei sixiang he xinli de chongji." *Hanxue Yanjiu*, 11(1), June 1993, pp. 103–134.

———. "Zhongguo jindai wenxueshi de tupo: Wang Guowei de wenxueguan." *Hanxue Yanjiu*, 13(1), June 1995, pp. 239–279.

Cua, A. S. "Reason and Principle in Chinese Philosophy." In *A Companion to World Philosophies*, ed. Eliot Deutsch and Ron Bontekoe. Oxford: Blackwell, 1997.
Fo, Chu. *Wang Guowei shixue yanjiu*. Beijing: Beijing daxue chubanshe, 1987.
Tang, Junyi. "Lun Zhongguo zhexue zhong *Li* zhi liuyi." *Xinya xuebao*, No. 1, August 1955, pp. 45–98.
Wang, Guowei. *Luo Zhenyu Wang Guowei wanglai shuxin*, annot. Wang Qingxiang and Xiao Liwen. Beijing: Dongfang chubanshe, 2000. (Examined with further annotations by Luo Jizu.)
———. *Wang Guowei mei lunwen xuan*, ed. Liu Gangqiang. Changsha, Hunan: Hunan renmin, 1987.
———. *Wang Guowei wenxue meixue lunwenji*, ed. Zhou Yangshan. Taiyuan, Shansi: Beiyue wenyi, 1987.
———. *Wang Guowei quanji: Shuxin*, ed. Wu Ze. Beijng: Zhonghua shuju, 1984.
———. *Wang Guowei xiansheng quanji*, 25 vols. Taipei: Datong shuju, 1976.
———. *Wang Guowei zhexue meixue lunwen jiyi*, comp. and ed. Fo Chu. Shanghai: Huadong shihfan daxue chubanshe, 1993.
Wu, Ze, ed. *Wang Guowei xueshu yanjiu lunji*, 3 vols. Shanghai: Huadong shifan daxue chubanshe, 1983, 1987, 1990.
Yeh, Chia-ying. *Wang Guowei ji qi wenxue piping*. Jiulong: Zhonghua Shuju, 1980.

Wang Yangming (Wang Yang-ming)

A. S. CUA

Any attempt to present the thought of Wang Yangming (1472–1529) is beset by a major problem, for the dynamic character of his works appears to resist systematic formulation. It behooves the student to pay heed to Wing-tsit Chan's reminder: "The philosophy of Wang Yangming is a vigorous philosophy born of serious searching and bitter experience. It is no idle speculation or abstract theory developed for the sake of intellectual curiosity" (*Instructions*, xix). In his letters and conversations recorded by his disciples, we find a recurrent emphasis on personal realization as a key to understanding his teachings. Indeed, it is plausible to maintain that his central teachings, such as the unity of knowledge and action and the vision of the sage as "forming one body with heaven, earth, and the myriad things," are intended not as theoretical doctrines but as compendious statements of the culmination of his quest for understanding the spirit of Confucian learning and tradition. Wang's doctrine of the unity of knowledge and action, for example, may be regarded as a forceful and concise way of stating the unity of his life and teaching during his formative years. Appreciating this unity suggests, as Tu Weiming points out, that "unlike the unity of speculative construct or epistemological system, the integrity of Yangming's teaching is based on his life experiences rather than an objectifiable structure of propositions" (Tu 1976, 3).

Wang's quest for the spirit of Confucian learning may be characterized as a quest for the spirit and meaning of Confucian sagehood, the ideal embodiment of the unity and harmony of man and nature. We may see this quest as the search for an answer to the question, "How can one become a Confucian sage?"—parallel to Kierkegaard's "How can one become a Christian?" (1959). Obviously such a question is intelligible only in the light of a firm commitment to the actuating or transformative significance of the notion of sagehood. According to the *Chronological Biography* (*Nianpu*), at age seventeen Wang had a strong desire to "study to become a sage." Possibly his desire was foreshadowed at an earlier age. As a precocious boy of ten, Wang asked his tutor, "What is the most important task in life?" The tutor responded, "It is to pass the civil examinations." Wang commented in a doubtful tone, "I am afraid that passing the civil examinations cannot be considered as the most important task in life. Perhaps, it is to study to become a sage or a worthy." Wang's vision of sagehood seems to have acquired a definite shape when he was thirty-three and first met Zhan Ruoshui, who was to become his best friend. The biography informs us that both resolved "to promote and clarify the teachings of the sages." In Zhan Ruoshui's eulogy for Wang, we are told that they had "agreed to adhere to Cheng Hao's teaching: 'the man of humanity (*jen*) forms one body with all things without differentiation' " (Tu 1976, 93). In his *Inquiry on the Great Learning*, written a little over a year before his death, we find a comprehensive statement of this Confucian vision. It is reasonable to presume that his youthful commitment to the realization of sagehood was more a commitment to clarifying the concrete significance of the vision, a sort of an ideal theme to be developed in thought and action, rather than an ideal norm with preceptive import. The ideal theme is more a perspective or focal point than a fixed principle of conduct (Cua 1978, ch. 8; 1982, 32–35, passim.)

At any rate, in Wang's teaching the importance of commitment in learning to become a sage is often stressed. In one of the instructions to his disciples at Longchang, Wang says:

> If the will is not [firmly] established (*lizhi*), nothing in the world can be accomplished. Though there may be hundreds of professions, there is not a single one that does not depend on such a determination.

He goes on to point out that "if one establishes one's will to become a sage, one can become a sage; if one establishes one's will to become a worthy, one can become a worthy." A lack of willful commitment or decision is compared to a ship without a rudder or a horse without a bit (*Yangming quanshu*, ch. 26, 5B). Elsewhere, Wang remarks: "The way of learning is a task of creating something out of nothing. . . . All depends on making up one's mind (*lizhi*). If the student makes up his mind to have one thought to do good, his mind will be like the seed of a tree." With tender care, cultivation, and nourishment, the vitality of the tree "will be increasingly great and its branches and leaves more luxuriant" (*Instructions*, Sec. 115). This commitment or decision is to be made with one's *xin* (mind and heart) or, in Kierkegaard's language, with the whole inwardness of one's personality (171). It is a decision that furnishes a basis and a point of departure (*tounao*) for learning to become a sage (*Instructions*, Secs. 31, 102, 168).

The principal aim of this essay is to offer a critical introduction to some basic ideas of Wang's philosophy. After dealing with the problem of methodology, I discuss the vision of *ren* (the Confucian ideal of humanity) as an object of ethical commitment and then the nature of self-confidence expressed in Wang's doctrine of mind. I turn next to Wang's famous doctrines of the unity of knowledge and action (*zhixing heyi*) and *liangzhi* as a mediation between the ideal of *ren* and the actual world. I conclude with a brief discussion of problems that arise out of the general characterization of *liangzhi*. This order of exposition is adopted mainly for convenience of exposition, for in Wang's mature philosophy all these topics are interdependent, and they deserve a more comprehensive study.

The Problem of Explication

Before proceeding to Wang's vision, let me make clear my approach by remarking on the problem of explication. Aside from Wang's recurrent stress on personal realization as the key to understanding his teachings, from the point of view of communication, there is a fundamental problem of interpretation. Wang's own explanations of his basic tenets use standard terms derived from Song Confucianism and the classics. These terms are often used in a novel way without explicit warning. It is quite possible that the terms function as "satellite" notions that revolve around the central theme of *ren* or *dao*. Terms such as *tianli* (heavenly reason) and *xin zhi benti* (mind in itself) serve as satellites or complements for elucidating the central theme of *ren* as the ultimate concern of human endeavors. From the perspective of practical understanding, these terms have no explanatory value in theoretical discourse. In other words, the terms are best construed as indicative of practical understanding. They give alternative emphases to the actuating or transformative significance of the vision of *ren*.

Apart from the difficulty of translating and interpreting major terms such as *tianli* or *liangzhi*, Wang also tends to collapse the significance of various distinctions such as *wu* (things) and *shi* (affairs or events), *xin* (mind) and *li* (reason). I have chosen not to translate some of these terms, not because available translations are completely inadequate, but because such translations, like those given in the preceding paragraph, may have connotations that mislead the readers into thinking that there exist exact English equivalents with the same philosophical import. Moreover, they appear to be somewhat contrary to my own understanding of Wang's intentions in using these terms. My uncertainty about the value of some translations possibly reflects a personal failure. In retaining the transcriptions, I believe that a coherent interpretation is possible and quite consistent with Wang's own stress on personal realization (*tiren*), though there is a special difficulty in reconciling such an attempt with Wang's claim that there is something which cannot be verbally transmitted.

Consider the following conversation recorded by Lu Zheng:

> *Passage A*
> I said, "Scholars of later generations have written a great deal. I am afraid some of it has confounded correct learning."
> The Teacher said, "The human mind and *tianli* are completely undifferentiated (*hunran*)." Sages and worthies wrote about them very much like a portrait painter painting the true likeness and transmitting the spirit. He shows only an outline of the appearance to serve as a basis for people to seek and find the true personality. Among one's spirit, feelings, expressions, and behavior, there is that which

> cannot be transmitted. Later writers have imitated and copied what the sages have drawn. (*Instructions*, Sec. 20)

Or more directly, responding to a student's report of his realization of the meaning or significance of the doctrine of the extension of knowledge, Wang said:

> *Passage B*
> From this we can know that knowledge acquired through personal realization is different from that acquired through listening to discussions. When I first lectured on the subject, I knew you took it lightly and were not interested. However, when one goes further and realizes this essential and wonderful thing personally to its very depth, he will see that it becomes different everyday and [its significance] is inexhaustible. (*Instructions*, Sec. 211)

If one takes the point of untransmittability seriously, Wang's utterances can only be construed as pointers toward appreciating the heart of his teachings. But at the same time, these pointers are often given in standard terminology that requires interpretation. Given the important role of self-realization, inevitably these pointers can be elucidated only in the light of personal understanding. Thus, while retaining the transcriptions, such as *liangzhi* and *tianli*, I often present what may be called focal indicators for their meanings; largely to facilitate my exposition, but also to indicate ways of interpretation without ascribing to Wang theoretical or systematic doctrines or using doctrinal labels familiar to students of western philosophy. In particular, because my exploration of Wang's works has been guided by my own interest in moral philosophy, I have refrained from ascribing metaphysical doctrines to Wang. This is not to deny that, with respect to some of Wang's central teachings, there are metaphysical presuppositions and implications. On the whole, however, I believe that, at least at first, Wang's insights are best appreciated without such a metaphysical focus. In sum, what follows is a personal report of what I learned from reflections on Wang's philosophy.

The Vision of *Ren*: The Universe as a Moral Community

Wang adopted Cheng Hao's vision of the man of *ren* as "forming one body (*yiti*) with all things without differentiation," a vision eloquently expressed in Zhang Zai's *Western Inscription* and also endorsed by Cheng Hao's younger brother Cheng Yi (1033–1107). This vision is a powerful version of the classical Confucian ideal of man "forming a triad (*can*) with heaven and earth" in the *Doctrine of the Mean*. Significantly, for Zhu Xi (1130–1200) the statements by the Cheng brothers failed to provide a clear and definitive guide to the realization of *ren*. According to Cheng Hao, "The student must first of all understand *ren*. The man of *ren* forms one body (*yiti*) with all things without differentiation. Righteousness (*yi*), wisdom (*zhi*), and faithfulness (*xin*) are [expressions of] *ren*" (Chan 1963, 523.) Zhu Xi points out that these are excellent sayings but are "too broad" and "it is difficult for the student to embark on" the road to *ren*. With regard to Cheng Yi's comment "the man of *ren* considers heaven and earth and all things as one body (*yiti*)," Zhu Xi complains that it is "too profound" and "there is nothing [definite] to be grasped" as a point of departure. The statement that the man of *ren* has the same body (*tongti*) as that of heaven and earth and all things is unobjectionable so long as one realizes that *ren* is something to be sought within the person himself. "*Ren* is the character of mind and the *li* (rationale) of love." It is through the extension (*tui*) of this mind and love that the vision of *ren* can be realized. In other words, the notion of "the same body" suggests an exclusively external rather than an internal approach to realizing *ren*. Furthermore, to talk about *ren* in terms of the self as having "the same body" as all things, "will lead people to be vague, confused, neglectful, and make no effort to be alert" (Qian 1982, 2:59–60).

Zhu Xi's dissatisfaction with the notion of "forming one body" (*yiti*) or "having the same body" (*tongti*) as a way of characterizing the vision of *ren* raises an issue that is crucial for any attempt to elucidate *ren* in general or abstract terms without a proper elaboration of its concrete significance, that is, an exemplification of the possibility of realizing the ideal in the actual world. Wang's own version of *ren*, though making use of the notions derived from the Cheng brothers, may be seen as a response to Zhu Xi's challenge. Wang's own version runs:

> *Passage C*
> The great man regards heaven, earth, and the myriad things as one body (*yiti*). He regards the world as one family and the country as one person. . . . Forming one body with heaven, earth, and the myriad things is not only true of the great man. Even the mind (*xin*) of the small man is no different. Only he makes it small. Therefore, when he sees a child about to fall into a well, he cannot help a feeling of alarm and commiseration (*Mencius*, 2A.6). This shows that his humanity (*ren*) forms one body with the child. Again, when he observes the pitiful cries and frightened appearance of the birds and animals about to be slaughtered, he cannot help feeling an "inability to bear" their suffering. This shows that his humanity forms one body with birds and animals. ("Inquiry on the *Great Learning*," *Instructions*, 195)

Wang goes on to point out that the man of *ren* also forms one body with plants, stones, tiles, mountains, and rivers.

When we ponder this vision, we can no longer say that the concept of "one body" (*yiti*) is devoid of concrete significance. The use of Mencius's doctrine of innate capacity for moral feeling—in particular, the inability to bear the suffering of all existent things—gives us some sense of concrete significance. The classical ideal of the harmony of man and nature is now understood as an ideal of the universe as a moral community. This ideal gives the committed agent a unifying perspective for experiencing and dealing with all persons, things, events, and human affairs. However, as an object of commitment, the possibility of realizing *ren* within the actual world depends on extending *xin* (mind-heart) to its utmost reaches. Love and active sympathy are characteristic expressions of *ren*, especially in the human world. *Ren* stresses the significance of the moral vision as residing in human relationships (*lun*), a habitat that is capable of indefinite expansion and ultimately embraces the whole universe. As Wang once rhetorically put it: "At bottom heaven and earth and all things are my body (*wushen*). Is there any suffering or bitterness of the great masses that is not disease or pain in my own body?" (*Instructions*, 179).

Since *ren* depends on extending *xin* (mind-heart), we may say that the possibility of realizing *ren* rests on the actualization of *renxin*, sometimes called *daoxin*. The notion of *xin* carries the connotation of "appreciation," which suggests a range of abilities or dispositions, such as awareness, cognition, perception, esteem, sensibility, and responsiveness to the states or conditions of existent things. For Wang, this *xin* is endowed by heaven and is naturally intelligent (*ling*), clear or shining (*zhao*). It is called the "clear character" (*mingde*) in the *Great Learning*. So long as it is not beclouded or obscured (*bi*) by selfish desires, the clear character will manifest itself and thus will attain the condition of forming one body (*yiti*) with the whole universe. The intrinsic quality (*benti*) of the clear character is also called *liangzhi*.

Let us set aside the notion of *liangzhi* for the moment and focus on the vision of *ren* in passage *C*. Presumably, when this vision is realized, one may also be said to have the "same body" (*tongti*) as all things. But notably, our understanding of the language of vision here is largely based on the idea of *ren* as a sort of diffuse affection. Other ways of characterizing the vision are also present in Wang. Later, we shall consider some examples. For the present, let us explore some possibilities for further elucidation of "one body" (*yiti*) or "same body" (*tongti*).

The primary meaning of *ti* is the human body. *Ti* is a generic term for the head, body, hands, and legs. Wang's notion of *yiti* appears to be an analogical extension of the idea of a living human body. This is suggested in his explanation of *yiti* in terms of sharing the same *qi*. *Qi* may be rendered as "vital force" or "energy." In Zhang Zai and in Song-Ming Confucianism, it is a technical term used, along with *li* (principle, reason), to explain material things, and so it can also be rendered as "material force." However, Wang rarely used the notion of *qi*. Like the *ti* in *yiti*, *qi* in *yiqi* appears to be an analogical or metaphorical extension of *qi*, which is believed to pervade the living human body. As A. C. Graham points out:

> *Ch'i* [*qi*], a common and elusive word in ordinary Chinese speech and philosophy, covers a number of concepts for which we have different names in English or none at all. Unlike the abstract *li* (represented as veins or grain only by metaphor), *ch'i* is quite concrete; it really is, among other things, the breath in our throats. It is the source of life, dispersing into the air at death. (1958, 3)

For further reflection on the notion of *yiti* (one body), particularly stressing *ren* as the *li* of creative vitality or energy, let us consider Wang's response to Lu Zheng's query on the difference between the notion of *ren* and Mozi's doctrine of universal love.

> *Passage D*
> It is very difficult to say. You gentlemen must find it out through personal realization (*tiren*). *Ren* is the *li* of unceasing creative and vital transformation (*zaohua shengsheng*). Although it is prevalent and extensive and there is no place where it does not exist, nevertheless there is an order in its operation and growth. . . . Take a tree, for example. When in the beginning it puts forth a shoot, there is the starting point of the tree's spirit (*shengyi*) of life. . . . The love between father and son and between the elder and younger brothers is the starting point of the human mind's (*xin*) spirit of life, just like the sprout of the tree. Mo Tzu's [Mozi's] universal love makes no distinction in human relationships and regards one's own father, son, elder brother or younger brother as being the same as a passer-by. That means that Mo Tzu's universal love has no starting point. It does not sprout. We thereby know that it has no roots (*wugen*). For that reason, it cannot be considered to be the process of unceasing transformation. How can it be called *ren*? (*Instructions*, Sec. 93, emended)

Clearly, *ren* or *yiti* is not an abstract concept but has concrete significance. The criticism of Mozi echoes Mencius's (3B.9), i.e., that Mozi denied the special parental relationship, but is expressed more vividly and persuasively in terms of Mozi's lack of appreciation or neglect of the human "need for roots" entailed by the commitment to the realization of *ren*. Mozi's doctrine of universal love (*jian'ai*) thus has "no roots" (*wugen*). Unlike the Confucian ideal of *ren* as diffuse affection, it has no starting point in familial relationships. "It has no sprouts." How can a purely abstract conception be understood without some exemplification of its concrete significance? *Ren*, as involving the *xin* (mind-heart) appreciative of the integrity of every existent thing and of concern for the preservation of its continuing spirit or vitality, may properly be said to be the *li* of unceasing creative transformation. Alternatively, it is our *xin* that manifests the *li* of things (*xinjili*)—a theme we shall explore later.

For a fuller appreciation of the practical import of *ren* as an object of ethical commitment, it is worthwhile to consider Wang's use of the distinction between *ti* (inward nature) and *yong* (function, expression). Here too, *ti* appears to be a metaphorical extension of *ti* in the sense of a living human body. Just as we cannot conceive of a body apart from its various functions (sensations, feelings, etc.), we cannot understand the *ti* of any concept without understanding its *yong* or operational significance. Thus for Wang, the distinction between *ti* and *yong* is relative, not a dichotomy:

> When we speak of *ti* as *ti, yong* (function) is already involved in it. When we speak of *yong* as *yong, ti* is already involved. This is the meaning of [Cheng Yi's] saying, "*Ti* and *yong* coming from the same source." (*Instructions*, Sec. 108, emended)

In the *Inquiry on the Great Learning*, we find the distinction between *ti* and *yong* in connection with *yiti* (one body), e.g., *yiti zhi ti* and *yiti zhi yong*. According to Wang, in the *Great Learning*:

> Manifesting clear character has to do with establishing (*li*) or setting forth the *ti* of man's forming one body (*yiti*) with heaven, earth, and the myriad things, whereas loving the people has to do with realizing (*da*) the function (*yong*) of [the ideal of] forming one body (*yiti*) with heaven, earth, and the myriad things. Thus manifesting clear character must necessarily involve loving people, and loving people is the way of manifesting clear character. (*Instructions*, Sec. 273, emended)

We may take Wang as saying that we cannot understand the *ti* of the vision of *ren* as forming one body with all things without appreciating it as having an expressive power (*yong*) or as having an intrinsically actuating or transformative significance within the moral life. Recall that *ren* is the *li* of creative vitality and transformation and has its "root" in the experience of human relationships. The *ti* or inward nature of the commitment to *ren* thus cannot be separated from the effort to realize its *yong* or expressive power, not only in the realm of human relationships but also in the universe as a whole. *Ren*, the ideal of the universe as a moral community, by virtue of its *ti* and *yong*, is an object of ethical commitment rather than of intellectual entertainment. And the realization of this commitment, while ultimately a matter of personal experience, presupposes a confidence in *xin* (mind-heart) as a point of departure.

Mind as the Locus for the Manifestation of *Li*

Appreciating the concrete significance of the vision of *ren* signifies no more than an initial understanding of the possibility of becoming a sage. For a committed agent (that is, one who is seriously committed to the vision) the urgent task is to search for ways and means of converting this possibility into an actuality. Following Cheng Yi, Zhu Xi taught that the starting point was the investigation of things (*gewu*), which means embarking on an inquiry into the *li* (principle, reason, rationale) of each thing. According to Zhu Xi, the human mind is intelligent and thus equipped with an ability to know, and not a single thing in the world is devoid of *li*. When a person has exerted himself for a long time in "exhausting the *li* of things" (*qiongli*), he will one day acquire an insight into their interconnection (*huoran guantong*). As a consequence of this experience, "the qualities of things, whether internal or external, refined or coarse, will be apprehended. Moreover, the mind's inward nature (*ti*) and function (*yong*) will become completely perspicuous" (Chan 1963, 89; *Sishu jizhu*, 6).

According to the *Chronological Biography*, at the age of twenty Wang, with his friend, tried to follow Zhu Xi's advice by investigating the *li* of the bamboos in front of his pavilion, but ended up in utter frustration and sickness. Seventeen years later, while in exile in Longchang, in the dead of night, Wang acquired an instantaneous insight (*wu*) into the true meaning of "investigation of things" (*gewu*) in the *Great Learning*. For the first time, he realized that "my own nature is quite sufficient to attain sagehood," and that he had erred in "seeking the *li* of things and affairs from the outside" (*Yangming quanshu*, 32:7A). In retrospect, Wang said of his sudden enlightenment:

> *Passage E*
> It was only after I had lived among the barbarians [in Longchang] for [almost] three years that I understood the meaning [of "investigation of things"]; that fundamentally, there is not a single thing in the world that can be investigated; and that the effort to investigate things is to be carried out only with one's mind and the wholeness of one's own person. If one is firmly committed to the teaching that everyone can become a sage, he can assume the responsibility [of fulfilling the commitment]. (*Intructions*, Sec. 319, emended)

Wang's doctrine of mind as the locus for the manifestation of the *li* of things (*xinjili*) may be construed as a compendious expression of his own experience in the efficacy of self-reliance; that is, the mind itself possesses its own capabilities and resources for realizing the vision of *ren*. The doctrine may be regarded as an expressive symbol of Wang's self-confidence in attaining sagehood. However, his use of *li* in stating the doctrine appears to presuppose an established usage familiar to his audience. For clarification, it is important to explore Zhu Xi's uses, particularly in view of the fact that Wang's doctrine was taught as a direct critical response to Zhu Xi's conception of the investigation of things. There is also a problem of coherent explication of the doctrine, because of a series of highly perplexing claims based on the doctrine, for example, such claims as "outside the mind there is no *li*" (*xinwai wuli*) and "outside the mind there are no things or affairs" (*xinwai wuwu, xinwai wushi*). More centrally, there is an apparent inconsistency between his views that "knowledge is the intrinsic quality (*benti*) of the mind" and "the mind has no inward nature (*ti*) of its own." While one must respect Wang's appeal to personal realization for the meanings of these tenets, such an appeal is helpful only when there is a prior discursive understanding. One must first have some idea of Wang's teachings before one can tell whether or not his experience constitutes a personal corroboration of their acceptability. In what follows, I shall deal with these difficulties with a view of offering a coherent though critical reconstruction of Wang's conception of mind.

Let us first attend to Wang's own explanation of his doctrine of *xinjili*, i.e., mind is the locus for the manifestation of *li*. According to Wang, Zhu Xi's teaching, adopted from Cheng Yi, that *li* is inherent in things external to the human mind has been obscuring people's minds for a long time. It is difficult to dispel this obscuration by a single saying such as *xinjili*. Nevertheless, he proceeded to elucidate this saying by way of examples.

> *Passage F*
> For instance, in the matter of serving one's parents, one cannot seek for the *li* of filial piety in the parent. In serving one's ruler, one cannot seek for the *li* of loyalty in the ruler. In the intercourse with friends and in governing the people, one cannot seek for the *li* of faithfulness and humanity (*ren*) in friends and the people. They are all in the mind. It is the mind that manifests *li* (*xinjili*). When the mind is free from the obscuration of selfish desires, it is the embodiment of *tianli* (heavenly *li*), which requires not an iota added from the outside. When this mind is completely invested with *tianli* and manifests itself in serving parents, there is filial piety. When it manifests itself in serving the ruler, there is loyalty. And when it manifests itself in dealing with friends or in governing the people, there are faithfulness and humanity (*ren*). (*Instructions*, Sec. 3)

Note that the passage involves two distinct but closely connected terms: *li* and *tianli*. *Li* appears as a generic term subject to specification in particular contexts, such as the *li* of filial piety or the *li* of friendship. Presumably one can also speak of the *li* of tables and chairs. *Tianli*, on the other hand, is explicitly contrasted with selfish desires (*yu*); and significantly it does not admit of specification.

To understand Wang's use of *li* in passage *F*, we may make a brief excursion to Zhu Xi's uses, some of which are also implicit in the works of Cheng Yi (Graham 1958, ch. 1). Sometimes, Zhu Xi used *li* in the sense of "what is naturally so" (*ziran*), suggesting a description. On one occasion, responding to a query on the distinction between *dao* (way) and *li*, Zhu Xi remarked that "*dao* is a collective term (*zongming*); *li* is a term that refers to the detailed items." To put this differently, "The word *dao* is all-encompassing; the *li* are so many veins inside the *dao*" (*Zhuzi yulei*, 6:1A). This use suggests the notion of pattern (*wenli*). Thus he also said that *li* "can be compared to the patterns (*wenli*) of bamboos and trees" (*Zhuzi yulei*, 6:2A). In this sense, the *li* of a thing or state of affair consists of its pattern or orderly arrangement of elements. More significantly, we find in Zhu Xi a use of *li* that is functionally equivalent to "reason," in two distinctive ways. In the one case, *li* refers to the "reason why a thing is as it is" (*soyiran zhi gu*). In another context (Chen 1983, 481) *li* is said to refer to the "standard or norm for what is right and proper" (*dangran zhi ze*). And by extension in familiar ethical contexts, that is, in contexts that involve Confucian notions of virtue, we may use *li* to refer to judgments and actions. In light of this distinction in some of Zhu Xi's remarks, it seems plausible to ascribe to him a distinction between reasons for existence and reasons for action. Since reasons for existence have primarily explanatory force in accounting for the existence of things or states of affairs, quite properly their use conveys Zhu Xi's metaphysical interest in speculating on the nature of existence. Thus in Zhu Xi's system, *li* cannot be separated from *qi* in accounting for the nature of individuals. Reasons for action, on the other hand, have primarily normative force. But on the whole, the ideal standard is implicit rather than explicit. Thus its justificatory force remains an important subject for further inquiry.

This sketch of Zhu Xi's uses of *li* does not ascribe to him a clear conceptual distinction. Because of their fundamental ethical inclination, for the most part Confucian thinkers, with Xunzi as a possible exception, do not clearly distinguish descriptive, explanatory, and normative uses of terms (Cua 1985). In general, what are commonly considered descriptive terms like "father" and "son" are terms used with implicit normative force. As Graham points out, for them, "one is truly a father only if one is compassionate, truly a son only if one is filial" (18). Factual statements, in the context of ethical discourse, are generally regarded as invested with moral import (Cua 1979).

For our purposes, the sketch of Zhu Xi's uses of *li* is a preliminary framework for understanding Wang's doctrine of *xinjili* (mind). Unlike Zhu Xi, Wang has no metaphysical interest in accounting for the existence of things. Thus the explanatory and descriptive uses of *li* do not help us interpret his doctrine; only the normative use of *li* is at issue. The *li* of filial piety in passage *F*, for instance, is quite properly construed as a reason for acting in accordance with the requirement or standard of "filiality." *Li* in this sense is a reason for action, since it expresses an agent's active concern for his parents. The formula *xinjili*, which I have rendered as "the mind manifests *li*," is a concise way of stating a truism—as we shall see later, an important truism (Cua 1982). Alternatively, we may render *xinjili* as "it is the mind that renders *li* manifest." In this manner, it is absurd to say that one can "seek for the *li* of filial piety in the parents." The same truism may be stated more forcefully but provocatively in such remarks of Wang's as these (*Instructions*, Secs. 3 and 33): "Outside the mind, there is no *li* (*xinwai wuli*)"; "Outside the mind, there are no things (*wu*) or affairs (*shi*)." In light of the vision of *ren*, we can now appreciate that Wang's quest for sagehood is basically internal rather than external. Reasons for actions (*li*) are those informed by the spirit of the vision and can be sought only within oneself or, in Wang's term, within the mind (*xin*). Thus we may say with Julia Ching (1976, 58) that *xinjili* initially "represents Yangming's attempt to internalize the moral quest." But ultimately, it embodies an important truism with practical import. As Wang said of the basic purpose of his doctrine, it is proposed as a remedy for rectifying moral faults and misconduct.

> *Passage G*
> Why do I maintain that it is the mind that manifests *li*? Simply because people of the world have divided the mind (*xin*) and *li* into two, thus giving rise to many defects and evils. For instance, the five despots drove out the barbarians and honored the house of Zhou all because of their selfishness, and therefore they did not act, as they should, in accord with *li* (*budangli*). (*Instructions*, Sec. 322, emended)

Wang goes on, as in passage *F*, to invoke the distinction between *tianli* and selfish desires. Let us now turn to this distinction.

Tianli (heavenly *li*), along with other "binomials" involving *li*—e.g., *daoli, tiaoli*, and *yili*—is part of the standard neo-Confucian conceptual apparatus (Cua 1982, ch. 2). But significantly, whether implicit or explicit, *tianli* is often contrasted with human desires (*renyu*), which are generally regarded as selfish or self-serving desires oblivious of ethical requirements. The *locus classicus* of this distinction is found in the "Record of Music" (*Yueji*) in the *Book of Rites* (*Liji*):

> To be still at birth is man's Heavenly endowed nature. Man acts as he is affected by external things, and thus develops desires (*yu*) incidental to his nature. As he confronts things, he becomes conscious [of his internal states] and thereupon displays his likes and dislikes. When these likes and dislikes are not regulated from within, his consciousness [of the states] will be beguiled by external things. If he does not turn back to himself and engages in reflection, his *tianli* will be eclipsed. In general, there is no end to things affecting men. But if man's likes and dislikes are not regulated, he will be subjected to transformation according to the occurrence of external things. In this manner, he will eclipse *tianli* and gives free rein to his desires. As a consequence, we have rebellious and deceitful hearts, along with licentious and violent disorder. For this reason, the strong oppresses the weak, the multitude tramples upon the few, the clever deceives the ignorant and stupid, the audacious makes the timid suffer; the sick are not cared for; the old, young, orphans, and the lonely are neglected and cannot find a proper home. (Legge 1966, 2:96–97; Wang Mengou 1977, 2:491)

In this passage, the distinction between *tianli* and human desires (*renyu*) does not strictly represent a dichotomy. Man's likes and dislikes and the desires that arise from them are not always problematic. Desires *qua* desires are not good or bad. As Xunzi points out: "Beings that possess desires and those that do not belong to two different categories—the categories of the living and the dead. But the possession or non-possession of desires has nothing to do with good government or bad" (Watson 1963, 150). The author of our passage in the *Liji* was probably influenced by Xunzi. He condemns not self-regarding desires in general but only unregulated desires. Significantly, *tianli* is the standard for regulation. Problematic desires are those which are selfish and self-serving in a manner that deviates from *tianli*. Thus Wang, like neo-Confucians in general, uses the term *siyu* (selfish desires) in lieu of *renyu* (human desires), though the latter's contrast with *tianli* is often sharply drawn, as for example in Zhang Zai's saying: "Those who understand the higher things return to *tianli*, while those who understand lower things follow human desires" (Chan 1963, 509).

In our passage from the *Liji, tianli*, as a norm or standard, is to be discovered by reflection or introspection. There is a suggestion that *tianli* is inherent in the human mind, rather than something like the natural law inherent in the nature of things, as these things are regarded as external to the human mind. Thus we can appreciate Cheng Hao's famous saying, "Although my learning is indebted to others, the two words *tianli* represent something that I personally realized" (Chan, 520); and Wang's response to a query on the meaning of *zhong* (equilibrium or centrality) in the *Doctrine of the Mean*, "It (*zhong*) is a matter of personal realization of one's own mind. It cannot be explained by words. *Zhong* is nothing but *tianli*" (*Instructions*, Sec. 76, emended). While I do not know the reason for the use of *tianli* instead of *li*, as in the *Xunzi* (Cua 1985, 20–30), we may conjecture that since *tian* (heavenly) in the "binomial" *tianli* has the connotation of something supreme, vast, and awe-inspiring, *tianli* may be construed as a supreme standard of ethical life and conduct.

When we construe *li* as functionally equivalent to reason, *tianli* is a term for the "reason for moral reasons." However, *tianli*, particularly in Wang, is not a supreme standard or ideal norm as exemplified in the familiar western doctrine of the hierarchy of values, inspired perhaps by Plato's *Philebus*. For Wang, as I have suggested elsewhere (1982), it is more an alternative expression for the vision of *ren* as an ideal theme, but it has a special use in focusing on selfish desires as obstructing the realization of the vision (this is as evident in passage *F*). Thus if "the mind is free from the obscuration of selfish desires, it is the embodiment of *tianli*" and when this mind is completely pervaded by the concern with *tianli*, it will become evident in serving one's parents. Thus passage *F* is accompanied by the following remark:

> *Passage H*
> If the mind (*xin*) is free from selfish human desires and is completely invested with *tianli*, and if it is the mind that is sincere in performing filial acts, then in the winter it will naturally think of the cold of parents and seek a way to provide warmth for them, and in the summer it will naturally think of the heat of the parents and seek a way to provide coolness for them. These are all offshoots of the mind that is sincere in its filial piety. Nevertheless, there must first be such a mind before there can be these offshoots. (*Instructions*, Sec. 3)

Wang's doctrine of mind as the locus for the manifestation of *li* (*xinjili*) cannot thus be understood without his conception of mind as a moral mind (*daoxin*), i.e., a human mind animated by a commitment to the vision of *ren*, in the comprehensive sense, as an ideal of the universe as a moral community. In pursing its actualization with sincerity and self-examination, a committed person will experience joy. In Wang's words:

> *Passage I*:
> Joy is the intrinsic characteristic (*benti*) of the mind. Although only the sages can experience true joy, it is an experience which ordinary persons can have, except that ordinary persons are not aware [of the ethical significance] of this experience. Instead they bring on themselves a great deal of anxiety and suffering, and in addition, bewilderment and self-abandonment. Even in the midst of these, this joy is present. As soon as a single thought is enlightened, and one examines oneself with utmost sincerity, the joy is present. (*Instructions*, Sec. 166, emended)

Let us turn to Wang's tenet that "the mind has no *ti* (inward nature) of its own." Consider the following remark:

> *Passage J*
> The eye has no inward nature (*ti*) of its own. Its inward nature consists of the colors of all things. The ear has no inward nature of its own. Its inward nature consists of the sounds of all things. . . . Likewise, the mind has no inward nature of its own (*xin wu ti*). Its inward nature consists in the right and wrong of the influences and responses of heaven, earth, and all things. (*Instructions*, Sec. 277, emended)

One way to interpret this perplexing remark is to recall that for Wang, as I have indicated earlier, the *ti* (inward nature) of a thing cannot be conceived or characterized apart from its *yong* (function). Therefore, the *ti* of the mind cannot be grasped apart from its function. There is an implicit presupposition that any attempt to describe the nature of a thing in purely abstract or conceptual terms cannot capture its *ti*. We may thus regard passage *J* as a reminder of the inadequacy of any abstract approach to the nature of things. This interpretation suggests that Wang's attitude toward any abstract inquiry is purely pragmatic. In light of his preoccupation with the vision of *ren* and personal realization, this attitude is intelligible. However, the appeal to the correlation of *ti* and *yong* (function) throws no light on the plausibility of passage *J*. For even if a thing's inward nature cannot be conceived apart from its function, the latter can still be intelligently described in abstract terms. To describe a thing's function, after all is to indicate its possible rather than actual operation. Thus we speak intelligibly of a thing's failure to carry out its function or malfunction. But observe that in doing so, we presuppose an understanding of its function. Similarly, the human mind can sensibly be said to have a function, quite distinct from its actualization. In terms of Wang's notion of *tianli* the mind can fail to comply with its own requirements. Wang would remind us, as in passage *H*, that this is because the mind is obscured (*bi*) by selfish desires. This explanation, as we shall see at the end of this essay, is inadequate to account for moral failure. But even if the explanation is sound, it is uninformative, unless something can be said about the *ti* of *tianli* in relation to the mind. In fact, Wang explicitly maintained that *tianli* is the fundamental *ti* of the mind, *xin zhi benti*

(*Instructions*, Sec. 48). But this tenet is inconsistent with that in passage *J*.

A closer examination of passage *J* reveals a deeper problem. Wang's use of *ti* is highly misleading. If one follows his frequent insistence on the significance of the correlation of *ti* (inward nature) and *yong* (function), one would expect him to say that the *ti* of the eyes and the *ti* of the ears involve their *yong*, i.e., as consisting of seeing and hearing rather than colors and sounds, which are the objects and not the functions of eyes and ears. Zhu Xi is quite clear that the distinction between *ti* and *yong* is relative. When queried about *dao* with respect to *ti* and *yong*, Zhu replied, "Let us suppose that the ear is *ti*, its *yong* is hearing. Likewise, if the eye is considered *ti*, its *yong* is seeing." For Zhu, *ti* and *yong*, while inseparable, comprise a relative distinction. "Consider our body as *ti*, seeing and hearing, as well as the movements of our hands and legs, are its *yong*. But if we consider our hand as *ti*, then the movement of the fingers is its *yong*." Moreover, the *ti* of a thing cannot be understood apart from its *li* in the explanatory sense, particularly in accounting for the distinction between individuals. The trouble with Wang, with respect to the distinction and relationship between *ti* and *yong* distinction, is his failure to attend to *li* as having an explanatory force, i.e., as accounting for the existence of particular things. This difficulty, I believe, stems from his preoccupation with the realization of the vision of *ren* and thus prevents him from seeing that one cannot appreciate the integrity of individual things without pursuing a factual inquiry into their nature. I will deal with an aspect of that problem in the conclusion of this essay (Qian 1982, 1: 429–431).

Even if *ti* is inseparable from *yong*, as Wang claims, *yong* still cannot be construed in terms of objects. *Yong* is a term used to indicate the capacity of an object to function in a certain way, not a term designating objects as such. Passage *J* thus contains a series of misdescriptions founded on a categorial confusion between objects and functions. This elementary conceptual error prevents us from understanding the *ti* of the mind through an analogy with the *ti* of the senses, i.e., that the *ti* of the mind consists of the "right and wrong of the influences and responses of heaven, earth, and all things." Even if it is considered independently, this characterization of the mind is hardly intelligible. Perhaps Wang was simply proposing another way of saying that faith in the capacity of the mind to realize the vision of *ren* lies ultimately in the success of one's efforts, and this success would constitute the *ti* of the mind committed to realizing *ren*. But such a restatement creates an insuperable difficulty in understanding his doctrine of mind as the locus for the manifestation of *li* (*xinjili*). Perhaps passage *J*, which was recorded by a disciple without any indication of its context, was an occasional remark in response to a less than serious query and thus cannot be considered a contribution to coherent explication of Wang's conception of mind, particularly in view of its inconsistency with Wang's various characterizations of the nature of mind by way of his notion of *benti*, which suggests a conception of intrinsic property (e.g., *Instructions*, Secs. 2, 6, 101, 118, and 228). Below I shall take up one of these characterization in connection with *liangzhi*.

The preceding exposition of *xinjili* in passage *F* focuses largely on *li* and *tianli*. *Tianli* plays the central role in Wang's thought. Frequently, *li* appears as a stand-in for *tianli*. But it must be noted that the distinction is philosophically important. In the case of *li* it is quite natural to say "the *li* of *X*," but one cannot sensibly say "the *tianli* of *X*." "The *li* of *X*," construed as "reasons for actions," can be analyzed as different types of reason depending on the notion of virtue deemed appropriate to the context of discourse, e.g., "the *li* of filial piety" or "the *li* of loyalty" as in passage *F*. *Tianli*, on the other hand, is unanalyzable. As I suggested above, it is an alternative term for Wang's vision of *ren* but stresses primarily, as in the *Liji*, its opposition to selfish desires. Thus Wang once reminded a student that *li* does not admit of "splitting up" (*Instructions*, Sec. 35). Wang has a tendency to collapse important philosophical distinctions, fearing that distinctions can too easily be made into into mutually exclusive dichotomies. This fear is sometimes apparent in his strange interpretation of Zhu Xi's view. For instance, Zhu Xi's interpertation of "the investigation of things (*gewu*) in terms of investigating the *li* of things to the utmost (*qiongli*)" was said to be a matter of abiding by *tianli* at all times and places. "*Tianli* is clear character, and to investigate the *li* of things to the utmost is to manifest clear character" (*Instructions*, Sec. 7). This tendency to collapse valuable distinctions accounts for a great deal of difficulty in a sympathetic appreciation of Wang's works, but it can perhaps itself be accounted for in terms of his own preoccupation with the realization of the vision of *ren*. In the case of *li*, he did not seem to have any interest in *li* in the explanatory sense, that is, in accounting for the existence of things (*soyiran zhi li*) as is evident in Zhu Xi; however, it must be admitted that some of his sayings may be interpreted as having metaphysical import or even as proposing a conception of things akin to some version of metaphysical idealism as expounded by Carsun Chang. But in terms of Wang's avowed interest in the quest for becoming a sage, it is best to see his doctrine of *xinjili* as an expressive symbol of a culmination of a stage in his quest; that is, the human mind by itself is quite sufficient for pursuing the realization of *ren* without relying on the quest for *li* inherent in external things. Indeed, for Wang, things (*wu*), like affairs or events (*shi*), are but the objects of human will (*yi*), particularly the will to attain the highest good (*Instructions*, Sec. 6). And the *li* of things have no intrinsic epistemic status; they are the manifestation of the mind's concern with *tianli*. This view raises an important problem pertaining to the role of factual knowledge and inquiry in his moral theory.

Given the mind's concern with the vision of *ren* or *tianli*, an urgent question arises for a committed agent: "In what sense or respect can the mind attain the vision?" Perhaps, late in life, Wang realized that it is not satisfactory to answer that so long as the mind is completely free from obscuration by selfish desires, *tianli* will manifest itself (passage *H*). Were this the concrete content of self-reliance, the committed agent would need to do nothing but perform negative actions. Something positive must be said about the characteristic capacity of the human mind to realize the vision. Wang's conception of *liangzhi*, a term adopted from Mencius, is a response to our agent's question. The doctrine that the mind is the locus of where *li* is manifested (*xinjili*) can at most serve as an expressive symbol of self-reliance. It is useful as a word of encouragement, but it can suggest misleadingly that sagehood is a condition of utter tranquillity rather than activity. Also, it can easily be translated into a theoretical doctrine subject to analytical examination abstracted from Wang's commitment to the vision.

Before we turn to Wang's conception of *liangzhi*, something must be said about his use of *dao* (the Way). Like *tianli*, it is an alternative term for *ren*, the ideal of the universe as a moral community. But we have in *dao* a focus on the ongoing course of changing circumstances that requires, as we shall see, an agent's sense of rightness (*yi*) in coping with changes. In Wang's words, *dao* "has neither restrictions nor physical form, and cannot be pinned down to any particular" (*Instructions*, Sec. 66). As suggested at the beginning of this essay, a commitment to the Confucian vision is a commitment to an ideal theme rather than an ideal norm or set of precepts. This means that the vision itself has an inexhaustible significance within the moral life. As Wang put it, "*dao* cannot be exhausted with finality," *dao wu zhongqiong* (*Instructions*, Sec. 64, emended; Sec. 342). One cannot deduce from *dao* any specific precepts for resolving moral perplexities. The realization of *dao* depends basically on one's effort, and ultimately on extending one's *liangzhi*.

Liangzhi as the Basis of Mediation

According to the *Chronological Biography*, a year after Wang's sudden enlightenment on the meaning of the "investigation of things and the extension of knowledge," he began teaching the unity of knowledge and action, *zhixing heyi* (*Yangming quanshu*, 32:8A). His concern with this theme, apart from his later conception of *liangzhi*, may be seen as a response to the question of understanding the actuating force or transformative significance of moral knowledge as a form of practical knowledge (Cua 1982). In terms of his vision of *ren*, this teaching has a distinctive place in focusing on the unity of self and action. A sincere commitment to *ren* involves an active will (*yi*) to self-transformation in the light of the ideal. This means that the agent has a conscientious regard for the quality of his thoughts and interests as they affect the pursuit of *ren*. The ideal self to be realized is fundamentally constituted by one's acts. Thus the agent must exercise constant vigilance in surveying his thoughts as they affect the quality of his actions. This point applies also to moral knowledge derived from learning. When asked about the unity of knowledge and action, Wang said:

> *Passage K*
> You need to understand the basic purpose of my doctrine. In their learning people of today separate knowledge and action into two different sorts of task. As a consequence, when a thought arises, although it is evil, they do not stop it, because it has not been translated into action. I advocate the doctrine of the unity of knowledge and action precisely because I want people to understand that when a thought is aroused it is already action. If there is anything evil when the thought is aroused, one must overcome the evil thought. One must go to the root and go the bottom and not allow the evil thought to lie latent in his mind. This is the basic purpose of my doctrine. (*Instructions*, Sec. 226, emended)

Indeed, knowing what is good or evil, right or wrong, is an intrinsic characteristic (*benti*) of the mind concerned with *ren*. Given that the mind is the locus where *li* is manifested, especially in the sense of *tianli*, moral knowledge may be construed as an outcome of ideal achievement, i.e., retrospective rather than prospective knowledge (Cua 1982, ch. 1). In Wang's formulation, "Knowledge is the intelligent locus (*lingchu*) of *li*" or "Knowledge is the intelligence (*lingming*) of the mind" (*Instructions*, Secs. 118 and 78). Retrospective knowledge is the fruit of the successful exercise of intelligence, that is, cognizance of matters at hand, and particularly discernment of the import of good and evil thoughts. In this manner, prospective knowledge informed by the vision of *ren*, through the active will (*yi*), can be translated into action, thus transforming an actual self into an ideal self, and gives rise to retrospective knowledge. In Wang's words, "Knowledge is the beginning of action and action is the completion of knowledge" (*Instructions*, Sec. 5). Wang's later conception of *liangzhi*, a "binomial" in which *zhi* (knowledge) is a component, appears as a simple linguistic modification. But this conception, while it incorporates some of the insights of this doctrine of the unity of knowledge and action, offers a deeper, firmer grasp of the concrete significance of the vision of *ren*. *Liangzhi* plays a central role in Wang's mature philosophy, especially in providing the basis for mediation between the ideal of *ren* and the actual world of human experience. Unlike his doctrine of mind as the locus of where *li* is manifested (*xinjili*), which at most serves as an expressive symbol of self-confidence in one's quest for sagehood, his conception of *liangzhi* directs the committed agent to the seat of self-sufficiency as a point of departure (*tounao*).

Again, Wang's *liangzhi* (like his other doctrines) requires personal realization (passage *B*). In the *Chronological Biography* we are told that at age forty-nine, Wang began teaching the doctrine of extension of *liangzhi*. He was reported to have made the following remarks:

> *Passage L*
> My doctrine of *liangzhi* was arrived at through a hundred deaths and a thousand sufferings. I cannot help but concisely express it by a single utterance. Only I fear that when a student receives this teaching, it is all too easy for him to regard the teaching as something to play with occasionally without any real understanding, as it involves concrete and substantial effort. (*Yangming quanshu*, 33: 16B)

However, Wang gives various explanations of his notion of *liangzhi*. From the standpoint of explication, it is difficult to set forth a simple and coherent view without reconstruction. While we have no evidence that Wang would encourage such an attempt, he did admit that *liangzhi* has diverse compatible interpretations. Consider a conversation recorded by Huang Mianzhi:

> I [Wang] said, "There is only one *liangzhi*. King Wen wrote the explanations of hexagrams in the *Book of Changes*, Duke Zhou wrote the explanations of the lines of the hexagrams, and Confucius wrote the commentaries and 'Appended Remarks.' Why did each view the *li* (rationale) differently?" The teacher said, "How could these sages be confined to a rigid pattern. So long as they all proceeded from *liangzhi*, what harm is there in each one's explaining in his own way? Take for example a garden of bamboos. So long as they all have branches and joints, they are similar in general. If it were rigidly insisted upon that each and every branch or joint had to be of the same size or height, that would not be the wonderful handiwork of creation. You people should just go ahead and cultivate *liangzhi*. If all have the same *liangzhi*, there is no harm in their being different here and there. But if you are not willing to exert effort, you don't even sprout. What branches or joints are there to talk about?" (*Instructions*, Sec. 293, emended)

In what follows, I offer a general characterization of *liangzhi* under different headings. The order of exposition represents an attempt at a coherent reading of Wang's varying remarks. At the end of this essay, I point to some problems arising from our characterization, particularly the relation between *liangzhi* and factual knowledge.

Moral discrimination. In Wang's major works, there is a recurrent emphasis on *liangzhi* as inherent in every person's mind. It is inborn rather than acquired, that is, its presence in the human mind does not depend on deliberation or on learning (*Instructions*, Secs. 152, 171, 208). It is indestructible and omnipresent (Sec. 162), though subject to obscuration (*bi*) by one's insistent selfish desires. Fundamentally *liangzhi* is a native ability to distinguish right from wrong, as well as good from bad (Sec. 162). However, the notion of rightness is subordinate to that of goodness. As Wang put it:

> *Passage M*
> *Liangzhi* is only the sense of right and wrong (*Mencius*, 6A.6), and this sense of right and wrong is nothing but the love [of good] and the hate [of evil]. With these love and hate, one can exhaust [the meanings] of right and wrong. . . . The words "right" and "wrong" refer to general standards of conduct. How to deal with them depends on human ingenuity. (*Instructions*, Sec. 288, emended)

This remark also applies to such words as "should" and "must." Significantly, as we shall see, moral notions do not encapsulate fixed standards of conduct.

In the basic sense, then, *liangzhi* refers to a native, peculiar ability of human beings to discern moral distinctions, especially in particular situations that call for an appropriate response in terms of positive actions. For further elucidation on the nature of this ability and the sense of knowledge (*zhi*) involved in *liangzhi*, we may consider the following:

> *Passage N*
> Knowledge (*zhi*) is the intrinsic characteristic (*benti*) of the mind. The human mind is naturally able to know. When it perceives (*jian*) the parents, it naturally knows that one should be filial. When it perceives the elder brother, it naturally knows that one should be respectful. And when it perceives a child about to fall into a well, it naturally knows that it should intervene (*Mencius*, 2A.6). This is *liangzhi* and need not be sought outside. (*Instructions*, Sec. 8, emended)

This translation may imply misleadingly that the sense of knowledge at issue is "knowing that," e.g., knowing that a statement or proposition is true or false. Here, knowledge (*zhi*) is closely tied to perception. But perception here is more than just sense perception. It is closer to recognition or acknowledgment, though it may suggest, again misleadingly, that past experience is required for the exercise of *liangzhi*. To understand Wang's use of *zhi*, "knowledge," it is better to borrow Wittgenstein's notion of "seeing as" or "aspect-seeing" (1969, 197f). *Jian*, rendered as "perceives," can also be rendered as "sees," much in the sense in which one sees a friend in the street, or sees someone as a friend, as a parent, or as an elder brother (in Wang's examples). Of course, one must be cautious in imputing this ability to the outcome of learning, for *liangzhi* is inborn. The use of *liang* in *liangzhi* clearly implies *liang* in the sense of innateness, though it also conveys some sense of goodness that cannot be understood apart from Wang's vision. (Thus *liangzhi* is commonly translated as "innate knowledge of the good.") We shall pursue this notion below. For our present purposes, in order to convey the nonpropositional character of knowledge (*zhi*) involved in the exercise of *liangzhi*, it is perhaps best to adopt Russell's term "knowledge by acquaintance," but with an explicit warning against construing it as an epistemological concept. According to Russell, "we have *acquaintance* with anything of which we are directly aware, without the intermediary of any process of inference of any knowledge of truths" (1950, 48). The exercise of *liangzhi* as moral discrimination does yield knowledge (*zhi*) in this sense of acquaintance. And in this sense also, knowledge (*zhi*) may be seen as the intrinsic characteristic (*benti*) of the mind, and this ability to know is *liangzhi*.

In view of this close tie to sense perception and to internal perception of one's mental states, it is unsurprising that Wang, earlier in explaining his doctrine of the unity of knowledge and action, drew what may be called aesthetic and psychological analogies. Knowing filial piety is compared to seeing and loving beautiful colors, and to one's knowledge of pain (*Instructions*, Sec. 8). Such analogies suggest that Wang's *liangzhi*, because of its affinity with Francis Hutcheson's moral theory, may be rendered as "moral sense"; though again, one must not ascribe to Wang any interest in moral epistemology. For Hutcheson, moral sense is a form of perception of "immediate goodness" of some actions, whether one's own or another's, completely free from any view on their bearing for self-interest or selfish desires. Moreover, this notion of moral sense does not presuppose any propositional knowledge and is akin to the aesthetic perception of objects with harmonious form or composition (Raphael 1969, 1:269). The affinity of *liangzhi* with Hutcheson's moral sense does suggest a topic worthy of exploration in comparative ethics.

Moral consciousness. Liangzhi, in the sense of the capacity for moral discrimination, while basic, cannot capture the depth of Wang's concern in his teaching of extending *liangzhi*. The human mind is, in the rudimentary sense, consciousness (*Instructions*, Sec. 323); but without a commitment to the vision of *ren*, or alternatively to *dao* or *tianli*, it would be indifferent to moral concerns. Possessed of *liangzhi*, the mind as informed by the vision will be distinctively marked as moral consciousness. Moreover, the vision can no longer appear as a mere object of intellectual entertainment; it can be a proper subject only of serious discourse. As Wang once remarked, "*Dao* is public and belongs to the whole world, and the doctrine is public and belongs to the whole world. They are not the private properties of Master Chu [Zhu Xi] or even Confucius" (*Instructions*, Sec. 176). A discussion of Wang's vision and the central role of *liangzhi* is thus consonant with this spirit of Wang's teachings.

Above, I indicated that *liangzhi* provides the basis for mediation between Wang's vision and the actual world. *Liangzhi* is the seat of self-reliance in the pursuit of the vision. More especially, *liangzhi* makes clear the possibility of realizing the ideal of "forming one body" with all things in the universe. As Wang was wont to say, *liangzhi* manifests *tianli* or *liangzhi* manifests *dao* (*Instructions*, Secs. 165, 169, 265, and 284). *Liangzhi* is the locus where *tianli* naturally and clearly is revealed in consciousness, and "There is only one *liangzhi*. In its manifestation and operation, it is then and there quite self-sufficient" (*Instructions*, Sec. 189, emended). As the intrinsic quality (*benti*) of the moral mind, *liangzhi* is "naturally intelligent, clear, and unbeclouded" (*Instructions*, 274). When the mind is devoid of any selfish desires, *tianli* will be evident (passage *H*).

This notion of *liangzhi* as the seat of moral consciousness does involve *liangzhi* in the sense of moral discrimination, and it significantly stresses the exercise of clear intelligence in discerning the moral import of particular situations. As suggested above, moral knowledge is the "intelligent locus of *li*." When *li* is construed as a stand-in for *tianli*, we have a supreme standard guiding the intelligent exercise of *liangzhi*. Inspired by the *Book of Rites* (*Liji*), like most of his Confucian predecessors, Wang often urged his students to get rid of selfish desires and preserve *tianli* (*Instructions*, Sec. 4). As embodying the concern for *tianli, liangzhi* is properly considered a personal standard, that is, a standard for autonomous judgments of the moral quality of thought and actions, as well as feelings (*Instructions*, Secs. 44, 206, 290, 292, 297). But as we shall see, as an alternative expression for the vision of *ren*, it does not involve precepts. Thus

Wang's notion of *liangzhi* cannot be understood apart from his vision and confidence in the mind as possessing its own capability of realizing the vision—topics I elaborated above.

Before we turn to the nonpreceptive standard in *liangzhi*, a word must be said about its implicit volitional character. *Liangzhi*, being an active concern of the moral mind with *tianli*, clearly involves the will to its actualization. Thus, in addition to the cognitive sense as moral discrimination, *liangzhi* cannot be understood apart from the earnest endeavor in actual performance. Passage *N* clearly points to the volitional element involved. The sense of knowledge by acquaintance is quite remote from that of passive appreciation of the situations described. This point, given our discussion thus far, is fairly evident in the following:

> *Passage O*
> The mind is the master of the body, and the capacious and clear consciousness (*xuling mingjue*) of the mind is the meaning of *liangzhi*, as naturally inherent [in the mind]. When this *liangzhi* in its capacious intelligence and clear consciousness is activated in response to external challenges, I call it the will (*yi*), knowledge (*zhi*) must be present before the will. Without knowledge, there will be no will. Is knowledge, then, not the inward nature (*ti*) of the will? (*Instructions*, Sec. 137, emended)

Deliberation and changing circumstances. Tianli, as an alternative term for *ren*, is basically an ideal theme rather than a preceptive norm. As a standard for conduct, it is a unifying perspective on changing circumstances, a standard of inspiration rather than a standard of aspiration, i.e., an ideal animated by the committed agent's concern for its actualization in the real world. The agent, by his or her active endeavors, endows *tianli* with a vital spirit. As embodying this active concern with *tianli, liangzhi* cannot be rendered as "intuition" as this term is used in ethical intuitionism. For *liangzhi* has nothing to do with the claim of immediate knowledge of self-evident propositions concerning the meanings of the terms "right," "good," or "obligation" in moral discourse (Cua 1966, 163–182). As we have seen, *liangzhi* has a volitional character not present in the use of "intuition" in western ethical theory. Especially in the context of exigent and changing circumstances of human life, *liangzhi* is not the repository of universal principles or rules to guide the perplexed moral agent. In terms of one of its functions (*yong*), it is akin to that of conscience in Butler's sense, but without the implication that human nature is a sort of an ordered system of particular passions, affections, and appetites subordinate to the governance of principles of self-love and benevolence under the supreme aegis of the authority of reflection or conscience. For Wang, *liangzhi* is a supreme moral authority, but there is no suggestion that *liangzhi* occupies a preeminent position which can inform us as to how the various demands of the elements of human nature are to be met, as stipulated by a hierarchy of values intimated in Butler's moral theory. There is an agility or flexibility in the exercise of *liangzhi* that is absent from Butler's notion of conscience. For this reason, rendering *liangzhi* as "conscience" may be highly misleading, though it is useful in conveying the idea of personal autonomy. But it must be admitted that Wang, to my knowledge, gives us no clue as to how this idea is to be explicated.

To appreciate Wang's attitude toward the role of deliberation in the exercise of *liangzhi*, we may begin by recalling passage *M*, where human ingenuity is stressed in the application of presumably established general standards of conduct. The question of what to do can arise in both normal and changing or exigent circumstances of human life. Deliberation with a view to doing the right thing is thus necessary, "so as to provide a basis for the proper handling of affairs" (*Instructions*, Sec. 139). For an ordinary agent the question in the normal situation can probably be answered with relative ease, so long as he or she has a good sense of what conventional morality requires. Moreover, past experience, whether one's own or another's, can provide sufficient guidance. In such a situation, *liangzhi* need not be invoked. Genuine perplexity arises in changing or exigent circumstances, where established standards do not provide clear guidance (Cua 1982, ch. 3.) Wang mentioned two cases: Shun's "marrying without first telling his parents" and King Wu's "launching a military expedition before burying his father." Both these actions are for Wang unprecedented and represent the outcome of a direct deliberative exercise of *liangzhi* in exigent situations. Established standards, which are appropriate to normal situations, cannot be invoked in exigent cases. Shun and Wu could not help doing what they did, given the lack of guidance from past experience or the paradigmatic actions of others in similar circumstances. Each could only search into his *liangzhi* "in an instant thought in his own mind," weigh "all factors as to what was proper," and act accordingly (*Instructions*, Sec. 139).

While *liangzhi* is inherent in all minds, the distinguishing characteristic of the sage is his attitude toward study and reflection. Unlike ordinary persons, he does not worry about "minute details and varying circumstances" with a view to preparing himself to deal with all possible human situations. "What he studies is precisely the extension of *liangzhi* in order to examine [the import of] *tianli* in the mind carefully" (*Instructions*, Sec. 139, emended). As invested with *tianli, li-*

angzhi is indeed a standard, but it does not issue recipes for coping with changing circumstances. This is because "minute details and varying circumstances" cannot be predetermined. Indeed, moral reasons (*yili*) cannot be categorized in advance of a confrontation with particular circumstances (*Instructions*, Sec. 52). The thing to do is to keep the mind as clear as a mirror and engage in moral reflection. "The sage does a thing when the time comes. . . . The study of changing conditions and events is to be done at the time of response" (*Instructions*, Sec. 21). Wang has faith that *liangzhi* can provide unerring guidance without prior factual inquiry. This faith poses a problem that I will take up in my conclusion.

Extension and achievement. The vision of *ren* is an ideal of the universe as a moral community. For a committed agent, "*ren* is the *li* of unceasing creative and vital transformation" (passage *D*). Given *liangzhi* as the basis of the mediation between the ideal and the actual world, the extension of *liangzhi*, i.e., the increasing expansion of the scope of one's moral concern, is an urgent task. The committed agent sees his *liangzhi* as the "spirit of creation" (*Instructions*, Sec. 261). Presumably, the utmost achievement is a complete realization of the vision. This interpretation is suggested in a rather perplexing passage on *liangzhi* as inherent not only in men but in all things in the universe.

> *Passage P*
> *Liangzhi* of man is the same as that of plants and trees, tiles and stones. This is not true of them only. Without man's *liangzhi* there cannot be heaven and earth. For at bottom, heaven, earth, and the myriad things form one body (*yiti*). The point at which this unity is manifested in its most refined and excellent form is the clear intelligence (*liangming*). Wind, rain, dew, thunder, sun and moon, stars, animals and plants, mountains and rivers, earth and stones are essentially of one body with man. It is for this reason that such things as the rains and animals can nourish man and that such things as medicine and minerals can heal diseases. Since they all share the same *qi*, they can penetrate into one another. (*Instructions*, Sec. 272, emended)

I have commented earlier on the notion of *qi*. One way to construe this passage is as a retrospective report of Wang's own experience of the extension and achievement of *liangzhi* (passage *L*). Were it to be taken in the prospective sense, his notion of extending *liangzhi* as a task would seem pointless. Consistent with much of my reading, the passage can also be read as an exaltation or glorification of the vision of *ren*. But I must admit that a metaphysical reading is possible, and this sort of reading does deserve careful exploration (Mou 1979).

This discussion of Wang's conception of *liangzhi* has presented a sketch of its role in relation to Wang's vision and cannot pretend to be a comprehensive exposition; but I hope it serves as an introduction to further inquiry.

Conclusion

I have dealt here with some principal aspects of Wang's philosophy. In effect, I have charted the *dao*, the journey from commitment to *ren*, the vision of the universe as a moral community, to its possible realization through the extension of *liangzhi*. For a committed agent, the path will be difficult and at times tortuous, as in Wang's own case, since *dao* is essentially a course of changing events that cannot be expressed in determinate formulas. Without persistent self-reliance and effort, the agent is bound to experience nothing but anguish and frustration. But in Wang's belief, when he becomes a sage, while equipped with no foreknowledge, he knows "the incipient and activating force of things and handles it in accordance with the circumstance (*Instructions*, Sec. 281). For a practical student of ethics, Wang's vision may appear to be high moral idealism. Though lending itself to lofty and exalted redescription, it is more usefully regarded as an object of imaginative entertainment rather than a serious candidate for moral commitment. Arguably, there are good reasons for adopting Wang's vision (Cua 1982, ch. 4). For a philosophical thinker who shares Wang's vision, there is an intimation of a profound human responsibility toward the cosmos. He will, perhaps, proclaim with William James, "Whether we are empiricists or rationalists, we are ourselves parts of the universe and share the same one deep concern in its destinies. We crave alike to feel more truly at home with it, and to contribute our mite to its amelioration." In addition to these possible responses to Wang's vision, there will undoubtedly be others, whether genial or hostile, sincere or pretentious, serious or amusing, or, of course, completely indifferent.

For a contemporary Confucian philosopher, however, our study gives rise to problems that require careful consideration. By way of conclusion, I focus briefly on two problems that arise from our general characterization of *liangzhi*. The aim is to formulate these problems and to suggest their importance for further inquiry, rather than to propose solutions. In the final analysis, these problems, along with others, deserve attention, not only because they are important to the evaluation of Wang's philosophy as a whole but also because they raise disturbing questions for one concerned, as the present writer is, with the critical development of Confucian ethics.

The first problem that comes to mind pertains to moral failure. Wang's insistence on selfish desires as the one and only source of the obscuration of the mind (i.e., that so long as the mind is free from the obscuration of selfish desires, *tianli* will manifest itself) cannot be considered an adequate explanation of moral failure (passage *F*). For the mind at issue is a moral mind (*daoxin*), informed by the moral vision of *ren* in the sense of "moral" as involving concern for others; thus the value of this tenet is limited to a way of spelling out the meaning of moral commitment. As an account of moral failure, the view is simplistic. As Xunzi has shown, owing to its ability to draw distinctions, the moral mind committed to *dao* as a holistic vision can be obscured (*bi*) in many different ways. In general, the mind can be obscured by distinctions such as desire and aversion, the beginning and the end of human affairs and endeavors, immediate and distant consequences of action, and past and present experiences, as well as the breadth and shallowness of knowledge. Unless the mind is guided by reason (*li*), it cannot cope with changing circumstances (Cua, 1985, 138–45; Watson 1963, 121–138). Because of this liability to diverse sources of obscuration, the *liangzhi* of the moral mind cannot be an unerring guide to resolving moral perplexities and dilemmas. Wang's lack of interest in the notion of *li* in the explanatory and descriptive senses prevents him from paying close attention to Xunzi's insight. More important, even if the mind is divested of selfish desires, for a reflective agent, this is a condition preparatory to the exercise of *liangzhi*, not a condition of moral achievement.

As Wang is well aware, moral failure may also result from insincerity of the will. *Liangzhi* as involving will pertains quite properly to the sincerity of the will, or in Wang's words, "A sincere will is in accordance with *tianli*" (*Instructions*, Sec. 101). This aspect of Wang's philosophy deserves further study. However, it is unclear how Wang would deal with conditions of the will that may well be beyond the agent's control, for example, lack of will or weakness of will. On this question, I believe that a careful examination of the works of Mencius will provide materials for the construction of an adequate answer (Cua 2002). And related to these internal conditions, there are external ones that affect the exercise of *liangzhi*, again, those that are not subject to the agent's control. *Liangzhi* can successfully mediate between the vision of *ren* and the actual world only if the natural and cultural orders cooperate. There are natural and cultural constraints on the exercise of *liangzhi*, and these constraints may well prevent the agent from realizing that vision in toto. In exploring this question, again, we can learn much from Xunzi and Mencius, and Confucius's attitude toward human fate (*ming*). A contemporary Confucian must thus inquire into the connection between *liangzhi* and fate (*ming*). This inquiry involves a complex, difficult question concerning the relation between *liangzhi* and factual knowledge: in standard neo-Confucian terms, "knowledge of moral nature" (*dexing zhi zhi*) and "knowledge of hearing and seeing" (*wenjian zhi zhi*). Here I shall formulate this as a problem of the relation between moral knowledge and factual knowledge. What Wang says on this problem is quite incisive, but rather incomplete.

According to Wang, "*liangzhi* does not come from hearing and seeing, and yet all hearing and seeing are functions (*yong*) of *liangzhi*. Therefore *liangzhi* is not impeded by seeing and hearing. Nor is it separated from hearing and seeing" (*Instructions*, Sec. 168). In other words, "*liangzhi* is the basis (*tounao*) of learning and inquiry" (Sec. 140). This remark points to a connection between moral knowledge and factual knowledge, but significantly assigns a secondary status to the latter. In this view, factual knowledge or inquiry is relevant to the proper exercise of *liangzhi*, and in turn can yield moral knowledge in the retrospective sense, i.e., the knowledge that an action is in accord with the *tianli* of *liangzhi*. In other words, the moral relevance of factual knowledge is determined by *liangzhi*. From the moral point of view, then, inquiry has an indispensable role in the quest for factual information, and the outcome of this quest will provide the necessary data for deliberation at the time of response to changing circumstances. However, in light of *ren*, the vision of the universe as a moral community, the secondary status assigned to factual knowledge and inquiry may well be questioned. That vision expresses a concern for the existence of things. How, then, can such a concern be indifferent to the need of inquiry into their nature, even if such an inquiry has no direct relevance to moral problems and perplexities? In this connection, one would also think that prior factual knowledge is an indispensable aid in dealing with the changing circumstances of human life. Only the sage can dispense with such knowledge; for ordinary committed agents, factual knowledge is an invaluable aid in dealing with exigent cases. Wang seemed to be aware of this point (passage *O*), but on the whole was uninterested in pursuing the connection between moral knowledge and factual knowledge. It is, however, to his credit to have suggested that *liangzhi* cannot be exercised apart from factual knowledge. (For a perceptive discussion of this issue, see Tang 1978.)

See also Mou Zongsan; *Quan*; *Ren*; *Ti*; *Ti* and *Yong*; *Yi* and *Li*; Zhan Ruoshui; *Zhixing Heyi*.

Bibliography

Note: All quotations from Wang Yangming's *Quanxilu* are translations from Wing-tsit Chan's *Instructions*; some have been emended.

Butler, Joseph. *Fifteen Sermons Preached at Rolls Chapel*. London: Bell, 1953.
Chan, Wing-tsit, trans. *A Source Book in Chinese Philosophy*. Princeton, N.J.: Princeton University Press, 1963.
Chang, Carsun. *Wang Yangming: Idealist Philosopher of Sixteenth Century China*. Jamaica: St. John's University Press, 1962.
Chen, Rongjie (Wing-tsit Chan). "*Li*." In *Zhongguo zhexue cidian daquan*, ed. Wei Zhengtong. Taipei: Shuiniu, 1983
Ching, Julia. *To Acquire Wisdom: The Way of Wang Yangming*. New York: Columbia University Press, 1976.
Cua, A. S. *Dimensions of Moral Creativity: Paradigms, Principles, and Ideals*. University Park: Pennsylvania State University Press, 1978.
———. *Ethical Argumentation: A Study in Hsün Tzu's Moral Epistemology*. Honolulu: University of Hawaii Press, 1985.
———. *Reason and Virtue: A Study in the Ethics of Richard Price*. Athens: Ohio University Press, 1966.
———. "Tasks of Confucian Ethics." *Journal of Chinese Philosophy*, 6(1), 1979.
———. *The Unity of Knowledge and Action: A Study in Wang Yang-ming's Moral Psychology*. Honolulu: University of Hawaii Press, 1982.
———. "*Xin* and Moral Failure: Notes on an Aspect of Mencius's Moral Psychology." In *Mencius: Contexts and Interpretations*, ed. Alan Chan. Honolulu: University of Hawaii Press, 2002.
Graham, A. C. *Two Chinese Philosophers: Ch'eng Ming-tao and Ch'eng Yi-ch'uan*. London: Lund Humphries, 1958.
Kierkegaard, Søren. *Either/Or*, Vol. 2. New York: Anchor, 1959.
Legge, James. *The Li Ki or Collection of Treatises on the Rules of Propriety or Ceremonial Usages*, Vol. 2. Delhi: Moltilal Barnasidass, 1966.
Mou, Zongsan. *Cong Lu Xiangshan dao Liu Jishan*. Taipei: Xuesheng, 1979.
Qian, Mu. *Zhuzi xin xue'an*, Vol. 2. Taipei: Sanmin, 1982.
Raphael, D. D., ed. *British Moralists: 1650–1800*, Vol. 1. Oxford: Clarendon, 1969.
Russell, Bertrand. *Problems of Philosophy*. Oxford: Oxford University Press, 1950.
Tang, Junyi. *Zhongguo zhexue yuanlun, daolun pian*. Taipei: Xuesheng, 1978.
Tu, Weiming. *Neo-Confucian Thought in Action: Wang Yangming's Youth (1472–1509)*. Berkeley: University of California Press, 1976.
Wang, Mengou. *Liji jinzhu jinyi*, Vol. 2. Taipei: Commercial Press, 1977.
Wang, Yangming. *Instructions for Practical Living and Other Neo-Confucian Writings*, trans. with notes Wing-tsit Chan. New York: Columbia University Press, 1963.
———. *Yangming quanshu*. In *Sibu beiyao*. Taipei: Zhonghua, 1970.
———. *Quanxilu xiangzhu jiping*, ed. with annot. Chen Rongjie (Wing-tsit Chan). Taipei: Xuesheng, 1983.
Watson, Burton, trans. *Hsün Tzu: Basic Writings*. New York: Columbia University Press, 1963.
Wittgenstein, Ludwig. *Philosophical Investigations*. New York: Macmillan, 1969.
Zhu, Xi. *Zhuzi yulei*. Taipei: Zhengzhong, 1962.

Wang Yangming (Wang Yang-ming): Rivals and Followers

William Yau-nang Ng

The introduction of the philosophy of Wang Yangming (1472–1529) in the fifteenth century no doubt brought about a climax of neo-Confucianism, a branch of Confucianism that aimed at a revival of Confucius's teaching and had emerged as an identifiable philosophical movement which flourished from the Song dynasty (960–1126) to the Ming (1368–1644). However, Wang rose to prominence in a time when the Cheng-Zhu (or Ch'eng-Chu) school, named after its supposed founders—Cheng Hao (1032–1085), Cheng Yi (1033–1108), and Zhu Xi (1130–1200)—still dominated intellectual life and the school of Chen Xianzhang (1428–1500) had just begun to enjoy growing acceptance in Guangdong Province in southern China. Wang had to face challenges from rivals in both schools.

The major rivals of Wang Yangming were Zhan Ruoshui (1463–1557), Luo Qinshun (1465–1547) and Lu Nan (1479–1542). Zhan, better known as Zhan Ganquan, was a native of Guangtong Province and a disciple of Chen Xianzhang. In 1505, Zhan passed the *jinshi* examination and entered Hanlin Academy, where he met Wang Yangming. The two philosophers soon became friends. However, they differed sharply in their ontology and their ideas of spiritual cultivation. Following the teaching of Chen Xianzhang, his mentor, Zhan carried out a long debate with Wang Yangming over the objective existence of *li* (principle). He criticized Wang's identification of the mind with principle, as having the "internal" (subjectivity) but denying the "external" (objectivity). This ontological difference is reflected in their different approaches to spiritual cultivation. Wang advocated an inner quest for one's own *liangzhi* (innate knowledge of the good), the foundation of spiritual self-perfection; Chan, by contrast, emphasized the "realization everywhere of the heavenly principle" (*suichu tiren tianli*), a phrase that is almost an imprint of Chan's philosophy. Accordingly, the object of reflection in spiritual cultivation was not *liangzhi* alone, but everything under heaven.

Because almost all neo-Confucian scholars wanted to return to the original teaching of the classics, their controversies usually concern textual interpretation; in the case of Wang's philosophy they center on the *Great Learning* (*Daxue*), which together with the *Analects*, the *Mencius*, and the *Doctrine of the Mean* forms the Confucian Four Books. The difference between Wang and Chan stems mainly from their conflicting interpretations of *gewu*, a term established in the *Great Learning*. For Wang, *gewu* means "to rectify one's thought at its very beginning" (*zheng niantou*) and refers to the moral rectification of one's mind. Chan, however, held that it should be interpreted as "to arrive at the principle" (*zhiqili*). Thus, instead of concentrating retrospectively on one's own *xin* (mind-and-heart) as Wang had suggested, Chan emphasized investigating external things in order to grasp the principle. In fact, he offered a different interpretation of *xin*:

> The learning of the sages has always been the learning of mind-and-heart. What we call mind-and-heart does not mean something within us, something in our inner hearts, as opposed to external things. There is nothing that is not mind-and-heart. When Yao and Shun held to the mean, this does not mean only in regard to things: it means that mind-and-heart and things were joined as one.

Wang criticized Chan's position as looking outward for the principle in external things instead of looking inward to one's own mind-and-heart. Chan rejected that position, on the ground that Wang's interpretation had little textual support in the classics. The idea of rectifying one's mind-and-heart, as Chan understood it, was already covered by *chengyi* (making the will sincere), a term that also appears in the *Great Learning*. Wang's interpretation would make repetition in the text unavoidable. More important, Chan held that Wang disregarded the fact that the mind-and-heart as such or by itself does not supply any proof of its correctness. Wang and Chan also contradicted each other over the relation between knowledge (*zhi*) and action (*xing*). Wang maintained the unity of knowledge and action, while Chan believed in the dialectical development of the two.

Both Chan and Wang attracted followers from all over the country. It was recorded in the *Mingshi*, the official history of the Ming dynasty, that all scholars became followers of either Chan or Wang; the only exceptions were Lu Nan and Luo Qinshun, who remained faithful to the teachings of the school of Cheng-Zhu.

Luo Qinshun was a native of Taihe in Jiangxi Province. As mentioned earlier, he was generally regarded as a follower of the school of Cheng-Zhu, though there are significant differences between Luo and Zhu. Luo studied Chan Buddhism in his early years but later attacked it, having become a professed follower of Confucianism. In 1518, Luo wrote to Wang Yangming, voicing some disagreements with Wang. In his debate with Wang over the interpretation of the *Great Learning*, Luo kept close to Zhu Xi's position. The crucial difference lies in Luo's disagreement with Wang's interpretation of *gewu* as the "rectification of mind-and-heart" (*zhengxin*). Luo argued that while it is possible to rectify one's own mind-and-heart, it is impossible to "rectify" mountains, rivers, hawks, and fish. However, these are things, among many others, that also are counted as *wu* in the Confucian classics and thus should also be rectified if one follows Wang's teaching. Luo remarked that Wang's emphasis on the mind-and-heart alone left out all these other *wu* and would thus contradict the *Great Learning*. Such an approach, as Luo understood it, would result in limiting oneself to the interior while "abandoning the exterior" and would come dangerously close to the teachings of Chan Buddhism.

Basically, Luo refused to interpret *wu* as "mind-and-heart" and thus was unwilling to accept Wang's position in taking *gewu* as a kind of introspection—that is, as rectifying one's own mind-and-heart. Rather, he maintained that *gewu* referred to a spiritual horizon which was *tongche wujian*: completely free from any interval and distinction. Following Zhu Xi, Luo also maintained the distinctions between *xin* (mind-and-heart) and *xing* (nature) and resisted Wang's idea of identifying the *xin* with *li* (principle).

In his reply, Wang Yangming insisted that introspection should not be taken as limiting ourselves to the mind-and-heart. Since there is no difference between the principle within ourselves and the principle of the external world, it follows that introspection should not be taken as seeking the principle only within oneself. What Wang Yangming is referring to here as principle is not anything that resembles natural law. He means, instead, moral norms that originate in our mind-and-heart and can also be found in the external world.

Whereas Zhan and Luo focused mainly on *gewu* in their discussions with Wang, Lu Nan disagreed with Wang's doctrine of the "extension of *liangzhi*" (*zhi liangzhi*). Following Zhu Xi's teaching, Lu maintained the doctrine of *gewu* (investigation of things) and *qungli* (exhausting the principles of things).

Lu Nan came from the Guanzhong area, where Zhang Zai (Chang Tsai, 1020–1077), one of the founders of neo-Confucianism in the Song dynasty, still exerted considerable influence during the Ming period. Scholars from this area were collectively referred to as the Guanzhong school in some neo-Confucian writings. Most of the scholars of the Guanzhong school during the Ming remained faithful to the teaching of the Cheng-Zhu school or to a combination of the teachings of the Cheng-Zhu and Zhang Zai schools. Few were convinced by Wang Yangming's teaching.

To repeat, in spite of all this opposition Wang exerted tremendous influence and attracted thousands of followers. However, shortly after the death of the master, the Wang Yangming school split into at least eight "subschools." Huang Zongxi (1610–1695) classified these subschools according to the place of origin of their principal representatives. The following seven are particularly important:

1. Zhezhong (central Zhejiang) school, which included scholars like Xu Ai (1487–1517), Qian Dehong (1497–1574), and Wang Ji (1498–1583).
2. Jiangyou (Jiangxi) school, with Zou Shouyi (1491–1562), Ouyang De (1496–1554), Luo Hongxian (1504–1564), and Nie Bao (1487–1563) as its major figures.
3. Nanzhong (southern Zhili) school, which included scholars like Tang Shunzhi (1507–1560), who came from southern Zhili, the region that comprises much of today's Jiangsu, Zhejiang, and Anhui.
4. Chuzhong (Huguang region) school, which included scholars like Jiang Xin (1483–1559).
5. Beifang (Northern) school, with Mu Konghui (1479–1539) and Meng Huali (fl. 1580) as its major figures.
6. School of Yue and Min (Guangtong and Fujian), which included scholars like Fang Xianfu (d. 1543) and Xie Kan (1486–1545).
7. Taizhou school, which included scholars from Jiangsu. Wang Geng (1483–1588), Luo Rufang (1515–1588), and Geng Dingxiang (1524–1596), among others, are representative thinkers.

Huang's classification became a tradition in neo-Confucian writings, but his regional categories do not necessary reflect philosophical positions. If we look at philosophical variations, the most significant differences are between the Jiangyou school on the one hand and the Zhezhong school and the Taizhou school on the other. Modern scholars usually refer to them as *youpai* (rightist) and *zuopai* (leftist), respectively. That is, the Jiangyou school was "rightist" whereas the Zhezhong school and the Taizhou school were both "leftist."

The most important debate within the Wang Yangming school was, however, initiated by two Zhezhong scholars—Wang Ji and Qian Dehong—who disputed over Wang's well-known "four maxims" (*sijujiao*):

- The absence of good and evil characterizes the *xin*-in-itself.
- The presence of good and evil characterizes the movement of its intentions.
- Knowing good and evil is the capacity of *liangzhi*.
- To do good and to remove evil is *gewu* (the act of rectifying affairs).

These four maxims are certainly abstruse and are open to varying interpretations. In 1527, Wang Ji and Qian Dehong proposed different interpretations and, naturally, asked Wang Yangming for advice. Wang Ji was interested in maintaining the consistency of the four maxims. He held that if *xin*-in-itself (*xinti*) is devoid of good and evil, then its intention would be absent from good and evil as well. Thus Wang Ji declared:

> If we say that *xin*-in-itself is characterized by the absence of good and evil, then [we should be able] to say the same of intentions, of knowledge, and of things [or acts]. And if we say that the [movements of] the intentions are characterized by the presence of good and evil, then [we should also] say the same of *xin*-in-itself.

Clearly, in order to maintain consistency with the assertion that *xin*-in-itself is "neither good nor evil," the idea of the first maxim, Wang Ji had developed the understanding that its intention, its knowledge, and all its acts should be "neither good nor evil."

Qian focused not so much on ontology, the nature of mind-and-heart, as on self-cultivation. He held that neither good nor evil characterized *xin*-in-itself, which was beyond such a distinction. However, one's intentions could be said to be good or evil, and this was the reason why self-cultivation—preserving the good while eradicating the evil—was necessary. The first maxim teaches the innocence and purity of the original state of the mind-and-heart; the other three maxims teach self-cultivation for those whose hearts no longer possess this innocence and purity. Qian emphasized exercises of self-cultivation that, in a sense, accorded with Wang Yangming's doctrine of *zhiliangzhi*.

When presented with this controversy, Wang Yangming declared that both interpretations were correct and should complement each other. Wang Yangming pointed out that Wang Ji's interpretation suited the needs of gifted minds, whereas Qian's was good for those less endowed. Wang Yangming's response was a pedagogical expedient rather than a real answer to the question. After his death, Wang Ji and Qian Dehong continued to develop their philosophies, each along his own lines, and the differences between them became more apparent.

Wang Ji had also asserted that—just like the nature of the mind-and-heart—intentions, knowledge, and things were all devoid of good and evil. The mind-and-heart was thus independent of moral judgments and at the same time the ultimate origin of such judgments. This is known as the theory of the "four negatives" (*siwu*). That position led him to teach what is known as the doctrine of the "ready-made *liangzhi*" (*xiancheng liangzhi*): *liangzhi* is already perfect, and thus no effort at improvement is necessary. What is needed is not an effort to perfect it but efforts to awaken it, and this awakening is best attained by faith in *liangzhi*. Although he continued the neo-Confucian attacks on Buddhism and Daoism, Wang Ji borrowed terminology freely from both religions. He even went so far as to take *liangzhi* as the focal point for integrating the "three teachings." This of course aroused controversy and criticism among his fellow neo-Confucians, including his friends and disciples.

Although Wang Yangming had accepted the "four negatives," he had also reminded Wang Ji that few people in the world have the gift or talent of perceiving the highest reality without considerable effort at spiritual self-cultivation. Wang Yangming had added that concentrating only on meditation would lead to "emptiness and the void," another term for Buddhism and Daoism in neo-Confucian writings. Thus Wang Yangming warned Wang Ji to be cautious in guiding students.

Other criticism came mainly from Ouyang De, Zou Shouyi, Nie Bao, and Luo Hongxian, all members of the Jiangyou school. However, it would be an oversimplification to assume that they took similar positions in their disagreements with Wang Ji. Zou and Ouyang sought to remedy what they saw as abuses of Wang Ji's teaching: the danger of overemphasizing sudden inner illumination of the mind-and-heart while overlooking the importance of efforts at self-cultivation. Luo Hongxian and Nie Bao had a different emphasis: they taught tranquillity in meditation, with the ultimate goal of grasping *liangzhi*. Thus we can see that differences existed even within the Jiangyou school, which, according to Huang Zhongxi, had the honor of being the only true transmission of the way of Wang Yangming. Basically, two lines of thought can be distinguished within the Jiangyou school. Zou and Ouyang can be called the school of *xiuzheng* ("cultivation so as to testify"), since they both emphasized the teaching of cultivation; Luo and Nie can be called the school of *guiji* ("returning to tranquillity").

Wang Ji's teaching became very popular, especially when it was joined with the work of an exceptionally devoted Confucian scholar, Wang Geng, the founder of the Taizhou school, to whom we must now turn.

Wang Geng was perhaps the most charismatic of Wang Yangming's disciples. His life is worth mentioning here, for it is a good illustration of his thought. He came from a family of salt farmers or small salt dealers in Taizhou. His given name was Yin (silver), but he was better-known by a name his mentor Wang Yangmin bestowed on him in 1521: Geng, one of the eight trigrams.

Wang Geng had actually formed his own philosophy before he met Wang Yangming. When he was told there were great similarities between his thought and Wang Yangming's, he set out almost at once to visit Wang Yangming, who was then the governor of Jiangxi. Wearing his archaic costume, Wang Geng met Wang Yangming. He sat in the place of honor, discoursing with Wang Yangming for a long while. Then, feeling abashed, he moved to a lower seat; finally, he begged to become Wang Yangming's disciple. But when he withdrew, he had second thoughts, decided that he must have heard everything there was to hear from Wang Yangming, and regretted his request. The next day, he went to see Wang Yangming again and once more took the seat of honor. Only after a long discussion was Wang Geng fully convinced that he was no match for Wang Yangming. Thus he became Wang Yangming's disciple for the rest of his life.

In 1522, Wang Geng visited Beijing, the capital. There, his bizarre appearance and behavior attracted attention, so Wang Yangming admonished him and told him to return to the south. Wang Yangming censured him severely for his lofty attitude but finally forgave him. Thereafter, Wang Geng then studied closely with Wang Yangming and at the same time helped his master instruct new students. Wang Geng had a talent for bringing others to insights and awakening. He returned to Taizhou after the death of Wang Yangming in 1529 and established a school there, attracting many followers; among them, He Xinyin (1517–1579, original name Liang Ruyuan), Luo Rufang (1515–1588), and Li Zhi (1527–1602) were the most famous.

In spite of the differences between Wang Geng and his followers, their teachings broadly advocated a sort of natural freedom; they encouraged or at least did not hinder the spontaneous expression of feelings. This kind of teaching, in practical terms, led to a deliberate refusal to study, especially for the sake of passing the civil service examinations. These thinkers preferred to approach the classics directly, with no reference to the old commentaries. They valued their intuitive understanding of the classics more than any academic achievement based on scholarly efforts. Because this attitude toward scholarship resembled Chan Buddhism, the Taizhou school was called "Wild Chan" (*kuang chan*). Wild Chan, in a sense, can also be seen as a reaction against the insincerity and corruption that prevailed among Confucian scholars and officials in the late Ming. Some thinkers had a strong will to live as genuine Confucian gentlemen and tried hard to fight against these currents, but quite a number showed no respect whatever for any established tradition.

Li Zhi, a man of independent character noted for his eccentricities, can be counted as a member of the Taizhou school, though he became a follower of Buddhism in his later years. While many people disliked the hypocrisy and injustice of their society, few dared to challenge it openly; but Li Zhi was one of the few. According to legend, Li held that Guan Zhong (d. 645 B.C.E.) was more virtuous than Confucius (551–479 B.C.E.), and that Feng Dao (882–954) was a loyal minister—judgments that went directly against traditional orthodox Confucianism. Later on, when Li became a Buddhist, he went so far as to have his head shaved. His bold teachings and unconventional conduct won him great popularity among the common people but frightened the ruling scholar-officials. He was sent to jail, where he commited suicide. After his death, his thought continued to spread.

It is commonly held that the Taizhou school soon became so popular and so influential that it produced a mass movement of social protest. The teachings of Wang Geng and Wang Zhi provoked critical thinking and eccentric individual conduct in the late Ming. This critical spirit became part of the foundation of the Tonglin movement, which produced the best political critics up to the end of the Ming dynasty. However, the eccentric behavior of these "Confucian scholars" of the late Ming was also severely criticized by the scholars of the Tonglin school. Gu Xianzheng (1550–1612), for example, was worried about the scholars at his time, who strove for the easy and the natural, which did not require any true effort of self-cultivation. Other important followers of the Wang Yangming school, such as Liu Zongzhou (1578–1645) and Huang Zongxi, shared these objections.

Though not completely satisfied with Wang Yangming's teaching, Liu Zongzhou stood in direct opposition to any dualistic thought, especially that of Zhu Xi. He emphasized the priority or primacy of willing over knowing in the moral activities of the mind-and-heart. The emphasis thus shifted from rectification of the mind, the focus of Yangming's interpretation of *gewu*, to sincerity of the will. Liu's teaching of "vigilance in solitude" (*shendui*) also brought about a new understanding of the concept of "substance of nature" (*xingti*).

Liu's disciple Huang Zongxi was a great intellectual historian, perhaps the last great philosopher of the Ming dynasty. After the fall of Beijing, Huang took part in several heroic but vain attempts to restore the Ming empire. The rapid success of the Manchu put an end to his dream of restoration, and Huang spent the rest of his life in almost purely academic pursuits. After compiling the *Mingru xue'an* (*Records of Ming Scholars*) he turned to the *Song Yuan xue'an* (*Records of the Song and Yuan Scholars*). He was unable to finish the *Song Yuan xue'an* before he died, and it was completed at the hands of his son and disciples. These two works are a comprehensive account of neo-Confucian scholars, presenting their biographies and excerpts from their writings. The two works remained the sources most frequently consulted by modern scholars of neo-Confucianism.

Shocked by the collapse of the Ming empire, Huang tried to find an explanation. The result was another important work, his *Mingyi daifanglu* (*Waiting for the Dawn: A Plan for the Prince*), in which he attacked selfish traditional political ideas such as considering the country the possession of the ruler. This work was banned during the Qing dynasty, but it exerted great influence toward the end of the empire, when reformers such as Liang Qichao (1873–1929) made use of it for their political propaganda.

The early Qing period also witnessed a renewed interest in the Cheng-Zhu school. The teaching of Wang Yangming declined in influence, as some scholars held it responsible for the collapse of the Ming. Emperor Kangxi supported research into, and the spread of, Zhu Xi's philosophy. Leading scholars of the time, such as Li Guangdi (1642–1718), Lu Longqi (1630–1693), Lu Shiyi (1611–1741), and Zhang Liuxiang (1611–1674), devoted themselves to studying and disseminating Zhu's work.

Before long, the rise of a kind of scholarship known as *shixue* (evidential research) marked a shift of interest from philosophy to philology among Chinese intellectuals. Scholars who engaged in *shixue* used philology, textual criticism, and epigraphy to study history and the classics. They lost interest in philosophical thinking in general. This also contributed to the decline of Wang Yangming's influence—indeed, Wang's thought did not regain the attention of Chinese intellectuals until perhaps the beginning of the twentieth century.

It is difficult to identify Wang Yangming's followers in the twentieth century. However, there is no doubt that his philosophy is very influential among modern Chinese scholars. He Lin (1902–1995), in his famous *Wushi nianlai di zhongguo zhexue* (*Fifty Years of Chinese Philosophy*), stated that there had been a significant development of the Wang Yangming school in the first half of the twentieth century, and in fact that Wang's teaching was the mainstream of modern Chinese philosophy. He Lin—who himself had once been a follower of Wang Yangming's philosophy—identified Kang Youwei (1858–1927) and Liang Shuming (1893–1988) as other followers and described Xiong Shili (1885–1968) as the great synthesizer of the master's teaching. There is no doubt that these philosophers drew heavily on Wang Yangming's teachings in constructing their own. However, it would certainly be a mistake to overlook the important influence of Zhu Xi on modern Chinese scholars such as Feng Youlan (1895–1990) and Qian Mu (1895–1990).

The period after World War II witnessed the rise of the *dangdai xinruxue*, "contemporary new Confucians," in Hong Kong and Taiwan. Mou Zongsan (1909–1995) and Carsun Chang (1886–1969), among others, were noted for their sympathy and support for Wang Yangming's teaching. Mou's teaching, in particular, inspired a whole generation of young scholars in Hong Kong and Taiwan. Nowadays, Wang Yangming's teaching continues to influence Chinese philosophers and is becoming better understood in the English-speaking world, owing to the contributions of scholars like Wing-tsit Chan, Tu Weiming, Julia Ching, and A. S. Cua.

See also Chen Xianzhang; Liu Zongzhou; Luo Qinshun; Wang Yangming; *Xin*; *Xing*; Zhan Ruoshui; *Zhi*; *Zhixing heyi*.

Bibliography

Note: This bibliography is confined mainly to works in English.

Araki, Kengo, Okada Takehiko, et al. *Yomeigaku benran* (A User's Guide to the Yangming School), Vol. 12 of *Yomeigaku taikei* (A Compendium of the School of Wang Yangming). Tokyo: Meitoku, 1974.

Bloom, Irene, trans. *Knowledge Painfully Acquired: The K'un-chih chi of Lo Ch'in-shun*. New York: Columbia University Press, 1987.

Chan, Wing-tsit, trans. and annot. *Instructions for Practical Living and Other Neo-Confucian Writings by Wang Yangming*. New York: Columbia University Press, 1963.

———. *Religious Trends in Modern China*. New York: Columbia University Press, 1953.

Chang, Carsun. *The Development of Neo-Confucian Thought*, 2 vols. New York: Bookman, 1957, 1962.

———. *Wang Yang-ming: The Idealist Philosopher of Sixteenth-Century China*. Jamaica: St. John's University Press, 1970.

Cheng, Chung-ying. "The Consistency and Meaning of the Four-Sentence Teaching in *Ming Ju Hsueh An*." In *New Dimensions of Confucian Philosophy*. Albany: State University of New York Press, 1991, pp. 481–503.

Ching, Julia. *To Acquire Wisdom: The Way of Wang Yangming*. New York: Columbia University Press, 1976. (See apps. 1 and 2 for a brief discussion of Wang Yangming's philosophy in Korea and Japan. When Wang's teaching spread to those countries, Korean scholars remained almost completely faithful to Chu Hsi, but there were important developments of the Yangming school in Japan.)

Cleary, J. C., trans. and ed. *Worldly Wisdom: Confucian Teachings of the Ming Dynasty*. Boston, Mass.: Shambhala, 1991.

Cua, A. S. "Between Commitment and Realization: Wang Yang-ming's Vision of the Universe as a Moral Community." *Philosophy East and West*, 43(4), 1993, pp. 611–649. (This essay also appears in Cua's *Moral Vision and Tradition: Essays in Chinese Ethics*. Washington: Catholic University of America Press, 1998.)

———. *The Unity of Knowledge and Action: A Study in Wang Yang-ming's Moral Psychology*. Honolulu: University of Hawaii Press, 1982.

de Bary, William Theodore. "Neo-Confucian Cultivation and the Seventeenth-Century Enlightenment." In *The Unfolding of Neo-Confucianism*, ed. W. T. de Bary. New York: Columbia University Press, 1975.

———, ed. *Self and Society in Ming Thought*. New York: Columbia University Press, 1970.

———, ed. *The Unfolding of Neo-Confucianism*. New York: Columbia University Press, 1975.

de Bary, William Theodore, and Irene Bloom, eds. *Principle and Practicality: Essays in Neo-Confucianism and Practical Learning*. New York: Columbia University Press, 1979.

Fung, Yu-lan (Feng Youlan). *A History of Chinese Philosophy*, 2 vols., trans. Derk Bodde. Princeton, N.J: Princeton University Press, 1953.

———. *A Short History of Chinese Philosophy*. New York: Macmillan, 1948.

Goodrich, L. Carrington, and Fang Chaoying, eds. *Dictionary of Ming Biography 1368–1644*. New York: Columbia University Press, 1976.

Huang, Zongxi. *Mingru xue'an. SPPY*. (For selected English translations of this work see Julia Ching, ed. *The Records of Ming Scholars*. Honolulu: University of Hawaii Press, 1987.)

Ji, Wenfu. *Zuopai Wangxue* (The Leftists of the School of Wang Yang-ming). Shanghai: Kaiming 1934. Taipei: Guowen tiandi, 1990. (Reprinted.)

Mou, Zongsan. *Cong Lu Xiangshan dao Liu jishan* (From Lu Xiangshan to Liu Jishan). Taipei: Xuesheng shuju, 1979.

Okada, Takehiko. *O Yomei to Minmatsu no Jugaku* (Wang Yangming and Late Ming Confucianism). Tokyo: Komeisha, 1970.

Shimada, Kenji. *Chugoku ni okeru kindai shii no zazetsu* (The Frustration of Thinking in Early Modern China). Tokyo: Chikuma shobo, 1970.

———. *Shushigaku to Yomeigaka* (The Zhu Xi School and the Wang Yangming School). Tokyo: Iwanami shoten, 1967.

Tang, Junyi. "The Criticism of Wang Yang-ming's Teachings as Raised by His Contemporaries." In *Essays on Chinese Philosophy and Culture*. Taipei: Xuesheng, 1988.

———. "The Development of the Concept of Moral Mind from Wang Yangming to Wang Ji." In *Self and Society in Ming Thought*, ed. W. T. de Bary. New York: Columbia University Press, 1970, pp. 93–120.

Tu, Weiming. "An Inquiry into Wang Yang-ming's Four Sentence Teaching." In *Humanity and Self-Cultivation: Essays in Confucian Thought*. Berkeley, Calif.: Asian Humanities Press, 1979.

———. *Neo-Confucian Thought in Action: Wang Yang-ming's Youth (1472–1509)*. Berkeley: University of California Press, 1976.

———. *Way, Learning, and Politics: Essays on the Confucian Intellectual*. Albany: State University of New York Press, 1993.

Yamashita, Ryuji. *Yomeigaku no kenkyu* (Studies on Wang Yangming: Development of the School). Tokyo: Gendai johosha 1971.

The *Wenzi* (*Wen Tzu*) Treatise

Paul Van Els

The *Wenzi* (*Master Wen*) is a treatise with Daoist hues that consists of 12 chapters with a total of nearly 40,000 graphs. Little is known of the master after whom the book is named. Ban Gu (32–92 C.E.) states in his *Hanshu* that Wenzi was a disciple of Laozi (according to tradition, sixth century B.C.E.), the patriarch of Daoism. Whether or not there existed a Master Wen among the disciples of Laozi, whose historical identity also remains shrouded in mystery, the author or authors of the *Wenzi* certainly felt inspired by Laozi's teachings. Not only is a large portion of the *Wenzi* explicitly attributed to its spiritual mentor (many sections start with the phrase "Laozi said . . ."), but the text also includes numerous citations from the *Daodejing*. The *Wenzi* explains these citations or uses them as authoritative statements to reinforce its own argument. In its development of Laozi's thought, the *Wenzi* readily borrows concepts of pre-Qin texts of entirely different philosophical leanings, including *Mengzi, Xunzi*, and *Guanzi*. The *Wenzi* thus exudes the atmosphere of a text of the late Warring States period or the Han dynasty, as it represents a new, syncretic form of Daoism that is based on the philosophy of Laozi and, to a lesser extent, Zhuangzi, but is also informed by ideas of other philosophical schools.

Textual History of the *Wenzi*

The initial creation of the *Wenzi* took place more than 2,000 years ago, perhaps even in the Warring States period, as many contemporary scholars believe. Between the moment of its creation and the third century C.E., this original *Wenzi* underwent major revisions, in which large amounts of external material (mainly from the *Huainanzi*) were blended into the text. In this new form, the text was transmitted to the present day.

In the centuries following these revisions, the *Wenzi* provoked widely differing opinions among its readers. It was praised for its "sparkling clarity" by the literary critic Liu Xie (c. 465–522) and granted the honorific title *Tongxuan zhenjing* (*True Scripture on Penetrating the Mysteries*) by the Tang emperor Xuanzong (r. 712–756). Soon afterward, however, scholars started focusing on its frequent quotation of other texts and noted that no less than three-quarters of the content of the *Wenzi* also appeared in the *Huainanzi*. Since the vast majority of scholars argued for the historical priority of the *Huainanzi*, the *Wenzi* was commonly branded a forgery and became a marginalized text.

The centuries of neglect abruptly ended in 1973, when a fragmentary bamboo manuscript was discovered in Ding County (Hebei Province), in a tomb dated 56 B.C.E. The unearthed slips contain a copy of the original *Wenzi*, that is, as it had existed before its revision. The manuscript proves that the transmitted *Wenzi* was not a third-century forgery but the revision of an authentic Han or even pre-Han work.

Relationship between *Wenzi* and *Huainanzi*

The discovery made in 1973 also shed light on the relationship between the transmitted *Wenzi* and the *Huainanzi*. It proved what many scholars already suspected, that the former was partially copied from the latter. However, despite a striking mutual correspondence of phrases and even full paragraphs, the *Wenzi* is markedly different from the *Huainanzi*. The *Wenzi* contains original material not found in the *Huainanzi*; what is more, its editors carefully selected those passages from the *Huainanzi* that they deemed suitable for inclusion. Five chapters of *Huainanzi* were thus left untouched. Also, material from *Huainanzi* selected for inclusion was thoroughly revised. Through stylistic and rhetorical changes, such as replacing difficult and dialect words with more common synonyms; deleting, changing, or adding grammatical particles; turning dialogue into monologue; and removing historical anecdotes, the arguments taken from *Huainanzi* were radically transformed, and a new text with its own style and philosophy was created.

Philosophy of the *Wenzi*

The *Wenzi* discusses a wide range of topics, including those now classified as warfare, culture, psychology, ecology, and law. Its overall concern, however, is political. The book's central issue is the one that motivated virtually all pre-Qin masters: how to turn a disorderly society into a well-organized one.

The *Wenzi* resembles other ancient Chinese philosophical texts by displaying a belief in a time when everything was perfect. In Master Wen's eyes, this "golden age" took place in high antiquity, well before the reigns of the (legendary) rulers Fu Xi, Shennong, and Huangdi (*Wenzi*, 12.1). This was the age when the Way (*dao*) reigned supreme: all living creatures dwelled together in peaceful harmony and human beings were still "innocent like children and did not know west from east" (1.10). When culture and intelligence arose, craftiness and desire also cropped up. As a consequence, society gradually deteriorated and ended up in the chaotic situation Wenzi found himself in. Although Wenzi wishes for his world to be more like his ideal, he does not advocate an actual return to this primordial situation of natural order, for that would require one to abandon society and culture and retreat as a recluse to the wilds. Instead, he promotes the application of the principle that ruled the golden age (i.e., the Way) within the framework of present-day society. The obvious person to implement this is the sage, or the exemplary ruler.

According to Wenzi, the ruler is to the state what the heart is to the body. Since a calm body requires a stable heart, an important precondition for good government is to have a healthy ruler. As to the importance of his physical health, the *Wenzi* states that "when his body is not calm, right or wrong have nowhere to be formed" (2.6) and "when his body labors without resting, it collapses" (3.3). More important yet is the ruler's mental condition. If his spirit is not clear and his mind not calm, he will be led by emotions. As a result, influence and profit will entice him, music and sex seduce him, eloquent speakers easily persuade him, and courageous people overawe him. Instead of directing others, he will then be directed by them. Therefore, the *Wenzi* asserts that "being a sage is not in governing others, it is in organizing oneself" (1.4).

The essence of government lies in the interaction between ruler and subjects. As to the latter, Wenzi maintains that "the people are the foundation of the state" (10.8), an idea also upheld by Mengzi and Xunzi, but much less by the early Daoist masters Laozi and Zhuangzi. The importance of the people to the state is stressed throughout the *Wenzi*. Since the people are the source of political authority, the sage, according to Wenzi, loves his people as a father loves his child, worries about their poverty, and has an inborn desire to benefit them. Actions by the sage always correspond to the minds of the people; they are never undertaken out of self-interest. For example, annexing a neighboring state for wealth and natural resources is clearly an act of self-interest, and as such unjustifiable; military expeditions are allowed only when a ruler wants to aid suffering people abroad by deposing their tyrannical sovereign. Thus if a ruler does not attune his actions to the demands of the common people, he undermines his own authority.

As befits a true student of Laozi, Wenzi regards the Way as the most important concept in his philosophical system. In words reminiscent of the four silk manuscripts discovered at Mawangdui, the Way is described as being "too high to reach and too deep to fathom" (1.1); it is an invisible yet all-embracing entity that bestows life on all things. Since the Way can change what has already been carved and polished (i.e., culturally and politically refined) back to its original, uncarved state, it is this principle that the ruler must rely on when organizing his chaotic (carved and polished) nation. To change society, he "instructs the masses by means of the Way and guides them by its power (*de*)" (11.12). In instructing the common people—unlike other types of teaching—no words are used, for the function of words is limited. Facial expressions (*rongmao*) reach where words cannot go, and imperceptible instructions (*ganhu*) reach even further. Therefore, the sage spiritually transforms the masses.

This "spiritual transformation" (*shenhua*) constitutes a type of ruling in which the subjects are unaware of the fact that they are being ruled. Governing through spiritual transformation, the ruler bases all his actions on the Way and executes them with "pure sincerity" (*jingcheng*), i.e., without any hidden motives. This impresses the people, who spontaneously follow his exemplary behavior. Should this prove insufficient, the ruler may then turn to "humaneness" (*ren*) and "righteousness" (*yi*), or even to "rites" (*li*) and "music" (*yue*) and, if absolutely necessary, to arms and weapons. By adopting humaneness and righteousness as key terms in his philosophical system, Wenzi again deviates from his mentor Laozi, in whose text these terms play only a marginal role.

Humaneness and righteousness are expressed mainly through reward and punishment. These should be fair and equal and above all, they should correspond to what the people expect them to be. For example, to punish an entire group for the crime of one of its members is generally considered unfair, and the people will resent a ruler who decides to implement this punishment. Since the expectations of the common people differ across times and cultures, it would be wrong for the ruler to stick persistently to measures such as laws, rules, rites, or punishments that fail to match the particularities of his own time and culture. The ruler may be perfectly humane and righteous, but if he does not adapt these qualities to contemporary needs, he has not yet attained the Way. Sages of the past who did attain the Way used different measures to organize society, and still each was called a sage. This is because they realized that such measures are mere tools for the creation of order and are not that which makes order order. Therefore, on the outside they attuned their measures to the needs of the people of their times, whereas inside they remained forever focused on the unchanging Way.

But the *Wenzi* is not an exclusively political treatise. Its relatively simple style and the universal character of many of its sayings make the book accessible to a broad audience: "When affairs are sparse, they are easy to manage; when desires are few, they are easy to satisfy" (10.6). "When you realize that a fan on a winter day or a fur coat in summer is of no use to you, then all things will turn into dust and dirt" (12.4). "What is charming to the eye or pleasing to the heart, is what the fool considers profitable, but what those who have the Way avoid" (7.14). The scope of sayings such as these easily exceeds theories and practices of politics. In general, the *Wenzi* argues for a lifestyle in accordance with the Way, focusing on important problems rather than insignificant issues, reducing one's desires, and being sincere in one's actions—in other words, a lifestyle of potential appeal to many, both then and now.

See also *Huainanzi*.

Bibliography

Cleary, Thomas. *Wen-Tzu: Understanding the Mysteries*. Boston, Mass.: Shambhala, 1992.

Ding, Yuanzhi. *Huainanzi yu Wenzi kaobian* (Critical Examination of the *Huainanzi* and the *Wenzi*). Taipei: Wan juan lou, 1999.

———. *Wenzi xin lun* (New Essays on the *Wenzi*). Taipei: Wan juan lou, 1999.

———. *Wenzi ziliao tansuo* (Critical Analysis of the *Wenzi* Material). Taipei: Wan juan lou, 1999.

Ho, Che Wah. *Chutu Wen zi xinzheng* (A Study of the *Wenzi* Excavated in Ding County in 1973). *Renwen Zhongguo Xuebao* (Sino-Humanitas), 5, 1998, pp. 151–187.

Kandel, Barbara. *Wen Tzu-Ein Betrag zur Problematik und zum Verständnis eines taoistischen Textes*. Frankfurt: Peter Lang, 1974.

Lau, D. C. *A Concordance to the Wenzi*. Chinese University of Hong Hong (CUHK) ICS, Ancient Chinese Text Concordances Series. Hong Kong: Commercial Press, 1993.

Le Blanc, Charles. *Le Wenzi à la lumière de l'histoire et de l'archéologie*. Montréal: Presses de l'Université de Montréal, 2000.

Li, Dingsheng, and Xu Huijun. *Wenzi yaoquan* (Explaining the Essence of the *Wenzi*). Shanghai: Fudan daxue chubanshe, 1988.

Ryden, Edmund. "The 1996 *Wenzi* Conference held at Fujen University." *Early China News*, 9, 1996, pp. 24–26, 28, 29.

Wuwei (*Wu-wei*): Taking No Action

Chad Hansen

Laozi's famous slogan has puzzled interpreters for centuries and has given rise to numerous interpretations. Arguably, Laozi knew it was paradoxical, since the complete slogan is *wuwei* and yet *wu* not-*wei*. The first character is not the main problem. *Wu* is simply "does not exist." In this phrase, however, interpreters treat it as a negative prescription: "avoid *wei*." Chinese texts include many similar uses, and we commonly read other declarative sentences in the *Laozi* as prescriptions. So let us take it as saying that one should lack *wei*—whatever that is. The harder problem is to understand *wei*.

Textbook interpretations say that *wei* means "purpose." In modern Mandarin, the character has two different tones. The fourth tone reading is usually translated as "for the sake of." In the second tone reading, the character would normally be translated as "to act." Thus, translators argue, *wuwei* (or *wu-wei*) really means no purposive action. The whole slogan is "no purposive action and yet do act."

The second tone reading, however, has another important use. Grammar textbooks call it the putative sense—"to deem, regard, or interpret." *Wei* functions in this sense in belief ascriptions. In classical Chinese, unlike English, belief and knowledge, as contexts, did not entail grammatically parallel constructions such as "believe that *P*" and "know that *P*." In Chinese, the grammatical object of "to know" was either a noun phrase, "he knew Kelly's-having-eaten-the-rice," or a verb phrase: "he knew (how) to defer to authority." The closest counterpart of a claim about belief like "*A* believed that *T* was *P*" was the structure: "*A yi* (with, using) *T wei* (interprets, regards, deems it as) *P*." A more common way of asserting the same thing was simply to write "*A P*s *T*" where *P* becomes a transitive verb. (In Chinese, no inflection marks such changes in parts of speech.)

Wei also figures, in a related way, in some contexts involving knowledge. Usually the counterpart of propositional knowledge is "*A zhi* (knows) *T*'s *P*-ing." However, when the embedded predicate is a noun phrase, the form changes to "*A zhi* (knows) *T*1's *wei*-ing (counting as, or perhaps amounting to) *T*2." The tempting parallel to verbal contexts is "*A* knows-to interpret (deem) *T*1 as *T*2."

A related variant adds a "human" radical to *wei*. Typical translations of this character include "artificial" and "false." It corresponds to the important contrast between *tian* (nature) and *ren* (humanenss). *Wei* is something done by humans rather than something "natural." This variant is central particularly in the Confucian text *Xunzi*, which contrasts the conventional *dao* handed down through tradition with natural behavior. The *si* (thought) of the sage kings is *wei* (a product of artifice, not nature). Other homophones related in meaning include the archaic linking verb *wei* (only-is) and the verb *wei* (to call, to name).

If we think of "to deem or regard" as a component of Laozi's use of *wei*, it will help us explain his doctrine better than the analysis in terms of purpose. Little in the *Laozi* suggests any theory of voluntary, deliberate, or purposive action that could motivate one's objecting to it. The translators' glosses (and later tradition) import a Buddhist or western opposition of reason versus desire or emotion. Emotions disrupt rational processing. Thus, in Indo-European thought giving mind and ideas a privileged position over heart and feelings normally implies a favorable attitude toward intellect and knowledge. Laozi, however, attacks knowledge as much as (or more than) he attacks desires. Indo-European thought links mind or ideas to language and stresses the incommensurability of feelings. Laozi, by contrast, opposes desires precisely because of their link to language.

The key to understanding the slogan, then, may be to study the suggestive links between *wei*, knowledge, desires, and names. The *Zhuangzi* portrays Laozi as following Shen Dao in opposing knowledge. Shen Dao, however, does so on what looks like a Stoic or fatalistic ground. The *Zhuangzi* suggests that Laozi accepted the slogan "abandon knowledge" but rejected the fatalistic basis.

The *Zhuangzi* also notes a paradox in Shen Dao's position. It was a *dao* that could not *dao* (guide us); that is, logical determinism has no implications for behavior. "Abandon knowledge" is itself knowledge of the type it seemingly rejects, i.e., guidance or advice. To follow it is to disobey it. The "inner chapters" of the *Zhuangzi* mostly avoid the slogan *wuwei*. It is far more frequent in the "outer chapters," which were influenced by the *Laozi*.

We will, accordingly, develop Laozi's alternative reason for using the slogan "abandon knowledge": his theory of names. The core idea is that ordinary (guiding) knowledge is based on names and thus relies on social conventions. Daoism is suspicious of social conventions (favored by Confucianism). Allowing conventions to control us amounts to losing our natural spontaneity.

The basic Confucian model required that to follow conventions, we have to "rectify" names. That is, we must interpret things in the environment as being of the type mentioned in the *Book of Rites*. The model of "knowledge" combined mastery of a text of instructions with the ability to apply its names in guiding our action. Interpreting (*wei*) is done in acting (*wei*).

Laozi's analysis uses his famous contrast theory of "names" (descriptive terms). Learning a word requires learning its opposite. To learn a name (*X*) is to learn how to make a distinction between what is *X* and what is not-*X*. For each distinction, there are two "names." Laozi highlights the distinctions between beautiful and ugly, good and not good, and existing and not existing. The model arouses suspicion that the way we divide the world up into things reflects social convention. When our parents teach us a name, they correct our usage until we make the distinction in the accepted, inherited, conventional way. We come to regard those distinctions as natural, but looking at their genesis provokes doubt.

Notice, further, that we do not count terms as having been learned unless we guide our action in the "normal" way with them. For example, merely using "beautiful" and "ugly" in describing works of art the same way our parents and teachers do will invite further "teaching." If we prefer the ugly, our teachers will correct us. Learning a name implicitly draws learning to desire properly in its wake.

Along with the distinctions, then, we learn socially appropriate desires. This is most clear when we consider purely evaluative distinctions like good and not good. The guidance is more context-dependent when it involves more "world-guided" evaluative terms such as "beautiful," "brave," and "wise." We could make the same observation about seemingly nonevaluative distinctions such as "before-after" and "elder-younger," since they figure in descriptions of appropriate ritual action.

Laozi's metaphor for this complex analysis is his invitation to be like the "nameless, uncarved, *pu*" (block, wood, simplicity) that he says is simply freedom from desire. The antidote to socialization is to reverse the process that instills the names, distinctions, and desires. To pursue learning is to add to every day; to pursue *dao* is to forget every day. We forget and forget until we return to the simplicity of a newborn child.

Therefore, mastering a language is learning an appropriate set of unnatural desires and distinctions. The socially constituted desires ruffle our natural tranquillity and engender competition and strife. They distort and constrain our natural spontaneity. A Daoist's objection to desires is not that they interfere with intellect but that they are conventional. The objection stems from the contrast between nature and convention rather than from a contrast between reason and emotion. Implicitly, unlike Buddhism, Laozi does not object to such "natural" desires as the desire for food, sex, and physical comfort. The "cultured" or "sophisticated" desires cause the trouble.

"Knowledge" is the combined result of names, distinctions, desires, and *wei*—acting toward a thing according to conventional categories. We deem or interpret it to be something mentioned in a learned rule and treat it accordingly. To *wei* is thus to act on social conventions. To lack *wei* is to escape the constraints of socialization of our desires, distinctions, and names. We are to avoid acting toward something on the basis of the name we give it or the conventional category to which we assign it. Implicitly, natural actions are acceptable.

Laozi's "solution" may avoid fatalism, but it still conceals a paradox. As suggested above, Laozi probably noticed this and adopted the more complicated formula: *wuwei* yet *wu* not-*wei*. The paradox arises because Laozi, like Shen Dao, is trying to advise us to avoid linguistic-based advice. Following Laozi's advice requires that we apply contrasting terms ("conventional" and "natural") in a particular way. We identify language with conventions rather than nature. Then we adopt an unnatural desire (valuing the natural) and finally act out of that desire.

The action is seeking to "forget" knowledge and return to the state of the uncarved block. The problem arises when we try to not-*wei*. We must interpret or deem something to count as *wei* and something else as not-*wei*. Laozi's philosophy thus can work only like Wittgenstein's ladder. When you have seen the point, you have to throw it away. To avoid *wei* we must avoid avoiding *wei*. The famous opening of the *Laozi* may be a rationalization that the paradox is inescapable for any *dao* that guides us (*dao* used as a verb). "Any *dao* that can *dao* is not a constant *dao*, [because] any name that can name is not a constant name."

What we should do after we get the *wuwei* insight and throw it away is hard to say—which is probably why Laozi did not say it.

As we have noted, the early parts of *Zhuangzi* hardly mention the slogan. However, its use in the later writings in the text invites us to construct a *Zhuangzi* version of the slogan. This usual view associates *wuwei* with the *Zhuangzi*'s ideal of skillful behavior that becomes second nature. The most famous model was the butcher who had the grace of a dancer when he carved oxen. Such behavior requires a focus and absorption that is incompatible with ordinary self-consciousness, purpose, and rehearsal of instructions. We experience mastery as "becoming one with the activity."

The *wuwei* ideal also informs the neo-Daoist slogan "Sage within; king without." It suggests (following Zhuangzi) that the Daoist *wuwei* may be consistent with being a good Confucian. Being a scholar-official is as much a skill as being a butcher, and one may practice it with the same attitude of inner emptiness. As long as one takes the "right" attitude, one may pursue any activity consistent with Daoism. Neo-Daoists conform to Confucian roles without regarding or interpreting them as ultimately right—or as anything else.

With the importation of Indo-European Buddhism from India, *wuwei* started to be interpreted by means of the western conceptual apparatus contrasting desire or purpose and reason. This shaped the modern Chinese interpretation and probably undermined the ideal. It became a target of attacks from "modern" Chinese who regarded Daoist "nonstriving" or "purposelessness" as the source of Chinese passivity. The activist reformer Kang Youwei (Kang "have-*wei*") took the denial of the slogan as his scholarly name.

See also Daoism: Classical; Daoism: Neo-Daoism; Kang Youwei; Laozi; Shen Dao; *Shifei*; *Xu*; *Youwu*; Zhuangzi.

Bibliography

Chan, Wing-tsit, trans. *A Source Book in Chinese Philosophy*. Princeton, N.J.: Princeton University Press, 1963.

Chen, Guying. *Laozi: Text, Notes, and Comments*. San Francisco, Calif.: Chinese Materials Center, 1977.

Fung, Yu-lan (Feng Youlan). *The Spirit of Chinese Philosophy*. London: Routledge and Kegan Paul, 1947.

Hansen, Chad. *A Daoist Theory of Chinese Thought*. New York: Oxford University Press, 1992.

Lau, D. C., trans. *Laozi: Tao Te Ching*. Baltimore: Penguin, 1963.

Wu, Yi. *Chinese Philosophical Terms*. Lanham, Md.: University Press of America, 1986.

Wuxing (Wu-hsing): Five Phases

John B. Henderson

Like the more famous duality *yin-yang*, the mature concept of *wuxing* was concerned mainly with describing and explaining processes of change in various realms ranging from the human body to the body politic to the heavenly bodies. The active nature of the *xing* is suggested by its etymology as a verb that means "to do," "to act," "to move," "to set in motion." But the superficial similarity between the *wuxing*—wood, fire, earth, metal, and water—and the "four elements" of the ancient Greek philosophy of Empedocles (c. 495–435 B.C.E.) led some earlier western sinologists to conceive of them simply as material substances corresponding more or less to their counterparts in the state of nature. This misconception, in turn, made it hard to appreciate the dynamic qualities of the *wuxing*, as well as their wide use in areas of human endeavor ranging from natural science to political science. An "interdisciplinary" idea of comparable range and importance (as well as malleability) in the modern west might be the theory (or theories) of evolution.

The mature cosmological conception of the five phases did not proceed fully formed from the brow of Zou Yan (c. 305–240 B.C.E.) or some other cosmologist of the late classical period. Its antecedents, in the form of quinary sets, may be traced as far back as the Shang era (c. 1700–1045 B.C.E.), for example in the set of the four quarters plus the center. Throughout the subsequent Zhou period (c. 1045–256 B.C.E.), however, sets based on five by no means dominated the cosmological landscape. Such classical sources as the "*Zuo* Commentary" (*Zuozhuan*) and the *Documents Classic* (*Shujing*) record numerologies based on three, four, six, eight, nine, ten, and twelve as well. Working from Durkheimian assumptions regarding the social basis of cosmological thought, the great French sinologist Marcel Granet (1950) went so far as to link some of these orders with particular social groups or classes: five with the peasants, six with the nobility, and three with the urban military class. Although peasants did not triumph in classical China, quinary sets did overshadow their classical rivals by early Han times. These quinary sets, however, were not at first necessarily subsumed under the *wuxing*. As John Major (1993) has pointed out, in the thought of late-classical cosmologists of the third century B.C.E., fives were usually specified as "five materials" (*wucai*) or "five powers" (*wude*).

Although *wuxing* as used by Chinese cosmologists of the Han and later refers most commonly to phases or processes of change, early occurrences of the term do seem to point more concretely to material constituents. In the enormously influential chapter "Great Norms" (*Hongfan*) in the *Documents Classic, wuxing* apparently refers to substances which are conceived in terms of their functional attributes: "Water is said to soak and descend; fire is said to blaze and ascend; wood is said to curve or be straight; metal is said to obey and change, earth is said to take seeds and give crops." Such a characterization of material substances, such as metal, in terms of their functional attributes, however, opened the way for a more abstract (or operational) rendering of *wuxing*. For example, various entities, ranging from dynasties to medicines, which had the quality of "obeying and changing," could be categorized as "metal," even though they might lack any material resemblance to the texture or substance of metal.

The *wuxing* having been characterized more abstractly in terms of their functional attributes, they could be more easily and generally linked with one another to describe and explain processes and cycles of change. To give a simple example from the "Great Norms" quoted above, "water" and "fire" could be linked as the "descending" and "ascending" phases of natural (or historical) processes. Cosmologists of the Han era (202 B.C.E.–220 C.E.) linked all five of the phases in series that they used to describe an ordered sequence or complete cycle of changes, such as the succession of ruling dynasties from high antiquity to the present. Two of the most popular of these sequential orders were the "mutual production" and "mutual conquest" series; cosmologists used both of them to account for the sequence by which dynasties succeeded one another.

According to the "mutual production" order, wood produced fire, fire produced earth, earth produced metal, metal produced water, and water produced wood. In the "mutual conquest" series, on the other hand, wood conquered earth, metal conquered wood, fire conquered metal, water conquered fire, and earth conquered water. Thus a dynasty whose emblem was water, for example, might expect to be overcome by one whose emblem was of earth. But while the water-borne dynasty remained afloat, it was supposed to adopt rituals, emblems, and even policies that were properly correlated with its patron phase, all of which could be mapped out in complex tables of correspondence. Hence, the determination of the one of the five phases corresponding to a reigning dynasty could be a matter of considerable political and ritual import. Under the Han dynasty, debates over the proper phase correlate of that dynasty led to four changes in its patron phase. On two of these occasions, the Han actually adopted a different color of ritual paraphernalia and a calendar beginning in a different month, both of which had to correspond to the newly inaugurated phase. Such maneuvers, in turn, enhanced the dynasty's aura of legitimacy. In fact, one of the advantages the five-phases conception had over rival numeric-cosmological orders in the Qin-Han era (221 B.C.E.–220 C.E.) was that it offered a convincing way to legitimize a new dynasty. What might appear on the surface to be a case of political usurpation could be more reasonably presented as a change brought about by an ineluctable and predictable cosmological process based on the order of nature.

Dynastic politics and ritual were not the only fields in which five-phases conceptions found practical applications. They were also applied in areas ranging from family relations to medical remedies. For example, the *Comprehensive Discussions in White Tiger Hall* (*Baihu tongyi*, c. 80 C.E.), a cosmological compendium of the Han era, provides the following explanation for why a mature son should remain with his parents while a daughter should leave home, based on the mutual production order of the five phases:

> The son not leaving his parents models himself on what? He models himself on fire that does not depart from wood. The daughter leaving her parents models herself on what? She models herself on water which by flowing departs from metal.

On the other hand, the "mutual conquest" series of the five phases was generally more favored in medicine. A disease associated with a certain energetic phase might be overcome by a medicine correlated with the phase that conquered it. Thus, for example, a "cooling" drug associated with water, which "conquered" fire, might neutralize a febrile disease.

While the more striking and significant use of the *wuxing* in postclassical Chinese thought was in explaining configurations and processes of change in various realms, it remained the basis for quinary numerological arrangements by which various entities, ranging from colors to seasons to plants to planets, were classified into sets of five. The canonical *Record of Rites* (*Liji*), in fact, mentions sixty-two such quinary sets, even the five turnings of the royal boat. These quinary sets, moreover, were sometimes correlated with one another in ways that were more or less natural or commonsensical. For example, cosmologists paired the wood phase with the color green and the spring season, fire with red and summer, and so forth. Inasmuch as such paired members of different sets shared a common vital force (*qi*), they could even resonate or interact with one another, much like two separate sets of pitch pipes. This opened up the possibility that humans could affect the natural order by performing appropriately harmonizing acts. For example, by wearing ritual vestments of green and eating from vessels of wood, the sovereign might promote the generative powers of spring.

In sum, the *wuxing*, in addition to providing a description and explanation of processes of change in various realms, also furnished an energetic field that related these realms to one another in a way that prescribed how man might harmonize them. Although some of the relations and harmonies of the world may strike us as rather forced or artificial, they were one of the chief bases of a sense of cosmos that endured from late classical times to the twentieth century. The demise of this cosmos, this "good order," or its devolution into mere "superstition," is one of the most pervasive and traumatic cultural changes of the modern era of Chinese history.

See also Cosmology.

Bibliography

Allan, Sarah. *The Shape of the Turtle: Myth, Art, and Cosmos in Early China*. Albany: State University of New York Press, 1991.

Bodde, Derk. *Chinese Thought, Society, and Science: The Intellectual and Social Background of Science and Technology in Pre-Modern China*. Honolulu: University of Hawaii Press, 1991.

Granet, Marcel. *La pensée chinoise*. Paris: Éditions Albin Michel, 1950.

Henderson, John B. *The Development and Decline of Chinese Cosmology*. New York: Columbia University Press, 1984.

Karlgren, Bernhard, trans. *The Book of Documents*. Göteborg: Elanders Boktryckeri Artiebolog, 1950. (Reprinted from *Bulletin of the Museum of Far Eastern Antiquities*, No. 22.)

Major, John S. *Heaven and Earth in Early Han Thought: Chapters Three, Four, and Five of the Huainanzi*. Albany: State University of New York Press, 1993.

Needham, Joseph. *Science and Civilisation in China*, Vol. 2, *History of ScientificThought*. Cambridge: Cambridge University Press, 1956.

Sivin, Nathan. *Traditional Medicine in Contemporary China*. Science, Medicine, and Technology in East Asia, No. 2. Ann Arbor: Center for Chinese Studies, University of Michigan, 1987.

Tjan, Tjoe Som, trans. *Po Hu T'ung: The Comprehensive Discussions in White Tiger Hall*. Sinica Leidensia, Vol. 6. Leiden: Brill, 1949. (See also reprint, Westport, Conn.: Hyperion, 1973.)

中國哲學

X

Xi Kang (Hsi K'ang)

Alan K. L. CHAN

Xi Kang (223–262 or 224–263 C.E.; the surname Xi is commonly pronounced "Ji" in modern Chinese) cuts a striking figure in the history of Chinese philosophy. A brilliant musician and poet, a master of "pure conversation" (*qingtan*), an iconoclast, a model of integrity and a tall, handsome man by all accounts, Xi was one of the most influential neo-Daoist thinkers of his age. Leader of the "seven worthies of the bamboo grove," a group of prominent intellectuals who challenged the Confucian orthodoxy during the Wei-Jin transition, Xi played a significant role in shaping the neo-Daoist agenda in the second phase of its development.

The initial flowering of neo-Daoist philosophy may be said to have come to an end in 249 C.E., when a power struggle between the two main factions at court came to a head, resulting in the death of He Yan—a dean of the "learning of the mysterious" or "profound learning" (*xuanxue*), as neo-Daoism is known properly in Chinese—and scores of others. Wang Bi, the star of the early neo-Daoist movement, died in the same year. The Wei government then fell under the control of the Sima clan, at the expense of the imperial house of Cao. A series of bloody but futile revolts against the Sima regime followed, until the establishment of the Jin dynasty in 265. In the words of a later historian, this was a time when few intellectuals of note (*mingshi*) were spared a violent end.

Xi Kang was related to the Cao family by marriage. Not once did he bow to the dictates of the Sima government. Likened to a "sleeping dragon" threatening the regime, he was eventually imprisoned and sentenced to death. Several thousand students of the imperial academy reportedly petitioned for his release. Before the execution, as traditional sources further relate, Xi remained calm and perfectly composed; as the final hour approached, he asked for a *qin* (zither, or lute according to some translators) and gave a parting performance, lamenting only that the tune he played would now die with him. Later scholars throughout Chinese history who found themselves similarly engulfed by forces of disorder would often look to Xi and draw inspiration from his courage and integrity.

Xi Kang's extant writings include a collection of sixty poems, the influential essay "Rhapsody on the Zither" (*Qinfu*), and fourteen other essays. These last—the most important of which are available in English in a fine translation by Robert Henricks—not only are crucial to an understanding of Xi's thought but provide a good introduction to the third-century Chinese intellectual scene as a whole. It is worth noting that Xi did not leave behind any commentaries on the Daoist classics, although he openly acknowledged Laozi and Zhuangzi as his "teachers." Most of Xi's extant essays originated in the context of debates, which gained currency in "pure conversation" as a genre of philosophical discourse rivaling the more established medium of commentary. Xi's corpus also includes a biographical work, or rather an anthology of legends: *Shengxian gaoshi zhuan* (*Biographies of Sages and Extraordinary Men*), which survives in an edition reconstituted during the Qing dynasty. This work is of greater historical than philosophical interest but nonetheless should not be overlooked, for it bears indirectly on Xi's famous discourse on "nourishing life."

The key to Xi Kang's neo-Daoist philosophy lies in the concept of *ziran*, naturalness, spontaneity, or literally "what is of itself so." This is a general concept, which serves to depict the perceived inherent order of the Daoist universe. While it is central to *xuanxue* as a whole, different interpretations can be discerned that help demarcate the internal division within neo-Daoism.

There is no disagreement that the order of *ziran* stems from the *dao*, the source of all creation. What this means, however, invites debate. Unlike Wang Bi, who has a stronger metaphysical bent and traces the created order to the fundamental concept of "non-being," Xi's approach remains essentially cosmological, making use of ideas long established since the Han dynasty.

Put simply, the origin of the Daoist cosmos is to be understood in terms of *qi*, the vital energy that creates and sustains life. Undifferentiated yet complete, the "original energy" (*yuanqi*) gave rise to the transformation of *yin* and *yang*, from which heaven and earth, the five phases or elements (*wuxing*), and the "ten thousand things" in turn ensued. Boundless and formless, the *dao* can indeed be described as "no-thing" or "nonbeing" (*wu*). The more important point, however, is that the emptiness of *dao* is now shown to mean the fullness of *qi*.

This basic understanding extends to all aspects of Xi's thinking. Things are what they are because of the quality and quantity of *qi*-energy they possess. The doctrine of *ziran* suggests that at birth, all individuals receive an endowment of energy of varying abundance and richness, which defines their nature and capacity. This explains why some people are blessed with long life or exceptional talents, while others must endure certain natural disadvantages. The fact that one may be gifted in some ways but deficient in others testifies to the presence of different powers informing each individual.

In his essay "On Intelligence and Courage" (*Mingdan lun*), Xi thus disputes the claim that those who possess intelligence or discernment are sure to have courage. Arising from a different determination of *qi*, the two "cannot produce each other." Although these words do not refer explicitly to the larger debate on the relationship between talent or capacity (*cai*) and nature (*xing*)—one of the most important in "profound learning"—they address the same issue. Undoubtedly, Xi Kang would have distanced himself from the view that nature and capacity are "identical" or that they "coincide." This is all the more evident because the main proponents of that view aligned themselves politically with the Sima camp.

While most people are born with a mix of strengths and weaknesses, the logic of *ziran* does allow the possibility of perfect endowment. Viewed in this light, sages and worthies must be regarded as extraordinary beings energized by the purest form of *qi*. For the same reason, Xi defended the possibility of immortality, a popular ideal in religious Daoism. Any hasty reduction of the Daoist vision to a skeptical naturalism devoid of spiritual significance must be resisted. Nevertheless, while perfect destiny (*ming*) cannot be ruled out, in no way should it be attributed to the hidden hand of an omnipotent divine agent. Rather, the argument is that "naturalism" should be expanded to include the "supernatural"; or more precisely, that such a distinction collapses in the realm of *dao*, that both the sacred and the mundane spring from the transformation of *ziran*.

So defined, neither sagehood nor immortality can be achieved through effort or learning. But the doctrine of *ziran* does not necessarily entail a kind of "fatalism" that dismisses all effort. Immortality may be beyond reach, but as Xi Kang explains in his essay "On Nourishing Life" (*Yangsheng lun*), self-cultivation can substantially enhance one's physical and spiritual well-being. Specifically, breathing exercises, dietary measures, and the use of drugs can help maximize the limits of one's natural endowment and bring about rejuvenation and long life. Incidentally, the use of drugs was widespread among the literati during the Wei-Jin period. Historical sources unanimously report that Xi Kang was a connoisseur of drugs.

Thus, in terms of self-cultivation, significant differences in degree can be pursued even if they do not amount to differences in kind. This same insight underlies Xi's debate with his friend Ruan Kan on whether good and bad fortune are associated with one's place of residence. The debate arose when Xi objected to Ruan's claim that destiny has little to do with one's dwelling. A total of four exchanges (probably out of six) between the two are preserved in Xi's collected writings.

Xi did not set out to defend geomancy. The debate is not about whether houses can be built in such a way as to ensure good fortune. In rejecting any link between destiny and one's residence—i.e., that residence can alter the course of destiny—Ruan was in fact affirming the belief that destiny is entirely predetermined. In contrast, reflecting a more dynamic view of *ziran*, Xi's argument is twofold.

First, since the Daoist universe as a whole is constituted of essences of *qi*, some places presumably have a stronger concentration than others. For example, the fertility of the soil in any given area is a measure of its allotment of energy. Thus it is conceivable that some places are so rich—in terms of the quality of thie air or water, for example—that they can contribute directly to the well-being of residents. In any event, given our lack of knowledge, a point that Xi emphasizes in these and other essays, one should not arbitrarily close one's mind to the possible wonders of nature.

Environmental conditions can play a positive role in the determination of fortune. But the more important argument is that such conditions can be made more conducive to personal and social development. Having fertile soil alone is not sufficient; one must constantly ensure that it is not overrun with weeds, that the young shoots are not harmed by insects, and so on. To take a modern example, although some may argue that creativity cannot be taught, it does not follow that the conditions for creativity cannot be made more favorable. In this way, Xi sought to work out an ethical theory recognizing the facticity of *ziran*, but nonetheless not repudiating the place of human effort.

Effort must not be confused with artificial discipline or self-assertive control. From the neo-Daoist perspective, effort is always defined in the light of *ziran*. This brings into view Xi's critique of Confucian orthodoxy. Restrictive, and therefore unnatural, Confucian learning and other practices will only prove counterproductive to the project of nourishing life. Xi Kang in fact devoted an essay to refuting the widely held view that people "naturally delight in learning" (*ziran haoxue*). Fondness for learning, which presupposes diligence and wilful restraint, is an acquired trait; it does not come naturally to ordinary human beings, whose need to preserve energy predisposes them to repose.

From this essay, it also becomes clear that the concept of *ziran* is closely tied to a Daoist philosophy of history, which envisages a process of decline from a pristine "beginning" of simplicity and wholesome goodness. Echoing the *Laozi*, Xi Kang writes, it is only when the "great *dao*" fell into disuse—i.e., when selfishness and strife rendered natural, prereflective kindness something out of the ordinary—that benevolence and rightness came to govern human consciousness. In this sense, Confucian learning reflects a loss of naturalness in a world dominated by self-interest. In another essay, "On Dispelling Self-Interest" (*Shisi lun*), Xi brings out further the practical implications of a philosophy of *ziran*.

Being without self-interest means at the very least that one is completely open about one's feelings and intentions. This does not guarantee moral purity—truthfulness may be accompanied by arrogance, for example—but it reflects a mind-heart (*xin*) no longer burdened by praise or blame, approval or censure, and other self-centered concerns. Conversely, veiled motives and hidden feelings invariably involve a calculus of gain and loss, and this calculus corrupts nature even if it involves moral ventures.

Ideally, in the case of a Daoist sage endowed with perfect nature, complete openness and purity coincide. For the majority, however, self-interest poses an obstacle to the realization of *ziran*. From this perspective, nourishing life thus takes on a deeper ethical meaning. Although breathing exercises and the use of drugs to enhance *qi* may be useful, ultimately all "effort" must be directed at dispelling self-interest. To dispel self-interest and in this sense attain utmost "emptiness," it is necessary to confront the root problem of desire. The way of naturalness means precisely freedom from the tyranny of desire.

Desires are harmful to both body and mind. Purity of being, in contrast, entails the absence of desire or any form of emotional disturbance. In this context, Xi Kang can hardly avoid the question whether all desires are unnatural. His essay on nourishing life in fact led to a critique by Xiang Xiu, the celebrated commentator on the *Zhuangzi* and a fellow member of the "seven worthies of the bamboo grove," for whom desires arise naturally from the mind-heart. As such, they cannot be eradicated; rather, affects and appetites can only be regulated by means of ritual action and rules of propriety.

In reply, Xi Kang points out that although anger and joy, and the desire for fame and beauty, may stem from the self, like a tumor they do not serve the interest of personal well-being. Basic needs are of course not to be denied, but desires are shaped by objects and reflect cognitive distortions that blind and consume the self. To quench one's thirst, one does not desire to drink the whole river. This is fundamentally different from the desire for power and wealth, which allows no rest.

Further, the suppression of desire by artificial means may remove certain symptoms, but it does not cure the disease. Only by recognizing the harmful influences of desire can one begin to seek calmness and emptiness of mind. Ultimately, nourishing life is not only a matter of health and longevity; it sets its sight on a higher—and to Xi Kang, more authentic—mode of being characterized by dispassion.

It is in this sense that Xi Kang advocated going beyond the norms of tradition—especially the orthodox teachings of Confucianism (*mingjiao*)—and relying on *ziran*. Far from giving rein to desire, and equally opposed to any repressive regime to rein in one's natural impulses, naturalness offers an alternative that purports to, as it were, throw out the dirty bath water of self-interest without harming the baby, i.e., the authentic core within.

The emphasis on nourishing life means that careful tending is required to preserve one's nature. Extending the metaphor of the bath water, not taking baths is not a genuine Daoist option, for neglect breeds corruption and disease. Yet radical surgery is also not the answer, for it is predicated on the wrong assumption that destiny can be altered at will. Nature as a whole conforms to general laws, or what Xi Kang calls "necessary principles" (*biran zhi li*), which reflect the very workings of the *dao*. In the final analysis, notwithstanding differences in degree which can be cultivated, it is nature that dictates who we are and what we ought to do.

Xi Kang's thesis of "nourishing life" wielded considerable influence among neo-Daoists. The same is true of his theory that emotions are foreign to music—or literally, that "sounds do not have [in them] sorrow or joy" (*sheng wu aile*). If emotions and desires are not intrinsic to nature, and since sounds are naturally produced by the vibration of *qi*-energy, it cannot be maintained that music embodies sorrow or joy, as traditional Chinese musical theory generally assumed. Subjective and cognitive reactions, in other words, should be distinguished from what is natural and objective; otherwise, Xi argues, one can hardly account for the fact that the same piece of music may invoke different responses from different audiences.

At the ethical level, music can be a powerful aid to nourishing life. This is because music can articulate harmony, which would render conditions more favorable for the mind-heart to dispel self-interest. If music is intrinsically tied to desire and emotion, it cannot be of much therapeutic value to Xi Kang's ethics of naturalness.

Later neo-Daoists were to identify "nourishing life," *sheng wu aile*, and "words and meaning" as the three main topics of "profound learning." That Xi was at the center of the first two provides additional proof of his stature.

Concerning the last, the debate has to do with whether "words can fully express meaning" (*yan jin yi*). Many neo-Daoists considered language insufficient for understanding, in the sense that words and images remain on the surface and do not exhaust the deeper meaning of a text. Indeed, as Wang Bi puts it, the words must be forgotten before meaning can be understood; otherwise, understanding would stop short at the level of signs pointing to the real destination.

Xi Kang did make use of the same idea in his essays, but his focus is always on the fact of *ziran*. Words are but signifiers; contingent and culture-specific, they are not fixed entities. What must be brought to light is the order of nature that stands beyond the vagaries of interpretation and subjective experience. This is closely related to his musical theory, and it is somewhat different—family resemblances notwithstanding—from the emphasis on direct illumination, a sudden apprehension of meaning, which some neo-Daoists appear to favor.

Xi Kang is often depicted as a radical iconoclast. Whether this translates into a reclusive and "antipolitical" stance remains a question. Compared with Wang Bi and Guo Xiang, another important neo-Daoist, Xi certainly seems less inclined to accommodate Confucian insights in his vision of *ziran*. There is also little question that he was politically frustrated and disillusioned. Yet the impression that nourishing life stands in direct opposition to political involvement may not be entirely accurate.

The natural order encompasses basic social institutions such as the family and the state. In his "Family Admonition" (*Jia jie*), Xi instructs his children to uphold integrity in both private and public life. In an essay devoted to the teachings of government (*Taishi zhen*), Xi admits that rulership has a basis in the natural order. Respect for elders and abiding by kindness are not contrary to *ziran*; that is, so long as they do not become deliberate acts with a view to personal gain.

There is thus no evidence to suggest that Xi supported anarchism, a view to which not a few neo-Daoists were attracted. Xi might have preferred a life of "free and easy wandering," to borrow a metaphor from the *Zhuangzi*—historical sources do relate that he sought the company of recluses and "extraordinary men"—but this does not mean that he was unconcerned with the politics of his day.

In another essay (*Guan Cai lun*), Xi attempts to rehabilitate two nobles of the Zhou dynasty—lords Guan and Cai—who had been condemned by orthodox historians for their opposition to the duke of Zhou. No reader would fail to detect the real criticism beneath the historical pretext, directed at the Sima regime. This is not the work of a man who rejected politics as a matter of principle; rather, it suggests an engaged intellectual who would stop at nothing to make known the truth as he saw it.

In the end, if the natural order were allowed to flourish, if desire and self-interest were uprooted, and if careful nourishing were applied to remove interference especially of the Confucian and legalist variety, society would attain harmony of its own accord. Despite the tragic circumstances of his life, Xi Kang proves, in his faith in the power of *ziran*, far more sanguine than some scholars may allow.

See also Daoism: Neo-Daoism; Daoism: Religious; Guo Xiang; Wang Bi.

Bibliography

Balazs, Etienne. "Nihilistic Revolt or Mystical Escapism: Currents of Thought in China during the Third Century A.D." In *Chinese Civilization and Bureaucray*, ed. H. M. Wright. New Haven, Conn., and London: Yale University Press, 1964, pp. 226–254.

Bauer, Wolfgang. "The Hidden Hero: Creation and Disintegration of the Ideal of Eremitism." *Individualism and Holism: Studies in Confucian and Taoist Values*, ed. Donald Munro. Ann Arbor: Center for Chinese Studies, University of Michigan, 1985, pp. 157–197.

Dai, Ming-yang. *Xi Kang ji jiao-zhu* (Critically Annotated Edition of Xi Kang's Collected Works). Peking: Renmin chubanshe, 1962.

Henricks, Robert G. "Hsi K'ang and Argumentation in the Wei." *Journal of Chinese Philosophy*, 8, 1981, pp. 169–221.

———, trans. *Philosophy and Argumentation in Third-Century China: The Essays of Hsi K'ang*. Princeton, N.J.: Princeton University Press, 1983.

Holzman, David. "La poésie de Ji Kang." *Journal Asiatique*, 248(1–2), 1980, pp. 107–177; 248(3–4), 1980, pp. 323–378. (Reprinted in David Holzman. *Immortals, Festivals, and Poetry in Medieval China*. Aldershot Ashgate Variorum, 1998.)

———. "Les sept sages de la forêt des bambous et la société de leur temps." *T'oung Pao*, 44, 1956, pp. 317–346.

———. *La vie et la pensée de Hsi K'ang*. Leiden: Brill, 1957.

van Gulik, R. H., trans. *Hsi K'ang and His Poetical Essay on the Lute*. Tokyo: Sophia University in cooperation with Tuttle, 1968.

Mather, Richard. "The Controversy over Conformity and Naturalness during the Six Dynasties." *History of Religions*, 9, 1969–1970, pp. 160–180.

———, trans. *Shih-shuo Hsin-yü: A New Account of Tales of the World*. Minneapolis: University of Minnesota Press, 1976.

Yin, Xiang, and Guo Quan-zhi. *Xi Kang ji zhu* (Annotated edition of Xi Kang's Collected Works). Anhui: Huangshan shushe, 1986.

Yü, Ying-shih. "Individualism and the Neo-Daoist Movement in Wei-Chin China." In *Individualism and Holism: Studies in Confucian and Taoist Values*, ed. Donald Munro. Ann Arbor: Center for Chinese Studies, University of Michigan, 1985, pp. 121–155.

Xiao (*Hsiao*): Filial Piety

Kwong-loi SHUN

Xiao, or filial piety, describes a relation to parents that the Confucians regard as the basis for both self-cultivation and the political order. It is highlighted in the three major pre-Qin Confucian texts: the *Lunyu* (*Analects*, recording Confucius's teachings), the *Mengzi* (*Mencius*), and the *Xunzi*. Two collections of essays probably dating from the early Han—the *Xiaojing* (*Treatise on Filial Piety*) and the *Liji* (*Record of Rites*)—as well as the *Zhongyong* (*Centrality and Commonality*), which was originally a chapter in the *Liji*, also contain detailed discussions of *xiao*. As presented in these texts, *xiao* is based on a sense of continuity with one's parents and ancestors and a devotion to furthering such continuity. It involves a heightened awareness that one not only owes one's existence to parents and ancestors but also has been shaped by them to become the kind of person one is. It involves a devotion to further the continuity by looking after one's body and by having offspring, as well as by carrying out the wishes and projects of parents and ancestors.

The attitudes toward parents, *qin*, involved in *xiao* are characterized in terms of love, *ai* (*Mengzi*, 7A.15) and seriousness or reverence, *jing* (*Lunyu*, 2.7; cf. *Mengzi*, 4A.19). *Ai* involves a concern to promote the well-being of parents as well as affective responses to their condition, and *jing* involves constantly treating them with attention, caution, and reverence. While such attitudes should also be directed to other human beings, they take a special form when directed to one's parents. This special form of the attitudes is sometimes characterized as *qinqin*, "treating as parents one's parents" (*Mengzi*, 7A.15, 7A.45). It involves constantly bearing one's parents in mind in one's daily life. For example, one keeps in mind the parents' ages, both taking joy in their living to an old age and being concerned about their deteriorating health (*Lunyu*, 4.21).

One does not act in any way that endangers them (*Mengzi*, 4B.30), and one avoids traveling far and keeps them informed of one's whereabouts so as to avoid causing them unnecessary concern (*Liji*, 1.4A–5A; *Lunyu*, 4.19). One provides for their daily necessities with respect (*Lunyu*, 2.7; *Mengzi*, 4A.19) and devotes oneself to serving them in other ways (*Lunyu*, 1.7), such as taking up chores for them so that they do not exhaust themselves (*Lunyu*, 2.8). One seeks to please them (*Mengzi*, 4A.12, 4A.28, 5A.1) and to ensure that they are contented in their daily life (*Liji*, 8.23A–23B).

The special obligations one has toward one's parents are defined by *li* (rites), rules that regulate conduct between people in different social positions. The rules of *li* also extend to the way children treat their parents after the parents' death, including burying them properly, mourning them sorrowfully shortly after their death, and subsequently continuing to offer regular sacrifices to them with reverence (*Liji*, 14.18B; *Lunyu*, 2.5; *Mengzi*, 3A.2). One's obligations to parents also extend to the way one conducts oneself throughout one's life. One should care for one's own physical body, which one has received from parents and ancestors (*Liji*, 14.14B–15A; *Xiaojing*, 1.2A) and should have offspring to ensure the continuation of the family line (*Mengzi*, 4A.26, 5A.2). One should also seek to continue the way of one's parents (*Lunyu*, 1.11, 4.20). One should love and respect those whom one's parents love and respect (*Liji*, 8.23A–B); in the case of a ruler who has succeeded his father, *xiao* involves continuing the father's past policies as well as employing the officials that the father employed, when appropriate (*Lunyu*, 19.18; cf. *Zhongyong*, chs. 18, 19). One should cultivate oneself and conduct oneself properly to avoid causing disgrace to one's parents and ancestors (*Liji*, 1.5A, 14.6A, 14.13B, 14.14B–15A; *Xiaojing*, 8.1B). More positively, one should conduct oneself in a way that brings honor to them, such as through achievements that will be remembered by later generations (*Xiaojing*, 1.1B–2B); the greatest honor one can bring to one's parents is to establish oneself as a true king, bringing peace and order to the empire (*Mengzi*, 5A.4; cf. *Zhongyong*, ch. 17).

While emphasizing serving and obeying parents, the Confucians also stress that one's relation to parents should be regulated by a sense of what is proper (*yi*). One should remonstrate with parents when they are in the wrong, although one should do this gently and without offending them (*Liji*, 14.14AB, 15.17A; *Lunyu*, 4.18; *Xiaojing*, 7.2B). So genuine *xiao* is not a matter of blind obedience; it involves being ready to dissent when obedience would involve improper behavior, especially behavior that endangered or disgraced one's parents (*Xunzi*, 29.2–6). One may even violate a rule of *li* in exigencies. The legendary sage king Shun, for example, did not observe the *li* of informing his parents before marrying because, if he had done so, he would not have received permission to marry and so would not have been able to have offspring, this being itself a serious violation of *xiao* (*Mengzi*, 4A.26, 5A.2). In this regard, one's relation to parents is like an official's relation to the ruler—while the Confucians advocate devotion (*zhong*) to the ruler, the devotion is regulated by a sense of what is proper (*yi*) in that one should be ready to remonstrate with and even disobey a ruler who is in the wrong. A difference, though, is that while one may quit office when the ruler does not heed one's remonstrations, the parent-child relation is inescapable. If one's parents are not responsive to one's remonstrations, one should continue to be respectful to them, although one will at the same time be moved by sorrow and may even be reduced to tears (*Liji*, 1.27A).

The importance the Confucians attach to *xiao* can be partly explained by their belief that special affection for parents is a natural response to the care and nourishment one has received from them. In response to a question about prolonged mourning for deceased parents, Confucius explained that one naturally has affection for one's parents from whom one has received care and nourishment, and that one simply cannot enjoy good food or clothing for a certain period after their death (*Lunyu*, 17.21). Mencius also referred to the natural affection young children have for their parents (*Mengzi*, 7A.15), and even Xunzi, who emphasized the self-regarding desires of human beings, acknowledged that human beings share love for those of their own kind as well as remembrance of and longing for the deceased (*Xunzi*, 19.93–127). Such affection for parents is deep-rooted and difficult to alter; it is also a respectable part of the human psychology that the ideal human life should accommodate.

Another reason for the Confucians' emphasis on *xiao* is that they regard it as a basis for both self-cultivation and the political order. Given the actual social setup, the family is the place in which one first acquires love and respect for others; self-cultivation involves nurturing such attitudes toward parents and other family members and then extending them to others outside the family. Thus Confucius described *xiao* and *ti* (obedience to elder brothers) as the basis of humaneness, *ren* (*Lunyu*, 1.2); and Mencius described affection for parents and respect for elder brothers as the basis of *ren* and propriety, *yi* (*Mengzi*, 7A.15). The *Xiaojing* (7.1A) also describes *xiao* and *ti* as not confined to the family but as manifested in one's daily interactions with others, because their natural extension leads to respect for others' parents and elder brothers.

Xiao is also the starting point for developing proper attitudes in government, such as devotion to the ruler (*Xiaojing*, 7.1B) and not being arrogant when in a high position or disorderly when in a low position (*Xiaojing*, 6.1A–B). Furthermore, Confucius and Mencius believed that the proper purpose of government is to "rectify" people in the sense of transforming their character, and this purpose is achieved through the transformative power that pertains to a good character (*Lunyu*, 2.1, 2.3, 12.17, 12.19, 13.4, 13.13; *Mengzi*, 4A.20; cf. *Mengzi*, 4A.4, 7A.19). As the starting point for cultivating one's own good character, *xiao* is also the basis for political order. The close link between proper attitudes toward parents and the political order is emphasized by both Confucius and Mencius (*Lunyu*, 1.2, 8.2; *Mengzi*, 4A.11, 4A.28; cf. *Mengzi*, 4A.5, 4A.12) and is reflected in the remark by Zengzi, a disciple of Confucius's, that the people will be transformed as long as those in power attend cautiously and properly to the burial of parents and sacrifices to ancestors (*Lunyu*, 1.9). The link is also reflected in Confucius's own observation that participation in government need not involve actually taking office but can be a matter of exerting one's influence through *xiao* (*Lunyu*, 2.21).

See also *Li*: Rites or Propriety; *Ren*; *Yi (I)* and *Li*.

Bibliography

Liji (Record of Rites). (References are by volume and page numbers to the text in Zheng Xuan's commentary in the *Sibu beiyao* Series.)

Lunyu (Analects). (References are by book and passage numbers to Yang Bojun, trans. *Lunyu yizhu*. Beijing: Zhonghua shuju, 1980; modern Chinese. See also D. C. Lau, trans. *Confucius: The Lun Yü*, London: Penguin, 1979.)

Mengzi (Mencius). (References are by book and passage numbers—with book numbers 1A to 7B substituted for 1 to 14—to Yang Bojun, trans. *Mengzi yizhu*. Beijing: Zhonghua shuju, 1984; modern Chinese. See also D. C. Lau, trans. *Mencius*. London: Penguin, 1970.)

Xiaojing (Treatise on Filial Piety). (References are by volume and page numbers to *Xiaojing Zhushu* in the *Sibu beiyao* Series.)

Xunzi. (References are by chapter and line numbers to the text in Harvard-Yenching Institute Sinological Index Series. See also John Knoblock, trans. *Xunzi: A Translation and Study of the Complete Works*, 3 vols. Stanford, Calif.: Stanford University Press, 1988–1994.)

Zhongyong (Centrality and Commonality, or Doctrine of the Mean). (References are by chapter numbers, following Zhu Xi's division of the text, to James Legge, trans. *Confucius: Confucian Lun Yü, The Great Learning and the Doctrine of the Mean*, 2nd ed. Oxford: Clarendon, 1893.)

Xin (*Hsin*): Heart and Mind

John BERTHRONG

Xin, or the mind-heart, is at the center of many diverse aspects and philosophic schools of the Chinese intellectual world. Although the graph for *xin* has not yet been found on any oracle bone inscriptions, the term occurs in bronze castings and other archaic forms of early Chinese script. The bronze rendition of the mind-heart is truly graphic, representing the mind-heart as a physical organ; and the *Shuowen*, the most ancient Chinese dictionary, confirms the reading of *xin* as a physical organ. The term is also found in some of the earliest classical texts, such as the *Book of Poetry* and the *Yijing* (*Yi jing*, *I Ching*). Because of these ancient origins, it is not surprising that *xin* became a significant and debatable philosophic concept among the various schools of the Warring States period, and among the Confucians, Daoists (Taoists), and Buddhists who inherited and expanded the philosophic heritage of classical China.

In fact, the whole range of later meanings were latent in the way the mind-heart was discussed in the early classical literature. As the eclectic *Lüshi chunqiu* notes, the mind-heart is the central organ or repository for the human being. Very quickly the mind-heart becomes identified with the emotions and volition, the will to maintain a course of action, the notion of being in charge of the person's ability to make appropriate decisions, and the notion of being the seat of wisdom as well as emotion. In fact, the term becomes identified with both the emotional and the cognitive aspects of human life early in its philosophic career. This is the reason that it is now often translated as "mind-heart"—an English neologism that captures the dual role of *xin*.

The *Yijing* views the mind-heart as the organ of volition, including resolve or agreement. The *Book of Poetry*, as one would expect, often highlights the emotional nature of the mind-heart, although it means more than just the identification of a particular emotional state and depicts the motions of the mind-heart as emotions and judgments. What is developed from these early usages is the root metaphor of the mind-heart as responsive emotionally and intellectually to the world and all its pleasant and unpleasant vicissitudes.

Furthermore, the *Yijing* also notes that the mind-heart can be decisive, so that two people share an intention or commitment. It is easy to see how this idea of resolve shades off into the emotion of commonality or agreement between people. A person is moved to agree with someone else; this agreement is founded on an emotional movement, empathy, even reciprocity or concord between the people. Again, it is not then hard to see, on the basis of the responsiveness and resolve of the mind-heart, that the idea of intelligence, wisdom, and discernment as choice or purpose became part of the intentional mix. The mind-heart was not only an organ of emotion, response, and will but also the seat of deliberation. Here the emotional flavor of intention fuses with the discrimination of response to suggest the future history of the mind-heart as the human organ capable of rational discourse and wise self-cultivation as well as the seat of sentiments, both tranquil and agitated.

As Benjamin Schwartz notes, even in the earliest stratum of Chinese philosophical literature, the mind-heart combines the intellectual qualities of rationality, deliberation, and emotional response that become themes of the mind as agent of reason and the heart as the organ of the emotions. Schwartz cites two examples from the *Analects* to demonstrate the great semantic range of *xin*. First, Confucius noted that Yan Hui, his favorite disciple, did not allow his mind-heart to stray from humaneness for three months (*Analects*, 6, Sec. 5). This indicates that the mind-heart is a repository for human virtue. Second, Confucius affirmed that "at seventy I followed my mind-heart's desire without overstepping the line" (*Analects*, 2, Sec. 4; modified from Lau 1992). Hence the mind-heart is the reservoir of human desire as well as virtue; and both, as Confucius also explains, need to be guided by careful thought.

While Confucius points toward the well-conducted mind-heart that is at the center of Confucian reflection, the *Guanzi* shows that *xin* was also part of early Chinese medical and physical lore, and hence intimately connected to the dynamics of *qi* (or *ch'i*). The *Guanzi* is an eclectic work, and its various sections provide the foundation for both Confucian and Daoist notions of the mind-heart as the mysterious prince of the senses, the place where the emotions and thought are regulated and wherein the entire psychophysical reality is guided. "The magical *ch'i* [*qi*] in the heart/Now comes, now passes away,/If the heart is capable of maintaining stillness,/The Way of itself will be fixed" (Graham 1989, 102). Within the main line of the Confucian tradition, Mencius later pondered and extended the idea, found first in texts such as the *Guanzi*, that the four good seeds of mind-heart can be successfully cultivated so as to control the power of the floodlike *qi* as the dynamic, passionate aspect of human nature.

Of course, Zhuangzi rejects this Confucian search for the mind-heart as a sort of fundamental ruler of the person. The mind-heart is able to respond to the things of the world, but why should that ability make it a fit master of the other sense organs or of the person? Zhuangzi makes the point that although we seek a ruler for the self, and although the mind-heart is the Confucian choice for such a ruler, this quest does not make it the ruler. In fact, everything is spontaneously so of itself, and this holds true for Zhuangzi's view of the mind-heart, a view that informs most later philosophic Daoist views of *xin*.

In a typical Confucian response to Zhuangzi's Daoist vision, Xunzi wrote about the mind-heart as part of his theory of self-cultivation. His carefully crafted discussion about how to dispel the obstructions of the mind-heart skillfully mixes elements he learned from the Mohist logicians with the Confucian traditions and Zhaungzi's naturalism. Xunzi argues that we need to overcome our tendency to be distracted by the two pulls which dominate our mental and emotional lives: the external world and the wonderful machinations of our own reactions to the world. For Xunzi, heart-mind is the "ruler of the body and master of godlike intelligence." Responding to the question "What do men use to know the Way?" Xunzi says, "It is the mind. How does the mind know? I say by emptiness, unity, and stillness" (Knoblock 1994, 3:104). The mind is empty because it never ceases to entertain new thoughts and old memories; it is unified because it does not allow the understanding of one thing to obstruct the understanding of another; and it is still because it does not allow dreams and illusions to disturb its proper functioning. Ultimately the mind-heart is free to balance right and wrong and cannot be compelled to accept something the way the body can be physically coerced.

When the Chinese philosophic tradition creatively confronted the Buddhist challenge to its world after the second century C.E., it produced uniquely Buddhist readings of the perennial question of the functioning of the mind-heart. Of course, ideas analogous to the mind-heart were at the core of pan-Buddhist philosophies imported into China from central and south Asia. For instance, there is a whole tradition called the "mind-only" or "consciousness-only" school that became a staple of Chinese Buddhist speculation.

The Awakening of Faith, a fundamental Chinese philosophic text, picks up where Xunzi leaves off; it argues that we must learn to deal with the mind-heart before we can even contemplate the wonders of liberation for the sake of *nirvana*. The treatise points out that our normal human consciousness is deluded and needs to be purged of false thinking in order for the person to understand the role of the undeluded, fundamental "one" mind or consciousness of liberation. Only when we have identified the dualistic, defiled mind-heart can we understand that our true mind-heart, the mind of enlightenment, is no different from the root cause of suchness, liberation itself. The treatise teaches that our fundamental mind-heart is pure in terms of its own ultimate self-reference, but it is always conjoined with defiled states of the mind-heart in need of the medicine of enlightenment.

The great neo-Confucian reformer Zhu Xi (1130–1200) provided a considered Confucian response to the Chinese Buddhist interpretation of the mind-heart. His response was based on a careful consideration of the teachings of his masters of the Northern and Southern Song (Sung). According to Zhu, the mind-heart unifies human emotions and normative principles within the person. Countering the Buddhists' claims, Zhu and the neo-Confucians see the mind-heart as part of the mundane world, although they mean the special part of the world that is capable of understanding moral principles. In fact, the mind-heart mediates between what heaven (*tian, t'ien*) gives as our essential human nature and the various portions of matter-energy randomly allotted to us as individual human beings.

Zhu says that the mind-heart resides at the center of our being as a unifying force balanced between emotion and principle. "Nature consists of principles embraced in the mind, and the mind is where these principles are united. Nature is principle. The mind is its embracement and reservoir, and issues it forth into operation" (Chan 1963, 631). The mind-heart is the true master of the person whether in stillness or action, and never more so than when it recognizes and carries out the true moral principles of the *dao* (*tao*).

Dai Zhen (1724–1777) believed that Zhu Xi's understanding of the Confucian mind-heart was too abstract. According to Dai, the mind-heart is not linked to some realm of abstract principle. Rather, the mind-heart finds its proper balance when it responds to concrete things and does so in terms of the virtue of reciprocity. Principle is found nowhere else than in the events and affairs of daily life. The role of the mind-heart is to clarify our fundamental human emotions and to bring them into accord with the virtues of humanity and righteousness.

Debates about the nature of the mind-heart continue even now, as the peoples of east Asia ponder their extensive philosophic heritage. Modern Daoists, Buddhists, and Confucians still speculate on the nature of the mind-heart even as they engage in dialogue with western philosophic, religious, and psychological traditions.

See also Confucianism: Constructs of Classical Thought.

Bibliography

Chan, Wing-tsit. *A Source Book in Chinese Philosophy*. Princeton, N.J.: Princeton University Press, 1963.

Graham, A. C. *Disputers of the Tao: Philosophical Argument in Ancient China*. La Salle, Ill.: Open Court, 1989.

Hakeda, Yoshito S., trans. *The Awakening of Faith, Attributed to Asvaghosa*. New York: Columbia University Press, 1967.

Knoblock, John. *Xunzi: A Translation and Study of the Complete Works*, 3 vols. Stanford, Calif.: Stanford University Press, 1988–1994.

Lau, D. C., trans. *Confucius: The Analects* (*Lun yü*). Hong Kong: Chinese University Press, 1992.

Schwartz, Benjamin I. *The World of Thought in Ancient China*. Cambridge, Mass.: Belknap Press of Harvard University, 1985.

Xing (*Hsing*): Human Nature

Kwong-loi SHUN

The character *xing*, often translated as "nature," was derived from the character *sheng*, meaning "life," "growth," or "to give birth." The earlier use of *xing* probably referred to the direction of growth (*sheng*) of a thing, and in pre-Qin texts *xing* and *sheng* are sometimes used interchangeably. Later, *xing* came to acquire other related meanings. In the historical records *Zuozhuan* and *Guoyu*, there are several references to enriching the *xing* or the *sheng* of the common people, often in the context of talking about their material well-being; also, material deprivation is described as a failure to protect the *xing* of the common people. This shows that *xing* is used also in early texts to refer to livelihood, understood in terms of basic human needs and desires. In addition, there are references to certain aggressive tendencies as the *xing* of the petty person (*xiaoren*) and to a desire to rise to a high position as the *xing* of certain people, as well as a reference to the *xing* of those who enjoy fat meat and millet. In these occurrences, *xing* refers to particular tendencies characteristic of the things under consideration. In all these usages, *xing* has a dynamic connotation, referring not to fixed qualities but to directions of growth, to desires, or to tendencies characteristic of a thing.

Among pre-Qin philosophical texts, *xing* occurs only rarely in the *Lunyu* and the *Mozi*, though it was a prominent notion in the Yangist movement, of which Yangzhu (fifth to fourth century B.C.E.) is a representative figure. Scholars have identified five chapters of the *Lushi chunqiu* as recording ideas belonging to later developments of the Yangist movement, and these chapters use *xing* interchangeably with *sheng*. On the basis of these chapters, we can see that the Yangists viewed *xing* or *sheng* primarily in terms of health and longevity and regarded it as the proper course of development of human beings, to which other activities should be subordinated. Different views about *xing* emerged in the late fourth and early third century B.C.E. One, represented by the chapter *Jie* in the *Guanzi*, retained a conception of *sheng* as constituted by the life forces but saw it as without direction and advocated giving it a direction by imposing on it propriety (*yi*), probably understood in Confucian terms. Another, represented by the chapters *Neiye* and *Xinshuxia* in the *Guanzi*, regarded the vital energies (*qi*)—the energies that fill and give life to the body—as already having an ethical direction, probably understood in Confucian terms, and advocated quieting the heart (*xin*) through Confucian practices to allow the vital energies to respond freely. Two other views of *xing* during that period are found in the *Mengzi* (*Mencius*) and the *Zhuangzi*.

In the *Mengzi*, *xing* is often used interchangeably with *qing* (fact, what is genuine, emotions). Although *qing* later acquired the meaning "emotions," it was used in the *Mengzi* primarily to refer to certain features characteristic of things of a kind, revealing what such things are really like. When the features are tendencies of each individual thing of that kind, such tendencies can also be referred to as *xing*. The difference between *qing* and *xing* is that *qing* emphasizes the fact that these things have certain characteristic tendencies, which are difficult to alter and reveal what these things are really like, whereas *xing* emphasizes the presence of such tendencies—tendencies that are subject to all kinds of influences and can be nourished or harmed—as part of the constitution of these things. Mencius, in opposition to the Yangists and his contemporary and adversary Gaozi, advocated viewing *xing* primarily in terms of an ethical direction that the heart already has. This ethical direction of the heart is realized in the Confucian way of life, which involves abiding by and shaping one's life in accordance with the norms and values that govern traditional social arrangements. The *xing* of all human beings is good (*shan*) in that it already points in an ethical direction, and this distinguishes Mencius's position from other views current during his time, including Gaozi's view that *xing* comprises biological tendencies (including eating and having sex) and is ethically neutral, the view that the *xing* of human beings comprises both good (*shan*) and bad (*bushan*) elements, or the view that some human beings have a good *xing* and some a bad *xing*.

Xing does not occur in the seven "inner chapters" of the *Zhuangzi*, which are generally agreed to represent the teachings of Zhuangzi of the fourth century B.C.E. It does occur in other chapters, and *xing* is supposed to be preserved by making the heart vacuous in the sense that the heart does not give direction to the vital energies (*qi*), allowing those energies to respond freely. Confucian teachings, which uphold the existing social setup, are seen as doing violence to *xing*, just like the kind of preoccupation with worldly goods that the Confucians themselves opposed; ideally, one should free people from moral teachings as well as from desires for worldly goods so as to preserve their *xing*. *Qing* is often used in conjunction with *xing* to refer to what human beings are really like, although it is also used occasionally to refer to the kind of emotional responses that can harm oneself.

When *xing* is used to refer to tendencies characteristic of a thing, as in the *Mengzi*, it need not connote that the thing is born with such tendencies. For example, the aggressive tendencies that constitute the *xing* of the petty person may well be something this person acquired in the process of becoming petty. However, although the character *xing* itself does not have this connotation, the *xing* of human beings probably does comprise tendencies that human beings are born with—if such tendencies are truly characteristic of human beings, then human beings would already have such tendencies at birth. The *Zhuangzi* on one occasion refers to *xing* as what a thing is born with, and this characterization of *xing* becomes explicit in the *Xunzi*, which describes *xing* as that which is as it is from birth, is due to *tian* (heaven, nature), and is not learned or acquired by effort. *Qing*, though also used in the *Xunzi* to refer to characteristic features of a thing revealing what the thing is really like, is frequently used to refer to emotions, such as liking and disliking, pleasure and anger, sorrow and joy. Xunzi emphasized self-regarding desires and emotions in his characterization of *xing*, describing *xing* as evil (*e*) in the sense that, when not regulated by the heart, the pursuit of satisfaction of such desires and expression of such emotions will lead to strife and disorder. The traditional social arrangements that the Confucians advocate are justified as serving to regulate and transform such desires and emotions, thereby bringing about order and making possible the appropriate satisfaction of desires and expression of emotions.

By the Han dynasty (206 B.C.E.–220 C.E.), it had become common to view *xing* as what pertains to human beings by birth and *qing* as the emotions, though there were extensive disagreements about how the two are related and whether *xing* and *qing* are good (*shan*) or evil (*e*). Dong Zhongshu (c.179–104 B.C.E.) held that, just as the natural order operates through the interaction of the two forces *yin* and *yang*, there are both greed and humanity (*ren*) in human beings. He sometimes wrote as if humanity can be traced to *xing* and greed to *qing*, implying that *xing* is directed to goodness and *qing* to evil. This view was opposed by several Han thinkers, including Liu Xiang (c.79–8 B.C.E.), Wang Chong (first century B.C.E.), and Xun Yue (148–209 C.E.). Liu Xiang argued that *xing* and *qing* are related rather as the inner to the outer—*xing* is what is in a person and not yet manifested, while *qing* is the outward manifestation of *xing* when human beings come into contact with things. Whereas Xun Yue endorsed Liu Xiang's view, Wang Chong opposed it, arguing that *xing* also concerns the way human beings respond to situations. Regarding whether *xing* is good or evil, Dong held that *xing* is not yet good but has the beginnings of goodness, whose realization depends on awakening by the king. Yang Xiong (53 B.C.E.–18 C.E.) believed that there is both good and evil in *xing*. Both Wang Chong and Xun Yue believed that different human beings have different *xing*, some good and some evil. Despite these differences, the Han thinkers shared an emphasis on the changeability of most people, advocating education to transform the people and edicts and punishment to control the evil tendencies.

In the Wei dynasty (220–265 C.E.) and the Jin dynasty (265–420), the thinking of several scholars was developed on the basis of a study of early Daoist texts. One representative is Guo Xiang (d. 312), who wrote an influential commentary on the *Zhuangzi*, either borrowing from or building on a commentary by Xiang Xiu (fl. 250). Developing ideas in the *Zhuangzi*, Guo Xiang advocated letting everything follow its *xing* without interference. However, different human beings have different *xing* suited to different roles in society; for example, some have a *xing* appropriate to rulers and some a *xing* appropriate to officials. Accordingly, it is in the *xing* of human beings to occupy different social positions, and the inner calm and contentedness depicted in the *Zhuangzi* is seen as resulting from following one's *xing* by occupying the social position to which one is suited. Thus, while Guo Xiang formed his views from a study of the *Zhuangzi*, the ideal that he advocated is compatible with the kind of social and political engagement that the Confucians defended.

In the Tang dynasty (618–907), the Confucian thinkers Han Yu (768–824) and Li Ao (eighth–ninth century) characterized *qing* in terms of the seven emotions—pleasure, anger, sorrow, fear, love, hatred, desire—and regarded *qing* as the activation of *xing* when it comes into contact with external things. Han Yu, while regarding Mencius as the true transmitter of Confucius's teachings, distinguished between three grades of *xing*. Higher people have an unchangeably good *xing*, which can be developed by education; lower people have an unchangeably evil *xing*, which can be restrained by edicts and punishment; intermediate people have a *xing* such that they can become either good or evil. According to Han Yu, Mencius's, Xunzi's, and Yang Xiong's views all describe the intermediate people: Mencius described those who begin with a good *xing* but can become evil, Xunzi described those who begin with an evil *xing* but can become good, and Yang Xiong described those who begin with a mixed *xing* and can become either good or evil. Li Ao, on the other hand, described *xing* as good. *Qing*, understood in terms of emotions, is the manifestation of *xing*, and whether one is manifestly good depends on whether this activation is of the right balance. If not, *qing* is impure and obscures one's good *xing*. The relation between *xing* and *qing* is like that between water and sediment; water itself is pure, but it can become impure because of sediment. Just as water can be made pure again by stilling it, the purity of *xing* can be restored by stilling the heart.

Li Ao's view of the relation between *xing* and *qing* was retained by Confucians of the Song dynasty (960–1279) such as Cheng Yi (1033–1107) and Zhu Xi (1130–1200), and it was incorporated into their cosmological framework of *li* (pattern, principle) and *qi* (material force). *Li* is abstract, runs through everything, and is that which explains why things operate as they do and to which the behavior of things should conform. It is *li* that plants flourish in the spring and fade in the autumn, or that a boat travels on water but not on land. In the human realm, *li* includes all norms of human behavior, such as affection between parents and children. *Qi* is the stuff of which things are composed, and it is supposed to be fluid, freely flowing, and active. According to Cheng Yi, everything is composed of *li* and *qi*, and *li* in human beings is identical to the Confucian virtues; however, a person may not be manifestly ethical, because *li* in human beings can be obscured by impure *qi*. *Xing* refers primarily to *li*; thus *xing* is good, but impure *qi* can distort its manifestation as *qing*, so that *qing* can be good or evil depending on the endowment of *qi*. Zhu Xi retained this view of the relation between *xing* and *qing* and regarded *qing* as due to the activation of the heart. The heart in its original state has insight into *li*, which is identical to *xing*, and ideally this insight should guide human conduct. However, this insight can be obscured because of impure *qi*; this results in bad *qing* and accounts for a failure to be ethical.

The view that *xing* is good and that Mencius was the true transmitter of the Confucian way became Confucian orthodoxy after Zhu Xi, although different views of *xing* and its relation to *qing* continued to be developed. In opposition to Zhu Xi, Wang Yangming (1472–1529) of the Ming dynasty (1368–1644) denied that the heart in its original state has an insight into *li* which guides its responses. Instead, the heart in its original state responds appropriately to situations without guidance from such insight. An analogy is the taste for food: while one's taste may move one to respond favorably to certain kinds of food, and while such responses may be accompanied by the thought that such food is delicious, the thought is part of the response and does not guide it. And just as what constitutes delicious food resides in the way the human taste for food is structured, what constitutes *li* resides in the responses of the heart in the original state. *Xing*, which is identical to *li*, is therefore not separate from the heart and its responses.

Another kind of reaction to Zhu Xi is found among scholars of the Qing dynasty (1644–1912). One representative figure is Dai Zhen (1724–1777). According to Dai, the *xing* of human beings comprises *qing* (emotions) and *yu* (desires), and *li* (pattern, principle) is the proper structuring of these. By the application of a form of golden rule, one comes to know how one's own and other people's desires can be appropriately satisfied and emotions can be appropriately expressed. This constitutes a grasp of *li; li* is not something already in the heart that can be obscured but is a matter of the appropriate satisfaction of desires and the appropriate expression of emotions. *Xing* is good not in the sense that the heart originally has insight into *li*, but in the sense that *li* is a completion of the emotions and desires natural to human beings.

See also Cheng Yi; Dai Zhen; Dong Zhongshu; Guo Xiang; Han Yu; *Li*: Principle, Pattern, Reason; Li Ao; Mencius; Philosophy of Human Nature; *Qi*; *Qing; Sheng*: Life or Creativity; Wang Chong; Wang Yangming; Yang Xiong; Yang Zhu; Zhu Xi; Zhuangzi.

Bibliography

Chan, Wing-tsit, trans. and comp. *A Source Book in Chinese Philosophy*. Princeton, N.J.: Princeton University Press, 1963.

Dai, Zhen. *Mengzi Ziyi Shuzheng*, 2nd ed. Beijing: Zhonghua shuju.

Dong, Zhongshu. *Chunqiu fanlu*. (In the *Sibu beiyao* Series.)

Guanzi. (See also W. Allyn Rickett, trans. *Kuan-tzu*, Vol. 1. Hong Kong: Hong Kong University Press, 1965, pp. 151–172; and *Guanzi: A Study and Translation*, Vol. 1, Princeton, N.J.: Princeton University Press, 1985, pp. 376–386.)

Guo, Xiang. *Zhuangzi zhu*. (In the *Sibu beiyao* Series.)

Han, Yu. *Han Changli Chuanji*. (In the *Sibu baiyao* Series.)

Li, Ao. *Li Wengong ji*. (In the *Siku chuanshu* Series.)

Lunyu (Analects). (See also D. C. Lau, trans. *Confucius: The Analects*. London: Penguin, 1979.)

Lushi chunqhiu. (See also Xu Weiyu. *Lushi chunqiu jishi*. Beijing: Shangwu yinshuguan, 1955, chs. 1.2, 1.3, 2.2, 2.3, 21.4.)

Mengzi (Mencius). (See also D. C. Lau, trans. *Mencius*. London: Penguin, 1970.)

Mozi. (See also Burton Watson, trans. *Mo Tzu: Basic Writings*. New York: Columbia University Press, 1963.)

Wang, Chong. *Lunheng*. (In the *Sibu beiyao* Series.)

Wang, Yangming. *Quanxilu*. In *Yangming Chuanshu, Sibo beiyao* Series. (See also Wing-tsit Chan, trans. *Instructions for Practical Living and Other Neo-Confucian Writings by*

Wang Yang-ming. New York: Columbia University Press, 1963.)
Xun, Yue. *Shenjian*. (In the *Sibu beiyao* Series.)
Xunzi. (See also John Knoblock, trans. *Xunzi: A Translation and Study of the Complete Works*, 3 vols. Stanford, Calif.: Stanford University Press, 1988–1994.)
Yang, Xiang. *Fayan*. (In the *Sibu Beiyao* series.)
Zhu Xi. *Zhuzi yulei*. Beijing: Zhonghua shuju, 1986.
Zhuangzi. (See also A. C. Graham, trans. *Chuang-tzu: The Seven Inner Chapters and Other Writings from the Book Chuang-tzu*. London: Allen and Unwin, 1981.)
Zuozhuan. (See also James Legge, trans. *The Ch'un Ts'ew with the Tso Chuen*, rev. ed. Taipei: Wen-shih-che ch'u-pan-she, 1972.)

Xiong Shili (Hsiung Shih-li)

Shu-hsien Liu

Xiong Shili (1885–1968) is commonly regarded as the founder of contemporary neo-Confucianism; among his disciples were Tang Junyi (1909–1978), Mou Zongsan (1909–1995), and Xu Fuguan (1903–1982).

Xiong was raised in a poor family. When he was young, he joined the army and participated in revolutionary activities. In middle age, he was puzzled by the problem of life and experienced a spiritual crisis of some sort, so he entered the Institute of Buddhism at Nanjing to study under Ouyang Jingwu (1871–1943). In 1922 he was asked to lecture on *weishi* ("consciousness-only") Buddhism at Peking University; this was the start of a lifelong association with the university. Xiong's lecture notes on *weishi* Buddhism were published by the university, but he soon became dissatisfied with *weishi* and developed a new "consciousness-only" doctrine based on his understanding of the philosophy of creativity implied in the *Yijing* (*Book of Changes*). Thus he opened up a new direction for contemporary neo-Confucian philosophy. As the new doctrine was a challenge to the old theory, it created a stir in Buddhist circles. The Institute of Buddhism published a book intended to refute this new doctrine, but Xiong countered with a refutation of the refutation. The originality of Xiong's approach and the depth of his thought attracted a group of students to him; some of them developed into leading figures in the vital movement later called contemporary neo-Confucianism.

When the People's Republic of China was established in 1949, Xiong Shili chose to remain on the mainland. It was considered a miracle that he continued to publish works about his own philosophy and his own thought after the revolution, though their circulation was very small; for example, *Yuanru* (*An Inquiry on Confucianism*) was published in 1956. Wing-tsit Chan was of the opinion that Xiong had not altered the fundamental thesis of his new doctrine of consciousness-only. Although from a metaphysical point of view Xiong's later thought changed very little, as he still rejected materialism, he did take a very different perspective on the development of Confucian thought, especially its social and political ideals. During the Cultural Revolution, Xiong was an object of abuse by the Red Guards, and he lived miserably in his later years.

Xiong was a prolific writer. His writings may be divided into two groups: before and after 1949. In the first group, the more important works are *Xin weishi lun* (*New Consciousness-Only Doctrine*) and *Shili yuyao* (*Important Sayings by Xiong Shili*). In the second group, after *Yuanru*, he published *Tiyong lun* (*A Treatise on Substance and Function*, 1958), *Mingxin pian* (*On Enlightenment of the Mind*, 1959), and *Qiankun yan* (*An Explication of the Meanings of Hexagrams Qian and Kun*, 1961). Although he himself was convinced that his earlier writings should be replaced by his later work, the quality of the latter is no match for the former. Therefore, for his metaphysical and epistemological thought, it is better to rely on his earlier publications. For his social and political thought, however, we have no choice but to follow his later works.

Epistemology and Methodology

Throughout his life Xiong wanted to develop an epistemological theory. His attempt was never successful, but his general approach was nevertheless clear; below, I give a summary of his thought. Xiong was greatly interested in methodology and often expressed a wish to write a book on *lianglun* (epistemology and methodology) in addition to *jinglun* (metaphysics and cosmology), which he had already covered in *Xin weishi lun*.

From the terminology he used, we know that his approach was very much influenced by the school of Nyaya and consciousness-only Buddhism in Indian thought. The term *liang* refers to means of knowledge. According to Nyaya, there are four means of knowledge: perception, inference, analogy, and testimony. The Buddhist tradition never trusts perception and inference, which start from something phenomenal and can never get to the bottom of things; and analogy, though helpful, is never precise. Thus only testimony from an enlightened person can guide us to follow the right way. There is no doubt that Xiong was in this tradition, which presupposed a source of knowledge higher than the empirical knowledge built on sense perception and logical inference. Xiong tells us that throughout his career he never opposed the intellect, but he felt deeply that apart from the pursuit of external knowledge there is the world to which we can gain access only through meditation beyond thought and self-realization beyond words. Thus he endorsed the Buddhist distinction between two levels of truth: the worldly truth (*laukikasatya*) or common or relative truth that things exist provisionally as dependent beings or temporary names; and the absolute truth (*paramarthasatya*) that surpasses expression and conceptualization in language. Xiong appreciated the Buddhist wisdom intended to deliver us from the evil consequences of clinging to unreal fabrications of consciousnesses; but he refused to see absolute truth as *sunyata* (emptiness), as taught by the Buddhists.

According to Xiong, a philosophical approach must be radically different from a scientific approach. Science needs to postulate the external reality of objects in order to investigate them and discover the principles that govern their actions, but such an approach can capture only manifestations. Philosophy, by contrast, is intended to capture the reality behind phenomena. When objects are taken to be substantially real, philosophy enters a blind alley or becomes deluded, with dire consequences. Xiong appreciated the Buddhist critique of this philosophically untenable position.

Xiong identified two streams of thought in Indian Buddhism; after they were imported to China, they became the "consciousness-only" school (*weishi zong*) and the "three treatises" school (*sanlun zong*). "Consciousness-only" was devoted to explaining the phenomenal world and so can be called *youzong* (school of being). "Three treatises" was devoted to showing that in the final analysis all *dharma* (elements) are empty; it can thus be called *kongzong* (school of nonbeing or emptiness).

Through a rather elaborate analysis, the consciousness-only school concluded that the phenomenal world as we know it results from the transformation of eight "consciousnesses": the five sense-consciousnesses, the sixth or sense-center consciousness (*manovijnana*), the seventh or thought-center consciousness (*manasvijnana*), and the eighth or storehouse consciousness (*alaya*). Although Xiong would agree that there is no world apart from the transformation of consciousnesses, he finds fault with the consciousness-only school because it tends to separate the manifestation or *yong* (function) from its source or *ti* (foundation). According to his understanding of the doctrine, generation and destruction can be traced to seeds stored in *alaya*, whereas *zhenru* (*tathata*, ultimate reality or thusness) has nothing whatsoever to do with them. This dualism is totally unacceptable to him. Xiong praises the approach of the *kongzong* ("three treatises) school: sweeping aside *xiang* (appearance) in order to manifest *xing* (true nature) as *kong* (*sunyata* or emptiness). But he also finds fault with *kongzong*, as it leaves no room for genuine creativity. Therefore, he returns to Chinese tradition, specifically to its fountainhead, the *Yijing* (*Book of Changes*).

Xiong ranks *Yijing* first among the Six Classics, ahead of *Book of Poetry, Book of History, Book of Rites, Book of Music*, and *Spring and Autumn Annals*. Through the *Yijing*, we realize that the ultimate metaphysical principle is not the Daoist *wu* (nothingness) or the Buddhist *kong* (emptiness), but rather the Confucian "way" or Way, which is characterized by *shengsheng* (creative creativity) working ceaselessly in the universe.

How can we realize that the ultimate metaphysical principle is characterized by creativity? Surely we cannot arrive at this conclusion either through logical reasoning or by generalizing from experience. Here, Xiong introduces a pair of concepts that he calls *liangzhi* (wisdom from measurement) and *xingzhi* (original wisdom).

Liangzhi has to do with the functions of measurement of inference. It differentiates between the principles of things and our experience of things, and it evaluates experience. It may be called reason or the intellect. Empirical sciences can be established on this level, but no metaphysical theories can be constructed or conjectured through logical reasoning or empirical generalization. Furthermore, *liangzhi* depends on the senses to manifest its function, and so it can be misled by the senses to assume that external objects are metaphysically real.

Xingzhi refers to illumination through self-realization. The opening statements of the *Doctrine of the Mean* are: "What Heaven imparts to man is called human nature. To follow our nature is called the Way. Cultivating the Way is called education." Xiong firmly believed that we are endowed with our nature by the decree of heaven. There is no need to seek *xingzhi* from external sources. If we can realize the creativity within ourselves, then we can also realize the creativity of heaven. There is a correlation between microcosm and macrocosm. Xiong liked to use the ocean as a metaphor, saying that when you taste a drop of ocean water, you taste the whole ocean. Thus we have no need to look for a justification for *xingzhi*; it is originally with us. Only when we are misled by the senses do we chase after external objects, bcoming victims of our own delusions.

There is a dialectical relationship between *xingzhi* and *liangzhi*. In the final analysis, *liangzhi* has no other source than *xingzhi*, but *xingzhi* has to manifest itself through *liangzhi*. Unfortunately, however, sometimes the slave usurps the position of the master, and then we have to pay a heavy price. In this regard, according to Xiong, the Buddhists tend to emphasize the ills and suffering caused by deep-seated ignorance (*avidya*), whereas the Confucians choose to emphasize the affirmative side of life.

Metaphysics and Cosmology

For Xiong there is no clear line dividing epistemological and metaphysical issues. Just as he distinguished between *xingzhi* and *liangzhi*, he also distinguished between what he called *benxin* (original mind) and *xixin* (habitual mind).

The original mind, *benxin*, is ontologically prior. It has the following characteristics. In the first place, it is empty and silent: silent because it transcends all confusion and anxiety and hence has a divine function; empty because it is not embodied in any concrete forms and hence has inexhaustible creative power. In the second place, it is illuminating and thus is the origin of all genuine knowledge. The original mind is therefore the ontological principle of our own being as well as of all beings. This view was a development of Mencius's view that we need to "realize our mind in order to realize our nature as well as to realize heaven," which is the symbol for the origin of all beings.

The habitual mind, *xixin*, distinguishes between the self and other phenomena, and between what is internal and what is external. It takes the "small self" as the only true self. If we rely solely on *xixin*, it will be impossible for us to discover our true nature and the ontological principle of all beings.

The original mind (*benxin*) should not be seen as the opposite of matter; rather, the habitual mind (*xixin*) is the opposite of matter and the correlate of matter. The original mind is "nothing," if we take things as particular physical objects in time and space; it is the creative power that operates in things without being limited by them. It has to manifest itself as matter and through matter, but it is not to be dominated by matter. It is the absolute. Only through the realization of our original mind can we establish any metaphysical knowledge at all.

If we grant this distinction between the original mind and the habitual mind, we can divide human learning into two branches: metaphysics, which has its foundation in the original mind; and sciences, which have their foundation in the habitual mind. The sciences use the analytic method; they investigate particular aspects of the phenomenal world. Metaphysics relies on the method of testimony or inner illumination to comprehend the universe as a whole. As a practical matter, the sciences take "things" as having an independent objective existence, and so the intellect always directs its attention outward. Metaphysics, however, takes the ultimate as immaterial and inherent within our being. The ultimate cannot be reached through intellectual inferences; it can be realized only through inner illumination, budding forth from our reason.

To sum up, according to Xiong, scientific truths, as distinct from metaphysical truths, have six characteristics:

1. They have to postulate the objective existence of a physical universe that is subject to observation and it is not a product of our subjective imagination or mental construction.
2. The discovery of scientific truths must be based on and verified by sense experience.
3. The results of scientific investigation must be intersubjectively verifiable and, once established, will be recognized by all men to certain extent.
4. These truths, under existing conditions, must be relatively stable; they will invariably hold unless the conditions change or disappear altogether. It does not matter whether these principles are exemplified by concrete examples, so long as the conditions persist.
5. Although these truths are relatively stable, they are not absolutely unchangeable. Their objects are particular existing things or events, which are relative to one another. The sciences are instrumental in discovering correlations between phenomena or events through experience. Hence scientific truths are always many, never one.
6. The sciences rely heavily on hypotheses. They need to postulate many concepts that are subjective in origin but nevertheless find correspondences in an objective world.

Metaphysical truth has entirely different characteristics, which may be summarized as follows:

1. It is the ontological principle for all beings.
2. It is absolute and hence needs no further reasons to justify its existence. It cannot be reached by inferences of the intellect and cannot be adequately expressed in human language.
3. It can be realized only through inner illumination or testimony. The subject and the object are united. There is no longer a distinction between the internal and the external, between the thing and the self, and so forth. Metaphysical truth transcends all relational concepts and false conjectures of the mind. In short, it is the easiest and the simplest of all truths.

Once the two levels of truths are properly distinguished, the next task for Xiong is to relate them. First, negatively speaking, scientific truths cannot possibly contradict metaphysical truth, since they belong to two entirely different universes of discourse. They are both valuable studies to be pursued vigorously on the level of human understanding. Second, positively speaking, the two levels of truth are complementary. The sciences study the functional aspect and metaphysics studies the ontological aspect of the same principle. Every phenomenon or function must be the phenomenon or function of a substance; and every substance must manifest itself as a phenomenon or function. Thus the sciences and metaphysics are complementary because only by combining them can we hope to apprehend both the functional aspect and the substantial aspect of any principle. Consequently, philosophy does not contradict reason or the intellect, although it must transcend the intellect if it is to establish any metaphysical truth. The intellect would be rejected only when it tries to undertake metaphysics by itself and alienates from its origin.

Here, we need not elaborate on Xiong's metaphysical system; it will suffice to introduce the guiding principles of his metaphysics and cosmology: *tiyong bu'er* (substance and function are nondual) and *xipi chengbian* (transformation through closing and opening).

Tiyong is a pair of concepts often used in traditional Chinese philosophy. Cheng Yi said in the preface to his *Commentary on Yijing*: "*Ti* and *yong* come from the same source, and there is no gap between the manifest and the hidden." Xiong further developed such insights in his own way, and indeed raised them to a new height. There is no exact equivalent in English for *ti* and *yong*; perhaps we have no choice except to render them as "substance" and "function," but we must realize that in this context substance does not mean something eternal which has nothing to do with change. For Xiong, *ti* means the creative ontological principle that works incessantly in the universe. Apart from its function (*yong*) or manifestation, there is no way to realize the creativity of the substance except through the illumination of the original mind. For Xiong, manifestations must be many, and philosophy must not follow science by postulating the external reality of objects in order to investigate them; on the contrary, the task of philosophy is to identify the creative source amid the many manifestations. In other words, the principle is one, while its manifestations are many (*liyi fenshu*). Hence there is a difference between knowledge and wisdom. To acquire knowledge, we must postulate external objects; but for wisdom to function, we must realize the one reality. Science can capture only the manifestations; and only philosophy can capture the one reality that is the source of these manifestations. Because there are no manifestations apart from substance and there is no substance apart from manifestations, *ti* and *yong* are nondual. But one question remains. Why do we find all kinds of obstructions in the world instead of the "great functioning everywhere" that would be implied by this metaphysics?

To answer this question, Xiong relied on another pair of concepts, which he had borrowed from the *Yijing* to develop his cosmology: *xi* (closing) and *pi* (opening). As the ultimate source of creativity, substance is never static or stagnant but ever-changing; from instant to instant, it leaves the past behind and creates anew. As substance manifests itself in various activities, they are referred to as its function. According to Xiong, substance comprises complexities such as what we call as "matter" and "mind" and therefore manifests itself in activities that are apparently opposed to each other. Through *xi*, the materializing tendency, the "myriad things" are created, but none of them are substantially real. They come and they go, and as the new instantaneously replaces the old, they merely give an impression of continuity, even permanence. When these objects are taken as something real in themselves, they are cut off from their source. Obstruction—that is, illusory obstruction—ensues, function ceases to be function, and the principle of creativity cannot be seen. In other words, in the creative process principle must manifest itself in phenomena that appear to be material things, and this tends to conceal its creative nature.

Meanwhile, however, the opposing tendency, *pi*—the spiritualizing tendency—is also at work. It does not allow *xi* to become dominant; thus the materializing tendency is reversed and the creative nature of the principle is recovered. Through the continual interaction of *xi* and *pi*, we can discern a creative universe in which substance and function are interdependent or, as noted above, nondual.

The same cosmic forces are at work in human lives; we can experience these opposing tendencies within ourselves. We have a materializing tendency to chase after external things, and this can cause us great trouble unless we recover our mind and restore our creative nature. In this regard, sages and worthies set an example for us to follow. Once we recover our creative nature, we can participate in the creative process of the universe, as envisaged in the *Doctrine of the Mean*. Xiong never sees the origin of the universe as "dark forces," because we can personally realize, within ourselves, a creative nature that is consonant with the creative universe. Although these concepts may seem highly speculative, Xiong claims that all individuals may reach these insights as soon as they realize the inner depth of their being. A true ontology is established not by external cosmological speculation but by inner realization of human depths.

Social and Political Philosophy

Xiong was firmly in the Confucian tradition. He cared not only for *neisheng* (inward sageliness), which emphasizes personal cultivation, but also for *waiwang* (outward kingliness), which has to do with maintaining a stable, just social and political order. For Xiong, the ideal situation—borrowed from the hexagram *qian* in *Yijing*—would be a number of dragons without a leader, a symbol of democracy and socialism. In real life, such a lofty ideal can hardly be realized. Therefore, sages must devise a system to bring about peace and harmony throughout the world.

In *Yuanru*, Xiong advanced the bold thesis that the Six Classics were the work of Confucius in his later years and had been revised, after Confucius's death, by what he called "slave-scholars" in order to support the rule of the emperors. As a result, the true teachings of Confucius were not available to later scholars. This radical view stirred up considerable controversy, and very few scholars—not even Xiong's disciples—accepted it.

Xiong, as we have seen, ranked *Yijing* first among the Six Classics, as having laid the philosophical foundation of the entire Confucian tradition. The two most important hexagrams in *Yijing* were *qian* and *kun*, so he wrote a book to expound their meaning. Xiong believed that the *Book of Poetry* and the *Book of History* had been edited by Confucius. These works preserved some ancient documents. The *Book of Poetry* contained poems telling of the plight of the common people, but later scholars had tampered so much with the *Book of History* that it was no longer of much use. The *Book of Music* was no longer extant. Xiong praised the *Zhouguan* (*Chou Rituals*) highly, believing that its lofty ideals could not have been conceived by anyone other than Confucius; he rejected the view that the work was spurious, even though he could not provide any evidence for his thesis. He saw the guiding principles of the *Zhouguan* as equality and unity. It espoused an elaborate system of government under which the welfare of the people was the primary concern; industries would be developed, private property (including private ownership of land) would be abolished, and large businesses would be run by the government. Such ideas remain relevant and deserve study even today.

In the *Book of Rites* Xiong singled out the essay on the "great unity" as preserving certain authentic insights from Confucius. This essay made a sharp distinction between *datong* ("great unity") and *xiaogang* ("small peace"). Xiong felt that it should be read together with *Chunqiu* (*Spring and Autumn Annals*). Supposedly, Confucius was the author of *Chunqiu*, commenting on events in Lu, his native state. Xiong believed that Confucius followed the tradition of teaching the rites to his students until age fifty, when his thinking underwent a radical conversion. Instead of teaching only *xiaogang*, he now also taught *datong*, under which social classes and private property were to be abolished. Xiong theorized that the succession of "three ages" taught by commentators on *Chunqiu* in the Gongyang school had originated with Confucius himself. An "age of disorder" would be followed by an "age of rising peace" and finally by the "age of great peace," in which all boundaries between races would be eliminated. In this final stage the world would become one family, with each person in control of his own life; all human beings would be equal and would render mutual aid, totally ignoring the distinction between "self" and "other." This "great unity" should be emphasized, Xiong held, but later scholars had wrongly emphasized the practice of "small peace," thus lending support to dynastic rulers. Xiong's radical views led him to accuse Mencius of betraying Confucius's lofty ideals and promoting filial piety as a means of helping rulers consolidate their power. Thereafter, Dong Zhongshu (c. 170–104 B.C.E.) in the Han dynasty had wrongly emphasized the loyalty of subjects toward the ruler. Such distorted teaching of Confucius's ideas had dominated the thinking of Confucian scholars throughout the ages; even Kang Youwei (1858–1927) was still trapped within it, despite his talk of the great unity.

Conclusion

There is no question that Xiong was the most original thinker of his generation, and he is regarded as the fountainhead of contemporary neo-Confucianism. But his influence was limited to a small circle of scholars, and none of his famous disciples can be counted as faithful followers of his philosophical system. His thought can be divided into two periods: before and after 1949. Some scholars emphasize continuity in his thought, but others accuse him of making too many accommodations to the communist revolution.

Actually, the truth is somewhere in between. There is certainly continuity in his thought, and he showed great courage in maintaining his philosophical position after 1949–the position that the ultimate metaphysical principle is neither matter nor mind, as both are functions of the principle. Throughout his life he refused to accept materialism, even though he tried to draw certain insights from Marxian dialectics, which emphasizes the unity of opposites and does not appear to be greatly different from traditional Chinese thought. His social and political philosophy changed more, however: his condemnation of Mencius was new, and he showed greater enthusiasm for and sympathy toward revolutionary ideals, more forcefully advocating socialism and democracy as he understood them through his creative interpretation of the classics. Still, it would be untrue to say that there is no continuity in this respect; Xiong always had a high regard for *Chunqiu* and *Zhouguan* and always believed in the principles of equality, justice, and socialism.

Xiong did not have the slightest idea of democracy in the western sense. He was deeply rooted in the Chinese tradition, and it was through his reinterpretation of this tradition that he attempted to find a rapprochement with the Indian tradition earlier in his career and with Marxism in his later years. In either case, though, he found no followers. Rather, his greatest contribution was that he recognized the inner creativity in human beings and that he dared to follow his own independent thinking and maintain unpopular positions. Perhaps inadvertently, he pointed out a new direction for the neo-Confucian scholars who came after him.

See also *Sheng*: Life or Creativity; *Ti; Ti* and *Yong; Ti-Yong* Metaphysics.

Bibliography

Cai, Renhou. *Xiong Shili xiansheng xuexing nianbiao* (Chronology of Master Xiong Shili's Learning and Practice). Taipei: Mingwen, 1987.

Chan, Wing-tsit. *Religious Trends in Modern China*. New York: Columbia University Press, 1953.

——. trans. and comp. *A Source Book in Chinese Philosophy*. Princeton, N.J.: Princeton University Press, 1963.

Furth, Charlotte, ed. *The Limits of Change: Essays on Conservative Alternatives in Republican China*. Cambridge, Mass.: Harvard University Press, 1976.

Guo, Jiyong. *Xiong Shili sixiang yanjiu* (A Study of Xiong Shili's Thought). Tianjian People's Publications, 1993.

Jing, Haifeng. *Xiong Shili*. Taipei: Dongda, 1991.

Liu, Shu-hsien "The Contemporary Development of a Neo-Confucian Epistemology." *Inquiry*, 14, 1971, pp. 19–40. (Republished as the second chapter in *Invitation to Chinese Philosophy*, ed. Arne Naess and Alastair Hannay. Oslo: Universitetsforlaget, 1972, pp. 19–40.)

——. *Xiong Shilili yu Liu Jingzhuang lunxue shujian* (Correspondences between Xiong Shili and Liu Jingzhuang). Taipei: China Times, 1984.

——. "Hsiung Shih-li's Theory of Causation." *Philosophy East and West*, 12(4), October 1969, pp. 399–407.

——. "The Religious Import of Confucian Philosophy: Its Traditional Outlook and Contemporary Significance." *Philosophy East and West*, 21(2), April 1971, pp. 151–175.

——. "Postwar Neo-Confucian Philosophy: Its Development and Issues." *Religious Issues and Interreligious Dialogues*, ed. Charles Wei-hsun Fu and Gerhard E. Spiegler. New York: Greenwood, 1989.

Mou, Zongsan. *Shenming de xuewen* (The Learning of Life). Taipei: Sanmin, 1970.

Tang, Junyi. *Zhongguo wenhua zhi jingshen jiazhi* (The Spiritual Values of the Chinese Culture). Taipei: Zhengzhong, 1953.

Xiong, Shili. *Mingxin pian* (On Enlightenment of the Mind). Taipei: Xuesheng, 1976.

——. *Qiankun yan* (An Explication of the Meanings of Hexagrams Qian and Kun). Taipei: Xuesheng, 1976.

——. *Shili yuyao* (Important Sayings by Xiong Shili). Taipei: Gongwen, 1962.

——. *Tiyong lun* (A Treatise on Substance and Function). Taipei: Xuesheng, 1976.

——. *Xin weishi lun* (New Consciousness-Only Doctrine). Shanghai: Commercial Press, 1947.

——. *Yuanru* (An Inquiry on Confucianism). Hong Kong: Longmen, 1970.

Xiushen (*Hsiu-shen*): Self-Cultivation

Kwong-loi Shun

Xiushen, or self-cultivation, is the process of improving oneself, out of a reflection on the kind of person one is; this process is a primary concern of Confucian thinkers. Among early Confucian texts, the combination *xiushen* occurs three times in the *Mengzi* (*Mencius*), is the title of a chapter in the *Xunzi* and is used to refer to one of the eight items of adult learning in the *Daxue* (*Great Learning*). Although the combination does not occur in the *Lunyu* (*Analects*), which records Confucius's teachings, *xiu* (cultivating) is used in conjunction with *ji* (oneself) (14.42) and *zheng* (rectifying) in conjunction with *shen* (the person) to refer to a similar phenomenon (13.6, 13.13).

The goal of Confucian self-cultivation is to embody various ideal ethical attributes, including *ren* (humaneness, benevolence), *yi* (righteousness, propriety), *li* (observance of rites), and *zhi* (wisdom). *Ren* involves an affective concern for all, although the degree and nature of this concern vary, depending on one's social relation to others. *Yi* is a commitment to live up to certain ethical standards; it entails regarding whatever falls below such standards as something that is beneath oneself and from which one should distance oneself. *Li* is a commitment to follow various traditional rules (themselves also referred to as *li*) governing the interaction between people in recurring social contexts; one should follow such rules with reverence (*jing*) for those with whom one is dealing and should be prepared to suspend such rules in exigencies when appropriate. *Zhi* involves an ability to assess what is proper in a way that is not bound by rigid rules but is sensitive to particular circumstances.

The process of self-cultivation affects the person as a whole. It affects the heart (*xin*), the site of both cognitive and affective activities; and the physical body (*ti*) and its parts, such as the four limbs and the senses. It also affects *qi*, the vital energies that fill and flow freely in the body, giving life to the person and being responsible for the emotions. For example, Xunzi emphasized that following *li* (rites) can give order to *qi* and nourish the heart (*Xunzi*, ch. 2); Mencius spoke of nourishing the floodlike *qi* (*Mengzi*, 2A.2). These different aspects of a person interact. The heart can focus itself in certain directions (*zhi*), and these directions of the heart, which include general aims in life as well as specific intentions, both shape *qi* and can be affected by the condition of *qi*. *Qi* can be affected by what happens to the body, such as the tastes that the mouth takes in and the sounds that the ears hear; conversely, *qi* can generate speech in the mouth and sight in the eyes. It follows from the interaction between the heart and *qi*, and between *qi* and the body, that the heart and the body are also intimately related. For example, Mencius spoke of how the condition of the heart is manifested in the body, not just in action and speech, but in the face, the look of the eyes, the four limbs, and one's physical bearing in general; indeed, only through self-cultivation can one give complete fulfilment to the body (*Mengzi*, 4A.15, 7A.21, 7A.38). Likewise, the *Daxue* (ch. 6) speaks of how virtue (*de*) adorns the body just as riches adorn a house, and how when the heart is expanded the body is also at ease.

Not only does self-cultivation affect one's whole person; it also has the power to attract and transform others, a power that the Confucians regard as the ideal basis for government. For Confucius and Mencius, the goal of government is to transform people's character, and the way to accomplish this is to first cultivate oneself and then let the transforming power of one's cultivated character take effect (*Lunyu*, 2.1, 2.3, 12.19, 13.4, 13.13, 15.5; *Mengzi*, 4A.20, 7A.19). This does not mean that governmental policies are unimportant; in fact, both Confucius and Mencius discussed details of government. But proper policies are themselves a manifestation of the cultivated character of those in power, and properly carrying out policies transmitted from the past also requires a cultivated character (*Mengzi*, 2A.6, 4A.1; cf. 7B.5). So the ultimate basis for order is cultivating oneself (*Mengzi*, 4A.5, 4A.12, 7B.32), an idea that the *Daxue* expresses by describing self-cultivation as the basis for regulating the family, giving order to the state, and ultimately bringing peace to the whole empire.

Because a cultivated character has such power, it can lead to personal advantages. A cultivated character is likely to be appreciated by others, resulting in employment and a high rank in government. The associated power of attracting and transforming enables a ruler to win the allegiance of the people, and to become invincible in the sense of confronting little or no hostility. However, the Confucians say emphatically that one should not engage in self-cultivation for such purposes. Confucius said that in self-cultivation one should be concerned not with others' appreciation but with one's own character and ability as such; learning should be for oneself, not for others (*Lunyu*, 14.24; cf. 1.1, 1.16, 4.14, 14.30, 15.19). Mencius, elaborating on Confucius's ideas, criticized the honest villager whose way of life is determined by social opinion (*Mengzi*, 7B.37; cf. *Lunyu*, 13.21, 13.24, 17.13, 17.18). The honest villager aims at having others regarding him as good, and since he adjusts his way of life accordingly it is difficult to find fault with him. But he lacks a genuine concern for goodness, and what he has attained is not genuine goodness but at best a semblance of it.

The Confucians also advocate a total commitment to the ethical life, a life characterized by the attributes *ren*, *yi*, *li*, and *zhi*. Mencius emphasized that one should not be led to deviate the ethical life by the prospect of adversity or of profit, and the heart should be "unmoved" in that one is not subject to fear, uncertainty, or any kind of distorting influences (*Mengzi*, 2A.2, 3B.2, 7A.9). Instead, one should willingly accept any material disadvantages, including the loss of one's life, that result from one's ethical pursuits. This attitude of acceptance is conveyed through the notion *ming* (decree, destiny), and it involves not being worried by the adverse outcomes and not engaging in improper conduct to alter them (*Mengzi*, 7A.1, 2).

Willingly accepting material disadvantages and not being led astray by them requires a complete inclination toward the ethical, and this inclination is expressed by the notion *cheng*, highlighted in the *Daxue* (*Great Learning*) and the *Zhongyong* (*Centrality and Commonality*). *Cheng* connotes being real and complete; it refers to a state in which one fully embodies ethical attributes. There are no discrepancies between the way one is and one's outward appearances and behavior, or within the heart itself. Not a single thought or inclination is incongruent with the ethical attributes; there is nothing that could cause the slightest reluctance or hesitation about acting properly. The *Zhongyong* describes *cheng* as the ideal basis of government. It emphasizes that what is on the inside will inevitably be manifested on the outside, and only when one is fully *cheng* can one have the transforming effect on others that provides the basis for the political order (*Zhongyong*, chs. 1, 20–25). Indeed, since this transforming effect is a natural outgrowth of one's cultivated character, a failure to transform others indicates a failure in self-cultivation. Accordingly, one's concern for cultivating oneself cannot be separated from a concern for cultivating others.

Regarding the method of self-cultivation, there have been significant differences in emphasis among Confucian thinkers. Confucius (*Lunyu*, 2.15) stressed both learning (*xue*) and reflection (*si*). *Xue* involves drawing moral lessons from the cultural heritage, including poetry, history, rites (*li*), music, and archery, and embodying such lessons in one's life. *Si* involves pondering what one has learned so as to adapt it to one's present circumstances. Xunzi, who regarded human beings as naturally inclined to strife and disorder unless transformed by social norms, emphasized learning as a lifelong process. What one has learned from *li* (rites) and other aspects of the cultural heritage permeates the whole person, and their accumulated effects redirect the person toward ethics.

On the other hand, Mencius, who believed that all human hearts share such ethical tendencies as compassion and shame, emphasized reflection in the sense of directing attention to these tendencies and nourishing them. Everyone is able to attain the ethical ideal through such reflection, and ethical failure is due to a failure to reflect.

Other methods of self-cultivation include the idea, found in both the *Daxue* and the *Zhongyong*, of cautiously watching over the minute, subtle tendencies of the heart to ensure that they are properly inclined, thereby attaining *cheng*. Another example is the emphasis on *jing* (seriousness, reverence) found in the *Yijing* (*Book of Changes*), where *jing* is understood in the sense of concentrating or gathering one's attention so that one is not distracted by distorting influences.

Differences in emphasis regarding methods of self-cultivation are also found among later Confucians. Zhu Xi (1130–1200) held that the heart in its original state has an insight into *li* (pattern, principle), which ideally should guide human conduct. This insight can be obscured by erroneous thoughts and distorting desires, leading to a failure to be ethical. To restore this insight, one needs to examine daily affairs, such as how parents and children should interact, as well as study the classics and history to draw moral lessons from them. By doing so and by constantly acting on what one derives from this process, one can restore the heart's original insight into *li*. Although Zhu Xi also considered other methods of self-cultivation, such as cautiously watching over the subtle, minute tendencies of the heart to ensure that they are properly inclinced, or nourishing the self through *jing* (seriousness, reverence), his emphasis on learning distinguishes him from Wang Yangming (1472–1529), another influential Confucian thinker.

According to Wang Yangming, although the heart in its original state will respond appropriately to situations, its responses are not guided by an insight into *li* (pattern, principle); instead, *li* simply resides in the way the heart responds to situations. An analogy is the taste for food. While one's taste may move one to respond favorably to certain kinds of food, such responses are not guided by prior knowledge of what is delicious; instead, what is delicious is itself determined by the way one responds to food. According to Wang Yangming, the goal of self-cultivation is not to regain insight into *li* but to free the heart from the influence of certain distorting desires that prevent it from responding as it would in its original state. Thus, he advocated attending directly to the heart, constantly watching out for and eliminating the influence of distorting desires. He acknowledged the need to learn certain things such as music, rites, and the institutions of government, and allowed room for reading the basic classics for the purpose of stimulating the heart. However, since *li* itself resides in the heart and does not need to be learned from the outside, he discouraged the kind of extensive commentaries on and analysis of classics that Zhu Xi advocated.

Disagreements about the methods of self-cultivation continued in subsequent developments of Confucian thought. However, despite such disagreements, Confucians share an emphasis on self-cultivation as something to which one should be devoted for a lifetime, with the inner goal of improving oneself rather than for the external advantages that it brings. There is also general agreement on the goal of self-cultivation—which involves a complete transformation of the self and a total commitment to the ethical life, as characterized by the ethical attributes—and on the importance of self-cultivation to the political order.

See also *Cheng*; *Chengyi*; Confucianism: Confucius; Mencius; Wang Yangming; Xunzi; Zhu Xi.

Bibliography

Daxue (Great Learning). (References are by chapter numbers, following Zhu Xi's division of the text, to James Legge, trans. *Confucius: Confucian Analects, The Great Learning, and the Doctrine of the Mean*, 2nd ed. Oxford: Clarendon, 1893.)

Lunyu (Analects). (References are by book and passage numbers to Yang Bojun, trans. *Lunyu Yizhu*. Beijing: Chung-hua shu-che, 1980; modern Chinese. See also D. C. Lau, trans. *Confucius: The Analects*. London: Penguin, 1979.)

Mengzi (Mencius). (References are by book and passage numbers—with book numbers 1A to 7B substituted for 1 to 14—to Yang Bojun, trans. *Mengzi yizhu*. Beijing: Zhonghua shuju, 1984; modern Chines. See also D. C. Lau, trans. *Mencius*. London: Penguin, 1970.)

Xunzi. (See also John Knoblock, trans. *Xunzi: A Translation and Study of the Complete Works*, 3 vols. Stanford, Calif.: Stanford University Press, 1988–1994.)

Yijing (Book of Changes). (See James Legge, trans. *The I Ching: The Book of Changes*, 2nd ed. Oxford: Clarendon, 1899.)

Zhu, Xi. *Zhuzi yulei*. Beijing: Zhonghua shuju, 1986. (See also Wing-tsit Chan, trans. and comp. *A Source Book in Chinese Philosophy*. Princeton, N.J.: Princeton University Press, 1963, ch. 34.)

Zhongyong (Centrality and Commonality, or Doctrine of the Mean). (References are by chapter numbers, following Zhu Xi's division of the text, to James Legge, trans. *Confucius: Confucian Analects, The Great Learning, and the Doctrine of the Mean*, 2nd ed. Oxford: Clarendon, 1893.)

Xu (*Hsü*): Emptiness

Xiaogan LIU

The philosophical meaning and importance of the term *xu* began with Laozi, the founder of Daoism, and the term was further developed by Zhuangzi. This term has been widely used among Chinese literati and has exerted enormous influence in all aspects of Chinese culture, from philosophy, aesthetics, literature, art, and calligraphy to personal cultivation, physical exercise, and medicine.

Literally, the word *xu* suggests emptiness, weakness, softness, and unreality; its antonym *shi* roughly indicates fullness, strength, solidness, and reality. *Xu* is difficult to translate but is often rendered as "empty, "emptiness," "vacuous," "vacuity." In philosophical circles, it is used, often as a pair with its antonym, in connection with quasi-cosmological or quasi-ontological issues, and with theories of the mind and self-cultivation. I use the prefix "quasi" as a reminder that in Chinese philosophy there is no exact counterpart of western metaphysics, which emphasizes, for example, the separation of or distinction between the metaphysical and the physical, the material and the spiritual, or reality and appearance.

The two aspects of the term are found in the *Laozi* or *Daodejing*. Laozi thinks of the original space between heaven and earth as like a huge bellows: it is internally empty but without being exhausted; the more it works, the more it swells out (ch. 5). The idea of *xu* or emptiness is also expressed through another word, *chong*. "The Way is empty (*chong*)," Laozi says, "yet its use will not drain it. Deep, it is like the ancestor of the myriad creatures. . . . I know not whose son it is. It images the forefather of God" (ch. 4). An empty *dao* or Way, before even God, is the origin or the source of the universe; this is a unique idea, and an important contribution to Chinese cosmology. In this sense, *xu* also means the profound and deep continuum in which there is no obstruction.

Like the emptiness (*xu*) of the ultimate root of universe, the human mind—including the sage's mind—should also be empty. Chapter 16 reads: "I do my utmost to attain complete emptiness; I hold firmly to stillness. The myriad creatures all rise together and I watch their return. . . . All return to their roots." Emptiness here is the state of mind, the necessary condition for apprehending the roots of the world.

The idea of emptiness as a significant state of mind is dramatically advanced by Zhuangzi, the second most important Daoist. Zhuangzi explicitly views the emptiness of mind as essential for both transcendent experience and worldly life, presenting a new concept of *xinzhai*, meaning "fasting of the mind." Fasting of the mind is explained in the following statement:

> To make one's will one, don't listen with ears; listen with mind. Don't listen with mind, but listen with spirit. Listening stops with the ears, the mind stops with recognition, but spirit is empty and waits on all things. Then the Way rests on emptiness alone. Emptiness is the fasting of the mind.

The essence of fasting of the mind is a state of spiritual emptiness, which is fundamental to the realization or experience of union with the Way. It is also the best way to get rid of conflicts and protect one's life.

The importance of emptiness in Zhuangzi's philosophy lies in pursuing the mysterious intuition and self-cultivation. Xunzi adopts the concept as a precondition for knowing the Way. Xunzi argues:

> The beginning of good government lies in understanding the Way through the mind. And how can the mind understand it? Because it is empty (*xu*), unified (*yi*), and still (*jing*). The mind is constantly storing up things, and yet it is said to be empty [*xu*]. . . . Man is born with an intellect, and where there is intellect there is memory. Memory is what is stored up in the mind. Yet the mind is said to be empty because what has already been stored up in it does not hinder the reception of new impressions. (Watson 1963, 127–128)

Xunzi teaches a technique for achieving the best or most accurate knowledge of the external world, including the political Way. A man needs practice in keeping the mind focused on the one object that he seeks to know, without letting it stray to another object (*yi*) or go off into reveries about another object (*jing*), and he must not allow an impression already stored to interfere with the reception of a new one (*xu*).

Similarly, when the authors of the *Guanzi* discuss the desirable state of the mind, they also emphasize *xu*, the connection of the Way with one's spiritual condition. They carry on Laozi's idea, claiming that the Way is empty, nonbeing, and formless. They also maintain that *tian* or heaven is empty and formless, and that the earth is peaceful. Emptiness both in the Way or heaven and in the state of the mind suggests "no-desires" or "no-pursuing," which is necessary to let spirits (*shen*) come and stay, and to let the intellect do its utmost in spiritual cultivation (ch. 36, *Xinshu shang*). The authors give this wonderful mental condition with the name *xu*, emptiness.

The most important legalist philosopher, Han Feizi, develops the idea of *xu* in his interpretation of the *Laozi* (*Hanfeizi*, ch. 20). He identifies *xu* or emptiness with two other Daoist concepts, nonaction (*wuwei*) and nonthinking (*wusi*), and claims that the advantage of *xu* is its emphasis on free will. A man of true emptiness takes no action while unaware of doing so. According to Han Feizi, emptiness is great virtue.

Whereas latter-day Daoists, like Huainanzi and Wang Bi, develop the concept of *xu* along with the theory that the universe comes from emptiness and nonbeing, some neo-Confucians use the term to describe a state of mind: absolute peacefulness, purity, freedom from worry, freedom from selfish desires, and freedom from disturbance by incoming impressions. However, *xu* is not to be equated with the Buddhist term *kong* (also translated as "empty"). The distinction may be partly explained in this way. *Kong* means the absence of specific characters. Although it does not really imply nihilism, *kong* is a negative concept. *Xu* is a more positive concept, but neo-Confucians use it sparingly (Chan 1963, 788).

In discussing the origin or reality of the universe, neo-Confucians often use the concept of *taixu* (great emptiness or great void). They argue about the reality of *taixu*, or the relationship of *taixu* and *qi* (material and vital force). For Zhang Zai, *taixu* is full of *qi*, the shapeless stuff that makes up the universe. Wang Yangming speaks of *liangzhi* (innate knowledge of the good) as somehow one with *taixu*, thus endowing *taixu* not only with life and vitality but also with consciousness and a certain intelligence and spirituality. He speaks, for example, of *liangzhi benti* (the original substance of the innate knowledge of the good) as *taixu*, describing it as a self-transcending state of *xin* or mind-and-heart (Ching 1987, 284).

See also Laozi; *Xin*; Xunzi; Zhuangzi.

Bibliography

Chan, Wing-tsit. *A Source Book in Chinese Philosophy*. Princeton, N.J.: Princeton University Press, 1963.

Ching, Julia. "Glossary of Technical Terms." In *The Records of Ming Scholars by Huang Tsung-hsi*, trans. Julia Ching. Honolulu: University of Hawaii Press, 1987.

Cua, A. S. "The Possibility of Ethical Knowledge: Reflections on a Theme in the *Hsün Tzu*." In *Epistemological Issues in Ancient Chinese Philosophy*, ed. Hans Lenk and Gregor Paul. Albany: State University of New York Press, 1993.

Lau, D. C., trans. *Lao Tzu Tao Te Ching*. New York: Penguin, 1963. (Basis of the translations in the present article.)

Munro, Donald J. *The Concept of Man in Early China*. Stanford, Calif.: Stanford University Press, 1969.

Watson, Burton, trans. *The Complete Works of Chuang Tzu*. New York: Columbia University Press, 1968. (Basis of the translations in the present article.)

———, trans. *Hsün Tzu: Basic Writings*. New York: Columbia University Press, 1963.

Zhang, Dainian. *Zhongguo gudian zhexue gainian fanchou yaolun* (An Outline of Concepts and Categories in Classic Chinese Philosophy). Peking: Zhongguo shehui kexue chubanshe, 1989.

Xu Fuguan (Hsü Fu-kuan)

Su-san Lee

Xu Fuguan (Hsü Fu-kuan, 1904–1982) was a second-generation new Confucian (*xin rujia*). Xu's remarkably multifaceted life can be divided into three phases: in mainland China (1904–1949), in Taiwan (1949–1969), and in Hong Kong (1969–1982).

Born into a poor family in a destitute village of the Hubei Province, Xu identified himself with the rural masses, in defiance of the urbanity of most modern Chinese intellectuals. He received the classical Chinese education of a schoolteacher, but poverty forced him to join the army. Lu Xun's works made him an iconoclast, and he was converted to socialism by reading Kawakami Hajime during two years of study in Japan. His antipathy to the brutal class struggle kept him from joining the Chinese Communist Party (CCP); ironically, though, after serving as a liaison counselor in Yan'an, he wrote an insightful report on the CCP in 1943 that won over the Nationalist (KMT) leader Chiang Kai-shek. Xu's life took another turn in 1944, when he met the ingenious, eccentric new-Confucian master Xiong Shili. Xiong's powerful personality and unconventional interpretations of Chinese culture dissolved Xu's long-held hostility to Confucianism. But Xu did not commit himself to serious scholarship until his aspirations for reforming the KMT were frustrated.

As the CCP rose to power in 1949, Xu fled to Taiwan, along with a million other refugees. His military and political career came to a halt, and his public life as an intellectual began. During his twenty-year stay in Taiwan, Xu was the publisher of the *Democratic Review* (*Minzhu pinglun*, 1949–1966) and a professor of Chinese literature at Tunghai University (1955–1969), an institution founded by American missionaries. His sharp political-cultural commentaries made him famous, as did his heated debates with rivals on all fronts: the KMT's propagandists, westernized liberals (e.g., Hu Shi, Yin Haiguang, and Li Ao), abstract artists, mainstream historians, and others.

If the confusion created by the fall of the imperial order and the May Fourth Movement constituted the quandary of first-generation modern Confucians such as Liang Shuming and Xiong Shili, the triumph of communism in China constituted an even deeper cultural crisis for the second-generation new Confucians. In his soul-searching on the fall of the Nationalist China, Xu not only blamed the corrupt ruling party, with its political and military blunders, but also found the nonchalance of the westernized liberal intellectuals inexcusable. Xu's sense of a predicament (*youhuan yixia*, a term he coined) impelled him to ponder a fundamental question: other than radical communism, conservative fascism, and impotent liberalism, what alternative polity and culture could modern Chinese envision? In his book *Between Scholarship and Politics* (*Xueshu yu zhengzhi zhijian*, 1956), he proposed building democracy and science on the basis of Confucianism. In 1958, together with Tang Junyi, Mou Zongsan, and the senior Zhang Junmai (Carsun Chang), Xu announced a "Manifesto for a Reappraisal of Sinology and Reconstruction of Chinese Culture" (*Wei Zhongguo wenhua jinggao shijie renshi xuanyan*); its aim was to rejuvenate China through modern Confucianism.

Instead of a totalistic, organic view of culture, Xu argued that every nation consisted of multiple layers of traditions to be treated separately and analytically. He portrayed China as an innocent, diligent rural society suffering from exploitation by the monarchy and the gentry; authentic Confucians were the peasants' only ally. Therefore, neither an all-out attack on Chinese culture nor an unconditional embrace of that culture was justifiable. Even Confucianism per se needed to be examined critically. For example, the Confucian faith in human nature had fostered the great doctrines of "dominion through virtue" (*dezhi*) and "governing on behalf of the people" (*minben*), yet in reality these doctrines had hardly succeeded in ridding China of despotism or dynastic cycles. Xu agreed with his mentor Xiong that the ruler-focused approach rendered Confucian political philosophy wishful thinking. Instead of regulating the ruler's power, Confucians always expected the emergence of a sage king. Rather than actively fighting for their rights from below, the Chinese people accommodated themselves to whatever the ruler decreed from above. Moreover, the Confucian focus on ethics and politics prevented the development of a tradition of "knowledge for knowledge's sake"—a tradition conducive to modern science.

In countering the traditionalists, Xu argued that, historically, democracy and science had not evolved in China, yet currently Chinese culture needed both of these modern (not just "western") developments, so that the invisible, subjective Confucian morality could be reinforced by an objective rule of law and measurable knowledge. To meet the liberals' skepticism about the compatibility of Confucianism with democracy and science, Xu argued that, unlike the Christian church, Confucianism had a rational, worldly character with no antiscience elements. In addition, if it adopted the old formula *zhongti xiyong*—Chinese learning for essence, western learning for function—Confucianism could well fit into democracy. Xu differed from his new-Confucian colleagues in that his political experiences seemed to give him a deeper faith in the "western function." Indeed, if one understood Confucianism as a set of timeless values transcending history, and democracy as a neutral form or procedure open to competition among ideologies (this is similar to Joseph A. Schumpeter's idea of democracy), then a scenario in which "quintessential Confucianism" would operate as an alternative ideology in that democratic procedure was to some extent feasible. Such eclecticism seems to have helped alleviate the tension between Xu's early iconoclasm and his later Confucian convictions.

However, except for science and democracy, Xu saw western civilization as full of flaws. Besides the oppressive western colonialism, he was highly critical of other prevalent western ideas—Christianity, communism, Freudianism, existentialism, logical empiricism, and even modern art. This attitude was based primarily on his interpretation of Confucian "human nature." As Xu reveals in his preface to *The History of the Chinese Philosophy of Human Nature: The Pre-Qin Period* (*Zhongguo renxinglun shi: Xianqin pian*, 1959), he considered the philosophy of human nature the key of all culture. He characterized the Confucian idea (or more specifically, the Mencian idea) of humanity as follows. Human mind (*xin*) contained both cognitive and moral faculties: the cognitive faculties were neutral, passive, and susceptible to being driven by sensual desires, whereas the moral faculties, embodied one's moral nature (*xing*), were conferred by heaven and as divine as heaven. Though rudimentary at its inception, moral nature could be mastered and expanded to distinguish humans from animals. In terms of this moral endowment, everyone was equal. Belief in this immanent morality implied not looking for the ultimate value elsewhere (e.g., in God or in Platonic "ideas"), but rather fostering one's own moral responsibility and thus guaranteeing the meaning of one's life in this world.

Seen in this light, the Christian postulation of sin and the Christian belief in transcendence were the root of the lapse of the west. Despite their atheism, the Marxists' materialist interpretation of history implied a negation of humanity similar to the Judeo-Christian denial of human moral autonomy. By the same token, in Xu's eyes, the Freudians' stress on a subconscious driven by *eros*, the existentialists' emphasis on unconsciousness as genuine human existence, and even the logical empiricists' colorless thought all verged on a rejection of human moral accountability. It seems that, while Xu denounced a holistic organic approach to the study of Chinese culture, his view of western culture was an oversimplified generalization.

Xu's "moral aesthetics" and his critique of modern art reflected the same propensity. In *The Spirit of Chinese Art* (*Zhongguo yishu jingshen*, 1966), he paid tribute to the Daoist Zhuangzi's quasi-aesthetic outlook on life. By renouncing sensual desires and intellectual bias, Zhuangzi had achieved an egalitarian view of the world. Moreover, as the boundary between subject and object dissolved, extraordinary art emerged. In Xu's opinion, traits of Chinese landscape paintings—such as the beauty of plainness (*dan*) and the tranquil appreciation of nature—derived from Zhuangzi. However, despite Xu's praise of Daoist aesthetics, his own philosophy of art was, perhaps unwittingly, more Confucian than Daoist. Xu's controversy with young artists in Taiwan over modernist painting revealed that he thought of art as an instrument of morality rather than as something free from utilitarian concerns. Whereas Daoism affirms all values equally, Xu asserted that only the virtuous could create the beautiful. Although he realized that aesthetic activity and moral cultivation were categorically different, he still expected the artist to incorporate public-spiritdness into self-expression. He believed that innate, universal human goodness was the reason why individuality and society could converge.

Xu argued that along with its idiosyncratic negation of natural images, modern art (e.g., Dada, surrealism, and abstract art) was characterized by desperation, skepticism, and a strongly destructive impulse. Avant-garde artists aspired to liberate human beings from mechanical civilization by invoking the power of the subconscious and the unconscious. In fact, though, they secluded themselves from society and from nature, and so they could hardly affect the ethos of scientific rationality—instead, they were really threatening humanity and morality. According to Xu, western culture was strong in cognitive reason but weak in moral reason; to check the afflictions resulting from overrationalization, westerners should transform their lives through moral reason rather than turn to the libido. Xu believed that in this sense Confucianism offered a remedy to the west.

Xu's impetuous style as well as his Confucian convictions made him a controversial figure in Taiwan. Probably because of his former tie with Chiang Kai-shek, Xu escaped being purged during the "white terror." Yet eventually his strong nationalism disturbed his Christian colleagues, and the KMT's secret agency conspired to force him to leave Tunghai University, and leave Taiwan as well.

Xu was at first dismayed by his move to Hong Kong, but gradually he began to appreciate the British colony as a vantage point from which to watch China, as well as a place where free expression was possible. He now shifted his target from Chiang's Taiwan to Mao's China. Xu's strong critique of the Cultural Revolution irritated the CCP but won him great respect among the general public. In Hong Kong he completed his last major work, the three-volume *Intellectual History of the Han Dynasty* (*Lianghan sixiangshi*, 1972–1979). As an adherent of Lu-Wang neo-Confucianism, Xu wrote this book to refute the Qing scholars' claim that the essence of Han learning was philology, though he too studied philology and applied solid textual scholarship. According to Xu, Chinese intellectuals had fared tragically after the unified, despotic Qin-Han rule replaced the decentralized, feudal Chou (Zhou) dynasty. Xu admired the Han scholars' efforts to keep Confucianism alive under despotism, but he felt that their syncretism amounted to deterioration, compared with the intellectual creativity of the pre-Qin era. As usual, Xu's contemporary concerns permeated his academic research—for example, one can read his critique of the Cultural Revolution between the lines of *Intellectual History of the Han Dynasty*. This flawed his work but fascinated his readers.

Xu never considered himself a philosopher. His strong sense of reality and his impulse to action distinguished him from his new-Confucian colleagues, who took a more metaphysical approach. At the end of his life, Xu conceded that the Confucian cause was lost, though he himself remained an unyielding warrior. People admired his moral courage as a political dissenter, but neither China, Hong Kong, nor Taiwan was likely to build a democracy along Confucian lines. Xu endeavored to explore the universal meaning of Confucianism in modern terms and to scrutinize modernity in terms of Confucian criteria, but this effort found little response among the general public and academicians. However, as a soldier, politician, historian, democratic activist, and political-cultural critic, Xu was concerned with important human values in every phase of his life. Whether or not Confucianism revives in the public sphere, we find in Xu Fuguan an embodiment of Confucian self-fulfillment that will be meaningful for many in the years to come.

See also Philosophy: Recent Trends in Taiwan.

Bibliography

Cao, Yongyang, ed. *Xu Fuguan jiashou jinian wenji* (Essays in Memory of Professor Xu Fuguan). Taipei: Shibao Culture, 1984.

Li, Weiwu, ed. *Xu Fuguan yu zhongguo wenhua* (Xu Fuguan and Chinese Culture). Wuhan: Hubei People's Publishing House, 1997.

Xu, Fuguan. *Lianghan sixiangshi* (Intellectual History of the Han Dynasty). Taipei: Xuesheng Bookstore, 1985. (Reprint of 1972–1979 edition.)

———. *Xu Fuguan wenlu xuancui* (Selected Miscellaneous Essays of Xu Fuguan), ed. Xiao Xinyi. Taipei: Xuesheng Bookstore, 1980.

———. *Xu Fuguan zawen* (Commentaries by Xu Fuguan), ed. Xiao Xinyi. Taipei: Shibao Culture, 1980.

———. *Xueshu yu zhengzhi zhijian* (Between Scholarship and Politics). Taipei: Xuesheng Bookstore, 1980. (Reprint of 1956–1957 edition.)

———. *Zhongguo renxinglun shi: Xianqin pian* (The History of the Chinese Philosophy of Human Nature: The Pre-Qin Period). Taipei: Shangwu Bookstore, 1990. (Reprint of 1967 edition.)

———. *Zhongguo sixiangshi lunji* (Treatises on Chinese history of idea). Taipei: Xuesheng Bookstore, 1993. (Reprint of 1959 edition.)

———. *Zhongguo wenxue lunji* (Treatises on Chinese Literature). Taipei: Xuesheng Bookstore, 1974.

———. *Zhongguo yishu jingshen* (The Spirit of Chinese Art). Taipei: Xuesheng Bookstore, 1976. (Reprint of 1966 edition.)

Yang, Xiugong, ed. *Tunghai (Donghai) daxue Xu Fuguan xueshu sixiang guoji yantaohui lunwenji* (An International Symposium on Xu Fuguan's Scholarship and Ideas, Held at Tunghai University). Taichung: Tunghai University, 1992.

Xuanzang (Hsüan-tsang)

Bruce Williams

Xuanzang (Hsüan-tsang, c. 602 or 603–664) was known for the record of his travels to India, as well as for numerous influential translations of Indian Buddhist texts. Xuanzang has not left us any explicit, detailed discussion of his philosophical position. Any attempt to reconstruct his philosophical outlook must proceed by culling information from three main areas. First are his *Record of the Western Regions* (*Xiyu ji*, T. 2057), completed in 646 C.E., and the three extant biographies written by his contemporaries: (1) *Biography of the Dharma Master Xuanzang* (*Xuanzang fashi xingzhuang*, T. 2052) by Ming Xiang (dates unknown); (2) the biography of Xuanzang that occupies the bulk of fascicle (*juan*) 4 of *Continuation of the Biographies of Eminent Monks* (*Xu Gaoseng zhuan*, T. 2060) by Daoxuan (596–667); and (3) *Biography of Tripitaka, the Dharma Master of the Great Ci'en Monastery under the Great Tang* (*Da Tang da Ci'en sanzang fashi zhuan*, T. 2053) by Huili (615–c. 675) and Yancong (fl. 649–688), with a preface by Yancong dated to 688. Ming Xiang's biography, although undated, predates the other two, since they both utilize it. The biography by Huili and Yancong has been traditionally regarded as Xuanzang's standard biography. Second are the types of texts Xuanzang translated. Third, according to tradition, is his translation of *Thirty Stanzas* (*Trimsika*) by Vasubandhu (c. 420–500) and his editing of ten commentaries to these stanzas, all compiled under the title *Discourse on the Accomplishment of Consciousness Only* (*Cheng weishi lun*, T. 1585), or *Vijnaptimatrata siddhi*.

Despite discrepancies among the three biographies, the dates of certain events in Xuanzang's life can be ascertained reasonably well. Xuanzang, originally surnamed Chen, was the youngest of four children from an elite northern Chinese family; his grandfather, Chen Kang, served at the court of the Northern Qi dynasty (561–577). Xuanzang grew to adulthood during the last years of the Sui dynasty (581–618) and the beginning of the Tang dynasty (618–906). He became a novice monk while young, and traveled with his second oldest brother, Chen Su, who had previously been fully ordained as the *bhiksu* Changjie at the Jingtu Monastery in Luoyang. In the fifth year of the Wude reign period (622), at age twenty or twenty-one, Xuanzang was ordained as a *bhiksu* in Chengdu. He established himself early on as a talented monk. He was particularly interested in clarifying problems he encountered in reading the *Mahayana samgraha* (*She dacheng lun*, T. 1592, 1593), attributed to Asanga, and was well-versed in the *Abhidharma*, most likely of the Indian Sarvastivada school. He was not satisfied with the answers he received from other Chinese monks to his questions regarding the *Mahayana samgraha*. Furthermore, he felt that some of the problems he encountered were the result of faulty translations. Since he heard that in India there was another text by Asanga, the *Yogacarabhumi sastra*, which laid out the Yogacara approach fully, he decided to go to India to obtain this teaching and resolve his doubts. According to tradition, he left the capital, Chang'an, in the eighth lunar month of 629. However, his departure more likely took place in the autumn of 627, because in the fourth or fifth lunar month he met with the Turkish Yagbu Kagan Tong, who died before the eighth lunar month of 628. Because of the interdiction on travel in the early, unsettled years of the Tang dynasty, he left illegally. Shortly after he arrived in Khotan in 644, after his extended stay in India, he sent a letter to Emperor Taizong of the Tang. He apologized for his illegal departure and announced that he was returning to China with a large number of Buddhist scriptures, but no longer had the means to transport them further. After a wait of seven or eight months he received an imperial decree supplying him with horses and supplies. He arrived in Chang'an on the seventh day of the first lunar month of 645. He brought with him 150 relic bones, and numerous images, of the Buddha. In addition, twenty horses carried 657 (sic) books in 520 bundles: 224 Mahayana sastras, 192 Mahayana treatises, 15 treatises and works on the disciplinary rules of the Sthavira school, 15 treatises and works on the disciplinary rules of the Mahasamghikas, 15 treatises and works on the disciplinary rules of the Sammitiyas, 22 treatises and works on the disciplinary rules of the Mahisasakas, 17 treatises and works on the disciplinary rules of the Kasyapiyas, 42 treatises and works on the disciplinary rules of the Dharmaguptakas, 67 treatises and works on the disciplinary rules of the Sarvastivadas, 36 texts on logic (*Hetuvidya*), and 13 texts on grammar (*Sabdavidya*).

Xuanzang had audiences with Emperor Taizong in Luoyang on the twenty-third of that month, and again on the first of the second month. During his second audience he declined the emperor's offer of an official post in the government and requested that he be allowed to translate the texts he had brought back to China. The emperor not only acceded to his request but also granted him the use of Hongfu Monastery, built in 634 in Chang'an to commemorate the death of Taizong's mother. This began the steady imperial patronage that Xuanzang was to enjoy for the rest of his life. Xuanzang took up residence at the monastery immediately upon his return to Chang'an and in the sixth lunar month of that year consolidated his translation bureau. Translation began on the first day of the seventh month and continued uninterrupted, first at Hongfu Monastery and then at other monasteries, until Xuanzang's death at midnight of the fifth day of the second lunar month, 668.

In the middle of the first lunar month of 668, shortly before he died, Xuanzang had a monk make a list of his translations and accomplishments. In addition to his translation of 75 works in 1,335 fascicles, he had painted 1,000 pictures each of Maitreya and Bhrkuti; made 10 *kotis* of clay statues; transcribed 1,000 times each such sutras as the *Diamond Sutra*, the *Bhaisajyaguru sutra*, and the *Sadmukhadharani sutra*; given alms to more than 10,000 poor people; made offerings to more than 10,000 monks; lit hundreds of thousands of lamps; and redeemed the lives of tens of thousands of living creatures. He was a longtime devotee of Maitreya, and immediately before dying he expressed his certainty that he would be born in the presence of Maitreya in the Tusita heaven.

Xuanzang's biographers state repeatedly that he viewed himself primarily as a translator and viewed his translations as his legacy. These biographies, especially his standard biography, attest to his devotion to Sakyamuni Buddha, Avalokitesvara (e.g., through his recitations of the *Xinjing*, or *Heart Sutra*), Manjusri (e.g., in prophetic dreams), and especially Maitreya. His devotion to Maitreya predated his meeting with Silabhadra (c. 529–645) in India. This is demonstrated, in his standard biography, by the meditative visualization Xuanzang performed when he was preparing to meet his death at the hands of pirates soon after he arrived in India. Such Maitreya meditations are also detailed in the writings of Ci'en Kuiji (632–682), Xuanzang's most famous disciple and the founder of the *Faxiang*, or *Dharma-laksana*, lineage of Chinese Buddhism, and of the Korean monk Wonhyo (617–686). In addition to the importance that Maitreya had for Asanga and his brother Vasubandhu and the lineages that developed from them—e.g., through Dharmapala (c. 530–561) and his disciple Silabhadra—as early as Dao'an (312–385) in China we see Maitreya approached not only as a compassionate bodhisattva and the next buddha, but also as the patron of exegetes.

To ascertain Xuanzang's philosophical views, we need to survey the following issues: his abiding allegiance to the Mahayana, and, in particular, to the Yogacara tradition; his interest in the literature of *prajnaparamita*, or perfection of wisdom; his persistent interest in *Abhidharma*, particularly that of the non-Mahayana Sarvastivada school; his standardization of the number of "consciousnesses" in Yogacara at eight; his continuation of Dharmapala's interpretation of *vijnana parinama* in preference to Sthiramati's interpretation; his interpretation of the three natures; and his association with the issue that there are *icchantika*, or beings who never attain buddhahood.

The biographies of Xuanzang and the texts he both brought back to China and chose to translate attest to his lifelong commitment to the Mahayana. His standard biography provides examples, in fact, of his belittling non-Mahayana Buddhist monks; one of them was Prajnadeva in India—who, despite this ridicule, still held Xuanzang in high regard. Xuanzang's interest in both Yogacara and *prajnaparamita* likewise predated his departure for India. We have already noted the role of the *Mahayana samgraha* and the *Yogacarabhumi sastra* in Xuanzang's decision to go to India. Before he left he also had already studied the *prajnaparamita* literature. He learned the *Heart Sutra* while in Shu, in southwestern China, from an old monk; while traveling in Central Asia he often recited this sutra to dispel evils and troubles. In India, Xuanzang is recorded as having written the *Nikaya samgraha sastra* (*Huizong lun*)—in 3,000 stanzas—to demonstrate the fundamental harmony of Yogacara and Madhyamaka. Unfortunately, since this work has not survived, we have no clear statement by him on this issue. Another of Xuanzang's disciples, however, the Korean monk Wonch'uk (612–696), did write on this issue in his commentary to the *Sandhinirmocana sutra*, the *Arya gambira samdhinirmocana sutra tika*, now preserved in Tibetan translation. Unfortunately, there seems to have been considerable friction between Wonch'uk's chief disciple, Tojung (dates unknown), and Huizhao (d. 714), Kuiji's successor in the *Faxiang* lineage, and possibly even between Kuiji and Wonch'uk themselves. Moreover, Wonch'uk frequently championed Sthiramati's interpretation of certain issues, e.g., on the *icchantika*, over Dharmapala's. Thus we can only speculate about to what extent Wonch'uk's views on this issue reflect Xuanzang's. Twenty-three of the seventy-five works Xuanzong translated were related to Yogacara. Toward the end of his life Xuanzang again focused on the *prajnaparamita* literature. Between the middle of 660 and the end of 663, while at Yuhua Palace, he translated the *100,000-line Mahaprajnaparamita sutra* in 600 fascicles, and lectured on it.

Xuanzang's study of the *Abhidharma* literature parallels his study of Yogacara. The form of Yogacara elucidated in the *Cheng weishi lun* shows strong affiliations with Sarvastivada *Abhidharma* in both terminology and conceptual structure. His interest in *Abhidharma* may go beyond a simple interest in what might be called the "background" of Indian Yogacara. One suspects—from his long study of (Sarvastivada) *Abhidharma* treatises in China, Central Asia, and India; from his frequent discussions of *Abhidharma* with non-Mahayana, and especially Sarvastivada, monks and his study of *Abhidharma* treatises with them; and from the significant number of important Sarvastivada *Abhidharma* works he translated—that Xuanzang had a solid interest in this literature in its own right. While Mahayana sutras, Mahayana treatises, and Sarvastivada works account for 81 percent of the texts he translated and 73 percent of the texts he brought back from India, Sarvastivada works alone account for 11 percent of the texts he brought back, and 19 persent of what he translated—remarkable numbers for a devout Mahayanist.

Traditional and modern scholars of Buddhism in east Asia have usually regarded the *Cheng weishi lun* as an exposition of Xuanzang's philosophical position. This stance is problematic for at least two reasons. First is the problem of the work's structure. It has two main parts: a translation of Vasubandhu's *Trimsika*, or *Thirty Stanzas*; and a summary, by Xuanzang, of ten commentaries to the *Trimsika*. In his introductory remarks to his abbreviated commentary to this work, *The Pivotal Essentials, As If in the Palm of Your Hand, to the Cheng weishi lun* (*Cheng weishi lun zhangzhong shuyao*, T. 1831) in four fascicles, Kuiji tells us that Xuanzang originally planned to translate each of the ten commentaries separately. Kuiji threatened to leave the translation project, and Xuanzang, if Xuanzang did so. Kuiji argued that a straightforward translation of the verses together with ten different commentaries, each with its own point of view, would only confuse those who wanted to know the profound meaning of the *Trimsika*. He suggested that Xuanzang combine the ten commentaries into a single text and arrange it so that the import of the verses would be clear. Xuanzang finally relented. Of the ten commentators used—Dharmapala, Sthiramati, Cittrabhana, Nanda, Gunamati, Jinamitra, Jnanacandra, Vandhusri, Suddhacandra, and Jinapura—only the commentary by Sthiramati has survived, and in Sanskrit. It has treaditionally been thought that Xuanzang used Dharmapala's commentary as a framework to organize and synthesize the other nine into a single text, and that Dharmapāla's interpretation was taken as the standard. Although we depend almost entirely on Kuiji's commentaries to the *Cheng weishi lun* to identify the various commentators and their positions, certain of these attributions can be checked through reference to Sthiramati's commentary.

It is in the synthesis of the commentaries and in the promotion of Dharmapala's views as correct, following Kuiji's identifications, that any assessment of Xuanzang's philosophy lies. Central to this assessment is the degree to which one determines that a disciple reflects accurately the views of his teacher (or teacher's teacher). This is a problem that involves both Xuanzang and Kuiji and indicates our second problem with the *Cheng weishi lun*: it appears to have been a much more important work for Kuiji than for Xuanzang.

Kuiji wrote three commentaries to the *Cheng weishi lun*: his large twenty-fascicle *Exposition of the Cheng weishi lun* (*Cheng weishi lun shuji*, T. 1830); the *Pivotal Essentials*, mentioned earlier; and *Separate Notes on the Cheng weishi lun* (*Cheng weishi lun bichao*, ZZ 1.77.5), of which only four somewhat defective fascicles (1, 5, 9, and 10) out of ten survive. Kuiji states (in the introductory remarks to the *Pivotal Essentials*) that he was the only assistant Xuanzang had during the translation of this work, and thus the only person to whom Xuanzang revealed its true meaning; he also says (in the introductory remarks to the *Exposition*) that his commentary on the *Cheng weishi lun* was done under Xuanzang's guidance. The *Cheng weishi lun* formed the central text of the *Faxiang* lineage founded by Kuiji, and his commentaries provided the orthodox interpretation of this text. This contrasts sharply with the absence of any mention of the *Cheng weishi lun* in Xuanzang's standard biography. There the important text is the voluminous *Yogacarabhumi sastra* (and the *Mahayana samgraha*).

Despite these qualifications the *Cheng weishi lun* can be used effectively on occasion to gauge Xuanzang's views. For example, together with the *Yogacarabhumi sastra*, the *Cheng weishi lun* determined finally for Chinese Buddhists whether there were eight or nine consciousnesses. Before the introduction of these two works, certain Chinese Buddhist scholars argued for nine consciousnesses: (1–6) the six sense consciousnesses, including the (sixth) mental consciousness (*manovijnana*); (7) the *manas*, or continually discriminating mind, that objectifies the next consciousness, the *alayavijnana*, as an abiding, permanently existing self; (8) the *alayavijnana*, or "storage" consciousness; and (9) the *amalavijnana*, or unstained consciousness. This last consciousness was sometimes also called the *tathagatagarbha* (*rulai zang*), or "womb of the Tathagata." While this ninth consciousness was completely pure and devoid of any defilement, the *alayavijnana* was regarded as defiled. These two works stated that there were only eight consciousnesses and denied the existence of a ninth, undefiled consciousness.

The *Cheng weishi lun* presented a fourfold classification of purity and impurity: defiled, undefiled, and nondefined, itself divided into defiled nondefined, and nondefiled nondefined. In this system the *alayavijnana* was classified as nondefiled nondefined, since in its essence the *alayavijnana* was the result of karmic retribution (*vipakaphala*) and, by definition, karmic retribution was neither pure nor impure. While this perspective on the *alayavijnana* did not finally resolve the debate in China, or the rest of east Asia, over the purity or impurity of the *alayavijnana* and such issues as the status of the *tathagatagarbha*, such debates now took place within the framework of eight consciousnesses. Even Wonch'uk, who frequently advocated Sthiramati's position as opposed to Dharmapala's, followed Dharmapala's theory of an eightfold division rather than Sthiramati's ninefold division.

The organization of the *Cheng weishi lun* also allows us to see Xuanzang's position on *vijnana-parinama*, or the transformations of consciousness. All Indian Yogacarins agreed that for those beings not yet liberated—i.e., beings below the eighth *bhumi*, or stage, of ten—the eight (or nine) consciousnesses were permanently split into a component that grasps (*grahaka*), the subject; and a component that is grasped (*grahya*), the object. Disagreement arose, however, about the status of this distinction for those who were liberated, i.e., the buddhas and those bodhisattvas of the eighth through the tenth *bhumi*, who have removed all the obstructions due to defilements (*klesavarana*), but who (in the case of bodhisattvas) may not have yet removed all obstructions to knowledge (*jneyavarana*). In line with the logicians Dignaga (c. 480–540) and Dharmakirti (c. 600–660), Dharmapala claimed that the consciousnesses of all beings, including buddhas, were characterized by a threefold division: the perceived division (*nimittabhaga*); the perceiving division (*darsanabhaga*); and the self-witnessing division (*svasamvittibhaga*). This last division is the apperception that a cognition has taken place, i.e., having perceived the color blue, one is aware that one has perceived the color blue. This division was also a crucial component in establishing the idealist position: it eliminated the need for external objects to explain cognition, since the mind just knows its own subjective and objective components.

In India after Dharmakirti this position was called *sakaravada*, or the view (*vada*) that consciousness is always endowed with (*sa*) an image (*akara*). Conversely, Indian Yogacarins such as Vasubandhu and Sthiramati state that for enlightened beings of the eighth *bhumi* and above, this bifurcation into "grasper" and "grasped" is seen to be pure fabrication or imagination. This group of Yogacarins does not use the terminology of the threefold division. Since, in the final stages, consciousness, pure and radiant, is fundamentally without an image, this position was also called the *nirakaravada*, or the view that consciousness is fundamentally devoid of (*nir*) an image.

Dharmapala presents his interpretation of *vijnana-parinama* in his commentary to verse 17 of the *Trimsika*. It reads, in Sanskrit:

> *Vijnana-parinamo 'yam vikalpo yad vikalpyate*
> *tena tannasti tenedam sarvam vijnaptimatrakam.*

Following Dharmapala's commentary, Xuanzang translated this verse as:

> *Shi zhushi zhuanbian,*
> *Fenbie suofenbie;*
> *Youci bi jie wu,*
> *Gu yiqie weishi.*

Or, in English:

> The various transformations of consciousness (are split into) the distinguishing and what is distinguished;
> Because of this, those (dharmas and the self) all do not exist;
> Therefore everything is consciousness only.

Sthiramati, arguably closer to the grammar and Vasubandhu's position, interprets the Sanskrit verse as follows:

> These transformations of consciousness are false discrimination; what is falsely discriminated,
> That, by reason of this, does not exist; therefore all is representation-only.

Both Dharmapala and Sthiramati take verse 17 as the conclusion to the first sixteen verses, which have dealt with the three transformations of consciousness first enumerated at the end of verse 1 and the beginning of verse 2: *alayavijnana, manas*, and the six sense consciousnesses. Each uses this conclusion to establish the truth of *vijnaptimatrata*, or "representation only." Dharmapala's interpretation establishes this truth based on the fundamental bifurcation of consciousness (*vijnana*) into perceiving and perceived divisions. Since these are two aspects of the same fundamental consciousness, the self and the dharmas, taken by deluded beings to be existing separately, perduring entities, do not exist as such. Sthiramati, in his commentary, interprets this verse to mean that, for the unenlightened, the basic split of various consciousnesses into "grasper" and "grasped," self and dharmas, does not actually exist but is a result of false discrimination.

The telling aspect of the *Cheng weishi lun* at this point is that Sthiramati's interpretation of the verse is absent from the summary in Xuanzang's commentary. Unless the commentary by Sthiramati in Xuanzang's possession differed significantly from that now extant, we must conclude that Xuanzang made a conscious decision to exclude it from the apparatus for this verse, and that this decision was based on Xuanzang's philosophical position on *vijnana-parinama*.

The difference between Dharmapala and Sthiramati is also reflected in their treatment of the three natures: (1) the imagined nature (*parikalpita-svabhava*); (2) the "other-dependent" nature (*paratantra-svabhava*); (3) and the totally pure and tranquil nature (*parinispanna-svabhava*). Yogacara thinkers in India disagreed with the Madhyamakas over the range of application of *sunyata* (*kong*), or emptiness. For the Madhyamakas everything was characterized as empty. The Yogacarins argued that, while everything that had an imagined nature (*parikalpita-svabhava*) was empty, *parinispanna-svabhava* was not. Within Yogacara, however, there was disagreement over whether *paratantra-svabhava*—in Yogacara synonymous with codependent origination (*pratityasamutpada*)—was empty or not. In general, only by realizing *parinispanna-svabhava* could one see *paratantra-svabhava* correctly, unobscured by the false imputations of *parikalpita-svabhava*. For Sthiramati, *paratantra-svabhava* was the matrix characterized by "grasper" and "grasped." Since this split was the result of false discrimination, *paratantra-svabhava* itself was empty. For Dharmapala, *paratantra-svabhava* was the matrix characterized by the threefold division. To the extent that it is discriminated falsely as the existent self and dharmas, it participates in *parikalpita-svabhava*, and is empty. As the actual nondual structure of consciousness based on *parinispanna-svabhava*, it was not empty. The commentary to verse 22 of the *Cheng weishi lun*, in fact, states that *paratantra-svabhava* and *parinispanna-svabhava* are neither different nor not different. If *parinispanna-svabhava*, synonymous with *tathata* (suchness), were not different from *paratantra-svabhava, tathata* would not be eternal; if they were not not different, *tathata* would not be the real nature of *paratantra-svabhava*. For Dharmapala, if *paratantra-svabhava* were not real, the threefold division of perceived, perceiving, and self-witnessing, as the tripartite, nondual structure of consciousness, would not be real.

Perhaps no position associated with Xuanzang was so hotly contested in East Asia as his position on the *icchantika* (*yichanti*), beings who never attain enlightenment. Although among those associated with Xuanzang the clearest, most complete early statements on the existence of the *icchantika* come from Kuiji's writings, evidence that Xuanzang himself personally held that there was such a class of beings can be gathered from two areas: Xuanzang's inquiry before an image of Avalokitesvara (Guanyin) in India whether he was an *icchantika* or not; and the criticism of the monk Lingrun (d. c. 649), one of Xuanzang's earliest assistants in the translation bureau.

In China the issue of the *icchantika* is linked to two related debates over a fivefold division of sentient beings into (1) those (*sravaka*) who were destined to become *arhat*; (2) those destined to become *pratyekabuddha*, or solitary buddhas; (3) those (bodhisattvas) destined to become buddhas; (4) those whose destiny (as 1, 2, or 3) was not yet determined; and (5) those (*icchantika*) who never would, or never could, attain enlightenment. On the one hand there was a debate that first surfaced in China in the early fifth century over whether the first three divisions constituted distinct, exclusive spiritual paths, the three vehicles; or whether there was just one, the Buddha vehicle. On the other hand there was the debate over whether the *icchantika*, who were mentioned in the sutras, could ever attain enlightenment. The problem was whether this class was composed of beings who do not attain enlightenment, but could if they met with the right conditions; or whether it was composed of beings who could never attain enlightenment, presumably because they were so evil. The influence of a translation by Dharmaksema (385–431) of the *Mahaparinirvana sutra* (T. 374, 375), completed in 421, as well as the influence of translations of the *Saddharmapundarika sutra*, or *Lotus Sutra*, had long resolved both issues for most Chinese Buddhists before Xuanzang's return from India. There was only one vehicle, the Buddha vehicle; the three vehicles were only a metaphor, and all beings were capable of attaining buddhahood, since all beings possessed the Buddha-nature (*foxing*).

Xuanzang's standard biography indicates that he accepted the existence of the *icchantika*, and thus the distinctness of the three vehicles. Since the first event that demonstrates his acceptance of the *icchantika* doctrine occurs after his meeting with Silabhadra, this suggests that Silabhadra may have been influential in Xuanzang's adoption of this theory. After studying the *Yogacarabhumi sastra* with Silabhadra at Nalanda, Xuanzang set out eastward for Iranyaparvata. On the way, two or three *li* (Chinese miles) south of Kapotika Monastery, Xuanzang paid homage before an image of Avalokitesvara in the central temple, and made three requests. In his third request he noted that in the Buddhist teachings there were mentions of beings who had no Buddha-nature, and that he had doubts and did not know if he were such a being. He asked that if he were a being endowed with Buddha-nature and could attain buddhahood through spiritual practice, a garland might fall around the neck of Avalokitesvara's statue. After making the three requests, he scattered flowers from a distance; the flowers fell just as he had asked.

Lingrun was a noted *Dilun* and *Shelun* scholar, or scholar of the *Dasabhumika vyakhyana* (*Shidi jing lun*), and *Mahayana samgraha* (*She dacheng lun*). In 634, when Emperor Taizong founded Hongfu Monastery, Lingrun was summoned to live there. When Hongfu Monastery was chosen as the site for Xuanzang's translation bureau early in 645, Lingrun was chosen as one of Xuanzang's first twelve verifiers (*zhengyi*). By 648 he had left the translation bureau. Sometime between mid–645 and around 649, when Lingrun probably died, he wrote a short treatise criticizing Xuanzang's positions. It is divided into fourteen sections; only quotations from the first section have survived in the *Hokke shuku*, composed in 821 by Saicho (767–822), a Japanese monk and the founder of the Tendai sect in Japan. Since these quotations present a detailed attack against the existence of *icchantika* soon after Xuanzang's return from India, the target of these attacks is very probably a position espoused by Xuanzang himself.

With the exception of the *Faxiang* lineage, and its Japanese counterpart, the Hosso, there has been sustained opposition to the existence of the *icchantika* in East Asia from the early fifth century to the present. The most obvious reason for this opposition is that the concept challenged the basic Mahayana Buddhist mission of saving and liberating all sentient beings. The *icchantika* posed a significant challenge in another area as well. It struck at the heart of the theory of the universality of the Buddha-nature (*foxing*) as a strategy for the acculturation of Buddhism in China. The theory of the Buddha-nature is concerned not just with the nature of buddhahood itself, but also with how sentient beings, especially human beings, participate in this Buddha-nature. Consequently, debates over the Buddha-nature are generally debates over human nature, a long-standing issue in Chinese philosophy. Medieval Daoists entered this debate through their treatments of the "nature of the Way" (*daoxing*). Later, through the influence of the writings of the Tiantai patriarch Zhanran (711–782), the theory was expanded to include the insentient as well as the sentient. In general Buddha nature theory increasingly determined the dimensions of both spiritual practice and doctrinal discourse in Chinese and East Asian Buddhism.

A final issue involves how to characterize Yogacara idealism. In East Asia after Xuanzang, Yogacara has almost universally been interpreted as a form of what might be called in western philosophy "ontological idealism": the world is consciousness and is generated through the activity of the *alayavijnana*. Scholars of the "Critical Buddhism" movement have recently attacked this "essentialist" position. Recent research suggests that in India, Yogacara was more commonly, if not universally, interpreted as a form of "epistemological idealism": all we can know is consciousness, and the apprehension of the world is solely as representation. It is still unresolved how Xuanzang, that most Indianized of all recorded premodern Chinese Buddhists, regarded Yogacara. Finally, in light of traditional Indian Buddhist schema of meditation, treating Indian Yogacara as a form of "epistemological idealism" presents us with a further question. Does the attainment of buddhahood take place within the framework of this "epistemological idealism," or is that attainment, rather, a release from its confines?

The legacy of Xuanzang is as a monk, pilgrim, translator, devotee, practitioner, and philosopher. As a pilgrim he has gone down in history with his travelogue, biographies, and translations, and also in literary and artistic legend with, for example, the seventeenth-century novel *Journey to the West* (*Xiyou ji*). The works he produced as a translator served to standardize Buddhist terminology and allowed Chinese monks and scholars to clarify and refine the Yogacara model. Although the *Faxiang* lineage founded by Kuiji died out in China around the middle of the eighth century, it lives on in Japan. Through the Huayan and Chan (Zen) lineages the Yogacara system became almost the universal model in East Asia for interpreting Buddhism and Buddhist teachings. Ironically, Xuanzang is most enigmatic as a philosopher. It is still unresolved whether we should attempt to approach him as a philosopher in his own right, or, as the East Asian traditions have done, read his philosophy through that of his students, especially Kuiji.

See also Buddhism in China.

Bibliography

Chatterjee, K. N., trans. *Vasubandhu's Vijnapti-matrata-siddhi (With Sthiramati's Commentary)*. Varanasi: Kishor Vidya Niketan, 1980, pp. 27–157. (Text with English translation.)

Dai Nihon zokuzokyo. (Cited as ZZ. Reference is to series, case, and volume.)

Groner, Paul. *Saicho: The Establishment of the Japanese Tendai School*. Berkeley Buddhist Studies Series, Vol. 7. Berkeley: Center for South and Southeast Asian Studies, University of California at Berkeley and The Institute of Buddhist Studies, 1984.

Hubbard, Jamie, and Paul L. Swanson, eds. *Pruning the Bodhi Tree: The Storm over Critical Buddhism*. Nanzan Library of Asian Religion and Culture. Honolulu: University of Hawaii Press, 1997.

Kajiyama, Yuichi. "Controversy between the Sakara- and Nirakara-vadins of the Yogacara School: Some Materials." *Journal of Indian and Buddhist Studies*, 14(1), 1965.

La Vallée Poussin, Louis de, trans. "*Vijnaptmatrata, La Siddhi de Hiuan-tsang*." *Buddhica*, Premiere Serie, Mémoires: 1, 1928; 5, 1929. (8 fascicules.)

Lévi, Sylvain. *Materiaux pour l'etude du systeme vijnaptmatrata Bibliotheque de L'Ecole des Hautes Etudes: Sciences Historique et Philologiques*, 260, 1932.

———. "*Vijnaptmatrata siddhi: Deux traites de Vasubandhu—Vimsatika* et *Trimsika. Bibliotheque de L'Ecole des Hautes Etudes: Sciences Historique et Philologiques*, 245, 1925.

Li, Rongxi, trans. *A Biography of the Tripitaka Master of the Great Ci'en Monastery of the Great Tang Dynasty*, by Sramana Huili and Shi Yancong. BDK English Tripitaka, Vol. 77. Berkeley: Numata Center for Buddhist Translation and Research, 1995.

———. *The Great Tang Dynasty Record of the Western Regions*, by Xuanzang. BDK English Tripitaka, Vol. 79. Berkeley.: Numata Center for Buddhist Translation and Research, 1996.

Lusthaus, Dan. "A Philosophic Investigation of the *Ch'eng wei-shih lun*: Vasubandhu, Hsüan-tsang, and the Transmission of *Vijnaptmatrata* (Yogacara) from India to China." Ph.D. dissertation, Temple University, 1989.

———. *Buddhist Phenomenology: A Philosophical Investigation of Yopacara Buddhism and to Ch'eng Wei-shih Lun*. Routledge Curgon Critical Studies in Buddhism, No. 13. New York: Taylor & Francis, 2002.

Mayer, Alexander Leonhard. *Xuanzangs Leben und Werk*, Teil 1, *Xuanzang: Übersetzer und Heiliger*. Veröffentlichungen der Societas Uralo-Altaica, herausgegeben von Annemarie v. Gabain und Wolfgang Veenker, Band 34. Wiesbaden: Otto Harrassowitz, 1992.

Penkower, Linda. "T'ien-t'ai during the T'ang Dynasty: Chan-jan and the Sinification of Buddhism." Ph.D. dissertation, Columbia University, 1993.

Rhodes, Robert F. "A Controversy over the Buddha-Nature in T'ang China: The Initial Debate between Ling-jun, Shen-t'ai, and I-yung." *Otani Gakuho* 73(4), April 1994, pp. 1–23.

Sponberg, Alan. "Meditation in Fa-hsiang Buddhism." In *Traditions of Meditation in Chinese Buddhism*, ed. Peter N. Gregory. Kuroda Institute, Studies in East Asian Buddhism, No. 4. Honolulu: University of Hawaii Press, 1986, pp. 15–43.

———. "Wonhyo on Maitreya Visualization." In *Maitreya, the Future Buddha*, eds. Alan Sponberg and Helen Hardacre. Cambridge: Cambridge University Press, 1988, pp. 94–109.

Takakusu, Junjiro, and Watanabe Kaigyoku, eds. *Taisho shinshu Daizokyo*, 85 vols. Tokyo: Taisho Issaikyo Kankokai, 1925–1932. (Cited as T. References are to the text sequence number.)

Tillemans, Tom J. F. *Materials for the Study of Aryadeva, Dharmapala, and Candrakirti*. Wiener Studien zur Tibetologie und Buddhismuskunde, Heft 24(2), 2 vols. Vienna: Universität Wien, 1992.

Ueda, Yoshifumi. "Two Main Streams of Thought in Yogacara Philosophy." *Philosophy East and West*, 17(1–4), January–October 1967, pp. 155–165.

Wei, Tat, trans. *Ch'eng Wei-Shih Lun: Doctrine of Mere Consciousness*, trans. and comp. Hsüan Tsang. Hong Kong: Ch'eng Wei-Shih Lun Publication Committee, 1973.

Weinstein, Stanley. "A Biographical Study of Tz'u-en." *Monumenta Nipponica*, 15, 1959–1960, pp. 119–149.

———. "The Concept of *Alayavijnana* in Pre-T'ang Chinese Buddhism." In *Essays on the History of Buddhist Thought Presented to Professor Reimon Yuki*. Tokyo: Daizo shuppan, 1964, pp. 33–50.

Willis, Janice Dean. "Introduction." In *On Knowing Reality: The Tattvartha Chapter of Asanga's Bodhisattvabhumi*. New York: Columbia University Press, 1979, pp. 3–66.

Xunzi (Hsün Tzu)

A. S. Cua

Xunzi (Master Xun, c. 298–238 B.C.E.), also known as Xun Qing and Xun Kuang, was an important exponent of classical Confucianism. Very little is known of his life. According to the earliest biography, by Sima Qian (c. 145–87 B.C.E.), *Historical Record* (*Shiji*), completed in 91 B.C.E., Xunzi was a native of the state of Zhao (in north China), went to Qi (in modern Shantung) at age fifty to spread his teachings, and became the most eminent among senior scholars. He was thrice appointed chief libationer, a position generally occupied by men of exemplary scholarship and virtue. When some men of Qi slandered him, he went to Chu and was a magistrate in Lanling. He later lost the position, but he remained there and taught until his death. His fundamental doctrines are contained in the *Xunzi*, consisting of thirty-two sections, compiled by Liu Xiang of the Former Han (206 B.C.E.–8 C.E.). While the authorship of many sections is disputed, most of the self-contained essays give a remarkably coherent and reasoned statement of the key aspects of the Confucian ethical and political vision of a well-ordered society.

Xunzi was perhaps one of the most brilliant Confucian thinkers of ancient China. His works display a wide-ranging interest in such topics as the relation between morality and human nature, moral agency, the ideal of the good human life, the nature of ethical discourse and argumentation, the ethical uses of history, moral education, and personal cultivation. Because of the comprehensive and systematic character of his philosophical concerns, Xunzi is sometimes compared to Aristotle.

Noteworthy is Xunzi's emphasis on *li* or rules of proper conduct, and the holistic character of *dao*, the Confucian ideal of the good human life. He criticized other philosophers not because of their mistakes but because of their preoccupation with one aspect of *dao* to the exclusion of others. In forming his ideal of a well-ordered society, Xunzi—like Confucius and Mencius—focused on government by an enlightened ruler (*mingzhu*), whose private and public life would exemplify the *dao* (the Way), that is, a concern with *ren* (benevolence), *yi* (rightness, righteousness), and *li* (rites, rules of proper conduct). Unlike Mencius, Xunzi was staunchly opposed to hereditary titles. For him, a good ruler must be able to attract worthy, talented persons to government service and promote or demote them in accordance with the merits or demerits of their performance. Moreover, he must provide the state and its people with a strong military defense and, more important, promulgate and efficiently administer ethically legitimate laws and institutions. Thus an enlightened ruler is one who is good at organizing society in accordance with the requirements expressed in *ren, yi*, and *li*.

This essay focuses on three important aspects of Xunzi's moral philosophy: (1) human nature, (2) the functions of *li* and its connection with *yi* and *ren*, and (3) moral epistemology as comprising concerns with the possibility of ethical deliberation, knowledge, and argumentation.

Human Nature (*Xing*)

Xunzi is best-known for his thesis that "human nature is bad" (*e*). This was proposed in opposition to Mencius's thesis that "human nature is originally good." For a critical appreciation of the issue, it is quite unproductive to regard these remarks as simple assertions. One should look for the reasons supporting these statements (Lau 1953, 558). Because many Chinese thinkers tend to use simple expressions "only as convenient labels and pivots of debate," a question properly arises "whether they may have had some inkling that the formulae unduly simplify what they were trying to say." And in the case of Xunzi's remark that "human nature is bad," it is quite inadequate as it stands for distinguishing his view from that of Mencius (Graham 1967, 258). However, while acknowledging that such simple remarks are misleading, we can profitably deal with them by attending to the notions and distinctions used.

More important, we should also consider their supporting arguments. A thesis expressed in a simple remark can be illuminating, if it is seen as a compendious way of expressing a set of arguments or observations about human nature. Arguments have an essential and dual role in explicating a thesis. The obvious role concerns the inference of a thesis as a conclusion of a given set of premises. The less obvious role pertains to their function in elucidating the meaning of the thesis. The two roles of argument cannot be separated in understanding philosophical discourse. More fundamental is an understanding of the problem that the thesis is proposed as a solution. Below I present an abbreviated account of an extensive study on this topic (Cua 1977, 1978).

To understand Xunzi's conception of human nature (*xing*), let us consider the first and principal passage in his essay on human nature (Book 23):

> The nature (*xing*) of man is bad (*e*); his goodness (*shan*) is the result of constructive effort (*wei*). The nature of man today is such that he is born with the desire for gain (*haoli*). If this tendency is followed, strife and rapacity will result and courtesy and modesty will disappear. Man is born with envy and hatred. If he yields to these feelings, injury and destruction will result and loyalty and faithfulness will disappear. Man is born with the possession of the desires (*yu*) of the ears and eyes and liking (*hao*) for sound and beauty. If he indulges in these desires lewdness and licentiousness will result, and *li* (propriety) and *yi* (righteousness) as well as cultural pattern and order (*wenli*) will disappear. Therefore, to follow man's nature and his feelings will inevitably result in strife and rapacity, combined with rebellion and disorder, and end in violence. Therefore, humans must be guided by the transformative influence of teachers and laws and the guidance of *li* and *yi*. Only then will they be able to observe the rules of deference and modesty, comply with the requirements of cultural refinement (*wenli*), and return to the social, political order (*zhi*). From this point of view, it is evident that the nature of man is bad (*e*) and that his goodness (*shan*) is the result of constructive effort (*wei*). (Book 23; Knoblock 1994, 3: 151; cf. Watson 1963, 157)

Before we explicate this passage, which is also Xunzi's principal argument, let us attend to Xunzi's use of terms such as *xing* (nature), *shan* (good) and *e* (bad). For Xunzi, *xing* pertains to whatever can be characterized as having its origin from birth. Says Xunzi, "that which is as it is from the time of birth is called the nature (*xing*) of man. That which is harmonious from birth, which is capable of perceiving through the senses and of responding to stimulus spontaneously, is also called *xing*" (Book 22, Watson 139). What is attributable to *xing* is something originally "endowed by heaven" (*tian*), something that can neither be learned nor acquired though work (Book 23, Watson 158).

Xing, the original human nature, is the opposite of *wei*: constructive effort, that which can be learned and completed by work or effort. Xunzi gives the following definitions of *shan* (good) and *e* (bad), presumably reporting the usage current in his time:

> All men in the past and the present use the term "good" (*shan*) to characterize conduct that is upright, reasonable (*li*), and conducive to peace and order (*zhiping*); and "bad" (*e*) to characerize what is arbitrarily partial (*pian*), heedless of dangerous consequences (*xian*), and conducive to chaos (*luan*). (Book 23; cf. Watson 162)

It is important to note that these definitions of "good" and "bad," while purporting to report current usage, are for Xunzi a statement of ethical norms or standards, standards such as *li* (rules of propriety, rituals; a different character from *li*, reasonable, above) and *yi* (rightness) for defining a well-ordered and peaceful society, and the opposite chaos is contrary to *li and yi* (Book 2, Knoblock 1988, 1:176).

In light of the foregoing explanations of Xunzi's use of such terms as *xing* (human nature), *wei* (productive effort), *shan* (good), and *e* (evil), we can give an analysis of the principal passage or argument. Let us restate the argument for elucidation and support by other considerations.

- *P*1: Man's nature today is such that he is born with a desire for gain (*haoli*), that is, a general desire or characteristic tendency to obtain personal benefit or satisfaction of a range of desires (*yu*). If these desires are followed, strife and rapacity will result, and deference and compliance, pattern and order of propriety (*li*) will disappear.
- *P*2: Man's nature today is such that he is born with a variety of feelings (*qing*), e.g., envy and hate. If these feelings are followed, injury and destruction will result, and all sense of loyalty and faithfulness will disappear.
- Conclusion: Given *P*1 and *P*2, it is clear that man's nature (*xing*) is bad (*e*), and that his goodness (*shan*) is the result of constructive effort (*wei*).

Alternatively stated, Xunzi's thesis amounts to the following: "Man's nature is bad because the characteristic tendency (*haoli*) of his basic motivational structure (for example, his desires and feelings) inevitably leads to strife and disorder, consequences which are undesirable from the moral point of view understood in terms of *ren* (benevolence), *li* (ritual propriety), and *yi* (rightness)." This reformulation requires a qualification: the characteristic tendency (*haoli*) is a self-seeking tendency, an inclination or readiness of the individual to satisfy a range of his desires as responses to his feelings. This self-seeking tendency marks, however, a positive characteristic of man's basic motivational structure. Xunzi quite clearly also recognizes a negative characteristic, that is, a tendency to dislike and avoid what is injurious or harmful (for example, Book 4). In effect, Xunzi recognizes both the appetitive and the aversive characteristics of man's purposive behavior. With this qualification in mind, we can now attend to Xunzi's supporting arguments.

The supporting arguments can be seen as answers to the following question: "What will the human situation be like when humans indulge in their basic nature without regard to moral requirements?" However, one may ask about this notion of the human situation. For our present purpose, the relevant sense of "situation" refers to a state of affairs in which human beings find themselves. A situation may thus be regarded as a human situation, in Dewey's words, an affair of doing, enjoying, and suffering. A situation is a state of affairs in which our basic nature plays an essential role. There are situations in our experience that attain, so to speak, their natural completion, for example, cases where our desires terminate in quiescence without much effort on our part, that is, when the objects of our desires are immediately accessible or available. No problem arises in these situations. But for the most part, human life is marked by interpersonal situations in which competing feelings and desires are involved. In noting their problematic character, we are focusing on the relations of humans to one another.

To a large extent, our notion of situation here is a moral notion (Kovesi 1967, 119.). To view a state of affairs as a situation, in part, reflects a moral concern, that is, a concern with the proper relations between humans as actuated by their basic nature. In this way, Xunzi's normative claim is already an implicit feature of the quasi-empirical claim. Strife is a conflicting relation between men, and disorder is regarded more properly as a consequence of strife. It may be said that not all strife leads to disorder. But for Xunzi the strife at issue is to be regarded as a strife outside the institutional setting of rules and regulations. And in this setting, the strife itself is ungoverned by rules, and to say that it is also a state of disorder is the same as to say that it is ungoverned by rules. As we shall see shortly, the *li* or ritual rules are basically procedures for guiding human activities. In the quasi-empirical claim we are dealing with brute facts and not institutional facts about men (Searle 1964). As far as institutional facts are concerned, the relations between human beings are, to Xunzi, social relations defined in terms of moral distinctions. A human society is in effect a moral society.

Thus, supporting arguments are best construed as thought experiments for answering our question: "What will the human situation be like when men indulge in their basic nature without regard to moral requirements?" These thought experiments may be characterized as a two-stage process: (1) an imaginary situation is set up for consideration and reflective judgment, and (2) a justification of the reflective judgment is proferred in terms of empirical plausibility in the sense of its coherence with a set of current beliefs about human behavior. The normative claim is the further judgment based on the moral point of view. Consider one of the three arguments in Xunzi's essay on human nature (Book 23):

> Let us suppose that there is a property to be divided among elder and younger brothers. If they follow their sensory emotional nature (*qingxing*), loving profit (*haoli*) and seeking gain, they will quarrel and wrangle. But if they are transformed by *li* and *yi*, they will even yield to complete strangers. (Watson 1963, 61, modified)

This argument does exhibit the two-stage process of a thought experiment. The supposition of the situation, in effect, requires us to envisage imaginatively the situation as an ordinary or relatively familiar situation in human experience. The plausibility of the argument thus, in part, depends on envisaging a possible human situation. The reflective judgment is revealed in the last half of the passage. This judgment clearly depends on Xunzi's moral point of view. Thus both statements in the passage show the two-stage process.

In evaluating Xunzi's argument, one may first ask whether it is a just representation of this type of human situation, for it appears equally plausible to imagine situations of division of properties or inheritance in which the parties in question willingly accept an arrangement. But then the question arises whether the acceptance of any given arrangement can be justified without regard to moral considerations. Given the self-seeking tendency of man's basic nature, it is unlikely that an orderly situation would obtain without the parties' paying regard to certain moral considerations. As support for Xunzi's thesis, this argument throws light on the sort of situations relevant to man's basic nature—problematic rather than determinate situations. Undoubtedly, the quasi-empirical claim embodies a contingent statement. But when one attends to problematic situations of this sort, it is not unreasonable to claim that strife and disorder will inevitably ensue from the unrestrained pursuit of men's desires in the absence of moral regulation. The inevitability at issue more directly pertains to our confidence in the outcome of strife and disorder. Thus, when one reflects on man's self-seeking tendency (*haoli*), one can properly claim that its actualization will lead to strife and disorder. More often as a matter of common experience, brothers, without regard to moral considerations, will fall into a state of disaffection, if not vengefulness, when a settlement of property is not according to their wishes.

Suppose, on the other hand, we take the imagined situation in the light of the brothers' heeding moral requirements in moderating, in particular, their demands, that is, by consideration of *li* and *yi*; we can be confident that their desires and feelings will be expressed in a manner amenable to the influence of even complete strangers. This is not confidence in a general empirical hypothesis but confidence founded on our experiences of human situations in general, that is, a sort of expectation, in Hume's words, a "belief" that carries weight and influence in our conduct in relation to other people (1955, 63). At times this expectation is frustrated, but given our belief that morality must have a transforming influence on our basic nature, the expectation can be regarded as reasonably justified.

Xunzi's argument supports his basic thesis. The reflective judgment on strife and wrangling is particularly plausible as a judgment coherent with our general beliefs about human situations of the sort envisaged. The situation—an inheritance—is an effective component in this thought experiment, for it is a situation of personal relations disrupted by the self-seeking tendency and demands of the parties. When we accept the quasi-empirical claim, we may then pronounce the judgment that disorder and strife are morally undesirable. And to accept this judgment is, in part, to appreciate a basic function of morality as establishing orderly procedures for regulating man's pursuit of desires in the context of interpersonal relations. In this respect, man's basic nature is bad from the moral point of view; his goodness is due to the transforming influence of morality. (For Xunzi's other arguments from thought experiment, see Cua 1978.)

The Tradition of *Li*: Ritual, Rites, Rules of Proper Conduct

For governing human action, Xunzi emphasizes the *li* and *yi* (righteousness), especially *li* as a set of formal prescriptions or rules of proper conduct. While the *li* represent an inherited ethical tradition, they do not always provide adequate guidance in perplexing, exigent situations of human life. As markers of *dao* (the Way), "the *li* provide models, but no explanations" (*Xunzi* Book 1; Watson 1963, 20). The *li* provide general guidelines delimiting proper behavior and individual responsibility. Perhaps even more important, the *li* provide for satisfaction of people's pursuit of their individual desires or interests (Book 19). In this respect, the *li* may be compared to the laws of contracts or of wills, enabling the agents to fulfill their desires effectively. Of course the key question, whether the existing *li* in fact perform their proper functions, depends on whether they satisfy the requirements of *yi* (that is, whether they are the right sort of rules) and the extent to which they ennoble human character in terms of *ren* (benevolence) and cultural refinement (*wen*; Cua 1989). For Xunzi, the regulative or delimiting function of *li* is important in ensuring a good, stable social and political order. The necessity of the *li* is due to the problematic motivational structure of human nature. This is the force of his rather misleading remark that "human nature is bad; human goodness is the product of constructive efforts" (Book 23; cf. Watson 1963, 157). In terms of an inborn motivational structure, consisting of feelings and desires, every human is a self-seeking animal actuated by fondness for personal gain. In the absence of regulative rules, this propensity may be viewed as bad or evil because it tends to lead to social conflict and disorder. What is good is "upright, reasonable, and orderly"; what is bad is "partial, irresponsible, and chaotic" (Book 23; cf. Watson 1963, 162). More fundamental is a scarcity of resources to satisfy everyone's desires, which creates the problem of competition and wrangling. Without *li* as regulations as well as a sense of *yi* (rightness), the human condition is likely to be unsettled and even chaotic.

In this light, inborn human nature (*xing*) is value-neutral, not intrinsically bad or evil but requiring regulation and molding. This nature provides the basic materials for ethical transformation, as clay provides the material for pottery. Indeed, with respect to human nature, the sage and ordinary humans are alike. Every person in the street can become a sage. "What makes the sage emperor Yu a Yu was the fact that he practiced *ren* and *yi* and complied with proper rules and standards of conduct." Moreover, the rationales of *ren, yi,* and proper rules and standards can be known and practiced by ordinary persons, because they are capable of obtaining such knowledge and acting accordingly. It must be admitted that not every person can actually become a sage, for not everyone is willing to make the effort, especially in moral learning (*Xunzi*, 23).

Xunzi's essay "Encouraging Learning" (Book 1) presents a sketch of his conception of moral learning as a continuing process that ceases only with death. Principally, learning is devoted to acquiring knowledge of various classics such as the *Shijing* (*Book of Songs*), the *Shujing* (*Book of Documents*), the *Lijing* (*Classic of Rites*), and the *Spring and Autumn Annals*, as well as the established musical text. While recitation is stressed, Xunzi calls attention to understanding and insight concerning the concrete significance of these works in human life. Initially, learning to be an ethical person depends on having teachers of exemplary ethical character, but this learning continues throughout one's life. The proximate objective is to become a scholar-official (*shi*); the ultimate objective is to become a sage (*sheng*).

Notably, the classics provide an introduction to what Xunzi considers the best Ru or Confucian tradition. In this light, historical knowledge of the tradition is indispensable. Xunzi's own writings attest to the importance of acquiring historical knowledge (Cua

1985b). As we shall see toward the end of this essay, special stress is given to different functions of the ethical use of history in discourse.

For Xunzi, the ethical uses of history provide better guidance than religious beliefs and superstitions about *tian* (heaven) as dispensing fortunes and misfortunes. *Tian* is a natural order of regularity, not an order governed by a supreme personal being. The proper attitude toward strange events or phenomena is wonder and awe (Book 17). Practices such as prayer and divination are based on superstition. However, the *li* or rites of mourning and sacrifice are ethically acceptable and, in fact, to be encouraged. Their significance lies in their function of satisfying human yearnings and providing an avenue for the proper expression of reverence, honor, and affection for the dead. Moreover, these rites contribute to the Confucian conception of cultural refinement, *wen* (Book 19). Moral learning culminates in the attainment of completeness and purity, that is, a state of ethical integrity.

Ethical Knowledge, Deliberation, and Argumentation

In ancient Chinese thought, *dao* is a term of art used by different schools of thought for propounding competing solutions to the common problem of ordering the state and personal life. In the *Xunzi, dao* is often used as a generic term (*gongming*) for a holistic ethical vision, the ideal standard of thought, speech, and action. The concrete significance of *dao* may be specified in terms of *ren* (benevolence), *li* (ritual propriety), and *yi* (rightness). Says Xunzi:

> The *dao* of the former [sage] kings is the magnificent display of *ren* (*ren zhi long ye*), for they follow what is fitting and appropriate (*zhong*). What do the fitting and appropriate mean? It is *li* and *yi*. The *dao* is neither the *dao* of heaven nor the *dao* of the earth. It is the *dao* humans [should] use as a guide to conduct, the *dao* the superior man (*junzi*) follows. (Book 8; cf. Knoblock 2:71)

Xunzi is well aware of the difficulty of persuading the uncommitted to follow *dao*. Unlike Mencius, Xunzi ascribes to the human mind (*xin*) not only a capacity for thought and deliberation but also a capacity to approve or disapprove and, crucially, to approve or disapprove of *dao* as the end of human life. Says Xunzi, "This is the salient feature of *xin* (*xinrong*): Its choices are not subject to any external control. Inevitably it manifests its own choices" (Book 21; cf. Watson, 129). For *xin* to approve or disapprove of *dao* as the ideal balance or weighing standard (*heng*) for all thought and action, *xin* must first know and understand *dao*. Ideally, for *xin* to understand *dao*, it must attain the state of great purity and clarity, *da qingming* (Book 21).

More fundamentally, knowing and understanding *dao* requires clarity (*ming*) of mind (*xin*). In particular, the clear mind must be free from obsession with ideas or matters that tend to becloud (*bi*) its proper function. When a clear mind is guided by reason, it will be free from all sorts of factors that obscure (*bi*) vision. One must be especially watchful of the contextual significance of distinctions such as those between desires and aversions, immediate and distant consequences, and the past and the present. Failure to weigh the relevance of one item in a distinction is likely to blind the agent to the significance of the other item.

Basically, distinctions are relative to the purpose and context of discourse; they are not exclusive disjunctions or absolute dichotomies. Since distinctions in general are products of the mind's intellectual function at the service of cognition and action, their utility in a particular situation is also relative to purpose and context. Even in cases where the utility of the distinction is not in question, the agent must render a reasoned judgment concerning the significance of each item in the distinction. Obscuration (*bi*) of the mind arises when the mind attends exclusively to the significance of one item without proper regard for the other. Even philosophers are susceptible to *bi*. Mozi, for example, exaggerates the importance of utility without understanding the importance of culture or the beauty of forms; Zhuangzi is preoccupied with *tian* (heaven) without regard for humanity. In general, ordinary people as well as philosophers tend to see only "one corner" of *dao* and thus fail to appreciate its holistic character. Only an enlightened sage "confronts all things and weighs them impartially on a balance" (Book 21; Cua 1993).

Suppose an agent knows and adopts *dao* as an ideal unifying perspective. How is he or she to apply or specify its significance in dealing with the problem of choice (*ze*) in particular situations? In dealing with this question, it is best to attend to Xunzi's conception of *zhilü*, which may be rendered as "wise and informed deliberation." *Zhilü* performs two different but related functions: (1) resolution of perplexities concerning right or wrong conduct that arise in present, particular situations, and (2) preparation for response to changing circumstances (Book 12). For elucidation of its nature and method, let us consider the component characters, *zhi* and *lü*, focusing primarily on their epistemic import.

Lü may be rendered as "thought," "reflection," "careful consideration," or "deliberation." Xunzi's definition explicitly connects it with choice or selection (*ze*): "love, hate, pleasure, anger, sorrow, and joy in our original nature (*xing*) are called feelings (*qing*). When these feelings arise and the mind (*xin*) makes a selection, this is called *lü*" (Book 22; Watson, 129). Since our original nature (*xing*), in the sense of a basic motivational structure, also comprises desires and aversions, which are natural responses to feelings, *lü* is properly considered to have its principal function in the choice of the desires. This interpretation is suggested by the following passage:

> The nature (*xing*) of man is what he receives from heaven; his feelings (*qing*) are constitutive of his nature; his desires are the responses to these feelings. . . . Although a person cannot completely satisfy all his desires, he can come close to satisfying them, and although he cannot do away with all desires, by means of *lü*, he can regulate his pursuit. . . . The man of *dao* will advance his pursuit when he can and will regulate his pursuit when he cannot satisfy his desires. (Book 22)

Note that the regulation of the pursuit of desires by means of *lü* (henceforth, deliberation) entails a choice (*ze*) or decision on which desire is to be preferred as the end of action. However, given that a person is a self-determining agent, deliberation can be viewed as aiming at the formation of second-order or reflective desires (Frankfurt 1971; Liang 1988). A natural desire, if directed by the mind (*xin*) and in accord with reason, can be transformed into reflective desires in such a way that it is difficult to assign it to the same category as natural desire (Book 22; Watson, 151, modified). In light of the commitment to *dao*, ethical autonomy is the ideal autonomy of will as constituted by second-order desires, the product of reasoned deliberation.

For performing the dual task of *zhilü*, the agent must adopt a method for evaluating or weighing (*quan*) the relative merits and demerits of desires and aversions, as well as alternative options in terms of their beneficial and harmful consequences. Guided by *dao* as a holistic perspective, the proper method is *jianquan*, that is, thoughtful consideration of all relevant factors before arriving at a decision. In Xunzi's words:

> When one sees something desirable, he must carefully consider (*lü*) whether or not it will lead to a detestable consequence; when he sees something beneficial, he must carefully consider (*lü*) whether or not it will lead to a harmful consequence. All these consequences must be weighed together (*jianquan*) and taken into account in any mature plan before one determines which desire or aversion, choice or rejection is to be preferred. (Book 3)

Deliberation, at its inception, addresses a current perplexity. Its primary concern is the immediate consequence of pursuing concurrent desires. But the present situation, as one posing a problem of choice, may well be an exigent situation, i.e., a novel circumstance in which past experience does not provide sufficient guidance. Also, it may be one in which the decision to be rendered is a plan of action. In this case, the agent cannot be content with mere examination of the immediate consequences of the contemplated actions but must attend to distant consequences—in Xunzi's words, "consider the long view of things and think of their consequences," *changlü guhou* (Book 4; Knoblock 1:193–194). In this case, the dual task of *zhilü* represents a single process of thought. Nevertheless, the focus is the present problem of choice. Like most judicial decisions in an Anglo-American higher court, which observes the doctrine of precedent, the emergent decision settles a case at hand but at the same time indicates its significance for like cases in the future.

Implicit in this characterization of *zhilü* is cost-benefit analysis; but, significantly, such a deliberation must be guided by *dao*, specifiable in terms of *ren*, *li* (rules of proper conduct), and *yi* (rightness), especially *yi*, since it is through the use of *yi* that one responds to changing circumstances (Books 3 and 14). It is interesting to note that when we focus on the present, the object of deliberation may be said, Dewey put it, to be a "unified preference": "Choice is not the emergence of preference out of indifference. It is the emergence of a unified preference out of competing preferences" (1922, 193). Similarly, Xunzi remarks:

> Of all the methods of controlling the vital breath (*qi*) and nourishing the mind (*xin*), none is more direct than proceeding according to the *li*, none more essential than obtaining a good teacher, and none more intelligent than unifying one's likes. (Book 2; Knoblock 1:154)

For deliberation (*lü*) to be adequate in resolving the problem of choice, it must be qualified by *zhi*. As a component of *zhilü*, I suggest that *zhi* be construed as "wise and well-informed." To elaborate its nature, let us consider *zhi* as a cognitive term with a range of uses corresponding somewhat to "know" or "knowledge." Implicit in Xunzi's definition of *zhi*, as Liang Qixiong points out, is a distinction between the natural ability to know (*benneng zhizhi*) and its achievement (*chenggong zhizhi*). "That in man by which he knows, *zhi*, is called *zhi*; the *zhi* that corresponds (*he*) to actuality is called wisdom, *zhi*" (the second *zhi* is a homophone; Book 22; cf. Watson, 140). For present purposes, we may regard the range of achievement as comprising two broad types of knowledge: perceptual and ethical. In both types of knowledge, discrimination (*bian*) is involved. The content of perceptual knowledge is provided by the data of the five senses. Each sense has its proper object, for example, the eye can distinguish differences in "shape, color, or marking," the ear can distinguish differences in "tone, timbre, pitch, or modulation." While each sense has its proper object, it cannot provide any classification (*lei*) of, say, the different types of color or tones. Strictly speaking, perceptual knowledge is possible because the mind (*xin*) possesses *zhengzhi*, i.e., the ability to identify and reidentify sense content as belonging to different sorts, as well as to synthesize these data and explain the grounds of perceptual judgments (Book 22; cf. Watson, 142–143).

Since explanation is a phase of argumentation, it must satisfy certain standards. In general, according to Xunzi, "before one can profitably engage in any discussion, there must first be established just and proper standards. Without such standards, right and wrong (*shifei*) cannot be distinguished and disputes cannot be settled" (Book 18). Among the standards of competence, accord with evidence (*fuyan*) is crucial in determining the reliability of perceptual judgments. Equally important, especially in the case of direct perception, is evidence that the claimant's state of mind is clear and settled. Says Xunzi:

> In general, when doubts arise in the course of observing things, and one's mind is unsettled, then one's perception of the external things will become unclear. When our thoughts (*lü*) are unclear, one cannot be in a position to determine whether a thing is so or is not so. (Book 21)

Xunzi goes on to cite and explain numerous examples of perceptual illusions: for example, how darkness can distort vision as in the case of a man walking in the dark and mistaking a stone for tiger; or how excessive consumption of wine can impair our normal vision, as in the case of a drunkard who stoops to go through a city gate, mistaking its height. Apart from these cases of illusion, Xunzi discusses cases of delusion, e.g., double image, mirror reflection, and the blind man's mistaken judgment concerning the existence or nonexistence of stars. In the light of Xunzi's discussion of perceptual deceptions, it is plausible to ascribe to him the notion of a standard observer, though we do not find much textual material for reconstructing a Confucian theory of perception.

Like perceptual knowledge, ethical knowledge involves facts and thus also requires *zhengzhi*, that is, evidential judgments concerning matters of fact. Ethical judgments are interpretive judgments informed by *dao* as an ideal unifying perspective. Reliable claims to ethical knowledge must be supported by accurate information concerning the *li* (rules of proper conduct) or institutional facts. This accounts for one frequent use of *zhi*, in the sense of acquisition of information or knowledge of right and wrong (*shifei*) and of the noble and the base (*guijian*). However, in the case of a person committed to *dao*, the use of *zhi* in *zhidao* (knowing *dao*) also involves knowledge in the sense of acknowledgement, that is, an assent to *dao*—as well as the sense of *zhi* as realization, that is, the successful effort to make *dao* an actual object of deliberation. If we distinguish between *zhi* as a task word and *zhi* as an achievement word, implicit, for example, in Wang Yangming's doctrine of the unity of knowledge and action (*zhixing heyi*), then *zhi* in *zhidao* may be construed as embracing the distinction between prospective and retrospective knowledge (Cua 1982, ch. 1).

In terms of *zhidao*, the definition of *zhi* (the homophone), cited earlier as the "*zhi* that corresponds to actuality," can now be understood as *zhi* in the sense of retrospective knowledge, an achievement of the effort to realize *dao* in the actual world. Since *zhi* (homophone) and *zhi* are often used interchangeably in the classical literature, *zhi* can be properly rendered as "wisdom." The *zhi* in *zhilü* may thus be construed as "wise and well-informed," embracing both prospective and retrospective knowledge of *dao*. Sound ethical judgements responsive to the problem of choice in *zhilü* are not only well-informed, as they are grounded in available factual knowledge of the living, historical tradition; they are also wise in the sense of being prudent, since they reflect a reasoned assessment of desires and aversions, as well as of competing options in the light of their beneficial and harmful consequences. Such wisdom, as an achievement of *zhi* or retrospective knowledge, may be viewed as a depository of ethical judgments and insights derived from the exercise of *yi* in deliberation (*lü*) coping with changing circumstances in human life. Much in the spirit of Xunzi is Zhu Xi's notion of wisdom (*zhi*, homophone) as *shoulian*, the gathering of the fruits of reflective ethical activities (Cua 1987).

Like perceptual judgments, ethical judgments are fallible, for in the ideal case, they are judgments rendered, all things considered, as the best solutions to the problems of choice. Factors germane to deliberation may well be neglected or mistakenly consigned to irrelevance. More important, as Xunzi urges, the agent may not possess the clarity of mind (*xin*) indispensable to wise and well-informed deliberation (*zhilü*). Given the autonomy of mind, even if the agent has access to knowledge of *dao*, adequate to resolving the problem of choice, he may willfully act in a manner contrary to *dao*, perhaps owing to weakness of will or to lack of a genuine, wholehearted commitment to realizing *dao*. More likely, the agent's mind, though guided by practical reason, is beset with preconceptions of good and evil or of right and wrong, as well as unexamined prejudices. Xunzi's technical term for these liabilities is *bi*, a condition of a mind cluttered up with extraneous preconceptions and preferences—a common affliction of humanity. This is a theme discussed earlier. In general, the problem of *bi* is the problem of replacing bad habits (of mind) with good, flexible habits. Freedom from *bi* is an ethical transformation of the basic autonomy of mind, through reflection and self-cultivation, into moral autonomy—Xunzi's ideal of moral agency.

Ethical judgments, as implicit throughout our discussion of *zhilü*, are not only liable to errors but also revisable in the light of our historical understanding of an ethical tradition and its prospective significance. In this respect, even if the mind (*xin*) is completely free from *bi*, its ethical judgments have only the status of plausible presumptions. They are to be qualified in such terms as "adequate in so far as our experience goes." Nevertheless, given the conception of wisdom (*zhi*, homophone) as a depository of insights, they may be viewed as "intuitions." And in so far as such wisdom provides sufficient guidance for resolving the problem of choice, *zhilü* will appear to be a facile proceeding. Our intuitions will always be the starting point in *zhilü*, as an articulation of wisdom, even if in the end they may be deemed inadequate to resolving the problem of choice.

Since ethical judgments are at best plausible presumptions, they are are defeasible—always open to challenge in discourse or argumentation. One of Xunzi's contributions is to provide materials for reconstructing a Confucian theory of ethical argumentation (Cua 1985a). Confucian argumentation is a cooperative activity of reasonable persuasion addressed to a particular rather than a universal audience. Apart from the requirement of satisfying certain standards of competence such as conceptual clarity, consistency, coherence, respect for linguistic practices, and accord with reason and experience, it is expected that participants will possess and display certain qualities of character conducive to the proceeding. Ideally, these are the qualities of a *junzi* (an ethically superior person) or paradigmatic individual who governs his or her life by *dao*, the ideal of the good human life as a whole. The *dao* of the *junzi* is the *dao* of humanity embodying *ren, li*, and *yi*.

In the light of ethical argumentation, we can appreciate the common Confucian appeal to historical events in discourse. There are four uses of historical appeals: pedagogical, rhetorical, elucidative, and evaluative. (1) The pedagogical use stresses the study of the classics in terms of the standards of *ren, yi*, and *li*. As noted earlier, however, learning is not a mere acquisition of knowledge; it requires understanding and insight. Also, the companion study of paradigmatic individuals is important, not only because they are models to follow but also because they are exemplary personifications of the spirit of *ren, yi*, and *li*. Moreover, they also function as reminders of moral learning and conduct that appeal especially to what is deemed in the real interest of the learner. (2) The rhetorical use of historical appeals is basically an appeal to plausible presumptions, or shared beliefs and trustworthiness. These presumptions are subject to further challenge, but they can be accepted as starting points in discourse. (3) The elucidative use of historical appeals purports to clarify the relevance of the past for the present. (4) Perhaps most important for argumentative discourse is the evaluative function of historical appeals. It focuses on our knowledge and understanding of our present problematic situations as a basis for evaluating the unexamined claims that the past is guidance for the present. Thus, both the elucidative and the evaluative uses of historical appeals are critical and attentive to evidential grounding of ethical claims.

Conclusion

This discussion has presented only a few key aspects of Xunzi's philosophy. Other aspects have been explored in recent scholarship (Cua 2003; Kline and Ivanhoe 2000; Vittinghoff 2001). Xunzi is widely acknowledged to be one of the greatest Chinese philosophers. Apart from his critical and coherent exposition of ancient Confucianism, he is also distinguished for his insights into the nature of ethical knowledge and argumentation (Cua 1985a).

See also Confuciansim: Ethics; Confucianism: Rhetoric; Confucianism: Tradition; Confucianism: Vision; *Li*: Rites or Propriety; *Quan*; *Yi* and *Li*.

Bibliography

Chan, Wing-tsit, and Charles Fu. *Guide to Chinese Philosophy*. Boston, Mass.: Hall, 1978. (A contemporary bibliography.)

Cheung, Leo K. C. "The Way of the *Xunzi*." *Journal of Chinese Philosophy*, 28(3), 2001, pp. 301–320.

Cua, A. S. "The Concept of *Li* in Confucian Moral Theory." In *Understanding the Chinese Mind: The Philosophical Roots*, ed. Robert E. Allinson. Hong Kong: Oxford University Press, 1989.

———. "The Conceptual Aspect of Hsün Tzu's Philosophy of Human Nature." *Philosophy East and West*, 27(4), 1977, pp. 373–389.

———. "Dimensions of *Li* (Propriety): Reflections on an Aspect of Hsün Tzu's Ethics." *Philosophy East and West*, 29(4), 1979, pp. 373–394.

———. *Ethical Argumentation: A Study in Hsün Tzu's Moral Epistemology*. Honolulu: University of Hawaii Press, 1985a.

———. "The Ethical and the Religious Dimensions of *Li*." *Review of Metaphysics*, 65(3), 2002.

———. "Ethical Significance of Shame: Insights of Aristotle and Xunzi." *Philosophy East and West*, 53(2), 2003.

———. "Ethical Uses of the Past in Early Confucianism: The Case of Hsün Tzu." *Philosophy East and West*, 35(2), 1985b, pp. 133–156. (Reprinted with pinyin transcriptions in T. C. Kline and Philip J. Ivanhoe, eds. *Virtue, Nature, and Moral Agency in the Xunzi*. Indianapolis, Ind., and Cambridge: Hackett, 2000.)

———. "Feature Review: John Knoblock, *Xunzi—A Translation and Study of the Complete Works*, Volume I, Books 1–6." *Philosophy East and West*, 41(2), 1991, pp. 215–227.

———. "Hsün Tzu and the Unity of Virtues." *Journal of Chinese Philosophy*, 14(4), 1987, pp. 81–400.

———. "Hsün Tzu's Theory of Argumentation: A Reconstruction." *Review of Metaphysics*, 36(2), 1983, pp. 867–892.

———. *Moral Vision and Tradition: Essays in Chinese Ethics*. Washington: Catholic University of America Press, 1998.

———. "Morality and Human Nature." *Philosophy East and West*, 32(3), 1982, pp. 279–294.

———. "The Possibility of Ethical Knowledge: Reflections on a Theme in the Hsün Tzu." In *Epistemological Issues in Ancient Chinese Philosophy*, ed. Hans Lenk and Gregor Paul. Albany: State University of New York Press, 1993. (A study of the possibility of knowing *dao* and the problem of cognitive blindness.)

———. "The Problem of Conceptual Unity in Hsün Tzu and Li Kou's Solution." *Philosophy East and West*, 39(2), 1989.

———. "The Quasi-Empirical Aspect of Hsün Tzu's Philosophy of Human Nature." *Philosophy East and West*, 28(1), 1978, pp. 3–19.

———. *The Unity of Knowledge and Action: A Study in Wang Yang-ming's Moral Psychology*. Honolulu: University of Hawaii Press, 1982.

Dewey, John. *Human Nature and Conduct*. New York: Modern Library, 1922.

Dubs, H. H. *Hsüntze: The Moulder of Ancient Confucianism*. London: Arthur Probsthain, 1927. (The first comprehensive English study of Hsün Tzu.)

———, trans. *The Works of Hsüntze*. Taipei: Chengwen, 1966.

Fung, Yu-lan (Feng Youlan). *History of Chinese Philosophy*, Vol. 1, trans. Derk Bodde. Princeton, N.J.: Princeton University Press, 1952.

Frankfurt, Harry. "Freedom of the Will and the Concept of a Person." *Journal of Philosophy*, 68(1), 1971, pp. 5–20.

Goldin, Paul Rakita. *Ritual of the Way: The Philosophy of Xunzi*. La Salle, Ill.: Open Court, 1999.

Graham, A. C. "The Background of the Mencian Theory of Human Nature." *Tsing Hua Journal of Chinese Studies*, New Series 7(1–2), 1967. (Reprinted in T. C. Kline and Philip J. Ivanhoe, eds. *Virtue, Nature, and Moral Agency in the Xunzi*. Indianapolis, Ind., and Cambridge: Hackett, 2000.)

———. *Disputers of the Tao*. La Salle, Ill.: Open Court, 1989.

———. *Studies in Chinese Philosophy and Philosophical Literature*. Singapore: Institute of East Asian Philosophies, 1986.

Hume, David. *An Inquiry Concerning Human Understanding*. Indianapolis: Bobbs-Merrill Co., 1955.

Kline, T. C., and Philip J. Ivanhoe, eds. *Virtue, Nature, and Moral Agency in the Xunzi*. Indianapolis, Ind., and Cambridge: Hackett, 2000. (The bibliography is a good supplement to Knoblock's first and third volumes.)

Knoblock, John. *Xunzi Tzu: A Translation and Study of the Complete Works*, 3 vols. Stanford, Calif.: Stanford University Press, 1988, 1990, 1994. (Contains valuable introductions in Vols. 1 and 2, and extensive bibliographies in Vols. 1 and 3.)

Kovesi, Julius. *Moral Notions*. London: Routledge and Kegan Paul, 1967.

Lau, D. C. "Theories of Human Nature in Mencius and Shyuntzyy." *Bulletin of the School of Oriental and African Studies*, 15, 1953, pp. 541–565. (Reprinted in T. C. Kline and Philip J. Ivanhoe, eds. *Virtue, Nature, and Moral Agency in the Xunzi*. Indianapolis, Ind., and Cambridge: Hackett, 2000.)

Li, Disheng, *Xunzi jishi*. Taipei: Xuesheng, 1979. (A good modern Chinese annotated edition.)

Liang, Qixiong. *Xunzi jianshi*. Taipei: Muduo, 1988.

Machle, Edward J. *Nature and Heaven in the Xunzi*. Albany: State University of New York Press, 1993.

Searle, John. "How to Derive 'Ought' from 'Is'?" *Philosophical Review*, 73(1), 1964.

Vittinghoff, Helmolt. "Recent Bibliography in Classical Chinese Philosophy." *Journal of Chinese Philosophy*, 28(1–2), 2001, pp. v–xi, 1–208.

Wang, Xianqian. *Xunzi jijie*. Taipei: World, 1961.

Watson, Burton, trans. *Hsün Tzu: Basic Writings*. New York: Columbia University Press, 1963.

中國哲學

Y

Yan Fu (Yen Fu)

Kirill O. Thompson

Yan Fu (1853–1921) was an eminent intellectual of the late Qing and early republican era. He was a consummate translator of the vital texts that, in his view, set forth the constellation of ideas which explained the formation of a prosperous and powerful Victorian England. He was also a capable disseminator of Herbert Spencer's social Darwinism and the modern theory of political economy. To underscore the seriousness of the subject matter, Yan rendered his translations in elegant classical Chinese. He also provided commentaries with discussions on the ramifications of the new ideas and principles for understanding the history, culture, present conditions, and prospects of China. Moreover, in essays and lectures, Yan gave prescient assessments of various conditions—cultural, political, educational, economic, etc.—that had to be met for China to begin to develop in earnest. Through Yan's works, Darwinian nomenclature took a root as significant explanatory categories in Chinese discourse. Viewing the tumultuous last century of Chinese history, one cannot help thinking that China would have developed more smoothly had Yan's forward-looking views been made policy by Chinese officialdom at the start. An interesting feature of Yan's philosophic overview was that he grounded his ideas and principles in a Spencerian cosmology adorned with concepts adopted from Laozi, Zhuangzi, Song neo-Confucianism, and Chinese Buddhism.

"One truth is manifest: creation, at root, evolves flawlessly." Yan Fu was born in 1853 in Houkuan, Fujian, China (in present-day Linshen County, Fujian). He was a precocious child who by age fourteen had studied the Chinese classics and Han classical commentaries for four years and had mastered some basic texts of Song neo-Confucianism. Thus Yan in childhood was deeply immersed in traditional Chinese thought and culture. Moreover, these studies in Han classicism and Song neo-Confucianism provided him with experience in factual inquiry and theoretical speculation. At the same time, he nurtured an inimitable writing style by undertaking a serious study of traditional essays and poems.

Yan Fu's attainments in traditional learning served him well when he applied to the Fuzhou Shipyard School. He received the highest score on the entrance examination for his classical essay "Lifelong Filial Devotion to One's Parents." At the Shipyard School, Yan studied modern mathematics, science, and engineering. He excelled in classes in geometry, algebra, analytic geometry, trigonometry, physics, mechanics, chemistry, geology, astronomy, and navigation. He also learned English and took some courses in the Chinese humanities. In 1871, after five years, Yan graduated at the top of his class and put out to sea.

In 1874, Yan Fu set off for England to study navigation, engineering, and naval strategy and tactics. He studied first at the Portsmouth Academy and later at Greenwich Naval College. Impressed by the wealth, power, and vitality of Victorian England, Yan endeavored to understand its political, economic, and social institutions. He carefully studied books that explained the empirical outlook and logical methods which had supported England's robust development into a great power in the nineteenth century.

In 1881, Yan read with interest Herbert Spencer's *The Study of Sociology* (1873); he was to publish a translation in 1903. He was impressed that, as in the theory of learning presented in *The Great Learning* and *The Doctrine of the Mean*, Spencer emphasized emotional and ethical as well as intellectual factors in the acquisition of knowledge: the pursuit of knowledge includes overcoming emotional biases and moral shortcomings by making oneself detached and morally perspicacious. In other words, one must possess a certain moral fiber to engage in significant scientific inquiry. Yan was also excited to discover that western knowledge was not just instrumental; it was obtained through systematic methods of inquiry aimed at discovering truths about the world. He drew the moral that scientific training was a valid way to clarify the mind.

Given Yan's concern for discovering the rudiments of a vital society and a strong nation, he was taken with Spencer's view of sociology as the queen of the sciences and, especially, with Spencer's application of Darwin's theory of natural evolution and its constituent principles—e.g., the struggle for survival, natural selection, and survival of the fittest—to human society. Yan thought this provided a solid basis for understanding human relationships, interpersonal conduct, and the formation of society. In 1903, as mentioned above, he published a translation of Spencer's *The Study of Sociology*, thoroughly annotated. Notably, he modified Spencer's descriptive account of the principles of social evolution into a prescriptive guide to social regeneration and nation building with his country and countrymen in mind.

China's unsuccessful prosecution of the Sino-Japanese war led to a national outcry in 1895, but people could not agree on what China's problems were or on how to revitalize China. Yan Fu joined the fray by publishing several essays in which he explained and applied to China the worldview and principles he had acquired during his sojourn in England. In "On the Speed of Change in the World," "On Power," "On Our Salvation," and "Refutation of Han Yu," he sought to explain that westerners were not merely barbarians with advanced technology: they had been shaped in a dynamic, competitive environment, and their power reflected a healthy, vital approach to life. In contrast, the Chinese outlook was dominated by sentimentality over the past, disdain for innovation, and a closed, cyclic view of history. Ostensibly, this mind-set had crippled China's ability to meet the challenge of the western powers in the nineteenth century.

Spencer described the operation of evolution in societies as deterministic and left little space for individual initiative. Yan's cross-cultural perspective enabled him to see through Spencer's deterministic fallacy to the vital role played by thought and culture, concepts and will, in driving social evolution. He saw ideas as a catalyst in individual, social, and national life. On this basis, he argued that China's failure to evolve significantly for several centuries resulted, in large part, from the closed, cyclic vision of life that characterized its traditional thought and culture: in their predilection for tranquillity and ritual, the Chinese sages had not grasped the energizing notion of evolution and, thus, had consigned posterity to generations of stagnation. On this basis, Yan attempted to reassure his countrymen that China's malaise had resulted not from unalterable factors like geography, climate, or racial inheritance but from repressive cultural beliefs that had stifled its natural evolution.

Yan Fu's most influential book was his translation of Thomas Henry Huxley's *Evolution and Ethics and Other Essays* (1894; translation published in 1898). Ironically, this was a contentious translation. Yan accepted Huxley's account of evolution but rejected his qualification that societies produce humane ethics which work to counteract the pitiless laws of evolution. Yan even dropped the term "ethics" from the title in his Chinese rendering, *On Evolution*. What commended the book to Yan was its elegant compendium of Darwinian natural tenets and vivid illustrations of evolution in nature. Moreover, Huxley did not limit himself to natural science but took up a spectrum of cross-cultural themes: the history of thought, the philosophy of life and death, the problems of evil and suffering, etc. For example, he juxtaposed Greek, Stoic, Indian, and Buddhist responses to the problem of suffering: whereas the Greeks had chosen to focus on the joy in life, the Stoics sought relief in *apatheia*, the Indians turned away from nature, and the Buddhists sought to deny the existence of a substantive material realm. Huxley thus presented various philosophies as forming a spectrum of responses to the perennial problems of human existence. Yan drew on this reflection to argue that Chinese thought and culture were not discontinuous with other traditions, that the Chinese belonged to the family of humankind.

Notably, where Huxley argued that human ethics counteracted the laws of evolution, Yan, in his commentary, forcefully presented Spencer's view of man and human society as part and parcel of the cosmic process and fully subject to the laws of evolution. Yan's position was the more consistent in that he asserted the universal applicability of Darwinian law, whereas Huxley had to argue that human society created exceptions. Yan recalled that in traditional China similar debates centered on whether or not ethics was an expression of human nature, a reflection of the total process of nature. On this issue, he aligned Spencer with Mencius, Laozi, and Zhu Xi for finding the roots of ethics in man and the cosmos, and Huxley with Xunzi and Liu Zongyuan for treating ethics as a human artifact.

By persuasively laying out his Spencerian outlook and ethics in his commentary on *Evolution and Ethics*, Yan instigated a transformation of values among Chinese readers taken with the challenge and promise of social Darwinism. The theory of political economy addressed the problem of how to create a wealthy and powerful state in a Darwinian universe; thus Yan translated Adam Smith's capitalist manifesto *An Inquiry into the Nature and Causes of the Wealth of Nations* (1776, translation published in 1901–1902). Yan was particularly interested in Smith's celebration of the entrepreneur's release of egoistic energies; he believed that these energies can propel a nation's economy and, by extension, stimulate its society. Yan often stressed that a state's wealth and power spring from unleashing the economic vitality of individuals, and thus that economic liberalization generally leads to economic expansion.

In pressing Smith's case, Yan had to address conflicts in values between tradition and modernity. He argued as follows: it appears that the Confucian Way, benevolence, and righteousness are completely inconsistent with capitalist free competition, self-interest, and profit; but, since success in business depends on moral factors, such as honesty, reliability, and fairness, Smith's capitalist values must presuppose traditional values akin to the Confucian values. Nonetheless, Yan retained the Spencerian view that egoism is man's primary motivating force; e.g., people form societies for personal security and advantage, and thus altruistic values like sympathy are, and must be, derivative.

Believing that economic liberalism could flourish only under political liberalism, rule of law, and democracy, Yan also translated several texts in these fields: Montesquieu's "Spirit of the Laws" (*L'esprit des lois*, 1743; translation published in 1904–1909), E. Jenks's *A History of Politics* (1900; translation published in 1904), and John Stuart Mill's *On Liberty* (1859; translation published in 1903).

Through Montesquieu's *Spirit of the Laws*, Yan sought to convey the idea that law forms an impartial, universal system divided into several branches. He believed that the inherent fairness of legal systems of this cast fosters social equality, public-spiritedness, patriotism, and a vital sense of liberty, which in turn contribute to economic expansion. In contrast, China's authoritarian, paternalistic Confucian system was full of inconsistencies and loopholes and gave too much discretion to a biased judiciary. Moreover, matters defined as public were understood to be solely the concern of officials, so that the common people were advised just to look after their own interests and not be public-spirited.

Yan decried Montesquieu's lack of an evolutionary perspective. Montesquieu had treated various political systems as forming discrete patterns rather than as phases in evolutionary development. In *A History of Politics*, Jenks applied the evolutionary perspective to political systems, seeing a development in which capitalist-based democracy, such as that embodied in Victorian England, was the highest advancement. Jenks's book provided Yan with grounds for arguing that China's Confucian system was an anachronism which should have receded into history centuries earlier.

Intriguingly, Yan also translated Mill's *On Liberty*. He accepted Mill's faith that through the proliferation of ideas in a free market of opinions, more truths will be discovered, more innovations will be made, and more people will be able to realize themselves. Still, whereas Mill regarded the free exercise of thought as an intrinsic good, Yan valued it for its effect of vitalizing the state—by encouraging individuals to develop their thought and knowledge. Mill's *On Liberty* contained a litany of revolutionary doctrines and recommendations: that freedom of thought is a catalyst in finding new truths; that one should refuse to accept any opinions uncritically, even those held sacrosanct by tradition and the pronouncements of authority figures; that one should acknowledge truths, even those uttered by monsters, and reject falsehoods, even those uttered by saints. These sentiments were a breath of fresh air to readers in a society where thought had been stifled for millennia by self-righteous, authoritarian, tradition-bound officials.

Yan saw in logic a universal method of critical inquiry for distinguishing truth from falsehood and for extending knowledge. Accordingly, he taught seminars on logic and translated the first half of Mill's *A System of Logic* (1843; translation published in 1905) and W. S. Jevons's *Logic: A Primer* (translated in 1909). Given his background in engineering and science, Yan focused on Mill's empiricist methods of induction more than on formal deduction. He thus viewed logic as starting from discrete impressions and states of consciousness to build up, by inductive steps, the various sciences. Yan used this conception to critique the ethical intuitionism of Mencius, Lu Xiangshan, and Wang Yangming, which postulated a priori moral knowledge. He praised Zhu Xi's inductive notion of "investigating things to acquire knowledge" adapted from *The Great Learning*, but lamented Zhu's tendency to apply the method more to textual studies than to natural phenomena.

Yan did not adopt the narrow phenomenalist outlook that attended Mill's logical method but retained a speculative Spencerian vision of the cosmos as a patterned order evolving out of a nameless ultimate—*dao*. To Yan, Mill's logic was valuable as a guide for discovering truths about nature through induction. As Bacon affirmed, knowledge yields power, and Mill's method provided a strategy for discovering nature's secrets to be utilized in creating more wealth and power in the state. Interestingly, Yan also wrote a commentary on Wang Bi's rendition of the *Laozi* (published in 1931) that revealed salient aspects of Yan's outlook on human destiny, philosophy, and religion. He read the *Laozi* as partly compatible with the thought of Darwin, Spencer, and Montesquieu. (See, for example, *Laozi*, chs. 5, 14, 25, 51, and 80.) Yan also saw in the *Laozi*'s formless politics the roots of a democratic position and took delight in Laozi's sharp critique of Confucian values. The preface to Yan's *Lectures on Politics* (1906) reads:

> Copernicus's theory . . . relativized the absolute notion of the "high" and the "low" and thus . . . struck a mortal blow to artificial notions of status. This was one of the roots of the theory of liberty and equality. In a free and equal society, a man's place is determined by his actual worth as determined in the crucible of natural selection, without appeal to any preordained, absolute hierarchical social order. Laozi, however, already had relativized all the antitheses of the phenomenal world long before Copernicus.

Living in an archaic tradition-bound society structured on artificial inequalities sanctioned by Confucian values, Yan reveled in Laozi's iconoclasm toward a "Way" and "high culture" that repressed society and stifled the people's will to realize themselves in a dynamic, competitive environment.

See also Intercultural Hermeneutics; Translation and Its Problems.

Bibliography:

Grieder, Jerome. *Intellectuals and Modern China: A Narrative History*. New York: Free Press, 1981.

Lin, Bao-chun. *Yan Fu: Zhangguo jindai sixiang qimeng zhe*. (Yan Fu: Herald of Modern Chinese Thought). Taipei: Yushi, 1990.

Schwartz, Benjamin. *In Search of Wealth and Power: Yen Fu and the West*. Cambridge, Mass.: Belknap Press of Harvard University Press, 1964.

Yang, Y. C. *Chinese Intellectuals and the West 1872–1949*. Chapel Hill: University of North Carolina Press, 1966.

Yan Yuan (Yen Yüan)

Ying-shih Yü

Yan Yuan (Yen Yüan, 1635–1704), the founder of the famous "pragmatic" Yan-Li school, was a native of Boye County near Beijing. His was an uneventful life wholly devoted to study and teaching in his residential neighborhood. At the same time, however, he also began to develop a radically new conception of Confucian learning. He would have remained an obscure local scholar had it not been for the fact that he found a most faithful and fervent disciple in the distinguished Li Gong (1659–1733). From the 1690s on, Li was determined to present his teacher's ideas to the intellectual world by taking up periodic residence in the capital (Beijing) as well as traveling to the lower Yangtze (Chang) region. Among the leading scholars he made friends with were Mao Qiling (1623–1716), Yan Roju (1636–1704), Wan Sitong (1638–1702), Yao Jiheng (b. 1647), and Fang Bao (1668–1749). As a result the Yan-Li school won a nationwide recognition.

By general consensus the importance of Yan Yuan in early Qing thought lies not so much in his philosophical originality as in his redefinition of Confucianism with regard to its nature and function. The best way to introduce him is, therefore, to present his basic views in their historical context.

According to Yan Yuan, the true spirit of *dao* as embodied in the noble deeds of ancient sages and distilled in the plain words of Confucius and Mencius had been obscured, if not wholly lost, since the end of the classical age. In its long journey Confucianism had taken two wrong turns: the textual exegesis of the Han period (206 B.C.E.–220 C.E.) and the metaphysical speculation of the Song period (960–1279 C.E.), each leading to a disastrous consequence uniquely its own. Textual exegesis produced impractical bookworms whereas metaphysical speculation bred idle talkers. As a result the so-called Confucians in the past two thousand years were either bookworms or idle talkers or both. None of them proved to be of any practical use to society.

In this connection, however, Yan's revolt against Cheng-Zhu neo-Confucianism merits special attention. For a decade, from 1658 to 1668, Yan was a true believer in Cheng-Zhu philosophy. During this period his admiration for Zhu Xi was unbounded; sometimes he even followed the master to a fault. Observing the mourning rules for his grandmother in 1668, he followed the *Family Rituals*, a handbook attributed to Zhu Xi, in its minutest detail. These rules turned out to be so harsh that he inflicted much damage on his own health. This traumatic experience provided him with an occasion to reexamine his Confucian faith; the result was a complete break not only with Cheng-Zhu philosophy but with the neo-Confucian tradition as a whole. He singled out the teaching of Zhu Xi for attack because, in his eyes, it embraced at once the weaknesses of both textual exegesis and metaphysical speculation. In response to Zhu Xi's instruction that one ought to spend half a day in "quiet-sitting" and half a day in "book-reading," he objected that this amounted to requiring a student to divide his time equally between being a Buddhist monk and a Han exegete, altogether a senseless waste of time.

Immediately after his open revolt against Cheng-Zhu neo-Confucianism, Yan set out in 1669 to write a treatise on "Preservation of Human Nature" and another on "Preservation of Learning"—two of his well-known "Four Preservations" (the third and fourth being on "governance" and "humanity" respectively). In these two philosophical works he vehemently argued against a variety of dualism in the Cheng-Zhu system. In the space available here, two of his arguments may be briefly mentioned.

First, he seriously questioned the distinction between "moral nature" as the source of good and "physical nature" as source of evil. Human nature consists basically of physical nature out of which goodness is developed. He took evil to be extrinsic to human nature; the source must be traced to society. Thus he agreed with Mencius that human physical nature, including feeling and ability, is always good and located the origin of evil in such external forces as "attraction," "obscuration," "habit," and "contagion"—all of which are socially formed.

Second, and similarly, he also repudiated the distinction between *li* ("principle") and *qi* ("matter"). In his view, *li* and *qi* are not two separate entities that, when joined together, produce all things in the world. Nor is it the case that *li*, being "above shapes," exists in the transcendent world whereas *qi*, being "below shapes," exists in the material world. On the contrary, *li* and *qi* form a single continuum, distinguishable in conception but inseparable in reality. However, between *li* and *qi* he accorded *qi* a more basic status: *li* is inherent in *qi* in the same way as "moral nature" stands in relation to "physical nature." For this reason, *qi* cannot be identified as the source of evil.

Yan's philosophical criticism of neo-Confucianism, especially the Cheng-Zhu school, may be better understood as a strategic move to clear the way for his new Confucian project. We have seen that he was in principle against metaphysical speculation, dismissing it as a useless mental exercise. Why then did he spend so much time debating metaphysical questions, such as *li* versus *qi*, with neo-Confucian philosophers in their own terms? A reasonable explanation, perhaps, would be that he needed to demolish various dualistic presuppositions of the Cheng-Zhu school and establish in their stead a monism that would ground his own project. The monism he espoused turned out to be none other than the monism of *qi* that had been gradually on the rise since the sixteenth century: neo-Confucians of both the Cheng-Zhu and the Lu-Wang schools such as Luo Qinshun (1465–1547) and Liu Zongzhou (1578–1645) developed it, each in his own way. In metaphysics, Yan was more an ordinary consumer than a creative producer.

Now, a brief description of Yan's new conception of Confucianism is in order. His central concern was with "practice" (*xi*) as opposed to theory. To begin with, it is desirable to know why he came to take such a position and how he managed to justify it. In a sense he may well have been pushed into this position by a movement of "returning to the sources" during the Ming-Qing intellectual transition. As his theory of the "two wrong turns of *dao*," mentioned earlier, suggests, he distrusted not only Song-Ming metaphysical speculation but also Han textual exegesis. This is exactly why he insisted more emphatically than any of his contemporaries that a true understanding of *dao* can be obtained only by returning directly to the sacred texts of Confucius and pre-Confucian sages. He argued forcefully that ancient sages including Confucius rarely, if ever, discussed *dao* in abstract, theoretical terms. Instead, they taught people to do concrete, practical things ranging from housework to management of public affairs. Since adequate performance of all these tasks requires technical skills, constant "practice" is the only way to acquire them. It was by no means an accident that he changed the name of his studio from *Sigu* (Thinking on the Ancients) to *Xi* (Practice) in 1669, the year his break with neo-Confucianism was complete. He justified the change in these words: "I feel that thinking (*si*) is not as good as learning (*xue*), and learning must depend on practicing (*xi*)," a clear reference to Confucius's ideas in the *Analects* (1.1, 15.31).

Yan's emphasis on the central importance of "practice," however, is predicated on his new interpretation of *dao*. As he saw it, the *dao* in pre-Confucian antiquity was no more than the ideal political-social-economic arrangements made by a long line of sage kings beginning with Yao and Shun and ending with the duke of Zhou. It was also the very same *dao* to which Confucius wanted to return when it had ceased to prevail in his time. This original Confucian *dao* bore no resemblance whatsoever to the neo-Confucian *dao* conceived under the influence of Buddhism and Daoism as a metaphysical entity. In ancient times, Yan further surmised, members of the intellectual elite (*shi*) were all trained for technical competence in the "six arts" (rituals, music, archery, charioteering, writing, and mathematics) and other useful crafts, and in the end each settled into a special art as a lifelong vocation. Thus in the original Confucian curriculum there was little room left for "book-reading" as a means of seeking the Way. "Quiet-sitting" in quest of *dao* as transcendent reality was simply inconceivable. In those early days the *dao* was directly shown to everyone through the deeds and words of the sage kings and therefore could not possibly have become something subject to different interpretations. Free from the burden of seeking to know *dao*, all a student needed to do was to concentrate on learning and practicing the art of his chosen specialization. As a result, the *shi* as a group contributed enormously to the actualization of *dao* in ancient times. Fully aware of this ideal past, Confucius continued to train his disciples in the "six arts" and rarely, if ever, discussed such abstract topics as "human nature" or the "Way of heaven."

It was this imagined Confucian *dao*, before its two wrong turns, that Yan hoped to introduce to his own age. He quoted two passages, one from a chapter ("The Counsels of the Great Yü") in the *Book of History* and one from the *Institutes of Zhou*, to support his point about the nature of *dao* as well as his contention that authentic Confucian education consists largely of technical competence in various practical "arts." Ironically, owing to his isolation from mainstream classical scholarship of his day, he was unaware that the authenticity of the two texts he quoted was being called into question.

It is not difficult, as has been so often done, to dismiss Yan with a shrug either as a philosophical thinker or as a classical scholar; but that is rather beside the point. What cannot be easily dismissed is the question why his thought drew so much attention from Qing Confucians, especially in the last decades of the Qing dynasty? To answer this question we need to place him in the historical context of Qing Confucianism.

From many of the autobiographical accounts in his writings, it is clear that, like most Confucians of the early Qing, Yan never fully recovered from the shock of the fall of the Ming dynasty. Throughout his life he retained a deep sense of political and social crisis that redirected his thinking about Confucianism. He blamed the collapse of the Ming squarely on neo-Confucianism, which, in his eyes, had been all along too much disposed to contemplation rather than action. As he vividly characterized late Ming neo-Confucians:

> In times of leisure they discoursed with folded hands on the abstract ideas of mind and human nature; when they were confronted with a real dynastic crisis, they could repay the throne only by committing suicide.

Determined to remedy this pathetic situation, he began a new project in the hope of turning Confucianism from quietism to activism. Thus he redefined the Confucian *dao* as follows:

> The "five emperors," the "three kings," the duke of Zhou, and Confucius are all sages who taught the world how to move forward. They are all sages who shaped *dao* of the world through movement.

Here, he not only identified *dao* as the ideal political-social-economic order but also interpreted its actualization as resulting directly from the intelligent design and dynamic action of the ancient sages. Viewed in this way the primary function of Confucianism must of necessity be understood as setting the world in good order. This leads naturally to the Confucian notion of *jingshi* ("ordering the world"), which often came to the surface in times of crisis. In his writings Yan repeatedly refers to the idea of *jingshi*. The central values stressed in his Confucian project—such as "activeness," "practicality," "utility" (*yong*), and "technical competence"—are all justified on the ground that they are absolutely instrumental to "setting the world in order." It is therefore safe to conclude that of all of Qing Confucians Yan alone gave the idea of *jingshi* its fullest intellectual expression. This is precisely why his project was rediscovered in the late nineteenth century when a more powerful *jingshi* movement returned to the intellectual world. With the publication in 1869 of *Yanshi xueji* (*Scholarly Records of Yan Yuan*) by Dai Wang (1837–1873), ideas of Yan Yuan became widely and increasingly influential among reform-minded Confucians in the late Qing. They have been subject to various interpretations to this day.

See also Confucianism: Qing; *Li*: Principle, Pattern, Reason; *Qi*; Zhu Xi.

Bibliography

Chan, Wing-tsit. *A Source Book in Chinese Philosophy*. Princeton, N.J.: Princeton University Press, 1963. (See ch. 37, "Practical Confucianism of Yen Yuan.")

Fung, Yu-lan (Feng Youlan). *History of Chinese Philosophy*, trans. Derk Bodde, Vol. 2. Princeton, N.J.: Princeton University Press, 1953. (See ch. 15, "The Ch'ing Continuation of Neo-Confucianism," Sec. 2, "Yen Yuan, Li Kung, and One Group in Neo-Confucianism.")

Liang, Ch'i-ch'ao. *Intellectual Trends in the Ch'ing Period*, trans. Immanuel C. Y. Hsü. Cambridge, Mass.: Harvard University Press, 1959. (See Part 1.2, "Yen Yüan. 1635–1704.")

Qian, Mu. *Zhongguo jin sanbainian xueshu shi* (Chinese Intellectual History of the Past Three Hundred Years). Shanghai: Commercial Press, 1937. (See ch. 5, "Yan Xizhai, Li Shugu.")

Weiming, Tu. "Yen Yüan: From Inner Experience to Lived Concreteness." In *The Unfolding of Neo-Confucianism*, ed. William Theodore de Bary. New York and London: Columbia University Press, 1975.

Yang Xiong (Yang Hsiung)

Michael Nylan

Yang Xiong (Yang Hsiung, 53 B.C.E.–18 C.E.), having achieved his youthful ambition to become a court poet, spent his late thirties and forties producing the occasional poetry required by the throne to commemorate major events. Sometime around Yang's fiftieth year, perhaps in reaction to the increasingly factional politics at the capital, Yang came to disparage his own genius for composing *fu* (rhapsodic poems). By Yang's own account, the verbal pyrotechnics expected with the *fu* made them seem a childish game; even worse, he felt that the *fu* as entertainment were not merely devoid of moral content but injurious to the moral process. In consequence, Yang became preoccupied with composing and then defending three subsequent works: the *Taixuan jing* (*Canon of Supreme Mystery*), the *Fayan* (*Model Sayings*), and the *Fangyan* (*Dialect Words*). Creating the first two of these three new "classics" (*jing*) required, if anything, still greater ingenuity on Yang's part than writing *fu*, for Yang sought to capture not only the inner message but also the outer form of canonical works taught in the Confucian curriculum in Han times: The *Mystery* was patterned after the *Yijing* (*Classic of Changes*), the *Fayan* after the *Lunyu* (*Analects*). The *Fangyan*, which claimed inspiration from the ancient Zhou (Chou) transcriptions of the *Book of Odes*, possibly was also fashioned after the *Erya*, an early word list ascribed in Han times to Confucius. By such bold attempts at "renewing the old," Yang hoped to rejuvenate and restore the authentic teachings associated with the true Confucian Way.

In imitation of the *Yijing*, an abstruse divination text turned philosophical work by the addition of *Ten Wings*, the *Taixuan jing* unfolds on at least two levels simultaneously. For the ordinary reader, its divinatory formulas prescribe certain social virtues, especially humility, respect, and cautiousness, that make for good order in the empire while keeping the individual from serious harm. (On this level, the *Mystery* pays tribute to Yang's early mentor, Yan Junping, who saw in his own profession as diviner an opportunity to persuade unthinking clients fearful of the future to adopt the wisest courses of action.) For the more sophisticated reader, however, the *Mystery* represents a larger challenge: A series of vignettes drawn from daily life and keyed to the calendar are to be pieced together with graphic emblems, cryptic summaries, and Yang's own "autocommentaries" in such a way as to form meaningful patterns that illustrate the complex relation between human conduct and preordained fate—an obvious subject for a divination text.

According to Yang's vision of the triadic realms of heaven, earth, and man, the interaction of four main factors determines the quality of each person's existence: time, tools, position, and virtue. Although the workings of fate (*ming*), equated in Yang's work with time or "timely opportunity" (*shi*), lie completely outside human control, the effects of time may be offset to some extent by three other factors under better human control: (1) the individual's comparative skill in handling certain tools at hand (not only physical tools, like the boat and the ax, but also human institutions, such as the family, rites, and the penal code); (2) his relative position (meaning his geographic location, as well as his rank); and, most important, (3) his behavior, or virtue. Since Yang traced all distinctively human achievements to the ability to "move diligently according to the time," the *Mystery* emphasizes, on the negative side, the need for the careful alignment with prevailing trends that will "keep oneself intact" and, more positively, the concurrent need to be, like Confucius, "stingy with one's time," so that one's limited time on earth is used to maximum advantage to attain the only form of true happiness that is perfectly secure: the moral life.

In reconstructing the underlying forces that propel human existence, Yang invariably puts human life within the larger cosmological context of heaven and earth. Using the most advanced scientific theories of his time, Yang sketches the finely tuned cycles of *yin, yang*, and the "five phases" in the universe, relating them to the regular movements of the heavenly bodies. In the course of outlining these cosmic patterns, Yang touches on many of the usual topics in Han philosophy: whether and in what sense ghosts exist, how to imagine the role of divination and the divine, the origins and cosmogonic stages of the universe, its influence on the hierarchical orders invented for human civilization, and the definition of "good government." Key to such discussions is one passage in Yang's autocommentaries that seeks to explain the central double paradox (natural-artificial; human-divine) of early Confucian philosophy in terms of *jing* (single-minded dedication to the good): the absolute realization of human potential through total dedication to the arduous process of self-cultivation results in the acquisition of a virtual second nature that is godlike in its powers. As Yang writes:

> The sage would match his body with heaven-and-earth, aim for the numinosity of the ghosts and gods, push his transformations to the limit with yin and yang, and participate in the four seasons. Contemplating heaven, he becomes heaven. . . . To draw out the infinitude of all-under-heaven, to dispel the confusion and chaos of all-under-heaven, what else but single-minded concentration [of the good] can accomplish it?

Building on that central paradox, Yang began refining his insights in a new work, the *Fayan*, started soon after the untimely death of his most beloved son. If the single most important theme of Yang Xiong's *Mystery* is the interaction between human will and divine fate, the single most important idea of the *Fayan* is that this single-minded devotion to the Good leads to an exquisite appreciation of the cosmic order which itself constitutes the highest happiness of which human beings are capable. A dialogue in the style of the *Analects* of Confucius, the *Fayan* constructs a compelling argument in favor of this inherently unprovable assertion by a curious but highly effective method: Yang arranges a series of seemingly disparate interchanges weighing the value of famous lives in such a way that the fictional dialogue suggests the underlying interconnection of otherwise isolated beliefs and observations. Yang's choice of the dialogue form was fortunate, for the extensive conversations between Yang and an unnamed interlocutor in the *Fayan* encourage the reader to face initial bewilderment, then to arrive at syntheses by deducing relations from incomplete information—in short, to re-create the "feel" of mundane experience as it applies to moral problems. Believing that moral preferences can only be taught only by example, rather than by force or rhetorical argument (ch. 2), Yang juxtaposes hypothetical cases with references to historical personages, all reinforced by his ironical remarks, to induce the reader to undertake the extremely complex practices of self-shaping and "self-analysis" (ch. 10) that rely on questioning conventions and developing significant patterns in one's personal connections.

Yang Xiong ultimately intends the *Fayan* to convince the reader of four linked propositions. The first is that a crucial distinction exists between the "vulgar" *Ru*, exemplified by many popular "heroes" and current office-holders, and the "true" *Ru*, defined as those who are faithful to the original vision of the sage-master Confucius. Second, that the vulgar Ru badly misperceive the Confucian life. Insofar as they mistake its pursuit for material (bureaucratic) success, they tend to reduce its subtle signposts to overly simplistic formulas; and insofar as they confuse the Confucian Way with either factual knowledge or rule making, they fail to undertake the therapeutic journey toward goodness that entails identification with historical and contemporary examples of the "worthy man." For Yang, only guided study of the ancients, followed by consistent practice of their Way (which demands full "immersion" in the hermeneutic model provided by the sages) can lift a person beyond bestiality or mediocrity. Third, that the very process of learning to intuit the sages' intent embodied in the "true" *Ru* vision so hones the learner's being that he is gradually able to experience for the first time the most exquisite form of pleasure known to humankind, a pleasure akin to, but more sublime, than aesthetic connoisseurship—what Yang describes (ch. 6) as the "ultimate in discrimination" (*zhishi*). Only this immersion in true Confucian models can satisfy all aspects of human nature, with its mixture of good and evil (ch. 3), for the immersion suits both a person's best instincts (defined as the impulse to admire and identify with those greater than oneself) and his worst (those of greed, envy, and the egotistical insistence upon ever keener pleasures). Fourth, that this kind of pleasure is the only sure reward available to humans for a comparable expenditure of effort.

Unfortunately, neither study of the Confucian classics nor practice of the Confucian Way can ever be made entirely "easy," since truly great entities, such as heaven, earth, and the Five Classics, must be comprehensive enough to encompass all the lesser things (chs. 5, 8). Also, this same compulsion to become greater than oneself is as much a source of agonizing frustration as of ineffable joy. Nevertheless, Yang promises that the pursuit of goodness is "easy" in other ways: it entails no trickery or treachery; it imparts a kind of mental equilibrium, along with an enhanced ability to understand and predict human behavior (chs. 2, 9). Moreover, final mastery of the process of immersion into the minds of the sages reveals an entire world of marvelous, if delicate, balances binding heaven, earth, and man.

Yang's *Fayan* is quite remarkable, then, for the authority with which it presents an idea embedded equally in the Confucian and Daoist traditions: that true virtue elicits supreme pleasure, an "immeasurable joy" reserved for the discriminating few. In effect, the *Fayan* issues a challenge to members of the Han sociopolitical elite (all nominal "Confucians," or *Ru*, in that they have been trained in the Five Classics) to transform themselves into a genuine elite of real nobility, whose proclivities and sensitivities would far excel those of ordinary mortals. Yang therefore portrays himself as a latter-day Mencius determined to save the Confucian tradition not only from its outspoken critics but also from some of its nominal adherents, those sloppy thinkers who blame Confucian teachings for the essential emptiness of their lives. Decrying the attractions of alchemy, numerology, and the occult sciences, Yang offers different enticements to his readers, namely, "essential words and marvelous doctrines."

Given the broad strokes of the *Mystery* and the sweeping claims of the *Fayan*, it is hard to see how Yang's third great work, the *Fangyan*, fits with his mature vision, for the *Fangyan* is a meticulous record of dialect expressions found in particular regions within the extended Chinese cultural sphere. It helps to remember that Han philosophers generally assumed that the melodic patterns of human speech, as well as musical rhythms, the calligraphic forms of written characters, and the geographical configurations of the earth, all served as intimations of the divine order. One passage in the *Fayan* (ch. 5), in fact, quite specifically explains Yang's lifelong fascination with words, wordplay, and variants in terms of his moral vision:

> To understand men's longings, there is nothing so good as words. [Words] fully order matters in all-under-heaven; they record events of long ago; they show what will happen far [in the future]. To elucidate what is closed [to us] in great antiquity, to transmit [one's] sorrows over [the space of] 1,000 *li*, there is nothing so good as writing. Thus, words are the music of the heart-mind (*xin*); and writings, its painting. As soon as music and painting assume form, the noble and petty men are seen! And music and painting are the means whereby to move the emotions of noble and petty men.

For Yang, the supreme goal was to use artistic forms to spark the imagination in a precise manner so that its excited sensibilities might be more receptive to the serious business of moral edification. Accordingly, Yang was the first philosopher to develop detailed theories of important aesthetic concepts and the hermeneutic enterprise, and then demonstrate their emotive power through the language of his own literary masterpieces. In the *Mystery*, archaistic rhymes and graphic forms were coupled in such a way as to allow the reader to glimpse the central core of existence. And in the *Fayan*, Yang's deft use of various dramatic devices (even stage directions) conveys a sense of the dizzying whirl of competing, commensurate claims upon the individual psyche that occasion terrible swings between crass calculation and reckless hedonism, preparing the chastened reader to welcome the quiet wisdom that informs Yang's holistic vision.

During Yang's own lifetime, the *Mystery* and the *Model Sayings* earned Yang the title of Confucian master within a devoted circle of disciples (among them the philosophical masters Huan Tan and Hou Ba), though there were clearly those who mistrusted Yang's incredible versatility in creating new Confucian "classics." Liu Xin, for example, reportedly derided Yang's philosophical labors as "self-imposed torture to no purpose" (*kongziku*). Following his death, Yang was elevated still higher in the minds of many scholars, including the professed skeptic Wang Chong (27–97 C.E.) and the Eastern Han exegete Song Zhong. The critic Liu Xie, of the Six Dynasties period, called Yang "most profound, both in the language he employs and in the themes he treats." Han Yu (768–842) named Yang Xiong, not Xunzi, as the single philosopher qualified to "transmit the [Confucian] Way" after Mencius; and Sima Guang (1018–1086) insisted that neither Mencius nor Xunzi could compare with Yang Xiong in understanding the Way of the ancients. Thus Yang occupied a prominent place in the orthodox roster of Confucian sages for more than a millennium after his death, despite the abstruse character of the *Mystery*.

A mere century after Sima Guang, some Song thinkers, especially Zhu Xi (1130–1200), applying their recently formulated standards of morality retroactively to Yang's works, proceeded to condemn them on four principal grounds: (1) Yang's open eclecticism, which embraced numerous tenets proposed by philosophers of the Warring States period whom they judged "heterodox"; (2) his evident arrogance in daring to compose classics in imitation of the Supreme Master Confucius; (3) his presumed disloyalty in continuing to serve at court after the "usurpation" by Wang Mang; and (4) his outright rejection of the theory of human nature proposed by Mencius. Yang's phenomenal ability to project a coherent cosmology based on very different principles than those favored by Southern Song theorists must have struck his critics as equally objectionable. Although Yang's cosmology was seldom singled out for explicit attack by Zhu Xi and his followers, this may explain the special ire Zhu's adherents reserved for the *Canon of Supreme Mystery*. In any case, not until the Qing evidential school, which looked to overturn many Cheng-Zhu commonplaces, was Yang partially restored to his rightful place in the history of Chinese thought as one of the few thinkers who successfully reconciled the many scholastic impulses revered in the Han, thereby epitomizing the syncretic spirit of his age. Recent scholars have celebrated the independence of mind that led Yang to insist that the state sponsorship of Confucian ethics, rather than promoting the vision of the Sage-master, was exerting a deleterious effect on the community of classical scholars. A renewed interest in Han studies in general will surely prompt more evenhanded assessments of Yang's unique contributions in future.

See also Confucianism: Han; Wang Chong.

Bibliography

Knechtges, David R. *The Han Rhapsody: A Study of the Fu of Yang Hsiung*. Cambridge: Cambridge University Press, 1976.

——. *The Han Shu Biography of Yang Xiong: 53 B.C. to A.D. 18* Tempe: Arizona State University Press, 1982.

Pan, Ku. *The Han shu Biography of Yang Hsiung (53 B.C.–A.D. 18)*, trans. and annot.

Yang, Hsiung. *The Canon of Supreme Mystery*, trans. with commentary by Michael Nylan. Albany: State University of New York Press, 1993.

——. *Fang-yen*. (See *The Chinese Dialects of Han Time According to Fang Yen*, trans. and annot. Paul L-M Serruys. Berkeley: University of California Press, 1959.)

——. *Fayan*, trans. Michael Nylan. (Forthcoming.)

——. *Fayan yishu*, comp. Wang Rongbao. Beijing: Zhonghua, 1987.

——. *Fayan zhu*, annot. Han Jing. Beijing: Zhonghua, 1992.

——. *Taixuan jiaoyi*, comp. Zheng Wangeng. Beijing: Shifan daxue, 1989. (The best edition of the *Taixuan jing*.)

Yang Zhu (Yang Chu)

Vincent SHEN

The proper name Yang Zhu can be understood as referring to a person, to a school of thought, or to a group of works. Nothing certain is known about the person Yang Zhu, except that, together with Mozi (Mo Di), he was someone very influential in pre-Qin thought. The school of thought Yang Zhu is mentioned in the works of many pre-Qin and later authors, such as the *Mencius, Xunzi, Han Feizi, Lushi Chunqiu, Huainanzi*, and *Lunheng*. We find in the *Liezi* a chapter called *Yang Zhu*, though many scholars regard it as a forgery by much later authors. As a body of works, Yang Zhu was quite influential during the time of the Warring States or even earlier. According to Mencius, Yang Zhu and Mozi represented the most influential currents of thought during this time:

> The words of Yang Zhu and Mo Di flourish under heaven. Opinions of the world follow either Yang or Mo. Yang exists only for his own self, and pays no special regard to the ruler. Mo advocates universal love, and pays no special regard for one's father.

This is intended as a criticism of Yang Zhu's emphasis on the self and what Mencius considers its "anarchist" consequences, but it is also documentary proof of the powerful influence of Yang Zhu's thought, along with Mozi's, in a period before Mencius.

Besides objecting to his anarchism, Mencius criticized Yang Zhu for selfishness and indifference to the public interest: "Yang Zhu chooses to exist only for his own self, and does nothing for the world, not even by drawing out one hair of his head." But in the chapter *Yang Zhu* in the *Liezi*, there is quite a different story. We read there that Yang Zhu was asked by Qinzi whether he would agree to lose one hair in order to help the whole world. Yang Zhu answered by saying, "In principle, the world could not be helped by one hair." Also, in the *Lushi chunqiu*, it is said that "the scholar Yang elevates the self." And in the *Huainanzi*, we read: "To keep the totality of his life and cherish the authenticity of his self, and not to burden his bodily life with external things—this is that on which Yang Zhu stands, yet it is criticized by Mencius." From such textual evidence we can conclude, disregarding ideological biases and critiques of ideologies, such as Mencius's, that Yang Zhu concentrates on the value of life or existence and on the self.

What does Yang Zhu mean by keeping the "totality of life" and cherishing the "authenticity of the self"? Some hermeneutic work is needed in reading texts such as the chapter *Yang Zhu* in the *Liezi* and other relevant texts such as *Lushi chunqiu*, although it is best not to become too entangled with the question of authorship. In Yang Zhu's case, the totality of life always refers to bodily human life; we can say that there is a philosophy of the body in Yang Zhu. Keeping the totality of one's life refers to economizing on bodily energy and to properly satisfying one's desires. In the *Lushi Chunqiu* we find, " 'Keep the totality of one's life' means that all six desires are appropriately attained." We also find:

> A man who has attained the level of *dao* can live long, still experiencing the joy of sound, color, and taste. Why? Because he has set up, from the beginning, his position in life. If he has set up his position early on, then he knows from the outset that he should economize his energy in order to endure for a long time without becoming exhausted.

Yang Zhu's philosophy of the body is thus defined with respect to satisfying desires in a proper way and spending energy wisely.

As to the authenticity of the self, Yang Zhu emphasizes autonomy relative to all external determinants. Here, autonomy does not mean positing norms of action or rules of behavior through one's own will. It means, rather, a spontaneous unfolding of one's own nature. This is not to be determined by external entities, either real or ideal; it is determined internally by oneself. Yang Zhu believed that people could not enjoy a restful or quiet life, because they were ceaselessly running after four things: longevity, fame, position, and goods. When people long for these four things, they will be afraid of ghosts, other people, power, and punishment. And then they are no longer free men; they can be called *dunren*, "escapists"—people who have fled from or abandoned their natural selves. They are at the mercy of others, who could kill them or keep them alive; their destiny depends on external factors.

By contrast, if one does not act against one's own destiny, one need not covet longevity. If one is not proud of having a high position, one need not covet fame. If one does not play with power, one need not covet position. If one is not greedy for wealth, one need not covet goods. In this case, a person is called *shunmin*, "conformist," and "there will be no opposition under heaven to his life, and his destiny is determined internally, by himself." It is clear that for Yang Zhu the authenticity of one's life is closely related to the autonomy of the self, which means self-determination.

With regard to philosophical anthropology, it seems that for Yang Zhu, human intellect, the most precious element in human life, is developed out of biological weakness. Biologically, a human being is much weaker than other animals or natural forces:

> His nails and teeth are not strong enough for self-defense. His skin and muscle are not strong enough for self-protection. His running is not fast enough to allow him to flee from any harmful force. He has no fur or feathers to protect himself against heat and cold.

Therefore, a human being "should use things to nourish his own nature, and let his own intellect develop without appealing to physical force." Human intellect can be applied to conserve the self by utilizing natural resources, without appealing to violence:

> That which is precious about the human intellect consists of self-conservation, and that which is despicable in physical force consists of its aggressive violence to other things.

Finally, a few words should be said about Yang Zhu's philosophy of learning. In the chapter *Yang Zhu* in the *Liezi*, there is an image of losing sheep along roads that diverge in too many ways. The message being conveyed is that "just as one cannot find one's lost sheep because of too many deviations along a road, one can lose his own life if there are too many deviations in learning." Here, life is taken as a basic value, and one is counseled not to get lost by embarking on too many directions of learning. The passage also suggests the authenticity of life as the final unity of all learning:

> Learning in its origin is not diverse, is not without unity, yet people in the end come to be very different; only by returning to that sameness and unity can they avoid getting lost in confusion.

Yang Zhe seems to value a certain pragmatism in learning: we learn for the purpose of conserving life and the authenticity of the self. The conservation of life and its development according to the principle of authenticity seem to be, for Yang Zhu, the ultimate values in human existence and also the final unity of all learning.

See also Egoism in Chinese Ethics.

Bibliography

Chan, Wing-tsit, trans. *A Source Book in Chinese Philosophy*. Princeton, N.J.: Princeton University Press, 1963.

Fang, Thomé (Fang Dongmei). *Chinese Philosophy: Its Spirit and Its Development*. Taipei: Linking, 1981.

———. *Yuanshi rujia daojia zhexue* (Philosophies of Primordial Confucianism and Daoism). Taipei: Li-ming, 1983.

Fung, Yu-lan (Feng Youlan). *A History of Chinese Philosophy*, 2 vols., trans. Derk Bodde. Princeton, N.J.: Princeton University Press, 1952–1953.

Graham, A. C. *Chuang Tzu: The Inner Chapters*. London: Allen and Unwin, 1981.

Han, Feizi. *The Complete Works of Han Fei Tzu*, 2 vols., trans. W. K. Liao. London: Probsthain, 1939, 1960.

Huainanzi. *Huainanzi* (The Book of the Master of Huai-nan), annot. GaoYu. Taipei: Shijie Book Store, 1985. (8th printing.)

———. *Tao: The Great Luminant*, trans. Evan Morgan. Shanghai: Kelly and Walsh, 1934.

Liezi. *The Book of Lieh Tzu*, trans. A. C. Graham. London: Murray, 1960.

———. *Liezi*. In *Ershi'er zi*, Vol. 2. Taipei: Prophet, 1976. (Reprint.)

Mencius. *The Sayings of Mencius*, trans. James Ware. New York: New American Library, 1960.

Wang, Chong. *Lunheng*. In *Sibu beiyao*. Taipei: Chung Hua Book Store, 1981.

Xu, Weiyu. *Lushi Chunqiu*, 3 vols. Taipei, Shijie Book Store, 1988.

Xunzi. *The Works of Hsüntze*, trans. H. H. Dubs. London: Probsthain, 1928.

Zhuangzi. *Zhuangzi jishi*, ed. Guo Qingfan. Taipei: Shih-chieh, 1985. (12th reprint.)

Yi (*I*) and *Li*: Rightness and Rites

A. S. Cua

The ethical significance of *yi*, in part, is an attempt to provide a rationale for the acceptance of *li*. *Yi* focuses principally on what is right or fitting. The equation of *yi* with its homophone meaning "appropriateness" is explicit in *Zhongyong* (Sec. 20) and generally accepted by Confucian thinkers, e.g., Xunzi, Li Gou, and Zhu Xi. However, what is right or fitting depends on reasoned judgment. As Xunzi puts it: "The person concerned with *yi* follows reason" (Li 1979, 605). Thus, *yi* may be construed as reasoned judgment concerning the right thing to do in particular exigencies. Recall Li Gou's plausible statement that *yi* is "decisive judgment" appropriate to the situation at hand (Cua 1989). While both *ren* and *li* have been closely studied, *yi* is largely neglected (Cheng 1972; Cua 1971; Hall and Ames 1987). Below I offer a fuller explication for appreciating the ethical significance of *yi* and its connection with *li*.

The Interdependence of *Yi* and *Li*

In dealing with the distinction and relation between *yi* and *li*, the following scheme for analysis of *yi* may be helpful. The scheme is a conceptual proposal for *yi* as rightness independent of issues in textual scholarship. (S stands for "statement.")

- S1. An action is *right* if either of the following is true:
  - a. It conforms to the requirement of an established rule.
  - b. It conforms to the agent's judgment of what is appropriate or fitting to the requirements of the situation at hand.
- S2. A person is *righteous* if he is conscientious in performing the right action as indicated in S1.

- S3. A person's *judgment* concerning what is right (S1) is correct (i.e., has a reasoned justification) if either of the following is true:

    a. It can be shown to be a correct judgment of the relevance of an established rule to his action (S1a).
    b. It can be shown to be consonant with other ethical values, which, in the situation, are considered relevant and not open to question (S1b).

- S4. A person has *moral sense* if either of the following is true:

    a. He appreciates the distinction between right and wrong (moral distinction).
    b. He is actuated by a sense of duty as pertaining to what he ought or ought not to do in a particular situation.

In contemporary idiom, *yi* as an ethical notion can be explicated as (S1) a deontic, (S2) an aretaic, (S3) an epistemic, or (S4) a psychological term. Thus *yi* is a distinct plurisign adaptable to a range of meaning or significance in the various contexts of discourse.

With the foregoing scheme, along with the assumption that the *li* comprise a set of ritual rules, let us first take up the question of *li* and *yi* as distinct notions. We may proceed by inquiring into the respect in which they differ. In other words, let us focus on each sense of *yi* and see what can be plausibly said about *li* and *yi* as distinct notions.

In general, both *li* and *yi* have the same objective in ensuring the performance of right conduct. This is the strength of the functional-equivalence thesis that *li* and *yi* have the same regulative function, that is, the same purpose in indicating standards of conduct (Chen 1954). In our scheme, with respect to S1, S1a is functionally equivalent to *li*, since the *li* collectively represent the established rules for proper conduct. Plausibly, it is this thesis that explains Xunzi's frequent association of *li* and laws (*fa*), rules, and regulations. But for him, the *li* collectively constitute the foundation for all rulelike requirements. According to S1a, a right action is one that accords with an established rule, and unproblematically this rule may be said to be a part of *li*. But this leaves us open to action in accord with S1b, that is, to the case of right conduct that falls outside the scope of *li*. This is the merit of the delimitation thesis, that *yi* in the sense of S1b fixes the boundary or the scope of *li* in particular situations (Wei 1974, 7), which are deemed exigent rather than normal (Cua 1989). Xunzi recognizes the real possibility of this sort of situation, as is evident in his remark:

> Where there are established rules of conduct [*fa*], comply with them. Where there are no such rules, act in the spirit of analogy [*lei*]. (Li 163; Watson 1963, 34, emended)

Thus the *li* cannot deal with situations envisaged by S1b.

Our scheme suggests that *li* and *yi* can be properly distinguished along the line indicated by the distinction between S1a and S1b. Alternatively, the distinction depicts a difference in the direction of focus. *Li* is rule-focused and *yi* situation-focused. Thus even if an action is described as conforming to a rule of *li*, this description presupposes that the rule in question is relevant to the action in a particular situation. Now S1b clearly points out that the action in a particular situation may be adjudged by the agent to be outside the operative scope of *li*. This judgment, of course, has to be justified as required by S3. Thus both S1a and S1b imply S3, which is the distinctive function of *yi*. Let us briefly look at S2.

S2 depends for clarification on S1, which in turn depends on S3. The focus of S2 is *yi* as an aretaic term with reference to a virtue, a desirable character trait, or a virtuous disposition. Confucius and major Confucian thinkers contrast *yi* with the concern for personal gain or profit. To act in the spirit of *yi* is to display a conscientious regard for moral distinctions (S4) in considering whether one should carry out one's self-serving projects. In this sense *yi* is an aretaic term. *Li* can also be construed as an aretaic term referring to the virtue of rule responsibility or compliance, that is, to the ethically commendable disposition (*meide*) to conform to established requirements. *Li* is a first-order virtue; *yi* as conscientiousness is a second-order virtue. As William Frankena points out:

> Besides first order virtues such as these [e.g., honesty, fidelity, benevolence, and justice], there are certain other moral virtues that ought to be cultivated, which are in a way more abstract and general and may be called second-order virtues. Conscientiousness is such a virtue; it is not limited to a certain sector of the moral life, as gratitude and honesty are, but a virtue covering the whole of the moral life. (1973, 46)

Of course, Confucians will add that the ultimate significance of *yi* lies in its connection with *dao* or *ren* as an ideal of extensive affection for all things in the world. Also, they will emphasize such dependent virtues as integrity, courage, circumspection, and informed and wise deliberation—a common theme in both Confucian and western ethical thought.

In connection with S3, it is important to note that *yi* as a virtue implicitly presupposes impartiality (Cua 1985, ch. 1). *Yi* in the sense of S2 implies the likely divergence of and opposition between morality and personal advantage. When a conflict occurs, concern for *yi* must take precedence. Although this contrast is sometimes present in a *li*-performance, there the emphasis is on the importance of compliance with conventional standards of conduct. In the case of *yi*, the emphasis is on detachment from the desire for personal gain as required by consideration of situational appropriateness. Again, Xunzi is emphatic on this point: "A clear system of rules and regulations, weights and measures, exists for the sake of proper employment; they are not conventions to be blindly followed" (Li, 286). *Li* and *yi* in S2 are thus distinct notions, for compliance with *li* may be based on consideration of personal gain rather than on conscientious regard for established standards of conduct. It is also possible for a committed person to perform a conscientious action devoid of a reasoned judgment of appropriate action in a particular situation. Thus S2 depends on the force of S3.

Let us now turn to S3, which lies at the heart of *yi* as a distinct ethical notion. It is essentially the notion of reasoned or correct judgment or ruling. In S3a, *yi* pertains to the judgment of the relevance of a rule to a particular situation; in S3b, it pertains to the judgment that appeals to the relevance of other ethical notions. This sense of *yi* is hardly detachable from *quan*, the exercise of moral discretion. Within Confucian ethics, such notions as *ren*, in the narrow sense of benevolence, may be deemed operative in particular cases. It cannot be denied that if *li* is broadly construed as a comprehensive ethical term in Confucian ethics, *ren* and *yi* would be subsumed under *li* (Dubs 1927, 66; Fingarette 1972). The plausibility of this interpretation of the *Analects* presupposes that *li* is a set of ideal-embedded rules rather than a mere set of established rules. This means that this use of *li* entails its connection with *ren*. Also, *li* in the primary regulative sense depends on *yi* for assessing the relevance of rules to particular cases. *Yi* in the distinctive sense of S3, as a focus on reasoned judgment, is essentially an epistemic notion, thus involving explanation and justification of ethical judgments (Cua 1985, 51–86).

Again, *yi* in S4 cannot be equated with *li* in the regulative sense. Moral sense is essentially a cognitive appreciation of moral distinction (S4a) and more especially a sense of duty (S4b). It is this notion of *yi* that renders plausible a basic aspect of Wang Yangming's Mencian conception of *liangzhi* as the native ability of humans to distinguish right from wrong conduct. One can perform a *li*-action without appreciating its rationale. As a cognitive ability for appreciating ethical distinctions, *yi* presupposes the capacity to form reasoned judgment (*yi* in S3) or to engage in informed deliberation (*zhilü*)—a theme that pervades Xunzi's concern with reasoned response to changing circumstances (*yiyi bianying*). Our analytic scheme for the analysis of *yi* in relation to *li* thus provides us a way for locating *li* and *yi* as distinct ethical notions.

The preceding remarks, however, pertain to the distinction between *li* and *yi*. While we acknowledge that in terms of S1a, *li* and *yi* are functionally equivalent (Chen 1954), it is also important to inquire into their connection. As specific terms for the elaborating the concrete significance of the generic term *dao*, *li* and *yi* are partners in the same enterprise of morality. They are focal, complementary notions in Confucian ethics. Generally, within Confucian ethical thought, the distinction between notions is important only because some connection can be made out in appropriate contexts of discourse. Let us now go through the various senses of *yi* and exhibit, if possible, their connection.

With respect to S1a, we may construe the connection as the priority of *li* as an ethical consideration over *yi*, for S1a clearly implies such a thesis. That is, we need to appeal to our own judgment of the appropriate thing to do in a particular situation only when the *li*, as embodying the established rules, in some sense fail to guide us in resolving our current problem. In other words, this is the sort of situation in which a *li*-requirement is considered but, on reflection, the agent deems it inoperative or inapplicable to a case at hand. As Xunzi points out, "Just as weights and measures are the standard for things, the *li* are the standard for rules and regulations. Weights and measures establish quantity; the *li* fix the different sorts of human relationship" (Li, 397). The *li*, always in the first instance, provide ethical considerations as reasons for action, although in a particular situation they may not furnish sufficient guidance. In the sense of *li* as the first consideration, *yi* is thus dependent on *li*.

However, in another sense *yi* in S3 is prior to *li* as an ethical consideration. In S3a, *yi* in the sense of reasoned judgment on the relevance of rule to a particular case is presupposed by any application of *li*. For Xunzi, just as there are no rules or laws that can establish their own efficacy without men to carry them out, so also there are no kinds (*lei*) of rules that contain their own rules for application (263). Thus *yi* in S3a can claim a priority in moral consideration for determining the relevance of rules to particular cases. If the *li* are deemed applicable to particular cases, they must be adjudged to be the right sort of rule. In S3b, this claim of priority of yi over *li* is even more obvious, for *li* has to be declared irrelevant to exigent situations. This is the basis for our earlier idea that *yi* may be construed as reasoned judgment concerning the right thing to do in particular exigencies. Thus, while the *li* always present a claim to attention in ethical thinking, it is *yi* in S3 that decisively establishes their relevance or irrelevance. The same sort of priority may be said of *yi* in S2 as a second-order virtue, for acting ethically requires not only following rules (S1a) but also a disposition to do the right thing in a particular situation. Whether the disposition is properly guided depends on a judgment of appropriateness (S1b), which, in turn, requires reasoned justification (S3). Moreover, as we have earlier observed, acting from a virtuous disposition is quite different from mere responsibility to rules, for it requires the willingness to forgo one's personal interests for the sake of the requirement of righteousness. As Xunzi puts it: "A *junzi* (paradigmatic or exemplary individual) must be able to overcome his private desires in favor of impartiality (*gong*) and rightness (*yi*)" (Li, 2).

When we turn to *yi* in S4, the appreciation of moral distinctions and sense of duty, we can again claim the priority of *yi* in moral consideration over *li*. The former (S4a) implies, in particular, that one possesses an enlightened understanding of the significance of *li*. In Xunzi's words, "A *junzi* engages in extensive learning and daily examines himself, so that his understanding will be enlightened and his conduct be without fault" (Li, 2; Watson, 15, emended). This enlightened understanding essentially involves an appreciation of the rationale of *li* and related matters, i.e., the connection of *li* with other moral values (S3b), principally *ren*. Indeed, a profound insight into the living significance of *dao* and the interconnection of basic ethical notions depends on preserving clarity of mind. This clarity of mind is a prerequisite to reflection and reasoned justification of ethical judgments and decisions in exigent situations. We may thus conclude that, with the exception of *yi* in S1a, which is functionally equivalent to *li*, in all other cases, *yi* is prior to *li* in moral thought and action.

This claim of priority of *yi* as a moral consideration over *li* is not an absolute claim. If it were a claim to absolute priority, it might misleadingly suggest that *li* could be ignored when one judges that a particular rule is irrelevant to an exigent circumstance. After all, given the functional equivalence of *li* and *yi* (S1a) in some contexts, they have the same objective in governing conduct. This sense of *yi* is exemplified in the expression *shiyi* in the *Liji* (*Book of Rites*), the ten duties of the classical five human relationships (Wang 1977, vol. 1, ch. 9). Given *yi* in S3, for instance, *li* may again become relevant in communicating our reasoned judgments to others as they affect others' well-being. In so doing, the *li*, as rules of civility, need to be attended to, for they are an essential requirement for participation in traditional ethical life and argumentation (Cua 1985, 8–11). Consequently, the question of priority regarding *li* and *yi* does not admit of an absolute and final answer. It is a contextual question that has varying answers depending on the nature of the situation, which may be either a normal or changing or exigent circumstance of human life. In this light, while *li* in *yi* are distinct focal notions, in a particular context they may be mutually dependent for their actuating import for moral conduct. In this way, we may regard *li* and *yi* as partners in the same human enterprise.

Conclusion

In light of the foregoing discussion, we may state the interdependence of Confucian basic notions in this way. Given *dao* as the ideal of the good human life as a whole, *ren*, *li*, and *yi*, the basic, interdependent Confucian virtues (*de*), are constitutive rather than mere instrumental means to the fulfillment of *dao*. In other words, the realization of *dao* requires the concurrent satisfaction of the standards expressed in *ren, li*, and *yi*. Since these focal notions pertain to different but related fields of ethical interest, we may also say that the realization of *dao* requires a coordination or harmonious interaction of three equally important centers of ethical interest and endeavor. The connection between these foci is interdependence rather than subordination. Thus, in the ideal case, *ren, li*, and *yi* are mutually supportive and adhere to the same ideal of *dao*. When *dao* is in fact realized, *ren, li*, and *yi* would be deemed constituents of this condition of achievement. On the other hand, when one attends to the prospect of *dao*-realization, *ren, li*, and *yi* would be regarded as complementary foci and means to *dao* as an ultimate end. In this light, *ren, li*, and yi are complementary aspects of *dao*.

See also Confucianism: Ethics; Confucianism: Tradition; *Quan*.

Bibliography

Chen, Daqi. *Xunzi xueshuo*. Taipei: Zhonghua wenhua she, 1954.

Cheng, Chung-ying. "*Yi* as a Universal Principle of Specific Application." *Philosophy East and West*, 22(3), 1972.

Cua, A. S. "The Concept of Paradigmatic Individuals in the Ethics of Confucius." *Inquiry*, 14, 1971, pp. 41–55.

———. *Ethical Argumentation: A Study in Hsün Tzu's Moral Epistemology*. Honolulu: University of Hawaii Press, 1985.

———. "Hsün Tzu and the Unity of Virtues." *Journal of Chinese Philosophy*, 14(4), 1987, pp. 381–400.

———. "The Problem of Conceptual Unity in Hsün Tzu and Li Kou's Solution." *Philosophy East and West*, 39(2), 1989, pp. 115–134.

Dubs, Homer H. *Hsüntze: The Moulder of Ancient Confucianism*. London: Probsthain, 1927.

Fingarette, Herbert. *Confucius: The Secular as Sacred*. New York: Harper and Row, 1972.
Frankena, William. *Ethics*, 2nd ed. Englewood Cliffs, N.J.: Prentice-Hall, 1973.
Hall, David L., and Roger T. Ames. *Thinking through Confucius*. Albany: State University of New York Press, 1987.
Li, Disheng. *Xunzi jishi*. Taipei: Xuesheng, 1979.
Wang, Meng'ou. *Liji jinzhu junyi*, Vol. 1. Taipei: Shangwu, 1977.
Watson, Burton, trans. *Hsün Tzu: Basic Writing*. New York: Columbia University Press, 1963.
Wei, Zhengtong. *Xunzi yu gudai zhexue*. Taipei: Commercial Press, 1974.

Yin and *Yang*

Roger T. Ames

Yin and *yang* are terms used to express a contrastive relationship that obtains between two or more things. The image is captured in the etymology of the two characters: *yin* is the shady side of a hill, and *yang* is the sunny side. Since classical Chinese natural cosmology begins from the presumption of the uniqueness and the processional nature of all things, this *yinyang* vocabulary describes how things hang together in their dynamic and always changing relationships. Importantly, these relationships that define things are intrinsic and constitutive. Persons, for example, are radically situated within their natural, cultural, and social environments; they *are* their relationships. They are spouses and parents and neighbors. When they divorce or relocate, they are, as persons, surgically diminished to the extent that the abandoned relationships were important in their lives.

When this analogy of shade and sun is applied to the relationship between two particular things in respect of some characteristic or attribute, one thing at this particular point in time and in this particular situation will necessarily "overshadow" the other, and hence will be *yang* to the other's *yin*. In some other respect or at some other time and place, however, the opposite might well be true.

For example, with regard to wisdom younger persons might generally (but certainly not always) be *yin* in their relationship to some older person, who is thus *yang* in this particular relationship. But when it comes to physical strength or virility or endurance, the opposite might well be the case (although again, not always). And as the young themselves grow old, the relationships that locate them in the world will change accordingly.

Yinyang explains how one thing stands in relation to another, and hence can be described as expressing a correlation between them. Given that *yinyang* must always refer to a particular time and place, such correlations are always unstable. In fact, the *Book of Changes* appeals to *yinyang* as a way of articulating the process of ceaseless change within which the human experience is played out: "It is the succession of and alternation between *yin* and *yang* that is called the way (*dao*)." This propensity of things to move through different phases across their careers aligned *yinyang* with the "five phases" (*wuxing*) cosmology that emerged in the early Han dynasty. This "*yinyang* five phases" cosmology would track the correlations that constitute things as they make their way through their narratives in the world as a way of maximizing the harmony that can be achieved by taking best advantage of these interdependent relationships.

In addition to being a vocabulary of contrast within particular contexts, *yin* and *yang* suggest the interdependence of proximate things in the world. A teacher (*yang*) stands in contrast to her student (*yin*), but they are interdependent in that she can be a great teacher only to the extent that she has great students. This is what the *Daodejing* (42) means when it says: "The myriad things shouldering the *yin* and embracing the *yang*; blend these energies to constitute a harmony."

In this "correlative" cosmology of classical China, *yinyang* became a pervasive way of understanding how all things are related to each other, and it sets a pattern for the vocabulary used to articulate this understanding. Opposition within this tradition is understood as correlative rather than dualistic. Dualism, familiar in classical western metaphysical thinking, arises when a transcendent, determinative principle creates and sustain a world that stands independent of itself. This sets up a "two worlds" theory in which there is a putative "reality" behind changing appearances, a "being" behind the beings, a "one" behind the many. Thus the mind or soul is the real person; the body is a passing shade. Objective knowledge is truth; subjective knowledge is mere opinion.

In classical China, on the other hand, there is no counterpart to this distinction between "reality" and "appearance." Divinity and humanity, for example, are correlative and mutually entailing categories. Gods are dead people; they are the ancestors and cultural heroes who have defined the values of the tradition, and as such, become the objects of communal deference. This *yinyang* relationship in the Chinese religious sensibility is captured in the expression *tianren heyi*: "the continuity between divinity and human beings." Mind and body are on a continuum in a world in which psychophysical *qi* is its basic category. And given the radical embeddedness of the human experience, all knowledge is from some perspective or other, and thus is only in degree either objective or subjective.

Two important clarifications need to be made. First, as should be clear from what has been said above, *yin* and *yang* are explanatory rather than ontological categories. That is, the language of "principle" and "essences" that we often find associated with *yinyang* is inappropriate, and at best misleading. There is nothing that is "essentially" *yin* or *yang*; whether something is *yin* or *yang* depends on what particular relationship is being expressed. This does not preclude the cultural assumptions that have come to associate *yin* with female and *yang* with male, thereby generating generalizations that reinforce these same assumptions.

Secondly the usual pattern of classical Chinese correlative categories is that dominance is given to the first member of the pair. For example, *tianren* gives divinity a privileged place over the human being in their interdependent relationship; "knowing and doing" (*zhixing*) gives the privileged place to "knowing" in their relationship. There have been various explanations for why *yinyang* violates this pattern, from linguistic convenience (it is easier to say "*yinyang*" than "*yangyin*") to the idea that the proto-Chinese society was matriarchal. Certainly, the correlative way of understanding relatedness that has come to be characterized as *yinyang* thinking predates the use of this particular "binomial" expression, which does not become prominent until the late Warring States period (403–221 B.C.E.), and perhaps the application of this term as it evolved was purposely directed at challenging persistent cultural assumptions.

See also *Qi*; *Wuxing*.

Bibliography

Ames, Roger T. and David L. Hall. *A Philosophical Translation of the Daodejing: Making this Life Significant*. New York: Ballantine, 2002.

Black, Alison H. "Gender and Cosmology in Chinese Correlative Thinking." In *Gender and Religion: On the Complexity of Symbols*, ed. C. W. Bynum, S. Harrell, and P. Richman. Boston, Mass.: Beacon, 1989.

Graham, A. C. *Disputers of the Tao*. La Salle, Ill.: Open Court, 1989.

Major, John S. *Heaven and Earth in Early Han Thought: Chapters Three, Four, and Five of the Huainanzi*. Albany: State University of New York Press, 1993.

Youwu (*Yu-wu*): Being and Nonbeing

Chad HANSEN

You behaves roughly like an existential quantifier in classical Chinese and *wu* like its negation. So *you X* says simply that *X* exists and *wu X* denies it. The most elegant grammatical treatment, however, is an extension of the use of this pair as two-place predicates (transitive verbs). *S you X* says that *S* has *X*; *S wu X* says that *S* lacks *X*. This analysis neatly generates the straightforward existential sentence because preverbal terms (e.g., topic or subject) are optional even in assertions. Where the context signals that the topic or subject is *S*, *you X* could be thought of as "With regard to *S*, there is *X*." Alternatively, in the "pure" case, one might think of *you X* as "The world (universe of discourse) has *X*."

The pair *you-wu* features in the question whether or not Chinese philosophy has a concept of being—

and if so what it is. A related question concerns rules for interpreting western philosophy into Chinese: into what Chinese concept should we translate "being"? The two main rivals are *youwu* and *shifei*. We will approach the question from a different angle: should we use the word "being" in translating or interpreting Chinese philosophy? Angus Graham suggests that we should avoid "being" and "essence" because the western concept is the abstract object linked to the verb "to be" (or its translations in Indo-European languages).

Graham's analysis drew on Aristotle's response to Parmenides's doctrine that forbade saying anything about being other than "it is." Parmenides was committed to metaphysical monism, the doctrine that there is only permanent, all-embracing being with no distinctions, properties, or change. He treated being and identity as the same thing because he confused two distinct meanings of "to be": existence and predication. On the one hand, "is" has the meaning "exists"—"What is simply is and cannot not be." On the other hand, "is" links a thing to its predicates or properties. If we focus merely on the verb and the principle "what is not cannot become what is," then it will seem to entail that "what is not old cannot become old." Parmenides concludes that things cannot change. Similar arguments supposedly motivated his conclusion that there could be no motion.

Aristotle's categories distinguished a number of different senses of "being" that underlay the different ways we can predicate things of a subject (what it can be said to be). One of these is what came to be known as the essence or essential predication. Graham seemed to conclude that we should avoid either term in discussing Chinese philosophy. This indeed gives us reason to worry that Aristotle's rich concept of "being" (including all the categories) would not coincide exactly with either *youwu* or *shifei*. However, Aristotle's doctrine is similarly difficult for modern western students. For most of us, the concept of being coincides roughly with existence, not predication. It does not, therefore, appear to be misleading to translate the pair *you-wu* as being and nonbeing. (Of course, whether doing so in a translation of Aristotle will help or hinder intelligibility is a distinct issue.)

By an interesting coincidence, an argument by the neo-Daoist Guo Xiang almost paraphrases Parmenides—*wu* is simply *wu* and cannot become *you*. The contrast is immediate: "*You*, though it goes through endless transformation, never becomes *wu*." Where Parmenides moved inexorably to permanence, Guo Xiang did not see change as any kind of philosophical problem. Things change, but they do not cease to exist. What the grammar of Chinese explains is not the absence of the concept of being but the absence of a problem of permanence and change.

The question of "essence" in Chinese is complicated by combining the problem of identity and change with Aristotle's grammatical analysis of truths into subject (substance) and predicate (attribute) structure. The analysis (and the concept of a sentence) was unattested to in Chinese thought. Aristotle then drew a further distinction between accidental attributes and those without which the thing would not be what it is. Graham was right in the sense that there was no similarly structured metaphysical theory, but it is not clear that it has anything to do with *you* and *wu*. Its roots lie in the absence of anything sufficiently resembling subject-predicate grammatical analysis or its corollary, substance-property metaphysics. (Graham, however, does attribute a concept like "essence" to ancient thinkers.)

You and *wu* pose problems in Chinese philosophy primarily in theory of language and metaphysics. Mozi presents a theory of language under which he justifies, including in public discourse, the claims "there are spirits" and "there is no fate." He justifies this by a series of arguments that we should use words in ways corresponding to historical exemplars (arguably the coiners of terms), to the testimony of people using their eyes and ears, and to the utility of such use in promoting good behavior. He identifies his conclusion as "knowing the way to *youwu*."

The pair emerges in philosophy again in Laozi's *Daodejing*. There Laozi speaks of *youwu* "arising together." Lacking any marking that distinguishes use from mention, his slogan allows two interpretations. One says that the terms *you* and *wu* arise together and the other that existence arises with nonexistence. It is hard to say, offhand, what the latter amounts to. The more natural linguistic reading is buttressed by the fact that the claim arises in the context of a series of similar claims about many opposites: beautiful-ugly, good not good, before-after, etc. Laozi operates with an implicit contrast theory of language. A word has meaning only by virtue of contrasting with its opposite. To know any term *X*, to know how to use it, is to know not only what to call *X* but also what to call not-*X*.

Applying this analysis to *youwu* yields a puzzle like the puzzle of the reference of "nothing." It treats *you* and *wu* as referring expressions with an extension. Ancient Chinese linguistic theory tended to analyze all such words as names, *ming*. In Laozi's analysis, the puzzle is trying to think of the two names "emerging together." Supposedly, to do so is to think of making a distinction in things. However, if we divide anything off from being, it appears that we then "have" whatever has been divided off, so it must count as part of *you* rather than *wu*. Thus it seems impossible to imagine the pair of "names" emerging from a single distinction. Laozi declares this the "gateway to a myriad of mysteries."

In other passages, Laozi seems to favor *wu*. *Wu* symbolizes his *dao* of reversal, which favors what convention usually disfavors. In one passage, he says that *wu* gives rise to *you*. This has led many to conclude that *dao* is *wu*.

The puzzle emerges in cosmological form in neo-Daoism, which arose following the decline of the superstitious and cosmological Han. It called itself "mysterious learning" (*xuanxue*). Wang Bi (226–249) read Laozi's discussions alongside the *yinyang* cosmology contained in the *Yijing*. He postulated that *wu* was the "original reality" while *you* was merely a functional state of *wu*. His dichotomy between "substance" and "function" (*tiyong*) was influential in Buddhism and neo-Confucianism, though it was never explained with any clarity. The effect was to treat *wu* not only as real but as the most basic reality. This eventually leads to understanding the Buddhist *nirvana* as a positive notion. Neo-Confucians objected to the implication that reality had no moral content—a view they attributed to both Buddhism and Daoism.

The alternative neo-Daoist analysis came from Guo Xiang. He insisted that *wu* simply was not and could not be the gateway to anything. Therefore, he concluded, *you* must be self-engendered and eternal. What there was could change into other things that exist, but it never ceased to exist. He analyzed the unity of cosmology as arising from the fact that in its arising, all of *you* interacts with all the rest of *you*. Guo Xiang, perhaps drawing on Zhuangzi's perspectivalism, relativizes *wu*. All *wu* makes sense only relative to some other term. There is no *wu simpliciter*.

The issue of *youwu* extends into the theory of Buddhism mainly in the theory of the "emptiness" of all *dharma*, or the emptiness of the Buddha-nature, *nirvana* or *satori*. It is not clear that anyone subsequently focused on the linguistic version of the puzzle about *you-wu*.

See also Daoism: Neo-Daoism; Guo Xiang; Language and Logic; Laozi; Mohism: The Founder, Mozi; Philosophy of Language; *Qing*; *Shifei*; *Ti* and *Yong*; *Ti-Yong* Metaphysics; Wang Bi; Zhuangzi.

Bibliography

Chan, Wing-tsit. *A Source Book in Chinese Philosophy*. Princeton, N.J.: Princeton University Press, 1963.

Chao, Y. R. "Notes on Chinese Grammar and Logic." *Philosophy East and West*, 5(1), 1955, pp. 31–41.

Chen, Ku-ying. *Laozi: Text, Notes, and Comments*. San Francisco, Calif.: Chinese Materials Center, 1977.

Fung, Yu-lan (Feng Youlan). *The Spirit of Chinese Philosophy*. London: Routledge and Kegan Paul, 1947.

Graham, Angus. "Being in Western Philosophy Compared with *Shih/Fei* and *You/Wu* in Chinese Philosophy." *Asia Major*, New Series, 7(1–2), 1959.

———. *Disputers of the Tao: Philosophical Argument in Ancient China*. La Salle, Ill.: Open Court, 1989.

Lau, D. C., trans. *Laozi: Tao Te Ching*. Baltimore, Md.: Penguin, 1963.

Wu, Yi. *Chinese Philosophical Terms*. Lanham, Md.: University Press of America, 1986.

中國哲學

Z

Zhan Ruoshui (Chan Jo-shui)

Annping Chin

Zhan Ruoshui (1466–1560, also known as Zhan Ganquan), was a Confucian thinker of the Ming dynasty (1368–1644) who made important contributions in scholarship, public service, and education. His Ganquan school, during the sixteenth century, was second only to the Wang Yangming school in size and influence. Zhan Ruoshui was a direct disciple of Chen Xianzhang (Chen Baisha, 1428–1500) and a close friend of Wang Yangming (1472–1529). Together with Chen and Wang, he gave Ming thought its particular characteristics; he also anticipated certain issues that would become more pressing in the late Ming as the Yangming school attracted more followers and as these followers became less restrained in their thinking and behavior.

Zhan Ruoshui was a native of Zengcheng, Guangdong. His family was from the village of Shabei, in a section of Zengcheng known as Ganquan; thus Zhan's contemporaries honored him as Master Ganquan. His ancestors were originally from Fujian Province. His great-grandfather became a local hero when he bravely defended Shabei village against bandits and rival factions at the fall of the Yuan dynasty. His grandfather accumulated most of the family wealth. His father, however, was implicated in a robbery case and died early, when Zhan was only nine.

As a young man, Zhan Ruoshui was stubbornly independent; he shunned the metropolitan examination after only one try. His mother was probably eager for him to attain the degree of *jinshi* (an advanced scholar), since that would have helped to restore the honor of the Zhan family, but she respected his decision. By the time Zhan made up his mind to become a private scholar—when he was nearly thirty—he was already under the influence of Chen Xianzhang. He was to become Chen's most devoted follower. Zhan referred to Chen as his "moral teacher," the person "who cultivated me and gave me life." And Chen, the year before he died, wrote a poem to Zhan, making it clear that he was handing the lamp of his Jiangmen school over to Zhan to transmit. When Chen died in 1500, Zhan observed the three-year mourning rites as would a son.

Zhan emerged from his mourning in 1503 with a change of heart regarding his future. In 1505, he took the metropolitan examination once again and passed. With a *jinshi* degree in hand, he plunged into the life of an official—first as a Hanlin compiler and then as an assistant examiner. It was around this time, in 1506, that he met Wang Yangming in the capital. The two immediately took a liking to each other. Wang had just spent two years in a grotto at his native place in Yuyao, Zhejiang, practicing the Daoist art of nourishing life. Zhan, similarly, had also just returned to the world of men after an extended period of study and contemplation in his native *Guangdong*. Their withdrawal had made them both eager for public service and more convinced than ever that the Confucian way was the correct path to follow. They formed a covenant in 1506, pledging to defend the Confucian teachings together. By the end of that year, Wang Yang-ming would rise to the challenge by giving a memorandum to the throne, asking for the emperor's protection of more than thirty officials who had been wrongfully arrested by the eunuch Liu Jin. As a result of this action, Wang was imprisoned for two months, publicly flogged, and then banished to Longchang in Guizhou Province.

By comparison Zhan Ruoshui had a rather quiet career. After a stint as an assistant examiner, he was sent as court emissary first to Jiangxi and then to Annam. In 1515, he was back in Guangdong, in mourning after his mother's death. He did not return to the capital after his three years of seclusion. It is possible that he had grown wary of court politics and had become discouraged by the conduct of the emperor, who, having essentially given up his imperial responsibilities, preferred instead to spend his time in his pleasure palace and on the northwest frontier, where he could indulge his pretense of being a military commander. Under these conditions, Zhan found it more peaceful to be in Guangdong, where his reputation as a teacher of Confucian learning attracted scores of followers. With generous endowments from the local gentry, he founded the first of what would eventually be thirty-six academies. The Dake Academy, as it was called, gave Zhan a quiet place to reflect and write. It was during this period that he refined his teaching of "personally realizing the principles of heaven wherever one may be" and formulated his philosophy of the natural (*ziran*). It was also during this period that he and Wang Yangming engaged in a series of debates over the "investigation of things" (*gewu*).

In 1521, the Zhengde emperor died; his cousin Zhu Houcong (r. 1521–1567) ascended the throne. By 1522, Zhan Ruoshui was back in Beijing, hoping that the new emperor would be more attentive than his predecessors to court duties and more receptive to the advice and admonitions of his Confucian officials. Things did not go exactly as Zhan had wanted. The Jiajing reign was consumed by questions regarding rites, which the emperor himself had instigated. It is not clear where Zhan stood on these matters. But in the late 1520s and early 1530s, while he was holding the posts of junior minister and senior minister of rites, Zhan, on two separate occasions, was pressured into siding with the emperor when the latter altered the traditional practices of the rites to suit his own interpretation.

Beginning with Confucius, Chinese scholars-officials, for two millennia, had resisted any attempt to tinker with the rites without sound reason or historical precedent. Any change in the rites might rattle the sociopolitical order, even though, as Confucius had made quite plain in the *Analects*, some questions about the rites had greater importance than others. The Jiajing emperor wanted to sacrifice to heaven and earth at separate altars on different dates, and he also wanted to include Daoist liturgy in court rituals. Most officials regarded these ideas as gross transgressions, but Zhan acquiesced in them.

From 1521 until his retirement in 1540, Zhan had two periods of reprieve from the politics in Beijing. In 1524, he was appointed chancellor of the National University in Nanjing. This was the year when he completed the *Diagram of Mind and Nature*, a broad metaphysical reflection on the principles underlying his teachings. In 1533, he was back in Nanjing. For the next seven years he headed the ministries of rites, personnel, and war, and he also founded three major academies in the Nanjing area. Zhan was to live for another twenty years after his retirement in 1540. He remained active, teaching primarily in his native Guangdong until his death in 1560 at age ninety-five.

Zhan Ruoshui's debate with Wang Yangming over *gewu* (investigation of things) was a celebrated event in Chinese intellectual history. From the letters and recorded conversations of the period from 1515 to 1521, we learn that the central issue in this debate was the concept of *li* (principle). Wang Yangming describes the investigation of things as a process of purifying the mind of cloudiness and errors until it becomes identical with its original substance (*benti*), which is *li*. He regards the investigation of things as a personal quest, requiring only that the individual hold on to his innate sense of the good (*liangzhi*) as he does everything and applies himself everywhere. Zhan Ruoshui, on the other hand, explains the investigation of things as "personally realizing the principle of heaven wherever one may be" (*suichu tiren tianli*). In their debate, Wang criticized Zhan's theory as "chasing after principles in things that are outside the mind," the implication being that it was no different from Cheng Yi's and Zhu Xi's original formulation. Zhan, in response, charged that Wang mistook his teaching of *gewu* for Zhu Xi's because Wang never understood his notion of principle. Zhan maintained that his notion of principle pointed to something supple and living (*huode*) while Zhu Xi's notion of principle denoted something rigid and reified (*yingde*).

In Zhan Ruoshui's thought, principle is both the principle of production (*shengli*) and the principle of heaven (*tianli*). The principle of production is the individual nature (*xing*); it is the life-giving impulse (*shengyi*) in the mind. Zhan also describes it in Mencian terms as the "floodlike *qi*." The principle of production is *qi* because *qi* is the basis of life. It is floodlike (*haoran*)—great and unyielding—because *qi* as human nature has the power of perfecting itself. Following Mencius, Zhan explains man's moral potential as his inborn ability to arrive at rightness (*yi*), or "the appropriate measure in every thing and every matter," and rightness, for him, implies both impartiality (*zhigong*) and no transgression (*buguo*). He said, "What is inherent in the mind is principle. When applied to things, [principle] becomes rightness. The two are the substance and function [of the mind]."

One could regard Zhan Ruoshui's teaching of "personally realizing the principle of heaven wherever one may be" as his quest for the meaning of rightness as it appears in Mencius's explanation to Gongsun Chou that "*qi*, when coupled with rightness and the way, will never starve." According to Zhan's reading of this passage, rightness refers to the appropriate amount of effort we should apply in tending our *qi* or in realizing our nature, and for Mencius an appropriate amount means "not forgetting that this is the most important project of our life and not forcibly helping the project along." The theory that "in between not-forgetting and not-helping lies the principle of heaven" is one Zhan had refined out of this particular aspect of Mencius's teachings, and it became the basis of his philosophy of the natural (*ziran*). In a letter to a friend, Nie Bao (Wenwei, 1487–1563), he explains why this is the most subtle point in the learning of the heart-and-mind (*xinxue*): "in between not-forgetting and not-helping" (*wuwang wuzhu*) approximates what is most natural because "not the slightest effort is exerted," yet it describes a precise standard that is not predetermined or normative. The standard is placed in the middle (*zhong*), but the mind must find this for itself. For this reason, Zhan Ruoshui insisted that his notion of principle was something living and was not fixed. He used Zeng Can and Confucius as examples of the difference between understanding principle as fixed and as living. According to a Confucian text of the second century, the *Kongzi jiayu* (*Home Sayings of Confucius*), Zeng Can, who had committed a minor offense, let his father beat him to the point of unconsciousness because he thought that it was incorrect for a son to run away from his father under any circumstances. Confucius, however, deemed that this was not a filial act. He said, "When the parent uses a small stick, the son should accept the beating, but when the parent uses a large stick, the son should run away." In Zhan Ruoshui's view, Confucius's judgment showed an understanding of the principle of heaven.

To Zhan, profound understanding, such as that of Confucius, is possible only when the mind is clear and discerning, which means that the mind must make an effort to learn. Zhan Ruoshui tells Wang Yangming in a letter that "if a person does not learn, he will die as a fool" and that "even Confucius encouraged himself to learn and worried that he had not learned enough." Zhan believed that the act of rectifying intentions alone could not restore the mind to its original substance. Just as rightness feeds the spirit, learning safeguards the mind against obsessions and against the delusion that one is not making a mistake. Learning is another issue that Zhan Ruoshui and Wang Yangming could not agree on in their debate.

The debate between Zhan and Wang over the investigation of things is important because it sharpened the differences in their teachings. Who was right in this debate? Were the accusations the two made against each other fair? Whose argument was more persuasive? Who had reason on his side? One way of assessing the debate is to regard the philosophies of Zhan and Wang as two aspects of Mencius's teachings. Both thinkers rejected principle as normative; thus both rejected the basic premise of Zhu Xi's method of *gewu*. Wang approached the investigation of things as a process of rectifying intentions, and so he told Zhan that if one was sincerely committed to living a moral life, all one needed to do was "always be doing something." Wang saw no point in searching for the principle lying in between not-forgetting and not-helping, and he regarded Zhan's method of *gewu* as "having nothing to hang on to." Wang's own method shows a profound appreciation of what Mencius said in Book 7:

> Seek and you will get it; let go and you will lose it. If this is the case, then seeking is of use to getting, and what you sought is within yourself. But if there is a proper way to seek it and whether you get it or not depends on destiny, then seeking is of no use to getting and what is sought lies outside of yourself.

Zhan, on the other hand, was drawn to the living impulse in things, and he was fascinated by the idea that this impulse was fed by an internal order, a principle of the natural that exerted not the slightest effort on a thing. He pointed out that it was Mencius who first suggested the idea in a remark about nourishing the flood-like *qi*, and his formulation of "personally realizing the principle wherever one may be" never veered from Mencius's original insight.

Zhan Ruoshui's writings include three exegetical studies: the *Guwen xiaoxue* (the "old text" version of *Elementary Learning*), the *Erlijing zhuance* (a study of the two ritual classics and their commentaries), and the *Chunqiu zhengzhuan* (an exegesis of the *Spring and Autumn Annals*). His magnum opus was the *Shengxue gewutong*, a work in 100 *juan* on the investigation of things, which he presented to the Jiajing emperor in 1529. He also wrote three philosophical treatises: the *Xinxing tu shuo* (*An Explanation of the*

Diagram of Mind and Nature), the *Ziran ming* (*Inscriptions on the Concept of the Natural*), and the *Zundao lu* (*On Following the Way*). His recorded conversations are collected in several volumes, the best-known being the *Qiaoyu* (*Recorded Sayings from Mount Xiqiao*), *Xinquan wenbianlu* (*Recorded Questions and Responses from the Xinquan Academy*), *Tianguan wenda* (*Recorded Questions and Answers from the Tianguan Academy*), and *Jinling wenda* (*Recorded Questions and Answers from the Jinling Academy*). These conversations together with his lectures, letters, and philosophical essays can be found in the *Zhan Ganquan xiansheng wenji* (*Literary Works of Master Zhan Ganquan*).

See also Chen Xianzhang; *Li*: Principle, Pattern, Reason; Mencius; Reason and Principle; Wang Yangming; Wang Yangming: Rivals and Followers.

Bibliography

Araki Kengo. "Tan Kansen to O Yomei" (Zhan Ganquan and Wang Yangming)." *Tetsugaku Nempo*, 26–27, 1967–1968, pp. 275–305.

Chan, Wing-tsit. "Chan Jo-shui's Influence on Wang Yang-ming." *Philosophy East and West*, 23, 1973, pp. 9–30.

Chin, Annping. "Chan Kan-ch'üan and the Continuing Neo-Confucian Discourse on Mind and Principle." Ph.D. dissertation, Columbia University, 1985.

Ching, Julia. *To Acquire Wisdom*. New York: Columbia University Press, 1976.

Cua, A. S. *The Unity of Knowledge and Action: A Study in Wang Yang-ming's Moral Psychology*. Honolulu: University of Hawaii Press, 1982.

de Bary, William Theodore, ed. *Self and Society in Ming Thought*. New York: Columbia University Press, 1970.

Goodrich, L. Carrington, and Fang Chao-ying. *Dictionary of Ming Biography 1368–1644*. New York: Columbia University Press, 1976.

Huang, Zongxi. *Mingru xue'an* (The Records of Ming Scholars). SPPY.

Jen, Yu-wen. *Baishazi yenjiu* (A Study of the Thought of Master Pai-sha). Hong Kong: 1970.

Mencius, trans. D. C. Lau. London: Penguin, 1970.

Shiga, Ichiro. *Tan Kansen no kenkyu* (A Study of the Thought of Zhan Ganquan). Tokyo, 1981.

Tu, Weiming. *Neo-Confucian Thought in Action*. Berkeley: University of California Press, 1976.

Wang, Yangming. *Instructions for Practical Learning and Other Neo-Confucian Writings by Wang Yang-ming*, trans. Wing-tsit Chan. New York: Columbia University Press, 1964.

Zhan, Ruoshui. *Zhan Ganquan xiansheng wenji*. 1580. (Edition in 35 *jian*.)

Zhang Binglin (Chang Ping-lin)

Fan-sen Wang

Zhang Binglin (1868–1936), also known as Taiyan, was one of the most influential scholars and political propagandists in modern China. He played an important role in both the political and the academic world. Zhang might have remained a scholar involved in evidential research if China had not been defeated by Japan in 1895. From then on, however, he decided to leave *Gujing jingshe* ("Refined study for the Explication of the Classics") and his life of pure scholarship; he joined and became active in propagandist and reformist groups. However, Zhang eventually left these groups because of his intense hostility toward the Manchu government. This hostility had two sources: first, late Ming and early Qing records of the Manchus' conquest of Ming China and the cruel ensuing slaughter; and second, the more current internal and external failures of the Qing government. Zhang was firmly convinced that the Manchus were alien rulers: that all Manchus, including the emperor, were the enemies of the Han Chinese and should be expelled. Thus although he joined various activist groups, he was soon to break away from them because of their support of the Manchu regime. Zhang felt that the Chinese were not impelled to act because they did not fully recognize the Manchu rulers as aliens. He championed a revolutionary goal—nourishing Han patriotism by stimulating or awakening a sense of history. He later described this approach as using "national essence" to instigate patriotism. He organized a meeting in Tokyo on 1 May 1902 to mark the 250th anniversary of China's fall to the Manchu conquerors. This meeting later developed into Guangfu hui (Restoration Party).

Zhang summed up his career as a revolutionary as having been "jailed thrice and arrested seven times."

His was a heroic career dedicated to overthrowing Manchu rule. With the "Supao incident" in 1903, Zhang's fame as a rebel rose tremendously. In his famous article "Refutation of Kang Youwei's Political Views," Zhang denounced the Qing emperor in words that might have been supposed unthinkable: Zaitian (the emperor Guangxu) "is a young clown who could not tell beans from barley." The legal proceedings brought against Zhang immediately afterward were unprecedented in that they were held in a mixed court in Shanghai. In these proceedings, the Qing government and Zhang Binglin were viewed as two separate political entities. The judge referred to trying the "Qing government" against "Zhang Binglin," and this was astonishing to many people who had never held a single thought of the Chinese people as an entity separate from the Manchu government.

Zhang staunchly opposed the prophetic "new text" school represented by Kang Youwei. In the late Qing, Kang held that Confucius was a political reformer, a religious leader, and an unthroned king, and that the Six Classics were mostly made up by Confucius as outlines for his vision of political reform. Zhang developed his strategies against Kang in two ways. First, Zhang insisted that Confucius was no more than a historian, and thus that Kang's contributions were groundless. Second, Zhang emphasized that the Confucian classics were historical documents with no subtle, hidden meanings, and he rejected any radical use of Chinese tradition.

Zhang was, then, a very rigorous scholar. He was famous for his philological studies. For him, the ideal role of the literati was not to be scholar-statesmen as Kang Youwei believed but to be detached specialists. Zhang was famous for his criticism of the old dictum "Fully grasp the meaning of the classics, then put them to practical use" (*tongjing zhiyong*), a dictum that had helped form a trend toward making learning a separate concern in the early republican period.

Zhang did not view modern western civilization as the sole stairway on which all civilizations of the world should climb. He believed, instead, in different ways for different civilizations, and in this he was sharply distinct from most thinkers of his time. Accordingly, he did not believe it appropriate for the Chinese to take up western standards for assessing values: Chinese values differed from those of other civilizations. This belief gave him and a group of other traditional thinkers, such as Liang Shuming, a theoretical weapon for resisting the naively optimistic attitude toward westernization.

Zhang's theoretical weapons enabled him to be consistently negative about things western. It is not too much to characterize Zhang as a negative philosopher in general, for his philosophical system was based on negatives. We can discern this in the titles of several influential articles he published between 1900 and 1911, all of which include negative terms, such as "The Five-Without Theory" (*Wuwu lun*), "The Four Illusions" (*Sihuo lun*), and "Atheism" (*Wusheng lun*).

Zhang Binglin had a very clear idea of what he opposed, and a rather vague idea of what he supported. Here I shall analyze his negative ideas. These stemmed mostly from his opposition to what China adopted as a result of westernization.

First, Zhang opposed the parliamentary system. It was widely believed in China during his time that the parliamentary system was the secret of the power of the west. Zhang held that the parliamentary system was a way of legitimizing local villains and crowning lions. The institution was a parliament in name, but in reality it was a group of evildoers.

Second, he was opposed to any religion, especially Christianity, which was gradually gaining in popularity. He insisted that prostrating oneself before a supreme god was tantamount to sacrificing one's individuality. He viewed God as he did any authority. In this way, of course, he was opposing Kang Youwei's intention to transform Confucianism into a state religion.

Third, Zhang was very skeptical toward Darwinism. He contended that progress is an illusion. In his famous article "The Theory of Dual Evolution" (*Jufen jinhua lun*), he maintained that he did not necessarily see the theory of progress as wrong but that this theory was unusable as a measure of human morality, goodness, or pleasure. He repeatedly emphasized that evil kept pace with good; when good progresses, evil progresses as well. Mankind is more progressive than animals are, but mankind is also more cruel in war than animals are. Westerners are more progressive, but they are also imperialists who slaughter backward peoples in unforeseeably cruel ways. To denounce Darwinism, Zhang also wrote his essay "The Five-Without Theory," in which he saw the ideal world as "without government," "without territory," "without the human race," "without life," and "without worlds." His first two "without's" betray the influence of the anarchist movement, which was very much in vogue while Zhang was in Japan. The last three "without's," however, were his strategies for stopping evolution by stopping life. He hoped to block any possibility for small organisms to evolve into human beings. He looked for biological extinction.

Fourth, Zhang wanted to redirect the Chinese bureaucracy-centered culture. He was a radical plebeianist, an anarchic individualist. He berated local despots (*haomin*) and merchants. He pronounced severe criticisms and called for a general strike. He felt special contempt for the building up of business clans under the slogan "commercial warfare" (*shangzhan*).

Fifth, he opposed any plan to industrialize China. He complained that the number of merchants was increasing while the number of farmers was decreasing.

More positively, Zhang was an equalizer. He believed that if all land could be equally distributed to the people, numerous problems could be solved. He espoused traditional Chinese legalist ideas and believed that if the Chinese government and people followed laws sincerely, Chinese society would be harmonious. Therefore, no western political theory was needed in present China.

Zhang Binglin played an important role in the period between 1906 and 1911. He joined the Tokyo Chinese revolutionary group led by Sun Yat-sen and became editor of the influential *Minbao*. He became the most powerful propagandist dismantling the discourse undertaken by the reform group of Kang Youwei and Liang Qichao. At least two factors were involved in this. First, Zhang's negative points were mostly diametrically opposed to Liang Qichao's political points, especially regarding parliamentary institutions. Second, Zhang held the seemingly monomaniacal belief that the Manchu people—not traditional political systems—should be blamed for all of China's failures in the modern world. Thus he disagreed with Sun Yat-sen, Kang, Liang, and many others who were convinced of the necessity of reforming traditional political systems and introducing as many western democratic institutions as possible. According to Zhang, every cause of failure would be eliminated once the Manchus were overthrown. The new post-Manchu government should then devote itself to retaining good traditional Chinese institutions, keeping them as intact as possible.

Culturally, Zhang Binglin's major influence was his contribution to the iconoclasm of the late Qing. This influence had two aspects. For one thing, he denounced several progenitors of the Confucian school. He singled out Confucius and Mencius for special scorn and sarcasm. For example, in his famous article "Brief Discussions of Noncanonical Philosophers" (*Zhuzixue lueshuo*), he characterized Confucius as a politician of expediency and Mencius as a man who never lived up to his faith. In his *Qiushu* (*A Book of Emergency*), Zhang never hesitated to criticize Confucius and Mencius. He believed that Xunzi had transmitted the authentic legacy of ancient Chinese philosophy. He exalted Liu Xin to an unprecedented height; by contrast, Kang Youwei singled Liu Xin out as the great forger of the Guwen school.

Second, Zhang Binglin's iconoclasm was also evident in various writings in which he gave the pre-Qin philosophers equal standing with Confucius and Mencius. This influenced Hu Shi's *History of Ancient Chinese Philosophy* (*Zhongguo gudai zhexue shi*)—Hu made the pathbreaking announcement that he would treat pre-Qin philosophers equally. Zhang revered legalist and Daoist philosophy more highly than Confucianism. According to Zhang, the philosophic value of the *Zhuangzi* was higher than that of Confucianism. As for politics, legalist philosophy was more valuable than Confucianism.

What, then, was left for Confucianism? According to Zhang, in terms of philosophic value Buddhism far surpassed all traditional Chinese philosophies. He also used Buddhism to evaluate the Chinese philosophical tradition and insisted that Chinese philosophical schools were on the very low end of the scale. He can be seen as someone who believed that the Chinese philosophical world should be Indianized, in contrast with Hu Shi, who held that the Indianization of medieval China had seriously hindered the healthy development of Chinese thought.

Although he was a veteran of the revolution of 1911, and although his telegrams were always considered "as powerful as a division of troops," Zhang never entered the core echelons of the new regime. He held only trivial positions in the early republican period: special adviser to the president; frontier defense commissioner for the three northeastern provinces. In the latter post, which he held for just a few months, he had a staff of about ten, and his major achievement was drawing a set of new maps for two of the three provinces.

One thing stands out as an indicator of Zhang's political influence in republican China. The name Republic of China (*Zhonghua minguo*), assumed after the success of the revolution of 1911 and still retained by the Nationalist government on Taiwan, was first coined by Zhang, in his landmark article "Explanation of the National Title 'Republic of China' " (*Zhonghua minguo jie*).

See also Confucianism: Rhetoric; Confucianism: Tradition; Hu Shi; Kang Youwei; Legalism; Liang Qichao; Philosophy in China: Historiography; Sun Yat-sen; Xunzi.

Bibliography

Boorman, Howard, ed. *Biographical Dictionary of Republican China*. New York: Columbia University Press, 1967, Vol. 1, pp.92–98.

Chang, Hao. "Chang Ping-lin." In *Chinese Intellectual in Crisis: Search for Order and Meaning*. Berkeley: University of California Press, 1989.

Furth, Charlotte. "The Sage as Rebel: The Inner World of Chang Ping-lin." In *The Limits of Change*, ed. Charlotte Furth. Cambridge, Mass.: Harvard University Press, 1976.

Kawata, Teiichi. "Hitei teki shiso ka: Sho Hei-rin." In *Chugoku kindai shiso to Gendai*. Tokyo: Kenbun, 1987.

Pusey, James. *China and Charles Darwin*. Cambridge, Mass.: Harvard University Press, 1976.
Wang, Fan-shen. *Chang T'ai-yen te Ssu-hsiang*. Taipei: Shih-pao, 1985.
Wong, Young-tsu. *Search for Modern Nationalism: Zhang Binglin and Revolutionary China (1869–1936)*. Hong Kong: Oxford University Press, 1989.

Zhang Dongsun (Chang Tung-sun)

Key-chong YAP (YEH Ch'i-chung)

Zhang Dongsun (1886–1973, also known as Zhang Dong-sheng) came from a prominent Zhejiang family with a long scholarly tradition and received a solid grounding in the Chinese classics under the guidance of his elder brother, the famous scholar Zhang Ertian. Zhang's penchant for philosophy began in either 1902 or 1904, when he was in his late teens and read the *Mahayanasraddhotpada sastra* and the *Surangama sutra*. He then became a lay Buddhist; and in 1904 he went to Japan, where he studied Buddhism, western philosophy, and psychology—the three subjects that were to become the principal, though by no means easily comparable, ingredients of his thought. He returned to China in 1911.

On the whole, up to 1949, Zhang's career seems to have gone through three stages. In the beginning, he was both a journalist and a politician, writing numerous articles with a strong philosophical bent, mainly on constitutional, social, political, and cultural problems of the time. Then, in 1924, he entered the academic community as a formidable philosopher and educationalist, serving simultaneously or successively as a professor of philosophy, head of a department of philosophy, and dean of a college. At this second stage he expressed his philosophical thought, voluminously, in many articles and books. The third stage, precipitated by the "September eighteenth incident" of 1931, and accelerated especially after the Sino-Japanese war of 1937, then became a long, gradual fusion of his careers as a politician and as an academic.

Immediately after the communist takeover, Zhang was given numerous posts, including membership on the Central Committee of the People's Government. In 1951 he came under communist censure and was removed from the faculty of Yenjing University, where he had served since 1930. He then suffered several episodes of self-criticism in private and in public during the "three antimovements" (*sanfan*) and the "five antimovements" (*wufan*). In 1952 he was accused of spying for the United States and was charged with treason, but he was later reprieved by Mao Zedong. He was put in a sort of confinement, a treatment he found spiritually intolerable. (This had also been the main cause of his four attempts at suicide in a Japanese prison during 1941–1942.) During the Cultural Revolution, the communist functionary for unspecified political causes in some undisclosed place (a hospital) again put Zhang under house (hospital) confinement (roughly between early 1968 and early 1973) until its very last phase. Zhang died at the Sixth Peking Hospital on 2 June 1973, at age eighty-seven.

An elaboration of Zhang's epistemological cosmology, moral philosophy, and sociopolitical thought would be beyond the scope of this article. However, we can note, first of all, that philosophically Zhang Dongsun was a self-proclaimed eclectic who wanted to develop an independent epistemology on the basis of mostly western sources, with some insights from Buddhism and Chinese tradition. His highest ambition in philosophy was to expound a new theory of knowledge, an epistemological synthesis that he ultimately called a multiple-factors theory of knowledge.

Following is an outline of some salient features of his major achievements in epistemology. Although Zhang's name is well-known to students of Chinese politics before the ascendancy of the communists, his philosophical contribution—especially in epistemology, the field to which he devoted most of his intellectual energy—has been neglected in both traditional and modern Chinese thought. In fact, the neglect or disregard of epistemology in Chinese philosophy has been a major difference between Chinese and western traditions.

Zhang's epistemology can be found in numerous articles and books he wrote from the 1920s to the 1940s. Drawing heavily on western sources, but by no means always understanding them in a western sense, Zhang produced three major epistemological syntheses. In each synthesis, transcendental elements were diminished and sociocultural factors were increased.

Zhang acknowledged that his first epistemological synthesis was a kind of "objective idealism" (or "skeptical idealism," to use Ting Wen-chiang's term), but he himself preferred to call it "pragmatic rationalism" as opposed to Royce's "empirical idealism." According to this doctrine, the ability to "cognize" (i.e., know or understand) and the "cognized" (known, understood) object or act are two aspects of a single cognition. In any cognition, there is inevitably a "naked" given. The unfolding of the given is knowledge, and the establishment of knowledge implies the existence of an ordered world. In terms of the unfolding of knowledge, this viewpoint constitutes "idealism"; in terms only of the given, that given is unknowable—it cannot be traced back to its origin.

Zhang initially called his second epistemological synthesis "epistemological pluralism" but soon began to call it a "multiple-factors" theory of knowledge. The description "multiple-factors" applies to his third epistemological synthesis as well, but for the third synthesis Zhang also applied yet another term, "pluralistic interactionism." By "pluralistic interactionism" he meant that knowledge is subject to biological and cultural limitations, which are are understood through knowledge; this implies that our understanding of these limitations is itself limited by our knowledge. In other words, biologically based knowledge—as well as other forms of knowledge, such as sociology and philosophy—is limited by the nature of knowledge itself. This point has long been appreciated by physicists and also applies to other sciences.

Each of Zhang's syntheses is unique and deserves its own exposition and critique. Here, however, I shall focus on "pluralistic interactionism," his last but by no means final synthesis, because it encapsulates most of his previous epistemology.

Zhang believed that an "epistemological principle" always had to be adopted, meaning that in a discussion of, say, physics or society, epistemology should always be taken up first. However, this "priority" is not absolute. Physics, sociology, and other domains of knowledge can complement epistemology, which in turn can complement them. By adopting this broad view, Zhang merges the problem of cognition into the theory of knowledge and, sociologically, stresses cognition as a constraint on personal knowledge.

Zhang noted that all epistemologists after Kant had contributed to discovering limitations on knowledge, but he wanted to go further into the "epistemic determination of reality." Once we have discovered that there is a limit to knowledge, it follows that the final object of knowledge must be regarded as unknowable, or at least as not completely knowable. This leads one toward agnosticism and phenomenalism; for that reason, Zhang does not discuss the final object of knowledge to any great extent. He adopts a theory of immanence rather than a theory of transcendence. He stresses the nature of knowledge itself and maintains that this nature determines the nature of the "object within knowledge." This theory is, he insists, neither subjectivism nor pragmatism, because subjectivism absorbs "the known" into "the knower," while pragmatism confounds knowledge with "utility."

Zhang insisted that his is neither sociological epistemology nor philosophical (that is, metaphysical) epistemology; nor is it a "psychological theory of the intellect" as such. Mainly, he tells us, it is a confluence of these three sources. Zhang considered epistemology different from traditional epistemology, which paid attention to the problem of the validity of knowledge—i.e., attempted to establish the relation between "knowing" and "the known." Zhang does not confine himself to this; he felt that if epistemology was to become an independent study, it had to eliminate the process of knowing (the activity of thinking), relegating that process to psychology. Also, it had to eliminate the "object" of knowledge, relegating that to metaphysics—i.e., letting the metaphysicians pursue the question whether the object is in some sense a "true" facet of an external thing or a mental image. Then, what remains for us to study is knowledge itself, a *tertium quid*: a hybrid produced by the activity of knowing and the object of knowledge. From this viewpoint, epistemology is neither psychology nor metaphysics. Traditional epistemology considers knowledge a "relation," but Zhang sees knowledge as a resultant. Thus, it is permissible to see the relation as an independent construction, which will accordingly become a kind of existent and, to repeat, a resultant. That resultant is the hybrid Zhang calls "pluralistic interactionism." He describes it as follows:

> My epistemology is neither idealism nor materialism (realism) but is only a kind of multifactors interactionism. In essence, it is advocated that these four entities, or constructions, of the "external," the "sensation," the "perception," and the "concept" have, respectively, their own independent properties, but intermingle together and cannot be separated. In the meantime, they are interacting, interinfluencing, that is to say that, on the one hand, the external influences the senses and perception, which in turn influence concepts. On the other hand, the concept interprets

> the senses and perception, which in turn fuses with the external. But it should be noted that sensation is after all nearer to the external. Though perception is relatively farther from the external, it still contains sensation in it, and thus it does not depart from the external. This is not so in the case of the concept; for the concept can . . . truly depart from the external.

Zhang uses "pluralistic interactionism" to refer not only to the interaction within the structure of knowledge but also to the relationship between (1) knowledge and culture, and (2) various elements of culture. He says:

> Between knowledge and culture there is also an interaction. Knowledge is constrained by culture in such forms as language, which is capable of both constraining and fostering thought. Various aspects of culture influence one another as well: thus language is capable of influencing logic; logic is capable of dominating philosophy; and philosophy is capable of directing social and political thought. On the other hand, social and political thought can determine philosophy, and philosophy implicitly guides logic; and logic is capable of reforming language.

In sum, for Zhang, knowledge itself is a "projective construct," but it must have a ground; this is called the "given." Knowledge does not consist only of the given, for various "influences" are capable of dictating it. So we have three interacting concepts: "construct," "given," and "influence." Knowledge itself is a construct based on the given and subject to influence. Therefore, knowledge is certainly not determined by just one factor. Many factors interact to constitute knowledge: sensation, the correlate behind sensation, the concept, and the development of some concepts into "categories." Interaction is not confined to what lies within the structure of knowledge, such as sensation or conception. Things outside the structure of knowledge, such as various cultural influences that implicitly dictate knowledge, are another kind of factor.

Knowledge thus has three aspects. The first aspect concerns knowledge itself, which is a construct. The second concerns the object of knowledge, or the material of knowledge, which is the immediate datum (the given). The third concerns influences on knowledge. Although the direct influence on knowledge is only personal experience, patterns of thought and attitudes are without exception derived from society. An individual's social attitude is wholly created by cultural patterns such as folkways, tradition, and thought; at the same time, these cultural patterns are embodied in the social attitude of each individual and cannot exist independent of individuals.

According to Zhang, all our knowledge moves from a lower "level of sensation" to a higher "level of concept," which is a sort of construct. We project constructs onto the external realm, supposing that all of them are contained in it. This is the "projective" character of knowledge. When sensations, perceptions, and concepts arise in us, we regard them as belonging to the external realm. But from their nature we cannot completely know what their objective correlates are; we can know only the three orders discussed above. Meanwhile, every perception immediately detaches itself to become a concept, so that behind a concept there is a perception, and behind the perception there is a correlate. They seem to be three layers, but in effect they are unified. This unification of three layers into one is called a "three-layered folding." Because there is an external behind a perception, perceptual knowledge is originally a joint product. The development of a perception into a concept forms the second layer of this joint product, because there is a perception behind the concept. This is also true of the emergence of "categories" (i.e., Zhang's general concepts or postulates) from the concept, which is the third layer. Thus knowledge is a multilayered joint product, in which the higher layer has considerable power to determine the lower layer. This may be regarded as an epistemological law, which we ordinarily call the determination of the parts by the whole. Nevertheless, the lower layers may, within certain limits, resist the interpretations of the higher layer. That is, external objects permeate into our perception and then into our concepts. However, the more a concept has been influenced by the nature of perception, the further it is from the (apparent) external object (as first revealed by the senses).

Therefore, regarding the knowledge of things, Zhang suggests that we must move from direct sensation and perception to indirect inference, because what has been obtained from the senses is not the true nature of things and seems less reliable than inferences. What we really know about things are only certain mathematical formulas; however, such a formula can guide our control of external objects to such an extent that we regard it as really obtained from external things. In sum, what we know about things are only physical laws, not "things in themselves." It is a defect of the neorealists' panobjectivism to regard external correlates as "rigid." It is also a defect of the idealists' subjectivism to take these scattered external grounds or correlates as nonexistent.

Zhang's thinking was influenced by Madhyamika Buddhism, and so to him what is external is only an empty structure, without any real nature. That is, structure must subsist in sensation; on the basis of changes in sensation, we can know that there is a difference in the state of the structure. In this respect, Zhang is really not idealistic: he acknowledges that the subsisting structure is external. But he is not materialistic either: he does not advocate the existence of "matter." The matter that is studied by epistemology is not the nature of this external source.

In the Buddhist terminology that Zhang sometimes adopted, knowledge is the pursuit of common phenomena (universals) in particular phenomena (particulars). Knowledge itself takes the form of a sensation, then of a perception, and then of a concept. This is a cycle in which universals are abstracted from particulars, concepts in turn embed universals, and concepts then return to illumine particulars. Sensation, perception, and conception are stages in a continuous process of the unfolding of experience—as William James put it, the changing of "that's" into "what's." This unfolding establishes cognition. Cognition is, therefore, a use of universals as forms to be embedded in given particulars, for what appears only once cannot be established as knowledge, and what is established as knowledge must be transferable. Accordingly, knowledge is a kind of abstraction, designed to change what is concrete into what is abstract, for without abstraction no universals can be obtained from particulars.

Philosophers doubt everything, Zhang says, but they cannot doubt knowledge itself. The mission of philosophy is to trace back the properties of knowledge to discover the values and ideal forms of human life. If we study the nature of knowledge thoroughly, we will understand that the "naked" given has no meaning to be talked about: meaning is produced by the mind. Every judgment is a pursuit of the universal amid particulars, and the use of universals is to be subsequently embedded in particulars. Purely particular facts are chaotic and cannot be combined with judgments to form terms; the transformation of crude facts into ordered facts is the transformation of facts into meanings.

In brief, human beings are weird. They cannot survive apart from legends, faith, ordinary ideas, and other such constructs and interpretations that work on the basis of subconscious "self-deception." The reason is that the genuine orders of the external realm are too scarce, obliging us, in Zhang's view, to construct various kinds of entities. Having constructed these numerous entities, human beings then use theories to "explain" them; however, these theories are sometimes destroyed, either before or after they are used for explanation. Either way, humans are still in the grip of their own constructs.

It has been noted by Wing-tsit Chan (1963):

> The number of scholars advocating Western philosophy has been far greater than those oriented toward Chinese thought, although they cannot match the latter group either in originality or in influence until Marxism overcame China. . . . The one who has assimilated the most of Western thought, established the most comprehensive and well coordinated system, and exerted the greatest influence among the Western oriented Chinese philosophers, however, is indisputably Chang Tung-sun [Zhang Dongsun]. . . . He shows not only the influence of Kant and Hume, but also that of Dewey, Russell, and Lewis. During World War II he shifted more and more from metaphysics to the sociology of knowledge and thus was drawn closer to Marxism. This is a far cry from his anti-Marxian stand in 1934 when he edited a symposium mostly critical of dialectical materialism. But his theory of concepts as products of culture made it easy, if not inevitable, for him to accept the Marxian philosophy.

Chan's assessment of Zhang's acceptance of Marxism and Chinese communism must be treated with great reservation, because a detailed study of all Zhang's works and of his last years points to a different conclusion. For various reasons, until very recently, Zhang was largely forgotten—philosophically, politically, and in the world of scholarship. Today there is every sign that his thought will become important, when the Chinese once again reflect on their intellectual encounter with the west in the past hundred years.

See also Philosophy of Knowledge.

Bibliography

Chan, Wing-tsit, trans. and comp. *A Source Book in Chinese Philosophy*. Princeton, N.J.: Princeton University Press, 1963, pp. 744–750.

Howard L. Boorman, ed. *Biographical Dictionary of Republican China*. New York: Columbia University Press, 1967, Vol. 1, pp. 129–133.

Yap, Key-chong. "Culture-Bound Reality: The Interactionistic Epistemology of Chang Tung-sun." *East Asian History*, No. 3, June 1992, pp. 77–120.

———. "Western Wisdom in the Mind's Eye of a Westernized Chinese Lay Buddhist: The Thought of Chang Tung-sun (1886–1962)." Ph.D. dissertation, Oxford University, 1991.

Zhang, Dongsun. "A Chinese Philosopher's Theory of Knowledge," trans. Li An-chi. *Yenching Journal of Social Studies*, 1(1), 1938. (See also *A Review of General Semantics*, Vol. 9, 1952, pp. 203–226.) Reprinted in S. I. Hayakawa, ed. *Our Language and Our World: Selections from etc.: A Review of General Semantics*. New York: Harper, 1959, pp. 299–323.

———. "Duoyuan renshi lun chongshu (Epistemological Pluralism Restated)." In *Zhang Jusheng xiansheng qishi sheng-ri jinian lunwen ji* (A Collection of Essays Commemorating Mr. Zhang Jusheng's Seventieth Birthday), ed. Hu Shi, Cai Yuan-pei, and Wang Yunwu. Shanghai: Shang-wu yin-shu-kuan, 1937.

———. *Epistemological Pluralism*, trans. C. Y. Chang. Author, c. 1932.

———. *Kexua yu zhexue* (Science and Philosophy). Shanghai: Shangwu yinshu guan, 1924, 1928.

———. *Lixing yu minzhu* (Reason and Democracy). Shanghai: Shangwu yinshu guan, 1946.
———. *Sixiang yu shehui* (Thought and Society). Shanghai: Shangwu yinshu guan, 1946.
———. *Xin zhexue longcong* (Collected Essays on New Philosophy). Shanghai: Shangwu yinshu guan, 1929.
———. *Zhang Dongsun de duoyuan renshi lun ji piping* (Zhang Dongsun's Epistemological Pluralism and Its Criticisms), ed. Zhan Wenhu. Shanghai: Shijieh shuju, 1936.
———. *Zhishi yu wenhua* (Knowledge and Culture). Shanghai: Shangwu yinshu guan, 1946.

Zhang Xuecheng (Chang Hsüeh-ch'eng)

David S. Nivison

Zhang Xuecheng (*Shizhai*, 1738–1801) was born in Shaoxing, Zhejiang Province, to a family of modest status in the local gentry. His father, Chang Biao (d. 1768), attained the *jinshi* (the highest civil service degree) in 1742; in 1751 the father became magistrate of Yingcheng in Hubei, but he was dismissed in 1756, and thereafter the family was financially pressed. The elder Zhang then supported himself by teaching and occasionally writing local histories on commission, with his son's assistance.

In 1760 Zhang traveled to Beijing, in the first of many unsuccessful attempts to pass the *juren* examination. He finally succeeded in 1777, and he attained the *jinshi* in 1778, ten years after his father's death. Zhang never held a government appointment himself beyond being enrolled as a student in the Guozijian (National Academy in Beijing) from 1762 to 1771. He supported himself in his later years by tutoring, serving as master of local academies (such appointments were controlled by local officials), accepting commissions to compile local histories and family histories, and securing the patronage of distinguished and wealthy officials, notably Zhu Yun in Beijing, whom he acknowledged as teacher, and later Bi Yuan in Hubei (1787–1788, 1790–1793). Under Bi's patronage, Zhang compiled a history of Hubei Province, which barely failed of publication, and worked on a massive "Critical Study of Historical Writings" (*Shiji kao*), never finished (the manuscript probably was lost in the Taiping rebellion). Its distinctive feature was to treat all types of writing, even poetry, as material for history.

A small selection of Zhang's essays and letters, which he published himself in 1796 to attract the support of patrons, does not survive. His major collections of essays, *Wenshi tongyi* (*General Principles of Literature and History*) and the shorter *Jiaochou tongyi* (*General Principles of Bibliography*) remained unpublished for three decades after his death, when one of his sons secured financing for a printing in Kaifeng, Henan (1832–1833). The literal translations of these titles do not adequately convey Zhang's guiding concept: in both collections he moves from the text and bibliography to an evaluative history of traditions and kinds of writing. Zhang took the term *jiaochou* from the title of the survey of the history of letters in Zheng Qiao's *Tong zhi*, which he much admired; *wenshi* is a bibliographer's term of art at least as old as the Tang dynasty, intended to include critical works such as Liu Xie's *Wenxin diaolong* and Liu Zhiji's *Shi tong* (a book that had fascinated Zhang when he was a young man).

The greater part of Zhang's surviving manuscripts was not published until the twentieth century. The basic essay collections were reprinted several times in the nineteenth century, but Zhang did not receive wide attention until 1920, when the Japanese journalist and scholar Naito Torajiro (Naito Konan) published a short chronological biography. This was followed in 1922 by a publication of most of the surviving manuscripts of Zhang's many letters and occasional writings, and (based on this) Hu Shi's much larger chronological biography, expanded and republished by Yao Mingda in 1931. The secondary literature on Zhang, both books and articles, is now quite large.

Zhang in his own lifetime was much less well known. He did live close to the center of intellectual activity in the late eighteenth century. Zhu Yun, who took Zhang into his own house, was a close friend of the leading writers and scholars in the capital, who thus became Zhang's acquaintances. And Zhu was highly placed; his brother Zhu Gui was tutor to the succeeding Jiaqing emperor, and Zhu himself was the author of the historic memorandum to the throne that initiated the project to compile the *Siku quanshu* (Four Treasuries Complete Books, an imperial manuscript library; there were seven copies of this manuscript library in different locations) and its widely used published catalog. The conception and formulation of this massive project were the joint work of Zhu and his students, including Zhang.

In 1766, while he was a student under Zhu Yun's tutelage in Beijing, Zhang met Dai Zhen (1724–1777). Dai and Zhang are now regarded as the leading philosophers of their age; but at the time Dai was famous and Zhang almost unknown. Dai's reputation was for his achievements in classical philosophy; in 1766, he had just finished his first philosophical essays, including his *Yuanshan* ("An Analysis of Goodness"). Some of Zhang's most important later essays can be seen as reactions to the challenge of Dai's ideas in *Yuanshan* and (probably) also in Dai's *Mengzi ziyi shuzheng* (*A Study of the Philosophical Terms in Mencius*), published in 1777.

Intellectually, the eighteenth century was reacting to a turn, in the preceding century, away from self-cultivationist ethics, coupled with disturbing discoveries in philology, such as Yen Ruoju's proof that parts of the *Shangshu* (*Classic of Documents*) which had been basic to earlier moral philosophy and Confucian moral-religious cultivation were in fact fabrications done in the third century C.E. The effect of such shocking discoveries was to force a reexamination of everything, a search for an exact account of origins. Two things can be expected among thinkers honest enough to accept such a revolutionary challenge to sacred tradition, while still remaining faithful: one can redouble philological efforts to establish what still can (one hopes) be known for certain; or one can stop trying to plumb partly sacred writings for literal truth, and see them in the perspective of intellectual history, as showing the development (perhaps under transhuman guidance) of human understanding. Dai exemplifies the first tendency, Zhang the second. For Dai, the "classics" are books written by the sages, which state what the "Way" (*dao*) is; to understand this all-important information, one must understand the language of the texts, and for this one needs a trained, skilled philologist (such as Dai himself). For Zhang, these books are the residue of ancient government, the "documents of the sage kings," which "illustrate" the Way rather than stating it, requiring the insight of a historian (such as Zhang). This idea is summed up at the beginning of Zhang's *Wenshi tongyi* in an epigrammatic sentence that became famous: "The Six Classics are all history" (*liujing jieshi*).

Zhang's distinctive viewpoint seems to have developed some time before 1770, to judge from a poem addressed to him in that year by his teacher and patron Zhu Yun. Zhu refers to Zhang's vigorous defense, in discussions in Zhu's circle in Beijing, of the "insights of the Lius," i.e., the Han bibliographers (father and son) Liu Xiang and Liu Xin. Their work on the history of "literature" (in the broadest sense) survives in the form of a catalog of books, *Yiwen zhi*, included in Ban Gu's *Hanshu*. In it, writings are sorted into categories, and at the end of each there is the comment that this kind of work developed in such-and-such an "office" in the ancient state, becoming the writings of such-and-such a "school" when the ancient political order disintegrated in Warring States China. Zhang expands the idea into an ideal theory of intellectual history: in the earliest stages of human society, there was no distinction between society and government; all "learning" was functional, developing as the specialty of the occupants of this or that government office, these "officials" being at the same time the only "teachers" there were. Thus writings were not "private" and so did not serve to bolster the vanity of individual authors. This ended in the age of the "philosophical schools," whose writings are the prototypes of later categories of writing, when "officials were no longer teachers" and "government (*zhi*) and teaching (*jiao*) were no longer unified" (an idea Zhang owes to the Song historian Ouyang Xiu).

The schema is evaluative: the privatization of writing not only corrupts its intent but also destroys its unity. The ancient philosophers, battling with each other, each grasped only a limited vision of the truth (Zhang echoes the final chapter of the *Zhuangzi*); and in a larger sense beyond this, successive ages are marked by one-sided interests: the ancient philosophers are followed by the great masters of philology in the Han era, followed by a flowering of literary art in the poets and essayists of the Six Dynasties and the Tang. Then the cycle repeats, with philosophy in the Song, Yuan, and Ming and philology in the Qing. This explanatory concept of a triad of tendencies—thought, the cult of facts, art—was especially stressed by the "Tongcheng" school of mid-Qing writers (which included Fang Bao and Yao Nai), some of them friends of Zhang; but it was quite common in expansive "discussions of learning" in this period.

All his life, Zhang kept reworking this vision. It first finds expression in internal prefaces in his *Local History of Hezhou* in 1774 (only these parts of that book survive). Zhang finished a first version of his *Jiaochou tongyi* in 1779; the manuscript was stolen in 1781, and the work was reconstituted and much altered by Zhang in 1788. The obvious totalitarian implications of his vision led him in this work to propose a system of public libraries, which would make books available to the public and would also keep track of writings wherever they might be, so as to expedite the government's always necessary task of weeding out and destroying objectionable matter; thus by implication Zhang endorsed the "literary inquisition" of the late Qianlong.

In the spring of 1789, visiting a magistrate friend in Anhui, Zhang wrote, rapidly, the most evocative essays of what became the *Wenshi tongyi*, including a monograph-length three-part essay "Historical Analysis of the Way" (*Yuandao*), greatly expanding a short essay of that title in the *Jiaochou tongyi*. This essay sets forth his basic philosophical position. The source of the Way is "heaven," conceived as the necessity of the natural development of order in the world. The Way is not a set of rules; it is rather what underlies all the formal rules of morality and law that take explicit shape as human society develops, from simple households to small communities to collections of communities organized under a formal government. All norms of morality and society that can be stated in words are not the Way itself but historical products born very gradually of the social needs of human beings: "The Way is the 'why' (*suoyi ran*) of all things; it is not the 'ought' (*dangran*) of things." As the human world developed, each creating "sage" ruler simply responded to the needs of the time, without realizing that he was creating or intending to create so as to be a sage. In doing this, he simply studied the behavior of the common people, which alone is where the process of the Way reveals itself. Perhaps reflecting Dai Zhen's distinction between the "natural" (*ziran*), distilled by the enlightened mind into the "necessary" (*biran*), Chang says: "In the Way there is the natural; for the sage there is what cannot be otherwise" (*bude buran*).

Zhang sees two sages as unique. One, the duke of Zhou, happened on the historical scene at a time when the cumulative creative process had reached completeness and synthesized it in the institutions of the Zhou order—but without thereby intending to be a sage of sages. In him was the culmination of "government." The other, Confucius, happened on the scene at a time when the primal social-political order was breaking up (when "government" and "teaching" were separating); but being himself without authority to create or enact institutions, his function was and could only be to preserve the heritage of the past for all future ages, thus becoming the epitome of "teaching." (This dichotomy between action and knowledge, which underlies much of Zhang's thinking, is expressed also by the Tang essayist Han Yu in *Yuandao*, which Zhang cites.)

Zhang (unlike Dai Zhen) accepted the Song metaphysics of *li* (principle) and *qi* (material embodiment); but he insisted that the two are inseparable, like a shadow and the material form that casts it. Therefore, attempts to treat the Six Classics as "books that record the Way" are mistaken, leading to the misconception that the Way can be separated from its unifying matrix, and to talking about the Way in "empty words" (*kongyan*). The result is different partial understandings of the Way by bitterly opposed rival schools—such as the partisans of Cheng-Zhu and Lu-Wang. The best sort of writing and scholarship is history, which sees that "principles" (*li*) and events (*shi*) are inseparable; it sees that the classics must be continued in historical narratives that plumb the "great Way" as it takes shape in later times, the historian's work being controlled by the same conditions that controlled the creative work of the sage kings: "first some need and then the satisfying of it, first some anxiety and then the expression of it, first some evil and then the remedying of it." One does not use words just to gain a reputation for being an artistic writer or an original thinker. The same point of view guides Zhang's critique of the philological "fashion" of his age: moderns lack the advantage of the ancients, whose lives were embedded in the social embodiment of the Way; so out of what the ancients learned easily, the modern scholar can grasp only a fraction, even in a lifetime of arduous study; but in this overconcentration on a partial area of "fact" the modern will miss the Way itself. However, Zhang in effect embraces the philologist's ideal of letting the "facts" speak for themselves. As he argues in later essays, an implication of the unity of "principle" and "fact" is that the historian must withhold judgments of persons in his work that might express his own bias.

A large part of Zhang's professional energy was spent in compiling local histories (*difang zhi*) and family histories, and in writing vigorously argued essays defending his own views on how such works ought to be researched and organized. His holistic tendency of thought led him to stress the place of such writings in the larger whole of historical writing. A man's literary collection (which should be organized chronologically and according to content, not sorted out by literary genres) can be thought of as the "history" of an individual, supplying material for family histories, in turn providing material for the history of a locality. The last (this was done in the late Qianlong) can then be requisitioned by the appointed compilers of histories of the state. Although most of his own work in these forms has vanished in the storms of time, Zhang is probably justly credited with elevating local historiography to a respected place in the endeavors of Chinese historians.

Zhang's call for philosophical peace sits badly with his character: he was combative, and more so as he aged. Throughout the nineteenth century he was probably best-known (when he was known at all) for a handful of animated, even vituperative, essays attacking the poet Yuan Mei, written shortly after Yuan's death in 1798. (The demise of Heshen, a notoriously corrupt favorite of the Qianlong emperor, provoked from Zhang equally spirited public denunciations, after the emperor's death in 1799.) Zhang found Yuan's personal morals disgusting and was appalled by Yuan's liberated views about women, some of whom he accepted as students; and in such diatribes Zhang expresses a violent prejudice that a woman's place is where it always had been. (To be sure, though, in sketches of women among his own relatives or those of his friends, Zhang can show a warm and appealing sensitivity.) In 1800, the year before his death, he wrote a final essay, "The Learning of Eastern Zhejiang," aligning himself with such local famous forerunners as the Ming philosopher Wang Yangming, and in the Qing era Liu Zongzhou, and the philosopher-historian Huang Zongxi and Huang's followers. The connections made in this "lifetime's afterthought" are stretched, if not entirely without point. This essay has led to the misleading convention of calling Zhang Xuecheng a member of a putative "eastern Zhejiang school" of historians.

See also Confucianism: Ethics; Dai Zhen; *De*; Huang Zongxi; Liu Zongzhou; Philosophy of History; Wang Yangming.

Bibliography

Cang, Xiuliang. *Zhang Xuecheng he wenshi tongyi* (Zhang Xuecheng and the *Wenshi Tongyi*). Peking: Zhonghua shuju, 1984.

Cang, Xiuliang, with Ye Jianhua. *Zhang Xuechang Ping Zhuan*, Nanjing Daxue Chubanshe, 1996.

Demieville, Paul. "Chang Hsüeh-ch'eng and His Historiography." In *Historians of China and Japan*, ed. W. G. Beasley and E. G. Pulleyblank. London: Oxford University Press, 1961, pp. 167–185.

Hu, Shi. *Zhang Shizhai nianpu* (A Chronological Biography of Zhang Xuecheng), rev. Yao Mingda. Shanghai: Commercial Press, 1931.

Mann, Susan. "Women in the Life and Thought of Zhang Xuecheng." In *Chinese Language, Thought, and Culture: Nivison and His Critics*, ed. P. J. Ivanhoe. LaSalle, Ill.: Open Court, 1996.

Momose, Hiromu. "Chang Hsüeh-ch'eng." In *Eminent Chinese of the Ch'ing Period*, ed. Arthur W. Hummel. Washington, D.C.: Library of Congress, 1943, pp. 38–41.

Naito, Torajiro (Naito Konan). "Ko Tekishi no Kincho *Sho Jitsusai Nempu* wo Yomu (On Reading Hu Shih's Recent Chronological Biography of Chang Hsüeh-ch'eng)." *Shinagaku*, 3, 1922. (Included in Torajiro Naito, *Kenki shoroku*. Kyoto, 1928, pp. 113–157.)

———. "Sho Jitsusai nempu (A Chronological Biography of Chang Hsüeh-ch'eng)." *Shinagaku*, 1, 1920. (Included in Torajiro Naito, *Kenki shoroku*. Kyoto, 1928, pp. 113–157.)

Nivison, David S. *The Life and Thought of Chang Hsüeh-ch'eng (1738–1801)*. Stanford, Calif: Stanford University Press, 1966.

Qian, Mu. *Zhongguo jin sanbainian xueshu shi* (A History of Chinese Thought in the Past Three Centuries), 2 vols. Taipei: Commercial Press, 1937, 1957. (See "Dai Dongyuan," pp. 306–379; "Zhang Shizhai," pp. 380–452.)

Yü,Ying-shih. *Lun Dai Zhen yü Zhang Xuecheng* (An Evaluation of Dai Zhen and Zhang Xuecheng). Hong Kong: Longmen shudian, 1976.

———. "Zhang Xuecheng versus Dai Zhen: A Study in Intellectual Challenge and Response in Eighteenth-Century China." In *Chinese Language, Thought, and Culture: Nivison and His Critics*, ed. P. J. Ivanhoe. La Salle, Ill.: Open Court, 1996.

Zhang, Xuecheng. *Zhang Shi yishu* (The Remaining Writings of Zhang Xuecheng), 8 vols. Shanghai: Commercial Press, 1936. (Typeset punctuated reprint of 1922 wood-block edition by Liu, Chenggan; Jiayetang Library).

Zhang Zai (Chang Tsai)

Chung-ying CHENG

Zhang Zai (Zhang Hengqu, 1020–1077) was born in Kaifeng, Henan Province. For most of his life he lived in a small town, Hengqu, in Mei County in modern Shensi; hence he took Henqu as his style name. When he was twenty-one, he was encouraged by Fang Zhongyan to study the *Zhongyong* (*Doctrine of the Mean*), and so he went back to the Confucian classics, after a few years of strenuous study of Daoism and Buddhism. This means that his thought had gone beyond Daoism and Buddhism in a quest for a perennial philosophy of the Confucian *dao*. Like Zhou Dunyi, Zhang Zai finally became engrossed with the *Yijing* and set his mind on the philosophy of change (*yi*) as the essence of the *dao* learning. Because he disagreed in general with Wang Anshi's political reform, Zhang resigned his official post and then devoted his life to thinking, writing, and teaching in the tradition of classical Confucianism. During this period of seclusion he produced the famous work *Zhengmeng* (*Rectifying Obscurations*), in which his metaphysics of the *qi* was fully developed. In writing this treatise, he became the first philosopher to expound *qi* as the essence of the *dao* and thus provide a systematic foundation for understanding and developing the cosmology and ontology of changes in the Confucian tradition.

In comparison with Zhou Dunyi, who developed the cosmology of changes in terms of the abstract notion of *taiji* and the nature of *li* (principle, reason), Zhang Zai arrived at a newer, more unified, and yet more detailed description of the formation and transformation of all things in the world. Again like Zhou, Zhang Zai applied his cosmology to his own life; he wanted to learn to become a Confucian sage. In his own words, the ideal of a Confucian sage was "to establish the heart-mind of heaven and earth, to create a destiny for people who live, to inherit the spiritual teachings of past sages, and to found peace for a thousand generations." In his work *Zhengmeng* we can single out the essay *Ximing* ("Western Inscription") as a deeply felt statement of his view on the cosmos, human life, and ideal practice. We may characterize Zhang Zai's philosophy as a metaphysics of the ubiquitous *qi*, which inspires and justifies the theory of human mind-nature endowed with epistemological and ethical powers.

The influence of Zhang Zai is both deep and wide. He is known as the founder of the Guan school of Song neo-Confucianism, and he inspired many others after him, such as Zhu Xi and Wang Fuzhi, to pursue the neo-Confucian philosophy of the world and man. Zhang's cosmic organism also set the tone for Wang Yangming's philosophy of the unity of man and cosmos.

Metaphysics of *Qi* and Dialectics of *Qi* Transformation

Zhang's primary proposition regarding the *qi* is: "The great void (*taixu*) is *qi*." By *taixu* Zhang meant the original source of all things, to which all things would also return. Whereas the Daoists would identify the *taixu* as an ontologically different *wu* (emptiness) from the material of which things are made, and whereas the Buddhists identified it with absolute nothingness, Zhang Zai saw the great void as nothing other than what we would call the *qi*, the vital or material force from which things are made. In this regard we may suspect that he was influenced by the Daoists: in the *Laozi* and the *Zhuangzi*, one does not need to interpret the *wu* as an entity different from the *qi*. In fact, Laozi left the notion of the *wu* open, so that we may indeed identify *wu* with the *qi*; and this view is even more conspicuous in the *Zhuangzi*.

To understand the *taixu* in Zhang's sense, we must see *qi* as capable of assuming two forms: (1) In the state of dispersion (*shan*), *qi* is not yet formed into things—this is the state to which all things will return after being destroyed. (2) In the state of concentration (*ju*), *qi* is formed into things. *Taixu*, being void, is no doubt the *qi* that is dispersed, the *qi* that is yet to be formed into things; we may call this a state of preformation of things. Zhang Zai says that "*qi* disperses and coalesces in the great void, and this is like ice dissolving into water. Hence we know that the void is the *qi*, and there is no emptiness (*wuwu*)."

If *qi* disperses and coalesces in the great void, one may think that the great void is the place where dispersion and concentration of *qi* take place. However, the example of ice dissolving into water makes it clear that the great void is only the vast unformed *qi* wherein things are formed from the *qi* and can dissolve into the *qi*. This also means that the great void, being unformed and hence invisible, is both the material source of things in the world and the place where things are materially formed and transformed. The reason why things are formed and transformed is again to be found in the great void of the *qi*. The great void has powers of dispersion and concentration that are exhibited in the movement and rest, the firmness and softness, and the brightness and darkness of the *qi*. Zhang says:

> The *qi* as the vast great void ascends, descends, and flows. There is no cessation of this process. This is what the *Book of Change* has called "fermentation" and what Zhuangzi has called "breathing among living things" or the "wild force." This is just a mechanism of the void and substantiation, movement and rest, and the beginning of *yin-yang* and *kang-ruo*.

Thus described, the great void can be called heaven (*tian*), which is the source of life for all things.

The *qi*, then, has intrinsic powers of movement and rest. This conforms to what is described in the *Yijing* and leads to the idea of principle (*li*) as inherent in the movement and rest of things. *Li* as the way in which *qi* naturally moves and rest, disperses and coalesces, is part and parcel of the *qi* and cannot be separated from it. Thus *li* could be described as the very nature of the *qi*, as a process, and as having all the characteristics of the two polarities (*liangduan* or *liangji*) of *yin* and *yang*. Zhang recognizes the ceaseless circulation of the formation and transformation of things within the polarity of *yin* and *yang* as the fundamental principle of things.

To say that this is the principle of things, and especially to say that it is the principle of their nature (*xing*) and destiny (*ming*), is to recognize its universality and its necessity, although the universality and necessity of *li* have to be manifested in a multitude of forms of changes of things. We recognize this unity of principle in the variety of things because we are capable of abstracting and concretizing, of separating and uniting. Zhang Zai insisted on the primary unity of *li* and *qi*, on the primacy of *qi*, and on *qi* as source, so that metaphysically *li* has no independent ontological status apart from the *qi*. This was an important insight.

Zhang Zai also recognized that because of the nature of *qi*, anything can be said to have two polarities of *yin* and *yang* in a unity; thus anything is both unity in duality and duality in unity. As unity in duality it is not static but is subject to unpredictable changes (because of its uniqueness); as duality in unity, it is again not static—it is the dynamic basis of continuing unity. This concept brings out both the opposed and the complementary functions of *yin* and *yang*; because of them, there is a unity of oneness and duality in the intrinsic nature of the great void or the heaven, and there is continuous production of new things in the world. Zhang Zai says:

> That a thing has two polarities is due to its being the *qi*. Because it is one, it is capable of being divine [Zhang Zai's note: because two are present it is hence unpredictable in its changes]; and because it is two, it is capable of transformation [Zhang's note: enforcing oneness]. This is how heaven participates (*can*) in the world of things.

Zhang Zai uses *can* to mean both the participation of heaven as the principle of creativity and the production of new things based on the interplay of the unity of duality and the duality of unity of the *yinyang*. The process of *qi*-creativity or productivity is called a process of "subtle transformation of the *qi*," which is also called the *dao*.

This important passage summarizes the creativity of the great void of *qi*: it is the constant interplay of the *yin* and *yang* and hence the constant interplay of the one (the complementing or uniting force of *yinyang*) and the two (the differentiating and oppositional force of *yinyang*) that gives rise to changes—the formation of new things and the transformation of old things. The universe is a process of never-ending change simply because it is the nature of the universe understood as the great void of the *qi*.

Seen in terms of this creative aspect of *qi*, the great void is also called the "great harmony" (*taihe*). Zhang Zai says:

> The great harmony is what is called the *dao*, in which is contained the nature of the interflow of floating and sinking, rising and descending, moving and resting. It is the beginning of begetting fermentation, interaction, winning and defeating, contracting and stretching (of the *qi*). . . . When it is differentiated and becomes visible in form, it is the material force (*qi*); when it is penetrating and not capable of being seen in a form, it is the spirit (*sheng*).

Zhang Zai wants to describe the process of creativity of *qi* so as to suggest the "*Duan* Commentary" to the *Yijing* on the hexagram of the "creative" (*qian*).

Whereas the term *taixu* comes from *Zhuangzi*, the term *taihe* comes from the *Yizhuan* (*Ten Commentaries*) of the *Yijing*. Ontologically, these two terms refer to the same ultimate reality of *qi*, but they nevertheless can be distinguished as referring to two different aspects of *qi*. *Taixu* refers to the original or primordial state of *qi* before any differentiation between *yin* and *yang* takes place, to which the dispersion of formed things pertains. *Taihe* refers to the state of *qi* when the nondifferentiation of *yin* and *yang* is in a process of differentiation; this is the state in which the differentiated *yin* and *yang* of *qi* interact and interpenetrate to produce new things in the world. *Taixu* stands for the *yin* of the *qi*: rest. *Taihe* stands for the *yang* of the *qi*: motion. *Taixu* corresponds to the notion of the *wuqi* and *taihe* to the notion of the *taiji* in Zhou Dunyi's *Discourse on the Diagram of the Great Ultimate*.

Human Nature, Mind, and Understanding

On the basis of his theory of *taihe*, Zhang Zai developed his views on the formation and transformation of human nature and the human mind. He says:

> From the *taixu* we come to have the name of heaven; from the *qi*-transformation we come to have the name of *dao*. To unite the void with the *qi*, we have the name of human nature (*xing*); to unite human nature with perception, we have the name of heart-mind (*xin*).

Heaven is a name for the formless nature of the *qi*, and *dao* is a name to describe the creative process of the *qi*. Similarly, the name *xin* describes the human capacity for feelings and *xing* describes human creativity. For Zhang Zai, whereas the human being has a "*qi* origin" and a "*qi* structure," his nature is not confined to the human form or body but combines that physical structure with the creative *dao*, which is indicated by the term "void" (*xu*).

Zhang Zai suggests a notion of the human being as representing, within the finite body, the infinite creativity of the *dao* or the *taixu* and the *taihe*. In its formation, human nature participates in heaven—a view originating in the *Zhongyong* and the *Yizhuan*. The human heart-mind is that part of human nature which, through perception, becomes self-conscious and conscious of other things. Just as human nature is an extension or elevation of the *dao*, so the human heart-mind is an extension or elevation of human nature and hence also of the *dao*. This takes place as a result of the creative functions of the *dao* and thus can be regarded as a creative act of the self-transcendence of the *dao*.

When human nature and the human mind are understood in this way, it is not difficult to see how human nature can reach a full understanding of the creativity of the *dao*, which consists in creating all things in the world and in preserving life by universal or benevolent love (*ren*). Nor is it difficult to see how human understanding, through the human mind, can contribute to continuous cultivation along the path toward sagehood, or sagely vision. The mind must choose and remain on the right path; this explains the need for learning and understanding, which Confucianism stressed from its beginnings in the time of Confucius.

With regard to human nature, Zhang Zai distinguishes between the "nature of heaven and earth" (*tiandi zhixing*) and the "nature of temperament and desires" (*qizhi zhixing*). Both are sources of human nature, because it consists of the physical (the formed *qi*) and the nonphysical or the spiritual (the unformed *dao*). One source gives rise to the desire for food and sex; the other source gives rise to the virtues of love, righteousness, propriety, and wisdom. More profoundly, one source is rooted in the nondifferentiating nature of heaven and earth or the *dao*, whereas the other comes from the differentiation and formation of things. Zhang Zai, as a Confucian, does not advocate eliminating all human desires; instead, he advocates controlling and restraining desires so that they will not get in the way of realizing the deeper nature of all things and embracing all things without selfishness, possessiveness, or ignorance due to the limitations of one's natural condition.

One's physical nature is the source of moral evil; one's spiritual nature is the source of moral good. If one restrains one's physical nature in light of one's spiritual nature, one will not fall into evil. This implies that the physical and the spiritual can coexist harmoniously if a human being is able to exercise self-control and self-restraint in light of deep self-reflection on his cosmological and ontological roots. Zhang Zai says:

> Once formed, a human being has a physical nature; but through careful self-reflection one will come to see one's nature as of heaven and earth. Hence in speaking of the nature of the physical, the superior man sees something he would not call his nature. (*Zhengming*)

One can discern in this statement a trace of Mencius, who first distinguished between what is capable of being actively cultivated and what is passively received. This is a distinction between nature, which Zhang Zai calls the nature of "heaven and earth"; and fate, which he calls "temperament and desires."

Zhang Zai thus distinguishes between "knowledge of virtues" (*dexing zhizhi*) and "knowledge of seeing and hearing" (*jianwen zhizhi*). Knowledge of virtues comes not from seeing and hearing but from reflection on one's nature of heaven and earth so that one sees the functions and powers of the *dao* as well as how one embodies these functions and powers for a creative transformation of the self toward virtues and sageliness. One needs to learn things of the world by perception and experience, which are important for maintaining a correct understanding of the physical order of things. Regarding the knowledge of virtues, we can say that one's nature contains the "heavenly principle" (*tianli*), which is not simply an object to be reflected on but also a motive for pursuing the supreme good and a way of distinguishing moral evil from moral goodness. This idea led, four centuries later, to Wang Yangming's concept of an active knowledge of innate goodness (*liangzhi*).

How does one transform one's nature to conform more with the heavenly principle (*tianli*)? Or—what amounts to the same thing—how does one develop one's knowledge of virtues without being hindered and fettered by empirical knowledge? The answer is that one must look into the function and ability of *xin*, the human heart-mind. As we have seen, the heart-mind comes from a combination of human nature with perception; this means that it is human nature becoming self-conscious, becoming conscious of the outside world, and becoming creatively self-controlling and self-determining.

This is a subtle point. Zhang articulates it, in a way, in *Xingli shiyi*, in his famous characterization of the human mind: "The mind unifies and commands human nature and human feelings" (*xintong xingqing*). However, it is not anywhere expounded or elaborated. Zhu Xi gave equal importance to this statement and to Cheng Yi's concept that "Human nature is principle" (*xingjili*) and proceeded to develop a theory of the heart-mind and its integration of human nature and feelings. Zhu says: "Human nature is considered as principle, and feelings are the activation of nature. Heart-mind on the other hand is that which controls and integrates nature and feelings" (*Zhuzi yulei*, Vol. 5). The essence of Zhu's doctrine is that the human heart-mind contains and penetrates both nature and feelings in their various forms, realized or virtual. Furthermore, spurred on by Zhang Shi, he comes to perceive the meaning of ruling or commanding in the relationship between mind and nature and feelings. *Xin tong xingqing* seems to echo Xunzi's remark: "*Xin* is the ruler of the body" (*xingzhe xingzhi junye*) in *Jiebe pian* (Cua 1993).

In other words, Zhu Xi comes to interpret *xin tong xingqing* as *xin zhu xingqing*, "The heart-mind rules and commands (*zhuzai*) nature and feelings." From this recognition Zhu develops his theory of moral preservation and nourishing (*cunyang*), scrutiny and apprehension (*chashi*). One needs to preserve and nourish one's nature before it is activated, and one needs to scrutinize and apprehend one's feelings and desires when they are activated from one's nature.

Both *cunyang* and *chashi* are essential functions and abilities and thus *gongfu* of the heart-mind, necessary for moral cultivation and moral self-control. But for the heart-mind to be able to exercise supervision and control, it must be able to perceive the principle of nature that represents the criteria of rightness and goodness. That is, the heart-mind must acquire moral knowledge through active learning and reflection. Even more important, the heart-mind must have the will to decide to pursue right actions and good character, and to enforce and implement its decision freely and effectively. There is good evidence that Zhu Xi achieved this further insight into the heart-mind and thus good reason to say that his was the first neo-Confucian philosophy to emphasize the will as an aspect of the heart-mind.

The question is whether what Zhu Xi claimed for the heart-mind can be identified in Zhang Zai's view, not just with reference to the statement about the heart-mind commanding nature and feelings but elsewhere as well. In his reinterpretation of the *Yizhuan*, Zhang Zai stressed "inheriting the goodness of heaven and accomplishing human nature" by cultivating and transforming one's nature in accordance with one's understanding of the principle of heaven. This seems to presuppose that the heart-mind has the active function of knowing the principle and acting on the transformation of one's nature, and that the heart-mind must pay close attention to learning.

For Zhang Zai, if one is able to learn to the extent of being like heaven he has "accomplished nature." This idea of accomplishing nature does not contradict the Mencian thesis that one has to exhaust one's heart-mind in order to know one's nature fully. Nor does this interpretation of the *xin* and *xing* contradict the thesis that nature becomes conscious in developing one's heart-mind; in fact, it goes a long way toward completing an ontohermeneutic circle, which is necessary for understanding the intricate relationship between the heart-mind and the heavenly *dao*. Human nature gives rise to the heart-mind, but Zhang Zai also tells us that the heart-mind can contribute to the transformation and even the formation of one's nature. Zhang Shih takes Zhang Zai's position on accomplishing nature by the heart-mind; Zhu Xi objected to this, but nothing is said in Zhu Xi's work that would contradict the view described here regarding the active function of the heart-mind.

Zhang Zai suggested that by "emptying one's heart-mind" (*xuxin*) one can transform one's nature. *Xuxin* is required for opening oneself to learning and for gaining insight into the principle that underlies an understanding of the world. The actual transformation comes with the insistence that the heart-mind has the power of transformation and self-transformation. Apart from *xuxin*, Zhang Zai also speaks of "broadening one's heart-mind" (*daxin*). In the chapter *Daxin*, Zhang says:

> Broaden one's heart; then one can experience the things under heaven. If there is anything not yet experienced, then one's heart has something beyond its scope. The mind of common people stops at the narrow views of hearing and seeing. The sage fulfils his nature and thus does not shackle his heart with hearing and seeing. When the sage looks at the world, he cannot find anything identifiable with himself. Mencius says that one fulfills one's mind so that one comes to know one's nature and to know heaven. . . . Heaven has no exterior; hence any mind having an exterior is not sufficient to go together with the heart of heaven.

How does one broaden one's heart? Again, there is no other way than by opening one's eyes to things of the world and then reflecting on their source and not confining the mind to experience alone. This implies that one has to discover or rediscover oneself as a moral agent and as a source of moral goodness.

Human Stations and Sociopolitical Philosophy

On the basis of his cosmology, Zhang Zai can be said to have achieved and articulated the most vivid organismic Confucian vision of the human station in the cosmos and human society and government since the chapter *Datong* in the *Liji*. For this aspect of his thought we may refer to his short essay "Western Inscription" (*Ximing*), which originally had the title "Rectifying Stubbornness" (*Tingwan*). Here Zhang Zai uses the first person to speak of heaven and earth as parents of the human person. He says:

> Consequently, I can regard that which fills the cosmos as my own body, and that which leads the cosmos as my nature. All people are my siblings and all things are my

> friends. The great ruler is the oldest son and his grand ministers are his stewards.

The cosmos is like a great family organized in the Confucian spirit of mutual love, care, and respect. One can therefore apply all the Confucian virtues to all things in the cosmos. We must respect not only our own parents but also the parents of others; we must care not only for our children but also for the children of others. This attitude and this understanding would eliminate all borders between races and nations.

Our care for people and things would include a concern for protecting our environment and preserving our natural resources, as advocated in modern environmental ethics. Thus human virtues acquire a cosmological significance. When a human being fulfills the virtues given to him as part of his nature, he can be said to identify his parents with heaven and earth. The very nature of the human being is to live in harmony with heaven and earth and to cultivate that harmony to its fullest extent. For Zhang Zai the basic virtue making this harmony possible is filial piety; of six examples he gives for caring and love, five have to do with filial piety. Thus his view of a good society and good government reflects an important proposition of the *Analects*: "Filial piety and brotherhood are the roots of benevolence" (*ren*). For Zhang, as for Confucius and Mencius, benevolence is the inspiration and source of good government. But Zhang Zai, unlike Mencius, did not deal with the requirements of a good ruler. Zhang focused strictly on cultivating the human being as a member of the family of heaven and earth.

The question has been raised (by Yang Shi, for one) whether Zhang Zai's position here is essentially the Mohist doctrine of universal love (*jianai*). In response, both Cheng Yi and Zhu Xi stressed that here, benevolent love is not universal love; rather, it is love based on one principle and many applications or many manifestations (*liyi fenshu*). The same benevolent love is not applied to everything with no distinctions or differentiation. For the Confucian, the cosmos is a highly differentiated order, like a family, in which each member deserves virtuous treatment. Although this argument is not worked out in detail, it seems clear that the human being must take account of concrete circumstances in order to act fittingly.

Zhang Zai's point about the whole cosmos being "my body" implies that one should tend to different parts of the body in different ways. Hence in treating heaven and earth as our parents, we are not to give up our duties as children to our actual biological parents; rather, we extend filial respect and care to our natural abode. We may construe "one principle with many manifestations" (*liyi fenshu*) as "one body with many applications" (*tiyi yongshu*), which is based on the essential neo-Confucian distinction between substance and function in our world and our life.

Conclusion

No doubt Zhang Zai's "Western Inspiration" indicates the deep-set cosmic piety of the Confucian tradition, which is both ethical and religious in spirit. In lieu of an explicit organized religion, Confucianism reaches for a cosmic sentiment of piety rooted in one's self-cultivation of the bond between the human and the cosmic, a bond that would transcend and dissolve the problems of life and death. Hence Zhang's final statement in "Western Inscription": "In life I feel at ease; in death I will be at peace."

See also Zhou Dunyi.

Bibligraphy

Note: For works of Zhang Zai, see *Hengzhu yishuo, Qingxue li gu, Xingli shiyi, Zhangshi quanshu* (in *Guoxue jiben congshu*), and *Zhengmeng*. In *Zhang Zai ji*. Beijing: Zhonghua, 1978.

Chan, Wing-tsit. *A Source Book in Chinese Philosophy*. Princeton, N.J.: Princeton Uiversity Press, 1963.

Cheng, Chung-ying. "On Transformation as Harmony: Paradigms from the Philosophy of the I Ching." In *Philosophy of Harmony and Strife*, ed. Liu Shu-hsien and Robert Allinson. Hong Kong: Chinese University of Hong Press, 1988.

———. "Reality and Divinity in Chinese Philosophy." In *Companion to World Philosophy*, ed. Eliot Deutsch and Ron Bontekoe. London: Blackwell, 1997.

———. "Religious Reality and Religious Understanding in Confucianism and Neo-Confucianism." *International Philosophical Quarterly*, 13(1), 1973, pp. 33–61.

———. "The Trinity of Cosmology, Ecology, and Ethics in the Confucian Personhood." In *Confucianism and Ecology*, ed. Mary Evelyn Tucker and John Berthrong. Cambridge, Mass.: Harvard University Press, 1998.

Cua, A. S. "The Possibility of Ethical Knowledge: Reflections on a Theme in the *Hsün Tzu*." In *Epistemological Issues in Ancient Chinese Philosophy*, ed. Hans Lenk and Gregor Paul. Albany: State University of New York Press, 1993.

Fung, Yu-lan (Feng Youlan). *A History of Chinese Philosophy*, Vol. 2, trans. Derk Bodde. Princeton, N.J.: Princeton University Press, 1953.

Kasoff, Ira. *The Thought of Chang Tsai (1020–1077)*. Cambrdige: Cambridge University Press, 1984.

Needham, Joseph. *Science and Civilization in China*, Vol. 2. Cambridge: Cambridge University Press, 1956.

Wang, Fuzhi. *Commentary on the Zheng Meng*.

Xunzi. In *Sibu beiyao* series.

Zhu, Xi. *Zhuzi yulei*.

Zhengming (*Cheng-ming*): Rectifying Names

Chung-ying CHENG

"Rectifying names" (*zhengming*) occupies an important position in classical Confucianism. This doctrine begins with Confucius, is fully developed in the writings of Xunzi, and can be said to be applied in all Confucian writings since Confucius.

Zhengming in Confucius

To "rectify names" is to establish a social order by identifying and defining moral relationships among human beings in the family, society, and the state. In fact, we might say that family, society, and state are possible only through a commitment to this identification and definition of human moral relationships. When Confucius's disciple Zilu asked what Confucius would do first in starting a government, the master replied with his idea of "rectifying names" (*Lunyu*, *Analects*, 13.3).

The doctrine of rectifying names has two main parts: (1) the reasons for rectifying names, and (2) an account of the content of names and the rationale for rectification.

1. What are the reasons for "rectifying names"? To give such reasons is equivalent to accounting for the significance of this doctrine in securing a well-ordered society. In other words, the attainment of a well-ordered society is the quintessential function of rectifying names. Confucius gives the following account:

> If names are not rectified, then speech would not be smooth (consistent). If speech is not smooth, then there would be no flourishing of ritual or music. If there is no flourishing of ritual and music, then punishment would not hold right. If punishment does not hold right, then people would not know how to act rightly. Therefore, for a governing person, a name must be used in speech, and speech must be practiced. For a governing person, there is nothing unserious in his speech. (*Analects*, 13.3)

What Confucius proposes here is insightful and to the point: to rectify names is to make names that identify and define social relationships by marking out what is required in such relationships in our common understanding. This means that names have to be used in speech, and speech—apart from communicating ideas—is meant to identify and define a situation or event and a norm for action. Confucius's insight is that speech or language is not a simple matter of description but a matter of prescription. It is in fact intended to prescribe—to set a norm—and hence to normalize, to organize, and to order by means of correct, acceptable actions and behavior. Systems of ritual and music and punishments all have to do with normative behavior and action. Thus if there were no recognition of the prescriptive-normative function and capacity of names and speech, no such systems—and hence no actual social order or social transactions—could be obtained.

Given this normative nature of language (names and speech), Confucius is able to bring out the holistic nature of names and speech as they are used. Names cannot do without speech, and speech cannot do without systems of social norms and social control. By the same token, systems of social norms and social control require the use of names and language, which represent the rational activities of our minds as we recognize reality and judge values. Confucius emphasizes the practical implications of language and speech and the cognitive sources of institutions. This is the core of the Confucian doctrine of the unity of theory and practice, and of knowledge and action.

2. We now come to the substantial part of the doctrine of *zhengming*. In *Analects* 12.11, Confucius replies to Duke Qiqing's question about how to govern: "The ruler should be like a ruler, the subject should be like a subject, the father should be like a father, the son should be like a son." Undoubtedly, Confucius is stating how the name of a position is to be rectified: it is to be rectified by the norm or requirement governing that position. The goal of such rectification is for the name to live up to a standard and a standard to apply to a name, where the name is the name of an actuality. Names for actualities—that is, the names of the most basic relationships among humans in society and the state—correspond with reality and standards. Although the passage lists the political relationship of ruler and subject first, we may consider the moral relationship of father and son as primary: as the basis of society and state.

The term "father" normally denotes a male biological progenitor, but the biological fact of procreation does not cover the social and moral rights and obligations of a father to his son. These rights and obligations are invoked because there are social and moral contexts in which such rights and obligations are attributed to and required of a biological father. Hence in the statement "a father should be like a father" the first "father" refers to the biological description and the second "father" to a moral or normative definition. To rectify the name "father" is to hold the biological father responsible for his duties and obligations as a moral custodian. These duties and obligations could be derived from a moral community or could be established by rational reflection on what social order would require.

Hence the project of rectifying names involves clarifying and articulating the connoted values and the substantive duties of a term for a human relationship as based on history, reason, or both. For Confucius, connoted values and the substantive duties of "father" are no doubt founded on both the tradition of the *Zhouli* and rational reflection about an orderly, moral society. This point also applies to rectifying the name "son."

Along the same lines, we may recognize the fact of a person's political rulership, but to rectify the appellation "ruler" requires the de facto ruler to conform to the moral requirements of being a ruler. Confucius speaks of many moral virtues required of a ruler. However, because the ruler is a sovereign—a powerful person in a dominant position—the name "ruler" (unlike "father" or "son") cannot be rectified unless the ruler is willing to engage in a moral transformation of his political power. Confucius teaches self-cultivation of virtues; we have to count on a process of moral education of the ruler beginning in his youth and continuing with moral advice during his reign.

Rectification is easier in the case of the subjects; here the requirement of rectification is loyalty to one's lord or to the state. A disloyal subject has the name "subject" without the moral substance. In this case, the rectification of the name "subject" may be controlled by, or under the power of, a ruler or the state. But one may suspect that Confucius's intention in this regard was moral discipline, not political control.

Thus "rectifying names," in Confucius, has several features. First, it is a holistic program; it is not to be effected piecemeal. Second, it is primarily a moral program or a program of moral education; in this regard, we should note that it may not be feasible in the case of rulers. Third, the moral practice of rectification may work by requiring moral examples. Fathers and rulers might be the best examples, and their moral rectification will probably best secure the moral rectification of sons and subjects. As we can see in Mencius, however, moral rectification may sometimes take place through sons' setting examples: a filial, pious son, such as Shun, may have a moral impact on his father. Regarding subjects, Mencius's dictum is that if a ruler is not benevolent, his subjects need not be loyal to him; in fact, a bandit ruler deserves to be overthrown by his subjects. In extreme cases, a moderate program of political reform by moral rectification may evolve into a more radical program of political revolt.

Zhengming in Xunzi

When we come to Xunzi, what began as a moral and political project is developed as an epistemological and logical doctrine of the origins and use of language. That is no surprise, in light of the political and social disintegration of Xunzi's time: this was a period of moral decline because the central authority of the Zhou has disappeared and dukes had usurped the power and the name of kings. Moreover, there were philosophical doctrines that in Xunzi's eyes explicitly defied and distorted logic and reason. Hence Xunzi felt an urgent need to consider, profoundly, the origin and nature of language as an institution, to show what is wrong with wrong uses of language, and to show how corrections could be made. He could then argue for a restoration or reconstruction of the rules of proper behavior on the basis of the rules of proper speech. We see, therefore, that the doctrine of rectifying names can be expanded to embrace Xunzi's entire social and political philosophy, which would eventually lead to the legalistic takeover and unification of China by the ambitious Qin state.

In his essay on *zhengming*, Xunzi points out that specialized names always have a special tradition. Common names, by contrast, are established and evolved through custom and convention. Xunzi cites as examples some key philosophical terms. According to him, the name *xing* (human nature) would explain the possibility of a special life-form. In this sense one would seek a natural or naturalistic understanding of how a term is given. Hence *xing*, as vested in the abilities of seeing and hearing, feeling and thinking, is a product of the harmony of the natural forces of *yin* and *yang*, without human intervention. What follows from the feelings of human nature is called *qing* (emotions). When a person ponders on his feelings and decides on an action, we have *lü* (deliberation). When we act not simply in accordance with our nature but rather after deliberation in the mind, that is called *wei* (human action). If such an action is done correctly and directed toward the common good of human society, it is called *shi* (deed). If such an action is directed toward justice, it is called *xing* (conduct).

What I have conveyed is how Xunzi regards all common terms in our language as having their essential meaning and reference, which he believed could be clarified in his reconstructed definitions. This process of reconstructing definitions may be then regarded as the essence of effecting the doctrine of rectifying names. But the doctrine of rectifying names also acquired from Xunzi a historical and theoretical foundation. Besides, Xunzi felt that intelligent rulers could see the need for reforming our names and therefore could institute new names and assign meanings to old names in order to effect enlightened political changes. This point of Xunzi's is innovative but was based on historical observation.

Xunzi makes three cardinal points about how names are created and come to prevail: (1) the ground for instituting names, (2) explanations of reasons or causes for identity and differences among names, and (3) the essentials of instituting names.

See also Confucianism: Confucius; Language and Logic; Philosophy of Language; Xunzi.

Bibliography

Note: For classic texts, see *Lunyu, Xunzi, Han Feizi, Gongsun Longzi*. In *Sibu beiyao* Series.

Cheng, Chung-ying. "Chinese Philosophy and Contemporary Human Communication Theory." In *Theory of Communication in East-West Perspectives*, ed. Larry Kincaid. New York, 1987.

———. "Human Rights in Chinese History and Chinese Philosophy." *Comparative Civilizations Review*, No.1, 1979, pp. 1–20.

———. "Kung-sun Lung: White Horse and Other Issues." *Philosophy East and West*, 33(4), 1983, pp. 341–354.

———. "Legalism versus Confucianism: A Philosophical Appraisal." *Journal of Chinese Philosophy*, 8(3), 1981, pp. 271–302.

———. "Rectifying Names (Cheng-Ming) in Classical Confucianism." In *Essays in Asian Studies*, ed. Harry Lambly. University of Hawaii Asian Studies Publications, 1969, pp. 82–96.

Cua, A. S. "The Conceptual Framework of Confucian Ethical Thought." *Journal of Chinese Philosophy*, 23(2), 1996, pp. 153–174.

———. *Ethical Argumentation: A Study in Hsün Tzu's Moral Epistemology*. Honolulu: University of Hawaii Press, 1985.

Djamouri, Redouane. "Théorie de la 'rectification des dénominations' et reflexion linguistique chez Xunzi." *Extreme-Orient/Extreme Occident*, 15, 1993, pp. 55–74.

Duyvendak, Jan J. L. "Hsün-tzu on the Rectification of Names." *T'oung Pao*, 26, 1929, pp. 73–95.

Fingarette, Herbert. "Reason, Spontaneity, and the *Li*: A Confucian Critique of Graham's Solution to the Problem of Fact and Value." In *Chinese Texts and Philosophical Contexts: Essays Dedicated to Angus C. Graham*, ed. Henry Rosemont, Jr. Open Count: La Salle, Ill., 1991.

Hansen, Chad D. "Classical Chinese Philosophy as Linguistic Analysis." *Journal of Chinese Philosophy*, 14, 1987, pp. 309–330.

Zhenren (Chen-jen): The True, Authentic Person

Vincent SHEN

Zhenren, the authentic person, represents a Daoist ideal of the best human being or, in the words of Antonio Cua (1978, 1998), a paradigmatic individual. This concept was developed mainly in the *Zhuangzi*, although we can also find it in the *Huainanzi* and other more religious writings of Daoism.

In the *Zhuangzi*, we find several concepts representing the ideal human being, such as *zhiren* (supreme person), *shenren* (marvelous person), *shengren* (sagely person), and *zhenren* (authentic person). In Chapter 1, *Xiaoyao you* ("Self-Distancing and Free Wandering"), Zhuangzi says, "Therefore, it is said that the ultimate person has no self, the marvelous person has no particular achievements, and the sagely person has no name." Thus *zhiren, shenren*, and *shengren* are described in essentially negative terms: *zhiren* is defined negatively with respect to the self; *shenren* is defined negatively with respect to particular achievements; *shengren* is defined negatively with respect to name. We could conclude that Zhuangzi presents these types of "negative paradigmatic individuals" in relation to those of other schools of thought, such as Confucianism, Mohism, and the school of names.

Only for *zhenren*, the authentic individual, do we find a positive description, or a "positive paradigmatic individual." In the chapter *Tianxia* ("Under Heaven"), Zhuangzi specifically names Guan Yin and Lao Dan as consummate "authentic persons" of old. We also find positive descriptions of the authentic person in Chapter 6 of the *Zhuangzi*, *Da Zongshi* ("The Great Master"), which focuses on the relation between *dao* and man. Interestingly, for Zhuangzi *dao* is not something separate from authentic person or from human praxis directed toward realization of the *dao*. *Dao* is that which is grasped by an authentic person, and an authentic person is one who has grasped *dao* in his praxis. Authentic knowledge of *dao* presupposes someone who can truly manifest *dao*—the authentic person. Zhuangzi says, "We must, moreover, have an authentic person before we can have authentic knowledge," that is, knowledge of the *dao*. Thus an authentic person can make a synthesis of the human and the natural. It seems that there is a hermeneutic circle between *dao* and authentic person.

Zhuangzi describes an authentic person's spiritual achievement in terms of both social behavior and self-cultivation. The spiritual achievement of man, according to Zhuangzi, is not an abstract matter as it is in Hegel's *Phenomenology of Spirit*. Rather, it is concretely realized; the *dao* is incarnated in the actual body and in social contexts:

> The authentic men of old did not override the weak, did not attain their ends by brute strength, and did not gather counselors around themselves. Thus failing was no cause for regret, and succeeding was no cause for self-satisfaction. And thus they could soar to great heights without trembling, enter water without becoming wet, and go through fire without feeling hot. This is the kind of knowledge that reaches to the depth of *dao*.

Or, again:

> The authentic men of old slept without dreams and awakened without worries. When they ate, they were indifferent to flavor; and they drew deep breaths—the authentic person drew breath from the heels. . . . When men's attachments to lustful desire are deep, their divine endowments are shallow.

This text describes an authentic person's self-control through the praxis of breathing and thereby reducing desire even to the point of being able to master it in the state of unconsciousness, and even to the point of not manifesting it through the act of eating or in dreams.

Transcending all constraints of life and death, the authentic person can be free in mind and calm in demeanor. A human being need not be aware of his own authenticity by being conscious of and anxious about his unique death, as Heidegger proposes in *Sein und Zeit*. In his complete spiritual freedom, he only follows the natural rhythm of birth and death:

> The authentic persons of old did not know what it was to love life or to hate death. They did not rejoice in birth, or strive to put off their dissolution. Unconcerned they came and unconcerned they went. That was all.

In achieving these corporeal, mental, and social states, the authentic person can synthesize the human and the natural. Zhuangzi says of the "authentic men of old":

> In that which was "one," they were of nature; in that which was not one, they were of man. And so between the human and the natural no conflict ensued. This was what it meant to be an authentic man.

In thus achieving harmony between the human and the natural, and transcending all finitude in playing with the infinite, an authentic person could manifest *dao* and enjoy a profound sense of beauty.

But even if *dao* is manifested by an authentic person, Zhuangzi would not say that the authentic person is to be identified with *dao*. It is by being authentic that a person can manifest *dao*. *Dao* transcends all things and all human experience, even if it is also immanent in them. Therefore, *dao* could not be absorbed totally in the experience and achievement of an authentic person. On the contrary, when revealed by an authentic person, *dao* manifests some attributes totally independent of any determination by all things, including the authentic person himself. *Dao* is the origin of all things and the ultimate cause of all becoming. It manifests itself through all things and also through the authentic person, but *dao* itself is invisible and formless. It has no other cause than itself. It is infinite in space and time. In playing with it and wandering within it, an authentic person can perceive the ontological beauty of all things. Therefore the meaning of *dao* and the meaning of man mutually determine each another, but this does not mean that we can reduce *dao* to human experience and thereby determine it through mere humanistic considerations.

In the *Huainanzi*, the concept of the authentic person has to do more with a state of mind achieved through self-cultivation. Negatively, the authentic persons rids himself of all influence of desire and all instrumental calculation, to the point of arriving at a state of "nothingness." Positively, he plays and wanders in the realm of nothingness and conforms totally to *dao*. The *Huainanzi* says, "The so-called *zhenren* is he who by nature conforms to *dao*; therefore he seems to be in nothingness, even if in being; he seems to be in vacuity, even if in fullness." Spiritual nothingness therefore mediates between the negative and positive aspects of *zhenren*. By way of spiritual nothingness, an authentic person leads a quiet, simple, and thought-free life, following the *dao*.

Later, in religious Daoism, *zhenren* means two things. First, it means a state of divinity attained by individuals because of their spiritual achievement. According to the *Taiping jing* (Vol. 42), the status of *zhenren* is "above the immortals but under the great God." After the Tang dynasty, some emperors would confer the title *zhenren* on certain historical figures or famous Daoists. For example, Tang Xuansong gave Zhuangzi the title *Nan Hua zhenren*. Religious Daoists would also call their ancient masters *zhenren*. Second, *zhenren* represents the original spirit of human beings (*yuanshen*), which is the original source of all Daoist practices, including breathing (as in the *Zhouyi cantong qi*) and alchemy (as in the *Jindan dachengji*).

We can say that the philosophical concept of *zhenren* is even more important and more meaningful than the religious concept, because the philosophical concept represents the Daoist image of a perfect man or an ideal human being—the goal of the Daoists' meditative way of life, or praxis. It therefore implies the Daoist concept of the perfectibility of human nature, which unfolds through praxis.

See also Daoism: Religious; The *Huainanzi* Text; *Sheng*: Sage; Zhuangzi.

Bibliography

Chan, Wing-tsit. *A Source Book in Chinese Philosophy*. Princeton, N.J.: Princeton University Press, 1963.

Cua, A. S. *Dimensions of Moral Creativity: Paradigms, Principles, and Ideals*. University Park: Pensylvannia State University Press, 1978.

———. *Moral Vision and Tradition: Essays in Chinese Ethics*. Washington, D.C.: Catholic University of America Press, 1998. (See Essay 8.)

Fang, Thomé (Fang Dongmei). *Chinese Philosophy: Its Spirit and Its Development*. Taipei: Linking, 1981.

———. *Yuanshi rujia daojia zhexue* (Philosophies of Primordial Confucianism and Daoism). Taipei: Li-ming, 1983.

Huainanzi. *Dao, The Great Luminant*, trans. Evan Morgan. Shanghai: Kelly and Walsh, 1934.

———. *Huainanzi* (The Book of the Master of Huainan), annot. Gao Yu. Taipei: Shih-chieh, 1985. (8th reprint.)

Le Blanc, Charles. *Huai-nan Tzu: Philosophical Synthesis in Early Han Thought*. Hong Kong: Hong Kong University Press, 1958.

Lin, Yutang. *The Wisdom of Laotze*. New York: Modern Library, 1948.

Maspero, Henri. *Le Daoïsme et les religions chinoises*. Paris: Gallimard, 1971.

Schipper, Kristofer. *Le corps daoïst*. Paris: Arthème Fayard, 1982.

Shen, Vincent. "Annäherung an das daoistische Verständnis von Wissenschaft: Die Epistemologie des Lao Tses und Tschuang Tses." In *Grenz ziehungen zum Konstruktiven Realismus*, ed. F. Wallner, J. Schimmer, and M. Costazza. Vienna: WUV Universitätsverlag, 1993.

———. "Zhuangzi di Daolun: Dui dangdai xingshang kunhuo di yige jieda (Zhuangzi's Discourse on *Dao*: Answers to Contemporary Metaphysical Questions)." *National Chengchi University Philosophical Journal*, No.1, 1994, pp.19–34. (Taipei: National Chengchi University.)

———. "Zhuangzi di renguang (Zhuangzi's Concept of Man)." *Zhexue Yu Wenhua*, 14(6), 1987, pp. 13–23.

Zhuangzi. *The Complete Works of Zhuangzi*, trans. Burton Watson. New York: Columbia University Press, 1968.

———. *Zhuangzi jishi*, 12th ed., ed. Kuo Ch'ing-pan (Guo Qingfan). Taipei: Shih-chieh, 1985.

Zhi (*Chih*): To Know, To Realize

Roger T. Ames

The conventional English translation for *zhi* is "to know," "knowledge." This translation does do some of the work needed to communicate this complex idea, but it is inadequate in several important respects.

First, the classical Chinese language does not distinguish between "knowledge" and "wisdom." There is no sharp dichotomy between theory and practice, and so the assumption is that "knowledge" must be authenticated in action in order to qualify as knowledge. It must be practically efficacious. *Zhi* thus has an important pragmatic connotation.

Since *zhi* involves practice, it is always local knowledge. There is no putative "view from nowhere" or "God's-eye view" that would provide an "objective" perspective. This being the case, knowing a world is reflexive and evaluative: it is to recommend this world from this point of view. It is a normative world-making.

The pragmatic aspect of *zhi* leads to a second observation: *zhi* is meliorative—it seeks to make the world better. In the *Analects* (6.20) Confucius says: "To truly love it is better than to just know it, and to enjoy it is better than to simply love it." As suggested here, *zhi* certainly has a cognitive dimension. In fact, in Mencius, *zhi* as an initial cognitive capacity is one of the four "beginnings" distinguishing the human being from the beast. But the expectation is that this cognitive capacity must be cultivated into a quality of understanding that is productive of human happiness. The kind of knowledge that is directed and purposeful is given a privileged place over simple cognition, and the kind of knowledge that actually conduces to communal enjoyment is better yet.

We can say that "knowing" thus understood not only is informative but also has "performative" force. This means that "knowing" does something; it changes the world. *Zhi* can also be translated as "realizing" in order to highlight this sense of "making something real"—that is, bringing a particular world into being.

Again, as in Austin (1962), *zhi* has "perlocutionary" force: "knowing" has a direct and significant affect on the feelings, beliefs, and mood of those who come to know. It literally changes their minds.

In the classical Chinese world, the person (*ren*) is irreducibly social. Situation has priority over individual agency; where an individual person is always an abstraction from a natural, social, and cultural context. Knowledge thus resides not in an individual knower but in a knowing community, where knowledge is an immediate resource for communal happiness.

An analysis of the etymology of the character *zhi* gives us "an arrow" and "a mouth." The "mouth" element appears in many key philosophical terms in classical Chinese philosophy, reflecting the importance of the social, communicative aspect. And the philologist Bernhard Karlgren has speculated that the "arrow" element in the character *zhi* was originally "person" or "persons" (*ren*), reinforcing the sense that *zhi* connotes a sociology of knowledge rather than simply a solitary knower.

In the *Analects* (6.23) Confucius uses suggestive metaphors to shed light on *zhi*:

> The wise (*zhi*) enjoy water; those authoritative in their conduct (*ren*, a homophone) enjoy mountains. The wise are active; the authoritative are still. The wise find enjoyment; the authoritative are long-enduring.

The association between acting wisely and water is instructive. As a metaphor, water is dynamic: it is life and growth, a source of nutrition and purification. Water assumes its shape according to context, only to be recontextualized as it moves on. It challenges the distinction between noun and verb, and it vitiates the categories of solid, liquid, and gas.

The communal aspect is also highlighted in this passage, where wisdom is a source not of joy but of enjoyment—joy that is shared. This passage also associates knowing and becoming wise with authoritative conduct (*ren*, homophone), an association that we find recurring in the philosophical literature. Knowledge and virtue are coterminous and entail each other.

In fact, the correspondence model of object and idea that has been a main theme in classical western epistemology has little relevance for China. The western vocabulary of knowing reflects this sense of discerning the real world behind appearances: "to grasp," "to get," "to comprehend," "to understand"—that is, to seize on some formal unchanging reality behind the passing shades.

By contrast, the Chinese epistemic vocabulary suggests "mapping out" and "finding the way" (*dao*) as its dominant image. The language of knowing is "to unravel the pattern" (*lijie*), "to break through" (*tongda*). To know is to cultivate productively the patterned regularity that gives one context. It is to function effectively within an always fluid reality. This sense of mapping carries over into modern Chinese, in which the expression for "I know" is literally "I know the way" (*wo zhidao*). To know is to be cognizant of prevailing conditions, to have enough imagination to see their possibilities, and to have achieved enough respect within one's own community to rally support for a chosen future.

Importantly, "the way" (*dao*) is not the "object" of knowledge as such but rather a qualitative way of being in the world that entails both subject and object, the attributes of the subject as well as the modality of the actions being carried out. Knowing tells us as much about the quality of the person who knows as it does about something known, as much about action as it does about a state of mind. To know in the classical Chinese world is to be an effective communicator, to be a focus of communal deference, and to be a beacon for other members of the community who would find their way.

Perhaps this reflection on *zhi* might end with a Daoist qualification on the efficacy of knowledge: after all, the *Daodejing* repeatedly exhorts us to be "without knowledge" (*wuzhi*). The thrust of the Daoist caution, however, is not to recommend ignorance. On the contrary, it is to recommend a certain quality of knowing. The concern here is that, to the extent we can, we must always entertain novel situations without prejudice or presuppositions. In order to understand a situation thoroughly, we must strive to take it on its own terms without imposing preexisting structures or values on it. *Wuzhi* is thus better understood positively as "unprincipled knowing"—a kind of knowing that abjures a final vocabulary in favor of an ironic sensibility, a readiness to relinquish this way of understanding the situation for another, better way.

See also Philosophy of Knowedge; *Quan*; *Zhixing Heyi*.

Bibliography

Ames, Roger T. "Confucius and the Ontology of Knowing." In *Interpreting Across Boundaries*, ed. Gerry Larson and Eliot Deutsch. Princeton, N.J.: Princeton University Press, 1988.

———. "Prolegomena to a Confucian Epistemology." In *Culture and Modernity: East-West Philosophical Perspectives*, ed. Eliot Deutsch. Honolulu: University of Hawaii Press, 1991.

Ausitn, J. L. *How to Do Things with Words*. Cambridge, Mass.: Harvard University Press, 1962.

Cua, A. S. *Ethical Argumentation: A Study in Hsun Tzu's [Xunzi's] Moral Epistemology*. Honolulu: University of Hawaii Press, 1985.

Zhang, Dongsun. *Lixing yu liangzhi: Zhang Dongsun wenxuan* (The Ideal and Efficacious Knowing), ed. by Zhang Rolun. Shanghai: Shanghai Yuandong chubanshe, 1995.

———. *Zhishi yu wenhua: Zhang Dongsun wenhua lunzhu jiyao* (Knowledge and Culture: Key Selections from Zhang Dongsun's Cultural Essays), ed. Zhang Yaonan. Peking: Zhongguo Guangbo dianshi chubanshe, 1995.

Zhixing Heyi (Chih-hsing Ho-i): Unity of Knowledge and Action

A. S. Cua

The connection between moral knowledge and practice is an important topic in Confucian ethics. Various sayings of Confucius recorded in the *Analects* suggest different, though not contradictory, conceptions. First, Confucius stresses the importance of applying one's moral learning, and the delight of so doing (*Analects* 1.1). Characteristically, a wise person is joyous and actively exercises moral learning or knowledge (6.23).

Second, moral practice in accord with one's learning and knowledge is not blind compliance, for it presupposes consideration of the distant consequences of action. Says Confucius, "Learning without thinking will lead to perplexity [about right and wrong conduct]; thinking without learning will put one's life in jeopardy" (2.15). Thus a wise person is free from perplexity (9.29, 14.28). Thoughtful deliberation about the nonimmediate consequences of actions is especially important to right and good conduct. In the words of Confucius, "If a person has no thought for the future, he is sure to be troubled by what is near at hand" (15.12). As one of Confucius's disciples points out, moral thinking is essentially "reflection on things at hand" rather than reflection on the application of moral theory to practice (19:6). In Confucius's conception of the *junzi* (superior or noble man), the ethically paradigmatic individual, such reflection must be free from preconceptions and catholic, i.e., impartial and broad-minded.

Third, and even more important, Confucius emphasizes the harmony of words and action, especially in "suiting the word to the action." A moral person, in relation to others, keeps his or her words or commitments. Indeed, "without knowing the force of words, one cannot know another person's moral character" (20.3).

Because of the various uses of *zhi*, often rendered as "knowledge," different views of the relation between moral learning or knowledge and action are possible. Roughly speaking, there are two senses of *zhi* corresponding to two senses of "knowledge." For convenience, we will use the distinction between prospective and retrospective moral knowledge, i.e., knowledge acquired before action and knowledge acquired after action. Both prospective and retrospective ethical knowledge seem implicit in the *Analects*. These uses of *zhi* also imply other uses of *zhi* in the sense of learning or acquiring information, and of realization. Thus, apart from the use of *zhi* as "knowledge," in the *Ana-*

lects, *zhi* is also used in the sense of acknowledgment, understanding, or appreciation, and "knowing how." In the various uses of *zhi*, the foundation is learning *li* (rites, propriety), a basic component of the Confucian ethical tradition.

After the *Analects*, there are different views on the connection between moral knowledge and action. Since moral knowledge is based primarily on learning, some thinkers stress the importance of learning prior to practice, whereas others stress the primacy of practice over learning. In classical Confucianism, two philosophical views deserve attention. On the one hand, Mencius maintains that every ordinary person has an innate capacity for acquiring knowledge of right and good conduct. If the natural environment and the human environment are congenial to the development of inborn moral dispositions, these dispositions will flourish and become virtues such as *ren* (benevolence), *yi* (righteousness), *li* (propriety), and wisdom. In this view, traditional learning is secondary to the exercise of moral sense. Moral failure is often viewed as a result of corruption of the moral sense and of innate moral dispositions owing to an uncongenial environment or self-destructive conduct. On the other hand, Xunzi attributes moral failure principally to a lack of moral knowledge derived from learning the Confucian tradition of *li* or rules of proper behavior. Whereas Mencius has faith in the innate goodness of human nature, Xunzi maintains that human nature is problematic, considered in terms of its inborn ego-centered motivational structure, for example, unlearned feelings and desires. For Xunzi, human nature must be disciplined by a traditional education. Apart from recitation of the classics, the student must understand the texts to appreciate the interconnected ideas forming the Confucian tradition of rules of proper conduct (*li*), especially the rationales for these rules.

The doctrine of the unity of knowledge (*zhixing heyi*) is a basic component of Wang Yangming's philosophy. In his later years Wang stressed the role of the Mencian *liangzhi* (innate awareness of the good) in the moral life; earlier, however, he proposed the doctrine of the unity of knowledge and action as a pedagogical solution or remedy to a "disease." We are told that "the idea arose as an urgent remedial measure" (1963, Sec. 133). Once, in his letters, he laments over the sick world of his times: "The world today has been morally degenerate. It does not differ from a sick man, approaching death." Whether or not the diagnosis is correct, Wang undoubtedly arrived at his attitude through reflection on his own experience and moral struggle. Regarding the nature of the disease, Wang is quite explicit:

> People today distinguish between knowledge and action and pursue them separately, believing that one must know before he can act. They will discuss and learn the business of knowledge first, they say, and wait till they truly know before they put their knowledge into practice. Consequently, to the last day of life, they will never act and also will never know. This doctrine of knowledge first and action later is not a minor disease and it did not come about only yesterday. My present advocacy of the unity of knowledge and action is precisely the medicine for that disease. (Sec. 5)

Wang's analogy between moral knowledge and practical knowledge is a useful reminder that both forms of knowledge are practical, not theoretical. Although the cognitive content of practical knowledge is a product of learning, adequate performance depends more fundamentally on appreciating the actuating import of practical knowledge. Thus, for Wang, the doctrine of *zhixing heyi* (the unity of moral knowledge and action) is not, strictly speaking, a doctrine of applying knowledge or theory to practice.

To understand Wang's doctrine, we turn to his two famous compendious remarks:

1. "Knowledge is the direction (*zhuyi*) of action and action the effort (*gongfu*) of knowledge."
2. "Knowledge is the beginning of action and action the completion of knowledge."

Wang continues: "If this is understood, then when only knowledge is mentioned, action is included, and when only action is mentioned, knowledge is included" (Sec. 5). Applying the distinction between prospective and retrospective knowledge (*zhi*), let us consider these remarks, first separately, then together, and see whether we have a coherent doctrine.

In statement 1, the notion of knowledge (*zhi*) is prospective rather than retrospective. As prospective knowledge, by virtue of its cognitive content acquired through learning, it provides a *direction* (*zhuyi*) for actual conduct. Since *zhuyi* can also be rendered as "leading idea," the first half of statement 1 can thus be restated: "Prospective moral knowledge, by virtue of its cognitive content, is a leading idea of action." Since *gongfu*, apart from effort, can also be rendered as work or accomplishment, the second half of statement 1 can be restated as "action is the work or accomplishment of knowledge, in the sense of successful effort devoted to carrying out moral requirements." For a committed agent, effort is involved in prospective moral knowledge, because this knowledge is fundamentally an acknowledgment of the actuating import of moral requirements. The acknowledgment is an acceptance that also involves a conative attitude in the sense of an effort to carry out, say, one's duty in actual conduct. The hope is to be successful in the effort. And when one achieves this, one can also be said to have retrospective moral knowledge, which is the focus of statement 2.

In statement 2, both senses of moral knowledge appear to be involved. Prospective knowledge is the beginning of action, and action is the completion of knowledge, but this knowledge is retrospective. Using the point in statement 1, prospective knowledge is a task and retrospective knowledge is an accomplishment, or the experience of actual practice. Thus Wang once explained his doctrine by drawing an analogy with the experience of pain: "Only after one has experienced pain can one know pain. The same is true of cold and hunger. How can knowledge (*zhi*) and action (*xing*) be separated?" (Sec. 5). If we regard the cognitive content of prospective knowledge as a by-product of learning, we may conceive of statements 1 and 2 together as putting forth a conception of moral learning. Moral learning, if it is deemed successful, is learning that has a transforming effect on the student's life. Moral requirements—the cognitive content of moral knowledge—are a component of the moral life. When such learning has been fulfilled in our life, we have retrospective knowledge of the course of our moral experience. Thus statements 1 and 2 together can be viewed as a plausible attempt to elucidate moral agency and, particularly, as a doctrine concerning the proper ascription of the successful exercise of moral agency.

Statements 1 and 2 differ in emphasis, however, if we focus on mere effort rather than successful effort or retrospective moral knowledge. In this light, while 1 stresses the process, 2 stresses moral achievement. The process for Wang is not a temporal process consisting of discrete stages ordered in terms of before and after but a continuum of prospective moral knowledge through successful efforts eventuating in retrospective moral knowledge. This continuum of moral knowledge and action may be described more succinctly as the "original substance" (*benti*) that expresses the intrinsic nature of both knowledge and action—or, if one prefers, the noncontingent connection between prospective and retrospective moral knowledge. It is a noncontingent connection in that moral knowledge and action are mutually dependent notions. Prospective moral knowledge involves actual, conscientious effort. When such effort is successful, our action is in retrospect an accomplishment of what we set out to do in accord with prospective moral knowledge. When the effort fails—owing, for example, to the interference of selfish desires—our moral knowledge and action become separated. When this occurs, we may end up in two separate independent pursuits.

According to Wang, for pedagogical purposes, particularly for rectifying character defects, knowledge and action may be emphasized separately to restore their proper balance as two aspects of the same moral process. But if one pursues the cognitive content exclusively, regardless of its actuating import, one may, in Wang's words, be chasing after "shadows and echoes, as it were." Equally, if one focuses exclusively on actuating force without regard for the cognitive content, one is likely to become "confused and act on impulse without any sense of deliberation or self-examination, and . . . thus also behave blindly and erroneously." The pursuit of moral knowledge, mindful of both cognitive content and its actuating import, is thus an intelligent and concerned, not an empty and irresponsible, occupation. Wang assures his pupils, as indicated earlier, that his doctrine is not a product of baseless imagination; it has the principal aim of being a "medicine for that disease" of pursuing moral knowledge and action separately.

See also *Junzi*; Wang Yangming; *Zhi*.

Bibliography

Chan, Wing-tsit, trans. *A Source Book in Chinese Philosophy*. Princeton, N.J.: Princeton University Press, 1963.

Chang, Carsun. *Wang Yang-ming: Idealist Philosopher of Sixteenth-Century China*. Jamaica: St. John's University Press, 1962.

Cua, A. S. *Moral Vision and Tradition: Essays in Chinese Ethics*. Washington, D. C.: Catholic University of America Press, 1998.

———. "The Possibility of Ethical Knowledge: Reflections on a Theme in the *Hsün Tzu*." In *Epistemological Issues in Ancient Chinese Philosophy*, ed. Hans Lenk and Gregor Paul. Albany: State University of New York Press, 1993.

———. *The Unity of Knowledge and Action: A Study in Wang Yang-ming's Moral Psychology*. Honolulu: University of Hawaii Press, 1982.

———. "*Xin* and Moral Failure: Notes on an Aspect of Mencius's Moral Psychology." In *Mencius: Contexts and Interpretations*, ed. Alan Chan. Honolulu: University of Hawaii Press, 2002.

Kierkegaard, Søren. *Either/Or*, Vol. 1. New York: Anchor, 1959.

Tu, weiming. *Neo-Confucian Thought in Action: Wang Yangming's Youth (1472–1509)*. Berkeley: University of California Press, 1976.

Wang, Yangming. *Instructions for Practical Living and Other Neo-Confucian Writings*, trans. with notes Wing-tsit Chan. New York: Columbia University Press, 1963.

Zhiyi (Chih-i)

David CHAPPELL

Zhiyi (Chih-i, 538–597) ranks as one of China's foremost Buddhist thinkers and is included with Thomas Aquinas and al-Ghazali as one of the great systematizes of religious thought and practice in world history. During Zhiyi's lifetime the Sui dynasty (589–618) united China politically after centuries of division, and sponsored Zhiyi's similar efforts to integrate the diversity of Buddhist texts and practices that had emerged in China during the previous four centuries. By balancing the critical philosophy of emptiness with his positive religious experience under the tutelage of Huisi (515–577) and the *Lotus Sutra*, Zhiyi provided a synthesis of theory and practice, of the critical and the constructive, that became the first enduring Chinese Buddhist school and the foundation for Buddhism in eastern Asia.

In China the Madhyamika philosophy of Nagarjuna (known as Sanlun) became focused only on doctrine, and its disciples went elsewhere to learn meditation. Like all east Asians, Zhiyi took the Sanlun tradition as fundamental in clarifing meditation, but he also argued that meditation was necessary to advance wisdom. This balance of practice and wisdom was symbolized as the two wheels of a cart, or the two wings of a bird, and Zhiyi discussed it most fully under the heading *zhiguan*, "calming and insight." Zhiyi's genius was to integrate practice and wisdom so effectively that the need for, and viability of, an independent "perfection of wisdom" and Madhyamika tradition in China ended soon after the formation of Tiantai. Although in the eighth century Chan (Zen) inherited the Tiantai balance of meditation and wisdom (but substituted the phrase *dinghui* for *zhiguan*), in fact Chan stressed wisdom while continuing to rely on Zhiyi's meditation manuals.

In contrast to later Chan, Zhiyi's view of enlightenment did not eliminate practical distinctions in an emphasis on emptiness. While giving priority to "sudden and complete enlightenment" that awakened to the incomprehensible and ineffable "true reality of all things" (*zhufa shixiang*), Zhiyi also emphasized gradual practice and the necessity of words. The device he invented to contain this tension was his unique teaching of "threefold contemplation" (*sanguang*) and "three truths" (*sandi*): emptiness, temporariness, and the middle. For Zhiyi the liberating experience of emptiness (*kong*) must be followed by the rise of compassion for others and a return to the mundane world, which is then experienced as temporary (*jia*). Since true realization cannot be separated from ordinary life, and compassion cannot be separate from emptiness, the experience of their integration is the middle truth (*zhong*). Zhiyi emphasized that enlightenment is not a synthesis in which the truths of emptiness and temporary worldly distinctions are unified (the middle alone), but an integration in which all three dimensions continue to be present (an inclusive middle). In terms of the *yin-yang* symbol, the middle truth would be symbolized by the outer circle that embraces the dialectic of emptiness and temporariness, sudden and gradual, *yin* and *yang*. While these "three truths" remain faithful to the understanding of Nagarjuna, their formulation as an ongoing process provided a foundation for many of Zhiyi's distinctive philosophical contributions.

A major achievement of Zhiyi was to organize the vast array of Indian Buddhist doctrines and practices into a single system of "four teachings" (*sijiao*). To do this, Zhiyi added a fourth category to the three truths to include conventional religion before practitioners had experienced the truth of emptiness. Zhiyi called this new category the *tripitaka* teaching (*zangjiao*), meaning those Buddhist teachings that do not assume an insight into emptiness, such as morality, ritual, cosmology, history, and some meditation. The second teaching, called the "shared teaching" (*tongjiao*), refers to the teaching of emptiness (*kong*) that is shared by both pre-Mahayana and Mahayana. The third teaching is distinctive (*biejiao*) to Mahayana, since it emphasizes the bodhisattva's compassionate return to the mundane world that is then seen through the insight into emptiness as temporary (*jia*). Finally, the three teachings of conventional Buddhism, emptiness, and the temporary world are all integrated in an inclusive middle (*zhong*) that Zhiyi called the "complete teaching" (*yuanjiao*).

Experientially, the complete teaching could be seen gradually, but Zhiyi stressed realizing it completely and suddenly (*yuandun*). This was often expressed as being aware of the "three thousand worlds in a single moment of consciousness" (*yinian sanqian*).

Nevertheless, rather than emphasizing the complete teaching exclusively, Zhiyi maintained the importance of all four teachings. Unlike Chan, he made many conceptual structures and affirmed the necessity of using language to symbolize the infinite diversity of reality. On the other hand, he also emphasized the ultimate inadequacy of language and thought to capture suddenly and completely (*dunyuan*) the true reality of all things (*zhufa shixiang*). Zhiyi used the phrase *shixiang* to express what is seen by those who are enlightened, which he also called the "middle path" (*zhongdao*) and "marvelous existence" (*miaoyou*), positive terms that contrast with the later Chan emphasis on emptiness (*wu*).

For Zhiyi, the importance of using language while recognizing its inadequacy was justified by the doctrine of four *siddanta* (four perspectives or approaches to teaching) found in the *Dazhidulun*: (1) teaching the worldly understanding of interdependent causes and conditions, (2) teaching according to the experience and capacities of the individual, (3) therapeutic teaching of what is helpful, and (4) teaching the ultimate truth that is beyond words and distinctions. "The benefits obtained from the first three siddhantas are called 'having a limit,' while the benefit obtained from the ultimate siddânta is called 'neither being limited nor being unlimited.' "

Zhiyi combined an emphasis on inner realization with the obligation to study the scriptures and to teach others. This frequently took the form not only of lectures but also of developing effective rituals, including popular devotions within a larger framework of "fourfold meditation": constantly sitting (adopted by Chan), constantly walking while reciting the name of Amitabha Buddha (Pure Land), half-sitting and half-walking (repentance and rituals), and freestyle. As it evolved, Chan Buddhism was based on the constantly sitting meditation, whereas an independent Pure Land tradition that developed in northern China during the Sui-Tang dynasties became totally integrated with Tiantai in the Song dynasty.

Zhiyi's integration of various lists of bodhisattva practices into a structure of fifty-two stages has been widely adopted, while the "four great bodhisattva vows" that he formulated have been used liturgically ever since in east Asia, especially in Zen:

> Beings are infinite in number, I vow to save them all. Attachments are endless in number; I vow to end them all. Helpful teachings are innumerable; I vow to learn them all. Buddhahood is supreme; I vow to attain it.

The four great vows and the four *siddanta* directly reflect the four teachings, which are based on the more primary structure of threefold contemplation and three truths constituting Zhiyi's core philosophy.

Zhiyi also invented a fourfold way of interpreting the "four noble truths": as "arising and perishing," as "neither arising nor perishing," as immeasurable, and as unconditioned. Nevertheless, he grouped all Indian Buddhist scriptures into five flavors (*wuwei*) by adding the *Huayanjing* of sudden enlightenment to the fourfold teachings to express the full enlightenment of Buddha without regard to developmental stages expressed by the threefold and fourfold schemes. Zhiyi justified the division of all Buddhist texts into five flavors as a device developed by Buddha to meet the different needs and capacities of his audience. By proposing this idea, Zhiyi integrated the obviously disparate Buddhist tradition by quoting the Indian Buddhist analogy of different flavors of milk (whole milk, cream, curds, butter, and ghee), while echoing the fivefold categories in the *yinyang wuxing* (five phases) of classical Chinese cosmology. Accordingly, it is not surprising that later Chinese Buddhists readily accepted this doctrine and added that the five flavors of scriptures were taught by Buddha in five different periods of his life.

Although Zhiyi invented a fivefold exegetical method for interpreting scriptures that was designed to penetrate their inner meaning (*xuanyi*), he did not subsume all reality within the mind (as stressed by Huayan and Yogacara philosophy, the apocryphal *Shoulengyanjing*, and the "off the mountain" Tiantai school of the Song dynasty). Instead, for Zhiyi, mind did not subsume the Buddha and sentient beings but functioned in a coequal trinity; theory was always balanced by ritual and meditative practice, principle by phenomena (*lishi*), inherent Buddha-nature with the reality of evil, and sudden and complete realization with the need for daily repentance.

Zhiyi asserted that enlightened awareness included all ten levels of rebirth, from hell through hungry ghosts, animals, humans, demons, gods, *sravaka, pratyekabuddha*, bodhisattvas, and buddhas. Since they were all interdependent and interfused, this led to the philosophical problem of reconciling evil with buddhahood or including it in buddhahood. Conceptually, Zhiyi may seem contradictory, since by definition Buddhahood involves liberation from all ignorance and bad karma; but experientially, he maintained that they were not separate, since the awareness of ignorance, attachment, and anger can be an important occasion for insight and liberation. While emphasizing meditation on evil and the nonduality of demons and the Buddha, of addictions and enlightenment, and of *samsara* and nirvana, Zhiyi did not set up antinomian extremes; he instituted repentance for wrong actions, attitudes, and ideas as a prominent, daily feature of Tiantai practice. Many later Chan masters regarded evil and delusion as accidental, added features not inherent in one's original "mind-nature." However, Zhiyi affirmed the enduring presence of both evil and good as necessary for buddhahood: a buddha's personal evil may be extinguished, but he is not separate from others' realms of hell but is responsive to them. A person able to do only good is not as complete as someone who embodies all reality, both good and evil.

In contrast to the Huayan and Chan theory of mind as the source of all, Zhiyi taught a communicative, responsive relationship (*ganying daojiao*) between practitioners and reality. Ritual practices assumed the character of supernatural responses to confirm and guide practitioners. By initiating practice, a stimulus (*gan*) was made that solicited a response (*ying*) in accordance with the occasion (*ji*). That response is none other than the *tathagata dharmakaya*, which in itself is otherwise changeless and formless:

> The water never ascends, and the moon never descends, but the moon shines everywhere simultaneously over the water. The Buddha never comes, and sentient beings never go, but the compassionate power of the Buddha pervades them all.

Even though mind, Buddha, and sentient beings were equally empty and one, they also had provisional existence in relation to each other. Accordingly, true reality (*shixiang*) is not just empty stillness but is also dynamic and responsive, as expressed in the three truths. Zhiyi symbolized the three truths by using the metaphor of light, images, and the surface of a mirror as their integration. Later Chan thinkers such as Zongmi (780–841) gave priority to the "mirror mind," whereas Zhiyi had specifically warned against focusing on "the middle only" and instead taught that the complete middle included all three truths equally. Accordingly, Tiantai differs from Huayan and Chan, which emphasize that mind is the primary reality and that the three realms of birth and death are "mind only." Instead, Zhiyi favored a passage from the *Huayan Scripture* that emphasized the equal balance of Buddha, sentient beings, and mind. Each moment of thought is identical to being empty, provisional, and the middle at once, which is the true reality (*shixiang*) of all things.

Zhiyi's greatest philosophical achievement was his nuanced presentation of the dialectic of principle-phenomena (*lishi*) by creating the three truths, four teachings, and five flavors. Instead of regarding life as mundane phenomena (*shi*), Zhiyi showed that ordinary life could be viewed either conventionally (as in the *tripitaka* teaching and by pre-Mahayana practitioners) or as provisional existence (*jia*) for the bodhisattva who returns to the world from emptiness out of compassion for others. Similarly, true reality (*li*) is not simply empty (*kong*) but must include provisional existence (*jia*) in the middle way (*zhongdao*) lived in compassion for others. This not only made the transcendent immanent but emphasized the process of transforming oneself and others. Tiantai philosophy cannot be understood apart from these meditative and compassionate practices, just as these practices cannot be adequately understood without the insights of impermanence and interdependence.

Zhiyi's elegant Buddhist synthesis was sponsored by and closely identified with the Sui dynasty; therefore, the political elite of the Tang (618–907) avoided Tiantai and replaced it with Chan Buddhism. As a result, scarcely a single work of Zhiyi's survived by the end of the Tang dynasty. However, since Tiantai was successfully transported to Korea and received imperial sponsorship in Japan, after the fall of the Tang his writings were recovered from Korea and Japan and a Tiantai revival blossomed in the Song dynasty.

Zhiyi's work was the most complete and satisfying integration of the diversity of Indian Buddhism in east Asia. Fortunately, with the help of his disciple Guanding (561–632), Zhiyi's thought has been preserved in several major works, especially his magnum opus, the *Moho zhiguan* (*The Great Calming and Awareness Treatise*) and the *Fahua xuanyi* (*The Inner Meaning of the Lotus Sutra*). Because the Tiantai synthesis became the first enduring Chinese Buddhist school and laid the foundation for later east Asian Buddhism, Zhiyi is often considered China's most influential Buddhist thinker.

See also Buddhism in China; Buddhism: Chan (Zen).

Bibliography

Chappell, David, ed. *Tiantai Buddhism: An Outline of the Fourfold Teachings*. Tokyo: Daiichi shobô, 1983.

Donner, Neal, and Daniel B. Stevenson, *The Great Calming and Contemplation: A Study and Annotated Translation of the First Chapter of Zhiyi's Mo-ho zhiguan*. Honolulu: University of Hawaii Press, 1933.

Hurvitz, Leon. "Zhiyi (538–597): An Introduction to the Life and Ideas of a Chinese Monk." *Mélanges Chinois et Bouddhiques*, 12, 1960–1962, pp. 1–372.

Penkower, Linda. *Tiantai during the T'ang Dynasty: Chan-jan and the Sinification of Buddhism*. Ann Arbor, Mich.: University Microfilms, 1993.

Shinohara, Koichi. "Guanding's Biography of Zhiyi, the Fourth Chinese Patriarch of the Tiantai Tradition." In *Speaking of Monks: Religious Biography in India and China*, ed. Phyllis Granoff and Koichi Shinohara. New York: Mosaic, 1992, pp. 97–232.

Stevenson, Daniel. *The Tiantai Four Forms of Samâdhi and Late North-South Dynasties, Sui, and Early T'ang Buddhist Devotionalism*. Ann Arbor, Mich.: University Microfilms, 1987.

Swanson, Paul. *Foundations of Tiantai Philosophy: The Flowering of the Two Truths Theory in Chinese Buddhism*. Berkeley, Calif.: Asian Humanities, 1989.

Zhong (*Chung*) and *Shu*: Loyalty and Reciprocity

David S. Nivison

The classic text for *zhong* and *shu* as a related pair of concepts is *Lunyu* (*Analects*) 4.15:

> The master said, "Shen! In my *dao* (Way) there is one [idea] threading it together." Zengzi said, "Quite so." The master left. The disciples asked, "What did he mean?" Zengzi replied, "The master's Way consists of *zhong* and *shu* and nothing more."

This text is an insertion at least half a century, perhaps nearly two centuries, after Confucius's death, invented by followers of Zeng Shen, designed to enhance Zeng's status in the Confucian community—effective because mysterious (Brooks 1999). The vexing question left to the Confucian tradition has been, What are these two concepts, so important that they could be called the "one thread" of Confucius's Way?

Another text in the *Analects*, 15.24, which is also probably a late insertion (c. 300 B.C.E.), identifies *shu*:

> Zi Gong asked, "Is there one maxim that may be used as a guide for conduct throughout life?" The master replied, "Surely, *shu*! What you don't want done to yourself, do not inflict on others."

One concludes that *shu* is a (negative) formulation of the golden rule. This narrows the focus for *zhong*: it must denote an idea, at least as the word is used here, that can be in some sense appropriately mated with a form of the golden rule. There have been at least five theories.

1. The dominant explanation in the Confucian tradition in recent centuries was formulated in the Song dynasty by the philosopher Zhu Xi (1130–1200), commenting on *Analects* 4.15:

> Fully realizing the self is called *zhong*; extending the self is called *shu*. . . . Someone has said that "center disposition" (*zhongxin*, "center-heart") is *zhong*; "congruent disposition" (*ruxin*, "like-heart") is *shu*.

Zhu Xi goes on to apply Song metaphysical categories, identifying *zhong* as *ti* (substance) and *shu* as *yong* (function). This comment is at least in tune with ancient ways of thinking. There is the view in the *Mencius* (6A) that our moral dispositions are "inner" (*nei*), expressed in overt behavior. Confucians appropriate the ideal in the chapter *Tian xia* in *Zhuangzi*, of "the Way of sage inside, king outside" (*nei sheng wai wang*). Zhu thinks, probably, of *Zhongyong* (1), and its distinction between *zhong*, the central and inner, unexpressed; and *he*, the harmoniously manifested, in human emotions.

The obvious difficulty with Zhu Xi's solution is that *zhong* had, and continues to have, a very common meaning: it means "loyalty." Zhu has ignored this, seeing *shu* as "mental likeness"), an ideal of how I should behave toward you, or some other "like" myself, and (with suspect philology) *zhong* as "mental innerness," and so the inner cultivated state of character that manifests itself in *shu*. There is no easy way of connecting this imagined meaning with "loyalty."

2. Another theory is offered by a modern philosopher and historian of Chinese philosophy, Feng Youlan. Feng notices that the formulation of *shu* in the *Analects* is cast in the negative. He is no doubt aware that western missionary students of things Chinese had noticed this too, and in fact had invidiously contrasted Confucius with Jesus, whose statement of the golden rule in the Gospels is positive: "Do unto others what you would have others do to you." Surely, thought Feng, there must be positive statements in ancient Chinese philosophy too. Indeed there are, and Feng finds some of them:

> The term *ren* (benevolence) means that when you desire getting established (being received at court) for yourself, you help others to get established; and when you desire success for yourself, you help others to succeed. The ability to make a comparison (with the other person) from what is near at hand (from your own case) can simply be called the method of (attaining) *ren*. (*Analects* 6.30)

Feng finds more in the *Zhongyong*:

> *Zhong* and *shu* are not far from the Way (*dao*). If you would not be willing to have something done to yourself, then don't do it to others. The ways of the morally noble man (*junzi*) are four, and I (Confucius) have not yet mastered even one of them: What you would require of your son, use in serving your father; . . . what you would require of your subordinate, use in serving your prince; . . . what you would require of your younger brother, use in serving your elder brother; . . . what your would require of your friend, first apply in your treatment of him. . . . (13)

Feng concludes that since *shu* is a negative statement of the rule, here repeated first, *zhong* must be the positive statement of it, here exemplified in the "four ways."

Feng's solution in part has the defect of Zhu Xi's: it splits the artificially constructed philosopher's meaning of *zhong* off from its ancient and modern ordinary meaning, "loyalty." (Although some of the examples do look like loyalty, Feng's analysis easily admits instances that do not.) And it has another defect. Zhu at least was moving within a Chinese framework of thought; but Feng's problem—to find in the Chinese material a positive as well as a negative statement of the rule—is a modern western problem imposed on the analysis of Chinese philosophy.

And it is not even an ancient western problem; in fact, arguably it is no problem at all, outside the minds of modern Christian missionaries. If one examines ancient western religious literature, it is easy to find negative statements of the rule, as in Tertullian (*Adversus Marcionem*): "Even as you wish it to be done to you by other men, so also do you to them." But in the next breath, "Even as you wish it not to be done to you by other men, so also let you not do to them." The guiding intuition here is right. "Doing something" can be refraining from doing something. I am "doing" to you what I would have you "do" to me, i.e., behaving toward you as I would have you behave toward me, when I refrain from hitting you. The "problem" seems purely verbal.

3. Another (very interesting) attack on the difficulty starts from a reflection that is at least as old as Kant—whose "categorical imperative" would seem to have something of the golden rule in it: act so that you can will the maxim guiding your action to be a universal law. Kant thinks otherwise and sniffs at "the trivial *quod tibi non vis fieri*" maxim; it would have the absurd consequence that a judge must let a criminal off, because if in the criminal's position he would want to be let off himself. This is but one of a class of cases where mindlessly treating the other as you would want to be treated without taking into account the difference in your situations, and what is appropriate and right for each, would lead to obviously wrong action.

In brief, Confucius's *shu*, taken by itself *tout court*, needs help; and this must be so whether or not the ancient Chinese moralists were consciously aware of it. Herbert Fingarette sees this and argues that just as Jesus' summary of the law contains two propositions—"Love thy neighbor" preceded by "Love God"—so must Confucius's "one thread": be considerate (*shu*), but follow the substantive moral rules, which must be the meaning of *zhong* in Zeng Shen's statement; *zhong* Fingarette takes as *zhongxin*, "loyalty-faithfulness" (to principles of right, which Confucians would have granted are ordained by heaven—the equivalent, perhaps, of God).

It cannot be fairly charged against this ingenious solution that the concept inspiring it, the problem of the consistency and completeness of a set of rules, is a modern western one: the problem is real. But the solution does require that a meaning has to be assigned to *zhong* which is (probably) at best derivative rather than primary: loyalty is primarily to persons, and only after reflection to principles (which can conflict with loyalty to persons). But in fairness to Fingarette, it must be granted that *zhong* does sometimes have the meaning he needs.

Fingarette's idea also seems to require that *shu* be thought of as a decision procedure or (more precisely) that *zhong* and *shu* together be a decision procedure. The early modern Chinese philosopher Dai Zhen (1724–1777) did take *shu* this way. Dai's idea was that what at a refined stage of moral understanding one can conclude to be right, and therefore necessary (*biran*), must be based on what we sense naturally (*ziran*) to be good or desirable; the refining consists in using *shu* as a criterion: what seems good to me does not qualify as right unless you, and everyone, would feel the same way about it if our positions were reversed. But ancient Confucians probably thought of *shu* as an ideal quality of a cultivated character. Confucius is less likely to have felt the need of a moral decision procedure than to have sensed a need for a program of self-improvement (as *Analects* 6.30 suggests). Nonetheless, in the *Daxue* (10) we find a restatement of the ideal of reversability, which is actually called the (moral) "measuring square."

4. D. C. Lau has offered another interesting attempt to solve the problem of *zhongshu*. Lau explicitly takes *shu* as a decision procedure; *shu* by itself is, in his picture of Confucius, a procedure for answering the question "What ought I to do?" Lau thus ignores the difficulty Fingarette sees (since for Lau *shu* alone suffices) and fixes on another one: there is still the problem of being effectively moved to act. One must not object that Lau is sounding like Hume ("Facts alone can never sway me"), because in China the problem is ancient, from times much earlier than Confucius. Lau is thus led to propose that *zhong* completes *shu* in his required sense; it is a general injunction "Do your best." The problem again is that one has to squeeze, implausibly, to get this meaning out of *zhong*; it seems rather to be constructed to satisfy the analyst's need.

5. One more theory has been proposed (by the present author, Nivison); it does accept "loyalty" close to the ordinary sense as the meaning of *zhong*. This theory notices that *zhong* and *shu* are hierarchic opposites: ordinarily one thinks of "consideration" as applying to persons at one's social level or below, while "loyalty" applies to persons at one's level or above. Confucius's maxim was that one is not to "do to" or "inflict on" (*shu*) another what one would not want for oneself; and the word *shu* normally has this *downward* direction. In contrast, consider the use of *zhong* in *Analects* 5.19:

> Zi Zhang (the disciple Zhuansun Shi) asked the following question: "Zi Wen, the *lingyin* (prime minister of Chu) was three times appointed *lingyin*, and showed no sign of delight. He was three times dismissed, and showed no sigh of resentment. He always informed the incoming *lingyin* of the past administrative business of the *lingyin*'s office. What would you say of him?" The Master replied, "He was indeed *zhong*." Zi Zhang continued, "But was he *ren* (benevolent)?" Confucius answered, "I do not know yet (from what you have said) how he would qualify as *ren*."

If one recalls how *ren* is linked with the idea of *shu* in 6.30, here, it seems, Confucius himself is in effect contrasting *zhong* and *shu*. The contrast seems to be this. *Shu* bids me to be kind to *another* in an equal or lower position, consulting my own feelings and not hurting the other if I can avoid it, any more than I would want to be hurt if our positions were reversed. But *zhong* bids me to be strict with *myself* in dealing with another in an equal or higher position, disregarding my own feelings about myself if I must, and holding myself to at least the same high standard of behavior toward the other that I would expect him to observe toward me if our positions were reversed. The "ways" in *Zhongyong* (13) easily illustrate this analysis of *zhong*. We might think that one of the lines in the "measuring square" of *Daxue* (10) is even more obviously applicable: "What you would dislike in the one who precedes you, do not use in dealing with the one who comes after you." But this would seem to be *shu*, reciprocal considerateness. Zi Wen was *zhong*—he showed a principled loyalty to his ruler, in his selfless attitude toward office.

This analysis vindicates Fingarette in one way: *zhong* does imply an objective and public standard. One could even say that if *zhong* is *zhongxin*, it combines adherence to the public standard with being bound (in *xin*, being true to one's word) by any special responsibilities one has created for oneself by making promises. But Fingarette would have *zhong* and *shu* apply to the same case in combination, checking each other, whereas for Nivison they apply primarily to different socially contrasting cases. Thus Fingarette seems committed to the view that if one treats an inferior with both *zhong* and *shu*—considerately, but according to objective moral standards—one is being "loyal" to that person (if *zhong* somehow still means "loyal").

Does this solution overlook the difficulty that prompted Fingarette's analysis, the need to put spine into "consideration" lest it lead to morally wrong action? Perhaps not, for when we look at Chinese explications of the ideal of reversability (as in *Zhongyong* 13; and *Daxue* 10), we find that the ideal is not abstract but is typically thought of as embedded in specific social relationships which will supply by implication the needed objective standards. Both Nivison's and Fingarette's concepts of *zhong*, furthermore, can be given a philological backing: *zhong* must be, not "mental innerness," as Zhu Xi thought, but "mentally being on the mark," taking the root *zhong* in a common ancient sense of hitting the center of a target.

A striking formulation by another of the Song philosophers seems at first to establish conclusively the solution under review. Zhang Zai (1020–1077) has *Zhongyong* (13) before him (*Zhengmeng*, ch. 2, Sec. 8) and so must be thinking of *zhong* and *shu*:

> If one holds oneself responsible just as one is disposed to hold others responsible, then one realizes the Way completely. This is illustrated by the words "the ways of the morally noble man are four; and I, Confucius, have not yet been able to attain even one of them." If one loves others just as one is disposed to love oneself, then one realizes benevolence (*ren*) completely. This is illustrated by the words "if something were done to you and you wouldn't want it, then for your part don't do it to others."

"Holding oneself responsible" was in effect the proposed sense of *zhong*. And "loving others as oneself" is (as also in western religion) often and easily thought of as a formulation of what Confucius called *shu*, "consideration."

But in the end Nivison's solution too is not satisfactory. While *Analects* 5.19 (on Zi Wen) does illustrate the analysis of *zhong* as "holding oneself responsible," none of the Chinese analyses in terms of "holding oneself responsible" clearly and explicitly labels this idea *zhong*. Even Zhang Zai could be saying that *zhong* and *shu* together—to be distinguished in some other way, if at all—have the two aspects of kindness toward others and strictness with oneself. Worse, at least one ancient Chinese analysis explicitly gives the label *shu* to the idea of being strict with oneself. Consider the following passage from *Xunzi*, in the chapter *Fa xing* ("Law and Practice"):

> Confucius said, "The noble man has three (rules of) *shu*: (1) To have a ruler one cannot serve (properly), and yet to have a subject one seeks to employ (i.e., holding him to a proper standard of service), is not *shu*. (2) To have parents one cannot repay, and yet to have a son and to require filial piety of him, is not *shu*. (3) To have an elder brother and be unable to give him proper respect, and yet to have a younger brother and to require obedience of him, is not *shu*. If a gentleman understands these three kinds of *shu*, then he will be able to straighten himself.

The writer (perhaps later than Xunzi) is obviously rephrasing *Zhongyong* (13), or he is a source for the author of that text. Thus Nivison's proposal too is doubtable. Pseudo-Zengzi's challenge remains: the exact proper analysis of *zhong* and *shu* is still an open problem.

See also Confucianism: Vision; *Zhong* and *Xin*.

Bibliography

Alton, Bruce Scott. "An Examination of the Golden Rule." Ph.D. dissertation, Stanford University, 1966. Ann Arbor, Mich.: University Microfilms (67–4315).

Brooks, E. Bruce, with the assistance of A. Taeko Brooks. *The Original Analects: Sayings of Confucius and His Successors, 479–249*. New York: Columbia University Press, 1999.

Dai, Zhen. *Menzi ziyi shuzheng*, 1777. (Reprinted in Hu Shi. *Dai Dongyuan di zhexue*. Shanghai: Shangwu, 1927. See especially Secs. 1.2 and 1.5, pp. 41 and 46.)

Fingarette, Herbert, "Following the 'One Thread' in the *Analects*." *Journal of the American Academy of Religion*, 47(3S), 1979, pp. 373–405. (Thematic Issue: Studies in Classical Chinese Thought.)

Fung, Yulan (Feng Youlan). *A Short History of Chinese Philosophy*. New York: Macmillan, 1948. (See also paperback reprint, New York: Free Press, 1966, pp. 43–44.)

Kant, Immanuel. *Groundwork of the Metaphysic of Morals*, trans. H. J. Paton. New York: Harper Torchbooks, 1964, p. 97 (See also original 2nd ed. and Royal Prussian Academy ed., pp. 68, 430.)

Lau, D. C., trans. *Confucius: The Analects*. Harmondsworth: Penguin, 1979, pp. 15–16. (See also reprint, 1984.)

Nivison, David S. "Golden Rule Arguments in Chinese Moral Philosophy." In *The Ways of Confucianism: Investigations in Chinese Philosophy*, ed. Bryan W. Van Norden. La Salle, Ill.: Open Court, 1996, pp. 97–130.

Zhong (*Chung*) and *Xin* (*Hsin*): Loyalty and Trustworthiness

Kwong-loi Shun

Zhong (devotion, loyalty) and *xin* (trustworthiness) often occur in combination in Confucian texts. Three passages in the *Lunyu* (*Analects*), which records Confucius's teachings, advocate *zhongxin* as a guiding principle in one's life (1.8, 9.25, 12.10), and other passages also mention the two together (1.4, 5.28, 7.25, 15.6). The combination *zhongxin* occurs in other early Confucian texts such as the *Mengzi*, or *Mencius* (1A.5, 6A.16, 7A.32, 7B,37), and the *Xunzi* (e.g., 2.22, 7.33, 8.19), showing that *zhong* and *xin* are closely related.

Zhong can refer to an attitude directed to superiors, and it is often translated as "loyalty" in such contexts. However, even in such contexts, *zhong* is not a matter of blind obedience to superiors but is guided by a sense of what is proper. For example, while the *Lunyu* sometimes speaks of serving a ruler with *zhong* (e.g., 3.19), it also advocates remonstrating with the ruler when appropriate (14.22; cf. 14.7) and emphasizes serving a ruler with the Way, *dao* (11.24). Similarly, the historical text *Guoyu* idealizes *zhong* in the sense of following propriety (*yi*) in serving the ruler, rather than blindly obeying the ruler (7.5B.9–12). The *Xunzi* observes that *zhong* may involve disobeying the ruler when appropriate, though it also emphasizes that if one is to be successful in one's remonstrations, one should remonstrate gently to avoid angering the ruler (ch. 13). It also makes explicit that what one follows in government is the Way rather than the ruler, just as what one follows in the family is propriety rather than one's father (29.1–2).

So, even when directed to the ruler, *zhong* is guided by a sense of one's proper responsibilities. Sometimes, *zhong* is mentioned in relation to one's responsibilities in government, without specifically mentioning one's superiors. For example, the *Lunyu* describes Lingyin Ziwen's devotion to his responsibilities in government as *zhong* (5.19) and links *zhong* to devotion to one's responsibilities in government (12.14). Besides devotion to one's proper responsibilities in government, *zhong* can also describe one's dealings with others that are not set in a governmental context. For example, the *Lunyu* refers to *zhong* in connection with working for other people's interests (1.4) and observes that one should be *zhong* in dealing with others even when among barbarians (13.19). It refers to *zhong* in properly guiding one's friends (12.23), and the *Mengzi* also refers to *zhong* in connection with guiding others to goodness (3A.4). In these examples, *zhong* has to do with wholehearted devotion to serving or guiding others, in a way that is regulated by a sense of what is proper.

Xin has the meaning "to trust," and it is often used in connection with one's words (*yan*). For example, the *Lunyu* speaks of *xin* in one's words when one is interacting with friends (1.7), and it observes that *xin* enables one to repeat one's words (1.13). Words in turn are often mentioned in connection with one's actions, with an emphasis on the match between words and actions (*Lunyu* 5.10, 13.3, 14.27; cf. *Mengzi* 7B: 37 and *Zhongyong*, ch. 13); since it is difficult to live up to one's words, one should always be cautious with them (*Lunyu* 1.14, 4.22, 4.24, 14.20). So one important aspect of *xin* has to do with a match between one's words and actions, and such a match links up with the idea of trust, in that one's words about one's actions can be trusted when the match obtains.

It is likely, though, that *xin* has to do more generally with the quality of being worthy of trust, which includes but goes beyond a match between words and actions. The *Lunyu* observes that the superior person should be *xin* before working the common people hard or remonstrating with superiors; if he is without *xin*, the common people will regard him as being harsh to them and superiors will regard him as slandering them (19.10). Although the superior person's words are involved in issuing orders to the common people or remonstrating with superiors, *xin* in this case is a matter not of the superior person's matching his own actions to his words, but of whether he can be trusted with regard to what he represents to others by his words. In working the people hard, he represents the situation as one in which hard work is in the people's own interest; in remonstrating with superiors, he represents himself as doing so for the good of the state. He can be trusted with regard to such representations if he is *xin*, but he will be viewed as exploiting the people and slandering superiors if he is not *xin*.

So *xin* is the quality of being worthy of trust, a quality that one attains through a history of matching one's representation of things to the way things are. To have this quality is not necessarily to be actually trusted by others but only to be deserving of trust (e.g., *Xunzi* 6.38–41). Sometimes *xin* is paired with *cheng* (wholeness, sincerity) in early texts (e.g., *Xunzi* 2.23). The difference between *cheng* and *xin* is that whereas *cheng* emphasizes one's truly and fully having something in oneself, *xin* emphasizes the match between the way things are and one's outward representation of things. To put this differently, whereas *xin* emphasizes that there is no discrepancy between the way one represents things outwardly and the way things are, *cheng* emphasizes that there are no discrepancies in the inner workings of the heart. *Cheng* involves being fully devoted to what is ethical and not being subject to the slightest influence that might lead one to deviate from what is proper.

Just like *zhong*, *xin* is important both in the political context and in one's daily interactions with others. The *Lunyu* stresses the importance of *xin* among those in power (e.g., 1.5, 19.10; cf. *Zhongyong*, chs. 29, 31) and describes trust by the common people as more important than military preparedness or adequate provisions (12.7); it also emphasizes the importance of *xin* in one's dealings with friends (1.4, 1.7, 5.26; cf. *Mengzi* 3A.4, 4A.12). The *Daxue* stresses the need for *xin* in one's interactions with people in the state (ch. 3). The difference between *zhong* and *xin* is that whereas *zhong* emphasizes devotion to fulfilling one's proper responsibilities and to working for the good of others, *xin* emphasizes trustworthiness in one's dealings with others. The contrast is highlighted in the *Lunyu*, which links *zhong* to working for others' interests and *xin* to interaction with friends (1.4).

There is one important difference in the way *zhong* and *xin* are described in the *Lunyu*. As we have seen, *zhong* already involves a conception of what is proper in that, to be really *zhong*, one has to be guided by such a conception in serving others. *Xin*, on the other hand, is presented in the *Lunyu* as something that requires supplementation by such a concept. For example, it is said that one who is insistent on *xin* in words and on carrying actions to the end is a petty person

(13.20; cf. *Mengzi* 4B.11). Likewise, the *Xunzi* contrasts *xin* with *yi* (propriety) in the political context and describes *xin* as second in importance to *yi* (16.79–80); it also contrasts a true king (*wang*) who bases himself on *yi* with an overlord (*ba*) who bases himself on *xin* (11.3–4). So while *xin* is generally desirable, it has to be regulated by a conception of what is proper.

Zhong and *xin* continue to be key concepts for later Confucian thinkers, although there have been significant changes in the way they are understood. For example, partly owing to the influence of the theory of the five processes (*wuxing*), Han Confucian thinkers such as Yang Xiong (53 B.C.E.–18 C.E.; 3.2A–2B) and Xun Yue (C.E. 148–209; 1.1B) both listed *xin* along with *ren* (humaneness), *yi* (propriety), *li* (observance of rites), and *zhi* (wisdom), the four attributes highlighted in Mencius's thinking; and Xun Yue explicitly referred to them as five virtues (*de*). Later, Han Yu (768–824) listed the five as five aspects of nature, *xing* (11.6A), and Zhou Dunyi (1017–1073) referred to them as the five norms that are based on *cheng*—wholeness, sincerity (14–15). Thus *xin* gradually came to be regarded as an aspect of the highest Confucian ideal, rather than as something that, though generally desirable, can still be problematic unless regulated by a sense of what is proper.

The way *zhong* and *xin* are understood and related has also undergone significant changes, as illustrated by the way Zhu Xi (1130–1200) viewed them. Citing a saying of Cheng Yi (1033–1107) that "being single-hearted is what is meant by *cheng*, and fully devoting one's heart is what is meant by *zhong*," Zhu explained *zhong* in terms of fully devoting one's heart. In the sage, *cheng* involves fully cultivating the ethical attributes in oneself so that one is able to respond appropriately and without effort to the situations one confronts. *Zhong*, on the other hand, is the function (*yong*) of *cheng*; it is the outward manifestation of *cheng* in one's fully and properly devoting oneself when dealing with affairs. That is, *cheng* emphasizes the full or real (*shi*) presence of the ethical attributes within oneself while *zhong* emphasizes one's total devotion when dealing with affairs on the outside. The two are related because it is owing to *cheng*, the real presence of the ethical attributes, that one is *zhong* in dealing with things.

A similar distinction can be drawn for specific areas of life. For example, with regard to filial piety, to be *cheng* means that the appropriate attitude toward parents is fully present in oneself, without a single incongruous thought or inclination. To be *zhong*, on the other hand, means that one is fully and properly devoted to observing one's responsibilities to parents and in one's dealings with them generally (*Daxue zhangju*, ch. 10; *Zhongyong zhangju*, ch. 13; *Lunyu jizhu* 1.4; *Zhuzi yulei*, 485–490, 2486).

As for *xin*, Zhu Xi contrasted it with *zhong* by saying that whereas *zhong* involves fully devoting oneself, *xin* involves making real (*shi*) the things and affairs one deals with. *Xin* is the function (*yong*) of *zhong* in that *zhong* describes the attitude of fully devoting oneself while *xin* describes the way one deals with things on the basis of such devotion. For example, in telling someone about certain things, *zhong* is a matter of being devoted to informing the other person of the relevant details. Given this devotion, one will accurately represent what is the case and what is not the case, and this is *xin*. To take another example, in employing officials in government, *zhong* involves being devoted to employing those most suited to the office. Given this devotion, one will employ those who are able and worthy and dismiss those who are not, and this is *xin* in that one's employment and dismissal of officials matches the officials' ability and worth. So while *zhong* emphasizes one's state of mind, *xin* emphasizes how one deals with things and affairs in a way that conforms to the way they are, making one deserving of trust by others (*Daxue zhangju*, ch. 10; *Lunyu jizhu* 1.4; *Zhuzi yulei*, 485–490).

For Zhu Xi, just as *zhong* is a manifestation of *cheng*, *xin* is also a manifestation of *cheng*. *Cheng* emphasizes the real presence of the ethical attributes, *zhong* the full devotion to others that flows from *cheng*, and *xin* the match between the way things are and one's way of dealing with things, which flows from this devotion. This conception of the relation between the three illustrates how key concepts from early Confucian texts are dramatically transformed in later Confucian thought.

See also *Cheng*; Confucianism: Vision; *Zhong* and *Shu*.

Bibliography

Daxue (Great Learning). (References are by chapter numbers, following Zhu Xi's division of the text, to James Legge, trans. *Confucius: Confucian Analects, The Great Learning, and the Doctrine of the Mean*, 2nd ed. Oxford: Clarendon, 1893.)

Guoyu. (References are by volume, page, and line numbers to *Tiansheng mingdao ben* edition.)

Han, Yu. *Han Changli Chuanji*. In the *Sibu beiyao* Series. (References are by volume and page numbers.)

Lunyu (Analects). (References are by book and passage numbers to Yang Bojun, trans. *Lunyu yizhu*. Beijing: Zhonghua shuju, 1980; modern Chinese. See also D. C. Lau, trans. *Confucius: The Analects*. London: Penguin, 1979.)

Mengzi (Mencius). (References are by book and passage numbers—with book numbers 1A to 7B substituted for 1 to 14—to Yang Bojun, trans. *Mengzi yizhu*. Beijing: Zhonghua shuju, 1984; modern Chinese. See also D. C. Lau, trans. *Mencius*. London: Penguin, 1970.)

Xun, Yue. *Shenjian*. In the *Sibu beiyao* Series. (References are by volume and page numbers.)

Xunzi. (References are by chapter and line numbers to the text in Harvard-Yenching Institute Sinological Index Series. See also John Knoblock, trans. *Xunzi: A Translation and Study of the Complete Works*, 3 vols. Stanford, Calif.: Stanford University Press, 1988–1994.)

Yang, Xiong. *Fayan*. In *Sibu beiyao* Series. (References are by volume and page numbers.)

Zhou, Dunyi. *Zhou Dunyi ji*. Beijing: Zhonghua shuju, 1990. (References are by page numbers.)

Zhongyong (Centrality and Commonality, or Doctrine of the Mean). (References are by chapter numbers, following Zhu Xi's division of the text, to James Legge, trans. *Confucius: Confucian Analects, The Great Learning, and the Doctrine of the Mean*, 2nd ed. Oxford: Clarendon, 1893.)

Zhu, Xi. *Daxue zhangju* (Commentary on the *Daxue*). (References follow the chapter numbering of the *Daxue*.)

———. *Lunyu jizhu* (Commentary on the Analects). (References follow the passage numbering of the *Lunyu*. See also Wing-tsit Chan, trans. and comp. *A Source Book in Chinese Philosophy*. Princeton, N.J.: Princeton University Press, 1963, ch. 34.)

———. *Zhongyong zhangju* (Commentary on the *Zhongyong*). (References follow the chapter numbering of the *Zhongyong*.)

———. *Zhuzi yulei*. Beijing: Zhonghua shuju, 1986. (References are by passage numbers.)

Zhongyong (*Chung yung*): The Doctrine of the Mean

Yanming AN

Zhongyong (*Zhong yong*, *Chung yung*)—*The Doctrine of the Mean* or *Centrality and Commonality*—is one of the most important Confucian classics. Originally it was a relatively obscure chapter (ch. 31) in the *Liji* (*Records of Ritual*) that Dai Sheng compiled in the Former Han dynasty (206 B.C.E.–8 C.E). Later, in the Song dynasty (960–1279), it was selected by Zhu Xi (1130–1200) as part of the Four Books, along with *Lunyu* (the *Analects* of Confucius), *Mengzi* (*Mencius*), and *Daxue* (*The Great Learning*). From 1313 until 1905, it was a basic text for the national civil service examination.

Despite *Zhongyong*'s lofty position in premodern China, dispute about its authorship has never ceased. Sima Qian (born c. 135 B.C.E.), the author of *Shiji* (*Records of the Grand Historian*), first stated that Zi Si, the grandson of Confucius, had "composed *Zhongyong*." This opinion was widely accepted by mainstream scholars, including the classicists Zheng Xuan (127–200) and Kong Yingda (574–648) and the philosophers Li Ao (772–841) and Zhu Xi. Ouyang Xiu (1007–1072) in the Song dynasty may have been the first major scholar to begin to question the legitimacy of this opinion. He was then echoed by other Song scholars, such as Ye Shi (1150–1223) and Wang Bo (1197–1274). Later in the Qing dynasty, more scholars, including Yuan Mei (1716–1798) and Cui Shu (1740–1816), joined the skeptics. They carefully examined the *Zhongyong*, textually and in terms of its intellectual content, and found that contradictions and inconsistencies arose when Zi Si was taken to be its author. In the present era, the majority of scholars, including Feng Youlan and Qian Mu, have sided with the skeptics. They generally agree that *Zhongyong* was composed by more than one person, and its composition might be dated roughly from the third century B.C.E.

Zhongyong is unusual in the Confucian tradition because it deals systematically (if briefly) with two subjects, human nature and the Way of heaven, on which Confucius's disciples "could hardly hear his views" (*Analects* 5.12). This may account for the fact that, in comparison with other Confucian classics, it elicited more enthusiastic commentaries and exegeses from the Confucian circle, as well as from certain Buddhist schools. The most notable were by Zheng Xuan and Zhu Xi.

Zheng Xuan was the first commentator on *Zhongyong*. Because he lived close in time to the composition of the text, his commentary preserved the original meanings of many characters, phrases, expressions, and paragraphs. Thus it has been regarded as a solid foundation on which all the later interpretations and exegeses developed. Zhu Xi is important in *Zhongyong* scholarship for other reasons: as a great thinker, he creatively synthesized what his neo-Confucian predecessors had done with the text, and he also introduced new philosophical insights as part of his own interpretation. Zhu rearranged the chapters of *Zhongyong*, outlined its central theses, and reinterpreted a number of crucial terms, providing a highly consistent elucidation of the text. Since 1313, when Zhu's commentary was decreed a standard interpretation, its authoritative position has never been seriously challenged.

Zhongyong may be divided into four parts, according to its intellectual content.

1. The first part (ch. 1), as Zhu Xi indicated, is the "quintessence" (*tiyao*) of the whole text. It explicitly defines five key concepts: "human nature" (*xing*), "Way" (*dao*), "education" (*jiao*), "equilibrium" (*zhong*), and "harmony" (*he*). They jointly constitute a philosophical framework regarding the relationship of heaven and humans, or the heavenly Way and human nature. Human nature is something imparted by heaven, so its substance is unchangeable. Humans have a mandate or obligation to follow the guidance of this nature. Nevertheless, as earthly beings, they may frequently depart from it to satisfy their desires. Herein lies the necessity of education. In essence, education means an endeavor to teach people the propriety of maintaining their nature, and to prevent them from taking a wrong direction. By the same token, a gentleman (*junzi*) should be always watchful over his innermost mind, to prevent it from straying from human nature.

Zhongyong indicates that human nature contains all kinds of potential feelings: pleasure, anger, sorrow, and joy. The state before the feelings are aroused is called "equilibrium," and the state in which the feelings arise and attain their due measure and degree is called "harmony." "Equilibrium" is a "great root" (*daben*), because all human activities in the world grow from it. "Harmony" is a universal path (*dadao*), because it has been taken by all the great figures from antiquity until now. According to *Zhongyong*, when "equilibrium" and "harmony" are realized to their high degree, heaven and earth will attain their proper order and all things will flourish.

2. The second part of *Zhongyong* (chs. 2–11) quotes a number of statements from Confucius to explain the term *zhongyong* (the mean) and people's various attitudes toward it. "The mean" refers to a perfect virtue whereby a person will be neither one-sided nor extreme. As Confucius observed, for a long time few people have been able to hold to this virtue. Intelligent and worthy people went beyond it; stupid and unworthy people did not come up to it. If some people might happen to choose the mean, they could not maintain it long—not even for a month. Confucius sighed, "The empire, the states, and the families can be put in order. Ranks and emolument can be declined. A bare, naked weapon can be tramped upon. But the mean cannot [easily] be attained" (ch. 9; Chan 1963, 99). Despite this difficulty, however, the mean is not unreachable. As both evidence and encouragement, Confucius introduced two exemplars, Yan Hui (his disciple) and Shun (one of the sage kings), who practiced the mean through their lives. His point is that people should model themselves on these ethically superior individuals, who are "in accord with the mean." These exemplars, "though retired from the world and . . . unknown to their age" still have no regrets (Sec. 11; Chan, 100)

3. The third part of *Zhongyong* (chs.12–19), in a miscellaneous manner, quotes Confucius's words to explain the universality of the way. The central thesis is that the Way functions everywhere and yet is hidden. It is so great that nothing in the world can contain it; and it is so small that nothing in the world can split it. It lies in the private relationship between man and woman and, at the same time, shines brightly through heaven and earth. Confucius insisted that "the Way is not far from man" (ch. 13). Thus, one who truly pursues it should pay particular attention to things at hand rather than what is remote and difficult. Specifically, he needs to apply the principles of "conscientiousness" (*zhong*) and "reciprocity" (*shu*) consistently in his daily life: to do what is proper to his position and never want to go beyond it; and not to do to others what he does not wish them to do to him.

Furthermore, according to Confucius, the Way exists in any situation in which a man lives. No matter what the man is—whether he is wealthy and honorable or poor and humble, whether he is sorrowful or in difficulties, even if he is entangled with a barbarian tribe—he can still find, pursue, and practice the Way. The practice of the Way and its final achievement can be compared to traveling a long distance or ascending a high mountain. To reach a distant goal or climb to a great height, one needs to starts from the nearest point or the lowest ground (ch. 15). The ancient sages—Shun, King Wen, King Wu, and Duke Zhou—were men who finally attained the greatest goal and the loftiest height. And because they occupied a position of rulership, their personal success was necessarily translated into a prevalence of the Way during their own time.

4. The final part of *Zhongyong* (chs. 20–33) extensively explores the content of *cheng*, a pivotal idea in the text. In general, *cheng* has two meanings, which can be roughly rendered by two English terms, "sincerity" and "reality." The first meaning designates a psychological effort to be sincere to oneself and to others.

The second signifies the substance shared by humans and heaven. The textual sequence of *Zhongyong* shows that the idea of *cheng* first emerged from people's social-ethical life and then was applied to describe what is in nature.

According to *Zhongyong, cheng* is the ultimate source or origin of all moral behavior. There are five "universal paths" (*dadao*), which refer, respectively, to five human relationships: ruler and minister, father and son, husband and wife, elder and younger brother, friend and friend. We are enabled to handle these five relationships properly by three "universal virtues" (*dade*): wisdom (*zhi*), humaneness (*ren*), and courage (*yong*). What underlies these three virtues is "one" principle: *cheng* (ch. 20). For those in superior positions, *cheng* is a key to directing an empire, a state, or a family. There are "nine standards" (*jing*) for governing "the empire, its states, and families": (1) cultivating one's own character, (2) honoring the worthy, (3) having affection for one's relatives, (4) respecting the great ministers, (5) treating the whole body of officers considerately, (6) dealing with the common people as if they were one's own children, (7) attracting all classes of artisans, (8) showing tenderness to foreigners, and (9) kindly cherishing the feudal lords. Here, as with the "five universal paths," *cheng* is the principle that leads to the implementation of "nine standards" (ch. 20). Finally, for those in inferior positions, *cheng* is a key to successfully fulfilling their social duties. The reasoning in *Zhongyong* is that if a person who knows the good (*shan*) is sincere with himself (*chengshen*), then he will be obedient to his parents, and then he will be trusted by his friends, and then he will have the confidence of his superiors, and then he will be able to govern people. This is reminiscent of similar reasoning in the *Mencius* (4B.12).

Zhongyong distinguishes two categories: "*cheng* as such" (*chengzhe*), which is the "Way of heaven"; and "striving to be *cheng*" (*chengzhizhe*), which is the "way of humans" (ch. 20). In other words, "*cheng* as such" refers to the reality of heaven, whereas "striving to be *cheng*" refers to a moral effort to live in accordance with the reality of heaven, and to retain the human nature imparted by heaven. Accordingly, the text distinguishes two kinds of good persons: the sage, who embodies "*cheng* as such"; and the worthy, who embodies "striving to be *cheng*."

The sage stands as a spiritual link between humans and heaven. As a man, he lives with ordinary people and shares their earthly feelings. Concurrently, as a morally perfect man, he hits on what is right without effort, apprehends without thinking, and is naturally and easily in harmony with the way (ch. 20). Because he can fully develop or completely preserve his own nature, he is able to develop fully the nature of others and that of things, to assist in the transforming and nourishing process of heaven and earth, and thus to form a trinity with heaven and earth (ch. 22). For the same reason, the sage can order and adjust relations in the world and establish a foundation for the world (ch. 32). Nor is this all: he can even foretell if a nation or family will flourish or perish, or experience calamity or happiness. He is as great as spirit (ch. 24).

The sage is illustrated in *Zhongyong* as a spring from which a great river flows to transform (*hua*) people. Moreover, since all humans are endowed with the same nature, they all possess a capacity for being transformed. Because of this correspondence between the two sides—the sage and humanity—the transformation itself is a natural process, which originates with the sage and is gradually realized in the people. As for the sage's achievement, the key is not political techniques, such as reward and punishment, but the development or preservation of his own nature. After all, as *Zhongyong* stresses, "in influencing people, the use of sound or appearance (*shengse*) is of secondary importance" (ch. 33). What people really need is simply a silent but morally perfect model that they can imitate.

In contrast, the slightly lesser "worthies" are a group of people who are first transformed. They study *cheng* extensively, inquire into it accurately, ponder it and sift it carefully, and practice it earnestly (ch. 20). Because of the enlightenment (*ming*) they acquire through their education at the hands of the sage, they may eventually attain the realm of "*cheng* as such" (ch. 21).

Cheng originates in people's social life but then extends to what is in nature. In this new context, *cheng* primarily refers to an attribute that may be roughly rendered by a combination of three English terms: "consistency," "constancy," and "regularity." *Cheng* manifests itself in the regular motions of heavenly bodies, the predictable changes of four seasons, the constant flowing of rivers, and the life cycle of plants. *Zhongyong* emphasizes that *cheng* is the reality of a thing, even the reality of nature as a whole: "*Cheng* is the beginning and end of things. Without *cheng* there would be nothing" (ch. 25). Because of *cheng*, heaven always overshadows and embraces all things, earth always supports and contains all things, and categories of things, such as trees, always retain their identity. At the same time, *cheng* is described as a source of production and reproduction of a "myriad of things." Because heaven and earth possess *cheng* as their reality, "so they produce things in an unfathomable way" (ch. 26).

To elucidate what *cheng* in nature is and why it is responsible for production and reproduction, *Zhong-*

yong introduces many graphic terms: "ceaselessness" (*wuxi*), as in the flowing of a river; "everlasting" (*buyi*), as in the motions of heavenly bodies; "nondoubleness" (*bu'er*), as in the impression we have when comparing a mountain today with the same mountain ten years ago. It is noteworthy that these terms are also used to identify the sage. Thus *Zhongyong* conveys a deep belief in the unity of heaven-nature and humans, represented by the sage. The two parts of the unity are combined by *cheng*, and the unity itself is realized through *cheng*. People can understand the *cheng* of heaven-nature through that of the sage, and the *cheng* of the sage through that of heaven-nature.

This throws light on the connection between the two uses of *cheng*: "sincerity" and "reality." Now "to be sincere" is no longer a matter of personal choice. Instead, it is a mandate from heaven (nature), a moral imperative that people are duty-bound to comply with, and an act through which they can prove and exhibit their reality as human beings. *Cheng* in heaven (nature) serves as a great mirror reminding people to be sincere, while the *cheng* of the sage provides them with a concrete model of the desirability of being sincere. Both aspects of *cheng* encourage universal sincerity among people. In the final analysis, this also means that people are not alienated from their reality, and that social harmony will eventually materialize throughout the world.

See also *Cheng*; Confucianism: Constructs of Classical Thought.

Bibliography

Cua, A. S. "Confucian Vision and Experience of the World." *Philosophy East and West*, 25(3), 1975, pp. 319–333. (Reprinted in *Moral Vision and Tradition: Essays in Chinese Ethics*. Washington, D.C.: Catholic University of America Press, 1998.)

Tu, Weiming. *Centrality and Commonality*. Honolulu: University of Hawaii Press, 1976.

Wang, Fuzhi. *Du sishu daquan shuo*. Beijing: Zhonghua shuju, 1975.

Wu, Yi. *Zhongyong cheng de zhexue*. Taipei: Dongda tushu gongsi, 1976.

Zhao, Shunsun. *Zhongyong zhuanshu*. Shanghai: Huadong shifan daxue chubanshe, 1992.

Zheng, Xuan, and Kong Yingda. "Liji zhushu." In *Shisan jing zhushu*. Beijing: Zhonghua shuju, 1980.

Zhu, Xi. *Zhongyong zhangju*. In *Sishu jizhu*, Beijing: Zhonghua shuju, 1986. (See Wing-tsit Chan, trans. and comp. *The Doctrine of the Mean*. In *A Source Book in Chinese Philosophy*. Princeton, N.J.: Princeton University Press, 1969. See also James Legge, trans. *The Doctrine of the Mean*. In *Confucius: Confucian Analects, The Great Learning, and The Doctrine of the Mean*. New York: Dover, 1971.)

———. *Zhuzi yulei*. Beijing: Zhonghua shuju, 1986.

Zhou Dunyi (Chou Tun-i)

Tze-ki Hon

Zhou Dunyi (Chou Tun-i, 1017–1073)—also known as Zhou Lianxi and Zhou Maoshu—was a pioneer of neo-Confucianism. Zhou was a native of Daozhou in present-day Hunan. He spent most of his life working as a minor official at the provincial level. During one of his postings in southwestern China, he tutored the young Cheng brothers—Cheng Hao (1032–1085) and Cheng Yi (1033–1107)—who later became the leading neo-Confucian thinkers of their time. In the last few years of his life, Zhou retired to the picturesque Mount Lu in central China. He named his study at his home there after the stream Lianxi ("stream of waterfalls"), hence his courtesy name Lianxi and his posthumous honorific Master Lianxi.

Zhou Dunyi is generally considered the first eleventh-century thinker who redefined Confucian ethics and metaphysics. He is credited particularly with making a sophisticated argument for the inseparability of ethics and metaphysics. His two writings—*Taiji tushuo* (*An Explanation of the Diagram of the Great Ultimate*) and *Tongshu* or *Yi tongshu* (*Penetrating the Book of Changes*)—are regarded by many as the major neo-Confucian statements on moral metaphysics.

In the *Taiji tushuo*, as the title indicates, Zhou comments on a diagram of the "great ultimate," *taiji tu* (Fung 1953, 436; *Song Yuan xue'an* 12.1A), depicting the evolution of the universe. This diagram consists of five circles, as follows.

The top circle, symbolizing the universe as a whole, is empty. The figure of a circle indicates that the universe is an organic entity with no beginning and no end. Also, like a bouncing ball, the universe is always in motion. Movement and self-regeneration are the two hallmarks of the universe.

The second circle contains three intersecting semicircles, colored dark and light. The dark semicircles represent the *yin* (the yielding cosmic force); the light semicircles represent the *yang* (the active cosmic force). The intersections of the semicircles symbolize the dynamics of the *yin* and the *yang* as a bipolar, complementary pair. In their pushing and pulling, the *yin* and the *yang* provide the source of motion for the universe's self-regeneration.

The third circle is the most complicated. It is a group of five small circles, each symbolizing one of the "five phases" (*wuxing*)—water, fire, wood, metal, and earth. These five small circles represent the five material forces driving all activities and revitalizing all beings in the universe. To highlight the interconnection among the five material forces, the five circles are arranged in a rectangle with lines linking each circle to the others. The circle for "earth" is at the center of the rectangle; the other four circles are at the corners. This arrangement signifies that the "earth force" is the source of the other four forces. One interesting feature of the group in the third circle is that it is linked to the second circle by a tiny "V" sign. This sign shows that the five phases are products of the interaction of *yin* and *yang*.

Like the first circle, the fourth and fifth circles are empty. Together these two empty circles symbolize the organic process by which *yin* and *yang* produce the "myriad beings." Focusing on biological reproduction, the fourth circle depicts how the *yin* moves the female and the *yang* moves the male. The fifth circle likens the process by which the myriad beings are produced to the union of the two sexes. Also in these last two circles, the intangible cosmic forces in the universe are manifested in the creation of the multitude of beings.

On the basis of this diagram of the "great ultimate," Zhou Dunyi makes three important statements about the universe. First, the universe has material existence. It creates and propels itself by the dynamics of the *yin* and the *yang*, and their derivatives, the five phases. The universe is not, as the Buddhists claim, nonexistence. Second, the universe is organic. It is constantly in motion to renew itself—so much so that one may say its being is its becoming. Its essence is its inner propensity to transform itself. Third, the universe and the myriad beings are interdependent as part and whole. In essence, the universe and the myriad beings are the same, because both are the products of the *yin* and the *yang*. But their functions are different. The universe is the whole that brings the myriad beings together as a family of beings. The myriad beings, each unique in its own right, are the parts that make the universe alive. Part and whole—like sound and echo, shape and shadow—require each other. While the universe unifies the myriad beings, the myriad beings enliven the universe.

Zhou's last point is particularly important in the development of Confucian metaphysics. Medieval Confucian metaphysics, summarized in a commentary by Kong Yingda (574–648) on the *Book of Changes*, gives preference to the whole at the expense of the part. The universe, the whole, is seen as a life-giving organism whose existence precedes that of the myriad beings. The universe (or the *wu*, the invisible) "begets" the myriad beings (or the *you*, the visible) by assigning them specific roles in a system. Without the preexistence of a gigantic system of relationships, the medieval Confucian metaphysicians argue, the myriad beings have no way to exist, let alone to be productive members of the universe.

For Zhou Dunyi, how the universe comes about is not as important as making sure that the universe continues its self-transformation. Shifting the focus of metaphysical discussion, he is interested less in locating the ontological ground of the universe than in explaining the dynamics of its self-transformation. By focusing on cosmogony rather than cosmology, he underscores the partnership of the part and the whole in the universe's continuous self-renewal. By putting the part and the whole on the same footing, he ushers in a new way of metaphysical thinking, which is often referred to as neo-Confucian metaphysics.

In explaining the diagram of the "great ultimate," Zhou helps his reader visualize the two-way flow between the whole and the part, the one and the many. He suggests reading the diagram from top to bottom as well as from bottom to top. Reading from top to bottom, he shows how the one gives rise to the many: the diagram illustrates how the great ultimate (*taiji*) produces the *yin* and the *yang*, the five phases, and the multitude of beings. Reading from bottom to top, he shows how the many are in fact one: the diagram explains how the multitude of beings are products of the five phases and the *yin* and the *yang*, which in turn are products of the great ultimate. Whether we envision proceeding from one to many or from many to one, the diagram shows that the universe is an organic system in which part and whole depend on each other.

Despite its importance in shaping neo-Confucian metaphysics, the *Taiji tushuo* has been the subject of a long-standing debate, focusing on the origin of the diagram. To some scholars, the diagram is undoubtedly Daoist. It is believed to be modeled after the Daoist diagrams for obtaining elixir such as the *Xiantian taiji tu* (*Diagram of the Primordial Great Ultimate*) and the *Wuji tu* (*Diagram of the Ultimate of Nonbeing*). Some scholars in the Qing dynasty (1644–1911) went so far as to identify eleventh-century Daoist priests, such as Chen Tuan (c. 906–989), as having transmitted the Daoist diagrams to Zhou. Other scholars took Zhou to task for using Daoist terms such as "ultimate of nonbeing" (*wuji*) and "tranquillity" (*jing*). The bone of contention in this controversy is Zhou himself: scholars debate whether he was too Daoist to be considered an early neo-Confucian thinker.

Possible Daoist influences notwithstanding, one should not underestimate Zhou's originality in transforming the diagram of the great ultimate from a diagram for obtaining an elixir into a diagram about cosmogony. His transformation of the diagram includes two parts. First, as we have seen, he reads the diagram both top-down and bottom-up: this is contrary to the Daoist practice of reading elixir diagrams bottom-up so as to trace the cosmic forces in one's body back to the cosmic forces in the universe. This change of sequence in reading the diagram radically alters its nature. It is no longer a manual for an individual quest for immortality but a graphic depiction of the universe as a family of beings.

Second, Zhou devotes only half of *Taiji tushuo* to explaining the diagram; in the rest, he goes beyond the diagram to argue for a direct link between ethics and metaphysics. He argues that human beings, given their sensibility and consciousness, are the most intelligent among the myriad beings. As free agents in this universe who have the power to decide on their actions, human beings can be active participants in or stubborn obstructors of its self-renewal. The active participants are called "superior men," and the stubborn obstructors "inferior men." Hence, the daily moral practices of human beings (e.g., humanity, righteousness, propriety, wisdom, and faithfulness) are more than simply ethical. They are metaphysical as well, because they involve a conscious decision to participate in the universe's self-renewal (*Song Yuan xue'an* 12.1B).

In the last part of *Taiji tushuo*, to drive home his point, Zhou mediates on the meaning of being a sage. As the ideal human being, a sage does his utmost to facilitate the universe's self-renewal from his given position in the human community. Characteristic of a sage is his double understanding: understanding his particular role in human community, and understanding how his particular role in human community is connected to the universe's self-renewal. With his double understanding, a sage is half human and half cosmic. Zhou writes:

> The virtue of a sage is identical with that of heaven and earth; his brilliance is identical with that of the sun and moon; his order is identical with that of the four seasons; and his fortunes and misfortunes are identical with those of spiritual beings. (*Song Yuan xue'an* 12.1B)

In short, a sage is half human and half cosmic because he, as a part, has embodied the whole.

Although the two halves of *Taiji tushuo* differ in emphasis, we may consider them two parts of the same argument about the inseparability of metaphysics and ethics. The first half is about how metaphysics is linked to ethics. From the perspective of the whole, the first half clarifies the web of relationships by which the myriad things (including humans) are joined as a family of beings. As part of a huge and organic system, human beings are responsible not only for themselves but for all beings in this universe. They have to liberate themselves from anthropocentrism. From the opposite perspective—that of human beings—the second half is about how ethics is linked to metaphysics. The second half discusses the possibility of a human being's embodying the entire universe. As an integral part of the universe, human beings have an impact not only on the human community but on the entire universe. The two halves of *Taiji tushuo*, like the *yin* and the *yang* in constant alternation, suggest the two-way flows in the part-whole partnership between human beings and the universe.

Zhou's other work, the *Tongshu* (also known as *Yi tongshu*), is much longer than *Taiji tushuo*. In terms of its subject matter, *Tongshu* is similar to the second half of *Taiji tushuo*. It discusses how a human being embodies the whole in his or her daily ethical practices. Because it directly addresses the method of moral cultivation, a major concern of neo-Confucianism, *Tongshu* is usually presented before *Taiji tushu* in neo-Confucian anthologies, to indicate its importance. In terms of its format, part of *Tongshu* was written like a commentary on the *Book of Changes* (*Yijing*). Zhou quoted frequently from the classic and devoted tremendous effort to elucidating the meanings of the quoted statements. It was probably for this reason that he also called this work *Yi tongshu—Penetrating the Book of Changes*.

Zhou had ample reason to quote from and comment on the *Book of Changes*. First, the *Book of Changes* is a Confucian classic dealing specifically with the relationship between human beings and the universe. Using trigrams and hexagrams, the *Book of Changes* describes the relationship between human beings and the universe as a trinity (or *sancai*, "three materials"): the heavens at the top, humankind in the middle, and the earth at the bottom. The three members of the trinity share the same essence and shape each other's destiny. Graphically, the *Book of Changes* gives support to the argument that human beings and the universe are interrelated as part and whole. Second, many hexagram statements, line statements, and especially statements from the "Great Appendix" (*Xici*) are particularly germane to the metaphysical nature of moral cultivation. They are useful in elucidating the inseparability of ethics and metaphysics. As a matter of fact, many neo-Confucians commented on the *Book of Changes* because its worldview was so similar to their own. Zhou was certainly among the first group of neo-Confucian commentators.

In *Tongshu*, Zhou addresses two issues: the possibility of learning to embody the universe, and the nature of that learning. Concerning the first issue, he concentrates on sincerity (*cheng*), a concept originally from the *Doctrine of the Mean* (a chapter in the *Book of Rites*). "Sincerity" refers to the innate human goodness endowed by nature. Since it is an endowment from nature, innate human goodness is not just a human ability; it is also the crucial link between humankind and the universe. Innate human goodness is the ground on which humankind may embody the universe.

For Zhou, there are three reasons why innate human goodness is called sincerity. First, innate human goodness, although available to every human being, is hidden. One has to uncover it by being honest and true to oneself. Sincerity therefore is the means of activating this innate goodness. Second, since all beings in the universe are intricately connected as a family, to be true to oneself requires being true to others. To be true to oneself at the expense of others is not sincerity but selfishness. So sincerity has to be rooted in altruism. It demands an understanding of the universe as a web of relationships, and a recognition that the existence of an individual is partially shaped by the existence of others. In calling innate human goodness sincerity, Zhou wants to emphasize that fully realizing sincerity requires the participation of all members of the universe. Third, just as one is true to oneself by being altruistic, the universe is true to itself by giving birth to the myriad beings and nurturing them in its ceaseless self-renewal. The universe gives rather than takes, nourishes rather than demands returns. It achieves through helping others to achieve; it completes itself through completing others. This goodness of the universe is the same as the innate human goodness that one uncovers when one is sincere. Thus in calling innate human goodness sincerity, Zhou also wants to emphasize that this is the same goodness the universe has manifested in giving birth to the myriad things (*Song Yuan xue'an* 11.1A–3B).

According to Zhou, Yan Hui—Confucius's favorite student—proved that it is possible to embody the universe by uncovering one's innate human goodness. Yan is depicted in the *Analects* as an extremely self-motivated student who earned Confucius's praise by engaging himself wholeheartedly in learning to be a sage. Yan was so self-critical that he earned a reputation for never committing the same mistake twice. For Zhou Dunyi, Yan Hui's embodiment of the universe could be seen in Yan's spiritual peace despite his brief, impoverished life. Materially, Yan had almost nothing—a single bamboo dish of rice, a single gourd of drink, a home in a mean, narrow lane. But spiritually, Yan had much. Every day he studied the classics, debated with his classmates, and asked Confucius for advice; and he was always hopeful in his constant quest to transcend himself (*Song Yuan xue'an* 11.7A).

Zhou attributes Yan Hui's joy in his impoverished life to the broadening of his mind. Yan did not see human destiny in terms of material comforts or personal gain; he saw it, instead, in terms of reaching a noble state of mind in which one considered oneself part of the universe. Because Yan saw human destiny in this broad perspective, he treasured whatever would benefit all beings in this world rather than what would benefit him alone (*Song Yuan xue'an* 11.7A). Cheng Yi recollected that Zhou often asked his students to seek Yan Hui's joy in his quest for sagehood. Cheng Yi's famous essay "A Treatise on What Yanzi Loved to Learn" is in many respects a systematic response to Zhou's advice. It is important to notice that this search for Yan's joy is tantamount to uncovering one's roots in the universe. What Zhou wanted his students to achieve is a sense of connection with all beings in the universe. Yan's joy, according to Zhou, is the joy of seeing the universe as a vast family of beings. This feeling of intimate connection with all beings in this universe is what Zhou means by embodying the universe.

In paying tribute to Yan Hui, Zhou Dunyi not only demonstrates that human beings are capable of learning to embody the universe but also defines the nature of that learning. In earlier times, Confucians understood learning as learning to be a loyal government official. Serving the human community by assuming a high political post was regarded as the direct way to realize the Confucian goal. Hence, successful prime ministers (such as Yi Yin of the Shang dynasty in the seventeenth century B.C.E.) rather than the solitary souls like Yan Hui were considered exemplary students of Confucius. By extolling Yan as the true student of Confucius, Zhou redefined learning as an individual quest to broaden the mind. Perfecting himself in a shabby lane, Yan personified the spiritual learning that one must undertake by oneself.

Of course, Zhou continued to hold that serving the human community was a good way to connect with the universe, but for him the starting point of learning had changed. Instead of encouraging his students to become prominent government officials, he called on them to "desire what Yi Yin desired and learn what Yanzi [Hui] learned" (*Song Yuan xue'an* 11.5A). He told them that to connect with the universe, they first needed to act properly in the human community—and to act properly, they first needed to have a proper perspective. A learned person, then, is not just a person of action. He is also a right-minded person who recognizes the inherent connections among all beings in the universe. This "inward turning," as some scholars call it, makes cultivation of the mind the most important part of human learning.

With regard to cultivating the mind, Zhou emphasizes concentration, a seemingly trivial point. He calls attention to the most difficult aspect of cultivating the mind: freeing it from distractions and focusing it on one thing at a time. The purpose of mental concentration is not to make us narrow-minded but to set us free from human desires (*Song Yuan xue'an* 11.6B). By "having no desire," Zhou does not mean the cessation of human craving stated in the Buddhist "four noble truths." What he means is focusing one's mind on one thing at a time, so that one will not be swayed by other competing claims.

As a pioneer of neo-Confucianism, Zhou Dunyi did not spell out clearly his method of cultivating the mind; besides setting "having no desires" as the goal of moral cultivation, he did not offer any specific guidelines. For this reason, despite his contributions to founding neo-Confucian metaphysics and defining the nature of neo-Confucian learning, he is not generally regarded as a full-fledged neo-Confucian. For many scholars, neo-Confucianism as a movement did not begin until Cheng Hao and Cheng Yi appeared on the scene.

See also Cheng Hao; Cheng Yi; *Wuxing; Yin* and *Yang*.

Bibliography

Chan, Wing-tsit, trans. *A Source Book in Chinese Philosophy*. Princeton, N.J.: Princeton: Princeton University Press, 1963.

Fung, Yu-lan (Feng Youlan). *A History of Chinese Philosophy*, Vol. 1, trans. Derk Bodde. Princeton, N.J.: Princeton University Press, 1953.

Graham, A. C. *Two Chinese Philosophers: Ch'eng Ming-tao and Ch'eng Yi-chuan*. La Salle, Ill.: Open Court, 1992.

Huang, Zongxi. *Song Yuan xue'an*. Taipei: Taiwan Zhonghua shuju. (Reprint.)

Mou, Zongsan. *Xinti yu xingti* (The Substance of the Mind and the Substance of Human Nature), Vol. 1. Taipei: Zhengzhong shuju, 1969.

Zhou, Dunyi. *Zhouzi quanshu* (The Complete Works of Master Zhou), ed. Dong Rong. Taipei: Guangxue she yinshu guan, 1975. (Reprint.)

Zhu Xi (Chu Hsi)

Shu-hsien Liu

Zhu Xi (Chu Hsi, Yuanhui, 1130–1200) has commonly been regarded as the greatest neo-Confucian philosopher since Confucius and Mencius. His commentaries on the Four Books—the *Analects, Book of Mencius, Great Learning*, and *Doctrine of the Mean* (the last two of these were chapters of the *Book of Rites*)—became the basis of the civil service examinations in 1313, during the Yuan dynasty, and remained so until they were abolished in 1905, in the late Qing dynasty. Zhu gave Confucianism a new meaning and for centuries dominated not only Chinese thought but Korean and Japanese thought as well.

Zhu Xi was born in the Southern Song period, in Fujian; his father was not happy with the political situation at the time and had chosen to move to this remote coastal province. Zhu Xi himself, over his lifetime, served at court for only forty-nine days, for he was strongly opposed to concluding peace with the Jin, who occupied northern China, and he repeatedly sent memorandums to the throne in which he criticized officials and policies. Apart from a short period when he was minor official, he spent most of his life, off and on, as a guardian of one temple or another, using the peace and quiet to study, write, carry on extensive discussions of philosophical and social issues with fellow scholars, and—last but not least—devote himself to teaching and educational matters. For neo-Confucians, study is not a means for getting a position; from the very beginning, promising young scholars must set their minds on the Way. Zhu Xi made great efforts to revive some of the *shuyuan* (colleges); his influence became widespread, and so he incurred the jealousy and hatred of certain people in power. When he died, his teachings were denounced as "false learning." Nevertheless, almost a thousand people attended his funeral; he was subsequently rehabilitated; and his reputation continued to grow. In the Yuan dynasty (1271–1368), the school of Cheng (Yichuan, 1033–1107) and Zhu was honored as orthodoxy. Its supremacy remained unchallenged until the last dynasty. The influence of Zhu's thought even survived the revolution; it became the foundation of Feng Youlan's new rationalism in the 1930s. Nor was Zhu's influence limited to China: it became an orthodoxy in Korea and the outstanding school of thought in the history of Japan.

Zhu Xi's Search for Equilibrium and Harmony

It is impossible to understand Zhu Xi's thought without identifying the problems he considered most important. Basically, the traditional Chinese approach to philosophy was somewhat different from the traditional western approach, as can be seen in the title of the book *Jinsi lu* (*Reflections on Things at Hand*)—a neo-Confucian anthology compiled by Zhu Xi and his friend Lu Zuqian that exerted a profound influence on the Chinese mind for more than 700 years (Zhu 1967). The term *jinsi* comes from the *Analects* (19.6), where it is suggested that reflecting on things at hand is a way to approach humanity (*ren*). Zhu and Lu's anthology does not lack cosmological speculation similar to what we find in the west, but such speculation was definitely not the starting point for Chinese philosophy. Rather, the primary concerns of Chinese philosophers were existential problems of the self. Zhu Xi was firmly in the Chinese tradition; at a tender age he had already set his mind on "learning for one's self" (de Bary 1991), although he was also attracted by Buddhism and Daoism until he studied under Li Tong (Yanping, 1095–1163), who urged him to look for the right Way through the Confucian classics. That gave Zhu his general direction, but before he could formulate his own thought he devoted many years, after Li died, to a quest to realize *zhonghe* (equilibrium and harmony). The term *zhonghe* comes from the *Doctrine of the Mean*:

> Before the feelings of pleasure, anger, sorrow, and joy are aroused it is called equilibrium (*zhong*, centrality, mean). When these feelings are aroused and each and all attain due measure and degree, it is called harmony (*he*). Equilibrium is the great foundation of the world, and harmony its universal path. When equilibrium and harmony are realized to the highest degree, heaven and earth will attain their proper order and all things will flourish. (Chan 1963, 98)

According to Zhu Xi, in his early years Li Tong taught him the *Doctrine of the Mean*, and the master usually instructed his students to meditate and examine the prevailing spirit before arousing pleasure, anger, sorrow, and joy in order to seek equilibrium—so that when they dealt with affairs and responded to things they would attain "due measure and degree" naturally. This was the formula transmitted by the followers of Yang Shi (Gueishan, 1053–1135). Zhu did not pay enough attention to such matters; and when, after Li Tong's death, he was disturbed in his mind, he searched desperately to recover the master's teachings, to no avail. The master had seemed to teach that one must first practice self-cultivation before one examined and reflected. This approach appeared directly opposed to that of the Hunan school, transmitted by Hu Hong (Wufeng, 1100–1155), which Zhu learned from his friend Zhang Shi (Jingfu, 1133–1180); according to the Hunan school, one must first examine and reflect before one can practice self-cultivation. According to Mou Zongsan, Li Tong's and Hu Hong's approaches were two possible ways of realizing equilibrium, developed from the teachings of the two major disciples of the Cheng brothers (Mingdao, 1032–1085; Yichuan, 1033–1107): Yang Gueishan and Xie Shangcai (Liangzuo, 1050–1103). But Zhu failed to appreciate the depth of these approaches and was determined to develop his own approach, based on his understanding of Yichuan's teachings.

According to Mou, Li's approach was "to realize equilibrium through temporary separation from daily activities." Li strongly emphasized practicing meditation until one had achieved an equilibrium that could resist all interference from selfish desires. Once this was achieved, one could easily realize equilibrium in daily life and achieve an ultimate sense of unity—like ice melting in water and leaving no visible trace. Zhu did not particularly like this approach; he was the kind of person who diligently studied classical texts and carried out all his duties in life, so he would hardly care to divorce himself from the world, even temporarily. He perhaps did not fully realize that for Li, sitting still actually meant much more than calming the mind; it was a way to find a correlation with the ultimate creative ontological principle, which manifested itself in an equilibrium realizable through discipline of the mind. This would explain why Zhu chose not to follow Li Tong while Li was still alive.

After Li died, however, Zhu Xi began to experience doubt. How to realize equilibrium and harmony seemed to have become a puzzling, and urgent, problem for him. He then sought the advice of his friend Zhang Shi, who told him about Hu Hong's teaching. This approach seemed to accord with Zhu's temperament; in one letter to Zhang, Zhu wrote that if a scholar devoted himself to examining and preserving the mind, he could gain a comprehensive understanding of the Way and recover his original nature. But before long, Zhu changed his mind again, telling Zhang:

> I thought that I had gotten hold the right thing, but in fact I had not thought through the implications of "how to attend equilibrium and harmony," I felt that I did not have a solid ground under my feet to practice self-discipline, the atmosphere resembled the violent torrents of the sea, and I felt every day that I was driven by a great transforming process, as if I was under huge waves, and did not get a moment of rest. (Liu 1988, 260)

Zhu seems not to have realized that for the Hunan school, examining and reflecting meant specifically the way to recover the original mind; he erroneously interpreted this to mean examining external things and affairs. It is no wonder, then, that when he responded to things, he felt twice as coarse as before and experienced no sense of magnanimity.

Zhu was thus driven to appreciate the merit of Li Tong's approach. He wavered between the two approaches for some time without being able to settle his mind. Later, he described his correspondence from this period as documents that preserve his old view of equilibrium and harmony, according to which the mind (as the state after feelings are aroused) and nature (as the state before feelings are aroused) are two consecutive stages.

After much struggle, Zhu reached his mature understanding of the problem. In his "First Letter to the Gentlemen from Hunan on Equilibrium and Harmony," he came to realize what Cheng Yi taught in his discussions of the problem. There is a state of mind before there is any sign of thought or deliberation, before the arrival of external things (stimuli), and before pleasure, anger, sorrow, and joy are aroused. That state is identical with the substance of the mind, which is absolutely tranquil and inactive, and the nature endowed by heaven should be completely embodied in it. It is neither excessive nor insufficient, neither unbalanced nor one-sided, and so it is called equilibrium. When it is acted on and immediately penetrates all things, the feelings are then aroused. In this second state, the functioning of the mind can be seen. Because it never fails to attain the proper measure and degree and has never deviated from what is right, it is called harmony (Chan 1963, 401). Thus the mind encompasses both the state before and the state after the feelings are aroused. Therefore, a two-pronged approach is required, as Cheng Yi said: "Self-cultivation requires seriousness (*jing*); the pursuit of learning depends on the extension of knowledge" (Chan 1963, 562). Self-cultivation by maintaining seriousness is required before the feelings are aroused, and the extension of knowledge through the examination of things is required after the feelings are aroused.

Zhu Xi believed that by following Cheng Yi he could work out a synthesis that would balance the approaches of Li Tong and the Hunan school. He compared them to the two wings of a bird or the two wheels of a cart. This was his mature view; once he formulated it, he never changed his course again.

Later on, Zhu wrote another long letter to Zhang Shi, further developing his views on the problem. A man's body and the functioning of perception, Zhu said, must depend on the action of the mind; the mind has to be the master of the body, regardless of the difference between motion and rest, speaking and silence. When the mind is tranquil, things have not yet come into contact with it, thoughts have not yet begun, and nature remains undifferentiated, embodying all principles. Here we find a form of equilibrium demonstrating that the mind is the substance which is tranquil and inactive. When there is activity, things crowd together, thoughts begin to emerge, and the seven emotions alternate with one another, each going its own way. Then there is a form of harmony that demonstrates the functioning of the mind: when acted on, it immediately penetrates all things. As it circulates, substance and function never separate from each other, and there is no moment in which it is not inspired with humanity. Humanity is the Way of the mind; seriousness is the firmness of the mind. This is the Way that encompasses both the transcendent and the immanent, reflecting the fundamental teachings of the sages (Liu 1988, 267).

From then on, Zhu formulated his grand system of philosophy. He made a tripartite division between the mind (*xin*), human nature (*xing*), and feelings (*qing*); he also developed a metaphysics of *li* (principle) and *qi* (material force). These will be discussed in some detail here.

The Tripartite Division of the Mind, Human Nature, and Feelings

Zhu had started with an existential concern, which forced him to develop a metaphysics of mind and nature by following Cheng Yi's thought. The mind is the agent that carries out disciplines according to principles inherent in human nature. The contrast between the two is that nature is transcendent while mind is immanent. But there is also a correlation between the two. Nature provides a solid foundation for the mind to act, so that the mind will not go astray and become lost; the mind has the ability to put principles in nature to work in real life. In his famous essay "A Treatise on *Ren*" (humanity), Zhu said:

> "The mind of Heaven and Earth is to produce things." In the production of man and things, they receive the mind of Heaven and Earth as their mind. Therefore, with reference to the character of the mind, although it embraces and penetrates all and leaves nothing to be desired, nevertheless, one word will cover all of it, namely, *ren*. (Chan 1963, 593–594)

Here Zhu Xi explicitly stated that *ren* is the character of the mind, and that the human mind is essentially the same as the creative mind of Heaven and Earth. He elaborated:

> . . . *Ren* as constituting the Way (*dao*) consists of the fact that the mind of Heaven and Earth to produce things is present in everything. Before feelings are aroused, this substance is already existent in its completeness. After feelings are aroused, its function is infinite. If we can truly practice love and preserve it, then we have in it the spring of all virtues and the root of all good deeds. This is why in the teachings of the Confucian school, the student is always urged to exert anxious unceasing efforts in the pursuit of *ren*.

This thought was thoroughly consistent with Zhu's understanding of *zhonghe*. Zhu also endorsed Cheng Yi's view that "love is feeling whereas humanity is nature." He summed up his own views as follows:

> Some time ago I read statements by Wufeng (Hu Hong) in which he spoke of the mind only in contrast to nature, leaving the feelings unaccounted for. Later when I read Hengqu's (Zhang Zai's) doctrine that "the mind commands (unites) man's nature and feelings," I realized that it was a great contribution. Only then did I find a satisfactory account of the feelings. His doctrine agrees with that of Mencius. In the words of Mencius, "the feeling [mind-heart] of commiseration is the beginning of humanity." Now humanity is nature, and commiseration is feeling. In this, the mind can be seen through the feelings. He further said, "Humanity, righteousness, propriety, and wisdom are rooted in the mind." In this the mind is seen through nature. For the mind embraces both nature and the feelings. Nature is substance and feelings are function. (Chan 1963, 631)

Interestingly, Mencius himself never made a sharp distinction between mind-heart (*xin*) and feelings (*qing*), or between mind and nature—on the contrary, the essential goodness of nature was to be seen through the essential goodness of mind-heart. For Zhu, however, only the transcendent nature (principle) is necessarily good; the empirical mind can be either good, by following principles, or evil, by acting against principles. Zhu's tripartite division of mind, nature, and feelings was something new and quite original.

Zhu also distinguished between physical nature and moral nature, and between *renxin* (the human mind) and *daoxin* (the mind of *dao*). To appreciate these rather complex matters, we should first consider Zhu's metaphysics of *li* (principle) and *qi* (material force), a comprehensive philosophy he developed in order to understand the universe and human life.

The Metaphysics of *Li* and *Qi*

Li (principle) was not an important philosophical concept in ancient Confucian thought; Mencius, for example, barely referred to it and never elaborated on its implications. But in Huayan Buddhism, *li* became philosophically significant. Apparently influenced by Buddhist thought, Song philosophers gave new meanings to the term and made it probably the most important concept in Song-Ming neo-Confucian philosophy; posterity has referred to it as Song-Ming *lixue* (study of principle). Cheng Hao (1032–1085) was the first to emphasize the personal realization of *tianli* (principle of Heaven) within the self. His brother Cheng Yi made the famous assertion that nature (*xing*) is principle, which became the cornerstone of Zhu Xi's philosophy.

Another important concept in Song-Ming neo-Confucian philosophy was *qi* (material or vital force). Mencius was the first to urge us to cultivate this vital force in ourselves, implicitly assuming a correlation between Heaven and man, or macrocosm and microcosm. The *yin-yang* school then understood *yin* and *yang* as two vital forces explaining the formation of the natural universe and human society. Some of these ideas found expression in the *Commentaries* on the *Yijing* (*Book of Changes*) and were inherited by Song philosophers such as Zhou Dunyi (1017–1073) and Zhang Zai. Zhang in particular developed a comprehensive cosmology that made extensive use of the concept of *qi* and made a most important distinction between physical nature and moral nature. Although the Cheng brothers had reservation about Zhang's cosmology, they fully endorsed his approach to nature. The Chengs said:

> It would be incomplete to talk about the nature without referring to material force and unintelligible to talk about material force without referring to nature. It would be wrong to consider them apart from each other. (Chan 1963, 552)

This is exactly Zhu Xi's point of departure.

In his search for equilibrium and harmony of the mind Zhu recognized the transcendent character of human nature; if it did not have this character, there would be no place to rest on. This was why he took to heart Cheng Yi's assertion that nature is principle. However, without the material force and concrete stuff of the universe, principle would have nothing in which to inhere. When material force is received in its state of clarity, there will be no obscurity or obstruction and principle will express itself freely. If there is no obscurity or obstruction, or if the only obstruction is small, the principle of Heaven will dominate. But selfish human desires will dominate if the obstruction is great. From this we know that the original nature is perfectly good. This is the nature described by Mencius as "good" and by Cheng Yi as "the fundamental character of our nature" and "the nature traced to the source of our being." However, Zhang Zai said, "In physical nature there is that which the superior man denies to be his original nature," and "If one learns to return to the original nature endowed by Heaven and Earth, then it will be preserved" (Chan 1963, 511). We must, then, include physical nature before our discussion of nature can be complete.

Zhu's understanding of nature presupposes a metaphysics of *li* and *qi*. Zhu, assimilating Zhou Dunyi's concept of the "great ultimate" (*taiji*) and combining it with the Chengs' concept of principle, held that the "great ultimate" has no physical form but consists entirely of principle: all actual and potential principles are contained in it (Chan 1963, 590). Zhu envisioned one great ultimate for the whole universe, but the same principle can be manifested in the "myriad things" in the world. Hence we can also say that there is a great ultimate in everything and in every human being. The relationship between the great ultimate in the universe and the great ultimate in each individual thing is not one of whole and part; rather, it is like the moonlight shining on ten thousand streams—the moon is the same, but each reflection is unique. Thus the one principle (*li*) has innumerable manifestations, which may be called principles inherent in the universe.

Chan (1963, 590) gives us a general picture of Zhu Xi's philosophy. In the ongoing process of creation principles must find their concrete embodiment, and actualization requires principle as its substance and material force as its actuality. Thus the great ultimate involves both principle and material force; the two are inseparable though not combined. Principle is necessary to explain the reality and universality of things. It is incorporeal, one, eternal, unchanging, uniform, constituting the essence of things, always good; but it does not contain a dichotomy of good and evil, and it does not create things. Material force is necessary to explain physical form, individuality, and the transformation of things. It is physical, many, transitory, changeable, unequal in things, constituting their actual existence, involving both good and evil; and it is the agent of creation.

Zhu's dualism should not be understood as either Platonic or Cartesian, because *li* (principle) and *qi* (material force) are inseparable. Principle needs material force in order to have something to adhere to, and material force needs principle as its form or essence. But principle and material force are not reducible to each other; each will maintain its own identity and special characteristics. Thus, Zhu may be said to have taught a constitutional dualism or functional monism. In actuality, we can never find a state in which principle and material forces are separate from each other. But in theory, principle is still regarded as ontologically prior to material force. In a sense, Zhu could still say that principle is the ultimate, which generates (*sheng*) material force. But we must not understand Zhu to mean that principle gives birth to material force as a mother gives birth to a child. What he meant was that the great ultimate (*taiji*) is the principle of creativity; for the principle to manifest its great function of creativity, it must be set in motion by material force—i.e., *yin* and *yang*. Thus *li* is not chronologically prior to *qi*; the two coexist even before the cosmic order comes into being. However, concrete things exist because of principle, and nothing can exist without principle. It is in this sense that principle is considered the origin of all things, which are composed of material force as required by principle. Paradoxically, even though principle is the ultimate reality, it has no concrete existence and can take no action—it must depend on the function of material force. Zhu therefore saw *li* as weak and *qi* as strong. Some later scholars vividly compared the relationship between *li* and *qi* to a dead man riding a living horse.

Xing, *Qing*, and *Xin*: Further Complications

Zhu Xi made full use of the concepts of *li* and *qi* to offer fresh interpretations of *xing* (nature), *qing* (feelings and emotions), and *xin* (mind-heart). He endorsed Cheng Yi's statements that *xing* is *li* and that *renxing aiqing*, "humanity pertains to nature while love pertains to feeling." Everyone is endowed with humanity, which constitutes our moral nature; but love is the expression of feelings (*qing*), which are inseparable from the function of material force. We must make an effort to command our feelings and emotions in accordance with principles, and to be our own master; and that effort must depend on the discipline of the *xin* (mind-heart). Thus, *xin* occupied a pivotal position in Zhu Xi's philosophy.

While it is clear that *xing* is *li* and *qing* is *qi*, where Zhu would place *xin* becomes an interesting problem. Zhu greatly admired Zhang Zai's insight that the mind-heart unifies nature and feeling. This might suggest that *xin* may serve a bridge between *li* and *qi*. But Zhu refused to take *xin* as something other than *li* and *qi*. His solution was to see *xin* as composed of the subtlest kind of material force, which has the ability to unify with principle. Thus the relation between the two is that the mind-heart comprises principle. Zhu also greatly appreciated an insight by Shao Yong (1011–1077) that "nature is the concrete embodiment of the Way and the mind is the enclosure of the nature" (Chan 1963, 620). The Way itself has no physical form or body; it finds form and embodiment only in man's nature. If there were no mind, where could nature be? There must be mind before nature can be gotten hold of and put forth into operation, for the principles contained in nature are humanity, righteousness, propriety, and wisdom, and these are concrete principles. Zhu saw the relation between nature and mind as exactly parallel to that between principle and material force; they are not to be mixed with each other, and yet they are not to be separated from each other. According to him, nature is comparable to the great ultimate, and the mind to *yin* and *yang*. The great ultimate exists only in *yin* and *yang* and cannot be separated from them. In the final analysis, however, the great ultimate is the great ultimate and *yin* and *yang* are *yin* and *yang*. So it is with nature and mind.

The metaphysics of *li* and *qi* certainly had implications far richer than a theory of nature and mind. Indeed, Zhu had developed a comprehensive cosmology to deal with related problems. It is from principle and material force that the "myriad things" in the world come into being. Zhu admitted that all things have nature, so the question he had to face was whether the nature of things differed from or was the same as the nature of human beings. His answer was complex. Zhu theorized that if we are talking about the origin of things, principle is one while material forces are different; but if we are talking about the existence of the myriad things, the material force is similar while the principles embodied are very different. Zhu elaborated this as follows. When we trace the universe to its origin, there is just one principle; it is the same principle that serves as the ground for the myriad things to come into being and is shared by all with no discrimination. As the myriad things are constituted by the material forces of *yin* and *yang* and further differentiated into the "five agents"—metal, wood, water, fire, and Earth—the vast differences between them must be accounted for by material force. Human beings are different from other things because only humans receive the kind of material force that resonates the comprehensive, creative way of Heaven. From another perspective, however, it can be seen that the material forces of *yin* and *yang* constituting human beings and the myriad things are the same, although the principles embodied in human beings, such as humanity, righteousness, propriety, and wisdom, cannot be shared by other animals.

Zhu followed Zhang Zai in giving ghosts and spirits a naturalistic explanation. He never denied the popular belief in the existence of ghosts and gods, but he felt that they could also be explained in terms of *yin* and *yang*. The contraction of *yin* results in ghosts, and the expansion of *yang* results in gods. Human beings are situated between ghosts and gods.

Zhu also debated with scholars about whether withered things have nature. From his point of view, all things have nature because they share the same principle as their origin. Human beings and animals have blood, vital force, and perceptions; plants lack these but still have life; withered things do not even have life but still have shapes and smells. Human beings, animals, plants, and withered things differ greatly from each other, but they all come from the same origin. Once they become concrete existents, then the principles they embody are also different. Human beings are the most intelligent; they have a moral nature that comprises five moral principles (humanity, righteousness, propriety, wisdom, and faithfulness). Animals do not have them all; plants and withered things do not even have perceptions, but there must be principles in order for them to exist in the world. If there are things without nature, then there is vacuity in the universe; this is tantamount to saying that they exist without a ground (reason or principle) for existence. Such a position is unacceptable, indeed absurd. Clearly, Zhu's theory is miles away from Mencius, who was concerned only to identify the distinct human nature setting humans apart from other animals. Zhu's rival in his own day, Lu Xiangshan (1139–1193), certainly did not care to talk about the nature of withered things; perhaps this is why he complained that Zhu Xi had been led astray by too many distractions and had failed to concentrate on what was most essential in personal cultivation. This difference in metaphysical outlooks also led to difference regarding learning and education.

Learning and Education

Lu Xiangshan identified the mind with principle. The Ming philosopher Wang Yangming (1472–1529) further developed this view—hence the term "school of Lu-Wang." This school was also called *xinxue*, the "school of mind." Zhu Xi's perspective was different;

he maintained that the mind comprises principles, a view that was a further development of Cheng Yi's thought—hence the term "school of Cheng-Zhu." That school is also called *lixue*, the "school of principle." We must not be misled by these labels: the difference between the two schools is certainly not that one school emphasizes mind exclusively and the other emphasizes principle exclusively. As we have seen, the mind occupies a pivotal position in Zhu Xi's philosophy. But the two schools did have a rather different understanding of the relation between the mind and principle.

The mind referred to by Lu-Wang was *benxin* (the original mind); it is actually nondual relative to *benxing* (the original nature), moral nature as distinct from animal nature; actions coming out of this mind can only be in accordance with *li* (principles). Lu-Wang strictly followed the Mencian approach that in learning one must first establish the greater or the nobler part, i.e., the mind, which has *liangzhi liangneng* (innate knowledge and innate ability). Under its guidance, the lesser parts—i.e., the sense organs—would function properly. The primary purpose of learning is to recover the lost mind.

Zhu also professed to follow Mencius, but his approach was different. As Mou Zongsan pointed out, Zhu's starting point is the empirical mind, which has to work hard to conform to principles. After a long, difficult, gradual process, the mind and principle can finally be said to be one, in the sense that they become unified. Through discipline, the mind composed of material force can be transformed to the mind of *dao* and can conform to the principles comprised by the mind; they are inseparable from each but must not be mixed up with each other.

Zhu found the Confucian learning program in the *Great Learning* (*Daxue*). There are the famous eight items; the starting point is *gewu*. According to Zhu's interpretation, it means investigating things; thus the text reads:

> When things are investigated, knowledge is extended; when knowledge is extended, the will becomes sincere; when the will is sincere, the mind is rectified; when the mind is rectified, the personal life is cultivated; when the personal life is cultivated, the family will be regulated; when the family is regulated, the state will be in order; and when the state is in order, there will be peace throughout the world. From the son of Heaven to the common people, all must regard cultivation of the personal life as the root and foundation. (Chan 1963, 86–87)

But Zhu Xi believed that the commentary explaining the meaning of investigation of things and the extension of knowledge had been lost. He ventured to take the view of Cheng Yi and supplement it as follows.

> The meaning of the expression "The perfection of knowledge depends on the investigation of things" is this: If we wish to extend our knowledge to the utmost, we must investigate the principles of all things we come into contact with, for the intelligent mind of man is certainly formed to know, and there is not a single thing in which its principles do not inhere. It is only because all principles are not investigated that man's knowledge is incomplete. For this reason, the first step in the education of the adult is to instruct the learner, in regard to all things in the world, to proceed from what knowledge he has of their principles, and investigate further until he reaches the limit. After exerting himself in this way for a long time, he will achieve a wide and far-reaching penetration. Then the qualities of all things whether internal or external, the refined or the coarse, will all be apprehended, and the mind, in its total substance and great functioning, will be perfectly intelligent. This is called the investigation of things. This is called the perfection of knowledge. (Chan 1963, 89)

Zhu's interpretation of *gewu* is not without its difficulties. Some scholars, such as Wang Yangming, did not believe that any texts at all had been lost from the commentary; and Wang questioned Zhu Xi's interpretation of *gewu*. For Wang, *gewu* means to rectify that which is not correct so as to get rid of evil and return to correctness so as to do good; the extension of knowledge means to extend innate knowledge of the mind to things (affairs) in the world. Zhu did not make a clear distinction between moral knowledge and empirical knowledge, and so Wang (who was then quite young) questioned Zhu Xi's approach, asking how the investigation of a bamboo tree in the courtyard could help one cultivate the personal life as urged in the *Great Learning*. In fairness to Zhu, however, he surely did not mean that one can know everything or that an accumulation of empirical knowledge can bring about moral enlightenment. What he firmly believed was that there are principles in all the things in the world, and that through the investigation of things one would somehow recognize all principles in the world as having the same origin—as manifestations of the same principle. Hence he declared that there is a great ultimate in everything and in every person. Evidently, Zhu's problem was not realizing that without a leap of faith, a gradual accumulation of knowledge will not necessarily lead to seeing a single principle in the whole universe. And he freely admitted that Lu's approach of "honoring the moral nature" had a much more direct impact on personal cultivation than his own approach of "following the path of study and inquiry," even though he insisted that his approach also had a place in the pursuit of learning. Zhu simply believed that sudden enlightenment was the approach of Chan (Zen) Buddhism; the Confucian approach had to start with the investigation of things and the study of classics and proceed to the stage of realizing that the same principle governs human life as well as the whole universe.

Actually, for Zhu, in the educational process one must go through a preparatory stage of "small learning" before being ready for "great learning." One must learn how to follow daily routines in a proper way and how to conduct oneself properly before one is ready to reflect on the self or to set one's mind on following the sagely way so as to find resonance with the way of Heaven. In developing a curriculum, Zhu followed the lead of the Cheng brothers. The purpose of learning was not to get an official position or to gain profit for oneself. As the Five Classics were difficult to study, they were replaced by the Four Books. It is ironic that Zhu's commentaries on the Four Books became the basis for the civil service examination from the Yuan dynasty on.

Conclusion

Zhu Xi was indeed the most influential Confucian philosopher after Confucius and Mencius. He established the orthodox line of the Way. After Mencius, the line had been broken until it was revived in the Song dynasty by Zhou Dunyi, Zhang Zai, and the Cheng brothers. Zhu naturally saw himself as a successor of that line. But Mou Zongsan noted that *li* for Zhou, Zhang, and Cheng Hao is a principle in action, whereas Zhu Xi, following Cheng Yi, took *li*, as principle, as the ultimate ground for being which is not engaged in action. Hence Mou considers Zhu the side branch diverging from orthodoxy. Whether or not one agrees with Mou, one cannot deny the important role Zhu Xi played in the history of Chinese philosophy. He transmitted a pattern of thought that dominated the Chinese way of thinking for 700 years, until it was challenged by influences from the west.

See also Cheng Hao; Cheng Yi; *Daxue*: The Great Learning; Hu Hong; *Li*: Principle, Pattern, Reason; Lu Xiangshan; *Qi*; Shao Yong; Wang Yangming; *Yin* and *Yang*; Zhang Zai.

Bibliography

Chan, Wing-tsit. *Chu Hsi: Life and Thought*. Hong Kong: Chinese University Press, 1987.

——. ed. *Chu Hsi and Neo-Confucianism*. Honolulu: University of Hawaii Press, 1986.

——. *Chu Hsi: New Studies*. Honolulu: University of Hawaii Press, 1989.

——. trans. and comp. *A Source Book in Chinese Philosophy*. Princeton, N.J.: Princeton University Press, 1963.

Chang, Carsun. *The Development of Neo-Confucian Thought*, 2 vols. New York: Bookman Associates, 1957–1962.

de Bary, William Theodore. *Learning for One's Self: Essays on the Individual in Neo-Confucian Thought*. New York: Columbia University Press, 1991.

Liu, Shu-hsien. "The Function of the Mind in Chu Hsi's Philosophy." *Journal of Chinese Philosophy*, 5(2), June 1978, pp. 195–208.

——. "On Chu Hsi as an Important Source for the Development of the Philosophy of Wang Yang-ming." *Journal of Chinese Philosophy*, 11(1), March 1984, pp. 83–107.

——. "On Chu Hsi's Search for Equilibrium and Harmony." In *Harmony and Strife: Contemporary Perspectives East and West*, ed. Shu-hsien Liu and Robert E. Allinson. Hong Kong: Chinese University of Hong Kong Press, 1988, pp. 249–270.

——. "On Chu Hsi's Understanding of *Hsing* (Nature)." *Tsing-hua Journal of Chinese Studies*, New Series, 17(1–2), December 1985, pp. 127–148.

——. "The Problem of Orthodoxy in Chu Hsi's Philosophy." *Chu Hsi and Neo-Confucianism*, ed. Wing-tsit Chan. Honolulu: University of Hawaii Press, 1986, pp. 437–460.

——. *Understanding Confucian Philosophy: Classical and Sung-Ming*. Westport, N.J.: Greenwood, 1998.

——. *Zhuzi zhexue sixiang di fanzhen yu wancheng* (The Development and Completion of Master Zhu's Philosophical Thought), 3rd ed. Taipei: Xuesheng, 1995.

Mou, Zongsan. *Xinti yu xingti* (The Substance of the Mind and the Substance of the Nature), 3 vols. Taipei: Zhengzhong, 1968–1969.

Munro, Donald J. *Images of Human Nature: A Sung Portrait*. Princeton, N.J.: Princeton University Press, 1988.

Percy, Bruce, J. *Chu Hsi and His Masters*. London: Probsthain, 1923. (Reprint, New York: AMS, 1973.)

Qian, Mu. *Zhuzi xinxuean* (A New Study of Zhu Xi), 5 vols. Taipei: Sanmin, 1971.

Zhu, Xi. *Learning to Be a Sage: Selections from the Conversations of Mater Chu, Arranged Topically*, trans. Daniel K. Gardner. Berkeley: University of California Press, 1990.

——. *Zhuzi daquan* (Complete Literary Works of Zhu Xi), SPPY ed., 12 vols. Taipei: Zhonghua, 1970.

——. *Zhuzi yulei* (Classified Conversations of Zhu Xi), 8 vols., comp. Li Jingde. Beijing: Zhonghua, 1986.

Zhu, Xi, and Lü Tsu-ch'ien, eds. *Reflections on Things at Hand: The Neo-Confucian Anthology*, trans. Wing-tsit Chan. New York: Columbia University Press, 1967.

Zhu Xi (Chu Hsi): Rivals and Followers

Hoyt Cleveland TILLMAN

From the perspective of scholars in later centuries, Zhu Xi (1130–1200) has assumed such stature that his contemporaries appear as dwarfs. When the Chinese government, in 1241, enshrined Zhu in the Confucian temple, the emperor singled him out as the twelfth-century thinker who had contributed most profoundly to the culmination and transmission of what was now promulgated as the mainstream of Confucian teachings. The emperor also declared that Zhu's commentaries on the classical Four Books would henceforth be basic texts for those preparing in government schools for the civil service examinations. Emperors of later dynasties would enhance the prominence of Zhu's interpretation of Confucianism and complete the institutional structure of state orthodoxy, but it was in 1241 that Zhu became the official cornerstone of this orthodoxy. Thus, soon after his death, Zhu began to overshadow his rivals and provide the focal point for his followers.

Nonetheless, during his own day Zhu Xi faced several rivals and groups who challenged his authority and interpretations. Zhu's exchanges with some of his rivals had a considerable impact on the development of his own thought. Moreover, his own followers sometimes made subtle shifts of emphasis that affected the legacy of his school and system of thought. Exploring the ideas and actions of several major critics and followers should augment our understanding of how Zhu's philosophy itself developed, how the literati class of officials and other scholars gradually embraced it as intellectual orthodoxy, and why the state eventually centered its orthodoxy on Zhu Xi's reconstruction of the Confucian tradition. Before we take up his followers and his symbolic triumph in 1241, a discussion of his rivals will provide a contemporaneous context for his thought and actions.

Zhu Xi's Rivals

Zhu Xi's rivals arose from numerous directions and challenged him from various points of view; thus they cannot be reduced to a single voice or position. Four crucial groups will be discussed in turn.

1. Some of Zhu Xi's rivals maintained allegiance to other intellectual leanings within Confucianism of the Song (960–1279), particularly to the philosophies of either Wang Anshi (1021–1086) or Su Shi (1036–1101). Zhu was often critical of these Confucians of the Northern Song (960–1279); besides, he championed a different tradition, a Confucian fellowship called *daoxue*, "*dao* learning" or "learning of the Way." From the perspective of the twelfth century, this "*dao* learning" fellowship included not only the "four masters"—Zhou Dunyi (1017–1073), Cheng Hao (1032–1086), Cheng Yi (1033–1107), and Zhang Zai (1020–1077)—but also Sima Guang (1019–1086) and their associates, especially from the prominent Lü and Hu families. These thinkers, within and outside the fellowship, represented a diverse spectrum of Song Confucianism, and there were philosophical differences among them, but they all participated in the Confucian renaissance of the Northern Sung.

As we learn from such renaissance figures as Ouyang Xiu (1007–1072), all these "Song Confucians" assumed that they could read the Confucian classics of antiquity directly, without depending on scholastic commentaries from the Han (206 B.C.E.–220 C.E.) or the Tang (618–906). They were also highly critical of Han and Tang scholars, who they believed had missed much of the larger meaning of the ancient classics, especially the more profound philosophical ideas and empowering vision of true spiritual self-cultivation. With renewed confidence in their own culture, they proclaimed that they had the same mind-and-heart (*xin*) as the ancient sages; therefore, they could strive to understand the *dao* (Way) and learn to become sages.

Although the various schools of Song Confucianism differed over approaches to the *dao*, methods of spiritual and cultural cultivation, and sociopolitical and economic programs, they generally shared certain assumptions about the classics, the mind, sagehood, and the *dao*. These shared assumptions are quite evident when the schools are viewed collectively against the backdrop of Han Confucian scholarship. It was during the Han that Confucians first synthesized their ethics so successfully with prevailing views of the natural world, philosophy, social and family norms, and political institutions that Confucianism became recognized as orthodoxy by the state. Confucian orthodoxy enhanced the position of the imperial throne and the emperor's role and initiative in improving the sociopolitical order, thereby enabling people to cultivate themselves as better persons and ensuring harmony between the sociopolitical order and the natural realm of earth and cosmos. The Han synthesis integrated some Daoist philosophical ideas, legalist assumptions about authority and political institutions, and diverse notions about psychophysical energy (*qi*), the five phases (*wuxing*), and *yin* and *yang* polarities in all things. In contrast, Song Confucianism was enriched by borrowing from Buddhism—in particular, the Buddhist philosophy, regimen for self-cultivation, educational discipline, rules for monastic communities, and charitable institutions. Compared with the Han synthesis, the new Song Confucian synthesis incorporated more additional external elements, and so it was more centered on the ethical initiative and cultural creativity of individual literati and less focused on the initiative and role of the ruler.

In addition to a number of significant studies of Wang Anshi and Su Shi, considerable work has been done on Zhu Xi's criticisms of these two Northern Song thinkers; however, modern scholars have largely ignored Wang's and Su's followers during the Southern Song (1127–1279). Even scholars who have explored Wang's and the Su family's influence in the Southern Song have generally focused on their ideas about institutions or their belles lettres. Unfortunately, these topics have seldom been linked to their overall philosophies or integrated into systematic studies of philosophy. Thus modern researchers need to pay much more attention to these major schools.

Two examples of scholar-officials in the Southern Song who sought to integrate the teachings of Wang Anshi and Su Shi might suggest some reasons why these intellectual trends failed to compete successfully with Zhu Xi. These two examples happen to be the only men from Jinhua (in the central part of modern province of Zhejiang) who managed to pass the "erudite literati examination" (*boxue hongci ke*), the highest certified degree of mastery of all literary genres. One of them, Tang Zhongyou (1136–1188), was an external critic of the "*dao* learning" fellowship; the other, Lü Zuqian (1137–1181), was a leader within the fellowship.

Tang Zhongyou was, like Wang Anshi, a specialist on statecraft who had considerable faith in solving sociopolitical problems by reforming social, political, and economic institutions. Like Su Shi, he was also critical of the fellowship's claim to special understanding of the *dao* of heaven and earth, and he emphasized creative literary expression rather than abstract philosophical treatises on the *dao*. However, most modern scholars concentrate on Tang's personal clash with Zhu Xi and its impact on Zhu's political career. Soon after the emperor gave Zhu supervisory authority over an area where Tang served as a local official, Zhu impeached Tang for corruption and other alleged crimes. One of the two chief chancellors in the capital presented the case as simply arising from petty squabbles between rival intellectuals. The emperor, apparently agreeing with this assessment, decided merely to deny Tang's recently designated promotion to another bureaucratic post and to accept Zhu's resignation from the supervisory office. But especially after Zhu's version of *dao* learning came to be recognized as orthodoxy, Tang's guilt was taken for granted and his appreciation of Wang's and Su's ideas tarnished them.

Lü Zuqian was probably Zhu Xi's closest personal friend and benefactor from the early 1160s to 1181, when Lü died. By 1170, Lü had emerged as the most influential intellectual within the fellowship. For instance, the emperor commissioned Lü to select for an official compilation the greatest literary pieces written during the Northern Song. Wang Anshi, Su Shi, and Ouyang Xiu were the dominant figures in Lü's *Mirror to Song Prose* (*Song wenjian*). Although Cheng Yi had elevated learning the *dao* over studying literary culture (*wen*), Lü sought to reverse this trend toward polarizing *dao* and *wen* and to achieve a harmonious balance between them. Elsewhere in his own writings, when he commented on literary models, Lü often advocated studying Su Shi. His appreciation of Su Shi's emphasis on literary culture elicited strong criticism from Zhu Xi, who complained that Lü was vigorously defending Su Shi despite Su's heterodox ideas. Zhu also argued that Lü's excessive attention to teaching students how to pass the civil service examinations was the reason why Lü was so fond of Su's clever artfulness—which, according to Zhu, was achieved without adequate regard for ethical considerations. After Lü died, his reputation was damaged by attacks from Zhu and Zhu's followers. As a result, Lü has been widely regarded as merely a historian; only a few modern scholars, and only recently, have begun to take him seriously as a philosopher.

2. Other rivals of Zhu Xi considered themselves more true to the views of Mencius (Mengzi, c. 371–289 B.C.E.) on the original mind, innate virtues, and human nature.

The most famous of Zhu's contemporary rivals representing this Mencian tradition was Lu Jiuyuan (1139–1193), more widely known by his courtesy name, Lu Xiangshan. The Lu family came from an area near the border of Jiangxi Province; it grew into an extended family with considerable landholdings, an herbal drug business, and its own militia. Growing up in a relatively open frontier region, and as the youngest of several sons within a protective family environment, Lu developed a strong sense of his personal capacities and of the possibility of being good. Moreover, because he had no educational mentors outside his own family circle, he developed an especially keen sense of reading and understanding the *Mencius* directly, without the mediation of teachers or commentaries.

Lu Jiuyuan's self-confidence was evident in the relaxed manner in which he approached the civil service examinations and government service. He passed the examinations in 1172; the chief examiner who recognized Lu's genius and passed him was Lü Zuqian. (Lü also wrote laudatory letters introducing Lu Jiuyuan to Zhu Xi and others within the fellowship.) After passing the examination, Lu spent most of his remaining twenty-one years accepting whatever opportunities were offered for public service. With his exceptionally strong Mencian confidence in his own moral will and actions, he apparently experienced none of the anguish that beset Zhu Xi regarding the government of the time and made Zhu reluctant to accept government appointments.

Lu's intuitive concept of the Mencian original mind was graphically illustrated in 1172, when Yang Jian (1141–1226), a local magistrate adjudicating a lawsuit, asked him about the character of the original mind. Yang's insight into which litigant was right had come directly from his own original mind, rather than from the legal code or any other external factors, and so he asked if this clarity of perception was all that was necessary. Lu barked, "What else could there be?" Yang immediately withdrew to meditate, attained enlightenment, and became one of Lu's earliest and most notable followers.

In 1175 Lu Jiuyuan and Zhu Xi met for discussions at the Goose Lake Monastery, where they could address their differences in person. Lü Zuqian had arranged this meeting; Zhu had frequently written to Lü to complain that the Lu brothers were too Buddhist in seeking enlightenment of the mind without adequate reading of the Confucian classics. At the meeting, Zhu's suspicions about Lu Jiuyuan were confirmed. Early in the discussion, poems composed by the Lu brothers satirized Zhu Xi to such a degree that he suddenly turned pale, and Lü Zuqian called a recess. The poetry belittled Zhu's scholarship as fragmented and aimless. Instead of becoming mired in Zhu's exhaustive book learning and his externally directed striving for sagehood, the Lu brothers proposed that to regain the Mencian original mind, firm resolve and daily practice were needed. Thus the Lu brothers were presenting the quest for sagehood as a natural, spontaneous, uncomplicated process.

To counter Zhu's insistence on close, extensive reading of the classics, Lu Jiuyuan proposed a rather brazen retort. He planned to ask, "What classics had the ancient sage kings read?" His point was that even without the benefit of the classics, these early sage kings were still able to perceive their original minds and express their moral will in action. When Han and Tang classical scholarship flourished and produced the officially recognized commentaries on the classics, academic inquiry eclipsed both the Mencian quest for sagehood and the Mencian original mind. Similarly, Zhu's obsession with writing commentaries had apparently distracted him from realizing the original mind and achieving the ultimate Confucian ethical goals. Lu's elder brother stopped him from confronting Zhu so blatantly; but the planned retort was circulated among Lu Jiuyuan's students and was preserved in his collected works.

Later scholars regarded the meeting at Goose Lake as the dividing moment between Zhu's and Lu's schools of thought; however, the interactions among the participants over the next ten years suggest that this is a considerable overstatement. At least until Lü Zuqian died in 1181, Lu Jiuyuan moved steadily toward Lü's and Zhu's insistence on the importance of reading and studying the classics. Also, in his eulogy to Lü Zuqian, Lu expressed appreciation for Lü's instruction, which had enabled the Lu brothers to correct some of the wild ideas they had expressed at Goose Lake. In a letter to another friend, Lu observed that the *Doctrine of the Mean* talked about taking action only after study, inquiry, and reflection; thus, as in Zhu's philosophy, knowledge was the prerequisite for action. Zhu, for his part, writing to Lü actually praised Lu Jiuyuan for actually teaching students how to read texts. Moreover, when Lu visited Zhu's White Deer Grotto Academy in 1181, Zhu invited him to deliver a lecture to the students there. So pleased was Zhu with Lu's lecture—which was about the need to be mindful of Mencius's distinction between integrity and profit—that he had it engraved in stone.

Still, differences over pedagogy remained. Zhu had a specific curriculum in which certain classical texts should be read before others, and he wrote commentaries to guide students through his particular reading of the classics. Furthermore, he and Lü Zuqian compiled *Reflections on Things at Hand* (*Jinsi lu*), an anthology of the Northern Song masters, to prescribe and structure the way students entered the works of those Zhu considered the philosophical mentors of the fellowship. In such works, Zhu implicitly made himself the authoritative reader of the Confucian tradition. By contrast, Lu Jiuyuan was less structured, willingly allowing students to follow their own interests in reading a wider range of texts, although he did insist on a careful reading of the classics to discover their implicit meaning. He sometimes encouraged students to consult early commentaries to aid their understanding of the classics, but he was generally suspicious of recent commentaries and warned students against becoming overburdened by them; and unlike Zhu, he did not write commentaries himself. Another pedagogical difference was that beginning in 1188, Zhu Xi strongly criticized Lu Jiuyuan for not reprimanding students who had a penchant for Chan (Zen) Buddhism.

With regard to Zhu's and Lu's pedagogy, we should note that some of the differences between them reflected the audiences being addressed. Most of Zhu's famous comments about reading were addressed to an elite—the literati—whereas Lu was famous for his lectures to mass audiences, and some of his comments about reading also appear to be meant for a larger audience. Other qualifications may also be necessary. For instance, Lu Jiuyuan occasionally made spectacular statements, as when he claimed that the classics were footnotes to himself. But in the case of this particular statement, many modern scholars leave off its first half, which makes it dependent on comprehending what is truly fundamental while studying the classics. The idea that Lu disregarded the classics arises from some of Zhu's sharp condemnations of Lu after the mid–1180s. But at the same time, Zhu also criticized Lu for quoting the classics at wearisome length and for adhering too closely to literal readings of the texts. Thus it is problematic to regard Lu as having neglected the classics or as having tried to transcend them.

However, even if the Goose Lake meeting between Zhu and Lu was not a watershed, and even if we must qualify some of their differences over pedagogy, there were other important disputes. For example, Zhu was outraged by Lu's essay commemorating the renovation of Wang Anshi's memorial hall near Lu's home; Lu had evaluated Wang very positively and had said that the founders of the "*dao* learning" fellowship were largely responsible for the failure of Wang's reforms.

Also, in the late 1180s Zhu and Lu became embroiled in a debate over Zhou Dunyi's *Diagram of the Supreme Ultimate*. Zhu's philosophical synthesis linked Zhou's concepts of the "supreme ultimate" (*taiji*) and the "ultimate of nonbeing" (*wuji*) with the Cheng brothers' concept of principle (*li*) to produce a metaphysics that would counter the Buddhists. But Lu pointed out that the origins of the diagram and the term "ultimate of nonbeing" were Daoist; moreover, even if Zhou had adopted the diagram, he must certainly have realized that it was mistaken, because he never referred to the "nonultimate" in his other writings. This challenge seriously undermined Zhu's claim to represent the most authentic, purest Confucian tradition. Zhu objected strongly to what he regarded as Lu's slander of Zhou but could not refute the suspicion that the origins of the term and diagram were Daoist. This part of the debate was inconclusive, but it became very famous and drew so much attention that almost no notice was given to another aspect of Lu's challenge.

In his letters about Zhou's diagram, Lu also questioned Zhu's authority to redefine the Confucian tradition. Lu said that both he and Zhu were adrift amid diverse opinions and asked how Zhu could be so sure that his perception of principle was anything more than just another opinion. Lu considered such certainty unfounded and said that it arose because scholars like Zhu pursued literary culture, broad erudition, and abstract theorizing instead of seeking the truth from concrete facts. Zhu had gone even further astray by building a philosophical synthesis on overly erudite texts and on some mysterious secret about the "ultimate of nonbeing" that Zhou Dunyi had purportedly been the first sage to discover.

Although Zhu and Lu did not directly debate human nature and the mind when they confronted each other in their letters, that was historically the most important issue dividing their schools of thought, and scholars have focused on it for centuries. Zhu identified human nature with principle and the mind with psychophysical energy (*qi*). Only because mind was pure energy could it enclose and command human nature and the feelings. Since the mind easily drifted and pursued passions, the way to morality lay in disciplining the mind through study and cultivation in order to submit it to principle. Lu equated mind with principle; thus, one's mind could directly perceive and follow principle without such an intensive quest for learning and investigating texts and for other things outside one's own heart-and-mind.

3. Some of Zhu's rivals had once participated in the fellowship but became alienated from it beginning in the early 1180s, when it became increasingly exclusive and Zhu claimed its leadership after Lü Zuqian's death.

The most famous dissenter in this category is now Chen Liang (1143–1194). In the late 1160s and 1170s, he had studied under the direction of the fellowship's leaders. One of his writings during this period, his preface (1173) to comments by three of the Northern Song masters on governmental affairs (*San xiansheng lunshi lu xu*), is so characteristic of the fellowship that after Lü Zuqian passed it along to Zhu Xi, it became mixed with Zhu's own writings and was included in printings of Zhu's collected works. By the late 1170s, however, Chen became more radical, having repeatedly failed the civil service examinations. Also, he felt frustrated because philosophical discussions were distracting the fellowship, and the country, from a pressing need to liberate North China from the rule imposed in 1127 by the Jurchen from the forests of Manchuria. After venting his frustrations in memorandums to the emperor in 1178, and under Lü's admonitions, Chen quieted down. But less than a year after Lü's death, Chen voiced his radical views in a series of ten essays that he sent to Zhu Xi in 1182.

In these essays, Chen advocated flexibly following expediency or weighing situations (*quan*) to address current problems. Zhu found the essays so disturbing that he said he dared not show them to his students, lest they stray from standard ethical principles. Chen was going beyond the traditional Confucian awareness of the need to adjust the standard (*jing*) to varying situations and times. He equated integrity or what is right (*yi*) with expediency, and so in his synthesis what is right evolved in accord with time and situation. Whereas Chen felt that the concepts could be unified into a utilitarian ethics of end results, Zhu continued to uphold a more polar relationship in which what was right should always take precedence over any consideration of practical results. Actually, Chen was critical of past governments as well as of policies of his day, and he upheld norms that he considered inherent in the proper functioning of institutions. But Zhu condemned Chen's ethics as endorsing any successful power—a caricature of Chen's position that still dominates most perceptions of Chen's utilitarian ethics.

Taking a holistic view of integrity and utility, Chen Liang sought to revise the historical narrative of selected Han and Tang rulers to transform them into positive models for solving the country's problems. Many members of the fellowship vehemently condemned these past heroes on ethical grounds, but Chen argued that he was following the example of Kongzi (Confucius, 551–479 B.C.E.). Because Daoists were opposed to active participation by governments in society, Confucius had, in editing the classics, washed the historical records clean in order to provide examples of and encouragement for government action and community service. Unfortunately, later Confucians ignored the master's high-minded purpose and misrepresented the bowdlerized records as an actual historical standard by which to criticize the honest efforts of later generations of statesmen.

Some of Zhu's private comments to students suggest that he was aware that antiquity was not as ideal as classical reconstructions presented it; thus he could not directly answer Chen's bold assertion that Confucius had deliberately altered the classical records. Instead, Zhu shifted the focus of the issue: since Chen's Han and Tang rulers and statesmen had obvious failings, Chen surely must be willing to embrace any expedient wielders of power as long as they achieved something. Zhu also maintained that Chen and other Zhejiang literati were obsessed with expediency and so had been led to make unethical concessions on matters of principle.

Zhu felt that Chen had willfully concealed the imperfections of the Han and Tang heroes; Zhu himself, by contrast, insisted on judging all times and all persons by the same standard—a standard that remained even though the *dao* had not been realized or put into practice for at least fifteen centuries, including the Han and Tang periods. Both Zhu and Chen spoke of the standard as the *dao* in their debate on whether or not the *dao* had been eclipsed during the course of history. As a result, later scholars took this discussion of the *dao* as speculative nonempirical philosophy—that is, metaphysics. In part, this confusion arose because scholars focused only on the letters Zhu and Chen exchanged, when they should also have taken Chen's ten essays into account. Those essays had impelled Zhu to address the issue of a changing, even transitory, *dao*.

Zhu perceived, accurately, that the thrust of Chen's arguments about the impact of changes over time was to make values historical, or relative to time and context. Chen's relative values were grounded in his surmise that there was no qualitative difference between unidealized high antiquity and later dynasties. Thus Chen's concept of the *dao* as inherent in historical change provoked a debate over the enduring nature of cultural values. As a philosopher, Zhu was committed to classical truths transcending time; as a historian, Chen traced changes through time and circumstances in order to understand present problems. Zhu himself had studied history, but to him it was a handmaiden in the service of philosophical doctrines and polemics; indeed, he complained that Chen had been corrupted by historical studies.

Chen's close friend Ye Shi (1150–1223) provides an example of a more prominent scholar-official who broke with the fellowship because of its growing exclusiveness. Ye's contemporaries had considered him a leader of the fellowship, largely because of his political activism on its behalf, including his famous defense of Zhu Xi to the emperor in 1188. In his later years, however, Ye became famous for his stinging criticisms of the speculative philosophy and intellectual assumptions associated with the fellowship. For instance, he said that even the early disciples of Confucius had forsaken the master's practical ideas about serving one's country and society; moreover, whereas Confucius had simply sought to preserve antiquity through the classics, his professed disciples in later centuries wanted to interject philosophical profundities so as to gain fame for their creative genius. Ye was not only attacking members of the fellowship for their creative reconstructions of antiquity; he was also undermining the basis for Chen Liang's efforts to provide an alternative to the fellowship's value system. In his vitriolic attacks against the creative Song reformulations of Confucianism, Ye might have been partly influenced by attitudes current in the fourth category of opponents to Zhu Xi.

4. Still other rivals of Zhu Xi's rejected the major philosophical assumptions that Ouyang Xiu and other Northern Song Confucians had developed. These individuals might best be called "conventional Confucians" (*shiru*) because, although they lived during the Song, they did not embrace eleventh-century reconstructions of the classical tradition. They consistently held that various schools of Song Confucianism were no more than the narrow views and concoctions of recent thinkers. Whereas the Song Confucians focused on the mind and the quest for sagehood, these "conventional Confucians," like their predecessors in the Han and the early Tang, concentrated on textual studies, especially studies of the Confucian classics. Indeed, the conventional Confucians deliberately and closely followed Han and Tang classical scholarship.

The best-known scholarly family associated with the conventional Confucians was that of Zhou Mi (1232—after 1308). Almost all the other conventional Confucians, such as Qin Gui (1090–1155), Lin Li (1142 *chin-shih*), Gao Wenhu (1134–1212), and Han Tuozhou (1152–1207), have tended to be totally rejected as "anti-intellectual" because they used governmental power in an effort to suppress the fellowship. Zhou Mi was not alive during the twelfth-century government prohibitions against the fellowship, but the others actively called for such bans. Since they ended up on the losing side of the struggle when Zhu Xi's views became state orthodoxy in 1241, these conventional Confucians lost their voice; and for centuries almost no one has been interested in preserving their writings or looking for the philosophical reasons underlying their opposition to the fellowship and to Zhu Xi.

Zhu Xi's Followers

Zhu Xi's followers provided one impetus for giving Zhu Xi the status of state orthodoxy in 1241. One of his contemporaries mentioned in passing that Zhu had about a thousand students, and modern scholars have identified the names of 467 literati who sought his instruction or advice (or both) at one time or another. Between one-third and one-half of these men came from Fujian; most of the rest lived in either Zhejiang or Jiangxi. Hence, Zhu's circle had a solid base in the prosperous southeastern coastal province where Zhu himself had spent most of his life, and it also had a significant presence in the two provinces where his major rivals lived.

Of Zhu's students, 28 percent held government office at some time; clearly, then, they were as a group very successful in entering government service despite the hostility of the government to the fellowship during at least part of their lifetime. Notwithstanding Zhu's focus on pursuing moral cultivation and scholarship instead of government careers, at least 131 of his students were not content with the fellowship's program of moral cultivation as the basis of their identity and social status as literati. In other words, dedication to moral cultivation alone would not have given them the public status, social prestige, or recognition that they gained through government service.

Huang Gan (1152–1221) held government posts in several areas where he disseminated Zhu Xi's teachings; when he retired, students from various areas traveled to Fujian for further study with him. Besides having a reputation for government service, Huang was Zhu's son-in-law and designated successor. Huang encouraged Zhu's followers to hold regular regional meetings and to build networks among themselves. As Zhu's literary executor, Huang wrote one of the first biographies of Zhu and also coedited the first collection of Zhu's recorded conversations. In these activities, Huang focused conservatively on faithfully maintaining and preserving Zhu's doctrines.

According to Huang Gan, the succession in the *dao* tradition culminated with Zhu Xi. In his biography of Zhu, he said that very few individuals could transmit the *dao*, but Zhu had done so and indeed had done something even more profound and rare: Zhu and Mencius were the two men who, after Confucius, were able to make the *dao* prominent and clear. By placing Zhu and Mencius in the same category, Huang gave Zhu a much higher place than was occupied by the "four masters" of the Northern Song, whose ideas were so important in Zhu's philosophic synthesis. Huang further claimed that henceforth all people should simply follow the *dao* elucidated by Zhu; to deviate from it was to err.

Chen Chun (1159–1223) also considered Zhu Xi the culmination of the Confucian tradition and the only gateway to the learning of the sages; and he too exalted Zhu above the four Northern Song masters, because Zhu had been able to refine and clarify their ideas and unify them with the good points of other schools of thought. Chen's major work was *Terms Explained* (*Beixi ziyi*), a systematic exposition of twenty-five of Zhu's major philosophical concepts. The clarity of Chen's presentation has made this work a crucial guide to Zhu's philosophical system. Chen felt that he had received unique instruction from Zhu Xi and had a special mission to pass it down to future generations. During his first period of study with Zhu, in

1190–1191, the master had taught him to seek the source (*genyuan*) of principle—a doctrine that, according to Chen, had been entrusted to no one else. In 1199, during his second and final period of study with Zhu, the master encouraged him to seek within himself and thus take a more independent and leading role in Fujian. However, most of Zhu's followers recognized Huang Gan rather than Chen Chun as the master's authoritative successor.

When He Ji (1188–1268) returned to Jinhua in Zhejiang to establish Zhu's teachings there, he and Wang Bo (1197–1274) and their successors presented Huang Gan as Zhu's successor and themselves as thereby inheriting the most orthodox of Zhu's teachings. Most later followers of Zhu acquiesced in this claim, and in He's and Wang's relegation of others, like Chen Chun, to branch lineages. Moreover, whereas Chen focused on *Reflection of Things at Hand*, Zhu Xi and Lü Zuqian's anthology of the writings of the Northern Song masters, He Ji and his successors turned their attention to Zhu's commentaries on the Four Books. As a result, Zhu's followers in Zhejiang made him even more prominent relative to the Northern Song masters. Although He Ji presented himself as Huang Gan's successor, some of Huang's own statements indicate that he had looked primarily to other scholar-officials to carry his teachings to the next generation.

Zhen Dexiu (1178–1235) was apparently the person in whom Huang Gan placed most confidence as the leader of the next generation. As an official, Huang realized that Zhen's political career would be an asset to the Zhu school. Zhen replaced Zhang Zai with Zhu as one of the "four masters" to whom heaven had entrusted long-lost secrets of the *dao*. In his *Classic on the Mind-and-Heart* (*Xinjing*), Zhen quoted Zhu, along with Zhou Dunyi and the Cheng brothers, as classic thinkers in their own right. In his *Extended Meaning of the Great Learning* (*Daxue yanyi*), Zhen drew heavily on Zhu's comments on the *Daxue* (one of the Four Books) in an effort to establish a program for the spiritual cultivation of the emperor as the foundation for governance. When he presented these writings to the emperor in 1234, Zhen had an opportunity to urge Licong (r. 1224–1264) to give Zhu's version of *dao* learning the status of orthodoxy.

Seven years later, in 1241 (as we have seen), the emperor reversed the government's policy, recognized the legitimacy of the fellowship, enshrined Zhu Xi in the Confucian temple, and ordered that Zhu's commentaries be used by government students preparing for the civil service examinations. Thereafter, some people within Zhu's tradition claimed that Zhen had almost singlehandedly influenced the emperor to change the dynastic policy. Actually, however, the pleas of Zhen Dexiu, Wei Liaoweng (1178–1237), and other followers of Zhu probably had less effect than the pressures created by the Mongol conquest of North China, and especially by the Mongols' efforts in the 1230s to present themselves, culturally and politically, as the legitimate rulers of China. Also, other individuals—such as Lü Zuqian's student Qiao Xingjian (1156–1241)—apparently played a more crucial role at the imperial court in advocating this kind of pragmatic policy to support the dynasty in its struggle against the Mongols. Ever since the fellowship first emerged on the national level in the 1080s, its fortunes had waxed and waned largely in conjuction with the presence or absence of sympathetic officials at the top of the bureaucracy who had access to the emperor. Politics and expediency were thus factors in the ascendancy of this school of Confucian learning. Nevertheless, the claim about Zhen's role was accepted in the official Song dynastic history (*Song shi*) compiled in the 1340s.

The *Song shi* completed the long process of transforming *dao* learning and reducing it to the boundaries of the Zhu Xi school. The official dynastic history reserved *daoxue* to designate a very narrow line of thinkers, beginning with the Northern Song masters, culminating with Zhu Xi, and passed down to Huang Gan and a few selected disciples. In official biographies, even such leading figures in the fellowship as Zhen Dexiu and Lü Zuqian were excluded from this special category; their biographies were consigned to a large "forest of scholars" that included, among others, Zhu's rivals. Zhu Xi's victory over his rivals and his dominance over his followers—thus enshrined in official history—became the authoritative narrative.

Although Zhu Xi's followers presented themselves as faithfully maintaining his doctrines, they did make some significant modifications. Huang Gan, Chen Chun, and Zhen Dexiu subtly shifted the center of Zhu's system away from speculative philosophy and toward cultural values and spiritual cultivation. For instance, Chen Chun's *Terms Explained* did not even include the concept of psychophysical energy (*qi*), which was crucial to Zhu's metaphysics. Although Chen was hostile to the Lu Jiuyuan school, Zhen Dexiu encouraged dialogue with Lu's followers and incorporated some of their emphasis on the "learning of the mind-and-heart" (*xinxue*) into his expositions of Zhu's tradition. Regarding statecraft, some of Zhen Dexiu's and Wang Bo's discussions of governance and institutions suggest borrowings from Lü Zuqian and other thinkers from Zhejiang.

Conclusion

Ideas from some of the Zhu Xi's friends and rivals contributed to the development of his version of Confucianism and continued, after his death, to influence his followers and draw his school of thought back somewhat toward the center of the twelfth-century "*dao* learning" fellowship. Thus, studying Zhu's rivals and followers is crucial to understanding Zhu's philosophical synthesis and its historical development.

See also Lu Xiangshan; Zhu Xi.

Bibliography

Adler, Joseph A. "Chu Hsi and Divination." In *Sung Dynasty Uses of the I Ching*, ed. Kidder Smith, Jr., Peter K. Bol, Joseph Adler, and Don J. Wyatt. Princeton, N.J.: Princeton University Press, 1990.

Bol, Peter K. "Chu Hsi's Redefinition of Literati Learning." In *Neo-Confucian Education: The Formative State*, ed. William Theodore de Bary and John Chaffee. Berkeley: University of California Press, 1989.

———. *"This Culture of Ours": Intellectual Transitions in T'ang and Sung China*. Stanford, Calif.: Stanford University Press, 1992.

Chan, Wing-tsit. *Chu Hsi: New Studies*. Honolulu: University of Hawaii Press, 1989.

———, trans. *Neo-Confucian Terms Explained: (The Pei-hsi Tzu-i) by Ch'en Ch'un, 1159–1223*. New York: Columbia University Press, 1986.

———, trans. *Reflections on Things at Hand: The Neo-Confucian Anthology Compiled by Chu Hsi and Lü Tsu-ch'ien*. New York: Columbia University Press, 1967.

Chu, Ron-Guey. "Chen Te-hsiu and the 'Classic on Governance': The Coming of Age of Neo-Confucian Statecraft." Ph.D. dissertation, Columbia University, 1988.

de Bary, William Theodore. "Chen Te-hsiu and Statecraft." In *Ordering the World: Approaches to State and Society in Sung Dynasty China*, ed. Conrad Schirokauer and Robert Hymes. Berkeley: University of California Press, 1993.

Gardner, Daniel K., trans. *Learning to Be a Sage: Selections from the Conversations of Master Chu, Arranged Topically*. Berkeley: University of California Press, 1990.

Huang, Chin-shing. "Chu Hsi versus Lu Hsiang-shan: A Philosophical Interpretation." *Journal of Chinese Philosophy* 14.2 (1987): 179–208.

Hymes, Robert P. "Lu Chiu-yüan, Academies, and the Problem of the Local Community." In *Neo-Confucian Education: The Formative State*, ed. William Theodore de Bary and John Chaffee. Berkeley: University of California Press, 1989.

Kim, Oaksook Chun. "Chu Hsi and Lu Hsiang-shan: A Study of Philosophical Achievements and Controversy in Neo-Confucianism." Ph.D. dissertation, University of Iowa, 1980.

Kim, Yung Sik. *The Natural Philosophy of Chu Hsi (1130–1200)*. Philadelphia, Pa.: American Philosophical Society, 2000.

Liu, James T. C. *China Turning Inward: Intellectual-Political Changes in the Early Twelfth Century*. Cambridge, Mass.: Council on East Asian Studies, Harvard University, 1988.

———. "Wei Liao-weng's Thwarted Statecraft." In *Ordering the World: Approaches to State and Society in Sung Dynasty China*, ed. Conrad Schirokauer and Robert Hymes. Berkeley: University of California Press, 1993.

Liu, Ts'un-yan. "The Disciples of Zhu Xi as Seen in Yi Hwang's *Songgye Won Myong Ihak T'ongnok*." *T'oung Pao*, 73(1–3), 1987, pp. 16–32.

Lo, Winston Wan. *The Life and Thought of Ye Shih*. Hong Kong: Chinese University of Hong Kong Press, 1974.

Mao, Huaixin. "The Establishment of the School of Chu Hsi and Its Propagation in Fukien." In *Chu Hsi and Neo-Confucianism*, ed. Wing-tsit Chan. Honolulu: University of Hawaii Press, 1989.

Tillman, Hoyt Cleveland. *Ch'en Liang on Public Interest and the Law*. Monographs of the Society for Asian and Comparative Philosophy, No. 12. Honolulu: University of Hawaii Press, 1994.

———. *Confucian Discourse and Chu Hsi's Ascendancy*. Honolulu: University of Hawaii Press, 1992.

———. *Utilitarian Confucianism: Ch'en Liang's Challenge to Chu Hsi*. Cambridge, Mass.: Harvard University, Council on East Asian Studies, 1982.

Wilson, Thomas A. *Genealogy of the Way: The Construction and Uses of the Confucian Tradition in Late Imperial China*. Stanford, Calif.: Stanford University Press, 1995.

Yü, Ying-shih. "Morality and Knowledge in Chu Hsi's Philosophical System." In *Chu Hsi and Neo-Confucianism*, ed. Wing-tsit Chan. Honolulu: University of Hawaii Press, 1986.

Zhuangzi (Chuang Tzu)

Chad Hansen

Zhuangzi (c. 360 B.C.E.), also known as Zhuang Zhou, along with Laozi, is a defining figure in Chinese Daoism. Zhuangzi probably wrote only parts of the first seven chapters, the so-called inner chapters, of the present text of the *Zhuangzi*. The rest was written by thinkers of related but distinct theoretical leanings, who often expand on themes in the "inner chapters."

The relation between the two founding figures of Daoism is an enduring and growing puzzle. According to Chinese tradition, Zhuangzi inherited Daoism—a monist view of reality and a mystical theory of knowledge—from Laozi. What we know of Zhuangzi's life is mainly what we can surmise from the text. It hardly confirms that traditional story. On the contrary, the text, along with recent archaeological discoveries, makes it equally plausible that Zhuangzi was the original Daoist. In fact, A. C. Graham (1981) speculated that he may have been responsible for Laozi's being regarded as a Daoist. Zhuangzi used Laozi as a fictional figure in his dialogues in order to "talk down" to Confucius. The doctrines put into Laozi's mouth sounded enough like the popular (then anonymous) *Daodejing* that Chinese tradition subsequently came to call it the *Laozi*.

I will assume some theoretical connection between Laozi and the *Zhuangzi* but not necessarily that of teacher and student. This simplifies our interpretive task, since it need not settle the even more difficult interpretive questions surrounding the *Laozi*. I will simply treat Zhuangzi as someone dealing with the philosophical issues that preoccupied others in ancient China. He shares both terminology and background assumptions with most other major philosophical figures. In particular, I will not presuppose that Zhuangzi changed the meaning of *dao* from its usual ethical sense to a distinctively Daoist sense or that he had a mystical or religious experience and tried to describe it. The various metaphysical statuses that a *dao* can have will be the same for other thinkers and will be conceptually linked to the role of a *dao* as a guide to action—to its irreducible normative character.

Zhuangzi's familiarity with and confident handling of the technical language of ancient Chinese semantics makes it probable that he had studied the arguments closely. The best indicator of this intellectual influence on Zhuangzi is his long-standing friendship and interaction with the relativist and monist dialectician Hui Shi (370–319 B.C.E.). Zhuangzi lamented that Hui Shi's death had deprived him of the person "on whom he sharpened his wits." Arguably, Zhuangzi's crucial strategy for combating the ancient Chinese version of realism comes from Hui Shi. This article will therefore start with Hui Shi's theses (which are not included within those of the later Mohists). In any case, our only source of information about them is from the *Zhuangzi*.

Zhuangzi, despite his obvious affection for Hui Shi, is often critical of Hui's optimistic faith that debate and analysis can resolve philosophical issues. Traditional accounts have taken this as the haughty disdain of a mystic, Zhuangzi, for Hui's "logic." However, Hui's theses deal with language, not logic, and they undermine rather than support drawing distinctions. Therefore, if we resist regarding Zhuangzi as Laozi's mystical disciple, we get a strikingly different view of the dynamics between the two philosophical friends. Hui (probably busy with politics) emerges as an erudite, enthusiastic, loquacious but somewhat confused, rather mystical, semantic dilettante. Zhuangzi, by contrast, appears to be an accomplished and consistently rigorous linguistic analyst. Zhuangzi reports enjoying debating with Hui—supposedly because Hui had enough learning to be worth refuting. Still, Hui was ultimately a soft target for a dialectician of Zhuangzi's caliber.

Hui Shi's Teaching

The chapter "Empire" in the *Zhuangzi* contains an account of Hui Shi's doctrines, at the end of its "history of philosophy." The history traces the progression of different *dao* (guiding doctrines) leading up to Zhuangzi. We can understand Hui's motivation best by viewing these passages against the background of the realist theory of language given in the *Mohist Canon*. The realists' doctrine was motivated by the idea that real-world similarities and differences provide the basis for the conventional "carving" or "picking out" that divides the "stuff" of the world into "thing kinds." They advanced a rudimentary theory of natural kinds (natural distinctions in reality). It purported to explain how words and language could reliably guide action.

Hui Shi tried to undermine the Mohists' semantic proposal by drawing attention to comparatives. Comparatives also mark distinctions, but it is less plausible that the distinctions are "in the world." Where we draw a comparison or contrast is relative to our purpose and point of view. Whether, say, this ant is large or small varies as we compare it with other ants or other animals. Hui focuses on distinctions such as large-small, thick-thin, high-low, south-north, and today-yesterday. The common feature of these pairs is that from different standpoints we can assign either member of a pair to the same object. His typical paradox makes sense as a comment about how we might redescribe familiar examples from different perspectives:

> Heaven is as low as the earth; mountains are level with marshes.
> The sun from one perspective is in the middle; from another, declining.
> Natural kinds are from one perspective living and from another perspective dying.
> I go to Yue today and arrive yesterday.

The most important implication for theory of language strikes at the Achilles' heel of Mohist realism—the construction of similarity classes, i.e., "The ten-thousand thing-kinds are ultimately alike and ultimately different. Call this the great similarity-difference."

As the *Zhuangzi* develops this insight, it amounts to the claim that we can find a difference between any two things no matter how alike they are, and we can also find a similarity between any two things no matter how different they are. Therefore, even if there are objective similarities and differences, they do not justify any particular way of distinguishing between thing-kinds. For every category and name we use, we could have had conventions that just as consistently, and with equal "world-guidedness," divide stuff up differently.

The list of Hui's sayings, however, begins and ends with claims about reality. He presupposes an ultimate perspective and a concept of "everything." Since distinctions are not in things, reality must be "one." His formulation invites the view (usually attributed to Daoists) that reality is a single, indivisible totality:

> The ultimately great, which has nothing outside it, call it the "great one"!
> The ultimately small, which has nothing inside it, call it the "small one"!
> Universally love the ten-thousand thing-kinds; the cosmos is one *ti* (substantive part).

This concluding statement echoes the Mohists' ethical doctrine of universal love and uses their technical term *ti*. The account in the *Zhuangzi* does not give us Hui's reasoning, nor can we be sure of the implications he drew from these formulas. However, the list exhibits a common tendency toward the "relativist fallacy," drawing absolute conclusions from relative premises. Most translators, for example, agree with Hui that it is rational to conclude that all distinctions distort reality. (The fact that judgments are relative to some perspective gives us no reason to conclude anything about absolute reality.)

Since interpreters commonly treat all Daoists as committing this fallacy, we should start out by noting that the presentation of Hui's views in the *Zhuangzi* concludes: "He had many perspectives and his library would fill five carts. His doctrine was self-contradictory and his language did not hit the target: his intent to make sense of things." This suggests a hypothesis that Zhuangzi understood the later Mohists' proof of the incoherence of denying all distinctions. Consider also Graham's speculation about Gongsun Long's "Pointing and Things" and the argument that we cannot point to an ultimate one. Whether or not Gongsun Long rejected the inference of a concept of "everything," Zhuangzi clearly rejected it. The text almost paraphrases Hui in Zhuangzi's skeptical rebuttal:

> "The cosmos and I were born together; the ten-thousand things and I are one." Now, having already constructed a "one," is it possible to say something about it? Having already called it a "one," can we fail to say something about it? "One" and saying it make two. Two and one make three and, going from here, even a skilled calculator cannot keep up with us—let alone an ordinary person.

Zhuangzi: Skeptical Perspectivalism

Zhuangzi had a unique philosophical style that has contributed to the tendency to treat him as an irrationalist. He wrote philosophical fantasy rather than direct argument. Some western readers interpret this style as romantic, as rejecting reason for emotion. A more plausible hypothesis is that Zhuangzi presents his positions in fantasized dialogues in order to illustrate and conform to a pluralist perspective. He puts positions up for consideration as if endorsing them and then, after reflection, abandons them. He does this either in an imagined conversation among fantastic creatures (rebellious thieves, distorted freaks, or converted Confucians) or as an internal monologue. In his fantasized dialogues, Zhuangzi seems to challenge us to identify his voice. Even his monologues typically end with a double rhetorical question in place of a conclusion, e.g., "Then is there really any *X*? Or is there no *X*?"

One key to Zhuangzi's adaptation of Hui Shi's relativism is his treatment of "useful." Everything is useful from some position or other, and there are positions from which even the most useful thing is useless or useful precisely in being useless. Zhuangzi illustrates this theme with his famous parables of a huge "useless" tree that, consequently, no one ever chopped down and a huge gourd—it was useless to eat but made a great boat. Pragmatic arguments (like those of Mozi) will always be relative to some implicit (and possibly controversial) value. This observation does not justify our abandoning pragmatic arguments (which, as we will see below, Zhuangzi uses repeatedly). It only prompts us to be aware that our assumptions about pragmatic "success" might be controversial.

Zhuangzi develops his perspectivalism in a more consistent direction than Hui's. Possibly because of his knowledge of the Mohist refutation, he does not fall into the trap of rejecting all language (as, arguably, Laozi did). Being natural does not require abandoning words. Human speaking, from empty greetings and small talk to the disputes of philosophers, is as natural a noise as birdsong. Disputing philosophers are "pipes of nature." Zhuangzi's use of this metaphor signals that nothing he is going to say entails that disputation should stop, any more than that brooks must stop babbling. Then he considers an objection to his opening metaphor: "Language is not blowing breath; language users have language. That which it 'languages', however, is never fixed."

He develops this critique with his own analysis of all linguistic distinctions as indexical. His argument relies heavily on some core terms of Chinese philosophical analysis: *shi* (is this, right) and *fei* (not this, wrong). He starts by highlighting the indexical content of *shi* by contrasting it with *pi* (that). Zhuangzi asks if anything is inherently "this" or "that" or cannot be "this" or "that." He then shifts to the contrast *shi-fei* (right-wrong), which governs all linguistic distinctions. Relative to a name, any object is either *shi* (is this, right) or *fei* (is not this, wrong). These keys to language analysis illustrate the claim that it does not have any rigid, naming relation to the world. Language traces our changing position relative to reality as much as its joints and fissures.

This perspectival pluralism differs from western subjectivity. Zhuangzi does not highlight the perspectives of continuing individual consciousness or internal representations—the private mental world. Arguably, Chinese thinkers did not generate anything comparable to western folk psychology. Zhuangzi seems as fascinated by the shifting perspectives within the same person at different times or in different moods as he is by interpersonal differences in viewpoint. His main theoretical focus, however, is on the slants arising from using language differently, e.g., being influenced by a different moral discourse. Thus he concludes that the dispute between Confucians and Mohists is irresolvable.

Zhuangzi does reflect, in some passages, on the perspective of "self." Recalling Laozi's emphasis on contrasts, he thinks this perspective arose as a contrast with "other." He suggests that the deep motive for the distinction is our inability to identify the source of pleasure, anger, sadness, joy, forethought, regret, change, and immobility. They "alternate day and night" and, not knowing whence they come, we give up and merely accept them. Without them there would be no "self," and without "self" there would be no "choosing of one thing over another." He notes the inevitability of our assumption that there is some "true ruler" harmonizing and organizing the self, then adds, skeptically, that we never find any sign of it.

Intuitionism

Confucians, particularly innatists (e.g., Mencius) do presuppose a "natural ruler"—the moral heart. Zhuangzi wonders how it can be any more natural than the other "hundred joints, nine openings, and six viscera are." Do they need a ruler? Cannot each rule itself? Or take turns? To identify one organ as supreme conflicts with the intention to give a natural basis for morality. (Mencius addresses this problem in connection with the distinction between nature and fate.)

Zhuangzi observes that all the bodily organs grow together in encountering and adapting to life. As the heart does this, it is *cheng* (completed)—a term Zhuangzi uses somewhat ironically as suggesting that any completion leaves some defect in its wake. Translators frequently render *cheng* as "biased." That translation effectively emphasizes this implicit criticism of idealistic Confucianism. It suggests that the heart does acquire a *shi-fei* direction from its upbringing. The translation, however, loses Zhuangzi's ironic twist. *Cheng*, like "success" and "accomplishment," denotes something we all seek. Zhuangzi's use suggests that our natural and common goal of growth and maturity is not possible without some kind of skewing and loss. In a striking illustration, Zhuangzi observes that playing a note requires a zither player to "not-play" all the others.

Thus, all hearts equally achieve *cheng*. They grow up just as the rest of the body does. For the heart, this amounts to acquiring a pattern of tendencies to *shi-fei* judgment. Every person's heart acquires some pattern or other. Hence, if this heart, which grows with the body, is the authority, then we all equally have one. Confucian innatists make a question-begging assumption about which pattern of *cheng* (completion) is really right. They advocate a program of cultivating the *xin* (heart-mind) so that it will give the correct *shi-*

fei judgments. Without such cultivation, they imply, we lose our heart's natural potential. The sage's heart-mind is the ultimate Mencian standard for right judgment. The sage is supposedly one who has fully cultivated his natural moral potential. Zhuangzi wonders what standard we use to distinguish a sage's heart-mind from a fool's. Each has a heart that makes *shi-fei* judgments. If we use *A*'s heart as a guide, *A* will look like a sage and *B* like a fool, and vice versa. There appears to be no way to identify the proper way to cultivate all existing heart-minds. The innatists beg another question in favor of their acquired leaning when they advocate cultivation. An appeal to the "natural ruler" should simply result in the empty injunction to act as we decide to act.

Zhuangzi's analysis of the *chengxin* (completed heart-mind) echoes Laozi's view that knowledge and attitudes are unconsciously acquired in the process of learning language. Attitudes that seem natural and spontaneous simply reflect an early upbringing that has become second nature. No innate or spontaneous dispositions survive without *cheng* influences. Zhuangzi says that the heart lacks a *shi-fei* unless it has been put there in the process of *cheng*. To deny that is "like going to Yue today and arriving yesterday!"

Interpretive Issues

At this point, we face serious interpretive controversies. Traditional interpretations take Zhuangzi as believing in a God-like mystical *dao*. As we have seen, Zhuangzi's stylistic use of fantasy and parables makes him unusually malleable; interpreters can bend him to their own philosophical perspective. (Perhaps Zhuangzi intended this outcome to illustrate the vagaries of discourse.) We can either attribute perspectival pluralism to him (or what actually follows from this doctrine) or suppose that Zhuangzi was prone to the relativist fallacy. Most translators inadvertently do the latter because they assume that an absolute conclusion does follow from the relative premises. That is a philosophical, but not necessarily an interpretive, error. Zhuangzi may have been no clearer a thinker than your average translator.

The only evidence is his text. If we can read it in a philosophically coherent way, then, lacking independent evidence of his ineptitude, the translator's argument begs an important question. The translation tradition thus relies on the old myth that Zhuangzi learned Daoist monism from Laozi. If he was philosophically more clever than Hui Shi, the usual translations do him an injustice.

Interpreters who accept the affiliation with Laozi tend to read Zhuangzi's pluralism as leading to a dogmatic monism linked to an "error theory," i.e., the view that everyone else's commonsense picture of a pluralistic world is absolutely wrong. A minority read it as classic relativism—everyone is right. Neither conclusion, however, follows merely from the plurality of perspectives. One can argue that each conclusion explains certain passages. Still, given Zhuangzi's style, it is hard to rule out the idea that he intended certain passages as ironical or merely as opening lines of thought to further reflection.

Some of Zhuangzi's most memorable images and parables illustrate this interpretive ambiguity. Zhuangzi tells us of an encounter between a giant sea turtle and a frog in a well. It is natural to suppose the giant sea turtle represents some ultimate truth not accessible to the frog (as the Chinese adage derived from the parable does). However, in Zhuangzi's account, the sea turtle cannot even get one flipper into the frog's well. He is as incapable of appreciating the frog's joys and insights as the frog is of appreciating his. Similar analysis applies to the parables of the great bird and the small chickadee, the great fish, etc. Zhuangzi is the least likely thinker of the period to take "great" and "small" as signs of absolute value.

The dogmatic reading also presupposes a mystical epistemology. Zhuangzi gives no account of a route to any purported metaknowledge that everyone else lacks. This interpretation has the burden of showing that Zhuangzi's arguments do not undermine its envisioned conception of the required special route to knowledge. The refutation of Mencius looks perfectly general. It should apply to any view of a special transcendent insight or intuition. It is not clear how Zhuangzi could be astute enough to see the fallacy in Mencius's view and naive enough to turn around and adopt its epistemic twin.

The classic relativist interpretation is plausible only to the extent that Zhuangzi clearly views all existing points of view as natural. To say that (to smooth them on the sandpaper of nature) is neither to approve them nor to judge them equal. Zhuangzi removes the traditional authority of *tian* (nature) as a standpoint. Other schools (except for the later Mohists) took as a goal the identification of which *dao* (guide) was *tian* (natural or heavenly). Zhuangzi's argument, as we saw, was that we achieve this goal all too easily for it to be a useful guide. All we can say "equally" of an existing point of view is "it is"—which applies to the perspectives of other animals as well.

Zhuangzi infers that we can rank perspectives only by assuming some background *dao*. He sees that all authority is based on *dao*, not on *tian*. (Dogmatists make this point using "the *dao*.") Any judgment that different daos are equal in value must be (1) a result of taking some standard for granted or (2) a misleading way to say "make no judgment." The problem with the latter is that, given Zhuangzi's view of the relation of language and judgment, it amounts to saying that we should stop speaking—which, as I argued above, we should avoid attributing to Zhuangzi.

What is the alternative? Zhuangzi thinks we must judge from a standpoint, and his is a perspective on perspectives. He advocates something he calls *ming* (discrimination), but what is it? Is it a mystical total insight or a mere awareness of the plurality of perspectives? Zhuangzi, wary of Hui Shi's error, generally avoided contrasting our limited perspectives with any cosmic or total perspective. He contrasted perspectives mainly with other perspectives. *Ming* is not "the" viewpoint, although Zhuangzi is implicitly recommending it. That stance, furthermore, does allow judgments about other perspectives (e.g., that of Mencius). Zhuangzi is not caught in a "Hitler problem." Nazism was a result of the operation of nature, but a perspectivalist can (and presumably would) disapprove (as Zhuangzi does of even less cruel rulers).

The safest solution, then, is to assume that Zhuangzi does make judgments from his perspective on perspectives. In doing so, he need not presume that his is an absolute, total, or cosmic angle of vision. It is, as he admits, "of a type with the others." One must have some perspective, and adopting the *ming* view gives him no reason to stop registering his reactions. Saying that it is a perspective is not a condemnation. It requires only the realization that there are other perspectives.

We do not need to presuppose some absolute or total view to recognize that our views are partial. We need only appreciate that another outlook offers something ours does not. (Opponents of a perspectival interpretation may point out that this interpretation leaves something out. That would be fine—as long as they acknowledge that theirs does too.) Nor does the fact that perspectives have limitations entail that they are mistaken.

Zhuangzi's focus is epistemological more than metaphysical. His frequent suggestion that there could be a fantastically adept and successful *dao* (e.g., that one might reach the point of being able to endure fire, cold, lightning, and wind; harness natural powers; and travel immense distances) appears to require two things. One is an actual world with real features that some daos reflect better than others do. The other is that we rely on our present standards of success (desires, fantasies, goals, delights, etc.) to evaluate alternative perspectives.

Skepticism versus Dogmatic Monism

The linguistic nature of perspectivalism comes more to the fore when Zhuangzi responds to the later Mohists. He notes that their term of analysis, *ke* (assertable), is obviously relative to a conventional, linguistic perspective. Different and changing patterns and principles of usage still constitute conventions and generate a language and a viewpoint. Single schools of thought may split, and disputing factions may combine again. Any language that people actually speak is assertable. Any moral discourse for which there is a rival is (from the rival's standpoint) not assertable.

Zhuangzi hints that the confidence we feel in the appearance of right and wrong in our language is a function of how fully we can elaborate and embellish. How well can we continue with our way of speaking? We argue for a point of view mainly by spelling it out in greater detail. This encourages the illusion that it may be a total point of view. The seemingly endless disputes between Mohists and Confucians arise from their highly elaborated systems for assigning "is this" and "not this." As we saw, each can build hierarchies of standards that guide their different choices. They come to consider the errors of rivals "obvious."

Zhuangzi introduces *ming* (discrimination) again in presenting his "perspective" on the relativity of language. In the same section he hints at imagining an "absolute" viewpoint—he calls it the axis of *dao*. We extrapolate, imaginatively reversing our historical path back to the axis from which we began. At the axis, he says, no limit can be drawn on what we could treat as "is this" or "is not this." All *shifei* patterns are possible, none actual.

From that axis, however, we make no judgment. It is not a relevant alternative to the disputing perspectives. If we succumb to the absolute interpretive temptation, we fall back into the antilanguage abyss. The absolute viewpoint neither advocates nor forbids any espousal of *dao*. From the perspective of *ming*, the absolute is not a point of view. Any practical guide is somewhere an actual path that takes us from the axis in one direction rather than another, one particular (indefinitely expandable) way of making distinctions.

Zhuangzi emphasizes the unlimited possibility of these standpoints. Occasionally, however, he presents it as almost a tragic inevitability. Once we have started on a *dao*, we seem doomed to elaborate and develop it in a kind of "race to death." Youth is the state of being comparatively open to many possible systems of *shi-fei*. As we grow and gain "knowledge," we close off possibilities in a rush toward old age and death. Zhuangzi exploits the analogy of youth and flexibility. Nothing can free us from the headlong rush to complete our initial commitments to *shi* and *fei* as if they were oaths or treaties. We rush through life clinging to the alternative we judge as winning. "Is life really as stupid as this? Or is it that I am the only stupid one and there are others not so stupid?"

Given all the possible systems of guiding discourse, practical knowledge is potentially unlimited. No matter how much we advance and promote a guide, a way of dealing with things, we will be deficient at something else. To have any developed viewpoint is to leave something out. This, however, gives us no reason either to avoid language or to prefer other forms of discourse. It is the simple corollary of the fact that knowledge is limitless and our lives are not.

So-called sages project their point of view and prejudices onto *tian* (nature), and then treat it as an authority. "Those who have arrived" purportedly know that they are to deem everything one—they dismiss the multiplicity of viewpoints as biased. Does Zhuangzi recommend that we take this attitude? Instead of trying to transcend and abandon our usual or conventional ways of speaking, Zhuangzi recommends that we rest with treating them as pragmatically useful. They enable us to communicate and get things done. That, moreover, is all one can sensibly ask of them.

Beyond what is implied in the fact that our language is useful (from the standards within our discourse), we do not know the way things are in themselves. We merely signal that lack of ultimate metaphysical knowledge when we call reality *dao*. Treating it as an irreducible "one" (mysticism) differs from saying nothing about it (skepticism) only in attitudinal ways. In the end, neither has anything to say. Only the different attitudes one takes in saying (essentially) nothing distinguish them.

Zhuangzi's contrast between skepticism and monism surfaces in a number of places. In one passage he traces the "devolution" of the knowledge of old from knowing "nothing exists" to knowing "one" to knowing things but no distinctions or boundaries and finally to knowing *shi-fei*. In another passage, notoriously obscure, one of his characters is skeptical about skepticism. However, he does not appeal to our familiar sentential grounds, i.e., he does not ask how he knows that he does not know. The Mohists ask how he can know what we do not know. Zhuangzi's question centers on the grounds of distinction. He wonders if he knows how to distinguish between "knowing" and "ignorance."

Zhuangzi's treatment of dreams also highlights his different approach to skepticism. He does not use dreaming to motivate sensory skepticism. His doubts arise mainly from semantics. (Is there any real relation between our words and things?) Dreaming then becomes a further illustration of a skepticism rooted in worries about whether there is a right way to distinguish or "pick out" by using a word. We use the distinction between dreaming and waking to organize "what happens" (in the broadest sense). We have learned to use that distinction to bring greater unity or coherence to our experience.

In a dream we can still make the distinction between dreaming and waking. Ultimately we can wonder about other ways (the pragmatic advantages) of making that distinction. Zhuangzi fulfills his heart's desire in dreaming of a butterfly. He does not know how to distinguish Zhuangzi's dream of the butterfly from the butterfly's dream of Zhuangzi. (Translators typically convert the "distinction point" into a propositional point.)

Practical Implications

Zhuangzi's perspectivalism arises in a form of discourse that expects a philosophy to have some moral. None seems to follow from absolute skepticism, monism, or relativism. In any case, we should take Zhuangzi as reflectively aware that his advice comes from one perspective—his *ming* approach to discourse. What follows from that insight into the nature of knowledge? We should expect any advice to be tenuous and hedged.

We have already hinted at some of the useful recommendations. First, Zhuangzi "mildly" recommends a kind of perspective flexibility. He "recommends" it in the sense that one can "recommend" being young. To be young at heart-mind is to be open to new ways of thinking and conceptualizing. The more committed you are to a scheme, as we saw, the "older" you become intellectually, until you are "dead" from learning.

This practical line is paradoxical on several grounds. First, any reason we may have for being flexible in adopting or tolerant to other points of view has to be a reason that motivates us to depart from our present point of view. We must now be able to envision that the alternative ways of thinking will help us more with goals we now have than our present scheme does. Not just any other point of view will be a candidate for such openness. So this could not be an abstract argument for total openness. Similarly, it advises tolerance only within certain limits, and where we draw these limits depends on our present moral stance. Thus Zhuangzi is not, as I argued above, required to be "tolerant" of Nazism. From a the standpoint of *ming*, judgment is not only still possible but inescapable.

Second, the motivation for being open to other schemes of knowledge presupposes the potential value of acquiring them. The openness of youth is valuable only because it represents the possibility of mature sophistication. If we were to take the invitation to openness as antiknowledge in principle, then perspectivalism would give us no reason to value it.

The second moral is negative. One reaction to dissatisfaction with some normative conventions is a blanket rejection. As we have noted, the later Mohists showed that this negative posture, as applied to language at least, is incoherent. Zhuangzi recognizes that we need not avoid conventions. The second bit of "advice" is simply not to waste useful conventions. Again, we must judge usefulness from some standpoint, some values, and standards.

The third bit of advice comes in a famous parable. In it, Zhuangzi draws an uncharacteristically favorable portrait of specialization. His example reminds us of Aristotle's observation that the exercise of acquired skill is fulfilling to humans. Highly honed skills invite paradoxical, almost mystical, descriptions. In performance we seem to experience a unity of actor and action. Such practice is a way of losing oneself, as one might lose oneself in contemplation or a trance. We can mystify ourselves by the fluid accuracy of our own actions. We do not understand how we did it—we certainly cannot explain it to others.

We all recognize a state of responsive awareness that suspends consciousness of "self" and "other" when we are totally absorbed in a skillful activity. This feature of *dao* mastery explains the temptation to read the Daoist use as propounding a metaphysical thesis. It is natural to express this ideal of mastery of skills in language that suggests mystical awareness. It does normally involve suspension of self-consciousness or ratiocination and seems like surrender to an external force. That language should not confuse us, however. The experience is compatible with Zhuangzi's window on perspectives. Here is Zhuangzi's account:

> Cook Ding was slicing an ox for Lord Wenhui. At every push of his hand, every angle of his shoulder, every step with his feet, every bend of his knee—Zip! Zoop! He slithered the knife along with a zing, and all was in perfect rhythm, as though he were dancing at Mulberry Grove or keeping time to *qingshou* music.
>
> "Ah, this is marvelous!" said Lord Wenhui. "Imagine skill reaching such heights!"
>
> Cook Ding laid down his knife and replied, "What I care about is a *dao* which advances my skill. When first I began cutting up oxen, I could see nothing that was not oxen. After three years, I never saw a whole ox. And now—now I go at it by spirit and do not look with my eyes. Controlling knowledge has stopped and my spirit wills the performance. I depend on the natural makeup, cut through the creases, guide through fissures. I depend on things as they are. So I never touch the smallest ligament or tendon, much less bone.
>
> "A good cook changes his knife once a year—because he cuts. A mediocre cook changes his knife once a month—because he hacks. I have had this knife of mine for nineteen years and I've cut up thousands of oxen with it. Yet the blade is as good as if it had just come from the grindstone . . .
>
> "Despite that, I regularly come to the limit of what I am used to. I see its being hard to carry on. I become alert; my gaze comes to rest. I slow down my performance and move the blade with delicacy. Then zhrup! it cuts through and falls to the ground. I stand with the knife erect, look all around, deem it wonderfully fulfilling, strop the knife and put it away."

Traditional interpreters stress the mystical flavor and the reference to *dao*. One can read the claim that *dao* advances skill as saying that it surpasses skill. This traditional commitment to a mystical, monistic *dao* suggests that there is a shortcut to the butcher's accomplishment. The reading detaches achievement from its ordinary connection with effort. It comes from some sudden and inexplicable insight, mystical experience, or attitude. This interpretation coincides with a familiar Zen puzzle about "sudden" enlightenment. The absolutist monistic interpretation needs to avoid the suggestion that Ding knows his *dao* and still can improve. How can you have some of a *dao* that has no parts? When you have it, you suspend entirely all thought and sensation.

Cook Ding's story thus clashes slightly with this religious or mystical view of Zhuangzi's advice. His description implies that Ding has a hold on a particular way of doing only one thing. Further, Ding's way is still "developing." He continues to progress in pursuing his skill by tracing his *dao* to points beyond his previous training. When he comes to a hard part, he has to pay attention, make distinctions, try them out, and then move on. The focus required for a superb performance may not be compatible with deliberating self-consciousness. This supports the view that developing a skill eventually goes beyond what we can explain using concepts, distinctions, or language, but it is not consistent with sudden, total, "mystical" perfection.

Cook Ding clearly sees his skills as related to his learning—what in other places Zhuangzi calls a *cheng* (completion). Ding does not report any sudden conversion where some mystical insight flowed into him. He does not suggest that he found a mystical shortcut which revealed his practice to be a mistake. Nor does he hint that by being a master butcher, he is in command of all the skills of life. He could not use his "awareness" of *dao* to be a master archer. His account is compatible with perspectivalism. He has mastered one particular *dao*.

Note, furthermore, that Cook Ding's activity is cutting—dividing something into parts. When he is mastering his guiding *dao*, he perceives a world in which the ox is already cut up. He comes to see the holes and fissures and spaces as inherent in nature. That seems a perfect metaphor for our coming to see the world as divided into the natural kinds that correspond to our mastery of terms. When we master a *dao*, we must be able to execute it in a real situation. It requires finding the distinctions (concepts) used in instruction as mapping onto nature. We no longer have time to read the map; we begin to see ourselves as reading the world. Mastering any *dao* thus yields this sense of harmony. It is as if the world, not the instructions, guides us.

Cook Ding can be aware that others may have different ways to dissect an ox. He simply cannot exercise his skill while also trying to choose among them. In realizing a *dao* of some activity in us, we make it second nature. The sense of being "pulled" is neither a mere, inert, cognition of external force nor a surrender to a structure already innate in us.

The choice of a butcher for this parable is pivotal. Cultures seldom consider butchering a noble profession. Even "Ding" may be significant—it may not be the cook's name but a sign of relatively low rank, something like an also-ran. Other popular examples of the theme include the cicada catcher and the wheelwright. Zhuangzi probably intends to signal that this level of expertise is available in any activity.

We may achieve this absorption in performance by achieving skill at any *dao*—dancing, skating, playing music, butchering, chopping logic, making love, skiing, using language, programming computers, throwing pottery, or cooking. At the highest levels of skill, we reach a point where we seem to transcend our own self-consciousness. What once felt like a skill developing inside us begins to feel like control from the natural structure of things. Our normal ability to respond to complex feedback bypasses conscious processing. In our skilled actions, we have internalized a heightened sensitivity to the context.

Traditional interpretations, however, rule out some activities. The examples above, together with Zhuangzi's obvious delight in parable, fantasy, and poetry, invite the common analogy to a western romantic. Is Zhuangzi suspicious of direct, reasoned, logical discourse in favor of the more "emotional" arts? At least, one should eschew "intellectual" activities. However, it is hard to find a motivation for this dichotomy in the Chinese philosophical context. We find no counterpart of the human faculty of reason (or its logical correlate), still less a contrast between reason and emotion.

The romantic interpretation seeks to explain why Zhuangzi criticizes Hui Shi, the alleged logician. The problem is that along with his comments about Hui, Zhuangzi offers similar observations about a zither player. Furthermore, he criticizes the search for total know-how but not the search for know-how in a specific activity. Zhuangzi's "criticism" is that in being good at *X*, these paradigms of skill are miserably inept at *Y*. These are his examples of how *hui* (defect) always accompanies *cheng* (completion).

These reflections lead us to a problem with "achieve *dao* mastery" as a prescription. As we have noted, Zhuangzi is ambivalent about mastery. Any attainment, he notes, must leave something out. Most particularly, to exercise any skill is to ignore others. Masters are frequently not good teachers. They fail with their sons or disciples. We trade accomplishment at one skill for ineptitude at some other. If the renowned practitioners reach completion, he says, then so does everyone. If they do not, no one can.

Thus, the three parts in Zhuangzi's *dao* pull in separate directions, and we must treat each as tentative and conditional. The advice about flexibility seems hard to follow if we also accept convention and work for single-minded mastery. That, in the end, may be the message of Zhuangzi's perspectivalism. We have limits—but we might as well get on with life.

See also Hui Shi; Laozi; Mencius; Mohism: Later; Philosophy of Mind; *Shifei*; Zhuangzi: Schools.

Bibliography

Cua, A. S. "Forgetting Morality: Reflections on a Theme in *Chuang Tzu*." *Journal of Chinese Philosophy*, 4(4), 1977, pp. 305–328. (Reprinted in A. S. Cua. *Moral Vision and Tradition: Essays in Chinese Ethics*. Washington, D.C.: Catholic University of America Press, 1998.)

Giles, Herbert A. *Zhuangzi: Mystic, Moralist, and Social Reformer*. London: Allen and Unwin, 1981.

Graham, Angus. "Zhuang-tzu's Essay on Seeing Things as Equal." *History of Religions*, 9, 1969, pp. 137–159.

———. *Zhuangzi: The Inner Chapters*. London: Allen and Unwin, 1981.

Hansen, Chad. *A Daoist Theory of Chinese Thought*. New York: Oxford University Press, 1992.

Liu, Xiaogan. *Classifying the Zhuangzi Chapters*. Michigan Monograph in Chinese Studies. Ann Arbor: University of Michigan, 1994.

Mair, Victor, ed. *Experimental Essays on Zhuangzi*. Honolulu: University of Hawaii Press, 1983.

Watson, Burton. *Zhuangzi: Basic Writings*. New York: Columbia University Press, 1964.

Wu, Kuang-ming. *Chuang Tzu: World Philosopher at Play*. American Academy of Religion, Studies in Religion. New York, 1982.

Zhuangzi (Chuang Tzu): Schools

Xiaogan LIU

The idea of a school of Zhuangzi (Chuang Tzu) derived from textual analyses of the *Zhuangzi*, which concluded that the book was a general collection of works of Zhuangzi and his followers, although there was no evidence for an organized school continuing after his death.

There are different views about the features and authors of *Zhuangzi,* especially about the outer chapters (*waipian*) and miscellaneous chapters (*zapian*), in addition to the inner chapters (*neipian*). For example, according to Feng Youlan (Fung Yu-lan), it is a compilation of Daoist writings, not only of the Zhuangzi school. A. C. Graham (1981, 1990) considered it a collection of Daoist works and works by other groups, such as primitivists, Yangists, and syncretists. Nevertheless, on the basis of a detailed textual examination, relatively complete statistics, and comparison with corresponding linguistic materials, Liu Xiaogan (1994) argues that the parts at issue are essentially the work of a Zhuangzi school, with the sole exception of Chapter 30. The authors of the book include Zhuangzi (the author of the inner chapters) and his followers. The authors of the outer and miscellaneous chapters (*waizapian*) are divided into three groups, implying that Zhuangzi's followers can be described as three branches.

The Nucleus and Foundation of the School

Zhuangzi's philosophical thought has been an inspiration and a spiritual source for Chinese culture for more than 2,000 years. In particular, it is a document involving individual freedom, intellectual criticism, artistic imagination, literary romanticism, and philosophical speculation. Although Zhuangzi adopted the key concepts of *dao* (the Way), *ziran* (natural or naturalness), *wuwei* (no-action) from Lao Tzu (Laozi), he propounded a new spiritual insight, including a philosophy of life and a philosophical methodology.

"Free and Easy Wandering" (*Xiaoyao yu*), the title of his first chapter, characterizes Zhuangzi's philosophy of life. It is not about the journey of immortals in heaven (as in later Daoist religious teachings); nor is it about the affairs of common, human life. Free and easy wandering means "Just go along with things and let the mind move freely"; it describes an ideal state of mind completely devoid of concern with the mundane world. When the ideal of freedom is attained, the individual will experience unity with the Way or *dao*, the *summum bonum* of Daoism. Zhuangzi's ideal of freedom is purely personal and spiritual and is based on adaptation to natural surroundings and on "destiny" (*ming*), which is supposed to be determined by heaven (*tian*) or *dao*. On one reading, Zhuangzi seems to be "passive" in counseling adjustment to the circumstances of earthly life. A more plausible reading would point to his lively concern with pursuing personal freedom in both the human realm and the spiritual realm.

The second chapter, on the equality of all things (*Qiwulun*), is representative of Zhuangzi's methodology. As the earliest and most important skeptic in the Chinese philosophical tradition, Zhuangzi taught that because of human limitations, people cannot attain full cognition of the world. People cannot reach the truth, because there is no incontestable standard for evaluating claims about what is right or wrong, or true or false (*shifei*). For example, if a man sleeps in a damp place, his back may ache and he may end up half paralyzed, but can one truly ascribe the same condition to a roach? If a man lives in a tree, he may be terrified and shake with fright, but does the same obtain in the case of a monkey? Of these three creatures, then, which one knows the proper place to live? Men eat meat, deer eat grass, centipedes find snakes tasty, and hawks relish mice. Of these four, which knows what is the proper food? (Watson 1968, 45–46). Therefore, people cannot tell what is right or wrong, and all arguments about good or evil are implausible. Zhuangzi was not interested in making value judgments; rather, his purpose was to urge his readers to pursue what he thought to be the ultimate destination—transcendent freedom, which is identical with *dao*.

Here we find the seeds of cultural relativism, which may lead to multiculturalism. Zhuangzi emphasizes that opposites—"that" and "this," "right" and "wrong," birth and death, unacceptability and acceptability—always depend on each other and are transformed into each other; thus there are no important differences between such opposites, and people should consider "that" and "this," "right" and "wrong," as having the same status. People can then move beyond the conflict between that and this, right and wrong; or, to change the image, they can stand in the center of the circle of conflict and respond indifferently, without any sense of inadequacy. This is an important stage in transcending the empirical world and reaching the end, which is union with *dao*.

There would have been no such thing as the school of Zhuangzi if there were no latter-day developers of Zhuangzi's teachings. The first group consists of transmitters or expositors among Zhuangzi's followers (*shu Zhuang pai*) who lived nearest in time to Zhuangzi and whose thought most closely resembles that of the "inner chapters." Chapters 17–27 and 32 should be assigned to them, Chapter 17 (*Qiushui*, "Autumn Floods") and Chapter 22 (*Zhi beiyu*, "Knowledge Wandered North") being especially good examples. A second group consists of "anarchists." The third groups is the Huang-Lao school.

Expositors

The first group, the expositors, inherited the concept of the Way from Laozi and Zhuangzi and created a metaphorical concept of "original root" (*bengen*) to indicate and describe the Way. In Chapter 22 we read:

> North, south, east, west, heaven and earth have never passed beyond its border; things as tiny as the tip of a hair must wait for it to achieve bodily form. The *yin* and *yang*, the four seasons follow one another in succession, each keeping to its proper place. Dark and hidden, it seems not to exist and yet it is there; lush and unbounded, it possesses no form but functions mysteriously; myriad things (*wanwu*) are shepherded by it, though they are not aware of it—this is what is called *bengen*, the original root. (Watson 1968, 237)

The metaphor of a root suggests that the relationship between the Way and the "myriad things" (*wanwu*) is similar to that between root and twig: they are in a continuous world, not separated into two realms as in western Platonic metaphysical theories.

The same authors also account for the view that the Way is radically different from the "myriad things." They argue:

> There is that which was born before heaven and earth, but is it a thing? That which makes things things cannot be a thing (*wuwu zhe fei wu*). Things that come forth can never precede all other things, because there were already things existing then; and before that, too, there were already things existing, so on without end. (Watson, 246)

Thus they believe "that which makes things things" (*wuwu zhe*) makes things full and empty without itself filling or emptying; and that which makes things wither and decay does so without itself withering or decaying. It establishes trunk and twig but is itself neither trunk nor twig itself; it determines when to store up or scatter but does not itself store or scatter (Watson, 242). Therefore, the Way or "that which makes things things" cannot be a thing among the myriad things: it must be different or transcendent, although not necessarily isolated from them.

The expositors also consciously develop Zhuangzi's theory of the equality of things and relativism. Chapter 17 maintains:

> From the point of view of the Way, things are neither noble nor mean. From the point of view of the individual things, each thing would consider itself noble, and [things] would demean one another. Furthermore, from the point of view of difference, if we choose to call something great because it is greater than something else, then there is nothing in the world that is not great; and if we choose to call something small because it is smaller than something else, then there is nothing which is not small. Also, from the point of view of preference, if we regard a thing as right because there is a certain right to it, then among the ten thousand things there are none that are not right. If we regard a thing as wrong because there is a certain wrong to it, then among the ten thousand things there are none that are not wrong. (Watson, 179–180)

This argument is in line with Zhuangzi's skepticism.

In addition, the disciples carry on Zhuangzi's idea of "no mind" and "no emotion" but direct it toward creative work instead of transcendent freedom. They were convinced that the creation of extraordinary art required an exceptional state of mind, which meant that the artist should concentrate on nothing but the natural conception of the object to be created. They tell a story about the sculptor Qing, who created a bell stand that looked demonic and ghostly and amazed everyone who saw it. When he was asked for his secret, he replied that when he was going to make a bell stand, he first made sure to fast in order to still the heart. After fasting three days, he was no longer concerned about congratulations and reward or honors and payment. After fasting five days, he became oblivious of any blame or praise, skill or clumsiness. After fasting seven days, he became so intent that he forgot he had a body and four limbs. Only then was he able to go into the mountain forest and observe the nature of the wood as heaven makes it grow. The aptitude of the body had attained its peak; only then did he have a complete vision of the bell stand, and only then did he put his hand to it. This is "joining what is heaven's to what is heaven's." The group thus extended Zhuangzi's doctrine of spiritual freedom into the realm of aesthetics. Their theory has had great influence on literary and artistic creation in China.

Anarchists

Whereas the first group of Zhuangzi's followers, the expositors, took as its main purpose the task of following along the lines of his thought and further developing his ideas, the second group—the anarchists (*wujun pai*, "school of no sovereign")—attempted some major revisions of his doctrines. (This group is roughly equivalent to Graham's "primitivist" and "Yangist" schools.)

Instead of the transcendence preferred by Zhuangzi, the anarchists advocated a direct confrontation with reality and radically attacked monarchical power as well as important concepts of Confucianism and Mohism. Their approach is found in Chapters 8–10, 28–29, and 31 and the first part of Chapter 11; it is especially well illustrated in Chapter 8, *Pianmu*.

The anarchists of course inherited some ideas from Zhuangzi, but they developed those ideas in a new direction. For example, they carried on the master's theory of the equality of things and applied it to intensive political criticism. Zhuangzi himself had addressed some social problems, but the outstanding characteristic of his philosophy is its focus on transcending reality and its longing for spiritual freedom; the anarchists, by contrast, attacked current social and political conditions, directing their criticism not only against the monarchs of their own time but also against the legendary sagely rulers. Generally, we might assume that people will oppose a tyrant or an inept ruler but not a good and wise ruler. Yet the anarchists opposed all monarchical rule. Consequently, they equated a bad ruler and a good one. They said:

> Long ago, when the sage Yao governed the world, he made the world bright and gleeful; men delighted in their nature, and there was no calmness anywhere. When the tyrant Jie governed the world, he made the world weary and vexed; men found bitterness in their nature and there was no contentment anywhere. Either to lack calmness or to lack contentment is to go against Virtue, and there has never been any society in the world that could go against Virtue and survive for long. (Watson, 114)

Here, what is most important and most valuable is neutral human nature; thus the preservation of original human nature becomes the criterion of an ideal society.

To preserve original human nature, the concept of any difference between a mean person and a sage should also be eliminated. The anarchists' argument appeals to undesirable consequences: the mean person will risk death for the sake of profit; the gentry will risk it for the sake of fame; the high official will risk it for his clan; the sage will risk it for the world. All these men go about their business in different ways, but they are the same in risking their lives and blighting their inborn nature (Watson, 101.) The anarchists were the first to attack social and political realities by applying Zhuangzi's theory of equality of things—they are an example of combining an inheritance with reforms.

Similarly, while maintaining Zhuangzi's spirit of following naturalness (*ziran*), they took it in a new direction: preserving internal nature instead of accompanying external natural (unforced) movement. Therefore, their key concept was the primary nature of the human being. They argued that the way a trainer manages horses is against the natural life of horses and totally destroys the nature of horses; the trainer therefore sins against the horses. For the same reason, the potter and carpenter destroy the nature of clay and wood, and they deserve to be criticized. The mangers of the world ruin the true nature of people, although every ruler would like to say that he greatly benefits them (Watson, 104).

Huang-Lao School

The third group among Zhuangzi's followers, the Huang-Lao school, differed from the anarchists by incorporating rather than criticizing concepts and theories of Confucianism and legalism. The members of the Huang-Lao school moved from Zhuangzi's romantic style to a new social-political inclination. Their new style was described by Sima Qian, who considered it a criterion of this school.

The Huang-Lao school originated in the middle Warring States period and prevailed in the early Han dynasty. Its outstanding feature, according to Sima Qian, was that it "selected the good parts of Confucianism and Mohism and gathered the essentials of the school of names and legalism" to create a new form of Daoist thought. In the *Zhuangzi*, this school of thought is expressed in Chapters 12–16 and 33, and the latter part of Chapter 11. (Graham's closest match is "syncretists.")

One of the best examples of the Daoist comprehensiveness or inclusiveness is Chapter 13 (*Tiandao*, "The Way of Heaven"). According to this text, in ancient times those who sought to understand the "great way" started by understanding heaven (*tian*), and then the (Daoist) Way (*dao*) and its virtue (*de*). Once they understood the Way and its virtue, then (Confucian) benevolence (*ren*) and righteousness (*yi*) would follow. Once they understood benevolence and righteousness, then the notion of keeping one's place and obedience (*fenshou*) would follow. Once they understood the notion of keeping one's place and obedience, then an understanding of the proper forms and names of things (*xingming*) would follow. Once they understood the proper forms and names of things and situations, they would know what causes things to happen and how to use things with trust (*yinren*). Once what is right and what is wrong (*shifei*) were clear, then proper reward and punishment (*shangfa*) would follow (a legalist concept). Once people were clear about rewards and punishments, the foolish and the wise, the noble and the mean would put themselves in the appropriate place, position, or rank. We must have knowledge and wisdom and stratagems, but not use them. A person who does this is surely reverting to heaven. This is what is called the great peace (a Daoist social ideal), and it is the best governance of all (Watson, 146–147). These antecedents and consequences are a systematic arrangement, ranking the concepts of Daoism, Confucianism, and legalism in a hierarchical structure, which is common in other passages of the works of the group and a typical feature of Huang-Lao school.

Another characteristic of this group is its new theory of *wuwei*, or taking no action: nonaction by rulers and zealous action by ministers. This is different from Laozi's nonaction of the sage and Zhuangzi's nonaction of the superior man. The Huang-Lao school emphasized the distinction between the principle and method of a ruler and of ministers. To rest in inaction and command respect—this is the Way of heaven. To engage in action and become entangled in it—this is the way of man. The ruler practices the Way of heaven; his subjects practice the way of man. The Way of heaven and the way of man are far apart. Accordingly, the highest ruler does nothing and is respected; the officials are wearied by managing everything. The Way of the ruler, taking no action (*wuwei*), and the way of ministers, taking action (*youwei*), should be clearly distinguished (Watson, 125).

There are also detailed arguments. For example, the virtue of an emperor or a king takes nonaction as its constant rule. With nonaction, you may make the world work for you and have leisure to spare; with action, you will find yourself working for the world, and never will your work be enough. If a superior adopts nonaction and his inferiors adopt it as well, there will be none to act as minister. If the inferiors adopt action and the superior adopts it as well, there will be none to act as lord. Superiors must adopt nonaction and make the world work for them; inferiors must adopt action and work for the world. This is an unvarying truth (Watson, 144). "Superior" here indicates the sovereign; "inferiors" indicates the ministers. The sovereign does nothing; hence he has no faults or insufficiencies and makes no mistakes. Thus he can be the ruler of the world. The ministers, on the other hand, have to do something or everything. They have faults, insufficiencies, and shortcomings. The concept of *wuwei* (taking no action) is no longer a general principle of management or rulership but the unique characteristic of a king or an emperor. *Wuwei* becomes the private benefit of royalty, but at the same time it restrains the sovereign, which may explain why few rulers accepted the privilege of *wuwei*. Although it is common knowledge that Daoists insisted that the ruler should practice *wuwei* and that the ministers should exert themselves, we cannot find more detailed and direct statements of this Daoist principle in other documents or texts, even in the "Huang-Lao silk manuscript" (*Huang Lao boshu* or *Huangdi sijing*).

In addition, the Huang-Lao school brought up the idea of following and obeying the trend of the times and the prevailing tendencies of things. They argue:

> If one is traveling by water, there is nothing better than using a boat; if one is traveling by land, there is nothing better than using a carriage. That is because the boat can travel easily in the water, but if you tried to push it on the land, then to the end of the age you would still not be able to make it travel a few feet. Now, is not the difference between the past and the present like the difference between the water and the land? And is the difference between State of Zhou and State of Lu not like the difference between the boat and the carriage? If you wanted to exercise the ways of Zhou in the State of Lu, would that not be like trying to push a boat on land? There will be no reward for such labor; and there will be some harm to the body. (Watson, 159)

The difference here between the water and the land is an objective difference; the difference between the boat and the carriage is a difference in ways of transportation. The method of enterprise must correspond to the prevailing conditions and trends. With changes in time and place, the method of ruling the world must also be adaptive and must be revised accordingly. This idea of changing in compliance with the trends of the times is particularly valuable in an age of great transformation such as the Warring States period. The authors might have been influenced by the earlier legalist Shang Yang.

This essay has given a brief account of the schools of Zhuangzi. Although the classification of Zhuangzi's followers is based on theoretical analysis, it can be further justified by linguistic and statistical analysis of the texts (for details, see Graham 1990; Liu 1994).

See also Daoism: Neo-Daoism; *Wuwei*; Zhuangzi.

Bibliography

Graham, A. C., trans. *Chuang-tzu: The Inner Chapters*. London: Allen and Unwin, 1981.

Graham, A. C. "How Much of *Chuang-tzu* Did Chuang-tzu Write?" In *Studies in Classical Chinese Thought*, ed. Henry Rosemont, Jr., and Benjamin I. Schwartz, *Journal of the American Academy of Religion*, 47(3), September 1979, pp. 459–502. (Reprinted in A. C. Graham. *Studies in Chinese Philosophy and Philosophical Literature*. Albany: State University of New York Press, 1990.)

Guan, Feng. *Zhuangzi neipian yijie he pipan* (Translation and Criticism of the Inner Chapters in the *Zhuangzi*). Beijing: Zhonghua, 1961.

Liu, Xiaogan. *Classifying the Zhuangzi Chapters*, trans. William E. Savage. Ann Arbor: Center for Chinese Studies University of Michigan, 1994.

———. "The Evolution of Three Schools of Later-Day Zhuang Zi Philosophy (I, II)." *Chinese Studies in Philosophy*, 23(2, whole issue), 1991; and 24(2), 1992, pp. 3–54.

———. "Wu-wei (Non-Action): From *Laozi* to *Huainanzi*." *Daoist Resources*, 3(1), 1991, pp. 41–56.

Munro, Donald J. "Foreword." In Liu Xiaogan, *Classifying the Zhuangzi Chapters*, trans. William E. Savage. Ann Arbor: Center for Chinese Studies University of Michigan, 1994.

Watson, Burton, trans. *The Complete Works of Chuang Tzu*. New York: Columbia University Press, 1968.

Zhang, Hengshou. *Zhuangzi xintan* (A New Investigation into the *Zhuangzi*). Wuhan: Hubei renmin, 1983.

中國哲學

GLOSSARY

Notes: 1. Family (and dynastic) names are alphabetized preceding other words spelled the same.
2. A single romanization (such as *li* or *shu*) may represent different Chinese characters that are homophones.

abhidharma (Indian Buddhism.) Genre of texts; analysis and insights; also, schools of thought. *Abhidharma* involves classifying factors in experience.

Ai Siqi (1910–1966.) Popularizer of Chinese Marxism.

ai Love.

ai wanwu Sense of being "one with all things"; dictum to openly love all things.

aizhili (Also *ai zhi li*.) *Li* of love; rationale or principle of love.

akara (Indian Buddhism.) Image.

Akbar (r. 1542–1605.) Mogul emperor who promoted dialogues and exchange among different religions.

alaya (Indian Buddhism.) Eighth or storehouse consciousness.

alayavijnana (Sanskrit.) Deep stratum of consciousness where all experiences and forms of knowledge are stored.

amalavijnanna (Indian Buddhism.) Unstained consciousness; also called *tathagatagarbha* (*rulai zang*), or "womb of the *tathagata*" (i.e., of those who know the truth).

An Shigao Translator (c. 150) who left a literary trace of the Buddhist tradition.

an 1. Calm happiness; peace and security. 2. Settling an issue.

Analects See *Lunyu*.

anatman (Sanskrit; *wushen* in Chinese.) Selflessness; no soul; no self.

anjun Muddleheaded ruler.

ao Subtle mystery.

arhat Buddhist who has reached the stage of enlightenment.

Aryadeva (c. 163–263.) Developed Madhyamika Buddhism; wrote the *Hundred Treatise*.

Arya gambira samdhinirmocana sutra tika Commentary by Wonch'uk (612–696) to the *Sandhinirmocana sutra*.

Asanga (4th–5th century C.E.) Founder of the Yogacara school of Indian Buddhist idealism.

asunya (Sanskrit.) Not empty.

atman (Sanskrit.) Self, soul.

Avalokitesvara (Guanyin, Kuan-yin.) "Lord who looks down," Mahayana buddhist meditational deity, also considered a bodhisattva and a buddha; correlated and later merged with the female deity Guanyin in China.

Avatamsaka (Sanskrit.) Garland, wreath; Buddhist corpus compiled in Central Asia.

avidya (Sanskrit.) Ignorance.

ba (Also *pa*.) Hegemon, hegemonist.

bagua (Also *baqua*, *pakua*.) Eight basic symbols (trigrams) of the *Yijing* (*Book of Changes*).

baguwen (Also *bagu-wen*.) "Eight-legged" essay.

baohe taihe To cherish and embrace primal harmony.

Bai Zhongxi Official influenced by the legalist thinking of Guanzi in the 600s B.C.E..

bai White.

baihua wen Folk prose.

Baihu tongi *Comprehensive Discussion in White Tiger Hall* (c. 80 C.E.), a cosmological compendium.

Baima (Also *Bai ma*.) "White Horse," a chapter in *Gongsun Longzi*.

baima fei ma "White horse is not horse," paradox formulated by Gongsun Long.

Baima lun "White Horse Discourse," by Gongsun Long.

Baiyuhai shihua Work by Chen Yan-chao; the title means "poetic talk," with Chen's style name.

Ban Gu (32–92.) Historian of neo-Daoism, author of *Standard History of the Han* (*Hanshu*).
Bao Jingyan (Dates unknown.) Neo-Daoist thinker, author of *Treatise on Not Having Rulers* (*Wu jun lun*).
baobian Praise and blame.
Baodang School located in Sichuan (Szechwan); Mazu Daoyi may have come out of it.
baojun Cruel ruler.
Baolinzhuan *Record of the Baolin Temple*, text of the Hongzhou (or Hangzhou) school.
Baopuzi *The Master Who Embraces Simplicity*, by Ke Hong.
Basho no Gororku *The Recorded Sayings of Mazu*, compilation by Iriya Yoshitaka.
Beifang school (Also Northern school.) Subschool of the Wang Yangming school.
Bei li Section of *Lüshi chunqiu*.
Beixi ziyi *Terms Explained*, by Chen Chun.
ben Foundation, root.
bencao Materia medica, pharmacopeia.
benneng zhizhi Natural ability to know.
benti Essence, original substance of life and nature.
Benti yu quanshi *Ontology and Interpretation*, by Chung-ying Cheng.
benwu Daoist concept of original nothingness or nihilistic void, challenged by Mindu's notion of *xinwu*.
benxin Original mind.
benxing Original nature.
benyou Originates in.
bhiksu In Buddhism, an ordained monk (male, a female being *bhiksuni*).
Bhrkuti "Fierce-eyed," name of a famous Nepali Buddhist princess, and an epithet given to several Buddhist deities.
bhumi (Indian Buddhism.) Stage of consciousness.
Bi Yuan (18th century.) Patron of Zhang Xuecheng.
bi 1. Mind. 2. Truth. 3. Obscuration or blindness of the mind (literally, a screen or cover). 4. Other.
bian 1. Discernment, ability to discriminate; functionally similar to *logos* in western philosophy. 2. Change; that which changes. 3. Distinction, dispute; in Mohist thought, especially philosophical dispute.
bianhua Changes and transformations of heaven and earth.
bianyi Interpenetrating cyclic changes.
bian zhe Disputers, those who argue out alternatives; pre-Qin alternative term for *mingjia* (or *ming jia*), the school of names.
biao Standard, gnomon.
biejiao Distinctive teaching, in Mahayana Buddhism; emphasizes the bodhisattva's compassionate return to the mundane world.
bieming Specific or discriminating names or terms.
Bifaji *Note on the Art of the Brush* by Jing Hao (c. 870–930).
biguan (Chinese.) Wall gazing, method of sitting meditation practiced and popularized by Bodhidharma; it is characteristic of Chan Buddhism in China, Japan, and Korea.
biji Jottings.
bing Disease.
biran Necessity.
biran zhi li General laws, necessary principles.
bixue Record or omit.
Bi zhen tu *Strategic Plan of Battle for the Brush*, early theory of calligraphy by Madam Wei.
Bodhidharma (d. 532.) Twenty-eighth partiarch of Chan Buddhism in India, regarded as the first patriarch of Chan in China.
Bohu tongyi See *Baihu tongyi*.
boqian (Also *bojian*.) Breadth and shallowness of knowledge.
Boruo wuzhi "*Prajna* without Knowledge," essay by Sengzhao.
boshi Official scholars in charge of teaching the five Confucian classics in the Han court; the term means "erudite."
boshu Silk manuscripts.
boxue hongci ke Erudite literati examination, highest certified degree of mastery of all literary genres.
Boyangfu (fl. c. 781 B.C.E.) Zhou master.
brahma (Sanskrit.) Ultimate ground of all being.
Bu Shang (Zixia, Tzu hsia.) Disiple of Confucius who was instrumental in establishing the classical Confucian canon.
bu (Also *pu*.) 1. Not, no (word that negates a predicate). 2. Divination.
budangli To act in accord with *li*.
bude buran What cannot be otherwise.
bu dongxin (Also *budong xin*, *bu tongxin*.) "Being not moved in heart," holding to the beginnings and principles of the good that emerge from the heart-mind so as not to be carried away by external temptations and forces.
buer (Also *bu er*, *bu'er*.) Nondoubleness, nonduality. Title of a chapter in *Lüshi chunqiu*.
bugou (Also *buguo*.) No transgression.
Bugou (Also *Pukou*, *Pu-kou*.) "Nothing Indecorous"; part of the *Xunzi*, Yang Liang's ninth-century commentary.
buqiu zhitian Not to know heaven.
buping Harmony.
buren To be unfeeling.
bu shan Bad.

bushi Lack of genuine conviction.
bushi shi Not losing time.
bu tongxin See *bu dongxin*.
buwei Refusal to do certain things.
buxie Disdain.
buyan No speech; Daoist position that the speech aspect of language has no ontological import.
buyi Timeless, unchanging.
Bu zhenkong "Emptiness of the Non-Absolute," essay by Sengzhao.
bu zhi qi ran er ran Unself-conscious behavior.

Cai (Zhou dynasty.) Lord condemned by orthodox historians for his opposition to the duke of Zhou.
Cai Lun Eunuch in charge of the office responsible for manufacturing instruments and weapons in the second century C.E.; said (erroneously) to have invented paper.
cai Faculty or faculties; capacity.
can 1. Triad. 2. Participation.
can tiante Humans forming a triad with heaven and earth.
can tianti Humanity.
can wu Checks and matches, phrase used characterize *mingjia* (*ming jia*, school of names).
Cang Ji (Cang Jie, Ts'ang chi.) Sage said to have created a paradigm and tied it up in the knot of an ideograph or character; he can perhaps be identified with the Yellow Emperor's minister (2697–2598 B.C.E.).
Canglang shihua Work by Yan Yu; the title means "poetic talk," with Yan's style name.
Cantong qi *Tally to the Yijing*, by Wei Boyang (2nd century C.E.), representative text of alchemical Daoism.
Cao Cao of Wei (Three Kingdoms period.) Resembled the legalists in valuing talent and merit over morality.
Cao Pi (187–226.) Brother of Cao Zhi; author of *Lun wen* or *Dianlun lunwen* (*Essay on Literature*).
Cao Zhi (192–232.) Poet.
Carsun Chang (1886 or 1887–1969; the senior Zhang Junmai.) With others, issued *Manifesto for a Reappraisal of Sinology and Reconstruction of Chinese Culture* (1958), critical of communist China.
Cengzi See Zengzi.
cha Careful observation.
Chan (Also Chan Buddhism, Chanzong, Ch'an; in Japanese, Zen.) From *ch'an-na*, a Chinese phonetic rendering of the Sanskrit *dhyana*, "meditation." School of Buddhism said to have been introduced into China by Bodhidharma during the reign of Emperor Wu (502–549) and emphasizing meditation.
Chan, Wing-tsit (Chen Rongjie, 1901–1994.) Scholar well known for his translation and compilation of a sourcebook of Chinese philosophy.
Chang Bejia (20th century.) Economist, a founder of New Asia College, which became part of the Chinese University of Hong Kong.
Chang Biao (Chang Piao, Zhang Piao, d. 1768.) Father of Zhang Xuecheng.
Chang Hao (b. 1937.) Chinese-American scholar interested in the modern transformation of Confucianism.
Chang Xuecheng See Zhang Xuecheng.
chang Constancy; that which is constant.
changde Constant virtue.
changlü guhou To consider the long view of things and consequences.
changshi Common sense or common knowledge.
Chanzong zhengdaoge Songs testifying to truth in Chan.
Chao Chuo Legalist of the early Han who proposed policies undermining noblemen's profit.
chap sinh (Vietnamese.) Philosophy of engagement (Nguyen Cong Tru).
chashi Scrutiny and apprehension.
ch'e (Korean; *ti* in Chinese.) Substance.
Chen Boda (1904–1989.) Wrote articles on Confucius and Mozi, which were discussed by Mao Zedong.
Chen Chixu (Shangyangzi, c. 1330). Integrator of the northern and southern schools of Song alchemical Daoism, author of *Jindan dayao* (*Great Principles of the Golden Elixir*, 1067).
Chen Chun (1159–1223.) Disciple of Zhu Xi.
Chen Daqi (Ch'en Ta'ch'i, 1887–1983.) Confucian who took a logical and ethical approach.
Chen Duxiu (1879–1942.) Intellectual leader of Chinese Marxism following World War I; a representative of materialistic scientism.
Chen Guying Contemporary thinker important in the Daoist revival.
Chen Jian (1497–1567.) Adherent of the Cheng-Zhu school.
Chen Kang (Northern Qi dynasty.) Grandfather of Xuanzang; served at court.
Chen Kuide (b. 1946.) Challenged dialectical materialism.
Chen Lai Contemporary scholar of new Confucianism.
Chen Liang (1143–1194.) Propounded the equal necessity of righteousness and profit; was involved in a famous controversy with Zhu Xi.

Chen Lifu (Ch'en Li-fu.) In the debate about science in the 1920s, advocated vitalist and antirationalist theories.

Chen Que (Ch'en Ch'üeh, 1604–1677.) Confucian philosopher of the Qing dynasty.

Chen Shou (233–297.) Historian; author of the *Sanguo zhi* (*Chronicles of the Three Kingdoms*).

Chen Su Brother of Xuanzang; ordained as the *bhiksu* Changjie at the Jingtu Monastery in Luoyang.

Chen Tuan (c. 906–989.) Daoist priest, identified by some Qing scholars as having transmitted Daoist diagrams of the great ultimate to Zhou Dunyi.

Chen Xianzhang (Baisha, 1428–1500.) Confucian scholar who devised *jingzuo* (quiet sitting) for self-cultivation.

Chen Yan-chao (1853–1892.) Wrote *Baiyuhai shihua* (the title means ''poetic talk,'' with Chen's style name).

chen Hour.

chendao pian Essays on the ways of ministers.

Cheng Gongsheng (fl. late 3rd century B.C.E.) Writer from the *mingjia* (*ming jia*, school of names); *Cheng Gongsheng*, which is no longer extant, was attributed to him.

Cheng Hao (Ch'eng Hao, Mingdao, 1032–1085.) Neo-Confucian who wrote ''On Understanding the Nature of *Ren*''; brother of Cheng Yi.

Cheng Minzheng (1445–c. 1499.) Neo-Confucian, compiled the anthology *Daoyi pian* (*The Way Is Open*).

Cheng Yi (Yichuan, 1033–1107 or 1108.) Neo-Confucian who wrote ''A Treatise on What Yanzi (Yan Hui) Loved to Learn''; brother of Cheng Hao.

Cheng Xuan (127–200.) Han scholar of ancient rituals and classical philology.

Cheng-Zhu (Also Cheng Zhu.) 1. School of Cheng Yi and Zhu Xi, one of two neo-Confucian schools of the early Ming, investigating the mind-heart. 2. One of three trends discerned by Mou Zongsan in Song-Ming neo-Confucian philosophy (the others are Hu-Liu and Lu-Wang).

cheng (Also *ch'eng*, *chen.*) True nature; sincerity or wholeness; completion.

Cheng-chih hsueh kang-yao *Outline of Political Science*, by Gao Yihan.

chengde Perfection of virtue.

chengde zhi xue Confucian doctrine of perfect virtue.

chenggong zhizhi Realization of the innate ability to know.

cheng qiyi (Also *cheng qi yi, chengyi.*) To make one's thought sincere.

chengren Perfect person.

chengshen Sincere with oneself.

Chengshilun (Sanskrit, *Satyasiddhi.*) *Treatise on Establishing the Real*, by Harivarman.

chengti Body of *cheng* (true nature, sincerity).

Cheng weishi lun (Also *Vijnaptimatrata siddhi.*) *Discourse on the Accomplishment of Consciousness Only*, compilation of Xuanzang's editing of ten commentaries to *Trimsika* (*Thirty Stanzas*), by Vasubandhu (4th or 5th century C.E.).

Cheng weishi lun bichao *Separate Notes on the Cheng weishi lun*, commentary to *Cheng weishi lun* by Ci'en Kuiji.

Cheng weishi lun shuji *Exposition of the Cheng weishi lun*, commentary to *Cheng weishi lun* by Ci'en Kuiji.

Cheng weishi lun zhangzhong shuyao *The Pivotal Essentials, As If in the Palm of Your Hand, to the Cheng weishi lun*, abbreviated commentary by Ci'en Kuiji.

chengyi (Also *ch'eng-i, cheng qi yi, cheng qiyi.*) Making one's thoughts or will sincere; a central concept of the *Daxue* (*Great Learning*).

chengzhe Truthful, sincere person.

chengzhi 1. Evidential learning. 2. *Cheng* as such, the way of heaven.

chenwei zhi xue (Also *chenwei zhi hsüeh.*) Prophetic signs.

chengzhizhe Striving to be *cheng*, the way of humans.

chi Shame, reaction to a situation one considers beneath oneself.

Chia Yi (Early Han.) Scholar who synthesized Confucianism and Daoism.

Chiang Ching-kuo See Jiang Jingguo.

Chiang Kai-shek (Jiang Jieshi, Jiang Zhongzheng, 1887–1975.) Leader of Nationalist China; author of *China's Destiny* (1949) and *Soviet Russia in China* (1956).

chichi (Also *chi chi.*) Already completed; hexagram in the *Yijing*.

chilchong (Korean; *qiqing* in Chinese.) The seven emotions: pleasure, anger, sorrow, fear, love, hatred, and desire.

chin-shi (Also *chin-shih, jinshi, qin shi.*) Highest attainment in the imperial examination.

chinyong (Also *qin yong.*) Familiarity with practical usage.

chizi zhixin Human nature (''original mind'' of man, ''mind of a newborn child'').

chong 1. (Korean; *qing* or *ching* in Chinese.) Human feelings. 2. (Chinese.) Empty, emptiness.

chongxing (Also *chongxin.*) Revival.

Chongyou lun "Extolling the Virtue of Being," treatise by the Jin Daoist Pei Wei.

Chu Hsi (Yüan-hui; 1130–1200.) Proponent, with Cheng Yi, of the mind-heart school (*lixue*) of neo-Confucianism.

chu (Also *zhu.*) Host.

chuandeng Transmission of the lamp, in Chan Buddhism.

Chuang-tzu See Zhuangzi.

chuanti Holistic character.

Chuanxi lu (Also *Ch'üan-hsi lu.*) *Instructions*, by Wang Yangming.

Chuanzhen *dao* True Purity sect, which proposed an integration of three teachings—Daoism, Confucianism, and Buddhism.

Chu ci (*Chu ci*[*xishi*].) Anthology of poetry from the southern province of Chu, possibly by Qu Yua (c. 340–278 B.C.E.).

Chu Han chunqiu *Spring and Autumn Annals of Chu and Han*, by Lu Jia.

Chung yung See *Zhongyong*.

Chunqiu (Also *Ch'un Ch'iu*, *Chun Qiu*, *Zhun Qiu.*) *Spring and Autumn Annals*, text in the classical Confucian canon.

Chunqiu fanlu (Also *Chunqiufanlu.*) *Luxuriant Dew of the Spring and Autumn* [*Annals*], attributed to Dong Zhongshu (c. 179–104 B.C.E.).

***Chunqiu* school** Group of Tang Confucian scholars—Dan Zhu (d. 770), Zhao Kuang (fl. c. 770), and Lu Chun (d. 805)—who restored the text Liu Zhiji had questioned and emphasized *quan*, expedient action.

Chunqiu shilun *General Treatise on Chun Qiu*, by Wang Fuzhi.

Chunqiu zhengzhuan Exegesis by Zhan Ruoshui of the *Spring and Autumn Annals*.

churipa (Korean.) Primacy of *i*, a central feature of T'oegye's Korean neo-Confucian philosophy.

Chuzhong school (Also Huguang region school.) Subschool of the Wang Yangming school.

ci 1. Discourse, used to understand the *dao* (way). 2. Judgments. 3. Politely declining.

Ci'en Kuiji (632–682.) Disciple of Xuanzang; founder of *faxiang*, or *dharmaa-laksana*, Chinese Buddhism; wrote commentaries on the *Cheng weishi lun*.

cihua Talk on *ci* poetry.

Ciming (986–1040.) Chan master known for his unconventional techniques for effecting enlightenment in his disciples.

Cittrabhana Author of a commentary to *Trimsika* (*Thirty Stanzas*).

Cixi (1835–1908.) Dowager empress.

cizhang Literary art.

classics (Also Chinese Classics, Confucian Classics.) Texts of divination, history, philosophy, poetry, ritual, and lexicography; since the Song dynasty they have been: (1) *Shujing* (*Book of Documents*), (2) *Yijing* (*Book of Changes*), (3) *Shijing* (*Book of Songs*), (4) *Yili* (*Ceremony and Rites*), (5) *Zhouli* (*Rites of Zhou*), (6) *Liji* (*Book of Rites*), (7) *Zuozhuan* (*Zuo Annals*), (8) *Guliangzhuan* (*Guliang Annals*), (9) *Gongyangzhuan* (*Gongyang Annals*), (10) *Lunyu* (*Analects of Confucius*), (11) *Xiaojing* (*Book of Filial Piety*), (12) *Erya* (*Graceful and Refined*), (13) *Mengzi* (*Mencius*). Texts 4, 5, and 6 make up the *Lijing* (*Classic of Rites*). Texts 7, 8, and 9 are commentaries to *Chunqiu* (*Spring and Autumn Annals*).

Confucius (Kongzi, K'ung Tzu, Chung-ni, 551–479 B.C.E.) Chinese philosopher of the Zhou dynasty whose teachings emphasize ethics and developing moral character cultivated by practicing the six arts: propriety and ceremony, music making, archery, charioteering, writing, and mathematics.

Cua Khong san trinh "Gate to Kong and the garden of the Chengs," Vietnamese phrase referring to Confucianism.

Cui Jian (d. 290 C.E.) Quoted in *Jingdian shiwen* (*Comments on the Classics and Other Prose Literature*).

Cui Shu (1740–1816.) Scholar who questioned Zi Si's authorship of the *Zhongyong*.

cui 1. Purity. 2. Hexagram in the *Zhouyi*.

cunyang Moral preservation and nourishing.

da To realize.

daben Great root.

Da Dai liji (Also *Da Tai Liji.*) *Rites of Great Dai* (1st century C.E.).

dadao Universal path.

dade Universal virtues.

da gong-ming Highest general name, encompassing all things in the same class.

dahua Endless changes.

Dai Sheng (Former Han dynasty.) Compiler of the *Liji* (*Records of Ritual*).

Dai Wang (1837–1873.) Wrote *Scholarly Records of Yan Yuan* (*Yanshi xueji*).

Dai Zhen (Tai Chen, Dai Dongyuan, 1723 or 1724–1777.) Neo-Confucian of the Qing era who advocated philology as a path to understanding the wisdom of the ancients.

Daigakuryo National university in Japan that promoted Confucianism.

Dai-Nihon-shi *History of Great Japan*, a national history; the project began in the mid-seventeenth century and lasted two centuries.

Daju *The Greater Taking* or *The Greater Choosing*, neo-Mohist text (c. 4th century B.C.E.).

dali 1. "Large" or comprehensive reason; term used by Xunzi to indicate a systematic order of things. 2. Warp and woof of heaven and earth.

Damei (8th century.) Student of Mazu.

Dan Zhu (d. 770.) One of the Chunqiu school of Tang Confucian scholars.

dan Plainness, beauty of plainness.

dangdai xinrujia Contemporary new Confucians.

dangran What ought to be.

dangran zhi ze (Also *dangran zhizhe*.) Standard or norm (*ze*) for determining what ought to be, or what is right and proper.

dangxing Party (communist) viewpoint.

dao (Also *tao*.) 1. The way or Way; way of life. 2. To guide, to offer guidance on the way. *Dao* is perhaps the most basic term in Chinese philosophy, designating ultimate reality, truth, method, and the essence of all things.

Dao'an (312–385.) Chinese Buddhist who criticized the *prajna* schools and established a cult of Maitreya.

daode Moral virtue.

daode benti Moral substance.

daode de xingshangxue Moral metaphysics of Confucianism.

Daodejing (Also *Daode jing*, *Dao dejing*, *Dao de jing*, *Laozi*.) *Classic of Dao and De*—that is, of "the way" and "virtue" (c. 6th century B.C.E.). Influential treatise attributed to Laozi.

Daode zhenjing guangsheng yi *Wide Sage Meaning of the Perfect Scripture of the Dao and Virtue*, work by Du Guangting that systematizes and interprets the *Daodejing*.

Daofu (Dao Fu, Taofu, Tao Fu.) Disciple of Bodhidharma.

Daoism (Also Taoism.) The classical version was founded by Laozi in the *Daodejing* (6th century B.C.E.) and developed by Zhuangzi.

Dao jia (Also *Tao chia*.) Classical Daoism.

daojiao Religious Daoism.

Daojiao yishu *The Pivotal Meaning of the Daoist Teaching*, by Meng Anpai; late seventh-century systematization of Daoist lives and thinking.

Daojia wenhua yanjiu *Study of Daoist Culture*, journal founded in 1992.

daoli Moral norm, principle.

daoquan Thread of *dao*.

Daosheng (c. 360–430.) Chinese Buddhist teacher who advocated the concept of sudden enlightenment; one of the last neo-Daoist Buddhists.

daotong (Also *tao-t'ung*.) Transmission or tradition of *dao*: moral tradition, tradition of interpretation.

dao tongyu yi *Dao* among things.

daowenxue Following the path of inquiry and study; one of two ways to seek the *dao* offered in the *Doctrine of the Mean*.

dao wu zhongqiong (Also *dao wu chongqiong*.) *Dao* cannot be exhausted with finality.

Daoxin (Tao-hsin, 580–635 or 651.) Fourth Chan patricarch; he emphasized living and practicing in the world rather than the asceticism of his predecessors, the forest monks.

daoxin Moral mind.

Daoxuan (596–667.) Wrote a biography of Xuanzang in *Xu Gaoseng zhuan* (*Continuation of the Biographies of Eminent Monks*).

daoxue Song Confucianism, neo-Confucianiam; its followers were devoted to manifestation of the *dao* (way).

Daoxue zhengzong *Orthodox Lineage of Dao Learning*, anthology meant to refute the lineage claims made by Zhou Rudeng for Wang Yangming.

Daoyu (Taoyu.) Disciple of Bodhidharma.

da qing ming Great and pure enlightenment.

Daren xiansheng zhuan "Biography of Master Great Man," treatise by the neo-Daoist Ruan Ji.

darsanabhaga (Indian Buddhism.) Perceiving division, one of the three divisions characterizing consciousnesses.

Dasabhumika sutra sastra (Also *Shidi jing lun*.) Buddhist text.

Da Tai liji See *Da Dai Liji*.

Da Tang da C'ien sanzang fashi zhuan *Biography of Tripitaka, the Dharma Master of the Great C'ien Monastery under the Great Tang*, by Huili and Yancong, with a preface by Yancong dated to 688; biography of Xuanzang.

Da Tang jiaosi lu *Record of Suburban and Sacrificial Offerings in the Tang*, history of several state rites compiled by Wang Jing.

Da Tang Kaiyuan li (732.) Codification of the Kaiyuan ritual of the Tang period; the first complete such code in China to survive.

Da Tang liudian *Sixfold Compendium of Government of the Tang*, compilation accounting for the institutions of government.

dati Large whole.

datong Grand union; grand unity and harmony. Title of a chapter in the *Liji*.

Datong shu *Book on the Great Unity*, by Kang Youwei.

daxin Broadening one's heart-mind.

daxu Hexagram in the *Zhouyi*.

Daxue (Also *Da xue*, *Ta hsüeh*.) *The Great Learning*, text in the classical Confucian canon, originally a chapter in the *Book of Rites* (*Liji*).

Daxue bian *Distinguishing the Great Learning,* critique of the *Daxue* by Chen Que in which the text is attributed to a Han scholar propagating Chan Buddhism.

Daxue yanyi *Extended Meaning of the Great Learning*, by Zhen Dexiu.

Daxue zhangju Commentary on *the Great Learning*, by Zhu Xi.

da yitong One world.

Dayu (9th century.) Chan master.

Dazhidulun *Treatise on the Great Perfection of Wisdom*, a commentary on the *Prajnaparamita sutra*.

da zhuan One of two seal script styles that came to prominence in the Shang, Zhou, and Qin periods.

Da zhuang lun (Also *Da Zhuang lun*.) "Discourse Reaching Fully the *Zhuangzi*," essay by Ruan Ji.

de (Also *te*.) 1. Virtue, power; the propensity to behave in a certain way when provided with an inspiring model. The five Confucian *de* (virtues) are *ren*, *yi*, *li*, *zhi*, and *xin*. 2. Settled. 3. Insight. 4. Virtuosity.

dechao Integrity.

defa Moral norm.

Deng Chun Wrote *Huaji* (*On Painting*, c. 1167).

Deng Liqun During the post-Mao period, a president of the Chinese Academy of Social Science (CASS).

Deng Xi (Dengxi, late 6th century–early 5th century B.C.E.) Official in the state of Zheng, reputed to have drawn up a code of penal laws and argued for the admissibility of contradictory propositions.

Deng Xiaoping (Teng Hsiao-p'ing, 1904 or 1905–1997.) Chinese communist leader from 1977 until his death.

Dengxi (Also *Deng Xi*.) Pre-Qin writing associated with the school of names.

de re Attitude consisting in projecting a mental category or concept onto an actual thing.

de xiansheng "Mr. Democracy," slogan of the May Fourth movement of 1919.

dexing zhizhi Knowledge of moral nature.

deyi wangyan One forgets language once meaning is obtained; a famous phrase of Zhuangzi.

dezhi Dominion through virtue (a Confucian doctrine).

dharma (Sanskrit; in Chinese, *fa*.) 1. Teaching, dispassion. 2. (Buddhism) Phenomena. 3. Divine law.

dharmadhatu (Sanskrit.) Space of *dharma*; in Huayan, infinite interconnectedness of part and whole; also the vision of a Buddha-kingdom on earth.

Dharmaguptakas Buddhist school or sect that had a great influence in China in the second and third centuries C.E.

Dharmakaya (Sanskrit.) *Body of Law*.

Dharmakirti (c. 600–660). Logician who propounded a theory of consciousness.

Dharmaksema (385–431.) Translator of the Mahayana *Nirvana sutra*.

Dharmapala (c. 530–561.) Author of a commentary to *Trimsika* (*Thirty Stanzas*) summarized by Xuanzang; propounded a theory of consciousnesses.

dharmata (Sanskrit; in Chinese, *faxing*, *fa-hsing*.) The one form of the real underlying all things, as distinguished from perspectives on it.

dhyana In Indian Chan Buddhism, meditation.

di 1. Lord, emperor. 2. God. 3. Brotherly respect. 4. Earth-sustenance.

Dianlun lunwen (Also *Lun wen*.) *On Literature*, by Cao Pi.

Diao Qu Yuan "Lament for Qu Yuan," attributed to Jia Yi (200–168 B.C.E.).

difang zhi Local histories.

Dignaga (c. 480–540.) Traditionally considered the founder of a school of Indian Buddhism that emphasized logic and epistemology rather than the study of scriptures and scriptural commentaries.

Dilun Scholar of the *Dasabhumika sutra sastra* (*Shidi jing lun*).

Ding Cook or butcher, a figure in a famous passage of the *Zhuangzi*.

ding 1. Fixed, confined. 2. Idea, ideal.

dingfa Fixing the standards, a theory attributed to the legalist Shang Yang.

dinghui (Also *zhiguan*.) Calming and insight.

dingli Theorem.

di zhi xuanjie Zhuangzi's concept of resolution of the ultimate.

Doba Wei (Also Tuoba Wei, Northern Wei.) Dynasty, 386–534, that united the north of China.

Dogen (12th century.) Japanese Zen master.

Dong Guozi Figure in the *Zhuangzi* who asks Zhuangzi about *dao*.

Dong Qichang (1555–1636.) Contributor to the Chinese discourse on the aesthetics of painting.

Dong Zhongshu (Tung Chung-shu, c. 195–105 or 170 or 179–104 B.C.E.) Han Confucian thinker instrumental in establishing Confucianism as state ideology; author of *Chunqiu fanlu* (*Luxuriant Dew of the Spring and Autumn Annals*) and an interpreter of the *Gongyang Commentary* to the *Spring and Autumn Annals*.

dong Motion, movement, to move; activity.

Donglin (Also Tonglin.) Seventeenth-century political movement.

Dongshan (807–869.) Chan master.

Dongxi wenhua ji qi zhexue (Also *Dong Xi wenhua ji qi zhexue.*) *Eastern and Western Cultures and Their Philosophies*, by Liang Shuming.

Dou Mo (1196–1280.) Neo-Confucian scholar of the north.

Du Guangting (850–933.) Daoist who synthesized diverse teachings; author of *Daode zhenjing guangsheng yi* (*Wide Sage Meaning of the Perfect Scripture of the Dao and Virtue*).

Du You (735–812.) Tang scholar who compiled a major work on government, the *Comprehensive Compendium* (*Tongdian*).

du 1. Solitude, privacy. 2. Subtle activities of the heart in response to a situation; such activities are not yet outwardly manifested and thus are known only to oneself.

Duan Yucai (1735–1815.) Disciple of Dai Zhen.

duan 1. (Also *duanni.*) Inborn "sprouts" of the *xin* (heart-mind), postulated by Mencius. 2. (Also *tuan.*) "Judgment" about a hexagram in the *Yijing*.

Duanzhuan (Also *Duan, Tuan.*) *Commentary on the Judgments*; its two sections form two of the *Ten Wings* (*Yizhuan* or *Shiyi*), commentaries on the *Yijing*.

dunren Escapists, people who have fled from or abandoned their natural selves.

dunyuan Suddenly and completely.

Du sishu daquan shuo *Discourse on Reading the Great Collection of Commentaries on the Four Books*, by Wang Fuzhi.

Du tongjian lun *Treatise on Reading Tongjian*, by Wang Fuzhi.

dyana (Also *samadhi.*) Term adopted by Chinese Buddhists, who merged the meanings of comprehensive observation and inner meditation.

e Evil.

en Kindness.

er ben wu fen Two foundations without distinctions; doctrine implied by the Mohist teaching of universal love without distinction, as opposed to the Confucian teaching of graded love.

Er Cheng "The two Chengs": Cheng Hao (1032–1085) and his younger brother, Cheng Yi (1033–1108).

Er Cheng quanshu *The Complete Work of the Two Cheng Brothers.*

erdi Twofold truth: conventional or relative truth, and ultimate or absolute truth.

Erdi yi (Also *Erdiyi.*) *The Meaning of the Twofold Truth*, by Jizang (c. 549–623 C.E.).

erdi zhongdao Middle way of the twofold truth.

Erlijing zhuance Study by Zhan Ruoshui of the two ritual classics (*Da Dai liji* and *Liji*) and their commentaries.

Erya *Graceful and Refined*, a book of glosses of Zhou dynasty terms, ascribed in Han times to Confucius; one of the Confucian classics.

eryong Dual function.

fa 1. Law, rule, model, doctrine; in the Warring States period (403–221 B.C.E.) *fa* came to mean penal law. 2. Standard, gnomon.

Fa fa "On Conforming to the Law," legalist chapter in *Guanzi*.

Faguo (c. 344–416.) Buddhist from the northern *sangha* in China who advocated the right of a king to demand homage of a monk.

Fahua xuanyi *The Hidden Meaning of the Dharma Flower*, text by Zhiyi.

fajia (Also *fa jia, fa chia.*) Legalists; legalist school, legalist thought.

Fajin (Also *Fa jin.*) "On Laws and Prohibitions," legalist chapter in *Guanzi*.

Falang (506–581.) Promoter of Sanlun Madhyamika Buddhism at the Xinghuang Temple in Sheshan, and teacher of Jizang.

falun gong Popular religious movement practicing *qigong*.

Fan Chi Figure in the *Analects* who asks Confucius about wisdom.

Fan Xuanzi Wrote *The Book of Penalty*, to which Confucius objected.

Fang Bao (1668–1749.) Scholar, friend of Li Gong.

Fang Dongmei (Thomé H. Fang, 1899–1977.) Synthesizer of western and Chinese metaphysics, author of *The Chinese View of Life* (1957) and many other works.

Fang Keli Contemporary scholar; a dean of the graduate school of China Academy of Social Sciences (CASS).

Fang Lizhi (b. 1936.) Physicist, former Chinese Communist Party member who openly abandoned belief in Marxism.

Fang Xianfu (d. 1543.) Member of the school of Yue and Min.

Fang Xiaoru (1357–1402.) Disciple of Song Lian who was executed by dismemberment for refusing to serve a usurping emperor.

Fang Zhongyan (11th century.) Contemporary of Zhang Zai who encouraged Zhang to study the *Zhongyong* (*Doctrine of the Mean*).

fang "Dikes," used metaphorically in the *Liji* (*Book of Rites*); e.g., *fangde*, a dike to conserve virtues.

fangbian Skillful measure; balance of mind, nature, and wisdom, which may open one to enlightenment.

fanguan Reflective perception.

Fangyan *Dialect Words*, by Yang Xiong.

fawai chuanxin Transmission from mind to mind, without a mediating text.

faxiang (Sanskrit, *dharma-laksana*.) Forms of things; teaching from India that views essence and form as separate and stresses "consciousness only."

Faxiang Essay on the laws of nature by Dai Zhen; it became part of the first section of his *Yuanshan*.

faxing (Also *fa-hsing*; Sanskrit, *dharmata*.) Essence of mind; the one form of the real underlying all things (*dharma*); teaching that views the fluid interrelation of mind and world by analogy with water and waves (things of the world).

Fa xing (Also *Faxing*.) "Law and Practice," chapter in the *Xunzi*.

Fayan *Moral Discourses* or *Model Sayings*, by Yang Xiong; dialogue in the style of the *Analects* of Confucius.

fayan wei ming "For the ancient people names arise from speech."

Fazang (Fa-tsang, 643–712.) Systematizer of Huayan thought, sometimes considered the founder of the Huayan school, which elaborated and propagated the teaching of the *Huayan jing* (*Garland Sutra*).

fazhi Rule of standards.

fei "Non-"; wrong; is not, not-this (as opposed to *shi*, "this").

fei fei To reject distinctions; literally, to not "this-not this"(Mohist term).

Fei shi'erzi "Against the Twelve Philosophers," a chapter of the *Xunzi*.

fen 1. Division, distinction. 2. Allotment.

Feng Dao (882–954.) Considered by Li Zhi to be a loyal minister, a judgment counter to traditional orthodox Confucianism.

Feng Lanrui Theoretician of the post-Mao period who provided a renewed defense of humanism.

Feng Qi (1915–1995.) Epistemologist who focused on how to transform knowledge into wisdom.

Feng Youlan (Fung Yu-lan, 1885, 1895, or 1889–1990.) Author of *History of Chinese Philosophy* (1932); integrated pragmatism, logical positivism, and neorealism into neo-Confucianism.

fengjian Feudal system.

Fengjian lun "Essay on Feudalism," by Liu Zongyuan.

fengshan Sacrificial ritual performed as a public announcement that a new ruler had received the mandate of heaven.

fengshui Geomancy or siting.

fenli Differentiated order (Dai Zhen).

fenshu Differing manifestations or roles.

fenye "Field allocation," astrological system sometimes referred to as "disastrous geography," in which the classical nine or twelve provinces of China had corresponding heavenly "fields" (Han era).

Five Classics *Yijing* (*Book of Changes*), *Shijing* (*Book of Odes*), *Shujing* (*Book of History*), *Liji* (*Book of Rites*), and *Chungqiu* (*Spring and Autumn Annals*).

Fotudeng (d. 349.) Founder of the northern *sangha* in China, responsible for converting much of the population of northern China to Buddhism.

Four Books *Analects* (*Lunyu*), *Mencius* (*Mengzi*), *Great Learning* (*Daxue*), and *Doctrine of the Mean* (*Zhongyong*); Confucian texts.

foxing Buddha-nature.

Fu Weixun (Charles Fu, 1933–1996.) Scholar who devoted himself to Chinese Buddhism and Chinese religions.

Fu Xi (Fuxi, possibly 2852–2738 B.C.E.) Legendary sage who claimed that writing originated as a mnemonic device of tying knots in a cord and is said to have invented the system of *gua* or *yi* symbols in the *Yijing*.

Fu Yi (fl. 600.) Wrote on the texts of Laozi during the Tang dynasty.

fu 1. Prose poems; originally developed to reflect reality mimetically but later tending toward language rich in imagery and rhyme. 2. To restore balance, through ritual propriety, after a disturbance by feelings. 3. Man, adult. 4. Treasury, storehouse. 5. Orb. 6. Talisman; with *yao* (cinnabar) and *qi* (vital breath), one of the three techniques of Daoism. 7. Hexagram in the *Zhouyi*.

Fukuzawa Yukichi (1835–1901.) Japanese journalist and educator, a modernizer during the Meiji era (1868–1912).

fuli Return to ritual propriety, realignment with heavenly principles.

Fuli lun *On Returning to Ritual Propriety*, by Ling Ting-kan.

Fu'niao fu "The Owl," attributed to Jia Yi.

Fushe Seventeenth-century reform movement.

fushi zhiwei "This is what is meant by . . . ," formula for explaining the meaning of terms.

Fuxing shu *Essay on Restoring Nature* or *Writings on Returning to One's True Nature*, by the Confucian Li Ao.

fuyan Accord with evidence.

Gan Yang Contemporary postmodernist.

gan 1. Stimulus. 2. Feeling.

gang Hard, firm, strong.
ganhu Imperceptible instructions.
Ganquan School of Zhan Ruoshui, whose family was from Ganquan, a section of Zengcheng, Guangdong.
ganxian Falling on objectivization, process by which the infinite mind manifests itself and in which it restricts itself (Mou Zongsan).
ganying (Also *kanying*.) Stimulus and response; mutual sympathy or resonance of macrocosm and microcosms.
ganying daojiao Communicative, responsive relationship.
Ganying pian *Tract on Action and Response* (c. 1164), text of the *gongguo* (merit and demerit) movement, compiled by Li Zhiji.
Gao Ertai Theoretician who provided a renewed defense of humanism during the reforms of the post-Mao period.
Gao Panlong (1562–1626.) Leader of the Donglin Academy who attempted to promote a return to Cheng-Zhu doctrine.
Gao Wenhu (1134–1212.) Conventional Confucian who used governmental power in an effort to suppress the "*dao* learning" fellowship.
Gao Yihan (1884–1968.) Involved in the debate over *quanli* (rights); wrote *Cheng-chih hsueh kang-yao, Outline of Political Science*.
Gao You (c. 168–212.) Author of a commentary on the *Huainanzi*.
Gaozi (Also Gao Zi.) Contemporary of Mencius; Gaozi maintained that human nature is neutral and therefore malleable by outside forces.
Gaozu (Xiaowendi, r. 471–500.) Sinicized emperor who initiated a cultural renaissance in the north of China.
Gaudapada (6th century.) Indian philosopher who commented on the Upanishads.
Gautama Siddharta Buddha (Sakyamuni Buddha, "enlighened wise man of the Sakya clan," 563–483 B.C.E.) Indian prince who, after attempting to become enlightened through following Hindu and ascetic practices, attained enlightenment and spent his life teaching. He is considered the founder of Buddhism.
Ge Hong (Baopuzi.) During the Eastern Jin dynasty, modified primitive religious Daoism to assimilate Confucianism and legalism without absorbing Buddhism.
geli Investigation of ritual propriety.
gen 1. Roots. 2. Hexagram in the *Yijing*, "mountain," "keeping still."
Geng Dingxiang (1524–1596.) Member of the Taizhou school.
genyuan Source.
gewu (Also *kewu*, *ke-wu*, *ku-wu*.) Investigation of things.
gewu xiongli Investigating things and exhausting the *li* (principle).
gewu zhizhi 1. Interpreted by Zhu Xi as investigation of things and extension of knowledge. 2. Interpreted by Wang Yangming as our effort to rectify things, in order to extend our innate moral knowledge (*liangzhi*) to events or affairs.
geyi Practice of matching concepts.
Gido Shushin (1325–1388.) Monk who spread Confucian ideas among the aristocracy of Kyoto.
goko Local schools in Japan.
Gong He (Zhou dynasty.) Regent who exiled Li, the tenth king of the Zhou.
Gong Yuzhi Recorded Mao Zedong's conversation about the problem of the three categories at the lectures of 1937; later vice president of the Central Party School.
Gong Zizhen (1782–1841.) Qing philologist who advocated a harmonious relation between the two strands of Confucian thought, *zundexing* (honoring the moral nature) and *daowenxue* (path of inquiry and study), but favored the latter.
gong (Also *kong*.) 1. Impartiality. 2. Public spirit. 3. Extendable realm of public and global values, the general. 4. Respectfulness. 5. Handicrafts.
gongan (Also *gong'an*, Chinese; in Japanese, *koan*.) 1. Chan scriptures indigenous to China, hence not translated from Indian sutras; they are used not only for transmitting *dharma* but also for achieving enlightenment. 2. Late Ming school of writing, a literary extension of Yangming thought.
gongde Virtue that promotes public well-being.
gongfu Moral exertion; mental efforts.
Gonggong Mythical giant.
gongguo Merit and demerit; Song Daoist movement that kept ledgers in order to assess one's standing in otherworldly realms.
gongguo ge Manuals for moral self-improvement.
gonghuan Common affliction.
gongli Axiom.
gongming Generic or common names or terms.
Gongsun Chou Recipient of an explanation from Mencius about *qi*.
Gongsun Long (Kung-sun Lung, Gongsun Longzi, b. 380 B.C.E.) Figure in the school of names; propounded the paradox "white horse is not horse." *Gongsun Longzi* (*Book of Master Gongsun Long*) is attributed to him.
Gongsun Qiao (Zichan.) Promulgated *The Canons of Penalty* in 536 B.C.E. in the Zheng state.

Gongxi Chi (Zihua.) Disciple of Confucius known for his diplomacy and concise, decorous speech.

gongyang School of exegesis later known as the "new text" school; it claimed that Confucius's teachings had been transmitted orally, thus allowing nonliteral readings of a classical text.

Gongyang (Also *Gongyongzhuan.*) *Gongyong Annals*, one of three commentaries on the Confucian text *Spring and Autumn Annals* (*Chunqiu*).

Gonsun Hong (Han dynasty.) Confucian scholar; first Confucian to rise from the status of commoner to prime minister at the court.

grahaka That which grasps.

grahya That which is grasped.

Gu Kaizhi (c. 345–406.) Wrote *Lunhua* (*Discussing Painting*).

Gu Xiancheng (1550—1612.) Founder of the Donglin (or Tonglin) Academy.

Gu Yanwu (Ku Yen-wu, Tinglin, 1613–1682.) Historian and founder of a less speculative, more text-focused Qing classical scholarship; author of *Rizhi lu* (*Record of Knowledge Gained Daily*), on Confucian statecraft.

gu 1. Past. 2. Reason, cause.

gua 1. To cut, to diminish. 2. To expand, to boast. 3. (Also *yi*.) Trigram (plural, *guan*).

Guafu Lunar titan, in a myth from the *Shanhaijing* (*Book of Mountains and Seas*).

guai Weird.

Guamati (Gunamati, 5th–6th century C.E.) Author of a commentary to *Trimsika* (*Thirty Stanzas*) summarized by Xuanzang.

Guan 1. (Zhou dynasty.) Lord condemned by orthodox historians for his opposition to the duke of Zhou. 2. School of Song neo-Confucianism founded by Zhang Zai.

Guan Yin (Yin Si, Yin Xi.) Legendary barrier keeper at whose demand the *Laozi* was said to have been written. See also Guanyinzi.

Guan Zhong (d. 645 B.C.E.) Minister of state in Qi, erroneously considered by some to be the author of *Guanzi*; called the father of legalism.

guan 1. Observation, perception, understanding. 2. "Retracing regard," intuition of essences of things in letting things be themselves.

Guan Cai lun Essay by Xi Kang rehabilitating lords Guan and Cai of the Zhou dynasty.

Guanding (561–632.) Disciple of Zhiyi.

guangde Expansive virtue.

Guangfuhui (Also Guangfu hui.) Restoration Society, revolutionary group in Japan that supported Sun Yat-sen.

Guangxiao Buddhist temple; the name means "enlarging filial piety."

Guangxu (Guang Xu, personal name Zaitian, 1871–1908.) Ninth emperor of the Qing dynasty; during much of his reign he was dominated by his aunt, the dowager empress Cixi.

guanjing Observing purity.

guantong Wide and far-reaching (cognitive) penetration.

guantong zhixue Learning in order to acquire comprehensive insights.

Guanwu "Contemplating Things," the chapter titles in Shao Yong's *Supreme Ultimate Ordering the World* (*Huangji jingshi*).

Guanyin See Avalokitesvara.

Guanyinzi Ancient Daoist identified with Guan Yin (Yin Xi, Yin Si); his work *Guanyinzi* was reedited and possibly rewritten in the Yuan dynasty; it appears in the commentary *Wenshi zhenjing* (*Perfect Scripture of Master Wenshi*).

Guanzi (Also *Kuan Tzu*.) *Book of Master Guan* (c. 26 B.C.E.), collection of early Chinese materials put together from various sources by Liu Xiang (77–6 B.C.E.); its title is the name of a minister of the state of Qi, Guan Zhong (d. 645 B.C.E.).

gufa yongbi Bone method; use the brush.

guiji Returning to tranquillity, school of Nie Bao and Luo Hongxian.

guijian The noble and the base.

guishen Ghosts, spirits.

gujin Past and present.

gujing jingshe Refined study for explication of the classics.

Guliang (Also *Guliangzhuan*.) *Guliang Annals*, one of three commentaries on the *Spring and Autumn Annals* (*Chunqiu*).

Guo Moruo (1894–1979.) Intellectual leader of Chinese Marxism following World War I.

Guo Qiyung Contemporary scholar of new Confucianism.

Guo Ruoxu Wrote *Tuhua jianwen zhi* (*Record of Things Seen and Heard with Regard to Painting*, c. 1080).

Guo Si (d. after 1123.) Guo Xi's son.

Guo Xi (after 1000–c. 1090.) Court painter and author of a compilation on mountain and water painting, *Linquan gaozhi* (*The Lofty Truth of Forests and Streams*).

Guo Xiang (Kuo Hsiang, Zixuan, c. 252–312.) Advocate of a neo-Daoist movement called "profound learning"; important interpreter of the *Zhuangzi* who also wrote a commentary on the *Analects* of Confucius.

Guodian zhujian Guodian bamboo slips, excavated in the village of Guodian (Kuo-tien) in 1993, containing pre-Qin texts; officially published as *Guo-*

dian Chumu Zhujian (*Guodian Chu Tomb Bamboo Slips*) in 1998.
Guo Qin lun "Discussion of the Faults of the Qin," by Jia Yi.
guoshi State history.
guoxing (Also *kuo-hsing*.) National character.
Guoyu (Also *Guo Yu*.) *Records of States*, c. 500 B.C.E.
guwen 1. Archaic or ancient prose; a terse prose style complemented by tacit imagery and rhyme. 2. "Old texts" of the Confucian tradition, preserved in an ancient style of calligraphy. 3. Name of a school that included Liu Xin.
Guwen longhu jing *Old Text Dragon and Tiger Scripture*, by Wei Boyang (2nd century C.E.).
Guwen xiaoxue "Old text" version of *Elementary Learning*, by Zhan Ruoshui.

Han Dynasty, 202 B.C.E.–220 C.E.
Han Feizi (Han Fei, Han Fei Zi, Han Fei Tzu, 281–233 B.C.E.) Legalist, a student of Xunzi.
Han Tuozhou (1152–1207.) Conventional Confucian often considered anti-intellectual.
Han Yu (Han Yü, 768–824.) Confucian who wrote a treatment of aesthetics, *Song Meng Dongye shu* (*Letter to Meng Tung-yeh*); the poem "Xie Ziran"; and "Essentials of the Moral Way" or "The Origin of the Way" (*Yuan dao*).
Han Zhuo (fl. c. 1095–1125.) Wrote *Shanshui Chunquan ji* (*Chunquan's Collected Notes on Landscape*).
Hanfeizi (Also *Han Feizi*.) *Book of Master Han Fei*, a collection of Han's writings; it was compiled by his disciples, who substantially altered some of his essays and added others.
Hanji (Also *Han ji*.) *Chronicles of the Former Han*, by Xun Yue; treatise critical of the Han dynasty.
hanko Prefectural school in Japan.
Hanlin Academy Institution whose name refers to a member of the Imperial Academy.
Hanshu (Also *Han shu*.) *Standard History of the Han* or *History of Han*, by Ban Gu.
Hanxue Han learning.
hanyang Quietude.
Hao Jing (1223–1275.) Neo-Confucian scholar of the north.
hao Likes, preferences.
haoli Desire for gain; self-seeking tendency.
haomin Local despots.
haoran Floodlike; great and unyielding.
haoran zhiqu 1. Great flood of the vital force, the *qi* that generated, filled, and sustained the cosmos. 2. Situation or instance of the cosmic breath; that which living letters (poems or poetry) represent or give a sense of.
haotian Majestic or august heaven.
Harivarman (c. 250–350 C.E.) Buddhist scholar, author of *Chengshilun* (*Satyasiddhi* in Sanskrit, *Treatise on Establishing the Real*).
He Hangzhou Modern scholar who has contributed to the discourse on rights.
He Ji (1188–1268.) Song neo-Confucian who received Huang Gan's teachings.
He Liangchun (1506–1573.) Wrote *Qulun* (*On Drama*).
He Lin (1902–1995.) Wrote *Wushi nianlai di zhongguo zhexue* (*Fifty Years of Chinese Philosophy*).
He Xinyin (Liang Ruyuan, 517–1579.) Taizhou thinker and lecturer who publicly advocated righting social injustices.
He Xiu (129–182.) Commentator on the *Chunqiu* (*Springs and Autumns* or *Spring and Autumn Annals*.)
He Yan (c. 190–249.) Neo-Daoist thinker and author who also wrote a commentary on Confucius's *Analects*.
he Harmony.
Heguanzi (Also *Ho Kuan Tzu*, late 3rd century B.C.E.) Daoist political treatise attributed to the otherwise unknown "Pheasant Cap Master," rejected as a forgery; its core was probably written in the southern state of Chu.
hehe xue Theory of harmony and integration formulated by Zhang Liwen.
heng 1. Balance or weighing standard. 2. Hexagram in the *Zhouyi*.
heqi Harmonious relationship.
Heshang Gong (Probably 3rd–4th century C.E.) Wrote commentary on texts of Laozi.
Heshen Corrupt favorite of the Qianlong emperor (the emperor died in 1799).
Hetuvidya (Indian Buddhism.) Texts on logic.
Heze Chan school founded by Shenhui (c. 670–762).
Hinayana (Sanskrit, small or narrow vehicle.) The more conservative of three main paths of Buddhism.
Hokke shuku *Superlative Passages of the Lotus Sutra*, work by the Japanese monk Saicho.
Hongfan "Great Norms," chapter in the *Shangshu* (*Book of Documents*).
Honglou meng *Dream of the Red Chamber*, mid-eighteenth-century novel.
Hongloumeng pinglun *On "The Dreams* [or *Dream*] *of the Red Chamber"*; a work of literary criticism by Wang Guowei.
Hongren (Hong Ren, Hung-jen, c. 601–674.) Disciple of Daoxin; fifth patriarch of Chan in China; teacher of Huineng.
hong Ru Great Ru.

Hongzhou (Also Hangzhou.) School of Chan Buddhism.

Hosso Japanese counterpart of the *faxiang* lineage, which stresses "consciousness only."

hotoku (Japanese.) Repayment.

Hou Ba (c. 1st century.) Disciple of Yang Xiong.

houtian Posterior to heaven.

Hsi ming (Also *Xi ming*, *Ximing*.) *Western Inscription*, by Zhang Zai.

Hsün Tzu See Xunzi.

Hu Feng Figure of the 1940s, favored continuing the May Fourth movement by advocating "modern" and "international" arts and literature.

Hu Hai (d. 207 B.C.E.) Qin emperor.

Hu Hong (Hu Hung, Renzhong, Wufeng xiansheng, 1105–1161, or 1100 or 1110–1155.) Song neo-Confucian said to have founded the Hu-Xiang (Hunan) school; author of *The Great Records of Emperors and Kings* (*Huangwang daji*) and *Understanding Words* (*Zhiyan*).

Hu Jie Song scholar who commented on Jia Yi.

Hu Juren (1434–1484.) Student of Wu Yubi and author of *Juyelu*.

Hu Lingyi Confucian general.

Hu-Liu One of three trends discerned by Mou Zongsan in Song-Ming neo-Confucian philosophy (the others are Cheng-Zhu and Lu-Wang). Hu-Liu is centered on the thought of Hu Hong and Liu Qishan.

Hu Qiaomu During the post-Mao period, a president of the Chinese Academy of Social Science (CASS).

Hu Shi (Hu Shih, Shizhi, 1891–1962.) Proponent of John Dewey's pragmatism.

Hu Yaobang (1915–1989.) General secretary of the Chinese Communist Party from 1981 to 1987, a leader of post-Mao reforms.

Hu Yin (1098–1156.) Song neo-Confucian, brother of Hu Hong.

Hu Yuan (993–1056.) Teacher of Cheng Yi.

Hua Guofeng (b. 1921.) Successor of Mao Zedong in 1976, leader of the People's Republic of China and the Chinese Communist Party from 1976 to 1981.

Hua Tuo Possibly legendary figure of the Eastern Han, said to have been the first Chinese to perform surgery; became a god of medicine.

hua 1. Moral transformation. 2. Beauty or outward appearance. 3. Measuring. 4. Speech (in modern Chinese, as opposed to literature).

huahu Debate on whether Laozi was a reincarnation of Buddha or vice versa.

Huainanzi (d. 122 B.C.E.) Syncretic Daoist.

Huainanzi (Also *Huai-nan Tzu*, c. 139 B.C.E.) Han political treatise by a group of scholars in the court of Liu An (r. 164–122 B.C.E.).

Huairang (677–744.) Chan master.

Huaji *On Painting* (c. 1167), by Deng Chun.

Huan Kuan (Early Han.) Confucian, compiler of *Yan tie lun* (*Discourses on Salt and Iron*).

Huan Tan (c. 1st century C.E.) Han Confucian master, disciple of Yang Xiong.

Huang Daoist master in the time of Emperor Qing (r. 158–141 B.C.E.).

Huang Dapo (Mistress Huang, late 13th century.) Introduced a cotton gin and other devices in the lower Yangtze (Chang) valley and was worshiped as a goddess.

Huang Di (Huangdi.) Yellow Emperor, Yellow Thearch.

Huang Gan (1152–1221.) Most advanced disciple of Zhu Xi.

Huang Gong (fl. late 3rd century B.C.E.) *Huang Gong*, pre-Qin writing attributed to him that is no longer extant, was sometimes classified as representative of the school of names (*mingjia*, *ming jia*).

Huang-Lao School of *Zhuangzi* scholarship that integrated Confucian and legalist positions.

Huang Tingjian (Huang Ting-jian, 1045–1105.) Painter, poet, and calligrapher.

Huang Zongxi (Huang Chung-Hsi, Huang Lizhou, Huang Tsunghi, c. 1605–1695.) Qing scholar, author of *Mingyi daifang lu* (*Waiting for the Dawn: A Plan for the Prince*, 1662).

Huang Zunsu Ming official; father of Huang Zongxi.

Huang Zuo (1490–1566.) Wrote about ritual in the Ming period.

huang 1. Waste. 2. Sage.

Huangchao jingshi wenbian (1827.) Collection of Qing writings edited by Huo Changlin and Wei Yuan.

Huangdi neijing suwen *Plain Questions of the Yellow Sovereign's Inner Classic* or *Basic Questions of the Inner Canon of the Yellow Sovereign* (Han era).

Huangdi zhaijing *Yellow Sovereign's Site Classic* (5th–1st century B.C.E.).

Huangji jingshi *Supreme Ultimate Ordering the World*, by Shao Yong.

Huangji jingshi guanwu neipian Inner chapter of *Huangji jingshi*.

Huanglao boshu (Also *Huang Lao boshu*; *Huangdi sujing*, "Huang-Lao silk manuscript.") Text of the Huang-Lao school, found within the Mawangdui silk texts of Laozi discovered in 1973; it shows an intermingling of Daoist and legalist thought.

Huangpo (d. 847.) Chan master.

Huangwang daji *The Great Records of Emperors and Kings*, historical work by Hu Hong (1105–1161).

Huanjin shu *The Art of Reverting Gold*, early work of inner alchemical Daoism.

Hua shanshui jue *The Secrets of Painting Landscapes* by Li Chengsou (c. 1150–after 1221).

Hua shanshui xu *Introduction to the Painting of Landscape* by Zong Bing (375–443).

Huashi *A History of Painting*, by Mi Fu (1052–1107).

huatou "Heading words," abbreviated from the *gongan*.

Huaxinghui China Arise Society, revolutionary group in Japan that supported Sun Yat-sen.

huaxing qiwei Trasformation through human efforts.

Huayan (Hua Yen, *Garland*, *Avatamsaka*.) School of Chinese Buddhism patronized by Empress Wu; it propagated the teaching of the *Huayan jing* (*Garland Sutra*).

Huayanjing (Also *Huayan jing*.) *Garland Sutra*, mid-Mahayana text first translated into Chinese in its entirety by Buddhabhadra (359–429).

Hua yulu *Enlightening Remarks on Painting*, by Shitao (1642–c. 1707).

Hui 1. Emperor (r. 195–188 B.C.E.). 2. King of Wei (c. 340–320 C.E.) who employed Hui Shi as chief minister.

Hui Shi (Hui Shih, 370–319 or 380–305 B.C.E.). Logician of the school of names.

hui 1. Wisdom (Chinese equivalent of the *prajna* of Indian Chan). 2. Epoch.

huidian Official compendiums of statutes and edicts.

Huiguan (fl. c. 400 C.E.) Chinese Buddhist who argued that enlightenment comes gradually, not suddenly.

Huili (615–c. 675.) Coauthor of *Da Tang da C'ien sanzang fashi zhuan* (*Biography of Tripitaka, the Dharma Master of the Great C'ien Monastery under the Great Tang*), a biography of Xuanzang.

Huike (Hui-k'o, 487–593.) Disciple of Bodidharma and extreme ascetic (*dhuta*), or forest monk; second patriarch of Chan in China.

Huineng (Hui-neng; 638–713.) Chan (Zen) master, sixth patriarch in the southern *sangha* in China; advocate of the doctrine of sudden enlightenment. His teachings are collected in *Sutra Spoken by the Sixth Patriarch from the High Seat of the Treasure of the Law*.

Huisi (515–577.) Tutor of Zhiyi.

huiyi Principle of deciphering meaning by associative understanding, i.e., by noting family relationships among similar character shapes or sounds.

Huiyuan (Hui-yüan, 334–416.) Buddhist monk from the southern *sangha* in China who advocated spiritual autonomy based on a strict division between the mundane and the spiritual.

Huizhao (d. 714.) Ci'en Kuiji's successor in the *faxiang* lineage.

Huizi (Also *Hui zi*.) *Book of Master Hui*, attributed to Hui Shi; pre-Qin writing, no longer extant, sometimes classified as representative of the school of names (*mingjia*, *ming jia*).

Huizong lun (Also *Nikaya samgraha sastra*.) Work said to have been written by Xuanzang; it no longer survives.

hun The human spirit.

Hunan School transmitted by Hu Hong.

hundun (Also *huntun*.) Chaos. A personification, Hundun, figures in a story of Zhuangzi.

hunran Undifferentiated.

Huo Changlin (1785–1848.) During the Qing, editor of *Huangchao jingshi wenbian*.

huo Mislead, delude.

huoqi Fire-vapor.

huoran guangtong Sudden opening up and breaking through; insight into interconnections; comprehensive understanding.

Hwadam See So Kyong-dok.

huo-te Supple and living.

i (Korean; *li* in Chinese.) Principle.

icchantika (Also *yichanti*.) Beings who never attain buddhahood.

Ichiro Kaneyoshi (1403–1481.) Developed a Shinto-Confucian synthesis.

ikihobal (Korean; *liqi hufa* in Chinese.) Mutual alternate manifestation of *i* and *ki* in T'oegye's four-seven theory.

Inoue Tetsujiro (1856–1944.) Philosopher at Tokyo University who promoted Confucianism.

insim (Korean; *renxin* in Chinese.) Human mind.

Iriya Yoshitaka Compiled *Basho no Gororku* (*The Recorded Sayings of Mazu*).

Ishida Baigan (1685–1744.) Japanese Confucian.

Ito Hirobumi (1841–1909.) Japanese Confucian politician who helped draft a constitution balancing citizens' rights and imperial power.

Ixing (683–727.) Tang court astronomer.

ji 1. In Daoist aesthetics, inchoate, indescribable budding. 2. For early Confucians, subtle incipient action or tendency that activates *cheng* (sincerity, wholeness). 3. Fortunate, beneficial, auspicious.

4. Enlightenment; ultimate. 5. Moment. 6. Oneself; one's relation to oneself (in contrast to to *zi*, oneself as distinguised from others).

Jia Yi (Chia I, 200–168 B.C.E.) Classical scholar, philosopher, and poet.

jia Temporary.

jiajie Lending the meaning of complex characters.

Jia jie ''Family Admonition,'' essay by Xi Kang.

jian 1. Beings that hold humanity in common. 2. Whole. 3. Hard (as of the blade of a sword). 4. Compounding. 5. Diligence. 6. To perceive.

jian'ai (Also *jian ai*, *jianai*.) Love of *jian* (members of one's own species); universal love; indiscriminate concern.

jian bai Separation of hard and white, concept of Gongsun Long.

Jianbei lun Essay by Gongsun Long on hardness and whiteness.

jiande (Also *jian-de*, *jian de*.) Firm virtue.

Jiang Jingguo (Chiang Ching-kuo.) Son and successor of Chiang Kai-shek.

Jiang Kui (c. 1155–1221.) Literary critic.

Jiang Qing (Blue River, born Li Yunhe, 1913–1991.) Wife of Mao Zegong, leader of the Gang of Four, force behind the Cultural Revolution of the 1960s and 1970s.

Jiang Xin (1483–1559) Member of the Chuzhong (or Huguang region) school, a subschool of the Wang Yangming school.

Jiangmen School of Chen Xianzhang, mentor of Zhan Ruoshui.

jiangxue Learned discussion.

Jiangyou school (Also Jiangxi school.) Subschool of the Wang Yangming school.

jianming Compound terms.

jianquan Weighed together.

jianqishi ru jianqiren Seeing a person's poetry is like seeing the person.

jianshu (Also *jian-shu*.) Art of accommodation.

jianwen zhizhi Knowledge of seeing and hearing.

jianyi (Also *jenyi*.) Ascent or descent through different levels.

Jiao Hong (1540–1620.) Ming neo-Confucian.

Jiao Xün (1763–1820.) Wrote *Qushuo* (*On Drama*).

jiao Teachings; formative education.

Jiaochou tongyi *General Principles of Bibliography*, collection of essays by Zhang Xuecheng.

jiaocuo Crisscrossing of paradigmatic shapes that, togther with rhythmic sounds, define literature.

jiaoji Sacrificial ritual to petition heaven for successful agriculture.

jia shi Family histories.

jiazhi benti Value *benti*.

Jicang See Jizang.

Jie ''Admonitions,'' chapter in *Guanzi*.

jie bi Factors that obscure discernment of right and wrong.

Jiebe pian (Also *Jiebe*.) ''Removing Obscuration,'' essay by Xunzi.

Jiefang *Liberation*, periodical publication of Mao Zedong's time.

jieju zhi dao Reciprocity.

jienyi See *jianyi*.

jieqi Climatic change.

jietuo di xingshangxue Liberation metaphysics of Daoism and Buddhism.

Jin Guantao (b. 1947.) Elaborated a theory of China as culturally determined as a ''superstable system,'' in which Marxism fitted the need for a centralized ideology.

Jin Lüxiang (1232–1303.) Yuan neo-Confucian who received Huang Gan's teachings.

Jin Shengtan (1608–1661.) Wrote *Pingdian Shuihuzhuan* (*Commentaries on ''Water Margins*,'' a work of literary criticism.

Jin Yuelin (1895–1984.) Analytical philosopher.

jin 1. Present. 2. Proximity; near consequences. 3. Caution, circumspection.

Jinamitra Author of a commentary to *Trimsika* (*Thirty Stanzas*) summarized by Xuanzang.

Jinapura Author of a commentary to *Trimsika* (*Thirty Stanzas*) summarized by Xuanzang.

Jindan dachengji Daoist alchemical text.

Jindan dayao *Great Principles of the Golden Elixir* (1067), by Shangyangzi; work integrating the southern and northern schools of Song alchemical Daoism.

Jing Hao (c. 870–c. 930). Wrote *Bifaji* (*Note on the Art of the Brush*).

jing 1. Normal situations. 2. Invariable rule or a standard of conduct; something constant or recurring. 3. Reverence, respect, seriousness. 4. Tranquillity, stillness, quietude, rest. 5. Concentration, focus. 6. Fulfillment. 7. Classic, classical canon. 8. Hexagram forms in the original *Yijing* (*Book of Changes*). 9. Material world or scene. See also *jingjie*.

Jing *Canons*, neo-Mohist text.

Jin-gang jing *Diamond Sutra*.

jingchang zhi dao Normal, constant requirements of *dao*.

jingcheng Pure sincerity.

jingde To revere virtue.

Jingdian shiwen (Also *Jing dian shi wen*.) *Comments on the Classics and Other Prose Literature*, by Lu Deming.

jingjie (Also *jing*.) Critics' response to questions about the relationship between emotion and the material scene (*jing*, a homophone). This term is sometimes rendered as "world" or "realm" but is really untranslatable. Literally it means "spectacle," "vista"—a piece of reality under the human eye. In criticism it refers primarily to the metaphysical relationship between observer and observed.

jingjing Association of *jing* (material world) and *jingjie*.

jinglun Metaphysics and cosmology.

jingqi Quintessential *qi*.

jingshen Soul, consciousness, human spirit.

jingshi 1. Ordering the world, a principle of action in Confucianism. 2. Practical statesmanship, the dominant concept among Chinese scholars in the latter Qing dynasty.

Jingshuo *Discourse on Canons*, neo-Mohist text.

jingwai zhi jing Scene beyond scene.

Jingwei Mythical bird.

jingxin Fulfillment of the mind or heart-mind.

jingxing Fulfillment of human nature; fulfillment of the nature of a thing.

jingxue Classical scholarship; period of classical learning from Dong Zhongshu (c. 179–104) to Kang Youwei (1858–1927).

jingyanzhi Speaking more accurately.

jingzuo Quiet sitting.

Jinling wenda *Recorded Questions and Answers from the Jinling Academy*, volume of conversations of Zhan Ruoshui.

jinshi (Also *chin-shi*.) Course of study that valued the art of writing and was a prestigious way of entering officialdom during most of the Tang era.

jinsi To reflect on things at hand.

Jinsilu *(Also Jinsi lu.) Reflections on Things at Hand*, neo-Confucian anthology compiled by Zhu Xi and Lu Zuqian.

Jin taikang diji *Record of the Topography of the Jin Dynasty Tai Kang Period.*

jinwen pai (Also *jin-wen pai*.) "New text" school of Confucianism.

jinxin To fulfill one's heart-mind.

jishen (Also *ji shen*.) Worshiping spirits.

jitsugaku (Japanese.) Practical learning.

jiu Regret.

jiujing Nine realms or horizons of reality.

Jiuyuan jueyi lun "On Ontological Inquiry and the Perplexities of Life," by Liang Shuming.

Jiuzhang suanshu *Computational Canon in Nine Chapters*, classic of mathematics from the mid-Han.

Jizang (Jicang, c. 549–623 C.E.) Master of Sanlun ("three treatises") Madhyamika Buddhism in China.

jizhuan Annal-biographical form.

Jnanacandra Author of a commentary to *Trimsika* (*Thirty Stanzas*) summarized by Xuanzang.

jneyavarana (Indian Buddhism.) Obstructions to knowledge.

ju 1. Pick out. 2. State of concentration (as opposed to dispersion).

juan (Also *chüan*, *quan*.) Chapter.

Ju chia See *Ru jia* (Confucianism).

Judi Master who taught one-finger Chan; i.e., by apprehending one device we can apprehend many devices.

judong Roundabout.

jue Capacity for enlightenment.

Jufen jinhua lun "The Theory of Dual Evolution," article by Zhang Binglin.

Juge Liang During the Three Kingdoms, a premier of Shu; synchronized Confucianism, Daoism, and legalism.

jundao pian Essays on the ways of a ruler.

junzi (Also *chün-tzu*.) Moral person; ethically superior person; gentleman; paragon. In Mencian thought *junzi* is potentially attainable by anyone, regardless of class.

juren Academic degree.

jusha (Japanese.) Confucian scholar in Japan.

juso Buddhist-Confucian monks.

Juyelu Work by Hu Juren (1434–1484).

Kabara Ekken (1630–1714.) Japanese intellectual concerned with practical learning (*jitsugaku*) who spread Confucian moral teachings in Japan; author of *Precepts for Daily Life in Japan*, *Onna Daigaku* (*Learning for Women*), and *Yojokun* (*Precepts for Health Care*).

Kaicheng shijing *Canon of the Kaich'eng Period Engraved in Stone* (837). Attempt to provide definitive answers to textual questions.

kaiduan Beginnings or presence.

kai shu Standard script that arose in the Tang (618–907).

kakun House code in a Japanese temple school.

Kamakura Period from c. 1185 to 1336 in Japan.

Kamalasila (c. 740–797.) Adherent of Madhyamaka Buddhism; went to Tibet in 794; opposed the "sudden enlightenment" doctrine of the Chinese Chan Buddhists.

kan Decisive impact.

Kang Sheng Asked about the problem of three categories at Mao Zedong's lectures on dialectical materialism in 1938.

Kang Xi (Kangxi, r. 1662–1723.) Qing emperor.

Kang Youwei (K'ang Yu-wei, 1858–1927.) Qing scholar of the "new text" school, author of

Xinxue weijing kao (a treatise on forged classics) and *Kongzi gaizhi kao* (*Confucius as a Reformer*).
kangakko Government school in Japan.
kang-ruo Firm-soft.
kangxian Abnegate.
Kangzi neiwai pian *The Esoteric and Exoteric Essays of Master Kang*, by Kang Youwei.
kanying (Also *ganying*.) Feeling and response; stimulus and response.
Kaogong ji *Records of the Artisans*, in the last section of the *Zhouli* (*Rites of the Zhou*); *Kaogong ji* was an independent work that may have originated c. fifth century B.C.E..
kaozheng Evidential investigation; philology; methodological principle of Qing scholarship.
karma (Sanskrit.) Fate, work.
Kasyapiyas Indian Buddhist school of thought.
Kawakami Hajime (1879–1946.) Japanese Marxist theoretician; introduced Marxism to Japan.
ke Assertable (Mohism).
Ke Hong (c. 283–363.) Neo-Daoist whose work contains the little we know of Bao Jingyan; author of *Baopuzi* (*The Master Who Embraces Simplicity*).
Keian Genju (1427–1508.) Japanese monk who established a Confucian school in Satsuma.
keji fuli "To subdue oneself and return to propriety is perfect virtue" (Confucius).
keji fuli wei ren "To overcome oneself and restore the practice of proprieties is benevolent love" (Confucius).
kejin renyu, fujin tianli Eradicating all selfish desires and returning completely to heavenly principles.
ken (Also *gen*.) Hexagram in the *Yijing*, "mountain," "keeping still."
k'e-pen Textbooks.
keren zhi qiu (Also *geiren zhi qiu*.) To provide opportunity for the satisfaction of desires.
keti World of objects; objective existence.
kexuan zhizheng Debate on science in the 1920s, polemic between science and metaphysics.
kexue Science, a neologism.
keyi 1. (Also *ko yi*, "extending the idea"; *keyi zhi xue*, "matching concepts.") Understanding by analogy, a method of understanding Buddhist concepts by relating them to Daoist terms as used in the fourth century. 2. Admissibility of an interpretation. 3. Capacity.
keyi zhi xue Matching concepts, used as a means of clarifying ideas.
keyu Desirability.
khi (Vietnamese; *qi* in Chinese). Energy.
Ki Tae-song (Kobong, 1529–1592.) Korean neo-Confucian.
ki (Korean; *qi* or *chi* in Chinese.) Material force.
kijilchisong (Korean; *qichizhixing* in Chinese.) Nature of physical disposition, which is connected to *ki* in the philosophy of T'oegye.
klesavarana (Indian Buddhism.) Defilement.
kogaku Ancient learning in Japan; *kokugaku* is based on the Confucian and neo-Confucian classics.
Kojikii Early history of Japan compiled in the eighth century; promoted Confucian morality and statecraft.
kokugaku National learning in Japan; *kokugaku* is based on Shinto and Japanese historical and literary texts.
Kong Yingda (574–648.) Tang Confucian scholar who oversaw a review of the entire tradition of Confucian commentary and produced a subcommentary series, *Wu jing zhengyi*.
kong 1. Empty; emptiness; to empty one's mind. 2. Terrifying events or phenomena.
kongde (Also *kong-de*.) Large virtue.
Kongjia King, seventh ruler of the Xia dynasty; a figure in myth and legend.
Kongjiao Chinese state religion, "Confucian teaching," advocated by Kang Youwei.
kongli Buddhist principle of *sunyata* (emptiness).
kongqi Air in empty space.
kongyan Empty words.
Kongzi (K'ung Tzu.) See Confucius.
Kongzi gaizhi kao *Confucius as a Reformer*, by Kang Youwei.
Kongzi jiayu *Home Sayings of Confucius* (2nd century).
kongziku Self-imposed torture to no purpose (Liu Xin; phrase deriding the philosophical work of Yang Xiong).
Kongzi xueshuo *Doctrines of Confucius*, critical work by Chen Daqi.
kongzong (Also Sanlun Zong, *sanlun zong*, "three treatises" school.) School of nonbeing or emptiness.
kotis Large number.
Kou Qienzhi (365–448.) Merged Tianshi *dao* with Taiping *dao*, forming a single sect.
Ku Hung-ming (1856–1928.) One of the first few ethnic Chinese translators of selective English versions of the Confucian canon.
kuan Magnanimous.
kuang chan "Wild Chan," describing the Taizhou school (which valued intuitive understanding of the classics more than scholarship).
kuangju False representation of things.

Kueishan (Kuei-shan, Quishan, 771–853.) Chan master who taught by silence and absenting himself.
Kumarajiva (343 or 344–413.) Translated numerous Buddhist texts from Sanskrit into Chinese.
kun 1. Mythical giant fish from the *Zhuangzi*. 2. Earth. 3. Trigram or hexagram in the *Yijing*, "the creative."
Kung-yang tradition Concept of "three ages," the last being an age of universal peace (*taiping shi*).
kunlun Daoist cosmological practice.
Kunzhi ji (Also *K'un-chih chi*, *Kunzhi ji*.) *Knowledge Painfully Acquired*, by Luo Qinshun.
kuochong Full extension, by which good human nature can be discerned.
kuo-hsing (Also *quoxing*.) National character, a nation's sense of identity.

Lankavatara sutra Describes the relation between calm "storehouse" consciousness and active consciousness.
Lao Dan Alleged to be the same person as Laozi, i.e., to have written the *Daodejing*.
Laozi (Lao Tzu, Li Erh, c. 6th century B.C.E.) Name referring to one or a few questionable historical figures and a group of texts, the *Laozi* or *Daodejing*. 1. As a historical figure, Laozi was the founder of Daoism. 2. Traditional texts exist in commentaries by Yan Zun (53–24 B.C.E.), Wang Bi (226–249 C.E.), and Heshang Gong (probably 3rd–4th century C.E.) and Fu Yi's version (Tang dynasty); as silk texts found at Mawangdui in 1973; and as Guodian bamboo slip texts discovered in 1993.
Laozi See *Daodejing*.
laukikasatya (Buddhist.) Worldly truth; common or relative truth that things exist provisionally as dependent beings or temporary names.
le Ethics of utilitarian happiness.
lei Kind, class.
Li (Zhou dynasty.) Tenth king of the Zhou, exiled by the regent Gong He.
Li Ao (Style name Xizhi, c. 772 or 774–836 or 841.) Confucian disciple of Han Yu; author of *Fuxing shu*, "Essay on Returning to (or Restoring) Nature."
Li Buyun Modern scholar who has contributed to the discourse on rights.
Li Chengsou (c. 1150–after 1221.) Wrote *Hua shanshui jue* (*The Secrets of Painting Landscapes*).
Li Da (1889–1966.) Popularizer of Chinese Marxism following World War I; later persecuted.
Li Dazhao (1883–1927.) Leading figure of the "new culture: movement, who began to study and publicize Marxism after the May Fourth movement of 1919.
Li Diao-yüan (1734–1803.) Wrote *Yuchun quhua* (*Talk on Drama*).
Li Gong (1659–1733.) Confucian purist; disciple of Yan Yuan.
Li Gou (Northern Song.) Influenced by legalism; with his disciple Wang Anshi, emphasized seeking profit for the people.
Li Guangdi (1642–1718.) Scholar who studied and disseminated Zhu Xi's work.
Li Honglin Theoretician who defended humanism during the post-Mao reforms.
Li Ji (20th century.) Trotskyite who developed a thesis of "precapitalism" to explain the nature of imperial China; during the Cultural Revolution, Li was wrongly identified as as a legalist.
Li Ke Figure identified as a Confucian in *Lüshi chunqiu* and *Hanshu* (*History of Han*).
Li Kui (c. 453–395 B.C.E.) Legalist thinker; premier and mentor of Marquis Wen in the state of Wei, who concentrated on education and the development of agriculture. Often erroneously identified with Li Ke.
Li Linfu (d. 752.) Minister of the Tang period; author of a commentary to *Da Tang liudian*.
Li Shizeng (Li Shicen, 20th century.) Nietzschean supporter of Chinese Marxism; praised by Mao Zedong in 1920 for sending students to France to learn "cosmopolitanism" (*shijie zhuyi*).
Li Si (c. 3rd century B.C.E.) Disciple of Xunzi.
Li Tong (Yanping, 1093 or 1095–1163.) Teacher of Zhu Xi and advocate of the dictum *liyi fenshu*—"principle is one but its manifestations are many."
Li Yong (1627–1705.) Qing neo-Confucian scholar who advocated *jingshi*.
Li Yü (1611–1679.) Wrote *Xian Qingou ji* (*A Casual Record of Idle Feelings*).
Li Zehou (b. 1930 or 1940.) Theoretician who defended humanism during the post-Mao reforms but distanced himself from socialist humanists; an advocate of "Chinese post-Marxism."
Li Zhi (1527–1552 or 1602.) Taizhou thinker who wrote *Piping Pipaji* (*A Critique of "The Story of Pipa"*).
Li Zhicai (11th century.) Teacher of Shao Yong.
Li Zhiji (d. 1182.) Confucian official who compiled the *Ganying pian*.
li 1. Ritual propriety; rites. 2. Principle, pattern, reason. 3. Benefit. 4. Social roles and moral intentions within a cultural lifestyle; conventional behavior. 5. (Also *lifa*.) Mathematical astronomy. 6. Perilous. 7. Chinese miles.
lian Link.

Liang Hui King who had an encounter with Mencius concerning self-profit as an unsound principle for strengthening a nation or a family.
Liang Huixing Modern scholar who has contributed to the discourse on rights.
Liang Ji Father of Liang Shuming.
Liang Qichao (Liang Ch'i-ch'ao, Zhuoru, Renfu, Rengong, 1873–1929.) Scholar, reformer, and journalist.
Liang Ruyuan Original name of He Xinyin.
Liang Shuming (Liang Shu-ming, Huanding, 1893–1988.) One of the founders of ''new Confucianism'' (*xin Rujia*).
Liang Xiang King who asked a question to which Mencius replied that the world would be settled in peace by being ''settled in oneness.''
liang Means of knowledge.
liangdao Good doctrines.
Lianghan jingxue jinguwen pingyi (Also *Liang-Han jingxue jinguwen pingyi*.) *Assessment of the Han Old and New Text Controversy*, by Qian Mu.
Lianghan sixiangshi *Intellectual History of the Han Dynasty*, by Xu Fuguan.
liangji (Also *liangduan*.) Polarities.
lianglun Epistemology and methodology.
liangming Clear intelligence.
Liang Qichao nianpu changpian Biography of Liang Qichao.
liangxin Root-mind, good mind.
liang xing Letting be.
liangyi Forces produced by the *taiji* (supreme ultimate).
liangzhi (Also *liang-chih*.) Innate knowledge of the good; moral sense or moral intuition; innate goodness or knowledge; sense of rightness; ability to distinguish right from wrong.
liangzhi benti Original substance of the innate knowledge of the good.
liangzhi liangneng Innate knowledge and innate ability.
li ben tian zhi ziran Heaven's spontaneous, natural course.
Licong (r. 1224–1264.) Emperor who enshrined Zhu Xi in the Confucian temple and ordered that Zhu's commentaries be used in preparing for the civil service examinations.
Lidai minghua ji *Record of Famous Painters through the Dynasties* (c. 847), by Zhang Yanyuan.
lide Establishing virtues; one of three components of the Confucian view of immortality.
Liezi (Also *Lieh tzu*.) Neo-Daoist work, introduced in the late fourth century by the scholar Zhang Zhan; apart from his own commentary the text was probably by his father (Zhang Kuang) or his grandfather (Zhang Yi), perhaps incorporating some ancient sources.
ligong Establishing accomplishments; one of three components of the Confucian view of immortality.
liguan Concept of *li* as the thread running through things, events, and human affairs.
li-hai (Mohist term.) Consequences in terms of benefit and harm.
Liji (Also *Li ji*, *Li chi*.) *Book of Rites*, *Book of Ritual*, *Record of Rites*. Classical Confucian text, a Han work containing the *Daxue* (*Great Learning*), a central text of neo-Confucianism.
lijiao Ritualist ethics, doctrine of ritual propriety.
lijie Understanding order; understanding the world in terms of the *li* or order of reality.
li ji li Heavenly principles.
Lijing *Classic of Rites*. It consists of three of the Confucian classic texts: *Yili* (*Ceremony and Rites*), *Zhouli* (*Rites of Zhou*), and *Liji* (*Book of Rites*).
Liji zhangju *Textual Annotation on the Book of Rites*, by Wang Fuzhi.
Lik Kuen Tong See Tang Liquan.
Liming ''Effort and Destiny,'' chapter of *Book of Liezi*, described by Liu Xiang in 14 B.C.E..
Liming pian *Determining Your Own Fate* (c. 1550), guide to moral self-improvement by Yungu (a Chan master) and Yuan Huang (a scholar-official).
Lin Biao (1907–1971.) Military leader of the Chinese Communist Party, killed in an alleged attempted coup.
Lin Li (1100s.) Conventional Confucian, often considered anti-intellectual.
Lin Yusheng (b. 1934.) Chinese-American scholar.
Lin Yutang (1895–1976.) Author of *My Country and My People*, *The Importance of Living*, and many other works; important popularizer of Chinese thought.
Ling Ting-kan (Ling Tingkan, Ling T'ing-k'an, 1757–1809.) Exponent of the ritualist ethics of the ''Han learning'' classicists in the high Qing.
ling 1. Luminous, luminosity; spiritual; profound, intellectual, intelligence; vitality. 2. Small error.
Lingbao bifa *Ultimate Methods of Numinous Treasure*, text of the northern school of Song alchemical Daoism.
lingming Intelligence.
Lingrun (d. c. 649.) Monk, assistant of Xuanzang in the translation bureau.
lingyin Prime minister.
Linji (d. 867.) Monk, disciple of Huangpo and Dayu who founded the Linji Chan (in Japanese, Rinzai) school.

Linquan gaozhi *The Lofty Truth of Forests and Streams* (11th century), work on painting compiled by Guo Xi.

liqi Combination in Song Confucian moral metaphysics: reason (or principle) and vital force.

liquan Thread that runs through the rationales of things.

lishi Phenomena.

li shu Clerical script style that arose in the Han (206 B.C.E.–220 C.E.).

Liu Baonan (1791–1895.) Wrote *Lunyu zhengyi* (*Correct Meanings of the Analects*).

Liu Bang (d. 195 B.C.E.) Patron of Lu Jia.

Liu Fenglu (1776–1829.) Qing scholar who drew attention to the esoteric work of Zhuang Cunyu and *gongyang*.

Liu Guan (1270–1342.) Late Yuan Confucian who emphasized codifying laws and legal expertise for government officials.

Liu Jin (d. 1510.) Powerful eunuch who deprived Luo Qinshun of rank and office.

Liu Qishan (1578–1645.) Thinker who emphasized sincerity of the will; studied by Mou Zongsan.

Liu Shao (16th–17th century.) Son and disciple of Liu Zongzhou.

Liu Shaoqi (1898–1969.) Chairman of the People's Republic of China from 1959 to 1969.

Liu Shipei (1884–1919.) Linguist who believed that meaning arises from the sound of a word, not the shape of its character.

Liu Xi Wrote *Shiming* (*Interpretation of Names*).

Liu Xiang (79 or 77–8 or 6 B.C.E.) Compiler of *Guanzi* (*Book of Master Guan*).

Liu Xiaobo Figure of the post-Mao period who openly abandoned Marxism.

Liu Xiaofeng (b. 1956.) Advocate of Christianity as an intellectual pursuit.

Liu Xie (c. 465–522.) Author of *Wenxin diaolong* (*Literary Mind-Heart Etching Dragon* or *The Literary Mind: Elaborations*).

Liu Xin (46 B.C.E.–23 C.E.) Han scholar, who Kang Youwei claimed had inserted forged entries into most of the traditional Confucian classics.

Liu Yimin (Li Yimin Shu.) Corresponded with Sengzhao, who collected the letters in *Zhaolun* (*The Book of Zhao*, 413).

Liu Yin (1249–1293.) Neo-Confucian scholar of the north.

Liu Yuxi (772–842.) Tang scholar who was critical of correlative astronomy but advocated a numerical understanding of natural (including human) processes.

Liu Zhi (c. 1662–1736.) Chinese Muslim scholar who advocated understanding Islam in a Confucian framework by incorporating Buddhist and Daoist teachings.

Liu Zhiji (661–721.) Tang historian and critic; author of *Generalities on History* or *General Principles of Historiography* (*Shitong*, 710).

Liu Zongyuan (773–819.) Author of ''Essay on Feudalism'' (*Fengjian lun*); wrongly identified as a legalist during the Cultural Revolution.

Liu Zhongzhou (Liu Zongzhou, Liu Tsung-chou, Liu Xianzhang, Liu Jishan, 1576 or 1578–1645). Neo-Confucian thinker; student of Wang Yangming and teacher of Huang Zongxi.

liu Flow.

Liufa (Also *Liu fa.*) *Six Principles* by Xie He (fl. c. 500–535).

liujing jieshi ''The Six Classics are all history,'' famous epigrammatic sentence at the beginning of Zhang Xuecheng's *Wenshi tongyi* (*General Principles of Literature and History*).

liupo Old ladies (implying medical charlatans).

liuyi The six arts in the curriculum taught by Confucius.

Liuzu tanjing Work by Huineng.

lixing ''Reason'' inherent in the evolution of the material universe toward higher and more complex forms.

lixing zhexue Philosophy of action, advocated by Chiang Kai-shek.

lixue School of *li* (principle, reason); rationalistic school of thought, one of the two schools of neo-Confucianism; represented by Cheng Yi and Zhu Xi.

liyan Establishing words; one of three components of the Confucian view of immortality.

liyi Rites and propriety.

liyi fenshu (Also *li yi fen shu*, *li-i fen-shu*, *liyi er fenshu.*) One principle, diverse manifestations; ''the principle is one but its function is differentiated into the many.''

liyong ''It is advantageous to act,'' paradigm in the *Yijing*.

liyou Modern term for reason, ground, or rationale.

liyue Ritual and music, central approach of Confucius to moral cultivation and social order.

Liyun ''Evolution of the Rites,'' chapter in the *Liji* (*Book of Rites*).

lizhe Principle.

li zhe tianli zhi jiewen ''Ritual is the particular manifestation of heavenly principle'' (Zhu Xi).

lizhi 1. Intellect. 2. To make up one's mind. 3. Ritualist approach to government.

lizhiben Foundation of *li* (rites or propriety).

lizhili (Also *li zhi li.*) Rationale of *li*; *li* of rites.

lizhishu Plurality or numerousness of *li*.

lizhiyi Significance of *li*.
lizi jingmi *Li* is a word for details.
Lo Guang See Luo Guang.
loji Logic.
long Glorious, exalted; to glorify or exalt.
Lotus ekayana (Sanskrit; also, Mahayana.) The one vehicle, recognized by Jizang.
Lü Dowager empress (c. 188–180 B.C.E.).
Lu Ban Engineer of the Warring States period who invented a siege ladder (*yunti*).
Lu Chun (d. 805.) One of the *Chunqiu* school of Tang Confucian scholars.
Lu Deming Wrote *Jingdian shiwen* (*Comments on the Classics and Other Prose Literature*).
Lu Ji (261–303.) Author of *Wenfu* (*Rhyme-Prose on Letters* or *Discourse on Literature*), first work of Chinese literary criticism; Lu also first articulated the idea *shi yuan qing* (poetry traces emotions).
Lu Jia (Lu Chia, d. 178 B.C.E.) Influential Chinese scholar-official of the early Han dynasty, notable for his attempts to integrate concepts such as *wuwei* and *yinyang* into the Confucian mainstream.
Lu Jiuling (Fuzhai, 1100s.) Brother of Lu Xiangshan.
Lu Jiushao (Suoshan, 1100s.) Brother of Lu Xiangshan.
Lü Liuliang Essayist.
Lu Longqi (1630–1693.) Studied and disseminated Zhu Xi's work.
Lü Kun (1536–1618.) Neo-Confucian, wrote about ritual in the Ming period.
Lu Nan (1479–1542.) Rival of Wang Yangming; member of the Cheng-Zhu school.
Lu Shiyi (17th–18th century.) Scholar who advocated strengthening kinship bonds as a basic social institution.
Lu-Wang One of three trends discerned by Mou Zongsan in Song-Ming neo-Confucian philosophy (the others were Cheng-Zhu and Hu-Liu). The focus of Lu-Wang was moral and intuitive.
Lu Xiangshan (Lu Xiang-shan, Lu Chiu-yüan, Lu Jiuyuan, Lu Hsiang-shan, 1139–1192 or 1193.) Proponent, with Wang Yangming, of the idealistic "mind and heart" school of neo-Confucianism.
Lu Xiujing (406–477.) Religious Daoist; reorganized the Celestial Masters, who presented Laozi as a deified creator-savior.
Lu Xun (Zhou Shouren, 1881–1936.) Leading man of letters who wrote sardonic, and very popular, social commentary.
Lu Zheng (1500s.) Disciple of Wang Yangming.
Lu Zuqian (Lü Zuqian, 1137–1181.) Compiler, with Zhu Xi, of *Jinsi lu* (*Reflections on Things at Hand*); author of *Mirror to Song Prose* (*Song wenjian*).
lü 1. Deliberating, deliberation. 2. Mathematical harmonics.
luan Turmoil, disorder.
lue Summary.
lun Human relationships.
Lunheng *Balanced Discussions* or *On Constancy*, moral treatise by Wang Chong.
Lunhua *Discussing Painting* by Gu Kaizhi (c. 345–406).
lunli Ethics; principles of human relationships (*lun*).
lunli xue 1. Inquiry concerning the rationales of human relationships. 2. Ethics.
Lun wen (Also *Dianlun lunwen*.) *On Literature* or *Essay on Literature*, by Cao Pi.
Lunyu *Analects*, literally "discourses." Authoritative collection of the teachings of Confucius as assembled by his disciples; one of the Confucian classic texts.
Lunyu bijie *Random Notes on the Analects*, commentary attributed to Han Yu and Li Ao but of uncertain authorship.
Lunyu jizhu Commentary on the *Analects*, by Zhu Xi.
Lunyu zhengyi *Correct Meanings of the Analects*, by Liu Baonan (1791–1895).
Luo Guang (Lo Guang, Lo Kuang.) Contemporary historian, representative of the Chinese neoscholastic synthesis.
Luo Hongxian (1504–1564) Major figure of the Jiangyou school who emphasized tranquillity in meditation.
Luo Mengda Modern scholar who has contributed to the discourse on rights.
Luo Qinshun (Luo Qin-shun, Lo Ch'in-shun, 1465–1547.) Neo-Confucian scholar in the Ming dynasty; his works include *Zhengan cunkao* (*Occasional Writings*) and *Kunzhi ji* (*Knowledge Painfully Acquired*).
Luo Rufang (1515–1588.) Taizhou thinker who concieved of inherent goodness as a vast shoreless sea.
Luo Zhenyu Wang Guowei wanglai shuxin Correspondence of Wang Guowei.
Luo Zinshun (1465–1547.) Neo-Confucian whose metaphysical dispute with Wang Yangming resulted in high-quality textual scholarship.
Lüshi chunqiu (Also *Lushi chunqiu*, *Lü shi chun qiu*, *Lü-shi chunqiu*, *Lü shi chun qiu jishi*, *Lüshi qunqiu*.) *Spring and Autumn Annals of Master Lu Buwei*, a commentary dating from 241–238 B.C.E. Lu was a prime minister of Qin from 249 to 237

B.C.E., and the work was completed by guest scholars at his estate.

[Lu] *Xiangshan* [*Xiansheng*] *quanji* *The Complete Works of Lu Xiangshan.*

ly (Vietnamese; in Chinese, *li.*) Principle, pattern.

Ma Duanlin (1254–1324 or 1325.) Yuan historian, author of the encyclopedic institutional history *Comprehensive Survey of Literary Remains.*

Ma Rong (79–166.) Han commentator on the *Yijing.*

ma Horse.

Madhyamaka (Also Madhyamika.) "Middle doctrine" or "middle way," school of Buddhist thought; one of two main schools of Mahayana Buddhism, the other being Yogacara.

Madhyamika-karika *Middle Treatise*, by Nagarjuna (c. 100–200).

Mahakasyapa Said to have been a disciple and appointed successor to Buddha; the transmission to Mahakasyapa is taken by many as the origin of the Chan school.

Maha-parinirvana sutra Work of teachings by Buddha.

Mahasamhikas (Also Mahasanghikas.) "Greater assembly," one of the two earliest sects of Hinayana; it influenced the development of Mahayana Buddhism.

Mahayana (Sanskrit, "great vehicle.") One of the three main paths of Buddhism, which emphasizes emptiness (*xu*; *sunyata* in Sanskrit) and includes Chan (Japanese, Zen).

Mahayana samgraha (In Chinese, *She dacheng lun.*) Attributed to Asanga; an important *sastra* text of Yogacara Buddhism.

Mahayanasraddhotpada sastra Buddhist text.

Mahisasakas Two schools of Indian Buddhism, at different times; they split from the Sarvastivadins c. third century B.C.E.

Maitreya Future buddha living in Tusita heaven (the abode of satisfied bodhisattvas); sometimes held to have been an actual human teacher.

Makesizhuyi de zhongguohua Sinification of Marxism, slogan put forth by Mao Zedong, 1938.

manas (Indian Buddhism.) Continually discriminating mind.

manasvijnana (Indian Buddhism.) Seventh or thought-center consciousness.

Manjusri Figure associated with wisdom and intellectual acuity; he is considered a bodhisattva, a buddha, and a meditational deity.

manovijnana (Indian Buddhism.) Sixth or sense-center consciousness.

Mao Gong (Mao Kung.) Contemporary of Gongsun Long, associated with the school of names (*mingjia, mingjia.*) *Mao Gong*, attributed to him, is a pre-Qin writing sometimes classified as representative of *mingjia*; it is no longer extant.

Mao Qiling (1623–1716.) Qing scholar who attempted to refute Yan Roju's thesis on the authenticity of parts of the *Shujing* (*Book of History*).

Mao Zedong (Mao Tse-tung, 1893–1976.) Chinese communist, leader of the People's Republic of China from 1949 until his death.

Mao Zonggang (c. early Qing dynasty.) Wrote *Sanguo yanyi pingdian* (*Commentaries on "The Three Kingdoms"*).

Maoshi xu *Great Preface* by an anonymous author of the Han dynasty.

Mao Zedong zhuyi Article written in 1942 by one of Mao Zedong's secretaries in praise of "Maoism."

May Fourth Movement of 1915–1923 and especially 1919 that advocated antitraditionalism and westernization.

Mazu Daoyi (Ma-tsu Tao-i, 709–788.) "Patriarch Ma." Headed the Hongzhou school of Chan Buddhism.

mei Beauty.

meide Beautiful virtues.

Mencius (Mengzi, Meng Zi, Meng Tzu, Meng Ke, c. 371–289 B.C.E.) Classical Confucian scholar known for his argumentation and ethical thinking focusing on *xin* (heart-mind); author of the *Mencius* (*Mengzi*, *Book of Master Meng*).

Meng Anpai (late 7th century.) Daoist, author of *Daojiao yishu* (*The Pivotal Meaning of the Daoist Teaching*), which responds to Buddhist criticisms of Daoism.

Meng Hualii (fl. 1580.) Member of the Beifang (or Northern) school, a subschool of the Wang Yangming school.

Mengzi (Also *Mencius.*) Book of *Master Meng*, one of the Confucian classics; it records dialogues between Mencius and his students, several rulers, and various philosophers and rhetoricians.

Mengzi shishuo *My Teacher's Teachings on the Mencius* by Huang Zongxi.

Mengzi ziyi suzheng (Also *Mengzi ziyi shuzheng.*) *Commentaries and Annotations on Concepts and Words from Mencius*, by Dai Zhen.

Mi Fu (1052–1107.) Painter, calligrapher, connoisseur, and scholar; author of *Huashi* (*A History of Painting*).

mianzi Self-esteem, "face."

miaoji Sacrificial ritual acknowledging heaven as the origin of the "myriad things" on earth.

miaowu Intuitive awakening, a theory formulated by Yan Yu.

miaoyou Marvelous existence.

min People, as opposed to separate bodily selves.

Minamimura Baiken Japanese monk who taught a Zen-Confucian sycretism.

Minbao *People's Tribune*, organ of Sun Yat-sen's Revolutionary Alliance in Tokyo.

minben Governing on behalf of the people (a Confucian doctrine).

Mindu (fl. 340.) Chinese Buddhist monk who, against contemporary orthodoxy, denied the existence of the soul.

Ming Dynasty, 1368–1644.

Ming, emperor r. 57–75 C.E.

Ming Xiang (Dates unknown.) Author of *Xuanzang fashi xingzhuang* (*Biography of the Dharma Master Xuanzang*).

ming 1. Name; to name. 2. Discrimination, insight, clarity. 3. To understand, to illuminate, to reflect. 4. In calligraphy, a sounding forth (said of writing as evocative of the cosmic harmony). 5. Destiny, fate. 6. Accident.

Mingdan lun "On Intelligence and Courage," essay by Xi Kang.

mingdao Way to the light.

mingde Clear character, term used by Wang Yangming to describe *xin*.

Ming fa "On Making the Law Clear," legalist chapter in *Guanzi*.

mingfen Social station.

mingjia (Also *ming jia*, *ming chia*.) School of names; actually, individual thinkers who were retrospectively identified as a school by virtue of their perceived common approach to disputation or discrimination (*bian*).

mingjiao Orthodox teachings.

mingjun sage; enlightened person.

mingli Principle in logical reasoning and philosophical speculation.

ming mingde Clear exemplification of the virtues (*de*).

mingqi *Qi* of reputation, quintessence of *qi* that gives rise to all life, flows between heaven and earth as spirits, and resides in the minds of sages.

Mingru xue'an *Records of Ming Scholars* or *Cases in Ming Confucianism*, by Huang Zongxi (1676).

mingshen Manifested spirits.

mingshi 1. (Also *ming shi*.) Names and actualities. 2. Noted intellectuals.

Mingshi Official history of the Ming dynasty.

Mingtang "Bright Hall" of the Zhou kings.

Ming wenan Anthology of Ming prose by Huang Zongxi.

Ming wenhai Anthology of Ming prose by Huang Zongxi; his *Mingwen shoudu* is a distillation from it.

Mingxin pian *On Enlightenment of the Mind*, by Xiong Shili.

mingxue Logical analysis; logic practiced by Xunzi.

ming-yan Language (literally, "name-speech").

Mingyi daifang lu *Waiting for the Dawn: A Plan for the Prince* by Huang Zongxi.

mingzhu Government by an enlightened ruler.

minquan zhuyi People's rights.

minsheng zhuyi People's livelihood.

minzhu Democracy.

Minzhu pinglun *Democratic Review*, journal published by Xu Fuguan, 1949–1966.

minzu jingshen National spirit, invoked by Chiang Kai-shek.

minzu zhuyi Nationalism, national consciousness.

mo 1. Branch or branches. 2. Triviality.

mofa Stages, last stages.

Moho zhiguan *The Great Calming and Awareness Treatise*, by Zhiyi.

Mojia (Also *Mo jia*, *Mo chia*.) Later Mohism, neo-Mohism, dialectical Mohism. Wing of the school of Mozi whose central work is the *Mohist Canon*; this and two later writings make up Chapters 40–45 of the *Mozi*. The later Mohists focused on theory of language.

Mojing Work written by Mozi.

Motoda Eifu (1818–1891.) Japanese Confucian tutor; author of the Confucian moral treatises *Fundamentals of Education for the Young* (1882) and *Imperial Rescript on Education* (1890).

Mou Zongsan (Mou Tsung-san, 1909—1995.) Influential figure in the second generation of contemporary neo-Confucianism (*xin Ruxue*).

Mozi (Mo Tzu, personal name Di, fl. 470–391 B.C.E.) Founder of Mohism.

Mozi Text consisting of ten essays propounding ten central doctrines of Mohism; different versions of the essays may correspond to Mohist sects.

Mu Konghui (1479–1539.) Member of the Beifang (or Northern) school, a subschool of the Wang Yangming school.

Nagarjuna (c. 100–200.) Mahayana commentator on the discourses of the Buddha; author of *Madhyamika-karika* (*Middle Treatise*).

Naito Torajiro (Naito Konan.) Japanese journalist and scholar; published a biography of Zhang Xuecheng in 1920.

najia Correlative system based on the *Yijing*; lines of the hexagrams were correlated with the twelve months of the year, the twenty-four solar periods, etc.

Nangong Kuo (Zirong.) Disciple of Confucius praised by the master as a gentleman and man of virtue.

Nangong Yue (fl. c. 705–733.) Tang court astronomer.

Nan Hua zhenren "True man of southern China," title given to Zhuangzi by Tang Xuanzong.

Nanquan (748–834). Chan master who taught by silence.

Nanwei Section in *Lüshi chunqiu.*

Nanyue Huairang (677–744.) Disciple of Huineng and tutor of Mazu.

Nanzhong school (Also southern Zhili school.) Subschool of the Wang Yangming school.

nei Inner.

neidan Internal alchemy.

Neijing *Inner Classic*, contains the theory of bodily *qi.*

neisheng Inward sageliness.

neisheng waiwang (Also *nei sheng wai wang.*) Sageliness within and kingliness without; internal sagehood and external kingship.

Neiye "Inner Workings," chapter in the *Guanzi.*

nengdongxin de fanying lun Dynamic, revolutionary reflection theory; theory of knowledge corresponding to Marxist social practice.

neng 1. Abilites. 2. Actually possible.

neo-Confucianism (Also Neo-Confucianism.) Attempt to revive Confucian thought prominent in the eleventh century and associated with the "five masters"—Cheng Hao, Cheng Yi, Zhou Dunyi, Shao Yong, and Zhang Zai—and with a canon called the Four Books: *Great Learning*, *Doctrine of the Mean*, *Analects*, and *Mencius*.

neo-Daoism (Also Neo-Daoism or Taoism, *xuanxue*, *hsüan-hsüeh.*) Revival of Daoist thought in the third century C.E.

nhan (Vietnamese; in Chinese, *ren.*) Benevolence.

nian 1. Willing. 2. "Thought moment." 3. To keep certain things in mind.

Nianpan wuming "Nirvana without Name," essay by Sengzhao.

Nianpu *Chronological Biography* (of Wang Yangming).

Nie Bao (Wenyou, 1487–1563.) Member of the Jiangyou school; emphasized tranquil meditation.

Nihongi One of the two earliest histories of Japan, compiled in the eighth century; promoted Confucian morality and statecraft.

Nikaya samgraha sastra (In Chinese, *Huizong lun.*) Work said to have been written by Xuanzang; it no longer survives.

nimittabhaga Perceived division, one of the three divisions characterizing consciousnesses.

Ninomiya Sontoku (1685–1744.) Japanese Confucian who advocated repayment (*hotoku*) for what one receives from heaven and earth.

nir (Indian Buddhism.) To be devoid of.

nirakaravada (Indian Buddhism.) Concept of consciousness as fundamentally devoid of an image.

nirvana (Sanskrit; in Chinese, *nianpan.*) Apprehension and practice of emptiness.

Nirvana sutra Mahayana *sutra* emphasizing the Buddha-nature.

niu Ox.

Northern Qi (Also Ch'i.) Dynasty, 550–577.

Northern Wei (Also Doba Wei, Tuoba Wei.) Dynasty, 386–534.

Nuwa Mythical emperor's daughter who changed into the bird Jingwei.

Onna Daigaku *Learning for Women*, by Kabara Ekken (1630–1714).

On'yoryo Bureau of Yin and Yang established in Japan c. 675 to divine and prognosticate events.

Ouyang De (1496–1554.) Member of the Jiangyou school, a subschool of the Wang Yangming school.

Ouyang Jingwu (1871–1943.) Taught Xiong Shili at the Institute of Buddhism in Nanjing.

Ouyang Jiong (896–971.) Wrote *Yizhou minghua lu* (*Record of Famous Painters of Yizhou*).

Ouyang Xiu (1007–1072.) Song statesman and poet who practiced and reflected on calligraphy and collaborated on a history of the Tang.

Pan Gu Commentator on legalism.

Pan Tongzhou (20th century.) Associated with *New Trends* (*Xin si chao*), a leftist magazine.

Pancavimsati Buddhist scripture.

paramarthasatya In Indian Buddhism, ultimate or absolute truth.

paratantra-svabhava (Indian Buddhism.) "Other-dependent" nature.

parikalpita-svabhava (Indian Buddhism.) Imagined nature.

parinispanna-svabhava (Indian Buddhism.) Totally pure and tranquil nature.

Pei Wei (Jin dynasty.) Daoist, author of the treatise "Extolling (the Virtue of) Being" (*Chongyou lun*).

Peng Meng Figure, possibly legendary, mentioned in the *Zhuangzi* as a precursor of Laozi and Zhuangzi.

Peng Pu (b. 1928.) Researcher at China Academy of Social Sciences (CASS).

peng Mythical bird from the *Zhuangzi.*

phong trao van than (Vietnamese.) Nineteenth-century "movement of literates."

pi 1. (Also *yang*.) Opening function of ultimate reality. 2. The creative. 3. Hexagram in the *Zhouyi*.
pian 1. Partiality. 2. Section or part of a work.
piannian Chronological.
pianwen Parallel prose, a highly lyrical form.
ping 1. Illness. 2. Peace.
pingchang Everyday mind, at peace (*ping*) with itself and forever constant (*chang*).
pingdeng Equality.
pingdian Commentary on fiction.
Pingdian Shuihuzhuan (Also *Pingdian Shuihuchuan*.) Work by Jin Shengtan; the title means *Commentaries on "Water Margins."*
po Animal soul present at conception.
ponyonchisong (Korean; *benranzhixing* in Chinese). Nature of original disposition, which is connected with *i* in the philosophy of T'oegye.
poxie Refutation of erroneous views.
poxie xianzheng Refutation of erroneous views as the illumination of right views.
prajna In Indian Chan, wisdom.
Prajnadeva (Sthavira Prajnadeva.) Indian Buddhist scholar who helped develop Chinese Buddhism c. 654 C.E.
prajnaparamita (Indian Buddhism.) Perfection of wisdom.
Prajnaparamita sutras *Transcendental Wisdom* sutras.
pratityasamutpada (Indian Buddhism.) Codependent origination.
pratyekabuddha (Indian Buddhism.) Solitary buddha, a level of rebirth.
pu 1. Block, wood. 2. Simplicity.
Puji (651–739.) Disciple of Shenxiu (a figure of the northern Chan).
Pukou See *Bugou*.

Qi (Also Ch'i.) Dynasty: Northern Qi (550–577), Southern Qi (479–502).
qi (Also *ch'i*.) 1. Vital force, life force. 2. Corporeal aspect of human nature, according to Chen Que. 3. Breath. 4. Literary thrust; intertextual dynamics. 5. In metaphysics, implements or ontic things. 6. Deceive.
Qian Positivist school (*jia*) of thought.
Qian Dehong (1497–1574.) Ming neo-Confucian who emphasized moral practice.
Qian Mu (Ch'ien Mu, 1895–1990 or 1991.) Scholar, author and teacher, a master of classical Chinese humanities.
qian Hexagram in the *Book of Changes* (*Yijing*); "the creative," "modesty," "heaven."
Qianfu lun *Discourses by a Recluse*, by Wang Fu; treatise critical of contemporary conditions.
qiangquan Social Darwinist concept of might as right.
Qianlong (d. 1799.) Emperor.
qianming Compound Chinese character or graph.
Qiankun yan *An Explication of the Meanings of Hexagrams Qian and Kun*, by Xiong Shili.
Qiao Xingjian (1156–1241.) Student of Lu Zuqian; advocated change of dynastic policy in enshrining Zhu Xi's teachings as a pragmatic response to the Mongol conquest of North China.
qiao Skill, sometimes with the pejoritive connotation of craftiness.
Qiaoyu *Recorded Sayings from Mount Xiqiao*, volume of conversations of Zhan Ruoshui.
qiaozhe Skillful men.
qigong Energy exercises; medical application of inner alchemical techniques.
Qin Dynasty, 221–206 B.C.E.
Qin Gui (1090–1155.) Conventional Confucian, often considered anti-intellectual.
Qin Jiayi (Julia Ching, 1935–2001.) Scholar of neo-Confucianism and Chinese culture.
qin 1. Chinese seven-stringed zither. 2. Parents, relatives, intimates.
Qinfu "Rhapsody on the Zither," essay by Xi Kang.
Qing (Also Ch'ing, Manchu.) Dynasty, 1644–1911.
qing (Also *ch'ing*). 1. Sentiments, emotions, feelings, desires. 2. Facts, reality. 3. Input.
qingjing heyi Emotion and scene become one.
qingjing jiaorong Emotion and scene melt together.
qingli Morally pure; (literally) pure criticism.
Qingmu (Pingala.) Author of a commentary in Nagarjuna's *Middle Treatise*.
Qingru xue'an *Case Studies of the Qing Literati*, by Qian Mu.
qingsuan Liquidate.
qingtan Pure conversations.
qingxing Sensory emotional nature.
Qingyuan (d. 740.) Chan master who held that enlightenment consisted not in gaining or apprehending something external but in a change of outlook.
qinmin Loving the people.
qinqin Treating as parents one's parents; term describing the special form taken by attitudes that should be directed to all other human beings when these attitudes are directed to one's parents.
qinshou Lower animals.
qin yong (Also *chinyong*.) Familiarity with practical usage.
qiongli (Also *qiong qi li*, *xiongli*, *ch'iung-li*.) Thorough realization of *li* (i.e., of pattern, order, reason, or principle). Exhaustive inquiry into princi-

ples, i.e., rationales for the existence of things; exhausting the principles of things.

qiongli gewu Investigation of things (*gewu*) in terms of exhaustively investigating their principles (*qiongli*).

Qiqing Duke who asked Confucius about how to govern.

Qiu Jun (1420–1495.) Wrote about ritual in the Ming period.

Qiushu *A Book of Emergency*, by Zhang Binglin.

Qiwulun "On Making All Things Equal," a chapter of *Zhuangzi*.

qiyun 1. Spiritual consonance, harmony, or responsiveness. 2. Rhythmic vitality.

qiyun shengdong shi ye Animating power inherent in nature, in all things, and in a painting.

qizhi zhixing Imbalance of physical constitution; Zhang Zai saw this as the cause of a partial rupture between humans and the cosmos.

qi zhi yi li To standardize.

qi zhuzhu Daily "actions and repose" of a sovereign, officially recorded.

Qu Qiubai (1879–1942.) Intellectual leader of Chinese Marxism following World War I.

Qu Yuan Figure wrongly identified as a legalist during the Cultural Revolution.

qu Choose.

quan 1. (Also *ch'üan*, literally steelyard or balance.) Moral discretion; weighing of circumstances; exigency; adaptive behavior. 2. To weigh, estimate, or consider. 3. Integrity. 4. Completeness. 5. "Fish trap," a device to attract people to Buddha's *dharma* (used to describe language). 6. (Also *chüan*, *juan*.) Chapter.

quancui State of integrity, completeness, purity.

quanli (Also *ch'üan-li*.) Rights.

quanshi lilü Power and profit.

quanti Grasp the larger picture.

quantong (Also *guantong*.) Comprehensive understanding of the meaning and practical import of texts.

Quan xiu "On the Cultivation of Political Power," legalist chapter in *Guanzi*.

quhua $Talk on drama.

Quishan See Kueishan.

qujie Periods.

Quli (Also *Qu li*.) Chapter in the *Book of Rites* maintaining that proprieties must not apply downward to ordinary people, and penalties for ordinary people should not apply upward to officials.

Qulun *On Drama* by He Liangchun.

qun Group, to group, to form groups; association.

Qushuo *On Drama* by Jiao Xün.

quzhi zhi xing Physical embodiment.

ran Pollution of nothingness, said to be the origin of things and life.

rang Yielding to others.

Ren Shu (20th century.) Associated with the magazine *New Life* (*Xin sheng ming*).

ren (Also *jen*.) Benevolence, goodness, love; humaneness, humanity. For Confucius, authoritative conduct or becoming a person.

rendao (Also *ren dao, jentao*.) 1. Ultimate reality. 2. Way of humanity. 3. Personal moral disposition.

Ren fa "Reliance on Law," legalist chapter in *Guanzi*.

renge Personality of an individual or group.

Renjian cihua *Poetic Talks in the World of Men*, by Wang Guowei.

Renpu *Manual for Humankind*, by Liu Zongzhou.

Renshixin zhi pipan *A Critique of the Cognitive Mind*, by Mou Zongsan.

renti (Also *jenti*.) Reality of *ren* (Mou Zongsan).

renxin Human mind; sense of care and concern.

Renxin yu rensheng *The Human Heart-Mind and Human Life*, by Liang Shuming.

renxing Human nature.

renxing aiqing Humanity pertains to nature while love pertains to feeling (Cheng Yi).

Renxue *An Exposition of Benevolence* (1897–1899), by Tan Sitong.

renyu Personal human desires.

renzhe Humane man.

renzheng Humane government.

ren zhi dao *Dao* of the human person.

ren zhi long ye Magnificent display of *ren*.

reqi Sensation of heat.

ri Day.

ritsuryo (Japanese.) Administrative codes based on Chinese (Confucian) models.

Rizhi lu *Record of Knowledge Gained Daily*, by Gu Yanwu.

rongmao Facial expressions.

rou Soft, yielding, weak.

ru 1. Naturalness, thusness, suchness, so-ness; Chinese translation of *tathata*. 2. Character consisting of *ren* (benevolence) and *xu* (emptiness) and implying "the weak people." 3. Disgrace. 4. Similar.

Ru (Also *Ju*.) Confucians.

Ru jia (Also *Ju chia*.) Confucianism. Lineage of scholars who ponder and elaborate on the canonical texts. By the mid-nineteenth century it had four major fields: *jingshi* (ordering the world; action), *yili* (philosophy), *kaozheng* (philology), *cizhang* (literary art).

Ru jiao Religious Confucian.

Ruan Ji (Juan Chi, Sizong, 210–263.) Neo-Daoist; leader of the seven worthies of the bamboo grove; author of commentaries on the *Zhuangzi* and the *Laozi* and of "Biography of Master Great Man" (*Daren xiansheng zhuan*).
Ruan Kan (3rd century.) Friend of Xi Kang who debated with Xi on whether good and bad fortune are associated with one's place of residence.
Ruan Yuan (1764–1849.) Founded Xuehaitang, a famous private academy.
rui Intelligence.
ruode Virtue approved (by the spirits).
Rupakaya (Sanskrit.) *Body of Form.*
Ruxiao "Teachings of the Confucians," a chapter in *Xunzi*.
ruxin Congruent disposition.
ruxue Genuine follower of Confucianism.
Ruyao jing *Mirror of Entering the Divine Drug*, early work of inner alchemical Daoism.

sa To be endowed with.
Sabdavidya (Indian Buddhism.) Texts on grammar.
sadan (Korean.) See *siduan* (Chinese).
Saddharmapundarika sutra *Lotus of the Good Law Sutra*, Buddhist text.
Saicho (767–822.) Japanese monk, founder of the Tendai sect.
sai xiansheng "Mr. Science," slogan of the May Fourth movement of 1919.
sakaravada (Indian Buddhism.) Concept of consciousness as always endowed with an image (*akara*).
Sammitiyas Indian Buddhist school of thought.
samsara (Sanskrit.) World or cycle of life and death as we know it.
samvrtisatya (Sanskrit.) Conventional or relative truth.
sancai Three materials, a concept in the *Yijing*: heavens at the top, humankind in the middle, and earth at the bottom.
sandi Three truths (emptiness, temporariness, the middle).
Sandong zhunang *A Bag of Pearls from the Three Caverns*, by Wang Xuanhe; systematization of Daoist lives and thinking.
sanfan Three antimovements.
Sang Hongyang (Early Han.) Representative of profit-minded ministers during a dispute between Confucianism and legalism.
san'gang Three principal items.
sangha (Sanskrit.) Congregation, community (Buddhism).
Sanghadeva Indian Buddhist monk who traveled to China and taught Sarvastivadin literature.
sanguang Threefold contemplation.
Sanguo yanyi pingdian Work of literary criticism by Mao Zonggang; the title means *Commentaries on "The Three Kingdoms."*
Sanguo zhi *Chronicles of the Three Kingdoms*, by Chen Shou.
sanjiao Three great traditions (Daoism, Buddhism, Confucianism).
sankang Three canons.
Sankara Indian philosopher who commented on the Upanishads.
sanlun (Also *san lun*.) "Three-logies," cybernetics, systems theory, and futurology.
Sanlun (Also Sanlun Zong, *sanlun zong*, *kongsong*.) "Three treatises" school of Madhyamika Buddhism in China.
Sanlun xuanyi *The Profound Meaning of Three Treatises*, by Jizang.
sanmin zhuyi Three principles of the people: livelihood, nationalism, and democracy.
sanshi Historical progression in "three ages."
Santian neijie jing *Inner Explanation of the Three Heavens*, text of religious Daoism.
sanwen Free prose, a terse discourse favored by the essayists of the Tang and Sang eras, contrasting with the lyrical *pianwen*.
San xiansheng lunshi lu xu Comments by three Northern Song masters on governmental affairs, with a preface (1173) by Chen Liang.
Sanxuan (Also *San xuan*.) *Three Profound Treatises*, the neo-Daoist canon: *Yijing*, *Laozi*, and *Zhuangzi*. (A fourth work, *Liezi*, is sometimes also considered canonical.)
Sarvastivada Hinayana atomist school which claims that everything conceivable must be real in itself.
sastra (Sanskrit.) Scholarly commentary on the words of Buddha in the sutras.
satori (Japanese.) Zen (Chan) notion of sudden enlightenment; emptiness of the Buddha-nature; *nirvana*.
sekiten (Japanese.) Seasonal sacrifices.
Senglang (494–512.) Sanlun master.
Sengquan (d. 528.) Sanlun master.
Sengrui (352–446.) Sanlun scholar, disciple of Kumarajiva.
Sengzan (Seng-ts'an, d. 606.) Disciple of Huike; third patriarch of Chan in China.
Sengzhao (Seng-chao, 374–414.) Chinese philosopher of the early Sanlun Madhyamika Buddhist school.
shan 1. Goodness; excellence. 2. To complete (Shao Yong). 3. State of dispersion.
Shang (Also Yin.) Dynasty, c. 1600–1045 B.C.E.

Shang Yang (Gongsun Yang, Wei Yang, c. 390–338 or 339 B.C.E.) Statesman and legalist scholar of the pre-Han period; traditionally but probably erroneously considered the author of *The Book of Lord Shang*.

shangde (Also *shang-de.*) Upper virtue.

shangdi 1. Lord on high. 2. God (a controversial translation).

Shangfang si Office responsible for manufacturing instruments and weapons (2nd century C.E.).

Shang jun shu (Also *Shangjun shu.*) *Book of Lord Shang*, attributed to Shang Yang.

Shangshu (Also *Shang shu, Shujing.*) *Book of Documents* or *Book of History*.

Shangshu yinyi *Extended Meaning of the Book of History*, by Wang Fuzhi.

Shangyangzi See Chen Chixu.

shangzhan Commercial warfare.

Shanhaijing *Book of Mountains and Seas*, text containing the myth of Guafu.

shanhao Excellence or goodness.

Shanshui Chunquan ji *Chunquan's Collected Notes on Landscape* by Han Zhuo (active c. 1095–1125).

shanshui hua Landscape painting, literally ''mountain and water'' painting.

Shao Yong (Shao Yung, style name Yaofu, honorific Kangjie, 1011 or 1012–1077). Called Teacher Peace-and-Happiness (*Anle xiansheng*); one of the founders of neo-Confucianism, best-known for his ideas on numerology and foreknowledge.

She dacheng lun (Also *Mahayana samgraha, Shelun.*) Work attributed to Asanga.

sheji (Mencian term.) Placement of people over land and grains.

Shelun Scholar of the *Mahayana samgraha* (in Chinese, *She dacheng lun*).

Shen Buhai (Shen Pu-hai, d. 337 B.C.E.). Legalist who emphasized statecraft, prestige, and power.

Shen Dao (Shen Tao, c. 350–275 B.C.E.) Thinker who influenced both Daoism and legalism; said to have orginated the legalist theory of *shi* (circumstance, power, charisma).

Shen Nong ''Divine Farmer,'' said to have been an early emperor.

Shen Yue (Shen Yüe, Shen-yüeh, 441–513.) Wrote *Songshu xie Lingyun chuanlun* (*Life of Hsieh Ling-yün in the ''Sung History''*); commented on Emperor Wu's *Awakening of Faith*.

shen 1. Spirit; divinity. 2. With the appropriate possessive pronoun, oneself or one's own person; self.

shencai (Also *shen cai.*) Vivacity of spirit of calligraphy (as distinguished from *xi xing*, the shapes of the characters).

Shendao (Also *Shen Dao.*) Fragmentary texts attributed to Shen Dao.

shendu 1. Ultimate solitariness. 2. Absolute subjectivity.

shendui Vigilance in solitude.

sheng 1. Life, creativity, growth; to live; to give birth, engender. 2. Sage; sageliness; a state of comprehensive wisdom.

shengli Principle of production.

shengming benti Life *benti*.

shengren (Also *shenren.*) Sage; Laozi's ideal human; one aspect of Zhuangzi's ideal human.

shengsheng (Also *sheng sheng.*) Creative creativity; productivity of life.

sheng wu aile Sounds do not contain sorrow or joy (Xi Kang's theory that emotions are foreign to music).

Shengxian gaoshi zhuan *Biographies of Sages and Extraordinary Men*, anthology of legends by Xi Kang.

shengxian yuqi Voices of sages and worthies.

Shengxue gewutong *Learning to Become a Sage through Comprehending the Investigation of Things*, by Zhan Ruoshui.

shengyi Spirit of life.

shengyun Sound or phonetic realization of a word that is assigned to a character.

shenhua Spiritual transformation, rule in which the subjects are unaware of being ruled.

Shenhui (Shen-hui, c. 670–762.) Founder of the Heze Chan school; disciple of and advocate for Huineng. Shenhui strengthened the southern lineage of Chan and helped make sudden enlightenment (*satori*) available to unlettered laypersons.

Shenjian *Extended Reflections*, by Xun Yue, a work of speculative philosophy suggesting that a subtle mystery (*ao*) or something darkly known (*xuan*) lies beneath the rational mind.

shenming (Also *shen-ming.*) 1. Variously translated as gods, godlike intelligence, godlike insight, superhuman knowledge, and mental resources. 2. Images of gods in Daoist or Buddhist temples.

Shennong Legendary king, considerably earlier than high antiquity.

shenqi Radiation of lively energy, or being angry.

shenxian fangshu Magical arts for becoming an immortal.

Shenxiu (d. 762, or 605–706.) Figure of the northern Chan who caused a schism in the Chan school by insisting on a doctrine of gradual enlightenment (as opposed to instant enlightenment, advocated by Huineng).

shenyun Divine resonance, a theory formulated by Wang Shizhen.

shenzhu Ancestral tablets.
Shenzi *Book of Master Shen*, traditionally credited to the legalist Shen Buhai but not extant.
shezhun Presuppositions.
shi 1. Fully, really; reality, genuineness; to be. 2. Circumstances, times. 3. Timeliness. 4. Forces, power, charisma. 5. Generation. 6. Business. 7. Events, deeds. 8. Ethically responsible scholar or official. 9. Physical things. 10. Classic poetry. 11. This (as opposed to *fei*, not or not-this.) 12. Insight; seeing.
shide Virtue in a historian.
Shidi jing lun (Also *Dasabhumika sutra sastra*). Buddhist text.
shi er buxiu Immortality.
shifa Arising from time.
shifei (Also *shih-fei.*) 1. This-not, right-wrong. Analogous to the western concept of judgment. 2. Gossip (modern usage).
shih See *shi*.
shihua Poetic discourse, a form of critical writing.
Shihua liuyi Work by Ouyang Xiu. It was originally titled simply *Shihua* (''poetic talk''); a later compiler adding *liuyi* (Six-One, the author's style name) to distinguish it from imitations.
Shiji *Records of the Historian* of Sima Qian (Han era).
shijian Practice; knowledge and experience.
shijie zhuyi Cosmopolitanism.
Shiji gao ''Critical Study of Historical Writings,'' unfinished work of Zhang Xuecheng.
Shijing (Also *Shi jing.*) *Book of Poetry*, *Book of Odes*, *Book of Songs*; one of the classical texts of Confucianism. It contains 305 poems said to have been collected by Confucius.
shili 1. Principles inherent in events or affairs; concrete principle. 2. To fail in the exercise of reason.
Shili gongfa *Substantial Truths and General Laws*, by Kang Youwei.
Shilin shihua Work by Ye Mengde; the title means ''poetic talk,'' with the author's style name.
Shili yuyao *Important Sayings of Hsiung Shih-li* (*Xiong Shili*).
shilu True record.
Shiming *Interpretation of Names*, by Liu Xi.
shingaku (Japanese.) Learning of the mind and heart; Japanese syncretism of Buddhist and Confucian notions of self-cultivation.
Shinto Indigenous religion of Japan.
shipin 1. Poetic moods. 2. Title of a work by Zhong Rong, translated as *Poets Graded.*
shiqida Greatness of time.
shirong Extrinsic honor, drived from a person's circumstances.
shiru Shame derived from a person's circumstances.
shi Ru (Also *shiru.*) Classicist or conventional Confucians.
Shisanjing zhusu *Commentaries on Commentaries*, a basic work of Chinese philology.
shishi Losing time.
shishi qiushi Seeking truth in actual facts.
Shisi lun ''On Dispelling Self-Interest,'' essay by Xi Kang.
Shitao (Dao Ji; Yuan Ji, 1642–c. 1707.) Author of *Hua yulu* (*Enlightening Remarks on Painting*).
Shitong (Also *Shi tong.*) *Generalities on History*, by Liu Zhiji.
shixiang True reality, seen by those who are enlightened.
shixing Moving from time.
shixue Evidential research.
shi yan zhi Poetry expresses intent (a Confucian idea).
shiye Affairs and accomplishments.
Shiyi (*Yizhuan.*) *Ten Wings* or *Ten Commentaries*, commentary on the *Yijing* dating from the Warring States period. See also *Yizhuan*.
shiyi zhida Greatness of the meaning of time.
shiyong zhida Greatness of the function of time.
shi yuan qing Poetry traces emotions, first articulated by Lu Ji (261–303)
shiyu xingshang xue Substance metaphysics.
shizhong (Also *shih-chung.*) Timeliness; timely equilibrium.
Shotoku Taishi (573–621.) Japanese regent who issued the *Seventeen Article Constitution*; his thought blended Buddhism and Shinto with Confucianism.
shou To receive.
Shoulengyanjing Apocryphal Buddhist text.
shoulian Gathering of the fruits of reflective ethical activities.
shu 1. Reciprocity; reciprocal consideration; compassion; conscientiousness; regard for others. 2. Method, art, technique. 3. Calligraphy. 4. History, ancient history. 5. Numbers.
shui Water; emptiness that extinguishes the burning fire of desires.
Shujing (Also *Shu jing, Shangshu, Shu.*) *Documents*, *Book of Documents*, *Book of History*, *Book of Historical Documents*. Contains historical documents mostly dating from the fourth century B.C.E., said to have been compiled by Confucius; one of the Five Classics.
Shun 1. Sage king who figures in myth, in an argument about partiality in the *Mencius* (*Mengzi*), and in an analysis by Wang Yangming of someone

who married without first telling his parents. 2. Emperor (r. 126–144 C.E.).

shun Fit, correct.

shunmin Conforming; describes one whose life is not determined by externals such as longevity, fame, position, or goods.

Shuo (Also *Shuogua, Shuo gua.*) *Explaining the Trigrams*; one of the *Ten Wings* (*Yizhuan* or *Shiyi*), commentaries on the *Yijing*.

Shuofu "Explaining Matching," chapter of *Leizi*.

Shuogua See *Shuo*.

Shuowen jiezi *Thirteen Classics: Commentaries* (dating from the Eastern Han), by Xu Shen; first etyomological dictionary in China.

Shupu (Also *Shu pu.*) *Treatise on Calligraphy*, by Sun Guoting.

shushigaku One of two schools of neo-Confucianism in Japan; this school followed the teachings of Zhu Xi.

shushu Numbers and techniques.

Shuyan "Cardinal Sayings," a chapter of *Guanzi*.

shuyuan Colleges.

si 1. Thinking; to reflect on. 2. Mimesis, formal likeness. 3. Self-centeredness, partiality, selfishness.

siddanta Perspectives on or approaches to teaching.

side Virtue that governs personal conduct.

siduan The four beginnings (from the *Mencius* or *Megnzi*): the heart-mind of commiseration is the beginning of benevolence, the heart-mind of shame is the beginning of righteousness, the heart-mind of courtesy is the beginning of propriety, and the heart-mind of right and wrong is the beginning of wisdom.

sifu Four treasuries.

sigu Thinking on the ancients.

Sihuo lun "The Four Illusions," article by Zhang Binglin.

sijiao "Four teachings," Zhiyi's organization of Indian Buddhist doctrines and practices into a single system.

sijujiao Four maxims.

Sikong Tu (837–908.) Critic during the Tang who used *jing* as a critical concept, a complete poetic concept.

Siku quanshu Four Treasuries Complete Books or Complete Library of the Four Branches of Books, a Qing imperial manuscript library, conceived and formulated by Zhu Yun and his students, including Zhang Xuecheng.

sila In Indian Chan, morality.

Silabhadra (c. 529–645.) Disciple of Dharmapala.

siliang Thought.

sim (Korean; *xin* in Chinese.) Mind-heart.

Sima Biao (c. 240–306 C.E.) Wrote *Xu Han shu* (*Extension of Han History*), a work that is now lost.

Sima Chengzhen (647–735.) Daoist and Highest Purity patriarch who tried to systematize and simplify Daoist teachings.

Sima Guang (1018 or 1019–1086.) Neo-Confucian who continued the anti-Buddhist rhetoric of Han Yu.

Sima Qian (c. 145–90 B.C.E.) Daoist scholar, author of *Records of the Historian* or *Historical Records* (*Shiji*).

Sima Tan (died c. 110 B.C.E.) Father of Sima Qian. Sima Tan began *Shiji*, which was then finished by his son; Sima Tan's *Discussion of the Essentials of the Six Schools* (in *Shiji*) is the earliest extant writing to use the term *mingjia* (*ming jia*), "school of names."

Sima Yi General who seized control of the government in 249 C.E.; Ruan Ji served under him.

Simgyong (Korean.) See *Xinjing*.

Sishu Four Books.

Sishu jichu (Also *Sishu jizhu.*) *Collected Commentaries on the Four Books*, by Zhu Xi.

Sishu xunyi *Contemporary Interpretation of the Meaning of the Four Books*, by Wang Fuzhi.

siwu Four nothingnesses.

Six Dynasties Period from the fall of the Han (220 or 222 C.E.) to the unification of China under the Sui (589 C.E.). The six dynasties were the Wu (222–280), Eastern Jin (317–419 or 420), Song (420–479), Qi (Southern, 479–502), Liang (502–557), and Chen (557–589).

sixiang Four images produced by the two *liangyi* (forces), which are in turn produced by the *taiji* (supreme ultimate).

siyu 1. Personal interest or preference. 2. Selfish desires.

siyu jing xie Unity of ideas and *jing* (principle pioneered by Sikong Tu).

So Kyong-dok (Hwadam, 1489–1546.) Korean neo-Confucian, a follower of Zhang Zai.

Song (Also Sung.) Dynasty, 960–1279: Northern Song, 960–1127; Southern Song, 1127–1279.

Song Hon (Also Ugye; 1536–1598.) Korean neo-Confucian who defended T'oegye's thinking.

Song Jiaoren Sun Yat-sen's assistant, assassinated in 1913.

Song Lian (1310–1381.) Neo-Confucian of the early Ming; a court adviser.

Song Xianfeng (1776–1860.) Qing scholar who drew attention to the nonmainstream work of Zhuang Cunyu and *gongyang*.

Song Xing (475–221 B.C.E.) Thinker from the state of Song, during the Warring States period; he was attacked by Xunzi for his view that *qing* desires are few.

Song Zhong (Eastern Han.) Exegete who praised Yang Xiong.

song 1. (Chinese.) Property. 2. (Korean; *xing* in Chinese.) Human nature.

Songlun (Also *Song lun.*) *Treatise on the Song Dynasty*, by Wang Fuzhi.

Song-Ming lixue kaishu *Introduction to Song-Ming Neo-Confucianism*, by Qian Mu.

Songnidaejon (Korean.) See *Xingli daquan* (*Xingli dazhun*).

Songshi (Also *Song shi.*) Official Song dynastic history compiled in the 1340s.

Songshu xie Lingyun chuanlun *Life of Hsieh Lingyün in the* "*Sung History*," by Shen Yüe.

Song wenjian *Mirror to Song Prose*, by Lu Zuqian.

Song Yuan xue'an *Learned Records of the Song and Yuan Dynasties*, by Huang Zongxi.

Southern Qi Dynasty, 479–502.

soyiran zhigu Reason or cause (*gu*) for something's being as it is.

soyiran zhi li Existence of things.

Spring and Autumn Period from 770 to 476 B.C.E.

sravaka In Buddhism, a level of rebirth; those destined to become *arhat*.

Sthavira School of Indian Buddhism.

Sthiramati (510–570 C.E.) Author of a commentary to *Trimsika* (*Thirty Stanzas*) summarized by Xuanzang.

Su Shaozhi (b. 1923.) Director of the Institute for Marxism-Leninism in the Chinese Academy of Social Science (CASS) who formulated a theory of a "primary stage of socialism."

Su Shi (1036 or 1037–1101.) Calligrapher, painter, poet, and essayist of the Song dynasty whose work incorporated many Buddhist ideas and images.

suan Mathematics.

Suddhacandra Author of a commentary to *Trimsika* (*Thirty Stanzas*) summarized by Xuanzang.

sudi Conventional or relative truth.

Sui Dynasty, 581–618.

sui Year.

suichu tiren tianli Realization everywhere of the heavenly principle.

suishi Following time.

Suiliao (8th century.) Monk, student of Mazu.

Suiyüan shihua Work by Yüan Mei; the title means "poetic talk," with the author's style name.

Sun Guoting (Tang dynasty.) Author of *Shu Pu* (*Treatise on Calligraphy*).

Sun Simiao (601–693.) Thinker who systematized and simplified Daoist teachings.

Sun Yat-sen (Sun Wen, Sun Zhongshan, 1866–1925.) Revolutionary leader and founder of the Chinese republic.

Sun Yirang (1848–1908.) Recovered the text of the *Mohist Canon.*

Sung Yuan xue'an *Records of the Sung* [*Song*] *and Yuan Scholars*, by Huang Zongxi (completed after his death by his son and disciples).

sunya (Sanskrit). Empty.

sunyata (Sanskrit). Emptiness; as a doctrine it is typical of Mahayana Buddhism.

sunyi Harm and benefit.

suowei you-ming How names are introduced into language.

suoyi ran The "why" of all things.

sutra (Sanskrit.) Scripture; precept; discourse on Buddhist doctrines.

Suvarnaprabhasa Mahayana scripture.

svabhava (Theravada Buddhism.) Self; inherent nature of a thing.

svasamvittibhaga (Indian Buddhism.) Self-witnessing division, one of the three divisions characterizing consciousnesses.

t'aeguk (Korean; *taiji* in Chinese). Great ultimate.

t'aeh taixu (Korean; also *taixu.*) Great vacuity, identified with *ki* (Chinese *qi*) in the neo-Confucian philosophy of Hwadam.

Taiche Great Pool in mythology.

taifu Tutor.

taihe Great harmony.

taiji Great or supreme ultimate; unity of the great ultimate; category of nonbeing.

taijiao Fetal education, e.g., by exposure of a pregnant woman to the correct music and food.

taiji tu Diagram of the great ultimate.

Taiji tushuo (Also *Taijitushuo, Taiji tushuo.*) *An Explanation of the Diagram of the Great Ultimate*, by Zhou Dunyi.

taiping Grand peace, great peace.

Taiping *dao* Grand Peace, a Daoist sect.

Taiping jing *Scripture of Great Peace*, early Daoist text that was lost after the Yellow Turban rebellion of 184 and reconstituted in the sixth century.

taiping shi Age of universal peace, last of three ages in the Kung-yang tradition.

Taishi zhen Essay by Xi Kang on the teachings of government.

taixu (Also *t'aeh taixu.*) Great vacuity.

Taixuan jing *Canon of Supreme Mystery*, divination text by Yang Xiong.

taiyi Supreme spirit; astral body; the *dao*. In the Daoist *Taiyi sheng shui* it generates time and the universe.

Taiyi sheng shui *The Ultimate Generating Water*, previously unknown Daoist text found in the Guodian bamboo slips (*Guodian zhujian*).
taizhong daifu Palace grandee.
Taizhou Subschool of the Wang Yangming school.
Taizo (r. 386–409.) Northern Wei emperor.
Taizong Tang emperor who founded the Hongfu Monastery in 634 and supported Xuanzang's work translating texts.
Tan Sitong (T'an Ssu-t'ung, 1865–1898.) Eclectic philosopher; author of *Renxue* (*An Exposition of Benevolence*, 1897); brother of Kang Youwei.
Tang (Also T'ang.) Dynasty, 618–907.
Tang Junyi (T'ang Chün-i, 1909–1978.) Neo-Confucian; his writings include *A Comparison of Chinese and Western Culture and Philosophy*, *On the Establishment of the Moral Self*, *The Spirit of Value of Chinese Culture*, and *The Reestablishment of the Spirit of Humanism*.
Tang Liquan (Lik Kuen Tong, b. 1935.) Scholar who has been president and executive director of the International Society for Chinese Philosophy.
Tang Shunzhi (1507–1560.) Member of the Nanzhong school.
Tang Xuanzong (Tang Xuansong.) Emperor during the Tang dynasty.
Tang Yijie Contemporary scholar; a president of the Academy of Chinese Culture in Beijing.
Tang Yongtong (20th century.) Classmate of Liang Shuming.
Tang Zhongyou (1136–1188.) Sought to integrate the teachings of Wang Anshi and Su Shi.
tango-kazoku Word families.
Tangwu Founder of the ancient Shang dynasty.
tanming Single Chinese character or graph.
Tantai Mieming (Ziyu.) Disciple of Confucius and protégé of Zengzi who emphasized protocol.
Tanxian Chan master.
tanzhu In aid of conversation.
tao See *dao*.
Tao-an (Tao An, 312–388.) Monk who advocated a purer version of *abhidharma*.
Tao-fu See Daofu.
Tao Hongjing (456–536.) Codified the scriptures of Highest Purity Daoism in *Zhengao* (*Declarations of the Perfected*).
Tao Qian (372–427.) Poet, author of *Biography of Teacher Five Willows*.
Tao Xisheng (1893–1988.) Associated with the magazine *New Life* (*Xin sheng ming*).
Taoyu See Daoyu.
tathagata One who knows the truth.
tathagatagarbha (Sanskrit; in Chinese, *ju-lai tsang*.) Embryo or seed of the Buddha; Buddha-nature.
tathata (Sanskrit.) Thusness, suchness, so-ness; translated into Chinese as *ru*, "naturalness."
Tendai Sect founded in Japan by Saicho.
terakoya (Japanese.) Temple school.
thien ly (Vietnamese; in Chinese, *tianli*.) Heavenly principle.
ti (Also *t'i*.) 1. Body, embodiment, substance, form. 2. Metaphysical reality. 3. Part. 4. Obedience; obedience to elder brothers.
Tian Pian Precursor of Laozi and Zhuangzi who studied Huang-Lao doctrines and *daode*.
tian (Also *t'ien*.) 1. Heaven; nature. 2. In Confucius, revered but faceless amalgam of ancestors.
tiandao (Also *tian dao, t'ien tao*.) Heavenly *dao*; the way of heaven.
tiandi Cosmos.
tiandi zhixin Mind of heaven and earth.
tiandi zhixing Nature of heaven and earth.
Tianguanshu "Treatise on the Celestial Offices" in the *Records of the Historian* (*Shiji*) of Sima Qian (Han era).
Tianguan wenda *Recorded Questions and Answers from the Tianguan Academy*, volume of conversations of Zhan Ruoshui.
tianli (Also *t'ien-li*.) Principle of heaven, reason of heaven.
Tianlun *Discourse on Heaven*, by Xunzi.
tianming Mandate of heaven.
tianren ganying Interplay of *tian* and humans, as exemplified in *Mozi*.
tianren hede Vision in the *Mengzi* of achieving unity and harmony of *tian* (heaven) and humans through the perfection of ethical character and virtues.
tianren heyi Unity and harmony of man and nature; unity of heaven and humanity.
Tianrui "Heaven's Gifts," first chapter of *Leizi*.
tiansheng rencheng Xunzi's vision of *tian* as providing materials for humans to complete their proper tasks.
Tianshi *dao* (Also Wudoumi *dao*.) Sect of the Heavenly Masters.
Tiantai (Also *tiantai*, Lotus, Saddharmapundarika.) First Mahayana school in China, patronized by the Sui rulers.
tianwen Astrology.
tianxia (Also *tian xia*.) 1. Ideal of a universal community; Confucian concept of "all under heaven"; the world. 2. Part of the *Zhuangzi*.
tianxia weigong "A public spirit ruling all under the heavens," phrase used by Confucius to describe the ancient golden age.
tianxing Comprehension of heaven in how things are conditioned.
tian zhi dao *Dao* of heaven or of heaven and earth.

tianzi Son of heaven.
tiaoli Pattern, order.
t'ien-li (Also *tianli*.) Heavenly principle.
tifa Theoretical norms of the Chinese Communist Party.
Ting Wen-chiang (Ding Wenjiang, V. K. Ting, 1887–1936.) Western-trained geologist, an influential intellectual who advocated modernization through science.
Tingwan "Rectifying Stubbornness," original title of the essay *Ximing* (*Western Inscription*), by Zhang Zai.
tiren Personal realization, self-realization; to embody *ren*.
tishu Form numbers, assigned by Saho Yong to categories of *qi*.
tiyan Coming to know by intimate, personal experience.
tiyi yongshu One body with many applications; concept based on the essential neo-Confucian distinction between substance and function.
tiyao Quintessence.
tiyong (Also *ti-yong*.) Substance-function; sensible forms and activities of heaven and earth.
tiyong bu'er Inseparability or nonduality of substance and function.
tiyong heyi Unity of substance and function.
Tiyong lun *A Treatise on Substance and Function*, by Xiong Shili.
tizhi Embodied knowledge.
Todo Akiyasu Developed frames of shapes and sounds to organize synonyms and etymologically related characters into word families.
T'oegye (Yi Hwang, 1501–1570.) Important Korean Confucian scholar.
Tojung (Dates unknown.) Disciple of Wonch'uk.
Tokugawa Mitsukuni (17 century.) Responsible for launching the *Dai-Nihon-shi* (*History of Great Japan*).
tong 1. Unity, coherence. 2. Similarity.
tongche wujian Completely free from any interval or distinction.
tongda To break through.
Tongdian *Comprehensive Compendium*, Tang work on government compiled by Du You (735–812).
tongjiao Shared teaching, the teaching of emptiness shared by pre-Mahayana and Mahayana Buddhism.
tongjing zhiyong Fully grasp the meaning of the classics, then put them to practical use; dictum of the early republican period.
Tong Lao lun *On Comprehending Lao-tzu*, essay on the *Laozi* by Ruan Ji; it survives only in fragments.
tonglei Rational coherence.
Tonglin See Donglin.
Tongmenghui Revolutionary Alliance, founded by Sun Yat-sen in Tokyo.
tongming Unifying term.
tongren Polymath.
Tongshu (Also *Yi tongshu*.) *Penetrating the Book of Changes*, by Zhou Dunyi.
tongti Unifying substance.
tongxu Continuity.
Tongxuan zhenjing *True Scripture on Penetrating the Mysteries*, honorific title bestowed on the *Wenzi* by the Tang emperor Xuanzong.
Tong yi lun *Comprehending Change*, essay on the *Yijing* by Ruan Ji.
tong yu guishen To have intercourse with ghosts and spirits.
tong yu shenming Have intercourse with *shenming* (gods); become as wise as the gods, partake of godlike intelligence.
Tongzheng School of mid-Qing writers, which included Fang Bao and Yao Nai.
Tong zhi Work by Zheng Qiao.
tosim (Korean; *daoxin* in Chinese.) Moral mind.
tounao Point of departure, basis.
Trimsika (Also *Trimsikakarikavrtti*.) *Thirty Stanzas* or *Thirty-Verse Treatise*, by Vasubandhu (4th or 5th century B.C.E.).
tripitaka Buddhist teaching that does not assume an insight into emptiness.
Tsou Yen See Zou Yan.
Tuhua jianwen zhi *Record of Things Seen and Heard with Regard to Painting* (c. 1080), by Guo Ruoxu.
tui To extend.
tui lei Analogical projection.
tunhu ren Cultivating benevolence.
tuqi *Qi* of earth.
Tusita heaven (Indian Buddhism.) Abode of satisfied bodhisattvas.

upaya (Sanskrit.) Expedient, or formula, for attaining wisdom. Five loosely connected *upaya* informed early Chan practice.

vada (Indian Buddhism.) View, belief.
Vandhusri Author of a commentary to *Trimsika* (*Thirty Stanzas*) summarized by Xuanzang.
Vasubandhu (Vasu, Shih-ch'in, 4th or 5th century B.C.E.) Indian scholar, brother or half-brother of Asanga. Vasubandhu wrote *Trimsika* (*Thirty Stanzas*) and *Abhidharma-kosa-sastra*, a commentary on the Hinayana *Abhidharma-Pitaka*. According to one theory, there were two Vasubandus: the earlier figure was Asanga's brother; the second

lived in the late fifth century and was the author of *Abhidharma-kosa-sastra*.

vijnana (Indian Buddhism.) Consciousness.

vijnana parinama (Also *vijnana-parinama.*) In Indian Buddhism, transformations of consciousness.

vijnaptimatrata (Also *vijnaptmatrata.*) Consciousness only or representation only.

Vijnaptimatrata siddhi (Also *Cheng weishi lun.*) *Discourse on the Accomplishment of Consciousness Only*, compilation of Xuanzang's editing of ten commentaries to *Trimsika* (*Thirty Stanzas*), by Vasubandhu (4th or 5th century C.E.).

Vimalakirti Wealthy *bodhisattva* of Vaisali who realized a *keyi*, or conceptual combination, of *dao* and nonabiding *nirvana*; author of the *Vimalakirti sutra*.

Vimalakirti Mahayana Buddhist scripture; Sengzhao wrote a commentary on it.

vinaya (Sanskrit.) 1. Belief that enlightenment, *wu*, comes as a result of gradual discipline (not, as in *satori*, suddenly); doctrine typical of Hinayana Buddhism. 2. Rules of a Buddhist monastic order.

vipakaphala (Indian Buddhism.) Karmic retribution.

wai Outer.

waidan External alchemy.

waishu ''Outer books,'' term used by Liu Xiang apparently describing portions of *Liezi*, in private hands.

waiwang Outward kingliness.

waku Frames of shapes and sounds developed by Todo to organize synonyms and etymologically related characters into *tango-kazoku*, or word families.

Wan Sitong (1638–1702.) Author of *Rulin zongpai* (*Lineages of the Confucians*).

Wang Anshi (1021–1086.) Disciple of Li Gou in the Northern Song.

Wang Bi (Wang Pi, Fusi, 226–249.) Neo-Daoist who claimed that nonbeing is the substance of being; wrote a commentary on the *Analects* of Confucius.

Wang Bo (1197–1274.) Scholar who disseminated Zhu Xi's teachings.

Wang Chong (Wang Ch'ung, 27–97 C.E..) Han Confucian scholar, author of *Lunheng* (*Balanced Discussions* or *Discourses Weighed*); a skeptical, materialist thinker of striking originality.

Wang Daiyu (1580–1650.) Chinese Muslim scholar who saw a commonality of virtues in Islam and Confucianism.

Wang Fu (c. 90–165.) Confucian scholar critical of political, socioeconomic, and spiritual conditions in the Later Han (c. 190–220); author of *Qianfu lun* (*Discourses by a Recluse*).

Wang Fuzhi (Wang Fu-chih, Wang Chuanshan, 1619–1692.) Wang devoted his life to studying the classics. His son collected and organized Wang's manuscripts posthumously; they were finally put into print in 1842, but some were lost.

Wang Geng (Wang Gen, 1483–1541 or 1588.) Confucian scholar, founder of the Taizhou school, disciple of Wang Yangming.

Wang Guowei (Wang Kuo-wei, Jing'an, Guantang, 1877–1927.) Pioneer student of western philosophy; his philosophical and scholarly writings are collected in *Wang Guowei xiansheng quanji*.

Wang Hui Contemporary representative of the ''new left.''

Wang Ji (Wang Zhi, 1498–1583.) Ming neo-Confucian who argued that the four nothingnesses (mind, intentions, knowledge, and things) are one and neither good nor evil.

Wang Jing Compiled *Da Tang jiaosi lu* (*Record of Suburban and Sacrificial Offerings in the Tang*).

Wang Mang (c. 1st century.) Usurper at the time of Yang Xiong.

Wang Meng Writer and former minister of cultural affairs, author of an influential article, ''Steer Clear of Being Noble'' (1993).

Wang Pan (1202–1293.) Scholar and teacher at the Mongol court in Yanjing (Beijing); helped establish neo-Confucianism in the north.

Wang Po (1197–1274.) Song Neo-Confucian who received Huang Gan's teachings.

Wang Ruoshui (Wang Roshui, b. 1926.) Theoretician who defended humanism during the post-Mao reforms.

Wang Shizhen (1634–1590.) Propounded a theory of divine resonance (*shenyun*).

Wang Shuo Controversial popular writer of the 1990s, defended by Wang Meng.

Wang Tingxiang (1474–1544.) Daoist thinker who wanted to revive Zhang Zhi's doctrine of primal *qi* (*yuanqi*).

Wang Wei (415–443.) Wrote *Xuhua* (*Discussing Painting*).

Wang Wei (699–759.) Poet.

Wang Xi Influential figure of the contemporary new left.

Wang Xizhi (321–379.) Calligrapher. *Bizhen tu* (*Diagram of the Battle Formation of the Brush*) is sometimes attributed to him.

Wang Xuanhe (7th century.) Daoist, author of *Sandong zhunang* (*A Bag of Pearls from the Three Caverns*).

Wang Xuewen (20th century.) Associated with the leftist magazine *New Trends* (*Xin si chao*).

Wang Yan (256–311.) Author whose escapist notion of *qingtan* (pure conversations) is similar to Wang Yangming's *liangzhi*.

Wang Yangming (Wang Yang-ming, Wang Shouren, 1472–1529.) Confucian sycretist; wrote *Chuanxi lu*, *Zhu Xi's Final Conclusions Arrived at Late in Life*, and *Inquiry on the Great Learning*.

Wang Yi (1303–1354.) Late Yuan Confucian who applied Confucian doctrines of magnanimity and impartiality to local fiscal reform.

Wang Yuanhua (b. 1920.) Marxist who came to advocate the western Enlightenment and then traditional Chinese values.

Wang Yun (1227–1304.) Jin statesman who served Khubilai (Kublai Khan, r. 1260–1294) after the Mongols conquered the north; emphasized politicocultural values rather than speculative metaphysics.

Wang Zhi See Wang Ji.

Wang Zhong See Wang Chong.

wang 1. Deceptive, misleading. 2. Ruined. 3. King.

wangdao (Also *wang dao*.) Way of a virtuous king.

Wang Guowei quanji: Shuxin Correspondence of Wang Guowei.

Wang Guowei xiansheng quanji Philosophical and scholarly writings of Wang Guowei.

wangyan "Forgetting language"; Daoist doctrine of Zhuangzi.

Wang guowei zhexue meixue lunwen jiyi Early essays on the philosophy and aesthetics of Wang Guowei.

Wangzhi "Regulations of the King," a chapter of the *Xunzi*.

wanwu Myriad things, ten thousand things, all things.

Warring States Period from 475 to 221 B.C.E.

Wei Boyang (2nd century C.E.) Wrote *Cantong qi* (*Tally to the Yijing*) and *Guwen longhu jing* (*Old Text Dragon and Tiger Scripture*).

Wei-Jin Thought that attempted to blend the ideas of Confucianism, Daoism, and the school of names.

Wei Liaoweng (1178–1237.) Supporter of Zhu Xi's teachings.

Wei, Madam (272–349.) Author of *Bi zhen tu*, a theory of calligraphy.

Wei Yuan (1794–1856.) In the Qing era, editor of *Huangchao jingshi wenbian*.

wei 1. False appearance. 2. Conscious effort or acquired ability. 3. Human doing; to act. 4. Manifested. 5. Position, status. 6. To call, to name. 7. Archaic linking verb. 8. Deems, regards.

weichi (Also *wei chi*.) Not completed; last of the sixty-four hexagrams in the *Yijing*.

weifa Mind's activation.

Weishi Buddhism (Also *weishi lun*, *weishi zong*.) "Consciousness only": Vijnaptimatra or Yogacara.

weiwei Err.

wei wo Egoism.

weiyan Subtle choices of words.

Wei Zhongguo wenhua jinggao shijie renshi xuanyan "Manifesto for a Reappraisal of Sinology and Reconstruction of Chinese Culture" (1958), by Xu Fuguan, Tang Junyi, Mou Zongsan, and Carsun Chang.

Wei zhu Ruler of (Northern) Wei.

Wen 1. King, legendary figure whose wisdom Mencius sought to continue. 2. Emperor (r. 180–157 B.C.E.) who employed Lu Jia.

wen 1. Tapestry; hence, pattern. 2. Literature; letters; prose. 3. Cultural refinement; elegant conduct. 4. Civil or literary aspect of Chinese culture.

wenbi yu daoju Literature must have the *dao*.

wende *De* of literary art; moral ideal for a writer.

Wenfu *Rhyme-Prose on Letters* or *Discourse on Literature*, by Lu Ji, the first Chinese work of "literary criticism" (appreciative discernment rather than judgment or evaluation).

Wenji *Collected Writings*, miscellaneous prefaces, letters, poems, etc., by Hu Hong.

wenjian zhi zhi Knowledge of hearing and seeing.

wenli (Also *wen-li*.) 1. Principle in cultural activities. 2. Pattern.

wen ru qiren Writing is like the person.

wenshi Bibliographic term dating from the Tang dynasty or earlier, intended to include critical works.

Wenshi tongyi *General Principles of Literature and History*, a collection of essays by Zhang Xuecheng.

Wenshi zhenjing *Perfect Scripture of Master Wenshi*, commentary including the *Guanyinzi*.

Wenxin diaolong *Literary Mind-Heart Etching Dragon* or *The Literary Mind and the Carving of Dragons*, by Liu Xie (Liu Hsieh, c. 465–523); first systematic treatise on literature in China. Also translated as *The Literary Mind: Elaborations*.

Wenxuan Influential literary collection of early imperial China.

Wenyan (Also *Wen yan*.) *Commentary on the Words of the Text*; one of the *Yizhuan* or *Shiyi* (*Ten Wings*), commentaries on the *Yijing*.

wen yi guandao Literature for implementing the *dao*.

wen yi mingdao Literature for illuminating the *dao*.

wen yi zaidao Literature for carrying the *dao*.

Wenzhang liubie lun *On Genre*, by Zhi Yü.
Wenzi (Also *Wen tzu.*) *Book of Master Wen*, treatise with Daoist aspects; little is known of Master Wen, but he may have been a disciple of Laozi. The text may have originated as early as the Warring States period; between its initial creation and the third century C.E., it underwent revisions in which much external material (mainly from the *Huainanzi*) was incorporated.
wo zhidao I know (literally, "I know the way"); a modern Chinese expression.
Wonch'uk (612–696.) Wrote *Arya gambira sandhinirmocana sutra tika*, a commentary on the *Sandhinirmocana sutra*.
Wonhyo (617–686.) Korean monk.
Wu 1. Sage king (c. 1122 B.C.E.), founder of the Zhou dynasty; he launched a military expedition before burying his father, a circumstance analyzed by Wang Yangming. 2. Emperor (r. 140–87 B.C.E.) of the Western Han dynasty. 3. Emperor (r. 502–549) of the Liang dynasty and patron of Daoism and Buddhism; wrote *Awakening of Faith*. 4. (Wu Zetian, Wu Tse-t'ien, Wu Caho, 627–705.) Empress (r. 684–705).
Wu Cheng (1249–1333.) Confucian scholar in the Yuan; edited the *Veritable Record of the Yingzong Emperor* (r. 1311–1324) and further developed the philosophy of mind (*xinxue*).
Wu Ding (Wuding, late 13th century.) Shang king.
Wu Jingxiong (20th century.) Representative of the Chinese neoscholastic synthesis.
Wu Lai (1297–1340.) Late Yuan Confucian who emphasized codifying laws.
Wu Liping (20th century.) Associated with the leftist magazine *New Trends* (*Xin si chao*).
Wu Qi of Wei (Wei dynasty.) Legalist who studied under Confucius's disciple Zeng Shen.
Wu Qihui (20th century.) Proponent of technological determinism.
Wu Wang Zhou conqueror who Mencius believed had achieved victory without bloodshed.
Wu Yubi (1397–1469.) Founder of the Chongren school.
Wu Yun (d. 778.) Poet whose work helped to systematize and simplify Daoist teachings.
Wu Zetian (627–705.) Empress; see Wu.
Wu Zhihui (1864–1953.) Advocate of modernization that would include technological process.
wu 1. (In Sanskrit, *nirvana*.) Enlightenment, awakening. 2. Emptiness, void. 3. Unreal. 4. Nonbeing; opposite of *you*. 5. Things. 6. Aversion. 7. Military aspect of Chinese culture.
Wu buqian "Things Do Not Shift," essay by Sengzhao.
wucai Five materials needed for human subsistence (fire, earth, metal, and water); later developed into the concept of the "five phases" (*wuxing*).
Wu cheng *Completion of the War*, text that became a chapter in the classic *Book of History* (*Shangshu*).
wude Five powers.
Wuding See Wu Ding.
Wudoumi *dao* (Also Tianshi *dao*.) Sect of the Heavenly Masters.
wufan Five antimovements.
wugen Without roots.
wuji Without ultimate; cosmological state before *taiji* (supreme ultimate); category of being.
Wu jing zhengyi *True Meaning of the Five Classics*, subcommentary series produced in the early Tang period.
Wujing sishu daquan *Great Collection on the Five Classics and Four Books* (1415), authoritative version of the Confucian and neo-Confucian canons compiled under the Yongle emperor.
Wuji tu *Diagram of the Ultimate of Nonbeing* (Daoist); possible origin of the diagram of the great ultimate (*taiji tu*).
Wu jun lun *Treatise on Not Having Rulers*, anarchic work by Bao Jingyan.
wuli 1. Principles of physics or empirical sciences. 2. Physical studies. 3. No principle.
wuli xue Physics.
Wumazi In the *Mozi*, a participant in a dialogue with Mozi.
Wumenguan *Gateless Gate*, Chan writing.
wuming 1. "No names," namelessness; Daoist position of Laozi that the naming aspect of language has no ontological import. 2. (Also *wu-ming*.) Lack fate.
Wuming gong zhuan *Biography of Master No Name*, of uncertain authorship but traditionally attributed to Shao Yong.
wunien No-thought; freedom from delusions.
wushen My body, my person.
Wusheng lun "Atheism," article by Zhang Binglin.
Wushi nianlai di zhongguo zhexue *Fifty Years of Chinese Philosophy*, by He Lin (1902–1995).
wusi Nonthinking.
wuti No substance.
wuwang Freedom from falsity.
wuwang wuzhu In between not-forgetting and not-helping; Zhan Ruoshui's description of what approximates the most natural.
wuwe Five flavors.
wuwei (Also *wu-wei*.) 1. Nondoing, nonaction, taking no action; a famous slogan of Laozi. 2. Effortlessness.

wuwei er wubuwei Capacity of the *dao* to do everything.

wuwo (Also *wu wo*.) No self; to abandon the self, to have no desires.

wuwu No emptiness.

Wuwu lun "The Five-Without Theory," article by Zhang Binglin.

wuxi Ceaselessness, as in the flowing of a river.

wuxin No mind.

wuxing (Also *wu-hsing*.) 1. The five elementary forces or elements: fire, water, wood, metal, and soil. 2. "No nature," "without nature," "elimination of nature"; translation of the Sanskrit *sunyata*.

Wuxing The five Confucian classics: *Lunyu* (*Analects*); *Shijing* (*Book of Poetry* or *Book of Odes*); *Spring and Autumn Annals* (*Chunqiu*); *Book of Rites* (*Liji*); *Zhongyong* (*Doctrine of the Mean*).

wuxing xiangke The five elements overcome one another (symbolizes the rise of a new dynasty).

wuyan "No language."

wuyu "No desires"; Daoist doctrine of Laozi that if we are devoid of desires, we are able to see the true nature of the *dao*.

wuzhi 1. Without knowledge; kind of knowing that entertains a novel situation without prejudice or presuppositions. 2. Ontology free from clinging (Mou Zongsan).

Xi Kang (Hsi K'ang, 223–262 or 224–263 C.E.) Influential neo-Daoist, a leader of the seven worthies of the bamboo grove, author of *On Nourishing Life* (*Yangsheng lun*).

xi 1. (Also *yin*.) Closing functions of ultimate reality. 2. The receptive. 3. Practice (as opposed to theory).

Xia Dynasty, twenty-first to sixteenth centuries B.C.E.

Xia Yong Modern scholar who has contributed to the discourse on rights.

xian 1. Manifest. 2. Dangerous consequences. 3. Penal statute. 4. Hexagram in the *Zhouyi*.

xiancheng liangzhi Ready-made *liangzhi*, doctrine of Wang Ji that *liangzhi* (innate knowledge of the good) is already perfect.

Xiang Linping Figure of the 1940s, in favor of the "traditional" and the "national."

Xiang Xiu (c. 227–280.) Neo-Daoist with strongly Confucian leanings.

xiang Images; basic symbols in the *Yijing*.

xiangfan Opposition.

xiangke Mutual conquest.

xiangsheng Mutual generation.

xiangshu (Also *xiang-shu*.) "Image-number" school of interpretation of the *Yijing*.

xiangshu xue Learning of images and numbers.

xiangwai zhi xiang Image beyond image.

xiangxing Shaping or painting of a character; graphic representation of a character.

xiang-xu See *xiang-shu*.

xiangyin Filling and cohering with each other as opposed to being separate; e.g., separate impressions such as hardness and whiteness can cohere into one thing.

Xiangzhuan (Also *Xiang*.) *Commentary on the Images*; its two sections form two of the *Yizhuan* or *Shiyi* (*Ten Wings*), commentaries on the *Yijing*.

Xian Qingou ji *A Casual Record of Idle Feelings*, by Li Yü.

Xianqin zhuzi yinian (Also *Xian-Qin zhuzi yinian*.) *Chronological Studies of the Pre-Qin Philosophers*, by Qian Mu.

Xiantian taiji tu *Diagram of the Primordial Great Ultimate* (Daoist).

xiantian xue "Prior to heaven" learning (Shao Yong).

xianxue Learning.

xianzheng Illumination of right views.

Xianzhi (c. 4th century B.C.E.) Calligrapher, son of Wang Xizhi.

Xiao Jefu (Hsiao Jefu, b. 1924.) Intellectual historian.

Xiao Tong (501–531.) Compiled *Zhaoming wenxuan* (*The Zhao-Ming Anthology of Literature*).

xiao (Also *hsiao*.) Filial piety, filiality.

xiaogang Small peace (contrasts with *datong*, "great unity.")

Xiaojing *Classic of Filial Piety* or *Book of Filial Piety*, a Confucian canonical (classic) text consisting of a dialogue between Confucius and a disciple.

xiaokang "Lesser peace."

Xiaolian xia *A Sheathed Sword for Nocturnal Practice*, by Zhu Dezhi.

Xiaoqu (Also *Xiaoju*.) *The Smaller Taking*, neo-Mohist text.

xiaoren (Also *hsiao-ren*.) Small-minded person, opposite of *junzi*.

xiaoxue Elementary learning.

xiaoxue wenzi Linguistic study of texts and language, used to form the discourse (*ci*) applied to understand *dao*.

xiao zhi li *Li* of filiality.

Xiaoyao you "Self-Distancing and Free Wandering," first chapter of the *Zhuangzi*.

xiao zhuan One of two seal script styles that came to prominence in the Shang, Zhou, and Qin periods; the other is *da zhuan*.

Xici *Commentary on the Appended Phrases*; also *Dazhuan* (*Great Commentary*), *Great Appendix*; its two sections are two of the *Yizhuan* or *Shiyi* (*Ten Wings*), commentaries on the *Yijing*.
Xici shang First part (''above'') of *Xici*.
Xici xia Second part (''below'') of *Xici*.
Xie He (fl. c. 500–535.) Wrote *Liufa* (*Six Principles*).
Xie Kan (1486–1545.) Member of the school of Yue and Min.
Xie Liangzuo (1050–1103.) Regarded *li* and *yu* as opposites, insisting that *li* contains the ultimate moral principle.
Xie Ling-yun (385–433.) Poet.
Xie Shangcai (Liangzuo, 1050–1103.) Disciple of Cheng Hao and Cheng Yi.
xiejue zhi dao Principle of the measuring square (concept in the *Daxue*).
xiesheng Homophones.
xie yi Writing intent.
xilun Conceptual game (Jizang's concept of language).
Ximing (Also *Hsi ming*, *Xi ming*.) *Western Inscription*, by the neo-Confucian Zhang Zai, an essay in the *Zhengmeng*.
xin (Also *hsin*.) 1. Mind; heart; mind-heart; heart-mind. 2. Trustworthiness. 3. Sense of belief or faith; confidence. 4. Feelings.
Xing Fensi Present-day expositor of official Marxism.
xing (Also *hsing*.) 1. Nature, the nature of a thing; human nature. 2. Conduct. 3. Virtuous deeds. 4. Penalty, penalties; rules or laws that discourage or punish disorderly or destructive conduct. 5. Material and observable forms, shapes, appearances. 6. Inspired expression.
xinge (Also *xing'e*.) Evil nature.
xing er shang (Also *xing'ershang*.) Before or above forms.
xing er shang xue (Also *xingshangxue*.) Metaphysics.
xing er xia (Also *xing'erxia*.) Within form.
Xingjie *Explaining Human Nature*, treatise by Chen Que that synthesizes thoughts from the *Book of Changes* (*Yijing*) and *Mencius* (*Mengzi*).
xingjili Nature is principle; premise of Zhu Xi's neo-Confucianism.
xingli Principles of nature.
Xingli daquan)(Also *Xingli dazhun*.) *Great Collection on Nature and Principle* or *Great Compendium of Human Nature and Principle*, anthology of writing by Song-Yuan neo-Confucians.
xingling Inspired sensibility, a theory formulated by Yüan Mei.
Xingli shiyi Work by Zhang Zai.
xingli zhi xue Studies of principle of nature.
xingming 1. Thinkers associated retrospectively with the school of names. 2. Method of administrative accountability designed to ensure that the ''shape'' or outcome of a functionary's words matches the evidence of his deeds. 3. (Also *xing-ming*.) Shape and name.
xingshang xue ''Above form.''
xingshu (Also *xing shu*.) Running script devised in the fourth century and still in use.
xingsi Likeness of appearance or form.
xingti Fundamental reality (substance) of our nature.
xingzhe xingzhi junye *Xin* is the ruler of the body.
xingzhi Original wisdom.
Xingzhonghui Revive China Society, founded by Sun Yat-sen in Honolulu in 1894.
xin ji Mind is principle; premise of Wang Yang-ming's neo-Confucianism.
xinjili Heart-mind is principle.
Xinjing *Classic for the Mind-Heart*, by the neo-Confucian Zhen Dexiu of the Cheng-Zhu school.
Xin lixue *A New Doctrine of Li*, by Feng Youlan.
xinli xue Psychology.
xinmin Liang Qichao's ''new citizenry.''
Xinquan wenbianlu *Recorded Questions and Responses from the Xinchuan Academy*, volume of conversations of Zhan Ruoshui.
xinrong Salient feature of *xin*.
xin Rujia (Also *xinrujia*.) New Confucianism, New Confucians.
xin Ruxue (Also *xin Ru xue*.) ''New'' neo-Confucians of the second half of the twentieth century; contemporary neo-Confucianism.
Xinshengming *New Life*, magazine of the 1920s.
xin-shu Heart-mind methods, in the thought of Shen Buhai.
Xinshu *New Writings*, with fifty-eight chapters attributed to Jia Yi.
Xinshu shang First part (''above'') of *Xinshu*, a chapter of the *Guanzi*.
Xinshu xia Second part (''below'') of *Xinshu*, a chapter of the *Guanzi*.
Xinsi chao *New Trends*, leftist magazine.
xinti (Also *xin-ti*.) Fundamental reality of heart-mind; substance of mind.
xintong xingqing The mind unifies and commands human nature and human feelings (Zhang Zai).
xinwai wuli Outside the mind there is no *li*.
xinwai wuwu, xinwai wushi Outside the mind there are no things or affairs.
Xin weishi lun *New Consciousness-Only Doctrine*, by Xiong Shili.
xinwu Mindu's concept of emptiness of mind.

xin wu ti No inward nature of its own.

xinxia xue "Within form."

xinxing (Also *xin-xing*.) Mind-nature.

Xinxing tu shuo *An Explanation of the Diagram of Mind and Nature*, by Zhan Ruoshui.

xinxue 1. Mind and heart school, one of the two schools of neo-Confucianism, represented by Wang Yangming, Lu Xiangshan, and Cheng Hao. 2. Philosophy of mind.

Xinxue weijing kao *A Study of the Forged Classics of the Xin Period*, by Kang Youwei.

Xinyu *New Discussions*, by Lu Jia; its authenticity is disputed, but several sections are regarded as probably genuine.

xin zhi benti Mind in itself, fundamental *ti* of the mind.

xinzhide Virtue of *xin* or heart-mind.

xin zhu xingqing The heart-mind rules and commands nature and feelings (Zhu Xi).

Xiong Cili (17th century.) Official who favored dogmatism.

Xiong Shili (Xiong Shiyi, Hsiung Shih-li, Xung Shili, 1885–1968.) Commonly regarded as the founder of contemporary neo-Confucianism.

xiong Disastrous, harmful.

xipi chengbian Transformation through closing and opening; a guiding principle of Xiong Shili's metaphysics and cosmology.

Xisheng jing *Scripture of Western Ascension*, medieval Daoist writing attributed to the northern Celestial Masters; it presents a syncretism of Buddhist and Daoist concepts and cosmology.

xiu To cultivate.

xiushen (Also *hsiu-shen*, *xiuji*.) Self-cultivation; the process of improving oneself.

xiuzheng Cultivation so as to testify, school of Ouyang De and Zou Shouyi.

xixin Habitual mind; distinguishes between the self and other phenomena.

xi xing Shapes of characters in calligraphy.

Xiyu ji (Also *Xiyou ji*.) 1. *Record of the Western Regions*, by Xuanzang. 2. *Journey to the West* (17th century), novel in which the legend of Xuanzang figures.

Xu Ai (1487–1517.) Member of the Zhezhong school.

Xu Fuguan (Hsü Fu-kuan, 1903 or 1904–1982.) Second-generation new Confucian (*xin Rujia*).

Xu Fuyuan (1530–1604.) Neo-Confucian adherent of Wang Yangming.

Xu Heng (1209–1281.) Neo-Confucian scholar who taught the ideas of Cheng Yi and Zhu Xi in the north.

Xu Qian (1270–1337.) Yuan neo-Confucian who received Huang Gan's teachings.

Xu Shen (30–124.) Author of the *Shuowen jiezi*, the first etymological dictionary in China.

Xu Shen (c. 55–149.) Author of a commentary on the *Huainanzi*.

Xu Youyu Outspoken liberal of the 1990s.

xu (Also *hsü*.) 1. Emptiness. 2. To interfere with the reception of a new impression.

Xu (Also *Xugua*, *Xu gua*.) *Providing the Sequence of the Hexagrams*; one of the *Ten Wings* (*Yizhuan* or *Shiyi*), commentaries on the *Yijing*.

xuan Something darkly known; blackness or darkness, symbolizing depth or profound wisdom.

Xuancang See Xuanzang.

xuande (Also *xuan-de*.) Supreme virtue.

xuanli In Daoism, reason transcending wordly reason.

Xuanxue (Also *Hsüan-hsüeh*.) Myterious or dark learning: neo-Daoism.

xuan xue gui "Metaphysicians," a nickname rather than a strict academic term.

xuanyi Inner meaning.

Xuanzang (Hsüan-tsang, Xuancang, Master Tripitaka, c. 602 or 603–664.) Known for the record of his travels to India and for his influential translations of Indian Buddhist texts, a member of the "consciousness-only" school.

Xuanzang fashi xingzhuang *Biography of the Dharma Master Xuanzang*, by Ming Xiang.

Xuanzong (r. 712–756.) Tang emperor.

xue Learning.

xueqi Blood forces or physiological force, term used by Dai Zhen.

Xueshu yu zhengzhi zhijian *Between Scholarship and Politics*, by Xu Fuguan.

xuetong Tradition of learning.

xuezin Patience or receptivity.

Xu Gaoseng zhuan *Continuation of the Biographies of Eminent Monks*, including a biography of Xuanzang, by Daoxuan (596–667).

Xugua See *Xu*.

Xuhua *Discussing Painting*, by Wang Wei (415–443).

xuling mingjue Capacious and clear consciousness.

Xun Can (c. 212–240.) Neo-Daoist who claimed that words are an imperfect medium of transmission and that the classics are mere remains of the masters' teachings.

Xun Yue (148–209 C.E.) Confucian thinker, author of *Han Ji* (*Chronicles of the Former Han*) and the speculative philosophical work *Shenjian* (*Extended Reflections*).

xundexing Honoring moral nature; one of two ways to seek the *dao* offered in the *Doctrine of the Mean*.

Xunzi (Hsün Tsu, Hsüntze, Master Xun, Xun Qing, Xun Kuang, c. 313, 310, or 298–244, 238, or 210 B.C.E.) Classical Confucian scholar known for logical analysis (*mingxue*) and argumentation; author of *Zidao* (*Way of the Son*) and *Lilun pian* (*Discussion of Rites*).

Xunzi *The Book of Master Xun*, work in thirty-two sections containing the fundamental doctrines of Xunzi, compiled by Liu Xiang in the Former Han (206 B.C.E.–8 C.E.).

xuwei Pretense.

xuxin Emptying one's heart-mind.

Xuyan *Prefatory Words*, by Dai Zhen (1723–1777).

xu yi er jing (Also *xuyi er jing*.) Vacuity, unity, and stillness; empty, united, and still.

xuzi gua Numerical hexagrams.

Yan Fu (Yen Fu, 1853 or 1854–1921.) Eminent intellectual and translator of the late Qing and early republican era.

Yan Jiaqi (b. 1942.) Member of a younger generation of systems theorists who emerged from the Cultural Revolution conversant with contemporary science.

Yan Junping (c. 1st century.) Diviner; early mentor of Yang Xiong.

Yan-Li Pragmatic school founded by Yan Yuan.

Yan Roju (1636–1704.) Qing textual scholar who challenged the authenticity of sixteen chapters of the *Book of History*.

Yan Shigu (581–645.) Tang Confucian who determined a correct version of the five Confucian classics.

Yan Yu (c. 1195–1264.) Wrote *Canglang shihua*; the title means "poetic talk," with Yan's style name.

Yan Yuan (Yen Yüan; 1635–1704.) Founder of the "pragmatic" Yan-Li school.

Yan Zhenqing (709–784.) Author of *Directives for the Yuanling Mausoleum* (*Yuanling yizhhu*).

Yan Zun (53–24 B.C.E.) Commentator on the texts of Laozi.

yan 1. Speech or "saying"; words; language. 2. Ethical doctrines.

Yancong (fl. 649–688.) Coauthor of *Da Tang da C'ien sanzang fashi zhuan* (*Biography of Tripitaka, the Dharma Master of the Great C'ien Monastery under the Great Tang*), a biography of Xuanzang.

yan bu jinyi Language cannot fully convey meaning; a famous phrase by Zhuangzi.

Yandi In mythology, the Fiery Emperor.

Yang Chao (20th century.) Member of Mao Zedong's philosophical study group in Yan'an.

Yang Gongyi (1225–1294.) Neo-Confucian scholar of the north.

Yang Gueishan See Yang Shi.

Yang Jian (1141–1226.) Local magistrate who asked Lu Xiangshan about the original mind and became one of his followers.

Yang Liang (9th century.) Wrote *Bugou*, a commentary on *Xunzi*.

Yang Shi (Yang Gueishan, 1053–1135.) Disciple of Cheng Hao and Cheng Yi; questioned the treatment of *ren* in *Hsi ming* (*Ximing, Western Inscription*), by Zhang Zai.

Yang Weizhong (1205 or 1206–1260.) Chinese military commander serving the Mongols who recruited scribes and scholars to collect classical and historical works.

Yang Xi (364–370.) Said to be a medium who first received the scriptures of Highest Purity Daoism.

Yang Xianzhen In the post-Mao period, target of attacks concerning "one dividing into two" versus "two combining into one."

Yang Xiong (Yang Hsiung, 53 B.C.E.–18 C.E.) Han Confucian thinker and commentator, author of *Fayan* (*Moral Discourses*).

Yang Zhu (Yangzhu, Yang Chu.) Proper name that can be understood as referring to a person, school of thought, or group of works. 1. The person Yang Zhu (c. 440–360 B.C.E.), with Mozi, was influential in pre-Qin thought and is a representative figure of the Yangist movement, which viewed *xing* or *sheng* primarily in terms of health and longevity. 2. The school of thought Yang Zhu is mentioned by pre-Qin and later authors. 3. The *Liezi* has a chapter called *Yang Zhu*, which may, however, be a later forgery.

yang 1. Positive. 2. (Also *pi*.) Opening function of ultimate reality. To the fourth century B.C.E., *yang* meant "sunshine," particularly the sunny side of a slope, in contrast to *yin*, "shade." In the late-classical and Han eras *yang* and *yin* became a complementary duality signifying the active and latent phases of a process. These are relative (not absolute) concepts. 3. To educate, to nourish.

yangqi 1. Masculine *qi*. 2. Nourishing *qi* (Mencius). 3. One's vital force.

yangru yinshi Confucians who are secretly Buddhists; said of other Confucians by proponents of the neo-Confucian Cheng-Zhu school.

yangsheng Daoist practice that is physical (e.g., *qigong*).

Yangsheng lun "On Nourishing Life," by Xi Kang, treatise on the physical and spiritual benefits of self-cultivation (*xiushen*).

Yangsheng zhu "Secret of Caring for Life" or "Secret of Nourishing Life," section of the *Zhuangzi* containing a famous passage about Cook (or Butcher) Ding.

yangxing Nourishment of one's nature; in Cheng Yi's view, the outward aspect of moral cultivation.

Yangzhu See Yang Zhu.

yan jin yi Words can fully express meaning; refers to a neo-Daoist debate about whether or not language is sufficient for understanding.

Yanshi xueji *Scholarly Records of Yan Yuan*, by Dai Wang (1837–1873).

Yantielun (Also *Yan tie lun.*) *Discourses on Salt and Iron*, compiled by Huan Kuan.

yanwai zhi yan Language beyond language.

yanxing heyi Correspondence of words and deeds.

Yanzi (Yan Hui, Yan Yuan.) Favored student of Confucius; Yanzi's death at age thirty-one devastated the master.

Yao Sage king; mythical predynastic ruler, the predecessor of Shun.

Yao Jiheng (b. 1647.) Scholar, friend of Li Gong.

Yao Mingda Expanded and republished Hu Shi's biography of Zhang Xuecheng in 1931.

Yao Nai (1731–1815.) Literary critic; member of the Tongzheng school of writers.

Yao Shu (1203–1280.) Recruited scribes and scholars to collect classical and historical works; helped establish the Academy of the Supreme Ultimate in Yanjing.

yao 1. Medicine. 2. Line (in the *Yijing*). 3. Cinnabar; with *fu* (talisman) and *qi* (vital breath), one of the three techniques of Daoism.

yaobian Phase structure of process or change.

Yaojiang school Named after the Yaojiang area west of Ningbo, one of the two regions of China where Wang Yangming learning retained its most dedicated following.

Yaoshan Weiyan (751–834.) Chan (Zen) master, sometimes wrongly said to have been a teacher of Li Ao.

ya Ru Refined Confucian.

Ye Mengde (1077–1148.) Wrote *Shilin shihua*; the title means "poetic talk," with Ye's style name.

Ye Qing (Ren Zhuoxuan, b. 1896.) Popularizer of Chinese Marxism following World War I.

Ye Shi (1150–1223.) Friend of Chen Liang; Ye was famous for his stinging criticism of the "*dao* learning" fellowship.

ye Assertion marker.

yeh Particle that is an assertion marker.

Yen Lingfeng (Yan Lingfen, 20th century.) Associated with the magazine *New Life* (*Xinshengming*).

Yen Ruozhu (17th–18th century.) Proved that parts of the *Shangshu* (*Classic of Documents*) were third-century fabrications.

Yi He Figure quoted in the *Zuozhuan* as speaking of the six *qi* of nature.

Yi Hwang See T'oegye.

Yi I (Yulgok, 1536–1584.) Korean Neo-Confucian.

Yi On-jok (Hoejae; 1491–1553.). Korean neo-Confucian follower of Zhu Xi's theory of *i* (*yi*) and *ki* (*qi*).

Yi Yin (17th century B.C.E.) Prime minister of the Shang dynasty.

Yi Zhi Mohist who figures in an argument in the *Mencius* (*Mengzi*).

yi 1. (Also *i.*) Change. 2. (Also *gua.*) Trigrams. 3. Righteousness; appropriateness; propriety; the right thing to do; justice; morality. 4. Dislike of what is dishonorable. 5. Thought, opinion. 6. Will, intent, purpose, meaning. 7. Reflect clearly. 8. Medicine. 9. Unified. 10. With regard to.

yi'an Case histories.

yichanti (Also *icchantika.*) Beings who never attain buddhahood.

Yichuan jirang ji *Yi River Teacher's Beating the Rang*, collection of poetry of Shao Yong.

yici shuyi Intention and meanings.

yigu Antiquity.

yihua Singular brush stroke.

yijian Personal opinions.

Yijing (Also, *Yi Jing*, *I Ching.*) *Book of Changes*, *Record of Changes*, or *Classic of Changes*. One of the thirteen Confucian classics and one of the two basic texts of Daoism, the other being Laozi's *Daodejing*; the oldest parts of *Yijing* are thought to have come into their present form c. 650 C.E. *Yijing* is a work of divination consisting of sixty-four hexagams and related texts. Its two parts are *Zhouyi* (*Zhou Changes*) and *Shiyi* (or *Yizhuan*, *Ten Wings* or *Ten Commentaries*).

Yijing Xici shang *Xici* commentary on the *Yijing*, first part ("above").

yileiju (Also *yileiyui.*) Examples from the same class of things.

yili 1. Underlying principles; philosophy. 2. "Meaning-principle" school of interpretation of the *Yijing*.

Yili *Book of Etiquette and Decorum*, or *Ceremony and Rites*, a Confucian classic; one of the three extant ancient texts on *li* (propriety). It dates from the Warring States period.

Yili jingzhuan tongjie *General Exposition of the Book of Etiquette and Decorum and Its Commentaries*, by Zhu Xi.

yi li wei jiao Teaching morality through ritual, pedagogical method of Zhang Zai.
yili xue Learning of moral principles.
yimin Treating the people as one, a theory attributed to the legalist Shang Yang.
yiming 1. Zhuangzi's concept of "by-illumination." 2. Possible prototype of Xunzi's concept of *da qingming* ("great clarity").
Yin Haiguang (1919–1969.) Westernized liberal in Taiwan debated by Xu Fuguan.
Yin Si (Guan Yin, Yin Xi.) In legend, barrier keeper at whose demand Laozi wrote a text.
Yin Wen (Yinwenzi, 350–270 B.C.E.) Gongsun Long's teacher. *Yin Wen* or *Yin Wenzi*, attributed to him, is a pre-Qin writing sometimes classified as representative of the school of names (*mingjia*, *ming jia*); however, the received text is considered a forgery of c. 200 C.E.
yin 1. Negative. 2. Latent. 3. (Also *xi*.) Closing function of ultimate reality. Originally (until 4th century B.C.E.) "shade," particularly the shady side of a slope, as opposed to *yang*, sunshine. Late-classical and Han cosmologists conceptualized *yin* and *yang* as a complementary duality—the active and latent phases of a process. *Yin* and *yang* are not absolutes but relational.
Yin binshi heji Collected works of Liang Qichao.
yingde Rigid and reified.
yinge Following and changing.
yingu Ground-consequence, a schema of reason (Mou Zongsan).
yinguo Cause-effect, a schema of reason (Mou Zongsan).
yinian sanqian Three thousand worlds in a single moment of consciousness; phrase expressing complete, sudden teaching.
yinli Lunar calendar.
yinming jushi Things in reality.
yinren ziran Daoist vision, in *Laoziu* and *Zhuangzi*, of humans' harmony with the natural order of events.
Yinwenzi See Yin Wen.
yirong Intrinsic or justly deserved honor.
yiru (Also *i-ju*.) Shame justly deserved, intrinsic shame.
yishi Soul, consciousness.
yishuo chugu Explanations of things.
yisi Intention.
yitai Ether.
yiti (Also *yi-t'i*.) One body, one entity.
yitong Unity.
Yi tongshu (Also *Tongshu*) *Penetrating the Book of Changes*, by Zhou Dunyi.
Yiwen zhi Catalog of books; included in Ban Gu's *Hanshu* (*Standard History of the Han*).
Yixue xiangshu lun *On Image and Number in Studies of the Classic of Changes* by Huang Zongxi; critique of various theories about meanings in the *Yijing*.
yiyi bianying 1. Changing or exigent circumstances of human life. 2. Sense of rightness or discretion.
yiyin yiyang Matching and exchange of *yin* and *yang*.
yizhi yiluan One prosperous era followed by one chaotic era, cyclical pattern of history.
Yizhou minghua lu *Record of Famous Painters of Yizhou*, by Ouyang Jiong (896–971).
Yizhuan (Also *Yi zhuan*, *Shiyi*.) *Ten Wings* or *Commentaries of Change*, commentary on the *Yijing*. All ten "wings" were attributed to Confucius, but only the first four seem to be products of Confucius or his school, the others being later. The "wings" are: (1–4) *Duan* (*Tuan*, i.e., *Commentary on the Judgments*) and *Xiang* (*Commentary on the Images*), in two sections each; (5) *Wenyan* (*Commentary on the Words of the Text*); (6–7) *Xici* (*Commentary on the Appended Phrases*) or *Dazhuan* (*Great Commentary*), in two sections; (8) *Shuo* (or *Shuogua*, *Explaining the Trigrams*); (9) *Xu* (or *Xugua*, *Providing the Sequence of the Hexagrams*); (10) *Zha* (or *Zagua*, *Hexagrams in Irregular Order*).
yizhidao (Also *yi zhi dao*.) *Dao* of the change.
Yizi (Yi Zhi, Yi Chih.) Mohist who figures in an argument in the *Mengzi* over his elaborate burial of his parents.
Yogacara Idealist school of Yoga masters who accept the notion of universal emptiness while claiming that this emptiness is due to its being known only through representations, that is, only by means of the mind (*vijnaptmatrata*).
Yojokun *Precepts for Health Care*, by Kabara Ekken (1630–1714).
yomeigaku One of two schools of neo-Confucianism in Japan; followed the teachings of Wang Yangming.
yong (Also *yung*.) 1. Function, activity. 2. Courage.
Yongle dadian *Great Canon of the Yongle Era*, neo-Confucian writings collected in the Ming era.
yongshe dachuan "Act to cross the great river," judgment in the *Yijing*.
yongshu Activity numbers, assigned by Shao Yong to categories to *qi*.
Yoshida Kanetomo (1434–1511.) Developed a Shinto-Confucian synthesis.
you 1. Real. 2. Being.

youhuan yixia Predicament, term coined by Xu Fuguan.
youpai Rightist.
youshi Having time.
youwu (Also *yu-wu*, *you-wu*.) 1. Being and nonbeing, being and nothingness. In Daoism *you* (being) signifies the moment of manifestation, realization, completion, embodiment, while *wu* (nonbeing) represents the moment of dissimulation, possibility, potentiality, and transcendence. 2. Have-lack.
you wu hun cheng Thing of undifferentiated wholeness.
youzong School of being, alternative description of the "consciousness-only" school (*weishi zong*).
Yu 1. Sage king, possibly a dragon, from whom the Xia dynasty was said to be descended. 2. (Yü, Yü Ruo, Yu Ruo, Ziyu, "Great Yu.") Disciple praised by Confucius for his reverence to ancestors; Yu emphasized performance of rites and rituals (*li*).
yu (Also *yü*.) 1. Desire, inclination. 2. Dislike, disinclination.
Yuan (Also Yüan, Mongol.) Dynasty, 1279–1368.
Yuan Haowen (1190–1257.) Jin poet who refused to serve the Mongols when they defeated the north.
Yuan Huang (1500s.) Scholar-official from northern Zhejiang; with Yungu, wrote *Liming pian* (*Determining Your Own Fate*).
Yuan Mei (Yüan Mei, 1716–1798.) Poet, attacked on moral grounds by Zhang Xuecheng. Yuan wrote *Suiyüan shihua* (the title means "poetic talk," with the author's style name) and propounded a theory of "inspired sensibility" (*xingling*).
Yuan Shikai (1859–1916.) First president of the Chinese republic.
yuan 1. Circle, cycle. 2. Distance; distant consequences. 3. Origin; coorigination (of things and life from nothingness). 4. Fundamental, essential. 5. Protest.
Yuandao 1. "Essentials of the Moral Way" or "The Origin of the Way," essay by Han Yu arguing for Confucianism, rather than Daoism or Buddhism, as a guide to conduct. 2. "Historical Analysis of the Way," essay by Zhang Xuecheng.
yuande Preeminent virtue; efficacious prestige of a king.
yuandun Completely and suddenly.
Yuangu (Yuan-ku.) Confucian master in the time of Emperor Qing (r. 158–141 B.C.E.); argued publicly in favor of revolution.
yuanjiao Complete teaching; integration of the three teachings of conventional Buddhism, emptiness, and the temporary world.
yuanjin Distance and nearness.
yuanli Principle.
Yuanling yizhhu *Directives for the Yuanling Mausoleum*, instructions regarding the death rites for the emperor Daizong, a practicing Buddhist, in 779; they demonstrate scholars' concern to demarcate the three traditions in China.
yuanqi 1, Primal *qi*; doctrine promoted first by Zhang Zhi and later by Wang Tingxiang. 2. Cloud-vapor.
Yuanru *An Inquiry on Confucianism*, by Xiong Shili.
yuanshen Original spirit of human beings.
yuanshi Daojia Primordial Daoist philosophy (Feng Youlan).
yuanshi Rujia Primordial Confucian philosophy (Feng Youlan).
Yuanshan *Inquiry into Goodness*, by Dai Zhen (1723–1777).
Yuanxiang *Inquiry into Solar Movements and Seasons*, by Dai Zhen (1723–1777).
yuanyi Original meanings.
yuanzhe Principle.
Yuchun quhua *Talk on Drama*, by Li Diao-yüan.
Yue Guang (252–304.) Neo-Daoist; he was critical of efforts to lead a fulfilling life, believing that *mingjiao* (orthodox teachings) sufficed for bliss.
Yue and Min (Also Guangtong and Fujian.) Subschool of the Wang Yangming school.
yue 1. Month. 2. Music.
Yueji "Record of Music," chapter of *Liji*.
yueqi Cloudy vapor around the moon.
Yuelun "Discourse on Music," essay by Ruan Ji.
Yulgok See Yi I.
yulu Chinese vernacular scriptures specific to Chan.
Yulu *Recorded Sayings*, compilation of the life and deeds of Mazu by his disciples.
Yun Richu (c. 1600.) Disciple of Liu Zongzhou.
yun 1. Rhythm; poetic rhythm; rhyming or phonemic coupling of words in a poem. 2. Resonance, consonance, harmony. 3. Revolution.
Yungu (1500s.) Chan master; with Yuan Huang, wrote *Liming pian* (*Determining Your Own Fate*).
yunti Siege ladder ("ladder that flies to the clouds") invented by Lu Ban in the Warring States period.
Yuqiao wendui Conversation *between the Fisherman and the Woodcutter*, of uncertain authorship but traditionally attributed to Shao Yong.
yuqishi Strive and reach for time.
yushi jieji To reach the limit with time.
yushi jiexing To move with time.

yushi xiuxi Rising and resting together with time.
yuwu Desire and aversion.
yuzhou benti Cosmos *benti*.

Zagua See *Zha*.
Zai Yu (Also Zai Wo, Ziwo.) Disciple of Confucius who was criticized by the master for his lack of character.
Zaitian Personal name of Emperor Guangxu (1871–1908).
zangfu (Also *zang*.) Orbs.
zangjiao *Tripitaka* teaching, i.e., does not assume an insight into emptiness.
zaohua shengsheng Vital transformation.
zaowuzhe Creator; maker of the phenomenal world.
zazen (Korean.) See *zuochan* (Chinese.)
ze 1. Choice, selection. 2. (Also *zhe*.) Standard, norm.
Zen See Chan.
Zeng Guofan (1811–1872.) Confucian general, a Han official who formed the Hunan army (*Xiangjun*) during the late Qing; as a scholar, he helped establish *jingshi* as one of the four major fields of Confucian studies.
Zengzi (Tseng Tzu, Cengzi, Zeng Can, Zeng Zan, Zeng Shen, Ziyu.) Disciple of Confucius who emphasized filial piety and its extension, friendship. He figures in a parable about fixed and living principle in a Confucian text, *Home Sayings of Confucius* (*Kongzi jiayu*).
Zha (Also *Zagua*, *Za gua*.) *Hexagrams in Irregular Order*; one of the *Ten Wings* (*Yizhuan* or *Shiyi*), commentaries on the *Yijing*.
Zhan Ruoshui (Chan Jo-shui, Zhan Ganquan, Zuan Ruoshui, 1463 or 1466–1557 or 1560.) Zhan's Ganquan school, during the sixteenth century, was second only to the Wang Yangming school in size and influence. *Zhan Ganquan xiansheng wenji* (*Literary Works of Master Zhan Ganquan*) is a compilation of Zhan's lectures, letters, philosophical essays, and recorded conversations.
Zhang Emperor at the time of Wang Chong.
Zhang Binglin (Chang Ping-lin, Tai-yan, 1868–1936.) Influential scholar and political propagandist.
Zhang Dainian (b. 1909.) Intellectual historian.
Zhang Dongsun (Chang Tung-sun, Zhang Dongsheng, 1886–1973.) Journalist and politician who later became a philosopher and educationalist.
Zhang Ertian Scholar, elder brother of Zhang Dongsun.
Zhang Huaiguan (9th century.) Theorist of Chinese writing who defined calligraphy as the art of movement captured in script and distinguished between *zi* (the character) and *shu* (the gesture of writing).
Zhang Junmai See Carsun Chang.
Zhang Ling Established Wudoumi (Tianshi) *dao*, the sect of the Heavenly Masters.
Zhang Liuxiang (1611–1674.) Studied and disseminated Zhu Xi's work.
Zhang Liwen (b. 1935.) Scholar of neo-Confucianism.
Zhang Mou (1436–1521.) Chancellor of Imperial University in Nanjing, where Luo Qinshun taught.
Zhang Piao See Chang Biao.
Zhang Shi (Jingfu, 1133–1180.) Student of Hu Hong and friend of Zhu Xi; proponent of self-cultivation.
Zhang Songnian (20th century.) Classmate of Liang Shuming.
Zhang Xuecheng (Chang Hsüeh-ch'eng, Chang Xuecheng, Shizhai, 1738 or 1739–1801.) Qing scholar who promoted original scholarship, not speculation, as a way of understanding the *dao*; author of *Wenshi tongyi* (*General Principles of Literature and History*).
Zhang Yanyuan (c. 815–after 875.) Author of *Lidai minghua ji* (*Record of Famous Painters through the Dynasties*, c. 847).
Zhang Zai (Chang Tsai, Zhang Hengqu, 1020–1077.) Neo-Confucian philosopher, author of *Hsi ming* (*Western Inscription*) and "Reply to Master Hengzhu's Letter on Calming Human Nature."
Zhang Zhan (c. 330–400.) Neo-Daoist commentator on the *Liezi* who included Buddhism in his concept of profound learning.
Zhang Zhitong (Zhang Zhidong, 1837–1909.) Reformer who coined the slogan "Chinese culture as substance and western learning as function" (*zhongxue weiti xixue weiyong*).
zhang Chapter or subsection of a work.
Zhanguo ce *Records of the Warring States* (period from 475 to 221 B.C.E.)
Zhanran (711–782.) Tiantai patriarch.
Zhao Fu (fl. 1235–1257.) Scholar at the Mongol court in Yanjing (Beijing); popular teacher of Cheng-Zhu neo-Confucianism.
Zhao Jie (fl. 1271.) Late Yuan Confucian who applied Confucian doctrines of magnanimity and impartiality to local fiscal reform.
Zhao Kuang (fl. c. 770.) One of the *Chunqiu* school of Tang Confucian scholars.
Zhao Mengfu (Yuan dynasty.) Calligrapher who combined calligraphy and pictoral forms.
zhao Radiation; shining.
Zhaolun *The Book of Zhao*, by Sengzhao.

Zhaoming wenxuan *The Zhaoming Anthology of Literature*, compiled by Xiao Tong.

zhe 1. (Also *zhi*.) Wisdom. 2. Then (as in "if-then"). 3. (Also *ze*.) Standard, rule, procedure. 4. Thorn tree (a kind of mulberry).

Zhe daoti hao-hao wu qiongchong "This substance of *dao* is vast and inexhaustible" (Zhu Xi).

Zhen Dexiu (Chen Dexiu, 1178–1235.) Adherent of the Cheng-Zhu school of neo-Confucianism, author of *Xinjing* (*Classic for the Mind-Heart*).

zhen Reality; truthfulness.

zhendi Ultimate or absolute truth.

Zheng Qiao (1104–1160.) Song historian, author of *Tong zhi*.

Zheng Xuan (127–200.) Wrote the first commentary on the *Daxue* (*Great Learning*).

Zheng Jiadong (b. 1956.) Scholar of new Confucianism.

zheng 1. Rectified; represented correctly. 2. Signs, characteristics.

Zhengan cunkao *Occasional Writings*, by Luo Qinshun.

Zhengao *Declarations of the Perfected*, by Tao Hongjing; codifies the scriptures of Highest Purity Daoism.

zhengdao The way of politics.

Zhengmeng *Rectifying Obscurations*, by Zhang Zai.

Zhengmeng zhu *Commentary on Zhang Zai's Zhengmeng*, by Wang Fuzhi.

zhengming (Also *cheng-ming*.) Rectifying names; right use (or rectification) of terms (or names); strongly emphasized in the classical Confucian tradition. Title of an essay by Xunzi.

zheng niantou To rectify one's thought at its very beginning.

Zhengren Society Forum founded in Shanyin by Liu Zhongzhou.

Zheng shi "Rectifying the Age," legalist chapter in *Guanzi*.

zhengtong 1. Tradition of politics. 2. Correct succession.

Zhenguan zheng yao *Essentials of the Good Government of the Zhenguan Period*, Tang anthology of open exchanges between the emperor and officials on political morality.

zhengxin Rectification of mind-heart.

zhengyi Verifier.

zhengzhi Evidential judgments concerning matters of fact.

zhengzong Orthodox lineage.

zhenren (Also *chen-jen*.) Authentic man, true person; one who maintains his intrinsic nature; the Daoist ideal of the best human being (a paradigmatic individual).

zhenru Ultimate reality or thusness (*tathata*).

zhenshi wuwang State of truthfulness, genuineness, and freedom from falsity.

zhenzhi Knowing by evidence.

zhexue Philosophy, philosophical learning.

Zhexue cidian Chinese dictionary of philosophy, first published in 1925.

zhexue shidai Period of the philosophers from Confucius (551–479 B.C.E.) to Huainanzi (d. 122).

Zhezhong school (Also central Zhejiang school.) Subschool of the Wang Yangming school.

Zhi Dun (Zhi Daolin, 314–366.) Chinese Buddhist who synthesized contemporary Buddhist and Daoist ideas on emptiness.

Zhi Yü (d. 311.) Wrote *Wenzhang liubie lun* (*On Genre*).

zhi (Also *zhe*, *chih*.) 1. Wisdom, knowledge, realization. 2. To know, to realize. 3. Cognition. 4. Sense of right and wrong. 4. Intentions, aims, will, commitment, directions of the heart. 5. Act of reference. 6. Substance. 7. Simplicity. 8. Ontology of clinging (Mou Songsan). 8. Government.

zhibi Recording the truth.

zhidao (Also *zhitao*.) 1. The way of government. 2. Knowing *dao*.

zhide (Also *zhi-de*.) Authentic virtue.

zhi de zhijiao (Also *zhi di zhijue*.) Intellectual intuition.

zhide zhi shi Age of ultimate virtue brought about by nondoing, according to Zhuangzi.

zhigong Impartiality.

zhiguan 1. Straightforward. 2. Calming and insight.

zhihzhong Perfect balance.

zhijiao Governing and teaching.

zhili Knowing rites.

zhi liangzhi Extension of innate knowledge of the good, doctrine of Wang Yangming.

zhilü Informed deliberation.

zhiming Knowing destiny.

zhimin zhizhan (Mencian term.) Social plan for protecting the property of the people.

zhi-ming-zhi-shu-yao How names are instituted or formulated as they are used.

zhinan xingyi To know is difficult, to act is easy.

zhiping Utmost peace and order.

zhiqili To arrive at the principle.

zhiren 1. Supreme man; one aspect of Zhuangzi's ideal human. 2. Ability to know other humans. 3. Knowing benevolence.

zhishan Ethical excellence.

zhisheng Knowing life.

zhishi 1. Ultimate in discrimination; a quality more sublime than aesthetic connoisseurship. 2. Actualities.

zhisi Knowing death.
zhitian To know heaven.
zhi tianming Knowing the mandate of heaven.
zhiwei Quasi-definitional locution used by Xunzi.
zhiwo Knowing myself.
Zhiwu (Also *Zhi wu*, *Zhiwu lun.*) ''Pointing to Things,'' chapter in *Gongsun Longzi*, attributed to Gongsun Long.
zhixing To know one's nature.
zhixing heyi (Also *zhixin heyi*, *zhi-hsing heyi*, *chih-hsing ho-i.*) Unity of action and knowledge.
zhiyan To know *yan* (speech or ''saying''); to seek and value knowledge as formulated in the language of reason.
Zhiyan *Understanding Words*, by Hu Hong.
zhiyanzhi Speaking plainly.
Zhiyi (Chih-i, 538–597.) Third patriarch of the Tiantai school; author of *Fahua xuanyi* (*The Hidden Meaning of the Dharma Flower*); one of China's foremost Buddhist thinkers.
zhiyong Knowing things in order to ''reach'' their use.
zhizhe Men of wisdom.
zhizhi (Also *chih-chih.*) 1. Extension of knowledge. 2. Reaching knowledge. 3. Event.
Zhizhi ''The Extreme Limit of Knowledge,'' chapter of the *Liezi.*
zhi zhonghe Fulfillment of centrality and harmony.
zhizhong wu-quan Moral discretion.
Zhong Hui (225–264.) Neo-Daoist thinker; his work has not survived.
Zhong Rong (c. 468–518.) Wrote *Shipin* (*Poets Graded*).
Zhong Yu (Zilu.) Favored disciple of Confucius.
zhong (Also *chung.*) 1. Centeredness, centrality; pertinent principle. 2. Doing one's best. 3. Loyalty. 4. Mean or balance of various factors.
zhongdao Middle way.
Zhonggong (Also Ran Yong.) Penurious but regal and refined disciple of Confucius who was much admired by the master.
zhonggua Hexagrams.
Zhongguo gudai zhexue shi *History of Ancient Chinese Philosophy*, by Hu Shi.
Zhongguohun Soul of China, invoked by Chiang Kai-shek.
Zhongguo renxinglun shi: Xianqin pian *The History of the Chinese Philosophy of Human Nature: The Pre-Qin Period*, by Xu Fuguan.
Zhongguo sixiang shi *History of Chinese Thought*, by Qian Mu.
Zhongguo wenhua yaoyi *The Essence of Chinese Culture*, by Liang Shuming.
Zhongguo yishu jingshen *The Spirit of Chinese Art*, by Xu Fuguan.
zhonghe Equilibrium and harmony.
Zhonghua minguo Republic of China.
Zhonghua minguo jie ''Explanation of the National Title 'Republic of China,''' article by Zhang Binglin.
Zhonghua minzu Chinese race, concept advocated by Sun Yat-sen.
zhongli To succeed in the exercise of reason.
Zhongling (Also *Zhong ling.*) ''On the Importance of Orders,'' legalist chapter in *Guanzi.*
Zhong-Lü chuandao ji *Record of Zhong and Lü's Transmission of the Dao*, text of the northern school of Song alchemical Daoism.
zhongquegong Duke of loyalty and sincerity, honorific bestowed posthumously on Wang Guowei.
zhongshi Cycles.
zhongshu Loyalty and reciprocity.
zhongti xiyong Chinese learning for essence, western learning for function.
zhongxin Loyalty, faithfulness to principles; centeredness.
Zhongyong (Also *Zhong yong*, *Chung yung.*) *Doctrine of the Mean* or *Centrality and Commonality*, attributed to Zisi (Zi Si, Confucius's grandson). Text in the classical Confucian canon; originally a chapter in the *Book of Rites* (*Liji*).
Zhongyong zhangju Commentary on the *Zhongyong*, by Zhu Xi.
Zhou Dynasty, 1045–206 B.C.E.
Zhou, duke (Chou.) Regent in the early Zhou dynasty whose wisdom Mencius sought to continue.
Zhou Dunyi (Chou Tun-yi, Chou Tun-i, Zhou Tunyi, Zhou Lianxi, Zhou Maoshu, 1017–1073.) Pioneer of neo-Confucianism; wrote *An Explanation of the Diagram of the Great Ultimate.*
Zhou Enlai (Chou En-lai, 1898–1976.) Premier of People's Republic of China from 1949 to 1976.
Zhou Mi (1232–after 1308.) Head of a scholarly family associated with the conventional Confucians.
Zhou Rudeng (1547–c. 1629.) Neo-Confucian thinker and historian, author of *Shengxue zongchuan* (*Transmission of the Sage's Learning*).
Zhou Yan See Zou Yan.
Zhou Yang Champion of the Chinese Communist Party line in literature in the 1960s.
Zhou Yong Author of the Madhyamika treatise *Three Schools of Two Truths.*
Zhou bisuan jing *Zhou Dynasty Canon of Gnomonic Computations.*
Zhouli (Also *Zhou li.*) *Rites of the Zhou*, *Rites of Zhou*; also known as *Zhouguan*, *Offices of the*

Zhou. One of the Confucian classics, and one of three Confucian canons of ritual; it dates from the Warring States period.

Zhouyi (Also *Zhou Yi*.) *Zhou Changes*, *Book of Changes from the Zhou* (c. 1200 B.C.E.). Divinitory manual that is one of the two parts of the *Yijing* (the other part is *Shiyi* or *Yizhuan*).

Zhouyi cantong qi Daoist alchemical text (7th century) that discusses breathing.

Zhouyi neizhuan *Internal Commentary on the Book of Changes*, by Wang Fuzhi.

Zhouyi waizhuan *External Commentary on the Book of Changes*, by Wang Fuzhi.

Zhouyu Section of *Guoyu* (*Records of States*).

Zhouzi quanshu *The Complete Works of Master Zhou [Dunyi]*.

Zhozhuan *Zuozhuan*; see *Zuo*.

Zhu (Also Chu.) State.

Zhu Dezhi Author of *Xiaolian xia* (*A Sheathed Sword for Nocturnal Practice*).

Zhu Gui (1700s.) Brother of Zhu Yun; served as an imperial tutor.

Zhu Houcong (r. 1521–1567.) Emperor who altered traditional rites to suit his own interpretation.

Zhu Xi (Zhuxi, Chu Hsi, Yuanhui, 1130–1200.) Neo-Confucian scholar who completed the establishment of the canonical Four Books; author of *Family Rituals* and *Zhuxi yulei*.

Zhu Yun (1700s.) Compiled *Siku quanshu* (Four Treasuries Complete Books, an imperial manuscript library), with his students, who included Zhang Xuecheng.

zhu 1. Self-controlling. 2. (Also *chu*.) Host.

zhuan Explanations, commentaries.

Zhuang Cunyu (1719–1788.) Qing scholar instrumental in the rise of the *gongyang* (new text) school.

zhuangdao ruo xing As if it were one's nature.

Zhuangzi (Chuang Tzu, Zhuang Zhou; c. 360, or between 399 and 295, or c. 369–286 B.C.E.) Along with Laozi, a defining figure in Chinese Daoism; author of parts of the first seven (''inner'') chapters of the *Zhuangzi*, *The Great Master*, and *On Making All Things Equal*.

Zhuangzi Major Daoist text; parts of the first seven chapters (the ''inner chapters'') have been reliably attributed to Zhuangzi; the rest consists of critical commentary by later Daoists.

zhuanshen Transmit the spirit.

Zhuansun Shi (Zi Zhang.) Disciple of Confucius.

zhuanzhu Extending the meaning of especially complex characters.

Zhubing yuanhou fang *On the Cause and Course of All Illnesses* (610), compiled by Chao Yuanfang and others.

zhufa shixiang True reality of all things.

Zhun qiu See *Chunqiu* (*Spring and Autumn Annals*).

zhuti 1. Subjectivity. 2. Host substance or ruling substance.

Zhutian jiang *Lectures on the Heavens*, by Kang Youwei.

Zhuxi yulei *Classified Conversations of Zhu Xi*.

zhuyi Direction, leading idea.

zhuzai Role of primary will as the self-guide and self-control of heart-mind.

Zhuzi daquan *Great Compendium of Master Zhu Xi*, teachings by the neo-Confucian Zhu Xi.

Zhuzixue lueshuo ''Brief Discussions of Noncanonical Philosophers,'' article by Zhang Binglin.

Zhuzi yulei *Master Zhu's Categorized Conversations* (13th century), anthology that formed the basis for *Xingli daquan*.

Zi Chan Legalist.

Zi Gong Appears in a discussion of *shu* in the *Analects* (the passage is probably a late insertion).

Zi Lu (Zilu.) Figure in the *Analects*; asked Confucius how a *junzi* (paragon) behaves.

Zi Si (Zisi, Kong Ji, c. 483–402 B.C.E.) Grandson of Confucius; according to Sima Qian, Zi Si composed the *Zhongyong*.

Zi Wen (Ziwen.) Mentioned in the *Analects* as a prime minister devoted to his responsibilities.

Zi Zhang (Zhuansun Shi.) Disciple of Confucius.

zi 1. Characters of Chinese writing, as distinguished from *shu*, calligraphy. 2. Onself, especially as distinguished from others (in contrast to *ji*, oneself in relation to oneself.) 3. ''Self-'' as a prefix or reflexive form; e.g., *zibao* (self-violence, do violence to oneself).

Zidao *Way of the Son*, by Xunzi.

zide Realize *dao* in oneself.

zifan Self-examination, examine oneself.

Zigong (Duanmu Si.) Wealthy disciple of Confucius whose eloquent words were judged by the master as lagging behind his ungenerous, superior behavior.

zijue de nengdongxing Conscious activity.

zimei Beautify itself.

ziming ye Naming oneself.

ziqi Self-deception.

Ziqian (Min Sun.) Disciple of Confucius much admired by the master for his scrupluous behavior and direct manner of speaking.

ziqian (In Zhu Xi, *ziqie*.) Self-satisfaction; self-respect.

ziran (Also *zijan*.) Naturalness; the natural; spontaneity; natural delight in learning.

Ziran ming *Inscriptions on the Concept of the Natural*, by Zhan Ruoshui.

ziru Disgrace oneself.
Zisi See Zi Si.
zisong Reproach oneself; self-reproach.
zixing Examine oneself; self-examination.
zixiu Self-cultivation.
zixue shidai See *zhexue shidai.*
ziyang Self-nourishment, nourish oneself.
ziyou Freedom.
zizhi Self-knowledge.
zizu Self-contentment or self-satisfaction.
Zong Bing (375–443.) Wrote *Hua shanshui xu* (*Introduction to the Painting of Landscape*).
zongfa Descent-line system.
Zongmi (780–841.) Chan thinker.
zongming Collective term.
Zong shi "The Great Master," sixth chapter of the *Zhuangzi.*
zongzhi Main idea or aim.
Zou Yan (Tsou Yen, Zhou Yan, c. 305–240 B.C.E.) Cosmologist who systematized the *yinyang* and "five processes" (*wuxing*) philosophy.
Zou Shouyi (1491–1562.) Important figure of the Jiangyou school.
zu 1. Patriarch. 2. Satisfaction, contentment.
zui 1. Purity. 2. Sin (controversial translation).
Zuigen pin *The Roots of Sin*, scripture of the Numinous Treasure school of medieval Daoism.
Zundao lu *On Following the Way*, by Zhan Ruoshui.
zundexing Honoring the moral nature.
Zuo (Also *Zuozhuan, Zuo zhuan, Zuojuan, Zuochuan, Zuo Chuan.*) *Zuo Commentary* on *Chunqiu* (*Spring and Autumn Annals*). *Zuo* is of debatable date and authorship.
zuochan (Chinese; in Japanese, *zazen.*) Sitting meditation practiced by Chan (Zen) Buddhists.
Zuojuan See *Zuo.*
zuopai Leftist.
zuoren Developing one's personality or being a person; term applied to individuals and groups.
zuowang Oblivion.
Zuowang lun *Discourse on Sitting in Oblivion*, by Sima Chengzhen.
Zuozhuan See *Zuo.*

中國哲學

PERMISSION ACKNOWLEDGMENTS

Permission has been granted, as appropriate, by publishers and journals for the use of materials for the following entries in the *Encyclopedia of Chinese Philosophy*.

''Confucianism: Confucius (Kongzi, K'ung Tzu)'' by Roger T. Ames. Based on Roger T. Ames's Introduction to *Confucius Speaks* by Tsai Chih-chung, trans. Brain Bruya (Anchor). By permission of Random House, Inc.

''Confucianism: Ethics'' by A. S. Cua. Based on portions of ch. 13, ''Basic Concepts of Confucian Ethics,'' in A. S. Cua, *Moral Vision and Tradition: Essays in Chinese Ethics*. Washington, D.C., Catholic University of America Press, 1998; and also on ''Confucian Philosophy, Chinese,'' by A. S. Cua in *Routledge Encyclopedia of Philosophy*, ed. Edward Craig, Routledge, London and New York, 1998, Vol. 2. By permission of Catholic University of America Press and Routledge.

''Confucianism: Humanism and the Enlightenment'' by Weiming Tu. Revised and condensed from ''Beyond the Enlightenment Mentality'' by Weiming Tu in *Worldviews and Ecology: Religions, Philosophy, and the Environment*, ed. Mary Ellen Tucker and Patrick Grim, pp. 19–29. Maryknoll, N.Y.: Orbis Books, 1994, copyright by and used by permission of Associated University Presses, Inc. (Another version of this article, under the same title, appeared in *Confucianism and Ecology*, ed. Mary Evelyn Tucker and John Berthrong, distributed by Harvard University Press for Harvard University Center for the Study of World Religions, Cambridge, Mass., 1998.)

''Confucianism: Rhetoric'' by A. S. Cua. Adapted from ''The Possibility of a Confucian Theory of Rhetoric'' in A. S. Cua, *Moral Vision and Tradition: Essays in Chinese Ethics*. Washington: Catholic University of America Press, 1998. By permission of Catholic University of America Press.

''Confucianism: Tradition—*Daotong* (*Tao-t'ung*)'' by A. S. Cua. Based on ch. 12, ''The Confucian Tradition (*Tao-t'ung*),'' in A. S. Cua, *Moral Vision and Tradition: Essays in Chinese Ethics*, Washington, D. C., Catholic University of America Press, 1998; and also on ''Confucian Philosophy, Chinese'' in *Routledge Encyclopedia of Philosophy*, ed. Edward Craig, Routledge, London and New York, 1998, Vol. 2. By permission of Catholic University of America Press and Routledge.

''Confucianism: Vision'' by A. S. Cua. Adapted from ''Confucian Vision and the Human Community'' by A. S. Cua in *Journal of Chinese Philosophy*, 11(3), 1984. By permission of *Journal of Chinese Philosophy*.

''*Junzi* (*Chün-tzu*): The Moral Person'' by A. S. Cua. Revised and extended treatment of the topic, drawn from materials in A. S. Cua, *Dimensions of Moral Creativity: Paradigms, Principles, and Ideal*, published by Pennsylvania State University Press, 1978; copyright A. S. Cua.

''*Li*: Rites or Propriety'' by A. S. Cua. Adapted from ''Ethical and Religious Dimensions of *Li* (Rites),'' in *Review of Metaphysics*, 55(3), March 2002. By permission of *Review of Metaphysics*.

''Mou Zongsan (Mou Tsung-san)'' by Shu-hsien Liu. Some sections of this entry were freely paraphrased from the author's article ''Postwar Neo-Confucian Philosophy'' in a volume published by Greenwood Press, 1989.

''Philosophy in China: Historiography'' by A. S. Cua. Adapted from ''Emergence of the History of Chinese Philosophy,'' in *International Philosophical Quarterly* 40(4), December 2000. By permission of *International Philosophical Quarterly*.

''*Quan* (*Ch'üan*): Weighing Circumstances'' by A. S. Cua. Based on a portion of ''The Idea of Confucian Tradition,'' in *Review of Metaphysics*, 45(4), 1992. By permission of *Review of Metaphysics*.

''Reason and Principle'' by A. S. Cua. Adapted from ''Reason and Principle in Chinese Philosophy,'' in *A Companion to World Philosophies*, ed. Eliot Deutsch and Ron Bontekoe. Oxford: Blackwell, 1997. By permission of Blackwell Publishing.

''Self-Deception'' by A. S. Cua. Adapted from ''A Confucian Perspective on Self-Deception'' by A. S. Cua in *Self and Deception: A Cross-Cultural Philosophical Inquiry*, ed. Roger T. Ames and Wimal Dissanayake, by permission of State University of New York Press, ©1996 State University of New York. All rights reserved.

''Wang Yangming (Wang Yang-ming)'' by A. S. Cua. Adapted from ''Between Commitment and Realization: Wang Yang-ming's Vision of the Universe as a Moral Community'' by A. S. Cua in *Philosophy East and West*, 43(4), 1993. By permission of University of Hawaii Press.

''Xiong Shili (Hsiung Shih-li)'' by Shu-hsien Liu. Some sections of this entry were freely paraphrased from the author's article ''Postwar Neo-Confucian Philosophy'' in a volume published by Greenwood Press, 1989.

''*Yi* (*I*) and *Li*: Rightness and Rites'' by A. S. Cua. Based on portions of ch. 13, ''Basic Concepts of Confucian Ethics,'' in A. S. Cua, *Moral Vision and Tradition: Essays in Chinese Ethics*. Washington: Catholic University of America Press, 1998. By permission of Catholic University of America Press.

''*Zhixing heyi* (*Chih-hsing ho-i*): Unity of Knowledge and Action'' by A. S. Cua. Based on A. S. Cua, *The Unity of Knowledge and Action: A Study in Wang Yang-ming's Moral Psychology*. University of Hawaii Press, 1982; copyright A. S. Cua.

中國哲學

INDEX

Note: Page numbers in **boldface** indicate primary discussion of the topic.

Abhidharma literature, 816
absolutes
  ethics and, 72–73
  God as, 92–93
  Qing Confucianism on, 123
Academy of the Supreme Ultimate, 183
Acker, William B., 513
action
  Confucius on harmony of words and, 876
  in the *junzi*, 334–335
  Mao on, 428, 430
  Mencius on connection between moral knowledge and, 877
  philosophy of, 50–51
  philosophy of mind and, 582
  situations leading to, 732
  unity of knowledge and, 760, 769, **876–878**
  yi and, 245–246
  Yijing as basis for, 521–522
aesthetics, **1–5, 511–517**
  calligraphy and, 25–27
  of culture, 532
  Fang on, 250–251, 609
  li in, 373–374
  Marxism on, 432
  Xu Fuguan on, 812–813
age, reverence for, 34, 59
agriculture, 659, 660
ai (love), filial piety and, 793. *See also jian ai* (universal love)
Ai Siqi, 434
alchemy, 193
  inner, 222–223, 226–227, 228, 658–659
  outer, 659
  as science, 661
al-Gahazali, 879
Allan, Sarah, 487
Althusser, Louis, 665
American Chinese Philosophers Association, 607
Ames, Roger, 171, 607
  on self-deception, 676–677
Analects (Confucius). *See Lunyu* (*Analects*) (Confucius)
analytical philosophy, 718
anarchists, followers of Zhuangzi, 920–921
Andronicus of Rhodes, 449
An Lushan rebellion, 140, 143
An Shigao, 7–8
argumentation. *See also* rhetoric
  of Jizang, 324–326
  Kang Youwei on, 337–341
  Mencius on, 445–447, 460
  neo-Daoist, 215–216
  neo-Mohist, 353–354
  rhetoric and, 128–130
  school of names, 491–497
  Xunzi on, 825–828
Aristotle, 848
  in comparative philosophy, 52
  Confucius compared with, 134
  on egoism, 242
  epistemology in, 558
  ethics of, 626
  humanism in, 663
  metaphysics of, 449
  on moral person, 330
  rhetoric in, 127–128
  Xunzi compared to, 821
  Zhuangzi and, 917
art, 714, 812–813. *See also* calligraphy; painting
Ārya gambīra saṁdhinirmocaṅa sūtra ṭīka (Wŏnch'ŭk), 816
asceticism, Zen school, 17–18
Ashikaga school, 99
Asiatic mode of production, 433–434
Assessment of the Han Old and New Text Controversy (Qian), 619
astrology. *See* cosmology
astronomy, 547–548
Austin, J. L., 334, 722
  on *li*, 381
  on *zhi*, 875
authoritarianism. *See also* Marxism
  familial, 90–91
  Huang Zongxi on, 122–123

authoritarianism. *See also* Marxism (*Continued*)
in Ling Ting-kan, 404
Qin, 240
western vs. Chinese concepts of, 93
Avatamsaka, 13
Awakening of Faith, The, 796
Awakening of Faith in Mahayana (Wu), 11–12, 13, 16

Bacon, Francis, 393, 834
bagu wen (eight-legged essay), 109, 272–273
Baigan, Ishida, 100
baihua wen (folk prose), 2–3
Baiken, Minamimura, 99
Baisha Shuyuan, 36
Bai Yuchan, 227
Ba Jin, 90–91
Bamboo Annals, 545
Bangkok Declaration, 630
Ban Gu, 321, 862
"Treatise on Bibliography," 492
on Wenzi, 781
Zheng and, 552
baohjuan (precious scrolls), 228
Baolinzhuan (*Record of the Baolin Temple*), 439
Baopuzi. *See* Ge Hong (Baopuzi)
Baopuzi (*The Master Who Embraces Simplicity*) (Ge), 660
Bao Shichen, 125
beauty. *See* aesthetics
behaviorism, 363
Beifang (Northern) school of neo-Confucianism, 777
being. *See youwu* (*yu-wu*)*:* being and nonbeing
benevolence, 709
bengen (original root), 920
Benjijing (*Scripture of the Genesis Point*), 225
Bennett, Steven, 193
Bentham, Jeremy, 390
benti, 718–720, 723, 725
benxin (original mind), 165–166
Lu-Wang school's mind as, 901
Xiong Shili on, 803
Bergson, Henri, 598, 665
in Fang, 250
in Kang, 340
Liang on, 396
Berkeley, George, 418
Berling, Judith, 112
Between Scholarship and Politics (*Xueshu yu zhengshi shijian*) (Xu Fuguan), 812
Between Zhouyi and Whitehead—Introduction to the Philosophy of Field-Being (Tong), 605
bian (distinctions), in language philosophy, 571–572
Bibliography of Dai Dongyan Xiansheng (Duan), 195
binomials, 635–637
bi (obscuration), 379–380
self-deception and, 673–675
Xunzi on, 634
Biography of Master No Name (*Wuming Gong zhuan*) (Shao), 683
Biography of the Dharma Master Xuanzang (*Xuanzang fashi xingzhuang*) (Ming Xiang), 814
Biography of Tripitaka, the Dharma Master of the Great C'ien Monastery under the Great Tang (*Da Tang da C'ien sanzang fashi zhuan*) (Huili, Yancong), 814
Bi Yuan, 861
Bi zhen tu (*Strategic Plan of Battle for the Brush*) (Wei), 26–27
Bluntschli, Johann Kaspar, 389, 391
Bodde, Derk, 657
Bodhidharma, 17, 18, 699
on nature, 23
as Zen patriarch, 19–20
Bodin, Jean, 394
body. *See ti:* body or embodiment
Bohu tongyi (*Comprehensive Discussions in White Tiger Hall*), 188, 189, 787
Book of Lord Shang, The (Shang), 247
Book of Poetry. See Shijing
Book of Rites. See Liji (*Book of Rites*)
Book of the Mean. See Zhongyong (*Chung Yung*)*:* the doctrine of the mean
Book of Yin and Yang (*Yin yang shu*) (Lu), 142
Borodin, Mikhail, 707
Boston school of Confucianism, 171
Boxer Rebellion (1899), 163, 706
breathing, Zhuangzi on, 212–213
Bridgman, Elijah, 735
"Brief Discussions of Noncanonical Philosophers" (*Zhuzixue lueshuo*) (Zhang), 856
Buddha, 8, 9–10, 880
Buddha-nature, 8–9
Mazu Daoyi on, 439
paradism shifts on, 11–12
Buddha-Nature, The (Mou), 484
Buddhism
argumentation in, 55
Cheng Hao on, 39
Cheng Yi on, 44–45
Chinese schools of, 13–18
in comparative philosophy, 53–54
Confucian dialogues with, 69–72
on culture, 527–528
Fazang in, 252–258
geyi (matching concepts) in, 365–366
Han Yu on, 289–290
Hinayana (Small Vehicle), 19
Huayan (Garland, Avatamsaka) school of, 15–17
influence on interpretation of *wuwei*, 786
influence on Tan Sitong, 709
in Japan, 97
on language, 345, 569
Mahayana (Great Vehicle), 19
in neo-Confucianism, 60
neo-Daoism and, 221
persecution of, 23–24
philosophy of the mind in, 586–587
on *qing*, 622

as religion, 641
religious Daoism and, 224–225
ritualism and, 650–651
ritual practice of *tiantai*, 881
on sagehood, 698
Sanlun Madhyamika, 323–328
Sengzhao in, 678–680
Song Confucianism and, 135–136
Tang Confucianism and, 140, 143
texts divided into five flavors by Shiyi, 880
Tiantai, 13–15
in twentieth-century Confucianism, 171
ultimate substance as state of emptiness and nothingness, 725
in Vietnam, 173–177
worldview of, 548
on *xin* (mind-heart), 796
Zhang Binglin on, 856
Zhang Dongsun and, 857
Zhou dynasty, 640
Buddhism, Zen (Chan), 17–18, **19–24**, 880
asceticism in, 17–18
in Cheng, 137–138
Chen Que on, 33–34
Gu on, 273
Huineng in, 312–314
in Japan, 98–99
Li Ao in, 385–387
Luo Qinshun and, 776
Mazu Daoyi in, 438–440
one-finger, 21–22
paradox in, 22–23
philosophy of the mind in, 586
Sanlun philosophy in, 328
Shenhui in, 699–700
Tiantai and, 879
in Zhang, 121, 137–138
Zhu Xi and, 901
Buddhism in China: a historical survey, **7–19**
Bugou, 493–494
Bureau of Yin and Yang, 98
Bush, Susan, 512, 515
Bu Shang, 63
Butler, Joseph, 772
bu tongxin (being not moved in heart), 443–444

Cahill, James, 513
Cai Lun, 661
Cai Tingji, 322
Cai Yuanbei, 502
cai (capacity), 44
calligraphy, **25–29**
aesthetics in, 1, 2–3
Kang Youwei on, 338
philosophy of art and, 511–517
philosophy of mind and, 582–583
phonetics and, 3
Cang Jie, 2, 516
Canon Explanations, 462
Canon of Filial Piety (*Xiao jing*) (Xuanzong), 144
Canon of the Kaich'eng Period Engraved in Stone (*Kaicheng shijing*), 145
Cao Pi, 4, 576
capitalism
ethics and, 93
family/community and, 92
Cases on Jurisprudence (Wu), 610
Case Studies of the Qing Literati (Qian), 619
cauldrons of Shang, 235–236
causation, 257–258
Celestial Masters (Tianshi), 222, 223–224, 225
Cengzi, 75–76
Chan, Wing-tsit, 36, 170, 599–600, 736, 737, 760, 780, 860
on human nature, 756
intercultural hermeneutics and, 317–318
on Laozi, 355
on *li*, 631
Moore and, 598
A Source Book in Chinese Philosophy, 500
translation of *ti* and *yong*, 720
on Xiong Shili, 801
on Zhu Xi, 155, 899
Chang, Carson, 168, 768, 780
Marxism of, 433
Mou and, 480
Xu Fuguan and, 812
Chang Bejia, 712
Chang Chunmai, 168
Chang Hao, 388
Confucianism interpreted by, 590
on Liang Qichao, 390
as one of the four masters, 903
on personal realization of *tianli*, 898
Chang Heng, 193
Chang Jie, 287
Chang Tsai. *See* Zhang Zai (Chang Tsai)
Chang Xuecheng, 550–551
Wenshitongyi, 551
chang (the constant), 156–157
change. *See* philosophy of change
Chao Chuo, 363
Chao Yuanfang, 659
"Chart of the Four Images of Heaven and Earth That Order the World," 684–685
chashi (scrutiny and apprehension), 868
Chen Baisha. *See* Chen Xianzhang (Ch'en Hsien-chang)
Chen Boda, 426
Chen Chixu, 227
Chen Chun, 158, 671
Zhu Xi and, 908–909
Chen Daqi (Ch'en Ta-ch'i), **29–32**, 611
Kongzi xueshuo (*Doctrines of Confucius*) (Chen), 74–75, 611
Chen Di, 275
Chen Duxiu, 433, 629, 666
Chen Jian, 112
Chen Kuide, 591

Chen Lai, 114, 590
Chen Liang, 184, 363, 906–907
Chen Lifu (Ch'en Li-fu), 668
Chen Minzheng, 112
Chen Nan, 227
Chen Qiyou, 285
Chen Qiyun (Chi-yun Chen), 83
Chen Que (Ch'en Ch'üeh), **32–35**
  classical scholarship by, 117
  on desire, 123
  Huang Zongxi and, 307
Chen Rongjie. *See* Chan, Wing-tsit
Chen Tuan, 136, 893
Chen Tuxiu, 163
Chen Xianzhang (Ch'en Hsien-chang), **35–37**, 688, 775
  Hu Juren on, 110
  Wang Yangming and, 110–111
  Zhan Roshui disciple of, 851
Chen Zilong, 124
Cheng, King, 235
Cheng Chung-ying, 590
Cheng Hao, 767, 775
  and orthodox line of the Way, 902
  tutored by Zhou Dunyi, 891
  Wang Yangming and, 762
Cheng Hao (Ch'eng Hao), 35, **39–43**
  Cheng Yi compared with, 43, 45
  on *Daxue*, 232
  Feng on, 261
  Hu Hong and, 294
  in Korean Confucianism, 106
  on *li*, 383
  Mou on, 483–484
  as Northern Song master, 136
  on *ren*, 137–138
  Vietnam and, 174
Cheng Ruoyong, 186
Cheng Shaokai, 186
Cheng Xuan, 650
Cheng Xuanying, 225
Cheng Yi (Ch'eng I), **43–46**, 762, 775
  on ancestor worship, 34
  on *cheng*, 38
  Chen Que on, 34
  compared with Cheng Hao, 41–42
  on *Daxue*, 232
  on egoism, 246
  Feng on, 261
  on heaven, 750
  Hu Hong and, 294
  on human nature, 556
  in Korean Confucianism, 106
  on *li* and *qi*, 366–367, 725
  on *li* and *yu*, 757
  on *liyi fenshu*, 409, 633
  Mou on, 483–484
  in neo-Confucianism, 39
  as Northern Song master, 136
  as one of the four masters, 903
  and orthodox line of the Way, 902
  on reflection, 179
  ritualism and, 651
  on *ti* and *yong*, 804
  "Treatise on What Yanzi Loved to Learn, A," 42
  tutored by Zhou Dunyi, 891
  Vietnam and, 174
  on *xing*, 800, 898
  Zen and, 138
  on Zhang Zai, 867, 869
  on *zhonghe* (equilibrium and harmony), 897
  on Zhou Dunyi, 894
  Zhu Xi and, 899
Cheng Zhongying. *See* Chung-ying Cheng
Cheng Gongsheng, 492
Chengshilun (*Satyasiddhi, Treatise on Establishing the Real*) (Harivarman), 9
Cheng weishi lun (*Discourse on the Accomplishment of Consciousness Only*) (Xuanzang), 814, 816
  commentaries to by Kuiji, 816
chengxin, Zhuangzi on, 914
chengyi: making one's thoughts sincere, **47–48**
  Liu Zongzhou on, 406–407
  self-deception and, 671–673
Chengzhi wenzhi (*Completing and Hearing*), 150, 151
Cheng-Zhu Confucianism, 750, 751, 775, 777, 901
  Chen Que and, 33
  established, 108–109
  Kangxi revival of, 652
  in Korea, 103–104, 106
  Lu Xiangshan on, 413, 414
  Ming, 107–115, 113
  Qing, 116
  universal love and, 246
  Wang Fuzhi and, 749
  Yan Yuan's revolt against, 835
  Zhang genealogy, 120–121
cheng: wholeness or sincerity, **37–39**
  in classical Confucianism, 68
  li and, 374, 379
  paired with *xin*, 886
  self-cultivation and, 808
  self-deception and, 670–673
  zhongyong on, 889–890
  Zhou Dunyi on, 894
  Zhuangzi on, 913–914
chi. See qi (*ch'i*)*:* vital force
Chiang Kai-shek (Jiang Jieshi), **48–51**, 668, 811
China Academy of Social Sciences (CASS), 589
China's Destiny (Chiang), 49, 50
Chinese Academy of Science (CAS), 434–435
Chinese Academy of Social Science (CASS), 435–436
Chinese Classics (Legge), 735, 737
Chinese-English Dictionary of Modern Usage (Lin), 401
Chinese Nationalist Party, 47–51, 707
Chinese Philosophy: Its Spirit and Its Development (Fang), 249, 250

Chinese Philosophy and Modernization (Liu), 605
Chinese Philosophy in Classical Times (Hughes), 736
Chinese Renaissance, The (Hu), 297
Chinese Repository (Bridgman and Williams, eds.), 735
Chinese University of Hong Kong, 712
Chinese View of Life (Fang), 169, 250
Ching, Julia, 171, 606, 766, 780
chong, 810
Chow, Kai-wing, 112
Christianity
  Confucianism and, 70–71, 598
  influence of on language, 276
  Jesuit missionaries, 90
  opposed by Zhang Binglin, 855
  recent Chinese philosophy and, 591
  translations and, 735
  in Vietnam, 176
Chronological Biography (*Nianpu*), 760, 764, 769, 770
Chronological Studies of the Pre-Qin Philosophers (Qian), 619
Chuanzhen dao, 641
Chu Hsi. *See* Zhu Xi (Chu Hsi)
Chung-ying Cheng, 170–171, 598–599, 601–603
  benti in, 718
Chung Yung. *See Zhongyong* (*Chung Yung*): the doctrine of the mean
Chunqiu fanlu (*Spring and Autumn Annals*)
  authorship of, 238
  cosmology in, 188
  forged classics school and, 125
  Gongyang Commentary on, 163
  history of, 546–547
  modern text of, 84
  new text school on, 124
  in Song Confucianism, 135
  translation by Legge, 735
  Xiong Shili on, 805
Chunqiu school, 145–148
Chunqiu zhengzhuan (Zhan Roshui), 853
Chuzhong (Huguang region) school of neo-Confucianism, 777
Cicero, 737
Ci'en Kuiji, 815
Ciming, Master, 22
civil service
  democracy and, 92
  established, 85–86
  in Japan, 98
  Ming, 108–109
  in Tang Confucianism, 140
classical scholarship
  Dai Zhen in, 196–204
  Qing, 115–125
  Tang canon revision, 143–145
Classic of Spring and Autumn. *See Chunqiu fanlu* (*Spring and Autumn Annals*)
Classic on the Mind-and-Heart (*Xinjing*) (Zhen Dexiu), 909
classification
  in language and logic, 347–348
  in neo-Mohism, 353–354
clerical script, 26
Collected Works Concerning Han Fei, 285
Collection of Hu Shih's English Writings, 297
Collie, David, 735
colonialism, 90–91
commentaries. *See also individual works*
  Chunqiu, 145–146, 546
  Han, 215
  neo-Daoist, 215
  Tang, 141–142, 143–144
  Ten Wings, 517–524
  on the *Yijing*, 732
communism. *See also* Marxism
  Chiang Kai-shek and, 47–51
  Soviet Union's collapse and, 90
  in Vietnam, 176
community
  aesthetics and, 4
  cheng in, 38
  Confucius on, 61–62, 181–182
  Enlightenment on, 91–96
  Mencius on, 442
  tradition and, 154
  yi and, 76
comparative philosophy, **51–58**, 126–135
Comparison of Chinese and Western Culture and Philosophy, A (Tang Junyi), 712
Complete Perfection (Quanzhen) school, 222, 227
Complete Works of Han Fei Tzu (Liao), 285
Comprehensive Compendium (*Tongdian*) (Du), 146
Comprehensive Discussions in White Tiger Hall (*Baihu tongyi*), 188, 189, 787
comprehensive harmony, 249–252
Comprehensive Survey of Literary Remains, 185
Comte, Auguste, 668
concentration, 895
Confucianism. *See also* neo-Confucianism
  argumentation in, 55
  Boston school, 171
  Buddhism compared with, 18–19
  Buddhist influence on, 18, 24
  Chen Daqi in, 29–32
  Cheng on, 602
  Chen Que on, 32–35
  Chen Xianzhang on, 35–37
  contextuality of, 456
  on culture, 527–528
  on *dao*, 204–206
  epistemology in, 563–568
  on the heart, 477–478
  humanism and, 667–668
  Laozi on, 207–209
  legalism compared with, 362–363
  market economics and government in, 92–96
  modern interpretations of, 589–590

Confucianism. *See also* neo-Confucianism (*Continued*)
outside China, 169–170
as religion, 71–72, 164
the self in, 675–677
in Taiwan, 609–610
Tang era, 13
tian in, 727–728
total commitment to the ethical life, 808
xin as an aspect of highest ideal, 887
Confucianism: Confucius (Kongzi), **58–64**. *See also* Confucius
Confucianism: Confucius's classical thought, **64–69**
Confucianism: dialogues, **69–72**
Confucianism: ethics, **72–79**
Confucianism: ethics and law, **80–81**
Confucianism: Han, **82–89**
Dong Zhongshu in, 238–240
scholarship, 903–904
Confucianism: humanism and the Enlightenment, **89–96**
Confucianism: Japan, **97–102**
Confucianism: Korea, **102–107**
Confucianism: Ming, **107–115**
Chan on, 600–601
Qing compared with, 115–117
Confucianism: Qing (Ch'ing), **115–125**
Confucianism: rhetoric, **126–135**
Confucianism: Song
and *benti*, 719
importance of *li* in, 898
on *ti-yong*, 721
Confucianism: Song (Sung), **135–139**
art and, 511–513
Chan on, 600–601
Dai Zhen on, 195–202
on *li*, 632
Qing compared with, 115–117
as revival, 108–109
Confucianism: Tang, **140–149**
Confucianism: texts in Guodian Bamboo slips, **149–153**, 643–645
Confucianism: tradition—*daotong* (*tao-t'ung*), **153–160**
Confucianism: twentieth century, **160–172**
Confucianism: Vietnam, **173–177**
Confucianism: vision, **177–182**
Confucianism: Yuan, **182–187**
Confucianism and Christianity (Ching), 606
Confucius, **58–64**
aesthetics and, 4
as agnostic, 640
argumentation in, 54
Aristotle compared with, 134
and Confucian ethics, 729
on culture, 529–530
as god, 59–60
on government, 807
on human nature, 756
on importance of applying one's moral learning, 876
influence of, 60–61
intercultural hermeneutics and, 317–318
on *junzi*, 331–332, 333, 529–530
on law, 80–81
on literature, 576
Li Zhi on, 779
Mao on, 426
on metaphysics, 40
on moral philosophy and philosophy of time, 733
on natural affection for parents, 794
new text school on, 124
order of canon, 737
on philosophy of mind, 583
pregnant phrase and, 1–2
on proper purpose of government, 795
on rectifying names, 570–571
relation with Zhuangzi, 911
on *ren*, 643
on ritualism, 647–648
on sagehood, 697
on self-cultivation, 730, 808
on self-regard, 180
on society, 553
as teacher, 59
on *tian*, 727
on universality of the Way, 889
Wang Bi on, 741
on *wuwei*, 695–696
on *yi*, 843
Yijing and, 522–523
Zhang Binglin on, 856
Zhang Xuecheng on, 863
on *zhengming*, 365, 870–871
Confucius: The Sacred as the Secular (Fingarette), 171
Confucius the Philosopher, 598
conquest series, 488–490
consciousnesses, number of, 817
Consciousness of Culture and Moral Reason (Tang Junyi), 713
consciousness-only Buddhism, 366, 802
consumerism, 596
context, 456. *See also quan* (*ch'üan*)*:* weighing circumstances
Continuation of the Biographies of Eminent Monks (*Xu Gaoseng Zhuan*) (Daoxuan), 814
coordinative reasoning, 131–132
correlative thinking
in cosmology, 187–194
Han dynasty, 545–548
cosmogony, 892
cosmology, **187–194**, 487–490
Cheng Hao on, 40–42
Dong Zhongshu on, 239–240
in Guodian bamboo slips, 231
Han, 585
Huainanzi on, 304–306
human nature and, 557
imperial rule in, 238–240
Laozi on, 204, 210–211, 224, 357–358

of Liang Shuming, 395–397
in *Liezi*, 398–399
Lu Jia on, 411–412
Lu Xiangshan on, 415–416
Mou on, 480
Numinous Treasure school on, 224–225
philosophy of the mind and, 585
religious Daoism and, 223–224
Tang, 142–146
of time, 730–732
Wang Fuzhi and, 749–750
Xiong Shili and, 803–805
in the *Yijing*, 518–519, 523
Zhang Zai on, 41, 137–138
in Zhuangzi, 210–211
of Zhu Xi, 900
cosmopolitanism, 424
creativity, 695–697. *See also sheng:* life or creativity
Cua on, 603–604
Fang on, 250–252
Laozi on, 358–359
neo-Confucianism on, 410
semantic, 3–4
Creativity in Man and Nature (Fang), 250
creator, *tian* as, 727
Creel, H. G., 362, 690
"Critical Buddhism" movement, 819
Critique of Pure Reason, The (Kant), 756
cross-cultural exchange, 69–72
C Theory: Philosophy of Management from the Yijing (Cheng), 603
Cua, Antonio S., 171, 603–604, 780, 872
Confucianism interpreted by, 590
on egoism, 242, 243
Cui Shu, 197, 888
cultural radicals of the May Fourth period, 758
cultural relativism, 126
in Zhuangzi, 919
Cultural Revolution, 430
Chiang Kai-shek and, 50
Liang Shuming and, 396–397
Mou in, 480–486
qigong (energy exercises) in, 228
scientism and, 667
Xu Fuguan's critique of, 813
Zhang Dongsun during, 857
culture
benti in philosophy of, 718
civilization and, 551–552
great debate on, 593–594
mass, 596
of representation, 252
Cummings, Robert, 607
curriculum developed by Zhu Xi, 902

Dadai liji, 199
Dai Dongyuan. *See* Dai Zhen (Tai Chen)
Dai-Nihon-shi (*History of Great Japan*) (Mitsukuni), 101
Dai Sheng, 888
Dai Tai liji (*Rites of Great Tai*), 344
Dai Wang, 837
Dai Zhen (Tai Chen), 119, 121, **195–202**
classical studies of, 117–118
on *daotong*, 159
on desire, 123
on *li*, 367, 369
Ling Ting-kan on, 403
on ritualism, 652
Wang Fuzhi's influence on, 754
on *xing*, 800
on *xin* (mind-heart), 797
Zhang Xuecheng and, 862, 863
on *zhong* and *shu*, 883
Daizong, Emperor, death rites of, 145
Dake Academy, 852
Dan Fu, King, 244, 245
Danto, Arthur C., 129–130
Dan Zhu, 145
Dao-an, 8
Dao Ji, 511
Daodejing
aesthetics and, 4–5
commentaries written by Wang Bi, 741
on community, 4
on culture, 527–528
dao in, 203–206
de in, 236–237
on government, 536
Guodian bamboo slip texts, 150, 229–231, 355–356
on the heart, 477–478
on history, 543
on language, 572
persuasion in, 54–55
on *qing*, 621
Ruan on, 654
Wang Bi commentary on, 216
and Western thought, 834
Yan's commentary on Wang Bi's rendition of, 834
on *yinyang*, 846
Daode zhenjing guangsheng yi (*Wide Sage Meaning of the Perfect Scripture of the Dao and Virtue*) (Du), 226
Daoism: classical, **206–214**
aesthetics and, 4–5
argumentation in, 55
Buddhism influenced by, 8
Cheng Hao on, 39
Chen Xianzhang and, 35–36
in comparative philosophy, 53–54
compared with Confucianism, 204–206
comprehensiveness or inclusiveness, 921–922
Confucian dialogues with, 69–72
on culture, 527–528
geyi (matching concepts) in, 365–366
Guanzi on, 278–279
Han Yu on, 290
on the heart, 477–478
Heguanzi in, 291–294

Daoism: classical (*Continued*)
huahu controversy in, 10
immortal soul in, 9
influece on Zhang Zai, 865
on language, 345
Laozi in, 355–361
Liezi in, 397–400
literature in, 578–579
modern interpretations of, 589, 590–591
moral philosophy and, 470–472
origin of cosmos in, 742, 790
religious, 874
on sagehood, 698
Shen Dao in, 692–694
shenming in, 700–701
Song Confucianism and, 135–136
Tang Confucianism and, 140, 144
tian in, 728
in Vietnam, 173–177
virtues in, 731
wuming in, 348–349
Yijing in, 523–524
on *zhengming*, 365
Daoism: neo-Daoism (*xuanxue, hsüan-hsüeh*), **214–222**, 789
Guo Xiang in, 280–284
influence of Xi Kang's thesis of "nourishing life," 792
Ruan Ji and, 653–656
Wang Bi and, 741
and *you-wu*, 849
Daoism: religious, **222–229**, 641–642, 874
Daoism: texts in Guodian bamboo slips, 150–151, **229–231**, 355–356
Daojiao yishu (*The Pivotal Meaning of the Daoist Teaching*) (Meng), 226
Daojia wenhua yanjiu (*Study of Daoist Culture*), 591
Dao Learning school, 108–109, 112–113
Daosheng, 8–9
dao (*tao*): the way, **202–206**
and authentic persons, 873
benti compared to, 718
Chen Daqi on, 30
Chen Liang's concept of, 907
Chen Xianzhang on, 35–36
in Confucian vision, 177–178
Confucian vs. Daoist view of, 204–206
Confucius on, 61–62
Dai on, 119
de and, 236
defining, 73–77, 450–451
government and, 549–550
in Guodian bamboo slips, 230–231
Guo Xiang on, 281
Han Feizi on, 285–286
holistic character in Xunzi, 821
Hu Hong on, 295
Laozi on, 356–361
literature and, 578–579
Mazu on, 439–440
in metaphysics, 449–452
namelessness of, 348–349
neo-Daoists on, 215–216
as "nonbeing," 742
not object of knowledge, 875
original versus neo-Confucian concept, 836
philosophy of mind and, 581–583
in Qing Confucianism, 122
quan and, 626–627
and *ren*, 721–722
rhetoric in, 127–135
Shao Yong on, 687–688
shifei and, 704
Wang on, 743
Xunzi on, 67
Yan Yuan's interpretation of, 836
Zhang on, 120–121
in *Zhongyong*, 889
Zhuangzi and, 919
daotong (*tao-t'ung*) (tradition), **153–160**, **706–708**
in aesthetics, 3
Cheng-Zhu on, 108–109
Han Yu on, 290
Mencius on, 440–448
Mou on, 480–481
Zhao on, 183
Daoxin, 17
Daoxuan, 814
daoxue (Dao school, learning), 108–109, 112–113
Dardess, John, 108
Daren xiansheng zhuan (Biography of Master Great Man) (Ruan), 654, 655
Darwin, Charles
in Hu Shu, 298
Hu Shu on, 302
influence of, 716
Liang Qichao and, 388–390
Darwinism, 855
Dasheng Qixin Lun (*Awakening of Faith in the Mahayana*), 253
Datong shu (*The Book on the Great Unity*) (Kang), 338, 339–340
Davis, John Francis, 735
daxin, Zhang Zai on, 868
Daxue (*Ta Hsüeh*): the Great Learning
altered by Zhu Xi, 110–111
cheng in, 37–38, 808
chengyi in, 47
Cheng Yi on, 46
Chen Que on, 33–34
in classical Confucianism, 68
on *du*, 48
on knowledge, 566–568
on learning, 832, 901
on *li*, 632–633
Ling Ting-kan on, 403–405
Luo Qinshun and Wang Yangming's debate, 776
in neo-Confucianism, 46

principle of reciprocity, 729
on *qiongli* (reality), 624
on self-cultivation, 806
on self-deception, 670–673
seven feelings in, 104
on *ti-yong*, 721
Wang commentary on, 112, 116
on *xin*, 886
xiushen in, 807
in Yuan Confucianism, 183–184
on *zhong*, 884
Dazhidulun, 880
death
Buddhism on, 641
mourning, Mozi on, 454, 460
mourning and *li*, 380–383
Tang views on, 147
de Bary, William Theodore, 72, 171, 607
on Wang Yangming, 112
on Zhu Xi, 155
debates
on culture, 593–594
Gaozi and Mencius, 446
on *gewu* (investigation of things), 852
Shenhui debates on *dharma*, 699
Xi Kang and, 789–790
"Declaration on Chinese Culture to People in the World," 168
"Declaration toward a Global Ethic," 410
deductivism, 130–131
deliberation, 772–773, 824–826, 876
democracy
Hu Shu on, 300–302
Liang on, 392–394
new left and, 596–597
in twentieth-century Confucianism, 163
Democratic League, 396
Democratic Review (*Minzhu pinglun*), 811
Deng Chun, 511
Deng Liqun, 437
Deng Xi, 492
Deng Xiaoping, 435–437, 594–597
Derrida, Jacques, 665
Descartes, René
epistemology in, 558–559
Tang Junyi and, 713
descent-line system. *See* lineages
Descent of Man (Darwin), 716
desire
Chen Que on, 123
in Confucian vision, 179–180
Dai Zhen on, 199
Hu Hong on, 296
human nature and, 555
Laozi on, 349
li in, 372–373
Lu Xiangshan on, 417
Mencius on, 443
in neo-Daoism, 218–220
Qing theory on, 123
Wang Fuzhi on, 751
Xunzi on, 526
Zhang Zai on, 867
destiny
and commitment to ethical life, 808
Guo Xiang on, 282
Mencius on, 442–445, 458–460
de (*te*): virtue or power, **234–237**, 731
Chen Daqi on, 31
cheng in, 38
Confucius on, 62
Daoism compared with Confucian, 208–209
defining, 73–77
female, 112
Han Feizi on, 286
Heguanzi on, 292
Laozi on, 208–209, 358–359
Liang Qichao on, 389
moral psychology and, 478–479
paradox in, 236–237
philosophy of mind and, 583
self-deception and, 673
deus abscontitus, 251
Development and Completion of Zhu Xi's Philosophical Ideas (Liu), 605
Development of the Logical Method in Ancient China, The (Hu), 502–503
Dewey, John, 598
Chinese study of, 598
on culture, 531
on deliberation, 508
Feng and, 249, 503
Hu Shi and, 297–303, 502–503
influence on Chinese thinkers, 716, 736
DeWoskin, Kenneth, 190, 193
dharma
Cheng Hao on, 40
date of demise of, 10
Huineng on, 314
Jizang on, 326–327
kings and, 9–10
law and, 248
Mazu Daoyi on, 439
Shenhui debates on, 699
Zen school on, 20–22
Dharmakaya (*Body of Law*), 14
Dharmakīrti, 817
Dharmakṣema, 819
Dharmapāla, 817, 818
Diagram of Mind and Nature (Zhan), 852
Diagram of the Mind Commanding Human Nature and Feelings (T'oegye), 106
Diagram of the Transmission of the Way (Zhao), 183
dialectical materialism, 425–429
"Dialectical materialism" (Mao), 434

Diamond Sutra
Huineng and, 312
Zen school and, 17–18
Dianlun lunwen (*On Literature*) (Cao), 576
Dignāga, 817
Dimensions of Moral Creativity (Cua), 603–604
ding fa (fixing the standards), 680–681
Directives for the Yuanling mausoleum (*Yuanling Yizhhu*) (Yan), 145
disastrous geography, 189
discipline
in calligraphy, 27–28
"Discourse on Music" (*Yuelun*) (Ruan), 654
Discourse on Sitting in Oblivion (*Zuowang lun*) (Sima), 386
Discourses of the States (*Guoyu*) (Liu), 145
Discourses on Salt and Iron, 86
"Discussions on Humanism and Alienation," 593
"Discussions on the Criteria of Truth," 593
Disenchantment of the World (Shen), 612
Distinguishing the Great Learning (*Daxue bian*) (Chen), 33–34
divination, 519–520
doctrine of the mean. *See Zhongyong* (*Chung Yung*)*:* the doctrine of the mean
Dogen, 730
dominator, *tian* as, 727
Dong Qichang, 511
Dong Zhongshu (Tung Chung'shu), **238–240**, 805
on Confucius, 547
cosmology of, 188
on ethics and law, 81
on history, 552
on human nature, 556
hundred schools and, 640
new text school and, 124
on ritualism, 649–650
Vietnam and, 173
on *xing*, 799
drama, 577
Wang Guowei and, 758–759
Dream of the Red Chamber (*Jonglou meng*), 193, 759
dreams, 193
Freud on, 212
Zhuangzi on, 212, 916
dualism, 368, 679
Duan Yucai
on Dai Zhen, 195
new text school and, 118
duan (moral sprouts), 104, 457–458, 530, 644
in comparative philosophy, 56
Duanmu Siu, 63
Duan (*Tuan*) *Commentary*, 517, 561, 733
and time ontocosmology, 732
Du Guangting, 226
Duo Mo, 183
Durkheim, Émile, 93
du (solitude, privacy), 287
in *Daxue*, 47–48
watching over (*shendu*), 404, 406–407, 477
duty
comparative philosophy on, 52
Mencius on, 457–458
Du You, 146
Dworkin, Ronald, 126, 501, 628
dynasties
concept of, 553
five-phases conception and legitimization on new, 787

Eastern and Western Cultures and Their Philosophies (Liang), 395–396
e (bad), Xunzi's use of, 822
Economic Manuscripts (Marx), 436
Economic Problems of Socialism in the USSR (Stalin), 428
economics
in *Analects*, 238–239
Guanzi on, 277–280
laissez-faire, 390
Liang Qichao on, 390
Tang on, 714
in twentieth-century Confucianism, 161–162
Yan Fu on, 831
education. *See jiao* (education)
egoism in Chinese ethics, **241–246**
Eifu, Motoda, 101
Eight Laws of Yong, 27
Ekken, Kaibara, 100
Elegant Rocks and Sparse Trees (Zhao), 28
Elements of International Law (Wheaton), 628
Elman, Benjamin, 108
Emerson, Rupert, 391
emotion. *See also qing* (*ch'ing*)*:* reality or feeling
in Confucian rhetoric, 133–134
Li Ao on, 386
Ling Ting-kan on, 403–404
Mencius on, 442
moral psychology and, 475–479
mourning and *li*, 380–383
in neo-Daoism, 218–219, 220
Ruan on, 655
of sages, 217
Shao Yong on, 687
Xunzi on, 526
Empedocles, 786
empirical scientism, 664, 665
emptiness. *See xi* (*hsü*)*:* emptiness; *kong:* emptiness
"Encouraging Learning" (Xunzi), 824
Engels, Friedrich, 664
enlightenment. *See wu* (enlightenment)
Enlightenment, the
Chinese, 668–669
Confucianism and, 89–96
Enni, Ben'en, 99
epistemology, 558–569
Chinese, 559–560
comparitive philosophy on, 54–57
Mohist, 462–463
ontoepistemology, 560–562
western, 558–559

Xiong Shili and, 801–803
Zhang Dongsun and, 857–860
equality of all things, 919, 920, 921
equilibrium and harmony. *See zhong* (equilibrium or centrality)
Er Cheng quanshu (*The Complete Work of the Two Cheng Brothers*), 39
Erdiyi (*The Profound of the Twofold Truth*) (Jizang), 324, 326
Erli jing zhuan ce (Zhan), 853
eschatology, 223
"Essay on Restoring Nature" (Li), 38, 267
"Essay on Returning to the Nature" (*Fu xing shu*) (Li), 147–148
essays
aesthetics of, 2–3
bagu wen (eight-legged), 109, 272–273
"essence," in Chinese, 848
Essence of Chinese Culture, The (Liang), 396
Essentials of the Good Government of Zhenguan Period (*Zhenguan zheng yao*), 142
ether, concept of (*yitai*), 710
Ethical Argumentation: A Study in Hsün Tzu's Moral Epistemology (Cua), 604
ethical intuitionism
criticized by Yan Fu, 834
"Ethical Uses of History in Early Confucianism" (Cua), 604
"Ethical Values in Classic Eastern Texts" (North), 126, 127
ethics
aesthetics and, 3–4
Chen Daqi on, 30–32
Cheng Hao on, 40–41
Chen Que on, 32–34
Chung-ying Cheng on, 603
comparitive philosophy on, 51–54
global, 410
Heguanzi on, 292–293
human nature and, 555
Mohist, 462
moral philosophy and, 470–475
neo-Daoist, 219
of situations vs. ethics of principles, 728
in twentieth-century Confucianism, 162
Zhou Dunyi on link with metaphysics, 893
ethnocentrism, 96, 317
Eucken, Rudolf, 665
evidential learning, 272–276
evil
Cheng Yi on, 43–44
Huayan school on, 16
Hu Hong on, 296
Huineng on, 313–314
human nature and, 556
Lu Xiangshan on, 415
origin of, 713
philosophy of the mind and, 587
Tiantai school on, 14
evolution, 298, 302
Evolution and Ethics and Other Essays (Huxley), 716, 832–833
existentialism, 611
Existing Life and Aspects of the Understanding of the Human Mind (Tang), 715
"Experimentalism" (Hu), 297
experimental logic, 502–503
Explaining Human Nature (Chen), 33
"Explanation of the Diagram of the Great Ultimate, An" (Zhou), 41, 136
"Explanation of the National Title 'Republic of China' " (*Zhonghua minguo jie*) (Zhang Binglin), 856
Exposition of the Cheng weishi lun (*Cheng weishi lun shuji*) (Kuiji), 816
Extended Meaning of the Great Learning (*Daxue yanyi*) (Zhen), 184, 909

fa: model, law, doctrine, **247–248**
li in, 373
quanli (rights) and, 628–630
Shang Yang on, 680–682
Shen Buhai on, 689–692
Tang, 142
in Yang Confucianism, 184
Faguo, 9
Fahua Jing (*Lotus sutra*), 8–9, 12–13, 14, 254
Fahua xuanyi (*The Hidden Meaning of the Dharma Flower*) (Zhiyi), 14
Fahua xuanyi (*The Inner Meaning of the Lotus Sutra*) (Zhiyi), 881
Falang, 323
family
authoritarianism in, 90–91
Buddhism on, 641
Confucius on, 61–62
egoism and, 242–243
in ethics and law, 81
Guo Xiang on, 282
primacy of, 76
Tang on, 713–714
Family, The (Ba), 90–91
"Family Admonition" (*Jia jie*) (Xi Kang), 792
Family Ritual by Master Zhu, 34, 651, 652
Fan Feizi, 680
Fan Xuanzi, 363
Fan Zhen, 11
Fang Bao, 834, 862
Fang Chaoying, 275
Fang Dongmei (Thomé H. Fang), 168–169, **249–252**
on *li*, 78
organicist synthesis of, 609
Fang Keli, 590
Fang Lizhi, 437
Fang, Thomé H. *See* Fang Dongmei (Thomé H. Fang)
Fang Xianfu, 777
Fang Xiaoru, 108
Fang Xuanling, 141
Fangyan (*Dialect Words*) (Yang Xiong), 837, 839

fate
  and commitment to ethical life, 808
  Guo Xiang on, 282
  Mencius on, 442–445, 458–460
  Wang Chong on, 745–746
Faxiang, or *Dharma-lakśaṅa*, lineage of Chinese Buddhism, 815, 819
Fayan (*Model Discourses*) (Yang), 87–88
Fayan (*Model Sayings*) (Yang Xiong), 837, 838–839
Fazang (Fa-tsang), 16–17, **252–258**
Feng Congwu, 113
Feng Dao, 779
Feng Qi, 589
Feng Youlan (Fung Yu-lan), 7, **258–261**, 716, 736, 737
  on authorship of *Zhongyong*, 888
  on authorship of *Zhuangzi*, 919
  on Gongsun, 270
  as historian, 503–505
  A History of Chinese Philosophy, 139
  ideology approach of, 83
  Lao on, 505–506, 507–509
  Mou on, 484–485
  New Learning of Li, 168
  works on the history of Chinese philosophy, **261–265**
  on *zhong* and *shu*, 882–883
  Zhu Xi's influence on, 780, 896
Fengdu, 224
Fengjian lun ("Essay on Feudalism") (Liu), 548–549
Fengjian lun (On Decentralized Administration) (Gu), 273
fengshui, 660. *See also* geomancy
field allocation system, 189
filial piety. *See xiao* (*hsiao*)*:* filial piety
Fingarette, Herbert, 171
  on the *junzi*, 334
  on *li*, 382
  on philosophy of mind, 581
  "The Problem of the Self in the *Analects*," 676
  on *zhong* and *shu*, 883, 884
"First Interview in Qin" (Han), 285
"First Letter to the Gentlemen from Hunan on Equilibrium and Harmony" (Zhu Xi), 897
Five Classics
  ancient and modern texts of, 84
  classical Confucianism on, 65
  in Han Confucianism, 84
  Tang commentary on, 141–142, 143–144
five phases. *See wuxing*
five-stage theory, 433–434
five universal paths (*dadao*), 890
"Five Vermin" (Han), 285, 287
"Five-Without Theory, The" (Zhang Binglin), 855
forged classics, 125, 338
Fotudeng, 9
Fountain of Justice (Wu), 610
four beginnings, 457–458, 530, 644
Four Books (*Sishu*). *See also Daxue* (*Ta Hsüeh*)*:* the Great Learning; *Lunyu* (*Analects*) (Confucius); *Mengzi* (Mencius); *Zhongyong* (*Chung Yung*)*:* the doctrine of the mean
  Cheng Yi and, 46
  commentary by Wang Fuzhi, 749
  on *daotong*, 154–155
  defined, 135
  early translations by missionaries, 735
  forged classics and, 125
  Ling Ting-kan on, 404–405
  philosophical studies focused on, 736
  translation by Legge, 735
  in Yuan Confucianism, 183–184
  Zhu Xi on, 155–156, 895, 903
fourfold classification of purity and impurity, 817
"four great bodhisattva vows," 880
Four Noble Truths, 11, 880
Four Periods, 14
"Four-Sentence Teaching of Wang Yangming," 406–407
four *siddanta*, doctrine of
  Zhiyi and, 880
four sprouts, 56, 104, 457–458, 530, 644
Fourteen Lectures on the Encounter and Synthesis of Chinese and Western Philosophy (Mou), 610
Frankena, William, 843
"Free and Easy Wandering" (*Xiaoyao yu*) (Zhiangzi), 919
freedom
  Liang on, 389–390, 392–394
  new left and, 596–597
  Wang Guowei on, 758
  Zhuangzi on, 919
Freud, Sigmund, 212
friendship, 242. *See also* relationships
Fuli lun (*On Returning to Ritual Propriety*) (Ling), 403–404
function, *yong* as, 723–724
Fundamentals of Education for the Young (Eifu), 101
Fundamentals of National Reconstruction (Sun), 708
Fung Yu-lan. *See* Feng Youlan (Fung Yu-lan)
Fu Wei-hsun, Charles, 590, 605
Fu Weixun. *See* Fu Wei-hsun, Charles
Fu Xi, 684
  cosmology of, 518, 524
  ideographs invented by, 2
Fu Yi, 355, 357
fu (treasury, storehouse, orb), 686
Fuxing shu (*Writings on Returning to One's True Nature*) (Li), 385–387
Fuzhou Shipyard School, 831

Gai Kuanrao, 87
Ganquan school, 851
Gan Yang, 591
Ganying pian (*Tract on Action and Response*) (Li), 227–228
Gao Panlong, 113, 114, 651
Gao Wenhu, 908
Gao Yihan, 629
Gao You, 305
Gaozi
  on human nature, 756
  Mencius debates with, 446
  on *xing*, 798
Gaozu (Xiaowendi), 12, 141

Garland Sutra, 17, 252–258
Ge Hong (Baopuzi), 363, 660
genealogies, 652
  Ming, 112–113
  Zhang on, 120–121
Generalities on History (*Shitong*) (Liu), 143–144
genetic method, 299–300
Geng Dingxiang, 777
Genju, Keian, 99
geomancy, 193, 660
  Tang, 142–146
gewu (*ke-wu*) and *zhizhi* (*chih-chih*): investigation of things and extension of knowledge, **267–269**, 776
  Cheng Yi on, 46
  Dai Zhen and, 196–197
  in *Daxue*, 47
  Ling Ting-kan on, 404–405
  Luo Qinshun on, 421
  Wang Yangming and Zhan Roshui debates over, 852
  Zhu Xi on, 901
geyi (matching concepts), 8, 365–366
Giles, Herbert, 322, 735
Giles, Lionel, 330
globalization, 95–96, 601–603
gods. *See also shenming:* gods or godlike intelligence
  absolutes as, 92–93
  city, 189
  in Confucianism, 71–72
  Confucius, 59–60
  Laozi on, 358
  Shang dynasty, 638–639
  technology as, 661
  western humanism on, 92–93
golden rule
  global ethics and, 410
  negative statement of, 317–318
  self-interest and, 91–92
gong'an (*koan*), 24, 439–440
Gong Zizhen, 118, 124
gong (impartiality). *See also jian ai* (universal love)
  Confucian vision of, 180–182
  in the *junzi*, 333–334
  in Mozi, 453–456
  rhetoric on, 129
  Tang theory on, 146–147
  Zhuangzi on, 212
Gongsun Long (Kung-sun Lung), **270–271**, 912
  Hui Shi compared with, 309–310
  on language, 573
  "Left and Right," 494
  Mohist theory on, 465–467
  Platonism in, 346, 350–352
  as prime minister, 85
  separating hardness and white, 310–311, 494–497
  "white horse is not horse," 495–497
  on *yan*, 345
Gongsun Yang. *See* Shang Yang
Gongsun Longzi, 492
Gongxi Chi (Zihua), 64
Gongyang Commentary, 238, 546
gongyang (new text) school, 118
  on Confucius as king, 141–142
  Kan Youwei in, 337–341
  opposed by Zhang Binglin, 855
  Qing era, 124–125
  Tan Sitong and, 710
  in twentieth-century Confucianism, 162–163
good. *See shan* (good)
government. *See also* political order; rulers
  Daoism on, 4–5
  philosophy of, 534–540
  rectifying names and, 571
  ritualism and, 648–650
  self-cultivation as basis of, 807
Graham, Angus C., 187, 188, 236, 763, 766
  on "being" and "essence," 848
  on egoism, 241–242
  on Gongsun, 270, 493, 912
  on the *Heguanzi*, 293
  Later Mohist Logic, Ethics, and Science, 462
  on *li*, 632
  on *Liezi*, 399
  on Mencius, 460
  on Mohist theory, 467
  on *shifei*, 704
  on Yang Zhu, 243
  on Zhuangzi, 911
Gramsci, Antonio, 665
Granet, Marcel, 234–235, 786
Great Appendix. *See Xici*
"great debate on culture," 593–594
Great Leap Forward, 430
Great Learning. See Daxue (*Ta Hsüeh*): the Great Learning
"Great Norms" (*Hongfan*) in *Documents Classic*, 787
Great Peace movement, 222, 223
"Great Preface of the Book of Songs" (*Maoshi daxu*), 142
great ultimate. *See taiji*
"Great Union of the Popular Masses, The" (Mao), 424
great unity, 338, 339–340
Gu Kaizhi, 511, 512
Gu Xianzheng, 113, 651, 779
Gu Yanwu (Ku Yen-wu), **272–276**
  on civil service exams, 109
  classical scholarship of, 116–117
  on *dao*, 122
  economic theory of, 123
  on human nature, 123
  on moral principles, 118
  on political order, 146
  on ritualism, 652
Guafu, story of, 488–489
Guan Yin, 873
Guan Zhong
  Guanzi and, 277
  legalism and, 361
  Li Zhi on, 779

guan (comprehensive and contemplative observation), 518–519, 602
Guan Cai lun (Xi Kang), 792
Guanding, 881
Guangfu hui (Restoration Party), 854
Guangxu, Emperor, 162–163
Guantang. *See* Wang Guowei
guantong (comprehensive understanding), 633
Guanzhong school of neo-Confucianism, 777
Guanzi (*Kuan Tzu*): the book of Master Chan, **277–280**
  on government, 534
  on human nature, 555
  influence on *Wenzi*, 781
  legalism and, 361
  on *sheng*, 798
  shenming in, 701
  on *xu*, 810
Guided Readings in Han Feizi (Chen, Zhang), 285
Guliang Commentary, 546
Guodian bamboo slips
  Confucian texts in, 149–153
  Daodejing, 355–356
  Daoist texts in, 150–151, 229–231
  on *ren*, 643–644, 644–645
Guodian Chumu Zhujian (*Guodian Chu Tomb Bamboo Slips*), 150
Guoji Ruxue Lianhehui, 171
Guomindang, 707
Guo Moruo, 433–434
Guo Qiyung, 590
Guo Rouxu, 511
Guo Xi, 511, 512, 515
Guo Xiang (Kuo Hsiang), **280–284**
  commentaries by, 216
  on human nature, 555–556
  neo-Daoism of, 216–218
  and Parmenides, 848
  on self-transformation, 219
  Xi Kang compared to, 792
  on *xing*, 799
  on *you-wu*, 849
  Zhuangzi and, 209
Guo Qin lun (Discussion of the Faults of the Qin) (Jia), 322
guoxue re (national studies fever), 595
Guoyu
  on enriching the *xing/sheng* of common people, 798
  on *zhong*, 885
guwen (ancient prose) movement, 289
Guwen xiaoxue (Zhan Roshui), 853

Hall, David, 171, 607
Hamberger, Max, 134
Han Feizi (Han Fei Tzu), **285–288**
  on ethics and law, 81
  fa and, 247–248
  on history, 543–544
  on language, 575
  legalism of, 83, 84–85, 362, 363
  on *li*, 365
  Lu Xiangshan on, 417–418
  Shen Dao and, 693–694
  Vietnam and, 173
  on *xingming*, 492
  on *xu*, 810
Han Tuozhou, 908
Han Yu, 18, **288–291**
  on Buddhism, 70
  Daxue commentary, 232
  on human nature, 556
  Li Ao and, 387
  neo-Confucianism and, 135–136
  "On the Dao," 237
  "Origin of the Way," 549
  on political order, 146
  on *ren*, 645
  on self-cultivation, 147–148
  Song Meng Dongye xu (*Letter to Meng Tungyeh*), 3
  on *xin*, 887
  on *xing*, 799–800
  on Yang Xiong, 839
  Yuan dao (An inquiry on the Way), 135–136, 289–290, 549, 551
Han Zhuo, 511
Han dynasty
  Buddhism in, 7–8
  Confucianism in, 82–89
  cosmology of, 585
  learning, 403–405, 652
  religions in, 640–642
  the shouls in, 10–11
  tian after, 728
  Vietnam and, 173–174
Han Feizi, 538
Hang, Thaddeus, 611
Han Ji (*Chronicles of the Former Han*) (Xun), 88–89
Hansen, Chad, 270
Hanshu (Ban Gu)
  on Wenzi, 781
  Yiwen zhi included in, 862
Hanxue (Han learning), 403–405, 652
Hao Jing, 183
Harivarman
  Chengshilun (*On Establishing the Real*), 11
  on enlightenment, 9
  on two truths, 11
harmony. *See he* (harmony); *zhong* (equilibrium or centrality)
heart-mind. *See xin* (*hsin*): heart and mind
Heavenly Masters, 641–642
hedonism, 337–341
Hegel, Georg Wilhelm Friedrich
  intercultural hermeneutics and, 319–320
  Phenomenology of Spirit, 873
Heidegger, Martin
  on knowledge, 359
  Mou on, 484–485
  Sein und Zeit, 873
He Ji, 184, 909

He Lin, 168, 716, 780
He Xiu, 547
He Yan, 215, 217
  death of, 789
  ontology of, 216
He Xinyin (Liang Ruyuan), 112, 778
he (harmony). *See also zhong* (equilibrium or centrality)
  aesthetics and, 1–5
  comprehensive, 249–252
  defined in *Zhongyong*, 889
  Tiantai school on, 14–15
  universal, 391
he tongyi (identifying similarity with difference)
  Feng on, 260–261
Henricks, Robert, 789
Hequanzi (*Ho Kuan Tzu*) treatise, **291–294**
hermeneutics
  Cheng on, 602–603
  creative, 605
  Dai Zhen in, 196–197
  Han, 215
  intercultural, 315–320, **315–320**
  onto-, 590, 602–603
  Yijingi and, 520–521
Hermeneutics (Palmer), 315
Heshang Gong, 355
Highest Purity (Shangqing), 222, 224
Hirobumi, Ito, 101
"Historical Analysis of the Way" (*Yuan dao*) (Zhang Xuecheng), 863
"Historical Background and Present Difficulties of Hegelian Philosophy, The" (Fang), 249–250
Historical Record (*Shiji*) (Sima Qian), 546–547, 821
history
  Feng Youlan on, 258–261, 261–264
  historiography, **499–510**
  Hu Shu on, 299–301
  intercultural hermeneutics and, 320
  Mao on, 426
  Marxism on, 432, 436
  philosophy of, 540–554, **540–554**
  Tang theory of, 142–143
  Wang Fuzhi on, 752–753
  Yuan, 184–185
History of Ancient Chinese Philosophy (*Zhongguo gudai zhexue shi*) (Hu Shi)
  Zhang Binglin's influence on, 856
History of Chinese Philosophical Thought (Lo), 509
History of Chinese Philosophy, A (Feng), 258, 261–264, 503–505, 736
  on Lu and Zhu, 139
History of Chinese Philosophy (*Lao*), 505–509
History of Chinese Thought of the Last Three Hundred Years (Qian), 619, 620
History of Politics, A (Jenks), 833
History of the Chinese Philosophy of Human Nature, The: The Pre-Qin Period (*Zhongguo renxinglun shi: Xianqin pian*) (Xu Fuguan), 812
Hobbes, Thomas, 380, 390, 529
Hoejae, 103
Hohfeld, Wesley, 628
Hokke shūku (Saichō), 819
Holin Bobo, 9
Hong Kong, twentieth-century Confucianism in, 168–169
Hongren, 17, 20–21, 699
Hotokusha (Society for Returning Virtue), 100
Hou Ba, 839
Hshih-hsio Yen, 512
Hsia, C. T., 759
Hsiao Kung-chuan, 392, 394
Hsi ming (Western Inscription) (Zhang), 41
Hsüan-tsang. *See* Xuanzang (Hsüan-tsang)
Hsün Tzu, 382
Hu Feng, 667
Hu Hai, 321–322
Hu Hong (Hu Hung), 43, **294–297**
  Mou on, 483–484
  on *zhonghe* (equilibrium and harmony), 896
Hu Juren
  on Cheng Yi, 109–110
  on Chen Xianzhang, 110
  Juyelu, 36
  on Zhu Xi, 109–110
Hu Lingyi, 50
Hu Qiaomu, 437, 669
Hu Shi (Hu Shih), **297–303**, 716, 759, 861
  as historian, 501–503
  Lao on, 507–508
  Mao on, 434
  Marxism of, 433
  on morality, 163
  on rights, 629
  Zhang Binglin's influence on, 856
Hu Weiyong, 107
Hu Yaobang, 435
Hu Yin, 294
Hu Yuan, 43
Hua Tuo, 661
huahu controversy, 10
Huainanzi (*Huai-nan Tzu*) text, **303–306**
  cosmology in, 188, 189
  Daoism of, 206
  on *qi*, 616–617
  shenming in, 701
  Wenzi and, 781–782
  on *xu*, 810
  on Yang Zhu, 841
  zhenren in, 872, 873–874
Huairang, Master, 21
Huaji (*On Painting*) (Deng), 511
Huan Kuan, 363
Huan Tan
  Wang Chong and, 748
  on Yang Xiong, 839
Huang Daopo, 661
Huang Di, 542, 658

Huang Gan, 184
  on *daoong*, 185, 186
  Zhu Xi and, 908, 909
Huang Lizhou. *See* Huang Zongxi
Huang Mianzhi, 770
Huang Quan, 515
Huang Rucheng, 274
Huang Ting-Jian, 28, 511, 512
Huang Zongxi (Huang Chung-hsi), **306–309**, 777, 778, 779
  compared with Gu Yanwu, 272
  on *dao*, 122
  on *despotism*, 122–123
  economic theory of, 123
  on government, 539
  in lineage, 113
  Mingru Xue'an (*Records of Ming Scholars*), 36
  on Shao, 688
  Zhang Xuecheng and, 864
Huang Zunsu, 114, 306
Huang Zuo, 651
Huangchao jingshi wenbian, 124
Huangdi neijing suwen (*Plain Questions of the Yellow Sovereign's Inner Classic*), 188, 193
Huangdi zhaijing (*Yellow Sovereign's Site Classic*), 193
Huang Gong, 492
Huangji jingshi (*Supreme Ultimate Ordering the World*) (Shao), 683–684
Huang-Lao school, 223, 921–922
  on government, 538
  Wang Chong and, 748
Huang Ming jingshi wenbian, 124
Huangpo, 21, 294
Huangwang daji (*Great Records of Emperors and Kings*) (Hu), 294
Huanjin shu (*The Art of Reverting Gold*), 227
Hua shanshui xu (*Introduction to the Painting of Landscape*) (Zong), 511, 512, 514
Huashi (*A History of Painting*) (Mi), 511
Huayan (Garland, Avatamsaka) Buddhism, 15–17, 898
  Fazang in, 252–258
Huayan jing (*Garland Sutra*), 17, 252–258
Huayan Jing Tanxuan Ji (*Inquiry into the Profound Meaning of the Garland Sutra*) (Fazang), 253
Hua yulu (*Enlightening Remarks on Painting*) (Shitao), 511, 512, 513
Hughes, Ernest Richard, 736, 737
Hui Shi (Hui Shih), **309–311**, 911–912
  on language, 573
  ten propositions of, 493–495
  Zhuangzi and, 209–210
Huiguan, 8–9
Huike, 17, 20
Huili, 814
Huineng: the sixth patriarch, 17–18, 18, **312–314**
  on enlightenment, 21
  Mazu Daoyi and, 438–440
  on middle way, 22–23
  Platform Sutra of the Sixth Patriarch, 23
  as Zen patriarch, 20–21
Huisi, 879
huiyi (associative understanding), 2
Huiyuan, 9
Huizhao, 816
Hui Zi, 493
Human Heart-Mind and Human Life (Liang), 397
humanism
  anthropocosmic Confucian, 590
  Confucianism and, 89–96
  Lin Yutang and, 401–402
  Marxist, 588–590, 592–594, 595–596, 665, 667
  neotraditionalism and, 595–596
  scientism and, **663–669**
  in Tang, 167–168
  Tang Junyi on, 712–713, 714
humanity. *See ren* (*jen*): humanity
human nature, **554–558**
  Chen Daqi on, 30, 31
  cheng and, 38
  Cheng Hao on, 42
  Cheng Yi on, 43–44
  Chen Que on, 32–34
  civil service examinations and, 109
  in classical Confucianism, 67
  classical Confucianism on, 65
  in comparative philosophy, 56
  Dai Zhen on, 196, 197–204
  de and, 235
  Dong Zhongshu on, 239
  effect of on moral learning (*xue*), 746
  egoism and, 242–244
  Fang on, 251, 609
  Fazang on, 254–256
  Guodian bamboo slips on, 151–152
  Gu on, 123
  Han Feizi on, 286
  Heguanzi on, 292–293
  Japanese views of, 100
  Li Ao on, 386–387
  Ling Ting-kan on, 403–404
  Liu Zongzhou on, 406
  Mencius on, 31, 441–442, 446–447
  moral philosophy and, 470–475
  rhetoric and, 133–134
  talent and, 219–221
  Tang theories on, 147
  universal love and, 456–567
  Wang Fuzhi on, 750–751
  Wang Guowei on, 756–757
  Xiong on, 165–166
human situation, notion of, 823
Hume, David, 55, 824, 884
humility, *li* and, 374–375
Hunan school
  on *zhonghe* (equilibrium and harmony), 896
Huo Changlin, 124
Hu Shi wencun, 297

Husserl's Concept of Epoqué (Woo), 612
Hutcheson, Francis, 771
Hu-Xiang school (school of thought), 294–297
Huxley, Thomas
  Evolution and Ethics and Other Essays, 832–833
  Hu Shu on, 298, 300, 301
  Liang Qichao and, 388–389
Hwadam, 103

Iberhim, Anway, 96
icchāntika (*yichanti*), 818
I Ching. See Yijing (*Book of Changes*)
iconoclasm, 668, 856
idealism, 420–421
  Marxism and, 435
  Mencius on, 440–448
  in Mou, 451–452
  objective, 420–421
  of Tang Junyi, 712–713, 715
ideographs, 2–3. *See also* calligraphy
ideology aproach, 83
immanence, theory of, 858
immortality, 10–11
  Daoism on, 9, 226
  li and, 381
  Xi Kang on, 790
impartiality. *See gong* (impartiality); *jian ai* (universal love)
Imperial Rescript on Education (Eifu), 101
Importance of Living, The (Lin), 400, 401
India
  Buddhism in, 7, 8, 13, 19
  history in, 540–541
  logic in, 29, 366
  rhetoric in, 126
  Zen and, 23
individuality
  Confucius on, 61–62
  egoism and, 241–246
  Guo Xiang on, 282, 283
  Hu Shu on, 302
  Lu Xiangshan on, 416
  Mao on, 423–424
  Marxist humanism and, 593–594
  Tang philosophy of, 143
  in twentieth-century Confucianism, 162
  western vs. Chinese concepts of, 92
industrialization, 856. *See also* modernization
inner realization (Buddhist), 879
Inquiry into the Nature and Causes of the Wealth of Nations, An (Smith), 833
Inquiry on the Great Learning (Wang Yangming), 760
Institute of Buddhism, 801
Instructions for Practical Living (Chan), 600
Intellectual History of the Han Dynasty (*Lianghan sixiangshi*) (Xu Fuguan), 813
intellectual inquiry, 118–119
intercultural hermeneutics, **315–320**
International Conferences on Chinese Philosophy, 607
International Confucian Association, 171
International Society for Chinese Philosophy, 170–171, 598, 599, 607
Introduction to the Original Discussion on Chinese Traditional Philosophy, An (Tang), 715
intuition
  intellectual, 451–452
  Zhuangzi and, 913–914
Islam, Confucianism and, 70

Jaikong jing (*Scripture of Master Haikong*), 225
James, William, 378, 504, 773, 860
Jao Tsung-i, 234
Japan
  Confucianism in, 97–102
  defeat of China by, 162, 164, 666
  market economics and government in, 92–96
  Zen in, 24
Jen Yu-wen, 35–36
jen. See ren (jen): humanity
Jenks, E., 833
Jevons, W. S., 833
Jia Yi (Chia I), 85, **321–323**
jian ai (universal love), 243–244
  egoism and, 241–242
  liyi fenshu compared with, 409–410
  in Mozi, 453–456
Jiang, Paul Yun-ming, 36
Jiang Jieshi. *See* Chiang Kai-shek (Jiang Jieshi)
Jiang Qing, 60–61
Jiang Xin, 777
Jiang Yong, 275
Jiang Zhongzheng. *See* Chiang Kai-shek (Jiang Jieshi)
Jiangmen school, 851
Jiangyou (Jiangxi) school of neo-Confucianism, 777
Jiao Hong
  classical scholarship by, 117
  on Jesuits, 276
jiao (education). *See also* knowledge; learning
  defined in *Zhongyong*, 889
  ethical, 472–473
  Han Confucianism and, 84–85
  Han Feizi on, 287
  in Japan, 97, 98, 100–101
  Jia Yi on, 322
  li in, 373–374
  Tang, 141
  in Tang Confucianism, 140
  zhengming and, 871
  Zhu Xi on, 900–902
jiaochou, 861
Jiaochou tongyi (*General Principles of Bibliography*) (Zhang Xuecheng), 861, 862
Jiaxiang Dashi. *See* Jizang (Chi-tsang)
Jin Guantao, 436, 591, 669
Jin Lüxiang, 184
Jin Qunfeng, 83
Jin Yuelin, 168, 718
Jindan dayao (*Great Principles of the Golden Elixir*) (Chen), 227

Jin dynasty, 221
Jing Hao, 515
Jing'an. *See* Wang Guowei
jing (constant)
  "nine standards" for governing, 890
  quan and, 157–159, 625–626
  Shao Yong and, 684–685
Jingguo (Chiang Ching-kuo), 49
jingjie (material world) criticism, 580
jing (seriousness or reverence)
  filial piety and, 793
  Yang Xiong on, 838
jingshi (ordering the world), 124
  Liang Qichao on, 388–394
  in Qing Confucianism, 122
  reformism and, 125
  Yan Yuan and, 836–837
Jingwei, story of, 489–490
Jinling wenda (*Recorded Questions and Answers from the Jinling Academy*) (Zhan Roshui), 854
Jinsai, Ito, 101
Jinsi lu (*Reflections on Things at Hand*) (Zhu Xi, Lu Zuqian), 896, 905
jinsi (reflection), 179, 477, 896
Jizang (Chi-tsang), **323–328**
  on Buddha-nature, 12
  on two truths, 11
  two truths of, 225
Johnston, Henry, 130
Journal of Chinese Philosophy, 170, 598, 599
Journey to the West (*Xiyou ji*), 193, 819
Juan Chi. *See* Ruan Ji (Juan Chi)
judge, *tian* as, 727
judgment. *See quan* (judgment); *shifei* (*shih-fei*): this and not, right and wrong
Judi, Master, 21–22
Juge Liang, 363
Junxian lun (On Centralized Administration) (Gu), 273
junzi (*chün-tzu*): the moral person, **329–335**
  in Confucian vision, 178, 179
  Confucius on, 529–530
  as counselors, 132–134
  Cua on, 604
  in *Daxue*, 232
  educational role of, 74
  Heguanzi on, 292
  Mencius on, 443
  quan and, 626
  rhetoric on, 128–130
  ritualism and, 648
  sage compared with, 132–134
Juyelu (Hu), 36

Kaiyuan ritual code, 144
Kamakura period, 24
Kanetomo, Yoshida, 99
Kaneyoshi, Ichiro, 99
Kang Sheng, 429
Kang Youwei (K'ang Yu-wei), **337–341**, 710, 711, 805, 856
  on family, 91
  forged classics and, 125
  on history, 552
  influence of Wang Yangming on, 780
  on *jingshi*, 124
  Liang Qichao and, 388
  opposed by Zhang Binglin, 855
  reform of a hundred days and, 162–163
  on *ren*, 646
  Tan Sitong and, 709
  universal harmony, 391
Kant, Immanuel, 883
  epistemology in, 558–559
  Hu Shu on, 302
  influence of, 663–664
  intellectual intuition in, 451
  intercultural hermeneutics and, 317
  Li Zehou on, 436, 589
  on morality, 54
  moral philsophy and, 473–474
  Mou on, 480, 483, 485, 508
  Wang Guowei and, 755, 756, 757, 758, 759
Kanzi neiwai pian (*The Esoteric and Exoteric Essays of Master Kang*) (Kang), 337
Karlgren, Bernhard, 735, 875
karma
  Numinous Treasure view of, 225
  religious Daoism on, 227–228
Kawakami Hajime, 811
keti, 718
Ke Xiongwen, 171
Khubilai (Kublai Khan), 182, 183, 274
Khuong Cong Phu, 173
Ki Taesong, 104–105
Kierkegaard, Søren, 760
Kim Dinh, 175, 176
Kimarajiva, 678
knowledge. *See also gewu* (*ke-wu*) and *zhizhi* (*chih-chih*): investigation of things and extension of knowledge; *qiongli* (*ch'iung-li*): exhaustive inquiry into principles; *zhi* (*chih*): to know, to realize
  Buddhist terminology on, 860
  Cheng Yi on, 45–46
  innate, 367
  Laozi on, 359
  Lu Jia on, 412
  Lu Xiangshan on, 417
  not distinguished from wisom in classical Chinese, 874
  philosophy of, **558–569**
  self-deception and, 672–673
  Shen Dao on, 694
  of virtues (*dexing zhi zhi*), 867
  Wang Fuzhi on, 751–752
  and *wuwei*, 785
  Xunzi on, 825–828, 827
  Zhang Dongsun on, 859–860
Kobong, 104–105
Kojikii, 98

Kong Yingda, 141–142
  on authorship of *Zhongyong*, 888
  commentary on the *Book of Changes*, 892
  neo-Daoism in, 142
kong (emptiness). *See also* xi (*hsü*): emptiness
  Bodhidharma on, 20
  in Mahayana (Great Vehicle) Buddhism, 23
  Mindu on, 10
  Nagarjuna on, 15
  Sengzhao on, 10–11
  taixu (great emptiness or great void), 810
  ultimate substance as, 725
  xu distinguished from, 810
  in Zhiyi, 879
Kongjia, King, 486–487
Kongzi gaizhi kao (*Confucius as a Reformer*) (Kang), 338
Kongzi jiayu (*Home Sayings of Confucius*), 853
Kongzi xueshuo (*Doctrines of Confucius*) (Chen), 29, 74–75, 611
Korea
  Confucianism in, 102–107
  market economics and government in, 92–96
Köster, Herrmann, 700–701
Ku Hung-ming, 736
Kuhn, Thomas S., 759
Kuiji, 816, 818
Kumarajiva, 8, 12
Kunzhi ji (Luo), 420, 421
Kuo Hsi, 515
Kuo Hsiang. *See* Guo Xiang (Kuo Hsiang)
Kwong-loi Shun, 607

laboratory attitude, 298
Lacouperie, Terrien de, 738
laissez-faire theory, 390
"Lament for Qu Yuan" (Jia), 322–323
language and logic, **343–355**. *See also* philosophy of language
  ancient theory on, 848
  Heguanzi on, 292–293
  Huineng on, 313
  Hu Shu on, 299
  Jesuit influence on, 276
  Jizang on, 326–327
  in Ling Ting-kan, 404
  Lu Xiangshan on, 415–416
  Mohist theory of, 462–468
  in neo-Daoism, 215–216
  philosophy of mind and, 582–583
  and prescription in Confucius, 870
  rhetoric and, 126–135
  shenming and, 379–380
  shifei in, 703–706
  words and meaning debate in, 215–216
  in Xunzi, 72–73
  Zhiyi on necessity of, 879, 880
  Zhuangzi on, 210–211
Lankavatara sutra, 16
Lao Dan, 230, 873. *See also Laozi*
Lao Szu-Kwang (Lao Siguang), 505–509
Laozi. See Daodejing
Laozi (Lao Tzu), **355–361**. *See also Daodejing;* Daoism
  birth of, 224
  as Buddha, 10
  Celestial Masters on, 223
  in classical Daoism, 207–209
  Confucius's visit to, 60
  cosmogony of, 210–211
  cosmology of, 204
  on *dao*, 210–211
  influence on the *Wenzi* treatise, *781*
  life praxis in, 212–213
  on literature, 576
  on namelessness, 348–349
  on nonbeing, 8, 357–358
  on philosophy of mind, 584
  on *qing*, 621
  on the sage, 211
  on sagehood, 698
  on *sheng*, 695
  Tang emperors descended from, 143
  on *tian*, 728
  on *wuwei*, 784
  on *xu*, 809, 810
  on *you-wu*, 848–849
Later Mohist Logic, Ethics, and Science (Graham), 462
Lau, D. C., 76, 330, 736
  on moral discretion, 626
  on *zhong* and *shu*, 883–884
law. *See fa:* model, law, doctrine
learning. *See also* education
  Cheng Hao on, 39, 41–42
  Chen Xianzhang on, 35–36
  classical Confucianism on, 65
  evidential, of Gu Yanwu, 272–276
  Lu Xiangshan on, 414
  Qin era, 83–84
  Yang Zhu on, 841–842
  Zhan Roshui and Wang Yangming on, 853
  Zhu Xi on, 155–156, 900–902
learning movement, 32–34
"Learning of Eastern Zhejiang, The" (Zhang Xuecheng), 864
Le Blanc, Charles, 304
Lecture Notes on Dialectical Materialism, 427
Lectures on Politics (Yan Fu), 834
Lectures on the Heavens (*Zhutian jiang*) (Kang), 340
"Left and Right" (Gongsun), 494
legalism, **361–364**. *See also fa:* model, law, doctrine
  on culture, 527–528
  Guanzi on, 278
  Han Feizi and, 83, 285–288
  on language, 575
  Lu Xiangshan on, 417–418
  Shang Yang in, 680–682
  Shen Buhai on, 689–692
  Shen Dao in, 692–694
  in Vietnam, 173–177

Legge, James, 329, 331, 598, 735
on self-deception, 671
Leibniz, Gottfried, 598
lei (nature, correspondences), 515–516
Lenin, Vladimir, on Asiatic mode of production, 433–434
Levenson, Joseph R., 160, 392
Li Ao, 18, **385–387**
on authorship of *Zhongyong*, 888
on *cheng*, 37
du in, 47
"Essay on Restoring Nature," 38
Fuxingshu, 267
on self-cultivation, 147–148
on *xing*, 799, 800
Li Da, 433, 437
Li Daochun, 227
Li Dazhao, 163
Li Gong, 652, 834
Li Guangdi, 549–550, 779
Li Guo, 76–77, 842
Li Kui, 362
Li Linfu, 144
Li Qunfu, 182
Li Rong, 225
Li Shenzi, 592
Li Si, 83, 285, 363
Li Tien, 173
Li Tong, 896, 897
Li Yong, 122
Li Zhehou, 90, 436, 589
benti in, 718
on *ren*, 593
scientism and humanism and, 669
Li Zhi, 111, 779
Li Zhiji, 227–228
li: principle, pattern, reason, **364–370**, **631–638**
central to Wang Yangming and Zhan Roshui's debate on *gewu*, 852
Cheng Hao on, 39–42, 41
Cheng Yi on, 43, 45–46
defining, 72–73, 74–77.
kungli, 365–366
mingli, 365
Mou on, 171
rhetoric and, 130–132
shili, 367
and *ti-yong*, 721
Wan Guowei on, 757–758
wenli, 364–365
wuli, 367
xingli, 366–367
Yan Yuan on, 835
Zhang Xuecheng and, 863
Zhang Zai on, 865–866
Zhu Xi on, 898–899
li: rites or propriety, 369, **370–385**
classical Confucianism on, 65–66
in comparative philosophy, 53
in Confucian vision, 178–179
Confucius on, 62
culture as, 528
Dai on, 119
Dai Zhen on, 196–197, 199–200, 201–202
daotong and, 156
defining special obligations toward one's parents, 794
ennobling function of, 78
in ethics and law, 80–81
government and, 537–538
Guo Xiang on, 281–282
Han Feizi on, 286
heaven and, 206
Hu Shu on, 300
junzi and, 332–333
justification of, 78–79
in Korea, 102–106
Laozi on, 208
Ling Ting-kan and, 403–405
Luo Qinshun on, 420–421
Lu Xiangshan on, 414–415
metaphysical meaning in the Song period, 757
in Ming Confucianism, 113
moral philosophy and, 471–473
Mozi on, 454
in philosophy of the mind, 587
religions and, 640
in religious Daoism, 226, 227
rhetoric on, 129, 130–132
self-cultivation and, 807
supportive function of, 77–78
Tang, 143–144
Wang Yangming on, 765
Xunzi on, 67, 821, 824–825
Yijing and, 522–523
Zhu Xi on, 898–899
Liang Qichao (Liang Ch'i-ch'ao), **388–394**, 779, 856
on Gu, 116, 272
Kang and, 339
Levenson on, 160
Marxism of, 433
on morality, 163
Tan Sitong and, 709
Liang Qixiong, 826
Liang Shuming, 165, 166, **395–397**, 716, 855
benti in, 718
influence of Wang Yangming on, 780
Mao on, 434
on nature, 665
liangzhi (intuitive goodness), 844, 877–878
Liu Zongzhou on, 406–407
as seat of moral consiousness, 771
taixu and, 810–811
Wang Yangming and, 769–773, 770–771
liangzhi (intuitive goodness)
Xiong Shili and, 802–803
Liao, W. K., 285
Libbrecht, Ulrich, 658

liberalism, 592, 594–597, 596–597
liberation metaphysics, 451–452
Licong, 909
Lidai minghua ji (*Record of Famous Painters through the Dynasties*) (Zhang), 511, 512, 513
Liezi (Lieh Tzu), 206, **397–400**
Liezi, 397–400
  on Yang Zhu, 841
  Zhang and, 221
"Lifelong Filial Devotion to One's Parents" (Yan Fu), 831
life praxis, 212–213
li jianbai (separating hardness from whiteness), 260–261, 310–311, 465–467, 494–497
Liji (*Book of Rites*)
  on aesthetics, 4
  commentary by Wang Fuzhi, 749
  community in, 181
  cosmology in, 146
  Daxue from, 232
  Guodian bamboo slip text, 150
  influence on Wang Yangming, 771
  Kang on, 339–340
  on *li*, 77–79, 372
  "Monthly Commands," 146
  quinary sets in, 787
  seven feelings in, 104
  on *shiyi*, 845
  on *tianli* and *renyu*, 766
  on *xiao*, 793
  Xiong Shili on, 805
  Zhongyong originally part of, 888
Lik Kuen Tong, 605–606
Lil Zhi, 778
Lin Biao, 363
Lin Li, 908
Lin Yusheng, 590, 592
Lin Yutang, **400–402**, 736, 737
lineages, 34, 113, 155
Ling Qichaeo, 629
Ling Ting-kan, **403–405**
Lingbao bifa (*Ultimate Methods of Numinous Treasure*), 227
Lingrun
  and *icchāntika*, 818
  and Xuanzang, 819
linguistic theory. *See* language and logic
Linji, 21
Linji Chan school, 21
Linquan gaozhi (*The Lofty Truth of Forests and Streams*) (Guo), 511, 512, 515
Lin Yutang Trilogy, 401
lishi (dialectic of pinciple-phenomena), 881
literary criticism, 3, 577
  cosmology and, 193
  jingjie (material world), 580
  qingjing jiaorong (emotion and scene melt together), 579–580
  shihua (poetic talk), 577
  Tang, 142
literature
  aesthetics of, 2–3
  art writing, 515
  Lin Yutang and, 401–402
  scientism and, 667
  semantic creativity in, 3–4
  Tang on, 714
Liu, James J. Y., 758
Liu Bang, 240, 411
Liu Baonan, 317–318
Liu Bingzhong, 183, 185
Liu Cao, 227
Liu Fengli, 124
Liu Guan, 184
Liu Ji, 186
Liu Jin, 420
Liu Jishan. *See* Liu Zongzhou (Liu Tsung-chou)
Liu Qishan, 483–484
Liu Shao, 220, 307
Liu Shipei, 2, 629
Liu Shu-hsien. *See* Shu-hsien Liu
Liu Shuxian. *See* Shu-hsien Liu
Liu Xi, 340
Liu Xiang, 547, 821
  Guanzi and, 277–280
  on Liezi, 398
  on *xing*, 799
  on *xingming*, 492
Liu Xianzhang. *See* Liu Zongzhou (Liu Tsung-chou)
Liu Xiaobo, 437
Liu Xiaofeng, 591
Liu Xiaogan, 919
Liu Xie, 2
  on *de*, 237
  Wenxin diaolong (*Literary Mind-Heart Etching Dragon*), 4, 193, 576, 577, 861
  on *Wenzi*, *781*
  on Yang Xiong, 839
Liu Xin, 125, 338, 547–548
  Kang and, 552
  on Yang Xiong, 839
  Zhang Binglin on, 856
Liu Yiming, 228
Liu Yin, 183, 184, 688
Liu Yuxi, 146
Liu Zhi, 70
Liu Zhiji, 143–144, 548
  Shi tong, 861
Liu Zhuo, 144
Liu Zongyuan
  Chunqiu school and, 145–147
  history of, 548–549
  on literature, 147
Liu Zongzhou (Liu Tsung-chou), 32, **405–408**, 779, 835
  and *benti*, 719
  Huang Zongxi and, 307–308
  Hu Hong and, 296
  in lineage, 113

Liu Zongzhou (Liu Tsung-chou) (*Continued*)
on Wang, 114
Zhang Xuecheng and, 864
Liude (*Six Virtues*), 150, 152
liuxiang (six characteristics), 257
live universe theory, 395–397
lixue (principle) school
Chengs on, 41
compared with *xinxue*, 139
Dai Zhen and, 196–197
emergence of, 136
li in, 364–370
Liu Zongzhou and, 405–406
on *qiongli* (reality), 624
in Vietnam, 174
Lixue school. *See* Cheng-Zhu Confucianism
liyi fenshu: principle and manifestations, 369, **409–410**, 633
Mou on, 485
in Taiwan, 610
liyue (ritual and music), 647–648
Lo Guang (Lo Kuang), 609, 610, 611
Local History of Hezhou (Zhang Xuecheng), 862
Locke, John, 663
logic. *See also* language and logic
Chen Daqi and, 29–32
experimental, 502–503
Gongsun Long on, 270–271
Jizang on, 324–326
Yan Fu on, 833–834
Logic: A Primer (Jevons), 833
Lotus sutra
ekayana (one vehicle), 12–13
on enlightenment, 8–9
one vehicle on, 12–13, 254
Tiantai school on, 14
Zhiyi and, 879
Lu Ban, 661
Lu Cai, 142
Lu Chun, 145
Lu Ji, 3, 576
Lu Jia (Lu Chia), **411–413**
Lu Jiuling, 413–414
Lu Jiushao, 413–414
Lu Jiuyuan. *See* Lu Xiangshan (Lu Hsiang-shan)
Lü Kun, 112, 651
Lü Liuliang, 308
Lu Longpi, 779
Lu Nan, 775, 776, 777
Lü Qi, 34
Lu Shiyi, 652, 779
Lu Xiang, 834
Lu Xiangshan (Lu Hsiang-shan), **413–420**, 749, 900, 904–905
debate with Zhu Xi, 138–139
differences with Zhu Xi over pedagogy, 905–906
Luo Qinshun on, 420–422
meeting with Zhu Xi at Goose Lake Monastery, 905, 906
on mind identified with principle, 900
Mou on, 483–484
on *qiongli* (reality), 625
as Southern Song master, 136
Wang Yangming and, 112–113
on *Zhongyon*, 905
Lu Xiujing, 223
Lu Xuangong, 145
Lu Xun, 91
Lu Zheng, 761
Lü Zuqian, 184, 896, 904, 905
lü (deliberation), 772–773, 824–826, 825–826, 876
Lu Mu Gong wen Zisi (*Duke Mu of Lu Asking Zisi*), 150, 151
lunar myths, 488–490
Lunheng (*Balanced Discussions*) (Wang), 87–88, 745–747
Lunheng (*On Constancy*) (Wang), 576
Lunhua (*Discussing Painting*) (Gu), 511, 512
Lun wen (*Essay on Literature*) (Cao), 4
Lunyu (*Analects*)(Confucius), 61
classical Confucianism on, 65–66
on *dao*, 205
economic policy in, 238–239
encounter with Chu in, 69
ethical vocabulary in, 74–77
on government, 535–536
on *junzi*, 329–331
on law, 80–81, 248
on literature, 576
on metaphysics, 40
persuasion in, 54
on *qing*, 620
on the self, 675
on self-deception, 672
on *sheng*, 695
translation by Lau, 736
versions of, 61
Wang Bi on, 741
on Xia, 541–542
on *xiao*, 793
on *xin*, 886
xin (mind-heart) in, 796
Yang Xiong's *Fayan* patterned after, 837
zhengming in, 870
on *zhi*, 875
on *zhong*, 886
zhong and *shu* in, 882
on *zhongxin*, 885
Lun Yu bijie (*Random Notes on the Analects*), 291
Lunyu zhengyi (*Correct meanings of the Analects*) (Liu), 317–318
Luo Hongxian, 777, 778
Luo Longji, 629
Luo Qinshun (Lo Ch'in-shun), **420–422**, 775, 776, 835
on *li*, 113
textual scholarship of, 116
Zhu Xi and, 112
Luo Rufang, 111, 777, 778
Luo Zhenyu Wang Guowei wanglai shuxin, 755
Lüshi qunqiu, 545

xin in, 795
and Yangist movement, 798
on Yang Zhu, 841
Lu-Wang Confucianism, 749, 750, 900
criticized by Wang Fuzhi, 750
He Lin on, 168
li in, 368–369
Qing, 116
Xu Fuguan and, 813
Zhang genealogy, 120–121
Ly, Gabriel, 611
Ly Cam, 173
lyrical philosophy, 400–402

Machle, Edward J., 379, 380
MacIntyre, Alasdair, 501
Madhyamika Buddhism, 323–328
influence on Zhang Dongsun, 859
Zhiyi and, 879
Madhyamika-karika (*Middle Treatise*) (Nagarjuna), 14
Ma Duanlin, 185
Ma Rong, 742
Ma Su, 363
Mahakasyapa, 19
Mahayana (Great Vehicle) Buddhism
emptiness in, 23
Xuangzang's commitment to, 815
Zen as, 19–24
Mahayana samgraha (*She dacheng lun*) (attr. Asanga), 814
Maitreya, 815
Major, John, 190, 192, 787
Makra, Mary Lelia, 700–701
management, 603
"Manifesto for a Reappraisal of Sinology and Reconstruction of Chinese Culture," 480, 812
Manquan, Master, 22
manufacturing processes, 660
Mao Gong, 492
Mao Qiling, 834
Yan Roju and, 117
Mao Zedong (Mao Tse-tung), **423–431**. *See also* Marxism in China
Chiang Kai-shek and, 50
on class, 434–435
family under, 91
Feng on, 263
Liang Shuming and, 395, 396–397
Mou on, 480–481
twentieth-century Confucianism and, 166
Maoshi xu (*Great Preface*), 576
Marshman, Joshua, 735
martial arts, 4
Martin, W. A. P., 628–629
Marx, Karl, 663
Marxism
on history, 552–553
humanist, 588–590
influence of on Chinese thinkers, 736
sinification of, 425–427
in Vietnam, 176
Marxism in China, **431–438**
Confucianism and, 71
Confucianism in, 60
family/community and, 92
in Feng, 505
on history, 552–553
humanist, 592–594, 595–596, 665, 667, 669
Mao on, 424–430
neo-, 592
new left and, 596–597
philosophical self-transformation of, 588–590
philosophy of the mind of, 587
propositions in, 592–596
quanli (rights) and, 629–630
scientism and, 664–665, 667
Sun Yat-sen on, 707–708
twentieth-century Confucianism and, 166–168
mass culture, 596
Master Yichuan. *See* Cheng Yi (Ch'eng I)
materialism, 589
scientism and, 664–665
mathematics, 449–450
Mauss, Marcel, 235
Mawangdui silk texts, 355, 356, 538–539
May Fourth movement
as Chinese Enlightenment, 594
Chinese Enlightenment and, 668–669
Liang Qichao and, 388–394
Mao and, 423–431
neotraditionalism and, 591–592
twentieth-century Confucianism and, 163–164
westernization of, 90–91, 598
Mazu Daoyi (Ma-tsu Tao-i), 18, **438–440**
meditation of, 21
McGee, Douglas, 331
meaning
aesthetics and, 2–3
calligraphy and, 2–3
creativity in, 3–4
Medhurst, Walter, 735
medicine, 659–660
cosmology and, 192
Guanzi on, 279–280
"mutual conquests" series of the five phases and, 787
meditation
Huineng on, 313–314
Shenhui on, 700
Zen, 20–24
meide (beautiful, commendable), 73
Mencius (Menzi, Heng-Tzu), **440–449**
aesthetics and, 4
antinomianism of, 542–543
argumentation in, 55
and *benti*, 719
Chen Daqi on, 29, 30, 31
in classical Confucianism, 66–67
on connection between moral knowledge and action, 877

Mencius (Menzi, Heng-Tzu) (*Continued*)
critical of Yang Zhu, 841
on culture, 530
Dai Zhen on, 196–197, 199, 200–201
on *dao*, 205
egoism and, 244–245
epistemology of, 564
ethical intuitionism criticized by Yan Fu, 834
four beginnings in, 104, 530, 644
on government, 795, 807
on human nature, 31, 757
influence on Wang Fuzhi's political thinking, 753
Jia Yi influenced by, 321
on justifying *li*, 78
in *Liezi*, 398–399
on life or creativity, 696
Lu Xiangshan on, 414
on natural affection for parents, 794
on philosophy of mind, 583–584
on principle of reciprocity, 729
on *qi*, 616
on *qing*, 621
on *quan*, 159
on *ren*, 643–645, 729
on rights, 53
on sagehood, 697
on self-cultivation, 730, 808
on *shifei*, 704
syncretism of, 69–70
on *tian*, 727–728
on *xin*, 796
on *xing*, 798
on *yan*, 344
on *yi*, 729
Zhang Binglin on, 856
Zhan Roshui and, 853
on *zhi*, 875
on *zhong* and *shu*, 882
Mencius-Lu Xiangshan-Wang Yangming school and *benti*, *719*
Mencius on the Mind (Richards), 131
Meng Anpai, 226
Meng Huali, 777
Mengru xuean (Huang), 308
Mengzi (*Mencius*)
cheng in, 37
on egoism, 242
four beginnings in, 104
on government, 535–536
influence on *Wenzi*, 781
mentioning *xiushen*, 807
moral psychology and, 477
on people being the foundation of the state, 782
on *qiongli* (reality), 623–624
on the self, 675
translation by Lau, 736
on *xiao*, 793
on *xing*, 798
on *zhong*, 886
on *zhongxin*, 885
Mengzi shishuo (Huang), 307–308
Mengzi ziyi shuzheng (*A Study of the Philosophical Terms in Mencius*) (Dai Zhen), 201–202, 862
Mengzi ziyi shuzheng (*Verification of the Literal Meanings of Mencius*) (Dai), 403
mentality approach, 83
metaphysics, **449–452**, **723–726**
Cheng Hao on, 40–41
comparitive philosophy on, 54–57
Feng on, 259–261
in Jizang, 325
liberation, 451–452
moral vs. of morality, 508
in twentieth-century Confucianism, 164–166, 171
Xiong Shili and, 803–805
in Zhang, 137–138
Zhou Dunyi on link with ethics, 893
methodology
Xiong Shili and, 801–803
of Zhuangzi, 919
Mi Fu, 28, 511, 512
middle path
Huineng on, 312–314
Nagarjuna on, 8
paradigm shifts on, 12–13
Sengzhao on, 10–11
in Zen, 22–23
Mill, John Stuart, 393
On Liberty, 833
System of Logic, A, 833
Min Sun (Ziqian), 63
Minbao (*People's Tribune*), 706, 707
mind. *See* philosophy of mind
mind-heart. *See xin* (*hsin*): heart and mind
mind-substance philosophy, 167–168
Mindu, 10
Ming Taizu, Emperor, 107–108
syncretism of, 111–112
Ming Xiang, 814
ming chia. See names, school of (*ming chia, ming jia*)
ming (decree, destiny), 808
Mingi daifanglu (*Waiting for the Dawn: A Plan for the Prince*) (Huang Zongxi), 779
ming (names)
Hui Shi on, 310–311
language and logic and, 343–355
in Mohism, 460
Wang Chong on, 746
wuwei and, 785
yan compared with, 343–344
Zhuangzi on, 915
Mingru Xue'an (*Records of Ming Scholars*) (Huang), 36, 779
Ming wenan, 308
Ming wenhai, 308
Mingwen shoudu, 308
Mingxin pian (*On Enlightenment of the Mind*) (Xiong), 801

Mingyi daifanglu (*Plan for a Prince*) (Huang), 272, 308–309
Mirror to Song Prose (*Song wenjian*) (Lü Zuqian), 904
Mitin doctrine, 434
Mitsukuni, Tokugawa, 101, 660–661
modernization, 594–597. *See also* western culture
  Cheng on, 601–603
  in Japan, 101–102
  Liang Qichao on, 388–394
  tradition and, 94
modern texts school, 87–88
Mohism
  argumentation in, 491–497
  Confucian dialogues with, 69–72
  on culture, 527–528
  Hui Shi and, 911–912
  on language, 346, 571–573
  liyi fenshu compared with, 409–410
  on political disorder, 469–470
  Qian on, 618
  shifei in, 704–705
  on *tian*, 727–728
  on warfare, 543
  on *yan*, 345
  Zhou Dynasty, 640
Mohism: later (*jo jia, mo chia*), **461–469**
Mohism: the founder, Mozi (Mo Tzu), **453–461**, 825
  on human nature, 556–557
  on language, 571–572
  on philosophy of mind, 583
  on *qing*, 620–621
  on *you-wu*, 848
Mohist Canon, 461–469
Moho zhiguan (*The Great Calming and Awareness Treatise*) (Zhiyi), 881
monarchy, 754, 921
monism, 418
  versus skepticism in Zhuangzi, 915–916
  of Yan Yuan, 835
Montague, William P., 503
Montesquieu, Charles Louis de Secondat, 833
Moore, Charles, 598
Moore, G. E., 721
moral consciousness, 771–772
moral cultivation. *See also xioshen* (*hsiu-shen*): self-cultivation
  Cheng Yi on, 43–44
  Qing, 118–119
  Tongshu on, 893
moral discrimination, 770–771
moral failure, 877
  Wang Yangming on, 774
Moral Idealism (Mou), 480
morality
  aesthetics and, 3–4
  Chen Que on, 33
  comparative philosophy on, 52–53
  in ethics and law, 80–81
  four sprouts of, 56, 104, 457–458, 530, 644
  in the *junzi*, 333–335
  metaphysics of, 451–452
  Tang on, 714
  Tong on, 605–606
  in twentieth-century Confucianism, 162
moral philosophy, **469–475**
moral praxis, 452
moral psychology, **475–479**
moral self-cultivation, 729–730, 731–732
Morrison, Robert, 735
Mote, Friedrich, 607
Mou Zongsan (Mou Tsung-san), 15, **480–486**, 714, 716, 726
  benti in, 718
  Chen Daqi on, 29–30, 30–31
  on *dao*, 211
  disciple of Xiong Shili, 801
  Fang and, 249, 251
  Hu Hong and, 296
  Kant and, 31
  on *li*, 367–368, 369
  moral metaphysics of, 451–452
  on moral reason, 171
  on *ren*, 644
  twentieth-century Confucianism and, 166, 167
  on Wei-Jin, 365
  Xu Fuguan and, 812
  on *zhonghe* (equilibrium and harmony), 896
  on Zhu Xi, 901, 902
Mou Zongsan (Mou Tsung-san)(second), 590, 610
mourning, 380–383, 454, 460
Mozi (Mo Tzu), **453–461**, 840
  on egoism, 241–242
  on government, 534–535
  Hu Shu on, 300
  Mao on, 426
  on *shenming*, 700
  universal love and, 241–244, 763–764
Mu Konghui, 777
"multiple-factors" theory of knowledge of Zhang Dongsun, 858
Munakata, Kiyohiko, 514
Munro, Donald, 73, 235, 607
Murphy, Arthur, 633
Murray, D. L., 249
music. *See yue* (music)
"mutual conquest" order of the five phases, 787
"mutual production" order of the five phases, 787
My Country and My People (Lin), 400, 401
mysterious intuition, 810
mysticism, 55
  Han Feizi on, 285–286
  Shen Buhai on, 691
mythology and early Chinese thought, **486–490**. *See also* cosmology

Nagarjuna
  on emptiness, 15
  Madhyamika-karika (*Middle Treatise*), 14
  middle path of, 8

Nagarjuna (*Continued*)
two truths of, 11
Zhiyi and, 879
Naito Torajiro (Naito Konan), 861
names. *See ming* (names); *zhengming* (*cheng-ming*): rectifying names
names, school of (*ming chia, ming jia*), 461–469, **491–497**. *See also* Mohism
Gongsun Long and, 270–271
Hui Shi in, 309–311
on language, 573
Qian on, 618
Zhuangzi and, 209–210
Nangong Kuo (Zirong), 64
Nangong Yue, 144
Nanquan, Master, 23
Nanyue Huairang, 438–439
Nanzhong (southern Zhili) school of neo-Confucianism, 777
nationalism
Japanese, 101–102
Liang Qichao on, 390–392
Qian Mu on, 617–618
nation-building, 617–618
natural. *See ziran* (naturalness)
nature. *See also ziran* (naturalness)
in Buddhism, 8
calligraphy and, 26–27
Dai Zhen on, 196, 197–198
li and, 375–378
Li Ao on, 386
Shao Yong on, 684–685
in Zen, 23
nature vs. nurture
Cheng Hao on, 42
Cheng Yi on, 44
in Jia Yi, 321–323
Needham, Joseph, 188, 293, 657, 658
nei and *wai*, 722
neidan (inner alchemy), 222–223, 226–227, 228
Neijing (*Inner Classic*), 617
neo-Confucianism
benti in, 718, 719
canon redefined in, 135
Cheng Hao in, 39–43
Cheng on, 602
Cheng Yi in, 43–46
Ching in, 606
classic texts in, 46
and commentaries on the *Book of Changes*, 894
cosmology, 187
on culture, 531
Dai Zhen in, 195–202
on egoism, 246
Hu Hong and, 294–297
Hu Shu on, 301–302
in Japan, 97, 98–99, 99–100
in Korea, 102–107
Liang Shuming in, 395–397
on life or creativity, 696
li in, 366–367, 725
Liu on, 605
on *liyi fenshu*, 410
Luo Qinshun in, 420–422
metaphysics of *li* (principle) and *qi* (vital force), 725
Mou Zongsan in, 480–486
philosophy of the mind in, 586–587
on *qing*, 622
ritualism and, 650–651
on sagehood, 698
Shao Yong in, 683–689
Song, 135–139
Tang Junyi and, 716
twentieth-century, 164–166
in Vietnam, 174–177
Wang Fuzhi as summation of, 754
Wang Yangming's philosophy as climax of, 775
xinxue compared with *lixue*, 41
Xiong Shili as founder of, 801
Yijing in, 523
Yuan, 182–187
neo-Daoism, 789
Guo Xiang in, 280–284
influence of Xi Kang's thesis of "nourishing life," 792
Ruan Ji and, 653–656
Wang Bi and, 741
and *you-wu*, 849
neo-Marxism, 592
neo-Mohism, 352–354. *See also* Mohism: later (*jo jia, mo chia*)
neotraditionalism, 591–592, 594–597
Neville, Robert, 171
New Anthology and Critical Inquiry into Zhu Xi (Qian), 619–620
New Asia College, 712
New Asia Institute of Advanced Chinese Study and Research, 712
New Culture movement, 433
New Discussions (*Xinyu*) (Lu), 411–413
New Learning of Li (*Xin Lixue*) (Feng), 168
new life movement, 50
New Life (*Xin sheng ming*), 666
New manual for Women (*Bu xinfu pu*) (Lü), 34
"new text" classicism, 649–650
new text school. *See gongyang* (new text) school
New Trends (*Xin si chao*), 666
New Vienna School, 612
Nguhen Anh, 174
Nguyen Cong Tru, 175
Nguyen Hue, 174
Nguyen Khac Kieu, 176
Nguyen Lo Trach, 176
Nguyen Nhac, 174
Nguyen Truong To, 175–176
Nichomachean Ethics (Aristotle), 242
Nie Bao, 777, 778, 853
Nienhauser, William H., Jr., 2–3

Nietzsche, Friedrich
  Daoism and Buddhism and, 53–54
  Wang Guowei and, *755*
nihilism, 10–11
Nihongi, 98
"Nine Explanations" (Zhou), 114
nine-level aspectism, 715–716
"Nine Queries (Xu), 113–114
Ni Pu, 184
nirvana
  Jizang on, 326
  Mahayana idea of, 8
  in Zen, 22
Nirvana Sutra, 8, 9, 11, 12
Nivison, David S., 884
nominalism, 345, 346, 349–350
nonbeing. *See youwu* (*yu-wu*): being and nonbeing
norms, 474. *See also li:* rites or propriety
North, Helen, 126, 127, 133, 134
"no self" (*wu wo*), 710
noumenon, 756
numerology, 786
  cosmology and, 189–190
  Huang Zongxi on, 309
  of Shao Yong, 136, 137, 683–689
  Shen Buhai on, 691
Numinous Treasure (Lingbao), 222, 224–225

objective idealism, 420–421
Odin, Steve, 257
old text school, 125
Oliver, Robert, 126, 129
"On Contradiction" (Mao), 425, 426–428, 429, 434
"On Dispelling Self-Interest" (*Shisi lun*) (Xi Kang), 791
one-vehicle teaching, 12–13, 254
On Five Virtues, 644–645
"On Intelligence and Courage" (*Mingdan lun*) (Xi Kang), *790*
On Liberty (Mill), 833
On Making All Things Equal (Zhuangzi), 210–211
Onna Daigaku (*Learning for Women*) (Ekken), 100
"On Nourishing Life" (*Yangsheng lun*) (Xi), 790, 791
"On Ontological Inquiry and the Perplexities of Life" (Liang), 395
"On Our Salvation" (Yan Fu), 832
"On Power" (Yan Fu), 832
"On Practice" (Mao), 425, 426–428, 434
On Protracted War (Mao), 425
On Summum Bonum (Mou), 485
"On the Correct Handling of Contradictions among the People" (Mao), 434
On the Development of the Spirit of Chinese Humanism (Tan), 714
On the Establishment of the Moral Self (Tang Junyi), 712–713
"On the Speed of Change in the World" (Yan Fu), 832
On the Spirit of Chinese and Western Philosophies (Cheng), 603
ontohermeneutics, 602–603, 690
ontology
  Guo Xiang on, 281
  language and logic and, 349–350
  Lu Xiangshan on, 414–415
  Marxist, 435
  in neo-Daoism, 216
Ontology and Interpretation (Cheng), 603
"On Understanding the Nature of *Ren*" (Cheng), 40, 41, 42, 137
Open Society and Its Enemies (Popper), 509
Opium War (1842), 162
organic solidarity, 93
Original Discussion on Dao in Chinese Traditional Philosophy, An (Tang Junyi), 715
Original Discussion on Education in Traditional Chinese Philosophy, An (Tang Junyi), 715
Original Discussion on Human Nature in Chinese Traditional Philosophy, An (Tang Junyi), 715
Origin of Species (Darwin), 716
Outline of the History of Chinese Philosophy, An (Hu), 501–503
  Lao on, 505–506
Ouyang De, 777, 778
Ouyang Jiong, 515
Ouyang Xiu
  on authorship of *Zhongyong*, 888
  on history, 549
  on Song Confucians, 903
Ouyang Xun, 27–28
"Owl, The" (Jia), 322–323

painting
  calligraphy influences on, 28
  philosophy of, 511–517
Palmer, Richard, 315
Pan Gu, 362
panjiao (classification of teachings), 253–254
pan-naturalism, 716
pan-scientism, 716
paper, calligraphy and, 26
paradoxes
  of Hui Shi, 310–311
  in virtue, 236–237
  in Zen Buddhism, 22–23
parliamentary system, 855
Parliament of the World's Religions, 410
Parmenides, 558, 848
Parsons, Talcott, 90, 594
Passmore, John, 499
pathos, 133–134
pedagogy, 905–906
Peirce and Lewis's Theories of Induction (Cheng), 601
Peiyuan meng, 36
Peking University, 801
Pelikan, Jaroslav, 153
Peng Meng, 693
Peng Pu, 590
People's Republic of China. *See also* Marxism in China
  emigration from, 95
  internal migration in, 95

People's Tribune, 706, 707
perceptual illusions/deceptions, 827
perfection, 87
personal realization, 770
perspectival pluralism, 913
perspective flexibility, 916
persuasion, 54–55. *See also* argumentation
Phan Boi Chau, 176
Phan Chu Trinh, 176
Pheasant Cap master, 291
phenomenology, 612
Phenomenology of Spirit (Hegel), 873
Phenomenon and the Thing-in-Itself (Mou), 485
Philebus (Plato), 767
philosophical anthropology, 841
philosophical fantasy of Zhuangzi, 912
philosophical terms
  problems of translation, 737, 761
  use of transliterations, 737–738
"Philosophical Thought of Mozi, The" (Chen), 426
philosophy: recent trends in China since Mao, **588–597**
philosophy: recent trends in Taiwan, **608–613**
philosophy: recent trends overseas, **598–608**
philosophy in China: historiography, **499–510**
philosophy of action, 50–51
philosophy of art, **511–517**
philosophy of change, **517–524**
  Guo Xiang on, 282–283
  Han Yu on, 551
  Lo Guang on, 611
philosophy of culture, **525–533**
philosophy of governance, **534–540**
philosophy of history, **540–554**
Philosophy of History (Mou), 480, 482
philosophy of human nature, **554–558**
  Wang Fuzhi and, 750–751
philosophy of knowledge, **558–569**
philosophy of language, **569–575**, 665
  in comparative philosophy, 56
  qing in, 621
philosophy of literature, **576–581**
Philosophy of Man (Hang), 611
philosophy of mind, **581–588**
  benxin (original mind), 165–166, 803, 901
  Wang Yangming on, 764–769
  xu and, 810
  Zhang Zai on, 866–868
  Zhu Xi on, 897–898
"Philosophy of the Table" (Wang), 436
phonology, 275–276
physical appearance, 478–479
Physical Nature and Speculative Reason (Mou), 480, 482–483
pi, 804
Piaget, Jean, 190
Pirketh Abot, 316
Pivotal Essentials, As If in the Palm of Your Hand, to the Cheng weishi lun, The (Cheng weishi lun zhangzhong shuyao) (Kuiji), 816
Plaks, Andrew, 193
Platform Sutra of the Sixth Patriarch, 18, 23
Plato
  on egoism, 242
  epistemology in, 558
  humanism in, 663
  metaphysics of, 449
  Philebus, 767
  Republic, 56
Platonism, 345, 346, 350–352
plausible presumptions, 73, 131
"pluralistic interactionism" of Zhang Dongsun, 858
Poetics (Aristotle), 759
poetry, 576–581
  aesthetics of, 2–3
  calligraphy and, 28
  of Jia Yi, 322–323
  Lu Jia and, 411–413
  Ruan Ji and, 653–656
  Tang philosophy of, 142
"Pointing and Things" (Gongsun Long), 912
political economy, 831
political order
  cheng in, 38
  Chinese Enlightenment and, 668–669
  classical Confucianism on, 65
  Confucius influence on, 59
  Dong Zhongshu on, 239
  ethics and, 73–74
  Guanzi on, 277–280
  Gu Yanwu on, 272, 273–275
  Han Confucianism on, 84–89
  Heguanzi on, 292
  Huainanzi on, 304–306
  Huang Zongxi on, 308–309
  in Japan, 98
  Jia Yi on, 321–322
  junzi in, 132–134
  Laozi on, 359–360
  Liang Qichao on, 388
  Liang Shuming on, 395–397
  Lu Jia on, 411–413
  Lu Xiangshan on, 417–418
  Mao on, 428–429
  Mencius on, 440–441, 447–448, 458–460
  Ming, 107–115
  moral philosophy and, 469–471
  neo-Daoism on, 216–217, 219
  Qing theory on, 122–125
  quanli (rights) and, 628–630
  religious Daoism and, 223
  of Shang Yant, 680–681
  Shen Buhai on, 690–692
  Shen Dao on, 693–694
  Tang, 142–146, 146–147
  in twentieth-century Confucianism, 161–162
  western humanism and, 92–95
  xiao as basis for, 794

political philosophy
of Confucianism, 812
Wang Fuzhi and, 753–754
political reform, 709
politicization, 665
politics
Tang on, 714
Wang Bi and, 743–744
Wenzi on, 782
Popper, Karl, 509
Porkert, Manfred, 193
positivism, 610
postmodernism
comprehensive harmony and, 249–252
humanism and, 596, 667
recent Chinese philosophy and, 591
scientism and humanism and, 665
Powers, Martin, 513
practice (*xi*). *See also* action
linked to moral knowledge, 876
Yan Yuan's concern with, 835–836
in *zhi*, 874
Zhiyi and, 879
"pragmatic rationalism" of Zhang Dongsun, 858
pragmatism
Hu Shi and, 297–303
in Hu Shu, 298–303
Prajna (Mou), 484
praxis materialism, 589
Precepts for Daily Life in Japan (Ekken), 100
pregnant phrase, 1–2
"Preservation of Human Nature" (Yan Yuan), 835
"Preservation of Learning" (Yan Yuan), 835
Primordial Confucianism and Taoism (Fang), 250
Principia Ethica (Moore), 721
privacy. *See du* (solitude, privacy)
"Problem of the Self in the *Analects*, The" (Fingarette), 676
Process Metaphysics and Hua-yen Buddhism (Odin), 257
prognostication, cosmology and, 189–190, 192
Program of National Reconstruction (Sun), 708
"Prominent Learning" (Han), 287
psychology, moral, 475–479
Pure Land Buddhism, 13, 16–17, 880
Pyrrho of Elis, 558

Qian Dehong, 111, 777
Qian Mu (Ch'ien Mu), **617–620**, 712
on authorship of *Zhongyong*, 888
legalism and, 681
on *li*, 375
zeitgeist approach of, 83
Zhu Xi's influence on, 780
Qianfu Lun (Discourses by a Recluse) (Wang), 88
Qian Han shu (History of the Former Han Dynasty), 277
Qiankun yan (An Explication of the Meanings of Hexagrams Qian and Kun) (Xiong Shili), 801, 805
Qiao Xingjian, 909
Qiaoyu (Recorded Sayings from Mount Xiqiao) (Zhan Roshui), 854
qi (ch'i): vital force, **615–617**, 863
art and, 515
in beauty, 1
cheng and, 38
Cheng Hao on, 42
Cheng Yi on, 44
in cosmology, 190
Dai Zhen on, 198
Heguanzi on, 292–293
Huang Zongxi on, 308
in Korea, 102–106
li and, 366–367, 632
Luo Qinshun on, 420–421
Lu Xiangshan on, 414–415
in metaphysics, 449
in Ming Confucianism, 113
moral psychology and, 475–479
in neo-Daoism, 218–220
in philosophy of the mind, 585, 587
as science, 660–661
Shao Yong and, 684–685
Yan Yuan on, 835
Zhang Zai on, 865–866
Zhu Xi on, 898–899
qigong (energy exercises), 228
Qin Gui, 908
Qin Jiayi. *See* Ching, Julia
Qin regime, destruction of, 83–84
qing (ch'ing): reality or feeling, **620–622**. *See also* emotion; reality
in neo-Daoism, 217
of sages, 217
Zhu Xi on, 899–900
Qingda yi shi (Adversity and Success by Fortune), 150, 152
Qing imperial collection of the Complete Library of the Four Branches of Books, 737
qingjing jiaorong (emotion and scene melt together), 579–580
qingtan (pure conversation) movement, 214–215, 218–221
qingyi (pure criticism) movement, 214
Qingyuan, Master, 22
qiongli (ch'iung-li): exhaustive inquiry into principles, **623–625**
Qiu Jun, 651
Qiushu (A Book of Emergency) (Zhang Binglin), 856
qiyun (spirit consonance), 512–515, 516
Qu Qiubai, 433
Quan Deyu, 147
quan (ch'üan): weighing circumstances, **625–627**
quan (judgment), 157–159
quanli (ch'üan-li): rights, **628–630**
Chiang on, 50–51
in comparative philosophy, 52–53, 54
government and, 539–540
Hu Shu on, 302
Kang Youwei on, 337–338
legalism and, 681–682
Liang Qichao on, 390

quanli (*ch'üan-li*): rights (*Continued*)
in Marxist humanism, 593
Mencius on, 447–448
western vs. Chinese concepts of, 93, 94
Quanzi, 796
Queen Srimala Sutra, 8
Quine, W. V., 559
qun (group), 388–389

Radahkrishnan, S., 250
Ran Yong, 63
rationality
in comparative philosophy, 56
in Jizang, 325
philosophy of mind and, 583
rhetoric and, 130–132
western vs. Chinese, 90
Razan, Hayashi, 99
"Reading Notes" (Mao), 428–429
ready-made *liangzhi*, doctrine of the, 778
realism
in Dai Zhen, 198–200
language and, 345, 346
in neo-Mohism, 352–354
New Vienna School of Constructive, 612
reality
in comparative philosophy, 55–56
Fazang on, 256–257
knowledge and, 560, 561–562
language and logic and, 343–355
Mencius on, 623–624
Sengzhao in, 679
Wang Yangming on, 625
Zhiyi on, 881
Zhu Xi on, 624–625
reason and principle, **631–638**. *See also li:* principle, pattern, reason
Mou on, 480
in neo-Mohism, 353–354
Reason and Virtue: A Study of the Ethics of Richard Price (Cua), 603
reciprocity. *See zhong* (*chung*) and *shu:* loyalty and reciprocity
recommendations of Zhuangzi, 916–918
Record of Suburban and Sacrificial Offerings in the Tang (*Da Tang jiaosi lu*) (Wang), 145
Record of the Loyang Temples, 17
Record of the Western Regions (*Xiyu ji*) (Xuanzang), 814
Records of the Historian (Qian)
cosmology in, 188–189
on legalism, 361
on Zhuangzi, 209
"Rectifying Stubborness" (*Tingwan*) (Zhang Zai), 868
Reestablishment of the Spirit of Humanism, The (Tang), 714
reflection, 179, 477, 896
Reflections on Things at Hand (Chan), 600
reform of a hundred days, 162–163, 666, 706
"Refutation of Han Yu" (Yan Fu), 832
"Refutation of Kang Youwei's Political Views" (Zhang), 855
regicide, 448
Reischauer, Edwin, 95
relationships
Lu Xiangshan on, 414–415
ren and, 644–645
self-deception and, 672
relativity, theory of, 559
reliabilism, 562
religions, **638–642**
Daoism, 222–229
Hu Shu on, 301
li as, 375–380
Tang on, 714
in twentieth-century Confucianism, 161–162
Ren Jiyu, 263
Ren Zhouxuan, 433
Renfu. *See* Liang Qichao (Liang Ch'i-ch'ao)
Rengong. *See* Liang Qichao (Liang Ch'i-ch'ao)
ren (*jen*): humanity, **643–646**
Chan on, 600
Chen Daqi on, 30–31
Cheng Hao on, 40–42, 137–138
classical Confucianism on, 65
in Confucian vision, 178–181
Confucius and, 729
Confucius on, 62–63
Dai Zhen on, 198
daotong and, 156
defining, 72–73, 74–77
Hu Hong on, 296
human nature and, 554–555
junzi and, 331–332
Laozi on, 207–208
li and, 371
Lu Jia on, 412–413
in Marxist humanism, 593–594
Mencius on, 440–448
Mohist theory on, 462
in moral philosophy, 469–475
moral philosophy and, 471–473
rhetoric on, 128–129
self-cultivation and, 807
in Song Confucianism, 135
Wang Yangming and, 762–764, 773
Wenzi and, 783
Xu Fuguan on Confucian idea of, 812
Yijing and, 522–523
Zhu Xi on, 409–410
Renpu manual, 407
Renshixin zhi pipan (*A Critique of the Cognitive Mind*) (Mou), 480
Renwu zhi (*The Study of Human Abilities*) (Liu), 220
renxin (*daoxin*), 763
Renxue (*An Exposition of Benevolence*) (Tan Sitong), 709
Renzhong. *See* Hu Hong (Hu Hung)
"Reply to Master Hengzhu's Letter on Calming Human Nature" (Cheng), 42
Republic (Plato), 56, 242

Rescher, Nicholas, 73, 507
revealer, *tian* as, 727
Revive China Society, 706
Revolutionary Alliance, 706, 707
Revolutionary Strategy (Sun), 708
"Rhapsody on the Zither" (*Qinfu*) (Xi Kang), 789
rhetoric, 126–135
Rhyme-Prose about Meditations on the Mystery, 193
Ricci, Matteo, 90, 275, 610
Richards, I. A., 131
rightness. *See yi* (rightness, appropriateness)
rights. *See quanli* (*ch'üan-li*): rights
Rinzai school, 21
ritualism, **646–653**. *See also li:* rites or propriety
River Elegy, 594
Rizhi lu (*Record of Knowledge Gained Daily*) (Gu), 274
Rousseau, Jean-Jacques, 389, 663
Royce, Josiah, 154, 634, 858
Ruan Ji (Juan Chi), **653–656**
  on freedom, 220
  neo-Daoism of, 218
Ruan Kan, 790–791
Ruan Yuan, 124, 652, 737
rulers. *See also* government
  Guanzi on, 277–280
  Guo Xiang on, 283
  Huainanzi on, 304–306
  Liang on, 392–394
  Lu Jia on, 411–413
  mandate of heaven and, 541–545
  Mao on, 423–424
  Mencius on, 447–448
  monarchy, 754, 921
  Mozi on, 454
  mythology and early thought on, 486–487
  sagehood and, 698
  Shao Yong on, 686–687
  Wang Bi on sage ruler, 743
  Xunzi on, 821
ru (naturalness)
  classical Confucianism on, 64–65
  distinction between "vulgar" and "true," 838
running script, 26
Rupakaya (*Body of Form*), 14
rural reconstruction movement, 396
Russell, Bertrand, 598, 736, 771
Ruyao jing (*Mirror of Entering the Divine Drug*), 227

Sacred Books of China (Legge), 735
sage. *See sheng:* sage; *shengren* (sage)
Said, Edward, 596
salvation, 224–225
sameness in nature, theory of, 751
Sandong zhunang (*A Bag of Pearls from the Three Caverns*) (Wang), 226
Sang Hongyang, 363
Sanlun Madhyamika Buddhism, 678–680
Sanlun Xuanyi (*The Profound Meaning of Three Treatises*) (Jizang), 324
sanmin zhuyi (three people's principles), 50, 707–708
Santian neijie jing (*Inner Explanation of the Three Heavens*), 224
sanwen (free prose), 2–3
San Wui Commercial Society (SWCS), 36
Schiller, Friedrich, 758
scholastic debates, 747–748
school of Chen Xianzhang (neo-Confucianism), 775
school of mind, 622
school of names. *See* names, school of (*ming chia, ming jia*)
school of Nyaya, 802
school of thought, 294–297
School of Yue and Min (Guangtong and Fujian), 777
Schopenhauer, Arthur
  in Liang, 395–396
  Wang Guowei and, 755, 756, 757, 759
Schumacher, E. F., 360
Schumpeter, Joseph A., 812
Schwarcz, Vera, 90
Schwartz, Benjamin, 171, 424–425, 593, 607, 796
Science, Philosophy, and Life (Fang), 249
Science and Civilisation in China (Needham), 658
science and technology, **657–663**. *See also* cosmology
  Confucianism and, 71
  Hu Shu on, 300–302
  in Taiwan, 612
  Tang on, 714
  Tang view of, 144
  in twentieth-century Confucianism, 163
  Yijing in, 523–524
scientific method, 300–302
scientific realism, 345, 346, 352–354
scientism and humanism, **663–669**
  pan-scientism, 716
sculpture, 324
seal scripts, 26
Sein und Zeit (Heidegger), 873
self
  in calligraphy, 27–28
  in Confucianism, 674–677
  "no self" (*wu wo*), 710
  as primary concern of Chinese philosophers, 896
  Tang on, 713–714
  Yang Zhu on, 841
  Zhunagzi on, 913
self-control, 211
self-cultivation. *See xioshen* (*hsiu-shen*)*:* self-cultivation
self-deception, **670–678**
  in *Daxue*, 232–233
self-interest. *See also* egoism in Chinese ethics
  Confucian golden rule on, 91–92
  selfishness vs., 242
selfishness
  Dai Zhen on, 200–201, 201–202
  gewu and *zhizhi* and, 269
  Huainanzi on, 305
  self-interest vs., 242
self-transformation, 219, 281–282

semiotics, 531–532
Sengzan, 17
Sengzhao (Seng-chao), 8, **678–680**
  on enlightenment, 9
  middle path of, 10–11
senses
  Gongsun on, 351–352
  moral psychology and, 475–476
  philosophy of mind and, 582
Separate Notes on the Cheng weishi lun (*Cheng weishi lun biechao*) (Kuiji), 816
separating hardness and white, 310–311, 494–497
  Mohist theory on, 465–467
separating hardness from whiteness, 260–261, 310–311, 465–467, 494–497
Seventeen Article Constitution, 97, 98
"seven worthies of the bamboo grove," 789, 791
sexuality, 235
Shagshu (*Book of History*), 753–754
shamanism, 700–701
shame (*chi*)
  li and, 375
  moral philosophy and, 472, 474
  self-deception and, 673
shan (good)
  Chen Que on, 33
  Xunzi's use of, 822
Shang Yang, **680–682**
  on ethics and law, 81
  fa and, 247
  on history, 544
  legalism of, 362
  Mao on, 423
  "Six Lice," 287
Shangqing (Highest Purity) school, 222, 224
Shangshu. See Shujing
Shangun shu, 536–537
Shanshui Chunquan ji (*Chunquan's Collected Notes on Landscape*) (Han), 511
Shao Jinhan, 552
Shao Yong (Shao Yung), **683–689**, 900
  Daoism in, 136
  Huang Zongxi on, 309
  in neo-Confucianism, 39
  as Northern Song master, 136–137
  numerology of, 136, 137
Shen Buhai (Shen Pu-hai), **689–692**
  on government, 537
  legalism of, 362
  on *xingming*, 492
Shen Dao (Shen Tao), **692–695**
  legalism of, 362
  on *wuwei*, 784
Shen Nong, 542
Shen, Vincent, 612
Shen Yue, 12
shendu (vigilance in solitude), 404
  Liu Zongzhou on, 406–407
  moral psychology and, 477
sheng: life or creativity, **695–697**
sheng: sage, **697–699**
  Feng on, 260
  Hu Hong on, 295
  in neo-Daoism, 217
  ren and, 644–645
  Shao Yong on, 686–687
  Wang Bi on, 744
  Wang Yangming vision of, 760
  Wenzi on, 782
  in *Zhongyong*, 890
  Zhou Dunyi on, 893
shengren (sage)
  Huainanzi on, 305
  junzi compared with, 132–134, 335
  Laozi on, 211
  Li Ao on, 385–387
  Lu Jia on, 412
  Mencius on, 460
  shenming in, 701
  Zhuangzi on, 211–212
shengren (sagely person), 872
Shengxian gaoshi zhuan (*Biographies of Sages and Extraordinary Men*) (Xi Kang), 790
Shengxue gewu tong (Zhan Roshui), 853
shengyun (assigned sounds)
  aesthetics and, 2
Shenhui, 17, **699–700**
  on middle way, 22–23
Shenjian (*Extended Reflections*) (Xun), 89
shenming: gods or godlike intelligence, **701–703**
  li and, 378–380
shenren (marvelous person), 872
shen (spirit-energy)
  li and, 378–380
  in philosophy of the mind, 585
Shenxiu, 17
  on *dharma*, 20–21
  on enlightenment, 21
  Huineng and, 312
  Zen school and, 18
Shenzi (Shen), 689
Shi ben (Han), 286–287
shifei (*shih-fei*)*:* this and not, right and wrong, **703–706**, 848
  in language philosophy, 571–572
  philosophy of mind and, 584
  Xunzi on ethical, 827–828
  Zhuangzi on, 913
shi (genuineness)
  as antonym of *xu*, 809
  self-deception and, 670–671
Shih-hsio Yen, 515
shihua (poetic talk) criticism, 577
Shijing (*Book of Poetry* or *Book of Odes*)
  aesthetics and, 1–2, 4
  commentary by Wang Fuzhi, 749

translation by Davis, 735
translation by Legge, 735
use of term *tian* in, 727
xin in, 795, 796
Shiji (Sima), 546–547, 821
Shili gongfa (*Substantial truths and General Laws*) (Kang), 337–338
Shili yuyao (*Important Sayings by Hsiung Shih-li*) (Xiong Shili), 801
Shils, Edward, 154
shingaku (heart and mind), 99–100
Shinto, 97, 99
Shipin (Zhong), 577
Shitao, 511, 512, 513
Shitong (*General Principles of Historiography*) (Liu), 548
Shi tong (Liu Zhiji), 861
shixiang (true reality), 881
shixue (evidential research), 779
Shiyan zhuyi (*Pragmatism*) (Murray), 249
Shizhi. *See* Hu Shi (Hu Shih)
shu. *See zhong* (*chung*) and *shu:* loyalty and reciprocity
Shu-hsien Liu, 155, 171, 604–605, 610
Shujing (*Book of Documents/Book of History/Book of Historical Documents*)
on numerology, 786
translation by Medhurst, 735
use of term *tian* in, 727
Wang Fuzhi commentary on, 749
shu (methods), 690
Shun, 542
life and creativity and, 695
practicing the mean through his life, 889
wuwei and, 217
"Shuo Commentary," 517
Shuogua (Discourse Commentary), 623
Shuowen jiezi (*Discourse on Language*) (Xu), 2, 340, 371, 639, 795
shu (reciprocal consideration with compassion), 68
Shushin, Gido, 99
sijiao (four teachings), 879
sijujiao (four maxims), 777
Śīlabhadra, 815, 819
silk manuscripts, 355, 356, 538–539
"silver rule," 729
Sima Chengzen, 226, 386
Sima Guang, 549, 840, 903
Sima Qian, 821, 888
on Buddhism, 148
cosmology in, 188–189
on ethics and law, 81
on Han, 285–286
on Huang-Lao school, 921
on Laozi, 355
on legalism, 361
Records of the Historian, 209
Shiji, 546–547
on Wuji, 237
on Zhuangzi, 209
Sima Yi, 653
Singer, Marcus, 180
Singer, Peter, 455
Si Nhiep, 173–174
"Sinic World in Perspective, The" (Reischauer), 95
Sivin, Nathan, 190, 657, 658
siwu (four nothingnesses), 111, 778
six arts of Confucius, 59
Sixfold Compendium of Government of the Tang (*Da Tang liudian*), 144
"Six Lice" (Shang), 287
"Sixteen-Character Transmmission of the Mind-and-Heart," 105
"Sixty Articles on Work Methods" (Mao), 429
skeptical perspectivalism, 912–913
skepticism
versus dogmatic monism in Zhuangzi, 915–916
Wang Chong and, 745
Zhunagzi and, 919
slavery, 553
Smith, Adam, 390, 833
Smith, Huston, 96
Smith, Richard, 191
social and political philosophy. *See* political order; social order
social class
in Japan, 100
Mao on, 434–435
Marxist theory on, 431–438
social contract, 389
social Darwinism, 388–390
socialism, 811. *See also* communism; Marxism
social order. *See also* government; political order
cheng in, 38
Gu Yanwu on, 274–275
Han Feizi on, 286–287
Hu Shu on, 302
Laozi on, 207–208, 359–360
law in, 247–248
li in, 372
Lu Xiangshan on, 416–417
ritualism and, 647–653
Shao Yong on, 686–687
in twentieth-century Confucianism, 162
So Kyong-dok, 103
"Solitary Indignation" (Han), 285
Song Hon, 105–106
Song Jiaoren, 707
Song Lian, 107–108
Song Meiling, 50
Song Xiangfeng, 124
Song Zhong, 839
Song Confuciansim, 903–904
Song Meng Dongye xu (*Letter to Meng Tungyeh*) (Han), 3
Song shi, 909
Sontoku, Niomiya, 100
Sorai, Ogyu, 101

soul
Buddha-nature and, 11–12
Buddhism on, 10–11
immortal, 9, 10–11, 381, 790
Source Book in Chinese Philosophy, A (Chan), 500, 600, 720, 736
Sources of Chinese Tradition (de Bary, Chan, Watson), 736
Soviet Russia in China (Chiang), 49
Soviet Union, collapse of, 90
specialization, 917
Spencer, Herbert, 300
Yan Fu and, 831, 832
Spirit of Chinese Art, The (*Zhongguo yishu jingshen*) (Xu Fuguan), 812–813
Spirit of Laws (Montesquieu)
translated by Yan Fu, 833
Spirit of Value of Chinese Culture, The (Tang Junyi), 713
spirits, 640, 700
spiritual transformation (*shenshua*), 782–783
spontaneity
in calligraphy, 28
Chen Xianzhang on, 36
human nature and, 555–556
Laozi on, 349, 358–359
Spring and Autumn Annals. See Chunqiu fanlu (*Spring and Autumn Annals*)
Stalin, Joseph
five-stage theory, 433–434
Standard History of the Han (*Hanshu*) (Ban), 321
standard script, 26
state analogy of cosmology, 188–189
state Buddhism, 9–10. *See also* Buddhism
"Steer Clear of Being Noble" (Wang), 595–596
Sthiramati, 818
stoicism, 693–694
story telling, 2–3
Study of Sociology, The (Spencer), 832
Su Shaozhi, 436, 588–589
Su Shi, 2, 28, 511–512, 515, 903–904
on Buddhism, 70
on calligraphy, 27
Lü Zuqian and, 904
in Yuan Confucianism, 182
substance, translation of *ti* as, 721
Substance of Mind and the Substance of Nature, The (Mou), 483
Sun Bin, 362
Sun Guoting, 26, 27
Sun Simiao, 226
Sun Wen. *See* Sun Yat-sen
Sun Wu, 362
Sun Yat-sen, 163, **706–708**
Chiang Kai-shek and, 48, 49, 50, 51
on rights, 629
Zhang Binglin and, 856
Sun Yirang, 462
Sun Zhongshan. *See* Sun Yat-sen
Sung Yuan xuean (*Records of the Sung and Yan Scholars*) (Huang Zongxi), 779
superstition, 377–378
Supreme Principles Governing the World (Shao), 137
sustainable development, 96
sustainer, *tian* as, 727
Sutra Spoken by the Sixth Patriarch from the High Seat of the Treasure of the Law, 21, 314
syncretism
Dong Zhongshu in, 238
Heguanzi on, 293
in Japan, 101
of Ming Taizu, Emperor, 111–112
in religious Daoism, 222–223, 227–228
Tang Confucianism, 140
in Vietnam, 173–177
in Warring States era, 83
synonyms, 3
System of Logic, A (Mill), 833

taihe (great harmony), 866
taiji (the great ultimate), 724
knowledge and, 563
Lo Guang on, 611
time and timeless and, 730
Tong on, 605
Wang Fuzhi on, 750
in the *Xici* of the *Yizhuan*, 718
in Yuan Confucianism, 186
Zhou on, 41, 136
Zhu Xi and, 899
Taiji tushuo (*An Explanation of the Diagram of the Great Ultimate*) (Zhou), 891–893, 906
Taijitushuo (Zhou), 719
Taika reforms, 98
Taiping Dao, 88, 641–642
taiping (great peace), 222, 223, 874
Taiping jingi (*Scripture of Great Peace*), 223, 641
taiping shi (age of universal peace), 391–393
Taishi, Shotoku, 97, 98
Taishi zhen (Xi Kang), 792
Taiwan
Chiang Kai-shek and, 49–51
market economics and government in, 92–96
recent philosophy in, **608–613**
twentieth-century Confucianism in, 168–169
Taixuan jing (*Canon of Supreme Mystery*) (Yang Xiong), 837–838
Taixue (Grand Imperial Academy), 85–86
taixu (great emptiness or great void), 810, 865
Tai-yan. *See* Zhang Binglin (Chang Ping-lin)
Taiyi jinhua zongzhi (*Secret of the Golden Flower of Great Unity*), 228
Taiyi sheng shui (*The Ultimate Generating Water*), 230, 231, 356, 357–358
Guodian bamboo slip text, 150
Taizhou school, 111–112, 777, 779
Taizong, Emperor, 141
Taizu, Emperor, 9
Takehiko, Okada, 111

talent
  neo-Daoism on, 219–220
  Tong on, 605–606
Tan Sitong (T'an Ssu-t'ung), **709–712**
  on family, 91
  Kang and, 339
  legalism of, 363
  on *ren*, 391, 646
  Wang Fuzhi's influence on, 754
Tang Junyi, 168, 609–610, **712–716**
  Chen Daqi on, 29–30
  disciple of Xiong Shili, 801
  Fang and, 249, 251
  on *li*, 367, 369, 383, 631, 635
  Mou and, 480
  twentieth-century Confucianism and, 166, 167–168
  Wang Fuzhi's influence on, *754*
  Xu Fuguan and, 812
Tang Shu, 113
Tang Shunzhi, 777
Tang Yijie, 590
Tang Zhen, 123
Tang Zhongyou, 184, 904
Tang era
  Buddhism in, 13, 15–17
  Confucianism in, 13
  Daoism in, 225–226
Tang Yu zhi dao (*The Way of Tang Yao and Yu Shun*), 150, 152
Tantai Mieming (Ziyu), 63
tao. See dao (*tao*)*:* the way
Tao-fu, 20
Tao Hongjing, 224, 660
tathagatagarbha (pure mind), 253–258
technological determinism, 665
temporal theory of ontocosmology, 730–732
Temür, 183
tendency (*shi*), 753
Terms Explained (*Beixi ziyi*) (Chen Chun), 908, 909
Tertullian, 883
Tetsujiro, Inoue, 101
Tetsuro, Watsuji, 97
"Theory of Dual Evolution, The" (*Jufen jinhua lun*) (Zhang Binglin), 855
theory of harmony and integration, 589
theory of the "four negatives" (*siwu*), 111, 778
Theses on Feuerbach (Marx), 436
Thirty Stanzas (Vasubandhu), 814
Thomas Aquinas, 879
Thousand-Character Essay, 26
"three ages" theory, 711
three eras theory, 338–339
"threefold contemplation" (*sanguang*), 879
three natures, 818
"Three Peoples' Principles" (Sun), 50, 707–708
"Three Profound Treatises" (Ruan), 654
Three Schools of Two Truths (Zhou), 11
"Three Traditions of Philosophical Wisdom" (Fang), 249
three treatises school, 366
"three treatises" school of Buddhism, 802
"three truths" (*sandi*), 879
three "universal virtues," 890
ti: body or embodiment, **717–720**
  benti as, 718–719
  entailing *yong*, 724
  moral psychology and, 475–479
  Wang Yangming use of, 768
  Xiong Shili on, *804*
  Yang Zhu on, 841
  and *yong* (*t'i* and *yung*)*:* substance and function, **720–723**
  zhong identified as, by Zhu Xi, 882
Tianguan wenda (*Recorded Questions and Answers from the Tianguan Academy*) (Zhan Roshui), 854
tianli (heavenly principle)
  as alternative term for *ren*, 772
  contrasted with human desires (*renyu*), 766
  li and, 636
  ritualism and, 651
  Wang Yangming and, 768
Tian lun (Xunzi), 526
tianming (mandate of heaven)
  gods and, 639–640
  life and creativity and, 695–696
  as mandate to rule, 541–542
  Mencius on, 441–442, 447–448
  in neo-Daoism, 217
Tian Pian, 693
tianren heyi, 847
Tianshi dao, 641–642
Tiantai (Lotus, Saddharmapundarika) Buddhism, 13–15, 879
tian (*t'ien*)*:* heaven, **726–728**
  in classical Confucianism, 67–68, 205–206
  Dai Zhen on, 199
  de and, 235
  Dong Zhongshu on, 239–240
  government and, 534–540
  in Han Confucianism, 85
  li and, 374, 375–376
  Liu Zongzhou on, 406
  Lu Jia on, 411–413
  Lu Xiangshan on, 415
  mechanistic theory of, 411–413
  Mencius on, 458–460
  as nature, 375–378
  Shen Dao on, 693–694
  in Tang Confucianism, 140–142, 142–146
  in Vietnamese Confucianism, 174
  Wang Chong on, 747
  Wang Fuzhi on, 750
  Xunzi on, 825
  Zhou dynasty on, 639–640
Tianxia junguo libing shu (Gu), 274
time and timeliness (*shizhong, shih-chung*), **728–734**
Ting Weng-chiang, 858
tiyan (coming to know by intimate, personal experience), 717
tiyong heyi or *tiyong buer*, 725, 804

Tiyong lun (*A Treatise on Substance and Fuction*) (Xiong Shili), 801
ti yong (*t'i-yung*) metaphysics, **723–726**, 764–765
T'oegye, 103–104, 105–106
Togai, Ito, 101
Toghon Temür, 185
Tojung, 816
"Tongcheng" school of mid-Qing writers, 862
tong (continuity, unity), 550
Tonghu or *Yi tongshu* (*Penetrating the Book of Changes*) (Zhou Dunyi), 891
Tonglin movement, 779
Tong zhi (Zheng Qiao), 861
totalism, 15–17
Toulmin, Stephen, 674–675
tradition. *See daotong* (*tao-t'ung*) (tradition)
Tradition (Shils), 154
Tran Te Xuong, 176
transcendence
  Ly on, 611
  in neo-Daoism, 216–217
Transcendental Wisdom Sutras, 8
translation
  of *cheng*, 913
  and its problems, **734–739**
  of philosophical terms, 737, 761
  of Sanskrit Buddhist texts, 814
  Yan Fu as translator, 831
  of Zhuangzi, 914
"Treatise on Bibliography" (Ban), 492
Treatise on Calligraphy (*Shu Pu*) (Sun), 26
"Treatise on *Ren*, A" (Zhu Xi), 898
"Treatise on What Yanzi Loved to Learn, A" (Cheng), 42, 43, 894
trend of the times, following
  Huang-Lao school and, 922
Triṁśīkā, 817–818
True Meaning of the Five Classics (*Wu jing zhengyi*), 141–142, 143
True Purity sect, 641
truth
  characterictics of metaphysical truth, 804
  in comparative philosophy, 55–56
  Jizang on, 326–327
  Xiong Shili on, 803–804
Tu Weiming, 102, 171, 606–607, 760, 780
  anthropocosmic Confucian humanism of, 590
  on Cheng Hao, 40–42
  on the self, 676
Tuhua jianwen zhi (*Record of Things Seen and Heard with Regard to Painting*) (Guo), 511
Tunghai University, 811
Twofold Mystery (Chongxuan) school, 225–226
twofold truth
  Huineng on, 313
  Jizang on, 325, 326–327

Ugye, 105–106
Understanding Words (Hu), 294, 295
United Front, 49
United Nations World Conference on Human Rights, 630
United States, twentieth-century Confucianism in, 169
unity
  of heaven-nature and human, 890
  of knowledge and action (*zhixing heyi*), 760, 769
  of substance and function, 724–725
universal love. *See jian ai* (universal love)
universals, 351–352
universe. *See also* cosmology
  xu ultimate root of, 810
  Zhou Dunyi on, 892
"useful," 912–913
utilitarianism
  in Kan Youwei, 340–341
  of language, 571–572
  Liang Qichao on, 390
  in Mozi, 453–456

values, Mencius on, 446–447
Vasubandhu, 814, 818
Vatican II, 71
Veritable Record of the Yingzong Emperor (Wu), 185
Vienna Circle, 508–509
Vietnam, Confucianism in, 173–177
Viet Nho, 174–177
Vimalakirti, 8
Vimalakirti Sutra, 8
virtue. *See de* (*te*): virtue or power
virtue ethics
  comparative philosophy on, 52–53
  Confucianism as, 72–79
  of Cua, 604

Waiting for the Dawn: A Plan for the Prince (Huang), 122–123
Waley, Arthur, 76, 330, 371, 735
Wan Sitong, 113, 834
Wang Anshi, 363, 903, 904
  Lu Jiuyuan on, 906
  Lu Xiangshan on, 418
  Zhang Zai disagreement with, 865
Wang Bi (Wang Pi), 8, 718, **741–745**
  Cheng Hao and, 40
  commentaries by, 215–216, 355
  death of, 789
  neo-Daoism of, 215–219
  on words and meaning, 215
  Xi Kang compared to, 792
  on *xu*, 810
  yi-li (meaning-principle) school and, 520–521
  on *youwu*, 849
Wang Bo, 909
  on authorship of *Zhongyong*, 888
  follower of Zhu Xi, 909
Wang Chong (Wang Ch'ung), **745–748**
  on ethics, 87–88
  on human nature, 556
  Lunheng (*On Constancy*), 576

philosophy of the mind of, 585
on *qi*, 617
on *xing*, 799
on Yang Xiong, 839
Wang Daiyu, 70
Wang Fu, 88
Wang Fuzhi (Wang Fu-chih), **748–755**
compared with Gu Yanwu, 272
on *dao*, 122
economic theory of, 123
on *li*, 367
on *qi*, 617
on Shao, 688
Tan Sitong and, 709
Wang Gen, 406–407, 777, 778
Wang Guowei (Wang Kuo-wei), **755–760**
humanism in, 665
literary criticism by, 580
Wang Hui, 592
Wang Ji, 777, 778
on four nothingnesses, 111
Liu Zongzhou on, 406–407
Wang Jing, 145
Wang Mang, 87
Wang Meng, 595–596
Wang O, 185
Wang Pan, 183
Wang Po, 184
Wang Ruoshui, 588–590, 668
"Philosophy of the Table," 436
Wang Ruoxu, 182
Wang Shizhen, 580
Wang Shouren. *See* Wang Yangming
Wang Tingxiang, 113
Wang Wei, 2, 511
Wang Xi, 597
Wang Xianzhi, 27
Wang Xizhi, 27
Wang Xuanhe, 226
Wang Yan, 273
Wang Yangming, 32, 749, **760–775**
and *benti*, 719
on *cheng*, 37
Chen Que on, 33, 34
Chen Xiangshang and, 36, 110–111
coordinative reasoning in, 131
A. S. Cua on, 604
ethical intuitionism criticized by Yan Fu, 834
"Four-Sentence Teaching of," 406–407
on *gewu* and *zhizhi*, 268–269, 901
Gu on, 273
on history, 551
in Japan, 99
the *junzi* and, 334
in Korean Confucianism, 106
on *li*, 383, 636, 757
on *li* and *qi*, 725
Liu Zongzhou on, 406–407
Luo Qinshun on, 420–422
Lu Xiangshan and, 112–113, 413, 418
metaphysics and pragmatics in, 56
mind and heart school under, 139
on mind identified with principle, 900
Mou on, 483–484
promulgation of in Ming, 112
on *qing*, 622
on *qiongli* (reality), 625
on *quan*, 626
on *ren*, 646
on self-cultivation, 808–809
on selfishness, 269
on *taixu*, 810–811
on *ti-yong*, 722
Wang Fuzhi compared to, 750, 752
on *xing*, 800
and *yi*, 844
Zhang Xuecheng and, 864
Zhang Zai's influence on, 867
Zhan Roshui close friend of, 851
on *zhixing heyi*, 827, 877–878
on Zhu Xi, 901
Wang Yangming: rivals and followers, **775–781**
Chiang Kai-shek, 50
Wang Yi, 184
Wang Yuanhua, 589
Wang Yun, 183
Wang Guowei quanji: Shuxin, 755
Wang Guowei xiansheng quanji, 755
Wang Guowei zhexue meixue lunwen jiyi, 755
Wanli emperor, 108
war
Heguanzi on, 293
Mohism on, 543
Warring States era
Dong Zhongshu and, 238
fa in, 246
legalism in, 84–85
syncretism in, 83
water
associated with acting wisely, 875
Laozi on, 357–358
Mencius on, 446
Watson, Burton, 636
Watson, J. B., 363
Way of Politics and the Way of Government, The (Mou), 480, 482
Ways of Chinese Philosophy (Hang), 611
Weber, Max, 594, 663
Wei Liaoweng
and Zhu Xi, 909
Wei Boyang, 659–660
Wei Cheng-t'ung, 157, 626
Wei, Madam, 26–27
Wei Yuan, 124
new text school and, 124
reformism of, 125

Wei Zheng, 141
Wei Zhongxian, 114
Wei dynasty, 214–216
wei (false appearance), 36
Wei-Jin era
  Daoism in, 8
  Ruan Ji and, 653–656
wei wo (egoism). *See* egoism in Chinese ethics
Wellek, René, 299
Wen, King, 517
Wen Fong, 28
Wenfu (*Rhyme-Prose on Letters*) (Lu), 3, 576
Wenfu (*Rhyme-Prose on Literature*) (Gu), 275
Wenshi tongyi (*General Principles of Literature and History*) (Zhang), 551, 861, 862, 863
Wenxin diaolong (*Literary Mind-Heart Etching Dragon*) (Liu), 4, 193, 576, 577, 861
  cosmology in, 193
Wenxuan, 322
Wenyan Commentary. *See Xici*
Wen Yan Commentary, 733
Wenzhang liubie lun (*On Genre*) (Zhi), 576
Wenzi treatise, the, **781–783**
western culture
  Cheng on, 601
  community in, 91–96
  Confucianism and, 70–72
  egoism in, 241–242
  the Enlightenment, 89–96
  epistemology in, 558–559
  Fang on, 249–252
  in Hu Shi, 297–303
  in Japan, 101–102
  Liang on, 392–394, 396
  Lin Yutang on, 400–402
  Marxism in China and, 431–438
  metaphysics in, 449
  principles of things in, 367–368
  Qian on, 618
  recent Chinese philosophy and, 591–592
  scientism and humanism and, **663–669**
  in Taiwan, 608–613
  Wang Guowei and scholarship, 755–756
  Xu Fuguan on, 812
  Zhang Binglin negative about, 855
"Western Inscription" (*Ximing*) (Zhang Zai), 762, 865, 868–869
Western Zhou period, 726–727
Wheaton, Henry, 628
Wheelwright, Philip, 72
White Deer Grotto Academy, 905
Whitehead, Alfred North, 257–258
"white horse is not horse," 270–271, 495–497
  language philosophy and, 573
  Mohist theory on, 464–465
  neo-Mohism on, 354
  Platonism in, 350–352
White Paper on Human Rights, 630
Wieman, Henry N., 605
Wilde, Oscar, 316
Wilhelm, Richard, 598, 735
Williams, Samuel Wells, 735
Windelband, Wilhelm, 502
wisdom
  Confucius on, 62
  xingzhi (original wisdom), 802–803
Wisdom, John, 131–132
Wisdom of China, The (Lin), 736
Wisdom of Confucius, The (Lin), 736
withered things, debate on nature of, 900
Wittgenstein, Ludwig, 504, 771, 785
women
  Chen Que on, 34
  in Ming Confucianism, 112
Wŏnhyo, 815, 816
Woo, Peter, 612
words. *See also* language and logic
  Yang's fascination with, 839
  Zhuangzi on, 912–913
words and meaning
  debate on, 215–216
  Wang Bi on, 742, 792
  Xi Kang on, 792
World's Religions, The (Smith), 96
Wu, Emperor (Liang)
  Awakening of Faith in Mahayana, 11–12
  Doctrine of the Mean commentary, 12
  reforms of, 85
Wu, Empress
  Buddhism and, 15, 17
  ritual under, 143
Wu Cheng, 185–186, 186
Wu Di, Emperor, 81
Wu Ding, 234
Wu Jingxiong (Wu Ching-hsiung), 610–611
Wu Kang, 421
Wu Lai, 184
Wu Qi, 362
Wu Qihui, 666
Wu Yubi, 35, 109
Wu Yun, 226
Wu Zhihui, 668
Wufeng xiansheng. *See* Hu Hong (Hu Hung)
Wuji, Lord Xing, 237
wujiao (five teachings), 253–254
Wujiao Zhang (*Treatise on the Five Teachings*) (Fazang), 253, 256–257
Wujing sishu daquan (*Great Collection on the Five Classics and Four Books*), 108–109
Wujinzang, 313
Wuji tu (*Diagram of the Ultimate of Nonbeing*), 892
wuji (ultimateless), 719
Wu jun lun (*Treatise on Not Having Rulers*) (Bao), 218
wujun pai "school of no sovereign." *See* anarchists
Wumazi, 241–242
Wumenguan (*Gateless Gate*), 20

wuming (no names no saying), 345–346, 348–349
Wushang biyao (*Esoteric Essentials of the Most High*), 226
Wushi nianlai di zhongguo zhexue (*Fifty Years of Chinese Philosophy*) (He Lin), 780
wuwang (freedom from falsity), 671
wuwei: taking no action, 731, **783–786**
aesthetics and, 4–5
government and, 536
in Guodian bamboo slips, 230–231
Guo Xiang on, 282–283
in Han Confucianism, 83–84
Han Feizi on, 286
Huang-Lao school and, 922
Laozi on, 359–360
moral psychology and, 478
neo-Daoism on, 217
Shen Buhai on, 690–691
Wang Bi on, 743
Zhuangzi and, 919
Wuxing (*Five Moral Principles*)
Guodian bamboo slip text, 150
wuxing (*wu-hsing*)*:* five phases, **786–788**
in aesthetics, 1–2
combinations of natural forces as, 730
in cosmology, 190–192
de in, 236
Dong Zhongshu on, 239–240
Guanzi on, 279–280
history of, 545
Ling Ting-kan on, 403–404
mythology of, 487–490
ritualism and, 649–650
as science, 660–661
Yang Xiong on, 838
yinyang, 239–240
yinyang and, 846
Wuzhen pian (*Awakening to Perfection*), 227
wuzhi (without knowledge), 875–876
wu (enlightenment)
cessation of thought in, 12
Chen Daqi on, 30
Fazang on, 253–258
gradual vs. sudden, 8–9
Huineng on, 314
Mazu Daoyi on, 439–440
trigger in, 439–440
in Zen, 20–24
wucai (five materials), 787
wude (five powers), 787

Xhiming (*Interpretation of Names*) (Liu), 340
Xi Kang (Hsi K'ang), **789–793**
on freedom, 220
neo-Daoism of, 218–219
Ruan Ji and, 653
Xia dynasty, 541
mythology of, 486–487
Xiang Xiu, 791, 799
Guo Xiang and, 280
in neo-Daoism, 218, 219, 220
"Xiang Comentaries," 517
Xiangshan quanji (*Complete Works of Lu Xiangshan*), 413
xiang-shu (image-number) school, 520–521
xiangxing (painting), 2, 3
Xiantian taiji tu (*Diagram of the Primordial Great Ultimate*), 892
Xianzong, Emperor, 289
Xiao Jefu, 589
Xiao Gongzhuan, 388
xiao (*hsiao*): filial piety, **793–795**
Zhang Zai on, 869
zhong and *cheng* in, 887
Xiaojing (*Treatise on Filial Piety*), 793, 794–795
Xiaolian xia (*A Sheathed Sword for Nocturnal Practice*) (Zhu), 227
Xici (*Commentary on the Appended Phrases*), 517, 718, 719
and *benti*, 719
on comprehensive observation, 560–562
dao in, 203
guan (comprehensive and contemplative observation) in, 518–519
and *ti*, 717–718
time ontocosmology in, 732
Xie He, 513
Xie Kan, 777
Xie Liangzuo, 757
Xie Shangcai, 896
"Xie Ziran" (Han), 290
xi (*hsü*): emptiness, **809–811**. *See also kong* (emptiness)
Buddhism on, 10–11
Jizang on, 324–326, 327–328
Li Ao on, 386
Nagarjuna on, 15
Xiong Shili on, 804
in Zen, 20
Xing Fensi, 437
xing (*hsing*): human nature, **554–558**, **798–801**
Cheng Yi on, 44
Dai Zhen on, 199
defined in *Zhongyong*, 889
Hu Hong on, 295–296
Laozi on, 208–209
Luo Qinshun on, 420–421
original human nature as criterion of an ideal society, 921
Xu Guguan on, 812
Xunzi on, 821–824
Zhang Zai on, 866–868
zhengming and, 871
Zhu Xi on, 899–900
Xingli daquan (*Great Collection on Nature and Principle*), 108–109
Xingli shiyi (Zhang Zai), 867
xing (material form), 449–450
xing (mind), 23
xing ming (performance and title), 492, 691
xingshangxue. *See* metaphysics
xingzhi (original wisdom), 802–803

Xingzhonghui, 706
Xing zi mingchu (*Human Nature from Destiny*), 150, 151–152
xin (*hsin*): heart and mind, **581–588**, **795–797**
  in calligraphy, 26–27
  cheng compared with, 37
  Chen Xianzhang on, 35
  in Confucian vision, 180–181
  culivation of, 913–914
  Huainanzi on, 305
  Hu Hong on, 295
  human nature and, 556
  in Japan, 99–100
  in Korea, 102–103, 105–106
  Liang Shuming on, 397
  Liu Zongzhou on, 406
  Luo Qinshun on, 420–421
  Mencius on, 442
  Mohist theory of, 462–463
  moral psychology and, 476–479
  paired with *cheng*, 886
  Shao Yong and, 683–684
  Shen Buhai on, 691
  used in connection with one's words (*yan*), 886
  Xu Guguan on, 812
  Zhang on, 121
  Zhang Zai on, 866–868
  Zhu Xi on, 867–868, 899–900
xinjili (heart-mind is principle), 765
xin lixue (new theory of *li*), 259–261
Xinquan wen bian lu (*Recorded Questions and Responses from the Xinquan Academy*) (Zhan Roshui), 854
Xin shilun (*A New Treatise on Human Affairs*) (Feng), 259–260
Xin weishi lun (*New Consciousness-Only Doctrine*) (Xiong Shili), 801
Xinxing tu shuo (*An Explanation of the Diagram of Mind and Nature*) (Zhan Roshui), 853–854
xinxue (mind and heart) school. *See also* Lu-Wang Confucianism
  Chengs on, 41
  compared with *lixue*, 139
  emergence of, 136
  He Lin on, 168
  Huang Zongxi and, 307–309
  Liu Zongzhou and, 405–406
  Lu Xiangshan in, 413–420
  philosophy of the mind and, 587
  under Wang, 139
  Wu Cheng in, 186
  Zhan Roshui on, 853
Xinxue weijing kao (*A Study of the Forged Classics of the Xin Period*) (Kang), 338
xinzhai (fasting of the mind), 810
Xiong Shili (Hsiung Shih-li), 165–166, 716, **801–806**
  on *benti*, 718, 725
  Confucianism interpreted by, 590
  on life or creativity, 696
  Mou and, 480, 485
  Xu Fuguan and, 811
xioshen (*hsiu-shen*): self-cultivation, **807–809**, 810
  in Buddhism, 641
  Cheng Yi on, 44–45
  culture and, 532
  Dai Zhen on, 200–202
  in *Daxue*, 232–233
  Daxue on, 710
  Han Yu on, 290–291
  Huainanzi on, 305
  Hu Hong on, 296
  in Japan, 99–100
  knowledge and, 566–568
  Li Ao on, 385–387
  Ling Ting-kan on, 404
  Liu Zongzhou on, 406–407
  Lu on, 138–139
  Lu Xiangshan on, 417
  Mencius on, 442–445, 458–460
  moral philsophy and, 473–474
  in neo-Daoism, 218–220
  in Tang Confucianism, 141, 147–148
  xiao as basis for, 794
  in Yang Confucianism, 183–184
  Zhu on, 138–139
Xipi chengbian (transformation through closing and opening)
  Xiong Shili and, 804
Xisheng jing (*Scripture of Western Ascension*), 225
xixin (habitual mind), 803
Xizhi. *See* Li Ao
Xu Ai, 777
Xu Fuguan (Hsü Fu-kuan), 714, **811–814**
  disciple of Xiong Shili, 801
  in lineage, 113
  mentality approach of, 83
  Mou and, 480
Xu Heng, 183–184, 184
Xu Qian, 184
Xu Shen
  Huainanzi commentary, 305
  Shuowen jiezi, 2, 340
Xu Youyu, 597
Xuan, Emperor, 87
xuanxue (*hsüan-hsüeh*) (mysterious learning), 741. *See also* neo-Daoism
  Han Yu and, 290
  on *youwu*, 849
Xuanzang (Hsüan-tsang), 15–16, 143, **814–820**
  Canon of Filial Piety, 144
  on *Wenzi*, 781
"Xu Commentary," 517
Xuhua (*Discussing painging*) (Wang), 511
Xun Can, 215, 220
Xun Kuang. *See* Xunzi (Hsün Tzu)
Xun Qing. *See* Xunzi (Hsün Tzu)
Xun Shuang, 88

Xun Yue
Han Ji (*Chronicles of the Former Han*), 88–89
on *xin*, 887
on *xing*, 799
Xung Shili, 780
Xunzi, 725, 821
du in, 47, 48
on egoism, 243
on government, 537–538
influence on *Wenzi*, 781
quanli (rights) in, 628
on the self, 675
on *shenming*, 700
on wei, 784
on *xiao*, 793
on *xin* and *yi*, 887
in *xing*, 799
xiushen in, 807
on *zhong* and *shu*, 885
on *zhongxin*, 885
Xunzi (Hsün Tzu), 500–501, 710, 722, 766, **821–829**, 868
argumentation in, 55
on *bi*, 634
Chen Daqi on, 29, 30
in classical Confucianism, 67
on connection between moral knowledge and action, 877
coordinative reasoning in, 132
Cua on, 604
on culture, 525–527, 530–531
on *dao* and change, 156
epistemology of, 564–566
on generic vs. specific terms, 370–371
on Gongsun, 575
on history, 543–544
on Hui Shi, 310
on human nature, 56, 756–757
on lli *and* yi, 844
Jia Yi influenced by, 321
on *junzi*, 132–133, 330, 331
Kang Youwei on, 339
on language, 574–575
language of, 72–73
on *li*, 77, 372, 631–632, 843
on *li* and *yi*, 845
on the mind, 584–585
on mourning, 380–383
on natural affection for parents, 794
on people being the foundation of the state, 782
on *qing*, 621–622
on *quan*, 626
rhetoric in, 127–135
on rights, 53
on ritualism, 648–649
on sages, 379–380, 698
on self-cultivation, 808
on self-deception, 673–675
syncretism of, 70
on *tian*, 728
on *xin* (mind-heart), 796
on *xu*, 810
on *yi*, 76, 78–79, 842
on *zhengming*, 347–348
zhengming in, 871–872
xuxin, 868
Xuyan (*Prefatory Words*) (Dai), 196

Yamanoi Yu, 36, 421
Yan Fu (Yen Fu), 433, 716, **831–834**
Yan Hui. *See* Xunzi (Hsün Tzu)
Yan Jiaqi, 436
Yan Junping, 837
Yan Lingfeng, 285
Yan Mijian, 184
Yan Roju, 117, 834
Yan Shigu, 141
Yan Yu, 580
Yan Yuan (Yen Yüan), 122, 652, 754, **834–837**
Yan Zhenqing, 28, 145
Yan Zun, 355
Yancong, 814
Yang Chao, 429
Yang Gongyi, 183
Yang Gueishan, 896
Yang Guorong, 589
Yang Haowen, 185
Yang Huan, 182, 185
Yang Jian, 905
Yang Kueisong, 430
Yang Shi
on *liyi fenshu*, 409
on *zhonghe* (equilibrium and harmony), 896
Yang Weizhong, 183
Yang Xi, 224
Yang Xianzhen, 436
Yang Xiong (Yang Hsiung), **837–840**
on grand unity, 87–88
on human nature, 556
Wang Chong and, 748
on *xin*, 887
Zhongguo meixueshi, 26
Yang Zhu (Yang Chu), 798, **840–842**
Yangist movement, 470, 798
yangqi (nourishing vital force), 445
Yangsheng zhu (Lordly Principle of Nourishing Life), 4
Yan-Li school, 834
yan (saying), 343–345
Yanshi xueji (*Scholarly Records of Yan Yuan*) (Dai Wang), 837
Yan tie lun (*Discourses on Salt and Iron*), 363
Yanzi (Yan Hui), 796, 889, 894
Cheng Yi on, 44
Confucius and, 59
as Confucius disciple, 63
Yao, Emperor, 542
Yao Jiheng, 834
Yao Mingda, 861
Yao Nai, 862

Yaoshan Weiyan, 386
Yao Shu, 183
Yaojiang school, 405–408
Ye Qing, 433
Ye Shi, 184, 888, 907–908
Yehlü Chucai, 182
Yellow Turban uprising, 88, 223
Yen Ruoju, 862
Yi Hwang, 103–104
Yi I, 103–104, 105–106
Yi On-jok, 103
Yi Zhi, 242
yi (change)
  action and, 245–246
  dao and, 203
  junzi and, 332–333
  li and, 371–372
  Lu Jia on, 412–413
  Mencius on, 440–448
  moral philosophy and, 471–473
  in Mozi, 456
  quan and, 626
  rhetoric on, 129, 130–132
  self-cultivation and, 807
  self-deception and, 671
yi (i) and *li:* rightness and rites, **842–846**
yi (rightness, appropriateness)
  as beauty, 1–3
  in calligraphy, 28
  Chen Daqi on, 30–31
  in comparative philosophy, 52–53
  Dai Zhen on, 198
  daotong and, 156
  defining, 72–73, 74–77
  Liang Qichao on, 390
  in *quan* and *jing*, 158
  Xunzi on, 67
yijian (opinions), 201–202
Yijing (*Book of Changes*). *See also Yizhuan* (*Ten Wings*)
  aesthetics and, 1, 3–5
  cheng in, 38
  cosmology in, 189, 192
  dao in, 203
  de in, 73
  divination in, 519–520
  example of ethics of timeliness, 732
  Kong Yingda commentary on, 892
  on life or creativity, 696
  li in, 366–367
  Liu Zongzhou on, 405–408
  Mou on, 480
  numerology in, 683
  ontocosmology of time in, 730
  philosophy of change and, 517–524
  Qian hexagram, 489–490
  ranked first by Xiong Shili, 802
  in religious Daoism, 226–227
  San Sitong and, 711
  on self-deception, 672
  Shiong Shili on, 805
  on *ti*, 717
  Tongshu as commentary on, 893
  in twentieth-century Confucianism, 163
  Wang Bi on, 216, 741, 742
  Wang Fuzhi's commentaries on, 749
  xin in, 795, 796
  Xun commentary on, 88
  Yang Xiong's *Mystery* patterned after, 837
  on *yinyang*, 846
  Zhang Zai and, 864
Yijing Xici shang, 717
Yili jingzhuan tongjie (*General Exposition of the Book of Etiquette and Decorum and Its Commentaries*) (Zhu), 404–405, 651, 652
yi-li (meaning-principle) school, 520–521
yi min (treating the people as one), 680, 682
Yin Si, 355
yin and *yang*, **846–847**
  aesthetics and, 3–5
  in beauty, 1–2
  in cosmology, 190–192
  Dai Zhen on, 197–198
  dao and, 203, 204
  function of the *taiji*, 724
  human history reflecting movement of, 752–753
  in mythology, 488–490
  philosophy of the mind in, 585
  in religious Daoism, 226–227
  Shao Yong and, 684
  things as natural combinations of natural forces represented by, 730
  ti/yong distinction and, 722
  Yang Xiong on, 838
  Zhang Zai on, 866
  in Zhou Dunyi's *Taiji tushuo*, 892
  Zhou dynasty school of, 640
  Zhu Xi and, 900
Yin binshi jehi (Liang), 388
Yin Wen, 492
Yinwenzi, 346, 349–350
Yinxue wushu (*Five Treatises on Phonology*) (Gu), 275
Yi River Teacher's Beating the Rang (*Yichuan jirang ji*) (Shao), 683
yiti (one body), 763
Yiwen zhi, 862
Yixue xiangshu lun (On image and number in studies of the Classic of Changes) (Huang), 309
Yizhuan (*Ten Wings*), 517–524, 724
  ben and *ti* in, 718
  in classical Confucianism, 67–68
  on *dao*, 523–524
  dao in, 203
  on *qiongli* (reality), 623
  and *ti*, 717
Yizi (Yi Zhi; Yi Chih), 460
  Mencius on, 457–458
Yogacara philosophy, 15–16, 815, 816

Yojokun (*Precepts for Health Care*) (Ekken), 100
Yolgok, 105–106
yong (courage)
  shu identified as, by Zhu Xi, 882
  Xiong Shili on, 804
  in the *Yijing*, 723
Yongle dadian (*Great Canon of the Yongle Era*), 108
Yongle emperor, 108
Young Men's Christian Association (YMCA), 50
youwu (*yu-wu*): being and nonbeing, 8, **847–849**
  in comparative philosophy, 56
  dao on, 742
  Fang on, 251
  Guo Xiang on, 281
  Laozi on, 8, 357–358
  in neo-Daoism, 216–217
  Wang Bi on, 742–743
  Wang Fuzhi on, 750
Yu Ruo (Ziyu), 64
Yü Yingshih, 155, 759
Yuan, Emperor, 86
Yuan Haowen, 182
Yuan Huang, 407
Yuan Ji, 511
Yuan Mei, 864, 888
Yüan Mei, 580
Yuan Shikai, 48, 707
Yuan dao (An inquiry on the Way) (Han), 135–136, 289–290, 549, 551
yuanli (principle), 635
Yuanru (*An Inquiry on Confucianism*) (Xiong Shili), 801, 805
Yuanshan (*Inquiry into Goodness*) (Dai), 195, 862
Yu Cong (*Collection of Sayings*), 150, 152
Yue Guang, 221
yue (music)
  Confucius on, 62
  cosmology and, 189–190
  liyue (ritual and music), 647–648
  Mozi on, 454
  Wenzi and, 783
  Xi Kang on, 792
Yukichi, Fukuzawa, 424
Yulu (*Recorded Sayings*), 439–440
Yun Richu, 307
Yungu, 407
Yushima Seido school, 101

Zai Yu, 63
zeitgeist approach, 83
Zen Buddhism. *See* Buddhism, Zen (Chan)
Zeng Can (Ziyu), 63–64
Zeng Guofan, 50, 124
Zeng Shen, 882, 883
"Zha Commentary," 517
Zhai Yi, 272
Zhan Ganquan. *See* Zhan Roshui (Chan Jo-shui)
Zhan Ganquan xiansheng wenji (*Literary Works of Master Zhan Ganquan*), 854
Zhang Binglin (Chang Ping-lin), 272, **854–857**
Zhang Boduan, 227
Zhang Dainian, 589
Zhang Dong-sheng. *See* Zhang Dongsun (Chang Tung-sun)
Zhang Dongsun (Chang Tung-sun), **857–861**
Zhang Ertian, 857
Zhang Huaiguan, 25–26
Zhang Jue, 285
Zhang Junmai. *See* Chang, Carson
Zhang Kuang, 398–399
Zhang Liwen, 589
Zhang Lüxiang, 34
Zhang Lyuxiang, 779
Zhang Rong, 11
Zhang Shi, 296, 868
  on *zhonghe* (equilibrium and harmony), 896, 897
  Zhu Xi and, 847
Zhang Wenda, 111
Zhang Xuecheng (Chang Hsüeh-ch'eng), 119–122, 237, **861–864**
Zhang Yanyuan, 511, 512, 513
Zhang Yi, 398–399
Zhang Zai (Chang Tsai), 710, 762, 766, 777, **864–869**
  Cheng Hao on, 41, 42
  cosmology of, 898
  influence on Zhu Xi, 900
  on *liyi fenshu*, 409–410
  metaphysics in, 137–138
  Mou on, 483–484
  in neo-Confucianism, 39
  as Northern Song master, 136
  as one of the four masters, 903
  and orthodox line of the Way, 902
  on *qi*, 617
  on *ren*, 645
  ritualism and, 650
  on *taixu*, 810
  use of *ti* by, 720
  Wang Fuzhi and, 749, 750
  on *zhong* and *shu*, 884–885
  Zhu Xi and, 899
Zhang Zhan, 221, 398–399
Zhang Zhi, 867
Zhang Zhidong, 428, 725
Zhanran, 819
Zhan Roshui (Chan Jo-shui), 35, 775–776, **851–854**
  Chen Xianzhang and, 36
  in lineage, 113
  Wang Yangming and, 760
Zhao Bingwen, 182
Zhao Fu, 183
Zhao Jie, 184
Zhao Kuang, 145
Zhao Mengfu, 28
Zhao yu zhi (Gu), 274
Zhen Dexiu, 184
  and dialogue with Lu Jiuyuan school, 909
  follower of Zhu Xi, 909

Zhen Dexiu (*Continued*)
  modifications to Zhu Xi's doctrines, 909
  T'oegye on, 103
Zheng Jiadong, 590
Zheng Qiao, 552, 861
Zheng Xuan, 232, 888
Zhengao (*Declarations of the Perfected*), 224
Zhengmeng (*Rectifying Obscurations*) (Zhang Zai), 865
zhengming (*cheng-ming*)*:* rectifying names, 501, **870–872**
  Dong Zhongshu in, 239
  in ethics and law, 80–81
  the *junzi* and, 334
  knowledge and, 563–566
  language and logic and, 343–355, 570–571
  Mencius on, 445–447
  Mohist theory of, 462–468
  Mou on, 482–483
  rhetoric and, 130–131
zhengxin (rectification of the heart), 47–48
Zhengzi, 730
zhenren (*chen-jen*)*:* the true, authentic person, **872–874**
zhexue (philosophy), 499
Zhezhong (central Zhejiang) school of neo-Confucianism, 777
Zhi Dun (Zhi Daolin), 10
Zhi Xi, 835
Zhi Yü, 576
zhi (*chih*): to know; to realize, **874–876**
  Cheng Yi on, 45–46
  Confucian epistemology of, 563–568
  Mencius on, 444–445
  neo-Mohists on, 352–354
  philosophy of mind and, 584
  prospective versus retrospective knowledge, 876
  self-cultivation and, 807
  Xunzi on, 826
zhidao, 827
zhi-hsing heyi (unity of knowledge), 877–878
zhilü (informed deliberation), 825–826
zhiren (supreme person), 872
zhixing heyi (*chih-hsing ho-i*)*:* unity of knowledge and action, 827, **876–878**
zhixing (to know one's nature), 847
zhiyan (knowing language), 445
Zhiyi (Chih-i), **879–882**
  Tiantai school and, 13–15
  Zhuangzi compared with, 15
zhizhi (extension of knowledge), 47
Zhong Hui, 220
Zhong Rong, 577
Zhong Yu, 63
zhong (*chung*) and *shu:* loyalty and reciprocity, 51–52, **882–885**
  in Confucian vision, 179–181
  Dai Zhen on, 201
  in *Daxue*, 233
  Mencius on, 457–458
zhong (*chung*) and *xin* (*hsin*): loyalty and trustworthiness, **885–888**
zhong (equilibrium or centrality), 403–404, 896
  defined in *Zhongyong*, 889
  Wang Yangming on, 767
  Zhu Xi on, 896–897
Zhongguo meixueshi, 25–26
Zhongguo zhexue fazhan shi (*The History of the Development of Chinese Philosophy*) (Ren), 263
Zhongguo zhexue shi bu (*Supplement to the History of Chinese Philosophy*) (Feng), 262
Zhongguo zhexueshi dagang (Hu), 297
Zhongguo zhexue shi xinbian (*New Version of the History of Chinese Philosophy*) (Feng), 262–264
Zhongguo zhexue xiaoshi (*Short History of Chinese Philosophy*) (Feng), 262
Zhonghe ji (*Collection of Central Harmony*), 227
Zhong-Lü school. *See* Complete Perfection (Quanzhen) school
zhong (the mean), in rhetoric, 134
Zhongyong (*Chung Yung*)*:* the doctrine of the mean, 718, 724, 884, **888–891**
  on *cheng*, 37–38, 808
  in classical Confucianism, 68
  on culture, 525, 530
  on *dao*, 205
  du in, 47–48
  on *junzi*, 329, 332
  on knowledge, 566–568
  Li Ao on, 385–386
  on life or creativity, 696
  li in, 366–367
  philosophy of the mind in, 585
  on self-cultivation, 808
  studied by Zhang Zai, 864
  Tang theories on, 147
  and term *zhonghe*, 896
  theory of learning in compared to Spencer by Yan Fu, 832
  Tu Weiming on, 606
  Wu commentary on, 12
  on *xiao*, 793
  yi in, 76–77, 842
Zhou, duke of, 863
Zhou Dunyi (Chou Tun-i), 719, 750, **891–895**, 898
  on *cheng*, 37, 38
  Cheng Hao and, 41
  Daoism in, 136
  great ultimate and, 563
  on *ji*, 47
  Luo Qinshun and, 420
  Mou on, 483–484
  in neo-Confucianism, 39
  as Northern Song master, 136
  as one of the four masters, 903
  and orthodox line of the Way, 902
  on *ren*, 645
  on *xin*, 887
  Zhang Zai compared to, 864, 865
Zhou Enlai, 60–61
Zhou Gong, 173–174

Zhou Lianxi. *See* Zhou Dunyi (Chou Tun-i)
Zhou Maoshu. *See* Zhou Dunyi (Chou Tun-i)
Zhou Mi, 908
Zhou Rudeng, 112–113, 114
Zhou Yan, 616
Zhou Yang, 429
Zhou Yi, 517
Zhou Yong, 11
Zhou Zumo, 275
Zhou dynasty, 58, 60, 541–542
  Han Confucianism and, 84
  religions in, 640
Zhouguan (*Offices of the Zhou*), 660, 805
Zhouli (*Rites of the Zhou*), 643, 660–661, 871
Zhou Yi (*Book of Changes from the Zhou*)
  ontoepistemology in, 560–562
Zhu Dezhi, 227
Zhu Si, 7
Zhu Xi (Chu Hsi), 750, 768, 775, 779, **895–902**
  on authorship of *Zhongyong*, 888
  and *benti*, 719
  on Buddhism, 148
  Chan on, 600–601
  on *cheng*, 37, 38
  on *chengyi*, 47
  Chen Liang and, 363
  Chen Que on, 34
  civil service examinations and, 109
  commentary on *Zhongyong*, 888–889
  critical of Chang Hao and Chen Yi's explanation of *ren*, 762
  on *daotong*, 154–159
  on the *Daxue*, 232, 267–268
  Daxue altered by, 110–111
  debate with Lu, 138–139
  differences with Lu Jiuyuan over pedagogy, 905–906
  on distinction of *ti* and *yong*, 768
  on egoism, 246
  Family Rituals, 34
  followers, 908–909
  Four Books and, 154–155
  on *gewu* and *zhizhi*, 268
  Gu on, 273
  on heaven, 750
  on history, 549
  Huang Zongxi on, 307–308
  influence on modern Chinese scholars, 780
  in Japan, 99
  Kang Youwei on, 339
  on *li*, 632–633, 757
  on *li* and *qi*, 725
  on *li* and *yu*, 757
  lineage of, 155
  liyi fenshu and, 409–410
  Lu Xiangshan and, 413
  Lu Xiangshan on, 417
  meeting with Lu Jiuyuan at Goose Lake Monastery, 905, 906
  metaphysics and pragmatics in, 56
  on the moral mind, 105–106
  Mou on, 167, 483–484
  notion of wisdom as *shoulien*, 827
  praised by Yan Fu, 834
  on *qi*, 36
  Qian on, 618
  on *qiongli* (reality), 624–625
  on *quan* and *jing*, 157–159, 626
  on reflection, 179
  on *ren*, 645–646, 722
  on ritualism, 651
  rivals, 903–908
  on self-cultivation, 808
  on self-deception, 671–672, 673
  on selfishness, 269
  as Southern Song master, 136
  on *ti-yong*, 720–721
  T'oegye on, 103–104
  use of *li*, 764–765
  Wang Fuzhi and, 749
  on *xi*, 796
  on *xing*, 800
  on Yang Xiong, 840
  on Zhang Zai, 867, 869
  on *zhong* and *cheng*, 887
  on *zhong* and *shu*, 882, 884
  on *zhong* and *xi*, 887
  Zongyong included in the *Four Books*, 888
Zhu Xi (Chu Hsi): rivals and followers, **903–910**
Zhu Ying, 35
Zhu Yuanzhang, 107–108
Zhu Yun, 861, 862
Zhuang Cunyu, 124–125
Zhuang Zhou. *See* Zhuangzi (Chuang Tzu)
Zhuangzi (Chuang Tzu), 710, 825, **911–918**
  butterfly dream of, 318
  in classical Daoism, 206–207, 209–210
  cosmogony of, 210–211
  on *dao*, 204, 210–211
  on *de*, 236
  on emptiness as significant state of mind, 810
  influence on *Wenzi*, 781
  interpretations of, 914–915
  on language, 573–574
  life praxis in, 212–213
  on literature, 576, 579
  mythology of, 487
  on nature, 8
  Nietzsche compared with, 53–54
  on philosophy of mind, 584
  on *qing*, 621
  on the sage, 211–212
  on *shifei*, 704–705
  on *tian*, 728
  on virtue, 5
  on *xu*, 809
  Xu Fuguan on, 812–813
  Zhiyi compared with, 15

Zhuangzi (Chuang Tzu): schools, **919–923**
Zhuangzi
authorship of, 919
on culture, 527–528
dao on, 451
egoism in, 243
on government, 536
Guo Xiang on, 280–284
on human nature, 555–556
moral psychology and, 477
persuasion in, 54–55
on sagehood, 698
Shen Dao in, 692–694
shenming in, 701–702
on *wuwei*, 785–786
wuwei in, 784
on *xing*, 798, 799
Zhang Binglin on, 856
zhenren developed in, 872
on *zhong* and *shu*, 882
Zhuangzi as author of, 911
Zhubing yuanhou fang (*On the Cause and Course of All Illnesses*), 659
Zhunagzi, 796
commentary by Guo Xiang, 799
Zhun Qiu, 749
Zhuoru. *See* Liang Qichao (Liang Ch'i-ch'ao)
zhuti, 718
Zhu Xi's Final Conclusions Arrived at Late in Life (Wang), 116
Zhuzi julei (*Master Zhu's Categorized Conversations*), 109
on *dao*, 156
Zi Si, 888
Zi Wen, 884
Zi Chan, 361
Zigong. *See* Duanmu Siu
Zilu. *See* Zhong Yu
Ziran ming (*Inscriptions on the Concept of the Natural*) (Zhan Roshui), 854
ziran (naturalness)
Chen Xianzhang on, 35–36
in cosmology, 188–190
eight trigrams and, 730
in Guodian bamboo slips, 230–231
Guo Xiang on, 283
Lu Jia on, 412
in neo-Daoism, 218–220
in Ruan Ji, 654–655
Wang Bi on, 743
Xi Kang and, 790, 791
Zhan Roshui on, 853
Zhuangzi and, 919
Zisi (Kong Ji), 150, 151
Ziwo. *See* Zai Yu
Zixia. *See* Bu Shang
Ziyi (*Black Gown*), 150, 151
Zi zhi tongjian (*Comprehensive Mirror for Aid in Government*) (Sima), 549
Zizhuan, 868
Zon Yan, 786
Zong Bing, 511, 512, 514
Zongchi, 20
Zonggong. *See* Ran Yong
Zongmi, 881
Zongxin zhi dao (*The Way of Loyalty and Trustworthiness*), 150, 152
Zou Shouyi, 777, 778
Zou Yan, 545
Zouping experiment, 396
Zu Fuguan, 166–167
Zuigen pin (*The Roots of Sin*), 225
Zundao lu (*On Following the Way*) (Zhan), 854
Zun deyi (*Revering Virtue and Righteousness*), 150, 151
Zuo, 546
de in, 234, 235–236, 236
on enriching the *xing/sheng* of common people, 798
on history, 544–545
on numerology, 786
on *qi*, 616
on *shenming*, 700
shenming in, 701